W9-BBL-429

The Torah
A Women's
Commentary

Dr. Tamara Cohn Eskenazi
*Editor*

Rabbi Andrea L. Weiss, Ph.D.
*Associate Editor*

New York • 2008

URJ Press • 633 Third Avenue • New York, NY 10017-6778
(212) 650-4124 • press@urj.org



*Masoretic Hebrew Text Editor* Rabbi David E. S. Stein (2005)

*Translations:*
*Genesis* Rabbi Chaim Stern ז"ל (1999)
*Exodus–Deuteronomy* Jewish Publication Society (1999)
Rabbi David E. S. Stein, revising translator (2005–06)
Dr. Carol Meyers, consulting editor
Dr. Adele Berlin, consulting editor

*Design* Rabbi David E. S. Stein
*Artwork* Rabbi Me'irah Iliinsky
*Composition* El Ot Pre Press & Computing, Ltd., Tel Aviv
*Cover Design* Michael Silber

*Project Manager* Rabbi David E. S. Stein

*Library of Congress Cataloging-in-Publication Data*

The Torah : a women's commentary / Tamara Cohn Eskenazi, editor ; Andrea L. Weiss, associate editor.
p. cm.
Includes the text of the Pentateuch in Hebrew and English.
Includes bibliographical references and index.
ISBN 978-0-8074-1081-3 (alk. paper)
1. Bible. O.T. Pentateuch–Commentaries. 2. Bible. O.T. Pentateuch–Feminist criticism. 3. Women in the Bible. I. Eskenazi, Tamara Cohn. II. Weiss, Andrea L. III. Bible. O.T. Pentateuch. Hebrew. 2008. IV. Bible. O.T. Pentateuch. English. 2008.
BS1225.53.T675 2008
222'.1077082–dc22

2007040500

Printed in the United States of America. This book is printed on acid-free paper.
1 2 3 4 5 6 7 8 9 10

## *Joanne B. Fried*

In memory of

Winifred F. Fried,

Sylvia S. Fox,

and Helen F. Strauss,

my mother,

grandmother,

and great-grandmother,

all of blessed memory.

In memory of those who came before us,

and in honor of those still to come.

Let this be my legacy to them.

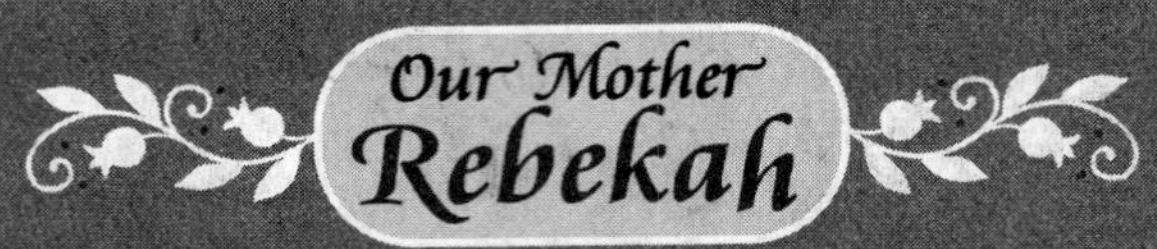


## Alan Gover

In gratitude to the Almighty,

*B'reishit* For the lives of my parents, Beatrice and Norman, and my parents-in-law, Frances and Philip and Gloria and Leonard.

*Lech L'cha* For the Outstretched Hand that guides me.

*Vayeira* For the life of my beloved wife, Ellen, of blessed memory.

*Chayei Sarah* For the life of my beloved wife, Janine.

*V'zot Hab'rachah* For the lives of my dear children, Maxwell and Mary, and Janine's, Greg, Amanda and Zac, and her grandchildren, Joshua and Julia.

## Sheila and Bill Lambert

In memory of the women who were pioneers
and in honor of the women of valor
who are the future of the Jewish people.

# Our Mother Leah

## Betty B. Golomb

In memory of my loving father, I. Mose Brenner, who, despite economic difficulties and being amidst a highly assimilated family, saw that I went to religious school and was confirmed. The joy of my early experience established a lifelong dedication to Jewish learning and a love of Torah.

## Linda L. Henderson

In memory of my parents, Robert M. and Lucille R. Levin, whose legacy included tzedakah, study, and a responsibility for Tikkun Olam.

## Judith and Martin Hertz

In loving tribute to Marjory Hess. It was her steadfast insistence that Jewish women use their life experiences as an interpretive lens when studying sacred Jewish texts that kindled the sparks that inspired us.

## Carol and Alan LeBovidge

In honor of our children, Andrew, Larissa, Jason, and Jennifer, and our grandchildren, Audrey, Claire, Elise, Abigail, and Ethan.

## Daryl Messinger, Rabbi Sarah Messinger, Alice Messinger, and Lisa Messinger

In honor of our parents and families.

## Women of Reform Judaism of Temple Israel, Boston, Massachusetts

We honor and celebrate *The Torah: A Women's Commentary.* Thank you for bringing these blessed words into our synagogues, our homes, and our hearts.

## The Women of Temple Israel Sisterhood, Minneapolis, Minnesota

In continued support of Women of Reform Judaism and in recognition of the value of women's role in Judaism.

## Dolores Kosberg Wilkenfeld

In loving memory of my parents, Cy and Dorothy Kosberg, and my husband, J.H. "Buddy" Wilkenfeld. In honor of my children and grandchildren, Lewis, Serena, Melody, and Jesse Wilkenfeld.

# Our Mother Rachel

### Julie, Drew, Kevin, and Amy Alexander

In honor of my mother, Davna Brook.

### Drs. Kenneth and Ofelia Averack

In honor of our dear children: Pamela, Peter, Kyle, and Brittany Averack.

### Judy Bernstein Bunzl and Nick Bunzl

In honor of our daughters Alexandra Rachel and Natasha Hannah and all the very special teachers of Torah and Jewish life who have helped our family learn the meaning of leading a true Jewish life.

### Patti and Louis Grossman

We honor and remember our parents, Barbara, Aaron, Morton, and Sylvia; our children, Joel, David, Jacob and Debra; our teachers, Rabbis Gittelsohn, Fields, Sonsino, Perlman, Markley and Lenke, who continually guide and inspire us.

### Susan and William Hess

### Lynn Magid Lazar and Dale Lazar

In honor of Bernice Friedland and Ethel Lazar.

### Eleanor Rachel Schwartz

To honor the memory of my mother, Gertrude, an independent, compassionate, and faithful daughter of Zion; to honor her granddaughters, my nieces, Laura, Joanne, and Jane, and their daughters Carmit, Emma, Hannah, Sophie, and Molly.

### Rodef Shalom Sisterhood, Pittsburgh, Pennsylvania

In honor of the women of Rodef Shalom Sisterhood—our past, our present, and our future.

### Congregation Schaarai Zedek Sisterhood, Tampa, Florida

To those women of Congregation Schaarai Zedek who left us their legacy, and to those women whom we precede, we proudly share our love of Torah and dedicate this Commentary to them.

### Women of Reform Judaism Temple Kol Emeth, Marietta, Georgia

In honor of our past, present, and future sisterhood members.

### Women of Reform Judaism District 3

We honor all District 3 women and are proud to have inspired Cantor Sager at our 1992 Convention to initiate the creation of *The Torah: A Women's Commentary*. Generations can now celebrate the women of Torah.

# Parashot

| | | |
|---|---|---|
| NOACH | *Sigrid and Alan Belinkoff* | In memory of Minna Silverglade |
| TOL'DOT | *Helen L. Gold* | In honor of Women of Reform Judaism |
| VAYISHLACH | *Betty and Arthur Roswell* | In memory of our mothers Hilda Blaustein and Florence Roswell |
| VAYIGASH | *Judith O. Rosenkranz* | In loving memory of Stanley W. Rosenkranz |
| VAY'CHI | *Temple Israel Sisterhood, Women of Reform Judaism Memphis, Tennessee* | In honor of the women on whose shoulders we stand |
| SH'MOT | *Franklin M. Fisher and Ellen Paradise Fisher* | In honor of Abigail S. Fisher |
| VA-EIRA | *The Lehman Family* | Dedicated in honor of Brenda Lehman |
| B'SHALACH | *Women of Reform Judaism Southeast District* | In honor of the incredible women of the Southeast District |
| YITRO | *Rosanne and David Selfon* | To honor all those who shape our lives: past, present, and future |
| KI TISA | *Diane and Howard Kaplan* | In honor of our children and our grand-children |

| | | |
|---|---|---|
| P'KUDEI | *Members of Congregation Rodeph Sholom Sisterhood, New York, New York* | In honor of our beloved Rabbi Lisa Grushcow |
| VAYIKRA | *Women of Reform Judaism District 1* | In honor of the women of District 1 |
| K'DOSHIM | *Joan and Peter Weidhorn* | In honor of our Jewish future: our children and grandchildren |
| NASO | *Linda Wimmer* | In memory of my gentle and loving mother, Isabel Philip |
| B'HAALOT'CHA | *Women of Reform Judaism Atlantic District* | In honor of the consolidation of Districts 4 and 5. |
| PINCHAS | *Shelley Lindauer* | In honor of my children, Carly and Joshua |
| VA-ET'CHANAN | *G. Leonard Teitelbaum* | In honor of Bessie Teitelbaum; Dorothy Teitelbaum; Karen Teitelbaum Buckner |
| R'EIH | *The Bergman Family— New York, London,and South Africa* | In memory of Ruth Bergman, pioneer Reform Jewess in South Africa |
| SHOF'TIM | *Sally B. Frank* | In honor of and in memory of my parents, Dr. Herman I. Frank and Claire B. Frank |

# Contents

## לך לך • *Lech L'cha* 12:1–17:27



## וירא • *Vayeira* 18:1–22:24



## חיי שרה • *Chayei Sarah* 23:1–25:18



## תולדת • *Tol'dot* 25:19–28:9



## ויצא • *Vayeitzei* 28:10–32:3

## שמיני • *Sh'mini* 9:1–11:47



## תזריע • *Tazria* 12:1–13:59



## מצרע • *M'tzora* 14:1–15:33



## אחרי מות • *Acharei Mot* 16:1–18:30



## קדשים • *K'doshim* 19:1–20:27

## נשא • *Naso* 4:21–7:89



## בהעלתך • *B'haalot'cha* 8:1–12:16



## שלח לך • *Sh'lach L'cha* 13:1–15:41



## קרח • *Korach* 16:1–18:32



## חקת • *Chukat* 19:1–22:1

## האזינו • *Haazinu* 32:1–52



## וזאת הברכה • *V'zot Hab'rachah* 33:1–34:12

## האזינו Haazinu 32:1–52



## וזאת הברכה V'zot Hab'rachah 33:1–34:12

# Foreword

Women of Reform Judaism (WRJ) is immensely proud to have nurtured the creation of *The Torah: A Women's Commentary.* This book began when one woman, Cantor Sarah Sager, challenged WRJ to produce a Torah commentary that would help women re-claim Torah by gathering together the scholarship and insights of women across the Jewish spectrum and around the world. When Cantor Sager served in 1992 as Scholar-in-Residence at the biennial convention of District 3 of the WRJ (then called NFTS, National Federation of Temple Sisterhoods), she planted a seed, claiming that women could create a Torah commentary that would incorporate women's experiences and women's history into the living memory of our people.

One year later, at the 1993 NFTS Biennial Assembly in San Francisco, Cantor Sager challenged the entire national delegate assembly to "imagine... women being permitted, for the first time, feeling able, feeling legitimate in their study of Torah... and imagine Sisterhood as the empowering agent for this transformation of what *is* into what *should be.*"

The Board of Directors of Women of Reform Judaism responded enthusiastically to Cantor Sager's challenge. Then-president Judith Rosenkranz asked past-president Judith Hertz and board member Elaine Merians to chair a committee that would assess the feasibility of creating a women's Torah commentary. Dr. Sherry Blumberg and other scholars worked with various WRJ districts over the following years, leading women in Torah study and helping to spark an interest in this project. In the spring of 1995, WRJ convened a gathering in Elizabeth, New Jersey, that brought together WRJ lay leaders, scholars, and clergy to begin to envision what this sort of commentary might look like. Enthusiasm for the project was contagious. Less than one month later, WRJ Board member Dayna Brook put forth a motion to the WRJ Board of Directors that WRJ should publish a Torah commentary authored by women. The motion passed unanimously amidst tears of joy and celebration.

From that point on, WRJ was committed to funding fully the publication of this commentary, which aimed to bring new insights to the Torah, hopefully engaging thousands of women and men in study. We recognized the extraordinary promise this project held, for it would be an opportunity to bring representations of women, in ancient Israel as well as in our modern world, into the public arena. It would offer a way into Torah study for women who previously felt excluded or marginalized. And it would provide an opportunity to highlight the outstanding work of Jewish women scholars and community leaders. In its distinguished 94-year history, WRJ has been involved in countless important projects; but this is certainly one of its most ambitious and most historically significant.

Many conversations and meetings followed in which the content and form of the commentary began to take shape. We explored many far-reaching questions: What would be the look and tone of the book? Who would be invited to participate? How would the commentary handle gender issues in Hebrew and English? How could we meet the high standards of scholarly integrity yet also succeed in engaging students just beginning Torah study? And, of primary importance, who could possibly gather together and lead the dynamic women who would make these critical decisions?

Understanding that leadership for the project held the key to its success, WRJ invited Dr. Tamara Cohn Eskenazi (Professor of Bible at HUC–JIR) to serve as Editor. Dr. Eskenazi, whose expertise, contacts, and academic standing are widely recognized and respected, possessed a clear vision of the book's promise; and she approached collaboration with WRJ with open arms. In an early meeting with WRJ leaders, Dr. Eskenazi commented, "Women of Reform Judaism brings a sophistication of judgment and commitment to learning. . . . Partnering together will allow us to put Torah back into the hands of the community, especially the women."

Dr. Eskenazi immediately went to work assembling an editorial board of leading women scholars and clergy: Dr. Rachel Adler, Dr. Judith Baskin, Dr. Sherry Blumberg, Dr. Tikva Frymer-Kensky ז״ל, Rabbi Sue Levi Elwell, Ph.D., Dr. Carol Meyers, Dr. Carol Ochs, Dr. Judith Plaskow, Cantor Sarah Sager, Rabbi Judith Schindler, Rabbi Ruth Sohn, Dr. Ellen Umansky, and Rabbi Andrea L. Weiss, Ph.D., who later took on the role of Associate Editor.

This volume is a testament to the generous spirit of women working together and supporting each other. Each step toward publishing the commentary was the result of determination and diligent teamwork on many different levels. Over the years, hundreds of women—lay leaders as well as Jewish professionals and scholars—collectively labored to birth *The Torah: A Women's Commentary.* Rabbi Emily Feigenson edited an early pilot edition entitled *Beginning the Journey: Toward A Women's Commentary on Torah*, which was released at the 1997 WRJ Assembly. A sample parashah, *Parashat Pinchas*, edited by Dr. Eskenazi, followed in 2003. Both of these early samples stimulated feedback from readers that was crucial in determining the final content and design of the book. Further refinement came in 2006 after nearly 15,000 women and men around the world took part in the opportunity to study from *Parashat Chayei Sarah* sample booklets.

Members of WRJ hosted commentary salons in order to raise the significant funds required to publish this book. A very special thank you is due to WRJ Board member Joanne Fried for her generous gift that initiated our successful fundraising campaign. To all the women and men whose solicitations and contributions enabled WRJ to publish *The Torah: A Women's Commentary*, I say a heartfelt thank you.

Special acknowledgment must be given to WRJ Honorary President Norma U. Levitt and Past Presidents Betty Benjamin, Constance Kreshtool, Dolores K. Wilkenfeld, Judith M. Hertz, Judith O. Rosenkranz, Judith Silverman, and Helene Waranch. Their commitment to the *Commentary* kept the project on the WRJ agenda.

Several former staff members deserve recognition for their important roles in the genesis of this project. These include Executive Director Emeritae Dr. Jane Evans ז״ל, Eleanor Schwartz, and Ellen Y. Rosenberg, under whose leadership the project began. Eve Roshevsky and Alison Lee were also instrumental in advancing the *Commentary* in its early days.

WRJ Executive Director Shelley Lindauer shepherded this project to its conclusion and deserves unlimited thanks. WRJ Manager of Development and Special Projects Lindsay Bellows kept accurate donor records. I leave it to the Acknowledgments (p. xxix) to formally recognize the contributions of the many individuals involved in the actual production of the present book.

May God bless us as we inaugurate a new era of Torah study.

בָּרוּךְ אַתָּה יְיָ, אֱלֹהֵינוּ מֶלֶךְ הָעוֹלָם,
שֶׁהֶחֱיָנוּ וְקִיְּמָנוּ וְהִגִּיעָנוּ לַזְּמַן הַזֶּה.

Praise to You, Eternal our God,
Sovereign of the universe, for giving us life,
sustaining us, and enabling us to reach this season.

—*Rosanne M. Selfon*
President
Women of Reform Judaism

# Preface

THE INVITATION CAME during the week of *parashat Vayeira.* At the time, I had been struggling with a *d'var Torah* I was preparing for the monthly board of trustees meeting at my synagogue. The central story of that portion is *Akedat Yitzchak*, the binding and near sacrifice of Isaac (Genesis 22:1–19). As I thought about the horrifying image of Abraham with arm uplifted against his son, I suddenly thought about Sarah. For the very first time, it occurred to me that Sarah was part of this story, that her feelings and her reactions mattered, that if she had been asked to sacrifice her child, the story might have ended right there. I realized that in her absence and her silence there was room for commentary; therefore, I accepted the invitation to be the Scholar-in-Residence for the 1992 District 3 National Federation of Temple Sisterhoods (NFTS; now Women of Reform Judaism) biennial convention as a way to further explore Sarah's experience.

As I began my research, I soon found that I was not the first to think about the silent women of our tradition. I discovered that there were women—and men—at work in diverse fields of study who were uncovering and recovering a far more complex understanding of the ancient world than the Torah narrative suggests. Their work was opening the door to restoring a sense of women's presence at the most important moments of our history and in our most sacred text. In various settings and circumstances, these individuals were beginning to add to and expand Torah.

I was awed and overwhelmed by the scholarship and creative work going on in all parts of the Jewish world. However, I realized that there was no organized, cohesive way in which to access this groundbreaking work. It occurred to me that the time had come to gather the best minds of our generation, to apply all that they had researched and discovered, all that they could now interpret and imagine, to create an egalitarian commentary to the Torah, a volume that would allow women, as well as men, to find themselves in the pages of the sacred text of our people.

I first issued the charge at the 1992 District 3 NFTS convention and repeated it at the NFTS National Biennial Assembly in San Francisco in 1993. The *Commentary* you now hold in your hands is WRJ's response to that challenge. What follows is an excerpt from my presentation, "Sarah's Hidden Voice: Recovering and Discovering Women's Spirituality":

"In every generation, our people have turned to the Torah to seek answers to their needs, their problems, their contemporary challenges. We are here today, in large measure, because the Torah has yielded meaning and truth to every generation that has sought its wisdom. We can do no less. It is our responsibility to make this book live for us. As men have done throughout the centuries, we must stretch the words, we must invest them with our needs and our imagination. We must struggle with the plain sense of stories, laws, and attitudes that exclude, de-value, and indict women. We must incorporate women's history and women's experience as part of the living memory of the Jewish people.

"The past fifteen years have seen an explosion of scholarship and creative work that will help us do this.... The work that feminist scholars are doing is changing our assumptions and conceptions of the world out of which Judaism emerged.... What is so important about this understanding is that it gives us a sense that there is much to uncover and recover in our history that speaks to us directly as women and restores to us a sense of our presence in and at the most important moments in our history. This insight also encourages us to proceed with this process of adding to and expanding Torah, of building upon the intimations that peek through the patriarchal gloss of the text, of prodding our communal memory and inventing what we have forgotten, of remembering and inventing together in order to recover the hidden half of Torah, reshape Jewish memory, and allow women to speak. [See Judith Plaskow, *Standing Again at Sinai*, 1990, p. 56, who quotes Monique Wittig's novel *Les Guerilleres*: "You say you have lost all recollection of it, remember.... Make an effort to remember. Or, failing that, invent."] . . .

"I present this final charge to you not as a theoretical proposal of something women ideally ought to do and somehow will be accomplished 'out there' by women rabbis and scholars. I present this idea of re-claiming Torah as a very specific proposal to this great gathering of Jewish women, to this unique organization dedicated to the spiritual life and religious empowerment of Reform Jewish women. If we are really serious about women's spirituality, about re-claiming our history and our voices, about liberating the concepts of God and community, of integrating the Torah of our tradition into the Torah of our lives [a concept that I learned from Rabbi Laura Geller], then there is something very concrete that we can do. We can commission the creation of the first women's commentary to the Torah!"

Since my first encounter with Women of Reform Judaism in 1979 (when they were still NFTS), I have been awed by the power of this organization and the ability of the women who lead it. I am profoundly grateful to every member of WRJ for undertaking this project with courage and resolve, with an understanding of its potential to transform our tradition, with willingness to embrace a dream and make it a reality. Working together, women have funded, designed, researched, written, edited, and critiqued this unprecedented volume. We have done all of this in historic fashion: a woman's voice inspired a community of women to undertake this project in which women scholars, rabbis, cantors, teachers and poets bring their voices, their unique perspective to the ancient text of our overwhelmingly patriarchal tradition. This extraordinary volume, the result of the efforts of so many, is a veritable symphony of women's voices—beautiful, powerful, inspirational, transformative.

As we open these pages, with excitement and anticipation, we hear the sound of Sarah's laughter, triumphant: "My daughters have discovered me, my children have given me new life and new hope. I am reborn for a future as infinite and as radiant as the stars in the heavens of God's promise to Abraham and me, to Isaac and Rebecca, to Jacob, Rachel, and Leah, and to *all* of our descendants."

*Kein y'hi ratzon*—may this be God's desire!

—*Sarah Sager*

# Acknowledgments

THE TORAH: A WOMEN'S COMMENTARY has been a labor of love for the many women associated with this project from its inception to publication. Those of us who are fortunate to have been a part of the process in any way know that we are indeed blessed to have had this opportunity. Special thanks must go to Rosanne Selfon, WRJ President, who has steadfastly and selflessly worked to ensure the funding for *The Torah: A Women's Commentary.* The dedication of all involved in this publication will leave a lasting impact on our daughters and granddaughters, sons and grandsons, and all future generations.

—*Shelley Lindauer*
Executive Director
Women of Reform Judaism

I DEDICATED THIS WORK with love to my children and grandchildren who are both the source and the reason for this *Commentary*: Willa Eskenazi, Kay Eskenazi, Joanne Cohn with Martin and Alex White; Naomi, Michael, Erika, and Nicole Eskenazi; Devon, David, Miranda, and Jeremy Cohn. I also dedicate the book with love and gratitude to the late David Eskenazi and Bill Whedbee, from whom I learned *torah* in its fullest sense; to the memory of Howie Cohn; and to my fabulous sister Sylvia Wildenstein and dear friends for their unfailing support (especially Rachel Adler, Annette Aronowicz, Eleanore Judd, Barbara Lehman, Marilyn Levy, Evely Shlensky, and Sheila Teitlebaum). Many thanks to my colleagues and students at Hebrew Union College, Los Angeles, who were involved (sometimes unknowingly) in this enterprise. Finally, I thank my friend and colleague, the amazing Andrea Weiss, for being a peerless partner in this enterprise; Hara Person, for wisely, skillfully, and cheerfully navigating all of us; David Stein, for his devotion to the text and to its interpreters; Barbara Koppel, for going well beyond the call of duty; and the splendid Editorial Board for reading and re-reading (especially Carol Meyers, who helped with the large biblical entries). This remarkable team, together with the contributors to the *Commentary*, made this project a joyous and inspiring dialogue.

—*Tamara Cohn Eskenazi*

MY EDITING OF THE COMMENTARY was enhanced by the feedback of many individuals who studied drafts of this material, in particular the members of the Beth David Torah study class (Susan Dein Bricklin, Dinah Engel, Lynne Glasser, Anita Lichtenberg, Francine Pearlman-Storch, Stacey Polan, Val Rossman, Roberta Ruvin, Lynn Scott, Nancy Streim) and my Fall 2006 elective at the Hebrew Union College–Jewish Institute of Religion in New York (Debra Bennet, Heather Borshof, Jesse Gallop, Shira Ginsburg, Alissa Goodkin, Zoe Jacobs, Marcy Kadin, Sharon Kunitz, Katie Oringel, Daniel Sikowitz, Jill Perlman, Jennifer Strauss-Klein). I thank all of my students and colleagues at HUC–JIR, New York, for the many ways they contributed to the completion of this volume. I am grateful to have worked with and learned from the many contributors and editors of this *Commentary*, especially my cherished teacher and mentor Tamara Eskenazi, as well as Carol Meyers, Hara Person, David Stein, and Barbara Koppel. Finally, I could not have devoted the time this project required without the help of three wonderful au pairs

(Lisa Kornhauser, Ana Bakija, Einav Margalit) and the love and support of my husband, Alan Tauber, and our children, Rebecca and Ilan Tauber, to whom I dedicate this *Commentary*.

*—Andrea L. Weiss*

IN ADDITION TO the individuals mentioned in the *Preface* and above, there are many others who are deserving of recognition and thanks. Significant early support for this project came from Rabbi Danny Freelander. Thanks also to the URJ Business Board, Mort Finkelstein, Jane Aronoff, Austin Beutel, Myrna Beyer, Allan Hirsh III, Bob Koppel, Anne Molloy, and Gary Weinberger, as well as URJ colleagues Rabbi Elliot Kleinman, Rabbi Sue Ann Wasserman, Emily Grotta, and Donny Cohen-Cutler. Thanks go to all the congregations who participated in the pilot *Chayei Sarah* Study Shabbat in November 2006. I am also indebted to my colleagues from the Women's Rabbinic Network who allowed us to study with them and provided helpful feedback at the 2007 WRN conference. Thanks also to Dr. Phil Miller at HUC–JIR in New York, Rabbi Debra Hachen, Rabbi Micky Boyden, Rabbi Bill Cutter, Jessica Greenbaum, Clare Kinberg, Chana Bloch, and Linda Zisquit.

My colleagues at the URJ Press all lent their considerable individual talents and enthusiasm to make this project a reality, including Debra Hirsch Corman, Ben Farber, Leah Barak, and Amy Nichols. In addition to the whole staff's overall support and dedication, special thanks to Victor Ney and Zack Kolstein who share my passion for this project and generously provided their financial and marketing acumen, Ron Ghatan for valiantly taking on various aspects of production, Chris Aguero for keeping on top of the printing and paper issues, Michael Silber for handling some design issues and creating a beautiful cover, and Rebecca Baer for tackling the Voices permissions and bio process started by Elizabeth Gutterman. We were also helped by dedicated rabbinic interns: Jocee Hudson (Voices), Leah Berkowitz (Voices), Cari Bricklin (cross-references), Owen Gottlieb (About the Authors, and the Bibliography), and Judith Bacharach (About the Voices Contributors).

A special pleasure during the development of this book was the opportunity to study excerpts from it with the Women's Study Group of the Brooklyn Heights Synagogue, namely Jessica Brown, Susan Chadick, Fran Gottfried, Ida Gutterman, Randi Jaffe, Karen Moshman, Robbin Slade, and Carol Ziegler. The encouragement of Rabbi Serge Lippe is also deeply appreciated.

Working on this book was a delight and a pleasure in no small part because of the opportunity to work closely with and learn from Tamara Eskenazi, Andrea Weiss, Sue Levi Elwell, Sherry Blumberg, Barbara Koppel, and David Stein, as well as the whole Editorial Board. I continue to be inspired by the vision and tenacity of Shelley Lindauer and Rosanne Selfon. Most of all, heartfelt thanks and love to Diane Person, Jenni Person, and Chaim Lieberperson, and especially to Yigal, Liya, and Yoni Rechtman for understanding and patience way beyond the call of duty.

*—Hara E. Person*

MY THANKS GO to Rabbi Me'irah Iliinsky, whose illustrations have given this book a special sparkle, and to Emily Law (proofreader), Leslie Rubin (associate copy editor, and indexer), and Joysa Winter (proofreader), as well as the first-rate team at El Ot (compositors).

*—David E. S. Stein*

# Introduction: About This Book

The book of Proverbs, a collection of wisdom texts ascribed to King Solomon, instructs its audience: "Keep your father's commandments, / And do not forsake your mother's *torah* (teaching, wisdom)" (6:20; similarly 1:8). From the biblical period onward, women have played important roles in transmitting Jewish teachings, values, and practices; however, until recently, little of this wisdom has been preserved in written form. *The Torah: A Women's Commentary* collects and showcases the teachings of Jewish women in the first comprehensive commentary on the Torah written entirely by women.

This *Commentary* examines the entirety of the Torah, yet it focuses most sharply on women in the Torah and on texts particularly relevant to women's lives. In this volume, biblical scholars illustrate what the Torah probably meant in its own cultural milieu and literary context. Then, scholars of rabbinic Judaism, Jewish thought, and other academic disciplines, along with clergy and other Jewish professionals, augment the exegesis (interpretation) of the biblical text to show how the Torah continues to have new meanings for later generations.

### Our Guiding Principles

From its inception, *The Torah: A Women's Commentary* was envisioned as a contemporary Torah commentary written by Jewish women. Three words reflect our guiding principles: contemporary, Jewish, and women.

*Contemporary:* In this *Commentary*, distinguished women scholars, clergy, and poets illumine the meanings of the Torah by using both traditional tools and innovative approaches. Our authors bring new insights and new questions to our sacred tradition, all the while placing their words within the ongoing stream of Jewish interpretation. Our scholars apply contemporary scholarly approaches—such as literary analysis, historical criticism, comparative linguistics, philology, archeology, anthropology, and sociology—to clarify and interpret the Torah, thus helping to show what the text meant to its own early audience and what it can teach us today. Particularly in the "Contemporary Reflection" and "Voices" sections, our contributors regularly address issues of concern in the 21st century and explore how this ancient text connects to our modern lives.

> *"Do not forsake your mother's torah."*
> —*Proverbs 6:20*

*Jewish:* Judaism can be seen as an ongoing dialogue between ever-changing circumstances and Jewish texts invested with enduring authority. This is especially true with respect to our most sacred text, the Torah. The Torah has always been central to the life of the Jewish people. It is embedded within a wide web of interpretations, written and oral, that provided guidance for how to understand it in new contexts. As the Rabbis of the Talmud wisely note, each generation produces its own interpreters (BT *Avodah Zarah* 5a). We have brought together interpreters for the 21st century, so that the voices of the entire Jewish people at last would be fully represented.

One of the many things that make this book a distinctly Jewish commentary is that it follows the centuries-old liturgical division of the Torah into 54 portions. Long before computers and the Internet, Jews were connected through a World Wide Web of sorts, based on the division of the Torah into weekly readings so that the complete Torah—Genesis through Deuteronomy—is read sequentially each year. To this day, Jews in Melbourne, Manhattan, or Marrakech share the same story by reading the same weekly Torah portion (*parashah* in Hebrew) in the synagogue. Jewish communities may differ as to which sections of the parashah they read or discuss, what they say about it, or how they apply the Torah to their lives, but this sacred text unites us.

One of the hallmarks of Jewish interpretation is that it embraces a range of approaches and viewpoints, preserving a diversity of voices. Our *Commentary* emulates the style of the *Mikraot G'dolot* (also called the Rabbinic Bible), a popular format for Jewish Bible commentary since the 16th century. In such a work, the text of the entire Torah is accompanied by a translation and by running commentaries from a variety of sages who interpreted the text for their own generation. In our *Commentary*, however, we have replaced the classic Aramaic translation with an English translation (described below), and the sages are all women.

Another feature that makes this a Jewish commentary is that our contributors represent the full spectrum of the Jewish community: in addition to Reform, we include Conservative, Orthodox, and Reconstructionist scholars as well as unaffiliated and secular ones. We invited clergy and academics from diverse streams of Jewish life so that the work can speak on behalf of *klal Israel*, "the entirety of the Jewish people." Our writers span the globe, hailing from North America, South America, Europe, and Israel.

*Women:* The distinguishing feature of this commentary is that it is written entirely by women. In the past, commentaries by learned men spoke on behalf of our people, even when they did not represent the insights of women. By providing commentary authored by women, we expect to represent the wider community, with qualified women interpreters who illuminate much that has been overlooked. In doing so, we are bringing women out of the shadows—the women in the text as well as the women in the Jewish world.

We deliberately sought to cast as wide a net as possible to show how women trained in various aspects of Bible and Jewish studies are thinking about the Torah on the basis of their professional training. Our commentators include academics, rabbis, cantors, educators, and poets, all of whom offer different lenses though which to view the biblical text. Their commentaries show how women's experiences can shed light both on the text of the Torah and the *torah* of our lives.

This book could not have been written fifty or even twenty years ago. We are fortunate to have in the present generation, at last, hundreds of qualified women whose teaching and insights are having a profound influence on our evolving understanding of the Torah. While we bring together the work of one hundred writers (not including the Voices sections), we are fully aware of the many gifted women who are not included in this volume.

In the course of compiling and editing this *Commentary*, we were repeatedly asked why we include only women commentators. Even after much deliberation, we could not see a way of inviting male colleagues without having their voices be mere tokens. We concluded that this would not adequately represent men's scholarship, and also it would detract from giving women a full representation. Although we invited only women contributors, we draw upon the work of all scholars—women and men, Jewish and non-Jewish—many of whom do not appear in these pages by name but who are indispensable to any study of the Torah.

### *Gender and the Translation of the Torah*

One issue about which there was unanimous agreement from the start was the importance of including both the complete Hebrew text of the Torah and an English translation. But which translation would we use? The endeavor of translating the Bible into one's everyday language began centuries before the Common Era. Jewish communities of the time used and transmitted versions of the Torah in Greek (referred to as the Septuagint) and in Aramaic (referred to as Targum), which are still studied today. The best known early English translation of the Bible (the King James Version), which relied at times upon rabbinic commentaries, dates to the 17th century and in turn it has influenced a variety of Jewish translations. Today the most widely used translation in liberal circles is the New Jewish Publication Society (NJPS) version.

The art of translation has always been challenging. For us, gendered language posed yet an additional challenge. Although some Christian "gender sensitive" or "gender neutral" Bibles have been published since the mid-1980s, the only comparable Jewish translation first appeared in 2005, when the URJ Press published a revised edition of *The Torah: A Modern Commentary* (edited by W. Gunther Plaut). We have incorporated the 2006 version of that URJ translation, with some minor modifications, in *The Torah: A Women's Commentary.*

The URJ translation combines the work of two translators. The late Rabbi Chaim Stern prepared a fresh translation of Genesis. Following his death in 2001, Rabbi David Stein stepped in as revising translator for Exodus through Deuteronomy, creating an updated and "gender-accurate" version of the NJPS translation.

The most innovative aspect of Stern's translation is its gender-neutral treatment of language for God. Consider first the divine name composed of four Hebrew consonants (י-ה-ו-ה) and referred to as the tetragrammaton (see at Genesis 2:4 and Exodus 3:15). It has been typically translated since antiquity as forms of the word "Lord" (becoming "the LORD" in the King James Version and elsewhere, such as NJPS). In Jewish circles, God's name has been read aloud in the synagogue using the substitution *Adonai,* the Hebrew word for "Lord" or "Lords"; some Jewish translations substitute the word "*Hashem*" (meaning "the Name") instead. However, Stern rendered God's name as "the Eternal," a choice that dates back to Moses Mendelssohn's 1783 translation of the Torah into German, and one that reflects a biblical understanding of this divine name as related to the Hebrew verb "to be."

In the present translation, we decided not to translate God's name at all, but to preserve it the way the Torah itself does, using the same four Hebrew letters. Every instance of the ineffable name thus poses a challenge; in this way, we encourage our readers to share in the struggle with how we address the Divine.

The Hebrew Bible typically uses masculine verb forms, adjectives, and pronouns when referring to God; and customarily such language is mechanically reproduced in English. Therefore, speaking about God in a gender-neutral way requires making adjustments not only to God's name, but also to all related wording. In his translation, Stern resorted to a variety of techniques, such as recasting sentences to avoid the need for pronouns, replacing "He" with "[God]" and "His" with "[God's]," and the like. Like German and French—but unlike English—Hebrew is a gender-inflected language. That is, all Hebrew nouns grammatically are either masculine or feminine; no neutral form exists. Even inanimate objects (like a chair or a table) are assigned a grammatical gender; however, there is no fixed correlation between the grammatical gender of a noun and its social gender (or biological reality). In the Bible, God is referred to in masculine language. This raises the question: Does this grammatically masculine language mean that the Torah depicts God as a male deity? While some scholars answer this question in the affirmative, others argue that the God of the Torah is implicitly beyond the biological categories that distinguish female and male; God is "beyond gender" (see at Deuteronomy 33:5).

Even if ancient Israelites imagined Israel's God primarily as male, the Torah and the rest of the Hebrew Bible do enable readers to understand God in gender-inclusive terms. Support for thinking about God not only in masculine terms comes in part from the metaphors that depict Israel's God. The biblical writers sometimes refer to God using male imagery: for example, as a warrior (see at Exodus 15:3), father (see at Deuteronomy 32:6), or king (see at Deuteronomy 33:5). But biblical texts also portray God with female imagery, as one who gives birth (see at Numbers 11:12; Deuteronomy 32:13, 18; Exodus 15:22–17:16; 15:26). In addition, they utilize animals and inanimate objects to characterize God as, for instance, an eagle (see at Exodus 19:4; Deuteronomy 32:11) or a rock (see at Deuteronomy 32:4)—none of which is to be taken literally. We find an even greater array of divine metaphors outside of the Torah, which suggests that the gender of a particular image does not correlate to the perceptions of Israel's God.

Different questions emerge when translating the Torah's references to human beings. When a verse uses masculine language, is it exclusively addressing or speaking about men? When does that grammatical form refer to women and men alike? Furthermore, when do Hebrew personal nouns like *ish* or *adam*, often rendered as "man" in older translations, refer specifically to men, or to both men and women?

As Stein set about adapting the NJPS translation of Exodus through Deuteronomy, he needed to interpret how certain grammatical forms and vocabulary were operating in each instance. Stein examined the text methodically in light of the most up-to-date conclusions about the way the Hebrew language operates in the Torah, and about the roles that women and men played in ancient Israel. He did so by drawing on published research as well as by conducting extensive correspondence with leading biblical scholars. Readers of *The Torah: A Women's Commentary* will become more familiar with how the resulting translation functions when they read the Central Commentary, for numerous comments explain—and sometimes challenge—Stein's impressive achievement in biblical translation and biblical scholarship.

The URJ calls its translation a "gender accurate" translation, not a "gender neutral" or "gender sensitive" version. In other words, it does not render all grammatically masculine language in gender-inclusive terms but instead attempts to convey what was meant in a given context. For example, it sometimes translates the word *avot* as "fathers" and sometimes as "ancestors," depending whether that Hebrew noun functions inclusively or not in that particular passage (for instance, see at Deuteronomy 7:12). Likewise in regard to personal nouns such as *ish*: sometimes the translation construes this noun in a gender-inclusive sense (see at Exodus 21:7), but elsewhere as referring specifically to a man (see at Deuteronomy 8:5).

For more on the URJ's Torah translation, see Stein, "Preface to the Revised Edition," in *The Torah: A Modern Commentary*, 2005, p. xxv–xxxi; and "Preface," *The Contemporary Torah*, 2006, pp. v–xxxv.

### *The Five Components of the Commentary*

In selecting the more than one hundred contributors for the *Commentary*, the Editorial Board resisted the temptation to let a single type of voice dominate the interpretation of the Torah. The editors, in turn, aimed to achieve consistency only insofar as it would facilitate readers' use of the commentary; the particular ideas and styles remain those of the individual authors. On occasion, the editors have inserted a note in square brackets (like this: [ —*Ed.*]) either to supplement the commentator's work or to juxtapose a different opinion. We consider the act of preserving a multiplicity of voices not only a defining feature of the Jewish interpretive tradition, but also an explicit feminist endeavor.

The multi-vocal nature of this commentary is also evident from the five elements that address each Torah portion in turn:

*Central Commentary.* Written by a scholar of Bible, this section begins with an introduction and outline that provide an overview of the Torah portion. The commentary then accompanies the Hebrew text and the English translation, providing a running exegesis (explanation) of the parashah. Its main objective is to help readers understand the plain sense of the text in its own cultural context as well as in ours.

*Another View.* This short essay, also by a biblical scholar, focuses on a specific aspect of the parashah, in a way that supplements or challenges the Central Commentary.

*Post-biblical Interpretations.* In this section, a scholar of rabbinic literature discusses a selection of past responses to the Torah—typically, rabbinic teachings and classical commentaries. (See Women and Post-biblical Commentary, p. xlix.)

*Contemporary Reflection.* In this section, an author—a scholar of contemporary Jewish thought and life, rabbi, cantor, or educator—reflects on the parashah and what meanings it holds for Jews today. (See Women and Contemporary Revelation, p. lvi.)

*Voices.* This section contains creative responses to the parashah, mainly in the form of poetry. (See The Poetry of Torah and the Torah of Poetry, p. lx.)

At times different parts of the *Commentary* treat similar topics, or they approach the same topic from divergent standpoints—just as various biblical verses interrelate. Therefore the commentary frequently includes cross-references that enable the reader to engage more deeply in the study of the Torah. By looking up a cross-reference, a reader can examine how related biblical passages compare and contrast, and explore texts in other parts of the Bible. The reader can also trace the evidence that leads an interpreter to draw a certain conclusion, and weigh the author's opinion against divergent views elsewhere in the book. When the notation "see" precedes a biblical citation, it points to a passage in the text itself, whereas the notation "see at" refers to the commentary on that cited passage.

Another convention in the commentary similarly reflects the many levels on which it treats the text: the occasional use of a vertical line (|) between sentences. This indicates the start of a new thought that is still based on the same lemma (the biblical passage being commented upon).

For more about this book, see its Web page online via www.urjbooksandmusic.com.

Space constraints required our contributors and editors to be highly selective. In general, the *Commentary* focuses on three aspects of the text: that which relates to women, that which is obscure to contemporary readers (at least at first glance), and that which remains particularly significant for Jews today. Inevitably this means that not everything that flows from the inexhaustible fountain of wisdom we call Torah is included in this *Commentary.* We trust that what we have included will guide new as well as seasoned readers of the Torah as they explore the sacred texts of our tradition.

—*Tamara Cohn Eskenazi*
*Andrea L. Weiss*

# *Women and Interpretation of the Torah*

THE WORD *torah*, or "teaching," can mean different things in different contexts. In Proverbs 6:20, which states "do not forsake your mother's *torah*," the term denotes human wisdom in general. Elsewhere in the Bible, the word refers to particular divine precepts (see Exodus 13:9), certain priestly instructions (see at Leviticus 6:2), or the core of the book of Deuteronomy (see at Deuteronomy 31:9).

While in the Bible the word *torah* (translated variously as "Teaching," "Instruction," "ritual," or "Law") refers to a number of different kinds of teachings, in time "*the* Torah" came to mean the books of Genesis, Exodus, Leviticus, Numbers, and Deuteronomy (in Hebrew: *B'reishit*, *Sh'mot*, *Vayikra*, *B'midbar*, and *D'varim*). Together, those five books constitute the first of the three parts of the Jewish Scriptures, or the Hebrew Bible, namely: Torah, Prophets, and Writings (or *Torah*, *N'viim*, and *K'tuvim*, which combine to produce an acronym that is pronounced *Tanach*). A common Jewish name for any published volume of the Torah is *Chumash*, which is related to the Hebrew word for "five." The term "Pentateuch" (from the Greek word for "five") is commonly used as well, especially in scholarly circles.

The word "Torah," then, refers to the foundation of authoritative teachings in Judaism and the repository of God's teachings for Israel. From antiquity, Jewish (and subsequently Christian) traditions typically considered the Torah—in the sense of the first five books of the Bible—to have been written by Moses and to represent a record of God's words to Moses; hence the customary reference to "the Five Books of Moses." However, this title is misleading, because nothing in the Torah claims that Moses wrote the entire collection. Genesis and Exodus mention no author; and although most of Leviticus and major parts of Exodus and Numbers purport to represent God's words to Moses or Israel, only Deuteronomy claims to quote Moses extensively and states that he wrote those sections.

Some Rabbis noted early on that certain statements in the Torah could not have been written by Moses (such as the report about his death in Deuteronomy 34). Nevertheless, a widespread presumption that Moses wrote the whole Torah at God's dictation prevailed until the modern era.

In the modern era, academic scholars began to challenge the view of the Torah as the unified work of Moses. The theory that became most widely accepted in scholarly circles, beginning in the 19th century, claims that the Torah is composed of four major sources that were combined gradually over many centuries. In general, this "Documentary Hypothesis" (associated with the German biblical scholar Julius Wellhausen) posits that the source labeled "J" (or "Yahwist," marked by the prominence of God's name, *YHVH*) was the earliest (10th or 9th century B.C.E.) and represented the interests and traditions of the kingdom of Judah. (Prior to that time traditions were transmitted orally.) Source "E" (or "Elohist," distinguished by its preference for referring to God as Elohim) represented northern traditions, that is, the kingdom of Israel, from about a century later. Source "D" (or "Deuteronomist") refers primarily to the book of Deuteronomy, a work that becomes influential in the 7th century B.C.E. Finally, the "P" (or "Priestly") source represented the concerns of the priests from the period when Israel was exiled in Babylon or shortly after, in the post-exilic period of the 6th to 5th centuries B.C.E.

Proponents of the Documentary Hypothesis describe the particular literary characteristics and concerns of each source; and some have sought to identify the actual authors as well. Harold Bloom and David Rosenberg speculated that the author of J was in fact a woman living in King David's court (*The Book of J*, 1990), an idea that Richard Friedman first proposed in *Who Wrote the Bible?* (1987, p. 86). However, the speculation that J was a woman has not been widely accepted for a number of reasons. First, while the idea that women had a role in the composition of the Torah (or other parts of the Bible) remains theoretically possible, the very notion of a single individual author of J is no longer accepted. Second, Bloom's criteria for what he identifies as a woman's voice are highly flawed (even sexist). Third, as scholars in a variety of fields demonstrate, identifying the gender of an author even in a modern setting is extremely difficult; how much more so in an ancient setting when we have no supporting evidence! Therefore, most scholars question our ability to recover such precise information about the origins of the sources.

The Documentary Hypothesis maintains that the entire Torah as we know it only came into being in the 5th century B.C.E. with the work of Ezra the priest and scribe. Nehemiah 8 depicts the dramatic moment when Ezra reads the book of the Torah (*sefer ha-torah*) in Jerusalem in the presence of all the people, "men and women and all who could listen with understanding" (8:2). Some regard the enthusiastic affirmation of the Torah by the entire community at the time of Ezra as a "second Sinai." For many scholars, this moment represents the time that the Torah was finally complete.

Many aspects of the Documentary Hypothesis no longer represent scholarly consensus; others remain influential. Its enduring contribution is the claim that the Torah is the fruit of a long process and contains diverse sources, often shaped by responses to new crises. This conclusion continues to be important and often guides scholarly interpretation, but along lines that differ from the Documentary Hypothesis itself. Moreover, two of the sources, J and E, no longer seem to be widely recognized. References to P, the distinctive priestly traditions, remain useful insofar as such material has a coherent world view (as in Genesis 1) and often focuses on the sanctuary and its personnel, as well as on genealogies. But some scholars now distinguish between two types of priestly writings: one priestly school labeled "P" and another whose work is referred to as "H" (for the Holiness Code; see the introduction to Leviticus 19:1–37, p. 703).

Deuteronomy seems to have a separate history. For the purpose of this *Commentary* the discovery of the "book of the Torah," which scholars equate with Deuteronomy, is particularly relevant. According to II Kings 22:8–20 (also II Chronicles 34:14–30), a book of the *torah* (*sefer ha-torah*) is found in the Temple during the course of renovations (at about 622 B.C.E.). When the king hears the book's messages, he instructs his highest officials: "Go, inquire of יהוה . . . concerning the words of this scroll that has been found" (II Kings 22:13). The commissioned leaders then go to the prophet Huldah, wife of Shallum, who is sitting at the Mishneh section in Jerusalem. (The so-called Huldah Gates at the Temple's southern wall excavation in today's Jerusalem are named after her, probably because of a tradition that placed her in this location.) Huldah responds to the delegation by confirming the authenticity of the book's messages. Her authority goes unchallenged. According to II Kings, her authentication of the book leads King Josiah to undertake major reforms. Since these reforms conform to Deuteronomy's laws and not other biblical texts, many scholars maintain that the "book of the *torah*" found and implemented is actually a version of Deuteronomy. References in Deuteronomy to a *torah* written by Moses further strengthen this conclusion. If so, then this major book of the Torah assumed a prominent place in Israel's sacred tradition because Huldah affirmed its reliability.

* * *

For most of its history, Jewish interpretation of sacred texts did not represent the knowledge and insights of women, for authoritative interpretation long remained the domain of men. (See "Women and Post-biblical Commentary," p. xlix.) A notable change—a landmark, really—can be found with the work of the English writer Grace Aguilar (1816–1847). Prior to her death at age 31, she wrote and published essays, novels, and poetry. Her magisterial book on women in the Bible and the Talmud (576 pages) was published in 1845, preceding by fifty years the celebrated *Woman's Bible* of Elizabeth Cady Stanton, a work usually credited as the first feminist interpretation of the Bible. The full title of Aguilar's book amply describes her goals: *The Women of Israel or Characters and Sketches from the Holy Scriptures and Jewish History Illustrative of the Past History, Present Duty, and Future Destiny of the Hebrew Females, as Based on the Word of God.*

An English Jew of Converso/Spanish descent, Aguilar considered it her special task to encourage Jews, especially women, to go back to the Bible for sources of Jewish identity. She explicitly wanted to counter two troublesome issues: first, the view expressed in her time that "Christianity was the sole source of female excellence"; and second, the allegations that the Hebrew Bible shows how "the law of Moses sunk the Hebrew female to the lowest state of degradation." Although Aguilar's book is not technically a commentary, it examines all the major women in the Bible and also lingers on minor characters and obscure references to women. She hardly misses a note. For instance, she discusses the female workers of the Tabernacle (Exodus 38:8), Caleb's daughter Achsah (Joshua 15:16–19; Judges 1:10–15), and laws concerning wives, widows, and female servants.

Aguilar cites the story about the Israelite slave girl who directs the foreigner Naaman to the prophet Elisha (II Kings 5) to advocate the training of Jewish women of all classes. After all, she argues, even lower-class women, such as this Israelite servant, were obviously educated religiously in ancient Israel! In her discussion of this episode as well as others, Aguilar's attention to issues of class, religion, and gender is impressive and comports well with insights that are rediscovered today.

> *In the last forty years, Jewish women have become truly visible as biblical interpreters.*

Aguilar was probably not the first Jewish woman to engage in the study of the Bible in a publicly influential way. From the Middle Ages, there is evidence of women scribes who copied biblical manuscripts, and some interpreters have suggested that Rashi's daughters were important transmitters of his teachings. In addition, we know that in 1288, Paula Dei Mansi of Verona translated her father's Bible commentaries from Hebrew into Italian, adding her own explanations as well (see *JPS Guide to Jewish Women*, 2003, p. 111). But Aguilar is the first whose work is fully preserved and boldly made an impact.

In recent years, a book in Yiddish known as *Tzenah U-r'enah* (alternatively transliterated as *Tsenerene*, "Go Out and See") has been touted as the first "feminist" Bible. The title alludes to the charge to women to go out and see (Song of Songs 3:11), thus suggesting that the intended audience was female; moreover the interpretations focus heavily on women. The book is a retelling of biblical tales. However, although the book frequently highlights stories concerning women, it cannot be claimed as an early feminist work or a "women's Bible." It aims to transmit and popularize selected traditional rabbinic teachings, and its author-compiler-translator was Rabbi Yaakov son of Isaac Ashkenazi, not a woman interpreter. Still, first published in the 16th century, this book became the most popular written source of Bible stories for the next two centuries, and it brought female characters in the Bible to the attention of generations of women and men who did not have access to texts in Hebrew.

Also from the Middle Ages there is evidence that Jewishly educated women in some prominent, learned families led other women in prayer and taught them songs and biblical passages; some wrote commentaries that were circulated privately among the family members but for reasons of modesty were not published.

Only since the last third of the 20th century, however, have Jewish women become truly visible in both the academic arena of biblical scholarship and in specifically Jewish circles. One need mention only Nehama Leibowitz and Sara Japhet—two Israeli scholars of unrivaled international reputation—to realize the great contribution that Jewish women have began to make to biblical studies. The late Nehama Leibowitz, widely acclaimed as one of the foremost Bible teachers in Israel, brought together classical rabbinic sources and traditional Jewish commentaries to help her students delve into Torah study (see her *Studies in Bereshit–Devarim*, 1976–1993). Sara Japhet's impeccable biblical scholarship, especially her work on Chronicles and the Restoration Period, proved a milestone in the field of biblical studies, as recognized by the prestigious Israel Prize she was awarded in 2004. The impact of their work demonstrated the unquestionable quality and value of women's contribution to biblical studies and thereby opened the door for subsequent to women scholars.

Neither Leibowitz nor Japhet identifies herself—or her approach—explicitly as feminist. Other scholars, such as the Israeli scholar Athalya Brenner, who edited 19 volumes of the *Feminist Companion to the Bible* (1993–2001), write as feminists but do not typically identify a specific Jewish agenda. Some, like the late Tikva Frymer-Kensky, explicitly combine both feminist and Jewish perspectives. The contributors to this *Commentary* reflect these different approaches and others as well.

Feminist scholars also vary in their perception of the Bible's presentation of women and women's interests. The first influential feminist study of the Bible in the late 20th century was "Depatriarchalizing in Biblical Interpretation" by the Protestant scholar Phyllis Trible (1973). Trible argues that key biblical texts do not promote patriarchal subordination of women but that later (mis)interpretations of them imposed such meanings on the Bible. She uses a literary approach that has since become widespread in biblical scholarship as a whole, influencing Jewish and feminist studies. The Jewish scholar Carol Meyers has employed a different approach to feminist scholarship, using her expertise in Bible and in archeology. Her groundbreaking work (which began in 1978 with "Roots of Restriction" and includes *Discovering Eve: Israelite Woman in Context*, 1988) incorporates social-scientific methodologies in order to uncover the roles and status of women in ancient Israel (see her introduction "Women in Ancient Israel—An Overview," p. xli). Her research suggests that in many respects the Bible reflects a high regard for women. Indeed, some interpreters argue that the Bible should be lauded as a resource for feminism and for women in general. In contrast, others argue that the Bible is detrimental to women and is best disregarded or opposed as a resource for women. In between these two perspectives, one finds a spectrum of views that acknowledge some problems in the Bible when it comes to the depiction and treatment of women and offer an array of responses for addressing those problems. (For a good survey of such positions, see

Alice Ogden Bellis, *Helpmates, Harlots, and Heroes: Women's Stories in the Hebrew Bible*, 1994.)

Interpreters of the Bible for whom this text carries defining authority, Jews and non-Jews alike, have developed a number of ways of responding to the seeming tension between feminist concerns and the Bible. In facing certain problematic passages, some interpreters hold the major messages of the Bible as key for determining the text's authority; that is, central teachings are given greater weight over peripheral ones. For example, the story of the Exodus illustrates that God opposes the oppression of Israelites. Given that the Exodus story is foundational to Israel's identity, those biblical teachings that conflict with the message of the Exodus by calling for the oppression of members of society are considered less authoritative. Thus, the command to love the resident alien because of the experience of slavery in Egypt (Leviticus 19:33–34) is used to challenge teachings elsewhere that disadvantage non-Israelites.

When confronting various troubling texts, some interpreters place the Bible in its own historical context and evaluate its perspectives in light of the ancient world to which the Bible responds. This approach thus distances those teachings from contemporary circumstances in which they may no longer seem to make sense. For instance, comparisons with other ancient Near Eastern legal collections provide perspective on the numerous laws about slavery in the Bible (see at Exodus 21:2–11). Likewise, evidence about surrogate motherhood in the ancient Near East helps the reader understand Sarah's attempt to have a child through her handmaid and her subsequent treatment of Hagar (see at Genesis 16:1–6).

Others use contemporary modern or postmodern values to prioritize women's experiences as a criterion to adjudicate between teachings that deserve allegiance and those that do not. Such an approach means that the interpreter refuses to grant authority to teachings that appear to degrade women or other persons. (See, for example, how Judith Plaskow responds to certain laws about sexuality and sanctity in her Contemporary Reflection on *parashat Acharei Mot*, p. 696.)

In reproducing the variety of Torah interpretations, past and present, we envision our readers joining the centuries-old dialogue through their own personal and communal study. We hope that *The Torah: A Women's Commentary* will inspire and invigorate a lifelong exploration that will go beyond these pages and will shape women and men in our communities well into the future. In this way, all of us will rightly pay tribute, at last, to the *torah* of our mothers and fathers.

—*Tamara Cohn Eskenazi*

*Andrea L. Weiss*

# Women in Ancient Israel—An Overview

Because the Torah—the first five books of the Bible—is the center of Jewish liturgical life, our perception of Israelite women tends to be determined largely by what we read in the synagogue.* Yet women are mentioned throughout the Bible, and many passages in Prophets and Writings provide additional information about their lives. Still, the Bible alone is not a sufficient or adequate source for recovering the lives of Israelite women in the biblical period. For one thing, it deals more with national concerns and leaders than the lives of ordinary people; and even when addressing individuals, it focuses on the responsibilities and (mis)deeds of the male heads of the households in which most people lived. Men are thus mentioned far more often than are women. Moreover, much of the Bible originated in and reflects the urban setting of Jerusalem, whereas most Israelites lived in agrarian households in small villages or walled towns that were not true cities.

Fortunately, modern scholarship has been able to overcome many of these difficulties by using extra-biblical sources in addition to the biblical text. Archeological materials from Israelite sites—including dwellings, remnants of foodstuffs, tools and implements, tombs, jewelry, and ancient art—provide important data. Ethnographic studies of traditional cultures in the Middle East and elsewhere help us relate the archeological materials to various aspects of daily life in biblical antiquity. And anthropological models dealing with gender dynamics in premodern cultures allow us to understand the interactions of Israelite men and women and also the significance of women's roles. In addition, texts from other ancient Near Eastern cultures can supplement or illumine the information in biblical texts. All together, these sources provide a fuller and more accurate view of the women of ancient Israel than could be obtained by using the Bible alone.

*Evidence negates the stereotype that women were confined to the household.*

### *Marriage and Children*

The Hebrew noun *ishah* means both "woman" and "wife." This signals the fact that a woman's identity was virtually inseparable from her status as a married woman. It was inconceivable that a woman might willingly live on her own apart from a family; widows and divorcées often led precarious lives. Marriage was the norm for both women and men, but it was not usually the kind of love-based companionate relationship that is the ideal in the modern world (and in some biblical stories such as Rachel and Jacob in Genesis 29). Rather, it was a heterosexual pairing meant to provide offspring and thus assure generational continuity in the ownership of family land. The conjugal pair with their children would also constitute a work force sufficient to meet household needs in an agrarian society. In addition, adult children would be the ones

* This essay is a modified and abridged version of the biblical section of the entry "Woman," *Encyclopaedia Judaica*, 2nd edition, edited by Michael Berenbaum and Fred Skolnik (2007), Volume 21, pp. 156–161.

to care for aging parents. Having children was a non-negotiable necessity.

The Bible does not have a term for "marriage" as such. The term *chatan*, translated "groom," denotes a man with a father-in-law, thus indicating the conception of marriage as a union of two families. The Bible typically indicates the formation of a marital bond by saying that a man "takes" a woman. The courtship narrative of Rebekah, for example, culminates in the statement that Isaac "took Rebekah and she became his wife" (Genesis 24:67). This expression reflects the patrilocality of Israelite households. That is, a bride would move to the household of the groom, who usually continued to reside in the same household where he was raised. An extended family would thus be formed, although each constituent nuclear family might have its own abode within a family compound.

Financial arrangements generally accompanied marriage except among the poorest families. Although there are no "marriage laws" as such in the Bible, information in narratives indicates that a bride's family typically provided a dowry, usually consisting of moveable property such as jewelry, clothing, and household utensils. In wealthier families, livestock and servants might also be included (see Genesis 24:59; 29:24, 29); and the groom and his family could supplement it (Genesis 24:53). The dowry theoretically remained the possession of the woman for the duration of the marriage, although her husband sometimes may have had access to it.

Another marital payment was made by the groom's family to that of the bride. This betrothal gift, sometimes erroneously called "bride-price" (*mohar*; see Genesis 34:12; Exodus 22:15–16; I Samuel 18:25), has often been interpreted as evidence that a man purchased a woman. The fact that a word sometimes used for "husband" is *baal*, which can (but does not always) mean "master," has also been adduced to claim that a woman was the property of her husband. And the use of the verb *kanah*, which can mean "to buy" but more generally "to acquire," to describe Boaz's marriage to Ruth (Ruth 4:10) has been similarly interpreted.

However, anthropological analysis of these exchanges shows that such assertions are flawed. Instead, the dowry and betrothal gift are understood to function in overlapping ways to maintain the viability of a family. The betrothal gift would provide some compensation to a woman's family, which would lose the labor of a daughter upon her marriage. The dowry would constitute a woman's economic safety net in the event of widowhood or divorce, especially if she had no sons or if her father was deceased. Moreover, the two payments together served to establish and solidify alliances between a woman's natal family and her marital one. Such connections were important in agrarian communities; they increased the likelihood of mutual aid in the event of economic or other difficulties, not unusual in Israelite households living in marginal environments. Thus betrothal and dowry payments together had important economic, social, and legal functions.

To say that a husband did not own his wife is not to claim that there was equality between spouses. Perhaps the greatest gender asymmetry was in the area of sexuality. The patrilineal nature of Israelite society, with land and property transferred across generations via the male line, is likely the reason for the stringency of biblical legal precepts dealing with female sexuality. A woman's fiancé and then her husband had exclusive rights to her sexuality; and her parents guarded it before betrothal. Her virginity at marriage was valued, at least in part, as a means of assuring the groom of his paternity of his bride's first child. For similar reasons, women and men are treated differently in biblical adultery laws (Leviticus 20:10; Deuteronomy 22:22–28), where sex between a married man and an unmarried woman is discouraged but not proscribed. Concern for heirs is also a factor in the institution known as levirate marriage, in which a childless widow would marry her deceased husband's brother, with the first child (or son, according to some interpreters) produced by that liaison considered the dead man's heir (Deuteronomy 25:5–10; see the narrative of Tamar in Genesis 38). The case of the daughters of Zelophehad (Numbers 26:33; 27:1–11; 36:1–12) would seem to modulate the absolute nature of Israelite patrilineal inheritance; note, however, that in that case, inheritance of land by daughters is accompanied subsequently by provisions that the land would remain within the clan (Numbers 36).

The existence of polygyny (more than one wife) in ancient Israel, as in other Near Eastern lands, must also be understood in light of powerful communal interest in stabilizing households by transmitting property to biological heirs. The multiple wives of a monarch (such as David and Solomon) signified his high status and his ability to establish political alliances with diplomatic marriages, and wealthy individuals had several wives as a sign of affluence. But in most instances a man took a second wife or a concubine when the first wife failed to produce offspring. The Genesis narratives give the impression that polygyny was common. However, shorter life spans for women than for men, which meant a shortage of women of childbearing age, and the fact that most people probably lived near the poverty level, would have precluded polygyny for all but the wealthy. Indeed, many biblical texts, such as Genesis 2:24, the Song of Songs, several passages in wisdom literature, and even legal rulings such as Exodus 21:4–5, reflect a monogamous norm.

Although dissolution of a marriage was sometimes unavoidable, very little is known about provisions for divorce. Malachi 2:14 refers to a marriage contract, and Isaiah 50:1 mentions a bill of divorce, indicating that formal documents were used for establishing and dissolving a marriage, although probably only for people of means. The sole biblical text with divorce rulings, Deuteronomy 24:1–4, addresses a particular situation, the case of a man seeking to remarry a woman to whom he had once been married. Unfortunately, it gives the impression that only men could initiate divorce in the biblical period. However, that notion can be contested in light of the narrative of a Levite's secondary wife leaving him (Judges 19:2) and because the Elephantine papyri, which are documents from a community founded by Judeans in Egypt in the 6th century B.C.E., mention a woman divorcing her husband.

### *Women in Household Life*

It would be incorrect to assume, on the basis of gender asymmetry in matters of sexuality, that women were subordinate to and dominated by men in all other aspects of life. Indeed, with few resources available from outside the household, the relationship between a woman and her husband was one of interdependence and complementarity in most household functions. As the primary social and economic unit, the family household was the locus of all the activities, in addition to procreation, that were necessary for the maintenance and continuity of life. Family life was task-oriented; without the labor of both women and men, and also children, survival in the marginal habitat of the Israelite highlands would not have been possible. But in meeting a household's economic, educational, and religious needs, the responsibilities of all family members were not the same. The division of labor by gender, albeit with some overlap, was the most efficient way to accomplish the myriad household tasks.

In the contemporary world we tend to think of households as private realms, distinct from the public, male-dominated arena. However, this private-public dichotomy is based on the structure of large, industrialized societies and is not an accurate characterization of small, premodern agrarian communities, where the boundaries between households and the larger communities in which they were enmeshed were blurred. Both men and women, although probably in different ways, took part in the discussions and decisions affecting community life that took place within most households. Realizing this, along with recognizing the significant household roles of women as described below, helps us understand the folly of referring to Israelite women as "only wives and mothers."

*Economic Roles.* Women's economic roles were manifold and complex. Women sometimes participated in the male-dominated tasks of growing grains and tending orchards and vineyards, especially in labor-intensive harvest periods (see Ruth 2:2–9). They also had their own agricultural activities, especially the cultivation of garden vegetables and herbs. Both genders shared in the care of livestock and of work animals. However, women's major contributions to the household economy were the time-consuming food- and fiber-processing jobs. They transformed agricultural products into edible and wearable forms through their expertise and labor.

Cereal crops, the most important food source in the biblical period, provided an estimated 50% of a person's daily calories. A series of arduous processes, including grinding and kneading, were necessary to make grains edible. It is estimated that three hours of work would have been required each day to produce enough bread or gruel for an average family of six. Women, with the help of older children, not only produced bread but also processed and prepared many other foodstuffs, mainly fruits, vegetables, legumes, and dairy products. Some of these were eaten raw; but many were variously churned, pressed, pickled, roasted, or dried on a seasonal basis. Meat would have been eaten rarely, probably only at festivals.

Several positive features offset the onerous nature of women's food preparation responsibilities. Unlike male crop-growing tasks, in which yields could be drastically affected by periodic droughts or infestations of insects, food preparation always yielded a finished product. Thus, women would have experienced a consistent sense of accomplishment from their daily work. Another source of gratification lay in a woman's mastery of the considerable technical skills required by the diverse food-processing procedures.

Social and political aspects added to the individual benefits, for women, of food preparation. Archeologists often find grinding tools in clusters in Israelite dwellings. This indicates that women from neighboring households gathered together, undoubtedly to chat and sing during the long hours spent preparing grains and other foods. The time spent together helped forge women into informal social networks in a way that the more solitary tasks performed by men did not. These networks constituted a social safety net—women would know of an illness or emergency in a neighboring household and would find ways to help. These networks also operated on a political level; women gained and shared information that influenced community decisions made by male officials. Such indirect female political power is typically unrecognized but nonetheless real.

Women had other economic roles. They concocted potions and salves from wild or homegrown herbs and plants to use in folk remedies. Although rural households did procure sophisticated terracotta vessels and metal implements from urban workshops, some village women likely produced simple ceramic pots and stone grinding tools for everyday use. However, the most important household activity besides food processing was textile production, perhaps because of its potential for commercial activity beyond the household (see Proverbs 31:13, 24).

Archeologists have discovered tools—spindle whorls, loom weights, weaving shuttles, and needles—that testify to the production of fabrics in Israelite households. Like the steps involved in grain processing, the procedures for making textiles were often time-consuming and tedious. It takes several hours of spinning, for example, to produce the amount of yarn or thread needed for an hour of weaving. Women in pre-modern cultures typically do textile work together; indeed, some of the tasks are done most efficiently by women working in tandem. The personal, social, and political benefits accruing to women as food-producers were intensified by their experience of working together to make garments and coverings for their families and perhaps also for barter or sale.

*Educational and Managerial Roles.* The primary care of young children was the mother's responsibility. Child care was integrated into a woman's daily routines, no doubt with the assistance of older children and elderly parents. Women were assisted in most household tasks by their children; and they supervised offspring of both genders until boys were old enough to accompany their fathers into the fields. Fathers surely taught sons the tasks and activities performed mainly by men. Because there were no schools in the biblical period, except perhaps for a small number of upper-class urban youth, women were the chief educators and socializers of both boys and girls in their early years, and for girls into adolescence.

Women as educators are not very visible in the Bible, where the mention of sages and elders gives the impression of a male monopoly in teaching skills and inculcating traditional practices and beliefs. However, an understanding of the dynamics of an agrarian household indicates the prominence of women in this role, which involved instruction in the technologies of household life, in appropriate behavior, and also in the transmission of culture and values more generally. The frequent parallelism of "mother" and "father" in the book of Proverbs (1:8; 4:3; 6:20; 15:20; 19:26; 20:20; 23:22, 25; 28:24; 30:11, 17) indicates that both parents taught their children. Proverbs 31:1 singles out King Lemuel's mother as the source of his instruction.

Because women had more contact hours with children, their interactions with offspring were essential for transmitting many aspects of Israelite culture from one generation to the next. The very notion of "wisdom," which includes technical expertise as well as social sagacity, has important female aspects, arguably rooted in the broad role of women in caring for and socializing their children. Note that the wisdom is frequently personified as a woman in Proverbs (1:20–33; 3:13–18; 4:5–9; 7:4–5; 8:1–36; 9:1–6; 14:1). Also, the "strong woman" (*eshet chayil*) of Proverbs 31 is characterized as speaking wisdom and teaching kindness (v. 26). And two narratives feature an *ishah chachamah* ("wise woman"; II Samuel 14:1–20; 20:14–22).

A woman's educative role involved more than the instruction of children. In the complex, multigenerational Israelite households, older women served as household managers, instructing (depending upon the household's particular composition) daughters, daughters-in-law, nieces, slaves, servants, and other dependents in the array of women's tasks, as well as in appropriate behavior. The fifth commandment (Exodus 20:12; Deuteronomy 5:16) and the parent laws of Exodus 21:15, 17 and Leviticus 20:9, which were likely concerned with the behavior of adult children in multi-generational households, underscore the authority of both parents over both female and male offspring. In contrast, other ancient Near Eastern societies apparently favored men over women in assigning parental authority. Another indication of female authority in household life is the fact that mothers predominate in the Bible as the ones who name their children.

In light of women's extensive educative and managerial roles, the appearance of the phrase "mother's household" (*beit eim*) rather than the usual "father's household" (*beit av*) several times in the Bible is noteworthy. "Mother's household" appears in several women-centered texts (Genesis 24:28; Ruth 1:8; Songs 3:4; 8:2; see also Proverbs 14:1) and suggests that women controlled most internal household activities (as does Rebekah, Genesis 27:5–17; and the woman of Shunem, II Kings 4:8–37; 8:1–6), whereas men dealt with supra-household, lineage-related matters. Near Eastern documents attest to the managerial authority of royal women over certain aspects of palace life; women in ordinary households would likely have had similar control on a smaller scale, especially if there were slaves or servants in their households. Thus a senior woman would have had some authority over male servitors as well as over children, as when the woman of Shunem gives instructions to "her [male] servant" (II Kings 4:24).

*Religious Roles.* Women also had major roles in household religious life. Biblical texts focus on national and communal practices yet reveal that family celebrations punctuated the annual religious calendar. For example, Passover in its origins was likely a home-based spring festival involving specific kinds of food preparation; the other major festivals, similarly grounded in the agricultural calendar, no doubt involved family feasting. Household Sabbath traditions are difficult to trace back to the biblical period; but the story of the manna provisions for the seventh day (Exodus 16:21–30), as well as post-biblical sources, indicate festal meals on the seventh day. The food component of festivals and Sabbath is inconceivable without female culinary expertise and labor.

Women also participated in celebrations at shrines near their homes and even initiated cultic activity. The Hannah narrative (I Samuel 1–2) is instructive in this regard. The childless Hannah journeys regularly with her family to the cultic center of Shiloh to share in an annual sacrificial offering; she comes "before יהוה" to make a vow in the hope of ending her barrenness; and later, having given birth to Samuel, she fulfills her vow by bringing sacrificial offerings to Shiloh. Also, several passages in Deuteronomy (12:12; 16:11, 14; 31:10–12) are gender inclusive in their instructions for bringing sacrifices and celebrating at the central shrine, although in other texts (Exodus 23:17; Deuteronomy 16:16) only men are specifically required to do so. Finally, dozens of priestly passages use the common-gender term *nefesh,* indicating that both women and men were commanded to offer certain sacrifices (see Leviticus 2:1 and Numbers 5:6–10).

In addition to family festivals and communal celebrations and sacrifices mentioned in the Bible, certain household religious activities—carried out *only* by women—are known from archeological and ethnographic evidence. These practices, which are related to childbearing, may well have been the most important part of women's religious lives. Women in pre-modern cultures typically cope with the many problems related to reproduction, which today would be handled by medicine, through behaviors that might now be considered "magic" but were clearly religious in nature. Facing the possibility of barrenness, childbirth complications, difficulty in lactation, and high infant mortality rates (for as many as one in two infants did not survive to the age of five), Israelite women carried out various practices meant not only to keep away the evil spirits thought to cause problems but also to attract benevolent ones believed to bring reproductive success. Many of these practices—such as wearing amulets to avert the "evil eye," tying a red thread around the limb of a newborn, keeping a light burning in a birthing or sleeping room, salting and swaddling a newborn (see Ezekiel 16:4)—continued into the post-biblical period and are found in Jewish,

Christian, and Muslim families well into the 20th century.

These household religious activities, which focused on the welfare of their families and dealt with life-and-death matters, would have been empowering. Women were ritual experts in household practice much as priests were at the Temple, for they possessed the requisite knowledge to perform rituals in a prescribed and, they believed, efficacious way. Moreover, household rituals dealing with childbirth were carried out *for* women *by* women, including neighbors, relatives, and sometimes midwives (I Samuel 4:20; see also Ruth 4:13–17) in intimate settings that further contributed to female bonding and solidarity. Women's religious practices were profoundly important components of their adult lives.

### *Professional Women*

Women in the Bible appear in nearly twenty different community roles beyond those we often associate with the household. These particular roles correspond in a large measure to what we know about women's lives from extra-biblical sources. These professional activities are noteworthy because they show that some Israelite women did hold professional positions that served their communities directly, thus negating the notion that women were confined to the household (a stereotype itself in that it often conjures the household in contemporary terms rather than a household as a pre-modern locus of economic and social power).

The role mentioned most frequently is prostitution, perhaps a recourse for marginalized women unable to support themselves in any other way. This occupation is condemned in priestly texts but viewed matter-of-factly in the narratives about Rahab, the heroic prostitute of Jericho (Joshua 2, 5), and about the two women who brought their dispute to Solomon (I Kings 3:16–28).

Other roles were much less controversial and contributed in important ways to Israelite communities. Women practiced trades or crafts, working in palace workshops to produce items (perfume, food, baked goods) for the royal family or state events (I Samuel 8:13) and to produce fabrics for religious shrines (Exodus 35:25; II Kings 23:7). Some women marketed textiles produced at home (Proverbs 31:24); and the archeological discovery of women's stamp seals, which were used for commercial transactions, attests to female activity in the business world. According to Nehemiah 3:12, women were construction workers in the post-exilic effort to rebuild the walls of Jerusalem. Women served in the communication arena as couriers, usually carrying dispatches from women to other women (Proverbs 9:3–4) but occasionally bearing messages between men (II Samuel 17:17); and they were heralds, making announcements to the wider public (Isaiah 40:9; Psalm 68:12). Women served as midwives; they assist Rachel and Tamar in childbirth, and the midwives Shiphrah and Puah are heroes of the Exodus narrative. Wet-nurses are also mentioned, usually only for elites; Rebekah has one, as probably did most princes (II Kings 11:2–3), with Moses' own mother (Jochebed) hired to nurse him.

Midwives were also religious specialists, since prayers and potions are part of the culture of childbirth in traditional societies. Other female religious specialists included minor temple servitors (Exodus 38:8; I Samuel 2:22). Some female religious specialists are condemned, as in the gender-inclusive denunciations of various kinds of divination (including consulting the dead) in Leviticus (19:31; 20:6, 27) and Deuteronomy (18:10–11), a sure sign that women's divinatory services were being utilized. Although necromancy is condemned, I Samuel 28:7–25 depicts a female medium consulting the dead Samuel for King Saul effectively and without the narrator's criticism. Women also in some cases were perceived as sorcerers and are specifically censured as such (Exodus 22:17; see also Isaiah 57:3). The prophet Ezekiel reviles women performing a Temple ritual (8:14–15) as well as a group of female prophets engaged in divination (13:17–23). But other women prophets are heroic figures. Two of the most prominent women in the Bible, Miriam and Deborah, are called prophets (Exodus 15:20; Judges 4:4), as are Huldah, the first person to rule on the authenticity of a text as God's word (II Kings 22:14–20), and Noadiah, a leader of the postexilic community (Nehemiah 6:14).

Other female professionals, less explicitly religious, include Deborah in her role as a resolver of disputes and as a charismatic military leader ("judge"), and the "wise women" of Tekoa and Abel, who help resolve national crises. The wives of kings managed palace-related tasks; and a few also exercised political power, some even bearing a title (*g'virah*) signifying that they were royal functionaries (see I Kings 15:13 and II Kings 10:13). Female musicians led the celebrations for military victories attributed to divine intervention (Exodus 15:21; I Samuel 18:6–7; Psalm 68:26; Jeremiah 31:4, 13); their performances reflect a women's musical genre that involved drumming, dancing, and singing. Other women are mentioned as professional singers (II Samuel 19:36; Ezra 2:65; Nehemiah 7:67; Ecclesiastes 2:8) and perhaps even Temple singers (I Chronicles 25:5–6). Also, as in many traditional societies, women more than men were experts in mourning rituals (Jeremiah 9:16–19; Ezekiel 32:16).

Recognizing women's community roles has important implications for understanding the lives of the women engaged in these occupations. Many of these professional specialists, including musicians and singers, mourning women, "wise women," and even midwives and prophets, functioned in groups or were connected to each other in guild-like associations. The "daughters" learning dirges in Jeremiah 9:19 and wailing over Saul in II Samuel 1:24 are analogous to "sons" in the phrase "sons [or: company, disciples] of the prophets" (as in II Kings 5:22; 6:1); they constituted a guild (loosely speaking) of professional mourning women. The existence of other such groups can safely be assumed; informal organizations of women with technical expertise in certain areas, such as birthing or healing, are widely found in pre-modern cultures, including Israel's neighbors. These women would have gathered occasionally to share knowledge, train new members, and, in the case of musical professions, compose songs and rehearse in preparation for performances.

Membership in such groups, which typically are organized hierarchically with senior or more talented members earning the respect of the others, provided women with opportunities to experience prestige and status. Also, whether they functioned in groups or as individuals, female professionals provided services to their communities, thereby reaping the benefits of contributing to the public weal. It is noteworthy that societies in which women have rich opportunities for extra-household association with each other are generally considered the least repressive with respect to gender.

Finally, the existence of such groups, with their own hierarchies, calls into question the very notion (held by some readers today) of ancient Israel as completely patriarchal, with women dominated by men. As in every society, there were multiple loci of power in ancient Israel. Women's professional services and groups, along with the informal networks of women in neighboring households (described above) and the senior wife's managerial authority within the household (described above), cut across the male-dominated hierarchies that prevailed in other aspects of family and community life. Recognizing these three aspects of ancient Israelite society allows a more nuanced reading of Israelite women's lives.

—*Carol Meyers*

# Women and Post-biblical Commentary

Jews have traditionally believed that each of the books that comprise the Hebrew Bible reflects God's word in some way. As a "religion of the book," Judaism has looked to these revealed writings for guidance in every aspect of human life. Yet a religion based upon static texts, however holy, cannot easily adjust to the ever-varying conditions of human life. That Judaism has endured is due, in large part, to our traditions of biblical interpretation. In every generation, expositors of the divine message have discovered new meanings in the Hebrew Scriptures and demonstrated their relevance to an ever-evolving Jewish community.

For each parashah, *The Torah: A Women's Commentary* includes a section titled Post-biblical Interpretations. Rabbinic biblical commentaries, written from the 3rd through the 19th centuries, have played a central role in shaping how Jews have understood the Torah. Like *The Torah: A Women's Commentary*, these interpretations endeavored to keep biblical teachings alive, relevant, and compelling. The authors of our Post-biblical Interpretations have chosen from this vast treasury those passages that they believe will illuminate our contemporary understandings of biblical texts. Wherever possible, these selections focus on female characters and larger issues concerning women in Jewish law and Jewish life.

This essay presents an historical overview of the Jewish commentaries and commentators cited in the Post-biblical Interpretations sections.

### Written Torah and Oral Torah

Jewish biblical interpretation is already present in the Bible, since later biblical books often (directly or indirectly) interpret earlier writings. Following the destruction of the Second Temple (70 C.E.), textual scholars and interpreters, generally referred to as "the Rabbis," emerged as Jewish spiritual leaders. During the rabbinic period (from the beginning of the Common Era to the end of the 6th century), much of their intellectual endeavors concentrated on recording, preserving, and expanding the biblical interpretations that they deemed essential for the conduct of day-to-day Jewish life.

*The Rabbis adapted the Bible to their own world—a society oriented toward men.*

The word "*torah*" can be understood broadly as "teaching" or "revelation." Rabbinic teachers enlarged the meaning of Torah itself to include the entire body of rabbinic interpretive literature. Thus, "Written Torah" came to refer to the Bible, and "Oral Torah" became a designation for the voluminous rabbinic texts that grew up around the Bible. The oral tradition of Torah interpretation assumed the sanctity and inviolability of the written word. The Rabbis taught that both components of divine revelation were delivered to the people of Israel at Mt. Sinai and subsequently passed down through later prophets and other recognized authoritative figures (Mishnah *Avot* 1).

Rabbinic interpretation begins with the premise that Torah in all of its parts, both written and oral, is of divine origin and authority. Sometimes God's will is evident in the plain sense of the words, what is called the *p'shat.* This term refers to the contextual meaning of a biblical passage that is evident through a straightforward reading of a text. More frequently, the Rabbis believed, the actual import of biblical words can be discerned only by those who know how to penetrate to the *d'rash*, the deeper sense that lies beneath the surface. They sought to discover and elucidate those inner meanings, and in this way they maintained continuity with the past while adapting law to the changing conditions of the present and the needs of the future.

### *Rabbinic Literature*

The rabbinic method of biblical interpretation is called *midrash*, frequently translated as "exposition" or "elucidation." There are two types of midrash, legal and non-legal. Legal midrash contains a composite of ceremonial ordinances, ritual teachings, ethical rulings, and civil, criminal, and domestic laws that generally find their origin in a biblical statement or commandment. Since biblical laws are often vague or incomplete, rabbinic elaboration provides the details to allow for their implementation in a variety of particular situations. As later generations sought to follow the laws and teaching of the Bible, many topics required elucidation, such as the proper way of keeping Shabbat or how to solemnize a marriage or write a bill of divorce. Thus, rabbinic law enlarged and clarified the biblical text, applying scriptural principles and contemporary practices to an ever-broader variety of cases, while also considering a greater number of contingencies.

The other type of rabbinic biblical interpretation is non-legal in nature and includes expansions of biblical narratives, folktales, and anecdotes about the Rabbis themselves. These rabbinic writings also contain homilies (sermons) that teach religious beliefs and ethical behavior, and that comfort the downcast of Israel with promises of future redemption. Convinced that biblical texts contained neither contradiction nor repetition, the Rabbis creatively exercised their interpretive powers to demonstrate that this was so. Most of the "Post-biblical Interpretations" in this volume focus on this second type of interpretation, known as *midrash aggadah*.

Eventually, the Rabbis collected what is known as the "Oral Torah" into compilations that preserve competing interpretations and opinions; while majority views are generally honored, minority opinions are recorded as well. These complex texts interweave traditions, motifs, and influences from a variety of sources, time periods, and diverse environments, reflective of the extended duration of their composition and editing. Those texts from the Land of Israel incorporated and responded to Greco-Roman and early Christian cultural influences. Other texts were shaped in the very different world of mostly pre-Islamic Iraq, known in Jewish tradition as Babylon. The main collections are the Mishnah and the Talmud (usually cited as BT or JT, see below for details).

### *Women in Rabbinic Writings*

The shapers and expositors of rabbinic Judaism were men, and the ideal human society that they imagined was decidedly oriented towards men. Nevertheless, women were a part of these men's lives and a number of rabbinic writings address issues involving women. An entire division of the key rabbinic texts, the Mishnah and Talmuds, is entitled *Nashim* ("Women"), and its seven tractates deal with women in their legal relationships to men in matters of betrothal, marriage, levirate marriage, divorce, suspected adultery, and women's limited ability to make vows of various kinds. Another section, *Niddah* ("The Menstruating Woman"), one of the twelve tractates in the division *Tohorot* ("Ritual Purity"), is mainly concerned with strict definitions of female impurity during and after menstruation and following childbirth, in order to prevent communication of this ritual impurity to men.

With few exceptions, female voices are not heard in rabbinic literature. When they are, they are usually mediated through rabbinic assumptions about women's lesser intellectual, spiritual, and moral capacities, reflecting set views of women's appropriate roles in life, which were believed to differ from those of men. Rabbinic texts do not grant women a significant role in any aspect of rabbinic Judaism's communal life of leadership, study, and worship. Neither women's religious rituals—which undoubtedly existed—nor female understandings of their lives, experiences, and spirituality are retrievable in any significant way from rabbinic Judaism's androcentric writings that became so central to a millennium-and-a-half of Jewish existence. From rabbinic literature alone, a reader would never know, for example, that in various parts of the Roman Empire, some Jewish women held leadership roles in synagogue life and other public arenas. (Archeological evidence shows that such was the case in the first six or seven centuries of the Common Era. Some of the women involved, who appear to have been independent and wealthy, may have been converts to Judaism. See Bernadette Brooten, *Women Leaders in the Ancient Synagogue*, 1982.)

In their interpretive writings, the Rabbis praised biblical women who played central roles in the destiny of the people of Israel, including the matriarchs (*imahot*). According to the Babylonian Talmud (abbreviated as BT), Sarah, Miriam, Deborah, Hannah, Abigail, Huldah, and Esther have the status of prophets (*M'gillah* 14a); and the midrash collection *B'reishit Rabbah* declared that all four mothers of Israel were prophets (67.9 and 72.6). The Rabbis also lauded the women whose supportive roles in the domestic realm enabled husbands and sons to participate in public worship and communal study. For example, they extol Rachel, wife of Rabbi Akiva, as an exemplary woman who sacrificed her own comfort for her husband's scholarship (Judith Baskin, *Midrashic Women*, 2002, pp. 101–3). On the other hand, the Rabbis condemned as immodest women who appeared unveiled in public or gathered in groups with other women, or those whose voices the Rabbis considered too strident. Similarly, some sages criticized women who asserted themselves as public leaders. Thus, the Babylonian Talmud goes on to denigrate the judge Deborah as a hornet and the prophet Hulda as a weasel (the meaning of their respective names), since they held powerful positions usually associated with men (*M'gillah* 14b; Baskin, *Midrashic Women*, 2002, pp. 31–32, 109–14, 140–54).

The *midrash* about Rahab the harlot is a good example of the creative and transformative powers of rabbinic commentary when applied positively to a biblical woman. Rahab appears in Joshua 2 as a prostitute who lived independently in the city of Jericho. She is a righteous woman who hides Joshua's two spies in her house and saves them from capture. According to Joshua 2:9–11, Rahab recognizes the overwhelming power of God and foresees the future victory of Israel.

The Rabbis taught that Rahab became a convert to Judaism; and her statement of faith in Joshua 2:11 earned her the highest place among all biblical proselytes (*M'chilta Amalek* 3; *D'varim Rabbah* 2.26–27). A midrash recounts that she became the ancestor of priests and prophets in Israel (*B'midbar Rabbah* 8.9). According to the Rabbis, Joshua himself married her. Thus, his illustrious descendants were also hers (BT *M'gillah* 14b). (On how priests and prophets could be descended from a non-Israelite prostitute, see *Sifrei B'midbar* 78 and the discussion in Baskin, *Midrashic Women*, 2002, pp. 154–60.) Her rabbinic rehabilitation as a wife and mother demonstrates how the Rabbis preferred to imagine women, even as it provides a firm precedent for our own contemporary reconstructions of biblical women and men in ways that reveal meanings from the ancient text that speak to our own lives and concerns.

Rabbinic literature also preserves anecdotes about contemporaneous admirable women. These include Imma Shalom (1st century C.E.), whose husband was Rabbi Eliezer ben Hyrcanus and whose brother was the Patriarch Gamliel II (BT *Shabbat* 116a, BT *Bava M'tzia* 59b); she mediated a bitter quarrel between those two men. Traditions associated with Beruriah (2nd century C.E.), whose father and husband were rabbis, acknowledge the possibility of a learned female. A number of passages depict Beruriah as having a profound knowledge of rabbinic biblical exegesis and outstanding intelligence (for instance, BT *P'sachim* 62b, BT *B'rachot* 10a, and BT *Eiruvin* 53b–54a). However, beyond one very early attribution, which is repeated nowhere else, no actual legal rulings are ever credited to her (Tosefta *Keilim, Bava M'tzia* 1:6). Moreover, Beruriah's reputed scholarly expertise became a problem for rabbinic Judaism. In a medieval reference, which may reflect earlier sources, she reaps the tragic consequences of the "light-mindedness" supposedly inherent in women. Rashi (see below) relates a tradition that Beruriah was seduced by one of her husband's students and subsequently committed suicide (Rashi's commentary on BT *Avodah Zarah* 18b; Baskin, *Midrashic Women*, 2002, pp. 81–83).

Seven aggadic narratives in the Babylonian Talmud discuss Yalta, an aristocratic Jewish woman of notable learning who exercised significant communal authority in the Jewish community in Babylon. Clearly, the Rabbis were aware of women like Yalta whose strong personalities, control of significant financial resources, and exalted lineage afforded them far more communal respect and power than ordinary women could imagine. While several of the stories about Yalta report her ability to act independently against Jewish rabbinic and political rulings when necessary, at least two of the anecdotes (BT *Kiddushin* 70a–b and BT *B'rachot* 51b) demonstrate a rabbinic desire to curtail such female pretensions to independence and power (Baskin, *Midrashic Women*, 2002, pp. 83–87).

### *Why Rabbinic Literature Is Included Here*

The Rabbis adapted the Hebrew Bible to their own circumstances and attitudes, but always with the conviction that they were proceeding with divine authority. The traditions they established about the inappropriateness of women's presence in the communal domains of worship, study, and leadership were continued, with few exceptions, in medieval and early modern Judaism. They persist in some Jewish communities up to the present day. Although the patriarchal approach toward women that is typical of rabbinic and medieval biblical commentary was never unique to the Jewish community, the consequences of this attitude have been long lasting in stifling female intellectual, spiritual, and leadership roles in Judaism. Contemporary women may well ask what this androcentric literature, written and transmitted by men, has to offer and why they should read it. Why have we included "Post-biblical Interpretations" in this volume at all?

For one thing, this complex and multifaceted literature is a rich part of our Jewish heritage. The Rabbis and later exegetes were profoundly immersed in biblical literature and had considered deeply its wide range of meanings and possible applications. The many dimensions they read into and out of the biblical text over the centuries have shaped the course of Jewish intellectual and spiritual history—and continue to amaze and enlighten us today. Moreover, rabbinic exegesis has always been sensitive to the multilayered and multivocal qualities of the Hebrew Scriptures. While the majority of exegetical teachings about women's intellectual capacities and public roles tend to be negative, differing points of view have also been preserved. One example that acknowledges the injustice of arbitrary limitations on female roles appears in the midrash collection *Sifrei Numbers* 133, in a discussion of the redoubtable daughters of Zelophehad (Numbers 26): "The compassion of God is not like human compassion. Human rulers favor males over females but the One who spoke and brought the world into being is not like that. Rather, God shows mercy to every living thing" (see *parashat Pinchas*, p. 984). Thus, our commentary includes "Post-biblical Interpretations" because they are part of our legacy of Oral Torah, because they have a great deal to teach us about biblical writings, and because they represent the diverse points of view that have always been a part of the way Jews read the Torah.

When thinking about women, it is especially important that we pay attention to this immense body of post-biblical interpretive literature which is a central part of Jewish tradition. Contemporary interpretations of Jewish texts have played a leading role in bringing about positive changes in women's status in Judaism and in the larger world, and in enlarging women's access to the realms of Jewish learning. Indeed, the many scholars who have contributed "Post-biblical Interepretations" to this volume demonstrate that women are now expert in rabbinic writings. As educated women and men advocate for a Judaism that is egalitarian and forward looking, it is essential that we become knowledgeable about all aspects of our heritage and build on those teachings of the past.

### *Documents of Rabbinic Judaism*

The Mishnah is the earliest written document of rabbinic Judaism. It is a legal compilation based on biblical law, actual practice, and spiritual vision. This work, edited in the early 3rd century C.E., is written in Hebrew and is organized according to six subject divisions, which are further separated into a total of sixty-three tractates. The Tosefta, generally held to be a slightly later collection of legal rulings, follows the order of the Mishnah and supplements it. These works are attributed to the rabbinic sages from the 1st to 3rd centuries C.E. In the following centuries, rabbinic scholars in the land of Israel and in Babylonia (today's Iraq) produced extensive commentaries on the Mishnah, known as Gemara. Much of the Gemara is written in Aramaic, a language close to Hebrew that was dominant in Western Asia in that period. In the 6th century C.E., the Mishnah and this more extensive Gemara were combined and edited by several generations of Rabbis to form the Babylonian Talmud (cited here as BT). This work became the definitive compilation of Jewish law and tradition for many centuries to come. The Talmud of the Land of Israel (cited here as JT), completed at the end of the 4th century C.E., although less comprehensive than the Babylonian Talmud, also became an important part of the larger body of rabbinic literature.

Parallel to the Mishnah, Tosefta, and Talmuds are midrash collections that either provide a running commentary on a specific biblical book or are organized according to cycles of scriptural readings. These midrash compilations, typically named after biblical books (for example, *B'reishit Rabbah*, also known as *Genesis Rabbah*), are mainly in Hebrew and share numerous interpretations and rulings in common with the Mishnah and Talmuds. The dates of composition for these midrashic documents extend from the period of the Mishnah into the early Middle Ages and are often difficult to determine with any exactitude.

### *Medieval Biblical Interpretation*

During the medieval period (from 600 C.E. to 1500 C.E.), many important biblical commentaries were written by scholars throughout the Jewish world. Several of these exegetes are cited in the "Post-biblical Interpretations" entries in this volume. The most famous medieval commentator is Rabbi Solomon ben Isaac (known by the acronym Rashi), who lived in France between 1040 and 1105. Best known for his commentaries on both the Babylonian Talmud and most of the biblical books, Rashi's exegesis has long been admired for its clarity and for his attention to the *p'shat* or contextual meaning of a biblical passage. Only after he had explicated the plain sense of a text as he understood it, did Rashi turn to *d'rash*, using *midrash aggadah* to expand his readers' understanding of the Bible. Rashi had only daughters and they were apparently well educated. Most of his grandsons became important interpreters of Jewish texts.

Rabbi Abraham Ibn Ezra (died 1165), a native of Spain whose first language was Arabic, is often considered the most original of medieval Jewish biblical interpreters. He composed commentaries on all the biblical books, as well as Hebrew poetry and works on astronomy and science. As a scientist and philosopher, Ibn Ezra used his knowledge of Hebrew and Arabic grammar to demonstrate the contextual meaning (*p'shat*) of biblical words and phrases; he had little interest in the elaborations of *midrash aggadah* that appealed so much to Rashi. His approach to the Bible is in many ways a precursor to modern biblical scholarship. Another important Spanish exegete was Rabbi Moses ben Nachman (1194–1270), also known as Nachmanides or by his acronym, Ramban. He lived most of his life near Barcelona, spending his final days in the Land of Israel. He is well known for his commentary on the five books of the Torah and for the strong influence from Jewish mysticism that infuses his interpretation.

The *Mikraot G'dolot* ("Rabbinic Bible") became a popular repository of medieval biblical commentary for later generations. Published with the vocalized text of the Bible, an Aramaic translation, and selected Masoretic notes, the typical volume of *Mikraot G'dolot* contains the commentaries of Rashi; Rabbi Samuel ben Meir (1085–1158), one of Rashi's grandsons who is also known as Rashbam; Abraham ibn Ezra; Nachmanides; and Obadiah Sforno (1475–1550), an Italian rabbi, physician, and commentator.

### Pre-modern Jewish Women and Hebrew Scriptures

Most Jewish women in rabbinic and medieval times lacked access to the Torah and interpretive writings, since very few women learned to read Hebrew. The greatest Jewish philosopher of the Middle Ages, Moses Maimonides (1135–1204), who was born in Spain and spent most of his life in Cairo, discouraged girls' education in traditional texts, on the grounds that women had no halachic obligation to study. He also believed that women were deficient in the mental skills required for serious Torah learning. In his famous law code the *Mishneh Torah*, Maimonides wrote, "Our sages said: 'Whoever teaches his daughter Torah, it is as if he taught her frivolity [or: lasciviousness]' (Mishnah *Sotah* 3:4). This all refers to the Oral Torah. However, regarding the Written Torah he should not set out to teach her; but, if he does teach her, it is not considered as if he taught her frivolity" (*Mishneh Torah*, Study of Torah 1:13). The French scholar Moses of Coucy (early 13th century) explained that although "a woman is exempt from both the commandment to learn Torah and to teach her son, even so, if she aids her son and husband in their efforts to learn [by supporting them financially], she shares their reward for the fulfillment of that commandment" (*Sefer Mitzvot Gadol*, Positive Commandment 12).

The invention of printing in the 15th century and the spread of printed works in vernacular languages transformed Jewish women's educational opportunities. Most rabbinic leaders agreed with Maimonides that the rabbinic injunctions against female study applied to the Talmud but not to the Bible or the legal rulings necessary for women's everyday activities. It is no accident that translations and paraphrases of portions of the Bible into Yiddish were among the first printed Jewish books intended for a female audience. (These were also important works for the large number of Jewish men who also lacked a good understanding of Hebrew.) Particularly popular were the *Taytsh-khumesh* ("Yiddish Five Books of Moses") by Sheftl Hurwitz of Prague and first published in 1590, and the *Tsenerene* (or *Tzenah U'renah*, "Go Out and See"), by Rabbi Yaakov son of Isaac Ashkenazi. Both of these biblical paraphrases included homilies on the weekly biblical readings from the Torah and Prophets, as well as stories, legends, and parables from rabbinic literature, the *Zohar*, and other mystical texts. The *Tsenerene* was particularly popular and appeared in more than three hundred editions. As Chava Weissler has written, "Women read it for inspiration and catharsis, often weeping over the text, as a regular part of their Sabbath afternoon activities" (*Voices of the Matriarchs*, 1998, p. 6). In this way, for the first time, large numbers of women became familiar with the Torah and haftarah portions of the week, a wide variety of *midrash aggadah*, and the teachings of the best-known commentators. Aspects of this knowledge, particularly about biblical women, was also incorporated contemporaneously into women's vernacular supplicatory prayers (*tkhines*), at least some of which were composed by women (see *Voices of the Matriarchs*). Thus, a new technology in the larger culture (namely, printing) transformed the piety and possibilities of Jewish women, just as the technological and social changes of the past hundred years have profoundly altered the opportunities available for Jewish women at the beginning of the 21st century.

—*Judith R. Baskin*

# Women and Contemporary Revelation

In the section for each parashah titled "Contemporary Reflection," Jewish thinkers, rabbis, cantors, educators, and other Jewish interpreters respond to the Torah through a personal or professional lens in order to articulate an ongoing encounter with God. In Hebrew, there is no single word for revelation. Rather, revelation is described as both *matan Torah* (the giving of Torah) and *kabbalat Torah* (the receiving of Torah). Revelation occurs when these two intersect and the voice of God is heard, directly or indirectly. Drawing on Deuteronomy 30:12 (in which Moses states that the Torah is "not in the heavens that you should say: 'Who among us can go up can go up to the heavens and get it for us and impart it for us . . .'"), later rabbinic sages asserted that the will of God, as represented in the Torah, was no longer in Heaven but is entrusted to human interpreters (BT *Bava M'tzia* 59b). In the rabbinic context this meant that the community could discern God's voice by wrestling with the text, that is, by intensely engaging with Torah. Thus, Torah study replaced prophecy as the source of revelation.

Even when women were exempt (or excluded) from Torah study, the Rabbis did not exclude women as bearers of revelation. They acknowledged that in ancient Israel, God spoke to female prophets as well as male prophets, who consequently served as divine messengers. Indeed, whereas the Bible identifies by name only four female prophets (see at Deuteronomy 13:2), the Rabbis expand this list considerably. According to one source, seven women were prophets. Acknowledging Miriam (Exodus 15:20), Deborah (Judges 4:4), and Huldah (II Kings 22:14), but ignoring Noadiah (Nehemiah 6:14), rabbinic sages add Sarah (Genesis 11–25), Hannah (I Samuel 1–2), Abigail (I Samuel 25), and Esther (BT *M'gillah* 14a). The Midrash also emphasizes the prophetic qualities of all four matriarchs (Sarah, Rebecca, Rachel, and Leah; *B'reishit Rabbah* 67.9; 72.6) and maintains that "just as sixty myriads of male prophets arose for Israel, so there arose for them sixty myriads of female prophets" (*Shir HaShirim Rabbah* 4.11).

> *God continues to speak to each generation; in this one, we hear women's voices.*

Who hears the divine voice? The rabbinic sages did not understand one's relationship to God as connected primarily to gender, but rather, as Barry Holtz notes, to "talent, inclination and strength" (*Finding Our Way*, 1990, p. 102). For example, one midrash enjoins its readers, "Come and see how the voice [of God] went forth [at Sinai]—coming to each Israelite according to his individual strength—to the old, according to their strength; to the young according to their strength; to the children according to their strength; to the infants according to their strength; *and to the women according to their strength*" (*Sh'mot Rabbah* 5.9, emphasis added).

New and challenging scholarly theories in the 19th century about the historical formation of the Bible led Reform Jews, and later Conservative and Reconstructionist Jews, to rethink the concept of divine revelation and to reevaluate women's religious roles. This created new opportunities for women to see themselves as bearers of revelation. Reform Judaism's notion of progressive revelation particularly encouraged women and men to recognize the many ways in which one could hear God's voice. In a sermon delivered in 1918, Lily Montagu, founder of the Liberal Jewish movement in England and of the World Union for Progressive Judaism, maintained that "we [Liberal Jews] are no longer worried by the claims of tradition when these clash with our conception of truth. We have boldly enunciated our belief in progressive revelation, and this faith has quickened our hope for the future and intensified our reverence for the past" ("Kinship With God," in Ellen M. Umansky, ed., *Lily H. Montagu*, 1985, p. 113).

In line with this new understanding, Reform Judaism made religious education equally available to girls and boys, and the ceremony of confirmation, which initially replaced bar mitzvah, marked the end of one's formal Jewish studies. Unlike the celebration of one's becoming a bar or bat mitzvah, which is usually held on or soon after one's 13th birthday, confirmation is held on Shavuot, the holiday traditionally marking the revelation at Sinai. Confirmation was at first an individual or small group ceremony, with girls confirmed at a temple in Berlin as early as 1817. In the U.S., confirmation became a group or class celebration, taking place at the end of 10th grade. Becoming a confirmand on Shavuot serves as a reminder of the centrality of the Torah (whether equated with God's moral teachings or including ritual observance as well); it also reenacts symbolically for each person the receiving of the Torah and living in covenantal relationship with God. By the 20th century, the notion of continuing revelation—the idea that God continues to speak to each and every generation—was largely accepted. Indeed, for many if not most Jews today, the concept of Torah has expanded to mean Jewish learning or learning in general.

In his 1955 book *God in Search of Man*, Rabbi Abraham Joshua Heschel asked, "How did Israel know that what their eye and ear perceived in the desert of Sinai was not a phantom?" Was it truly a moment of revelation, or was such a perception only an illusion? "*What* we see," he concluded, "may be an illusion; *that* we see can never be questioned" (p. 196). Speaking before members of the Central Conference of American Rabbis in 1986, Reform rabbi Laura Geller similarly emphasized the importance of lived experience. Describing revelation as a moment of connection with God, she, like Heschel, emphasized the transformative nature of this moment. Yet moving beyond what he identified as Torah, she came to realize that although she had not noticed, God is always present. She asserted:

> I wasn't looking, or perhaps I was looking in the wrong places. . . . I needed to listen to the gentle whisper, the still small voice, the Presence one encounters by diving deep and surfacing. . . . I suddenly realized that my experience is Jewish experience. There is a Torah of our lives as well as the Torah that was written down. Both need to be listened to and wrestled with: both unfold through interactive commentary (*Four Centuries of Jewish Women's Spirituality: A Sourcebook*, 1992, pp. 244–45).

Like Geller, Judith Plaskow advocates expanding our understanding of Torah to include not just the first five books of the Hebrew Bible and traditional Jewish learning, "but women's words, teachings, and actions hitherto unseen." Plaskow asserts that Jewish feminists must "reclaim Torah as our own" in order to make visible the "presence, experience, and deeds of women erased in traditional sources," telling the "stories of women's encounters with God and captur[ing] the texture of their religious experience." She also insists upon reconstructing history to include women's history, not by changing the past, but by altering the shape of Jewish memory (*Standing Again at Sinai: Judaism from a Feminist Perspective*, 1990, p. 28).

Rachel Adler has identified such efforts as "engendering Judaism." She also calls for models of thinking about and practicing Judaism in a way that enables both women and men to "recreate and renew together as equals" (*Engendering Judaism: An Inclusive Theology and Ethics*, 1998, p. xiv). In so doing, Adler draws heavily on narrative as a tool of critique and vision, while advocating among liberal or progressive Jews the re-appropriation of halachah (the traditional authoritative legal tradition) as a source of meaning, rather than one of power. This means, among other things, retaining those laws that remain grounded in the practice of the progressive Jewish community while adding new laws, grounded in new stories, that reflect new communal practices.

In "We All Stood Together," poet Merle Feld re-envisions both women and men at Mt. Sinai, ready to receive the words of God. In her creative remembering, her brother kept a journal of what he saw and heard while she, always holding a baby, was never able to write anything down. Consequently, she came to forget the particulars of this revelatory moment, until she was left with nothing but the feeling that something important had occurred. At the poem's conclusion, she writes that if Jews could somehow remember that moment at Sinai as it was experienced by men *and women*, that sacred moment could be recreated (see *Yitro*, Voices, p. 425).

In this *Commentary*, the section called Contemporary Reflection contains responses by women who, in a variety of ways, explore the continuing meanings of the revelation of Torah. Written by Jewish professionals from a variety of fields, these pieces represent new, individual wrestlings with the biblical text. Explicitly or implicitly revealing an awareness of both biblical and post-biblical interpretations, the brief essays reflect a contemporary, often feminist, perspective. They not only focus on women's roles and concerns, but also attempt to draw on women's lived experiences (what Geller describes as "the Torah of our lives") in order to create to recreate Jewish memory (as articulated by Plaskow and Feld) and, in the process, engender Judaism (as suggested by Adler).

Many of the topics explored in these reflections are identical to those found in other sections of this *Commentary*, including notions of covenant, peoplehood, religious leadership, free will, social justice, purity, pollution, sacrifice, forgiveness, and mercy. Yet instead of reading the text within a post-biblical or early rabbinic context, these reflections offer readings that are clearly in the present and have implications for the future. Some underscore the contemporary relevance of the Torah's teachings, like Noa Kushner's reflection on *parashat P'kudei* and God's earthly presence, and Alice Shalvi's on *parashat Ki Tavo* and the Israelites' settling in the land of Israel. Others, like Suzanne Singer's reflection on the hardening of Pharaoh's heart in *parashat Bo*, suggest reading against the text—creating counter-narratives that provoke new theological questions and problems. Many of the pieces move beyond the text altogether, using words, phrases, or concepts within a particular parashah as a means of exploring issues and ideas that are of particular interest to contemporary readers, including women. Judith Plaskow, for example, draws on the priestly evaluation of sexual behavior in *parashat Acharei Mot* to discuss the persistence of homophobia as well as sexual and family violence in today's society; in my reflection on *parashat Haazinu*, I reject the text's imagery of God as Rock and Warrior, and instead offer new images that, in my view, better convey the love and justice of God. Writing more personally, Zoë Klein, in her reflection on *parashat Ki Tisa*, draws upon similarities to her husband's proposing marriage to her at Mount Sinai and God's continual revelation to Israel there, using one to view the other as moments of "eternal, loving joining," while Blu Greenberg explores the impact of sudden loss, as she grapples with *parashat Sh'mini.*

The importance of the Contemporary Reflection sections of this *Commentary* is that they enable us to hear women's voices that reckon with divine revelation. The reflections in this *Commentary* represent different attitudes toward the Torah and the many ways in which its teachings can be appropriated into our lives. While some authors defend its teachings, others challenge them. Yet each essay shows the significance of Torah as a record of God's revelation to Israel: it is a repository of Jewish memory, however incomplete, from which we, as individuals and as members of contemporary Jewish communities, can attempt to hear and understand the voice of God.

—*Ellen M. Umansky*

# The Poetry of Torah and the Torah of Poetry

THIS COMMENTARY INVITES the reader to meet the Torah text on new terms and to read the text through new eyes. In addition to more traditional modes of interpretation, this *Commentary* includes poetry, an innovative mode of expanding and extending the Torah text. In the Voices section at the conclusion of each parashah, we have collected poetry, along with selected prose pieces, to invite you to consider how issues and themes in each Torah portion reflect and illuminate women's lives and experiences. This essay will explore the intention and the process of collecting the poems included in this volume.

### Poetry and the Oral Tradition

The Torah is a living document. While some contemporary Jews may think of the Torah as a static, fixed "book," the Torah has always been read aloud or chanted as an essential part of weekly, Shabbat, and holiday synagogue ritual. This declamatory aspect of Torah reading invites response, and the rich history of Torah commentary has developed from and continues to depend upon listeners' familiarity with the oral text. Public reading brings together the intensely personal encounter with sacred text with the shared experience of hearing the text chanted or read aloud. Mirroring the communal experience of prayer, which, for Jews, always frames the public reading of Torah, each person is challenged to listen with concentrated attention: both as a member of the community and as an individual, hearing the words each time as if for the first time.

Poetry, too, demands oral recitation. By complementing each Torah portion with poetry, we are continuing the oral tradition of intentional listening and of challenging the "listener" to make connections between the text and your own life through the medium of commentary—in this case, in the form of poetry. As the poet Adrienne Rich

*We invite you to meet the Torah text on new terms and to read it through new eyes.*

writes, "What poetry is made of is so old, so familiar, that it's easy to forget that it's not just the words." Rather, "every poem breaks a silence that had to be overcome." Furthermore, "in the wash of poetry, the old, beaten, worn stones of language take on colors." But these "colors," or meanings, may also "disappear when you sieve them up out of the streambed and try to sort them out" (*What Is Found There: Notebooks on Poetry and Politics*, 1993, p. 84). This is the challenge of poetry.

### The Challenges and Pleasures of Poetry

For many readers, poetry is a particularly demanding medium. Whether deprived of teachers who welcomed us into the rich and exciting world of poetic language, or bored as children by memorizing poetry that seemed to have no meaning or relevance, some of us draw away from a poem that meets us on the page, hesitating, perhaps even ashamed of what we misinterpret as our lack of skills to approach or unpack the poem. Perhaps we hesitate to approach poetry because we feel the poem beckoning and we are unsure how to respond. The poet Muriel Rukeyser writes, "A poem does invite, it does require. What does it invite? A poem invites you to feel. More than that: it invites you to respond. And better than that: a poem invites a total response" (*The Life of Poetry*, 1996, p. 11). When we move beyond our fears, we can begin to respond to the poem—and to the Torah.

The Voices section invites you to give poetry a chance, to open your heart to the invitation to feel, to hear, to respond. We invite you to read each poem once, and then again, silently and aloud. Each reading will reveal new sounds, new meanings, new insights. Share your reading, and your interpretations with others. How does the poem illuminate the Torah text? How does the Torah text illuminate the poem? How does the poem serve as midrash, providing a deeper or broader reading of the text? If a poem is not immediately clear or understood, return to it at a later point. Read it again. Discuss the poem with your study partner, your friends, your teachers. In most cases we include references to verses in the Torah that we consider relevant to the poem; elsewhere we omit these because the poem relates to the parashah as a whole. Give each poem an opportunity to speak to you, opening a powerful and fresh perspective into the timeless Torah text. You may be surprised and delighted with your response.

### *Poetry and Women's Experience*

Since ancient times, women have collected and recorded their stories, their dreams, their fears, and their hopes. While their fathers and brothers may have bent over sacred texts, women composed songs and poems to welcome new life, to celebrate weddings, to mourn the dead. Some of these works were passed down from mother to daughter, orally or in writing. While some compositions were preserved, other writings—like many precious belongings—were lost as our people wandered from continent to continent, changing location, language, and worldview.

Women's poetry begins in the Torah, with the Song of Miriam (Exodus 15:20–21), perhaps even the Song at the Sea (see at Exodus 15:1–19). Several other biblical poems are associated with women, namely the Song of Deborah (Judges 5), the Song of Hannah (I Samuel 2) and most of Song of Songs; and women were known to compose and perform victory songs and laments (see the introduction to *parashat Haazinu*, p. 1251). However, we know of few writings by Jewish women between ancient times and the 16th century, when Deborah Ascarelli composed and translated liturgy for her community in Rome. In the next century, Gluckel of Hameln composed her memoirs and Sarah Copio Sullam wrote poetry for her family and friends in Venice. Another kind of poetic text that has been preserved are numerous *tkhines*, petitionary prayers, some of which were written by women, including Rebecca Tiktiner of Prague (16th century) and Sarah daughter of Tovim of Podolia, Ukraine (18th century). For many years, these prayers served as a primary liturgical resource for many women, particularly for those whose language skills did not include Hebrew. In the wake of the Haskalah (the so-called Jewish Enlightenment, beginning in the late 18th century), we begin to see published works and essays by women, including poetry, first by Rachel Morpurgo in Trieste (1790–1871; see *Balak*, Voices, p. 964), Grace Aguilar (1816–1847) in Britain, and Penina Moise (1797–1880) and Emma Lazarus (1849–1887) in the United States, among others. These poets made their voices heard by a wider audience, writing primarily in their native tongues. (See *The JPS Guide to Jewish Women: 600 BCE–1900 CE*, edited by Emily Taitz, Sondra Henry, and Cheryl Tallan, 2003.) Although considerably limited in quantity, women's diaries, *tkhines*, memoirs, and poetry form a parallel tradition to the rich body of codes, commentary, and discursive literature composed by Jewish men throughout the ages.

The poetry collected in this *Commentary*'s Voices section reflects the writings of Jewish women across a wide chronological and geographical span. Whereas some poems date back as far as the 17th century, the majority were written in the last half century, largely by American, Israeli, and European poets. Although all the poetry in this volume appears in English, many poems have been translated from Hebrew, Yiddish, German, Russian, and other languages. The poets include both well-known, award-winning poets, as well as new, emerging poets. While a number of the poems were written as responses to specific parts of the Torah, others were not. In fact, many of the poets included in this volume were surprised and delighted to discover their work being juxtaposed as Torah commentary. A poem is the poet's gift to the world; once released from the pen, the words enter hearts and minds in ways that the poet might never have dreamed or imagined. The wide range of poetry in this volume reflects the elasticity, the expansiveness, and the timelessness of a Torah that is open to continued and continual interpretation.

### *The Process*

In keeping with the larger goals of this *Commentary*, the Voices section contains poems that, in some way, illuminate the experience of Jewish women as participants in, readers of, and heirs to the Torah and biblical history. The poems in Voices add depth to the four other types of commentary in each parashah by complementing, strengthening, and opening new readings of each portion. The poems fill in some of the lacunae of the biblical text by considering questions such as: Who were the women of the Bible? What might have they thought about and felt? What were the nature and the boundaries of their relationships with other women, with the men in their lives, with their children, and with their neighbors? When no women are mentioned in a story, where *are* the women? Who might they have been? While some of the poems give voice to the experiences and emotions of women mentioned in the Torah, others address broader topics and themes raised explicitly or implicitly in a given parashah, such as approaching the holy, sexual awakening, risk taking, creating and sustaining families and communities, pregnancy and childbirth, infertility, loss and mourning, and more.

For the other four sections that accompany each parashah, contributors were invited to write for this volume. In contrast, the Voices section was assembled by a small working group made up of the Editors (Tamara Cohn Eskenazi and Andrea L. Weiss), two members of the Editorial Board (Sherry Blumberg and Sue Levi Elwell), the Managing Editor (Hara Person), the Project Coordinator (Barbara Koppel), and our Rabbinic Student Interns (Jocelyn Hudson and Leah Berkowitz). Because our group included women who lived across the United States, we conducted our work on the telephone through conference calls, often meeting once a week for two hours at a time. This diverse group included women of different ages and diverse journeys. We discovered that we brought to our conversations a rich range of Jewish women's experiences—as daughter, sister, friend, beloved, partner, mother of children by birth and by adoption, grandmother, and widow. The poetry that we considered challenged, comforted, and changed us. We hope you will share those experiences.

As we started gathering potential Voices material, we cast a wide net. We read widely, networking with poets, writers, teachers of literature, and our own friends and colleagues, sharing favorite books and poets, and spending countless hours in the stacks of libraries and bookstores and on the Internet. We found ample material for the narrative portions of the Torah; other genres presented a greater challenge.

As we evaluated material, we asked: How might a woman's perspective enable us to ask new questions of the Torah? How are our understandings of gender and sexuality challenged by biblical texts, and how might biblical text be challenged by our growing understandings of these topics? What is the message of this poem, and how does it intersect with the biblical text? How far can we push the text, and also push each poem? What happens when we read and interpret familiar signs and symbols in new and powerfully different ways? How does an innovative reading of the text make that text more accessible and meaningful for contemporary readers?

During our phone calls, we read the selections aloud and discussed whether they merited inclusion and, if so, where they might fit. As our process continued, our understanding of our task deepened. We aimed to find, or, when necessary, commission or compose, poems that could act as spotlights on different aspects of each parashah. We hoped that together, these poems would reveal several distinct points of entry into each Torah portion. Additionally, for each parashah we attempted to balance poems that readers might find more accessible with those that might prove more challenging and require greater interpretive effort.

The Torah, which weaves together narrative, law, and song, is our people's essential poetic expression. It calls to each of us, inviting attention and response. Poetry is a resource for facing challenges. As Muriel Rukeyser writes, "In this moment when we face horizons and conflicts wider than ever before, we want our resources, the ways of strength. We look again to the human wish, its faiths, the means by which the imagination leads us to surpass ourselves. If there is a feeling that something has been lost, it may be because much has not yet been used, much is still to be found and begun" (*The Life of Poetry*, 1996, p. 8). The time has come for all of us to hear women's songs that echo, respond to, and challenge the themes of our ancient texts: celebrating the victory of the human spirit, crying out with the pain of loss, reflecting upon the quiet joy, and feeling the ecstasy of standing in the presence of holiness. Rukeyser observes that "much is still to be found and begun." The Voices sections begin this process of restoring, renewing, and invigorating the study of—and delight in—the Torah of poetry and the poetry of Torah. May these poems open paths of insight and joy.

*—Sue Levi Elwell*

#  בראשית ✦ *B'reishit*

# GENESIS

GENESIS IS A BOOK OF beginnings, birthings, and blessings. It depicts the origin of humankind as a family, and then it follows the development of one particular family. Genesis serves as the "prequel" to the Exodus story that the Bible repeatedly presents as Israel's founding event. Tracing the people's origin back to its beginning, Genesis identifies who the Israelites are and how they came to be in Egypt.

After a brief yet crucial description of how God creates an orderly world and its inhabitants (1:1–2:3), the book persistently focuses on families. The first part (Genesis 1–11) provides an overview of the human family as a whole, establishing the unity of all people while also accounting for diversity and dispersion. These early chapters depict human development as a series of transgressions and transformations in which both God and humankind discover and develop their relationship. The rest of the book focuses on Israel's ancestors: Abraham, Sarah and Hagar (Genesis 12–23); Rebekah and Isaac (Genesis 24–26); Jacob, Leah, and Rachel (Genesis 27–35, with a genealogy of Esau in 36); Joseph, Judah, and

*Resourceful women are central to Genesis.*

their brothers (Genesis 37–50)—each generation with its trials, tribulations, and triumphs. In these accounts, women play an active and integral role.

Although many traditional interpreters (both Jewish and non-Jewish) believe that these stories depict the actual lives of our ancestors, most contemporary scholars consider the historical information in Genesis to be more oblique. Such scholars consider Genesis to be a tapestry woven from several sources, sometimes labeled as J, E, and P (see Women and Interpretation of the Torah, p. xxxvi); they suppose that the book is the work of later generations who retroject into the past the tensions and circumstances of their own time. Thus, a careful reading of Genesis offers insights into how ancient Israel constructed its identity at different points in its history. For example, Jacob's sons apparently represent clans that at some point banded together and then sought to account for this later unity by constructing a shared genealogy. Likewise, stories such as the tale about Lot's daughters (Genesis 19) try to account for both affinity and tension with surrounding cultures.

Considering Genesis in its broader ancient Near Eastern and Mediterranean context—where stories of origin feature violent creation and heroic and semi-divine figures—highlights Genesis' distinctive worldview. Genesis begins with a peaceful creation and then concentrates on an ordinary, aged couple (Sarah and Abraham, who become extraordinary as their story unfolds), with whom God enters into a covenant, and on their somewhat fumbling offspring. Far from promoting fame and fortune through great feats of might, Genesis illustrates how persons walk with God (17:1) dialogue with God (Genesis 18), and also wrestle with God (Genesis 32) in the pursuit of blessings.

The theme of sibling rivalry runs through Genesis from beginning to end (in contrast with Greek mythology, in which intergenerational conflict often occupies center stage). Beginning with the first murder (Abel by Cain; Genesis 4), competition between siblings plagues every generation. Eventually, the persistent, murderous impulse is channeled into repentance and reconciliation when Joseph unites tearfully with his brothers (see 45:1–15 and 50:18–22). Sibling rivalry and competition also characterize the story of the book's two prominent sisters, Leah and Rachel (Genesis 29–30 and 35:16–20). Remarkably, however, their competition results in producing children, jointly building the "House of Israel" (as the community affirms in Ruth 4:11).

Beginning with daring Eve, resourceful women are central to the book of Genesis. Women are key, not merely because they give birth, but because they shape their family's destiny; there would be no "Israel" without the matriarchs. Their stories belie any claim that Genesis privileges males at the expense of females. Rather, the book privileges the ones who secure the continuity of the family and perpetuate God's blessings. In addition to Eve (Genesis 1–4), Sarah (Genesis 12–23), Hagar (Genesis 16 and 21), Rebekah (Genesis 24–28), Leah, Rachel, and their handmaids Bilhah and Zilpah (Genesis 29–31), Genesis devotes attention to the dilemma of Lot's daughters (Genesis 19), the tragic fate of Dinah (Genesis 34), the triumph of Tamar (Genesis 38), and the seductive Potiphar's wife (Genesis 39). Together, these women represent the biblical understanding of humans as God's partners in maintaining God's good world.

—*Tamara Cohn Eskenazi*

# בראשית ✦ *B'reishit*

## GENESIS 1:1–6:8

## *Creation and Transformation*

WHO ARE WE? The question is answered in the first portion of Genesis as follows: We are God's prized creation, inhabiting a good world that God has made. We are a constellation of four relationships: with the earth from whence we came and whither we return (Genesis 2), with each other as women and men equally blessed and jointly commissioned to care for the world (Genesis 1), with the animal world toward which we have responsibility (Genesis 1 and 2), and with God in whose image we are made (Genesis 1) and whose breath animates us (Genesis 2). Human disobedience complicates these relationships but does not destroy them.

Genesis 1 emphasizes the power of language and the reality of goodness. Humankind is embedded in a larger world over which God reigns supreme, but within which human beings can and do play a unique, decisive role.

A wide-angle lens that encompasses the whole world in Genesis 1 is augmented in Genesis 2–3 with a zoom lens that discloses an "up close and personal" relationship with God. This split-screen view characterizes the Torah as a whole and introduces a biblical practice of offering more than one perspective on important events.

The subsequent narratives, through Genesis 11, continue to respond to universal human questions about origins. They account for human suffering and inequality while affirming the sovereignty of a God who deeply cares for the world and its creatures.

Genesis 1–11 depicts God as still discovering the qualities of the material at hand (humankind) and (re)assessing its potential. Despite repeated disappointments, God remains faithful and hopeful, adjusting expectations and offering humankind new tools and guidance.

> *No biblical story has had more influence on women's lives and identity.*

The parashah concludes at a nadir, with God's disappointment in humankind when violence corrupts goodness (6:6). However, the text also makes clear the possibility of renewal despite decline (a theme throughout the Bible). Goodness and connectedness persist.

No biblical story has had more influence on women's lives and identity—and none has been more often reinterpreted through later cultural biases—than the creation of woman in Genesis 2 and the expulsion from the Garden in Genesis 3. The version of creation of humankind in 1:26–28, which portrays equality between the sexes and their shared reflection of God's image, is typically overlooked in favor the more ambiguous one in Genesis 2, which is typically read as one in which man precedes woman in time. Consequently, the first woman has been cast by later interpreters as an afterthought: second and therefore secondary in value, not essential to God's plan. She has also been held solely or at least primarily responsible for human suffering.

However, a close reading of Genesis 1–3 indicates that such (mis)readings overlook the context and nuances of the depiction of woman. Suffice it to say here that the first woman is depicted as a discerning, responsible person who despite transgression (Genesis 3) maintains a creative partnership with both God and the first man. She is rightly recognized by her man as a source of life (3:20).

Other named women make cameo appearances: Ada, Zillah, and Naamah (4:19–23). The parashah concludes with a mysterious account about the illegitimate seizing of women, a prelude to the flood story that will follow (see at 6:1–8).

—*Tamara Cohn Eskenazi*

## Outline

I. The First Creation Story
*Creation of World, Time, and Life* (1:1–2:3)

II. The Second Creation Story
*From the "Human" to "Woman and Man"* (2:4–25)

A. The first human (vv. 4–7)
B. Humankind's first home: the Garden of Eden (vv. 8–17)
C. The creation of human partnership (vv. 18–25)

III. Temptation, Transgression, and Transformation
*In the Garden of Eden* (3:1–24)

A. Temptation and transgression (vv. 1–6)
B. The transformation (vv. 7–21)
C. The expulsion (vv. 22–24)

IV. Life Outside the Garden (4:1–6:8)

A. Eve and Adam reunite: childbirth and naming (4:1–2)
B. The first sin: Cain and Abel (4:3–24)
C. Eve and Adam reunite: childbirth and naming (4:25–26)
D. The recapitulation of human origins, and their genealogy to Noah (5:1–32)
E. The marriage between heavenly beings and earthly women (6:1–4)
F. Conclusion: God's regret (6:5–8)

1:1

When God was about to create heaven and
earth, [2]the earth was a chaos, unformed,
and on the chaotic waters' face there was darkness.
Then God's spirit glided over the face of the waters,
[3]and God said, "Let there be light!"—and there was
light. [4]And when God saw how good the light was,

א בְּרֵאשִׁית בָּרָא אֱלֹהִים אֵת הַשָּׁמַיִם
וְאֵת הָאָרֶץ׃ 2 וְהָאָרֶץ הָיְתָה תֹהוּ וָבֹהוּ
וְחֹשֶׁךְ עַל־פְּנֵי תְהוֹם וְרוּחַ אֱלֹהִים מְרַחֶפֶת
עַל־פְּנֵי הַמָּיִם׃ 3 וַיֹּאמֶר אֱלֹהִים יְהִי אוֹר
וַיְהִי־אוֹר׃ 4 וַיַּרְא אֱלֹהִים אֶת־הָאוֹר כִּי־

## *The First Creation Story*

### CREATION OF WORLD, TIME, AND LIFE (1:1–2:3)

Genesis 1 unfolds in a rhythmic, poetic fashion, depicting an orderly creation of the world and life in six days. Genesis does not offer a scientific account of creation but an interpretation and a system of values that encodes from the start three essential ideas: the power of language, especially God's word; the goodness of God's world; and the orderly nature of the world. Creating the world begins with a series of separations—from chaos to differentiated bodies—that, with one exception (day 2), are pronounced as "good." In the first three days God creates a context for life. In the last three God creates heavenly and earthly bodies to inhabit the space. The movement of each day, from evening to morning, replicates a journey from darkness to light.

*1.* ***When God was about to create.*** The more familiar expression "In the beginning" has been replaced by the more accurate translation. As Rashi noted, the opening verses do not claim creation out of nothing.

*2.* ***chaotic waters'.*** The feminine noun *t'hom*, often translated as "the deep," echoes the name of the Mesopotamian goddess Tiamat. According to the Babylonian creation myth, Tiamat was brutally killed by her rebellious offspring in the process of creating the world. See also at 7:11, "great deep."

*3.* ***God said.*** God's use of language contrasts with some other ancient Near East creation stories that emphasize battles among the gods. By privileging language as a source of creative power, the Torah identifies tools for renewal in times of military defeat.

***"Let there be light!"*** As the first of God's creative acts, light becomes not only a physical phenomenon but also a symbol of clarity and illumination that extend beyond the physical.

*4.* ***God saw how good.*** This phrase repeats in similar form six times in this passage, expressing the basic goodness of God's creation.

◗ A woman would have up to eight pregnancies to provide the optimum family size.

ANOTHER VIEW ➤ *27*

◗ Our sexualities seem to point toward some element in the divine nature.

CONTEMPORARY REFLECTION ➤ *29*

◗ For the Rabbis, the female also shares in the divine image.

POST-BIBLICAL INTERPRETATIONS ➤ *28*

◗ Your hands create my body / your mouth breathes life in me / my face shines.

VOICES ➤ *32*

God divided the light from the darkness; 5God
then called the light Day, and called the darkness
Night, and there was evening and there was morning, [the] first day.
6God then said, "Let there be an expanse in the
midst of the waters, and let it divide water from
water!" 7So God made the expanse, separating the
waters beneath the expanse from the waters above
the expanse—and so it was. 8God then called the
expanse Sky, and there was evening and there was
morning, a second day.
9God then said, "Let the waters beneath the sky
be collected in one place, so that the dry ground
may be seen!"—and so it was. 10And God called the
dry ground Earth, and called the collected waters
Seas. And when God saw how good it was, 11God
said, "Let the earth grow vegetation, seed-bearing
plants, fruit trees on the earth that bear fruit, each
true to its type, with its seed in it!"—and so it was.
12The earth brought forth vegetation, seed-bearing
plants, each true to its type, and trees bearing fruit,
each true to its type, with its seed in it. And God
saw how good it was, 13and there was evening and
there was morning, a third day.
14God then said, "Let there be lights in the expanse of the sky, to separate day from night, to be
markers for sacred seasons, for days and years, 15and
to be lights in the expanse of the sky, spilling light
upon the earth!"—and so it was. 16Thus God made
the two great lights: the greater light to govern the
day, and the lesser light to govern the night and the
stars. 17God set them in the sky's expanse to spill
light upon the earth, 18to govern the day and the

טוֹב וַיַּבְדֵּל אֱלֹהִים בֵּין הָאוֹר וּבֵין הַחֹשֶׁךְ׃
5 וַיִּקְרָא אֱלֹהִים ׀ לָאוֹר יוֹם וְלַחֹשֶׁךְ קָרָא
לָיְלָה וַיְהִי־עֶרֶב וַיְהִי־בֹקֶר יוֹם אֶחָד׃ פ
6 וַיֹּאמֶר אֱלֹהִים יְהִי רָקִיעַ בְּתוֹךְ הַמָּיִם
וִיהִי מַבְדִּיל בֵּין מַיִם לָמָיִם׃ 7 וַיַּעַשׂ
אֱלֹהִים אֶת־הָרָקִיעַ וַיַּבְדֵּל בֵּין הַמַּיִם אֲשֶׁר
מִתַּחַת לָרָקִיעַ וּבֵין הַמַּיִם אֲשֶׁר מֵעַל
לָרָקִיעַ וַיְהִי־כֵן׃ 8 וַיִּקְרָא אֱלֹהִים לָרָקִיעַ
שָׁמָיִם וַיְהִי־עֶרֶב וַיְהִי־בֹקֶר יוֹם שֵׁנִי׃ פ
9 וַיֹּאמֶר אֱלֹהִים יִקָּווּ הַמַּיִם מִתַּחַת
הַשָּׁמַיִם אֶל־מָקוֹם אֶחָד וְתֵרָאֶה הַיַּבָּשָׁה
וַיְהִי־כֵן׃ 10 וַיִּקְרָא אֱלֹהִים ׀ לַיַּבָּשָׁה אֶרֶץ
וּלְמִקְוֵה הַמַּיִם קָרָא יַמִּים וַיַּרְא אֱלֹהִים
כִּי־טוֹב׃ 11 וַיֹּאמֶר אֱלֹהִים תַּדְשֵׁא הָאָרֶץ
דֶּשֶׁא עֵשֶׂב מַזְרִיעַ זֶרַע עֵץ פְּרִי עֹשֶׂה פְּרִי
לְמִינוֹ אֲשֶׁר זַרְעוֹ־בוֹ עַל־הָאָרֶץ וַיְהִי־כֵן׃
12 וַתּוֹצֵא הָאָרֶץ דֶּשֶׁא עֵשֶׂב מַזְרִיעַ זֶרַע
לְמִינֵהוּ וְעֵץ עֹשֶׂה־פְּרִי אֲשֶׁר זַרְעוֹ־בוֹ
לְמִינֵהוּ וַיַּרְא אֱלֹהִים כִּי־טוֹב׃ 13 וַיְהִי־
עֶרֶב וַיְהִי־בֹקֶר יוֹם שְׁלִישִׁי׃ פ
14 וַיֹּאמֶר אֱלֹהִים יְהִי מְאֹרֹת בִּרְקִיעַ
הַשָּׁמַיִם לְהַבְדִּיל בֵּין הַיּוֹם וּבֵין הַלָּיְלָה
וְהָיוּ לְאֹתֹת וּלְמוֹעֲדִים וּלְיָמִים וְשָׁנִים׃
15 וְהָיוּ לִמְאוֹרֹת בִּרְקִיעַ הַשָּׁמַיִם לְהָאִיר
עַל־הָאָרֶץ וַיְהִי־כֵן׃ 16 וַיַּעַשׂ אֱלֹהִים אֶת־
שְׁנֵי הַמְּאֹרֹת הַגְּדֹלִים אֶת־הַמָּאוֹר הַגָּדֹל
לְמֶמְשֶׁלֶת הַיּוֹם וְאֶת־הַמָּאוֹר הַקָּטֹן
לְמֶמְשֶׁלֶת הַלַּיְלָה וְאֵת הַכּוֹכָבִים׃ 17 וַיִּתֵּן
אֹתָם אֱלֹהִים בִּרְקִיעַ הַשָּׁמָיִם לְהָאִיר
עַל־הָאָרֶץ׃ 18 וְלִמְשֹׁל בַּיּוֹם וּבַלַּיְלָה

***God divided.*** God brings order out of chaos by separating the swirling mass into coherent bodies (land, contained water, sky), which will provide a habitat and sustenance for life.

***10. collected.*** The noun *mikveh* is rendered here as an adjective to suit English idiom. It is the usual word for a reservoir or other bodies of water (Exodus 7:19, Leviticus 11:36), including eventually a ritual bath. On the *mikveh* as ritual bath, see *Tazria*, Contemporary Reflection, p. 652.

night, to separate the light from the darkness; and
God saw how good it was. 19And there was evening
and there was morning, a fourth day.
20God then said, "Let the waters bring forth
swarms of living creatures, and let the birds fly over
the earth, across the face of the expanse of the sky!"
21God then formed the great sea monsters, and
every living creature that creeps, with which the
waters swarm, all true to their types, and every
winged bird, each true to its type; and God saw
how good it was. 22God then blessed them, saying,
"Be fruitful and multiply, fill the waters of the seas,
and let the birds multiply in the earth!" 23And there
was evening and there was morning, a fifth day.
24God then said, "Let the earth bring forth
living creatures of every type: domestic animals
and creeping things and wild animals, each true
to its type!"—and so it was. 25Thus God made the
wild animals, each true to its type, and the domestic
animals, each true to its type, and every creature
that creeps on the ground, each true to its type; and
God saw how good it was. 26God now said, "Let us
make human beings in our image, after our likeness;

וּֽלְהַבְדִּ֔יל בֵּ֥ין הָא֖וֹר וּבֵ֣ין הַחֹ֑שֶׁךְ וַיַּ֥רְא
אֱלֹהִ֖ים כִּי־טֽוֹב׃ 19 וַֽיְהִי־עֶ֥רֶב וַֽיְהִי־בֹ֖קֶר
י֥וֹם רְבִיעִֽי׃ פ
20 וַיֹּ֣אמֶר אֱלֹהִ֔ים יִשְׁרְצ֣וּ הַמַּ֔יִם שֶׁ֖רֶץ נֶ֣פֶשׁ
חַיָּ֑ה וְעוֹף֙ יְעוֹפֵ֣ף עַל־הָאָ֔רֶץ עַל־פְּנֵ֖י רְקִ֥יעַ
הַשָּׁמָֽיִם׃ 21 וַיִּבְרָ֣א אֱלֹהִ֔ים אֶת־הַתַּנִּינִ֖ם
הַגְּדֹלִ֑ים וְאֵ֣ת כׇּל־נֶ֣פֶשׁ הַֽחַיָּ֣ה ׀ הָֽרֹמֶ֡שֶׂת
אֲשֶׁר֩ שָׁרְצ֨וּ הַמַּ֜יִם לְמִֽינֵהֶ֗ם וְאֵ֨ת כׇּל־ע֤וֹף
כָּנָף֙ לְמִינֵ֔הוּ וַיַּ֥רְא אֱלֹהִ֖ים כִּי־טֽוֹב׃ 22 וַיְבָ֧רֶךְ
אֹתָ֛ם אֱלֹהִ֖ים לֵאמֹ֑ר פְּר֣וּ וּרְב֗וּ וּמִלְא֤וּ אֶת־
הַמַּ֙יִם֙ בַּיַּמִּ֔ים וְהָע֖וֹף יִ֥רֶב בָּאָֽרֶץ׃ 23 וַֽיְהִי־
עֶ֥רֶב וַֽיְהִי־בֹ֖קֶר י֥וֹם חֲמִישִֽׁי׃ פ
24 וַיֹּ֣אמֶר אֱלֹהִ֗ים תּוֹצֵ֨א הָאָ֜רֶץ נֶ֤פֶשׁ חַיָּה֙
לְמִינָ֔הּ בְּהֵמָ֥ה וָרֶ֛מֶשׂ וְחַֽיְתוֹ־אֶ֖רֶץ לְמִינָ֑הּ
וַֽיְהִי־כֵֽן׃ 25 וַיַּ֣עַשׂ אֱלֹהִים֩ אֶת־חַיַּ֨ת הָאָ֜רֶץ
לְמִינָ֗הּ וְאֶת־הַבְּהֵמָה֙ לְמִינָ֔הּ וְאֵ֛ת כׇּל־רֶ֥מֶשׂ
הָֽאֲדָמָ֖ה לְמִינֵ֑הוּ וַיַּ֥רְא אֱלֹהִ֖ים כִּי־טֽוֹב׃
26 וַיֹּ֣אמֶר אֱלֹהִ֔ים נַֽעֲשֶׂ֥ה אָדָ֛ם בְּצַלְמֵ֖נוּ
כִּדְמוּתֵ֑נוּ וְיִרְדּוּ֩ בִדְגַ֨ת הַיָּ֜ם וּבְע֣וֹף הַשָּׁמַ֗יִם

*26–30.* Day six, the most complex and detailed, first describes the emergence of land creatures from the earth (vv. 24–25). Thus far, each species has been endowed with the capacity of reproduction and renewal (vv. 12, 21, 25). The narration now dwells the most on the creation of humankind (vv. 26–27), indicating its importance in the created realm.

***26. "Let us make."*** God is speaking to the divine entourage; compare Genesis 6:4 and Job 1:6, which envision *b'nei Elohim* (literally "sons of God") as divine beings subordinate to God.

***"human beings."*** Heb. *adam,* a singular noun, stands here for a collective, like the English words "fish" or "fowl." It refers to humankind as a whole, including both females and males (compare 5:1–2). Older translations render it as "man," often meant in its gender-neutral sense—a usage that is sometimes misunderstood and thereby misleading. In fact, the noun *adam* is almost always a generic term, employed when gender is not germane. Apart from the thirty references to the particular *adam* of the Eden story (who gives rise to the name "Adam") and one to the progenitor of a lineage (Joshua 14:15), none of the Bible's 530 other occurrences of *adam* refers to a particular individual (David Stein, "What Does It Mean to Be a 'Man'?" 2006–7, § VI.B; "*adam,*" *Semantic Dictionary of Biblical Hebrew,* 2007; Alison Grant, "*'adam* and *'ish*: Man in the OT," 1977, pp. 5, 11).

Here, the preceding verses have narrated the generic creation of other earthly creatures, a context that now evokes the correspondingly generic sense of *adam.* Thus, the Hebrew text unambiguously presents female and male as co-created and equal.

***"our image, after our likeness."*** These tantalizing attributes are uniquely bestowed upon human-

and let them hold sway over the fish of the sea and
the birds of the sky, over the beasts, over all the
earth, over all that creeps upon the earth." 27So
God created the human beings in [the divine]
image, creating [them] in the image of God, creating them male and female. 28God then blessed
them, and God said to them, "Be fruitful and
multiply; fill the earth and tame it; hold sway over
the fish of the sea and the birds of the sky, and
over every animal that creeps on the earth." 29And
God said, "Look, I have given you all the seed-
bearing plants on the face of the earth, and every
tree that has in it seed-bearing fruit—these are
yours to eat. 30And to every land animal, and to
every bird of the sky, and to all that creeps on the
earth in which is the breath of life, I [give] all green

וּבַבְּהֵמָה וּבְכָל־הָאָרֶץ וּבְכָל־הָרֶמֶשׂ הָרֹמֵשׂ
עַל־הָאָרֶץ׃ 27 וַיִּבְרָא אֱלֹהִים ׀ אֶת־הָאָדָם
בְּצַלְמוֹ בְּצֶלֶם אֱלֹהִים בָּרָא אֹתוֹ זָכָר
וּנְקֵבָה בָּרָא אֹתָם׃ 28 וַיְבָרֶךְ אֹתָם אֱלֹהִים
וַיֹּאמֶר לָהֶם אֱלֹהִים פְּרוּ וּרְבוּ וּמִלְאוּ אֶת־
הָאָרֶץ וְכִבְשֻׁהָ וּרְדוּ בִּדְגַת הַיָּם וּבְעוֹף
הַשָּׁמַיִם וּבְכָל־חַיָּה הָרֹמֶשֶׂת עַל־הָאָרֶץ׃
29 וַיֹּאמֶר אֱלֹהִים הִנֵּה נָתַתִּי לָכֶם אֶת־כָּל־
עֵשֶׂב ׀ זֹרֵעַ זֶרַע אֲשֶׁר עַל־פְּנֵי כָל־הָאָרֶץ
וְאֶת־כָּל־הָעֵץ אֲשֶׁר־בּוֹ פְרִי־עֵץ זֹרֵעַ זָרַע
לָכֶם יִהְיֶה לְאָכְלָה׃ 30 וּלְכָל־חַיַּת הָאָרֶץ
וּלְכָל־עוֹף הַשָּׁמַיִם וּלְכֹל ׀ רוֹמֵשׂ עַל־הָאָרֶץ
אֲשֶׁר־בּוֹ נֶפֶשׁ חַיָּה אֶת־כָּל־יֶרֶק עֵשֶׂב

kind as a whole. They introduce a new way for the divine to be manifested in the world through every human being. The notion that all humans are in the divine image is in sharp contrast to ancient Near East traditions where only kings represent the divine. This radical idea from the Hebrew Bible proved to be a fundamental notion in Western history.

***"hold sway."*** See at 1:28 and 9:1–7.

*27.* ***human beings.*** This translation resorts to the plural to avoid using misleading masculine pronouns later in the verse. Literally the Hebrew has: "And God created the *adam*. In the image of God he created him/it; male and female he created them" (shifting the object pronoun from singular to plural). By referring to *adam,* the text is not describing an individual but a new class of beings that comprises female and male from the start, both of them in God's image. This idea is repeated more clearly in 5:1–2. The shift from singular to plural does not convey that man was created before woman. (That the singular pronoun is masculine can be explained as necessary for grammatical gender agreement in the Hebrew language.) Rather, it seems to say that our humanity, as *adam*, precedes our division into sexual categories. Our humanity comes first; our sexual identity next.

***male and female.*** This passage explicitly proclaims the co-creation of female and male, both in God's image. It establishes the goodness and gender balance as the foundation for all that follows. The terms male (*zachar*) and female (*n'kevah*) designate biological categories, thus relevant to fertility, a major theme in this passage. The word *zachar* evokes the Hebrew word for "remembering," and *n'kevah* evokes the word for being pierced.

***God then blessed them.*** Female and male receive the same blessings.

*28.* ***"Be fruitful and multiply."*** The harsh conditions and the fragility of life in the ancient world make fertility a most valued gift and necessity. The plain sense of the text is that this "first commandment" is issued to both female and male.

***"hold sway."*** This promise surely brought comfort to early readers who lived at the mercy of the natural world, who were vulnerable to its unpredictability, and who had reason to fear becoming prey to wild beasts. It is not a mandate to exploit nature. See 9:1–7 where this dominion is altered.

*29.* ***"I have given you."*** See at 9:2–4.

vegetation for food."—and so it was. ³¹God then surveyed all that [God] had made, and look—it was very good! And there was evening and there was morning, the sixth day.

2 Completed now were heaven and earth and all their host. ²On the seventh day, God had completed the work that had been done, ceasing then on the seventh day from all the work that [God] had done. ³Then God blessed the seventh day and made it holy, and ceased from all the creative work that God [had chosen] to do.

⁴This is the chronicle of heaven and earth when they were created, on the day God יהוה made earth

לְאָכְלָ֑ה וַֽיְהִי־כֵֽן: 31 וַיַּ֤רְא אֱלֹהִים֙ אֶת־כָּל־אֲשֶׁ֣ר עָשָׂ֔ה וְהִנֵּה־ט֖וֹב מְאֹ֑ד וַֽיְהִי־עֶ֥רֶב וַֽיְהִי־בֹ֖קֶר י֥וֹם הַשִּׁשִּֽׁי: פ

ב וַיְכֻלּ֛וּ הַשָּׁמַ֥יִם וְהָאָ֖רֶץ וְכָל־צְבָאָֽם: 2 וַיְכַ֤ל אֱלֹהִים֙ בַּיּ֣וֹם הַשְּׁבִיעִ֔י מְלַאכְתּ֖וֹ אֲשֶׁ֣ר עָשָׂ֑ה וַיִּשְׁבֹּת֙ בַּיּ֣וֹם הַשְּׁבִיעִ֔י מִכָּל־מְלַאכְתּ֖וֹ אֲשֶׁ֥ר עָשָֽׂה: 3 וַיְבָ֤רֶךְ אֱלֹהִים֙ אֶת־י֣וֹם הַשְּׁבִיעִ֔י וַיְקַדֵּ֖שׁ אֹת֑וֹ כִּ֣י ב֤וֹ שָׁבַת֙ מִכָּל־מְלַאכְתּ֔וֹ אֲשֶׁר־בָּרָ֥א אֱלֹהִ֖ים לַעֲשֽׂוֹת: פ

4 אֵ֣לֶּה תֽוֹלְד֧וֹת הַשָּׁמַ֛יִם וְהָאָ֖רֶץ בְּהִבָּֽרְאָ֑ם בְּי֗וֹם עֲשׂ֛וֹת יְהוָ֥ה אֱלֹהִ֖ים אֶ֥רֶץ וְשָׁמָֽיִם:

---

**31.** *it was very good.* The final survey, which affirms the goodness of all that God has created, comes only after humankind appears.

**2:2.** *the seventh day.* The number seven in the Bible signifies completeness. Only the seventh day, not yet designated as Shabbat, is holy. Time, not space, is thus consecrated, which (as A. J. Heschel notes) becomes a hallmark of Judaism. The sequence from lesser to greater, culminating with the Sabbath, is relevant to assessing the creation of woman. Last does not mean least in Genesis.

## The Second Creation Story
### FROM THE "HUMAN" TO "WOMAN AND MAN" (2:4–25)

Genesis 2 offers a second perspective on creation, focusing on humankind. Genesis is unique in ancient Near Eastern literature in giving special attention to the formation of woman. In Greece, however, Hesiod (8th century B.C.E.) claimed that the first woman, Pandora, was created to ensnare men to their death. In contrast, Genesis 2 envisions the creation of woman and man for mutual benefit: "It is not good for the *adam* to be alone" (2:18). In contrast to Genesis 1, here the gen-

der identity of the first *adam* is ambiguous (see at "the man," v. 7); therefore, the status of woman in Genesis 2 remains open to different interpretations.

Many Jews and Christians over the centuries have interpreted the early portions of Genesis to mean that woman was secondary and thus subordinate, created merely for man's benefit. Three factors argue against such interpretations. (*1*) The term *adam* is generic, not specifically "a man," complicating the notion of the gender identity of the first person. (*2*) Even if one interprets this particular *adam* as male, last does not mean least. (Indeed, in Genesis 1 human beings are created last, a sequence that some interpreters consider a sign of superiority.) (*3*) God creates human partnership, not hierarchy, in Genesis 2. (For a different interpretation, see Contemporary Reflection, p. 29.)

### THE FIRST HUMAN (2:4–7)

**4.** This verse bridges the text's first two units. (The present translation places it with the second one.) Its first clause concludes the first story of Creation, and its second begins the story that follows.

**יהוה.** The first time in the Bible that God's name—YHVH, liturgically read as *Adonai*—appears. Later traditions consider this name to repre-

and heaven. 5No shrub of the field was yet on the
earth, no plant of the field had yet sprung up—
for God יהוה had not poured rain down upon the
earth, and there was not a soul to till the soil—
6though a flow would emerge from the earth and
water the surface of the soil. 7Then God יהוה
fashioned the man—dust from the soil—and
breathed into his nostrils the breath of life, so that
the man became a living being.

5 וְכֹל ׀ שִׂיחַ הַשָּׂדֶה טֶרֶם יִהְיֶה בָאָרֶץ וְכָל־
עֵשֶׂב הַשָּׂדֶה טֶרֶם יִצְמָח כִּי לֹא הִמְטִיר
יְהֹוָה אֱלֹהִים עַל־הָאָרֶץ וְאָדָם אַיִן לַעֲבֹד
אֶת־הָאֲדָמָה׃ 6 וְאֵד יַעֲלֶה מִן־הָאָרֶץ
וְהִשְׁקָה אֶת־כָּל־פְּנֵי הָאֲדָמָה׃ 7 וַיִּיצֶר
יְהֹוָה אֱלֹהִים אֶת־הָאָדָם עָפָר מִן־הָאֲדָמָה
וַיִּפַּח בְּאַפָּיו נִשְׁמַת חַיִּים וַיְהִי הָאָדָם
לְנֶפֶשׁ חַיָּה׃

sent specific qualities of God, such as compassion (in contrast to the term "God," which emphasizes justice). Most translations use "the LORD" (so the New JPS) or "the Eternal" (*The Torah: A Modern Commentary,* revised edition). Some translations have used "Jehovah" or "Yahweh" in an attempt to capture the sound of the name. Like *The Contemporary Torah* (2006), we have chosen to retain the original Hebrew name. In the post-biblical period, Jews came to believe that God's name is too sacred to be pronounced. This has led to substituting the reverential euphemism *Adonai* (a grander form of the word for "my Lord") for God's actual name. The name itself shows no marks of gender. Some scholars have understood it as a form of the verb "to be," although this explanation is now disputed and far from certain. An abbreviated form of the name appears as "Yah" in names (Jeremiah) or words such as "Hallelujah." (See also at Exodus 3:15.)

5. ***there was not a soul.*** Literally, "no *adam*"—no human being.

7. ***man . . . from the soil.*** Or, "soul . . . from the soil," to express the word play between *adamah* (soil; earth) and *adam* (a human being, an "earthling"). In contrast to Genesis 1, *adam* is created before the animals and set in a fertile place to care for it.

***God . . . breathed.*** The human being is infused with divine breath (literally "in-spired").

***breath.*** Heb. *n'shamah,* often translated as "soul," is the life force that comes from God.

***the man.*** The word *adam* functioned in v. 5 in its usual role as a collective noun designating human beings of both genders, as also earlier in 1:26–27 and later in 5:1–2. But now in 2:7–3:30, *ha-adam* ("the *adam*") refers to a particular individual. And this second creation story is ambiguous with respect to this person's gender. On the one hand, it can be presumed that early readers understood *ha-adam* to designate the first human being as male: all patrilineages originated in this first human being, and in biblical genealogies, the typical initiator of any lineage is male. In other words, as David Stein suggests, *ha-adam* in this story functions as an etiology "not of human biology but rather of lineage" (*The Contemporary Torah,* 2006, p. 394). This presumption works well with the narrative flow—in which even after the creation of woman, the term *ha-adam* continues to be used to refer to the man.

According to this view, woman—in terms of lineage, but only in those terms—is indeed presented as second and derivative. Nonetheless, this story presents, as Phyllis Bird notes, "a portrait of humankind in which the two sexes are essential to the action and are bound together in mutual dependence" (*Theology Today* 50/4, 1994, p. 524).

On the other hand, when viewing the individual designated by the term *adam*, the usual inclusive meaning of that term (see at 1:26) cannot be ignored. A gender-neutral or non-gendered progenitor was not unknown in the ancient world; it appears, for example, in Sumerian literature and in the work of Plato. (Plato's *Symposium* describes humans as not gendered initially but divided later into three types of pairs: man and woman; man

[8]To the east, God יהוה planted a garden in Eden, setting the man there whom [God] had formed. [9]Then, out of the soil, God יהוה grew trees alluring to the eye and good for fruit; and in the middle of the garden, the Tree of Life and the Tree of All Knowledge. [10]A river went forth from Eden to water the garden; from there it divided and became four branches. [11]The first was named Pishon—that one flows around the land of Havilah, where there is gold. [12]The gold of that land is fine; bdellium is there, and onyx stone. [13]The second was named Gihon—that one flows around the land of Cush. [14]The third was named Tigris—that one flows east of Assyria. And the fourth river is the Euphrates.

[15]So God יהוה took the man, placing him in the Garden of Eden to work it and keep it. [16]God יהוה then commanded the man, saying, "You may eat all you like of every tree in the garden—

8 וַיִּטַּע יְהוָה אֱלֹהִים גַּן־בְּעֵדֶן מִקֶּדֶם וַיָּשֶׂם
שָׁם אֶת־הָאָדָם אֲשֶׁר יָצָר׃ 9 וַיַּצְמַח יְהוָה
אֱלֹהִים מִן־הָאֲדָמָה כָּל־עֵץ נֶחְמָד לְמַרְאֶה
וְטוֹב לְמַאֲכָל וְעֵץ הַחַיִּים בְּתוֹךְ הַגָּן וְעֵץ
הַדַּעַת טוֹב וָרָע׃ 10 וְנָהָר יֹצֵא מֵעֵדֶן
לְהַשְׁקוֹת אֶת־הַגָּן וּמִשָּׁם יִפָּרֵד וְהָיָה
לְאַרְבָּעָה רָאשִׁים׃ 11 שֵׁם הָאֶחָד פִּישׁוֹן
הוּא הַסֹּבֵב אֵת כָּל־אֶרֶץ הַחֲוִילָה אֲשֶׁר־
שָׁם הַזָּהָב׃ 12 וּזֲהַב הָאָרֶץ הַהִוא טוֹב שָׁם
הַבְּדֹלַח וְאֶבֶן הַשֹּׁהַם׃ 13 וְשֵׁם־הַנָּהָר הַשֵּׁנִי
גִּיחוֹן הוּא הַסּוֹבֵב אֵת כָּל־אֶרֶץ כּוּשׁ׃
14 וְשֵׁם הַנָּהָר הַשְּׁלִישִׁי חִדֶּקֶל הוּא הַהֹלֵךְ
קִדְמַת אַשּׁוּר וְהַנָּהָר הָרְבִיעִי הוּא פְרָת׃
15 וַיִּקַּח יְהוָה אֱלֹהִים אֶת־הָאָדָם וַיַּנִּחֵהוּ
בְגַן־עֵדֶן לְעָבְדָהּ וּלְשָׁמְרָהּ׃ 16 וַיְצַו יְהוָה
אֱלֹהִים עַל־הָאָדָם לֵאמֹר מִכֹּל עֵץ־הַגָּן

and man; woman and woman. The Greek myth thus accounts for different sexual affinities, as persons seek their specific "other half.") In Genesis 2, the generic term in the text creates ambiguity regarding that character's gender. This *adam* is at the same both a single individual and "the human being."

Through this gender ambiguity, the text seems to be expressing complex ideas about the position of female and male in God's plan, and about the tension perceived in cultural reality. The immediate emphasis falls on the earthiness of the person (*adamah* means "earth").

### HUMANKIND'S FIRST HOME: THE GARDEN OF EDEN (2:8–17)

***8. a garden in Eden.*** The place name *eden* (pleasure) evokes a moist, luxurious garden.

***9. good for fruit.*** The Hebrew words *maachal* (fruit, literally "food") and *achal* (eat) together appear more than twenty times in the Eden narrative, evidence of an overriding concern among the text's earliest audience with procuring food.

***Tree of All Knowledge.*** The familiar, literal translations "knowledge of good and evil" or "knowledge of good and bad" preserve an ambiguity that seems intentional. The phrase "good and bad" could stand for "everything," but it also could imply intellectual comprehension (everything from *A* to *Z*, or from good to bad), moral judgment, or —perhaps best—experience, meaning a direct encounter with good and bad. It is the latter that seems to have befallen humankind as a result of eating. Elsewhere, "to know" refers to intimate, often sexual relations (see at 4:1).

***10–14.*** The four rivers express the superabundance of the garden. In the land of Israel, water was a scarce and precious commodity. The names recall actual rivers but the locations of some is problematic. Pishon and Gihon are small rivers in the land of Israel.

[17]but of the Tree of All Knowledge you may not
eat, for the moment you eat of it you shall be
doomed to die."
[18]Then God יהוה considered, "It is not good
that the man be alone—I will make him a helpmate." [19]So God יהוה formed the wild animals
and the birds of the sky out of the soil, and brought
the man to see what he would call each one; and
whatever the man called it, that became the creature's name. [20]The man gave names to every domestic animal and to the birds of the sky, and
to all the wild animals, but for [himself] Adam
found no helpmate. [21]Then, throwing the man
into a profound slumber, so that he slept, God
יהוה took one of his ribs and closed up the flesh
in that place. [22]Now God יהוה built up the rib
taken from the man into a woman, and brought
her to the man, [23]and the man said, "This time— /



אָכֹל תֹּאכֵל׃ 17 וּמֵעֵץ הַדַּעַת טוֹב וָרָע לֹא
תֹאכַל מִמֶּנּוּ כִּי בְּיוֹם אֲכָלְךָ מִמֶּנּוּ מוֹת
תָּמוּת׃
18 וַיֹּאמֶר יְהֹוָה אֱלֹהִים לֹא־טוֹב הֱיוֹת
הָאָדָם לְבַדּוֹ אֶעֱשֶׂה־לּוֹ עֵזֶר כְּנֶגְדּוֹ׃
19 וַיִּצֶר יְהֹוָה אֱלֹהִים מִן־הָאֲדָמָה כָּל־
חַיַּת הַשָּׂדֶה וְאֵת כָּל־עוֹף הַשָּׁמַיִם וַיָּבֵא
אֶל־הָאָדָם לִרְאוֹת מַה־יִּקְרָא־לוֹ וְכֹל אֲשֶׁר
יִקְרָא־לוֹ הָאָדָם נֶפֶשׁ חַיָּה הוּא שְׁמוֹ׃
20 וַיִּקְרָא הָאָדָם שֵׁמוֹת לְכָל־הַבְּהֵמָה
וּלְעוֹף הַשָּׁמַיִם וּלְכֹל חַיַּת הַשָּׂדֶה וּלְאָדָם
לֹא־מָצָא עֵזֶר כְּנֶגְדּוֹ׃ 21 וַיַּפֵּל יְהֹוָה אֱלֹהִים ׀
תַּרְדֵּמָה עַל־הָאָדָם וַיִּישָׁן וַיִּקַּח אַחַת
מִצַּלְעֹתָיו וַיִּסְגֹּר בָּשָׂר תַּחְתֶּנָּה׃ 22 וַיִּבֶן
יְהֹוָה אֱלֹהִים ׀ אֶת־הַצֵּלָע אֲשֶׁר־לָקַח מִן־
הָאָדָם לְאִשָּׁה וַיְבִאֶהָ אֶל־הָאָדָם׃ 23 וַיֹּאמֶר

*17. you may not eat.* The momentous prohibition concerns only the tree of knowledge.

### THE CREATION OF HUMAN PARTNERSHIP (2:18–25)

*18. "It is not good."* God proclaims (discovers?!) the first "not good": human isolation.

*"man."* Heb. *adam*; see at v. 7, "the man."

*"helpmate."* Heb. *ezer k'negdo*, literally "a helper as if opposite [or: in front of] him/it," that is, "a helpful counterpart." In the Bible the word *ezer* (helper) typically refers to God and thus lacks any overtone of inferiority. And *negdo* (opposite him/it) suggests a spatial and metaphorical otherness, someone whom one confronts. Psalm 16:8 envisions God in this position, illustrating the positive sense of the word.

Some scholars who assume that God seeks a remedy for human loneliness conclude that God creates woman to comfort and ease man's life. But God's solution implies that what is not good about aloneness concerns the human need for a counterpart. Since the *adam* both is inferior to God and superior to the animals, neither suffices as a partner. Only an equal who is both "other" and "alike" provides the necessary dialogue for human maturation, meaning, and joy.

*20.* The first human task is naming the world. God's unsuccessful experiment to discover a partner reveals God as one who learns from experience in the interaction with humankind, not one who foresees and plans all with precision.

*21. ribs.* The word more accurately means "sides," meaning a more substantial part of the *adam*. Elsewhere in the Bible, the term typically designates a side of a building, a large section necessary for stability.

*23. the man.* Although the word *ha-adam* ("the *adam*") is still utilized here, context indicates a reference to the male. It will be used that way until 3:22, when the inclusive, generic sense—the human being—briefly resumes.

*"This time."* Human encounter elicits human speech. The man's exclamation is poetic, celebrating both similarity and difference.

bone of my bone, flesh of my flesh! / Let this one be called woman, / for this one is taken from man."
24So it is that a man will leave his father and mother and cling to his wife, and they become one flesh.

25Now the two of them were naked, the man and his wife, and they were not ashamed. **3** Of all the wild animals that God יהוה made, the

הָאָדָם זֹאת הַפַּעַם עֶצֶם מֵעֲצָמַי וּבָשָׂר
מִבְּשָׂרִי לְזֹאת יִקָּרֵא אִשָּׁה כִּי מֵאִישׁ לֻקֳחָה־
זֹּאת׃ 24 עַל־כֵּן יַעֲזָב־אִישׁ אֶת־אָבִיו וְאֶת־
אִמּוֹ וְדָבַק בְּאִשְׁתּוֹ וְהָיוּ לְבָשָׂר אֶחָד׃

25 וַיִּהְיוּ שְׁנֵיהֶם עֲרוּמִּים הָאָדָם וְאִשְׁתּוֹ
וְלֹא יִתְבֹּשָׁשׁוּ׃ ג וְהַנָּחָשׁ הָיָה עָרוּם
מִכֹּל חַיַּת הַשָּׂדֶה אֲשֶׁר עָשָׂה יְהוָה אֱלֹהִים

*"Let this one be called."* This is not an act of naming or domination but rather an acknowledgement and interpretation of the man's perception.

*"woman... taken from man."* Only after surgery in Genesis 2 do woman (*ishah*) and man (*ish*) appear, marked by gender-specific terms. If one understands *ha-adam* ("the *adam*") beforehand to refer to a non-gendered person, then this remark describes the division into two human categories: woman and man. Here *ish* designates "a (male) member of the human species," and *ishah* "a (female) member of the human species." Both are fully and equally human. The man's proclamation indicates what the woman means to him; it also serves as an etiology to explain how women and men are related to each other. In addition, the etiology explains why *ishah* and *ish* sound so much alike.

*24.* ***a man will leave his father and mother.*** Typically in biblical texts, women join their husband's household. Most likely this statement does not refer to a man's residence but to his establishing a new alignment, with the couple as a new unity that supersedes the relation to parents. In the ancient world such a separation from a man's parents frees the woman from the control of her husband's family.

***wife.*** Heb. *ishah*. The Hebrew word for "wife" is identical to the word for "woman" (v. 23).

*25.* Nakedness describes the human couple's ease with their bodies—and sets the stage for the next scene in the garden.

## *Temptation, Transgression, Transformation*

### IN THE GARDEN OF EDEN (3:1–24)

Genesis 3, one of the most controversial passages in the Bible, seeks to explain why a wholly good world, created by a caring God, is nonetheless rife with hardship and inequality. It resolves the problem by placing responsibility on humankind. In this drama, woman plays a leading role. Yet she and her mate are equally held responsible.

The story reflects two possible theologies about God and knowledge. God may be perceived as a protective parent, ambivalent about exposing vulnerable humans to the full range of experience that knowledge brings; but God could be understood also as a protector of divine prerogatives against the human desire to have more than is permitted. Either way, the story also cautions about the danger of "premature knowledge"—a message especially pertinent to our own day, where knowledge (as information) is easily separable from maturity.

Although most later interpreters have made this story of transgression the turning point in human events, in Genesis this is but the first of several encounters between God and human beings in which both sides learn about the perils and possibilities of the human condition. There is no mention of an original sin, perpetually present in humankind. The word "sin" does not appear here at all in this episode. Nowhere does the writer imply that humanity

וַיֹּאמֶר אֶל־הָאִשָּׁה אַף כִּֽי־אָמַר אֱלֹהִים לֹא
תֹֽאכְלוּ מִכֹּל עֵץ הַגָּֽן׃ 2 וַתֹּאמֶר הָֽאִשָּׁה
אֶל־הַנָּחָשׁ מִפְּרִי עֵֽץ־הַגָּן נֹאכֵֽל׃ 3 וּמִפְּרִי
הָעֵץ אֲשֶׁר בְּתוֹךְ־הַגָּן אָמַר אֱלֹהִים לֹא
תֹֽאכְלוּ מִמֶּנּוּ וְלֹא תִגְּעוּ בּוֹ פֶּן־תְּמֻתֽוּן׃
4 וַיֹּאמֶר הַנָּחָשׁ אֶל־הָֽאִשָּׁה לֹֽא־מוֹת
תְּמֻתֽוּן׃ 5 כִּי יֹדֵעַ אֱלֹהִים כִּי בְּיוֹם אֲכָלְכֶם
מִמֶּנּוּ וְנִפְקְחוּ עֵֽינֵיכֶם וִהְיִיתֶם כֵּֽאלֹהִים
יֹדְעֵי טוֹב וָרָֽע׃ 6 וַתֵּרֶא הָֽאִשָּׁה כִּי טוֹב
הָעֵץ לְמַאֲכָל וְכִי תַֽאֲוָה־הוּא לָעֵינַיִם
וְנֶחְמָד הָעֵץ לְהַשְׂכִּיל וַתִּקַּח מִפִּרְיוֹ

serpent was the most cunning. It said to the woman,
"Did God really say, 'You may not eat of any tree in
the Garden'?" 2The woman said to the serpent, "Of
any tree in the Garden we may eat the fruit; 3but
God said, 'Of the fruit of the tree in the middle of
it do not eat, and do not [even] touch it, or you will
die.'" 4But the serpent said to the woman, "You
most certainly will not die! 5On the contrary: God
knows that when you do eat of it, your eyes will
be opened and you will be like gods, knowing all
things." 6So when the woman saw how good to eat
the tree's fruit would be, and how alluring to the
eyes it was, and how desirable the insight was that

is doomed to make bad choices. There is no "Fall of Man." Nor does God curse humankind. Rather, the story makes clear that transgression, namely disobedience, carries consequences.

TEMPTATION AND TRANSGRESSION (3:1–6)

*1. serpent.* Its role here is perhaps a polemic against other traditions, where serpents—representing healing wisdom—become objects of idolatry. Compare the bronze serpent in Numbers 21:6–9 and its destruction in II Kings 18:4. (Note also the ancient roots of our modern medical symbol, the caduceus, with its intertwined serpents.)

***cunning.*** The word (in the singular here) is the same as the one for "naked" in 2:25, one of several puns that run through the narrative.

***"Did God really say . . . ?"*** The Hebrew is ambiguous, but the intent is clear: a question to draw attention to the one prohibited tree.

***"You may not."*** The "you" is plural, including the man who (according to 3:6) is with her. Why the man remains silent is left to the reader's imagination.

*3.* ***"God said."*** The woman is the first human to speak of God and to engage in dialogue. She will invoke God in almost every one of her statements (also 4:1, 25). In contrast, the man does not mention God in his speeches.

***"do not [even] touch it."*** God does not prohibit touching the tree in 2:17. If the woman adds this element herself, she anticipates the Rabbis whose rulings later create a "fence around the Torah," meaning additional prohibitions to prevent an accidental violation of Torah laws.

*4.* ***"You . . . will not die!"*** The woman and man live long after their transgression.

*5.* ***"God knows . . . you will be like gods."*** This new information will prove true—God confirms it in v. 22. Those who criticize the woman argue that the wish to be like God—a usurpation of divine power—prompts her to transgress God's command. The next verse, however, debunks this claim by offering a rare biblical description of a person's motive. Hers includes a desire for wisdom.

***"all things."*** Literally, "good and bad." See at 2:9.

*6.* ***the woman saw.*** Genesis lists three reasons why the woman reaches for the fruit: it is good to eat (healthful); visually attractive; and a source for wisdom. (No motive is ascribed to the man. He will simply take and eat.) The desire for knowledge, rather than immortality, distinguishes this story from other ancient traditions such as Gilgamesh.

the tree would bring, she took some of its fruit and ate; and then she gave some to her man who was with her, and he ate. [7]Then the eyes of both of them were opened, and, realizing that they were naked, they sewed fig leaves together and made themselves skirts.

[8]At the breezy time of the day, they heard the sound of God יהוה walking about in the Garden; and the man and his woman hid themselves from God יהוה among the trees. [9]But God יהוה called out to the man, saying, "Where are you?" [10]He said, "I heard the sound of You in the Garden; I was afraid because I was naked, so I hid myself." [11]Then [God] said, "Who told you that you were naked? Did you eat the fruit of the tree that I forbade you to eat?" [12]The man said, "The woman whom You gave me, she gave me the fruit of the tree,

וַתֹּאכַל וַתִּתֵּן גַּם־לְאִישָׁהּ עִמָּהּ וַיֹּאכַל׃
7 וַתִּפָּקַחְנָה עֵינֵי שְׁנֵיהֶם וַיֵּדְעוּ כִּי עֵירֻמִּם
הֵם וַיִּתְפְּרוּ עֲלֵה תְאֵנָה וַיַּעֲשׂוּ לָהֶם
חֲגֹרֹת׃
8 וַיִּשְׁמְעוּ אֶת־קוֹל יְהֹוָה אֱלֹהִים מִתְהַלֵּךְ
בַּגָּן לְרוּחַ הַיּוֹם וַיִּתְחַבֵּא הָאָדָם וְאִשְׁתּוֹ
מִפְּנֵי יְהֹוָה אֱלֹהִים בְּתוֹךְ עֵץ הַגָּן׃ 9 וַיִּקְרָא
יְהֹוָה אֱלֹהִים אֶל־הָאָדָם וַיֹּאמֶר לוֹ אַיֶּכָּה׃
10 וַיֹּאמֶר אֶת־קֹלְךָ שָׁמַעְתִּי בַּגָּן וָאִירָא כִּי־
עֵירֹם אָנֹכִי וָאֵחָבֵא׃ 11 וַיֹּאמֶר מִי הִגִּיד לְךָ
כִּי עֵירֹם אָתָּה הֲמִן־הָעֵץ אֲשֶׁר צִוִּיתִיךָ
לְבִלְתִּי אֲכָל־מִמֶּנּוּ אָכָלְתָּ׃ 12 וַיֹּאמֶר
הָאָדָם הָאִשָּׁה אֲשֶׁר נָתַתָּה עִמָּדִי הִוא

***its fruit.*** The type is not identified; the fig is the only kind of tree specified in the story (v. 7). Some later traditions championed the apple, which has since come to the fore in the popular imagination.

***she gave . . . to her man who was with her.*** Only now does the reader learn that the man was with the woman all along (note also "*her* man"). The silence concerning the man's motive is all the more problematic if he (alone) was directly warned by God in 2:17. Most earlier translations unfortunately omit "with her," letting readers assume that the man was ignorant of the exchange and thereby innocent. Genesis, however, portrays both woman and man as culpable. The woman takes the first step toward what modern interpreters call consciousness-raising. If the tree entails "knowing all things," then woman is bringer of civilization, not death. As for giving the fruit to the man, Carol Meyers observes that this reflects Israelite agrarian families, where women doled out the food. Note the emphasis on eating in this etiological tale. (See *Discovering Eve: Ancient Israelite Woman in Context*, 1988.)

## THE TRANSFORMATION (3:7–21)

The four relationships that constitute the human being—with the land, the animals, each other, and God—suffer a severe blow but prove enduring nevertheless.

*7.* ***they were naked.*** As the serpent promised, their eyes open, leading to a new awareness.

***made themselves skirts.*** Possibly modesty and shame resulted from eating the fruit. At any rate, knowledge discloses to them their vulnerability, exposing them to the precariousness of life and to consequent fear.

*9.* ***"Where are you?"*** God's first question is more than a mere request for location; it is an opportunity to accept responsibility.

*10.* ***"I was afraid because I was naked."*** The fear could imply a moral awareness stemming from transgression, an awareness of vulnerability, or both.

*12.* ***"The woman whom You gave me."*** An opportunity for repentance ("I did so, and I am sorry") is used instead for double blame: the man blames the woman and also God. As a result of his

so I ate." [13]God יהוה then said to the woman,
"What is this that you have done?" And the woman
said, "The serpent tricked me into eating it."
[14]Then God יהוה said to the serpent, "Because
you did this, you—out of all the beasts, all the wild
animals—are under a curse: on your belly shall you
crawl, eating dust all the days of your life. [15]And
between you and the woman, / and between her
seed and your seed, / I am setting enmity: / They
shall strike at your head, / and you shall strike at
their heel." [16]And to the woman, [God] said, "I am
doubling and redoubling your toil and your pregnancies; / with anguish shall you bear children, /

נָתְנָה־לִּי מִן־הָעֵץ וָאֹכֵל׃ 13 וַיֹּאמֶר יְהוָה
אֱלֹהִים לָאִשָּׁה מַה־זֹּאת עָשִׂית וַתֹּאמֶר
הָאִשָּׁה הַנָּחָשׁ הִשִּׁיאַנִי וָאֹכֵל׃
14 וַיֹּאמֶר יְהוָה אֱלֹהִים ׀ אֶל־הַנָּחָשׁ כִּי
עָשִׂיתָ זֹּאת אָרוּר אַתָּה מִכָּל־הַבְּהֵמָה
וּמִכֹּל חַיַּת הַשָּׂדֶה עַל־גְּחֹנְךָ תֵלֵךְ וְעָפָר
תֹּאכַל כָּל־יְמֵי חַיֶּיךָ׃ 15 וְאֵיבָה ׀ אָשִׁית
בֵּינְךָ וּבֵין הָאִשָּׁה וּבֵין זַרְעֲךָ וּבֵין זַרְעָהּ
הוּא יְשׁוּפְךָ רֹאשׁ וְאַתָּה תְּשׁוּפֶנּוּ עָקֵב׃ ס
16 אֶל־הָאִשָּׁה אָמַר הַרְבָּה אַרְבֶּה עִצְּבוֹנֵךְ
וְהֵרֹנֵךְ בְּעֶצֶב תֵּלְדִי בָנִים וְאֶל־אִישֵׁךְ

refusal to accept responsibility, his disobedience alienates him from both God and the woman.

*13. "The serpent tricked me."* The woman likewise shifts the blame, but not to God.

*14. "you . . . are under a curse."* While all three culprits pay a price for their transgression (and the humans' unwillingness to own up to it), only the serpent is explicitly cursed. The narrator presents God as one who considers the serpent the most culpable. This emphasis is overlooked by later interpreters who focus on the woman as cause.

*15. "between you and the woman."* Enmity destroys a harmony between humankind and animals.

*16.* God's words to the woman have been misinterpreted in ways that disadvantaged women dramatically. The pronouncements to the woman (v. 16) and to the man (v. 17) are largely parallel, which implies parallel consequences. But for several centuries the key term has been typically rendered one way regarding the woman and another regarding the man, in a manner that intensifies the punishment for the woman, prompting the claim that her culpability must have been greater than the man's.

*"your toil and your pregnancies."* Older translations and some recent ones translate this pair of nouns differently. The New JPS version has "your pangs in childbirth," and Chaim Stern's translation of Genesis in *The Torah: A Modern Commentary*, revised edition, has "your pains of pregnancy." (This verse and the next are the only places in this book where we have changed Stern's translation.) The Hebrew noun *itzavon* (from *etzev*), is here translated as "toil." In ancient Israel women regularly worked long hours—in food preparation and storage, in the manufacture of clothing, in farming alongside of men, and more. For the Torah's original audience, this story would have brought such labors readily to mind. The word can also be rendered as either "sorrow," "hardship," or "anguish." All these meanings appear elsewhere in Genesis (for example, "hard labor," 5:29). Indeed, *itzavon* does not mean "pain" elsewhere in the Bible. For more details, see Another View, p. 27.

The writer in vv. 16–17 is accounting for the hardships of human existence and especially the creative aspects of life: procreation and production of food. Earlier ease is now mingled with hardship: "good" comes with "bad."

*"anguish."* The word here is *etzev*, a term related to *itzavon* in the previous line; it predominantly means "sorrow." Those whose experience is conveyed by *etzev* include: God, when humankind does not meet expectations (Genesis 6:6); Jonathan, when his father humiliates him (I Samuel 20:34);

תְּשׁוּקָתֵךְ וְהוּא יִמְשָׁל־בָּךְ׃ ס 17 וּלְאָדָם
אָמַר כִּי־שָׁמַעְתָּ לְקוֹל אִשְׁתֶּךָ וַתֹּאכַל
מִן־הָעֵץ אֲשֶׁר צִוִּיתִיךָ לֵאמֹר לֹא תֹאכַל
מִמֶּנּוּ אֲרוּרָה הָאֲדָמָה בַּעֲבוּרֶךָ בְּעִצָּבוֹן
תֹּאכְלֶנָּה כֹּל יְמֵי חַיֶּיךָ׃ 18 וְקוֹץ וְדַרְדַּר
תַּצְמִיחַ לָךְ וְאָכַלְתָּ אֶת־עֵשֶׂב הַשָּׂדֶה׃

yet your desire shall be for your man, / and he
shall rule over you." 17 Now to the man, [God] said,
"Because you hearkened to your wife and ate of the
tree about which I commanded you, saying, 'Do
not eat of it,' the soil is now cursed on your account: Only through anguish shall you eat of it,
as long as you live. 18 It shall sprout thorns and
thistles for you, when you would eat the plants of

and David, when his son dies (II Samuel 19:3). Most instances of this verb in narrative pertain to sorrow in connection with family members.

Our translation as "anguish" rather than "toil" (as for *itzavon*) aims at differentiating the nuances between two related Hebrew terms. (The King James Version of 1611, which has been authoritative for centuries in English-speaking countries, translates both *etzev* and *itzavon* as "sorrow." Other translations, including Chaim Stern's, substituted forms of "pain" for "sorrow," presumably in recognition that childbirth is often painful.)

Genesis 3:16 neither imposes physical pain upon the woman nor condones it. The passage describes the hardship that often accompanies birthing and raising children. Unlike the pronouncements to the serpent, which speak of perpetual enmity, nothing suggests that this *etzev* is a continual condition. Thus along with her joy in being a parent (4:1), the first woman will herself experience—and express—sorrow and the need for comfort after her first-born kills his brother (4:25). On the etiological function of this pronouncement, see Another View, p. 27.

***"desire."*** Heb. *t'shukah*. The word appears only three times in the entire Bible—twice in Genesis (see also 4:7) and once in Song of Songs (7:11). Here it acknowledges woman's desire or passion. It may seek to account for why women are able and willing to overcome (or overlook) the hardship of childbirth. It may also suggest that the woman's desire is what places the woman under the man's control; compare God's warning in 4:7. (Song of Songs, which celebrates equality and mutuality between man and woman, reverses the relationship, describing in 7:11 the man's desire for the woman.)

***"he shall rule over you."*** God's words should not be read (as they have in both Jewish and Christian traditions) as an unqualified mandate for males' general control over females. In this verse, "ruling" is confined to situations in which desire is at work. The writer may be communicating the power of desire to make one person subservient to another.

Another view is that in the ancient context the writer acknowledges a husband's responsibility for his wife's sexuality.

*17.* ***"Because you hearkened to your wife."*** Literally, ". . . to your wife's voice." In 21:12 God will command Abraham to hearken to his wife's voice; thus this notice is not meant as a blanket objection to obeying one's wife. Oddly, there is no indication earlier that the woman said anything to the man.

***"I commanded you."*** God accuses only the man of disobedience (the "you" is singular).

***"the soil is now cursed."*** The land has done nothing to deserve punishment. But for Israelite farmers the etiology explained why their land was not fertile. Again, neither the woman nor the man is cursed.

***"anguish."*** Heb. *itzavon*; see at 3:16. Initially, working the land was presented as creative and satisfying labor, and now it also becomes a hardship.

the field! <sup>19</sup>By the sweat of your brow shall you eat bread, till you return to the earth—that earth you were taken from; / for dust you are, / and to dust you shall return."

<sup>20</sup>The man called his wife's name Eve, for she would be the mother of all the living. <sup>21</sup>And God יהוה made outfits out of skin for Adam and his wife, and clothed them. <sup>22</sup>God יהוה then said, "Look, the humans are like us, knowing all things. Now they may even reach out to take fruit from the Tree of Life and eat, and live forever." <sup>23</sup>So God יהוה drove them out of the Garden of Eden to work the soil from which they had been taken, <sup>24</sup>expelling the humans and stationing Cherubim to the east of Eden, and the flaming blade of a flashing sword to guard the way to the Tree of Life.

19 בְּזֵעַת אַפֶּ֫יךָ תֹּ֣אכַל לֶ֔חֶם עַ֤ד שֽׁוּבְךָ֙ אֶל־הָ֣אֲדָמָ֔ה כִּ֥י מִמֶּ֖נָּה לֻקָּ֑חְתָּ כִּֽי־עָפָ֣ר אַ֔תָּה וְאֶל־עָפָ֖ר תָּשֽׁוּב׃

20 וַיִּקְרָ֧א הָֽאָדָ֛ם שֵׁ֥ם אִשְׁתּ֖וֹ חַוָּ֑ה כִּ֛י הִ֥וא הָֽיְתָ֖ה אֵ֥ם כָּל־חָֽי׃ 21 וַיַּ֩עַשׂ֩ יְהֹוָ֨ה אֱלֹהִ֜ים לְאָדָ֧ם וּלְאִשְׁתּ֛וֹ כָּתְנ֥וֹת ע֖וֹר וַיַּלְבִּשֵֽׁם׃ פ

22 וַיֹּ֣אמֶר ׀ יְהֹוָ֣ה אֱלֹהִ֗ים הֵ֤ן הָֽאָדָם֙ הָיָה֙ כְּאַחַ֣ד מִמֶּ֔נּוּ לָדַ֖עַת ט֣וֹב וָרָ֑ע וְעַתָּ֣ה ׀ פֶּן־יִשְׁלַ֣ח יָד֗וֹ וְלָקַח֙ גַּ֚ם מֵעֵ֣ץ הַֽחַיִּ֔ים וְאָכַ֖ל וָחַ֥י לְעֹלָֽם׃ 23 וַֽיְשַׁלְּחֵ֛הוּ יְהֹוָ֥ה אֱלֹהִ֖ים מִגַּן־עֵ֑דֶן לַֽעֲבֹד֙ אֶת־הָ֣אֲדָמָ֔ה אֲשֶׁ֥ר לֻקַּ֖ח מִשָּֽׁם׃

24 וַיְגָ֖רֶשׁ אֶת־הָֽאָדָ֑ם וַיַּשְׁכֵּן֩ מִקֶּ֨דֶם לְגַן־עֵ֜דֶן אֶת־הַכְּרֻבִ֗ים וְאֵ֨ת לַ֤הַט הַחֶ֙רֶב֙ הַמִּתְהַפֶּ֔כֶת לִשְׁמֹ֕ר אֶת־דֶּ֖רֶךְ עֵ֥ץ הַֽחַיִּֽים׃ ס

- - - - - - - - - - - - - - - - - - - - - - - - - - - - - - -

*19. to dust.* Presumably, eating from the Tree of Life would have enabled them to live forever.

*20. The man called his wife's name.* In the Bible names often disclose the hopes and reality of the naming person, not the named. The man, significantly, becomes aware of the woman as a source of life precisely when the prospect of death is made comprehensible. Faced with inevitable disintegration, he recognizes—and celebrates—her life-bearing ability.

*Eve.* Heb. *Chavah*, a play on *chai* (life). The narrator explains the word-play and accounts for the woman's role as child-bearer. The designation confirms the text's positive depiction of the woman's role in Eden and beyond.

*21. God . . . clothed them.* Far from displaying anger, God appears as a concerned protector, replacing the couple's flimsy covering with sturdy material. Such solicitude indicates God's continued commitment.

## THE EXPULSION (3:22–24)

*22. "the humans."* Literally, "the *adam*," the singular generic term referring to both woman and man. Whatever the ambiguity of the term beginning with 2:7, where it could refer to "the man," here it is an inclusive category.

*"are like us."* The serpent's words in 3:5 are confirmed. On the plural "us," see at 1:26.

*"knowing all things."* See at 2:9 and 2:17.

*"they may even."* Anticipating more dire consequences, God bars human beings from the Tree of Life, the source of perpetual renewal.

*24. the humans.* Literally, "the *adam*," referring to the woman and the man.

*stationing Cherubim.* These mythological creatures appear elsewhere as God's entourage. Their sculpted form decorates the holy ark (Exodus 25:18). The gateway to the garden is closed, but the world has opened up.

4 The man now was intimate with his wife;
she became pregnant and gave birth to Cain, saying, "Both I and יהוה have made a man." 2 She then
continued, giving birth to his brother Abel. Abel
became a shepherd, while Cain tilled the soil.
3 [One day,] in the course of time, Cain brought
some of his harvest as an offering to יהוה, 4 and
Abel, too, brought [an offering] from among the
choice lambs of his flock and their fattest parts.
יהוה approved Abel and his offering, 5 but did

ד וְהָ֣אָדָ֔ם יָדַ֖ע אֶת־חַוָּ֣ה אִשְׁתּ֑וֹ וַתַּ֙הַר֙
וַתֵּ֣לֶד אֶת־קַ֔יִן וַתֹּ֕אמֶר קָנִ֥יתִי אִ֖ישׁ אֶת־
יְהֹוָֽה׃ 2 וַתֹּ֣סֶף לָלֶ֔דֶת אֶת־אָחִ֖יו אֶת־הָ֑בֶל
וַֽיְהִי־הֶ֙בֶל֙ רֹ֣עֵה צֹ֔אן וְקַ֕יִן הָיָ֖ה עֹבֵ֥ד
אֲדָמָֽה׃
3 וַיְהִ֖י מִקֵּ֣ץ יָמִ֑ים וַיָּבֵ֨א קַ֜יִן מִפְּרִ֧י הָֽאֲדָמָ֛ה
מִנְחָ֖ה לַֽיהֹוָֽה׃ 4 וְהֶ֨בֶל הֵבִ֥יא גַם־ה֛וּא
מִבְּכֹר֥וֹת צֹאנ֖וֹ וּמֵֽחֶלְבֵהֶ֑ן וַיִּ֣שַׁע יְהֹוָ֔ה אֶל־
הֶ֖בֶל וְאֶל־מִנְחָתֽוֹ׃ 5 וְאֶל־קַ֥יִן וְאֶל־מִנְחָת֖וֹ

## *Life Outside the Garden* (4:1–6:8)

### EVE AND ADAM REUNITE: CHILDBIRTH AND NAMING (4:1–2)

Most readers pay little attention to Eve and Adam once they leave the garden. But here, in fact, the Torah gives new, important lessons. The first couple turns back—not back to the garden, but to one another and to God. The man who earlier blamed the woman now enters into an intimate relationship with her, and the woman names their first child in honor of her partnership with God. With these halting steps, they begin to repair the damage of earlier acts.

*1. **The man now was intimate with his wife.*** Literally, "the *adam* knew his woman/wife." Here *adam* can only mean the man. In Hebrew "to know" includes sexual intercourse; fundamentally it expresses intimate knowledge of the other.

***saying.*** The woman is the one who names the children and records the history and meaning of the family's life, both here and again after the death of Abel (see at 4:25).

***"Both I and יהוה."*** Eve is the very first human being to use God's personal name, just as she was the first human to mention God (3:3).

***"made a man."*** Commentators consider this "man" a reference to the son—whose name, Cain (*kayin*), is a pun on "made" (*kaniti*). If so, then Eve acknowledges here that giving birth involves God and celebrates the mystery of female creativity. However, Eve could also be referring to her husband as one who became hers with God's help. The verb *k-n-h* elsewhere often means "acquired" and typically refers to a man acquiring a wife (see Ruth 4:10). In a surprising reversal here, the woman is acquiring "a man."

*2.* ***his brother Abel.*** The name Abel (*hevel*) means "mist" or "vapor," hinting at transience.

### THE FIRST SIN: CAIN AND ABEL (4:3–24)

In the Torah, the word "sin" only enters with sibling rivalry and the murder that follows (not with Eve and Adam). Murderous conflict among brothers runs throughout Genesis as a theme that finally finds its resolution with the reconciliation between Joseph and his brothers (Genesis 50). Sisterly conflicts result in births (see 30:1–24). | In an ancient Sumerian story about the goddess Inanna, a farmer and shepherd compete for her affection; and she chooses to marry the shepherd. Competition between two modes of life may also account for this story in Genesis. The emphasis on "brother," which appears seven times in this narrative, may be a literary ploy, a way to say that all humans are "brothers" and thus all murder is "fratricide."

*4–5.* No reason is given for God's acceptance of Abel's offering and not Cain's.

not approve Cain and his offering. Cain was filled with rage; his face fell. 6יהוה then said to Cain, "Why are you so angry? / Why your fallen face? / 7Would you not do well to lift it? / For if you do not do well— / sin is a demon at the door; / you are the one it craves, / and yet you can govern it."

8Cain now thought about his brother Abel.... Then, when they were in the field, Cain turned on his brother Abel and killed him. 9Then יהוה said to Cain, "Where is your brother Abel?" And he replied, "How should I know; am I my brother's keeper?" 10And [God] said, "What have you done? Your brother's blood is shrieking to Me from the ground! 11Now you are cursed by this very soil, which has opened its mouth to receive your brother's blood from your hands. 12When you till the soil, no longer shall it give you its yield. You shall become a rootless wanderer on the earth." 13Cain then said to יהוה, "My punishment is too heavy to bear! 14Seeing as now You have expelled me from the face of the soil and I must hide from Your face, I am become a rootless wanderer on the earth, and anyone who finds me might kill me!" 15"Not so," said יהוה. "Should anyone kill Cain, he would

לֹא שָׁעָה וַיִּחַר לְקַיִן מְאֹד וַיִּפְּלוּ פָּנָיו׃
6 וַיֹּאמֶר יְהֹוָה אֶל־קָיִן לָמָּה חָרָה לָךְ וְלָמָּה
נָפְלוּ פָנֶיךָ׃ 7 הֲלוֹא אִם־תֵּיטִיב שְׂאֵת וְאִם
לֹא תֵיטִיב לַפֶּתַח חַטָּאת רֹבֵץ וְאֵלֶיךָ
תְּשׁוּקָתוֹ וְאַתָּה תִּמְשָׁל־בּוֹ׃
8 וַיֹּאמֶר קַיִן אֶל־הֶבֶל אָחִיו וַיְהִי בִּהְיוֹתָם
בַּשָּׂדֶה וַיָּקָם קַיִן אֶל־הֶבֶל אָחִיו וַיַּהַרְגֵהוּ׃
9 וַיֹּאמֶר יְהֹוָה אֶל־קַיִן אֵי הֶבֶל אָחִיךָ
וַיֹּאמֶר לֹא יָדַעְתִּי הֲשֹׁמֵר אָחִי אָנֹכִי׃
10 וַיֹּאמֶר מֶה עָשִׂיתָ קוֹל דְּמֵי אָחִיךָ צֹעֲקִים
אֵלַי מִן־הָאֲדָמָה׃ 11 וְעַתָּה אָרוּר אָתָּה מִן־
הָאֲדָמָה אֲשֶׁר פָּצְתָה אֶת־פִּיהָ לָקַחַת אֶת־
דְּמֵי אָחִיךָ מִיָּדֶךָ׃ 12 כִּי תַעֲבֹד אֶת־הָאֲדָמָה
לֹא־תֹסֵף תֵּת־כֹּחָהּ לָךְ נָע וָנָד תִּהְיֶה
בָאָרֶץ׃ 13 וַיֹּאמֶר קַיִן אֶל־יְהֹוָה גָּדוֹל עֲוֺנִי
מִנְּשֹׂא׃ 14 הֵן גֵּרַשְׁתָּ אֹתִי הַיּוֹם מֵעַל פְּנֵי
הָאֲדָמָה וּמִפָּנֶיךָ אֶסָּתֵר וְהָיִיתִי נָע וָנָד
בָּאָרֶץ וְהָיָה כׇל־מֹצְאִי יַהַרְגֵנִי׃ 15 וַיֹּאמֶר
לוֹ יְהֹוָה לָכֵן כׇּל־הֹרֵג קַיִן שִׁבְעָתַיִם יֻקָּם

*6. "Would you not do well to lift it?"* The Hebrew is difficult. What seems clear is that God urges Cain to control the temptation to succumb to sin.

*"sin is a demon."* Or "sin is crouching." The image is of a personified evil ready to pounce; it is external to humans.

*"you are the one it craves / and yet you can govern it."* The sentence echoes closely God's pronouncement to the woman in 3:16. The idea is similar: the thing or person desired has control over the one who desires. God warns Cain about the danger of succumbing to rage. See at 3:16, "desire."

*8. thought about.* Literally, "and Cain said"; however, Cain's fatal words to Abel are missing.

*killed him.* The laconic statement only intensifies the horror of this first murder.

*9. "am I my brother's keeper?"* Cain rejects responsibility, as did his parents before him (3:11–13).

*11. "you are cursed."* This is the first curse uttered against a human being.

*14.* The mention of other people reminds us that this story is mythic rather than historical or realistic. On the literal side, one could conclude that Cain and Abel are not the only children of Adam and Eve. Compare v. 17.

*15.* The sign that God gives Cain as protection is unspecified. Like God's protection of Eve and Adam, so too God's actions toward Cain show an

be avenged sevenfold." And יהוה gave Cain a sign, that none who came upon him would kill him. ¹⁶Cain then went away from before יהוה, and settled in the Land of Nomads, east of Eden.

¹⁷Cain then was intimate with his wife, who became pregnant and gave birth to Enoch; he became the founder of a city, and he named the city after his son, Enoch. ¹⁸To Enoch was born Irad, and Irad begot Mehiyael, and Mehiyael begot Metushael, and Metushael begot Lamech. ¹⁹Lamech took two wives: one was named Adah and the other was named Zillah. ²⁰Adah bore Jabal—he was the progenitor of tent dwellers and herders. ²¹And his brother's name was Jubal—he was the progenitor of all who play the lute and the long flute. ²²As for Zillah, she too bore: Tubal-Cain, a smith, progenitor of every artisan who makes copper and iron tools; and Naamah was Tubal-Cain's sister. ²³Now Lamech said to his wives Adah and Zillah, "Hearken to me, wives of Lamech, / give ear to my speech: / because of my bruise I've slain a man, / because of my wound, a lad. / ²⁴Cain is avenged sevenfold, / and Lamech seventy-seven!"

וַיָּ֨שֶׂם יְהֹוָ֤ה לְקַ֙יִן֙ א֔וֹת לְבִלְתִּ֥י הַכּוֹת־אֹת֖וֹ כׇּל־מֹצְא֑וֹ: 16 וַיֵּ֥צֵא קַ֖יִן מִלִּפְנֵ֣י יְהֹוָ֑ה וַיֵּ֥שֶׁב בְּאֶֽרֶץ־נ֖וֹד קִדְמַת־עֵֽדֶן:

17 וַיֵּ֤דַע קַ֙יִן֙ אֶת־אִשְׁתּ֔וֹ וַתַּ֖הַר וַתֵּ֣לֶד אֶת־חֲנ֑וֹךְ וַֽיְהִי֙ בֹּ֣נֶה עִ֔יר וַיִּקְרָא֙ שֵׁ֣ם הָעִ֔יר כְּשֵׁ֖ם בְּנ֥וֹ חֲנֽוֹךְ: 18 וַיִּוָּלֵ֤ד לַֽחֲנוֹךְ֙ אֶת־עִירָ֔ד וְעִירָ֕ד יָלַ֖ד אֶת־מְחֽוּיָאֵ֑ל וּמְחִיָּיאֵ֗ל יָלַד֙ אֶת־מְת֣וּשָׁאֵ֔ל וּמְתֽוּשָׁאֵ֖ל יָלַ֥ד אֶת־לָֽמֶךְ: 19 וַיִּקַּֽח־ל֥וֹ לֶ֖מֶךְ שְׁתֵּ֣י נָשִׁ֑ים שֵׁ֤ם הָֽאַחַת֙ עָדָ֔ה וְשֵׁ֥ם הַשֵּׁנִ֖ית צִלָּֽה: 20 וַתֵּ֥לֶד עָדָ֖ה אֶת־יָבָ֑ל ה֣וּא הָיָ֔ה אֲבִ֕י יֹשֵׁ֥ב אֹ֖הֶל וּמִקְנֶֽה: 21 וְשֵׁ֥ם אָחִ֖יו יוּבָ֑ל ה֣וּא הָיָ֔ה אֲבִ֕י כׇּל־תֹּפֵ֥שׂ כִּנּ֖וֹר וְעוּגָֽב: 22 וְצִלָּ֣ה גַם־הִ֗וא יָֽלְדָה֙ אֶת־תּ֣וּבַל קַ֔יִן לֹטֵ֕שׁ כׇּל־חֹרֵ֥שׁ נְחֹ֖שֶׁת וּבַרְזֶ֑ל וַֽאֲח֥וֹת תּֽוּבַל־קַ֖יִן נַֽעֲמָֽה: 23 וַיֹּ֨אמֶר לֶ֜מֶךְ לְנָשָׁ֗יו עָדָ֤ה וְצִלָּה֙ שְׁמַ֣עַן קוֹלִ֔י נְשֵׁ֣י לֶ֔מֶךְ הַֽאֲזֵ֖נָּה אִמְרָתִ֑י כִּ֣י אִ֤ישׁ הָרַ֙גְתִּי֙ לְפִצְעִ֔י וְיֶ֖לֶד לְחַבֻּֽרָתִֽי: 24 כִּ֥י שִׁבְעָתַ֖יִם יֻקַּם־קָ֑יִן וְלֶ֖מֶךְ שִׁבְעִ֥ים וְשִׁבְעָֽה:

overriding compassion toward the newly created, fallible humans.

*17.* Like his father, upon leaving his home, Cain turns to his wife. Where did she come from? The writer is unconcerned with the question, another clue that this is not history but a myth attempting to account for the beginning of humankind and its consequences.

*17–18.* The genealogy of Cain resembles that of Seth (5:1–32), perhaps preserving old traditions or attempting to suggest parallel lines.

*19–24.* The vignette about Lamech and his wives Adah and Zillah breaks the genealogical list to describe the origins of music and crafts in the emerging civilization. The mention of the names of Lamech's wives and daughter suggests their importance.

*22.* ***and Naamah was Tubal-Cain's sister.*** Naamah is the first female whose mother, Zillah, is also named. Her name may mean "tuneful" and might represent her as the muse of song (so Carol Meyers, *Women in Scripture*, 2000, p. 129).

*23–24.* Lamech addresses his boast specifically to his wives. The bravado with which Lamech flaunts his superior worth vis-à-vis his forefather suggests a tradition about a figure that in time faded from memory. (Should one call him the first "macho man"?) In a second genealogy he features as Noah's father (5:28).

25Adam once again was intimate with his wife,
and she bore a son and gave him the name "Seth"—
"since God has given me another offspring in place
of Abel"—for Cain had slain him! 26As for Seth, to
him too was born a son, and he named him Enosh.
Then it was that people began to invoke יהוה.

25 וַיֵּדַע אָדָם עוֹד אֶת־אִשְׁתּוֹ וַתֵּלֶד בֵּן
וַתִּקְרָא אֶת־שְׁמוֹ שֵׁת כִּי שָׁת־לִי אֱלֹהִים
זֶרַע אַחֵר תַּחַת הֶבֶל כִּי הֲרָגוֹ קָיִן׃
26 וּלְשֵׁת גַּם־הוּא יֻלַּד־בֵּן וַיִּקְרָא אֶת־שְׁמוֹ
אֱנוֹשׁ אָז הוּחַל לִקְרֹא בְּשֵׁם יְהוָה׃ ס

5 This is the written record of the human line
from the day God created human beings, making
[them] in the likeness of God, 2creating them male
and female, blessing them, and naming them

ה זֶה סֵפֶר תּוֹלְדֹת אָדָם בְּיוֹם בְּרֹא
אֱלֹהִים אָדָם בִּדְמוּת אֱלֹהִים עָשָׂה אֹתוֹ׃
2 זָכָר וּנְקֵבָה בְּרָאָם וַיְבָרֶךְ אֹתָם וַיִּקְרָא

### EVE AND ADAM REUNITE: CHILDBIRTH AND NAMING (4:25–26)

The narrative returns to the story of Eve and Adam and their response to the tragedy that has befallen their household. Once again, the first man is intimate with ("knew") his wife and she conceives. Nothing in these reports of life outside the garden suggests that the woman was subservient to the man. To the contrary: she is the one who speaks; she is the one who names; and she has the power to interpret and preserve the family's history.

*25. she…gave him the name.* As in 4:1, the woman names the child and interprets the significance of the experience.

*"given."* Heb. *shat*, a word play on the name *shet* (Seth).

*"God has given me."* Once again, the woman acknowledges God. Note, in contrast, that the man has not uttered a word since leaving the garden. While affirming her unique role as mother, she nonetheless proclaims God as the bestower of the gift of a child. Later interpreters consider this formulation to be more modest than her earlier claim in 4:1, suggesting that her confidence may have been tempered by loss.

*26. people began to invoke* **יהוה***.* The beginning of an ongoing relation with God is thus linked with the grandson of Eve and Adam.

### THE RECAPITULATION OF HUMAN ORIGINS, AND THEIR GENEALOGY TO NOAH (5:1–32)

Like other ancient records, Genesis includes distant ancestors who lived extraordinarily long lives. (The biblical account is modest compared to the Babylonians, who recorded life spans in the tens of thousands of years.) The unrealistic numbers express the conviction that the flood constitutes a watershed in human longevity.

*1. the human…human beings.* In this verse, the word *adam* appears twice. The present translation takes both of these instances in the word's inclusive sense (as in v. 2, where *adam* explicitly means both female and male). Alternatively, the first instance could refer to the first man and is often translated as the name Adam (as in v. 3).

*2. creating them male and female, blessing them.* The co-creation of humans as both female and male is reiterated here (as in 1:27–28).

*"Humans."* Heb. *adam*, making it absolutely clear that this noun is generic and inclusive of both female and male.

"Humans" on the day they were created. 3 Adam
had lived 130 years, when he begot in his likeness,
after his image; and he named him Seth. 4 After
begetting Seth, Adam lived 800 years; and he begot
sons and daughters. 5 The years of Adam's life came
to 930; then he died.

6 Seth had lived 105 years when he begot Enosh.
7 After begetting Enosh, Seth lived 807 years; and he
begot sons and daughters. 8 The years of Seth's life
came to 912; then he died.

9 Enosh had lived 90 years when he begot
Kenan. 10 After begetting Kenan, Enosh lived 815
years; and he begot sons and daughters. 11 The years
of Enosh's life came to 905; then he died.

12 Kenan had lived 70 years when he begot
Mahalalel. 13 After begetting Mahalalel, Kenan lived
840 years; and he begot sons and daughters. 14 The
years of Kenan's life came to 910; then he died.

15 Mahalalel had lived 65 years when he begot
Jared. 16 After begetting Jared, Mahalalel lived 830
years; and he begot sons and daughters. 17 The years
of Mahalalel's life came to 895; then he died.

אֶת־שְׁמָם֙ אָדָ֔ם בְּי֖וֹם הִבָּֽרְאָֽם׃ 3 וַיְחִ֣י אָדָ֗ם
שְׁלֹשִׁ֤ים וּמְאַת֙ שָׁנָ֔ה וַיּ֥וֹלֶד בִּדְמוּת֖וֹ כְּצַלְמ֑וֹ
וַיִּקְרָ֥א אֶת־שְׁמ֖וֹ שֵֽׁת׃ 4 וַיִּהְי֣וּ יְמֵי־אָדָ֗ם
אַֽחֲרֵי֙ הוֹלִיד֣וֹ אֶת־שֵׁ֔ת שְׁמֹנֶ֥ה מֵאֹ֖ת שָׁנָ֑ה
וַיּ֥וֹלֶד בָּנִ֖ים וּבָנֽוֹת׃ 5 וַיִּֽהְי֞וּ כָּל־יְמֵ֤י אָדָם֙
אֲשֶׁר־חַ֔י תְּשַׁ֤ע מֵאוֹת֙ שָׁנָ֔ה וּשְׁלֹשִׁ֖ים שָׁנָ֑ה
וַיָּמֹֽת׃ ס

6 וַֽיְחִי־שֵׁ֕ת חָמֵ֥שׁ שָׁנִ֖ים וּמְאַ֣ת שָׁנָ֑ה וַיּ֖וֹלֶד
אֶת־אֱנֽוֹשׁ׃ 7 וַֽיְחִי־שֵׁ֗ת אַֽחֲרֵי֙ הוֹלִיד֣וֹ אֶת־
אֱנ֔וֹשׁ שֶׁ֣בַע שָׁנִ֔ים וּשְׁמֹנֶ֥ה מֵא֖וֹת שָׁנָ֑ה וַיּ֥וֹלֶד
בָּנִ֖ים וּבָנֽוֹת׃ 8 וַיִּֽהְיוּ֙ כָּל־יְמֵי־שֵׁ֔ת שְׁתֵּ֤ים
עֶשְׂרֵה֙ שָׁנָ֔ה וּתְשַׁ֥ע מֵא֖וֹת שָׁנָ֑ה וַיָּמֹֽת׃ ס

9 וַיְחִ֥י אֱנ֖וֹשׁ תִּשְׁעִ֣ים שָׁנָ֑ה וַיּ֖וֹלֶד אֶת־קֵינָֽן׃
10 וַיְחִ֣י אֱנ֗וֹשׁ אַֽחֲרֵי֙ הוֹלִיד֣וֹ אֶת־קֵינָ֔ן חֲמֵ֤שׁ
עֶשְׂרֵה֙ שָׁנָ֔ה וּשְׁמֹנֶ֥ה מֵא֖וֹת שָׁנָ֑ה וַיּ֥וֹלֶד
בָּנִ֖ים וּבָנֽוֹת׃ 11 וַיִּֽהְיוּ֙ כָּל־יְמֵ֣י אֱנ֔וֹשׁ חָמֵ֣שׁ
שָׁנִ֔ים וּתְשַׁ֥ע מֵא֖וֹת שָׁנָ֑ה וַיָּמֹֽת׃ ס

12 וַיְחִ֥י קֵינָ֖ן שִׁבְעִ֣ים שָׁנָ֑ה וַיּ֖וֹלֶד אֶת־
מַֽהֲלַלְאֵֽל׃ 13 וַיְחִ֣י קֵינָ֗ן אַֽחֲרֵי֙ הוֹלִיד֣וֹ אֶת־
מַֽהֲלַלְאֵ֔ל אַרְבָּעִ֣ים שָׁנָ֔ה וּשְׁמֹנֶ֥ה מֵא֖וֹת שָׁנָ֑ה
וַיּ֥וֹלֶד בָּנִ֖ים וּבָנֽוֹת׃ 14 וַיִּֽהְיוּ֙ כָּל־יְמֵ֣י קֵינָ֔ן
עֶ֚שֶׂר שָׁנִ֔ים וּתְשַׁ֥ע מֵא֖וֹת שָׁנָ֑ה וַיָּמֹֽת׃ ס

15 וַיְחִ֣י מַֽהֲלַלְאֵ֔ל חָמֵ֥שׁ שָׁנִ֖ים וְשִׁשִּׁ֣ים שָׁנָ֑ה
וַיּ֖וֹלֶד אֶת־יָֽרֶד׃ 16 וַיְחִ֣י מַֽהֲלַלְאֵ֗ל אַֽחֲרֵי֙
הוֹלִיד֣וֹ אֶת־יֶ֔רֶד שְׁלֹשִׁ֣ים שָׁנָ֔ה וּשְׁמֹנֶ֥ה
מֵא֖וֹת שָׁנָ֑ה וַיּ֥וֹלֶד בָּנִ֖ים וּבָנֽוֹת׃ 17 וַיִּֽהְיוּ֙
כָּל־יְמֵ֣י מַֽהֲלַלְאֵ֔ל חָמֵ֤שׁ וְתִשְׁעִים֙ שָׁנָ֔ה
וּשְׁמֹנֶ֥ה מֵא֖וֹת שָׁנָ֑ה וַיָּמֹֽת׃ ס

---

*3.* The divine image is now perpetuated through the line of Seth.

*4. **he begot sons and daughters.*** Those who take the story literally understand the wives of Cain, Seth, and others to come from among such unnamed daughters. This formulaic language about sons and daughters repeats for each subsequent generation (vv. 7, 10, 13, 16, 19, 22, 26, 30). Carol Meyers observes that the "presence of daughters conveys the requisite notion of demographic increase, which depends on the reproductive role of women" (*Women in Scripture*, 2000, p. 176). Compare at 10:1.

18 Jared had lived 70 years when he begot Enoch.
19 After begetting Enoch, Jared lived 800 years; and
he begot sons and daughters. 20 The years of Jared's
life came to 962; then he died.

21 Enoch had lived 65 years when he begot
Methuselah. 22 After begetting Methuselah, Enoch
walked with God 300 years; and he begot sons and
daughters. 23 The years of Enoch's life came to 365.
24 Enoch walked with God and then was no more,
for God had taken him.

25 Methusaleh had lived 187 years when he begot
Lamech. 26 After begetting Lamech, Methuselah
lived 782 years; and he begot sons and daughters.
27 The years of Methuselah's life came to 969; then
he died.

28 When Lamech had lived 182 years he begot a
son, 29 and he named him Noah, saying, "This one
shall console us for our work, for the hard labor of
our hands, and for the soil that יהוה has condemned." 30 After begetting Noah, Lamech lived
595 years; and he begot sons and daughters. 31 The
years of Lamech's life came to 777; then he died.

18 וַיְחִי־יֶרֶד שְׁתַּיִם וְשִׁשִּׁים שָׁנָה וּמְאַת
שָׁנָה וַיּוֹלֶד אֶת־חֲנוֹךְ׃ 19 וַיְחִי־יֶרֶד אַחֲרֵי
הוֹלִידוֹ אֶת־חֲנוֹךְ שְׁמֹנֶה מֵאוֹת שָׁנָה
וַיּוֹלֶד בָּנִים וּבָנוֹת׃ 20 וַיִּהְיוּ כָּל־יְמֵי־יֶרֶד
שְׁתַּיִם וְשִׁשִּׁים שָׁנָה וּתְשַׁע מֵאוֹת שָׁנָה
וַיָּמֹת׃ ס

21 וַיְחִי חֲנוֹךְ חָמֵשׁ וְשִׁשִּׁים שָׁנָה וַיּוֹלֶד אֶת־
מְתוּשָׁלַח׃ 22 וַיִּתְהַלֵּךְ חֲנוֹךְ אֶת־הָאֱלֹהִים
אַחֲרֵי הוֹלִידוֹ אֶת־מְתוּשֶׁלַח שְׁלֹשׁ מֵאוֹת
שָׁנָה וַיּוֹלֶד בָּנִים וּבָנוֹת׃ 23 וַיְהִי כָּל־יְמֵי
חֲנוֹךְ חָמֵשׁ וְשִׁשִּׁים שָׁנָה וּשְׁלֹשׁ מֵאוֹת
שָׁנָה׃ 24 וַיִּתְהַלֵּךְ חֲנוֹךְ אֶת־הָאֱלֹהִים
וְאֵינֶנּוּ כִּי־לָקַח אֹתוֹ אֱלֹהִים׃ ס

25 וַיְחִי מְתוּשֶׁלַח שֶׁבַע וּשְׁמֹנִים שָׁנָה
וּמְאַת שָׁנָה וַיּוֹלֶד אֶת־לָמֶךְ׃ 26 וַיְחִי
מְתוּשֶׁלַח אַחֲרֵי הוֹלִידוֹ אֶת־לֶמֶךְ שְׁתַּיִם
וּשְׁמוֹנִים שָׁנָה וּשְׁבַע מֵאוֹת שָׁנָה וַיּוֹלֶד
בָּנִים וּבָנוֹת׃ 27 וַיִּהְיוּ כָּל־יְמֵי מְתוּשֶׁלַח
תֵּשַׁע וְשִׁשִּׁים שָׁנָה וּתְשַׁע מֵאוֹת שָׁנָה
וַיָּמֹת׃ ס

28 וַיְחִי־לֶמֶךְ שְׁתַּיִם וּשְׁמֹנִים שָׁנָה וּמְאַת
שָׁנָה וַיּוֹלֶד בֵּן׃ 29 וַיִּקְרָא אֶת־שְׁמוֹ נֹחַ
לֵאמֹר זֶה יְנַחֲמֵנוּ מִמַּעֲשֵׂנוּ וּמֵעִצְּבוֹן יָדֵינוּ
מִן־הָאֲדָמָה אֲשֶׁר אֵרְרָהּ יְהוָה׃ 30 וַיְחִי־
לֶמֶךְ אַחֲרֵי הוֹלִידוֹ אֶת־נֹחַ חָמֵשׁ וְתִשְׁעִים
שָׁנָה וַחֲמֵשׁ מֵאֹת שָׁנָה וַיּוֹלֶד בָּנִים וּבָנוֹת׃
31 וַיְהִי כָּל־יְמֵי־לֶמֶךְ שֶׁבַע וְשִׁבְעִים שָׁנָה
וּשְׁבַע מֵאוֹת שָׁנָה וַיָּמֹת׃ ס

*22.* ***Enoch walked with God.*** The expression denotes a special relationship with God, granted to a righteous person such as Noah (see 6:9).

*24.* ***and then was no more, for God had taken him.*** This report, one of the most tantalizing in the Torah, is obscure. Compare the ascent to heaven of the prophet Elijah (II Kings 2:11–18).

*28–32.* Noah is the tenth generation.

*29.* Noah's name is a pun on the word "to comfort" (*n'chamah*). He represents the hope of reprieve from the original cursing of the ground.

***"hard labor."*** The word *itzavon* is the same one used earlier to describe the future fates of woman (3:16) and man (3:17). Here it could also mean "anguish" or "sorrow," as it does elsewhere.

[32]When Noah had lived 500 years, he begot Shem, Ham, and Japheth.

6 Now as people began to multiply on the earth, daughters were born to them, [2]and when the divine beings saw how fair were the human women, they took wives for themselves, as they chose. [3]Then יהוה said, "My spirit will not forever endure the humans, as they are but fallible flesh—their lifespan shall be [only] 120 years." [4]The Nephilim were on earth in those days; and afterward, too, when the divine beings mated with the human women, they bore for them those heroes who from of old enjoyed great renown.

32 וַיְהִי־נֹחַ בֶּן־חֲמֵשׁ מֵאוֹת שָׁנָה וַיּוֹלֶד נֹחַ
אֶת־שֵׁם אֶת־חָם וְאֶת־יָפֶת׃
ו וַיְהִי כִּי־הֵחֵל הָאָדָם לָרֹב עַל־פְּנֵי
הָאֲדָמָה וּבָנוֹת יֻלְּדוּ לָהֶם׃ 2 וַיִּרְאוּ בְנֵי־
הָאֱלֹהִים אֶת־בְּנוֹת הָאָדָם כִּי טֹבֹת הֵנָּה
וַיִּקְחוּ לָהֶם נָשִׁים מִכֹּל אֲשֶׁר בָּחָרוּ׃
3 וַיֹּאמֶר יְהוָה לֹא־יָדוֹן רוּחִי בָאָדָם
לְעֹלָם בְּשַׁגַּם הוּא בָשָׂר וְהָיוּ יָמָיו מֵאָה
וְעֶשְׂרִים שָׁנָה׃ 4 הַנְּפִלִים הָיוּ בָאָרֶץ בַּיָּמִים
הָהֵם וְגַם אַחֲרֵי־כֵן אֲשֶׁר יָבֹאוּ בְּנֵי
הָאֱלֹהִים אֶל־בְּנוֹת הָאָדָם וְיָלְדוּ לָהֶם
הֵמָּה הַגִּבֹּרִים אֲשֶׁר מֵעוֹלָם אַנְשֵׁי
הַשֵּׁם׃ פ

*32.* In contrast to the other genealogical references in this section, which name only one son and mention anonymous "sons and daughters," all of Noah's three sons are named.

***Shem, Ham, and Japheth.*** In 10:2, Shem will be described as the ancestor of the Semitic peoples, Ham of the Africans, and Japheth of the Greeks.

## THE MARRIAGE BETWEEN HEAVENLY BEINGS AND EARTHLY WOMEN (6:1–4)

The brief story about divine beings and earthly women is unique in the Bible. It reminds one of Greek mythology, which it indirectly opposes. Whereas Zeus' marriage with women produces heroes such as the venerated Hercules, the Bible portrays such unions as a calamity to be eradicated. The penalty affects human beings alone. Far from gaining immortality, the marriage of heaven and earth reduces human life span. Tikva Frymer-Kensky notes that in the Mesopotamian tradition, the reverse takes place: "Goddesses choose powerful men, particularly kings, as lovers" (*Women in Scripture*, 2000, p. 177).

*1.* ***daughters were born to them.*** Only daughters are mentioned, not sons (who surely were born as well). This detail illustrates the terse biblical style, which focuses only on what is directly relevant to the story at hand.

*2.* ***fair.*** Heb. *tovot*. The word can describe goodness, beauty, health, a source of pleasure, or moral quality. The precise nuance here is not clear, although most interpreters presume that the divine beings were viewing the women lustfully.

***they took.*** This is the verb used in the Bible for marriage.

*3.* While God's exact meaning is obscure, the consequences are clear-cut: human lifespan is to be reduced. The purpose, Tikva Frymer-Kensky suggests, is "to keep human and divine separated" (*Women in Scripture*, 2000, p. 177).

*4.* Heavenly males continue to mate with earthly women and produce giants. (Elsewhere, the Bible equates Nephilim with giants.) Later stories refer to the early inhabitants of Canaan as Nephilim; thus this story serves to cast aspersion on Israel's predecessors in the land. Here, the great renowned heroes meet with God's disapproval. Their exploits are not preserved.

***in those days.*** The writer makes clear the distance between the present account and these ancient stories, another indication that we are reading about the mythic past.

[5]When יהוה saw how great was the wickedness of human beings in the earth, that the direction of their thoughts was nothing but wicked all the time, [6]יהוה regretted having made human beings on earth, and was heartsick. [7]So יהוה thought: "I will wipe the humans whom I created from off the face of the earth—the humans, [and with them] the beasts, the reptiles, the birds of the sky—for I rue the day I made them." [8]But Noah found favor in יהוה's sight.

5 וַיַּרְא יְהֹוָה כִּי רַבָּה רָעַת הָאָדָם בָּאָרֶץ
וְכׇל־יֵצֶר מַחְשְׁבֹת לִבּוֹ רַק רַע כׇּל־הַיּוֹם׃
6 וַיִּנָּחֶם יְהֹוָה כִּי־עָשָׂה אֶת־הָאָדָם בָּאָרֶץ
וַיִּתְעַצֵּב אֶל־לִבּוֹ׃ 7 וַיֹּאמֶר יְהֹוָה אֶמְחֶה
אֶת־הָאָדָם אֲשֶׁר־בָּרָאתִי מֵעַל פְּנֵי הָאֲדָמָה
מֵאָדָם עַד־בְּהֵמָה עַד־רֶמֶשׂ וְעַד־עוֹף
הַשָּׁמָיִם כִּי נִחַמְתִּי כִּי עֲשִׂיתִם׃ 8 וְנֹחַ מָצָא
חֵן בְּעֵינֵי יְהֹוָה׃ פ

## CONCLUSION: GOD'S REGRET (6:5–8)

The parashah that began with the glorious creation of light and life ends with a disappointed God who prepares to start anew. The great experiment has failed, and God has second thoughts. Once again this parashah portrays God as one who learns through interaction with humankind rather than as an all-knowing God.

*5. the wickedness of human beings.* The narrator does not specify here what the evil deeds were, although later they are called "violence" (6:13). The forcible taking of earthly women could be one example of such condemned acts.

*human beings.* Heb. *adam.* See at 1:26.

*direction.* Heb. *yetzer,* which also means "inclination." Later traditions will speak of *yetzer hatov* and *yetzer hara* (usually but somewhat inadequately translated as "the good *yetzer*" and "the evil *yetzer*") as dual or even complementary human impulses. The verbal root *y-tz-r* means "to create."

*their thoughts.* God's words do not imply that human beings are innately evil.

*6. יהוה regretted.* Human evil causes God to repent, grieve, and destroy. Far from being infallible and all-knowing, God confronts unexpected results and has a change of heart. (Many passages, especially in prophetic literature, illustrate God's capacity to change in response to changing circumstances. For example, God regrets having chosen Saul to be king; I Samuel 15:11, 35.)

*was heartsick.* Literally, "his heart was sorrowing." In Genesis 3:16–17, God's pronouncements to the woman and man used noun forms of this verb, *e-tz-b.* Here, God's capacity for sorrow (pathos, as A. J. Heschel has put it) mirrors the sorrow or anguish that God proclaims for the humans after they eat the forbidden fruit. This acknowledgement that God can grieve also binds human and divine experience. The Bible portrays God not as a detached figure but rather as deeply responsive to humankind.

*7.* Elsewhere in the Bible we find the idea that human sin contaminates the whole of creation. Here, however, God's determination to destroy utterly seems excessive. God, again, is portrayed as one who struggles with humankind, this time losing patience with it.

*8. But Noah found favor.* Noah, whose name bears the hope of the people (5:29), now also becomes the hope of God—the one whom God favors. This ray of hope will provide a link to the future for both humankind and God.

*—Tamara Cohn Eskenazi*

# Another View

PERHAPS THE MOST DIFFICULT biblical verse for contemporary readers is Genesis 3:16. Traditional translations understand it to mandate painful pregnancies and the domination of women by men. However, that four-line poetic passage can be understood in a different way.

In Hebrew the first line of the poetry has four words: *harbah arbeh itz'vonech v'heronech*. The first two words constitute a double verbal form that asserts that the following two words—subjects of the verb—will be more intense, more plentiful, or more numerous than would be expected. The present translation "I will greatly increase" is a satisfactory rendering of the double verb.

The usual translation of the two nouns *itz'vonech v'heronech*—"your pains in [or: of] pregnancy"—is problematic. First, as stated, both nouns are objects of the verb "increase." That is, the Hebrew speaks about two distinct conditions that are subject to increase, joined by the Hebrew conjunction "and." Second, the word "pain" is inaccurate. For one thing, it suggests that pregnancy itself is painful, which is not the case in most normal gestations (in contrast to giving birth, which is often painful). Furthermore, the uninflected noun *itzavon* otherwise often refers to the "hard work" of physical labor, which it almost certainly does in the next verse in reference to the agricultural work of men: "through *toil* shall you eat of it."

For these reasons, our translation for the first line of 3:16 is "I will greatly increase your *toil* and your *pregnancies*." Not only does this rendering better reflect the Hebrew wording, but also it reflects the agrarian life situation of the Israelites. The highlands of the Land of Israel were not very fertile or well watered. Therefore, the hard work of both women and men was required for households to survive. Moreover, children were needed for the family labor force. With as many as one in two children dying before the age of five, a woman needed to have up to eight pregnancies to provide the optimum family size of four offspring.

The other three lines of the verse expand on the theme of procreation. The second line ("in anguish you will bear children") conveys the difficulty of childbirth itself, that is, the mental and also the physical anguish of giving birth. The third line ("to your man is your desire") refers to the passion—emotional as much as sexual—that a woman feels for her husband. Such passion allows her to succumb to the dominance mentioned in the last line: "And he will rule over you." In keeping with the focus of this verse on childbearing, that line probably speaks about a husband's ultimate responsibility for his wife's sexuality and not for her entire person. Because of the risks of death in childbirth, many Israelite women would have been reluctant to have numerous pregnancies. Yet, passion toward their spouses serves to prompt women to respond to male sexual urges and thus accept the possibility of another pregnancy. Indeed, some medieval commentaries understood it this way.

> *Perhaps the most difficult biblical verse for today's readers is Genesis 3:16.*

The translation as "rule"—though accurate in a limited way—remains inadequate because it implies general male dominance over women—and has usually been interpreted that way for millennia. Unfortunately, no single word in English precisely conveys the meaning of the Hebrew term in this context.

Like many biblical passages, Genesis 3:16 is an etiology, helping people to accept the difficult realities of life by viewing them as having been mandated by God. For Israelite women this meant hard work and many children as well as enduring the risks of procreation. Although their sexuality may have belonged to their husbands, women in other ways were autonomous individuals who controlled important aspects of household life.

—*Carol Meyers*

# Post-biblical Interpretations

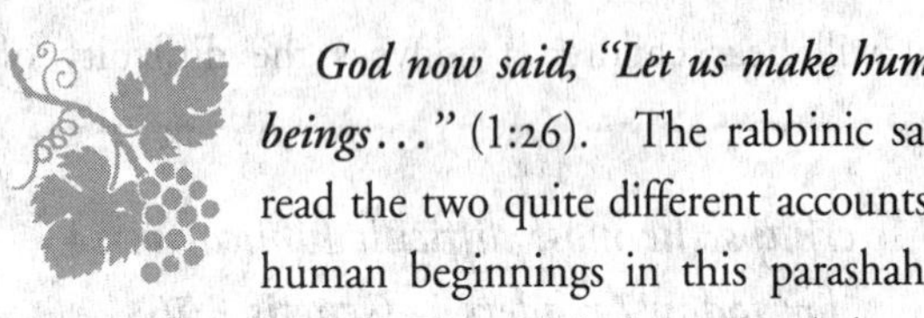

***God now said, "Let us make human beings…"*** (1:26). The rabbinic sages read the two quite different accounts of human beginnings in this parashah as one continuous text. They took for granted that the male and female creations of Genesis 1 were the Adam and Eve of Genesis 2–3. However, the Rabbis were skeptical that men and women were created simultaneously in the divine image as stated in 1:26; they generally insisted that the first woman was formed later, from the first human being, as in Genesis 2:4–25. In Midrash *B'reishit Rabbah* 8.1, Rabbi Jeremiah ben Leazar suggested the compromise position that initially God created one entity with both male and female sexual characteristics. Only afterward, as described in Genesis 2:22, did God separate the female "side" to form the first woman from an essentially male entity. This midrash makes the powerful point that man and woman were initially created as a united being to which they revert when they become *one flesh* (Genesis 2:24) in marriage.

***"In our image, after our likeness"*** (1:26). Parallel comments in *B'reishit Rabbah* 8.9 and 22.2 maintain the precedence of the man in human creation, while stressing the crucial role of marriage and procreation in human life: "In the past, Adam was created from the ground, and Eve from Adam; but henceforth [with the birth of offspring] it shall be *in our image, after our likeness.* Neither man without woman, nor woman without man, nor both of them without the *Shechinah.*" This invocation of the *Shechinah*—the indwelling nurturing aspect of the Divine, designated by a feminine noun—indicates that for the Rabbis, the female also shares in the divine image when she is joined to the male in a fruitful marriage.

***God then blessed them*** (1:28). Continuing the strong connection between Creation and marriage, *B'reishit Rabbah* 8.13 records the tradition that God "took up a cup of blessing and blessed them." Then it adds: "Rabbi Judah ben Rabbi Simon said: [The angels] Michael and Gabriel were Adam's 'best men.' Rabbi Simlai said: We find that the Holy One blesses bridegrooms, adorns brides, visits the sick, buries the

*Man and woman were initially created as a united being.*

dead, and recites the blessing for mourners. God blesses bridegrooms, as it is written: *God then blessed them*; and adorns brides, as it is written: *Now God* יהוה *built up the rib taken from the man into a woman* (Genesis 2:22)."

***Then God* יהוה *considered, "It is not good that the man be alone—I will make him a helpmate"*** (2:18). *B'reishit Rabbah* 17.2 teaches: "A man without a wife lives without good, without help, without joy, without blessing, and without atonement.... Some even say he falls short of the divine image, since immediately following *For human beings were made in the image of God* (Genesis 9:6) it is written, *As for you, be fruitful and multiply* (9:7). For the Rabbis, humankind is like God in its ability to create human beings, yet reproduction requires both females and males. According to

BT *Y'vamot* 63a, women also help men in pragmatic ways; there the prophet Elijah meets Rabbi Yosi and asks him rhetorically: "If a man brings in wheat, does he chew on the wheat? If flax, does he put on the flax? [No, he must wait until his wife sees to the processing of the wheat into bread, and of the flax into clothing!] Does she not, then, bring light to his eyes and put him on his feet?"

***and the man said, "This time— / bone of my bone, flesh of my flesh!*** (2:23). Prompted by *This time,* several rabbinic passages mention a previous time—a "first Eve," who fled from Adam and was replaced with a second female creation (*B'reishit Rabbah* 17.7, 18.4, 22.7). This legend was later combined with ancient folk traditions about the night spirit Lilith. In the *Alphabet of Ben Sira* (possibly 8th century C.E.), Lilith's rebelliousness is attributed to her equal creation with Adam. Refusing to be subservient in sexual intercourse or in any other way, she became a demon rather than endure Adam's domination. Jewish folklore attributed nocturnal emissions to Lilith, who was said to set upon sleeping men. She was also blamed for maternal deaths in childbirth and for infant mortality. One popular remedy was amulets bearing the names of angels. Lilith is further demonized in Jewish mystical traditions where she and her satanic husband Samael become the evil counterparts of Adam and Eve. (On Lilith, see further Judith R. Baskin, *Midrashic Women*, 2002, pp. 58–60.)

***And to the woman,* [*God*] *said*** (3:16). Some Rabbis blame Eve for the expulsion from the Garden of Eden and its consequences. While Adam was punished for his participation in divine disobedience, none of the pronouncements against him in Genesis 3:17–19 apply only to males. But Eve, and through her all women, received additional gender-specific punishments—and rabbinic literature discusses them frequently. The inventory found in *Avot D'Rabbi Nathan* B 42 includes: menstruation, "when she is driven from her house and banned from her husband"; childbirth; nursing her children; and being subject to her husband's authority and his jealousy. Moreover, she ages quickly and ceases to give birth, while "men never cease being able to beget children." Also, a woman stays indoors; and when she goes out, her head must be covered like a mourner: "That is why women precede the funeral bier, saying, 'We have brought death upon all the inhabitants of the world.'" Such harsh views permeate rabbinic commentary on Eve's creation and her role in the Garden of Eden, and they had a long and pernicious afterlife in shaping Jewish and Christian views of women.

*—Judith R. Baskin*

• • • • •

# Contemporary Reflection

THE ANCIENT BABYLONIAN MYTH (or foundational story) that strongly resembles Genesis 1 has one great dissimilarity from it: in that myth, creation begins with a murder. The goddess Tiamat—cognate to our word *t'hom* (watery chaos, 1:2)—is slain by the hero-god Marduk; and the universe is carved out of her body. Violence there is inextricable from the process of creation. In Genesis 1, however, creation entails no destruction. Even the primal watery abyss is not completely obliterated but lingers at the bottom of the sea to reappear in many a psalm or story. The drawing of distinctions and boundaries that marks both accounts is in Genesis 1 peaceful and harmonious.

God distinguishes elements of the original watery chaos by drawing boundaries between them and naming them: light and darkness, day and night. Created elements are not simple oppositions. They are both distinct and akin. Juxtaposed verses emphasize the parallels between elements. There are waters above and waters below. Between them stretch a solid expanse of earth and a solid expanse of firmament. The earth brings forth grasses and trees. The sky is strewn with lights. The sea and the air bring forth swarms of living things, schools of fish, flocks of birds, clouds of insects. The earth births its many creatures, joyously productive, mirroring the water and the air.

The creation of humankind continues these dual themes of distinction and similarity. Not one but two words underline the likeness between *adam* (the earthling) and its Maker. Humankind bears the *tzelem* (image) and *d'mut* (resemblance) of the divine Creator, although in contrast to God's oneness, they are several. They are also distinguished from one another: *zachar* (which means "male" but is also a word related to "remember"), the bearer of the male member, and *n'kevah* (which means "female" but is also a word related to "piercing"), the pierced one. In Genesis 3 the two will become a hierarchy, but in Genesis 1, they are presented as equals. Both bear the divine image and semblance, both are adjured to "be fruitful and multiply, fill the earth and tame it, and hold sway . . . over all the earth" (1:28).

*Adam* is the only creature whose sexuality the text notes—that is, describes as male and female. This suggests a sexuality unlike that of the animals. Moreover in both 1:27 and a summary in 5:1–3, the mention of *adam*'s maleness and femaleness is immediately followed by the proclamation of its divine image, as if our diverse sexualities and our kinship with God were linked. Rather than our sexualities being *dissimilar* to God or excluded from the divine image, they seem to *point toward* some element in the divine nature, some divine attribute—creativity or delight, perhaps, or the longing for an Other—for which our embodied sexuality is the metaphor.

Genesis 2 and 3 tell a darker tale. Here we learn why *adam* is called *adam*. Multiple puns are evoked by the name: kinship with *adamah* (earth or soil) out of which *adam* is fashioned, association with the color red (*adom*) like the ruddy sunburnt skin of the worker and the red earth he was created to till, and resonance with blood (*dam*), the red life-fluid. Unlike in Genesis 1, however, in 2:7–3:20 the term *adam* refers to the man. The woman is never called *adam* but only *ishah* (woman), "for this one is taken from man" (2:23). Together they are *ha-adam v'ishto*, "the human and his woman," for the first man represents both the male particular and the generically human.

As the verb "built" (2:22) attests, the creation of woman differs from other creations. The dual *adam* of Genesis 1 is created (*bara*) by divine word, and the *adam* of Genesis 2 is fashioned or molded (*yatzar*) by a divine potter. The woman is constructed (*banah*) out of part of an existing creation. An afterthought, created when *adam* finds the animals unsatisfactory for mating, she is meant to be *ezer k'negdo*, literally "a helper over against him," that is, opposite him or corresponding to him. The ambiguity in the expression foreshadows an ambivalent relationship. Is she against him or for him? A challenger or an "other" who mirrors him and merges with him? Awakening, *adam* claims her as part of himself: "bone of my bone, flesh of my flesh" (2:23). He does not appear to recognize her otherness, nor does he address her. Her only recorded conversations are first with the serpent and then with God. Finally, at the end of the chapter, *adam* names her as he previously named the animals. It does not occur to him to ask her what she calls herself.

*The world of patriarchy cries out for mending.*

Genesis 1 is an account of the Creation, whereas

Genesis 2–3 is an account of the creation of patriarchy—a remarkably truthful account. The world brought about by Genesis 2–3 is one in which desire is no longer joyful but oppressive. Even before the disobedience, relations between man and woman and world are commodified and function-based. *Adam* is created to till the soil. Woman is created to help *Adam*. However lush, the garden is a workplace. Created things are good, not intrinsically as in Genesis 1, but because they are resources. The Garden is described as prime real estate, rich in water and in trees, and adjacent to lands rich in gold and gemstones. Everything is viewed extractively. The forbidden fruit is presented as the epitome of desire in terms not of intrinsic value but of what it is good *for:* "good to eat," "alluring to the eyes," "desirable for insight" (3:6).

Woman's desire for man ensures her subjugation and her anguish (3:16). Man's desire is not even mentioned. He is exhausted by the effort to pull from the ground what can be consumed before descending into the ground and being consumed by it. Adam and Eve are alienated from each other, from the earth, from their labors, from the rest of creation.

The world of patriarchy cries out for mending. A mending world would commit itself to equality and power-sharing, to working cooperatively in order to fill needs and solve problems. At one again with the rest of Creation, perhaps we would even learn not to resent our mortality so bitterly. Reunited also with the rest of creation, men and women could learn again to be "loving friends"—as the traditional rabbinic wedding blessing portrays them.

—*Rachel Adler*

# Voices

## *Awakening*

Lynn Gottlieb

*Genesis 1:26–28; 2:18–24*

Shekinah gazed upon the sleeping form of
HeShe.
"I shall divide this being
So HeShe can find loving companionship
Like the other creatures in the garden."
HeShe lay asleep in the grass
Curled up like a snake in the warm sun
Dreaming of angels.
Shekinah thought,
"Which part of the body
Shall I take to form the woman?
Perhaps from the mouth
So she can tell stories like Serach,
The woman who smells of time.
Perhaps the eyes
So she sees the inside truth of things
Like Soft Eyes Woman Leah.
Perhaps from the neck
So she walks with pride
Like the daughters of Zelophehad
Who are Mahlah, Noah, Hoglah, Milcah, and
Tirzah.
Perhaps the ears
So she hears my laughter
Like See Far Woman Sarah.
Perhaps the heart
So she flows with tender mercies
Like Soft Hearted Woman Rachel.
Perhaps the arms
So she heals and restores with touch
Like the Hebrew midwife women.
Perhaps the legs
So she goes out seeking wisdom
Like Truth Seeking Woman Dinah.
Perhaps from the flower of her passion
So she enjoys the fruits of her body
Like Shulamit."
Then Shekinah blessed every part of woman's
body, saying,
"Be pure of heart
and always know you are created in My
image."
Then she awoke, first woman.

NOTES

***Serach.*** The daughter of Jacob's son Asher (Genesis 46:17, Numbers 26:46). See pp. 276, 984.

***Soft Eyes Woman Leah.*** In Genesis 29:17, Leah's eyes are called *rakot*, which some medieval rabbis understood to mean "soft" or "tender."

***daughters of Zelophehad.*** They ask to inherit their father's land and receive it (Numbers 27:1–11).

***laughter.*** Sarah laughs when she hears that she will bear a child (Genesis 18:10–15).

***See Far Woman Sarah.*** There is a rabbinic legend that Sarah was also known as Yiscah (Genesis 11:29), from the root *s-k-h* (to gaze), because she was able to see the holy spirit (BT *M'gillah* 14a).

***Rachel.*** She first appears in Genesis 29:10.

***Hebrew midwife women.*** Who disobey Pharaoh's orders to kill male infants (Exodus 1:15–22).

***Dinah.*** Leah's daughter, whose story appears in Genesis 34:1–31.

***Shulamit.*** The name of the woman in the sensual love poems of the Song of Songs (7:1).

## *from* Shirat Ishah

Esther Raab (transl. Harold Schimmel)

*Genesis 1:26–28; 2:18–24*

Blessed be the One who made me a woman—
that I'm earth and Adam
and a tender rib;
Blessed who made me
circles upon circles—
like wheels of planets
and like circles of fruits—
who gave me a living flesh
which blossoms
and made me like plant of the field—
that bears fruit.

## In the Beginning

Shirley Kaufman

*Genesis 2:18–24*

When he wakes, he turns
on his side. Something
is missing.

already she's out in the garden
smelling the lilacs, naming
the pterodactyls.

Already she's claiming
the strange face rippled
in the pond,

a terrible eagerness, trying
to scoop the pale shape
into her hands.

It's only water.
she wants it to tell her
who she is, or

what he lost.

## Genesis

Eva Tóth (transl. Peter Jay)

*Genesis 1:26–28; 2:18–24*

Your hands create my body
your mouth breathes life in me
my face shines in your eyes
you call me by my name

Alone how should I shine?
Alone I am in darkness
Alone unshapely clod of earth
Alone I do not exist

## A God Once Commanded Us

Lea Goldberg (transl. Robert Friend)

*Genesis 3*

A god once commanded us to stand strong
under the terrible tree of life.
And in the black wind of the years we stood,
stricken with expectation—
perhaps the fruit would fall at our feet.
But nothing happened.

And on the day of secret reckoning
between him and us
we saw a hunched landscape, brown leaves
falling,
and felt on our faces
a cold wind blowing.

Then said a Voice: this is your day of freedom.
This is everything. And this is good.

Now towards the flame of cutting cold, alone,
I take
a few steps only
until I meet
that flickering lantern
at the corner of the street.

## *Aspects of Eve*
Linda Pastan

*Genesis 2:21–22*

To have been one
of many ribs
and to be chosen.
To grow into something
quite different
knocking finally
as a bone knocks
on the closed gates of the garden—
which unexpectedly
open.

## *Eve's Birth*
Kim Chernin

*Genesis 2:18–24*

Was I summoned
or did I rise
from my own emergency?
Dreaming of a dark and formless thing
that had no eyes
and fashioned mine.
Remembering:
waters, the disquieting wind,
dark earth and dismembering fire:
a servile arc
that roared disquietude,
weakened from slumber;
and breath,
ribbed with mortality.

## *Where Did Its Redness Come From?*
Rivka Miriam (transl. Linda Stern Zisquit)

*Genesis 3:6*

Where did the apple's redness come from,
Eve wondered—
did it put on makeup to seduce me
or did it blush
seeing my skin tight as a bud
and no shame yet absorbed in me?

## *The Apple Was a Northern Invention*
Eleanor Wilner

*Genesis 3:6*

When she ate the pomegranate,
it was as if every seed
with its wet red shining coat
of sweet flesh clinging to the dark core
was one of nature's eyes. Afterward,
it was nature that was blind,
and she who was wild
with vision, condemned
to see what was before her, and behind.

NOTE

***apple.*** The Torah does not specify that the fruit eaten in Eden was an apple; that identification comes from a later source.

# נח ✦ Noach

## GENESIS 6:9–11:32

### *Beginning Again*

PARASHAT NOACH (Noah), named after the head of the household that survives the Flood, continues the basic themes of Genesis 1–11, accounting for the human condition with its possibilities and perils. The stories express a conviction that God persists—despite repeated disappointments—in (re)adjusting expectations in response to human limitations.

Two individuals, living ten generations apart, frame the parashah: Noah (6:9) and Abram/Abraham (11:27–32). Each becomes a vehicle for God's persistence in "beginning again." Between these two looms the devastating flood in response to human transgression, followed by God's renewed effort to restore harmony through a covenant with Noah and all creation. The covenant redefines the relationship between God and humankind.

The tale of the Tower of Babel (Genesis 11) follows the flood story, as yet another case of human disobedience and divine response. It accounts for linguistic diversity and also demonstrates God's covenantal restraint when humankind once again seeks to go beyond bounds. Finally, the introduction of Abram and Sarai that concludes the parashah prepares the stage for stories about the ancestral family—and about the descendants, the Israelites, who are the subject of the rest of the Bible.

Women's presence in this parashah is more implicit than explicit until the very end, when Sarai/Sarah receives more attention than her husband Abram/Abraham (11:29–30). Her condition, that of a barren woman, introduces the challenge that propels the plot of the next several Torah portions, namely: How can God's promises of progeny be fulfilled? Noah's wife, the new mother of humankind, is mentioned several times but never named (though some rabbis later identify her as Naamah of Genesis 4:22). The virtual absence of women's stories and names is all the more striking given the emphasis on women in the previous parashah and the lengthy, patrilineal genealogies in this one. Feminine presence is detected, however, in three basic ways: the (unnamed) wives of Noah and "his" sons; the emphasis on the animals who embark the ark as male and female; and the overwhelming presence of *t'hom*, "the deep"—a feminine noun evoking the name of the Babylonians' salt-water goddess, Tiamat. *T'hom* first appears in Genesis 1:2 as a subdued presence. Riled into action by God, *t'hom* in this Torah portion unleashes its waters and destroys all that lives on land (see at 7:1).

—*Tamara Cohn Eskenazi*

*Feminine presence in this parashah is detected in three basic ways.*

## *Outline*

*I.* Transgression and Divine Response
*Noah and the Flood* (6:9–9:29)

*A.* The Flood (6:9–8:14)

*B.* Transformation, covenant, and renewal (8:15–9:17)

*C.* The aftermath: Noah and his sons (vv. 18–29)

*II.* The Table of the Nations (10:1–32)

*III.* Transgression and Divine Response
*The Tower of Babel* (11:1–9)

*IV.* The Ten Generations from Noah to Abram (11:10–26)

*V.* A New Beginning
*Abram/Abraham and Sarai/Sarah* (11:27–32)

This is Noah's chronicle. Noah was a righteous man; in his generation, he was above re-

9 אֵלֶּה תּוֹלְדֹת נֹחַ נֹחַ אִישׁ צַדִּיק תָּמִים
הָיָה בְּדֹרֹתָיו אֶת־הָאֱלֹהִים הִתְהַלֶּךְ־נֹחַ׃

## *Transgression and Divine Response*

### NOAH AND THE FLOOD (6:9–9:29)

The Flood Story draws upon other ancient Near Eastern traditions about disastrous floods, such as the Babylonian epics Gilgamesh and Atra Hasis (dated as early as the 18th century B.C.E.). The parallels between the biblical and Babylonian versions are extensive and striking. They share a basic plot: the divine anger leads to a flood aiming to eradicate humankind. Many details are strikingly similar: one individual is told to build a boat to carry a select few to safety; the instructions for the boat, including the requirement for a window, are often parallel; and a raven and a dove go out to test the conditions in the aftermath. There can be no doubt that Babylonian traditions influenced the biblical version. The most significant differences between the two lie in the cause for the flood: in the Babylonian myth, the gods unleash the flood because human noise angers them; in Genesis, human violence prompts God to unleash the flood. In the Babylonian versions, the hero receives immortality as a gift from the gods. What the biblical hero receives is a covenant from God that promises the "immortality" of humankind. According to Tikva Frymer-Kensky, the biblical flood is not primarily a punishment but "a means of getting rid of the thoroughly polluted world and starting again with a well-washed one" ("The *Atrahasis* Epic and Its Significance for Our Understanding of Genesis 1–9," *Studies in Bible and Feminist Criticism*, 2006, p. 62). The laws that God gives Noah in Genesis 9:1–7 seek to prevent the kind of bloodshed that pollutes the land.

The description of the flood shows an interweaving of separate versions, illustrating a commitment to more than one voice in telling the story. Scholars of the Torah's historical development identify two major strands: "J" (also called "Yahwist," a Judean source) and "P" (Priestly source), each with its own characteristics (see the introduction to Genesis, p. 1).

### THE FLOOD (6:9–8:14)

*9. **Noah was a righteous man.*** Already introduced in the previous parashah as the hope of both humankind (5:28–29) and God (6:8), Noah is the bearer of potential comfort. His father had named him as such, a bringer of *n'chamah* ("comfort," a pun on the name *Noach*) to reverse the cursed condition of the earth (5:29).

***in his generation.*** Whether this qualification intends to diminish his virtue (meaning, "only when compared to others in that era of utter violence") or enhance it (meaning "even in the midst of a corrupt generation") remains unspecified.


The theme of barrenness is emphasized in the story of the ancestors.

ANOTHER VIEW ➤ 53

God's words show us how we can use language to repair relationships.

CONTEMPORARY REFLECTION ➤ 55

One rabbi argues that Noah's wife was Naamah, a descendant of Cain.

POST-BIBLICAL INTERPRETATIONS ➤ 53

My mother and sisters— / there would be no room for them. . . .

VOICES ➤ 57

proach; Noah walked with God. [10]Noah begot three sons: Shem, Ham, and Japheth.

[11]The earth became corrupt before God; the earth was filled with violence, [12]and when God saw how corrupted the earth was, how all flesh was acting in a corrupt way upon the earth, [13]God said to Noah, "The end of all flesh has come [to mind] before Me, because the earth is full of violence on their account; look, now—I am going to wipe them off the earth. [14]Make yourself an ark of *gopher* wood; make the ark with rooms, and cover it with tar inside and out. [15]This is how to make it: 300 cubits long, 50 cubits wide, and 30 cubits high. [16]Make a roof for the ark, making it overhang from above by a cubit. Put the ark's door

10 וַיּ֥וֹלֶד נֹ֖חַ שְׁלֹשָׁ֣ה בָנִ֑ים אֶת־שֵׁ֖ם אֶת־חָ֥ם
וְאֶת־יָֽפֶת׃
11 וַתִּשָּׁחֵ֥ת הָאָ֖רֶץ לִפְנֵ֣י הָֽאֱלֹהִ֑ים וַתִּמָּלֵ֥א
הָאָ֖רֶץ חָמָֽס׃ 12 וַיַּ֧רְא אֱלֹהִ֛ים אֶת־הָאָ֖רֶץ
וְהִנֵּ֣ה נִשְׁחָ֑תָה כִּֽי־הִשְׁחִ֧ית כׇּל־בָּשָׂ֛ר אֶת־
דַּרְכּ֖וֹ עַל־הָאָֽרֶץ׃ ס 13 וַיֹּ֨אמֶר אֱלֹהִ֜ים
לְנֹ֗חַ קֵ֤ץ כׇּל־בָּשָׂר֙ בָּ֣א לְפָנַ֔י כִּֽי־מָלְאָ֥ה
הָאָ֛רֶץ חָמָ֖ס מִפְּנֵיהֶ֑ם וְהִנְנִ֥י מַשְׁחִיתָ֖ם אֶת־
הָאָֽרֶץ׃ 14 עֲשֵׂ֤ה לְךָ֙ תֵּבַ֣ת עֲצֵי־גֹ֔פֶר קִנִּ֖ים
תַּעֲשֶׂ֣ה אֶת־הַתֵּבָ֑ה וְכָֽפַרְתָּ֥ אֹתָ֛הּ מִבַּ֥יִת
וּמִח֖וּץ בַּכֹּֽפֶר׃ 15 וְזֶ֕ה אֲשֶׁ֥ר תַּעֲשֶׂ֖ה אֹתָ֑הּ
שְׁלֹ֧שׁ מֵא֣וֹת אַמָּ֗ה אֹ֚רֶךְ הַתֵּבָ֔ה חֲמִשִּׁ֤ים
אַמָּה֙ רׇחְבָּ֔הּ וּשְׁלֹשִׁ֥ים אַמָּ֖ה קוֹמָתָֽהּ׃
16 צֹ֣הַר ׀ תַּעֲשֶׂ֣ה לַתֵּבָ֗ה וְאֶל־אַמָּה֙ תְּכַלֶּ֣נָּה

---

***walked with God.*** The phrase indicates special intimacy. In the Bible, only Enoch (5:22) and Noah receive such a high compliment. God asks Abraham to "walk *before* me" (17:1), possibly an even more demanding request than walking *with* God.

*10.* ***Noah begot three sons.*** This information was first reported in 5:32. No mother is mentioned, for generational continuity and transmission of property in ancient Israel focused on the male lineage. However, in the context of lineages, it generally goes without saying that women are essential to the household and to society.

***Shem, Ham, and Japheth.*** Each of the three sons represents a general linguistic or ethnic group in existence when the Torah was composed. According to 10:1–26, Shem is ancestor of the Semites to which Israel and the Arab peoples belong. Ham is ancestor of the African peoples and Japheth of the Greeks. Noah will later establish a hierarchy among them (9:24–27).

*6:11–7:23.* In the Babylonian flood stories, the gods are angry at humankind because people have become a nuisance, disturbing the peace. Genesis, instead, makes unchecked human violence the reason for God's drastic action of wiping out all living creatures—returning the world to primeval chaos.

*11.* ***violence.*** Tikva Frymer-Kensky points out that this Hebrew word, *chamas*, "in the Bible encompasses almost the entire spectrum of evil" ("The *Atrahasis* Epic," *Studies in Bible*, 2006, p. 61). After the flood, God gives Noah prohibitions regarding bloodshed, which suggests that bloodshed was the main concern.

*13–22.* The ark that God instructs Noah to build is intended to provide for the future by saving Noah, his family, and the representative animals.

*13.* ***God said… "I am going to wipe them off."*** The narrator had first mentioned God's decision to destroy humankind in 6:5–7. The report that divine beings married earthly women in what seemed like a violation of the boundary between heaven and earth (6:1–4) may also be a factor in God's decision.

*14.* ***"Make yourself an ark."*** The word *tevah* (ark) literally means a box. It appears again only in Exodus 2:3–5, when Moses' mother makes one for her newborn. In both cases, the ark carries the future, as it were.

in its side, and make a bottom, a second, and a
third deck.
[17]"As for Me, I am going to bring the floodwaters upon the earth to destroy all that lives under
the heavens, [all] that has the breath of life in it.
Everything on earth shall expire. [18]With you,
though, I will establish My covenant: go then into
the ark—you, your wife, your sons, and their wives
with you. [19]And take two each of every living creature—of all flesh—into the ark, male and female,
to keep them alive along with you: [20]every type
of bird, every type of beast, every type of creeping
thing—let two of each come to you to keep them
alive, [21]and take along edible foodstuffs of every
kind; gather them up so that there is food for yourself and for them." [22]And Noah did just as God had
commanded him: that is what he did.
7 יהוה then said to Noah, "Go into the ark
with all your household, for I see that you [alone] in
this age are righteous before Me. [2]Take seven pairs
of every pure beast, a male and its mate, and two of
every impure beast, a male and its mate. [3]Of the
birds of the sky, too, take seven pairs, male and
female, to give life to offspring on the face of the
earth. [4]For in another seven days I will pour rain

מִלְמַעְלָה וּפֶתַח הַתֵּבָה בְּצִדָּהּ תָּשִׂים
תַּחְתִּיִּם שְׁנִיִּם וּשְׁלִשִׁים תַּעֲשֶׂהָ׃
17 וַאֲנִי הִנְנִי מֵבִיא אֶת־הַמַּבּוּל מַיִם עַל־
הָאָרֶץ לְשַׁחֵת כָּל־בָּשָׂר אֲשֶׁר־בּוֹ רוּחַ חַיִּים
מִתַּחַת הַשָּׁמָיִם כֹּל אֲשֶׁר־בָּאָרֶץ יִגְוָע׃
18 וַהֲקִמֹתִי אֶת־בְּרִיתִי אִתָּךְ וּבָאתָ אֶל־
הַתֵּבָה אַתָּה וּבָנֶיךָ וְאִשְׁתְּךָ וּנְשֵׁי־בָנֶיךָ
אִתָּךְ׃ 19 וּמִכָּל־הָחַי מִכָּל־בָּשָׂר שְׁנַיִם מִכֹּל
תָּבִיא אֶל־הַתֵּבָה לְהַחֲיֹת אִתָּךְ זָכָר וּנְקֵבָה
יִהְיוּ׃ 20 מֵהָעוֹף לְמִינֵהוּ וּמִן־הַבְּהֵמָה
לְמִינָהּ מִכֹּל רֶמֶשׂ הָאֲדָמָה לְמִינֵהוּ שְׁנַיִם
מִכֹּל יָבֹאוּ אֵלֶיךָ לְהַחֲיוֹת׃ 21 וְאַתָּה קַח־
לְךָ מִכָּל־מַאֲכָל אֲשֶׁר יֵאָכֵל וְאָסַפְתָּ אֵלֶיךָ
וְהָיָה לְךָ וְלָהֶם לְאָכְלָה׃ 22 וַיַּעַשׂ נֹחַ כְּכֹל
אֲשֶׁר צִוָּה אֹתוֹ אֱלֹהִים כֵּן עָשָׂה׃
ז וַיֹּאמֶר יְהוָה לְנֹחַ בֹּא־אַתָּה וְכָל־בֵּיתְךָ
אֶל־הַתֵּבָה כִּי־אֹתְךָ רָאִיתִי צַדִּיק לְפָנַי בַּדּוֹר
הַזֶּה׃ 2 מִכֹּל ׀ הַבְּהֵמָה הַטְּהוֹרָה תִּקַּח־לְךָ
שִׁבְעָה שִׁבְעָה אִישׁ וְאִשְׁתּוֹ וּמִן־הַבְּהֵמָה
אֲשֶׁר לֹא טְהֹרָה הִוא שְׁנַיִם אִישׁ וְאִשְׁתּוֹ׃
3 גַּם מֵעוֹף הַשָּׁמַיִם שִׁבְעָה שִׁבְעָה זָכָר
וּנְקֵבָה לְחַיּוֹת זֶרַע עַל־פְּנֵי כָל־הָאָרֶץ׃ 4 כִּי
לְיָמִים עוֹד שִׁבְעָה אָנֹכִי מַמְטִיר עַל־הָאָרֶץ

*18. "With you, though, I will establish My covenant."* This first mentioned covenant will encompass all of Noah's descendants, and thus all humankind, as well as the entire natural world (see Genesis 9:8–17).

***"go . . . you, your wife, your sons, and their wives with you."*** As sole survivors, they constitute all humankind.

For the first time, Noah's unnamed wife is mentioned, along with the wives of his sons (not *her* sons or *their* sons). The wording reflects the patrilineal nature of the ancient society; see above at v. 10.

*19. "male and female."* Provision for continued procreation involves female and male creatures.

*7:1.* Noah's righteousness merits the saving of his entire household, the basic unit of ancient Near Eastern society. Whereas the hero of the Babylonian flood story tries to warn his neighbors and persuade them to join him in the ark, Noah does not attempt to include or reform others.

*2.* God further provides for the future by ensuring the procreation of animals (rather than creating them anew). Pure animals are those fit for sacrifice.

***"male and its mate."*** Heb. *ish v'ishto*, words that are sometimes used in biblical language to designate members of a group, human or otherwise. (See further at 2:23.)

upon the earth for forty days and nights and wipe all that exists—all that I have made—off the face of the earth." [5]Noah then did just as יהוה had commanded him.

[6]Noah was 600 years old when the flood came—waters upon the earth. [7]Noah, with his sons, his wife, and his sons' wives came into the ark on account of the deluge. [8]Of the pure beasts and the beasts that were not pure, of the birds and all that creep on the earth, [9]two by two they came to Noah to the ark, male and female, as God had commanded Noah.

[10]After seven days, the floodwaters covered the earth. [11]In the six hundredth year of Noah's life, in the second month, on the seventeenth day of the month, on that day, all the springs of the great deep broke out, and the sky's floodgates opened. [12]Rain fell upon the earth for forty days and nights.

[13]That very day Noah and Shem and Ham and Japheth, Noah's sons, came to the ark, with Noah's

אַרְבָּעִים יוֹם וְאַרְבָּעִים לָיְלָה וּמָחִיתִי אֶת־
כׇּל־הַיְקוּם אֲשֶׁר עָשִׂיתִי מֵעַל פְּנֵי הָאֲדָמָה׃
5 וַיַּעַשׂ נֹחַ כְּכֹל אֲשֶׁר־צִוָּהוּ יְהֹוָה׃
6 וְנֹחַ בֶּן־שֵׁשׁ מֵאוֹת שָׁנָה וְהַמַּבּוּל הָיָה
מַיִם עַל־הָאָרֶץ׃ 7 וַיָּבֹא נֹחַ וּבָנָיו וְאִשְׁתּוֹ
וּנְשֵׁי־בָנָיו אִתּוֹ אֶל־הַתֵּבָה מִפְּנֵי מֵי
הַמַּבּוּל׃ 8 מִן־הַבְּהֵמָה הַטְּהוֹרָה וּמִן־
הַבְּהֵמָה אֲשֶׁר אֵינֶנָּה טְהֹרָה וּמִן־הָעוֹף
וְכֹל אֲשֶׁר־רֹמֵשׂ עַל־הָאֲדָמָה׃ 9 שְׁנַיִם
שְׁנַיִם בָּאוּ אֶל־נֹחַ אֶל־הַתֵּבָה זָכָר וּנְקֵבָה
כַּאֲשֶׁר צִוָּה אֱלֹהִים אֶת־נֹחַ׃
10 וַיְהִי לְשִׁבְעַת הַיָּמִים וּמֵי הַמַּבּוּל הָיוּ
עַל־הָאָרֶץ׃ 11 בִּשְׁנַת שֵׁשׁ־מֵאוֹת שָׁנָה
לְחַיֵּי־נֹחַ בַּחֹדֶשׁ הַשֵּׁנִי בְּשִׁבְעָה־עָשָׂר יוֹם
לַחֹדֶשׁ בַּיּוֹם הַזֶּה נִבְקְעוּ כׇּל־מַעְיְנוֹת תְּהוֹם
רַבָּה וַאֲרֻבֹּת הַשָּׁמַיִם נִפְתָּחוּ׃ 12 וַיְהִי
הַגֶּשֶׁם עַל־הָאָרֶץ אַרְבָּעִים יוֹם וְאַרְבָּעִים
לָיְלָה׃
13 בְּעֶצֶם הַיּוֹם הַזֶּה בָּא נֹחַ וְשֵׁם־וְחָם וָיֶפֶת
בְּנֵי־נֹחַ וְאֵשֶׁת נֹחַ וּשְׁלֹשֶׁת נְשֵׁי־בָנָיו אִתָּם

*7. **Noah, with his sons, his wife, and his sons' wives came into the ark.*** Noah's wife and his sons' wives are mentioned several times without names. See above at 6:18.

*7:11–8:14.* The Flood is more than an overflow of water; it represents a return to primeval chaos, with water breaking through the boundaries created in Genesis 1 to form and protect the earth. The floodgates open from above and below, letting the waters wipe out everything. The details of the story show inconsistencies that expose the seams where two accounts are woven together. The actual flood lasts 40 days (7:17), yet waters continue to rise for 150 days (7:24), subsiding for 40 days plus 14 (8:6).

*11. **the great deep.*** Heb. *t'hom*, a noun also found in 1:2, echoes the name of the Mesopotamian goddess Tiamat. But now she bursts forth with the ferocity familiar from the Babylonian Creation story Enuma Elish. Primordial *t'hom*, like the awesome goddess Tiamat, has been often maligned. According to the Enuma Elish, Tiamat's children, led by the god Marduk, provoke her wrath by killing her husband. When she tries to retaliate, they destroy her and use her body to form the world. In the Bible, *t'hom* is typically associated with the uncontrollable and immeasurable. Catherine Keller, however, shows the nuanced ways in which *t'hom* as "the deep," infinite and fertile, also functions as a partner with God in creation (*The Face of the Deep: A Theology of Becoming*, 2003, pp. 213–228). See also the positive reference to *t'hom* in Psalm 42:8, "deep (*t'hom*) calls to deep (*t'hom*)."

wife and with his sons' three wives. 14 They, and
every type of animal, every type of beast, every
type of creature that creeps on the earth, every type
of fowl, every bird, every winged creature—15 they
came to Noah, to the ark, two by two, all flesh that
had in it the breath of life. 16 Those who came were
male and female; some of every species entered, just
as God had ordered him; then יהוה shut [the door]
after him.

17 Forty days the flood was upon the earth; the
waters increased and lifted the ark, and so it rose
over the ground. 18 The waters gained in strength,
increasing upon the earth, as the ark coursed on
the waters' surface. 19 High, high above the earth
towered the waters, so that the tallest mountains
that stand beneath the heavens were submerged.
20 Fifteen cubits higher the waters towered, as the
mountains were submerged. 21 Then all flesh that
swarmed upon the earth perished—whether bird,
cattle, or wild animal, or that which teemed over
the earth, or human being. 22 Whatever on dry land
had the breath of life in its nostrils, died. 23 [God]
wiped out all that existed on the face of the earth—
human, beast, reptile, birds of the sky—they were
wiped off the earth; there remained only Noah and
those with him in the ark.

24 And the waters towered over the earth a hundred and fifty days. *8* God then remembered
Noah and all the animals and all the beasts that
were with him in the ark, so God caused a wind
to sweep over the earth, and the waters subsided.

אֶל־הַתֵּבָה׃ 14 הֵמָּה וְכָל־הַחַיָּה לְמִינָהּ
וְכָל־הַבְּהֵמָה לְמִינָהּ וְכָל־הָרֶמֶשׂ הָרֹמֵשׂ
עַל־הָאָרֶץ לְמִינֵהוּ וְכָל־הָעוֹף לְמִינֵהוּ כֹּל
צִפּוֹר כָּל־כָּנָף׃ 15 וַיָּבֹאוּ אֶל־נֹחַ אֶל־הַתֵּבָה
שְׁנַיִם שְׁנַיִם מִכָּל־הַבָּשָׂר אֲשֶׁר־בּוֹ רוּחַ
חַיִּים׃ 16 וְהַבָּאִים זָכָר וּנְקֵבָה מִכָּל־בָּשָׂר
בָּאוּ כַּאֲשֶׁר צִוָּה אֹתוֹ אֱלֹהִים וַיִּסְגֹּר יְהוָה
בַּעֲדוֹ׃

17 וַיְהִי הַמַּבּוּל אַרְבָּעִים יוֹם עַל־הָאָרֶץ
וַיִּרְבּוּ הַמַּיִם וַיִּשְׂאוּ אֶת־הַתֵּבָה וַתָּרָם מֵעַל
הָאָרֶץ׃ 18 וַיִּגְבְּרוּ הַמַּיִם וַיִּרְבּוּ מְאֹד עַל־
הָאָרֶץ וַתֵּלֶךְ הַתֵּבָה עַל־פְּנֵי הַמָּיִם׃
19 וְהַמַּיִם גָּבְרוּ מְאֹד מְאֹד עַל־הָאָרֶץ וַיְכֻסּוּ
כָּל־הֶהָרִים הַגְּבֹהִים אֲשֶׁר־תַּחַת כָּל־
הַשָּׁמָיִם׃ 20 חֲמֵשׁ עֶשְׂרֵה אַמָּה מִלְמַעְלָה
גָּבְרוּ הַמָּיִם וַיְכֻסּוּ הֶהָרִים׃ 21 וַיִּגְוַע כָּל־
בָּשָׂר ׀ הָרֹמֵשׂ עַל־הָאָרֶץ בָּעוֹף וּבַבְּהֵמָה
וּבַחַיָּה וּבְכָל־הַשֶּׁרֶץ הַשֹּׁרֵץ עַל־הָאָרֶץ וְכֹל
הָאָדָם׃ 22 כֹּל אֲשֶׁר נִשְׁמַת־רוּחַ חַיִּים
בְּאַפָּיו מִכֹּל אֲשֶׁר בֶּחָרָבָה מֵתוּ׃ 23 וַיִּמַח
אֶת־כָּל־הַיְקוּם ׀ אֲשֶׁר ׀ עַל־פְּנֵי הָאֲדָמָה
מֵאָדָם עַד־בְּהֵמָה עַד־רֶמֶשׂ וְעַד־עוֹף
הַשָּׁמַיִם וַיִּמָּחוּ מִן־הָאָרֶץ וַיִּשָּׁאֶר אַךְ־נֹחַ
וַאֲשֶׁר אִתּוֹ בַּתֵּבָה׃

24 וַיִּגְבְּרוּ הַמַּיִם עַל־הָאָרֶץ חֲמִשִּׁים וּמְאַת
יוֹם׃ ח וַיִּזְכֹּר אֱלֹהִים אֶת־נֹחַ וְאֵת
כָּל־הַחַיָּה וְאֶת־כָּל־הַבְּהֵמָה אֲשֶׁר אִתּוֹ
בַּתֵּבָה וַיַּעֲבֵר אֱלֹהִים רוּחַ עַל־הָאָרֶץ

*21–23.* The destruction of all land-based animal life on earth is vividly recorded. Words such as "perished" and "blotted out" make clear that no one survives except "Noah and those with him in the ark" (v. 23).

***8:1. God then remembered Noah.*** God turns attention to Noah and begins to restore the world to order by reversing the direction of the waters. Remembering connotes acting, as when God remembers Rachel (Genesis 30:22) and she conceives.

***wind.*** Heb. *ruach*, the same word as in 1:2 (where it was rendered "spirit"). The Flood reverses Creation, and the aftermath is a new Creation that recalls Genesis 1.

2 The springs of the deep and the sky's floodgates closed up, and the rain was stopped up from the sky. 3 The waters diminished apace, ebbing and flowing, [draining] from the earth, and at the end of a hundred and fifty days the waters had receded. 4 In the seventh month, on the seventeenth day of the month, the ark came to rest atop one of the mountains of Ararat. 5 The waters kept on ebbing away until the tenth month; on the first day of the tenth [month], the mountain peaks could be seen.

6 Forty days later, Noah opened the ark's window that he had made 7 and sent out the raven, who went winging to and fro waiting for the water to dry up from upon the earth's surface. 8 Then he sent out the dove, to see whether the water had eased from off the surface of the soil, 9 but the dove could not find a resting-place for her foot, so she returned to the ark, for [still] there was water on the face of the earth: he reached out his hand and took her, bringing her back to him into the ark. 10 He waited yet another seven days, and again sent the dove out of the ark. 11 Toward evening, the dove came to him, and look—a freshly-plucked olive branch in her beak! So Noah knew that the water had eased from off the earth's. 12 He waited yet another seven days and sent the dove out; this time she no longer came back to him.

13 In [Noah's] six hundred and first year, on the first day of the first month, the water had receded from over the earth. When Noah removed the covering of the ark, he saw that the earth's surface

וַיָּשֹׁכּוּ הַמָּיִם׃ 2 וַיִּסָּכְרוּ מַעְיְנֹת תְּהוֹם
וַאֲרֻבֹּת הַשָּׁמָיִם וַיִּכָּלֵא הַגֶּשֶׁם מִן־הַשָּׁמָיִם׃
3 וַיָּשֻׁבוּ הַמַּיִם מֵעַל הָאָרֶץ הָלוֹךְ וָשׁוֹב
וַיַּחְסְרוּ הַמַּיִם מִקְצֵה חֲמִשִּׁים וּמְאַת יוֹם׃
4 וַתָּנַח הַתֵּבָה בַּחֹדֶשׁ הַשְּׁבִיעִי בְּשִׁבְעָה־
עָשָׂר יוֹם לַחֹדֶשׁ עַל הָרֵי אֲרָרָט׃ 5 וְהַמַּיִם
הָיוּ הָלוֹךְ וְחָסוֹר עַד הַחֹדֶשׁ הָעֲשִׂירִי
בָּעֲשִׂירִי בְּאֶחָד לַחֹדֶשׁ נִרְאוּ רָאשֵׁי
הֶהָרִים׃

6 וַיְהִי מִקֵּץ אַרְבָּעִים יוֹם וַיִּפְתַּח נֹחַ אֶת־
חַלּוֹן הַתֵּבָה אֲשֶׁר עָשָׂה׃ 7 וַיְשַׁלַּח אֶת־
הָעֹרֵב וַיֵּצֵא יָצוֹא וָשׁוֹב עַד־יְבֹשֶׁת הַמַּיִם
מֵעַל הָאָרֶץ׃ 8 וַיְשַׁלַּח אֶת־הַיּוֹנָה מֵאִתּוֹ
לִרְאוֹת הֲקַלּוּ הַמַּיִם מֵעַל פְּנֵי הָאֲדָמָה׃
9 וְלֹא־מָצְאָה הַיּוֹנָה מָנוֹחַ לְכַף־רַגְלָהּ
וַתָּשָׁב אֵלָיו אֶל־הַתֵּבָה כִּי־מַיִם עַל־פְּנֵי
כָל־הָאָרֶץ וַיִּשְׁלַח יָדוֹ וַיִּקָּחֶהָ וַיָּבֵא אֹתָהּ
אֵלָיו אֶל־הַתֵּבָה׃ 10 וַיָּחֶל עוֹד שִׁבְעַת יָמִים
אֲחֵרִים וַיֹּסֶף שַׁלַּח אֶת־הַיּוֹנָה מִן־הַתֵּבָה׃
11 וַתָּבֹא אֵלָיו הַיּוֹנָה לְעֵת עֶרֶב וְהִנֵּה
עֲלֵה־זַיִת טָרָף בְּפִיהָ וַיֵּדַע נֹחַ כִּי־קַלּוּ
הַמַּיִם מֵעַל הָאָרֶץ׃ 12 וַיִּיָּחֶל עוֹד שִׁבְעַת
יָמִים אֲחֵרִים וַיְשַׁלַּח אֶת־הַיּוֹנָה וְלֹא־יָסְפָה
שׁוּב־אֵלָיו עוֹד׃

13 וַיְהִי בְּאַחַת וְשֵׁשׁ־מֵאוֹת שָׁנָה בָּרִאשׁוֹן
בְּאֶחָד לַחֹדֶשׁ חָרְבוּ הַמַּיִם מֵעַל הָאָרֶץ
וַיָּסַר נֹחַ אֶת־מִכְסֵה הַתֵּבָה וַיַּרְא וְהִנֵּה

*4. Ararat.* Tradition associates this name with a mountainous district near the intersection of Turkey and Armenia. Explorers who consider the Flood narrative to be history rather than story periodically claim (unconvincingly) to have found remnants of the ark there.

*6–10. raven . . . dove.* The same birds appear in the Mesopotamian flood stories. Their flight patterns indicate the scope of destruction—and portend renewal.

*11. olive branch.* Returning, the dove demonstrates that plant life is visible again. The olive branch becomes a symbol of renewal and peace in the aftermath of devastation.

*12. the dove . . . no longer came back.* A final sign that the world was habitable again.

was beginning to dry, 14 and by the twenty-seventh day of the second month, the earth had dried up.

15 God then spoke to Noah, saying, 16 "Go out of the ark with your wife, your sons, and their wives. 17 Take every animal that is in your care—bird and beast, and all that creep over the earth; let them swarm on the earth; let them be fruitful and multiply on the earth." 18 So Noah went out, together with his sons, his wife, and his sons' wives. 19 The animals, the reptiles, the birds, everything that teems upon the earth—all departed from the ark in family groups.

20 Noah then built an altar in honor of יהוה; taking some pure beasts and some pure birds, he offered up whole burnt-offerings on the altar. 21 יהוה, inhaling the soothing fragrance, thought: "Never again will I bring doom upon the world on account of what people do, though the human mind inclines to evil from youth onward; never again will I destroy all living beings, as I have [just] done. 22 As long as the world exists, / planting and

חָרְבוּ פְּנֵי הָאֲדָמָה׃ 14 וּבַחֹדֶשׁ הַשֵּׁנִי
בְּשִׁבְעָה וְעֶשְׂרִים יוֹם לַחֹדֶשׁ יָבְשָׁה
הָאָרֶץ׃ ס

15 וַיְדַבֵּר אֱלֹהִים אֶל־נֹחַ לֵאמֹר׃ 16 צֵא מִן־
הַתֵּבָה אַתָּה וְאִשְׁתְּךָ וּבָנֶיךָ וּנְשֵׁי־בָנֶיךָ
אִתָּךְ׃ 17 כָּל־הַחַיָּה אֲשֶׁר־אִתְּךָ מִכָּל־בָּשָׂר
בָּעוֹף וּבַבְּהֵמָה וּבְכָל־הָרֶמֶשׂ הָרֹמֵשׂ עַל־
הָאָרֶץ הוצא הַיְצֵא אִתָּךְ וְשָׁרְצוּ בָאָרֶץ
וּפָרוּ וְרָבוּ עַל־הָאָרֶץ׃ 18 וַיֵּצֵא־נֹחַ וּבָנָיו
וְאִשְׁתּוֹ וּנְשֵׁי־בָנָיו אִתּוֹ׃ 19 כָּל־הַחַיָּה כָּל־
הָרֶמֶשׂ וְכָל־הָעוֹף כֹּל רוֹמֵשׂ עַל־הָאָרֶץ
לְמִשְׁפְּחֹתֵיהֶם יָצְאוּ מִן־הַתֵּבָה׃
20 וַיִּבֶן נֹחַ מִזְבֵּחַ לַיהוָה וַיִּקַּח מִכֹּל ׀
הַבְּהֵמָה הַטְּהֹרָה וּמִכֹּל הָעוֹף הַטָּהֹר וַיַּעַל
עֹלֹת בַּמִּזְבֵּחַ׃ 21 וַיָּרַח יְהוָה אֶת־רֵיחַ
הַנִּיחֹחַ וַיֹּאמֶר יְהוָה אֶל־לִבּוֹ לֹא־אֹסִף
לְקַלֵּל עוֹד אֶת־הָאֲדָמָה בַּעֲבוּר הָאָדָם כִּי
יֵצֶר לֵב הָאָדָם רַע מִנְּעֻרָיו וְלֹא־אֹסִף עוֹד
לְהַכּוֹת אֶת־כָּל־חַי כַּאֲשֶׁר עָשִׂיתִי׃ 22 עֹד

## TRANSFORMATION, COVENANT, AND RENEWAL (8:15–9:17)

*15. "Go out . . . with your wife, your sons, and their wives."* God's instructions imply that the world again is hospitable to living beings. Whereas the narrator groups Noah with his sons, followed by his wife with the sons' wives (7:7 and 8:18), God pairs Noah with his wife and the sons with theirs.

*18. Noah went out, together with his sons, his wife, and his sons' wives.* The writer leaves it to the reader to imagine the feelings of Noah and his family as they disembark. Compare the order in v. 15.

*20–22.* God reassesses humankind's nature and accepts human limitations. The anthropomorphic description of a God who responds and recants at the pleasing smell of sacrifice makes some modern readers uneasy. More striking is the basis of God's change of heart. The reason for not destroying life again is virtually the same as the reason for the flood: human beings incline to evil from their youth. In other words, God—not humankind—changes as a result of the flood.

*21. "inclines to evil from youth onward."* God recognizes that the inclination to do evil is part of human beings. God's observation does not claim that humans are inherently sinful but rather recognizes human limitations. God's subsequent laws reflect God's new awareness.

*"never again will I destroy."* The promise is momentous. It will be reiterated in the covenant that follows (see especially 9:11).

harvesting, / cold and heat, / summer and winter, / day and night / will never end."

9 God then blessed Noah and his sons, saying to them, "Be fruitful and multiply, and fill the earth, [2]and let the awe and dread of you be upon all the land animals, and all the birds of the sky, and all that creep on the ground, and all the fish of the sea: they are given into your hands. [3]Any small animal that is alive shall be food for you, like green grasses—I give you [them] all. [4]But flesh whose lifeblood is [still] in it you may not eat. [5]Moreover, for your own bloodguilt I will require your lives; I will require it by means of beasts or by means of human beings—by means of a fellow human being will I require a [guilty] person's life. [6]The shedder of human blood, / that person's blood shall be shed by [another] human; / for human beings were made /

כָּל־יְמֵי הָאָרֶץ זֶרַע וְקָצִיר וְקֹר וָחֹם וְקַיִץ
וָחֹרֶף וְיוֹם וָלַיְלָה לֹא יִשְׁבֹּתוּ׃
ט וַיְבָרֶךְ אֱלֹהִים אֶת־נֹחַ וְאֶת־בָּנָיו וַיֹּאמֶר
לָהֶם פְּרוּ וּרְבוּ וּמִלְאוּ אֶת־הָאָרֶץ׃
2 וּמוֹרַאֲכֶם וְחִתְּכֶם יִהְיֶה עַל כָּל־חַיַּת
הָאָרֶץ וְעַל כָּל־עוֹף הַשָּׁמָיִם בְּכֹל אֲשֶׁר
תִּרְמֹשׂ הָאֲדָמָה וּבְכָל־דְּגֵי הַיָּם בְּיֶדְכֶם
נִתָּנוּ׃ 3 כָּל־רֶמֶשׂ אֲשֶׁר הוּא־חַי לָכֶם יִהְיֶה
לְאָכְלָה כְּיֶרֶק עֵשֶׂב נָתַתִּי לָכֶם אֶת־כֹּל׃
4 אַךְ־בָּשָׂר בְּנַפְשׁוֹ דָמוֹ לֹא תֹאכֵלוּ׃ 5 וְאַךְ
אֶת־דִּמְכֶם לְנַפְשֹׁתֵיכֶם אֶדְרֹשׁ מִיַּד כָּל־
חַיָּה אֶדְרְשֶׁנּוּ וּמִיַּד הָאָדָם מִיַּד אִישׁ אָחִיו
אֶדְרֹשׁ אֶת־נֶפֶשׁ הָאָדָם׃ 6 שֹׁפֵךְ דַּם הָאָדָם
בָּאָדָם דָּמוֹ יִשָּׁפֵךְ כִּי בְּצֶלֶם אֱלֹהִים עָשָׂה

*9:1–7.* The transgressions that led to the Flood transform God's expectations. They result in new rules to guide humankind and a promise of a perpetual covenant. God's blessings and God's new instructions signal a new beginning. Only the command to procreate unites this commissioning with the first one in Genesis 1:28.

New guidelines aim at channeling impulses and containing them. The values are inscribed in the laws: life is precious, human life especially so. Several notable elements differentiate this renewal from the earlier commissioning of humankind. Eating meat (with some qualifications) is now permitted, perhaps as a concession to human need for aggression (9:4). Bloodshed is to be controlled. In particular, the sanctity of human life is announced (9:6). The absence of women in this text contrasts with the earlier blessings in Genesis 1. In split-screen fashion, an inclusive vision is also present meanwhile in the references to *adam,* the generic human being who is (still) in God's image (9:6).

Later rabbinic tradition expanded the laws in this section into seven "Noachite laws" that are binding upon all humankind.

*1.* ***"Be fruitful and multiply."*** This exact repetition of the original command (1:28) takes on new poignancy in light of the destruction that preceded; now it stands for regenerating life after death-dealing disasters.

*4.* Eating meat appears as a concession, not a requirement. (The original diet for both humans and beasts was vegetarian in 1:29–30.)

*5.* ***"bloodguilt."*** God singles out human life for special care. God demands restitution for the shedding of human blood.

*6.* ***"The shedder of human blood. . . ."*** The very formulation expresses parity between crime and punishment: the first six words repeat in exact mirror image: *spill–blood–human / human–blood–spill.* The message is both simple and profound: complete parallel between deed and consequence—no more, no less. This formulation resembles the "eye for an eye" principle (Exodus 21:24). Less clear is how such a guideline is to be carried out.

in the image of God. ⁷As for you, be fruitful and multiply; populate the earth and increase in it."

⁸God then said to Noah and his sons who were with him, ⁹"As for Me, I am going to establish My covenant with you and with your descendants after you, ¹⁰and with every living being in your care—the birds, the beasts, and all the land animals in your care—all who have gone out of the ark, all earth's animals. ¹¹I am establishing My covenant with you; never again shall all flesh be cut off by the waters of the flood; never again shall there be a flood to destroy the earth."

¹²And God said, "Here is the sign I am giving you of the covenant between Me and you, and every living being with you, down to the last generation: ¹³I have placed My bow in the cloud—it will be a sign of the covenant between Me and the earth. ¹⁴And when I cause clouds to form over the earth, and the bow appears in the cloud, ¹⁵I will remember My covenant between Me and you and all living beings, all flesh, and never again shall the waters become a flood, to destroy all flesh. ¹⁶When the bow is in the cloud, and I see it, I will remember the everlasting covenant between God and all living beings, all that live upon the earth."

¹⁷And God said to Noah, "This is the sign of the covenant that I have established between Me and all that live upon the earth."

אֶת־הָאָדָֽם׃ ⁷ וְאַתֶּ֥ם פְּר֖וּ וּרְב֑וּ שִׁרְצ֥וּ בָאָ֖רֶץ וּרְבוּ־בָֽהּ׃ ס

⁸ וַיֹּ֤אמֶר אֱלֹהִים֙ אֶל־נֹ֔חַ וְאֶל־בָּנָ֥יו אִתּ֖וֹ לֵאמֹֽר׃ ⁹ וַאֲנִ֕י הִנְנִ֥י מֵקִ֖ים אֶת־בְּרִיתִ֑י אִתְּכֶ֕ם וְאֶֽת־זַרְעֲכֶ֖ם אַחֲרֵיכֶֽם׃ ¹⁰ וְאֵ֣ת כָּל־נֶ֣פֶשׁ הַֽחַיָּה֩ אֲשֶׁ֨ר אִתְּכֶ֜ם בָּע֧וֹף בַּבְּהֵמָ֛ה וּֽבְכָל־חַיַּ֥ת הָאָ֖רֶץ אִתְּכֶ֑ם מִכֹּל֙ יֹצְאֵ֣י הַתֵּבָ֔ה לְכֹ֖ל חַיַּ֥ת הָאָֽרֶץ׃ ¹¹ וַהֲקִמֹתִ֤י אֶת־בְּרִיתִי֙ אִתְּכֶ֔ם וְלֹֽא־יִכָּרֵ֧ת כָּל־בָּשָׂ֛ר ע֖וֹד מִמֵּ֣י הַמַּבּ֑וּל וְלֹֽא־יִהְיֶ֥ה ע֛וֹד מַבּ֖וּל לְשַׁחֵ֥ת הָאָֽרֶץ׃

¹² וַיֹּ֣אמֶר אֱלֹהִ֗ים זֹ֤את אֽוֹת־הַבְּרִית֙ אֲשֶׁר־אֲנִ֣י נֹתֵ֗ן בֵּינִי֙ וּבֵ֣ינֵיכֶ֔ם וּבֵ֛ין כָּל־נֶ֥פֶשׁ חַיָּ֖ה אֲשֶׁ֣ר אִתְּכֶ֑ם לְדֹרֹ֖ת עוֹלָֽם׃ ¹³ אֶת־קַשְׁתִּ֕י נָתַ֖תִּי בֶּֽעָנָ֑ן וְהָֽיְתָה֙ לְא֣וֹת בְּרִ֔ית בֵּינִ֖י וּבֵ֥ין הָאָֽרֶץ׃ ¹⁴ וְהָיָ֕ה בְּעַֽנְנִ֥י עָנָ֖ן עַל־הָאָ֑רֶץ וְנִרְאֲתָ֥ה הַקֶּ֖שֶׁת בֶּֽעָנָֽן׃ ¹⁵ וְזָכַרְתִּ֣י אֶת־בְּרִיתִ֗י אֲשֶׁ֤ר בֵּינִי֙ וּבֵ֣ינֵיכֶ֔ם וּבֵ֛ין כָּל־נֶ֥פֶשׁ חַיָּ֖ה בְּכָל־בָּשָׂ֑ר וְלֹֽא־יִֽהְיֶ֨ה ע֤וֹד הַמַּ֙יִם֙ לְמַבּ֔וּל לְשַׁחֵ֖ת כָּל־בָּשָֽׂר׃ ¹⁶ וְהָיְתָ֥ה הַקֶּ֖שֶׁת בֶּֽעָנָ֑ן וּרְאִיתִ֗יהָ לִזְכֹּר֙ בְּרִ֣ית עוֹלָ֔ם בֵּ֣ין אֱלֹהִ֔ים וּבֵין֙ כָּל־נֶ֣פֶשׁ חַיָּ֔ה בְּכָל־בָּשָׂ֖ר אֲשֶׁ֥ר עַל־הָאָֽרֶץ׃

¹⁷ וַיֹּ֥אמֶר אֱלֹהִ֖ים אֶל־נֹ֑חַ זֹ֤את אֽוֹת־הַבְּרִית֙ אֲשֶׁ֣ר הֲקִמֹ֔תִי בֵּינִ֕י וּבֵ֥ין כָּל־בָּשָׂ֖ר אֲשֶׁ֥ר עַל־הָאָֽרֶץ׃ פ

· · · · · · · · · · · · · · ·

"in the image of God." Because humankind is made in God's image, murder counts as a crime against God.

9:8–17. The covenant emphasizes renewal. It also offers the assurance of security to humankind. The covenant reiterates the perpetuity of its promise (9:9, 12) and its expansive scope, encompassing all living beings (9:9–10, 12, 15, 16, 17).

Only Noah and his sons are addressed (9:8). God guarantees that no flood will ever eradicate all life on earth.

13. "My bow." A weapon is transformed into a symbol of peace.

15. God promises to never cause another global flood.

[18]Noah’s sons who went out of the ark were Shem, Ham, and Japheth. And Ham—he was the father of Canaan. [19]These three were Noah’s sons; from these the whole earth was populated.

[20]Noah, a man of the soil, was the first to plant a vineyard. [21]He drank of the wine and grew drunk; and exposed himself under his tent. [22]Ham—Canaan’s father—saw his father’s nakedness, and, outside, told his two brothers. [23]Shem and Japheth took a cloak and put it on both their shoulders. They walked backward and covered their father’s nakedness. Facing backward, they did not see their father’s nakedness. [24]Noah awakened from his wine and understood what his youngest son had done to him, [25]so he said, “Damned be Canaan! / To his brothers he shall be / the basest of slaves!” [26]And he said, “Praised be יהוה, / God of Shem; / and Canaan shall be a slave to him. / [27]For Japheth, God will make ample room; / he shall dwell in the tents of Shem; / and Canaan shall be a slave to him.”

[28]After the flood Noah lived 350 years; [29]the years of Noah’s life came to 950; then he died.

18 וַיִּהְיוּ בְנֵי־נֹחַ הַיֹּצְאִים מִן־הַתֵּבָה שֵׁם
וְחָם וָיָפֶת וְחָם הוּא אֲבִי כְנָעַן׃ 19 שְׁלֹשָׁה
אֵלֶּה בְּנֵי־נֹחַ וּמֵאֵלֶּה נָפְצָה כָל־הָאָרֶץ׃
20 וַיָּחֶל נֹחַ אִישׁ הָאֲדָמָה וַיִּטַּע כָּרֶם׃
21 וַיֵּשְׁתְּ מִן־הַיַּיִן וַיִּשְׁכָּר וַיִּתְגַּל בְּתוֹךְ
אהלה אָהֳלוֹ׃ 22 וַיַּרְא חָם אֲבִי כְנַעַן אֵת
עֶרְוַת אָבִיו וַיַּגֵּד לִשְׁנֵי־אֶחָיו בַּחוּץ׃ 23 וַיִּקַּח
שֵׁם וָיֶפֶת אֶת־הַשִּׂמְלָה וַיָּשִׂימוּ עַל־שְׁכֶם
שְׁנֵיהֶם וַיֵּלְכוּ אֲחֹרַנִּית וַיְכַסּוּ אֵת עֶרְוַת
אֲבִיהֶם וּפְנֵיהֶם אֲחֹרַנִּית וְעֶרְוַת אֲבִיהֶם
לֹא רָאוּ׃ 24 וַיִּיקֶץ נֹחַ מִיֵּינוֹ וַיֵּדַע אֵת אֲשֶׁר־
עָשָׂה לוֹ בְּנוֹ הַקָּטָן׃ 25 וַיֹּאמֶר אָרוּר כְּנָעַן
עֶבֶד עֲבָדִים יִהְיֶה לְאֶחָיו׃ 26 וַיֹּאמֶר בָּרוּךְ
יְהוָה אֱלֹהֵי שֵׁם וִיהִי כְנַעַן עֶבֶד לָמוֹ׃
27 יַפְתְּ אֱלֹהִים לְיֶפֶת וְיִשְׁכֹּן בְּאָהֳלֵי־שֵׁם
וִיהִי כְנַעַן עֶבֶד לָמוֹ׃
28 וַיְחִי־נֹחַ אַחַר הַמַּבּוּל שְׁלֹשׁ מֵאוֹת שָׁנָה
וַחֲמִשִּׁים שָׁנָה׃ 29 וַיְהִי כָּל־יְמֵי־נֹחַ תְּשַׁע
מֵאוֹת שָׁנָה וַחֲמִשִּׁים שָׁנָה וַיָּמֹת׃ פ

## THE AFTERMATH: NOAH AND HIS SONS (9:18–29)

The misbehavior of Noah’s youngest son Ham leads to the cursing of Ham’s youngest son Canaan. Unfortunately, this episode has been used by white colonizers to justify the exploitation of Africans, since Ham (in Genesis) is the ancestor of the people of Africa. However, it is not God but Noah—one might even add “under the influence”—who utters the curse; and God does not legitimate it.

*9:22–25.* Realizing that his son Ham saw him naked, Noah utters a curse. The story aims at asserting the dignity of the father and rewards those who cover the father’s nakedness. Many details remain unexplained, leaving irresolvable problems that later interpreters attempt to excuse. Why is Canaan punished for his father’s indiscretion? The story does not answer such questions. Rather, it functions as an etiology for Canaanite-Israelite tensions that will appear in later biblical accounts. Contemporary scholars hold that, historically speaking, Israel emerged mainly out of, and sought to distinguish itself from, a Canaanite population. The present story may seek to justify such a separation (compare Deuteronomy 7).

***nakedness.*** Heb. *ervah*, which differs from the word for naked in Genesis 2:25 (*arumim*). *Ervah* always has sexual connotations; uncovering relatives’ *ervah* incurs severe punishment under the Sinai covenant (see, for example Leviticus 18:6–19 and 20:10–21).

*9:25–27.* The curse of Canaan and his enslavement by the other two families aims to discredit Canaan, a people who posed a challenge to Israel’s identity.

**10** This is the line of Noah's sons Shem, Ham, and Japheth: sons were born to them after the flood.

[2]Japheth's sons were Gomer, Magog, Madai, Javan, Tubal, Meshech, and Tiras. [3]Gomer's sons were Ashkenaz, Riphat, and Togarmah. [4]Javan's sons were Elishah, Tarshish, Kittim, and Dodanim. [5]From them the nations of the coastal islands spread out, each with its own tongue, in their clan and their peoples.

[6]Ham's sons were Cush, Mitzraim, Put, and Canaan. [7]Cush's sons were Seba, Havilah, Sabtah, Raamah, and Sabteca; and Raamah's sons were Sheba and Dedan. [8]And Cush begot Nimrod; he was first among the earth's heroes. [9]He was a mighty hunter before יהוה, for which reason it is said, "Like Nimrod, a mighty hunter before יהוה." [10]His choice domains were Babylon, Erech, and Akkad, all of them in the land of Shinar. [11]From that land came Ashur, who founded Nineveh, Rechovot-ir, and Calah, [12]and Resen, between Nineveh and Calah—the largest city. [13]Mitzraim begot Ludim, Anamim, Lehabim, Naphtuhim, [14]Pathrusim, and Casluhim, from whom descended

י וְאֵ֙לֶּה֙ תּוֹלְדֹ֣ת בְּנֵי־נֹ֔חַ שֵׁ֖ם חָ֣ם וָיָ֑פֶת
וַיִּוָּלְד֥וּ לָהֶ֛ם בָּנִ֖ים אַחַ֥ר הַמַּבּֽוּל׃
2 בְּנֵ֣י יֶ֔פֶת גֹּ֣מֶר וּמָג֔וֹג וּמָדַ֖י וְיָוָ֣ן וְתֻבָ֑ל וּמֶ֖שֶׁךְ
וְתִירָֽס׃ 3 וּבְנֵ֖י גֹּ֑מֶר אַשְׁכְּנַ֥ז וְרִיפַ֖ת וְתֹגַרְמָֽה׃
4 וּבְנֵ֥י יָוָ֖ן אֱלִישָׁ֣ה וְתַרְשִׁ֑ישׁ כִּתִּ֖ים וְדֹדָנִֽים׃
5 מֵ֠אֵלֶּה נִפְרְד֞וּ אִיֵּ֤י הַגּוֹיִם֙ בְּאַרְצֹתָ֔ם אִ֖ישׁ
לִלְשֹׁנ֑וֹ לְמִשְׁפְּחֹתָ֖ם בְּגוֹיֵהֶֽם׃
6 וּבְנֵ֖י חָ֑ם כּ֥וּשׁ וּמִצְרַ֖יִם וּפ֥וּט וּכְנָֽעַן׃ 7 וּבְנֵ֣י
כ֔וּשׁ סְבָא֙ וַחֲוִילָ֔ה וְסַבְתָּ֥ה וְרַעְמָ֖ה וְסַבְתְּכָ֑א
וּבְנֵ֥י רַעְמָ֖ה שְׁבָ֥א וּדְדָֽן׃ 8 וְכ֖וּשׁ יָלַ֣ד אֶת־
נִמְרֹ֑ד ה֣וּא הֵחֵ֔ל לִהְי֥וֹת גִּבֹּ֖ר בָּאָֽרֶץ׃
9 הֽוּא־הָיָ֥ה גִבֹּֽר־צַ֖יִד לִפְנֵ֣י יְהוָ֑ה עַל־כֵּן֙
יֵֽאָמַ֔ר כְּנִמְרֹ֛ד גִּבּ֥וֹר צַ֖יִד לִפְנֵ֥י יְהוָֽה׃
10 וַתְּהִ֨י רֵאשִׁ֤ית מַמְלַכְתּוֹ֙ בָּבֶ֔ל וְאֶ֖רֶךְ
וְאַכַּ֣ד וְכַלְנֵ֑ה בְּאֶ֖רֶץ שִׁנְעָֽר׃ 11 מִן־הָאָ֥רֶץ
הַהִ֖וא יָצָ֣א אַשּׁ֑וּר וַיִּ֙בֶן֙ אֶת־נִֽינְוֵ֔ה וְאֶת־
רְחֹבֹ֥ת עִ֖יר וְאֶת־כָּֽלַח׃ 12 וְאֶת־רֶ֕סֶן בֵּ֥ין
נִֽינְוֵ֖ה וּבֵ֣ין כָּ֑לַח הִ֖וא הָעִ֥יר הַגְּדֹלָֽה׃
13 וּמִצְרַ֡יִם יָלַ֞ד אֶת־לוּדִ֧ים וְאֶת־עֲנָמִ֛ים
וְאֶת־לְהָבִ֖ים וְאֶת־נַפְתֻּחִֽים׃ 14 וְאֶת־
פַּתְרֻסִ֞ים וְאֶת־כַּסְלֻחִ֗ים אֲשֶׁ֨ר יָצְא֥וּ מִשָּׁ֛ם

## *The Table of Nations* (10:1–32)

Reflecting God's command to multiply, the list charts patterns of presumed kinship, as well as a linguistic and geographical "map" of the ancient world as understood in biblical times. Some of the information corresponds to known data; some conflicts with available information; and some cannot be identified. Roughly speaking, the divisions correspond to those in Asia (Shem), Europe (Japheth), and Africa (Ham), but the pattern is inconsistent. Seventy names represent the nations of the world.

*1. This is the line.* Biblical genealogies presume that the head of the household stands for the household as a whole, including its women (and subordinate men)—an assumption shared throughout the Bible and the ancient Near East. Thus biblical genealogies rarely mention mothers, wives, or daughters. (Exodus 6:14–25 is one exception.) In fact, however, the women cemented relationships among patrilineally defined groups via marriage.

Women must have been integral to Israelite kinship, for biblical stories take for granted that men who are related to each other only through a woman treat each other as kin (see Genesis 19:12, 14; Judges 9:1–3; II Samuel 13:37 in light of 3:3; 21:4–8). Nor is patrilineage always sufficient to identify oneself: Rebekah and Jacob each mention female ancestry (Genesis 24:24; 29:12). As for biblical law, see at Leviticus 18:10. While female-mediated kinship ties are not recounted in standard genealogical lists, they nevertheless formed part of the social structure (David Stein, personal communication).

[the] Philistines and Cretans. [15]Canaan begot
Sidon his first-born and Heth, [16]and the Jebusites,
the Amorites, and the Girgashites, [17]and the
Hivites, the Arkites, and the Sinites, [18]and the
Arvadites, the Zemarites, and the Hamathites;
afterwards the Canaanite clans spread out. [19]The
Canaanite border reached from Sidon, as far as
Gerar, up to Gaza, as far as Sodom, and Gomorrah,
and Admah, and Zeboim up to Lasha. [20]These are
Ham's sons by their clans, their tongues, in their
lands and their nations.

[21]And Shem too had progeny; [he was] the
ancestor of all the sons of Eber, brother of Japheth
the Great. [22]Shem's sons were Elam, Ashur,
Arpachshad, Lud, and Aram. [23]Aram's sons were
Utz, Hul, Gether, and Mash. [24]Arpachshad begot
Shelah, and Shelah begot Eber. [25]And to Eber
were born two sons; the first was named Peleg
["Division"], for in his time the earth was divided;
his brother's name was Joktan, [26]And Joktan begot
Almodad, Sheleph, Hazarmavet, Jerah, [27]Had-
oram, Uzal, Diklah, [28]Obal, Abimael, Sheba,
[29]Ophir, Havilah, and Jobab—all these were Joktan's sons. [30]Their dwelling was near Masha, as you
come to S'phara, the eastern mountain. [31]These are
Shem's sons by their clans, their tongues, in their
lands and their nations.

[32]These are the clans of Noah's sons by their
generations, by their peoples; from these the peoples of the earth spread out after the flood.

פְּלִשְׁתִּים וְאֶת־כַּפְתֹּרִים׃ ס 15 וּכְנַעַן
יָלַד אֶת־צִידֹן בְּכֹרוֹ וְאֶת־חֵת׃ 16 וְאֶת־
הַיְבוּסִי וְאֶת־הָאֱמֹרִי וְאֵת הַגִּרְגָּשִׁי׃
17 וְאֶת־הַחִוִּי וְאֶת־הַעַרְקִי וְאֶת־הַסִּינִי׃
18 וְאֶת־הָאַרְוָדִי וְאֶת־הַצְּמָרִי וְאֶת־הַחֲמָתִי
וְאַחַר נָפֹצוּ מִשְׁפְּחוֹת הַכְּנַעֲנִי׃ 19 וַיְהִי
גְּבוּל הַכְּנַעֲנִי מִצִּידֹן בֹּאֲכָה גְרָרָה עַד־
עַזָּה בֹּאֲכָה סְדֹמָה וַעֲמֹרָה וְאַדְמָה וּצְבֹיִם
עַד־לָשַׁע׃ 20 אֵלֶּה בְנֵי־חָם לְמִשְׁפְּחֹתָם
לִלְשֹׁנֹתָם בְּאַרְצֹתָם בְּגוֹיֵהֶם׃ ס
21 וּלְשֵׁם יֻלַּד גַּם־הוּא אֲבִי כָּל־בְּנֵי־עֵבֶר
אֲחִי יֶפֶת הַגָּדוֹל׃ 22 בְּנֵי שֵׁם עֵילָם וְאַשּׁוּר
וְאַרְפַּכְשַׁד וְלוּד וַאֲרָם׃ 23 וּבְנֵי אֲרָם עוּץ
וְחוּל וְגֶתֶר וָמַשׁ׃ 24 וְאַרְפַּכְשַׁד יָלַד אֶת־
שָׁלַח וְשֶׁלַח יָלַד אֶת־עֵבֶר׃ 25 וּלְעֵבֶר יֻלַּד
שְׁנֵי בָנִים שֵׁם הָאֶחָד פֶּלֶג כִּי בְיָמָיו נִפְלְגָה
הָאָרֶץ וְשֵׁם אָחִיו יָקְטָן׃ 26 וְיָקְטָן יָלַד אֶת־
אַלְמוֹדָד וְאֶת־שָׁלֶף וְאֶת־חֲצַרְמָוֶת וְאֶת־
יָרַח׃ 27 וְאֶת־הֲדוֹרָם וְאֶת־אוּזָל וְאֶת־
דִּקְלָה׃ 28 וְאֶת־עוֹבָל וְאֶת־אֲבִימָאֵל וְאֶת־
שְׁבָא׃ 29 וְאֶת־אוֹפִר וְאֶת־חֲוִילָה וְאֶת־
יוֹבָב כָּל־אֵלֶּה בְּנֵי יָקְטָן׃ 30 וַיְהִי מוֹשָׁבָם
מִמֵּשָׁא בֹּאֲכָה סְפָרָה הַר הַקֶּדֶם׃ 31 אֵלֶּה
בְנֵי־שֵׁם לְמִשְׁפְּחֹתָם לִלְשֹׁנֹתָם בְּאַרְצֹתָם
לְגוֹיֵהֶם׃
32 אֵלֶּה מִשְׁפְּחֹת בְּנֵי־נֹחַ לְתוֹלְדֹתָם
בְּגוֹיֵהֶם וּמֵאֵלֶּה נִפְרְדוּ הַגּוֹיִם בָּאָרֶץ אַחַר
הַמַּבּוּל׃ פ

*15–20. Canaan.* The spread of Canaan is especially relevant to Israel's history, and the cities listed play a role in subsequent narratives.

*19. Sodom, and Gomorrah.* Genesis 19 reports that these cities were destroyed because of their inhabitants' wickedness.

*21–31. Shem too had progeny.* Abraham—and thus Israel—belong to his line. The ancient Torah translation into Greek recorded his name as Sem (because Greek does not have a *sh* sound), leading to the English word "Semites." Shem's genealogy will be recounted more fully starting at 11:10.

11 All the earth had the same language and the same words. 2 As they wandered from the east, they came upon a valley in the land of Shinar and settled there. 3 Then people said to one another: "Come, let us make bricks and fire them hard." So they had bricks to build with, and tar served them as mortar. 4 Then they said, "Come, let us build a city with a tower that reaches the sky, so that we can make a name for ourselves and not be scattered over all the earth!" 5 Then יהוה came down to look at the city and tower the people had built, 6 and יהוה said, "Look—these are all one people with one language, and this is just the beginning of their

יא וַיְהִי כָל־הָאָרֶץ שָׂפָה אֶחָת וּדְבָרִים
אֲחָדִים׃ 2 וַיְהִי בְּנָסְעָם מִקֶּדֶם וַיִּמְצְאוּ
בִקְעָה בְּאֶרֶץ שִׁנְעָר וַיֵּשְׁבוּ שָׁם׃ 3 וַיֹּאמְרוּ
אִישׁ אֶל־רֵעֵהוּ הָבָה נִלְבְּנָה לְבֵנִים
וְנִשְׂרְפָה לִשְׂרֵפָה וַתְּהִי לָהֶם הַלְּבֵנָה
לְאָבֶן וְהַחֵמָר הָיָה לָהֶם לַחֹמֶר׃ 4 וַיֹּאמְרוּ
הָבָה ׀ נִבְנֶה־לָּנוּ עִיר וּמִגְדָּל וְרֹאשׁוֹ
בַשָּׁמַיִם וְנַעֲשֶׂה־לָּנוּ שֵׁם פֶּן־נָפוּץ עַל־פְּנֵי
כָל־הָאָרֶץ׃ 5 וַיֵּרֶד יְהוָה לִרְאֹת אֶת־
הָעִיר וְאֶת־הַמִּגְדָּל אֲשֶׁר בָּנוּ בְּנֵי הָאָדָם׃
6 וַיֹּאמֶר יְהוָה הֵן עַם אֶחָד וְשָׂפָה אַחַת
לְכֻלָּם וְזֶה הַחִלָּם לַעֲשׂוֹת וְעַתָּה לֹא־יִבָּצֵר

## *Transgression and Divine Response*

### THE TOWER OF BABEL (11:1–9)

Oddly, this story of the nations' dispersion follows the uncontroversial spread of nations described in the previous passage. This interlude, which interrupts the genealogy of Shem, accomplishes a number of things in very few lines: it reiterates the theme of humankind trying to go too far (again), accounts for linguistic diversity, and establishes the ignominious beginning of Babylon, Israel's eventual oppressor.

Less obviously, the story also expresses a significant theological message about God's new relationship with humankind. The story's taut, concise structure depicts divine response as mirroring human action very precisely. In sharp contrast to the indiscriminating response with the Flood, God's measured retribution demonstrates a system in which the "punishment" fits the "crime" (as noted in 9:6).

The word play on "name" (*shem*), "sky" (*shamaim*), "there" (*sham*) cannot be reproduced in English but pinpoints the issues: humankind attempts to reach the sky *(shamaim)* thereby to make a name (*shem*) for itself, instead of spreading out as God has demanded. A contrast with the line of Shem (which also means "name") is also at work (v. 10).

Contrary to some expectations, God prefers diversity to unity and uniformity (v. 6) and, in this story, actively promotes it.

*1. language . . . words.* "Language" in Hebrew is a feminine noun also meaning "lip." Contemporary discussions about the tension between the written and the oral traditions use such distinctions to differentiate between a female culture ("language" as oral) and a male one ("word" as written).

*3. "let us."* This language will be repeated when God responds, measure for measure.

*4. "a tower that reaches the sky."* The goal, to reach the sky (*shamaim*) and make a name (*shem*) for the builders, doubly offends divine prerogative: it is an incursion into God's physical domain and also usurps God's role in bestowing a name, which implies honor and legacy. The tower reflects and ridicules the Babylonian ziggurat, a massive "holy mountain" constructed of bricks that was the hallmark of Mesopotamian cities: it marked the meeting point of heaven and earth.

doings; now no scheme of theirs will be beyond their reach! [7]Let us go down there and confuse their speech, so that no one understands what the other is saying." [8]So it came about that יהוה scattered them over all the earth, and they stopped building the city. [9]That is why it was called Babel, because there יהוה confused the speech of all the earth; and from there יהוה scattered them over the face of the earth.

[10]This is the line of Shem: Shem was 100 years when he begot Arpachshad, 2 years after the flood. [11]After begetting Arpachshad, Shem lived 500 years; and he begot sons and daughters. [12]Arpachshad had lived 35 years when he begot Shelah. [13]After begetting Shelah, Arpachshad lived 403 years; and he begot sons and daughters. [14]Shelah had lived 30 years when he begot Eber. [15]After begetting Eber, Shelah lived 403 years; and he begot sons and daughters. [16]Eber had lived 34 years when he begot Peleg. [17]After begetting Peleg, Eber lived 430 years;

מֵהֶ֔ם כֹּ֛ל אֲשֶׁ֥ר יָזְמ֖וּ לַעֲשֽׂוֹת׃ [7] הָ֚בָה נֵֽרְדָ֔ה וְנָבְלָ֥ה שָׁ֖ם שְׂפָתָ֑ם אֲשֶׁר֙ לֹ֣א יִשְׁמְע֔וּ אִ֖ישׁ שְׂפַ֥ת רֵעֵֽהוּ׃ [8] וַיָּ֨פֶץ יְהֹוָ֥ה אֹתָ֛ם מִשָּׁ֖ם עַל־פְּנֵ֣י כׇל־הָאָ֑רֶץ וַֽיַּחְדְּל֖וּ לִבְנֹ֥ת הָעִֽיר׃ [9] עַל־כֵּ֞ן קָרָ֤א שְׁמָהּ֙ בָּבֶ֔ל כִּי־שָׁ֛ם בָּלַ֥ל יְהֹוָ֖ה שְׂפַ֣ת כׇּל־הָאָ֑רֶץ וּמִשָּׁם֙ הֱפִיצָ֣ם יְהֹוָ֔ה עַל־פְּנֵ֖י כׇּל־הָאָֽרֶץ׃ פ

[10] אֵ֚לֶּה תּוֹלְדֹ֣ת שֵׁ֔ם שֵׁ֚ם בֶּן־מְאַ֣ת שָׁנָ֔ה וַיּ֖וֹלֶד אֶת־אַרְפַּכְשָׁ֑ד שְׁנָתַ֖יִם אַחַ֥ר הַמַּבּֽוּל׃ [11] וַֽיְחִי־שֵׁ֗ם אַֽחֲרֵי֙ הוֹלִיד֣וֹ אֶת־אַרְפַּכְשָׁ֔ד חֲמֵ֥שׁ מֵא֖וֹת שָׁנָ֑ה וַיּ֥וֹלֶד בָּנִ֖ים וּבָנֽוֹת׃ ס [12] וְאַרְפַּכְשַׁ֣ד חַ֔י חָמֵ֥שׁ וּשְׁלֹשִׁ֖ים שָׁנָ֑ה וַיּ֖וֹלֶד אֶת־שָֽׁלַח׃ [13] וַֽיְחִ֣י אַרְפַּכְשַׁ֗ד אַֽחֲרֵי֙ הוֹלִיד֣וֹ אֶת־שֶׁ֔לַח שָׁלֹ֣שׁ שָׁנִ֔ים וְאַרְבַּ֥ע מֵא֖וֹת שָׁנָ֑ה וַיּ֥וֹלֶד בָּנִ֖ים וּבָנֽוֹת׃ ס [14] וְשֶׁ֖לַח חַ֣י שְׁלֹשִׁ֣ים שָׁנָ֑ה וַיּ֖וֹלֶד אֶת־עֵֽבֶר׃ [15] וַֽיְחִי־שֶׁ֗לַח אַֽחֲרֵי֙ הוֹלִיד֣וֹ אֶת־עֵ֔בֶר שָׁלֹ֣שׁ שָׁנִ֔ים וְאַרְבַּ֥ע מֵא֖וֹת שָׁנָ֑ה וַיּ֥וֹלֶד בָּנִ֖ים וּבָנֽוֹת׃ ס [16] וַֽיְחִי־עֵ֕בֶר אַרְבַּ֥ע וּשְׁלֹשִׁ֖ים שָׁנָ֑ה וַיּ֖וֹלֶד אֶת־פָּֽלֶג׃ [17] וַֽיְחִי־עֵ֗בֶר אַֽחֲרֵי֙ הוֹלִיד֣וֹ אֶת־

---

**6.** *"no scheme . . . beyond their reach."* God identifies human ambition and complete unity as a dangerous mix. Diversity seems to be by divine design.

**7.** *"Let us."* In language that closely parallels the human words in v. 3, God dismantles the human project point by point (brick by brick?). God uses the people's words but with different meanings—most of which cannot be adequately reproduced in English, such as the use of *l-b-n*, which permutates as *libnot* (build), *l'benah* (brick), and *n'belah* (confuse). (On "us" in God's speech, see at 1:26.) God's point-by-point response to human action expresses a new pattern for God's interaction with humankind, replacing the wholesale destruction by the Flood and confirming God's covenantal promise in Genesis 9.

**9.** Ridicule aimed at Babylon is unmistakable, accented in the word play of "confuse" (*balal*) and Babel (*bavel*).

## The Ten Generations from Noah to Abram (11:10–26)

Ten generations spanned the time from Adam and Eve to Noah (Genesis 5), and now another ten take us from Noah to Abram/Abraham. Coming immediately after another disappointing human act, this genealogy leads to the next attempt by God to "begin anew."

Until we come to Abraham, this genealogy mentions no wives, whereas it mentions the birth of (unnamed) daughters along with sons (until v. 26).

and he begot sons and daughters. [18]Peleg had lived 30 years when he begot Reu. [19]After begetting Reu, Peleg lived 209 years; and he begot sons and daughters. [20]Reu had lived 32 years when he begot Serug. [21]After begetting Serug, Reu lived 207 years; and he begot sons and daughters. [22]Serug had lived 30 years when he begot Nahor. [23]After begetting Nahor, Serug lived 200 years; and he begot sons and daughters. [24]Nahor had lived 29 years when he begot Terah. [25]After begetting Terah, Nahor lived 119; and he begot sons and daughters. [26]Terah had lived 70 years when he begot Abram, Nahor, and Haran.

[27]This is the chronicle of Terah: Terah begot Abram, Nahor, and Haran; and Haran begot Lot. [28]Then Haran died in the presence of Terah his father, in the land of his birth, in Ur of the Chaldeans. [29]Then Abram and Nahor took wives: Abram's wife was named Sarai, and Nahor's wife

פֶּ֫לֶג שְׁלֹשִׁ֤ים שָׁנָה֙ וְאַרְבַּ֣ע מֵא֣וֹת שָׁנָ֑ה וַיּ֖וֹלֶד בָּנִ֥ים וּבָנֽוֹת׃ ס 18 וַֽיְחִי־פֶ֗לֶג שְׁלֹשִׁ֥ים שָׁנָ֖ה וַיּ֥וֹלֶד אֶת־רְעֽוּ׃ 19 וַֽיְחִי־פֶ֗לֶג אַֽחֲרֵי֙ הוֹלִיד֣וֹ אֶת־רְע֔וּ תֵּ֥שַׁע שָׁנִ֖ים וּמָאתַ֣יִם שָׁנָ֑ה וַיּ֖וֹלֶד בָּנִ֥ים וּבָנֽוֹת׃ ס 20 וַיְחִ֣י רְע֔וּ שְׁתַּ֥יִם וּשְׁלֹשִׁ֖ים שָׁנָ֑ה וַיּ֖וֹלֶד אֶת־שְׂרֽוּג׃ 21 וַיְחִ֣י רְע֗וּ אַֽחֲרֵי֙ הוֹלִיד֣וֹ אֶת־שְׂר֔וּג שֶׁ֥בַע שָׁנִ֖ים וּמָאתַ֣יִם שָׁנָ֑ה וַיּ֖וֹלֶד בָּנִ֥ים וּבָנֽוֹת׃ ס 22 וַיְחִ֣י שְׂר֔וּג שְׁלֹשִׁ֖ים שָׁנָ֑ה וַיּ֖וֹלֶד אֶת־נָחֽוֹר׃ 23 וַיְחִ֣י שְׂר֗וּג אַֽחֲרֵי֙ הוֹלִיד֣וֹ אֶת־נָח֔וֹר מָאתַ֣יִם שָׁנָ֑ה וַיּ֖וֹלֶד בָּנִ֥ים וּבָנֽוֹת׃ ס 24 וַיְחִ֣י נָח֔וֹר תֵּ֥שַׁע וְעֶשְׂרִ֖ים שָׁנָ֑ה וַיּ֖וֹלֶד אֶת־תָּֽרַח׃ 25 וַיְחִ֣י נָח֗וֹר אַֽחֲרֵי֙ הוֹלִיד֣וֹ אֶת־תֶּ֔רַח תְּשַֽׁע־עֶשְׂרֵ֥ה שָׁנָ֖ה וּמְאַ֣ת שָׁנָ֑ה וַיּ֖וֹלֶד בָּנִ֥ים וּבָנֽוֹת׃ ס 26 וַֽיְחִי־תֶ֖רַח שִׁבְעִ֣ים שָׁנָ֑ה וַיּ֙וֹלֶד֙ אֶת־אַבְרָ֔ם אֶת־נָח֖וֹר וְאֶת־הָרָֽן׃

27 וְאֵ֙לֶּה֙ תּֽוֹלְדֹ֣ת תֶּ֔רַח תֶּ֖רַח הוֹלִ֣יד אֶת־אַבְרָ֔ם אֶת־נָח֖וֹר וְאֶת־הָרָ֑ן וְהָרָ֖ן הוֹלִ֥יד אֶת־לֽוֹט׃ 28 וַיָּ֣מׇת הָרָ֗ן עַל־פְּנֵי֙ תֶּ֣רַח אָבִ֔יו בְּאֶ֥רֶץ מֽוֹלַדְתּ֖וֹ בְּא֣וּר כַּשְׂדִּֽים׃ 29 וַיִּקַּ֨ח אַבְרָ֧ם וְנָח֛וֹר לָהֶ֖ם נָשִׁ֑ים שֵׁ֤ם אֵֽשֶׁת־אַבְרָם֙

---

In both respects it resembles the pre-Flood genealogy of Genesis 5. Such mention of daughters is atypical of other ancient Semitic genealogies. On women and biblical genealogies, see at 5:4 and 10:1.

## A New Beginning
### ABRAM/ABRAHAM AND SARAI/SARAH
### (11:27–32)

The family of Abram and Sarai represents a new beginning, and women emerge for the first time in this parashah as named individuals. Although Abram will become the chief protagonist

later in Genesis, Sarai (later called Sarah) receives more attention in this introduction. Her condition of barrenness creates the challenge that will propel the rest of this couple's story.

**28. *Ur.*** Either the Mesopotamian city (in today's southeastern Iraq) with a sophisticated culture dating as early as 2500 B.C.E., or another Ur mentioned in ancient tablets from Ebla in Syria, as located near the Aramean city of Haran (mentioned in v. 31).

**29. *Abram's wife was named Sarai.*** Her name echoes the word for prince (*sar*) and could mean "princess." Savina Teubal (*Sarah the Priestess: the First Matriarch of Genesis*, 1984), who reads the text as reflecting history, speculates that Sarah was indeed

was named Milcah daughter of Haran father of
Milcah and of Yiscah. [30]And Sarai was barren; she
had no offspring.
[31]Then Terah took his son Abram and his
brother's son Lot son of Haran and his daughter-
in-law Sarai, and they all left Ur of the Chaldeans to
go to the land of Canaan; but they got as far as
Haran and settled there. [32]The years of Terah's life
came to 205; then Terah died in Haran.

שָׂרָי וְשֵׁם אֵשֶׁת־נָחוֹר מִלְכָּה בַּת־הָרָן אֲבִי־
מִלְכָּה וַאֲבִי יִסְכָּה׃ 30 וַתְּהִי שָׂרַי עֲקָרָה
אֵין לָהּ וָלָד׃
31 וַיִּקַּח תֶּרַח אֶת־אַבְרָם בְּנוֹ וְאֶת־לוֹט בֶּן־
הָרָן בֶּן־בְּנוֹ וְאֵת שָׂרַי כַּלָּתוֹ אֵשֶׁת אַבְרָם
בְּנוֹ וַיֵּצְאוּ אִתָּם מֵאוּר כַּשְׂדִּים לָלֶכֶת
אַרְצָה כְּנַעַן וַיָּבֹאוּ עַד־חָרָן וַיֵּשְׁבוּ שָׁם׃
32 וַיִּהְיוּ יְמֵי־תֶרַח חָמֵשׁ שָׁנִים וּמָאתַיִם
שָׁנָה וַיָּמָת תֶּרַח בְּחָרָן׃ פ

a princess, as well as a priestess, who continued to uphold a tradition that was both matriarchal (women as leaders) and matrilineal (genealogy traced through the mother).

Abraham claims in 20:12 that Sarah is his sister through a different wife of his father. If she were his half sister, however, one would expect that information to appear here, especially since Milcah's genealogical connection to her husband is recorded (see below).

***Nahor's wife was named Milcah.*** Her name, like Sarai's, evokes royalty (*malcah* means "queen").

***daughter of Haran father of Milcah.*** The double identity markers for Milcah draw attention to her unique position in the ancestral lineage. It also discloses that she married her uncle. Rebekah, the second matriarch, will identify herself as Milcah's granddaughter (24:24), in the Bible's sole unambiguous mention of someone's grandmother. This reference highlights her importance.

***Yiscah.*** Presumably a sister, not brother, of Milcah. However, we learn nothing further about her.

*30.* ***Sarai was barren.*** Fertility stands out as a paramount concern in biblical tales, starting with Genesis 1:28. Sarai's lack of children will become the pivot around which the stories from Genesis 12–21 revolve. | In Genesis 16:2, Sarai will attribute her condition to God. However, the narrator nowhere suggests that God afflicted her with such a condition or that it is a stigma. Fertility of the barren women becomes a symbol of God's special blessing, without implying necessarily that lack of fertility is a punishment. | Stories about barren women subordinate the role of human beings in fertility and instead highlight God's role. See further Another View, p. 53. | This first mention of Sarah/Sarai, portraying her as a barren woman, contrasts with the Bible's final mention of Sarah, invoking her as a message of hope for a "barren" people in exile: "Look back to Abraham your father / And to Sarah who brought you forth" (Isaiah 51:2).

*31.* ***his daughter-in-law Sarai.*** The Hebrew actually adds also "wife of Abram." This double mention of Sarai's identity emphasizes her role in the family and prepares the reader for her continued prominence in the stories that follow. The report about the family's journey from Ur sets the stage for God's attempt to "begin anew," this time with the family of Abram and Sarai.

—*Tamara Cohn Eskenazi*

# Another View

A GENEALOGY IS a typical narrative strategy to account for the long passage of time and also to express the relationships among groups. In this parashah, the concluding genealogy leads to Abram and Sarai (11:27–32). It is shocking that this genealogy ends with the information that Sarai is barren, a statement that counters the very notion of genealogy, namely, family connectedness across generations.

The theme of barrenness is emphasized in the story of the ancestors, beginning with Sarah, the first matriarch; and it recurs in the next two generations, with Rebekah (25:21) and then Rachel (29:31). The idea of a barren woman giving birth highlights the importance of the offspring, calling attention to God's role in the child's birth—and thus to the significance of the child.

At the same time, the presence of the barrenness theme in matriarchal narratives signifies the values and concerns of an agrarian people. Most Israelites were self-sufficient farmers, requiring a team of people to work the land; having offspring therefore meant survival. It also meant the opportunity to raise an heir who would intimately know and maintain that parcel of land. Family lands were held as patrimonies and passed down across generations. Not surprisingly, legal precepts in the Torah aimed at helping families retain their property (see Leviticus 25:23–28).

In light of the great importance of land as inheritance, barrenness was a grave problem. Archeology has produced artifacts, such as small female figurines, that arguably were used, along with prayers, in household rituals women surely performed to deal with infertility. Also, potions and remedies to overcome barrenness are known from the texts of other ancient Near Eastern peoples and later Jewish folklore; and surely they were used by Israelite women (see the mandrake of Genesis 30:14–16).

In addition, like other ancient peoples, the Israelites solved this problem by allowing for adoption or

*The idea of a barren woman giving birth highlights the importance of the offspring.*

polygyny (multiple wives). A householder could take a second wife or secondary wife (a servant or a concubine), and the resulting offspring would allow the lineage—reckoned along the male line—to continue and the land to remain in the family. For elite families, especially royalty, having multiple wives was a sign of status; in ordinary families it was a solution to the dire predicament of the barrenness of a man's initial wife.

—*Carol Meyers*

# Post-biblical Interpretations

***"your wife"*** (6:18). Noah's wife is mentioned five times in the Flood story (Genesis 6:18; 7:7, 13; 8:16, 18) but she is never named. While she is not the only woman (or man) to go unnamed in Hebrew Scriptures, the Rabbis were curious about her identity. Midrash *B'reishit Rabbah* 23.3 preserves a dispute about her name, in which one rabbi argues that Noah's wife was Naamah, the "sister of Tubal-Cain," a descendant of Adam and Eve's son Cain, who is listed in the genealogies in Genesis 4:22. He justifies his view with the explanation that the name derives from the word "pleasant" and that Noah's wife's actions were pleasing (*n'imim*) to God. However, the majority opinion in *B'reishit Rabbah* 23.3 rejects the identification of Noah's wife with the Naamah of 4:22 since "her name indicates that she sang (*man'emet*) to the timbrel in honor of idolatry."

***Noah, with his sons, his wife, and his sons' wives came into the ark*** (7:7). Noah's family and the animals were chosen for preservation on the ark in male-female pairs, in order to ensure the continuation of their species after the Flood. However, a midrash in the Talmud (BT *Sanhedrin* 108b) teaches that this process of "continuation" did not begin on the ark. Careful attention to the word order shows that the genders were separated at the boarding of the ark. The midrash contrasts this with the wording of Genesis 8:16 where the instructions for disembarking are given to marriage groupings. That is, Noah was instructed that he should leave first with his wife, and then his sons with their wives. Thus, the authors of this midrash demonstrate that the sexes were segregated on board, at least enough that they did not have sexual contact on the ark. However, when they disembarked, each male, together with the appropriate female, they were to resume normal sexual relations.

***Abram's wife was named Sarai... Haran father of Milcah and of Yiscah*** (11:29). The text introduces us to Abraham, who at this point is still referred to by his pre-covenantal name, Abram. Similarly, his wife Sarah is also referred to here by her pre-covenantal name, Sarai. However, the Rabbis noticed that the first time Sarai is mentioned, her family is not identified. Yet in the same verse, Milcah—the wife of Abram's brother Nahor—is identified as the daughter of Haran; in addition and for no obvious reason, *her* sister Yiscah is then mentioned. The following verse (Genesis 11:30) resumes Sarai's story once again. It is probably the juxtaposition of all of these characters, as well as the rabbinic desire to link Sarai to the larger family, that explains a midrashic tradition that Sarai and Yiscah were in fact the same person. (The idea of marrying a niece would not have seemed unusual in the biblical or rabbinic eras. It is not one of the incestuous relationships forbidden in Leviticus 18.) The Talmud explains this conflation of Sarah with Yiscah (BT *M'gillah* 14a) linguistically. The Hebrew letters that spell the name

*Sarai and Yiscah were in fact the same person.*

Yiscah are similar to the Hebrew verb "to look" (*s-c-h*). Thus, based on midrashic traditions of Sarah's great beauty, the Rabbis explain that Sarai was called Yiscah because everyone wanted to *look* at her. A second explanation offered is that Sarai was called Yiscah because she was a prophet and could *look* into the future.

***And Sarah was barren; she had no offspring*** (11:30). The Talmud (BT *Y'vamot* 64b) understands this double description of Sarah's infertility to have two meanings. The first phrase, *was barren*, means Sarah did not have children; and the second phrase, *she had no offspring*, indicates she was missing the vital internal organs necessary for conception and pregnancy. Thus, the later birth of Isaac was doubly miraculous.

—*Anna Urowitz-Freudenstein*

# Contemporary Reflection

GENESIS BEGINS with God's creation of the world by word alone: *God said, "Let there be light!"* (1:3). At the end of Genesis 1, *God surveyed all that [God] had made, and look—it was very good!* With language God created the world, separated the waters above from the waters below, named, judged, and expressed great satisfaction with the results. But by the end of *parashat B'reishit*, we read that יהוה *saw how great was the wickedness of human beings.... So* יהוה *thought: "I will wipe the humans whom I created from off the face of the earth"* (6:5–7).

In *parasht Noach*, what sin had the people committed to warrant the Flood? The fact that so many different answers have been offered suggests that there is no clear answer. Some interpreters say that the wrongdoing was miscegenation: the interbreeding between the sons of God and the daughters of mankind (6:1–4). Others in traditional sources postulate that it was the sin of refusing to have children—indeed, even Noah waited until he was 500 years old to have his first child.

For all the various theories about the precise nature of the sin, it is clear that the Flood's essential purpose was to cleanse Creation of the flaw that led to its corruption. And yet, from the time of the Ark's landing on dry land, God demonstrates an awareness that some essential flaw persists. God says: *Never again will I bring doom upon the world on account of what people do, though the human mind inclines to evil from youth onward* (8:21). Why does the human mind incline to evil? What is the flaw in the human mind? While the questions are not explicitly answered, we can nevertheless find answers in our tradition.

Many commentators have criticized Noah for not challenging God about the planned destruction, as Abraham later does when God reveals the plan to destroy Sodom and Gomorrah (18:17–33). Readers over the ages have been puzzled by Noah's silence. But his silence is precisely the point. Nearly the entire portion of *Noach* is filled with God's speech and Noah's actions—but not words. From his building the ark through the entire Flood, Noah utters not a single word. When Noah finally speaks after being *awakened from his wine* (9:24), his words disclose the problem: he *understood what his youngest son had done to him, so he said "Damned be Canaan! To his brothers he shall be the basest of slaves!"* (9:24–25).

So Noah's first words neither praise God, nor express gratitude, nor ask for help, nor proclaim justice. Instead, he uses language to curse and to set up the differentiated love that will plague all the offspring of Genesis—from Ishmael and Isaac to Esau and Jacob, and to Joseph and his brothers. By "differentiated love" I mean love that is given to one person and withheld from another.

> *Noah's first words show what might be an essential flaw in creation.*

Noah's first words show what might be an essential flaw in creation, leading to destruction in this parashah. As we read in Proverbs 18:21, *death and life are in the power of the tongue.* We have already seen the creative power of language in Genesis 1. Now it becomes clear that one sin causing the Flood was the abuse of language. In a way, we have always known that, as the Confession for the Day of Atonement lists many forms of language: idle talk, offensive speech, foolish talk, slander, passing judgment, plotting, talebearing, and swearing falsely. Each of these offenses involves some abuse of language.

In *parashat Noach*, the inherent flaw is made clear. Noah's words form a curse; moreover, even when he comes to bless (9:27), he does so comparatively, blessing one son at the expense of another son's son, relegating his grandson Canaan to the role of slave. But love should not be comparative, quantifiable, or conditional.

God acknowledges the power of human language in the very next story, the episode of the Tower of Babel (Genesis 11). This time God, in order to restrain the people who are reaching out to heaven, confuses the language. God is thus undermining their capacity to use language in a destructive fashion (11:1–6).

From Noah's words and the people's words when they attempt to build their tower, we learn that the language that survives the devastation of the Flood is that of differentiated love, competition, hatred, cursing, and revenge across generations. God's action at Babel is an attempt to heal the flaw of the sin at Babel by multiplying languages: perhaps somewhere among the new tongues would emerge a vision of reality that transcends the destructive, condemning words carried forward in the ark.

Our own experience verifies the lesson of the sin of the Flood. We know how language can kill. We have seen the medical charts on which a doctor has scribbled "untreatable," thereby sealing a patient's fate. We have labeled a plant in our garden a "weed," thus sealing its fate.

Silence, then, might be a virtue. During the long days of the Flood and its aftermath, Noah did well, being silent. His silence reminds us of the better part of Job's comforters who initially *sat with him on the ground seven days and seven nights. None spoke a word to him for they saw how very great was his suffering* (Job 2:13). Once they began to speak, though, their words brought only discomfort, and finally God rebuked them: *for you have not spoken the truth about Me as did My servant Job* (42:7).

What lessons may we draw from this juxtaposition of silence and language? Is human speech invariably destructive? Where can we find the language that blesses, heals, and even creates? Again, the model is within this parashah, when God responds.

God restricts divine power, saying: *Never again will I bring doom upon the world on account of what people do* (Genesis 8:21); God restores blessings: *God then blessed Noah and his sons saying to them, "Be fruitful and multiply and fill the earth"* (9:1); and God enters into covenant with all living creatures: *I am going to establish My covenant with you and your descendants after you, and with every living being in your care* (9:9–10).

God's words and actions in the aftermath of destruction show us how we can use language to repair relationships, instruct others, forgive, and bless.

—*Carol Ochs*

# *Voices*

## *Parashat Noach*

Elaine Rose Glickman

*Genesis 6:18; 7:1–9*

I.
My mother and sisters—
there would be no room for them.
God had been very specific,
my husband said, on this point
as on all the others—
how long, how tall, how deep
how many windows (one)
how many animals (lots)
and how everyone else would die.

II.
At nine, my youngest sister is brown-haired,
plain, eyes quick and curious,
lips filled with laughter and secrets.
I will not go without her, I say,
trying to sound fierce and certain
against the darkening sky and gathering wind,
but I can hear my voice betray me,
high-pitched, cracking, muted by thunder
not so very far away.

## *from* The Flood

Chana Bloch

*Genesis 7*

The ark noisy with children,
angels, birds—dim, stuffy,
close, the nest of home
where Noah broods,
at sea.

How can one think
in such a place? The world
presses around, and God
breathes down his neck.

## *Family Reunion*

Shirley Blumberg

*Genesis 7:1–8:19*

Survivors of a storm
of more than forty days
and forty nights,
we turn to each other
more amazed than Noah
at our safe passage
and the fresh green branches
alive above the flood.
In wonderment,
we touch the spreading boughs,
caress each shining leaf.

This day was only dimly dreamed
when two by two
we climbed aboard the leaky ark
to abandon that accursed land,
those standing on the shore
weeping, fearing for our lives;
none of us foretelling
that we would find this sanctuary,
and they would perish in the storm.

## *How Much Water Is Inside a Tear?*

Zoë Klein

How much water is inside a tear,
And how long does it take to dry them?
As long as there is misery and fear
In the people who continue to cry them.

How much water is inside a flood
And how long does it take to recede?
As long as it takes to restore hope
To the people in desperate need.

How much water is inside a storm
And how long does it take to clear?
As long as it takes to rebuild a home
And restore everything that is dear.

How much water is inside a city
When a levee suddenly breaks?
As many as are the tears that are cried
When so many million hearts break.

## *Noah*

Rivka Miriam (transl. Linda Stern Zisquit)

*Genesis 8:1–19*

Noah installed wheels on his ark
dragging it after him
in case the flood suddenly returned.
Grapevines, noticing fins and his temples
and shiny scales at the opening of his shirt,
turned into raisins, dried out their juices
to ease his fear of their drowning wetness.
Noah installed wheels on his ark
and when children hung from its side-poles
for a ride
Noah lovingly offered them brittle clods
of Ararat.

## *from Scatter Us in the Sea*

Zoë Klein

*Genesis 11:1–9*

This is the generation that follows the devastating Flood. Perhaps the members of that generation were building a tower to make war upon the heavens. But didn't they deserve to be angry? They knew that in an instant the individual can be swept away. They remembered it. The blood of an entire generation cried to them from the bitter and sopping ground. The earth was a grave, and so they built a ladder out of it.

This is no tower, God! It is a lighthouse, tall as the heavens so that it cannot be drowned by Your billows and breakers, set to guide the arks that we will build ourselves next, our vain attempt to avoid your death sentence. Can you blame us?

## *Open Earth*

Clarisse Nicoïdski (transl. Stephen Levy)

*Genesis 8:13–14*

open earth
drinking water from
clouds
dry earth
everywhere opening up your ancient hands
torn earth
like the stomach of a woman who just gave
birth
each stone on your roads speaks to us of the
beating of
your heart

# לך לך ✦ Lech L'cha

GENESIS 12:1–17:27

## *Covenantal Promise and Cultural Self-Definition*

PARASHAT LECH L'CHA ("Go forth!") is about relationships: relationships between God and Israel, relationships among the Israelites, and relationships between Israelites and non-Israelites. The question "Who are we?"—which the first part of Genesis answered in universal terms—now begins to be explored by focusing on one family, the subject of the rest of the Torah.

The ideas are expressed in traditional biblical forms, such as scenes of covenant-making (Genesis 15 and 17); the annunciation to the mother of a future hero (Genesis 16); and the story of the patriarch who tells the foreign ruler that his wife is his sister (12:10–13; a version of such a story recurs in Genesis 20:1–18 and again in 26:1–16). All of these tales contribute to Israelite "founding myths," that is, stories of the people's origins, and to the process of self-definition.

As for its gender orientation, on one hand this parashah seems strongly androcentric. Divine conversation is primarily with Abraham, the patriarch. He is the party to the important scenes of covenant-making so central to the people's identity. Only males can undergo circumcision, the sign of the covenant with God. Much of the parashah's interest is in the birth of male children who will carry on the line of the patriarch and fulfill divine promises.

On the other hand, the women featured in this parashah, Sarah and Hagar, exhibit a power in the household that is also critical to the identity and development of the people. It is the barren woman—Sarah—who must bear the child in Abraham's line. The difficulty with which such women conceive further marks their sons' importance. Sarah is Abraham's co-trickster in Genesis 12, where he enlists her help in deceiving Pharaoh, thereby saving his life and improving his lot. Sarah, like Abraham, undergoes a name change marking her participation in God's covenant.

*Sarah and Hagar exhibit a power . . . that is critical to the people's development.*

Women are portrayed as essential for men's livelihood and for procreation, and also as keepers of their children's futures. To be sure, such roles are circumscribed and betoken a world politically dominated by men, but women do have important roles to play within the contours of this system. The tale of Hagar in Genesis 16 is particularly interesting in this respect. (On women's role in the covenant with God, see also Contemporary Reflection, p. 80.)

*—Susan Niditch*

## *Outline*

*I.* The Formation of a Relationship with God
*Abram and Sarai Begin the Journey* (12:1–9)

*II.* Relations within the Group and Outside (12:10–14:24)

- *A.* Abram and Sarai as tricksters (12:10–20)
- *B.* Abram and Lot: dispute and separation (13:1–13)
- *C.* Covenant promises: land and progeny (13:14–18)
- *D.* Abram as a warrior hero (14:1–24)

*III.* A Deepening Covenant (15:1–21)

*IV.* The Tale of Hagar (16:1–16)

- *A.* Barrenness and surrogate motherhood (vv. 1–6)
- *B.* Annunciation of the birth of a son (vv. 7–16)

*V.* Covenant and Circumcision (17:1–27)

- *A.* Covenant and implications of circumcision (vv. 1–14)
- *B.* Reiteration of promises of a child by Sarah (vv. 15–22)
- *C.* Adoption of the sign of circumcision (vv. 23–27)

יהוה said to Abram, "Go forth from your
land, your birthplace, your father's
house, to the land that I will show you. 2 I will make
of you a great nation, and I will bless you; I will
make your name great, and it shall be a blessing.
3 I will bless those who bless you, and I will pro-

יב וַיֹּאמֶר יְהוָה אֶל־אַבְרָם לֶךְ־לְךָ
מֵאַרְצְךָ וּמִמּוֹלַדְתְּךָ וּמִבֵּית אָבִיךָ אֶל־
הָאָרֶץ אֲשֶׁר אַרְאֶךָּ׃ 2 וְאֶעֶשְׂךָ לְגוֹי גָּדוֹל
וַאֲבָרֶכְךָ וַאֲגַדְּלָה שְׁמֶךָ וֶהְיֵה בְּרָכָה׃
3 וַאֲבָרְכָה מְבָרְכֶיךָ וּמְקַלֶּלְךָ אָאֹר וְנִבְרְכוּ

## *The Formation of a Relationship with God*

### ABRAM AND SARAI BEGIN THE JOURNEY (12:1–9)

*Parashat Lech L'cha* begins with a transformation in identity and status through a physical, geographical passage. Abraham, here called Abram, is instructed by God to leave the land of his birth and go to the land God shows him (12:1). Two other key players in this early Israelite foundation myth, who like Abram were introduced at the end of the previous parashah, are Sarah (Sarai), who is married to Abraham, and Lot, their nephew (12:4–5). The Deity establishes a relationship with the patriarch through blessings, grounded in covenantal promises of land and descendants (12:1–2, 7). God's words demarcate who is inside the group versus outside (12:3), as Abraham and his household are pictured wandering and migrating, stopping to set up key markers of presence and possession: the altars that link Abraham and his descendants with God (12:7, 8). Critical aspects of Israelite identity thus emerge from this initial sketch. God reaches out to Abraham, who in turn reaches out to God.

Abraham is treated as the blessed founding father of subsequent generations. Divine blessings are also possible for non-kin who may be "blessed in/by" Abraham (v. 3). A modern appropriator might consider the notion of being blessed through Abraham to be universalistic, perhaps referring to the ethos modeled by Abraham's life. Within its ancient Israelite setting, however, the phrase more likely affirmed the centrality and importance of Abraham as founder of Israel, covenant partner of God. As portrayed in Genesis, he is the mediator par excellence.

***12:1–3.*** These opening verses of this critical passage are rhythmic and rhyming, with repetition on the second person. The words catch the eye and ear as demarcating an important beginning.

*1.* ***Abram.*** Variant of Abraham, meaning "exalted father."

*3.* Blessing and curse depend upon regard for Abraham and his descendants. One thinks also of late-biblical works that imagine an ingathering to Jerusalem at the end-time, or an attempt by foreigners to latch onto Jews as a means of reaching

▶ The cycle of abuse can be broken if children refuse to continue the system of abuse.

ANOTHER VIEW ➤ 78

▶ The impassioned voices of Jewish women bring forth Sarah's voice in our own time.

CONTEMPORARY REFLECTION ➤ 80

▶ Rabbi Aha claims, "... God tells Abraham to obey all of Sarah's directives."

POST-BIBLICAL INTERPRETATIONS ➤ 78

▶ Smell the fragrance / Which spreads across the land / As you roam and wander....

VOICES ➤ 82

בְּךָ כֹּל מִשְׁפְּחֹת הָאֲדָמָה׃ 4 וַיֵּלֶךְ אַבְרָם
כַּאֲשֶׁר דִּבֶּר אֵלָיו יְהוָה וַיֵּלֶךְ אִתּוֹ לוֹט
וְאַבְרָם בֶּן־חָמֵשׁ שָׁנִים וְשִׁבְעִים שָׁנָה
בְּצֵאתוֹ מֵחָרָן׃ 5 וַיִּקַּח אַבְרָם אֶת־שָׂרַי
אִשְׁתּוֹ וְאֶת־לוֹט בֶּן־אָחִיו וְאֶת־כָּל־רְכוּשָׁם
אֲשֶׁר רָכָשׁוּ וְאֶת־הַנֶּפֶשׁ אֲשֶׁר־עָשׂוּ בְחָרָן
וַיֵּצְאוּ לָלֶכֶת אַרְצָה כְּנַעַן וַיָּבֹאוּ אַרְצָה
כְּנָעַן׃ 6 וַיַּעֲבֹר אַבְרָם בָּאָרֶץ עַד מְקוֹם
שְׁכֶם עַד אֵלוֹן מוֹרֶה וְהַכְּנַעֲנִי אָז בָּאָרֶץ׃
7 וַיֵּרָא יְהוָה אֶל־אַבְרָם וַיֹּאמֶר לְזַרְעֲךָ אֶתֵּן
אֶת־הָאָרֶץ הַזֹּאת וַיִּבֶן שָׁם מִזְבֵּחַ לַיהוָה
הַנִּרְאֶה אֵלָיו׃ 8 וַיַּעְתֵּק מִשָּׁם הָהָרָה מִקֶּדֶם
לְבֵית־אֵל וַיֵּט אהלה אָהֳלוֹ בֵּית־אֵל מִיָּם
וְהָעַי מִקֶּדֶם וַיִּבֶן־שָׁם מִזְבֵּחַ לַיהוָה וַיִּקְרָא
בְּשֵׁם יְהוָה׃ 9 וַיִּסַּע אַבְרָם הָלוֹךְ וְנָסוֹעַ
הַנֶּגְבָּה׃ פ

nounce doom on those who curse you; through you
all the families of the earth shall be blessed." [4]So
Abram went forth as יהוה had told him, and Lot
went with him. Abram was 75 years old when he
left Haran. [5]Abram took his wife Sarai, his brother's son Lot, all the possessions they had amassed,
and the people they had acquired in Haran. They
set forth for the land of Canaan, and they arrived in
the land of Canaan. [6]Abram then traversed the land
as far as the sacred site of Shechem, as far as the Oak
of Moreh. (At that time the Canaanites were present in the land.)

[7]יהוה now appeared to Abram and said, "I am
giving this land to your descendants." Abram then
built an altar there to יהוה who had appeared to
him. [8]From there he moved on to the hill country
east of Beth El. He pitched his tent between Beth
El on the west and Ai on the east. There he built
another altar to יהוה and called upon the Name of
יהוה. [9]And then Abram continued his journey—
toward the Negev.

salvation (as in Zechariah 8:20–23). The founding myth dealing with Abraham is thus perceived to have cosmic significance, but the message is meant less to encourage or convert foreigners than to assure the group of its own importance.

*4–9.* In this Israelite self-portrayal, the ancestors are pictured as a family group of marginal wanderers from "elsewhere" who travel in response to a divine command and who are not native to the land. Upon arrival, Abram's first act is to build an altar.

*5. Sarai.* The name means "Princess," a variant of Sarah. It has been proposed that the name reflects her high status (see at Genesis 11:29).

*6. Shechem.* Located forty miles north of Jerusalem, the city is later associated with covenant renewal in Joshua 24. However, it will also be the place of the so-called rape of Dinah (see Genesis 34). Originally Shechem was a sacred city to the Canaanites. Sacred groves were an important feature of cultic sites (note the tree under which Deborah sits in Judges 4:5). Here the "oak of *moreh*" (literally, the tree "of the teacher") is apparently a divinatory site where humans gain knowledge with help from the divine. Abraham is thus portrayed as establishing an altar at this ancient sacred space where people encountered God at a time long before Israelite kings, priests, and the great temple in Jerusalem.

*Canaanites.* Ancient inhabitants of the eastern Mediterranean region (modern-day Lebanon, southern Syria, Israel, and Jordan). Their sophisticated culture shared much with that of ancient Israel, although Israel's writers attempted to distinguish themselves from Canaanites, whom the Bible portrays as the pre-Israelite population of the land.

*7.* A way of marking the land as God's gift and as the future possession of the people of Israel.

*8. Beth El.* An ancient town north of Jerusalem and an important locus for Israelite foundation myths (see, for example, Jacob's dream at Beth El in Genesis 28).

[10]There was a famine in the land, and because
the famine in the land was severe, Abram went
down to stay in Egypt. [11]When he had almost
reached Egypt, he said to his wife Sarai, "Look,
now—I know what a beautiful woman you are!
[12]So when the Egyptians see you, and say: 'This is
his wife,' they may kill me; but you they shall keep
alive. [13]Please say then that you are my sister, so
that on your account it may go well for me, and that
my life may be spared because of you."

[14]And, indeed, when Abram arrived in Egypt
the Egyptians saw how exceptionally beautiful the

10 וַיְהִי רָעָב בָּאָרֶץ וַיֵּרֶד אַבְרָם מִצְרַיְמָה
לָגוּר שָׁם כִּי־כָבֵד הָרָעָב בָּאָרֶץ׃ 11 וַיְהִי
כַּאֲשֶׁר הִקְרִיב לָבוֹא מִצְרָיְמָה וַיֹּאמֶר
אֶל־שָׂרַי אִשְׁתּוֹ הִנֵּה־נָא יָדַעְתִּי כִּי אִשָּׁה
יְפַת־מַרְאֶה אָתְּ׃ 12 וְהָיָה כִּי־יִרְאוּ אֹתָךְ
הַמִּצְרִים וְאָמְרוּ אִשְׁתּוֹ זֹאת וְהָרְגוּ אֹתִי
וְאֹתָךְ יְחַיּוּ׃ 13 אִמְרִי־נָא אֲחֹתִי אָתְּ
לְמַעַן יִיטַב־לִי בַעֲבוּרֵךְ וְחָיְתָה נַפְשִׁי
בִּגְלָלֵךְ׃
14 וַיְהִי כְּבוֹא אַבְרָם מִצְרָיְמָה וַיִּרְאוּ
הַמִּצְרִים אֶת־הָאִשָּׁה כִּי־יָפָה הִוא מְאֹד׃

## *Relations within the Group and Outside* (12:10–14:24)

This unit continues to explain how the descendants of Abraham formed as a distinct group. The shaping of what constitutes "inside the group" entails the description of—and separation from—the "other," as variously defined.

### ABRAM AND SARAI AS TRICKSTERS (12:10–20)

This section is a variant of a tale in which the patriarch deceives a foreign ruler by telling him that his wife is his sister. A similar episode is found twice more in Genesis (Abraham and Sarah in 20:1–18; Isaac and Rebekah in 26:1–16). The deception leads to an improvement in the tricksters' status, but the deception is uncovered and they are summarily dismissed. They depart, however, with their newly acquired goods intact. The tale portrays Pharaoh as a dupe and deals with the "us-them" theme in a humorous and thoroughly traditional way.

This passage is not a tale about unethical behavior, but a story of marginalized persons who succeed in roundabout, unorthodox ways. In both such stories that involve Abraham and Sarah, Sarah proves to be the reason for Abraham's increased wealth.

*10. famine.* Departure in response to famine is a recurring biblical motif that reflects the ecological reality and agrarian concerns of the biblical writers.

*11. "I know what a beautiful woman you are!"* The biblical writer provides a reason for Pharaoh's interest in Sarai. While the Song of Songs is rich in poetic expressions of admiration for the lover's physical beauty, such overt observations about characters' beauty are limited and terse in the rest of the Bible. Their presence calls special attention to the relationship between the husband and wife.

*12.* Pharaoh, the despot, has no right simply to steal a man's wife if the woman pleases him, as he himself realizes (v. 18). Abram, as "brother," is treated as the man in charge of Sarai's sexuality. (Typically in the ancient Near East, a woman's reproductive capacity was controlled by a particular man, whether father, brother, or husband.) Here as in the Dinah story (Genesis 34), a special role is envisioned for a "brother."

*13. "Please say."* The request is polite. Sarai is asked rather than ordered.

15 וַיִּרְאוּ אֹתָהּ שָׂרֵי פַרְעֹה וַיְהַלְלוּ אֹתָהּ
אֶל־פַּרְעֹה וַתֻּקַּח הָאִשָּׁה בֵּית פַּרְעֹה׃
16 וּלְאַבְרָם הֵיטִיב בַּעֲבוּרָהּ וַיְהִי־לוֹ צֹאן־
וּבָקָר וַחֲמֹרִים וַעֲבָדִים וּשְׁפָחֹת וַאֲתֹנֹת
וּגְמַלִּים׃ 17 וַיְנַגַּע יְהוָה ׀ אֶת־פַּרְעֹה נְגָעִים
גְּדֹלִים וְאֶת־בֵּיתוֹ עַל־דְּבַר שָׂרַי אֵשֶׁת
אַבְרָם׃ 18 וַיִּקְרָא פַרְעֹה לְאַבְרָם וַיֹּאמֶר
מַה־זֹּאת עָשִׂיתָ לִּי לָמָּה לֹא־הִגַּדְתָּ לִּי
כִּי אִשְׁתְּךָ הִוא׃ 19 לָמָה אָמַרְתָּ אֲחֹתִי
הִוא וָאֶקַּח אֹתָהּ לִי לְאִשָּׁה וְעַתָּה הִנֵּה
אִשְׁתְּךָ קַח וָלֵךְ׃ 20 וַיְצַו עָלָיו פַּרְעֹה
אֲנָשִׁים וַיְשַׁלְּחוּ אֹתוֹ וְאֶת־אִשְׁתּוֹ וְאֶת־
כָּל־אֲשֶׁר־לוֹ׃

יג וַיַּעַל אַבְרָם מִמִּצְרַיִם הוּא וְאִשְׁתּוֹ
וְכָל־אֲשֶׁר־לוֹ וְלוֹט עִמּוֹ הַנֶּגְבָּה׃ 2 וְאַבְרָם
כָּבֵד מְאֹד בַּמִּקְנֶה בַּכֶּסֶף וּבַזָּהָב׃ 3 וַיֵּלֶךְ
לְמַסָּעָיו מִנֶּגֶב וְעַד־בֵּית־אֵל עַד־הַמָּקוֹם
אֲשֶׁר־הָיָה שָׁם אהלה אָהֳלוֹ בַּתְּחִלָּה בֵּין
בֵּית־אֵל וּבֵין הָעָי׃ 4 אֶל־מְקוֹם הַמִּזְבֵּחַ
אֲשֶׁר־עָשָׂה שָׁם בָּרִאשֹׁנָה וַיִּקְרָא שָׁם

woman was; 15when Pharaoh's ministers saw her,
they lauded her to Pharaoh, and the woman was
taken to Pharaoh's palace. 16Through her it did go
well for Abram, as he acquired sheep, cattle, and
asses, male and female slaves, she-asses and camels.
17יהוה then struck Pharaoh and his household with
severe afflictions because of Sarai, Abram's wife.
18Pharaoh now summoned Abram and said, "What
have you done to me? Why did you not tell me that
she was your wife? 19Why did you say that she was
your sister, so that I took her as a wife for myself?
Look, now that it turns out that she is your wife:
take [her] and begone!" 20Pharaoh then issued
orders and they drove him away, with his wife
and all that he owned.

13 Abram went up out of Egypt into the
Negev with his wife and all that he owned; and
Lot accompanied him. 2Abram was very rich, with
livestock, silver, and gold. 3On his [continuing]
march, he hiked from the Negev as far as Beth
El, up to the place where earlier his tent had been,
between Beth El and Ai, 4where he had first
built an altar. There Abram called upon the Name

*15–16.* As Abram anticipated, beautiful Sarai is transported to Pharaoh's harem; and wealth is transferred to Abram. An exchange of a woman has taken place. The tricksters' economic status has increased, explicitly because of Sarai.

*17.* Although Abram and Sarai are willing to overlook her predicament for his sake, God intervenes to protect her—another sign that she is crucial to God's plans. The plagues upon the Egyptians here prefigure the plagues of the Exodus, but without the latter's world-altering significance.

*18. What have you done to me.* A formulaic expression of wrong-doing. (See the parallels in Genesis 20:9; 26:10.)

*19. take [her] and begone.* The Hebrew is even more abrupt—literally, "Take! Go!"

*20.* The trickster never fully succeeds in emerging from his marginal status. Revelation of the deception brings a new reduction in status.

### ABRAM AND LOT: DISPUTE AND SEPARATION (13:1–13)

Abram and his nephew part ways. The writer thereby provides an explanation to the Israelite audience for the proximity of those nations that were understood to have descended from Lot (see 19:36–38). This passage alludes both to the kinship group that defines Israel and to the "Other" occupiers of land, while foreshadowing the tales of Sodom and Gomorrah that follow in Genesis 19.

of יהוה. [5]Now Lot, who had gone with Abram, also
had flocks and herds and tents, [6]so that the land
could not support them both; they had so much
property that they could not remain together. [7]A
quarrel [now] broke out between Abram's cattle
herders and Lot's cattle herders. (At that time the
Canaanites and the Perizzites were inhabiting the
land.) [8]Then Abram said to Lot, "There should be
no quarrel between you and me, and your herds-
men and mine, for we are close kin. [9]The whole
land lies before you! Pray part from me: if [you] go
north, I will turn south; and if [you] go south, I
will turn north." [10]Lot looked around and saw the
whole Jordan plain; all of it was well-watered, [this
being] before יהוה's destruction of Sodom and
Gomorrah; [it was] like a divine Garden, like the
land of Egypt as you get to Zoar. [11]So Lot chose the
whole Jordan plain for himself and moved away
toward the east. They parted, then, each from the
other. [12]Abram stayed in the land of Canaan, while
Lot settled among the cities of the plain, pitching
his tents as far as Sodom—[13]whose people were
wicked, hardened sinners against יהוה.

[14]יהוה now said to Abram, after Lot had parted
from him, "Look around from where you are, to
the north and the south, to the east and the west,
[15]for all the land that you see I am giving to you and
your descendants, forever. [16]I will make your de-

אַבְרָם בְּשֵׁם יְהוָה: 5 וְגַם־לְלוֹט הַהֹלֵךְ
אֶת־אַבְרָם הָיָה צֹאן־וּבָקָר וְאֹהָלִים:
6 וְלֹא־נָשָׂא אֹתָם הָאָרֶץ לָשֶׁבֶת יַחְדָּו כִּי־
הָיָה רְכוּשָׁם רָב וְלֹא יָכְלוּ לָשֶׁבֶת יַחְדָּו:
7 וַיְהִי־רִיב בֵּין רֹעֵי מִקְנֵה־אַבְרָם וּבֵין רֹעֵי
מִקְנֵה־לוֹט וְהַכְּנַעֲנִי וְהַפְּרִזִּי אָז יֹשֵׁב
בָּאָרֶץ: 8 וַיֹּאמֶר אַבְרָם אֶל־לוֹט אַל־נָא
תְהִי מְרִיבָה בֵּינִי וּבֵינֶךָ וּבֵין רֹעַי וּבֵין רֹעֶיךָ
כִּי־אֲנָשִׁים אַחִים אֲנָחְנוּ: 9 הֲלֹא כָל־הָאָרֶץ
לְפָנֶיךָ הִפָּרֶד נָא מֵעָלָי אִם־הַשְּׂמֹאל
וְאֵימִנָה וְאִם־הַיָּמִין וְאַשְׂמְאִילָה: 10 וַיִּשָּׂא־
לוֹט אֶת־עֵינָיו וַיַּרְא אֶת־כָּל־כִּכַּר הַיַּרְדֵּן כִּי
כֻלָּהּ מַשְׁקֶה לִפְנֵי | שַׁחֵת יְהוָה אֶת־סְדֹם
וְאֶת־עֲמֹרָה כְּגַן־יְהוָה כְּאֶרֶץ מִצְרַיִם
בֹּאֲכָה צֹעַר: 11 וַיִּבְחַר־לוֹ לוֹט אֵת כָּל־כִּכַּר
הַיַּרְדֵּן וַיִּסַּע לוֹט מִקֶּדֶם וַיִּפָּרְדוּ אִישׁ מֵעַל
אָחִיו: 12 אַבְרָם יָשַׁב בְּאֶרֶץ־כְּנָעַן וְלוֹט יָשַׁב
בְּעָרֵי הַכִּכָּר וַיֶּאֱהַל עַד־סְדֹם: 13 וְאַנְשֵׁי
סְדֹם רָעִים וְחַטָּאִים לַיהוָה מְאֹד:
14 וַיהוָה אָמַר אֶל־אַבְרָם אַחֲרֵי הִפָּרֶד־לוֹט
מֵעִמּוֹ שָׂא נָא עֵינֶיךָ וּרְאֵה מִן־הַמָּקוֹם
אֲשֶׁר־אַתָּה שָׁם צָפֹנָה וָנֶגְבָּה וָקֵדְמָה וָיָמָּה:
15 כִּי אֶת־כָּל־הָאָרֶץ אֲשֶׁר־אַתָּה רֹאֶה לְךָ
אֶתְּנֶנָּה וּלְזַרְעֲךָ עַד־עוֹלָם: 16 וְשַׂמְתִּי אֶת־

*13:5–13.* The amicable separation between the extended household of Lot and that of Abram continues the pattern of separation, distinguishing one group from another. Abram seeks to avoid enmity between kin.

*7. the Canaanites and the Perizzites.* This formulaic twosome is frequently employed to refer to the "native peoples" of the land encountered by Abram and his descendants (for example, Exodus 3:8, 17; 23:3).

*13. wicked, hardened sinners.* An anticipation of their city's destruction (Genesis 19).

## COVENANT PROMISES: LAND AND PROGENY (13:14–18)

This passage underscores the importance of the land-promise theme in Israelite self-understanding. Whatever Israel's actual, complex origins in the land, the tradition here insists upon both Israel's outsider status and the land as a divine boon.

*15–16. "land . . . descendants like the dust of the earth."* Each of the patriarchs hears similar language of promise (again Abraham in 22:17, Isaac in 26:3–4, and Jacob in 28:13–14). In this case, it rein-

scendants like the dust of the earth. Only if one can
count the dust of the earth will it be possible to
count your descendants. [17]Get up and walk about
the land—its length and its breadth—for it is to
you that I am giving it." [18]Moving his tent, Abram
went to dwell by the oaks of Mamre, in Hebron;
there he built an altar to honor יהוה.

14 In the time of Amraphel king of Shinar,
Arioch king of Ellasar, Chedarlaomer king of Elam,
and Tidal king of Goiim, [2]these [four] waged war
against Bera king of Sodom, Birsha king of Gomorrah, Shinab king of Admah, Shemeber king of
Zeboim, and the king of Bela (that is, Zoar). [3]These
all joined forces at the Valley of Siddim, now the
Dead Sea. [4]For twelve years they had been subject
to Chedarlaomer, but in the thirteenth year they
rebelled. [5]In the fourteenth year Chedarlaomer and
his allied kings came and subdued the Rephaim in
Ashterot-karnaim, the Zuzim in Ham, the Emim
in Shaveh-kiriata'im, [6]and the Horites in their hill
country of Seir as far as Eil Paran by the edge of
the wilderness. [7]They then returned, coming to Ein
Mishpat (that is, Kadesh), where they subdued the
whole country of Amalek and the Amorites who

זַרְעֲךָ כַּעֲפַר הָאָרֶץ אֲשֶׁר | אִם־יוּכַל אִישׁ
לִמְנוֹת אֶת־עֲפַר הָאָרֶץ גַּם־זַרְעֲךָ יִמָּנֶה׃
17 קוּם הִתְהַלֵּךְ בָּאָרֶץ לְאָרְכָּהּ וּלְרָחְבָּהּ כִּי
לְךָ אֶתְּנֶנָּה׃ 18 וַיֶּאֱהַל אַבְרָם וַיָּבֹא וַיֵּשֶׁב
בְּאֵלֹנֵי מַמְרֵא אֲשֶׁר בְּחֶבְרוֹן וַיִּבֶן־שָׁם
מִזְבֵּחַ לַיהוָה׃ פ

יד וַיְהִי בִּימֵי אַמְרָפֶל מֶלֶךְ־שִׁנְעָר אַרְיוֹךְ
מֶלֶךְ אֶלָּסָר כְּדָרְלָעֹמֶר מֶלֶךְ עֵילָם וְתִדְעָל
מֶלֶךְ גּוֹיִם׃ 2 עָשׂוּ מִלְחָמָה אֶת־בֶּרַע מֶלֶךְ
סְדֹם וְאֶת־בִּרְשַׁע מֶלֶךְ עֲמֹרָה שִׁנְאָב | מֶלֶךְ
אַדְמָה וְשֶׁמְאֵבֶר מֶלֶךְ צביים צְבוֹיִם וּמֶלֶךְ
בֶּלַע הִיא־צֹעַר׃ 3 כָּל־אֵלֶּה חָבְרוּ אֶל־עֵמֶק
הַשִּׂדִּים הוּא יָם הַמֶּלַח׃ 4 שְׁתֵּים עֶשְׂרֵה
שָׁנָה עָבְדוּ אֶת־כְּדָרְלָעֹמֶר וּשְׁלֹשׁ־עֶשְׂרֵה
שָׁנָה מָרָדוּ׃ 5 וּבְאַרְבַּע עֶשְׂרֵה שָׁנָה בָּא
כְדָרְלָעֹמֶר וְהַמְּלָכִים אֲשֶׁר אִתּוֹ וַיַּכּוּ אֶת־
רְפָאִים בְּעַשְׁתְּרֹת קַרְנַיִם וְאֶת־הַזּוּזִים בְּהָם
וְאֵת הָאֵימִים בְּשָׁוֵה קִרְיָתָיִם׃ 6 וְאֶת־
הַחֹרִי בְּהַרְרָם שֵׂעִיר עַד אֵיל פָּארָן אֲשֶׁר
עַל־הַמִּדְבָּר׃ 7 וַיָּשֻׁבוּ וַיָּבֹאוּ אֶל־עֵין מִשְׁפָּט
הִוא קָדֵשׁ וַיַּכּוּ אֶת־כָּל־שְׂדֵה הָעֲמָלֵקִי וְגַם

forces the message of fullness and the predictions' certainty.

*18. oaks of Mamre.* See 12:6.

ABRAM AS A WARRIOR HERO (14:1–24)

Throughout the rest of Genesis, Abraham is portrayed as a peaceful patriarch, protected by God: He migrates with family and flocks, establishing ties to the land. Although he has retainers, his major tactic in confrontations is withdrawal under divine protection. This story, however, is different—more like tales in the books of Judges and Samuel than like the stories that surround it. Here Abram is portrayed as an epic hero who skillfully fights to rescue captured kin.

*14:1–9.* Scholars used to seek historical information in these names of kings, but they have largely abandoned the search. This detailed war description includes an intriguing and fanciful mixture of the real, the unverifiable, and the richly mythic. While none of the named kings is known from biblical or extra-biblical sources, some of the places certainly existed, such as Seir, Kadesh, Shinar, and Elam.

*5. Rephaim . . . Zuzim . . . Emim.* Terms applied to the legendary giants and superheroes that pre-date Israel's history in the land according to the biblical chronology (see at Genesis 6:4).

*7. Amalek.* A people assigned by biblical tradition to the Negev region and treated as an arch-

dwell in Hazazon-tamar. [8]Then the king of Sodom, the king of Gomorrah, the king of Admah, the king of Zeboim, and the king of Bela (that is, Zoar) went out and arrayed themselves in battle formation against the [enemy] in the Valley of Siddim—[9]against Chedarlaomer king of Elam, Tidal king of Goiim, Amraphel king of Shinar, and Arioch king of Ellasar—four kings against five.

[10]Now the Valley of Siddim was studded with tar pits, and when the kings of Sodom and Gomorrah fled, some tumbled into them, and the rest fled to the hills. [11]So they took all the possessions of [the kings of] Sodom and Gomorrah and their food, and they went off; [12]and as they went off they took Lot, Abram's brother's son, with his possessions; he was a resident of Sodom.

[13]A fugitive then came and told Abram the Hebrew, who was living by the oak trees of Mamre the Amorite, brother of Eshkol and Aner, who were allied to Abram by treaty. [14]Hearing that his kinsman had been taken captive, Abram mustered his retainers, born into his household, 318 of them, going in pursuit as far as Dan. [15]At night he deployed himself and his forces against them and defeated them, pursuing them as far as Hobah, north of Damascus. [16]He then brought back all the possessions; his nephew Lot, too, and his possessions; [he restored] the women, too, and the [other]

אֶת־הָאֱמֹרִי הַיֹּשֵׁב בְּחַצְצֹן תָּמָר׃ 8 וַיֵּצֵא
מֶלֶךְ־סְדֹם וּמֶלֶךְ עֲמֹרָה וּמֶלֶךְ אַדְמָה וּמֶלֶךְ
צביים צְבוֹיִם וּמֶלֶךְ בֶּלַע הִוא־צֹעַר וַיַּעַרְכוּ
אִתָּם מִלְחָמָה בְּעֵמֶק הַשִּׂדִּים׃ 9 אֵת
כְּדָרְלָעֹמֶר מֶלֶךְ עֵילָם וְתִדְעָל מֶלֶךְ גּוֹיִם
וְאַמְרָפֶל מֶלֶךְ שִׁנְעָר וְאַרְיוֹךְ מֶלֶךְ אֶלָּסָר
אַרְבָּעָה מְלָכִים אֶת־הַחֲמִשָּׁה׃
10 וְעֵמֶק הַשִּׂדִּים בֶּאֱרֹת בֶּאֱרֹת חֵמָר וַיָּנֻסוּ
מֶלֶךְ־סְדֹם וַעֲמֹרָה וַיִּפְּלוּ־שָׁמָּה וְהַנִּשְׁאָרִים
הֶרָה נָּסוּ׃ 11 וַיִּקְחוּ אֶת־כָּל־רְכֻשׁ סְדֹם
וַעֲמֹרָה וְאֶת־כָּל־אָכְלָם וַיֵּלֵכוּ׃ 12 וַיִּקְחוּ
אֶת־לוֹט וְאֶת־רְכֻשׁוֹ בֶּן־אֲחִי אַבְרָם וַיֵּלֵכוּ
וְהוּא יֹשֵׁב בִּסְדֹם׃
13 וַיָּבֹא הַפָּלִיט וַיַּגֵּד לְאַבְרָם הָעִבְרִי וְהוּא
שֹׁכֵן בְּאֵלֹנֵי מַמְרֵא הָאֱמֹרִי אֲחִי אֶשְׁכֹּל
וַאֲחִי עָנֵר וְהֵם בַּעֲלֵי בְרִית־אַבְרָם׃
14 וַיִּשְׁמַע אַבְרָם כִּי נִשְׁבָּה אָחִיו וַיָּרֶק
אֶת־חֲנִיכָיו יְלִידֵי בֵיתוֹ שְׁמֹנָה עָשָׂר וּשְׁלֹשׁ
מֵאוֹת וַיִּרְדֹּף עַד־דָּן׃ 15 וַיֵּחָלֵק עֲלֵיהֶם ׀
לַיְלָה הוּא וַעֲבָדָיו וַיַּכֵּם וַיִּרְדְּפֵם עַד־חוֹבָה
אֲשֶׁר מִשְּׂמֹאל לְדַמָּשֶׂק׃ 16 וַיָּשֶׁב אֵת כָּל־
הָרְכֻשׁ וְגַם אֶת־לוֹט אָחִיו וּרְכֻשׁוֹ הֵשִׁיב

enemy and rival for the land (Exodus 17:8–16; Numbers 14:43–45).

***Amorites.*** A frequent biblical designation for the land's indigenous population (see Deuteronomy 1:4, 7).

*8.* ***Sodom ... Gomorrah.*** Treated as two ancient kingdoms or city-states without reference to ethical breaches associated with Genesis 18–19.

***Admah ... Zeboim.*** Like Sodom and Gomorrah, these cities are places of destruction (see Deuteronomy 29:22).

*13.* ***Hebrew.*** In Exodus, this word—perhaps related to *apiru,* a Semitic-language term for stateless folk—may refer to social status rather than to ethnic identity. Here, the term may well have ethnic connotations.

***oak trees of Mamre.*** Compare 12:6.

*14.* ***his kinsman.*** In biblical parlance, the head of a household stands for the entire household, including its women. (See also at 10:1.)

*15–16.* Quick narrative strokes cover the battle and victory. Note that the women are listed separately after the possessions, among the spoils of all-too-frequent war.

people. 17The king of Sodom came out to meet him
after his return to the Valley of Shaveh (that is, the
King's Valley) from fighting Chedarlaomer and his
allied kings. 18Now Melchizedek king of Salem
brought out bread and wine—he was a priest of
God Most High—19and blessed him, saying,
"Blessed be Abram by God Most High, maker of
heaven and earth, 20and blessed is God Most High,
who has given your foes into your hands." Then he
[Abram] gave him a tenth of everything.

21The king of Sodom now said to Abram, "Let
me have the people and keep the goods for
yourself." 22But Abram said to the king of Sodom,
"I have raised my hand to יהוה, God Most High,
maker of heaven and earth, 23that I would take
nothing of yours, not even a thread or a sandal-
strap—you shall not say, 'I enriched Abram'—24ex-
cept what the troops have eaten, and the share due
the leaders who went with me: Aner, Eshkol, and
Mamre; let them take their share."

15 After these things, the word of יהוה came
to Abram in a vision, saying, "Have no fear, Abram;
I am giving you an abundant reward as a gift."

וְגַם אֶת־הַנָּשִׁים וְאֶת־הָעָם׃ 17 וַיֵּצֵא מֶלֶךְ־
סְדֹם לִקְרָאתוֹ אַחֲרֵי שׁוּבוֹ מֵהַכּוֹת אֶת־
כְּדָרְלָעֹמֶר וְאֶת־הַמְּלָכִים אֲשֶׁר אִתּוֹ אֶל־
עֵמֶק שָׁוֵה הוּא עֵמֶק הַמֶּלֶךְ׃ 18 וּמַלְכִּי־צֶדֶק
מֶלֶךְ שָׁלֵם הוֹצִיא לֶחֶם וָיָיִן וְהוּא כֹהֵן לְאֵל
עֶלְיוֹן׃ 19 וַיְבָרְכֵהוּ וַיֹּאמַר בָּרוּךְ אַבְרָם
לְאֵל עֶלְיוֹן קֹנֵה שָׁמַיִם וָאָרֶץ׃ 20 וּבָרוּךְ אֵל
עֶלְיוֹן אֲשֶׁר־מִגֵּן צָרֶיךָ בְּיָדֶךָ וַיִּתֶּן־לוֹ מַעֲשֵׂר
מִכֹּל׃

21 וַיֹּאמֶר מֶלֶךְ־סְדֹם אֶל־אַבְרָם תֶּן־לִי
הַנֶּפֶשׁ וְהָרְכֻשׁ קַח־לָךְ׃ 22 וַיֹּאמֶר אַבְרָם
אֶל־מֶלֶךְ סְדֹם הֲרִמֹתִי יָדִי אֶל־יְהֹוָה אֵל
עֶלְיוֹן קֹנֵה שָׁמַיִם וָאָרֶץ׃ 23 אִם־מִחוּט
וְעַד שְׂרוֹךְ־נַעַל וְאִם־אֶקַּח מִכָּל־אֲשֶׁר־לָךְ
וְלֹא תֹאמַר אֲנִי הֶעֱשַׁרְתִּי אֶת־אַבְרָם׃
24 בִּלְעָדַי רַק אֲשֶׁר אָכְלוּ הַנְּעָרִים וְחֵלֶק
הָאֲנָשִׁים אֲשֶׁר הָלְכוּ אִתִּי עָנֵר אֶשְׁכֹּל
וּמַמְרֵא הֵם יִקְחוּ חֶלְקָם׃ ס

טו אַחַר ׀ הַדְּבָרִים הָאֵלֶּה הָיָה דְבַר־
יְהֹוָה אֶל־אַבְרָם בַּמַּחֲזֶה לֵאמֹר אַל־תִּירָא
אַבְרָם אָנֹכִי מָגֵן לָךְ שְׂכָרְךָ הַרְבֵּה מְאֹד׃

**18. *Melchizedek.*** This name, which associates the term for "king" with "righteousness," becomes symbolically important in the Dead Sea Scrolls and in later Jewish literature. Melchizedek is one of the many enigmatic biblical figures—probably rooted in a richer oral tradition—who appear briefly in the written tradition, and then go on to a fuller post-biblical afterlife. Serah daughter of Asher is another such figure (see Numbers 26:46).

***Salem.*** Perhaps to be identified with Jerusalem.

**20. *a tenth of everything.*** Abram appears to engage in an act of tithing, anticipating the Torah's later prescriptions (as in Leviticus 27:30–33).

**22–24.** In contrast to the usual practice of warrior heroes in Judges and I–II Samuel (see Joshua 8:1–3; Judges 8:24–26), Abram refuses to enjoy any of the spoil obtained through his military victory. As in the Book of Esther (9:10), battle is not for material gain but for the righteous cause.

## *A Deepening Covenant* (15:1–21)

This passage is a version of covenant-formation (see also Genesis 9, 12, 17; Exodus 6, 12). In this literary form, God appears or speaks; the recipient of the message is promised blessings of land and progeny; the Deity self-identifies; and a sign is provided to mark and seal the relationship. Of special note in this scene are the name of the Deity

[2]Abram then replied, "God יהוה, what can You give me, when I am going [to die] childless, and the heir to my household is Damascene Eliezer?" [3]Abram added, "Look—to me You have given no offspring, and one of my slaves is my heir!" [4]But יהוה's word to him was, "That one shall not be your heir; rather, one who comes from your own body—he shall be your heir!"

[5]Taking him outside, [God] said, "Turn your gaze toward the heavens and count the stars, if you can count them!" And [God] promised him: "So shall your seed be!" [6]And he put his trust in יהוה, who reckoned that as loyalty in him, [7]saying to him: "I am יהוה who brought you out of Ur of the Chaldeans, to give you this land as an inheritance." [8]He then said, "God יהוה, how can I know that I shall take possession of it?"

[9][God] answered, "Bring Me a three-year-old calf, a three-year-old kid, a three-year-old ram, and a young turtledove." [10]So he took all these and split them—all but the bird—in the middle, placing each half opposite the other. [11]Vultures descended upon the carcasses, but Abram chased them away.

2 וַיֹּאמֶר אַבְרָם אֲדֹנָי יהוה אֱלֹהִים מַה־
תִּתֶּן־לִי וְאָנֹכִי הוֹלֵךְ עֲרִירִי וּבֶן־מֶשֶׁק בֵּיתִי
הוּא דַּמֶּשֶׂק אֱלִיעֶזֶר׃ 3 וַיֹּאמֶר אַבְרָם הֵן
לִי לֹא נָתַתָּה זָרַע וְהִנֵּה בֶן־בֵּיתִי יוֹרֵשׁ
אֹתִי׃ 4 וְהִנֵּה דְבַר־יְהוָה אֵלָיו לֵאמֹר לֹא
יִירָשְׁךָ זֶה כִּי־אִם אֲשֶׁר יֵצֵא מִמֵּעֶיךָ הוּא
יִירָשֶׁךָ׃
5 וַיּוֹצֵא אֹתוֹ הַחוּצָה וַיֹּאמֶר הַבֶּט־נָא
הַשָּׁמַיְמָה וּסְפֹר הַכּוֹכָבִים אִם־תּוּכַל לִסְפֹּר
אֹתָם וַיֹּאמֶר לוֹ כֹּה יִהְיֶה זַרְעֶךָ׃ 6 וְהֶאֱמִן
בַּיהוָה וַיַּחְשְׁבֶהָ לּוֹ צְדָקָה׃ 7 וַיֹּאמֶר אֵלָיו
אֲנִי יְהוָה אֲשֶׁר הוֹצֵאתִיךָ מֵאוּר כַּשְׂדִּים
לָתֶת לְךָ אֶת־הָאָרֶץ הַזֹּאת לְרִשְׁתָּהּ׃
8 וַיֹּאמַר אֲדֹנָי יהוה אֱלֹהִים בַּמָּה אֵדַע
כִּי אִירָשֶׁנָּה׃
9 וַיֹּאמֶר אֵלָיו קְחָה לִי עֶגְלָה מְשֻׁלֶּשֶׁת וְעֵז
מְשֻׁלֶּשֶׁת וְאַיִל מְשֻׁלָּשׁ וְתֹר וְגוֹזָל׃ 10 וַיִּקַּח־
לוֹ אֶת־כָּל־אֵלֶּה וַיְבַתֵּר אֹתָם בַּתָּוֶךְ וַיִּתֵּן
אִישׁ־בִּתְרוֹ לִקְרַאת רֵעֵהוּ וְאֶת־הַצִּפֹּר לֹא
בָתָר׃ 11 וַיֵּרֶד הָעַיִט עַל־הַפְּגָרִים וַיַּשֵּׁב

(v. 7); the ritual (vv. 9–17); the prophecy offered (vv. 13–16); and the lack of explicit conditions laid upon the patriarch as covenant partner.

*15:1–6.* Twin promises of land and children are central to Israelite tales of self-definition; perhaps they reflect the importance of male lineages and patrimonies.

*1.* The divine communication comes in a vision, so that what is "seen" is a poetic blessing that verbally reassures Abram.

*2–3.* Abram confronts God, calling attention to the grand yet unfulfilled promises of progeny. Abram has not resorted to the variety of customs in ancient times that enabled householders to ensure their posterity (such as taking an additional wife). See at 16:1–3.

*7–19.* Known as the "covenant of the pieces," this eerie scene testifies to the strongly experiential dimension of the numinous, as Abram encounters the Deity.

*7.* "יהוה." God self-identifies by this name, which source critics have long considered to be a marker of a particular biblical thread or layer. See also at 2:4.

*10.* ***split them.*** In Hebrew idiom, to make a covenant is literally to "cut" one. Drawing parallels with ancient Near Eastern custom and Jeremiah 34:17–22, scholars have suggested that the division of the animal is an implied threat, symbolizing the result of a failure to keep the covenant. An alternate view is that the covenant's parties belong to one unit, one body; each half is incomplete without its counterpart. Bonds are affirmed through participation in sacrificial ritual—in a common mode of cultural expression.

¹²Then, as the sun was setting, Abram fell into a deep sleep, and lo! a powerful dark dread was falling upon him!

¹³[God] said to Abram, "Know now that your descendants shall be strangers in a land not theirs; they shall be enslaved and afflicted for four hundred years. ¹⁴But then I will bring judgment upon the nation they are serving; after that they shall go out with many possessions. ¹⁵And you—you shall go to your ancestors in peace; you shall be buried in good old age. ¹⁶The fourth generation shall return here, for not until then shall the iniquity of the Amorites be repaid."

¹⁷Now, when the sun had set and it was dark, lo—a smoking oven and a fiery torch were what passed between these pieces! ¹⁸On that day יהוה made a covenant with Abram, saying, "To your descendants I have given this land, from the river of Egypt to the great river, the Euphrates, ¹⁹[the land of] the Kenites, the Kenizzites, the Kadmonites, ²⁰the Hittites, the Perizzites, the Rephaim, ²¹the Amorites, the Canaanites, the Girgashites, and the Jebusites."

16 Now Abram's wife Sarai, who had not borne him a child, had an Egyptian slave named Hagar. ²So Sarai said to Abram: "Seeing as יהוה has

אֹתָ֖ם אַבְרָֽם׃ ¹² וַיְהִ֤י הַשֶּׁ֙מֶשׁ֙ לָב֔וֹא
וְתַרְדֵּמָ֖ה נָפְלָ֣ה עַל־אַבְרָ֑ם וְהִנֵּ֥ה אֵימָ֛ה
חֲשֵׁכָ֥ה גְדֹלָ֖ה נֹפֶ֥לֶת עָלָֽיו׃ ¹³ וַיֹּ֣אמֶר לְאַבְרָ֗ם יָדֹ֨עַ תֵּדַ֜ע כִּי־גֵ֣ר ׀ יִהְיֶ֣ה
זַרְעֲךָ֗ בְּאֶ֙רֶץ֙ לֹ֣א לָהֶ֔ם וַעֲבָד֖וּם וְעִנּ֣וּ אֹתָ֑ם
אַרְבַּ֥ע מֵא֖וֹת שָׁנָֽה׃ ¹⁴ וְגַ֧ם אֶת־הַגּ֛וֹי אֲשֶׁ֥ר
יַעֲבֹ֖דוּ דָּ֣ן אָנֹ֑כִי וְאַחֲרֵי־כֵ֥ן יֵצְא֖וּ בִּרְכֻ֥שׁ
גָּדֽוֹל׃ ¹⁵ וְאַתָּ֛ה תָּב֥וֹא אֶל־אֲבֹתֶ֖יךָ בְּשָׁל֑וֹם
תִּקָּבֵ֖ר בְּשֵׂיבָ֥ה טוֹבָֽה׃ ¹⁶ וְד֥וֹר רְבִיעִ֖י יָשׁ֣וּבוּ
הֵ֑נָּה כִּ֧י לֹא־שָׁלֵ֛ם עֲוֺ֥ן הָאֱמֹרִ֖י עַד־הֵֽנָּה׃
¹⁷ וַיְהִ֤י הַשֶּׁ֙מֶשׁ֙ בָּ֔אָה וַעֲלָטָ֖ה הָיָ֑ה וְהִנֵּ֨ה
תַנּ֤וּר עָשָׁן֙ וְלַפִּ֣יד אֵ֔שׁ אֲשֶׁ֣ר עָבַ֔ר בֵּ֖ין
הַגְּזָרִ֥ים הָאֵֽלֶּה׃ ¹⁸ בַּיּ֣וֹם הַה֗וּא כָּרַ֧ת יְהֹוָ֛ה
אֶת־אַבְרָ֖ם בְּרִ֣ית לֵאמֹ֑ר לְזַרְעֲךָ֗ נָתַ֙תִּי֙ אֶת־
הָאָ֣רֶץ הַזֹּ֔את מִנְּהַ֣ר מִצְרַ֔יִם עַד־הַנָּהָ֥ר
הַגָּדֹ֖ל נְהַר־פְּרָֽת׃ ¹⁹ אֶת־הַקֵּינִי֙ וְאֶת־הַקְּנִזִּ֔י
וְאֵ֖ת הַקַּדְמֹנִֽי׃ ²⁰ וְאֶת־הַֽחִתִּ֥י וְאֶת־הַפְּרִזִּ֖י
וְאֶת־הָרְפָאִֽים׃ ²¹ וְאֶת־הָֽאֱמֹרִי֙ וְאֶת־
הַֽכְּנַעֲנִ֔י וְאֶת־הַגִּרְגָּשִׁ֖י וְאֶת־הַיְבוּסִֽי׃ ס
טז וְשָׂרַי֙ אֵ֣שֶׁת אַבְרָ֔ם לֹ֥א יָלְדָ֖ה ל֑וֹ וְלָ֛הּ
שִׁפְחָ֥ה מִצְרִ֖ית וּשְׁמָ֥הּ הָגָֽר׃ ² וַתֹּ֨אמֶר שָׂרַ֜י

- - - - - - - - - - - - - - - - - - - - - - - - - - - - - -

**12. deep sleep.** The trance-like state signals important transformations. In Genesis 2:21, the first human being was likewise placed in deep sleep prior to the formation of woman.

**13–16.** A premonition of the later enslavement in Egypt and the Exodus.

**16. "iniquity of the Amorites."** The indigenous peoples are declared deserving of displacement. The author apparently seeks to justify biblical tradition concerning the Israelites' later conquest of the land.

**17. smoking oven...fiery torch.** The Deity is often associated with fire imagery (see Exodus 3:2; 19:18). [The text's ancient audience perceived certain artifacts to be associated with a particular gender. Ovens, torches, or both may well have been linked with women in particular, as those who bake

bread (Leviticus 26:26), or as with Deborah, who is said to be affiliated with *lapidot*, "torches" (Judges 4:4). Here, such items represent the divine Presence (David Stein, personal communication). —*Ed.*]

**passed between these pieces.** See at 15:10. The divine being passes between the halves, demonstrating reliability as a covenant partner.

## The Tale of Hagar  (16:1–16)

This passage returns to a problem mentioned earlier (11:30): the barrenness of the patriarch's wife. That topic is a recurring motif foreshadowing the birth of a hero (see the story of Hannah, mother of Samuel, in I Samuel 1–2). Here, Sarai

kept me from bearing a child, have intercourse with my slave: maybe I will have a son through her."

אֶל־אַבְרָם הִנֵּה־נָא עֲצָרַנִי יְהֹוָה מִלֶּדֶת בֹּא־נָא אֶל־שִׁפְחָתִי אוּלַי אִבָּנֶה מִמֶּנָּה

takes matters into her own hands by giving her husband her female slave as wife. The slave's children will belong to her mistress by adoption. The passage reveals the ethical and practical difficulties of this sort of surrogate motherhood, and the political dimensions of reproduction in a traditional patrilineal society. Nevertheless, in a world in which having children is a major source of status, Hagar is emboldened by her pregnancy (16:4). Sarai "treat(s) her harshly," and the girl runs away. The annunciation that follows is a traditional marker of the biography of a hero. Here, as in Genesis 21, the reader briefly feels immersed in a non-Israelite nation's founding myth.

### BARRENNESS AND SURROGATE MOTHERHOOD (16:1–6)

The theme of the barren wife recurs throughout tales of the matriarchs and of the mothers of other heroes—including Rebekah, Rachel, Samson's unnamed mother, and Hannah. The motif implies that a boy born under such circumstances is truly sent by God, his mother's condition having received special attention by the Deity. In the Bible, reproductive problems typically concern women, whereas in other traditions either parent may be regarded as infertile. This is another of the Bible's double-edged swords regarding the status of women. On the one hand, to be infertile is to be marginal, possibly afflicted by God; on the other hand, annunciations of a child's birth account for most of the few biblical passages in which God communicates with and empowers women. Here the biblical writers deftly draw out the ways in which children connote status in this society. Implicitly, they also point to the powerlessness of slave women whose reproductive capacity belongs to another. Both women—mistress and slave—have their options expanded and yet are also constrained by their cultural roles.

*16:1. an Egyptian slave.* Hebrew has several terms for female servants or slaves. The term here refers to the lowest level of servitude. Slavery was an accepted part of ancient Near Eastern cultures, Israel included. Although certain biblical laws ameliorate the plight of slaves, especially male Hebrews (see at Exodus 21:2–11 and Leviticus 25:35–54), they do not overtly oppose the institution. According to the Sinai covenant, a daughter sold into slavery was normally not released in the seventh year (Exodus 21:2, 7). In addition to the usual hardships that they shared with male counterparts, women slaves were also used by males in the household for sexual or procreative purposes. Typically, their masters or mistresses had extensive control over their fate. In the story of Rachel and Leah, their father Laban gives a woman slave to each of his daughters (Genesis 29:24, 29); in turn, they assign those slaves—named Zilpah and Bilhah—to their husband, Jacob, in order to produce children (Genesis 29–30). Here, when Hagar becomes Abram's wife (v. 3), she does not cease to be Sarai's slave; when Abraham surrenders Hagar to Sarai's authority (v. 6), he acknowledges that his wife has prior claims that supersede his. (In Genesis 25:6, Hagar appears to be counted among Abraham's concubines—a status higher than that of a slave but lower than a wife.)

*2.* Sarai acknowledges that fertility is ultimately in the hands of the Deity (see Genesis 30:2), but nevertheless takes matters into her own hands.

***"maybe I will have a son through her."*** The Hebrew is more ambiguous since the word "son" does not appear. Instead, Sarai is using a verb that can mean either "I will have a child" or "I will be built" —that is, established—which refers to creating a family and continuity with no reference to the offspring's gender. | Sarai's motive is not clear. Is it to ensure her own position, to fulfill Abram's dream of having a child as an heir (Genesis 15:2–3), or both? |

Abram heeded Sarai's voice. 3 Ten years after Abram had settled in the land of Canaan, Abram's wife Sarai took her slave Hagar the Egyptian and gave her to her husband Abram as a wife. 4 He came to Hagar and she became pregnant; and when she saw that she had become pregnant, her mistress became for her an object of scorn.

5 Sarai then said to Abram, "My wrong is on your head! I put my slave in your arms; no sooner did she see that she was pregnant, I became for her an object of scorn. Let יהוה judge between us!" 6 So Abram said to Sarai, "Look, your slave is in your hands; do to her as you please." Sarai then so af-

וַיִּשְׁמַע אַבְרָם לְקוֹל שָׂרָי׃ 3 וַתִּקַּח שָׂרַי
אֵשֶׁת־אַבְרָם אֶת־הָגָר הַמִּצְרִית שִׁפְחָתָהּ
מִקֵּץ עֶשֶׂר שָׁנִים לְשֶׁבֶת אַבְרָם בְּאֶרֶץ כְּנָעַן
וַתִּתֵּן אֹתָהּ לְאַבְרָם אִישָׁהּ לוֹ לְאִשָּׁה׃
4 וַיָּבֹא אֶל־הָגָר וַתַּהַר וַתֵּרֶא כִּי הָרָתָה
וַתֵּקַל גְּבִרְתָּהּ בְּעֵינֶיהָ׃
5 וַתֹּאמֶר שָׂרַי אֶל־אַבְרָם חֲמָסִי עָלֶיךָ אָנֹכִי
נָתַתִּי שִׁפְחָתִי בְּחֵיקֶךָ וַתֵּרֶא כִּי הָרָתָה
וָאֵקַל בְּעֵינֶיהָ יִשְׁפֹּט יְהוָה בֵּינִי וּבֵינֶיךָ׃
6 וַיֹּאמֶר אַבְרָם אֶל־שָׂרַי הִנֵּה שִׁפְחָתֵךְ
בְּיָדֵךְ עֲשִׂי־לָהּ הַטּוֹב בְּעֵינָיִךְ וַתְּעַנֶּהָ שָׂרַי

Modern scholars have long pointed to extra-biblical evidence for varieties of surrogate motherhood in the ancient Near East, such as was regulated in the Laws of Hammurabi (¶ 146). Sarai participates in an unspecified version of that widely practiced system and seeks to be empowered within its contours.

***Abram heeded Sarai's voice.*** In Genesis 3:17, the first man was chastised for heeding the woman's voice. In contrast, in Genesis 21:12, God will need to explicitly instruct Abraham to obey Sarah: "Do whatever Sarah tells you"—more literally "All that Sarah tells you, heed her voice." Here, however, Abram shows no reluctance to follow his wife's instructions. In household matters, women exercised authority.

*3.* ***gave her to her husband Abram as a wife.*** An ancient contract from Nuzi (Mesopotamia, 14th century B.C.E.) prescribes a similar response to barrenness: "Kelim-ninu [a woman] has been given in marriage to Shennima [a man]. . . . If Kelim-ninu does not bear, Kelim-ninu shall acquire a woman of the land of Lulu, and Kelim-ninu may not send the offspring away" (*ANET*, 1969, p. 220; see also at v. 1).

***wife.*** Heb. *ishah*; see at 2:24.

*4.* ***became for her an object of scorn.*** Literally, "became lightweight in her eyes." The status of childless women in antiquity was precarious, socially and economically. Pregnant, and as Abram's new wife, Hagar has reason to feel that her position has been elevated.

*5.* ***Sarai then said.*** The biblical writers are psychologically astute in describing the tension between husband and wife over difficult reproductive issues (see also Genesis 30:1–2).

*6.* The principal wife clearly has certain rights in these situations involving reproduction, as Abram —unquestioning—implicitly recognizes. From a much later Jewish community in Egypt (5th century B.C.E.) we have a document in which one man's slave becomes another's wife, and another document in which her master frees her. Such conflicting lines of authority create complexities of which the stories here and in Genesis 21 are a dramatic, even tragic, example. Meanwhile, from a literary perspective, one observes Abram's frustration and feelings of powerlessness, as well as his desire not to become involved in this world of women.

***Sarai then so afflicted her.*** [Tikva Frymer-Kensky suggests that this may mean that Sarai simply starts treating her like an ordinary slave (*Reading the Women of the Bible*, 2002, p. 229). The verb *innah* ("afflicted") refers to various forms of coercion. The same verb describes the treatment of the Israelites in Egypt (Exodus 1:11). On the long-term impact of the relationship between Sarah and Hagar, see at Genesis 21:10. —*Ed.*]

flicted her that she ran away, 7 and an angel of יהוה found her at a spring of water in the wilderness, at the spring on the road to Shur.

8 [The angel] said, "Hagar, slave of Sarai: Whence have you come and where are you going?" She answered, "I am running away from my mistress Sarai." 9 The angel of יהוה said to her, "Return to your mistress and submit to her ill-treatment." 10 The angel of יהוה went on to say to her, "I will greatly multiply your descendants; they shall be too numerous to count." 11 And then the angel of יהוה continued: "Look—you are pregnant and shall bear a son; call him Ishmael, for יהוה has heard your affliction. 12 He shall be a wild ass of a man; his hand shall be against all and the hand of all shall be against him; he shall dwell in [permanent] opposition to all his kin."

וַתִּבְרַח מִפָּנֶיהָ׃ 7 וַיִּמְצָאָהּ מַלְאַךְ יְהוָה עַל־
עֵין הַמַּיִם בַּמִּדְבָּר עַל־הָעַיִן בְּדֶרֶךְ שׁוּר׃
8 וַיֹּאמַר הָגָר שִׁפְחַת שָׂרַי אֵי־מִזֶּה בָאת
וְאָנָה תֵלֵכִי וַתֹּאמֶר מִפְּנֵי שָׂרַי גְּבִרְתִּי אָנֹכִי
בֹּרַחַת׃ 9 וַיֹּאמֶר לָהּ מַלְאַךְ יְהוָה שׁוּבִי
אֶל־גְּבִרְתֵּךְ וְהִתְעַנִּי תַּחַת יָדֶיהָ׃ 10 וַיֹּאמֶר
לָהּ מַלְאַךְ יְהוָה הַרְבָּה אַרְבֶּה אֶת־זַרְעֵךְ
וְלֹא יִסָּפֵר מֵרֹב׃ 11 וַיֹּאמֶר לָהּ מַלְאַךְ יְהוָה
הִנָּךְ הָרָה וְיֹלַדְתְּ בֵּן וְקָרָאת שְׁמוֹ יִשְׁמָעֵאל
כִּי־שָׁמַע יְהוָה אֶל־עָנְיֵךְ׃ 12 וְהוּא יִהְיֶה
פֶּרֶא אָדָם יָדוֹ בַכֹּל וְיַד כֹּל בּוֹ וְעַל־פְּנֵי כָל־
אֶחָיו יִשְׁכֹּן׃

### ANNUNCIATION OF THE BIRTH OF A SON (16:7–16)

The "Annunciation" is a biblical literary pattern (or "type-scene") in which a mother-to-be receives information from God or a divine messenger concerning the future birth of a male child. Often instructions or information are given about the hero's future. The female recipient of this knowledge frequently reacts with fear or wonder (see Genesis 18:9–15 where Sarah learns indirectly about her forthcoming pregnancy, and Judges 13:1–7 where Samson's mother-to-be learns that she shall have a son).

*7. **an angel of יהוה.*** This is the first report of a personal encounter between an individual woman and a divine being since Genesis 3; it is also the first time in the story that anyone addresses Hagar.

***at a spring of water.*** Water sources in the Bible are associated with fertility.

***8.*** For the first time, Hagar speaks and tells her story, which she does succinctly.

*9. **"Return."*** The ethical stance in the scene is one of accommodation to the existing power structure rather than encouragement to acts of self-liberation. In this system, the reward for submission is the promise of progeny.

***"I will greatly multiply your descendants."*** The formulaic blessing elsewhere offered only to patriarchs such as Abraham is here also promised to the heroine Hagar (see 13:16; 15:5; 26:4; 28:14). She thus receives a promise that parallels those to the patriarchs. She is the only woman in the Torah to be informed directly that her descendants (literally "her seed") will be numerous.

*11. **"Ishmael."*** The name means "God will listen"; it is a good omen for the boy, and a comment on God's attentiveness to Hagar's plight.

*12.* To be equated with a virile strong male animal is usually a positive metaphor in the ancient Near East (see the references to the bull and the wild-ox in Deuteronomy 33:17). The rest of the blessing should likewise be construed as positive, although this translator understood it differently.

***"he shall dwell."*** Ishmael will be the father of a people neighboring Israel.

13 So she called יהוה who had been speaking to her, "You are El Ro'i"—meaning by this, "Even here I have seen the back of the *One who looks upon me*!" 14 That is why that well—the one located between Kadesh and Bered—is called Be'er-lachai-ro'i.

15 Hagar bore to Abram a son, and Abram called his son whom Hagar had borne Ishmael. 16 When Hagar bore Ishmael to Abram, Abram was 86 years old.

17 When Abram was 99 years old, יהוה appeared to Abram and said to him, "I am El Shaddai —walk along before Me and be pure of heart, 2 and I will set a covenant between us, and multiply you exceedingly." 3 Abram fell on his face.

God spoke with him, saying, 4 "As for Me, here is My covenant with you: You shall be the father of a multitude of peoples. 5 No longer are you to be called Abram: your name is to be Abraham, for I

13 וַתִּקְרָא שֵׁם־יְהוָה הַדֹּבֵר אֵלֶיהָ אַתָּה אֵל
רֳאִי כִּי אָמְרָה הֲגַם הֲלֹם רָאִיתִי אַחֲרֵי
רֹאִי׃ 14 עַל־כֵּן קָרָא לַבְּאֵר בְּאֵר לַחַי רֹאִי
הִנֵּה בֵין־קָדֵשׁ וּבֵין בָּרֶד׃
15 וַתֵּלֶד הָגָר לְאַבְרָם בֵּן וַיִּקְרָא אַבְרָם שֶׁם־
בְּנוֹ אֲשֶׁר־יָלְדָה הָגָר יִשְׁמָעֵאל׃ 16 וְאַבְרָם
בֶּן־שְׁמֹנִים שָׁנָה וְשֵׁשׁ שָׁנִים בְּלֶדֶת־הָגָר
אֶת־יִשְׁמָעֵאל לְאַבְרָם׃ ס

יז וַיְהִי אַבְרָם בֶּן־תִּשְׁעִים שָׁנָה וְתֵשַׁע
שָׁנִים וַיֵּרָא יְהוָה אֶל־אַבְרָם וַיֹּאמֶר אֵלָיו
אֲנִי־אֵל שַׁדַּי הִתְהַלֵּךְ לְפָנַי וֶהְיֵה תָמִים׃
2 וְאֶתְּנָה בְרִיתִי בֵּינִי וּבֵינֶךָ וְאַרְבֶּה אוֹתְךָ
בִּמְאֹד מְאֹד׃ 3 וַיִּפֹּל אַבְרָם עַל־פָּנָיו
וַיְדַבֵּר אִתּוֹ אֱלֹהִים לֵאמֹר׃ 4 אֲנִי הִנֵּה
בְרִיתִי אִתָּךְ וְהָיִיתָ לְאַב הֲמוֹן גּוֹיִם׃
5 וְלֹא־יִקָּרֵא עוֹד אֶת־שִׁמְךָ אַבְרָם וְהָיָה

*13. "El Ro'i."* Literally, "God of my seeing." *"Even here . . . who looks upon me."* The clause is difficult to parse precisely. It seems to mean that Hagar feels lucky to be alive after a direct encounter with the Deity.

*14. Be'er-lachai-ro'i.* Literally, "the well of the living one of my seeing." The naming of a place after a theophany is a common biblical motif (cf. 28:19). However, Hagar is the only woman whose experience is enshrined in a place name. None of the matriarchs receive this honor. Such a privilege for the marginalized slave-woman—the outsider—is striking; the narrative views Hagar with sympathy and as having value.

## *Covenant and Circumcision* (17:1–27)

The Abrahamic covenant (Genesis 15) is now sealed by the rite of circumcision. The incising of the covenant on male bodies is a critical feature of Israelite self-identification and may perhaps be linked with the importance of male lineages in this ancient culture.

### COVENANT AND IMPLICATIONS OF CIRCUMCISION (17:1–14)

Motifs of progeny and land appear as the patriarch's transformation is effected by a name change and bodily marking.

*1. "El Shaddai."* An ancient name of the Deity, apparently meaning "God of the mountains" or "God of my breasts." Ancient Near Eastern and other deities are frequently associated with the mountains. The alternate meaning of *shaddai* as "breasts" perhaps hints at aspects of the feminine contained in the Deity. This name of God often appears in the Bible in a context where fertility is an issue. For example, Naomi uses this name in Ruth 1:20.

*5. "Abram . . . Abraham."* The name change marks a change in status. Abram and Abraham are variants, meaning "exalted father."

שְׁמְךָ אַבְרָהָם כִּי אַב־הֲמוֹן גּוֹיִם נְתַתִּיךָ׃
6 וְהִפְרֵתִי אֹתְךָ בִּמְאֹד מְאֹד וּנְתַתִּיךָ לְגוֹיִם
וּמְלָכִים מִמְּךָ יֵצֵאוּ׃ 7 וַהֲקִמֹתִי אֶת־בְּרִיתִי
בֵּינִי וּבֵינֶךָ וּבֵין זַרְעֲךָ אַחֲרֶיךָ לְדֹרֹתָם
לִבְרִית עוֹלָם לִהְיוֹת לְךָ לֵאלֹהִים וּלְזַרְעֲךָ
אַחֲרֶיךָ׃ 8 וְנָתַתִּי לְךָ וּלְזַרְעֲךָ אַחֲרֶיךָ אֵת ׀
אֶרֶץ מְגֻרֶיךָ אֵת כָּל־אֶרֶץ כְּנַעַן לַאֲחֻזַּת
עוֹלָם וְהָיִיתִי לָהֶם לֵאלֹהִים׃
9 וַיֹּאמֶר אֱלֹהִים אֶל־אַבְרָהָם וְאַתָּה אֶת־
בְּרִיתִי תִשְׁמֹר אַתָּה וְזַרְעֲךָ אַחֲרֶיךָ
לְדֹרֹתָם׃ 10 זֹאת בְּרִיתִי אֲשֶׁר תִּשְׁמְרוּ בֵּינִי
וּבֵינֵיכֶם וּבֵין זַרְעֲךָ אַחֲרֶיךָ הִמּוֹל לָכֶם כָּל־
זָכָר׃ 11 וּנְמַלְתֶּם אֵת בְּשַׂר עָרְלַתְכֶם וְהָיָה
לְאוֹת בְּרִית בֵּינִי וּבֵינֵיכֶם׃ 12 וּבֶן־שְׁמֹנַת
יָמִים יִמּוֹל לָכֶם כָּל־זָכָר לְדֹרֹתֵיכֶם יְלִיד
בָּיִת וּמִקְנַת־כֶּסֶף מִכֹּל בֶּן־נֵכָר אֲשֶׁר לֹא
מִזַּרְעֲךָ הוּא׃ 13 הִמּוֹל ׀ יִמּוֹל יְלִיד בֵּיתְךָ
וּמִקְנַת כַּסְפֶּךָ וְהָיְתָה בְרִיתִי בִּבְשַׂרְכֶם
לִבְרִית עוֹלָם׃ 14 וְעָרֵל ׀ זָכָר אֲשֶׁר לֹא־
יִמּוֹל אֶת־בְּשַׂר עָרְלָתוֹ וְנִכְרְתָה הַנֶּפֶשׁ
הַהִוא מֵעַמֶּיהָ אֶת־בְּרִיתִי הֵפַר׃ ס

am making you the father of a multitude of nations. 6 I am making you exceedingly fruitful, and turning you into nations; kings shall come forth from you; 7 I will establish My covenant with you, and with your descendants after you, for all their generations, an everlasting covenant: to be God to you and to your descendants after you. 8 I will give you and your descendants after you the land where you have sojourned, the whole land of Canaan, as an everlasting possession, and I will be their God."

9 God then said to Abraham, "As for you, observe My covenant—you and your descendants after you—in all your generations. 10 This is My covenant that you and your descendants after you are to observe: let every male among you be circumcised. 11 When the flesh of your foreskin has been circumcised, it shall become a sign of the covenant between us. 12 And in all your generations let every eight-day-old boy among you be circumcised, [whether it be] a homeborn slave or bought from foreigners, not of your own descent. 13 Let your homeborn slave and the one you buy be circumcised, so that My covenant may be in your flesh as an everlasting covenant. 14 An uncircumcised male who has not circumcised the flesh of his foreskin—that person shall be cut off from his people; he has broken My covenant."

*7–10.* Five times in this passage, God refers to the covenant's other party as "you and your descendants" (literally "seed"); this indicates that membership in the covenant is not limited to males, although every male is to bear circumcision as a mark of the covenant. This covenant is with Abraham and Sarah's offspring regardless of gender. Likewise the entire Israelite people is a party to the Covenant at Sinai, where Shabbat—not circumcision—is the covenantal *ot* (sign or mark), a sign that explicitly applies to all members of the community (Exodus 31:12–17).

*11.* ***"the flesh of your foreskin."*** That the key ritual for inclusion involves the male procreative organ reflects the male-oriented bent of the material and the worldview behind it. (See also Contemporary Reflection, p. 80.)

*12.* ***"slave."*** As in v. 27, circumcision marks a man as being inside the group, which includes slaves. (On slavery in Israelite culture, see at Exodus 21:1–11 and Leviticus 25:39–46.)

*14.* ***cut off.*** See at Leviticus 7:20.

***people.*** Heb. *ammim.* On the gender-inclusive sense of this term, see at Genesis 25:8.

[15]God then said to Abraham, "Sarai your wife—call her Sarai no more, for her name is [now] Sarah. [16]I will bless her and, too, I will give you a son through her; I will bless her and she shall become nations; rulers of peoples shall come from her."

[17]Abraham fell flat on his face and laughed, thinking: "Can a child be born to a man of 100? Can 90-year-old Sarah bear a child?" [18]Abraham then said to God: If only You would let Ishmael live [happily] before You! [19]But God said, "Nonetheless, your wife Sarah shall bear you a son, whom you shall call Isaac, and I will establish My covenant with him and his descendants after him as an everlasting covenant. [20]As for Ishmael, I have heard you. See, I have blessed him and made him fruitful and made him exceedingly numerous—he will father twelve princes; I will make him into a great nation. [21]But it is with Isaac, whom Sarah will bear for you at this time next year, that I will establish My covenant." [22]Done speaking with him, God ascended, away from Abraham.

[23]Abraham then took Ishmael his son and all his homeborn slaves and those who had been bought,

15 וַיֹּאמֶר אֱלֹהִים אֶל־אַבְרָהָם שָׂרַי אִשְׁתְּךָ
לֹא־תִקְרָא אֶת־שְׁמָהּ שָׂרָי כִּי שָׂרָה שְׁמָהּ׃
16 וּבֵרַכְתִּי אֹתָהּ וְגַם נָתַתִּי מִמֶּנָּה לְךָ בֵּן
וּבֵרַכְתִּיהָ וְהָיְתָה לְגוֹיִם מַלְכֵי עַמִּים מִמֶּנָּה
יִהְיוּ׃
17 וַיִּפֹּל אַבְרָהָם עַל־פָּנָיו וַיִּצְחָק וַיֹּאמֶר
בְּלִבּוֹ הַלְּבֶן מֵאָה־שָׁנָה יִוָּלֵד וְאִם־שָׂרָה
הֲבַת־תִּשְׁעִים שָׁנָה תֵּלֵד׃ 18 וַיֹּאמֶר
אַבְרָהָם אֶל־הָאֱלֹהִים לוּ יִשְׁמָעֵאל יִחְיֶה
לְפָנֶיךָ׃ 19 וַיֹּאמֶר אֱלֹהִים אֲבָל שָׂרָה
אִשְׁתְּךָ יֹלֶדֶת לְךָ בֵּן וְקָרָאתָ אֶת־שְׁמוֹ יִצְחָק
וַהֲקִמֹתִי אֶת־בְּרִיתִי אִתּוֹ לִבְרִית עוֹלָם
לְזַרְעוֹ אַחֲרָיו׃ 20 וּלְיִשְׁמָעֵאל שְׁמַעְתִּיךָ
הִנֵּה ׀ בֵּרַכְתִּי אֹתוֹ וְהִפְרֵיתִי אֹתוֹ וְהִרְבֵּיתִי
אֹתוֹ בִּמְאֹד מְאֹד שְׁנֵים־עָשָׂר נְשִׂיאִם יוֹלִיד
וּנְתַתִּיו לְגוֹי גָּדוֹל׃ 21 וְאֶת־בְּרִיתִי אָקִים
אֶת־יִצְחָק אֲשֶׁר תֵּלֵד לְךָ שָׂרָה לַמּוֹעֵד הַזֶּה
בַּשָּׁנָה הָאַחֶרֶת׃ 22 וַיְכַל לְדַבֵּר אִתּוֹ וַיַּעַל
אֱלֹהִים מֵעַל אַבְרָהָם׃
23 וַיִּקַּח אַבְרָהָם אֶת־יִשְׁמָעֵאל בְּנוֹ וְאֵת
כָּל־יְלִידֵי בֵיתוֹ וְאֵת כָּל־מִקְנַת כַּסְפּוֹ כָּל־

### REITERATION OF PROMISES OF A CHILD BY SARAH (17:15–22)

God's power over life is emphasized by the divine capacity to allow a ninety-year-old woman to bear a child. God's blessing of Sarah parallels that of Abraham, since both will be parents of many significant descendants. However, there are two striking differences. First, the promise is addressed directly to Abraham and not to Sarah. Second, only Sarah's son is the legitimate heir of the covenant, not any of Abraham's other sons. (See 25:1–5 for Abraham's additional sons.)

*15.* *"Sarah."* Sarai too receives a name change that marks an alteration in status. She is included in the covenant through her capacity to procreate.

*16.* *"I will bless her."* The blessing of Sarah is repeated twice in this verse. Like Abraham, she will be the founder of many nations and kings.

*17.* Like Abraham here, Sarah will laugh when she receives the promise of a son (see 18:12).

*18.* Abraham seems content with his son Ishmael as heir. It is God who insists that only Sarah's child will become the vehicle for God's covenant.

*19, 22.* The repetition of Sarah's unique role in both of these verses leaves no doubt that she is necessary for the covenant and its blessings. [In other words, the Torah conceives of the Israelite lineage not only in male terms. On women and lineage, see at 10:1 and the introduction to 22:20–24. *—Ed.*]

every male among Abraham's slaves, and on that
very day Abraham circumcised the flesh of their
foreskins as God had instructed him. 24Abraham
was 99 years old when he was circumcised in the
flesh of his foreskin, 25and Ishmael his son was 13
years old when he was circumcised in the flesh of
his foreskin. 26That very day both Abraham and
Ishmael his son were circumcised. 27And all the
people of his household—the homeborn slaves
and those bought from foreigners—were circumcised with him.

זָכָ֕ר בְּאַנְשֵׁ֖י בֵּ֣ית אַבְרָהָ֑ם וַיָּ֜מָל אֶת־בְּשַׂ֣ר
עָרְלָתָ֗ם בְּעֶ֙צֶם֙ הַיּ֣וֹם הַזֶּ֔ה כַּאֲשֶׁ֛ר דִּבֶּ֥ר אִתּ֖וֹ
אֱלֹהִֽים׃ 24 וְאַ֨בְרָהָ֔ם בֶּן־תִּשְׁעִ֥ים וָתֵ֖שַׁע
שָׁנָ֑ה בְּהִמֹּל֖וֹ בְּשַׂ֥ר עָרְלָתֽוֹ׃ 25 וְיִשְׁמָעֵ֣אל
בְּנ֔וֹ בֶּן־שְׁלֹ֥שׁ עֶשְׂרֵ֖ה שָׁנָ֑ה בְּהִ֨מֹּל֔וֹ אֵ֖ת
בְּשַׂ֥ר עָרְלָתֽוֹ׃ 26 בְּעֶ֙צֶם֙ הַיּ֣וֹם הַזֶּ֔ה נִמּ֖וֹל
אַבְרָהָ֑ם וְיִשְׁמָעֵ֖אל בְּנֽוֹ׃ 27 וְכָל־אַנְשֵׁ֤י בֵיתוֹ֙
יְלִ֣יד בָּ֔יִת וּמִקְנַת־כֶּ֖סֶף מֵאֵ֣ת בֶּן־נֵכָ֑ר נִמֹּ֖לוּ
אִתּֽוֹ׃ פ

## ADOPTION OF THE SIGN OF CIRCUMCISION (17:23–27)

The parashah concludes with membership in the group defined in terms of male circumcision. This should be read in light of the just-stated promise that the covenant will be bestowed only on Sarah's child, which makes clear how significant she in God's plan.

*—Susan Niditch*

# Another View

SARAH AND HAGAR neither speak to each other nor refer to each other by name, but their intertwined lives reflect both the systemic abuse women face and the combination of personal struggle and divine aid required to survive.

So that "it may go well for" him in Egypt, Abram asks Sarai to say she is his sister, and so the wife is taken into Pharaoh's house (Genesis 12). So that she may "have a son [or: child] through her" (16:2), Sarai places Hagar in Abram's bed. What the patriarch does to his wife, so the mistress does to her slave.

Like Sarai, the Egyptian Hagar—whose name echoes the word *ger* ("stranger")—is taken from her home to Canaan. This cycle of displacement and enslavement will continue: Hagar's descendants (the Ishmaelites) will sell Joseph into Egyptian slavery (37:27–28), and Hagar's people (the Egyptians) will "afflict" Sarah's descendants (Exodus 1:11–12) as Sarah "afflicted" Hagar (Genesis 16:6).

In Canaan, the women become rivals rather than companions. Rather than be "built up" through Hagar (see at 16:2), the post-menopausal Sarai "became light" (16:4) in the slave's eyes; Hagar grows weightier—both physically through pregnancy and emotionally as she recognizes her opportunity for advancement in Abram's household.

Abused by Sarai and ignored by Abram, Hagar flees to the wilderness. There an angel attends not to the Hebrew patriarch, but to the Egyptian slave: although sent back to her mistress, Hagar goes with the knowledge that "יהוה has heard (*shama*)" her affliction (16:11).

Similarly, Sarai herself—a foreign female trapped (enslaved?) in Pharaoh's house—receives divine aid. Her parallels to Hagar suggest that God acts not simply "because of Sarai" but specifically "upon Sarai's word" (*al d'var Sarai*, 12:17). Her crying out when

*In Canaan, the women become rivals rather than companions.*

Abram fails to act—for it is unclear how, or even if, Abram would extricate his wife—is what prompts God to send the plague (another Exodus foreshadowing) upon Pharaoh.

We later learn that the sons of Sarai and Hagar, although destined to be at odds (16:12), unite to bury their father (25:9): the cycle of abuse can be broken if children refuse to continue the system of abuse that entrapped their parents.

*—Amy-Jill Levine*

# Post-biblical Interpretations

***"I will make your name great"*** (12:2). Some midrashim describe the matriarchs as equal partners in God's covenant with Israel. Midrash *B'reishit Rabbah* 39.11 reports that "Abraham's coinage was widely distributed.... And what was on his coinage? An old man and an old woman (Abraham and Sarah) on one side, and a young man and a young woman (Isaac and Rebekah) on the other." This midrash also explained the repeated use of the words for "greatness" and "blessing": "greatness" refers to the patriarchs and "blessing" to the matriarchs.

***and the people*** [*nefesh*] ***they had acquired*** [*asu*, literally "made"] ***in Haran*** (12:5). According to *B'reishit Rabbah* 39.14, Sarah was an active agent of God's work in the world even when she and Abraham were still in Haran. Commenting on the literal sense, Rabbi Eleazar said in the name of Rabbi Yosi ben Zimra: "If all the inhabitants of the world got together to create [a living being], they would be unable to animate even a mosquito, but the Torah says *the people they had made*! These are the proselytes they converted." [The Midrash then asks:] If the verse refers to conversion, why does it employ the verb "made"? To teach you that when a person converts another, it is as if the one created the other. [The Midrash then points out a problem:] It should say, *he had made*—why does it say, *they had made*? Rav Huna said: "Abraham converted men and Sarah converted women."

**יהוה** ***then struck Pharaoh and his household with severe afflictions because of Sarai, Abram's wife*** (12:17). *B'reishit Rabbah* 41.2 imagines that when Sarai was trapped in Pharaoh's house, she prostrated herself "and said, 'Ruler of the Universe, Abram left [Haran] on the strength of promises, and I left on the strength of my faith. Now, Abram is outside this prison and I am inside!' The blessed Holy One said, 'All that I do, I do for you.'" This midrash suggests that Sarai's belief that she would share in Abram's blessings was called into question when she was trapped in Pharaoh's house while Abram walked free; however, she is reassured that it is precisely *because of Sarai, Abram's wife*, that Pharaoh is punished. Even more remarkably, Sarai reminds God that her willingness to leave Haran for an unknown destination is more praiseworthy than Abram's precisely because God has promised her nothing. Sarai serves here as a paradigm of a faithful follower of God, one who responds to God's call without the promise of reward.

***Now Abram's wife Sarai, who had not borne him a child, had an Egyptian slave named Hagar*** (16:1). The Rabbis gave Hagar an exalted lineage, identifying her as the daughter of Pharaoh. This tradition underscores Sarai's piety since it claims that when Pharaoh sees the wonders performed on her behalf, he exclaims, "Better my daughter be a servant in this household than mistress in another"; and later on, Sarai gives Hagar to Abram as a second wife, not as a concubine (*B'reishit Rabbah* 45.1). She also encourages Hagar to have sexual relations with Abram by emphasizing her husband's holiness (*B'reishit Rabbah* 45.3). According to *B'reishit Rabbah* 45.2, Sarai's decision that Abram should take Hagar as a wife is seen as an instance of her prophetic powers.

Still, the Rabbis are troubled by both Hagar's and Sarah's behavior. *B'reishit Rabbah* 45.4 relates that once Hagar became pregnant, she told other women that Sarah was clearly not the righteous woman she pretended to be, as evidenced by her infertility. Sarah, in turn, is criticized for harassing Hagar and for forcing Abraham to mediate between his wife and the mother of his unborn child (*B'reishit Rabbah* 45.5–6). While Hagar is criticized for treating her mistress disrespectfully, she is also worthy of divine protection. Five of God's messengers appear to Hagar as she flees Sarah's anger (*B'reishit Rabbah* 45.7). In naming God as the *One who looks upon me* (16:13), Hagar recognizes God as the One who sees the pain of the injured.

*The blessed Holy One said to Sarai, "All that I do, I do for you."*

***"Sarai your wife—call her Sarai no more, for her name is*** [*now*] ***Sarah"*** (17:15). *B'reishit Rabbah* 47.1 argues that Abraham and Sarah's relationship was unique. Rabbi Aha claims, "Abraham was crowned by Sarah rather than the reverse.... In most marriages, the husband commands, but in this case, God tells Abraham to obey all of Sarah's directives." At the age of ninety, Sarah is blessed with fertility—and, according to one tradition, God restored her youthful appearance (*B'reishit Rabbah* 47.2).

—*Dvora E. Weisberg*

# Contemporary Reflection

IS SARAH PART OF the *b'rit* (the covenant) that God establishes with Abraham? While our impulse might well be: "How can you ask such a question? *Of course* Sarah was part of the covenant," the details of the text force the question upon us. From the opening words calling Abraham to leave his homeland, and throughout this parashah, God speaks directly with Abraham, not with Sarah. Most dramatically, the sign of the *b'rit* in Genesis 17 is circumcision, clearly a male-only ritual.

One could argue that this ritual established a covenant only between God and Abraham, and Abraham's male descendants, and that women stood outside this religious cult altogether. Perhaps Sarah and the other matriarchs had their own religious practices and traditions, their own way of relating to God. Or, perhaps, they were passive members of this covenant between God and the men, valued as child-bearers, but otherwise on the periphery.

Let us consider another way to read the text. The critical element of the *b'rit* is the promise that Abraham will be fruitful and become the father of nations. Women's role as childbearers is therefore not ancillary but central to meaning of the covenant. And, while God does not address Sarah directly in Genesis 17, God refers to her and changes Sarah's name just like Abraham's—with the addition of the letter *heh* and with a parallel explanation: "she shall give rise to nations; rulers of peoples shall issue from her" (17:16).

Even when Abraham doubts Sarah's ability to bear children and suggests that God's covenant continue through Ishmael, God reassures him that the covenant will pass through Sarah's son, Isaac. Thus, God makes it clear that not *all* of Abraham's descendants are part of this covenant, *only the ones of Sarah.* This underscores Sarah's crucial role; it makes Sarah and Abraham, physically speaking, equal partners in the covenant.

In a sense, the greatest "sign" of this covenant is the fulfillment of God's promise that Sarah will bear a child. Sarah's pregnancy and Isaac's birth are tangible proof that God fulfills promises—and will similarly fulfill the other promises. Perhaps women after Sarah, as the ones bearing life, carry on the covenant between God and Abraham and Sarah's descendants in the most basic, physical way. Maybe circumcision is a male ritual to include men in a physical way in the covenant that women make real in their flesh when they bear the next generation.

This view has its own problems. Women of every nation bear children; how can childbearing be an essential characteristic or sign of a particular covenant?

## *Was Sarah part of the covenant?*

And what about women who will not bear children? Are they excluded from the covenant?

We need to look further. Scholars such as Savina Teubal argue that the world described in the Torah was preceded by a matriarchal system in which women held significant power, perhaps as priestesses. The decisive role of the matriarchs in determining the transmission of this male covenant (through Isaac and later Jacob) might be a trace from a time of greater female power (*Sarah the Priestess: The First Matriarch of Genesis,* 1984). Such intriguing possibilities open up different ways of understanding the Torah and our earliest history.

But regardless of its origins, Jews today understand the *b'rit* to include boys and girls, men and women. Numerous rituals have evolved to welcome baby girls into the covenant. Today, many Jews would not consider *not* having a *b'rit bat* ritual to welcome their daughter into the covenant. In some communities, a particular ritual provides the norm. In others, parents decide on the ritual, often together with the rabbi.

One covenant ceremony for girls is a simple foot-washing ritual often referred to as *B'rit R'chitzah* (the Covenant of Washing) or *B'rit N'tilat Raglayim* (the Covenant of Washing Feet). This ritual was first imagined into being by a small group of female rabbis and rabbinical students I participated in, at a retreat in Princeton in 1981. Eventually, this group crafted a ritual that continues to be used by individuals and communities in the United States, Israel, and other countries.

This idea—of washing a baby girl's feet to welcome her into the covenant between the Jewish people and God—grew out of our reading of Genesis 17–18. Immediately after the covenant in Genesis 17, when Abraham is circumcised, Abraham invites three visitors passing by for a meal (18:1–15). He washes their feet, a sign of welcome in his own day. Abraham's guests, who prove to be God's messengers, announce the future birth of Isaac.

Abraham's act of washing his guests' feet, as a sign of welcome, therefore, is closely associated with the original establishment of the *b'rit* in Genesis 17. Washing the baby's feet allows us to introduce water into the ritual, and to make the association with Miriam's Well, *mikveh* (ritual bath), and the healing, nurturing power of its *mayim chayim* (fresh water, literally "living waters"). The ritual includes readings and music that bring out these motifs and involves the parents as well. Usually the formal naming of the baby follows, with blessings over wine, as at a male circumcision. This ritual, simple and gentle, lends itself to individual adaptation and creativity (see "The Covenant of Washing: A Ceremony to Welcome Baby Girls Into the Covenant of Israel," *Menorah*, IV/3–4, May 1983).

Was Sarah part of the covenant? For centuries, Jews have looked to Sarah as the first of our foremothers. Women's *tekhines* (petitionary prayers) have called upon the God of Sarah, and pleaded in Sarah' name on women's behalf. As the covenant continues to be fulfilled by the commitment of every new generation of Jews, the impassioned voices of Jewish women bring forth Sarah's voice in our own time, with new clarity. Today we can celebrate a rediscovered Sarah as the mother of the covenant we the Jewish people share with God.

Even if *b'rit bat* rituals have not always been part of Jewish tradition, they are so today. Mothers who were welcomed into the covenant with such ceremonies now perform these same rituals with their own babies. Generations from now, Jews may be surprised to learn that baby girls were not always welcomed into the covenant with a ritual *b'rit bat*. As contemporary men and women today, we can look forward to seeing such rituals flourish and evolve in the years ahead.

—*Ruth H. Sohn*

# Voices

## L'chi Lach

Debbie Friedman

*Genesis 12:1*

*L'chi lach* to a land that I will show you
*Lech l'cha* to a place you do not know
*L'chi lach* on your journey I will bless you
And you shall be a blessing
You shall be a blessing *l'chi lach*

*L'chi lach* and I shall make your name great
*Lech l'cha* and all shall praise your name
*L'chi lach* to the place that I will show you
*L'simchat chayim l'chi lach*

NOTES

***L'chi lach.*** "Go forth" or "go forth to yourself," in a feminine address. These are the words of the male lover to the female lover in Song of Songs 2:10 and 13.

***Lech l'cha.*** "Go forth" or "go forth for yourself," in a masculine address. These are God's first words to Abram (Genesis 12:1).

## Lech L'cha

Andrea L. Weiss

*Genesis 12:1*

Go forth on a journey.

Go by yourself:
Standing at a crossroads
You venture from the known to the unknown.
Some journeys must be made alone.

Go to yourself:
Spiral inward and unwrap your past
And your potential.
Remember that the soul which you have made
Is unique and holy.

Go for yourself:
Smell the fragrance
Which spreads across the land
As you roam and wander.
Refresh yourself
Under the tree which grows by a spring
At the side of the road.
Make your name great and
Make your life a blessing.

## *Sarai*

Sherry Blumberg

*Genesis 12:5*

Leave my home?
My father, my mother?
Go with him
To this place unknown?

Follow this man
Who will cause me tears
Who may bring me laughter
Who says it's God's plan

So God, speak to me
That I may hear
Not just to him.
This is my plea!

## *My Freedom*

Else Lasker-Schüler (transl. Janine Canan)

*Genesis 16*

No one shall rob me
of my freedom.

If I die somewhere along the way,
you will come, dear Mother,

and lift me on your wing
to Heaven.

I know you were touched
by my lonely wandering,

the playful tick-tock
of my childlike heart.

## *At the Crossroads*

Hannah Senesh (transl. Ziva Shapiro)

*Genesis 12:1–5*

A voice called. I went.
I went, for it called.
I went, lest I fall.

At the crossroads
I blocked both ears with white frost
And cried
For what I had lost.

## *Fleeing*

Nelly Sachs (transl. Ruth and Matthew Mead)

*Genesis 16*

Fleeing,
what a reception
on the way—

Wrapped
in the wind's shawl
feet in the prayer of sand
which can never say amen
compelled
from fin to wing
and further—

The sick butterfly
will soon learn again of the sea—
This stone
with the fly's inscription
gave itself into my hand—

I hold instead of a homeland
the metamorphoses of the world—

## *Hagar*

Yocheved Bat-Miriam (transl. Zvi Jagendorf)

*Genesis 16*

Hanging her corals on the night she leaves
silent, possessing nothing.
A moon dives, a splash extinguished
in a wall of water.

Alone, just herself, the path
blown clean with white godhead
twists like a scrawled tattoo
trailing away from child and isolation.

—I won't come back, my country,
like Sphinx at the sun's door
I'll stay here to face
the fate and mystery of the desert land.

Branches rustle in imagined trees,
absent, a well burbles,
their mind-bound tranquility seeks
shelter in the moist shade of my eye,

and for him who stayed behind
who strayed and crossed the line
of a single love starred with silence,
parting and light.

With me, with me from far away
with myself bereft but free
I will be cloaked in make believe
in the drunken error of fantasy.

Wanderer, pursued by restlessness,
in love with impossible splendor,
he will gather us up forcefully to realize
the kingdom of his promised dream.

Stretch out the bow my son,
let the echo speak to the shaft,
so a quavering sound of welcome
may crown my diminishing path.

## *"And These Are Hagar's Poems to This Very Day"*

Anda Pinkerfeld-Amir (transl. Wendy Zierler)

*Genesis 16*

There in your tent, carpets are spread out,
caressed by the palms of your feet.
Every cord and thread, I wove myself,
every blossom raised from the mass of
threads—
my song of fingers for you.
Every flower, made magic by my love
to gladden your soul.

And how can these carpets soften for you,
how can your eyes drink the bounty of their
colors?
How is it that the petals don't burst
into blazing flame,
consuming your legs?
How can you walk complacently
on the blessing of my hands,
sent to you in my carpet,
your tranquility unconsumed by the wailing
of leaves,
weeping over my disgrace?

# וירא ◆ Vayeira

## GENESIS 18:1–22:24

### *Between Laughter and Tears*

PARASHAT VAYEIRA ("[he] appeared") describes several encounters between God and members of Abraham's household. In one sense, this parashah recounts the birth and survival of the next generation, Isaac and Rebekah: it begins with the announcement of Sarah's forthcoming pregnancy and Isaac's forthcoming birth (Genesis 18), continues with the challenges that stand in the way of the future, and concludes with Rebekah, Isaac's future wife (22:20–24).

Questions of identity and self-definition continue, as covenantal blessings demarcate the distinction between Sarah and Isaac on the one hand, and Hagar and Ishmael on the other. A subtext concerns Abraham's role in fulfilling God's plan. But the individual episodes do more than chart the hazards and successes that follow God's promises of progeny and land (see the previous parashah). Rather, they vividly depict the challenges, anguish, and joy that human beings experience as they create families and discover the complexities of multiple commitments.

The most famous of these episodes is the "Binding of Isaac," where Abraham is asked to sacrifice his beloved son (Genesis 22). This story has its counterpart in that of a mother with an imperiled child: the heart-wrenching story of Hagar and Ishmael in the wilderness (Genesis 21), in which Hagar despairs of her son's survival. Women are prominent throughout. At long last Sarah learns that she shall have a son (Genesis 18), and finally becomes a mother (Genesis 21). Tension between two mothers—Sarah and Hagar—each one seeking the welfare of her child, frames the story of Lot's daughters, who act together (Genesis 19). These tales offer glimpses into women's world and presumed concerns. The closing report about Rebekah's birth far from the land of Canaan sets the stage for when she becomes Isaac's wife (in the next parashah).

*These tales offer glimpses into women's world and presumed concerns.*

*—Tammi J. Schneider*

## Outline

I. Sarah Becomes a Mother
*Announcement of Isaac's Birth; Threats to Conception, Birth, and Survival* (18:1–21:7)

A. Divine messengers visit Abraham and Sarah, announcing that Sarah will become a mother (18:1–33)

B. Divine messengers visit Sodom and Lot, and Lot's daughters become mothers of nations (19:1–38)

C. Abraham and Sarah "visit" Abimelech (20:1–18)

D. Sarah becomes a mother (21:1–7)

II. First Threat to Isaac
*Two Mothers Clash Protecting Their Sons* (21:8–21)

A. Sarah seeks to protect Isaac: the expulsion of Hagar and Ishmael (vv. 8–13)

B. The rescue of Hagar and Ishmael in the wilderness (vv. 14–21)

III. Second Threat to Isaac
*Abraham's "Binding of Isaac," or "The Akedah"* (21:22–22:19)

A. Abraham settles in Beersheba (21:22–34)

B. Abraham's "test": the binding of Isaac (22:1–19)

IV. Preparation for the Future
*Rebekah's Birth* (22:20–24)

יהוה appeared to him by the oaks of
Mamre as he was sitting at the en-
trance of the tent at about the hottest time of the
day. 2Looking up, he saw: lo—three men standing
opposite him! Seeing [them], he ran from the entrance of the tent to meet them, and, bowing down
to the ground, 3he said, "My lords, if I have found
favor in your sight, please do not pass your servant
by. 4Let a little water be brought; then wash your
feet and recline under a tree, 5and let me bring a bit
of bread and you can restore yourselves. Then you
can go on—now that you have come across your
servant." And they responded: "Very well, do as
you propose."
6Abraham then hurried toward the tent, to
Sarah, and said, "Hurry, knead three measures of

יח וַיֵּרָא אֵלָיו יְהוָה בְּאֵלֹנֵי מַמְרֵא וְהוּא
יֹשֵׁב פֶּתַח־הָאֹהֶל כְּחֹם הַיּוֹם׃ 2 וַיִּשָּׂא
עֵינָיו וַיַּרְא וְהִנֵּה שְׁלֹשָׁה אֲנָשִׁים נִצָּבִים
עָלָיו וַיַּרְא וַיָּרָץ לִקְרָאתָם מִפֶּתַח הָאֹהֶל
וַיִּשְׁתַּחוּ אָרְצָה׃ 3 וַיֹּאמַר אֲדֹנָי אִם־נָא
מָצָאתִי חֵן בְּעֵינֶיךָ אַל־נָא תַעֲבֹר מֵעַל
עַבְדֶּךָ׃ 4 יֻקַּח־נָא מְעַט־מַיִם וְרַחֲצוּ רַגְלֵיכֶם
וְהִשָּׁעֲנוּ תַּחַת הָעֵץ׃ 5 וְאֶקְחָה פַת־לֶחֶם
וְסַעֲדוּ לִבְּכֶם אַחַר תַּעֲבֹרוּ כִּי־עַל־כֵּן
עֲבַרְתֶּם עַל־עַבְדְּכֶם וַיֹּאמְרוּ כֵּן תַּעֲשֶׂה
כַּאֲשֶׁר דִּבַּרְתָּ׃
6 וַיְמַהֵר אַבְרָהָם הָאֹהֱלָה אֶל־שָׂרָה וַיֹּאמֶר
מַהֲרִי שְׁלֹשׁ סְאִים קֶמַח סֹלֶת לוּשִׁי וַעֲשִׂי

## *Sarah Becomes a Mother*

### ANNOUNCEMENT OF ISAAC'S BIRTH; THREATS TO CONCEPTION, BIRTH, AND SURVIVAL (18:1–21:7)

Isaac's future was announced in Genesis 17 but only in this next section does Sarah learn that conception will soon occur (18:10).

### DIVINE MESSENGERS VISIT ABRAHAM AND SARAH, ANNOUNCING THAT SARAH WILL BECOME A MOTHER (18:1–33)

Because most of the angels' visit concerns the birth of Isaac—something Abraham knows about but Sarah does not—informing Sarah is likely the reason for the angels' appearance.

*1.* **יהוה** ***appeared to him.*** The text does not explicitly connect the events of this passage to the previous one where God tells Abraham that he and Sarah will have a child together (17:16), and where Abraham and his household are circumcised (17:23).

***him.*** [That is, Abraham; see 17:26. —*Ed.*]

*2.* ***three men.*** The reader knows that these are supernatural messengers. It is unclear whether Abraham recognizes this.

*6.* ***Abraham then hurried . . . to Sarah, and said, "Hurry, . . ."*** Sarah is 90 years old. It is the hottest part of the day and she is expected to do the baking. Is this because Abraham recognizes the

◗ The theme is threatened survival; and women ensure the safety of the next generation.

ANOTHER VIEW ➤ *105*

◗ . . . the only woman to whom God spoke directly, on account of her righteousness.

POST-BIBLICAL INTERPRETATIONS ➤ *105*

◗ The Torah provides us with opportunities to look honestly at ourselves.

CONTEMPORARY REFLECTION ➤ *107*

◗ But it was right that she / looked back. Not to be / curious . . .

VOICES ➤ *109*

wheat flour and bake some [bread-]cakes!” 7Abraham then ran to the herd and took a young calf, tender and sound, and gave it to the servant lad, who quickly prepared it. 8He took sour milk and [sweet] milk and the calf he had prepared and set [it all] before them; and as he stood over them under the tree, they ate.

9They then said to him, “Where is your wife Sarah?” “There, in the tent,” he replied. 10One of them then said, “Rest assured that I will return to you at this time next year, and your wife Sarah shall have a son.”

Now Sarah was listening at the entrance of the tent, behind him. 11Abraham and Sarah were old, well advanced in years; the way of women had ceased for Sarah—12so Sarah laughed inwardly, thinking: “Now that I am withered, will I have pleasure, with my lord so old!” 13But יהוה said to

עֻגוֹת׃ 7 וְאֶל־הַבָּקָר רָץ אַבְרָהָם וַיִּקַּח בֶּן־
בָּקָר רַךְ וָטוֹב וַיִּתֵּן אֶל־הַנַּעַר וַיְמַהֵר
לַעֲשׂוֹת אֹתוֹ׃ 8 וַיִּקַּח חֶמְאָה וְחָלָב וּבֶן־
הַבָּקָר אֲשֶׁר עָשָׂה וַיִּתֵּן לִפְנֵיהֶם וְהוּא־עֹמֵד
עֲלֵיהֶם תַּחַת הָעֵץ וַיֹּאכֵלוּ׃
9 וַיֹּאמְרוּ אֵלָיו אַיֵּה שָׂרָה אִשְׁתֶּךָ וַיֹּאמֶר
הִנֵּה בָאֹהֶל׃ 10 וַיֹּאמֶר שׁוֹב אָשׁוּב אֵלֶיךָ
כָּעֵת חַיָּה וְהִנֵּה־בֵן לְשָׂרָה אִשְׁתֶּךָ
וְשָׂרָה שֹׁמַעַת פֶּתַח הָאֹהֶל וְהוּא אַחֲרָיו׃
11 וְאַבְרָהָם וְשָׂרָה זְקֵנִים בָּאִים בַּיָּמִים
חָדַל לִהְיוֹת לְשָׂרָה אֹרַח כַּנָּשִׁים׃
12 וַתִּצְחַק שָׂרָה בְּקִרְבָּהּ לֵאמֹר אַחֲרֵי
בְלֹתִי הָיְתָה־לִּי עֶדְנָה וַאדֹנִי זָקֵן׃ 13 וַיֹּאמֶר

importance of these visitors and Sarah’s involvement raises the level of the meal? (On women as bakers, see at Exodus 16:3 and Leviticus 26:26.)

***9–10. “Where is your wife Sarah?” “There, in the tent.”*** The visitor knows of Abraham’s wife Sarah, asks where she is, and continues speaking in her hearing.

***10. “at this time next year . . . your wife Sarah shall have a son.”*** Since Abraham already knows that Sarah will have a son (17:16–19), the annunciation seems to be primarily for her benefit.

***Sarah was listening.*** For the first time, Sarah learns about her forthcoming pregnancy. Some use this verse to criticize Sarah for listening to other people’s conversations. But the speaker has asked specifically about Sarah, speaks knowing her proximity, and has information specifically designated for her. Clearly she is his audience.

***11. the way of women had ceased for Sarah.*** Sarah no longer menstruates, also meaning that she can no longer conceive. The reference highlights for the reader why she will be surprised by what she hears. [Rachel also refers to menstruation as “the way of women” (Genesis 31:35). See at Leviticus 15:19–24 for details about menstruation. —*Ed.*]

***12. Sarah laughed inwardly.*** Sarah, alone in the tent, responds with no outward sign—as opposed to Abraham, who fell on his face, laughing aloud, while he was in conversation with the Deity (17:17).

***“pleasure.”*** The word *ednah* is related to the word “Eden” (as in the Garden of Eden), alluding to a sense of “delight,” with a sexual connotation. Sarah is excited by the thought of an impending sexual encounter.

***“with my lord so old!”*** Sarah’s reaction reflects her delighted surprise in her husband’s abilities. God suggests a different reason (v. 13). This implies that Abraham and Sarah had stopped sexual relations, highlighting why the visitors inform her that the couple should renew them. Sarah does not doubt the Deity’s abilities, but rather Abraham’s.

Abraham, "Why is Sarah laughing so, thinking: 'Am I really going to bear a child, when I have grown so old?' 14 Is any wonder too difficult for יהוה? At this fixed time, next year, I will return to you, and Sarah shall have a son." 15 Sarah, then denied it, for she was afraid, and said, "I did not laugh"; but [God] said, "Ah, but you did laugh!"

יְהוָה אֶל־אַבְרָהָם לָמָּה זֶּה צָחֲקָה שָׂרָה
לֵאמֹר הַאַף אֻמְנָם אֵלֵד וַאֲנִי זָקַנְתִּי׃
14 הֲיִפָּלֵא מֵיְהוָה דָּבָר לַמּוֹעֵד אָשׁוּב אֵלֶיךָ
כָּעֵת חַיָּה וּלְשָׂרָה בֵן׃ 15 וַתְּכַחֵשׁ שָׂרָה ׀
לֵאמֹר לֹא צָחַקְתִּי כִּי ׀ יָרֵאָה וַיֹּאמֶר ׀ לֹא
כִּי צָחָקְתְּ׃

16 The men went up from there and gazed down upon Sodom, Abraham going along with them to send them off. 17 יהוה then thought: "Should I hide from Abraham what I am doing? 18 Yet Abraham is certain to become a great and populous nation, and through him all the nations of the earth shall be blessed! 19 For I have selected him, so that he may teach his children and those who come after him to

16 וַיָּקֻמוּ מִשָּׁם הָאֲנָשִׁים וַיַּשְׁקִפוּ עַל־פְּנֵי
סְדֹם וְאַבְרָהָם הֹלֵךְ עִמָּם לְשַׁלְּחָם׃
17 וַיהוָה אָמָר הַמְכַסֶּה אֲנִי מֵאַבְרָהָם
אֲשֶׁר אֲנִי עֹשֶׂה׃ 18 וְאַבְרָהָם הָיוֹ יִהְיֶה לְגוֹי
גָּדוֹל וְעָצוּם וְנִבְרְכוּ־בוֹ כֹּל גּוֹיֵי הָאָרֶץ׃
19 כִּי יְדַעְתִּיו לְמַעַן אֲשֶׁר יְצַוֶּה אֶת־בָּנָיו
וְאֶת־בֵּיתוֹ אַחֲרָיו וְשָׁמְרוּ דֶּרֶךְ יְהוָה

*13. "Why is Sarah laughing so."* Some interpreters have concluded, erroneously, that Sarah's laughter was derisive. When Abraham heard that he would have a child with Sarah, he "fell flat on his face and laughed, thinking: 'Can a child be born to a man of 100? Can 90-year-old Sarah bear a child?'" (17:17). Thus Sarah is actually now accused of Abraham's earlier actions. Since Sarah is alone in the tent when she laughs, is the Deity testing Abraham to determine if he will admit his own actions and protect Sarah? | [Tikva Frymer-Kensky, who considers Sarah's laughter as an expression of doubt, interprets God's response to Sarah this way: "God ignores Abraham's laughter but reacts to Sarah's. After all, Sarah should understand how important she is. . . . Sarah's importance in God's scheme means that God will have zero tolerance for skepticism from her" (*Women in Scripture*, 2000, p. 151). —*Ed.*]

*15. Sarah . . . was afraid.* Whom does Sarah fear? Most interpreters assume that Sarah is afraid of God. I contend that she fears Abraham. Sarah has no reason to fear God—who apparently comes to her rescue (in the house of the pharaoh, 12:10–18), blesses her and promises that she shall have a child (17:15–16), and has now sent messengers to tell her that she shall soon have her desired son. However, she does have reasons for fearing Abraham. He does not seem to object when she is taken to Pharaoh's palace (12:14–16); he allows Hagar to treat her with disrespect (16:3–4); and—insofar as the reader knows—has not informed her that they will be having a child.

*[God] said, "Ah, but you did laugh!"* The present translation adds "God" in brackets because the speaker is unnamed. The grammar supports the interpretation that the speaker is not God but Abraham (for details, see Tammi J. Schneider, *Sarah: Mother of Nations*, 2004, pp. 70–74). Another reason for doubting that God speaks here is that the Deity never speaks with Sarah before or after. And throughout 18:1–14 she is hidden from the visitors' sight, but not from Abraham's. Thus it is likely that it is Abraham who speaks these words, even though he has not heard her laugh.

*18:16–33.* The story of Abraham's attempted defense of Sodom follows directly the one in which he accuses his wife of his own actions.

keep the way of יהוה, doing what is right and just, so that יהוה may fulfill for Abraham all that has been promised him."

20 יהוה then said, "The outcry in Sodom and Gomorrah—how great it is; and their crime—how grave it is! 21 Let Me go down and determine whether they are wreaking havoc in equal measure to the shrieking that is coming to Me. If not, I will know."

22 The men now turned away and went toward Sodom, while Abraham remained standing before יהוה. 23 Abraham then came forward and said, "Will You indeed sweep away the innocent along with the wicked? 24 Suppose there are fifty innocent in the city—will You indeed sweep away the place, and not spare it for the sake of the fifty innocent who are in its midst? 25 Far be it from You to do such a thing, killing innocent and wicked alike, so that the innocent and the wicked suffer the same fate. Far be it from You! Must not the Judge of all the earth do justly?" 26 יהוה said, "If I find fifty innocent people in Sodom, I will pardon the whole place for their sake."

27 Again Abraham spoke: "Look now—let me undertake to speak up to my lord, though I am but dust and ashes: 28 What if the fifty innocent are five short; will you destroy the whole city because of five?" [God] answered, "If I find forty-five there, I will not destroy it."

29 Once more Abraham spoke up: "What if forty are found there?" And [God] answered, "For the sake of the forty, I will not do it."

30 Then he said, "Do not be angry, my lord, and let me speak: What if thirty are found there?" "If I find thirty there," said [God], "I will not do it."

31 And Abraham said, "Look now—let me undertake to speak up before my lord: What if twenty are found there?" And [God] said, "For the sake of the twenty, I will not destroy it."

לַעֲשׂוֹת צְדָקָה וּמִשְׁפָּט לְמַעַן הָבִיא יְהוָה
עַל־אַבְרָהָם אֵת אֲשֶׁר־דִּבֶּר עָלָיו׃
20 וַיֹּאמֶר יְהוָה זַעֲקַת סְדֹם וַעֲמֹרָה כִּי־רָבָּה
וְחַטָּאתָם כִּי כָבְדָה מְאֹד׃ 21 אֵרְדָה־נָּא
וְאֶרְאֶה הַכְּצַעֲקָתָהּ הַבָּאָה אֵלַי עָשׂוּ ׀ כָּלָה
וְאִם־לֹא אֵדָעָה׃
22 וַיִּפְנוּ מִשָּׁם הָאֲנָשִׁים וַיֵּלְכוּ סְדֹמָה
וְאַבְרָהָם עוֹדֶנּוּ עֹמֵד לִפְנֵי יְהוָה׃ 23 וַיִּגַּשׁ
אַבְרָהָם וַיֹּאמַר הַאַף תִּסְפֶּה צַדִּיק עִם־
רָשָׁע׃ 24 אוּלַי יֵשׁ חֲמִשִּׁים צַדִּיקִם בְּתוֹךְ
הָעִיר הַאַף תִּסְפֶּה וְלֹא־תִשָּׂא לַמָּקוֹם
לְמַעַן חֲמִשִּׁים הַצַּדִּיקִם אֲשֶׁר בְּקִרְבָּהּ׃
25 חָלִלָה לְּךָ מֵעֲשֹׂת ׀ כַּדָּבָר הַזֶּה לְהָמִית
צַדִּיק עִם־רָשָׁע וְהָיָה כַצַּדִּיק כָּרָשָׁע חָלִלָה
לָּךְ הֲשֹׁפֵט כָּל־הָאָרֶץ לֹא יַעֲשֶׂה מִשְׁפָּט׃
26 וַיֹּאמֶר יְהוָה אִם־אֶמְצָא בִסְדֹם חֲמִשִּׁים
צַדִּיקִם בְּתוֹךְ הָעִיר וְנָשָׂאתִי לְכָל־הַמָּקוֹם
בַּעֲבוּרָם׃
27 וַיַּעַן אַבְרָהָם וַיֹּאמַר הִנֵּה־נָא הוֹאַלְתִּי
לְדַבֵּר אֶל־אֲדֹנָי וְאָנֹכִי עָפָר וָאֵפֶר׃ 28 אוּלַי
יַחְסְרוּן חֲמִשִּׁים הַצַּדִּיקִם חֲמִשָּׁה הֲתַשְׁחִית
בַּחֲמִשָּׁה אֶת־כָּל־הָעִיר וַיֹּאמֶר לֹא אַשְׁחִית
אִם־אֶמְצָא שָׁם אַרְבָּעִים וַחֲמִשָּׁה׃
29 וַיֹּסֶף עוֹד לְדַבֵּר אֵלָיו וַיֹּאמַר אוּלַי
יִמָּצְאוּן שָׁם אַרְבָּעִים וַיֹּאמֶר לֹא אֶעֱשֶׂה
בַּעֲבוּר הָאַרְבָּעִים׃
30 וַיֹּאמֶר אַל־נָא יִחַר לַאדֹנָי וַאֲדַבֵּרָה אוּלַי
יִמָּצְאוּן שָׁם שְׁלֹשִׁים וַיֹּאמֶר לֹא אֶעֱשֶׂה
אִם־אֶמְצָא שָׁם שְׁלֹשִׁים׃
31 וַיֹּאמֶר הִנֵּה־נָא הוֹאַלְתִּי לְדַבֵּר אֶל־אֲדֹנָי
אוּלַי יִמָּצְאוּן שָׁם עֶשְׂרִים וַיֹּאמֶר לֹא
אַשְׁחִית בַּעֲבוּר הָעֶשְׂרִים׃

*23.* Abraham asks a daring question of God.

[32]Then Abraham said, "Let not my lord be angry, and let me speak up one last time: What if ten are found there?" And [God] said, "For the sake of the ten, I will not destroy it." [33]Then, done speaking to Abraham, יהוה departed; and Abraham returned to his place.

**19** That evening, the two [divine] emissaries came to Sodom, where Lot was sitting at the Sodom gate; seeing [them], Lot got up to greet them and, bowing all the way to the ground, [2]he said, "Come now, my lords, turn to your servant's house; stay there overnight and wash your feet; when you get up you can go on your way!" "No," said they, "we'll stay the night in the open." [3]He so pressed them, however, that they followed him and entered his house, where he made them a festive meal, baked unleavened bread, and they ate.

[4]They had yet to lie down when the townspeople, the people of Sodom, young and old alike, all the people, from every side, gathered around the house [5]and called to Lot, saying, "Where are the men who came to you tonight? Bring them out so we can have them." [6]Lot went out to them at the entrance and shut the door behind him. [7]He said, "Please, brothers, do no evil! [8]Look—I have two daughters who have never been intimate with a

32 וַיֹּאמֶר אַל־נָא יִחַר לַאדֹנָי וַאֲדַבְּרָה אַךְ־
הַפַּעַם אוּלַי יִמָּצְאוּן שָׁם עֲשָׂרָה וַיֹּאמֶר לֹא
אַשְׁחִית בַּעֲבוּר הָעֲשָׂרָה׃ 33 וַיֵּלֶךְ יְהוָה
כַּאֲשֶׁר כִּלָּה לְדַבֵּר אֶל־אַבְרָהָם וְאַבְרָהָם
שָׁב לִמְקֹמוֹ׃
יט וַיָּבֹאוּ שְׁנֵי הַמַּלְאָכִים סְדֹמָה בָּעֶרֶב
וְלוֹט יֹשֵׁב בְּשַׁעַר־סְדֹם וַיַּרְא־לוֹט וַיָּקָם
לִקְרָאתָם וַיִּשְׁתַּחוּ אַפַּיִם אָרְצָה׃ 2 וַיֹּאמֶר
הִנֶּה נָּא־אֲדֹנַי סוּרוּ נָא אֶל־בֵּית עַבְדְּכֶם
וְלִינוּ וְרַחֲצוּ רַגְלֵיכֶם וְהִשְׁכַּמְתֶּם וַהֲלַכְתֶּם
לְדַרְכְּכֶם וַיֹּאמְרוּ לֹּא כִּי בָרְחוֹב נָלִין׃
3 וַיִּפְצַר־בָּם מְאֹד וַיָּסֻרוּ אֵלָיו וַיָּבֹאוּ אֶל־
בֵּיתוֹ וַיַּעַשׂ לָהֶם מִשְׁתֶּה וּמַצּוֹת אָפָה
וַיֹּאכֵלוּ׃
4 טֶרֶם יִשְׁכָּבוּ וְאַנְשֵׁי הָעִיר אַנְשֵׁי סְדֹם
נָסַבּוּ עַל־הַבַּיִת מִנַּעַר וְעַד־זָקֵן כָּל־הָעָם
מִקָּצֶה׃ 5 וַיִּקְרְאוּ אֶל־לוֹט וַיֹּאמְרוּ לוֹ אַיֵּה
הָאֲנָשִׁים אֲשֶׁר־בָּאוּ אֵלֶיךָ הַלָּיְלָה הוֹצִיאֵם
אֵלֵינוּ וְנֵדְעָה אֹתָם׃ 6 וַיֵּצֵא אֲלֵהֶם לוֹט
הַפֶּתְחָה וְהַדֶּלֶת סָגַר אַחֲרָיו׃ 7 וַיֹּאמַר אַל־
נָא אַחַי תָּרֵעוּ׃ 8 הִנֵּה־נָא לִי שְׁתֵּי בָנוֹת
אֲשֶׁר לֹא־יָדְעוּ אִישׁ אוֹצִיאָה־נָּא אֶתְהֶן

*33. his place.* Either his dwelling-place (see v. 16), or his proper place of obeying—rather than debating with—the Deity.

### DIVINE MESSENGERS VISIT SODOM AND LOT, AND LOT'S DAUGHTERS BECOME MOTHERS OF NATIONS (19:1–38)

The visit to Sodom is a "test" of sorts (note Genesis 22) to determine the worthiness of the city and of Lot. Sodom has been mentioned several times already, and never positively (Genesis 13–14). Lot and his family are a major focus of this section. Since the parashah concerns establishing the next generation, and Lot is the nephew of Abraham and potential heir, then an evaluation of Lot is critical. [The story of Lot's daughters and their incestuous intercourse with their father (19:30–38) possibly seeks to account for why Isaac does not marry one of them, who as his nearby cousins would otherwise be prime candidates. —*Ed.*]

*5. "so we can have them."* Literally, "so we can know them," which carries a sexual connotation (see at 4:1).

*8.* Lot offers his daughters instead of the men. His effort to protect the visitors reflects his belief that male rape is worse than female rape, even of his own daughters. | Here, angels will save the women; in a similar incident in Judges 19, another woman is not so fortunate when she and her hus-

man; let me bring them out for you, and do to
them as you please. But do nothing to these men,
for they have come under the shelter of my roof."
9But they said, "Get out of the way!" And they said,
"This fellow comes here to stay a while, and now he
wants to act the judge! Well, we will make it worse
for you than for them!" They pressed the man Lot
hard as they advanced to break down the door,
10but the men reached out and pulled Lot toward
them into the house and shut the door, 11striking
every one of the men, large and small, who were
near the entrance of the house, with a blinding
light, so that they were unable to find the entrance.
12The men said to Lot, "Whoever is still with
you here—son-in-law, your sons and daughters, all
your property in the city—get them out of here,
13because we are going to destroy this place; the
outcry to יהוה against the people in it is so great,
that יהוה has sent us to destroy it." 14So Lot went
out and spoke to his sons-in-law, his daughters'
husbands, saying, "Up! Get out of this place, because יהוה is destroying the city"; but to his sons-
in-law he appeared to be joking.
15Just as dawn was rising the [divine] emissaries
rushed Lot, saying, "Up! Take your wife and your
two daughters who are here, or you will be caught
up in the city's punishment." 16As he vacillated, the
men, in יהוה's pity for him, seized his hand, his
wife's, and those of his two daughters, and took
them out, setting them down outside the city.
17Having taken them outside, one said, "Flee
for your life! Do not look behind you and do not
stand anywhere on the plain; flee to the hills or you

אֲלֵיכֶם וַעֲשׂוּ לָהֶן כַּטּוֹב בְּעֵינֵיכֶם רַק
לָאֲנָשִׁים הָאֵל אַל־תַּעֲשׂוּ דָבָר כִּי־עַל־כֵּן
בָּאוּ בְּצֵל קֹרָתִי׃ 9 וַיֹּאמְרוּ ׀ גֶּשׁ־הָלְאָה
וַיֹּאמְרוּ הָאֶחָד בָּא־לָגוּר וַיִּשְׁפֹּט שָׁפוֹט
עַתָּה נָרַע לְךָ מֵהֶם וַיִּפְצְרוּ בָאִישׁ בְּלוֹט
מְאֹד וַיִּגְּשׁוּ לִשְׁבֹּר הַדָּלֶת׃ 10 וַיִּשְׁלְחוּ
הָאֲנָשִׁים אֶת־יָדָם וַיָּבִיאוּ אֶת־לוֹט אֲלֵיהֶם
הַבָּיְתָה וְאֶת־הַדֶּלֶת סָגָרוּ׃ 11 וְאֶת־
הָאֲנָשִׁים אֲשֶׁר־פֶּתַח הַבַּיִת הִכּוּ בַּסַּנְוֵרִים
מִקָּטֹן וְעַד־גָּדוֹל וַיִּלְאוּ לִמְצֹא הַפָּתַח׃
12 וַיֹּאמְרוּ הָאֲנָשִׁים אֶל־לוֹט עֹד מִי־לְךָ פֹה
חָתָן וּבָנֶיךָ וּבְנֹתֶיךָ וְכֹל אֲשֶׁר־לְךָ בָּעִיר
הוֹצֵא מִן־הַמָּקוֹם׃ 13 כִּי־מַשְׁחִתִים אֲנַחְנוּ
אֶת־הַמָּקוֹם הַזֶּה כִּי־גָדְלָה צַעֲקָתָם אֶת־
פְּנֵי יְהוָה וַיְשַׁלְּחֵנוּ יְהוָה לְשַׁחֲתָהּ׃ 14 וַיֵּצֵא
לוֹט וַיְדַבֵּר ׀ אֶל־חֲתָנָיו ׀ לֹקְחֵי בְנֹתָיו וַיֹּאמֶר
קוּמוּ צְּאוּ מִן־הַמָּקוֹם הַזֶּה כִּי־מַשְׁחִית
יְהוָה אֶת־הָעִיר וַיְהִי כִמְצַחֵק בְּעֵינֵי
חֲתָנָיו׃
15 וּכְמוֹ הַשַּׁחַר עָלָה וַיָּאִיצוּ הַמַּלְאָכִים
בְּלוֹט לֵאמֹר קוּם קַח אֶת־אִשְׁתְּךָ וְאֶת־
שְׁתֵּי בְנֹתֶיךָ הַנִּמְצָאֹת פֶּן־תִּסָּפֶה בַּעֲוֺן
הָעִיר׃ 16 וַיִּתְמַהְמָהּ ׀ וַיַּחֲזִיקוּ הָאֲנָשִׁים
בְּיָדוֹ וּבְיַד־אִשְׁתּוֹ וּבְיַד שְׁתֵּי בְנֹתָיו בְּחֶמְלַת
יְהוָה עָלָיו וַיֹּצִאֻהוּ וַיַּנִּחֻהוּ מִחוּץ לָעִיר׃
17 וַיְהִי כְהוֹצִיאָם אֹתָם הַחוּצָה וַיֹּאמֶר
הִמָּלֵט עַל־נַפְשֶׁךָ אַל־תַּבִּיט אַחֲרֶיךָ וְאַל־
תַּעֲמֹד בְּכָל־הַכִּכָּר הָהָרָה הִמָּלֵט פֶּן־

band visit and she is offered in lieu of him to a mob. She is repeatedly molested by the mob and dies soon after. The incident triggers a civil war in retaliation.

*17–23.* After the city is destroyed, Lot—as leader of his family—appears overwhelmed by the enormity of the situation and unable to guide and protect his family. This seems to be what leads to his wife's immobilization and his daughters' risky actions.

*17. "Do not look behind you."* These words are addressed in masculine singular language; it may be construed that they were spoken only to Lot.

will be swept away!" [18]But Lot said to them, "No, please, my lords! [19]Look—your servant has found favor in your sight; the kindness with which you have treated me by keeping me alive has been great—but I cannot flee to the hills; the evil may take hold of me and I shall die. [20]Look—yonder town is near enough to escape to, and it is tiny; let me flee there and save my life—it is tiny." [21]He replied to him, "See, now, I am showing you favor in this matter too, not overthrowing the town you have spoken of. [22]Flee there quickly, for I can do nothing until you get there." (That is why the city is called Zoar.)

[23]The sun was rising over the land as Lot was going down to Zoar, [24]and יהוה rained upon Sodom and Gomorrah brimstone and fire—from יהוה—out of the heavens, [25]overthrowing these cities and the entire plain, all the cities' inhabitants and what grew in the soil. [26]And his wife looked behind him and became a pillar of salt.

[27]Abraham rose early in the morning and [went] to the place where he had previously stood before יהוה. [28]As he gazed down upon Sodom and Gomorrah and upon the whole face of the plain, lo—fumes were rising from the earth like fumes from a furnace. [29]But when God destroyed the cities of the plain, God remembered Abraham and, when overthrowing the cities in which Lot had lived, sent Lot away from the upheaval. [30]Together with his two daughters, Lot then went up from Zoar to live in

תִּסָּפֶה: 18 וַיֹּאמֶר לוֹט אֲלֵהֶם אַל־נָא אֲדֹנָי:
19 הִנֵּה־נָא מָצָא עַבְדְּךָ חֵן בְּעֵינֶיךָ וַתַּגְדֵּל
חַסְדְּךָ אֲשֶׁר עָשִׂיתָ עִמָּדִי לְהַחֲיוֹת אֶת־
נַפְשִׁי וְאָנֹכִי לֹא אוּכַל לְהִמָּלֵט הָהָרָה פֶּן־
תִּדְבָּקַנִי הָרָעָה וָמַתִּי: 20 הִנֵּה־נָא הָעִיר
הַזֹּאת קְרֹבָה לָנוּס שָׁמָּה וְהִוא מִצְעָר
אִמָּלְטָה נָּא שָׁמָּה הֲלֹא מִצְעָר הִוא וּתְחִי
נַפְשִׁי: 21 וַיֹּאמֶר אֵלָיו הִנֵּה נָשָׂאתִי פָנֶיךָ
גַּם לַדָּבָר הַזֶּה לְבִלְתִּי הָפְכִּי אֶת־הָעִיר
אֲשֶׁר דִּבַּרְתָּ: 22 מַהֵר הִמָּלֵט שָׁמָּה כִּי לֹא
אוּכַל לַעֲשׂוֹת דָּבָר עַד־בֹּאֲךָ שָׁמָּה עַל־כֵּן
קָרָא שֵׁם־הָעִיר צוֹעַר:
23 הַשֶּׁמֶשׁ יָצָא עַל־הָאָרֶץ וְלוֹט בָּא צֹעֲרָה:
24 וַיהוָה הִמְטִיר עַל־סְדֹם וְעַל־עֲמֹרָה
גָּפְרִית וָאֵשׁ מֵאֵת יְהוָה מִן־הַשָּׁמָיִם:
25 וַיַּהֲפֹךְ אֶת־הֶעָרִים הָאֵל וְאֵת כָּל־הַכִּכָּר
וְאֵת כָּל־יֹשְׁבֵי הֶעָרִים וְצֶמַח הָאֲדָמָה:
26 וַתַּבֵּט אִשְׁתּוֹ מֵאַחֲרָיו וַתְּהִי נְצִיב מֶלַח:
27 וַיַּשְׁכֵּם אַבְרָהָם בַּבֹּקֶר אֶל־הַמָּקוֹם
אֲשֶׁר־עָמַד שָׁם אֶת־פְּנֵי יְהוָה: 28 וַיַּשְׁקֵף
עַל־פְּנֵי סְדֹם וַעֲמֹרָה וְעַל כָּל־פְּנֵי אֶרֶץ
הַכִּכָּר וַיַּרְא וְהִנֵּה עָלָה קִיטֹר הָאָרֶץ כְּקִיטֹר
הַכִּבְשָׁן: 29 וַיְהִי בְּשַׁחֵת אֱלֹהִים אֶת־עָרֵי
הַכִּכָּר וַיִּזְכֹּר אֱלֹהִים אֶת־אַבְרָהָם וַיְשַׁלַּח
אֶת־לוֹט מִתּוֹךְ הַהֲפֵכָה בַּהֲפֹךְ אֶת־הֶעָרִים
אֲשֶׁר־יָשַׁב בָּהֵן לוֹט: 30 וַיַּעַל לוֹט מִצּוֹעַר

***26. his wife looked behind him.*** This is precisely what Lot is warned against. Nowhere does the text indicate that he passes this information to his wife and daughters. The question remains: Does Lot's wife not know about the warning—or does she look back in spite of it?

***and became a pillar of salt.*** She is reluctant to ignore what happens to those she leaves behind, and this concern costs her life.

***30–38.*** Lot's daughters become mothers of nations that—through him—are related to the line of Abraham. Fearful that humankind has been annihilated, the daughters (the same ones whom Lot offered to the town's men earlier?) take drastic measures to perpetuate life. Like Tamar (see Genesis 38), they break taboos. Their sons produce the nations Moab and Ammon, Israel's eastern neighbors.

the hill country, for he was afraid to live in Zoar; so he lived in a cave, he and his two daughters.

[31]The first-born now said to the younger, "Our father is old, and there is no man left on earth to couple with us in the way of all the earth. [32]Let us give our father wine to drink and lie with him, and give life to offspring through our father." [33]So that night they gave their father wine to drink; the first-born then went and lay with her father, who had no awareness of her lying down and getting up.

[34]On the morrow the first-born said to the younger, "Seeing that last night I lay with my father, let us give him wine to drink tonight as well; then you go and lie with him, so that we can give life to offspring through our father." [35]So that night too they gave their father wine to drink; the younger got up and lay with him, and he had no awareness of her lying down and getting up.

[36]Lot's two daughters became pregnant through their father. [37]The first-born bore a son and named him Moab; he is the ancestor of the present-day Moabites. [38]The younger, too, bore a son and named him Ben-ammi; he is the ancestor of the present-day Ammonites.

וַיֵּשֶׁב בָּהָר וּשְׁתֵּי בְנֹתָיו עִמּוֹ כִּי יָרֵא לָשֶׁבֶת
בְּצוֹעַר וַיֵּשֶׁב בַּמְּעָרָה הוּא וּשְׁתֵּי בְנֹתָיו׃
31 וַתֹּאמֶר הַבְּכִירָה אֶל־הַצְּעִירָה אָבִינוּ זָקֵן
וְאִישׁ אֵין בָּאָרֶץ לָבוֹא עָלֵינוּ כְּדֶרֶךְ
כָּל־הָאָרֶץ׃ 32 לְכָה נַשְׁקֶה אֶת־אָבִינוּ יַיִן
וְנִשְׁכְּבָה עִמּוֹ וּנְחַיֶּה מֵאָבִינוּ זָרַע׃
33 וַתַּשְׁקֶיןָ אֶת־אֲבִיהֶן יַיִן בַּלַּיְלָה הוּא
וַתָּבֹא הַבְּכִירָה וַתִּשְׁכַּב אֶת־אָבִיהָ וְלֹא־
יָדַע בְּשִׁכְבָהּ וּבְקוּמָהּ׃
34 וַיְהִי מִמָּחֳרָת וַתֹּאמֶר הַבְּכִירָה אֶל־
הַצְּעִירָה הֵן־שָׁכַבְתִּי אֶמֶשׁ אֶת־אָבִי נַשְׁקֶנּוּ
יַיִן גַּם־הַלַּיְלָה וּבֹאִי שִׁכְבִי עִמּוֹ וּנְחַיֶּה
מֵאָבִינוּ זָרַע׃ 35 וַתַּשְׁקֶיןָ גַּם בַּלַּיְלָה הַהוּא
אֶת־אֲבִיהֶן יָיִן וַתָּקָם הַצְּעִירָה וַתִּשְׁכַּב עִמּוֹ
וְלֹא־יָדַע בְּשִׁכְבָהּ וּבְקֻמָהּ׃
36 וַתַּהֲרֶיןָ שְׁתֵּי בְנוֹת־לוֹט מֵאֲבִיהֶן׃
37 וַתֵּלֶד הַבְּכִירָה בֵּן וַתִּקְרָא שְׁמוֹ מוֹאָב
הוּא אֲבִי־מוֹאָב עַד־הַיּוֹם׃ 38 וְהַצְּעִירָה
גַם־הִוא יָלְדָה בֵּן וַתִּקְרָא שְׁמוֹ בֶּן־עַמִּי הוּא
אֲבִי בְנֵי־עַמּוֹן עַד־הַיּוֹם׃ ס

*31.* The daughters are living in a cave and think they are the only ones on earth. It also means they do not know their great-uncle Abraham's family is nearby. The motive for what follows: ensure that life on earth continues.

*33–34. lay with her father.* Oddly, incest laws in Leviticus and Deuteronomy do not explicitly prohibit sexual relations between a father and his daughter (see at Leviticus 18:6–24). Technically speaking, the daughters break no biblical law. Nonetheless, the daughters do seem to break a taboo (which explains why they first get their father drunk), yet the text does not condemn their actions.

*"so that we can give life to offspring through our father."* The motive of the older daughter is clear: perpetuate life in a world that seems to them to have no other men.

*34.* The older daughter ensures that her younger sister is not without the opportunity to conceive a child. Their cooperation contrasts with the competition between Rachel and Leah (Genesis 29–30).

*37–38. Moabites . . . Ammonites.* Two nations that according to this story are related to Israel. Deuteronomy 23:4 excludes Ammonites and Moabites from joining the Israelite community. The Book of Ruth, however, offers a different perspective in that it portrays Ruth the Moabite as the ancestress of King David.

20 Abraham then journeyed from there toward the Negev and dwelt between Kadesh and Shur, settling in Gerar. 2Abraham said of his wife Sarah, "She is my sister," and Abimelech king of Gerar sent [men] to seize Sarah.

3God now came to Abimelech in a dream of the night, saying to him, "Look—you are a dead man because of the woman you have taken; she is a married woman!" 4Abimelech had not touched her and he said, "My lord, will you slay a completely innocent folk! 5Did he not tell me, 'She is my sister'? And she too said, 'He is my brother.' I did this with a pure heart and clean hands!" 6In the dream God said to him, "I do indeed know that you did this with a pure heart, and it is I who held you back from sinning against Me; therefore I did not let you touch her. 7Now return the man's wife—he is a prophet and will intercede for you, so that you may live. But if you do not return [her], know that you will most certainly die, you and yours."

8When Abimelech woke up early in the morning he summoned all his retainers and drummed the whole story into their ears, and they became filled with fear. 9He then summoned Abraham and said to him, "What have you done to us? How had I sinned against you that you brought a great sin upon me and my kingdom? You did things to me that should not be done!" 10Abimelech said to Abraham, "What were you thinking of, that you

כ וַיִּסַּ֨ע מִשָּׁ֤ם אַבְרָהָם֙ אַ֣רְצָה הַנֶּ֔גֶב וַיֵּ֥שֶׁב בֵּין־קָדֵ֖שׁ וּבֵ֣ין שׁ֑וּר וַיָּ֖גָר בִּגְרָֽר׃ 2 וַיֹּ֧אמֶר אַבְרָהָ֛ם אֶל־שָׂרָ֥ה אִשְׁתּ֖וֹ אֲחֹ֣תִי הִ֑וא וַיִּשְׁלַ֗ח אֲבִימֶ֙לֶךְ֙ מֶ֣לֶךְ גְּרָ֔ר וַיִּקַּ֖ח אֶת־שָׂרָֽה׃

3 וַיָּבֹ֧א אֱלֹהִ֛ים אֶל־אֲבִימֶ֖לֶךְ בַּחֲל֣וֹם הַלָּ֑יְלָה וַיֹּ֣אמֶר ל֗וֹ הִנְּךָ֥ מֵת֙ עַל־הָאִשָּׁ֣ה אֲשֶׁר־לָקַ֔חְתָּ וְהִ֖וא בְּעֻ֥לַת בָּֽעַל׃ 4 וַאֲבִימֶ֕לֶךְ לֹ֥א קָרַ֖ב אֵלֶ֑יהָ וַיֹּאמַ֕ר אֲדֹנָ֕י הֲג֥וֹי גַּם־צַדִּ֖יק תַּהֲרֹֽג׃ 5 הֲלֹ֨א ה֤וּא אָֽמַר־לִי֙ אֲחֹ֣תִי הִ֔וא וְהִֽיא־גַם־הִ֥וא אָֽמְרָ֖ה אָחִ֣י ה֑וּא בְּתָם־לְבָבִ֛י וּבְנִקְיֹ֥ן כַּפַּ֖י עָשִׂ֥יתִי זֹֽאת׃ 6 וַיֹּאמֶר֩ אֵלָ֨יו הָֽאֱלֹהִ֜ים בַּחֲלֹ֗ם גַּ֣ם אָֽנֹכִ֤י יָדַ֙עְתִּי֙ כִּ֤י בְתָם־לְבָֽבְךָ֙ עָשִׂ֣יתָ זֹּ֔את וָאֶחְשֹׂ֧ךְ גַּם־אָנֹכִ֛י אֽוֹתְךָ֖ מֵחֲטוֹ־לִ֑י עַל־כֵּ֥ן לֹא־נְתַתִּ֖יךָ לִנְגֹּ֥עַ אֵלֶֽיהָ׃ 7 וְעַתָּ֗ה הָשֵׁ֤ב אֵֽשֶׁת־הָאִישׁ֙ כִּֽי־נָבִ֣יא ה֔וּא וְיִתְפַּלֵּ֥ל בַּֽעַדְךָ֖ וֶֽחְיֵ֑ה וְאִם־אֵֽינְךָ֣ מֵשִׁ֗יב דַּ֚ע כִּי־מ֣וֹת תָּמ֔וּת אַתָּ֖ה וְכָל־אֲשֶׁר־לָֽךְ׃

8 וַיַּשְׁכֵּ֨ם אֲבִימֶ֜לֶךְ בַּבֹּ֗קֶר וַיִּקְרָא֙ לְכָל־עֲבָדָ֔יו וַיְדַבֵּ֛ר אֶת־כָּל־הַדְּבָרִ֥ים הָאֵ֖לֶּה בְּאָזְנֵיהֶ֑ם וַיִּֽירְא֥וּ הָאֲנָשִׁ֖ים מְאֹֽד׃ 9 וַיִּקְרָ֨א אֲבִימֶ֜לֶךְ לְאַבְרָהָ֗ם וַיֹּ֨אמֶר ל֜וֹ מֶֽה־עָשִׂ֤יתָ לָּ֙נוּ֙ וּמֶֽה־חָטָ֣אתִי לָ֔ךְ כִּֽי־הֵבֵ֧אתָ עָלַ֛י וְעַל־מַמְלַכְתִּ֖י חֲטָאָ֣ה גְדֹלָ֑ה מַעֲשִׂים֙ אֲשֶׁ֣ר לֹא־יֵֽעָשׂ֔וּ עָשִׂ֖יתָ עִמָּדִֽי׃ 10 וַיֹּ֥אמֶר אֲבִימֶ֖לֶךְ אֶל־אַבְרָהָ֑ם מָ֣ה רָאִ֔יתָ כִּ֥י עָשִׂ֖יתָ אֶת־הַדָּבָ֥ר

• • • • • • • • • • • • • • • • • • • • • • • •

ABRAHAM AND SARAH "VISIT"
ABIMELECH (20:1–18)

For a second time, Abraham hands over his wife to a king (see 12:10–20; compare 26:1–11). His actions here are more problematic both because he has done it before, and because his wife is supposed to bear him a child soon.

2. *Abraham said of his wife Sarah, "She is my sister."* In the earlier case, Abraham had been propelled by hunger, and by fear for his life on account of Sarah's beauty (12:10–13). Here the text provides no reason for Abraham's movements or for deceiving the king of Gerar, until vv. 11–13.

4. *Abimelech had not touched her.* Presumably sexually. But clearly that is his intention.

did this?" [11]Abraham replied, "I thought, 'There is
no fear of God at all in this place, and they will kill
me for my wife.' [12]And, as a matter of fact, she is
my sister, my father's daughter, though not my
mother's daughter, so she became my wife. [13]And
when God made me wander from my father's
house, I said to her: Do this kindness for me—
wherever we go, say of me, 'He is my brother.'"
[14]Abimelech then took sheep and oxen, male
and female slaves, and gave [them] to Abraham;
he also restored his wife Sarah to him. [15]And Abimelech said, "Look, my land is before you; settle
wherever you please." [16]And to Sarah he said,
"Look, I have given your brother a thousand pieces
of silver; thus it testifies to your unblemished virtue
to all who are with you; you are in the right with
[them] all." [17]Abraham then prayed to God and
God restored Abimelech, his wife, and his female
slaves, and they bore children—[18]for יהוה had completely shut every womb of Abimelech's household
on account of Abraham's wife Sarah.

הַזֶּה׃ 11 וַיֹּאמֶר אַבְרָהָם כִּי אָמַרְתִּי רַק
אֵין־יִרְאַת אֱלֹהִים בַּמָּקוֹם הַזֶּה וַהֲרָגוּנִי
עַל־דְּבַר אִשְׁתִּי׃ 12 וְגַם־אָמְנָה אֲחֹתִי בַת־
אָבִי הִוא אַךְ לֹא בַת־אִמִּי וַתְּהִי־לִי
לְאִשָּׁה׃ 13 וַיְהִי כַּאֲשֶׁר הִתְעוּ אֹתִי אֱלֹהִים
מִבֵּית אָבִי וָאֹמַר לָהּ זֶה חַסְדֵּךְ אֲשֶׁר תַּעֲשִׂי
עִמָּדִי אֶל כָּל־הַמָּקוֹם אֲשֶׁר נָבוֹא שָׁמָּה
אִמְרִי־לִי אָחִי הוּא׃
14 וַיִּקַּח אֲבִימֶלֶךְ צֹאן וּבָקָר וַעֲבָדִים
וּשְׁפָחֹת וַיִּתֵּן לְאַבְרָהָם וַיָּשֶׁב לוֹ אֵת שָׂרָה
אִשְׁתּוֹ׃ 15 וַיֹּאמֶר אֲבִימֶלֶךְ הִנֵּה אַרְצִי
לְפָנֶיךָ בַּטּוֹב בְּעֵינֶיךָ שֵׁב׃ 16 וּלְשָׂרָה אָמַר
הִנֵּה נָתַתִּי אֶלֶף כֶּסֶף לְאָחִיךְ הִנֵּה הוּא־לָךְ
כְּסוּת עֵינַיִם לְכֹל אֲשֶׁר אִתָּךְ וְאֵת כֹּל
וְנֹכָחַת׃ 17 וַיִּתְפַּלֵּל אַבְרָהָם אֶל־הָאֱלֹהִים
וַיִּרְפָּא אֱלֹהִים אֶת־אֲבִימֶלֶךְ וְאֶת־אִשְׁתּוֹ
וְאַמְהֹתָיו וַיֵּלֵדוּ׃ 18 כִּי־עָצֹר עָצַר יְהוָה
בְּעַד כָּל־רֶחֶם לְבֵית אֲבִימֶלֶךְ עַל־דְּבַר
שָׂרָה אֵשֶׁת אַבְרָהָם׃ ס

*11. "There is no fear of God at all in this place."* In the previous story, Abraham had argued with God to save a city for the sake of the righteous individuals that he wrongly thought it contained. Here, Abraham believes that a city contains no God-fearing persons, and he is wrong again. This time, however, his error almost causes "a great sin" (v. 9) to be committed.

*12. "she is my sister."* Abraham's statement is not confirmed either by the narrator, other dialogue, or genealogical source. Both Sarah's and Abraham's genealogy appear in 11:27–30, where this fact is not mentioned; see the comment there. The earlier episode (12:10–18) contains no reference to a real brother/sister relationship; if Abraham and Sarah were truly brother and sister, the perfect opportunity to mention it would have been then, before they entered Egypt. Yet unlike Isaac, who claims that his wife and first cousin Rebekah is his sister (26:1–11), Abraham here provides plausible specifics: he and Sarah are related through their father. Note that Deuteronomy 27:22 condemns a sexual relationship between such siblings.

*16. "it testifies to your unblemished virtue."* Despite Sarah and Abimelech's innocence, her reputation still needs to be cleared.

*18.* ***יהוה*** ***had completely shut every womb of Abimelech's household.*** Paradoxically, this information is imparted only after Abraham prays to the Deity—who heals Abimelech, his wife, and his slave girls so that they bear children. It raises questions: Did Abraham pray earlier for his own wife to conceive? Did she now benefit too from this prayer of Abraham's? (See the episode that follows.) The next matriarch, Rebekah, will be barren until Isaac pleads on her behalf (25:21).

***on account of Abraham's wife Sarah.*** Sarah—not Abraham—is God's primary concern.

21 יהוה now remembered Sarah; יהוה did for
Sarah as promised, 2so that she became pregnant
and bore a son to Abraham in his old age, at the
exact time God had told him. 3Abraham named his
newborn son, whom Sarah had borne to him, Isaac.
4When his son Isaac was eight days old, Abraham
circumcised him, as God had commanded him.
5Abraham was 100 years old when his son Isaac
was born.

6Sarah said, "God has brought me laughter; all
who hear will laugh with me." 7And she added,
"Who would have dared say to Abraham, 'Sarah
shall nurse children'? Yet I have borne a son in his
old age!" 8The child grew and was weaned, and on
Isaac's weaning day, Abraham held a great feast.

כא וַיהוָה פָּקַד אֶת־שָׂרָה כַּאֲשֶׁר אָמָר
וַיַּעַשׂ יְהוָה לְשָׂרָה כַּאֲשֶׁר דִּבֵּר׃ 2 וַתַּהַר
וַתֵּלֶד שָׂרָה לְאַבְרָהָם בֵּן לִזְקֻנָיו לַמּוֹעֵד
אֲשֶׁר־דִּבֶּר אֹתוֹ אֱלֹהִים׃ 3 וַיִּקְרָא אַבְרָהָם
אֶת־שֶׁם־בְּנוֹ הַנּוֹלַד־לוֹ אֲשֶׁר־יָלְדָה־לּוֹ
שָׂרָה יִצְחָק׃ 4 וַיָּמָל אַבְרָהָם אֶת־יִצְחָק
בְּנוֹ בֶּן־שְׁמֹנַת יָמִים כַּאֲשֶׁר צִוָּה אֹתוֹ
אֱלֹהִים׃ 5 וְאַבְרָהָם בֶּן־מְאַת שָׁנָה בְּהִוָּלֶד
לוֹ אֵת יִצְחָק בְּנוֹ׃
6 וַתֹּאמֶר שָׂרָה צְחֹק עָשָׂה לִי אֱלֹהִים כָּל־
הַשֹּׁמֵעַ יִצְחַק־לִי׃ 7 וַתֹּאמֶר מִי מִלֵּל
לְאַבְרָהָם הֵינִיקָה בָנִים שָׂרָה כִּי־יָלַדְתִּי בֵן
לִזְקֻנָיו׃ 8 וַיִּגְדַּל הַיֶּלֶד וַיִּגָּמַל וַיַּעַשׂ אַבְרָהָם
מִשְׁתֶּה גָדוֹל בְּיוֹם הִגָּמֵל אֶת־יִצְחָק׃

### SARAH BECOMES A MOTHER (21:1–7)

*1.* **יהוה *now remembered Sarah.*** God had spoken with Abraham (17:16, 21; 18:10) and, through the "messengers," with Sarah (18:10) about the forthcoming child; but God remembers only Sarah here.

*2.* ***she became pregnant and bore a son.*** After much discussion about this event (15:4; 17:16–19, 21; 18:9–15), Isaac's conception and delivery are reported in just three Hebrew words.

***to Abraham.*** The text is explicit here that the father is Abraham because the preceding episode with Abimelech might raise a doubt about the father's identity.

*3.* Abraham names the child "Isaac," a name that means "he laughs." Usually in the Bible it is the mother who names her son.

*6.* ***"all who hear will laugh with me."*** Sarah responds to maternity with laughter. Earlier the laughter was private (18:12). Now it embraces everyone else.

*7.* ***"Sarah shall nurse."*** Sarah is celebrating her capacity to nurture her child. (For details about the practice of nursing babies in the ancient world and in the Bible, see at Exodus 2:9.)

***"I have borne a son."*** In the book of Isaiah, the prophet urges the people to look "to Sarah who brought you forth" (Isaiah 51:2) as a source of hope and renewal. After the exile to Babylon in the 6th century B.C.E., Sarah's giving birth apparently exemplified the potential for renewal.

***"in his old age."*** Abraham's age seems to be more of a miracle to Sarah than her own, as she celebrates her capacity to bring forth life.

## *First Threat to Isaac*

### TWO MOTHERS CLASH PROTECTING THEIR SONS (21:8–21:21)

The tension in the family does not end with Isaac's birth, since there are potential threats to his longevity and success from both his brother and his father.

One of the most poignant parts of the parashah is the story of two mothers, each of whom desires the well-being of her son. Mother Sarah seeks to

[9]Now Sarah saw the son that Hagar the Egyptian had borne to Abraham, playing. [10]She said to Abraham, "Throw this slave girl and her son out. The son of this slave girl is not going to share in the inheritance with my son Isaac!" [11]This grieved

9 וַתֵּ֨רֶא שָׂרָ֜ה אֶֽת־בֶּן־הָגָ֧ר הַמִּצְרִ֛ית אֲשֶׁר־
יָלְדָ֥ה לְאַבְרָהָ֖ם מְצַחֵֽק׃ 10 וַתֹּ֙אמֶר֙
לְאַבְרָהָ֔ם גָּרֵ֛שׁ הָאָמָ֥ה הַזֹּ֖את וְאֶת־בְּנָ֑הּ
כִּ֣י לֹ֤א יִירַשׁ֙ בֶּן־הָאָמָ֣ה הַזֹּ֔את עִם־בְּנִ֖י
עִם־יִצְחָֽק׃ 11 וַיֵּ֧רַע הַדָּבָ֛ר מְאֹ֖ד בְּעֵינֵ֣י

secure her infant's future (a future that she will probably not live to see, given her age) by expelling a rival. Hagar then faces the near death of her son. The Torah is sympathetic to both mothers caught in the cross-currents.

The plight here of mother Hagar and son Ishmael will be mirrored by that of father Abraham and his son Isaac in the story immediately following. Certain details connect the stories: In both, the parent rises early, a child is imperiled; and a divine messenger intervenes at the last moment. (Both stories are read on Rosh HaShanah in traditional synagogues.)

### SARAH SEEKS TO PROTECT ISAAC: THE EXPULSION OF HAGAR AND ISHMAEL (21:8–13)

*8. on Isaac's weaning day.* I Samuel 1:23 and II Maccabees 7:27 indicate that in ancient Israel, children were weaned at about three years of age.

*great feast.* Weaning apparently was marked by a ritual, the details of which have not been preserved. This life-passage is obviously significant to mother and child.

*9. Sarah saw the son . . . playing.* Ishmael's precise action is at issue. All we know for sure is that it triggers a severe reaction in Sarah. The word *m'tzachek* ("playing") puns on the name Isaac (*yitzchak*). It can also mean "mocking," "fooling around," and toying with him sexually.

*10. "Throw this slave girl and her son out."* [From a feminist perspective, the call for the expulsion of Hagar raises troubling questions. The story portrays the oppression of one woman by another; it also places responsibility for the enmity between two peoples—the descendants of Isaac and those of Ishmael—upon women, especially Sarah. As a story about domestic relations, the narrative builds sympathy for Hagar at Sarah's expense. Some scholars respond by pointing out that Sarah's concern is legitimate. As an old woman she anticipates her young son's vulnerable position in the event of her death. She takes steps to protect him by removing the competition for Abraham's possessions—and possibly also for his affection. Rather than casting a human drama in simplistic terms, the story of Sarah, Hagar, and Abraham poignantly illustrates the dilemma of multiple commitments. Among other things, this passage may seek to sensitize the reader to the plight of the outsider. —*Ed.*]

***"The son of this slave girl is not going to share in the inheritance."*** Sarah raises inheritance as the issue, stressing meanwhile that Hagar is a slave. In 17:19, God had earmarked Isaac to receive the covenantal promise, and perhaps Sarah is acting with that knowledge. Ancient law collections from Mesopotamia address inheritance in similar cases, illustrating ancient customs that may lie in the background of this story. In the collection of Lipit Ishtar, the status of the second wife determines whether or not her son inherits. In the collection of Hammurabi, a child of a slave inherits only if the father claims him. The sons of Zilpah and Bilhah—women of a status similar to Hagar—do later inherit along with the children of the primary wives, Leah and Rachel. Perhaps Sarah objects to such an arrangement because her son is so young and she may not be around to protect him.

*11. This grieved Abraham greatly, on account of his son.* The text does not clarify what "this" is, or specify which son he refers to; therefore what bothers Abraham is open to interpretation. One might suppose here that Abraham is not concerned

Abraham greatly, on account of his son. 12 But God said to Abraham, "Do not be grieved over the boy or your slave. Do whatever Sarah tells you, for it is through Isaac that offspring shall be called yours. 13 Yet I will also make a nation out of the children of the slave's son, for he, too, is your offspring."

14 Early next morning, Abraham got up and took bread and a waterskin and handed them to Hagar, placing them and the boy on her shoulder. Then he cast her out; trudging away, she wandered aimlessly in the wilderness of Beersheba. 15 When the water in the skin was all gone, she cast the child away under a bush; 16 she walked away and sat down on the other side at a remove of about a bowshot, thinking: "Let me not see the child's death." There, on the other side, she sat and wept in a loud voice.

אַבְרָהָ֖ם עַ֥ל אוֹדֹ֖ת בְּנֽוֹ׃ 12 וַיֹּ֨אמֶר אֱלֹהִ֜ים
אֶל־אַבְרָהָ֗ם אַל־יֵרַ֤ע בְּעֵינֶ֙יךָ֙ עַל־הַנַּ֣עַר
וְעַל־אֲמָתֶ֔ךָ כֹּל֩ אֲשֶׁ֨ר תֹּאמַ֥ר אֵלֶ֛יךָ שָׂרָ֖ה
שְׁמַ֣ע בְּקֹלָ֑הּ כִּ֣י בְיִצְחָ֔ק יִקָּרֵ֥א לְךָ֖ זָֽרַע׃
13 וְגַ֥ם אֶת־בֶּן־הָאָמָ֖ה לְג֣וֹי אֲשִׂימֶ֑נּוּ כִּ֥י
זַרְעֲךָ֖ הֽוּא׃
14 וַיַּשְׁכֵּ֣ם אַבְרָהָ֣ם ׀ בַּבֹּ֡קֶר וַיִּֽקַּֽח־לֶחֶם֩
וְחֵ֨מַת מַ֜יִם וַיִּתֵּ֣ן אֶל־הָ֠גָר שָׂ֧ם עַל־שִׁכְמָ֛הּ
וְאֶת־הַיֶּ֖לֶד וַֽיְשַׁלְּחֶ֑הָ וַתֵּ֣לֶךְ וַתֵּ֔תַע בְּמִדְבַּ֖ר
בְּאֵ֥ר שָֽׁבַע׃ 15 וַיִּכְל֥וּ הַמַּ֖יִם מִן־הַחֵ֑מֶת
וַתַּשְׁלֵ֣ךְ אֶת־הַיֶּ֔לֶד תַּ֖חַת אַחַ֥ד הַשִּׂיחִֽם׃
16 וַתֵּלֶךְ֩ וַתֵּ֨שֶׁב לָ֜הּ מִנֶּ֗גֶד הַרְחֵק֙ כִּמְטַחֲוֵ֣י
קֶ֔שֶׁת כִּ֣י אָֽמְרָ֔ה אַל־אֶרְאֶ֖ה בְּמ֣וֹת הַיָּ֑לֶד
וַתֵּ֣שֶׁב מִנֶּ֔גֶד וַתִּשָּׂ֥א אֶת־קֹלָ֖הּ וַתֵּֽבְךְּ׃

about Hagar, but God's response in the next verse ("do not be grieved . . . over your slave") implies otherwise.

*12. "Do whatever Sarah tells you."* Abraham is instructed to obey his wife, literally "whatever Sarah says to you, listen to her voice." In 3:17 the man was chastised for listening to his wife's voice. [God's rebuke in 3:17 might lead readers to conclude that listening to a wife's voice is wrong. God's instruction in the present passage illustrates that this is not the case. —*Ed.*] | God supports Sarah's concern about inheritance. Abraham's distrust that the Deity will care for both his sons may be the background for the Deity's decision to test Abraham in the episode that follows this story of Ishmael.

## THE RESCUE OF HAGAR AND ISHMAEL IN THE DESERT (21:14–21)

Once again, Hagar is in the wilderness (compare 16:7–14). Earlier, she had been pregnant with Ishmael and had left of her own accord. This time she has her son on her back and is sent away.

***14. Early next morning, Abraham got up.*** Though not translated identically here, these words in Hebrew are the same as in 22:3, where Abraham rises to sacrifice Isaac. The common phrasing connects the two episodes, both of which deal with the potential death of a son of Abraham.

***took bread and a waterskin and handed them to Hagar, placing them and the boy on her shoulder.*** Placing the child on Hagar's back hints that Ishmael is a small child, though, according to the preceding notices (17:23–25; 21:5, 8), Ishmael at this point is at least fifteen years of age. The narrator uses poetic license to depict Ishmael as younger and more vulnerable to make the scene more poignant.

***cast her out.*** [The verb is used for divorce but more literally means "sent her out." It will be used when Pharaoh lets the Israelites go from slavery (Exodus 13:17). Tikva Frymer-Kensky points out that Hagar and Ishmael are not sold and suggests that they are freed. They leave Abraham's household as emancipated slaves (*Reading the Women of the Bible,* 2002, p. 235). See, however, at v. 10. —*Ed.*]

***16. "Let me not see the child's death."*** The scene is heartrending. Watching one's child die must be horrible; what might be worse is leaving one's child to die alone.

***she sat and wept in a loud voice.*** The verse

17 God heard the boy's cry, and from heaven an
angel of God called to Hagar and said, "What is
troubling you, Hagar? Have no fear, for God has
heard the cry of the lad where he is. 18 Get up, lift
the boy, and hold him with your hand, for I am
going to make of him a great nation." 19 God then
opened her eyes, and she saw a well. She went and
filled the skin with water and gave the boy to drink.
20 God was with the boy, and he grew up; he
lived in the wilderness and became a bowman. 21 He
lived in the wilderness of Paran, and his mother
took him a wife from the land of Egypt.
22 At that time Abimelech and Pichol the commander of his army said to Abraham, "God is with
you in all that you do. 23 Swear to me now that you
will not be false to me, my progeny, or my posterity; do me and the land in which you have been
staying as much kindness as I have done to you."
24 Abraham replied, "I will swear."
25 But Abraham rebuked Abimelech on account
of the water well that Abimelech's servants had

17 וַיִּשְׁמַע אֱלֹהִים אֶת־קוֹל הַנַּעַר וַיִּקְרָא
מַלְאַךְ אֱלֹהִים ׀ אֶל־הָגָר מִן־הַשָּׁמַיִם וַיֹּאמֶר
לָהּ מַה־לָּךְ הָגָר אַל־תִּירְאִי כִּי־שָׁמַע
אֱלֹהִים אֶל־קוֹל הַנַּעַר בַּאֲשֶׁר הוּא־שָׁם׃
18 קוּמִי שְׂאִי אֶת־הַנַּעַר וְהַחֲזִיקִי אֶת־יָדֵךְ
בּוֹ כִּי־לְגוֹי גָּדוֹל אֲשִׂימֶנּוּ׃ 19 וַיִּפְקַח אֱלֹהִים
אֶת־עֵינֶיהָ וַתֵּרֶא בְּאֵר מָיִם וַתֵּלֶךְ וַתְּמַלֵּא
אֶת־הַחֵמֶת מַיִם וַתַּשְׁקְ אֶת־הַנָּעַר׃
20 וַיְהִי אֱלֹהִים אֶת־הַנַּעַר וַיִּגְדָּל וַיֵּשֶׁב
בַּמִּדְבָּר וַיְהִי רֹבֶה קַשָּׁת׃ 21 וַיֵּשֶׁב בְּמִדְבַּר
פָּארָן וַתִּקַּח־לוֹ אִמּוֹ אִשָּׁה מֵאֶרֶץ
מִצְרָיִם׃ פ
22 וַיְהִי בָּעֵת הַהִוא וַיֹּאמֶר אֲבִימֶלֶךְ וּפִיכֹל
שַׂר־צְבָאוֹ אֶל־אַבְרָהָם לֵאמֹר אֱלֹהִים
עִמְּךָ בְּכֹל אֲשֶׁר־אַתָּה עֹשֶׂה׃ 23 וְעַתָּה
הִשָּׁבְעָה לִּי בֵאלֹהִים הֵנָּה אִם־תִּשְׁקֹר לִי
וּלְנִינִי וּלְנֶכְדִּי כַּחֶסֶד אֲשֶׁר־עָשִׂיתִי עִמְּךָ
תַּעֲשֶׂה עִמָּדִי וְעִם־הָאָרֶץ אֲשֶׁר־גַּרְתָּה בָּהּ׃
24 וַיֹּאמֶר אַבְרָהָם אָנֹכִי אִשָּׁבֵעַ׃
25 וְהוֹכִחַ אַבְרָהָם אֶת־אֲבִימֶלֶךְ עַל־אֹדוֹת
בְּאֵר הַמַּיִם אֲשֶׁר גָּזְלוּ עַבְדֵי אֲבִימֶלֶךְ׃

states that she placed her child at some distance, implying that they could not hear each other.

**17. *God heard the boy's cry, and from heaven an angel of God called to Hagar.*** Hagar weeps—but the Deity focuses on the boy's cry. The message of assurance comes to her, however, because she herself has moved so far from him that she cannot hear him.

**18. *"I am going to make of him a great nation."*** This statement reiterates the earlier divine promise that her "seed" will be numerous (16:10).

**21.** Unlike most biblical women, Hagar herself finds her son a wife. Ishmael's wife is from Egypt, like Hagar herself (16:1).

## *Second Threat to Isaac*

### ABRAHAM'S "BINDING OF ISAAC," OR "THE AKEDAH" (21:22–22:21)

#### ABRAHAM SETTLES IN BEERSHEBA (21:22–34)

**22. *At that time.*** Abraham's negotiations over wells near Beersheba seemingly have little to do with Ishmael or Isaac; yet this new residence is on the edge of the desert, not far from where the text just left Hagar and Ishmael (v. 21). Meanwhile, it is the same town to which Abraham will go (22:19) at the end of the next episode, which features Isaac.

stolen, [26]and Abimelech replied, "I do not know who did this; you certainly never told me, nor did I ever hear of it until today." [27]Abraham then took sheep and oxen and gave them to Abimelech, and the two of them forged a treaty. [28]Abraham then set aside seven lambs of the flock. [29]When Abimelech said, "What do these seven lambs that you have set aside signify?" [30]Abraham replied, "So that you take the seven lambs from me as my testimony that I dug this well." [31]That is why that place is called Beersheba, for there the two of them took an oath.

[32]They forged a treaty in Beersheba; then Abimelech and Pichol the commander of his army got up and returned to the land of the Philistines, [33]while Abraham planted a tamarisk and called upon the Name of יהוה, the everlasting God; [34]he stayed in the land of the Philistines a long time.

22 After these things, God tested Abraham, saying to him, "Abraham!" And he said, "Here I am." [2][God] said, "Take your son, your only one, the one you love, Isaac, and go forth to the land of Moriah. Offer him there as a burnt-offering, on one of the mountains that I will show you."

26 וַיֹּאמֶר אֲבִימֶלֶךְ לֹא יָדַעְתִּי מִי עָשָׂה
אֶת־הַדָּבָר הַזֶּה וְגַם־אַתָּה לֹא־הִגַּדְתָּ לִּי
וְגַם אָנֹכִי לֹא שָׁמַעְתִּי בִּלְתִּי הַיּוֹם׃ 27 וַיִּקַּח
אַבְרָהָם צֹאן וּבָקָר וַיִּתֵּן לַאֲבִימֶלֶךְ וַיִּכְרְתוּ
שְׁנֵיהֶם בְּרִית׃ 28 וַיַּצֵּב אַבְרָהָם אֶת־שֶׁבַע
כִּבְשֹׂת הַצֹּאן לְבַדְּהֶן׃ 29 וַיֹּאמֶר אֲבִימֶלֶךְ
אֶל־אַבְרָהָם מָה הֵנָּה שֶׁבַע כְּבָשֹׂת הָאֵלֶּה
אֲשֶׁר הִצַּבְתָּ לְבַדָּנָה׃ 30 וַיֹּאמֶר כִּי אֶת־
שֶׁבַע כְּבָשֹׂת תִּקַּח מִיָּדִי בַּעֲבוּר תִּהְיֶה־לִּי
לְעֵדָה כִּי חָפַרְתִּי אֶת־הַבְּאֵר הַזֹּאת׃
31 עַל־כֵּן קָרָא לַמָּקוֹם הַהוּא בְּאֵר שָׁבַע
כִּי שָׁם נִשְׁבְּעוּ שְׁנֵיהֶם׃
32 וַיִּכְרְתוּ בְרִית בִּבְאֵר שָׁבַע וַיָּקָם אֲבִימֶלֶךְ
וּפִיכֹל שַׂר־צְבָאוֹ וַיָּשֻׁבוּ אֶל־אֶרֶץ פְּלִשְׁתִּים׃
33 וַיִּטַּע אֵשֶׁל בִּבְאֵר שָׁבַע וַיִּקְרָא־שָׁם בְּשֵׁם
יְהוָה אֵל עוֹלָם׃ 34 וַיָּגָר אַבְרָהָם בְּאֶרֶץ
פְּלִשְׁתִּים יָמִים רַבִּים׃ פ

כב וַיְהִי אַחַר הַדְּבָרִים הָאֵלֶּה וְהָאֱלֹהִים
נִסָּה אֶת־אַבְרָהָם וַיֹּאמֶר אֵלָיו אַבְרָהָם
וַיֹּאמֶר הִנֵּנִי׃ 2 וַיֹּאמֶר קַח־נָא אֶת־בִּנְךָ אֶת־
יְחִידְךָ אֲשֶׁר־אָהַבְתָּ אֶת־יִצְחָק וְלֶךְ־לְךָ אֶל־
אֶרֶץ הַמֹּרִיָּה וְהַעֲלֵהוּ שָׁם לְעֹלָה עַל אַחַד
הֶהָרִים אֲשֶׁר אֹמַר אֵלֶיךָ׃

## ABRAHAM'S "TEST": THE BINDING OF ISAAC (22:1–19)

In this episode, one of the most famous in Genesis, Sarah the mother is completely absent—a striking absence given that her only son is the subject of God's instructions. Apparently she does not need to be tested.

*1. After these things.* What are "these things": Isaac's birth? Banishing Ishmael? The expulsion of Hagar? Settling near Ishmael?

*God tested Abraham.* The text never explains why Abraham needs to be tested. Perhaps his actions thus far have somehow not been adequate.

*2. "your only one, the one you love."* These touching words to describe Isaac can be challenged. Isaac is not Abraham's only son. [They might be explained as a recognition that Isaac is now the only legal son because Abraham has banished Ishmael. —*Ed.*] Nor have we been told that Abraham has expressed any feelings toward Isaac.

*"Offer him there as a burnt-offering."* Abraham, the man who advocates for Ishmael (17:18) and actively negotiates with the Deity for the people of Sodom (18:23–33), is surprisingly silent after receiving the command.

3 Abraham rose early, saddled his donkey,
chopped wood for the burnt-offering, took Isaac
his son and his two lads, and set out for the place
that God had spoken of to him. 4 On the third day,
Abraham lifted up his eyes and saw the place from
afar. 5 Abraham said to his servant lads, "Stay here
with the donkey; the lad and I will go yonder. We
will worship and return to you." 6 Abraham then
took the wood for the burnt-offering and laid it
on Isaac his son; in his own hand he held the firestone and the knife. And the two of them went on
together.

7 Isaac then said to Abraham his father, "Father!"
He answered: "Here I am, my son." And Isaac said,
"Here is the firestone and the wood, but where
is the lamb for the burnt-offering?" 8 Abraham
replied, "God will see to the lamb for the burnt-
offering, my son." And the two of them went on
together.

9 They came to the place that God had shown
him. There Abraham built the altar and arranged
the wood and bound Isaac his son and laid him on
the altar, upon the wood. 10 Abraham now reached
out and took the knife to slay his son, 11 but out
of heaven an angel of יהוה called to him, saying,
"Abraham, Abraham!" He replied: "Here I am."
12 [The angel] then said, "Do not lay your hand on
the lad; do nothing to him; for now I know that
you are one who fears God, as you did not withhold
your son, your only one, from Me."

3 וַיַּשְׁכֵּם אַבְרָהָם בַּבֹּקֶר וַיַּחֲבֹשׁ אֶת־חֲמֹרוֹ
וַיִּקַּח אֶת־שְׁנֵי נְעָרָיו אִתּוֹ וְאֵת יִצְחָק בְּנוֹ
וַיְבַקַּע עֲצֵי עֹלָה וַיָּקָם וַיֵּלֶךְ אֶל־הַמָּקוֹם
אֲשֶׁר־אָמַר־לוֹ הָאֱלֹהִים׃ 4 בַּיּוֹם הַשְּׁלִישִׁי
וַיִּשָּׂא אַבְרָהָם אֶת־עֵינָיו וַיַּרְא אֶת־הַמָּקוֹם
מֵרָחֹק׃ 5 וַיֹּאמֶר אַבְרָהָם אֶל־נְעָרָיו שְׁבוּ־
לָכֶם פֹּה עִם־הַחֲמוֹר וַאֲנִי וְהַנַּעַר נֵלְכָה
עַד־כֹּה וְנִשְׁתַּחֲוֶה וְנָשׁוּבָה אֲלֵיכֶם׃ 6 וַיִּקַּח
אַבְרָהָם אֶת־עֲצֵי הָעֹלָה וַיָּשֶׂם עַל־יִצְחָק
בְּנוֹ וַיִּקַּח בְּיָדוֹ אֶת־הָאֵשׁ וְאֶת־הַמַּאֲכֶלֶת
וַיֵּלְכוּ שְׁנֵיהֶם יַחְדָּו׃
7 וַיֹּאמֶר יִצְחָק אֶל־אַבְרָהָם אָבִיו וַיֹּאמֶר
אָבִי וַיֹּאמֶר הִנֶּנִּי בְנִי וַיֹּאמֶר הִנֵּה הָאֵשׁ
וְהָעֵצִים וְאַיֵּה הַשֶּׂה לְעֹלָה׃ 8 וַיֹּאמֶר
אַבְרָהָם אֱלֹהִים יִרְאֶה־לּוֹ הַשֶּׂה לְעֹלָה בְּנִי
וַיֵּלְכוּ שְׁנֵיהֶם יַחְדָּו׃
9 וַיָּבֹאוּ אֶל־הַמָּקוֹם אֲשֶׁר אָמַר־לוֹ
הָאֱלֹהִים וַיִּבֶן שָׁם אַבְרָהָם אֶת־הַמִּזְבֵּחַ
וַיַּעֲרֹךְ אֶת־הָעֵצִים וַיַּעֲקֹד אֶת־יִצְחָק בְּנוֹ
וַיָּשֶׂם אֹתוֹ עַל־הַמִּזְבֵּחַ מִמַּעַל לָעֵצִים׃
10 וַיִּשְׁלַח אַבְרָהָם אֶת־יָדוֹ וַיִּקַּח אֶת־
הַמַּאֲכֶלֶת לִשְׁחֹט אֶת־בְּנוֹ׃ 11 וַיִּקְרָא אֵלָיו
מַלְאַךְ יְהוָה מִן־הַשָּׁמַיִם וַיֹּאמֶר אַבְרָהָם ׀
אַבְרָהָם וַיֹּאמֶר הִנֵּנִי׃ 12 וַיֹּאמֶר אַל־תִּשְׁלַח
יָדְךָ אֶל־הַנַּעַר וְאַל־תַּעַשׂ לוֹ מְאוּמָה כִּי ׀
עַתָּה יָדַעְתִּי כִּי־יְרֵא אֱלֹהִים אַתָּה וְלֹא
חָשַׂכְתָּ אֶת־בִּנְךָ אֶת־יְחִידְךָ מִמֶּנִּי׃

*3. Abraham rose early.* See at 21:14.

*5. "We will . . . return to you."* Is Abraham afraid that the servants will try to stop him? Or does he know the Deity will not let him carry out the instructions?

*7. "Father!"* This is Isaac's first word in the Torah.

*"Here I am, my son."* Abraham's response—the first time in the Torah that he calls Isaac his son—are words of comfort.

*"but where is the lamb for the burnt-offering?"* Isaac is old enough to know what is necessary for a burnt-offering and that they do not have it. Does he sense how much is amiss? Commentators debate whether or not Isaac is aware of what is going to happen.

*9–10.* Abraham carries out his actions methodically, with no reported words or emotion—unlike when he lost Ishmael (21:11). Isaac, too, is silent.

[13]Abraham lifted his eyes: he now could see a ram [just] after it was caught by its horns in a thicket. Abraham went and took the ram and offered it as a burnt-offering in place of his son. [14]Abraham named that place *YHVH Yir'eh;* to this day people say: "On the mount of יהוה, [God] will be seen."

[15]Then out of heaven an angel of יהוה called to Abraham a second time, [16]saying, "By Myself I swear, says יהוה, that because you did this thing, and did not withhold your son, your only one, [17]I will bless you greatly, and make your descendants as numerous as the stars of heaven and the sands of the seashore, and your descendants shall take possession of the gates of their foes. [18]And through your descendants the nations of the earth shall be blessed, because you hearkened to My voice." [19]Abraham then returned to his servant lads; they got up and traveled together to Beersheba, and Abraham settled in Beersheba.

[20]And after all these things, Abraham was told the following: Milcah, she too has borne sons, to

13 וַיִּשָּׂא אַבְרָהָם אֶת־עֵינָיו וַיַּרְא וְהִנֵּה־אַיִל
אַחַר נֶאֱחַז בַּסְּבַךְ בְּקַרְנָיו וַיֵּלֶךְ אַבְרָהָם
וַיִּקַּח אֶת־הָאַיִל וַיַּעֲלֵהוּ לְעֹלָה תַּחַת
בְּנוֹ׃ 14 וַיִּקְרָא אַבְרָהָם שֵׁם־הַמָּקוֹם הַהוּא
יְהוָה ׀ יִרְאֶה אֲשֶׁר יֵאָמֵר הַיּוֹם בְּהַר יְהוָה
יֵרָאֶה׃

15 וַיִּקְרָא מַלְאַךְ יְהוָה אֶל־אַבְרָהָם שֵׁנִית
מִן־הַשָּׁמָיִם׃ 16 וַיֹּאמֶר בִּי נִשְׁבַּעְתִּי נְאֻם־
יְהוָה כִּי יַעַן אֲשֶׁר עָשִׂיתָ אֶת־הַדָּבָר הַזֶּה
וְלֹא חָשַׂכְתָּ אֶת־בִּנְךָ אֶת־יְחִידֶךָ׃ 17 כִּי־
בָרֵךְ אֲבָרֶכְךָ וְהַרְבָּה אַרְבֶּה אֶת־זַרְעֲךָ
כְּכוֹכְבֵי הַשָּׁמַיִם וְכַחוֹל אֲשֶׁר עַל־שְׂפַת
הַיָּם וְיִרַשׁ זַרְעֲךָ אֵת שַׁעַר אֹיְבָיו׃
18 וְהִתְבָּרְכוּ בְזַרְעֲךָ כֹּל גּוֹיֵי הָאָרֶץ עֵקֶב
אֲשֶׁר שָׁמַעְתָּ בְּקֹלִי׃ 19 וַיָּשָׁב אַבְרָהָם אֶל־
נְעָרָיו וַיָּקֻמוּ וַיֵּלְכוּ יַחְדָּו אֶל־בְּאֵר שָׁבַע
וַיֵּשֶׁב אַבְרָהָם בִּבְאֵר שָׁבַע׃ פ

20 וַיְהִי אַחֲרֵי הַדְּבָרִים הָאֵלֶּה וַיֻּגַּד
לְאַבְרָהָם לֵאמֹר הִנֵּה יָלְדָה מִלְכָּה גַם־

---

***16–17. "because you . . . did not withhold your son . . . I will . . . make your descendants . . . numerous."*** God had promised Abraham numerous progeny even before this test (12:2; 13:16; 15:5; 17:5). What then would have happened had Abraham not attempted to sacrifice Isaac?

***19.*** The text mentions Abraham and his servants, but not Isaac. Isaac and Abraham are never represented together again. When Isaac reappears in the text, he is near Be'er-lachai-ro'i (24:62), where pregnant Hagar had gone when she ran away from Sarah (16:14).

## *Preparation for the Future*

### REBEKAH'S BIRTH (22:20–24)

Sandwiched between the binding of Isaac and Sarah's death (in the next parashah) is a paragraph concerning Rebekah's family. This parashah ends with Isaac safe, and with his future wife born to the right woman from the right lineage. Rebekah, the matriarch for the next generation, appears immediately before the previous one, Sarah, dies. This passage emphasizes the women in the lineage and highlights the importance of women in the "patriarchal" line of the people of Israel. On the role of women in the Israelite lineage, see also at 17:19, 22.

***20. Milcah.*** We were told of her marriage to Nahor when she was first introduced with Sarai (11:29), before Abram's household left the city of Haran for Canaan. Now she is mentioned again—and once more in verse 23—just before Sarah dies (23:1–2). Rebekah will also mention her grandmother Milcah when she identifies herself (24:24, 47). It is not clear why Milcah merits her relative prominence.

הֽוּא בָּנִ֖ים לְנָח֥וֹר אָחִֽיךָ׃ 21 אֶת־ע֥וּץ בְּכֹר֖וֹ
וְאֶת־בּ֣וּז אָחִ֑יו וְאֶת־קְמוּאֵ֖ל אֲבִ֥י אֲרָֽם׃
22 וְאֶת־כֶּ֣שֶׂד וְאֶת־חֲז֔וֹ וְאֶת־פִּלְדָּ֖שׁ וְאֶת־
יִדְלָ֑ף וְאֵ֖ת בְּתוּאֵֽל׃ 23 וּבְתוּאֵ֖ל יָלַ֣ד אֶת־
רִבְקָ֑ה שְׁמֹנָ֣ה אֵ֗לֶּה יָלְדָ֤ה מִלְכָּה֙ לְנָח֖וֹר
אֲחִ֥י אַבְרָהָֽם׃ 24 וּפִילַגְשׁ֖וֹ וּשְׁמָ֣הּ רְאוּמָ֑ה
וַתֵּ֤לֶד גַּם־הִוא֙ אֶת־טֶ֣בַח וְאֶת־גַּ֔חַם וְאֶת־
תַּ֖חַשׁ וְאֶת־מַעֲכָֽה׃ פ

your brother Nahor—21Uz his first-born, his
brother Buz, Kemuel father of Aram, 22Chesed,
Hazo, Pildash, Jidlaph, and Bethuel. 23(Bethuel
fathered Rebekah.) These eight did Milcah bear
to Nahor, Abraham's brother. 24And his concubine
—her name was Reumah—she too bore: Tebah,
Gaham, Tahash, and Maacah.

*23. Bethuel fathered Rebekah.* The text highlights only Rebekah in her generation. Rebekah is important not only because she will marry Isaac (Genesis 24) but also because she proves to be decisive in arranging for the transfer of the covenantal blessing in the next generation (27:6–13). Although we know the name of Rebekah's grandmother, Milcah, we never learn the name of her mother.

*Milcah.* See at v. 20.

*24. Maacah.* [Probably referring to a daughter rather than a son. In the Bible, this name is borne by at least eight other individuals—all of whom are, or might be, women. Biblical genealogies do occasionally identify a lineage by a woman's name. Here it seems to represent an Aramean people who lived east of the Jordan (see Deuteronomy 3:14; *The Contemporary Torah*, 2006, pp. xxii–xxiv). Maacah's mention perhaps further anticipates the forthcoming union between Isaac and Rebekah in Genesis. —*Ed.*]

—*Tammi J. Schneider*

# Another View

LIKE THE PRECEDING PARASHAH, this one frames the theme of generational and genealogical continuity as a male affair. Women are constructed largely as sexual objects and procreative instruments with mostly a physical and corporeal relationship to the story of threatened birth and threatened survival. The two wife-sister episodes—in Genesis 12:10–20 and (in our parashah) 20:2–18—present Sarai/Sarah as a silent object of desire. Sarah is taken by Abimelech, king of Gerar, and later returned to her husband—as, one may say, a possession—while her husband is amply compensated for the king's error. In her role as barren wife, she is a figure discussed by, rather than addressed directly by, God, who questions her skeptical laughter (18:12–14). The announcement of a male child is not transmitted by God to Sarah, but rather to Abraham, as she eavesdrops on the conversation at the entrance of the tent (18:10). As a mother, however, Sarah is validated by God, who advises Abraham to obey her demand that her rival, Hagar, and Hagar's son, Ishmael, be removed from the household (21:12). Yet, beyond her protective role as mother, Sarah is neither consulted nor even mentioned in the story of the great test of faith that Abraham endures when God asks him to sacrifice his one and only remaining son at the altar (22:1–19).

It can be argued, then, that in this parashah the mother's role is limited to procreation, nurturance, and physical protectiveness. Sarah, in fact, disappears from the story as soon as Abraham is rewarded for the successful test and blessed with future progeny (22:16–19).

*Women have mostly a corporeal relationship to the story of threatened survival.*

Still, as God makes clear, it is Sarah's son, not merely Abraham's, who is God's chosen. Stories about Hagar and Ishmael, and about Lot's daughters, continue the theme of threatened survival in which women ensure the safety of the next generation: God responds to Hagar's cry for help (21:15–21); Lot's daughters, who first appear as silent sexual objects, and whose procreative role is temporarily threatened (19:1–8), daringly initiate incestuous sexual relations with their father and secure generational continuity (19:30–38).

—*Esther Fuchs*

# Post-biblical Interpretations

***"Why is Sarah laughing so...?"*** (18:13). In Genesis 18:12, Sarah's laughter at the prediction that she would soon bear a child was prompted as much by her husband's advanced age as her own. According to Midrash *B'reishit Rabbah* 48.18 and BT *Bava M'tzia* 87a, however, God's query omitted Sarah's reference to Abraham's age so as to preserve good will between husband and wife, demonstrating that truth may be compromised for the sake of peace. The Rabbis also noted that Sarah was the only woman to whom God spoke directly, on account of her righteousness. When God spoke to Hagar or Rebekah, it was through an angel or an intermediary (*B'reishit Rabbah* 48.20).

***his wife looked behind him and became a pillar of salt*** (19:26). According to one midrashic tradition, Lot's wife turned around to ensure that her daughters were still following—and inadvertently beheld the

*Shechinah*, who had descended to rain fire and brimstone on Sodom (*Pirkei D'Rabbi Eliezer* 25).

***God restored Abimelech, his wife, and his female slaves, and they bore children*** (20:17). The Rabbis appreciated Sarah's discomfort after Abimelech's wife and even his slave girls gave birth. The angels cried out to God on Sarah's behalf, claiming that it was only just that she too bear a child (*P'sikta Rabbati* 42). In other texts, the conception of Isaac is attributed to Sarah's enduring trust in God during this painful episode (*B'reishit Rabbah* 53.3).

***יהוה now remembered Sarah*** (21:1). According to *B'reishit Rabbah* 53.8 and *P'sikta Rabbati* 42, God rejoiced in Isaac's birth by showering gifts on the whole of Creation: infertile women gave birth; the blind were granted sight; the deaf could now hear; and the insane became sane. God was so exultant that the sun shone forth with a full radiant splendor not seen since Creation.

***Sarah shall nurse children*** (21:7). [The plural noun is surprising, given that Sarah has only one son. Rabbi Levi read this rhetorical flourish as a sign that Sarah had surplus milk and nursed others' children as well (BT *Bava M'tzia* 87a). —*Ed.*]

***Now Sarah saw the son . . . playing*** (21:9). Citing a series of verses linked by multiple usages of *m'tzachek* ("playing"), the Rabbis defend Sarah's culpability in the expulsions of Hagar and Ishmael by suggesting that Ishmael was actually "making sport" by seducing women, engaging in idolatrous practices, and even threatening Isaac by shooting arrows in his direction. These activities border on the three most serious public offenses in Jewish law: idolatry, rape, and murder. The Rabbis explained that God told Abraham to listen to Sarah's demand to expel Hagar and Ishmael because her perceptions were inspired by prophecy (BT *M'gillah* 14a; BT *Sanhedrin* 69b; *Seder Olam Rabbah* 2).

***God heard the boy's cry*** (21:17). The midrash notes that God answered Ishmael although it was Hagar who cried out. This is because "sick persons' prayers on their own behalf are more efficacious than those of anyone else" (*B'reishit Rabbah* 53.14).

***God then opened her eyes, and she saw a well*** (21:19). This was said to be Miriam's Well, created on the eve of the first Shabbat of Creation (*Pirkei D'Rabbi Eliezer* 30). Rabbi Benjamin suggested that the phraseology of the text teaches that "All are blind until God brings light to their eyes" (*B'reishit Rabbah* 53.19).

***After these things*** (22:1). *Sefer HaYashar, parashat Vayeira*, suggests that when God commanded Abraham to offer up his son, Abraham masked his intentions and informed Sarah that he was taking Isaac to study with the sages. Sarah agreed but begged Abraham to protect Isaac on the journey and not to keep him away for long, "for his soul is bound up with mine."

*Sick persons' prayers on their own behalf are more efficacious than those of anyone else.*

***after all these things*** (22:20). Strikingly, Sarah is never mentioned in Genesis 22, but Genesis 23 will begin with her death. This juxtaposition led to the tradition that when Sarah learned that Abraham planned to offer Isaac as a sacrifice to God, she died of grief, thinking her son dead (*B'reishit Rabbah* 58.5). Other versions suggest that when Satan (or the demon Samael) told Sarah that Isaac had been sacrificed, she began to weep and cried aloud three times, corresponding to the shofar's three sustained notes (*t'kiah*) on Rosh HaShanah, followed by three laments corresponding to the three disconnected short notes (*t'ruah*). Her soul then fled and she died (*Pirkei D'Rabbi Eliezer* 32). According to others, Sarah died of shock when she learned that Isaac had actually survived (*Tanchuma* on *Vayeira* 23; *Midrash HaGadol*).

—*Ruth H. Sohn*

# *Contemporary Reflection*

This extraordinarily rich parashah is filled with violence—not just the obvious and dramatic violence of the destruction of Sodom and Gomorrah and the incipient violence of the binding of Isaac, but also various, more ordinary, forms of violence against women. Half-buried in the vivid description of the people of Sodom gathering around Lot's house and demanding the strangers staying with him is Lot's reply, "Look—I have two daughters who have never been intimate with a man; let me bring them out for you, and do to them as you please. But do nothing to these men, for they have come under the shelter of my roof" (19:8). While a later midrash will see Lot's offer as evidence that he was infected by the wickedness of Sodom and picture him as having been punished (*Tanchuma Vayeira* 12), the biblical text offers no explicit judgment on his behavior. The violence of the people of Sodom merits the destruction of the city, but the willingness of Lot to see his daughters assaulted and raped is apparently unworthy of comment.

At the beginning of Genesis 20, we have another form of violence: the second of two stories (or two versions of the same story; see 12:10–20) in which Abraham seeks to pass off his wife Sarah as his sister in order to protect himself. In this passage, Abimelech, king of Gerar, seizes Sarah, but her potential rape is averted when God keeps Abimelech from touching her. The similar tale will be repeated once again in relation to Isaac and Rebekah (26:6–11). The three-fold reiteration of the narrative suggests that it might serve as a paradigm of the situation of Jewish women. The first two male ancestors of the Jews, perceiving themselves as "other" and therefore endangered in foreign lands, use their wives as buffers between themselves and the larger culture. The women become the "others' other," the ones whose safety and well-being can be sacrificed in order to save the patriarchs' skins. The story names a pattern that becomes a recurring part of Jewish history: male Jews, subordinated by the dominant culture, in turn subordinate women within their own cultures, doubling the otherness that partly mirrors their own. As in the case of Lot's offering his daughters to the people of Sodom, the biblical text offers no comment on or protest against this situation. Unlike when God appears to Abimelech in a dream and threatens him with death unless he releases Sarah (Genesis 12), God does not explicitly chastise Abraham or Lot.

Then, in Genesis 21, we meet still another form of violence—this time Sarah's violence against Hagar.

*Can we strengthen our resolve to hold both ourselves and God accountable?*

After Sarah bears Isaac in her old age, she tells Abraham to throw the slave girl Hagar and her son Ishmael out of the house, so that Ishmael will not share in his father's inheritance along with Isaac. The violence that is practiced by Abraham against Sarah, she now recapitulates in relation to the most vulnerable person in her own household. Thus, the cycle of abuse goes on. In this context, not only does the text not judge Sarah, but God is explicitly on her side, telling Abraham to listen to Sarah because her son Isaac will be the bearer of the covenantal line.

This Torah portion makes clear that our ancestors are by no means always models of ethical behavior that edify and inspire us. On the contrary, often the Torah holds up a mirror to the ugliest aspects of human nature and human society. It provides us with opportunities to look honestly at ourselves and the world we have created, to reflect on destructive patterns of human relating, and to ask how we might address and change them. In Lot's treatment of his daughters—and in the Torah's lack of comment on that treatment—can we see the casual acceptance, indeed the invisibility, of violence against women that is so ubiquitous in many cultures, including our own? In Abraham's seeming lack of concern about the fate of Sarah, can we see the ways in which marginalized peoples are all too liable to duplicate patterns of subordination from which they themselves have suffered? In Sarah's banishment of Hagar, can we see the horizontal violence that oppressed people visit on each other as they jockey for what seems to them limited resources, rather than making common cause against the forces that suppress them? And what do we do when we see ourselves enacting these patterns in our own personal and political lives? How do we respond to and interrupt them?

It is striking that throughout the portion, God is implicated in the violence in the text. Except in the case of Lot's willingness to sacrifice his daughters, God carries out or commands the violence (Sodom and Gomorrah; Isaac) or supports it (Abraham and Sarah; Sarah and Hagar). The representations of violence that the text holds up to us are ones on which the human and divine levels mirror each other. There is no cosmic relief, so to speak, from the reality of violence. Abraham's challenge to God over the destruction of Sodom and Gomorrah can thus be seen as a question to both God and ourselves. "Must not the Judge of all the earth do justly?" Abraham asks God. "Will You indeed sweep away the innocent along with the wicked?" (18:23). The implication of these questions is that it is the judge of all the earth who creates the ethical norms that Abraham reflects back to God and to which he holds God answerable. But the moral voice in this passage is Abraham's voice. What happens to that moral vision two chapters later when Abraham betrays his wife Sarah? Can we read these narratives in ways that strengthen our resolve to hold both ourselves and God accountable to standards of justice that we recognize and value—and yet continually violate?

*—Judith Plaskow*

# *Voices*

## *His Wife*

Shirley Kaufman (transl. Myra Glazer)

*Genesis 19:26*

But it was right that she
looked back. Not to be
curious, some lumpy
reaching of the mind
that turns all shapes to pillars.
But to be only who she was
apart from them, the place
exploding, and herself
defined. Seeing them melt
to slag heaps and the flames
slide into their mouths.
Testing her own lips then,
the coolness, till
she could taste the salt.

## *A Meditation in Seven Days*

Alicia Suskin Ostriker

*Genesis 21:1–21*

The lines of another story, inscribed
And reinscribed like an endless chain

A proud old woman, her face desert-bitten
Has named her son: laughter

Laughter for bodily pleasure, laughter for
 old age triumph
Hagar the rival stumbles away

In the hot sand, along with her son Ishmael
They nearly die of thirst, God pities them

But among us each son and daughter
Is the child of Sarah, whom God made to laugh.

## *Sarah*

Edna Aphek (transl. Yishai Tobin)

*Genesis 21:1–21*

*1*
Sarah
was a woman
soft and pliant
like a furrowed field
and he with
Hagar.

*2*
Sarah was
soft and pliant
quiet and kind
a woman
and he with
Hagar.

*3*
Sarah was
a woman
quiet and kind
crushed and cruel
and he with
Hagar.

*4*
Sarah was
crushed and cruel
a woman
when her womb
was soft with son
call her the
laughing one.

## *from* Sarah and Hagar

Linda Hirschhorn

*Genesis 21:1–21*

I am calling you, O Sarah;
This is your sister, Hagar,
calling through the centuries
to reach you from afar....

Oh yes, I am your Sarah.
I remember you, Hagar.
Your voice comes through the distance,
a cry upon my heart.

## With My Grandfather

Zelda (transl. Marcia Falk)

*Genesis 22:1–19*

Like our father Abraham
who counted stars at night,
who called out to his Creator
from the furnace,
who bound his son
on the altar—
so was my grandfather.
The same perfect faith
in the midst of the flames,
the same dewy gaze
and soft-curling beard.
Outside, it snowed;
outside, they roared:
*"There is no justice,*
*no judge."*
And in the shambles of his room,
cherubs sang
of the Heavenly Jerusalem.

## *from* The Sacrifice

Chana Bloch

*Genesis 22:1–19*

*2*

The patriarch in black takes
candle and knife
like cutlery,
rehearsing under his breath
the Benediction
on the Death of an Only Son.

Isaac stoops under the raw wood,
carries his father on his back,
candle, velvet and all.

*3*

On the woodpile
Isaac's body waits
as women wait,
fever trilling under his skin.

He will remember the blade's
white silence,
the waiting
under his father's eyes.

## I Will Not Offer

Ra'aya Harnik (transl. Ruth Kartun-Blum)

*Genesis 22:1–19*

I will not offer
My first born for sacrifice
Not I

At night God and I
Make reckonings
Who can claim what

I know and am
Grateful
But not my son
And not
for sacrifice

# חיי שרה ✦ *Chayei Sarah*

GENESIS 23:1–25:18

## *From Sarah to Rebekah*

PARASHAT CHAYEI SARAH ("the life of Sarah") opens with the death and burial of Sarah. It centers on the introduction of Rebekah as a wife to Isaac and concludes with the deaths of Abraham and of Ishmael. Within this framework, the Torah relates two incidents in detail: how Sarah's death prompts Abraham's purchase of a burial plot in the promised land; and how Rebekah agrees to leave her homeland and family in Aram-naharaim in order to marry Isaac.

With these two incidents, Abraham begins to realize the divine promises of land and progeny. It becomes evident that these divine promises are deeply connected to the lives of women, in particular to the matriarchs. To guarantee that Sarah has a permanent resting spot, Abraham purchases the cave of Machpelah. This purchase marks Abraham's first concrete step toward realizing the divine promise of land, for he acquires legitimate title to the field containing the cave. Second, Abraham achieves his goal that Isaac marry a woman from the land of his birth when Rebekah emerges as a more-than-suitable wife for Isaac. Through that marriage to Isaac, the future of the patriarch's family will be assured and, by extension, the covenant with God will be renewed.

The longest unit in the parashah, Genesis 24, is devoted to what has been called the Courting of Rebekah. It introduces Rebekah as an energetic young woman who, like Abraham (Genesis 12), embarks on a journey to a distant land.

*These divine promises are deeply connected to the lives of women.*

The closing unit accentuates Isaac's special standing. Abraham sends away the sons who were born to him through his subsequent wife, Keturah, and through the concubines he had taken (25:1–6). Isaac thus remains his sole heir. This accords both with God's promise that "My covenant I will maintain with Isaac" (Genesis 17:21) and with Sarah's demand that Ishmael (and presumably other of Abraham's sons) not inherit with her son, Isaac (21:10). This separation from Ishmael highlights the continuing question of identity formation in relation to other peoples.

—*Yairah Amit*

## Outline

*I.* SARAH'S DEATH LEADS ABRAHAM TO ACQUIRE LAND
*The Purchase of the Field of Machpelah* (23:1–20)

*A.* Sarah's death (vv. 1–2)

*B.* Abraham negotiates for a burial ground (vv. 3–18)

*C.* Conclusion: Sarah's burial (vv. 19–20)

*II.* ABRAHAM ENSURES THE COVENANT'S CONTINUITY
*Rebekah Becomes Isaac's Wife* (24:1–67)

*A.* Exposition: Abraham as blessed (v. 1)

*B.* Abraham commissions his servant to bring a wife for Isaac (vv. 2–10a)

*C.* The servant meets Rebekah at the well (vv. 10b–27)

*D.* The servant meets Laban (vv. 28–31)

*E.* Rebekah's betrothal (vv. 32–54a)

*F.* Rebekah agrees to go (vv. 54b–58)

*G.* Rebekah departs (vv. 59–61)

*H.* Rebekah meets Isaac (vv. 62–66)

*I.* Conclusion: Rebekah moves into Sarah's tent (v. 67)

*III.* ABRAHAM'S DESCENDANTS AND HIS DEATH (25:1–18)

*A.* The descendants of Keturah (vv. 1–4)

*B.* Isaac's status (vv. 5–6)

*C.* Abraham's death and burial (vv. 7–11)

*D.* Hagar's descendants (vv. 12–18)

23:1
Sarah lived to be 127 years old—such was the
span of Sarah's life. [2]Sarah died in Kiriath-
arba (that is, Hebron) in the land of Canaan, and

כג וַיִּהְיוּ חַיֵּי שָׂרָה מֵאָה שָׁנָה וְעֶשְׂרִים
שָׁנָה וְשֶׁבַע שָׁנִים שְׁנֵי חַיֵּי שָׂרָה׃
2 וַתָּמָת שָׂרָה בְּקִרְיַת אַרְבַּע הִוא חֶבְרוֹן

## *Sarah's Death Leads Abraham to Acquire Land*

### THE PURCHASE OF THE FIELD OF MACHPELAH (23:1–20)

Why does the Torah present such a lengthy description of the purchase of the cave of Machpelah? Biblical narrative is usually sparing of details about realia and daily life, yet the negotiations over the purchase of the field containing the cave of Machpelah are reported fully. It seems that the purchase of the field symbolizes Abraham and his family's legal ownership of the entire promised land.

Abraham does not wish to purchase just a cave, but rather a whole burial site. He is particularly interested in Ephron's plot since it is apparently located on the outskirts of the town (23:9 and 17). All this would limit potential friction with Hebron's residents and ensure him free access to the cave. Abraham struggles to find a resting place not only for Sarah, but also for the generations he hopes would descend from him. This reflects the tension between his presently temporary status (no land and no assurance of descendants in his central line) and the promise that God has repeatedly made to him (a divine promise of land and progeny).

According to the Bible, this site will also become the burial place of Abraham, Isaac, Rebekah, Jacob, and Leah (Genesis 25:9–10, 35:27–29, 49:29–32, 50:13); hundreds of years later, the nearby city of Hebron will also serve as capital of David's kingdom until he conquers Jerusalem.

### SARAH'S DEATH (23:1–2)

*1. Sarah lived.* Though beginning with her life, the chapter actually focuses on her death and burial. However, the notice that the marriage of Isaac and Rebekah is consummated in Sarah's tent (24:67) suggests that her life continues through the next matriarch.

*127 years old.* Sarah is the only matriarch whose age at death is reported. Her age surpasses the ideal 120 with the sacred number of 7.

*2. Sarah died.* No explanation is given as a cause of her death. It is reasonable to assume that it was her age, but as Abraham was last seen in Beersheba (22:19), some distance from where Sarah died, one may ask: Did Sarah know about Abraham's binding of Isaac (Genesis 22)? Was that a factor in her death? Perhaps Sarah had been living apart from Abraham.

*Kiriath-arba.* Another name for Hebron.

▶ Isaac's love for Rebekah is the first mention of spousal love in the Bible.

ANOTHER VIEW ➤ 127

▶ "The heart of her husband trusts in her" (Proverbs 31:11)—this is Sarah.

POST-BIBLICAL INTERPRETATIONS ➤ 127

▶ Consider the history of a significant yet often obscured tradition in women's discourse, namely, mourning.

CONTEMPORARY REFLECTION ➤ 129

▶ I remember the music... in the firelight....

VOICES ➤ 131

Abraham proceeded to mourn for Sarah and to bewail her.

³Then Abraham rose up from upon his dead [wife], and spoke to the Hittites, saying, ⁴"I am a foreigner living for a time among you; sell me a gravesite among you, that I may bury my dead here." ⁵The Hittites answered Abraham, saying, ⁶"Hear us, my lord; you are a mighty prince in our midst; bury your dead in any of our choicest graves. Not one of us will keep you from burying your dead by withholding a gravesite from you."

⁷Abraham then got up and bowed low to the people of the land, the Hittites, ⁸pressing them: "If you [really] are willing to let me bury my dead here, listen to me and entreat Ephron son of Zoar for me, ⁹and let him sell me the cave of Machpelah. He owns it—it is at the edge of his land. Let him sell it to me as an inalienable gravesite in your midst at the market price." ¹⁰Ephron [himself] was sitting among the Hittites, and, in the hearing of all the

בָּאָ֑רֶץ כְּנַ֖עַן וַיָּבֹא֙ אַבְרָהָ֔ם לִסְפֹּ֥ד לְשָׂרָ֖ה
וְלִבְכֹּתָֽהּ׃
3 וַיָּ֙קָם֙ אַבְרָהָ֔ם מֵעַ֖ל פְּנֵ֣י מֵת֑וֹ וַיְדַבֵּ֥ר אֶל־
בְּנֵי־חֵ֖ת לֵאמֹֽר׃ 4 גֵּר־וְתוֹשָׁ֥ב אָנֹכִ֖י עִמָּכֶ֑ם
תְּנ֨וּ לִ֜י אֲחֻזַּת־קֶ֙בֶר֙ עִמָּכֶ֔ם וְאֶקְבְּרָ֥ה מֵתִ֖י
מִלְּפָנָֽי׃ 5 וַיַּעֲנ֧וּ בְנֵי־חֵ֛ת אֶת־אַבְרָהָ֖ם
לֵאמֹ֥ר לֽוֹ׃ 6 שְׁמָעֵ֣נוּ ׀ אֲדֹנִ֗י נְשִׂ֨יא אֱלֹהִ֤ים
אַתָּה֙ בְּתוֹכֵ֔נוּ בְּמִבְחַ֣ר קְבָרֵ֔ינוּ קְבֹ֖ר אֶת־
מֵתֶ֑ךָ אִ֣ישׁ מִמֶּ֗נּוּ אֶת־קִבְר֛וֹ לֹֽא־יִכְלֶ֥ה מִמְּךָ֖
מִקְּבֹ֥ר מֵתֶֽךָ׃
7 וַיָּ֧קָם אַבְרָהָ֛ם וַיִּשְׁתַּ֥חוּ לְעַם־הָאָ֖רֶץ לִבְנֵי־
חֵֽת׃ 8 וַיְדַבֵּ֥ר אִתָּ֖ם לֵאמֹ֑ר אִם־יֵ֣שׁ אֶת־
נַפְשְׁכֶ֗ם לִקְבֹּ֤ר אֶת־מֵתִי֙ מִלְּפָנַ֔י שְׁמָע֕וּנִי
וּפִגְעוּ־לִ֖י בְּעֶפְר֥וֹן בֶּן־צֹֽחַר׃ 9 וְיִתֶּן־לִ֣י אֶת־
מְעָרַ֤ת הַמַּכְפֵּלָה֙ אֲשֶׁר־ל֔וֹ אֲשֶׁ֖ר בִּקְצֵ֣ה
שָׂדֵ֑הוּ בְּכֶ֨סֶף מָלֵ֜א יִתְּנֶ֥נָּה לִּ֛י בְּתוֹכְכֶ֖ם
לַאֲחֻזַּת־קָֽבֶר׃ 10 וְעֶפְר֥וֹן יֹשֵׁ֖ב בְּת֣וֹךְ בְּנֵי־
חֵ֑ת וַיַּ֩עַן֩ עֶפְר֨וֹן הַחִתִּ֤י אֶת־אַבְרָהָם֙ בְּאׇזְנֵ֣י

---

***Abraham proceeded to mourn for Sarah and to bewail her.*** This verse marks one of only two instances where the Torah uses the root *s-p-d*, to mourn. (The other is in Genesis 50:10, when Joseph mourns the passing of his father Jacob.) This is also the only place where the text mentions details of mourning in connection with a woman's death. Even Jacob's mourning over his beloved Rachel is not recorded (Genesis 35:19–20).

### ABRAHAM NEGOTIATES FOR A BURIAL GROUND (23:3–18)

As soon as Abraham rises from beside Sarah's body, he seeks out her burial place. Abraham addresses a representative body of town citizens that is called "the Hittites" but also "the people of the land" (v. 7) and "the town leaders" (literally "those who entered the gate of the city"; v. 10). Hittites

are associated with an ancient empire that was centered in today's Turkey.

As Abraham declares at the outset, he is a resident alien (a "foreigner living for a time" among the native population) and thus dependent upon the good will of the local landowners. He makes it clear that he wishes to acquire an entire burial site, including field, cave and trees—not only a cave. This language reflects Abraham's attempt to realize God's first promise to him, of land. It also foreshadows his steps to realize God's second promise, of progeny (Genesis 24).

*6. "a mighty prince in our midst."* The Hittites address Abraham with a respectful title.

*7–9.* The courtesy, respect, and ready response of the Hittites allow Abraham to specify that he is particularly interested in the cave within the plot of Ephron, and that he wishes to purchase it at whatever price they require.

Hittites and all the town leaders, Ephron the Hittite answered Abraham, saying, [11]"No, my lord; listen to me. I am giving you the field, and the cave that is in it I give to you; in the sight of my people I give it to you; go ahead—bury your dead."

[12]But Abraham bowed low before the landowning citizens, [13]and in their hearing he addressed Ephron the Hittite: "Oh, if only you would listen to me! I will pay the field's price; take it from me, and let me bury my dead there." [14]Ephron then made this reply to Abraham: [15]"My lord, hear me: land worth 400 shekels of silver—what is that between you and me? Go bury your dead!"

[16]Abraham listened to Ephron, and Abraham weighed out for Ephron the [amount of] silver he had named in the hearing of the Hittites—400 shekels of silver, [using weights] standard among traders. [17–18]So Ephron's land in Machpelah, looking out on Mamre—the field, its cave, and all the trees in the field within its boundaries—passed to Abraham by purchase, in the sight of the Hittites and of all the town leaders.

[19]Afterward, Abraham buried his wife Sarah in the cave of the field of Machpelah—facing Mamre (that is, Hebron)—in the land of Canaan. [20]Thus was confirmed Abraham's acquisition from the Hittites of the field and its cave as a fully owned gravesite.

בְּנֵי־חֵת לְכֹל בָּאֵי שַׁעַר־עִירוֹ לֵאמֹר׃
11 לֹא־אֲדֹנִי שְׁמָעֵנִי הַשָּׂדֶה נָתַתִּי לָךְ
וְהַמְּעָרָה אֲשֶׁר־בּוֹ לְךָ נְתַתִּיהָ לְעֵינֵי בְנֵי־
עַמִּי נְתַתִּיהָ לָּךְ קְבֹר מֵתֶךָ׃
12 וַיִּשְׁתַּחוּ אַבְרָהָם לִפְנֵי עַם הָאָרֶץ׃
13 וַיְדַבֵּר אֶל־עֶפְרוֹן בְּאָזְנֵי עַם־הָאָרֶץ
לֵאמֹר אַךְ אִם־אַתָּה לוּ שְׁמָעֵנִי נָתַתִּי
כֶּסֶף הַשָּׂדֶה קַח מִמֶּנִּי וְאֶקְבְּרָה אֶת־מֵתִי
שָׁמָּה׃ 14 וַיַּעַן עֶפְרוֹן אֶת־אַבְרָהָם לֵאמֹר
לוֹ׃ 15 אֲדֹנִי שְׁמָעֵנִי אֶרֶץ אַרְבַּע מֵאֹת
שֶׁקֶל־כֶּסֶף בֵּינִי וּבֵינְךָ מַה־הִוא וְאֶת־מֵתְךָ
קְבֹר׃
16 וַיִּשְׁמַע אַבְרָהָם אֶל־עֶפְרוֹן וַיִּשְׁקֹל
אַבְרָהָם לְעֶפְרֹן אֶת־הַכֶּסֶף אֲשֶׁר דִּבֶּר
בְּאָזְנֵי בְנֵי־חֵת אַרְבַּע מֵאוֹת שֶׁקֶל כֶּסֶף
עֹבֵר לַסֹּחֵר׃ 17 וַיָּקָם ׀ שְׂדֵה עֶפְרוֹן אֲשֶׁר
בַּמַּכְפֵּלָה אֲשֶׁר לִפְנֵי מַמְרֵא הַשָּׂדֶה
וְהַמְּעָרָה אֲשֶׁר־בּוֹ וְכָל־הָעֵץ אֲשֶׁר בַּשָּׂדֶה
אֲשֶׁר בְּכָל־גְּבֻלוֹ סָבִיב׃ 18 לְאַבְרָהָם לְמִקְנָה
לְעֵינֵי בְנֵי־חֵת בְּכֹל בָּאֵי שַׁעַר־עִירוֹ׃
19 וְאַחֲרֵי־כֵן קָבַר אַבְרָהָם אֶת־שָׂרָה אִשְׁתּוֹ
אֶל־מְעָרַת שְׂדֵה הַמַּכְפֵּלָה עַל־פְּנֵי מַמְרֵא
הִוא חֶבְרוֹן בְּאֶרֶץ כְּנָעַן׃ 20 וַיָּקָם הַשָּׂדֶה
וְהַמְּעָרָה אֲשֶׁר־בּוֹ לְאַבְרָהָם לַאֲחֻזַּת־קָבֶר
מֵאֵת בְּנֵי־חֵת׃ ס

*12–13.* Abraham makes it clear that he does not want a grant or gift; rather, he desires legal rights to the entire field through full purchase of the property.

*14–15.* Ephron takes advantage of the situation and demands an exorbitant sum.

*16–18.* Abraham does not haggle, but hastens to pay the required sum, high as it might be. The purchase is made according to legal custom in the presence of the town's leaders, at the city gate, which is the traditional seat of justice and place to notarize transactions. The text emphasizes that the purchase includes the field and all it contains. Similar declarations recur afterward (25:9–10, 49:29–32, 50:13), indicating the importance of the purchase.

## CONCLUSION: SARAH'S BURIAL (23:19–20)

More time is devoted to the negotiations than to the burial itself (on burial customs, see *Va-y'chi*, Another View, p. 297). After Sarah is buried, the text reiterates that the field and all within it became

24 Abraham was old, well advanced in years,
and יהוה had blessed Abraham in every way. [2]Abra-
ham now said to his slave, the elder of his household, who had oversight of all that was his, "Put
your hand under my thigh, [3]so that I may have you

כד וְאַבְרָהָם זָקֵן בָּא בַּיָּמִים וַיהוָה בֵּרַךְ
אֶת־אַבְרָהָם בַּכֹּל׃ 2 וַיֹּאמֶר אַבְרָהָם אֶל־
עַבְדּוֹ זְקַן בֵּיתוֹ הַמֹּשֵׁל בְּכָל־אֲשֶׁר־לוֹ שִׂים־
נָא יָדְךָ תַּחַת יְרֵכִי׃ 3 וְאַשְׁבִּיעֲךָ בַּיהוָה

Abraham's rightful possession. Thus Sarah's grave is the first permanent, legal presence in the land promised to Abraham and to their descendants.

## *Abraham Ensures the Covenant's Continuity*

### REBEKAH BECOMES ISAAC'S WIFE (24:1–67)

The major factor that motivates the story of Rebekah's betrothal is Abraham's concern with preventing his son Isaac, his designated heir to the divine promise, from establishing blood ties with the Canaanites in the land. The story turns upon divine providence and God's covert intervention. God is present behind the scenes, planning and directing the course of events.

Concerns with group identity and its relation to the surroundings continue throughout the patriarchal and matriarchal narratives, which repeatedly stress ties with the land of Israel. Thus Abraham takes pains to obtain his servant's promise not to allow Isaac to return to the land Abraham left behind. At the same time, Abraham sends his servant to bring a wife for Isaac from his extended family in the distant homeland, preferring family ties over those with the natives of the land. In contrast to this attitude, the story of Joseph will later report, with no hint of criticism, that he marries the Egyptian daughter of an Egyptian priest (Genesis 41:45). In other words, Genesis integrates apparently conflicting positions alongside each other—as is found throughout the Bible. One tendency calls for keeping separate from the other nations (see Deuteronomy 7:1–4, 23:4–9; Ezra 9–11), while the other outlook is universalistic and open to the stranger (see Exodus 12:38; Ruth 1–4).

This story also reflects the seemingly dual (even contradictory) positions that women hold throughout the *Tanach*: at times as passive characters, and at others as decision makers who assert their will on others. The text introduces Rebekah to the reader through a narrative account (24:15–16); but Rebekah introduces herself to the servant using her own words (24:24). At first, Rebekah's brother and father, Laban and Bethuel, give Rebekah to the servant so that she might marry Isaac (24:51). However, Rebekah is the one whose consent is needed before the caravan can depart (24:58). When Isaac wanders into the vicinity of Rebekah's camels (24:63), the story again focuses on Rebekah. At this point, she acts of her own volition.

This chapter, with 67 verses, is the longest in the book of Genesis. Its length is a direct result of the artistic use of repetition. Verses 15–20 report how all that the servant prayed for in vv. 13–14 actually transpired, and vv. 35–48 reiterate all that happened to the servant in vv. 2–26. The repetitions are not verbatim; rather, they display considerable alterations that shed light on the character of the servant, Rebekah, and the members of her family.

#### EXPOSITION: ABRAHAM AS BLESSED (24:1)

This verse emphasizes Abraham's wealth.

#### ABRAHAM COMMISSIONS HIS SERVANT TO BRING A WIFE FOR ISAAC (24:2–10a)

*2–3.* The thigh represents the male organ. Apparently, one who touches this member when

swear by יהוה, God of heaven and God of earth,
that you will not take a wife for my son from
among the daughters of the Canaanites, in whose
midst I dwell. 4Rather, you shall go to my land, my
birthplace, and get a wife for my son Isaac." 5The
slave replied, "Suppose the woman does not care
to follow me to this land—should I then bring
your son back to the land you came from?"

6Abraham then answered him, "Take great care
not to bring my son back there! 7יהוה, the God of
heaven—who took me from my father's house,
from the land of my birth, who spoke to me and
promised me, saying, 'To your descendants will I
give this land'—will send a [divine] emissary before you, and you shall take a wife for my son from
there. 8But if the woman does not care to follow
you, you are released from this oath of mine—only
do not bring my son back there!" 9The slave placed
his hand under his master Abraham's thigh and
swore to him concerning this matter.

10The slave then took ten of his master's camels
and, laden with an abundant store of his master's
goods, got up and went to Aram-naharaim, to the
city of Nahor. 11He made the camels kneel down
outside the city at the water-well, at eventide, at
the time when the girls who draw water go forth,
12and he prayed: "יהוה, God of my master Abraham, please bring me luck today, and do a kind-

אֱלֹהֵי הַשָּׁמַיִם וֵאלֹהֵי הָאָרֶץ אֲשֶׁר לֹא־
תִקַּח אִשָּׁה לִבְנִי מִבְּנוֹת הַכְּנַעֲנִי אֲשֶׁר
אָנֹכִי יוֹשֵׁב בְּקִרְבּוֹ׃ 4 כִּי אֶל־אַרְצִי וְאֶל־
מוֹלַדְתִּי תֵּלֵךְ וְלָקַחְתָּ אִשָּׁה לִבְנִי לְיִצְחָק׃
5 וַיֹּאמֶר אֵלָיו הָעֶבֶד אוּלַי לֹא־תֹאבֶה
הָאִשָּׁה לָלֶכֶת אַחֲרַי אֶל־הָאָרֶץ הַזֹּאת
הֶהָשֵׁב אָשִׁיב אֶת־בִּנְךָ אֶל־הָאָרֶץ אֲשֶׁר־
יָצָאתָ מִשָּׁם׃
6 וַיֹּאמֶר אֵלָיו אַבְרָהָם הִשָּׁמֶר לְךָ פֶּן־
תָּשִׁיב אֶת־בְּנִי שָׁמָּה׃ 7 יְהוָה ׀ אֱלֹהֵי
הַשָּׁמַיִם אֲשֶׁר לְקָחַנִי מִבֵּית אָבִי וּמֵאֶרֶץ
מוֹלַדְתִּי וַאֲשֶׁר דִּבֶּר־לִי וַאֲשֶׁר נִשְׁבַּע־לִי
לֵאמֹר לְזַרְעֲךָ אֶתֵּן אֶת־הָאָרֶץ הַזֹּאת הוּא
יִשְׁלַח מַלְאָכוֹ לְפָנֶיךָ וְלָקַחְתָּ אִשָּׁה לִבְנִי
מִשָּׁם׃ 8 וְאִם־לֹא תֹאבֶה הָאִשָּׁה לָלֶכֶת
אַחֲרֶיךָ וְנִקִּיתָ מִשְּׁבֻעָתִי זֹאת רַק אֶת־בְּנִי
לֹא תָשֵׁב שָׁמָּה׃ 9 וַיָּשֶׂם הָעֶבֶד אֶת־יָדוֹ
תַּחַת יֶרֶךְ אַבְרָהָם אֲדֹנָיו וַיִּשָּׁבַע לוֹ עַל־
הַדָּבָר הַזֶּה׃
10 וַיִּקַּח הָעֶבֶד עֲשָׂרָה גְמַלִּים מִגְּמַלֵּי אֲדֹנָיו
וַיֵּלֶךְ וְכָל־טוּב אֲדֹנָיו בְּיָדוֹ וַיָּקָם וַיֵּלֶךְ
אֶל־אֲרַם נַהֲרַיִם אֶל־עִיר נָחוֹר׃ 11 וַיַּבְרֵךְ
הַגְּמַלִּים מִחוּץ לָעִיר אֶל־בְּאֵר הַמָּיִם לְעֵת
עֶרֶב לְעֵת צֵאת הַשֹּׁאֲבֹת׃ 12 וַיֹּאמַר ׀ יְהוָה
אֱלֹהֵי אֲדֹנִי אַבְרָהָם הַקְרֵה־נָא לְפָנַי הַיּוֹם

swearing an oath is obliged to uphold that oath on pain of either sterility or death of offspring. That Abraham insists on such a grave oath illustrates the importance of the "right" wife for Isaac.

*3. "daughters of the Canaanites."* See at 28:1.

*4. "a wife for my son."* The word for "wife," *ishah*, also means "woman." It recurs frequently in these verses, emphasizing Abraham's fear that Isaac will marry the "wrong" woman.

*5. "Suppose the woman does not care to."* Literally, "perhaps the woman will be unwilling." The servant's question implies that the woman can legally choose to refuse. A woman cannot simply be "taken."

*6–8.* Abraham's response introduces a key biblical concept: the special bond between the family of the patriarchs and the land of Israel.

*8. does not care to follow.* See at v. 5 above.

### THE SERVANT MEETS REBEKAH AT THE WELL (24:10b–27)

*12. "יהוה, God of my master Abraham, please bring me luck today."* The turn of events is even better than the servant has reason to expect. The

וְעָֽשֵׂה־חֶ֕סֶד עִ֖ם אֲדֹנִ֥י אַבְרָהָֽם׃ 13 הִנֵּ֛ה
אָנֹכִ֥י נִצָּ֖ב עַל־עֵ֣ין הַמָּ֑יִם וּבְנוֹת֙ אַנְשֵׁ֣י הָעִ֔יר
יֹצְאֹ֖ת לִשְׁאֹ֥ב מָֽיִם׃ 14 וְהָיָ֣ה הנער הַנַּעֲרָ֗ה
אֲשֶׁ֨ר אֹמַ֤ר אֵלֶ֙יהָ֙ הַטִּי־נָ֤א כַדֵּךְ֙ וְאֶשְׁתֶּ֔ה
וְאָמְרָ֣ה שְׁתֵ֔ה וְגַם־גְּמַלֶּ֖יךָ אַשְׁקֶ֑ה אֹתָ֤הּ
הֹכַ֙חְתָּ֙ לְעַבְדְּךָ֣ לְיִצְחָ֔ק וּבָ֣הּ אֵדַ֔ע כִּֽי־עָשִׂ֥יתָ
חֶ֖סֶד עִם־אֲדֹנִֽי׃

15 וַֽיְהִי־ה֗וּא טֶ֘רֶם֮ כִּלָּ֣ה לְדַבֵּר֒ וְהִנֵּ֧ה רִבְקָ֣ה
יֹצֵ֗את אֲשֶׁ֤ר יֻלְּדָה֙ לִבְתוּאֵ֣ל בֶּן־מִלְכָּ֔ה
אֵ֥שֶׁת נָח֖וֹר אֲחִ֣י אַבְרָהָ֑ם וְכַדָּ֖הּ עַל־שִׁכְמָֽהּ׃
16 והנער וְהַנַּעֲרָ֗ה טֹבַ֤ת מַרְאֶה֙ מְאֹ֔ד בְּתוּלָ֕ה
וְאִ֖ישׁ לֹ֣א יְדָעָ֑הּ וַתֵּ֣רֶד הָעַ֔יְנָה וַתְּמַלֵּ֥א
כַדָּ֖הּ וַתָּֽעַל׃

17 וַיָּ֥רָץ הָעֶ֖בֶד לִקְרָאתָ֑הּ וַיֹּ֕אמֶר הַגְמִיאִ֥ינִי
נָ֛א מְעַט־מַ֖יִם מִכַּדֵּֽךְ׃ 18 וַתֹּ֖אמֶר שְׁתֵ֣ה

ness for my master Abraham. 13 Here I am standing
at the water-fount, and the daughters of the townspeople are going forth to draw water; 14 the girl to
whom I say, 'Tip your pitcher and let me drink,'
and who replies, 'Drink; and let me water your
camels, too'—let her be the one You have designated for Your servant Isaac; that is how I shall know
that You have done a kindness for my master."

15 Before he was done praying, Rebekah, who
had been born to Bethuel, son of Milcah, wife of
Abraham's brother Nahor, was going forth with
her pitcher on her shoulder. 16 She was an exceedingly beautiful girl, of marriageable age, whom no
man had yet known. She went down to the spring,
filled her pitcher, and went up.

17 The slave ran toward her and said, "Let
me sip a little water from your pitcher." 18 And
she replied, "Drink, sir!" Quickly she lowered

developments appear to be the result of chance, but actually the reader has enough signs to understand that they are directed by God.

*13. "the daughters of the townspeople are going forth to draw water."* A well figures in two other biblical stories as the meeting place where the hero encounters the woman he will marry (Jacob meets Rachel in Genesis 29:1–14; Moses meets Zipporah in Exodus 2:15–22). It is likely that this motif is rooted in ancient social reality, in which the well served as a place of meeting and assembly (Judges 5:11). In the framework of this motif, the characters' behavior by the well is tested. In the present story, the girl's hospitality surpasses the servant's expectations. [Drawing well water appears to be the task specifically of the households' daughters, who proceed unchaperoned (see also v. 11; I Samuel 9:11). *—Ed.*]

*15. Milcah.* See at 11:29 and 22:20.

*going forth.* As soon as Rebekah is introduced, she is an active character.

*16.* Rebekah possesses three virtues that neither Abraham nor the servant had stipulated.

*marriageable age.* The word *b'tulah* is often translated as "virgin" but has a broader meaning than a biological one. In the ancient world, women often married shortly after puberty; therefore, one can assume that Rebekah is very young. Isaac, her future husband, is forty years old (25:20).

*whom no man had yet known.* To "know" in the Bible often refers to sexual relationships. This phrase indicates that Rebekah is a virgin (see at 4:1).

*18–19.* Once the servant asks Rebekah for "a little water" from her jar (v. 17), she assumes the role of primary actor. Rebekah's response portrays her as an energetic and resourceful woman, one ready to engage in conversation with a total stranger rather than retreat from such an encounter. Nothing suggests that Rebekah, or other women, were expected to be in seclusion, away from men's gaze or contact, as would become customary later in the Middle East (see also 29:1–10).

*18. "Drink, sir!"* Rebekah instructs him gently.

her pitcher on her hand and let him drink.
[19]The drinking done, she said, "I will draw some
for your camels, too, till they are done drinking."
[20]Quickly she emptied her pitcher in the trough
and she again ran to the well to draw water, drawing water for all his camels.

[21]The man stood staring at her, silent, in order
to learn whether or not יהוה had cleared the way
for him. [22]When the camels were done drinking,
the man took a gold nose-ring, a half-shekel in
weight, and two bracelets for her wrists, ten gold
shekels in weight, [23]and said, "Please tell me:
whose daughter are you? Is there a place in your father's house for us to lodge?" [24]She said to him, "I
am Bethuel's daughter; [he is] the son of Milcah,
whom she bore to Nahor." [25]And she added, "We
have straw and fodder in abundance, as well as
room for lodging."

[26]The man kneeled and bowed down to יהוה,
[27]saying, "Blessed is יהוה, God of my master Abraham, whose faithful kindness has not deserted my
master; as for me, יהוה led me straightaway to my
master's brother's house!" [28]The girl then ran and
related these things to her mother's household.

[29]Now Rebekah had a brother named Laban,
and Laban ran outside to the man at the spring.

אֲדֹנִי וַתְּמַהֵר וַתֹּרֶד כַּדָּהּ עַל־יָדָהּ וַתַּשְׁקֵהוּ׃
19 וַתְּכַל לְהַשְׁקֹתוֹ וַתֹּאמֶר גַּם לִגְמַלֶּיךָ
אֶשְׁאָב עַד אִם־כִּלּוּ לִשְׁתֹּת׃ 20 וַתְּמַהֵר
וַתְּעַר כַּדָּהּ אֶל־הַשֹּׁקֶת וַתָּרָץ עוֹד אֶל־
הַבְּאֵר לִשְׁאֹב וַתִּשְׁאַב לְכָל־גְּמַלָּיו׃

21 וְהָאִישׁ מִשְׁתָּאֵה לָהּ מַחֲרִישׁ לָדַעַת
הַהִצְלִיחַ יְהוָה דַּרְכּוֹ אִם־לֹא׃ 22 וַיְהִי
כַּאֲשֶׁר כִּלּוּ הַגְּמַלִּים לִשְׁתּוֹת וַיִּקַּח הָאִישׁ
נֶזֶם זָהָב בֶּקַע מִשְׁקָלוֹ וּשְׁנֵי צְמִידִים עַל־
יָדֶיהָ עֲשָׂרָה זָהָב מִשְׁקָלָם׃ 23 וַיֹּאמֶר בַּת־
מִי אַתְּ הַגִּידִי נָא לִי הֲיֵשׁ בֵּית־אָבִיךְ מָקוֹם
לָנוּ לָלִין׃ 24 וַתֹּאמֶר אֵלָיו בַּת־בְּתוּאֵל
אָנֹכִי בֶּן־מִלְכָּה אֲשֶׁר יָלְדָה לְנָחוֹר׃
25 וַתֹּאמֶר אֵלָיו גַּם־תֶּבֶן גַּם־מִסְפּוֹא רַב
עִמָּנוּ גַּם־מָקוֹם לָלוּן׃

26 וַיִּקֹּד הָאִישׁ וַיִּשְׁתַּחוּ לַיהוָה׃ 27 וַיֹּאמֶר
בָּרוּךְ יְהוָה אֱלֹהֵי אֲדֹנִי אַבְרָהָם אֲשֶׁר
לֹא־עָזַב חַסְדּוֹ וַאֲמִתּוֹ מֵעִם אֲדֹנִי אָנֹכִי
בַּדֶּרֶךְ נָחַנִי יְהוָה בֵּית אֲחֵי אֲדֹנִי׃ 28 וַתָּרָץ
הנער הַנַּעֲרָה וַתַּגֵּד לְבֵית אִמָּהּ כַּדְּבָרִים
הָאֵלֶּה׃

29 וּלְרִבְקָה אָח וּשְׁמוֹ לָבָן וַיָּרָץ לָבָן אֶל־

*19. "I will draw some for your camels, too."* Given the amount of water a camel drinks, this is no easy task.

*22–27.* Based on this impressive display of character, the servant presents Rebekah with adornments even before she informs him that she is the granddaughter of Abraham's brother. Her lineage is additional and decisive proof of divine intervention.

***24. "I am Bethuel's daughter;*** [*he is*] ***the son of Milcah, whom she bore to Nahor."*** Rebekah introduces herself by naming her grandmother Milcah (compare v. 15). Rebekah's mother remains unnamed in the story, even though she plays a role in the marriage negotiations (24:53).

## THE SERVANT MEETS LABAN (24:28–31)

Rebekah's brother Laban is the negative counterpart to Rebekah's character. While she displays gracious hospitality toward the stranger, Laban is impressed first and foremost with the adornments she received from the stranger. Only then does Laban hasten to greet him.

***28. her mother's household.*** Although the servant asked about her *father's* house (24:23), Rebekah goes to her *mother's* house. At the end of this chapter she will move into Sarah's tent (24:67). The mention of women's domain (tent or house) occurs only in Genesis 24, the book of Ruth (1:8),

[30]When Laban saw the nose-ring and the bracelets on his sister's wrists, and heard his sister Rebekah say, "This is what the man told me," he went to the man, who was still standing by his camels at the spring. [31]"Come in, O blessed of יהוה!" said he. "Why stand outside when I have cleared the house, and [also made] space for the camels?" [32]So he ushered the man into the house, unsaddled the camels and gave them straw and fodder and brought water in to wash his feet and those of the men with him.

[33]But when food was put in front of him, the man said, "I will not eat until I have had my say." He [Laban] said, "Speak!" [34]"I am the slave of Abraham," said he, [35]"and יהוה has blessed my master exceedingly and made him rich, giving him sheep and cattle, silver and gold, male and female slaves, camels and donkeys. [36]Sarah, my master's wife, bore him a son in her old age, and my master has given him everything he owns. [37]My master adjured me, saying, 'You must not choose a wife for my son from among the daughters of the Canaanites, in whose land I now live. [38]Go, rather, to my father's people, to my relations, and take a wife for my son.' [39]I said to my master, 'What if the woman will not follow me?' [40]He answered, 'יהוה, before whom I have walked, will send an angel with you who will clear the way for you. You

הָאִישׁ הַחוּצָה אֶל־הָעָיִן׃ 30 וַיְהִי ׀ כִּרְאֹת
אֶת־הַנֶּזֶם וְאֶת־הַצְּמִדִים עַל־יְדֵי אֲחֹתוֹ
וּכְשָׁמְעוֹ אֶת־דִּבְרֵי רִבְקָה אֲחֹתוֹ לֵאמֹר
כֹּה־דִבֶּר אֵלַי הָאִישׁ וַיָּבֹא אֶל־הָאִישׁ וְהִנֵּה
עֹמֵד עַל־הַגְּמַלִּים עַל־הָעָיִן׃ 31 וַיֹּאמֶר בּוֹא
בְּרוּךְ יְהוָה לָמָּה תַעֲמֹד בַּחוּץ וְאָנֹכִי פִּנִּיתִי
הַבַּיִת וּמָקוֹם לַגְּמַלִּים׃ 32 וַיָּבֹא הָאִישׁ
הַבַּיְתָה וַיְפַתַּח הַגְּמַלִּים וַיִּתֵּן תֶּבֶן וּמִסְפּוֹא
לַגְּמַלִּים וּמַיִם לִרְחֹץ רַגְלָיו וְרַגְלֵי הָאֲנָשִׁים
אֲשֶׁר אִתּוֹ׃
33 ויישם וַיּוּשַׂם לְפָנָיו לֶאֱכֹל וַיֹּאמֶר לֹא
אֹכַל עַד אִם־דִּבַּרְתִּי דְּבָרָי וַיֹּאמֶר דַּבֵּר׃
34 וַיֹּאמַר עֶבֶד אַבְרָהָם אָנֹכִי׃ 35 וַיהוָה
בֵּרַךְ אֶת־אֲדֹנִי מְאֹד וַיִּגְדָּל וַיִּתֶּן־לוֹ צֹאן
וּבָקָר וְכֶסֶף וְזָהָב וַעֲבָדִם וּשְׁפָחֹת וּגְמַלִּים
וַחֲמֹרִים׃ 36 וַתֵּלֶד שָׂרָה אֵשֶׁת אֲדֹנִי בֵן
לַאדֹנִי אַחֲרֵי זִקְנָתָהּ וַיִּתֶּן־לוֹ אֶת־כָּל־
אֲשֶׁר־לוֹ׃ 37 וַיַּשְׁבִּעֵנִי אֲדֹנִי לֵאמֹר לֹא־
תִקַּח אִשָּׁה לִבְנִי מִבְּנוֹת הַכְּנַעֲנִי אֲשֶׁר
אָנֹכִי יֹשֵׁב בְּאַרְצוֹ׃ 38 אִם־לֹא אֶל־בֵּית־
אָבִי תֵּלֵךְ וְאֶל־מִשְׁפַּחְתִּי וְלָקַחְתָּ אִשָּׁה
לִבְנִי׃ 39 וָאֹמַר אֶל־אֲדֹנִי אֻלַי לֹא־תֵלֵךְ
הָאִשָּׁה אַחֲרָי׃ 40 וַיֹּאמֶר אֵלָי יְהוָה אֲשֶׁר־
הִתְהַלַּכְתִּי לְפָנָיו יִשְׁלַח מַלְאָכוֹ אִתָּךְ

and Song of Songs (3:4, 8:2)—texts in which we find women of strong character. The expression "mother's household" (*beit em*) emphasizes that the household is associated with women's activities. (For details about women's roles and households, see further Women in Ancient Israel—An Overview, p. xli.)

### REBEKAH'S BETROTHAL (24:32–54a)

All the members of Rebekah's family take part in this encounter.

*35–49.* The servant emphasizes divine intervention in order to convince his hosts that his mission is in accordance with divine will—so that they will entrust Rebekah to him. The servant is also aware of the human weaknesses of his hosts; he therefore expands his description of Abraham's wealth (v. 35) and stresses that Isaac is his master's sole heir (v. 36). He also reverses the order in which he asked the name of the girl and presented her with ornaments so they would not say, "How could you give her [the jewelry] when you did not yet know who she was?" (Rashi).

will take a wife for my son from my clan, from my father's family. [41]You will be free from your obligation only if you go to my relations and they refuse you. In that case, you will be free from your obligation.'

[42]"When I came to the well today, I prayed, 'יהוה, God of my master Abraham, if You truly intend to clear the way on which I am going, [43]here I am at the water-fount. When a young woman comes out to get water, I will say to her, "Please give me a drink of water from your pitcher." [44]If she answers, "Go ahead and drink, and I will draw water for your camels, too"—let her be the one You have designated as the wife for my master's son.' [45]Before I had finished rehearsing my thought, Rebekah came with a water pitcher on her shoulder and went down to the well to get water. I said to her: 'Please give me a drink.' [46]She quickly lowered her pitcher and said, 'Drink, and I will water your camels, too.' So I drank, and she gave water to the camels, too. [47]I asked her, 'Whose daughter are you?' And she answered, 'I am the daughter of Bethuel son of Nahor and Milcah.' Then I put the ring on her nose and the bracelets on her wrists. [48]I knelt down in worship of יהוה, and I praised יהוה, the God of my master Abraham, who had led me on the right path to get the daughter of my master's brother for his son. [49]And now, if you mean to treat my master with faithful kindness, tell me; if not, tell me, and I will turn in another direction."

[50]Laban and Bethuel responded by saying, "This matter has emanated from יהוה; we cannot answer you one way or another. [51]Look—Rebekah is before you; take [her] and go, and let her be your master's son's wife as יהוה has decreed!"

וְהִצְלִ֣יחַ דַּרְכֶּ֔ךָ וְלָקַחְתָּ֤ אִשָּׁה֙ לִבְנִ֔י
מִמִּשְׁפַּחְתִּ֖י וּמִבֵּ֥ית אָבִֽי׃ 41 אָ֤ז תִּנָּקֶה֙
מֵאָ֣לָתִ֔י כִּ֥י תָב֖וֹא אֶל־מִשְׁפַּחְתִּ֑י וְאִם־לֹ֤א
יִתְּנוּ֙ לָ֔ךְ וְהָיִ֥יתָ נָקִ֖י מֵאָלָתִֽי׃
42 וָאָבֹ֥א הַיּ֖וֹם אֶל־הָעָ֑יִן וָאֹמַ֗ר יְהֹוָה֙ אֱלֹהֵי֙
אֲדֹנִ֣י אַבְרָהָ֔ם אִם־יֶשְׁךָ־נָּא֙ מַצְלִ֣יחַ דַּרְכִּ֔י
אֲשֶׁ֥ר אָנֹכִ֖י הֹלֵ֥ךְ עָלֶֽיהָ׃ 43 הִנֵּ֛ה אָנֹכִ֥י נִצָּ֖ב
עַל־עֵ֣ין הַמָּ֑יִם וְהָיָ֤ה הָֽעַלְמָה֙ הַיֹּצֵ֣את
לִשְׁאֹ֔ב וְאָמַרְתִּ֣י אֵלֶ֔יהָ הַשְׁקִֽינִי־נָ֥א מְעַט־
מַ֖יִם מִכַּדֵּֽךְ׃ 44 וְאָמְרָ֤ה אֵלַי֙ גַּם־אַתָּ֣ה שְׁתֵ֔ה
וְגַ֥ם לִגְמַלֶּ֖יךָ אֶשְׁאָ֑ב הִ֣וא הָֽאִשָּׁ֔ה אֲשֶׁר־
הֹכִ֥יחַ יְהֹוָ֖ה לְבֶן־אֲדֹנִֽי׃ 45 אֲנִי֩ טֶ֨רֶם אֲכַלֶּ֜ה
לְדַבֵּ֣ר אֶל־לִבִּ֗י וְהִנֵּ֨ה רִבְקָ֤ה יֹצֵאת֙ וְכַדָּ֣הּ
עַל־שִׁכְמָ֔הּ וַתֵּ֥רֶד הָעַ֖יְנָה וַתִּשְׁאָ֑ב וָאֹמַ֥ר
אֵלֶ֖יהָ הַשְׁקִ֥ינִי נָֽא׃ 46 וַתְּמַהֵ֗ר וַתּ֤וֹרֶד כַּדָּהּ֙
מֵֽעָלֶ֔יהָ וַתֹּ֣אמֶר שְׁתֵ֔ה וְגַם־גְּמַלֶּ֖יךָ אַשְׁקֶ֑ה
וָאֵ֕שְׁתְּ וְגַ֥ם הַגְּמַלִּ֖ים הִשְׁקָֽתָה׃ 47 וָאֶשְׁאַ֣ל
אֹתָ֗הּ וָאֹמַר֮ בַּת־מִ֣י אַתְּ֒ וַתֹּ֗אמֶר בַּת־
בְּתוּאֵל֙ בֶּן־נָח֔וֹר אֲשֶׁ֥ר יָֽלְדָה־לּ֖וֹ מִלְכָּ֑ה
וָאָשִׂ֤ם הַנֶּ֙זֶם֙ עַל־אַפָּ֔הּ וְהַצְּמִידִ֖ים עַל־
יָדֶֽיהָ׃ 48 וָאֶקֹּ֥ד וָאֶֽשְׁתַּחֲוֶ֖ה לַֽיהֹוָ֑ה וָאֲבָרֵ֗ךְ
אֶת־יְהֹוָה֙ אֱלֹהֵי֙ אֲדֹנִ֣י אַבְרָהָ֔ם אֲשֶׁ֤ר הִנְחַ֙נִי֙
בְּדֶ֣רֶךְ אֱמֶ֔ת לָקַ֛חַת אֶת־בַּת־אֲחִ֥י אֲדֹנִ֖י
לִבְנֽוֹ׃ 49 וְעַתָּ֡ה אִם־יֶשְׁכֶם֩ עֹשִׂ֨ים חֶ֧סֶד
וֶֽאֱמֶ֛ת אֶת־אֲדֹנִ֖י הַגִּ֣ידוּ לִ֑י וְאִם־לֹ֕א הַגִּ֣ידוּ
לִ֔י וְאֶפְנֶ֥ה עַל־יָמִ֖ין א֥וֹ עַל־שְׂמֹֽאל׃
50 וַיַּ֨עַן לָבָ֤ן וּבְתוּאֵל֙ וַיֹּ֣אמְר֔וּ מֵיְהֹוָ֖ה יָצָ֣א
הַדָּבָ֑ר לֹ֥א נוּכַ֛ל דַּבֵּ֥ר אֵלֶ֖יךָ רַ֥ע אוֹ־טֽוֹב׃
51 הִנֵּֽה־רִבְקָ֥ה לְפָנֶ֖יךָ קַ֣ח וָלֵ֑ךְ וּתְהִ֤י אִשָּׁה֙
לְבֶן־אֲדֹנֶ֔יךָ כַּאֲשֶׁ֖ר דִּבֶּ֥ר יְהֹוָֽה׃

*50–51.* After the servant's speech, it is wholly fitting that those present admit that the matter is in accordance with divine will, and that they therefore agree to place Rebekah in the servant's care.

*50. **Laban and Bethuel.*** [The father and brother consent to Rebekah's marriage. The father's rare appearance here highlights his absence from what follows. —*Ed.*]

52 When Abraham's slave heard their words he bowed low to יהוה, 53 and brought out silver and gold objects, and articles of clothing, and gave them to Rebekah; and to her brother and mother he gave precious gifts. 54 So he and the men with him ate and drank and stayed overnight.

When they got up in the morning he said, "Send me off to my master." 55 Her brother and mother said, "Let the girl stay with us another few days—ten, perhaps—afterward she may go." 56 But he said to them, "Do not delay me, now that יהוה has cleared the way for me; send me off and let me go to my master." 57 They answered, "Let us call the girl and see what she has to say." 58 So they called Rebekah and asked her, "Will you go with this man?" And she said, "I will go."

59 They then sent their sister Rebekah off with

52 וַיְהִ֕י כַּאֲשֶׁ֥ר שָׁמַ֛ע עֶ֥בֶד אַבְרָהָ֖ם אֶת־
דִּבְרֵיהֶ֑ם וַיִּשְׁתַּ֥חוּ אַ֖רְצָה לַֽיהוָֽה׃ 53 וַיּוֹצֵ֨א
הָעֶ֜בֶד כְּלֵי־כֶ֨סֶף וּכְלֵ֤י זָהָב֙ וּבְגָדִ֔ים וַיִּתֵּ֖ן
לְרִבְקָ֑ה וּמִ֨גְדָּנֹ֔ת נָתַ֥ן לְאָחִ֖יהָ וּלְאִמָּֽהּ׃
54 וַיֹּאכְל֣וּ וַיִּשְׁתּ֗וּ ה֛וּא וְהָאֲנָשִׁ֥ים אֲשֶׁר
עִמּ֖וֹ וַיָּלִ֑ינוּ

וַיָּק֣וּמוּ בַבֹּ֔קֶר וַיֹּ֖אמֶר שַׁלְּחֻ֥נִי לַֽאדֹנִֽי׃
55 וַיֹּ֤אמֶר אָחִ֙יהָ֙ וְאִמָּ֔הּ תֵּשֵׁ֨ב הנער הַנַּעֲרָ֥ה
אִתָּ֛נוּ יָמִ֖ים א֣וֹ עָשׂ֑וֹר אַחַ֖ר תֵּלֵֽךְ׃ 56 וַיֹּ֤אמֶר
אֲלֵהֶם֙ אַל־תְּאַחֲר֣וּ אֹתִ֔י וַֽיהוָ֖ה הִצְלִ֣יחַ
דַּרְכִּ֑י שַׁלְּח֕וּנִי וְאֵלְכָ֖ה לַֽאדֹנִֽי׃ 57 וַיֹּאמְר֖וּ
נִקְרָ֣א לנער לַֽנַּעֲרָ֑ה וְנִשְׁאֲלָ֖ה אֶת־פִּֽיהָ׃
58 וַיִּקְרְא֤וּ לְרִבְקָה֙ וַיֹּאמְר֣וּ אֵלֶ֔יהָ הֲתֵלְכִ֖י
עִם־הָאִ֣ישׁ הַזֶּ֑ה וַתֹּ֖אמֶר אֵלֵֽךְ׃
59 וַיְשַׁלְּח֛וּ אֶת־רִבְקָ֥ה אֲחֹתָ֖ם וְאֶת־מֵנִקְתָּ֑הּ

## REBEKAH AGREES TO GO (24:54b–58)

*55. Her brother and mother.* [These two family members conduct the negotiations regarding the marriage that was approved in vv. 50–51. —*Ed.*]

*58. "I will go."* Rebekah's decision to leave her homeland and her family, go to a new place, and live with a man unknown to her, is reminiscent of Abraham, who left everything behind him in order to fulfill a divine command (12:1). Women's contribution to the fulfillment of national destiny finds its expression not only in their role as childbearers but also in their ability to take bold and vital action at critical moments. Rebekah's actions will later find an echo in Ruth's leaving her father, mother, and land of her own accord. When Ruth joins her fate with that of her mother-in-law, Naomi, and subsequently marries Naomi's kinsman Boaz, Ruth too contributes to fulfilling the national destiny, in that King David would be the future offspring of that union.

The apparent role of chance in both stories, as expressed by the Hebrew root *k-r-h*, links the book of Ruth and the story of Rebekah. The servant requests of God "please bring me luck today" (24:12), while of Ruth it is written "as luck would have it, it was the piece of land belonging to Boaz" (Ruth 2:3). Divine providence seems to direct the fate of both these women. Moreover, when the servant learns Rebekah's identity, he blesses God, saying, "Blessed is יהוה, God of my master Abraham, whose faithful kindness has not deserted my master" (Genesis 24:27). Likewise, when Naomi learns where Ruth gleaned, she pronounces a similar blessing, "Blessed be he of יהוה, who has not failed in kindness . . . !" (Ruth 2:20).

## REBEKAH DEPARTS (24:59–61)

The family's blessing of Rebekah serves to reinforce her role in fulfilling the divine promises God made to Abraham—not only the blessing of progeny, but also a continued blessing of land.

her nurse, with Abraham's slave, and with his men,
60bestowing this blessing upon Rebekah: "Sister,
may you become thousands of myriads; may your
descendants take possession of the gates of their
foes!" 61Rebekah and her servant girls got up and
mounted the camels and followed the man, as the
slave took Rebekah and went off.

62Now Isaac was coming from the approach to
Be'er-lachai-ro'i, for he was living in the area of
the Negev. 63Going out toward evening to stroll in
the field, Isaac looked up and saw—camels coming!
64And Rebekah looked up: seeing Isaac, she got off
the camel 65and said to the slave: "Who is this man
striding in the field coming to meet us?" "He is my
master," said the slave. Taking a veil, she covered
herself. 66The slave then told Isaac all that he had

וְאֶת־עֶ֥בֶד אַבְרָהָ֖ם וְאֶת־אֲנָשָֽׁיו׃ 60 וַיְבָרְכ֤וּ
אֶת־רִבְקָה֙ וַיֹּ֣אמְרוּ לָ֔הּ אֲחֹתֵ֕נוּ אַ֥תְּ הֲיִ֖י
לְאַלְפֵ֣י רְבָבָ֑ה וְיִירַ֣שׁ זַרְעֵ֔ךְ אֵ֖ת שַׁ֥עַר
שֹׂנְאָֽיו׃ 61 וַתָּ֨קָם רִבְקָ֜ה וְנַעֲרֹתֶ֗יהָ וַתִּרְכַּ֙בְנָה֙
עַל־הַגְּמַלִּ֔ים וַתֵּלַ֖כְנָה אַחֲרֵ֣י הָאִ֑ישׁ וַיִּקַּ֥ח
הָעֶ֛בֶד אֶת־רִבְקָ֖ה וַיֵּלַֽךְ׃
62 וְיִצְחָק֙ בָּ֣א מִבּ֔וֹא בְּאֵ֖ר לַחַ֣י רֹאִ֑י וְה֥וּא
יוֹשֵׁ֖ב בְּאֶ֥רֶץ הַנֶּֽגֶב׃ 63 וַיֵּצֵ֥א יִצְחָ֛ק לָשׂ֥וּחַ
בַּשָּׂדֶ֖ה לִפְנ֣וֹת עָ֑רֶב וַיִּשָּׂ֤א עֵינָיו֙ וַיַּ֔רְא וְהִנֵּ֥ה
גְמַלִּ֖ים בָּאִֽים׃ 64 וַתִּשָּׂ֤א רִבְקָה֙ אֶת־עֵינֶ֔יהָ
וַתֵּ֖רֶא אֶת־יִצְחָ֑ק וַתִּפֹּ֖ל מֵעַ֥ל הַגָּמָֽל׃
65 וַתֹּ֣אמֶר אֶל־הָעֶ֗בֶד מִֽי־הָאִ֤ישׁ הַלָּזֶה֙
הַהֹלֵ֤ךְ בַּשָּׂדֶה֙ לִקְרָאתֵ֔נוּ וַיֹּ֥אמֶר הָעֶ֖בֶד ה֣וּא
אֲדֹנִ֑י וַתִּקַּ֥ח הַצָּעִ֖יף וַתִּתְכָּֽס׃ 66 וַיְסַפֵּ֥ר
הָעֶ֖בֶד לְיִצְחָ֑ק אֵ֥ת כָּל־הַדְּבָרִ֖ים אֲשֶׁ֥ר

***59. her nurse.*** [Heb. *menekta* (her wet nurse). From Exodus 2—where Moses' mother is hired to nurse him for Pharaoh's daughter—we learn that wet nurses were sometimes paid (see at Exodus 2:9–10). Carol Meyers points out that most Israelite women (and their ancestors) probably nursed their own children, except perhaps for women in elite classes (*Exodus*, 2005, p. 41). | In this account, the nurse apparently has remained in the household long after Rebekah was weaned, implying that they have a special bond; she might function as a surrogate mother or companion for young Rebekah in a foreign land. Genesis 35:8 will mention this nurse again by name, with a notice of her death and burial in Beth El; see comment there. —*Ed.*]

***60. "may you become thousands of myriads."*** Jews traditionally use this first part of the blessing in the *bedeken* ceremony before a wedding, when the groom places the veil upon the bride's face.

***"may your descendants."*** [The family blesses Rebekah with the identical blessing that God's messenger used for Abraham in 22:17. —*Ed.*]

***61. servant girls.*** [Their mention, like that of a wet nurse, implies that Rebekah's family is affluent. —*Ed.*]

## REBEKAH MEETS ISAAC (24:62–66)

The text re-introduces Isaac by explaining that he had returned from the vicinity of Beer-lahai-roi, the place where God has been revealed to Hagar (16:13–14). Yet as soon as Isaac sees the approaching camels (24:63), it is she who becomes the subject of the verbs (24:64).

***65. "my master."*** This is the first time that the servant calls Isaac "my master" and not "my master's son."

***Taking a veil, she covered herself.*** Rebekah's action may signal modesty. Is it because of her new status as a married woman? Not enough is known about the role of veils in ancient Israel.

***66.*** As if the presence of Rebekah as wife elevates Isaac to the role of master, the servant tells Isaac (not Abraham) all that had occurred. Isaac is now fully established as the legitimate successor to his father.

done. [67]And Isaac brought her into the tent of
his mother Sarah; he took Rebekah, and she became his wife and he loved her. Thus did Isaac take
comfort after [the death of] his mother.
25 Abraham went on and took a wife named
Keturah. [2]She bore to him Zimran, Jokshan,
Medan, Midian, Ishbak, and Shuah. [3]Jokshan begot Sheba and Dedan, and Dedan's sons were
Ashurim, Letushim, and Leummim. [4]Midian's

עָשָׂה׃ 67 וַיְבִאֶהָ יִצְחָק הָאֹהֱלָה שָׂרָה אִמּוֹ
וַיִּקַּח אֶת־רִבְקָה וַתְּהִי־לוֹ לְאִשָּׁה וַיֶּאֱהָבֶהָ
וַיִּנָּחֵם יִצְחָק אַחֲרֵי אִמּוֹ׃ פ
כה וַיֹּסֶף אַבְרָהָם וַיִּקַּח אִשָּׁה וּשְׁמָהּ
קְטוּרָה׃ 2 וַתֵּלֶד לוֹ אֶת־זִמְרָן וְאֶת־יָקְשָׁן
וְאֶת־מְדָן וְאֶת־מִדְיָן וְאֶת־יִשְׁבָּק וְאֶת־שׁוּחַ׃
3 וְיָקְשָׁן יָלַד אֶת־שְׁבָא וְאֶת־דְּדָן וּבְנֵי דְדָן
הָיוּ אַשּׁוּרִם וּלְטוּשִׁם וּלְאֻמִּים׃ 4 וּבְנֵי מִדְיָן

### CONCLUSION: REBEKAH MOVES INTO SARAH'S TENT (24:67)

The appearance of Rebekah, who is brought to his mother's tent, comforts Isaac for the death of his mother and hints to the reader to expect the continued fulfillment of the divine promises to the line of Abraham, through Isaac and Rebekah. This final verse, which focuses on Isaac's emotional connections to his mother and to his new wife, reasserts the central role that women play in realizing God's covenantal promises. Sarah's death had inspired Abraham to purchase the field of Machpelah as a burial site (chapter 23), while Rebekah's marriage to Isaac will soon allow the family to be blessed with more children.

***tent of his mother.*** The combination of "tent" with "mother" appears only here. (On the similar combination of "household" with "mother," see at 24:28.)

***she became his wife and he loved her.*** This is the first time that we read about a man's love for a woman. Biblical literature only twice mentions women's love of men (Michal's love for David in I Samuel 18:20 and 28; and the Song of Songs). Men's love appears more frequently, as for example Jacob's love for Rachel (Genesis 29:18), Shechem's love of Dinah (34:3), and Jonathan's love for David (I Samuel 18:1, 3). In many of those cases, as in ours, the use of the verb "love" implies a sexual relationship.

## *Abraham's Descendants and His Death* (25:1–18)

The final unit reports Abraham's additional marriage to Keturah, his additional offspring by Keturah, and their settling in the land of the East (vv. 1–4); Isaac's favored position (vv. 5–6); the length of Abraham's life, his death, and his burial (vv. 7–11); and finally the genealogy of Ishmael's descendants, their dwelling-place, the length of Ishmael's life, and his death (vv. 12–18).

In the previous story, Abraham's concern was providing Isaac with a wife. In this unit, he takes steps to ensure that his other sons shall have no portion in the inheritance of the land of Canaan, which is destined for Isaac's hands alone. In this manner, he fulfills Sarah's demand that others will not inherit with her son Isaac (21:10).

### THE DESCENDANTS OF KETURAH (25:1–4)

Some interpreters see Keturah as one of Abraham's concubines, since v. 6 mentions "the sons of Abraham's concubines." Such is in fact stated in I Chronicles 1:32. The name Keturah is connected in Hebrew to incense and fragrant spices (see Song of Songs 3:6). The Bible gives no further information about her (but see Post-biblical Interpretations, p. 127).

***2–4.*** The names of the sons of Keturah are those of nomadic desert tribes.

sons were Ephah, Epher, Hanoch, Abida, and El-daah. All these were Keturah's sons. [5]Abraham gave all that he owned to Isaac, [6]but to the sons of Abraham's concubines, Abraham gave gifts; while he was still alive, he sent them away from Isaac, eastward to the land of Kedem.

[7]These are the days of the years of Abraham's life: he lived 175 years. [8]Abraham breathed his last and died in good old age, full of age, and was gathered to his people. [9]His sons Isaac and Ishmael buried him in the cave of Machpelah, facing Mamre, in the field of Ephron son of Zoar the Hittite, [10]the field that Abraham had bought from the Hittites; there Abraham and his wife Sarah were buried. [11]After the death of Abraham, God blessed his son Isaac, and Isaac lived near Be'er-lachai-ro'i.

עֵיפָ֣ה וָעֵ֔פֶר וַחֲנֹ֥ךְ וַאֲבִידָ֖ע וְאֶלְדָּעָ֑ה כָּל־
אֵ֖לֶּה בְּנֵ֥י קְטוּרָֽה: 5 וַיִּתֵּ֧ן אַבְרָהָ֛ם אֶת־כָּל־
אֲשֶׁר־ל֖וֹ לְיִצְחָֽק: 6 וְלִבְנֵ֤י הַפִּֽילַגְשִׁים֙ אֲשֶׁ֣ר
לְאַבְרָהָ֔ם נָתַ֥ן אַבְרָהָ֖ם מַתָּנֹ֑ת וַֽיְשַׁלְּחֵ֞ם
מֵעַ֨ל יִצְחָ֤ק בְּנוֹ֙ בְּעוֹדֶ֣נּוּ חַ֔י קֵ֖דְמָה אֶל־אֶ֥רֶץ
קֶֽדֶם:
7 וְאֵ֗לֶּה יְמֵ֛י שְׁנֵֽי־חַיֵּ֥י אַבְרָהָ֖ם אֲשֶׁר־חָ֑י
מְאַ֥ת שָׁנָ֛ה וְשִׁבְעִ֥ים שָׁנָ֖ה וְחָמֵ֥שׁ שָׁנִֽים:
8 וַיִּגְוַ֨ע וַיָּ֧מָת אַבְרָהָ֛ם בְּשֵׂיבָ֥ה טוֹבָ֖ה זָקֵ֣ן
וְשָׂבֵ֑עַ וַיֵּאָ֖סֶף אֶל־עַמָּֽיו: 9 וַיִּקְבְּר֨וּ אֹת֜וֹ
יִצְחָ֤ק וְיִשְׁמָעֵאל֙ בָּנָ֔יו אֶל־מְעָרַ֖ת הַמַּכְפֵּלָ֑ה
אֶל־שְׂדֵ֞ה עֶפְרֹ֤ן בֶּן־צֹ֨חַר֙ הַֽחִתִּ֔י אֲשֶׁ֖ר עַל־
פְּנֵ֥י מַמְרֵֽא: 10 הַשָּׂדֶ֛ה אֲשֶׁר־קָנָ֥ה אַבְרָהָ֖ם
מֵאֵ֣ת בְּנֵי־חֵ֑ת שָׁ֛מָּה קֻבַּ֥ר אַבְרָהָ֖ם וְשָׂרָ֥ה
אִשְׁתּֽוֹ: 11 וַיְהִ֗י אַֽחֲרֵי֙ מ֣וֹת אַבְרָהָ֔ם וַיְבָ֥רֶךְ
אֱלֹהִ֖ים אֶת־יִצְחָ֣ק בְּנ֑וֹ וַיֵּ֣שֶׁב יִצְחָ֔ק עִם־
בְּאֵ֥ר לַחַ֖י רֹאִֽי: פ

- - - - - - - - - - - - - - - - - - - - - - -

## ISAAC'S STATUS (25:5–6)

The fact that Abraham wills what he owns to Isaac, while only leaving gifts to the sons he had with his concubines, further asserts Rebekah's central role as replacing Sarah (see 24:67).

*6.* Abraham's grant of gifts to his sons is reported before his death is, indicating that he took care to dispose of the inheritance in his lifetime.

*concubines.* [The reference seems to be to Hagar and Keturah. Hagar is also described as Sarah's slave (25:12). The Hebrew word *pilegesh* (concubine) may derive from Greek. It refers to women with a status between a wife and a slave: technically independent, with sustenance coming from the man or men in the household, yet free to leave (compare Judges 19:1–3). A 3rd-century-B.C.E. Greek source (Demosthenes) observes that men have concubines "for the care of the body," namely, for sexual relations. Often the children of concubines were excluded from inheriting, as here. —*Ed.*]

## ABRAHAM'S DEATH AND BURIAL (25:7–11)

*7–10.* The description of Abraham's burial emphasizes the cooperation between Isaac and Ishmael. If the two half-brothers had felt some emotional distance from each other beforehand, we can presume that they reconciled at this point.

*8. gathered to his people.* [In this expression the text's original audience would have understood the kinship term *ammim* in a gender-inclusive sense, as the translation here reflects ("people"). Despite the Bible's reliance on patrilineal genealogies and on patronymics, female relatives counted as kin. See at Genesis 10:1 and Numbers 31:2; see also *The Contemporary Torah*, 2006, s.v. "predecessors," p. 408. —*Ed.*]

*10. there Abraham and his wife Sarah were buried.* The reiterated note about the legitimate purchase of the cave of Machpelah emphasizes the importance of acquiring property through purchase

12This is the line of Ishmael son of Abraham,
borne by Hagar the Egyptian, Sarah's slave, to
Abraham: 13Here are the names of Ishmael's sons
in their birth order: Ishmael's first-born Nebaioth,
Kedar, Adbeel, and Mibsam; 14Mishma, Duma,
and Massa; 15Hadad and Tema; Jetur, Naphish,
and Kedmah. 16These then are Ishmael's sons, and
these are their names, by their villages and encampments—twelve princes by their tribes. 17and
these are the years of Ishmael's life: 137; he then ex-
pired and died and was gathered to his people.
18They occupied the area from Havilah to Shur,
which is near Egypt on the way to Ashur. He settled
in the presence of all his kin.

12 וְאֵלֶּה תֹּלְדֹת יִשְׁמָעֵאל בֶּן־אַבְרָהָם
אֲשֶׁר יָלְדָה הָגָר הַמִּצְרִית שִׁפְחַת שָׂרָה
לְאַבְרָהָם׃ 13 וְאֵלֶּה שְׁמוֹת בְּנֵי יִשְׁמָעֵאל
בִּשְׁמֹתָם לְתוֹלְדֹתָם בְּכֹר יִשְׁמָעֵאל נְבָיֹת
וְקֵדָר וְאַדְבְּאֵל וּמִבְשָׂם׃ 14 וּמִשְׁמָע וְדוּמָה
וּמַשָּׂא׃ 15 חֲדַד וְתֵימָא יְטוּר נָפִישׁ
וָקֵדְמָה׃ 16 אֵלֶּה הֵם בְּנֵי יִשְׁמָעֵאל וְאֵלֶּה
שְׁמֹתָם בְּחַצְרֵיהֶם וּבְטִירֹתָם שְׁנֵים־עָשָׂר
נְשִׂיאִם לְאֻמֹּתָם׃ 17 וְאֵלֶּה שְׁנֵי חַיֵּי
יִשְׁמָעֵאל מְאַת שָׁנָה וּשְׁלֹשִׁים שָׁנָה
וְשֶׁבַע שָׁנִים וַיִּגְוַע וַיָּמָת וַיֵּאָסֶף אֶל־עַמָּיו׃
18 וַיִּשְׁכְּנוּ מֵחֲוִילָה עַד־שׁוּר אֲשֶׁר עַל־פְּנֵי
מִצְרַיִם בֹּאֲכָה אַשּׁוּרָה עַל־פְּנֵי כָל־אֶחָיו
נָפָל׃ פ

in the land of Israel. The mention of Sarah's burial is a reminder of the critical role that she played not only in Abraham's life, but also in his realization of the divine promise of land.

HAGAR'S DESCENDANTS (25:12–18)

*12. borne by Hagar the Egyptian, Sarah's slave.* Ishmael's line is credited to his mother, whose identity is fully recalled. The sons of Ishmael are nomadic tribal peoples who dwelt on the southwest and southeast fringes of the land of Israel.

*—Yairah Amit*

# Another View

Isaac's love for Rebekah (24:67) is the first mention of spousal love in the Bible. Like other ancient Near Eastern sources, the Bible shows a concern with preserving family possessions, both tangible (land) and intangible (blessings and identity). Arranged marriages serve this purpose. Love, however, is also mentioned as a motive for marriage: Jacob loves Rachel (Genesis 29:30), and Michal loves David (I Samuel 18:20). With Isaac, love follows rather than precedes marriage. We do not know whether Rebekah loves Isaac. Reports of a woman's love for a man are rare, found only with Princess Michal (I Samuel 18:20 and 48) and in sensual terms in Song of Songs (see, for example, 1:7).

The Bible is largely silent about marriage procedures. In fact, Genesis 24 remains the most detailed biblical source on this subject. The customs it describes largely correspond to information from ancient Mesopotamian texts. According to both sources, parents usually arrange the marriage (as when Shechem's father negotiates a marriage with Dinah in Genesis 34, or when Samson asks his father *and* mother to get him a wife in Judges 14:2–3). Brothers sometimes act in this role (see Laban in Genesis 24). The groom or his family brings gifts for the bride's family. In the Bible these gifts are called *mohar*, a term without the misleading commercial overtones of its usual English translation as "bride-price." The servant's gifts in Genesis 24 may represent the *mohar*. In some Babylonian documents, the bride's father also gives gifts. (See Women in Ancient Israel—An Overview, p. xli.)

Genesis 24 emphasizes Rebekah's role in the marriage negotiations. The servant bestows expensive gifts mostly on Rebekah herself ("objects of silver and gold, and garments"), with only some for her brother and mother (24:53; note the silence about the father). Moreover, she chooses when to go to her husband (24:55–58). In contrast, the groom, Isaac, plays no role in the arrangements. These details emphasize the union of Rebekah and Isaac as one in which the woman is assertive and the man compliant. This depiction sets the stage for Rebekah's prominence in subsequent episodes (25:22–23, 28; 27:1–28:5).

> *Genesis 24 remains the most detailed biblical source on marriage procedures.*

—*Tamara Cohn Eskenazi*

# Post-biblical Interpretations

***Sarah died*** (23:2). A 13th-century Yemenite Midrash collection begins its interpretations of this parashah with an extended commentary on Proverbs 31, the description of a "woman of valor." The midrash connects the various exemplary qualities of the outstanding wife of Proverbs 31 to twenty-three biblical women, in order of their scriptural appearance. The second woman discussed (after Noah's wife) is Sarah: "'The heart of her husband trusts in her' (Proverbs 31:11)—this is Sarah, in whom Abraham's heart trusted. 'And lacks no good thing' (same verse)—for she used to bring guests [converts] under the wings of the Shechinah" (*Midrash HaGadol*). | Commenting on "the sun rises, and the sun sets" (Ecclesiastes 1:5), another midrash notes the Torah's juxtaposition of the mention of Rebekah's lineage at the end of Genesis 22 and the death of Sarah at the beginning of Genesis 23; that midrash praises the divine omniscience that plans for all things: "Before allowing Sarah's sun to set, the Holy One caused Rebekah's sun to rise" (Midrash *B'reishit Rabbah* 58.2).

***Abraham was old, well advanced in years*** (24:1). Abraham was profoundly affected by Sarah's death, according to the Rabbis. While she was alive, he felt himself young and vigorous, but after she had passed away, old age suddenly overtook him (*Tanchuma* 4). | According to the Talmud, "Until Abraham there was no physical aging; people would confuse Abraham with his son Isaac because they looked so similar. Thereupon Abraham prayed and the physical manifestations of old age came into existence" (BT *Bava M'tzia* 87a).

*Before allowing Sarah's sun to set, the Holy One caused Rebekah's sun to rise.*

***So they called Rebekah and asked her. . . . And she said, "I will go"*** (24:58). One midrash connects this episode with "She is good to him, never bad" (Proverbs 31:12) and comments, "It was customary in the world that when a man would wed his daughter to someone . . . she would be too embarrassed to say anything [either in affirmation or rejection]" (*Midrash HaGadol*). Rebekah, however, made clear that she was willing to go with a stranger to become Isaac's wife. | Another midrash derives from this narrative the legal ruling that "a fatherless maiden may not be given in marriage without her consent" (*B'reishit Rabbah* 60.12).

***Sister, may you become thousands of myriads*** (24:60). Rabbinic tradition harbors great suspicion toward Rebekah's brother, Laban, as an enemy of the people of Israel. Therefore, some rabbis strongly denied that his blessing could have had any positive effect: "Why was Rebekah not remembered [with children] until Isaac prayed for her (Genesis 25:21)? So that the heathen should not say, 'Our prayer bore fruit'" (*B'reishit Rabbah* 60.13).

***Isaac brought her into the tent of his mother Sarah*** (24:67). One midrash claims that this verse proves that "Rebekah's deeds were [praiseworthy] like Sarah's" (*Midrash HaGadol*). A cloud signifying the divine Presence had hovered over Sarah's tent throughout her lifetime. It disappeared when she died—"but when Rebekah came, it returned" (*B'reishit Rabbah* 60.16). Similarly, Rebekah continued all the positive activities that Sarah had initiated, "separating her *challah* in ritual purity" (see Numbers 15:18–21) and keeping the Sabbath lamp kindled.

***Abraham went on and took a wife named Keturah*** (25:1). This marriage is mentioned following Isaac's marriage to Rebekah. One midrash learns from this that "if a man has grown-up sons, he must first see that they marry, and only then take a wife himself" (*B'reishit Rabbah* 60.16). | The Rabbis wondered who Keturah was, since no information is given about her origins or lineage. Some of the sages insisted she was actually Hagar, who, they argued, had returned to Abraham after Sarah's death (*Pirkei D'Rabbi Eliezer* 30, among others). And lest anyone be concerned about Hagar's chastity during her absence from Abraham's household, another midrash explains, based on the linguistic similarities between the Hebrew root *k-t-r* (to "tie up" or "seal") and the name Keturah, "that she was like one who seals up a treasure and produces it with its seal" (*B'reishit Rabbah* 61.4). An alternate and late midrashic tradition understands Keturah to be a separate individual from Hagar. This midrash relates that Abraham married three wives and that each was a descendant of one of the sons of Noah: Sarah was of the line of Shem, Keturah descended from Japheth, and Hagar was from the family of Ham (*Yalkut Reuveni,* Genesis 26.2, 36c).

—*Judith R. Baskin*

# Contemporary Reflection

"AND ABRAHAM PROCEEDED to mourn for Sarah and to bewail her" (Genesis 23:2). With this verse, our parashah invites us to consider the history of a significant yet often obscured tradition in women's discourse, namely, mourning.

In this parashah we have the first account of mourning (even though death has figured prominently earlier). Here a woman, Sarah, is mourned, and the mourner is a man, Abraham her husband. Yet sources disclose that in the ancient world the act of mourning was typically associated with women. Margaret Alexiou's landmark study, *The Ritual Lament in Greek Tradition* (1974), calls attention to the gendered characteristics of mourning practices and language. Throughout antiquity, in both Greek and Middle Eastern cultures, the lament—a standard feature of ritual life—belonged largely to women who gathered to lead the community in the rites of grief. In the Bible, just as in the Classical tradition, the lament was associated with the feminine. The book of Jeremiah lets us hear the bitter weeping of Rachel, mourning over her absent children (Jeremiah 31:15). That book also conspicuously presents songs of communal loss as a maternal legacy; because of disaster, the prophet instructs the women thus: "Teach your daughters wailing, and one another lamentation" (Jeremiah 9:19). When the world splits open, when history fails, the feminine voice is made audible.

The Bible does not preserve actual descriptions of mourning rituals or women's laments. What we do have is the book of Lamentations, a national lament, in which—as is common in laments—the poet repeatedly appropriates a female persona, singing as if a woman: "My children are forlorn, / For the foe has prevailed" (1:16). Composed in response to the destruction of Jerusalem (586 B.C.E.) at the hands of the Neo-Babylonian army, Lamentations chronicles a nation's effort to know itself in the aftermath of a profound severing of its relation to God—the divine principle that confers meaning upon the social order. And in this book, catastrophe is repeatedly gendered. The female is the subject reciting the lament; she is also the object of exploitation, since to the poet the feminine body represents the site of social disrepair. In this way, Lamentations provides yet another textual example of the widespread symbol of nation-as-woman, ever vulnerable to foreign invasion. Women are cast as the ideal speakers of loss and rupture, for that is a condition which they embody.

Lamentations opens with a cluster of images figuring Jerusalem as an abandoned woman; she is likened

*Women poets explore the power of mourning.*

variously to a slave, a fallen princess, and a widow—an *almanah*, a term Alan Mintz points out "designates not so much a woman who has lost her husband as the social status of a woman who has no legal protector and who may thus be abused with impunity" (*Reading Hebrew Literature*, 2002, p. 24). Indeed, *almanah* may be etymologically linked to the Hebrew verb that means to be mute or dumb (with the letters *aleph*, *lamed*, and *mem*). This association deepens our sense of the widow as one who cannot speak on her own behalf. Focusing on the structures of meaning in the Hebrew Bible, Elaine Scarry identifies a crucial division between God manifested as a *voice* and humanity as *embodied*: "To have a body is to be creatable, . . . and woundable. To have no body, to have only a voice, is to be none of these things; it is to be the wounder but not oneself woundable" (*The Body in Pain*, 1985, p. 206). The distinction is central to Lamentations, where "daughter Zion" is represented, especially in the first chapters, as virtually all body, broken and disabled.

Turning to the post-biblical period, women continue

to dominate in the mention of laments. Rabbinic tractates include a few such references. For example, in Mishnah *K'tubot* (4:4), Rabbi Yehuda rules that even the poorest husband must provide one lament-singing woman for his wife's funeral, as a minimum display of honor. In the Talmud, we find a suite of poetic fragments which suggest that the lament, as a standard feature of ritual life, belonged largely to the women who gathered to lead the community in the rites. Attributed to the sage Raba, we read: "The women of Shkanziv say: 'Woe for his leaving / woe for our grieving'" (BT *Moed Katan* 28b). To this day, Yemenite and Kurdistani women living in Israel continue to assume a large role in mourning the dead in their communities. (See Susan Sered, *Women as Ritual Experts*, 1992.)

In Western culture, meanwhile, the genre of lament has become a useful frame for women poets. Dahlia Ravikovitch, who emerged as an important Israeli poet during the 1950s, has been described as a "lamenting poetess in the ancient biblical tradition" (Shirley Kaufman et al., eds., *Hebrew Feminist Poems,* 1999, p. 13). A particularly beautiful and haunting example of Ravikovitch's contribution to the genre may be found in her poem "They Required a Song of Us." The poem begins with a line from another well-known Israeli poet, Lea Goldberg, who asks: "How shall we sing a song of Zion / when we have not even begun to hear?" Like Goldberg's query, Ravikovitch's poem meditates on Psalm 137, a famous expression of exilic despair in the Bible, where the speaker asks: "How can we sing a song of יהוה on alien soil?" Ravikovitch answers this ancient query by recognizing the need for a new kind of utterance: "Sing intimate songs / that the soul shies away from singing..." (Tal Nizan, ed., *With an Iron Pen: Hebrew Protest Poetry 1984–2004*, 2005).

Turning to twentieth-century Jewish American poetry, we find new variations on the lament in the work of Adrienne Rich. Wrestling with the expressive limitations of other forms of poetic mourning, Rich writes of her frustration in "A Woman Dead In Her Forties." Here the speaker first confronts the genre of lament's potential inadequacy, feeling "half-afraid" to write a lament for one who did not "read it much"—and then gropes for an alternative: "from here on I want," she writes, "more crazy mourning, more howl, more keening" (*Facts on a Doorframe*, 2002, p. 255). This discontent compels Rich to reactivate the lament in her 1991 volume *An Atlas of the Difficult World.* In a later collection, written in the aftermath of the Gulf War crisis (1991–92), Rich longs to convey what she knows to be true: that poetry can be a powerful, socially constitutive force for reconfiguring community (*What is Found There*, 1993, p. xiv). Poets such as Merle Feld, Esther Broner, and Penina Adelman also explore the power of mourning. Their versions of lament, along with Rich's, alert us to the reconstructive possibilities of an ancient biblical form.

—*Maeera Shreiber*

# Voices

## *Undo It, Take It Back*

Nessa Rapoport

*Genesis 23:1–2*

Undo it, take it back, make every day the previous one until I am returned to the day before the one that made you gone. Or set me on an airplane traveling west, crossing the date line again and again, losing this day, then that, until the day of loss still lies ahead, and you are here instead of sorrow.

## *Isaac*

Rivka Miriam (transl. Linda Stern Zisquit)

*Genesis 24:62–67*

Rebecca has married the dusks
that are the essence of in-betweens,
a gray so sensitive it easily forgives.
On a noble camel she rode toward her dusks
and seeing them across from her
so restrained, serious as jasmine severed from
    its fragrance,
she fell off the camel
like a joyous vat of wine
whose hoops have been loosened.

## *Rebecca*

Amy Blank

*Genesis 24*

I left home easily
(as when the ready seed drops from the tree),
Carefree—for I knew not what...

I stuffed my toys into the saddle-bag
braided my hair and for that dusty journey
wore my broidered gown.
I chose my camel and set out, light-hearted,
to enjoy adventure—scarcely a pang
as tents and trees of home faded into
    wilderness.
But this I wondered:
how would it befit to ask that awesome man,
Abraham's servant, what manner
was he to whom I was betrothed?
Better to hold the question, I decided.
Isaac, after all was also kinsman—one more—
fabulous Abraham's son—and I,
I would be his daughter... daughter? sister?
    wife?
Hardly a difference in my young mind.

## *Chayei Sarah*

Laurie Patton

*Genesis 25:9*

ISHMAEL:
I was thirteen,
and I remember the music
and my mother whispering,
"Why such a party, when
it is only a weaning?"
And the smell of lamb
and the hand-drums;
and the involuntary sound
coming from my own throat—
half laughter, half-sob—
after I saw my mother's face
in the firelight;
and I knew
my little brother
was now my rival.
But God was still good to us—

ISAAC:
—and I was three,
and I remember
staring out in the dark
of the morning
and seeing two shadows
and then the clear outline
of your mother
clutching a water bottle,
and watching her wave
in the air,
as if she were talking
to Someone.
But God was still good to us—

ISHMAEL:
—and now we stare together
into the cave
that holds our father—

ISAAC:
—our father's bones
and his memory,
in the place before Mamre—

ISHMAEL:
—and yet I fear
for the future—

ISAAC:
—since perhaps
the only thing
we can do together

ISHMAEL AND ISAAC:
is to bury
and to mourn
our dead.

# תולדת ✦ Tol'dot

## GENESIS 25:19–28:9

## *Shaping Destiny: The Story of Rebekah*

PARASHAT TOL'DOT ("generations") begins with Isaac but focuses heavily on Rebekah as the more active member of this family. Rebekah runs the family and undertakes the task of determining the destiny of God's blessings. As the one who blesses, Isaac has authority; but in determining who gets blessed—seemingly against Isaac's intentions—Rebekah has the power. She independently seeks God and alone receives God's answer about the future.

This parashah recounts a family story. A mother gives birth to twins, Esau and Jacob; and from the beginning, the brothers vie for prominence and their parents' favor. Like other biblical narratives in Genesis, this parashah is also concerned with self-definition—with the identity of the Israelite community in relation to surrounding peoples and cultures. Rebekah's twins represent two distinct nations: Israel and Edom.

Rebekah occupies center stage in several key scenes. Energetically, Rebekah ensures that the covenantal blessings will be bestowed on the more suitable son. Isaac, eclipsed by his parents, wife, and offspring, simply goes along—passively and gently surviving.

As Alice Bellis observes, interpreters often object to Rebekah's manipulations of her husband, comparing her unfavorably with Sarah's treatment of Hagar in Genesis 16 and 21, as if

*Rebekah occupies center stage in several key scenes.*

"[abusing] a woman servant is acceptable; deceiving a man, even to achieve God's mission, is not" (*Helpmates, Harlots, and Heroes: Women's Stories in the Hebrew Bible*, 1994, p. 83). The Torah, however, presents Rebekah as a figure without whom the covenant will not continue properly, the necessary link between Abraham's blessing and Jacob's.

—*Tamara Cohn Eskenazi*
*Hara E. Person*

## *Outline*

*I*. Rebekah Becomes the Mother of Twins (25:19–26)

*II*. Favoritism and the Selling of the Birthright (25:27–34)

*III*. Isaac and Rebekah "Visit" Abimelech
*Isaac at the Center* (26:1–33)

- *A*. Isaac receives the covenant promise (vv. 1–5)
- *B*. Isaac passes his wife off as his sister (vv. 6–11)
- *C*. Isaac digs wells, loses them, persists, and prospers (vv. 12–33)

*IV*. Esau Marries Canaanite Wives (26:34–35)

*V*. Rebekah Ensures the Transmission of the Covenantal Blessings to Jacob (27:1–28:9)

- *A*. Isaac prepares to bless Esau (27:1–4)
- *B*. Rebekah arranges for Jacob to receive Isaac's blessing instead (27:5–17)
- *C*. Jacob steals Esau's blessing (27:18–29)
- *D*. Esau discovers the deception (27:30–40)
- *E*. Rebekah convinces Isaac to send Jacob away (27:41–28:9)

25:19

This is the line of Isaac son of Abraham: Abraham begot Isaac. [20]Isaac was 40 years old when he took as his wife Rebekah daughter of Bethuel the Aramean of Paddan-aram, the sister of Laban the Aramean. [21]Isaac pleaded with יהוה on behalf of his wife, for she was childless, and יהוה acceded to his entreaty, so his wife Rebekah became pregnant.

כה 19 וְאֵ֛לֶּה תּוֹלְדֹ֥ת יִצְחָ֖ק בֶּן־אַבְרָהָ֑ם
אַבְרָהָ֖ם הוֹלִ֥יד אֶת־יִצְחָֽק׃ 20 וַיְהִ֣י יִצְחָ֗ק
בֶּן־אַרְבָּעִ֣ים שָׁנָ֔ה בְּקַחְתּ֣וֹ אֶת־רִבְקָ֗ה בַּת־
בְּתוּאֵל֙ הָֽאֲרַמִּ֔י מִפַּדַּ֖ן אֲרָ֑ם אֲח֛וֹת לָבָ֥ן
הָאֲרַמִּ֖י ל֥וֹ לְאִשָּֽׁה׃ 21 וַיֶּעְתַּ֨ר יִצְחָ֤ק לַֽיהֹוָה֙
לְנֹ֣כַח אִשְׁתּ֔וֹ כִּ֥י עֲקָרָ֖ה הִ֑וא וַיֵּעָ֤תֶר לוֹ֙ יְהֹוָ֔ה
וַתַּ֖הַר רִבְקָ֥ה אִשְׁתּֽוֹ׃

## *Rebekah Becomes the Mother of Twins* (25:19–26)

The opening unit focuses on Rebekah's pregnancy: how it came about, what was its nature, what steps she took, and what was the result. Twenty years after we first meet her in Genesis 24, Rebekah again proves resourceful and energetic, as she seeks God to inquire about her distressing situation.

*19. **Abraham begot Isaac.*** The last mention of Isaac highlighted his bond with his mother (24:67), yet the formulaic genealogical note here does not reflect Sarah's importance in Isaac's life.

*20. **he took as his wife Rebekah daughter of Bethuel the Aramean of Paddan-Aram, the sister of Laban the Aramean.*** Rebekah has been identified several times in Genesis 24. By adding place names, her personal lineage emphasizes that she is now far from home. Absent from this list is Milcah, Rebekah's grandmother, whom Rebekah herself mentions when she first identifies herself (24:24; see also 24:15).

*21. **Isaac pleaded.*** We do not learn about Rebekah's feelings concerning her childlessness, nor are we told that she does anything to try to change the situation. Isaac could have taken other wives to solve the problem of continuity (see at "childless," below), but he apparently does not. Isaac's sensitivity to Rebekah stands out in contrast to Jacob, who chastises his barren wife Rachel when she asks for children (30:2).

***on behalf of his wife.*** Literally, "in front of his wife," implying that Rebekah is present. Why does she not pray herself? Hannah is the exemplar of a woman who prays to have a child (I Samuel 1).

***childless.*** Heb. *akarah*, the same word translated as "barren" in describing Sarah's condition (11:30) and Rachel's (29:31). In contrast to stories about these other matriarchs or Hannah, we are not told that Rebekah resorts to "extreme measures" to ensure fertility. Ancient Near Eastern documents describe adoption as one of the strategies for handling the social and economic problems resulting from lack of progeny. Another potential solution is reflected in Genesis 16, where Sarah gives Abraham

▶ Rebekah . . . pays a very high price for her determination.

ANOTHER VIEW ➤ *150*

▶ The emotional reaction to infertility has remained largely unchanged.

CONTEMPORARY REFLECTION ➤ *152*

▶ The Rabbis . . . observe that Rebekah experienced divine revelation twice.

POST-BIBLICAL INTERPRETATIONS ➤ *150*

▶ Jacob is Isaac's son in tenderness . . . / And Esau in lustiness is mine. . . .

VOICES ➤ *154*

22The children pressed against each other inside
her. She thought: "If this is so, why do I exist?" So
she went to inquire of יהוה. 23יהוה said to her:

Two peoples are in your belly;
two nations shall branch off from each other
[as they emerge] from your womb.
One people shall prevail over the other;
the elder shall serve the younger.

24When the time came for her to give birth,
lo—she had twins in her belly! 25The first came out

22 וַיִּתְרֹצְצוּ הַבָּנִים בְּקִרְבָּהּ וַתֹּאמֶר אִם־כֵּן
לָמָּה זֶּה אָנֹכִי וַתֵּלֶךְ לִדְרֹשׁ אֶת־יְהֹוָה׃
23 וַיֹּאמֶר יְהֹוָה לָהּ
שְׁנֵי גיים גוֹיִם בְּבִטְנֵךְ
וּשְׁנֵי לְאֻמִּים מִמֵּעַיִךְ
יִפָּרֵדוּ וּלְאֹם מִלְאֹם יֶאֱמָץ
וְרַב יַעֲבֹד צָעִיר׃
24 וַיִּמְלְאוּ יָמֶיהָ לָלֶדֶת וְהִנֵּה תוֹמִם
בְּבִטְנָהּ׃ 25 וַיֵּצֵא הָרִאשׁוֹן אַדְמוֹנִי כֻּלּוֹ

her handmaid Hagar in order to produce an offspring. Elsewhere in the Bible, women resort to prayer (Hannah in I Samuel 1) or a presumed fertility plant (see Rachel bargaining with Leah for mandrakes in Genesis 30:14). For more on barrenness, see *Noach*, Another View, p. 53.

*22. **The children pressed... She thought.*** Although there is no mention that Rebekah turned to God when she could not conceive, she does so in response to her pregnancy.

***"why do I exist?"*** Literally, "why am I?" Interpreters often say that Rebekah is bemoaning her physical pain. However, the text mentions only that the pregnancy is unsettling, not that it is painful. Instead, what prompts her question may be the prospect of multiple children, which in the Bible typically signals a special destiny. Far from complaining about her condition, Rebekah is wondering about her role in such destiny. God's answer (v. 23) confirms such a reading, since it refers to the children's future.

***inquire.*** Heb. *lidrosh*, a verb that usually designates a formal consultation, in this case with God. The text pointedly omits any mention of mediated communication, which suggests that Rebekah addresses God directly, and that God responds to her with equal directness (v. 23). The earlier picture of Rebekah as gutsy, independent, and resourceful (Genesis 24) thus continues. Yet many interpreters both ancient and modern have distanced Rebekah from a direct contact with God. One rabbinic commentator claimed, for example, that she went to a house of study (see Post-biblical Interpretations, p. 150). Some modern feminist commentators have speculated that she receives the information in a dream (see citations in Alice Bellis, *Helpmates, Harlots, and Heroes*, 1994, pp. 82–83).

*23. **יהוה said to her.*** God replies to Rebekah directly, informing her—not Isaac—about their sons' future. Two other biblical mothers to whom God discloses their son's future are Hagar (16:10–12, 21:17–18) and Samson's mother (Judges 13:3–5).

***the elder shall serve the younger.*** The poetic Hebrew is more ambiguous than the translation indicates—literally "elder serve younger," which could also mean that the younger shall serve the elder. The text may seek to suggest that Jacob's subsequent preeminence results from Rebekah's interpretation. | The election of the younger over the elder is a theme that pervades Genesis. It may reflect a conflict relating to the audience's national identity and the formation of a people in which newer traditions are integrated with older ones.

*24. **When the time came for her to give birth.*** The focus remains on Rebekah's experience. The description of Isaac's role in the conception has been limited to pleading.

***lo—she had twins in her belly!*** A nearly identical expression appears again with the birth of Tamar's twins (38:27). Each of these women eventually uses subterfuge in order to ensure what she believes is the right outcome: Tamar, in order to have

reddish all over, as though covered with a hairy mantle, so they named him Esau; 26his brother, following, came out holding Esau's heel, so they named him Jacob. Isaac was 60 years old when they were born. 27When the boys grew up, Esau became a skillful hunter, a man of the outdoors; but Jacob was a homespun man, keeping to the tents. 28Isaac favored Esau, because he [Esau] put game in his mouth, but Rebekah favored Jacob.

29[One day,] when Jacob was cooking a stew, Esau came in from the [hunting] field. He was famished, 30and he said to Jacob, "I'm famished; let me gulp down some of that red stuff!" (That is

כְּאַדֶּ֣רֶת שֵׂעָ֑ר וַיִּקְרְא֥וּ שְׁמ֖וֹ עֵשָֽׂו׃ 26 וְאַֽחֲרֵי־
כֵ֞ן יָצָ֣א אָחִ֗יו וְיָד֤וֹ אֹחֶ֙זֶת֙ בַּעֲקֵ֣ב עֵשָׂ֔ו וַיִּקְרָ֥א
שְׁמ֖וֹ יַעֲקֹ֑ב וְיִצְחָ֛ק בֶּן־שִׁשִּׁ֥ים שָׁנָ֖ה בְּלֶ֥דֶת
אֹתָֽם׃ 27 וַֽיִּגְדְּלוּ֙ הַנְּעָרִ֔ים וַיְהִ֣י עֵשָׂ֗ו אִ֛ישׁ
יֹדֵ֥עַ צַ֖יִד אִ֣ישׁ שָׂדֶ֑ה וְיַעֲקֹב֙ אִ֣ישׁ תָּ֔ם יֹשֵׁ֖ב
אֹהָלִֽים׃ 28 וַיֶּאֱהַ֥ב יִצְחָ֛ק אֶת־עֵשָׂ֖ו כִּי־צַ֣יִד
בְּפִ֑יו וְרִבְקָ֖ה אֹהֶ֥בֶת אֶֽת־יַעֲקֹֽב׃
29 וַיָּ֥זֶד יַעֲקֹ֖ב נָזִ֑יד וַיָּבֹ֥א עֵשָׂ֛ו מִן־הַשָּׂדֶ֖ה
וְה֥וּא עָיֵֽף׃ 30 וַיֹּ֨אמֶר עֵשָׂ֜ו אֶֽל־יַעֲקֹ֗ב
הַלְעִיטֵ֤נִי נָא֙ מִן־הָאָדֹ֤ם הָאָדֹם֙ הַזֶּ֔ה כִּ֥י
עָיֵ֖ף אָנֹ֑כִי עַל־כֵּ֥ן קָרָֽא־שְׁמ֖וֹ אֱדֽוֹם׃

a child (Genesis 38); Rebekah, to secure the future of the son she considers most worthy (Genesis 27).

*25. Esau.* The etymology of this name is unclear. Esau is also known as Edom (25:30, 36:8), which relates to "red" (*adom*). He will become the ancestor of the Edomites (36:9), a nation with which Israel has frequent conflict, according to later books of the Bible.

*26. Jacob.* Heb. *Yaakov*, which echoes the word "heel" (*akev*) and can also be translated as "he will act crookedly."

## *Favoritism and the Selling of the Birthright* (25:27–34)

Beginning with the story of Cain and Abel (Genesis 4), favoritism plagues the subsequent generations (see Noah's sons, 9:18–27; Isaac and Ishmael, 21:9–14; Joseph and his brothers, 37:3–35).

*28. favored.* Literally, "loved" (*ahav*). We are told why Isaac loves Esau: His son the hunter brings Isaac his favored meal of fresh game.

***Rebekah favored Jacob.*** Rebekah's love is left unexplained. Her favoritism of Jacob does not appear to depend on any self-gratification. Possibly her love serves as a compensation for Isaac's preference of Esau, or perhaps is a response to Jacob's nature as a "homespun man" who apparently stays close to home (v. 27). Her preference may also be related to how she interprets God's words in 25:23; she favors the son she thinks has been selected by God.

There is only one other biblical narrative that mentions a woman's love. In I Samuel 18, we read, "Michal, daughter of Saul, loved David" (I Samuel 18:20, 28). In both instances, the women eventually resort to deception to protect the one they love. (Michal rescues David from her father's wrath and lies to her father about it; see I Samuel 19.) Love will soon spur Rebekah into deceiving Isaac in order to secure Jacob's destiny (see Genesis 27).

*30–33.* Jacob's manipulation of his short-sighted brother reflects poorly on both characters. Of the two, Jacob places value on what endures—a quality that may, in part, account for Rebekah's machinations on his behalf. | Possessing the birthright, Jacob is now entitled to Isaac's special blessings. The Hebrew term *b'chorah* ("birthright") usually refers to the status of successor as head of the corporate household, which entails special economic and religious responsibilities as well as privileges. Normally in the ancient Near East, a first-born son possessed this status automatically, although he could barter it away or be stripped of it by the paterfamilias. Deuteronomy 21:15–17 presumes that the first-born son receives a disproportionate share of the inheritance.

why he was named Edom.) [31]Jacob said, "Sell me
your birthright here and now." [32]And Esau said,
"Here I am going to die; what good is the birthright
to me?" [33]But Jacob said, "Confirm it to me by
oath here and now." So he swore it to him, and sold
his birthright to Jacob. [34]Jacob then gave Esau
bread and lentil stew. He ate, drank, got up, and
left. Thus did Esau disdain his birthright.

31 וַיֹּאמֶר יַעֲקֹב מִכְרָה כַיּוֹם אֶת־בְּכֹרָתְךָ
לִי׃ 32 וַיֹּאמֶר עֵשָׂו הִנֵּה אָנֹכִי הוֹלֵךְ לָמוּת
וְלָמָּה־זֶּה לִי בְּכֹרָה׃ 33 וַיֹּאמֶר יַעֲקֹב
הִשָּׁבְעָה לִּי כַּיּוֹם וַיִּשָּׁבַע לוֹ וַיִּמְכֹּר אֶת־
בְּכֹרָתוֹ לְיַעֲקֹב׃ 34 וְיַעֲקֹב נָתַן לְעֵשָׂו לֶחֶם
וּנְזִיד עֲדָשִׁים וַיֹּאכַל וַיֵּשְׁתְּ וַיָּקָם וַיֵּלַךְ וַיִּבֶז
עֵשָׂו אֶת־הַבְּכֹרָה׃ פ

*26* There was a famine in the land, apart
from the earlier famine that had occurred in the
time of Abraham; Isaac therefore traveled to Abimelech king of the Philistines, to Gerar. [2]יהוה then
appeared to him, saying, "Do not go down to
Egypt; reside in the land that I will point out to
you. [3]Stay in this land and I will be with you and
bless you; for to you and your descendants will I
give all these lands, fulfilling the oath that I swore
to your father Abraham. [4]I will multiply your seed
as the stars of heaven, giving your descendants all
these lands; and through your seed all the peoples
of the earth shall be blessed—[5]because Abraham

כו וַיְהִי רָעָב בָּאָרֶץ מִלְּבַד הָרָעָב
הָרִאשׁוֹן אֲשֶׁר הָיָה בִּימֵי אַבְרָהָם וַיֵּלֶךְ
יִצְחָק אֶל־אֲבִימֶלֶךְ מֶלֶךְ־פְּלִשְׁתִּים גְּרָרָה׃
2 וַיֵּרָא אֵלָיו יְהוָה וַיֹּאמֶר אַל־תֵּרֵד
מִצְרָיְמָה שְׁכֹן בָּאָרֶץ אֲשֶׁר אֹמַר אֵלֶיךָ׃
3 גּוּר בָּאָרֶץ הַזֹּאת וְאֶהְיֶה עִמְּךָ וַאֲבָרְכֶךָּ
כִּי־לְךָ וּלְזַרְעֲךָ אֶתֵּן אֶת־כָּל־הָאֲרָצֹת הָאֵל
וַהֲקִמֹתִי אֶת־הַשְּׁבֻעָה אֲשֶׁר נִשְׁבַּעְתִּי
לְאַבְרָהָם אָבִיךָ׃ 4 וְהִרְבֵּיתִי אֶת־זַרְעֲךָ
כְּכוֹכְבֵי הַשָּׁמַיִם וְנָתַתִּי לְזַרְעֲךָ אֵת כָּל־
הָאֲרָצֹת הָאֵל וְהִתְבָּרְכוּ בְזַרְעֲךָ כֹּל גּוֹיֵי
הָאָרֶץ׃ 5 עֵקֶב אֲשֶׁר־שָׁמַע אַבְרָהָם בְּקֹלִי

## *Isaac and Rebekah "Visit" Abimelech*

### ISAAC AT THE CENTER (26:1–33)

The Torah repeatedly portrays Isaac as a passive figure; he is largely overshadowed by other members of his family. Only in this passage does Isaac appear as the chief actor. Even here, however, his father looms large. In all these episodes Isaac walks in his father's footsteps, performing deeds similar to his father's but with different results. First, God's blessings are bestowed upon him due solely to his father's merit. Second, his lie that Rebekah is his sister (repeating Abraham's "wife-sister" deceptions in Genesis 12 and 21) backfires. Third, the wells he digs are repeatedly taken away (Genesis 26:15; contrast with Abraham who stands his ground in Genesis 21). And yet, Isaac gains a moral victory and comes away blessed (see 26:29). In this fashion, he represents another mode of Jewish survival: compliance rather than confrontation.

### ISAAC RECEIVES THE COVENANT PROMISE (26:1–5)

Isaac receives the covenant only on account of his father's merit.

*1.* ***Abimelech.*** This is the name also of the king whom Abraham had deceived with the "wife-sister" ruse in Genesis 20.

*3–5.* ***"I will be with you . . . because Abraham hearkened to My voice and kept My charge."*** God bestows blessings upon Isaac because of Abraham's (not Isaac's) merit, further underscoring his stature vis-à-vis his more distinguished father.

hearkened to My voice and kept My charge, My
commands, My statutes, and My laws." [6]Isaac
[therefore] settled in Gerar. [7]And when the people
of that place asked about his wife, he answered,
"She is my sister," because he was afraid to say:
"My wife," [thinking,] "Lest the local people kill
me on account of Rebekah, since she is so good-looking."

[8]As his days there stretched out, Abimelech king
of the Philistines happened [one day] to look out of
a window and he saw—Isaac fondling his wife
Rebekah! [9]So Abimelech summoned Isaac and said,
"Look—she must be your wife; why then did you
say, 'She is my sister'?" Isaac said to him, "I spoke
that way for fear of dying on her account." [10]But
Abimelech said, "What is this that you have done
to us? One of the people nearly lay with your wife;
you would have brought [suffering] upon us for our
guilt!" [11]The king thereupon instructed all the
people: Anyone who touches this man or his wife
will be put to death!

וַיִּשְׁמֹר מִשְׁמַרְתִּי מִצְוֺתַי חֻקּוֹתַי וְתוֹרֹתָי׃
6 וַיֵּשֶׁב יִצְחָק בִּגְרָר׃ 7 וַיִּשְׁאֲלוּ אַנְשֵׁי
הַמָּקוֹם לְאִשְׁתּוֹ וַיֹּאמֶר אֲחֹתִי הִוא כִּי
יָרֵא לֵאמֹר אִשְׁתִּי פֶּן־יַהַרְגֻנִי אַנְשֵׁי הַמָּקוֹם
עַל־רִבְקָה כִּי־טוֹבַת מַרְאֶה הִוא׃
8 וַיְהִי כִּי אָרְכוּ־לוֹ שָׁם הַיָּמִים וַיַּשְׁקֵף
אֲבִימֶלֶךְ מֶלֶךְ פְּלִשְׁתִּים בְּעַד הַחַלּוֹן וַיַּרְא
וְהִנֵּה יִצְחָק מְצַחֵק אֵת רִבְקָה אִשְׁתּוֹ׃
9 וַיִּקְרָא אֲבִימֶלֶךְ לְיִצְחָק וַיֹּאמֶר אַךְ הִנֵּה
אִשְׁתְּךָ הִוא וְאֵיךְ אָמַרְתָּ אֲחֹתִי הִוא
וַיֹּאמֶר אֵלָיו יִצְחָק כִּי אָמַרְתִּי פֶּן־אָמוּת
עָלֶיהָ׃ 10 וַיֹּאמֶר אֲבִימֶלֶךְ מַה־זֹּאת עָשִׂיתָ
לָּנוּ כִּמְעַט שָׁכַב אַחַד הָעָם אֶת־אִשְׁתֶּךָ
וְהֵבֵאתָ עָלֵינוּ אָשָׁם׃ 11 וַיְצַו אֲבִימֶלֶךְ אֶת־
כָּל־הָעָם לֵאמֹר הַנֹּגֵעַ בָּאִישׁ הַזֶּה וּבְאִשְׁתּוֹ
מוֹת יוּמָת׃

## ISAAC PASSES HIS WIFE OFF AS HIS SISTER (26:6–11)

This "wife-sister" episode, like those of Abraham and Sarah (Genesis 12 and 20), portrays a patriarch fearful for his life, protecting himself by posing his wife as his sister. The difference from Abraham and Sarah's story is that Isaac thinks his wife is irresistibly attractive, but apparently no one else does. Nonetheless, Isaac and Rebekah receive royal protection.

*7.* Like his father (20:11), Isaac pretends—out of fear—that Rebekah is his sister in order to protect himself.

*"she is so good-looking."* The same description of Rebekah appears when the narrator introduces her in 24:16 (translated there as "exceedingly beautiful"). Narrative sequence implies that this visit takes place decades later. Apparently Isaac still considers Rebekah alluringly beautiful.

*8. his days there stretched out.* Sarah's beauty prompted kings to take her to their palace (12:14–15; 20:2). However, in this episode, contrary to Isaac's fears, no one takes Rebekah. Is it because she is not as attractive as Isaac supposes, or because King Abimelech learned his lesson with Abraham and Sarah? What follows indicates that Isaac continues to find his wife appealing and cannot keep himself away from her as time passes.

*Isaac fondling.* In an ironic twist, Isaac is caught "playing" with his wife. The verb *m'tzachek* is a pun on his name, *Yitzchak*. Here the term connotes laughter and playfulness of the sort that spouses engage in. It is identical with the verb used of Ishmael with Isaac in 21:9, where the connotations were less clear (see there).

*11.* Rebekah's position is not compromised. Isaac's wealth results from his efforts and from God's blessings.

<sup>12</sup>In that area Isaac sowed seed, and in that year he received a hundredfold, for יהוה blessed him. <sup>13</sup>The man grew rich, and he went on growing all the richer until he was exceedingly rich. <sup>14</sup>He had herds of sheep and herds of cattle, and a large body of servants, so that the Philistines envied him, <sup>15</sup>and the Philistines stopped up all the wells that his father's servants had dug in the time of his father Abraham, filling them with rubble. <sup>16</sup>Abimelech now said to Isaac, "Leave us; you have become much too numerous for us." <sup>17</sup>So Isaac went away from there, encamping in the wadi of Gerar. There he settled.

<sup>18</sup>Isaac then turned to digging anew the water-wells they had dug in the time of his father Abraham—which the Philistines had stopped up after Abraham's death—and he gave them the same names as his father had given them. <sup>19</sup>And when Isaac's servants dug in the wadi, they discovered there a well of living waters, <sup>20</sup>and the shepherds of Gerar quarreled with Isaac's shepherds, saying, "The water is ours!" So he named the well Wrangle, for they had wrangled with him. <sup>21</sup>They then dug another well, but they quarreled over this one, too, so he named it Animosity. <sup>22</sup>He then moved from there and dug another well, and over this one they did not quarrel, so he named it Rehoboth, meaning: Now יהוה has granted us *ample room* and will make us fruitful in the land. <sup>23</sup>And from there he went up to Beersheba.

<sup>24</sup>That very night יהוה appeared to him, saying, "I am the God of your father Abraham; have no fear, for I am with you! I will bless you and make your descendants numerous for the sake of My ser-

יב וַיִּזְרַ֤ע יִצְחָק֙ בָּאָ֣רֶץ הַהִ֔וא וַיִּמְצָ֛א בַּשָּׁנָ֥ה הַהִ֖וא מֵאָ֣ה שְׁעָרִ֑ים וַֽיְבָרֲכֵ֖הוּ יְהוָֽה: יג וַיִּגְדַּ֖ל הָאִ֑ישׁ וַיֵּ֤לֶךְ הָלוֹךְ֙ וְגָדֵ֔ל עַ֥ד כִּֽי־גָדַ֖ל מְאֹֽד: יד וַֽיְהִי־ל֤וֹ מִקְנֵה־צֹאן֙ וּמִקְנֵ֣ה בָקָ֔ר וַעֲבֻדָּ֖ה רַבָּ֑ה וַיְקַנְא֥וּ אֹת֖וֹ פְּלִשְׁתִּֽים: טו וְכָל־הַבְּאֵרֹ֗ת אֲשֶׁ֤ר חָֽפְרוּ֙ עַבְדֵ֣י אָבִ֔יו בִּימֵ֖י אַבְרָהָ֣ם אָבִ֑יו סִתְּמ֣וּם פְּלִשְׁתִּ֔ים וַיְמַלְא֖וּם עָפָֽר: טז וַיֹּ֥אמֶר אֲבִימֶ֖לֶךְ אֶל־יִצְחָ֑ק לֵ֚ךְ מֵֽעִמָּ֔נוּ כִּֽי־עָצַ֥מְתָּ מִמֶּ֖נּוּ מְאֹֽד: יז וַיֵּ֥לֶךְ מִשָּׁ֖ם יִצְחָ֑ק וַיִּ֥חַן בְּנַֽחַל־גְּרָ֖ר וַיֵּ֥שֶׁב שָֽׁם: יח וַיָּ֨שָׁב יִצְחָ֜ק וַיַּחְפֹּ֣ר ׀ אֶת־בְּאֵרֹ֣ת הַמַּ֗יִם אֲשֶׁ֤ר חָֽפְרוּ֙ בִּימֵי֙ אַבְרָהָ֣ם אָבִ֔יו וַיְסַתְּמ֣וּם פְּלִשְׁתִּ֔ים אַחֲרֵ֖י מ֣וֹת אַבְרָהָ֑ם וַיִּקְרָ֤א לָהֶן֙ שֵׁמ֔וֹת כַּשֵּׁמֹ֕ת אֲשֶׁר־קָרָ֥א לָהֶ֖ן אָבִֽיו: יט וַיַּחְפְּר֥וּ עַבְדֵֽי־יִצְחָ֖ק בַּנָּ֑חַל וַיִּ֨מְצְאוּ־שָׁ֔ם בְּאֵ֖ר מַ֥יִם חַיִּֽים: כ וַיָּרִ֜יבוּ רֹעֵ֣י גְרָ֗ר עִם־רֹעֵ֤י יִצְחָק֙ לֵאמֹ֔ר לָ֖נוּ הַמָּ֑יִם וַיִּקְרָ֤א שֵֽׁם־הַבְּאֵר֙ עֵ֔שֶׂק כִּ֥י הִֽתְעַשְּׂק֖וּ עִמּֽוֹ: כא וַֽיַּחְפְּרוּ֙ בְּאֵ֣ר אַחֶ֔רֶת וַיָּרִ֖יבוּ גַּם־עָלֶ֑יהָ וַיִּקְרָ֥א שְׁמָ֖הּ שִׂטְנָֽה: כב וַיַּעְתֵּ֣ק מִשָּׁ֗ם וַיַּחְפֹּר֙ בְּאֵ֣ר אַחֶ֔רֶת וְלֹ֥א רָב֖וּ עָלֶ֑יהָ וַיִּקְרָ֤א שְׁמָהּ֙ רְחֹב֔וֹת וַיֹּ֗אמֶר כִּֽי־עַתָּ֞ה הִרְחִ֧יב יְהוָ֛ה לָ֖נוּ וּפָרִ֥ינוּ בָאָֽרֶץ: כג וַיַּ֥עַל מִשָּׁ֖ם בְּאֵ֥ר שָֽׁבַע: כד וַיֵּרָ֨א אֵלָ֤יו יְהוָה֙ בַּלַּ֣יְלָה הַה֔וּא וַיֹּ֕אמֶר אָֽנֹכִ֕י אֱלֹהֵ֖י אַבְרָהָ֣ם אָבִ֑יךָ אַל־תִּירָא֙ כִּֽי־אִתְּךָ֣ אָנֹ֔כִי וּבֵֽרַכְתִּ֨יךָ֙ וְהִרְבֵּיתִ֣י אֶת־זַרְעֲךָ֔

---

## ISAAC DIGS WELLS, LOSES THEM, PERSISTS, AND PROSPERS (26:12–33)

Isaac's peaceful disposition is apparent in the patience with which he digs and re-digs wells. When his ownership of wells is challenged, he relinquishes them, whereas Abraham had stood his ground (Genesis 21). Later, Isaac's passivity and persistence pay off when Abimelech recognizes his merit and concludes a treaty with him (26:29).

vant Abraham." 25So there he built an altar and called upon the Name of יהוה; there he pitched his tent and there Isaac's servants dug out a well.

26Abimelech now went to him from Gerar with Ahuzzath his confidant, and Pichol, commander of his troops. 27Isaac said to them, "Why have you come to me, when you hate me and drove me away from your midst?" 28They replied, "We see clearly now that יהוה has been with you, so we thought: Pray let there be a sworn treaty between us—between you and us; we will make a compact with you. 29Would you ill-treat us, seeing that we never did you an injury and did only good to you and sent you away in peace? You are now the blessed of יהוה!" 30So he made them a [covenantal] feast; they ate and drank.

31When they got up in the morning they made a vow, each to the other; then Isaac sent them away and they parted from him in harmony. 32That same day Isaac's servants came and told him about the well they had dug, saying to him, "We have found water!" 33So he called it Shiba, which is why the town is called Beersheba to this day.

34When Esau was 40 years old he took to wife Judith daughter of Beeri the Hittite and Basemath daughter of Elon the Hittite. 35They were a bitterness of spirit to Isaac and Rebekah.

בַּעֲב֖וּר אַבְרָהָ֥ם עַבְדִּֽי׃ 25 וַיִּ֧בֶן שָׁ֣ם מִזְבֵּ֗חַ
וַיִּקְרָא֙ בְּשֵׁ֣ם יְהוָ֔ה וַיֶּט־שָׁ֖ם אָהֳל֑וֹ וַיִּכְרוּ־
שָׁ֥ם עַבְדֵי־יִצְחָ֖ק בְּאֵֽר׃
26 וַאֲבִימֶ֕לֶךְ הָלַ֥ךְ אֵלָ֖יו מִגְּרָ֑ר וַאֲחֻזַּת֙
מֵֽרֵעֵ֔הוּ וּפִיכֹ֖ל שַׂר־צְבָאֽוֹ׃ 27 וַיֹּ֤אמֶר אֲלֵהֶם֙
יִצְחָ֔ק מַדּ֖וּעַ בָּאתֶ֣ם אֵלָ֑י וְאַתֶּם֙ שְׂנֵאתֶ֣ם
אֹתִ֔י וַתְּשַׁלְּח֖וּנִי מֵאִתְּכֶֽם׃ 28 וַיֹּאמְר֗וּ רָא֣וֹ
רָאִ֘ינוּ֮ כִּֽי־הָיָ֣ה יְהוָ֣ה ׀ עִמָּךְ֒ וַנֹּ֗אמֶר תְּהִ֨י
נָ֥א אָלָ֛ה בֵּינוֹתֵ֖ינוּ בֵּינֵ֣ינוּ וּבֵינֶ֑ךָ וְנִכְרְתָ֥ה
בְרִ֖ית עִמָּֽךְ׃ 29 אִם־תַּעֲשֵׂ֨ה עִמָּ֜נוּ רָעָ֗ה
כַּאֲשֶׁר֙ לֹ֣א נְגַֽעֲנ֔וּךָ וְכַאֲשֶׁ֨ר עָשִׂ֤ינוּ עִמְּךָ֙
רַק־ט֔וֹב וַנְּשַׁלֵּחֲךָ֖ בְּשָׁל֑וֹם אַתָּ֥ה עַתָּ֖ה בְּר֥וּךְ
יְהוָֽה׃ 30 וַיַּ֤עַשׂ לָהֶם֙ מִשְׁתֶּ֔ה וַיֹּאכְל֖וּ
וַיִּשְׁתּֽוּ׃
31 וַיַּשְׁכִּ֣ימוּ בַבֹּ֔קֶר וַיִּשָּׁבְע֖וּ אִ֣ישׁ לְאָחִ֑יו
וַיְשַׁלְּחֵ֣ם יִצְחָ֔ק וַיֵּלְכ֥וּ מֵאִתּ֖וֹ בְּשָׁלֽוֹם׃
32 וַיְהִ֣י ׀ בַּיּ֣וֹם הַה֗וּא וַיָּבֹ֙אוּ֙ עַבְדֵ֣י יִצְחָ֔ק
וַיַּגִּ֣דוּ ל֔וֹ עַל־אֹד֥וֹת הַבְּאֵ֖ר אֲשֶׁ֣ר חָפָ֑רוּ
וַיֹּ֥אמְרוּ ל֖וֹ מָצָ֥אנוּ מָֽיִם׃ 33 וַיִּקְרָ֥א אֹתָ֖הּ
שִׁבְעָ֑ה עַל־כֵּ֤ן שֵׁם־הָעִיר֙ בְּאֵ֣ר שֶׁ֔בַע עַ֖ד
הַיּ֥וֹם הַזֶּֽה׃ ס
34 וַיְהִ֤י עֵשָׂו֙ בֶּן־אַרְבָּעִ֣ים שָׁנָ֔ה וַיִּקַּ֥ח אִשָּׁה֙
אֶת־יְהוּדִ֔ית בַּת־בְּאֵרִ֖י הַחִתִּ֑י וְאֶת־בָּ֣שְׂמַ֔ת
בַּת־אֵילֹ֖ן הַֽחִתִּֽי׃ 35 וַתִּהְיֶ֖יןָ מֹ֣רַת ר֑וּחַ
לְיִצְחָ֖ק וּלְרִבְקָֽה׃ ס

## *Esau Marries Canaanite Wives*

(26:34–35)

The marriage of Esau brings consternation to both his parents. In 27:46, Rebekah claims that Esau's marriages cause her despair. Isaac does nothing. One gathers that the fact the women are Canaanite is problematic (see at 28:1). Is this marriage one of the reasons why Rebekah chooses the drastic measures to pass the blessings to Jacob? Is it Isaac's passivity in the face of what both consider a problem that moves her to take action?

*34. Judith.* This name's debut in Esau's family is surprising in light of its subsequent use: The masculine form, Judah, will come to designate the main tribe in Israelite history, becoming the basis of the Hebrew word for "Jew." (The enduring popularity among Jews of the name Judith comes from a different source: the heroic central character in an ancient Jewish post-biblical book of the same name.)

27 When Isaac had grown old and his eyesight had dimmed, he called his elder son Esau,
saying to him, "My son!" "Here I am," he answered. 2"Look now," said he. "I have grown old,
[and] for all I know I may die any day. 3So pick up
your weapons—your quiver and your bow—and
go out to the countryside and hunt me some game.
4Then you can make me tasty dishes such as I like
and bring [them] to me and I will eat, so that I can
give you my heartfelt blessing before I die."
5As Isaac was speaking to his son Esau, Rebekah
was listening; and when Esau went to the countryside to hunt for some game to bring [him],

כז וַיְהִי כִּי־זָקֵן יִצְחָק וַתִּכְהֶיןָ עֵינָיו
מֵרְאֹת וַיִּקְרָא אֶת־עֵשָׂו ׀ בְּנוֹ הַגָּדֹל וַיֹּאמֶר
אֵלָיו בְּנִי וַיֹּאמֶר אֵלָיו הִנֵּנִי׃ 2 וַיֹּאמֶר הִנֵּה־
נָא זָקַנְתִּי לֹא יָדַעְתִּי יוֹם מוֹתִי׃ 3 וְעַתָּה
שָׂא־נָא כֵלֶיךָ תֶּלְיְךָ וְקַשְׁתֶּךָ וְצֵא הַשָּׂדֶה
וְצוּדָה לִּי צידה צָיִד׃ 4 וַעֲשֵׂה־לִי מַטְעַמִּים
כַּאֲשֶׁר אָהַבְתִּי וְהָבִיאָה לִּי וְאֹכֵלָה בַּעֲבוּר
תְּבָרֶכְךָ נַפְשִׁי בְּטֶרֶם אָמוּת׃
5 וְרִבְקָה שֹׁמַעַת בְּדַבֵּר יִצְחָק אֶל־עֵשָׂו בְּנוֹ
וַיֵּלֶךְ עֵשָׂו הַשָּׂדֶה לָצוּד צַיִד לְהָבִיא׃

## *Rebekah Ensures the Transmission of the Covenantal Blessings to Jacob*

(27:1–28:9)

Rebekah appears to be in charge of the events in this episode, actively putting her plan into action. In order to implement what she understands as the divine plan, she must ensure that it is Jacob who receives the blessing from Isaac. Not being the head of the household, she lacks the authority to give Jacob the blessing directly. Rebekah thus works through Isaac, albeit without his explicit knowledge or consent. She creates a way to usurp his authority and use it for her own ends. If Rebekah had possessed the authority to work through the formal structures of inheritance, she would not have needed to use subterfuge and to pit brother against brother, son against father. Subterfuge is what women and men in positions of powerlessness, or of limited power, use to meet their rightful needs. See, for example, Tamar's daring encounter with Judah (Genesis 38), and young David's deception of King Achish (I Samuel 21:11–16). Because women generally lack certain authority in biblical narrative, they sometimes work out unusual tactics to resolve problems and achieve results. They take on the daring plots that dramatically alter the course of events. In biblical narratives, their acts are usually recognized as beneficial: lives are saved, the right side wins, the right son inherits, the family line continues.

Although the rabbinic sages primarily praise Rebekah for her actions, modern biblical scholars are more mixed in their readings of her actions. Some see her as a laudable trickster who must use stratagems to bend the male power structure to her purpose. Others see her as a manipulating schemer whose actions here fit into stereotyped expectations of female behavior, and who is punished for her behavior by never seeing her favorite child again. Adrien Bledstein offers an alternate reading of the episode, suggesting that Isaac is in fact the trickster: he is not deceived by Rebekah but rather has her do his dirty work for him ("Binder, Trickster, Heel...," 1993). (For a range of opinions on Rebekah, see Bellis, *Helpmates, Harlots, and Heroes*, 1994, pp. 80–84.)

### ISAAC PREPARES TO BLESS ESAU (27:1–4)

*1. **Isaac had grown old.*** Isaac's growing incapacity may play a role in Rebekah's decision to shape the course of events.

***his elder son.*** Throughout this episode, Esau is repeatedly identified in relation to his father and brother, and less so to his mother (see 27:6, 11, 42, 44).

6 Rebekah said this to her son Jacob, "Look—I
heard your father speaking to your brother Esau,
saying, 7 'Bring me game and make me tasty dishes,
that I may eat—and [then] bless you before יהוה
before my death.'
8 "Now, son, listen to me, to what I am instructing you: 9 Go to the flock and bring me two tender
kids, and I will make them into tasty dishes for
your father, such as he likes. 10 You will bring them
to your father and he will eat, so that he may bless
you before his death." 11 But Jacob said to his
mother Rebekah, "Look—my brother Esau is a
hairy man and I am a smooth-skinned man;
12 should my father feel me I will seem to him like
a cheat, and I will bring a curse on myself, not a
blessing!"

6 וְרִבְקָה֙ אָֽמְרָ֔ה אֶל־יַעֲקֹ֥ב בְּנָ֖הּ לֵאמֹ֑ר הִנֵּ֤ה
שָׁמַ֙עְתִּי֙ אֶת־אָבִ֔יךָ מְדַבֵּ֛ר אֶל־עֵשָׂ֥ו אָחִ֖יךָ
לֵאמֹֽר׃ 7 הָבִ֨יאָה לִּ֥י צַ֛יִד וַעֲשֵׂה־לִ֥י
מַטְעַמִּ֖ים וְאֹכֵ֑לָה וַאֲבָרֶכְכָ֛ה לִפְנֵ֥י יְהוָ֖ה
לִפְנֵ֥י מוֹתִֽי׃
8 וְעַתָּ֥ה בְנִ֖י שְׁמַ֣ע בְּקֹלִ֑י לַאֲשֶׁ֥ר אֲנִ֖י מְצַוָּ֥ה
אֹתָֽךְ׃ 9 לֶךְ־נָא֙ אֶל־הַצֹּ֔אן וְקַח־לִ֣י מִשָּׁ֗ם
שְׁנֵ֛י גְּדָיֵ֥י עִזִּ֖ים טֹבִ֑ים וְאֶֽעֱשֶׂ֨ה אֹתָ֧ם
מַטְעַמִּ֛ים לְאָבִ֖יךָ כַּאֲשֶׁ֥ר אָהֵֽב׃ 10 וְהֵבֵאתָ֥
לְאָבִ֖יךָ וְאָכָ֑ל בַּעֲבֻ֥ר אֲשֶׁ֛ר יְבָרֶכְךָ֖ לִפְנֵ֥י
מוֹתֽוֹ׃ 11 וַיֹּ֣אמֶר יַעֲקֹ֔ב אֶל־רִבְקָ֖ה אִמּ֑וֹ
הֵ֚ן עֵשָׂ֣ו אָחִ֔י אִ֣ישׁ שָׂעִ֔ר וְאָנֹכִ֖י אִ֥ישׁ
חָלָֽק׃ 12 אוּלַ֤י יְמֻשֵּׁ֙נִי֙ אָבִ֔י וְהָיִ֥יתִי בְעֵינָ֖יו
כִּמְתַעְתֵּ֑עַ וְהֵבֵאתִ֥י עָלַ֛י קְלָלָ֖ה וְלֹ֥א
בְרָכָֽה׃

### REBEKAH ARRANGES FOR JACOB TO RECEIVE ISAAC'S BLESSING INSTEAD (27:5–17)

*6. her son.* In contrast to Esau, Jacob is referred to several times as "her son" (see also v. 17). The language used here seems to exclude Esau from the kind of close relationship that Jacob has with Rebekah.

*"your father."* In this chapter Isaac is never referred to in relation to Rebekah; he is called "father" (vv. 6, 9, 10, 14), but not Rebekah's husband. Isaac's importance to Rebekah seems to recede into the background, and her most primary relationship is with Jacob her son. Rebekah and Isaac converse only at the very end of the tale, when Rebekah intervenes (again) for Jacob's sake (27:46). While Isaac is reported to have loved Rebekah upon seeing her (24:67), the narrative never states that Rebekah returns this love. The language in this section of the text connects her directly to her son Jacob, but not to Isaac.

*8. "listen to me."* Rebekah will tell Jacob twice more to listen to her (vv. 13 and 43). She repeats herself to make sure that she has his attention. Carol Meyers notes that *authority* is the ability to control situations and decision-making through official channels and systems, whereas *power* involves doing so through more informal and unofficial avenues (*Discovering Eve: Ancient Israelite Women in Context,* 1988, p. 41). Here, Rebekah does not have the proper authority, but she has power. She cannot formally bestow the blessing upon Jacob, but she can ensure he listens to her.

*"instructing."* Heb. *m'tzavah,* literally "command." Because of their close relationship, Jacob is one person over whom Rebekah can exert some limited power—and, as his mother, also authority. She commands him to do as she directs.

*9. "likes."* Heb. *ahav,* literally "loves"; compare 25:28.

*12.* In going along with Rebekah's plan, Jacob knowingly takes on the role of trickster vis-à-vis Isaac; in the process, Jacob learns from his mother how to achieve a goal by the use of subterfuge. Later, he himself will be tricked by Laban, his father-in-law, who will again use the ploy of covering up the truth to manipulate Jacob into marrying not his

13 His mother then said to him, "Any curse that you get will be on me, son—just listen to me and go get [them] for me!" 14 So he went and got them and brought [them] to his mother, and his mother made tasty dishes, such as his father liked.

15 Rebekah now took the finest of her elder son Esau's garments that she had in the house, and dressed up her younger son Jacob. 16 The skins of the kids she wrapped on his hands and over the smooth part of his neck, 17 and she put the tasty food and the bread that she had made into her son Jacob's hand.

13 וַתֹּאמֶר לוֹ אִמּוֹ עָלַי קִלְלָתְךָ בְּנִי אַךְ
שְׁמַע בְּקֹלִי וְלֵךְ קַח־לִי׃ 14 וַיֵּלֶךְ וַיִּקַּח וַיָּבֵא
לְאִמּוֹ וַתַּעַשׂ אִמּוֹ מַטְעַמִּים כַּאֲשֶׁר אָהֵב
אָבִיו׃
15 וַתִּקַּח רִבְקָה אֶת־בִּגְדֵי עֵשָׂו בְּנָהּ הַגָּדֹל
הַחֲמֻדֹת אֲשֶׁר אִתָּהּ בַּבָּיִת וַתַּלְבֵּשׁ אֶת־
יַעֲקֹב בְּנָהּ הַקָּטָן׃ 16 וְאֵת עֹרֹת גְּדָיֵי הָעִזִּים
הִלְבִּישָׁה עַל־יָדָיו וְעַל חֶלְקַת צַוָּארָיו׃
17 וַתִּתֵּן אֶת־הַמַּטְעַמִּים וְאֶת־הַלֶּחֶם אֲשֶׁר
עָשָׂתָה בְּיַד יַעֲקֹב בְּנָהּ׃

beloved Rachel, but her sister Leah (29:25). In turn, Jacob will refine his trickster status by convincing Laban to agree to an arrangement by which Jacob will depart with a significant percentage of Laban's flock (Genesis 30).

*13. "Any curse that you get will be on me, son."* Rebekah assures Jacob that if anyone is blamed or punished for what he is about to do, it will be she and not he. Her readiness to take responsibility can be seen as her understanding that what she is doing is not deception for personal gain, but the fulfillment of God's plan as revealed to her during her pregnancy (25:23). The deception they are about to carry out is for the greater good, a case of "the ends justifies the means."

*15. that she had in the house.* Images of domesticity fill Rebekah's story. As Carol Meyers notes, women in ancient Israel held major roles within the household. They had the primary responsibility for educating the young as well as for transforming unprocessed ingredients into cooked, consumable food (*Discovering Eve*, 1988, pp. 145–146). Rebekah moves confidently throughout her family's domain. She is in control of its clothing and of the preparation of its food. She decides when its livestock is to be slaughtered. Her tools for survival are the items immediately and easily available to her. Such things mark this as a woman's story.

*dressed up her younger son Jacob.* The covering up of Jacob is the central element of Rebekah's act of subterfuge. Like Tamar in Genesis 38, who covers herself with a veil, Rebekah can be successful only through the act of covering up, not by acting directly and out in the open.

*16. she wrapped.* The narrator repeatedly emphasizes Rebekah's actions.

*17. she put the tasty food and the bread that she had made.* As with the clothing in v. 15, Rebekah uses what is on hand in the female sphere. The seemingly harmless domestic items of food or bread become the tools she uses to influence the course of events. The verse is clear that these are items whose preparation Rebekah has personally directed (and perhaps has undertaken herself), emphasizing her purposefulness in executing the plan.

## JACOB STEALS ESAU'S BLESSING (27:18–29)

The climax of this episode occurs when Jacob goes to Isaac posing as Esau and receives the blessing intended for his brother. In a dramatic scene between father and son, Isaac asks several times for reassurance that this is indeed Esau before him. Isaac, who cannot see well, uses all his other senses in trying to make sure this is the right son: he touches Jacob (vv. 22, 26), he listens to his voice (v. 22), he tastes his food (v. 25), and he smells him (v. 27). Isaac's blessing of Jacob in this scene establishes Jacob as the heir to the covenantal promises. Although Isaac is depicted as a weak and passive

[18]Going then to his father, he said, "Father!" and he replied: "Here I am; which son of mine are you?"

[19]Jacob said to his father, "I am Esau your first-born; I have done as you told me; pray get up and sit and eat of my game so that you can give me your heartfelt blessing." [20]Isaac then said to his son: "How is it that you were able to find [game] so quickly, my son?" And he replied, "Your God יהוה made it happen for me." [21]"Pray come near me," said Isaac to Jacob, "so that I can feel you, son. Are you really my son Esau, or are you not?"

[22]Jacob approached his father Isaac, who felt him and said, "The voice is the voice of Jacob, but the hands are the hands of Esau!" [23]He did not recognize him, however, because his hands were hairy, like the hands of his brother Esau—and as he was [preparing to] bless him, [24]he said, "Are you really my son Esau?" "I am," he answered. [25]He said, "Bring [it] near me and I will eat of my son's game, so that I can give you my heartfelt blessing." He brought [it] to him and he ate; he brought him wine and he drank. [26]His father Isaac then said to him, "Pray come near and kiss me, son."

[27]As he came near and kissed him, [Isaac] smelled the scent of his clothes and blessed him, saying:

18 וַיָּבֹא אֶל־אָבִיו וַיֹּאמֶר אָבִי וַיֹּאמֶר הִנֶּנִּי
מִי אַתָּה בְּנִי׃
19 וַיֹּאמֶר יַעֲקֹב אֶל־אָבִיו אָנֹכִי עֵשָׂו בְּכֹרֶךָ
עָשִׂיתִי כַּאֲשֶׁר דִּבַּרְתָּ אֵלָי קוּם־נָא שְׁבָה
וְאָכְלָה מִצֵּידִי בַּעֲבוּר תְּבָרְכַנִּי נַפְשֶׁךָ׃
20 וַיֹּאמֶר יִצְחָק אֶל־בְּנוֹ מַה־זֶּה מִהַרְתָּ
לִמְצֹא בְּנִי וַיֹּאמֶר כִּי הִקְרָה יְהוָה אֱלֹהֶיךָ
לְפָנָי׃ 21 וַיֹּאמֶר יִצְחָק אֶל־יַעֲקֹב גְּשָׁה־נָּא
וַאֲמֻשְׁךָ בְּנִי הַאַתָּה זֶה בְּנִי עֵשָׂו אִם־לֹא׃
22 וַיִּגַּשׁ יַעֲקֹב אֶל־יִצְחָק אָבִיו וַיְמֻשֵּׁהוּ
וַיֹּאמֶר הַקֹּל קוֹל יַעֲקֹב וְהַיָּדַיִם יְדֵי עֵשָׂו׃
23 וְלֹא הִכִּירוֹ כִּי־הָיוּ יָדָיו כִּידֵי עֵשָׂו אָחִיו
שְׂעִרֹת וַיְבָרְכֵהוּ׃ 24 וַיֹּאמֶר אַתָּה זֶה בְּנִי
עֵשָׂו וַיֹּאמֶר אָנִי׃ 25 וַיֹּאמֶר הַגִּשָׁה לִּי
וְאֹכְלָה מִצֵּיד בְּנִי לְמַעַן תְּבָרֶכְךָ נַפְשִׁי
וַיַּגֶּשׁ־לוֹ וַיֹּאכַל וַיָּבֵא לוֹ יַיִן וַיֵּשְׁתְּ׃
26 וַיֹּאמֶר אֵלָיו יִצְחָק אָבִיו גְּשָׁה־נָּא וּשְׁקָה־
לִּי בְּנִי׃
27 וַיִּגַּשׁ וַיִּשַּׁק־לוֹ וַיָּרַח אֶת־רֵיחַ בְּגָדָיו
וַיְבָרְכֵהוּ וַיֹּאמֶר

dupe, the overly exaggerated and repetitive details presented here beg the question of how complicit Isaac is in the ruse.

*18. "which son of mine are you?"* Isaac asks the critical question. Rebekah has worked hard to cover up Jacob's identity, dressing him in Esau's clothes and putting in his hands the food made under her supervision (vv. 15–17).

*21. "Are you really my son Esau?"* Isaac is not only physically blind, but on a deeper level he refuses to recognize what would be clear to any parent. Can his knowledge of his children truly be so superficial that he can only distinguish between them visually? His question indicates doubt, yet he seems to want to believe this son before him.

*25. and he ate.* Although a lover of Esau's hunt and cooking (25:28; 27:4, 9), Isaac seems unable to distinguish Esau's cooking from Rebekah's.

*26. "Pray come near and kiss me, son."* For the third time, Isaac wants to make sure this is the right son. Is he really being fooled by the costume, as he was fooled by the food in the previous verse, or is he willingly allowing himself to be led through a charade? Perhaps Isaac is allowing himself to be misled; he is blind to what he chooses not to see.

*27. scent of his clothes.* Isaac smells not the son before him, but the clothes in which Jacob has disguised himself.

"See, my son's scent is like the scent of a field
blessed by יהוה.
28 God give you of heaven's dew,
of earth's bounty;
abundant grain and new wine.
29 Let peoples serve you,
nations bow down to you.
Be a ruler to your brothers,
and let your mother's sons bow down to you.
May those who curse you be cursed;
may those who bless you be blessed."
30 Just as Isaac finished blessing Jacob, at the
very moment that Jacob was in the act of leaving
his father Isaac's presence, his brother Esau came in
from his hunt. 31 He too made tasty dishes that he
brought to his father and he said to his father, "Let
my father get ready to eat of his son's game, so that
you can give me your heartfelt blessing." 32 But
his father Isaac said to him, "Who are you?" So
he replied, "I am your son, your first-born, Esau!"
33 Isaac now began to shudder—a shuddering exceedingly great—and he said, "Who then hunted
game and brought [it] to me and I ate of it all before
you came? I blessed him—and blessed he will
remain!"
34 When Esau heard his father's words, he
broke into an exceedingly loud and bitter howl
and said to his father, "Bless me! Me too, Father!"

רְאֵה רֵיחַ בְּנִי כְּרֵיחַ שָׂדֶה
אֲשֶׁר בֵּרֲכוֹ יְהוָה׃
28 וְיִתֶּן־לְךָ הָאֱלֹהִים מִטַּל הַשָּׁמַיִם
וּמִשְׁמַנֵּי הָאָרֶץ
וְרֹב דָּגָן וְתִירֹשׁ׃
29 יַעַבְדוּךָ עַמִּים
וישתחו וְיִשְׁתַּחֲוֻו לְךָ לְאֻמִּים
הֱוֵה גְבִיר לְאַחֶיךָ
וְיִשְׁתַּחֲווּ לְךָ בְּנֵי אִמֶּךָ
אֹרְרֶיךָ אָרוּר
וּמְבָרֲכֶיךָ בָּרוּךְ׃
30 וַיְהִי כַּאֲשֶׁר כִּלָּה יִצְחָק לְבָרֵךְ אֶת־יַעֲקֹב
וַיְהִי אַךְ יָצֹא יָצָא יַעֲקֹב מֵאֵת פְּנֵי יִצְחָק
אָבִיו וְעֵשָׂו אָחִיו בָּא מִצֵּידוֹ׃ 31 וַיַּעַשׂ גַּם־
הוּא מַטְעַמִּים וַיָּבֵא לְאָבִיו וַיֹּאמֶר לְאָבִיו
יָקֻם אָבִי וְיֹאכַל מִצֵּיד בְּנוֹ בַּעֲבֻר תְּבָרֲכַנִּי
נַפְשֶׁךָ׃ 32 וַיֹּאמֶר לוֹ יִצְחָק אָבִיו מִי־אָתָּה
וַיֹּאמֶר אֲנִי בִּנְךָ בְכֹרְךָ עֵשָׂו׃ 33 וַיֶּחֱרַד יִצְחָק
חֲרָדָה גְּדֹלָה עַד־מְאֹד וַיֹּאמֶר מִי־אֵפוֹא
הוּא הַצָּד־צַיִד וַיָּבֵא לִי וָאֹכַל מִכֹּל בְּטֶרֶם
תָּבוֹא וָאֲבָרֲכֵהוּ גַּם־בָּרוּךְ יִהְיֶה׃
34 כִּשְׁמֹעַ עֵשָׂו אֶת־דִּבְרֵי אָבִיו וַיִּצְעַק
צְעָקָה גְּדֹלָה וּמָרָה עַד־מְאֹד וַיֹּאמֶר לְאָבִיו

*28–29.* Isaac's blessing to Jacob fulfills the prophecy given to Rebekah during her pregnancy (25:23), in accord with her apparent earlier interpretation of it: Jacob will be the primary son.

The manner in which the story is narrated up to this moment leaves open the possibility that Isaac not only knows that Jacob has the qualities needed for proceeding with the covenantal plan but also lets Rebekah arrange for Jacob to received his blessing. He could, however, be genuinely deceived.

## ESAU DISCOVERS THE DECEPTION
(27:30–40)

The narration spotlights Esau's heartbreaking cry as he begs his father for a blessing, which evokes the reader's sympathy for the eldest son's plight.

*34. "Me too, Father!"* Esau's cry here echoes Jacob's answer to Isaac in v. 18. They are both his sons; they both deserve his blessing.

35But he said, "Your brother came with deceit and
took away your blessing!"
36He replied, "Is he not named Jacob? Twice
now he has cheated me—he took my birthright
and now, look, he has taken my blessing!" And he
added, "Did you not reserve a blessing for me?"
37Isaac responded by saying to Esau, "Look—I
have appointed him your master, and given him
all his kin to be his servants, and have supported
him with grain and new wine; come, now, what am
I to do, my son?"
38"Do you have but one blessing, Father?" said
Esau to his father. "Bless me! Me too, Father!" And
Esau cried out and wept. 39His father Isaac then
responded and said to him:

"Lo, among the fat places of the earth shall your
dwelling be,
and with heaven's dew from above.
40By your sword shall you live,
your brother shall you serve.
But when you move away,
You shall break his yoke off your neck."

41Esau now bore a grudge against Jacob because
of the blessing his father had conferred upon him,
and Esau formed this resolve: "The days of mourning for my father are approaching; then I will kill
my brother Jacob." 42When Rebekah was told her

בֵּרֲכֵנִי גַם־אָנִי אָבִי׃ 35 וַיֹּאמֶר בָּא אָחִיךָ
בְּמִרְמָה וַיִּקַּח בִּרְכָתֶךָ׃
36 וַיֹּאמֶר הֲכִי קָרָא שְׁמוֹ יַעֲקֹב וַיַּעְקְבֵנִי
זֶה פַעֲמַיִם אֶת־בְּכֹרָתִי לָקָח וְהִנֵּה עַתָּה
לָקַח בִּרְכָתִי וַיֹּאמַר הֲלֹא־אָצַלְתָּ לִּי
בְּרָכָה׃ 37 וַיַּעַן יִצְחָק וַיֹּאמֶר לְעֵשָׂו הֵן
גְּבִיר שַׂמְתִּיו לָךְ וְאֶת־כָּל־אֶחָיו נָתַתִּי לוֹ
לַעֲבָדִים וְדָגָן וְתִירֹשׁ סְמַכְתִּיו וּלְכָה אֵפוֹא
מָה אֶעֱשֶׂה בְּנִי׃
38 וַיֹּאמֶר עֵשָׂו אֶל־אָבִיו הַבְרָכָה אַחַת
הִוא־לְךָ אָבִי בָּרְכֵנִי גַם־אָנִי אָבִי וַיִּשָּׂא עֵשָׂו
קֹלוֹ וַיֵּבְךְּ׃ 39 וַיַּעַן יִצְחָק אָבִיו וַיֹּאמֶר
אֵלָיו

הִנֵּה מִשְׁמַנֵּי הָאָרֶץ יִהְיֶה מוֹשָׁבֶךָ
וּמִטַּל הַשָּׁמַיִם מֵעָל׃
40 וְעַל־חַרְבְּךָ תִחְיֶה
וְאֶת־אָחִיךָ תַּעֲבֹד
וְהָיָה כַּאֲשֶׁר תָּרִיד
וּפָרַקְתָּ עֻלּוֹ מֵעַל צַוָּארֶךָ׃

41 וַיִּשְׂטֹם עֵשָׂו אֶת־יַעֲקֹב עַל־הַבְּרָכָה אֲשֶׁר
בֵּרְכוֹ אָבִיו וַיֹּאמֶר עֵשָׂו בְּלִבּוֹ יִקְרְבוּ יְמֵי
אֵבֶל אָבִי וְאַהַרְגָה אֶת־יַעֲקֹב אָחִי׃ 42 וַיֻּגַּד
לְרִבְקָה אֶת־דִּבְרֵי עֵשָׂו בְּנָהּ הַגָּדֹל וַתִּשְׁלַח

*35.* Although Rebekah had assured Jacob that any blame would be on her (v. 12), Isaac holds Jacob responsible for his actions. Adrien Bledstein reads this as Isaac's acknowledgement that Jacob is, like himself, a fellow trickster ("Binder, Trickster, Heel . . . ," 1993, p. 288).

***"deceit."*** Heb. *mirmah*, which appears only once more in the Torah, when Jacob's sons deceive Shechem and Hamor in Dinah's story (34:13).

*36.* ***"Jacob . . . cheated."*** Heb. *yaakov . . . vayakveini*, an obvious play on Jacob's name (*Yaakov*). In using this specific word, Esau, too, places the blame squarely on Jacob's shoulders. According to Esau, his sibling has not merely tricked him; Jacob is—as his name implies—a cheater by nature.

## REBEKAH CONVINCES ISAAC TO SEND JACOB AWAY (27:41–28:9)

The immediate consequences of the theft include Esau's hatred of Jacob, Rebekah's clever rescue of Jacob, and Esau's marriage to an Ishmaelite woman. This will also be the only time in this episode that Rebekah addresses Isaac directly.

elder son Esau's words, she sent for her younger son
Jacob and said to him, "Look—your brother Esau
is plotting to avenge himself by killing you. [43]Now,
son, listen to me: get going and flee to my brother
Laban in Haran. [44]You can stay there a while until
your brother's rage cools down; [45]when your brother's anger turns away from you and he forgets what
you did to him, I will send to bring you back from
there—why should I be bereft of the two of you in
a single day?"
[46]So Rebekah said to Isaac, "I abhor my life because of the daughters of the Hittites; if Jacob takes
a wife from the daughters of the Hittites—like
these from among the daughters of the land—what
would my life be worth?" *28* Isaac then summoned Jacob and blessed him and gave him this
instruction: "Do not take a wife from among the
daughters of Canaan. [2]Get ready, go to Paddan-
aram, to the house of Bethuel your mother's father,
and take yourself a wife from among the daughters
of Laban your mother's brother. [3]And may God
Almighty bless you, and make you fruitful and
numerous, so that you become a host of peoples,

וַתִּקְרָא לְיַעֲקֹב בְּנָהּ הַקָּטָן וַתֹּאמֶר אֵלָיו
הִנֵּה עֵשָׂו אָחִיךָ מִתְנַחֵם לְךָ לְהָרְגֶךָ׃
43 וְעַתָּה בְנִי שְׁמַע בְּקֹלִי וְקוּם בְּרַח־לְךָ
אֶל־לָבָן אָחִי חָרָנָה׃ 44 וְיָשַׁבְתָּ עִמּוֹ יָמִים
אֲחָדִים עַד אֲשֶׁר־תָּשׁוּב חֲמַת אָחִיךָ׃
45 עַד־שׁוּב אַף־אָחִיךָ מִמְּךָ וְשָׁכַח אֵת
אֲשֶׁר־עָשִׂיתָ לּוֹ וְשָׁלַחְתִּי וּלְקַחְתִּיךָ מִשָּׁם
לָמָה אֶשְׁכַּל גַּם־שְׁנֵיכֶם יוֹם אֶחָד׃
46 וַתֹּאמֶר רִבְקָה אֶל־יִצְחָק קַצְתִּי בְחַיַּי
מִפְּנֵי בְּנוֹת חֵת אִם־לֹקֵחַ יַעֲקֹב אִשָּׁה
מִבְּנוֹת־חֵת כָּאֵלֶּה מִבְּנוֹת הָאָרֶץ לָמָּה לִּי
חַיִּים׃ כח וַיִּקְרָא יִצְחָק אֶל־יַעֲקֹב
וַיְבָרֶךְ אֹתוֹ וַיְצַוֵּהוּ וַיֹּאמֶר לוֹ לֹא־תִקַּח
אִשָּׁה מִבְּנוֹת כְּנָעַן׃ 2 קוּם לֵךְ פַּדֶּנָה אֲרָם
בֵּיתָה בְתוּאֵל אֲבִי אִמֶּךָ וְקַח־לְךָ מִשָּׁם
אִשָּׁה מִבְּנוֹת לָבָן אֲחִי אִמֶּךָ׃ 3 וְאֵל שַׁדַּי
יְבָרֵךְ אֹתְךָ וְיַפְרְךָ וְיַרְבֶּךָ וְהָיִיתָ לִקְהַל

*43.* ***"get going."*** Rebekah gives up what she loves most, her son Jacob. Like so many mothers, she sacrifices her own desires to ensure her child a future.

*45.* ***"I will... bring you back from there."*** As this episode comes to a close, Rebekah remains a woman with a plan. Her hope is that Jacob leaves only temporarily, until it is safe to return. Yet once Jacob leaves home, they never meet again.

***"why should I be bereft of the two of you...?"*** Rebekah encourages her son to leave by saying that it is better for her if he does, a statement calculated to release Jacob from the fear that he is abandoning her.

*46.* Rebekah addresses her words to Isaac, providing a reason to for him to send Jacob away. This way, Jacob is able to leave with Isaac's blessing and permission. Once again, Rebekah has created a situation in which it seems that Isaac is in control, while she pulls the strings. She has done what had to be done, but now her beloved Jacob will be gone.

*28:1.* As the people of Israel formulates its own identity in tension with surrounding cultures, its traditions frequently express anxiety about Israelite men marrying Canaanite women. Thus with regard to Isaac, Genesis 24 strongly advocated endogamy—that is, marriage within the family's kinship group. In this parashah, Esau's marriage to Canaanite women upsets his parents (26:35, 27:46, 28:8). The concern seems less when the foreign woman comes from a non-Canaanite family (see, for example, Deuteronomy 21:10–14).

*2.* ***"your mother's father . . . your mother's brother."*** Isaac's way of referring to Jacob's destination further highlights the bond between mother and son.

4 and give you the blessing of Abraham—you along with your descendants—to possess the land in which you have sojourned, that God gave to Abraham!" 5 Thus did Isaac send Jacob away; he went to Paddan-aram, to Laban son of Bethuel the Aramean, brother of Rebekah, mother of Jacob and Esau.

6 When Esau saw that Isaac had blessed Jacob and sent him away to Paddan-aram, there to take a wife for himself, blessing him and instructing him: Do not take a wife from among the daughters of Canaan, 7 and that Jacob had heeded his father and mother and gone to Paddan-aram, 8 Esau understood that his father Isaac looked with disfavor at the daughters of Canaan, 9 so he went to Ishmael and took as his wife Mahalath daughter of Ishmael, Abraham's son, sister of Nebaioth, adding her to his [other] wives.

עַמִּים׃ 4 וְיִתֶּן־לְךָ אֶת־בִּרְכַּת אַבְרָהָם לְךָ
וּלְזַרְעֲךָ אִתָּךְ לְרִשְׁתְּךָ אֶת־אֶרֶץ מְגֻרֶיךָ
אֲשֶׁר־נָתַן אֱלֹהִים לְאַבְרָהָם׃ 5 וַיִּשְׁלַח
יִצְחָק אֶת־יַעֲקֹב וַיֵּלֶךְ פַּדֶּנָה אֲרָם אֶל־לָבָן
בֶּן־בְּתוּאֵל הָאֲרַמִּי אֲחִי רִבְקָה אֵם יַעֲקֹב
וְעֵשָׂו׃
6 וַיַּרְא עֵשָׂו כִּי־בֵרַךְ יִצְחָק אֶת־יַעֲקֹב וְשִׁלַּח
אֹתוֹ פַּדֶּנָה אֲרָם לָקַחַת־לוֹ מִשָּׁם אִשָּׁה
בְּבָרְכוֹ אֹתוֹ וַיְצַו עָלָיו לֵאמֹר לֹא־תִקַּח
אִשָּׁה מִבְּנוֹת כְּנָעַן׃ 7 וַיִּשְׁמַע יַעֲקֹב אֶל־
אָבִיו וְאֶל־אִמּוֹ וַיֵּלֶךְ פַּדֶּנָה אֲרָם׃ 8 וַיַּרְא
עֵשָׂו כִּי רָעוֹת בְּנוֹת כְּנָעַן בְּעֵינֵי יִצְחָק
אָבִיו׃ 9 וַיֵּלֶךְ עֵשָׂו אֶל־יִשְׁמָעֵאל וַיִּקַּח אֶת־
מָחֲלַת ׀ בַּת־יִשְׁמָעֵאל בֶּן־אַבְרָהָם אֲחוֹת
נְבָיוֹת עַל־נָשָׁיו לוֹ לְאִשָּׁה׃ ס

***6–9. When Esau saw.*** The text portrays Esau as one who still wants parental approval. Whereas Jacob leaves on the advice of his mother and his father (28:7), Esau seeks only his father's approval (28:8) in choosing a non-Canaanite wife. At the end of this parashah, Rebekah recedes to the shadows, now that she has seen to the continuation of the Covenant.

*—Tamara Cohn Eskenazi*
*Hara E. Person*

# Another View

IN THIS TORAH PORTION, our foremother Rebekah takes matters into her own hands in order to secure Isaac's blessing for her favorite son, Jacob. She is encouraged to do so by the prophecy she receives when she inquires of God during her pregnancy (25:23). God answers Rebekah's inquiry about her pregnancy with the ambiguity inherent in every oracle. The oracle specifies that Rebekah is carrying twins and that each child will develop into a nation. Their future relationships, however, remain ambiguous (see at v. 23). Which of the two peoples shall overcome the other? Who will serve whom?

What if Rebekah misinterprets the prophecy? What if its ambiguity is part of the divine purpose? What if, by eliminating the ambiguity—by urging Jacob to steal the blessing meant for his brother—Rebekah is not acting in harmony with the will of God?

In that case we would expect the text to show dire consequences. Indeed, such consequences ensue. First, the fruits of the stolen blessing do not come easily to Jacob. The blessing that he gains by guile refers to material benefits (27:28–29). He later secures his wealth—the promise in this stolen blessing—in an environment of stealth (Genesis 29–31). Second, he soon loses something far more precious than material abundance: his beloved wife dies in childbirth (35:19). Third, there is consequently Rebekah's pain. She sends Jacob away for his protection (27:43–44) and dies without seeing him again. Rebekah must have suffered deeply in separating from her beloved son Jacob. She pays a very high price for her determination to ignore the ambiguity of God's word.

*What if the ambiguity of the oracle is part of the divine purpose?*

The outcome of Rebekah's story may, perhaps, teach us to allow the divine process to unfold for a while, before we decide to take action on God's behalf. Perhaps the gift from our biblical mother Rebekah in this parashah is her prompting us to sense ambiguity, to appreciate nuance—and to have the wisdom and patience to let divine intention blossom in its own time. *—Diane M. Sharon*

# Post-biblical Interpretations

***This is the line of Isaac*** (25:19). In *parashat Tol'dot* the reader is re-introduced to Rebekah, the second of the matriarchs, whom the Rabbis extolled for resisting the temptations of idolatry and unrighteous behavior that characterized her childhood home. Moreover, when God's intention to maintain the covenant through Jacob was made known to her, she single-mindedly fulfilled the divine will, even when it meant deceiving her husband and disinheriting her older son. The Rabbis' high regard for her reminds us that this portion is as much about Rebekah as it is about her husband. According to the Rabbis, her virtuous behavior merited that the twelve tribes would spring directly from her through her son Jacob (Midrash *B'reishit Rabbah* 63.6).

***daughter of... the Aramean*** (25:20). This verse describes Rebekah as the daughter of Bethuel "the Aramean," of Paddan Aram, and as the sister of Laban "the Aramean." Given the name of the city, both mentions of "the Aramean" (*ha-arami*) appear superfluous. By means of word play, *B'reishit Rabbah* 63.4 explains that the first "Aramean" comes to teach us that her father was a *ram'ai*—a deceiver. Her brother was also a deceiver, as were all her neighbors. Rebekah was surrounded by deception, living among bad influences on her behavior. But she set herself apart and stood out like "a lily among the thorns" (Song of Songs 2:2).

***Isaac pleaded with* יהוה *on behalf of his wife, for she was childless*** (25:21). According to rabbinic tradition, there were seven infertile biblical women for whom prayer was efficacious. *P'sikta D'Rav Kahana* 20.1 lists the first six as Sarah, Rebekah, Leah, Rachel, the wife of Manoah (Samson's mother in Judges 13), and Hannah. The seventh is personified Israel, based on the characterization of Zion as a childless woman whose hopes for offspring will be fulfilled by God at the time of redemption (Isaiah 54).

***The children pressed against each other inside her*** (25:22). *B'reishit Rabbah* 63.6 relates that whenever Rebekah stood near synagogues or schools, Jacob struggled to come out; and when she passed idolatrous temples, Esau eagerly endeavored to emerge.

**יהוה *said to her: "Two peoples are in your belly"*** (25:22). The Rabbis dignified both Sarah and Rebekah with the title of prophet. They further observed that Rebekah experienced divine revelation twice, once when God informed her that she was pregnant with twins, and again when Rebekah learned about Esau's decision to kill Jacob (27:42). In the first instance, she learns of the two nations struggling in her womb when she visits the study house of Shem and Eber (see Genesis 11:10–26; *B'reishit Rabbah* 63.6). Here, the Rabbis reaffirmed the need for intercession between the Divine and humans, a notion found also in *B'reishit Rabbah* 82.3 with reference to Jacob. Thus gender does not seem to be the issue as much as the notion of how one makes contact with God. Similarly, in the second case, the Rabbis stated that the matriarchs were prophets—and Rebekah was a matriarch. Thus, despite her less than reputable pedigree, Rebekah joins her husband in meriting prophetic status; in fact, it is Rebekah rather than Isaac who executes the divine will in ensuring that Jacob receive the status of first-born son (*B'reishit Rabbah* 63.7; 67.9).

***but Rebekah favored Jacob*** (25:28). According to *B'reishit Rabbah* 63.10, "The more she heard his voice [engaged in study, reciting his lessons aloud], the stronger grew her love for him."

***They were a bitterness of spirit to Isaac and Rebekah*** (26:34–35). The Rabbis invoked Rebekah's idolatrous pedigree when they considered this reference to Isaac's and Rebekah's unhappiness over Esau's choice of wives. They concluded that Isaac is mentioned first

*It is Rebekah rather than Isaac who executes the divine will.*

in this verse because he was far more disturbed over Esau's marriages to idolators than Rebekah. This is because, "as the daughter of idolatrous priests, Rebekah was more accustomed to the pollution of idolatry and did not object—but Isaac, the son of holy parents, did object" (*B'reishit Rabbah* 65.4). The Rabbis were also struck by the focus on Isaac in a passage concerned with domestic matters. Ordinarily one would have expected Rebekah to be more aware of what went on in her household than her husband. The Rabbis extrapolated this assumption to women in general, positing "another reason why Isaac is mentioned first: It is a woman's habit to stay at home [and do productive work], and a man's to go out in public and learn understanding from people; but as Isaac's eyes were dim he stayed at home; therefore [the matter was disturbing] to Isaac first" (*B'reishit Rabbah* 65.4).

—*Carol Bakhos*

# *Contemporary Reflection*

THIS TORAH PORTION PRESENTS the second of three matriarchs who suffer barrenness. In this episode Rebekah and Isaac are unable to conceive for the first twenty years of their marriage (25:20, 26). The Torah uses barren couples as a literary device to demonstrate the miraculous nature of the conception of the patriarchs and the beneficence of God. Infertility in the twenty-first century tells a different story: overworked and overstressed women, late marriage, and perhaps environmental toxins that inhibit reproduction.

The economy and culture of Rebekah's Canaan and our society are worlds apart, yet the emotional reaction to infertility has remained largely unchanged. While suffering from her difficult pregnancy, Rebekah cries out, "*Im ken lamah zeh anochi?* (If this is so, why do I exist?)" Rebekah herself utters these words after she becomes pregnant. But many Jews ask such a question earlier, when they face difficulty conceiving and bringing a pregnancy to term. Aspiring parents today often suffer a crisis of meaning. Women and men who face infertility may experience devastating depression, anger, jealousy, and deep existential angst. It might seem that feminism would have liberated women from expectations of motherhood. After all, feminists of our age take pride that we are not limited by the narrow definitions of womanhood that characterized Rebekah's milieu. Yet even in our liberated modern age, women and men usually see biological parenthood as a necessary rite of passage without which they are not considered full adults. Generating a child is a signifier of "true womanhood" and "real manhood" to many. Barrenness remains a social stigma—particularly in the Jewish community, which holds that the first *mitzvah* in the Torah is *p'ru u-rvu* (be fruitful and multiply).

Full integration and acceptance in the Jewish community often revolve around family life. The Jewish community has grown more open to gay and lesbian families in recent years largely because many such couples have been able to become parents—some through adoption or prior heterosexual reproduction, and more recently through artificial insemination. Yet adults in their thirties, forties, and fifties without children—regardless of their marital status and sexual orientation—remain outsiders in all but the most avant-garde synagogues and activist Jewish organizations. Childless adults treated as full participants in Jewish life remain the exception, and thus the Jewish community tends to lose these people from the rolls of temple membership.

> *Rebekah's question continues to bedevil Jewish adults who hope to parent.*

What of the Jewish championing of classic feminist ideas that a woman is much more than a baby machine; that anatomy is not destiny; that a woman defines herself not primarily through her family but through her deeds and ideas? Even today, motherhood and fatherhood in the Jewish community are both idealized and romanticized. Now as much as ever, family and parenthood are the primary cultural institution where individuals look to find personal fulfillment, happiness, and love. Most contemporary Jews cannot imagine finding such rewards without children; many find it difficult to consider doing so without their own genetic children to realize the wish to pass Judaism, love, and genes *mi-dor l'dor* (from generation to generation).

Our community has done only an adequate job providing support for the infertile. Chapters on infertility in mainstream Jewish parenting books remain either absent or in the non-normative category even though infertility is rife. Nina Beth Cardin has written *Tears of Sorrow, Seeds of Hope* (second edition, 2007), a spiritual companion for those grieving infertility, pregnancy loss, or stillbirth. This book belongs in every Jewish library, and in time, its messages will perhaps pervade Jewish culture. Yet even in this book adoption is discussed only as a last and unfavorable alternative.

Meanwhile, responsa literature and halachic interpretations have strongly supported artificial insemination and *in vitro* fertilization for heterosexual couples facing infertility because of the strong drive for Jewish continuity. Such a notion of Jewish continuity is not only religious, but also biological. There is more support in the Jewish institutional world than in Christian communities for reproductive technologies, apparently because many Jews believe Judaism is inherited as much as taught.

The definition of family in the Jewish world, it seems, clings to a model of parents who have genetic offspring. For example, in a study reported in 1991, researchers who surveyed a sample of male college students found that the Jews considered it more important than did the Christians that children be conceived by themselves and their spouse, rather than adopted.

Bonnie Ellen Baron and Lawrence Baron refer to that survey in the ground-breaking book *Lifecycles*, edited by Rabbi Debra Orenstein (1994). In their article "On Adoption" they explain that while there are some biblical precedents for adoption (Mordecai was guardian of Esther; Sarah initially seeks to adopt Hagar's son), Judaism never has strongly encouraged it. They speculate that "Jewish law lacks a formal procedure for adoption because of the primacy it accords biological kinship in determining a child's inheritance rights and religious and tribal status" (p. 28). This is true in spite of the primacy of *tikkun olam* as a deeply embedded value among Jews. How can we identify ourselves as a community of *tikkun* (repair) without a commitment to adopt children who languish around the world without loving parents?

Adoption support is rarely modeled by Jewish leaders. A remarkable exception is Yosef Abramowitz and Rabbi Susan Silverman, a couple who direct Jewish Family and Life! and began a family with biological offspring but also fulfilled a dream to adopt two children born in Ethiopia.

"*Im ken lamah zeh anochi?* (If this is so, why do I exist?)" was Rebekah's question that continues to bedevil Jewish adults who hope to parent but are unable to carry a pregnancy to term. Has feminism not brought us better questions and better answers? Have modern, forward-thinking Jewish communities failed to provide real alternatives to a dilemma of meaninglessness in the absence of genetic heirs?

*Tol'dot* poses the question of meaning. If we answer that we exist only to fulfill impulses through our children, we have failed Judaism and feminism. If we answer that we exist for *tikkun*, to nurture children—biological, adoptive, and those we teach, mentor and support—then we will have succeeded far more in realizing the sacred goal of *mi-dor l'dor*, from generation to generation.

—*Valerie Lieber*

# *Voices*

## *from* I Know Four

Amy Blank

III.
Now that I am big with child
—so big, I think with twins—
I chuckle: will our silence be maintained?
Womanhood is set on me, I have grown
    strong,
and I will hold two tumbling sons in check
whilst Isaac dreams—
Yes, and sometimes shrieks in dream.
(What was done to him?
He does not say . . .) When he wakes
he goes into the fields
listens to the bubbling well
the ewe calling from the hill,
the wind . . . and he is comforted.
I will be mother—and father too—
to those hotheaded sons.
(I feel them kicking, struggling
in the womb.) They will be silent
before Isaac.

IV.
Jacob and Esau grown . . .
Jacob is Isaac's son in tenderness;
for this I love him.
And Esau in lustiness is mine;
Isaac loves him for this.
Isaac, blind and patient
is fulfilled in blessing.

I stole the blessing,
I sent Jacob to Haran,
I saved Esau from Cain's sin.

Though I yearn for Jacob
and tremble for his return
I am still strong enough
to draw this house together.
The tent cords must not slacken;
I will hold taut.

## *Dear Descartes: Creativity*

Ada Aharoni

*Genesis 25:22–26*

Dear Descartes,
Not only *"I think, therefore I am,"*
but mostly:
I create, therefore I am.

I am me for having given birth
to them, this, and you.

I gaze intently at my offspring,
my oeuvre,
launched for life, for death?
Vibrating sharp soft sparks
of magnetic birth,
marvelously quenching my desire
and thirst—
pure essence
    of fresh vitality.

## *Enwombed*

Edna Aphek (transl. Yishai Tobin)

*Genesis 25:22–23*

Not to be enwombed,
Not to touch from within
To know
That
We are embryos
In the uterus of death.

The children of Jacob and Esau
Keep killing the dead
From death to death.

## *Jacob and Esau*

Edna Aphek (transl. Yishai Tobin)

*Genesis 25:27–28*

I hear the smell of your garments
Esau coming from the field
The yelling of your eyes
A kneeling
And Jacob keeps reading the book

## *from* Comfort Me

Rahel (transl. Maurice Samuel)

*Genesis 27:42–45*

Comfort my tears with words, my only one;
    My heart is dark with pain.
You know and I know that the wandering son
    Will never see his mother's door again.

## *Rebecca*

Shirley Kaufman

It's the duplicity that sticks—
that I would trick my husband when
he couldn't see. Rocking, he hugged
his knees and heard the meat already
ticking in its grease.
                    Oh
we were quick about it then,
though Jacob was slow to move.
He used to squat all day in the tent,
feeding the fire with me. I watched
the blood run when he stripped the goats,
and helped him carry the skins behind
the trees. I wound the pelts around
his wrists, his smooth girl's neck,
and dressed him in his brother's clothes,
smelling of woods and wind, the wild
grass after a rain.
                  I plotted
merely for a gift. Like any
clever woman at her stew. A pot
of deer, salt and fresh herbs.
It wasn't easy pacing inside my flesh
while Isaac ate, sucking my breath
between the cracks of my small teeth,
hotness climbing over my face, the way
I waited for him as a bride.
I listened still to water at the well,
an arm uplifted to the jug.

Clumsy at noontime in his night,
he wiped his mouth and shook the light
outside him, touching the wrong one.
His fingers, delicate as leaves,
dropped in the false skin.

*Let people serve and nations bow*
*to thee.*
        and all the rest. It stays
in my ear like cramps. Blessed, Blessed.

## *there is the river*

Ona Siporin

*Genesis 25:21–24*

every day
i go to the river
to gather the smooth stones

i run through the forest
dropping them
one by one
down my breasts
over my belly
    i chant
        these stones fall easily
        make the child fall
        like these stones

i stroke myself
my hand    the stream
over my belly
        let the child come
        like this

i let small eels    chips of wood    berries
fall over me

i know there are those
who will help me

## *A Prayer for My Sons*

Elaine Feinstein

*Genesis 27:43–45*

Forgive me    bright sons    if I have hobbled
you, put my fear into you, I will
suck it out    with my    lips

spit it out    look    I will stop hiding,
see without dreaming, take the nag of
that into my spirit, live without miracles,
    humbly.

I want you to puzzle this planet out, this
brown planet, so you can
move with your eyes open, without lying

Please be free of me    you will
lose nothing, the dark trees will be
there at the garden's end for you still, and many
    songs.

# ויצא ✦ *Vayeitzei*

## GENESIS 28:10–32:3

## *The Journey Within*

PARASHAT VAYEITZEI ("he went out") is the Torah's greatest love story. In it the lovers—Rachel and Jacob—figure as doubles. Their lives are in many ways parallel. Each of them works as a shepherd, flees from home, steals a father's legacy, contends with sibling and God alike, tricks others and is in turn tricked, and bargains for the blessing of having children. The stories of Rachel and Jacob illustrate the distinct but intersecting male and female journey cycles that characterize Genesis 12–35. In the male journey cycle a hero departs from home, gains intimacy with God by wandering promised and unpromised lands, has visions while exposed in the outdoors, and struggles to fulfill God's blessing by engendering children.

For their part, the matriarchal heroines also wander across external terrain. However, their journey toward intimacy with God takes place in the internal terrain of the body. Three of the four matriarchs experience a state of barrenness; two of them (Sarah and Rachel) reverse it by articulating their discontent or taking direct action in order to signal their intentions to create life. The often extreme measures they take in order to give birth alert God to their drive. This leads to a divine encounter that results in conception.

Genesis acknowledges that conception ensues from sexual relations. But the subtext of the female journey cycle indicates that its success requires intimacy not only between a man and a woman but also between a woman and God. Following the birth of a child, the mother encodes the memory of her specific path from barrenness to fertility in the name that she bestows as a legacy to her child. This paradigm is apparent as Rachel and her sister, Leah, compete for the love of both Jacob and God while simultaneously birthing the people of Israel. Their achievement is celebrated in the book of Ruth when the people praise "Rachel and Leah, both of whom built the house of Israel" (Ruth 4:11).

*She encodes the memory of her journey in the name she bestows on her child.*

—*Rachel Havrelock*

## Outline

*I.* Departure of the Hero Jacob (28:10–22)

*II.* Temporary Home for Jacob, Leah, and Rachel (29:1–30)

- *A.* Jacob at the well (vv. 1–8)
- *B.* Meeting Rachel (vv. 9–21)
- *C.* Jacob's marriage to Leah and Rachel (vv. 22–30)

*III.* From Barrenness to Fertility
*Leah and Rachel Birth the People of Israel* (29:31–30:24)

- *A.* Competition between sisters (29:31–30:13)
- *B.* Exchange between sisters (30:14–24)

*IV.* Leaving Laban
*Jacob, Leah, and Rachel Journey Toward a Home in Canaan* (30:25–31:42)

- *A.* Competition between men (30:25–31:3)
- *B.* Sisterly collaboration (31:4–16)
- *C.* Flight, theft, and pursuit (31:17–42)

*V.* Reconciliation and Separation of Jacob and Laban (31:43–32:3)

And Jacob left Beersheba and set out for Haran.
11Coming upon a [certain] place, he passed
the night there, for the sun was setting; taking one
of the stones of the place, he made it his head-rest
as he lay down in that place. 12He dreamed, and
lo—a ladder was set on the ground, with its top
reaching to heaven, and lo—angels of God going
up and coming down on it. 13And lo—יהוה stood

כח 10 וַיֵּצֵא יַעֲקֹב מִבְּאֵר שָׁבַע וַיֵּלֶךְ
חָרָנָה׃ 11 וַיִּפְגַּע בַּמָּקוֹם וַיָּלֶן שָׁם כִּי־בָא
הַשֶּׁמֶשׁ וַיִּקַּח מֵאַבְנֵי הַמָּקוֹם וַיָּשֶׂם
מְרַאֲשֹׁתָיו וַיִּשְׁכַּב בַּמָּקוֹם הַהוּא׃ 12 וַיַּחֲלֹם
וְהִנֵּה סֻלָּם מֻצָּב אַרְצָה וְרֹאשׁוֹ מַגִּיעַ
הַשָּׁמָיְמָה וְהִנֵּה מַלְאֲכֵי אֱלֹהִים עֹלִים
וְיֹרְדִים בּוֹ׃ 13 וְהִנֵּה יְהוָה נִצָּב עָלָיו וַיֹּאמַר

## *Departure of the Hero Jacob*

(28:10–22)

Jacob's flight and return serve as the frame of this parashah, which recounts how the people of Israel were built up through the intersecting struggles and wills of Rachel, Leah, and Jacob. When Jacob departs from home with the intangible gifts of the blessing and the birthright, he exhibits his youthful adaptability by using a stone for a pillow and sleeping alone in the mountains blanketed in darkness. These mountains—which form the western boundary of the Jordan River Valley—serve as a threshold to the realm of the Divine that Jacob recognizes as he sleeps. As he awakes and speaks, the confidence and self-certainty of the young Jacob become apparent. This vision where Jacob sees the angels of God will be balanced and extended by his nocturnal wrestling with a divine being on the east side of the Jordan prior to his eventual return home (32:4–33). The transformation that he undergoes is evident in the change of tone in which he speaks to God on either side of the Jordan. The youthful Jacob stipulates a list of terms (28:20–21) while the older Jacob pleads to God to save his family despite his unworthiness (32:10–13). A parallel transformation is evident in Rachel and Leah, who initially employ language as the means of their competition, but ultimately speak with one voice when deciding to embark on a journey away from home.

*10–11.* The journey begins. Previously, Jacob's mother, Rebekah, had secured his father's blessing for him through a stratagem; then she had ensured her son's safe passage from home. In so doing, Rebekah had voiced two intentions for Jacob's departure: safety and a wife (27:4–28:4). Thus he now journeys with the dual intent of finding safety in his uncle Laban's house and finding a suitable wife. On his way from Beersheba to his uncle's in Haran, Jacob stops at an unidentified place.

*12–15.* Scholars have noted that the ladder in Jacob's dream is most likely a ziggurat, a tower known from the temples of Mesopotamia. This "ladder" serves as a bridge between heaven and earth upon which angels ascend and descend—thus

➤ The Deity sympathized with Leah.

ANOTHER VIEW ➤ *176*

➤ Leah's prayer was powerful enough to alter her fate.

POST-BIBLICAL INTERPRETATIONS ➤ *176*

➤ What are these *t'rafim* that Rachel risks so much to steal?

CONTEMPORARY REFLECTION ➤ *178*

➤ . . . I swim raging / against the stream.

VOICES ➤ *180*

up above it, and said, "I, יהוה, am the God of your father Abraham and God of Isaac: the land on which you are lying I will give to you and to your descendants. 14 And your descendants shall be like the dust of the earth, and you shall spread out to the west and the east and the north and the south. Through you and your descendants all the families of the earth shall find blessing. 15 And here I am, with you: I will watch over you wherever you go, and I will bring you back to this soil. I will not let go of you as long as I have yet to do what I have promised you."

16 Waking from his sleep, Jacob said, "Truly, יהוה is in this place, and I did not know it!" 17 He was awestruck, and said, "How awe-inspiring is this place! This is none other than the house of God, and this is the gate of heaven!"

18 Rising early that morning, Jacob took the stone that he had put under his head and set it up as a monument. He then poured oil on its top. 19 He named that place Beth El. (But originally the town's name was Luz.) 20 Jacob then made this vow: "If God is with me and watches over me on this path that I am taking and gives me bread to eat and clothes to wear, 21 and if I return safely to my

אֲנִי יְהֹוָה אֱלֹהֵי אַבְרָהָם אָבִיךָ וֵאלֹהֵי
יִצְחָק הָאָרֶץ אֲשֶׁר אַתָּה שֹׁכֵב עָלֶיהָ לְךָ
אֶתְּנֶנָּה וּלְזַרְעֶךָ׃ 14 וְהָיָה זַרְעֲךָ כַּעֲפַר
הָאָרֶץ וּפָרַצְתָּ יָמָּה וָקֵדְמָה וְצָפֹנָה וָנֶגְבָּה
וְנִבְרְכוּ בְךָ כָּל־מִשְׁפְּחֹת הָאֲדָמָה וּבְזַרְעֶךָ׃
15 וְהִנֵּה אָנֹכִי עִמָּךְ וּשְׁמַרְתִּיךָ בְּכֹל אֲשֶׁר־
תֵּלֵךְ וַהֲשִׁבֹתִיךָ אֶל־הָאֲדָמָה הַזֹּאת כִּי לֹא
אֶעֱזָבְךָ עַד אֲשֶׁר אִם־עָשִׂיתִי אֵת אֲשֶׁר־
דִּבַּרְתִּי לָךְ׃
16 וַיִּיקַץ יַעֲקֹב מִשְּׁנָתוֹ וַיֹּאמֶר אָכֵן יֵשׁ
יְהֹוָה בַּמָּקוֹם הַזֶּה וְאָנֹכִי לֹא יָדָעְתִּי׃
17 וַיִּירָא וַיֹּאמַר מַה־נּוֹרָא הַמָּקוֹם הַזֶּה
אֵין זֶה כִּי אִם־בֵּית אֱלֹהִים וְזֶה שַׁעַר
הַשָּׁמָיִם׃
18 וַיַּשְׁכֵּם יַעֲקֹב בַּבֹּקֶר וַיִּקַּח אֶת־הָאֶבֶן
אֲשֶׁר־שָׂם מְרַאֲשֹׁתָיו וַיָּשֶׂם אֹתָהּ מַצֵּבָה
וַיִּצֹק שֶׁמֶן עַל־רֹאשָׁהּ׃ 19 וַיִּקְרָא אֶת־
שֵׁם־הַמָּקוֹם הַהוּא בֵּית־אֵל וְאוּלָם לוּז
שֵׁם־הָעִיר לָרִאשֹׁנָה׃ 20 וַיִּדַּר יַעֲקֹב נֶדֶר
לֵאמֹר אִם־יִהְיֶה אֱלֹהִים עִמָּדִי וּשְׁמָרַנִי
בַּדֶּרֶךְ הַזֶּה אֲשֶׁר אָנֹכִי הוֹלֵךְ וְנָתַן־לִי לֶחֶם
לֶאֱכֹל וּבֶגֶד לִלְבֹּשׁ׃ 21 וְשַׁבְתִּי בְשָׁלוֹם

indicating the dialogic nature of communication between the two realms. Thus Jacob has begun a double journey: a dream journey toward increasing proximity to God parallels his physical wanderings across the horizontal plane of space. Jacob encounters his angels while traveling. The stations between home and exile have a corollary in the rungs between heaven and earth.

*16–22.* Jacob's deal with God follows his dream.

*19. He named that place Beth El.* The vision results in a new perception of his environment as "the house of God" and "the gate of heaven." Accordingly, Jacob names it *Beit El* (House of God). Beth El—as it is known in English—later became the national sanctuary of the Northern Kingdom of Israel, although one that some prophets maligned (Amos 3:14; 4:4; 5:5–6; Hosea 10:15). In ancient Israel the account of Jacob's vision likely justified and sanctified the Beth El temple.

*20–21.* Jacob drives a hard bargain with God. Jacob wants real-life indicators that God will watch over him wherever he goes, and will return him to his native soil. He pledges that if he meets with success on his journey, then the God of his father's household will be his God, his pillow will become the cornerstone of a temple, and he will sacrifice a tenth of his bounty.

father's house, then will יהוה be my God; 22and this
stone that I have set up as a monument shall be a
house of God. And [of] all that You give me, I will
dedicate a tenth to You."

29 Jacob then moved on and headed for the
land of the people of Kedem. 2He looked and lo—a
well in the field, with three flocks of sheep lying at
rest by it, because this was the well from which they
watered the flocks; a good-sized rock lay on the
mouth of the well. 3When all the flocks were
gathered there, they [the shepherds] would roll
the stone off the well's mouth and water the flocks.
Then they would put the stone back in place over
the well's mouth.

4Jacob said to them, "My friends, where are you
from?" "We are from Haran," they said. 5He said
to them, "Do you know Laban son of Nahor?" And
they said, "We do know [him]." 6"Is he well?" said
he to them. "He is well," said they, "and there is his
daughter Rachel, coming with the flock." 7He said,
"Since the day is still young, [and] not yet the time
for rounding up the livestock, why don't you water
the flock and then take them out to pasture?" 8But
they said, "We can't do that until all the flocks are
rounded up and they [the shepherds] roll the stone
off the well's mouth; then we water the sheep."

אֶל־בֵּית אָבִי וְהָיָה יְהוָה לִי לֵאלֹהִים׃
22 וְהָאֶבֶן הַזֹּאת אֲשֶׁר־שַׂמְתִּי מַצֵּבָה יִהְיֶה
בֵּית אֱלֹהִים וְכֹל אֲשֶׁר תִּתֶּן־לִי עַשֵּׂר
אֲעַשְּׂרֶנּוּ לָךְ׃

כט וַיִּשָּׂא יַעֲקֹב רַגְלָיו וַיֵּלֶךְ אַרְצָה בְנֵי־
קֶדֶם׃ 2 וַיַּרְא וְהִנֵּה בְאֵר בַּשָּׂדֶה וְהִנֵּה־שָׁם
שְׁלֹשָׁה עֶדְרֵי־צֹאן רֹבְצִים עָלֶיהָ כִּי מִן־
הַבְּאֵר הַהִוא יַשְׁקוּ הָעֲדָרִים וְהָאֶבֶן גְּדֹלָה
עַל־פִּי הַבְּאֵר׃ 3 וְנֶאֶסְפוּ־שָׁמָּה כָל־הָעֲדָרִים
וְגָלְלוּ אֶת־הָאֶבֶן מֵעַל פִּי הַבְּאֵר וְהִשְׁקוּ
אֶת־הַצֹּאן וְהֵשִׁיבוּ אֶת־הָאֶבֶן עַל־פִּי
הַבְּאֵר לִמְקֹמָהּ׃
4 וַיֹּאמֶר לָהֶם יַעֲקֹב אַחַי מֵאַיִן אַתֶּם
וַיֹּאמְרוּ מֵחָרָן אֲנָחְנוּ׃ 5 וַיֹּאמֶר לָהֶם
הַיְדַעְתֶּם אֶת־לָבָן בֶּן־נָחוֹר וַיֹּאמְרוּ יָדָעְנוּ׃
6 וַיֹּאמֶר לָהֶם הֲשָׁלוֹם לוֹ וַיֹּאמְרוּ שָׁלוֹם
וְהִנֵּה רָחֵל בִּתּוֹ בָּאָה עִם־הַצֹּאן׃ 7 וַיֹּאמֶר
הֵן עוֹד הַיּוֹם גָּדוֹל לֹא־עֵת הֵאָסֵף הַמִּקְנֶה
הַשְׁקוּ הַצֹּאן וּלְכוּ רְעוּ׃ 8 וַיֹּאמְרוּ לֹא נוּכַל
עַד אֲשֶׁר יֵאָסְפוּ כָּל־הָעֲדָרִים וְגָלְלוּ אֶת־
הָאֶבֶן מֵעַל פִּי הַבְּאֵר וְהִשְׁקִינוּ הַצֹּאן׃

## *Temporary Home for Jacob, Leah, and Rachel* (29:1–30)

It is one of the Torah's great paradoxes that the divine imperative to engender descendants and produce a great nation reaches fruition first in the land of Aram (Syria) and later in Egypt. In this episode, Jacob finds refuge in his uncle's home and meets his counterpart, Rachel, thereby satisfying the wishes of his mother. In a foreign land he also engenders a family and becomes wealthy, thereby bringing God's promises into being.

### JACOB AT THE WELL (29:1–8)

The well is the Torah's famed meeting place, a romantic topos. Here Abraham's servant finds Isaac's bride, Rachel and Jacob meet, and Moses first encounters his future wife, Zipporah. (On wells as symbols of fertility, see at 16:7 and 24:11.) It is also the place where Jacob goes to seek information about his relatives.

*6.* In the midst of Jacob's inquiry, Rachel appears guiding the flock.

⁹While he was still talking with them, Rachel arrived with her father's sheep—she was a shepherd. ¹⁰When Jacob saw Rachel daughter of Laban, his mother's brother, with his uncle Laban's flock, Jacob went over, rolled the stone off the well's mouth, and watered his uncle Laban's flock. ¹¹Now Jacob kissed Rachel, and began to cry in a loud voice. ¹²Jacob then told Rachel that he was her father's kinsman, that he was Rebekah's son, and she ran and told her father.

¹³Upon hearing the news of his sister's son Jacob, Laban ran to greet him; hugging and kissing him, he brought him into his house. Then [Jacob] told Laban everything that had happened, ¹⁴and Laban said to him, "Truly, you are my bone and my flesh!" So he stayed with him a whole month.

¹⁵Laban then said to Jacob, "Just because you are my kin, should you serve me for nothing? Tell me what you want to be paid." ¹⁶Now Laban had two daughters; the elder was named Leah, and the

9 עוֹדֶ֙נּוּ֙ מְדַבֵּ֣ר עִמָּ֔ם וְרָחֵ֣ל | בָּ֗אָה עִם־הַצֹּאן֙
אֲשֶׁ֣ר לְאָבִ֔יהָ כִּ֥י רֹעָ֖ה הִֽוא: 10 וַיְהִ֡י כַּאֲשֶׁר֩
רָאָ֨ה יַעֲקֹ֜ב אֶת־רָחֵ֗ל בַּת־לָבָן֙ אֲחִ֣י אִמּ֔וֹ
וְאֶת־צֹ֥אן לָבָ֖ן אֲחִ֣י אִמּ֑וֹ וַיִּגַּ֣שׁ יַעֲקֹ֗ב וַיָּ֤גֶל
אֶת־הָאֶ֙בֶן֙ מֵעַל֙ פִּ֣י הַבְּאֵ֔ר וַיַּ֕שְׁקְ אֶת־צֹ֥אן
לָבָ֖ן אֲחִ֥י אִמּֽוֹ: 11 וַיִּשַּׁ֥ק יַעֲקֹ֖ב לְרָחֵ֑ל וַיִּשָּׂ֥א
אֶת־קֹל֖וֹ וַיֵּֽבְךְּ: 12 וַיַּגֵּ֨ד יַעֲקֹ֜ב לְרָחֵ֗ל כִּ֣י אֲחִ֤י
אָבִ֙יהָ֙ ה֔וּא וְכִ֥י בֶן־רִבְקָ֖ה ה֑וּא וַתָּ֕רָץ וַתַּגֵּ֖ד
לְאָבִֽיהָ:

13 וַיְהִי֩ כִשְׁמֹ֨עַ לָבָ֜ן אֶת־שֵׁ֣מַע | יַעֲקֹ֣ב בֶּן־
אֲחֹת֗וֹ וַיָּ֤רָץ לִקְרָאתוֹ֙ וַיְחַבֶּק־לוֹ֙ וַיְנַשֶּׁק־ל֔וֹ
וַיְבִיאֵ֖הוּ אֶל־בֵּית֑וֹ וַיְסַפֵּ֣ר לְלָבָ֔ן אֵ֥ת כָּל־
הַדְּבָרִ֖ים הָאֵֽלֶּה: 14 וַיֹּ֤אמֶר לוֹ֙ לָבָ֔ן אַ֛ךְ
עַצְמִ֥י וּבְשָׂרִ֖י אָ֑תָּה וַיֵּ֥שֶׁב עִמּ֖וֹ חֹ֥דֶשׁ יָמִֽים:

15 וַיֹּ֤אמֶר לָבָן֙ לְיַֽעֲקֹ֔ב הֲכִי־אָחִ֣י אַ֔תָּה
וַעֲבַדְתַּ֖נִי חִנָּ֑ם הַגִּ֣ידָה לִּ֔י מַה־מַּשְׂכֻּרְתֶּֽךָ:
16 וּלְלָבָ֖ן שְׁתֵּ֣י בָנ֑וֹת שֵׁ֤ם הַגְּדֹלָה֙ לֵאָ֔ה

## MEETING RACHEL (29:9–21)

*9. she was a shepherd.* The first description of Rachel does not emphasize her beauty—as is sometimes the case when a female character is introduced (Rebekah, Genesis 24:16; Abigail, I Samuel 25:3; Bathsheba, II Samuel 11:2). Rather, it declares her occupation. Rachel's very name means "ewe."

*10. rolled the stone off the well's mouth.* In this occasion of biblical humor, Jacob is so overwhelmed when Rachel appears that—in superhero fashion—he single-handedly rolls the stone cover off the mouth of the well. The reader is particularly impressed with this, having just been informed that the act required the efforts of all Haran's shepherds.

*11.* One cannot help but wonder about Rachel's response to the stranger who kisses her, weeps, and then declares that he is her cousin.

*12. he was Rebekah's son.* Jacob identifies himself only as Rebekah's son, not Isaac's. (On the place

of women in the kinship ties of Israelite social structure, see at 10:1.)

*she ran.* The text, tending toward silence about emotions, speaks only of her acts of running and announcing the arrival, as did Rebekah when Abraham's servant revealed his identity at the same well (24:28). Rebekah, however, ran to her mother's house.

*14. "Truly, you are my bone and my flesh!"* Laban's effusive statement of recognition and solidarity will soon become ironic as uncle and nephew prove equal in chicanery.

*16. Now Laban had two daughters.* In the pasture Rachel had been identified as a shepherd, but at home she is marked as the younger of two sisters. When Leah is introduced, Rachel's beauty becomes a cause for further distinction in the face of Leah's "weak eyes" (v. 17). Jacob has fallen in love with Rachel and soon attests to his willingness to sustain the love for seven years (v. 18). In the

younger was named Rachel. [17]Leah's eyes were weak, but Rachel was beautiful of form and of face. [18]Jacob was in love with Rachel, so he said, "I will work for you seven years for your younger daughter Rachel."

[19]Laban answered, "I would rather give her to you than to any other man; stay [here] with me." [20]So Jacob labored seven years for Rachel; yet in his love for her they seemed to him but a few days. [21]Jacob then said to Laban, "Let me have my wife; I have filled my term; now I want to make love to her."

[22]So Laban invited all the people of the place and made a feast. [23]In the evening, he took his daughter Leah and brought her to [Jacob], who made love to her. [24](And Laban gave his maid Zilpah to his daughter Leah to be her maid.) [25]In the morning, look—it was Leah! and [Jacob] said

וְשֵׁ֥ם הַקְּטַנָּ֖ה רָחֵֽל׃ 17 וְעֵינֵ֥י לֵאָ֖ה רַכּ֑וֹת
וְרָחֵל֙ הָֽיְתָ֔ה יְפַת־תֹּ֖אַר וִיפַ֥ת מַרְאֶֽה׃
18 וַיֶּאֱהַ֥ב יַעֲקֹ֖ב אֶת־רָחֵ֑ל וַיֹּ֗אמֶר אֶֽעֱבָדְךָ֙
שֶׁ֣בַע שָׁנִ֔ים בְּרָחֵ֥ל בִּתְּךָ֖ הַקְּטַנָּֽה׃
19 וַיֹּ֣אמֶר לָבָ֗ן ט֚וֹב תִּתִּ֣י אֹתָ֣הּ לָ֔ךְ מִתִּתִּ֥י
אֹתָ֖הּ לְאִ֣ישׁ אַחֵ֑ר שְׁבָ֖ה עִמָּדִֽי׃ 20 וַיַּעֲבֹ֧ד
יַעֲקֹ֛ב בְּרָחֵ֖ל שֶׁ֣בַע שָׁנִ֑ים וַיִּהְי֤וּ בְעֵינָיו֙
כְּיָמִ֣ים אֲחָדִ֔ים בְּאַהֲבָת֖וֹ אֹתָֽהּ׃ 21 וַיֹּ֨אמֶר
יַעֲקֹ֤ב אֶל־לָבָן֙ הָבָ֣ה אֶת־אִשְׁתִּ֔י כִּ֥י מָלְא֖וּ
יָמָ֑י וְאָב֖וֹאָה אֵלֶֽיהָ׃
22 וַיֶּאֱסֹ֥ף לָבָ֛ן אֶת־כָּל־אַנְשֵׁ֥י הַמָּק֖וֹם וַיַּ֥עַשׂ
מִשְׁתֶּֽה׃ 23 וַיְהִ֣י בָעֶ֔רֶב וַיִּקַּח֙ אֶת־לֵאָ֣ה בִתּ֔וֹ
וַיָּבֵ֥א אֹתָ֖הּ אֵלָ֑יו וַיָּבֹ֖א אֵלֶֽיהָ׃ 24 וַיִּתֵּ֤ן לָבָן֙
לָ֔הּ אֶת־זִלְפָּ֖ה שִׁפְחָת֑וֹ לְלֵאָ֥ה בִתּ֖וֹ שִׁפְחָֽה׃
25 וַיְהִ֣י בַבֹּ֔קֶר וְהִנֵּה־הִ֖וא לֵאָ֑ה וַיֹּ֣אמֶר אֶל־

ensuing scenes, the focus falls on Rachel and Leah; Laban's sons are not mentioned until they voice their resentment at Jacob's success (31:1).

*17.* Leah and Rachel are described as different in appearance. Earlier, the text had contrasted Jacob and Esau also on the basis of their respective occupations (25:27, where *yoshev ohalim* seems to mean "raising livestock"; compare 4:20).

***18. "seven years for your younger daughter."*** In the social world of the Bible, a bridegroom or his family needed to compensate his bride's household. Apparently, part of this payment would normally accrue to the bride herself. (See *Chayei Sarah*, Another View, p. 127, and at 31:15.)

Two biblical motifs are evident here: of love directed to a younger child (Rachel), and of seven (years) as a number of wholeness.

*19.* Laban speaks of Rachel as a gift that he will bestow on his nephew and says nothing about the work extracted from Jacob. Laban's manipulation of Jacob begins with his appeal to familial bonds, asserting that it is within his power to "give" Rachel to whomever he desires.

***20. a few days.*** Heb. *ke-yamim achadim.* Jacob's perception of his seven years of labor as "a few days" recalls the *yamim achadim* ("a while," literally "a few days") that his mother, Rebekah, had recommended that he spend with Laban (27:44).

## JACOB'S MARRIAGE TO LEAH AND RACHEL (29:22–30)

In Jacob's mind the marital relationship with Rachel will be enacted by his initiation of the sexual act. Where Jacob imagines an act of intimacy, Laban plans a public feast.

Laban substitutes his older daughter for the younger. The provocative question that arises from this bed-trick is the same as that raised by Rebekah and Jacob's earlier deception of Isaac: does human subterfuge disrupt the divine plan—or advance it? In this case Laban's trick enables the building of the house of Israel through the combined efforts of the two sisters and their two maids. It is precisely the interfamilial competition that renders the household productive.

to Laban, "What have you done to me? Wasn't it for Rachel that I [agreed to] serve you? Why did you deceive me?"

²⁶And Laban replied, "This is not done in our region, to give the younger before the first-born. ²⁷Fulfill this [additional] seven-year term, and that one, too, will be given you in exchange for the additional seven years of work that you will do for me." ²⁸Jacob did so; he fulfilled this [additional] term of seven years; whereupon [Laban] gave him his daughter Rachel as a wife.

²⁹Laban then gave his maid Bilhah to his daughter Rachel to be her maid. ³⁰[Jacob] made love with Rachel, too; he loved Rachel—for whom he had served [Laban] yet another seven years—so much more than Leah.

לָבָ֔ן מַה־זֹּ֥את עָשִׂ֖יתָ לִּ֑י הֲלֹ֤א בְרָחֵל֙ עָבַ֣דְתִּי עִמָּ֔ךְ וְלָ֖מָּה רִמִּיתָֽנִי׃ ²⁶ וַיֹּ֣אמֶר לָבָ֔ן לֹא־יֵעָשֶׂ֥ה כֵ֖ן בִּמְקוֹמֵ֑נוּ לָתֵ֥ת הַצְּעִירָ֖ה לִפְנֵ֥י הַבְּכִירָֽה׃ ²⁷ מַלֵּ֖א שְׁבֻ֣עַ זֹ֑את וְנִתְּנָ֨ה לְךָ֜ גַּם־אֶת־זֹ֗את בַּעֲבֹדָה֙ אֲשֶׁ֣ר תַּעֲבֹ֣ד עִמָּדִ֔י ע֖וֹד שֶֽׁבַע־שָׁנִ֥ים אֲחֵרֽוֹת׃ ²⁸ וַיַּ֤עַשׂ יַעֲקֹב֙ כֵּ֔ן וַיְמַלֵּ֖א שְׁבֻ֣עַ זֹ֑את וַיִּתֶּן־ ל֛וֹ אֶת־רָחֵ֥ל בִּתּ֖וֹ ל֥וֹ לְאִשָּֽׁה׃ ²⁹ וַיִּתֵּ֤ן לָבָן֙ לְרָחֵ֣ל בִּתּ֔וֹ אֶת־בִּלְהָ֖ה שִׁפְחָת֑וֹ לָ֖הּ לְשִׁפְחָֽה׃ ³⁰ וַיָּבֹא֙ גַּ֣ם אֶל־רָחֵ֔ל וַיֶּאֱהַ֥ב גַּֽם־אֶת־רָחֵ֖ל מִלֵּאָ֑ה וַיַּעֲבֹ֣ד עִמּ֔וֹ ע֖וֹד שֶֽׁבַע־ שָׁנִ֥ים אֲחֵרֽוֹת׃

· · · · · · · · · · · · · · · · · · · · · · · · · · · · · · · · · · · · · · ·

**26–29.** The unfolding scenario—in which Jacob weds two sisters—is an instance where a biblical law (the prohibition against marrying a woman's sister during her lifetime, Leviticus 18:18) is contradicted by an episode in biblical narrative.

**30.** [*Jacob*] *made love with Rachel, too.* Literally, "he also came into Rachel," which is a biblical way of indicating a sexual intercourse. At long last Jacob is united with his beloved Rachel.

*he loved Rachel . . . so much more than Leah.* The preference of one wife over the other reintroduces the theme of favoritism that begins with Cain and Abel (Genesis 4) and continues as sibling rivalry throughout Genesis. Such preference, while promoting strife within the family, leads in the sisters' case to productivity and the realization of the divine blessing in the human realm.

## From Barrenness to Fertility
### LEAH AND RACHEL BIRTH THE PEOPLE OF ISRAEL (29:31–30:24)

The narrative focuses on how each matriarch negotiates the terrain between barrenness and fertility, which offers cherished insight into the individual characters of these biblical women. Where the male heroes seek to conquer, claim, and sanctify land, the female heroes strive to inscribe their memory on the bodies of their heirs; the acts of birthing and naming function as the counterpart to those of inaugurating and settling territory. The matriarchs go to extreme lengths in order to initiate and improvise their own Covenant. The female journey spans the poles from barrenness to fertility and affords the matriarch the opportunity to wrestle with other persons, God, and social position. The steps of this journey are: barrenness, statement of protest, direct action, encounter with God, conception, birth, and naming.

### COMPETITION BETWEEN SISTERS
(29:31–30:13)

Whereas Jacob has split from his brother, Rachel must live alongside her sister as co-wife. Previously, the narrator has emphasized that Jacob "loves" Rachel by mentioning it three times (29:18, 20, 30). In this section, according to the narrator, God infers that Leah is in contrast "disfavored" (in Hebrew, literally "hated"; v. 31) and intervenes by making Leah fertile.

[31]Now, seeing that Leah was disfavored, יהוה opened her womb, while Rachel was childless. [32]Leah thus became pregnant and bore a son and named him Reuben, for she said, "יהוה *saw* my plight; yes, now my husband will love me." [33]Again she became pregnant and bore a son and said, "יהוה *heard* that I am despised and has given me this one too"; so she named him Simeon. [34]Again she became pregnant and bore a son and said, "Now, this time, my husband will be *attached* to me, for I have borne to him three sons." She therefore named him Levi. [35]Again she became pregnant and bore a son and said, "This time I *give thanks* to יהוה." She therefore named him Judah. Then she stopped bearing.

**30** When Rachel saw that she was not bearing [children] to Jacob, Rachel came to envy her sister. She said to Jacob, "Let me have children; otherwise I am a dead woman!" [2]Jacob grew angry with Rachel and said, "Am I in place of God who

31 וַיַּרְא יְהוָה כִּי־שְׂנוּאָה לֵאָה וַיִּפְתַּח אֶת־
רַחְמָהּ וְרָחֵל עֲקָרָה׃ 32 וַתַּהַר לֵאָה וַתֵּלֶד
בֵּן וַתִּקְרָא שְׁמוֹ רְאוּבֵן כִּי אָמְרָה כִּי־רָאָה
יְהוָה בְּעָנְיִי כִּי עַתָּה יֶאֱהָבַנִי אִישִׁי׃
33 וַתַּהַר עוֹד וַתֵּלֶד בֵּן וַתֹּאמֶר כִּי־שָׁמַע
יְהוָה כִּי־שְׂנוּאָה אָנֹכִי וַיִּתֶּן־לִי גַּם־אֶת־זֶה
וַתִּקְרָא שְׁמוֹ שִׁמְעוֹן׃ 34 וַתַּהַר עוֹד וַתֵּלֶד
בֵּן וַתֹּאמֶר עַתָּה הַפַּעַם יִלָּוֶה אִישִׁי אֵלַי
כִּי־יָלַדְתִּי לוֹ שְׁלֹשָׁה בָנִים עַל־כֵּן קָרָא־
שְׁמוֹ לֵוִי׃ 35 וַתַּהַר עוֹד וַתֵּלֶד בֵּן וַתֹּאמֶר
הַפַּעַם אוֹדֶה אֶת־יְהוָה עַל־כֵּן קָרְאָה שְׁמוֹ
יְהוּדָה וַתַּעֲמֹד מִלֶּדֶת׃
ל וַתֵּרֶא רָחֵל כִּי לֹא יָלְדָה לְיַעֲקֹב וַתְּקַנֵּא
רָחֵל בַּאֲחֹתָהּ וַתֹּאמֶר אֶל־יַעֲקֹב הָבָה־לִּי
בָנִים וְאִם־אַיִן מֵתָה אָנֹכִי׃ 2 וַיִּחַר־אַף
יַעֲקֹב בְּרָחֵל וַיֹּאמֶר הֲתַחַת אֱלֹהִים אָנֹכִי

*32.* ***bore.*** As the translation reflects, the directness of the Hebrew root *y-l-d* points to the action of birthing. It thus emphasizes the agency and volition of the matriarchs. In contrast, the usual English idiom "to give birth" focuses more on the *outcome* of birthing, namely, the child.

*32–35.* Rachel's infertility becomes doubly bitter in the shadow of Leah's celebrations of the births of her first four sons. Through the names, Leah exults that "יהוה *saw* my plight" (Reuben, a pun on "See, a son!") and "יהוה *heard* that I am despised and has given me this one too" (Simeon, a pun on "hearing"); she speculates that "this time my husband will be *attached* to me" (Levi, a pun on "Accompany"), and resolves that "this time I *give thanks* to יהוה" (Judah, a pun on "thanks"). While marking her triumphs and articulating her desire for marital love in the names of her sons, Leah bequeaths them sibling rivalry, an inheritance that drives the story of Joseph and his brothers.

***30:1.*** ***"me . . . I."*** Heb. *li . . . anochi.* Rachel emphasizes her personal need for children through first person pronouns (see also at v. 3); she is concerned with her vitality and her own lineage. Let Jacob have his sons with Leah, but he must—at the same time—preserve Rachel's individual legacy.

***"otherwise I am a dead woman!"*** Rachel equates her inability to give birth with death, implying that her story will never be told if not condensed in the name of a child; ironically, she will eventually die giving birth to her second child (35:18). In effect she protests not only the state of barrenness, but also the limits that her society sets on female autonomy. In this case, Rachel speaks to the threat of her negation should she not reproduce. Perceiving the limits of her own authority, she turns to a person with immediate authority over her—her husband, Jacob.

*2.* Jacob deflects responsibility and in fury directs Rachel's protest toward God. However, had Rachel not spoken out, her journey would have had no beginning and no fulfillment.

has withheld from you the fruit of the womb?"
[3]But she said, "Here is my maid Bilhah; couple
with her and let her give birth on my knees, so that
I too may have a son, through her." [4]So she gave
him her maid Bilhah as a wife, and Jacob coupled
with her. [5]Bilhah became pregnant and bore a son
to Jacob. [6]Rachel said, "God has *judged* me and has
also listened to my plea and given me a son." She
therefore named him Dan. [7]Again Rachel's maid
Bilhah became pregnant; she bore a second son to
Jacob. [8]Rachel then said, "A mighty *rivalry* have I
waged with my sister; moreover, I have prevailed."
She therefore named him Naphtali.

אֲשֶׁר־מָנַע מִמֵּךְ פְּרִי־בָטֶן׃ 3 וַתֹּאמֶר הִנֵּה
אֲמָתִי בִלְהָה בֹּא אֵלֶיהָ וְתֵלֵד עַל־בִּרְכַּי
וְאִבָּנֶה גַם־אָנֹכִי מִמֶּנָּה׃ 4 וַתִּתֶּן־לוֹ אֶת־
בִּלְהָה שִׁפְחָתָהּ לְאִשָּׁה וַיָּבֹא אֵלֶיהָ יַעֲקֹב׃
5 וַתַּהַר בִּלְהָה וַתֵּלֶד לְיַעֲקֹב בֵּן׃ 6 וַתֹּאמֶר
רָחֵל דָּנַנִּי אֱלֹהִים וְגַם שָׁמַע בְּקֹלִי וַיִּתֶּן־
לִי בֵּן עַל־כֵּן קָרְאָה שְׁמוֹ דָּן׃ 7 וַתַּהַר
עוֹד וַתֵּלֶד בִּלְהָה שִׁפְחַת רָחֵל בֵּן שֵׁנִי
לְיַעֲקֹב׃ 8 וַתֹּאמֶר רָחֵל נַפְתּוּלֵי אֱלֹהִים ׀
נִפְתַּלְתִּי עִם־אֲחֹתִי גַּם־יָכֹלְתִּי וַתִּקְרָא שְׁמוֹ
נַפְתָּלִי׃

*3. But she said, "Here is my maid Bilhah."* That is, her slave; see at 16:1. The space between barrenness and fertility is a gap in the relationship between Rachel and God that she must bridge through symbolic acts. By employing her slave, Bilhah, as a surrogate, Rachel performs a kind of imitative magic in which she plays the Deity—causing a woman to conceive in the hopes that the Creator will likewise fertilize her. Like Sarah (16:1–3) and Leah (below, v. 9), Rachel relies on surrogacy also to bypass the obstacles to conception more directly. She achieves her goal by claiming the body of another woman as an extension of her own. In biblical narrative, birth is a moment of female collaboration when the boundaries between distinct bodies collapse, an occasion in which multiple female bodies operate in tandem. All females on the narrative stage at the moment of birth function as a collective body absorbed in the process and implication of birthing. This is evident in the surrogacy scenes, as well as in the birth scenes of Rachel and of Tamar—in which midwives take part in the naming of the child (35:17–18; 38:29; see also I Samuel 4:19–22). It is also clear when the midwives defy Pharaoh in order to save the lives of Hebrew babies (Exodus 1). Birth as a collective female action even transcends ethnic difference, as in the book of Ruth. There, Ruth the Moabite pledges to bind her body and her fate to her Israelite mother-in-law, Naomi—who has declared herself "too old to be married" (Ruth 1:12). Following the birth of Ruth's son, a chorus of women blesses Naomi with the pronouncement that "a son is born to Naomi" (4:17). (On surrogacy see also at Genesis 16:2.) | Viewed from a more individualistic perspective, it is deeply problematic that the matriarchs potentially force their servants into undesired sexual relations.

***"my . . . I too."*** Heb. *gam anochi.* Rachel emphasizes her personal volition when spelling out the surrogacy procedure to Jacob, adding an extra first-person singular pronoun.

***"I . . . may have a son."*** Heb. *ibaneh,* the same term that Sarah had used (16:2); on its meaning, see there.

*6–8.* As Bilhah twice gives birth, Rachel has the opportunity to thrust her own jabs at her sister through the names of sons: Dan (a pun on "judge") because "God has *judged* me and has also listened to my plea"; and Naphtali (a pun on "struggle") because "a mighty *rivalry* have I waged with my sister."

*8. **"I have prevailed."*** Heb. *yacholti.* As she engages in sibling rivalry, Rachel also struggles with God in order to win the ability to give birth. Her naming of Naphtali is verbally linked with God's later renaming of Jacob as Israel: "for you have

[9]When Leah saw that she was no longer bearing children, she took her maid Zilpah and gave her to Jacob as a wife. [10]And Zilpah, Leah's maid, bore a son to Jacob. [11]Leah said, "*Fortune* has come!" She therefore named him Gad. [12]And Zilpah, Leah's maid, bore a second son to Jacob. [13]Leah then said, "How *happy* I am—yes, women will call me happy!" She therefore named him Asher.

[14]In the time of the wheat harvest, Reuben went out and found mandrakes in the field. When he brought them to his mother Leah, Rachel said to Leah, "Pray give me some of your son's mandrakes." [15]She replied, "Isn't it enough that you took my husband, and now you want to take my son's mandrakes!" And Rachel said, "Very well, let him sleep with you tonight in exchange for your son's mandrakes." [16]When Jacob came in from the field [that] evening, Leah went out to meet him and said, "I am the one you will bed [tonight], for I have bought you with my son's mandrakes." That night he slept with her, [17]and God now listened to Leah; she became pregnant and bore a fifth son to Jacob. [18]Leah said, "God has given me my *reward* for

9 וַתֵּ֣רֶא לֵאָ֔ה כִּ֥י עָמְדָ֖ה מִלֶּ֑דֶת וַתִּקַּח֙ אֶת־זִלְפָּ֣ה שִׁפְחָתָ֔הּ וַתִּתֵּ֥ן אֹתָ֛הּ לְיַעֲקֹ֖ב לְאִשָּֽׁה: 10 וַתֵּ֗לֶד זִלְפָּ֛ה שִׁפְחַ֥ת לֵאָ֖ה לְיַעֲקֹ֥ב בֵּֽן: 11 וַתֹּ֥אמֶר לֵאָ֖ה בגד בָּ֣א גָ֑ד וַתִּקְרָ֥א אֶת־שְׁמֹ֖ו גָּֽד: 12 וַתֵּ֗לֶד זִלְפָּה֙ שִׁפְחַ֣ת לֵאָ֔ה בֵּ֥ן שֵׁנִ֖י לְיַעֲקֹֽב: 13 וַתֹּ֣אמֶר לֵאָ֔ה בְּאָשְׁרִ֕י כִּ֥י אִשְּׁר֖וּנִי בָּנֹ֑ות וַתִּקְרָ֥א אֶת־שְׁמֹ֖ו אָשֵֽׁר:

14 וַיֵּ֨לֶךְ רְאוּבֵ֜ן בִּימֵ֣י קְצִיר־חִטִּ֗ים וַיִּמְצָ֤א דֽוּדָאִים֙ בַּשָּׂדֶ֔ה וַיָּבֵ֣א אֹתָ֔ם אֶל־לֵאָ֖ה אִמֹּ֑ו וַתֹּ֤אמֶר רָחֵל֙ אֶל־לֵאָ֔ה תְּנִי־נָ֣א לִ֔י מִדּֽוּדָאֵ֖י בְּנֵֽךְ: 15 וַתֹּ֣אמֶר לָ֗הּ הַמְעַט֙ קַחְתֵּ֣ךְ אֶת־אִישִׁ֔י וְלָקַ֕חַת גַּ֥ם אֶת־דּוּדָאֵ֖י בְּנִ֑י וַתֹּ֣אמֶר רָחֵ֗ל לָכֵן֙ יִשְׁכַּ֤ב עִמָּךְ֙ הַלַּ֔יְלָה תַּ֖חַת דּוּדָאֵ֥י בְּנֵֽךְ: 16 וַיָּבֹ֨א יַעֲקֹ֣ב מִן־הַשָּׂדֶה֮ בָּעֶרֶב֒ וַתֵּצֵ֨א לֵאָ֜ה לִקְרָאתֹ֗ו וַתֹּ֨אמֶר֙ אֵלַ֣י תָּבֹ֔וא כִּ֚י שָׂכֹ֣ר שְׂכַרְתִּ֔יךָ בְּדוּדָאֵ֖י בְּנִ֑י וַיִּשְׁכַּ֥ב עִמָּ֖הּ בַּלַּ֥יְלָה הֽוּא: 17 וַיִּשְׁמַ֥ע אֱלֹהִ֖ים אֶל־לֵאָ֑ה וַתַּ֛הַר וַתֵּ֥לֶד לְיַעֲקֹ֖ב בֵּ֥ן חֲמִישִֽׁי: 18 וַתֹּ֣אמֶר לֵאָה֒

---

struggled with God and with human beings, and you have prevailed (*vatuchal*)" (32:29). Both Rachel and Jacob prevail in contests doubly waged with people and with God.

**9. Leah saw that she was no longer bearing children.** Leah is never called barren, but she does experience a period of infertility.

**10–13.** Leah stresses her good fortune as she names the sons of Zilpah. *Gad* means literally "good fortune" and *Asher* is a name based on a verb form ("Fortunate is...") that anticipates that other women will declare Leah fortunate.

### EXCHANGE BETWEEN SISTERS (30:14–24)

The turning point in the sisters' relationship comes with their readiness to enter into an exchange—to give each what the other lacks. Symbolically, Leah is willing to give fertility (via man-

drakes) to her barren sister and, in turn, Rachel gives Jacob to Leah, who longs for his love. | Whereas Jacob will first draw a truce with God (32:25–31) and then negotiate an icy peace with his brother (33:1–17), Rachel first strikes a deal with her sister and then wins the ability to create from God.

**14. mandrakes.** Or "love fruits," known as an aphrodisiac as well as an aid to conception.

**15.** Leah's acerbic response exposes her pain. Rachel turns her sister's complaint into terms of negotiation by giving Leah "back" her husband for one night in exchange for the mandrakes. In the meantime, she increases her request for a portion of the mandrakes to a demand for all of them.

**18.** As she names her fifth biological son, Leah attests that she is rewarded by God: Issachar (a pun on "reward" or "hire"), saying, "God has given me my reward because I gave my maidservant to my husband" (30:18). The name also puns on Leah's

giving my maid to my husband." She therefore
named him Issachar. 19 Again Leah became pregnant; she bore a sixth son to Jacob. 20 Leah then
said, "God has *given me a fine gift*. Now my husband will [finally] *give me the* [wedding] *gift* due
me, for I have borne him six sons." She therefore
named him Zebulun. 21 Afterward she bore a
daughter and named her Dinah.

22 God now remembered Rachel; God listened
to her and opened her womb, 23 so she became pregnant and bore a son. She said, "God has *removed*
my disgrace." 24 She therefore named him Joseph,
saying, "May יהוה *add on* another son for me."

25 Now, after Rachel bore Joseph, Jacob said to
Laban, "Release me; let me go to my [own] place,
my [own] land. 26 Let me have my wives and children for whom I toiled under you, and let me go,
for you know the service I have rendered you."

נָתַ֤ן אֱלֹהִים֙ שְׂכָרִ֔י אֲשֶׁר־נָתַ֥תִּי שִׁפְחָתִ֖י
לְאִישִׁ֑י וַתִּקְרָ֥א שְׁמ֖וֹ יששכר יִשָּׂכָֽר׃ 19 וַתַּ֤הַר
עוֹד֙ לֵאָ֔ה וַתֵּ֥לֶד בֵּן־שִׁשִּׁ֖י לְיַעֲקֹֽב׃ 20 וַתֹּ֣אמֶר
לֵאָ֗ה זְבָדַ֨נִי אֱלֹהִ֥ים ׀ אֹתִי֮ זֵ֣בֶד טוֹב֒ הַפַּ֙עַם֙
יִזְבְּלֵ֣נִי אִישִׁ֔י כִּֽי־יָלַ֥דְתִּי ל֖וֹ שִׁשָּׁ֣ה בָנִ֑ים
וַתִּקְרָ֥א אֶת־שְׁמ֖וֹ זְבֻלֽוּן׃ 21 וְאַחַ֖ר יָ֣לְדָה בַּ֑ת
וַתִּקְרָ֥א אֶת־שְׁמָ֖הּ דִּינָֽה׃

22 וַיִּזְכֹּ֥ר אֱלֹהִ֖ים אֶת־רָחֵ֑ל וַיִּשְׁמַ֤ע אֵלֶ֙יהָ֙
אֱלֹהִ֔ים וַיִּפְתַּ֖ח אֶת־רַחְמָֽהּ׃ 23 וַתַּ֖הַר וַתֵּ֣לֶד
בֵּ֑ן וַתֹּ֕אמֶר אָסַ֥ף אֱלֹהִ֖ים אֶת־חֶרְפָּתִֽי׃
24 וַתִּקְרָ֧א אֶת־שְׁמ֛וֹ יוֹסֵ֖ף לֵאמֹ֑ר יֹסֵ֧ף יְהֹוָ֛ה
לִ֖י בֵּ֥ן אַחֵֽר׃
25 וַיְהִ֕י כַּאֲשֶׁ֛ר יָלְדָ֥ה רָחֵ֖ל אֶת־יוֹסֵ֑ף וַיֹּ֤אמֶר
יַעֲקֹב֙ אֶל־לָבָ֔ן שַׁלְּחֵ֙נִי֙ וְאֵ֣לְכָ֔ה אֶל־מְקוֹמִ֖י
וּלְאַרְצִֽי׃ 26 תְּנָ֞ה אֶת־נָשַׁ֣י וְאֶת־יְלָדַ֗י אֲשֶׁ֨ר
עָבַ֧דְתִּי אֹֽתְךָ֛ בָּהֵ֖ן וְאֵלֵ֑כָה כִּ֚י אַתָּ֣ה יָדַ֔עְתָּ

pre-coital statement to Jacob, "I have bought (or: hired) you with my son's mandrakes" (30:16).

***20.*** In this naming ceremony, Leah utters a pious word of thanks, which hints at the name Zebed. But then she expresses her true wish. The name Zebulun reflects her focus on improving her marriage.

***21.*** The exchange (v. 15) results not only in the birth of Leah's fifth and sixth sons but also in her first daughter, Dinah. The phrase "she conceived and she bore" associated with the birth of each son is absent here. Also absent is a naming declaration for Dinah, although her name means "judgment that leads to justice."

***22.*** The mandrakes (vv. 14–15) do not cure Rachel's barrenness, but they do alert God to her desperation—and the lengths to which she will go in order to conceive. In other words, the actions that Rachel takes to reverse her situation function as self-initiation into a relationship with God. They also prove her to be an ambitious mother worthy of a heroic son. Rachel has followed a three-part course in protesting her infertility: articulation of discontent, surrogacy, and medicinal aid. God likewise responds with three actions: "God now remembered . . . listened . . . and opened her womb." Her struggle results in a response from God—such that her memory is assured, her voice heeded, and the barrier to conception lifted.

***God . . . remembered.*** The same idea appeared (in different Hebrew terms) when God "remembered" Sarah and she became pregnant (21:1). In the biblical accounts of the nation of Israel's loss or suffering, acts of memory (whether human or divine) are the first step toward redemption. In the stories of barren women, the occasion of divine remembrance signals that their actions have led to acknowledgment—and the reversal of their situation.

***24.*** The giving of a name affords the new mother an opportunity to tell her story of movement from barrenness to fertility, and to perpetuate her experience through the child's ascribed identity. Although Rachel uses a pious statement that "God has removed (Heb. *asaf*) my disgrace," she calls her son Joseph (*yosef*), meaning "may God add on (*yosef*) another child for me." Celebrating her victory, Rachel already begins strategizing for another.

[27]Laban then said to him, "Please [hear this]: I have prospered and יהוה has blessed me on your account." [28]He added, "Indicate your wages to me, and I will pay them."

[29][Jacob] said to him, "You know [the result] of my labors for you and how your livestock fared with me: [30]What little you had before I came along has increased greatly; יהוה has blessed you at my every step; but now, when shall I provide for myself, for my own household?" [31][Laban] said, "What should I pay you?"

Jacob replied: "Do not pay me a thing; if you do this for me, I shall return to shepherding, to keeping your flock. [32]Let me pass by all your flock today, removing from it every spotted and speckled kid and every dark lamb among the rams and every speckled and spotted goat; that will be my payment. [33]My honesty shall answer for me on the morrow. When you give me my wages, in your presence [I affirm] that any animal that is not either spotted among the goats or speckled or dark among the young rams is stolen if found in my possession." [34]"Agreed," said Laban, "let it but be as you have said."

[35]But that day he [Laban] removed the streaked and speckled he-goats, and all the spotted and speckled she-goats, every one that had white on it and every one of the young rams that was dark, and handed them over to his sons; [36]he then set a distance of three days' journey between himself and Jacob, and Jacob tended what remained of Laban's flock.

[37]Jacob now took fresh rods of poplar, almond, and plane, and peeled off white strips of bark,

אֶת־עֲבֹדָתִי אֲשֶׁר עֲבַדְתִּיךָ׃ 27 וַיֹּאמֶר אֵלָיו
לָבָן אִם־נָא מָצָאתִי חֵן בְּעֵינֶיךָ נִחַשְׁתִּי
וַיְבָרְכֵנִי יְהֹוָה בִּגְלָלֶךָ׃ 28 וַיֹּאמַר נָקְבָה
שְׂכָרְךָ עָלַי וְאֶתֵּנָה׃
29 וַיֹּאמֶר אֵלָיו אַתָּה יָדַעְתָּ אֵת אֲשֶׁר
עֲבַדְתִּיךָ וְאֵת אֲשֶׁר־הָיָה מִקְנְךָ אִתִּי׃ 30 כִּי
מְעַט אֲשֶׁר־הָיָה לְךָ לְפָנַי וַיִּפְרֹץ לָרֹב וַיְבָרֶךְ
יְהֹוָה אֹתְךָ לְרַגְלִי וְעַתָּה מָתַי אֶעֱשֶׂה גַם־
אָנֹכִי לְבֵיתִי׃ 31 וַיֹּאמֶר מָה אֶתֶּן־לָךְ
וַיֹּאמֶר יַעֲקֹב לֹא־תִתֶּן־לִי מְאוּמָה אִם־
תַּעֲשֶׂה־לִּי הַדָּבָר הַזֶּה אָשׁוּבָה אֶרְעֶה
צֹאנְךָ אֶשְׁמֹר׃ 32 אֶעֱבֹר בְּכָל־צֹאנְךָ הַיּוֹם
הָסֵר מִשָּׁם כָּל־שֶׂה ׀ נָקֹד וְטָלוּא וְכָל־שֶׂה־
חוּם בַּכְּשָׂבִים וְטָלוּא וְנָקֹד בָּעִזִּים וְהָיָה
שְׂכָרִי׃ 33 וְעָנְתָה־בִּי צִדְקָתִי בְּיוֹם מָחָר כִּי־
תָבוֹא עַל־שְׂכָרִי לְפָנֶיךָ כֹּל אֲשֶׁר־אֵינֶנּוּ נָקֹד
וְטָלוּא בָּעִזִּים וְחוּם בַּכְּשָׂבִים גָּנוּב הוּא
אִתִּי׃ 34 וַיֹּאמֶר לָבָן הֵן לוּ יְהִי כִדְבָרֶךָ׃
35 וַיָּסַר בַּיּוֹם הַהוּא אֶת־הַתְּיָשִׁים הָעֲקֻדִּים
וְהַטְּלֻאִים וְאֵת כָּל־הָעִזִּים הַנְּקֻדּוֹת
וְהַטְּלֻאֹת כֹּל אֲשֶׁר־לָבָן בּוֹ וְכָל־חוּם
בַּכְּשָׂבִים וַיִּתֵּן בְּיַד־בָּנָיו׃ 36 וַיָּשֶׂם דֶּרֶךְ
שְׁלֹשֶׁת יָמִים בֵּינוֹ וּבֵין יַעֲקֹב וְיַעֲקֹב רֹעֶה
אֶת־צֹאן לָבָן הַנּוֹתָרֹת׃
37 וַיִּקַּח־לוֹ יַעֲקֹב מַקַּל לִבְנֶה לַח וְלוּז
וְעַרְמוֹן וַיְפַצֵּל בָּהֵן פְּצָלוֹת לְבָנוֹת מַחְשֹׂף

## *Leaving Laban*

### JACOB, LEAH, AND RACHEL JOURNEY TOWARD A HOME IN CANAAN (30:25–31:42)

#### COMPETITION BETWEEN MEN (30:25–31:3)

*32. "speckled and spotted goat."* These animals are worth less than solid-colored goats. Jacob makes a modest request—although his intentions, along with Laban's, are surreptitious throughout this negotiation. The completion of Rachel's internal journey motivates Jacob to prepare for his return home.

*37–39.* How peeled rods can determine the color of sheep is anyone's guess, but Jacob later explains to Rachel and Leah that the technique was revealed to him during a dream communication with an angel (31:10–13).

stripping the white on the surface of the rods. 38He
set the rods he had just peeled by the water troughs,
by the trenches filled with water where the flock
was wont to drink, opposite the sheep; and they
went into heat as they approached to drink.
39When the flocks conceived in front of the rods,
[they] brought forth young that were striped,
speckled, and spotted. 40And the young rams Jacob
kept for himself, turning the faces of the flocks
toward all those sheep of Laban's that were streaked
or dark; he set apart herds for himself and did not
join them to Laban's flocks. 41So when the hardy
among the flocks went into heat, Jacob placed the
rods in the direct view of the sheep at the water
troughs, to bring them into heat by virtue of the
rods. 42But he did not put them among the sickly of
the flocks, so that the sickly ones became Laban's
and the hardy, Jacob's. 43Thus the man prospered
more and more; he had abundant flocks, female
slaves and male slaves, camels and donkeys.

הַלָּבָ֔ן אֲשֶׁ֖ר עַל־הַמַּקְלֽוֹת׃ 38 וַיַּצֵּ֗ג אֶת־
הַמַּקְלוֹת֙ אֲשֶׁ֣ר פִּצֵּ֔ל בָּרְהָטִ֖ים בְּשִֽׁקְת֣וֹת
הַמָּ֑יִם אֲשֶׁר֩ תָּבֹ֨אןָ הַצֹּ֤אן לִשְׁתּוֹת֙ לְנֹ֣כַח
הַצֹּ֔אן וַיֵּחַ֖מְנָה בְּבֹאָ֥ן לִשְׁתּֽוֹת׃ 39 וַיֶּחֱמ֥וּ
הַצֹּ֖אן אֶל־הַמַּקְל֑וֹת וַתֵּלַ֣דְןָ הַצֹּ֔אן עֲקֻדִּ֥ים
נְקֻדִּ֖ים וּטְלֻאִֽים׃ 40 וְהַכְּשָׂבִים֮ הִפְרִ֣יד יַעֲקֹב֒
וַ֠יִּתֵּן פְּנֵ֨י הַצֹּ֧אן אֶל־עָקֹ֛ד וְכָל־ח֖וּם
בְּצֹ֣אן לָבָ֑ן וַיָּֽשֶׁת־ל֤וֹ עֲדָרִים֙ לְבַדּ֔וֹ וְלֹ֥א
שָׁתָ֖ם עַל־צֹ֥אן לָבָֽן׃ 41 וְהָיָ֗ה בְּכָל־יַחֵם֮
הַצֹּ֣אן הַמְקֻשָּׁרוֹת֒ וְשָׂ֨ם יַעֲקֹ֧ב אֶת־הַמַּקְל֛וֹת
לְעֵינֵ֥י הַצֹּ֖אן בָּרְהָטִ֑ים לְיַחְמֵ֖נָּה בַּמַּקְלֽוֹת׃
42 וּבְהַעֲטִ֥יף הַצֹּ֖אן לֹ֣א יָשִׂ֑ים וְהָיָ֤ה
הָעֲטֻפִים֙ לְלָבָ֔ן וְהַקְּשֻׁרִ֖ים לְיַעֲקֹֽב׃ 43 וַיִּפְרֹ֥ץ
הָאִ֖ישׁ מְאֹ֣ד מְאֹ֑ד וַֽיְהִי־לוֹ֙ צֹ֣אן רַבּ֔וֹת
וּשְׁפָחוֹת֙ וַעֲבָדִ֔ים וּגְמַלִּ֖ים וַחֲמֹרִֽים׃

31 [Jacob] now heard the words of Laban's
sons. They were saying, "Jacob has taken all that
belongs to our father; it is from our father's possessions that he has gained all this wealth!" 2And Jacob saw Laban's countenance—plainly, it was no
longer [favorable] to him as before. 3So יהוה said
to Jacob, "Return to the land of your ancestors, to
your birthplace, and I will be with you."

4Jacob therefore summoned Rachel and Leah to
the field, to his flocks, 5and said to them, "When I
look at your father's countenance, it no longer is
[favorable] to me as in days gone by; but the God of
my father has been with me. 6Now, you are aware

לא וַיִּשְׁמַ֗ע אֶת־דִּבְרֵ֤י בְנֵֽי־לָבָן֙ לֵאמֹ֔ר
לָקַ֣ח יַעֲקֹ֔ב אֵ֖ת כָּל־אֲשֶׁ֣ר לְאָבִ֑ינוּ וּמֵאֲשֶׁ֣ר
לְאָבִ֔ינוּ עָשָׂ֕ה אֵ֥ת כָּל־הַכָּבֹ֖ד הַזֶּֽה׃ 2 וַיַּ֥רְא
יַעֲקֹ֖ב אֶת־פְּנֵ֣י לָבָ֑ן וְהִנֵּ֛ה אֵינֶ֥נּוּ עִמּ֖וֹ
כִּתְמ֥וֹל שִׁלְשֽׁוֹם׃ 3 וַיֹּ֤אמֶר יְהוָה֙ אֶל־יַעֲקֹ֔ב
שׁ֛וּב אֶל־אֶ֥רֶץ אֲבוֹתֶ֖יךָ וּלְמוֹלַדְתֶּ֑ךָ וְאֶֽהְיֶ֖ה
עִמָּֽךְ׃
4 וַיִּשְׁלַ֣ח יַעֲקֹ֔ב וַיִּקְרָ֖א לְרָחֵ֣ל וּלְלֵאָ֑ה
הַשָּׂדֶ֖ה אֶל־צֹאנֽוֹ׃ 5 וַיֹּ֣אמֶר לָהֶ֗ן רֹאֶ֤ה
אָנֹכִי֙ אֶת־פְּנֵ֣י אֲבִיכֶ֔ן כִּֽי־אֵינֶ֥נּוּ אֵלַ֖י כִּתְמֹ֣ל
שִׁלְשֹׁ֑ם וֵאלֹהֵ֣י אָבִ֔י הָיָ֖ה עִמָּדִֽי׃ 6 וְאַתֵּ֖נָה
יְדַעְתֶּ֑ן כִּ֚י בְּכָל־כֹּחִ֔י עָבַ֖דְתִּי אֶת־אֲבִיכֶֽן׃

*31:1. "Jacob has taken all that belongs to our father."* In fact, Jacob has acquired his wealth by usurping his own brother's blessing. Resentment on the part of the host culture toward Hebrew successes is likewise evident at the start of Exodus and later comprises a familiar trope in Jewish history.

*4. Rachel and Leah.* Here and in v. 14, the narrator places Rachel before Leah, consistent with the larger theme of the displaced first-born in Genesis. As with Jacob, Rachel's preeminent position in the family implies that hierarchies can be unsettled by action. Ruth 4:11 also lists Rachel prior to Leah, suggesting that Ruth's mode of contending with barrenness most closely parallels Rachel's journey to fertility.

that I have labored with all my strength for your father; 7 but your father has deceived me, changing my pay ten times—though God has not let him harm me: 8 so that if he said, 'The spotted shall be your pay,' the flocks bore spotted; and if he said, 'The streaked shall be your pay,' the flocks bore streaked. 9 God has taken away your father's livestock and given them to me. 10 One time, when the flocks were in heat, in a dream I looked up and saw that the male goats mounting the flock were streaked, spotted, and dappled. 11 In that dream an angel of God said to me: 'Jacob!' 'Here I am!' said I. 12 [The angel] said, 'Pray look up; see how the male goats mounting the flocks are striped, spotted, and mottled, for I have seen all that Laban has done to you. 13 I am the God of Beth El, where you anointed a monument, where you made Me a vow; now get up, leave this land and return to your native land.'"

14 Rachel and Leah made this response to him, "Have we any longer a portion or inheritance in our father's house? 15 Are we not like foreigners to him? He sold us and has completely eaten up our money! 16 Since all the wealth that God has taken away from our father is ours and our children's, so now do just what God has commanded you!"

17 Jacob then got up and mounted his sons and his wives on camels. 18 He drove all his livestock and all his possessions that he had acquired—the live-

7 וַאֲבִיכֶן הֵתֶל בִּי וְהֶחֱלִף אֶת־מַשְׂכֻּרְתִּי
עֲשֶׂרֶת מֹנִים וְלֹא־נְתָנוֹ אֱלֹהִים לְהָרַע
עִמָּדִי׃ 8 אִם־כֹּה יֹאמַר נְקֻדִּים יִהְיֶה
שְׂכָרֶךָ וְיָלְדוּ כָל־הַצֹּאן נְקֻדִּים וְאִם־כֹּה
יֹאמַר עֲקֻדִּים יִהְיֶה שְׂכָרֶךָ וְיָלְדוּ כָל־
הַצֹּאן עֲקֻדִּים׃ 9 וַיַּצֵּל אֱלֹהִים אֶת־מִקְנֵה
אֲבִיכֶם וַיִּתֶּן־לִי׃ 10 וַיְהִי בְּעֵת יַחֵם הַצֹּאן
וָאֶשָּׂא עֵינַי וָאֵרֶא בַּחֲלוֹם וְהִנֵּה הָעַתֻּדִים
הָעֹלִים עַל־הַצֹּאן עֲקֻדִּים נְקֻדִּים וּבְרֻדִּים׃
11 וַיֹּאמֶר אֵלַי מַלְאַךְ הָאֱלֹהִים בַּחֲלוֹם
יַעֲקֹב וָאֹמַר הִנֵּנִי׃ 12 וַיֹּאמֶר שָׂא־נָא עֵינֶיךָ
וּרְאֵה כָּל־הָעַתֻּדִים הָעֹלִים עַל־הַצֹּאן
עֲקֻדִּים נְקֻדִּים וּבְרֻדִּים כִּי רָאִיתִי אֵת כָּל־
אֲשֶׁר לָבָן עֹשֶׂה לָּךְ׃ 13 אָנֹכִי הָאֵל בֵּית־אֵל
אֲשֶׁר מָשַׁחְתָּ שָּׁם מַצֵּבָה אֲשֶׁר נָדַרְתָּ לִּי
שָׁם נֶדֶר עַתָּה קוּם צֵא מִן־הָאָרֶץ הַזֹּאת
וְשׁוּב אֶל־אֶרֶץ מוֹלַדְתֶּךָ׃

14 וַתַּעַן רָחֵל וְלֵאָה וַתֹּאמַרְנָה לוֹ הַעוֹד לָנוּ
חֵלֶק וְנַחֲלָה בְּבֵית אָבִינוּ׃ 15 הֲלוֹא נָכְרִיּוֹת
נֶחְשַׁבְנוּ לוֹ כִּי מְכָרָנוּ וַיֹּאכַל גַּם־אָכוֹל
אֶת־כַּסְפֵּנוּ׃ 16 כִּי כָל־הָעֹשֶׁר אֲשֶׁר הִצִּיל
אֱלֹהִים מֵאָבִינוּ לָנוּ הוּא וּלְבָנֵינוּ וְעַתָּה כֹּל
אֲשֶׁר אָמַר אֱלֹהִים אֵלֶיךָ עֲשֵׂה׃

17 וַיָּקָם יַעֲקֹב וַיִּשָּׂא אֶת־בָּנָיו וְאֶת־נָשָׁיו
עַל־הַגְּמַלִּים׃ 18 וַיִּנְהַג אֶת־כָּל־מִקְנֵהוּ
וְאֶת־כָּל־רְכֻשׁוֹ אֲשֶׁר רָכָשׁ מִקְנֵה קִנְיָנוֹ

## SISTERLY COLLABORATION (31:4–16)

*13.* Jacob determines Rachel and Leah's readiness to depart from their home by introducing them to the divine voice that guides him.

*14. Rachel and Leah made this response.* Previously the sisters have employed language as a mode of competition; but here they speak with one voice, indicating their common desire and alliance with Jacob—and, implicitly, with each other. (Rachel continues to display her individual will in v. 19.)

*15. "Are we not like foreigners to him?"* By acknowledging their outsider status in the household, Leah and Rachel prepare themselves to journey to an unknown land. They distinguish themselves from their father, citing the egregious manner in which he married them off and then denied them their due; see at 29:18.

stock in his possession that he had acquired in Paddan-aram—to go to his father Isaac in the land of Canaan. ([19]While Laban had gone to shear his sheep, Rachel had stolen her father's household gods, [20]and Jacob had deceived Laban the Aramean, by not informing him that he was fleeing.) [21][Jacob] fled with all that was his, going up and crossing the river and setting his face toward the hill country of Gilead.

[22][Not until] the third day was Laban told that Jacob had fled. [23]He then took his kin with him and pursued [Jacob], a seven-day trek, and caught up with him in the hill country of Gilead. [24]God then came to Laban the Aramean in a dream of the night, saying to him, "Beware lest you speak to Jacob, beginning well but ending ill."

[25]When Laban caught up to Jacob, Jacob had pitched his tent by the mountain. Laban then drove in his tent-pegs among his kinsmen near Mount Gilead. [26]Laban said to Jacob, "What have you done, deceiving me and driving my daughters off like prisoners of war? [27]Why did you flee by stealth and deceive me by not informing me? I would have sent you off with festive songs, with hand-drum and lyre! [28]Nor did you give me a chance to kiss my sons and daughters—how fool-

אֲשֶׁר רָכַשׁ בְּפַדַּן אֲרָם לָבוֹא אֶל־יִצְחָק
אָבִיו אַרְצָה כְּנָעַן׃ 19 וְלָבָן הָלַךְ לִגְזֹז אֶת־
צֹאנוֹ וַתִּגְנֹב רָחֵל אֶת־הַתְּרָפִים אֲשֶׁר
לְאָבִיהָ׃ 20 וַיִּגְנֹב יַעֲקֹב אֶת־לֵב לָבָן
הָאֲרַמִּי עַל־בְּלִי הִגִּיד לוֹ כִּי בֹרֵחַ הוּא׃
21 וַיִּבְרַח הוּא וְכָל־אֲשֶׁר־לוֹ וַיָּקָם וַיַּעֲבֹר
אֶת־הַנָּהָר וַיָּשֶׂם אֶת־פָּנָיו הַר הַגִּלְעָד׃
22 וַיֻּגַּד לְלָבָן בַּיּוֹם הַשְּׁלִישִׁי כִּי בָרַח יַעֲקֹב׃
23 וַיִּקַּח אֶת־אֶחָיו עִמּוֹ וַיִּרְדֹּף אַחֲרָיו דֶּרֶךְ
שִׁבְעַת יָמִים וַיַּדְבֵּק אֹתוֹ בְּהַר הַגִּלְעָד׃
24 וַיָּבֹא אֱלֹהִים אֶל־לָבָן הָאֲרַמִּי בַּחֲלֹם
הַלָּיְלָה וַיֹּאמֶר לוֹ הִשָּׁמֶר לְךָ פֶּן־תְּדַבֵּר עִם־
יַעֲקֹב מִטּוֹב עַד־רָע׃
25 וַיַּשֵּׂג לָבָן אֶת־יַעֲקֹב וְיַעֲקֹב תָּקַע אֶת־
אָהֳלוֹ בָּהָר וְלָבָן תָּקַע אֶת־אֶחָיו בְּהַר
הַגִּלְעָד׃ 26 וַיֹּאמֶר לָבָן לְיַעֲקֹב מֶה עָשִׂיתָ
וַתִּגְנֹב אֶת־לְבָבִי וַתְּנַהֵג אֶת־בְּנֹתַי כִּשְׁבֻיוֹת
חָרֶב׃ 27 לָמָּה נַחְבֵּאתָ לִבְרֹחַ וַתִּגְנֹב אֹתִי
וְלֹא־הִגַּדְתָּ לִּי וָאֲשַׁלֵּחֲךָ בְּשִׂמְחָה וּבְשִׁרִים
בְּתֹף וּבְכִנּוֹר׃ 28 וְלֹא נְטַשְׁתַּנִי לְנַשֵּׁק לְבָנַי

FLIGHT, THEFT, AND PURSUIT (31:17–42)

*19. Rachel had stolen her father's household gods.* We can gain a hint of Rachel's presumed motive from the 14th-century-B.C.E. tablets of Nuzi, an ancient city in Iraq. Evidence from there suggests that possession of the household gods was associated with clan leadership or inheritance rights. Thus Rachel, like Jacob before her, deceives the father in order to gain tokens of power and authority. Once again, Rachel is a counterpart to Jacob (Ilana Pardes, *Countertraditions in the Bible*, 1992, p. 61). She may also have sought the *t'rafim* to serve as fertility gods, hoping for a second child (see Contemporary Reflection, p. 178). | The Torah includes a number of trickster stories like this, showing how marginalized men and women outwit the powerful in order to survive or safeguard justice (for example, Genesis 12:10–20; 38:1–30).

*24. God then came to Laban the Aramean in a dream.* This is the third in a series of dreams where God guides and protects Jacob.

*26. "driving my daughters off like prisoners of war."* After Rachel and Leah have voiced their desire to extricate themselves from their father and his manipulations (vv. 14–16), Laban's claim of concern for his daughters' well-being strikes the reader as hollow.

*28. "sons and daughters."* That is, his grandchildren and his daughters.

ishly you acted! 29 It is well within my power to do
you an injury, but the God of your fathers said to
me last night: Beware lest you speak to Jacob, beginning well but ending ill. 30 Now, then—you
have gone away because you yearn so desperately
for your father's house, but why did you steal my
gods?"

31 Jacob responded by saying to Laban, "Because
I was afraid—because I said [to myself]—suppose
you steal your daughters from me. 32 But the one
with whom you find your gods shall not live; see for
yourself—in front of our kin—what I have with me
and take it back!" Jacob did not know that Rachel
had stolen them.

33 Laban then entered Jacob's tent and Leah's
tent and the tent of the two maids and found nothing. He then left Leah's tent and entered Rachel's
tent. 34 Rachel had taken the household gods and
put them in the camel's saddlebag and was sitting
on them as Laban rummaged through everything
in the tent and found nothing. 35 She now said to
her father, "May my lord not take offense that I
cannot get up in your presence, for the way of
women is upon me." He searched but did not find
the household gods.

36 Jacob then grew angry and berated Laban;
Jacob spoke up by saying to Laban, "What is my
transgression? What is my sin, that you pursued me
so hotly, 37 that you felt all my goods? What did you
find of all your household goods? Put it here before
my kin and yours, and let them decide between us!
38 These twenty years that I have been with you

וְלִבְנֹתָ֑י עַתָּ֖ה הִסְכַּ֥לְתָּ עֲשֽׂוֹ׃ 29 יֶשׁ־לְאֵ֣ל יָדִ֔י
לַעֲשׂ֥וֹת עִמָּכֶ֖ם רָ֑ע וֵאלֹהֵ֨י אֲבִיכֶ֜ם אֶ֣מֶשׁ ׀
אָמַ֧ר אֵלַ֣י לֵאמֹ֗ר הִשָּׁ֧מֶר לְךָ֛ מִדַּבֵּ֥ר עִֽם־
יַעֲקֹ֖ב מִטּ֥וֹב עַד־רָֽע׃ 30 וְעַתָּה֙ הָלֹ֣ךְ הָלַ֔כְתָּ
כִּֽי־נִכְסֹ֥ף נִכְסַ֖פְתָּה לְבֵ֣ית אָבִ֑יךָ לָ֥מָּה גָנַ֖בְתָּ
אֶת־אֱלֹהָֽי׃
31 וַיַּ֥עַן יַעֲקֹ֖ב וַיֹּ֣אמֶר לְלָבָ֑ן כִּ֣י יָרֵ֔אתִי
כִּ֣י אָמַ֔רְתִּי פֶּן־תִּגְזֹ֥ל אֶת־בְּנוֹתֶ֖יךָ מֵעִמִּֽי׃
32 עִ֠ם אֲשֶׁ֨ר תִּמְצָ֣א אֶת־אֱלֹהֶ֘יךָ֮ לֹ֣א יִֽחְיֶה֒
נֶ֣גֶד אַחֵ֧ינוּ הַֽכֶּר־לְךָ֛ מָ֥ה עִמָּדִ֖י וְקַֽח־לָ֑ךְ
וְלֹֽא־יָדַ֣ע יַעֲקֹ֔ב כִּ֥י רָחֵ֖ל גְּנָבָֽתַם׃
33 וַיָּבֹ֨א לָבָ֜ן בְּאֹ֥הֶל־יַעֲקֹ֣ב ׀ וּבְאֹ֣הֶל לֵאָ֗ה
וּבְאֹ֛הֶל שְׁתֵּ֥י הָאֲמָהֹ֖ת וְלֹ֣א מָצָ֑א וַיֵּצֵא֙
מֵאֹ֣הֶל לֵאָ֔ה וַיָּבֹ֖א בְּאֹ֥הֶל רָחֵֽל׃ 34 וְרָחֵ֞ל
לָקְחָ֣ה אֶת־הַתְּרָפִ֗ים וַתְּשִׂמֵ֛ם בְּכַ֥ר הַגָּמָ֖ל
וַתֵּ֣שֶׁב עֲלֵיהֶ֑ם וַיְמַשֵּׁ֥שׁ לָבָ֛ן אֶת־כָּל־הָאֹ֖הֶל
וְלֹ֥א מָצָֽא׃ 35 וַתֹּ֣אמֶר אֶל־אָבִ֗יהָ אַל־יִ֙חַר֙
בְּעֵינֵ֣י אֲדֹנִ֔י כִּ֣י ל֤וֹא אוּכַל֙ לָק֣וּם מִפָּנֶ֔יךָ כִּי־
דֶ֥רֶךְ נָשִׁ֖ים לִ֑י וַיְחַפֵּ֕שׂ וְלֹ֥א מָצָ֖א אֶת־
הַתְּרָפִֽים׃
36 וַיִּ֥חַר לְיַעֲקֹ֖ב וַיָּ֣רֶב בְּלָבָ֑ן וַיַּ֤עַן יַעֲקֹב֙
וַיֹּ֣אמֶר לְלָבָ֔ן מַה־פִּשְׁעִי֙ מַ֣ה חַטָּאתִ֔י כִּ֥י
דָלַ֖קְתָּ אַחֲרָֽי׃ 37 כִּֽי־מִשַּׁ֣שְׁתָּ אֶת־כָּל־כֵּלַ֗י
מַה־מָּצָ֙אתָ֙ מִכֹּ֣ל כְּלֵי־בֵיתֶ֔ךָ שִׂ֣ים כֹּ֔ה נֶ֥גֶד
אַחַ֖י וְאַחֶ֑יךָ וְיוֹכִ֖יחוּ בֵּ֥ין שְׁנֵֽינוּ׃ 38 זֶה֩
עֶשְׂרִ֨ים שָׁנָ֤ה אָנֹכִי֙ עִמָּ֔ךְ רְחֵלֶ֥יךָ וְעִזֶּ֖יךָ לֹ֣א

32. ***"the one with whom you find your gods shall not live."*** Through law and story alike, the Torah as well as later Jewish tradition warns against oath-taking. Jacob's oath here is often cited by commentators as the reason for Rachel's untimely death (35:18). (For a different perspective, see Contemporary Reflection, p. 178.) | This verse provides further evidence of Rachel's concern for her own status and survival.

35. ***"the way of women is upon me."*** With poetic euphemism, Rachel staves off her father by playing on masculine fears about menstruation. The irony is that these same fears result in the type of purity laws and prohibitions concerning menstruating women that would categorize bleeding on gods as an act of contamination (Leviticus 15:20). The ruse displays Rachel's cleverness. (On menstruation, see at Leviticus 15:19–32.)

your ewes and your she-goats never miscarried, and I never ate the rams of your flocks; [39]I never brought you an animal torn up by wild beasts; I made good the loss from my own possessions, when you demanded it [for] a sheep stolen by day or by night. [40]For me it was: by day the heat consumed me, and the cold by night—and sleep fled from my eyes. [41]Thus it was for me: twenty years I served you in your house—fourteen years for your two daughters, and six years for your flocks; and you changed my pay ten times! [42]Had not the God of my father—the God of Abraham, the Fear of Isaac—been for me, you would right now be driving me away empty-handed; but God saw my affliction and hard labor and warned [you] last night!"

[43]Laban then responded by saying to Jacob, "The daughters are my daughters and the sons are my sons and the flocks are my flocks; everything that you see is really mine! But as for my daughters, what can I now do about them or the sons that they have borne? [44]So now, come, let us make a pact, you and I, and let it be a witness between us!"

[45]Jacob then took a stone and raised it up as a monument. [46]And Jacob said to his kin, "Gather stones"; so they took stones and made a mound; they then ate there by the mound. [47]Laban called it Yegar-sahadutha, while Jacob called it Galeid.

[48]Laban said, "This mound is a witness between us today"; therefore he [Jacob] had named it Galeid, [49]and [this is] the Mitzpah about which he [Laban] said, "May יהוה keep watch between you and me, when we are hidden one from the other! [50]Should you mistreat my daughters or take wives in addition to my daughters, [though] no one else is

שִׁכֵּלוּ וְאֵילֵי צֹאנְךָ לֹא אָכָלְתִּי׃ 39 טְרֵפָה
לֹא־הֵבֵאתִי אֵלֶיךָ אָנֹכִי אֲחַטֶּנָּה מִיָּדִי
תְּבַקְשֶׁנָּה גְּנֻבְתִי יוֹם וּגְנֻבְתִי לָיְלָה׃
40 הָיִיתִי בַיּוֹם אֲכָלַנִי חֹרֶב וְקֶרַח בַּלָּיְלָה
וַתִּדַּד שְׁנָתִי מֵעֵינָי׃ 41 זֶה־לִּי עֶשְׂרִים שָׁנָה
בְּבֵיתֶךָ עֲבַדְתִּיךָ אַרְבַּע־עֶשְׂרֵה שָׁנָה בִּשְׁתֵּי
בְנֹתֶיךָ וְשֵׁשׁ שָׁנִים בְּצֹאנֶךָ וַתַּחֲלֵף אֶת־
מַשְׂכֻּרְתִּי עֲשֶׂרֶת מֹנִים׃ 42 לוּלֵי אֱלֹהֵי אָבִי
אֱלֹהֵי אַבְרָהָם וּפַחַד יִצְחָק הָיָה לִי כִּי
עַתָּה רֵיקָם שִׁלַּחְתָּנִי אֶת־עָנְיִי וְאֶת־יְגִיעַ
כַּפַּי רָאָה אֱלֹהִים וַיּוֹכַח אָמֶשׁ׃
43 וַיַּעַן לָבָן וַיֹּאמֶר אֶל־יַעֲקֹב הַבָּנוֹת בְּנֹתַי
וְהַבָּנִים בָּנַי וְהַצֹּאן צֹאנִי וְכֹל אֲשֶׁר־אַתָּה
רֹאֶה לִי־הוּא וְלִבְנֹתַי מָה־אֶעֱשֶׂה לָאֵלֶּה
הַיּוֹם אוֹ לִבְנֵיהֶן אֲשֶׁר יָלָדוּ׃ 44 וְעַתָּה לְכָה
נִכְרְתָה בְרִית אֲנִי וָאָתָּה וְהָיָה לְעֵד בֵּינִי
וּבֵינֶךָ׃
45 וַיִּקַּח יַעֲקֹב אָבֶן וַיְרִימֶהָ מַצֵּבָה׃
46 וַיֹּאמֶר יַעֲקֹב לְאֶחָיו לִקְטוּ אֲבָנִים וַיִּקְחוּ
אֲבָנִים וַיַּעֲשׂוּ־גָל וַיֹּאכְלוּ שָׁם עַל־הַגָּל׃
47 וַיִּקְרָא־לוֹ לָבָן יְגַר שָׂהֲדוּתָא וְיַעֲקֹב
קָרָא לוֹ גַּלְעֵד׃
48 וַיֹּאמֶר לָבָן הַגַּל הַזֶּה עֵד בֵּינִי וּבֵינְךָ הַיּוֹם
עַל־כֵּן קָרָא־שְׁמוֹ גַּלְעֵד׃ 49 וְהַמִּצְפָּה אֲשֶׁר
אָמַר יִצֶף יְהֹוָה בֵּינִי וּבֵינֶךָ כִּי נִסָּתֵר אִישׁ
מֵרֵעֵהוּ׃ 50 אִם־תְּעַנֶּה אֶת־בְּנֹתַי וְאִם־תִּקַּח
נָשִׁים עַל־בְּנֹתַי אֵין אִישׁ עִמָּנוּ רְאֵה אֱלֹהִים

## *Reconciliation and Separation of Jacob and Laban* (31:43–32:3)

In the parashah's concluding scene, Jacob sets a border between himself and his Syrian relative and thereby ratifies a peace treaty. The tension that suffuses their dialogue will erupt into future hostilities between the nations of Israel and of Aram, but this first treaty makes them equal partners. The scene itself is composed of doublets: two stones, two meals, two maps, two Gods, and two levels to the treaty—one familial and one political.

with us, consider! God is witness between you and
me." 51And Laban said [additionally] to Jacob,
"Behold this mound and behold this monument
that I have raised between us. 52This mound is a
witness, this monument is a witness, that I shall
never pass this mound toward you [intending
harm], and that you shall never pass this mound
and this monument toward me, intending harm.
53Let [both] the god of Abraham and the god of
Nahor—the god of each one's father—judge between us!" And Jacob swore by the Fear of his
father Isaac. 54Jacob then offered a sacrifice by the
mountain, inviting his kin to eat bread. They ate
bread and stayed the night by the mountain.

32 In the morning Laban got up early, kissed
his sons and his daughters and blessed them; then
he went home. So Laban returned to his place.
2Now Jacob went on his way and angels of God
met him. 3And when he saw them, Jacob said,
"This is the camp of God!" So he named that place
Mahanaim.

עֵ֖ד בֵּינִ֥י וּבֵינֶֽךָ׃ 51 וַיֹּ֥אמֶר לָבָ֖ן לְיַעֲקֹ֑ב הִנֵּ֣ה ׀
הַגַּ֣ל הַזֶּ֗ה וְהִנֵּה֙ הַמַּצֵּבָ֔ה אֲשֶׁ֥ר יָרִ֖יתִי בֵּינִ֥י
וּבֵינֶֽךָ׃ 52 עֵ֚ד הַגַּ֣ל הַזֶּ֔ה וְעֵדָ֖ה הַמַּצֵּבָ֑ה אִם־
אָ֗נִי לֹֽא־אֶעֱבֹ֤ר אֵלֶ֙יךָ֙ אֶת־הַגַּ֣ל הַזֶּ֔ה וְאִם־
אַ֠תָּה לֹא־תַעֲבֹ֨ר אֵלַ֜י אֶת־הַגַּ֥ל הַזֶּ֛ה וְאֶת־
הַמַּצֵּבָ֥ה הַזֹּ֖את לְרָעָֽה׃ 53 אֱלֹהֵ֨י אַבְרָהָ֜ם
וֵאלֹהֵ֤י נָחוֹר֙ יִשְׁפְּט֣וּ בֵינֵ֔ינוּ אֱלֹהֵ֖י אֲבִיהֶ֑ם
וַיִּשָּׁבַ֣ע יַעֲקֹ֔ב בְּפַ֖חַד אָבִ֥יו יִצְחָֽק׃ 54 וַיִּזְבַּ֨ח
יַעֲקֹ֥ב זֶ֙בַח֙ בָּהָ֔ר וַיִּקְרָ֥א לְאֶחָ֖יו לֶאֱכָל־לָ֑חֶם
וַיֹּ֣אכְלוּ לֶ֔חֶם וַיָּלִ֖ינוּ בָּהָֽר׃

לב וַיַּשְׁכֵּ֨ם לָבָ֜ן בַּבֹּ֗קֶר וַיְנַשֵּׁ֛ק לְבָנָ֥יו
וְלִבְנוֹתָ֖יו וַיְבָ֣רֶךְ אֶתְהֶ֑ם וַיֵּ֛לֶךְ וַיָּ֥שָׁב לָבָ֖ן
לִמְקֹמֽוֹ׃ 2 וְיַעֲקֹ֖ב הָלַ֣ךְ לְדַרְכּ֑וֹ וַיִּפְגְּעוּ־ב֖וֹ
מַלְאֲכֵ֥י אֱלֹהִֽים׃ 3 וַיֹּ֤אמֶר יַעֲקֹב֙ כַּאֲשֶׁ֣ר
רָאָ֔ם מַחֲנֵ֥ה אֱלֹהִ֖ים זֶ֑ה וַיִּקְרָ֛א שֵֽׁם־הַמָּק֥וֹם
הַה֖וּא מַחֲנָֽיִם׃ פ

---

*52.* ***"This mound is a witness."*** That is, to the treaty that stipulates that Jacob must not mistreat Rachel or Leah, and that neither Jacob nor Laban will cross the border to attack the other. The stone monument of Rachel's tomb (Genesis 35:20) will likewise mark the boundary of the territory of Benjamin (I Samuel 10:2). Rachel and Jacob are both figures associated with borders.

*54.* Peacefully camping side by side affords Laban the good-bye kisses that he claimed he was denied (v. 28).

*32:2–3.* ***Now Jacob went on his way and angels of God met him.*** As Jacob retreats from the border and heads homeward, he crosses an additional boundary guarded by angels.

***Mahanaim.*** In the company of angels, Jacob recognizes the place as "the camp of God" and himself as the dweller in Mahanaim, "Two Camps." This encounter with angels indicates that he crosses the threshold between home and exile, as well as that between heaven and earth.

*—Rachel Havrelock*

# Another View

For many, the love story between Rachel and Jacob shows the text's preference for Rachel over Leah. If one reads the story through modern eyes, where love conquers all, then Rachel seems to be more important than Leah. However, if one reads this parashah with an eye toward its own biblical concerns, then Rachel and Leah look very different.

The love story begins with Jacob seeing Rachel (29:10). The text notes that Rachel is "beautiful of form and of face" (v. 17). To modern readers beauty is positive, but in the Hebrew Bible it is dangerous for women. Abram charges that Sarai's beauty threatens his life (12:11–12), and Amnon rapes Tamar, supposedly because of her beauty (II Samuel 13). In other places in the Bible, when people make choices because of what they see, those choices prove to be misguided. For example, Lot chooses to live in the Jordan plain because it looks nicer than Canaan (Genesis 13:10–11). Samson marries a Philistine woman because of her appearance (Judges 14:1–3), and the results are disastrous. Clearly the Bible does not recommend judging a book by its cover.

The text notes that "seeing Leah was disfavored, יהוה opened her womb" (Genesis 29:31). This clearly means that the Deity sympathized with Leah. Leah names her first child Reuben because of a play on words that the Deity saw her plight, but she adds what she hopes it will bring her: the love of her husband (v. 32). The second child follows the same pattern; Simeon is so named because God "heard" of her plight (v. 33). The third son, Levi, is named in the hope that her husband will be attached to her (v. 34). All three names reflect not only thankfulness but also a need for more—namely, Jacob's love. With her fourth son, something finally changes and she names him Judah because, "This time I give thanks to יהוה" (v. 35). Thus Judah, who becomes the forefather of most of the Jewish people, is so named because his mother was simply thankful to the Deity to have him.

*In the Hebrew Bible, beauty is dangerous for women.*

*—Tammi J. Schneider*

# Post-biblical Interpretations

***Now Laban had two daughters*** (29:16). Midrash *B'reishit Rabbah* 70.15 portrays the sisters Rachel and Leah as equal partners in building the Jewish people: "Both produced chieftains and kings. . . . Both produced prophets and judges." Leah was "greater in gifts," in that her sons were the ancestors of the priests and the Davidic kings.

***Leah's eyes were weak*** (29:16). In *B'reishit Rabbah* 70.16, Rabbi Yohanan explains that Leah's eyes had grown weak from weeping. It had been expected that Rebekah's two sons would marry Laban's two daughters—and Esau was intended for Leah. Hearing negative reports about Esau's conduct, Leah had wept, praying that her destiny would change. Rabbi Huna observes that Leah's prayer had been powerful enough to alter her fate, but in the process her eyes were permanently affected.

***In the morning*** (29:25). The commentators are amazed that Leah fooled Jacob. After living in Laban's house for seven years, surely Jacob could tell Rachel and Leah apart! Furthermore, how did Laban prevent Rachel from warning Jacob of the deception? Midrash *Eichah Rabbah*, proem 24, explains that Rachel was a willing—albeit unhappy—partner to Laban's plan. In this midrash, Rachel recounts her version of the events of Genesis 29. Aware that her father was plotting to deceive Jacob, she warned her future husband of Laban's plans. Jacob and Rachel agreed upon a sign to allow Jacob to distinguish between the sisters. But then, Rachel changed her mind, realizing that if Laban's plan failed, Leah would be shamed. Instead of thwarting her father's plot, Rachel aided her sister in the deception: "That evening, my sister took my place with Jacob and I taught her the signs I had given him

> *"I showed kindness to my sister; I saved her from disgrace."*

so that he would think she was Rachel. I also hid under the bed upon which they lay, and when Jacob spoke to my sister, I responded while she was silent so that he would not recognize her voice. In this way, I showed kindness to my sister; I did not act on my jealousy and saved her from disgrace."

***Laban then gave his maid Bilhah*** (29:29). According to the 11th-century commentator Rashi, the slaves Bilhah and Zilpah were Laban's daughters by his concubine, thus suitable mothers of four of the tribes of Israel (on 31:50). The childless Rachel's use of Bilhah parallels Sarah's earlier use of Hagar in 16:1–3 (*B'reishit Rabbah* 71.7). Leah's motives in giving Zilpah to Jacob are less clear; some commentators suggest that Leah acted to ensure that Jacob would father twelve sons. The Midrash *Tanna D'Vei Eliyahu Rabbah* 25 (Ish-Shalom edn., p. 138) counts Rachel's and Leah's willingness to offer their maidservants to Jacob as among the righteous acts of the matriarchs that led to Israel's redemption from Egypt. Some traditions include Bilhah and Zilpah among the matriarchs (*B'midbar Rabbah* 12; *Shir HaShirim Rabbah* 6; *P'sikta D'Rav Kahana* 1.10).

***"Let me have children"*** (30:1). Rachel's demand is understood by rabbinic tradition as a complaint against Jacob. She expects him to pray on her behalf, as his father Isaac did for Rebekah. Jacob was criticized by some rabbis for his harsh reply (*B'reishit Rabbah* 71.7). Isaac Arama, a 15th-century commentator in Spain, attributed Jacob's frustration to Rachel's insistence that a childless woman is worthless. He argues that women have two functions: like men, they can develop their intellectual and spiritual qualities, and they can also bear and raise children. Jacob wants Rachel to recognize that she can have a meaningful life even if she has no children (*Akedat Yitzchak* on Genesis 3:20).

***Afterwards she bore a daughter*** (30:21). The power of Leah's prayers is again emphasized in BT *B'rachot* 60a. Commenting on "afterwards," Rav suggests that after she discovered she was pregnant, "Leah reasoned, 'Jacob is destined to father twelve tribes. I have given birth to six sons, and the handmaidens have borne four. If this child is a son, my sister Rachel won't be equal even to the handmaidens.' Immediately, the child [in her womb] was transformed to a female." In other versions of this miraculous demonstration of the efficacy of prayer, the handmaidens, Bilhah and Zilpah, join Leah in prayers on Rachel's behalf (*B'reishit Rabbah* 72.6).

***Reuben went and found mandrakes*** (30:14). In *B'reishit Rabbah* 72.5, the sages explain that through these mandrakes two additional tribes came into being, Issachar and Zebulun. Leah's willingness to barter with her sister allowed her to attain precedence as the mother of six tribes and to merit burial at Jacob's side (*B'reishit Rabbah* 72.3).

*—Dvora E. Weisberg*

# Contemporary Reflection

In Genesis 31, Jacob calls his wives Rachel and Leah out to the field and confidentially expresses his desire to return to Canaan. *Vataan Rachel v'Leah* (31:14): Rachel and Leah respond in one voice—as indicated by the singular verb form—expressing a shared anger against their father and a willingness to leave Haran. Jacob then gets up, places his wives and sons on camels, carries off his cattle and other property, and departs.

At first, Jacob appears as the central actor in this narrative. Everything is said and done in relation to him, stated in masculine possessive terms. In 31:19, however, Rachel seizes the opportunity afforded by Laban's going off to shear his sheep to steal her father's *t'rafim.* Until this point, Rachel and Leah have followed a course initiated by Jacob and his concerns. Here, however, Rachel initiates and plots her own destiny. So much so that in the next verse Jacob is seen as following Rachel's lead: Rachel stole the *t'rafim* (v. 19) and Jacob "stole the mind (literally: heart) of Laban the Aramean" (v. 20).

Jacob re-assumes center stage in the narrative when Laban overtakes him on his journey and the two men begin to air their respective grievances. But from the moment Rachel steals the *t'rafim,* Jacob ceases to control the action or facts. It is in a condition of ironic ignorance that Jacob makes his rash pronouncement (v. 32): "But the one with whom you find your gods shall not live." (Compare Jephthah's vow in Judges 11:30 to sacrifice the first to come out to meet him, a vow that leads him to sacrifice his daughter.)

Several midrashic sources contend that Jacob's death sentence for the theft of Laban's *t'rafim* is borne out in Rachel's tragic death after giving birth to Benjamin (for example, *B'reishit Rabbah* 74.32). According to a plain reading of Genesis 31, however, Rachel emerges from the episode victorious and unscathed. After all, Jacob's curse is conditioned upon Laban actually finding the *t'rafim* in someone's possession—something that Laban never accomplishes.

Laban conducts a thorough search of Jacob's camp: Jacob's tent, Leah's, the two maidservants', and Rachel's—*v'lo matza* (and he finds nothing), a verb construction that appears three times (31:33, 34, 35). What has Rachel done to elude her father? She has placed the *t'rafim* in a camel's saddle (echoing how Jacob put his wives and sons onto camels in v. 17) and conceals them by sitting on this same saddle. She then shrewdly apologizes to her father for not obeying usual custom and rising before him as he searches her tent. "The way of women is upon me" (31:35), Rachel claims, cunningly manipulating the (male) menstruation taboo to her own advantage.

*The theft is a story about women's potential to use and craft language.*

What are these *t'rafim* that Rachel risks so much to steal? What did they stand for in Rachel's time, and what do they mean for us today?

According to Rashi, the 11th-century commentator, the *t'rafim* were household idols that Rachel steals from her father for pious, monotheistic reasons: "in order to distance him from the practice of idol worship." This interpretation clearly stems from rabbinic discomfort with the idea of Rachel as idol worshipper. But if Rachel were so angry with her father as to be willing to leave his house forever without so much as a goodbye, would she really care about his spiritual fate?

Based on other instances in the Bible where the same word appears, other traditional exegetes identify the *t'rafim* with the practice of divination. Thus, Rachel steals the *t'rafim,* which were used by ancient magicians as a means of telling the future, in order to prevent Laban from knowing Jacob's plans or whereabouts. If that were the case, however, Rachel should have simply broken them. Why does she go to the trouble of stealing them, hiding them in a saddle, and tricking her father?

Several contemporary biblical scholars have argued that possession of the "household gods" was related to issues of clan leadership or inheritance. Accordingly, the *t'rafim* are symbolic tokens that indicate Rachel's right to take her children and possessions away from her father and hand them over to her husband. And yet, Rachel's decision not to inform Jacob of her theft of the *t'rafim* suggests that she acts for her own sake, not Jacob's.

Along these lines, feminist biblical scholar J. E. Lapsley argues that Rachel steals the *t'rafim* because her status as a woman in a patriarchal household prevents her from confronting her father with her own grievances about her rightful inheritance. "Therefore, she goes about getting justice from her father through devious and extra-legal means" ("The Voice of Rachel," *Genesis: A Feminist Companion to the Bible (Second Series)*, ed. Athalya Brenner, 1998, p. 238). In telling her father that she cannot "rise before" him because the "way of women is upon her," Rachel is "speaking two languages simultaneously." Laban hears Rachel as saying that she cannot honor him by standing because she is menstruating. But Rachel's speech also reads as a complaint that she has no forum for rising before her father and pleading her case for inheritance; the social "way of women" constrains her possibilities for speech, advocacy, and direct action. According to Lapsley, Rachel's "subversive action in stealing the *t'rafim* is matched by her equally subversive undermining of male definitions of women and her creation of new meanings out of male-generated language" (p. 242). According to this interpretation, Rachel steals not only the *t'rafim* but also the *language* that has been used by this patriarchy to define her as woman and limit her access to culture and law.

Rachel thus emerges from this story as an archetypal feminist writer, who dares to steal across the border of masculine culture, seize control of her cultural inheritance, and make it her own. Understood this way, the theft of the *t'rafim* becomes a story about women's potential to use and craft language, both holy and mundane, in all of its many meanings, to speak potently—and cause others to listen.

—*Wendy Zierler*

# Voices

## Posit

Linda Stern Zisquit

*Genesis 29–30*

Had Rachel not looked up
Jacob would not have seen her.
There would have been no water,
no winding dream,
no tribe or unrelenting
portion of sadness
dispersed on his land, his Jerusalem,
and I would not have promised
to gather them home. But Rachel
saw him and he loved her.
She was barren and she suffered
and she followed him.
So I have this heaviness
to bear. Her life before him
had also the dailiness of lives,
an hour at which she would rise and go
to the well. Then out of the blue
her future came crashing against her lids
when she looked up, those hours changed,
and I was moved to his, another well.

## The Tune to Jacob Who Removed the Stone from the Mouth of the Well

Rivka Miriam (transl. Linda Stern Zisquit)

*Genesis 29*

He didn't know I was Leah
and I—I was Leah.
Rachel, he said, Rachel, like a lamb
the grass becomes part of, stems are part of you.
Flocks of sheep hummed between our blankets,
tent-flies were pulled to the wind.
Rachel, he said, Rachel—
and my eyes, they were weak
the bottom of a dark swamp.
The whites of his eyes melted
to the whites of my eyes.
The cords of his tent held fast to the ground
while the wind was blowing from the palms
of my hands.

And he didn't know I was Leah
and flocks of sons broke through my womb
to his hands.

## At the Well

Malka Heifetz Tussman (transl. Marcia Falk)

*Genesis 29:1–8*

My whole life straining—
and but a crack
I've moved the stone from the well
where in darkness
the water is clear.
And now, when a star
blinks there,
at once
I taste tomorrow's tears.

## *Leah*

Shirley Kaufman

*Genesis 29*

I do what I have to
like an obedient daughter
or a dog. Not for your fingers
in my flesh. I watch you
every day as you watch her.
Since I'm the ugly one,
the one pushed into your bed
at night when you can't
tell the difference.

I've got another
son inside me, and still
you watch her. She doesn't
sag as I do after each birth
until you fill me again.

Why can't you look at me
in daylight, or take
my hand and press it
against your mouth?
I'm not a stone, a shell
your foot rolls over
in the sand. The life
gone out of it.
Maybe I am.
Your sons have sucked me
empty and dull.

I leave your tent at dawn
and walk to the river where I
throw my clothes off,
and the water shows me
my body floating
on the surface. It shivers
when I touch the blue dome
of your unborn child.

I touch my unwanted self
where the smooth skin
stretches over my breasts,
the silver veins. I'm cold.

I enter the water
as you enter me. Quick.
Like insects doing it while
they fly. The shock of it
lifts me,
and I swim raging
against the stream.

## *from* Leah to Her Sister

Sherry Blumberg

*Genesis 29:17*

My eyes are weak
But my body is strong
I'm not afraid to work
I have worked and will work
And someday will bear children

My eyes are weak
But my resolve is strong
I shall have my due
First to be married
First to bear children
Yet I'll not be as loved as you

My eyes are weak
But my love is strong
For I have loved you
You shall become a legend
I will always be second
Even in memory and in prayer

## *Zilpah*

Jill Hammer

*Genesis 30:9–13*

Rachel called me your friend;
we both hated that. We were more than girls
giggling at shepherds.
We were two hours in a day.
Night yielding to the sun.
Two voices twining to make song.

Laban found us once, my hair
falling over your body like leaves
swept into the stream. Afraid
he could never get rid of you,
he made you lie with Jacob
on Rachel's wedding night.
You threatening you'd tell everything
unless he brought me to you.
So we were together
while you bore child after child.

I was jealous. Maybe you were jealous too,
that I was still high-breasted.
One night you braided my hair and took me
to him.
When the blood burst out of me,
you squeezed my hand and wept:
"Here I am; I am sorry." Then you went
back to him
and bore a daughter.

Now I have my own tent: not what we wanted.
Our hair is grayer. On rare mornings
we slide, infant-laden, onto the same pillow
and touch each other's faces. Sun yielding
to night.

## *Rachel Solo*

Alicia Suskin Ostriker

*Genesis 31:19, 31–35*

Not getting mad, just getting even,
Papa, I'll say goodbye to you,
I'll load my camel with my goods
And take your household idols too,
And should you come in search of them
With indignation red and blue,
I'll sit upon your statuettes
And make good use of a bad taboo.
*Papa,* I'll say, *forgive me but*
*My monthly's here; don't misconstrue*
*This failure to get up*. . . . And you'll
Back off in dread. That's what you'll do.

## *Sorrow Song*

Rahel (transl. Wendy Zierler)

*Genesis 29:20–28*

Will you hear my voice, my distant one,
will you hear my voice, wherever you are—
a voice calling strong, a voice crying silently
and above time, commanding blessing?

This world is wide with many paths.
They meet narrowly, part forever.
A man seeks, but his feet fail,
he cannot find what he has lost.

Maybe my last day is already near,
already near, the day of tearful parting,
I shall wait for you until my life dims,
as Rachel awaited her lover.

# וישלח ✦ Vayishlach

## GENESIS 32:4–36:43

### *From Jacob to Israel*

PARASHAT VAYISHLACH ("And he sent") features Jacob—the third and final patriarch—as he becomes the last individual to receive a personal covenant with God. In a life-transforming event, Jacob meets God face to face, and his name is changed to "Israel," which may reflect his own struggles with God. After Jacob, all future covenant renewals will be made between God and *B'nei Yisrael* (literally "the children of [the patriarch] Israel")—the Israelites as a whole, who will continue the struggle.

All of the women in this parashah (except for those in the genealogy of Esau in Genesis 36) are members of Jacob's immediate family. What stands out is the troubling story of Dinah and Shechem (Genesis 34), although Dinah's role in the narrative is revealingly minor. While she functions as a trigger for the event, the tale focuses on the relations between the men of the family of Jacob and the Canaanites among whom they have settled. The major concern in the story as told is not the personal fate of an individual woman (or man) but the political relationship between Israel and the other inhabitants in the land. Dinah becomes a symbol in the exploration of the theme of identity—of self and of other—that began with the story of Abraham.

The other women in Jacob's household appear in passing in this parashah, with Rachel's death as a poignant conclusion. In general, these passages enable us to view the women of the story as intermediaries linking together groups of men, while moving about in the social world of the male characters—who have the authority to represent both the women and the subordinate men in their households.

*Dinah becomes a symbol in the exploration of the theme of identity.*

*—Shawna Dolansky*
*Risa Levitt Kohn*

## Outline

*I.* Settling Accounts
*Jacob's Struggles with God and Men* (32:4–33:20)

- *A.* Jacob sets out to meet Esau (32:4–16)
- *B.* Jacob struggles with God (32:17–33)
- *C.* The brothers reconcile (33:1–20)

*II.* Dinah and Shechem
*Sex and Social Status* (34:1–31)

- *A.* Rape? (vv. 1–4)
- *B.* Brothers' interpretation: An outrage against Israel (vv. 5–24)
- *C.* Brothers' revenge (vv. 25–31)

*III.* Israel and B'nei Yisrael
*Covenant Renewal, Death, and Life* (35:1–36:43)

- *A.* Beth El and the renaming of Jacob/Israel (35:1–15)
- *B.* Rachel's second son and her death (35:16–21)
- *C.* Jacob's wives and children (35:22–26)
- *D.* Isaac's death (35:27–29)
- *E.* The line of Esau (36:1–43)

32:4

Jacob now sent messengers ahead of him to his brother Esau in the land of Seir, in the countryside of Edom. [5]He instructed them as follows: "Say this to my lord Esau: 'Thus says your servant Jacob: With Laban have I stayed and have lingered until just now. [6]I came to own cattle, donkeys, sheep, and male and female slaves, and I am sending my lord this message [in the hope] of pleasing you.'" [7]When the messengers came back to Jacob, they said, "We went to your brother Esau, and he, too—accompanied by four hundred men—is marching to meet you."

לב 4 וַיִּשְׁלַח יַעֲקֹב מַלְאָכִים לְפָנָיו אֶל־
עֵשָׂו אָחִיו אַרְצָה שֵׂעִיר שְׂדֵה אֱדוֹם׃ 5 וַיְצַו
אֹתָם לֵאמֹר כֹּה תֹאמְרוּן לַאדֹנִי לְעֵשָׂו כֹּה
אָמַר עַבְדְּךָ יַעֲקֹב עִם־לָבָן גַּרְתִּי וָאֵחַר עַד־
עָתָּה׃ 6 וַיְהִי־לִי שׁוֹר וַחֲמוֹר צֹאן וְעֶבֶד
וְשִׁפְחָה וָאֶשְׁלְחָה לְהַגִּיד לַאדֹנִי לִמְצֹא־חֵן
בְּעֵינֶיךָ׃ 7 וַיָּשֻׁבוּ הַמַּלְאָכִים אֶל־יַעֲקֹב
לֵאמֹר בָּאנוּ אֶל־אָחִיךָ אֶל־עֵשָׂו וְגַם הֹלֵךְ
לִקְרָאתְךָ וְאַרְבַּע־מֵאוֹת אִישׁ עִמּוֹ׃

## *Settling Accounts*

### JACOB'S STRUGGLES WITH GOD AND MEN (32:4–33:20)

Even before birth, Jacob was portrayed as a character who struggles. He struggled in the womb (25:22). He struggled with Esau for birthright and blessing (Genesis 25 and 27). After twenty years of living in Aram he struggled with Laban (Genesis 31) and, ever since he has headed back toward the land of Canaan, he has been facing a potentially dangerous encounter with his estranged brother Esau. Now, on the way home, Jacob endures a physical confrontation with God—and as a result, has his name changed to Israel. The struggle between humans and God is a prevalent theme in the Hebrew Bible that culminates not with Jacob/Israel, but with *B'nei Yisrael*, his descendants—who continually engage in either avoidance of, or confrontation with, their God.

### JACOB SETS OUT TO MEET ESAU (32:4–16)

According to the preceding narrative, Jacob had wronged his brother, Esau, and then left home (27:1–28:5). Now Esau comes to meet Jacob with four hundred men, and Jacob is terrified. Jacob responds by making use of his two greatest assets: a wily mind, and God's covenant with his ancestors.

*4. **messengers.*** Heb. *malach*, the same word as in v. 2 (just before this parashah begins), where it was translated "angels."


◗ How to account for Jacob's prominence over Esau? It begins with their mother's decision.

ANOTHER VIEW ➤ *202*

◗ Dinah's story challenges us to be also the voices for all of our sisters.

CONTEMPORARY REFLECTION ➤ *204*

◗ Because Rebekah's life ended in such a lonely way, the Torah only hints at her passing.

POST-BIBLICAL INTERPRETATIONS ➤ *202*

◗ Dinah tried to imagine having a story of her own to tell, of connections she had made.

VOICES ➤ *206*

[8]Jacob was terrified. So anxious was he, that he divided the people who were with him—and the flocks, the herds, and the camels—into two camps. [9]He thought: "If Esau advances on the first camp and strikes it, the remaining camp will be able to escape." [10]Then Jacob said, "God of my father Abraham and God of my father Isaac, יהוה who says to me, 'Return to your native land and I will make things go well with you'! [11]I am unworthy of all the proofs of mercy and all the faithfulness that You have shown Your servant. For I crossed this Jordan with [nothing but] my walking stick, and now I have become [these] two camps! [12]Save me, I pray, from my brother's hand, from Esau's hand! I am afraid of him, lest he advance on me and strike me, mother [falling] on child. [13]Yet You said, 'I will make things go well with you and make your descendants like the grains of sand along the seashore, which are too many to be counted.'"

[14]After spending the night there, he chose an offering for his brother Esau from what was at hand—[15]200 goats and 20 he-goats, 200 ewes and 20 rams, [16]30 milch camels and their young, 40 cows and 10 bulls, 20 she-asses and 10 he-asses. [17]He put his slaves in charge of each drove separately, saying to his slaves, "Pass before me and leave some distance between one drove and the next." [18]He instructed the first as follows, "If my brother Esau meets you and asks you, 'To whom do

8 וַיִּירָא יַעֲקֹב מְאֹד וַיֵּצֶר לוֹ וַיַּחַץ אֶת־
הָעָם אֲשֶׁר־אִתּוֹ וְאֶת־הַצֹּאן וְאֶת־הַבָּקָר
וְהַגְּמַלִּים לִשְׁנֵי מַחֲנוֹת׃ 9 וַיֹּאמֶר אִם־יָבוֹא
עֵשָׂו אֶל־הַמַּחֲנֶה הָאַחַת וְהִכָּהוּ וְהָיָה
הַמַּחֲנֶה הַנִּשְׁאָר לִפְלֵיטָה׃ 10 וַיֹּאמֶר יַעֲקֹב
אֱלֹהֵי אָבִי אַבְרָהָם וֵאלֹהֵי אָבִי יִצְחָק יְהוָה
הָאֹמֵר אֵלַי שׁוּב לְאַרְצְךָ וּלְמוֹלַדְתְּךָ
וְאֵיטִיבָה עִמָּךְ׃ 11 קָטֹנְתִּי מִכֹּל הַחֲסָדִים
וּמִכָּל־הָאֱמֶת אֲשֶׁר עָשִׂיתָ אֶת־עַבְדֶּךָ כִּי
בְמַקְלִי עָבַרְתִּי אֶת־הַיַּרְדֵּן הַזֶּה וְעַתָּה
הָיִיתִי לִשְׁנֵי מַחֲנוֹת׃ 12 הַצִּילֵנִי נָא מִיַּד
אָחִי מִיַּד עֵשָׂו כִּי־יָרֵא אָנֹכִי אֹתוֹ פֶּן־יָבוֹא
וְהִכַּנִי אֵם עַל־בָּנִים׃ 13 וְאַתָּה אָמַרְתָּ הֵיטֵב
אֵיטִיב עִמָּךְ וְשַׂמְתִּי אֶת־זַרְעֲךָ כְּחוֹל הַיָּם
אֲשֶׁר לֹא־יִסָּפֵר מֵרֹב׃

14 וַיָּלֶן שָׁם בַּלַּיְלָה הַהוּא וַיִּקַּח מִן־הַבָּא
בְיָדוֹ מִנְחָה לְעֵשָׂו אָחִיו׃ 15 עִזִּים מָאתַיִם
וּתְיָשִׁים עֶשְׂרִים רְחֵלִים מָאתַיִם וְאֵילִים
עֶשְׂרִים׃ 16 גְּמַלִּים מֵינִיקוֹת וּבְנֵיהֶם
שְׁלֹשִׁים פָּרוֹת אַרְבָּעִים וּפָרִים עֲשָׂרָה
אֲתֹנֹת עֶשְׂרִים וַעְיָרִם עֲשָׂרָה׃ 17 וַיִּתֵּן
בְּיַד־עֲבָדָיו עֵדֶר עֵדֶר לְבַדּוֹ וַיֹּאמֶר אֶל־
עֲבָדָיו עִבְרוּ לְפָנַי וְרֶוַח תָּשִׂימוּ בֵּין עֵדֶר
וּבֵין עֵדֶר׃ 18 וַיְצַו אֶת־הָרִאשׁוֹן לֵאמֹר כִּי
יִפְגָשְׁךָ עֵשָׂו אָחִי וּשְׁאֵלְךָ לֵאמֹר לְמִי־אַתָּה

*12. "Save me, I pray, from my brother's hand."* Jacob's prayer (vv. 10–13) is one of the few prayers recorded in the narrative books of the Bible. (Another is Hannah's prayer of victory; I Samuel 2.) The prayer opens and closes with direct allusions to God's covenant with Abraham (vv. 10 and 13).

## JACOB STRUGGLES WITH GOD (32:17–33)

Separated from all his recent acquisitions and now alone, Jacob wrestles with a mysterious being. This is a life-altering event for him. He demands a blessing, and receives a name change that signifies a permanent change in Jacob's character.

*17–22.* Forms of the word "face" (Heb. *panim*) occur seven times in this passage (at times translated as "in front of" or "ahead of"), providing a verbal link to the life-altering theme in the events that are about to occur. The repetition conveys the force of this moment in Jacob's life and of all that he must face—including his brother. Two encounters, first with his God and then with his brother, will be united when he eventually says to Esau, "I've seen your face—like seeing God's face!" (33:10).

you belong, where are you going, and whose are these ahead of you?’ 19say, ‘These are your servant’s, Jacob’s; it is an offering sent to my lord Esau; and in fact he is following close behind us.’” 20He instructed the second, too, and third as well, and all [the others] who were to follow the droves, saying, “This is what you shall tell Esau when you find him. 21And say as well, ‘And in fact your servant Jacob is [coming] behind us.’” For he reasoned, “I will win him over with an offering in advance; then, when I face him, he may pardon me.” 22And so the offering went on ahead, while he remained in camp that night.

23That same night, he got up, took his two wives, his two maidservants, and his eleven children, and crossed at a ford of the Jabbok [river]. 24After taking them across the stream, he sent across all that he owned.

25Now Jacob was left alone, and a man wrestled with him until the rise of dawn. 26When [the man] saw that he could not overcome him, he struck Jacob’s hip-socket, so that Jacob’s hip-socket was wrenched as [the man] wrestled with him. 27Then he said, “Let me go; dawn is breaking!” But [Jacob] said, “I will not let you go unless you bless me!”

28The other said to him, “What is your name?” and he said, “Jacob.” 29“No more shall you be called Jacob, but Israel,” said the other, “for you

וְאָ֣נָה תֵלֵ֔ךְ וּלְמִ֖י אֵ֥לֶּה לְפָנֶֽיךָ׃ 19 וְאָמַרְתָּ֙
לְעַבְדְּךָ֣ לְיַעֲקֹ֔ב מִנְחָ֥ה הִוא֙ שְׁלוּחָ֔ה לַֽאדֹנִ֖י
לְעֵשָׂ֑ו וְהִנֵּ֥ה גַם־ה֖וּא אַחֲרֵֽינוּ׃ 20 וַיְצַ֞ו גַּ֣ם
אֶת־הַשֵּׁנִ֗י גַּ֚ם אֶת־הַשְּׁלִישִׁ֔י גַּ֚ם אֶת־כׇּל־
הַהֹ֣לְכִ֔ים אַחֲרֵ֥י הָעֲדָרִ֖ים לֵאמֹ֑ר כַּדָּבָ֤ר
הַזֶּה֙ תְּדַבְּר֣וּן אֶל־עֵשָׂ֔ו בְּמֹצַאֲכֶ֖ם אֹתֽוֹ׃
21 וַאֲמַרְתֶּ֕ם גַּ֛ם הִנֵּ֛ה עַבְדְּךָ֥ יַעֲקֹ֖ב אַחֲרֵ֑ינוּ
כִּֽי־אָמַ֞ר אֲכַפְּרָ֣ה פָנָ֗יו בַּמִּנְחָה֙ הַהֹלֶ֣כֶת
לְפָנָ֔י וְאַחֲרֵי־כֵן֙ אֶרְאֶ֣ה פָנָ֔יו אוּלַ֖י יִשָּׂ֥א
פָנָֽי׃ 22 וַתַּעֲבֹ֥ר הַמִּנְחָ֖ה עַל־פָּנָ֑יו וְה֛וּא לָ֥ן
בַּלַּֽיְלָה־הַה֖וּא בַּֽמַּחֲנֶֽה׃
23 וַיָּ֣קׇם ׀ בַּלַּ֣יְלָה ה֗וּא וַיִּקַּ֞ח אֶת־שְׁתֵּ֤י נָשָׁיו֙
וְאֶת־שְׁתֵּ֣י שִׁפְחֹתָ֔יו וְאֶת־אַחַ֥ד עָשָׂ֖ר יְלָדָ֑יו
וַֽיַּעֲבֹ֔ר אֵ֖ת מַעֲבַ֥ר יַבֹּֽק׃ 24 וַיִּקָּחֵ֔ם וַיַּעֲבִרֵ֖ם
אֶת־הַנָּ֑חַל וַֽיַּעֲבֵ֖ר אֶת־אֲשֶׁר־לֽוֹ׃
25 וַיִּוָּתֵ֥ר יַעֲקֹ֖ב לְבַדּ֑וֹ וַיֵּאָבֵ֥ק אִישׁ֙ עִמּ֔וֹ עַ֖ד
עֲל֥וֹת הַשָּֽׁחַר׃ 26 וַיַּ֗רְא כִּ֣י לֹ֤א יָכֹל֙ ל֔וֹ וַיִּגַּ֖ע
בְּכַף־יְרֵכ֑וֹ וַתֵּ֙קַע֙ כַּף־יֶ֣רֶךְ יַעֲקֹ֔ב בְּהֵאָבְק֖וֹ
עִמּֽוֹ׃ 27 וַיֹּ֣אמֶר שַׁלְּחֵ֔נִי כִּ֥י עָלָ֖ה הַשָּׁ֑חַר
וַיֹּ֙אמֶר֙ לֹ֣א אֲשַֽׁלֵּחֲךָ֔ כִּ֖י אִם־בֵּרַכְתָּֽנִי׃
28 וַיֹּ֥אמֶר אֵלָ֖יו מַה־שְּׁמֶ֑ךָ וַיֹּ֖אמֶר יַעֲקֹֽב׃
29 וַיֹּ֗אמֶר לֹ֤א יַעֲקֹב֙ יֵאָמֵ֥ר עוֹד֙ שִׁמְךָ֔ כִּ֖י
אִם־יִשְׂרָאֵ֑ל כִּֽי־שָׂרִ֧יתָ עִם־אֱלֹהִ֛ים וְעִם־

*23. eleven children.* Heb. *y’ladim* here must actually refer to “boys” only, because the narrator specifies eleven of them. Dinah, Jacob’s daughter (30:21), is not included in this count. [Apparently the narrator here relates to Jacob’s children in genealogical terms, their being the ancestors of the future tribes of Israel. On women and biblical genealogies, see at 10:1. *—Ed.*]

*25. a man wrestled with him.* In Hosea 12:5–6, the prophet states specifically that Jacob “strove with a divine being (*elohim*); he strove with an angel (*malach*) and prevailed.” However, here the mysterious being that appears suddenly as Jacob’s adversary is described only as an *ish*, translated here as “a man,” as is conventional. However, given the flexibility in biblical Hebrew of the term *ish*, it can mean a challenging figure that need not be human but could be divine.

*27. “I will not let you go unless you bless me!”* Jacob insists that the struggle lead to blessing.

*29. “Israel.”* The original meaning of this two-part name cannot be stated definitively. In most cases, *el* is a noun meaning “God,” but sometimes it has a more general sense of “divine” or “superlative.” Also unclear is whether *el* is subject or object of the name’s verbal portion, which itself is ambigu-

have struggled with God and with human beings, and you have prevailed." [30]Then Jacob asked, "Pray tell me now your name." But he said, "Why do you ask my name?" And then he took his leave of him.

[31]Jacob therefore named that place Peni'el—"For I have seen *God face*-to-face, yet my life has been spared." [32]The sun shone on him as he was leaving Penu'el, and he was limping on account of his thigh. [33]To this day that is why the people of Israel do not eat the thigh muscle that is in the socket of the hip, because he struck Jacob's hip-socket at the thigh muscle.

33 When Jacob was looking into the distance, he beheld Esau coming with his four hundred men, so he divided the children among Leah, Rachel, and the two maids. [2]He placed the maids

אֲנָשִׁים וַתּוּכָל׃ 30 וַיִּשְׁאַל יַעֲקֹב וַיֹּאמֶר
הַגִּידָה־נָּא שְׁמֶךָ וַיֹּאמֶר לָמָּה זֶּה תִּשְׁאַל
לִשְׁמִי וַיְבָרֶךְ אֹתוֹ שָׁם׃
31 וַיִּקְרָא יַעֲקֹב שֵׁם הַמָּקוֹם פְּנִיאֵל כִּי־
רָאִיתִי אֱלֹהִים פָּנִים אֶל־פָּנִים וַתִּנָּצֵל
נַפְשִׁי׃ 32 וַיִּזְרַח־לוֹ הַשֶּׁמֶשׁ כַּאֲשֶׁר עָבַר
אֶת־פְּנוּאֵל וְהוּא צֹלֵעַ עַל־יְרֵכוֹ׃ 33 עַל־כֵּן
לֹא־יֹאכְלוּ בְנֵי־יִשְׂרָאֵל אֶת־גִּיד הַנָּשֶׁה
אֲשֶׁר עַל־כַּף הַיָּרֵךְ עַד הַיּוֹם הַזֶּה כִּי נָגַע
בְּכַף־יֶרֶךְ יַעֲקֹב בְּגִיד הַנָּשֶׁה׃
לג וַיִּשָּׂא יַעֲקֹב עֵינָיו וַיַּרְא וְהִנֵּה עֵשָׂו בָּא
וְעִמּוֹ אַרְבַּע מֵאוֹת אִישׁ וַיַּחַץ אֶת־הַיְלָדִים
עַל־לֵאָה וְעַל־רָחֵל וְעַל שְׁתֵּי הַשְּׁפָחוֹת׃
2 וַיָּשֶׂם אֶת־הַשְּׁפָחוֹת וְאֶת־יַלְדֵיהֶן רִאשֹׁנָה

---

ous. Thus this name can be construed as "he struggles with God," or "God struggles," or "God rules," or "his struggle is mighty," and more. The present story turns on the first of those possible meanings.

A name change often signifies a change in character. Jacob is no longer simply the "deceiver/supplanter" (27:36). Abraham and Sarah have their names changed permanently and consistently (Genesis 17); Jacob, on the other hand, will be called both Jacob and Israel after this name change.

***"struggled with God."*** Or "... with divine beings" (compare Judges 13:22). It is not clear whether this statement is intended literally to describe the recent wrestling match, or figuratively in reference to Jacob's general life circumstances.

***31. Peniel—"For I have seen God face-to-face."*** Explaining the place name as if it meant "face of God" (*p'nei-el*), suggesting that Jacob understands his overnight struggle as a direct encounter with God. [Because the Bible—as in the ancient Near East generally—considers the actions of messengers to be largely inseparable from the principal who sent them, Jacob may perhaps be referring to an encounter with a divine messenger as agent. —*Ed.*]

***32.*** Jacob leaves the encounter with a serious injury. He thus sets out to meet his brother while physically limping and vulnerable, but with new internal strength.

***33. the people of Israel do not eat the thigh muscle.*** This dietary restriction is not mentioned in the laws of *kashrut* in either Leviticus 11 or Deuteronomy 14:3–21. It is presented as a matter of ethnic identification rather than of ritual purity.

### THE BROTHERS RECONCILE
### (33:1–20)

***1–2.*** After his encounter with God, Jacob turns back to the confrontation with his brother, Esau. He divides the women and children, situating the women most likely according to personal preference: maids and their children first, then Leah and her children, and then, Rachel and Joseph—his favorites—in back. The status of Jacob's sons depends apparently upon their mothers' favor with Jacob, not their birth order or even their personalities. Joseph is the only child specifically cited. These spatial and narrative details spotlight Jacob's preference of Rachel, an attitude that later proves to undermine harmony within the household.

and their children in front, Leah and her children next, with Rachel and Joseph last. 3He himself went on ahead of them and bowed down to the ground seven times as he approached his brother.

4Esau, though, ran to meet him, and embraced him, and fell on his neck and kissed him. And they burst into tears.

5When Esau looked around and saw the women and the children, he said, "Who are these? Yours?" [Jacob] answered, "The children with whom God has favored your servant." 6Then the lesser wives with their children approached and bowed down; 7Leah, too, approached with her children and bowed down; afterward, Joseph and Rachel approached and bowed down.

8Esau said, "What, is all this camp that I came across *yours*?" And Jacob replied, "Yes, [it is all meant] to find favor in the sight of my lord." 9Esau said, "I have an abundance, my brother; let what is yours be yours." 10Jacob said, "No, please, if I have truly found favor in your sight, take the offering from my hand; for to see your face is like seeing the face of God; and you have [already] shown me favor. 11Please accept my gift of blessing that has been presented to you; God has been gracious to me, and I have all [that I need]." [Jacob] kept on pressing him until [Esau] accepted.

12[Esau] then said, "Let us start on our way. I will go at your side." 13But [Jacob] answered, "My lord knows that the children are delicate, and that I have to think about the sheep and cattle that are nursing. If they drive them hard a single day, the small cattle will perish! 14Let my lord go on ahead of his servant; as for myself, let me proceed on my way at my own pace, [following] the footsteps of

וְאֶת־לֵאָה וִילָדֶיהָ אַחֲרֹנִים וְאֶת־רָחֵל
וְאֶת־יוֹסֵף אַחֲרֹנִים׃ 3 וְהוּא עָבַר לִפְנֵיהֶם
וַיִּשְׁתַּחוּ אַרְצָה שֶׁבַע פְּעָמִים עַד־גִּשְׁתּוֹ
עַד־אָחִיו׃
4 וַיָּרָץ עֵשָׂו לִקְרָאתוֹ וַיְחַבְּקֵהוּ וַיִּפֹּל עַל־
צוארו צַוָּארָיו וַיִּשָּׁקֵהוּ וַיִּבְכּוּ׃
5 וַיִּשָּׂא אֶת־עֵינָיו וַיַּרְא אֶת־הַנָּשִׁים וְאֶת־
הַיְלָדִים וַיֹּאמֶר מִי־אֵלֶּה לָּךְ וַיֹּאמַר
הַיְלָדִים אֲשֶׁר־חָנַן אֱלֹהִים אֶת־עַבְדֶּךָ׃
6 וַתִּגַּשְׁןָ הַשְּׁפָחוֹת הֵנָּה וְיַלְדֵיהֶן
וַתִּשְׁתַּחֲוֶיןָ׃ 7 וַתִּגַּשׁ גַּם־לֵאָה וִילָדֶיהָ
וַיִּשְׁתַּחֲווּ וְאַחַר נִגַּשׁ יוֹסֵף וְרָחֵל וַיִּשְׁתַּחֲווּ׃
8 וַיֹּאמֶר מִי לְךָ כָּל־הַמַּחֲנֶה הַזֶּה אֲשֶׁר
פָּגָשְׁתִּי וַיֹּאמֶר לִמְצֹא־חֵן בְּעֵינֵי אֲדֹנִי׃
9 וַיֹּאמֶר עֵשָׂו יֶשׁ־לִי רָב אָחִי יְהִי לְךָ אֲשֶׁר־
לָךְ׃ 10 וַיֹּאמֶר יַעֲקֹב אַל־נָא אִם־נָא מָצָאתִי
חֵן בְּעֵינֶיךָ וְלָקַחְתָּ מִנְחָתִי מִיָּדִי כִּי עַל־כֵּן
רָאִיתִי פָנֶיךָ כִּרְאֹת פְּנֵי אֱלֹהִים וַתִּרְצֵנִי׃
11 קַח־נָא אֶת־בִּרְכָתִי אֲשֶׁר הֻבָאת לָךְ
כִּי־חַנַּנִי אֱלֹהִים וְכִי יֶשׁ־לִי־כֹל וַיִּפְצַר־בּוֹ
וַיִּקָּח׃
12 וַיֹּאמֶר נִסְעָה וְנֵלֵכָה וְאֵלְכָה לְנֶגְדֶּךָ׃
13 וַיֹּאמֶר אֵלָיו אֲדֹנִי יֹדֵעַ כִּי־הַיְלָדִים רַכִּים
וְהַצֹּאן וְהַבָּקָר עָלוֹת עָלָי וּדְפָקוּם יוֹם אֶחָד
וָמֵתוּ כָּל־הַצֹּאן׃ 14 יַעֲבָר־נָא אֲדֹנִי לִפְנֵי
עַבְדּוֹ וַאֲנִי אֶתְנָהֲלָה לְאִטִּי לְרֶגֶל הַמְּלָאכָה

*5.* The narrator pointedly relates that Esau asks, "Who are these with you?" only after he has noticed "the women and the children." Yet Jacob's reply mentions only "the children," not the women.

*11.* ***"Please accept my gift of blessing."*** Literally, "please take my blessing," which suggests that Jacob is attempting to compensate for having appropriated Esau's blessing twenty years earlier.

*14–15.* Jacob wants reconciliation, but not closeness. He tells Esau that he will meet him in one place—but travels to another.

אֲשֶׁר־לְפָנַי וּלְרֶגֶל הַיְלָדִים עַד אֲשֶׁר־אָבֹא
אֶל־אֲדֹנִי שֵׂעִירָה׃
15 וַיֹּאמֶר עֵשָׂו אַצִּיגָה־נָּא עִמְּךָ מִן־הָעָם
אֲשֶׁר אִתִּי וַיֹּאמֶר לָמָּה זֶּה אֶמְצָא־חֵן
בְּעֵינֵי אֲדֹנִי׃ 16 וַיָּשָׁב בַּיּוֹם הַהוּא עֵשָׂו
לְדַרְכּוֹ שֵׂעִירָה׃ 17 וְיַעֲקֹב נָסַע סֻכֹּתָה וַיִּבֶן
לוֹ בָּיִת וּלְמִקְנֵהוּ עָשָׂה סֻכֹּת עַל־כֵּן קָרָא
שֵׁם־הַמָּקוֹם סֻכּוֹת׃ ס

18 וַיָּבֹא יַעֲקֹב שָׁלֵם עִיר שְׁכֶם אֲשֶׁר בְּאֶרֶץ
כְּנַעַן בְּבֹאוֹ מִפַּדַּן אֲרָם וַיִּחַן אֶת־פְּנֵי הָעִיר׃
19 וַיִּקֶן אֶת־חֶלְקַת הַשָּׂדֶה אֲשֶׁר נָטָה־שָׁם
אָהֳלוֹ מִיַּד בְּנֵי־חֲמוֹר אֲבִי שְׁכֶם בְּמֵאָה
קְשִׂיטָה׃ 20 וַיַּצֶּב־שָׁם מִזְבֵּחַ וַיִּקְרָא־לוֹ אֵל
אֱלֹהֵי יִשְׂרָאֵל׃ ס
לד וַתֵּצֵא דִינָה בַּת־לֵאָה אֲשֶׁר יָלְדָה
לְיַעֲקֹב לִרְאוֹת בִּבְנוֹת הָאָרֶץ׃ 2 וַיַּרְא אֹתָהּ

the livestock in front of me and [following] the footsteps of the children, until I catch up to my lord near Seir."

15 Esau said, "Pray let me then leave behind with you a portion of the force that accompanies me." But [Jacob] said, "Why should my lord show me
such favor?" 16 So that day Esau started back on his
way to Seir, 17 while Jacob went on to Succoth, where
he built a house for himself and shelters for his livestock; that is why the place was called Succoth.

18 Thus Jacob, in his journey from Paddan-aram, arrived safely in the city of Shechem, in the
land of Canaan; he made camp facing the city. 19 He
bought the portion of the field where he had pitched his tent from the sons of Hamor, Shechem's father, for a hundredweight. 20 He then set
up an altar, calling it El-Elohei-Yisrael.

34 [One day] Dinah, Leah's daughter whom she had borne to Jacob, went out to see the women
of the locality, 2 and Shechem son of Hamor the

## *Dinah and Shechem*

### SEX AND SOCIAL STATUS
(34:1–31)

Dinah, acting independently and of her own initiative, goes out to visit "the women of the locality." In the span of just two verses, the local Hivite prince, Shechem, spots Dinah, has sex with her, falls in love with her, and wants to marry her. Her brothers react violently and destroy Shechem and his city.

Dinah's status and her standing in society steadily decline as the story progresses. She moves from fulfilling the proper role in the proper place (virgin-daughter in father's house) to a socially ambiguous role with no proper corresponding physical place. Her story serves as a warning in the larger—and probably overriding—issue of the political and ethnic identity of the Israelites in relation to the other people in the land.

Throughout the story, Dinah's location corresponds directly to her perceived position in society and illustrates the precarious state of the daughter in biblical Israel. Though she seems free to move about, she is not secure anywhere. One need only consider the plight of Jephthah's daughter in Judges 11, the concubine in Judges 19, and the daughters of Shiloh in Judges 21, to get the message that women, or at least daughters, are vulnerable to calamity when they "go out."

### RAPE? (34:1–4)

A crucial question for modern interpreters is whether or not Dinah was raped. When considering the modern concept of rape—characterized by an aggressive act and lack of mutual consent—there

Hivite, the local prince, saw her; he took her and lay her down and raped her. [3]He was then capti-

שְׁכֶם בֶּן־חֲמָוֹר הַחִוִּי נְשִׂיא הָאָרֶץ וַיִּקַּח אֹתָהּ וַיִּשְׁכַּב אֹתָהּ וַיְעַנֶּהָ׃ 3 וַתִּדְבַּק נַפְשׁוֹ

is little question as to what happens to Dinah; the author tells us that Shechem saw her, took her, lay with her, and humiliated her. To us, this string of verbs screams "rape" (and is in fact even translated that way in v. 2). The assumption made by most interpreters is that Dinah did not consent to the sexual act. However, the question of consent, so central to the modern notion of rape and of women's rights in general, is entirely ignored in this text. Dinah's consent is not the issue. The ambiguity of the Hebrew verbs describing Shechem's actions toward Dinah compounds the difficulty of interpretation.

If we contemporary interpreters are sensitive to the ancient context in which the story was recorded, we need to entertain the possibility that there is a fundamental difference between our modern concept of rape and what may represent rape in the biblical text. In our society, forcing a woman to have sex against her will is seen as terrible both for its emotional and psychological consequences, and for the humiliation and debasement suffered by the woman as an individual. The Bible, even in its rape laws, was primarily concerned with the juridical and social-status consequences of the tort involved in sleeping with a virgin without either marrying her or compensating her father. As with adultery, the problem was not treated as an emotional or psychological one. When Amnon rapes Tamar in II Samuel 13, the violation that has taken place is made clear when Tamar begs Amnon not to reject her but to request her for his wife. It is his rejection subsequent to the sexual act that damages Tamar's life the most, because as an unmarried non-virgin princess, she has completely lost status in her society. In contrast to Tamar, Dinah is not granted a voice in the story; instead, her body and life form a site for settling issues between men.

If Shechem marries Dinah after having sex with her, she would have full status as a wife in his household. The story, however, aims at excluding such a union with the other peoples in the land. Thus Jacob ignores his obligation to protect the women of his household when he does not subsequently negotiate Dinah's marriage to Shechem. (For a different perspective on this episode, see Another View, p. 202.)

*1. Dinah, Leah's daughter.* Dinah is introduced as the daughter of Leah, the wife that Jacob did not want. (On the status of offspring as a function of Jacob's favoring Rachel, see at 33:1–2.)

Dinah is referred to as "daughter" seven times in this story. See also at v. 4, s.v. "girl."

***went out to see the women of the locality.*** Dinah goes out of her father's house to a public space, literally "to see the daughters of the land." Dinah seems free to leave, but she does so at her own risk. She is going out to "see" her peers, but she is ultimately "seen"—with dramatic consequences. Nowhere in the text is she criticized for her action.

*2. Shechem.* The name both of the prince and of the settlement (today's Nablus). In the book of Joshua, this locale becomes the site of a special covenant ceremony for the Israelites (Joshua 24). Later it rivaled Jerusalem; this rivalry may account for the hostility with which the city is portrayed in the present story.

***he took her and lay her down and raped her.*** Interpretive debates about the story and its import revolve around the meaning of the word *innah*, here rendered as "rape." The meaning of the other verbs as well is both affected by, and in turn influences, how one interprets the actions involved in this episode.

Deuteronomy 22 contains several laws about sexual offenses with terminology similar to what appears here. From the usage in Deuteronomy one can conclude that *innah* means "violate," not

vated by Jacob's daughter Dinah and, falling in love with the young woman, spoke tenderly to the young woman. [4]So Shechem said to his father Hamor, "Obtain this girl for me as [my] wife."

[5]At the time that Jacob heard that his daughter Dinah had been defiled, his sons were in the field with his livestock, so he kept quiet until they came back. [6]Shechem's father Hamor now went to Jacob to speak with him, [7]and meanwhile Jacob's sons had returned from the field. When they heard, the men were grieved and became extremely angry, for he had committed an outrage against Israel by

בְּדִינָ֖ה בַּֽת־יַעֲקֹ֑ב וַיֶּ֙אֱהַב֙ אֶת־הנער הַֽנַּעֲרָ֔ה
וַיְדַבֵּ֖ר עַל־לֵ֥ב הנער הַֽנַּעֲרָֽה׃ 4 וַיֹּ֣אמֶר שְׁכֶ֔ם
אֶל־חֲמ֥וֹר אָבִ֖יו לֵאמֹ֑ר קַח־לִ֛י אֶת־הַיַּלְדָּ֥ה
הַזֹּ֖את לְאִשָּֽׁה׃
5 וְיַעֲקֹ֣ב שָׁמַ֗ע כִּ֤י טִמֵּא֙ אֶת־דִּינָ֣ה בִתּ֔וֹ וּבָנָ֛יו
הָי֥וּ אֶת־מִקְנֵ֖הוּ בַּשָּׂדֶ֑ה וְהֶחֱרִ֥שׁ יַעֲקֹ֖ב עַד־
בֹּאָֽם׃ 6 וַיֵּצֵ֛א חֲמ֥וֹר אֲבִֽי־שְׁכֶ֖ם אֶל־יַעֲקֹ֑ב
לְדַבֵּ֖ר אִתּֽוֹ׃ 7 וּבְנֵ֨י יַעֲקֹ֜ב בָּ֤אוּ מִן־הַשָּׂדֶה֙
כְּשָׁמְעָ֔ם וַיִּֽתְעַצְּבוּ֙ הָֽאֲנָשִׁ֔ים וַיִּ֥חַר לָהֶ֖ם

"rape" (22:23–24). The expression "he took hold of her" *is* apparently the one used for rape in Deuteronomy (22:25) as well in the Tamar/Amnon story (II Samuel 13:14)—and it is not used here in the present verse. Consequently, the word *innah* should not be translated as rape, and what happened to Dinah certainly should not to be understood as an act of rape in the modern sense of the word. Rather, the term demonstrates in this passage, as elsewhere, a downward movement in a social sense, meaning to "debase" or "humiliate" (Genesis 16:6). Though an affront to the woman's family, the term does not carry with it the psychological and emotional implications for the woman that the contemporary notion of rape suggests. In this particular text, the woman has no voice, and the narrator has no interest in whether or not she consented to the sexual act. Bear in mind that according to ancient Near Eastern mores, Dinah would have been considered to have been disgraced even if she had consented.

**4. *"girl."*** Heb. *yaldah*; literally, "a (female) child," which suggests that she is rather young. Similar terms such as *bat* (daughter) and *naara* (girl or young woman) appear repeatedly in this passage (see at v. 1). Taken together, these descriptors suggest that Dinah's youth was relevant to the events that follow.

***"girl . . . wife."*** Heb. *yaldah . . . ishah*. The transition from childhood to adulthood (for *ishah* can also mean "woman") is brought on by a change in status involving sexual relations.

## BROTHERS' INTERPRETATION: AN OUTRAGE AGAINST ISRAEL (34:5–24)

Jacob hears what has happened to Dinah and, somewhat uncharacteristically, waits until the return of his sons. There is irony here in that on the Canaanite side the son (Shechem) goes to his father (Hamor) to negotiate on his behalf, while Jacob remains silent throughout the entire story until v. 30, when he chastises his sons for having made trouble for him in his new land.

**5. *defiled.*** Heb. *timei*, indicating that Dinah's status has changed for the worse. Other forms of this word are used in Leviticus for "pollution" or "impure," a condition that can be temporary (as in 11:44; 15:31; 18:20). Something defiled can often be rendered pure with proper ritual purification. In the case of Dinah, it appears that marriage to Shechem could potentially change her status from "defiled" to "pure."

**7. *an outrage against Israel.*** The sons are angry because of the "outrage against Israel." The only "Israel" in this story is Jacob himself; but he is not the one outraged. Rather, it is his sons, the *B'nei Yisrael*, who are affected and who take action in response.

lying with Jacob's daughter—such things were not done.

8Hamor now spoke with them, saying, "My son Shechem has set his heart on your daughter; pray give her to him to be [his] wife. 9Make marriages with us—give us your daughters and you yourselves take our daughters. 10Live among us and the land will be before you; settle and trade here and acquire property here." 11And Shechem said to [Dinah's] father and brothers, "Let me but find favor in your sight, and I will give you whatever you ask. 12Exact from me bridal money and gifts to excess, yet I will pay whatever you demand of me; only give me the girl to be [my] wife!"

13The sons of Jacob answered Shechem and his father Hamor deceptively, speaking thus because he had defiled their sister Dinah. 14They said to them, "We cannot do this thing, giving our sister to a man who has a foreskin, for this is a shame to us. 15Only on this condition will we consent to you: if you become like us by having every one of your males circumcised. 16Then we would give you our daughters and would take your daughters and settle among you and become one people. 17But if you do not listen to us [and consent] to be circumcised, we shall take our daughter and leave."

מְאֹד כִּי־נְבָלָה עָשָׂה בְיִשְׂרָאֵל לִשְׁכַּב אֶת־
בַּת־יַעֲקֹב וְכֵן לֹא יֵעָשֶׂה׃
8 וַיְדַבֵּר חֲמוֹר אִתָּם לֵאמֹר שְׁכֶם בְּנִי
חָשְׁקָה נַפְשׁוֹ בְּבִתְּכֶם תְּנוּ נָא אֹתָהּ לוֹ
לְאִשָּׁה׃ 9 וְהִתְחַתְּנוּ אֹתָנוּ בְּנֹתֵיכֶם תִּתְּנוּ־
לָנוּ וְאֶת־בְּנֹתֵינוּ תִּקְחוּ לָכֶם׃ 10 וְאִתָּנוּ
תֵּשֵׁבוּ וְהָאָרֶץ תִּהְיֶה לִפְנֵיכֶם שְׁבוּ וּסְחָרוּהָ
וְהֵאָחֲזוּ בָּהּ׃ 11 וַיֹּאמֶר שְׁכֶם אֶל־אָבִיהָ
וְאֶל־אַחֶיהָ אֶמְצָא־חֵן בְּעֵינֵיכֶם וַאֲשֶׁר
תֹּאמְרוּ אֵלַי אֶתֵּן׃ 12 הַרְבּוּ עָלַי מְאֹד מֹהַר
וּמַתָּן וְאֶתְּנָה כַּאֲשֶׁר תֹּאמְרוּ אֵלָי וּתְנוּ־לִי
אֶת־הנער הַנַּעֲרָה לְאִשָּׁה׃
13 וַיַּעֲנוּ בְנֵי־יַעֲקֹב אֶת־שְׁכֶם וְאֶת־חֲמוֹר
אָבִיו בְּמִרְמָה וַיְדַבֵּרוּ אֲשֶׁר טִמֵּא אֵת דִּינָה
אֲחֹתָם׃ 14 וַיֹּאמְרוּ אֲלֵיהֶם לֹא נוּכַל
לַעֲשׂוֹת הַדָּבָר הַזֶּה לָתֵת אֶת־אֲחֹתֵנוּ
לְאִישׁ אֲשֶׁר־לוֹ עָרְלָה כִּי־חֶרְפָּה הִוא לָנוּ׃
15 אַךְ־בְּזֹאת נֵאוֹת לָכֶם אִם תִּהְיוּ כָמֹנוּ
לְהִמֹּל לָכֶם כָּל־זָכָר׃ 16 וְנָתַנּוּ אֶת־בְּנֹתֵינוּ
לָכֶם וְאֶת־בְּנֹתֵיכֶם נִקַּח־לָנוּ וְיָשַׁבְנוּ אִתְּכֶם
וְהָיִינוּ לְעַם אֶחָד׃ 17 וְאִם־לֹא תִשְׁמְעוּ
אֵלֵינוּ לְהִמּוֹל וְלָקַחְנוּ אֶת־בִּתֵּנוּ וְהָלָכְנוּ׃

***lying with Jacob's daughter—such things were not done.*** The reason Jacob's sons give for their rage is clearly expressed. The "thing not to be done" is to have sex with Jacob's daughter.

*8–17.* ***Hamor now spoke with them.*** The negotiation occurs only among men. They alone discuss the details involved in changing Dinah's status from unmarried virgin in her father's house to married wife and future mother in her husband's house. The negotiations as stated do not convey Dinah's consent or desire. It is Shechem's wish that was expressed (v. 4), and it is his father's negotiation that now takes place on his behalf.

*12.* ***"girl."*** Shechem here refers to Dinah as a *naara* rather than as *yaldah* (child, girl); see at v. 4.

*13.* ***deceptively.*** Heb. *b'mirmah*; here this word is applied to "Jacob's sons," a reminder that earlier it referred to Jacob himself (see at 27:35). On subterfuge as a recourse for both women and men who face abuses of authority, see at 27:1–28:9 (introduction).

*14–24.* Entering into a binding marriage requires both negotiation and sex (not necessarily in that order); so Dinah and Shechem are already halfway there. For their part of the negotiation, the brothers tell Shechem that they cannot give Dinah to him in marriage until he is circumcised. In a surprising move, Shechem is able to convince the males of the town to become circumcised in order to benefit from contact with Jacob's family.

18Their words seemed good to Hamor and
Hamor's son Shechem, 19and the youth did not
delay doing this thing, for he yearned for Jacob's
daughter, and he was preeminent in his father's
household. 20So Hamor and his son Shechem went
to the gate of their city and spoke to their fellow-
citizens, saying, 21"These people are peaceably disposed toward us; they will settle in the land and
trade here; plainly, the land is open wide on every
side before them. We will take to wife their daughters and give our daughters to them. 22But only
on this condition have these people agreed to settle among us and become one people: every male
among us must be circumcised as they are circumcised. 23Their livestock and their possessions—all
their animals—will be ours; let us consent to them,
that they may settle among us." 24All who went out
of the city gate listened to Hamor and his son Shechem; and every male, every able-bodied man, was
circumcised.

25On the third day, when they were in [the
greatest] pain, the two sons of Jacob Simeon and
Levi, Dinah's brothers, each took his sword; they
went undisturbed into the city and killed every
male. 26And they also killed Hamor and his son
Shechem by the sword; then, taking Dinah from
Shechem's house, they left. 27Jacob's [other] sons
went over the slain and plundered the city, whose
inhabitants had defiled their sister, 28taking their
sheep, their cattle, and their donkeys, and all that

18 וַיִּיטְב֥וּ דִבְרֵיהֶ֖ם בְּעֵינֵ֣י חֲמ֑וֹר וּבְעֵינֵ֖י שְׁכֶ֥ם
בֶּן־חֲמֽוֹר׃ 19 וְלֹֽא־אֵחַ֤ר הַנַּ֙עַר֙ לַעֲשׂ֣וֹת
הַדָּבָ֔ר כִּ֥י חָפֵ֖ץ בְּבַֽת־יַעֲקֹ֑ב וְה֣וּא נִכְבָּ֔ד מִכֹּ֖ל
בֵּ֥ית אָבִֽיו׃ 20 וַיָּבֹ֥א חֲמ֛וֹר וּשְׁכֶ֥ם בְּנ֖וֹ אֶל־
שַׁ֣עַר עִירָ֑ם וַיְדַבְּר֛וּ אֶל־אַנְשֵׁ֥י עִירָ֖ם לֵאמֹֽר׃
21 הָאֲנָשִׁ֨ים הָאֵ֜לֶּה שְֽׁלֵמִ֧ים הֵ֣ם אִתָּ֗נוּ
וְיֵשְׁב֤וּ בָאָ֙רֶץ֙ וְיִסְחֲר֣וּ אֹתָ֔הּ וְהָאָ֛רֶץ הִנֵּ֥ה
רַֽחֲבַת־יָדַ֖יִם לִפְנֵיהֶ֑ם אֶת־בְּנֹתָם֙ נִקַּֽח־לָ֣נוּ
לְנָשִׁ֔ים וְאֶת־בְּנֹתֵ֖ינוּ נִתֵּ֥ן לָהֶֽם׃ 22 אַךְ־
בְּ֠זֹאת יֵאֹ֨תוּ לָ֤נוּ הָֽאֲנָשִׁים֙ לָשֶׁ֣בֶת אִתָּ֔נוּ
לִהְי֖וֹת לְעַ֣ם אֶחָ֑ד בְּהִמּ֥וֹל לָ֙נוּ֙ כָּל־זָכָ֔ר
כַּאֲשֶׁ֖ר הֵ֥ם נִמֹּלִֽים׃ 23 מִקְנֵהֶ֤ם וְקִנְיָנָם֙ וְכָל־
בְּהֶמְתָּ֔ם הֲל֥וֹא לָ֖נוּ הֵ֑ם אַ֚ךְ נֵא֣וֹתָה לָהֶ֔ם
וְיֵשְׁב֖וּ אִתָּֽנוּ׃ 24 וַיִּשְׁמְע֤וּ אֶל־חֲמוֹר֙ וְאֶל־
שְׁכֶ֣ם בְּנ֔וֹ כָּל־יֹצְאֵ֖י שַׁ֣עַר עִיר֑וֹ וַיִּמֹּ֙לוּ֙ כָּל־
זָכָ֔ר כָּל־יֹצְאֵ֖י שַׁ֥עַר עִירֽוֹ׃
25 וַיְהִי֩ בַיּ֨וֹם הַשְּׁלִישִׁ֜י בִּֽהְיוֹתָ֣ם כֹּאֲבִ֗ים
וַיִּקְח֣וּ שְׁנֵֽי־בְנֵֽי־יַ֠עֲקֹב שִׁמְע֨וֹן וְלֵוִ֜י אֲחֵ֤י דִינָה֙
אִ֣ישׁ חַרְבּ֔וֹ וַיָּבֹ֥אוּ עַל־הָעִ֖יר בֶּ֑טַח וַיַּֽהַרְג֖וּ
כָּל־זָכָֽר׃ 26 וְאֶת־חֲמוֹר֙ וְאֶת־שְׁכֶ֣ם בְּנ֔וֹ הָרְג֖וּ
לְפִי־חָ֑רֶב וַיִּקְח֧וּ אֶת־דִּינָ֛ה מִבֵּ֥ית שְׁכֶ֖ם
וַיֵּצֵֽאוּ׃ 27 בְּנֵ֣י יַעֲקֹ֗ב בָּ֚אוּ עַל־הַ֣חֲלָלִ֔ים וַיָּבֹ֖זּוּ
הָעִ֑יר אֲשֶׁ֥ר טִמְּא֖וּ אֲחוֹתָֽם׃ 28 אֶת־צֹאנָ֥ם
וְאֶת־בְּקָרָ֖ם וְאֶת־חֲמֹרֵיהֶ֑ם וְאֵ֧ת אֲשֶׁר־בָּעִ֛יר

### BROTHERS' REVENGE (34:25–31)

Rather than framing their sister's loss of virginity in the context of marriage, "Jacob's sons" had arranged marriage deceptively (v. 13). Rather than following through with the terms they had negotiated, Simeon and Levi—now also identified as "Dinah's brothers" (v. 25)—exact revenge.

***26. taking Dinah from Shechem's house.*** After her initial encounter with Shechem, Dinah does not return to her father's house. But in Shechem's house, her status is equally problematic as she is not officially his wife. An alien in a foreign household, lacking a negotiated marriage and children, Dinah is literally on the social fringe. Her removal from Shechem's house at this point in the story does nothing to improve the situation. With a voided marriage but the sexual status of wife, there is no acceptable place for her in society.

***28–29.*** The brothers kill all the men but spare women and children, taking them captive instead.

was in the city and in the countryside. 29 And all their wealth, their little ones, and their wives, and all that was in the houses, they seized as captives and as spoil.

30 Jacob then said to Simeon and Levi, "You have made trouble for me by making me odious to the land's inhabitants—the Canaanites and the Perizzites. Since I am few in number, they will gather themselves against me and strike at me, and I and my household will be destroyed." 31 But they said, "Should he then have been allowed to treat our sister like a whore?"

35 God now said to Jacob, "Get up, go up to Beth El and settle there; erect an altar there to the God who appeared to you when you fled from the presence of your brother Esau." 2 Jacob thereupon said to his household and all who were with him, "Get rid of the foreign gods in your midst; purify yourselves and change your clothing. 3 Let us get moving and go up to Beth El, that I may build an altar there to the God who responds to me in my time of distress, who has been with me on the road that I have traveled." 4 So they gave Jacob all the foreign gods they were holding and the rings in

וְאֶת־אֲשֶׁר בַּשָּׂדֶה לָקָחוּ׃ 29 וְאֶת־כָּל־חֵילָם
וְאֶת־כָּל־טַפָּם וְאֶת־נְשֵׁיהֶם שָׁבוּ וַיָּבֹזּוּ וְאֵת
כָּל־אֲשֶׁר בַּבָּיִת׃
30 וַיֹּאמֶר יַעֲקֹב אֶל־שִׁמְעוֹן וְאֶל־לֵוִי
עֲכַרְתֶּם אֹתִי לְהַבְאִישֵׁנִי בְּיֹשֵׁב הָאָרֶץ
בַּכְּנַעֲנִי וּבַפְּרִזִּי וַאֲנִי מְתֵי מִסְפָּר וְנֶאֶסְפוּ
עָלַי וְהִכּוּנִי וְנִשְׁמַדְתִּי אֲנִי וּבֵיתִי׃ 31 וַיֹּאמְרוּ
הַכְזוֹנָה יַעֲשֶׂה אֶת־אֲחוֹתֵנוּ׃ פ

לה וַיֹּאמֶר אֱלֹהִים אֶל־יַעֲקֹב קוּם עֲלֵה
בֵית־אֵל וְשֶׁב־שָׁם וַעֲשֵׂה־שָׁם מִזְבֵּחַ לָאֵל
הַנִּרְאֶה אֵלֶיךָ בְּבָרְחֲךָ מִפְּנֵי עֵשָׂו אָחִיךָ׃
2 וַיֹּאמֶר יַעֲקֹב אֶל־בֵּיתוֹ וְאֶל כָּל־אֲשֶׁר עִמּוֹ
הָסִרוּ אֶת־אֱלֹהֵי הַנֵּכָר אֲשֶׁר בְּתֹכְכֶם
וְהִטַּהֲרוּ וְהַחֲלִיפוּ שִׂמְלֹתֵיכֶם׃ 3 וְנָקוּמָה
וְנַעֲלֶה בֵּית־אֵל וְאֶעֱשֶׂה־שָּׁם מִזְבֵּחַ לָאֵל
הָעֹנֶה אֹתִי בְּיוֹם צָרָתִי וַיְהִי עִמָּדִי בַּדֶּרֶךְ
אֲשֶׁר הָלָכְתִּי׃ 4 וַיִּתְּנוּ אֶל־יַעֲקֹב אֵת כָּל־
אֱלֹהֵי הַנֵּכָר אֲשֶׁר בְּיָדָם וְאֶת־הַנְּזָמִים אֲשֶׁר

*30. "You have made trouble for me."* Jacob chastises his sons for their violent response (compare 49:5–6), predicting the destruction of his own household as a result.

*31. "Should he then have been allowed to treat our sister like a whore?"* The brothers choose to view the offer of money in compensation for Dinah's virginity not as an elevation of her status, but rather as a statement about Dinah's availability as a prostitute. Their explanation for their behavior makes clear that Dinah herself is not culpable. This position stands in stark contrast to tendencies in the ancient (and modern) world to blame the woman for the family's shame.

## *Israel and B'nei Yisrael*

### COVENANT RENEWAL, DEATH, AND LIFE (35:1–36:43)

This unit begins with the covenant renewal at Beth El, and then it takes the reader through a transition in Jacob's life and character. Jacob now plays a more passive role than before, and his sons slowly take over the limelight.

#### BETH EL AND THE RENAMING OF JACOB/ISRAEL (35:1–15)

*4.* Jacob's household buries all the foreign gods and the earrings from their ears—presumably also

their ears, and Jacob hid them under the Oak near Shechem. 5As they journeyed, the dread of God fell upon the cities around them, so they did not pursue Jacob's clan.

6And Jacob came to Luz in the land of Canaan—that is, Beth El—he and all the folk with him. 7There he build an altar, and called that sacred site El of Beth El, for there, in his flight from his brother, God had been revealed to him. 8And Deborah, Rebekah's nurse, died and was buried below Beth El under the Oak, so he named it the Oak of Weeping.

9God appeared to Jacob again on his return from Paddan-aram, and blessed him. 10God said to him, "Jacob is your name; but Jacob are you called no more, for Israel is your name!" Thus [God] named him Israel. 11And God said to him, "I am El Shaddai; be fruitful and multiply. A people and a host of peoples shall come from you, and kings shall go forth from your loins. 12And the land that I gave to Abraham and to Isaac I will give to you; and to your descendants after you will I give the land." 13And [the presence of God] ascended from him, at that sacred site where [God] had spoken to him.

14Jacob set up a monument in that sacred site where [God] had spoken to him, a pillar of stone; he then poured out a libation upon it and anointed it with oil. 15Jacob named the place where God had spoken to him Beth El.

בְּאָזְנֵיהֶ֑ם וַיִּטְמֹ֤ן אֹתָם֙ יַעֲקֹ֔ב תַּ֥חַת הָאֵלָ֖ה
אֲשֶׁ֥ר עִם־שְׁכֶֽם׃ 5 וַיִּסָּ֑עוּ וַיְהִ֣י ׀ חִתַּ֣ת
אֱלֹהִ֗ים עַל־הֶֽעָרִים֙ אֲשֶׁר֙ סְבִיב֣וֹתֵיהֶ֔ם וְלֹ֣א
רָֽדְפ֔וּ אַחֲרֵ֖י בְּנֵ֥י יַעֲקֹֽב׃
6 וַיָּבֹ֨א יַעֲקֹ֜ב ל֗וּזָה אֲשֶׁר֙ בְּאֶ֣רֶץ כְּנַ֔עַן הִ֖וא
בֵּֽית־אֵ֑ל ה֖וּא וְכָל־הָעָ֥ם אֲשֶׁר־עִמּֽוֹ׃ 7 וַיִּ֤בֶן
שָׁם֙ מִזְבֵּ֔חַ וַיִּקְרָא֙ לַמָּק֔וֹם אֵ֖ל בֵּֽית־אֵ֑ל כִּ֣י
שָׁ֗ם נִגְל֤וּ אֵלָיו֙ הָאֱלֹהִ֔ים בְּבָרְח֖וֹ מִפְּנֵ֥י
אָחִֽיו׃ 8 וַתָּ֤מָת דְּבֹרָה֙ מֵינֶ֣קֶת רִבְקָ֔ה וַתִּקָּבֵ֛ר
מִתַּ֥חַת לְבֵֽית־אֵ֖ל תַּ֣חַת הָֽאַלּ֑וֹן וַיִּקְרָ֥א שְׁמ֖וֹ
אַלּ֥וֹן בָּכֽוּת׃ פ
9 וַיֵּרָ֨א אֱלֹהִ֤ים אֶֽל־יַעֲקֹב֙ ע֔וֹד בְּבֹא֖וֹ מִפַּדַּ֣ן
אֲרָ֑ם וַיְבָ֖רֶךְ אֹתֽוֹ׃ 10 וַיֹּֽאמֶר־ל֥וֹ אֱלֹהִ֖ים
שִׁמְךָ֣ יַעֲקֹ֑ב לֹֽא־יִקָּרֵא֩ שִׁמְךָ֨ ע֜וֹד יַעֲקֹ֗ב כִּ֤י
אִם־יִשְׂרָאֵל֙ יִהְיֶ֣ה שְׁמֶ֔ךָ וַיִּקְרָ֥א אֶת־שְׁמ֖וֹ
יִשְׂרָאֵֽל׃ 11 וַיֹּאמֶר֩ ל֨וֹ אֱלֹהִ֜ים אֲנִ֨י אֵ֤ל שַׁדַּי֙
פְּרֵ֣ה וּרְבֵ֔ה גּ֛וֹי וּקְהַ֥ל גּוֹיִ֖ם יִהְיֶ֣ה מִמֶּ֑ךָּ
וּמְלָכִ֖ים מֵחֲלָצֶ֥יךָ יֵצֵֽאוּ׃ 12 וְאֶת־הָאָ֗רֶץ
אֲשֶׁ֥ר נָתַ֛תִּי לְאַבְרָהָ֥ם וּלְיִצְחָ֖ק לְךָ֣ אֶתְּנֶ֑נָּה
וּֽלְזַרְעֲךָ֥ אַחֲרֶ֖יךָ אֶתֵּ֥ן אֶת־הָאָֽרֶץ׃ 13 וַיַּ֥עַל
מֵעָלָ֖יו אֱלֹהִ֑ים בַּמָּק֖וֹם אֲשֶׁר־דִּבֶּ֥ר אִתּֽוֹ׃
14 וַיַּצֵּ֨ב יַעֲקֹ֜ב מַצֵּבָ֗ה בַּמָּקוֹם֙ אֲשֶׁר־דִּבֶּ֣ר
אִתּ֔וֹ מַצֶּ֖בֶת אָ֑בֶן וַיַּסֵּ֤ךְ עָלֶ֙יהָ֙ נֶ֔סֶךְ וַיִּצֹ֥ק עָלֶ֖יהָ
שָֽׁמֶן׃ 15 וַיִּקְרָ֨א יַעֲקֹ֜ב אֶת־שֵׁ֣ם הַמָּק֗וֹם
אֲשֶׁר֩ דִּבֶּ֨ר אִתּ֥וֹ שָׁ֛ם אֱלֹהִ֖ים בֵּֽית־אֵֽל׃

the *t'rafim* (household gods) that Rachel stole from her father (31:19). The reason for specifying earrings is not clear. In Exodus 32 (the Golden Calf story) and Judges 8:24–27, earrings are used to fashion an idol.

***8. Deborah, Rebekah's nurse.*** See at 24:59.

***died.*** Rebekah's own death is never mentioned, so it is strange that her nurse's death is worth noting.

***the Oak.*** Presumably a tree near Beth El that served as a landmark. A more famous Deborah—the prophet—is also associated with a tree, for she would sit under a palm and render judgment (Judges 4:4–5).

***10. "Jacob are you called no more, for Israel is your name!"*** The story in vv. 9–15 is a doublet on the name change from Jacob to Israel (32:17–33), one of several episodes in the Torah that appear twice in similar form (see the sister/wife story of Abraham and Sarah in Genesis 12 and 20).

16 וַיִּסְעוּ מִבֵּית אֵל וַיְהִי־עוֹד כִּבְרַת־הָאָרֶץ
לָבוֹא אֶפְרָתָה וַתֵּלֶד רָחֵל וַתְּקַשׁ בְּלִדְתָּהּ׃
17 וַיְהִי בְהַקְשֹׁתָהּ בְּלִדְתָּהּ וַתֹּאמֶר לָהּ
הַמְיַלֶּדֶת אַל־תִּירְאִי כִּי־גַם־זֶה לָךְ בֵּן׃
18 וַיְהִי בְּצֵאת נַפְשָׁהּ כִּי מֵתָה וַתִּקְרָא שְׁמוֹ
בֶּן־אוֹנִי וְאָבִיו קָרָא־לוֹ בִנְיָמִין׃ 19 וַתָּמָת
רָחֵל וַתִּקָּבֵר בְּדֶרֶךְ אֶפְרָתָה הִוא בֵּית
לָחֶם׃ 20 וַיַּצֵּב יַעֲקֹב מַצֵּבָה עַל־קְבֻרָתָהּ
הִוא מַצֶּבֶת קְבֻרַת־רָחֵל עַד־הַיּוֹם׃

16 They then journeyed from Beth El, and there was still some ground to cover before reaching Ephrath, when Rachel went into labor, and her labor was difficult. 17 And as her labor was difficult for her, the midwife said to her, "Don't be afraid; this one, too, will be a son for you." 18 And as her life was leaving her—for she was dying—she named him Ben-oni, but his father called him Benjamin. 19 Rachel died and was buried on the road to Ephrath, that is, Bethlehem, 20 and Jacob set up a pillar by her burial site; it is the monument at Rachel's tomb to this day.

## RACHEL'S SECOND SON AND HER DEATH (35:16–21)

On the road from Beth El, Rachel dies in childbirth. Earlier, when Laban had charged Jacob with stealing the household gods (Genesis 31), Jacob had countered, "the one with whom you find your gods shall not live" (31:32). It is unclear whether according to the text's composer(s) Rachel's death is an unwitting result of Jacob's rash curse (after all, Laban did not find his household gods). Deaths during childbirth were a widespread phenomenon in the ancient world. Rachel's demise may implicitly be connected to her former barrenness and desperate attempts to have a child. Ironically, the woman who so longed for children dies in childbirth.

This is one of only two stories in the Bible about such deaths. In the other (I Samuel 4:18–22), a woman's premature labor is triggered by the shock of Israel's defeat in war and of the deaths of her father-in-law and husband; and she, like Rachel, dies after naming the child (but see at 30:3).

*17. "Don't be afraid; this one, too, will be a son for you."* Rachel—who embedded her longing for another son already in the name of her first son, Joseph (30:24)—is dying; but her midwife tries to comfort her with the knowledge that she is giving up her life for a living (male) child. A similar attempt at comfort is recorded in I Samuel 4:18.

*18. Ben-oni.* An ambiguous name that can mean "son of my suffering" or "son of my strength."

*Benjamin.* That is, "son of the right [hand]." Perhaps Jacob is changing Rachel's sense of the futility of her life into an affirmation of her importance to Jacob as his favorite wife.

***19. buried on the road to Ephrath, that is, Bethlehem.*** According to I Samuel 10:2, the tomb of Rachel was in the territory of (or at the boundary of) Benjamin, as might be expected, and not near Bethlehem, which is in Judah. In Jeremiah 31:15, Rachel weeps for her children in Ramah, a city in Benjamin. The later status accorded to Bethlehem under David's influence might account for the present note that Rachel's tomb was near Bethlehem. According to the biblical accounts, Rachel is the only one of the four matriarchs not buried in the cave of Machpelah, purchased by Abraham for Sarah (Genesis 23)—which is also Jacob's final resting place (50:13). Such perpetual separation is sadly ironic, given his intense love for Rachel.

*20.* Just as he had set up a pillar to commemorate his encounter with God (35:14), Jacob sets up one to mark Rachel's grave. Although no emotions are expressed here, on his deathbed Jacob will poignantly recall this loss and burial (48:7).

21Israel then resumed his journey, and pitched
his tent beyond the tower of Eder. 22Now, while
Israel was residing in that area, Reuben went and
lay with his father's concubine Bilhah, and Israel
heard of it.

The sons of Jacob were twelve in number.
23Leah's sons were Jacob's first-born Reuben, Simeon, Levi, Judah, Issachar, and Zebulun. 24Ra-
chel's sons were Joseph and Benjamin. 25The sons
of Bilhah, Rachel's maid, were Dan and Naphtali.
26And the sons of Zilpah, Leah's maid, were Gad
and Asher. These are the sons of Jacob, born to him
in Paddan-aram.

27Jacob came to his father Isaac at Mamre [near]
Kiriath-arba (that is, Hebron), where Abraham and
Isaac had sojourned. 28The years of Isaac's life came
to 180. 29Isaac then breathed his last and died; he

21 וַיִּסַּע יִשְׂרָאֵל וַיֵּט אהלה אָהֳלוֹ מֵהָלְאָה
לְמִגְדַּל־עֵדֶר׃ 22 וַיְהִי בִּשְׁכֹּן יִשְׂרָאֵל בָּאָרֶץ
הַהִוא וַיֵּלֶךְ רְאוּבֵן וַיִּשְׁכַּב אֶת־בִּלְהָה
פִּילֶגֶשׁ אָבִיו וַיִּשְׁמַע יִשְׂרָאֵל* פ
וַיִּהְיוּ בְנֵי־יַעֲקֹב שְׁנֵים עָשָׂר׃ 23 בְּנֵי לֵאָה
בְּכוֹר יַעֲקֹב רְאוּבֵן וְשִׁמְעוֹן וְלֵוִי וִיהוּדָה
ויששכר וְיִשָּׂשכָר וּזְבֻלוּן׃ 24 בְּנֵי רָחֵל יוֹסֵף
וּבִנְיָמִן׃ 25 וּבְנֵי בִלְהָה שִׁפְחַת רָחֵל דָּן
וְנַפְתָּלִי׃ 26 וּבְנֵי זִלְפָּה שִׁפְחַת לֵאָה גָּד
וְאָשֵׁר אֵלֶּה בְּנֵי יַעֲקֹב אֲשֶׁר יֻלַּד־לוֹ בְּפַדַּן
אֲרָם׃
27 וַיָּבֹא יַעֲקֹב אֶל־יִצְחָק אָבִיו מַמְרֵא קִרְיַת
הָאַרְבַּע הִוא חֶבְרוֹן אֲשֶׁר־גָּר־שָׁם אַבְרָהָם
וְיִצְחָק׃ 28 וַיִּהְיוּ יְמֵי יִצְחָק מְאַת שָׁנָה
וּשְׁמֹנִים שָׁנָה׃ 29 וַיִּגְוַע יִצְחָק וַיָּמָת וַיֵּאָסֶף

*For the latter part of this verse, Masoretic tradition also preserves an alternative cantillation pattern:
וַיֵּלֶךְ רְאוּבֵן וַיִּשְׁכַּב אֶת־בִּלְהָה פִּילֶגֶשׁ אָבִיו וַיִּשְׁמַע יִשְׂרָאֵל׃

**22. *Reuben went and lay with his father's concubine Bilhah.*** Sleeping with one's father's wife was a great offense (Leviticus 18:8; 20:11). It is possible that this is why Bilhah is called a concubine (*pilegesh*) here, while she appears as "wife" in other instances (see Genesis 37:2). Intercourse with the father's concubine, although a less severe offense than with his wife, is apparently tantamount to a declaration of rebellion against the father. When Adonijah asks for Abishag, the woman who shared David's bed when he was old (I Kings 1:1–4), Solomon takes this as a bid for the throne, and has Adonijah executed for treason (I Kings 2:13–25). Note also Absalom's sleeping with David's concubines as a sign of displacing his father, David (II Samuel 16:22–23).

***and Israel heard.*** As with Dinah in Genesis 34, Jacob takes no immediate action. However, he will bypass Reuben for the birthright in his deathbed blessing (Genesis 49:3–4).

## JACOB'S WIVES AND CHILDREN (35:22–26)

The summary list of Jacob's twelve sons is given according to their mothers. Dinah, and any other possible daughters, are omitted. The mothers' mention presumably indicates the relative status of the sons. The mothers are listed in a different order than seen previously. In 33:2, fearing Esau's wrath, Jacob had placed the maids Bilhah and Zilpah and their children first, Leah and her children next, and Rachel and her son closest to the rear. That order reflects their importance to Jacob, from the most to the least expendable. Here, the women's order corresponds to the order in which Jacob married them: Leah; Rachel; Rachel's maid, Bilhah; and Leah's maid, Zilpah.

## ISAAC'S DEATH (35:27–29)

Jacob returns to see his father Isaac (who may have been on his deathbed for two decades; 27:1–2,

was gathered to his people old and full of years, and
his sons Esau and Jacob buried him.
36 This is the line of Esau (that is, Edom).
2 Esau took his wives from the daughters of Canaan
—Adah daughter of Elon the Hivite and Oholibamah daughter of Anah daughter of Zibeon the
Hivite, 3 and Basemath, Ishmael's daughter, Nebaioth's sister. 4 Adah bore Eliphaz to Esau, and
Basemath bore Reuel. 5 Oholibamah bore Jeush,
Jalam, and Korah—these are the sons of Esau born
to him in the land of Canaan.
6 Esau took his wives and sons and all the people
of his household, his livestock, his cattle, and all his
possessions acquired in the land of Canaan, and
went to [another] region because of his brother
Jacob; 7 for their wealth was too abundant for them
to dwell together; the land where they were staying
could not support them both, because of their livestock. 8 So Esau settled in the hill country of Seir;
Esau is [also called] Edom. 9 This, then, is the line
of Esau, progenitor of the Edomites, of the hill
country of Seir:
10 These are the names of Esau's sons: Eliphaz
son of Adah, Esau's wife; Reuel son of Basemath,
Esau's wife. 11 The sons of Eliphaz were Teman,

אֶל־עַמָּיו זָקֵן וּשְׂבַע יָמִים וַיִּקְבְּרוּ אֹתוֹ עֵשָׂו
וְיַעֲקֹב בָּנָיו׃ פ
לו וְאֵלֶּה תֹּלְדוֹת עֵשָׂו הוּא אֱדוֹם׃ 2 עֵשָׂו
לָקַח אֶת־נָשָׁיו מִבְּנוֹת כְּנָעַן אֶת־עָדָה בַּת־
אֵילוֹן הַחִתִּי וְאֶת־אָהֳלִיבָמָה בַּת־עֲנָה בַּת־
צִבְעוֹן הַחִוִּי׃ 3 וְאֶת־בָּשְׂמַת בַּת־יִשְׁמָעֵאל
אֲחוֹת נְבָיוֹת׃ 4 וַתֵּלֶד עָדָה לְעֵשָׂו
אֶת־אֱלִיפָז וּבָשְׂמַת יָלְדָה אֶת־רְעוּאֵל׃
5 וְאָהֳלִיבָמָה יָלְדָה אֶת־יעיש יְעוּשׁ וְאֶת־
יַעְלָם וְאֶת־קֹרַח אֵלֶּה בְּנֵי עֵשָׂו אֲשֶׁר יֻלְּדוּ־
לוֹ בְּאֶרֶץ כְּנָעַן׃
6 וַיִּקַּח עֵשָׂו אֶת־נָשָׁיו וְאֶת־בָּנָיו וְאֶת־בְּנֹתָיו
וְאֶת־כָּל־נַפְשׁוֹת בֵּיתוֹ וְאֶת־מִקְנֵהוּ וְאֶת־
כָּל־בְּהֶמְתּוֹ וְאֵת כָּל־קִנְיָנוֹ אֲשֶׁר רָכַשׁ
בְּאֶרֶץ כְּנָעַן וַיֵּלֶךְ אֶל־אֶרֶץ מִפְּנֵי יַעֲקֹב
אָחִיו׃ 7 כִּי־הָיָה רְכוּשָׁם רָב מִשֶּׁבֶת יַחְדָּו
וְלֹא יָכְלָה אֶרֶץ מְגוּרֵיהֶם לָשֵׂאת אֹתָם
מִפְּנֵי מִקְנֵיהֶם׃ 8 וַיֵּשֶׁב עֵשָׂו בְּהַר שֵׂעִיר
עֵשָׂו הוּא אֱדוֹם׃ 9 וְאֵלֶּה תֹּלְדוֹת עֵשָׂו אֲבִי
אֱדוֹם בְּהַר שֵׂעִיר׃
10 אֵלֶּה שְׁמוֹת בְּנֵי־עֵשָׂו אֱלִיפַז בֶּן־עָדָה
אֵשֶׁת עֵשָׂו רְעוּאֵל בֶּן־בָּשְׂמַת אֵשֶׁת עֵשָׂו׃
11 וַיִּהְיוּ בְּנֵי אֱלִיפָז תֵּימָן אוֹמָר צְפוֹ וּגַעְתָּם

31:41). Nothing is said about his mother Rebekah, whose death is never reported. Isaac dies and is buried by both Esau and Jacob. This brief report recalls that of Abraham's death and burial (25:8–10). In both cases estranged brothers come together to bury their father. Nothing is recorded as to whether they also bury their differences.

### THE LINE OF ESAU (36:1–43)

This section provides the genealogy of Esau's line. Esau's Canaanite wives figure prominently. While the women in Jacob's list above are mentioned only in connection with their sons, Esau's wives are identified by the name and ethnicity of their fathers. Esau acquires power by establishing a series of marriage alliances corresponding to the later relationship of the nation Edom with these other nations. Here the movement of women from the house of their father to the house of their husband serves to establish political and social relations between two groups of previously unrelated men.

The passage's inconsistent genealogies must have been compiled from a variety of sources. The names of Esau's wives in vv. 2–3 do not correspond to the names of his wives given earlier (26:34, 28:9). Prominent in this list are wives Adah, Basemath, Timna, Oholibamah, and Zibeon.

Omar, Zepho, Gatam, and Kenaz. [12]Timna was a
concubine of Eliphaz, Esau's son. She bore Amalek
to Eliphaz. These were the descendants of Adah,
Esau's wife. [13]And these are the sons of Reuel:
Nahath, Zerah, Shammah, and Mizzah. These
were the descendants of Basemath, Esau's wife.
[14]And these were the sons of Oholibamah daughter
of Anah daughter of Zibeon, Esau's wife—she bore
Jeush, Jalam, and Korah to Esau.

[15]These are the clans of Esau's descendants: the
descendants of Eliphaz, Esau's first-born—the clan
of Teman, the clan of Omar, the clan of Zepho,
the clan of Kenaz; [16]the clan of Korah, the clan
of Gatam, the clan of Amalek; these are the clans
of Eliphaz in the land of Edom; these are the descendants of Adah. [17]And these are the descendants
of Reuel, Esau's son: the clan of Nahath, the clan of
Nahath, the clan of Zerah, the clan of Shammah,
the clan of Mizzah; these are the clans of Reuel in
the land of Edom; these are the descendants of
Basemath, Esau's wife. [18]And these are the descendants of Oholibamah, Esau's wife: the clan of
Jeush, the clan of Jalam, the clan of Korah; these
are the clans of Oholibamah daughter of Anah,
Esau's wife. [19]These are the descendants of Esau,
that is, Edom, and these are their clans.

[20]These are the descendants of Seir the Horite,
who dwelt in the land—Lotan, Shobal, Zibeon,
Anah, [21]Dishon, Ezer, and Dishan. These are the
Horite clans, the descendants of Seir in the land of
Edom. [22]The sons of Lotan were Hori and He-
mam; Lotan's sister was Timna. [23]And these are the
sons of Shobal—Alvan, Manahath, Ebal, Shepho,
and Onam. [24]And these are the sons of Zibeon—
Aiah and Anah. This is the Anah who discovered
the hot springs in the wilderness as he was tending
his father Zibeon's donkeys. [25]And these are the
children of Anah—Dishon, and Oholibamah,
Anah's daughter. [26]And these are the sons of Dishon—Hemdan, Eshban, Ithran, and Cheran.
[27]And these are the sons of Ezer—Bilhan, Zaavan,

וּקְנַז׃ 12 וְתִמְנַע ׀ הָיְתָה פִילֶגֶשׁ לֶאֱלִיפַז בֶּן־
עֵשָׂו וַתֵּלֶד לֶאֱלִיפַז אֶת־עֲמָלֵק אֵלֶּה בְּנֵי
עָדָה אֵשֶׁת עֵשָׂו׃ 13 וְאֵלֶּה בְּנֵי רְעוּאֵל נַחַת
וָזֶרַח שַׁמָּה וּמִזָּה אֵלֶּה הָיוּ בְּנֵי בָשְׂמַת
אֵשֶׁת עֵשָׂו׃ 14 וְאֵלֶּה הָיוּ בְּנֵי אָהֳלִיבָמָה
בַת־עֲנָה בַּת־צִבְעוֹן אֵשֶׁת עֵשָׂו וַתֵּלֶד לְעֵשָׂו
אֶת־יעיש יְעוּשׁ וְאֶת־יַעְלָם וְאֶת־קֹרַח׃
15 אֵלֶּה אַלּוּפֵי בְנֵי־עֵשָׂו בְּנֵי אֱלִיפַז בְּכוֹר
עֵשָׂו אַלּוּף תֵּימָן אַלּוּף אוֹמָר אַלּוּף צְפוֹ
אַלּוּף קְנַז׃ 16 אַלּוּף־קֹרַח אַלּוּף גַּעְתָּם אַלּוּף
עֲמָלֵק אֵלֶּה אַלּוּפֵי אֱלִיפַז בְּאֶרֶץ אֱדוֹם
אֵלֶּה בְּנֵי עָדָה׃ 17 וְאֵלֶּה בְּנֵי רְעוּאֵל בֶּן־
עֵשָׂו אַלּוּף נַחַת אַלּוּף זֶרַח אַלּוּף שַׁמָּה
אַלּוּף מִזָּה אֵלֶּה אַלּוּפֵי רְעוּאֵל בְּאֶרֶץ אֱדוֹם
אֵלֶּה בְּנֵי בָשְׂמַת אֵשֶׁת עֵשָׂו׃ 18 וְאֵלֶּה בְּנֵי
אָהֳלִיבָמָה אֵשֶׁת עֵשָׂו אַלּוּף יְעוּשׁ אַלּוּף
יַעְלָם אַלּוּף קֹרַח אֵלֶּה אַלּוּפֵי אָהֳלִיבָמָה
בַּת־עֲנָה אֵשֶׁת עֵשָׂו׃ 19 אֵלֶּה בְנֵי־עֵשָׂו
וְאֵלֶּה אַלּוּפֵיהֶם הוּא אֱדוֹם׃
20 אֵלֶּה בְנֵי־שֵׂעִיר הַחֹרִי יֹשְׁבֵי הָאָרֶץ לוֹטָן
וְשׁוֹבָל וְצִבְעוֹן וַעֲנָה׃ 21 וְדִשׁוֹן וְאֵצֶר וְדִישָׁן
אֵלֶּה אַלּוּפֵי הַחֹרִי בְּנֵי שֵׂעִיר בְּאֶרֶץ אֱדוֹם׃
22 וַיִּהְיוּ בְנֵי־לוֹטָן חֹרִי וְהֵימָם וַאֲחוֹת לוֹטָן
תִּמְנָע׃ 23 וְאֵלֶּה בְּנֵי שׁוֹבָל עַלְוָן וּמָנַחַת
וְעֵיבָל שְׁפוֹ וְאוֹנָם׃ 24 וְאֵלֶּה בְנֵי־צִבְעוֹן
וְאַיָּה וַעֲנָה הוּא עֲנָה אֲשֶׁר מָצָא אֶת־הַיֵּמִם
בַּמִּדְבָּר בִּרְעֹתוֹ אֶת־הַחֲמֹרִים לְצִבְעוֹן
אָבִיו׃ 25 וְאֵלֶּה בְנֵי־עֲנָה דִּשֹׁן וְאָהֳלִיבָמָה
בַּת־עֲנָה׃ 26 וְאֵלֶּה בְּנֵי דִישָׁן חֶמְדָּן וְאֶשְׁבָּן
וְיִתְרָן וּכְרָן׃ 27 אֵלֶּה בְּנֵי־אֵצֶר בִּלְהָן וְזַעֲוָן

and Akan. [28]And these are the sons of Dishan—Uz and Aran. [29]These, then, are the Horite clans—the clan of Lotan, the clan of Shobal, the clan of Zibeon, the clan of Anah, [30]the clan of Dishon, the clan of Ezer, the clan of Dishan; clan by clan, these are the Horite clans in the land of Edom.

[31]And these are the kings who reigned in the land of Edom, before a king reigned over the people of Israel—[32]Bela son of Beor reigned in Edom, and his city's name was Dinhabah. [33]When Bela died, Jobab son of Zerah, of Bozrah, reigned in his place. [34]When Jobab died, Husham of the land of the Temanites reigned in his place. [35]When Husham died, Hadad son of Bedad, who defeated Midian in the countryside of Moab, reigned in his place; his city's name was Avith. [36]When Hadad died, Samlah of Masrekah reigned in his place. [37]When Samlah died, Saul of Rehoboth-on-the-River reigned in his place. [38]When Saul died, Baal-hanan of Achbor reigned in his place. [39]When Baal-hanan of Achbor died, Hadar reigned in his place; his city's name was Pau, and his wife's name was Mehetabel daughter of Matred daughter of Me-zahab.

[40]These, then, are the names of Esau's clans, by their families, their locations, their names—the clan of Timna, the clan of Alvah, the clan of Jetheth, [41]the clan of Oholibamah, the clan of Elah, the clan of Pinon, [42]the clan of Kenaz, the clan of Teman, the clan of Mibzar, [43]the clan of Magdiel, and the clan of Iram. These are the clans of Edom (that is, of Esau the progenitor of the Edomites) in their settlements in the land they possessed.

וַעֲקָן׃ 28 אֵלֶּה בְנֵי־דִישָׁן עוּץ וַאֲרָן׃ 29 אֵלֶּה
אַלּוּפֵי הַחֹרִי אַלּוּף לוֹטָן אַלּוּף שׁוֹבָל אַלּוּף
צִבְעוֹן אַלּוּף עֲנָה׃ 30 אַלּוּף דִּשֹׁן אַלּוּף אֵצֶר
אַלּוּף דִּישָׁן אֵלֶּה אַלּוּפֵי הַחֹרִי לְאַלֻּפֵיהֶם
בְּאֶרֶץ שֵׂעִיר׃ פ

31 וְאֵלֶּה הַמְּלָכִים אֲשֶׁר מָלְכוּ בְּאֶרֶץ אֱדוֹם
לִפְנֵי מְלָךְ־מֶלֶךְ לִבְנֵי יִשְׂרָאֵל׃ 32 וַיִּמְלֹךְ
בֶּאֱדוֹם בֶּלַע בֶּן־בְּעוֹר וְשֵׁם עִירוֹ דִּנְהָבָה׃
33 וַיָּמָת בָּלַע וַיִּמְלֹךְ תַּחְתָּיו יוֹבָב בֶּן־זֶרַח
מִבָּצְרָה׃ 34 וַיָּמָת יוֹבָב וַיִּמְלֹךְ תַּחְתָּיו חֻשָׁם
מֵאֶרֶץ הַתֵּימָנִי׃ 35 וַיָּמָת חֻשָׁם וַיִּמְלֹךְ
תַּחְתָּיו הֲדַד בֶּן־בְּדַד הַמַּכֶּה אֶת־מִדְיָן
בִּשְׂדֵה מוֹאָב וְשֵׁם עִירוֹ עֲוִית׃ 36 וַיָּמָת
הֲדָד וַיִּמְלֹךְ תַּחְתָּיו שַׂמְלָה מִמַּשְׂרֵקָה׃
37 וַיָּמָת שַׂמְלָה וַיִּמְלֹךְ תַּחְתָּיו שָׁאוּל
מֵרְחֹבוֹת הַנָּהָר׃ 38 וַיָּמָת שָׁאוּל וַיִּמְלֹךְ
תַּחְתָּיו בַּעַל חָנָן בֶּן־עַכְבּוֹר׃ 39 וַיָּמָת בַּעַל
חָנָן בֶּן־עַכְבּוֹר וַיִּמְלֹךְ תַּחְתָּיו הֲדַר וְשֵׁם
עִירוֹ פָּעוּ וְשֵׁם אִשְׁתּוֹ מְהֵיטַבְאֵל בַּת־מַטְרֵד
בַּת מֵי זָהָב׃

40 וְאֵלֶּה שְׁמוֹת אַלּוּפֵי עֵשָׂו לְמִשְׁפְּחֹתָם
לִמְקֹמֹתָם בִּשְׁמֹתָם אַלּוּף תִּמְנָע אַלּוּף
עַלְוָה אַלּוּף יְתֵת׃ 41 אַלּוּף אָהֳלִיבָמָה
אַלּוּף אֵלָה אַלּוּף פִּינֹן׃ 42 אַלּוּף קְנַז אַלּוּף
תֵּימָן אַלּוּף מִבְצָר׃ 43 אַלּוּף מַגְדִּיאֵל אַלּוּף
עִירָם אֵלֶּה ׀ אַלּוּפֵי אֱדוֹם לְמֹשְׁבֹתָם בְּאֶרֶץ
אֲחֻזָּתָם הוּא עֵשָׂו אֲבִי אֱדוֹם׃ פ

*39. Mehetabel.* [The mention of this woman's mother and her maternal grandparent is unusual, especially since nothing further is known about her—and even less is known about her husband. —*Ed.*]

*40–43.* The concluding list of clans in Esau's line, here identified as Edom, Israel's neighbor, includes women—Timna and Oholibamah—each as the head of a clan.

—*Shawna Dolansky*
*Risa Levitt Kohn*

# Another View

VAYISHLACH BEGINS AND ENDS with references to Esau, Jacob's twin brother. At the beginning of this parashah, it is to Esau whom Jacob sends messengers (32:4), who return with a report that he is on the move, coming to meet his brother (32:7). The parashah concludes with Esau going to another region "because of his brother Jacob" (36:6–8) and with Esau's genealogical line, the Edomite people (36:9–42).

Esau is thus highlighted in this parashah by being the subject of the beginning and ending units. Even so, Jacob is clearly the more important character—a fate Esau has had to endure from early on. Esau is a touching figure because no matter how hard he tries, he cannot measure up to his younger brother who—though not always honest and fair in his dealings—outmaneuvers him.

What distinguishes the two brothers? How to account for Jacob's prominence over Esau? The difference between the two begins with their mother's decision and continues with their choices of marriage partners. God informs Rebekah—not Isaac—about their yet-to-be-born twins that "the older shall serve the younger" (25:23). Rebekah acts on this information by supporting Jacob at the expense of her other son.

Then Esau marries two Hittite women, causing his parents distress (26:34–35), whereas Jacob is sent (at his mother's instigation) to find a wife from her own people (27:46–28:5), which he does (29:21–30). Attempting to please his parents, Esau tries again by marrying Mahalath, also a cousin like Jacob's wives; she is the daughter of Ishmael, his father's brother (28:8–9).

The Dinah story occurs in the middle, in between the references to Esau that frame this parashah. After Shechem—a Canaanite prince—rapes Jacob's daughter, Jacob is indecisive about their marriage (34:5).

*Jacob's prominence over Esau is due to their mother and wives.*

Dinah's two oldest full brothers, however, respond by killing all the Shechemites so that the marriage between Dinah and Shechem does not happen, thereby keeping their sister from marrying the people in the land.

Genesis 34 reaffirms the importance of marrying the right people within the family. Together these incidents illustrate the importance of mother and wife, and not only father, in determining a person's destiny.

—*Tammi J. Schneider*

# Post-biblical Interpretations

***his eleven children*** (32:23). Benjamin was not yet born, but didn't Jacob already have twelve children? Midrash *B'reishit Rabbah* 76.9 and 80.4 suggest that Jacob hid Dinah in a box so that Esau would not see her and seek to marry her. On that basis, Jacob is castigated for lack of compassion toward his brother; as Rashi explains, perhaps by such a marriage, Esau would have returned to a path of good (on 32:23).

***Dinah, Leah's daughter . . . went out*** (34:1). *B'reishit Rabbah* 80.1 (also 8.12, 18.2, 45.5) and JT *Sanhedrin* 2:6 (20d) are among numerous sources that judge both Dinah and Leah harshly based on this verse. Both are seen to act inappropriately for women simply by going out unattended—Dinah here, and Leah when she likewise "went out" to inform Jacob, "I am the one you will bed [tonight]" (30:16).

***to see the women of the locality*** (34:1). *Pirkei D'Rabbi Eliezer* 38 claims that they were a ruse, sent by Shechem to play timbrels outside Dinah's tent, in order to lure her outside—where he could lay hold of her.

***then, taking Dinah*** (34:26). Dinah is mentioned only once more in Torah, among Jacob's descendants in 46:15. What became of her? In *B'reishit Rabbah* 80.11, Rabbi Huna puts into Dinah's mouth the words of Tamar—King David's daughter who was raped by her half-brother Amnon: "Where will I carry my shame...?" (II Samuel 13:13); he suggests that Dinah

*Dinah became pregnant when raped by Shechem, and she bore a daughter.*

agreed to leave Shechem's house only after her brother Simeon promised to marry her himself. Thus—based on her involvement with Shechem—Dinah is identified as the otherwise unnamed "Canaanite woman" who was the mother of Simeon's son Saul (46:10). It was also taught that when she died, Simeon buried her in Canaan.

Another tradition found in *B'reishit Rabbah* 19.12 (also 57.4, 76.9, 80.4) and BT *Bava Batra* 15b, among other sources, is that Dinah became the wife of Job. Some versions of this tradition view Dinah's subsequent marriage to a non-Israelite (namely, Job) as part of Jacob's punishment for having withheld her from Esau (see the first entry, above). Alternatively, *Pirkei D'Rabbi Eliezer* 38 states that Dinah became pregnant when raped by Shechem, and she bore a daughter. Afraid of the shame that the presence of this child would bring on their community, Dinah's brothers sought to kill the infant. Jacob, however, put an amulet with the name of God around the girl's neck and sent her away; she was taken by the archangel Michael to Egypt, where she was adopted by a childless Egyptian priest and raised as his daughter. Dinah's daughter, "Asenath daughter of Potiphera, priest of On" (Genesis 41:45), later became Joseph's wife. A further embellishment on this legend tells the story as follows: Joseph was exceedingly handsome, and when he went out, women would throw jewelry to attract his notice. Asenath tossed her amulet and when Joseph saw it, he realized their relationship and married her (*Chizz'kuni* to 41:45).

***Deborah, Rebekah's nurse, died... and was buried ... under the... Oak of Weeping*** (35:8). The word *bachut*, "weeping," is similar to the plural term *b'chiyot*, "weepings," suggesting to the Rabbis that *two* deaths were being mourned here: the death of Deborah, and the death of Rebekah—an event not otherwise mentioned in the Torah. According to *B'reishit Rabbah* 81.5, this is why the next verse (35:9) relates that *God appeared to Jacob... and blessed him*: God performed the kindness of visiting and comforting Jacob while he mourned his mother. But why is Rebekah's death not related directly? Midrash *Tanchuma, Ki Teitzei* 4, explains that it was impossible to have an honorable funeral for her. Abraham was dead; Isaac, blind and weakened, could not leave his tent; and Jacob had gone abroad and could not return in time. Only Esau remained, and the continued ill feeling between him and his mother made it unlikely that he would come. Because Rebekah's life ended in such a lonely way, the Torah hints at her passing only obliquely (see also the medieval commentator Ramban on 35:8).

***as her life was leaving her... she named him Ben-oni, but his father called him Benjamin*** (35:18). Commentators generally agree that by the word *oni*, Rachel meant "my pain" or "my sorrow." Rabbi Moses ben Nachman (1194–1270)—usually known as "Nachmanides" or by his initials as "Ramban"—notes here that another meaning of *on* is "strength," as in 49:3, in which Jacob blesses Reuben as "first fruit of my vigor (*reishit oni*)." So too *y'min*, the right hand, stands for strength in the biblical world. Thus, Jacob does not actually change the name given by Rachel—for all Jacob's children bear names given to them by their mothers—but rather "translates" it to its most positive interpretation.

—*Gail Labovitz*

# *Contemporary Reflection*

After twenty years, Jacob is coming home. Anticipating that the reunion with the brother he cheated all those years ago will be disastrous, he sends messengers laden with presents ahead to his brother. But just to be on the safe side, he divides his camp in order to minimize the losses should he come under attack. The story continues: "That same night, he got up, took his two wives, his two maidservants, and his eleven children, and crossed at a ford of the Jabbok [river]. . . . Jacob was left alone, and a man wrestled with him" (32:23–25). The nocturnal wrestler wounds and blesses him and gives him a new name—our name: Yisrael, one who wrestles with God.

Jacob's wrestling with God is a powerful image and legacy. We never know with whom Jacob is wrestling: is it himself, his conscience, his brother, God, or all of these parts of himself and of his life? Jacob names the place Peniel, meaning "Face of God," for, as he states, "I have seen God face-to-face" (32:31). Somehow, alone, separated from his "two wives" and his "eleven children," Jacob discovers the face of God in his adversary—and Jacob is blessed.

Eleven children cross the river? But Jacob already at this point has twelve children. What about Dinah, his daughter? What happened to her? Rashi, quoting a midrash, explains: "He placed her in a chest and locked her in." While many commentaries understand that by locking Dinah in a box Jacob intends to protect her from marrying his brother Esau, we know the truth of the story. Hiding Dinah—locking her up—is a powerful image about silencing a woman. And that silence echoes loudly through the rest of the Torah.

What happens next? Dinah gets raped (Genesis 34).

In an ultimate act of silencing, the commentaries understand Dinah's rape as Jacob's punishment for withholding her from Esau. Dinah's rape is *Jacob's* punishment? What about Dinah? What has she done? How does she feel? Our text is silent. We only know what her brothers and father think: that she has been defiled (34:5–7), that she must not be treated as a whore (34:31). No one in the Torah or the midrashic accounts asks her what she wants, what she needs, or how she can be comforted.

*No one asks Dinah what she wants, what she needs, or how she can be comforted.*

Her silence is loud enough to reverberate through the generations. We hear it in the reports of other fathers who perceive their daughter's rape as their dishonor, their punishment. Fortunately for Dinah, in Genesis the blame and punishment fall entirely on the perpetrator and his people, not on her. Other women are not as lucky. In 1998, in Pakistan, Arbab Khatoon was raped by three men in a village in Jacobabad district. She was murdered seven hours later. According to local residents, she was killed by her relatives for bringing dishonour to the family by going to the police. In 1999, Lal Jamilla Mandokhel, a 16-year-old mentally retarded girl, was reportedly raped several times by a junior clerk of the local government department of agriculture in a hotel in Parachinar, Pakistan. The girl's uncle filed a complaint about the incident with police—who took the accused into protective custody but then handed over the girl to her tribe. The elders decided that she had brought shame to her tribe and that the honor could only be restored by her death; she was killed in front of a tribal gathering.

Similar stories are reported not only in Pakistan but also in Bangladesh, Great Britain, Brazil, Ecuador, Egypt, India, Israel, Italy, Jordan, Pakistan, Morocco, Sweden, Turkey, Uganda—as well as Afghanistan, Iraq, and Iran. No wonder women are silent!

This outrage is only part of a much larger problem of violence against women. For example, according to the United Nations Children's Fund (UNICEF), more than five thousand brides die annually in India because their dowries are considered insufficient. Widney Brown, advocacy director for Human Rights Watch, says that "in countries where Islam is practiced, they're called honor killings, but dowry deaths and so-called crimes of passion have a similar dynamic in that the women are killed by male family members and the crimes are perceived as excusable or understandable." The practice, she said, "goes across cultures and across religions." In the few cases when public outcry around the world and international pressure were used, a woman's life was spared. But stories that capture the headlines do not begin to address the scope and range of the problem.

Another form that violence takes is sexual slavery and human trafficking, which even happens in Israel. According to a recent Knesset report, thousands of women are illegally smuggled into Israel and sold into sexual slavery. These young women—typically in their early twenties—are raped, abused, incarcerated and threatened, "servicing" 15–25 clients over 14–18 hours a day, 7 days a week. The women become indentured slaves with an ever-growing debt to their owners. Israeli men from all walks of life pay approximately a million visits to brothels per month and the profits from this illicit activity are estimated at $750 million annually. Sexual slavery and human trafficking remain a global problem, taking place in nearly every corner of the world. It is estimated that 600,000–800,000 people—mostly women and children—are trafficked across borders worldwide every year. (For ways to get information—and to get involved in this issue—please contact the Task Force on Human Trafficking through its Web site.)

We hear Dinah's silence as well in the challenges to reproductive rights happening right now in the United States. If Dinah were raped and became pregnant while living in South Dakota in 2007, she might not be able to get an abortion.

What happens to Dinah in the aftermath of her ordeal? We do not know. We never hear from her, just as we may never hear from the women and girls in our generation who are victims of violence and whose voices are not heard. But the legacy of Jacob as Israel, the one who wrestles, demands that we confront the shadowy parts of ourselves and our world—and not passively ignore these facts. The feminist educator Nelle Morton urged women to hear each other "into speech." Dinah's story challenges us to go even further and be also the voices for all of our sisters.

*—Laura Geller*

# *Voices*

## *Dinah*

Ruth Fainlight

*Genesis 34*

Holding up my hands in warning,
I want to call, "No! No! Don't do it!",
to Shechem and Dinah, to Simeon and Levi,
but most of all, to every able-bodied male
of Hamor's tribe. "Don't consent, it's a trap."

Swollen tender flesh:
Shechem's, aching with lust and love
(he told his father, "Get me this damsel to wife",
he "spoke comfortingly unto the damsel");
Dinah's broken maidenhead;
Hamor's guards, weakened by pain,
three days after circumcision.

That was the moment chosen to destroy them,
spoil the city, take their flocks and herds,
enslave their wives and little ones, while
Dinah's brothers led her back to Jacob's tents,
ancient honour satisfied.

Jacob chided his sons, fearful
that Canaanites and Perizzites
would now combine against him.
Not until he lay dying
did he curse them for that wild vengeance.
Whether Dinah was saddened by
Shechem's death is never mentioned.

"No, no, don't do it!",
I want to call out,
palms upward, heart pounding.
"Choose another future!"
But it's always too late or too soon.
So much still must happen.
The story has only started.

## *from* *Dina's Own Story*

Vanessa Ochs

*Genesis 34*

Dina tried to imagine having a story of her own to tell, of connections she had made that could widen their world. Her story would make her brothers lean forward with curiosity and jealousy, their elbows on their knees, their faces lit orange by the fire.

What if it were she, and not her father, who had encountered angels of God ascending and descending a ladder? She would have learned the name of each angel. She would have held on to their wings, climbed on their backs, and followed them homeward—and then she'd reciprocate, inviting them to her home. If she could only meet people outside her world, hear their languages, eat their foods, shop for red ribbon in their bazaars, wear their clothes, style her hair as they did. She would make a friend, who would reach for her hand. . . .

## *The Struggle*

Amy K. Blank

*Genesis 32:17–33*

God: I am that which is not.
Search and you shall find
about your universe of thought
only my shadow; grasp
only to hold the measure of your grip.
So am I God—therefore let go!

Jacob: I will not let you go.

## *Leah at Benjamin's B'rit Milah*

Hara E. Person

*Genesis 35:16–20*

How will I explain to you how all this came
to be?
Someday you will ask, and what will I tell you?
My sister, your mother, his beloved—Rachel.
How happy she was, in the midst of that pain,
to bring forth one more son.
How I had gloated, son after son,
carrying your brothers past her,
complaining loudly about the discomforts of
pregnancy,
turning a cold shoulder to her pain.
She had his love, but I had his sons.
One after another they streamed forth out
of me,
as I was blessed by God for my suffering.
She dreamed and prayed, day after day,
to have a child.
Finally Joseph arrived.
And then, so many years later,
when she thought it was all over,
she grew big with you—oh, Benjamin, her
happiness!

But now it is me, standing here today,
watching from the tent as the men perform
their ritual,
not your mother but me,
and I remember.
I remember how we came together at Joseph's
*b'rit*,
how finding it possible to put aside the hurt and
the jealousy,
I walked over to her and held her,
keeping her steady as they prepared the blade.
She wanted to scream but refused to look away
and I, the mother of so many sons, tried to
comfort her.
And now here I stand, at your *b'rit milah*,
taking her place.
She wanted so much.
She always wanted too much.
Not just her husband's God,
but her father's too, just in case.
She wanted everything.

Rachel, my sister, it has always been your face
I see when I look in the mirror.

## *The Death of Rachel*

Shirley Kaufman

*Genesis 35:16–20*

All day she stirs the soup
while the tourists park their cars
on the side of the road to visit
her tomb. Soldiers stand guard.
Barren women sway in their scarves
and pray for a child.
She stirs bitter lumps
from the dry riverbed
where the sheep feed on anything
that grows. She keeps her eyes
on the pot so it won't boil over.

When she stole her father's idols
and he chased after them,
she sat on the gods. She told him
the slit moon under her skirt
spilled blood and she couldn't rise.

She's run out of lies.
She has been ready for a long time
listening to the calm of the desert
between her pains.
She strains till the last one in her
forces his dark head out.
She stirs the dust into dust.

## *Like Rachel*

Dahlia Ravikovitch
(transl. Chana Bloch and Chana Kronfeld)

*Genesis 35:16–20*

To die like Rachel
when the soul shudders like a bird,
wants to break free.
Behind the tent, in fear and dread,
Jacob and Joseph speak of her,
all a-tremble.
All the days of her own life
turn head over heels inside her
like a baby that wants to be born.

How grueling. How
Jacob's love ate away at her
greedily,
with open mouth.
Now, as the soul takes leave,
she has no use for any of that.

Suddenly the baby screeches
and Jacob comes into the tent,
but Rachel does not even sense it.
Rapture washes over her face,
her head.

And then did a great repose descend upon her.
The breath of her nostrils would not stir a
feather.
They laid her to rest among mountain stones
and made her no lament.
To die like Rachel,
that's what I want.

## *Rachel Cried There for Her Children*

Rivka Miriam (transl. Linda Stern Zisquit)

*Genesis 35:16–20*

Rachel cried there for her children not yet born
not yet soft-faced infants whose mothers melt
to them.
In the field she stood to the wind,
transparent as her shadow,
and her flesh was with the soil.
Joseph and Benjamin already clods
and she cried for her children against the hills.
Rachel cried for her children
before they knew how to cry
before they burst from the dust
to return to it.

NOTE
***Rachel cried . . . for her children.*** Jeremiah 31:15–17.

## *Timna's Revenge*

Sherry Blumberg

*Genesis 36:12*

Lessen my status,
Deny me as wife
Think you are wise
My hate is my life

And I shall give it
Freely to the one
Who will plague you forever
To Amalek, my son

# ויישב ◆ *Vayeishev*

GENESIS 37:1–40:23

## *Trials, Tribulations, and Changing Circumstances*

PARASHAT VAYEISHEV ("he settled") begins the so-called "Joseph story cycle," which goes on until the end of Genesis. In this first portion, the personal drama of Jacob and his family incorporates questions of national identity and survival outside the Promised Land. The reader follows Joseph's external and internal journey as he grows through hardships and tribulations from a spoiled son—favored by his father but hated by his brothers—into a wiser youth in an Egyptian jail.

Two stories of a woman and sex stand literally at the center of the parashah. One is the story of Tamar and her father-in-law Judah (Genesis 38), in which she eventually gives birth to two sons, one of whom will be a forefather of King David; in this episode Tamar takes extraordinary risks to secure the family's future (if not her own) by getting pregnant by her father-in-law. In the second story, the wife of Potiphar—Joseph's Egyptian master—attempts to seduce Joseph; he resists, she lies about the circumstances, and he is sent to prison (Genesis 39).

The two stories present the men's behavior as contrasts: Judah eagerly has sex with the veiled Tamar, whereas Joseph resists Potiphar's wife. (The contrast displays a bias for Joseph tribes as Genesis retrojects a much later, ongoing rivalry between the tribes of Joseph in the north and Judah in the south.) In both cases the text presumes that women can be sexually dangerous to men; but Tamar, unlike Potiphar's wife, is pronounced righteous for ensuring—by using her body—that Judah's family is not "written out of history."

Structurally, the parashah is symmetrical: the first and last episodes portray Joseph in relations to dreams and dream solving. Joseph's development, the structure suggests, revolves around his dreams, and it is generated by his own actions as well as the behavior of others (his father, brothers, master, Potiphar's wife). God, though involved, remains in the background.

*Two stories of a woman and sex stand literally at the center of the parashah.*

These themes surround two stories about a woman's desire and its consequences. In both, the woman uses a garment to deceive. In both, she furthers the education and development of a man. Yet her actions, while advancing the plot—and the divine plan, so it seems—are not transformational; Judah and Joseph will each have to struggle further to transform self-centeredness into leadership. Tamar's desire and action are rewarded: she becomes a mother of twins—and is invoked in the book of Ruth within a blessing (4:12). In contrast, the desire of Potiphar's wife remains unfulfilled and she disappears unnamed. (In early Christian interpretation, Jewish post-biblical sources, and Islamic re-tellings including the Qur'an [sura 12], she endures as a symbol of the dangerous foreign woman.)

*—Athalya Brenner*

## Outline

*I.* JOSEPH THE DREAMER
*His Journey from Home to Slavery in Egypt* (37:1–36)

*II.* AN INTERLUDE: TAMAR AND JUDAH
*Judah Is Educated through Deception and Sex* (38:1–30)

- *A.* Introduction: Judah and his family (vv. 1–5)
- *B.* Tamar loses her husbands and position (vv. 6–11)
- *C.* Tamar evolves from victim to agent: deception, sex, and pregnancy (vv. 12–23)
- *D.* Tamar is vindicated: trial, birth, and education (vv. 24–30)

*III.* JOSEPH AND MADAM POTIPHAR
*Sex and Deception* (39:1–23)

- *A.* Joseph succeeds in Potiphar's house (vv. 1–6)
- *B.* Joseph resists seduction (vv. 7–12)
- *C.* Madam Potiphar lies and Joseph is arrested (vv. 13–20)
- *D.* Conclusion: Joseph succeeds in jail (vv. 21–23)

*IV.* JOSEPH'S EDUCATION CONTINUES
*The Dream Interpreter in Jail* (40:1–23)

37:1

Jacob now settled in the land of his father's
sojourning, in the land of Canaan.
[2]This is the family history of Jacob: when Joseph was 17 years old, he would tend the flock
alongside his brothers; he was an attendant along
with the sons of Bilhah and Zilpah, his father's
wives, and Joseph would bring malicious reports
about them to their father. [3]Yet Israel loved Joseph
better than his other sons, for he was to him the son
of his old age; he therefore made him a coat of
many colors. [4]When his brothers saw that he was

לז וַיֵּ֣שֶׁב יַעֲקֹ֔ב בְּאֶ֖רֶץ מְגוּרֵ֣י אָבִ֑יו בְּאֶ֖רֶץ
כְּנָֽעַן׃
2 אֵ֣לֶּה ׀ תֹּלְד֣וֹת יַעֲקֹ֗ב יוֹסֵ֞ף בֶּן־שְׁבַֽע־עֶשְׂרֵ֤ה
שָׁנָה֙ הָיָ֨ה רֹעֶ֤ה אֶת־אֶחָיו֙ בַּצֹּ֔אן וְה֣וּא נַ֗עַר
אֶת־בְּנֵ֥י בִלְהָ֛ה וְאֶת־בְּנֵ֥י זִלְפָּ֖ה נְשֵׁ֣י אָבִ֑יו
וַיָּבֵ֥א יוֹסֵ֛ף אֶת־דִּבָּתָ֥ם רָעָ֖ה אֶל־אֲבִיהֶֽם׃
3 וְיִשְׂרָאֵ֗ל אָהַ֤ב אֶת־יוֹסֵף֙ מִכָּל־בָּנָ֔יו כִּֽי־
בֶן־זְקֻנִ֥ים ה֖וּא ל֑וֹ וְעָ֥שָׂה ל֖וֹ כְּתֹ֥נֶת פַּסִּֽים׃
4 וַיִּרְא֣וּ אֶחָ֗יו כִּֽי־אֹת֞וֹ אָהַ֤ב אֲבִיהֶם֙

## *Joseph the Dreamer*

### HIS JOURNEY FROM HOME TO SLAVERY IN EGYPT (37:1–36)

*1. **Jacob now settled.*** The opening lines begin with Jacob. However, the subject is really Joseph, whose mother Rachel—beloved by his father—had died upon giving birth to Benjamin (35:16–20).

*2. **sons of Bilhah and Zilpah.*** These sons of Jacob's secondary wives seem less valued than the sons of Leah and Rachel. Joseph's young age (seventeen) and his status as an eleventh son would justify his family status as similar to theirs.

*3. **Israel.*** That is, Jacob. Even after receiving this new designation (32:29; 35:9–15), he continues to be known by both names.

***he was to him the son of his old age.*** This is the reason given for Jacob's favoring Joseph, although the younger Benjamin would have been a better candidate for that. No reason is given, although presumably this reflects Jacob's intense love for Rachel, Joseph's (and Benjamin's) deceased mother.

***coat of many colors.*** Or "long tunic." The book of Samuel uses the same expression for the garment worn by Tamar, daughter of King David, who tears it after her half-brother Amnon rapes her. It may have been an external marker of her status as a royal virgin daughter (II Samuel 13:18–19). That is, this garment functions as a symbol of its wearer's special status. (Compare the role of a garment in Tamar's and Madam Potiphar's stories, below.)

*4. **his brothers saw.*** Jacob's other sons have two reasons for hating Joseph: he is a telltale, and he is his father's favorite—as they can see, all the time, by looking at his distinctive attire.

◗ Potiphar's wife serves as a test in the initiation of Joseph, the young wisdom hero.

ANOTHER VIEW ➤ *226*

◗ Spousal loss should not force anyone into desperate acts.

CONTEMPORARY REFLECTION ➤ *228*

◗ Tamar herself was mindful of the important role her descendants would later play.

POST-BIBLICAL INTERPRETATIONS ➤ *226*

◗ Rachel sits in the tent / and gathers each curl . . . / of her little daughter Joseph. . . .

VOICES ➤ *230*

the one their father loved, more than any of his brothers, they hated him and could not bear to speak peaceably to him.

5 Joseph dreamt a dream [one time], and when he told it to his brothers, they hated him all the more. 6 He said to them, "Do hear this dream that I dreamt! 7 There we were, tying up sheaves of wheat in the field, when my sheaf rose up and stood up straight! Your sheaves then paraded in a circle around mine and bowed down to my sheaf." 8 His brothers said to him, "Are you so certain you will reign over us? Do you really expect to rule us?" So they hated him all the more for his dreams and for his words.

9 He dreamt yet another dream and recounted it to his brothers, saying, "Look now—I have dreamt another dream, and look: the sun, the moon, and eleven stars were bowing down to me." 10 But when he recounted it to his father and his brothers, his father rebuked him, saying, "What is this dream that you dreamt? Your mother, your brothers, and I—must we really come to bow down to the ground before you?" 11 His brothers detested him, but his father kept the matter in mind.

12 And when his brothers went to tend their father's flock at Shechem, 13 Israel said to Joseph, "Surely your brothers are tending the flock at Shechem [by now]. Come, let me send you to them." He answered, "Here I am!" 14 Israel then said to him, "Pray go see how your brothers are, and how the flock is doing, and bring me back word." So he sent him from the valley of Hebron and he came to Shechem.

15 [There] a man happened on him as he was wandering in the countryside. The man asked him:

מִכָּל־אֶחָיו וַיִּשְׂנְאוּ אֹתוֹ וְלֹא יָכְלוּ דַּבְּרוֹ
לְשָׁלֹם׃
5 וַיַּחֲלֹם יוֹסֵף חֲלוֹם וַיַּגֵּד לְאֶחָיו וַיּוֹסִפוּ
עוֹד שְׂנֹא אֹתוֹ׃ 6 וַיֹּאמֶר אֲלֵיהֶם שִׁמְעוּ־
נָא הַחֲלוֹם הַזֶּה אֲשֶׁר חָלָמְתִּי׃ 7 וְהִנֵּה
אֲנַחְנוּ מְאַלְּמִים אֲלֻמִּים בְּתוֹךְ הַשָּׂדֶה
וְהִנֵּה קָמָה אֲלֻמָּתִי וְגַם־נִצָּבָה וְהִנֵּה
תְסֻבֶּינָה אֲלֻמֹּתֵיכֶם וַתִּשְׁתַּחֲוֶיןָ לַאֲלֻמָּתִי׃
8 וַיֹּאמְרוּ לוֹ אֶחָיו הֲמָלֹךְ תִּמְלֹךְ עָלֵינוּ
אִם־מָשׁוֹל תִּמְשֹׁל בָּנוּ וַיּוֹסִפוּ עוֹד שְׂנֹא
אֹתוֹ עַל־חֲלֹמֹתָיו וְעַל־דְּבָרָיו׃
9 וַיַּחֲלֹם עוֹד חֲלוֹם אַחֵר וַיְסַפֵּר אֹתוֹ
לְאֶחָיו וַיֹּאמֶר הִנֵּה חָלַמְתִּי חֲלוֹם עוֹד
וְהִנֵּה הַשֶּׁמֶשׁ וְהַיָּרֵחַ וְאַחַד עָשָׂר כּוֹכָבִים
מִשְׁתַּחֲוִים לִי׃ 10 וַיְסַפֵּר אֶל־אָבִיו וְאֶל־
אֶחָיו וַיִּגְעַר־בּוֹ אָבִיו וַיֹּאמֶר לוֹ מָה הַחֲלוֹם
הַזֶּה אֲשֶׁר חָלָמְתָּ הֲבוֹא נָבוֹא אֲנִי וְאִמְּךָ
וְאַחֶיךָ לְהִשְׁתַּחֲוֹת לְךָ אָרְצָה׃ 11 וַיְקַנְאוּ־בוֹ
אֶחָיו וְאָבִיו שָׁמַר אֶת־הַדָּבָר׃
12 וַיֵּלְכוּ אֶחָיו לִרְעוֹת אֶת־צֹאן אֲבִיהֶם
בִּשְׁכֶם׃ 13 וַיֹּאמֶר יִשְׂרָאֵל אֶל־יוֹסֵף הֲלוֹא
אַחֶיךָ רֹעִים בִּשְׁכֶם לְכָה וְאֶשְׁלָחֲךָ אֲלֵיהֶם
וַיֹּאמֶר לוֹ הִנֵּנִי׃ 14 וַיֹּאמֶר לוֹ לֶךְ־נָא רְאֵה
אֶת־שְׁלוֹם אַחֶיךָ וְאֶת־שְׁלוֹם הַצֹּאן
וַהֲשִׁבֵנִי דָּבָר וַיִּשְׁלָחֵהוּ מֵעֵמֶק חֶבְרוֹן וַיָּבֹא
שְׁכֶמָה׃
15 וַיִּמְצָאֵהוּ אִישׁ וְהִנֵּה תֹעֶה בַּשָּׂדֶה
וַיִּשְׁאָלֵהוּ הָאִישׁ לֵאמֹר מַה־תְּבַקֵּשׁ׃

*5–11.* Two dreams of Joseph about his forthcoming dominance over other members of his family exacerbate the enmity.

*10–11.* Jacob chides Joseph for his dream but fails to defuse the situation.

*12–30.* Jacob again proves to be an ineffective father, for he does not act to protect Joseph—as he did not protect his daughter, Dinah (Genesis 34). Ignoring the tension among the siblings, he sends Joseph to the brothers alone and defenseless.

What are you looking for? [16]He said, "I'm looking for my brothers. Can you tell me please where they are tending the flock?" [17]The man said, "They left this place; yes, I heard them say, Let's go to Dothan." So Joseph went after his brothers and found them at Dothan.

[18]They saw him in the distance, and before he neared them, they wickedly plotted against him, to bring about his death. [19]They said to one another, "Here comes that master of dreams! [20]Now then, let us kill him and throw him into one of [these] pits and say, 'A wild animal devoured him.' Then we'll see what becomes of his dreams!"

[21]But when Reuben heard [this], he saved him from their hands by saying, "Let us not strike him a mortal blow!" [22]Reuben said to them, "Do not shed blood; throw him into this pit, [here] in the wilderness, but do not lay a hand against him"—in order to deliver him from their hands, to restore him to his father. [23]So when Joseph came to his brothers, they stripped Joseph of his coat, the coat of many colors that he had on; [24]then they took him and threw him into a pit. The pit was empty; there was no water in it.

[25]They had sat down to eat, when they looked up and saw a caravan of Ishmaelites traveling from Gilead. Their camels were loaded with laudanum, balm, and mastic; they were heading down to Egypt. [26]Judah then said to his brothers, "How will it profit [us] if we kill our brother and cover up his blood? [27]Let us [rather] sell him to the Ishmaelites; then our hand will not be on him; after all, he is our brother, our own flesh." And his brothers heeded [him].

[28]When the Midianite traders came through they pulled Joseph up out of the pit; they sold

16 וַיֹּ֕אמֶר אֶת־אַחַ֖י אָנֹכִ֣י מְבַקֵּ֑שׁ הַגִּֽידָה־נָּ֣א לִ֔י אֵיפֹ֖ה הֵ֥ם רֹעִֽים׃ 17 וַיֹּ֤אמֶר הָאִישׁ֙ נָסְע֣וּ מִזֶּ֔ה כִּ֤י שָׁמַ֙עְתִּי֙ אֹֽמְרִ֔ים נֵלְכָ֖ה דֹּתָ֑יְנָה וַיֵּ֤לֶךְ יוֹסֵף֙ אַחַ֣ר אֶחָ֔יו וַיִּמְצָאֵ֖ם בְּדֹתָֽן׃

18 וַיִּרְא֥וּ אֹת֖וֹ מֵרָחֹ֑ק וּבְטֶ֙רֶם֙ יִקְרַ֣ב אֲלֵיהֶ֔ם וַיִּֽתְנַכְּל֥וּ אֹת֖וֹ לַהֲמִיתֽוֹ׃ 19 וַיֹּאמְר֖וּ אִ֣ישׁ אֶל־אָחִ֑יו הִנֵּ֗ה בַּ֛עַל הַחֲלֹמ֥וֹת הַלָּזֶ֖ה בָּֽא׃ 20 וְעַתָּ֣ה ׀ לְכ֣וּ וְנַֽהַרְגֵ֗הוּ וְנַשְׁלִכֵ֙הוּ֙ בְּאַחַ֣ד הַבֹּר֔וֹת וְאָמַ֕רְנוּ חַיָּ֥ה רָעָ֖ה אֲכָלָ֑תְהוּ וְנִרְאֶ֕ה מַה־יִּהְי֖וּ חֲלֹמֹתָֽיו׃

21 וַיִּשְׁמַ֣ע רְאוּבֵ֔ן וַיַּצִּלֵ֖הוּ מִיָּדָ֑ם וַיֹּ֕אמֶר לֹ֥א נַכֶּ֖נּוּ נָֽפֶשׁ׃ 22 וַיֹּ֨אמֶר אֲלֵהֶ֥ם ׀ רְאוּבֵ֘ן אַל־תִּשְׁפְּכוּ־דָ֗ם הַשְׁלִ֤יכוּ אֹתוֹ֙ אֶל־הַבּ֤וֹר הַזֶּה֙ אֲשֶׁ֣ר בַּמִּדְבָּ֔ר וְיָ֖ד אַל־תִּשְׁלְחוּ־ב֑וֹ לְמַ֗עַן הַצִּ֤יל אֹתוֹ֙ מִיָּדָ֔ם לַהֲשִׁיב֖וֹ אֶל־אָבִֽיו׃ 23 וַֽיְהִ֕י כַּֽאֲשֶׁר־בָּ֥א יוֹסֵ֖ף אֶל־אֶחָ֑יו וַיַּפְשִׁ֤יטוּ אֶת־יוֹסֵף֙ אֶת־כֻּתָּנְתּ֔וֹ אֶת־כְּתֹ֥נֶת הַפַּסִּ֖ים אֲשֶׁ֥ר עָלָֽיו׃ 24 וַיִּ֨קָּחֻ֔הוּ וַיַּשְׁלִ֥כוּ אֹת֖וֹ הַבֹּ֑רָה וְהַבּ֣וֹר רֵ֔ק אֵ֥ין בּ֖וֹ מָֽיִם׃

25 וַיֵּשְׁבוּ֮ לֶֽאֱכָל־לֶחֶם֒ וַיִּשְׂא֤וּ עֵֽינֵיהֶם֙ וַיִּרְא֔וּ וְהִנֵּה֙ אֹרְחַ֣ת יִשְׁמְעֵאלִ֔ים בָּאָ֖ה מִגִּלְעָ֑ד וּגְמַלֵּיהֶ֣ם נֹֽשְׂאִ֗ים נְכֹאת֙ וּצְרִ֣י וָלֹ֔ט הוֹלְכִ֖ים לְהוֹרִ֥יד מִצְרָֽיְמָה׃ 26 וַיֹּ֥אמֶר יְהוּדָ֖ה אֶל־אֶחָ֑יו מַה־בֶּ֗צַע כִּ֤י נַהֲרֹג֙ אֶת־אָחִ֔ינוּ וְכִסִּ֖ינוּ אֶת־דָּמֽוֹ׃ 27 לְכ֞וּ וְנִמְכְּרֶ֣נּוּ לַיִּשְׁמְעֵאלִ֗ים וְיָדֵ֙נוּ֙ אַל־תְּהִי־ב֔וֹ כִּֽי־אָחִ֥ינוּ בְשָׂרֵ֖נוּ ה֑וּא וַֽיִּשְׁמְע֖וּ אֶחָֽיו׃

28 וַיַּֽעַבְרוּ֩ אֲנָשִׁ֨ים מִדְיָנִ֜ים סֹֽחֲרִ֗ים וַֽיִּמְשְׁכוּ֙ וַיַּֽעֲל֤וּ אֶת־יוֹסֵף֙ מִן־הַבּ֔וֹר וַיִּמְכְּר֧וּ אֶת־יוֹסֵ֛ף

---

**18. They saw him in the distance ... they wickedly plotted against him.** There is some confusion as to the sequence and participants of what follows, when the brothers act against Joseph; perhaps two accounts have been combined. The result, though, is clear. Joseph is taken to Egypt and is enslaved (v. 28).

Joseph for twenty pieces of silver to the Ishmaelites, who carried Joseph off to Egypt.

29 Reuben went back to the pit—but Joseph was not there in the pit! He tore his clothes. 30 Going back to his brothers, he said, "The boy is not there; where am I to go?"

31 So they slaughtered a goat, took Joseph's coat, and dipped the coat in the blood. 32 They carried the coat of many colors and brought it to their father. They said, "We found this; do you recognize it? Is it your son's coat?" 33 He recognized it, saying, "My son's coat! A wild animal has devoured him! Joseph has been ripped to shreds!" 34 Then Jacob tore his clothes, put sackcloth on his loins, and mourned his son many days. 35 His sons and daughters endeavored to console him, but he refused to be consoled, saying, "No, in mourning shall I go down to my son to Sheol!" Thus did his father bewail him.

36 Meanwhile, the Medanites sold him to Egypt, to Potiphar, one of Pharaoh's officers, Captain of the Guard.

לַיִּשְׁמְעֵאלִים בְּעֶשְׂרִים כָּסֶף וַיָּבִיאוּ אֶת־
יוֹסֵף מִצְרָיְמָה׃
29 וַיָּשָׁב רְאוּבֵן אֶל־הַבּוֹר וְהִנֵּה אֵין־יוֹסֵף
בַּבּוֹר וַיִּקְרַע אֶת־בְּגָדָיו׃ 30 וַיָּשָׁב אֶל־אֶחָיו
וַיֹּאמַר הַיֶּלֶד אֵינֶנּוּ וַאֲנִי אָנָה אֲנִי־בָא׃
31 וַיִּקְחוּ אֶת־כְּתֹנֶת יוֹסֵף וַיִּשְׁחֲטוּ שְׂעִיר
עִזִּים וַיִּטְבְּלוּ אֶת־הַכֻּתֹּנֶת בַּדָּם׃ 32 וַיְשַׁלְּחוּ
אֶת־כְּתֹנֶת הַפַּסִּים וַיָּבִיאוּ אֶל־אֲבִיהֶם
וַיֹּאמְרוּ זֹאת מָצָאנוּ הַכֶּר־נָא הַכְּתֹנֶת בִּנְךָ
הוּא אִם־לֹא׃ 33 וַיַּכִּירָהּ וַיֹּאמֶר כְּתֹנֶת בְּנִי
חַיָּה רָעָה אֲכָלָתְהוּ טָרֹף טֹרַף יוֹסֵף׃
34 וַיִּקְרַע יַעֲקֹב שִׂמְלֹתָיו וַיָּשֶׂם שַׂק בְּמָתְנָיו
וַיִּתְאַבֵּל עַל־בְּנוֹ יָמִים רַבִּים׃ 35 וַיָּקֻמוּ כָל־
בָּנָיו וְכָל־בְּנֹתָיו לְנַחֲמוֹ וַיְמָאֵן לְהִתְנַחֵם
וַיֹּאמֶר כִּי־אֵרֵד אֶל־בְּנִי אָבֵל שְׁאֹלָה וַיֵּבְךְּ
אֹתוֹ אָבִיו׃
36 וְהַמְּדָנִים מָכְרוּ אֹתוֹ אֶל־מִצְרָיִם לְפוֹטִיפַר
סְרִיס פַּרְעֹה שַׂר הַטַּבָּחִים׃ פ

*31–35.* Jacob draws his own conclusion about Joseph's "death" by looking at the garment that signified Joseph's favorite status, now immersed in a goat's blood. The goat whose blood stains the tunic recalls the kids' skins that Rebekah had placed on Jacob to dupe his father, Isaac, into believing Jacob was Esau (27:16). The allusion is unmistakable: Jacob is deceived by his sons in the same manner he deceived his father—for the same practice of favoring a son. A kid will be part of Tamar's negotiation with Judah in 38:17, yet another play on the same theme.

*32. "Is it your son's coat?"* The brothers do not *tell* Jacob that Joseph is dead—that is, they do not formally lie to him. Instead, they present the fabricated evidence and let him reach his own conclusions. An invitation to recognize items signifying identity is also important later in Tamar's message to Judah (38:25).

*35. he refused to be consoled.* This, like his death wish, shows disregard for the rest of the family.

*36.* At the end of this passage, Joseph is in Egypt as a slave; Jacob is in mourning; and the text gives no sign that Joseph's brothers feel remorse. Perhaps the family's dysfunction can be explained by the void left after Rachel's death (35:16–19). Also Leah is no longer in view and has perhaps died, too. (The text never reports her demise, only that Jacob eventually buried her body in the family's burial site, the cave at Machpelah; 49:31.)

38 Around that time, Judah parted from his
brothers, and fell in with an Adullamite named
Hirah. 2 There Judah saw the daughter of a Canaanite named Shua; he took her [to wife] and coupled
with her. 3 She became pregnant and bore a son,
and he named him Er. 4 Again she became pregnant
and bore a son, and she named him Onan. 5 Yet
again she became pregnant and bore a son, and she
named him Shelah; when she gave birth to him, he
[Judah] was in Chezib.

לח וַיְהִי בָּעֵת הַהִוא וַיֵּרֶד יְהוּדָה מֵאֵת
אֶחָיו וַיֵּט עַד־אִישׁ עֲדֻלָּמִי וּשְׁמוֹ חִירָה׃
2 וַיַּרְא־שָׁם יְהוּדָה בַּת־אִישׁ כְּנַעֲנִי וּשְׁמוֹ
שׁוּעַ וַיִּקָּחֶהָ וַיָּבֹא אֵלֶיהָ׃ 3 וַתַּהַר וַתֵּלֶד בֵּן
וַיִּקְרָא אֶת־שְׁמוֹ עֵר׃ 4 וַתַּהַר עוֹד וַתֵּלֶד בֵּן
וַתִּקְרָא אֶת־שְׁמוֹ אוֹנָן׃ 5 וַתֹּסֶף עוֹד וַתֵּלֶד
בֵּן וַתִּקְרָא אֶת־שְׁמוֹ שֵׁלָה וְהָיָה בִכְזִיב
בְּלִדְתָּהּ אֹתוֹ׃

## *An Interlude: Tamar and Judah*

### JUDAH IS EDUCATED THROUGH DECEPTION AND SEX (38:1–30)

Readers who wish to learn what will happen to Joseph must wait, because now Tamar and Judah take center stage. This passage disrupts the plotline—just as Tamar and Judah disrupt each other's lives—and it even seems to be placed out of chronological sequence. We do not know when these events happen. As some early rabbis and Rashi pointed out, however, this episode has literary (thematic and verbal) links to the episodes that precede and follow it, despite the ostensible interruption. For example, Judah deceives his father in the previous episode and is deceived by Tamar (for a good purpose) here; garments—Joseph's and then Tamar's—play a central role in both stories, as status markers as well as vehicles of deceit; and the issue of group survival is present in both. This story also looks forward to the next episode. Tamar's bold desire and the resulting sexual transgression here is comparable (positively or negatively) with Madam Potiphar's desire for Joseph in the story that follows, in which a garment again figures prominently.

The present story is part of the ongoing history that leads to King David, founder of Israel's most illustrious dynasty. According to the Bible, David's pre-history started when Lot's daughters, believing that the rest of humankind has been destroyed, deceived their drunken father in order to get pregnant. Two sons, Moab and Ammon, were born (19:25–38). In the second (present) installment, Tamar deceives Judah and gives birth to twins. In the third installment, Ruth the Moabite (a descendant of Lot's daughter) marries Boaz (a descendant of Tamar's son Perez), making her the great-grandmother of David. All three stories involve transgression of norms inscribed elsewhere in the Bible. In all three cases a younger female relative prompts a male to engage in a sexual liaison; the woman initiates the action at considerable risk to herself; and the woman dupes the man to some extent. All three cases result in the birth of one or more sons, which signals divine approval and brings benefit to Israel. Although Tamar is not explicitly identified as foreign, the context suggests that she might be. Thus foreign women become mothers of Israel's most illustrious dynasty.

### INTRODUCTION: JUDAH AND HIS FAMILY (38:1–5)

*1.* Judah seems to be fully integrated in the Canaanite environment.

*2. the daughter.* On her name, see at v. 12.

*3–5.* Judah's Canaanite wife is credited with giving birth to three sons for Judah, and with naming the two younger ones.

[6]Judah now took a wife for Er, his first-born; her name was Tamar; [7]but Er, Judah's first-born, was wicked in the sight of יהוה, and יהוה brought about his death. [8]Judah then said to Onan, "Couple with your brother's widow, unite with her, and raise up offspring for your brother!" [9]But Onan knew that the offspring would not be his, so whenever he coupled with his brother's wife, he would waste [his seed] on the ground, in order not to produce offspring for his brother. [10]What he did was wicked in the sight of יהוה, who brought about his death, as well. [11]Judah then said to his daughter-in-law Tamar, "Stay as a widow in your father's house until my son Shelah grows up." He thought: "Lest he too die like his brothers." So Tamar went and stayed in her father's house.

6 וַיִּקַּח יְהוּדָה אִשָּׁה לְעֵר בְּכוֹרוֹ וּשְׁמָהּ
תָּמָר׃ 7 וַיְהִי עֵר בְּכוֹר יְהוּדָה רַע בְּעֵינֵי
יְהוָה וַיְמִתֵהוּ יְהוָה׃ 8 וַיֹּאמֶר יְהוּדָה לְאוֹנָן
בֹּא אֶל־אֵשֶׁת אָחִיךָ וְיַבֵּם אֹתָהּ וְהָקֵם זֶרַע
לְאָחִיךָ׃ 9 וַיֵּדַע אוֹנָן כִּי לֹּא לוֹ יִהְיֶה הַזָּרַע
וְהָיָה אִם־בָּא אֶל־אֵשֶׁת אָחִיו וְשִׁחֵת
אַרְצָה לְבִלְתִּי נְתָן־זֶרַע לְאָחִיו׃ 10 וַיֵּרַע
בְּעֵינֵי יְהוָה אֲשֶׁר עָשָׂה וַיָּמֶת גַּם־אֹתוֹ׃
11 וַיֹּאמֶר יְהוּדָה לְתָמָר כַּלָּתוֹ שְׁבִי אַלְמָנָה
בֵית־אָבִיךְ עַד־יִגְדַּל שֵׁלָה בְנִי כִּי אָמַר פֶּן־
יָמוּת גַּם־הוּא כְּאֶחָיו וַתֵּלֶךְ תָּמָר וַתֵּשֶׁב
בֵּית אָבִיהָ׃

### TAMAR LOSES HER HUSBANDS AND POSITION (38:6–11)

*6. Judah now took a wife for Er.* As is common in the Bible, the father finds a wife for his son. (But Hagar takes a wife for her son, 21:21.)

*Tamar.* The name means "a palm tree," a tree used in the ancient Near East as a royal symbol. The context implies that Tamar is Canaanite, although this is never stated.

*7. his death.* Er dies without offspring.

*8.* In agreement with the custom of levirate marriage, Judah gives Tamar to his next son, Onan. In levirate marriage (see at Deuteronomy 25:5–10), the wife of a deceased, childless man bears a son for the dead husband by being impregnated by his living brother. The practice applies when brothers live together. The son of such a union inherits the deceased brother's property. Although this is not stated in the current passage, presumably the son also takes care of his mother, who otherwise—with neither a son nor an inheritance—would have no economic resources apart from what she brought into the marriage.

*9. waste [his seed] on the ground.* Onan's "sin" is refusing to impregnate his sister-in-law. His fate does not serve to condemn either masturbation or coitus interruptus, two definitions for "onanism" in English dictionaries. Onan's selfish reasoning is logical (but condemned): he has no interest in producing an heir for his dead brother's (land) portion, which is in the interest of the household's structure but not in his own personal interest.

*10.* Onan dies because he refuses to cooperate. Like his brother Er before him, Onan is presented as responsible for his own demise. The reader thus knows that Tamar does not cause these deaths.

*11. "Stay as a widow."* Judah disposes of Tamar by sending her to her father's home while keeping her legally bound to his own. His subterfuge is Shelah's youth. As with Joseph in the previous episode (37:26–27), Judah rids himself of a person whose presence vexes him.

*"Lest he too die like his brothers."* Judah removes Tamar because he blames her for his sons' death (compare at v. 10). While his reluctance is humanly understandable, his deception of Tamar is objectionable—and will, eventually, incite her to act.

*So Tamar went.* Tamar is obedient. We learn nothing about Tamar's response or feelings through-

[12]Time passed; and Shua's daughter, Judah's wife, died, and [after] Judah was consoled, he went up to his sheepshearers—he and his friend Hirah the Adullamite—toward Timnah. [13]When Tamar was told, "Look—your father-in-law is going up toward Timnah to shear his sheep," [14]she discarded her widow's garb, covered herself up with a veil, wrapped herself up, and stationed herself at the entrance to Enaim on the way to Timnah—for she saw that Shelah had grown up, yet she had not been given to him as a wife. [15]When Judah saw her, he took her for a prostitute, for she had covered her face; [16]so he turned toward her on the road and said, "Pray let me couple with you"—he was not

12 וַיִּרְבּוּ הַיָּמִים וַתָּמָת בַּת־שׁוּעַ אֵשֶׁת־
יְהוּדָה וַיִּנָּחֶם יְהוּדָה וַיַּעַל עַל־גֹּזְזֵי צֹאנוֹ
הוּא וְחִירָה רֵעֵהוּ הָעֲדֻלָּמִי תִּמְנָתָה׃
13 וַיֻּגַּד לְתָמָר לֵאמֹר הִנֵּה חָמִיךְ עֹלֶה
תִמְנָתָה לָגֹז צֹאנוֹ׃ 14 וַתָּסַר בִּגְדֵי
אַלְמְנוּתָהּ מֵעָלֶיהָ וַתְּכַס בַּצָּעִיף וַתִּתְעַלָּף
וַתֵּשֶׁב בְּפֶתַח עֵינַיִם אֲשֶׁר עַל־דֶּרֶךְ תִּמְנָתָה
כִּי רָאֲתָה כִּי־גָדַל שֵׁלָה וְהִוא לֹא־נִתְּנָה לוֹ
לְאִשָּׁה׃ 15 וַיִּרְאֶהָ יְהוּדָה וַיַּחְשְׁבֶהָ לְזוֹנָה
כִּי כִסְּתָה פָּנֶיהָ׃ 16 וַיֵּט אֵלֶיהָ אֶל־הַדֶּרֶךְ
וַיֹּאמֶר הָבָה־נָּא אָבוֹא אֵלַיִךְ כִּי לֹא יָדַע כִּי

out these occurrences. She is twice widowed (or at least bereft of a partner) in a short time, denied her third man and thus the possibility of all-important motherhood. Moreover, she loses her place in Judah's household by being sent back to her father but is not released of her duty to this same household. Up to this point, Tamar has no voice but only a passive presence.

### TAMAR EVOLVES FROM VICTIM TO AGENT: DECEPTION, SEX, AND PREGNANCY (38:12–23)

Tamar finally takes matters into her own hands and ensures that she will have a child by deceiving her father-in-law Judah into having sex with her. This would be incest according to the stipulation in the book of Leviticus ("you shall not uncover the nakedness of your daughter-in-law," Leviticus 18:15), and is punishable by death (Leviticus 20:12).

Tamar seems to be motivated by the wish to conceive for Judah's family: she endangers herself, because legally she is bound to Shelah. She deceives Judah by covering herself up—not by pretending to be anything she is not. She, then, falls in with his impulsive cupidity.

*12. Shua's daughter.* Heb. *bat shua*, which perhaps should be understood as a proper name ("Bathshua," akin to Bathsheba); however, her father's name is indeed Shua (v. 2). Like many other wives of named characters in the Bible, she seems to remain unnamed in this story.

*Judah's wife, died.* This remark might serve as partial justification for Judah's eagerness upon meeting Tamar.

*14–15. covered herself up with a veil.* Ironically, Judah sees Tamar only when she is covered. Whether a covered face indicated the garb of a prostitute in the ancient Near East is far from certain. That Judah does not recognize Tamar despite the veil—or at least by her voice when they negotiate—is a measure of his eager state. It may also signal a lack of familiarity with his daughter-in-law. She, in fact, does not pretend to anything apart from disguising herself and looking available. She leaves the rest to him. He jumps to the conclusion that she is a prostitute.

*14. entrance to Enaim.* The phrase is also a pun, meaning "opening of the eyes." Blind in this very spot to Tamar's plight and presence, Judah's eyes will soon open.

*for she saw.* Although Tamar's specific plan is not recorded, the incentive for her action is clear: Judah's failure to keep his promise and duty.

כַּלָּתוֹ הִוא וַתֹּאמֶר מַה־תִּתֶּן־לִי כִּי תָבוֹא
אֵלָי׃ 17 וַיֹּאמֶר אָנֹכִי אֲשַׁלַּח גְּדִי־עִזִּים מִן־
הַצֹּאן וַתֹּאמֶר אִם־תִּתֵּן עֵרָבוֹן עַד שָׁלְחֶךָ׃
18 וַיֹּאמֶר מָה הָעֵרָבוֹן אֲשֶׁר אֶתֶּן־לָּךְ
וַתֹּאמֶר חֹתָמְךָ וּפְתִילֶךָ וּמַטְּךָ אֲשֶׁר בְּיָדֶךָ
וַיִּתֶּן־לָהּ וַיָּבֹא אֵלֶיהָ וַתַּהַר לוֹ׃
19 וַתָּקָם וַתֵּלֶךְ וַתָּסַר צְעִיפָהּ מֵעָלֶיהָ
וַתִּלְבַּשׁ בִּגְדֵי אַלְמְנוּתָהּ׃ 20 וַיִּשְׁלַח יְהוּדָה
אֶת־גְּדִי הָעִזִּים בְּיַד רֵעֵהוּ הָעֲדֻלָּמִי לָקַחַת
הָעֵרָבוֹן מִיַּד הָאִשָּׁה וְלֹא מְצָאָהּ׃ 21 וַיִּשְׁאַל
אֶת־אַנְשֵׁי מְקֹמָהּ לֵאמֹר אַיֵּה הַקְּדֵשָׁה הִוא
בָעֵינַיִם עַל־הַדָּרֶךְ וַיֹּאמְרוּ לֹא־הָיְתָה בָזֶה
קְדֵשָׁה׃ 22 וַיָּשָׁב אֶל־יְהוּדָה וַיֹּאמֶר לֹא
מְצָאתִיהָ וְגַם אַנְשֵׁי הַמָּקוֹם אָמְרוּ לֹא־
הָיְתָה בָזֶה קְדֵשָׁה׃ 23 וַיֹּאמֶר יְהוּדָה תִּקַּח־
לָהּ פֶּן נִהְיֶה לָבוּז הִנֵּה שָׁלַחְתִּי הַגְּדִי הַזֶּה
וְאַתָּה לֹא מְצָאתָהּ׃

aware that she was his daughter-in-law—and she said, "What will you give me to couple with me?" 17He replied, "I will send you a kid from the flock." But she said, "Only if you give [me] a pledge until you send [it]." 18He asked, "What [sort] of pledge should I give you?" She then said, "Your signet seal, your cord, and the staff in your hand." So he gave [them] to her and coupled with her—and she became pregnant by him.

19When he got up and left, she discarded her veil and put on her widow's garb. 20But when Judah sent the kid by way of his Adullamite friend to redeem the deposit from the woman, he did not find her. 21And when he asked the people of her place, "Where is that courtesan, the one at the crossroads?" they replied, "There wasn't any courtesan here." 22He then returned to Judah and said, "I did not find her; moreover, the people of the place said, 'There never has been a courtesan here.'" 23Judah then said, "Let her keep it, lest we become a laughingstock! I did send this kid, though you could not find her!"

*16. she said, "What will you give me to couple with me?"* Has Tamar planned to have sex with Judah, as the text at least implies? Or did she have some other encounter in mind—and this is why she has disguised herself? At any rate, when Judah suggests having sex with her as a prostitute, she quickly bargains for her presumed wages. She demands a payment; and even if she had no previous such plan, she is quick-witted enough to devise one now.

*18. "Your signet seal, your cord, and the staff in your hand."* Judah characteristically suggests a delayed payment (a kid; see at 37:31–35). Tamar asks for a guaranty: she names Judah's signet, cord, and staff. In other words, she wants *all* his identity markers (equivalent today to all of one's major credit cards; see Robert Alter, *The Art of Biblical Narrative*, 1981, p. 9). While practical as a guaranty, these items also convey Tamar's goal of legitimating herself. Surprisingly, Judah agrees to this exaggerated request. Tamar, if she had no plan to conceive a child prior to the encounter, certainly has this possibility in mind at this point. Judah has now surrendered, symbolically, his identity and social status as patriarch to Tamar.

*21. "courtesan."* Heb. *k'deishah* ("hallowed one" or "one apart"), a word related to *kadosh* ("holy") and thus translated sometimes as "cult prostitute." While Judah previously assumes that Tamar is a *zonah* (prostitute), here his friend inquires using a different term. Some have suggested that cultic prostitution—namely, sexual activities connected to worship in shrines—existed in ancient Israel. But there is no evidence that this ever existed anywhere in the ancient Near East. Judah's friend may be attempting to add dignity to a simple sexual transaction by giving it a cultic meaning. The present translation presumes that he is using a more genteel term, with no cultic signification implied.

[24]Then, [after] about three months, Judah was told, "Tamar your daughter-in-law has played the whore; and now she has even become pregnant by whoring." And Judah said, "Bring her out and let her be burned!" [25]Brought out she was, but she sent to her father-in-law, saying, "The man to whom these belong made me pregnant. Acknowledge whose signet seal, cords, and staff these are!" [26]Judah recognized [them] and said, "She is more in the right than I, for certainly I did not give her to my son Shelah." And he never touched her again.

[27]When she was giving birth, lo—she had twins in her belly! [28]And just as she was giving birth, one put a hand out and the midwife took [it] and tied a

24 וַיְהִ֣י ׀ כְּמִשְׁלֹ֣שׁ חֳדָשִׁ֗ים וַיֻּגַּ֨ד לִֽיהוּדָ֤ה
לֵאמֹר֙ זָֽנְתָה֙ תָּמָ֣ר כַּלָּתֶ֔ךָ וְגַ֛ם הִנֵּ֥ה הָרָ֖ה
לִזְנוּנִ֑ים וַיֹּ֣אמֶר יְהוּדָ֔ה הוֹצִיא֖וּהָ וְתִשָּׂרֵֽף׃
25 הִ֣וא מוּצֵ֗את וְהִ֨יא שָׁלְחָ֤ה אֶל־חָמִ֙יהָ֙
לֵאמֹ֔ר לְאִ֙ישׁ֙ אֲשֶׁר־אֵ֣לֶּה לּ֔וֹ אָנֹכִ֖י הָרָ֑ה
וַתֹּ֙אמֶר֙ הַכֶּר־נָ֔א לְמִ֞י הַחֹתֶ֧מֶת וְהַפְּתִילִ֛ים
וְהַמַּטֶּ֖ה הָאֵֽלֶּה׃ 26 וַיַּכֵּ֣ר יְהוּדָ֗ה וַיֹּ֙אמֶר֙
צָֽדְקָ֣ה מִמֶּ֔נִּי כִּֽי־עַל־כֵּ֥ן לֹא־נְתַתִּ֖יהָ לְשֵׁלָ֣ה
בְנִ֑י וְלֹֽא־יָסַ֥ף ע֖וֹד לְדַעְתָּֽהּ׃
27 וַיְהִ֖י בְּעֵ֣ת לִדְתָּ֑הּ וְהִנֵּ֥ה תְאוֹמִ֖ים בְּבִטְנָֽהּ׃
28 וַיְהִ֣י בְלִדְתָּ֔הּ וַיִּתֶּן־יָ֑ד וַתִּקַּ֣ח הַמְיַלֶּ֗דֶת

## TAMAR IS VINDICATED: TRIAL, BIRTH, AND EDUCATION (38:24–30)

*24. "let her be burned!"* Judah's rash judgment highlights the gender double-standard that the story unmasks and probably critiques. Judah has the right, as head of household, to condemn Tamar to death for her "whoredom," which is how her pregnancy is seen. The usual biblical punishment for adultery, for both women and men, is by stoning; but Judah demands burning. In the Bible and the ancient Near East, "adultery" concerned only a married woman; and Tamar's status is still that because, in spite of being sent to her father's house, the marriage relationship is with the household (Judah's), not only with the dead husband; and Judah has not released her of this bond (as is possible to do according to the levirate marriage custom, Deuteronomy 25:7–10).

*25. Acknowledge.* Heb. *haker na,* the same words that Judah and his brothers had posed to their father when they deceived him ("do you recognize it," 37:32).

Tamar, discreetly, does not confront Judah but sends his symbols of identity and allows him to draw his own conclusion (as was done to Jacob upon Joseph's presumed death, 37:32–33). Such an indirect mode is risky but in this case effective; complete silence or a head-on confrontation would have been shameful, perhaps also counterproductive.

*26. Judah . . . said, "She is more in the right than I."* Judah recognizes that Tamar has behaved in a more moral fashion than he has. He does not comment on his own unchecked desire, on his having been deceived, or on the sudden prospect of progeny. The phrasing indicates relativization: according to Judah, Tamar is not *wholly* in the right but is better by comparison with him. Yet this is the first reported occasion where anyone has called Judah to account for his actions; he rises to the occasion by taking responsibility for his earlier words and actions—albeit indirectly. It marks a definite step in his maturation.

***he never touched her again.*** That he has no more sex with Tamar may be another attempt to whitewash his dubious behavior. At any rate, his response limits Tamar's success: she becomes a mother (of twins) but remains without a (sexual) partner. She saves Judah's household (and, historically, Israel) but does not transform her own position back into a married woman (as it should have been had Judah given her Shelah as promised).

*27–30.* Tamar's vindication by Judah is supplemented by what seems like divine vindication.

crimson thread on its hand, saying, "This one came
out first." [29]But when it pulled the hand back,
look—its brother came out! So she said, "What a
breach you have breached!" And she named him
Perez. [30]Afterward came his brother on whose hand
was the crimson thread, and she named him Zerah.

וַתִּקְשֹׁר עַל־יָדוֹ שָׁנִי לֵאמֹר זֶה יָצָא
רִאשֹׁנָה׃ 29 וַיְהִי ׀ כְּמֵשִׁיב יָדוֹ וְהִנֵּה יָצָא
אָחִיו וַתֹּאמֶר מַה־פָּרַצְתָּ עָלֶיךָ פָּרֶץ וַיִּקְרָא
שְׁמוֹ פָּרֶץ׃ 30 וְאַחַר יָצָא אָחִיו אֲשֶׁר עַל־
יָדוֹ הַשָּׁנִי וַיִּקְרָא שְׁמוֹ זָרַח׃ ס

*39* Now Joseph was brought down to Egypt,
and Potiphar, one of Pharaoh's officers, Captain of
the Guard, an Egyptian man, purchased him from
the Ishmaelites who had brought him down there.
[2]But יהוה was with Joseph: he was a man who prospered. Now that he was in the household of his
Egyptian master, [3]his master saw that יהוה was with
him, and that יהוה was prospering whatever he
touched. [4]Joseph [therefore] found favor in his
sight and ministered to him; he [Potiphar] gave
him authority over his household, and placed all
that he owned in his hand. [5]From the time he gave
him authority over his household and over all that
he owned, יהוה blessed the house of the Egyptian

לט וְיוֹסֵף הוּרַד מִצְרָיְמָה וַיִּקְנֵהוּ פּוֹטִיפַר
סְרִיס פַּרְעֹה שַׂר הַטַּבָּחִים אִישׁ מִצְרִי
מִיַּד הַיִּשְׁמְעֵאלִים אֲשֶׁר הוֹרִדֻהוּ שָׁמָּה׃
2 וַיְהִי יְהֹוָה אֶת־יוֹסֵף וַיְהִי אִישׁ מַצְלִיחַ
וַיְהִי בְּבֵית אֲדֹנָיו הַמִּצְרִי׃ 3 וַיַּרְא אֲדֹנָיו כִּי
יְהֹוָה אִתּוֹ וְכֹל אֲשֶׁר־הוּא עֹשֶׂה יְהֹוָה
מַצְלִיחַ בְּיָדוֹ׃ 4 וַיִּמְצָא יוֹסֵף חֵן בְּעֵינָיו
וַיְשָׁרֶת אֹתוֹ וַיַּפְקִדֵהוּ עַל־בֵּיתוֹ וְכָל־יֶשׁ־לוֹ
נָתַן בְּיָדוֹ׃ 5 וַיְהִי מֵאָז הִפְקִיד אֹתוֹ בְּבֵיתוֹ
וְעַל כָּל־אֲשֶׁר יֶשׁ־לוֹ וַיְבָרֶךְ יְהֹוָה אֶת־בֵּית

Tamar is amply rewarded for her deeds: she brings twin sons into the world (although she remains a single mother).

*29. she said.* Most likely the midwife, who has identified the baby and his actions (v. 28).

*she named him.* [Literally, "[he] named him"; but the verb's implied subject lacks a clear male antecedent. In such a construction the masculine verb does not necessarily imply a gendered referent; many translations render the verb impersonally: "he was named." The present translation, however, seems influenced by the fact that in the Bible, it is usually the mother or midwife who names a newborn, and that some ancient translations also state "she named him," as if that was perhaps the reading in their Hebrew source manuscripts. —*Ed.*]

*Perez.* The name means "Breach." It describes not only the circumstances of his birth, but also, indirectly, of his conception.

## *Joseph and Madam Potiphar*

### SEX AND DECEPTION (39:1–23)

The story of Joseph resumes right where it left him in 37:36—brought down to Egypt and sold as a slave there. While much in this narrative remains ambiguous, it does continue the theme of self-definition in relation to the other peoples, this time focusing on the danger awaiting a male Israelite in a foreign land.

### JOSEPH SUCCEEDS IN POTIPHAR'S HOUSE (39:1–6)

*1. Potiphar.* The name of Joseph's new master resembles Potiphera, the name of the father of Asenath, Joseph's future wife (41:45). If there is a connection, the Torah does not describe it.

on account of Joseph; the blessing of יהוה was on
all that he owned in the house and in the field. 6He
left all that was his in Joseph's hands and gave
no thought to what he had, other than the food
he ate.

Now Joseph happened to be fair of form and
fair of appearance, 7and after all this, his master's
wife set her sights on Joseph and said, "Lie with
me!" 8But he refused, saying to his master's wife,
"Look, my master gives no thought to what is in
this house; all that he owns he has put into my
hands. 9There is none greater than I in this house;
he has withheld nothing from me, other than you,
inasmuch as you are his wife; how then could I do
this great evil, and thus sin against God?" 10And so
she would sweet-talk Joseph day after day, but he
did not heed her plea to lie by her and be with her.

הַמִּצְרִי בִּגְלַל יוֹסֵף וַיְהִי בִּרְכַּת יְהוָה בְּכָל־
אֲשֶׁר יֶשׁ־לוֹ בַּבַּיִת וּבַשָּׂדֶה׃ 6 וַיַּעֲזֹב כָּל־
אֲשֶׁר־לוֹ בְּיַד־יוֹסֵף וְלֹא־יָדַע אִתּוֹ מְאוּמָה
כִּי אִם־הַלֶּחֶם אֲשֶׁר־הוּא אוֹכֵל
וַיְהִי יוֹסֵף יְפֵה־תֹאַר וִיפֵה מַרְאֶה׃ 7 וַיְהִי
אַחַר הַדְּבָרִים הָאֵלֶּה וַתִּשָּׂא אֵשֶׁת־אֲדֹנָיו
אֶת־עֵינֶיהָ אֶל־יוֹסֵף וַתֹּאמֶר שִׁכְבָה עִמִּי׃
8 וַיְמָאֵן ׀ וַיֹּאמֶר אֶל־אֵשֶׁת אֲדֹנָיו הֵן אֲדֹנִי
לֹא־יָדַע אִתִּי מַה־בַּבָּיִת וְכֹל אֲשֶׁר־יֶשׁ־לוֹ
נָתַן בְּיָדִי׃ 9 אֵינֶנּוּ גָדוֹל בַּבַּיִת הַזֶּה מִמֶּנִּי
וְלֹא־חָשַׂךְ מִמֶּנִּי מְאוּמָה כִּי אִם־אוֹתָךְ
בַּאֲשֶׁר אַתְּ־אִשְׁתּוֹ וְאֵיךְ אֶעֱשֶׂה הָרָעָה
הַגְּדֹלָה הַזֹּאת וְחָטָאתִי לֵאלֹהִים׃ 10 וַיְהִי
כְּדַבְּרָהּ אֶל־יוֹסֵף יוֹם ׀ יוֹם וְלֹא־שָׁמַע אֵלֶיהָ
לִשְׁכַּב אֶצְלָהּ לִהְיוֹת עִמָּהּ׃

*one of Pharaoh's officers.* Heb. *s'ris paroh*; the noun *saris* means either "a eunuch" or "an official." Potiphar's wife's attraction to Joseph and her attempted seduction of him (see below) might seem different if her husband were understood to be a eunuch.

*2–5.* God intervenes directly for the first time in this parashah. And undoubtedly Joseph—as a young man in a strange land—would need this divine help.

*6. the food he ate.* This might be a playful reference to his wife, given that in v. 9 below, Joseph tells Madam Potiphar that his master has "withheld nothing from me but you."

*fair of form and fair of appearance.* Literally, "good looking and good to look at." The same words described his mother Rachel in 29:17 (translated there as "beautiful of form and of face"). Implicitly, his beauty would serve as Madam Potiphar's motivation for what follows.

## JOSEPH RESISTS SEDUCTION (39:7–12)

*7. set her sights on Joseph.* Literally, "lifted her eyes up to Joseph."

*"Lie with me!"* Madam Potiphar falls for Joseph and approaches him with this blatant bid. She is painfully direct. We have no details as to her motivation apart from Joseph's beauty: is it lust only, or love as well? Is her husband a eunuch (see at v. 1), thus justifying her adulterous thought somewhat?

*8–9. But he refused.* Joseph cites his master's trust and God as the two reasons for his refusal. He does *not* say whether or not he desires his mistress. Indeed, in the absence of data about her—name, looks, age, and attractiveness are all lacking—we may read his refusal either as lack of interest or, conversely, as control of desire due to loyalty to his earthly and divine masters.

*10. she would sweet-talk Joseph day after day.* The seduction attempts are still only verbal.

11 On one such day, when he came into the house to do his work—and not one of the people of the household was there in the house— 12 she took hold of him by his garment, saying, "Lie with me!" He left his garment in her hand, fled, and ran outside. 13 When she saw that he had left his garment in her hand and fled outside, 14 she summoned her household servants and spoke to them, saying, "See! He brought us a Hebrew man to toy with us. He came to me to lie with me, and I cried out in a loud voice; 15 when he heard me raise my voice and cry out, he left his garment with me and fled and ran outside!" 16 And she kept his garment with her until his master came home.

17 She spoke to him in this manner, saying, "The Hebrew slave whom you brought to us came

11 וַיְהִי כְּהַיּוֹם הַזֶּה וַיָּבֹא הַבַּיְתָה לַעֲשׂוֹת
מְלַאכְתּוֹ וְאֵין אִישׁ מֵאַנְשֵׁי הַבַּיִת שָׁם
בַּבָּיִת׃ 12 וַתִּתְפְּשֵׂהוּ בְּבִגְדוֹ לֵאמֹר שִׁכְבָה
עִמִּי וַיַּעֲזֹב בִּגְדוֹ בְּיָדָהּ וַיָּנָס וַיֵּצֵא הַחוּצָה׃
13 וַיְהִי כִּרְאוֹתָהּ כִּי־עָזַב בִּגְדוֹ בְּיָדָהּ וַיָּנָס
הַחוּצָה׃ 14 וַתִּקְרָא לְאַנְשֵׁי בֵיתָהּ וַתֹּאמֶר
לָהֶם לֵאמֹר רְאוּ הֵבִיא לָנוּ אִישׁ עִבְרִי
לְצַחֶק בָּנוּ בָּא אֵלַי לִשְׁכַּב עִמִּי וָאֶקְרָא
בְּקוֹל גָּדוֹל׃ 15 וַיְהִי כְשָׁמְעוֹ כִּי־הֲרִימֹתִי
קוֹלִי וָאֶקְרָא וַיַּעֲזֹב בִּגְדוֹ אֶצְלִי וַיָּנָס וַיֵּצֵא
הַחוּצָה׃ 16 וַתַּנַּח בִּגְדוֹ אֶצְלָהּ עַד־בּוֹא
אֲדֹנָיו אֶל־בֵּיתוֹ׃
17 וַתְּדַבֵּר אֵלָיו כַּדְּבָרִים הָאֵלֶּה לֵאמֹר בָּא־
אֵלַי הָעֶבֶד הָעִבְרִי אֲשֶׁר־הֵבֵאתָ לָּנוּ לְצַחֶק

---

*11.* Why does Joseph go inside when no one else is around, when he knows the mistress should be inside and waiting to pursue him, as she does "day after day"? What is the unspecified "work"? And where are all the household members? The text is ambiguous, as is Joseph's behavior.

*12.* ***she took hold of him.*** For the first time, Madam attempts something physical: she gets hold of Joseph's garment.

***he left his garment in her hand.*** As when his brothers took his robe (37:23), Joseph here is divested of his garment. This time we have no idea what garment it is, although once again it will be used to deceive.

***fled, and ran outside.*** Joseph votes with his feet, so to speak. His verbal refusal is now backed by action.

### MADAM POTIPHAR LIES AND JOSEPH IS ARRESTED (39:13–20)

To protect herself, Madam Potiphar accuses Joseph of intending to or actually forcing himself on her. The woman who kept saying laconically, "Lie with me!" now becomes a great rhetor as well as an accomplished liar. She presents her case skillfully to the menservants and to her husband, emphasizing different things in each instance.

*13–15.* Somehow the menservants are now available again to Madam. In this, her first version of the story, she enlists their sympathy against an upstart foreign (Hebrew) man, brought in by "him"—her husband.

*14.* ***"to toy."*** Heb. *l'tzachek*, which has a sexual connotation—such as when Isaac "toys" with his wife Rebekah, whereby Abimelech understands that the pair is married (26:8, where this verb is translated as "fondling").

***"with us."*** She includes the menservants as intended victims. The "us" versus "he" places her on the side of the menservants, against her unnamed husband.

*16.* She then keeps the garment, presumably as proof of her story.

*17.* ***"The Hebrew slave."*** In this second version, delivered to the master, she emphasizes Joseph's slave status.

***"whom you brought to us."*** Given that no one else seems to be present, the "us" here presumably refers only to her and her husband, thus empha-

to me to toy with me; 18 but when I raised my voice and cried out, he left his garment near me and fled and ran outside!" 19 When his master heard his wife's words, namely, "Your slave did these things to me!" he was enraged. 20 So Joseph's master took him and gave him over to the prison, the place where the Pharaoh's prisoners are kept; and there he remained, in the prison.

21 Yet יהוה was with Joseph, and extended kindness to him, and lent him grace in the prison warden's sight. 22 The prison warden put all the prisoners of the jail in Joseph's hands, and whatever was done there was his doing. 23 The prison warden never saw anything amiss with him, because יהוה was with him, and because whatever he did יהוה prospered.

40 After all this, the cupbearer of the king of Egypt and the baker offended against their master,

בִּי׃ 18 וַיְהִי כַּהֲרִימִי קוֹלִי וָאֶקְרָא וַיַּעֲזֹב
בִּגְדוֹ אֶצְלִי וַיָּנָס הַחוּצָה׃ 19 וַיְהִי כִשְׁמֹעַ
אֲדֹנָיו אֶת־דִּבְרֵי אִשְׁתּוֹ אֲשֶׁר דִּבְּרָה אֵלָיו
לֵאמֹר כַּדְּבָרִים הָאֵלֶּה עָשָׂה לִי עַבְדֶּךָ וַיִּחַר
אַפּוֹ׃ 20 וַיִּקַּח אֲדֹנֵי יוֹסֵף אֹתוֹ וַיִּתְּנֵהוּ אֶל־
בֵּית הַסֹּהַר מְקוֹם אֲשֶׁר־אסורי אֲסִירֵי הַמֶּלֶךְ
אֲסוּרִים וַיְהִי־שָׁם בְּבֵית הַסֹּהַר׃
21 וַיְהִי יְהֹוָה אֶת־יוֹסֵף וַיֵּט אֵלָיו חָסֶד וַיִּתֵּן
חִנּוֹ בְּעֵינֵי שַׂר בֵּית־הַסֹּהַר׃ 22 וַיִּתֵּן שַׂר
בֵּית־הַסֹּהַר בְּיַד־יוֹסֵף אֵת כָּל־הָאֲסִירִם
אֲשֶׁר בְּבֵית הַסֹּהַר וְאֵת כָּל־אֲשֶׁר עֹשִׂים
שָׁם הוּא הָיָה עֹשֶׂה׃ 23 אֵין ׀ שַׂר בֵּית־
הַסֹּהַר רֹאֶה אֶת־כָּל־מְאוּמָה בְּיָדוֹ בַּאֲשֶׁר
יְהֹוָה אִתּוֹ וַאֲשֶׁר־הוּא עֹשֶׂה יְהֹוָה
מַצְלִיחַ׃ פ
מ וַיְהִי אַחַר הַדְּבָרִים הָאֵלֶּה חָטְאוּ
מַשְׁקֵה מֶלֶךְ־מִצְרַיִם וְהָאֹפֶה לַאֲדֹנֵיהֶם

---

sizing Potiphar's responsibility in this shared concern of wife and husband to uphold the husband's honor.

***"to toy with me."*** The "us" from her previous statement is reconfigured as "me."

***19.*** The wife manages to anger her husband, but we readers remain in the dark: does he believe her? He sends Joseph to prison (v. 20), but this is the royal prison where accused persons await decisions concerning their fate. Potiphar does not punish his wife, which would indicate more clearly that he believes Joseph. The ambiguity remains.

### CONCLUSION: JOSEPH SUCCEEDS IN JAIL (39:21–23)

At first it appears that Joseph has merely moved from one pit (in the ground in Canaan) to another (in prison in Egypt). Yet the end of this episode links with its beginning. God again has blessed Joseph; the chief jailer likes him and puts him in charge (vv. 21–22) and leaves "everything" to Joseph's management. Once again, God makes Joseph "succeed."

## *Joseph's Education Continues*

### THE DREAM INTERPRETER IN JAIL (40:1–23)

In this concluding unit of the parashah, Joseph grows further in stature. From a callous youth, he becomes a person who cares. He asks two jail mates why they look sad after their dreams and is prepared to help (vv. 7–8). He protests his innocence but forgoes the chance to blame anybody specifically (v. 15). From being a mere dreamer, he becomes a dream interpreter. He is coming closer to the ancient Near East's "wise man" or "wise courtier" ideal type, which is present also in the portrayals of Mordecai (in the book of Esther) and of Daniel.

the king of Egypt, 2and Pharaoh was furious at his two officers, at the chief cupbearer and at the chief baker. 3He placed them under guard in the house of the Captain of the Guard, in the prison, the [very] place where Joseph was confined. 4The Captain of the Guard assigned Joseph to them; he waited on them, and they were [some] time under guard.

5They dreamt a dream, the two of them—the cupbearer and the baker of the king of Egypt who were held in the prison—each one's dream falling on the same night, each one's dream with its own meaning. 6When Joseph came to them in the morning, he saw that they seemed out of sorts. 7He asked Pharaoh's officers who were with him under guard, "Why are you so downcast today?"

8So they said to him, "We each dreamt a dream, but there is no one to interpret it." Joseph then said to them, "Surely interpretations are in God's domain; but go ahead and tell them to me." 9The chief cupbearer then recounted his dream to Joseph, saying to him, "In my dream, there was a vine in front of me, 10and on that vine were three branches. Barely had it budded when its blossoms flowered; its clusters ripened with grapes. 11Pharaoh's cup was in my hand, and I took the grapes and squeezed them into Pharaoh's cup and put the cup in Pharaoh's palm."

12Joseph then said to him, "This is its meaning—the three branches are three days; 13in three days' time, Pharaoh will lift up your head and restore you to your post; you shall [again] place Pharaoh's cup in his hand, as you used to do when you were his cupbearer. 14Only call me to mind when it goes well for you, and keep faith with me: commend me to Pharaoh and get me out of this place! 15For I was stolen from the land of the Hebrews, and here, too, I did nothing, that they consigned me to [this] pit!"

לְמֶלֶךְ מִצְרָיִם׃ 2 וַיִּקְצֹף פַּרְעֹה עַל שְׁנֵי
סָרִיסָיו עַל שַׂר הַמַּשְׁקִים וְעַל שַׂר הָאוֹפִים׃
3 וַיִּתֵּן אֹתָם בְּמִשְׁמַר בֵּית שַׂר הַטַּבָּחִים
אֶל־בֵּית הַסֹּהַר מְקוֹם אֲשֶׁר יוֹסֵף אָסוּר
שָׁם׃ 4 וַיִּפְקֹד שַׂר הַטַּבָּחִים אֶת־יוֹסֵף אִתָּם
וַיְשָׁרֶת אֹתָם וַיִּהְיוּ יָמִים בְּמִשְׁמָר׃
5 וַיַּחַלְמוּ חֲלוֹם שְׁנֵיהֶם אִישׁ חֲלֹמוֹ בְּלַיְלָה
אֶחָד אִישׁ כְּפִתְרוֹן חֲלֹמוֹ הַמַּשְׁקֶה וְהָאֹפֶה
אֲשֶׁר לְמֶלֶךְ מִצְרַיִם אֲשֶׁר אֲסוּרִים בְּבֵית
הַסֹּהַר׃ 6 וַיָּבֹא אֲלֵיהֶם יוֹסֵף בַּבֹּקֶר וַיַּרְא
אֹתָם וְהִנָּם זֹעֲפִים׃ 7 וַיִּשְׁאַל אֶת־סְרִיסֵי
פַרְעֹה אֲשֶׁר אִתּוֹ בְמִשְׁמַר בֵּית אֲדֹנָיו
לֵאמֹר מַדּוּעַ פְּנֵיכֶם רָעִים הַיּוֹם׃
8 וַיֹּאמְרוּ אֵלָיו חֲלוֹם חָלַמְנוּ וּפֹתֵר אֵין
אֹתוֹ וַיֹּאמֶר אֲלֵהֶם יוֹסֵף הֲלוֹא לֵאלֹהִים
פִּתְרֹנִים סַפְּרוּ־נָא לִי׃ 9 וַיְסַפֵּר שַׂר־
הַמַּשְׁקִים אֶת־חֲלֹמוֹ לְיוֹסֵף וַיֹּאמֶר לוֹ
בַּחֲלוֹמִי וְהִנֵּה־גֶפֶן לְפָנָי׃ 10 וּבַגֶּפֶן שְׁלֹשָׁה
שָׂרִיגִם וְהִוא כְפֹרַחַת עָלְתָה נִצָּהּ הִבְשִׁילוּ
אַשְׁכְּלֹתֶיהָ עֲנָבִים׃ 11 וְכוֹס פַּרְעֹה בְּיָדִי
וָאֶקַּח אֶת־הָעֲנָבִים וָאֶשְׂחַט אֹתָם אֶל־כּוֹס
פַּרְעֹה וָאֶתֵּן אֶת־הַכּוֹס עַל־כַּף פַּרְעֹה׃
12 וַיֹּאמֶר לוֹ יוֹסֵף זֶה פִּתְרֹנוֹ שְׁלֹשֶׁת
הַשָּׂרִגִים שְׁלֹשֶׁת יָמִים הֵם׃ 13 בְּעוֹד |
שְׁלֹשֶׁת יָמִים יִשָּׂא פַרְעֹה אֶת־רֹאשֶׁךָ
וַהֲשִׁיבְךָ עַל־כַּנֶּךָ וְנָתַתָּ כוֹס־פַּרְעֹה בְּיָדוֹ
כַּמִּשְׁפָּט הָרִאשׁוֹן אֲשֶׁר הָיִיתָ מַשְׁקֵהוּ׃
14 כִּי אִם־זְכַרְתַּנִי אִתְּךָ כַּאֲשֶׁר יִיטַב לָךְ
וְעָשִׂיתָ־נָּא עִמָּדִי חָסֶד וְהִזְכַּרְתַּנִי אֶל־
פַּרְעֹה וְהוֹצֵאתַנִי מִן־הַבַּיִת הַזֶּה׃ 15 כִּי־
גֻנֹּב גֻּנַּבְתִּי מֵאֶרֶץ הָעִבְרִים וְגַם־פֹּה לֹא־
עָשִׂיתִי מְאוּמָה כִּי־שָׂמוּ אֹתִי בַּבּוֹר׃

*15.* For the first time, the story depicts Joseph telling someone in Egypt how he came to be there. The version he tells the cupbearer is notable for its heavily edited contents. There is not a word about his brothers, or the events in Potiphar's house. He blames nobody and names no culprit. All he does is

16 When the chief baker saw how well he had interpreted, he said to Joseph, "In my dream, too, look, there were three—baskets of bread on my head, 17 and in the topmost basket was every kind of food for Pharaoh, baked goods, and birds eating them from the basket on my head."

18 Joseph then responded, saying, "This is its meaning—the three baskets are three days. 19 In three days' time, Pharaoh will lift your head from your body and hang you on a pole, and birds will eat your flesh from upon you."

20 The third day was Pharaoh's birthday, and he gave a feast for all his officials. He singled out the chief cupbearer and the chief baker among his officials: 21 He restored the chief cupbearer to his office; [again] he placed the cup in Pharaoh's palm. 22 The chief baker he hanged, as Joseph had interpreted for them. 23 But the chief cupbearer did not remember Joseph; [instead] he forgot him.

16 וַיַּ֥רְא שַֽׂר־הָאֹפִ֖ים כִּ֣י ט֣וֹב פָּתָ֑ר וַיֹּ֙אמֶר֙
אֶל־יוֹסֵ֔ף אַף־אֲנִי֙ בַּחֲלוֹמִ֔י וְהִנֵּ֗ה שְׁלֹשָׁ֛ה
סַלֵּ֥י חֹרִ֖י עַל־רֹאשִֽׁי׃ 17 וּבַסַּ֣ל הָעֶלְי֔וֹן מִכֹּ֥ל
מַאֲכַ֛ל פַּרְעֹ֖ה מַעֲשֵׂ֣ה אֹפֶ֑ה וְהָע֗וֹף אֹכֵ֥ל
אֹתָ֛ם מִן־הַסַּ֖ל מֵעַ֥ל רֹאשִֽׁי׃
18 וַיַּ֤עַן יוֹסֵף֙ וַיֹּ֔אמֶר זֶ֖ה פִּתְרֹנ֑וֹ שְׁלֹ֙שֶׁת֙
הַסַּלִּ֔ים שְׁלֹ֥שֶׁת יָמִ֖ים הֵֽם׃ 19 בְּע֣וֹד ׀
שְׁלֹ֣שֶׁת יָמִ֗ים יִשָּׂ֨א פַרְעֹ֤ה אֶת־רֹֽאשְׁךָ֙
מֵעָלֶ֔יךָ וְתָלָ֥ה אוֹתְךָ֖ עַל־עֵ֑ץ וְאָכַ֥ל הָע֛וֹף
אֶת־בְּשָׂרְךָ֖ מֵעָלֶֽיךָ׃
20 וַיְהִ֣י ׀ בַּיּ֣וֹם הַשְּׁלִישִׁ֗י י֚וֹם הֻלֶּ֣דֶת אֶת־
פַּרְעֹ֔ה וַיַּ֥עַשׂ מִשְׁתֶּ֖ה לְכָל־עֲבָדָ֑יו וַיִּשָּׂ֞א אֶת־
רֹ֣אשׁ ׀ שַׂ֣ר הַמַּשְׁקִ֗ים וְאֶת־רֹ֛אשׁ שַׂ֥ר
הָאֹפִ֖ים בְּת֥וֹךְ עֲבָדָֽיו׃ 21 וַיָּ֛שֶׁב אֶת־שַׂ֥ר
הַמַּשְׁקִ֖ים עַל־מַשְׁקֵ֑הוּ וַיִּתֵּ֥ן הַכּ֖וֹס עַל־כַּ֥ף
פַּרְעֹֽה׃ 22 וְאֵ֛ת שַׂ֥ר הָאֹפִ֖ים תָּלָ֑ה כַּאֲשֶׁ֥ר
פָּתַ֛ר לָהֶ֖ם יוֹסֵֽף׃ 23 וְלֹֽא־זָכַ֧ר שַֽׂר־הַמַּשְׁקִ֛ים
אֶת־יוֹסֵ֖ף וַיִּשְׁכָּחֵֽהוּ׃

establish his innocence so that, upon his restoration, the cupbearer would remember and mention him to the pharaoh. This is also the first time we are told that Joseph actively seeks freedom, or an improvement of his lot, since coming to Egypt.

* * *

From an arrogant and gossipy boy, Joseph has grown into a young man who refuses adultery with his master's wife, who suffers in prison, who does not tell on his brothers when the opportunity arises. Clearly, he can now exercise control over his own behavior and emotions, which he could not do earlier—and which is a prerequisite for his future role. In addition, from a dreamer he has evolved into a dream interpreter. He is poised to act on dreams to the benefit of all: his adopted land, his own self, and his original family.

*—Athalya Brenner*

# Another View

Potiphar's wife and Tamar provide two models of the feminine and help to forge the contrasting characterizations of Joseph and Judah.

Potiphar's wife is overtly sensual and verbally aggressive. Like the negative archetype of the feminine in one passage of the book of Proverbs (7:1–23), she tempts the young man into sexual impropriety. Potiphar's wife serves as a test in the initiation of Joseph, the young wisdom hero who refuses to allow a woman to make him unfaithful to his master.

Tamar, a young childless widow, becomes a trickster, a marginal figure who succeeds in indirect ways, by deceiving those in power. The trickster's marginality may be rooted in gender, age, economic or social status. Biblical tricksters include Abraham (Genesis 12:1–10), Jacob (Genesis 27), Rebekah (Genesis 27), and Tamar. Tales of tricksters appeal to the underdog side of each of us, but they may have special appeal among groups who feel themselves out of power—for example, women in a world dominated by men.

In Genesis 38, the qualities of the feminine that limited Tamar become her source of strength. When Judah sends her back to her father with empty promises of giving her his third son in good time, Tamar, like other marginal females in ancient Israelite social structure, is caught betwixt and between social categories available to women—as virgins or as child-producing, faithful wives. Eventually, Tamar takes matters into her own hands. Dressing as a prostitute and standing at the crossroads in a double symbolization of her marginality, she becomes pregnant by Judah. Wisely she has demanded and then kept his pledges, symbols of his identity and status. Judah—who is no more appealing in this tale than in the selling of Joseph—orders that Tamar be burned alive

*The qualities of the feminine that limited Tamar become her source of strength.*

when he hears she is pregnant, dismissing her with two words. But she—clever girl—produces the tokens that identify Judah as the father, and even he must admit he has been bested. Judah, coconspirator in the exile of Joseph, is one of the many biblical males, including Samson, Sisera, and Isaac, who are tricked by women's wiles. It is Tamar's right to bear children in Judah's line, and the twins indicate abundant fertility. She will be the ancestress of kings. Tamar's power is indirect, circumscribed by the realm of procreation and supported by tricksterism. It is a power, nevertheless, that is celebrated in the biblical tale.

—*Susan Niditch*

# Post-biblical Interpretations

***Around that time*** (38:1). Pondering why the story of Joseph is interrupted by events in the life of his brother Judah, the Rabbis draw our attention to the pivotal roles women play in the lives of both men. Midrash *B'reishit Rabbah* 85.2 explains that Judah's and Joseph's adventures are juxtaposed "to bring the stories of Tamar and Potiphar's wife into close proximity, in order to teach that as the former was actuated by a pure motive, so was the latter. For Rabbi

Joshua ben Levi said: Potiphar's wife saw by her astrological arts that she was to produce a child by Joseph, but she did not know whether it was to be from her—or from her daughter." In fact, as related in *B'reishit Rabbah* 86.3, the Rabbis believed that the woman whom Joseph eventually married was none other than the daughter of Potiphar and his wife, since they identified Potiphar with "Potiphera priest of On," Joseph's future father-in-law (41:45).

***covered herself up with a veil*** (38:14). For the Rabbis, Tamar's heroic actions displayed the wherewithal, foresight, and fortitude of a matriarch such as Rebekah. They allude to this association in *B'reishit Rabbah* 60.15 and 85.7: "Two covered themselves with a veil, and each gave birth to twins—Rebekah and Tamar." Tamar's behavior is considered a praiseworthy response to a situation of injustice.

*Potiphar's wife saw by her astrological arts that she was to produce a child by Joseph.*

***he turned toward her*** (38:16). The Rabbis saw Tamar's deception as foreordained since they believed that the messiah will ultimately arise from her long-ago union with Judah. *B'reishit Rabbah* 85.8 recounts that an angel intervened on Tamar's behalf in order to make sure that Judah did not pass her by: "Rabbi Yohanan said: He wished to go on, but the blessed Holy One made the angel who is in charge of desire appear before him and say to him: 'Where are you going, Judah? From where are kings and redeemers to arise?' Thus: *he turned toward her.*"

***a kid from the flock*** (38:17). *B'reishit Rabbah* 85.9 makes clear that Judah received his comeuppance: "The blessed Holy One said to Judah, 'You deceived your father with a kid of goats [when you hid the truth about Joseph's disappearance, 37:31–32], thus Tamar will deceive you with a kid of goats.'"

***"Your signet seal, your cord, and the staff in your hand"*** (38:18). In *B'reishit Rabbah* 85.9, the Rabbis further express their support for Tamar's actions by interpreting the pledges that Judah gives her as emblems of (future) royalty.

***she became pregnant by him*** (38:18). Even Tamar herself was mindful of the important role her descendants would later play. During her pregnancy, "she would pat her belly and exclaim, 'I am big with kings and redeemers'" (*B'reishit Rabbah* 85.10).

A 1st-century-C.E. Jewish work known as *Biblical Antiquities* (by an unknown author usually referred to as Pseudo-Philo) presents Tamar as a role model for the Israelites in Egypt. In that account, Amram, Moses' father, speaks of her as "our mother Tamar." The emphasis falls on her determination to perpetuate the line of Judah despite risk—which Amram uses to encourage the people to continue to perpetuate life despite their slavery (*Biblical Antiquities* 9.5–6).

***Judah . . . said, "She is more in the right than I"*** (38:26). According to *B'reishit Rabbah* 97, Judah was rewarded for his confession that he had wronged Tamar, since God delivers those who admit their misdeeds—and promises them a life in the world to come.

***after all this, his master's wife*** (39:7). Tamar and Potiphar's wife are both presented in midrashic texts as powerful, beautiful, clever, and seductive women. However, while Tamar is universally praised because she ensured the future destiny of the tribe of Judah—from which the Davidic dynasty would eventually spring—Potiphar's wife emerges as a more ambiguous figure. She is most often depicted as both seducer and seduced. She is portrayed as an immoral woman who meant to taunt and tease Joseph but was overwhelmed by his great beauty. According to *B'reishit Rabbah* 87.10, when Joseph was in prison, she would say to him: "See how I have made you suffer. By your life, I will persecute you in other ways too." The midrash continues: "She went so far as to place an iron fork under his neck so that he should have to lift up his eyes and look at her. Yet in spite of that he would not look at her." Rabbi Huna explains that Jacob's outcry—"a wild animal has devoured him" (37:33)—was actually a moment of clairvoyance in which the distraught father perceived Mrs. Potiphar's wicked ways and her obsession with Joseph (*B'reishit Rabbah* 84.19). Indeed, the more depraved and seductive she acted, the more commendable was Joseph's resistance and display of honor.

—*Carol Bakhos*

• • • • •

# *Contemporary Reflection*

In terms of the biblical worldview, Tamar's tragedy is evident: she has lost her husband, and she has no offspring to secure her status as a widow and give her life purpose. Tired of leaving her fate to male relatives, Tamar takes action to secure her own position, thereby joining the circle of matriarchs who exemplify action to protect Israelite destiny.

*When the Family Constellation Changes.* As the Bible tells the story, Judah and Tamar are in-laws who have reached a crisis point in their relationship. Why? As Carol Meyers explains (*Discovering Eve: Ancient Israelite Women in Context,* 1988, pp. 133, 183), a young woman typically married into her husband's extended family household. The new wife was expected to conform to household norms.

At first, Judah is more than willing to support Tamar's rights. It is he who prompts Onan to perform his duty (38:8); however, when Onan dies in turn, Judah inwardly blames Tamar (38:11), although the reader knows that she is innocent (38:7, 10). Clearly, there is a failure of communication. Judah tells Tamar he will eventually allow her access to Shelah, while he privately intends no such thing. For her part, Tamar correctly surmises Judah's true intentions, but she never confronts him, discusses it with him, or attempts less radical measures, such as mediation. Evidently, Judah's abiding sense of loss and resentment are blocking his reconciliation with Tamar. Because of Judah's failure to heal, Tamar is also unable to move on.

Even now, any new family member—whether spouse, in-law, or child—begins as an outsider. The attendant changes in family dynamics bring accompanying stresses. If conversion or adoption is involved, the difficulties of adjustment may be compounded, requiring increased patience and sensitivity. Recriminations, too, have never been uncommon when premature death occurs in a family.

*Recovering from the Loss of a Husband.* Tamar's actions following the loss of her spouse involve extreme risk, but they are not reckless; she has a plan. Spousal

> *Tamar's courage in the face of adversity may reduce our fear to realistic proportions.*

loss should not force anyone into desperate acts. In modern terms, Tamar's predicament cautions women today not to abdicate their financial security to others. They should be aware of and involved in household decisions concerning retirement plans, mortgages, and taxes. Too many widows emerge from mourning to discover financial troubles they had not known existed, and, apart from any monetary crisis that may ensue, are left with a tainted memory of their loved one and an ensuing anger that is hard to resolve.

On a less dire note, entering widowhood nowadays may not be dangerous, but it can be frightening to face life as a single after years of partnership. Tamar's courage in the face of genuine adversity serves as a model for those who fear entering a social situation alone for the first time, and it may help reduce that fear to realistic proportions. After all, no one in America today will try to burn them for exiting their fathers' houses, even were they to turn up pregnant.

Widows today should remember that they are not genuinely alone. Just as Tamar could fall back on her family of origin, the bereaved should not avoid turning to their support networks of family and friends. If these do not exist or are inadequate, there are communal resources—and new interests and people yet to explore.

Tamar eventually rises from her mourning and responds to her loss by taking action that will produce meaning for her life. Producing an heir is not the only way to create a legacy. Many are the widows and widowers who have responded to their loss through volunteer work and community involvement. Victor Frankl, in his work *Man's Search for Meaning* (1959), taught that while we may have no control over circumstances in which we find ourselves, we have utter freedom in how we respond to those circumstances, even if only in the attitude we choose to assume in response. Tamar teaches us not to become immobilized by loss. Mourn—but then move to find ongoing purpose.

*The Role of the Foreigner.* Had Tamar been kin, mention of her lineage would be expected; thus it seems that she was foreign. Yet this matters little to Judah: he resents Tamar because he associates her with the loss of his sons, not because of her ethnic identity. Judah had himself been married to a Canaanite, and it is he who arranged Er's marriage with Tamar in the first place (38:6). Moreover, in Tamar's time, no conversion rite, as such, existed; she makes her affiliation clear by aligning herself with the destiny of Judah's household—and thus with the destiny of Israel.

Non-Israelite origin connects Tamar to the story of Potiphar's wife that follows in Genesis 39. Placing the story of a good woman next to that of a bad woman clarifies, from a biblical standpoint, the meaning of both goodness and badness in women. This juxtaposition of good and bad models, known to literary structuralists as "binary opposition," is found again in the case of the widow of Zarephath (in Phoenicia), who aids Elijah in I Kings 17 and is in counterpoint to that other Phoenician woman, Jezebel, who hounds Elijah. Women are not the only foreign exemplars: the good Kenites are repeatedly balanced with the hated Amalekites (Exodus 17–18; Judges 4; and I Samuel 15:6). Such stories provide examples of how a foreigner or foreign people should behave, and another less edifying one of how they often did behave. In the context of the Bible, such passages represent ethnic tensions of the past and highlight the uncertainty of trusting outsiders. For the modern world, they serve as a reminder for us to judge individuals by their actions and attitudes, rather than by labels and assumptions.

—*Carol Selkin Wise*

# Voices

## Tamar's Lament

Hara E. Person

*Genesis 38:11*

The man of my dreams was brave, true, a hero.
Handsome, yes, but more,
a provider, someone to listen to me.
Not a trickster against man or God.
Not a rebellious son.
Not a defiant man.

Why did it go so wrong?
Why was all that I had learned in my mother's
house
not any use with these brothers?
Their sneers, their spite.
No children would they give me.
They robbed me.
They stole my innocence and my hope.
And every month, when their mother would
ask,
what could I say?

But there is also Shelah.
Ah, Shelah, their baby.
*Shelah*, hers, mine.
Shelah, *sheli*.
My husband-in-waiting.
The soft-skinned, gentle, beautiful boy,
waiting for me.

Can I take Shelah, *sheli*,
before he grows up to be like them?
Can I take this beautiful boy
before he becomes hardened and bitter and
angry?
But they won't let me,
he is only a small boy after all,
and if I am to be his wife I cannot also be
his mother.

And so they send me,
with no baby in my arms,
no baby at my breast—
in shame they send me back to my father's
house.
There I will sit, and wait—and sit, and wait,
for Shelah, for mine,
and try over and over again to tell myself
that it wasn't me,
that I did nothing wrong.

NOTES

***Shelah.*** In Hebrew, the name Shelah sounds like the word *shelah* ("hers").

***sheli.*** In Hebrew, "mine."

## *from* The Five Books of Miriam

Ellen Frankel

*Genesis 38:13–19*

*Tamar answers*: I regarded this entire episode as my final test of Judah's character. He'd already failed to enforce his family's levirate obligation. He'd sent me home in disgrace to my father's house. Now, by his cavalier surrender of his name and power, he conclusively proved his unworthiness as paterfamilias. And so once the bargain was sealed, it was *I* who left *him* and went on my way; he remained behind, stripped of his identity. From that moment on, the family birthright passed to me, the mother of Judah's heir.

## *The Stripes in Joseph's Coat*

Rivka Miriam (transl. Linda Stern Zisquit)

*Genesis 37:3–4*

The stripes in Joseph's coat
were like the rungs in the ladder of Jacob's
dream.
The cloak was warm from the sun moon
and stars,
sheaves flew off from it as Joseph walked.
He was in the pit as if in the arms of his mother
Rachel of the Well.
Ishmaelites roamed above, their bells ringing
and on the humps of their camels they moved
him
as in the heart of seas.
The camel rolls up its neck like a long arm
and bracelets leap in Joseph's eyes.
On the camel his mother hid the idols under her
pressing them close like large dolls,
he touched them with a small finger
and with a larger finger they stabbed him
shooting him to Egypt.
The God of the Hebrews slept under him the
whole way
like a large stone lumped together from many
stones.

## *from* Potiphar's Wife

Linda Hepner

*Genesis 39*

Joseph, your raven locks have made me mad—
On moonlit nights I dream awake
My soul red-hot that you with snake-like tread
Enter my courtyard. Had I summoned you
For bread, for wine, I should have been
prepared,
But nightly you pass by and nightly I
Leap trembling at your trespass.

Potiphar lies snoring at my side.
Goats cannot wake him. Daylight calls his
chores
From furrows in his mind and he jolts up
With shouts of "Joseph, my cloak!" You appear,
Eyes low with lack of sleep.

Sweet boy your body gleams,
Your tunic ripples. Motes of light reflect
And I beneath my sheet observe.
Girls of your land avert their gaze
And well they might, for gossips shock:
Barbaric brothers once they say
Slaughtered a city in revenge
For loving of their sister.
She like me desired a stranger.

Here I shall stand bejeweled
And naked; our embrace
Shall touch our mouths our toes—
Together we shall encircle
All the world with our desire.

## *She Is Joseph*

Nurit Zarchi (transl. Shirley Kaufman)

*Genesis 37:3–10*

Rachel sits in the tent
and gathers each curl closer
to hide them under the silken cap
of her little daughter Joseph,

because if you wanted a son
and your time was running out,
what else would you do but lie
to alter what God had done.

The little one sits in the tent
in a coat of colored stripes.
Revealed to all—a boy,
a girl whose sex is hidden.

And now the whole world knows
her shame is gone. For his father
Rachel brought forth a son
and she is her mother's daughter.

And the mother reads the future
in the dark hair of her daughter:
dreams will cast you in a pit,
a foreign court soon after.

The little one sits in the tent,
she hears the words of her mother,
and she is caught in a spell,
and she is caught in horror,

while Rachel continues, stunned,
the shocks grow more extreme:
you will be locked in prison
and freed once more by dreams.

Dreams will save you, daughter,
will cast you in a pit.
But Rachel's time is short
for the riddle of her daughter.

The little one sits in the tent,
holds her breath and listens.
Revealed to all—a boy,
a girl whose sex is hidden.

## *A Word before the Last about Loss*

Linda Stern Zisquit

*Genesis 37:35*

Precisely because you are alive
there is no comfort in this world.
Because wherever you are not
I search, and where I hear your step
you have not been or left a mark.
So the roads are trampled by one,
not two. And the past is maimed
by remembering more. Just as
an old man cannot live at peace
clutching a rag of stripes as proof
without a swish of snakes underneath,
without imagining profoundest disease that follows him—a body
of bones, a soul clanking around—
it is asking for comfort where
there is none, possessing the one
thing alive that has no end.

# מקץ ✦ *Mikeitz*

## GENESIS 41:1–44:17

### *When Dreams Come True*

PARASHAT MIKEITZ ("at the end of") marks the end of Joseph's time in prison, traces his rise to power in Pharaoh's court, and concludes when his brothers stand before him fearful for their fate. Earlier, in Genesis 37, Joseph's dreams had provoked the envy of his brothers. In this parashah, dreams enable him to leave prison when he uses his gifts to interpret Pharaoh's dreams. Joseph's own dreams come true when his brothers—not knowing who he is—bow to him in supplication. How will Joseph respond? Have the brothers changed? The parashah concludes with the key question still unanswered: *is this family doomed to relive a violent past, or will it show that transformation and growth are possible?* In this parashah, Judah takes the lead as representative of the brothers. His rise to responsibility can be linked to his encounter with Tamar in Genesis 38 (see below).

Favoritism in Jacob's household continues to propel the narrative. Jacob's undying love for Rachel has led him to favor her sons, Joseph and Benjamin, over those of Leah, Bilhah, and Zilpah—resulting in virulent sibling rivalry for Jacob's affection (Genesis 37). Years later, the brothers still must cope with Jacob's blatant favoritism while he remains oblivious to the effect of his behavior.

In this parashah, women appear mostly indirectly. Unlike Sarah and Rebekah—who actively appeared in the earlier episodes about Abraham, Isaac, and their offspring—Jacob's wives remain in the background and do not act. Rachel has already died (35:19), and Leah, whose burial is retrospectively recorded later (49:31), goes unmentioned. Nothing further is said about Zilpah or Bilhah. Only Asenath plays a direct role, as Joseph's Egyptian wife and as mother of his sons. The name of her

> *Judah's rise now to responsibility can be linked to his earlier encounter with Tamar.*

father, the priest Potiphera, echoes Potiphar's name—evoking memories of Potiphar's wife, the cause for Joseph's incarceration in the previous parashah (Genesis 39).

At the same time, one notes several allusions or connections with the encounter between Tamar and Judah in Genesis 38. For example, in both stories, clothing serves as a disguise, hiding the true identity of Judah's interlocutor; in both, the same verb (translated as "acknowledge" in 38:25–26 and "recognize" in 42:8) marks a pivotal moment; in both, also, the notion of pledge plays a role (see at 43:9). Possibly, Judah's rise to prominence in this parashah results from the transformation he had undergone when Tamar quietly called him to account.

—*Naomi Steinberg*

## *Outline*

*I.* Joseph Interprets Pharaoh's Dreams and Rises to Power (41:1–57)

- *A.* Pharaoh dreams about cows and corn (vv. 1–8)
- *B.* The chief cupbearer recalls Joseph, interpreter of dreams (vv. 9–13)
- *C.* Joseph interprets Pharaoh's dreams (vv. 14–36)
- *D.* Joseph is elevated to high office and marries Asenath (vv. 37–49)
- *E.* Asenath bears Manasseh and Ephraim to Joseph (vv. 50–52)
- *F.* Famine causes "all lands" to travel to Egypt for grain (vv. 53–57)

*II.* Ten Brothers Journey to Egypt (42:1–25)

- *A.* Jacob sends ten brothers to Egypt for food (vv. 1–5)
- *B.* The brothers appear before Joseph (vv. 6–17)
- *C.* Joseph demands that they bring Benjamin (vv. 18–25)

*III.* Nine Brothers Return to Canaan (42:26–38)

- *A.* One brother discovers money in his sack (vv. 26–28)
- *B.* The brothers report to Jacob (vv. 29–35)
- *C.* Jacob is dismayed mostly over the prospective loss of Benjamin (vv. 36–38)

*IV.* The Second Journey to Egypt, with Benjamin (43:1–44:13a)

- *A.* Continuing famine forces Jacob to let Benjamin go (43:1–14)
- *B.* The brothers appear before Joseph (43:15–34)
- *C.* Joseph tests the brothers (44:1–2)
- *D.* The brothers are charged with theft (44:3–13a)

*V.* The Third appearance before joseph
*The Final Test* (44:13b–17)

- *A.* The brothers appear before Joseph (vv. 13b–15)
- *B.* Judah's confession (v. 16)
- *C.* Joseph demands only Benjamin (vv. 17)

At the end of two years' time, Pharaoh had a dream: there he was, standing by the Nile, [2]when seven cows came up out of the Nile, handsome and fat. They grazed among the reeds. [3]And now seven other cows came up after them from the Nile—repulsive and gaunt. They stood beside the [other] cows at the bank of the Nile. [4]The cows that were repulsive and gaunt then ate the cows that were handsome and fat, and Pharaoh woke up.

[5]He fell asleep and dreamt a second time: this time, seven ears of grain were growing on a single stalk; they were healthy and good; [6]and then seven

מא וַיְהִי מִקֵּץ שְׁנָתַיִם יָמִים וּפַרְעֹה חֹלֵם
וְהִנֵּה עֹמֵד עַל־הַיְאֹר׃ 2 וְהִנֵּה מִן־הַיְאֹר
עֹלֹת שֶׁבַע פָּרוֹת יְפוֹת מַרְאֶה וּבְרִיאֹת
בָּשָׂר וַתִּרְעֶינָה בָּאָחוּ׃ 3 וְהִנֵּה שֶׁבַע פָּרוֹת
אֲחֵרוֹת עֹלוֹת אַחֲרֵיהֶן מִן־הַיְאֹר רָעוֹת
מַרְאֶה וְדַקּוֹת בָּשָׂר וַתַּעֲמֹדְנָה אֵצֶל הַפָּרוֹת
עַל־שְׂפַת הַיְאֹר׃ 4 וַתֹּאכַלְנָה הַפָּרוֹת רָעוֹת
הַמַּרְאֶה וְדַקֹּת הַבָּשָׂר אֵת שֶׁבַע הַפָּרוֹת
יְפֹת הַמַּרְאֶה וְהַבְּרִיאֹת וַיִּיקַץ פַּרְעֹה׃
5 וַיִּישָׁן וַיַּחֲלֹם שֵׁנִית וְהִנֵּה ׀ שֶׁבַע שִׁבֳּלִים
עֹלוֹת בְּקָנֶה אֶחָד בְּרִיאוֹת וְטֹבוֹת׃ 6 וְהִנֵּה

## *Joseph Interprets Pharaoh's Dreams and Rises to Power*

(41:1–57)

As the parashah opens, Joseph is in Egypt, where he is not only a slave but also indefinitely detained in a prison—and no one in his family knows his whereabouts. For readers the situation would seem grim but for the narrator's note that "יהוה was with Joseph" (39:21). In his youth, Joseph's dreams had provided the pretext for his enslavement (see 37:19–20); now—in a turn of poetic justice—the dreams of others provide the context for solving his problem both of enslavement and of imprisonment: the ruler of Egypt awakens from a pair of disturbing premonitory dreams; upon hearing this, his chief cupbearer recalls how he once received help with his own troubling dream. And this leads back to Joseph.

Although Pharaoh's dreams strictly relate to famine in Egypt, as the story later unfolds we will see the famine extending to the land where Jacob resides. Thus, the famine will make it possible for Joseph to be reunited with his family.

### PHARAOH DREAMS OF COWS AND CORN (41:1–8)

After Joseph interpreted the dreams of the chief cupbearer and the chief baker (Genesis 40), he has another opportunity to demonstrate his dream interpretation skills.

*2–7. cows . . . ears of grain.* The cows and the corn symbolize the fertility of the land.

▶ If a single dream would have sufficed, why are there two, and why do they follow so closely?

ANOTHER VIEW ➤ *252*

▶ Power rests not in the dream itself, but in the wisdom of the interpreter.

POST-BIBLICAL INTERPRETATIONS ➤ *252*

▶ They made peace with their father's favoritism.

▶ Jewish lineage is not shaped by genetics alone.

CONTEMPORARY REFLECTION ➤ *254, 255*

▶ For you dear father, I plant today a garden of grain. . . .

VOICES ➤ *257*

ears of grain—thin, scorched by the east wind—
grew after them! 7The seven ears of grain that were
thin and scorched by the east wind then swallowed
the seven ears of grain that were healthy and full,
and Pharaoh woke up; behold—it was a dream!
8In the morning his spirit was troubled; he put
out a call for all the soothsayer-priests and sages of
Egypt; Pharaoh related his dream to them, but no
one could interpret them for Pharaoh.
9The chief cupbearer then spoke to Pharaoh,
saying, "This day I [must] acknowledge my sins!
10Pharaoh had grown angry at his servants, so he
put me under guard in the house of the Captain of
the Guard—me and the chief baker. 11We dreamt a
dream on a single night, he and I, each dream of
ours with its own meaning. 12Now, there with us
was a Hebrew lad, a slave of the Captain of the
Guard; when we related our dreams to him, he
interpreted for us, interpreting each one's dream
according to its own meaning. 13And as he interpreted for us, so it came to be—[Pharaoh] restored
me to my position, and him [Pharaoh] hanged."
14So Pharaoh sent to summon Joseph; they hurried
him from the pit: he shaved, changed his clothing,
and came to Pharaoh.
15Pharaoh said to Joseph, "I dreamt a dream and
there is no one to interpret it; but I have heard this

שֶׁבַע שִׁבֳּלִים דַּקּוֹת וּשְׁדוּפֹת קָדִים צֹמְחוֹת
אַחֲרֵיהֶן׃ 7 וַתִּבְלַעְנָה הַשִּׁבֳּלִים הַדַּקּוֹת אֵת
שֶׁבַע הַשִּׁבֳּלִים הַבְּרִיאוֹת וְהַמְּלֵאוֹת וַיִּיקַץ
פַּרְעֹה וְהִנֵּה חֲלוֹם׃
8 וַיְהִי בַבֹּקֶר וַתִּפָּעֶם רוּחוֹ וַיִּשְׁלַח וַיִּקְרָא
אֶת־כׇּל־חַרְטֻמֵּי מִצְרַיִם וְאֶת־כׇּל־חֲכָמֶיהָ
וַיְסַפֵּר פַּרְעֹה לָהֶם אֶת־חֲלֹמוֹ וְאֵין־פּוֹתֵר
אוֹתָם לְפַרְעֹה׃
9 וַיְדַבֵּר שַׂר הַמַּשְׁקִים אֶת־פַּרְעֹה לֵאמֹר
אֶת־חֲטָאַי אֲנִי מַזְכִּיר הַיּוֹם׃ 10 פַּרְעֹה קָצַף
עַל־עֲבָדָיו וַיִּתֵּן אֹתִי בְּמִשְׁמַר בֵּית שַׂר
הַטַּבָּחִים אֹתִי וְאֵת שַׂר הָאֹפִים׃
11 וַנַּחַלְמָה חֲלוֹם בְּלַיְלָה אֶחָד אֲנִי וָהוּא
אִישׁ כְּפִתְרוֹן חֲלֹמוֹ חָלָמְנוּ׃ 12 וְשָׁם אִתָּנוּ
נַעַר עִבְרִי עֶבֶד לְשַׂר הַטַּבָּחִים וַנְּסַפֶּר־לוֹ
וַיִּפְתׇּר־לָנוּ אֶת־חֲלֹמֹתֵינוּ אִישׁ כַּחֲלֹמוֹ
פָּתָר׃ 13 וַיְהִי כַּאֲשֶׁר פָּתַר־לָנוּ כֵּן הָיָה אֹתִי
הֵשִׁיב עַל־כַּנִּי וְאֹתוֹ תָלָה׃ 14 וַיִּשְׁלַח פַּרְעֹה
וַיִּקְרָא אֶת־יוֹסֵף וַיְרִיצֻהוּ מִן־הַבּוֹר וַיְגַלַּח
וַיְחַלֵּף שִׂמְלֹתָיו וַיָּבֹא אֶל־פַּרְעֹה׃
15 וַיֹּאמֶר פַּרְעֹה אֶל־יוֹסֵף חֲלוֹם חָלַמְתִּי
וּפֹתֵר אֵין אֹתוֹ וַאֲנִי שָׁמַעְתִּי עָלֶיךָ לֵאמֹר

## THE CHIEF CUPBEARER RECALLS JOSEPH, INTERPRETER OF DREAMS (41:9–13)

*9. "This day I [must] acknowledge my sins!"* In 40:14 Joseph had asked the cupbearer to mention him to Pharaoh and to help free him. The cupbearer is only doing that now, two years later. His offense this time is forgetting Joseph.

*12. "he interpreted for us."* The cupbearer attributes the ability to interpret dreams to Joseph, while Joseph had claimed that dream interpretation comes from God (40:8), a view that he articulates consistently (see below at v. 16).

## JOSEPH INTERPRETS PHARAOH'S DREAMS (41:14–36)

*14. he shaved.* In the ancient Near East, only the Egyptians were clean shaven, so as Joseph prepares to go before Pharaoh his appearance is made distinctively Egyptian, reflecting Egyptian protocol—and foreshadowing Joseph's rise from a slave to one who has authority over Egyptians.

*changed his clothing.* Joseph's clothes have served to signal his fate (his special coat from his father, 37:3, 33; his garment in the hands of his master's wife, 39:12–18). In this case, new clothing is a sign of a positive shift in identity.

about you: you have but to hear a dream to interpret it." [16]Joseph answered Pharaoh by saying, "Not I—it is God who will account for Pharaoh's well-being."

[17]Pharaoh then spoke to Joseph, "In my dream I stood on the bank of the Nile, [18]and lo—seven cows went up out of the river; fat and handsome, they grazed among the reeds. [19]And lo—seven other cows—poor, truly repulsive, emaciated—came up after them. Never have I seen any so repulsive in all the land of Egypt! [20]The emaciated and repulsive cows then ate up the first cows, the fat ones. [21]Once they had digested them, one could not tell that they had digested them; they were as repulsive as before—whereupon I awoke. [22]Then in my [other] dream I saw that seven ears of grain were growing on one stalk, full and good. [23]Then sprouting after them were seven ears of grain—dried up, thin, scorched by the east wind! [24]The seven thin ears of grain swallowed up the seven goodly ears. But when I told the soothsayer-priests, none could explain [it] to me."

[25]Joseph then said to Pharaoh, "Pharaoh's dream is one: what God is doing, [God] has revealed to Pharaoh. [26]The seven goodly cows are seven years, and the seven goodly ears of grain are seven years: it is all one dream. [27]The seven cows coming up after them that were emaciated and repulsive are seven years; and the seven ears of grain [that were] thin and scorched by an east wind—they are seven years of famine. [28]This is the very thing I told Pharaoh: what God is doing, [God] has shown to Pharaoh. [29]Look—seven years are

תִּשְׁמַע חֲלוֹם לִפְתֹּר אֹתוֹ׃ 16 וַיַּעַן יוֹסֵף
אֶת־פַּרְעֹה לֵאמֹר בִּלְעָדָי אֱלֹהִים יַעֲנֶה
אֶת־שְׁלוֹם פַּרְעֹה׃
17 וַיְדַבֵּר פַּרְעֹה אֶל־יוֹסֵף בַּחֲלֹמִי הִנְנִי
עֹמֵד עַל־שְׂפַת הַיְאֹר׃ 18 וְהִנֵּה מִן־הַיְאֹר
עֹלֹת שֶׁבַע פָּרוֹת בְּרִיאוֹת בָּשָׂר וִיפֹת
תֹּאַר וַתִּרְעֶינָה בָּאָחוּ׃ 19 וְהִנֵּה שֶׁבַע־פָּרוֹת
אֲחֵרוֹת עֹלוֹת אַחֲרֵיהֶן דַּלּוֹת וְרָעוֹת תֹּאַר
מְאֹד וְרַקּוֹת בָּשָׂר לֹא־רָאִיתִי כָהֵנָּה בְּכָל־
אֶרֶץ מִצְרַיִם לָרֹעַ׃ 20 וַתֹּאכַלְנָה הַפָּרוֹת
הָרַקּוֹת וְהָרָעוֹת אֵת שֶׁבַע הַפָּרוֹת
הָרִאשֹׁנוֹת הַבְּרִיאֹת׃ 21 וַתָּבֹאנָה אֶל־
קִרְבֶּנָה וְלֹא נוֹדַע כִּי־בָאוּ אֶל־קִרְבֶּנָה
וּמַרְאֵיהֶן רַע כַּאֲשֶׁר בַּתְּחִלָּה וָאִיקָץ׃
22 וָאֵרֶא בַּחֲלֹמִי וְהִנֵּה ׀ שֶׁבַע שִׁבֳּלִים עֹלֹת
בְּקָנֶה אֶחָד מְלֵאֹת וְטֹבוֹת׃ 23 וְהִנֵּה שֶׁבַע
שִׁבֳּלִים צְנֻמוֹת דַּקּוֹת שְׁדֻפוֹת קָדִים
צֹמְחוֹת אַחֲרֵיהֶם׃ 24 וַתִּבְלַעְןָ הַשִּׁבֳּלִים
הַדַּקֹּת אֵת שֶׁבַע הַשִּׁבֳּלִים הַטֹּבוֹת וָאֹמַר
אֶל־הַחַרְטֻמִּים וְאֵין מַגִּיד לִי׃
25 וַיֹּאמֶר יוֹסֵף אֶל־פַּרְעֹה חֲלוֹם פַּרְעֹה
אֶחָד הוּא אֵת אֲשֶׁר הָאֱלֹהִים עֹשֶׂה הִגִּיד
לְפַרְעֹה׃ 26 שֶׁבַע פָּרֹת הַטֹּבֹת שֶׁבַע שָׁנִים
הֵנָּה וְשֶׁבַע הַשִּׁבֳּלִים הַטֹּבֹת שֶׁבַע שָׁנִים
הֵנָּה חֲלוֹם אֶחָד הוּא׃ 27 וְשֶׁבַע הַפָּרוֹת
הָרַקּוֹת וְהָרָעֹת הָעֹלֹת אַחֲרֵיהֶן שֶׁבַע שָׁנִים
הֵנָּה וְשֶׁבַע הַשִּׁבֳּלִים הָרֵקוֹת שְׁדֻפוֹת
הַקָּדִים יִהְיוּ שֶׁבַע שְׁנֵי רָעָב׃ 28 הוּא הַדָּבָר
אֲשֶׁר דִּבַּרְתִּי אֶל־פַּרְעֹה אֲשֶׁר הָאֱלֹהִים
עֹשֶׂה הֶרְאָה אֶת־פַּרְעֹה׃ 29 הִנֵּה שֶׁבַע

*16. "Not I—it is God who will account for Pharaoh's well-being."* Joseph's deference to God marks his humility.

*25–32.* Joseph brilliantly interprets dreams that foretell upcoming events of great magnitude. Through his interpretation, we discover that both cows and ears of corn are symbols of food that express the fertility of land. However, in the next parashah, Joseph will be the one to provide nourishment when he is in charge of distributing grain during the famine.

coming, [of] great plenty in all the land of Egypt. [30]But seven years of famine are coming up after them, and all the plenty in the land of Egypt will be forgotten; the famine will consume the land. [31]The plenty will no longer be known in the land, because of the famine that will follow, so harsh will it be. [32]Pharaoh's dream was repeated—two times—because the matter has been fixed by God, and God is making haste to accomplish it.

[33]"Let Pharaoh now select a man who is discerning and wise and set him over the land of Egypt; [34]let Pharaoh act and appoint administrators over the land, and let him take one-fifth of [the produce of] the land of Egypt during the seven years of plenty. [35]Have them gather up all the [surplus] food of these good years that are coming, and let them store up grain in the cities under Pharaoh's control, and put it under guard. [36]The food will then be a reserve for the land during the seven years of famine that will prevail in the land of Egypt; thus the land will not perish through famine." [37]This advice seemed good to Pharaoh and his officials, [38]and Pharaoh said to his officials, "Is there anyone like this to be found, a man with the spirit of God in him?"

[39]Pharaoh then said to Joseph, "Since God has made all this known to you, there is no one as discerning and wise as you! [40]You shall be in charge of my household, and all my people shall obey your word; only I, The Throne, shall be greater than you."

[41]And Pharaoh said to Joseph, "Observe, I have placed you in charge of the entire land of Egypt." [42]Pharaoh removed his signet ring from his hand

שָׁנִים בָּאוֹת שָׂבָע גָּדוֹל בְּכָל־אֶרֶץ מִצְרָיִם׃
30 וְקָמוּ שֶׁבַע שְׁנֵי רָעָב אַחֲרֵיהֶן וְנִשְׁכַּח
כָּל־הַשָּׂבָע בְּאֶרֶץ מִצְרָיִם וְכִלָּה הָרָעָב אֶת־
הָאָרֶץ׃ 31 וְלֹא־יִוָּדַע הַשָּׂבָע בָּאָרֶץ מִפְּנֵי
הָרָעָב הַהוּא אַחֲרֵי־כֵן כִּי־כָבֵד הוּא מְאֹד׃
32 וְעַל הִשָּׁנוֹת הַחֲלוֹם אֶל־פַּרְעֹה פַּעֲמָיִם
כִּי־נָכוֹן הַדָּבָר מֵעִם הָאֱלֹהִים וּמְמַהֵר
הָאֱלֹהִים לַעֲשֹׂתוֹ׃

33 וְעַתָּה יֵרֶא פַרְעֹה אִישׁ נָבוֹן וְחָכָם
וִישִׁיתֵהוּ עַל־אֶרֶץ מִצְרָיִם׃ 34 יַעֲשֶׂה פַרְעֹה
וְיַפְקֵד פְּקִדִים עַל־הָאָרֶץ וְחִמֵּשׁ אֶת־אֶרֶץ
מִצְרַיִם בְּשֶׁבַע שְׁנֵי הַשָּׂבָע׃ 35 וְיִקְבְּצוּ אֶת־
כָּל־אֹכֶל הַשָּׁנִים הַטֹּבֹת הַבָּאֹת הָאֵלֶּה
וְיִצְבְּרוּ־בָר תַּחַת יַד־פַּרְעֹה אֹכֶל בֶּעָרִים
וְשָׁמָרוּ׃ 36 וְהָיָה הָאֹכֶל לְפִקָּדוֹן לָאָרֶץ
לְשֶׁבַע שְׁנֵי הָרָעָב אֲשֶׁר תִּהְיֶיןָ בְּאֶרֶץ
מִצְרָיִם וְלֹא־תִכָּרֵת הָאָרֶץ בָּרָעָב׃ 37 וַיִּיטַב
הַדָּבָר בְּעֵינֵי פַרְעֹה וּבְעֵינֵי כָּל־עֲבָדָיו׃
38 וַיֹּאמֶר פַּרְעֹה אֶל־עֲבָדָיו הֲנִמְצָא כָזֶה
אִישׁ אֲשֶׁר רוּחַ אֱלֹהִים בּוֹ׃

39 וַיֹּאמֶר פַּרְעֹה אֶל־יוֹסֵף אַחֲרֵי הוֹדִיעַ
אֱלֹהִים אוֹתְךָ אֶת־כָּל־זֹאת אֵין־נָבוֹן וְחָכָם
כָּמוֹךָ׃ 40 אַתָּה תִּהְיֶה עַל־בֵּיתִי וְעַל־פִּיךָ
יִשַּׁק כָּל־עַמִּי רַק הַכִּסֵּא אֶגְדַּל מִמֶּךָּ׃
41 וַיֹּאמֶר פַּרְעֹה אֶל־יוֹסֵף רְאֵה נָתַתִּי אֹתְךָ
עַל כָּל־אֶרֶץ מִצְרָיִם׃ 42 וַיָּסַר פַּרְעֹה אֶת־
טַבַּעְתּוֹ מֵעַל יָדוֹ וַיִּתֵּן אֹתָהּ עַל־יַד יוֹסֵף

## JOSEPH IS ELEVATED TO HIGH OFFICE AND MARRIES ASENATH (41:37–49)

Here Joseph is given signs of his authority in the Egyptian court. With this clothing and associated goods, Joseph moves from an outsider to an insider status in Egypt. Ironically, a slave has risen to the second-highest post. It has been suggested that such a role for the foreigner would have been historically possible during the time when the Asiatic Hyksos reigned in Egypt (the 17th and 16th centuries B.C.E.).

***42. signet ring.*** A ring with the royal symbol of Pharaoh.

and put it on Joseph's hand; he dressed him in linen trappings and placed the gold chain [of office] around his neck. [43]He gave him his viceroy's chariot to ride; they cried out "Royal Steward!" before him; he placed him in charge of all the land of Egypt.

[44]Pharaoh now said to Joseph, "I am Pharaoh, and without you none shall lift hand or foot in all the land of Egypt." [45]Pharaoh called Joseph Zaphenath-paneah and gave him Asenath daughter of Potiphera priest of On as a wife; thus Joseph came to be in charge of the land of Egypt. [46]When Joseph began to serve Pharaoh, king of Egypt, he was 30 years old; Joseph left Pharaoh's presence and traversed the whole land of Egypt.

[47]In the seven years of plenty the land produced to overflowing. [48]He gathered all the [surplus] food

וַיַּלְבֵּשׁ אֹתוֹ בִּגְדֵי־שֵׁשׁ וַיָּשֶׂם רְבִד הַזָּהָב עַל־צַוָּארֽוֹ: 43 וַיַּרְכֵּב אֹתוֹ בְּמִרְכֶּבֶת הַמִּשְׁנֶה אֲשֶׁר־לוֹ וַיִּקְרְאוּ לְפָנָיו אַבְרֵךְ וְנָתוֹן אֹתוֹ עַל כָּל־אֶרֶץ מִצְרָֽיִם: 44 וַיֹּאמֶר פַּרְעֹה אֶל־יוֹסֵף אֲנִי פַרְעֹה וּבִלְעָדֶיךָ לֹא־יָרִים אִישׁ אֶת־יָדוֹ וְאֶת־רַגְלוֹ בְּכָל־אֶרֶץ מִצְרָֽיִם: 45 וַיִּקְרָא פַרְעֹה שֵׁם־יוֹסֵף צָֽפְנַת פַּעְנֵחַ וַיִּתֶּן־לוֹ אֶת־אָֽסְנַת בַּת־פּֽוֹטִי פֶרַע כֹּהֵן אֹן לְאִשָּׁה וַיֵּצֵא יוֹסֵף עַל־אֶרֶץ מִצְרָֽיִם: 46 וְיוֹסֵף בֶּן־שְׁלֹשִׁים שָׁנָה בְּעָמְדוֹ לִפְנֵי פַּרְעֹה מֶֽלֶךְ־מִצְרָיִם וַיֵּצֵא יוֹסֵף מִלִּפְנֵי פַרְעֹה וַיַּֽעֲבֹר בְּכָל־אֶרֶץ מִצְרָֽיִם: 47 וַתַּעַשׂ הָאָרֶץ בְּשֶׁבַע שְׁנֵי הַשָּׂבָע לִקְמָצִֽים: 48 וַיִּקְבֹּץ אֶת־כָּל־אֹכֶל | שֶׁבַע

- - - - - - - - - - - - - - - - - - - - - - - - - - - - - -

**43.** *"Royal Steward!"* Heb. *avrech*; it appears nowhere else in the Bible and its meaning is unclear. It has also been translated "bow the knee." The term may have Egyptian origins.

**45.** *Zaphenath-paneah.* Egyptian for "God speaks and lives."

*On.* The ancient city of Heliopolis, north of modern Cairo.

*Asenath.* Egyptian for "the one belonging to Neith." Neith was an Egyptian creator goddess seen as both the mother of the king and the mother of Re, the ancient Egyptian creator god and god of the sun.

*daughter of Potiphera.* When Joseph had encountered Potiphar's wife, he wound up in jail (Genesis 39); but now, when he encounters Potiphera's daughter, Joseph becomes fully integrated into Egyptian society. Perhaps the author is subtly contrasting the "evil woman" versus the "good woman" here. Biblical women characters in Genesis are often presented in pairs: Sarah and Hagar, Rachel and Leah, Bilhah and Zilpah, and now, Potiphar's wife and Asenath.

*Potiphera.* In Egyptian, "the one whom [the god] Re gave." As just noted, this name evokes that of Pharaoh's officer, Potiphar (Genesis 39), which is obviously similar; but the distinctions between professions suggest different figures.

*as a wife.* This, like his new name, indicates Joseph's acceptance into Egyptian society and a shift in his identity. One may understand Joseph now to be not only an Egyptian, but also a fully adult male (age 30, according to v. 46). Comparative evidence, not only from other ancient Near Eastern cultures but also from anthropological data regarding patrilineally organized societies, makes clear that in the biblical period, a male was not considered a man until he had a wife (if not also children). Similarly, a female in ancient Israel was not fully accepted as a woman until she was married and had borne children to her husband (think of Sarah in Genesis 12–21; see further Naomi Steinberg, *Kinship and Marriage in Genesis*, 1993).

Joseph's marriage to a woman of Egyptian descent is an example of *exogamous* marriage, that is, marriage outside the patrilineal (male line) kinship group. This prefigures Moses' marriage to a foreign woman (Exodus 2:21) and is in stark contrast to the postexilic marriage restrictions in Ezra 9–10. (See further Another Contemporary Reflection, p. 255.)

there was in the land of Egypt from the seven years. He placed food in the cities; the food that came from a city's surrounding fields he placed in its midst. [49]Thus Joseph heaped up grain as plentiful as the sands of the sea, until he left off measuring—for it was beyond measure.

[50]Two sons were born to Joseph before the years of famine arrived, born to him by Asenath daughter of Potiphera, priest of On. [51]Joseph named the first-born son Manasseh, "For God has *made me forget* all the troubles I endured in my father's house." [52]And he named the second one Ephraim, "For God has *made me fruitful* in the land of my affliction."

[53]The seven years of plenty that prevailed in the land of Egypt came to an end, [54]and the seven years of famine began, as Joseph had foretold. There was famine in all the lands, but all over the land of Egypt there was food; [55]yet all the land of Egypt was starving, so that the people cried out to Pharaoh for food. Pharaoh said to all Egypt, "Go to Joseph; do whatever he tells you." [56]The famine had spread across the land, so Joseph opened up all that was in [the stores] and he provided for Egypt, for the famine had gained strength in the land of Egypt. [57]And all lands came to Egypt to buy provisions from Joseph, for the famine had taken hold in every land.

שָׁנִים אֲשֶׁר הָיוּ בְּאֶרֶץ מִצְרַיִם וַיִּתֶּן־אֹכֶל
בֶּעָרִים אֹכֶל שְׂדֵה־הָעִיר אֲשֶׁר סְבִיבֹתֶיהָ
נָתַן בְּתוֹכָהּ׃ 49 וַיִּצְבֹּר יוֹסֵף בָּר כְּחוֹל הַיָּם
הַרְבֵּה מְאֹד עַד כִּי־חָדַל לִסְפֹּר כִּי־אֵין
מִסְפָּר׃

50 וּלְיוֹסֵף יֻלַּד שְׁנֵי בָנִים בְּטֶרֶם תָּבוֹא
שְׁנַת הָרָעָב אֲשֶׁר יָלְדָה־לּוֹ אָסְנַת בַּת־פּוֹטִי
פֶרַע כֹּהֵן אוֹן׃ 51 וַיִּקְרָא יוֹסֵף אֶת־שֵׁם
הַבְּכוֹר מְנַשֶּׁה כִּי־נַשַּׁנִי אֱלֹהִים אֶת־כָּל־
עֲמָלִי וְאֵת כָּל־בֵּית אָבִי׃ 52 וְאֵת שֵׁם הַשֵּׁנִי
קָרָא אֶפְרָיִם כִּי־הִפְרַנִי אֱלֹהִים בְּאֶרֶץ
עָנְיִי׃

53 וַתִּכְלֶינָה שֶׁבַע שְׁנֵי הַשָּׂבָע אֲשֶׁר הָיָה
בְּאֶרֶץ מִצְרָיִם׃ 54 וַתְּחִלֶּינָה שֶׁבַע שְׁנֵי
הָרָעָב לָבוֹא כַּאֲשֶׁר אָמַר יוֹסֵף וַיְהִי רָעָב
בְּכָל־הָאֲרָצוֹת וּבְכָל־אֶרֶץ מִצְרַיִם הָיָה
לָחֶם׃ 55 וַתִּרְעַב כָּל־אֶרֶץ מִצְרַיִם וַיִּצְעַק
הָעָם אֶל־פַּרְעֹה לַלָּחֶם וַיֹּאמֶר פַּרְעֹה לְכָל־
מִצְרַיִם לְכוּ אֶל־יוֹסֵף אֲשֶׁר־יֹאמַר לָכֶם
תַּעֲשׂוּ׃ 56 וְהָרָעָב הָיָה עַל כָּל־פְּנֵי הָאָרֶץ
וַיִּפְתַּח יוֹסֵף אֶת־כָּל־אֲשֶׁר בָּהֶם וַיִּשְׁבֹּר
לְמִצְרַיִם וַיֶּחֱזַק הָרָעָב בְּאֶרֶץ מִצְרָיִם׃
57 וְכָל־הָאָרֶץ בָּאוּ מִצְרַיְמָה לִשְׁבֹּר אֶל־
יוֹסֵף כִּי־חָזַק הָרָעָב בְּכָל־הָאָרֶץ׃

### ASENATH BEARS MANASSEH AND EPHRAIM TO JOSEPH (41:50–52)

The names of Joseph's sons reflect their father's circumstances and embody his longing to forget his past (Manasseh) and his hope of success (Ephraim). In contrast to Jacob's sons, whose names bear the hopes and circumstances of their mothers Leah and Rachel (29:31–30:24; 35:18), these sons' names say nothing about Asenath's aspirations. Her sons, progenitors of the tribes of Manasseh and Ephraim, are not only linked to the family of Israel but also are descendants of an Egyptian priestly heritage. Jacob later recognizes both of these sons as full heirs to the Israelite lineage (48:5).

### FAMINE CAUSES "ALL LANDS" TO TRAVEL TO EGYPT FOR GRAIN (41:53–57)

Presumably due to its reliable water supply from the Nile, Egypt is a destination for food; see Abraham and Sarah's visit there for that reason (12:10). In Genesis (contrary to Exodus) the Israelites find sustenance in Egypt.

**42** When Jacob realized that there was grain for sale in Egypt, Jacob said to his sons, "Why are you staring at each other?" [2]He said, "Look—I have heard that there are provisions for sale in Egypt; go down that way and buy us provisions from there, that we may live and not die." [3]So Joseph's brothers went down—ten of them—to buy grain from Egypt. [4]But Jacob did not send Benjamin, Joseph's [full] brother, with his brothers, for he thought: "Lest a deadly mishap befall him."

[5]Israel's sons came to buy provisions in the midst of those who came, for the famine prevailed over the [whole] land of Canaan. [6]Now Joseph was the one who held sway over the land; he was the one selling provisions to all the people of the land; Joseph's brothers therefore came and bowed down to him with their faces to the ground. [7]When Joseph saw his brothers he recognized them, but he pretended to be a stranger to them and spoke roughly to them; he said to them, "Where have you come from?" They said, "From the land of Canaan to buy food." [8]Joseph recognized his brothers, but they did not recognize him. [9]Joseph then remem-

מב וַיַּרְא יַעֲקֹב כִּי יֶשׁ־שֶׁבֶר בְּמִצְרָיִם
וַיֹּאמֶר יַעֲקֹב לְבָנָיו לָמָּה תִּתְרָאוּ׃ 2 וַיֹּאמֶר
הִנֵּה שָׁמַעְתִּי כִּי יֶשׁ־שֶׁבֶר בְּמִצְרָיִם
רְדוּ־שָׁמָּה וְשִׁבְרוּ־לָנוּ מִשָּׁם וְנִחְיֶה וְלֹא
נָמוּת׃ 3 וַיֵּרְדוּ אֲחֵי־יוֹסֵף עֲשָׂרָה לִשְׁבֹּר בָּר
מִמִּצְרָיִם׃ 4 וְאֶת־בִּנְיָמִין אֲחִי יוֹסֵף לֹא־
שָׁלַח יַעֲקֹב אֶת־אֶחָיו כִּי אָמַר פֶּן־יִקְרָאֶנּוּ
אָסוֹן׃
5 וַיָּבֹאוּ בְּנֵי יִשְׂרָאֵל לִשְׁבֹּר בְּתוֹךְ הַבָּאִים
כִּי־הָיָה הָרָעָב בְּאֶרֶץ כְּנָעַן׃ 6 וְיוֹסֵף הוּא
הַשַּׁלִּיט עַל־הָאָרֶץ הוּא הַמַּשְׁבִּיר לְכָל־עַם
הָאָרֶץ וַיָּבֹאוּ אֲחֵי יוֹסֵף וַיִּשְׁתַּחֲווּ־לוֹ אַפַּיִם
אָרְצָה׃ 7 וַיַּרְא יוֹסֵף אֶת־אֶחָיו וַיַּכִּרֵם
וַיִּתְנַכֵּר אֲלֵיהֶם וַיְדַבֵּר אִתָּם קָשׁוֹת וַיֹּאמֶר
אֲלֵהֶם מֵאַיִן בָּאתֶם וַיֹּאמְרוּ מֵאֶרֶץ כְּנַעַן
לִשְׁבָּר־אֹכֶל׃ 8 וַיַּכֵּר יוֹסֵף אֶת־אֶחָיו וְהֵם
לֹא הִכִּרֻהוּ׃ 9 וַיִּזְכֹּר יוֹסֵף אֵת הַחֲלֹמוֹת

• • • • • • • • • • • • • • • • • • • • • • • • • • • • • • • • • • • • • • •

## *Ten Brothers Journey to Egypt*

(42:1–25)

This unit explores what it means to be a member of a family: what it means to be a brother, what it means to be a father (especially one who plays favorites among his children), and what it means to take responsibility for one's past actions toward other family members.

The words "brother" and "recognize" are abundant in this unit; they remind us of when Jacob recognized a bloodied coat as belonging to Joseph (37:31–33). Likewise, they recall Tamar's words to Judah, inviting him to recognize ("acknowledge") and take responsibility for his actions (38:25). This is one of several connections to the episode of Tamar and Judah in Genesis 38.

### JACOB SENDS TEN BROTHERS TO EGYPT FOR FOOD (42:1–5)

*3–4.* ***Joseph's brothers . . . ten of them . . . Joseph's [full] brother . . . his brothers.*** The differing status of the brothers' relationship to Jacob—depending on their different mothers—is emphasized in the wording that separates Joseph's ten half-brothers from Benjamin, Joseph's brother by the same mother Rachel.

### THE BROTHERS APPEAR BEFORE JOSEPH (42:6–17)

*7.* ***recognized . . . pretended to be a stranger.*** There is a wordplay at this point because the same Hebrew root, *n-k-r*, is behind both verbs. The word

bered the dreams he had dreamt about them, and he said to them, "You are spies who have come to see the land's nakedness!" [10]"No, my lord," they said to him. "Your servants have come to buy food; [11]we are all of us sons of the same man; we are honest; your servants have never been spies." [12]He said to them, "No, indeed: it is the land's nakedness that you have come to see!" [13]They then said, "Your servants are twelve brothers, sons of a man in the land of Canaan; the youngest is with our father right now, and one is no more." [14]But Joseph said to them, "It is as I have said to you—you are spies! [15]This is how you shall be put to the test: as Pharaoh lives, you shall not get out of this unless your youngest brother comes here! [16]Send forth one of you and let him fetch your brother while [the rest of] you are confined; thus your words will be put to the test [to see] whether you are being truthful; if not, as Pharaoh lives, you are indeed spies!" [17]And he placed them under guard for three days.

[18]On the third day Joseph said to them, "Do this, and live—I am a god-fearing man! [19]If you are honest men, let one of your brothers be confined in your place of custody, while [the rest of] you go bring provisions [to relieve the] starvation of your

אֲשֶׁר חָלַם לָהֶם וַיֹּאמֶר אֲלֵהֶם מְרַגְּלִים
אַתֶּם לִרְאוֹת אֶת־עֶרְוַת הָאָרֶץ בָּאתֶם׃
10 וַיֹּאמְרוּ אֵלָיו לֹא אֲדֹנִי וַעֲבָדֶיךָ בָּאוּ
לִשְׁבָּר־אֹכֶל׃ 11 כֻּלָּנוּ בְּנֵי אִישׁ־אֶחָד נָחְנוּ
כֵּנִים אֲנַחְנוּ לֹא־הָיוּ עֲבָדֶיךָ מְרַגְּלִים׃
12 וַיֹּאמֶר אֲלֵהֶם לֹא כִּי־עֶרְוַת הָאָרֶץ
בָּאתֶם לִרְאוֹת׃ 13 וַיֹּאמְרוּ שְׁנֵים עָשָׂר
עֲבָדֶיךָ אַחִים ׀ אֲנַחְנוּ בְּנֵי אִישׁ־אֶחָד בְּאֶרֶץ
כְּנָעַן וְהִנֵּה הַקָּטֹן אֶת־אָבִינוּ הַיּוֹם וְהָאֶחָד
אֵינֶנּוּ׃ 14 וַיֹּאמֶר אֲלֵהֶם יוֹסֵף הוּא אֲשֶׁר
דִּבַּרְתִּי אֲלֵכֶם לֵאמֹר מְרַגְּלִים אַתֶּם׃
15 בְּזֹאת תִּבָּחֵנוּ חֵי פַרְעֹה אִם־תֵּצְאוּ מִזֶּה
כִּי אִם־בְּבוֹא אֲחִיכֶם הַקָּטֹן הֵנָּה׃ 16 שִׁלְחוּ
מִכֶּם אֶחָד וְיִקַּח אֶת־אֲחִיכֶם וְאַתֶּם הֵאָסְרוּ
וְיִבָּחֲנוּ דִּבְרֵיכֶם הַאֱמֶת אִתְּכֶם וְאִם־לֹא חֵי
פַרְעֹה כִּי מְרַגְּלִים אַתֶּם׃ 17 וַיֶּאֱסֹף אֹתָם
אֶל־מִשְׁמָר שְׁלֹשֶׁת יָמִים׃
18 וַיֹּאמֶר אֲלֵהֶם יוֹסֵף בַּיּוֹם הַשְּׁלִישִׁי זֹאת
עֲשׂוּ וִחְיוּ אֶת־הָאֱלֹהִים אֲנִי יָרֵא׃ 19 אִם־
כֵּנִים אַתֶּם אֲחִיכֶם אֶחָד יֵאָסֵר בְּבֵית
מִשְׁמַרְכֶם וְאַתֶּם לְכוּ הָבִיאוּ שֶׁבֶר רַעֲבוֹן

---

also figures prominently in the story of Tamar and Judah—when Tamar confronts Judah with his responsibility for her pregnancy (38:25).

*9.* Joseph's identity is masked from his brothers, enabling him to confine them, just as he was earlier confined by them. This is a case of role reversal between the brothers. Joseph may have had one or more motives at this time: punishment, testing, teaching a lesson, or fulfillment of his earlier dream of having all his brothers bow down to him.

*"nakedness."* Heb. *ervah,* which brings to mind that in the Bible nakedness is usually connected with sexual misconduct. (See Leviticus 18:6–20.)

*11.* *"we are all of us sons of the same man."* The brothers' statement is intended to refute the charge that they are a band of unrelated individuals plotting against Egyptian bounty, but on another level it reminds us of the emphasis on family unity that characterizes the tension of the narrative.

*15–16.* Joseph asks to see the other son borne by his mother, Rachel. In light of how Leah's sons had mistreated him, Joseph may fear that a similar fate has met his only full brother, Benjamin.

*17.* ***he placed them under guard for three days.*** The brothers are confined just as Joseph was (40:3).

### JOSEPH DEMANDS THAT THEY BRING BENJAMIN (42:18–25)

*19–20.* ***"let one of your brothers be confined in your place of custody . . . then bring your youngest brother to me."*** We are not told what motivates

families; [20]then bring your youngest brother to me, and let your words be proven trustworthy, so that you do not die." They went to do this. [21]The brothers said to one another, "Oh, we are being punished on account of our brother! We saw his soul's distress when he pleaded with us, but we didn't listen—on that account this distress has come upon us." [22]Reuben now responded to them, saying, "Didn't I say to you, 'Do not sin against the lad'! But you wouldn't listen, and so his blood-payment, see—it has come due."

[23]They did not know that Joseph understood, for the interpreter had been between them. [24]He left them and wept; then he came back to them, spoke to them, took Simeon from them, and bound him before their eyes. [25]Joseph gave the command: they were to fill their bags with grain and [his men were] to return each one's silver to his sack and give them provisions for the road; thus he did to them. [26]They loaded their provisions on their asses and went away.

בָּתֵּיכֶם׃ 20 וְאֶת־אֲחִיכֶם הַקָּטֹן תָּבִיאוּ אֵלַי
וְיֵאָמְנוּ דִבְרֵיכֶם וְלֹא תָמוּתוּ וַיַּעֲשׂוּ־כֵן׃
21 וַיֹּאמְרוּ אִישׁ אֶל־אָחִיו אֲבָל אֲשֵׁמִים ׀
אֲנַחְנוּ עַל־אָחִינוּ אֲשֶׁר רָאִינוּ צָרַת נַפְשׁוֹ
בְּהִתְחַנְנוֹ אֵלֵינוּ וְלֹא שָׁמָעְנוּ עַל־כֵּן בָּאָה
אֵלֵינוּ הַצָּרָה הַזֹּאת׃ 22 וַיַּעַן רְאוּבֵן אֹתָם
לֵאמֹר הֲלוֹא אָמַרְתִּי אֲלֵיכֶם ׀ לֵאמֹר אַל־
תֶּחֶטְאוּ בַיֶּלֶד וְלֹא שְׁמַעְתֶּם וְגַם־דָּמוֹ הִנֵּה
נִדְרָשׁ׃
23 וְהֵם לֹא יָדְעוּ כִּי שֹׁמֵעַ יוֹסֵף כִּי הַמֵּלִיץ
בֵּינֹתָם׃ 24 וַיִּסֹּב מֵעֲלֵיהֶם וַיֵּבְךְּ וַיָּשָׁב
אֲלֵהֶם וַיְדַבֵּר אֲלֵהֶם וַיִּקַּח מֵאִתָּם אֶת־
שִׁמְעוֹן וַיֶּאֱסֹר אֹתוֹ לְעֵינֵיהֶם׃ 25 וַיְצַו יוֹסֵף
וַיְמַלְאוּ אֶת־כְּלֵיהֶם בָּר וּלְהָשִׁיב כַּסְפֵּיהֶם
אִישׁ אֶל־שַׂקּוֹ וְלָתֵת לָהֶם צֵדָה לַדָּרֶךְ
וַיַּעַשׂ לָהֶם כֵּן׃ 26 וַיִּשְׂאוּ אֶת־שִׁבְרָם עַל־
חֲמֹרֵיהֶם וַיֵּלְכוּ מִשָּׁם׃

---

Joseph's change in plans. Joseph must realize that the separation of Benjamin and Jacob will cause great distress to his father.

*22. Reuben now responded to them, saying, "Didn't I say to you, 'Do not sin against the lad!'"* Reuben's remark indicates that the brothers' actions toward Joseph still haunt them.

*24. He left them and wept.* This is the first of four times in this parashah and the next that Joseph weeps with emotion over his brothers (see also 43:30; 45:1–2, 14–15; and in 46:29, Joseph weeps when he is reunited with his father).

*took Simeon from them.* Leah's second son is taken hostage until Benjamin, Rachel's second son, comes down to Egypt and appears before Joseph. Not knowing for sure that Benjamin is alive and well, Joseph may think that his brothers will care more for money than for Simeon—a repetition of their past actions toward him. However, the significance of Joseph's actions can have more than one meaning: while earlier the brothers judged him, now he stands in judgment over them and attempts to make them feel the desperation that they once made him feel.

## *Nine Brothers Return to Canaan*

(42:26–38)

The vizier has detained Simeon and dismissed the rest of the brothers (vv. 24–25). Ten had left for Egypt to procure food (v. 3), but only nine now make it back home to their father. As these ostensibly free family members react to their situation, it reveals to the reader that they are, as it were, trapped in a confinement of their own: the family is constrained by unacknowledged favoritism, betrayal, and guilt. Thus even what might otherwise be greeted with glee—the surprise discovery of money—is received with dismay (vv. 28, 35).

[27]When, at the night-lodging, one of them opened his sack to give fodder to his ass, he saw his silver—it was in the mouth of his bag! [28]When he said to his brothers, "My silver has been returned; look—it's in my bag!" their hearts gave out, and trembling they turned to each other and said, "What is this that God has done to us?"

[29]They then came to Jacob their father in the land of Canaan and told him all that had befallen them, saying, [30]"The man who is lord of the land spoke roughly to us; he treated us as though we were spying out the land. [31]We said to him, 'We are honest men, we have never been spies; [32]we are twelve brothers, sons of the same father; one is no more and the youngest is with our father right now, in the land of Canaan.' [33]That man, the lord of the land, said to us, 'This is how I will know that you are honest—leave one of your brothers with me; take [relief for the] starvation of your families, and go [34]and bring your youngest brother to me. Then I will indeed know that you are not spies, that you are honest; I will give you back your brother and you can pass through the land.'"

[35]When they emptied their sacks, each one's money-bag was in his sack; and when they caught sight of their money-bags, they and their father, they were struck with fear. [36]Their father Jacob said to them, "You have left me bereft—Joseph is no

27 וַיִּפְתַּח הָאֶחָד אֶת־שַׂקּוֹ לָתֵת מִסְפּוֹא
לַחֲמֹרוֹ בַּמָּלוֹן וַיַּרְא אֶת־כַּסְפּוֹ וְהִנֵּה־הוּא
בְּפִי אַמְתַּחְתּוֹ׃ 28 וַיֹּאמֶר אֶל־אֶחָיו הוּשַׁב
כַּסְפִּי וְגַם הִנֵּה בְאַמְתַּחְתִּי וַיֵּצֵא לִבָּם
וַיֶּחֶרְדוּ אִישׁ אֶל־אָחִיו לֵאמֹר מַה־זֹּאת
עָשָׂה אֱלֹהִים לָנוּ׃
29 וַיָּבֹאוּ אֶל־יַעֲקֹב אֲבִיהֶם אַרְצָה כְּנָעַן
וַיַּגִּידוּ לוֹ אֵת כָּל־הַקֹּרֹת אֹתָם לֵאמֹר׃
30 דִּבֶּר הָאִישׁ אֲדֹנֵי הָאָרֶץ אִתָּנוּ קָשׁוֹת
וַיִּתֵּן אֹתָנוּ כִּמְרַגְּלִים אֶת־הָאָרֶץ׃ 31 וַנֹּאמֶר
אֵלָיו כֵּנִים אֲנָחְנוּ לֹא הָיִינוּ מְרַגְּלִים׃
32 שְׁנֵים־עָשָׂר אֲנַחְנוּ אַחִים בְּנֵי אָבִינוּ
הָאֶחָד אֵינֶנּוּ וְהַקָּטֹן הַיּוֹם אֶת־אָבִינוּ בְּאֶרֶץ
כְּנָעַן׃ 33 וַיֹּאמֶר אֵלֵינוּ הָאִישׁ אֲדֹנֵי הָאָרֶץ
בְּזֹאת אֵדַע כִּי כֵנִים אַתֶּם אֲחִיכֶם הָאֶחָד
הַנִּיחוּ אִתִּי וְאֶת־רַעֲבוֹן בָּתֵּיכֶם קְחוּ וָלֵכוּ׃
34 וְהָבִיאוּ אֶת־אֲחִיכֶם הַקָּטֹן אֵלַי וְאֵדְעָה
כִּי לֹא מְרַגְּלִים אַתֶּם כִּי כֵנִים אַתֶּם אֶת־
אֲחִיכֶם אֶתֵּן לָכֶם וְאֶת־הָאָרֶץ תִּסְחָרוּ׃
35 וַיְהִי הֵם מְרִיקִים שַׂקֵּיהֶם וְהִנֵּה־אִישׁ
צְרוֹר־כַּסְפּוֹ בְּשַׂקּוֹ וַיִּרְאוּ אֶת־צְרֹרוֹת
כַּסְפֵּיהֶם הֵמָּה וַאֲבִיהֶם וַיִּירָאוּ׃ 36 וַיֹּאמֶר
אֲלֵהֶם יַעֲקֹב אֲבִיהֶם אֹתִי שִׁכַּלְתֶּם יוֹסֵף

### ONE BROTHER DISCOVERS MONEY IN HIS SACK (42:26–28)

*28. "What is this . . . ?"* The brothers, like the reader, do not know why the money is in each of their sacks. Will it be the source of economic relief or cause them trouble?

### THE BROTHERS REPORT TO JACOB (42:29–35)

*35. each one's money-bag was in his sack.* As also in v. 27, above, the Hebrew word *hinneh* (untranslated here, but rendered as "lo" or "behold" elsewhere in this translation) appears at the beginning of this phrase to emphasize the drama of the discovery of the money. Here it also indicates a shift from the narrator's to the character's point of view.

### JACOB IS DISMAYED MOSTLY OVER THE PROSPECTIVE LOSS OF BENJAMIN (42:36–38)

*36. "Joseph is no more, Simeon is no more, and now you would take Benjamin from me."* Jacob may think that the brothers sold Simeon for the money that now appears in their sacks—and that

more, Simeon is no more, and now you would take
Benjamin from me—all these things have come
down on me!" [37]Reuben then said to his father,
"Put my two sons to death if I do not bring him
back to you; give him into my hands, and I will return him to you." [38]But [Jacob] said, "My son shall
not go down with you—his brother is dead and he
alone remains; if a disaster should befall him on the
way that you will be going, you would cause my
gray head to go down in anguish to Sheol."

אֵינֶנּוּ וְשִׁמְעוֹן אֵינֶנּוּ וְאֶת־בִּנְיָמִן תִּקָּחוּ עָלַי
הָיוּ כֻלָּנָה׃ 37 וַיֹּאמֶר רְאוּבֵן אֶל־אָבִיו
לֵאמֹר אֶת־שְׁנֵי בָנַי תָּמִית אִם־לֹא אֲבִיאֶנּוּ
אֵלֶיךָ תְּנָה אֹתוֹ עַל־יָדִי וַאֲנִי אֲשִׁיבֶנּוּ
אֵלֶיךָ׃ 38 וַיֹּאמֶר לֹא־יֵרֵד בְּנִי עִמָּכֶם כִּי־
אָחִיו מֵת וְהוּא לְבַדּוֹ נִשְׁאָר וּקְרָאָהוּ אָסוֹן
בַּדֶּרֶךְ אֲשֶׁר תֵּלְכוּ־בָהּ וְהוֹרַדְתֶּם אֶת־
שֵׂיבָתִי בְּיָגוֹן שְׁאוֹלָה׃

43 The famine bore heavily on the land, [2]and
when they had consumed the provisions they had
brought from Egypt, their father said to them, "Go
back and buy us a bit of food!" [3]But Judah said to
him, "The man adjured us most definitely, saying,
'You shall not see my face unless your brother is

מג וְהָרָעָב כָּבֵד בָּאָרֶץ׃ 2 וַיְהִי כַּאֲשֶׁר כִּלּוּ
לֶאֱכֹל אֶת־הַשֶּׁבֶר אֲשֶׁר הֵבִיאוּ מִמִּצְרָיִם
וַיֹּאמֶר אֲלֵיהֶם אֲבִיהֶם שֻׁבוּ שִׁבְרוּ־לָנוּ
מְעַט־אֹכֶל׃ 3 וַיֹּאמֶר אֵלָיו יְהוּדָה לֵאמֹר
הָעֵד הֵעִד בָּנוּ הָאִישׁ לֵאמֹר לֹא־תִרְאוּ פָנַי

they plan the same fate for Benjamin. Benjamin is Jacob's youngest son and, as far as Jacob knows, his only surviving son from his beloved wife Rachel, who died in childbirth (35:16–19).

*38. But [Jacob] said, "My son shall not go down with you—his brother is dead and he alone remains."* Jacob's speech illustrates that he cannot be consoled after losing the sons Rachel bore to him, while the loss of his other sons is acceptable. Note the shifting familial language: Jacob refers to Benjamin as "my son" and then Joseph as "his brother," relating them both back to his love for the deceased Rachel. Jacob is still oblivious to the alienation that such favoritism causes among the brothers. His response—that only Benjamin remains—denies the other ten brothers any place in their father's family or feelings. It is as if they do not exist for their father.

*"cause my gray head to go down in anguish to Sheol."* Jacob uses a Hebrew idiom for dying due to grief—rather than in a good old age—and descending to the realm of the dead. Earlier, Jacob had said he would go down to Sheol in mourning for the loss of Joseph, presumably to seek out his son there (37:35). Although Sheol is the underworld—a place below the ground—it is not to be equated with notions of Hell or a judgment after death. Such ideas did not exist in ancient Israelite thought; going to Sheol was the fate of all human beings.

## *The Second Journey to Egypt, with Benjamin* (43:1–44:13a)

Eventually even in Jacob's enormously wealthy household (30:43), the economic situation in Canaan gets desperate. Judah, the fourth oldest son, is at first as reactive as the rest, but eventually he rises to the occasion and shows real leadership. This enables the family to move forward with a plan.

### CONTINUING FAMINE FORCES JACOB TO LET BENJAMIN GO (43:1–14)

*3. Judah said to him.* Now Judah functions as spokesman for the brothers; previously Reuben had spoken up ineffectually on their behalf (42:37). It may be that Reuben was afraid to challenge his

with you.' [4]If you're willing to let our brother go with us, we'll go down and buy food for you, [5]but if you are not willing to let [him] go, we will not go down; the man said to us: 'You shall not see my face unless your brother is with you.'"

[6]Israel then said, "Why did you do me this wrong, answering the man['s question], 'Have you yet another brother'?" [7]They answered, "The man questioned us closely about ourselves and our family, saying, 'Is your father still alive? Do you have a brother?' So we answered as required by these questions. How on earth could we have known that he would say, 'Bring your brother down'?"

[8]Judah then said to his father Israel, "Let the lad go with me and let us get up and be on our way, that we may live and not die—we ourselves, and you, and our little ones, as well. [9]I will be responsible for him: from my hand you may demand him; and if I do not bring him back to you and plant him

בִּלְתִּי אֲחִיכֶם אִתְּכֶם׃ 4 אִם־יֶשְׁךָ מְשַׁלֵּחַ
אֶת־אָחִינוּ אִתָּנוּ נֵרְדָה וְנִשְׁבְּרָה לְךָ אֹכֶל׃
5 וְאִם־אֵינְךָ מְשַׁלֵּחַ לֹא נֵרֵד כִּי־הָאִישׁ
אָמַר אֵלֵינוּ לֹא־תִרְאוּ פָנַי בִּלְתִּי אֲחִיכֶם
אִתְּכֶם׃
6 וַיֹּאמֶר יִשְׂרָאֵל לָמָה הֲרֵעֹתֶם לִי לְהַגִּיד
לָאִישׁ הַעוֹד לָכֶם אָח׃ 7 וַיֹּאמְרוּ שָׁאוֹל
שָׁאַל־הָאִישׁ לָנוּ וּלְמוֹלַדְתֵּנוּ לֵאמֹר הַעוֹד
אֲבִיכֶם חַי הֲיֵשׁ לָכֶם אָח וַנַּגֶּד־לוֹ עַל־פִּי
הַדְּבָרִים הָאֵלֶּה הֲיָדוֹעַ נֵדַע כִּי יֹאמַר
הוֹרִידוּ אֶת־אֲחִיכֶם׃
8 וַיֹּאמֶר יְהוּדָה אֶל־יִשְׂרָאֵל אָבִיו שִׁלְחָה
הַנַּעַר אִתִּי וְנָקוּמָה וְנֵלֵכָה וְנִחְיֶה וְלֹא
נָמוּת גַּם־אֲנַחְנוּ גַם־אַתָּה גַּם־טַפֵּנוּ׃ 9 אָנֹכִי
אֶעֶרְבֶנּוּ מִיָּדִי תְּבַקְשֶׁנּוּ אִם־לֹא הֲבִיאֹתִיו

father directly due to his apparently unsuccessful attempt to usurp Jacob's role as head of the family when Reuben lay with Bilhah (35:22). However, based on his experience that followed upon his unjust treatment of Tamar (Genesis 38; see further below, v. 9), Judah has meanwhile developed the resolve to speak directly to his father of what needs to be done in order for the family to survive.

*6–7. "Why did you do me this wrong… 'Bring your brother down'?"* Jacob blames his sons for disclosing the existence of Benjamin. They innocently and honestly respond that they could hardly have foreseen that they would be asked to bring Benjamin with them on their next trip to Egypt. Imagine how Jacob would have felt if he learned at this point of their earlier treatment of Joseph.

*9.* Judah now takes responsibility for the safe return of Benjamin from Egypt. He introduces the religious language of sin (*ch-t-a*), here translated as "condemned," which emphasizes the gravity of Judah's offer to his father. Judah promises Jacob that he will answer for Benjamin in Egypt. Through their statements we can perceive the concern that the brothers have for their father's emotional well-being, as well as the depth of Jacob's love for Benjamin. Although the family of Jacob has been torn apart in many respects, specific sons struggle to keep the family intact as best they can.

***"I will be responsible for him."*** Heb. *e'ervenu*, based on the same root (*e-r-v*) as *eravon* ("pledge"), found in the Bible only in Genesis 38 (vv. 17, 18, 20). The use of such a rare term suggests a deliberate link to the Tamar and Judah story in Genesis 38—and to Judah's earlier, hasty responses in that episode. If so, the author may imply that Judah's more mature behavior results from his encounter with Tamar at "the entrance to Enaim" (38:14), a locale that also can be read as "the opening of the eyes." The transformation of Judah from a callous son in Genesis 37 to a responsible man who can rise to leadership can be understood, then, as a consequence of his eye-opening experience with Tamar.

in front of you, I shall stand condemned before you for all time. [10]If we hadn't dallied, we could have returned twice by now!" [11]Their father Israel then said to them, "If that's the way it must be, do this: take from among the land's choice products in your bags, and bring the man an offering—a bit of balm, a bit of honey, some laudanum, mastic, pistachios, and almonds. [12]And take double the silver with you, and hand over the silver that was returned in your bags—it may have been a mistake. [13][Yes,] take your brother, get going, and go back to the man! [14]May El Shaddai give you mercy before that man, so that he lets you and your other brother and Benjamin go! And as for me—if I am bereaved, I am bereaved!"

[15]The men then took this offering, and taking in hand the double portion of silver, along with Benjamin, they got going and went down to Egypt, and stood before Joseph. [16]When Joseph saw Benjamin with them, he said to the one in charge of his household, "Bring the men into the house and slaughter an animal and prepare [it], for [these] men are going to eat with me at noon." [17]The man did as Joseph said; the man brought the men into Joseph's house. [18]The men were frightened when they were brought into Joseph's house; they thought: "It is on account of the silver that came back in our bags the first time that we're being brought [here]—in order to fall upon us, to pounce on us, to take us as slaves, along with our asses." [19]They therefore approached the man in charge of Joseph's household and spoke to him at the entrance of the house, [20]saying, "By your leave, my lord, the last time we came down to buy food,

אֵלֶיךָ וְהִצַּגְתִּיו לְפָנֶיךָ וְחָטָאתִי לְךָ כָּל־
הַיָּמִים׃ 10 כִּי לוּלֵא הִתְמַהְמָהְנוּ כִּי־
עַתָּה שַׁבְנוּ זֶה פַעֲמָיִם׃ 11 וַיֹּאמֶר אֲלֵהֶם
יִשְׂרָאֵל אֲבִיהֶם אִם־כֵּן ׀ אֵפוֹא זֹאת עֲשׂוּ
קְחוּ מִזִּמְרַת הָאָרֶץ בִּכְלֵיכֶם וְהוֹרִידוּ
לָאִישׁ מִנְחָה מְעַט צֳרִי וּמְעַט דְּבַשׁ נְכֹאת
וָלֹט בָּטְנִים וּשְׁקֵדִים׃ 12 וְכֶסֶף מִשְׁנֶה
קְחוּ בְיֶדְכֶם וְאֶת־הַכֶּסֶף הַמּוּשָׁב בְּפִי
אַמְתְּחֹתֵיכֶם תָּשִׁיבוּ בְיֶדְכֶם אוּלַי מִשְׁגֶּה
הוּא׃ 13 וְאֶת־אֲחִיכֶם קָחוּ וְקוּמוּ שׁוּבוּ אֶל־
הָאִישׁ׃ 14 וְאֵל שַׁדַּי יִתֵּן לָכֶם רַחֲמִים לִפְנֵי
הָאִישׁ וְשִׁלַּח לָכֶם אֶת־אֲחִיכֶם אַחֵר וְאֶת־
בִּנְיָמִין וַאֲנִי כַּאֲשֶׁר שָׁכֹלְתִּי שָׁכָלְתִּי׃
15 וַיִּקְחוּ הָאֲנָשִׁים אֶת־הַמִּנְחָה הַזֹּאת
וּמִשְׁנֶה־כֶּסֶף לָקְחוּ בְיָדָם וְאֶת־בִּנְיָמִן וַיָּקֻמוּ
וַיֵּרְדוּ מִצְרַיִם וַיַּעַמְדוּ לִפְנֵי יוֹסֵף׃ 16 וַיַּרְא
יוֹסֵף אִתָּם אֶת־בִּנְיָמִין וַיֹּאמֶר לַאֲשֶׁר עַל־
בֵּיתוֹ הָבֵא אֶת־הָאֲנָשִׁים הַבָּיְתָה וּטְבֹחַ
טֶבַח וְהָכֵן כִּי אִתִּי יֹאכְלוּ הָאֲנָשִׁים
בַּצָּהֳרָיִם׃ 17 וַיַּעַשׂ הָאִישׁ כַּאֲשֶׁר אָמַר יוֹסֵף
וַיָּבֵא הָאִישׁ אֶת־הָאֲנָשִׁים בֵּיתָה יוֹסֵף׃
18 וַיִּירְאוּ הָאֲנָשִׁים כִּי הוּבְאוּ בֵּית יוֹסֵף
וַיֹּאמְרוּ עַל־דְּבַר הַכֶּסֶף הַשָּׁב בְּאַמְתְּחֹתֵינוּ
בַּתְּחִלָּה אֲנַחְנוּ מוּבָאִים לְהִתְגֹּלֵל עָלֵינוּ
וּלְהִתְנַפֵּל עָלֵינוּ וְלָקַחַת אֹתָנוּ לַעֲבָדִים
וְאֶת־חֲמֹרֵינוּ׃ 19 וַיִּגְּשׁוּ אֶל־הָאִישׁ אֲשֶׁר
עַל־בֵּית יוֹסֵף וַיְדַבְּרוּ אֵלָיו פֶּתַח הַבָּיִת׃
20 וַיֹּאמְרוּ בִּי אֲדֹנִי יָרֹד יָרַדְנוּ בַּתְּחִלָּה

*14. "if I am bereaved, I am bereaved!"* [Jacob expresses his resignation in a manner resembling that of Queen Esther when Mordechai convinces her to risk her life. Her words: "If I am to perish, I shall perish" (Esther 4:16). —*Ed.*]

### THE BROTHERS APPEAR BEFORE JOSEPH (43:15–34)

Joseph's generous hospitality toward his brothers—who still do not know who he is—takes them off guard. Possibly he is trying to lull them into a false sense of security.

<sup>21</sup>when we got to the night lodging and opened our bags, each one's silver was in the mouth of his bag—the exact amount that had been weighed out, and we have brought it back with us. <sup>22</sup>And we have brought other money to buy food—we don't know who put our silver in our bags." <sup>23</sup>He replied, "You're all right; have no fear. Your god and your father's god has given you a hidden treasure in your bags—your money reached me!" And he brought Simeon out to them.

<sup>24</sup>The man then ushered the men into Joseph's house; he supplied water and they washed their feet, and he gave fodder to their asses. <sup>25</sup>They laid out the offering for the arrival of Joseph at noon, for they had heard that they would eat food there. <sup>26</sup>When Joseph entered the house they presented to him the offering they had brought into the house, and they bowed down before him to the ground. <sup>27</sup>He asked them how they were, and said, "How is your aged father of whom you spoke? Is he still alive?" <sup>28</sup>They said, "Your servant our father is well; he is still alive." And they knelt and bowed down.

<sup>29</sup>He looked up and saw his [full] brother Benjamin, his mother's son, and he said, "Is this your youngest brother you told me about?" And he added, "God be gracious to you, my son!" <sup>30</sup>Joseph hurried [out], for he was so deeply stirred with tender warmth toward his brother that he wanted to weep; he went into an [inner] chamber and there he wept. <sup>31</sup>He washed his face, and when he came out, he held himself in check and said, "Serve food!" <sup>32</sup>They served him separately and them separately and the Egyptians who usually ate with him separately, for the Egyptians could not eat food with the Hebrews, since it was an abomination to the Egyptians.

לְשַׁבֶּר־אֹֽכֶל: 21 וַֽיְהִי כִּֽי־בָאנוּ אֶל־הַמָּלוֹן וַנִּפְתְּחָה אֶת־אַמְתְּחֹתֵינוּ וְהִנֵּה כֶֽסֶף־אִישׁ בְּפִי אַמְתַּחְתּוֹ כַּסְפֵּנוּ בְּמִשְׁקָלוֹ וַנָּשֶׁב אֹתוֹ בְּיָדֵֽנוּ: 22 וְכֶסֶף אַחֵר הוֹרַדְנוּ בְיָדֵנוּ לִשְׁבָּר־אֹכֶל לֹא יָדַעְנוּ מִי־שָׂם כַּסְפֵּנוּ בְּאַמְתְּחֹתֵֽינוּ: 23 וַיֹּאמֶר שָׁלוֹם לָכֶם אַל־תִּירָאוּ אֱלֹֽהֵיכֶם וֵֽאלֹהֵי אֲבִיכֶם נָתַן לָכֶם מַטְמוֹן בְּאַמְתְּחֹֽתֵיכֶם כַּסְפְּכֶם בָּא אֵלָי וַיּוֹצֵא אֲלֵהֶם אֶת־שִׁמְעֽוֹן:

24 וַיָּבֵא הָאִישׁ אֶת־הָֽאֲנָשִׁים בֵּיתָה יוֹסֵף וַיִּתֶּן־מַיִם וַיִּרְחֲצוּ רַגְלֵיהֶם וַיִּתֵּן מִסְפּוֹא לַחֲמֹֽרֵיהֶֽם: 25 וַיָּכִינוּ אֶת־הַמִּנְחָה עַד־בּוֹא יוֹסֵף בַּֽצָּהֳרָיִם כִּי שָֽׁמְעוּ כִּי־שָׁם יֹאכְלוּ לָֽחֶם: 26 וַיָּבֹא יוֹסֵף הַבַּיְתָה וַיָּבִיאוּ לוֹ אֶת־הַמִּנְחָה אֲשֶׁר־בְּיָדָם הַבָּיְתָה וַיִּשְׁתַּחֲווּ־לוֹ אָֽרְצָה: 27 וַיִּשְׁאַל לָהֶם לְשָׁלוֹם וַיֹּאמֶר הֲשָׁלוֹם אֲבִיכֶם הַזָּקֵן אֲשֶׁר אֲמַרְתֶּם הַעוֹדֶנּוּ חָֽי: 28 וַיֹּאמְרוּ שָׁלוֹם לְעַבְדְּךָ לְאָבִינוּ עוֹדֶנּוּ חָי וַֽיִּקְּדוּ וישתחו וַיִּֽשְׁתַּחֲוֽוּ:

29 וַיִּשָּׂא עֵינָיו וַיַּרְא אֶת־בִּנְיָמִין אָחִיו בֶּן־אִמּוֹ וַיֹּאמֶר הֲזֶה אֲחִיכֶם הַקָּטֹן אֲשֶׁר אֲמַרְתֶּם אֵלָי וַיֹּאמַר אֱלֹהִים יָחְנְךָ בְּנִֽי: 30 וַיְמַהֵר יוֹסֵף כִּֽי־נִכְמְרוּ רַחֲמָיו אֶל־אָחִיו וַיְבַקֵּשׁ לִבְכּוֹת וַיָּבֹא הַחַדְרָה וַיֵּבְךְּ שָֽׁמָּה: 31 וַיִּרְחַץ פָּנָיו וַיֵּצֵא וַיִּתְאַפַּק וַיֹּאמֶר שִׂימוּ לָֽחֶם: 32 וַיָּשִׂימוּ לוֹ לְבַדּוֹ וְלָהֶם לְבַדָּם וְלַמִּצְרִים הָאֹכְלִים אִתּוֹ לְבַדָּם כִּי לֹא יֽוּכְלוּן הַמִּצְרִים לֶאֱכֹל אֶת־הָֽעִבְרִים לֶחֶם כִּֽי־תוֹעֵבָה הִוא לְמִצְרָֽיִם:

— — — — — — — — — — — — — — — — — — — — — — — — — — — —

27. Joseph's first concern is his father. But when he sees Benjamin, he most deeply reacts.

30. *with tender warmth.* Heb. *rachamim* (literally "innards"—taken as the bodily locus of compassion) is not gender specific, unlike *rechem* (womb), which only women possess.

*there he wept.* This is the second time we are told that Joseph weeps; see at 42:24, above.

33 As they were seated before him, the first-born
according to his seniority and the youngest according to his youth, the men looked at each other in
amazement. 34 He presented portions [of food] to
them from what was in front of him—Benjamin's
portion exceeded all of theirs fivefold—and they
drank and grew drunk with him. 44 [After-
ward,] he commanded the one in charge of his
household, saying, "Fill the men's bags with food,
as much as they can carry, and put each man's silver
in the mouth of his bag. 2 And put my goblet—the
silver goblet—in the mouth of the youngest one's
bag along with the silver for his grain." He did just
as Joseph instructed.

3 At morning light, the men were sent off—they
and their asses. 4 They had left the city [but] had
not gone far, when Joseph said to the one in charge
of his household, "Get going, pursue the men;
when you overtake them, say to them: 'Why did
you repay good with evil? 5 This is what my master
drinks from and with which he constantly practices
divination! Have you not caused harm by what you
have done?'"

33 וַיֵּשְׁבוּ לְפָנָיו הַבְּכֹר כִּבְכֹרָתוֹ וְהַצָּעִיר
כִּצְעִרָתוֹ וַיִּתְמְהוּ הָאֲנָשִׁים אִישׁ אֶל־רֵעֵהוּ׃
34 וַיִּשָּׂא מַשְׂאֹת מֵאֵת פָּנָיו אֲלֵהֶם וַתֵּרֶב
מַשְׂאַת בִּנְיָמִן מִמַּשְׂאֹת כֻּלָּם חָמֵשׁ יָדוֹת
וַיִּשְׁתּוּ וַיִּשְׁכְּרוּ עִמּוֹ׃ מד וַיְצַו אֶת־
אֲשֶׁר עַל־בֵּיתוֹ לֵאמֹר מַלֵּא אֶת־אַמְתְּחֹת
הָאֲנָשִׁים אֹכֶל כַּאֲשֶׁר יוּכְלוּן שְׂאֵת וְשִׂים
כֶּסֶף־אִישׁ בְּפִי אַמְתַּחְתּוֹ׃ 2 וְאֶת־גְּבִיעִי
גְּבִיעַ הַכֶּסֶף תָּשִׂים בְּפִי אַמְתַּחַת הַקָּטֹן
וְאֵת כֶּסֶף שִׁבְרוֹ וַיַּעַשׂ כִּדְבַר יוֹסֵף אֲשֶׁר
דִּבֵּר׃
3 הַבֹּקֶר אוֹר וְהָאֲנָשִׁים שֻׁלְּחוּ הֵמָּה
וַחֲמֹרֵיהֶם׃ 4 הֵם יָצְאוּ אֶת־הָעִיר לֹא
הִרְחִיקוּ וְיוֹסֵף אָמַר לַאֲשֶׁר עַל־בֵּיתוֹ קוּם
רְדֹף אַחֲרֵי הָאֲנָשִׁים וְהִשַּׂגְתָּם וְאָמַרְתָּ
אֲלֵהֶם לָמָּה שִׁלַּמְתֶּם רָעָה תַּחַת טוֹבָה׃
5 הֲלוֹא זֶה אֲשֶׁר יִשְׁתֶּה אֲדֹנִי בּוֹ וְהוּא נַחֵשׁ
יְנַחֵשׁ בּוֹ הֲרֵעֹתֶם אֲשֶׁר עֲשִׂיתֶם׃

34. ***Benjamin's portion exceeded all of theirs fivefold.*** Joseph's overt favoritism of Benjamin may indicate his own affection for the only other son borne by his mother Rachel. But Joseph may be testing his brothers to determine whether or not their jealousy toward Jacob's favorite now applies to Benjamin, now the perceived favorite son. Joseph treats his full brother differently from his half-brothers. By the brothers' and the narrator's identifying the sons not only through their father but also by their mother (see also v. 29), we understand that the mother matters, not only the father.

## JOSEPH TESTS THE BROTHERS (44:1–2)

Genesis 42 had begun a reenactment of scenes from Joseph's early experience with his brothers. Now begins the concluding episode that addresses these issues.

2. *"silver goblet."* The cup to be placed in Benjamin's sack is made of silver, recalling that Joseph was sold to the Ishmaelites for silver (37:28).

## THE BROTHERS ARE CHARGED WITH THEFT (44:3–13a)

3–5. Joseph instructs his steward to charge the brothers with theft.

5. ***"This is what my master drinks from and with which he constantly practices divination!"*** In the ancient Near East, divination by liquids involved interpreting the liquid in a bowl or cup as an indicator of events to come, comparable to reading tea leaves today.

[6]He overtook them and spoke all these words to
them, [7]and they said to him, "Why is my lord
speaking such words? Far be it from your servants
to do such a thing! [8]Look—we brought you back
the silver that we found in the mouth of our bags
[all the way] from the land of Canaan; why would
we steal silver or gold from your master's house?
[9]Let anyone caught with it among your servants
die, and we for our part will become my lord's
slaves." [10]He replied, "Yes, right away, just as you
say, so shall it be—but while he who is caught with
it shall be my slave, the rest of you shall be cleared."
[11]They hastened to lower their bags to the ground,
and each opened his bag. [12]He began searching
with the eldest and ended with the youngest, until
he found the goblet in Benjamin's bag. [13]They tore
their mantles; each then reloaded his ass and they
went back to the city.

6 וַיַּשִּׂגֵם וַיְדַבֵּר אֲלֵהֶם אֶת־הַדְּבָרִים
הָאֵלֶּה׃ 7 וַיֹּאמְרוּ אֵלָיו לָמָּה יְדַבֵּר אֲדֹנִי
כַּדְּבָרִים הָאֵלֶּה חָלִילָה לַעֲבָדֶיךָ מֵעֲשׂוֹת
כַּדָּבָר הַזֶּה׃ 8 הֵן כֶּסֶף אֲשֶׁר מָצָאנוּ בְּפִי
אַמְתְּחֹתֵינוּ הֱשִׁיבֹנוּ אֵלֶיךָ מֵאֶרֶץ כְּנָעַן
וְאֵיךְ נִגְנֹב מִבֵּית אֲדֹנֶיךָ כֶּסֶף אוֹ זָהָב׃
9 אֲשֶׁר יִמָּצֵא אִתּוֹ מֵעֲבָדֶיךָ וָמֵת וְגַם־
אֲנַחְנוּ נִהְיֶה לַאדֹנִי לַעֲבָדִים׃ 10 וַיֹּאמֶר גַּם־
עַתָּה כְדִבְרֵיכֶם כֶּן־הוּא אֲשֶׁר יִמָּצֵא אִתּוֹ
יִהְיֶה־לִּי עָבֶד וְאַתֶּם תִּהְיוּ נְקִיִּם׃ 11 וַיְמַהֲרוּ
וַיּוֹרִדוּ אִישׁ אֶת־אַמְתַּחְתּוֹ אָרְצָה וַיִּפְתְּחוּ
אִישׁ אַמְתַּחְתּוֹ׃ 12 וַיְחַפֵּשׂ בַּגָּדוֹל הֵחֵל
וּבַקָּטֹן כִּלָּה וַיִּמָּצֵא הַגָּבִיעַ בְּאַמְתַּחַת
בִּנְיָמִן׃ 13 וַיִּקְרְעוּ שִׂמְלֹתָם וַיַּעֲמֹס אִישׁ
עַל־חֲמֹרוֹ וַיָּשֻׁבוּ הָעִירָה׃

*9. "Let anyone caught with it among your servants die."* The brothers' rash statement, like Jacob's in 31:32, condemns the "thief" to death, but it will have bearing on the fate of all the brothers.

*10.* The steward agrees that the harsh sentence is just, but he promises a lighter punishment.

*12. eldest . . . youngest.* This search scene continues to recall the one in which Laban searched throughout the tents of his nephew's family, ending up in the tent of his youngest daughter, Rachel (31:30–35). Now the present search ends with her youngest son, Benjamin.

*13. They tore their mantles.* The tearing of the clothing reflects the brothers' concern that Benjamin would be torn from their family. (The custom of tearing one's clothes as an act of mourning is still followed today.) His fate appears to have been sealed by his brothers' own words (v. 9). Thus once again they have set up one of Rachel's offspring to become a slave. Indeed, these brothers had caused their father likewise to tear his garment—more than two decades earlier (37:34).

## *The Third Appearance before Joseph*

### THE FINAL TEST (44:13b–17)

The vizier's missing goblet has been found in Benjamin's bag (v. 12), suggesting that he stole it. Benjamin stands accused but lacks the ability to prove his innocence. Surely he will be enslaved and remain in Egypt, presumably for the rest of his life. Benjamin's voice is heard nowhere in the entire narrative. Although he is now at the heart of the story, it is not really about him, but rather about the relationship of his brothers to each other and to their father. (In this regard he resembles his half-sister Dinah in Genesis 34.)

At this point the rest of the brothers—having narrowly escaped slavery themselves—are free to return home. Remarkably, they do not do so. Instead, they return with Benjamin to face the vizier (Joseph), who challenges them to account for their deed. Judah replies, and a dialogue ensues.

At this juncture, the psychological dynamics of

14 וַיָּבֹא יְהוּדָה וְאֶחָיו בֵּיתָה יוֹסֵף וְהוּא
עוֹדֶנּוּ שָׁם וַיִּפְּלוּ לְפָנָיו אָרְצָה׃ 15 וַיֹּאמֶר
לָהֶם יוֹסֵף מָה־הַמַּעֲשֶׂה הַזֶּה אֲשֶׁר עֲשִׂיתֶם
הֲלוֹא יְדַעְתֶּם כִּי־נַחֵשׁ יְנַחֵשׁ אִישׁ אֲשֶׁר
כָּמֹנִי׃ 16 וַיֹּאמֶר יְהוּדָה מַה־נֹּאמַר לַאדֹנִי
מַה־נְּדַבֵּר וּמַה־נִּצְטַדָּק הָאֱלֹהִים מָצָא אֶת־
עֲוֺן עֲבָדֶיךָ הִנֶּנּוּ עֲבָדִים לַאדֹנִי גַּם־אֲנַחְנוּ
גַּם אֲשֶׁר־נִמְצָא הַגָּבִיעַ בְּיָדוֹ׃
17 וַיֹּאמֶר חָלִילָה לִּי מֵעֲשׂוֹת זֹאת הָאִישׁ
אֲשֶׁר נִמְצָא הַגָּבִיעַ בְּיָדוֹ הוּא יִהְיֶה־לִּי עָבֶד
וְאַתֶּם עֲלוּ לְשָׁלוֹם אֶל־אֲבִיכֶם׃ פ

14 Judah and his brothers entered Joseph's house; he was still there. They fell to the ground before him. 15 Joseph said to them, "What is this deed that you have done? Did you not know that a man like me constantly practices divination?" 16 Judah replied, "What can we say to my lord? How speak and how justify ourselves? God has found out the iniquity of your servants; here we are, my lord's slaves—both we and the one who was caught with the goblet in his possession!"

17 But he said, "Far be it from me to do this! The man in whose possession the goblet was found, he shall be my slave, and the rest of you—go up in peace to your father."

these events operate on multiple levels. Thus we may speculate that Judah is haunted by guilt over what the brothers (without Benjamin's involvement) did to Joseph long ago—and he feels that they must finally pay for their actions (see 42:21). Judah's remarks can then refer both to the present unfortunate reality of the goblet in Benjamin's sack and to the brothers' past behavior toward Joseph.

### THE BROTHERS APPEAR BEFORE JOSEPH (44:13b–15)

*14. **Judah and his brothers.*** Contrast this designation with 43:15–44:4. Since they left Canaan for Egypt, this party has been referred to—ten times in a row—only as *ha-anashim* (traditionally rendered as "the men"). The shift in language is significant; it may hint at the fraternal solidarity that forces on Judah the role of spokesperson for the brothers.

### JUDAH'S CONFESSION (44:16)

Judah acknowledges that all of the brothers are guilty before God, although he presumably believes that none of them is guilty of the crime in question.

### JOSEPH DEMANDS ONLY BENJAMIN (44:17)

Joseph sets up the brothers in order to test them. He intends to find out whether or not they have changed since when they threw him in a pit. In other words, Joseph intends to determine if the brothers will abandon Benjamin as earlier they had abandoned Joseph himself. He is also trying to set them up to face the prospect of their father's grief over the loss of a favorite son.

***"go up in peace to your father."*** The last words of this parashah remind us of the peace that Jacob had lost when his ten oldest sons showed him Joseph's bloodied coat (37:32). The parashah ends as a cliff-hanger, with the story's resolution still to come in the parashah that follows.

—*Naomi Steinberg*

# Another View

"PHARAOH'S DREAM WAS REPEATED—two times—because the matter has been fixed by God, and God is making haste to accomplish it" (41:32).

Why are there so many repetitions in the Hebrew Bible—and in the Torah especially? The Bible usually does not spell out its poetic principles, so that readers are obliged to deduce them from the text itself. Scholars since the 19th century have explained repetition in the Bible as due to its editors having drawn from different sources. But in this parashah, Genesis 41:32 uniquely offers what amounts to a poetic statement, explaining the need for narrative repetition.

The reader wonders why Pharaoh dreams twice—first of cows, then of ears of grain. Joseph explains that "Pharaoh's dream is one: what God is doing, [God] has revealed to Pharaoh" (41:25). Thus the two dreams have a single solution: God is informing Pharaoh that seven years of abundance will be followed by seven years of famine. But if a single dream would have sufficed, why are there two, and why do they follow so closely? Verse 32 explains that repetition right away means that God had decided the matter and would shortly carry it out.

A close reading reveals that the repetition is not confined to Pharaoh's dreams but recurs throughout the Joseph story. Joseph himself has two dreams (37:5–9), though not close together—meaning that they would not be realized immediately. Moreover, this story cycle's use of repeated occurrences—not necessarily dreams—justifies characterizing its plot as advancing by paired structures. For example: Joseph escapes being killed by his brothers thanks to two rescue attempts (37:18–30); the brothers go to Egypt twice to procure rations (42:1–43:25); Joseph twice acts like a stranger to them and punishes them (42:7–28, 44), and more. We may conclude that repetition does not necessarily indicate a plurality of sources or traditions; it may also represent a poetical principle, a device that indicates a fixed divine intention—and sometimes its imminent actualization. In this manner, *parashat Mikeitz* offers an interpretation of more than Pharaoh's dreams. It holds a key to the literary and theological use of repetition throughout the Hebrew Bible.

*This parashah explains why the Bible so often resorts to narrative repetition.*

—*Yairah Amit*

# Post-biblical Interpretations

***Pharaoh woke up*** (41:7). Many ancient Jews used to reflect on a passage from the Torah by juxtaposing it with a passage from the Prophets—called a haftarah—that contains similar themes, turns of phrase, or both. A widely attested haftarah with *parashat Mikeitz* is I Kings 3:15–4:1, which is the norm even today. Royal dreams form one connection between the two biblical passages. The haftarah echoes the parashah verbally by opening with the words "Solomon woke up," and then it relates that Israel's new king had been dreaming.

***no one could interpret them*** (41:8). In *B'reishit Rabbah* 89.6, the Rabbis explain that Pharaoh's magicians interpreted his dreams incorrectly. According to the sorcerers, the healthy cows foretold that Pharaoh would sire seven daughters; the starving cows signified that he would bury seven daughters.

***"as he interpreted for us, so it came to be"*** (41:13). Rabbi Eliezer states that "all dreams follow the mouth"; that is, a dream comes true according to how it is interpreted (BT *B'rachot* 55b). As an example, *B'reishit Rabbah* 89.8 recounts that a woman came to him and told him of a recurring dream in which her house split open. The first two times she came to the sage, he told her she would give birth to a boy. The third time the rabbi was away; his students told the woman that her husband would die and this immediately came to pass.

*"All dreams follow the mouth."*

When the rabbi heard her laments, he accused his students of killing the husband, and cited this verse as his proof. As the anecdote indicates, power rests not in the dream itself, but in the skill, wisdom, and righteousness of the interpreter.

***"Since God has made all this known to you, there is no one as discerning and wise as you!"*** (41:39). The haftarah cited above reiterates the parashah's mention of wisdom when it recounts how two prostitutes come before King Solomon. Each had recently given birth, but one of the babies had died during the night. Now each woman insists that the living boy is hers. Solomon orders that the surviving baby be cut in two, to be divided between the claimants. When one woman pleads for the child's life by agreeing to give the baby to the other woman, Solomon declares her to be the true mother. Thereupon, we read, the people "held the king in awe, seeing that he had within him divine wisdom" (I Kings 3:15–4:1).

***and gave him Asenath daughter of Potiphera priest of On as a wife*** (41:45). Uncomfortable with the Bible's implication that Joseph married a non-Israelite, Jews of the Hellenistic period composed a romance (*Joseph and Asenath*) in which Asenath, the most beautiful young virgin in Egypt, converts to belief in the one true God before her marriage to Joseph. During the seven years of plenty, Joseph—as second-in-command to Pharaoh—would travel throughout Egypt to collect corn. He stopped at the home of Pentephres (Potiphera, Asenath's father), where he met the bejeweled and richly attired Asenath. Upon her first sighting of Joseph, the haughty Asenath is smitten by the beauty of this man whom she first considered to be a common Israelite shepherd. Asenath's parents suggest that the two beautiful virgins kiss, but Joseph declines to kiss a woman who eats the sacrificial meat of idols. Asenath retires to her chambers (a high tower) to don sackcloth and ashes and repent before God for her sins of idol worship and selfishness. She throws away her idols, fasts, prays, and humbles herself. On the eighth day of her self-flagellation, an angel appears in Asenath's room and converts her to Judaism in an otherwise unknown ceremony involving a honeycomb and bees. Joseph returns, sees that Asenath is even more beautiful than before, and—having been informed by the angel of Asenath's conversion—agrees to marry her in a ceremony before Pharaoh.

Later midrashic traditions also demonstrate uneasiness with the implications of Joseph's marrying the daughter of an Egyptian priest. The sages told that Asenath was actually Dinah's daughter from her liaison with Shechem (Genesis 34). To prevent public disgrace to his family when the child was born out of wedlock, Jacob had placed an amulet engraved with the divine name around the baby's neck, and the angel Gabriel had carried her to Potiphar's house in Egypt—where Potiphar's childless wife raised her as her own daughter. (The Rabbis also insisted that Potiphar, Joseph's master, was identical to Potiphera, Joseph's father-in-law. See also *Vayishlach*, Post-biblical Interpretations, at 34:26.) Thus, according to this legend, Joseph ends up marrying his niece—a permitted marriage in Jewish law—and both are preserved from marrying outsiders.

—*Deborah Green*

# Contemporary Reflection

THE PAINFUL PAST casts a long shadow on *parashat Mikeitz.* A father's insensitive treatment of his sons—and the resulting sibling rivalry—form the backdrop to this tale. Though the women are never explicitly mentioned here, Jacob's relationship to his sons' mothers underlies his attitude toward their children. Among his wives, Jacob loves Rachel only, paying scant attention to Leah and the sisters' maidservants. Likewise, Jacob clearly favors Joseph—Rachel's firstborn—showing little evidence of affection toward his other children. Blind to the difficult family dynamic he engenders, Jacob had sent Joseph alone to check on his brothers (37:13–14), setting up a situation rife with the potential for disaster. Joseph's ensuing disappearance does nothing to stop Jacob from now favoring yet another son, Benjamin, Rachel's second (see 42:4).

But healing and transformation also begin here. A hint of what is to come is encapsulated in the name Joseph chooses for his first son, Manasseh, "For God has *made me forget* all the troubles I endured in my father's house" (41:51). Clearly Joseph has *not* forgotten his troubles if they form the basis of his son's name. Rather, it seems that the past is no longer a burden to him. He is able to thrive despite the horrors he suffered in the pit where his jealous brothers threw him (37:24). The name of Joseph's second son, Ephraim, expresses this forward movement: "For God has *made me fruitful* in the land of my affliction" (41:52). His marriage to Asenath indeed bears fruit: their children will become tribes of Israel.

Joseph soon enables his older brothers to achieve a new relationship with *their* past as well, creating a set of circumstances that provides them with the opportunity to respond to favoritism differently. That would represent true *t'shuvah* (literally "return"), as the medieval Spanish rabbi and philosopher Moses Maimonides describes it: *t'shuvah* has occurred when a person, confronted with the opportunity to commit a transgression anew, refrains from doing so—not out of fear of being caught or failure of strength (*Mishneh Torah, Hilchot T'shuvah* § 2.1). *T'shuvah* is, indeed, a primary theme of *parashat Mikeitz.* The word, too often mistranslated as "repentance," actually means "return"—to the right path. Whereas "repentance" connotes remorse and self-flagellation, "return" suggests a kind of joyous homecoming. Our mistakes, rather than serving solely as a source of guilt, become also a springboard of opportunity.

Perhaps unwittingly, the brothers had begun the process of *t'shuvah* before meeting Joseph again in Egypt. In 42:1, at home with their father, they are referred to as *Jacob's sons.* Two verses later, on their way to Egypt, we read, "So *Joseph's brothers* went down..." Restating classic midrashim, Rashi opines that "they set their hearts on conducting themselves toward him as brothers." This is an optimistic reading, but the language does suggest a change in their relationship to Joseph—though one that is undoubtedly buried beneath layers of guilt and denial.

> *They come to terms with their father's failings, choosing compassion over anger.*

Joseph manipulates the situation so that the brothers' feelings can rise to the surface. Simeon is held back as ransom. Alarmed at the prospect of returning home to their father one brother short, the brothers recall their cruelty of more than twenty years ago: "Oh, we are being punished on account of our brother! We saw his soul's distress when he pleaded with us, but we didn't listen..." (42:21). Perhaps because they could not hear him then, Joseph's pleading was not mentioned in the initial narrative (Genesis 37). Now, for the first time, the brothers exhibit empathy toward

Joseph. According to Marsha Pravder Mirkin, empathy is the key to *t'shuvah*: "Empathy... is valuing another person enough to listen and hear her voice. It is a halting that then allows us to take action... that brings us closer to becoming the best we can be" ("Hearken to Her Voice: Empathy as *Teshuva*," in Gail Twersky Reimer and Judith A. Kates, eds., *Beginning Anew: A Woman's Companion to the High Holy Days*, 1997, p. 70).

When the brothers return to their father in Canaan, a significant transformation has occurred. The first indication is their report of their time in Egypt: the brothers demonstrate a newfound sensitivity to their father's feelings, sparing Jacob some of the more disturbing details of their journey. Modern Israeli commentator Nehama Leibowitz points out, for example, that they omit Joseph's original plan to keep all but one of them in Egypt (42:16) and the threat of death (42:20) (*New Studies in Bereshit/Genesis*, undated, pp. 471–2). Then, in the face of their father's fear for Benjamin's life, Reuben offers his own sons' lives in pledge for Benjamin's (42:37). This is an impulsive and ill-conceived gesture—yet a marked change for the man whose idea it was to throw Joseph into the pit (37:22). Finally Judah, who had convinced his brothers to sell Joseph to the Ishmaelites (37:27), offers to take personal responsibility for the life of his youngest brother (43:9). Clearly, Judah is the brother who has matured and evolved the most.

He and his brothers have made peace with their father's favoritism. We might imagine that, after Joseph forces them to confront their guilt, they realize that their earlier violent response to their father's unequal love has not changed Jacob. Aware that hurting Jacob or Benjamin will not get them greater attention from their father, they come to terms with Jacob's failings, choosing compassion over anger in their dealings with him.

This parashah ends mid-action, leaving us to wonder: Will Joseph really enslave Benjamin? How will the brothers respond? Will Joseph reveal his identity? The answers are not clear—because neither Joseph's motivation for putting his brothers through this ordeal, nor their commitment to ethical behavior, are fully actualized until the next parashah. Perhaps the Rabbis broke off the story here to suggest that our choices are moment-to-moment decisions, the path never certain until the time comes to act. This cliffhanger ending is also a signal of hope, because *t'shuvah* is always open to us.

—*Suzanne Singer*

# *Another Contemporary Reflection*

ACCORDING TO *parashat Mikeitz*, Joseph marries an Egyptian. Their children, Ephraim and Manasseh (41:45–52), subsequently become progenitors of two Israelite tribes. A traditional blessing of children invokes these sons' names. Around the Sabbath table for many generations, parents of sons have been reciting (as one English translation renders it): "May you be like Ephraim and Manasseh." This biblical precedent, which recognizes the children of a non-Israelite mother as equal—even distinguished—members of Israel, invites an examination of assumptions as to who is counted as part of the people Israel and on what basis.

Most biblical texts implicitly reflect patrilineal descent: the child's membership is determined by that of the father, not the mother. A major exception is the book of Ezra, which excludes foreign wives with their children from the community (Ezra 10:3). The implication: these children, like the mother, do not belong to Israel even though their fathers are Israelites.

In the post-biblical era, rabbinic halachah determined what became normative in Judaism: a child of a Jewish mother is a Jew. (For a detailed discussion, see Shaye Cohen, *The Beginning of Jewishness*, 1999.)

In 1983, the Central Conference of American Rabbis voted to return to patrilineal descent while also retaining matrilineal descent. The resolution required that in the case of intermarriage, a child's Jewish identity must be confirmed through "acts of identification with the Jewish people" and "the performance of mitzvoth" (if either the mother or father is Jewish). According to this formulation, lineage is not determined by genetics alone but by identification with the Jewish people and by Jewish practice.

Rabbi Alexander Schindler, the visionary behind this effort, viewed this resolution as an extension of his vision of Outreach in response to the growing reality of intermarriage in American Jewish life. But he viewed the return to patrilineality also as an egalitarian issue. At a 1986 conference on Jewish unity he noted, "Why should a movement that from its birth-hour insisted on the full equality of men and women in religious life unquestioningly accept the principle that Jewish lineage is valid through the maternal line alone—all the more so because there is substantial support in our tradition for the validity of Jewish lineage through the paternal line!" (Princeton, New Jersey; March 16, 1986). (The Reconstructionist movement likewise adopted patrilineal descent as valid. The Conservative movement and Orthodox Jews do not accept patrilineal descent as defining who is a Jew.)

While patrilineal descent has been criticized harshly across the greater Jewish world for dividing the Jewish people, its supporters see its inclusion not as a movement away from tradition but as a transition back to certain biblical roots in light of changed circumstances. Thus Rabbi Bernard Zlotowitz writes that

*Who is counted as part of the people Israel?*

"the changes enacted in the Reform movement fall within the traditional parameters of Judaism as a living faith. In times of necessity and for the welfare of the people, halachah was revised and traditions set aside in favor of more adaptive ones" ("Patrilineal Descent," in *The Jewish Condition*, ed. Aron Hirt-Manheimer, 1995, p. 265). Zlotowitz notes several examples of adaptive changes that have become part of the halachah: the removal of the laws of the *sotah* (the wife suspected of adultery as in Numbers 5—see *Naso*, Contemporary Reflection, p. 838), and the abolition of the husband's right to divorce his wife without cause. These examples are similar in that the changed laws aim to provide for the Jewish community's preservation and continuity in the face of changing circumstances and values.

—*Judy Schindler*

# Voices

## Joseph and Pharaoh

Ruth Brin

*Genesis 41*

The nakedness of Joseph before Pharaoh
was the nakedness of an elm tree in the winter.

Not like the pine, whose branches hold the
snow,
and bend and break in the cold, stood Joseph,

But like the elm, stripped of his colored
garments,
the ornaments of his youthful summer,
stripped of his pride as favorite son,
of his pretensions to rule his brothers,

Yet rooted in the teachings of his fathers,
as the elm tree is rooted in the even temperature
of the deep earth,
Joseph stood before the king of Egypt.

The fine branches of his intellect
and the myriad fibers of his nerves
were exposed to the chilling air of the court.

The nakedness of Joseph before the Pharaoh
was a nakedness which both exposes and
protects.

It is the nakedness of Jacob before the
Wrestler—
for Jacob had sent his wealth, his family,
his pretensions and his pride, across the river.

It is the nakedness of Moses before God—
for Moses had left behind him the power
and the privilege of a prince in Egypt.

It is the nakedness of the Jew in history—
the nakedness of honesty and humility,
of innocence and abnegation, of deep roots and
bare branches,
of protection and exposure.

It is a nakedness neither to escape nor embrace,
but to accept, if it comes, as we have done
in every age.

## Pharaoh and Joseph

Else Lasker-Schüler (transl. Janine Canan)

*Genesis 41:39–40*

Pharaoh casts off his blossoming wives—
they smell of Amon's gardens.

His kingly head rests on my shoulder,
that emanates the scent of corn.

Pharaoh is made of gold.
His eyes come and go
like iridescent Nile waves.

But his heart lies in my blood—
ten wolves ran to my wells.

Pharaoh ruminates
about my brothers,
who threw me into the pit.

In sleep his arms become pillars—
threatening!

But his dreamy heart
thunders in my depths.

Therefore my lips compose
vast sweetnesses
in the wheat of our dawn.

## *Asenath's Plea to Her Husband Joseph*

Sherry Blumberg

*Genesis 41:45*

Joseph, you will bring these men
To the house we share.
They are your brothers, are they not?
Our steward will greet them,
I'll send water to wash their feet
We will do what is right and proper
You will test them
And I will support you.

But Joseph, I beg you
Do not ever ask me to love them
For they have meant you great harm
And I cannot forgive.
You will make yourself known one day
And I will do what is right and proper
For my love is towards you
The father of my sons

And Joseph, when in the future
Your sons are remembered
Please do not deny me—
Else the love that we shared
The lives we've created
Will be lessened by it.
I am the daughter of a priest
And I am your wife.

## *The Second Exodus*

Ada Aharoni

*Genesis 41:56–57*

Today, I again bring my grain vessel
to the docks of your granary, father—
while breathing the wheat smells you loved,
me in Dagon Silo in Haifa,
you far away back in Cairo.

Joseph in Egypt land, Canaanite jugs,
ritual bronze sickles from temples,
crushing-stones, mill-stones and mortars—
all link me back to you
on old rusty scales.
I remember your orange-beige office
in Cairo's Mouski,
with deaf Tohami weighing
the heavy sacks of flour and grain
on old rusty scales.
And me listening unaware
to the birds' chirped warning
on the beams of your ceiling:
"Wandering Jew, open your Jewish eyes,
you will soon have to spread your wings
again, and look for new nest."

Mighty Dagon's giant arms storing in bulk,
fill my own silo with tears
that you are not here with me
to view this wonder
deftly handling bread to Israel—
the land you so loved
but are not buried in.

For you dear father, I plant today a garden
of grain,
for you, who always taught us
how to sow.

NOTE

***Dagon.*** The ancient Philistine god of grain; also the name of an enormous grain silo in the modern-day port of Haifa.

# ויגש ✦ *Vayigash*

## GENESIS 44:18–47:27

## *Reunion and Reconciliation of Joseph, Jacob, and the Brothers*

THE HIGHLIGHT OF *parashat Vayigash* ("he approached") is when Joseph reveals his true identity to his brothers. This parashah starts with Judah's emotional plea to let Benjamin return to Jacob in Canaan. The plea revolves around the effect on Jacob of the brothers' returning without Benjamin. Unable to contain his feelings any longer, Joseph discloses his identity and sends his brothers home to bring his father to Egypt.

The brothers are both sorry and apprehensive about reprisal for what they did to Joseph long ago. But Jacob is happy to learn that Joseph, his elder son by his favorite wife Rachel, is still alive. He and the entire family move to Egypt. Family matters occupy center stage in *parashat Vayigash* as father and sons are reconciled with each other and forgive past behavior. The other brothers seem to set aside jealousies stemming from Jacob's favoring Rachel and her children.

On a deeper level, this parashah explores the dynamics of human growth. Robert Alter sums up the issues beautifully:

> What is it like, the biblical writers seek to know through their art, to be a human being with a divided consciousness—intermittently loving your brother but hating him even more; resentful or perhaps contemptuous of your father but also capable of the deepest filial regard; stumbling between disastrous ignorance and imperfect knowledge; fiercely asserting your own independence but caught in a tissue of events divinely contrived; outwardly a definite character and inwardly an unstable vortex of greed, ambition, jealousy, lust, piety, courage, compassion, and much more? (*The Art of Biblical Narrative*, 1981, p. 176)

The parashah, then, presents a study in the human capacity for lasting change. While not mentioned in this parashah, Tamar has been a pivotal figure in Judah's own growth. Their encounter in Genesis 38 best accounts for Judah's new capacity to sympathize with his father.

> *The parashah presents a study in the human capacity for lasting change.*

Women appear infrequently in this parashah. There are references to women in 44:20, 45:19, and among those who went to Egypt (46:5–27). The list of the descendants of Jacob who traveled to Egypt divides the entire family according to their mothers (46:8–27). Of the daughters of Jacob, only Dinah is mentioned by name (46:15). The total number of offspring of Jacob who traveled with him to Egypt does not count the wives of his sons (46:26).

—*Naomi Steinberg*

## Outline

I. Judah Pleads for Benjamin's Release (44:18–34)

II. Joseph Discloses His Identity
*Responses and Ramifications* (45:1–28)

- A. Joseph discloses his identity (vv. 1–3a)
- B. Joseph and his brothers reunite (vv. 3b–15)
- C. Pharaoh helps Joseph's family (vv. 16–24)
- D. Jacob learns that Joseph is alive (vv. 25–28)

III. Jacob/Israel Meets Joseph in Egypt (46:1–34)

- A. Preparations (vv. 1–7)
- B. The seventy members of Jacob's family who come to Egypt (vv. 8–27)
- C. Jacob and his sons reunite (vv. 28–34)

IV. Joseph and Jacob Meet with Pharaoh (47:1–10)

V. Further Details Regarding Joseph and Family (47:11–27)

- A. Joseph settles his father's household in Egypt (vv. 11–12)
- B. Joseph deals with the famine in Egypt (vv. 13–26)
- C. Conclusion: Israel/Jacob prospers in Egypt (v. 27)

44:18

Judah now approached him and said, "By your leave, my lord, please give your servant a hearing, and do not let your anger flare up at your servant—for you are like Pharaoh. 19My lord asked his servants, 'Do you have a father or a brother?' 20And we said to my lord, 'We have an aged father and a young boy of his old age, whose [full] brother is dead. He alone was left of his mother, and so his father loves him [all the more].' 21You then said to your servants, 'Bring him down here to me and let me lay my eyes on him.' 22But we said to my lord, 'The lad cannot leave his father; if he leaves his father, he will die!' 23You then said to your servants,

מד 18 וַיִּגַּשׁ אֵלָיו יְהוּדָה וַיֹּאמֶר בִּי אֲדֹנִי
יְדַבֶּר־נָא עַבְדְּךָ דָבָר בְּאָזְנֵי אֲדֹנִי וְאַל־יִחַר
אַפְּךָ בְּעַבְדֶּךָ כִּי כָמוֹךָ כְּפַרְעֹה׃ 19 אֲדֹנִי
שָׁאַל אֶת־עֲבָדָיו לֵאמֹר הֲיֵשׁ־לָכֶם אָב אוֹ־
אָח׃ 20 וַנֹּאמֶר אֶל־אֲדֹנִי יֶשׁ־לָנוּ אָב זָקֵן
וְיֶלֶד זְקֻנִים קָטָן וְאָחִיו מֵת וַיִּוָּתֵר הוּא
לְבַדּוֹ לְאִמּוֹ וְאָבִיו אֲהֵבוֹ׃ 21 וַתֹּאמֶר אֶל־
עֲבָדֶיךָ הוֹרִדֻהוּ אֵלָי וְאָשִׂימָה עֵינִי עָלָיו׃
22 וַנֹּאמֶר אֶל־אֲדֹנִי לֹא־יוּכַל הַנַּעַר לַעֲזֹב
אֶת־אָבִיו וְעָזַב אֶת־אָבִיו וָמֵת׃ 23 וַתֹּאמֶר

## *Judah Pleads for Benjamin's Release* (44:18–34)

This parashah picks up where the last one left off: Joseph's goblet had been found in Benjamin's sack, and Joseph had announced his plan to make Benjamin his slave. [Rather than using the occasion as an opportunity to eliminate a rival for his father's affection, Judah now strives to return Benjamin home. —*Ed.*]

*18. **Judah now approached him.*** Judah functions as a spokesman for the brothers.

*20. **"He alone was left of his mother, and so his father loves him [all the more]."*** Although the translator modifies the concluding mention of love with "[all the more]," the Hebrew can be understood to suggest that Jacob loves *only* Benjamin. Judah seems able to accept that state of affairs. The pathos of the story lies in this acknowledgement.

*22. **"if he leaves his father, he will die!"*** Judah's recollection of this filial concern both indicates psychological maturity on his part and foreshadows the unity of father and sons that will finally resolve the tensions that split the family apart in Genesis 37. A family that had been divided against itself is about to overcome the years of alienation and living a lie. The loss of two of his own sons (38:7–10) explains Judah's newfound sympathy, while his encounter with Tamar (38:12–26) seems to account for his willingness to take responsibility. (See at 43:9 and the introduction to *Mikeitz*, p. 233).

*23–34.* Judah makes several points in his eloquent speech to Joseph: (*1*) He retells the events

The renewed solidarity and cohesiveness do not include any of the family's female members.

ANOTHER VIEW ➤ *275*

Only by being open to what we learn from one another do we grow.

CONTEMPORARY REFLECTION ➤ *277*

Serah bat Asher "did not taste death" but entered Paradise alive.

POST-BIBLICAL INTERPRETATIONS ➤ *275*

I withdrew into the safety of silence, / learning to whisper through the music of my harp.

VOICES ➤ *279*

'If your youngest brother doesn't come down with you, you'll never see my face again!' [24]So when we went up to your servant my father, we related to him my lord's words. [25]And when our father said, 'Go back and buy us a bit of food,' [26]we said, 'We can't go down; only if our youngest brother is with us will we go down, for we won't be allowed to see the man's face unless our youngest brother is with us.' [27]Your servant my father then said to us, 'You know that of the two my wife bore me, [28]one is gone from my side, and I said, "Surely he's been ripped to shreds!" I haven't seen him to this day. [29]If you take this one too from me and some calamity befalls him, you will lower my gray head in woe to Sheol.'

[30]"And now, if I go to your servant my father and the lad—whose whole being is bound up in his—is not with us, [31]and he sees that the lad is not there, he will die, and your servants will have lowered your servant our father's gray head in anguish to Sheol. [32]For your servant made himself responsible for the lad to my father, saying, 'If I don't bring him back to you, I will stand guilty before my father for all time.' [33]So now, please let your servant remain as my lord's slave in place of the lad, and let the lad go home with his brothers; [34]for how can I

אֶל־עֲבָדֶ֑יךָ אִם־לֹ֥א יֵרֵ֛ד אֲחִיכֶ֥ם הַקָּטֹ֖ן אִתְּכֶ֑ם לֹ֥א תֹסִפ֖וּן לִרְא֥וֹת פָּנָֽי׃ [24]וַֽיְהִי֙ כִּ֣י עָלִ֔ינוּ אֶֽל־עַבְדְּךָ֖ אָבִ֑י וַנַּ֨גֶּד־ל֔וֹ אֵ֖ת דִּבְרֵ֥י אֲדֹנִֽי׃ [25]וַיֹּ֖אמֶר אָבִ֑ינוּ שֻׁ֖בוּ שִׁבְרוּ־לָ֥נוּ מְעַט־אֹֽכֶל׃ [26]וַנֹּ֕אמֶר לֹ֥א נוּכַ֖ל לָרֶ֑דֶת אִם־יֵ֩שׁ֩ אָחִ֨ינוּ הַקָּטֹ֤ן אִתָּ֨נוּ֙ וְיָרַ֔דְנוּ כִּי־לֹ֣א נוּכַ֗ל לִרְאוֹת֙ פְּנֵ֣י הָאִ֔ישׁ וְאָחִ֥ינוּ הַקָּטֹ֖ן אֵינֶ֥נּוּ אִתָּֽנוּ׃ [27]וַיֹּ֛אמֶר עַבְדְּךָ֥ אָבִ֖י אֵלֵ֑ינוּ אַתֶּ֣ם יְדַעְתֶּ֔ם כִּ֥י שְׁנַ֖יִם יָֽלְדָה־לִּ֥י אִשְׁתִּֽי׃ [28]וַיֵּצֵ֤א הָֽאֶחָד֙ מֵֽאִתִּ֔י וָאֹמַ֕ר אַ֖ךְ טָרֹ֣ף טֹרָ֑ף וְלֹ֥א רְאִיתִ֖יו עַד־הֵֽנָּה׃ [29]וּלְקַחְתֶּ֧ם גַּם־אֶת־זֶ֛ה מֵעִ֥ם פָּנַ֖י וְקָרָ֣הוּ אָס֑וֹן וְהֽוֹרַדְתֶּ֧ם אֶת־שֵֽׂיבָתִ֛י בְּרָעָ֖ה שְׁאֹֽלָה׃ [30]וְעַתָּ֗ה כְּבֹאִי֙ אֶל־עַבְדְּךָ֣ אָבִ֔י וְהַנַּ֖עַר אֵינֶ֣נּוּ אִתָּ֑נוּ וְנַפְשׁ֖וֹ קְשׁוּרָ֥ה בְנַפְשֽׁוֹ׃ [31]וְהָיָ֗ה כִּרְאוֹת֛וֹ כִּי־אֵ֥ין הַנַּ֖עַר וָמֵ֑ת וְהוֹרִ֨ידוּ עֲבָדֶ֜יךָ אֶת־שֵׂיבַ֨ת עַבְדְּךָ֥ אָבִ֛ינוּ בְּיָג֖וֹן שְׁאֹֽלָה׃ [32]כִּ֤י עַבְדְּךָ֙ עָרַ֣ב אֶת־הַנַּ֔עַר מֵעִ֥ם אָבִ֖י לֵאמֹ֑ר אִם־לֹ֤א אֲבִיאֶ֨נּוּ֙ אֵלֶ֔יךָ וְחָטָ֥אתִי לְאָבִ֖י כָּל־הַיָּמִֽים׃ [33]וְעַתָּ֗ה יֵֽשֶׁב־נָ֤א עַבְדְּךָ֙ תַּ֣חַת הַנַּ֔עַר עֶ֖בֶד לַֽאדֹנִ֑י וְהַנַּ֖עַר יַ֥עַל עִם־אֶחָֽיו׃ [34]כִּי־אֵיךְ֙ אֶֽעֱלֶ֣ה אֶל־אָבִ֔י וְהַנַּ֖עַר

that have led the brothers to be in their present circumstances. (2) He emphasizes how Benjamin's absence will break the heart of their father Jacob. (3) He demonstrates his sincere desire to spare their father the heartbreak and offers to serve in Benjamin's place in slavery.

**28. "Surely he's been ripped to shreds!"** Joseph now learns how Jacob interpreted Joseph's disappearance.

**29. "you will lower my gray head in woe to Sheol."** This near-quotation of Jacob's own words in 42:38 (reiterated in v. 31) leaves no doubt about the devastating effect on Jacob if Benjamin does not return to his father.

**31. "he will die."** Judah reveals his desperate concern for the effect on his father, thus demonstrating the love that now binds the sons to their father.

**32. "If I don't bring him back to you, I will stand guilty before my father for all time."** Judah holds himself responsible for Benjamin because he stood surety for him earlier (43:9–10). Judah's concern for his father's welfare at this time stands in direct contrast to the spirit that moved him to participate in the brothers' plot to rid them of Joseph back in 37:26. Previously self-centered, Judah emerges now as self-sacrificing.

go home to my father without the lad, and thus see
the harm my father will suffer?"
45 Joseph could no longer restrain himself
before all who were standing in attendance on him,
so he cried, "Send everyone away from me!" so that
no one else was there when Joseph made himself
known to his brothers. 2He gave voice to a loud
wail, and the Egyptians heard—Pharaoh's palace
heard! 3Joseph then said to his brothers, "I am
Joseph—is my father [really] alive?" But his brothers were unable to answer him—they recoiled in
fear of him.
4Joseph then went on to say to his brothers,
"Come, draw near to me!" so they drew near. He
said, "I am Joseph your brother, whom you sold to
Egypt; 5and now, don't be troubled, don't be cha-
grined because you sold me here, for it was to save

אֵינֶנּוּ אִתִּי פֶּן אֶרְאֶה בָרָע אֲשֶׁר יִמְצָא
אֶת־אָבִי׃
מה וְלֹא־יָכֹל יוֹסֵף לְהִתְאַפֵּק לְכֹל
הַנִּצָּבִים עָלָיו וַיִּקְרָא הוֹצִיאוּ כָל־אִישׁ
מֵעָלָי וְלֹא־עָמַד אִישׁ אִתּוֹ בְּהִתְוַדַּע יוֹסֵף
אֶל־אֶחָיו׃ 2 וַיִּתֵּן אֶת־קֹלוֹ בִּבְכִי וַיִּשְׁמְעוּ
מִצְרַיִם וַיִּשְׁמַע בֵּית פַּרְעֹה׃ 3 וַיֹּאמֶר יוֹסֵף
אֶל־אֶחָיו אֲנִי יוֹסֵף הַעוֹד אָבִי חָי וְלֹא־יָכְלוּ
אֶחָיו לַעֲנוֹת אֹתוֹ כִּי נִבְהֲלוּ מִפָּנָיו׃
4 וַיֹּאמֶר יוֹסֵף אֶל־אֶחָיו גְּשׁוּ־נָא אֵלַי וַיִּגָּשׁוּ
וַיֹּאמֶר אֲנִי יוֹסֵף אֲחִיכֶם אֲשֶׁר־מְכַרְתֶּם
אֹתִי מִצְרָיְמָה׃ 5 וְעַתָּה ׀ אַל־תֵּעָצְבוּ וְאַל־
יִחַר בְּעֵינֵיכֶם כִּי־מְכַרְתֶּם אֹתִי הֵנָּה כִּי

## *Joseph Discloses His Identity*

### RESPONSES AND RAMIFICATIONS (45:1–28)

Judah's speech to Joseph has brought the suspense between the brothers to a climax, and it prompts Joseph's self-revelation to his brothers. Joseph's statements reveal that he too has undergone a transformation. Joseph's emotional maturity matches the emotional maturity demonstrated in Judah's speech on behalf of Benjamin, as well as Judah's filial concern for Jacob's well-being.

### JOSEPH DISCLOSES HIS IDENTITY (45:1–3a)

Judah's speech, and his concern for his father's well-being, push Joseph to reveal himself—and proclaim his own identity and loyalties.

*2. wail.* This is the third of four times that Joseph weeps with emotion over his brothers (earlier: 42:24 and 43:30).

The Hebrew root *b-k-h* is often used also for female emotional distress, with a prominent example being the imagined weeping of Joseph's mother, Rachel, for her lost children after the destruction of the northern tribes of Israel (Jeremiah 31:15).

*3. "I am Joseph—is my father [really] alive?"* The story reaches its climax when Joseph finally discloses his true identity to his brothers. This is the pinnacle of the emotional build-up that has been developing in Joseph. His outburst of emotions and self-revelation stands out as one of the most moving expressions of family ties in the Torah.

### JOSEPH AND HIS BROTHERS REUNITE (45:3b–15)

***5–7. "don't be troubled . . . God sent me ahead of you."*** The assurance that God sent Joseph is so important here that it is repeated twice (in vv. 5 and 7). The arc that spans the stories of Joseph and his brothers serves to explain the will of God to bring about good for the people. The story perpetuates the idea that faithfulness results in divine action and ultimate relief for the people. Moreover, it affirms that God works through ordinary human

lives that God sent me ahead of you. [6]There have
already been two years of famine in the land, and
[there remain] five more years without plowing or
harvesting. [7]So God sent me ahead of you to assure
your survival in the land, and to keep you alive for a
great deliverance.
[8]"So it's not you who sent me here but the God
who made me a father to Pharaoh, a lord of all his
household, a ruler of the whole land of Egypt.
[9]Hurry back up to my father and say to him: 'Thus
says your son Joseph, God has made me a lord of all
Egypt; come down to me, do not delay! [10]You can
settle in the land of Goshen and be near to me—
you, your children, and your children's children,
your flocks and herds, and all that you own. [11]I will
sustain you there, for there remain five more years
of famine—so that you and your household and
all that you own are not impoverished.' [12]Look—
you can see with your own eyes, and so can my
brother Benjamin, that it's my mouth speaking

לְמִֽחְיָ֔ה שְׁלָחַ֥נִי אֱלֹהִ֖ים לִפְנֵיכֶֽם׃ 6 כִּי־זֶ֛ה
שְׁנָתַ֥יִם הָרָעָ֖ב בְּקֶ֣רֶב הָאָ֑רֶץ וְעוֹד֙ חָמֵ֣שׁ
שָׁנִ֔ים אֲשֶׁ֥ר אֵין־חָרִ֖ישׁ וְקָצִֽיר׃ 7 וַיִּשְׁלָחֵ֨נִי
אֱלֹהִים֙ לִפְנֵיכֶ֔ם לָשׂ֥וּם לָכֶ֛ם שְׁאֵרִ֖ית בָּאָ֑רֶץ
וּלְהַחֲי֣וֹת לָכֶ֔ם לִפְלֵיטָ֖ה גְּדֹלָֽה׃
8 וְעַתָּ֗ה לֹֽא־אַתֶּ֞ם שְׁלַחְתֶּ֤ם אֹתִי֙ הֵ֔נָּה כִּ֖י
הָאֱלֹהִ֑ים וַיְשִׂימֵ֨נִי לְאָ֜ב לְפַרְעֹ֗ה וּלְאָדוֹן֙
לְכָל־בֵּית֔וֹ וּמֹשֵׁ֖ל בְּכָל־אֶ֥רֶץ מִצְרָֽיִם׃
9 מַהֲרוּ֮ וַעֲל֣וּ אֶל־אָבִי֒ וַאֲמַרְתֶּ֣ם אֵלָ֗יו כֹּ֤ה
אָמַר֙ בִּנְךָ֣ יוֹסֵ֔ף שָׂמַ֧נִי אֱלֹהִ֛ים לְאָד֖וֹן לְכָל־
מִצְרָ֑יִם רְדָ֥ה אֵלַ֖י אַל־תַּעֲמֹֽד׃ 10 וְיָשַׁבְתָּ֣
בְאֶֽרֶץ־גֹּ֗שֶׁן וְהָיִ֤יתָ קָרוֹב֙ אֵלַ֔י אַתָּ֕ה וּבָנֶ֖יךָ
וּבְנֵ֣י בָנֶ֑יךָ וְצֹאנְךָ֥ וּבְקָרְךָ֖ וְכָל־אֲשֶׁר־לָֽךְ׃
11 וְכִלְכַּלְתִּ֤י אֹֽתְךָ֙ שָׁ֔ם כִּי־ע֛וֹד חָמֵ֥שׁ שָׁנִ֖ים
רָעָ֑ב פֶּן־תִּוָּרֵ֛שׁ אַתָּ֥ה וּבֵיתְךָ֖ וְכָל־אֲשֶׁר־לָֽךְ׃
12 וְהִנֵּ֤ה עֵינֵיכֶם֙ רֹא֔וֹת וְעֵינֵ֖י אָחִ֣י בִנְיָמִ֑ין

beings to accomplish salvation for the people of Israel, as represented by the family of Jacob and his children. Thus, despite the emphasis on Joseph in Genesis 37–50, the drama really concerns a father and all his sons. The family is only a family when all its members acknowledge their connection and unite to support each other. The travails of this family illustrate the messiness and unpredictability of human emotions. Rather than be angry at his brothers for what they did to him in the past, Joseph is now grateful for their presence in his life.

Moreover, the story establishes the importance of the capacity of human beings to forgive each other. The theme of family unity echoes the theme of God's unified control of events. By attributing all that has happened to the divine intention to save lives, Joseph provides psychological support for the brothers to rid themselves of guilt over what they had done earlier.

*8. "So it's not you who sent me here but the God who made me a father to Pharaoh."* Joseph uses the language of family relations as a way to explain to them his power over and ability to counsel Pharaoh. Although in the ancient Near East people expressed *all* interpersonal and political relationships in household terms, here such usage is poignant because another "father" (Jacob) is so much on the mind of his sons.

***10. "You can settle in the land of Goshen and be near to me—you, your children, and your children's children, your flocks and herds, and all that you own."*** The command from Joseph does not mention the women and wives traveling to Egypt with Jacob. This reflects the patrilineal concerns of the story. (See further at 6:10; 10:1.) However, in Genesis 45:19; 46:5 (see below) the wives of Jacob's sons are acknowledged as members of the family of Jacob who went with him to Egypt.

The precise location of Goshen is not known, but it is clear from the context that the name refers to a geographical spot that will be ideal for the extended family and its flocks (46:32–34; 47:6, 11).

to you! 13Tell my father how they honor me in Egypt, and all that you have seen; hurry up and bring my father down to here!" 14He then fell weeping upon his brother Benjamin's neck, and Benjamin wept on his neck. 15He kissed all his brothers and wept with them; only after this could his brothers respond to him.

כִּי־פִי הַמְדַבֵּר אֲלֵיכֶם׃ 13 וְהִגַּדְתֶּם לְאָבִי
אֶת־כָּל־כְּבוֹדִי בְּמִצְרַיִם וְאֵת כָּל־אֲשֶׁר
רְאִיתֶם וּמִהַרְתֶּם וְהוֹרַדְתֶּם אֶת־אָבִי הֵנָּה׃
14 וַיִּפֹּל עַל־צַוְּארֵי בִנְיָמִן־אָחִיו וַיֵּבְךְּ וּבִנְיָמִן
בָּכָה עַל־צַוָּארָיו׃ 15 וַיְנַשֵּׁק לְכָל־אֶחָיו וַיֵּבְךְּ
עֲלֵהֶם וְאַחֲרֵי כֵן דִּבְּרוּ אֶחָיו אִתּוֹ׃

16And the report was heard in Pharaoh's palace: "Joseph's brothers have arrived!" And this pleased Pharaoh and his courtiers, 17so Pharaoh said to Joseph, "Say to your brothers, 'Do this: load up your beasts and head straight for the land of Canaan, 18and take your father and your households and come to me; I will give you the best that the land of Egypt offers; [come] eat the fat of the land.' 19Moreover, you are instructed [to say], 'Do this: take wagons from the land of Egypt for your little ones and your wives, and convey your father, and come. 20And don't look with regret at your household goods, because the best that the whole land of Egypt offers is yours.'"

21Israel's sons set about doing this; Joseph provided them with wagons at Pharaoh's command, and he gave them provisions for the journey. 22To each he furnished a change of clothing; but to Benjamin he gave three hundred pieces of silver and five changes of clothing. 23And to his father he sent some ten asses laden with fine Egyptian goods and ten she-asses carrying grain, bread, and food to his

16 וְהַקֹּל נִשְׁמַע בֵּית פַּרְעֹה לֵאמֹר בָּאוּ אֲחֵי
יוֹסֵף וַיִּיטַב בְּעֵינֵי פַרְעֹה וּבְעֵינֵי עֲבָדָיו׃
17 וַיֹּאמֶר פַּרְעֹה אֶל־יוֹסֵף אֱמֹר אֶל־אַחֶיךָ
זֹאת עֲשׂוּ טַעֲנוּ אֶת־בְּעִירְכֶם וּלְכוּ־בֹאוּ
אַרְצָה כְּנָעַן׃ 18 וּקְחוּ אֶת־אֲבִיכֶם וְאֶת־
בָּתֵּיכֶם וּבֹאוּ אֵלָי וְאֶתְּנָה לָכֶם אֶת־טוּב
אֶרֶץ מִצְרַיִם וְאִכְלוּ אֶת־חֵלֶב הָאָרֶץ׃
19 וְאַתָּה צֻוֵּיתָה זֹאת עֲשׂוּ קְחוּ־לָכֶם
מֵאֶרֶץ מִצְרַיִם עֲגָלוֹת לְטַפְּכֶם וְלִנְשֵׁיכֶם
וּנְשָׂאתֶם אֶת־אֲבִיכֶם וּבָאתֶם׃ 20 וְעֵינְכֶם
אַל־תָּחֹס עַל־כְּלֵיכֶם כִּי־טוּב כָּל־אֶרֶץ
מִצְרַיִם לָכֶם הוּא׃
21 וַיַּעֲשׂוּ־כֵן בְּנֵי יִשְׂרָאֵל וַיִּתֵּן לָהֶם יוֹסֵף
עֲגָלוֹת עַל־פִּי פַרְעֹה וַיִּתֵּן לָהֶם צֵדָה
לַדָּרֶךְ׃ 22 לְכֻלָּם נָתַן לָאִישׁ חֲלִפוֹת שְׂמָלֹת
וּלְבִנְיָמִן נָתַן שְׁלֹשׁ מֵאוֹת כֶּסֶף וְחָמֵשׁ
חֲלִפֹת שְׂמָלֹת׃ 23 וּלְאָבִיו שָׁלַח כְּזֹאת
עֲשָׂרָה חֲמֹרִים נֹשְׂאִים מִטּוּב מִצְרָיִם וְעֶשֶׂר
אֲתֹנֹת נֹשְׂאֹת בָּר וָלֶחֶם וּמָזוֹן לְאָבִיו

*14–15. weeping… and wept.* This is the fourth time Joseph weeps over his brothers (see at 45:2); he also weeps when reunited with his father (46:29).

*15. only after this.* The gestures of Joseph's kissing his brothers and weeping over them is what gives the brothers confidence finally to respond. This very emotional scene clearly expresses the true fraternal affection felt by the brothers, who seem to have now made peace with the events of the past.

## PHARAOH HELPS JOSEPH'S FAMILY (45:16–24)

*18. "households."* Heb. *batim* (plural of *bayit,* literally "house"). The thrust of this term here is explained in the next verse: "little ones" and wives.

*22. To each he furnished a change of clothing.* The gift of clothing should remind the reader—and perhaps Joseph's brothers themselves—of their

father for the road. 24He sent his brothers forth, and
as they were going he said to them, "Don't be anxious along the way."
25They went up from Egypt and came to the
land of Canaan, to Jacob their father. 26When they
told him "Joseph is still alive"—and that he held
sway over the whole land of Egypt!—his heart
froze, for he could not believe them. 27But when
they told him all that Joseph had spoken to them,
and when he saw the wagons that Joseph has sent to
convey him, their father Jacob's spirit came alive.
28Israel said, "Enough! My son Joseph is alive! I
must go and see him before I die!"
46 Israel and all his company set off on their
journey and they came to Beersheba, where he offered sacrifices to the God of his father Isaac. 2God
addressed Israel in a night vision, saying, "Jacob,

לַדָּרֶךְ׃ 24 וַיְשַׁלַּח אֶת־אֶחָיו וַיֵּלֵכוּ וַיֹּאמֶר
אֲלֵהֶם אַל־תִּרְגְּזוּ בַּדָּרֶךְ׃
25 וַיַּעֲלוּ מִמִּצְרָיִם וַיָּבֹאוּ אֶרֶץ כְּנַעַן אֶל־
יַעֲקֹב אֲבִיהֶם׃ 26 וַיַּגִּדוּ לוֹ לֵאמֹר עוֹד יוֹסֵף
חַי וְכִי־הוּא מֹשֵׁל בְּכָל־אֶרֶץ מִצְרָיִם וַיָּפָג
לִבּוֹ כִּי לֹא־הֶאֱמִין לָהֶם׃ 27 וַיְדַבְּרוּ אֵלָיו
אֵת כָּל־דִּבְרֵי יוֹסֵף אֲשֶׁר דִּבֶּר אֲלֵהֶם וַיַּרְא
אֶת־הָעֲגָלוֹת אֲשֶׁר־שָׁלַח יוֹסֵף לָשֵׂאת אֹתוֹ
וַתְּחִי רוּחַ יַעֲקֹב אֲבִיהֶם׃ 28 וַיֹּאמֶר יִשְׂרָאֵל
רַב עוֹד־יוֹסֵף בְּנִי חָי אֵלְכָה וְאֶרְאֶנּוּ בְּטֶרֶם
אָמוּת׃
מו וַיִּסַּע יִשְׂרָאֵל וְכָל־אֲשֶׁר־לוֹ וַיָּבֹא
בְּאֵרָה שָּׁבַע וַיִּזְבַּח זְבָחִים לֵאלֹהֵי אָבִיו
יִצְחָק׃ 2 וַיֹּאמֶר אֱלֹהִים ׀ לְיִשְׂרָאֵל בְּמַרְאֹת

earlier jealousy of the special clothing that he had long ago received from their father, a sign of Jacob's favoritism (37:3–4). Whereas earlier, clothing had divided the brothers against Joseph, here it signifies the reconciliation between them.

### JACOB LEARNS THAT JOSEPH IS ALIVE (45:25–28)

*26–27.* ***When they told him "Joseph is still alive"... his heart froze,... But when they told him all that Joseph had spoken to them... their father Jacob's spirit came alive.*** Biblical narratives do not often describe how characters feel. Here, however, the vivid descriptions let readers see how shocked Jacob is upon discovering that his son Joseph—believed to have died twenty-two years earlier—is actually alive and well, and in a position of high authority and prestige in Egypt.

*28.* ***Israel said, "Enough! My son Joseph is alive! I must go and see him before I die!"*** Jacob's excitement about reuniting with Joseph overshadows all material complications that the prospect of life in Egypt would seem to present. Jacob's emotional outburst might have revived the brothers' jealousy, but we are not told that they express any such feelings.

## *Jacob/Israel Meets Joseph In Egypt* (46:1–34)

At this juncture—as Jacob sets out on his journey to Egypt—the narrative marks the occasion in two ways. The first is a revelation from God. This is the first reported divine communication to Jacob since the death of his wife Rachel more than twenty years before.

The second way that the text marks this moment's significance is with a genealogical list of all those who went down to Egypt with Jacob. Until now, Genesis has described the lineage of the patriarchs in what can be called a "vertical" genealogy that traces inheritance from father to one or more sons (11:27; 25:19; 37:2). In contrast, this unit emphasizes a "horizontal" genealogy that acknowledges the family relationship between Jacob and all of his offspring. (Compare Jacob's adoption and

Jacob!" And he said, "Here I am!" [3][God] said, "I am God, the God of your father; do not be afraid to go down to Egypt, for I will make you a great people there. [4]I Myself will go down with you to Egypt, and I will most surely bring you back up as well; and Joseph will lay his hand upon your eyes."

[5]Jacob then moved on from Beersheba; the sons of Israel lifted Jacob their father, their little ones, and their wives onto the wagons that Pharaoh had sent to carry him. [6]They took their livestock and the possessions they had amassed in the land of Canaan and they came to Egypt—Jacob and all his progeny with him. [7]His sons and his sons' sons were with him, his daughters and his sons' daughters—all his progeny that he brought with him to Egypt.

הַלַּ֔יְלָה וַיֹּ֖אמֶר יַעֲקֹ֣ב ׀ יַעֲקֹ֑ב וַיֹּ֖אמֶר הִנֵּֽנִי׃
3 וַיֹּ֕אמֶר אָנֹכִ֥י הָאֵ֖ל אֱלֹהֵ֣י אָבִ֑יךָ אַל־תִּירָא֙
מֵרְדָ֣ה מִצְרַ֔יְמָה כִּֽי־לְג֥וֹי גָּד֖וֹל אֲשִֽׂימְךָ֥ שָֽׁם׃
4 אָנֹכִ֗י אֵרֵ֤ד עִמְּךָ֙ מִצְרַ֔יְמָה וְאָנֹכִ֖י אַֽעַלְךָ֣
גַם־עָלֹ֑ה וְיוֹסֵ֕ף יָשִׁ֥ית יָד֖וֹ עַל־עֵינֶֽיךָ׃
5 וַיָּ֥קָם יַעֲקֹ֖ב מִבְּאֵ֣ר שָׁ֑בַע וַיִּשְׂא֨וּ בְנֵֽי־
יִשְׂרָאֵ֜ל אֶת־יַעֲקֹ֣ב אֲבִיהֶ֗ם וְאֶת־טַפָּם֙ וְאֶת־
נְשֵׁיהֶ֔ם בָּעֲגָל֕וֹת אֲשֶׁר־שָׁלַ֥ח פַּרְעֹ֖ה לָשֵׂ֥את
אֹתֽוֹ׃ 6 וַיִּקְח֣וּ אֶת־מִקְנֵיהֶ֗ם וְאֶת־רְכוּשָׁם֙
אֲשֶׁ֤ר רָֽכְשׁוּ֙ בְּאֶ֣רֶץ כְּנַ֔עַן וַיָּבֹ֖אוּ מִצְרָ֑יְמָה
יַעֲקֹ֖ב וְכָל־זַרְע֥וֹ אִתּֽוֹ׃ 7 בָּנָ֞יו וּבְנֵ֤י בָנָיו֙ אִתּ֔וֹ
בְּנֹתָ֛יו וּבְנ֥וֹת בָּנָ֖יו וְכָל־זַרְע֑וֹ הֵבִ֥יא אִתּ֖וֹ
מִצְרָֽיְמָה׃ ס

blessing of Ephraim and Manasseh in Genesis 48.) This shift in how the genealogy is established coincides with the conclusion of the ancestors' time in Canaan. The rest of the Torah will concern the people of Israel in circumstances outside their Promised Land.

### PREPARATIONS (46:1–7)

*1. Israel.* This is the name that was given to Jacob in 32:29 and 35:10. Jacob/Israel is an example of an eponym—a group's taking its name from (or: later attributing its name to) an individual. The shift here from Jacob (one man) to Israel (representing the people of God) may be occasioned by the fact that this is the only theophany—direct appearance of God—in the stories of Joseph.

***offered sacrifices.*** Eager though he is to see Joseph, Jacob nevertheless takes time to express gratitude and attend to his relationship with God.

*3. [God] said, "I am God, the God of your father."* Here is a reference to family religion, linking one generation of believers to the next. God's self-revelation emphasizes the overarching link between earlier stories of Jacob's ancestors and his own experiences of the divine.

***"do not be afraid to go down to Egypt."*** Only after God assures Jacob and blesses him does Jacob move on from Beersheba. This scene further reinforces the importance of God in Jacob's life.

*4. "Joseph will lay his hand upon your eyes."* A reference to the practice of a family member's closing the eyes of someone who has just died. God thereby promises Jacob that his favorite son not only will be present when he expires but also will properly care for his corpse. The latter was a matter of abiding concern in the Bible and ancient Near East. (On Israelite burial practices, see *Va-y'chi*, Another View, p. 297.)

***7. His sons and his sons' sons were with him, his daughters and his sons' daughters.*** The birth of only one daughter of Jacob—Dinah—is mentioned in Genesis. (She first appears in 30:21; see Genesis 34 for her story.) Both 37:35 and this verse indicate that Jacob had more than one daughter, but we have no other details about them apart from these references in passing. Likewise, 46:15 mentions "daughters" yet that passage identifies only Dinah.

<sup>8</sup>These are the names of Israel's sons who came to Egypt, Jacob and his sons: Jacob's first-born Reuben, <sup>9</sup>and Reuben's children Enoch, Pallu, Hezron, and Carmi. <sup>10</sup>Simeon's children were Jemuel, Jamin, Ohad, Jachin, Zohar, and Saul the son of a Canaanite woman; <sup>11</sup>Levi's children were Gershon, Kohath, and Merari; <sup>12</sup>Judah's children were Er, Onan, Shelah, Perez, and Zerah (but Er and Onan had died in the land of Canaan, and the sons of Perez were Hezron and Hamul); <sup>13</sup>Issachar's children were Tola, Puvah, Iob, and Shimron; <sup>14</sup>Zebulun's children were Sered, Elon, and Jahleel. <sup>15</sup>These were Leah's sons whom she bore to Jacob in Paddan Aram, along with Dinah his daughter. His sons and daughters were 33 persons in all, male and female.

<sup>16</sup>Gad's children were Ziphion, Haggi, Shuni, Ezbon, Eri, Arodi, and Areli. <sup>17</sup>Asher's sons were Imnah, Ishvah, Ishvi, and Beriah, and their sister Serah. Beriah's children were Heber and Malchiel.

‎8 וְאֵ֗לֶּה שְׁמ֤וֹת בְּנֵֽי־יִשְׂרָאֵל֙ הַבָּאִ֣ים מִצְרַ֔יְמָה יַעֲקֹ֖ב וּבָנָ֑יו בְּכֹ֥ר יַעֲקֹ֖ב רְאוּבֵֽן: ‎9 וּבְנֵ֖י רְאוּבֵ֑ן חֲנ֥וֹךְ וּפַלּ֖וּא וְחֶצְרֹ֥ן וְכַרְמִֽי: ‎10 וּבְנֵ֣י שִׁמְע֗וֹן יְמוּאֵ֧ל וְיָמִ֛ין וְאֹ֖הַד וְיָכִ֣ין וְצֹ֑חַר וְשָׁא֖וּל בֶּן־הַֽכְּנַעֲנִֽית: ‎11 וּבְנֵ֖י לֵוִ֑י גֵּרְשׁ֕וֹן קְהָ֖ת וּמְרָרִֽי: ‎12 וּבְנֵ֣י יְהוּדָ֗ה עֵ֤ר וְאוֹנָן֙ וְשֵׁלָ֣ה וָפֶ֔רֶץ וָזָ֑רַח וַיָּ֨מָת עֵ֤ר וְאוֹנָן֙ בְּאֶ֣רֶץ כְּנַ֔עַן וַיִּהְי֥וּ בְנֵי־פֶ֖רֶץ חֶצְרֹ֥ן וְחָמֽוּל: ‎13 וּבְנֵ֖י יִשָׂשכָ֑ר תּוֹלָ֥ע וּפֻוָּ֖ה וְי֥וֹב וְשִׁמְרֹֽן: ‎14 וּבְנֵ֖י זְבֻל֑וּן סֶ֥רֶד וְאֵל֖וֹן וְיַחְלְאֵֽל: ‎15 אֵ֣לֶּה | בְּנֵ֣י לֵאָ֗ה אֲשֶׁ֨ר יָֽלְדָ֤ה לְיַעֲקֹב֙ בְּפַדַּ֣ן אֲרָ֔ם וְאֵ֖ת דִּינָ֣ה בִתּ֑וֹ כָּל־נֶ֧פֶשׁ בָּנָ֛יו וּבְנוֹתָ֖יו שְׁלֹשִׁ֥ים וְשָׁלֹֽשׁ: ‎16 וּבְנֵ֣י גָ֔ד צִפְי֥וֹן וְחַגִּ֖י שׁוּנִ֣י וְאֶצְבֹּ֑ן עֵרִ֥י וַֽאֲרוֹדִ֖י וְאַרְאֵלִֽי: ‎17 וּבְנֵ֣י אָשֵׁ֗ר יִמְנָ֧ה וְיִשְׁוָ֛ה וְיִשְׁוִ֥י וּבְרִיעָ֖ה וְשֶׂ֣רַח אֲחֹתָ֑ם וּבְנֵ֣י בְרִיעָ֔ה

### THE SEVENTY MEMBERS OF JACOB'S FAMILY WHO COME TO EGYPT (46:8–27)

These verses are especially important because they make reference to the women who comprise the family of Jacob. This section reiterates that the totality of Jacob's family includes both women and men borne to Jacob by four different women. The members of the family are listed in relationship to the four women: Leah, Zilpah, Rachel, and Bilhah. The number of *banim* ("sons" or "children") attributed to each of the women includes not only the individuals they bore but also their grandchildren.

**8. *These are the names.*** The same words open the book of Exodus, which begins with a list of only the twelve sons of Israel/Jacob.

**10. *son of a Canaanite woman.*** Simeon's youngest son Saul is identified in the same unusual way in Exodus 6:15. Historically, the tribe of Simeon was later absorbed by the tribe of Judah. Not only Simeon married a Canaanite woman but also Judah (Genesis 38:2), reflecting both territorial expansion by these tribes and intermarriage with surrounding peoples.

**15. *These were Leah's sons.*** Leah's children are listed first, but she is not identified as a wife; compare v. 19.

**_along with Dinah his daughter._** On Dinah, see at v. 7. It may be significant that she is listed here as *Jacob's* daughter; she appeared in 34:1 as *Leah's* daughter.

**17. *their sister Serah.*** Zilpah, one of Jacob's wives, had borne him two sons, Gad and Asher; the latter became the father of four sons and one daughter, Serah. Serah is the only daughter of any of Jacob's sons mentioned in this genealogy of those who went to Egypt with Jacob. Serah's name appears again in Numbers 26:46—where she seems to be counted also among those leaving Egypt some

18These were Zilpah's children, whom Laban had
given to Leah his daughter. She bore these to Jacob
—16 persons.
19The sons of Jacob's wife Rachel were Joseph
and Benjamin. 20Born to Joseph in the land of
Egypt, whom Asenath daughter of Potiphera priest
of On bore to him, were Manasseh and Ephraim.
21Benjamin's children were Bela, Becher, Ashbel,
Gera, Naaman, Ehi, Rosh, Muppim, Huppim, and
Ard. 22These were Rachel's children who were born
to Jacob—14 persons in all.
23Dan's son was Hushim. 24Naphtali's sons
were Jahzeel, Guni, Jezer, and Shillem. 25These
were the children of Bilhah, whom Laban had
given to Rachel his daughter. She bore these to
Jacob—7 persons.
26All the people who came with Jacob to Egypt
—who came forth from his loins—apart from
the wives of Jacob's sons—were 66 people in all.
27And the sons of Joseph born to him in Egypt were

חֶבֶר וּמַלְכִּיאֵל׃ 18 אֵלֶּה בְּנֵי זִלְפָּה אֲשֶׁר־
נָתַן לָבָן לְלֵאָה בִתּוֹ וַתֵּלֶד אֶת־אֵלֶּה
לְיַעֲקֹב שֵׁשׁ עֶשְׂרֵה נָפֶשׁ׃
19 בְּנֵי רָחֵל אֵשֶׁת יַעֲקֹב יוֹסֵף וּבִנְיָמִן׃
20 וַיִּוָּלֵד לְיוֹסֵף בְּאֶרֶץ מִצְרַיִם אֲשֶׁר יָלְדָה־
לּוֹ אָסְנַת בַּת־פּוֹטִי פֶרַע כֹּהֵן אֹן אֶת־מְנַשֶּׁה
וְאֶת־אֶפְרָיִם׃ 21 וּבְנֵי בִנְיָמִן בֶּלַע וָבֶכֶר
וְאַשְׁבֵּל גֵּרָא וְנַעֲמָן אֵחִי וָרֹאשׁ מֻפִּים
וְחֻפִּים וָאָרְדְּ׃ 22 אֵלֶּה בְּנֵי רָחֵל אֲשֶׁר יֻלַּד
לְיַעֲקֹב כָּל־נֶפֶשׁ אַרְבָּעָה עָשָׂר׃
23 וּבְנֵי־דָן חֻשִׁים׃ 24 וּבְנֵי נַפְתָּלִי יַחְצְאֵל
וְגוּנִי וְיֵצֶר וְשִׁלֵּם׃ 25 אֵלֶּה בְּנֵי בִלְהָה
אֲשֶׁר־נָתַן לָבָן לְרָחֵל בִּתּוֹ וַתֵּלֶד אֶת־אֵלֶּה
לְיַעֲקֹב כָּל־נֶפֶשׁ שִׁבְעָה׃
26 כָּל־הַנֶּפֶשׁ הַבָּאָה לְיַעֲקֹב מִצְרַיְמָה יֹצְאֵי
יְרֵכוֹ מִלְּבַד נְשֵׁי בְנֵי־יַעֲקֹב כָּל־נֶפֶשׁ שִׁשִּׁים
וָשֵׁשׁ׃ 27 וּבְנֵי יוֹסֵף אֲשֶׁר־יֻלַּד־לוֹ בְמִצְרַיִם

400 years later—and in I Chronicles 7:30. [The Bible also mentions another of Jacob's granddaughters, Jochebed daughter of Levi; she is born in Egypt (Exodus 6:16–20; Numbers 26:59). —*Ed.*]

*18. **These were Zilpah's children, whom Laban had given to Leah his daughter. She bore these to Jacob.*** The sons are not reckoned as Leah's children but rather Zilpah's, her handmaid, even though Leah had named them and claimed them as her own (30:9–13). Despite the ostensibly lower status of the handmaids, their sons are acknowledged as equal members of the family—as "Israel's sons" (46:8). In this regard, it appears that the status of Jacob's secondary wives, Zilpah and Bilhah, is comparable to the status of his primary wives, Leah and Rachel.

*19. **Jacob's wife Rachel.*** Only she is explicitly identified as "Jacob's wife." And of the other wives, only her name appears twice (see v. 22), framing the list of her descendants.

*25. **These were the children of Bilhah, whom Laban had given to Rachel his daughter.*** These sons are not reckoned as Rachel's children but rather Bilhah's, even though Rachel had named them and claimed them as her own (30:3–8). As with Zilpah's children (see at v. 18), the handmaids' sons are acknowledged as equal members of the family.

*20. **whom Asenath daughter of Potiphera priest of On bore him.*** This reference repeats information first mentioned in 41:50. This is the Bible's third and final mention of Asenath; see also at 41:45. (The text does not censure Joseph for having married outside the kinship group, namely, for having an exogamous marriage.) Asenath is the only wife of the second generation to be named, perhaps a sign of her distinctive importance: Jacob's eventual adoption of Ephraim and Manasseh (48:5) will make her the mother of two tribes—by proxy, a seventh matriarch. Just as the other sons of Jacob are listed according to their mothers, so too here.

2 individuals; the members of Jacob's family who came to Egypt were 70 in all.

[28]Judah he sent ahead of him to Joseph, to show him the way to Goshen; so they came to the region of Goshen. [29]Joseph harnessed his chariot and went up to meet his father Israel in Goshen; he presented himself to him and threw himself on his neck, weeping all the time. [30]Israel said to Joseph, "Now that I've seen your face—for you're still alive!—I can die at last."

[31]Joseph said to his brothers and to his father's household, "I'm going to go up and tell Pharaoh; I will say to him: 'My brothers and my father's household who were in the land of Canaan have come to me. [32]The men are shepherds; in fact they are breeders of livestock, and they have brought their flocks and their herds and all that they own.' [33]Therefore, when Pharaoh sends for you and asks, 'What do you do?' [34]say: 'Your servants have been breeding livestock from youth onwards to now, both our households and our fathers' households'—in order that you may live in the region of Goshen; for Egyptians find shepherds abhorrent."

נֶפֶשׁ שְׁנָיִם כָּל־הַנֶּפֶשׁ לְבֵית־יַעֲקֹב הַבָּאָה
מִצְרַיְמָה שִׁבְעִים׃ ס

28 וְאֶת־יְהוּדָה שָׁלַח לְפָנָיו אֶל־יוֹסֵף
לְהוֹרֹת לְפָנָיו גֹּשְׁנָה וַיָּבֹאוּ אַרְצָה גֹּשֶׁן׃
29 וַיֶּאְסֹר יוֹסֵף מֶרְכַּבְתּוֹ וַיַּעַל לִקְרַאת־
יִשְׂרָאֵל אָבִיו גֹּשְׁנָה וַיֵּרָא אֵלָיו וַיִּפֹּל עַל־
צַוָּארָיו וַיֵּבְךְּ עַל־צַוָּארָיו עוֹד׃ 30 וַיֹּאמֶר
יִשְׂרָאֵל אֶל־יוֹסֵף אָמוּתָה הַפָּעַם אַחֲרֵי
רְאוֹתִי אֶת־פָּנֶיךָ כִּי עוֹדְךָ חָי׃
31 וַיֹּאמֶר יוֹסֵף אֶל־אֶחָיו וְאֶל־בֵּית אָבִיו
אֶעֱלֶה וְאַגִּידָה לְפַרְעֹה וְאֹמְרָה אֵלָיו אַחַי
וּבֵית־אָבִי אֲשֶׁר בְּאֶרֶץ־כְּנַעַן בָּאוּ אֵלָי׃
32 וְהָאֲנָשִׁים רֹעֵי צֹאן כִּי־אַנְשֵׁי מִקְנֶה הָיוּ
וְצֹאנָם וּבְקָרָם וְכָל־אֲשֶׁר לָהֶם הֵבִיאוּ׃
33 וְהָיָה כִּי־יִקְרָא לָכֶם פַּרְעֹה וְאָמַר מַה־
מַּעֲשֵׂיכֶם׃ 34 וַאֲמַרְתֶּם אַנְשֵׁי מִקְנֶה הָיוּ
עֲבָדֶיךָ מִנְּעוּרֵינוּ וְעַד־עַתָּה גַּם־אֲנַחְנוּ גַּם־
אֲבֹתֵינוּ בַּעֲבוּר תֵּשְׁבוּ בְּאֶרֶץ גֹּשֶׁן כִּי־
תוֹעֲבַת מִצְרַיִם כָּל־רֹעֵה צֹאן׃

*27.* *70 in all.* Seventy is a typological or symbolic number (a multiple of seven, equated with the seven days of Creation). Thus the text emphasizes the complete movement of the ancestral family from the Promised Land to Egypt, as the next step in their journey as God's chosen people.

JACOB AND HIS SONS REUNITE (46:28–34)

*29.* *weeping all the time.* Just as earlier Joseph wept over seeing his brothers (see at 45:14–15), he now weeps at being reunited with his father.

*30.* *Israel said to Joseph, "Now . . . I can die at last."* The poignancy of the reunion is stressed by Jacob's statement that he can now die a happy man (in contrast to going down to Sheol in grief; see at 42:38, 44:29), having seen Joseph alive again. One thinks here of the many tearful reunion scenes in our own day of family members reunited after being separated from each other for decades.

*31–34.* Joseph quickly becomes businesslike in telling his father how he and the brothers ought to respond when they are presented before Pharaoh.

*34.* *"Egyptians find shepherds abhorrent."* This statement is not supported by Egyptian records; moreover, even in the biblical account, Pharaoh has his own herds (see 47:6). Possibly it refers only to non-Egyptian shepherds. (Similarly, using the same Hebrew term as here, we are told that the Egyptians find it an "abomination" to eat together with Hebrews; 43:32.) The point seems to be that Jacob and his family will be allowed to live in a separate region from the Egyptian shepherds and maintain their own cultural identity.

47 Joseph then went and told Pharaoh, saying, "My father, my brothers, their flocks, their herds, and all that they own have arrived from the land of Canaan, and now they're in the region of Goshen." 2Out of all his brothers he picked five men and presented them before Pharaoh. 3When Pharaoh said to his brothers, "What do you do?" they said to Pharaoh, "Your servants are shepherds, both our households and our fathers' households." 4They went on to say to Pharaoh, "We have come to stay in the land because there is no pasture for your servants' flocks, for the famine is oppressive in the land of Canaan; now we ask you to let your servants settle in the region of Goshen." 5Pharaoh then said to Joseph, "[Now that] your father and brothers have reached you, 6the land of Egypt is before you—settle your father and brothers in the best part of the land. Let them settle in the region of Goshen; and if you know of any able men among them, make them overseers of my livestock."

7Joseph then brought his father Jacob and stood him before Pharaoh, and Jacob greeted Pharaoh. 8Pharaoh said to Jacob, "How many years have you

מז וַיָּבֹא יוֹסֵף וַיַּגֵּד לְפַרְעֹה וַיֹּאמֶר אָבִי
וְאַחַי וְצֹאנָם וּבְקָרָם וְכָל־אֲשֶׁר לָהֶם בָּאוּ
מֵאֶרֶץ כְּנָעַן וְהִנָּם בְּאֶרֶץ גֹּשֶׁן׃ 2 וּמִקְצֵה
אֶחָיו לָקַח חֲמִשָּׁה אֲנָשִׁים וַיַּצִּגֵם לִפְנֵי
פַרְעֹה׃ 3 וַיֹּאמֶר פַּרְעֹה אֶל־אֶחָיו מַה־
מַּעֲשֵׂיכֶם וַיֹּאמְרוּ אֶל־פַּרְעֹה רֹעֵה צֹאן
עֲבָדֶיךָ גַּם־אֲנַחְנוּ גַּם־אֲבוֹתֵינוּ׃ 4 וַיֹּאמְרוּ
אֶל־פַּרְעֹה לָגוּר בָּאָרֶץ בָּאנוּ כִּי־אֵין מִרְעֶה
לַצֹּאן אֲשֶׁר לַעֲבָדֶיךָ כִּי־כָבֵד הָרָעָב בְּאֶרֶץ
כְּנָעַן וְעַתָּה יֵשְׁבוּ־נָא עֲבָדֶיךָ בְּאֶרֶץ גֹּשֶׁן׃
5 וַיֹּאמֶר פַּרְעֹה אֶל־יוֹסֵף לֵאמֹר אָבִיךָ
וְאַחֶיךָ בָּאוּ אֵלֶיךָ׃ 6 אֶרֶץ מִצְרַיִם לְפָנֶיךָ
הִוא בְּמֵיטַב הָאָרֶץ הוֹשֵׁב אֶת־אָבִיךָ
וְאֶת־אַחֶיךָ יֵשְׁבוּ בְּאֶרֶץ גֹּשֶׁן וְאִם־יָדַעְתָּ
וְיֶשׁ־בָּם אַנְשֵׁי־חַיִל וְשַׂמְתָּם שָׂרֵי מִקְנֶה
עַל־אֲשֶׁר־לִי׃
7 וַיָּבֵא יוֹסֵף אֶת־יַעֲקֹב אָבִיו וַיַּעֲמִדֵהוּ לִפְנֵי
פַרְעֹה וַיְבָרֶךְ יַעֲקֹב אֶת־פַּרְעֹה׃ 8 וַיֹּאמֶר
פַּרְעֹה אֶל־יַעֲקֹב כַּמָּה יְמֵי שְׁנֵי חַיֶּיךָ׃

## *Joseph and Jacob Meet with Pharaoh* (47:1–10)

During his long years in Egypt and in service to the pharaoh, Joseph has become a master of court diplomacy. These verses bring out the split nature of Joseph's identity: he is aware of Egyptian court demeanor but also tied to his family of livestock herders. Throughout his time in Egypt, Joseph defies the "macho" stereotype; he uses diplomacy, rather than force, to raise his status in the Egyptian court. This is the characteristic maneuver of a minority people living in a majority culture; one thinks also of the biblical story of Esther and her dealings in the Persian court. However, standing in contrast to Joseph's subtle maneuvering is the later behavior of Moses, who dramatically cut his youthful ties with Pharaoh's palace when he "turned this way and that and, seeing no one about, he struck down the Egyptian and he hid him in the sand" (Exodus 2:12).

*2–4.* The text suggests a protocol that separates the pharaoh from the foreign brothers who are both ethnically and socially of a distinct status from the head of Egypt.

*6. "settle . . . in the best part of the land."* This instruction—in fulfillment of what Pharaoh said in 45:18—signals the success of the audience before the pharaoh.

*7. greeted.* Heb. *va-y'varech*, which can also be translated as "blessed" (see at v. 10).

*8. Pharaoh said to Jacob.* Possibly as a sign of respect both for Jacob's advanced age and for Joseph's authority within Egypt, Pharaoh speaks more directly to the aged father than to Joseph's brothers.

lived?” 9And Jacob said to Pharaoh, “The span of
the years of my lifetime has been 130; few and miserable have been the days of the years of my life.
They have not attained to the length of the days
of the years of my fathers when they were alive.”
10Jacob then gave Pharaoh a parting blessing, and
he left Pharaoh’s presence.

11Joseph settled his father and his brothers; he
gave them a holding in the land of Egypt, in the
best part of the land, in the region of Rameses, as
Pharaoh had commanded. 12Joseph also provided
food for his father and his brothers and all his
father’s household, according to the number of
their children.

13[At this time] no food was to be had in the

9 וַיֹּאמֶר יַעֲקֹב אֶל־פַּרְעֹה יְמֵי שְׁנֵי מְגוּרַי
שְׁלֹשִׁים וּמְאַת שָׁנָה מְעַט וְרָעִים הָיוּ יְמֵי
שְׁנֵי חַיַּי וְלֹא הִשִּׂיגוּ אֶת־יְמֵי שְׁנֵי חַיֵּי
אֲבֹתַי בִּימֵי מְגוּרֵיהֶם׃ 10 וַיְבָרֶךְ יַעֲקֹב אֶת־
פַּרְעֹה וַיֵּצֵא מִלִּפְנֵי פַרְעֹה׃
11 וַיּוֹשֵׁב יוֹסֵף אֶת־אָבִיו וְאֶת־אֶחָיו וַיִּתֵּן
לָהֶם אֲחֻזָּה בְּאֶרֶץ מִצְרַיִם בְּמֵיטַב הָאָרֶץ
בְּאֶרֶץ רַעְמְסֵס כַּאֲשֶׁר צִוָּה פַרְעֹה׃
12 וַיְכַלְכֵּל יוֹסֵף אֶת־אָבִיו וְאֶת־אֶחָיו וְאֵת
כָּל־בֵּית אָבִיו לֶחֶם לְפִי הַטָּף׃
13 וְלֶחֶם אֵין בְּכָל־הָאָרֶץ כִּי־כָבֵד הָרָעָב

*9.* Jacob responds to Pharaoh’s question with more than simple facts such as his age; he focuses on the sorrow in his life and acknowledges that his age does not compare with the longevity of his ancestors. Pharaoh’s request for personal information about Jacob establishes a bond between the two men who have in common that Joseph has been a central, life-sustaining figure for each of them.

***“fathers.”*** Heb. *avot*, which can mean “ancestors” (including females, as in v. 30, below), although here it seems that Jacob is intending only the male family heads: Terah died at 205, Abraham at 175, and Isaac at 180. He is, after all, older than his grandmother Sarah, who died at the age of 127. (The Bible does not disclose the longevity of the other matriarchs.)

***10. parting blessing.*** Heb. *va-y’varech*; compare v. 7. | The bond between the two elders becomes even clearer when Jacob blesses Pharaoh before departing from his presence. Jacob’s blessing is rooted in the blessing of life that Pharaoh made possible for Joseph’s family. Normally it would go without saying that one utters a benevolent wish when departing from a favorable audience before a monarch. What is noteworthy here is that such an utterance is mentioned—and described as a “blessing,” which in the Torah has an overtone of divine favor. Compare Bathsheba’s exit from an audience with her husband, King David, in I Kings 1:31.

## *Further Details Regarding Joseph and Family* (47:11–27)

### JOSEPH SETTLES HIS FATHER’S HOUSEHOLD IN EGYPT (47:11–12)

***11. in the region of Rameses.*** Up until this point, the text has repeatedly (eight times) referred to the place where Jacob would live with his family as “Goshen” (see also v. 27, below). A place named Rameses is mentioned also in Exodus 12:37 and Numbers 33:3, 5; it is identified as a settlement in Exodus 1:11. This is one of the many biblical passages where a merging of different stories may be responsible for the text.

### JOSEPH DEALS WITH THE FAMINE IN EGYPT (47:13–26)

The text has been focused on the reconciliation and reunion of the family. Now the narrator must remind the reader that despite these happy circum-

entire land, for the famine bore down very heavily. The land of Egypt and the land of Canaan languished on account of the famine. [14]Joseph now collected all the silver found in the lands of Egypt and Canaan as payment for the grain that the people were buying, and Joseph brought that silver into Pharaoh's palace. [15]When the silver in the lands of Egypt and Canaan was spent, all Egypt flocked to Joseph, saying, "Let us have food—why should we drop dead in front of you because the silver is exhausted?" [16]Joseph replied, "Bring your livestock and I will give it to you in exchange for your livestock, if the silver is exhausted." [17]They therefore brought their livestock to Joseph, and Joseph gave them food in exchange for horses, holdings of sheep and cattle, and asses; that year he kept them alive with food in exchange for all their livestock.

[18]That year ended, and they approached him in the following year and said to him, "We will not hide from my lord that the silver is spent and our animal holdings belong to my lord—there's nothing left before my lord but our bodies and our soil. [19]Why should we die before your eyes, both we and our soil? Buy us and our soil in exchange for food; we and our soil will be slaves to Pharaoh. Distribute seed, so we can live and not die, so the land is not deserted!" [20]Joseph then bought all the land in Egypt for Pharaoh, for each Egyptian had sold his field, because the famine had overwhelmed them. Thus the land came into Pharaoh's possession. [21]And thus he made serfs of the people from one end of the Egyptian border to the other. [22]Only the land belonging to the priests did he not buy, for the

מְאֹד וַתֵּ֫לַהּ אֶ֣רֶץ מִצְרַ֫יִם וְאֶ֣רֶץ כְּנַ֫עַן מִפְּנֵ֖י הָרָעָֽב: [14] וַיְלַקֵּ֣ט יוֹסֵף֮ אֶת־כָּל־הַכֶּ֣סֶף הַנִּמְצָ֣א בְאֶֽרֶץ־מִצְרַ֫יִם֮ וּבְאֶ֣רֶץ כְּנַ֫עַן֒ בַּשֶּׁ֖בֶר אֲשֶׁר־הֵ֣ם שֹֽׁבְרִ֑ים וַיָּבֵ֥א יוֹסֵ֛ף אֶת־הַכֶּ֖סֶף בֵּ֥יתָה פַרְעֹֽה: [15] וַיִּתֹּ֣ם הַכֶּ֗סֶף מֵאֶ֤רֶץ מִצְרַ֫יִם֙ וּמֵאֶ֣רֶץ כְּנַ֫עַן֒ וַיָּבֹ֩אוּ֩ כָל־מִצְרַ֜יִם אֶל־יוֹסֵ֣ף לֵאמֹר֙ הָֽבָה־לָּ֣נוּ לֶ֔חֶם וְלָ֥מָּה נָמ֖וּת נֶגְדֶּ֑ךָ כִּ֥י אָפֵ֖ס כָּֽסֶף: [16] וַיֹּ֤אמֶר יוֹסֵף֙ הָב֣וּ מִקְנֵיכֶ֔ם וְאֶתְּנָ֥ה לָכֶ֖ם בְּמִקְנֵיכֶ֑ם אִם־אָפֵ֖ס כָּֽסֶף: [17] וַיָּבִ֣יאוּ אֶת־מִקְנֵיהֶם֮ אֶל־יוֹסֵף֒ וַיִּתֵּ֣ן לָהֶ֣ם יוֹסֵ֣ף לֶ֗חֶם בַּסּוּסִ֤ים וּבְמִקְנֵ֤ה הַצֹּאן֙ וּבְמִקְנֵ֣ה הַבָּקָ֖ר וּבַֽחֲמֹרִ֑ים וַיְנַֽהֲלֵ֤ם בַּלֶּ֨חֶם֙ בְּכָל־מִקְנֵהֶ֔ם בַּשָּׁנָ֖ה הַהִֽוא:

[18] וַתִּתֹּם֮ הַשָּׁנָ֣ה הַהִוא֒ וַיָּבֹ֨אוּ אֵלָ֜יו בַּשָּׁנָ֣ה הַשֵּׁנִ֗ית וַיֹּ֤אמְרוּ לוֹ֙ לֹֽא־נְכַחֵ֣ד מֵֽאֲדֹנִ֔י כִּ֚י אִם־תַּ֣ם הַכֶּ֔סֶף וּמִקְנֵ֥ה הַבְּהֵמָ֖ה אֶל־אֲדֹנִ֑י לֹ֤א נִשְׁאַר֙ לִפְנֵ֣י אֲדֹנִ֔י בִּלְתִּ֥י אִם־גְּוִיָּתֵ֖נוּ וְאַדְמָתֵֽנוּ: [19] לָ֧מָּה נָמ֣וּת לְעֵינֶ֗יךָ גַּם־אֲנַ֫חְנוּ֙ גַּ֣ם אַדְמָתֵ֔נוּ קְנֵֽה־אֹתָ֥נוּ וְאֶת־אַדְמָתֵ֖נוּ בַּלָּ֑חֶם וְנִֽהְיֶ֞ה אֲנַ֤חְנוּ וְאַדְמָתֵ֨נוּ֙ עֲבָדִ֣ים לְפַרְעֹ֔ה וְתֶן־זֶ֗רַע וְנִֽחְיֶה֙ וְלֹ֣א נָמ֔וּת וְהָֽאֲדָמָ֖ה לֹ֥א תֵשָֽׁם: [20] וַיִּ֣קֶן יוֹסֵ֞ף אֶת־כָּל־אַדְמַ֤ת מִצְרַ֨יִם֙ לְפַרְעֹ֔ה כִּֽי־מָֽכְר֤וּ מִצְרַ֨יִם֙ אִ֣ישׁ שָׂדֵ֔הוּ כִּֽי־חָזַ֥ק עֲלֵהֶ֖ם הָרָעָ֑ב וַתְּהִ֥י הָאָ֖רֶץ לְפַרְעֹֽה: [21] וְאֶ֨ת־הָעָ֔ם הֶֽעֱבִ֥יר אֹת֖וֹ לֶֽעָרִ֑ים מִקְצֵ֥ה גְבֽוּל־מִצְרַ֖יִם וְעַד־קָצֵֽהוּ: [22] רַ֛ק אַדְמַ֥ת הַכֹּֽהֲנִ֖ים לֹ֣א קָנָ֑ה כִּ֣י חֹק֩ לַכֹּֽהֲנִ֨ים מֵאֵ֣ת פַּרְעֹ֗ה וְאָֽכְל֤וּ אֶת־חֻקָּם֙

· · · · · · · · · · · · · · · · · · · · · · · ·

stances, the reality of famine still plagues Egypt. This serves as a contrasting situation to that of Jacob's family, which is explicitly said to be given food by Joseph (v. 12). Due to the need to preserve human life, the Egyptian people first sell their grain, then their livestock, and finally both their land and themselves to the royal court.

*14.* The reminder of the famine allows the story to shift back to Joseph's role in Egypt as the one with a plan to avert death when the famine hits.

*20–21.* Joseph's authority as spokesperson for the Egyptian court is manifested when he buys all the land from the impoverished Egyptian population and accepts their servitude.

priests had an allotment from Pharaoh, and they ate
their allotted portion that Pharaoh had given them;
they therefore did not sell their land.
23Joseph then said to the people, "See, now that
I've bought you and your land for Pharaoh, here
is seed for you—sow the land. 24When harvest
comes, you must give Pharaoh a fifth, and the other
four portions will be yours for seeding the field and
to be food for you and your households, and for
your little ones to eat." 25And they said, "You have
given us life! May we find favor in my lord's sight
and be serfs to Pharaoh!" 26Joseph made this a law
to this day for Egypt's soil—one-fifth is Pharaoh's;
the priests' land alone did not become Pharaoh's.
27Israel thus settled in the land of Egypt, in the
region of Goshen. They struck roots in it, were
fruitful and multiplied greatly.

אֲשֶׁר נָתַן לָהֶם פַּרְעֹה עַל־כֵּן לֹא מָכְרוּ
אֶת־אַדְמָתָם׃
23 וַיֹּאמֶר יוֹסֵף אֶל־הָעָם הֵן קָנִיתִי אֶתְכֶם
הַיּוֹם וְאֶת־אַדְמַתְכֶם לְפַרְעֹה הֵא־לָכֶם זֶרַע
וּזְרַעְתֶּם אֶת־הָאֲדָמָה׃ 24 וְהָיָה בַּתְּבוּאֹת
וּנְתַתֶּם חֲמִישִׁית לְפַרְעֹה וְאַרְבַּע הַיָּדֹת
יִהְיֶה לָכֶם לְזֶרַע הַשָּׂדֶה וּלְאָכְלְכֶם וְלַאֲשֶׁר
בְּבָתֵּיכֶם וְלֶאֱכֹל לְטַפְּכֶם׃ 25 וַיֹּאמְרוּ
הֶחֱיִתָנוּ נִמְצָא־חֵן בְּעֵינֵי אֲדֹנִי וְהָיִינוּ
עֲבָדִים לְפַרְעֹה׃ 26 וַיָּשֶׂם אֹתָהּ יוֹסֵף לְחֹק
עַד־הַיּוֹם הַזֶּה עַל־אַדְמַת מִצְרַיִם לְפַרְעֹה
לַחֹמֶשׁ רַק אַדְמַת הַכֹּהֲנִים לְבַדָּם לֹא
הָיְתָה לְפַרְעֹה׃
27 וַיֵּשֶׁב יִשְׂרָאֵל בְּאֶרֶץ מִצְרַיִם בְּאֶרֶץ גֹּשֶׁן
וַיֵּאָחֲזוּ בָהּ וַיִּפְרוּ וַיִּרְבּוּ מְאֹד׃

## CONCLUSION: ISRAEL/JACOB PROSPERS IN EGYPT (47:27)

The parashah concludes by shifting attention back to the prosperity of Jacob in Egypt and the fruitfulness of the family line there.

*27. Israel thus settled.* By referring to the thriving of "Israel" rather than the individual Jacob, the text emphasizes that what was once a family of brothers (and sisters) and their father (and their mothers) has grown into a nation. (Compare at 46:1.) Both God's promise to Abraham in 12:2 ("I will make of you a great nation") and the blessing bestowed upon Rebekah in 24:60 ("Sister, may you become thousands of myriads") have begun to be fulfilled.

*—Naomi Steinberg*

# Another View

THIS PARASHAH DESCRIBES the successful deliverance of the extended family of Jacob from hunger in Canaan to prosperity in Egypt and the emergence of the tribal arrangement of the nation of Israel out of Jacob's twelve sons. The circumstances that enable the physical and social survival of the family are described in some detail. The physical survival of the family is made possible by the reconciliation of Joseph and his brothers—which leads to a reunion between Joseph and his father. Yet the family's renewed solidarity and cohesiveness does not include any of its female members. Thus for example, Dinah, whose rape and rescue by her brothers is described in some detail in Genesis 34, was omitted from the list of Jacob's offspring already in *parashat Vayishlach* (35:23–29).

Our parashah, which gives us insight into the emotional state of Jacob, Joseph, and his brothers, offers us no information about the emotional state of Dinah, the only daughter and sister to be explicitly mentioned here (46:15)—and no story of rehabilitation, reconciliation, nor restitution for her. Eliminated from the tribal list—whether by virtue of her gender, her rape, or association with a foreigner—Jacob's daughter is thereby punished in a way that his sons are not. Note that Joseph has two sons by Asenath, the daughter of the Egyptian priest Potiphera, and is not censored in any way by the narrator.

The detailed genealogical list in our parashah (46:8–27) makes only brief references to Rachel, Leah, Bilhah, and Zilpah—Jacob's four wives. To be sure,

*Women appear here as relatives of significant fathers, husbands, and sons.*

Rachel's special status is echoed somewhat in 44:20 and 27, and Asher's daughter Serah is mentioned by name in 46:17, but neither mothers nor daughters appear as significant names in the family or tribal genealogies. (On women in lineages, see also at 6:1, 6:10; 10:1; 17:19; 22:20–24.) Similarly, barely any information is offered at all about Asenath, Joseph's wife and the mother of Manasseh and Ephraim. Joseph fathers two tribes in the nation of Israel. In other words, women appear in our parashah as relatives of significant fathers, husbands, and sons, or as nameless relatives as in "your wives" (45:19) or "their wives" (46:5).

—*Esther Fuchs*

# Post-biblical Interpretations

***"give your servant a hearing"*** (44:18). In the Hebrew, what Judah literally asks is to speak a word in Joseph's ears. Midrash *B'reishit Rabbah* 93.6 understands this locution as implying that Judah was relaying a private caution to Joseph—warning him of violent consequences, both human and divine, if Benjamin were to be enslaved in Egypt. All of the examples Judah uses to back up his threats (according to the Rabbis) refer to episodes of retribution in the lives of female family members—starting with Sarah and Rachel: "Because Pharaoh took Benjamin's great-grandmother for only one night (12:15), he and his household were afflicted with plagues (12:17)." Moreover, "[Benjamin's] mother died only because of his father's curse, *But the one with whom you find your gods shall not live* (31:32). So take heed lest he hurl a curse against you—and you die!" Judah goes on to warn Joseph that two of his brothers once entered a large city and destroyed it (Genesis 34): "And if they did so much on account of a woman—their sister Dinah—how much the more so would they do when it is on account of a man [namely, their brother Benjamin], the beloved of the eyes, the one who gives hospitality to the blessed Holy One, as is said: *Of Benjamin he said: Beloved of the Eternal, / He rests securely beside* [*God*], */ Who protects him always, /* [*God*] *dwells amid his slopes* (Deuteronomy 33:12)." This valuing of a man over a woman is reflective of the social ordering of human beings in rabbinic literature, where women are seen as a secondary creation, both lesser and other than men. Nevertheless, the Rabbis did not view the women of Israel as nonentities; as each of the examples cited makes clear, their reputations, their words, and their actions were highly valued.

***"your servant made himself responsible for the lad. . . . how can I go home to my father without the lad . . . ?"*** (44:32–34). The Rabbis very much admired Judah's loyalty to Benjamin and to the pledge he had made to Jacob. Contrary to the biblical narrative, in which Judah speaks to Joseph with cautious and even obsequious words, the rabbinic sages imagined so mighty a confrontation between "Judah the lion and Joseph the bull" that even the angels descended from heaven to witness the dispute (Midrash *Tanchuma, Vayigash* 4, 5).

***His sons and his sons' sons were with him, his daughters and his sons' daughters*** (46:7). In *B'reishit Rabbah* 94.6, Rabbi Judah bar Ilai noticed that this verse includes both the sons and daughters of Jacob's sons but not his daughters' children, and commented: "The daughters of one's sons are as one's own children, whereas the sons of one's daughters are not as one's own sons." This statement reflects a frequent situation in ancient times where daughters left their birth families at marriage and became part of their husbands' households. Thus, their children were less likely to spend time with their maternal grandparents. In rabbinic halachah (that is, legal traditions), a married woman received a dowry from her father's resources at the time of marriage but did not automatically inherit anything from her father's estate.

***Asher's sons . . . and their sister Serah*** (46:17). This is the first biblical mention of Serah bat Asher. She reappears in Numbers 26:46 among Asher's descendants who participated in the Exodus. Some rabbis

*If they did so on account of a woman, how much more so on account of a man?*

linked these passages and imagined that Serah's lifetime spanned not only the four hundred years of Israel's captivity in Egypt but extended far beyond. Her remarkable longevity is attributed to a powerful blessing of praise that her grandfather Jacob bestowed on her when she informed him in song that Joseph was still alive (*Midrash HaGadol* and *Sefer HaYashar* on 46:8). At the time of the Exodus, Serah showed Moses where Joseph had been buried, so that his coffin might return with the Israelites to the land of Israel (*M'chilta, B'shalach* on 13:19; BT *Sotah* 13a). Other rabbis identify Serah with the "wise woman" who negotiated with David's general Joab in II Samuel 20:16–24, another four hundred years after the Exodus (*B'reishit Rabbah* 94.9; *Midrash HaGadol* on Genesis 23:1). In the 13th-century Yemenite compendium *Midrash HaGadol*, Serah is further linked with Proverbs 31:26, "Her mouth is full of wisdom, her tongue with kindly teaching" (on Genesis 23:1). Other medieval sources claim that Serah "did not taste death" but entered Paradise alive (*Alphabet of Ben Sira* 20–21).

—*Judith R. Baskin*

# *Contemporary Reflection*

AMERICANS LIVE in the kingdom of self-help books: *Five Steps to Overcoming Fear and Doubt*; *Five Steps to Emotional Healing*; *Five Steps to Spiritual Growth.* Every self-help book is marketed as the "ultimate one," or even as "the last self-help book you'll ever need." Over 300,000 self-help books are on the market. Typically, they promise a neatly outlined plan for self-transformation, for becoming free of a rooted sorrow or of deep-seated fears. They encourage the reader to believe that suffering is not worth the trouble, and gaining self-knowledge a routine affair—easily available for anyone with access to amazon.com and a credit card.

Thanks to the "self-help" industry, Americans—in particular—flee from mourning. We talk of going through the "grief process" until we experience "closure," as if we ourselves roll along an assembly line of emotion until we get to the final station: the packaging of our sorrow, the sealing it tight, the storing it away.

But the very notion of "closure" for grief is an illusion. Instead, there is only the tentative recognition that our anguish is endurable, that—despite ourselves—life goes on and engages us with new emotions, new situations and images, new challenges and changes. The remembrance of the people we miss gets tucked into our hearts to be revisited—perhaps when we least expect it. As for the process of true inner change, true self-transformation, we learn to forgive ourselves for the mistakes of the past by not making them again. If we are lucky, life "tenderizes" the heart, gives us hearts not of stone but of flesh.

*Vayigash* powerfully addresses this more authentic model of true emotional change via the character of Judah. In its very opening lines, we find Judah in the midst of responding in an impassioned voice to the demand of the Egyptian vizier that the youngest of Jacob and Rachel's sons, Benjamin, be left behind in Egypt. Not knowing, of course, that the forbidding vizier is none other than Rachel's other son, Joseph—whom Judah and his brothers threw into a pit years before—Judah pleads with him to change his mind. Losing Benjamin would break his father's heart, already broken because he believes his beloved Joseph is dead, says Judah. He begs to be kept behind in Benjamin's place. And then he speaks the most plaintive words of all: "For how can I go home to my father if the lad is not with me?" (44:34, my translation).

These words finally break Joseph's heart—and continue to reverberate through the ages. They signal to Joseph that he can finally trust his brothers, that there has been a profound sea-change in their character, that he can finally reveal himself to them. And so we need to ask ourselves what, in fact, has enabled Judah to come forth in this way? What has enabled the change?

The answer cannot be found in any self-help book. Judah most certainly did not take an instant course in "Five Steps to Become a Mensch." Instead, we can conclude that Judah is able to stand up to Joseph-the-Vizier's demand because he himself had gone through a painful, embarrassing experience of growth, one made possible through the courageous and determined intervention of his daughter-in-law Tamar.

Reflecting the Torah's brilliant narrative strategy, the story of Tamar appears right after the brothers have lied to their father Jacob, trying to make it appear as if Joseph has been killed. Jacob rends his garments, puts on sackcloth, and goes into mourning: "His sons and daughters endeavored to console him, but he refused to be consoled, saying, 'No, in mourning shall I go down to my son to Sheol!'" (37:35). No sooner does that happen than there is a break in the story, a seeming excursus: the scene switches to the tale of Tamar.

"Around that time," says the text (38:1), Judah marries the daughter of a man named Shua, and she then bears three sons. The oldest, Er, marries Tamar.

But Er dies, with no indication of an emotional reaction from Judah. Following Israelite law, he sends his second son, Onan, to marry Tamar, but Onan refuses to impregnate her and he, too, dies. The law dictates that the third son, Shelah, should now marry Tamar, but Judah delays fulfilling this law, afraid that Shelah, too, will die. Indeed, he waits so long that Tamar, hearing that he is going to a sheep-shearing, presents herself as a harlot on the road. He "couples" with her, not knowing who she is. When rumor later reaches him that his daughter-in-law is pregnant, he demands that she be taken out and burned. Only when she is brought to him and shows him the signet and staff that he had left with her in lieu of payment, does he realize what has transpired. He then admits: "She is more in the right than I, for certainly I did not give her to my son Shelah" (38:26).

Tamar's achievement lies in more than insisting that her father-in-law right his wrongdoing. Her act also becomes the galvanizing force that enables him to face, and thus finally overcome, the trauma of losing two of his sons and the paralyzing fear that he would lose his third, just as his own father Jacob had feared sending Benjamin to Egypt because he was the only son of Rachel left (42:38). Through the intervention of Tamar, Judah's heart is "tenderized" by his recognition of the wrong that his inchoate fear of loss had caused. That is why he is now able to plead for compassion before the seeming might of Egypt.

*Through the prior intervention of Tamar, Judah is now able to plead for compassion.*

Judah's experience illustrates that there are no instant transformations, no *Five Easy Self-Help Steps to Wisdom.* Instead, the Torah teaches that only by fully confronting ourselves—by being open to what we learn from one another—do we grow; only thus are we truly able to change.

*—Miriyam Glazer*

# Voices

## *Zilpah Speaks to Gad*

Elaine Rose Glickman

*Genesis 46:16–18*

To bear you but not to name you
was, I suppose, what I was born to do,
also to watch silently
while you learned a language that twisted my tongue
and swore allegiance to a God who was not mine.

Your children will not invoke my name
but still I send it with you, an echo,
my claim on you and on all that is to come—
the feasts of grain and lush pastures,
the smoldering heat and merciless bricks,
the clans and cities and prophets that shall be called after you.
You shall not hear my name again, but it will not matter.
I have entombed myself in you.

## *from And Jacob Blessed Pharaoh*

Amy Blank

*Genesis 47:7*

Above the silken river
Laden with moonlight and the drifting silt—
Quiet, heavy and simple,
Heedless of grandeur
Bent only by age
Jacob stood before the supple king,
The Pharaoh—
He also old and keen
And lean with polished wisdom
Of the ancient kingdom.
They stood together
Two old men who understood each other's
Separate earth and separate heaven.

The moonlight almost spent
Upon the river,
The stars spread far apart—
Jacob, the father, thought into the future:
"My hope is far removed."
The lissome Pharaoh thought:
"My hope is long fulfilled."

Deep silence fell
Upon the two old men who understood
Each other's separate earth and separate heaven.

## *Serah Bat Asher*

Hara E. Person

*Genesis 46:17*

Entranced by the swirling colors of his tunic
I crept behind Joseph when Grandfather sent
him to find his brothers.
Hidden behind a bush,
I watched my father and Reuben and the others.
Young and female and powerless
I could do nothing to stop them.
But I saw the cruel truth behind the lie.
Trapped between the responsibility of a
daughter's loyalty
and the heavy guilt of my secret knowledge,
I could not bring forth the words
that would have revealed my father and his
brothers
for what they became that day
and released my grandfather from his suffering.
Instead I withdrew into the safety of silence,
learning to whisper through the music of my
harp
while my refusal to speak
mocked my father's now empty authority.
They were relieved to let me stay with Jacob
in his tent,
hearing only the endless anguish of an old man
and the stubborn silence of a useless girl.
I played and he remembered,
recounting the travels and wanderings of our
family,
the pains and joys and dreams of each
generation.
He spoke of love and treachery and
misunderstanding,
and I created a soothing idiom of song.

It was I who was chosen to tell Jacob that
Joseph lives still.
Upon hearing the news he granted me eternal
life.
Endless life, for Joseph's life.
I became the family historian,
the keeper of tales,
the finder of bones,
the weaver of loose ends.
That is my gift from my grandfather,
to revisit sufferings and joys and wanderings
anew with each generation,
to observe endless cycles of loss and hope and
pain,
of births and deaths,
never to rest, never to finish, only to witness,
to drag these weary limbs through epoch after
epoch
and to wonder until the end of time
if this gift is a blessing of thanks for solace in
his loss
or a curse for having kept the truth from him all
those long years.

NOTE

***It was I who was chosen.*** According to rabbinic tradition, it was Serah bat Asher who informed Jacob that Joseph was alive; see Post-biblical Interpretations, p. 276.

# ויחי ✦ *Va-y'chi*

## GENESIS 47:28–50:26

## *Intimations of the Exodus: the Death of Jacob, the Birth of Israel*

PARASHAT VA-Y'CHI ("he lived," referring to Jacob's residing in Egypt) serves as a transition between the stories in Genesis about the patriarchs and Joseph, and the narrative in Exodus of the Egyptian slavery and exodus. It is both a conclusion and a foreshadowing. As the end of Jacob's life draws near, he wants to ensure the continuity of the family. Consequently, in this parashah the present points to both the past and the future. The past is represented by the patriarchal blessing, which features the divine promises of progeny made to Abraham, to Isaac, and to Jacob; the future, by Jacob's blessings for his own and for Joseph's sons.

Along with the concern for the family is the concern for the land, since both are part of the patriarchal blessing. In making arrangements for his own burial, Jacob insists that he must be laid to rest in the family plot established by Abraham in Canaan, in the cave of Machpelah purchased from Ephron the Hittite (see Genesis 23). Although the entire family now resides in Egypt, this will not be their final resting-place. The parashah foreshadows the Exodus: Jacob's burial procession from Egypt to Canaan anticipates the Israelites' march out of Egypt. But the family's return to Egypt, and Joseph's temporary burial there, show that the real exodus is yet to come.

Joseph plays the leading role among the brothers. He has matured, and he now takes responsibility for his family. He is the one first charged with Jacob's burial instructions, and he is the one who makes sure they are carried out. He also assures his brothers that he bears them no enmity for past deeds. With the death of their father, the brothers are now a reunited family.

The matriarchs are the only women mentioned in this parashah, and only in reference to their place of burial. Jacob recalls Rachel's death on the way to Canaan (48:7). While instructing that he be buried in the cave of Machpelah, Jacob mentions that Sarah (along with Abraham), Rebekah (along with Isaac), and Leah are already buried there (49:29–32). Rebekah's and Leah's deaths have not been mentioned previously, whereas Sarah's death received close attention (Genesis 23).

> *In burial, they represent the uniting of their family in the Promised Land.*

In death and burial, the matriarchs and patriarchs represent the uniting of the family in the Promised Land. Eventually, all Israel will reside in the land. But it will remain for the book of Exodus—where women once again will be very much in the foreground—to continue the story.

*—Adele Berlin*

## *Outline*

*I.* Jacob's Last Days (47:28–48:22)

- *A.* Jacob prepares for death and burial (47:28–31)
- *B.* Jacob blesses Ephraim and Manasseh (48:1–20)
- *C.* Jacob resumes his preparations for death (48:21–22)

*II.* Jacob's Deathbed Blessing (49:1–27)

*III.* Jacob Imparts Instructions for his Burial (49:28–33)

*IV.* Jacob's Funeral and Burial (50:1–13)

*V.* Joseph and His Brothers Return to Egypt (50:14–26)

- *A.* Brotherly reconciliation (vv. 14–21)
- *B.* Joseph's last days (vv. 22–26)

47:28

Jacob lived in the land of Egypt for 17 years;
Jacob's days—the years of his life—were 147.
29When Israel's time to die drew near, he summoned his son Joseph and said to him, "If I have

מז 28 וַיְחִי יַעֲקֹב בְּאֶרֶץ מִצְרַיִם שְׁבַע
עֶשְׂרֵה שָׁנָה וַיְהִי יְמֵי־יַעֲקֹב שְׁנֵי חַיָּיו שֶׁבַע
שָׁנִים וְאַרְבָּעִים וּמְאַת שָׁנָה׃ 29 וַיִּקְרְבוּ
יְמֵי־יִשְׂרָאֵל לָמוּת וַיִּקְרָא ׀ לִבְנוֹ לְיוֹסֵף

## *Jacob's Last Days* (47:28–48:22)

The patriarch turns his attention to his legacy. Jacob's first concern is his final resting-place (47:28–31); he insists that it be in the location that his grandfather Abraham had dedicated. Jacob's second concern for legacy involves assigning heirs, which prompts him to make special provisions for Joseph's two sons (48:1–20). His third concern, combining elements of the first two, is that his descendants return to their ancestral land and live there (48:21–22).

One aspect of the desires that Jacob expresses has since been echoed by pious Jews through the ages and in our own day: to be buried in the Land of Israel. On the ancient norm of burial in a family plot or cave, rather than in a communal cemetery, see Another View, p. 297.

### JACOB PREPARES FOR DEATH AND BURIAL (47:28–31)

***28. Jacob lived in the land of Egypt 17 years.*** The period is noted as if to say that it formed a separate chapter in his life.

***Jacob's days—the years of his life—were 147.*** The narration begins a formulaic summary of Jacob's lifetime, but it will not actually relate his demise until much later (49:33; compare 25:7–8; 35:28–29). This parashah thus zooms in on the relatively brief moment in Jacob's existence that lies in between.

***29.*** It is the duty of sons to bury their father: Isaac and Ishmael buried Abraham (25:9), and Esau and Jacob buried Isaac (35:29). But Jacob does not summon all his sons; he summons only Joseph—child of his beloved Rachel—his favorite son and the one of highest status in Egypt.

Later, when Joseph himself is about to die, he will utter a similar statement: "I am dying, but God will surely take care of you and bring you up out of this land to the land that [God] promised to Abraham, to Isaac, and to Jacob" (50:24).

***29–31.*** These burial instructions mention neither the locale of the ancestral resting-place nor even the country where it is located. What Jacob emphasizes is that burial must not be in Egypt (stated twice), and that Joseph must swear to carry out these instructions. Compare the reiterations at 49:29–32 and 50:5; see the comments there.

Burial in a cave conforms to actual interment practices in the Hebron region.

ANOTHER VIEW ➤ *297*

Ephraim and Manasseh are the first two siblings in the Bible who do not fight.

CONTEMPORARY REFLECTION ➤ *299*

One may alter another person's words for the sake of peace.

POST-BIBLICAL INTERPRETATIONS ➤ *297*

Surely, her blood flows in my blood, / Surely, her voice sings in mine....

VOICES ➤ *301*

but found favor in your sight, please put your hand under my thigh and treat me with faithful kindness; please do not bury me in Egypt. [30]When I [am laid to] rest with my ancestors, carry me out of Egypt and bury me in their burial-place." He replied, "I will do as you say." [31]He said, "Swear it to me!" so [Joseph] swore it to him; Israel then bowed down at the head of the bed.

48 After these things, they said to Joseph, "Look—your father is fading," so he took his two sons with him, Ephraim and Manasseh. [2]When they told Jacob, saying, "Look, your son Joseph has come," Israel rallied and sat up in the bed. [3]Jacob said to Joseph, "El Shaddai appeared to me in Luz in the land of Canaan and blessed me, [4]saying to me: 'Behold, I will make you fruitful and multiply you; I will make you a multitude of peoples and I will give this land to your seed after you as an everlasting possession.' [5]Now, then, your two sons born to you in the land of Egypt before my arrival

וַיֹּ֤אמֶר לוֹ֙ אִם־נָ֨א מָצָ֤אתִי חֵן֙ בְּעֵינֶ֔יךָ שִׂים־נָ֥א יָדְךָ֖ תַּ֣חַת יְרֵכִ֑י וְעָשִׂ֤יתָ עִמָּדִי֙ חֶ֣סֶד וֶאֱמֶ֔ת אַל־נָ֥א תִקְבְּרֵ֖נִי בְּמִצְרָֽיִם׃ [30]וְשָֽׁכַבְתִּי֙ עִם־אֲבֹתַ֔י וּנְשָׂאתַ֙נִי֙ מִמִּצְרַ֔יִם וּקְבַרְתַּ֖נִי בִּקְבֻרָתָ֑ם וַיֹּאמַ֕ר אָנֹכִ֖י אֶֽעֱשֶׂ֥ה כִדְבָרֶֽךָ׃ [31]וַיֹּ֗אמֶר הִשָּֽׁבְעָה֙ לִ֔י וַיִּשָּׁבַ֖ע ל֑וֹ וַיִּשְׁתַּ֥חוּ יִשְׂרָאֵ֖ל עַל־רֹ֥אשׁ הַמִּטָּֽה׃ פ

מח וַיְהִ֗י אַחֲרֵי֙ הַדְּבָרִ֣ים הָאֵ֔לֶּה וַיֹּ֣אמֶר לְיוֹסֵ֔ף הִנֵּ֥ה אָבִ֖יךָ חֹלֶ֑ה וַיִּקַּ֞ח אֶת־שְׁנֵ֤י בָנָיו֙ עִמּ֔וֹ אֶת־מְנַשֶּׁ֖ה וְאֶת־אֶפְרָֽיִם׃ [2]וַיַּגֵּ֣ד לְיַעֲקֹ֗ב וַיֹּ֙אמֶר֙ הִנֵּ֛ה בִּנְךָ֥ יוֹסֵ֖ף בָּ֣א אֵלֶ֑יךָ וַיִּתְחַזֵּק֙ יִשְׂרָאֵ֔ל וַיֵּ֖שֶׁב עַל־הַמִּטָּֽה׃ [3]וַיֹּ֤אמֶר יַעֲקֹב֙ אֶל־יוֹסֵ֔ף אֵ֥ל שַׁדַּ֛י נִרְאָֽה־אֵלַ֥י בְּל֖וּז בְּאֶ֣רֶץ כְּנָ֑עַן וַיְבָ֖רֶךְ אֹתִֽי׃ [4]וַיֹּ֣אמֶר אֵלַ֗י הִנְנִ֤י מַפְרְךָ֙ וְהִרְבִּיתִ֔ךָ וּנְתַתִּ֖יךָ לִקְהַ֣ל עַמִּ֑ים וְנָ֨תַתִּ֜י אֶת־הָאָ֧רֶץ הַזֹּ֛את לְזַרְעֲךָ֥ אַחֲרֶ֖יךָ אֲחֻזַּ֥ת עוֹלָֽם׃ [5]וְעַתָּ֡ה שְׁנֵֽי־בָנֶיךָ֩ הַנּוֹלָדִ֨ים לְךָ֜ בְּאֶ֣רֶץ מִצְרַ֗יִם עַד־בֹּאִ֥י אֵלֶ֛יךָ

. . . . . . . . . . . . . . . . . . . . . . . . . . . . . . . . .

**29.** *"put your hand under my thigh."* This act and the accompanying verbal oath (v. 31) comprise the swearing that Jacob requires; compare Abraham's procedure when he sent his slave to secure a wife for Isaac (24:2–3, 9).

**30.** *"ancestors."* [Heb. *avot*, often translated as "fathers." See at 25:8. —*Ed.*]

### JACOB BLESSES EPHRAIM AND MANASSEH (48:1–20)

**3–4.** Jacob repeats God's promise to the patriarchs of progeny and land. Both are in play here. Jacob's insistence on being buried in Canaan foreshadows the permanent settlement in the Promised Land. His "adoption" of Joseph's two sons points to progeny and family continuity.

**5.** *"your two sons . . . they are mine."* Another grandparent (or substitute grandparent) who is considered to be like a parent is Naomi in Ruth 4:17,

where the women declare of the son of Ruth and Boaz: "A son is born to Naomi." In our verse, Jacob equates Ephraim and Manasseh with Reuben and Simeon, his own first- and second-born sons.

Jacob has lifted Ephraim and Manasseh from the genealogy of Joseph and placed them in his own genealogical list. He does so in memory, as it were, of Rachel, Joseph's mother. This is a strong statement of family continuity—from Jacob to Joseph to Joseph's sons, a male genealogy inspired by a woman. In later biblical tradition Rachel is the mother of the northern tribes, symbolized by the "Joseph" tribes. Thus we read: "A voice is heard in Ramah / . . . Rachel is weeping for her children, / refusing to be comforted" (Jeremiah 31:14); the passage concludes with a promise that her children will be restored ("your children shall return to their own borders," v. 16).

If we view Genesis 48 as a late retrojection, reflecting the tribes that settled in Canaan, then this

in Egypt—they are mine; Ephraim and Manasseh will be to me like Reuben and Simeon. [6]But your progeny whom you engender after them are yours; they will be called by their brothers' names in their family allotment. [7]And I—as I was coming from Paddan, Rachel died in the land of Canaan, on the road, only a stretch of ground before reaching Ephrath. I buried her there on the way to Ephrath, that is, Bethlehem."

[8]When Israel saw Joseph's sons, he asked, "Who are these?" [9]And Joseph said to his father, "They are my sons, whom God has given me here." He [Jacob] said, "Bring them to me, pray, that I may bless them." [10]Israel's eyes had grown clouded with age; he could no longer see. Joseph brought them over to him, whereupon he kissed and hugged them.

[11]Israel then said to Joseph, "I never expected to see your face again, and here God has shown me your progeny as well!" [12]Joseph then removed them from his knees, and bowed down before him to the ground. [13]Then Joseph took the two of them, Ephraim with his right hand to Israel's left, and

מִצְרַיְמָה לִי־הֵם אֶפְרַיִם וּמְנַשֶּׁה כִּרְאוּבֵן
וְשִׁמְעוֹן יִהְיוּ־לִי׃ 6 וּמוֹלַדְתְּךָ אֲשֶׁר־הוֹלַדְתָּ
אַחֲרֵיהֶם לְךָ יִהְיוּ עַל שֵׁם אֲחֵיהֶם יִקָּרְאוּ
בְּנַחֲלָתָם׃ 7 וַאֲנִי | בְּבֹאִי מִפַּדָּן מֵתָה עָלַי
רָחֵל בְּאֶרֶץ כְּנַעַן בַּדֶּרֶךְ בְּעוֹד כִּבְרַת־אֶרֶץ
לָבֹא אֶפְרָתָה וָאֶקְבְּרֶהָ שָּׁם בְּדֶרֶךְ אֶפְרָת
הִוא בֵּית לָחֶם׃

8 וַיַּרְא יִשְׂרָאֵל אֶת־בְּנֵי יוֹסֵף וַיֹּאמֶר מִי־
אֵלֶּה׃ 9 וַיֹּאמֶר יוֹסֵף אֶל־אָבִיו בָּנַי הֵם
אֲשֶׁר־נָתַן־לִי אֱלֹהִים בָּזֶה וַיֹּאמַר קָחֶם־נָא
אֵלַי וַאֲבָרְכֵם׃ 10 וְעֵינֵי יִשְׂרָאֵל כָּבְדוּ מִזֹּקֶן
לֹא יוּכַל לִרְאוֹת וַיַּגֵּשׁ אֹתָם אֵלָיו וַיִּשַּׁק
לָהֶם וַיְחַבֵּק לָהֶם׃

11 וַיֹּאמֶר יִשְׂרָאֵל אֶל־יוֹסֵף רְאֹה פָנֶיךָ לֹא
פִלָּלְתִּי וְהִנֵּה הֶרְאָה אֹתִי אֱלֹהִים גַּם אֶת־
זַרְעֶךָ׃ 12 וַיּוֹצֵא יוֹסֵף אֹתָם מֵעִם בִּרְכָּיו
וַיִּשְׁתַּחוּ לְאַפָּיו אָרְצָה׃ 13 וַיִּקַּח יוֹסֵף
אֶת־שְׁנֵיהֶם אֶת־אֶפְרַיִם בִּימִינוֹ מִשְּׂמֹאל

is an etiology for how Ephraim and Manasseh—who were not sons of Jacob like the rest of the tribes' eponyms—came to be tribes. Jacob's bestowal on Ephraim of the birthright reflects the later reality: Ephraim the tribe became the largest and most influential in the northern kingdom.

*6. "progeny . . . after them."* No further progeny is known. If Joseph were to have subsequent sons, they would not form separate tribes bearing their names but would be included in the twelve tribes.

*7. "And I—."* In thinking about his own death and burial, Jacob suddenly recalls the death and burial of his beloved wife.

*"Rachel died in the land of Canaan."* Joseph's mother was not buried in the ancestral cave of Machpelah. (On its purchase and Sarah's burial there, see Genesis 23.) Her passing, first recounted in 35:16–20, is repeated here with the addition of this notice. This mention of Canaan re-emphasizes the idea of burial in Canaan that marked Jacob's earlier instructions.

*"Ephrath, that is, Bethlehem."* See Ruth 4:11, which mentions both Rachel and Leah as it links Ruth with Ephrathah, which is Bethlehem.

*8–20.* The bestowing of a blessing and a birthright, and bestowing it upon the "wrong" son, recalls Jacob's bargain to obtain the birthright from Esau (Genesis 25:29–34), his deception to obtain the blessing from his father, and the compensatory blessing granted to Esau (Genesis 27). The blessing here reiterates the patriarchal promise and again—as in the preceding passage—emphasizes the continuity from Abraham through Joseph's sons.

*8–10.* Jacob appears confused here, as if forgetting that he had just seen Joseph's sons and spoken about them at length. Modern critical scholars smooth the rough edges of this narrative sequence

Manasseh with his left hand to Israel's right, and he brought them close to him. 14But Israel stretched out his right hand and placed it on Ephraim's head, even though he was the younger, and his left hand on Manasseh's head, crossing his arms, though Manasseh was the first-born. 15He then blessed Joseph, saying, "The God before whom walked my fathers Abraham and Isaac, the God who has shepherded me ever since I came into being until this day—16the angel who has rescued me from all harm—bless these lads! Through them let my name and the name of my fathers Abraham and Isaac [ever] be recalled, and let them greatly multiply within the land!"

17When Joseph saw that his father had placed his right hand on Ephraim's head, it seemed wrong to him, so he took hold of his father's hand to move it from Ephraim's head onto the head of Manasseh. 18Joseph said to his father, "Not that way, Father! This is the first-born; put your right hand on his head." 19But his father refused, saying, "I know, my son, I know! He too shall become a people, and he too shall be great. Yet his younger brother shall be greater than he, and his seed shall become a multitude of nations." 20So he blessed them that day, saying, "By you shall [the people of] Israel give [their] blessing, saying, 'May God make you like Ephraim and Manasseh.'" And he put Ephraim ahead of Manasseh.

יִשְׂרָאֵל וְאֶת־מְנַשֶּׁה בִשְׂמֹאלוֹ מִימִין
יִשְׂרָאֵל וַיַּגֵּשׁ אֵלָיו׃ 14 וַיִּשְׁלַח יִשְׂרָאֵל
אֶת־יְמִינוֹ וַיָּשֶׁת עַל־רֹאשׁ אֶפְרַיִם וְהוּא
הַצָּעִיר וְאֶת־שְׂמֹאלוֹ עַל־רֹאשׁ מְנַשֶּׁה שִׂכֵּל
אֶת־יָדָיו כִּי מְנַשֶּׁה הַבְּכוֹר׃ 15 וַיְבָרֶךְ אֶת־
יוֹסֵף וַיֹּאמַר הָאֱלֹהִים אֲשֶׁר הִתְהַלְּכוּ אֲבֹתַי
לְפָנָיו אַבְרָהָם וְיִצְחָק הָאֱלֹהִים הָרֹעֶה אֹתִי
מֵעוֹדִי עַד־הַיּוֹם הַזֶּה׃ 16 הַמַּלְאָךְ הַגֹּאֵל
אֹתִי מִכָּל־רָע יְבָרֵךְ אֶת־הַנְּעָרִים וְיִקָּרֵא
בָהֶם שְׁמִי וְשֵׁם אֲבֹתַי אַבְרָהָם וְיִצְחָק וְיִדְגּוּ
לָרֹב בְּקֶרֶב הָאָרֶץ׃
17 וַיַּרְא יוֹסֵף כִּי־יָשִׁית אָבִיו יַד־יְמִינוֹ עַל־
רֹאשׁ אֶפְרַיִם וַיֵּרַע בְּעֵינָיו וַיִּתְמֹךְ יַד־אָבִיו
לְהָסִיר אֹתָהּ מֵעַל רֹאשׁ־אֶפְרַיִם עַל־רֹאשׁ
מְנַשֶּׁה׃ 18 וַיֹּאמֶר יוֹסֵף אֶל־אָבִיו לֹא־כֵן
אָבִי כִּי־זֶה הַבְּכֹר שִׂים יְמִינְךָ עַל־רֹאשׁוֹ׃
19 וַיְמָאֵן אָבִיו וַיֹּאמֶר יָדַעְתִּי בְנִי יָדַעְתִּי
גַּם־הוּא יִהְיֶה־לְּעָם וְגַם־הוּא יִגְדָּל וְאוּלָם
אָחִיו הַקָּטֹן יִגְדַּל מִמֶּנּוּ וְזַרְעוֹ יִהְיֶה מְלֹא־
הַגּוֹיִם׃ 20 וַיְבָרְכֵם בַּיּוֹם הַהוּא לֵאמוֹר בְּךָ
יְבָרֵךְ יִשְׂרָאֵל לֵאמֹר יְשִׂמְךָ אֱלֹהִים
כְּאֶפְרַיִם וְכִמְנַשֶּׁה וַיָּשֶׂם אֶת־אֶפְרַיִם לִפְנֵי
מְנַשֶּׁה׃

by suggesting that verse 8 is the continuation of verse 2, and that verses 3–7 are an insertion from a different source, interpreting the original scene.

*15. **He then blessed Joseph.*** He does so through his blessing of Ephraim and Manasseh (v. 16, "bless these lads").

*16. **"let them greatly multiply within the land."*** Jacob passes on the patriarchal blessing to the next generations: he recalls the names of Abraham and Isaac, and God's promises of land and progeny.

*19.* Jacob refuses Joseph's attempt to correct the order of precedence of the children. The same Jacob who supplanted his own older brother once again puts the younger before the older. The switching of places of Ephraim and Manasseh also invokes the common theme in Genesis of the younger sibling taking precedence over the older: Isaac over Ishmael (Genesis 21); Jacob over Esau (Genesis 27); Rachel over Leah (31:4); Tamar's son Perez over Zerah (38:27–30). (The theme is also a popular one elsewhere in the Bible. But in the story of Leah and Rachel, Laban reverses the theme, using the priority of Leah to trick Jacob; 29:26.)

[21]Israel then said to Joseph, "I am dying now, but God will be with you and bring you back to the land of your ancestors. [22]And I have given you—first among your brothers—the Shechem mountain-ridge, which I won from the Amorites with my sword and my bow."

21 וַיֹּאמֶר יִשְׂרָאֵל אֶל־יוֹסֵף הִנֵּה אָנֹכִי מֵת
וְהָיָה אֱלֹהִים עִמָּכֶם וְהֵשִׁיב אֶתְכֶם אֶל־
אֶרֶץ אֲבֹתֵיכֶם: 22 וַאֲנִי נָתַתִּי לְךָ שְׁכֶם
אַחַד עַל־אַחֶיךָ אֲשֶׁר לָקַחְתִּי מִיַּד הָאֱמֹרִי
בְּחַרְבִּי וּבְקַשְׁתִּי: פ

49 Jacob then summoned his sons, saying, "Gather 'round that I may tell you what shall befall to you in days to come:
[2]"Assemble and hearken, O sons of Jacob;
hearken to Israel your father.
[3]Reuben, my first-born,
you are my strength and first fruit of my vigor,
excessive in exalting [yourself],
excessive in strength.

מט וַיִּקְרָא יַעֲקֹב אֶל־בָּנָיו וַיֹּאמֶר הֵאָסְפוּ
וְאַגִּידָה לָכֶם אֵת אֲשֶׁר־יִקְרָא אֶתְכֶם
בְּאַחֲרִית הַיָּמִים:
2 הִקָּבְצוּ וְשִׁמְעוּ בְּנֵי יַעֲקֹב
וְשִׁמְעוּ אֶל־יִשְׂרָאֵל אֲבִיכֶם:
3 רְאוּבֵן בְּכֹרִי אַתָּה
כֹּחִי וְרֵאשִׁית אוֹנִי
יֶתֶר שְׂאֵת
וְיֶתֶר עָז:

### JACOB RESUMES HIS PREPARATIONS FOR DEATH (48:21–22)

*22. "Shechem mountain-ridge."* Heb. *sh'chem echad*, a difficult phrase. Many commentators understand it to mean "one portion," or the double portion assigned to the first-born (Deuteronomy 21:17). Others, including our translator, read it in terms of the walled town of Shechem, in the vicinity of which Jacob had once settled and even purchased land (Genesis 33:18–19). It is the locale where Jacob had sent Joseph when his brothers were pasturing flocks there (37:13), and where Joseph would eventually be buried (Joshua 24:32). According to the Bible's allotment of Canaan by tribe, Shechem sits in the territory of Manasseh—one of Joseph's sons—which would later become part of the northern kingdom of Israel. It is the same town where the story of Dinah takes place, and the name of the prince who lies with her (see at Genesis 34).

***"which I won . . . with my sword and my bow."*** This clause strengthens the argument that the previous phrase refers to a location. There is, however, no record of Jacob's having fought to obtain land.

***"Amorites."*** Another name for the indigenous inhabitants of Canaan.

## *Jacob's Deathbed Blessing* (49:1–27)

This is a laconic and therefore difficult poem; a number of verses remain poorly understood. In it, Jacob sets the future course of his sons—the eponyms of the tribes of Israel. It reflects a later time, after the tribes have settled in the land, but here its panoramic view is retrojected into a last will and testament of the patriarch. It has political overtones, putting some tribes in a more favorable light than others. Yet the overall effect—like so much in this parashah—is to foreshadow the fulfillment of the patriarchal promise: it depicts Israel settled in its land.

Such a testament is a well-known literary trope. A counterpart is found in Deuteronomy 33, in Moses' farewell blessing of Israel, in which the tribes are blessed as if they are his own sons. Ancient

⁴Licentious one, boil up like water no more—
Oh, you mounted your father's bed,
then defiled my couch—he mounted my couch!
⁵Simeon and Levi are partners;
instruments of violence are their plan.
⁶Let me not enter their council,
nor let my being join their assembly;
for they killed a man in their wrath,
and in their whim hamstrung an ox.
⁷Cursed is their wrath so fierce,
and their fury so harsh!
I will disperse them in Jacob,
scatter them in Israel.

⁴ פַּ֤חַז כַּמַּ֙יִם֙ אַל־תּוֹתַ֔ר
כִּ֥י עָלִ֖יתָ מִשְׁכְּבֵ֣י אָבִ֑יךָ
אָ֥ז חִלַּ֖לְתָּ יְצוּעִ֥י עָלָֽה׃ פ
⁵ שִׁמְע֥וֹן וְלֵוִ֖י אַחִ֑ים
כְּלֵ֥י חָמָ֖ס מְכֵרֹתֵיהֶֽם׃
⁶ בְּסֹדָם֙ אַל־תָּבֹ֣א נַפְשִׁ֔י
בִּקְהָלָ֖ם אַל־תֵּחַ֣ד כְּבֹדִ֑י
כִּ֤י בְאַפָּם֙ הָ֣רְגוּ אִ֔ישׁ
וּבִרְצֹנָ֖ם עִקְּרוּ־שֽׁוֹר׃
⁷ אָר֤וּר אַפָּם֙ כִּ֣י עָ֔ז
וְעֶבְרָתָ֖ם כִּ֣י קָשָׁ֑תָה
אֲחַלְּקֵ֣ם בְּיַעֲקֹ֔ב
וַאֲפִיצֵ֖ם בְּיִשְׂרָאֵֽל׃ פ

post-biblical literature elaborated on this genre, composing testaments for the Twelve Patriarchs—the twelve sons of Jacob—as well as for other biblical figures like Moses, Solomon, and Job.

The sons are listed roughly by the mothers who bore them. Leah's children appear first (Reuben, Simeon, Levi, Judah, Zebulun, Issachar) followed by Zilpah's and Bilhah's sons (Dan, Gad, Asher, Naphtali), and culminating in Rachel's sons (Joseph, Benjamin). But the order does not follow exactly the birth order in the stories in Genesis 29, 30, and 35. Despite the adoption of Ephraim and Manasseh in the foregoing section, they are not mentioned in this poem.

In some cases, the blessing includes the tribal totem or symbol. For example, Judah is a lion; Zebulun is associated with ships; Dan is a serpent; Benjamin is a wolf. (Through the ages, these symbols have been used by various artists, such as Chagall in his famous Hadassah Hospital windows in Jerusalem.) The poem often invokes wordplay on the sons' names.

Taken as a whole, this poem privileges Judah and Joseph—symbols of the later southern and northern Israelite kingdoms, respectively. It thereby looks beyond the tribal land allotments to the time of the divided monarchy, when the individual tribes had little significance, having been replaced by the two more centralized polities. Some scholars read the poem as promoting Judah over Joseph, implying an even later perspective when the northern kingdom had been destroyed and Judah alone was left (D. Carr, *Reading the Fractures of Genesis*, 1996, p. 250).

4.   *"you mounted your father's bed."*   An allusion to when Reuben slept with his father's concubine (35:22). Such an act is taken elsewhere as a sign of wishing to supplant the father (II Samuel 16:20–22; I Kings 2:20–22). This verse might be an attempt to explain why Reuben, although the firstborn of Jacob, was not to become a historically important tribe.

5–7.   The allusion is to Genesis 34, the Dinah story, in which Simeon and Levi arrange for the massacre of the men of Shechem. Here, as in the earlier account, Jacob's assessment differs from that of these two brothers.

7.   *"I will disperse them in Jacob, / scatter them in Israel."*   They would not remain distinct tribes. Simeon was absorbed into the tribe of Judah; and Levi—the tribe from which the Levites and priests would come—did not have landholdings.

8You, Judah:
your brothers shall heap praise on you—
your hand on the neck of your foes,
your father's sons shall bow down to you.
9Judah is a lion's cub:
you flourish, my son, from the prey.
He kneels, crouches like a lion,
like a lioness—who dare stir him up?
10The staff shall not depart from Judah,
nor the scepter from between his legs,
until he comes to Shiloh,
and the people's fealty is his.
11He tethers his ass to a vine,
his ass's foal to the choicest vine;
he cleanses his garments in wine,
his robe in the blood of grapes.
12Eyes that sparkle with wine!
Teeth whitened by milk!
13Zebulun shall dwell at the seashore,
he will be a harbor for ships,
with his farthest reach near Sidon.
14Issachar, a bony donkey,
lies between the folds,
15He saw how good was the resting-place,
and how pleasant the ground:
so he bent his shoulder to the burden,
to be subjected to forced labor.

8 יְהוּדָה אַתָּה יוֹדוּךָ אַחֶיךָ
יָדְךָ בְּעֹרֶף אֹיְבֶיךָ
יִשְׁתַּחֲווּ לְךָ בְּנֵי אָבִיךָ׃
9 גּוּר אַרְיֵה יְהוּדָה
מִטֶּרֶף בְּנִי עָלִיתָ
כָּרַע רָבַץ כְּאַרְיֵה
וּכְלָבִיא מִי יְקִימֶנּוּ׃
10 לֹא־יָסוּר שֵׁבֶט מִיהוּדָה
וּמְחֹקֵק מִבֵּין רַגְלָיו
עַד כִּי־יָבֹא שִׁילֹה
וְלוֹ יִקְּהַת עַמִּים׃
11 אֹסְרִי לַגֶּפֶן עירה עִירֹו
וְלַשֹּׂרֵקָה בְּנִי אֲתֹנוֹ
כִּבֵּס בַּיַּיִן לְבֻשׁוֹ
וּבְדַם־עֲנָבִים סותה סוּתֹו׃
12 חַכְלִילִי עֵינַיִם מִיָּיִן
וּלְבֶן־שִׁנַּיִם מֵחָלָב׃ פ
13 זְבוּלֻן לְחוֹף יַמִּים יִשְׁכֹּן
וְהוּא לְחוֹף אֳנִיֹּת
וְיַרְכָתוֹ עַל־צִידֹן׃ פ
14 יששכר יִשָּׂשכָר חֲמֹר גָּרֶם
רֹבֵץ בֵּין הַמִּשְׁפְּתָיִם׃
15 וַיַּרְא מְנֻחָה כִּי טוֹב
וְאֶת־הָאָרֶץ כִּי נָעֵמָה
וַיֵּט שִׁכְמוֹ לִסְבֹּל
וַיְהִי לְמַס־עֹבֵד׃ ס

*9–10.* The blessings of Reuben, Simeon, and Levi disqualify those three oldest sons, leaving Judah to serve as the leading tribe—securing the birthright, as it were.

*"lion's cub . . . lion . . . lioness."* The "king of beasts" is an appropriate emblem for Judah, the tribe linked with the Davidic kingship—an eternal dynasty.

*10. "until he comes to Shiloh."* This last part of the verse is obscure; it has been interpreted as having messianic meaning.

*11–12.* This blessing's emphasis on wine suggests agricultural fertility, as well as luxury and festive banqueting. Future royalty is surely implied.

*13.* This verse places the tribe of Zebulun on the northern coast of Israel.

*"Sidon."* A Phoenician port-town (now part of Lebanon).

*14.* Issachar is not portrayed positively; he is subjugated to those around him, probably the Canaanites.

16 Dan will plead his people's cause
as one of Israel's tribes.
17 Let Dan be a snake on the road,
a horned serpent on the path,
biting the horse's heels,
so its rider tumbles backward.
18 I await Your help, יהוה!
19 Gad shall be raided by raiders,
but shall raid their rearguard.
20 Asher—his food is fat,
he provides delicacies for a king.
21 Naphtali, a mountain-ewe born,
bears lovely lambs in the folds.
22 Joseph is a wild she-ass's son,
a wild she-ass's son by a spring,
the wild she-asses at Shur:
23 They harassed him,
shot arrows at him,
the archers were foes to him,
24 yet steady stayed his bow,
quick his arms!
Through the Mighty One of Jacob,
through the Shepherd, Israel's Rock,

16 דָּן יָדִין עַמּוֹ
כְּאַחַד שִׁבְטֵי יִשְׂרָאֵל׃
17 יְהִי־דָן נָחָשׁ עֲלֵי־דֶרֶךְ
שְׁפִיפֹן עֲלֵי־אֹרַח
הַנֹּשֵׁךְ עִקְּבֵי־סוּס
וַיִּפֹּל רֹכְבוֹ אָחוֹר׃
18 לִישׁוּעָתְךָ קִוִּיתִי יְהֹוָה׃
19 גָּד גְּדוּד יְגוּדֶנּוּ
וְהוּא יָגֻד עָקֵב׃ ס
20 מֵאָשֵׁר שְׁמֵנָה לַחְמוֹ
וְהוּא יִתֵּן מַעֲדַנֵּי־מֶלֶךְ׃ ס
21 נַפְתָּלִי אַיָּלָה שְׁלֻחָה
הַנֹּתֵן אִמְרֵי־שָׁפֶר׃ ס
22 בֵּן פֹּרָת יוֹסֵף
בֵּן פֹּרָת עֲלֵי־עָיִן
בָּנוֹת צָעֲדָה עֲלֵי־שׁוּר׃
23 וַיְמָרְרֻהוּ וָרֹבּוּ
וַיִּשְׂטְמֻהוּ בַּעֲלֵי חִצִּים׃
24 וַתֵּשֶׁב בְּאֵיתָן קַשְׁתּוֹ
וַיָּפֹזּוּ זְרֹעֵי יָדָיו
מִידֵי אֲבִיר יַעֲקֹב
מִשָּׁם רֹעֶה אֶבֶן יִשְׂרָאֵל׃

*16.* ***"Dan will plead."*** A wordplay on the name of Dan, linking it with the root *d-y-n*, "to judge."

*17.* This verse adds an apparently additional, unrelated portrait of Dan. It is not clear whether it is positive or negative.

*18.* This verse breaks away from the main poem and has been explained as an interpolation from elsewhere (see Psalm 119:166). In its present location, it might be seen as an aside by Jacob, calling on God's help.

*19.* This verse features repeated wordplay on the name of Gad, built on the root letters *g-w-d*.

*22.* ***"wild she-ass's son."*** Or, "a fruitful bough." Both interpretations have been offered for this difficult phrase. In either case, the image is one of vigor.

*23.* The poetry now transmutes the animal or floral image of the preceding verse into a human archer-warrior who, although having been set upon by enemies, was able to remain steady. We have no inkling of the referent of this image; the Bible nowhere else mentions Joseph as a warrior or archer. It may refer to the later history of the northern kingdom, given that the "Joseph" tribes of Ephraim and Manasseh settled in the central part of the country and dominated it politically.

*24–26.* Jacob heaps the greatest blessing upon Joseph.

*24.* ***"Mighty One of Jacob . . . Shepherd . . . Rock."*** The poetry invokes several ancient divine epithets.

25 by the God of your father, who helps you,
Shaddai, who blesses you,
blessings of heaven above,
blessings of the deep that lies below,
blessings of breasts and womb—
26 blessings of your father
surpass my parents' blessings—
the bounty of the timeless hills:
let them be on Joseph's head,
on the brow of the prince among his brothers.
27 Benjamin is a wolf that rends,
in the morning devouring the booty,
in the evening dividing the spoil."

28 All these are the twelve tribes of Israel, and
thus did their father speak to them as he blessed
them, blessing each one with a blessing that befit
him. 29 And he gave them a charge, saying, "When I

25 מֵאֵל אָבִיךָ וְיַעְזְרֶךָּ
וְאֵת שַׁדַּי וִיבָרְכֶךָּ
בִּרְכֹת שָׁמַיִם מֵעָל
בִּרְכֹת תְּהוֹם רֹבֶצֶת תָּחַת
בִּרְכֹת שָׁדַיִם וָרָחַם׃
26 בִּרְכֹת אָבִיךָ
גָּבְרוּ עַל־בִּרְכֹת הוֹרַי
עַד־תַּאֲוַת גִּבְעֹת עוֹלָם
תִּהְיֶיןָ לְרֹאשׁ יוֹסֵף
וּלְקָדְקֹד נְזִיר אֶחָיו׃ פ
27 בִּנְיָמִין זְאֵב יִטְרָף
בַּבֹּקֶר יֹאכַל עַד
וְלָעֶרֶב יְחַלֵּק שָׁלָל׃
28 כָּל־אֵלֶּה שִׁבְטֵי יִשְׂרָאֵל שְׁנֵים עָשָׂר
וְזֹאת אֲשֶׁר־דִּבֶּר לָהֶם אֲבִיהֶם וַיְבָרֶךְ אוֹתָם
אִישׁ אֲשֶׁר כְּבִרְכָתוֹ בֵּרַךְ אֹתָם׃ 29 וַיְצַו
אוֹתָם וַיֹּאמֶר אֲלֵהֶם אֲנִי נֶאֱסָף אֶל־עַמִּי

*25. "Shaddai."* One of God's names, often associated with fertility.

*"heaven above . . . deep . . . below."* The entire cosmos, from the heavens above to the primeval waters below, participates in the blessing.

*"blessings of breasts and womb."* This unusual reference signals fertility.

*26. "my parents' blessings."* The blessing on Joseph, says Jacob, will surpass the blessing he received from his own parents; that is to say, the blessing of Joseph will surpass the promise to the patriarchs. Interestingly, Jacob does not use the Hebrew word *avot* ("ancestors") but *horai*—here translated as "parents"—a term related to pregnancy.

## *Jacob Imparts Instructions for His Burial* (49:28–33)

The narrative returns to the issue of Jacob's instructions for his burial that has occupied so much of this parashah. Here, as opposed to 47:30, Jacob addresses all his sons—not Joseph alone—and he details the location of the burial place and the family members who have already been laid to rest in it. The deceased matriarchs figure as prominently as the patriarchs. Indeed, it was the death of Sarah that had necessitated acquiring this family plot. (Genesis 23:3–15 recounts the purchase of this site—the first land acquisition in the Promised Land, and the first step in the fulfillment of God's promise to Abraham.) In death, as in life, the matriarchs are the cement that provides family continuity.

*28. All these are the twelve tribes of Israel.* This summation acknowledges that the poem refers not to Jacob's sons themselves but to the future of the tribes. By putting the future of the tribes in the form of this testament, it suggests that what befell the tribes was fitting to the character of each; it was their destiny. The Bible often explains and justifies a current situation as if it had been predicted prophetically.

*29–32.* Jacob's words are not meant simply to provide instructions on how to find the burial plot.

am gathered to my people, bury me with my ancestors—in the cave that is in the field of Ephron the Hittite, [30]in the cave that is in the field of Machpelah, facing Mamre, in the land of Canaan, the field that Abraham bought from Ephron the Hittite as an inalienable gravesite. [31]There they buried Abraham and his wife Sarah, there they buried Isaac and his wife Rebekah, and there I buried Leah. [32]The purchase of the field and the cave in it was from the Hittites." [33]When Jacob was done charging his sons he drew his feet into the bed; he then breathed his last and was gathered to his people.

50 Joseph threw himself upon his father; he wept over him and kissed him. [2]Joseph then charged his servants the physicians to embalm his father, so the physicians embalmed Israel. [3]When his forty days were completed—for it took the embalmers that many days—Egypt bewailed him seventy days.

קִבְר֣וּ אֹתִי֮ אֶל־אֲבֹתָי֒ אֶל־הַמְּעָרָ֔ה אֲשֶׁ֖ר בִּשְׂדֵ֥ה עֶפְר֖וֹן הַֽחִתִּֽי: 30 בַּמְּעָרָ֞ה אֲשֶׁ֣ר בִּשְׂדֵ֣ה הַמַּכְפֵּלָ֗ה אֲשֶׁ֛ר עַל־פְּנֵֽי־מַמְרֵ֖א בְּאֶ֣רֶץ כְּנָ֑עַן אֲשֶׁר֩ קָנָ֨ה אַבְרָהָ֜ם אֶת־הַשָּׂדֶ֗ה מֵאֵ֛ת עֶפְרֹ֥ן הַֽחִתִּ֖י לַֽאֲחֻזַּת־קָֽבֶר: 31 שָׁ֣מָּה קָֽבְר֞וּ אֶת־אַבְרָהָ֗ם וְאֵת֙ שָׂרָ֣ה אִשְׁתּ֔וֹ שָׁ֚מָּה קָֽבְר֣וּ אֶת־יִצְחָ֔ק וְאֵ֖ת רִבְקָ֣ה אִשְׁתּ֑וֹ וְשָׁ֥מָּה קָבַ֖רְתִּי אֶת־לֵאָֽה: 32 מִקְנֵ֧ה הַשָּׂדֶ֛ה וְהַמְּעָרָ֥ה אֲשֶׁר־בּ֖וֹ מֵאֵ֥ת בְּנֵי־חֵֽת: 33 וַיְכַ֤ל יַֽעֲקֹב֙ לְצַוֹּ֣ת אֶת־בָּנָ֔יו וַיֶּֽאֱסֹ֥ף רַגְלָ֖יו אֶל־הַמִּטָּ֑ה וַיִּגְוַ֖ע וַיֵּאָ֥סֶף אֶל־עַמָּֽיו:

נ וַיִּפֹּ֥ל יוֹסֵ֖ף עַל־פְּנֵ֣י אָבִ֑יו וַיֵּ֥בְךְּ עָלָ֖יו וַיִּשַּׁק־לֽוֹ: 2 וַיְצַ֨ו יוֹסֵ֤ף אֶת־עֲבָדָיו֙ אֶת־הָרֹ֣פְאִ֔ים לַֽחֲנֹ֖ט אֶת־אָבִ֑יו וַיַּֽחַנְט֥וּ הָרֹֽפְאִ֖ים אֶת־יִשְׂרָאֵֽל: 3 וַיִּמְלְאוּ־לוֹ֙ אַרְבָּעִ֣ים י֔וֹם כִּ֛י כֵּ֥ן יִמְלְא֖וּ יְמֵ֣י הַֽחֲנֻטִ֑ים וַיִּבְכּ֥וּ אֹת֛וֹ מִצְרַ֖יִם שִׁבְעִ֥ים יֽוֹם:

* * * * * * * * * * * * *

By retelling the story of the site, Jacob appeals for family continuity—for the preservation of this burial tradition. (How often thoughts of family continuity and traditional practice come at the moment of death, when an important link in the chain is about to be lost!)

29. *"my people."* See at 25:8.

*"ancestors."* [Heb. *avot*, often translated as "fathers." See at 25:8. —*Ed.*]

33. *he drew his feet into the bed.* This action complements that of 48:2, when Jacob "sat up in the bed." His instructions are now complete; he can die in peace knowing that he has conveyed his wishes to his sons.

## Jacob's Funeral and Burial (50:1–13)

The narrative spotlight now shifts from Jacob to Joseph. He takes the lead in mourning for Jacob and in making arrangements to carry out his father's last wishes.

Some of the confusion in this unit—especially in reference to Joseph's acting alone versus all the brothers—is explained by modern critical scholars as the result of the combination of different sources, Priestly and non-Priestly accounts.

2. *his servants the physicians.* Apparently Joseph had his own staff of physicians. Knowledge of anatomy is necessary for embalming, during which the internal organs are removed.

*to embalm his father.* An Egyptian practice that conforms to Egyptian religious thought about the afterworld. This is one of several features in the Joseph story that reflects its Egyptian setting. Except for Jacob and Joseph, no other Israelites in the Bible are embalmed. Later Jewish law forbade attempts to preserve a corpse (except in extreme circumstances), since normally Jews are to be buried quickly.

3. The forty days of embalming were followed by thirty (or, per the present translation, seventy) days of public mourning: Jacob, because of his relation to Joseph, was treated as a quasi-royal figure.

4The days of bewailing him passed and Joseph
spoke to Pharaoh's household, saying, "If I have
found favor in your sight, please speak to Pharaoh
and say: 5"My father adjured me, saying, "See, I am
about to die; in my grave that I acquired for myself
in the land of Canaan, there must you bury me."
Now, then, give me leave to go up and bury my
father; then I will come back.''' 6Pharaoh said, "Go
up and bury your father as he adjured you."
7Joseph then went up to bury his father; with
him went all Pharaoh's officials, the elders of his
palace, all the [other] elders of Egypt, 8and all Joseph's household, and his brothers, and his father's

4 וַיַּעַבְרוּ יְמֵי בְכִיתוֹ וַיְדַבֵּר יוֹסֵף אֶל־בֵּית
פַּרְעֹה לֵאמֹר אִם־נָא מָצָאתִי חֵן בְּעֵינֵיכֶם
דַּבְּרוּ־נָא בְּאָזְנֵי פַרְעֹה לֵאמֹר׃ 5 אָבִי
הִשְׁבִּיעַנִי לֵאמֹר הִנֵּה אָנֹכִי מֵת בְּקִבְרִי
אֲשֶׁר כָּרִיתִי לִי בְּאֶרֶץ כְּנַעַן שָׁמָּה תִּקְבְּרֵנִי
וְעַתָּה אֶעֱלֶה־נָּא וְאֶקְבְּרָה אֶת־אָבִי
וְאָשׁוּבָה׃ 6 וַיֹּאמֶר פַּרְעֹה עֲלֵה וּקְבֹר אֶת־
אָבִיךָ כַּאֲשֶׁר הִשְׁבִּיעֶךָ׃
7 וַיַּעַל יוֹסֵף לִקְבֹּר אֶת־אָבִיו וַיַּעֲלוּ אִתּוֹ
כָּל־עַבְדֵי פַרְעֹה זִקְנֵי בֵיתוֹ וְכֹל זִקְנֵי אֶרֶץ־
מִצְרָיִם׃ 8 וְכֹל בֵּית יוֹסֵף וְאֶחָיו וּבֵית אָבִיו

*4–6.* Only after concluding the period of mourning does Joseph begin arrangements for the burial. Here Egyptian custom ends and Jacob's instructions begin to be carried out. Yet the Egyptian setting of the story is still in evidence in Joseph's carefully crafted words, seeking permission to bury his father in Canaan. Here—as often in the Bible—the narrative repeats a character's speech with changes that adjust it to its changing audience. Three times the text relates Jacob's burial instructions (47:29–30; 49:29–32; and here), and each time the wording is different, because both the purpose of the speech and the recipients of the information have changed. Joseph must obtain permission from Pharaoh, so he uses a strategy and language that will accomplish his goal.

*4. **Pharaoh's household.*** Joseph does not approach Pharaoh directly but through his official court, whom he asks to convey his request to Pharaoh. (This seems strange, given Joseph's high status as second only to Pharaoh.)

*5. **"My father adjured me, saying..."*** Joseph does not repeat the exact wording of the oath he swore to his father. He changes it so as to make it sound more positive: "bury me in Canaan" rather than "don't bury me in Egypt." It is not as if Jacob specifically rejected Egypt, but that he preferred Canaan. Joseph speaks here as a loyal Egyptian merely doing his filial duty.

***"'acquired.'"*** Heb. *kariti,* literally "dug" or perhaps "prepared." There is no prior notice that Jacob had prepared his grave in any way. This suggests that, as this translation reflects, it was the location that was important to Jacob himself—not the structure of the grave. (On the burial details, see Another View, p. 297.) But Joseph has designed *his* words to appeal to a pharaoh. High-ranking Egyptians had elaborate tombs prepared for themselves many years before their death. Therefore, we should take the word *kariti* literally: Joseph is making it sound as if his father, too, followed Egyptian custom, but with an Israelite twist—burial in the ground rather than in a pyramid. Pharaoh could predictably relate to this request of Joseph's, to honor his father by burying him in the "tomb" specially prepared for him.

***"then I will come back."*** Joseph's loyalty is again evident in these words. After the burial Joseph will resume his place in Egypt. Indeed, he and his brothers do return (v. 14), for although the funeral procession foreshadows the Exodus, it is, as it were, only a rehearsal for it (see below on vv. 8, 10).

*7–9.* Like the period of mourning, the funeral and burial involve a large entourage, including Egyptians. This is a state funeral. In fact, the Canaanites perceive it as "a solemn mourning for Egypt" (v. 11).

household. They left in Goshen only their little ones, their flocks, and their cattle. 9And with him went the chariots and charioteers, so the camp was very numerous.

10When they reached Goren ha-Atad on the other side of the Jordan, they held there a great and solemn lamentation; he observed a mourning ceremony of seven days for his father. 11When the land's inhabitants, the Canaanites, saw the mourning ceremony at Goren ha-Atad, they said, "This is a solemn mourning for Egypt," and they called [the place] Abel Mizraim; it is on the other side of the Jordan. 12Thus his sons did for [Jacob] exactly as he had commanded them. 13His sons conveyed him to the land of Canaan and buried him in the cave of the field of Machpelah, the field that Abraham had bought as an inalienable gravesite from Ephron the Hittite, facing Mamre.

רַק טַפָּם וְצֹאנָם וּבְקָרָם עָזְבוּ בְּאֶרֶץ גֹּשֶׁן׃
9 וַיַּעַל עִמּוֹ גַּם־רֶכֶב גַּם־פָּרָשִׁים וַיְהִי
הַמַּחֲנֶה כָּבֵד מְאֹד׃
10 וַיָּבֹאוּ עַד־גֹּרֶן הָאָטָד אֲשֶׁר בְּעֵבֶר הַיַּרְדֵּן
וַיִּסְפְּדוּ־שָׁם מִסְפֵּד גָּדוֹל וְכָבֵד מְאֹד וַיַּעַשׂ
לְאָבִיו אֵבֶל שִׁבְעַת יָמִים׃ 11 וַיַּרְא יוֹשֵׁב
הָאָרֶץ הַכְּנַעֲנִי אֶת־הָאֵבֶל בְּגֹרֶן הָאָטָד
וַיֹּאמְרוּ אֵבֶל־כָּבֵד זֶה לְמִצְרָיִם עַל־כֵּן קָרָא
שְׁמָהּ אָבֵל מִצְרַיִם אֲשֶׁר בְּעֵבֶר הַיַּרְדֵּן׃
12 וַיַּעֲשׂוּ בָנָיו לוֹ כֵּן כַּאֲשֶׁר צִוָּם׃ 13 וַיִּשְׂאוּ
אֹתוֹ בָנָיו אַרְצָה כְּנַעַן וַיִּקְבְּרוּ אֹתוֹ בִּמְעָרַת
שְׂדֵה הַמַּכְפֵּלָה אֲשֶׁר קָנָה אַבְרָהָם אֶת־
הַשָּׂדֶה לַאֲחֻזַּת־קֶבֶר מֵאֵת עֶפְרֹן הַחִתִּי
עַל־פְּנֵי מַמְרֵא׃

*8. They left in Goshen only their little ones, their flocks, and their cattle.* While this is not yet the Exodus, the language foreshadows the struggle to take the children and livestock in Exodus 10:9–11, 24. As for women, it seems likely that most remained with the children, while at least a few of them featured in the funeral and burial ceremonies (see at v. 10, "lamentation").

*10. Goren ha-Atad.* A place name not otherwise known.

*on the other side of the Jordan.* The route through Transjordan is not a direct route from Egypt to the cave of Machpelah. This route foreshadows that of the Israelite exodus, which also wound its way through Transjordan.

*they.* Presumably referring to the brothers and the Egyptians, or perhaps only the Egyptians.

*lamentation.* A specialty of women; the public voice of mourning in the ancient Near East was both female and male (see *Chayei Sarah*, Contemporary Reflection, p. 129, and at Leviticus 10:6).

*mourning ceremony.* The translation "ceremony" suggests that the mourning period observed by Joseph included still more lamentation. Alternatively, Joseph observed "a seven-day period of mourning" of an unspecified type.

*seven days.* A mourning period of seven days is known from the Mesopotamian epic of Gilgamesh, and in the Bible also from the mourning for Saul (I Samuel 31:13) and from Job's friends (Job 2:13). It became shivah, the traditional period for Jewish mourning that begins after the burial. Here, however, Jacob has not yet been buried (see v. 13). Alternatively, this verse reflects an alternate tradition which has Jacob buried at Goren ha-Atad, followed by the period of mourning. See also at vv. 12–13.

*11. Abel.* Which means "brook, watercourse" or "pasture, meadow, well-watered land." (Place names beginning with "Abel" are found in sites in Canaan dating from the transition between the Late Bronze and early Iron Ages. These sites originated among non-urban populations.) It is here given the false etymology of "mourning," deriving from this incident.

*Abel Mizraim.* This particular place name has been identified with several sites.

*12–13.* These verses give the impression that after the public mourning at Abel Mizraim, Jacob's

<sup></sup>

14 וַיָּ֤שָׁב יוֹסֵף֙ מִצְרַ֔יְמָה ה֖וּא וְאֶחָ֑יו וְכָל־
הָעֹלִ֥ים אִתּ֖וֹ לִקְבֹּ֣ר אֶת־אָבִ֑יו אַחֲרֵ֖י קָבְר֥וֹ
אֶת־אָבִֽיו: 15 וַיִּרְא֤וּ אֲחֵֽי־יוֹסֵף֙ כִּי־מֵ֣ת
אֲבִיהֶ֔ם וַיֹּ֣אמְר֔וּ ל֥וּ יִשְׂטְמֵ֖נוּ יוֹסֵ֑ף וְהָשֵׁ֤ב
יָשִׁיב֙ לָ֔נוּ אֵ֚ת כָּל־הָ֣רָעָ֔ה אֲשֶׁ֥ר גָּמַ֖לְנוּ אֹתֽוֹ:
16 וַיְצַוּ֕וּ אֶל־יוֹסֵ֖ף לֵאמֹ֑ר אָבִ֣יךָ צִוָּ֔ה לִפְנֵ֥י
מוֹת֖וֹ לֵאמֹֽר: 17 כֹּֽה־תֹאמְר֣וּ לְיוֹסֵ֗ף אָ֣נָּ֡א
שָׂ֣א נָ֡א פֶּ֣שַׁע אַחֶ֩יךָ֩ וְחַטָּאתָ֨ם כִּי־רָעָ֣ה
גְמָל֗וּךָ וְעַתָּה֙ שָׂ֣א נָ֔א לְפֶ֥שַׁע עַבְדֵ֖י אֱלֹהֵ֣י
אָבִ֑יךָ וַיֵּ֥בְךְּ יוֹסֵ֖ף בְּדַבְּרָ֥ם אֵלָֽיו: 18 וַיֵּלְכוּ֙
גַּם־אֶחָ֔יו וַֽיִּפְּל֖וּ לְפָנָ֑יו וַיֹּ֣אמְר֔וּ הִנֶּ֥נּֽוּ לְךָ֖
לַעֲבָדִֽים: 19 וַיֹּ֧אמֶר אֲלֵהֶ֛ם יוֹסֵ֖ף אַל־תִּירָ֑אוּ

<sup>14</sup>Joseph then returned to Egypt—he, his brothers, and all who had gone with him to bury his father—after burying his father. <sup>15</sup>Joseph's brothers, seeing that their father was dead, now said, "Perhaps Joseph [still] bears us enmity and intends to repay us for all the harm that we inflicted upon him!" <sup>16</sup>So they brought a charge to Joseph, saying, "Your father left this charge before his death, saying, <sup>17</sup>'Thus shall you say to Joseph: Please, I beg of you, forgive the transgression of your brothers and their sin, though they inflicted harm upon you'; yet now please forgive the transgression of the servants of your father's God." Joseph wept as they spoke to him. <sup>18</sup>His brothers also prostrated themselves before him and said, "Here we are, your slaves!" <sup>19</sup>Joseph said to them, "Have no fear, for am I in

family continued on to the cave of Machpelah for a private burial. Yet verse 14 mentions "all who had gone with him," as though the whole entourage was present at the burial. The present verses are, then, better understood as a conclusion, a frame bringing closure to Jacob's initial command, which has now been carried out as he wished. (See also at v. 10, "seven days.")

## Joseph and His Brothers Return to Egypt (50:14–26)

As he had promised Pharaoh (v. 5), Joseph—along with his brothers—returns to Egypt after the burial. The action of the Joseph story concludes as it began, with a confrontation between Joseph and his brothers.

### BROTHERLY RECONCILIATION (50:14–21)

Just as at the beginning of the story the brothers plotted against Joseph and fabricate a speech (Genesis 37), so they do at the end, although much more benignly. Worried now that after Jacob's death, Joseph will take revenge on them for all the trouble

they caused him, they introduce a hitherto unacknowledged deathbed speech of Jacob. The brothers claim that Jacob told them to tell Joseph that he should forgive his brothers.

The brothers' claim is implausible; why did Jacob not tell this directly to Joseph? It is better to conclude that Jacob never said this and that the brothers made it up. (Compare Bathsheba's making up a speech that her husband, King David, was supposed to have said, designating Solomon as heir; I Kings 1.) The language is overly formal, and one can imagine how stiffly and nervously the words were delivered.

But this lie is in essence true. The brothers have repented—and Joseph knows it. He cries when they say this. He will not hold their past actions against them.

*16.* *"Your father."* Not *our* father—to play on the special bond between Joseph and Jacob.

*17.* *"servants of your father's God."* The brothers refer to themselves via a phrase of humility and piety.

*17–18.* Joseph's weeping and the brothers' prostrating themselves and calling themselves "your slaves" is a replay of the earlier meetings between Joseph and his brothers (especially 45:1–5). But this

place of God? <sup>20</sup>Though you intended me harm, God intended it for good, in order to accomplish what is now the case, to keep alive a numerous people. <sup>21</sup>Now, therefore, have no fear—I will provide for you and your little ones." Thus did he comfort them and speak straight to their hearts.

<sup>22</sup>Joseph dwelt in Egypt, he and his father's household, and Joseph lived 110 years. <sup>23</sup>Joseph saw Ephraim's grandchildren; the children of Machir, too, Manasseh's son, were born on Joseph's knees. <sup>24</sup>Joseph then said to his kin, "I am dying, but God will surely take care of you and bring you up out of this land to the land that [God] promised to Abraham, to Isaac, and to Jacob." <sup>25</sup>Joseph adjured Israel's children, saying, "God will surely take care of you; bring my bones up from this place!" <sup>26</sup>Joseph died aged 110 years. They embalmed him and he was put into a coffin in Egypt.

כִּי הֲתַחַת אֱלֹהִים אָנִי: 20 וְאַתֶּם חֲשַׁבְתֶּם עָלַי רָעָה אֱלֹהִים חֲשָׁבָהּ לְטֹבָה לְמַעַן עֲשֹׂה כַּיּוֹם הַזֶּה לְהַחֲיֹת עַם־רָב: 21 וְעַתָּה אַל־תִּירָאוּ אָנֹכִי אֲכַלְכֵּל אֶתְכֶם וְאֶת־טַפְּכֶם וַיְנַחֵם אוֹתָם וַיְדַבֵּר עַל־לִבָּם: 22 וַיֵּשֶׁב יוֹסֵף בְּמִצְרַיִם הוּא וּבֵית אָבִיו וַיְחִי יוֹסֵף מֵאָה וָעֶשֶׂר שָׁנִים: 23 וַיַּרְא יוֹסֵף לְאֶפְרַיִם בְּנֵי שִׁלֵּשִׁים גַּם בְּנֵי מָכִיר בֶּן־מְנַשֶּׁה יֻלְּדוּ עַל־בִּרְכֵּי יוֹסֵף: 24 וַיֹּאמֶר יוֹסֵף אֶל־אֶחָיו אָנֹכִי מֵת וֵאלֹהִים פָּקֹד יִפְקֹד אֶתְכֶם וְהֶעֱלָה אֶתְכֶם מִן־הָאָרֶץ הַזֹּאת אֶל־הָאָרֶץ אֲשֶׁר נִשְׁבַּע לְאַבְרָהָם לְיִצְחָק וּלְיַעֲקֹב: 25 וַיַּשְׁבַּע יוֹסֵף אֶת־בְּנֵי יִשְׂרָאֵל לֵאמֹר פָּקֹד יִפְקֹד אֱלֹהִים אֶתְכֶם וְהַעֲלִתֶם אֶת־עַצְמֹתַי מִזֶּה: 26 וַיָּמָת יוֹסֵף בֶּן־מֵאָה וָעֶשֶׂר שָׁנִים וַיַּחַנְטוּ אֹתוֹ וַיִּישֶׂם בָּאָרוֹן בְּמִצְרָיִם:

time, at last, the relationship is wholly repaired: The brothers are fully reunited, not only physically, but also emotionally and psychologically. The next step, taken at the beginning of Exodus, is for this family to become a people.

### JOSEPH'S LAST DAYS (50:22–26)

**22.** *110 years.* This is the ideal life span in Egyptian culture; the Bible's ideal is 120 years (6:3).

**23.** *Ephraim's grandchildren.* In the Bible, to live to see one's grandchildren is one of the signs of blessing, along with living to a ripe old age (Psalm 128:6). Joseph is even more fortunate: he sees his great-grandchildren.

*Machir.* The eponym of the most important clan in the tribe of Manasseh. (In a genealogy else-

where in the Bible, his wife or sister is named as Maacah; I Chronicles 7:15–16.)

*born on Joseph's knees.* Joseph may have adopted Machir—as Jacob had adopted Ephraim and Manasseh (48:5–6, 12); alternatively, this is a figurative idiom for family continuity.

**24–26.** Joseph, too, like Jacob (49:1–28), makes a deathbed prophecy and extracts a promise from his survivors to bury him in Canaan.

**24.** *"take care."* Heb. *p-k-d,* literally "take notice." Moses will use the same verb and construction when he introduces the idea of the Exodus to the Israelites ("taken note," Exodus 3:16). The same verb appeared earlier in Genesis when God fulfilled a promise to Sarah: she became pregnant with Isaac ("remembered," 21:1).

—*Adele Berlin*



חֲזַק חֲזַק וְנִתְחַזֵּק

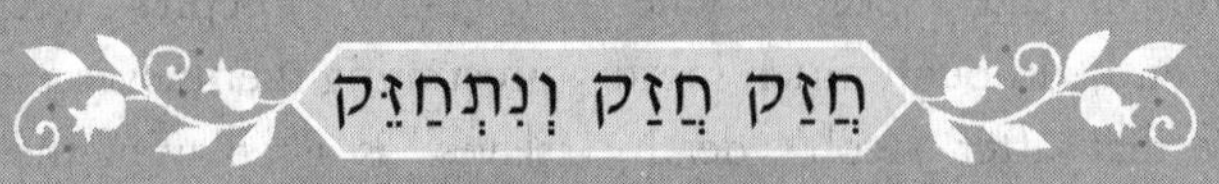

# Another View

ALTHOUGH IT IS NAMED VA-Y'CHI ("he lived"), this parashah details Jacob's death rather than his life. Here Jacob insists on being buried in the cave of Machpelah, near Hebron, where his ancestors and his wife Leah are already buried (49:29–32).

To flesh out the role of the dead in Israelite society, biblical testimony can be combined with archeological evidence. According to Jacob's statement, his family buried its members together: all the matriarchs and patriarchs were interred in the Cave of Machpelah, with the exception of Rachel. That tomb both substantiated the inheritance claim and served as a boundary marker; through his purchase of the field and cave, Abraham had established Israelite claim to territory near Hebron (Genesis 23).

Burial in a cave conforms to actual interment practices in the Hebron region from pre-Israelite times to the fall of the Davidic kingdom (ca. 1800–586 B.C.E.). The local residents indeed buried their family members—including children—together in either natural caves or roughly hewn chambers. Alongside their deceased, they placed ceramic vessels for food and drink, lamps, tools, and personal items. In the 8th and 7th centuries B.C.E., they occasionally provided also a clay female figurine—crudely formed, with little distinguished besides a head (sometimes schematic) and prominent breasts.

Grave goods suggest that the dead were considered to continue some form of existence. Many scholars—but by no means all—identify the female figurines with the fertility goddess Asherah, speculating that perhaps a figurine conveyed the wishes of the living for the dead to intercede on their behalf with God (and Asherah) to promote lactation for children's welfare. Biblical passages likewise attribute ongoing benevolent powers to the deceased. Repeated admonitions not to consult the dead—rather than God—on behalf of the living (Deuteronomy 18:11), the woman of En-dor conjuring up the deceased Samuel to foretell the future (I Samuel 28), and the Israelite householder's annual declaration that no tithed food had been given to the dead (Deuteronomy 26:14) are just three examples of belief in the continuing powers of the dead and the practices of reaching out to them.

*The dead were considered to continue some form of existence.*

*—Elizabeth Bloch-Smith*

# Post-biblical Interpretations

***"treat me with faithful kindness"*** (47:29). In giving his burial instructions, Jacob asks to be treated with *chesed v'emet.* The Midrash asks why Jacob uses this expression—is there really such a thing as *unfaithful* kindness? Rather, Jacob's words come to teach that truly faithful kindness is that which the living show the dead (*B'reishit Rabbah* 96.5). Consider that when a person shows kindness to someone living, no one knows for certain what that person's motivation is; perhaps there is a hope for a favor in return. Furthermore, the outcome of that action is uncertain; while intended to be kind, it may result in harm or pain. But the kindness shown to a dead person—in the form of burial and a eulogy—is always true kindness. In addition, it is disinterested; one expects no favors from the dead (*Itturei Torah*).

***"Rachel died... on the road"*** (48:7). Jacob had once before pressed Joseph to bury him in his ancestral burial plot (47:28–30). The commentators ask why Jacob only now—and not in that earlier scene—discusses his decision to bury Rachel at the roadside (rather than in the cave of Machpelah). One commentator argues that there was room in the cave of Machpelah only for Jacob and one of his wives. Up until now, Joseph had accepted the fact that Leah—as Jacob's senior wife and the mother of his oldest sons—was entitled to that place. However, Jacob has since adopted Joseph's sons, Ephraim and Manasseh, saying that they "will be to me as Reuben and Simeon" (48:5). With his sons recognized as the equals of his father's oldest sons, Joseph then must have inquired why his mother should not henceforth be viewed as Jacob's senior wife—and so be entitled to burial by his side. Therefore, Jacob now explains his decision to bury Rachel near Ephrath (*Itturei Torah*).

In defending his decision, Jacob explains that Rachel is destined to be an intercessor for her descendants (and, in fact, for all Israel). When the Israelites are conquered by the Babylonians, they will pass Rachel's tomb on their way into exile. Rachel will then mediate on their behalf, beseeching God to have compassion on her children (a rabbinic understanding of Jeremiah 31:15–17). Rachel, rather than any other matriarch, is chosen as Israel's intercessor because of her compassion for her sister, and her willingness to overcome her jealousy, when Leah married Jacob by subterfuge (*Itturei Torah*, citing Rashi and *Eichah Rabbah*, proem 24; see *parashat Vayeitzei* at 29:25, p. 176).

***"Rachel died."*** Heb. *metah alai Rachel*, literally "Rachel died on me" or "... upon me." According to *Rut Rabbah* 2, the preposition indicates that Jacob sees Rachel's death as a "greater grief than all his other misfortunes." Another rabbinic tradition construes the preposition as a reminder that a woman's death is painful especially to her husband (BT *Sanhedrin* 22b). The same teaching meanwhile derives the parallel lesson—that a man's death pains his wife more than anyone else—from Ruth 1:3, "And Elimelech, Naomi's husband, died..." because that verse identifies him in terms of her.

***"By you"*** (48:20). In his commentary on this parashah, Rashi cites this verse as the source for the custom of blessing sons with the words "May God make you like Ephraim and Manasseh."

***blessing each one*** (49:28). How could Jacob have "blessed" Simeon and Levi, given the harsh words he directed toward them (49:5–7)? One interpreter of this verse suggests that Jacob's rebuke of his sons

*Jacob explains that Rachel is destined to be an intercessor for all Israel.*

was, in fact, a blessing. In cursing their anger specifically—rather than his sons—Jacob sought to temper it, and to encourage them to distance themselves from their inappropriate behaviors. In this sense, his criticism was intended as a blessing, offering his sons a chance to renounce their past actions and become better people (*Itturei Torah*).

***"Please . . . forgive . . . your brothers"*** (50:17). Given that the narrative did not mention Jacob's having dispatched this exact message, Rabbi Eleazar son of Rabbi Simeon bar Yohai sees this verse as proof that one may alter another person's words for the sake of peace (BT *Y'vamot* 65b); the brothers' claim made it easier for them to approach Joseph and easier for him to respond positively.

***"I will provide"*** (50:21). Commentators wonder why Joseph promised to care for his brothers' children. The brothers believed that the compassion Joseph had shown them since their arrival in Egypt reflected his duty to them as his older brothers. They feared that when they died, Joseph's anger at them for selling him into slavery would emerge and be directed at their children. Joseph reassures them; not only does he have no intention of harming them, but he plans to care for their children even after their death (*Itturei Torah*).

—*Dvora E. Weisberg*

# *Contemporary Reflection*

VA-Y'CHI SPEAKS OF BLESSINGS, of a grandfather blessing his grandsons, a father blessing his sons. Imagine the scene at the end of the Torah portion: Jacob, whose name has been changed to Israel, calls his twelve sons to his deathbed and blesses each one of them. But his real concern, according to our rabbis, is that his sons will abandon his God after he has died. In the Midrash, his sons respond to this unstated fear with words that have become familiar to us: "*Sh'ma Yisrael* (Listen, [Dad—whose name is] Israel!): יהוה is our God, only יהוה." Hearing this, the dying patriarch sighs quietly: "*Baruch shem k'vod malchuto l'olam va'ed* (Blessed is the glorious Name whose kingdom is forever and ever)!" (Midrash *B'reishit Rabbah* 98.4). Each time we say the *Sh'ma*, we are rehearsing this moment. We are the children acknowledging the God of our own father, and we are pledging our own loyalty to the tradition of ancestors.

This farewell scene cannot fail to move us. But it is also confusing. Jacob also has daughters, and the one named Dinah is no longer in the story. Is she not worthy of blessing?

The question of blessing our daughters emerges by way of omission. Jacob and the rest of his family have been reunited with Joseph after many years (Genesis 46). The beloved child Joseph, whom Jacob thought was dead, is not only still alive, but he is a father, with children of his own!

Now, facing death, Jacob says: "I never thought I'd see your face again, and look, God has enabled me to see the face of your children!" (48:8–12). Joseph brings his sons close to his father, with Manasseh, the elder, first. Jacob crosses his arms, putting his right hand on Ephraim's head, and his left on Manasseh's. Joseph intervenes, "Not that way, Father! This is my first-born; put your right hand on his head." But Jacob wants to put Ephraim ahead of Manasseh. Then Jacob blesses them both together with these words: "By you shall the people of Israel give their blessing, saying, "May God make you like Ephraim and Manasseh" (48:18–20).

Why does Jacob bless his younger grandson first? It is hard to imagine this blessing without recalling the earlier moment when Jacob himself stole the blessing that his father Isaac meant for his older brother Esau. In blessing his grandsons, is Jacob repairing his own history, doing intentionally what Isaac did by accident? Is Jacob asserting through his act of blessing that birth order no longer determines one's destiny—and that blessing is an act of will as opposed to an accident of chance?

> *The question of blessing our daughters emerges by way of omission.*

The story raises other questions. Jacob's blessing of his grandsons has become over the centuries the blessing bestowed regularly upon boys; but what is it about Ephraim and Manasseh that merits our blessing our sons in their name? And what about our daughters?

We do not know much about these two young men. We meet them first when they are born (41:51–53), and we encounter them again at this moment of blessing. They are children of an Egyptian mother and a father who is one of the most powerful men in Egypt. They are children born in the Diaspora, not only Egyptian but also Israelite—children living in two worlds.

So why do we bless our sons in their name? Could it be because, like so many Jews throughout history, they grew up in the Diaspora and still remained Jews? Could it be because we imagine that they followed in their father's footsteps—being part of Egyptian culture and politics—and yet still connected to their grandfather, part of Israel's community?

Or perhaps we invoke Ephraim and Manasseh because these are the first two siblings in the Bible who do not fight. With Ephraim and Manasseh, the family pathology that unfolds in the book of Genesis, in which siblings struggle with each other, finally comes to an end. They teach us that we do not have to fight over blessings: there are enough of them to go around.

In the Middle Ages, the customary blessing of children took place before Kol Nidrei—the time when we are most aware of our mortality—a time reminiscent of Jacob's deathbed blessings. In recent centuries, the tradition expanded to include blessing the children every Shabbat evening and on the evening of holidays. Whereas we continue to bless sons by reference to Ephraim and Manasseh ("May God make you like Ephraim and Manasseh"), the tradition for our daughters is different; we bless them with these words: "May God make you like Sarah, Rebecca, Rachel, and Leah."

Why are the blessings so different? Rabbi Richard Levy suggests the following contemporary reason for interpreting the difference:

"Just as Ephraim and Manasseh received their merit not through any acts of their own but only because they were alive and were descendants of Jacob (as are we all), so Jewish boys need not feel that their parents' love is dependent on their accomplishments; they are beloved just because they are children. For Jewish girls, however, who might be inclined by society's prejudices to think that because they are girls they need not set their sights very high, the blessing holds them up to the highest models: May God make you like the greatest women the Torah knows—Sarah, Rebecca, Rachel, and Leah" ("Parashat Vayechi," in *Learn Torah With...*, 1996, Vol. 2, No. 12).

As our community mores continue to evolve, one might claim that we now expect *both* our daughters and our sons to set their sights high. We also hope to create an environment where *both* daughters and sons feel valued simply because they are alive—and are our children. So perhaps there is yet another way to interpret these blessings, one that accounts for changes we value in our contemporary world.

Maybe we can understand Jacob's blessing of his grandchildren this way: "Ephraim, may God help you become the best that Ephraim can be; Manasseh, may God help you become the best that Manasseh can be!" Maybe we should fill in the names of our own children as we bless them. So I would say to my daughter: "Elana, may you be fully Elana!" And to my son I would say: "Joshua, may you be fully Joshua!" Or, in the words of the modern Jewish poet Marcia Falk: "Be who you are... and may you be blessed in all that you are" (*The Book of Blessings*, 1996).

—*Laura Geller*

# *Voices*

## *Rachel*

Rahel (transl. Wendy Zierler)

*Genesis 48:7*

Surely, her blood flows in my blood,
Surely, her voice sings in mine—
Rachel who grazed Laban's flock,
Rachel—Mother of mothers.

Therefore, the house is narrow to me,
and the city—strange,
for her scarf once waved
to the winds of the desert;

and therefore, I shall hold firm to my way
with assurance such as this,
for safeguarded in my feet are the memories,
of back then, of back then!

## *Jacob Blesses Dinah*

Sue Levi Elwell

*Genesis 49*

I have wrestled with the words with which to
bless you,
Dinah, daughter of Leah.
A child, you went out to see the daughters of
the land.
You returned a woman.
Did you raise your voice? Your cries were not
heard.
Blood flowed through the streets of Shechem
and I was afraid.

Like your mother,
you walk among the people with head
unbowed.
May that strength and clarity of vision
continue in the generations to come.

To you, my daughter, belong the blessings
of the breast and the womb,
blessings of justice and care.
Your offspring will learn many tongues
and practice healing arts.
They will build cities of righteousness
and none shall make them afraid.

## *Leah's Last Words*

Sherry Blumberg

*Genesis 49:31*

So, in the end we will be together
Resting throughout time
In that piece of land
Abraham purchased long ago

Here, beautiful Sarah
And kind, strong-willed Rebekah
Lie with their mates, Abraham and Isaac
In the cave of Machpelah

Come, Jacob, let Joseph return you
Not to Rachel's side, but to mine
And here, with the ancestors we shall lie
In the cave of Machpelah

Yet I will miss Rachel, weeping for her children
Death puts to rest all jealousy and fear
And I think of Hagar and Bilhah and Zilpah
as our sons carry Jacob's bones home

This cave, now holy ground,
Open to receive Israel
Our bones wait for those who come
Let Jacob's long wrestling end in peace

## *There's Only One Question*

Merle Feld

*Genesis 50:1–13*

And the only answer
is to keep crying,
to cry daily,
the way one
is supposed to
write daily
or pray daily,
as a discipline.

## *I Know*

Else Lasker-Schüler (transl. Janine Canan)

*Genesis 49:28–33*

I know, that soon I must die.
Yet all the trees are glowing from July's
long-awaited kiss.

My dreams are fading—never
have I written a duller ending
in all my books of rhyme.

To greet me, you pick a flower—
I loved already in the bud.
Yes, I know, that soon I must die.

My breath hovers over God's river—
softly I set my foot
on the path to my eternal home.

## *Nearing the End*

Merle Feld

*Genesis 50:1–13*

One question is
should I save you
a place in my heart,
or should I work
to fill the emptiness,
or, alternatively,
allow the wild grasses
to grow over
the bald spot
naturally, as they will,
in their own good time.

# שמות ✦ *Sh'mot*

# EXODUS

FROM HIGH ATOP Mount Sinai, amidst thunder and lightning, comes a voice: "I יהוה am your God who brought you out of the land of Egypt, the house of bondage" (Exodus 20:2). The exodus from Egypt and the revelation at Mount Sinai form the heart of the book of Exodus and the foundation of biblical Israel and subsequent Judaism. This book contains some of the most memorable episodes in the Torah, including Moses' encounter with God at the Burning Bush, the ten signs and wonders ("plagues") that convince Pharaoh to free the Israelites, the Decalogue ("Ten Commandments"), and the Golden Calf.

The English name "Exodus," which derives from an ancient Greek title meaning "departure from Egypt," summarizes the dramatic events in the first part of the book. The Hebrew name *Sh'mot* ("names"), taken from the book's opening line ("These are the names of the sons of Israel who came to Egypt with Jacob . . ."), reflects the way in which Exodus continues the story that commenced in Genesis. In this second book of the Torah, the children of Israel/Jacob become the people of Israel. In fulfillment of the promises that God makes to the ancestors in Genesis, the patriarch's descendants substantially increase in number and eventually begin their journey to the land of Canaan, guided by the teachings transmitted at Sinai.

*Women take part in Israel's striving to maintain a connection with God.*

Exodus contains four main sections: (*1*) the story of the enslavement of the Israelites and the liberation from Egypt (1:1–15:21);

(*2*) the narrative of the journey from the shores of the Reed Sea to the wilderness of Sinai (15:22–18:27); (*3*) the account of Israel's entry into a covenant with God, including the precepts contained in the Decalogue and the Covenant Collection (19:1–24:18); and (*4*) detailed instructions for building the portable shrine (called the Tabernacle or Tent of Meeting), its furnishing, and the priestly vestments (25:1–40:38).

Many readers wrestle with the historical veracity of these events; but the book defies facile answers. While there is some evidence that enslavement and exodus were a core authentic experience, none of the names of the pharaohs is recorded (although the names of the midwives Shiphrah and Puah are preserved), no dates are given, and the biblical text does not correlate easily with archeological finds or extra-biblical evidence. The book itself does not focus on historical facts, but on the teachings derived from the episodes recounted. The main concern is how subsequent generations will answer the questions "What do you mean by this rite?" (12:26) and "What lessons can be derived from these narrative details?" (See also *Sh'mot*, Contemporary Reflection, p. 326.)

Women play a pivotal role in the Exodus account, especially in *parashat Sh'mot*, which records the heroic deeds of six women who take action to save Moses and the people Israel: the midwives Shiphrah and Puah (1:15–21), Moses' mother Jochebed and sister Miriam (2:1–10), Pharaoh's daughter (2:5–10), and Zipporah, Moses' wife (2:16–22; 4:24–26). Following the miraculous escape from Egypt, Miriam the prophet leads the women in a celebratory song and dance (15:20–21). (Some scholars consider her the probable author of the Song at the Sea as well; see pp. 386–87, 392.) Women figure prominently in the laws of Exodus (see p. 427); and four women are even mentioned in a Levite genealogy (6:14–25).

Yet in other parts of the book, women play a more elusive role. Moses' command before the revelation at Sinai not to go near a woman (19:15) and the grammatically masculine language of the laws have prompted questions about the extent to which women were included in the covenant between God and Israel, questions explored throughout this *Commentary* (see, in particular, *parashat Yitro*). Likewise, the account of the construction of the Tabernacle initially seems to largely exclude women. However, a close reading of the text reveals that women contributed directly to this sacred structure through their donations and their labor.

Thus, in various ways, women take part in the drama of the Exodus and in the people's striving to maintain a connection and covenant with God.

*—Andrea L. Weiss*

# שמות ✦ *Sh'mot*

EXODUS 1:1–6:1

## *The Birth of a Nation*

PARASHAT SH'MOT ("names of...") is both a new beginning and a continuation of the book of Genesis. In that first book, God made a twofold promise to Abraham of progeny and land (12:2–3, 7; 15:1–7, 18–21; 17:1–8). This second book amplifies the passing notice in Genesis (47:27) that part of the promise has been realized: the family of Jacob has "multiplied and increased very greatly" (1:7). Now the Torah turns to the acquisition of the Promised Land, which can begin only with an exodus from Egypt.

Four prominent themes appear in this parashah: the fertility of Israel; the oppression they suffer; God's decision to intervene; and the role of women in saving the nation. Israel's oppression is directly linked to Israel's fertility, for as the family of Jacob grows into the nation of Israel, Pharaoh becomes concerned that Israel will become too numerous and thereby too strong. Although he tries various ways to limit the population increase, he cannot stem Israel's growth. Thus begins the contest between God and Pharaoh that will play out in the story of the signs and wonders (in English parlance, commonly called "plagues") in the subsequent Torah portions.

Also intertwined with the theme of fertility is a more pervasive theme in the Bible: women save the nation. This conclusion emerges clearly from the stories of the matriarchs (Genesis 12–35) and the account of Tamar (Genesis 38), as well as in the book of Ruth: women ensure the continuity of the family—and ultimately the nation—through the birth or protection of a son through whom the line will continue. The beginning of Exodus explores this theme in unusual ways, through unnamed Israelite women and the agency of non-Israelite women. The fertile Israelite women increase the strength of the nation, fulfilling God's promise and threatening the pharaoh. The midwives Shiphrah and

*These heroic women are pivotal in Israel's eventual salvation.*

Puah disobey Pharaoh's command to kill the newborn boys. Moses' mother and sister (whose names are not yet disclosed), and later Pharaoh's own daughter, ensure that he is rescued and raised for future greatness. Finally, his wife, Zipporah, averts disaster by circumcising her son. Thus, while Moses and Aaron serve as the explicitly chosen instruments of God's deliverance, these heroic women are nevertheless pivotal in Israel's eventual salvation.

This parashah also marks a new stage in the national religion. In Genesis, the patriarchs had a personal relationship with God; in Exodus, the Israelites will enter into a communal relationship with the Divine. Previously, God was known to the patriarchs, and known in reference to them, as "the God of Abraham, Isaac, and Jacob" (Exodus 3:6, 16; 4:5). Now, as God hears the cries of the Israelites and resolves to rescue them, God's "official" or personal name, יהוה, will be revealed.

—*Adele Berlin*

## *Outline*

*I.* Israel Proliferates in Egypt (1:1–22)

- *A.* Transition from Genesis: Israelite fertility (vv. 1–7)
- *B.* Pharaoh's response: oppression and killing of the baby boys (vv. 8–16)
- *C.* Midwives' response: opposition to Pharaoh (vv. 17–22)

*II.* Moses' Birth, Upbringing, and Marriage (2:1–22)

- *A.* Moses' birth: women rescue and nurture Moses (vv. 1–10)
- *B.* Moses' flight to Midian (vv. 11–15)
- *C.* Moses' rescue of Reuel's daughters and marriage to Zipporah (vv. 16–22)

*III.* Moses' Mission Commences (2:23–6:1)

- *A.* Setting the stage: God takes note of Israel's suffering (2:23–25)
- *B.* The burning bush: God commissions Moses (3:1–10)
- *C.* Moses resists accepting God's mission (3:11–4:17)
- *D.* Moses accepts God's mission (4:18–23)
- *E.* Interlude: Zipporah rescues the "bridegroom of blood" (4:24–26)
- *F.* Moses and Aaron convince the Israelites of God's plan (4:27–31)
- *G.* Moses and Aaron fail to convince Pharaoh: oppression worsens (5:1–6:1)

1:1

These are the names of the sons of Israel who came to Egypt with Jacob, each coming with his household: 2Reuben, Simeon, Levi, and Judah; 3Issachar, Zebulun, and Benjamin; 4Dan and Naphtali, Gad and Asher. 5The total number of persons that were of Jacob's issue came to seventy, Joseph being already in Egypt. 6Joseph died, and all his brothers, and all that generation. 7But the Israelites were fertile and prolific; they multiplied and increased very greatly, so that the land was filled with them.

א וְאֵ֗לֶּה שְׁמוֹת֙ בְּנֵ֣י יִשְׂרָאֵ֔ל הַבָּאִ֖ים
מִצְרָ֑יְמָה אֵ֣ת יַעֲקֹ֔ב אִ֥ישׁ וּבֵית֖וֹ בָּֽאוּ׃
2 רְאוּבֵ֣ן שִׁמְע֔וֹן לֵוִ֖י וִיהוּדָֽה׃ 3 יששכר
יִשָּׂשכָ֥ר זְבוּלֻ֖ן וּבִנְיָמִֽן׃ 4 דָּ֥ן וְנַפְתָּלִ֖י גָּ֥ד
וְאָשֵֽׁר׃ 5 וַֽיְהִ֗י כָּל־נֶ֛פֶשׁ יֹצְאֵ֥י יֶֽרֶךְ־יַעֲקֹ֖ב
שִׁבְעִ֣ים נָ֑פֶשׁ וְיוֹסֵ֖ף הָיָ֥ה בְמִצְרָֽיִם׃ 6 וַיָּ֤מָת
יוֹסֵף֙ וְכָל־אֶחָ֔יו וְכֹ֖ל הַדּ֥וֹר הַהֽוּא׃ 7 וּבְנֵ֣י
יִשְׂרָאֵ֗ל פָּר֧וּ וַֽיִּשְׁרְצ֛וּ וַיִּרְבּ֥וּ וַיַּֽעַצְמ֖וּ בִּמְאֹ֣ד
מְאֹ֑ד וַתִּמָּלֵ֥א הָאָ֖רֶץ אֹתָֽם׃ פ

## *Israel Proliferates in Egypt* (1:1–22)

Fearful that the Israelites are "too numerous," the new ruler of Egypt tries several increasingly severe measures to reduce the population; yet his efforts produce the opposite effect.

### TRANSITION FROM GENESIS: ISRAELITE FERTILITY (1:1–7)

The names of the sons of Israel were listed in Genesis 46, so their repetition here provides a flashback to the descent into Egypt, which in turn becomes the preface to the exodus from Egypt. Exodus 1:6–7 also functions as an epilogue to the Joseph story. These verses introduce, or re-introduce (see Genesis 47:27), the theme of fertility, which dominates the first two units (Exodus 1:1–2:22).

*1.* ***These are the names.*** The identical expression in Genesis 46:8 introduces a list that includes Dinah, Leah, Serah, Zilpah, Rachel, Asenath, and Bilhah (46:15–25). [The list in Genesis also mentioned dozens of men who are not named here, which indicates that the men whose names *are* repeated here have been given a new role: each of them now represents a whole "house" (clan or tribe) of people—both women and men. —*Ed.*] Although these women do not appear here, named and unnamed women soon take on a central role in the narrative.

*7.* ***fertile and prolific . . . multiplied . . . the land was filled.*** Heb. *paru vayishr'tzu vayirbu . . . vatimalei ha-aretz*, which recalls the proliferation of life at the creation of the universe (Genesis 1:28) and also after the flood (9:1, 7)—particularly the teeming, swarming water creatures and the command to humans to "be fruitful and multiply and fill the earth" (1:28).

◗ The liberation of the people Israel from slavery begins with the saving acts of women.

ANOTHER VIEW ➤ *324*

◗ Why is it that the most unbelievable of Jewish stories is that which is most believed in?

CONTEMPORARY REFLECTION ➤ *326*

◗ This text is about a woman circumcising a child, which in early sources was not a problem.

POST-BIBLICAL INTERPRETATIONS ➤ *324*

◗ We were God's daughters, an army of re-sisters, with our weapons of love and faith.

VOICES ➤ *328*

[8]A new king arose over Egypt who did not
know Joseph. [9]And he said to his people, "Look,
the Israelite people are much too numerous for us.
[10]Let us deal shrewdly with them, so that they may
not increase; otherwise in the event of war they
may join our enemies in fighting against us and rise
from the ground." [11]So they set taskmasters over
them to oppress them with forced labor; and they
built garrison cities for Pharaoh: Pithom and Rameses. [12]But the more they were oppressed, the more
they increased and spread out, so that the [Egyp-
tians] came to dread the Israelites.

[13]The Egyptians ruthlessly imposed upon the
Israelites [14]the various labors that they made them
perform. Ruthlessly they made life bitter for them
with harsh labor at mortar and bricks and with all
sorts of tasks in the field.

8 וַיָּקָם מֶלֶךְ־חָדָשׁ עַל־מִצְרָיִם אֲשֶׁר לֹא־
יָדַע אֶת־יוֹסֵף׃ 9 וַיֹּאמֶר אֶל־עַמּוֹ הִנֵּה עַם
בְּנֵי יִשְׂרָאֵל רַב וְעָצוּם מִמֶּנּוּ׃ 10 הָבָה
נִתְחַכְּמָה לוֹ פֶּן־יִרְבֶּה וְהָיָה כִּי־תִקְרֶאנָה
מִלְחָמָה וְנוֹסַף גַּם־הוּא עַל־שֹׂנְאֵינוּ
וְנִלְחַם־בָּנוּ וְעָלָה מִן־הָאָרֶץ׃ 11 וַיָּשִׂימוּ
עָלָיו שָׂרֵי מִסִּים לְמַעַן עַנֹּתוֹ בְּסִבְלֹתָם
וַיִּבֶן עָרֵי מִסְכְּנוֹת לְפַרְעֹה אֶת־פִּתֹם וְאֶת־
רַעַמְסֵס׃ 12 וְכַאֲשֶׁר יְעַנּוּ אֹתוֹ כֵּן יִרְבֶּה וְכֵן
יִפְרֹץ וַיָּקֻצוּ מִפְּנֵי בְּנֵי יִשְׂרָאֵל׃
13 וַיַּעֲבִדוּ מִצְרַיִם אֶת־בְּנֵי יִשְׂרָאֵל בְּפָרֶךְ׃
14 וַיְמָרְרוּ אֶת־חַיֵּיהֶם בַּעֲבֹדָה קָשָׁה בְּחֹמֶר
וּבִלְבֵנִים וּבְכָל־עֲבֹדָה בַּשָּׂדֶה אֵת כָּל־
עֲבֹדָתָם אֲשֶׁר־עָבְדוּ בָהֶם בְּפָרֶךְ׃

### PHARAOH'S RESPONSE: OPPRESSION AND KILLING OF THE BABY BOYS (1:8–16)

*8. a new king arose over Egypt who did not know Joseph.* This notice indicates more than just the passage of time. Whereas in Joseph's time the pharaoh welcomed the family of Israel, now they face persecution by this new, unnamed king.

*9. "Israelite people."* Heb. *am b'nei yisrael*, which points to a significant transition. What in Joseph's time constituted "the *children* of Israel," that is, an extended family or clan, has now become a people. The shift in language marks a new era in Israel's history.

(Outside the Bible, the first extant mention of Israel as a people occurs in the Merneptah stele, a monument celebrating an Egyptian victory over various peoples in Canaan, including Israel. The pharaoh Merneptah, successor to Rameses II, ruled Egypt from 1213–1203 B.C.E.)

*"much too numerous for us."* Ironically, the king feels threatened by a people who remains a small minority.

*11. forced labor.* The Israelites were not forced into domestic slavery. Instead, they were conscripted for corvée labor, which entailed mandatory unpaid labor on large public projects.

*garrison cities.* These were not pyramids (royal tombs), a popular misconception.

*14. harsh labor at mortar and bricks.* In the ancient Near East, certain types of forced labor, such as building projects, were typically reserved for men. Brickmaking was understood to be men's work, even as voluntary labor. See also the next comment.

*made them perform . . . tasks in the field.* The biblical text speaks vaguely of "them"; thus it does not clearly indicate whether Israelite women were forced into working as slaves along with Israelite men. Women's participation may have been understood since historically in ancient Egypt, both women and men performed field work in state fields; and in ancient Israel, too, both genders regularly engaged in farm labor (see Ruth 2:8–9). More likely, it went without saying that the Egyptians drafted only Israelite men for the physical corvée labor.

15The king of Egypt spoke to the Hebrew midwives, one of whom was named Shiphrah and the other Puah, 16saying, "When you deliver the Hebrew women, look at the birthstool: if it is a boy, kill him; if it is a girl, let her live." 17The midwives, fearing God, did not do as the king of Egypt had told them; they let the boys live. 18So the king of Egypt summoned the midwives and said to them, "Why have you done this thing, letting the boys live?" 19The midwives said to Pharaoh, "Because the Hebrew women are not like the Egyptian women: they are vigorous. Before the midwife can come to

15 וַיֹּאמֶר מֶלֶךְ מִצְרַיִם לַמְיַלְּדֹת הָעִבְרִיֹּת
אֲשֶׁר שֵׁם הָאַחַת שִׁפְרָה וְשֵׁם הַשֵּׁנִית
פּוּעָה׃ 16 וַיֹּאמֶר בְּיַלֶּדְכֶן אֶת־הָעִבְרִיּוֹת
וּרְאִיתֶן עַל־הָאָבְנָיִם אִם־בֵּן הוּא וַהֲמִתֶּן
אֹתוֹ וְאִם־בַּת הִוא וָחָיָה׃ 17 וַתִּירֶאןָ
הַמְיַלְּדֹת אֶת־הָאֱלֹהִים וְלֹא עָשׂוּ כַּאֲשֶׁר
דִּבֶּר אֲלֵיהֶן מֶלֶךְ מִצְרָיִם וַתְּחַיֶּיןָ אֶת־
הַיְלָדִים׃ 18 וַיִּקְרָא מֶלֶךְ־מִצְרַיִם לַמְיַלְּדֹת
וַיֹּאמֶר לָהֶן מַדּוּעַ עֲשִׂיתֶן הַדָּבָר הַזֶּה
וַתְּחַיֶּיןָ אֶת־הַיְלָדִים׃ 19 וַתֹּאמַרְןָ הַמְיַלְּדֹת
אֶל־פַּרְעֹה כִּי לֹא כַנָּשִׁים הַמִּצְרִיֹּת
הָעִבְרִיֹּת כִּי־חָיוֹת הֵנָּה בְּטֶרֶם תָּבוֹא

*15. Hebrew midwives.* It is unclear from the wording of the Hebrew whether they are Hebrew women who work as midwives, or Egyptian midwives who serve the Hebrews. If the latter, the midwives are righteous gentiles who fear God (1:17).

*Shiphrah and... Puah.* The midwives' names are Semitic rather than Egyptian in origin. The name Shiphrah comes from the root meaning "to be beautiful" and has been found also in an a pre-biblical Egyptian document listing Asiatic slaves. The name Puah is attested in Ugaritic (Canaanite) literature and can be traced to a word for a fragrant blossom that came to mean "young girl."

Commentators question how two midwives could have served the entire burgeoning Israelite population. It has been suggested that this account only includes the names of the two midwives who disobeyed Pharaoh. Alternatively, it is possible that the narrator is here mentioning the names of the overseers of two guilds of midwives—or the names of the guilds themselves. Either way, it is significant that while the pharaoh's name is not mentioned, the names of these two women are preserved.

*"if it is a boy, kill him."* The reason is apparently so they could not become soldiers in an opposing army, which is what worries Pharaoh (see v. 10).

*16. "birthstool."* Literally, "two stones," referring to a pair of stones that women used for support as they squatted or kneeled during childbirth. (Not surprisingly, a kneeling woman was the Egyptian hieroglyphic sign for childbirth.) This practice allowed for an easier delivery than the contemporary practice of lying down, and gave access to the midwife; she sat facing a kneeling woman in labor, or behind a squatting woman. After the delivery, the midwife would cut the umbilical cord, bathe the baby, rub the child with salt, and wrap it in strips of cloth (see Ezekiel 16:4).

## MIDWIVES' RESPONSE: OPPOSITION TO PHARAOH (1:17–22)

Twice it is mentioned that the midwives are God-fearing (vv. 17, 21), which undoubtedly gives them the courage to countermand a direct order from Pharaoh by letting the Hebrew boys live. They cleverly make up the excuse that the Hebrew women delivered their children before the midwives could arrive. (See also Another View, p. 324.)

*19. "vigorous."* Heb. *chayot,* which also conveys the sense that the women are like wild animals (*chayot*) in that they gave birth naturally, without the assistance of a midwife. The midwives' resist-

them, they have given birth." 20And God dealt well
with the midwives; and the people multiplied and
increased greatly. 21And [God] established households for the midwives, because they feared God.
22Then Pharaoh charged all his people, saying,
"Every boy that is born you shall throw into the
Nile, but let every girl live."

אֲלֵהֶן הַמְיַלְּדֹת וְיָלָדוּ׃ 20 וַיֵּיטֶב אֱלֹהִים
לַמְיַלְּדֹת וַיִּרֶב הָעָם וַיַּעַצְמוּ מְאֹד׃ 21 וַיְהִי
כִּי־יָרְאוּ הַמְיַלְּדֹת אֶת־הָאֱלֹהִים וַיַּעַשׂ
לָהֶם בָּתִּים׃ 22 וַיְצַו פַּרְעֹה לְכָל־עַמּוֹ
לֵאמֹר כָּל־הַבֵּן הַיִּלּוֹד הַיְאֹרָה תַּשְׁלִיכֻהוּ
וְכָל־הַבַּת תְּחַיּוּן׃ פ

2 A certain member of the house of Levi
went and married a woman of Levi. 2The woman
conceived and bore a son; and when she saw how

ב וַיֵּלֶךְ אִישׁ מִבֵּית לֵוִי וַיִּקַּח אֶת־בַּת־לֵוִי׃
2 וַתַּהַר הָאִשָּׁה וַתֵּלֶד בֵּן וַתֵּרֶא אֹתוֹ

ance goes beyond non-cooperation to a direct defiance of Pharaoh through lies. On subterfuge as recourse for both women and men who face abuses of authority, see p. 142.

*21. [God] established households for the midwives.* The midwives are rewarded for their role in helping to increase the Israelite population by having progeny of their own. [Perhaps this notice means to suggest that a lineage was named after each midwife; elsewhere in the Bible, the word *batim* ("households") refers not merely to having progeny but to heading a lineage (see Ruth 4:11–12). Some scholars speculate that the biblical text mentions Shiphrah and Puah by name because those were lineage names known to the text's ancient audience (*The Torah: A Modern Commentary*, 2005, p. 347). In biblical genealogies, many of the names refer to a town or clan known also from later in Israelite history; occasionally—albeit rarely—the genealogies do mention women's names in this capacity. —*Ed.*]

*22. "throw."* Heb. *tashlichu*, which with regard to a child does not mean "to hurl" but "to abandon" (see Genesis 21:15; Ezekiel 16:5). The predictable—but not immediate—result would be the baby boy's death.

*"into the Nile."* Much as in ancient Greece, where unwanted female babies were left on hillsides, here the males are to be floated in baskets on the water—where they would die out of the sight of their parents, either by sinking into the water or from exposure. | Ironically, Moses will be saved, not killed, by the Nile. Later, a pharaoh will himself be killed with his troops by water in the Sea of Reeds as they pursue the Israelites (14:28).

## *Moses' Birth, Upbringing, and Marriage* (2:1–22)

Heroes in ancient traditions often have auspicious births. The Bible's typical special birth story involves a child born to a barren mother (Isaac, Jacob, Joseph, Samson, Samuel). However, given the emphasis on fertility in the Exodus account, a barren woman motif would be jarring, if not dissonant, so an alternate special birth theme was chosen: the young hero's abandonment and narrow escape from death. Similar stories were told about Sargon of Akkad (a king who established an empire in southern Mesopotamia) and Romulus and Remus (the founders of Rome). In both the Legend of Sargon and the Moses story, the child is born in secret, abandoned by his natural parents, set in a reed basket, and pulled out of the water by a rescuer. A distinctive feature of Exodus 2 is that the rescuers of the future hero are women.

### MOSES' BIRTH: WOMEN RESCUE AND NURTURE MOSES (2:1–10)

Moses' mother manages to keep his birth a secret for three months, until she is no longer able to hide

beautiful he was, she hid him for three months. [3]When she could hide him no longer, she got a wicker basket for him and caulked it with bitumen and pitch. She put the child into it and placed it among the reeds by the bank of the Nile. [4]And his sister stationed herself at a distance, to learn what would befall him.

[5]The daughter of Pharaoh came down to bathe in the Nile, while her maidens walked along the Nile. She spied the basket among the reeds and sent her slave girl to fetch it. [6]When she opened it, she saw that it was a child, a boy crying. She took pity on it and said, "This must be a Hebrew child." [7]Then his sister said to Pharaoh's daughter, "Shall I go and get you a Hebrew nurse to suckle the child for you?" [8]And Pharaoh's daughter answered, "Yes." So the girl went and called the child's mother. [9]And Pharaoh's daughter said to her,

כִּי־ט֣וֹב ה֔וּא וַֽתִּצְפְּנֵ֖הוּ שְׁלֹשָׁ֥ה יְרָחִֽים: [3]וְלֹא־יָֽכְלָ֣ה עוֹד֮ הַצְּפִינוֹ֒ וַתִּֽקַּֽח־לוֹ֙ תֵּ֣בַת גֹּ֔מֶא וַתַּחְמְרָ֥ה בַחֵמָ֖ר וּבַזָּ֑פֶת וַתָּ֤שֶׂם בָּהּ֙ אֶת־הַיֶּ֔לֶד וַתָּ֥שֶׂם בַּסּ֖וּף עַל־שְׂפַ֥ת הַיְאֹֽר: [4]וַתֵּֽתַצַּ֥ב אֲחֹת֖וֹ מֵֽרָחֹ֑ק לְדֵעָ֕ה מַה־יֵּֽעָשֶׂ֖ה לֽוֹ:

[5]וַתֵּ֤רֶד בַּת־פַּרְעֹה֙ לִרְחֹ֣ץ עַל־הַיְאֹ֔ר וְנַֽעֲרֹתֶ֥יהָ הֹֽלְכֹ֖ת עַל־יַ֣ד הַיְאֹ֑ר וַתֵּ֤רֶא אֶת־הַתֵּבָה֙ בְּת֣וֹךְ הַסּ֔וּף וַתִּשְׁלַ֥ח אֶת־אֲמָתָ֖הּ וַתִּקָּחֶֽהָ: [6]וַתִּפְתַּח֙ וַתִּרְאֵ֣הוּ אֶת־הַיֶּ֔לֶד וְהִנֵּה־נַ֖עַר בֹּכֶ֑ה וַתַּחְמֹ֣ל עָלָ֔יו וַתֹּ֕אמֶר מִיַּלְדֵ֥י הָֽעִבְרִ֖ים זֶֽה: [7]וַתֹּ֣אמֶר אֲחֹתוֹ֮ אֶל־בַּת־פַּרְעֹה֒ הַֽאֵלֵ֗ךְ וְקָרָ֤אתִי לָךְ֙ אִשָּׁ֣ה מֵינֶ֔קֶת מִ֖ן הָֽעִבְרִיֹּ֑ת וְתֵינִ֥ק לָ֖ךְ אֶת־הַיָּֽלֶד: [8]וַתֹּֽאמֶר־לָ֥הּ בַּת־פַּרְעֹ֖ה לֵ֑כִי וַתֵּ֨לֶךְ֙ הָֽעַלְמָ֔ה וַתִּקְרָ֖א אֶת־אֵ֥ם הַיָּֽלֶד: [9]וַתֹּ֣אמֶר

• • • • • • • • • • • • • • • • • • • • • • • • • • • • • • • • •

his existence. She then puts the baby in a basket on the Nile where he is rescued by Pharaoh's daughter and aided by his sister. The collaboration of these three women ensures that Moses will survive.

*1. A certain member of the house of Levi . . . married a woman of Levi.* Moses' parents remain anonymous in this story. (In 6:20, they are identified as Amram and Jochebed.) His father plays no further role; his mother and sister (see v. 4) take the initiative and do what is needed to protect Moses.

*2. bore.* See at Genesis 29:32.

*3. wicker.* That is, made from reeds growing along the Nile.

*basket.* Heb. *teivah,* the same word for Noah's ark (Genesis 6–9), another container designed to save special people from the water.

*caulked it with bitumen and pitch.* To make it watertight. Moses' mother thus takes special precautions to ensure the life of her son.

*4. his sister.* This is Miriam, although she is not referred to by name until 15:20, where she is called a prophet. | Although women were generally

not included in genealogical lists, Miriam's name appears in the list of Amram's three children in I Chronicles 5:29. Micah 6:4 mentions her along with Moses and Aaron as having played an equal role in saving Israel. (See also at Numbers 20:1.)

*stationed herself.* Here—and when she approaches Pharaoh's daughter in v. 7—the unnamed sister takes initiative. There is no indication that her mother or father sent her to watch over the baby. Thus this scene highlights Miriam's audacity and ingenuity.

*6. "Hebrew child."* It is significant that Pharaoh's daughter realizes that the baby is a Hebrew, because she probably knows about her father's injunction. If so, her rescue of the child constitutes another case in which a woman bravely defies Pharaoh's decree. (See also 1:17–22.)

*7. "Shall I go and get you a Hebrew nurse . . . ?"* Whereas Moses hesitates later before addressing Pharaoh, his sister displays no reluctance as she now approaches Pharaoh's daughter and enacts a clever plan to reunite Moses with his mother.

"Take this child and nurse it for me, and I will pay your wages." So the woman took the child and nursed it. 10When the child grew up, she brought him to Pharaoh's daughter, who made him her son. She named him Moses, explaining, "I drew him out of the water."

11Some time after that, when Moses had grown up, he went out to his kinsfolk and witnessed their labors. He saw an Egyptian beating a Hebrew, one of his kinsmen. 12He turned this way and that and, seeing no one about, he struck down the Egyptian and hid him in the sand. 13When he went out the next day, he found two Hebrews fighting; so he said to the offender, "Why do you strike your fellow?" 14He retorted, "Who made you chief and ruler over us? Do you mean to kill me as you killed

לָהּ בַּת־פַּרְעֹה הֵילִיכִי אֶת־הַיֶּלֶד הַזֶּה
וְהֵינִקִהוּ לִי וַאֲנִי אֶתֵּן אֶת־שְׂכָרֵךְ וַתִּקַּח
הָאִשָּׁה הַיֶּלֶד וַתְּנִיקֵהוּ׃ 10 וַיִּגְדַּל הַיֶּלֶד
וַתְּבִאֵהוּ לְבַת־פַּרְעֹה וַיְהִי־לָהּ לְבֵן וַתִּקְרָא
שְׁמוֹ מֹשֶׁה וַתֹּאמֶר כִּי מִן־הַמַּיִם
מְשִׁיתִהוּ׃

11 וַיְהִי ׀ בַּיָּמִים הָהֵם וַיִּגְדַּל מֹשֶׁה וַיֵּצֵא
אֶל־אֶחָיו וַיַּרְא בְּסִבְלֹתָם וַיַּרְא אִישׁ מִצְרִי
מַכֶּה אִישׁ־עִבְרִי מֵאֶחָיו׃ 12 וַיִּפֶן כֹּה וָכֹה
וַיַּרְא כִּי אֵין אִישׁ וַיַּךְ אֶת־הַמִּצְרִי וַיִּטְמְנֵהוּ
בַּחוֹל׃ 13 וַיֵּצֵא בַּיּוֹם הַשֵּׁנִי וְהִנֵּה שְׁנֵי־
אֲנָשִׁים עִבְרִים נִצִּים וַיֹּאמֶר לָרָשָׁע לָמָּה
תַכֶּה רֵעֶךָ׃ 14 וַיֹּאמֶר מִי שָׂמְךָ לְאִישׁ שַׂר
וְשֹׁפֵט עָלֵינוּ הַלְהָרְגֵנִי אַתָּה אֹמֵר כַּאֲשֶׁר

*9. "nurse it for me, and I will pay your wages."* Wet-nurse agreements like this one are attested in ancient Near Eastern documents, corroborating that a wet nurse might act as guardian for the infant during the first few years of its life. Here, the baby's mother is to be paid for nursing her own child. [In the ancient Near East, adoptive mothers often relied on wet nurses, as did birth mothers—particularly among the urban elite, and not only due to lack of milk or loss of the birth mother. See the mention of Rebekah's wet nurse in Genesis 24:59 and 35:8 and comments there. Similarly, one Mesopotamian document mentions that a woman had contracted to give her daughter to a team of two other women for wet-nursing; those nurses "received food and clothing for three years" plus a monetary payment (Mayer Gruber, "Breast-Feeding Practices . . . ," 1989, pp. 74–82). —*Ed.*]

*10. When the child grew up.* Extant documents suggest that in Egypt, as elsewhere in the ancient Near East, mothers usually weaned their children at around the age of three. [As long ago as the 18th century B.C.E., Mesopotamian contracts and other documents—including even lawsuits—mention a three-year period for wet-nursing (see previous note). —*Ed.*]

***She named him Moses.*** The narrator gives a Hebrew etiology for Moses' name, but the name is actually Egyptian, meaning "gave birth."

## MOSES' FLIGHT TO MIDIAN (2:11–15)

The young Moses is raised as a prince in the Egyptian court, yet upon his maturity he immediately identifies with his kin, an enslaved people. His first act is murder in defense of his kinsman, which prompts him to flee from Egypt; but after escaping, he almost immediately rescues seven Midianite shepherdesses. The narrative characterizes Moses here as heroic; although later known to be humble and modest, he shows leadership qualities from the start.

*11. kinsfolk.* Heb. *achim*, literally "brothers." Although raised in Pharaoh's palace, Moses considers the Israelite his "brother" and thus acts to defend him.

the Egyptian?" Moses was frightened, and thought: Then the matter is known! [15]When Pharaoh learned of the matter, he sought to kill Moses; but Moses fled from Pharaoh. He arrived in the land of Midian, and sat down beside a well.

[16]Now the priest of Midian had seven daughters. They came to draw water, and filled the troughs to water their father's flock; [17]but shepherds came and drove them off. Moses rose to their defense, and he watered their flock. [18]When they returned to their father Reuel, he said, "How is it that you have come back so soon today?" [19]They answered, "An Egyptian rescued us from the shepherds; he even drew water for us and watered the flock." [20]He said to his daughters, "Where is he then? Why did you leave the [Egyptian]? Ask him in to break bread." [21]Moses consented to stay in that household, and [Reuel] gave Moses his daughter Zipporah as wife. [22]She bore a son whom he named Gershom, for he said, "I have been a stranger in a foreign land."

[23]A long time after that, the king of Egypt died. The Israelites were groaning under the bondage

הָרַגְתָּ אֶת־הַמִּצְרִי וַיִּירָא מֹשֶׁה וַיֹּאמַר אָכֵן
נוֹדַע הַדָּבָר׃ 15 וַיִּשְׁמַע פַּרְעֹה אֶת־הַדָּבָר
הַזֶּה וַיְבַקֵּשׁ לַהֲרֹג אֶת־מֹשֶׁה וַיִּבְרַח מֹשֶׁה
מִפְּנֵי פַרְעֹה וַיֵּשֶׁב בְּאֶרֶץ־מִדְיָן וַיֵּשֶׁב
עַל־הַבְּאֵר׃

16 וּלְכֹהֵן מִדְיָן שֶׁבַע בָּנוֹת וַתָּבֹאנָה
וַתִּדְלֶנָה וַתְּמַלֶּאנָה אֶת־הָרְהָטִים לְהַשְׁקוֹת
צֹאן אֲבִיהֶן׃ 17 וַיָּבֹאוּ הָרֹעִים וַיְגָרְשׁוּם
וַיָּקָם מֹשֶׁה וַיּוֹשִׁעָן וַיַּשְׁקְ אֶת־צֹאנָם׃
18 וַתָּבֹאנָה אֶל־רְעוּאֵל אֲבִיהֶן וַיֹּאמֶר
מַדּוּעַ מִהַרְתֶּן בֹּא הַיּוֹם׃ 19 וַתֹּאמַרְןָ אִישׁ
מִצְרִי הִצִּילָנוּ מִיַּד הָרֹעִים וְגַם־דָּלֹה דָלָה
לָנוּ וַיַּשְׁקְ אֶת־הַצֹּאן׃ 20 וַיֹּאמֶר אֶל־בְּנֹתָיו
וְאַיּוֹ לָמָּה זֶּה עֲזַבְתֶּן אֶת־הָאִישׁ קִרְאֶן לוֹ
וְיֹאכַל לָחֶם׃ 21 וַיּוֹאֶל מֹשֶׁה לָשֶׁבֶת אֶת־
הָאִישׁ וַיִּתֵּן אֶת־צִפֹּרָה בִתּוֹ לְמֹשֶׁה׃
22 וַתֵּלֶד בֵּן וַיִּקְרָא אֶת־שְׁמוֹ גֵּרְשֹׁם כִּי
אָמַר גֵּר הָיִיתִי בְּאֶרֶץ נָכְרִיָּה׃ פ

23 וַיְהִי בַיָּמִים הָרַבִּים הָהֵם וַיָּמָת מֶלֶךְ
מִצְרַיִם וַיֵּאָנְחוּ בְנֵי־יִשְׂרָאֵל מִן־הָעֲבֹדָה

*15. Midian.* A region south of the Negev, which is beyond Egyptian jurisdiction.

***sat down beside a well.*** That is, a central gathering place.

MOSES' RESCUE OF REUEL'S DAUGHTERS AND MARRIAGE TO ZIPPORAH (2:16–22)

Meeting a future wife at a well is a narrative motif that recurs in betrothal type scenes in the Bible (see Genesis 24:10–27; 29:2–14). One difference about this scene is that here the man defends the women and waters their flocks, thus giving prominence to the hero, Moses.

***16. seven daughters.*** [With the five women mentioned earlier, this makes twelve women in Exodus 1–2, a parallel to the twelve tribes. —*Ed.*]

***They ... filled the troughs to water their father's flock.*** Although the seven sisters are not called "shepherds" (as was Rachel in Genesis 29:9), they are clearly acting in that capacity. In the ancient Near East, both females and males took care of the flocks.

***21. Zipporah.*** Her name means "bird." We are not told why she was selected from the seven daughters to marry Moses.

## *Moses' Mission Commences* (2:23–6:1)

The death of the pharaoh who had presumably sought to bring Moses to justice now paves the way for Moses' return to Egypt—but it does not end the oppression of the Israelites. Moses

and cried out; and their cry for help from the
bondage rose up to God. 24 God heard their moaning, and God remembered the covenant with Abraham and Isaac and Jacob. 25 God looked upon the
Israelites, and God took notice of them.

3 Now Moses, tending the flock of his father-
in-law Jethro, the priest of Midian, drove the flock
into the wilderness, and came to Horeb, the mountain of God. 2 An angel of יהוה appeared to him in a
blazing fire out of a bush. He gazed, and there was a
bush all aflame, yet the bush was not consumed.
3 Moses said, "I must turn aside to look at this
marvelous sight; why doesn't the bush burn up?"
4 When יהוה saw that he had turned aside to look,
God called to him out of the bush: "Moses!
Moses!" He answered, "Here I am." 5 And [God]
said, "Do not come closer! Remove your sandals
from your feet, for the place on which you stand is
holy ground!" 6 and continued, "I am the God of
your father's [house]—the God of Abraham, the
God of Isaac, and the God of Jacob." And Moses
hid his face, for he was afraid to look at God.

7 And יהוה continued, "I have marked well the
plight of My people in Egypt and have heeded their
outcry because of their taskmasters; yes, I am
mindful of their sufferings. 8 I have come down to

וַיִּזְעָ֑קוּ וַתַּ֧עַל שַׁוְעָתָ֛ם אֶל־הָאֱלֹהִ֖ים מִן־
הָעֲבֹדָֽה׃ 24 וַיִּשְׁמַ֥ע אֱלֹהִ֖ים אֶת־נַאֲקָתָ֑ם
וַיִּזְכֹּ֤ר אֱלֹהִים֙ אֶת־בְּרִית֔וֹ אֶת־אַבְרָהָ֖ם
אֶת־יִצְחָ֥ק וְאֶֽת־יַעֲקֹֽב׃ 25 וַיַּ֥רְא אֱלֹהִ֖ים
אֶת־בְּנֵ֣י יִשְׂרָאֵ֑ל וַיֵּ֖דַע אֱלֹהִֽים׃ ס

ג וּמֹשֶׁ֗ה הָיָ֥ה רֹעֶ֛ה אֶת־צֹ֛אן יִתְר֥וֹ חֹתְנ֖וֹ
כֹּהֵ֣ן מִדְיָ֑ן וַיִּנְהַ֤ג אֶת־הַצֹּאן֙ אַחַ֣ר הַמִּדְבָּ֔ר
וַיָּבֹ֛א אֶל־הַ֥ר הָאֱלֹהִ֖ים חֹרֵֽבָה׃ 2 וַ֠יֵּרָא
מַלְאַ֨ךְ יְהֹוָ֥ה אֵלָ֛יו בְּלַבַּת־אֵ֖שׁ מִתּ֣וֹךְ הַסְּנֶ֑ה
וַיַּ֗רְא וְהִנֵּ֤ה הַסְּנֶה֙ בֹּעֵ֣ר בָּאֵ֔שׁ וְהַסְּנֶ֖ה אֵינֶ֥נּוּ
אֻכָּֽל׃ 3 וַיֹּ֣אמֶר מֹשֶׁ֔ה אָסֻֽרָה־נָּ֣א וְאֶרְאֶ֔ה
אֶת־הַמַּרְאֶ֥ה הַגָּדֹ֖ל הַזֶּ֑ה מַדּ֖וּעַ לֹא־יִבְעַ֥ר
הַסְּנֶֽה׃ 4 וַיַּ֥רְא יְהֹוָ֖ה כִּ֣י סָ֣ר לִרְא֑וֹת וַיִּקְרָא֩
אֵלָ֨יו אֱלֹהִ֜ים מִתּ֣וֹךְ הַסְּנֶ֗ה וַיֹּ֛אמֶר מֹשֶׁ֥ה
מֹשֶׁ֖ה וַיֹּ֥אמֶר הִנֵּֽנִי׃ 5 וַיֹּ֖אמֶר אַל־תִּקְרַ֣ב
הֲלֹ֑ם שַׁל־נְעָלֶ֙יךָ֙ מֵעַ֣ל רַגְלֶ֔יךָ כִּ֣י הַמָּק֗וֹם
אֲשֶׁ֤ר אַתָּה֙ עוֹמֵ֣ד עָלָ֔יו אַדְמַת־קֹ֖דֶשׁ הֽוּא׃
6 וַיֹּ֗אמֶר אָנֹכִי֙ אֱלֹהֵ֣י אָבִ֔יךָ אֱלֹהֵ֧י אַבְרָהָ֛ם
אֱלֹהֵ֥י יִצְחָ֖ק וֵאלֹהֵ֣י יַעֲקֹ֑ב וַיַּסְתֵּ֤ר מֹשֶׁה֙
פָּנָ֔יו כִּ֣י יָרֵ֔א מֵהַבִּ֖יט אֶל־הָאֱלֹהִֽים׃
7 וַיֹּ֣אמֶר יְהֹוָ֔ה רָאֹ֥ה רָאִ֛יתִי אֶת־עֳנִ֥י עַמִּ֖י
אֲשֶׁ֣ר בְּמִצְרָ֑יִם וְאֶת־צַעֲקָתָ֤ם שָׁמַ֙עְתִּי֙ מִפְּנֵ֣י
נֹגְשָׂ֔יו כִּ֥י יָדַ֖עְתִּי אֶת־מַכְאֹבָֽיו׃ 8 וָאֵרֵ֞ד

reluctantly accepts that he has been chosen by God to deliver them from bondage.

### SETTING THE STAGE: GOD TAKES NOTE OF ISRAEL'S SUFFERING (2:23–25)

The covenant with the ancestors includes the promise of land; however, as predicted in Genesis 15:13–16, this promise would not be fulfilled until the Israelites endured enslavement and affliction. This report of God's resolve to respond to the Israelites' suffering signals the first step in their deliverance.

### THE BURNING BUSH: GOD COMMISSIONS MOSES (3:1–10)

Moses is first introduced to God through a modest vision of a burning bush—an object just odd enough to catch his attention. At first only curious about this unnatural phenomenon, he only gradually becomes aware that he stands before the divine presence.

*1. his father-in-law Jethro.* He was called Reuel in 2:18.

***Horeb.*** Another name for Sinai (see at 18:5).

rescue them from the Egyptians and to bring them
out of that land to a good and spacious land, a land
flowing with milk and honey, the region of the
Canaanites, the Hittites, the Amorites, the Perizzites, the Hivites, and the Jebusites. 9Now the cry
of the Israelites has reached Me; moreover, I have
seen how the Egyptians oppress them. 10Come,
therefore, I will send you to Pharaoh, and you shall
free My people, the Israelites, from Egypt."
11But Moses said to God, "Who am I that I
should go to Pharaoh and free the Israelites from
Egypt?" 12And [God] said, "I will be with you; that
shall be your sign that it was I who sent you. And
when you have freed the people from Egypt, you
shall worship God at this mountain."
13Moses said to God, "When I come to the Israelites and say to them, 'The God of your ancestors has sent me to you,' and they ask me, 'What is
his name?' what shall I say to them?" 14And God
said to Moses, "Ehyeh-Asher-Ehyeh," continuing,

לְהַצִּילוֹ ׀ מִיַּד מִצְרַיִם וּלְהַעֲלֹתוֹ מִן־הָאָרֶץ
הַהִוא אֶל־אֶרֶץ טוֹבָה וּרְחָבָה אֶל־אֶרֶץ
זָבַת חָלָב וּדְבָשׁ אֶל־מְקוֹם הַכְּנַעֲנִי וְהַחִתִּי
וְהָאֱמֹרִי וְהַפְּרִזִּי וְהַחִוִּי וְהַיְבוּסִי׃ 9 וְעַתָּה
הִנֵּה צַעֲקַת בְּנֵי־יִשְׂרָאֵל בָּאָה אֵלָי וְגַם־
רָאִיתִי אֶת־הַלַּחַץ אֲשֶׁר מִצְרַיִם לֹחֲצִים
אֹתָם׃ 10 וְעַתָּה לְכָה וְאֶשְׁלָחֲךָ אֶל־פַּרְעֹה
וְהוֹצֵא אֶת־עַמִּי בְנֵי־יִשְׂרָאֵל מִמִּצְרָיִם׃
11 וַיֹּאמֶר מֹשֶׁה אֶל־הָאֱלֹהִים מִי אָנֹכִי כִּי
אֵלֵךְ אֶל־פַּרְעֹה וְכִי אוֹצִיא אֶת־בְּנֵי יִשְׂרָאֵל
מִמִּצְרָיִם׃ 12 וַיֹּאמֶר כִּי־אֶהְיֶה עִמָּךְ וְזֶה־לְּךָ
הָאוֹת כִּי אָנֹכִי שְׁלַחְתִּיךָ בְּהוֹצִיאֲךָ אֶת־
הָעָם מִמִּצְרַיִם תַּעַבְדוּן אֶת־הָאֱלֹהִים עַל
הָהָר הַזֶּה׃
13 וַיֹּאמֶר מֹשֶׁה אֶל־הָאֱלֹהִים הִנֵּה אָנֹכִי
בָא אֶל־בְּנֵי יִשְׂרָאֵל וְאָמַרְתִּי לָהֶם אֱלֹהֵי
אֲבוֹתֵיכֶם שְׁלָחַנִי אֲלֵיכֶם וְאָמְרוּ־לִי מַה־
שְּׁמוֹ מָה אֹמַר אֲלֵהֶם׃ 14 וַיֹּאמֶר אֱלֹהִים
אֶל־מֹשֶׁה אֶהְיֶה אֲשֶׁר אֶהְיֶה וַיֹּאמֶר כֹּה

## MOSES RESISTS ACCEPTING GOD'S MISSION (3:11–4:17)

Like some later biblical prophets, Moses is reluctant to accept his prophetic commission, partially out of modesty and partially out of fear of how he will be received and whether he will be successful. Moses raises four objections (3:11, 13; 4:1, 10), each of which God addresses.

*11. "Who am I that I should go to Pharaoh . . . ?"* When Moses first objects to his prophetic calling, he expresses humility and lack of self-confidence. In response, God assures Moses that God will be with him (v. 12).

*13. "what shall I say to them?"* Moses' second objection concerns what proof to offer to the Israelites that God really sent him. The proof will be the knowledge of God's name (vv. 14–15), which is connected to the God of the ancestors, a deity already known to the Israelites. In the course of reassuring Moses, God foreshadows the events that will unfold: the people will be freed; they will return to the place where Moses stands now; Pharaoh will only let the Israelites go after God has smitten Egypt; and the Israelites will not leave Egypt empty-handed (vv. 16–22).

*14. "Ehyeh-Asher-Ehyeh."* God seems to proclaim this enigmatic phrase as a name, although it appears nowhere else in the Bible. Its first and third words derive from the Hebrew root *h-y-h* ("to be"). Thus, this divine name suggests pure existence, being—a presence that cannot be seen or touched but which is most certainly there. Left in transliteration here, the expression sometimes has been translated as "I Am That/Who I Am" or "I Will Be What I Will Be." The present verse may be explaining God's permanent name (see next comment) in terms of this one, as an instructive "folk"

"Thus shall you say to the Israelites, 'Ehyeh sent me to you.'" [15]And God said further to Moses, "Thus shall you speak to the Israelites: יהוה, the God of your ancestors—the God of Abraham, the God of Isaac, and the God of Jacob—has sent me to you:

This shall be My name forever,

This My appellation for all eternity.

[16]"Go and assemble the elders of Israel and say to them: יהוה, the God of your ancestors—the God of Abraham, Isaac, and Jacob—has appeared to me and said, 'I have taken note of you and of what is being done to you in Egypt, [17]and I have declared: I will take you out of the misery of Egypt to the land of the Canaanites, the Hittites, the Amorites, the Perizzites, the Hivites, and the Jebusites, to a land flowing with milk and honey.' [18]They will listen to you; then you shall go with the elders of Israel to the king of Egypt and you shall say to him, 'יהוה, the God of the Hebrews, became manifest to us. Now therefore, let us go a distance of three days into the wilderness to sacrifice to our God יהוה.' [19]Yet I know that the king of Egypt will let you go only because of a greater might. [20]So I will stretch out My hand and smite Egypt with various wonders which I will work upon them; after that he shall let you go. [21]And I will dispose the Egyptians favorably toward this people, so that when you

תֹּאמַ֖ר לִבְנֵ֣י יִשְׂרָאֵ֑ל אֶֽהְיֶ֖ה שְׁלָחַ֥נִי אֲלֵיכֶֽם׃
[15] וַיֹּאמֶר֩ ע֨וֹד אֱלֹהִ֜ים אֶל־מֹשֶׁ֗ה כֹּֽה־תֹאמַר֮ אֶל־בְּנֵ֣י יִשְׂרָאֵל֒ יְהֹוָ֞ה אֱלֹהֵ֣י אֲבֹֽתֵיכֶ֗ם אֱלֹהֵ֨י אַבְרָהָ֜ם אֱלֹהֵ֥י יִצְחָ֛ק וֵֽאלֹהֵ֥י יַעֲקֹ֖ב שְׁלָחַ֣נִי אֲלֵיכֶ֑ם זֶה־שְּׁמִ֣י לְעֹלָ֔ם וְזֶ֥ה זִכְרִ֖י לְדֹ֥ר דֹּֽר׃
[16] לֵ֣ךְ וְאָֽסַפְתָּ֞ אֶת־זִקְנֵ֣י יִשְׂרָאֵ֗ל וְאָֽמַרְתָּ֤ אֲלֵהֶם֙ יְהֹוָ֞ה אֱלֹהֵ֤י אֲבֹֽתֵיכֶם֙ נִרְאָ֣ה אֵלַ֔י אֱלֹהֵ֧י אַבְרָהָ֛ם יִצְחָ֥ק וְיַעֲקֹ֖ב לֵאמֹ֑ר פָּקֹ֤ד פָּקַ֨דְתִּי֙ אֶתְכֶ֔ם וְאֶת־הֶֽעָשׂ֥וּי לָכֶ֖ם בְּמִצְרָֽיִם׃
[17] וָֽאֹמַ֗ר אַעֲלֶ֣ה אֶתְכֶם֮ מֵֽעֳנִ֣י מִצְרַ֒יִם֒ אֶל־אֶ֤רֶץ הַֽכְּנַעֲנִי֙ וְהַ֣חִתִּ֔י וְהָֽאֱמֹרִי֙ וְהַפְּרִזִּ֔י וְהַֽחִוִּ֖י וְהַיְבוּסִ֑י אֶל־אֶ֛רֶץ זָבַ֥ת חָלָ֖ב וּדְבָֽשׁ׃
[18] וְשָֽׁמְע֖וּ לְקֹלֶ֑ךָ וּבָאתָ֡ אַתָּה֩ וְזִקְנֵ֨י יִשְׂרָאֵ֜ל אֶל־מֶ֣לֶךְ מִצְרַ֗יִם וַאֲמַרְתֶּ֤ם אֵלָיו֙ יְהֹוָ֞ה אֱלֹהֵ֤י הָֽעִבְרִיִּים֙ נִקְרָ֣ה עָלֵ֔ינוּ וְעַתָּ֗ה נֵֽלְכָה־נָּ֞א דֶּ֣רֶךְ שְׁלֹ֤שֶׁת יָמִים֙ בַּמִּדְבָּ֔ר וְנִזְבְּחָ֖ה לַֽיהֹוָ֥ה אֱלֹהֵֽינוּ׃ [19] וַאֲנִ֣י יָדַ֔עְתִּי כִּ֠י לֹֽא־יִתֵּ֥ן אֶתְכֶ֛ם מֶ֥לֶךְ מִצְרַ֖יִם לַֽהֲלֹ֑ךְ וְלֹ֖א בְּיָ֥ד חֲזָקָֽה׃
[20] וְשָֽׁלַחְתִּ֤י אֶת־יָדִי֙ וְהִכֵּיתִ֣י אֶת־מִצְרַ֔יִם בְּכֹל֙ נִפְלְאֹתַ֔י אֲשֶׁ֥ר אֶֽעֱשֶׂ֖ה בְּקִרְבּ֑וֹ וְאַֽחֲרֵי־כֵ֖ן יְשַׁלַּ֥ח אֶתְכֶֽם׃ [21] וְנָֽתַתִּ֛י אֶת־חֵ֥ן הָֽעָם־הַזֶּ֖ה בְּעֵינֵ֣י מִצְרָ֑יִם וְהָיָה֙ כִּ֣י תֵֽלֵכ֔וּן לֹ֥א

---

etymology—in much the same way that the Bible often portrays mothers as explaining via wordplay the name that she has given her child.

*15.* **יהוה, *the God of your ancestors.*"** God here proposes to be identified by an additional name, the more familiar יהוה (Y-H-V-H, *yud-hei-vav-hei*). Known in English as the tetragrammaton (from the Greek for "the four consonants"), Jews came to consider the pronunciation of this personal divine name so sacred that it was avoided and has been lost over time. In Jewish tradition, the convention developed in speech to substitute יהוה with *Adonai* (the Hebrew word meaning "my Lord") or *Hashem* ("the

name"), an even more indirect substitution. In 1783, Moses Mendelssohn proposed the translation "the Eternal," which has since become popular in certain Bible translations and religious circles. Meanwhile, modern academic scholars have widely accepted a reconstruction as "Yahweh," although there is only circumstantial evidence in its favor; many Jews avoid it. Whereas the word "Lord" invokes a masculine image, the divine name revealed in this verse is free of gendered associations (see at Genesis 2:4).

*21.* **"*I will dispose the Egyptians favorably toward this people.*"** That is, the Egyptians will willingly provide objects of value.

go, you will not go away empty-handed. [22]Each
woman shall borrow from her neighbor and the
lodger in her house objects of silver and gold, and
clothing, and you shall put these on your sons and
daughters, thus stripping the Egyptians."
4 But Moses spoke up and said, "What if
they do not believe me and do not listen to me, but
say: יהוה did not appear to you?" [2]יהוה said to him,
"What is that in your hand?" And he replied, "A
rod." [3][God] said, "Cast it on the ground." He cast
it on the ground and it became a snake; and Moses
recoiled from it. [4]Then יהוה said to Moses, "Put
out your hand and grasp it by the tail"—he put out
his hand and seized it, and it became a rod in his
hand—[5]"that they may believe that יהוה, the God
of their ancestors, the God of Abraham, the God of
Isaac, and the God of Jacob, did appear to you."

תֵלְכוּ רֵיקָם׃ 22 וְשָׁאֲלָה אִשָּׁה מִשְּׁכֶנְתָּהּ
וּמִגָּרַת בֵּיתָהּ כְּלֵי־כֶסֶף וּכְלֵי זָהָב וּשְׂמָלֹת
וְשַׂמְתֶּם עַל־בְּנֵיכֶם וְעַל־בְּנֹתֵיכֶם וְנִצַּלְתֶּם
אֶת־מִצְרָיִם׃
ד וַיַּעַן מֹשֶׁה וַיֹּאמֶר וְהֵן לֹא־יַאֲמִינוּ לִי
וְלֹא יִשְׁמְעוּ בְּקֹלִי כִּי יֹאמְרוּ לֹא־נִרְאָה
אֵלֶיךָ יְהֹוָה׃ 2 וַיֹּאמֶר אֵלָיו יְהֹוָה מזה מַה־
זֶּה בְיָדֶךָ וַיֹּאמֶר מַטֶּה׃ 3 וַיֹּאמֶר הַשְׁלִיכֵהוּ
אַרְצָה וַיַּשְׁלִכֵהוּ אַרְצָה וַיְהִי לְנָחָשׁ וַיָּנָס
מֹשֶׁה מִפָּנָיו׃ 4 וַיֹּאמֶר יְהֹוָה אֶל־מֹשֶׁה
שְׁלַח יָדְךָ וֶאֱחֹז בִּזְנָבוֹ וַיִּשְׁלַח יָדוֹ וַיַּחֲזֶק בּוֹ
וַיְהִי לְמַטֶּה בְּכַפּוֹ׃ 5 לְמַעַן יַאֲמִינוּ כִּי־
נִרְאָה אֵלֶיךָ יְהֹוָה אֱלֹהֵי אֲבֹתָם אֱלֹהֵי
אַבְרָהָם אֱלֹהֵי יִצְחָק וֵאלֹהֵי יַעֲקֹב׃

*22. "Each woman."* In these instructions, the women are the ones involved in the transfer of goods; but in 12:35–36, where the event takes place, women are not specifically mentioned. (Compare also 11:2, 3.)

*"borrow."* See at 11:2.

*"neighbor... lodger."* The Hebrew nouns are feminine, which may imply that Egyptian and Israelite women were on good terms, despite the subjugation of the Israelites. The wording of this verse suggests that both peoples lived in close proximity, not in segregated areas as depicted in the Joseph story (Genesis 46:34). Confirmation of this integration can be found later, in the need for the Israelites to mark their doorposts with blood so that their first-born sons will not be killed with those of the Egyptians (12:13; see also at 11:2).

*"lodger in her house."* This phrase is puzzling. Did Israelites have Egyptian servants in their homes? Some commentators suggest that the Israelites had Egyptian slave-women like Hagar (Genesis 16:1) who served as legally recognized concubines and could bear their master legitimate children.

*"silver and gold, and clothing."* That is, objects of value, in fulfillment of God's promise to Abraham that after four hundred years of servitude in a foreign land, God would bring judgment upon the nation they are serving and Israel "shall go out with many possessions" (Genesis 15:13–14).

*"on your sons and daughters."* Evidence from the ancient Near East suggests that men as well as women wore jewelry. Later, women and men will contribute to the Tabernacle their gold and silver jewelry and expensive textiles (35:21–29), presumably goods obtained from the Egyptians.

*"thus stripping the Egyptians."* Many commentators have been troubled by the implication that the Israelites would plunder the Egyptians. Commentators justify the taking of these valuable objects either as just payment for the years of slave labor, or as voluntary gifts from Egyptians who were eager to get rid of the Israelites.

*4:1. "What if they do not believe me?"* Moses' third objection expresses his concern that the Israelites will not believe him. At this point, Moses receives a set of more concrete signs to prove God's power: the rod that becomes a snake, the leprous hand, and the water that turns to blood.

<sup>6</sup>יהוה said to him further, "Put your hand into your bosom." He put his hand into his bosom; and when he took it out, his hand was encrusted with snowy scales! <sup>7</sup>And [God] said, "Put your hand back into your bosom."—He put his hand back into his bosom; and when he took it out of his bosom, there it was again like the rest of his body.—<sup>8</sup>"And if they do not believe you or pay heed to the first sign, they will believe the second. <sup>9</sup>And if they are not convinced by both these signs and still do not heed you, take some water from the Nile and pour it on the dry ground, and it—the water that you take from the Nile—will turn to blood on the dry ground."

<sup>10</sup>But Moses said to יהוה, "Please, O my lord, I have never been good with words, either in times past or now that You have spoken to Your servant; I am slow of speech and slow of tongue." <sup>11</sup>And יהוה said to him, "Who gives humans speech? Who makes them dumb or deaf, seeing or blind? Is it not I, יהוה? <sup>12</sup>Now go, and I will be with you as you speak and will instruct you what to say." <sup>13</sup>But he said, "Please, O my lord, make someone else Your agent." <sup>14</sup>יהוה became angry with Moses and said, "There is your brother Aaron the Levite. He, I know, speaks readily. Even now he is setting out to meet you, and he will be happy to see you. <sup>15</sup>You shall speak to him and put the words in his mouth—I will be with you and with him as you speak, and tell both of you what to do—<sup>16</sup>and he shall speak for you to the people. Thus he shall serve as your spokesman, with you playing the role of God to him, <sup>17</sup>and take with you this rod, with which you shall perform the signs."

6 וַיֹּ֩אמֶר֩ יְהֹוָ֨ה ל֜וֹ ע֗וֹד הָֽבֵא־נָ֤א יָֽדְךָ֙ בְּחֵיקֶ֔ךָ וַיָּבֵ֥א יָד֖וֹ בְּחֵיק֑וֹ וַיּ֣וֹצִאָ֔הּ וְהִנֵּ֥ה יָד֖וֹ מְצֹרַ֥עַת כַּשָּֽׁלֶג׃ 7 וַיֹּ֗אמֶר הָשֵׁ֤ב יָֽדְךָ֙ אֶל־חֵיקֶ֔ךָ וַיָּ֥שֶׁב יָד֖וֹ אֶל־חֵיק֑וֹ וַיּֽוֹצִאָהּ֙ מֵֽחֵיק֔וֹ וְהִנֵּה־שָׁ֖בָה כִּבְשָׂרֽוֹ׃ 8 וְהָיָה֙ אִם־לֹ֣א יַֽאֲמִ֣ינוּ לָ֔ךְ וְלֹ֣א יִשְׁמְע֔וּ לְקֹ֖ל הָאֹ֣ת הָרִאשׁ֑וֹן וְהֶֽאֱמִ֔ינוּ לְקֹ֖ל הָאֹ֥ת הָאַֽחֲרֽוֹן׃ 9 וְהָיָ֡ה אִם־לֹ֣א יַֽאֲמִ֡ינוּ גַּם֩ לִשְׁנֵ֨י הָֽאֹת֜וֹת הָאֵ֗לֶּה וְלֹ֤א יִשְׁמְעוּן֙ לְקֹלֶ֔ךָ וְלָֽקַחְתָּ֙ מִמֵּימֵ֣י הַיְאֹ֔ר וְשָֽׁפַכְתָּ֖ הַיַּבָּשָׁ֑ה וְהָי֤וּ הַמַּ֨יִם֙ אֲשֶׁ֣ר תִּקַּ֣ח מִן־הַיְאֹ֔ר וְהָי֥וּ לְדָ֖ם בַּיַּבָּֽשֶׁת׃

10 וַיֹּ֨אמֶר מֹשֶׁ֣ה אֶל־יְהֹוָה֮ בִּ֣י אֲדֹנָי֒ לֹא֩ אִ֨ישׁ דְּבָרִ֜ים אָנֹ֗כִי גַּ֤ם מִתְּמוֹל֙ גַּ֣ם מִשִּׁלְשֹׁ֔ם גַּ֛ם מֵאָ֥ז דַּבֶּרְךָ֖ אֶל־עַבְדֶּ֑ךָ כִּ֧י כְבַד־פֶּ֛ה וּכְבַ֥ד לָשׁ֖וֹן אָנֹֽכִי׃ 11 וַיֹּ֨אמֶר יְהֹוָ֜ה אֵלָ֗יו מִ֣י שָׂ֣ם פֶּה֮ לָֽאָדָם֒ א֚וֹ מִֽי־יָשׂ֣וּם אִלֵּ֔ם א֥וֹ חֵרֵ֖שׁ א֣וֹ פִקֵּ֑חַ א֣וֹ עִוֵּ֔ר הֲלֹ֥א אָֽנֹכִ֖י יְהֹוָֽה׃ 12 וְעַתָּ֖ה לֵ֑ךְ וְאָֽנֹכִ֤י אֶֽהְיֶה֙ עִם־פִּ֔יךָ וְהֽוֹרֵיתִ֖יךָ אֲשֶׁ֥ר תְּדַבֵּֽר׃ 13 וַיֹּ֖אמֶר בִּ֣י אֲדֹנָ֑י שְֽׁלַֽח־נָ֖א בְּיַד־תִּשְׁלָֽח׃ 14 וַיִּֽחַר־אַ֨ף יְהֹוָ֜ה בְּמֹשֶׁ֗ה וַיֹּ֙אמֶר֙ הֲלֹ֨א אַֽהֲרֹ֤ן אָחִ֨יךָ֙ הַלֵּוִ֔י יָדַ֕עְתִּי כִּֽי־דַבֵּ֥ר יְדַבֵּ֖ר ה֑וּא וְגַ֤ם הִנֵּה־הוּא֙ יֹצֵ֣א לִקְרָאתֶ֔ךָ וְרָֽאֲךָ֖ וְשָׂמַ֥ח בְּלִבּֽוֹ׃ 15 וְדִבַּרְתָּ֣ אֵלָ֗יו וְשַׂמְתָּ֥ אֶת־הַדְּבָרִ֖ים בְּפִ֑יו וְאָֽנֹכִ֗י אֶֽהְיֶ֤ה עִם־פִּ֨יךָ֙ וְעִם־פִּ֔יהוּ וְהֽוֹרֵיתִ֣י אֶתְכֶ֔ם אֵ֖ת אֲשֶׁ֥ר תַּֽעֲשֽׂוּן׃ 16 וְדִבֶּר־ה֥וּא לְךָ֖ אֶל־הָעָ֑ם וְהָ֤יָה הוּא֙ יִֽהְיֶה־לְּךָ֣ לְפֶ֔ה וְאַתָּ֖ה תִּֽהְיֶה־לּ֥וֹ לֵֽאלֹהִֽים׃ 17 וְאֶת־הַמַּטֶּ֥ה הַזֶּ֖ה תִּקַּ֣ח בְּיָדֶ֑ךָ אֲשֶׁ֥ר תַּֽעֲשֶׂה־בּ֖וֹ אֶת־הָֽאֹתֹֽת׃ פ

*10. "I have never been good with words."* Moses' fourth objection reflects his understanding that a prophet's success depends on his ability to speak, since he must represent God in a convincing manner. Again, God assures Moses about the source of prophetic power, though God also becomes annoyed with Moses' excuses and appoints Aaron as the official spokesperson (4:11–17).

<sup>18</sup>Moses went back to his father-in-law Jether and said to him, "Let me go back to my kinsfolk in Egypt and see how they are faring." And Jethro said to Moses, "Go in peace."

<sup>19</sup>יהוה said to Moses in Midian, "Go back to Egypt, for all the authorities who sought to kill you are dead." <sup>20</sup>So Moses took his wife and sons, mounted them on an ass, and went back to the land of Egypt; and Moses took the rod of God with him.

<sup>21</sup>And יהוה said to Moses, "When you return to Egypt, see that you perform before Pharaoh all the marvels that I have put within your power. I, however, will stiffen his heart so that he will not let the people go. <sup>22</sup>Then you shall say to Pharaoh, 'Thus says יהוה: Israel is My first-born son. <sup>23</sup>I have said to you, "Let My son go, that he may worship Me," yet you refuse to let him go. Now I will slay your first-born son.'"

<sup>24</sup>At a night encampment on the way, יהוה encountered him and sought to kill him. <sup>25</sup>So Zipporah took a flint and cut off her son's foreskin,

יח וַיֵּ֨לֶךְ מֹשֶׁ֜ה וַיָּ֣שָׁב ׀ אֶל־יֶ֣תֶר חֹֽתְנ֗וֹ וַיֹּ֤אמֶר ל֣וֹ אֵ֣לְכָה נָּ֗א וְאָשׁ֙וּבָה֙ אֶל־אַחַ֣י אֲשֶׁר־ בְּמִצְרַ֔יִם וְאֶרְאֶ֖ה הַעוֹדָ֣ם חַיִּ֑ים וַיֹּ֧אמֶר יִתְר֛וֹ לְמֹשֶׁ֖ה לֵ֥ךְ לְשָׁלֽוֹם׃

יט וַיֹּ֨אמֶר יְהֹוָ֤ה אֶל־מֹשֶׁה֙ בְּמִדְיָ֔ן לֵ֖ךְ שֻׁ֣ב מִצְרָ֑יִם כִּי־מֵ֙תוּ֙ כׇּל־הָ֣אֲנָשִׁ֔ים הַֽמְבַקְשִׁ֖ים אֶת־נַפְשֶֽׁךָ׃ כ וַיִּקַּ֨ח מֹשֶׁ֜ה אֶת־אִשְׁתּ֣וֹ וְאֶת־בָּנָ֗יו וַיַּרְכִּבֵם֙ עַל־הַ֣חֲמֹ֔ר וַיָּ֖שׇׁב אַ֣רְצָה מִצְרָ֑יִם וַיִּקַּ֥ח מֹשֶׁ֛ה אֶת־מַטֵּ֥ה הָאֱלֹהִ֖ים בְּיָדֽוֹ׃

כא וַיֹּ֣אמֶר יְהֹוָה֮ אֶל־מֹשֶׁה֒ בְּלֶכְתְּךָ֙ לָשׁ֣וּב מִצְרַ֔יְמָה רְאֵ֗ה כׇּל־הַמֹּֽפְתִים֙ אֲשֶׁר־שַׂ֣מְתִּי בְיָדֶ֔ךָ וַעֲשִׂיתָ֖ם לִפְנֵ֣י פַרְעֹ֑ה וַאֲנִי֙ אֲחַזֵּ֣ק אֶת־ לִבּ֔וֹ וְלֹ֥א יְשַׁלַּ֖ח אֶת־הָעָֽם׃ כב וְאָמַרְתָּ֖ אֶל־ פַּרְעֹ֑ה כֹּ֚ה אָמַ֣ר יְהֹוָ֔ה בְּנִ֥י בְכֹרִ֖י יִשְׂרָאֵֽל׃ כג וָאֹמַ֣ר אֵלֶ֗יךָ שַׁלַּ֤ח אֶת־בְּנִי֙ וְיַֽעַבְדֵ֔נִי וַתְּמָאֵ֖ן לְשַׁלְּח֑וֹ הִנֵּה֙ אָנֹכִ֣י הֹרֵ֔ג אֶת־בִּנְךָ֖ בְּכֹרֶֽךָ׃

כד וַיְהִ֥י בַדֶּ֖רֶךְ בַּמָּל֑וֹן וַיִּפְגְּשֵׁ֣הוּ יְהֹוָ֔ה וַיְבַקֵּ֖שׁ הֲמִיתֽוֹ׃ כה וַתִּקַּ֨ח צִפֹּרָ֜ה צֹ֗ר וַתִּכְרֹת֙ אֶת־

- - - - - - - - - -

## MOSES ACCEPTS GOD'S MISSION (4:18–23)

Moses asks for his father-in-law's permission to return to Egypt; yet he does not reveal the immense, divinely appointed task that awaits him.

**18. *Jether.*** An alternate form of the name Jethro (3:1).

**22–23.** If Pharaoh refuses to free God's first-born, Israel, then Pharaoh's first-born will suffer the consequences. Moses is never recorded as repeating these words to Pharaoh. Yet they set the tone for the long confrontation that will shortly ensue.

## INTERLUDE: ZIPPORAH RESCUES THE "BRIDEGROOM OF BLOOD" (4:24–26)

Moses' mission begins with an enigmatic episode. Perhaps an old, no-longer-understood story

was placed here because of the connection between the slaying of the first-born mentioned in the preceding verse and the blood of circumcision of Zipporah's son. Later blood will mark the Israelite homes, where the first-born will be spared (12:21–23). In both cases, blood is an apotropaic—warding off death.

**24. *sought to kill him.*** It is unclear who the intended victim is: Moses—or his and Zipporah's son, Gershom (2:22). Aside from God, the only name mentioned in this episode is Zipporah's.

**25. *So Zipporah took a flint and cut off her son's foreskin.*** This is the only place in the Bible that explicitly mentions a woman's performing the rite of circumcision. | Why was Gershom not circumcised before now? Commentators surmise that Zipporah's father might have prevented Gershom's

and touched his legs with it, saying, "You are truly a
bridegroom of blood to me!" 26And when [God]
let him alone, she added, "A bridegroom of blood
because of the circumcision."

27יהוה said to Aaron, "Go to meet Moses in the
wilderness." He went and met him at the mountain
of God, and he kissed him. 28Moses told Aaron
about all the things that יהוה had committed to
him and all the signs about which he had been
instructed. 29Then Moses and Aaron went and
assembled all the elders of the Israelites. 30Aaron
repeated all the words that יהוה had spoken to
Moses, and he performed the signs in the sight of
the people, 31and the people were convinced. When
they heard that יהוה had taken note of the Israelites
and that [God] had seen their plight, they bowed
low in homage.

5 Afterward Moses and Aaron went and said
to Pharaoh, "Thus says יהוה, the God of Israel: Let
My people go that they may celebrate a festival for

עָרְלַת בְּנָהּ וַתַּגַּע לְרַגְלָיו וַתֹּאמֶר כִּי חֲתַן־
דָּמִים אַתָּה לִי׃ 26 וַיִּרֶף מִמֶּנּוּ אָז אָמְרָה
חֲתַן דָּמִים לַמּוּלֹת׃ פ

27 וַיֹּאמֶר יְהוָה אֶל־אַהֲרֹן לֵךְ לִקְרַאת
מֹשֶׁה הַמִּדְבָּרָה וַיֵּלֶךְ וַיִּפְגְּשֵׁהוּ בְּהַר
הָאֱלֹהִים וַיִּשַּׁק־לוֹ׃ 28 וַיַּגֵּד מֹשֶׁה לְאַהֲרֹן
אֵת כָּל־דִּבְרֵי יְהוָה אֲשֶׁר שְׁלָחוֹ וְאֵת כָּל־
הָאֹתֹת אֲשֶׁר צִוָּהוּ׃ 29 וַיֵּלֶךְ מֹשֶׁה וְאַהֲרֹן
וַיַּאַסְפוּ אֶת־כָּל־זִקְנֵי בְּנֵי יִשְׂרָאֵל׃ 30 וַיְדַבֵּר
אַהֲרֹן אֵת כָּל־הַדְּבָרִים אֲשֶׁר־דִּבֶּר יְהוָה
אֶל־מֹשֶׁה וַיַּעַשׂ הָאֹתֹת לְעֵינֵי הָעָם׃
31 וַיַּאֲמֵן הָעָם וַיִּשְׁמְעוּ כִּי־פָקַד יְהוָה
אֶת־בְּנֵי יִשְׂרָאֵל וְכִי רָאָה אֶת־עָנְיָם וַיִּקְּדוּ
וַיִּשְׁתַּחֲוּוּ׃
ה וְאַחַר בָּאוּ מֹשֶׁה וְאַהֲרֹן וַיֹּאמְרוּ אֶל־
פַּרְעֹה כֹּה־אָמַר יְהוָה אֱלֹהֵי יִשְׂרָאֵל שַׁלַּח

circumcision, or Moses might have postponed it in anticipation of their difficult journey back to Egypt.

*26. "bridegroom of blood."* This baffling phrase may reflect an ancient custom (long since abandoned) of circumcision at the time of marriage.

### MOSES AND AARON CONVINCE THE ISRAELITES OF GOD'S PLAN (4:27–31)

As Aaron becomes Moses' assistant and spokesman, the two brothers must convince the Israelites of God's intentions before they can convince Pharaoh.

### MOSES AND AARON FAIL TO CONVINCE PHARAOH: OPPRESSION WORSENS (5:1–6:1)

The story returns to the reality of the Israelite suffering, which only gets worse after Moses and Aaron's initial meeting with Pharaoh. Pharaoh's pronouncement that the Israelite men must henceforth gather their own straw and still meet their quotas of bricks is reminiscent of the earlier pharaoh's decrees regarding "birth control" (1:16, 22); but here the pronouncement is also calculated to undermine the Israelites' acceptance of Moses and Aaron. The scene is now set, physically and psychologically, for a contest between the might of Pharaoh and the might of God.

*1–2.* Moses announces to Pharaoh the name of the God of Israel, whom Moses represents, but Pharaoh claims not to know this deity and therefore has no intention of heeding God's words. This is the main issue in the account that will follow of the signs and wonders: how and when will Pharaoh come to know God and understand that God's power trumps all other divine powers?

*1. "Let My people go that they may celebrate a festival for Me."* In God's name, Moses will repeatedly request to bring the people to the wilderness for a worship festival; he does not go so far as to ask to leave Egypt permanently.

Me in the wilderness." [2]But Pharaoh said, "Who is יהוה that I should heed him and let Israel go? I do not know יהוה, nor will I let Israel go." [3]They answered, "The God of the Hebrews has become manifest to us. Let us go, we pray, a distance of three days into the wilderness to sacrifice to our God יהוה, lest [God] strike us with pestilence or sword." [4]But the king of Egypt said to them, "Moses and Aaron, why do you distract the people from their tasks? Get to your labors!" [5]And Pharaoh continued, "The people of the land are already so numerous, and you would have them cease from their labors!"

[6]That same day Pharaoh charged the taskmasters and overseers of the people, saying, [7]"You shall no longer provide the people with straw for making bricks as heretofore; let them go and gather straw for themselves. [8]But impose upon them the same quota of bricks as they have been making heretofore; do not reduce it, for they are shirkers; that is why they cry, 'Let us go and sacrifice to our God!' [9]Let heavier work be laid upon the laborers; let them keep at it and not pay attention to deceitful promises."

[10]So the taskmasters and overseers of the people went out and said to the people, "Thus says Pharaoh: I will not give you any straw. [11]You must go

אֶת־עַמִּ֔י וְיָחֹ֥גּוּ לִ֖י בַּמִּדְבָּֽר׃ 2 וַיֹּ֣אמֶר פַּרְעֹ֔ה
מִ֤י יְהֹוָה֙ אֲשֶׁ֣ר אֶשְׁמַ֣ע בְּקֹל֔וֹ לְשַׁלַּ֖ח אֶת־
יִשְׂרָאֵ֑ל לֹ֤א יָדַ֙עְתִּי֙ אֶת־יְהֹוָ֔ה וְגַ֥ם אֶת־
יִשְׂרָאֵ֖ל לֹ֥א אֲשַׁלֵּֽחַ׃ 3 וַיֹּ֣אמְר֔וּ אֱלֹהֵ֥י
הָעִבְרִ֖ים נִקְרָ֣א עָלֵ֑ינוּ נֵ֣לְכָה נָּ֡א דֶּרֶךְ֩
שְׁלֹ֨שֶׁת יָמִ֜ים בַּמִּדְבָּ֗ר וְנִזְבְּחָה֙ לַיהֹוָ֣ה
אֱלֹהֵ֔ינוּ פֶּ֨ן־יִפְגָּעֵ֔נוּ בַּדֶּ֖בֶר א֥וֹ בֶחָֽרֶב׃
4 וַיֹּ֤אמֶר אֲלֵהֶם֙ מֶ֣לֶךְ מִצְרַ֔יִם לָ֚מָּה מֹשֶׁ֣ה
וְאַהֲרֹ֔ן תַּפְרִ֥יעוּ אֶת־הָעָ֖ם מִמַּֽעֲשָׂ֑יו לְכ֖וּ
לְסִבְלֹתֵיכֶֽם׃ 5 וַיֹּ֣אמֶר פַּרְעֹ֔ה הֵן־רַבִּ֥ים
עַתָּ֖ה עַ֣ם הָאָ֑רֶץ וְהִשְׁבַּתֶּ֥ם אֹתָ֖ם
מִסִּבְלֹתָֽם׃

6 וַיְצַ֥ו פַּרְעֹ֖ה בַּיּ֣וֹם הַה֑וּא אֶת־הַנֹּגְשִׂ֣ים
בָּעָ֔ם וְאֶת־שֹׁטְרָ֖יו לֵאמֹֽר׃ 7 לֹ֣א תֹאסִפ֞וּן
לָתֵ֨ת תֶּ֥בֶן לָעָ֛ם לִלְבֹּ֥ן הַלְּבֵנִ֖ים כִּתְמ֣וֹל
שִׁלְשֹׁ֑ם הֵ֣ם יֵֽלְכ֔וּ וְקֹשְׁשׁ֥וּ לָהֶ֖ם תֶּֽבֶן׃
8 וְאֶת־מַתְכֹּ֨נֶת הַלְּבֵנִ֜ים אֲשֶׁ֨ר הֵ֜ם עֹשִׂ֨ים
תְּמ֤וֹל שִׁלְשֹׁם֙ תָּשִׂ֣ימוּ עֲלֵיהֶ֔ם לֹ֥א תִגְרְע֖וּ
מִמֶּ֑נּוּ כִּֽי־נִרְפִּ֣ים הֵ֔ם עַל־כֵּ֗ן הֵ֤ם צֹֽעֲקִים֙
לֵאמֹ֔ר נֵלְכָ֖ה נִזְבְּחָ֥ה לֵאלֹהֵֽינוּ׃ 9 תִּכְבַּ֧ד
הָעֲבֹדָ֛ה עַל־הָאֲנָשִׁ֖ים וְיַעֲשׂוּ־בָ֑הּ וְאַל־יִשְׁע֖וּ
בְּדִבְרֵי־שָֽׁקֶר׃
10 וַיֵּ֨צְא֜וּ נֹגְשֵׂ֤י הָעָם֙ וְשֹׁ֣טְרָ֔יו וַיֹּאמְר֖וּ אֶל־
הָעָ֣ם לֵאמֹ֑ר כֹּ֚ה אָמַ֣ר פַּרְעֹ֔ה אֵינֶ֥נִּי נֹתֵ֛ן
לָכֶ֖ם תֶּֽבֶן׃ 11 אַתֶּ֗ם לְכ֤וּ קְחוּ֙ לָכֶ֣ם תֶּ֔בֶן

*6. **taskmasters and overseers.*** The "taskmasters" are Egyptians; the "overseers" are Israelite leaders of work-gangs who are supervised by the taskmasters (see v. 14).

*8.* Pharaoh claims repeatedly that the request for a three-day festival is an excuse to slack off from work (see also v. 17).

*9. **"laborers."*** Heb. *anashim*, a plural noun that can apply also to women in some contexts; but in the present context of brickmaking—considered to be men's work—it would go without saying that Pharaoh is placing an increased burden on the men in particular; see at 1:14. That Pharaoh would now single out males for harsh treatment is predictable, given that it is men (namely, Moses and Aaron, and presumably the elders for whom they are speaking) who openly challenge his authority. Furthermore, Pharaoh has been trying to get rid of the males all along (1:16, 22).

***"deceitful promises."*** Does Pharaoh refer here to the promise of a three-day festival vacation, or of liberation? Either way, he is trying to undermine Moses' credibility. Perhaps Pharaoh already senses that the request for a festival is a ruse.

and get the straw yourselves wherever you can find it; but there shall be no decrease whatever in your work." [12]Then the people scattered throughout the land of Egypt to gather stubble for straw. [13]And the taskmasters pressed them, saying, "You must complete the same work assignment each day as when you had straw." [14]And the overseers of the Israelites, whom Pharaoh's taskmasters had set over them, were beaten. "Why," they were asked, "did you not complete the prescribed amount of bricks, either yesterday or today, as you did before?"

[15]Then the overseers of the Israelites came to Pharaoh and cried: "Why do you deal thus with your servants? [16]No straw is issued to your servants, yet they demand of us: Make bricks! Thus your servants are being beaten, when the fault is with your own people." [17]He replied, "You are shirkers, shirkers! That is why you say, 'Let us go and sacrifice to יהוה.' [18]Be off now to your work! No straw shall be issued to you, but you must produce your quota of bricks!"

[19]Now the overseers of the Israelites found themselves in trouble because of the order, "You must not reduce your daily quantity of bricks." [20]As they left Pharaoh's presence, they came upon Moses and Aaron standing in their path, [21]and they said to them, "May יהוה look upon you and punish you for making us loathsome to Pharaoh and his courtiers—putting a sword in their hands to slay us." [22]Then Moses returned to יהוה and said, "O my lord, why did You bring harm upon this people? Why did You send me? [23]Ever since I came to Pharaoh to speak in Your name, he has dealt worse with this people; and still You have not delivered Your people."

מֵאֲשֶׁר תִּמְצָאוּ כִּי אֵין נִגְרָע מֵעֲבֹדַתְכֶם
דָּבָר׃ 12 וַיָּפֶץ הָעָם בְּכָל־אֶרֶץ מִצְרָיִם
לְקֹשֵׁשׁ קַשׁ לַתֶּבֶן׃ 13 וְהַנֹּגְשִׂים אָצִים
לֵאמֹר כַּלּוּ מַעֲשֵׂיכֶם דְּבַר־יוֹם בְּיוֹמוֹ
כַּאֲשֶׁר בִּהְיוֹת הַתֶּבֶן׃ 14 וַיֻּכּוּ שֹׁטְרֵי בְּנֵי
יִשְׂרָאֵל אֲשֶׁר־שָׂמוּ עֲלֵהֶם נֹגְשֵׂי פַרְעֹה
לֵאמֹר מַדּוּעַ לֹא כִלִּיתֶם חָקְכֶם לִלְבֹּן
כִּתְמוֹל שִׁלְשֹׁם גַּם־תְּמוֹל גַּם־הַיּוֹם׃
15 וַיָּבֹאוּ שֹׁטְרֵי בְּנֵי יִשְׂרָאֵל וַיִּצְעֲקוּ אֶל־
פַּרְעֹה לֵאמֹר לָמָּה תַעֲשֶׂה כֹה לַעֲבָדֶיךָ׃
16 תֶּבֶן אֵין נִתָּן לַעֲבָדֶיךָ וּלְבֵנִים אֹמְרִים
לָנוּ עֲשׂוּ וְהִנֵּה עֲבָדֶיךָ מֻכִּים וְחָטָאת עַמֶּךָ׃
17 וַיֹּאמֶר נִרְפִּים אַתֶּם נִרְפִּים עַל־כֵּן אַתֶּם
אֹמְרִים נֵלְכָה נִזְבְּחָה לַיהוָה׃ 18 וְעַתָּה לְכוּ
עִבְדוּ וְתֶבֶן לֹא־יִנָּתֵן לָכֶם וְתֹכֶן לְבֵנִים
תִּתֵּנוּ׃
19 וַיִּרְאוּ שֹׁטְרֵי בְנֵי־יִשְׂרָאֵל אֹתָם בְּרָע
לֵאמֹר לֹא־תִגְרְעוּ מִלִּבְנֵיכֶם דְּבַר־יוֹם
בְּיוֹמוֹ׃ 20 וַיִּפְגְּעוּ אֶת־מֹשֶׁה וְאֶת־אַהֲרֹן
נִצָּבִים לִקְרָאתָם בְּצֵאתָם מֵאֵת פַּרְעֹה׃
21 וַיֹּאמְרוּ אֲלֵהֶם יֵרֶא יְהוָה עֲלֵיכֶם וְיִשְׁפֹּט
אֲשֶׁר הִבְאַשְׁתֶּם אֶת־רֵיחֵנוּ בְּעֵינֵי פַרְעֹה
וּבְעֵינֵי עֲבָדָיו לָתֶת־חֶרֶב בְּיָדָם לְהָרְגֵנוּ׃
22 וַיָּשָׁב מֹשֶׁה אֶל־יְהוָה וַיֹּאמַר אֲדֹנָי לָמָה
הֲרֵעֹתָה לָעָם הַזֶּה לָמָּה זֶּה שְׁלַחְתָּנִי׃
23 וּמֵאָז בָּאתִי אֶל־פַּרְעֹה לְדַבֵּר בִּשְׁמֶךָ
הֵרַע לָעָם הַזֶּה וְהַצֵּל לֹא־הִצַּלְתָּ אֶת־
עַמֶּךָ׃

*14.* The Egyptian government now puts additional pressure on the overseers, who were responsible for meeting the quota of bricks. Their reaction is to seek redress from Pharaoh, and—when that fails—to blame Moses and Aaron.

*21.* This condemnation of Moses and Aaron is the first of a long list of Israelite complaints that will accompany and follow the Exodus.

*22.* As he will do many times, Moses turns to God to argue on behalf of the people. He also expresses despair at being sent on what seems to be a doomed mission.

6 Then יהוה said to Moses, "You shall soon see what I will do to Pharaoh: he shall let them go because of a greater might; indeed, because of a greater might he shall drive them from his land."

ו וַיֹּ֤אמֶר יְהֹוָה֙ אֶל־מֹשֶׁ֔ה עַתָּ֣ה תִרְאֶ֔ה אֲשֶׁ֥ר אֶעֱשֶׂ֖ה לְפַרְעֹ֑ה כִּ֣י בְיָ֤ד חֲזָקָה֙ יְשַׁלְּחֵ֔ם וּבְיָ֣ד חֲזָקָ֔ה יְגָרְשֵׁ֖ם מֵאַרְצֽוֹ׃ ס

*6:1.* Foreshadowing what is to come in the following three Torah portions, God assures Moses that Pharaoh will soon see God's might.

—*Adele Berlin*

# Another View

THE LIBERATION of the people Israel from slavery in Egypt begins with the saving acts of women. First, the midwives of the Hebrews refuse to follow Pharaoh's edict to destroy male Hebrew children. As Tikva Frymer-Kensky has noted, when the pharaoh confronts the midwives, they tell him just what he wants to hear (*Reading the Women of the Bible*, 2002, p. 26). To the ruler worried about a people that "swarms" and fills the land (1:7), Shiphrah and Puah claim that the Hebrew women are *chayot* ("vigorous"; or, like beasts)—creatures capable of giving birth by themselves, without the civilized intervention of professionals. When he buys their excuse, the incongruous encounter between the king-of-all-Egypt and the midwives-to-the-slaves exposes Pharaoh as a fool.

The next savior is Moses' mother, who defies Pharaoh by hiding her son and preparing a basket that saves him from death (2:3). When Pharaoh's own daughter discovers the crying boy among the reeds of the Nile (2:5–6), she recognizes immediately that this must be one of the Hebrew children doomed to death by her father. Moved by empathy and humanity, she too defies the king when she rescues the boy. The baby's sister then appears, offering to secure a nursemaid, who just happens to be Moses' own mother (2:7–9). Through this conspiracy of enterprising women who collaborate with each other across ethnic, class, and religious lines, the future leader of the Exodus is spared—and with him the entire people Israel.

The presence of these five women at the opening of this critical Israelite foundation myth is immensely significant. Deeply wise in fundamental, life-sustaining ways, these women understand instinctively that Pharaoh should be disobeyed; and, with initiative, they act on this knowledge. Ultimately, these women's defiance demeans the male tyrant. Thus, from these women filled with a power rooted in moral reason, an ethical concern for life, and the capacity to empathize, we learn a valuable lesson in political ethics: the very weakest in society can contribute to liberation by judiciously engaging in acts of civil disobedience.

> *From these women, we learn a valuable lesson in political ethics.*

—*Susan Niditch*

# Post-biblical Interpretations

***Shiphrah and... Puah*** (1:15). The Rabbis are worried about unnamed women and intrigued with the Hebrew midwives. They conclude that Shiphrah and Puah are actually designations for Jochebed and Miriam (Midrash *Sifrei B'midbar* 78). They explain this via wordplay on the meaning of the names: Shiphrah was associated with Jochebed because she made children beautiful, and Puah was linked with Miriam because she wept over Moses. This conflation of the characters limits the number of women involved in the salvation of Moses and, by association, all Israel.

***And his sister stationed herself*** (2:4). The Rabbis engage in creative midrash, claiming Miriam had prophetic powers. A midrash found in BT *Sotah* 12a–13a, among other sources, indicates that when Pharaoh decided to kill all Israelite male newborns, the

Israelites chose to cease procreating, and Amram—Moses's destined father—divorced his wife. His daughter Miriam rebuked him and described his decree as harsher than Pharaoh's, since Amram's action spelled disaster for females as well as males. Furthermore, Miriam prophesied that a son born to Amram would redeem Israel. Her father listened to her and remarried Jochebed, after which Moses was born. Yet, when they were forced to abandon Moses in the reeds, Amram no longer believed Miriam's prophecy and reprimanded her. To find out whether she was right, Miriam "stationed herself" to see what would befall her brother.

***The daughter of Pharaoh came down to bathe in the Nile*** (2:5). The Rabbis are also interested in naming Pharaoh's daughter. Using a verse from I Chronicles 4:18 ("These are the sons of Bithiah daughter of Pharaoh"), they identify Bithiah as her name and interpret it as a message from God: "Moses was not your son, yet you called him your son; so too you are not my daughter, yet I call you my daughter" (Bithiah, or *bat Yah*, means daughter of God) (*Vayikra Rabbah* 1.3). This very positive attitude to this Egyptian woman downplays her foreign background.

In BT *Sotah* 12b, the Rabbis transform Pharaoh's daughter into a prophet, claiming that the reason she could tell that the child in the basket was a Hebrew (2:5–6) was because of her unacknowledged prophetic capabilities. Since it is inconceivable to the Rabbis that such insight could be found in a non-Israelite woman, they thus conclude that Pharaoh's daughter had converted. To reach this conclusion, they interpret "the daughter of Pharaoh came down to bathe in the Nile" (2:5) with the words "she went down to wash away her father's idolatry." The Rabbis are also interested in presenting Moses' upbringing as untainted by heathen practices. They remark that a Hebrew wet nurse (ultimately his mother) was sought for Moses after he had turned down all the Egyptian wet nurses, their milk obviously not being kosher. Thus, the Rabbis are more concerned with a differentiation between Jews and Gentiles than the Bible seems to be.

***and [Reuel] gave Moses his daughter Zipporah as wife*** (2:21). Interestingly, Zipporah's foreign background does not seem to have been an issue for the Rabbis. When retelling the story of Moses' marriage to Zipporah, they make Moses a greater hero than in the Bible. They do so by suggesting that the shepherds from whom Moses saves Zipporah and her sisters had actually threatened to rape them (*B'reishit Rabbah* 70.11). In this stereotypical, patriarchal manner, they portray the man who is to become her husband as protecting the defenseless woman from sexual danger.

***יהוה encountered him and sought to kill him*** (4:24). In order to make sense of this mysterious story, the Rabbis fill in its gaps with the following details: Before encountering God in the desert, Moses had promised his heathen father-in-law to allow his first-born to be raised as a heathen. But God is merciless and will kill Moses unless he goes back on his word. Moses is placed in a difficult situation, which is resolved by Zipporah, who had herself made no such promise to her father. Thus, she is the one who circumcises the child (*M'chilta*, *Yitro* 1).

*Miriam prophesied that a son born to her father Amram would redeem Israel.*

***Zipporah . . . cut off her son's foreskin*** (4:25). This text is about a woman circumcising a child, which in early sources was not a problem (Tosefta *Shabbat* 15:8); yet for the Rabbis of the Babylonian Talmud it was. In a complicated halachic discussion they maintain that some Jews are not circumcised for medical reasons yet still are considered Jews, while some gentiles (such as Arabs) are circumcised but obviously are not Jews. In this context the Babylonian Talmud disqualifies women as circumcisors. This means that if a woman were to perform circumcision, her action would not be ritually valid. At this point, the Rabbis invoke the memory of Zipporah circumcising her son. To this seeming contradiction they respond with two alternative readings. One suggests that Zipporah only gave instructions and a man who was present performed the circumcision. The other claims that Zipporah took the knife, but that Moses actually circumcised his sons (*Avodah Zarah* 27a).

—*Tal Ilan*

• • • • •

# *Contemporary Reflection*

PARASHAT SH'MOT SETS THE STAGE for the drama that plays out not only in the rest of the book of Exodus but around tables worldwide as Jewish families gather year in and year out for Passover seders. The Exodus and the experiences connected with it—the slavery of the Israelites, their liberation from Egypt, the covenant at Sinai, and the journey in the wilderness toward the Promised Land—are indelibly stamped on the Jewish collective memory and imagination. North American Jews relish, arguably more than any other holiday, the festival of Passover whose symbolic foods serve as props for retelling the tale of Israelite bondage that ceases with God's redemptive miracles. The story is fantastic in every sense of the term: fanciful, remarkable, unreal, and superb. The biblical writers are at their best in these passages, crafting a gripping narrative inscribed with timeless ethical imperatives, such as "You shall not wrong nor oppress a stranger, for you were strangers in the land of Egypt" (Exodus 22:20), and theological conundrums, like why does God repeatedly harden Pharaoh's heart—thereby preventing the necessary redemption without plagues befalling Egypt? This story has sustained generations of Jews, from esteemed commentators of yore to today's questioning sons and daughters with mouths full of matzah and *maror*. Jews of all stripes rally to the Exodus cry; even those with mere peripheral knowledge of things Jewish resonate to "Let my people go!"

So why is it that the most unbelievable of Jewish stories is that which is most believed in? Why does the Exodus charm and beguile liberal Jews, even Reform Jews, who are products of a movement of leaders who early on dismissed what the 1885 Pittsburgh Platform calls "miraculous narratives" of the Bible as "reflecting the primitive ideas of its own age..."?

Indeed, on one level, the popularity of the Exodus is baffling. One might imagine that its lack of historical veracity would knock it off its pedestal. After all, biblical scholars, whose stock in trade is comparative materials of contemporaneous ancient Near Eastern cultures and archeology, inform us that few of the book's details can be substantiated by cold, hard facts.

*To my students' question, "But is it true?" I respond, "Yes!" and "No!"*

Take, for example, the matter of dating. Based on chronological indications in the text itself, the Hebrew Bible would have us believe that the Exodus took place in about 1446 B.C.E. One of the mathematical "proofs" for such a claim depends on the following information provided to the biblical reader in various places: Exodus 12:40 claims that the Israelite slavery in Egypt lasted 430 years (a figure that contradicts the prediction of an Egyptian sojourn of 400 years or four generations; Genesis 15:13, 16). I Kings 6:1 states that the Temple was constructed 480 years after the Exodus, during the fourth year of Solomon's forty-year reign (I Kings 11:42), which scholars date as 966 B.C.E. According to these calculations, the Israelites were enslaved in Egypt between 1876 and 1446 B.C.E. Moreover, if, as the text indicates, the Israelites wandered in the wilderness for forty years before entering the Promised Land, the conquest of Canaan would have begun in approximately 1406 B.C.E.

Besides the fact that the Torah texts do not agree with one another on the length of Israelite enslavement in Egypt, these numbers do not add up against the evidence of extra-biblical sources. In fact, the first clear historical proof of an Israelite presence in Canaan at all is the inscription on the so-called Israel Stele of the pharaoh Merneptah, dating to about 1207 B.C.E. In other words, the biblical claim of a 15th-century Exodus is off by 200 years when compared to the archeological evidence. Moreover, ancient records demonstrate that Egypt controlled Canaan in 1446, a fact that makes an escape from Egypt to Canaan at that time rather unlikely.

Another aspect of the story that troubles modern readers is the purported size of the Exodus. The biblical claim of 600,000 men (Exodus 12:37), which including their families would total nearly 2 million people, is hyperbolic at best. Plus, many of the sites appearing in the detailed itinerary of the Israelites' route from Egypt to Canaan (see Numbers 33) cannot be verified.

Certainly, scholars like the preeminent Nahum Sarna have argued convincingly that corroborating evidence suggests a "plausible context" for the Exodus story. Many have confidently asserted that a group of people who later became Israel went down to Egypt from Canaan, settled there, and became oppressed as foreigners. At some point, it can be presumed, they were conscripted into labor and oppressed as foreigners. Some of them later escaped and professed to a transcendent experience with a divine being in the desert. Still later, they or their descendants entered Canaan, where, according to Sarna, they were joined by other peoples and became the biblical nation of Israel.

From my perspective as a professor of Jewish history and a Reform rabbi, dismissing the story because it conflicts with historical data misses the point. Holding the Torah to critical standards of historiography is unfair, because it is not intended to be a history book containing scholars' attempts to re-create an impartial rendering of what occurred in the past. Instead, the Torah is a knitting together of narratives composed to cultivate a particular spiritual and moral point of view. So when God parts the Reed Sea, I can no more expect myself to nod in faithful assent like an open-mouthed child than when reading a book like *Harry Potter*.

As a non-literalist, non-fundamentalist, liberal, and committed Jew, I ascertain the message behind the medium. To me, the text asserts God's ability to subvert nature as a means of demonstrating God's vital interest in the welfare of the Israelites, which extends through time—indeed, I fervently hope, to our own time. To my students' question, "But is it true?" I respond, "Yes!" and "No!" The Exodus' visible and venerated place in the Jewish calendar assures that it will be believed in, year in and year out, to our rational consternation and spiritual delight.

—*Carole Balin*

# Voices

## Deliverance: Pu'ah Explains

Bonnie Lyons

*Exodus 1:15–21*

I would like to tell you
I acted out of deep faith
or that God sent me a dream
to prophesy this helpless baby
would grow up to deliver us
all out of Egypt.
But I can't.

Year after year
Shifrah and I struggled
to help mothers push newborns
out of their bodies and
into the world.
Hour after hour
we used the secret knowledge
of our sacred calling,
gentle words of encouragement,
our own powerful hands.
Oh the joy and triumph
when a wet head finally
crosses over, the transport
in every mother's eyes,
pain behind her now.

Besides, Jochebed
was my neighbor: could I
kill her son?

Hebrew cries were camel grunts
to Pharaoh's ears
so when we told him
our women delivered their babies
before we midwives could arrive
—that Hebrew women, unlike Egyptian
women,
poured babies from their bodies
like wine from a jug—
that stubborn, distrustful, arrogant man
naturally
believed us.

## *from* Yocheved's Own Story

Vanessa Ochs

*Exodus 2:1–2*

At the edge of the Nile, Yocheved gathered reeds, and exactly as her mother had taught her, she began to weave the basket to hold her baby son. She called him "my son, may God protect you," for she knew she could not give him the name that he would take with him. He would have to wait for the name to be given to him by his own life, by his own loves, and by his own pains....

Yocheved positioned the sleeping baby under the blanket so that his ear rested on her beating heart. She continued to weave as she spoke to her mother in heaven.

"You taught me to weave baskets for my babies so I could place them beside me when they were too large to carry. You never taught me how to make a basket strong enough to hold my child so he might float away from death."

## *from* Miriam

Marsha Pravder Mirkin

*Exodus 2:4–8*

I hid by the river, a young lioness, crouching, ready to jump, keeping myself still. And then she came—the princess dressed in her golden clothing. . . . That day changed my life and the life of the princess. I was no longer simply Moses' sister, and she was no longer simply Pharaoh's daughter. We were God's daughters, an army of resisters, with our weapons of love and faith.

## On Adoption

Lisa Hostein

*Exodus 2:10*

My new son did not come from the fruit of my womb, but he lives in the deepest recesses of my heart. Another woman gave birth to him, but with his adoption, his life is in my hands. He represents pure potential: the potential to grow and to blossom, to learn and to teach, to lead and to follow, to love and to be loved. He is a new life and a new beginning, a promise of what can be.

## Epitaph

Eleanor Wilner

*Exodus 2:1–10*

Though only a girl,
the first born of Pharaoh,
I was the first to die.

Young then,
we were bored already,
rouged pink as oleanders
on the palace grounds, petted
by the eunuchs, overfed
from gem-encrusted bowls, barren
with wealth, until the hours of the afternoon
seemed to outlast even
my grandmother's mummy, a perfect
little dried apricot
in a golden skin. We would paint
to pass the time, with delicate
brushes dipped in char
on clay, or on our own blank lids.
So it was that day we found him
wailing in the reeds, he seemed
a miracle to us, plucked
from the lotus by the ibis's beak,
the squalling seed of the sacred
Nile. He was permitted
as a toy; while I pretended play
I honed him like a sword.
For him, I was as polished and as perfect
as a pebble in a stutterer's mouth.

While the slaves' fans beat
incessantly as insect's wings,
I taught him how to hate
this painted Pharaoh's tomb
this palace built of brick
and dung, and gilded like a poet's
tongue; these painted eyes.

## *Miriam Argues for Her Place as Prophetess*

Chava Romm

*Exodus 2:1–10*

That morning when we left you
in the bulrushes,
scrubbed clean and freshly swaddled
in your simple basket,
I knew you were too precious
to abandon.

And when the princess
was taken by your innocence,
and claimed you for her own,
it was no mere fate that restored you
to the full breasts
of your rightful mother,

but your sister's cunning.

You lived a stranger
in the house of the oppressor.
I grew among midwives,
stubborn tribeswomen,
who spared the newborn sons
in rank defiance of the pharoah's orders.

You learned to speak for us
before kings and officials.
I coaxed children
from the narrows into light
with singing, tempered by our kin
laboring long in huts and brickyards.

My brother,
we have both been chosen.
What you witness on the mountain

cannot live without the miracles below.
Women draw water for the journey;
I have packed bells and timbrels.

Let us go.

## *The Wife of Moses*

Shirley Kaufman

*Exodus 2:21–22; 4:24–25*

Something went wrong
when he told her to pack
and went on listening
to voices she couldn't hear.

It wasn't her job,
this blood on her fingers,
this cut flesh, red love-bites
in the sand.

The desert widens between them
like an endless argument.
His mouth is too soft
for God's omnivorous rage,
fish will die, the river
stink and lice and flies
and boils and the rest.
Slice of the covenant: blood
on the doors.

He's off to his mountain.
She'll lose
what she saves,
fall out of the future
thankless, nothing to lean on
but her own arms,
holding the small face
unfathered anyway, crying
between her hands.

# ויארא ✦ *Va-eira*

EXODUS 6:2–9:35

## *Marvelous Signs and Destructive Wonders*

PARASHAT VA-EIRA ("I appeared") recounts how God, with the help of Moses and Aaron, endeavors to persuade the pharaoh to release his Hebrew slaves. Here we encounter a stubborn, resistant king not willing to concede an inch of ground to the beleaguered Israelites. This parashah begins the tale—continued in the two subsequent Torah portions—of how a reluctant, underdog prophet triumphs over a recalcitrant tyrant. The suspense-filled drama of the liberation from servitude is central to the Bible and to Judaism. This story is recalled with gratitude through the Passover seder, daily prayers, and identification with the oppressed. The exodus from Egypt has inspired resistance movements throughout the ages, as the downtrodden of many lands and faiths have invoked the potent phrase of self-determination: "Let my people go!"

The divine acts recounted in this parashah are commonly called "plagues," yet this term is used only rarely in the exodus narrative (see at 9:14). Instead, words like "signs" (*otot*), "marvels" (*moftim*), and "wonders" (*nifle'ot*) describe the events that devastate the land and attack the routine affairs of ordinary Egyptians. We read about the first seven signs in this parashah: bloody water, frogs, lice, swarms of insects, pestilence, boils, and hail. These episodes are intended to engender a specific kind of knowledge, teaching the Israelites that "I, יהוה, am your God" (6:7) and the Egyptian king "that there is none like יהוה" (8:6) and that "I יהוה am in the midst of the land" (8:18; see also 7:17; 9:14, 29).

Women figure far less prominently in this Torah portion than in the previous parashah,

*The movement of a people from slavery to liberation has wide-reaching consequences.*

yet the genealogy in 6:14–24 preserves the memory of four women: Moses' mother, Jochebed; Simeon's unnamed Canaanite wife; and two priestly wives, Elisheba and Putiel's daughter. The political clash that unfolds in *parashat Va-eira* is more destructive than the non-confrontational, non-violent resistance of the women in *parashat Sh'mot*. The events in this portion remind us that the movement of a people from slavery to liberation has wide-reaching consequences.

—*Rachel Havrelock*

## Outline

*I.* Prophetic Commission and Mission
*Covenant and Continuity* (6:2–7:7)

- *A.* Revelation of God's name and reaffirmation of the Covenant (6:2–9)
- *B.* Prophetic doubts (6:10–13)
- *C.* Genealogy listing four wives (6:14–25)
- *D.* Reiteration of the prophetic mission (6:26–7:7)

*II.* Moses and God versus Pharaoh
*Seven Signs and Marvels* (7:8–9:35)

- *A.* Prologue: snakes and spells (7:8–13)
- *B.* One: Nile turns to blood (7:14–24)
- *C.* Two: Egypt swarms with frogs (7:25–8:11)
- *D.* Three: dust turns to lice (8:12–15)
- *E.* Four: swarms invade the land (8:16–28)
- *F.* Five: pestilence attacks the animals (9:1–7)
- *G.* Six: soot brings about boils (9:8–12)
- *H.* Seven: hail rains down destruction (9:13–35)

God spoke to Moses and said to him, "I am יהוה.
3 I appeared to Abraham, Isaac, and Jacob as El
Shaddai, but I did not make Myself known to them

ו 2 וַיְדַבֵּר אֱלֹהִים אֶל־מֹשֶׁה וַיֹּאמֶר אֵלָיו
אֲנִי יְהוָה׃ 3 וָאֵרָא אֶל־אַבְרָהָם אֶל־יִצְחָק
וְאֶל־יַעֲקֹב בְּאֵל שַׁדָּי וּשְׁמִי יְהוָה לֹא

## *Prophetic Commission and Mission*

### COVENANT AND CONTINUITY (6:2–7:7)

Moses and Aaron's first appearance before Pharaoh (5:1–5) resulted only in harsher work conditions for the Israelites (5:6–19). The prior parashah ended with the Israelite overseers' condemnation of Moses and Aaron, and with Moses wondering why God had dispatched him. In response, God now reiterates the terms of the covenant and reassures Moses that he is God's chosen representative.

### REVELATION OF GOD'S NAME AND REAFFIRMATION OF THE COVENANT (6:2–9)

The name revealed to Moses is offered as proof of God's manifest presence. Moses initially asked for such evidence in order to assure the people that the Deity known to their ancestors had recognized their suffering (3:13). However, the desire to know God's name also can be seen as a gesture toward establishing a relationship. As the first piece of information we often give others about ourselves, a name enables interaction and serves as a substitute when we are not physically present, thus allowing for invocation and an extension of immanence.

2. ***"I am* יהוה."** The name revealed by God, with all its iconic power, is something of an enigma. On the history both of the pronunciation of this name and of its treatment in translations, see at 3:15.

***"El Shaddai."*** This complex title shares a root with the Akkadian word for mountain (*shadu*) and intersects with the Hebrew root *sh-d-d*, "to be powerful." Since *shad* also means "breast" in biblical Hebrew, some scholars have suggested that this divine name expresses the fertile, life-giving aspect of God. There is some evidence for this connotation in the book of Ruth, where Naomi invokes a shortened version of this name, Shaddai, when she refers to the Deity who claimed the lives of her husband and sons (Ruth 1:20–21; see also Genesis 17:1; 35:11). As the plot reveals, God also restores Naomi's fertility by providing her with an heir whom she is said to nurse (Ruth 4:16).

Historically speaking, El was the name of the chief god of the early Canaanite pantheon, and the Israelite forebears—who were largely Canaanite—would have worshipped El. Other divine names with El preserved in the ancestral stories include El Elyon (in our translation, "God Most High"; Genesis 14:18–22), El Ro'i (16:13), El-Elohei-Yisrael (33:20), and El Beth El ("El of Beth El," 35:7).

***"but I did not make Myself known to them by My name* יהוה."** The book of Genesis does in fact

Introducing a new divine name signals a new beginning for Israel.

ANOTHER VIEW ➤ 349

The Kabbalists taught that women have a monthly flow as the *Shechinah* menstruates.

CONTEMPORARY REFLECTION ➤ 351

Conflating several biblical personalities into one person is typical of rabbinic interpretation.

POST-BIBLICAL INTERPRETATIONS ➤ 349

One day I dared to put the O back / in G-d.

VOICES ➤ 353

by My name יהוה. ⁴I also established My covenant with them, to give them the land of Canaan, the land in which they lived as sojourners. ⁵I have now heard the moaning of the Israelites because the Egyptians are holding them in bondage, and I have remembered My covenant. ⁶Say, therefore, to the Israelite people: I am יהוה. I will free you from the labors of the Egyptians and deliver you from their bondage. I will redeem you with an outstretched arm and through extraordinary chastisements. ⁷And I will take you to be My people, and I will be your God. And you shall know that I, יהוה, am your God who freed you from the labors of the Egyptians. ⁸I will bring you into the land which I swore to give to Abraham, Isaac, and Jacob, and I will give it to you for a possession, I יהוה." ⁹But when Moses told this to the Israelites, they would not listen to Moses, their spirits crushed by cruel bondage.

¹⁰יהוה spoke to Moses, saying, ¹¹"Go and tell Pharaoh king of Egypt to let the Israelites depart from his land." ¹²But Moses appealed to יהוה, saying, "The Israelites would not listen to me; how then should Pharaoh heed me, me—who gets

נוֹדַ֖עְתִּי לָהֶֽם׃ ⁴ וְגַ֨ם הֲקִמֹ֤תִי אֶת־בְּרִיתִי֙ אִתָּ֔ם לָתֵ֥ת לָהֶ֖ם אֶת־אֶ֣רֶץ כְּנָ֑עַן אֵ֛ת אֶ֥רֶץ מְגֻרֵיהֶ֖ם אֲשֶׁר־גָּ֥רוּ בָֽהּ׃ ⁵ וְגַ֣ם ׀ אֲנִ֣י שָׁמַ֗עְתִּי אֶֽת־נַאֲקַת֙ בְּנֵ֣י יִשְׂרָאֵ֔ל אֲשֶׁ֥ר מִצְרַ֖יִם מַעֲבִדִ֣ים אֹתָ֑ם וָאֶזְכֹּ֖ר אֶת־בְּרִיתִֽי׃ ⁶ לָכֵ֞ן אֱמֹ֥ר לִבְנֵֽי־יִשְׂרָאֵל֮ אֲנִ֣י יְהֹוָה֒ וְהוֹצֵאתִ֣י אֶתְכֶ֗ם מִתַּ֙חַת֙ סִבְלֹ֣ת מִצְרַ֔יִם וְהִצַּלְתִּ֥י אֶתְכֶ֖ם מֵעֲבֹדָתָ֑ם וְגָאַלְתִּ֤י אֶתְכֶם֙ בִּזְר֣וֹעַ נְטוּיָ֔ה וּבִשְׁפָטִ֖ים גְּדֹלִֽים׃ ⁷ וְלָקַחְתִּ֨י אֶתְכֶ֥ם לִי֙ לְעָ֔ם וְהָיִ֥יתִי לָכֶ֖ם לֵֽאלֹהִ֑ים וִֽידַעְתֶּ֗ם כִּ֣י אֲנִ֤י יְהֹוָה֙ אֱלֹ֣הֵיכֶ֔ם הַמּוֹצִ֣יא אֶתְכֶ֔ם מִתַּ֖חַת סִבְל֥וֹת מִצְרָֽיִם׃ ⁸ וְהֵבֵאתִ֤י אֶתְכֶם֙ אֶל־הָאָ֔רֶץ אֲשֶׁ֤ר נָשָׂ֙אתִי֙ אֶת־יָדִ֔י לָתֵ֣ת אֹתָ֔הּ לְאַבְרָהָ֥ם לְיִצְחָ֖ק וּֽלְיַעֲקֹ֑ב וְנָתַתִּ֨י אֹתָ֥הּ לָכֶ֛ם מוֹרָשָׁ֖ה אֲנִ֥י יְהֹוָֽה׃ ⁹ וַיְדַבֵּ֥ר מֹשֶׁ֛ה כֵּ֖ן אֶל־בְּנֵ֣י יִשְׂרָאֵ֑ל וְלֹ֤א שָֽׁמְעוּ֙ אֶל־מֹשֶׁ֔ה מִקֹּ֣צֶר ר֔וּחַ וּמֵעֲבֹדָ֖ה קָשָֽׁה׃ פ

¹⁰ וַיְדַבֵּ֥ר יְהֹוָ֖ה אֶל־מֹשֶׁ֥ה לֵּאמֹֽר׃ ¹¹ בֹּ֣א דַבֵּ֔ר אֶל־פַּרְעֹ֖ה מֶ֣לֶךְ מִצְרָ֑יִם וִֽישַׁלַּ֥ח אֶת־בְּנֵֽי־יִשְׂרָאֵ֖ל מֵאַרְצֽוֹ׃ ¹² וַיְדַבֵּ֣ר מֹשֶׁ֔ה לִפְנֵ֥י יְהֹוָ֖ה לֵאמֹ֑ר הֵ֤ן בְּנֵֽי־יִשְׂרָאֵל֙ לֹֽא־שָׁמְע֣וּ אֵלַ֔י וְאֵיךְ֙ יִשְׁמָעֵ֣נִי פַרְעֹ֔ה וַאֲנִ֖י עֲרַ֥ל

---

portray the ancestors as using this divine personal name (as in 14:22, 15:2, 16:5), yet here God claims that the name יהוה was unknown to them.

7. *"I will take you to be My people, and I will be your God."* The covenantal language used in this verse indicates that God and Israel are entering into a binding relationship. This contractual, formulaic language also reflects the way marriage is spoken of in the Bible: God "takes" Israel the way that a man "takes" a wife. (On marriage in the Bible, see *Chayei Sarah*, Another View, p. 127.) There is a reciprocal devotion in this relationship: as God takes Israel, God becomes Israel's sole deity.

9. *they would not listen to Moses.* The Israelites responded positively to their first encounter

with Moses and Aaron, convinced that God had taken note of their plight (4:29–31). But since the first confrontation between Moses and Pharaoh resulted in more oppressive labor demands (5:6–23), the people's exhaustion and despondence prevent them from believing in the promise of redemption.

### PROPHETIC DOUBTS (6:10–13)

Moses has a herculean task on his hands. His own people reject him, and his request of Pharaoh is rebuffed. In this scene, Moses appears as the hesitant actor pushed onto the stage of history under God's reassuring direction.

12. *"who gets tongue-tied."* In response to his

tongue-tied!" [13] So יהוה spoke to both Moses and Aaron in regard to the Israelites and Pharaoh king of Egypt, instructing them to deliver the Israelites from the land of Egypt.

[14] The following are the heads of their respective clans.

The sons of Reuben, Israel's first-born: Enoch and Pallu, Hezron and Carmi; those are the families of Reuben. [15] The sons of Simeon: Jemuel, Jamin, Ohad, Jachin, Zohar, and Saul the son of a Canaanite woman; those are the families of Simeon. [16] These are the names of Levi's sons by their lineage: Gershon, Kohath, and Merari; and the span of Levi's life was 137 years. [17] The sons of Gershon: Libni and Shimei, by their families. [18] The sons of Kohath: Amram, Izhar, Hebron, and Uzziel; and the span of Kohath's life was 133 years. [19] The sons of Merari: Mahli and Mushi. These are the families of the Levites by their lineage.

שְׂפָתָֽיִם: פ 13 וַיְדַבֵּ֣ר יְהֹוָה֮ אֶל־מֹשֶׁ֣ה וְאֶֽל־אַהֲרֹן֒ וַיְצַוֵּם֙ אֶל־בְּנֵ֣י יִשְׂרָאֵ֔ל וְאֶל־ פַּרְעֹ֖ה מֶ֣לֶךְ מִצְרָ֑יִם לְהוֹצִ֥יא אֶת־בְּנֵֽי־ יִשְׂרָאֵ֖ל מֵאֶ֥רֶץ מִצְרָֽיִם: ס

14 אֵ֖לֶּה רָאשֵׁ֣י בֵית־אֲבֹתָ֑ם בְּנֵ֨י רְאוּבֵ֜ן בְּכֹ֣ר יִשְׂרָאֵ֗ל חֲנ֤וֹךְ וּפַלּוּא֙ חֶצְרֹ֣ן וְכַרְמִ֔י אֵ֖לֶּה מִשְׁפְּחֹ֥ת רְאוּבֵֽן: 15 וּבְנֵ֣י שִׁמְע֗וֹן יְמוּאֵ֨ל וְיָמִ֤ין וְאֹ֙הַד֙ וְיָכִ֣ין וְצֹ֔חַר וְשָׁא֖וּל בֶּן־הַֽכְּנַעֲנִ֑ית אֵ֖לֶּה מִשְׁפְּחֹ֥ת שִׁמְעֽוֹן: 16 וְאֵ֗לֶּה שְׁמ֤וֹת בְּנֵֽי־לֵוִי֙ לְתֹ֣לְדֹתָ֔ם גֵּֽרְשׁ֕וֹן וּקְהָ֖ת וּמְרָרִ֑י וּשְׁנֵי֙ חַיֵּ֣י לֵוִ֔י שֶׁ֧בַע וּשְׁלֹשִׁ֛ים וּמְאַ֖ת שָׁנָֽה: 17 בְּנֵ֥י גֵֽרְשׁ֖וֹן לִבְנִ֣י וְשִׁמְעִ֑י לְמִשְׁפְּחֹתָֽם: 18 וּבְנֵ֣י קְהָ֔ת עַמְרָ֣ם וְיִצְהָ֔ר וְחֶבְר֖וֹן וְעֻזִּיאֵ֑ל וּשְׁנֵי֙ חַיֵּ֣י קְהָ֔ת שָׁלֹ֧שׁ וּשְׁלֹשִׁ֛ים וּמְאַ֖ת שָׁנָֽה: 19 וּבְנֵ֥י מְרָרִ֖י מַחְלִ֣י וּמוּשִׁ֑י אֵ֛לֶּה מִשְׁפְּחֹ֥ת הַלֵּוִ֖י לְתֹלְדֹתָֽם:

* * *

being sent again to speak before Pharaoh, Moses claims to be literally "uncircumcised of lips" (the same protest he will raise in v. 30). His words echo the assertion at the burning bush that he is, literally "heavy of mouth and heavy of tongue" (4:10). While some commentators conclude that Moses claims to have some sort of speech impediment, others interpret these expressions to mean that Moses feels he is unworthy of transmitting the divine word.

**13.** *both Moses and Aaron.* In response to Moses' hesitation, God includes his brother Aaron—but not his sister Miriam—in the revelation. The Torah first mentioned Miriam (but not by name) at 2:4; see the comment there. Although she does not join her brothers during any of the revelatory moments in the Exodus narrative, she is referred to as a "prophet" (15:20), a title only metaphorically associated with Aaron (7:1). God speaks directly to all three siblings in Numbers 12:4–6.

## GENEALOGY LISTING FOUR WIVES (6:14–25)

The challenge presented by the Torah's genealogies for the female reader is the frequent omission of women's names. This genealogy stands out because it mentions four women. Carol Meyers claims that including Aaron's mother, wife, and daughter-in-law in this passage draws attention to Aaron and contributes to an aristocratic claim for the Aaronide priesthood (*Exodus*, 2005, p. 69).

**15.** *son of a Canaanite woman.* This unnamed mother gives birth to Saul, a Canaanite-Israelite half-breed who bears the same name as the future king of Israel; see at Genesis 46:10. Individuals of mixed origins trouble the juxtaposition of Israel and the other nations since they fall between ethnic categories. Nonetheless, it appears that some offspring of Israelite fathers and non-Israelite women assume positions of stature, as in the cases of Perez (son of Judah and Tamar; see Genesis 38; Ruth

20 וַיִּקַּח עַמְרָם אֶת־יוֹכֶבֶד דֹּדָתוֹ לוֹ לְאִשָּׁה
וַתֵּלֶד לוֹ אֶת־אַהֲרֹן וְאֶת־מֹשֶׁה וּשְׁנֵי חַיֵּי
עַמְרָם שֶׁבַע וּשְׁלֹשִׁים וּמְאַת שָׁנָה׃ 21 וּבְנֵי
יִצְהָר קֹרַח וָנֶפֶג וְזִכְרִי׃ 22 וּבְנֵי עֻזִּיאֵל
מִישָׁאֵל וְאֶלְצָפָן וְסִתְרִי׃ 23 וַיִּקַּח אַהֲרֹן
אֶת־אֱלִישֶׁבַע בַּת־עַמִּינָדָב אֲחוֹת נַחְשׁוֹן לוֹ
לְאִשָּׁה וַתֵּלֶד לוֹ אֶת־נָדָב וְאֶת־אֲבִיהוּא
אֶת־אֶלְעָזָר וְאֶת־אִיתָמָר׃ 24 וּבְנֵי קֹרַח
אַסִּיר וְאֶלְקָנָה וַאֲבִיאָסָף אֵלֶּה מִשְׁפְּחֹת
הַקָּרְחִי׃ 25 וְאֶלְעָזָר בֶּן־אַהֲרֹן לָקַח־לוֹ
מִבְּנוֹת פּוּטִיאֵל לוֹ לְאִשָּׁה וַתֵּלֶד לוֹ
אֶת־פִּינְחָס אֵלֶּה רָאשֵׁי אֲבוֹת הַלְוִיִּם
לְמִשְׁפְּחֹתָם׃
26 הוּא אַהֲרֹן וּמֹשֶׁה אֲשֶׁר אָמַר יְהוָה לָהֶם
הוֹצִיאוּ אֶת־בְּנֵי יִשְׂרָאֵל מֵאֶרֶץ מִצְרַיִם

20 Amram took to wife his father's sister Jochebed, and she bore him Aaron and Moses; and the
span of Amram's life was 137 years. 21 The sons of
Izhar: Korah, Nepheg, and Zichri. 22 The sons of
Uzziel: Mishael, Elzaphan, and Sithri. 23 Aaron took
to wife Elisheba, daughter of Amminadab and sister
of Nahshon, and she bore him Nadab and Abihu,
Eleazar and Ithamar. 24 The sons of Korah: Assir,
Elkanah, and Abiasaph. Those are the families of
the Korahites. 25 And Aaron's son Eleazar took to
wife one of Putiel's daughters, and she bore him
Phinehas. Those are the heads of the ancestral
houses of the Levites by their families.

26 It is the same Aaron and Moses to whom יהוה
said, "Bring forth the Israelites from the land of

4:11–22) and Phinehas (see v. 25). See also *Mikeitz*, Another Contemporary Reflection, p. 256.

***20. Jochebed.*** Moses' mother is the first person recorded in the Bible with a name containing elements of the tetragrammaton (see at 3:15), for her name means "Yo/Yah is glorified" (the first part of the name is a shortened form of יהוה). Her name thus gives weight to the tradition that identifies Moses as the first to know God's personal name (see 6:2). Jochebed is identified as her husband's aunt (the sister of Amram's father); note that Leviticus 18:12 and 20:19 ban marriages between family members so closely related.

***23. Elisheba, daughter of Amminadab and sister of Nahshon.*** The name of Aaron's wife may mean "My God is seven," alluding to the wholeness and perfection of the number seven that is evident in the story of Creation (Genesis 1) and the institution of the Jubilee (Leviticus 25). Alternatively, the name can be understood as "God of the oath," suggesting the promissory bond between God and her lineage. The names of Elisheba's father and brother indicate that she is from the tribe of Judah; her brother would become a distant ancestor of King David (see Numbers 2:3; Ruth 4:20–22).

***25. one of Putiel's daughters.*** The lineage of Eleazar's wife and Phinehas's mother is provided, yet not her name or her sisters' names. Putiel is a distinctly Egyptian name and is never otherwise mentioned in the Bible. If Putiel was an Egyptian, then this suggests that his grandson, the zealot priest Phinehas, was of mixed background (see Numbers 25:1–13). Note, however, Deuteronomy 23:8–9 considers the grandchildren of an Egyptian to be legitimate Israelites.

### REITERATION OF THE PROPHETIC MISSION (6:26–7:7)

The narrative resumes its focus on Aaron and Moses, as the major themes of Moses' commission are revisited. This section returns to various themes in 6:2–12, such as the declaration of the divine name (6:2, 29; 7:5), promise of deliverance from Egypt (6:6; 7:5), and the issue of Moses' "uncircumcised lips" (6:12, 30).

Egypt, troop by troop." 27 It was they who spoke
to Pharaoh king of Egypt to free the Israelites from
the Egyptians; these are the same Moses and
Aaron. 28 For when יהוה spoke to Moses in the land
of Egypt 29 and יהוה said to Moses, "I am יהוה;
speak to Pharaoh king of Egypt all that I will tell
you," 30 Moses appealed to יהוה, saying, "See, I get
tongue-tied; how then should Pharaoh heed
me!" 7 יהוה replied to Moses, "See, I place you
in the role of God to Pharaoh, with your brother
Aaron as your prophet. 2 You shall repeat all that I
command you, and your brother Aaron shall speak
to Pharaoh to let the Israelites depart from his land.
3 But I will harden Pharaoh's heart, that I may multiply My signs and marvels in the land of Egypt.
4 When Pharaoh does not heed you, I will lay My
hand upon Egypt and deliver My ranks, My people
the Israelites, from the land of Egypt with extraordinary chastisements. 5 And the Egyptians shall
know that I am יהוה, when I stretch out My hand
over Egypt and bring out the Israelites from their
midst." 6 This Moses and Aaron did; as יהוה commanded them, so they did. 7 Moses was eighty years
old and Aaron eighty-three, when they made their
demand on Pharaoh.

עַל־צִבְאֹתָם׃ 27 הֵם הַֽמְדַבְּרִים֙ אֶל־פַּרְעֹ֣ה
מֶֽלֶךְ־מִצְרַ֔יִם לְהוֹצִ֥יא אֶת־בְּנֵֽי־יִשְׂרָאֵ֖ל
מִמִּצְרָ֑יִם ה֥וּא מֹשֶׁ֖ה וְאַהֲרֹֽן׃ 28 וַיְהִ֗י בְּי֨וֹם
דִּבֶּ֧ר יְהוָ֛ה אֶל־מֹשֶׁ֖ה בְּאֶ֥רֶץ מִצְרָֽיִם׃ ס
29 וַיְדַבֵּ֧ר יְהוָ֛ה אֶל־מֹשֶׁ֥ה לֵּאמֹ֖ר אֲנִ֣י יְהוָ֑ה
דַּבֵּ֗ר אֶל־פַּרְעֹה֙ מֶ֣לֶךְ מִצְרַ֔יִם אֵ֛ת כָּל־אֲשֶׁ֥ר
אֲנִ֖י דֹּבֵ֥ר אֵלֶֽיךָ׃ 30 וַיֹּ֥אמֶר מֹשֶׁ֖ה לִפְנֵ֣י יְהוָ֑ה
הֵ֤ן אֲנִי֙ עֲרַ֣ל שְׂפָתַ֔יִם וְאֵ֕יךְ יִשְׁמַ֥ע אֵלַ֖י
פַּרְעֹֽה׃ פ ז וַיֹּ֤אמֶר יְהוָה֙ אֶל־מֹשֶׁ֔ה
רְאֵ֛ה נְתַתִּ֥יךָ אֱלֹהִ֖ים לְפַרְעֹ֑ה וְאַהֲרֹ֥ן אָחִ֖יךָ
יִהְיֶ֥ה נְבִיאֶֽךָ׃ 2 אַתָּ֣ה תְדַבֵּ֔ר אֵ֖ת כָּל־אֲשֶׁ֣ר
אֲצַוֶּ֑ךָּ וְאַהֲרֹ֤ן אָחִ֙יךָ֙ יְדַבֵּ֣ר אֶל־פַּרְעֹ֔ה וְשִׁלַּ֥ח
אֶת־בְּנֵֽי־יִשְׂרָאֵ֖ל מֵאַרְצֽוֹ׃ 3 וַאֲנִ֥י אַקְשֶׁ֖ה
אֶת־לֵ֣ב פַּרְעֹ֑ה וְהִרְבֵּיתִ֧י אֶת־אֹתֹתַ֛י וְאֶת־
מוֹפְתַ֖י בְּאֶ֥רֶץ מִצְרָֽיִם׃ 4 וְלֹֽא־יִשְׁמַ֤ע אֲלֵכֶם֙
פַּרְעֹ֔ה וְנָתַתִּ֥י אֶת־יָדִ֖י בְּמִצְרָ֑יִם וְהוֹצֵאתִ֨י
אֶת־צִבְאֹתַ֜י אֶת־עַמִּ֤י בְנֵֽי־יִשְׂרָאֵל֙ מֵאֶ֣רֶץ
מִצְרַ֔יִם בִּשְׁפָטִ֖ים גְּדֹלִֽים׃ 5 וְיָדְע֤וּ מִצְרַ֙יִם֙
כִּֽי־אֲנִ֣י יְהוָ֔ה בִּנְטֹתִ֥י אֶת־יָדִ֖י עַל־מִצְרָ֑יִם
וְהוֹצֵאתִ֥י אֶת־בְּנֵֽי־יִשְׂרָאֵ֖ל מִתּוֹכָֽם׃ 6 וַיַּ֥עַשׂ
מֹשֶׁ֖ה וְאַהֲרֹ֑ן כַּאֲשֶׁ֨ר צִוָּ֧ה יְהוָ֛ה אֹתָ֖ם כֵּ֥ן
עָשֽׂוּ׃ 7 וּמֹשֶׁה֙ בֶּן־שְׁמֹנִ֣ים שָׁנָ֔ה וְאַהֲרֹ֕ן
בֶּן־שָׁלֹ֥שׁ וּשְׁמֹנִ֖ים שָׁנָ֑ה בְּדַבְּרָ֖ם אֶל־
פַּרְעֹֽה׃ פ

*7:1. "I place you in the role of God to Pharaoh."* This astonishing analogy promotes Moses to the role of the Deity, lording over Pharaoh—who in Egyptian society was considered divine.

*3. "But I will harden Pharaoh's heart."* This aspect of the Exodus raises questions of theodicy. On one level, the obstacle of a hardened monarch and the ensuing portrait of Egypt's destruction seem unjust. Could God not have softened Pharaoh's heart and spared Egypt? The exodus narrative justifies the freedom won at the expense of the oppressors' devastation not as retribution, but as a means of impressing knowledge of divine power on Israel and Egypt alike. Pharaoh's opposition entails a clash of wills as well as a contest between the pantheon of Egypt and the lone God of Israel. Biblical narrative renders the victor indisputable and the powers of the Egyptian gods obsolete. The number ten is at work in this part of the plot: ten times God hardens Pharaoh's heart (4:21; 7:3; 9:12; 10:1, 20, 27; 11:10; 14:4, 8, 17); and another ten times Pharaoh is described as naturally resistant due to his own obstinacy (7:13, 14, 22; 8:11, 15, 28; 9:7, 34, 35; 13:15). (See also Another View, p. 349; and *Bo*, Contemporary Reflection, p. 374.)

8יהוה said to Moses and Aaron, 9"When Pharaoh speaks to you and says, 'Produce your marvel,'
you shall say to Aaron, 'Take your rod and cast it
down before Pharaoh.' It shall turn into a serpent."
10So Moses and Aaron came before Pharaoh and
did just as יהוה had commanded: Aaron cast down
his rod in the presence of Pharaoh and his courtiers,

8 וַיֹּאמֶר יְהֹוָה אֶל־מֹשֶׁה וְאֶל־אַהֲרֹן
לֵאמֹר׃ 9 כִּי יְדַבֵּר אֲלֵכֶם פַּרְעֹה לֵאמֹר
תְּנוּ לָכֶם מוֹפֵת וְאָמַרְתָּ אֶל־אַהֲרֹן קַח אֶת־
מַטְּךָ וְהַשְׁלֵךְ לִפְנֵי־פַרְעֹה יְהִי לְתַנִּין׃
10 וַיָּבֹא מֹשֶׁה וְאַהֲרֹן אֶל־פַּרְעֹה וַיַּעֲשׂוּ כֵן
כַּאֲשֶׁר צִוָּה יְהֹוָה וַיַּשְׁלֵךְ אַהֲרֹן אֶת־מַטֵּהוּ
לִפְנֵי פַרְעֹה וְלִפְנֵי עֲבָדָיו וַיְהִי לְתַנִּין׃

## *Moses and God versus Pharaoh*

### SEVEN SIGNS AND MARVELS (7:8–9:35)

Is there any logic behind the arrangement of the so-called ten plagues? Interpreters have indeed observed different types of organizing principles in this artfully crafted narrative. The events can be seen as a sequence of five pairs: two Nile transformations, two infestations of insects, two epidemics, two crop destructions, two conjurings of darkness and death. The narrative can also be divided into three triads topped by a climactic final plague: the 1st, 4th, and 7th signs begin with Moses "standing before" Pharaoh in the morning; the 2nd, 5th, and 8th start with Moses "coming before" Pharaoh; and the 3rd, 6th, and 9th are unleashed without warning. One line of rabbinic interpretation divides the signs according to the instigating agent: Aaron brings about the 1st, 2nd, and 3rd signs; Moses brings about the 7th, 8th, and 9th; God causes the 4th, 5th, and 10th; and the 6th is created by a collaboration of Aaron, Moses, and God (*Sh'mot Rabbah* 9.10; 20.1).

While the account in the book of Exodus enumerates ten separate episodes, two other accounts in Psalms 78:42–51 and 105:28–36 each list seven; and in those two poetic accounts, the signs are arranged in a different order than in the Torah. Interestingly, the designation "Ten Plagues" (*eser makkot*) is not found in the Bible; it is a later, rabbinic appellation. In fact, most of these divine acts are called "signs," not "plagues," thus highlighting that they were not considered punitive, but rather the means to convince Pharaoh, the Israelites, and the reader of God's might (see also at 9:14 and 11:1).

In straining to place the Exodus in an indisputably historical context—rather than a literary or religious one—some scholars have proposed naturalistic explanations of these events. For instance, the claim has been made that the Nile appeared red due to red sediment caused by uncommonly heavy rainfalls; this unusual flooding then disturbed the ecosystem of the Nile and caused a chain of events, including the invasion of frogs and disease-carrying insects that made cattle ill and caused boils. However, the rhetoric of Exodus emphasizes that these are unique preternatural occurrences intended to promote awareness of divine power; they are best understood as devices that heighten the contest between God and Pharaoh and drive the plot toward the liberation of Israel.

### PROLOGUE: SNAKES AND SPELLS (7:8–13)

Here and in several subsequent episodes, Aaron competes with the magicians of Egypt, showing how God bests Pharaoh and the Egyptian pantheon on their own terrain.

*9. "into a serpent."* During his earlier vision at Sinai, Moses was instructed to deploy a similar wonder as a means of authentication before the Israelites (4:2–5). Here Aaron's staff becomes a serpent (*tannin*), a large sea creature, as opposed to a snake in the prior episode. Since Aaron's staff later changes into an almond branch (Numbers 17:23), some scholars have identified a connection to the ancient Near Eastern goddess Asherah, who is associated with blooming trees, rods, and serpents.

and it turned into a serpent. 11Then Pharaoh, for
his part, summoned the sages and the sorcerers; and
the Egyptian magician-priests, in turn, did the
same with their spells: 12each cast down his rod,
and they turned into serpents. But Aaron's rod
swallowed their rods. 13Yet Pharaoh's heart stiffened
and he did not heed them, as יהוה had said.

11 וַיִּקְרָא גַּם־פַּרְעֹה לַחֲכָמִים וְלַמְכַשְּׁפִים
וַיַּעֲשׂוּ גַם־הֵם חַרְטֻמֵּי מִצְרַיִם בְּלַהֲטֵיהֶם
כֵּן׃ 12 וַיַּשְׁלִיכוּ אִישׁ מַטֵּהוּ וַיִּהְיוּ לְתַנִּינִם
וַיִּבְלַע מַטֵּה־אַהֲרֹן אֶת־מַטֹּתָם׃ 13 וַיֶּחֱזַק
לֵב פַּרְעֹה וְלֹא שָׁמַע אֲלֵהֶם כַּאֲשֶׁר דִּבֶּר
יְהוָה׃ ס

14And יהוה said to Moses, "Pharaoh is stubborn;
he refuses to let the people go. 15Go to Pharaoh in
the morning, as he is coming out to the water, and
station yourself before him at the edge of the Nile,
taking with you the rod that turned into a snake.
16And say to him, 'יהוה, the God of the Hebrews,
sent me to you to say, "Let My people go that they
may worship Me in the wilderness." But you have

14 וַיֹּאמֶר יְהוָה אֶל־מֹשֶׁה כָּבֵד לֵב פַּרְעֹה
מֵאֵן לְשַׁלַּח הָעָם׃ 15 לֵךְ אֶל־פַּרְעֹה בַּבֹּקֶר
הִנֵּה יֹצֵא הַמַּיְמָה וְנִצַּבְתָּ לִקְרָאתוֹ עַל־
שְׂפַת הַיְאֹר וְהַמַּטֶּה אֲשֶׁר־נֶהְפַּךְ לְנָחָשׁ
תִּקַּח בְּיָדֶךָ׃ 16 וְאָמַרְתָּ אֵלָיו יְהוָה אֱלֹהֵי
הָעִבְרִים שְׁלָחַנִי אֵלֶיךָ לֵאמֹר שַׁלַּח אֶת־
עַמִּי וְיַעַבְדֻנִי בַּמִּדְבָּר וְהִנֵּה לֹא־שָׁמַעְתָּ עַד־

*11. sages.* Given the plural language, women are conceivably included in this term. Historically speaking, "wise woman" was a well-known category in Egypt; and the Hebrew Bible also recognized women for their wisdom (II Samuel 14:2, 20:16; Proverbs 31:26).

***sorcerers.*** Again, given the plural term, women may be included: they were among Egypt's sorcerers since pre-dynastic times; and in the Bible, the practice of magic is specifically associated with women in Exodus 22:17 ("You shall not tolerate a sorceress") and Nahum 3:4.

***magician-priests.*** Unlike the preceding two Hebrew terms, this one comes directly from an Egyptian word that—in Egypt—applied only to men.

### ONE: NILE TURNS TO BLOOD (7:14–24)

The signs (often called "plagues" in later Jewish parlance) are framed by blood: They begin with the transformation of life-giving waters into deadly aquifers, and they end with blood smudged on Israelite doorposts to deflect the macabre visit of the Angel of Death (12:23). As both source of abundance and site of Egyptian divinity, the Nile is targeted first. Various water-related terms (such as rivers, canals, and ponds in v. 19) permeate this section, introducing a theme that will climax with the splitting of the Sea of Reeds.

*15. "at the edge of the Nile."* The spilling of Moses' blood was avoided when Pharaoh's daughter drew him from the Nile (2:5–10); now Moses faces another member of the Egyptian royal family on the banks of the river.

*16. "God of the Hebrews."* In the Bible, the Israelites tend to be called Hebrews (*ivrim*) by speakers outside of the group (Genesis 39:14; 41:12; Exodus 1:16, 19; 2:6) or when an Israelite speaks to an outsider (Genesis 14:13; Exodus 2:7; Jonah 1:9).

***"Let My people go."*** This resounding phrase first appeared in Exodus 5:1 (compare 4:23). God repeats it five more times in giving instructions to Moses (here; 7:26; 8:16; 9:1, 13), while Moses repeats it once more to Pharaoh (10:3)—a total of seven times.

***"that they may worship Me."*** The request for freedom from slavery is linked to the request for freedom to serve God. Linguistically speaking, the contrast could not be more pointed: the Hebrew narrative employs the same verb (*avod*) for the two

paid no heed until now. 17 Thus says יהוה, "By this
you shall know that I am יהוה." See, I shall strike
the water in the Nile with the rod that is in my
hand, and it will be turned into blood; 18 and the
fish in the Nile will die. The Nile will stink so that
the Egyptians will find it impossible to drink the
water of the Nile.'"

19 And יהוה said to Moses, "Say to Aaron: Take
your rod and hold out your arm over the waters of
Egypt—its rivers, its canals, its ponds, all its bodies
of water—that they may turn to blood; there shall
be blood throughout the land of Egypt, even in
vessels of wood and stone." 20 Moses and Aaron did
just as יהוה commanded: he lifted up the rod and
struck the water in the Nile in the sight of Pharaoh
and his courtiers, and all the water in the Nile was
turned into blood 21 and the fish in the Nile died.
The Nile stank so that the Egyptians could not
drink water from the Nile; and there was blood
throughout the land of Egypt. 22 But when the
Egyptian magician-priests did the same with their
spells, Pharaoh's heart stiffened and he did not heed
them—as יהוה had spoken. 23 Pharaoh turned and
went into his palace, paying no regard even to this.
24 And all the Egyptians had to dig round about the
Nile for drinking water, because they could not
drink the water of the Nile.

25 When seven days had passed after יהוה struck

כֹּה: 17 כֹּה אָמַר יְהוָה בְּזֹאת תֵּדַע כִּי אֲנִי
יְהוָה הִנֵּה אָנֹכִי מַכֶּה ׀ בַּמַּטֶּה אֲשֶׁר־בְּיָדִי
עַל־הַמַּיִם אֲשֶׁר בַּיְאֹר וְנֶהֶפְכוּ לְדָם:
18 וְהַדָּגָה אֲשֶׁר־בַּיְאֹר תָּמוּת וּבָאַשׁ הַיְאֹר
וְנִלְאוּ מִצְרַיִם לִשְׁתּוֹת מַיִם מִן־הַיְאֹר: ס
19 וַיֹּאמֶר יְהוָה אֶל־מֹשֶׁה אֱמֹר אֶל־אַהֲרֹן
קַח מַטְּךָ וּנְטֵה־יָדְךָ עַל־מֵימֵי מִצְרַיִם עַל־
נַהֲרֹתָם ׀ עַל־יְאֹרֵיהֶם וְעַל־אַגְמֵיהֶם וְעַל
כָּל־מִקְוֵה מֵימֵיהֶם וְיִהְיוּ־דָם וְהָיָה דָם
בְּכָל־אֶרֶץ מִצְרַיִם וּבָעֵצִים וּבָאֲבָנִים:
20 וַיַּעֲשׂוּ־כֵן מֹשֶׁה וְאַהֲרֹן כַּאֲשֶׁר ׀ צִוָּה
יְהוָה וַיָּרֶם בַּמַּטֶּה וַיַּךְ אֶת־הַמַּיִם אֲשֶׁר
בַּיְאֹר לְעֵינֵי פַרְעֹה וּלְעֵינֵי עֲבָדָיו וַיֵּהָפְכוּ
כָּל־הַמַּיִם אֲשֶׁר־בַּיְאֹר לְדָם: 21 וְהַדָּגָה
אֲשֶׁר־בַּיְאֹר מֵתָה וַיִּבְאַשׁ הַיְאֹר וְלֹא־יָכְלוּ
מִצְרַיִם לִשְׁתּוֹת מַיִם מִן־הַיְאֹר וַיְהִי הַדָּם
בְּכָל־אֶרֶץ מִצְרָיִם: 22 וַיַּעֲשׂוּ־כֵן חַרְטֻמֵּי
מִצְרַיִם בְּלָטֵיהֶם וַיֶּחֱזַק לֵב־פַּרְעֹה וְלֹא־
שָׁמַע אֲלֵהֶם כַּאֲשֶׁר דִּבֶּר יְהוָה: 23 וַיִּפֶן
פַּרְעֹה וַיָּבֹא אֶל־בֵּיתוֹ וְלֹא־שָׁת לִבּוֹ גַּם־
לָזֹאת: 24 וַיַּחְפְּרוּ כָל־מִצְרַיִם סְבִיבֹת הַיְאֹר
מַיִם לִשְׁתּוֹת כִּי לֹא יָכְלוּ לִשְׁתֹּת מִמֵּימֵי
הַיְאֹר:
25 וַיִּמָּלֵא שִׁבְעַת יָמִים אַחֲרֵי הַכּוֹת־יְהוָה

counterposed activities: "work as a slave" to Pharaoh, and "worship" God.

*20. all the water in the Nile was turned into blood.* This sign conveys a sense of measure-for-measure justice: the bloody river recalls the blood of Israelite infants spilled in the Nile (1:22).

A similar event is brought about by the goddess Inanna, "Queen of Heaven," in the Sumerian myth "Inanna and the Gardener": as a punishment, the goddess transforms all well water into blood.

*24. the Egyptians had to dig round about the Nile for drinking water.* Elsewhere the Bible portrays the hauling of water (for drinking and general use) as a woman's activity (Genesis 24:11; I Samuel 9:11). If this were also the case in Egypt, then one can imagine the particularly hard burden that this sign placed on Egyptian women.

### TWO: EGYPT SWARMS WITH FROGS (7:25–8:11)

In the course of the second sign, a creature that dwells mostly in water emerges to take over the human realm. This species invasion signals that the realms of creation—water, earth, and air—have been breached. The multiplication of frogs, like

the Nile, <sup>26</sup>יהוה said to Moses, "Go to Pharaoh and say to him, 'Thus says יהוה: Let My people go that they may worship Me. <sup>27</sup>If you refuse to let them go, then I will plague your whole country with frogs. <sup>28</sup>The Nile shall swarm with frogs, and they shall come up and enter your palace, your bed-chamber and your bed, the houses of your courtiers and your people, and your ovens and your kneading bowls. <sup>29</sup>The frogs shall come up on you and on your people and on all your courtiers.'"

8 And יהוה said to Moses, "Say to Aaron: Hold out your arm with the rod over the rivers, the canals, and the ponds, and bring up the frogs on the land of Egypt." <sup>2</sup>Aaron held out his arm over the waters of Egypt, and the frogs came up and covered the land of Egypt. <sup>3</sup>But the magician-priests did the same with their spells, and brought frogs upon the land of Egypt.

<sup>4</sup>Then Pharaoh summoned Moses and Aaron and said, "Plead with יהוה to remove the frogs from me and my people, and I will let the people go to sacrifice to יהוה." <sup>5</sup>And Moses said to Pharaoh, "You may have this triumph over me: for what time shall I plead in behalf of you and your courtiers and your people, that the frogs be cut off from you and your houses, to remain only in the

אֶת־הַיְאֹֽר׃ פ 26 וַיֹּ֤אמֶר יְהֹוָה֙ אֶל־מֹשֶׁ֔ה בֹּ֖א אֶל־פַּרְעֹ֑ה וְאָמַרְתָּ֣ אֵלָ֗יו כֹּ֚ה אָמַ֣ר יְהֹוָ֔ה שַׁלַּ֥ח אֶת־עַמִּ֖י וְיַֽעַבְדֻֽנִי׃ 27 וְאִם־מָאֵ֥ן אַתָּ֖ה לְשַׁלֵּ֑חַ הִנֵּ֣ה אָֽנֹכִ֗י נֹגֵ֛ף אֶת־כׇּל־גְּבֽוּלְךָ֖ בַּֽצְפַרְדְּעִֽים׃ 28 וְשָׁרַ֣ץ הַיְאֹר֘ צְפַרְדְּעִים֒ וְעָלוּ֙ וּבָ֣אוּ בְּבֵיתֶ֔ךָ וּבַֽחֲדַ֥ר מִשְׁכָּבְךָ֖ וְעַל־מִטָּתֶ֑ךָ וּבְבֵ֤ית עֲבָדֶ֙יךָ֙ וּבְעַמֶּ֔ךָ וּבְתַנּוּרֶ֖יךָ וּבְמִשְׁאֲרוֹתֶֽיךָ׃ 29 וּבְכָ֥ה וּֽבְעַמְּךָ֖ וּבְכׇל־עֲבָדֶ֑יךָ יַעֲל֖וּ הַֽצְפַרְדְּעִֽים׃

ח וַיֹּ֣אמֶר יְהֹוָה֮ אֶל־מֹשֶׁה֒ אֱמֹ֣ר אֶֽל־אַהֲרֹ֗ן נְטֵ֤ה אֶת־יָֽדְךָ֙ בְּמַטֶּ֔ךָ עַל־הַ֨נְּהָרֹ֔ת עַל־הַיְאֹרִ֖ים וְעַל־הָֽאֲגַמִּ֑ים וְהַ֥עַל אֶת־הַֽצְפַרְדְּעִ֖ים עַל־אֶ֥רֶץ מִצְרָֽיִם׃ 2 וַיֵּ֤ט אַֽהֲרֹן֙ אֶת־יָד֔וֹ עַ֖ל מֵימֵ֣י מִצְרָ֑יִם וַתַּ֙עַל֙ הַֽצְּפַרְדֵּ֔עַ וַתְּכַ֖ס אֶת־אֶ֥רֶץ מִצְרָֽיִם׃ 3 וַיַּֽעֲשׂוּ־כֵ֥ן הַֽחַרְטֻמִּ֖ים בְּלָֽטֵיהֶ֑ם וַיַּֽעֲל֥וּ אֶת־הַֽצְפַרְדְּעִ֖ים עַל־אֶ֥רֶץ מִצְרָֽיִם׃ 4 וַיִּקְרָ֨א פַרְעֹ֜ה לְמֹשֶׁ֣ה וּֽלְאַהֲרֹ֗ן וַיֹּ֙אמֶר֙ הַעְתִּ֣ירוּ אֶל־יְהֹוָ֔ה וְיָסֵר֙ הַֽצְפַרְדְּעִ֔ים מִמֶּ֖נִּי וּמֵֽעַמִּ֑י וַֽאֲשַׁלְּחָה֙ אֶת־הָעָ֔ם וְיִזְבְּח֖וּ לַֽיהֹוָֽה׃ 5 וַיֹּ֨אמֶר מֹשֶׁ֣ה לְפַרְעֹה֮ הִתְפָּאֵ֣ר עָלַי֒ לְמָתַ֣י ׀ אַעְתִּ֣יר לְךָ֗ וְלַֽעֲבָדֶ֙יךָ֙ וּֽלְעַמְּךָ֔ לְהַכְרִית֙ הַֽצְפַרְדְּעִ֔ים מִמְּךָ֖ וּמִבָּתֶּ֑יךָ רַ֥ק בַּיְאֹ֖ר

---

the appearance of the blood, conveys a sense of measure-for-measure justice: the "swarming" frogs (7:28) invoke Pharaoh's fear of the multiplying, "swarming" population of Israelites (1:7). In ancient Egypt, human reproduction was associated with Heqt, the frog goddess of childbirth who protected the mother and newborn infant. Other deities associated with fertility and childbirth include Bes (the hippo goddess) and Taweret (the female crocodile goddess).

**26.** *"Let My people go that they may worship Me."* Moses does not ask Pharaoh to liberate the Israelites permanently. Instead, following God's plan, Moses requests that the Israelites be allowed a

brief leave so they can take a three days' journey to the wilderness for a sacrificial celebration (3:18; 5:1–3; 8:21–24). Ancient Egyptian documents do attest to the practice of allowing free workers time off for various reasons, including participating in religious festivals.

**8:4.** *"I will let the people go to sacrifice to יהוה."* For the first time, the pharaoh seems to acknowledge the existence of God.

**5.** *"for what time shall I plead in behalf of you?"* In order to prove that the removal of the frogs is not incidental but rather an act of God, Moses lets Pharaoh name the time of their elimination.

Nile?" 6"For tomorrow," he replied. And [Moses]
said, "As you say—that you may know that there is
none like our God יהוה; 7the frogs shall retreat from
you and your courtiers and your people; they shall
remain only in the Nile." 8Then Moses and Aaron
left Pharaoh's presence, and Moses cried out to יהוה
in the matter of the frogs which had been inflicted
upon Pharaoh. 9And יהוה did as Moses asked; the
frogs died out in the houses, the courtyards, and
the fields. 10And they piled them up in heaps, till
the land stank. 11But when Pharaoh saw that there
was relief, he became stubborn and would not heed
them, as יהוה had spoken.

12Then יהוה said to Moses, "Say to Aaron: Hold
out your rod and strike the dust of the earth, and it
shall turn to lice throughout the land of Egypt."
13And they did so. Aaron held out his arm with the
rod and struck the dust of the earth, and vermin
came upon human and beast; all the dust of the
earth turned to lice throughout the land of Egypt.
14The magician-priests did the like with their spells
to produce lice, but they could not. The vermin remained upon human and beast; 15and the magician-
priests said to Pharaoh, "This is the finger of God!"

תִּשָּׁאַרְנָה׃ 6 וַיֹּ֖אמֶר לְמָחָ֑ר וַיֹּ֙אמֶר֙ כִּדְבָ֣רְךָ֔
לְמַ֣עַן תֵּדַ֔ע כִּי־אֵ֖ין כַּיהֹוָ֥ה אֱלֹהֵֽינוּ׃
7 וְסָר֣וּ הַֽצְפַרְדְּעִ֗ים מִמְּךָ֙ וּמִבָּ֣תֶּ֔יךָ וּמֵֽעֲבָדֶ֖יךָ
וּמֵֽעַמֶּ֑ךָ רַ֥ק בַּיְאֹ֖ר תִּשָּׁאַֽרְנָה׃ 8 וַיֵּצֵ֥א מֹשֶׁ֛ה
וְאַהֲרֹ֖ן מֵעִ֣ם פַּרְעֹ֑ה וַיִּצְעַ֤ק מֹשֶׁה֙ אֶל־יְהֹוָ֔ה
עַל־דְּבַ֥ר הַֽצְפַרְדְּעִ֖ים אֲשֶׁר־שָׂ֥ם לְפַרְעֹֽה׃
9 וַיַּ֥עַשׂ יְהֹוָ֖ה כִּדְבַ֣ר מֹשֶׁ֑ה וַיָּמֻ֙תוּ֙
הַֽצְפַרְדְּעִ֔ים מִן־הַבָּתִּ֥ים מִן־הַחֲצֵרֹ֖ת וּמִן־
הַשָּׂדֹֽת׃ 10 וַיִּצְבְּר֥וּ אֹתָ֖ם חֳמָרִ֣ם חֳמָרִ֑ם
וַתִּבְאַ֖שׁ הָאָֽרֶץ׃ 11 וַיַּ֣רְא פַּרְעֹ֗ה כִּ֤י הָֽיְתָה֙
הָֽרְוָחָ֔ה וְהַכְבֵּד֙ אֶת־לִבּ֔וֹ וְלֹ֥א שָׁמַ֖ע אֲלֵהֶ֑ם
כַּאֲשֶׁ֖ר דִּבֶּ֥ר יְהֹוָֽה׃ ס
12 וַיֹּ֣אמֶר יְהֹוָ֗ה אֶל־מֹשֶׁה֒ אֱמֹר֙ אֶֽל־אַהֲרֹ֔ן
נְטֵ֣ה אֶֽת־מַטְּךָ֔ וְהַ֖ךְ אֶת־עֲפַ֣ר הָאָ֑רֶץ וְהָיָ֥ה
לְכִנִּ֖ם בְּכָל־אֶ֥רֶץ מִצְרָֽיִם׃ 13 וַיַּֽעֲשׂוּ־כֵ֗ן וַיֵּ֨ט
אַהֲרֹ֤ן אֶת־יָדוֹ֙ בְמַטֵּ֙הוּ֙ וַיַּךְ֙ אֶת־עֲפַ֣ר הָאָ֔רֶץ
וַתְּהִי֙ הַכִּנָּ֔ם בָּאָדָ֖ם וּבַבְּהֵמָ֑ה כָּל־עֲפַ֥ר
הָאָ֛רֶץ הָיָ֥ה כִנִּ֖ים בְּכָל־אֶ֥רֶץ מִצְרָֽיִם׃
14 וַיַּֽעֲשׂוּ־כֵ֨ן הַחַרְטֻמִּ֧ים בְּלָטֵיהֶ֛ם לְהוֹצִ֥יא
אֶת־הַכִּנִּ֖ים וְלֹ֣א יָכֹ֑לוּ וַתְּהִי֙ הַכִּנָּ֔ם בָּאָדָ֖ם
וּבַבְּהֵמָֽה׃ 15 וַיֹּאמְר֤וּ הַֽחַרְטֻמִּם֙ אֶל־פַּרְעֹ֔ה

*6. "that you may know that there is none like our God* ***יהוה****."* The signs are expressly intended to engender knowledge of God among the Egyptians and Israelites, with differing effects on each. (See also Another View, p. 349.)

*10. the land stank.* Here and in 7:21, the text emphasizes the olfactory dimension of the first two signs. Measure-for-measure justice is again at work. In 5:21 the Israelites had condemned Moses and Aaron for literally "causing our breath to be malodorous" (in our translation: "making us loathsome"), meaning that Moses' demands have brought harsher labor requirements down on the slaves. As God proves through the signs, it is not the Israelites who stink, but rather the land of Egypt during its accelerated rate of decay.

THREE: DUST TURNS TO LICE (8:12–15)

During this third round, the Egyptian magician-priests drop out of the contest and—humbled—admit defeat, with a partial recognition of God's agency. The lice infest Egyptian bodies as the frogs would have disrupted their households.

*12. "Say to Aaron."* In the 3rd, 6th, and 9th signs (the last in each triad), the event occurs without any warning being given to Pharaoh.

*14. magician-priests . . . could not.* Having matched the signs performed by Moses and Aaron three times (rod in 7:11–12; blood in 7:22; frogs in 8:3), the Egyptians now fail to reproduce Aaron's actions.

*15. "This is the finger of God!"* Throughout

But Pharaoh's heart stiffened and he would not heed them, as יהוה had spoken.

16 And יהוה said to Moses, "Early in the morning present yourself to Pharaoh, as he is coming out to the water, and say to him, 'Thus says יהוה: Let My people go that they may worship Me. 17 For if you do not let My people go, I will let loose swarms of insects against you and your courtiers and your people and your houses; the houses of the Egyptians, and the very ground they stand on, shall be filled with swarms of insects. 18 But on that day I will set apart the region of Goshen, where My people dwell, so that no swarms of insects shall be there, that you may know that I יהוה am in the midst of the land. 19 And I will make a distinction between My people and your people. Tomorrow this sign shall come to pass.'" 20 And יהוה did so. Heavy swarms of insects invaded Pharaoh's palace and the houses of his courtiers; throughout the country of Egypt the land was ruined because of the swarms of insects.

אֶצְבַּע אֱלֹהִים הִוא וַיֶּחֱזַק לֵב־פַּרְעֹה וְלֹא־
שָׁמַע אֲלֵהֶם כַּאֲשֶׁר דִּבֶּר יְהֹוָה׃ ס
16 וַיֹּאמֶר יְהֹוָה אֶל־מֹשֶׁה הַשְׁכֵּם בַּבֹּקֶר
וְהִתְיַצֵּב לִפְנֵי פַרְעֹה הִנֵּה יוֹצֵא הַמָּיְמָה
וְאָמַרְתָּ אֵלָיו כֹּה אָמַר יְהֹוָה שַׁלַּח עַמִּי
וְיַעַבְדֻנִי׃ 17 כִּי אִם־אֵינְךָ מְשַׁלֵּחַ אֶת־עַמִּי
הִנְנִי מַשְׁלִיחַ בְּךָ וּבַעֲבָדֶיךָ וּבְעַמְּךָ וּבְבָתֶּיךָ
אֶת־הֶעָרֹב וּמָלְאוּ בָּתֵּי מִצְרַיִם אֶת־הֶעָרֹב
וְגַם הָאֲדָמָה אֲשֶׁר־הֵם עָלֶיהָ׃ 18 וְהִפְלֵיתִי
בַיּוֹם הַהוּא אֶת־אֶרֶץ גֹּשֶׁן אֲשֶׁר עַמִּי עֹמֵד
עָלֶיהָ לְבִלְתִּי הֱיוֹת־שָׁם עָרֹב לְמַעַן תֵּדַע
כִּי אֲנִי יְהֹוָה בְּקֶרֶב הָאָרֶץ׃ 19 וְשַׂמְתִּי פְדֻת
בֵּין עַמִּי וּבֵין עַמֶּךָ לְמָחָר יִהְיֶה הָאֹת הַזֶּה׃
20 וַיַּעַשׂ יְהֹוָה כֵּן וַיָּבֹא עָרֹב כָּבֵד בֵּיתָה
פַרְעֹה וּבֵית עֲבָדָיו וּבְכָל־אֶרֶץ מִצְרַיִם
תִּשָּׁחֵת הָאָרֶץ מִפְּנֵי הֶעָרֹב׃

the Exodus narrative, reference is made to God's outstretched hand (such as 3:20) or arm (such as 6:6) as the vehicle for punishing the Egyptians. Here, the magician-priests express their acknowledgment of God's power though a similarly anthropomorphic image. As in other ancient Near Eastern texts, the hand of a deity is an image that signifies her or his ability to act in the world.

## FOUR: SWARMS INVADE THE LAND (8:16–28)

*17. "if you do not let My people go."* God does not secure Israel's liberation in a non-violent manner, rather, each refusal entails a harsh consequence. Moses emphasizes the reciprocal damage that Pharaoh brings on himself and his people by using verbs that share the same root. A translation that captures the parallel is: "If you do not *send* my people, then I will *send* swarms against you."

*"swarms of insects."* Heb. *arov*, which stems from the root meaning "to mix." Some ancient and medieval commentators understood the word as referring to a mixture of wild beasts, while others interpreted the term as some sort of insect, perhaps a fly. The parallelism with "lice" in Psalm 105:31 supports the present translation.

*18. "I will set apart the region of Goshen."* God begins the process of separating the people of Israel from the Egyptian population while fulfilling the fantasy of the oppressed seeing their oppressors suffer. God wrenches Israel from Egypt in gradual stages of individuation during which Israel is free of suffering.

*19. "I will make a distinction."* The distinction that results from the Exodus is of two sorts: Israel becomes independent of Egypt and receives a legal code that marks it as different from other nations.

*20.* Like the frogs, the insects invade the houses of royalty and commoners alike.

21Then Pharaoh summoned Moses and Aaron and said, "Go and sacrifice to your God within the land." 22But Moses replied, "It would not be right to do this, for what we sacrifice to our God יהוה is untouchable to the Egyptians. If we sacrifice that which is untouchable to the Egyptians before their very eyes, will they not stone us! 23So we must go a distance of three days into the wilderness and sacrifice to יהוה as our God may command us." 24Pharaoh said, "I will let you go to sacrifice to your God יהוה in the wilderness; but do not go very far. Plead, then, for me." 25And Moses said, "When I leave your presence, I will plead with יהוה that the swarms of insects depart tomorrow from Pharaoh and his courtiers and his people; but let not Pharaoh again act deceitfully, not letting the people go to sacrifice to יהוה."

26So Moses left Pharaoh's presence and pleaded with יהוה. 27And יהוה did as Moses asked—removing the swarms of insects from Pharaoh, from his courtiers, and from his people; not one remained. 28But Pharaoh became stubborn this time also, and would not let the people go.

9 יהוה said to Moses, "Go to Pharaoh and say to him, 'Thus says יהוה, the God of the Hebrews: Let My people go to worship Me. 2For if you refuse to let them go, and continue to hold them, 3then the hand of יהוה will strike your livestock in the fields—the horses, the asses, the camels, the cattle,

21 וַיִּקְרָ֣א פַרְעֹ֗ה אֶל־מֹשֶׁ֥ה וּֽלְאַהֲרֹן֮ וַיֹּ֒אמֶר֒ לְכ֛וּ זִבְח֥וּ לֵֽאלֹהֵיכֶ֖ם בָּאָֽרֶץ: 22 וַיֹּ֣אמֶר מֹשֶׁ֗ה לֹ֤א נָכוֹן֙ לַעֲשׂ֣וֹת כֵּ֔ן כִּ֚י תּוֹעֲבַ֣ת מִצְרַ֔יִם נִזְבַּ֖ח לַיהֹוָ֣ה אֱלֹהֵ֑ינוּ הֵ֣ן נִזְבַּ֞ח אֶת־תּוֹעֲבַ֤ת מִצְרַ֙יִם֙ לְעֵ֣ינֵיהֶ֔ם וְלֹ֥א יִסְקְלֻֽנוּ: 23 דֶּ֚רֶךְ שְׁלֹ֣שֶׁת יָמִ֔ים נֵלֵ֖ךְ בַּמִּדְבָּ֑ר וְזָבַ֙חְנוּ֙ לַֽיהֹוָ֣ה אֱלֹהֵ֔ינוּ כַּאֲשֶׁ֖ר יֹאמַ֥ר אֵלֵֽינוּ: 24 וַיֹּ֣אמֶר פַּרְעֹ֗ה אָנֹכִ֞י אֲשַׁלַּ֤ח אֶתְכֶם֙ וּזְבַחְתֶּ֞ם לַֽיהֹוָ֤ה אֱלֹֽהֵיכֶם֙ בַּמִּדְבָּ֔ר רַ֛ק הַרְחֵ֥ק לֹֽא־תַרְחִ֖יקוּ לָלֶ֑כֶת הַעְתִּ֖ירוּ בַּעֲדִֽי: 25 וַיֹּ֣אמֶר מֹשֶׁ֗ה הִנֵּ֨ה אָנֹכִ֜י יוֹצֵ֤א מֵֽעִמָּךְ֙ וְהַעְתַּרְתִּ֣י אֶל־יְהֹוָ֔ה וְסָ֣ר הֶעָרֹ֗ב מִפַּרְעֹ֛ה מֵעֲבָדָ֥יו וּמֵעַמּ֖וֹ מָחָ֑ר רַ֗ק אַל־יֹסֵ֤ף פַּרְעֹה֙ הָתֵ֔ל לְבִלְתִּי֙ שַׁלַּ֣ח אֶת־הָעָ֔ם לִזְבֹּ֖חַ לַֽיהֹוָֽה: 26 וַיֵּצֵ֥א מֹשֶׁ֖ה מֵעִ֣ם פַּרְעֹ֑ה וַיֶּעְתַּ֖ר אֶל־יְהֹוָֽה: 27 וַיַּ֤עַשׂ יְהֹוָה֙ כִּדְבַ֣ר מֹשֶׁ֔ה וַיָּ֙סַר֙ הֶעָרֹ֔ב מִפַּרְעֹ֖ה מֵעֲבָדָ֣יו וּמֵעַמּ֑וֹ לֹ֥א נִשְׁאַ֖ר אֶחָֽד: 28 וַיַּכְבֵּ֤ד פַּרְעֹה֙ אֶת־לִבּ֔וֹ גַּ֖ם בַּפַּ֣עַם הַזֹּ֑את וְלֹ֥א שִׁלַּ֖ח אֶת־הָעָֽם: פ

ט וַיֹּ֤אמֶר יְהֹוָה֙ אֶל־מֹשֶׁ֔ה בֹּ֖א אֶל־פַּרְעֹ֑ה וְדִבַּרְתָּ֣ אֵלָ֗יו כֹּֽה־אָמַ֤ר יְהֹוָה֙ אֱלֹהֵ֣י הָֽעִבְרִ֔ים שַׁלַּ֥ח אֶת־עַמִּ֖י וְיַֽעַבְדֻֽנִי: 2 כִּ֛י אִם־מָאֵ֥ן אַתָּ֖ה לְשַׁלֵּ֑חַ וְעֽוֹדְךָ֖ מַחֲזִ֥יק בָּֽם: 3 הִנֵּ֣ה יַד־יְהֹוָ֗ה הוֹיָ֤ה בְּמִקְנְךָ֙ אֲשֶׁ֣ר בַּשָּׂדֶ֔ה בַּסּוּסִ֤ים בַּֽחֲמֹרִים֙ בַּגְּמַלִּ֔ים בַּבָּקָ֖ר

- - - - - - - - - -

**21.** *"sacrifice to your God within the land."* A clever negotiator, Pharaoh concedes to half of Israel's request by proposing that they sacrifice to their God *within* Egypt, a compromise Moses rejects.

**22.** *"what we sacrifice... is untouchable to the Egyptians."* According to classical sources, ancient Egyptians sacrificed animals to gods and to the dead, but the creatures they offered were not sheep and goats like the Israelites. This may account for the perception that Israelite sacrifices would be anathema to the Egyptians. This is a kind of "eth-

nic differentiation" in which the customs of one group are deeply disapproved of by another.

### FIVE: PESTILENCE ATTACKS THE ANIMALS (9:1–7)

Like the first two signs, this episode, too, seems to involve an element of measure-for-measure justice. Since Israel is not allowed to sacrifice its animals to God in Egypt, the animals of Egypt will suffer.

and the sheep—with a very severe pestilence. [4]But יהוה will make a distinction between the livestock of Israel and the livestock of the Egyptians, so that nothing shall die of all that belongs to the Israelites. [5]יהוה has fixed the time: tomorrow יהוה will do this thing in the land.'" [6]And יהוה did so the next day: all the livestock of the Egyptians died, but of the livestock of the Israelites not a beast died. [7]When Pharaoh inquired, he found that not a head of the livestock of Israel had died; yet Pharaoh remained stubborn, and he would not let the people go.

[8]Then יהוה said to Moses and Aaron, "Each of you take handfuls of soot from the kiln, and let Moses throw it toward the sky in the sight of Pharaoh. [9]It shall become a fine dust all over the land of Egypt, and cause an inflammation breaking out in boils on human and beast throughout the land of Egypt." [10]So they took soot of the kiln and appeared before Pharaoh; Moses threw it toward the sky, and it caused an inflammation breaking out in boils on human and beast. [11]The magician-priests were unable to confront Moses because of the inflammation, for the inflammation afflicted the magician-priests as well as all the other Egyptians. [12]But יהוה stiffened the heart of Pharaoh, and he would not heed them, just as יהוה had told Moses.

וּבַצֹּאן דֶּבֶר כָּבֵד מְאֹד׃ 4 וְהִפְלָה יְהֹוָה
בֵּין מִקְנֵה יִשְׂרָאֵל וּבֵין מִקְנֵה מִצְרָיִם וְלֹא
יָמוּת מִכׇּל־לִבְנֵי יִשְׂרָאֵל דָּבָר׃ 5 וַיָּשֶׂם
יְהֹוָה מוֹעֵד לֵאמֹר מָחָר יַעֲשֶׂה יְהֹוָה
הַדָּבָר הַזֶּה בָּאָרֶץ׃ 6 וַיַּעַשׂ יְהֹוָה אֶת־הַדָּבָר
הַזֶּה מִמׇּחֳרָת וַיָּמׇת כֹּל מִקְנֵה מִצְרָיִם
וּמִמִּקְנֵה בְנֵי־יִשְׂרָאֵל לֹא־מֵת אֶחָד׃
7 וַיִּשְׁלַח פַּרְעֹה וְהִנֵּה לֹא־מֵת מִמִּקְנֵה
יִשְׂרָאֵל עַד־אֶחָד וַיִּכְבַּד לֵב פַּרְעֹה וְלֹא
שִׁלַּח אֶת־הָעָם׃ פ
8 וַיֹּאמֶר יְהֹוָה אֶל־מֹשֶׁה וְאֶל־אַהֲרֹן קְחוּ
לָכֶם מְלֹא חׇפְנֵיכֶם פִּיחַ כִּבְשָׁן וּזְרָקוֹ מֹשֶׁה
הַשָּׁמַיְמָה לְעֵינֵי פַרְעֹה׃ 9 וְהָיָה לְאָבָק עַל
כׇּל־אֶרֶץ מִצְרָיִם וְהָיָה עַל־הָאָדָם וְעַל־
הַבְּהֵמָה לִשְׁחִין פֹּרֵחַ אֲבַעְבֻּעֹת בְּכׇל־אֶרֶץ
מִצְרָיִם׃ 10 וַיִּקְחוּ אֶת־פִּיחַ הַכִּבְשָׁן וַיַּעַמְדוּ
לִפְנֵי פַרְעֹה וַיִּזְרֹק אֹתוֹ מֹשֶׁה הַשָּׁמָיְמָה
וַיְהִי שְׁחִין אֲבַעְבֻּעֹת פֹּרֵחַ בָּאָדָם וּבַבְּהֵמָה׃
11 וְלֹא־יָכְלוּ הַחַרְטֻמִּים לַעֲמֹד לִפְנֵי מֹשֶׁה
מִפְּנֵי הַשְּׁחִין כִּי־הָיָה הַשְּׁחִין בַּחַרְטֻמִּם
וּבְכׇל־מִצְרָיִם׃ 12 וַיְחַזֵּק יְהֹוָה אֶת־לֵב
פַּרְעֹה וְלֹא שָׁמַע אֲלֵהֶם כַּאֲשֶׁר דִּבֶּר יְהֹוָה
אֶל־מֹשֶׁה׃ ס

## SIX: SOOT BRINGS ABOUT BOILS (9:8–12)

With Pharaoh as their witness, Moses and Aaron throw handfuls of soot into the air; the soot becomes dust and causes boils to break out on humans and animals. In James Frazer's typology of magic, this constitutes imitative magic, for the properties of one object (soot that has been *burnt*) resemble another (a *burning* rash on the skin) to the point of actual inflammation.

When stricken by boils, Job sits in ash and scratches himself with a potsherd (Job 2:7–8). This image conveys the misery of the affliction that, like the lice before it, affects the flesh of both humans and animals.

*8. "soot from the kiln."* The reason for this specification is not clear. Umberto Cassuto suggests that the kiln in view is one where bricks are forged; since the making and laying of bricks are the very labors forced on the Israelites, both symmetry and "poetic justice" would then be evident in this divine act (*Exodus*, 1967, p. 113). Arguing against that interpretation is the fact that in ancient Egypt, bricks were generally sun-dried rather than kiln-fired.

*10. Moses threw it.* Although both Aaron and Moses are instructed to take handfuls of soot, only Moses actually throws the soot into the sky. Aaron's role is fading, as Moses takes center stage along with God and Pharaoh.

[13]יהוה said to Moses, "Early in the morning present yourself to Pharaoh and say to him, 'Thus says
יהוה, the God of the Hebrews: Let My people go
to worship Me. [14]For this time I will send all My
plagues upon your person, and your courtiers, and
your people, in order that you may know that there
is none like Me in all the world. [15]I could have
stretched forth My hand and stricken you and your
people with pestilence, and you would have been
effaced from the earth. [16]Nevertheless I have spared
you for this purpose: in order to show you My
power, and in order that My fame may resound
throughout the world. [17]Yet you continue to thwart
My people, and do not let them go! [18]This time tomorrow I will rain down a very heavy hail, such as
has not been in Egypt from the day it was founded
until now. [19]Therefore, order your livestock and
everything you have in the open brought under
shelter; every human and beast that is found outside, not having been brought indoors, shall perish
when the hail comes down upon them!'" [20]Those
among Pharaoh's courtiers who feared יהוה's word
brought their slaves and livestock indoors to safety;
[21]but those who paid no regard to the word of יהוה
left their slaves and livestock in the open.

[22]יהוה said to Moses, "Hold out your arm toward the sky that hail may fall on all the land of

13 וַיֹּאמֶר יְהוָה אֶל־מֹשֶׁה הַשְׁכֵּם בַּבֹּקֶר
וְהִתְיַצֵּב לִפְנֵי פַרְעֹה וְאָמַרְתָּ אֵלָיו כֹּה־
אָמַר יְהוָה אֱלֹהֵי הָעִבְרִים שַׁלַּח אֶת־עַמִּי
וְיַעַבְדֻנִי׃ 14 כִּי ׀ בַּפַּעַם הַזֹּאת אֲנִי שֹׁלֵחַ
אֶת־כָּל־מַגֵּפֹתַי אֶל־לִבְּךָ וּבַעֲבָדֶיךָ וּבְעַמֶּךָ
בַּעֲבוּר תֵּדַע כִּי אֵין כָּמֹנִי בְּכָל־הָאָרֶץ׃
15 כִּי עַתָּה שָׁלַחְתִּי אֶת־יָדִי וָאַךְ אוֹתְךָ
וְאֶת־עַמְּךָ בַּדָּבֶר וַתִּכָּחֵד מִן־הָאָרֶץ׃
16 וְאוּלָם בַּעֲבוּר זֹאת הֶעֱמַדְתִּיךָ בַּעֲבוּר
הַרְאֹתְךָ אֶת־כֹּחִי וּלְמַעַן סַפֵּר שְׁמִי בְּכָל־
הָאָרֶץ׃ 17 עוֹדְךָ מִסְתּוֹלֵל בְּעַמִּי לְבִלְתִּי
שַׁלְּחָם׃ 18 הִנְנִי מַמְטִיר כָּעֵת מָחָר בָּרָד
כָּבֵד מְאֹד אֲשֶׁר לֹא־הָיָה כָמֹהוּ בְּמִצְרַיִם
לְמִן־הַיּוֹם הִוָּסְדָה וְעַד־עָתָּה׃ 19 וְעַתָּה
שְׁלַח הָעֵז אֶת־מִקְנְךָ וְאֵת כָּל־אֲשֶׁר לְךָ
בַּשָּׂדֶה כָּל־הָאָדָם וְהַבְּהֵמָה אֲשֶׁר־יִמָּצֵא
בַשָּׂדֶה וְלֹא יֵאָסֵף הַבַּיְתָה וְיָרַד עֲלֵהֶם
הַבָּרָד וָמֵתוּ׃ 20 הַיָּרֵא אֶת־דְּבַר יְהוָה
מֵעַבְדֵי פַּרְעֹה הֵנִיס אֶת־עֲבָדָיו וְאֶת־מִקְנֵהוּ
אֶל־הַבָּתִּים׃ 21 וַאֲשֶׁר לֹא־שָׂם לִבּוֹ אֶל־
דְּבַר יְהוָה וַיַּעֲזֹב אֶת־עֲבָדָיו וְאֶת־מִקְנֵהוּ
בַּשָּׂדֶה׃ פ
22 וַיֹּאמֶר יְהוָה אֶל־מֹשֶׁה נְטֵה אֶת־יָדְךָ
עַל־הַשָּׁמַיִם וִיהִי בָרָד בְּכָל־אֶרֶץ מִצְרָיִם

## SEVEN: HAIL RAINS DOWN DESTRUCTION (9:13–35)

This plague comes with an additional test of Pharaoh: he is forewarned that if he wants to preserve his remaining servants and livestock, then he will need to shelter them before the hail strikes. The warning divides Pharaoh's household into those who fear God's word and therefore bring the animals inside and those who do not heed the divine word and leave their animals exposed.

*14. "My plagues."* Prior to mention of the killing of the first-born (11:1), this is the one time that God uses a term of affliction: *mageifot* (plagues). While the other episodes are referred to as "signs," "marvels," or "wonders," here the term "plagues" may have been used because the hail will involve a loss of life for humans and animals. (See also at 11:1.)

***"in order that you may know that there is none like Me."*** The intended outcome of the increasingly severe signs is the recognition of the unequaled power of God. Such a sentiment is expressed in the Song at the Sea (15:11) and later intoned in Jewish liturgy as the prayer *Mi Chamochah*.

Egypt, upon human and beast and all the grasses of
the field in the land of Egypt." 23 So Moses held out
his rod toward the sky, and יהוה sent thunder and
hail, and fire streamed down to the ground, as יהוה
rained down hail upon the land of Egypt. 24 The
hail was very heavy—fire flashing in the midst of
the hail—such as had not fallen on the land of
Egypt since it had become a nation. 25 Throughout
the land of Egypt the hail struck down all that were
in the open, both human and beast; the hail also
struck down all the grasses of the field and shattered
all the trees of the field. 26 Only in the region of
Goshen, where the Israelites were, there was no hail.
27 Thereupon Pharaoh sent for Moses and Aaron
and said to them, "I stand guilty this time. יהוה is
in the right, and I and my people are in the wrong.
28 Plead with יהוה that there may be an end of God's
thunder and of hail. I will let you go; you need stay
no longer." 29 Moses said to him, "As I go out of the
city, I shall spread out my hands to יהוה; the thunder will cease and the hail will fall no more, so that
you may know that the earth is יהוה's. 30 But I know
that you and your courtiers do not yet fear God
יהוה."—31 Now the flax and barley were ruined, for
the barley was in the ear and the flax was in bud;
32 but the wheat and the emmer were not hurt, for
they ripen late.—33 Leaving Pharaoh, Moses went
outside the city and spread out his hands to יהוה:

עַל־הָאָדָם וְעַל־הַבְּהֵמָה וְעַל כָּל־עֵשֶׂב
הַשָּׂדֶה בְּאֶרֶץ מִצְרָיִם׃ 23 וַיֵּט מֹשֶׁה אֶת־
מַטֵּהוּ עַל־הַשָּׁמַיִם וַיהוָה נָתַן קֹלֹת וּבָרָד
וַתִּהֲלַךְ אֵשׁ אָרְצָה וַיַּמְטֵר יְהוָה בָּרָד עַל־
אֶרֶץ מִצְרָיִם׃ 24 וַיְהִי בָרָד וְאֵשׁ מִתְלַקַּחַת
בְּתוֹךְ הַבָּרָד כָּבֵד מְאֹד אֲשֶׁר לֹא־הָיָה
כָמֹהוּ בְּכָל־אֶרֶץ מִצְרַיִם מֵאָז הָיְתָה לְגוֹי׃
25 וַיַּךְ הַבָּרָד בְּכָל־אֶרֶץ מִצְרַיִם אֵת כָּל־
אֲשֶׁר בַּשָּׂדֶה מֵאָדָם וְעַד־בְּהֵמָה וְאֵת כָּל־
עֵשֶׂב הַשָּׂדֶה הִכָּה הַבָּרָד וְאֶת־כָּל־עֵץ
הַשָּׂדֶה שִׁבֵּר׃ 26 רַק בְּאֶרֶץ גֹּשֶׁן אֲשֶׁר־שָׁם
בְּנֵי יִשְׂרָאֵל לֹא הָיָה בָּרָד׃
27 וַיִּשְׁלַח פַּרְעֹה וַיִּקְרָא לְמֹשֶׁה וּלְאַהֲרֹן
וַיֹּאמֶר אֲלֵהֶם חָטָאתִי הַפָּעַם יְהוָה הַצַּדִּיק
וַאֲנִי וְעַמִּי הָרְשָׁעִים׃ 28 הַעְתִּירוּ אֶל־יְהוָה
וְרַב מִהְיֹת קֹלֹת אֱלֹהִים וּבָרָד וַאֲשַׁלְּחָה
אֶתְכֶם וְלֹא תֹסִפוּן לַעֲמֹד׃ 29 וַיֹּאמֶר אֵלָיו
מֹשֶׁה כְּצֵאתִי אֶת־הָעִיר אֶפְרֹשׂ אֶת־כַּפַּי
אֶל־יְהוָה הַקֹּלוֹת יֶחְדָּלוּן וְהַבָּרָד לֹא יִהְיֶה־
עוֹד לְמַעַן תֵּדַע כִּי לַיהוָה הָאָרֶץ׃ 30 וְאַתָּה
וַעֲבָדֶיךָ יָדַעְתִּי כִּי טֶרֶם תִּירְאוּן מִפְּנֵי יְהוָה
אֱלֹהִים׃ 31 וְהַפִּשְׁתָּה וְהַשְּׂעֹרָה נֻכָּתָה כִּי
הַשְּׂעֹרָה אָבִיב וְהַפִּשְׁתָּה גִּבְעֹל׃ 32 וְהַחִטָּה
וְהַכֻּסֶּמֶת לֹא נֻכּוּ כִּי אֲפִילֹת הֵנָּה׃ 33 וַיֵּצֵא
מֹשֶׁה מֵעִם פַּרְעֹה אֶת־הָעִיר וַיִּפְרֹשׂ כַּפָּיו

*23. thunder and hail, and fire.* Note the detailed language used to describe hail, rain, thunder, and lightning, which may foreshadow the revelation at Sinai (Exodus 19).

*27. "I stand guilty this time."* Pharaoh temporarily puts himself in the wrong, but he recants from this position when the marvel ceases (9:34–35). Pharaoh sometimes seems to peer beyond his stubbornness and grasp the inevitable conclusion of the struggle.

*31. Now the flax and barley were ruined.* This digression about the harvest emphasizes the loss of one season's yield as well as the survival of the late-blooming crops. This foreshadows more destruction to come.

*31–32. barley... wheat.* These grains are associated with the Exodus not only narratively but also ritually: the earliest celebrations of Passover marked the barley harvest; and Shavuot was, in its first form, the wheat harvest holiday. The practice of cleaning one's house of leaven before Passover recalls the farmers' clearing of stale remnants of a previous crop before the harvest of a new one.

*emmer.* A kind of wheat.

the thunder and the hail ceased, and no rain came pouring down upon the earth. [34]But when Pharaoh saw that the rain and the hail and the thunder had ceased, he became stubborn and reverted to his guilty ways, as did his courtiers. [35]So Pharaoh's heart stiffened and he would not let the Israelites go, just as יהוה had foretold through Moses.

אֶל־יְהֹוָה֙ וַֽיַּחְדְּל֣וּ הַקֹּל֔וֹת וְהַבָּרָ֖ד וּמָטָ֥ר לֹא־נִתַּ֖ךְ אָֽרְצָה׃ [34] וַיַּ֣רְא פַּרְעֹ֗ה כִּֽי־חָדַ֨ל הַמָּטָ֧ר וְהַבָּרָ֛ד וְהַקֹּלֹ֖ת וַיֹּ֣סֶף לַחֲטֹ֑א וַיַּכְבֵּ֥ד לִבּ֖וֹ ה֥וּא וַעֲבָדָֽיו׃ [35] וַֽיֶּחֱזַק֙ לֵ֣ב פַּרְעֹ֔ה וְלֹ֥א שִׁלַּ֖ח אֶת־בְּנֵ֣י יִשְׂרָאֵ֑ל כַּאֲשֶׁ֛ר דִּבֶּ֥ר יְהֹוָ֖ה בְּיַד־מֹשֶֽׁה׃ פ

35. The parashah ends with both Pharaoh's stone heart and the acknowledgment that all is going according to God's plan.
—*Rachel Havrelock*

# Another View

In the preceding parashah, Pharaoh challenged Moses: "Who is יהוה that I should heed him and let Israel go?" (5:2). Earlier, Moses had anticipated that the Israelites would pose a similar question: "When I come to the Israelites . . . and they ask me, 'What is his name?' what shall I say to them?" (3:13). Divine self-revelation in *parashat Va-eira* answers these questions in two ways.

First, God declares: "I am יהוה; I appeared to Abraham, Isaac, and Jacob as El Shaddai, but I did not make Myself known to them by My name יהוה" (6:2). This personal divine name validates the promises made to the ancestors in Genesis. It also evokes God's eternal nature (see at 3:14, 15). Moreover, introducing a new divine name signals a new beginning for Israel, as God prepares to bring them from slavery to freedom.

A second aspect of God becomes manifest in overpowering Pharaoh with the so-called plagues and even in controlling Pharaoh's heart. The text makes it clear that the signs and wonders are part of God's design—the means to demonstrate God's control of history. Had there only been one or two, they might have been dismissed as a chance occurrence. However, Israel's God is able both to inflict multiple signs and to withdraw them at a designated time.

Given the high status of Pharaoh as god in Egyptian culture, it is especially significant that Israel's God can also control and manipulate Pharaoh himself by hardening his heart in certain instances (4:21; 7:3; 9:12; 10:1, 20, 27; 11:10; 14:4, 8). Although hardening Pharaoh's heart creates tension regarding Pharaoh's culpability, it highlights God's supreme control.

*Divine self-revelation answers these questions in two ways.*

God's intentions are quite explicit: "I have spared you for this purpose: in order to show you my power, and in order that my fame may resound throughout the world" (9:16).

Thus, like the revelation at the burning bush (Exodus 3) and the revelation on Mt. Sinai (Exodus 19), the ten signs become a means of divine self-disclosure. They demonstrate God's supreme power, proving that the Creator of the universe controls even the most powerful of human rulers.

—*Naomi Steinberg*

# Post-biblical Interpretations

***Amram took to wife his father's sister Jochebed*** (6:20). While Moses' mother is mentioned several times in the Torah, her proper name, Jochebed, is stated only twice, here and in Numbers 26:59. Here, she is simply described in the Hebrew as her husband Amram's *dodah,* an imprecise term indicating a familial relationship. Numbers 26:59, however, makes clear that Jochebed was the daughter of Jacob's son Levi (and that she was born to Levi in Egypt). That information has been taken into account in the translation of the present verse: Jochebed (daughter of Levi) was the aunt of her husband, Amram (grandson of Levi; Exodus 6:16, 18).

The Rabbis were uncomfortable with this marriage, since it appeared to contradict the prohibition in

Leviticus 18:12 against an aunt-nephew sexual/marital relationship. One response to this dilemma was simply to point out that the relationship was pre-Sinaitic and therefore was not restricted to the law as stipulated in Leviticus (BT *Sanhedrin* 57b–58b). Another rabbinic approach rested on further investigation into the meaning of the word *dodah*. According to BT *Sanhedrin* 58b, Jochebed was only a "half-aunt." She and Amram's father were said to have shared the same father (Levi), but they were born of different (unnamed) mothers. Therefore, the marriage of Amram and Jochebed was not prohibited as it was between a man and his half-aunt.

***Aaron took to wife Elisheba, daughter of Amminadab*** (6:23). The Torah mentions Elisheba only once and defines her by her familial relationships. While it is standard for a biblical woman to be identified by her father's name, and even by her husband's or children's names, the mention of all of them in the same verse is unusual. The description of Elisheba is even more unusual in that she is also identified as the sister of Nahshon. *Vayikra Rabbah* 20.2 elaborates on these relationships by pointing to one day in Elisheba's life, which was also an important day in the lives of all the male relatives mentioned in this verse. According to narratives found later in the Torah, it occurred exactly one year after the Exodus took place; on that day, the Tabernacle was dedicated in the wilderness, and Elisheba experienced a number of joyous events—but then a disaster transformed her happiness into mourning. The joyous incidents were that her brother-in-law (Moses) took on a mantle of leadership that is compared to royalty; her brother (Nahshon) was made chief of the tribe of Judah; her husband (Aaron) was made high priest; her grandson (Phinehas) was anointed as a military leader; and two of her sons (Nadab and Abihu) were made assistants to the high priest. The circumstance for grief concerned these two sons. According to Leviticus 10:1–2, on that same day "they offered before יהוה alien fire... and fire came forth from יהוה and consumed them; thus they died at the instance of יהוה."

Even though Elisheba bat Amminadab is mentioned only once in the Torah, a rabbinic opinion in BT *Sotah* 11b equates her with Puah, one of the two midwives who saved the Israelite baby boys contrary to Pharaoh's decree (Exodus 1:15–22). These two midwives, Shiphrah and Puah, are identified by some rabbinic commentators as the mother-daughter team of Jochebed and Miriam, and by other rabbinic commentators as a mother–daughter-in-law team, namely, Jochebed and Elisheba. Such conflation of several biblical personalities into one person is typical of rabbinic interpretation.

***Aaron's son Eleazar took to wife one of Putiel's daughters*** (6:25). This verse is part of a longer priestly lineage recorded in Exodus 6. It is unusual, although not unique, in that it mentions a wife. The way that this woman is designated is also unusual, in that she is described as one of the daughters (plural) of Putiel, rather than simply a daughter (singular) of Putiel. The Rabbis derived from this plurality that *both* sides of her family may be seen as influences on her son, Phinehas (who plays a major, heroic role in events recorded in Numbers 25). They learned about her ancestors by analyzing the name of her father Putiel, since he is not mentioned elsewhere in the Bible, and nothing else is known about him. By examining the Hebrew root of his name they deduced that he (and therefore his daughter) is descended from Jethro (Moses' father-in-law) on one side of his family, and from Joseph on the other side (BT *Sotah* 43a).

*The way that this woman is designated is also unusual.*

—*Anna Urowitz-Freudenstein*

# Contemporary Reflection

THE SIGNS AND WONDERS (or "plagues") described in *parashat Va-eira* must have been extremely frightening for both the Egyptians who suffered and the Israelites who bore witness to God's might for the first time. Thirteenth-century Kabbalists believed that when the Children of Israel braved the agonies of slavery and the ten displays of divine might that devastated Egypt, they did not do so alone. Rather, the Israelites knew that the *Shechinah*, the pre-eminent feminine aspect of God, dwelled alongside them in Egypt. Medieval Kabbalists often portrayed the feminine *Shechinah* as a loving mother who suffers along with her children Israel in exile. She toils with her children while they are slaves in Egypt and protects them in the wilderness after they are liberated.

This association between the *Shechinah*, the supernal mother, and human mothers is given a biological dimension in the *Zohar*, the most popular work of medieval Kabbalah. The *Zohar* understands God as a power that is utterly transcendent and—at the same time—wholly immanent in our world. The Deity is comprised of the *Ein Sof* ("Without End"), which lies beyond the realm of human cognition, and ten lower *s'firot* (aspects) that emanate forth into the realm of being. Kabbalists believed that everything on earth reflects this divine realm.

The *Zohar* represents the realm of the *s'firot* in a myriad of different ways. It often compares the *s'firot* to an inverted tree or to the days of the week.

Perhaps the most popular symbol, however, is *gufa* (the body). Genesis 1:26 states that God made humans in God's image and after God's likeness. Kabbalists understood this verse literally. If human beings are in the form of an *anthropos* (human body), and if human beings were made in the image and likeness of God, then God must be an *anthropos* too. Human anatomy and physiology reflect this divine reality. Hence, women and men engage in sexual intercourse because two *s'firot*—*Tiferet* (the sixth *s'firah*, symbolically understood as the King and Groom) and *Shechinah* (the tenth *s'firah*, symbolically understood as the Queen and Bride)—desire harmony and union. Women conceive and give birth because the *Shechinah* receives the effluxes or emanative powers of the higher *s'firot*. And women have a monthly flow because the *Shechinah* menstruates when she comes under the influence of the demonic "other side" (*sitra achra*).

Medieval halachah (Jewish law) required women to separate from their husbands for twelve to fourteen days every month: the five- to seven-day period of menstruation plus another seven "clean" days. The *Zohar* traces the source of this halachah to the myth of the *Shechinah*. The *Zohar* considers Egypt to be the ultimate symbol of the *sitra achra*. When the *Shechinah* dwells with the Children of Israel in Goshen, She becomes influenced by the "other side" and begins to menstruate. Therefore she must separate from her husband, *Tiferet*, for the duration of her blood flow; as a consequence, she is exiled or banished (literally *niddah*) from the forces of the Holy. Although her flow ends as soon as the Children of Israel flee Egypt, the *Shechinah* is not ritually pure yet. In keeping with the dictates of halachah, she must separate from her husband for another seven clean days. The *Zohar* conceives of these seven "days" as seven weeks—the seven weeks of the counting of the *Omer* between Passover and Shavuot.

*Dairy meals on Shavuot recall the lactating Shechinah who nourishes Israel with Torah.*

After forty-nine days of travel, the *Shechinah* and her children rest at the foot of Mount Sinai, where she at last undergoes the final purificatory ritual: immersion in a supernal *mikveh* (pool). Like a newly adorned bride, the ritually pure *Shechinah* meets her husband, *Tiferet*, at the crest of Mount Sinai. They engage in divine union on the eve of Shavuot. On Shavuot day, the *Shechinah* gives birth to the two tablets of the Covenant. Ever the devoted mother, the *Shechinah* gives these tablets to Moses for her children Israel (*Zohar* 3:96b).

The *Shechinah* figures prominently throughout the *Zohar*. Consequently, many Jews understand Kabbalah to be the only haven for gender equality in rabbinic Judaism. Unfortunately, this is not the case. Indeed, it would be extraordinary if it were. The *Zohar* is the product of a 13th-century worldview. Its author, Moses de León, and his circle lived in a world in which women's physical and intellectual inferiority was believed to have been proven scientifically. It would have been inconceivable for them to develop a mythology of the *Shechinah* that defied societal norms. Hence, the *Shechinah* is most often represented as a passive vessel with "nothing of her own." When she acts righteously, she sometimes changes gender and becomes male; when she comes under the sway of the *sitra achra*, she always remains female.

There are passages, however, that we can read as more sympathetic to feminist views. When we read the *Zohar* through the prism of history, we can differentiate between the different shades of prejudice to create a new meaning. The Kabbalistic story of the *Shechinah*'s exodus from Egypt is a case in point. There are many troubling notions in this passage—the association between menstruation and demonic possession being one of the most egregious. Nonetheless, valuable insights that can enhance our spirituality are embedded in this story. The *Shechinah* as caring mother, basing the *Omer* on a female biological function, and the notion of the giving of Torah (*matan Torah*) as a birth are notions that we can reclaim and make our own. The notion that the *Shechinah* gave birth to the Torah tablets gives an entirely new meaning to the notion of "Torah from Sinai." Indeed, I believe that the custom of eating dairy on Shavuot can be traced to this very myth. After all, dairy foods symbolize the lactating *Shechinah* who nourishes her children Israel with the Torah.

—*Sharon Koren*

# Voices

## *Disquisition*

Chana Bloch

*Exodus 6:3*

One day I dared to put the O back
in G-d.
I watched Him bulge to God—
  paunchy, respectable
and sad.

I brooded about my heresy
until I guessed
that God who loves the circle best
  only to find
  our angularity
might after all not mind.

  He'd take it to heart, perhaps,
  if I chose to drop the caps.

But O that fine round O
  fleshed out from the scrawny spine
  of a minus sign—
  or would He object that O
  was zero,
  taking Him in vain?

God knows,
an O is an O is an O,
  and slyly checks
  our tic-tac-toe
with His wry X.

NOTE

*G-d.* God's sacred name is revealed to Moses in Exodus 6:3. In order to protect the sanctity of the divine name, some Jews write "G-d" rather than "God." The poet uses humor to challenge this custom.

## *I Spread Out God's Names in Front of Me*

Rivka Miriam (transl. Linda Stern Zisquit)

*Exodus 6:3*

I spread out God's names in front of me
on the floor of my chilly room.
The name by which I called him when his spirit
  breathed in me.
And the name by which I called him when
  I was a young girl.
The name by which I called him when I was
  given to a man.
And the name when I was again permissible
  to all.
The name by which I called him when my
  parents were a roof to me. And the name
  when I had no ceiling.
The name by which I called him so that I would
  fear him. And the name by which I called
  him so that I would not be afraid.
The name by which I called him so that he
  would remember me. And the name so
  that he would refrain from remembering.
In the heat of day I will prostrate myself
on the floor of my chilly room.

## *Elisheba Speaks*

Sue Levi Elwell

*Exodus 6:23*

Aaron bathes and anoints.
I prepare his priestly raiment.
I sew fine linen with bone needles, smoothing
the folds as I go.
I take great care to keep my bleeding fingers
from soiling the garments.

They teach that blood defiles.
He stays away from me when it flows.
I know that my bright blood is life.
In my strength, those nights, I sleep alone.

Aaron bathes and anoints. I, too, bathe.
I keep his priestly garments, and our sheets
white and pure.
Thus we each serve the Source of All.

## *God, Take Me By Your Hand*

Etty Hillesum (transl. Arnold J. Pomerans)

*Exodus 6:12*

God, take me by Your hand. I shall follow You dutifully, and not resist too much. I shall evade none of the tempests life has in store for me, I shall try to face it all as best I can. But now and then grant me a short respite. I shall never again assume, in my innocence, that any peace that comes my way will be eternal. I shall accept all the inevitable tumult and struggle. I delight in warmth and security, but I shall not rebel if I have to suffer cold, should You so decree. I shall follow wherever Your hand leads me and shall try not to be afraid. I shall try to spread some of my warmth, of my genuine love for others, wherever I go.

## *from* The Nursing Father

Alicia Suskin Ostriker

Child of compassion, child of wrath. Moses is Egyptian, he is Hebrew, he is both/neither, he is insider/outsider, he is compressed/torn. Child of the mothers in the world of the fathers. He is the locus of gain/loss, he is where another division begins. Between the God of the universe and the God of a tribe, between inclusion and exclusion, between the imperative of liberty and the imperative of law, explodes Moses. What we know about him is exactly nothing, exactly everything, he is a fierce mystery.

## *from* Passover

Linda Pastan

*Exodus 7:8–9:35*

Far from Egypt, I have sighted blood,
have heard the throaty mating of frogs.
My city knows vermin, animals loose in
hallways,
boils, sickness, hail.
In the suburban gardens
seventeen year locusts rise
from their heavy beds
in small explosions of sod.
Darkness of newsprint.
My son, my son.

# בא ✦ Bo

## EXODUS 10:1–13:16

### *Power, Plagues, Passover*

PARASHAT BO ("go") features three final signs from God (locusts, darkness, and the slaying of the first-born), following directly after the first seven signs in the previous parashah. (Although in English parlance this series of events is commonly called "the Ten Plagues," the Hebrew text refers to them mainly as "signs," "marvels," or "wonders"; see further at 11:1.) Then the narrative from which this book takes its English name reaches its climax as the Israelites' exodus from Egypt begins. Framing the account of the last sign and the hurried flight from Egypt are instructions for the (annual) passover sacrifice and the Festival of Matzot (Unleavened Bread).

An overriding theme in this Torah portion is God's omnipotence. The signs are meant to prove to Pharaoh, all Egypt, and the burgeoning people of Israel that Israel's God reigns supreme. Because of Pharaoh's stubborn willfulness, God's determination to respond to the outcry of the oppressed Israelites (3:7) ultimately leads to a loud cry in Egypt as the anguish of the death of every first-born male echoes in the night (11:6; 12:30).

The theme of remembrance also recurs throughout this parashah. Several passages emphasize the importance of teaching future generations about how God saved the Israelites (10:2; 12:26–27; 13:14–15). Also, a number of apparently existing rites—including the Festival of Matzot (12:14; 13:3), *t'fillin* (13:9, 16), and the redemption of the first-born (13:14–15)—are linked to the Exodus to institutionalize its memory.

Many readers of this parashah wonder about the historicity of the Exodus story. It is important to remember that these events are not recounted as verifiable history. Rather, the narrative describes a people's collective memory of their past. As such, the historical accuracy of the account is unimportant, for it has no bearing on the story's core message or themes. (See *Sh'mot*, Contemporary Reflection, p. 326.)

*The theme of remembrance recurs throughout this parashah.*

We find a few scattered references to women throughout this parashah. When Moses negotiates with Pharaoh, he insists that every Israelite—including the women—be permitted to leave Egypt to worship God (10:9). Further on, as the Israelites prepare to leave, women are instructed to "borrow" objects of silver and gold from their female Egyptian neighbors (11:2). (They will later donate such materials for the Tabernacle; 35:22–29.) In addition, Moses warns the people that every Egyptian first-born male will die—even the oldest child of "the slave girl who is behind the millstones" (11:5).

The image of her grinding grain into flour reflects the role women played in the complex production of bread (see at 11:5 and 12:8). Although we repeatedly read about unleavened bread in this parashah (12:8, 14–20, 39; 13:3–8), the text does not mention who makes the matzah. Textual and archeological evidence suggests that women would have baked the unleavened cakes of dough that are part of the story of the Israelites' fleeing from Egypt. As an integral part of each Israelite "family" and "household" (12:3), women experience the long-awaited Exodus, the unprecedented redemptive act that becomes the foundation for the relationship between God and Israel.

—*Sharon R. Keller*

## Outline

I. Moses and God versus Pharaoh, continued
*Two More Signs from God* (10:1–29)

A. Eight: locusts (vv. 1–20)
B. Nine: darkness (vv. 21–29)

II. Ritual Preparations for the Exodus (11:1–12:28)

A. Announcement of the tenth sign (11:1–10)
B. Instructions for the Passover sacrifice (12:1–13)
C. Regulations for the Feast of Matzot (12:14–20)
D. Instructions for the Passover sacrifice delivered to the elders (12:21–28)

III. The Tenth Sign
*Slaying of the First-born* (12:29–36)

IV. The Exodus from Egypt Begins (12:37–42)

V. Ritual Remembrances of the Exodus (12:43–13:16)

A. Laws of the Passover offering (12:43–51)
B. Consecration of first-born males, Feast of Matzot, and *t'fillin* (13:1–16)

10:1

Then יהוה said to Moses, "Go to Pharaoh. For I
have hardened his heart and the hearts of his
courtiers, in order that I may display these My signs
among them, 2and that you may recount in the
hearing of your children and of your children's children how I made a mockery of the Egyptians and

י וַיֹּאמֶר יְהוָֹה אֶל־מֹשֶׁה בֹּא אֶל־פַּרְעֹה
כִּי־אֲנִי הִכְבַּדְתִּי אֶת־לִבּוֹ וְאֶת־לֵב עֲבָדָיו
לְמַעַן שִׁתִי אֹתֹתַי אֵלֶּה בְּקִרְבּוֹ׃ 2 וּלְמַעַן
תְּסַפֵּר בְּאָזְנֵי בִנְךָ וּבֶן־בִּנְךָ אֵת אֲשֶׁר
הִתְעַלַּלְתִּי בְּמִצְרַיִם וְאֶת־אֹתֹתַי אֲשֶׁר־

## *Moses and God versus Pharaoh, continued*

### TWO MORE SIGNS FROM GOD (10:1–29)

The previous parashah ended after a series of seven signs of divine power. According to the narrator, Pharaoh reacted to these signs by "stiffening" his "heart" (that is, his will). Following the 5th sign, God began to "harden" Pharaoh's heart. Nevertheless, his free will remained (9:35).

Now, after Moses and Aaron again warn Pharaoh—and God once again hardens his heart—the east wind ushers in an unprecedented swarm of locusts. The grand scale of this 8th sign underscores that it is a one-time, cataclysmic event aimed to demonstrate God's supremacy.

Pharaoh is unable to relent. This will lead to a 9th sign—darkness—which is announced and performed without confrontation with, or warning to, Pharaoh (just like the 3rd and 6th signs; see 8:12–15 and 9:8–11).

### EIGHT: LOCUSTS (10:1–20)

*1. "I have hardened his heart."* A major theme of this parashah is God's omnipotence, especially in relation to the pharaoh. The narrator insists on showing that God completely controls all that is happening, as exemplified by the way God hardens Pharaoh's heart. (Earlier, Pharaoh hardens his own heart, as in 8:15.)

*"hardened."* Literally, God "made [Pharaoh's heart] heavy" (from the root *k-b-d*, "to be heavy"). The image of the heavy heart may relate to the ancient Egyptian conception that in the afterlife, when weighed on the scales of judgment, the virtuous soul is found to have a heart that is lighter than a feather, whereas the sinner has a heavy heart.

*2. "that you may recount."* The memory of the bondage in and redemption from Egypt is central to Israel's covenantal relationship with God, as seen in the prologue to the Decalogue (20:2). Moses is addressed in the singular here, as the one who will begin the process of the retelling of the


▸ Rituals . . . allow us to see a connection between blood, sacrifice, and family ties.

ANOTHER VIEW ➤ *372*

▸ God's hardening of Pharaoh's heart presents a theological problem on two levels.

CONTEMPORARY REFLECTION ➤ *374*

▸ The new mother's desperate cry was so great that it reached heaven.

POST-BIBLICAL INTERPRETATIONS ➤ *372*

▸ Miriam, her head hot in her hands, wept / as the city swelled / with the wail of Egypt's women.

VOICES ➤ *376*

how I displayed My signs among them—in order that you may know that I am יהוה." [3]So Moses and Aaron went to Pharaoh and said to him, "Thus says יהוה, the God of the Hebrews, 'How long will you refuse to humble yourself before Me? Let My people go that they may worship Me. [4]For if you refuse to let My people go, tomorrow I will bring locusts on your territory. [5]They shall cover the surface of the land, so that no one will be able to see the land. They shall devour the surviving remnant that was left to you after the hail; and they shall eat away all your trees that grow in the field. [6]Moreover, they shall fill your palaces and the houses of all your courtiers and of all the Egyptians—something that neither your fathers nor fathers' fathers have seen from the day they appeared on earth to this day.'" With that he turned and left Pharaoh's presence.

[7]Pharaoh's courtiers said to him, "How long shall this one be a snare to us? Let their notables go to worship their God יהוה! Are you not yet aware that Egypt is lost?" [8]So Moses and Aaron were brought back to Pharaoh and he said to them, "Go, worship your God יהוה! Who are the ones to go?" [9]Moses replied, "We will all go, regardless of social

שַׂמְתִּי בָם וִידַעְתֶּם כִּי־אֲנִי יְהוָה׃ 3 וַיָּבֹא
מֹשֶׁה וְאַהֲרֹן אֶל־פַּרְעֹה וַיֹּאמְרוּ אֵלָיו כֹּה־
אָמַר יְהוָה אֱלֹהֵי הָעִבְרִים עַד־מָתַי מֵאַנְתָּ
לֵעָנֹת מִפָּנָי שַׁלַּח עַמִּי וְיַעַבְדֻנִי׃ 4 כִּי אִם־
מָאֵן אַתָּה לְשַׁלֵּחַ אֶת־עַמִּי הִנְנִי מֵבִיא
מָחָר אַרְבֶּה בִּגְבֻלֶךָ׃ 5 וְכִסָּה אֶת־עֵין
הָאָרֶץ וְלֹא יוּכַל לִרְאֹת אֶת־הָאָרֶץ וְאָכַל
אֶת־יֶתֶר הַפְּלֵטָה הַנִּשְׁאֶרֶת לָכֶם מִן־
הַבָּרָד וְאָכַל אֶת־כָּל־הָעֵץ הַצֹּמֵחַ לָכֶם מִן־
הַשָּׂדֶה׃ 6 וּמָלְאוּ בָתֶּיךָ וּבָתֵּי כָל־עֲבָדֶיךָ
וּבָתֵּי כָל־מִצְרַיִם אֲשֶׁר לֹא־רָאוּ אֲבֹתֶיךָ
וַאֲבוֹת אֲבֹתֶיךָ מִיּוֹם הֱיוֹתָם עַל־הָאֲדָמָה
עַד הַיּוֹם הַזֶּה וַיִּפֶן וַיֵּצֵא מֵעִם פַּרְעֹה׃
7 וַיֹּאמְרוּ עַבְדֵי פַרְעֹה אֵלָיו עַד־מָתַי
יִהְיֶה זֶה לָנוּ לְמוֹקֵשׁ שַׁלַּח אֶת־הָאֲנָשִׁים
וְיַעַבְדוּ אֶת־יְהוָה אֱלֹהֵיהֶם הֲטֶרֶם תֵּדַע כִּי
אָבְדָה מִצְרָיִם׃ 8 וַיּוּשַׁב אֶת־מֹשֶׁה וְאֶת־
אַהֲרֹן אֶל־פַּרְעֹה וַיֹּאמֶר אֲלֵהֶם לְכוּ עִבְדוּ
אֶת־יְהוָה אֱלֹהֵיכֶם מִי וָמִי הַהֹלְכִים׃
9 וַיֹּאמֶר מֹשֶׁה בִּנְעָרֵינוּ וּבִזְקֵנֵינוּ נֵלֵךְ

enslavement and exodus to subsequent generations in order to ensure that these events do not fade from Israelite memory.

***"in order that you may know that I am יהוה."*** As with the other signs, part of God's stated motivation for these events is to demonstrate and authenticate the divine Presence, thus eliciting recognition of God's power from both the Egyptians and the Israelites.

*5.* ***no one will be able to see.*** This phrase refers not only to the 8th sign but also foreshadows the 9th sign (see next section). For further foreshadowing, see at v. 17, below.

*7.* ***"their notables."*** Heb. *ha-anashim* (traditionally "the men"), which the present translation understands as referring to a group's representatives. The courtiers' plea to Pharaoh is to dispatch the Israelite elders or officials—presumably men; thus Pharaoh asks for a specific list (v. 8).

*9.* ***"We will all go."*** In his reply, Moses shows that the courtiers' limited offer is unacceptable: he includes all the people as well as the livestock. Moses and Aaron had originally resorted to a ruse, telling Pharaoh that they wanted to leave only in order to worship their God at a distance of three days' journey into the wilderness (see 5:1, 3). Since they have no intention of returning to Egypt, no one and nothing can be left behind.

***"regardless of social station."*** Literally, "with our underlings and with our elders" or "with our youths and with our old folks"; the Hebrew terms can refer either to socioeconomic status or to age.

This type of expression is called a "merism," meaning that the figure of speech uses two extremes

station; we will go with our sons and daughters, our
flocks and herds—for we must observe יהוה's festival." 10But he said to them, "יהוה be with you the
same as I mean to let your dependents go with you!
Clearly, you are bent on mischief. 11No! You menfolk go and worship יהוה, since that is what you
want." And they were expelled from Pharaoh's
presence.

12Then יהוה said to Moses, "Hold out your arm
over the land of Egypt for the locusts, that they
may come upon the land of Egypt and eat up all the
grasses in the land, whatever the hail has left." 13So
Moses held out his rod over the land of Egypt, and
יהוה drove an east wind over the land all that day
and all night; and when morning came, the east
wind had brought the locusts. 14Locusts invaded all
the land of Egypt and settled within all the territory
of Egypt in a thick mass; never before had there
been so many, nor will there ever be so many again.
15They hid all the land from view, and the land was
darkened; and they ate up all the grasses of the field
and all the fruit of the trees which the hail had left,
so that nothing green was left, of tree or grass of the
field, in all the land of Egypt.

16Pharaoh hurriedly summoned Moses and
Aaron and said, "I stand guilty before your God
יהוה and before you. 17Forgive my offense just this
once, and plead with your God יהוה that this death
but be removed from me." 18So he left Pharaoh's
presence and pleaded with יהוה. 19יהוה caused a
shift to a very strong west wind, which lifted the
locusts and hurled them into the Sea of Reeds; not a

בְּבָנֵ֨ינוּ וּבִבְנוֹתֵ֜נוּ בְּצֹאנֵ֤נוּ וּבִבְקָרֵ֙נוּ֙ נֵלֵ֔ךְ כִּ֥י
חַג־יְהוָ֖ה לָֽנוּ׃ 10 וַיֹּ֣אמֶר אֲלֵהֶ֗ם יְהִ֨י כֵ֤ן
יְהוָה֙ עִמָּכֶ֔ם כַּאֲשֶׁ֛ר אֲשַׁלַּ֥ח אֶתְכֶ֖ם וְאֶֽת־
טַפְּכֶ֑ם רְא֕וּ כִּ֥י רָעָ֖ה נֶ֥גֶד פְּנֵיכֶֽם׃ 11 לֹ֣א כֵ֗ן
לְכֽוּ־נָ֤א הַגְּבָרִים֙ וְעִבְד֣וּ אֶת־יְהוָ֔ה כִּ֥י אֹתָ֖הּ
אַתֶּ֣ם מְבַקְשִׁ֑ים וַיְגָ֣רֶשׁ אֹתָ֔ם מֵאֵ֖ת פְּנֵ֥י
פַרְעֹֽה׃ ס
12 וַיֹּ֨אמֶר יְהוָ֜ה אֶל־מֹשֶׁ֗ה נְטֵ֨ה יָדְךָ֜ עַל־
אֶ֤רֶץ מִצְרַ֙יִם֙ בָּֽאַרְבֶּ֔ה וְיַ֖עַל עַל־אֶ֣רֶץ מִצְרָ֑יִם
וְיֹאכַל֙ אֶת־כָּל־עֵ֣שֶׂב הָאָ֔רֶץ אֵ֛ת כָּל־אֲשֶׁ֥ר
הִשְׁאִ֖יר הַבָּרָֽד׃ 13 וַיֵּ֨ט מֹשֶׁ֣ה אֶת־מַטֵּהוּ֮
עַל־אֶ֣רֶץ מִצְרַיִם֒ וַֽיהוָ֗ה נִהַ֤ג רֽוּחַ־קָדִים֙
בָּאָ֔רֶץ כָּל־הַיּ֥וֹם הַה֖וּא וְכָל־הַלָּ֑יְלָה הַבֹּ֣קֶר
הָיָ֔ה וְר֙וּחַ֙ הַקָּדִ֔ים נָשָׂ֖א אֶת־הָאַרְבֶּֽה׃
14 וַיַּ֣עַל הָֽאַרְבֶּ֗ה עַ֚ל כָּל־אֶ֣רֶץ מִצְרַ֔יִם וַיָּ֕נַח
בְּכֹ֖ל גְּב֣וּל מִצְרָ֑יִם כָּבֵ֣ד מְאֹ֔ד לְ֠פָנָיו לֹא־
הָ֨יָה כֵ֥ן אַרְבֶּ֙ה֙ כָּמֹ֔הוּ וְאַחֲרָ֖יו לֹ֥א יִֽהְיֶה־כֵּֽן׃
15 וַיְכַ֞ס אֶת־עֵ֣ין כָּל־הָאָ֘רֶץ֮ וַתֶּחְשַׁ֣ךְ הָאָרֶץ֒
וַיֹּ֜אכַל אֶת־כָּל־עֵ֣שֶׂב הָאָ֗רֶץ וְאֵת֙ כָּל־פְּרִ֣י
הָעֵ֔ץ אֲשֶׁ֥ר הוֹתִ֖יר הַבָּרָ֑ד וְלֹא־נוֹתַ֨ר כָּל־יֶ֧רֶק
בָּעֵ֛ץ וּבְעֵ֥שֶׂב הַשָּׂדֶ֖ה בְּכָל־אֶ֥רֶץ מִצְרָֽיִם׃
16 וַיְמַהֵ֣ר פַּרְעֹ֔ה לִקְרֹ֖א לְמֹשֶׁ֣ה וּֽלְאַהֲרֹ֑ן
וַיֹּ֗אמֶר חָטָ֛אתִי לַיהוָ֥ה אֱלֹהֵיכֶ֖ם וְלָכֶֽם׃
17 וְעַתָּ֗ה שָׂ֣א נָ֤א חַטָּאתִי֙ אַ֣ךְ הַפַּ֔עַם
וְהַעְתִּ֖ירוּ לַיהוָ֣ה אֱלֹהֵיכֶ֑ם וְיָסֵר֙ מֵֽעָלַ֔י רַ֖ק
אֶת־הַמָּ֥וֶת הַזֶּֽה׃ 18 וַיֵּצֵ֖א מֵעִ֣ם פַּרְעֹ֑ה
וַיֶּעְתַּ֖ר אֶל־יְהוָֽה׃ 19 וַיַּהֲפֹ֨ךְ יְהוָ֤ה רֽוּחַ־יָם֙
חָזָ֣ק מְאֹ֔ד וַיִּשָּׂא֙ אֶת־הָ֣אַרְבֶּ֔ה וַיִּתְקָעֵ֖הוּ

to convey a totality, as if it said "and everybody in between."

*"with our sons and daughters."* This is a second expression that Moses uses to signal inclusiveness in the proposed religious observance.

*13. east wind.* Later, when the Israelites cross the Sea of Reeds, God will again bring an east wind to turn the water into dry ground (see at 14:21; also Numbers 11:31).

*17. this death.* Thus the 8th sign anticipates the final and most crushing divine act, the death of the first-born sons (11:1–10; 12:29–36); compare at v. 5, above.

single locust remained in all the territory of Egypt. 20 But יהוה stiffened Pharaoh's heart, and he would not let the Israelites go.

21 Then יהוה said to Moses, "Hold out your arm toward the sky that there may be darkness upon the land of Egypt, a darkness that can be touched." 22 Moses held out his arm toward the sky and thick darkness descended upon all the land of Egypt for three days. 23 People could not see one another, and for three days no one could move about; but all the Israelites enjoyed light in their dwellings.

24 Pharaoh then summoned Moses and said, "Go, worship יהוה! Only your flocks and your herds shall be left behind; even your dependents may go with you." 25 But Moses said, "You yourself must provide us with sacrifices and burnt offerings to offer up to our God יהוה; 26 our own livestock, too, shall go along with us—not a hoof shall remain behind: for we must select from it for the worship of our God יהוה; and we shall not know with what we are to worship יהוה until we arrive there." 27 But יהוה stiffened Pharaoh's heart and he would not agree to let them go. 28 Pharaoh said to him, "Be gone from me! Take care not to see me again, for the moment you look upon my face you shall die." 29 And Moses replied, "You have spoken rightly. I shall not see your face again!"

יָ֣מָּה ס֑וּף לֹ֤א נִשְׁאַר֙ אַרְבֶּ֣ה אֶחָ֔ד בְּכֹ֖ל גְּב֥וּל
מִצְרָֽיִם׃ 20 וַיְחַזֵּ֥ק יְהֹוָ֖ה אֶת־לֵ֣ב פַּרְעֹ֑ה וְלֹ֥א
שִׁלַּ֖ח אֶת־בְּנֵ֥י יִשְׂרָאֵֽל׃ פ
21 וַיֹּ֨אמֶר יְהֹוָ֜ה אֶל־מֹשֶׁ֗ה נְטֵ֤ה יָֽדְךָ֙ עַל־
הַשָּׁמַ֔יִם וִ֥יהִי חֹ֖שֶׁךְ עַל־אֶ֣רֶץ מִצְרָ֑יִם וְיָמֵ֖שׁ
חֹֽשֶׁךְ׃ 22 וַיֵּ֥ט מֹשֶׁ֛ה אֶת־יָד֖וֹ עַל־הַשָּׁמָ֑יִם
וַיְהִ֧י חֹֽשֶׁךְ־אֲפֵלָ֛ה בְּכָל־אֶ֥רֶץ מִצְרַ֖יִם
שְׁלֹ֥שֶׁת יָמִֽים׃ 23 לֹֽא־רָא֞וּ אִ֣ישׁ אֶת־אָחִ֗יו
וְלֹא־קָ֛מוּ אִ֥ישׁ מִתַּחְתָּ֖יו שְׁלֹ֣שֶׁת יָמִ֑ים
וּֽלְכָל־בְּנֵ֧י יִשְׂרָאֵ֛ל הָ֥יָה א֖וֹר בְּמוֹשְׁבֹתָֽם׃
24 וַיִּקְרָ֨א פַרְעֹ֜ה אֶל־מֹשֶׁ֗ה וַיֹּ֙אמֶר֙ לְכוּ֙
עִבְד֣וּ אֶת־יְהֹוָ֔ה רַ֛ק צֹאנְכֶ֥ם וּבְקַרְכֶ֖ם יֻצָּ֑ג
גַּֽם־טַפְּכֶ֖ם יֵלֵ֥ךְ עִמָּכֶֽם׃ 25 וַיֹּ֣אמֶר מֹשֶׁ֔ה גַּם־
אַתָּ֛ה תִּתֵּ֥ן בְּיָדֵ֖נוּ זְבָחִ֣ים וְעֹלֹ֑ת וְעָשִׂ֖ינוּ
לַיהֹוָ֥ה אֱלֹהֵֽינוּ׃ 26 וְגַם־מִקְנֵ֜נוּ יֵלֵ֣ךְ עִמָּ֗נוּ
לֹ֤א תִשָּׁאֵר֙ פַּרְסָ֔ה כִּ֚י מִמֶּ֣נּוּ נִקַּ֔ח לַעֲבֹ֖ד אֶת־
יְהֹוָ֣ה אֱלֹהֵ֑ינוּ וַאֲנַ֣חְנוּ לֹֽא־נֵדַ֗ע מַה־נַּעֲבֹד֙
אֶת־יְהֹוָ֔ה עַד־בֹּאֵ֖נוּ שָֽׁמָּה׃ 27 וַיְחַזֵּ֥ק יְהֹוָ֖ה
אֶת־לֵ֣ב פַּרְעֹ֑ה וְלֹ֥א אָבָ֖ה לְשַׁלְּחָֽם׃
28 וַיֹּֽאמֶר־ל֥וֹ פַרְעֹ֖ה לֵ֣ךְ מֵעָלָ֑י הִשָּׁ֣מֶר לְךָ֗
אַל־תֹּ֙סֶף֙ רְא֣וֹת פָּנַ֔י כִּ֗י בְּי֛וֹם רְאֹתְךָ֥ פָנַ֖י
תָּמֽוּת׃ 29 וַיֹּ֣אמֶר מֹשֶׁ֔ה כֵּ֖ן דִּבַּ֑רְתָּ לֹא־אֹסִ֥ף
ע֖וֹד רְא֥וֹת פָּנֶֽיךָ׃ פ

### NINE: DARKNESS (10:21–29)

*23. People could not see one another... but all the Israelites enjoyed light.* Presumably the text's ancient audience would have understood such darkness as a reflection of the impotence of Re, the Egyptians' sun god. Thus this sign implicitly proves that the God of Israel is stronger than the gods of the Egyptians.

*24. "even your dependents may go with you."* Despite Pharaoh's earlier restriction that only the men leave (v. 11), he now relents and acquiesces to Moses' demand that all the people be allowed to leave (v. 9).

*"dependents."* Heb. *taf*, a flexible term whose sense depends on what it complements. Here it is counterposed with "the men" (see v. 10 and at vv. 7, 9) and so must include the women as well as children. Most individuals in this category would be economically productive members of their household.

*29. "You have spoken rightly. I shall not see your face again."* In spite of this statement, Moses continues speaking to Pharaoh (11:4–8). Moses and Aaron meet with Pharaoh again when Pharaoh gives his final permission for the Israelites to leave Egypt (12:31–32).

11 And יהוה said to Moses, "I will bring but
one more plague upon Pharaoh and upon Egypt;
after that he shall let you go from here; indeed,
when he lets you go, he will drive you out of here
one and all. 2Tell the people to borrow, each man
from his neighbor and each woman from hers,

יא וַיֹּאמֶר יְהֹוָה אֶל־מֹשֶׁה עוֹד נֶגַע אֶחָד
אָבִיא עַל־פַּרְעֹה וְעַל־מִצְרַיִם אַחֲרֵי־כֵן
יְשַׁלַּח אֶתְכֶם מִזֶּה כְּשַׁלְּחוֹ כָּלָה גָּרֵשׁ
יְגָרֵשׁ אֶתְכֶם מִזֶּה׃ 2 דַּבֶּר־נָא בְּאָזְנֵי הָעָם
וְיִשְׁאֲלוּ אִישׁ ׀ מֵאֵת רֵעֵהוּ וְאִשָּׁה מֵאֵת

## *Ritual Preparations for the Exodus*
(11:1–12:28)

Nine signs from God in dramatic escalation have led to the present impasse: Pharaoh is unwilling to relent. However, God has already hinted at a 10th sign (4:23), and now it is announced. But before describing the execution of that sign, the narrative will pause to embed in the story two ritual acts—a passover offering and a Feast of Matzot—that are to be commemorated annually.

### ANNOUNCEMENT OF THE TENTH SIGN
(11:1–10)

The final calamity, which is labeled a "plague" (see at 11:1), proves decisive. It is introduced at length and receives more narrative space than any of the others; the account is more dramatic and also more disturbing to modern readers. Although the Egyptians are condemned for inflicting bondage on the Israelites and attempting to kill Hebrew babies, God's killing of innocent Egyptians may still raise theological and ethical questions for a contemporary audience. However, these concerns are not central to the biblical account. From the Bible's perspective, the main purpose of the signs is to prove God's might and supreme control. While recognizing the literary function and ahistorical nature of these texts helps to provide perspective on the seeming injustice of God's actions, many nevertheless struggle with what remains for them a troubling biblical text.

*1.* ***יהוה said.*** This revelation to Moses interrupts the heated exchange between Moses and Pharaoh and begins the instructions to the Israelites regarding preparations for the impending exodus. This interruption heightens the tension preceding the actual exodus from Egypt.

***"plague."*** Heb. *nega,* a term of affliction like *mageifah* in 9:14 and *negef* in 12:13, which are all customarily translated by the same English word. Such terms appear only in connection with the killing of the first-born and the hail—both of which involve a loss of human life. However, as Carol Meyers has pointed out, whenever God or the narrator describes what these calamities are intended to mean to the story's Israelite characters—and to its Israelite audience—the term used is "signs" (*otot,* see 8:19), "marvels" (*mof'tim,* see 11:10), or "wonders" (*nifla'ot,* see 3:20) (*Exodus,* 2005, pp. 76–77). At the same time, the phrasing here ("one more plague") suggests that all ten events generally are "plagues," referring to how the Egyptians experience them.

*2.* ***"borrow."*** The Bible gives no indication of any intention to return the Egyptians' objects. The Hebrew word translated as "borrow" has a range of meanings, including "ask" or "demand" (see also at 3:22). To explain the Israelites' actions, commentators connect this verse with Deuteronomy 15:13, which states that a Hebrew slave should not be set free without payment. As early as the 2nd century B.C.E., the despoiling of the Egyptians was considered recompense for the labor of bondage (Jubilees 48:18).

***"each man from his neighbor and each woman from hers."*** In this context, the grammatically masculine language of the first phrase alone could have been understood as gender inclusive. God's

objects of silver and gold." 3יהוה disposed the Egyptians favorably toward the people. Moreover, their leader Moses was much esteemed in the land of Egypt, among Pharaoh's courtiers and among the people.

4Moses said, "Thus says יהוה: Toward midnight I will go forth among the Egyptians, 5and every [male] first-born in the land of Egypt shall die, from the first-born of Pharaoh who sits on his throne to the first-born of the slave girl who is behind the millstones; and all the first-born of the cattle. 6And there shall be a loud cry in all the land of Egypt, such as has never been or will ever be again; 7but not a dog shall snarl at any of the Israelites, at human or beast—in order that you may know that יהוה makes a distinction between Egypt and Israel.

8"Then all these courtiers of yours shall come down to me and bow low to me, saying, 'Depart,

רְעוּתָהּ כְּלֵי־כֶסֶף וּכְלֵי זָהָב׃ 3 וַיִּתֵּן יְהוָה
אֶת־חֵן הָעָם בְּעֵינֵי מִצְרָיִם גַּם ׀ הָאִישׁ
מֹשֶׁה גָּדוֹל מְאֹד בְּאֶרֶץ מִצְרַיִם בְּעֵינֵי
עַבְדֵי־פַרְעֹה וּבְעֵינֵי הָעָם׃ ס
4 וַיֹּאמֶר מֹשֶׁה כֹּה אָמַר יְהוָה כַּחֲצֹת
הַלַּיְלָה אֲנִי יוֹצֵא בְּתוֹךְ מִצְרָיִם׃ 5 וּמֵת
כָּל־בְּכוֹר בְּאֶרֶץ מִצְרַיִם מִבְּכוֹר פַּרְעֹה
הַיֹּשֵׁב עַל־כִּסְאוֹ עַד בְּכוֹר הַשִּׁפְחָה אֲשֶׁר
אַחַר הָרֵחָיִם וְכֹל בְּכוֹר בְּהֵמָה׃ 6 וְהָיְתָה
צְעָקָה גְדֹלָה בְּכָל־אֶרֶץ מִצְרָיִם אֲשֶׁר כָּמֹהוּ
לֹא נִהְיָתָה וְכָמֹהוּ לֹא תֹסִף׃ 7 וּלְכֹל ׀ בְּנֵי
יִשְׂרָאֵל לֹא יֶחֱרַץ־כֶּלֶב לְשֹׁנוֹ לְמֵאִישׁ וְעַד־
בְּהֵמָה לְמַעַן תֵּדְעוּן אֲשֶׁר יַפְלֶה יְהוָה בֵּין
מִצְרַיִם וּבֵין יִשְׂרָאֵל׃
8 וְיָרְדוּ כָל־עֲבָדֶיךָ אֵלֶּה אֵלַי וְהִשְׁתַּחֲווּ־לִי
לֵאמֹר צֵא אַתָּה וְכָל־הָעָם אֲשֶׁר־בְּרַגְלֶיךָ

instructions thus go out of their way to specify that the Israelite men are to interact with the Egyptian men, and the Israelite women are to deal with the Egyptian women.

*"neighbor."* Presumably Egyptians, not Israelites (see 12:35), thus implying that the Israelites lived in close proximity to at least some Egyptians. See also at 3:22.

*3. disposed the Egyptians favorably.* One of the main points of the account of the signs is that God is all-powerful: God rules heaven and earth and all therein, including the Egyptians. Each biblical reference to this episode underscores that the Egyptians willingly gave their belongings to the Israelites as a result of God's intervention, meaning that the silver and gold was not plunder, but freely given (see 3:19–22; 12:35–36; Psalm 105:36–38).

*5. "every [male] first-born."* This translation clarifies that the plague will target specifically first-born sons, not daughters.

*"from the first-born of Pharaoh . . . to the first-born of the slave girl."* Another merism (see at 10:9): the intent of this act is to affect all Egyptian households, from the highest male aristocracy to the lowest female slave. The Torah is not concerned with the guilt or innocence of any specific victim, nor with the ethical implications of blanket punishments; the focus remains resolutely on exemplifying God's supreme power.

*behind the millstones.* Grinding grain to make bread for household consumption was likely the task of free women, bondwomen, or bondmen. On some large estates in Egypt, men first would crush grain in a mortar to make it ready for the women who then would grind it into flour. In ordinary peasant households, women likely performed all the procedures necessary for transforming grain into bread. In the Bible, grinding stones are associated with women (Judges 9:53); when young men carry them, the world has gone topsy-turvy (Lamentations 5:13). (See at 12:8 for more on women's involvement in bread production.)

*6. "loud cry."* The cry of the Egyptians will parallel the earlier outcry of the Israelites that God heard (3:7), the event that precipitated their salvation.

you and all the people who follow you!' After that
I will depart." And he left Pharaoh's presence in hot
anger.
[9]Now יהוה had said to Moses, "Pharaoh will not
heed you, in order that My marvels may be multiplied in the land of Egypt." [10]Moses and Aaron had
performed all these marvels before Pharaoh, but
יהוה had stiffened the heart of Pharaoh so that he
would not let the Israelites go from his land.

וְאַחֲרֵי־כֵן אֵצֵא וַיֵּצֵא מֵעִם־פַּרְעֹה בָּחֳרִי־
אָף׃ ס
9 וַיֹּאמֶר יְהוָה אֶל־מֹשֶׁה לֹא־יִשְׁמַע אֲלֵיכֶם
פַּרְעֹה לְמַעַן רְבוֹת מוֹפְתַי בְּאֶרֶץ מִצְרָיִם׃
10 וּמֹשֶׁה וְאַהֲרֹן עָשׂוּ אֶת־כָּל־הַמֹּפְתִים
הָאֵלֶּה לִפְנֵי פַרְעֹה וַיְחַזֵּק יְהוָה אֶת־
לֵב פַּרְעֹה וְלֹא־שִׁלַּח אֶת־בְּנֵי־יִשְׂרָאֵל
מֵאַרְצוֹ׃ ס

12 יהוה said to Moses and Aaron in the land
of Egypt: [2]This month shall mark for you the beginning of the months; it shall be the first of the
months of the year for you. [3]Speak to the whole
community of Israel and say that on the tenth of
this month each of them shall take a lamb to a
family, a lamb to a household. [4]But if the house-

יב וַיֹּאמֶר יְהוָה אֶל־מֹשֶׁה וְאֶל־אַהֲרֹן
בְּאֶרֶץ מִצְרַיִם לֵאמֹר׃ 2 הַחֹדֶשׁ הַזֶּה לָכֶם
רֹאשׁ חֳדָשִׁים רִאשׁוֹן הוּא לָכֶם לְחָדְשֵׁי
הַשָּׁנָה׃ 3 דַּבְּרוּ אֶל־כָּל־עֲדַת יִשְׂרָאֵל לֵאמֹר
בֶּעָשֹׂר לַחֹדֶשׁ הַזֶּה וְיִקְחוּ לָהֶם אִישׁ שֶׂה
לְבֵית־אָבֹת שֶׂה לַבָּיִת׃ 4 וְאִם־יִמְעַט הַבַּיִת

INSTRUCTIONS FOR THE PASSOVER SACRIFICE (12:1–13)

The narrative is interrupted at this point, thus heightening the suspense and drama of the story. The account of the plague continues in v. 29, after God gives instructions for the preparation of the Passover sacrifice, the application of blood to the doorposts and lintels, and the Feast of Matzot—all means of remembering and commemorating God's signal acts.

*1–2.* This instruction depicts the exodus from Egypt as the start of a new epoch in Israelite history and in the relationship of the Israelites with God. This foundational event is memorialized by a reformation of the calendar so that the year starts in the spring, the time of the Exodus. Exactly one year later, the Tabernacle will be erected (40:17), again highlighting this date as one on which momentous events occurred.

*2. This month.* Although unnamed here, the month is later identified as Abib (13:4; 23:15; 34:18; Deuteronomy 16:1), meaning "month of new grain"; still later it is called Nisan (Esther 3:7).

*first of the months of the year.* Rosh HaShanah, the first day of the seventh month, is now celebrated as the Jewish New Year; however, the Bible simply refers to it as a holiday commemorated with a shofar blast (see Leviticus 23:24; Numbers 29:1). In an agricultural society, both the spring and the fall could be considered new years, so some scholars see these two festivals as a way of combining competing ancient beliefs regarding the beginning of the year.

*3–6.* The passover sacrifice is not a typical offering, for each family is to prepare, slaughter, and consume its own lamb (or kid—the Hebrew term applies to the young of both sheep and goats; see v. 5) as part of the offering. Some believe that this was an earlier apotropaic (or protective) custom that here becomes associated with the Exodus.

*3. family . . . household.* Heb. *beit avot* and *bayit*, both of which can refer to a small (6- to 12-person) family unit, as probably here, or to a larger clan or lineage group. The language here and in v. 21 (*mishpachot,* translated there as "families") signals that women were included in the passover sacrifice. See also Deuteronomy 16:16, in which only men are obligated to celebrate the Passover festival.

hold is too small for a lamb, let it share one with a neighbor who dwells nearby, in proportion to the number of persons: you shall contribute for the lamb according to what each household will eat. [5]Your lamb shall be without blemish, a yearling male; you may take it from the sheep or from the goats. [6]You shall keep watch over it until the fourteenth day of this month; and all the assembled congregation of the Israelites shall slaughter it at twilight. [7]They shall take some of the blood and put it on the two doorposts and the lintel of the houses in which they are to eat it. [8]They shall eat the flesh that same night; they shall eat it roasted over the fire, with unleavened bread and with bitter herbs. [9]Do not eat any of it raw, or cooked in any way with water, but roasted—head, legs, and entrails—over the fire. [10]You shall not leave any of it over until morning; if any of it is left until morning, you shall burn it.

[11]This is how you shall eat it: your loins girded, your sandals on your feet, and your staff in your

מִהְיֹ֣ת מִשֶּׂה֮ וְלָקַ֣ח ה֗וּא וּשְׁכֵנ֛וֹ הַקָּרֹ֥ב אֶל־בֵּית֖וֹ בְּמִכְסַ֣ת נְפָשֹׁ֑ת אִ֚ישׁ לְפִ֣י אָכְל֔וֹ תָּכֹ֖סּוּ עַל־הַשֶּֽׂה: [5] שֶׂ֧ה תָמִ֛ים זָכָ֥ר בֶּן־שָׁנָ֖ה יִהְיֶ֣ה לָכֶ֑ם מִן־הַכְּבָשִׂ֥ים וּמִן־הָעִזִּ֖ים תִּקָּֽחוּ: [6] וְהָיָ֤ה לָכֶם֙ לְמִשְׁמֶ֔רֶת עַ֣ד אַרְבָּעָ֥ה עָשָׂ֛ר י֖וֹם לַחֹ֣דֶשׁ הַזֶּ֑ה וְשָׁחֲט֣וּ אֹת֗וֹ כֹּ֛ל קְהַ֥ל עֲדַֽת־יִשְׂרָאֵ֖ל בֵּ֥ין הָעַרְבָּֽיִם: [7] וְלָֽקְחוּ֙ מִן־הַדָּ֔ם וְנָ֥תְנ֛וּ עַל־שְׁתֵּ֥י הַמְּזוּזֹ֖ת וְעַל־הַמַּשְׁק֑וֹף עַ֚ל הַבָּ֣תִּ֔ים אֲשֶׁר־יֹאכְל֥וּ אֹת֖וֹ בָּהֶֽם: [8] וְאָכְל֥וּ אֶת־הַבָּשָׂ֖ר בַּלַּ֣יְלָה הַזֶּ֑ה צְלִי־אֵ֣שׁ וּמַצּ֔וֹת עַל־מְרֹרִ֖ים יֹאכְלֻֽהוּ: [9] אַל־תֹּאכְל֤וּ מִמֶּ֙נּוּ֙ נָ֔א וּבָשֵׁ֥ל מְבֻשָּׁ֖ל בַּמָּ֑יִם כִּ֣י אִם־צְלִי־אֵ֔שׁ רֹאשׁ֥וֹ עַל־כְּרָעָ֖יו וְעַל־קִרְבּֽוֹ: [10] וְלֹא־תוֹתִ֥ירוּ מִמֶּ֖נּוּ עַד־בֹּ֑קֶר וְהַנֹּתָ֥ר מִמֶּ֛נּוּ עַד־בֹּ֖קֶר בָּאֵ֥שׁ תִּשְׂרֹֽפוּ: [11] וְכָ֘כָה֘ תֹּאכְל֣וּ אֹתוֹ֒ מָתְנֵיכֶ֣ם חֲגֻרִ֔ים נַֽעֲלֵיכֶם֙ בְּרַגְלֵיכֶ֔ם וּמַקֶּלְכֶ֖ם בְּיֶדְכֶ֑ם

**5. yearling male.** The male animal is selected for sacrifice not because it is considered more valuable than a female. Rather, the female animals are preserved for breeding purposes and for milk production.

**7–13.** Blood, as a vital force of life, has protective powers in biblical thought. Some scholars maintain that the blood is to be applied to the doorframe of the house to protect the point where evil might enter; therefore, no one is to pass through the doorway (v. 22). The blood must be applied to the doorway before nightfall so that the sign will be apparent to God, thus ensuring that the Israelites will remain safe.

**8. with unleavened bread and with bitter herbs.** No explanation is provided for the instruction to eat unleavened bread and bitter herbs along with the passover sacrifice. Hence, many scholars believe that this was a pre-existent custom that here becomes as-

sociated with the Exodus. The source of this custom is unknown, but many scholars associate the bitter herbs with a sharp seasoning that might have been used in ancient times. According to the Mishnah (*P'sachim* 10:5) and the Passover Haggadah, the bitter herbs symbolize the bitterness of the enforced labor (Exodus 1:14).

Although the Bible does not give much information about food preparation, several texts (Genesis 18:6; I Samuel 8:13; II Samuel 13:8; Ecclesiastes 12:3), as well as extra-biblical and ethnographic evidence, suggest that women usually prepared bread. See also at 11:5, 16:3, and Leviticus 26:26.

**11.** The instructions in this verse indicate that the Israelites are to be prepared for an imminent departure. A reference to speed appears again in vv. 33–34, which describe the Egyptians' impatience for the Israelites to leave, and in v. 39, which links the unleavened bread to the Israelites' hasty departure.

hand; and you shall eat it hurriedly: it is a passover offering to יהוה. [12]For that night I will go through the land of Egypt and strike down every [male] first-born in the land of Egypt, both human and beast; and I will mete out punishments to all the gods of Egypt, I יהוה. [13]And the blood on the houses where you are staying shall be a sign for you: when I see the blood I will pass over you, so that no plague will destroy you when I strike the land of Egypt.

[14]This day shall be to you one of remembrance: you shall celebrate it as a festival to יהוה throughout the ages; you shall celebrate it as an institution for all time. [15]Seven days you shall eat unleavened bread; on the very first day you shall remove leaven from your houses, for whoever eats leavened bread from the first day to the seventh day, that person shall be cut off from Israel.

[16]You shall celebrate a sacred occasion on the first day, and a sacred occasion on the seventh day; no work at all shall be done on them; only what every person is to eat, that alone may be prepared for you. [17]You shall observe the [Feast of] Unleavened Bread, for on this very day I brought your ranks out of the land of Egypt; you shall observe this day throughout the ages as an institution for all time. [18]In the first month, from the fourteenth day of the month at evening, you shall eat unleavened bread until the twenty-first day of the month at

וַאֲכַלְתֶּ֤ם אֹתוֹ֙ בְּחִפָּז֔וֹן פֶּ֥סַח ה֖וּא לַֽיהוָֽה: 12 וְעָבַרְתִּ֣י בְאֶֽרֶץ־מִצְרַ֘יִם֮ בַּלַּ֣יְלָה הַזֶּה֒ וְהִכֵּיתִ֤י כָל־בְּכוֹר֙ בְּאֶ֣רֶץ מִצְרַ֔יִם מֵֽאָדָ֖ם וְעַד־בְּהֵמָ֑ה וּבְכָל־אֱלֹהֵ֥י מִצְרַ֛יִם אֶֽעֱשֶׂ֥ה שְׁפָטִ֖ים אֲנִ֥י יְהוָֽה: 13 וְהָיָה֩ הַדָּ֨ם לָכֶ֜ם לְאֹ֗ת עַ֤ל הַבָּתִּים֙ אֲשֶׁ֣ר אַתֶּ֣ם שָׁ֔ם וְרָאִ֙יתִי֙ אֶת־הַדָּ֔ם וּפָֽסַחְתִּ֖י עֲלֵכֶ֑ם וְלֹֽא־יִֽהְיֶ֨ה בָכֶ֥ם נֶ֙גֶף֙ לְמַשְׁחִ֔ית בְּהַכֹּתִ֖י בְּאֶ֥רֶץ מִצְרָֽיִם: 14 וְהָיָה֩ הַיּ֨וֹם הַזֶּ֤ה לָכֶם֙ לְזִכָּר֔וֹן וְחַגֹּתֶ֥ם אֹת֖וֹ חַ֣ג לַֽיהוָ֑ה לְדֹרֹ֣תֵיכֶ֔ם חֻקַּ֥ת עוֹלָ֖ם תְּחָגֻּֽהוּ: 15 שִׁבְעַ֤ת יָמִים֙ מַצּ֣וֹת תֹּאכֵ֔לוּ אַ֚ךְ בַּיּ֣וֹם הָֽרִאשׁ֔וֹן תַּשְׁבִּ֥יתוּ שְּׂאֹ֖ר מִבָּֽתֵּיכֶ֑ם כִּ֣י ׀ כָּל־אֹכֵ֣ל חָמֵ֗ץ וְנִכְרְתָ֞ה הַנֶּ֤פֶשׁ הַהִוא֙ מִיִּשְׂרָאֵ֔ל מִיּ֥וֹם הָֽרִאשֹׁ֖ן עַד־י֥וֹם הַשְּׁבִעִֽי: 16 וּבַיּ֤וֹם הָֽרִאשׁוֹן֙ מִקְרָא־קֹ֔דֶשׁ וּבַיּוֹם֙ הַשְּׁבִיעִ֔י מִקְרָא־קֹ֖דֶשׁ יִֽהְיֶ֣ה לָכֶ֑ם כָּל־מְלָאכָה֙ לֹֽא־יֵֽעָשֶׂ֣ה בָהֶ֔ם אַ֚ךְ אֲשֶׁ֣ר יֵֽאָכֵ֣ל לְכָל־נֶ֔פֶשׁ ה֥וּא לְבַדּ֖וֹ יֵֽעָשֶׂ֥ה לָכֶֽם: 17 וּשְׁמַרְתֶּם֮ אֶת־הַמַּצּוֹת֒ כִּ֗י בְּעֶ֙צֶם֙ הַיּ֣וֹם הַזֶּ֔ה הוֹצֵ֥אתִי אֶת־צִבְאֽוֹתֵיכֶ֖ם מֵאֶ֣רֶץ מִצְרָ֑יִם וּשְׁמַרְתֶּ֞ם אֶת־הַיּ֤וֹם הַזֶּה֙ לְדֹרֹ֣תֵיכֶ֔ם חֻקַּ֥ת עוֹלָֽם: 18 בָּֽרִאשֹׁ֗ן בְּאַרְבָּעָ֣ה עָשָׂ֥ר י֛וֹם לַחֹ֖דֶשׁ בָּעֶ֑רֶב תֹּֽאכְל֖וּ מַצֹּ֑ת עַ֠ד י֣וֹם הָֽאֶחָ֤ד

---

*passover.* This is the first time the word *pesach* is used in the Torah; and, as with matzah and the bitter herbs, the text assumes that the Israelites will understand the term. A folk etymology for the name "Passover" connects it to the angel of death's passing over the houses of the Israelites (see at 12:27).

## REGULATIONS FOR THE FEAST OF MATZOT
(12:14–20)

Some scholars posit that the Feast of Unleavened Bread (*matzot*) and the passover sacrifice (*pesach*) originally were two distinct festivals; but there is no

consensus regarding their origins. Here the Bible connects the two and links them to the Exodus experience (see also Joshua 5:11; Ezekiel 45:21; II Chronicles 35:17), thereby making them part of the rite of remembrance.

*15. you shall eat unleavened bread.* The exact significance here of matzah is unclear. The Bible presents unleavened bread as both a festive food (Genesis 19:3) and a symbol of oppression, associating "the bread of distress" with the memory of the Exodus (Deuteronomy 16:3).

*person.* See at Leviticus 2:1.

*cut off from Israel.* See at Leviticus 7:20.

evening. [19]No leaven shall be found in your houses for seven days. For whoever eats what is leavened, that person—whether a stranger or a citizen of the country—shall be cut off from the community of Israel. [20]You shall eat nothing leavened; in all your settlements you shall eat unleavened bread.

[21]Moses then summoned all the elders of Israel and said to them, "Go, pick out lambs for your families, and slaughter the passover offering. [22]Take a bunch of hyssop, dip it in the blood that is in the basin, and apply some of the blood that is in the basin to the lintel and to the two doorposts. None of you shall go outside the door of your house until morning. [23]For יהוה, when going through to smite the Egyptians, will see the blood on the lintel and the two doorposts, and יהוה will pass over the door and not let the Destroyer enter and smite your home.

[24]"You shall observe this as an institution for all time, for you and for your descendants. [25]And when you enter the land that יהוה will give you, as promised, you shall observe this rite. [26]And when your children ask you, 'What do you mean by this rite?' [27]you shall say, 'It is the passover sacrifice to יהוה, who passed over the houses of the Israelites in

וְעֶשְׂרִ֛ים לַחֹ֖דֶשׁ בָּעָ֑רֶב: 19 שִׁבְעַ֣ת יָמִ֔ים שְׂאֹ֕ר לֹ֥א יִמָּצֵ֖א בְּבָתֵּיכֶ֑ם כִּ֣י | כָּל־אֹכֵ֣ל מַחְמֶ֗צֶת וְנִכְרְתָ֞ה הַנֶּ֤פֶשׁ הַהִוא֙ מֵעֲדַ֣ת יִשְׂרָאֵ֔ל בַּגֵּ֖ר וּבְאֶזְרַ֥ח הָאָֽרֶץ: 20 כָּל־מַחְמֶ֖צֶת לֹ֣א תֹאכֵ֑לוּ בְּכֹל֙ מוֹשְׁבֹ֣תֵיכֶ֔ם תֹּאכְל֖וּ מַצּֽוֹת: פ

21 וַיִּקְרָ֥א מֹשֶׁ֛ה לְכָל־זִקְנֵ֥י יִשְׂרָאֵ֖ל וַיֹּ֣אמֶר אֲלֵהֶ֑ם מִֽשְׁכ֗וּ וּקְח֨וּ לָכֶ֥ם צֹ֛אן לְמִשְׁפְּחֹתֵיכֶ֖ם וְשַׁחֲט֥וּ הַפָּֽסַח: 22 וּלְקַחְתֶּ֞ם אֲגֻדַּ֣ת אֵז֗וֹב וּטְבַלְתֶּם֮ בַּדָּ֣ם אֲשֶׁר־בַּסַּף֒ וְהִגַּעְתֶּ֤ם אֶל־הַמַּשְׁקוֹף֙ וְאֶל־שְׁתֵּ֣י הַמְּזוּזֹ֔ת מִן־הַדָּ֖ם אֲשֶׁ֣ר בַּסָּ֑ף וְאַתֶּ֗ם לֹ֥א תֵצְא֛וּ אִ֥ישׁ מִפֶּֽתַח־בֵּית֖וֹ עַד־בֹּֽקֶר: 23 וְעָבַ֣ר יְהֹוָה֮ לִנְגֹּ֣ף אֶת־מִצְרַיִם֒ וְרָאָ֤ה אֶת־הַדָּם֙ עַל־הַמַּשְׁק֔וֹף וְעַ֖ל שְׁתֵּ֣י הַמְּזוּזֹ֑ת וּפָסַ֤ח יְהֹוָה֙ עַל־הַפֶּ֔תַח וְלֹ֤א יִתֵּן֙ הַמַּשְׁחִ֔ית לָבֹ֥א אֶל־בָּתֵּיכֶ֖ם לִנְגֹּֽף: 24 וּשְׁמַרְתֶּ֖ם אֶת־הַדָּבָ֣ר הַזֶּ֑ה לְחָק־לְךָ֥ וּלְבָנֶ֖יךָ עַד־עוֹלָֽם: 25 וְהָיָ֞ה כִּֽי־תָבֹ֣אוּ אֶל־הָאָ֗רֶץ אֲשֶׁ֨ר יִתֵּ֧ן יְהֹוָ֛ה לָכֶ֖ם כַּאֲשֶׁ֣ר דִּבֵּ֑ר וּשְׁמַרְתֶּ֖ם אֶת־הָעֲבֹדָ֥ה הַזֹּֽאת: 26 וְהָיָ֕ה כִּֽי־יֹאמְר֥וּ אֲלֵיכֶ֖ם בְּנֵיכֶ֑ם מָ֛ה הָעֲבֹדָ֥ה הַזֹּ֖את לָכֶֽם: 27 וַאֲמַרְתֶּ֡ם זֶֽבַח־פֶּ֨סַח ה֜וּא לַֽיהֹוָ֗ה

. . . . . . . . . . . . . . . . . . . . . . . . . . . . . . . . . . . . . . . .

### INSTRUCTIONS FOR THE PASSOVER SACRIFICE DELIVERED TO THE ELDERS (12:21–28)

Earlier, God instructs Moses to "speak to the whole community of Israel" (12:3). Here, however, Moses speaks specifically to the elders of Israel, who then will disseminate the information about the passover sacrifice to the entire community.

22. *"None of you shall go outside the door of your house."* The blood applied to the doorway differentiates the Israelites from the Egyptians and symbolically protects any first-born male children in the house (see at 12:7–13).

23. *"Destroyer."* The one who brings the

plague is personified as an agent of God (see II Samuel 24:15–17; II Kings 19:32–37). Nonetheless, God's control remains complete, for it is God who will "not let the Destroyer" enter the Israelites' homes.

27. *"passed over."* In this verse, the root *p-s-ch* links the festival of Passover (*Pesach*) to God's passing over (*pasach*) the houses of the Israelites, thereby protecting them from this plague. Scholars debate the precise force of the verb here. Some focus on the apotropaic function of blood (see at vv. 7–13) and understand it to mean "protect." Others connect it with the leaping of the demons from which one needs protection, or they relate it to a rite of passage.

Egypt when smiting the Egyptians, but saved our houses.'"

The people then bowed low in homage. 28And the Israelites went and did so; just as יהוה had commanded Moses and Aaron, so they did.

29In the middle of the night יהוה struck down all the [male] first-born in the land of Egypt, from the first-born of Pharaoh who sat on the throne to the first-born of the captive who was in the dungeon, and all the first-born of the cattle. 30And Pharaoh arose in the night, with all his courtiers and all the Egyptians—because there was a loud cry in Egypt; for there was no house where there was not someone dead. 31He summoned Moses and Aaron in the night and said, "Up, depart from among my people, you and the Israelites with you! Go, worship יהוה as you said! 32Take also your flocks and your herds, as you said, and begone! And may you bring a blessing upon me also!"

33The Egyptians urged the people on, impatient to have them leave the country, for they said, "We shall all be dead." 34So the people took their dough before it was leavened, their kneading bowls wrapped in their cloaks upon their shoulders. 35The Israelites had done Moses' bidding and borrowed from the Egyptians objects of silver and gold, and clothing. 36And יהוה had disposed the Egyptians

אֲשֶׁר֩ פָּ֨סַח עַל־בָּתֵּ֤י בְנֵֽי־יִשְׂרָאֵל֙ בְּמִצְרַ֔יִם
בְּנׇגְפּ֥וֹ אֶת־מִצְרַ֖יִם וְאֶת־בָּתֵּ֣ינוּ הִצִּ֑יל
וַיִּקֹּ֥ד הָעָ֖ם וַיִּֽשְׁתַּחֲוֽוּ׃ 28 וַיֵּלְכ֥וּ וַֽיַּעֲשׂ֖וּ בְּנֵ֣י
יִשְׂרָאֵ֑ל כַּאֲשֶׁ֨ר צִוָּ֧ה יְהֹוָ֛ה אֶת־מֹשֶׁ֥ה וְאַהֲרֹ֖ן
כֵּ֥ן עָשֽׂוּ׃ ס

29 וַיְהִ֣י ׀ בַּחֲצִ֣י הַלַּ֗יְלָה וַֽיהֹוָה֮ הִכָּ֣ה כׇל־
בְּכוֹר֮ בְּאֶ֣רֶץ מִצְרַ֔יִם מִבְּכֹ֤ר פַּרְעֹה֙ הַיֹּשֵׁ֣ב
עַל־כִּסְא֔וֹ עַ֚ד בְּכ֣וֹר הַשְּׁבִ֔י אֲשֶׁ֖ר בְּבֵ֣ית
הַבּ֑וֹר וְכֹ֖ל בְּכ֥וֹר בְּהֵמָֽה׃ 30 וַיָּ֨קׇם פַּרְעֹ֜ה
לַ֗יְלָה ה֤וּא וְכׇל־עֲבָדָיו֙ וְכׇל־מִצְרַ֔יִם וַתְּהִ֛י
צְעָקָ֥ה גְדֹלָ֖ה בְּמִצְרָ֑יִם כִּֽי־אֵ֣ין בַּ֔יִת אֲשֶׁ֥ר
אֵֽין־שָׁ֖ם מֵֽת׃ 31 וַיִּקְרָא֩ לְמֹשֶׁ֨ה וּֽלְאַהֲרֹ֜ן
לַ֗יְלָה וַיֹּ֙אמֶר֙ ק֤וּמוּ צְּאוּ֙ מִתּ֣וֹךְ עַמִּ֔י גַּם־
אַתֶּ֖ם גַּם־בְּנֵ֣י יִשְׂרָאֵ֑ל וּלְכ֛וּ עִבְד֥וּ אֶת־יְהֹוָ֖ה
כְּדַבֶּרְכֶֽם׃ 32 גַּם־צֹאנְכֶ֨ם גַּם־בְּקַרְכֶ֥ם קְח֛וּ
כַּאֲשֶׁ֥ר דִּבַּרְתֶּ֖ם וָלֵ֑כוּ וּבֵֽרַכְתֶּ֖ם גַּם־אֹתִֽי׃
33 וַתֶּחֱזַ֤ק מִצְרַ֙יִם֙ עַל־הָעָ֔ם לְמַהֵ֖ר לְשַׁלְּחָ֣ם
מִן־הָאָ֑רֶץ כִּ֥י אָמְר֖וּ כֻּלָּ֥נוּ מֵתִֽים׃ 34 וַיִּשָּׂ֥א
הָעָ֛ם אֶת־בְּצֵק֖וֹ טֶ֣רֶם יֶחְמָ֑ץ מִשְׁאֲרֹתָ֛ם
צְרֻרֹ֥ת בְּשִׂמְלֹתָ֖ם עַל־שִׁכְמָֽם׃ 35 וּבְנֵֽי־
יִשְׂרָאֵ֥ל עָשׂ֖וּ כִּדְבַ֣ר מֹשֶׁ֑ה וַֽיִּשְׁאֲלוּ֙ מִמִּצְרַ֔יִם
כְּלֵי־כֶ֛סֶף וּכְלֵ֥י זָהָ֖ב וּשְׂמָלֹֽת׃ 36 וַיהֹוָ֞ה נָתַ֨ן

## *The Tenth Sign*

SLAYING OF THE FIRST-BORN (12:29–36)

The prior narrative—set aside since 12:1—picks up again here, after the Israelites carry out the instructions for the passover offering (v. 28).

*29. first-born of the captive.* When this sign is announced (11:5), a slave girl exemplifies the lowest member of society. Here a different figure, a male captive, is contrasted with Pharaoh to signify that all elements of Egyptian society are subject to the reach of God's wrath.

*30. loud cry.* See at 11:6.

*31. "Go, worship יהוה as you said."* The outcome predicted by God in 3:20 and 6:1 now comes to pass as Pharaoh finally recognizes God's supremacy.

*34. dough . . . kneading bowls.* The narrative may highlight these objects because the description of the unleavened cakes of dough baked on the journey out of Egypt (12:39) links the narrative of the Exodus to the festival of matzot (13:3).

favorably toward the people, and they let them have their request; thus they stripped the Egyptians.

<sup></sup>³⁷The Israelites journeyed from Rameses to Succoth, about six hundred thousand men on foot, aside from dependents. ³⁸Moreover, a mixed multitude went up with them, and very much livestock, both flocks and herds. ³⁹And they baked unleavened cakes of the dough that they had taken out of Egypt, for it was not leavened, since they had been driven out of Egypt and could not delay; nor had they prepared any provisions for themselves.

⁴⁰The length of time that the Israelites lived in Egypt was four hundred and thirty years; ⁴¹at the end of the four hundred and thirtieth year, to the very day, all the ranks of יהוה departed from the

אֶת־חֵ֤ן הָעָם֙ בְּעֵינֵ֣י מִצְרַ֔יִם וַיַּשְׁאִל֑וּם
וַֽיְנַצְּל֖וּ אֶת־מִצְרָֽיִם׃ פ
³⁷ וַיִּסְע֧וּ בְנֵֽי־יִשְׂרָאֵ֛ל מֵרַעְמְסֵ֖ס סֻכֹּ֑תָה
כְּשֵׁשׁ־מֵא֨וֹת אֶ֧לֶף רַגְלִ֛י הַגְּבָרִ֖ים לְבַ֥ד
מִטָּֽף׃ ³⁸ וְגַם־עֵ֥רֶב רַ֖ב עָלָ֣ה אִתָּ֑ם וְצֹ֣אן
וּבָקָ֔ר מִקְנֶ֖ה כָּבֵ֥ד מְאֹֽד׃ ³⁹ וַיֹּאפ֨וּ אֶת־
הַבָּצֵ֜ק אֲשֶׁ֨ר הוֹצִ֤יאוּ מִמִּצְרַ֨יִם֙ עֻגֹ֣ת מַצּ֔וֹת
כִּ֣י לֹ֣א חָמֵ֑ץ כִּֽי־גֹרְשׁ֣וּ מִמִּצְרַ֗יִם וְלֹ֤א יָֽכְלוּ֙
לְהִתְמַהְמֵ֔הַּ וְגַם־צֵדָ֖ה לֹא־עָשׂ֥וּ לָהֶֽם׃
⁴⁰ וּמוֹשַׁב֙ בְּנֵ֣י יִשְׂרָאֵ֔ל אֲשֶׁ֥ר יָשְׁב֖וּ בְּמִצְרָ֑יִם
שְׁלֹשִׁ֣ים שָׁנָ֔ה וְאַרְבַּ֥ע מֵא֖וֹת שָׁנָֽה׃ ⁴¹ וַיְהִ֗י
מִקֵּץ֙ שְׁלֹשִׁ֣ים שָׁנָ֔ה וְאַרְבַּ֥ע מֵא֖וֹת שָׁנָ֑ה
וַיְהִ֗י בְּעֶ֨צֶם֙ הַיּ֣וֹם הַזֶּ֔ה יָֽצְא֛וּ כָּל־צִבְא֥וֹת

**36. stripped.** Heb. root *n-tz-l*, meaning "to take away." Though in English "stripped" has a negative connotation, the Torah does not seem to give a pejorative spin to the "despoiling" of Egypt (see at 11:2).

## The Exodus from Egypt Begins
### (12:37–42)

The drama of the hurried flight from Egypt is followed by various details about the start of the journey, including where the Israelites traveled, how many left, and when the exodus occurred.

**37. from Rameses to Succoth.** The exact location of these cities, and therefore the route of the exodus itself, is unknown, perhaps because the biblical account is not an historical record but rather a story meant to dramatize and commemorate a formative experience.

**six hundred thousand men.** This large number is symbolic, perhaps representing all Israelites of generations to come. If taken literally, the estimates for the total number of people leaving Egypt range between two and three million, assuming each man was accompanied by a wife and between two and three children. The number here agrees with the ac-

counting in Numbers 11:21, but note the discrepancy with the census account in Numbers 26:51 (see also Exodus 38:26).

**dependents.** As in 10:24, this term presumably includes the women, children, and infirm or disabled men.

**38. mixed multitude.** Heb. *erev rav*, an expression implying that other people joined the Israelites when they fled Egypt; but these people are not identified.

**39.** The significance of eating matzah is given here, even though the initial directive for eating it had been given in connection with the regulations for the Passover Festival (v. 8).

**40. four hundred and thirty years.** It is impossible to reconcile this figure with the other dates for the sojourn in Egypt given in the Bible (see Genesis 15:13, 16). Large numbers like this need not be taken literally but can be read as indicating relative size (see at v. 37). In this case, the message conveyed is that the sojourn in Egypt lasted a long time. There is, as yet, not enough information available to posit any precise dating of the Exodus; any attempt to do so is, at best, speculation.

**41. to the very day.** This phrase indicates that the timing of the Exodus was either divinely preordained or miraculous. Either way, the implication

land of Egypt. [42]That was for יהוה a night of vigil to bring them out of the land of Egypt; that same night is יהוה's, one of vigil for all the children of Israel throughout the ages.

[43]יהוה said to Moses and Aaron: This is the law of the passover offering: No foreigner shall eat of it. [44]But any householder's purchased male slave may eat of it once he has been circumcised. [45]No bound or hired laborer shall eat of it. [46]It shall be eaten in one house: you shall not take any of the flesh outside the house; nor shall you break a bone of it. [47]The whole community of Israel shall offer it. [48]If a male stranger who dwells with you would offer the passover to יהוה, all his males must be circumcised; then he shall be admitted to offer it; he shall then be as a citizen of the country. But no uncircumcised man may eat of it. [49]There shall be one law for the citizen and for the stranger who dwells among you.

יְהֹוָ֖ה מֵאֶ֥רֶץ מִצְרָֽיִם׃ 42 לֵ֣יל שִׁמֻּרִ֥ים הוּא֙
לַֽיהֹוָ֔ה לְהוֹצִיאָ֖ם מֵאֶ֣רֶץ מִצְרָ֑יִם הֽוּא־
הַלַּ֤יְלָה הַזֶּה֙ לַֽיהֹוָ֔ה שִׁמֻּרִ֛ים לְכׇל־בְּנֵ֥י
יִשְׂרָאֵ֖ל לְדֹרֹתָֽם׃ פ

43 וַיֹּ֤אמֶר יְהֹוָה֙ אֶל־מֹשֶׁ֣ה וְאַהֲרֹ֔ן זֹ֖את חֻקַּ֣ת
הַפָּ֑סַח כׇּל־בֶּן־נֵכָ֖ר לֹא־יֹ֥אכַל בּֽוֹ׃ 44 וְכׇל־
עֶ֥בֶד אִ֖ישׁ מִקְנַת־כָּ֑סֶף וּמַלְתָּ֣ה אֹת֔וֹ אָ֖ז
יֹ֥אכַל בּֽוֹ׃ 45 תּוֹשָׁ֥ב וְשָׂכִ֖יר לֹא־יֹ֥אכַל בּֽוֹ׃
46 בְּבַ֤יִת אֶחָד֙ יֵאָכֵ֔ל לֹא־תוֹצִ֧יא מִן־הַבַּ֛יִת
מִן־הַבָּשָׂ֖ר ח֑וּצָה וְעֶ֖צֶם לֹ֥א תִשְׁבְּרוּ־בֽוֹ׃
47 כׇּל־עֲדַ֥ת יִשְׂרָאֵ֖ל יַעֲשׂ֥וּ אֹתֽוֹ׃ 48 וְכִֽי־
יָג֨וּר אִתְּךָ֜ גֵּ֗ר וְעָ֣שָׂה פֶ֘סַח֮ לַֽיהֹוָה֒ הִמּ֧וֹל ל֣וֹ
כׇל־זָכָ֗ר וְאָז֙ יִקְרַ֣ב לַעֲשֹׂת֔וֹ וְהָיָ֖ה כְּאֶזְרַ֣ח
הָאָ֑רֶץ וְכׇל־עָ֖רֵל לֹא־יֹ֥אכַל בּֽוֹ׃ 49 תּוֹרָ֣ה
אַחַ֔ת יִהְיֶ֖ה לָֽאֶזְרָ֑ח וְלַגֵּ֖ר הַגָּ֥ר בְּתוֹכְכֶֽם׃

is that God keeps all promises, thus continuing the theme of God's ultimate control over all events.

*42. vigil . . . vigil.* Heb. *shimurim*, literally "keeping watch," contains the root *sh-m-r*, which occurs a total of seven times in Exodus 12 (also "keep watch," v. 6; "observe," vv. 17 [twice], 24, 25). Just as God has kept watch to effectuate the Exodus, so the Israelites must vigilantly observe the various rites established to commemorate this extraordinary event. These rites are the subject of the remainder of the parashah.

## *Ritual Remembrances of the Exodus*

(12:43–13:16)

In returning to ritual considerations, the text now constructs a double frame around the climactic events just narrated. The first frame is focused on the passover sacrifice. The regulations enumerated earlier (vv. 3–6) discuss how the offering is to be prepared; here we are told who may partake of the offering and who is excluded. The topic of the second, outer frame is the importance of memory, a concern that not only began the parashah (10:2) but also appeared in the preparations for the Exodus (12:26–27); here we find a listing of rites that institutionalize the memory of the Exodus and God's redemptive power.

### LAWS OF THE PASSOVER OFFERING

(12:43–51)

*44. circumcised.* Inclusion in the covenantal relationship through circumcision is the dominant criterion for participation in the passover offering for foreigners who live in the community (see also v. 48). Mention of circumcision here links this episode to the circumcision performed by Zipporah, Moses' wife, in 4:24–26, and thus frames the story of the salvation of the Israelites.

50 And all the Israelites did so; as יהוה had commanded Moses and Aaron, so they did.

51 That very day יהוה freed the Israelites from the land of Egypt, troop by troop.

**13** יהוה spoke further to Moses, saying, 2 "Consecrate to Me every male first-born; human and beast, the first [male] issue of every womb among the Israelites is Mine."

3 And Moses said to the people,

"Remember this day, on which you went free from Egypt, the house of bondage, how יהוה freed you from it with a mighty hand: no leavened bread shall be eaten. 4 You go free on this day, in the month of Abib. 5 So, when יהוה has brought you into the land of the Canaanites, the Hittites, the Amorites, the Hivites, and the Jebusites, which was sworn to your fathers to be given you, a land flowing with milk and honey, you shall observe in this month the following practice:

6 "Seven days you shall eat unleavened bread, and on the seventh day there shall be a festival of יהוה. 7 Throughout the seven days unleavened bread shall be eaten; no leavened bread shall be found with you, and no leaven shall be found in all your territory. 8 And you shall explain to your child on that day, 'It is because of what יהוה did for me when I went free from Egypt.'

9 "And this shall serve you as a sign on your hand and as a reminder on your forehead—in order that

50 וַיַּעֲשׂוּ כׇּל־בְּנֵי יִשְׂרָאֵל כַּאֲשֶׁר צִוָּה יְהֹוָה
אֶת־מֹשֶׁה וְאֶת־אַהֲרֹן כֵּן עָשׂוּ׃ ס
51 וַיְהִי בְּעֶצֶם הַיּוֹם הַזֶּה הוֹצִיא יְהֹוָה
אֶת־בְּנֵי יִשְׂרָאֵל מֵאֶרֶץ מִצְרַיִם עַל־
צִבְאֹתָם׃ פ

יג וַיְדַבֵּר יְהֹוָה אֶל־מֹשֶׁה לֵּאמֹר׃ 2 קַדֶּשׁ־
לִי כׇל־בְּכוֹר פֶּטֶר כׇּל־רֶחֶם בִּבְנֵי יִשְׂרָאֵל
בָּאָדָם וּבַבְּהֵמָה לִי הוּא׃
3 וַיֹּאמֶר מֹשֶׁה אֶל־הָעָם
זָכוֹר אֶת־הַיּוֹם הַזֶּה אֲשֶׁר יְצָאתֶם מִמִּצְרַיִם
מִבֵּית עֲבָדִים כִּי בְּחֹזֶק יָד הוֹצִיא יְהֹוָה
אֶתְכֶם מִזֶּה וְלֹא יֵאָכֵל חָמֵץ׃ 4 הַיּוֹם אַתֶּם
יֹצְאִים בְּחֹדֶשׁ הָאָבִיב׃ 5 וְהָיָה כִי־יְבִיאֲךָ
יְהֹוָה אֶל־אֶרֶץ הַכְּנַעֲנִי וְהַחִתִּי וְהָאֱמֹרִי
וְהַחִוִּי וְהַיְבוּסִי אֲשֶׁר נִשְׁבַּע לַאֲבֹתֶיךָ לָתֶת
לָךְ אֶרֶץ זָבַת חָלָב וּדְבָשׁ וְעָבַדְתָּ אֶת־
הָעֲבֹדָה הַזֹּאת בַּחֹדֶשׁ הַזֶּה׃
6 שִׁבְעַת יָמִים תֹּאכַל מַצֹּת וּבַיּוֹם הַשְּׁבִיעִי
חַג לַיהֹוָה׃ 7 מַצּוֹת יֵאָכֵל אֵת שִׁבְעַת
הַיָּמִים וְלֹא־יֵרָאֶה לְךָ חָמֵץ וְלֹא־יֵרָאֶה לְךָ
שְׂאֹר בְּכׇל־גְּבֻלֶךָ׃ 8 וְהִגַּדְתָּ לְבִנְךָ בַּיּוֹם
הַהוּא לֵאמֹר בַּעֲבוּר זֶה עָשָׂה יְהֹוָה לִי
בְּצֵאתִי מִמִּצְרָיִם׃
9 וְהָיָה לְךָ לְאוֹת עַל־יָדְךָ וּלְזִכָּרוֹן בֵּין
עֵינֶיךָ לְמַעַן תִּהְיֶה תּוֹרַת יְהֹוָה בְּפִיךָ

CONSECRATION OF FIRST-BORN MALES, FEAST OF MATZOT, AND T'FILLIN (13:1–16)

*2. "first [male] issue of every womb."* Heb. *peter rechem*, from the root *p-t-r*, meaning "to separate" or "to open"; the phrase refers to a female's first offspring. | The reason for the consecration or separation of first-born males is explained in vv. 12–15.

*3–8.* This section connects the prior instructions for matzot (12:14–20) with the recounting of the events of the Exodus for future generations (see at 10:2).

*3. "house of bondage."* This is the Torah's first instance of this famous phrase, a depiction of Egypt that foreshadows the Decalogue (20:2). Literally a "house of slaves," it envisions all Egypt as one large slave quarters. Ancient workers' villages found in Egypt show that historically, laborers were housed in segregated areas near their building projects and given provisions according to their skills and the difficulty of their labor.

*5. fathers.* See at Deuteronomy 4:31.

*9. "sign . . . reminder."* Here and in other passages (see Deuteronomy 6:8; 11:18; Proverbs

the Teaching of יהוה may be in your mouth—that with a mighty hand יהוה freed you from Egypt. 10 You shall keep this institution at its set time from year to year.

11 "And when יהוה has brought you into the land of the Canaanites, as [God] swore to you and to your fathers, and has given it to you, 12 you shall set apart for יהוה every first issue of the womb: every male firstling that your cattle drop shall be יהוה's. 13 But every firstling ass you shall redeem with a sheep; if you do not redeem it, you must break its neck. And you must redeem every male first-born among your children. 14 And when, in time to come, a child of yours asks you, saying, 'What does this mean?' you shall reply, 'It was with a mighty hand that יהוה brought us out from Egypt, the house of bondage. 15 When Pharaoh stubbornly refused to let us go, יהוה slew every [male] first-born in the land of Egypt, the first-born of both human and beast. Therefore I sacrifice to יהוה every first male issue of the womb, but redeem every male first-born among my children.'

16 "And so it shall be as a sign upon your hand and as a symbol on your forehead that with a mighty hand יהוה freed us from Egypt."

כִּי בְּיָד חֲזָקָה הוֹצִאֲךָ יְהֹוָה מִמִּצְרָיִם׃
10 וְשָׁמַרְתָּ אֶת־הַחֻקָּה הַזֹּאת לְמוֹעֲדָהּ
מִיָּמִים יָמִימָה׃ פ
11 וְהָיָה כִּי־יְבִאֲךָ יְהֹוָה אֶל־אֶרֶץ הַכְּנַעֲנִי
כַּאֲשֶׁר נִשְׁבַּע לְךָ וְלַאֲבֹתֶיךָ וּנְתָנָהּ לָךְ׃
12 וְהַעֲבַרְתָּ כָל־פֶּטֶר־רֶחֶם לַיהֹוָה וְכָל־פֶּטֶר
׀ שֶׁגֶר בְּהֵמָה אֲשֶׁר יִהְיֶה לְךָ הַזְּכָרִים
לַיהֹוָה׃ 13 וְכָל־פֶּטֶר חֲמֹר תִּפְדֶּה בְשֶׂה
וְאִם־לֹא תִפְדֶּה וַעֲרַפְתּוֹ וְכֹל בְּכוֹר אָדָם
בְּבָנֶיךָ תִּפְדֶּה׃ 14 וְהָיָה כִּי־יִשְׁאָלְךָ בִנְךָ
מָחָר לֵאמֹר מַה־זֹּאת וְאָמַרְתָּ אֵלָיו בְּחֹזֶק
יָד הוֹצִיאָנוּ יְהֹוָה מִמִּצְרַיִם מִבֵּית עֲבָדִים׃
15 וַיְהִי כִּי־הִקְשָׁה פַרְעֹה לְשַׁלְּחֵנוּ וַיַּהֲרֹג
יְהֹוָה כָּל־בְּכוֹר בְּאֶרֶץ מִצְרַיִם מִבְּכֹר אָדָם
וְעַד־בְּכוֹר בְּהֵמָה עַל־כֵּן אֲנִי זֹבֵחַ לַיהֹוָה
כָּל־פֶּטֶר רֶחֶם הַזְּכָרִים וְכָל־בְּכוֹר בָּנַי
אֶפְדֶּה׃
16 וְהָיָה לְאוֹת עַל־יָדְכָה וּלְטוֹטָפֹת בֵּין
עֵינֶיךָ כִּי בְּחֹזֶק יָד הוֹצִיאָנוּ יְהֹוָה
מִמִּצְרָיִם׃ ס

6:20–21; 7:1–3) this sort of language refers metaphorically to the way certain ritual practices memorialize the Exodus experience. In late antiquity, some Jewish authorities understood this language literally, as referring to the wearing of *t'fillin* (phylacteries) on the hand and head. (See also at v. 16 and Deuteronomy 6:8.)

*15. "redeem every male first-born among my children."* Although animals are to be sacrificed to God, sons are to be redeemed by monetary means (Numbers 18:16) since human sacrifice is not tolerated. | This verse, together with Numbers 3:13 and 18:16, provide the biblical background for the Jewish ceremony of *pidyon haben*: on the thirty-first day after his birth, the parents redeem their first-born son, usually with silver coins, from a *kohein* (priest). Following v. 2, above, this ceremony is performed only if the son is the first issue of his mother's womb. Thus, exempt from redemption is a first-born son delivered by caesarean section, or a first-born son to a mother who had previously given birth to a daughter, or who had miscarried.

*16. "symbol."* Heb. *totafot*; the term's meaning is uncertain, but the context indicates that it refers to an amulet (an object thought to provide spiritual protection) worn "between the eyes" (that is, on the forehead). While some have attempted to connect *t'fillin* with specifically female ornaments or amulets, there is ample evidence that in the ancient Near East and Egypt both women and men wore forehead ornaments both for protection and for decoration. *T'fillin* are to serve as another type of reminder of the might of God and the redemption from Egypt. —*Sharon R. Keller*

# *Another View*

Parashat Bo describes a number of rituals surrounding the Exodus that allow us to see a connection between blood, sacrifice, and family ties. Sacrificial blood in 12:1–13 is protective, separating the Egyptians who are about to die from the Israelites who soon will hurriedly flee the "house of bondage." As an expression of the life force, the blood is also symbolic of the fertility of the family that offers it as a sacrifice and then applies it to the doorposts and the lintel of their house.

In addition, the blood symbolizes the connection between past and living generations. The living and the deceased should not be seen as mutually exclusive, but instead can be considered as part of a chain of human existence connecting ancestors and their descendants. Thus for readers of the story, the passover sacrifice acts as a link to generations past, a way to recognize the plight of those who first left Egypt and to offer gratitude to God for their liberation. The passover sacrifice also connects the past to the future, as one generation teaches the next the lessons of the Exodus: "And when your children ask you, 'What do you mean by this rite?' you shall say, 'It is the passover sacrifice to יהוה, who passed over the houses of the Israelites. . . .'" (12:26–27).

Furthermore, the consumption of the communal Passover meal provides a map of the social structure of the family network. Eating the roasted lamb (or kid) with unleavened bread and bitter herbs determines the boundaries of the people who share in the event, indicating who is inside and outside the group. With all family groups eating their paschal lamb on the same evening (vv. 6–8), the act of eating becomes symbolic of continuity and unity. However, the separate groups consume their own sacrifices, "a lamb to a household" (12:3), with no foreigners allowed to eat of it (12:43–45). Thus, the rite also symbolizes discontinuity and differentiation. In these various ways, the Passover sacrificial ritual is about identity and how we solidify family ties through this ancient ritual.

*The blood symbolizes the connection between past and living generations.*

—*Naomi Steinberg*

# *Post-biblical Interpretations*

***"the first-born of the slave girl who is behind the millstones"*** (11:5). According to the midrash collection *P'sikta D'Rav Kahana* 7.9, Egyptian slave women were proud to work beside well-born Israelite women like Serah bat Asher, Jacob's granddaughter (Genesis 46:17). Yet, despite their lowly status and their solidarity with Israelite slaves, the Torah makes clear that these women were still Egyptians—and their first-born children were not spared. According to midrashic tradition, Serah's life spanned the entire period of Israel's slavery in Egypt (see Numbers 26:46).

***"This month shall mark for you the beginning of the months"*** (12:2). Based on this verse, traditional Judaism ordains the celebration of Rosh Chodesh, the new month. Since the Jewish calendar is partially based on the lunar cycle, this observance corresponds with each new moon, and it has special connotations for women. In ancient times, Rosh Chodesh did not have the elevated status of a full holiday, but it was celebrated in a festive, sacred manner. According to JT *Taanit* 1:6, women customarily did not work on the day of the new moon. Later rabbinic sources explain that the Rosh Chodesh holiday was given to women as a reward, since—according to midrashim on Exodus 32—they refused to participate in the sin of the Golden Calf (*Pirkei D'Rabbi Eliezer* 45). The custom of special time for women on Rosh Chodesh, which persisted through the Middle Ages, has been renewed today in Rosh Chodesh groups for women and girls.

***In the middle of the night* יהוה *struck down all the [male] first-born in the land of Egypt*** (12:29). Even though the Egyptians had already been tortured with nine plagues, they continued to force the Israelites to work as slaves. One of the well-known, back-breaking tasks of the slaves was making bricks (1:14; 5:7). This involved the treading of clay to mix it with water and straw in order to prepare it for placing into molds to form bricks. A midrash in *Pirkei D'Rabbi Eliezer* 48 recounts the story of a specific woman, Rachel the granddaughter of Shuthelah, who is not actually named in the Torah although her grandfather appears in a genealogical list (Numbers 26:36). At this late stage in the Egyptian bondage, Rachel was pregnant and was treading clay for bricks along with her husband. She spontaneously gave birth to her baby in the midst of her work, and the newborn mistakenly fell into the clay and was mixed into it. The new mother's desperate cry was so great that it reached heaven. There, the angel Michael heard her, went down to earth, and took the clump of clay that had now been made into a brick with the infant inside it and brought it up to God's Throne of Glory, where the brick served as God's footstool. This outrage served as a reminder for God to proceed with the punishment of the Egyptians—and it was to that very same night that the present biblical verse refers.

***That was for* יהוה *a night of vigil*** (12:42). A rabbinic opinion states that first-born Egyptian females as well as males were killed in the tenth plague. According to this view, Pharaoh's daughter—who had rescued Moses and raised him as her son (2:5–10)—was a first-born and thus should have perished in this plague.

*First-born Egyptian females as well as males were killed in the tenth plague.*

*P'sikta D'Rav Kahana* 7.7 explains that Moses prayed for his adoptive mother, whose name was thought to be Bithiah. His prayer is said to have extolled Bithiah in the language of Proverbs 31, the biblical tribute to the "woman of valor." According to a verse in this poetic passage, the woman of valor's lamp does not go out at night (Proverbs 31:18). The midrash understands this statement as a metaphorical reference to the survival of Pharaoh's daughter, whose soul was not extinguished on the fateful night of death. Evidence is adduced from the unusual spelling of the Hebrew word for "night" as written in Proverbs 31:18 (without the final letter *heh*), which matches the spelling of a form of the same word in Exodus 12:42. Insisting on the connection between these two biblical verses, the midrash teaches that Pharaoh's first-born daughter was saved during the tenth plague due to Moses' prayer on her behalf.

—*Anna Urowitz-Freudenstein*

# Contemporary Reflection

GOD'S HARDENING OF PHARAOH'S HEART in Exodus 10:1 presents a theological problem on two levels. First, if God is the agent of Pharaoh's behavior, what does that imply about Pharaoh's free will? Second, if God hardens Pharaoh's heart in order to demonstrate God's power, we must ask: At what price the Israelites' liberation? Indeed, the ultimate result of Pharaoh's stubbornness is the murder of every first-born Egyptian male. Even if we consider this to be retributive justice, payback for Pharaoh's earlier order to kill all newborn Hebrew males, we still must ponder: Does one heinous crime justify another? And how do we come to terms with killing innocent children?

Commentators, equally bothered by this thorny moral dilemma, have provided inspired interpretations. With regard to the question of free will, some interpreters note that during the first five plagues, Pharaoh hardens his *own* heart. Only afterward does God take over, starting with the sixth plague (9:12), suggesting that Pharaoh has foregone the chance to operate independently. Modern psychoanalyst Erich Fromm writes, "The more man's heart hardens, the less freedom he has to change; the more he is determined by previous action . . . there comes a point of no return, when man's heart has become so hardened . . . that he has lost the possibility of freedom" (*You Shall Be as Gods*, 1966, p. 101). This is an astute insight into human behavior, but it begs the question of the text's plain meaning, which is that God causes Pharaoh's stubbornness.

The hardening of Pharaoh's heart might also be viewed as a paradigm for what Fran Burgess calls the "transformative power of adversity." According to this view, Pharaoh's stubborn resistance is the condition necessary for Moses and the Israelites to emerge from their straits (the Hebrew name for Egypt, *mitzrayim,* is very close to the Hebrew for "straits," *metzarim*). Indeed, it often takes facing overwhelming odds to make radical change. As Tour de France winner Lance Armstrong said, "Before cancer, I just lived. Now I live strong." Pharaoh thus serves as a tool for the Israelites' psychological and moral development. However keen, this interpretation too satisfies only on the level of metaphor.

Perhaps the most satisfactory approach is to keep the theological problems ever-present. In *The Particulars of Rapture: Reflections on Exodus* (1995), Avivah Gottlieb Zornberg suggests that the liberation story of

> *Just as women defied Pharaoh, so we must challenge troubling aspects of our sacred texts.*

the Israelites, what she calls the "master narrative," gives rise to "counter-narratives" that throw the justification of God's triumphal power into question. Indeed, as Zornberg argues, the master narrative of God as loving and benevolent redeemer of the Israelites is challenged by the killing of the Egyptians' first-born, including "the first-born of the captive who was in the dungeon" (12:29). This prompts a counter-narrative from the perspective of the plague's victims that asks: What sin could the babies and the captives possibly have committed to deserve this punishment? The answer posits an evil God. This narrative appears again later, in the story of the Golden Calf, when Moses convinces God not to murder the Israelites for their transgression, arguing that otherwise, the Egyptian story will prevail: "Let not the Egyptians say, 'It was with evil intent that he delivered them'" (32:12). Although the Midrash attempts to silence and "neutralize" potentially heretical answers to such queries, Zornberg maintains that "the Torah, even God's quoted words, gives rise to interpretations that radically contradict its own master-narrative, and that cannot, moreover, be totally repudiated by its accredited expositors" (p. 143).

For Zornberg, an alternative for dealing with the dissonance between narrative and counter-narrative is "the model of endless questioning, in which the answer does not totally silence the questioner" (p. 143). In fact, implicit and explicit questions play an important role in this parashah. God mandates that the story of the Exodus be told in response to children's queries: "And when your children ask you . . . , you shall say . . ." (12:26–27). This is the basis for the Passover *seder*'s custom of the Four Questions. Further, two more verses from this parashah and one from Deuteronomy instruct us to answer our children's questions about the Exodus. The Rabbis understood all these verses as referring to four kinds of children, the Haggadah's Four Sons, each with varying aptitudes, each eliciting a different perspective on the narrative: the Wise Son (Deuteronomy 6:20–21), the Wicked Son (Exodus 12:26), the Simple Son (13:14), and the One Who Is Unable to Ask (13:8).

Through questions, we might call forth another counter-narrative: the experience of women during the exodus and its subsequent retelling. Noting that the traditional Haggadah assumes a conversation between a father and four sons, contemporary feminist Haggadot fill in for the absence of women's voices. The *Ma'yan Haggadah*, for example, includes the Four Daughters. The daughter "in search of a usable past" asks, "Why did Moses say at Sinai, 'Go not near a woman,' addressing only men, as if preparation for revelation was not meant for us, as well?" The daughter "who wants to erase her difference" wonders about the importance of women's issues. The daughter "who does not know that she has a place at the table" asks, "What is this?" And the daughter "who asks no questions" is told: "From the moment Yocheved, Miriam, and the midwives questioned Pharaoh's edict until today, every question we ask helps us leave Egypt a little farther behind" (Tamara Cohen, Sue Levi Elwell, and Ronnie Horn, eds., *The Journey Continues: Ma'yan Passover Haggadah*, 1997).

Just as the women defied Pharaoh, so we too as readers must confront and challenge troubling aspects of our sacred narratives. The persistent hardening of Pharaoh's heart results in the Israelites' night of redemption, but we must never forget that this same night was one of horror for the Egyptians. We must continue to ask the questions that preserve our awareness of the Other's story. Did the Israelites hear the *tzaakah* (cry) of the Egyptians (12:30)? Did it remind them of their own cry—the *tzaakah* in 3:7, which brought God's attention to their plight? Year after year, as we recall at our seder table the wonders God performed for us, we must remember the price the Other paid for our liberation.

—*Suzanne Singer*

# *Voices*

## *Passover Love Song*

Hara E. Person

*Exodus 12:1–20*

The seder is a love song written
in the language of silver polish
and dishpan hands
freshly grated lemon zest
blanched almonds
ground pecans
shelled pistachios
pitted olives
sliced meat
matzah meal
white tablecloths
to-do lists
trips to Boro Park and Sahadi's

This is how it's done.

ashkenazi haroset
vegetarian chopped liver
my mother's real chopped liver
Bonnie's matzah ball soup
Israeli salad
gefilte fish terrine
chestnut farfel stuffing
tzimmes
leek and shallot kugel
salmon in grape leaves with pine nuts
turkey and brisket
coconut macaroons
sephardic lemon pistachio cookies
pecan meringues
chocolate dipped apricots

Remember.

tables stretched the length of the house
tulips on the mantle
my grandmother's blue glass plates
Aunt Hannah and Uncle Joe's silver
Nana's candlesticks
the silver salt bowls from my mother
Frieda and Solly's cut-glass horseradish pot
the wedding present seder plate
grape juice stains on the tablecloth
thin paperback haggadot
our mismatched family of friends
silly half-versions of songs
and don't lick the wine from your finger after
the plagues

Don't be fooled by the easy domesticity of
these words.
This is more than a recipe for nostalgia.
This is an urgent coded message of
survival
adaptation
love.

Read between the words.

## *Boiled Beet*

Anna Swanson

*Exodus 12:3–13*

Each seder is a retelling.
We come together and taste our way
through the story: Matzo,
unleavened because fleeing women
can't wait for bread to rise;
Charoset, the mortar used
to bind stone together;
Bitter herbs, the taste of slavery.

She passes me the haggadah
and I read out loud about the shank bone,
the blood which marked the doors
of Jewish houses with a message

to the angel of death
saying, *spare this home.*

This year we use a crooked beet
instead, smear beet juice on doorposts
and white picket fences.

I want to run around the city
with a boiled beet, mark the skin
of women everywhere, screaming
*may this body*
*this body*
*this body*
*be spared.*

## *Miriam's Song*

Eleanor Wilner

*Exodus 12:29–30*

Death to the first born sons, always—
The first fruits to the gods of men.
She had not meant it so, standing in the reeds
back then, the current tugging at her skirt
like hands, she had only meant to save
her little brother, Moses,
red-faced with rage when he was given
to the river. The long curve of the Nile
would keep their line, the promised land
around the bend. Years later
when the gray angel, like the smoke trail
of a dying comet, passed by their houses
with blood smeared over doorways,
Miriam, her head hot in her hands, wept
as the city swelled
with the wail of Egypt's women.
Then she straightened up, slowly plaited
her hair and wound it tight around her head,
drew her long white cloak with its deep blue
threads
around her, went out to watch the river
where Osiris, in his golden funeral barge,
floated by forever...

as if in offering, she placed a basket on the river,
this time an empty one, without the precious
cargo
of tomorrow. She watched it drift a little
from the shore. She threw one small stone in it,
then another, and another, till its weight
was too much for the water and it slowly turned
and sank. She watched the Nile gape and
shudder,
then heal its own green skin. She went
to join the others, to leave one ruler
for another, one Egypt for the next.
Some nights you still can see her, by some river
where the willows hang, listening to the heavy
tread
of armies, those sons once hidden dark
in baskets, and in her mind she sees her sister,
the black-eyed Pharaoh's daughter, lift the baby
like a gift from the brown flood waters
and take him home to save him, such a pretty
boy and so disarming, as his dimpled hands
reach up, his mouth already open
for the breast.

## *O the Night of the Weeping Children*

Nelly Sachs (transl. Michael Hamburger)

*Exodus 12:29–30*

O the night of the weeping children!
O the night of the children branded for death!
Sleep may not enter here.
Terrible nursemaids
Have usurped the place of mothers,
Have tautened their tendons with the false death,
Sown it on to the walls and into the beams—
Everywhere it is hatched in the nests of horror.
Instead of mother's milk, panic suckles those
little ones.

Yesterday Mother still drew
Sleep toward them like a white moon,
There was the doll with cheeks derouged by
kisses
In one arm,
The stuffed pet, already
Brought to life by love,
In the other—
Now blows the wind of dying,
Blows the shifts over the hair
That no one will comb again.

## *This Night*

Hara E. Person

*Exodus 12:29–30*

Outside there is only the pulsating darkness,
the terrified wails of other mothers' pain.
Death winds through nearby villages and
distant towns.
And I, I stand safe inside the light-filled shelter,
my arm wrapped tight around the narrow
shoulders
of my precious first-born.
In colorless gear the soldiers defend our
boundaries,
bursts of fire red in the shadows.
The cycle continues still.
Our sons fighting their sons,
too many children lost on the way to freedom.
In the morning the siren sounds the all-clear
and we emerge to a newly drawn landscape,
safe for now but still far from redemption.

## *Meditation for Tefillin*

Elizabeth Sarah

*Exodus 13:9, 16*

I cannot
bind myself
to You
I can only
unbind myself
continually and
free
Your spirit
within me

So why
this tender-cruel
parody of
bondage
black
leather
straps
skin
gut and
sacred litany of
power and
submission
which binds us
Your slave-people
still?

# בשלח ✦ *B'shalach*

## EXODUS 13:17–17:16

### *Crossing the Sea and Crises in the Wilderness*

PARASHAT B'SHALACH ("when [Pharaoh] let [the people] go") recounts the crossing of the sea, the culmination of the story of the Israelite sojourn in Egypt. From the beginning of the book of Exodus, the goal of leaving Egypt is part of the narrative thread describing the oppressive measures that Pharaoh uses to keep the Israelites in Egypt. That goal is finally realized once the Israelites traverse the Sea of Reeds. This climactic event is related in two versions: a prose account in 14:1–31, followed by a poetic account (called in rabbinic literature *Shirat HaYam*, "Song at the Sea") in 15:1–22. The latter is more of a celebratory or victory hymn than a record of the Exodus event. Without the prose version, the sequence and details of the crossing would be unclear. However, without the poetic one—which may be a female composition—the soaring emotion of escape and the realization of God's role in deliverance would be lost.

Fleeing from Egypt does not end the Israelites' woes. They are far from the Promised Land, and they must cross the uninviting Sinai Peninsula. The crises they face in the wilderness—military threats and shortages of food and water—are the focus of 15:22–17:16. These predicaments foreshadow the challenges they must deal with as an agrarian people living in the highlands of the land of Israel.

Just as women and water began the story of the liberation from Egypt (Exodus 2), so too they bring it to its fulfillment. Miriam, the sister who first stood by the water (the Nile River) to watch over her baby brother, now, as a prophet, leads the women in interpreting what crossing the water (the Sea of Reeds) means. Thus, women and water frame the story of Israel's beginnings, from servitude to freedom.

*Women and water frame the story of Israel's beginnings.*

—*Carol Meyers*

## *Outline*

*I.* Departing from Egypt (13:17–22)

*II.* Crossing the Sea (14:1–31)

- *A.* Egyptian pursuit (vv. 1–14)
- *B.* Splitting of the sea (vv. 15–25)
- *C.* Rejoining of the waters (vv. 26–31)

*III.* Celebrating Deliverance (15:1–21)

- *A.* Song at the Sea (vv. 1–19)
- *B.* Song of Miriam (vv. 20–21)

*IV.* Journeying in the Wilderness (15:22–17:16)

- *A.* Water crisis (15:22–27)
- *B.* Food crisis (16:1–36)
- *C.* Another water crisis (17:1–7)
- *D.* Military crisis (17:8–16)

Now when Pharaoh let the people go, God did
not lead them by way of the land of the
Philistines, although it was nearer; for God said,
"The people may have a change of heart when they
see war, and return to Egypt." 18So God led the
people round about, by way of the wilderness at
the Sea of Reeds.

Now the Israelites went up armed out of the
land of Egypt. 19And Moses took with him the
bones of Joseph, who had exacted an oath from
the children of Israel, saying, "God will be sure to
take notice of you: then you shall carry up my
bones from here with you."

יג 17 וַיְהִ֗י בְּשַׁלַּ֣ח פַּרְעֹה֮ אֶת־הָעָם֒ וְלֹא־
נָחָ֣ם אֱלֹהִ֗ים דֶּ֚רֶךְ אֶ֣רֶץ פְּלִשְׁתִּ֔ים כִּ֥י קָר֖וֹב
ה֑וּא כִּ֣י ׀ אָמַ֣ר אֱלֹהִ֗ים פֶּֽן־יִנָּחֵ֥ם הָעָ֛ם
בִּרְאֹתָ֥ם מִלְחָמָ֖ה וְשָׁ֥בוּ מִצְרָֽיְמָה׃ 18 וַיַּסֵּ֨ב
אֱלֹהִ֧ים ׀ אֶת־הָעָ֛ם דֶּ֥רֶךְ הַמִּדְבָּ֖ר יַם־ס֑וּף
וַחֲמֻשִׁ֛ים עָל֥וּ בְנֵֽי־יִשְׂרָאֵ֖ל מֵאֶ֥רֶץ מִצְרָֽיִם׃
19 וַיִּקַּ֥ח מֹשֶׁ֛ה אֶת־עַצְמ֥וֹת יוֹסֵ֖ף עִמּ֑וֹ כִּי֩
הַשְׁבֵּ֨עַ הִשְׁבִּ֜יעַ אֶת־בְּנֵ֤י יִשְׂרָאֵל֙ לֵאמֹ֔ר
פָּקֹ֨ד יִפְקֹ֤ד אֱלֹהִים֙ אֶתְכֶ֔ם וְהַעֲלִיתֶ֧ם אֶת־
עַצְמֹתַ֛י מִזֶּ֖ה אִתְּכֶֽם׃

## *Departing from Egypt* (13:17–22)

This parashah continues the account of the journey away from Egypt and into the wilderness that began in 12:37–42. God's involvement is apparent from the outset: God chooses the route, and God's presence as manifest in pillars of cloud and fire leads the people as they travel. Moses' role as human leader—so prominent in negotiations with the pharaoh that were featured in the previous three Torah portions—now gives way to divine leadership.

*17. way of the land of the Philistines.* This phrase refers to the coastal route from Egypt to Israel. The route derives its name from the Philistines, who settled the southern coast of Canaan in the early 12th century B.C.E. As such, it is anachronistic as a reference to the earlier migration from Egypt that this story is recounting.

*war.* This is perhaps a reference to the militarized way stations on the heavily traveled coastal route.

*18. by way of the wilderness at the Sea of Reeds.* This designates a more circuitous and difficult route. "Sea of Reeds" (or "Reed Sea") is a literal translation of *yam suf* and almost certainly does not refer to the Red Sea. It is a descriptive term for a body of water with an abundance of reedy plants rather than the designation of a specific sea. Attempts to identify the sea have proved fruitless, for this is an impressionistic recollection of escape rather than an accurate accounting of geographic places.

*19. bones of Joseph.* The Israelites comply

▸ Food can be called Israel's national obsession.

ANOTHER VIEW ➤ *400*

▸ In rabbinic literature, Miriam and Moses often appear in parallel, with Miriam given an equal status to Moses.

POST-BIBLICAL INTERPRETATIONS ➤ *400*

▸ There are moments that define us. . . . Crossroads come disguised in many forms.

CONTEMPORARY REFLECTION ➤ *402*

▸ . . . now, in the darkness, / there is only motion / and my mother's hand.

VOICES ➤ *404*

20 וַיִּסְעוּ מִסֻּכֹּת וַיַּחֲנוּ בְאֵתָם בִּקְצֵה
הַמִּדְבָּר׃ 21 וַיהוָה הֹלֵךְ לִפְנֵיהֶם יוֹמָם
בְּעַמּוּד עָנָן לַנְחֹתָם הַדֶּרֶךְ וְלַיְלָה בְּעַמּוּד
אֵשׁ לְהָאִיר לָהֶם לָלֶכֶת יוֹמָם וָלָיְלָה׃
22 לֹא־יָמִישׁ עַמּוּד הֶעָנָן יוֹמָם וְעַמּוּד
הָאֵשׁ לָיְלָה לִפְנֵי הָעָם׃ פ
יד וַיְדַבֵּר יְהוָה אֶל־מֹשֶׁה לֵּאמֹר׃ 2 דַּבֵּר
אֶל־בְּנֵי יִשְׂרָאֵל וְיָשֻׁבוּ וְיַחֲנוּ לִפְנֵי פִּי
הַחִירֹת בֵּין מִגְדֹּל וּבֵין הַיָּם לִפְנֵי בַּעַל
צְפֹן נִכְחוֹ תַחֲנוּ עַל־הַיָּם׃ 3 וְאָמַר פַּרְעֹה
לִבְנֵי יִשְׂרָאֵל נְבֻכִים הֵם בָּאָרֶץ סָגַר עֲלֵיהֶם
הַמִּדְבָּר׃ 4 וְחִזַּקְתִּי אֶת־לֵב־פַּרְעֹה וְרָדַף
אַחֲרֵיהֶם וְאִכָּבְדָה בְּפַרְעֹה וּבְכָל־חֵילוֹ
וְיָדְעוּ מִצְרַיִם כִּי־אֲנִי יְהוָה
וַיַּעֲשׂוּ־כֵן׃

[20]They set out from Succoth, and encamped at Etham, at the edge of the wilderness. [21]יהוה went before them in a pillar of cloud by day, to guide them along the way, and in a pillar of fire by night, to give them light, that they might travel day and night. [22]The pillar of cloud by day and the pillar of fire by night did not depart from before the people.

14 יהוה said to Moses: [2]Tell the Israelites to turn back and encamp before Pi-hahiroth, between Migdol and the sea, before Baal-zephon; you shall encamp facing it, by the sea. [3]Pharaoh will say of the Israelites, "They are astray in the land; the wilderness has closed in on them." [4]Then I will stiffen Pharaoh's heart and he will pursue them, that I may gain glory through Pharaoh and all his host; and the Egyptians shall know that I am יהוה.

And they did so.

with Joseph's deathbed request that his bones be buried in Israel (Genesis 50:24–26), thus making the Sinai journey a funeral procession as well as a trek to freedom.

***20. set out... encamped.*** Formulaic language —departing from *place A* and arriving at *place B*— introduces the second of what will be twelve stages of the wilderness journey. The symbolic number twelve suggests a set number of places and thus a purposeful journey rather than a period of random wandering. Most of the places mentioned in the account of the wilderness journey have not been firmly identified—nor is it likely that they ever will be, for the names have been gathered from various sources, or even invented by the storyteller, to give a sense of reality to the dimly remembered recollections of the journey.

***21. pillar of cloud... pillar of fire.*** Similar to signals that caravans use, these pillars represent God's presence. This imagery will recur in the account of the Tabernacle (Exodus 33:9–10) and elsewhere in the Torah (see 16:10).

## *Crossing the Sea* (14:1–31)

The sea crossing is set forth in three prose sections, each introduced by "יהוה said to Moses" (vv. 1, 15, 26). The literary structure thus emphasizes God's control of what happens.

### EGYPTIAN PURSUIT (14:1–14)

Having reached Etham, the Israelites are told to backtrack so that the pharaoh will think they are lost, thus setting the stage for one last appearance of the motif of the hardening of Pharaoh's heart. The Egyptians will attempt to capture the fleeing and frightened Israelites, but they will fail because of God's spectacular intervention.

***4. gain glory.*** The Heb. root is *k-b-d*, language that provides a sense of irony, for the "hardening" of the pharaoh's heart sometimes uses the same root (see at 10:1). The action caused by the Egyptian ruler's fateful stubbornness thus portends an event that will magnify God.

***Egyptians shall know that I am* יהוה.** Acknowledging the existence, and sometimes the su-

[5]When the king of Egypt was told that the people had fled, Pharaoh and his courtiers had a change of heart about the people and said, "What is this we have done, releasing Israel from our service?" [6]He ordered his chariot and took his force with him; [7]he took six hundred of his picked chariots, and the rest of the chariots of Egypt, with officers in all of them. [8]יהוה stiffened the heart of Pharaoh king of Egypt, and he gave chase to the Israelites. As the Israelites were departing defiantly, [9]the Egyptians gave chase to them, and all the chariot horses of Pharaoh, his riders, and his warriors overtook them encamped by the sea, near Pi-hahiroth, before Baal-zephon.

[10]As Pharaoh drew near, the Israelites caught sight of the Egyptians advancing upon them. Greatly frightened, the Israelites cried out to יהוה. [11]And they said to Moses, "Was it for want of graves in Egypt that you brought us to die in the wilderness? What have you done to us, taking us out of Egypt? [12]Is this not the very thing we told you in Egypt, saying, 'Let us be, and we will serve the Egyptians, for it is better for us to serve the Egyptians than to die in the wilderness'?" [13]But Moses said to the people, "Have no fear! Stand by, and witness the deliverance which יהוה will work for you today; for the Egyptians whom you see today you will never see again. [14]יהוה will battle for you; you hold your peace!"

5 וַיֻּגַּד לְמֶלֶךְ מִצְרַיִם כִּי בָרַח הָעָם וַיֵּהָפֵךְ
לְבַב פַּרְעֹה וַעֲבָדָיו אֶל־הָעָם וַיֹּאמְרוּ
מַה־זֹּאת עָשִׂינוּ כִּי־שִׁלַּחְנוּ אֶת־יִשְׂרָאֵל
מֵעָבְדֵנוּ׃ 6 וַיֶּאְסֹר אֶת־רִכְבּוֹ וְאֶת־עַמּוֹ
לָקַח עִמּוֹ׃ 7 וַיִּקַּח שֵׁשׁ־מֵאוֹת רֶכֶב בָּחוּר
וְכֹל רֶכֶב מִצְרָיִם וְשָׁלִשִׁם עַל־כֻּלּוֹ׃ 8 וַיְחַזֵּק
יְהֹוָה אֶת־לֵב פַּרְעֹה מֶלֶךְ מִצְרַיִם וַיִּרְדֹּף
אַחֲרֵי בְּנֵי יִשְׂרָאֵל וּבְנֵי יִשְׂרָאֵל יֹצְאִים בְּיָד
רָמָה׃ 9 וַיִּרְדְּפוּ מִצְרַיִם אַחֲרֵיהֶם וַיַּשִּׂיגוּ
אוֹתָם חֹנִים עַל־הַיָּם כָּל־סוּס רֶכֶב פַּרְעֹה
וּפָרָשָׁיו וְחֵילוֹ עַל־פִּי הַחִירֹת לִפְנֵי בַּעַל
צְפֹן׃

10 וּפַרְעֹה הִקְרִיב וַיִּשְׂאוּ בְנֵי־יִשְׂרָאֵל אֶת־
עֵינֵיהֶם וְהִנֵּה מִצְרַיִם ׀ נֹסֵעַ אַחֲרֵיהֶם
וַיִּירְאוּ מְאֹד וַיִּצְעֲקוּ בְנֵי־יִשְׂרָאֵל אֶל־יְהֹוָה׃
11 וַיֹּאמְרוּ אֶל־מֹשֶׁה הֲמִבְּלִי אֵין־קְבָרִים
בְּמִצְרַיִם לְקַחְתָּנוּ לָמוּת בַּמִּדְבָּר מַה־זֹּאת
עָשִׂיתָ לָּנוּ לְהוֹצִיאָנוּ מִמִּצְרָיִם׃ 12 הֲלֹא־זֶה
הַדָּבָר אֲשֶׁר דִּבַּרְנוּ אֵלֶיךָ בְמִצְרַיִם לֵאמֹר
חֲדַל מִמֶּנּוּ וְנַעַבְדָה אֶת־מִצְרָיִם כִּי טוֹב לָנוּ
עֲבֹד אֶת־מִצְרַיִם מִמֻּתֵנוּ בַּמִּדְבָּר׃ 13 וַיֹּאמֶר
מֹשֶׁה אֶל־הָעָם אַל־תִּירָאוּ הִתְיַצְּבוּ וּרְאוּ
אֶת־יְשׁוּעַת יְהֹוָה אֲשֶׁר־יַעֲשֶׂה לָכֶם הַיּוֹם
כִּי אֲשֶׁר רְאִיתֶם אֶת־מִצְרַיִם הַיּוֹם לֹא
תֹסִפוּ לִרְאֹתָם עוֹד עַד־עוֹלָם׃ 14 יְהֹוָה
יִלָּחֵם לָכֶם וְאַתֶּם תַּחֲרִשׁוּן׃ פ

premacy, of Israel's God is a recurring theme of the Exodus account (see 5:2 and 10:2).

*7. picked chariots . . . the rest of the chariots.* Given the elite nature of a chariot corps, such detail highlights the enormous social and military distance between the pursuers and their prey.

*8. defiantly.* Literally "with hand [held] high," this is an allusion to having an uplifted weapon. Thus it is an image of defiance.

*11–12.* The terrified Israelites pose three rhetorical questions, imbued with biting sarcasm. Their outcry is less a lack of faith in God than a sign of human anguish in the face of the perceived threat of death in the wilderness.

***13. "Have no fear! Stand by, and witness the deliverance."*** The people's three questions elicit three reassuring imperatives. The language here is used in military contexts to calm troops before battle and to denote battle readiness (see Deuteronomy 20:3; Joshua 10:25).

***14. "יהוה will battle for you."*** Moses' resolute and reassuring response introduces the "divine

[15]Then יהוה said to Moses, "Why do you cry
out to Me? Tell the Israelites to go forward. [16]And
you lift up your rod and hold out your arm over the
sea and split it, so that the Israelites may march into
the sea on dry ground. [17]And I will stiffen the hearts
of the Egyptians so that they go in after them; and
I will gain glory through Pharaoh and all his warriors, his chariots and his riders. [18]Let the Egyptians
know that I am יהוה, when I gain glory through
Pharaoh, his chariots, and his riders."

[19]The angel of God, who had been going ahead
of the Israelite army, now moved and followed
behind them; and the pillar of cloud shifted from
in front of them and took up a place behind them,
[20]and it came between the army of the Egyptians
and the army of Israel. Thus there was the cloud
with the darkness, and it cast a spell upon the night,
so that the one could not come near the other all
through the night.

[21]Then Moses held out his arm over the sea and
יהוה drove back the sea with a strong east wind all
that night, and turned the sea into dry ground. The
waters were split, [22]and the Israelites went into the
sea on dry ground, the waters forming a wall for

15 וַיֹּאמֶר יְהוָה אֶל־מֹשֶׁה מַה־תִּצְעַק אֵלָי
דַּבֵּר אֶל־בְּנֵי־יִשְׂרָאֵל וְיִסָּעוּ׃ 16 וְאַתָּה הָרֵם
אֶת־מַטְּךָ וּנְטֵה אֶת־יָדְךָ עַל־הַיָּם וּבְקָעֵהוּ
וְיָבֹאוּ בְנֵי־יִשְׂרָאֵל בְּתוֹךְ הַיָּם בַּיַּבָּשָׁה׃
17 וַאֲנִי הִנְנִי מְחַזֵּק אֶת־לֵב מִצְרַיִם וְיָבֹאוּ
אַחֲרֵיהֶם וְאִכָּבְדָה בְּפַרְעֹה וּבְכָל־חֵילוֹ
בְּרִכְבּוֹ וּבְפָרָשָׁיו׃ 18 וְיָדְעוּ מִצְרַיִם כִּי־אֲנִי
יְהוָה בְּהִכָּבְדִי בְּפַרְעֹה בְּרִכְבּוֹ וּבְפָרָשָׁיו׃
19 וַיִּסַּע מַלְאַךְ הָאֱלֹהִים הַהֹלֵךְ לִפְנֵי מַחֲנֵה
יִשְׂרָאֵל וַיֵּלֶךְ מֵאַחֲרֵיהֶם וַיִּסַּע עַמּוּד הֶעָנָן
מִפְּנֵיהֶם וַיַּעֲמֹד מֵאַחֲרֵיהֶם׃ 20 וַיָּבֹא בֵּין ׀
מַחֲנֵה מִצְרַיִם וּבֵין מַחֲנֵה יִשְׂרָאֵל וַיְהִי
הֶעָנָן וְהַחֹשֶׁךְ וַיָּאֶר אֶת־הַלָּיְלָה וְלֹא־קָרַב
זֶה אֶל־זֶה כָּל־הַלָּיְלָה׃
21 וַיֵּט מֹשֶׁה אֶת־יָדוֹ עַל־הַיָּם וַיּוֹלֶךְ יְהוָה ׀
אֶת־הַיָּם בְּרוּחַ קָדִים עַזָּה כָּל־הַלַּיְלָה
וַיָּשֶׂם אֶת־הַיָּם לֶחָרָבָה וַיִּבָּקְעוּ הַמָּיִם׃
22 וַיָּבֹאוּ בְנֵי־יִשְׂרָאֵל בְּתוֹךְ הַיָּם בַּיַּבָּשָׁה
וְהַמַּיִם לָהֶם חוֹמָה מִימִינָם וּמִשְּׂמֹאלָם׃

warrior" theme. Drawn from Canaanite mythology, the image of God doing battle with Israel's foes is a powerful expression of divine might and one of the most masculine biblical metaphors applied to God (see at 15:3). Military language suffuses the depiction of God's involvement in delivering the people.

### SPLITTING OF THE SEA (14:15–25)

The sea event takes the narrative to a new level. The signs and wonders performed in Egypt are intense versions of natural devastation, and the horrific slaying of the first-born is a counterpoint to the earlier Egyptian infanticide and an etiology for various Israelite rituals. But the splitting of the sea lies in the realm of cosmic battle.

*16. "your rod."* Moses' staff is a symbol of authority and an instrument of magical acts (see 4:2–3, 17).

*19. angel of God.* The narrator has not previously mentioned this divine messenger (compare 3:2), who appears to have been leading the Israelites along with the pillar of cloud, which contains God's presence (13:21). Both shift to the rear, forming a protective shield between the people and the advancing Egyptians (v. 20).

*21. his arm.* The narrative now refers to Moses' arm only and not his rod (compare v. 16).

*east wind.* Winds from the east, known today by the Arabic term *chamsin*, are notorious in the Levant for their suffocatingly hot gusts.

them on their right and on their left. [23]The Egyptians came in pursuit after them into the sea, all of Pharaoh's horses, chariots, and riders. [24]At the morning watch, יהוה looked down upon the Egyptian army from a pillar of fire and cloud, and threw the Egyptian army into panic. [25][God] locked the wheels of their chariots so that they moved forward with difficulty. And the Egyptians said, "Let us flee from the Israelites, for יהוה is fighting for them against Egypt."

[26]Then יהוה said to Moses, "Hold out your arm over the sea, that the waters may come back upon the Egyptians and upon their chariots and upon their riders." [27]Moses held out his arm over the sea, and at daybreak the sea returned to its normal state, and the Egyptians fled at its approach. But יהוה hurled the Egyptians into the sea. [28]The waters turned back and covered the chariots and the riders—Pharaoh's entire army that followed them into the sea; not one of them remained. [29]But the Israelites had marched through the sea on dry ground, the waters forming a wall for them on their right and on their left.

[30]Thus יהוה delivered Israel that day from the Egyptians. Israel saw the Egyptians dead on the shore of the sea. [31]And when Israel saw the wondrous power which יהוה had wielded against the Egyptians, the people feared יהוה; they had faith in יהוה and in God's servant Moses.

23 וַיִּרְדְּפוּ מִצְרַיִם וַיָּבֹאוּ אַחֲרֵיהֶם כֹּל סוּס
פַּרְעֹה רִכְבּוֹ וּפָרָשָׁיו אֶל־תּוֹךְ הַיָּם׃ 24 וַיְהִי
בְּאַשְׁמֹרֶת הַבֹּקֶר וַיַּשְׁקֵף יְהוָה אֶל־מַחֲנֵה
מִצְרַיִם בְּעַמּוּד אֵשׁ וְעָנָן וַיָּהָם אֵת מַחֲנֵה
מִצְרָיִם׃ 25 וַיָּסַר אֵת אֹפַן מַרְכְּבֹתָיו
וַיְנַהֲגֵהוּ בִּכְבֵדֻת וַיֹּאמֶר מִצְרַיִם אָנוּסָה
מִפְּנֵי יִשְׂרָאֵל כִּי יְהוָה נִלְחָם לָהֶם
בְּמִצְרָיִם׃ פ

26 וַיֹּאמֶר יְהוָה אֶל־מֹשֶׁה נְטֵה אֶת־יָדְךָ
עַל־הַיָּם וְיָשֻׁבוּ הַמַּיִם עַל־מִצְרַיִם עַל־רִכְבּוֹ
וְעַל־פָּרָשָׁיו׃ 27 וַיֵּט מֹשֶׁה אֶת־יָדוֹ עַל־הַיָּם
וַיָּשָׁב הַיָּם לִפְנוֹת בֹּקֶר לְאֵיתָנוֹ וּמִצְרַיִם
נָסִים לִקְרָאתוֹ וַיְנַעֵר יְהוָה אֶת־מִצְרַיִם
בְּתוֹךְ הַיָּם׃ 28 וַיָּשֻׁבוּ הַמַּיִם וַיְכַסּוּ אֶת־
הָרֶכֶב וְאֶת־הַפָּרָשִׁים לְכֹל חֵיל פַּרְעֹה
הַבָּאִים אַחֲרֵיהֶם בַּיָּם לֹא־נִשְׁאַר בָּהֶם
עַד־אֶחָד׃ 29 וּבְנֵי יִשְׂרָאֵל הָלְכוּ בַיַּבָּשָׁה
בְּתוֹךְ הַיָּם וְהַמַּיִם לָהֶם חֹמָה מִימִינָם
וּמִשְּׂמֹאלָם׃

30 וַיּוֹשַׁע יְהוָה בַּיּוֹם הַהוּא אֶת־יִשְׂרָאֵל
מִיַּד מִצְרָיִם וַיַּרְא יִשְׂרָאֵל אֶת־מִצְרַיִם מֵת
עַל־שְׂפַת הַיָּם׃ 31 וַיַּרְא יִשְׂרָאֵל אֶת־הַיָּד
הַגְּדֹלָה אֲשֶׁר עָשָׂה יְהוָה בְּמִצְרַיִם וַיִּירְאוּ
הָעָם אֶת־יְהוָה וַיַּאֲמִינוּ בַּיהוָה וּבְמֹשֶׁה
עַבְדּוֹ׃ פ

REJOINING OF THE WATERS (14:26–31)

The restoration of the divided waters brings deliverance for the Israelites but death for the Egyptian army.

***28.*** ***not one of them remained.*** Taken literally, the complete annihilation of the Egyptian army seems excessive and tragic. However, the story is more likely a literary way to emphasize divine might and God's concern for the oppressed. Realizing that it is not a historical record of the complete slaughter of many thousands of Egyptians partially ameliorates our modern revulsion at so many deaths. Yet we still must confront the reality of a tradition that recounts and even celebrates this extensive loss of human lives. (See the introduction to 11:1–10).

***31.*** ***wondrous power.*** Literally, "great hand (or: arm)." This translation masks the use of corporeal language for conveying divine might. God's arm, not Moses', becomes the instrument of destruction.

***had faith.*** The Hebrew word denotes trust rather than belief.

(*continued on p. 387*)

טו אָז יָשִׁיר־מֹשֶׁה וּבְנֵי יִשְׂרָאֵל אֶת־הַשִּׁירָה הַזֹּאת לַיהֹוָה וַיֹּאמְרוּ
לֵאמֹר אָשִׁירָה לַיהֹוָה כִּי־גָאֹה גָּאָה סוּס
וְרֹכְבוֹ רָמָה בַיָּם׃ 2 עָזִּי וְזִמְרָת יָהּ וַיְהִי־לִי
לִישׁוּעָה זֶה אֵלִי וְאַנְוֵהוּ אֱלֹהֵי
אָבִי וַאֲרֹמְמֶנְהוּ׃ 3 יְהֹוָה אִישׁ מִלְחָמָה יְהֹוָה
שְׁמוֹ׃ 4 מַרְכְּבֹת פַּרְעֹה וְחֵילוֹ יָרָה בַיָּם וּמִבְחַר

troops after battle (see at 15:20). Thus, the title "Song of Miriam" that is often used by modern scholars and interpreters for v. 21 might in fact be appropriate for this passage as well.

*1. Moses...sang this song.* The prose introduction mentions Moses, the chief human protagonist of the Exodus narrative, as the performer of the Song, along with the people. Hence it has traditionally been assumed that Moses is the author of the Song. Why would a woman's composition (see previous comment) be attributed to a man? Perhaps the centrality of Moses to the Exodus story meant that authorship of this hymnic masterpiece accrued to him.

*I will sing to* **יהוה**. Directed to God alone, human agency in the victory over the enemy disappears; neither Moses' rod nor outstretched arms, both prominent in the prose account (14:16, 21, 26–27), appear in the poem.

*He.* On the palpable masculinity of the poetic figure employed in vv. 1–4, see at v. 3, below.

*2.* **יהוה***... deliverance.* The first part of this verse is also found in Isaiah 12:2 and Psalm 118:14, suggesting a liturgical use of this resounding affirmation of God's power to save those in need.

*enshrine.* This term may allude to the building of an abode (shrine) for God, a project to which much of the second half of Exodus is devoted. However, because the poetry places it in parallel with "exalt," the Hebrew term might better be translated "glorify."

*ancestors.* Heb. *av*, which is sometimes translated "father." Yet here it does not refer to the poet's biological male parent; rather, it alludes to the ancestors of Genesis as a collective (see also Exodus 3:13, 15, 16; 4:5; 13:5, 11). The inclusive term "ancestor" best represents the poet's claim that the deity celebrated for deliverance at the sea is the same as the One who appeared to earlier generations.

*3. the Warrior.* As one of the most strikingly male metaphors applied to God in the Bible, this

(*continued on p. 389*)

15 Then Moses and the Israelites sang this song to יהוה.
They said:

I will sing to יהוה, for He has triumphed gloriously;
Horse and driver He has hurled into the sea.
2יהוה is my strength and might;
He is become my deliverance.
This is my God and I will enshrine Him;
The God of my ancestors, and I will exalt Him.
3יהוה, the Warrior—
יהוה is His name!
4Pharaoh's chariots and his army
He has cast into the sea;

## *Celebrating Deliverance* (15:1–21)

Most scholars understand the poetic celebration of Israel's miraculous rescue from the Egyptians to be a very ancient poem, dating to the late 12th or early 11th century B.C.E.—much older than the somewhat different prose account that precedes it. In form and content, the poetry draws from the mythological epics of ancient Canaan, in which the heroic deity Baal conquers the primordial forces of chaos, represented by surging waters, so that order can be established. The military imagery of that cosmic battle is echoed and historicized in the Song at the Sea (*Shirat HaYam*), in which the natural elements—water and wind—become God's weapons against human enemies. The miracle of deliverance is captured in exuberant language, making this passage the thematic centerpiece of Exodus.

Thus far the narrative movement of the book has taken us toward God's holy mountain, first mentioned in 3:1 and now again at the end of this poem (see also 3:12 and 4:27); most of the rest of Exodus focuses on God's revelation at this mountain. On its location, see at 18:5.

The poetic account of victory at the sea appears in two segments, a longer version (vv. 1–18, with a prose frame in vv. 1 and 19) followed by a much briefer version (v. 21, with a prose introduction in v. 20). On biblical poetry, see at Deuteronomy 32:1–43.

### SONG AT THE SEA (15:1–19)

Many modern scholars conclude that the Song was created and performed by women. Beginning in the mid-20th century, a considerable body of literary, historical, sociological, and musicological evidence has been amassed to suggest that the Song should be attributed to Miriam. For example, one ancient manuscript tradition calls it the Song of Miriam. Also, songs of military triumph belong to a victory song genre typically composed and performed by women—not men—to greet victorious

שָׁלִשָׁיו טֻבְּעוּ בְיַם־סוּף׃ 5 תְּהֹמֹת יְכַסְיֻמוּ יָרְדוּ בִמְצוֹלֹת כְּמוֹ־
אָבֶן׃ 6 יְמִינְךָ יְהֹוָה נֶאְדָּרִי בַּכֹּחַ יְמִינְךָ
יְהֹוָה תִּרְעַץ אוֹיֵב׃ 7 וּבְרֹב גְּאוֹנְךָ תַּהֲרֹס
קָמֶיךָ תְּשַׁלַּח חֲרֹנְךָ יֹאכְלֵמוֹ כַּקַּשׁ׃ 8 וּבְרוּחַ
אַפֶּיךָ נֶעֶרְמוּ מַיִם נִצְּבוּ כְמוֹ־נֵד
נֹזְלִים קָפְאוּ תְהֹמֹת בְּלֶב־יָם׃ 9 אָמַר
אוֹיֵב אֶרְדֹּף אַשִּׂיג אֲחַלֵּק שָׁלָל תִּמְלָאֵמוֹ
נַפְשִׁי אָרִיק חַרְבִּי תּוֹרִישֵׁמוֹ יָדִי׃ 10 נָשַׁפְתָּ
בְרוּחֲךָ כִּסָּמוֹ יָם צָלֲלוּ כַּעוֹפֶרֶת בְּמַיִם
אַדִּירִים׃ 11 מִי־כָמֹכָה בָּאֵלִם יְהֹוָה מִי

battle is often the booty gathered by the victors. This phrase probably implies the taking of humans as well as goods, since conquering soldiers took nubile women as spoil (see Judges 5:30). Young female captives were especially prized for their reproductive and labor potential, for the mortality rates for women due to death in childbirth meant a shortage of wives. (See at Deuteronomy 21:10–14.)

*11. Who is like You,* יהוה*, . . . ?* The proclamation of the incomparability of God is expressed in a resounding rhetorical question that has become part of daily Jewish liturgy and is known as the *Mi Chamochah*. The uniqueness of God flows from the divine might exemplified by the deliverance at the sea.

***among the celestials.*** The very declaration of uniqueness is witness to a polytheistic world: God is unique among the "celestials," a somewhat misleading translation of a word that means "gods." Because true monotheism did not emerge in ancient Israel until the 6th century B.C.E., this verse may well reflect an earlier period in which the existence of other divine beings was assumed. The reference to other gods also may denote the lesser heavenly beings, or "hosts," that were part of ancient Israel's (*continued on p. 391*)

And the pick of his officers
Are drowned in the Sea of Reeds.
5The deeps covered them;
They went down into the depths like a stone.
6Your right hand, יהוה, glorious in power,
Your right hand, יהוה, shatters the foe!
7In Your great triumph You break Your opponents;
You send forth Your fury, it consumes them like straw.
8At the blast of Your nostrils the waters piled up,
The floods stood straight like a wall;
The deeps froze in the heart of the sea.
9The foe said,
"I will pursue, I will overtake,
I will divide the spoil;
My desire shall have its fill of them.
I will bare my sword—
My hand shall subdue them."
10You made Your wind blow, the sea covered them;
They sank like lead in the majestic waters.

11Who is like You, יהוה, among the celestials;

term signifies divine power and asserts that human military victories must be attributed to God. It contributes to our contemporary notion that the biblical deity is male. However, although warriors were understood to be male, this imagery does not mean that the Torah's composer(s) believed God to be a male being. Note that female imagery for God also occasionally appears in the Bible, including in Exodus (see at 16:4, 19:4; Numbers 11:12; Deuteronomy 32:13, 18). In Isaiah 42:13–14, the image of God as a warrior is juxtaposed with the image of God as a woman in labor. The prophet uses both metaphors to convince the people of God's power.

*5. The deeps.* Heb. *t'homot,* the plural of *t'hom,* the deep waters of Genesis 1:2. This mention echoes the name of the Babylonian goddess Tiamat and represents primeval water and chaos.

*6. right hand... shatters.* This image depicts God's military might, for the right hand is the one used for holding a weapon in Near Eastern mythology.

*8. blast of Your nostrils.* Although God's flared nose usually means hot anger, here the anthropomorphic language for God depicts the ferocious winds that will reconfigure the waters.

*9. "I will divide the spoil."* An incentive for

כָּמֹכָה נֶאְדָּר בַּקֹּדֶשׁ נוֹרָא תְהִלֹּת עֹשֵׂה

פֶלֶא׃ 12 נָטִיתָ יְמִינְךָ תִּבְלָעֵמוֹ אָרֶץ׃ 13 נָחִיתָ

בְחַסְדְּךָ עַם־זוּ גָּאָלְתָּ נֵהַלְתָּ בְעָזְּךָ אֶל־נְוֵה

קָדְשֶׁךָ׃ 14 שָׁמְעוּ עַמִּים יִרְגָּזוּן חִיל

אָחַז יֹשְׁבֵי פְּלָשֶׁת׃ 15 אָז נִבְהֲלוּ אַלּוּפֵי

אֱדוֹם אֵילֵי מוֹאָב יֹאחֲזֵמוֹ רָעַד נָמֹגוּ

כֹּל יֹשְׁבֵי כְנָעַן׃ 16 תִּפֹּל עֲלֵיהֶם אֵימָתָה

וָפַחַד בִּגְדֹל זְרוֹעֲךָ יִדְּמוּ כָּאָבֶן עַד־

יַעֲבֹר עַמְּךָ יְהוָה עַד־יַעֲבֹר עַם־זוּ

קָנִיתָ׃ 17 תְּבִאֵמוֹ וְתִטָּעֵמוֹ בְּהַר נַחֲלָתְךָ מָכוֹן

לְשִׁבְתְּךָ פָּעַלְתָּ יְהוָה מִקְּדָשׁ אֲדֹנָי כּוֹנְנוּ

יָדֶיךָ׃ 18 יְהוָה ׀ יִמְלֹךְ לְעֹלָם וָעֶד׃ 19 כִּי

בָא סוּס פַּרְעֹה בְּרִכְבּוֹ וּבְפָרָשָׁיו בַּיָּם וַיָּשֶׁב יְהוָה עֲלֵהֶם

אֶת־מֵי הַיָּם וּבְנֵי יִשְׂרָאֵל הָלְכוּ בַיַּבָּשָׁה בְּתוֹךְ הַיָּם׃ פ

***16. ransomed.*** A better translation would be "created." The root *k-n-h* can mean "to acquire" (hence "ransomed"; compare "redeemed" in v. 13) or "to create." It was used when Eve, the archetypal mother, gave birth to her first child (Genesis 4:1), thus linking childbirth with divine creativity.

***17. Your own mountain . . . The sanctuary . . . which Your hands established.*** This verse reflects mythic language for God's sacred mountain and indicates that God has a hands-on role in the construction of this sanctuary. Like v. 13, the passage refers to God's imagined dwelling in the heavens.

***18. reign.*** The exultant closing line of the poem applies another masculine metaphor to God: kingship, an image commonly employed for deities in ancient Near Eastern literature (see at Deuteronomy 33:5).

(*continued on p. 392*)

Who is like You, majestic in holiness,
Awesome in splendor, working wonders!
12You put out Your right hand,
The earth swallowed them.
13In Your love You lead the people You redeemed;
In Your strength You guide them to Your holy abode.
14The peoples hear, they tremble;
Agony grips the dwellers in Philistia.
15Now are the clans of Edom dismayed;
The tribes of Moab—trembling grips them;
All the dwellers in Canaan are aghast.
16Terror and dread descend upon them;
Through the might of Your arm they are still as stone—
Till Your people cross over, יהוה,
Till Your people cross whom You have ransomed.

17You will bring them and plant them in Your own mountain,
The place You made to dwell in, יהוה,
The sanctuary, O Lord, which Your hands established.
18יהוה will reign for ever and ever!

19For the horses of Pharaoh, with his chariots and riders, went
into the sea; and יהוה turned back on them the waters of the
sea; but the Israelites marched on dry ground in the midst of
the sea.

understanding of divinity (see at Deuteronomy 6:4; Isaiah 3:1; Jeremiah 5:14; Zechariah 1:3).

*13. love.* Heb. *chesed*, a relational term. When applied to God, it indicates God's utter commitment and kindness to Israel. (See at Deuteronomy 7:12.)

***holy abode.*** Although some understand this to be a reference to the Jerusalem temple and thus consider the Song a composition of the monarchic period (beginning in the 10th century), the mythic nature of the hymn makes it more likely that "holy abode" refers to God's heavenly habitation. The Israelites, like their Canaanite neighbors, imagined a divine abode in heaven that became the model for God's earthly dwellings, the Tabernacle and the Temple (see at v. 17 and 25:9).

*14–15. dwellers in Philistia... Edom... Moab ... Canaan.* These four groups of people represent the Israelites' early enemies. The Song serves as a warning to them, anticipating or reflecting Israel's early struggles in the Promised Land.

[20]Then Miriam the prophet, Aaron's sister, picked up a hand-drum, and all the women went out after her in dance with hand-drums. [21]And Miriam chanted for them:

Sing to יהוה, for He has triumphed gloriously;
Horse and driver He has hurled into the sea.

20 וַתִּקַּח מִרְיָם הַנְּבִיאָה אֲחוֹת אַהֲרֹן אֶת־
הַתֹּף בְּיָדָהּ וַתֵּצֶאןָ כׇל־הַנָּשִׁים אַחֲרֶיהָ
בְּתֻפִּים וּבִמְחֹלֹת׃ 21 וַתַּעַן לָהֶם מִרְיָם
שִׁירוּ לַיהֹוָה כִּי־גָאֹה גָּאָה
סוּס וְרֹכְבוֹ רָמָה בַיָּם׃ ס

SONG OF MIRIAM (15:20–21)

Preceded by a prose introduction (v. 20), the single stanza of v. 21 is known in contemporary parlance as the Song of Miriam. This poetic verse is likely the title of the full poem, suggesting that the victory song in vv. 1–19 may have been composed by a woman (see at v. 1).

*20. Miriam the prophet.* Unnamed in Moses' birth narrative (2:4, 7–9), the woman mentioned in more biblical books (five) than any other female figure finally gets a name. She also gets a title, one that never appears for Moses in the book of Exodus. Miriam is the first of several biblical women—including Deborah (Judges 4:4), Huldah (II Kings 22:14), and Noadiah (Nehemiah 6:14)—to bear the title of prophet. The authority of prophets as conveyors of God's will to the people was gender inclusive both in the biblical world and in other parts of the ancient Near East. The 8th-century-B.C.E. prophet Micah acknowledges Miriam's leading role in the Exodus when he proclaims in God's name that to deliver Israel, "I sent you Moses, Aaron, and Miriam" (Micah 6:4). In the present verse, Miriam appears also as a singer and a leader of other singing women, a role familiar from other biblical texts and ancient cultures.

*hand-drum.* This translation of *tof* is more appropriate than either the anachronistic "tambourine" or the vague "timbrel" that appears in many English translations; tambourines are not attested until the Roman period, more than a thousand years later. The hand-drum, or frame-drum, is the only percussion instrument mentioned in the Bible, in contrast to other classes of instruments (such as string and wind instruments) for which there are many examples. Archeological evidence—such as terracotta statuettes of women (never men) playing the frame-drum—indicates that this was largely a woman's instrument. Thus, the mention of instrumental ensembles, including the frame-drum in other biblical texts (such as Psalm 150), suggests the presence of female musicians. Because of the rhythmic nature of ancient Hebrew music, drum playing—by women—would have been an essential part of most musical performances.

*all the women.* It was apparently customary in ancient Israel for women to welcome victorious armies with victory songs (see Judges 11:34; I Samuel 18:6–7). Accomplished female musicians would have earned the esteem of their community. Also, groups of female performers likely would have met together to practice their instruments and compose songs for specific occasions, which would have provided occasions for female bonding and for women to exert organizational skills and mentor younger performers.

*dance.* Along with singing and drum playing, dance was an integral part of this performance genre. It is likely that most musical performances in the biblical world involved movement as well as vocal and instrumental expression (see Psalms 149:3; 150:4).

[22]Then Moses caused Israel to set out from the Sea of Reeds. They went on into the wilderness of Shur; they traveled three days in the wilderness and found no water. [23]They came to Marah, but they could not drink the water of Marah because it was bitter; that is why it was named Marah. [24]And the people grumbled against Moses, saying, "What shall we drink?" [25]So he cried out to יהוה, and יהוה showed him a piece of wood; he threw it into the water and the water became sweet.

There [God] made for them a fixed rule; there they were put to the test. [26][God] said, "If you will heed your God יהוה diligently, doing what is upright in God's sight, giving ear to God's commandments and keeping all God's laws, then I will not bring upon you any of the diseases that I brought upon the Egyptians, for I יהוה am your healer."

22 וַיַּסַּע מֹשֶׁה אֶת־יִשְׂרָאֵל מִיַּם־סוּף
וַיֵּצְאוּ אֶל־מִדְבַּר־שׁוּר וַיֵּלְכוּ שְׁלֹשֶׁת־יָמִים
בַּמִּדְבָּר וְלֹא־מָצְאוּ מָיִם׃ 23 וַיָּבֹאוּ מָרָתָה
וְלֹא יָכְלוּ לִשְׁתֹּת מַיִם מִמָּרָה כִּי מָרִים הֵם
עַל־כֵּן קָרָא־שְׁמָהּ מָרָה׃ 24 וַיִּלֹּנוּ הָעָם עַל־
מֹשֶׁה לֵּאמֹר מַה־נִּשְׁתֶּה׃ 25 וַיִּצְעַק אֶל־
יְהוָֹה וַיּוֹרֵהוּ יְהוָֹה עֵץ וַיַּשְׁלֵךְ אֶל־הַמַּיִם
וַיִּמְתְּקוּ הַמָּיִם

שָׁם שָׂם לוֹ חֹק וּמִשְׁפָּט וְשָׁם נִסָּהוּ׃
26 וַיֹּאמֶר אִם־שָׁמוֹעַ תִּשְׁמַע לְקוֹל ׀ יְהוָֹה
אֱלֹהֶיךָ וְהַיָּשָׁר בְּעֵינָיו תַּעֲשֶׂה וְהַאֲזַנְתָּ
לְמִצְוֺתָיו וְשָׁמַרְתָּ כָּל־חֻקָּיו כָּל־הַמַּחֲלָה
אֲשֶׁר־שַׂמְתִּי בְמִצְרַיִם לֹא־אָשִׂים עָלֶיךָ כִּי
אֲנִי יְהוָֹה רֹפְאֶךָ׃ ס

## *Journeying in the Wilderness*

(15:22–17:16)

No sooner do the Israelites safely cross the sea than they are confronted with two universal problems of community survival. The first concerns sustenance: how will they secure enough to eat and drink? The second concerns safety: how will they deal with military threats? The provision of food and water and the protection from enemies signal God's beneficent presence. The deliverance from Egypt was depicted largely in masculine imagery—with God portrayed, for example, as a warrior defeating Israel's enemies. Now we come to accounts of divine resolution of food and water problems; arguably these episodes portray God with female imagery, insofar as women in ancient Israel were the ones who frequently drew water (see Genesis 24:11 and Exodus 2:16) and nearly always provided food.

### WATER CRISIS (15:22–27)

The trust in God and Moses established by the sea episode (14:31) gives way to bitter complaints in the face of life-threatening thirst.

***23. Marah.*** Like other places named in this parashah, this is an unknown locale and probably not a real place. Instead, its name, meaning "bitterness," indicates what happens there. In addition, the name connects the bitterness of wandering with the bitterness of work in Egypt (1:14), which the bitter herbs of the Passover ritual commemorate (12:8).

***25. piece of wood . . . the water became sweet.*** What might nowadays be considered magic and thus superstition was believed to be efficacious in the biblical world. Judging from Palestinian folklore, throwing wood into water may be akin to a modern European homeopathic procedure: a piece of wood with bitter-tasting bark removes the bitterness of impotable water.

***test.*** The theme of testing appears in all the food and water crises in this parashah.

***26. I יהוה am your healer.*** God as healer may evoke images of women as well as men as practitioners of folk medicine. Because women in ancient Israel prepared food and kept herb gardens, they possessed knowledge about the specific properties of various plant substances used in folk medicine.

27 And they came to Elim, where there were
twelve springs of water and seventy palm trees;
and they encamped there beside the water.
16 Setting out from Elim, the whole Israelite
community came to the wilderness of Sin, which is
between Elim and Sinai, on the fifteenth day of the
second month after their departure from the land
of Egypt. 2 In the wilderness, the whole Israelite
community grumbled against Moses and Aaron.
3 The Israelites said to them, "If only we had died
by the hand of יהוה in the land of Egypt, when we
sat by the fleshpots, when we ate our fill of bread!
For you have brought us out into this wilderness to
starve this whole congregation to death."
4 And יהוה said to Moses, "I will rain down
bread for you from the sky, and the people shall
go out and gather each day that day's portion—that
I may thus test them, to see whether they will follow My instructions or not. 5 But on the sixth day,
when they apportion what they have brought in, it
shall prove to be double the amount they gather
each day." 6 So Moses and Aaron said to all the Is-

27 וַיָּבֹאוּ אֵילִמָה וְשָׁם שְׁתֵּים עֶשְׂרֵה עֵינֹת
מַיִם וְשִׁבְעִים תְּמָרִים וַיַּחֲנוּ־שָׁם עַל־
הַמָּיִם׃
טז וַיִּסְעוּ מֵאֵילִם וַיָּבֹאוּ כָּל־עֲדַת בְּנֵי־
יִשְׂרָאֵל אֶל־מִדְבַּר־סִין אֲשֶׁר בֵּין־אֵילִם וּבֵין
סִינָי בַּחֲמִשָּׁה עָשָׂר יוֹם לַחֹדֶשׁ הַשֵּׁנִי
לְצֵאתָם מֵאֶרֶץ מִצְרָיִם׃ 2 וילינו וַיִּלּוֹנוּ
כָּל־עֲדַת בְּנֵי־יִשְׂרָאֵל עַל־מֹשֶׁה וְעַל־אַהֲרֹן
בַּמִּדְבָּר׃ 3 וַיֹּאמְרוּ אֲלֵהֶם בְּנֵי יִשְׂרָאֵל
מִי־יִתֵּן מוּתֵנוּ בְיַד־יְהוָה בְּאֶרֶץ מִצְרַיִם
בְּשִׁבְתֵּנוּ עַל־סִיר הַבָּשָׂר בְּאָכְלֵנוּ לֶחֶם
לָשֹׂבַע כִּי־הוֹצֵאתֶם אֹתָנוּ אֶל־הַמִּדְבָּר הַזֶּה
לְהָמִית אֶת־כָּל־הַקָּהָל הַזֶּה בָּרָעָב׃ ס
4 וַיֹּאמֶר יְהוָה אֶל־מֹשֶׁה הִנְנִי מַמְטִיר לָכֶם
לֶחֶם מִן־הַשָּׁמָיִם וְיָצָא הָעָם וְלָקְטוּ דְּבַר־
יוֹם בְּיוֹמוֹ לְמַעַן אֲנַסֶּנּוּ הֲיֵלֵךְ בְּתוֹרָתִי אִם־
לֹא׃ 5 וְהָיָה בַּיּוֹם הַשִּׁשִּׁי וְהֵכִינוּ אֵת אֲשֶׁר־
יָבִיאוּ וְהָיָה מִשְׁנֶה עַל אֲשֶׁר־יִלְקְטוּ יוֹם ׀
יוֹם׃ 6 וַיֹּאמֶר מֹשֶׁה וְאַהֲרֹן אֶל־כָּל־בְּנֵי

## FOOD CRISIS (16:1–36)

The next stage of the trek across Sinai is marked by food shortages, which are resolved by the provision of manna and quail in this somewhat repetitive narrative. The testing motif recurs, the complaining persists, and a strange ritual involving the manna is recounted.

*1. **wilderness of Sin.*** The place name Sin (unrelated to the English noun "sin") may be an alternative form of Sinai.

*2. **grumbled.*** This word of complaint occurs repeatedly in 16:1–12. The frequent use of "grumble" may be the narrator's way of expressing the intensity of the people's dissatisfaction with their lot.

*3. **"our fill of bread."*** Cereal products were so central to the diet of people in ancient Israel—providing approximately half of their daily caloric intake—that the Bible uses the term for bread (*lechem*) sometimes to denote to food more generally. Close examination of biblical texts mentioning bread production, and consideration of relevant archeological and ethnographic data, together indicate that women were the producers of bread in households in the Land of Israel. In an arduous series of operations—grinding, sifting, kneading, baking (which involved collecting wood and building fires)—taking several hours every day, women transformed grain into bread. This complex process was essential because human beings cannot digest the endosperm surrounding the grain nor the grains' nutritional starch in raw form. On women and bread-baking, see also at 11:5, 12:8, and Leviticus 26:26.

*4. **"I will rain down bread."*** In miraculously producing "bread" from on high, God assumes the female role of bread producer.

raelites, "By evening you shall know it was יהוה
who brought you out from the land of Egypt; 7and
in the morning you shall behold the Presence of
יהוה, because [God] has heard your grumblings
against יהוה. For who are we that you should grumble against us? 8Since it is יהוה," Moses continued,
"who will give you flesh to eat in the evening and
bread in the morning to the full—because יהוה has
heard the grumblings you utter—what is our part?
Your grumbling is against יהוה, not against us!"
9Then Moses said to Aaron, "Say to the whole
Israelite community: Advance toward יהוה, who
has heard your grumbling." 10And as Aaron spoke
to the whole Israelite community, they turned toward the wilderness, and there, in a cloud, appeared
the Presence of יהוה.
11יהוה spoke to Moses: 12"I have heard the
grumbling of the Israelites. Speak to them and say:
By evening you shall eat flesh, and in the morning
you shall have your fill of bread; and you shall
know that I יהוה am your God."
13In the evening quail appeared and covered the
camp; in the morning there was a fall of dew about
the camp. 14When the fall of dew lifted, there, over
the surface of the wilderness, lay a fine and flaky
substance, as fine as frost on the ground. 15When
the Israelites saw it, they said to one another,
"What is it?"—for they did not know what it was.
And Moses said to them, "That is the bread which
יהוה has given you to eat. 16This is what יהוה has
commanded: Gather as much of it as each of you
requires to eat, an *omer* to a person for as many of
you as there are; you shall each fetch for those in
your tent."

יִשְׂרָאֵל עֶרֶב וִידַעְתֶּם כִּי יְהוָה הוֹצִיא
אֶתְכֶם מֵאֶרֶץ מִצְרָיִם׃ 7 וּבֹקֶר וּרְאִיתֶם
אֶת־כְּבוֹד יְהוָה בְּשָׁמְעוֹ אֶת־תְּלֻנֹּתֵיכֶם
עַל־יְהוָה וְנַחְנוּ מָה כִּי תלונו תַלִּינוּ עָלֵינוּ׃
8 וַיֹּאמֶר מֹשֶׁה בְּתֵת יְהוָה לָכֶם בָּעֶרֶב בָּשָׂר
לֶאֱכֹל וְלֶחֶם בַּבֹּקֶר לִשְׂבֹּעַ בִּשְׁמֹעַ יְהוָה
אֶת־תְּלֻנֹּתֵיכֶם אֲשֶׁר־אַתֶּם מַלִּינִם עָלָיו
וְנַחְנוּ מָה לֹא־עָלֵינוּ תְלֻנֹּתֵיכֶם כִּי עַל־
יְהוָה׃
9 וַיֹּאמֶר מֹשֶׁה אֶל־אַהֲרֹן אֱמֹר אֶל־כָּל־
עֲדַת בְּנֵי יִשְׂרָאֵל קִרְבוּ לִפְנֵי יְהוָה כִּי שָׁמַע
אֵת תְּלֻנֹּתֵיכֶם׃ 10 וַיְהִי כְּדַבֵּר אַהֲרֹן אֶל־
כָּל־עֲדַת בְּנֵי־יִשְׂרָאֵל וַיִּפְנוּ אֶל־הַמִּדְבָּר
וְהִנֵּה כְּבוֹד יְהוָה נִרְאָה בֶּעָנָן׃ פ
11 וַיְדַבֵּר יְהוָה אֶל־מֹשֶׁה לֵּאמֹר׃ 12 שָׁמַעְתִּי
אֶת־תְּלוּנֹּת בְּנֵי יִשְׂרָאֵל דַּבֵּר אֲלֵהֶם לֵאמֹר
בֵּין הָעַרְבַּיִם תֹּאכְלוּ בָשָׂר וּבַבֹּקֶר תִּשְׂבְּעוּ־
לָחֶם וִידַעְתֶּם כִּי אֲנִי יְהוָה אֱלֹהֵיכֶם׃
13 וַיְהִי בָעֶרֶב וַתַּעַל הַשְּׂלָו וַתְּכַס אֶת־
הַמַּחֲנֶה וּבַבֹּקֶר הָיְתָה שִׁכְבַת הַטַּל סָבִיב
לַמַּחֲנֶה׃ 14 וַתַּעַל שִׁכְבַת הַטָּל וְהִנֵּה עַל־
פְּנֵי הַמִּדְבָּר דַּק מְחֻסְפָּס דַּק כַּכְּפֹר עַל־
הָאָרֶץ׃ 15 וַיִּרְאוּ בְנֵי־יִשְׂרָאֵל וַיֹּאמְרוּ אִישׁ
אֶל־אָחִיו מָן הוּא כִּי לֹא יָדְעוּ מַה־הוּא
וַיֹּאמֶר מֹשֶׁה אֲלֵהֶם הוּא הַלֶּחֶם אֲשֶׁר נָתַן
יְהוָה לָכֶם לְאָכְלָה׃ 16 זֶה הַדָּבָר אֲשֶׁר צִוָּה
יְהוָה לִקְטוּ מִמֶּנּוּ אִישׁ לְפִי אָכְלוֹ עֹמֶר
לַגֻּלְגֹּלֶת מִסְפַּר נַפְשֹׁתֵיכֶם אִישׁ לַאֲשֶׁר
בְּאָהֳלוֹ תִּקָּחוּ׃

*7. "you shall behold the Presence of* יהוה*."* Divine presence is signified by God's (female) role as bread provider.

*12. you shall know.* Ample food is seen as evidence of God's providence and relationship to Israel.

*13. quail.* These small, easily prepared birds serve as the evening meal, perhaps only this once (see Numbers 11). In ancient Israel, people rarely ate meat except at special occasions and festivals.

*15. "What is it?"* The Hebrew words of this question (*man hu*) provide a folk etymology for the term by which the bread from heaven will be known: *man* ("manna") (v. 31).

*16. "omer."* A measure of volume (see at v. 36).

[17]The Israelites did so, some gathering much, some little. [18]But when they measured it by the *omer,* anyone who had gathered much had no excess, and anyone who had gathered little had no deficiency: they had gathered as much as they needed to eat. [19]And Moses said to them, "Let no one leave any of it over until morning." [20]But they paid no attention to Moses; some of them left of it until morning, and it became infested with maggots and stank. And Moses was angry with them.

[21]So they gathered it every morning, as much as each one needed to eat; for when the sun grew hot, it would melt. [22]On the sixth day they gathered double the amount of food, two *omer*s for each; and when all the chieftains of the community came and told Moses, [23]he said to them, "This is what יהוה meant: Tomorrow is a day of rest, a holy sabbath of יהוה. Bake what you would bake and boil what you would boil; and all that is left put aside to be kept until morning." [24]So they put it aside until morning, as Moses had ordered; and it did not turn foul, and there were no maggots in it. [25]Then Moses said, "Eat it today, for today is a sabbath of יהוה; you will not find it today on the plain. [26]Six days you shall gather it; on the seventh day, the sabbath, there will be none."

[27]Yet some of the people went out on the seventh day to gather, but they found nothing. [28]And יהוה said to Moses, "How long will you all refuse to obey My commandments and My teachings? [29]Mark that it is יהוה who, having given you the sabbath, therefore gives you two days' food on the sixth day. Let everyone remain in place: let no one leave the vicinity on the seventh day." [30]So the people remained inactive on the seventh day.

[31]The house of Israel named it manna; it was

17 וַיַּעֲשׂוּ־כֵן בְּנֵי יִשְׂרָאֵל וַיִּלְקְטוּ הַמַּרְבֶּה
וְהַמַּמְעִיט׃ 18 וַיָּמֹדּוּ בָעֹמֶר וְלֹא הֶעְדִּיף
הַמַּרְבֶּה וְהַמַּמְעִיט לֹא הֶחְסִיר אִישׁ לְפִי־
אָכְלוֹ לָקָטוּ׃ 19 וַיֹּאמֶר מֹשֶׁה אֲלֵהֶם אִישׁ
אַל־יוֹתֵר מִמֶּנּוּ עַד־בֹּקֶר׃ 20 וְלֹא־שָׁמְעוּ
אֶל־מֹשֶׁה וַיּוֹתִרוּ אֲנָשִׁים מִמֶּנּוּ עַד־בֹּקֶר
וַיָּרֻם תּוֹלָעִים וַיִּבְאַשׁ וַיִּקְצֹף עֲלֵהֶם
מֹשֶׁה׃
21 וַיִּלְקְטוּ אֹתוֹ בַּבֹּקֶר בַּבֹּקֶר אִישׁ כְּפִי
אָכְלוֹ וְחַם הַשֶּׁמֶשׁ וְנָמָס׃ 22 וַיְהִי ׀ בַּיּוֹם
הַשִּׁשִּׁי לָקְטוּ לֶחֶם מִשְׁנֶה שְׁנֵי הָעֹמֶר
לָאֶחָד וַיָּבֹאוּ כָּל־נְשִׂיאֵי הָעֵדָה וַיַּגִּידוּ
לְמֹשֶׁה׃ 23 וַיֹּאמֶר אֲלֵהֶם הוּא אֲשֶׁר דִּבֶּר
יְהֹוָה שַׁבָּתוֹן שַׁבַּת־קֹדֶשׁ לַיהֹוָה מָחָר אֵת
אֲשֶׁר־תֹּאפוּ אֵפוּ וְאֵת אֲשֶׁר־תְּבַשְּׁלוּ בַּשֵּׁלוּ
וְאֵת כָּל־הָעֹדֵף הַנִּיחוּ לָכֶם לְמִשְׁמֶרֶת עַד־
הַבֹּקֶר׃ 24 וַיַּנִּיחוּ אֹתוֹ עַד־הַבֹּקֶר כַּאֲשֶׁר
צִוָּה מֹשֶׁה וְלֹא הִבְאִישׁ וְרִמָּה לֹא־הָיְתָה
בּוֹ׃ 25 וַיֹּאמֶר מֹשֶׁה אִכְלֻהוּ הַיּוֹם כִּי־שַׁבָּת
הַיּוֹם לַיהֹוָה הַיּוֹם לֹא תִמְצָאֻהוּ בַּשָּׂדֶה׃
26 שֵׁשֶׁת יָמִים תִּלְקְטֻהוּ וּבַיּוֹם הַשְּׁבִיעִי
שַׁבָּת לֹא יִהְיֶה־בּוֹ׃
27 וַיְהִי בַּיּוֹם הַשְּׁבִיעִי יָצְאוּ מִן־הָעָם לִלְקֹט
וְלֹא מָצָאוּ׃ ס 28 וַיֹּאמֶר יְהֹוָה אֶל־מֹשֶׁה
עַד־אָנָה מֵאַנְתֶּם לִשְׁמֹר מִצְוֺתַי וְתוֹרֹתָי׃
29 רְאוּ כִּי־יְהֹוָה נָתַן לָכֶם הַשַּׁבָּת עַל־כֵּן
הוּא נֹתֵן לָכֶם בַּיּוֹם הַשִּׁשִּׁי לֶחֶם יוֹמָיִם
שְׁבוּ ׀ אִישׁ תַּחְתָּיו אַל־יֵצֵא אִישׁ מִמְּקֹמוֹ
בַּיּוֹם הַשְּׁבִיעִי׃ 30 וַיִּשְׁבְּתוּ הָעָם בַּיּוֹם
הַשְּׁבִעִי׃
31 וַיִּקְרְאוּ בֵית־יִשְׂרָאֵל אֶת־שְׁמוֹ מָן וְהוּא

*21–25.* This anachronistic passage assumes that Sabbath regulations forbidding work on the seventh day are known even before the Sinai revelation (20:8–11).

*31. manna.* On the name, see at v. 15. Modern interpreters have tried but failed to show the historicity of the Exodus narrative by identifying manna with some known substance. Manna should be considered a non-natural substance, a miracle provided by God.

like coriander seed, white, and it tasted like wafers in honey. ³²Moses said, "This is what יהוה has commanded: Let one *omer* of it be kept throughout the ages, in order that they may see the bread that I fed you in the wilderness when I brought you out from the land of Egypt." ³³And Moses said to Aaron, "Take a jar, put one *omer* of manna in it, and place it before יהוה, to be kept throughout the ages." ³⁴As יהוה had commanded Moses, Aaron placed it before the Pact, to be kept. ³⁵And the Israelites ate manna forty years, until they came to a settled land; they ate the manna until they came to the border of the land of Canaan. ³⁶The *omer* is a tenth of an *eifah*.

17 From the wilderness of Sin the whole Israelite community continued by stages as יהוה would command. They encamped at Rephidim, and there was no water for the people to drink. ²The people quarreled with Moses. "Give us water to drink," they said; and Moses replied to them, "Why do you quarrel with me? Why do you try יהוה?" ³But the people thirsted there for water; and

כְּזֶ֣רַע גַּ֔ד לָבָ֑ן וְטַעְמ֖וֹ כְּצַפִּיחִ֥ת בִּדְבָֽשׁ׃
³² וַיֹּ֣אמֶר מֹשֶׁ֗ה זֶ֤ה הַדָּבָר֙ אֲשֶׁ֣ר צִוָּ֣ה יְהֹוָ֔ה מְלֹ֤א הָעֹ֙מֶר֙ מִמֶּ֔נּוּ לְמִשְׁמֶ֖רֶת לְדֹרֹתֵיכֶ֑ם לְמַ֣עַן ׀ יִרְא֣וּ אֶת־הַלֶּ֗חֶם אֲשֶׁ֨ר הֶאֱכַ֤לְתִּי אֶתְכֶם֙ בַּמִּדְבָּ֔ר בְּהוֹצִיאִ֥י אֶתְכֶ֖ם מֵאֶ֥רֶץ מִצְרָֽיִם׃ ³³ וַיֹּ֨אמֶר מֹשֶׁ֜ה אֶֽל־אַהֲרֹ֗ן קַ֚ח צִנְצֶ֣נֶת אַחַ֔ת וְתֶן־שָׁ֥מָּה מְלֹֽא־הָעֹ֖מֶר מָ֑ן וְהַנַּ֤ח אֹתוֹ֙ לִפְנֵ֣י יְהֹוָ֔ה לְמִשְׁמֶ֖רֶת לְדֹרֹתֵיכֶֽם׃ ³⁴ כַּאֲשֶׁ֛ר צִוָּ֥ה יְהֹוָ֖ה אֶל־מֹשֶׁ֑ה וַיַּנִּיחֵ֧הוּ אַהֲרֹ֛ן לִפְנֵ֥י הָעֵדֻ֖ת לְמִשְׁמָֽרֶת׃ ³⁵ וּבְנֵ֣י יִשְׂרָאֵ֗ל אָֽכְל֤וּ אֶת־הַמָּן֙ אַרְבָּעִ֣ים שָׁנָ֔ה עַד־בֹּאָ֖ם אֶל־אֶ֣רֶץ נוֹשָׁ֑בֶת אֶת־הַמָּן֙ אָֽכְל֔וּ עַד־בֹּאָ֕ם אֶל־קְצֵ֖ה אֶ֥רֶץ כְּנָֽעַן׃ ³⁶ וְהָעֹ֕מֶר עֲשִׂרִ֥ית הָאֵיפָ֖ה הֽוּא׃ פ

יז וַ֠יִּסְע֠וּ כׇּל־עֲדַ֨ת בְּנֵי־יִשְׂרָאֵ֧ל מִמִּדְבַּר־סִ֛ין לְמַסְעֵיהֶ֖ם עַל־פִּ֣י יְהֹוָ֑ה וַֽיַּחֲנוּ֙ בִּרְפִידִ֔ים וְאֵ֥ין מַ֖יִם לִשְׁתֹּ֥ת הָעָֽם׃ ² וַיָּ֤רֶב הָעָם֙ עִם־מֹשֶׁ֔ה וַיֹּ֣אמְר֔וּ תְּנוּ־לָ֥נוּ מַ֖יִם וְנִשְׁתֶּ֑ה וַיֹּ֤אמֶר לָהֶם֙ מֹשֶׁ֔ה מַה־תְּרִיבוּן֙ עִמָּדִ֔י מַה־תְּנַסּ֖וּן אֶת־יְהֹוָֽה׃ ³ וַיִּצְמָ֨א שָׁ֤ם הָעָם֙ לַמַּ֔יִם וַיָּ֤לֶן

---

**32–33.** This is probably the etiology of a ritual that did not survive into the post-biblical period.

**34.** *before the Pact.* This is an anachronistic and elliptical reference to the "Ark of the Pact," said to be the repository for the Covenant document (see at 25:16).

**35.** *forty years.* That is, a generation.

**36.** *eifah.* This seems to have been the most common dry measure in ancient Israel, yet its exact capacity is not known; perhaps it was between ten and twenty liters.

### ANOTHER WATER CRISIS (17:1–7)

Again the people claim they have nothing to drink, and Moses magically produces water by

striking a rock. Sufficient water was a persistent problem in ancient Israel. Thus, it is no wonder that two water crises appear in succession. This incident appears in other biblical books (such as Deuteronomy 33:8; Psalm 95:7–8) as an important example of how God provides for the people—and also as an illustration of the people's lack of trust that God will do so.

**1.** *Rephidim.* Because this place name is from a verb meaning "to help, support," it is probably not a real place name but rather a name that symbolizes what is said to happen there: God helps Israel with water. (Also, in the next episode—which takes place at this same locale—Moses receives support for his arms so as to effect military victory; see vv. 8, 12.)

the people grumbled against Moses and said, "Why did you bring us up from Egypt, to kill us and our children and livestock with thirst?" 4Moses cried out to יהוה, saying, "What shall I do with this people? Before long they will be stoning me!" 5Then יהוה said to Moses, "Pass before the people; take with you some of the elders of Israel, and take along the rod with which you struck the Nile, and set out. 6I will be standing there before you on the rock at Horeb. Strike the rock and water will issue from it, and the people will drink." And Moses did so in the sight of the elders of Israel. 7The place was named Massah and Meribah, because the Israelites quarreled and because they tried יהוה, saying, "Is יהוה present among us or not?"

8Amalek came and fought with Israel at Rephidim. 9Moses said to Joshua, "Pick some troops for us, and go out and do battle with Amalek. Tomor-

הָעָם עַל־מֹשֶׁה וַיֹּאמֶר לָמָּה זֶּה הֶעֱלִיתָנוּ
מִמִּצְרַיִם לְהָמִית אֹתִי וְאֶת־בָּנַי וְאֶת־מִקְנַי
בַּצָּמָא׃ 4 וַיִּצְעַק מֹשֶׁה אֶל־יְהֹוָה לֵאמֹר
מָה אֶעֱשֶׂה לָעָם הַזֶּה עוֹד מְעַט וּסְקָלֻנִי׃
5 וַיֹּאמֶר יְהֹוָה אֶל־מֹשֶׁה עֲבֹר לִפְנֵי הָעָם
וְקַח אִתְּךָ מִזִּקְנֵי יִשְׂרָאֵל וּמַטְּךָ אֲשֶׁר הִכִּיתָ
בּוֹ אֶת־הַיְאֹר קַח בְּיָדְךָ וְהָלָכְתָּ׃ 6 הִנְנִי
עֹמֵד לְפָנֶיךָ שָּׁם ׀ עַל־הַצּוּר בְּחֹרֵב וְהִכִּיתָ
בַצּוּר וְיָצְאוּ מִמֶּנּוּ מַיִם וְשָׁתָה הָעָם וַיַּעַשׂ
כֵּן מֹשֶׁה לְעֵינֵי זִקְנֵי יִשְׂרָאֵל׃ 7 וַיִּקְרָא שֵׁם
הַמָּקוֹם מַסָּה וּמְרִיבָה עַל־רִיב ׀ בְּנֵי יִשְׂרָאֵל
וְעַל נַסֹּתָם אֶת־יְהֹוָה לֵאמֹר הֲיֵשׁ יְהֹוָה
בְּקִרְבֵּנוּ אִם־אָיִן׃ פ

8 וַיָּבֹא עֲמָלֵק וַיִּלָּחֶם עִם־יִשְׂרָאֵל בִּרְפִידִם׃
9 וַיֹּאמֶר מֹשֶׁה אֶל־יְהוֹשֻׁעַ בְּחַר־לָנוּ
אֲנָשִׁים וְצֵא הִלָּחֵם בַּעֲמָלֵק מָחָר אָנֹכִי

---

*3. "us and our children and livestock."* That women are not listed separately indicates that they are part of "the people" registering the complaint. Clearly they have a voice in life-and-death matters affecting the community.

*5. "rod with which you struck the Nile."* Note the irony: the rod that had magically made the Nile undrinkable (7:14–24) will now provide potable water.

*6. "Horeb."* This is another name for Sinai (see 3:1, 12), perhaps reflecting a separate narrative tradition.

*7. Massah and Meribah.* Like so many of the places on the wilderness trek, these terms, meaning "Test" and "Quarrel," are probably symbolic rather than geographical names.

*"Is יהוה present . . . ?"* This agonizing query reveals a fundamental conundrum regarding the concept of divine presence. Because God's presence is equated with the provision of food and water (see, for example, 16:4–7), thirst and hunger seem to mean divine absence. (The same issue arises in the next episode regarding protection from enemies: military defeat would seem to indicate divine absence.) How can these facts be reconciled with the notion that God is everywhere? (See also Another View, p. 400.)

### MILITARY CRISIS (17:8–16)

The protective aspect of divine presence becomes immediately apparent in the confrontation with the Amalekites, who are defeated as long as Moses holds high his magical staff.

*8. Amalek.* The Amalekites are traditional enemies of the Israelites, especially in the premonarchic era. That they are also related to the Israelites—Amalek is a grandson of Esau (Genesis 36:11–12)—makes their traditional enmity all the more tragic.

*Rephidim.* See at v. 1.

*9. Joshua.* This is the first appearance of Moses' eventual successor.

row I will station myself on the top of the hill, with the rod of God in my hand." [10]Joshua did as Moses told him and fought with Amalek, while Moses, Aaron, and Hur went up to the top of the hill. [11]Then, whenever Moses held up his hand, Israel prevailed; but whenever he let down his hand, Amalek prevailed. [12]But Moses' hands grew heavy; so they took a stone and put it under him and he sat on it, while Aaron and Hur, one on each side, supported his hands; thus his hands remained steady until the sun set. [13]And Joshua overwhelmed the people of Amalek with the sword.

[14]Then יהוה said to Moses, "Inscribe this in a document as a reminder, and read it aloud to Joshua: I will utterly blot out the memory of Amalek from under heaven!" [15]And Moses built an altar and named it Adonai-nissi. [16]He said, "It means, 'Hand upon the throne of יהוה!' יהוה will be at war with Amalek throughout the ages."

נִצָּ֛ב עַל־רֹ֥אשׁ הַגִּבְעָ֖ה וּמַטֵּ֥ה הָאֱלֹהִ֖ים בְּיָדִֽי: 10 וַיַּ֣עַשׂ יְהוֹשֻׁ֗עַ כַּאֲשֶׁ֤ר אָֽמַר־לוֹ֙ מֹשֶׁ֔ה לְהִלָּחֵ֖ם בַּעֲמָלֵ֑ק וּמֹשֶׁה֙ אַהֲרֹ֣ן וְח֔וּר עָל֖וּ רֹ֥אשׁ הַגִּבְעָֽה: 11 וְהָיָ֗ה כַּאֲשֶׁ֨ר יָרִ֥ים מֹשֶׁ֛ה יָד֖וֹ וְגָבַ֣ר יִשְׂרָאֵ֑ל וְכַאֲשֶׁ֥ר יָנִ֛יחַ יָד֖וֹ וְגָבַ֥ר עֲמָלֵֽק: 12 וִידֵ֤י מֹשֶׁה֙ כְּבֵדִ֔ים וַיִּקְחוּ־אֶ֛בֶן וַיָּשִׂ֥ימוּ תַחְתָּ֖יו וַיֵּ֣שֶׁב עָלֶ֑יהָ וְאַהֲרֹ֨ן וְח֜וּר תָּֽמְכ֣וּ בְיָדָ֗יו מִזֶּ֤ה אֶחָד֙ וּמִזֶּ֣ה אֶחָ֔ד וַיְהִ֥י יָדָ֛יו אֱמוּנָ֖ה עַד־בֹּ֥א הַשָּֽׁמֶשׁ: 13 וַיַּחֲלֹ֧שׁ יְהוֹשֻׁ֛עַ אֶת־עֲמָלֵ֥ק וְאֶת־עַמּ֖וֹ לְפִי־חָֽרֶב: פ

14 וַיֹּ֨אמֶר יְהֹוָ֜ה אֶל־מֹשֶׁ֗ה כְּתֹ֨ב זֹ֤את זִכָּרוֹן֙ בַּסֵּ֔פֶר וְשִׂ֖ים בְּאׇזְנֵ֣י יְהוֹשֻׁ֑עַ כִּֽי־מָחֹ֤ה אֶמְחֶה֙ אֶת־זֵ֣כֶר עֲמָלֵ֔ק מִתַּ֖חַת הַשָּׁמָֽיִם: 15 וַיִּ֥בֶן מֹשֶׁ֖ה מִזְבֵּ֑חַ וַיִּקְרָ֥א שְׁמ֖וֹ יְהֹוָ֥ה | נִסִּֽי: 16 וַיֹּ֗אמֶר כִּֽי־יָד֙ עַל־כֵּ֣ס יָ֔הּ מִלְחָמָ֥ה לַיהֹוָ֖ה בַּעֲמָלֵ֑ק מִדֹּ֖ר דֹּֽר: פ

---

*10.* **Hur.** Along with Moses and Aaron, Hur is part of a triumvirate presented as Israel's leaders in the wilderness (see 24:14).

*14.* **"Inscribe this . . . as a reminder . . . and read it aloud."** This is the first explicit reference in the Bible to documents and to literacy. It takes for granted that Moses knew how to both read and write—the latter being a more elite skill in the ancient world.

**"utterly blot out the memory."** The total destruction of Amalek will not only be genocidal but will also preclude existence in memory. This is harsh and troubling language for expressing divine power.

*16.* **"'Hand upon the throne of יהוה!'"** Or, according to a frequent emendation of the text, ". . . the banner of יהוה (*nes* יהוה)." Either way, this etiology for the altar's name, Adonai-Nissi, is probably an ancient oath; it would be like swearing in God's name. Oaths in the biblical world were sworn while placing one's hand in a significant place.

**"throughout the ages."** If Amalek symbolizes Israel's enemies, this notice acknowledges the sad fact that military crises will always be part of Israelite life. With war in the ancient Near East being waged almost entirely by men, to the extent that the Bible is concerned for Israel's security it not surprisingly focuses on male characters, with little attention given to the lives of women.

—*Carol Meyers*

# Another View

By breaking through the waters of the Sea of Reeds and emerging through the narrow passage, Israel is born as a liberated nation. Like any newborn, Israel expresses the need for food and water—and voices the fear of their absence. In response, God behaves as a mother, sometimes nurturing, sometimes stern, often setting limits.

Israel first faces a lack of water. When they encounter bitter waters, Moses sweetens them by casting in a piece of wood. Later, panic ensues because no springs are discovered at Rephidim. God instructs Moses to bring forth water from a rock with the very staff that turned the Nile to blood. On this initial leg of the journey, the people interpret the lack of water and food as indicative of God's absence, much as an infant interprets a lack of nourishment as the absence of nurture.

Food can be called Israel's national obsession, and it is used to gauge the relative safety or danger of a situation. Raw foods that require less chewing (milk, honey, manna) indicate relative stability, while meat has the potential to cause trouble (Numbers 11). Although no mention is made of Israel eating anything in Egypt before the Passover celebration (Exodus 12:8–9, 15), the people salivate when remembering Egyptian delicacies (Exodus 16:3; Numbers 11:5). While God promises Israel a land of milk and honey, they accuse God of trying to starve them in the wilderness (Exodus 16:3; Numbers 21:5). God rains bread from heaven (Exodus 16:4) as a taste of what is to come: manna that is white as milk and resembles the promised honey (Exodus 16:31). But, as Moses later informs the Divine, not even manna can fill the bottomless pit of Israel's appetite (Numbers 11:21–22).

*Israel is born as a liberated nation; in response, God behaves as a mother.*

Why are the people so hungry? Perhaps the trauma of slavery has left a residue of deprivation, or perhaps meals allow for some regularity during the journey through an unknown wilderness. The plot of the Torah implies that the people can find satisfaction only when they partake of the homeland's fruits (Joshua 5:11–12). Hunger is indicative of exile; and Israel is not sated until it finds a home. —*Rachel Havrelock*

# Post-biblical Interpretations

***Then Moses and the Israelites sang this song*** (15:1). The Rabbis noted that the word *shirah* (song) appears ten times in the Hebrew Scriptures. The Song at the Sea (Exodus 15) is the second instance. According to *M'chilta*, an early commentary on Exodus, nine of these songs were sung in the past, but the tenth is for the "Age to Come." This passage also reports that "for all the songs referring to previous events the noun used (*shirah*) is in the feminine" (*Shirta* 1). In a revelatory exposition of rabbinic sexual politics, the sages explained that "even as a female gives birth, so the achievements of the past were followed by subjugation." That is, just as a woman who emerges from a successful labor is still subject to the authority of her husband, so Israel, despite small victories, has consistently been subjected to foreign conquest. However, in the case of the future song, predicted in "Sing unto

יהוה a new song" (Isaiah 42:10), the masculine noun *shir* is used. This indicates "that just as no male gives birth, so the triumph which is yet to come will not be succeeded by subjugation" (*M'chilta, Shirta* 1).

***Then Miriam the prophet*** (15:20). Miriam is called "the prophet" in this verse, although she never prophesies in the Bible. The *M'chilta* says she predicted the birth of Moses to her father, who praised her when Moses was born—but then blamed her when they were forced to expose him in the basket (*Shirta* 10; also BT *Sotah* 12a–13a, referring to Exodus 2:1–3).

***and all the women went out after her in dance with hand-drums*** (15:20). The Rabbis speculated as to where the women obtained the musical instruments they played when they danced at the sea. Like a mother who remembers to pack all the necessities for a family trip, the women's confidence that God would deliver them made them bring these instruments along: "But where did the Israelites get hand-drums and flutes in the wilderness? It was simply that the righteous were confident and knew that God would perform miracles and mighty deeds when they left Egypt, so they prepared hand-drums and flutes" (*M'chilta, Shirta* 10). Although the *M'chilta* calls the righteous *tzaddikim* (masculine plural), the medieval commentator Rashi, in his remarks on this verse, made a point of calling them *tzadkaniot* (feminine plural), referring to the women.

***And Miriam chanted for them*** (15:21). Interpreters visualized two choral groups at the sea chanting the same song, both led by prophets: the men by Moses, the women by Miriam. Just as Moses recited the Song among the men, so it was Miriam who recited among the women: "Sing to יהוה for He has triumphed gloriously" (*M'chilta, Shirta* 10).

In rabbinic literature, Miriam and Moses often appear in parallel, with Miriam given an equal status to Moses. In a midrash in the 13th-century-C.E. *Midrash HaGadol*, Joseph explains two dreams of Pharaoh in which the number three appears. According to Joseph's interpretation, the double appearance of this number refers to the three patriarchs and to the three leaders who would redeem the people from Egypt: Moses, Aaron, and Miriam. Furthermore, the miraculous well of Miriam, which accompanied the people of Israel though the wilderness and sustained them because of Miriam's righteousness (BT *Taanit* 9a; *B'midbar Rabbah* 1.2), was among the ten miraculous entities created by God during the twilight on the eve of the

*Where did the Israelites get hand-drums and flutes in the wilderness?*

first Sabbath (Mishnah *Avot* 5:6). This well complements the manna, which was given to the people because of Moses' righteousness. The Talmud (BT *Taanit* 9a, among many other sources) explains as follows: "Rabbi Yose the son of Rabbi Judah says, 'Three good leaders had arisen for Israel—namely, Moses, Aaron, and Miriam—and for their sake three good things were given: the well, the clouds of glory, and the manna. The first was given for the merits of Miriam, the second for those of Aaron, and the third for those of Moses.'" The well disappeared at Miriam's death, but one tradition says a vessel of water from Miriam's well is one of three concealed objects that Elijah will restore in the messianic age, along with vessels of manna and of sacred oil (*M'chilta, Vayassa* 6).

—*Claudia Setzer*

# *Contemporary Reflection*

THERE ARE MOMENTS that define us: unexpected or unplanned moments when the decisions we make, the actions we take, determine all that will follow. Crossroads come disguised in many forms. Many are unmarked, without a hint of what is ahead.

*B'shalach* describes such a crossroads. The crossing of the Sea of Reeds was not only the crossing out of Egypt and out of slavery, but also the entrance into an unknown future, made possible by a moment of extraordinary faith.

At the far bank of the sea, triumph rings out in instrumental music and in song, led by both Moses and Miriam. Yet earlier, with Egyptians in pursuit and the waters ahead, according to the Rabbis it was neither Moses nor Miriam who took center stage, but Nahshon ben Amminadab. Nahshon is a curious hero. Briefly mentioned as Aaron's brother-in-law (Exodus 6:23), the Torah neither notices nor lauds him. Yet the Rabbis praise him for his initiative, the one who first entered the billowing waves, leading all of Israel to safety.

Nahshon's heroism is a literary deduction. In Numbers 7:12, Nahshon, the prince of the tribe of Judah, brings the first offering to dedicate the Tabernacle. The Midrash surmises: "When it was time to dedicate the tabernacle, Moses confessed to the princes of the tribes, 'The Holy One has commanded you to bring offerings, but I do not know who should go first.' The princes looked at Nahshon, saying, 'This man has sanctified the name of the Holy One at the Sea of Reeds. He is worthy to bring the *Shechinah*. Let Nahshon go first'" (*B'midbar Rabbah* 12.21).

At the Sea of Reeds, according to midrashic tradition, Nahshon stood at a crossroads—whether to have faith and plunge into the water, or be gripped by fear and remain on the shore. What was that moment like? If we were on the shore of the sea that fateful day, how would we have acted? Confidently? Timidly? Would we have entered the water gingerly or with fury? Flailing or swimming? How do we approach the sea crossings in our own lives? Are we coerced by an army from behind, or pulled ahead by the unknown?

Some think of Nahshon as fearless, determined to be the first into the water. In *Midrash T'hillim* 114:8, Nahshon reputedly pelts his brothers with stones to assure his place of primacy. The daredevil confidence of this Nahshon contrasts sharply with another vision of this moment (*M'chilta, B'shalach* 5). Huddled together, a terrified crowd looks behind at the Egyptians

*Like Nahshon and Miriam, today's women face our own sea crossing.*

and forward toward water. As they yell, "I don't want to go into the sea!" Nahshon jumps up in fear; losing his footing, he falls into the waves. Overcome with terror, he cites Psalms, "Save me, O God, for the waters have reached my neck" (Psalm 69:2). Here, Nahshon—a fearful, drowning man—cries for God's help. The midrash alternately envisions Nahshon as hapless victim, brash show-off, or eager leader.

As she emerges from the water, Miriam, too, faces an array of alternatives—an internal sea crossing of her own. Was it the time to forge ahead, adrenaline still coursing from their narrow escape? Was it the occasion to mourn the loss of the known, the familiar if oppressive Egypt? Was it the instant to comfort those catching their breath, those who had needed to run and swim faster than they believed possible? Was it safer to hang back and let others take their rightful place as leaders? Or was this the moment to lift up the hand-drum and triumphantly sing and dance, giddy with gratitude for God's redemption?

Miriam had the foresight to bring her hand-drum.

Miriam had the wisdom to gather her sisters to acknowledge and affirm the miracle, to mark the moment when their tenuous hope broke forth in joy—the birth of her community as a people touched by God.

Like Nahshon, Miriam's leadership is surprising. *Kol ishah*, the voice of a woman, Miriam's strong voice, had been heard previously only as a sister and daughter. Yet, at her sea crossing, emerging from the waters, she does not wait for someone else to change the world. She does not demur that she was not bred for greatness. She does not blend into the crowd. Instead, Miriam's voice rings out for all to hear.

Miriam is a leader: a prophet who speaks to and binds others to God. Like a large *tallit* on small shoulders, she is one upon whom the mantle of authority does not fit snugly, one who might have been surprised at her own influence, but one who nevertheless conscientiously undertakes responsibility for contributing to God's purpose—much like contemporary women leaders. In the waters of transition, Miriam sparks innovation, creativity, and hope, rooted in the past yet focused on the future—just like contemporary women leaders. Like Nahshon before the waves and Miriam after them, we ask: how do we navigate waters never traversed before? How do we create rituals that reflect the tradition yet give voice to our experience? How do we speak new words that include the familiar in a Holy tongue?

Like Nahshon and Miriam, today's women face our own sea crossing. We too can choose to enter the water: with quiet certitude, brash impulsiveness, or terror at what lies ahead. Or, we may decide to hang back, looking around for someone else to go in first. Eventually, when we enter—however we enter—we, and our world, are transformed.

In our time, the sea crossing may be when we hear a cry for social justice, when we unexpectedly find our voice waxing prophetic; it may come as we read a book, converse with a friend, or witness a scene in which we are seized with understanding about our place in the world. As we enter the water, if we speak and act out of awe and gratitude, if we look around and trust our vision, we may discover that we are bathed in and buoyed by the presence of God.

*—Patricia Karlin-Neumann*

# *Voices*

## *Leaving Egypt*

Merle Feld

*Exodus 13:17–22*

The night is so dark
and I am afraid.
I see nothing, smell nothing,
the only reality—
I am holding my mother's hand.

And as we walk
I hear the sounds
of a multitude in motion—
in front, behind,
all around,
a multitude in motion.

I have no thought of tomorrow,
now, in the darkness,
there is only motion
and my mother's hand.

## *Miriam: The Red Sea*

Muriel Rukeyser

*Exodus 14:26–15:21*

High above shores and times,
I on the shore
forever and ever.
Moses my brother
has crossed over
to milk, honey,
that holy land.
Building Jerusalem.
I sing forever
on the seashore.
I do remember
horseman and horses,
waves of passage
poured into war,
all poured into journey.
My unseen brothers
have gone over,
chariots
deep seas under.
I alone stand here
ankle-deep
and I sing, I sing,
until the lands
sing to each other.

## *The Other Shore*

Shira Rubenstein

*Exodus 14:26–15:21*

The guilt begins on the other shore of the Reed Sea,
with us, drained from terror and excitement,
with the sun beating down,
seagulls swooping overhead,
waves lapping against the bodies on the sand,
so gently, now.
Children laugh or cry,
but the world is quiet,
afterwards.

Who is like you, O God?
We know about fear
and doubt,
resentment and guilt.
We thought we'd be leaving it behind.
How heavy a load can be carried out of Egypt?
How many in that army were blameless?

How many innocents will die for this freedom?

We don't know whether these questions are for God or us.
We try to drown them out with drums,
hoarse, harsh song,
the pounding of tired feet in a desperate dance.
We think of the cracks of the whip,
the insults,
every murdered child
—all the times we wished
something like this would occur.
We tell ourselves we have a right to rejoice.

It would be easier to believe
if the horses
hadn't had time
to
scream.

## *The Song of Miriam*

Ruth Sohn

I, Miriam, stand at the sea
and turn
to face the desert
stretching endless and
still.
My eyes are dazzled
The sky brilliant blue
Sunburnt sands unyielding white.
My hands turn to dove wings.
My arms
reach
for the sky
and I want to sing
the song rising inside me.
My mouth open
I stop.
Where are the words?
Where the melody?
In a moment of panic
My eyes go blind.
Can I take a step
Without knowing a
Destination?
Will I falter
Will I fall
Will the ground sink away from under me?

The song still unformed—
How can I sing?

To take the first step—
To sing a new song—
Is to close one's eyes
and dive
into unknown waters.
For a moment knowing nothing risking all—
But then to discover
The waters are friendly
The ground is firm.
And the song—
the song rises again.
Out of my mouth
come words lifting the wind.
And I hear
for the first
the song
that has been in my heart
silent
unknown
even to me.

## *Thirst IV*

Kadya Molodowsky (transl. Kathryn Hellerstein)

*Exodus 15:22–25*

My pitcher lies, dry and thirsty,
And I walk through all the streets
Seeking out a drop of water,
And I am spent
Near my pitcher.
I lay my lips
To the roots of the trees,
I stretch with eyes and mouth
To the sky's rains.
And my tongue is bitter from roots of the trees,
My mouth is thirsty,
And my eyes are tired from looking at the sky.
I seek my pitcher,
And it is dry.

# יִתְרוֹ ✦ *Yitro*

## EXODUS 18:1–20:23

### *The Birth of a Nation: Israel Becomes a Covenanted People*

PARASHAT YITRO ("Jethro") records the transformative encounter between God and Israel at Mount Sinai, the moment when God and the people Israel become wedded in an exclusive covenantal relationship. After experiencing how God bore them "on eagles' wings" (19:4) from Egypt, the people willingly accept God's proposal: If they listen to God's voice and obey the covenant, they will become God's "treasured possession," a "kingdom of priests and a holy nation" (19:5–6). The blare of a ram's horn and a spectacular display of smoke, thunder, and lightning herald the appearance of the Divine. Then, the revelation of the commandments stipulate what it means to walk in God's ways.

The teachings of the Decalogue, also known popularly as the Ten Commandments, guide the Israelites in their relationships with God and other human beings. The first four commandments charge the Israelites to worship God faithfully and to observe the Sabbath. The last five prohibit taking what is not yours: a human life, another man's wife, or someone else's property, either directly through stealing or indirectly through false testimony or coveting another's belongings. The fifth commandment—a bridge between the precepts focused on the Divine and those concerned with humans—mandates reverence of one's mother and father.

In the Decalogue, women are mentioned as mothers, wives, daughters, and servants. Elsewhere in the parashah, women play a more elusive role. Zipporah appears in the beginning of the portion, when Moses' father-in-law, Jethro, travels to the wilderness of Sinai in order to reunite Moses with his wife, Zipporah, and their two sons. What is puzzling about this scene is that an earlier passage in Exodus suggests that Moses brought his family with him to Egypt (4:20, 24–26). When and why had she "been sent home" (18:2) to Midian?

*Were women included in—or excluded from—the revelation at Sinai?*

Even more perplexing and disturbing for many contemporary readers is the question of whether women were included in, or excluded from, the revelation at Sinai. How should we interpret Moses' command to "not go near a woman" (19:15)? Does the masculine language of the laws address women? These issues are explored at 19:8, 15; introduction to 20:1–14; 20:10, 14, as well as in Another View (p. 421) and Contemporary Reflection (p. 423).

*—Elaine Goodfriend*

## *Outline*

*I.* Jethro's Advice to Moses (18:1–27)

*A.* Jethro, Zipporah, and sons with Moses at Sinai (vv. 1–12)

*B.* Jethro recommends delegating judicial authority (vv. 13–27)

*II.* Preparing for the Covenant and Divine Revelation (19:1–25)

*A.* Arriving at Sinai (vv. 1–2)

*B.* God proposes a covenant and Israel accepts (vv. 3–8)

*C.* Preparing for the divine revelation (vv. 9–25)

*III.* The Decalogue ("Ten Commandments") (20:1–14)

*A.* Introduction (vv. 1)

*B.* The commandments (vv. 2–14)

*IV.* The People's Response and the First Instruction (20:15–23)

**18:1**

Jethro priest of Midian, Moses' father-in-law, heard all that God had done for Moses and for Israel, God's people, how יהוה had brought Israel out from Egypt. [2]So Jethro, Moses' father-in-law, took Zipporah, Moses' wife, after she had been sent home, [3]and her two sons—of whom one was named Gershom, that is to say, "I have been a stranger in a foreign land"; [4]and the other was named Eliezer, meaning, "My ancestors' God was

יח וַיִּשְׁמַע יִתְרוֹ כֹהֵן מִדְיָן חֹתֵן מֹשֶׁה
אֵת כָּל־אֲשֶׁר עָשָׂה אֱלֹהִים לְמֹשֶׁה
וּלְיִשְׂרָאֵל עַמּוֹ כִּי־הוֹצִיא יְהֹוָה אֶת־
יִשְׂרָאֵל מִמִּצְרָיִם׃ 2 וַיִּקַּח יִתְרוֹ חֹתֵן מֹשֶׁה
אֶת־צִפֹּרָה אֵשֶׁת מֹשֶׁה אַחַר שִׁלּוּחֶיהָ׃
3 וְאֵת שְׁנֵי בָנֶיהָ אֲשֶׁר שֵׁם הָאֶחָד גֵּרְשֹׁם
כִּי אָמַר גֵּר הָיִיתִי בְּאֶרֶץ נָכְרִיָּה׃ 4 וְשֵׁם
הָאֶחָד אֱלִיעֶזֶר כִּי־אֱלֹהֵי אָבִי בְּעֶזְרִי וַיַּצִּלֵנִי

## *Jethro's Advice to Moses* (18:1–27)

Moses' Midianite father-in-law, Jethro, joins the Israelites at Sinai and advises Moses how to create a system for resolving internal disputes. This passage serves as a transition between the liberation from Egypt and the revelation of God's teachings. The positive relations between Israelite and non-Israelite at the start of this parashah stand in direct contrast to the conclusion of the preceding parashah, which expresses permanent hostility toward Amalek (17:16). The desire to contrast "good gentile" with "bad gentile" may have dictated the placement of this episode.

### JETHRO, ZIPPORAH, AND SONS WITH MOSES AT SINAI (18:1–12)

*1. **Jethro.*** Moses' father-in-law is referred to elsewhere as Jether (4:18), Hobab (Numbers 10:29; Judges 4:11), and Reuel (Exodus 2:18), though the latter may be the name of Jethro's father.

*2. **So Jethro . . . took Zipporah . . . after she had been sent home.*** The narration implies that Moses' wife and children were living in Midian while Moses returned to Egypt to free the Israelites. Yet no notice was given earlier that Zipporah and her sons were dispatched back to Midian. When last we encountered Zipporah, she was traveling with Moses and her sons from Midian to Egypt (4:20). On the way, she saved her family by circumcising her son, the mysterious "bridegroom of blood" incident (4:24–26).

***sent home.*** The Hebrew verb here can mean divorce, so some interpreters claim that Moses had divorced her; yet this explanation is not persuasive since Jethro refers to her as Moses' wife in v. 6. The reason for the separation is not explained.

*4. **Eliezer.*** While Gershom's birth is mentioned in 2:22, this is the first explicit reference to Eliezer, although 4:20 alludes to him.

***meaning.*** In the Torah, the explanation of a name by the mother or father is a standard feature of the birth of sons, but never of daughters. This may

What gives Moses the right to report God's words differently than originally delivered?

ANOTHER VIEW ➤ *421*

Moses renders women invisible as part of the congregation about to enter into the covenant.

CONTEMPORARY REFLECTION ➤ *423*

Neither gender, foreign origins, nor a dubious past is a barrier to joining the Jewish people.

POST-BIBLICAL INTERPRETATIONS ➤ *421*

. . . I was welcomed and more than welcome / among the women.

VOICES ➤ *425*

מֵחֶרֶב פַּרְעֹה׃ 5 וַיָּבֹא יִתְרוֹ חֹתֵן מֹשֶׁה
וּבָנָיו וְאִשְׁתּוֹ אֶל־מֹשֶׁה אֶל־הַמִּדְבָּר אֲשֶׁר־
הוּא חֹנֶה שָׁם הַר הָאֱלֹהִים׃ 6 וַיֹּאמֶר אֶל־
מֹשֶׁה אֲנִי חֹתֶנְךָ יִתְרוֹ בָּא אֵלֶיךָ וְאִשְׁתְּךָ
וּשְׁנֵי בָנֶיהָ עִמָּהּ׃ 7 וַיֵּצֵא מֹשֶׁה לִקְרַאת
חֹתְנוֹ וַיִּשְׁתַּחוּ וַיִּשַּׁק־לוֹ וַיִּשְׁאֲלוּ אִישׁ־
לְרֵעֵהוּ לְשָׁלוֹם וַיָּבֹאוּ הָאֹהֱלָה׃
8 וַיְסַפֵּר מֹשֶׁה לְחֹתְנוֹ אֵת כָּל־אֲשֶׁר עָשָׂה
יְהוָה לְפַרְעֹה וּלְמִצְרַיִם עַל אוֹדֹת יִשְׂרָאֵל
אֵת כָּל־הַתְּלָאָה אֲשֶׁר מְצָאָתַם בַּדֶּרֶךְ
וַיַּצִּלֵם יְהוָה׃ 9 וַיִּחַדְּ יִתְרוֹ עַל כָּל־הַטּוֹבָה
אֲשֶׁר־עָשָׂה יְהוָה לְיִשְׂרָאֵל אֲשֶׁר הִצִּילוֹ
מִיַּד מִצְרָיִם׃ 10 וַיֹּאמֶר יִתְרוֹ בָּרוּךְ יְהוָה
אֲשֶׁר הִצִּיל אֶתְכֶם מִיַּד מִצְרַיִם וּמִיַּד
פַּרְעֹה אֲשֶׁר הִצִּיל אֶת־הָעָם מִתַּחַת
יַד־מִצְרָיִם׃ 11 עַתָּה יָדַעְתִּי כִּי־גָדוֹל
יְהוָה מִכָּל־הָאֱלֹהִים כִּי בַדָּבָר אֲשֶׁר זָדוּ
עֲלֵיהֶם׃ 12 וַיִּקַּח יִתְרוֹ חֹתֵן מֹשֶׁה עֹלָה
וּזְבָחִים לֵאלֹהִים וַיָּבֹא אַהֲרֹן וְכֹל ׀ זִקְנֵי
יִשְׂרָאֵל לֶאֱכָל־לֶחֶם עִם־חֹתֵן מֹשֶׁה לִפְנֵי
הָאֱלֹהִים׃

my help, delivering me from the sword of Pharaoh." 5 Jethro, Moses' father-in-law, brought Moses' sons and wife to him in the wilderness, where he was encamped at the mountain of God. 6 He sent word to Moses, "I, your father-in-law Jethro, am coming to you, with your wife and her two sons." 7 Moses went out to meet his father-in-law; he bowed low and kissed him; each asked after the other's welfare, and they went into the tent.

8 Moses then recounted to his father-in-law everything that יהוה had done to Pharaoh and to the Egyptians for Israel's sake, all the hardships that had befallen them on the way, and how יהוה had delivered them. 9 And Jethro rejoiced over all the kindness that יהוה had shown Israel when delivering them from the Egyptians. 10 "Blessed be יהוה," Jethro said, "who delivered you from the Egyptians and from Pharaoh, and who delivered the people from under the hand of the Egyptians. 11 Now I know that יהוה is greater than all gods, yes, by the result of their very schemes against [the people]." 12 And Jethro, Moses' father-in-law, brought a burnt offering and sacrifices for God; and Aaron came with all the elders of Israel to partake of the meal before God with Moses' father-in-law.

---

be due to the patrilineal nature of Israelite society: the names of boys often become clan and tribal names, while girls' names did not.

***"My ancestors'."*** Heb. *avi*, literally "my father's." On the gender-inclusive sense, see at 15:2.

*5.* ***the mountain of God.*** Several passages in the Torah refer to this mountain as Sinai, while others call it Horeb (see 3:1). One explanation is that two different traditions existed about the name of this mountain; another possibility is that the term Horeb should be understood as the name of the larger region, while "wilderness of Sinai" and "Mount Sinai" refer to a specific area or peak in the boundaries of Horeb. People have long sought to locate this mountain, identifying it with Jebel Musa or other particular mountains in the Sinai Peninsula or northwestern Arabia. However, such efforts seem to misconstrue the way the Bible presents Sinai as a phenomenon that transcends space and time (Carol Meyers, *Exodus*, 2005, p. 144).

*7.* ***he bowed low and kissed him.*** Moses, acting as the host, warmly greets his father-in-law; but no mention is made of him welcoming his wife and sons. This imbalance may reflect the formal hospitality customs common in the biblical world. Or, rather than suggesting the neglect of his family, this may stem from the Torah's intent to highlight Moses' remarkable relations with his Midianite father-in-law.

[13]Next day, Moses sat as magistrate among the people, while the people stood about Moses from morning until evening. [14]But when Moses' father-in-law saw how much he had to do for the people, he said, "What is this thing that you are doing to the people? Why do you act alone, while all the people stand about you from morning until evening?" [15]Moses replied to his father-in-law, "It is because the people come to me to inquire of God. [16]When they have a dispute, it comes before me, and I decide between one person and another, and I make known the laws and teachings of God."

[17]But Moses' father-in-law said to him, "The thing you are doing is not right; [18]you will surely wear yourself out, and these people as well. For the task is too heavy for you; you cannot do it alone. [19]Now listen to me. I will give you counsel, and God be with you! You represent the people before God: you bring the disputes before God, [20]and enjoin upon them the laws and the teachings, and make known to them the way they are to go and the practices they are to follow. [21]You shall also seek out, from among all the people, capable individuals who fear God—trustworthy ones who spurn ill-gotten gain. Set these over them as chiefs of thousands, hundreds, fifties, and tens, and [22]let them judge the people at all times. Have them bring every major dispute to you, but let them decide every minor dispute themselves. Make it easier for yourself by letting them share the burden

13 וַיְהִי מִמָּחֳרָת וַיֵּשֶׁב מֹשֶׁה לִשְׁפֹּט אֶת־
הָעָם וַיַּעֲמֹד הָעָם עַל־מֹשֶׁה מִן־הַבֹּקֶר עַד־
הָעָרֶב׃ 14 וַיַּרְא חֹתֵן מֹשֶׁה אֵת כָּל־אֲשֶׁר־
הוּא עֹשֶׂה לָעָם וַיֹּאמֶר מָה־הַדָּבָר הַזֶּה
אֲשֶׁר אַתָּה עֹשֶׂה לָעָם מַדּוּעַ אַתָּה יוֹשֵׁב
לְבַדֶּךָ וְכָל־הָעָם נִצָּב עָלֶיךָ מִן־בֹּקֶר עַד־
עָרֶב׃ 15 וַיֹּאמֶר מֹשֶׁה לְחֹתְנוֹ כִּי־יָבֹא
אֵלַי הָעָם לִדְרֹשׁ אֱלֹהִים׃ 16 כִּי־יִהְיֶה לָהֶם
דָּבָר בָּא אֵלַי וְשָׁפַטְתִּי בֵּין אִישׁ וּבֵין
רֵעֵהוּ וְהוֹדַעְתִּי אֶת־חֻקֵּי הָאֱלֹהִים וְאֶת־
תּוֹרֹתָיו׃

17 וַיֹּאמֶר חֹתֵן מֹשֶׁה אֵלָיו לֹא־טוֹב הַדָּבָר
אֲשֶׁר אַתָּה עֹשֶׂה׃ 18 נָבֹל תִּבֹּל גַּם־אַתָּה
גַּם־הָעָם הַזֶּה אֲשֶׁר עִמָּךְ כִּי־כָבֵד מִמְּךָ
הַדָּבָר לֹא־תוּכַל עֲשֹׂהוּ לְבַדֶּךָ׃ 19 עַתָּה
שְׁמַע בְּקֹלִי אִיעָצְךָ וִיהִי אֱלֹהִים עִמָּךְ הֱיֵה
אַתָּה לָעָם מוּל הָאֱלֹהִים וְהֵבֵאתָ אַתָּה
אֶת־הַדְּבָרִים אֶל־הָאֱלֹהִים׃ 20 וְהִזְהַרְתָּה
אֶתְהֶם אֶת־הַחֻקִּים וְאֶת־הַתּוֹרֹת וְהוֹדַעְתָּ
לָהֶם אֶת־הַדֶּרֶךְ יֵלְכוּ בָהּ וְאֶת־הַמַּעֲשֶׂה
אֲשֶׁר יַעֲשׂוּן׃ 21 וְאַתָּה תֶחֱזֶה מִכָּל־הָעָם
אַנְשֵׁי־חַיִל יִרְאֵי אֱלֹהִים אַנְשֵׁי אֱמֶת שֹׂנְאֵי
בָצַע וְשַׂמְתָּ עֲלֵהֶם שָׂרֵי אֲלָפִים שָׂרֵי מֵאוֹת
שָׂרֵי חֲמִשִּׁים וְשָׂרֵי עֲשָׂרֹת׃ 22 וְשָׁפְטוּ אֶת־
הָעָם בְּכָל־עֵת וְהָיָה כָּל־הַדָּבָר הַגָּדֹל יָבִיאוּ
אֵלֶיךָ וְכָל־הַדָּבָר הַקָּטֹן יִשְׁפְּטוּ־הֵם וְהָקֵל

## JETHRO RECOMMENDS DELEGATING JUDICIAL AUTHORITY (18:13–27)

After noticing the cumbersome and inefficient nature of Moses' role as the sole judge of the people, Jethro makes a suggestion. Deuteronomy's version of this episode omits Jethro's role (Deuteronomy 1:9–18), which is hardly surprising since ascribing Israel's judiciary structure to a foreigner is quite remarkable.

*21. chiefs.* Heb. *sarim*, meaning officers with a range of administrative duties. The judicial system outlined by Jethro is hierarchical and quasi-military, which makes sense since Israel's organization in the wilderness is most akin to a military formation. The noun "judge" (*shofet*) is not used in this passage. While presumably women were excluded from such leadership positions, Judges 4–5 records that Deborah served as a judge and prophet.

with you. 23 If you do this—and God so commands you—you will be able to bear up; and all these people too will go home unwearied."

24 Moses heeded his father-in-law and did just as he had said. 25 Moses chose capable individuals out of all Israel, and appointed them heads over the people—chiefs of thousands, hundreds, fifties, and tens; 26 and they judged the people at all times: the difficult matters they would bring to Moses, and all the minor matters they would decide themselves. 27 Then Moses bade his father-in-law farewell, and he went his way to his own land.

**19** On the third new moon after the Israelites had gone forth from the land of Egypt, on that very day, they entered the wilderness of Sinai. 2 Having journeyed from Rephidim, they entered the wilderness of Sinai and encamped in the wilderness. Israel encamped there in front of the mountain, 3 and Moses went up to God. יהוה called to him from the mountain, saying, "Thus shall you say to the house of Jacob and declare to the children of Israel: 4 'You have seen what I did to the Egyptians, how

מֵעָלֶיךָ וְנָשְׂאוּ אִתָּךְ׃ 23 אִם אֶת־הַדָּבָר הַזֶּה
תַּעֲשֶׂה וְצִוְּךָ אֱלֹהִים וְיָכָלְתָּ עֲמֹד וְגַם כָּל־
הָעָם הַזֶּה עַל־מְקֹמוֹ יָבֹא בְשָׁלוֹם׃
24 וַיִּשְׁמַע מֹשֶׁה לְקוֹל חֹתְנוֹ וַיַּעַשׂ כֹּל אֲשֶׁר
אָמָר׃ 25 וַיִּבְחַר מֹשֶׁה אַנְשֵׁי־חַיִל מִכָּל־
יִשְׂרָאֵל וַיִּתֵּן אֹתָם רָאשִׁים עַל־הָעָם שָׂרֵי
אֲלָפִים שָׂרֵי מֵאוֹת שָׂרֵי חֲמִשִּׁים וְשָׂרֵי
עֲשָׂרֹת׃ 26 וְשָׁפְטוּ אֶת־הָעָם בְּכָל־עֵת אֶת־
הַדָּבָר הַקָּשֶׁה יְבִיאוּן אֶל־מֹשֶׁה וְכָל־הַדָּבָר
הַקָּטֹן יִשְׁפּוּטוּ הֵם׃ 27 וַיְשַׁלַּח מֹשֶׁה אֶת־
חֹתְנוֹ וַיֵּלֶךְ לוֹ אֶל־אַרְצוֹ׃ פ

יט בַּחֹדֶשׁ הַשְּׁלִישִׁי לְצֵאת בְּנֵי־יִשְׂרָאֵל
מֵאֶרֶץ מִצְרָיִם בַּיּוֹם הַזֶּה בָּאוּ מִדְבַּר סִינָי׃
2 וַיִּסְעוּ מֵרְפִידִים וַיָּבֹאוּ מִדְבַּר סִינַי וַיַּחֲנוּ
בַּמִּדְבָּר וַיִּחַן־שָׁם יִשְׂרָאֵל נֶגֶד הָהָר׃
3 וּמֹשֶׁה עָלָה אֶל־הָאֱלֹהִים וַיִּקְרָא אֵלָיו
יְהוָה מִן־הָהָר לֵאמֹר כֹּה תֹאמַר לְבֵית
יַעֲקֹב וְתַגֵּיד לִבְנֵי יִשְׂרָאֵל׃ 4 אַתֶּם רְאִיתֶם

## *Preparing for the Covenant and Divine Revelation* (19:1–25)

The encounter at Sinai forms the literary and ideological heart of the Torah. Israel's experience at "God's mountain" is presented as the determining factor in its spiritual and national identity. It is here that God proposes and Israel accepts the covenant (*b'rit*) that creates a legal and binding relationship between a people and its deity, a relationship not found elsewhere in the ancient world. This covenant also serves to bind individuals into a nation, for Israel's communal acceptance of the terms of the covenant (19:9) imposes upon the people collective rewards and punishments (Leviticus 26; Deuteronomy 28).

### ARRIVING AT SINAI (19:1–2)

This passage marks the Israelites' arrival in the wilderness of Sinai. According to Numbers 10:11–12, they remain there for nearly a year before briefly resuming their journey to the Promised Land.

### GOD PROPOSES A COVENANT AND ISRAEL ACCEPTS (19:3–8)

In contrast to the unconditional covenant with the ancestors in Genesis, the Sinai covenant requires the people to adhere to certain stipulations in order to receive God's promised benefactions. The people enthusiastically accept God's covenantal offer, although the exact terms of the covenant remain unspecified until Exodus 20–23.

I bore you on eagles' wings and brought you to Me.
[5]Now then, if you will obey Me faithfully and keep
My covenant, you shall be My treasured possession
among all the peoples. Indeed, all the earth is Mine,
[6]but you shall be to Me a kingdom of priests and a
holy nation.' These are the words that you shall
speak to the children of Israel."
[7]Moses came and summoned the elders of the
people and put before them all that יהוה had
commanded him. [8]All the people answered as
one, saying, "All that יהוה has spoken we will
do!" And Moses brought back the people's words
to יהוה. [9]And יהוה said to Moses, "I will come to
you in a thick cloud, in order that the people may
hear when I speak with you and so trust you ever

אֲשֶׁר עָשִׂיתִי לְמִצְרָיִם וָאֶשָּׂא אֶתְכֶם עַל־
כַּנְפֵי נְשָׁרִים וָאָבִא אֶתְכֶם אֵלָי׃ 5 וְעַתָּה
אִם־שָׁמוֹעַ תִּשְׁמְעוּ בְּקֹלִי וּשְׁמַרְתֶּם אֶת־
בְּרִיתִי וִהְיִיתֶם לִי סְגֻלָּה מִכָּל־הָעַמִּים כִּי־
לִי כָּל־הָאָרֶץ׃ 6 וְאַתֶּם תִּהְיוּ־לִי מַמְלֶכֶת
כֹּהֲנִים וְגוֹי קָדוֹשׁ אֵלֶּה הַדְּבָרִים אֲשֶׁר
תְּדַבֵּר אֶל־בְּנֵי יִשְׂרָאֵל׃
7 וַיָּבֹא מֹשֶׁה וַיִּקְרָא לְזִקְנֵי הָעָם וַיָּשֶׂם
לִפְנֵיהֶם אֵת כָּל־הַדְּבָרִים הָאֵלֶּה אֲשֶׁר
צִוָּהוּ יְהֹוָה׃ 8 וַיַּעֲנוּ כָל־הָעָם יַחְדָּו וַיֹּאמְרוּ
כֹּל אֲשֶׁר־דִּבֶּר יְהֹוָה נַעֲשֶׂה וַיָּשֶׁב מֹשֶׁה
אֶת־דִּבְרֵי הָעָם אֶל־יְהֹוָה׃ 9 וַיֹּאמֶר יְהֹוָה
אֶל־מֹשֶׁה הִנֵּה אָנֹכִי בָּא אֵלֶיךָ בְּעַב הֶעָנָן
בַּעֲבוּר יִשְׁמַע הָעָם בְּדַבְּרִי עִמָּךְ וְגַם־בְּךָ

*4. "I bore you on eagles' wings."* Whereas the prior parashah contains a number of masculine images of God (see at 14:14; 15:3, 18) and possibly some female divine imagery (see at 15:26; 16:4; and the introduction to 15:22–17:16), here we find God depicted as an eagle, a metaphor that evokes the way this majestic bird protectively carries its young while training them to fly.

*5. "treasured possession."* Heb. *s'gulah*, which normally refers to a private accumulation of valuable property (see Ecclesiastes 2:8). While this universal deity could potentially claim possession of any nation on earth, God chooses Israel as a personal treasure. The notion of Israel's exclusive relationship with God—found here and in the subsequent verse—is problematic for many modern readers. However, in the polytheistic world of the ancient Near East, it was assumed that a deity would have a special connection to a single people.

*6. "you shall be to Me a kingdom of priests and a holy nation."* These words clarify Israel's unique role as God's covenant partner. The words "kingdom" and "nation" express the idea that national autonomy and ethnic distinctiveness are essential for the fulfillment of Israel's mission. Further, just as the priests devote their lives to the service of the Divine and convey God's will to the people, so Israel is to assume this role among the nations. The word "holy" (*kadosh*) designates that which is set apart from the profane or ordinary. (For more on biblical notions of holiness, see *parashat K'doshim*.)

*8. All the people.* The presence of women in the *am* ("people") is not explicitly indicated by the text. Other public occasions where the Law is read, or covenants are made, expressly indicate the presence of women (Deuteronomy 31:9–13; Joshua 8:35; perhaps II Kings 23:2; Nehemiah 8:2–3). This is not the case at Sinai. However, since the event at Sinai represents the paradigmatic revelation to the Israelite nation, it seems unlikely that women would have been excluded.

## PREPARING FOR THE DIVINE REVELATION (19:9–25)

In this passage, the people prepare for God's self-manifestation, which is commonly associated with storm imagery (see Judges 5:4–5; Isaiah 29:6; 30:30; Nahum 1:3–6; Psalm 18:7–17). Here and in 20:15, the sight of lightning, dense clouds, and smoke,

after." Then Moses reported the people's words to
יהוה, 10and יהוה said to Moses, "Go to the people
and warn them to stay pure today and tomorrow.
Let them wash their clothes. 11Let them be ready
for the third day; for on the third day יהוה will
come down, in the sight of all the people, on
Mount Sinai. 12You shall set bounds for the people
round about, saying, 'Beware of going up the
mountain or touching the border of it. Whoever
touches the mountain shall be put to death 13with-
out being touched—by being either stoned or shot;
beast or person, a trespasser shall not live.' When
the ram's horn sounds a long blast, they may go up
on the mountain."

14Moses came down from the mountain to the
people and warned the people to stay pure, and
they washed their clothes. 15And he said to the people, "Be ready for the third day: [the men among]
you should not go near a woman."

יַאֲמִינוּ לְעוֹלָם וַיַּגֵּד מֹשֶׁה אֶת־דִּבְרֵי הָעָם
אֶל־יְהוָה׃ 10 וַיֹּאמֶר יְהוָה אֶל־מֹשֶׁה לֵךְ
אֶל־הָעָם וְקִדַּשְׁתָּם הַיּוֹם וּמָחָר וְכִבְּסוּ
שִׂמְלֹתָם׃ 11 וְהָיוּ נְכֹנִים לַיּוֹם הַשְּׁלִישִׁי
כִּי ׀ בַּיּוֹם הַשְּׁלִשִׁי יֵרֵד יְהוָה לְעֵינֵי כָל־
הָעָם עַל־הַר סִינָי׃ 12 וְהִגְבַּלְתָּ אֶת־הָעָם
סָבִיב לֵאמֹר הִשָּׁמְרוּ לָכֶם עֲלוֹת בָּהָר וּנְגֹעַ
בְּקָצֵהוּ כָּל־הַנֹּגֵעַ בָּהָר מוֹת יוּמָת׃ 13 לֹא־
תִגַּע בּוֹ יָד כִּי־סָקוֹל יִסָּקֵל אוֹ־יָרֹה יִיָּרֶה
אִם־בְּהֵמָה אִם־אִישׁ לֹא יִחְיֶה בִּמְשֹׁךְ
הַיֹּבֵל הֵמָּה יַעֲלוּ בָהָר׃

14 וַיֵּרֶד מֹשֶׁה מִן־הָהָר אֶל־הָעָם וַיְקַדֵּשׁ
אֶת־הָעָם וַיְכַבְּסוּ שִׂמְלֹתָם׃ 15 וַיֹּאמֶר אֶל־
הָעָם הֱיוּ נְכֹנִים לִשְׁלֹשֶׁת יָמִים אַל־תִּגְּשׁוּ
אֶל־אִשָּׁה׃

along with the sound of thunder and blaring horns, herald God's awesome revelation.

*10. "Go to the people and warn them to stay pure."* God instructs Moses to make sure that the people are in a pure state, expressed here by the root *k-d-sh*, "holy." Although this verse focuses only on washing clothes, other passages specify that attaining a physically holy state also involves washing oneself as well as avoiding sexual relations and contact with impurities (see at Leviticus 12–15; 17:15).

*15. "[the men among] you should not go near a woman."* In vv. 14–15, Moses implements the instructions received in vv. 10–13. He repeats God's charge to the Israelites to stay pure and launder their clothes, while he adds the command not to approach a woman. The prohibition seems to concern sexual intercourse (based on how the synonymous verb *k-r-v* is used in Leviticus 18:14; 20:16; Deuteronomy 22:14; Isaiah 8:3). According to Leviticus 15:18, sexual intercourse renders both parties ritually impure, so that they may not have access to the Sanctuary or objects deemed holy. By specifying a common action that would preclude individuals from participation in the sacred event of revelation, Moses amplifies God's directions to ensure the purity of the people.

The present translation inserts the phrase "[the men among]" in order to show that although the inclusion of women is generally assumed, in this particular verse the imperative must be addressed to men.

Some scholars infer from this that Moses spoke only to the men; they argue that if women were included in the covenant community, Moses would have phrased his warning in mutual terms, something akin to: "Men and women do not go near each other." However, this suggestion can be challenged by the fact that biblical Hebrew rarely addresses sexual relations in mutual terms. Instead, references to sexual relations usually contain a masculine subject and a female object: a man "knows" a woman, "lies" or "lies with" her, "approaches"

[16]On the third day, as morning dawned, there was thunder, and lightning, and a dense cloud upon the mountain, and a very loud blast of the horn; and all the people who were in the camp trembled. [17]Moses led the people out of the camp toward God, and they took their places at the foot of the mountain.

[18]Now Mount Sinai was all in smoke, for יהוה had come down upon it in fire; the smoke rose like the smoke of a kiln, and the whole mountain trembled violently. [19]The blare of the horn grew louder and louder. As Moses spoke, God answered him in thunder. [20]יהוה came down upon Mount Sinai, on the top of the mountain, and יהוה called Moses to the top of the mountain and Moses went up. [21]יהוה said to Moses, "Go down, warn the people not to break through to יהוה to gaze, lest many of them perish. [22]The priests also, who come near יהוה, must stay pure, lest יהוה break out against them." [23]But Moses said to יהוה, "The people cannot come up to Mount Sinai, for You warned us saying, 'Set bounds about the mountain and sanctify it.'" [24]So יהוה said to him, "Go down, and come back together with Aaron; but let not the priests or the people break through to come up to יהוה, lest [God] break out against them." [25]And Moses went down to the people and spoke to them.

16 וַיְהִי֩ בַיּ֨וֹם הַשְּׁלִישִׁ֜י בִּהְיֹ֣ת הַבֹּ֗קֶר וַיְהִי֩
קֹלֹ֨ת וּבְרָקִ֜ים וְעָנָ֤ן כָּבֵד֙ עַל־הָהָ֔ר וְקֹ֥ל שֹׁפָ֖ר
חָזָ֣ק מְאֹ֑ד וַיֶּחֱרַ֥ד כָּל־הָעָ֖ם אֲשֶׁ֥ר בַּֽמַּחֲנֶֽה׃
17 וַיּוֹצֵ֨א מֹשֶׁ֧ה אֶת־הָעָ֛ם לִקְרַ֥את הָֽאֱלֹהִ֖ים
מִן־הַֽמַּחֲנֶ֑ה וַיִּֽתְיַצְּב֖וּ בְּתַחְתִּ֥ית הָהָֽר׃
18 וְהַ֤ר סִינַי֙ עָשַׁ֣ן כֻּלּ֔וֹ מִ֠פְּנֵי אֲשֶׁ֨ר יָרַ֥ד עָלָ֛יו
יְהֹוָ֖ה בָּאֵ֑שׁ וַיַּ֤עַל עֲשָׁנוֹ֙ כְּעֶ֣שֶׁן הַכִּבְשָׁ֔ן וַיֶּחֱרַ֥ד
כָּל־הָהָ֖ר מְאֹֽד׃ 19 וַיְהִי֙ ק֣וֹל הַשֹּׁפָ֔ר הוֹלֵ֖ךְ
וְחָזֵ֣ק מְאֹ֑ד מֹשֶׁ֣ה יְדַבֵּ֔ר וְהָאֱלֹהִ֖ים יַעֲנֶ֥נּוּ
בְקֽוֹל׃ 20 וַיֵּ֧רֶד יְהֹוָ֛ה עַל־הַ֥ר סִינַ֖י אֶל־רֹ֣אשׁ
הָהָ֑ר וַיִּקְרָ֨א יְהֹוָ֧ה לְמֹשֶׁ֛ה אֶל־רֹ֥אשׁ הָהָ֖ר
וַיַּ֥עַל מֹשֶֽׁה׃ 21 וַיֹּ֤אמֶר יְהֹוָה֙ אֶל־מֹשֶׁ֔ה רֵ֖ד
הָעֵ֣ד בָּעָ֑ם פֶּן־יֶהֶרְס֤וּ אֶל־יְהֹוָה֙ לִרְא֔וֹת
וְנָפַ֥ל מִמֶּ֖נּוּ רָֽב׃ 22 וְגַ֧ם הַכֹּהֲנִ֛ים הַנִּגָּשִׁ֥ים
אֶל־יְהֹוָ֖ה יִתְקַדָּ֑שׁוּ פֶּן־יִפְרֹ֥ץ בָּהֶ֖ם יְהֹוָֽה׃
23 וַיֹּ֤אמֶר מֹשֶׁה֙ אֶל־יְהֹוָ֔ה לֹא־יוּכַ֣ל הָעָ֔ם
לַעֲלֹ֖ת אֶל־הַ֣ר סִינָ֑י כִּֽי־אַתָּ֞ה הַעֵדֹ֤תָה בָּ֙נוּ֙
לֵאמֹ֔ר הַגְבֵּ֥ל אֶת־הָהָ֖ר וְקִדַּשְׁתּֽוֹ׃ 24 וַיֹּ֨אמֶר
אֵלָ֤יו יְהֹוָה֙ לֶךְ־רֵ֔ד וְעָלִ֥יתָ אַתָּ֖ה וְאַהֲרֹ֣ן
עִמָּ֑ךְ וְהַכֹּהֲנִ֣ים וְהָעָ֗ם אַל־יֶהֶרְס֛וּ לַעֲלֹ֥ת
אֶל־יְהֹוָ֖ה פֶּן־יִפְרׇץ־בָּֽם׃ 25 וַיֵּ֥רֶד מֹשֶׁ֖ה אֶל־
הָעָ֑ם וַיֹּ֖אמֶר אֲלֵהֶֽם׃ ס

her, or "comes to" her. This language presents the male as the active figure and the female as the passive party. Although this linguistic pattern is problematic for contemporary readers, it means that the address to men in this verse cannot be used to argue that women were excluded from the revelation at Sinai. (See also Another View, p. 421, and Contemporary Reflection, p. 423.)

***19. in thunder.*** Heb. *b'kol*, literally "in a voice," is enigmatic. The identification of God's "voice" with thunder is found in several biblical passages (Psalm 18:14; 29:3); however, since the focus here is on God's discourse with Moses and Israel, "voice" is the more likely meaning. The content of Moses' conversation with God is unclear. Some commentators think that this verse refers to the Decalogue, while others identify it with God's instructions to Moses in vv. 21–22.

20 God spoke all these words, saying:

כ וַיְדַבֵּר אֱלֹהִים אֵת כָּל־הַדְּבָרִים הָאֵלֶּה לֵאמֹר׃ ס

## The Decalogue ("Ten Commandments") (20:1–14)

The unique status of the Decalogue is due to the tradition, found in the framework of Exodus 19–20 and Deuteronomy 4–5, that God recited these rules directly to the people, without the mediation of Moses. Only after the last commandment do the people demand Moses' intervention because they dread the terrifying display of divine power.

While Exodus 19–20 does not provide a specific title for this group of precepts, the label "Ten Words" (*aseret had'varim*) is found elsewhere (34:28; Deuteronomy 4:13; 10:4). The ancient Jewish Greek-speaking community in Egypt translated that Hebrew phrase as *deka logoi* ("ten words"), resulting in the alternative English name "Decalogue." The more common English title "Ten Commandments" is somewhat misleading since the Torah itself does not use the term "commandment" (*mitzvah*) in conjunction with this passage, nor is it clear that every one of its utterances constitutes a command (see at v. 2). Likewise, uncertainty exists as to how to divide these verses into ten discrete commandments. Verse 3 may be grouped with v. 2 or with vv. 4–5, while the prohibition against coveting in v. 14 may be considered a single law or two distinct commandments.

This passage has no specific target audience (such as priests or judges); nor does it refer to any societal institution (like kingship or the Temple) or any specific historical context (though v. 12 may reflect Israel's residence in Canaan). Reward for adherence is mentioned only once (v. 12), while punishments are largely omitted (except for v. 5). Recognition of divine authority and of prior acts of redemption, established in v. 2, seems to be the primary motivating factor for obeying these stipulations.

Exodus 20:2–14 consistently uses the second-person singular, perhaps to impress upon the audience their obligation as individuals to adhere to these teachings. Because the language of address is grammatically masculine, one might infer that these regulations address only men. However, in biblical Hebrew, masculine grammatical form does not specify social gender unless it is used to refer to a definite, particular person. So-called masculine forms often have a gender-neutral function. (See, for example, Deuteronomy 28:68, where masculine singular address at the start of the verse is equivalent to both masculine and feminine plurals at the end of the verse.) Therefore, the Decalogue's masculine singular address does not necessarily mean that only men were addressed. (See further at Exodus 21:2; *Mishpatim*, Another View, p. 445.)

The Torah later records that God also engraved the "Ten Words" upon two stone tablets, which Moses received on the top of Mount Sinai (31:18; Deuteronomy 4:13). Furthermore, these tablets were to be deposited in the Ark of the Covenant, which was to be placed in the "Holy of Holies" of the Tabernacle (25:16). This is akin to the ancient Near Eastern practice of storing a treaty document in the sanctuary of a temple so that the deity could serve as the guardian of its implementation. The medium of stone, as opposed to parchment or papyrus, underlines the permanent validity of these precepts.

### INTRODUCTION (20:1)

This verse establishes that God speaks the Decalogue directly to the people. In contrast, the precepts that follow in the Covenant Collection, like the Tabernacle instructions, are communicated through Moses (see 20:19; 25:2).

[2]I יהוה am your God who brought you out of the land of Egypt, the house of bondage: [3]You shall have no other gods besides Me.

[4]You shall not make for yourself a sculptured image, or any likeness of what is in the heavens above, or on the earth below, or in the waters under the earth. [5]You shall not bow down to them or serve them. For I your God יהוה am an impassioned God, visiting the guilt of the parents upon the

2*אָנֹכִי יְהוָה אֱלֹהֶיךָ אֲשֶׁר הוֹצֵאתִיךָ
מֵאֶרֶץ מִצְרַיִם מִבֵּית עֲבָדִים 3 לֹא־יִהְיֶה
לְךָ אֱלֹהִים אֲחֵרִים עַל־פָּנָי׃
4 לֹא־תַעֲשֶׂה לְךָ פֶּסֶל וְכָל־תְּמוּנָה אֲשֶׁר
בַּשָּׁמַיִם מִמַּעַל וַאֲשֶׁר בָּאָרֶץ מִתָּחַת וַאֲשֶׁר
בַּמַּיִם מִתַּחַת לָאָרֶץ׃ 5 לֹא־תִשְׁתַּחֲוֶה לָהֶם
וְלֹא תָעָבְדֵם כִּי אָנֹכִי יְהוָה אֱלֹהֶיךָ אֵל

*This accent pattern for the Decalogue is the one that is customarily used for private study. (Masoretic tradition also includes an accent pattern that is used for public reading.) Verses are numbered according to a modern convention.

## THE COMMANDMENTS
(20:2–14)

The "Ten Words" have a discernable arrangement, with a separation between those that dictate correct behavior regarding God and those that apply to the treatment of other human beings. Note, for instance, that the first statement opens with "your God," while the last one closes with "your neighbor." Further, the first five utterances mention "יהוה your God" five times, while the second five contain no references to God. The fifth commandment, which mandates honoring one's parents, serves as a bridge between the two halves; it contains both religious and social aspects, and both God and parents claim authority over the individual. Within each grouping of five, the directives are arranged in order of decreasing severity. (These foundational precepts are repeated, with minor variations, in Deuteronomy 5:6–18.)

*2. I יהוה am your God.* This verse, in which God is self-identified as the One who took Israel out of Egypt, serves as the introduction and basis for all that follows. It is because God redeemed Israel from Egypt that God reserves the right to command exclusive fidelity (v. 3).

*3. You shall have no other gods besides Me.* This command of fidelity to only one god is unique in the ancient Near East. Texts from this period present a generally tolerant religious environment: the gods did not mind the worship of their "peers" as long as their own needs (in the form of donations of precious goods, food, and drink) were not neglected. This precept does not negate the existence of other gods, and may be pre-monotheistic (see also Deuteronomy 6:4). Biblical scholars compare Israel's covenant with God to ancient Near Eastern international vassal–overlord treaties. Marriage is another, more familiar relationship that shared this kind of exclusivity; hence, the prophets develop the metaphor of God as husband and Israel as wife (see Isaiah 54, Jeremiah 3, Hosea 1–3).

*4. You shall not make for yourself a sculptured image.* Prevailing Jewish tradition understands vv. 4–6, forbidding the worship of images, as a continuation of v. 3. Yet if v. 3 is interpreted as the first stipulation, then v. 4 begins the second. The reason offered for the prohibition is that God communicated at Sinai only through a voice (Deuteronomy 4:12–16). Idols are therefore incompatible with the historic self-disclosure of God's nature. Further, the worship of God through fixed representations limits the range of the Deity's attributes.

*5. impassioned.* See at Deuteronomy 5:9.

*visiting the guilt of the parents upon the children.* While God may practice trans-generational reward and punishment, Israelite courts are forbidden to do so (Deuteronomy 24:16).

*parents.* Heb. *avot,* sometimes translated as "fathers." Here, however, the principle is more general: with regard to the covenant with God, the

children, upon the third and upon the fourth generations of those who reject Me, 6but showing kindness to the thousandth generation of those who love Me and keep My commandments.

7You shall not swear falsely by the name of your God יהוה; for יהוה will not clear one who swears falsely by God's name.

קַנָּ֔א פֹּ֠קֵד עֲוֺ֨ן אָבֹ֧ת עַל־בָּנִ֛ים עַל־שִׁלֵּשִׁ֥ים
וְעַל־רִבֵּעִ֖ים לְשֹׂנְאָֽי׃ 6 וְעֹ֥שֶׂה חֶ֖סֶד לַאֲלָפִ֑ים
לְאֹהֲבַ֖י וּלְשֹׁמְרֵ֥י מִצְוֺתָֽי׃ ס
7 לֹ֥א תִשָּׂ֛א אֶת־שֵׁם־יְהֹוָ֥ה אֱלֹהֶ֖יךָ לַשָּׁ֑וְא
כִּ֣י לֹ֤א יְנַקֶּה֙ יְהֹוָ֔ה אֵ֛ת אֲשֶׁר־יִשָּׂ֥א אֶת־שְׁמ֖וֹ
לַשָּֽׁוְא׃ פ

8Remember the sabbath day and keep it holy. 9Six days you shall labor and do all your work, 10but the seventh day is a sabbath of your God יהוה: you shall not do any work—you, your son or daughter, your male or female slave, or your cattle, or the stranger who is within your settlements. 11For in six days יהוה made heaven and earth and sea—and all that is in them—and then rested on the seventh day; therefore יהוה blessed the sabbath day and hallowed it.

8 זָכ֛וֹר אֶת־י֥וֹם הַשַּׁבָּ֖ת לְקַדְּשֽׁוֹ׃ 9 שֵׁ֤שֶׁת
יָמִים֙ תַּעֲבֹ֔ד וְעָשִׂ֖יתָ כׇּל־מְלַאכְתֶּֽךָ׃ 10 וְי֙וֹם֙
הַשְּׁבִיעִ֔י שַׁבָּ֖ת לַיהֹוָ֣ה אֱלֹהֶ֑יךָ לֹֽא־תַעֲשֶׂ֣ה
כׇל־מְלָאכָ֡ה אַתָּ֣ה ׀ וּבִנְךָ֣ וּבִתֶּ֗ךָ עַבְדְּךָ֤
וַאֲמָתְךָ֙ וּבְהֶמְתֶּ֔ךָ וְגֵרְךָ֖ אֲשֶׁ֥ר בִּשְׁעָרֶֽיךָ׃
11 כִּ֣י שֵֽׁשֶׁת־יָמִים֩ עָשָׂ֨ה יְהֹוָ֜ה אֶת־הַשָּׁמַ֣יִם
וְאֶת־הָאָ֗רֶץ אֶת־הַיָּם֙ וְאֶת־כׇּל־אֲשֶׁר־בָּ֔ם
וַיָּ֖נַח בַּיּ֣וֹם הַשְּׁבִיעִ֑י עַל־כֵּ֗ן בֵּרַ֧ךְ יְהֹוָ֛ה
אֶת־י֥וֹם הַשַּׁבָּ֖ת וַיְקַדְּשֵֽׁהוּ׃ ס

12Honor your father and your mother, that you may long endure on the land that your God יהוה is assigning to you.

12 כַּבֵּ֥ד אֶת־אָבִ֖יךָ וְאֶת־אִמֶּ֑ךָ לְמַ֙עַן֙ יַאֲרִכ֣וּן
יָמֶ֔יךָ עַ֚ל הָאֲדָמָ֔ה אֲשֶׁר־יְהֹוָ֥ה אֱלֹהֶ֖יךָ נֹתֵ֥ן
לָֽךְ׃ ס

deeds (and misdeeds) of both mothers and fathers will matter.

*7. You shall not swear falsely.* This verse prohibits the misuse of the divine name. Commentators debate whether this refers specifically to invoking God's name when taking an oath or more broadly to using God's name frivolously or improperly.

*10. sabbath.* This is an institution unique to ancient Israel.

*you shall not do any work.* This clause introduces a list of seven categories of individuals who are obligated to rest on the Sabbath, beginning with the word *atah*, the masculine singular second-person pronoun. On the scope of grammatically masculine address, see the introduction to the present unit (p. 416). Paradoxically, it is the conspicuous omission of the wife that signals her inclusion here: if she is not addressed by "you," then are we to assume that the verse burdens her with work—while her children, slaves, and draft animals rest? This can hardly be the case. As Tikva Frymer-Kensky writes, "the omission of a phrase 'and your wife' shows that the 'you' that the law addresses includes both women and men, each treated as a separate moral agent" ("Deuteronomy," *Women's Bible Commentary,* 1992, p. 59). Confirmation of a gender-inclusive "you" comes from comparing this verse to the similar construction in Deuteronomy 12:18, where logically and in light of 12:7 the word *atah* must have an inclusive sense.

*12. Honor your father and your mother.* The importance of respect for parents is underlined by its inclusion in the first five precepts, which concern proper behavior toward God. This command is the only one in the Decalogue for which a reward, extended residence in the land of Israel, is promised.

[13]You shall not murder. You shall not commit adultery. You shall not steal. You shall not bear false witness against your neighbor.

[14]You shall not covet your neighbor's house: you shall not covet your neighbor's wife, nor male nor female slave, nor ox nor ass, nor anything that is your neighbor's.

[15]All the people witnessed the thunder and lightning, the blare of the horn and the mountain

13 לֹ֥א תִּֿרְצָ֖ח ס לֹ֣א תִּֿנְאָ֑ף ס לֹ֣א
תִּֿגְנֹ֔ב ס לֹא־תַעֲנֶ֥ה בְרֵעֲךָ֖ עֵ֥ד שָֽׁקֶר׃ ס
14 לֹ֥א תַחְמֹ֖ד בֵּ֣ית רֵעֶ֑ךָ ס לֹֽא־תַחְמֹ֞ד
אֵ֣שֶׁת רֵעֶ֗ךָ וְעַבְדּ֤וֹ וַאֲמָתוֹ֙ וְשׁוֹר֣וֹ וַחֲמֹר֔וֹ וְכֹ֖ל
אֲשֶׁ֥ר לְרֵעֶֽךָ׃ פ

15 וְכָל־הָעָם֩ רֹאִ֨ים אֶת־הַקּוֹלֹ֜ת וְאֶת־
הַלַּפִּידִ֗ם וְאֵת֙ ק֣וֹל הַשֹּׁפָ֔ר וְאֶת־הָהָ֖ר עָשֵׁ֑ן

It may reflect the legal custom found in other ancient Near Eastern texts that inheritance of property is conditional upon proper treatment of parents in their old age. The Torah outlines various offenses against parents, some of which are considered capital crimes: striking, cursing, insulting, and insubordination (as in 21:15, 17; Deuteronomy 21:18; 27:16). The inclusion of the mother alongside the father is consistent in all of these laws. | The specific activities that constitute "honor" are enumerated in post-biblical Jewish texts, not in the Torah.

*13. **You shall not commit adultery.*** Adultery is defined in Israel and the ancient Near East as sexual relations between a betrothed or married woman and any man other than her fiancé or husband. A married man was guilty of adultery only if his sexual partner officially "belonged" to another, since a man could legitimately take another unmarried woman as wife. The Torah's legal texts consider adultery a capital offense and demand the execution of both the woman and her paramour (see Leviticus 18:20; 20:10; Deuteronomy 22:22–24; compare Hosea 2:4–9). Such harsh punishments reflect a concern for paternity and the transmission of property by men to their own offspring.

***false witness.*** See at Deuteronomy 5:17.

*14.* The traditional paragraphing in a Torah scroll properly breaks this verse into two clauses. In the first, the object of "covet" is "house," which should be understood as "household" (as in Genesis 7:1). As the present translation indicates, the second clause enumerates those objects that constitute an Israelite household, starting with the most important, one's wife.

***covet.*** This refers to an intense desire for an object, and perhaps the scheming to acquire it (34:24; Joshua 7:21). See also at Deuteronomy 5:18.

***your neighbor's wife.*** Some scholars have argued that if the Decalogue were addressed to women as well as men, it would have included a parallel prohibition against coveting "your neighbor's husband." But the lack of mutuality here does not rule out that the previous provisions of the Decalogue addressed themselves to both men and women. Rather, each provision is addressed to whomever it applies. In ancient Israel, marriage was not a symmetrical arrangement: typically a man was in a position to take a woman into the household as a wife, but typically a woman could not take a man into her household as a husband. That alone would seem to account for why "husband" is not mentioned in this verse, as Tikva Frymer-Kensky has pointed out ("Deuteronomy," *Women's Bible Commentary*, 1992, p. 59). (See also *Mishpatim*, Another View, p. 445.)

## *The People's Response and the First Instruction* (20:15–23)

The overwhelming display of divine might inspires such fear that the people withdraw and demand that Moses assume the role of mediator (vv. 15–16). The belief that seeing God could be lethal is found elsewhere in the Bible (Genesis 32:31;

smoking; and when the people saw it, they fell back and stood at a distance. [16]"You speak to us," they said to Moses, "and we will obey; but let not God speak to us, lest we die." [17]Moses answered the people, "Be not afraid; for God has come only in order to test you, and in order that the fear of God may be ever with you, so that you do not go astray." [18]So the people remained at a distance, while Moses approached the thick cloud where God was.

[19]יהוה said to Moses:

Thus shall you say to the Israelites: You yourselves saw that I spoke to you from the very heavens: [20]With Me, therefore, you shall not make any gods of silver, nor shall you make for yourselves any gods of gold. [21]Make for Me an altar of earth and sacrifice on it your burnt offerings and your sacrifices of well-being, your sheep and your oxen; in every place where I cause My name to be mentioned I will come to you and bless you. [22]And if you make for Me an altar of stones, do not build it of hewn stones; for by wielding your tool upon them you have profaned them. [23]Do not ascend My altar by steps, that your nakedness may not be exposed upon it.

וַיַּ֤רְא הָעָם֙ וַיָּנֻ֔עוּ וַיַּֽעַמְד֖וּ מֵֽרָחֹֽק׃ 16 וַיֹּֽאמְרוּ֙ אֶל־מֹשֶׁ֔ה דַּבֵּר־אַתָּ֥ה עִמָּ֖נוּ וְנִשְׁמָ֑עָה וְאַל־יְדַבֵּ֥ר עִמָּ֛נוּ אֱלֹהִ֖ים פֶּן־נָמֽוּת׃ 17 וַיֹּ֨אמֶר מֹשֶׁ֣ה אֶל־הָעָ֗ם אַל־תִּירָ֒אוּ֒ כִּ֣י לְבַֽעֲב֗וּר נַסּ֤וֹת אֶתְכֶם֙ בָּ֣א הָֽאֱלֹהִ֔ים וּבַֽעֲב֗וּר תִּֽהְיֶ֧ה יִרְאָת֛וֹ עַל־פְּנֵיכֶ֖ם לְבִלְתִּ֥י תֶֽחֱטָֽאוּ׃ 18 וַיַּֽעֲמֹ֥ד הָעָ֖ם מֵֽרָחֹ֑ק וּמֹשֶׁה֙ נִגַּ֣שׁ אֶל־הָ֣עֲרָפֶ֔ל אֲשֶׁר־שָׁ֖ם הָֽאֱלֹהִֽים׃ ס

19 וַיֹּ֥אמֶר יְהֹוָ֖ה אֶל־מֹשֶׁ֑ה כֹּ֤ה תֹאמַר֙ אֶל־בְּנֵ֣י יִשְׂרָאֵ֔ל אַתֶּ֣ם רְאִיתֶ֔ם כִּ֚י מִן־הַשָּׁמַ֔יִם דִּבַּ֖רְתִּי עִמָּכֶֽם׃ 20 לֹ֥א תַֽעֲשׂ֖וּן אִתִּ֑י אֱלֹ֤הֵי כֶ֨סֶף֙ וֵֽאלֹהֵ֣י זָהָ֔ב לֹ֥א תַֽעֲשׂ֖וּ לָכֶֽם׃ 21 מִזְבַּ֣ח אֲדָמָה֮ תַּֽעֲשֶׂה־לִּי֒ וְזָֽבַחְתָּ֣ עָלָ֗יו אֶת־עֹֽלֹתֶ֙יךָ֙ וְאֶת־שְׁלָמֶ֔יךָ אֶת־צֹֽאנְךָ֖ וְאֶת־בְּקָרֶ֑ךָ בְּכָל־הַמָּקוֹם֙ אֲשֶׁ֣ר אַזְכִּ֣יר אֶת־שְׁמִ֔י אָב֥וֹא אֵלֶ֖יךָ וּבֵֽרַכְתִּֽיךָ׃ 22 וְאִם־מִזְבַּ֤ח אֲבָנִים֙ תַּֽעֲשֶׂה־לִּ֔י לֹֽא־תִבְנֶ֥ה אֶתְהֶ֖ן גָּזִ֑ית כִּ֧י חַרְבְּךָ֛ הֵנַ֥פְתָּ עָלֶ֖יהָ וַתְּחַֽלְלֶֽהָ׃ 23 וְלֹֽא־תַֽעֲלֶ֥ה בְמַֽעֲלֹ֖ת עַל־מִזְבְּחִ֑י אֲשֶׁ֛ר לֹֽא־תִגָּלֶ֥ה עֶרְוָֽתְךָ֖ עָלָֽיו׃ פ

Exodus 33:20; Judges 6:22–23; 13:22). The revelatory experience at Sinai becomes the basis for the first instruction following the Decalogue (vv. 19–23): Because Israel's experience of God at Sinai was auditory and not directly visual, their worship of God should exclude physical representations. This passage introduces the precepts of the Covenant Collection that follow in the next parashah.

—*Elaine Goodfriend*

# Another View

When God tells Moses to command the people to sanctify themselves, wash their clothes, and be ready for the divine revelation, God emphasizes that the people should be instructed not to go up or touch the mountain (19:10–13). Moses begins by faithfully repeating God's commands, yet he concludes, not by reiterating God's warning not to touch the mountain, but instead by admonishing the Israelites not to go near a woman (19:15). Feminists have wrestled with this disturbing verse and its implications. Does this formulation mean that Moses was only speaking to the men? Moses seems to have subverted God's command to all the people by speaking only to half the Israelites.

Moses' striking deviation from God's command is troubling well beyond the feminist focus. Moses' alteration of God's command raises the central question of who is the final authority on what God really says. Which version of the command is authoritative? Is Moses faithfully transmitting God's words? Is the text accurately presenting God's instructions? And, ultimately, what gives Moses or the text the right to report God's words differently from the way in which they were originally delivered?

A clue can be found in the genre of this passage. Exodus 19:9–15 fits the ancient literary form of the Command/Performance formula, in which a divine command is expected to be transmitted by the messenger in identical language. According to this convention, any deviation from the initial command in the transmission draws attention to itself and is highly significant. What is the significance of Moses' alteration of the divine word here?

This text, with its deviation from the expected Command/Performance convention, cries out "*darsheini*" ("Interpret me!") and so invites readers—ancient as well as modern—to grapple with revelation. The entire history of interpretation of our sacred texts, from the Mishnah to modern feminist midrash, is empowered by Moses' audacious transformation of God's words. Exodus 19:9–15 subverts omniscient external authority and hands authority to the reader. This troubling passage empowers all of us to read, interpret, and find meaning in this parashah and its contradictions.

*Interpretation of sacred texts is empowered by Moses' transformation of God's words.*

—*Diane M. Sharon*

# Post-biblical Interpretations

***Jethro priest of Midian . . . heard*** (18:1). The Rabbis wondered what prompted Jethro, priest of Midian, father of Moses' wife, Zipporah, to visit Moses in the wilderness. One tradition concludes that Jethro learned of the revelation at Mt. Sinai. Another sage suggests that Jethro heard about the parting of the Sea of Reeds. The Rabbis go on to say that Jethro converted to Judaism because he was so impressed by God's power in redeeming Israel from Egypt (*M'chilta, Amalek* 3; *Sh'mot Rabbah* 27.6).

Discussion of Jethro's acceptance of Judaism in this passage in *M'chilta* reminded the Rabbis of another supposed convert, Rahab the harlot—who was said to have been, along with Sarah, Abigail, and Esther, one of the most beautiful women who ever lived (BT *M'gillah* 15a). In Joshua 2:10–11, Rahab tells Joshua's spies that when she heard of the parting of the Sea of Reeds, she became convinced that "your God יהוה is God in heaven above and here on earth" (Joshua 2:11). Rahab is said to have gone beyond all other converts in her recognition of God's great powers (*M'chilta, Amalek* 3). When she was fifty years old, she converted and asked God to forgive her for her life as a prostitute, reminding God that she had enabled Joshua's spies to escape from Jericho. According to some rabbinic sources, Rahab even married Joshua (BT *M'gillah* 14b) and was rewarded by having priests and prophets of Israel among her descendants (*Sifrei B'midbar* 78). Her story, like Jethro's, represents a powerful message that neither gender, foreign origins, nor a dubious past is a barrier to those who sincerely wish to join the Jewish people.

***So Jethro... took Zipporah, Moses' wife, after she had been sent home*** (18:2). The biblical text gives no information on when or why Moses sent Zipporah and her two sons back to Jethro. A tradition in *M'chilta, Amalek* 3, imagines that after Moses received the divine call to redeem Israel from slavery, he set out for Egypt with his family. When he encountered Aaron on the way (4:27), Moses introduced his wife and sons. Aaron responded, "We are worrying about those already there and now you bring upon us these newcomers!" At that moment, Moses said to Zipporah, "Go to your father's house." Based on the use of the verb "sent" (*shalach*) both here and in the description of divorce in Deuteronomy 24:1, the Rabbis concluded that Moses divorced his wife, though they debated whether he did so with a *get* (a bill of divorce) or simply by an oral statement (*M'chilta, Amalek* 3).

***Thus shall you say to the house of Jacob and declare to the children of Israel*** (19:3). The Rabbis were certain that divine words contained no repetition. Thus, *M'chilta, Bachodesh* 2, explains that *house of Jacob* refers to the Israelite women, while *children of Israel* refers to the men. (In 1917, Sarah Schenirer of Cracow, Poland, founded what is now a worldwide network of Orthodox schools for girls, which takes its name from the rabbinic interpretation of this verse: *Beis Yaakov*, The House of Jacob.) A second interpretation of this

*"House of Jacob" refers to the women; "children of Israel" refers to the men.*

juxtaposition suggests that *Thus shall you say* was a divine directive that Moses should instruct the women in a mild tone, while the parallel verb *declare* implied that Moses should be strict with the men. The result was that God's revelation was accessible to everyone.

***Honor your father and your mother*** (20:12). A statement in *M'chilta, Bachodesh* 8, observes that honoring parents is equal to honoring God. The Rabbis also noticed that this verse puts honoring father before honoring mother, while in Leviticus 19:3 fearing one's mother precedes fearing one's father. They explained this discrepancy as being the result of the parents' different gender roles: "a man honors his mother more than his father because she sways him with persuasive words," whereas "a man is more afraid of his father than of his mother because his father teaches him Torah."

—*Judith R. Baskin*

# Contemporary Reflection

READ FROM a feminist perspective, *Yitro* contains one of the most painful verses in the Torah. At the formative moment in Jewish history, when presumably the whole people of Israel stands in awe and trembling at the base of Mount Sinai waiting for God to descend upon the mountain and establish the covenant, Moses turns to the assembled community and says, "Be ready for the third day: do not go near a woman" (19:15). Moses wants to ensure that the people are ritually prepared to receive God's presence, and an emission of semen renders both a man and his female partner temporarily unfit to approach the sacred (see Leviticus 15:16–18). But Moses does not say, "Men and women do not go near each other." Instead, at this central juncture in the Jewish saga, he renders women invisible as part of the congregation about to enter into the covenant.

These words are deeply troubling for at least two reasons. First, they are a paradigm of the treatment of women as "other," both elsewhere in this portion and throughout the Torah. Again and again, the Torah seems to assume that the Israelite nation consists only of male heads of household. It records the experiences of men, but not the experiences of women. For example, the tenth commandment—"You shall not covet your neighbor's wife" (20:14)—presupposes a community of male hearers.

Second, entry into the covenant at Sinai is not just a one-time event, but an experience to be reappropriated by every generation (Deuteronomy 29:13–14). Every time the portion is chanted, whether as part of the annual cycle of Torah readings or as a special reading for Shavuot, women are thrust aside once again, eavesdropping on a conversation among men, and between men and God. The text thus potentially evokes a continuing sense of exclusion and disorientation in women. The whole Jewish people supposedly stood at Sinai. Were we there? Were we not there? If we were there, what did we hear when the men heard "do not go near a woman"? If we were not there originally, can we be there now? Since we are certainly part of the community now, how could we not have been there at that founding moment?

Given the seriousness of these questions, it is important to note the larger narrative context of Moses' injunction to the men not to go near a woman. When the Israelites arrive at Sinai on the third new moon after leaving Egypt, Moses twice ascends the mountain to talk with God. After he brings God the report

*There is no revelation without interpretation, and the process of interpretation is ongoing.*

that the people have agreed to accept the covenant, God gives Moses careful instructions for readying everyone for the moment of revelation: "Go to the people and warn them to stay pure today and tomorrow," God says. "Let them wash their clothes. Let them be ready for the third day; for on the third day יהוה will come down, in the sight of all the people, on Mount Sinai" (19:10–11). It is striking that *God's* instructions to Moses are addressed to the whole community. It is *Moses* who changes them, who glosses God's message, who assumes that the instructions are meant for only half the people. Thus, at this early stage in Jewish history, Moses filters and interprets God's commands through a patriarchal lens. His words are a paradigm of the treatment of women, but a complex one. They show how Jewish tradition has repeatedly excluded women, but also the way in which that exclusion must be understood as a *distortion* of revelation.

Interestingly, the Rabbis seem to have been disturbed by the implication of women's absence from

Sinai, because they read women into the text in a variety of ways. *B'reishit Rabbah* 28.2 understands Exodus 19:3 ("Thus shall you say to the house of Jacob and declare to the children of Israel") to mean that "the house of Jacob" refers to the women and "the children of Israel" refers to the men. According to the midrash, the order of the verse suggests that God sent Moses to the women with the Torah *first.* Perhaps, the sages speculate, God regretted the mistake of not directly giving Eve the commandment concerning the forbidden fruit and so resolved not to repeat it. Besides, the Rabbis note, women are more careful in observing religious precepts, and they are the ones who will instruct their children. Rashi, commenting on the Mishnah (*Shabbat* 9:3; BT *Shabbat* 86a), interprets Exodus 19:15 ("Do not go near a woman") as a stricture specifically designed to enable Israel's women to be present at Sinai. Since semen loses its power to create impurity after three days, Moses' instruction to the men guarantees that women will remain ritually pure, even if they discharge residual semen during the Revelation. In other words, without ever naming Moses' distortion of God's words directly, the Rabbis sought to reverse its effects.

Several lessons can be drawn from this. One is the inseparability of revelation and interpretation. There is no revelation without interpretation; the foundational experience of revelation also involves a crucial act of interpretation. Second, we learn that the process of interpretation is ongoing. What Moses does, the Rabbis in this case seek to undo. While they reiterate and reinforce the exclusion of women in many contexts, they mitigate it in others. Third, insofar as the task of interpretation is continuing, it now lies with us. If women's absence from Sinai is unthinkable to the Rabbis—despite the fact that they repeatedly reenact that absence in their own work—how much more must it be unthinkable to women and men today who function in communities in which women are full Jews? We have the privilege and the burden of recovering the divine words reverberating behind the silences in the text, recreating women's understandings of revelation throughout Jewish history.

—*Judith Plaskow*

# Voices

## The Ineffable Name

Hava Pincas-Cohen (transl. Miriyam Glazer)

*Exodus 19–20*

Everyone's gone to the mount already and
they're waiting,
waiting to see, waiting in great quiet—
even, strangely, the camels and the donkeys—
In this quiet not a bird twitters
or children on their fathers' shoulders.
An overwhelming quiet, as if before some
wondrous thing. Still—I wanted time
to hang out the laundry,
time for myself to freshen up
and I warmed the baby's milk so he won't get
hungry—
and God forbid, cry at the wrong moment,
however long till then. You can expect
the laundry to dry—but the baby?
No one knew.
And I saw that a soft breeze, like the breath of a
sleeping man, passed
through the laundry and ballooned the belly
of my nightgown and the Sabbath tablecloth
was a white sail in the middle of the desert
and we left there on the sky-blue
far away to the place where

we'll split open pomegranates and eat their juice
to the place where
love is
the ineffable name.

## We All Stood Together

Merle Feld

*Exodus 19–20*

My brother and I were at Sinai
He kept a journal
of what he saw,
of what he heard,
of what it all meant to him.

I wish I had such a record
of what happened to me there

It seems like every time I want to write
I can't—
I'm always holding a baby,
one of my own,
or one for a friend,
always holding a baby
so my hands are never free
to write things down.

And then
as time passes,
the particulars,
the hard data,
the who what when where why,
slip away from me,
and all I'm left with is
the feeling.

But feelings are just sounds
the vowel barking of a mute.

My brother is so sure of what he heard—
after all he's got a record of it—
consonant after consonant after consonant.

If we remembered it together
we could recreate holy time
sparks flying.

## *Zipporah's Return*

Bonnie Lyons

*Exodus 18:2–5*

Word of the divine events in Egypt reached us
and my father took us to Moses in the desert.
Now *I* was the stranger in an alien land
until Miriam told me
I was the fourth of the magic circle—
that his mother, and Pharaoh's daughter, and
Miriam herself had all saved him
and I was welcomed and more than welcome
among the women.

## *Prophet Miriam at Mount St. Helens, Washington, USA*

Helen Papell

*Exodus 19:14–15*

I was with the women at Mt. Sinai.
The cloud spoke out of a hole
but we were pushed away by my brother Moses.
He said Only I
am summoned by the voice. Only I
may climb the lava that spurts like semen.

I never asked Does the Eternal speak
only through men?
No woman had been made strong by boys'
games
my legs trembled like twigs
in the wind echoing the voice.

Other places, other volcanoes: always
lava erupted and dried over the body
of the mountain. I never asked
Does the Eternal speak only through men?

A postcard brought me here to Mount St.
Helens.
In the picture, tree trunks sprawl
like scorched bones
waiting for a mass grave

but where is the lava? My brother
would look for it.
A ranger says No lava flow. This volcano
kicked out her north top
screamed a birth of rock and ash.
She gives me ash hardened into pumice. Holes
sprinkle it. She says
Each hole to gather the dust of decayed wood,
a drop of rain, a seed
flying from beyond the dead trees.

Here at Mount St. Helens
I know the Eternal speaks also
through me: one of the holes shimmers water
like a well
from another a green stem pokes its head.

## *Mother*

Alicia Suskin Ostriker

*Exodus 20:12*

although I have put an ocean between us
still do you know how I lie awake at night
the eye in my right palm pictures you
sitting amid your litter, feet buried
by accumulated jars of buttons,
glasses lost beneath a decade of bank statements
and funny poems,
hands folded under your chin, staring
at nothing, preparing to be blind
and helpless, for fifty years
it has tortured me that I cannot save you from
madness
and that I do not love you enough

what is enough
nothing is enough

# משפטים ✦ *Mishpatim*

EXODUS 21:1–24:18

## *Rules for Life in a Covenant Community*

PARASHAT MISHPATIM ("rules") presents the culmination of the covenant process that began with the preparations for the revelation on Mount Sinai (Exodus 19). While the so-called Ten Commandments articulate the general principles of the covenant between God and Israel (20:1–14), this parashah presents specific stipulations. This collection of case rulings and rules, referred to as the "Book of the Covenant" (24:7), the "Covenant Code," or the "Covenant Collection," covers a range of topics—from criminal and civil matters like murder, assault, and theft, to moral and religious precepts, such as treatment of the stranger and observance of the festivals. Although the stipulations in this parashah address an array of subjects, they do not constitute a comprehensive legal code. Many essential aspects of life in biblical times, like marriage, adoption, or inheritance, do not appear here.

The contents of the Book of the Covenant can be divided into two groups of laws. The rules in the first group (21:2–22:16) are formulated mainly as case laws, meaning that the text describes a specific scenario and its legal consequences: "When an ox gores a man or a woman to death, the ox shall be stoned" (21:28).

As for the second group (22:17–23:19), many of its regulations are phrased as unconditional imperatives, similar to language of the Decalogue: "You shall not boil a kid in its mother's milk" (23:19).

*Parashat Mishpatim* refers to a remarkable number of women; however, like the men in this parashah, they are not named characters but rather different types of female figures who warranted legal consideration in certain situations. We read about the wife of the Hebrew slave (21:3–5), the daughter sold into slavery (21:7–11), the mother verbally or physically abused (21:15, 17), the female slave beaten by her master (21:20–21, 26–27), the pregnant woman who suffers a miscarriage and possible death because of a brawl (21:22–25), the woman gored by an ox (21:28–32), the unbetrothed young woman (22:15–16), the sorceress condemned to death (22:17), and the vulnerable widow (22:21–23). Furthermore, Exodus 21 repeatedly equates females and males regarding compensation for assault and injury (vv. 15, 16, 20, 26, 28, 29, 31, 32). This collection also treats other types of women implicitly, such as the slave owner (21:2, 10, and elsewhere), the debtor mother (21:7), the impudent daughter (21:15), the brawler (21:18, 22), the fatherless daughter (22:21), and more.

*This parashah refers to a remarkable number of women.*

After Moses communicates these stipulations to the people, they voice their enthusiastic acceptance of the terms of the covenant: "All that יהוה has spoken we will faithfully do! (*naaseh v'nishma*)" (24:7). The parashah ends with Moses' ascent of the mountain to receive two stone tablets, the physical symbol of the new legal relationship wedding God and Israel.

—*Elaine Goodfriend*

## *Outline*

I. The Covenant Collection (21:1–23:33)

- A. Introduction (21:1)
- B. Civil and criminal matters (21:2–22:16)
  1. Treatment of male and female Hebrew indentured servants (21:2–11)
  2. Capital crimes: murder, abuse of parents, kidnapping (21:12–17)
  3. Bodily injury caused by people and livestock (21:18–32)
  4. Property damage: injury to livestock, theft, crop damage, safeguarded property (21:33–22:14)
  5. Seduction of an unbetrothed woman (22:15–16)
- C. Assorted religious and social precepts (22:17–23:19)
  1. Prohibitions of sorcery, bestiality, and apostasy (22:17–19)
  2. Proper treatment of the disadvantaged (22:20–26)
  3. Obligations to God (22:27–30)
  4. Judicial conduct (23:1–3)
  5. Treatment of the enemy, needy, and stranger (23:4–9)
  6. Religious calendar with appended food prohibition (23:10–19)
- D. Divine promises and warnings (23:20–33)

II. The Covenant Ratification Ritual (24:1–18)

| | |
|---|---|
| These are the rules that you shall set before them: | כא וְאֵ֙לֶּה֙ הַמִּשְׁפָּטִ֔ים אֲשֶׁ֥ר תָּשִׂ֖ים לִפְנֵיהֶֽם׃ |

## *The Covenant Collection* (21:1–23:33)

In conveying the Decalogue (Exodus 20:2–14), God addressed the people directly; but because the people fear the terrifying display of divine might (20:18–21), Moses mediates the regulations that now follow. The Book of the Covenant exhibits numerous similarities in content, form, and organization to the law collections of Israel's neighbors. Yet biblical law departs from ancient Near Eastern jurisprudence in several ways. Israel was unique in its belief that God—not a king—authored the rules governing interactions with humans and the Divine. Another distinguishing feature is that all Israelites were charged with knowing the precepts in order to ensure their observance.

### INTRODUCTION (21:1)

The inclusive nature of Israelite law is seen in this verse, when God instructs Moses to set the rules before the people. In contrast, the Laws of Hammurabi stipulate that only the aggrieved party could have the laws read to him; in Mesopotamian society, public knowledge of the law was not assumed.

### CIVIL AND CRIMINAL MATTERS (21:2–22:16)

This section presents various cases involving the mistreatment of humans, livestock, or property, and the corresponding adjudications of those misdeeds. The Book of the Covenant commences with regulations concerning the emancipation of Hebrew indentured servants (21:2–11). While this arrangement might seem jarring at first glance—since it follows so closely after the story of the Israelites' deliverance from bondage—it makes sense when we understand it as an attempt to limit Israelite servitude.

In what comprises the bulk of this section (21:12–22:14), laws are arranged according to decreasing severity, with crimes against property in the last passage. The section closes with consideration of a case of seduction (22:15–16).

#### *Treatment of Male and Female Hebrew Indentured Servants* (21:2–11)

Whereas the Israelites were subject to corvée labor in Egypt (see at 1:11), this passage describes a more restricted form of indentured service, also called debt-slavery. An Israelite might be reduced to indentured servitude because of extreme poverty, debt, or in restitution for theft; the individual was not chattel owned by the master (see at v. 7).

In comparison to other ancient Near Eastern legal collections, several regulations in this parashah are somewhat protective of servants (see 21:2–11, 20–21, 26–27, 32). Most biblical rulings treat male and females slaves equally (see, for instance, 20:10

The English text now reflects the fact that many legal principles apply to women.
ANOTHER VIEW ➤ 445

Jews who translated the Bible in the 3rd century B.C.E. understood these verses differently.
POST-BIBLICAL INTERPRETATIONS ➤ 445

The Torah is truthful with us, although that truth does not always make us happy.
CONTEMPORARY REFLECTION ➤ 447

Help me say goodbye / to the child / who was growing within me, / to the dreams I bore.
VOICES ➤ 449

[2]When you acquire a Hebrew slave, that person shall serve six years—and shall go free in the seventh year, without payment. [3]If [a male slave] came single, he shall leave single; if he had a wife, his wife shall leave with him. [4]If his master gave him a wife, and she has borne him children, the wife and her children shall belong to the master, and he shall leave alone. [5]But if the slave declares, "I love my master, and my wife and children: I do not wish to go free," [6]his master shall take him before God. He shall be brought to the door or the doorpost, and

2 כִּי תִקְנֶה עֶבֶד עִבְרִי שֵׁשׁ שָׁנִים יַעֲבֹד
וּבַשְּׁבִעִת יֵצֵא לַחָפְשִׁי חִנָּם׃ 3 אִם־בְּגַפּוֹ
יָבֹא בְּגַפּוֹ יֵצֵא אִם־בַּעַל אִשָּׁה הוּא וְיָצְאָה
אִשְׁתּוֹ עִמּוֹ׃ 4 אִם־אֲדֹנָיו יִתֶּן־לוֹ אִשָּׁה
וְיָלְדָה־לוֹ בָנִים אוֹ בָנוֹת הָאִשָּׁה וִילָדֶיהָ
תִּהְיֶה לַאדֹנֶיהָ וְהוּא יֵצֵא בְגַפּוֹ׃ 5 וְאִם־
אָמֹר יֹאמַר הָעֶבֶד אָהַבְתִּי אֶת־אֲדֹנִי אֶת־
אִשְׁתִּי וְאֶת־בָּנָי לֹא אֵצֵא חָפְשִׁי׃ 6 וְהִגִּישׁוֹ
אֲדֹנָיו אֶל־הָאֱלֹהִים וְהִגִּישׁוֹ אֶל־הַדֶּלֶת אוֹ

or 21:20). Here, however, the text specifies that a male servant must be released at the end of six years, but not the indentured daughter (see at v. 7). [While this passage seems to present two contrasting laws, some interpretations—including the present translation—perceive that the unit has three parts: first, a general rule concerning the release of both female and male Hebrew indentured servants in the seventh year (v. 2, which is formulated in masculine language but represents an inclusive category); then two exceptions, one for males (vv. 3–6) and the other for daughters (vv. 7–11). This inclusive reading of v. 2 resembles Deuteronomy 15:12, which mandates the release of a Hebrew slave regardless of gender. —*Ed.*]

2. ***you.*** The Hebrew wording is grammatically masculine singular. The present translation presumes that such biblical language leaves the social gender unspecified whenever it refers to a nonspecific category of persons ("you who . . ." or "anyone who . . ."). Readers or listeners then determine the intended social gender from the topic under discussion, or from other clues in the context. Here, the topic is determinative: the sense is gender inclusive because in ancient Israel, some women as well as some men owned debt-slaves; and the law has no reason to discriminate according to the owner's gender.

***slave.*** Heb. *eved*, which can refer to either male or female servants or slaves. Here, the translation understands this noun in an inclusive way, on the grounds that the basic principle is not constrained by gender. This law would thus also cover the case of a desperate woman who—lacking familial assistance—sells herself into slavery (compare Deuteronomy 15:12, 28:68). Note, however, that this section takes pains not to be gender inclusive by differentiating between *eved* (v. 2) and *amah* (female slave) (v. 7) (see also vv. 20, 26–27, 32), as well as between *ish* (man) and *ishah* (woman) (v. 28) and between *ben* (son) and *bat* (daughter) (v. 31).

3. ***if he had a wife.*** This verse suggests that if a man was married before he became a debt slave, his wife accompanies him when he becomes an indentured servant and then is set free after six years. Presumably, the master provides for the man's wife and children during the years of servitude.

4. ***the wife and her children shall belong to the master.*** In this case, the master gives the bondsman a slave-wife, possibly of non-Israelite origin, in order to produce "house born" slaves. The mother's status determines the children's status, a practice that departs from the patrilineal norm in ancient Israel: if the mother is a slave, the children remain slaves. At the end of his indenture, the bondsman has to choose between continued servitude with his family or a lonely freedom. Perhaps because of the precariousness of his circumstances when freed, he might choose to stay. (For another perspective, see Contemporary Reflection, p. 447.)

his master shall pierce his ear with an awl; and he shall then remain his master's slave for life.

[7]When a parent sells a daughter as a slave, she shall not go free as other slaves do. [8]If she proves to be displeasing to her (male) master, who designated her for himself, he must let her be redeemed; he shall not have the right to sell her to outsiders, since he broke faith with her. [9]And if the master designated her for a son, he shall deal with her as is the practice with free maidens. [10]If he marries another,

אֶל־הַמְּזוּזָ֑ה וְרָצַ֨ע אֲדֹנָ֤יו אֶת־אׇזְנוֹ֙ בַּמַּרְצֵ֔עַ
וַעֲבָד֖וֹ לְעֹלָֽם׃ ס
7 וְכִֽי־יִמְכֹּ֥ר אִ֛ישׁ אֶת־בִּתּ֖וֹ לְאָמָ֑ה לֹ֥א תֵצֵ֖א
כְּצֵ֥את הָעֲבָדִֽים׃ 8 אִם־רָעָ֞ה בְּעֵינֵ֧י אֲדֹנֶ֛יהָ
אֲשֶׁר־לא ל֥וֹ יְעָדָ֖הּ וְהֶפְדָּ֑הּ לְעַ֤ם נׇכְרִי֙ לֹא־
יִמְשֹׁ֣ל לְמׇכְרָ֔הּ בְּבִגְדוֹ־בָֽהּ׃ 9 וְאִם־לִבְנ֖וֹ
יִֽיעָדֶ֑נָּה כְּמִשְׁפַּ֥ט הַבָּנ֖וֹת יַעֲשֶׂה־לָּֽהּ׃ 10 אִם־

*7–11.* This case concerns a daughter sold into debt servitude. Gregory Chirichigno observes that this passage applies to a female sold into marriage and specifically designated as a sexual partner, as opposed to a female dependent sold to perform only household or non-sexual labor; the latter case is treated in Deuteronomy 15:12–18 (*Debt-Slavery in Israel and the Ancient Near East*, 1993, p. 255).

*7. parent.* Heb. *ish* (traditionally translated as "man") in the Bible usually refers to a category of person ("anyone who . . ."). In the context of legal proceedings, when *ish* refers non-specifically to a plaintiff, defendant, or victim, the present translation understands the term as equivalent to the English word "party"; its social gender is determined not by the language but by the situation. Here, either a mother or a father could be in a position to sell a child; in the biblical world, impoverished families sometimes pledged a daughter or son in order to secure loans or land. The Bible tells of a widow who expects that a creditor will seize her children and force them into indentured servitude to pay off the family's debt (II Kings 4:1). In Nehemiah 5:5, the people complain about having to sell their children in order to survive.

*slave.* Heb. *amah*, which refers to a female servant and has a wide range of meanings. While designating a slave or servant (such as Bilhah in Genesis), it also can be a self-deprecating title for a woman when she wishes to show deference. (See how the term is repeatedly used by wealthy Abigail when speaking to David in I Samuel 25:24–31.)

*she shall not go free as other slaves do.* According to this passage, an indentured daughter does not go free in the seventh year (v. 2) but rather stays in her master's home where she becomes a wife or secondary wife of either the master or the master's son. In contrast, Deuteronomy 15:12 allows the Israelite woman to go free in the seventh year, but that verse may refer to a girl or woman who becomes an indentured servant with no intention of marriage. Here, marriage to the master or the master's son seems to be the condition the father makes for the daughter's indenture.

*8. If she proves to be displeasing.* What causes her to be seen, literally, as "bad in the eyes of her master"? Given the implicit focus on sexuality in this passage, some commentators infer that she is rejected because of something related to her status as a potential sexual partner or wife. However, reasons for the disapproval are not specified.

*he shall not have the right to sell her.* This law implies that if the master designates the girl as his wife but then finds her unsatisfactory for any reason, he has to allow her family to redeem her (compare Leviticus 25:47–49).

*outsiders.* The Hebrew phrase includes the word *am* (kin). While the woman changes hands without her choice, at least she remains among her people.

*9. he shall deal with her as is the practice with free maidens.* This verse suggests that the girl must be given the rights of a free Israelite bride, as explained in v. 10.

he must not withhold from this one her food, her clothing, or her conjugal rights. [11]If he fails her in these three ways, she shall go free, without payment.

[12]One who fatally strikes another person shall be put to death. [13]If [a male killer] did not do it by design, but it came about by an act of God, I will assign you a place to which he can flee.

[14]When a person schemes against another and kills through treachery, you shall take that person from My very altar to be put to death.

[15]One who strikes one's father or mother shall be put to death.

[16]One who kidnaps a person—whether having sold or still holding the victim—shall be put to death.

אַחֶרֶת יִקַּח־לוֹ שְׁאֵרָהּ כְּסוּתָהּ וְעֹנָתָהּ לֹא
יִגְרָע׃ 11 וְאִם־שְׁלָשׁ־אֵלֶּה לֹא יַעֲשֶׂה לָהּ
וְיָצְאָה חִנָּם אֵין כָּסֶף׃ ס
12 מַכֵּה אִישׁ וָמֵת מוֹת יוּמָת׃ 13 וַאֲשֶׁר לֹא
צָדָה וְהָאֱלֹהִים אִנָּה לְיָדוֹ וְשַׂמְתִּי לְךָ
מָקוֹם אֲשֶׁר יָנוּס שָׁמָּה׃ ס
14 וְכִי־יָזִד אִישׁ עַל־רֵעֵהוּ לְהָרְגוֹ בְעָרְמָה
מֵעִם מִזְבְּחִי תִּקָּחֶנּוּ לָמוּת׃ ס
15 וּמַכֵּה אָבִיו וְאִמּוֹ מוֹת יוּמָת׃ ס
16 וְגֹנֵב אִישׁ וּמְכָרוֹ וְנִמְצָא בְיָדוֹ מוֹת
יוּמָת׃ ס

---

*10. her food, her clothing, or her conjugal rights.* These three provisions comprise the basic entitlements of a married woman. The meaning of the third term (*onah*) is disputed; it appears nowhere else in the Bible. Some understand this word as a reference to a dwelling place (*ma'on*). Others translate the noun as "oil" or "ointment," a reading that is based not on linguistic evidence, but on the fact that the combination of food, clothing, and oil is found in several ancient Near Eastern texts concerned with the minimal requirements for supporting a dependent. Jewish tradition considers *onah* to refer to marital relations, either for the purpose of sexual gratification or procreation, hence the translation "conjugal rights." According to Nahum Sarna, if this interpretation is correct, "it would reflect a singular recognition in the laws of the ancient Near East that a wife is legally entitled to sexual gratification" (*Exodus*, 1991, p. 121).

*11. If he fails her in these three ways.* One interpretation of the phrase "three ways" is that she may leave as a free woman if the master does not allow her to be redeemed by her own family (v. 8), if he fails to treat her as a free maiden (v. 9), or if he neglects her maintenance (v. 10). Alternatively, "these three ways" could refer to "her food, her clothing, or her conjugal rights" (v. 10). In either case, if certain conditions are not met, the female servant has the ability to leave her master's home without one of her relatives paying a redemption fee.

### *Capital Crimes: Murder, Abuse of Parents, Kidnapping* (21:12–17)

This section enumerates crimes against persons for which the Book of the Covenant demands the execution of the guilty party.

*12. One.* Linguistically the social gender is unspecified (see at v. 2); here the same law—and the death penalty—would apply whether the killer was a man or a woman (compare at Genesis 9:5–6).

*13. If [a male killer].* The verse establishes that someone who commits involuntary homicide can flee to a city of refuge (see Numbers 35:9–29 and at Deuteronomy 19:1–13) to avoid vengeance being carried out by the deceased's family. The principle of asylum was applicable regardless of gender. However, it may have gone without saying—as the present translation presumes—that the case of a female killer would be somewhat more complicated than the case that the Torah outlines.

*15, 17. One who strikes one's father or mother . . . One who insults one's father or mother.* The

[17]One who insults one's father or mother shall be put to death.

[18]When [two] parties quarrel and one strikes the other with stone or fist, and the victim does not die but has to take to bed: [19]if that victim then gets up and walks outdoors upon a staff, the assailant shall go unpunished—except for paying for the idleness and the cure.

[20]When a person [who is a slave owner] strikes a slave, male or female, with a rod, who dies there and then, it must be avenged. [21]But if the victim survives a day or two, it is not to be avenged, since the one is the other's property.

[22]When [two or more] parties fight, and one of them pushes a pregnant woman and a miscarriage results, but no other damage ensues, the one responsible shall be fined according as the woman's

17 וּמְקַלֵּל אָבִיו וְאִמּוֹ מוֹת יוּמָת׃ ס
18 וְכִי־יְרִיבֻן אֲנָשִׁים וְהִכָּה־אִישׁ אֶת־
רֵעֵהוּ בְּאֶבֶן אוֹ בְאֶגְרֹף וְלֹא יָמוּת וְנָפַל
לְמִשְׁכָּב׃ 19 אִם־יָקוּם וְהִתְהַלֵּךְ בַּחוּץ עַל־
מִשְׁעַנְתּוֹ וְנִקָּה הַמַּכֶּה רַק שִׁבְתּוֹ יִתֵּן וְרַפֹּא
יְרַפֵּא׃ ס
20 וְכִי־יַכֶּה אִישׁ אֶת־עַבְדּוֹ אוֹ אֶת־אֲמָתוֹ
בַּשֵּׁבֶט וּמֵת תַּחַת יָדוֹ נָקֹם יִנָּקֵם׃ 21 אַךְ
אִם־יוֹם אוֹ יוֹמַיִם יַעֲמֹד לֹא יֻקַּם כִּי כַסְפּוֹ
הוּא׃ ס
22 וְכִי־יִנָּצוּ אֲנָשִׁים וְנָגְפוּ אִשָּׁה הָרָה וְיָצְאוּ
יְלָדֶיהָ וְלֹא יִהְיֶה אָסוֹן עָנוֹשׁ יֵעָנֵשׁ כַּאֲשֶׁר

physical or verbal abuse of father and mother is considered a capital offense, for these regulations are addressed to adult offspring upon whom senior family members are dependent for their survival. The word "insults" can refer to cursing or habitual rebellious behavior (see Deuteronomy 21:18–19), as well as treating parents with contempt; it is the opposite of "honor" in Exodus 20:12. Biblical law consistently mentions "mother" alongside "father" in its legislation regarding the honoring of parents, with father mentioned first in most cases (20:12; Deuteronomy 5:16; 21:18; 27:16) except for Leviticus 19:3, which lists the mother first. A similar provision in the Laws of Hammurabi (¶ 195) mentions only the father. See further at v. 20.

### *Bodily Injury Caused by People and Livestock* (21:18–32)

After treating the capital crimes, the text transitions to situations where the prescribed remedy can be execution but more typically is physical retaliation or financial compensation.

***20. A slave, male or female.*** A distinctive feature of the Covenant Collection is that eight among its first laws make the gender-inclusive sense explicit (vv. 15, 17, 20, 26, 28, 29, 31, 32). This may be due to the position of Exodus 21 as the first section of jurisprudence after the Decalogue. Thus, the equal protection of women is emphasized at the beginning of the covenant legislation.

***22. When** [two or more] **parties fight, and one of them pushes a pregnant woman and a miscarriage results.*** This verse contains two significant aspects of biblical and later Jewish law. First, this is the only Torah text that discusses the value of a fetal life, a subject crucial for the development of legislation concerning women. Further, it presents the statement of exact retaliation, "an eye for an eye" or "talion" law, from the Latin term *lex talionis.* | This verse does not explain how the woman became involved in the altercation. Was she simply an innocent bystander, or did she intervene to aid one of the parties? (The latter legal scenario is found in Deuteronomy 25:11–12.)

***damage.*** Heb. *ason*, which is used elsewhere in the Bible only in the Joseph narrative, when Jacob

husband may exact, the payment to be based on reckoning. 23 But if other damage ensues, the penalty shall be life for life, 24 eye for eye, tooth for tooth, hand for hand, foot for foot, 25 burn for burn, wound for wound, bruise for bruise.

26 When a person [who is a slave owner] strikes the eye of a slave, male or female, and destroys it, that person shall let the slave go free on account of the eye. 27 If the owner knocks out the tooth of a slave, male or female, that person shall let the slave go free on account of the tooth.

יָשִׁית עָלָיו בַּעַל הָאִשָּׁה וְנָתַן בִּפְלִלִים׃
23 וְאִם־אָסוֹן יִהְיֶה וְנָתַתָּה נֶפֶשׁ תַּחַת
נָפֶשׁ׃ 24 עַיִן תַּחַת עַיִן שֵׁן תַּחַת שֵׁן יָד
תַּחַת יָד רֶגֶל תַּחַת רָגֶל׃ 25 כְּוִיָּה תַּחַת
כְּוִיָּה פֶּצַע תַּחַת פָּצַע חַבּוּרָה תַּחַת
חַבּוּרָה׃ ס
26 וְכִי־יַכֶּה אִישׁ אֶת־עֵין עַבְדּוֹ אוֹ־אֶת־עֵין
אֲמָתוֹ וְשִׁחֲתָהּ לַחָפְשִׁי יְשַׁלְּחֶנּוּ תַּחַת עֵינוֹ׃
27 וְאִם־שֵׁן עַבְדּוֹ אוֹ־שֵׁן אֲמָתוֹ יַפִּיל
לַחָפְשִׁי יְשַׁלְּחֶנּוּ תַּחַת שִׁנּוֹ׃ פ

fears sending Benjamin down to Egypt lest an *ason*, meaning some sort of harm or mishap, befalls him (Genesis 42:4, 38; 44:29). Likewise the present translation understands that *ason* refers to harm in general, given the range of penalties mentioned in vv. 23–25. In this particular case, *ason* seems to refer specifically to the death of the mother as a result of the trauma of the assault and subsequent miscarriage. This assumption is corroborated by similar ancient Mesopotamian laws which speak first of the death of the fetus and then the death of the mother: "If a noble strikes a woman of the noble class and thereby causes her to miscarry her fetus, the perpetrator shall weigh and deliver ten shekels of silver for her fetus. If that woman should die, they shall kill the perpetrator's daughter" (Laws of Hammurabi ¶¶ 209–10). In the Hammurabi regulation, the one who kills the pregnant woman loses a daughter. In the Torah, the attacker is required to monetarily compensate the "owner" of the fetus, the woman's husband, with an amount of compensation to be negotiated.

*23. But if other damage ensues, the penalty shall be life for life.* Only if the mother dies (literally "if there is an *ason*") must the attacker pay "life for life" ("*nefesh* in place of *nefesh*"). The relatively permissive Jewish law regarding abortion is derived from the essential distinction between the fetus and its mother. While the mother is considered a *nefesh* and her death is a capital crime, the loss of a fetus carries a lesser penalty. Similar to other cases of physical injury (vv. 18–19), the miscarriage is punished by monetary compensation.

*24. eye for eye, tooth for tooth.* The legal formula for precise retribution, "eye for an eye," has little relevance here, as this case speaks only of the miscarriage of the fetus or of the mother's death (see at v. 22), not burns or injuries to eyes, hands, or feet. This expression was probably placed here to complete the beginning of the formula found in v. 23, "life for life," the one part of the phrase that fits this particular case. The talion formula recurs in different contexts in Leviticus 24:17–20 and Deuteronomy 19:21. According to Tikva Frymer-Kensky, this formula "must have been a judicial maxim to express the principles of equivalent retaliation" and not a mandate to inflict a penalty of bodily mutilation ("Israelite Law: State and Judiciary Law," *Encyclopedia of Religion*, 2nd ed., 2005, 7:4741). In other words, this language should not be interpreted literally. Measure-for-measure punishment is found not only in biblical law but also in narrative; this was considered God's own way of rendering justice.

*26. male or female.* On the mention of both genders, see at v. 20.

[28]When an ox gores a man or a woman to death, the ox shall be stoned and its flesh shall not be eaten, but the owner of the ox is not to be punished. [29]If, however, that ox has been in the habit of goring, and its owner, though warned, has failed to guard it, and it kills a man or a woman—the ox shall be stoned and its owner, too, shall be put to death. [30]If ransom is imposed, the owner must pay whatever is imposed to redeem the owner's own life. [31]So, too, if it gores a minor, male or female, [its owner] shall be dealt with according to the same rule. [32]But if the ox gores a slave, male or female, [its owner] shall pay thirty shekels of silver to the master, and the ox shall be stoned.

[33]When a person opens a pit, or digs a pit and does not cover it, and an ox or an ass falls into it, [34]the one responsible for the pit must make restitution—paying the price to the owner, but keeping the dead animal.

[35]When a person's ox injures a neighbor's ox and it dies, they shall sell the live ox and divide its price; they shall also divide the dead animal. [36]If, however, it is known that the ox was in the habit of goring, and its owner has failed to guard it, that person must restore ox for ox, but shall keep the dead animal.

[37]When a person steals an ox or a sheep, and slaughters it or sells it, that person shall pay five oxen for the ox, and four sheep for the sheep.—
**22** If the thief is seized while tunneling and beaten to death, there is no bloodguilt in that case. [2]If the sun had already risen, there is bloodguilt in that case.—The thief must make restitution, and if lacking the means, shall be sold for the theft. [3]But

28 וְכִֽי־יִגַּ֨ח שׁ֥וֹר אֶת־אִ֛ישׁ א֥וֹ אֶת־אִשָּׁ֖ה
וָמֵ֑ת סָק֨וֹל יִסָּקֵ֜ל הַשּׁ֗וֹר וְלֹ֤א יֵאָכֵל֙ אֶת־
בְּשָׂר֔וֹ וּבַ֥עַל הַשּׁ֖וֹר נָקִֽי׃ 29 וְאִ֡ם שׁ֣וֹר נַגָּח֩
ה֨וּא מִתְּמֹ֜ל שִׁלְשֹׁ֗ם וְהוּעַ֤ד בִּבְעָלָיו֙ וְלֹ֣א
יִשְׁמְרֶ֔נּוּ וְהֵמִ֥ית אִ֖ישׁ א֣וֹ אִשָּׁ֑ה הַשּׁוֹר֙ יִסָּקֵ֔ל
וְגַם־בְּעָלָ֖יו יוּמָֽת׃ 30 אִם־כֹּ֖פֶר יוּשַׁ֣ת עָלָ֑יו
וְנָתַן֙ פִּדְיֹ֣ן נַפְשׁ֔וֹ כְּכֹ֥ל אֲשֶׁר־יוּשַׁ֖ת עָלָֽיו׃
31 אוֹ־בֵ֥ן יִגָּ֖ח אוֹ־בַ֣ת יִגָּ֑ח כַּמִּשְׁפָּ֥ט הַזֶּ֖ה
יֵעָ֥שֶׂה לּֽוֹ׃ 32 אִם־עֶ֛בֶד יִגַּ֥ח הַשּׁ֖וֹר א֣וֹ אָמָ֑ה
כֶּ֣סֶף ׀ שְׁלֹשִׁ֣ים שְׁקָלִ֗ים יִתֵּן֙ לַֽאדֹנָ֔יו וְהַשּׁ֖וֹר
יִסָּקֵֽל׃ ס

33 וְכִֽי־יִפְתַּ֨ח אִ֜ישׁ בּ֗וֹר א֠וֹ כִּֽי־יִכְרֶ֥ה אִ֛ישׁ
בֹּ֖ר וְלֹ֣א יְכַסֶּ֑נּוּ וְנָֽפַל־שָׁ֥מָּה שּׁ֖וֹר א֥וֹ חֲמֽוֹר׃
34 בַּ֤עַל הַבּוֹר֙ יְשַׁלֵּ֔ם כֶּ֖סֶף יָשִׁ֣יב לִבְעָלָ֑יו
וְהַמֵּ֖ת יִֽהְיֶה־לּֽוֹ׃ ס

35 וְכִֽי־יִגֹּ֧ף שֽׁוֹר־אִ֛ישׁ אֶת־שׁ֥וֹר רֵעֵ֖הוּ וָמֵ֑ת
וּמָ֨כְר֜וּ אֶת־הַשּׁ֤וֹר הַחַי֙ וְחָצ֣וּ אֶת־כַּסְפּ֔וֹ
וְגַ֥ם אֶת־הַמֵּ֖ת יֶחֱצֽוּן׃ 36 א֣וֹ נוֹדַ֗ע כִּ֠י שׁ֣וֹר
נַגָּ֥ח הוּא֙ מִתְּמ֣וֹל שִׁלְשֹׁ֔ם וְלֹ֥א יִשְׁמְרֶ֖נּוּ
בְּעָלָ֑יו שַׁלֵּ֨ם יְשַׁלֵּ֥ם שׁוֹר֙ תַּ֣חַת הַשּׁ֔וֹר וְהַמֵּ֖ת
יִֽהְיֶה־לּֽוֹ׃ ס

37 כִּ֤י יִגְנֹֽב־אִישׁ֙ שׁ֣וֹר אוֹ־שֶׂ֔ה וּטְבָח֖וֹ א֣וֹ
מְכָר֑וֹ חֲמִשָּׁ֣ה בָקָ֗ר יְשַׁלֵּם֙ תַּ֣חַת הַשּׁ֔וֹר
וְאַרְבַּע־צֹ֖אן תַּ֥חַת הַשֶּֽׂה׃ כב אִם־
בַּמַּחְתֶּ֛רֶת יִמָּצֵ֥א הַגַּנָּ֖ב וְהֻכָּ֣ה וָמֵ֑ת אֵ֥ין
ל֖וֹ דָּמִֽים׃ 2 אִם־זָרְחָ֥ה הַשֶּׁ֛מֶשׁ עָלָ֖יו
דָּמִ֣ים ל֑וֹ שַׁלֵּ֣ם יְשַׁלֵּ֔ם אִם־אֵ֣ין ל֔וֹ וְנִמְכַּ֖ר
בִּגְנֵבָתֽוֹ׃ 3 אִם־הִמָּצֵא֩ תִמָּצֵ֨א בְיָד֜וֹ הַגְּנֵבָ֗ה

*28–32.* This case distinguishes between an animal that unexpectedly attacks someone and one that previously exhibited such aggressive behavior. The law's gender-inclusive sense is stressed via the repetition of "man or a woman" (vv. 28, 29) and "male and female" (vv. 31–32); see at v. 20.

### *Property Damage: Injury to Livestock, Theft, Crop Damage, Safeguarded Property* (21:33–22:14)

The regulations in this section deal with crimes against an individual's property. Penalties range

if what was stolen—whether ox or ass or sheep—is found alive and in hand, that person shall pay double.

4 When a person who owns livestock lets it loose to graze in another's land, and so allows a field or a vineyard to be grazed bare, restitution must be made for the impairment of that field or vineyard.

5 When a fire is started and spreads to thorns, so that stacked, standing, or growing grain is consumed, the one who started the fire must make restitution.

6 When a person gives money or goods to another for safekeeping, and they are stolen from that other person's house: if caught, the thief shall pay double; 7 if the thief is not caught, the owner of the house shall depose before God and deny laying hands on the other's property. (8 In all charges of misappropriation—pertaining to an ox, an ass, a sheep, a garment, or any other loss, whereof one party alleges, "This is it"—the case of both parties shall come before God: the one whom God declares guilty shall pay double to the other.)

9 When a person gives to another an ass, an ox, a sheep or any other animal to guard, and it dies or is injured or is carried off, with no witness about, 10 an oath before יהוה shall decide between the two of them that the one has not laid hands on the property of the other; the owner must acquiesce, and no restitution shall be made. 11 But if [the animal] was stolen from the guardian, restitution shall be made to its owner. 12 If it was torn by beasts, the guardian shall bring it as evidence—not needing to replace what has been torn by beasts.

13 When a person borrows [an animal] from another and it dies or is injured, its owner not being with it, that person must make restitution. 14 If its owner was with it, no restitution need be made; but if it was hired, that payment is due.

מִשּׁוֹר עַד־חֲמוֹר עַד־שֶׂה חַיִּים שְׁנַיִם
יְשַׁלֵּם׃ ס
4 כִּי יַבְעֶר־אִישׁ שָׂדֶה אוֹ־כֶרֶם וְשִׁלַּח אֶת־
בעירה בְּעִירוֹ וּבִעֵר בִּשְׂדֵה אַחֵר מֵיטַב
שָׂדֵהוּ וּמֵיטַב כַּרְמוֹ יְשַׁלֵּם׃ ס
5 כִּי־תֵצֵא אֵשׁ וּמָצְאָה קֹצִים וְנֶאֱכַל גָּדִישׁ
אוֹ הַקָּמָה אוֹ הַשָּׂדֶה שַׁלֵּם יְשַׁלֵּם הַמַּבְעִר
אֶת־הַבְּעֵרָה׃ ס
6 כִּי־יִתֵּן אִישׁ אֶל־רֵעֵהוּ כֶּסֶף אוֹ־כֵלִים
לִשְׁמֹר וְגֻנַּב מִבֵּית הָאִישׁ אִם־יִמָּצֵא הַגַּנָּב
יְשַׁלֵּם שְׁנָיִם׃ 7 אִם־לֹא יִמָּצֵא הַגַּנָּב וְנִקְרַב
בַּעַל־הַבַּיִת אֶל־הָאֱלֹהִים אִם־לֹא שָׁלַח יָדוֹ
בִּמְלֶאכֶת רֵעֵהוּ׃ 8 עַל־כָּל־דְּבַר־פֶּשַׁע עַל־
שׁוֹר עַל־חֲמוֹר עַל־שֶׂה עַל־שַׂלְמָה עַל־
כָּל־אֲבֵדָה אֲשֶׁר יֹאמַר כִּי־הוּא זֶה עַד
הָאֱלֹהִים יָבֹא דְּבַר־שְׁנֵיהֶם אֲשֶׁר יַרְשִׁיעֻן
אֱלֹהִים יְשַׁלֵּם שְׁנַיִם לְרֵעֵהוּ׃ ס
9 כִּי־יִתֵּן אִישׁ אֶל־רֵעֵהוּ חֲמוֹר אוֹ־שׁוֹר אוֹ־
שֶׂה וְכָל־בְּהֵמָה לִשְׁמֹר וּמֵת אוֹ־נִשְׁבַּר אוֹ־
נִשְׁבָּה אֵין רֹאֶה׃ 10 שְׁבֻעַת יְהוָה תִּהְיֶה בֵּין
שְׁנֵיהֶם אִם־לֹא שָׁלַח יָדוֹ בִּמְלֶאכֶת רֵעֵהוּ
וְלָקַח בְּעָלָיו וְלֹא יְשַׁלֵּם׃ 11 וְאִם־גָּנֹב יִגָּנֵב
מֵעִמּוֹ יְשַׁלֵּם לִבְעָלָיו׃ 12 אִם־טָרֹף יִטָּרֵף
יְבִאֵהוּ עֵד הַטְּרֵפָה לֹא יְשַׁלֵּם׃ פ
13 וְכִי־יִשְׁאַל אִישׁ מֵעִם רֵעֵהוּ וְנִשְׁבַּר
אוֹ־מֵת בְּעָלָיו אֵין־עִמּוֹ שַׁלֵּם יְשַׁלֵּם׃
14 אִם־בְּעָלָיו עִמּוֹ לֹא יְשַׁלֵּם אִם־שָׂכִיר
הוּא בָּא בִּשְׂכָרוֹ׃ ס

from financial compensation for loss of property to forced labor for the thief who cannot pay the penalty (22:2).

*21:37–22:3, 6–7.* On stealing, see at Leviticus 19:11.

[15]If a man seduces a virgin for whom the bride-price has not been paid, and lies with her, he must make her his wife by payment of a bride-price. [16]If her father refuses to give her to him, he must still weigh out silver in accordance with the bride-price for virgins.

[17]You shall not tolerate a sorceress.

15 וְכִֽי־יְפַתֶּ֣ה אִ֗ישׁ בְּתוּלָ֛ה אֲשֶׁ֥ר לֹא־אֹרָ֖שָׂה
וְשָׁכַ֣ב עִמָּ֑הּ מָהֹ֛ר יִמְהָרֶ֥נָּה לּ֖וֹ לְאִשָּֽׁה׃
16 אִם־מָאֵ֧ן יְמָאֵ֛ן אָבִ֖יהָ לְתִתָּ֣הּ ל֑וֹ כֶּ֣סֶף
יִשְׁקֹ֔ל כְּמֹ֖הַר הַבְּתוּלֹֽת׃ ס
17 מְכַשֵּׁפָ֖ה לֹ֥א תְחַיֶּֽה׃

*Seduction of an Unbetrothed Woman* (22:15–16)

This case concerns a young woman of marriageable age, as young as eleven or twelve, who loses her virginity to a man who did not seek her father's permission by entering into a formal engagement and paying a betrothal gift. While scholars generally differentiate between this case, which deals with the "persuasion" of the young girl, and Deuteronomy 22:28–29, which deals with rape, the distinction is not clear when dealing with young women who may be too naïve to offer real consent for sexual relations. This case is positioned after a series of laws regarding property loss (likewise remedied by monetary compensation), but before a series on disruptions to the social order; it seems to share aspects with both subjects. It may reflect an ancient Near Eastern view of a daughter's virginity as the father's or household's asset.

***bride-price.*** Heb. *mohar*, which indicates the customary transfer of property from the groom or his family to the bride's father (see also Genesis 34:12 and I Samuel 18:25–27), perhaps to compensate her family for the loss of her labor. The *mohar* is different from a dowry, the money or moveable property that the wife might bring to her husband and his family at marriage. Carol Meyers argues that the betrothal gift does not mean that the groom purchased the bride like chattel; therefore, the standard translation of *mohar* as "bride-price" is misleading. Instead, the dowry and betrothal gift (a better rendering of *mohar*) helped form alliances between the two families and provided security for the woman, who theoretically retained possession of the dowry (*Exodus*, 2005, p. 197).

***16. If her father refuses to give her to him.*** Although the law requires the man to take full responsibility for his actions and marry the woman, it is understandable that a father might refuse to allow his daughter to marry the man who evaded his parental authority and seduced his daughter. In that case, the law ensures that the father's household bears no financial loss and thus receives the betrothal gift of virgins, which would have been greater than that for widows or divorcees. The law underlines a father's responsibility for his daughter's sexuality.

## ASSORTED RELIGIOUS AND SOCIAL PRECEPTS (22:17–23:19)

The start of the second section of the Book of the Covenant is marked by a shift in content and style. Whereas the prior laws are formulated as hypothetical cases, many of the subsequent verses are phrased apodictically as categorical imperatives. These injunctions deal with various social and religious matters, such as questions of how to treat others and the proper way to approach God. One consequence of the notion of the divine authorship of the law is that the distinction between civil and religious law becomes blurred, as seen in this parashah.

*Prohibitions of Sorcery, Bestiality, and Apostasy* (22:17–19)

These three offenses all incur the death penalty. Sorcery and sacrificing to other gods conflict with the proper worship of Israel's God. Sexual relations with an animal are condemned elsewhere, along

18 Whoever lies with a beast shall be put to death.

19 Whoever sacrifices to a god other than יהוה alone shall be proscribed.

20 You shall not wrong nor oppress a stranger, for you were strangers in the land of Egypt.

21 You [communal leaders] shall not ill-treat any widow or orphan. 22 If you do mistreat them, I will heed their outcry as soon as they cry out to Me, 23 and My anger shall blaze forth and I will put you to the sword, and your own wives shall become widows and your children orphans.

24 If you lend money to My people, to the poor among you, do not act toward them as a creditor; exact no interest from them. 25 If you take your neighbor's garment in pledge, you must return it

18 כָּל־שֹׁכֵ֥ב עִם־בְּהֵמָ֖ה מ֥וֹת יוּמָֽת׃ ס
19 זֹבֵ֥חַ לָאֱלֹהִ֖ים יָחֳרָ֑ם בִּלְתִּ֥י לַיהוָ֖ה
לְבַדּֽוֹ׃
20 וְגֵ֥ר לֹא־תוֹנֶ֖ה וְלֹ֣א תִלְחָצֶ֑נּוּ כִּֽי־גֵרִ֥ים
הֱיִיתֶ֖ם בְּאֶ֥רֶץ מִצְרָֽיִם׃
21 כָּל־אַלְמָנָ֥ה וְיָת֖וֹם לֹ֥א תְעַנּֽוּן׃ 22 אִם־
עַנֵּ֥ה תְעַנֶּ֖ה אֹת֑וֹ כִּ֣י אִם־צָעֹ֤ק יִצְעַק֙ אֵלַ֔י
שָׁמֹ֥עַ אֶשְׁמַ֖ע צַעֲקָתֽוֹ׃ 23 וְחָרָ֣ה אַפִּ֔י
וְהָרַגְתִּ֥י אֶתְכֶ֖ם בֶּחָ֑רֶב וְהָי֤וּ נְשֵׁיכֶם֙ אַלְמָנ֔וֹת
וּבְנֵיכֶ֖ם יְתֹמִֽים׃ פ
24 אִם־כֶּ֣סֶף ׀ תַּלְוֶ֣ה אֶת־עַמִּ֗י אֶת־הֶֽעָנִי֙
עִמָּ֔ךְ לֹא־תִהְיֶ֥ה ל֖וֹ כְּנֹשֶׁ֑ה לֹֽא־תְשִׂימ֥וּן
עָלָ֖יו נֶֽשֶׁךְ׃ 25 אִם־חָבֹ֥ל תַּחְבֹּ֖ל שַׂלְמַ֣ת רֵעֶ֑ךָ

with incest and adultery (Leviticus 18:23, 20:15–16; Deuteronomy 27:21).

*17. **You shall not tolerate.*** Biblical authors treat an attempt to learn the future as permissible so long as it is accomplished through permissible means: consultation with prophets, dream interpretation, or an oracle via the high priest's breastplate (I Samuel 28:6). All other means—such as conjuring the spirits of the dead, interpreting the movements of clouds, or "reading" omens from the livers of sacrificial animals—fall into the category of intolerable sorcery (see next comment). Deuteronomy 18:13–14 suggests that sorcery violates Israel's obligation to wholeheartedly worship God.

***sorceress.*** Whereas many of the prior laws in this parashah mention both women and men, here the text focuses only on the former. Deuteronomy 18:9–14 enumerates various kinds of diviners and sorcerers, without distinguishing between male and female.

Women are associated with the occult in I Samuel 28, where the Woman of En-dor conjures up Samuel's ghost, and in Ezekiel 13:17–23, where the prophet denounces female soothsayers. (See also at Leviticus 20:27 and at Deuteronomy 18:10–11.)

### *Proper Treatment of the Disadvantaged* (22:20–26)

In this section, the Torah targets the oppression of the vulnerable members of society: the stranger, the widow, the fatherless, and the poor.

*21. **You [communal leaders].*** The Hebrew wording is masculine plural; on this language, see at 21:2. Here, the addressees are those with the authority and power to carry out this precept, namely, certain male leaders (see Isaiah 1:23; Jeremiah 22:2–3). This explains the reference to "your wives" in v. 23.

***widow or orphan.*** These two classes are recognized as deserving of compassion because they have no adult male provider and protector. The term *yatom* ("orphan") more precisely means "fatherless," since v. 23 makes it clear that the individual is bereft of a father, not both parents. The plight of a widow was often dire because she did not automatically inherit her husband's land. She was left at the mercy of her children, who might have been too young to support their mother, or, in the event that she had no children, her deceased husband's male relatives (Numbers 27:9–11). (On widows, see also *Eikev*, Another View, p. 1108.)

before the sun sets; 26 it is the only available clothing—it is what covers the skin. In what else shall [your neighbor] sleep? Therefore, if that person cries out to Me, I will pay heed, for I am compassionate.

27 You shall not revile God, nor put a curse upon a chieftain among your people.

28 You shall not put off the skimming of the first yield of your vats. You shall give Me the male first-born among your children. 29 You shall do the same with your cattle and your flocks: seven days it shall remain with its mother; on the eighth day you shall give it to Me.

30 You shall be holy people to Me: you must not eat flesh torn by beasts in the field; you shall cast it to the dogs.

23 You must not carry false rumors; you shall not join hands with the guilty to act as a malicious witness: 2 You shall neither side with the mighty to do wrong—you shall not give perverse testimony in a dispute so as to pervert it in favor of the mighty— 3 nor shall you show deference to a poor person in a dispute.

4 When you encounter your enemy's ox or ass wandering, you must take it back.

5 When you see the ass of your enemy lying under its burden and would refrain from raising it, you must nevertheless help raise it.

6 You shall not subvert the rights of your needy in their disputes. 7 Keep far from a false charge; do not bring death on those who are innocent and in the right, for I will not acquit the wrongdoer.

עַד־בֹּא הַשֶּׁמֶשׁ תְּשִׁיבֶנּוּ לוֹ׃ 26 כִּי הִוא
כסותה כְסוּתוֹ לְבַדָּהּ הִוא שִׂמְלָתוֹ לְעֹרוֹ
בַּמֶּה יִשְׁכָּב וְהָיָה כִּי־יִצְעַק אֵלַי וְשָׁמַעְתִּי
כִּי־חַנּוּן אָנִי׃ ס
27 אֱלֹהִים לֹא תְקַלֵּל וְנָשִׂיא בְעַמְּךָ לֹא
תָאֹר׃
28 מְלֵאָתְךָ וְדִמְעֲךָ לֹא תְאַחֵר בְּכוֹר בָּנֶיךָ
תִּתֶּן־לִּי׃ 29 כֵּן־תַּעֲשֶׂה לְשֹׁרְךָ לְצֹאנֶךָ
שִׁבְעַת יָמִים יִהְיֶה עִם־אִמּוֹ בַּיּוֹם הַשְּׁמִינִי
תִּתְּנוֹ־לִי׃
30 וְאַנְשֵׁי־קֹדֶשׁ תִּהְיוּן לִי וּבָשָׂר בַּשָּׂדֶה
טְרֵפָה לֹא תֹאכֵלוּ לַכֶּלֶב תַּשְׁלִכוּן
אֹתוֹ׃ ס
כג לֹא תִשָּׂא שֵׁמַע שָׁוְא אַל־תָּשֶׁת יָדְךָ
עִם־רָשָׁע לִהְיֹת עֵד חָמָס׃ 2 לֹא־תִהְיֶה
אַחֲרֵי־רַבִּים לְרָעֹת וְלֹא־תַעֲנֶה עַל־רִב
לִנְטֹת אַחֲרֵי רַבִּים לְהַטֹּת׃ 3 וְדָל לֹא
תֶהְדַּר בְּרִיבוֹ׃ ס
4 כִּי תִפְגַּע שׁוֹר אֹיִבְךָ אוֹ חֲמֹרוֹ תֹּעֶה הָשֵׁב
תְּשִׁיבֶנּוּ לוֹ׃ ס
5 כִּי־תִרְאֶה חֲמוֹר שֹׂנַאֲךָ רֹבֵץ תַּחַת
מַשָּׂאוֹ וְחָדַלְתָּ מֵעֲזֹב לוֹ עָזֹב תַּעֲזֹב
עִמּוֹ׃ ס
6 לֹא תַטֶּה מִשְׁפַּט אֶבְיֹנְךָ בְּרִיבוֹ׃ 7 מִדְּבַר־
שֶׁקֶר תִּרְחָק וְנָקִי וְצַדִּיק אַל־תַּהֲרֹג כִּי לֹא־

### *Obligations to God* (22:27–30)

These four verses prohibit cursing God or a chieftain, delaying gifts to the sanctuary, and consuming carrion. Their common concern is proper respect for tribal and especially religious authority.

### *Judicial Conduct* (23:1–3)

These admonitions warn judges, litigants, and witnesses not to undermine the integrity of the judicial system by offering false testimony or by favoring the poor, mighty, or majority opinion.

### *Treatment of the Enemy, Needy, and Stranger* (23:4–9)

After commands to kindly treat an enemy's animals, the focus returns to upholding justice and the rights of the poor and the stranger.

8 Do not take bribes, for bribes blind the clear-sighted and upset the pleas of those who are in the right.

9 You shall not oppress a stranger, for you know the feelings of the stranger, having yourselves been strangers in the land of Egypt.

10 Six years you shall sow your land and gather in its yield; 11 but in the seventh you shall let it rest and lie fallow. Let the needy among your people eat of it, and what they leave let the wild beasts eat. You shall do the same with your vineyards and your olive groves.

12 Six days you shall do your work, but on the seventh day you shall cease from labor, in order that your ox and your ass may rest, and that your home-born slave and the stranger may be refreshed.

13 Be on guard concerning all that I have told you. Make no mention of the names of other gods; they shall not be heard on your lips.

14 Three times a year you shall hold a festival for Me: 15 You shall observe the Feast of Unleavened Bread—eating unleavened bread for seven days as I have commanded you—at the set time in the month of Abib, for in it you went forth from Egypt; and none shall appear before Me empty-handed; 16 and the Feast of the Harvest, of the first fruits of your work, of what you sow in the field; and the Feast of Ingathering at the end of the year, when you gather in the results of your work from the field. 17 Three times a year all your males shall appear before the Sovereign, יהוה.

18 You shall not offer the blood of My sacrifice with anything leavened; and the fat of My festal offering shall not be left lying until morning.

19 The choice first fruits of your soil you shall bring to the house of your God יהוה.

You shall not boil a kid in its mother's milk.

אַצְדִּ֥יק רָשָֽׁע׃ 8 וְשֹׁ֖חַד לֹ֣א תִקָּ֑ח כִּ֤י הַשֹּׁ֙חַד֙
יְעַוֵּ֣ר פִּקְחִ֔ים וִֽיסַלֵּ֖ף דִּבְרֵ֥י צַדִּיקִֽים׃
9 וְגֵ֖ר לֹ֣א תִלְחָ֑ץ וְאַתֶּ֗ם יְדַעְתֶּם֙ אֶת־נֶ֣פֶשׁ
הַגֵּ֔ר כִּֽי־גֵרִ֥ים הֱיִיתֶ֖ם בְּאֶ֥רֶץ מִצְרָֽיִם׃

10 וְשֵׁ֥שׁ שָׁנִ֖ים תִּזְרַ֣ע אֶת־אַרְצֶ֑ךָ וְאָסַפְתָּ֖
אֶת־תְּבוּאָתָֽהּ׃ 11 וְהַשְּׁבִיעִ֞ת תִּשְׁמְטֶ֣נָּה
וּנְטַשְׁתָּ֗הּ וְאָֽכְלוּ֙ אֶבְיֹנֵ֣י עַמֶּ֔ךָ וְיִתְרָ֕ם
תֹּאכַ֖ל חַיַּ֣ת הַשָּׂדֶ֑ה כֵּֽן־תַּעֲשֶׂ֥ה לְכַרְמְךָ֖
לְזֵיתֶֽךָ׃
12 שֵׁ֤שֶׁת יָמִים֙ תַּעֲשֶׂ֣ה מַעֲשֶׂ֔יךָ וּבַיּ֥וֹם
הַשְּׁבִיעִ֖י תִּשְׁבֹּ֑ת לְמַ֣עַן יָנ֗וּחַ שֽׁוֹרְךָ֙ וַחֲמֹרֶ֔ךָ
וְיִנָּפֵ֥שׁ בֶּן־אֲמָתְךָ֖ וְהַגֵּֽר׃
13 וּבְכֹ֛ל אֲשֶׁר־אָמַ֥רְתִּי אֲלֵיכֶ֖ם תִּשָּׁמֵ֑רוּ
וְשֵׁ֨ם אֱלֹהִ֤ים אֲחֵרִים֙ לֹ֣א תַזְכִּ֔ירוּ לֹ֥א
יִשָּׁמַ֖ע עַל־פִּֽיךָ׃
14 שָׁלֹ֣שׁ רְגָלִ֔ים תָּחֹ֥ג לִ֖י בַּשָּׁנָֽה׃ 15 אֶת־חַ֣ג
הַמַּצּוֹת֮ תִּשְׁמֹר֒ שִׁבְעַ֣ת יָמִים֩ תֹּאכַ֨ל מַצּ֜וֹת
כַּאֲשֶׁ֣ר צִוִּיתִ֗ךָ לְמוֹעֵד֙ חֹ֣דֶשׁ הָֽאָבִ֔יב כִּי־ב֖וֹ
יָצָ֣אתָ מִמִּצְרָ֑יִם וְלֹא־יֵרָא֥וּ פָנַ֖י רֵיקָֽם׃
16 וְחַ֤ג הַקָּצִיר֙ בִּכּוּרֵ֣י מַעֲשֶׂ֔יךָ אֲשֶׁ֥ר תִּזְרַ֖ע
בַּשָּׂדֶ֑ה וְחַ֤ג הָֽאָסִף֙ בְּצֵ֣את הַשָּׁנָ֔ה בְּאָסְפְּךָ֥
אֶֽת־מַעֲשֶׂ֖יךָ מִן־הַשָּׂדֶֽה׃ 17 שָׁלֹ֥שׁ פְּעָמִ֖ים
בַּשָּׁנָ֑ה יֵרָאֶה֙ כָּל־זְכ֣וּרְךָ֔ אֶל־פְּנֵ֖י הָאָדֹ֥ן ׀
יְהֹוָֽה׃
18 לֹֽא־תִזְבַּ֥ח עַל־חָמֵ֖ץ דַּם־זִבְחִ֑י וְלֹֽא־יָלִ֥ין
חֵֽלֶב־חַגִּ֖י עַד־בֹּֽקֶר׃
19 רֵאשִׁ֗ית בִּכּוּרֵי֙ אַדְמָ֣תְךָ֔ תָּבִ֕יא בֵּ֖ית יְהֹוָ֣ה
אֱלֹהֶ֑יךָ
לֹֽא־תְבַשֵּׁ֥ל גְּדִ֖י בַּחֲלֵ֥ב אִמּֽוֹ׃ פ

*Religious Calendar with Appended Food Prohibition* (23:10–19)

These verses concern Israel's fixed times: the sabbatical year, Sabbath, and three pilgrimage festivals.

***19.*** While this verse is not directly addressed to women, few laws have had a greater impact on the domestic lives of Jewish women than this one, for it

[20]I am sending an angel before you to guard you on the way and to bring you to the place that I have made ready. [21]Pay heed to him and obey him. Do not defy him, for he will not pardon your offenses, since My Name is in him; [22]but if you obey him and do all that I say, I will be an enemy to your enemies and a foe to your foes.

[23]When My angel goes before you and brings you to the Amorites, the Hittites, the Perizzites, the Canaanites, the Hivites, and the Jebusites, and I annihilate them, [24]you shall not bow down to their gods in worship or follow their practices, but shall tear them down and smash their pillars to bits. [25]You shall serve your God יהוה, who will bless your bread and your water. And I will remove sickness from your midst. [26]No woman in your land shall miscarry or be barren. I will let you enjoy the full count of your days.

20 הִנֵּ֨ה אָנֹכִ֜י שֹׁלֵ֤חַ מַלְאָךְ֙ לְפָנֶ֔יךָ לִשְׁמָרְךָ֖
בַּדָּ֑רֶךְ וְלַהֲבִ֣יאֲךָ֔ אֶל־הַמָּק֖וֹם אֲשֶׁ֥ר הֲכִנֹֽתִי׃
21 הִשָּׁ֧מֶר מִפָּנָ֛יו וּשְׁמַ֥ע בְּקֹל֖וֹ אַל־תַּמֵּ֣ר בּ֑וֹ
כִּ֣י לֹ֤א יִשָּׂא֙ לְפִשְׁעֲכֶ֔ם כִּ֥י שְׁמִ֖י בְּקִרְבּֽוֹ׃
22 כִּ֣י אִם־שָׁמֹ֤עַ תִּשְׁמַע֙ בְּקֹל֔וֹ וְעָשִׂ֕יתָ כֹּ֖ל
אֲשֶׁ֣ר אֲדַבֵּ֑ר וְאָֽיַבְתִּי֙ אֶת־אֹ֣יְבֶ֔יךָ וְצַרְתִּ֖י
אֶת־צֹרְרֶֽיךָ׃
23 כִּֽי־יֵלֵ֣ךְ מַלְאָכִי֮ לְפָנֶ֒יךָ֒ וֶהֱבִֽיאֲךָ֗ אֶל־
הָֽאֱמֹרִי֙ וְהַ֣חִתִּ֔י וְהַפְּרִזִּי֙ וְהַֽכְּנַעֲנִ֔י הַחִוִּ֖י
וְהַיְבוּסִ֑י וְהִכְחַדְתִּֽיו׃ 24 לֹֽא־תִשְׁתַּחֲוֶ֤ה
לֵאלֹֽהֵיהֶם֙ וְלֹ֣א תָֽעָבְדֵ֔ם וְלֹ֥א תַעֲשֶׂ֖ה
כְּמַֽעֲשֵׂיהֶ֑ם כִּ֤י הָרֵס֙ תְּהָ֣רְסֵ֔ם וְשַׁבֵּ֥ר תְּשַׁבֵּ֖ר
מַצֵּבֹתֵיהֶֽם׃ 25 וַעֲבַדְתֶּ֗ם אֵ֚ת יְהֹוָ֣ה
אֱלֹֽהֵיכֶ֔ם וּבֵרַ֥ךְ אֶת־לַחְמְךָ֖ וְאֶת־מֵימֶ֑יךָ
וַהֲסִרֹתִ֥י מַחֲלָ֖ה מִקִּרְבֶּֽךָ׃ פ 26 לֹ֥א תִהְיֶ֛ה
מְשַׁכֵּלָ֥ה וַעֲקָרָ֖ה בְּאַרְצֶ֑ךָ אֶת־מִסְפַּ֥ר יָמֶ֖יךָ
אֲמַלֵּֽא׃

serves as the basis for the historic Jewish dietary practice of separating dairy and meat products. The kid, or young goat, is mentioned because it was the most common type of livestock; later Jewish law extended the prohibition to sheep and large cattle as well. In ancient Israel, meat was rarely consumed outside of special occasions—such as festivals, new moons, or perhaps the visit of an honored guest. Cooking the animal in milk instead of water would have made it tastier and more tender. (For a different theory, see at Deuteronomy 14:21.) Most commentators point to a humanitarian motivation for this law, like the other regulations in the Torah that express a sensitivity to animals and their young (see Exodus 22:29; Leviticus 22:27; Deuteronomy 22:6–7). Boiling a goat in its mother's milk, a plausible scenario on a small farm, represents the destruction of the young in the substance intended to sustain and nurture it. In order to prevent the accidental transgression of this original injunction, the rabbinic sages expanded this command into a general prohibition against mixing meat with dairy products.

### DIVINE PROMISES AND WARNINGS (23:20–33)

This epilogue reaffirms the divine promise to bring Israel to Canaan and articulates the blessings that will be enjoyed by those who keep the covenant. The blessings of food, water, health, and procreation were crucial for the Israelites to survive in the Promised Land.

***26. No woman in your land shall miscarry or be barren.*** Israel is admonished in vv. 24–25 to worship the God of Israel and not adopt the religious practices of the native Canaanite population. As a reward, they will receive an array of blessings, including absence of two kinds of women: those who are incapable of conception, and those who suffer miscarriages (or, according to Rashi, those who bury their children). Fertility was considered

27 I will send forth My terror before you, and
I will throw into panic all the people among whom
you come, and I will make all your enemies turn tail
before you. 28 I will send a plague ahead of you, and
it shall drive out before you the Hivites, the Canaanites, and the Hittites. 29 I will not drive them
out before you in a single year, lest the land become
desolate and the wild beasts multiply to your hurt.
30 I will drive them out before you little by little,
until you have increased and possess the land.
31 I will set your borders from the Sea of Reeds to
the Sea of Philistia, and from the wilderness to the
Euphrates; for I will deliver the inhabitants of the
land into your hands, and you will drive them out
before you. 32 You shall make no covenant with
them and their gods. 33 They shall not remain in
your land, lest they cause you to sin against Me; for
you will serve their gods—and it will prove a snare
to you.

*24* Then [God] said to Moses, "Come up to
יהוה, with Aaron, Nadab and Abihu, and seventy
elders of Israel, and bow low from afar. 2 Moses
alone shall come near יהוה; but the others shall not
come near, nor shall the people come up with
him."

27 אֶת־אֵימָתִי אֲשַׁלַּח לְפָנֶיךָ וְהַמֹּתִי אֶת־
כָּל־הָעָם אֲשֶׁר תָּבֹא בָּהֶם וְנָתַתִּי אֶת־כָּל־
אֹיְבֶיךָ אֵלֶיךָ עֹרֶף׃ 28 וְשָׁלַחְתִּי אֶת־הַצִּרְעָה
לְפָנֶיךָ וְגֵרְשָׁה אֶת־הַחִוִּי אֶת־הַכְּנַעֲנִי וְאֶת־
הַחִתִּי מִלְּפָנֶיךָ׃ 29 לֹא אֲגָרְשֶׁנּוּ מִפָּנֶיךָ
בְּשָׁנָה אֶחָת פֶּן־תִּהְיֶה הָאָרֶץ שְׁמָמָה
וְרַבָּה עָלֶיךָ חַיַּת הַשָּׂדֶה׃ 30 מְעַט מְעַט
אֲגָרְשֶׁנּוּ מִפָּנֶיךָ עַד אֲשֶׁר תִּפְרֶה וְנָחַלְתָּ
אֶת־הָאָרֶץ׃ 31 וְשַׁתִּי אֶת־גְּבֻלְךָ מִיַּם־סוּף
וְעַד־יָם פְּלִשְׁתִּים וּמִמִּדְבָּר עַד־הַנָּהָר כִּי ׀
אֶתֵּן בְּיֶדְכֶם אֵת יֹשְׁבֵי הָאָרֶץ וְגֵרַשְׁתָּמוֹ
מִפָּנֶיךָ׃ 32 לֹא־תִכְרֹת לָהֶם וְלֵאלֹהֵיהֶם
בְּרִית׃ 33 לֹא יֵשְׁבוּ בְּאַרְצְךָ פֶּן־יַחֲטִיאוּ
אֹתְךָ לִי כִּי תַעֲבֹד אֶת־אֱלֹהֵיהֶם כִּי־יִהְיֶה
לְךָ לְמוֹקֵשׁ׃ פ

כד וְאֶל־מֹשֶׁה אָמַר עֲלֵה אֶל־יְהוָה אַתָּה
וְאַהֲרֹן נָדָב וַאֲבִיהוּא וְשִׁבְעִים מִזִּקְנֵי
יִשְׂרָאֵל וְהִשְׁתַּחֲוִיתֶם מֵרָחֹק׃ 2 וְנִגַּשׁ מֹשֶׁה
לְבַדּוֹ אֶל־יְהוָה וְהֵם לֹא יִגָּשׁוּ וְהָעָם לֹא
יַעֲלוּ עִמּוֹ׃

crucial for both the individual and society for several reasons. Israel's agrarian economy depended upon large families to perform all necessary labors. Premature mortality due to disease therefore made it necessary for women to have many children in order to ensure that some lived to adulthood. Also, a woman's financial security depended upon having children, as seen in the book of Ruth, where the women rejoice that Ruth's son will provide for his grandmother Naomi in her old age (Ruth 4:14–15). If a woman was widowed without children and her husband made no provisions for her, she might have no means of support, for her deceased husband's property would be inherited by her husband's brothers (Numbers 27:9).

## *The Covenant Ratification Ritual*
(24:1–18)

Exodus 24 depicts the ratification of the covenant between God and Israel. The central components of this ceremony involve Moses' recitation of the terms of the covenant, the people's unanimous agreement to follow God's words, the construction of an altar and twelve pillars symbolizing the twelve tribes, and the offering of sacrifices, with half the blood dashed on the altar and the other half sprinkled on the people—perhaps a graphic symbol of their entry into the covenant.

This passage also describes an unusual scene in which the leaders and representatives of the people

[3]Moses went and repeated to the people all the commands of יהוה and all the rules; and all the people answered with one voice, saying, "All the things that יהוה has commanded we will do!" [4]Moses then wrote down all the commands of יהוה.

Early in the morning, he set up an altar at the foot of the mountain, with twelve pillars for the twelve tribes of Israel. [5]He designated some assistants among the Israelites, and they offered burnt offerings and sacrificed bulls as offerings of well-being to יהוה. [6]Moses took one part of the blood and put it in basins, and the other part of the blood he dashed against the altar. [7]Then he took the record of the covenant and read it aloud to the people. And they said, "All that יהוה has spoken we will faithfully do!" [8]Moses took the blood and dashed it on the people and said, "This is the blood of the covenant that יהוה now makes with you concerning all these commands."

[9]Then Moses and Aaron, Nadab and Abihu, and seventy elders of Israel ascended; [10]and they saw the God of Israel—under whose feet was the likeness of a pavement of sapphire, like the very sky for purity. [11]Yet [God] did not raise a hand against the leaders of the Israelites; they beheld God, and they ate and drank.

[12]יהוה said to Moses, "Come up to Me on the mountain and wait there, and I will give you the stone tablets with the teachings and commandments which I have inscribed to instruct them." [13]So Moses and his attendant Joshua arose, and

3 וַיָּבֹא מֹשֶׁה וַיְסַפֵּר לָעָם אֵת כָּל־דִּבְרֵי
יְהוָה וְאֵת כָּל־הַמִּשְׁפָּטִים וַיַּעַן כָּל־הָעָם
קוֹל אֶחָד וַיֹּאמְרוּ כָּל־הַדְּבָרִים אֲשֶׁר־דִּבֶּר
יְהוָה נַעֲשֶׂה׃ 4 וַיִּכְתֹּב מֹשֶׁה אֵת כָּל־דִּבְרֵי
יְהוָה

וַיַּשְׁכֵּם בַּבֹּקֶר וַיִּבֶן מִזְבֵּחַ תַּחַת הָהָר
וּשְׁתֵּים עֶשְׂרֵה מַצֵּבָה לִשְׁנֵים עָשָׂר שִׁבְטֵי
יִשְׂרָאֵל׃ 5 וַיִּשְׁלַח אֶת־נַעֲרֵי בְּנֵי יִשְׂרָאֵל
וַיַּעֲלוּ עֹלֹת וַיִּזְבְּחוּ זְבָחִים שְׁלָמִים לַיהוָה
פָּרִים׃ 6 וַיִּקַּח מֹשֶׁה חֲצִי הַדָּם וַיָּשֶׂם
בָּאַגָּנֹת וַחֲצִי הַדָּם זָרַק עַל־הַמִּזְבֵּחַ׃
7 וַיִּקַּח סֵפֶר הַבְּרִית וַיִּקְרָא בְּאָזְנֵי הָעָם
וַיֹּאמְרוּ כֹּל אֲשֶׁר־דִּבֶּר יְהוָה נַעֲשֶׂה
וְנִשְׁמָע׃ 8 וַיִּקַּח מֹשֶׁה אֶת־הַדָּם וַיִּזְרֹק
עַל־הָעָם וַיֹּאמֶר הִנֵּה דַם־הַבְּרִית אֲשֶׁר
כָּרַת יְהוָה עִמָּכֶם עַל כָּל־הַדְּבָרִים
הָאֵלֶּה׃

9 וַיַּעַל מֹשֶׁה וְאַהֲרֹן נָדָב וַאֲבִיהוּא וְשִׁבְעִים
מִזִּקְנֵי יִשְׂרָאֵל׃ 10 וַיִּרְאוּ אֵת אֱלֹהֵי יִשְׂרָאֵל
וְתַחַת רַגְלָיו כְּמַעֲשֵׂה לִבְנַת הַסַּפִּיר וּכְעֶצֶם
הַשָּׁמַיִם לָטֹהַר׃ 11 וְאֶל־אֲצִילֵי בְּנֵי יִשְׂרָאֵל
לֹא שָׁלַח יָדוֹ וַיֶּחֱזוּ אֶת־הָאֱלֹהִים וַיֹּאכְלוּ
וַיִּשְׁתּוּ׃ ס

12 וַיֹּאמֶר יְהוָה אֶל־מֹשֶׁה עֲלֵה אֵלַי הָהָרָה
וֶהְיֵה־שָׁם וְאֶתְּנָה לְךָ אֶת־לֻחֹת הָאֶבֶן
וְהַתּוֹרָה וְהַמִּצְוָה אֲשֶׁר כָּתַבְתִּי לְהוֹרֹתָם׃
13 וַיָּקָם מֹשֶׁה וִיהוֹשֻׁעַ מְשָׁרְתוֹ וַיַּעַל מֹשֶׁה

ascend partway up the mountain, where they collectively experience a vision of God and participate in a formal meal to solemnize the covenant. Various segments of Israel's leadership participate in this ceremony: prophetic (Moses), priestly (Aaron, his sons Nadab and Abihu), and judicial (seventy representative elders). Although women do not take part in this particular ritual, presumably they are included in the term "people" as everyone affirms, "All that יהוה has spoken we will faithfully do" (v. 7). The episode reaches its climax when Moses ascends the mountain and receives the stone tablets etched with God's precepts. The tablets are to be deposited eventually in the ark of the Tabernacle, the focus of most of the remaining portion of the book of Exodus.

*—Elaine Goodfriend*

Moses ascended the mountain of God. <sup>14</sup>To the elders he had said, "Wait here for us until we return to you. You have Aaron and Hur with you; let anyone who has a legal matter approach them."

<sup>15</sup>When Moses had ascended the mountain, the cloud covered the mountain. <sup>16</sup>The Presence of יהוה abode on Mount Sinai, and the cloud hid it for six days. On the seventh day [God] called to Moses from the midst of the cloud. <sup>17</sup>Now the Presence of יהוה appeared in the sight of the Israelites as a consuming fire on the top of the mountain. <sup>18</sup>Moses went inside the cloud and ascended the mountain; and Moses remained on the mountain forty days and forty nights.

אֶל־הַ֣ר הָאֱלֹהִֽים׃ 14 וְאֶל־הַזְּקֵנִ֤ים אָמַר֙ שְׁבוּ־לָ֣נוּ בָזֶ֔ה עַ֥ד אֲשֶׁר־נָשׁ֖וּב אֲלֵיכֶ֑ם וְהִנֵּ֨ה אַהֲרֹ֤ן וְחוּר֙ עִמָּכֶ֔ם מִי־בַ֥עַל דְּבָרִ֖ים יִגַּ֥שׁ אֲלֵהֶֽם׃ 15 וַיַּ֥עַל מֹשֶׁ֖ה אֶל־הָהָ֑ר וַיְכַ֥ס הֶעָנָ֖ן אֶת־הָהָֽר׃ 16 וַיִּשְׁכֹּ֤ן כְּבוֹד־יְהֹוָה֙ עַל־הַ֣ר סִינַ֔י וַיְכַסֵּ֥הוּ הֶעָנָ֖ן שֵׁ֣שֶׁת יָמִ֑ים וַיִּקְרָ֧א אֶל־מֹשֶׁ֛ה בַּיּ֥וֹם הַשְּׁבִיעִ֖י מִתּ֥וֹךְ הֶעָנָֽן׃ 17 וּמַרְאֵה֙ כְּב֣וֹד יְהֹוָ֔ה כְּאֵ֥שׁ אֹכֶ֖לֶת בְּרֹ֣אשׁ הָהָ֑ר לְעֵינֵ֖י בְּנֵ֥י יִשְׂרָאֵֽל׃ 18 וַיָּבֹ֥א מֹשֶׁ֛ה בְּת֥וֹךְ הֶעָנָ֖ן וַיַּ֣עַל אֶל־הָהָ֑ר וַיְהִ֤י מֹשֶׁה֙ בָּהָ֔ר אַרְבָּעִ֣ים י֔וֹם וְאַרְבָּעִ֖ים לָֽיְלָה׃ פ

## Another View

The title of parashat Mishpatim ("Rules") belies the diversity in form and content of its legal materials. For the most part, the principles of morality and ethical concern it contains reflect admirable humanitarian principles, especially when compared to similar legal materials from other ancient Near Eastern cultures. However, with respect to language, the consistent use of the masculine gender in verbal and nominal forms is problematic. Since Hebrew often uses masculine forms generically, how do we know when masculine language refers specifically to men as opposed to both men and women? The new translation in this volume is the result of scrupulous research conducted to identify masculine terms that should be understood inclusively. The English text now reads more accurately, for it reflects the fact that many legal principles apply to women as well as men.

Nonetheless, there is an important usage of the masculine singular that is not visible in this translation. The masculine singular pronoun *atah* is translated as "you." The word "you" is gender inclusive in English; but in Hebrew *atah* sometimes refers generically to men and women, at other times, just to men.

According to the Bible, a marital couple forms a unity. The classic evidence for this is Genesis 2:24, which presents the astonishing statement—given the patrilocal nature of Israelite society, with brides moving to the grooms' homes—that men are to leave their parents and become "one flesh" with their spouses. Despite a powerful concern with lineages and ancestry, the marital bond trumps the parental connection and expresses the merging of female and male.

Thus, many biblical passages using masculine language may refer to a conjugal pair. In such cases, masculine singular pronouns like *atah* or masculine singular imperatives ("you") are not simply inclusive terms, but reflect the special bond of husband and wife. For example, the injunction to cease from work on the seventh day (23:12) uses the masculine singular form but presumably applies to a man's wife as well. Similarly, the prohibition against cooking a kid in its mother's milk (23:19) is in the masculine singular but also applies to a man's spouse; after all, women were largely responsible for preparing food in ancient Israel.

*Many biblical passages that use masculine language may refer to a conjugal pair.*

—*Carol Meyers*

## Post-biblical Interpretations

***When you acquire a Hebrew slave*** (21:2–11). Slavery was an accepted part of life in biblical and post-biblical times. Numerous Roman Empire documents and inscriptions demonstrate that Jews were slaves and slave owners. Slaves could be emancipated, but mostly within ongoing structured relationships between freed persons and their master's/patron's household. The provisions for treatment of slaves outlined in our parashah do not appear to have been applied by Jews in the post-biblical period, even when their slaves were also Jews.

Thus, female slaves in the post-biblical period did not enjoy the protections of Exodus 21:9–11, which considers female slavery as leading to marriage and refers to a woman's conjugal rights. Rather, rabbinic legislation, like Roman law, considered slavery a deficient status. A Jewish slave woman could not form a legal marriage with her Jewish sexual partner, whether a slave or a free man, and the offspring of such a union were slaves (Mishnah *Kiddushin* 3:12). The likelihood of sexual relations between female slaves and various males in the master's household was assumed. Rabbinic texts tacitly recognized that women slaves were sexually available to their owners, as in the maxim "the more women slaves, the more unchastity" (Mishnah *Avot* 2:7). This warning addresses the distraction that female slaves posed to the male scholar.

Emancipation affected men and women differently. The Jewish historian Flavius Josephus (1st century C.E.) described a Jew who was taken as a slave to Rome and married a captive virgin at the command of his master, Emperor Vespasian (*Life* 414–15). At the moment that the male slave was freed, they separated, and later he married again. The first woman was apparently an appropriate wife for a slave, but not for a free man.

Rabbinic law presumed that female slaves and freed women were no longer virgins. Thus, even if a slave woman was emancipated, the legal minimum value of her marriage settlement (*k'tubah*) would be half that of an unmarried free woman. Although the liberation story of Exodus was always a central focus of Judaism, few commentators have struggled with the larger issues of enslavement that continued for centuries in Jewish societies.

Rabbinic Judaism did place a premium on *pidyon sh'vuyim*, the redemption of Jewish captives who were at risk of being sold into slavery. BT *Bava Batra* 8a–b asks: "Since Rabbi Samuel ben Judah has laid down that money for *tzedakah* is not to be levied from the fatherless 'even for the redemption of captives,' should we not conclude that redeeming captives is a religious duty of great importance?" The Rabbis insisted that in most cases women were to be redeemed from slavery before men, in order to preserve the women from dishonor (Mishnah *Horayot* 3:7; BT *Horayot* 13a). If a woman testified that a fellow female prisoner, the wife of a priest, was not raped in captivity, her testimony was believed, even though women's testimony was generally not admissible in rabbinic courts (Mishnah *K'tubot* 2:6; BT *K'tubot* 27b). This meant the undefiled woman could return to her husband.

***When* [*two or more*] *parties fight*** (21:22–25). The phrase *if other damage ensues* (v. 23) played a critical role in shaping rabbinic attitudes about abortion (Daniel Schiff, *Abortion in Judaism*, 2002). In the Torah, *a miscarriage results, but no other damage* (v. 22) is contrasted with the potential *other damage* (v. 23), an apparent reference to the death of the woman. This formulation suggests that only mortal injury to the pregnant woman is considered homicide. However, Jews who translated the Hebrew Bible into Greek (3rd century B.C.E.) understood the import of these verses differently. Instead of contrasting the death of the fetus and the death of the mother, the Septuagint (Greek translation) renders *ason* as "formed," distinguishing the death of an "imperfectly formed" fetus (v. 22) from that of a "perfectly formed" fetus (v. 23). Thus, this translation considers the violently induced miscarriage of a completely formed fetus as homicide.

*Few commentators have struggled with the larger issues of enslavement.*

Rabbinic interpretation, however, follows the Hebrew text; therefore, the Rabbis drew a clear distinction between the monetary penalty for one who kills a fetus, and the capital penalty for one who causes a woman's death. The Rabbis considered elsewhere the existence and formation of a fetus once it had reached forty days, but they stopped short of declaring it a *nefesh*, a legal human life. Despite the complexity and ambiguity in many of their discussions of abortion, the Rabbis specifically legislated aborting a fetus if its continued existence threatened the pregnant woman's life (Mishnah *Ohalot* 7:6 and BT *Sanhedrin* 72b).

—*Susan Marks*

# *Contemporary Reflection*

PARASHAT MISHPATIM CONTAINS the Torah's first law collection, which—unlike all other ancient Near-Eastern law collections—begins with regulations concerning slavery. The Torah seems unable to imagine an economy without slaves, but it frowns upon Hebrew slavery. Consequently, for Israelites in debt, Exodus 21:2–6 prescribes indentured servitude, but limited to six years. If a man enters debt-slavery while married, the master must let his wife go when he is released. However, if the master gives him a slave wife, the master retains the wife and children. What happens if the debt-slave declares, "I love my master and my wife and children: I do not wish to go free" (21:5)? He then has his earlobe pierced with an awl, and he becomes a slave in perpetuity, which the Rabbis interpret to mean until the Jubilee, or fiftieth, year.

Liberal readers are often sympathetic to this noble fellow who relinquishes his freedom to stay with his slave wife and children. But how would this case look from the perspective of the slave wife? I will argue that it looks much different. Who is this slave woman? She is not the *amah ivriyah* (Hebrew indentured servant) the text speaks about in 21:7–12. In that case, a girl has been sold by a presumably impoverished Israelite parent into a wealthier family on the understanding that she will eventually be married to the master or one of his sons as a free woman. This practice is well attested in other ancient Near Eastern documents. Should the man take another wife, he must continue to support her. An Israelite woman may not be resold if her owner is displeased with her; instead, she must go free without any compensation to the master. Her servitude, too, is time limited.

In contrast, the slave woman in Exodus 21:5–6 is most likely a foreign bondswoman. As a non-Israelite, she will not become part of the master's family, and her slavery is perpetual, not limited. As property, she and a male Israelite slave can be mated by the master to breed more slaves, which cannot be done to an Israelite handmaiden. The foreign bondswoman does not choose her husband and cannot reject him. Both he and her children can be taken from her. As we learn from Exodus 21:20, 26–27, her very body is at risk, for masters may beat their own slaves without legal interference as long as they do not kill them or destroy a major body part. (Slave narratives from different parts of the world confirm that slaves were, and are, routinely battered and then expected to work.

*How would this case look from the perspective of the slave wife?*

They may work less efficiently, but historically this has not been a sufficient disincentive to masters. The law cannot be said to permit battery of slaves; it is simply uninterested in such battery unless it results in major damage or death.)

While the Israelite slave must be freed at the start of the seventh year, how might the foreign bondswoman obtain her freedom? There are three options: First, she could save money given to her as a reward or a wage. If, with her owner's permission, she contracts herself out for pay after finishing her other work, she might be able to accumulate money to buy her freedom. Mesopotamian records show that slaves were able to gain extra money as artisans and agents (see Gregory Chirichigno, *Debt-Slavery in Israel and the Ancient Near East*, 1993, p. 54); this practice might have existed in ancient Israel as well. Second, she could run away. Deuteronomy 23:16–17 says that a fugitive slave may not be returned to the owner. Third, an Israelite slave husband once released could buy his slave wife and children and free them. African-American history shows examples of former slaves who bought spouses and children or arranged for them to be secretly stolen and led to freedom. Harriet Tubman, whose code name was "Moses," had a long career of gathering slaves and leading them North. Implicit in these narratives is a desperate determination to be free.

In contrast, what does the Israelite slave husband accomplish by pledging himself to perpetual slavery? When he declares that he loves his wife and children, it is not a happy, free family he is talking about. He cannot insure that his family will remain intact. His wife and children could be sold at any time. Even when his family is united, all will suffer the terrible humiliations of slavery: lack of choice, being objectified as property, being brutalized without recourse. Will the slave-wife appreciate his sinking into helplessness and hopelessness alongside her, especially if she was counting on his determination to free her once he was freed?

When the debt-slave professes his love for his master (whom he mentions before his slave family in v. 5), what kind of love is this? It is a love of dependency, of not having to make decisions, of not having to struggle for a living, to choose a wife, or take responsibility for one's children. Beyond that, embracing slavery undoes the liberation from Egypt and rejects the liberating God. In BT *Kiddushin* 22b, Rabbi Yochanan ben Zakkai explains why this man's ear is pierced with an awl: "The Holy One says, 'The ear that heard on Mount Sinai when I said, 'the people of Israel are my servants and not servants of servants' and went and got himself a human master, let that ear be pierced.'"

The bondswoman is not where she is because she volunteered to be a slave. Most likely, she is a captive taken in war, well schooled in the corrosive bitterness of slavery. She might see the Hebrew slave's renunciation of freedom not as a romantic gesture, but as a naïve, even stupid one. He has surrendered his power to free her or their children. He may have been her best chance for freedom.

The Torah is truthful with us, although that truth does not always make us happy. Ancient Near Eastern law could not imagine a world without slavery; yet Israelite law wanted the people to remain free of all human appropriation. That dilemma resulted in the preservation of this vignette about the conflicting loyalties of the Israelite slave. By highlighting the shadowy woman in the background, we get a rare, ironic glimpse of the dilemma from her usually invisible point of view.

—*Rachel Adler*

# Voices

## *from* After a Miscarriage: Hold Me Now

Vicki Hollander

*Exodus 21:22*

*Hayotzer,*
One who shapes,
Who formed us out of moistened clay,
Who rolled and pinched and sculpted the
world,
hold me now.

You who enable wisps of seeds to grow,
Who partnered the life which grew inside me,
shelter me.

Life was gifted.
Life removed.

*Hayotzer,*
shape me a place where I can weep,
and mourn the loss,
and let the blackness inside
cry.

Help me say goodbye
to the child
who was growing within me,
to the dreams I bore,
to the love I held within for that budding soul,
plucked away.

Let my voice ring,
a mother's call,
wild to the universe.

And You,
stand by me,
stand at my side,
and watch my tear fall and touch the earth.
Hear my pain and
hold me.

## Under the Spell of Miscarriage

Jessica Greenbaum

*Exodus 21:22*

whatever I touched took on a lifelessness
of its own, recomposed like a sentence
to its letters or partisans to their hiding places.
The corn bread came out—a stone tablet—
and the soup, puffing, grew as bland
as its original pearly beans. Molecules spilled
their promise like the string of beads
I was trying to clasp; bonds broke so fast
it seemed no two entities could have rapport;
in the metropolis of my body all the friends
en route to assignations turned for home,
and outside it, even our speech fell bewitched—
ideas skidded to a halt before they could
be loved, and nothing we said generated a laugh
or begot more conversation. How I wanted
to talk up a storm, to spin a yarn, to harvest,
like the fair's cotton candy, a wand of stuff
from the kindness farmed in the plot
between us
(because that is our defining nature).
A low bow to the one who forbids creation.
Now I see how powerful you are, and how
neglected.

## *Psalm 5: A Lullaby for Courage*

Debbie Perlman

*Exodus 23:25*

O Eternal, hold me with gentleness
Through this long night of pain;
Lay Your cool hand upon my body.
As a mother strokes the fevered brow
Of her beloved child,
Give me succor.

O Eternal, clasp me to Your bosom,
And rock me with quiet motion,
To and fro as the seconds pass,
Waiting, waiting for the next relief,
Stretching endlessly toward the dawn.

O Eternal, sing me to calm,
Humming a lullaby my grandmother sang
As she arranged the soup bowl on the tray,
And brought it to me with the warmth of
her smile.
Sing me that song to soothe my soul.

O Eternal, guard me through this darkness.
Wrap me in a soft, warm quilt of Your regard
That I might find a paragraph of flickering
comfort
To read and remember
Within this long, grim novel.

O Eternal, keep me safe through this night;
And let the morning come to renew me,
To turn me, to heal me,
To find me enfolded in the vigor of Your love.

## *Barren*

Rahel (transl. Maurice Samuel)

*Exodus 23:26*

Oh, if I had a son, a little son,
With black, curled hair and clever eyes,
A little son to walk with in the garden
Under morning skies
A son,
A little son!

I'd call him Uri, little, laughing Uri,
A tender name, as light, as full of joy
As sunlight on the dew, as tripping on the
tongue
As the laughter of a boy—
"Uri!"
I'd call him.

And still I wait, as mother Rahel waited,
Or Hannah at Shiloh, she, the barren one,
Until the day comes when my lips whisper,
"Uri, my son!"

# תרומה ✦ T'rumah

## EXODUS 25:1–27:19

### *A Place for God: Instructions for Building the Tabernacle*

Although God is theoretically everywhere, the Israelites needed assurance of God's constant accessibility and availability. They accomplished this—as did the other peoples of the ancient Near East—by constructing an earthly residence for God, one that would mirror the heavenly prototype in which God was presumed to dwell. With God in their midst in an earthly shrine, God's power to protect the people and provide for their well-being would be guaranteed. Beginning with *parashat T'rumah* ("gifts"), virtually all of the rest of Exodus focuses on the portable shrine known variously as the Tabernacle (*Mishkan*) or Tent of Meeting (*Ohel Mo'ed*). Even though some of its structure and objects are reflected in today's synagogue furnishings, the Tabernacle should not be compared to a synagogue. It was not a house of worship; and it was off limits to all but the upper echelons of the priesthood. Instead of being a place of communal worship, it was conceived of as an elaborate and costly residence for the divine presence. The word *Mishkan* comes from the root meaning "to dwell" (*sh-k-n*), which gave rise also to the well-known term *Shechinah* (see at 25:8).

The wealth of seemingly exact details in the instructions for the Tabernacle belies the fact that such a structure probably never existed. The early Israelites may have had a relatively simple tent shrine—perhaps the Tent of Meeting—that was later incorporated into the Jerusalem Temple during the monarchy. Memories of the original shrine likely were expanded as the Exodus Tabernacle account took shape centuries later, influenced by knowledge of the First and Second Temples. This is a highly constructed account, and very little of it seems to be historical.

The Tabernacle texts in Exodus—much like the sacred building texts of other ancient peoples—begin with elaborate instructions for

> *Behind the mass of arcane details lies a yearning for God's presence.*

making the *Mishkan*, its furnishings, and the priestly vestments (Exodus 25–31); some Bible scholars call these instructions the *prescriptive* Tabernacle texts. Much of this information is repeated in another lengthy section relating how the instructions were implemented (Exodus 35–40); its passages are called the *descriptive* Tabernacle texts. The Golden Calf episode (Exodus 32–34) separates these two pieces. It is helpful to remember that behind the mass of arcane details lies a yearning for God's presence and an attempt to establish a relationship between divine immanence and transcendence, in other words, between God's abilities to be "right here" and "everywhere" at the same time.

Aside from God and Moses, the only other actors in this parashah are the "people" who collectively provide the building materials. While women are not explicitly mentioned in this Torah portion, *parashat Vayak'heil* specifies that both women and men donated their possessions for the construction of the *Mishkan* (35:22, 29; 36:6) and that women were involved in producing textiles (35:25–26) and performing tasks at the entrance of the Tent of Meeting (38:8). Such passages challenge the popular impression that this holy edifice is the result of exclusively male efforts.

—*Carol Meyers*

## Outline

I. Instructions about Building Materials (25:1–9)

II. Instructions about Interior Furnishings (25:10–40)

- A. Ark and its cover (vv. 10–22)
- B. Table and menorah (vv. 23–40)

III. Instructions about the Tabernacle Structure (26:1–37)

- A. Coverings (vv. 1–14)
- B. Frames (vv. 15–30)
- C. Textile partitions (vv. 31–37)

IV. Instructions about the Courtyard (27:1–19)

- A. Altar (vv. 1–8)
- B. Enclosure (vv. 9–19)

יהוה spoke to Moses, saying: 2Tell the
Israelite people to bring Me gifts;
you shall accept gifts for Me from every person
whose heart is so moved. 3And these are the gifts
that you shall accept from them: gold, silver, and
copper; 4blue, purple, and crimson yarns, fine

כה וַיְדַבֵּר יְהֹוָה אֶל־מֹשֶׁה לֵּאמֹר׃ 2 דַּבֵּר
אֶל־בְּנֵי יִשְׂרָאֵל וְיִקְחוּ־לִי תְּרוּמָה מֵאֵת
כָּל־אִישׁ אֲשֶׁר יִדְּבֶנּוּ לִבּוֹ תִּקְחוּ אֶת־
תְּרוּמָתִי׃ 3 וְזֹאת הַתְּרוּמָה אֲשֶׁר תִּקְחוּ
מֵאִתָּם זָהָב וָכֶסֶף וּנְחֹשֶׁת׃ 4 וּתְכֵלֶת

## *Instructions about Building Materials* (25:1–9)

Because the Tabernacle is conceived of as God's abode, many of its features are highly symbolic. This is apparent in this introductory unit, which features seven categories of materials: metals, yarn, skins, wood, oil, spices, and gemstones. The number seven represents completeness in the Semitic world, so this group of materials signifies the totality of the supplies.

*1.* ***יהוה spoke to Moses.*** The directions for the Tabernacle are presented as being given to Moses at Sinai, thus linking the remainder of the book of Exodus to the preceding narrative about the exodus from Egypt and the revelation at Sinai.

*2.* ***gifts.*** Heb. *t'rumah,* a collective term, provides the designation for this parashah. The resources for the Tabernacle are to be donated, not elicited as taxes.

***people . . . every person.*** All members of the community, both female and male, are expected to contribute, as 35:22, 29 and 36:6 make explicit. This assumes that women had their own resources and control over them; presumably they could decide for themselves what to offer to the project.

*3.* ***gold, silver, and copper.*** Three metals will be used for the components of the Tabernacle according to their proximity to the most sacred space, the Holy of Holies. The most sacred objects will be made of gold, the most valuable metal.

***copper.*** The Hebrew term also designates bronze (a copper-based alloy), which, given its strength and hardness, is more likely the intended meaning with regard to the Tabernacle.

*4.* ***blue, purple, and crimson yarns.*** The three colors specified for the woolen yarns—indigo blue, sea-snail purple, and cochineal red—were the most desirable and expensive in ancient Israel and the wider Near East. These particular dyes were self-fixing, meaning that they were relatively impervious to light and remained bright. Dying woolen strands with these colors was costly because the raw materials were difficult to use or rare. These three colors are probably listed in order of costliness. Textile production was largely the domain of women, as the Torah reflects in 35:25–26 (see also Another View, p. 467; *P'kudei,* Another View, p. 560).

◗ Most women spun and wove to satisfy household needs: clothing, blankets, bags, and more.

ANOTHER VIEW ➤ *467*

◗ Imagine how these former slaves felt as they became builders of a dwelling for the Divine!

CONTEMPORARY REFLECTION ➤ *469*

◗ God is depicted as a father, longing to remain with his beloved daughter, Israel.

POST-BIBLICAL INTERPRETATIONS ➤ *468*

◗ one thing have I asked and it I seek / your dwelling in me your giving me a spirit. . .

VOICES ➤ *471*

linen, goats' hair; 5 tanned ram skins, dolphin skins,
and acacia wood; 6 oil for lighting, spices for the
anointing oil and for the aromatic incense; 7 lapis
lazuli and other stones for setting, for the ephod
and for the breastpiece. 8 And let them make Me a
sanctuary that I may dwell among them. 9 Exactly
as I show you—the pattern of the Tabernacle and
the pattern of all its furnishings—so shall you
make it.

וְאַרְגָּמָן וְתוֹלַעַת שָׁנִי וְשֵׁשׁ וְעִזִּים׃ 5 וְעֹרֹת
אֵילִם מְאָדָּמִים וְעֹרֹת תְּחָשִׁים וַעֲצֵי
שִׁטִּים׃ 6 שֶׁמֶן לַמָּאֹר בְּשָׂמִים לְשֶׁמֶן
הַמִּשְׁחָה וְלִקְטֹרֶת הַסַּמִּים׃ 7 אַבְנֵי־שֹׁהַם
וְאַבְנֵי מִלֻּאִים לָאֵפֹד וְלַחֹשֶׁן׃ 8 וְעָשׂוּ לִי
מִקְדָּשׁ וְשָׁכַנְתִּי בְּתוֹכָם׃ 9 כְּכֹל אֲשֶׁר אֲנִי
מַרְאֶה אוֹתְךָ אֵת תַּבְנִית הַמִּשְׁכָּן וְאֵת
תַּבְנִית כָּל־כֵּלָיו וְכֵן תַּעֲשׂוּ׃ ס

***linen.*** The word for linen is derived from an Egyptian term and denotes an especially fine grade of that fabric.

*5.* ***dolphin.*** The meaning of this term is uncertain; perhaps it represents a specific color—probably rust—of tanned and dyed sheep- or goatskin, rather than a sea animal.

***acacia.*** Wood from acacia trees is durable and relatively light in weight—ideal for a portable structure.

*6.* ***oil.*** Namely, olive oil to be used as lamp fuel, as explained later; see 27:20–21 and the comments there.

***spices for the anointing oil and... incense.*** The oil is to be used to anoint the sacred objects and the priests, as explained later; for the ingredients, see 30:22–38.

*7.* ***lapis lazuli.*** More likely onyx or possibly carnelian.

***ephod and . . . breastpiece.*** These are the paraphernalia of the vestments for the chief priestly official. (For more details, see at 28:6.)

*8.* ***sanctuary.*** Heb. *mikdash*, from the root *k-d-sh* ("to be hallowed"); the term emphasizes the Tabernacle's holiness.

***that I may dwell among them.*** This key statement articulates the purpose of the Tabernacle.

***dwell.*** The verb comes from the root *sh-k-n*. The usual word for "dwell" (*y-sh-b*) means to inhabit or live someplace. In contrast, the root *sh-k-n* indicates a moving, dynamic presence, not one tied to a fixed location. (The later concept of the *Shechinah* comes from the same root; see Post-biblical Interpretations, p. 468.)

***among them.*** Or, "in the midst of" the people. Such language helps negotiate the tension between the freedom of God to be everywhere and the need of humans to have tangible evidence of God's immanence and accessibility.

*9.* ***pattern.*** Heb. *tavnit*, a noun formed from the verb "to build" (*b-n-h*). It probably refers to an archetypal heavenly structure rather than to a plan an architect would use. Thus, God's imagined heavenly abode provides the model for the Tabernacle.

***Tabernacle.*** Heb. *mishkan*, from the root *sh-k-n* (see at v. 8 under "dwell"), which allows for the mobility inherent in the concept of a tent-shrine. The noun conveys the idea of a dwelling-place and is not simply a synonym for tent. The English word "Tabernacle" (which derives from Latin) refers only to this wilderness shrine, whereas *mishkan* is a more general term: when it refers to a structure occupied by human beings it is translated as "dwelling, abode, home" (for example, Leviticus 26:11; Numbers 16:24, 24:5). The Tabernacle is conceived of as a place on earth in which God will be readily accessible and from which God's protective power will emanate.

10 They shall make an ark of acacia wood, two
and a half cubits long, a cubit and a half wide, and a
cubit and a half high. 11 Overlay it with pure gold—
overlay it inside and out—and make upon it a gold
molding round about. 12 Cast four gold rings for it,
to be attached to its four feet, two rings on one of
its side walls and two on the other. 13 Make poles of
acacia wood and overlay them with gold; 14 then in-
sert the poles into the rings on the side walls of the
ark, for carrying the ark. 15 The poles shall remain in
the rings of the ark: they shall not be removed from
it. 16 And deposit in the Ark [the tablets of] the Pact
which I will give you.

10 וְעָשׂוּ אֲרוֹן עֲצֵי שִׁטִּים אַמָּתַיִם וָחֵצִי
אָרְכּוֹ וְאַמָּה וָחֵצִי רָחְבּוֹ וְאַמָּה וָחֵצִי
קֹמָתוֹ׃ 11 וְצִפִּיתָ אֹתוֹ זָהָב טָהוֹר מִבַּיִת
וּמִחוּץ תְּצַפֶּנּוּ וְעָשִׂיתָ עָלָיו זֵר זָהָב סָבִיב׃
12 וְיָצַקְתָּ לּוֹ אַרְבַּע טַבְּעֹת זָהָב וְנָתַתָּה עַל
אַרְבַּע פַּעֲמֹתָיו וּשְׁתֵּי טַבָּעֹת עַל־צַלְעוֹ
הָאֶחָת וּשְׁתֵּי טַבָּעֹת עַל־צַלְעוֹ הַשֵּׁנִית׃
13 וְעָשִׂיתָ בַדֵּי עֲצֵי שִׁטִּים וְצִפִּיתָ אֹתָם
זָהָב׃ 14 וְהֵבֵאתָ אֶת־הַבַּדִּים בַּטַּבָּעֹת עַל
צַלְעֹת הָאָרֹן לָשֵׂאת אֶת־הָאָרֹן בָּהֶם׃
15 בְּטַבְּעֹת הָאָרֹן יִהְיוּ הַבַּדִּים לֹא יָסֻרוּ
מִמֶּנּוּ׃ 16 וְנָתַתָּ אֶל־הָאָרֹן אֵת הָעֵדֻת אֲשֶׁר
אֶתֵּן אֵלֶיךָ׃

## *Instructions about Interior Furnishings* (25:10–40)

The prescriptive texts (those detailing what is to be done) begin with the contents of the Tabernacle, in contrast with the descriptive texts (those detailing what was done), which begin with its structure (see the introduction to *Vayak'heil*, p. 521). The first item in a series is arguably the most important. Here, the instructions for the furnishings begin with the most sacred object, the Ark, which will occupy the Holy of Holies, followed by the offering table and menorah in the outer room.

### ARK AND ITS COVER (25:10–22)

The term *aron* ("Ark") denotes a box or chest used as a container for valuables, probably similar to those known from ancient Egypt. The Ark is to contain a document understood to be the Decalogue ("Ten Commandments") or some form of the covenant between God and the people. At the same time, the Ark symbolically suggests a throne for the invisible deity and signifies God's presence in the Tabernacle's inner sanctum. (For the descriptive text later in Exodus that parallels this prescriptive section, see 37:1–9.)

*10. two and a half cubits . . . a cubit and a half . . . a cubit and a half.* The Ark is to be nearly 4 feet long (a little more than 1 meter) and a bit more than 2 feet wide and deep (about 2/3 meter). The cubit was a widely used measure in the ancient Near East but was never standardized.

*11. pure gold.* As part of the furnishings of the holiest zone, the Ark is to be covered with the most precious metal. The designation "pure" indicates that the highest quality of gold is to be used.

*12. its four feet.* The feet perhaps are added to ensure this sacred object will not rest directly on the ground.

*13–14. poles . . . for carrying.* Since the Ark was to be portable, it could be carried to battle to represent God's presence (see I Samuel 4–7; Numbers 10:35–36).

*16. [the tablets of] the Pact.* Heb. *edut*, meaning "pact" or "treaty," is likely an elliptical designation for "tablets of the Pact," the document on which the agreement between God and Israel was said to have been inscribed (31:18). Elsewhere in the Torah, the word *b'rit* ("covenant") is usually used for this treaty (as in 34:28).

17 You shall make a cover of pure gold, two and a half cubits long and a cubit and a half wide. 18 Make two cherubim of gold—make them of hammered work—at the two ends of the cover. 19 Make one cherub at one end and the other cherub at the other end; of one piece with the cover shall you make the cherubim at its two ends. 20 The cherubim shall have their wings spread out above, shielding the cover with their wings. They shall confront each other, the faces of the cherubim being turned toward the cover. 21 Place the cover on top of the Ark, after depositing inside the Ark the Pact that I will give you. 22 There I will meet with you, and I will impart to you—from above the cover, from between the two cherubim that are on top of the Ark of the Pact—all that I will command you concerning the Israelite people.

17 וְעָשִׂיתָ כַפֹּרֶת זָהָב טָהוֹר אַמָּתַיִם וָחֵצִי
אָרְכָּהּ וְאַמָּה וָחֵצִי רָחְבָּהּ׃ 18 וְעָשִׂיתָ שְׁנַיִם
כְּרֻבִים זָהָב מִקְשָׁה תַּעֲשֶׂה אֹתָם מִשְּׁנֵי
קְצוֹת הַכַּפֹּרֶת׃ 19 וַעֲשֵׂה כְּרוּב אֶחָד מִקָּצָה
מִזֶּה וּכְרוּב־אֶחָד מִקָּצָה מִזֶּה מִן־הַכַּפֹּרֶת
תַּעֲשׂוּ אֶת־הַכְּרֻבִים עַל־שְׁנֵי קְצוֹתָיו׃
20 וְהָיוּ הַכְּרֻבִים פֹּרְשֵׂי כְנָפַיִם לְמַעְלָה
סֹכְכִים בְּכַנְפֵיהֶם עַל־הַכַּפֹּרֶת וּפְנֵיהֶם אִישׁ
אֶל־אָחִיו אֶל־הַכַּפֹּרֶת יִהְיוּ פְּנֵי הַכְּרֻבִים׃
21 וְנָתַתָּ אֶת־הַכַּפֹּרֶת עַל־הָאָרֹן מִלְמָעְלָה
וְאֶל־הָאָרֹן תִּתֵּן אֶת־הָעֵדֻת אֲשֶׁר אֶתֵּן
אֵלֶיךָ׃ 22 וְנוֹעַדְתִּי לְךָ שָׁם וְדִבַּרְתִּי אִתְּךָ
מֵעַל הַכַּפֹּרֶת מִבֵּין שְׁנֵי הַכְּרֻבִים אֲשֶׁר עַל־
אֲרוֹן הָעֵדֻת אֵת כָּל־אֲשֶׁר אֲצַוֶּה אוֹתְךָ
אֶל־בְּנֵי יִשְׂרָאֵל׃ פ

*17.* ***cover.*** Heb. *kaporet*, whose meaning and etymology remain uncertain. Many understand it in relationship to the verb *k-p-r*, "to atone." It also is possible that it is derived from an Egyptian phrase that would make it equivalent to a place for one's feet to rest, a suggestion that gives it a tantalizingly close connection to the depiction of the ark in certain texts (I Samuel 4:4; Psalm 99:1–5), in which an invisible God seems to be present on a cherubim throne with a footstool.

*18.* ***cherubim.*** These fanciful beasts are well known in ancient Near Eastern culture. Composite creatures made up of human and animal features, they are not at all like the round-faced cherubs of Western art. Usually depicted with wings, they possessed the ability to move where humans cannot, which made them apt symbols of deities.

*19–21.* The placement of the cherubim on either side of the "cover" forms a throne, with the cover as a footstool for God's unseen presence (see at v. 17). The Ark, with its cover surmounted by cherubim, serves as the visible locus of God's invisible royal presence.

*22.* ***There I will meet with you.*** Another name for the Tabernacle, the Tent of Meeting (27:21 and frequently thereafter), is related to this concept of God's interaction with the people at the place where the divine Presence rests. In ancient Israel, such meetings probably took the form of divine oracles delivered via qualified priests (see *T'tzaveh*, Another View, p. 489), or via prophetic figures like Moses (see 34:34). While women did serve as prophets in Israel (see at 15:20), Israelite priests were male. In the Torah's depiction of the Tabernacle, oracular meetings held there to mediate God's will to the people are restricted to select male agents: only those from the family of Levi.

***concerning the Israelite people.*** In the ancient world, people typically sought oracles when they turned to a deity to resolve an otherwise intractable legal dispute (see, for example, Numbers 27:1–5). Oracles also aided with political decisions, such as determining whether or when to go to war or levy taxes. According to the Torah, oracular decisions are achieved by mechanical means; see comments about the ephod (Exodus 28:6), priestly "breastpiece of decision" (28:15), and Urim and Thummim (28:30).

23You shall make a table of acacia wood, two
cubits long, one cubit wide, and a cubit and a
half high. 24Overlay it with pure gold, and make a
gold molding around it. 25Make a rim of a hand's
breadth around it, and make a gold molding for its
rim round about. 26Make four gold rings for it, and
attach the rings to the four corners at its four legs.
27The rings shall be next to the rim, as holders for
poles to carry the table. 28Make the poles of acacia
wood, and overlay them with gold; by these the
table shall be carried. 29Make its bowls, ladles, jars
and jugs with which to offer libations; make them
of pure gold. 30And on the table you shall set the
bread of display, to be before Me always.

23 וְעָשִׂיתָ שֻׁלְחָן עֲצֵי שִׁטִּים אַמָּתַיִם אָרְכּוֹ
וְאַמָּה רָחְבּוֹ וְאַמָּה וָחֵצִי קֹמָתוֹ׃ 24 וְצִפִּיתָ
אֹתוֹ זָהָב טָהוֹר וְעָשִׂיתָ לּוֹ זֵר זָהָב סָבִיב׃
25 וְעָשִׂיתָ לּוֹ מִסְגֶּרֶת טֹפַח סָבִיב וְעָשִׂיתָ
זֵר־זָהָב לְמִסְגַּרְתּוֹ סָבִיב׃ 26 וְעָשִׂיתָ לּוֹ
אַרְבַּע טַבְּעֹת זָהָב וְנָתַתָּ אֶת־הַטַּבָּעֹת עַל
אַרְבַּע הַפֵּאֹת אֲשֶׁר לְאַרְבַּע רַגְלָיו׃
27 לְעֻמַּת הַמִּסְגֶּרֶת תִּהְיֶיןָ הַטַּבָּעֹת לְבָתִּים
לְבַדִּים לָשֵׂאת אֶת־הַשֻּׁלְחָן׃ 28 וְעָשִׂיתָ
אֶת־הַבַּדִּים עֲצֵי שִׁטִּים וְצִפִּיתָ אֹתָם זָהָב
וְנִשָּׂא־בָם אֶת־הַשֻּׁלְחָן׃ 29 וְעָשִׂיתָ קְּעָרֹתָיו
וְכַפֹּתָיו וּקְשׂוֹתָיו וּמְנַקִּיֹּתָיו אֲשֶׁר יֻסַּךְ בָּהֵן
זָהָב טָהוֹר תַּעֲשֶׂה אֹתָם׃ 30 וְנָתַתָּ עַל־
הַשֻּׁלְחָן לֶחֶם פָּנִים לְפָנַי תָּמִיד׃ פ

## TABLE AND MENORAH (25:23–40)

The Tabernacle's main, outer room is furnished with a table and a lampstand. A third object—an incense altar—will be mentioned in an addendum, in the next parashah (30:1–10). All three golden items are suitable furnishings for a royal abode; together they provide food and drink, light, and aromatic smells. (For the descriptive text later in Exodus that parallels this prescriptive section, see 37:10–24.)

The lampstand's significance seems to lie less in its functional role as the bearer of a light source and more in its iconic significance, for it resembles sacred trees of other Near Eastern culture. Such trees conveyed the idea of the fertility granted by divine powers (see also at v. 31). Because those powers were associated with both male and female deities, the menorah's presence in the Tabernacle perhaps conveyed the metaphoric female as well as male aspects of God.

*23. table.* Tables for food and drink offerings were typical furnishings of ancient Near Eastern shrines, as known from depictions in art.

*two cubits . . . one cubit . . . cubit and a half.* This rectangular table is to be about 3 feet (nearly 1 meter) long, $1\frac{1}{2}$ feet (nearly $\frac{1}{2}$ meter) wide, and a bit more than 2 feet (about $\frac{2}{3}$ meter) high.

*29. bowls, ladles, jars and jugs.* The Torah specifies four kinds of golden vessels for the table: "bowls" for serving the bread, cup-shaped "ladles" for the incense (frankincense), jars for pouring libations, and jugs into which the libations were poured.

*30. bread.* When the Israelites lived in the Land of Israel, roughly half of their caloric intake came from cereal products. Bread was the most important part of their diet, and so not surprisingly bread has primacy in the retrojected Tabernacle offerings. But the text does not tell us who baked the bread. As in most traditional societies, bread production in Israelite households was almost exclusively the task of women (see also at 16:3). However, in pre-modern cultures, male specialists were often responsible for baking and cooking in elite contexts (like palaces or temples)—just as master chefs today are predominantly male even though home cooks typically are female. Yet because I Samuel 8:13 indicates that royal bakers and cooks were women, it is possible that the text envisions women as preparing

³¹You shall make a lampstand of pure gold; the lampstand shall be made of hammered work; its base and its shaft, its cups, calyxes, and petals shall be of one piece. ³²Six branches shall issue from its sides; three branches from one side of the lampstand and three branches from the other side of the lampstand. ³³On one branch there shall be three cups shaped like almond-blossoms, each with calyx and petals, and on the next branch there shall be three cups shaped like almond-blossoms, each with calyx and petals; so for all six branches issuing from the lampstand. ³⁴And on the lampstand itself there

31 וְעָשִׂ֥יתָ מְנֹרַ֖ת זָהָ֣ב טָה֑וֹר מִקְשָׁ֞ה תֵּיעָשֶׂ֤ה הַמְּנוֹרָה֙ יְרֵכָ֣הּ וְקָנָ֔הּ גְּבִיעֶ֛יהָ כַּפְתֹּרֶ֥יהָ וּפְרָחֶ֖יהָ מִמֶּ֥נָּה יִהְיֽוּ: 32 וְשִׁשָּׁ֣ה קָנִ֔ים יֹצְאִ֖ים מִצִּדֶּ֑יהָ שְׁלֹשָׁ֣ה ׀ קְנֵ֣י מְנֹרָ֗ה מִצִּדָּהּ֙ הָֽאֶחָ֔ד וּשְׁלֹשָׁה֙ קְנֵ֣י מְנֹרָ֔ה מִצִּדָּ֖הּ הַשֵּׁנִֽי: 33 שְׁלֹשָׁ֣ה גְ֠בִעִים מְֽשֻׁקָּדִ֞ים בַּקָּנֶ֣ה הָֽאֶחָד֮ כַּפְתֹּ֣ר וָפֶרַח֒ וּשְׁלֹשָׁ֣ה גְבִעִ֗ים מְשֻׁקָּדִ֛ים בַּקָּנֶ֥ה הָֽאֶחָ֖ד כַּפְתֹּ֣ר וָפָ֑רַח כֵּ֚ן לְשֵׁ֣שֶׁת הַקָּנִ֔ים הַיֹּצְאִ֖ים מִן־הַמְּנֹרָֽה: 34 וּבַמְּנֹרָ֖ה אַרְבָּעָ֣ה גְבִעִ֑ים מְשֻׁקָּדִ֔ים

· · · · · · · · · · · · · · · · · · · · · · · · · · · · · · · · · · · · · · · · · ·

this sacred bread for the tent shrine, although in a Second Temple text, this task is assigned to a levitical clan (I Chronicles 9:31). Leviticus 24:5–8 describes how the bread offering is to be prepared and presented (see also at Leviticus 7:12).

*display.* Literally, "face." This term characterizes the bread offering. Because "face" indicates divine presence (see at 33:20), its association with the bread offering perhaps signifies that the bread is for God. (However, it is eventually eaten by priests; see Leviticus 24:9.)

*always.* The term *tamid* signifies that the loaves were to be on the table at all times, with fresh ones placed there weekly on the Sabbath (Leviticus 24:8).

*31. lampstand of pure gold.* The golden menorah has survived into post-biblical Judaism as one of the most recognizable Jewish symbols. The depiction of a single golden lampstand here conflicts with the description of ten lampstands in the First Temple (I Kings 7:49). It agrees, however, with the single lampstand of the Second Temple, which was carried off by the conquerors of Jerusalem and is depicted on the Arch of Titus in Rome. The lampstand of the Second Temple may recapture the single-menorah tradition of the pre-monarchic tent shrine. The terminology in the lampstand passage is replete with botanical terms, and its branched shape also implies a tree-like form. These features may signify the fertility provided by God or the idea of the eventual rise of a Davidic ruler as a

"shoot" or "branch" (see Isaiah 11:1, Jeremiah 23:5, and Zechariah 3:8). The form may even allude to the female aspect of God's presence, for female deities in the ancient Near East—such as the Canaanite goddess Asherah—may have been represented by sacred trees.

*hammered work.* According to the biblical description, the menorah seems to be made entirely of gold, but it is unclear whether it is solid gold or hollow. The translation "hammered" is conjectural, and the mode of the menorah's fabrication is not specified.

*its base and its shaft.* The menorah's central element is a thick cylinder or shaft, flared at the bottom to form a stable base, and not a slender one as in many depictions of the menorah from the post-biblical period.

*cups.* This term probably refers to a bulging shape (like the capital of a column): a decorative element of the shaft (v. 34) and its branches (v. 33).

*calyxes, and petals.* The first indication of botanical imagery, a calyx is the outer part of a flower.

*32. branches.* The term adds to the botanical imagery. The overall form likely would have looked like a tree, similar to depictions in Late Bronze and Iron Age Near Eastern art.

*33. almond-blossoms.* This additional information about the shape of the calyxes and petals provides another botanical term.

כַּפְתֹּרֶ֖יהָ וּפְרָחֶֽיהָ׃ 35 וְכַפְתֹּ֡ר תַּ֩חַת֩ שְׁנֵ֨י
הַקָּנִ֜ים מִמֶּ֗נָּה וְכַפְתֹּר֙ תַּ֣חַת שְׁנֵ֤י הַקָּנִים֙
מִמֶּ֔נָּה וְכַפְתֹּ֕ר תַּֽחַת־שְׁנֵ֥י הַקָּנִ֖ים מִמֶּ֑נָּה
לְשֵׁ֙שֶׁת֙ הַקָּנִ֔ים הַיֹּצְאִ֖ים מִן־הַמְּנֹרָֽה׃
36 כַּפְתֹּרֵיהֶ֥ם וּקְנֹתָ֖ם מִמֶּ֣נָּה יִהְי֑וּ כֻּלָּ֛הּ
מִקְשָׁ֥ה אַחַ֖ת זָהָ֥ב טָהֽוֹר׃ 37 וְעָשִׂ֥יתָ אֶת־
נֵרֹתֶ֖יהָ שִׁבְעָ֑ה וְהֶֽעֱלָה֙ אֶת־נֵ֣רֹתֶ֔יהָ וְהֵאִ֖יר
עַל־עֵ֥בֶר פָּנֶֽיהָ׃ 38 וּמַלְקָחֶ֥יהָ וּמַחְתֹּתֶ֖יהָ
זָהָ֥ב טָהֽוֹר׃ 39 כִּכָּ֛ר זָהָ֥ב טָה֖וֹר יַעֲשֶׂ֣ה
אֹתָ֑הּ אֵ֥ת כָּל־הַכֵּלִ֖ים הָאֵֽלֶּה׃ 40 וּרְאֵ֖ה
וַעֲשֵׂ֑ה בְּתַ֨בְנִיתָ֔ם אֲשֶׁר־אַתָּ֖ה מָרְאֶ֥ה
בָּהָֽר׃ ס
כו וְאֶת־הַמִּשְׁכָּ֥ן תַּעֲשֶׂ֖ה עֶ֣שֶׂר יְרִיעֹ֑ת שֵׁ֣שׁ
מָשְׁזָר֙ וּתְכֵ֤לֶת וְאַרְגָּמָן֙ וְתֹלַ֣עַת שָׁנִ֔י כְּרֻבִ֛ים

shall be four cups shaped like almond-blossoms, each with calyx and petals: 35 a calyx, of one piece with it, under a pair of branches; and a calyx, of one piece with it, under the second pair of branches, and a calyx, of one piece with it, under the last pair of branches; so for all six branches issuing from the lampstand. 36 Their calyxes and their stems shall be of one piece with it, the whole of it a single hammered piece of pure gold. 37 Make its seven lamps—the lamps shall be so mounted as to give the light on its front side—38 and its tongs and fire pans of pure gold. 39 It shall be made, with all these furnishings, out of a talent of pure gold. 40 Note well, and follow the patterns for them that are being shown you on the mountain.

26 As for the tabernacle, make it of ten strips of cloth; make these of fine twisted linen, of blue,

*37. seven lamps.* These were apparently not to be attached to the lampstand, nor is it specified that they were to be made of gold. According to Exodus 27:21 (see comment there), only one lamp may be involved. That is, the text may be describing a saucer lamp with seven spouts surmounting the central shaft, perhaps a simpler version of the complex visionary menorah of Zechariah 4:2.

*light.* The light-giving properties of the menorah are partly symbolic, connoting the cosmic power of God as the creator of heavenly lights.

*38. tongs and fire pans.* These were utensils for tending the lamp (or lamps).

*39. talent.* This term probably designates a weight of about 75 pounds (34 kilograms); see at 38:24.

## *Instructions about the Tabernacle Structure* (26:1–37)

With the directions for the Tabernacle's interior furnishings complete, the narrative turns to the dwelling itself, which consists of two internal sections. The structure will have three components: coverings of textiles and animal skins, wooden frames, and two textile partitions. Despite the plethora of details, the specifications are incomplete and the directions for assembling the structure are unclear. Thus, it is unlikely that this section contains actual directions for making a real shrine. Information about flooring is lacking; perhaps a dirt floor is assumed (see Numbers 5:17).

### COVERINGS (26:1–14)

The tent-like dwelling is to be made of two layers of fabric—decorated linen panels and unadorned goat-hair panels—which in turn will be covered with two layers of animal skins. (For the descriptive text later in Exodus that parallels this prescriptive section, see 36:8–19.)

*1. tabernacle.* The translation does not capitalize this word in this passage (vv. 1–14), to indicate that the Hebrew noun *mishkan* denotes only the inner fabric component of the dwelling, to be made of decorated linen. (Compare at 25:9.)

*fine twisted linen.* "Twisted" linen refers to

purple, and crimson yarns, with a design of cherubim worked into them. [2]The length of each cloth shall be twenty-eight cubits, and the width of each cloth shall be four cubits, all the cloths to have the same measurements. [3]Five of the cloths shall be joined to one another, and the other five cloths shall be joined to one another. [4]Make loops of blue wool on the edge of the outermost cloth of the one set; and do likewise on the edge of the outermost cloth of the other set: [5]make fifty loops on the one cloth, and fifty loops on the edge of the end cloth of the other set, the loops to be opposite one another. [6]And make fifty gold clasps, and couple the cloths to one another with the clasps, so that the tabernacle becomes one whole.

[7]You shall then make cloths of goats' hair for a tent over the tabernacle; make the cloths eleven in number. [8]The length of each cloth shall be thirty cubits, and the width of each cloth shall be four cubits, the eleven cloths to have the same measurements. [9]Join five of the cloths by themselves, and the other six cloths by themselves; and fold over the sixth cloth at the front of the tent. [10]Make fifty

מַעֲשֵׂה חֹשֵׁב תַּעֲשֶׂה אֹתָם׃ 2 אֹרֶךְ ׀
הַיְרִיעָה הָאַחַת שְׁמֹנֶה וְעֶשְׂרִים בָּאַמָּה
וְרֹחַב אַרְבַּע בָּאַמָּה הַיְרִיעָה הָאֶחָת מִדָּה
אַחַת לְכָל־הַיְרִיעֹת׃ 3 חֲמֵשׁ הַיְרִיעֹת
תִּהְיֶיןָ חֹבְרֹת אִשָּׁה אֶל־אֲחֹתָהּ וְחָמֵשׁ
יְרִיעֹת חֹבְרֹת אִשָּׁה אֶל־אֲחֹתָהּ׃ 4 וְעָשִׂיתָ
לֻלְאֹת תְּכֵלֶת עַל שְׂפַת הַיְרִיעָה הָאֶחָת
מִקָּצָה בַּחֹבָרֶת וְכֵן תַּעֲשֶׂה בִּשְׂפַת הַיְרִיעָה
הַקִּיצוֹנָה בַּמַּחְבֶּרֶת הַשֵּׁנִית׃ 5 חֲמִשִּׁים
לֻלָאֹת תַּעֲשֶׂה בַּיְרִיעָה הָאֶחָת וַחֲמִשִּׁים
לֻלָאֹת תַּעֲשֶׂה בִּקְצֵה הַיְרִיעָה אֲשֶׁר
בַּמַּחְבֶּרֶת הַשֵּׁנִית מַקְבִּילֹת הַלֻּלָאֹת אִשָּׁה
אֶל־אֲחֹתָהּ׃ 6 וְעָשִׂיתָ חֲמִשִּׁים קַרְסֵי זָהָב
וְחִבַּרְתָּ אֶת־הַיְרִיעֹת אִשָּׁה אֶל־אֲחֹתָהּ
בַּקְּרָסִים וְהָיָה הַמִּשְׁכָּן אֶחָד׃
7 וְעָשִׂיתָ יְרִיעֹת עִזִּים לְאֹהֶל עַל־הַמִּשְׁכָּן
עַשְׁתֵּי־עֶשְׂרֵה יְרִיעֹת תַּעֲשֶׂה אֹתָם׃ 8 אֹרֶךְ ׀
הַיְרִיעָה הָאַחַת שְׁלֹשִׁים בָּאַמָּה וְרֹחַב
אַרְבַּע בָּאַמָּה הַיְרִיעָה הָאֶחָת מִדָּה אַחַת
לְעַשְׁתֵּי עֶשְׂרֵה יְרִיעֹת׃ 9 וְחִבַּרְתָּ אֶת־חֲמֵשׁ
הַיְרִיעֹת לְבָד וְאֶת־שֵׁשׁ הַיְרִיעֹת לְבָד
וְכָפַלְתָּ אֶת־הַיְרִיעָה הַשִּׁשִּׁית אֶל־מוּל פְּנֵי
הָאֹהֶל׃ 10 וְעָשִׂיתָ חֲמִשִּׁים לֻלָאֹת עַל

the technique of spinning for preparing the linen thread. Women typically do this kind of work; compare 35:25–26.

*yarns.* Regally colored woolen yarns were apparently to be embroidered to make a design on the linen cloth.

*design of cherubim.* Images of these fanciful composite creatures would not only form the "throne" over the Ark (see at 25:18, 19–21) but also decorate the dwelling's fabric sides.

*2. twenty-eight cubits . . . four cubits.* Each fabric panel is to be about 14 yards (nearly 13 meters) by 2 yards (nearly 2 meters).

*3–6.* As specific as the directions for joining the fabric panels seem, the exact procedures remain elusive. It seems that five of the panels were joined together, perhaps by sewing, and then the two resulting larger panels were connected.

*7. cloths of goats' hair.* Goat hair can be spun into yarn and then woven into waterproof cloth. It has been used for tents in the Middle East for millennia.

*tent.* Heb. *ohel* denotes this second fabric layer, which is to cover and protect the linen tabernacle (vv. 1–6).

*8. thirty cubits . . . four cubits.* Each of the eleven panels is to be about 15 yards (nearly 14 meters) by 2 yards (nearly 2 meters).

loops on the edge of the outermost cloth of the one set, and fifty loops on the edge of the cloth of the other set. [11]Make fifty copper clasps, and fit the clasps into the loops, and couple the tent together so that it becomes one whole. [12]As for the overlapping excess of the cloths of the tent, the extra half-cloth shall overlap the back of the tabernacle, [13]while the extra cubit at either end of each length of tent cloth shall hang down to the bottom of the two sides of the tabernacle and cover it. [14]And make for the tent a covering of tanned ram skins, and a covering of dolphin skins above.

[15]You shall make the planks for the Tabernacle of acacia wood, upright. [16]The length of each plank shall be ten cubits and the width of each plank a cubit and a half. [17]Each plank shall have two tenons, parallel to each other; do the same with all the planks of the Tabernacle. [18]Of the planks of the Tabernacle, make twenty planks on the south side: [19]making forty silver sockets under the twenty planks, two sockets under the one plank for its two tenons and two sockets under each following plank for its two tenons; [20]and for the other side wall of the Tabernacle, on the north side, twenty planks, [21]with their forty silver sockets, two sockets under the one plank and two sockets under each following

שְׂפַת הַיְרִיעָה הָאֶחָת הַקִּיצֹנָה בַּחֹבָרֶת
וַחֲמִשִּׁים לֻלָאֹת עַל שְׂפַת הַיְרִיעָה הַחֹבֶרֶת
הַשֵּׁנִית׃ 11 וְעָשִׂיתָ קַרְסֵי נְחֹשֶׁת חֲמִשִּׁים
וְהֵבֵאתָ אֶת־הַקְּרָסִים בַּלֻּלָאֹת וְחִבַּרְתָּ
אֶת־הָאֹהֶל וְהָיָה אֶחָד׃ 12 וְסֶרַח הָעֹדֵף
בִּירִיעֹת הָאֹהֶל חֲצִי הַיְרִיעָה הָעֹדֶפֶת
תִּסְרַח עַל אֲחֹרֵי הַמִּשְׁכָּן׃ 13 וְהָאַמָּה מִזֶּה
וְהָאַמָּה מִזֶּה בָּעֹדֵף בְּאֹרֶךְ יְרִיעֹת הָאֹהֶל
יִהְיֶה סָרוּחַ עַל־צִדֵּי הַמִּשְׁכָּן מִזֶּה וּמִזֶּה
לְכַסֹּתוֹ׃ 14 וְעָשִׂיתָ מִכְסֶה לָאֹהֶל עֹרֹת
אֵילִם מְאָדָּמִים וּמִכְסֵה עֹרֹת תְּחָשִׁים
מִלְמָעְלָה׃ פ
15 וְעָשִׂיתָ אֶת־הַקְּרָשִׁים לַמִּשְׁכָּן עֲצֵי שִׁטִּים
עֹמְדִים׃ 16 עֶשֶׂר אַמּוֹת אֹרֶךְ הַקָּרֶשׁ וְאַמָּה
וַחֲצִי הָאַמָּה רֹחַב הַקֶּרֶשׁ הָאֶחָד׃ 17 שְׁתֵּי
יָדוֹת לַקֶּרֶשׁ הָאֶחָד מְשֻׁלָּבֹת אִשָּׁה אֶל־
אֲחֹתָהּ כֵּן תַּעֲשֶׂה לְכֹל קַרְשֵׁי הַמִּשְׁכָּן׃
18 וְעָשִׂיתָ אֶת־הַקְּרָשִׁים לַמִּשְׁכָּן עֶשְׂרִים
קֶרֶשׁ לִפְאַת נֶגְבָּה תֵימָנָה׃ 19 וְאַרְבָּעִים
אַדְנֵי־כֶסֶף תַּעֲשֶׂה תַּחַת עֶשְׂרִים הַקָּרֶשׁ
שְׁנֵי אֲדָנִים תַּחַת־הַקֶּרֶשׁ הָאֶחָד לִשְׁתֵּי
יְדֹתָיו וּשְׁנֵי אֲדָנִים תַּחַת־הַקֶּרֶשׁ הָאֶחָד
לִשְׁתֵּי יְדֹתָיו׃ 20 וּלְצֶלַע הַמִּשְׁכָּן הַשֵּׁנִית
לִפְאַת צָפוֹן עֶשְׂרִים קָרֶשׁ׃ 21 וְאַרְבָּעִים
אַדְנֵיהֶם כָּסֶף שְׁנֵי אֲדָנִים תַּחַת הַקֶּרֶשׁ
הָאֶחָד וּשְׁנֵי אֲדָנִים תַּחַת הַקֶּרֶשׁ הָאֶחָד׃

### FRAMES (26:15–30)

The structure's frame is to be constructed of a complex system of gilded boards and bars with metal fastenings; the frame is to be set into bases. (For the descriptive text later in Exodus that parallels this prescriptive section, see 36:20–34.)

***15. planks.*** The Hebrew word translated here as "planks" is used in the Bible only with regard to the Tabernacle; its precise nuance is not clear. Apparently the four layers of textiles and skins that comprise the tent will be hung on a frame made of acacia wood.

***16. ten cubits . . . a cubit and a half.*** The "planks" measure about 15 feet ($4\frac{1}{2}$ meters) by a bit more than 2 feet (about $\frac{2}{3}$ meter); their thickness is not specified. Despite the minutiae provided, it is not clear how the frame would be assembled.

***19. silver sockets.*** The sockets, which were probably bases in which the "planks" (see at v. 15) were set, were likely made of a less precious metal because they were to rest on the ground.

plank. [22]And for the rear of the Tabernacle, to the
west, make six planks; [23]and make two planks for
the corners of the Tabernacle at the rear. [24]They
shall match at the bottom, and terminate alike at
the top inside one ring; thus shall it be with both of
them: they shall form the two corners. [25]Thus there
shall be eight planks with their sockets of silver:
sixteen sockets, two sockets under the first plank,
and two sockets under each of the other planks.

[26]You shall make bars of acacia wood: five for
the planks of the one side wall of the Tabernacle,
[27]five bars for the planks of the other side wall of
the Tabernacle, and five bars for the planks of the
wall of the Tabernacle at the rear to the west. [28]The
center bar halfway up the planks shall run from end
to end. [29]Overlay the planks with gold, and make
their rings of gold, as holders for the bars; and overlay the bars with gold. [30]Then set up the Tabernacle
according to the manner of it that you were shown
on the mountain.

[31]You shall make a curtain of blue, purple, and
crimson yarns, and fine twisted linen; it shall have a

22 וּלְיַרְכְּתֵי הַמִּשְׁכָּן יָמָּה תַּעֲשֶׂה שִׁשָּׁה
קְרָשִׁים׃ 23 וּשְׁנֵי קְרָשִׁים תַּעֲשֶׂה לִמְקֻצְעֹת
הַמִּשְׁכָּן בַּיַּרְכָתָיִם׃ 24 וְיִהְיוּ תֹאֲמִם
מִלְּמַטָּה וְיַחְדָּו יִהְיוּ תַמִּים עַל־רֹאשׁוֹ אֶל־
הַטַּבַּעַת הָאֶחָת כֵּן יִהְיֶה לִשְׁנֵיהֶם לִשְׁנֵי
הַמִּקְצֹעֹת יִהְיוּ׃ 25 וְהָיוּ שְׁמֹנָה קְרָשִׁים
וְאַדְנֵיהֶם כֶּסֶף שִׁשָּׁה עָשָׂר אֲדָנִים שְׁנֵי
אֲדָנִים תַּחַת הַקֶּרֶשׁ הָאֶחָד וּשְׁנֵי אֲדָנִים
תַּחַת הַקֶּרֶשׁ הָאֶחָד׃

26 וְעָשִׂיתָ בְרִיחִם עֲצֵי שִׁטִּים חֲמִשָּׁה
לְקַרְשֵׁי צֶלַע־הַמִּשְׁכָּן הָאֶחָד׃ 27 וַחֲמִשָּׁה
בְרִיחִם לְקַרְשֵׁי צֶלַע־הַמִּשְׁכָּן הַשֵּׁנִית
וַחֲמִשָּׁה בְרִיחִם לְקַרְשֵׁי צֶלַע הַמִּשְׁכָּן
לַיַּרְכָתַיִם יָמָּה׃ 28 וְהַבְּרִיחַ הַתִּיכֹן בְּתוֹךְ
הַקְּרָשִׁים מַבְרִחַ מִן־הַקָּצֶה אֶל־הַקָּצֶה׃
29 וְאֶת־הַקְּרָשִׁים תְּצַפֶּה זָהָב וְאֶת־
טַבְּעֹתֵיהֶם תַּעֲשֶׂה זָהָב בָּתִּים לַבְּרִיחִם
וְצִפִּיתָ אֶת־הַבְּרִיחִם זָהָב׃ 30 וַהֲקֵמֹתָ
אֶת־הַמִּשְׁכָּן כְּמִשְׁפָּטוֹ אֲשֶׁר הָרְאֵיתָ
בָּהָר׃ ס

31 וְעָשִׂיתָ פָרֹכֶת תְּכֵלֶת וְאַרְגָּמָן וְתוֹלַעַת
שָׁנִי וְשֵׁשׁ מָשְׁזָר מַעֲשֵׂה חֹשֵׁב יַעֲשֶׂה אֹתָהּ

*22. west.* The rectangular interior space is to be oriented in an east-west direction, with its holiest rear wall at the west. If the entry partition (26:36–37) were open, the sun rising at the equinox would shine toward the Holy of Holies.

*26. bars.* Probably long horizontal rods or crossbars to stabilize the "planks" (see at v. 15).

*30. Tabernacle.* Now the term seems to refer to the entire structure, not just the tent coverings (see at v. 1).

### TEXTILE PARTITIONS (26:31–37)

The textile and skin coverings are to hang over a gilded wooden structure. The space thus created is to be divided into two parts by a textile partition hung on gilded posts. One of the areas is designated *kodesh* ("Holy") and the other *kodesh kodashim* ("Holy of Holies"). Another textile partition, also hung on gilded posts, is to separate the interior space from the surrounding courtyard. (For the descriptive text later in Exodus that parallels this prescriptive section, see 36:33–38.)

*31. make a curtain.* The curtain for the Tabernacle is to be made with the best grade of linen embroidered in cherubim designs with royally dyed woolen threads.

The word for "curtain" (*parochet*) survives in contemporary Jewish life as the designation for the fabric hung in front of a synagogue ark.

design of cherubim worked into it. [32]Hang it upon four posts of acacia wood overlaid with gold and having hooks of gold, [set] in four sockets of silver. [33]Hang the curtain under the clasps, and carry the Ark of the Pact there, behind the curtain, so that the curtain shall serve you as a partition between the Holy and the Holy of Holies. [34]Place the cover upon the Ark of the Pact in the Holy of Holies. [35]Place the table outside the curtain, and the lampstand by the south wall of the Tabernacle opposite the table, which is to be placed by the north wall.

[36]You shall make a screen for the entrance of the Tent, of blue, purple, and crimson yarns, and fine twisted linen, done in embroidery. [37]Make five posts of acacia wood for the screen and overlay them with gold—their hooks being of gold—and cast for them five sockets of copper.

27 You shall make the altar of acacia wood,

כְּרֻבִֽים: 32 וְנָתַתָּ֣ה אֹתָ֗הּ עַל־אַרְבָּעָ֤ה עַמּוּדֵ֣י שִׁטִּים֙ מְצֻפִּ֣ים זָהָ֔ב וָוֵיהֶ֖ם זָהָ֑ב עַל־אַרְבָּעָ֖ה אַדְנֵי־כָֽסֶף: 33 וְנָתַתָּ֣ה אֶת־הַפָּרֹ֗כֶת תַּ֣חַת הַקְּרָסִ֔ים וְהֵבֵאתָ֥ שָׁ֙מָּה֙ מִבֵּ֣ית לַפָּרֹ֔כֶת אֵ֖ת אֲר֣וֹן הָעֵד֑וּת וְהִבְדִּילָ֤ה הַפָּרֹ֙כֶת֙ לָכֶ֔ם בֵּ֣ין הַקֹּ֔דֶשׁ וּבֵ֖ין קֹ֥דֶשׁ הַקֳּדָשִֽׁים: 34 וְנָתַתָּ֙ אֶת־הַכַּפֹּ֔רֶת עַ֖ל אֲר֣וֹן הָעֵדֻ֑ת בְּקֹ֖דֶשׁ הַקֳּדָשִֽׁים: 35 וְשַׂמְתָּ֣ אֶת־הַשֻּׁלְחָן֮ מִח֣וּץ לַפָּרֹ֒כֶת֒ וְאֶת־הַמְּנֹרָה֙ נֹ֣כַח הַשֻּׁלְחָ֔ן עַ֛ל צֶ֥לַע הַמִּשְׁכָּ֖ן תֵּימָ֑נָה וְהַ֙שֻּׁלְחָ֔ן תִּתֵּ֖ן עַל־צֶ֥לַע צָפֽוֹן:

36 וְעָשִׂ֤יתָ מָסָךְ֙ לְפֶ֣תַח הָאֹ֔הֶל תְּכֵ֧לֶת וְאַרְגָּמָ֛ן וְתוֹלַ֥עַת שָׁנִ֖י וְשֵׁ֣שׁ מָשְׁזָ֑ר מַעֲשֵׂ֖ה רֹקֵֽם: 37 וְעָשִׂ֣יתָ לַמָּסָ֗ךְ חֲמִשָּׁה֙ עַמּוּדֵ֣י שִׁטִּ֔ים וְצִפִּיתָ֤ אֹתָם֙ זָהָ֔ב וָוֵיהֶ֖ם זָהָ֑ב וְיָצַקְתָּ֣ לָהֶ֔ם חֲמִשָּׁ֖ה אַדְנֵ֥י נְחֹֽשֶׁת: ס

כז וְעָשִׂ֥יתָ אֶת־הַמִּזְבֵּ֖חַ עֲצֵ֣י שִׁטִּ֑ים חָמֵשׁ֩

· · · · · ·   · · · · · ·   · · · · · ·

**32. gold...gold.** This precious metal is most appropriate for features of the holiest space.

**sockets of silver.** The bases for the gilded posts are silver perhaps because the bases touch the ground.

**33. carry the Ark of the Pact there.** The most sacred space, the Holy of Holies, is where the most sacred object—the Ark—will be placed.

**between the Holy and the Holy of Holies.** The interior is thus divided into two zones of holiness.

**35.** The offering table and the menorah are situated outside the Holy of Holies, the table on the north side and the menorah on the south. The space directly in the center of the curtain in front of the Ark seems to be vacant; but in 30:1–10 we will learn that a third item, the incense altar, is to occupy that spot.

**36. screen.** The fabric partition or "screen" between the interior and exterior spaces is to be similar to the *parochet* except without cherubim designs.

**37. gold ... copper.** The hooks and posts holding the screen are to be of gilded wood. The bases ("sockets") in which they are to be set, however, are "copper" (probably bronze; see at 25:3), the least precious of the three metals, because these foundation pieces are on the ground and border on the courtyard, the outer zone of holiness.

## Instructions about the Courtyard (27:1–19)

Like virtually every domicile in the ancient Near East, whether a village house or an urban palace, the Tabernacle is to have an unroofed outdoor space, a courtyard. Certain household functions, including roasting large pieces of meat, were performed more efficiently outdoors. Thus the altar for various types of offerings is to be placed in the courtyard.

five cubits long and five cubits wide—the altar is to be square—and three cubits high. [2]Make its horns on the four corners, the horns to be of one piece with it; and overlay it with copper. [3]Make the pails for removing its ashes, as well as its scrapers, basins, flesh hooks, and fire pans—make all its utensils of

אַמּוֹת אֹרֶךְ וְחָמֵשׁ אַמּוֹת רֹחַב רָבוּעַ יִהְיֶה
הַמִּזְבֵּחַ וְשָׁלֹשׁ אַמּוֹת קֹמָתוֹ׃ 2 וְעָשִׂיתָ
קַרְנֹתָיו עַל אַרְבַּע פִּנֹּתָיו מִמֶּנּוּ תִּהְיֶיןָ
קַרְנֹתָיו וְצִפִּיתָ אֹתוֹ נְחֹשֶׁת׃ 3 וְעָשִׂיתָ
סִּירֹתָיו לְדַשְּׁנוֹ וְיָעָיו וּמִזְרְקֹתָיו וּמִזְלְגֹתָיו
וּמַחְתֹּתָיו לְכָל־כֵּלָיו תַּעֲשֶׂה נְחֹשֶׁת׃

Whereas the other parts of the Tabernacle were restricted to certain priests, the courtyard was a place where the rest of the people—including women—could enter and present their offerings.

ALTAR (27:1–8)

Only the altar is mentioned in this section; but another courtyard installation, the laver (or basin), appears in 30:17–21. The instructions say nothing about how the altar is to be used, though the following parashah mentions grain, oil, wine, and animals as offerings to be made on the altar (29:38–42). Leviticus and other biblical texts presume that women, like men, would approach the altar to present their offerings (see the introduction to *Vayikra*, p. 569). (For the descriptive text later in Exodus that parallels this prescriptive section, see 38:1–8.)

*1. of acacia wood.* Because it is highly unlikely that a wooden altar, even one overlaid with metal, could have been functional, this must be a hypothetical item (see the parashah introduction, p. 451). A large-scale altar would have been made of stone, which would make it virtually impossible to build, dismantle, and transport. Features of known altars are integrated into the instructions for this somewhat imaginary wooden courtyard altar.

*five cubits . . . five cubits . . . three cubits.* At about $7\frac{1}{2}$ feet (more than 2 meters) square and $4\frac{1}{2}$ feet (almost $1\frac{1}{2}$ meters) high, the height would have required steps, thus making the altar conceptually different from stone or earthen altars (see 20:21–23), which can be built anywhere.

*2. horns on the four corners.* The most striking feature of the courtyard altar is that horns are to protrude from its four corners. How they are to be placed is not clear, but the positioning of the horns on stone altars discovered by archeologists suggests that the horns would have turned upward from the altar's corners. Most of the excavated horned altars are quite small, like the incense altar of 30:1–10; but two massive ones have been found at Beersheba and Arad. In the Tabernacle, the altar and its horns are to play a role in the consecration ceremony (see 29:12).

*copper.* Since the courtyard is the least holy zone, its furnishings, utensils, and carrying poles are to be made of bronze (see at 25:3).

*3. pails for removing its ashes.* This anticipates the function of the altar, for the ashy remains of the wood fuel and of the offerings consumed by fire would need to be removed.

*scrapers.* These are probably for cleaning the altar after the sacrifice has been burnt.

*basins.* The word for "basin" is from the verb *z-r-k* ("to sprinkle"), indicating that the basins are to be used to carry the blood to be sprinkled ("dashed") on the altar (see, for instance, Leviticus 7:2) or smeared on its horns (29:12).

*flesh hooks.* Probably long-handled meat forks for positioning the sacrificial flesh on the altar.

*fire pans.* These were used for carrying hot coals. The first step in preparing and using the altar comes last in the instructions, for the pails used for cleanup are specified first.

copper. 4 Make for it a grating of meshwork in copper; and on the mesh make four copper rings at its
four corners. 5 Set the mesh below, under the ledge
of the altar, so that it extends to the middle of the
altar. 6 And make poles for the altar, poles of acacia
wood, and overlay them with copper. 7 The poles
shall be inserted into the rings, so that the poles remain on the two sides of the altar when it is carried.
8 Make it hollow, of boards. As you were shown on
the mountain, so shall they be made.

9 You shall make the enclosure of the Tabernacle:
On the south side, a hundred cubits of hangings
of fine twisted linen for the length of the enclosure
on that side— 10 with its twenty posts and their
twenty sockets of copper, the hooks and bands of
the posts to be of silver.
11 Again a hundred cubits of hangings for its
length along the north side—with its twenty posts

4 וְעָשִׂיתָ לּוֹ מִכְבָּר מַעֲשֵׂה רֶשֶׁת נְחֹשֶׁת
וְעָשִׂיתָ עַל־הָרֶשֶׁת אַרְבַּע טַבְּעֹת נְחֹשֶׁת
עַל אַרְבַּע קְצוֹתָיו׃ 5 וְנָתַתָּה אֹתָהּ תַּחַת
כַּרְכֹּב הַמִּזְבֵּחַ מִלְּמָטָּה וְהָיְתָה הָרֶשֶׁת עַד
חֲצִי הַמִּזְבֵּחַ׃ 6 וְעָשִׂיתָ בַדִּים לַמִּזְבֵּחַ בַּדֵּי
עֲצֵי שִׁטִּים וְצִפִּיתָ אֹתָם נְחֹשֶׁת׃ 7 וְהוּבָא
אֶת־בַּדָּיו בַּטַּבָּעֹת וְהָיוּ הַבַּדִּים עַל־שְׁתֵּי
צַלְעֹת הַמִּזְבֵּחַ בִּשְׂאֵת אֹתוֹ׃ 8 נְבוּב לֻחֹת
תַּעֲשֶׂה אֹתוֹ כַּאֲשֶׁר הֶרְאָה אֹתְךָ בָּהָר כֵּן
יַעֲשׂוּ׃ ס

9 וְעָשִׂיתָ אֵת חֲצַר הַמִּשְׁכָּן לִפְאַת נֶגֶב־
תֵּימָנָה קְלָעִים לֶחָצֵר שֵׁשׁ מָשְׁזָר מֵאָה
בָאַמָּה אֹרֶךְ לַפֵּאָה הָאֶחָת׃ 10 וְעַמֻּדָיו
עֶשְׂרִים וְאַדְנֵיהֶם עֶשְׂרִים נְחֹשֶׁת וָוֵי
הָעַמֻּדִים וַחֲשֻׁקֵיהֶם כָּסֶף׃
11 וְכֵן לִפְאַת צָפוֹן בָּאֹרֶךְ קְלָעִים מֵאָה
אֹרֶךְ ועמדו וְעַמֻּדָיו עֶשְׂרִים וְאַדְנֵיהֶם

*4–5.* It is not clear whether the bronze "grating of meshwork" and the "ledge" are meant to be decorative or functional elements of the altar, or both.

*6. poles.* These bronze poles, inserted into rings attached at each of the corners, make the altar hypothetically portable.

*8. hollow.* This is another vague feature of the altar. Perhaps it is an attempt to deal with the conceptual problem of how an enormous object could be carried, or it may be related to the fact that no upper surface or top for the altar is specified.

## ENCLOSURE (27:9–19)

In the Land of Israel at the time of the Bible, people typically surrounded the courtyards of homes and palaces with enclosure walls that marked the limits of the premises. The enclosure also controlled the movement of animals and small children and protected the domestic and productive space and its contents from intruders. As the text describes the sacred Tabernacle precinct, its courtyard enclosure also serves as the boundary between holy space within and profane space outside. Despite the many details, directions for positioning the Tabernacle within the enclosure are not provided. (For the descriptive text later in Exodus that parallels this prescriptive section, see 38:9–20.)

*9. hangings of fine twisted linen.* Undecorated linen fabrics form the courtyard walls. They are to be made of the highest quality linen; but unlike the linen used for the interior fabrics (26:1, 31), they are not to be decorated with colored wool and designs. The least sacred zone, the courtyard has less elaborate materials.

*10. hooks . . . bands . . . silver.* It is not clear why these fastening devices use a higher grade of metal, while the poles are to be of bronze, a lesser grade substance.

and their twenty sockets of copper, the hooks and bands of the posts to be of silver.

12For the width of the enclosure, on the west side, fifty cubits of hangings, with their ten posts and their ten sockets.

13For the width of the enclosure on the front, or east side, fifty cubits: 14fifteen cubits of hangings on the one flank, with their three posts and their three sockets; 15fifteen cubits of hangings on the other flank, with their three posts and their three sockets; 16and for the gate of the enclosure, a screen of twenty cubits, of blue, purple, and crimson yarns, and fine twisted linen, done in embroidery, with their four posts and their four sockets.

17All the posts round the enclosure shall be banded with silver and their hooks shall be of silver; their sockets shall be of copper.

18The length of the enclosure shall be a hundred cubits, and the width fifty throughout; and the height five cubits—[with hangings] of fine twisted linen. The sockets shall be of copper: 19all the utensils of the Tabernacle, for all its service, as well as all its pegs and all the pegs of the court, shall be of copper.

עֶשְׂרִים֙ נְחֹ֔שֶׁת וָוֵ֧י הָֽעַמֻּדִ֛ים וַחֲשֻׁקֵיהֶ֖ם
כָּֽסֶף׃
12 וְרֹ֤חַב הֶֽחָצֵר֙ לִפְאַת־יָ֔ם קְלָעִ֖ים חֲמִשִּׁ֣ים
אַמָּ֑ה עַמֻּדֵיהֶ֣ם עֲשָׂרָ֔ה וְאַדְנֵיהֶ֖ם עֲשָׂרָֽה׃
13 וְרֹ֣חַב הֶֽחָצֵ֗ר לִפְאַ֛ת קֵ֥דְמָה מִזְרָ֖חָה
חֲמִשִּׁ֥ים אַמָּֽה׃ 14 וַחֲמֵ֨שׁ עֶשְׂרֵ֥ה אַמָּ֛ה
קְלָעִ֖ים לַכָּתֵ֑ף עַמֻּדֵיהֶ֣ם שְׁלֹשָׁ֔ה וְאַדְנֵיהֶ֖ם
שְׁלֹשָֽׁה׃ 15 וְלַכָּתֵף֙ הַשֵּׁנִ֔ית חֲמֵ֥שׁ עֶשְׂרֵ֖ה
קְלָעִ֑ים עַמֻּדֵיהֶ֣ם שְׁלֹשָׁ֔ה וְאַדְנֵיהֶ֖ם שְׁלֹשָֽׁה׃
16 וּלְשַׁ֨עַר הֶֽחָצֵ֜ר מָסָ֣ךְ ׀ עֶשְׂרִ֣ים אַמָּ֗ה
תְּ֠כֵלֶת וְאַרְגָּמָ֜ן וְתוֹלַ֧עַת שָׁנִ֛י וְשֵׁ֥שׁ מָשְׁזָ֖ר
מַעֲשֵׂ֣ה רֹקֵ֑ם עַמֻּדֵיהֶם֙ אַרְבָּעָ֔ה וְאַדְנֵיהֶ֖ם
אַרְבָּעָֽה׃
17 כָּל־עַמּוּדֵ֨י הֶחָצֵ֤ר סָבִיב֙ מְחֻשָּׁקִ֣ים כֶּ֔סֶף
וָוֵיהֶ֥ם כָּ֖סֶף וְאַדְנֵיהֶ֖ם נְחֹֽשֶׁת׃
18 אֹ֤רֶךְ הֶֽחָצֵר֙ מֵאָ֣ה בָֽאַמָּ֗ה וְרֹ֤חַב ׀ חֲמִשִּׁ֣ים
בַּחֲמִשִּׁ֔ים וְקֹמָ֖ה חָמֵ֣שׁ אַמּ֑וֹת שֵׁ֥שׁ מָשְׁזָ֖ר
וְאַדְנֵיהֶ֖ם נְחֹֽשֶׁת׃ 19 לְכֹל֙ כְּלֵ֣י הַמִּשְׁכָּ֔ן בְּכֹ֖ל
עֲבֹדָת֑וֹ וְכָל־יְתֵדֹתָ֛יו וְכָל־יִתְדֹ֥ת הֶחָצֵ֖ר
נְחֹֽשֶׁת׃ ס

*14–15. fifteen cubits . . . fifteen cubits.* The entrance space left between enclosure hangings is to be about 10 yards (9 meters) across.

*16. gate of the enclosure.* That is, the entrance to the sacred precinct.

*screen . . . embroidery.* The entrance to the courtyard is to be spanned by a textile panel of a more elaborate fabric, apparently the same as the screen for the entrance to the interior space (26:36).

*18. hundred cubits . . . fifty . . . five cubits.* Like the tent within, the courtyard is to be rectangular, about 50 yards (46 meters) by 25 yards (23 meters), with fabric walls more than 7 feet (more than 2 meters) high.

*19. utensils of the Tabernacle.* In this summary statement, the word *mishkan* seems to refer to the Tabernacle precinct—that is, the courtyard—and not the tent structure inside.

*service.* Heb. *avodah* can mean "labor" or "tasks" (as in 1:14), but it more often refers to devotional service such as the offerings on the courtyard altar.

*pegs . . . of copper.* Almost as an afterthought, the instructions mention copper stakes to which guy wires were presumably to be attached, to hold taut the enclosure fabrics and perhaps also the tent coverings.

*—Carol Meyers*

# Another View

Parashat T'rumah provides specifications for constructing the Tabernacle and its furnishings. Although the gender of the artisans is not mentioned, other biblical passages indicate that metallurgy was a male domain (I Samuel 8:12), while spinning and weaving were women's work (Judges 16:13–14; II Samuel 3:29; Proverbs 31:19). Producing and dyeing yarns, weaving, and embroidering textiles for the Tent of Meeting and officiating priests' clothing thus provided an avenue for women of the Exodus account to participate in this public and communal religious practice. According to II Kings 23:7, women continued producing textiles as devotional service also during the time of the Jerusalem Temple: while working in a room within the Temple precinct, "the women wove coverings" for the wooden pole of Asherah that stood in the Temple. (On worship of the goddess Asherah, see at Exodus 34:13.)

Archeological evidence of weaving abounds in both domestic and industrial contexts in the biblical period. Ceramic loom weights, indicative of an upright warp-weighted loom, stone or ceramic spindle whorls for twisting fibers into continuous yarn, and bone shuttles for weaving are common finds in domestic contexts. Loom weights found in rows suggest that looms, consisting of a crossbeam supported by two upright beams, rested against a room or courtyard wall. The weights pulled taut the vertical warp strings tied to the crossbeam above. Most women spun and wove to satisfy household needs: clothing, cloaks that also served as blankets, bags to transport grain, and waterproof coverings of goats' hair. Sheep and goats from one's flocks, the two most common domesticated animals, provided wool and hair; linen was produced from flax fibers.

While Israelite women wove cloth at home, the highly prized dye denoting sovereignty that was mandated for the Tabernacle curtains and vestments—*t'cheilet* (blue-violet) and *argaman* (purple)—was manufactured in specialized installations at coastal sites. A Mediterranean mollusk, *Murex*, secretes the main ingredient of the dye used to manufacture *t'cheilet* and *argaman*. Dye vats with accompanying mounds

*Biblical passages indicate that spinning and weaving were women's work.*

of broken murex shells have been uncovered in 9th-century-B.C.E. excavations at Tel Shiqmona, and in Persian Period Tel Dor, both located in Phoenician-controlled territory along the coast south of present-day Haifa. *Tolaat shani* (crimson/scarlet) was likely derived from the body of a female insect, *Kermococcus/Kermes*, or her eggs. Since wools took the dye but linen did not, those who produced the Tabernacle curtains and priests' ceremonial clothing likely combined decorative dyed wool with linen threads and then wove gold threads into the cloth (Exodus 39:2–3, 8). While mixing wool and linen was specified for Tabernacle draperies and curtains, the high priest's vestments, and for *tzitzit* (Exodus 26:1, 31, 36; 27:16; 28:4–5; Numbers 15:38; Deuteronomy 22:11–12), it was forbidden for common clothing and labeled *shaatnez* (see at Leviticus 19:19; Deuteronomy 22:9–11).

—*Elizabeth Bloch-Smith*

# Post-biblical Interpretations

***every person*** (25:2). Heb. *kol ish,* which is often translated as "every man," but as Nachmanides commented on "whole Israelite community" (35:1), the expression *kol ish* here includes women as well.

***whose heart is so moved*** (25:2). Sforno said that God specifically included the phrase "whose heart so moves" in order to differentiate this freely given offering from *tzedakah,* an obligation that everyone is obligated to fulfill.

***that I may dwell among them . . . the Tabernacle*** (25:8–9). The two key Hebrew words, *v'shachanti* ("that I may dwell") and *mishkan* ("Tabernacle"), are related linguistically to the feminine noun *Shechinah.* The Rabbis used that term for the indwelling and intimately felt presence of God, believing that the *Shechinah* was present in the Tabernacle and, later, in the Temple in Jerusalem. According to the Talmud, the *Shechinah* also accompanied Israel into exile (BT *M'gillah* 29a) and becomes manifest during communal worship (BT *Sanhedrin* 39a) and moments of individual need (BT *Shabbat* 12b). [As Sharon Faye Koren explains ("Shekhinah as Female Symbol," *Encyclopaedia Judaica,* 2nd ed., 2006), medieval Jewish mysticism (Kabbalah) often represented the *Shechinah* as a female aspect of God. The *Shechinah* mediated between heaven and earth and served as the passive eye or door through which a mystic could achieve divine vision. The mystics believed that sexual relations between the *Shechinah* and a male aspect of the divine brought about cosmic harmony. (Similarly, intercourse between a male mystic and his wife on earth, especially on Shabbat night, could foster both divine and mystical union.) Some contemporary Jewish feminists have reclaimed the symbol of the *Shechinah* to counter what they perceive to be the patriarchal bias of Jewish theology; they have reinterpreted mystical themes and emphasize the symbol of the feminine *Shechinah* in innovative new liturgies. —*Ed.*]

***so shall you make it*** (25:9). God's instructions concerning the building of the Tabernacle are recounted in the Torah prior to the incident of the Golden Calf (Exodus 32–34). However, some rabbinic commentators believed that these directions were given after that shameful event; and they interpret God's command to create the Tabernacle as a sign of divine forgiveness. According to Midrash *Sh'mot Rabbah* 51.4, the nations of the world had declared that God would never be reconciled with Israel after Israel

*All the Torah's commandments are in the form of the mystery of male and female.*

rejected God in favor of an idol. However, Moses successfully pleaded for mercy on the people's behalf. At that moment, God said to Moses, "I will let my *Shechinah* dwell among [the Israelites], so that all may know that I have forgiven Israel. My sanctuary in their midst will be testimony of My forgiveness—and from this time on may be called a 'Tabernacle of Testimony.'" (On the *Shechinah,* see the previous comment.) Nachmanides, however, did not accept this tampering with chronology. He suggested that the commandment to build the Tabernacle was divine acknowledgment of Israel's merit in having freely accepted the Decalogue (comment to 35:1).

*P'sikta D'Rav Kahana* 1.1–2 understands the Tabernacle as a sign of God's love for Israel and portrays it as a bridal chamber for the bride (Israel) and groom (God), patterned on the heavenly Tabernacle. A parable in *Sh'mot Rabbah* 33.1 utilizes somewhat different symbolism: When the beloved daughter of a king married another king, her father could not bear to part from her and so requested that his son-in-law build him a room so he could dwell with her. Here, God is depicted as a father and the Tabernacle as a place for the father to remain with his beloved daughter, Israel.

***Make two cherubim of gold*** (25:18). According to BT *Chagigah* 13b, the cherubim had the forms of winged human beings. One represented divine mercy and the other represented divine justice.

***There I will meet with you*** (25:22). The Rabbis acknowledged that God is everywhere. Nevertheless, they also understood that through an act of *tzimtzum*, contraction, God could meet with Moses from between the cherubim, which were ten spans above the earth (*Sh'mot Rabbah* 34.1).

***make fifty gold clasps, and couple the cloths to one another with the clasps, so that the Tabernacle becomes one whole*** (26:6). Ibn Ezra compared the interconnected components of the Tabernacle to the intricacies and interdependence of the parts of the human body, as well as to the similar interlocking segments of the entire world. The *Zohar* elaborates: "The mystery of the Tabernacle which is [composed of] limbs and joints—they all amount to the mystery of the human being, on the pattern of the commandments in the Torah, for all the commandments in the Torah are in the form of the mystery of the human being, male and female, for when they are joined together they are the single mystery of humanity" (*Zohar* 2:162b).

***You shall make the planks for the Tabernacle of acacia wood, upright*** (26:15). *Sh'mot Rabbah* 35.1 asks why the Hebrew reads "*the* planks" rather than just "planks." One answer is that God concealed some things after the Creation until they were specifically required. These particular cedar trees were hidden until they could be used to construct a dwelling place for the *Shechinah*. —*Ruth Gais*

• • • • •

# *Contemporary Reflection*

PARASHAT T'RUMAH FOCUSES on building the symbolic core of the Israelites: the Tabernacle (*Mishkan*), which will become the central shrine and sacred symbol of God's dwelling amidst the people. The *Mishkan* will be a physical entity, but it will spiritually link the Israelites into a nation through God's divine Presence. This portable structure is considered the forerunner of the Temple built in Jerusalem many generations after the wilderness experience. Today, the synagogue, with its distinct reminders of the Tabernacle and Temple, functions as the communal focal point for the Jewish people. It, too, serves as the spiritual center connecting Jews of all generations to our history, people, and covenant.

The building of the *Mishkan* will force the Israelites to work together in order to fulfill a common goal and prepare for a common future. Although they have just been given the Decalogue—the precepts that bind the Israelites to God and one another—the people's participation in the making of the Tabernacle will unify the nation in a different way. It will elevate the seemingly mundane work of construction into a sacred vocation, dedicated to the service of the One God who freed them from Egypt and revealed the terms of the covenant.

These former slaves are no strangers to building monuments and cities. The backbreaking labor of the Israelites in Egypt glorified the pharaoh and the Egyptian gods; but this certainly was not a sacred endeavor. In contrast, constructing the Tabernacle and all its finery will be holy work that aims to create sacred space and sacred instruments of worship.

*Parashat T'rumah* goes into great detail about the various parts of the Tabernacle, describing the Ark of the Covenant, the special table for the bread of display, the menorah, the curtains of the tent, the *parochet* (partition that screens off the sacred inner sanctum), and the altar for delivering offerings to God. In this Torah portion and the ones that follow, the design of the Tabernacle and its contents are laid out with precise measurements and great specificity. A number of these objects can be found in contemporary synagogues, reminders of the sacred structures of our biblical ancestors. Then and now, the ark stands as the epicenter of God's presence and the container for the divine word. Many arks contain a special curtain or partition called a *parochet*, as in the Tabernacle. In sanctuaries today, the menorah shines as a symbol of the Jewish people, just as the *ner tamid* (27:20; understood as an eternal light) provides a sign of God's indwelling presence.

According to *parashat T'rumah*, the Israelites—women and men alike—provide not only the labor, but also the raw materials for the *Mishkan*. Their gifts, brought as voluntary offerings, are gathered and transformed into a place for God to reside in their midst. Imagine how these former slaves felt as they became both builders of a nation and builders of a dwelling place for the Divine!

God instructs Moses: "Tell the Israelite people to bring Me gifts; you shall accept gifts for Me from every person whose heart is so moved" (25:2). This kind of giving, a freewill offering, does not come through guilt, coercion, or competition, but from the deepest recesses of the soul. The Israelites bring yarns, precious metals, cloth, and tanned skins—an array of earthly objects that will eventually become the sacred space where Israel can seek God's presence.

Today, it is important for all of us to continue to make freewill offerings to the institutions that unify the Jewish people. Along with *tzedakah* (required giving), *t'rumah* (voluntary giving) is vital for sustaining our community. Synagogues, Jewish centers, and Jewish communal agencies cannot survive on membership fees or dues alone. As they struggle to meet their financial needs, these institutions require our heartfelt support through the freewill gifts that are necessary to fulfill the good and holy work of these organizations.

The synagogue, in particular, lies at the intersection of the earthly and heavenly realms. The heir to the *Ohel Mo'ed* (Tent of Meeting), the contemporary synagogue is the place where Jews most often seek out God. Through study, prayer, and communal gatherings, the synagogue provides the necessary environment for Jewish connection, renewal, and survival. When we bring our voluntary gifts of money, time, and other resources, we bring the realm of the holy into our lives.

Just as our ancestors were transformed from ordinary slaves into builders of God's home on earth, we too are transformed through this sacred endeavor. We bring more peace, more hope, and more faith into our own lives and the life of our community when we support and build the synagogue. We strengthen the Jewish people even as we strengthen ourselves as Jews.

*When we bring our voluntary gifts, we bring the realm of the holy into our lives.*

Voluntary giving is different for each and every person; it is not simply a percentage or flat rate. A person of substantial means has the ability to give greater sums, while a person of more modest means might not have the capacity to give at such large levels. Nevertheless, each person can and should give significantly. The definition of a "meaningful gift" varies for each individual, depending on one's circumstances. But regardless of the *quantity* of the offering, the *quality* is the same: giving a meaningful voluntary offering to a synagogue or other Jewish institution is a privilege, not a burden. This kind of giving—be it of money or time and effort—is cheerful giving, giving that makes a difference, giving that matters. Our parashah teaches that the *t'rumah*-gift is an offering that comes from the deep recesses of the heart. Then and now, it is a privilege to be involved in the sacred work of building community and constructing a dwelling place for the Divine.

*—Denise L. Eger*

# Voices

## *Before*

Yokheved Bat-Miriam (transl. Wendy Zierler)

*Exodus 25:2–8*

Before, in this way, in bygone days,
Women, like me, in silence
Would bear supplications, hidden flames,
With a throbbing spirit.

They would—and in splintering wails
would prostrate themselves over ancestors'
graves.
And raise candles for the souls of the dead
with trembling hearts.

They would—for the holy arks
they would volunteer precious curtains.
On silk and velvet, in silver thread
were interwoven secret hopes.

Many and varied were the women
unfortunate, beaten, desolate.
Only one, only one nowadays is
close to my yearning heart:—

Hannah who went up for the festival
year after year to the tabernacle,
to pray, to speak her heart,
her prayer without sound and without tear.

Different from her am I
and different also is my expression
But like her longing among the shadows
I will stand and speak my heart.

## *T'rumah*

Laurie Patton

*Exodus 26:1–14*

We've always known
that clothing makes a world;
tents on our mother's beds,
earth and sky made of quilts
letting the light in
so that we are small makers
of tiny suns and miniature moons,
each requiring new stories.

We've always known
that our shawls
are second skins,
which, unlike snakes,
we have the blissful choice
of removing at will.

We've always known
that blankets
have an inch of heat
that can be the difference
between life and death
for someone newly nameless
searching for a subway vent.

We make
tiny worlds,
and shed skins,
and seek warm winds:
in these ways
we cry to You,
and You hear,
because You are gracious.

## *from please with gentleness*
Haviva Pedaya (transl. Harvey Bock)

*Exodus 25:8*

one thing have I asked and it I seek
your dwelling in me your giving me a spirit
one thing I cried when I remembered myself
for then when I prayed I lacked nothing
and now that I desire nothing
everything is trampled in me please be gracious
    to me and pity
bless my days purify them
raise them like a daughter crying over the apple
    of her eye
please if you can

## *Creation*
Nechama Gottschalk

*Exodus 25:8*

In this place I am filled with wonder and awe at
    Your Creation.

How can I feel such ecstasy when I know that
    babies starve daily;
    rulers abuse their peoples for the sake of
        power;
    species become extinct at each setting sun;
    and we humans spend our days destroying
        our world and its inhabitants,
        including ourselves?

Yet here I am and I see You in this place,
    and for the moment,
    my heart opens and I touch You
    and know Love for all Your Creation.

## *The Compassion of Shekhinah*
Ellen Frankel

*Exodus 25:8*

Esther the Hidden One Reveals: Shekhinah, the Holy-One-Who-Dwells-in-This-World, represents the mystical Community of Israel. All Israel constitutes her limbs. She is our intimate link with God-Who-Dwells-on-High and our companion as we wander in exile. As it is written: "*and let them make me a sanctuary that I may dwell among them* (Exodus 25:8). Not 'I will dwell below,' but *among* you—just as a wanderer would. In other words, wherever Israel wanders, I will go with them and I will dwell among them, but not in a permanent place." Mercifully, She holds back God's upraised hand when it threatens to harm Her children, but She does not hesitate to punish us Herself when we stray.

## *from An Interrupted Life*
Etty Hillesum (transl. Arnold J. Pomerans)

*Exodus 25:1–8*

There is a strange little melody inside me that sometimes cries out for words. But through inhibition, lack of self-confidence, laziness and goodness knows what else, that tune remains stifled, haunting me from within. Sometimes it wears me out completely. And then again it fills me with gentle, melancholy music. Sometimes I want to flee with everything I possess into a few words, seek refuge in them. But there are still no words to shelter me. That is the real problem. I am in search of a haven, yet I must first build it for myself, stone by stone. Everyone seeks a home, a refuge. And I am always in search of a few words.

# תצוה ✦ T'tzaveh

## EXODUS 27:20–30:10

## *Further Instructions: Consecration of Priests and Tabernacle*

PARASHAT T'TZAVEH ("you shall instruct") adds to the previous parashah's elaborate instructions for constructing the Tabernacle complex and furnishings, by giving detailed information about the vestments for the priests (28:1–43). Most of this information concerns the sacral garments for the chief priestly official, Aaron. As the one whose priestly functions bring him closest to the invisible presence of God in the Holy of Holies, his apparel must be of the same order of sanctity as the materials used for the holiest areas of the tent shrine.

The next order of business concerns the consecration service (29:1–37). An investiture (or ordination) ceremony will be necessary to confer upon Aaron and his subordinates the requisite sanctity for approaching God and performing their priestly tasks. A supplement (29:38–46) gives advance information about the regular sacrifices that will take place at the Tabernacle, and about God's availability there once the whole complex and its priests are sanctified.

Flanking the lengthy materials about vestments and consecration are two brief passages: one involves the oil for the daily ritual of lighting the lamps in the sacred tent (27:20–21), and the other the incense altar (30:1–10); both items are functionally related to the priests' role.

The wealth of detail about Aaron and his sons provides a stark portrayal of how males dominated the communal sacred lives of the ancient Israelites. Only later, in *parashat Vayak'heil,* will the minor presence of some female personnel at the communal religious shrine become apparent. There, we read about the women who are experts in making textiles (35:25–26) and "the women who performed tasks at the entrance of the Tent of Meeting" (38:8).

In contrast to the seemingly limited participation of women in the institutions of the Tabernacle or Temple, women did play a prominent role in household religious life—carrying

*Women did play a prominent role in household religious life.*

out religious practices deemed necessary for the well-being and survival of their families, such as rituals to achieve fertility, healthy pregnancy, and safe childbirth. Reproduction in the modern world has been medicalized; but traditional societies—including ancient Israel—addressed barrenness, difficult pregnancies and births, and infant mortality via religious practices carried out in the home. Although this information almost never emerges in the Bible, archeological and ethnographic data now provide strong evidence for these essential functions of Israelite women. (See further *Vayikra,* Another View, p. 587.) —*Carol Meyers*

## *Outline*

*I.* Instructions about Oil for Light (27:20–21)

*II.* Instructions about Priestly Vestments (28:1–43)

- *A.* Introduction (vv. 1–5)
- *B.* Ritual items for Aaron (vv. 6–30)
- *C.* Apparel for Aaron and other priests (vv. 31–43)

*III.* Instructions about Consecration (29:1–46)

- *A.* Installation rites (vv. 1–37)
- *B.* Directions for regular sacrifice (vv. 38–42a)
- *C.* Summation (vv. 42b–46)

*IV.* Instructions about the Incense Altar (30:1–10)

27:20

You shall further instruct the Israelites to bring
you clear oil of beaten olives for lighting, for
kindling lamps regularly. [21]Aaron and his sons shall

כז 20 וְאַתָּ֞ה תְּצַוֶּ֣ה ׀ אֶת־בְּנֵ֣י יִשְׂרָאֵ֗ל
וְיִקְח֨וּ אֵלֶ֜יךָ שֶׁ֣מֶן זַ֥יִת זָ֛ךְ כָּתִ֖ית לַמָּא֑וֹר
לְהַעֲלֹ֥ת נֵ֖ר תָּמִֽיד׃ 21 בְּאֹ֨הֶל מוֹעֵ֜ד מִח֣וּץ

## *Instructions about Oil for Light*
(27:20–21)

The instructions for making the menorah in Exodus 25 did not mention how it is to be used; instead, the directions for the lamp oil and its use appear here, as a prelude to the units on priestly vestments and investiture. Like the concluding unit of the parashah (instructions about the altar in 30:1–10), this passage might seem out of place. However, the arrangement makes sense since both passages concern specific rites to be performed inside the shrine by Aaron and his sons. (For the descriptive text later in Exodus that parallels this prescriptive unit, see 35:8, 28.)

*20. **clear oil of . . . olives.*** Olive oil was one of the major agricultural products of the Land of Israel. Not only did it serve as a clean-burning lamp fuel, but it provided the basic fat source for the ancient diet in the Mediterranean region. Olive oil also had cosmetic and medicinal uses; and it was used to consecrate objects and individuals (see at 29:7). Like blood and water, oil was a liquid associated with transformation and holiness. Olive trees provided relatively stable crops since they were not susceptible to the variations in rainfall and temperature that could harm other food supplies; thus they symbolize fertility in many biblical texts, like Psalm 128:3.

***beaten.*** Better, "crushed." Small quantities of oil, as in this context, were probably extracted from olives by placing them in a stone basin or a depression in a rock and then pounding them repeatedly with a stone tool. Because the technology for producing olive oil was similar to the grinding of grain for bread, which was done almost entirely by women (see at 16:3 and 25:30), and because women may have produced stone tools of this sort, the preparation of olive oil—at least in village settings in the Land of Israel—was likely a woman's task.

***lamps.*** Heb. *ner* (lamp), in the singular. The plural translation here may reflect an attempt to align this passage with the idea of seven lamps at the end of the branches of the menorah—perhaps a Second Temple reality, as opposed to a simpler single-lamp tradition for the pre-monarchic tent shrine (see at 25:37).

***regularly.*** Heb. *tamid*, which refers to the regular, daily ritual of lamp lighting. The term sometimes means "continually," but that is not its plain sense here (see next verse).

Later, Jews paired *tamid* ("regularly") with the preceding word *ner* ("lamp") to form the term *ner tamid*, the name for the ever-burning, or "eternal," light that is suspended in front of a synagogue's ark.

◗ There is no evidence of Israelite priestesses.

ANOTHER VIEW ➤ *489*

◗ The poet Yannai linked the priestly regulations for maintaining the Tabernacle's lights with women's kindling lamps for Shabbat.

POST-BIBLICAL INTERPRETATIONS ➤ *490*

◗ This parashah and the book of Esther, each in its own way, ask us to confront an absence.

CONTEMPORARY REFLECTION ➤ *491*

◗ we stand riveted before the lamp / as flame gutters in the wind. . . .

VOICES ➤ *493*

לְפָּרֹכֶת אֲשֶׁר עַל־הָעֵדֻת יַעֲרֹךְ אֹתוֹ אַהֲרֹן
וּבָנָיו מֵעֶרֶב עַד־בֹּקֶר לִפְנֵי יְהוָה חֻקַּת
עוֹלָם לְדֹרֹתָם מֵאֵת בְּנֵי יִשְׂרָאֵל׃ ס
כח וְאַתָּה הַקְרֵב אֵלֶיךָ אֶת־אַהֲרֹן אָחִיךָ
וְאֶת־בָּנָיו אִתּוֹ מִתּוֹךְ בְּנֵי יִשְׂרָאֵל לְכַהֲנוֹ־לִי
אַהֲרֹן נָדָב וַאֲבִיהוּא אֶלְעָזָר וְאִיתָמָר בְּנֵי

set them up in the Tent of Meeting, outside the curtain which is over [the Ark of] the Pact, [to burn] from evening to morning before יהוה. It shall be a due from the Israelites for all time, throughout the ages.

28 You shall bring forward your brother Aaron, with his sons, from among the Israelites, to serve Me as priests: Aaron, Nadab and Abihu,

*21. Tent of Meeting.* This designation for the sacred tent shrine appears here for the first time in Exodus. The term "meeting" (*mo'ed*) reflects the oracular function of such a shrine, in which God would "meet" with a human leader in order to communicate the divine will or provide answers to questions (see 33:7–11). The elaborate and costly Tabernacle (*Mishkan*) may be fictive, yet it seems to incorporate authentic traditions about a relatively small and simple tent shrine (Tent of Meeting) dating to the pre-monarchic era (see also the introduction to *T'rumah*, p. 451).

*the Pact.* An elliptical reference to the "tablets of the Pact"—the covenant document to be placed in the Ark (see at 25:16).

*[to burn] from evening to morning.* That is, overnight during the dark hours (see 30:7–8).

*for all time, throughout the ages.* In the Torah, such language usually signifies an etiology that would give divine sanction to an existing custom by attributing it to the era of Moses and the authority of the Sinai revelation (as in 12:14 and 40:15).

## Instructions about Priestly Vestments (28:1–43)

Like palaces, sacred shrines in the biblical world had coteries of servants to tend the needs of the occupant; in this case, the priests served God's unseen presence. Appropriate garb for entry into the sacred space of the Tabernacle structure is specified for Aaron, who functions as chief or head priest. Aaron's name appears many times in this priest-oriented text, in contrast to its virtual absence from the equivalent unit in the Tabernacle descriptive texts (see at 39:1–31). The focus here is on Aaron's garments; only three verses provide instructions for Aaron's sons' garments (28:40–43). Less elaborate clothing for the other priests, many of whom are to perform menial and messy tasks associated with the slaughter of animals in the courtyard, is also briefly mentioned.

The text does not indicate who will make the priestly apparel. However, because women were probably responsible for making textiles and clothing in ancient Israel, it is likely that they were responsible for producing the sacral garments, just as they were the ones who produced fabrics for the Tabernacle (see at 35:25).

### INTRODUCTION (28:1–5)

This brief introduction names the priestly family, calls for the services of skilled artisans, and lists the items of clothing and materials to be used to make the priestly vestments. (For the descriptive text later in Exodus that parallels this prescriptive section, see 39:1.)

*1. your brother Aaron . . . to serve Me as priests.* Although Aaron appears frequently in Exodus up to this point, this is the first place that his name is used together with the word "priest." Aaron's responsibilities as priest are said to include various matters of ritual (for example, 27:21; 28:35; 30:7–8), judicial proceedings (28:29–30), and instruction (Leviticus 10:11). The Bible never refers to Aaron by the title "high priest"—a term that seems to refer to an office

Eleazar and Ithamar, the sons of Aaron. 2Make sacral
vestments for your brother Aaron, for dignity and
adornment. 3Next you shall instruct all who are
skillful, whom I have endowed with the gift of skill,
to make Aaron's vestments, for consecrating him to
serve Me as priest. 4These are the vestments they are
to make: a breastpiece, an ephod, a robe, a fringed
tunic, a headdress, and a sash. They shall make
those sacral vestments for your brother Aaron and
his sons, for priestly service to Me; 5they, therefore,
shall receive the gold, the blue, purple, and crimson
yarns, and the fine linen.

6They shall make the ephod of gold, of blue,
purple, and crimson yarns, and of fine twisted

אַהֲרֹן׃ 2 וְעָשִׂיתָ בִגְדֵי־קֹדֶשׁ לְאַהֲרֹן אָחִיךָ
לְכָבוֹד וּלְתִפְאָרֶת׃ 3 וְאַתָּה תְּדַבֵּר אֶל־כָּל־
חַכְמֵי־לֵב אֲשֶׁר מִלֵּאתִיו רוּחַ חָכְמָה וְעָשׂוּ
אֶת־בִּגְדֵי אַהֲרֹן לְקַדְּשׁוֹ לְכַהֲנוֹ־לִי׃ 4 וְאֵלֶּה
הַבְּגָדִים אֲשֶׁר יַעֲשׂוּ חֹשֶׁן וְאֵפוֹד וּמְעִיל
וּכְתֹנֶת תַּשְׁבֵּץ מִצְנֶפֶת וְאַבְנֵט וְעָשׂוּ בִגְדֵי־
קֹדֶשׁ לְאַהֲרֹן אָחִיךָ וּלְבָנָיו לְכַהֲנוֹ־לִי׃
5 וְהֵם יִקְחוּ אֶת־הַזָּהָב וְאֶת־הַתְּכֵלֶת
וְאֶת־הָאַרְגָּמָן וְאֶת־תּוֹלַעַת הַשָּׁנִי וְאֶת־
הַשֵּׁשׁ׃ פ
6 וְעָשׂוּ אֶת־הָאֵפֹד זָהָב תְּכֵלֶת וְאַרְגָּמָן
תּוֹלַעַת שָׁנִי וְשֵׁשׁ מָשְׁזָר מַעֲשֵׂה חֹשֵׁב׃

---

that developed over time so that its responsibilities included also temple finance and management.

As the narrative presents it, Aaron seems to have become the head of the priestly line by virtue of being Moses' brother. Both are from the family of Levi, and their association with Sinai serves to legitimate the Aaronide priesthood. We know from Exodus 6:20 that Aaron's mother was Jochebed, and from 6:23 that his wife was "Elisheba, daughter of Amminadab and sister of Nahshon."

*3. all who are skillful.* More information about the textile workers appears in 35:25–26 and 36:6, where it is clear that female artisans are involved. "Skillful" is literally "wise of heart." In Israelite society, artisans were held in higher esteem than manual laborers; and their ability to apply unusual talent to create beautiful items was attributed to God.

*4.* Altogether, Aaron will wear seven items (the six mentioned here plus the frontlet in 28:36–37), seven being a symbol of perfection and totality. He will wear breeches too (v. 42), but they would not be visible and probably were not considered sacred. Note the absence of footwear, implying that priests wore no shoes on holy ground (see 3:5).

*5. gold, the blue, purple, and crimson yarns, and the fine linen.* The sumptuous materials to be used for the textiles of the Tabernacle and its partitions (see at 25:4) are also to be used for the garments worn by the one entering that holy space.

### RITUAL ITEMS FOR AARON (28:6–30)

Two highly specialized and somewhat enigmatic items of Aaron's apparel, the ephod and breastpiece, will have a role in ritual practice. Their collective importance is signaled by the length of the passages devoted to instructions for making these two items; but how they are to be used is never explained. (For the descriptive text later in Exodus that parallels this prescriptive section, see 39:2–21.)

*6. ephod.* The English noun is simply a transliteration of the Hebrew term. A number of diverse sources (Judges 8:24–27; I Samuel 2:18; II Kings 8:8–14) indicate that the ephod's appearance and function changed over time. It was a ritual garment, a divinatory device, or sometimes both—as seems to be the case here, because of the ephod's attachment to the "breastpiece of decision."

*of gold.* That is, using gold thread (Exodus 39:3). Fabrics with gold are known from Mesopotamian texts describing garments made to clothe statues of the gods. Golden garments are fit for deities or for their human attendants.

linen, worked into designs. [7]It shall have two shoulder-pieces attached; they shall be attached at its two ends. [8]And the decorated band that is upon it shall be made like it, of one piece with it: of gold, of blue, purple, and crimson yarns, and of fine twisted linen. [9]Then take two lazuli stones and engrave on them the names of the sons of Israel: [10]six of their names on the one stone, and the names of the remaining six on the other stone, in the order of their birth. [11]On the two stones you shall make seal engravings—the work of a lapidary—of the names of the sons of Israel. Having bordered them with frames of gold, [12]attach the two stones to the shoulder-pieces of the ephod, as stones for remembrance of the Israelite people, whose names Aaron shall carry upon his two shoulder-pieces for remembrance before יהוה.

[13]Then make frames of gold [14]and two chains of pure gold; braid these like corded work, and fasten the corded chains to the frames.

[15]You shall make a breastpiece of decision,

7 שְׁתֵּי כְתֵפֹת חֹבְרֹת יִהְיֶה־לּוֹ אֶל־שְׁנֵי
קְצוֹתָיו וְחֻבָּר׃ 8 וְחֵשֶׁב אֲפֻדָּתוֹ אֲשֶׁר עָלָיו
כְּמַעֲשֵׂהוּ מִמֶּנּוּ יִהְיֶה זָהָב תְּכֵלֶת וְאַרְגָּמָן
וְתוֹלַעַת שָׁנִי וְשֵׁשׁ מָשְׁזָר׃ 9 וְלָקַחְתָּ אֶת־
שְׁתֵּי אַבְנֵי־שֹׁהַם וּפִתַּחְתָּ עֲלֵיהֶם שְׁמוֹת
בְּנֵי יִשְׂרָאֵל׃ 10 שִׁשָּׁה מִשְּׁמֹתָם עַל הָאֶבֶן
הָאֶחָת וְאֶת־שְׁמוֹת הַשִּׁשָּׁה הַנּוֹתָרִים עַל־
הָאֶבֶן הַשֵּׁנִית כְּתוֹלְדֹתָם׃ 11 מַעֲשֵׂה חָרַשׁ
אֶבֶן פִּתּוּחֵי חֹתָם תְּפַתַּח אֶת־שְׁתֵּי
הָאֲבָנִים עַל־שְׁמֹת בְּנֵי יִשְׂרָאֵל מֻסַבֹּת
מִשְׁבְּצוֹת זָהָב תַּעֲשֶׂה אֹתָם׃ 12 וְשַׂמְתָּ
אֶת־שְׁתֵּי הָאֲבָנִים עַל כִּתְפֹת הָאֵפֹד אַבְנֵי
זִכָּרֹן לִבְנֵי יִשְׂרָאֵל וְנָשָׂא אַהֲרֹן אֶת־
שְׁמוֹתָם לִפְנֵי יְהוָה עַל־שְׁתֵּי כְתֵפָיו
לְזִכָּרֹן׃ ס
13 וְעָשִׂיתָ מִשְׁבְּצֹת זָהָב׃ 14 וּשְׁתֵּי שַׁרְשְׁרֹת
זָהָב טָהוֹר מִגְבָּלֹת תַּעֲשֶׂה אֹתָם מַעֲשֵׂה
עֲבֹת וְנָתַתָּה אֶת־שַׁרְשְׁרֹת הָעֲבֹתֹת עַל־
הַמִּשְׁבְּצֹת׃ ס
15 וְעָשִׂיתָ חֹשֶׁן מִשְׁפָּט מַעֲשֵׂה חֹשֵׁב

*worked into designs.* Like the fabrics of the Tabernacle (26:31, 36; 27:16), the ephod is to have embroidered work.

*7. shoulder-pieces.* Perhaps shoulder straps of a vest-like garment.

*9. lazuli stones.* More likely onyx or possibly carnelian.

*engrave on them the names of the sons of Israel.* Engraving gemstones with their owners' names, and sometimes with a design, was a highly developed craft in the ancient Near East. Engraved stones served as signets or seals and were used for legal or economic documents. Here, engraving the names of the twelve tribes—six on each stone—symbolizes the presence of all Israel in the decisions made with the ephod and gives authority to those rulings; it also carries the implicit hope for divine awareness of the people and their needs (see also at v. 12).

*10. in the order of their birth.* This implies knowledge of the matriarchal narratives of Genesis.

*11. lapidary.* Literally, a "cutter," meaning an engraver.

*12. stones for remembrance... names... for remembrance.* Ancient inscriptions asking that God "remember" supplicants for good attest to the implicit hope that God will always be mindful of the people and presumably bring them blessings.

*15. breastpiece.* This ornate pouch, square when viewed from the front (v. 16), is attached to the ephod. It contains the enigmatic Urim and Thummim, which probably were lots cast to determine God's will in legal, military, and other situations (see at v. 30).

*decision.* Heb. *mishpat,* meaning "judgment"; this term provides a clue to the breastpiece's ritual function. Like most ancient peoples, the Israelites

worked into a design; make it in the style of the
ephod: make it of gold, of blue, purple, and crimson yarns, and of fine twisted linen. [16]It shall be
square and doubled, a span in length and a span in
width. [17]Set in it mounted stones, in four rows of
stones. The first row shall be a row of carnelian,
chrysolite, and emerald; [18]the second row: a turquoise, a sapphire, and an amethyst; [19]the third
row: a jacinth, an agate, and a crystal; [20]and the
fourth row: a beryl, a lapis lazuli, and a jasper. They
shall be framed with gold in their mountings. [21]The
stones shall correspond [in number] to the names of
the sons of Israel: twelve, corresponding to their
names. They shall be engraved like seals, each with
its name, for the twelve tribes.

[22]On the breastpiece make braided chains of
corded work in pure gold. [23]Make two rings of gold
on the breastpiece, and fasten the two rings at the
two ends of the breastpiece, [24]attaching the two
golden cords to the two rings at the ends of the
breastpiece. [25]Then fasten the two ends of the cords
to the two frames, which you shall attach to the
shoulder-pieces of the ephod, at the front. [26]Make
two rings of gold and attach them to the two ends
of the breastpiece, at its inner edge, which faces the
ephod. [27]And make two other rings of gold and fasten them on the front of the ephod, low on the two
shoulder-pieces, close to its seam above the deco-

כְּמַעֲשֵׂה אֵפֹד תַּעֲשֶׂנּוּ זָהָב תְּכֵלֶת וְאַרְגָּמָן
וְתוֹלַעַת שָׁנִי וְשֵׁשׁ מָשְׁזָר תַּעֲשֶׂה אֹתוֹ׃
16 רָבוּעַ יִהְיֶה כָּפוּל זֶרֶת אָרְכּוֹ וְזֶרֶת
רָחְבּוֹ׃ 17 וּמִלֵּאתָ בוֹ מִלֻּאַת אֶבֶן אַרְבָּעָה
טוּרִים אָבֶן טוּר אֹדֶם פִּטְדָה וּבָרֶקֶת
הַטּוּר הָאֶחָד׃ 18 וְהַטּוּר הַשֵּׁנִי נֹפֶךְ סַפִּיר
וְיָהֲלֹם׃ 19 וְהַטּוּר הַשְּׁלִישִׁי לֶשֶׁם שְׁבוֹ
וְאַחְלָמָה׃ 20 וְהַטּוּר הָרְבִיעִי תַּרְשִׁישׁ וְשֹׁהַם
וְיָשְׁפֵה מְשֻׁבָּצִים זָהָב יִהְיוּ בְּמִלּוּאֹתָם׃
21 וְהָאֲבָנִים תִּהְיֶיןָ עַל־שְׁמֹת בְּנֵי־יִשְׂרָאֵל
שְׁתֵּים עֶשְׂרֵה עַל־שְׁמֹתָם פִּתּוּחֵי חוֹתָם
אִישׁ עַל־שְׁמוֹ תִּהְיֶיןָ לִשְׁנֵי עָשָׂר שָׁבֶט׃
22 וְעָשִׂיתָ עַל־הַחֹשֶׁן שַׁרְשֹׁת גַּבְלֻת מַעֲשֵׂה
עֲבֹת זָהָב טָהוֹר׃ 23 וְעָשִׂיתָ עַל־הַחֹשֶׁן שְׁתֵּי
טַבְּעוֹת זָהָב וְנָתַתָּ אֶת־שְׁתֵּי הַטַּבָּעוֹת עַל־
שְׁנֵי קְצוֹת הַחֹשֶׁן׃ 24 וְנָתַתָּה אֶת־שְׁתֵּי
עֲבֹתֹת הַזָּהָב עַל־שְׁתֵּי הַטַּבָּעֹת אֶל־קְצוֹת
הַחֹשֶׁן׃ 25 וְאֵת שְׁתֵּי קְצוֹת שְׁתֵּי הָעֲבֹתֹת
תִּתֵּן עַל־שְׁתֵּי הַמִּשְׁבְּצוֹת וְנָתַתָּה עַל־
כִּתְפוֹת הָאֵפֹד אֶל־מוּל פָּנָיו׃ 26 וְעָשִׂיתָ
שְׁתֵּי טַבְּעוֹת זָהָב וְשַׂמְתָּ אֹתָם עַל־שְׁנֵי
קְצוֹת הַחֹשֶׁן עַל־שְׂפָתוֹ אֲשֶׁר אֶל־עֵבֶר
הָאֵפוֹד בָּיְתָה׃ 27 וְעָשִׂיתָ שְׁתֵּי טַבְּעוֹת
זָהָב וְנָתַתָּה אֹתָם עַל־שְׁתֵּי כִתְפוֹת הָאֵפוֹד
מִלְּמַטָּה מִמּוּל פָּנָיו לְעֻמַּת מַחְבַּרְתּוֹ מִמַּעַל

---

turned to their deity to resolve judicial proceedings that had reached an impasse, often involving the word of one individual against another (see 22:8 and at 25:22).

*16. a span . . . a span.* The breastpiece is to be about nine by nine inches (a little more than 20 centimeters square).

*17–21.* A total of twelve stones, three each in four rows, are to adorn the breastpiece. The mineralogical identity of most of the stones is uncertain. (Thus, many of the names used in the translation are not necessarily accurate.) They seem to be the kind of semiprecious stones that were regularly engraved for use to mark the seals on official documents in the ancient world. Most of the Hebrew seals discovered in the Land of Israel by archeologists bear men's names; but a small percentage have women's names, attesting to the fact that some women performed legal or economic transactions.

*22–28.* Golden rings, chains, and frames along with a blue cord are to form an elaborate mechanism for securing the breastpiece to the ephod and for assuring the stability of this weighty item.

rated band. [28] The breastpiece shall be held in place by a cord of blue from its rings to the rings of the ephod, so that the breastpiece rests on the decorated band and does not come loose from the ephod. [29] Aaron shall carry the names of the sons of Israel on the breastpiece of decision over his heart, when he enters the sanctuary, for remembrance before יהוה at all times. [30] Inside the breastpiece of decision you shall place the Urim and Thummim, so that they are over Aaron's heart when he comes before יהוה. Thus Aaron shall carry the instrument of decision for the Israelites over his heart before יהוה at all times.

[31] You shall make the robe of the ephod of pure blue. [32] The opening for the head shall be in the middle of it; the opening shall have a binding of woven work round about—it shall be like the opening of a coat of mail—so that it does not tear. [33] On

לַחֵ֖שֶׁב הָאֵפֹ֑וד: 28 וְיִרְכְּס֣וּ אֶת־הַחֹ֗שֶׁן מִֽטַּבְּעֹתָיו֙ אֶל־טַבְּעֹ֣ת הָאֵפֹ֔וד בִּפְתִ֣יל תְּכֵ֔לֶת לִהְי֖וֹת עַל־חֵ֣שֶׁב הָאֵפֹ֑וד וְלֹֽא־יִזַּ֣ח הַחֹ֔שֶׁן מֵעַ֖ל הָאֵפֹֽוד: 29 וְנָשָׂ֣א אַֽהֲרֹ֡ן אֶת־שְׁמֹ֣ות בְּנֵֽי־יִשְׂרָאֵ֣ל בְּחֹ֣שֶׁן הַמִּשְׁפָּ֡ט עַל־לִבֹּ֡ו בְּבֹאֹ֣ו אֶל־הַקֹּ֗דֶשׁ לְזִכָּרֹ֛ן לִפְנֵֽי־יְהֹוָ֖ה תָּמִֽיד: 30 וְנָתַתָּ֞ אֶל־חֹ֣שֶׁן הַמִּשְׁפָּ֗ט אֶת־הָֽאוּרִים֙ וְאֶת־הַתֻּמִּ֔ים וְהָי֞וּ עַל־לֵ֤ב אַֽהֲרֹן֙ בְּבֹאֹ֣ו לִפְנֵ֣י יְהֹוָ֔ה וְנָשָׂ֣א אַֽהֲרֹ֡ן אֶת־מִשְׁפַּ֣ט בְּנֵֽי־יִשְׂרָאֵ֛ל עַל־לִבֹּ֖ו לִפְנֵ֥י יְהֹוָ֖ה תָּמִֽיד: ס

31 וְעָשִׂ֛יתָ אֶת־מְעִ֥יל הָאֵפֹ֖וד כְּלִ֥יל תְּכֵֽלֶת: 32 וְהָיָ֧ה פִֽי־רֹאשֹׁ֛ו בְּתֹוכֹ֖ו שָׂפָ֣ה יִֽהְיֶ֧ה לְפִ֛יו סָבִ֖יב מַֽעֲשֵׂ֣ה אֹרֵ֑ג כְּפִ֥י תַחְרָ֛א יִֽהְיֶה־לֹּ֖ו לֹ֥א יִקָּרֵֽעַ: 33 וְעָשִׂ֣יתָ עַל־שׁוּלָ֗יו רִמֹּנֵי֙ תְּכֵ֙לֶת

**28.** *cord of blue.* Blue seems to have been the most highly prized color—and thus the most fitting for priestly vestments—apparently because blue dyes were more difficult to obtain and prepare than those used for purple and crimson (see at 25:4; *T'rumah*, Another View, p. 467).

**29.** *over his heart.* The heart represents the identity of a human being in the Bible; it was considered the locus of various human functions, including memory.

**30.** *Urim and Thummim.* No translation is given for these terms because their meaning is so uncertain. They refer to stones, perhaps similar to dice or lots, to be kept in the breastpiece. Their function seems clear: they served as a medium for ascertaining a divine ruling on human problems. (See, for example, Numbers 27:21; I Samuel 14:41–42.)

**when he comes before יהוה.** That is, when he approaches the sacred space closest to God's invisible presence over the Ark.

### APPAREL FOR AARON AND OTHER PRIESTS (28:31–43)

The first two ritual vestments, a special robe and an adornment for the headgear, are for the chief priestly official alone. The other items—tunic, headdress, and sash—are for both the head of the priesthood and the next tier of priests. (For the descriptive text later in Exodus that parallels this prescriptive section, see 39:22–31.)

**31.** *robe of the ephod of pure blue.* Probably a full-length garment, the robe is blue, a color indicating an especially costly fabric. In other biblical texts, this kind of garment is associated with royalty or other high officials only.

**32.** Somewhat like a long vest (sleeves are not mentioned), the robe is pulled on through a reinforced opening for the head. According to I Samuel 2:19, Hannah made a new robe for her son Samuel each year while he served as a priest's assistant.

its hem make pomegranates of blue, purple, and
crimson yarns, all around the hem, with bells of
gold between them all around: 34a golden bell and
a pomegranate, a golden bell and a pomegranate,
all around the hem of the robe. 35Aaron shall wear
it while officiating, so that the sound of it is heard
when he comes into the sanctuary before יהוה
and when he goes out—that he may not die.

36You shall make a frontlet of pure gold and
engrave on it the seal inscription: "Holy to יהוה."
37Suspend it on a cord of blue, so that it may remain on the headdress; it shall remain on the front
of the headdress. 38It shall be on Aaron's forehead,
that Aaron may take away any sin arising from the
holy things that the Israelites consecrate, from any
of their sacred donations; it shall be on his forehead
at all times, to win acceptance for them before יהוה.

39You shall make the fringed tunic of fine linen.

וְאַרְגָּמָן וְתוֹלַעַת שָׁנִי עַל־שׁוּלָיו סָבִיב
וּפַעֲמֹנֵי זָהָב בְּתוֹכָם סָבִיב׃ 34 פַּעֲמֹן זָהָב
וְרִמּוֹן פַּעֲמֹן זָהָב וְרִמּוֹן עַל־שׁוּלֵי הַמְּעִיל
סָבִיב׃ 35 וְהָיָה עַל־אַהֲרֹן לְשָׁרֵת וְנִשְׁמַע
קוֹלוֹ בְּבֹאוֹ אֶל־הַקֹּדֶשׁ לִפְנֵי יְהֹוָה וּבְצֵאתוֹ
וְלֹא יָמוּת׃ ס

36 וְעָשִׂיתָ צִּיץ זָהָב טָהוֹר וּפִתַּחְתָּ עָלָיו
פִּתּוּחֵי חֹתָם קֹדֶשׁ לַיהֹוָה׃ 37 וְשַׂמְתָּ אֹתוֹ
עַל־פְּתִיל תְּכֵלֶת וְהָיָה עַל־הַמִּצְנָפֶת אֶל־
מוּל פְּנֵי־הַמִּצְנֶפֶת יִהְיֶה׃ 38 וְהָיָה עַל־מֵצַח
אַהֲרֹן וְנָשָׂא אַהֲרֹן אֶת־עֲוֺן הַקֳּדָשִׁים אֲשֶׁר
יַקְדִּישׁוּ בְּנֵי יִשְׂרָאֵל לְכָל־מַתְּנֹת קָדְשֵׁיהֶם
וְהָיָה עַל־מִצְחוֹ תָּמִיד לְרָצוֹן לָהֶם לִפְנֵי
יְהֹוָה׃

39 וְשִׁבַּצְתָּ הַכְּתֹנֶת שֵׁשׁ

*33. pomegranates of . . . yarns.* The pomegranate was a symbol of fertility and a well-known decorative element in ancient Near Eastern art. Here, they are to be made of woolen yarn that is colored with the same three dyes adorning both the Tabernacle fabrics and the ritual items of Aaron's garb. That is, these pomegranates would be elaborate tassels to be attached to the robe along with the golden bells.

*all around the hem.* The distinctive feature of this robe is its lower portion or "skirt" (rather than "hem"), which is to be specially embellished.

*35.* Bells, which incorporate the sense of hearing into the sensory array of the shrine's features, apparently had an apotropaic effect, meaning that they were intended to ward off evil. Sounds were believed to protect people, hence the notice that Aaron "will not die" as long as the noise can be heard. In this case, the danger would have been the intense holiness emanating from the presence of God as Aaron entered the holy zone of the Tabernacle.

*36. frontlet of pure gold.* All priests wore head coverings, but the chief priestly official also had an inscribed golden medallion hanging on the headdress, or perhaps an actual diadem surmounting it.

*frontlet.* Literally, "flower" or "blossom," referring perhaps to a rosette-shaped piece of metal. Rosettes, which are depicted as an ornament on the headdresses of deities in Assyrian art, perhaps indicate the high status of the one who wore it.

*"Holy to* יהוה*."* The intent of the inscribed phrase is ambiguous; the inscription may indicate the sanctity of the headdress, the priest, the priest's tasks in the shrine, or some combination of these.

*38. that Aaron may take away any sin.* This clause either suggests an apotropaic (protective) function for the frontlet, or it refers to the expiatory role of the head priest. The term "take away" can also mean "bear, carry"; that is, the priest either carries or removes any sinful aspect of what the Israelites bring as holy offerings to God.

*39. fringed.* The meaning of the Hebrew term is uncertain; it might represent some kind of decorative work.

*tunic.* This garment, mentioned many times in the Bible, was the main item of clothing worn by Israelite women as well as men.

You shall make the headdress of fine linen.
You shall make the sash of embroidered work.
[40]And for Aaron's sons also you shall make
tunics, and make sashes for them, and make turbans for them, for dignity and adornment. [41]Put
these on your brother Aaron and on his sons as well;
anoint them, and ordain them and consecrate them
to serve Me as priests.
[42]You shall also make for them linen breeches to
cover their nakedness; they shall extend from the
hips to the thighs. [43]They shall be worn by Aaron
and his sons when they enter the Tent of Meeting
or when they approach the altar to officiate in the
sanctuary, so that they do not incur punishment
and die. It shall be a law for all time for him and for
his offspring to come.

29 This is what you shall do to them in consecrating them to serve Me as priests: Take a young

וְעָשִׂיתָ מִצְנֶפֶת שֵׁשׁ
וְאַבְנֵט תַּעֲשֶׂה מַעֲשֵׂה רֹקֵם׃
40 וְלִבְנֵי אַהֲרֹן תַּעֲשֶׂה כֻתֳּנֹת וְעָשִׂיתָ לָהֶם
אַבְנֵטִים וּמִגְבָּעוֹת תַּעֲשֶׂה לָהֶם לְכָבוֹד
וּלְתִפְאָרֶת׃ 41 וְהִלְבַּשְׁתָּ אֹתָם אֶת־אַהֲרֹן
אָחִיךָ וְאֶת־בָּנָיו אִתּוֹ וּמָשַׁחְתָּ אֹתָם
וּמִלֵּאתָ אֶת־יָדָם וְקִדַּשְׁתָּ אֹתָם וְכִהֲנוּ
לִי׃
42 וַעֲשֵׂה לָהֶם מִכְנְסֵי־בָד לְכַסּוֹת בְּשַׂר
עֶרְוָה מִמָּתְנַיִם וְעַד־יְרֵכַיִם יִהְיוּ׃ 43 וְהָיוּ
עַל־אַהֲרֹן וְעַל־בָּנָיו בְּבֹאָם ׀ אֶל־אֹהֶל מוֹעֵד
אוֹ בְגִשְׁתָּם אֶל־הַמִּזְבֵּחַ לְשָׁרֵת בַּקֹּדֶשׁ
וְלֹא־יִשְׂאוּ עָוֺן וָמֵתוּ חֻקַּת עוֹלָם לוֹ
וּלְזַרְעוֹ אַחֲרָיו׃ ס

כט וְזֶה הַדָּבָר אֲשֶׁר־תַּעֲשֶׂה לָהֶם לְקַדֵּשׁ
אֹתָם לְכַהֵן לִי לְקַח פַּר אֶחָד בֶּן־בָּקָר

***40. tunics . . . sashes . . . turbans.*** The garb of the other priests does not include the special touches accorded to that of the chief priestly official. Their headdress is to be more of a "cap" than a turban.

***42. linen breeches.*** The text prescribes breeches to function as an undergarment worn by all priestly ranks, for reasons of modesty; the Bible does not mention breeches being worn by most people.

***43. incur punishment and die.*** Because of the great sanctity of the shrine, proper attire would be essential, and the consequences of having improper vestments would be dire.

***law for all time.*** See at 27:21.

## *Instructions about Consecration*

(29:1–46)

The ornate vestments provide the priests with authority for their roles only through elaborate and lengthy installation rituals. These instructions are not implemented until Leviticus 8–9, which parallels this prescriptive unit as a descriptive text: it records the investiture and consecration of the priests.

### INSTALLATION RITES (29:1–37)

The installation rites are to include three kinds of sacrifices: purgation offering (vv. 10–14), burnt offering (vv. 15–18), and elevation offering (vv. 22–26). The rites will also feature four procedures that focus on the persons involved: washing (v. 4), dressing (vv. 5–6, 8), anointing (v. 7), and carrying out a blood rite (vv. 19–21).

***1. you.*** The instructions are addressed to Moses, who himself is to act as priest in ordaining his brother and nephews.

***consecrating.*** The form of the verb *k-d-sh* that means "consecrate, make holy" appears seven times in this unit (vv. 1–46), thus indicating the complete sanctity endowed upon the priestly line. Holiness in the ancient world was not an abstract concept, as it is today. A highly positive quality linked with the

bull of the herd and two rams without blemish;
2 also unleavened bread, unleavened cakes with oil mixed in, and unleavened wafers spread with oil—make these of choice wheat flour.
3 Place these in one basket and present them in the basket, along with the bull and the two rams.
4 Lead Aaron and his sons up to the entrance of the Tent of Meeting, and wash them with water.
5 Then take the vestments, and clothe Aaron with the tunic, the robe of the ephod, the ephod, and the breastpiece, and gird him with the decorated band of the ephod.
6 Put the headdress on his head, and place the holy diadem upon the headdress.
7 Take the anointing oil and pour it on his head and anoint him.
8 Then bring his sons forward; clothe them with tunics
9 and wind turbans upon them. And gird both Aaron and his sons with sashes. And so they shall have priesthood as their right for all time.

You shall then ordain Aaron and his sons.
10 Lead the bull up to the front of the Tent of

וְאֵילִם שְׁנַיִם תְּמִימִם׃ 2 וְלֶחֶם מַצּוֹת
וְחַלֹּת מַצֹּת בְּלוּלֹת בַּשֶּׁמֶן וּרְקִיקֵי מַצּוֹת
מְשֻׁחִים בַּשָּׁמֶן סֹלֶת חִטִּים תַּעֲשֶׂה אֹתָם׃
3 וְנָתַתָּ אוֹתָם עַל־סַל אֶחָד וְהִקְרַבְתָּ אֹתָם
בַּסָּל וְאֶת־הַפָּר וְאֵת שְׁנֵי הָאֵילִם׃ 4 וְאֶת־
אַהֲרֹן וְאֶת־בָּנָיו תַּקְרִיב אֶל־פֶּתַח אֹהֶל
מוֹעֵד וְרָחַצְתָּ אֹתָם בַּמָּיִם׃ 5 וְלָקַחְתָּ אֶת־
הַבְּגָדִים וְהִלְבַּשְׁתָּ אֶת־אַהֲרֹן אֶת־הַכֻּתֹּנֶת
וְאֵת מְעִיל הָאֵפֹד וְאֶת־הָאֵפֹד וְאֶת־
הַחֹשֶׁן וְאָפַדְתָּ לוֹ בְּחֵשֶׁב הָאֵפֹד׃ 6 וְשַׂמְתָּ
הַמִּצְנֶפֶת עַל־רֹאשׁוֹ וְנָתַתָּ אֶת־נֵזֶר הַקֹּדֶשׁ
עַל־הַמִּצְנָפֶת׃ 7 וְלָקַחְתָּ אֶת־שֶׁמֶן הַמִּשְׁחָה
וְיָצַקְתָּ עַל־רֹאשׁוֹ וּמָשַׁחְתָּ אֹתוֹ׃ 8 וְאֶת־
בָּנָיו תַּקְרִיב וְהִלְבַּשְׁתָּם כֻּתֳּנֹת׃ 9 וְחָגַרְתָּ
אֹתָם אַבְנֵט אַהֲרֹן וּבָנָיו וְחָבַשְׁתָּ לָהֶם
מִגְבָּעֹת וְהָיְתָה לָהֶם כְּהֻנָּה לְחֻקַּת עוֹלָם
וּמִלֵּאתָ יַד־אַהֲרֹן וְיַד־בָּנָיו׃ 10 וְהִקְרַבְתָּ

nature of God, holiness could be acquired through ritual acts by people, animals, places, and things; only then could they approach the powerful sanctity of God, which paradoxically could be dangerous as well as beneficent because of its extreme power.

***bull of the herd and two rams.*** The Israelite custom of sacrificing these two kinds of animals is given extra significance by relating it to Sinai and the wilderness shrine. All three animals are male probably because killing females would jeopardize milk supplies and breeding.

*4.* ***wash them with water.*** Ablutions before approaching the sacred realm were meant to remove impurity. It is not certain whether washing was believed to actually wash off contaminating substances or only to signify their removal.

*7.* ***Take the anointing oil.*** Anointing with olive oil had cosmetic and even magical functions in daily life in ancient Israel and in the wider Near East (see also at 27:20). In ceremonial use, anointing served to formalize an elevation in status. Kings and priests were anointed as they took office. Eventually, the eschatological king is called the "messiah" (*mashiach*), meaning "anointed one."

*9.* ***priesthood as their right for all time.*** Making the priesthood the hereditary right of Aaron and his male offspring effectively precludes women from serving as officiants in the holy precinct. In this regard, the Israelites differed from other ancient peoples, for whom priestesses are mentioned. One possible explanation for the exclusion of women is a demographic one; that is, because infant mortality was high and women risked death in childbirth, women were needed for normal family life and thus were not separated out for Temple or Tabernacle service. (See further Another View, p. 489.) Establishing a hereditary priesthood meant that most males, those not from the tribe of Levi, were also denied the right to officiate.

***ordain.*** Literally, "to fill the hand" of Aaron and his sons. This idiom, known in other ancient texts, probably refers to the placing of a scepter in

Meeting, and let Aaron and his sons lay their hands upon the head of the bull. [11]Slaughter the bull before יהוה, at the entrance of the Tent of Meeting, [12]and take some of the bull's blood and put it on the horns of the altar with your finger; then pour out the rest of the blood at the base of the altar. [13]Take all the fat that covers the entrails, the protuberance on the liver, and the two kidneys with the fat on them, and turn them into smoke upon the altar. [14]The rest of the flesh of the bull, its hide, and its dung shall be put to the fire outside the camp; it is a purgation offering.

[15]Next take the one ram, and let Aaron and his sons lay their hands upon the ram's head. [16]Slaughter the ram, and take its blood and dash it against all sides of the altar. [17]Cut up the ram into sections, wash its entrails and legs, and put them with its quarters and its head. [18]Turn all of the ram into smoke upon the altar. It is a burnt offering to יהוה, a pleasing odor, an offering by fire to יהוה.

[19]Then take the other ram, and let Aaron and his sons lay their hands upon the ram's head. [20]Slaughter the ram, and take some of its blood and put it on the ridge of Aaron's right ear and on the ridges of his sons' right ears, and on the thumbs of their right hands, and on the big toes of their right feet; and dash the rest of the blood against every side of the altar round about. [21]Take some of the blood that is on the altar and some of the

אֶת־הַפָּ֔ר לִפְנֵ֖י אֹ֣הֶל מוֹעֵ֑ד וְסָמַ֨ךְ אַהֲרֹ֧ן
וּבָנָ֛יו אֶת־יְדֵיהֶ֖ם עַל־רֹ֥אשׁ הַפָּֽר׃ 11 וְשָׁחַטְתָּ֥
אֶת־הַפָּ֖ר לִפְנֵ֣י יְהֹוָ֑ה פֶּ֖תַח אֹ֥הֶל מוֹעֵֽד׃
12 וְלָקַחְתָּ֙ מִדַּ֣ם הַפָּ֔ר וְנָתַתָּ֛ה עַל־קַרְנֹ֥ת
הַמִּזְבֵּ֖חַ בְּאֶצְבָּעֶ֑ךָ וְאֶת־כָּל־הַדָּ֣ם תִּשְׁפֹּ֔ךְ
אֶל־יְס֖וֹד הַמִּזְבֵּֽחַ׃ 13 וְלָקַחְתָּ֗ אֶֽת־כָּל־
הַחֵ֘לֶב֮ הַֽמְכַסֶּ֣ה אֶת־הַקֶּ֒רֶב֒ וְאֵ֗ת הַיֹּתֶ֙רֶת֙
עַל־הַכָּבֵ֔ד וְאֵת֙ שְׁתֵּ֣י הַכְּלָיֹ֔ת וְאֶת־
הַחֵ֖לֶב אֲשֶׁ֣ר עֲלֵיהֶ֑ן וְהִקְטַרְתָּ֖ הַמִּזְבֵּֽחָה׃
14 וְאֶת־בְּשַׂ֤ר הַפָּר֙ וְאֶת־עֹר֣וֹ וְאֶת־פִּרְשׁ֔וֹ
תִּשְׂרֹ֥ף בָּאֵ֖שׁ מִח֣וּץ לַֽמַּחֲנֶ֑ה חַטָּ֖את הֽוּא׃
15 וְאֶת־הָאַ֥יִל הָאֶחָ֖ד תִּקָּ֑ח וְסָ֨מְכ֜וּ אַהֲרֹ֧ן
וּבָנָ֛יו אֶת־יְדֵיהֶ֖ם עַל־רֹ֥אשׁ הָאָֽיִל׃
16 וְשָׁחַטְתָּ֖ אֶת־הָאָ֑יִל וְלָֽקַחְתָּ֙ אֶת־דָּמ֔וֹ
וְזָרַקְתָּ֥ עַל־הַמִּזְבֵּ֖חַ סָבִֽיב׃ 17 וְאֶ֨ת־הָאַ֔יִל
תְּנַתֵּ֖חַ לִנְתָחָ֑יו וְרָחַצְתָּ֤ קִרְבּוֹ֙ וּכְרָעָ֔יו וְנָתַתָּ֥
עַל־נְתָחָ֖יו וְעַל־רֹאשֽׁוֹ׃ 18 וְהִקְטַרְתָּ֤ אֶת־
כָּל־הָאַ֙יִל֙ הַמִּזְבֵּ֔חָה עֹלָ֥ה ה֖וּא לַיהֹוָ֑ה רֵ֣יחַ
נִיח֔וֹחַ אִשֶּׁ֥ה לַיהֹוָ֖ה הֽוּא׃
19 וְלָקַחְתָּ֔ אֵ֖ת הָאַ֣יִל הַשֵּׁנִ֑י וְסָמַ֨ךְ
אַהֲרֹ֧ן וּבָנָ֛יו אֶת־יְדֵיהֶ֖ם עַל־רֹ֥אשׁ הָאָֽיִל׃
20 וְשָׁחַטְתָּ֣ אֶת־הָאַ֗יִל וְלָקַחְתָּ֣ מִדָּמוֹ֒ וְנָתַתָּ֡ה
עַל־תְּנ֨וּךְ אֹ֜זֶן אַהֲרֹ֗ן וְעַל־תְּנוּךְ֩ אֹ֨זֶן בָּנָ֜יו
הַיְמָנִ֗ית וְעַל־בֹּ֤הֶן יָדָם֙ הַיְמָנִ֔ית וְעַל־בֹּ֥הֶן
רַגְלָ֖ם הַיְמָנִ֑ית וְזָרַקְתָּ֧ אֶת־הַדָּ֛ם עַל־הַמִּזְבֵּ֖חַ
סָבִֽיב׃ 21 וְלָקַחְתָּ֞ מִן־הַדָּ֨ם אֲשֶׁ֥ר עַל־

the hands of an official who is being installed into office; it later comes to mean more generally "to install" or "ordain."

*10. lay their hands upon the head of the bull.* The purpose for this action is unclear. Laying hands upon the bull may transfer their impurity to the animal, which is then destroyed; or it may indicate the transfer of ownership of the bull to God, or both.

*12. take some of the bull's blood.* The significance of blood as the life force is apparent in many biblical texts; here it may purify the altar.

*14. purgation offering.* See Leviticus 6:17–23.

*15–32.* The first of the two rams is a "burnt offering" (vv. 15–18; see at Leviticus 1:3; 6:2); the second ram is the "ordination" offering (29:19–26, 31–32). Likewise, as documents from other ancient Near Eastern cultures indicate, the major sanctuaries of Israel's neighbors typically featured similarly complex and lengthy procedures using the blood and parts of animals along with cereal offerings.

anointing oil and sprinkle upon Aaron and his vestments, and also upon his sons and his sons' vestments. Thus shall he and his vestments be holy, as well as his sons and his sons' vestments.

22You shall take from the ram the fat parts—the broad tail, the fat that covers the entrails, the protuberance on the liver, the two kidneys with the fat on them—and the right thigh; for this is a ram of ordination. 23Add one flat loaf of bread, one cake of oil bread, and one wafer, from the basket of unleavened bread that is before יהוה. 24Place all these on the palms of Aaron and his sons, and offer them as an elevation offering before יהוה. 25Take them from their hands and turn them into smoke upon the altar with the burnt offering, as a pleasing odor before יהוה; it is an offering by fire to יהוה.

26Then take the breast of Aaron's ram of ordination and offer it as an elevation offering before יהוה; it shall be your portion. 27You shall consecrate the breast that was offered as an elevation offering and the thigh that was offered as a gift offering from the ram of ordination—from that which was Aaron's and from that which was his sons'—28and those parts shall be a due for all time from the Israelites to Aaron and his descendants. For they are a gift; and so shall they be a gift from the Israelites, their gift to יהוה out of their sacrifices of well-being.

29The sacral vestments of Aaron shall pass on to his sons after him, for them to be anointed and ordained in. 30He among his sons who becomes priest in his stead, who enters the Tent of Meeting to officiate within the sanctuary, shall wear them seven days.

הַמִּזְבֵּ֜חַ וּמִשֶּׁ֣מֶן הַמִּשְׁחָ֗ה וְהִזֵּיתָ֙ עַל־אַהֲרֹן֙
וְעַל־בְּגָדָ֔יו וְעַל־בָּנָ֛יו וְעַל־בִּגְדֵ֥י בָנָ֖יו אִתּ֑וֹ
וְקָדַ֥שׁ הוּא֙ וּבְגָדָ֔יו וּבָנָ֛יו וּבִגְדֵ֥י בָנָ֖יו אִתּֽוֹ׃
22 וְלָקַחְתָּ֣ מִן־הָ֠אַיִל הַחֵ֨לֶב וְהָֽאַלְיָ֜ה וְאֶת־
הַחֵ֣לֶב ׀ הַֽמְכַסֶּ֣ה אֶת־הַקֶּ֗רֶב וְאֵ֨ת יֹתֶ֤רֶת
הַכָּבֵד֙ וְאֵ֣ת ׀ שְׁתֵּ֣י הַכְּלָיֹ֗ת וְאֶת־הַחֵ֙לֶב֙ אֲשֶׁ֣ר
עֲלֵיהֶ֔ן וְאֵ֖ת שׁ֣וֹק הַיָּמִ֑ין כִּ֛י אֵ֥יל מִלֻּאִ֖ים
הֽוּא׃ 23 וְכִכַּ֨ר לֶ֜חֶם אַחַ֗ת וַֽחַלַּ֨ת לֶ֥חֶם שֶׁ֛מֶן
אַחַ֖ת וְרָקִ֣יק אֶחָ֑ד מִסַּל֙ הַמַּצּ֔וֹת אֲשֶׁ֖ר לִפְנֵ֥י
יְהוָֽה׃ 24 וְשַׂמְתָּ֣ הַכֹּ֔ל עַ֚ל כַּפֵּ֣י אַהֲרֹ֔ן וְעַ֖ל
כַּפֵּ֣י בָנָ֑יו וְהֵנַפְתָּ֥ אֹתָ֛ם תְּנוּפָ֖ה לִפְנֵ֥י יְהוָֽה׃
25 וְלָקַחְתָּ֤ אֹתָם֙ מִיָּדָ֔ם וְהִקְטַרְתָּ֥ הַמִּזְבֵּ֖חָה
עַל־הָעֹלָ֑ה לְרֵ֤יחַ נִיחוֹחַ֙ לִפְנֵ֣י יְהוָ֔ה אִשֶּׁ֥ה
ה֖וּא לַֽיהוָֽה׃
26 וְלָקַחְתָּ֣ אֶת־הֶחָזֶ֗ה מֵאֵ֤יל הַמִּלֻּאִים֙ אֲשֶׁ֣ר
לְאַהֲרֹ֔ן וְהֵנַפְתָּ֥ אֹת֛וֹ תְּנוּפָ֖ה לִפְנֵ֣י יְהוָ֑ה
וְהָיָ֥ה לְךָ֖ לְמָנָֽה׃ 27 וְקִדַּשְׁתָּ֞ אֵ֣ת ׀ חֲזֵ֣ה
הַתְּנוּפָ֗ה וְאֵת֙ שׁ֣וֹק הַתְּרוּמָ֔ה אֲשֶׁ֥ר הוּנַ֖ף
וַאֲשֶׁ֣ר הוּרָ֑ם מֵאֵיל֙ הַמִּלֻּאִ֔ים מֵאֲשֶׁ֥ר
לְאַהֲרֹ֖ן וּמֵאֲשֶׁ֥ר לְבָנָֽיו׃ 28 וְהָיָה֩ לְאַהֲרֹ֨ן
וּלְבָנָ֜יו לְחָק־עוֹלָ֗ם מֵאֵת֙ בְּנֵ֣י יִשְׂרָאֵ֔ל
כִּ֥י תְרוּמָ֖ה ה֑וּא וּתְרוּמָ֞ה יִהְיֶ֨ה מֵאֵ֤ת
בְּנֵֽי־יִשְׂרָאֵל֙ מִזִּבְחֵ֣י שַׁלְמֵיהֶ֔ם תְּרוּמָתָ֖ם
לַֽיהוָֽה׃
29 וּבִגְדֵ֤י הַקֹּ֙דֶשׁ֙ אֲשֶׁ֣ר לְאַהֲרֹ֔ן יִהְי֥וּ לְבָנָ֖יו
אַחֲרָ֑יו לְמָשְׁחָ֣ה בָהֶ֔ם וּלְמַלֵּא־בָ֖ם אֶת־
יָדָֽם׃ 30 שִׁבְעַ֣ת יָמִ֗ים יִלְבָּשָׁ֛ם הַכֹּהֵ֥ן תַּחְתָּ֖יו
מִבָּנָ֑יו אֲשֶׁ֥ר יָבֹ֛א אֶל־אֹ֥הֶל מוֹעֵ֖ד לְשָׁרֵ֥ת
בַּקֹּֽדֶשׁ׃

*28. those parts . . . to Aaron and his descendants.* Because priests had no land or herds, and thus no source of the agricultural products that provided sustenance, part of the sacrificial offerings were to be set aside as food for priests and their families. "Descendants" typically would include female as well as male offspring who were living in the priest's household, though vv. 31–34 specify that consumption of the sacral ordination sacrifice is limited to the priests themselves.

31 You shall take the ram of ordination and boil its flesh in the sacred precinct; 32 and Aaron and his sons shall eat the flesh of the ram, and the bread that is in the basket, at the entrance of the Tent of Meeting. 33 These things shall be eaten only by those for whom expiation was made with them when they were ordained and consecrated; they may not be eaten by a lay person, for they are holy. 34 And if any of the flesh of ordination, or any of the bread, is left until morning, you shall put what is left to the fire; it shall not be eaten, for it is holy.

35 Thus you shall do to Aaron and his sons, just as I have commanded you. You shall ordain them through seven days, 36 and each day you shall prepare a bull as a purgation offering for expiation; you shall purge the altar by performing purification upon it, and you shall anoint it to consecrate it. 37 Seven days you shall perform purification for the altar to consecrate it, and the altar shall become most holy; whatever touches the altar shall become consecrated.

38 Now this is what you shall offer upon the altar: two yearling lambs each day, regularly. 39 You shall offer the one lamb in the morning, and you shall offer the other lamb at twilight. 40 There shall be a tenth of a measure of choice flour with a quarter of a *hin* of beaten oil mixed in, and a libation of a quarter *hin* of wine for one lamb; 41 and you shall offer the other lamb at twilight, repeating with it the meal offering of the morning with its libation—an offering by fire for a pleasing odor to יהוה, 42 a regular burnt offering throughout the generations, at the entrance of the Tent of Meeting before יהוה.

31 וְאֵת אֵיל הַמִּלֻּאִים תִּקָּח וּבִשַּׁלְתָּ אֶת־
בְּשָׂרוֹ בְּמָקֹם קָדֹשׁ׃ 32 וְאָכַל אַהֲרֹן וּבָנָיו
אֶת־בְּשַׂר הָאַיִל וְאֶת־הַלֶּחֶם אֲשֶׁר בַּסָּל
פֶּתַח אֹהֶל מוֹעֵד׃ 33 וְאָכְלוּ אֹתָם אֲשֶׁר
כֻּפַּר בָּהֶם לְמַלֵּא אֶת־יָדָם לְקַדֵּשׁ אֹתָם
וְזָר לֹא־יֹאכַל כִּי־קֹדֶשׁ הֵם׃ 34 וְאִם־יִוָּתֵר
מִבְּשַׂר הַמִּלֻּאִים וּמִן־הַלֶּחֶם עַד־הַבֹּקֶר
וְשָׂרַפְתָּ אֶת־הַנּוֹתָר בָּאֵשׁ לֹא יֵאָכֵל כִּי־
קֹדֶשׁ הוּא׃
35 וְעָשִׂיתָ לְאַהֲרֹן וּלְבָנָיו כָּכָה כְּכֹל אֲשֶׁר־
צִוִּיתִי אֹתָכָה שִׁבְעַת יָמִים תְּמַלֵּא יָדָם׃
36 וּפַר חַטָּאת תַּעֲשֶׂה לַיּוֹם עַל־הַכִּפֻּרִים
וְחִטֵּאתָ עַל־הַמִּזְבֵּחַ בְּכַפֶּרְךָ עָלָיו וּמָשַׁחְתָּ
אֹתוֹ לְקַדְּשׁוֹ׃ 37 שִׁבְעַת יָמִים תְּכַפֵּר עַל־
הַמִּזְבֵּחַ וְקִדַּשְׁתָּ אֹתוֹ וְהָיָה הַמִּזְבֵּחַ קֹדֶשׁ
קָדָשִׁים כָּל־הַנֹּגֵעַ בַּמִּזְבֵּחַ יִקְדָּשׁ׃ ס
38 וְזֶה אֲשֶׁר תַּעֲשֶׂה עַל־הַמִּזְבֵּחַ כְּבָשִׂים
בְּנֵי־שָׁנָה שְׁנַיִם לַיּוֹם תָּמִיד׃ 39 אֶת־הַכֶּבֶשׂ
הָאֶחָד תַּעֲשֶׂה בַבֹּקֶר וְאֵת הַכֶּבֶשׂ הַשֵּׁנִי
תַּעֲשֶׂה בֵּין הָעַרְבָּיִם׃ 40 וְעִשָּׂרֹן סֹלֶת בָּלוּל
בְּשֶׁמֶן כָּתִית רֶבַע הַהִין וְנֵסֶךְ רְבִיעִת הַהִין
יָיִן לַכֶּבֶשׂ הָאֶחָד׃ 41 וְאֵת הַכֶּבֶשׂ הַשֵּׁנִי
תַּעֲשֶׂה בֵּין הָעַרְבָּיִם כְּמִנְחַת הַבֹּקֶר
וּכְנִסְכָּהּ תַּעֲשֶׂה־לָּהּ לְרֵיחַ נִיחֹחַ אִשֶּׁה
לַיהוָה׃ 42 עֹלַת תָּמִיד לְדֹרֹתֵיכֶם פֶּתַח
אֹהֶל־מוֹעֵד לִפְנֵי יְהוָה

DIRECTIONS FOR REGULAR SACRIFICE (29:38–42a)

Once the priests have been consecrated, they will be able to perform the obligatory daily offerings, which include meat, cereal, oil, and wine. The basic foodstuffs of the Israelite diet also become foods offered to God, the exalted resident of this resplendent earthly residence.

*38. yearling lambs.* Animals of this age are fully grown; they are sacrificed at this point, before additional investment in maintaining and feeding them is made. Thus, the more expendable male animal is to be used.

For there I will meet with you, and there I will speak with you, [43]and there I will meet with the Israelites, and it shall be sanctified by My Presence. [44]I will sanctify the Tent of Meeting and the altar, and I will consecrate Aaron and his sons to serve Me as priests. [45]I will abide among the Israelites, and I will be their God. [46]And they shall know that I יהוה am their God, who brought them out from the land of Egypt that I might abide among them, I their God יהוה.

30 You shall make an altar for burning incense; make it of acacia wood. [2]It shall be a cubit

אֲשֶׁ֨ר אִוָּעֵ֤ד לָכֶם֙ שָׁ֔מָּה לְדַבֵּ֥ר אֵלֶ֖יךָ שָֽׁם: 43 וְנֹעַדְתִּ֥י שָׁ֖מָּה לִבְנֵ֣י יִשְׂרָאֵ֑ל וְנִקְדַּ֖שׁ בִּכְבֹדִֽי: 44 וְקִדַּשְׁתִּ֛י אֶת־אֹ֥הֶל מוֹעֵ֖ד וְאֶת־הַמִּזְבֵּ֑חַ וְאֶת־אַהֲרֹ֧ן וְאֶת־בָּנָ֛יו אֲקַדֵּ֖שׁ לְכַהֵ֥ן לִֽי: 45 וְשָׁכַנְתִּ֕י בְּת֖וֹךְ בְּנֵ֣י יִשְׂרָאֵ֑ל וְהָיִ֥יתִי לָהֶ֖ם לֵאלֹהִֽים: 46 וְיָדְע֗וּ כִּ֣י אֲנִ֤י יְהֹוָה֙ אֱלֹ֣הֵיהֶ֔ם אֲשֶׁ֨ר הוֹצֵ֧אתִי אֹתָ֛ם מֵאֶ֥רֶץ מִצְרַ֖יִם לְשָׁכְנִ֣י בְתוֹכָ֑ם אֲנִ֖י יְהֹוָ֥ה אֱלֹהֵיהֶֽם: פ

ל וְעָשִׂ֥יתָ מִזְבֵּ֖חַ מִקְטַ֣ר קְטֹ֑רֶת עֲצֵ֥י שִׁטִּ֖ים תַּעֲשֶׂ֥ה אֹתֽוֹ: 2 אַמָּ֨ה אָרְכּ֜וֹ וְאַמָּ֤ה רָחְבּוֹ֙

---

## SUMMATION (29:42b–46)

Once the tent and its furnishings have been made and the priests consecrated, God will consecrate the Tent of Meeting and the whole establishment will become functional.

**42.** *there I will meet with you, and . . . speak with you.* God's communication with humans will take place at the shrine. The "you" in this verse is singular, referring to Moses. The location of this meeting place seems to be the courtyard altar, at the entrance to the Tent of Meeting, or in front of the curtain that screens off the Ark (see 30:6, 36).

**43.** *I will meet with the Israelites.* The verb "meet" from the previous verse is repeated, making it clear that God will be available to everyone there. The mechanism for the meeting is not clear; it is possible that Moses or Aaron is to be the intermediary.

**44.** *I will sanctify.* Here it is God who sanctifies; earlier, Moses is the one to do so (see 29:21, 35–36; 30:29–30). Is Moses the alter ego for God? Or are these variant traditions?

**45.** *I will be their God.* This is covenant language, the elliptical half of the statement that the people will be God's, and God will be their deity (see 20:2).

**46.** Again, covenant language appears in this succinct summary of the entire book of Exodus:

God has brought the people out of Egypt, as recounted in Exodus 1–24; then, the people construct a dwelling for God, who will then "dwell" (25:8; or, as the present translation has it here, "abide") among them, as set forth in Exodus 25–40.

## Instructions about the Incense Altar (30:1–10)

Why is the small gilded incense altar discussed here, rather than in Exodus 25 along with the lampstand and offering table that are also supposed to occupy the Holy place? Scholars have offered many answers, yet their explanations of this seemingly anomalous placement remain somewhat speculative. (For the descriptive text later in Exodus that parallels this prescriptive section, see 37:25–28.)

**1.** *altar for burning incense.* Incense altars were standard items in shrines in the ancient Near East, just as some mechanism for freshening the air was part of every household. This completes the sensory repertoire of items to be used in the interior space of the Tabernacle: sight, taste, sound, and now smell.

**2.** *a cubit . . . a cubit . . . two cubits.* The altar is to be about 1½ feet (½ meter) square and 3 feet (1 meter) high.

long and a cubit wide—it shall be square—and two cubits high, its horns of one piece with it. ³Overlay it with pure gold: its top, its sides round about, and its horns; and make a gold molding for it round about. ⁴And make two gold rings for it under its molding; make them on its two side walls, on opposite sides. They shall serve as holders for poles with which to carry it. ⁵Make the poles of acacia wood, and overlay them with gold.

⁶Place it in front of the curtain that is over the Ark of the Pact—in front of the cover that is over the Pact—where I will meet with you. ⁷On it Aaron shall burn aromatic incense: he shall burn it every morning when he tends the lamps, ⁸and Aaron shall burn it at twilight when he lights the lamps— a regular incense offering before יהוה throughout the ages. ⁹You shall not offer alien incense on it, or a burnt offering or a meal offering; neither shall you pour a libation on it. ¹⁰Once a year Aaron shall perform purification upon its horns with blood of the purgation offering of purification; purification shall be performed upon it once a year throughout the ages. It is most holy to יהוה.

רָב֧וּעַ יִהְיֶ֛ה וְאַמָּתַ֥יִם קֹמָת֖וֹ מִמֶּ֥נּוּ קַרְנֹתָֽיו׃ 3 וְצִפִּיתָ֨ אֹת֜וֹ זָהָ֣ב טָה֗וֹר אֶת־גַּגּ֤וֹ וְאֶת־ קִירֹתָ֙יו֙ סָבִ֔יב וְאֶת־קַרְנֹתָ֑יו וְעָשִׂ֥יתָ לּ֛וֹ זֵ֥ר זָהָ֖ב סָבִֽיב׃ 4 וּשְׁתֵּי֩ טַבְּעֹ֨ת זָהָ֜ב תַּֽעֲשֶׂה־לּ֣וֹ ׀ מִתַּ֣חַת לְזֵר֗וֹ עַ֚ל שְׁתֵּ֣י צַלְעֹתָ֔יו תַּעֲשֶׂ֖ה עַל־ שְׁנֵ֣י צִדָּ֑יו וְהָיָה֙ לְבָתִּ֣ים לְבַדִּ֔ים לָשֵׂ֥את אֹת֖וֹ בָּהֵֽמָּה׃ 5 וְעָשִׂ֥יתָ אֶת־הַבַּדִּ֖ים עֲצֵ֣י שִׁטִּ֑ים וְצִפִּיתָ֥ אֹתָ֖ם זָהָֽב׃

6 וְנָתַתָּ֣ה אֹת֗וֹ לִפְנֵ֤י הַפָּרֹ֙כֶת֙ אֲשֶׁ֣ר עַל־אֲרֹ֣ן הָעֵדֻ֔ת לִפְנֵ֣י הַכַּפֹּ֗רֶת אֲשֶׁר֙ עַל־הָ֣עֵדֻ֔ת אֲשֶׁ֛ר אִוָּעֵ֥ד לְךָ֖ שָֽׁמָּה׃ 7 וְהִקְטִ֥יר עָלָ֛יו אַהֲרֹ֖ן קְטֹ֣רֶת סַמִּ֑ים בַּבֹּ֣קֶר בַּבֹּ֗קֶר בְּהֵיטִיב֛וֹ אֶת־ הַנֵּרֹ֖ת יַקְטִירֶֽנָּה׃ 8 וּֽבְהַעֲלֹ֨ת אַהֲרֹ֧ן אֶת־ הַנֵּרֹ֛ת בֵּ֥ין הָעַרְבַּ֖יִם יַקְטִירֶ֑נָּה קְטֹ֧רֶת תָּמִ֛יד לִפְנֵ֥י יְהֹוָ֖ה לְדֹרֹתֵיכֶֽם׃ 9 לֹא־תַעֲל֨וּ עָלָ֜יו קְטֹ֤רֶת זָרָה֙ וְעֹלָ֣ה וּמִנְחָ֔ה וְנֵ֕סֶךְ לֹ֥א תִסְּכ֖וּ עָלָֽיו׃ 10 וְכִפֶּ֤ר אַהֲרֹן֙ עַל־קַרְנֹתָ֔יו אַחַ֖ת בַּשָּׁנָ֑ה מִדַּ֞ם חַטַּ֣את הַכִּפֻּרִ֗ים אַחַ֤ת בַּשָּׁנָה֙ יְכַפֵּ֤ר עָלָיו֙ לְדֹרֹ֣תֵיכֶ֔ם קֹֽדֶשׁ־קָֽדָשִׁ֥ים ה֖וּא לַֽיהֹוָֽה׃ פ

horns. Like the courtyard altar and the many small incense altars found in the Land of Israel by archeologists, the gilded incense altar's horns probably would be at the upper corners, projecting upward (see at 27:2).

6. The incense altar's central placement, directly in front of the textile panel that screens the Ark (and the unseen presence of God above it), will make it the most important of the three items of furniture in the room: incense altar, lampstand, and offering table. (On the latter two items, see at 25:23–40.)

7. aromatic incense. The wafting upward of the smoke of burning incense may represent a primitive metaphor in which God "smells" the incense in the earthly shrine and thereby notices the officiants and comes to meet them. Perhaps it also represents an attempt to communicate with the unseen Deity via something as ethereal as smoke. At the same time, the smoke conceals God's presence from the officiant, for seeing God can be lethal (see Leviticus 16:12–13). (For another perspective, see at 30:34–38.)

when he tends the lamps. Of the lampstand (menorah); see at 27:20–21.

10. blood of the purgation offering. This substance is to be brought from the courtyard altar, a less holy zone, and applied to the horns of the incense altar. Perhaps this is one reason that the instructions for the incense altar are separated from those prescribing the other items of utmost sanctity.
—Carol Meyers

# *Another View*

CERTAIN BIBLICAL PASSAGES show that women served in some capacity at the sanctuary. The clearest case is that of the women attendants at the Tent of Meeting (38:8; I Samuel 2:22). Yet, in contrast to some other ancient cultures, there is no evidence of priestesses in ancient Israel. Scholars have proposed several theories to explain this absence, but none solves the mystery.

One theory is that women could not be priests because they menstruated, making them periodically ritually unclean. However, menstruation is not considered any more defiling than other causes of ritual impurity (see Leviticus 15). Priests could become ritually impure on occasion, yet once the period of impurity passed, they could go back to their priestly duties after performing the necessary ablutions. If menstrual impurity were the issue, why could women not perform communal religious functions during the rather lengthy times in their lives when they were not menstruating?

A second theory is that the absence of women reflects a division of labor along gender lines and the needs of a pre-modern, agricultural community. Because women were needed to bear and raise children and to perform essential household tasks, they could not be spared for temple service. But then why did women function as priestesses in surrounding cultures?

A third theory suggests that the women were priestesses elsewhere because they served in the sanctuaries of goddesses; but since Israel's official religion did not sanction the worship of goddesses, there was no place in it for priestesses. However, a weakness of this theory is that priestesses in other ancient cultures served in sanctuaries of gods and goddesses alike.

A fourth theory suggests that excluding women from the priesthood meant to distinguish Israel from her neighbors, who often employed women in rituals of a sexual nature. Note, however, that in all the surrounding cultures, female functionaries filled a diverse number of roles, not all of which were sexual in nature. Some women functioned as priestesses; others filled maintenance and support roles or served as singers, dancers, and musicians.

A fifth theory is based on the claim that priestesses in the surrounding cultures did not conduct animal sacrifice—and that Israel followed its neighbors in this respect: women were not included because animal sacrifices constituted a central part of Israelite ritual. However, as Mayer Gruber notes, pictorial illustrations and written references to women slaughtering sacrifices are extant from all over the ancient Near East ("Women in the Cult According to the Priestly Code," 1987, n. 37).

*Scholars have proposed several theories, but none solves the mystery.*

In evaluating these theories, one should take into account the fact that many of the surrounding cultures where we find priestesses were more economically developed and socially complex than was Israel. The smaller sanctuary that likely existed in ancient Israel—and the simpler procedures there—would have limited the number of functionaries in general. Furthermore, while the Bible legitimizes only male priests (from Aaron's family), Israelite religion was surely more complex than what the text describes. Women probably had more roles in local sanctuaries than the Bible records.

—*Hilary Lipka*

# Post-biblical Interpretations

***You shall further instruct the Israelites to bring you clear oil...for kindling lamps regularly*** (27:20). Reflecting on this commandment about kindling lights, medieval commentators offered two possible interpretations of the phrase *ner tamid* (literally "light regularly" but understood to mean "eternal lamp"). Rashi suggested it meant "routinely kindled," while Nachmanides understood it as "continually burning." In general, the latter interpretation—the image of an eternal, rather than a regularly kindled, light—predominated. In the rabbinic imagination, the eternal lamp of the synagogue recalled the *menorah* of Temple times, since rabbinic tradition associated the *ner tamid* with the westernmost or central lamp of the *menorah* in the Temple (*Sifra Emor* 13.7). In a poem composed for the occasion of this Torah reading, the Byzantine Jewish liturgical poet Yannai drew a parallel between the synagogue's eternal lamp and that of the "woman of valor," whose "lamp never goes out at night" (Proverbs 31:18).

The Rabbis understood the eternal lamp as an important symbol with multiple meanings. First, they associated the light with Torah. For example, BT *B'rachot* 57a teaches: "If one sees olive oil in a dream, one may hope for the light of the Torah, as it is written, *You shall further instruct*..." This association derives from Proverbs 6:23, which states: *The commandment is a lamp / And the Torah is a light.* The song "*Torah Orah* (The Torah is a Light)," popular in many contemporary synagogues during the Torah services, reflects this symbolism.

The Rabbis frequently represented the eternal lamp as symbolic of the divine presence, or *Shechinah.* In BT *M'nachot* 87b, the Rabbis wonder why God would need a light; they then deduce that the eternal lamp commemorated the divine light that had led Israel through the wilderness. The reason the eternal lamp was the "western lamp" was because "the divine Presence will never depart from the Western Wall" (Midrash *Sh'mot Rabbah* 2.2). Over time, the ritual of the Temple lamp was transferred to the home. Thus, Mishnah *Shabbat* 2:1 offers instructions for kindling Shabbat lights, which 2:6 then characterizes as a specifically female commandment. Yannai read those Mishnaic passages back into Exodus, linking the priestly rules for maintaining the Tabernacle's lights with women's command of *hadlakat nerot,* kindling lamps.

The eternal lamp was also understood in post-biblical Judaism as foreshadowing the light of the messianic age. The lamps described in this parashah were popular in Byzantine and medieval synagogue art. These images, themselves multivalent, may have both memorialized the Temple destroyed in 70 C.E. and also anticipated a time when the Temple lamps would be rekindled. As the poet Yannai wrote of those days to come, "And our light will no longer be quenched / and our flames no longer extinguished / and You shall be our everlasting light."

*Together, soul and spirit represent a perfect union of masculine and feminine.*

The medieval mystical compilation *Zohar* (2:99b) offers a spiritual understanding of the *ner tamid* when it states that "*ner*" is an acronym for *n'shamah-ruach* ("soul-spirit"). Together, soul and spirit represent a perfect union of masculine and feminine. Together, they can bring forth light; but separated, they are powerless and in the dark.

***Make sacral vestments for your brother Aaron*** (28:2). The Rabbis taught that each item of the head priest's ritual garb possessed symbolic value. The fringed tunic atoned for bloodshed; the robe, for slander; the breeches, for sexual impropriety; the headdress, for arrogance; the frontlet, for brazenness;

the sash, for impure thoughts; the breastplate, for neglect of the civil laws; and the ephod, for idolatry (BT *Z'vachim* 88b; *Vayikra Rabbah* 10.6; *Shir HaShirim Rabbah* 4.8). According to BT *Sotah* 36b, it was Joseph's desire to have his name engraved upon the ephod (along with the names of his brothers) that restrained him from succumbing to temptation with Potiphar's wife (Genesis 39).

According to the *Zohar*, "All the priestly garments were emblematic of supernal mystery" (2:231a). This mystical reading focuses on the layered nature of the vestments, which indicate a balancing of dualities: left and right, soul and body, and male and female. The primordial human whom God created (Genesis 1)—this passage teaches—was a singular creature, both male and female, but the two halves were joined at the back, facing away from each other. God separated this single entity into two, and "thus they [the first woman and first man] were brought face to face, [and] love was multiplied in the world." Unfortunately, this physical division also led to emotional estrangement, jealousy, and strife. The unity of the ephod and breastplate (which were worn together) recalled the original unity of the first woman and the first man and, by extension, of all humankind.

—*Laura Lieber*

## *Contemporary Reflection*

MOST YEARS, this Torah portion is read during the week preceding Purim. The connection between the parashah and Purim is not immediately apparent. *T'tzaveh* is filled with exacting details about the assembly of the priestly garments and the ritual role Aaron and his sons are to perform as anointed priests. The book of Esther is a melodramatic tale of threat, intrigue, and ultimate redemption through plot twists and the reluctant heroism of a beautiful queen.

While the plots and purposes of these texts are vastly different, each in its own way, asks us to confront an absence. *T'tzaveh* is the only parashah from the beginning of the book of Exodus until the end of Deuteronomy where the name of Moses does not appear. And Esther is one of only two books of the Bible where the name of God does not appear. These absences are cause for abundant commentary in each individual case, but the relationship between the two texts seems to receive only passing mention.

What insight can this parallel *presence of absence* convey?

Many commentators speculate as to why Moses' name is absent from *parashat T'tzaveh*. One theory is that the omission is meant to acknowledge the anniversary of his death, which is said to be the seventh of Adar, just one week before Purim. Another theory is that Moses' name is left out as divine admonishment for his jealousy over Aaron's appointment as chief priest. Still others maintain that in his humility and self-effacement, Moses graciously cedes the role to his brother and absents himself from the narrative, so to speak, to make this clear.

Regardless of the reaction that Moses may or may not have experienced when his brother became the head priest instead of him, the narrative suggests that although his name is not mentioned, Moses remains God's agent—the enabler for all that is to happen. This is made evident through an unusual grammatical formulation found in the parashah's opening verses. Elsewhere in Torah, God's commands to Moses are stated in the simple imperative: "instruct" (*tzav*) or "speak" (*dabber*). In *T'tzaveh*, however, three instances of an additional pronoun appear, giving extra emphasis to the actor responsible for the actions. Translating the text more literally, the first verse of the parashah (27:20) reads: "And *you, yourself* shall command the children of Israel." Shortly thereafter, we read: "And *you*, bring near *to yourself* your brother Aaron, with his sons, from among the Israelites, to serve Me as priests" (28:1). The same grammatical form appears two lines later: "*You, yourself* speak to all who are skillful, whom I have endowed with the gift of skill, to make Aaron's vestments" (28:3). The 16th-century commentator Moshe Alshekh suggests that this repeated double emphasis is God's way of saying to Moses, "It's all really you. You have a greater share in it than anyone. All fulfill themselves through you" (cited in Nehama Leibowitz, *Studies in Shemot*, 1980, p. 526). Perhaps such language means to tell us that Moses is not absent at all. Rather, his presence is momentarily diminished so that other leaders can step forward to serve the broader needs of the community.

Just as we can see Moses as a behind the scenes mover in the parashah, so too, can we see God as filling a similar role in the Purim narrative. While many interpret the Purim story as an instance when the Jews achieved victory through their own actions—without waiting for divine intercession—the classic rabbinic interpretation is that God was hidden from view, but not absent. In BT *Chullin* 139b, the Rabbis made this point through a biblical proof text, asking: "Where is Esther indicated in the Torah? In the verse "I will surely hide (*astir*) My face" (Deuteronomy 31:18). The Hebrew word *astir* ("I will hide") serves as a wordplay on Esther's name.

We can extend the wordplay even further by considering that the Hebrew word *m'gillah* shares the same root as the verb "to reveal" (*g-l-h*). Thus, *M'gillat Ester* ("Scroll or Book of Esther") can be read playfully as "revealing the hidden." God's presence is revealed through Mordecai's conviction and Esther's courage. God's presence is revealed in the triumph of good over evil, in the flawed but ultimately responsible actions of human beings.

In a typical Purim twist, the biblical text also reinforces the *presence of God's absence* by pointing out the consequences of the *absence of God's presence.* The story opens with a drunken debauchery hosted by King Ahasuerus, where "he displayed the glory of his kingdom and the richness of his magnificent splendor for many days, for 180 days" (Esther 1:4). The words used to describe the "glory" and "splendor" of his kingdom are the same words, *kavod u'tiferet*, that are used in *T'tzaveh* to describe the priestly garments (28:2, 40; there translated as "dignity and adornment"). In *T'tzaveh*, the lavish garments are designed

*T'tzaveh and the book of Esther show us how to feel the glory of God's presence.*

to serve and honor God. In Esther, the King's wealth is evidence of his corruption. The midrash draws an even more powerful connection by claiming that the riches of Ahasuerus' kingdom were made up of the spoils of the Temple, including the priestly garments themselves (*Ester Rabbah* 2.1).

The Purim message that sometimes gets lost in all of the revelry is that a sense of God's presence in the world, even if hidden and obscure, gives us the strength and moral purpose to cope with uncertainties and imperfections. *Parashat T'tzaveh* paints a picture of the detail and exacting effort it took for the Israelites to feel God's presence in their midst. Today, we have no priests and no Temple. The only vestige we have of this experience is the *ner tamid*, the eternal light, the first thing that God instructs Moses to establish in the opening verses of the parashah. This light has come to symbolize the light of Torah. For us, then, the glory and splendor of God's presence must be felt through the study of Torah and the constant striving to live in its light.

—*Lisa D. Grant*

# *Voices*

## *from* This Tkhine Is Said before Kedushe

Beyle Hurvits (transl. Devra Kay)

*Exodus 27:20–21*

Near You, God, there is no night,
And candles are not needed beside You,
For You light up the whole world with Your
light.
And the morning speaks of Your mercy,
And the night speaks of Your truth,
And all creatures acknowledge Your wonder.
God, You help us every day.

## Baruch Hu

Amy Blank

*Exodus 27:20–21*

We look into the chambers of the Unknown
along a scimitar of light
and say, "Be blessed . . ."
It is our utmost flight.

## River of Light

Zelda (transl. unknown)

*Exodus 27:20–21*

To light candles in all the worlds—
that is Shabbat.
To light Shabbat candles
is a soul-leap pregnant with potential
into a splendid sea, in it the mystery
of the fire of sunset.
Lighting the candles transforms
my room into a river of light,
my heart sets in an emerald waterfall.

## Offering

Grace Schulman

*Exodus 27:20–21*

You said: "Driven from homes in the pogroms,
women took only their brass candlebra
for Sabbath lights." You never kindled them,
but kept a pair because their reedy limbs

promised to dance in flame. Dying, you yearned
for light to read by, to see roses burn
in a white bowl, to see what life was left.
I give you now June bugs, a sunlit leaf,

snowfalls in slanted lines, a great white egret's
scarflike wing flaps, and I laugh with your
laughter
at amber lamps that shone by seldom lit
the page, harsh neon signs that winked at night.
I give you metaphor in place of prayer:
May you hear "Let there be light!" where
there's light.

## *Menorah*

Jill Hammer

*Exodus 27:20–21*

as the high priest rises
to light the lamps
the tree of life comes to life
with seven branches like the seven days

again we are born in the flash of creation
we play in the dust of the garden
the snakes are our teachers
the sun and moon are our bellhops
carrying suitcases of light
to where we slumber on the grass

again we discover one another naked as twigs
the flowers opening are our twin siblings
the cherubim, still as noon, soak up gold in
their wings
we plant seeds of light and they grow into
people
the tree grows seven souls for each of us
we lack nothing

again one crumb of earth reigns over each of us
jealousy has not yet been invented
the night owl hoots like a ram's horn over the
land
no one has eaten anyone else yet
a bat has not swallowed a gnat
a human has not tasted fruit

we stand riveted before the lamp
as flame gutters in the wind
the high priest steps down
eden vanishes
the ritual of sacrifice begins

## *from* Letter to Mala Laaser, 1938

Regina Jonas (transl. Toby Axelrod)

*Exodus 29:9*

I hope a time will come for all of us in which there will be no more questions on the subject of "woman": for as long as there are questions, something is wrong. But if I must say what drove me as a woman to become a rabbi, two elements come to mind: My belief in the godly calling and my love for people. God has placed abilities and callings in our hearts, without regard to gender. Thus each of us has the duty, whether man or woman, to realize those gifts God has given. If you look at things this way, one takes woman and man for what they are: human beings.

NOTE

Regina Jonas was the first woman to be ordained as a rabbi. She was killed in Theresienstadt in 1944 at age 42.

## *from* Women Who Would Be Rabbis

Pamela S. Nadell

*Exodus 29:9*

On 3 June 1972, the high school junior of a decade before who had written, "Although I am a girl, I would like very much to study for a rabbinical degree," was ordained rabbi, teacher, and preacher in American Israel. When HUC President Alfred Gottschalk . . . placed his hands upon her head to confer ordination, [Sally] Priesand's classmates rose to honor the first woman rabbi. . . . The year 1972 thus came to stand then and forevermore as a benchmark for those crusading for gender equality in Judaism.

NOTE

Although Jonas was the first woman to be ordained, Priesand was the first to be ordained by a seminary.

# כי תשא ✦ Ki Tisa

EXODUS 30:11–34:35

## *Tablets, Calf, and Covenant: Mediating the Relationship with God*

PARASHAT KI TISA ("when you take") is the fulcrum of a larger portion of Exodus that is concerned with figuring out how God and Israel will co-exist. The parashah begins with instructions regarding census taking and the Tabernacle furnishings, moves on to the narrative of the Golden Calf, and concludes with a series of covenantal stipulations. While these units do not present a seamless narrative, they do contain a series of thematically related scenes that all negotiate the central issue catalyzed by the Sinai event: How can God and Israel maintain a relationship that takes into account the enormous disparities between the two parties—God, who is utterly holy, and Israel, a "stiffnecked" and backsliding nation that can achieve holiness but not maintain it?

By the end of the parashah, the text has affirmed three strategies for sustaining the relationship between God and Israel:

1. *Tabernacle*: The story of the Golden Calf is situated between the instructions for the Tabernacle (25:1–30:10) and the description of its construction (35:1–40:38). This arrangement affirms that the Tabernacle, unlike the calf, is an appropriate response to the people's needs for a physical location where they can gain access to God.
2. *Covenant*: The parashah concludes with a reiteration of the covenant, thus providing Israel with laws to help keep its conduct acceptable to God.
3. *Moses*: While the other two strategies are more permanent, Moses emerges as the most crucial mediating strategy between God and Israel, the go-between who repeatedly pleads to God on behalf of Israel. Although Moses is resoundingly human, the voices of this parashah conspire to identify Moses more and more closely with God until even his physical being is supernaturally transformed (34:29–35).

*How can God and Israel maintain a relationship given their disparities?*

The parashah refers to women directly in only a few places. In the account of the construction of the calf, Aaron directs the men to remove the jewelry from their wives, sons, and daughters (32:2). The legal section at the end of the parashah prohibits marriages between Israelite men and indigenous Canaanite women (34:16) and includes a polemic against *asherim* (34:13)—ritual objects probably related to the worship of the goddess Asherah.

Nevertheless, the parashah engages two issues that are central to feminist theology and theory. In wrestling with the question of how close God can be to humanity, the text raises the issue of divine immanence and transcendence, a central concern of contemporary feminist theology (see *Vayak'heil,* Another View, p. 538). The parashah also highlights the importance of narrative perspective and point of view. The crucial events of the Exodus and construction of the calf are described differently by different characters. These tellings not only highlight the disparate experiences of the speakers but also serve to articulate multiple perspectives on the text's central concerns.

*—Elsie R. Stern*

## *Outline*

I. INSTRUCTIONS FOR THE TABERNACLE (30:11–31:18)

- A. Census (30:11–16)
- B. Laver (30:17–21)
- C. Anointing oil (30:22–33)
- D. Incense (30:34–38)
- E. Artisans (31:1–11)
- F. Shabbat observance (31:12–17)
- G. Conclusion (31:18)

II. CRISIS: THE GOLDEN CALF EPISODE (32:1–35)

- A. Construction of the calf (vv. 1–6)
- B. God's anger and Moses' intercession (vv. 7–14)
- C. Moses' anger at the people and Aaron (vv. 15–29)
- D. Moses' intercession and God's response (vv. 30–35)

III. AFTERMATH (33:1–23)

- A. God's refusal to accompany the Israelites (vv. 1–6)
- B. God's concessions and forms of revelation (vv. 7–23)
  1. Tent of Meeting (vv. 7–11)
  2. Moses' request for revelation and God's response (vv. 12–23)

IV. RESTORATION OF THE COVENANT (34:1–35)

- A. Revelation of God's name (vv. 1–9)
- B. Terms of the Covenant (vv. 10–28)
- C. A visible change in Moses (vv. 29–35)

יהוה spoke to Moses, saying: [12]When you
take a census of the Israelite men according to their army enrollment, each shall pay
יהוה a ransom for himself on being enrolled, that no
plague may come upon them through their being
enrolled. [13]This is what everyone who is entered in
the records shall pay: a half-shekel by the sanctuary
weight—twenty *gerah*s to the shekel—a half-shekel
as an offering to יהוה. [14]Everyone who is entered in
the records, from the age of twenty years up, shall
give יהוה's offering: [15]the rich shall not pay more
and the poor shall not pay less than half a shekel
when giving יהוה's offering as expiation for your
persons. [16]You shall take the expiation money from
the Israelites and assign it to the service of the Tent
of Meeting; it shall serve the Israelites as a reminder
before יהוה, as expiation for your persons.

ל 11 וַיְדַבֵּר יְהוָה אֶל־מֹשֶׁה לֵּאמֹר׃ 12 כִּי
תִשָּׂא אֶת־רֹאשׁ בְּנֵי־יִשְׂרָאֵל לִפְקֻדֵיהֶם
וְנָתְנוּ אִישׁ כֹּפֶר נַפְשׁוֹ לַיהוָה בִּפְקֹד אֹתָם
וְלֹא־יִהְיֶה בָהֶם נֶגֶף בִּפְקֹד אֹתָם׃ 13 זֶה ׀
יִתְּנוּ כָּל־הָעֹבֵר עַל־הַפְּקֻדִים מַחֲצִית
הַשֶּׁקֶל בְּשֶׁקֶל הַקֹּדֶשׁ עֶשְׂרִים גֵּרָה הַשֶּׁקֶל
מַחֲצִית הַשֶּׁקֶל תְּרוּמָה לַיהוָה׃ 14 כֹּל
הָעֹבֵר עַל־הַפְּקֻדִים מִבֶּן עֶשְׂרִים שָׁנָה
וָמָעְלָה יִתֵּן תְּרוּמַת יְהוָה׃ 15 הֶעָשִׁיר לֹא־
יַרְבֶּה וְהַדַּל לֹא יַמְעִיט מִמַּחֲצִית הַשָּׁקֶל
לָתֵת אֶת־תְּרוּמַת יְהוָה לְכַפֵּר עַל־
נַפְשֹׁתֵיכֶם׃ 16 וְלָקַחְתָּ אֶת־כֶּסֶף הַכִּפֻּרִים
מֵאֵת בְּנֵי יִשְׂרָאֵל וְנָתַתָּ אֹתוֹ עַל־עֲבֹדַת
אֹהֶל מוֹעֵד וְהָיָה לִבְנֵי יִשְׂרָאֵל לְזִכָּרוֹן לִפְנֵי
יְהוָה לְכַפֵּר עַל־נַפְשֹׁתֵיכֶם׃ פ

## *Instructions for the Tabernacle*
(30:11–31:18)

The parashah starts with several supplemental instructions concerning the construction of the Tabernacle, an appendix to the detailed prescriptive texts in the prior two Torah portions.

### CENSUS (30:11–16)

Census taking, which was usually a prelude to military conscription or taxation, was considered an inherently dangerous act in the biblical world (see II Samuel 24). Its negative consequences must be pre-empted by paying a half-shekel ransom. Only the men of fighting age (twenty and older) are counted in the census and required to pay the tax, which in this case is to be used for the operation of the Tabernacle; women are not part of Israel's military and not counted in the census. The high concentration of expiation language in this passage (note the four-fold repetition of the root *k-p-r* [atone, propitiate], translated here as "ransom" or "expiation") underscores the text's anxiety about the supernatural and societal dangers of the census.

◗ The justification for prohibiting foreign wives . . . should be understood in broader terms.

ANOTHER VIEW ➤ *514*

◗ *Ki Tisa* is about a spectacular wedding feast between God and the people Israel.

CONTEMPORARY REFLECTION ➤ *516*

◗ This means that Bezalel was also Miriam's great-grandson.

POST-BIBLICAL INTERPRETATIONS ➤ *514*

◗ I haven't seen you in a long time God / where've you been keeping yourself?

VOICES ➤ *518*

17 יהוה spoke to Moses, saying: 18 Make a laver of copper and a stand of copper for it, for washing; and place it between the Tent of Meeting and the altar. Put water in it, 19 and let Aaron and his sons wash their hands and feet [in water drawn] from it. 20 When they enter the Tent of Meeting they shall wash with water, that they may not die; or when they approach the altar to serve, to turn into smoke an offering by fire to יהוה, 21 they shall wash their hands and feet, that they may not die. It shall be a law for all time for them—for him and his offspring—throughout the ages.

22 יהוה spoke to Moses, saying: 23 Next take choice spices: five hundred weight of solidified myrrh, half as much—two hundred and fifty—of fragrant cinnamon, two hundred and fifty of aromatic cane, 24 five hundred—by the sanctuary weight—of cassia, and a *hin* of olive oil. 25 Make of this a sacred anointing oil, a compound of ingredients expertly blended, to serve as sacred anointing oil. 26 With it anoint the Tent of Meeting, the Ark of the Pact, 27 the table and all its utensils, the lampstand and all its fittings, the altar of incense, 28 the altar of burnt offering and all its utensils, and the laver and its stand. 29 Thus you shall consecrate them so that they may be most holy; whatever touches them shall be consecrated. 30 You shall also anoint Aaron and his sons, consecrating them to serve Me as priests.

17 וַיְדַבֵּר יְהֹוָה אֶל־מֹשֶׁה לֵּאמֹר׃ 18 וְעָשִׂיתָ
כִּיּוֹר נְחֹשֶׁת וְכַנּוֹ נְחֹשֶׁת לְרָחְצָה וְנָתַתָּ
אֹתוֹ בֵּין־אֹהֶל מוֹעֵד וּבֵין הַמִּזְבֵּחַ וְנָתַתָּ
שָׁמָּה מָיִם׃ 19 וְרָחֲצוּ אַהֲרֹן וּבָנָיו מִמֶּנּוּ
אֶת־יְדֵיהֶם וְאֶת־רַגְלֵיהֶם׃ 20 בְּבֹאָם אֶל־
אֹהֶל מוֹעֵד יִרְחֲצוּ־מַיִם וְלֹא יָמֻתוּ אוֹ
בְגִשְׁתָּם אֶל־הַמִּזְבֵּחַ לְשָׁרֵת לְהַקְטִיר אִשֶּׁה
לַיהֹוָה׃ 21 וְרָחֲצוּ יְדֵיהֶם וְרַגְלֵיהֶם וְלֹא
יָמֻתוּ וְהָיְתָה לָהֶם חָק־עוֹלָם לוֹ וּלְזַרְעוֹ
לְדֹרֹתָם׃ פ

22 וַיְדַבֵּר יְהֹוָה אֶל־מֹשֶׁה לֵּאמֹר׃ 23 וְאַתָּה
קַח־לְךָ בְּשָׂמִים רֹאשׁ מָר־דְּרוֹר חֲמֵשׁ
מֵאוֹת וְקִנְּמָן־בֶּשֶׂם מַחֲצִיתוֹ חֲמִשִּׁים
וּמָאתָיִם וּקְנֵה־בֹשֶׂם חֲמִשִּׁים וּמָאתָיִם׃
24 וְקִדָּה חֲמֵשׁ מֵאוֹת בְּשֶׁקֶל הַקֹּדֶשׁ וְשֶׁמֶן
זַיִת הִין׃ 25 וְעָשִׂיתָ אֹתוֹ שֶׁמֶן מִשְׁחַת־קֹדֶשׁ
רֹקַח מִרְקַחַת מַעֲשֵׂה רֹקֵחַ שֶׁמֶן מִשְׁחַת־
קֹדֶשׁ יִהְיֶה׃ 26 וּמָשַׁחְתָּ בוֹ אֶת־אֹהֶל מוֹעֵד
וְאֵת אֲרוֹן הָעֵדֻת׃ 27 וְאֶת־הַשֻּׁלְחָן וְאֶת־
כָּל־כֵּלָיו וְאֶת־הַמְּנֹרָה וְאֶת־כֵּלֶיהָ וְאֵת
מִזְבַּח הַקְּטֹרֶת׃ 28 וְאֶת־מִזְבַּח הָעֹלָה וְאֶת־
כָּל־כֵּלָיו וְאֶת־הַכִּיֹּר וְאֶת־כַּנּוֹ׃ 29 וְקִדַּשְׁתָּ
אֹתָם וְהָיוּ קֹדֶשׁ קָדָשִׁים כָּל־הַנֹּגֵעַ בָּהֶם
יִקְדָּשׁ׃ 30 וְאֶת־אַהֲרֹן וְאֶת־בָּנָיו תִּמְשָׁח
וְקִדַּשְׁתָּ אֹתָם לְכַהֵן לִי׃

LAVER (30:17–21)

The laver, or basin, is to be placed in the Tabernacle courtyard, between the altar for burnt offerings and the entrance to the Tabernacle itself. It is to be used by the priests to wash their hands and feet, thus ensuring that they approach the altar in a state of ritual purity. According to 38:8, this basin was made from mirrors donated by "the women who performed tasks at the entrance of the Tent of Meeting."

***20. Tent of Meeting.*** See at 33:7–11.

ANOINTING OIL (30:22–33)

The oil used to anoint the sacred objects and the priests is to be made of four precious spices—myrrh, cinnamon, cane, and cassia—combined with olive oil. Because the oil conveys holiness to whatever it touches, there are severe penalties for its use on profane objects and laypeople.

[31]And speak to the Israelite people, as follows:
This shall be an anointing oil sacred to Me throughout the ages. [32]It must not be rubbed on any person's body, and you must not make anything like it
in the same proportions; it is sacred, to be held sacred by you. [33]Whoever compounds its like, or puts
any of it on a lay person, shall be cut off from kin.
[34]And יהוה said to Moses: Take the herbs stacte,
onycha, and galbanum—these herbs together with
pure frankincense; let there be an equal part of
each. [35]Make them into incense, a compound expertly blended, refined, pure, sacred. [36]Beat some
of it into powder, and put some before the Pact in
the Tent of Meeting, where I will meet with you; it
shall be most holy to you. [37]But when you make
this incense, you must not make any in the same
proportions for yourselves; it shall be held by you
sacred to יהוה. [38]Whoever makes any like it, to
smell of it, shall be cut off from kin.

31 יהוה spoke to Moses: [2]See, I have singled
out by name Bezalel son of Uri son of Hur, of the
tribe of Judah. [3]I have endowed him with a divine
spirit of skill, ability, and knowledge in every kind
of craft; [4]to make designs for work in gold, silver,
and copper, [5]to cut stones for setting and to carve
wood—to work in every kind of craft. [6]Moreover, I
have assigned to him Oholiab son of Ahisamach, of
the tribe of Dan; and I have also granted skill to all
who are skillful, that they may make everything

31 וְאֶל־בְּנֵי יִשְׂרָאֵל תְּדַבֵּר לֵאמֹר שֶׁמֶן
מִשְׁחַת־קֹדֶשׁ יִהְיֶה זֶה לִי לְדֹרֹתֵיכֶם׃
32 עַל־בְּשַׂר אָדָם לֹא יִיסָךְ וּבְמַתְכֻּנְתּוֹ לֹא
תַעֲשׂוּ כָּמֹהוּ קֹדֶשׁ הוּא קֹדֶשׁ יִהְיֶה לָכֶם׃
33 אִישׁ אֲשֶׁר יִרְקַח כָּמֹהוּ וַאֲשֶׁר יִתֵּן מִמֶּנּוּ
עַל־זָר וְנִכְרַת מֵעַמָּיו׃ ס
34 וַיֹּאמֶר יְהֹוָה אֶל־מֹשֶׁה קַח־לְךָ סַמִּים
נָטָף ׀ וּשְׁחֵלֶת וְחֶלְבְּנָה סַמִּים וּלְבֹנָה זַכָּה
בַּד בְּבַד יִהְיֶה׃ 35 וְעָשִׂיתָ אֹתָהּ קְטֹרֶת
רֹקַח מַעֲשֵׂה רוֹקֵחַ מְמֻלָּח טָהוֹר קֹדֶשׁ׃
36 וְשָׁחַקְתָּ מִמֶּנָּה הָדֵק וְנָתַתָּה מִמֶּנָּה לִפְנֵי
הָעֵדֻת בְּאֹהֶל מוֹעֵד אֲשֶׁר אִוָּעֵד לְךָ שָׁמָּה
קֹדֶשׁ קָדָשִׁים תִּהְיֶה לָכֶם׃ 37 וְהַקְּטֹרֶת אֲשֶׁר
תַּעֲשֶׂה בְּמַתְכֻּנְתָּהּ לֹא תַעֲשׂוּ לָכֶם קֹדֶשׁ
תִּהְיֶה לְךָ לַיהֹוָה׃ 38 אִישׁ אֲשֶׁר־יַעֲשֶׂה
כָמוֹהָ לְהָרִיחַ בָּהּ וְנִכְרַת מֵעַמָּיו׃ ס

לא וַיְדַבֵּר יְהֹוָה אֶל־מֹשֶׁה לֵּאמֹר׃ 2 רְאֵה
קָרָאתִי בְשֵׁם בְּצַלְאֵל בֶּן־אוּרִי בֶן־חוּר
לְמַטֵּה יְהוּדָה׃ 3 וָאֲמַלֵּא אֹתוֹ רוּחַ
אֱלֹהִים בְּחָכְמָה וּבִתְבוּנָה וּבְדַעַת וּבְכָל־
מְלָאכָה׃ 4 לַחְשֹׁב מַחֲשָׁבֹת לַעֲשׂוֹת בַּזָּהָב
וּבַכֶּסֶף וּבַנְּחֹשֶׁת׃ 5 וּבַחֲרֹשֶׁת אֶבֶן לְמַלֹּאת
וּבַחֲרֹשֶׁת עֵץ לַעֲשׂוֹת בְּכָל־מְלָאכָה׃ 6 וַאֲנִי
הִנֵּה נָתַתִּי אִתּוֹ אֵת אָהֳלִיאָב בֶּן־אֲחִיסָמָךְ
לְמַטֵּה־דָן וּבְלֵב כָּל־חֲכַם־לֵב נָתַתִּי חָכְמָה

INCENSE (30:34–38)

The incense contains three precious spices combined with frankincense. As v. 36 indicates, the incense created a cloud of smoke that was perceived as the manifestation or sign of God's presence. (See also at 30:7.)

ARTISANS (31:1–11)

This passage identifies the artisans—Bezalel and Oholiab—who are to make the Tabernacle and its furnishings. Their tasks will include directing and supervising the involvement of other artisans, including women (see 35:25–26; 36:1–4). The passage then gives a summary list of the components of the Tabernacle.

*3. divine spirit.* This phrase (*ruach elohim*) also appears in Genesis 1:2. Its use here strengthens the connection between the Tabernacle and the cosmos, and likewise between the creative work of God and of the artisans (see also at Exodus 40).

that I have commanded you: [7]the Tent of Meeting, the Ark for the Pact and the cover upon it, and all the furnishings of the Tent; [8]the table and its utensils, the pure lampstand and all its fittings, and the altar of incense; [9]the altar of burnt offering and all its utensils, and the laver and its stand; [10]the service vestments, the sacral vestments of Aaron the priest and the vestments of his sons, for their service as priests; [11]as well as the anointing oil and the aromatic incense for the sanctuary. Just as I have commanded you, they shall do.

[12]And יהוה said to Moses: [13]Speak to the Israelite people and say: Nevertheless, you must keep My sabbaths, for this is a sign between Me and you throughout the ages, that you may know that I יהוה have consecrated you. [14]You shall keep the sabbath, for it is holy for you. One who profanes it shall be put to death: whoever does work on it, that person shall be cut off from among kin. [15]Six days may work be done, but on the seventh day there shall be a sabbath of complete rest, holy to יהוה; whoever does work on the sabbath day shall be put to death. [16]The Israelite people shall keep the sabbath, observing the sabbath throughout the ages as a covenant for all time: [17]it shall be a sign for all time between Me and the people of Israel. For in six days יהוה made heaven and earth, and on the seventh day [God] ceased from work and was refreshed.

וְעָשׂוּ אֵת כָּל־אֲשֶׁר צִוִּיתִךָ׃ 7 אֵת | אֹהֶל
מוֹעֵד וְאֶת־הָאָרֹן לָעֵדֻת וְאֶת־הַכַּפֹּרֶת
אֲשֶׁר עָלָיו וְאֵת כָּל־כְּלֵי הָאֹהֶל׃ 8 וְאֶת־
הַשֻּׁלְחָן וְאֶת־כֵּלָיו וְאֶת־הַמְּנֹרָה הַטְּהֹרָה
וְאֶת־כָּל־כֵּלֶיהָ וְאֵת מִזְבַּח הַקְּטֹרֶת׃
9 וְאֶת־מִזְבַּח הָעֹלָה וְאֶת־כָּל־כֵּלָיו וְאֶת־
הַכִּיּוֹר וְאֶת־כַּנּוֹ׃ 10 וְאֵת בִּגְדֵי הַשְּׂרָד וְאֶת־
בִּגְדֵי הַקֹּדֶשׁ לְאַהֲרֹן הַכֹּהֵן וְאֶת־בִּגְדֵי
בָנָיו לְכַהֵן׃ 11 וְאֵת שֶׁמֶן הַמִּשְׁחָה וְאֶת־
קְטֹרֶת הַסַּמִּים לַקֹּדֶשׁ כְּכֹל אֲשֶׁר־צִוִּיתִךָ
יַעֲשׂוּ׃ פ
12 וַיֹּאמֶר יְהֹוָה אֶל־מֹשֶׁה לֵּאמֹר׃ 13 וְאַתָּה
דַּבֵּר אֶל־בְּנֵי יִשְׂרָאֵל לֵאמֹר אַךְ אֶת־
שַׁבְּתֹתַי תִּשְׁמֹרוּ כִּי אוֹת הִוא בֵּינִי
וּבֵינֵיכֶם לְדֹרֹתֵיכֶם לָדַעַת כִּי אֲנִי יְהֹוָה
מְקַדִּשְׁכֶם׃ 14 וּשְׁמַרְתֶּם אֶת־הַשַּׁבָּת כִּי
קֹדֶשׁ הִוא לָכֶם מְחַלְלֶיהָ מוֹת יוּמָת כִּי
כָּל־הָעֹשֶׂה בָהּ מְלָאכָה וְנִכְרְתָה הַנֶּפֶשׁ
הַהִוא מִקֶּרֶב עַמֶּיהָ׃ 15 שֵׁשֶׁת יָמִים יֵעָשֶׂה
מְלָאכָה וּבַיּוֹם הַשְּׁבִיעִי שַׁבַּת שַׁבָּתוֹן קֹדֶשׁ
לַיהֹוָה כָּל־הָעֹשֶׂה מְלָאכָה בְּיוֹם הַשַּׁבָּת
מוֹת יוּמָת׃ 16 וְשָׁמְרוּ בְנֵי־יִשְׂרָאֵל אֶת־
הַשַּׁבָּת לַעֲשׂוֹת אֶת־הַשַּׁבָּת לְדֹרֹתָם בְּרִית
עוֹלָם׃ 17 בֵּינִי וּבֵין בְּנֵי יִשְׂרָאֵל אוֹת הִוא
לְעֹלָם כִּי־שֵׁשֶׁת יָמִים עָשָׂה יְהֹוָה אֶת־
הַשָּׁמַיִם וְאֶת־הָאָרֶץ וּבַיּוֹם הַשְּׁבִיעִי שָׁבַת
וַיִּנָּפַשׁ׃ ס

SHABBAT OBSERVANCE (31:12–17)

The placement of the Shabbat commandment here connects the realms of holy space (the Tabernacle) and of holy time (Shabbat). A central concern of the Torah's priestly theology is the maintenance of these holy realms.

*14. person.* See at Leviticus 2:1.

*kin.* Heb. *ammim*; see at Genesis 25:8.

*16–17.* In rabbinic Judaism, these verses form the text of the *V'shamru* ("[they] shall keep") prayer, which is recited as part of the Shabbat liturgy and as a prelude to *Kiddush*, the blessing of the wine, on Shabbat morning.

18 Upon finishing speaking with him on Mount Sinai, [God] gave Moses the two tablets of the Pact, stone tablets inscribed with the finger of God.

18 וַיִּתֵּ֣ן אֶל־מֹשֶׁ֗ה כְּכַלֹּתוֹ֙ לְדַבֵּ֤ר אִתּוֹ֙ בְּהַ֣ר
סִינַ֔י שְׁנֵ֖י לֻחֹ֣ת הָעֵדֻ֑ת לֻחֹ֣ת אֶ֔בֶן כְּתֻבִ֖ים
בְּאֶצְבַּ֥ע אֱלֹהִֽים׃

32 When the people saw that Moses was so long in coming down from the mountain, the people gathered against Aaron and said to him,

לב וַיַּ֣רְא הָעָ֔ם כִּֽי־בֹשֵׁ֥שׁ מֹשֶׁ֖ה לָרֶ֣דֶת מִן־
הָהָ֑ר וַיִּקָּהֵ֨ל הָעָ֜ם עַֽל־אַהֲרֹ֗ן וַיֹּאמְר֤וּ אֵלָיו֙

### CONCLUSION (31:18)

*18. inscribed with the finger of God.* This image fits with the pervasive anthropomorphic depiction of God in this parashah. Functionally speaking, it portrays the tablets as concrete products and extensions of God's will.

## *Crisis: The Golden Calf Episode*

(32:1–35)

The Golden Calf episode reveals the challenge of maintaining a relationship between "stiff-necked" Israel and its holy God. For the Rabbis, this incident functions as a "fall" story (akin to how the Garden of Eden story in Genesis 3 functions for Christian and some later Jewish interpreters), meaning that this episode represents a rupture in the intimate connection between God and Israel and necessitates a more distant and mediated relationship.

The placement of this episode highlights the ironic link between the calf and the Tabernacle. In both instances, the people are invited to donate gold for the construction and do so willingly. The gold is then used to manufacture the ritual object and, upon its completion, the people offer sacrifices and celebrate. These similarities set into sharp relief the crucial difference between the Tabernacle, which is sanctioned by God, and the calf, which is condemned as a fatally inappropriate ritual object.

### CONSTRUCTION OF THE CALF (32:1–6)

The word *eigel* (commonly translated as "calf") refers to a young bull or ox (see Psalm 106:19–20), both of which were symbols of power and virility and associated with the God of Israel and other gods of the ancient Near East. According to I Kings 12:25–33, King Jeroboam—the first king of the northern kingdom of Israel—erected two golden calves, one at Bethel and one at Dan. Historically, these sacred objects probably functioned like the ark and cherubim in the Jerusalem Temple: as thrones or symbols for the God of Israel who was worshipped at those shrines (see at 25:17–21). However, in the biblical text, which reflects a Judean perspective and a later centralization of worship, the calves are condemned as inappropriate and idolatrous.

This biblical polemic provides a context for the Golden Calf episode and demonstrates the complexity of the question of "idolatry." The Bible and later rabbinic texts imagine that visual representations of God are "idols" that are worshipped as gods by their devotees. However, in most ancient and modern cases, images of gods are understood as symbols or accessories of the god, forms of mediation that help worshippers connect to the deity. Within the parashah, the calf shares many features of the Tabernacle: both are associated with the God of Israel and are constructed out of freewill offerings of the Israelites. However, the calf is condemned while the Tabernacle is legitimated. The overlap between these two forms of mediation demonstrates

"Come, make us a god who shall go before us, for
that fellow Moses—the leader who brought us
from the land of Egypt—we do not know what
has happened to him." 2Aaron said to them, "[You
men,] take off the gold rings that are on the ears of
your wives, your sons, and your daughters, and
bring them to me." 3And all the people took off
the gold rings that were in their ears and brought
them to Aaron. 4This he took from them and cast
in a mold, and made it into a molten calf. And
they exclaimed, "This is your god, O Israel, who
brought you out of the land of Egypt!" 5When
Aaron saw this, he built an altar before it; and
Aaron announced: "Tomorrow shall be a festival of
יהוה!" 6Early next day, the people offered up burnt
offerings and brought sacrifices of well-being; they
sat down to eat and drink, and then rose to dance.

קוּם ׀ עֲשֵׂה־לָ֣נוּ אֱלֹהִ֗ים אֲשֶׁ֤ר יֵֽלְכוּ֙ לְפָנֵ֔ינוּ
כִּי־זֶ֣ה ׀ מֹשֶׁ֣ה הָאִ֗ישׁ אֲשֶׁ֤ר הֶֽעֱלָ֙נוּ֙ מֵאֶ֣רֶץ
מִצְרַ֔יִם לֹ֥א יָדַ֖עְנוּ מֶה־הָ֥יָה לֽוֹ׃ 2 וַיֹּ֤אמֶר
אֲלֵהֶם֙ אַהֲרֹ֔ן פָּֽרְקוּ֙ נִזְמֵ֣י הַזָּהָ֔ב אֲשֶׁר֙ בְּאָזְנֵ֣י
נְשֵׁיכֶ֔ם בְּנֵיכֶ֖ם וּבְנֹתֵיכֶ֑ם וְהָבִ֖יאוּ אֵלָֽי׃
3 וַיִּתְפָּֽרְקוּ֙ כָּל־הָעָ֔ם אֶת־נִזְמֵ֥י הַזָּהָ֖ב אֲשֶׁ֣ר
בְּאָזְנֵיהֶ֑ם וַיָּבִ֖יאוּ אֶֽל־אַהֲרֹֽן׃ 4 וַיִּקַּ֣ח מִיָּדָ֗ם
וַיָּ֤צַר אֹתוֹ֙ בַּחֶ֔רֶט וַֽיַּעֲשֵׂ֖הוּ עֵ֣גֶל מַסֵּכָ֑ה
וַיֹּ֣אמְר֔וּ אֵ֤לֶּה אֱלֹהֶ֙יךָ֙ יִשְׂרָאֵ֔ל אֲשֶׁ֥ר הֶעֱל֖וּךָ
מֵאֶ֥רֶץ מִצְרָֽיִם׃ 5 וַיַּ֣רְא אַהֲרֹ֔ן וַיִּ֥בֶן מִזְבֵּ֖חַ
לְפָנָ֑יו וַיִּקְרָ֤א אַהֲרֹן֙ וַיֹּאמַ֔ר חַ֥ג לַיהוָ֖ה
מָחָֽר׃ 6 וַיַּשְׁכִּ֙ימוּ֙ מִֽמָּחֳרָ֔ת וַיַּעֲל֣וּ עֹלֹ֔ת
וַיַּגִּ֖שׁוּ שְׁלָמִ֑ים וַיֵּ֤שֶׁב הָעָם֙ לֶֽאֱכֹ֣ל וְשָׁת֔וֹ
וַיָּקֻ֖מוּ לְצַחֵֽק׃ פ

how complex the questions of divine mediation and religious representation are.

*1. "make us a god."* The word *elohim* (translated here as "god") is a plural noun (literally "gods") that can refer to either a single deity or more than one god. The God of Israel is often called *elohim,* but with singular verb forms used with that divine name. In this verse, the noun is paired with a plural verb, which might imply that the Israelites ask Aaron to make them more than one god. Or, as this translation suggests, the plural verb is used to signal that the Israelites are demanding *a* god, rather than *the* God.

***"that fellow Moses... who brought us from the land of Egypt."*** Elsewhere in the Torah, the identification of God as the agent of the Exodus is central to God's claim to authority over Israel (as in 20:2). But here Moses is identified as the one responsible for the Exodus.

*2.* ***"take off the gold rings that are on the ears of your wives, your sons, and your daughters."*** Aaron directs the men to take jewelry off the members of their household under their control.

*3.* ***all the people took off.*** This statement implicates everyone, not only the men, in the construction of the calf.

*4.* ***And they exclaimed, "This is your god... who brought you out of the land of Egypt!"*** While the ambiguity of the word *elohim* (see at v. 1) raises the possibility that the Israelites sought to worship another deity, the phrase "who brought you out of the land of Egypt" and Aaron's explicit mention of "יהוה" in v. 5 suggest that the people craved a visible symbol of God's presence. Nevertheless, by attributing these words to the Israelites, the authors of the text portray the people as idolators, who identify and worship the calf *as* a god.

*5.* Aaron's response is complex. By constructing an altar, he facilitates the inappropriate, idolatrous understanding of the calf. Yet by declaring a "festival of יהוה," he redirects the Israelites' attention to the God of Israel.

*6.* Of the three activities mentioned in this verse, sacrificial offerings and ritual feasting are part of authorized Israelite worship. However, dancing (literally "laughing") is non-normative and perhaps signals the deviant nature of this impromptu festival.

<sup>7</sup>יהוה spoke to Moses, "Hurry down, for your people, whom you brought out of the land of Egypt, have acted basely. <sup>8</sup>They have been quick to turn aside from the way that I enjoined upon them. They have made themselves a molten calf and bowed low to it and sacrificed to it, saying: 'This is your god, O Israel, who brought you out of the land of Egypt!'"

<sup>9</sup>יהוה further said to Moses, "I see that this is a stiffnecked people. <sup>10</sup>Now, let Me be, that My anger may blaze forth against them and that I may destroy them, and make of you a great nation." <sup>11</sup>But Moses implored his God יהוה, saying, "Let not Your anger, יהוה, blaze forth against Your people, whom You delivered from the land of Egypt with great power and with a mighty hand. <sup>12</sup>Let not the Egyptians say, 'It was with evil intent that he delivered them, only to kill them off in the mountains and annihilate them from the face of the earth.' Turn from Your blazing anger, and renounce the plan to punish Your people. <sup>13</sup>Remember Your servants, Abraham, Isaac, and Israel, how You swore to them by Your Self and said to them:

וַיְדַבֵּ֥ר יְהוָ֖ה אֶל־מֹשֶׁ֑ה לֶךְ־רֵ֕ד כִּ֚י שִׁחֵ֣ת 7 עַמְּךָ֔ אֲשֶׁ֥ר הֶעֱלֵ֖יתָ מֵאֶ֥רֶץ מִצְרָֽיִם׃ 8 סָ֣רוּ מַהֵ֗ר מִן־הַדֶּ֙רֶךְ֙ אֲשֶׁ֣ר צִוִּיתִ֔ם עָשׂ֣וּ לָהֶ֔ם עֵ֖גֶל מַסֵּכָ֑ה וַיִּשְׁתַּֽחֲווּ־לוֹ֙ וַיִּזְבְּחוּ־ל֔וֹ וַיֹּ֣אמְר֔וּ אֵ֤לֶּה אֱלֹהֶ֙יךָ֙ יִשְׂרָאֵ֔ל אֲשֶׁ֥ר הֶעֱל֖וּךָ מֵאֶ֥רֶץ מִצְרָֽיִם׃

וַיֹּ֥אמֶר יְהוָ֖ה אֶל־מֹשֶׁ֑ה רָאִ֙יתִי֙ אֶת־הָעָ֣ם 9 הַזֶּ֔ה וְהִנֵּ֥ה עַם־קְשֵׁה־עֹ֖רֶף הֽוּא׃ 10 וְעַתָּה֙ הַנִּ֣יחָה לִּ֔י וְיִֽחַר־אַפִּ֥י בָהֶ֖ם וַאֲכַלֵּ֑ם וְאֶֽעֱשֶׂ֥ה אוֹתְךָ֖ לְג֥וֹי גָּדֽוֹל׃ 11 וַיְחַ֣ל מֹשֶׁ֔ה אֶת־פְּנֵ֖י יְהוָ֣ה אֱלֹהָ֑יו וַיֹּ֗אמֶר לָמָ֤ה יְהוָה֙ יֶחֱרֶ֤ה אַפְּךָ֙ בְּעַמֶּ֔ךָ אֲשֶׁ֤ר הוֹצֵ֙אתָ֙ מֵאֶ֣רֶץ מִצְרַ֔יִם בְּכֹ֥חַ גָּד֖וֹל וּבְיָ֥ד חֲזָקָֽה׃ 12 לָ֩מָּה֩ יֹאמְר֨וּ מִצְרַ֜יִם לֵאמֹ֗ר בְּרָעָ֤ה הֽוֹצִיאָם֙ לַהֲרֹ֤ג אֹתָם֙ בֶּֽהָרִ֔ים וּ֨לְכַלֹּתָ֔ם מֵעַ֖ל פְּנֵ֣י הָֽאֲדָמָ֑ה שׁ֚וּב מֵחֲר֣וֹן אַפֶּ֔ךָ וְהִנָּחֵ֥ם עַל־הָרָעָ֖ה לְעַמֶּֽךָ׃ 13 זְכֹ֡ר לְאַבְרָהָם֩ לְיִצְחָ֨ק וּלְיִשְׂרָאֵ֜ל עֲבָדֶ֗יךָ אֲשֶׁ֙ר נִשְׁבַּ֣עְתָּ לָהֶם֮ בָּךְ֒ וַתְּדַבֵּ֣ר אֲלֵהֶ֔ם אַרְבֶּ֕ה

---

### GOD'S ANGER AND MOSES' INTERCESSION (32:7–14)

While the Golden Calf may be defensible as a legitimate, non-idolatrous religious object from the point of view of ancient Israelite history and theology (see above), the Torah unambiguously identifies its creation as transgressive. This is clear from the fury expressed by both God and Moses.

**8.** *"They have made themselves a molten calf."* This verse deflects blame for the calf from Aaron to the people. Throughout the parashah, the degree of blame attributed to Aaron fluctuates. In vv. 2–5, Aaron is portrayed as responsible for creating the calf. Yet here and in vv. 22–24, the people are identified as the creators of the calf. Some scholars have seen this contradiction as evidence for two earlier versions of this story, one pro-Aaron and the other

anti-Aaron. It is also possible to read the contradictions as a reflection of the difficulty involved in definitively identifying agency and responsibility.

**9.** *"stiffnecked people."* This epithet suggests that the calf is not a sign of Israelite fickleness, but rather of their stubbornness and their inability to adapt to the covenantal relationship with God that was established at Sinai (Avivah Gottlieb Zornberg, *The Particulars of Rapture*, 2001, pp. 408–9).

**11–14.** *But Moses implored.* Moses uses two rhetorical strategies to successfully dissuade God from destroying the people. First, he argues that God's reputation will be sullied if God annihilates the very people that God rescued from Egypt (vv. 11–12). Then, he reminds God of the covenant with the ancestors (v. 13). The success of Moses' intervention is underscored by the reference to Israel as God's people in v. 14.

I will make your offspring as numerous as the stars of heaven, and I will give to your offspring this whole land of which I spoke, to possess forever." [14]And יהוה renounced the punishment planned for God's people.

[15]Thereupon Moses turned and went down from the mountain bearing the two tablets of the Pact, tablets inscribed on both their surfaces: they were inscribed on the one side and on the other. [16]The tablets were God's work, and the writing was God's writing, incised upon the tablets. [17]When Joshua heard the sound of the people in its boisterousness, he said to Moses, "There is a cry of war in the camp." [18]But he answered,

"It is not the sound of the tune of triumph,
Or the sound of the tune of defeat;
It is the sound of song that I hear!"

[19]As soon as Moses came near the camp and saw the calf and the dancing, he became enraged; and he hurled the tablets from his hands and shattered them at the foot of the mountain. [20]He took the calf that they had made and burned it; he ground it to powder and strewed it upon the water and so made the Israelites drink it.

[21]Moses said to Aaron, "What did this people do to you that you have brought such great sin

אֶת־זַרְעֲכֶם כְּכוֹכְבֵי הַשָּׁמָיִם וְכָל־הָאָרֶץ
הַזֹּאת אֲשֶׁר אָמַרְתִּי אֶתֵּן לְזַרְעֲכֶם וְנָחֲלוּ
לְעֹלָם׃ 14 וַיִּנָּחֶם יְהוָה עַל־הָרָעָה אֲשֶׁר
דִּבֶּר לַעֲשׂוֹת לְעַמּוֹ׃ פ
15 וַיִּפֶן וַיֵּרֶד מֹשֶׁה מִן־הָהָר וּשְׁנֵי לֻחֹת
הָעֵדֻת בְּיָדוֹ לֻחֹת כְּתֻבִים מִשְּׁנֵי עֶבְרֵיהֶם
מִזֶּה וּמִזֶּה הֵם כְּתֻבִים׃ 16 וְהַלֻּחֹת מַעֲשֵׂה
אֱלֹהִים הֵמָּה וְהַמִּכְתָּב מִכְתַּב אֱלֹהִים הוּא
חָרוּת עַל־הַלֻּחֹת׃ 17 וַיִּשְׁמַע יְהוֹשֻׁעַ אֶת־
קוֹל הָעָם בְּרֵעֹה וַיֹּאמֶר אֶל־מֹשֶׁה קוֹל
מִלְחָמָה בַּמַּחֲנֶה׃ 18 וַיֹּאמֶר
אֵין קוֹל עֲנוֹת גְּבוּרָה
וְאֵין קוֹל עֲנוֹת חֲלוּשָׁה
קוֹל עַנּוֹת אָנֹכִי שֹׁמֵעַ׃
19 וַיְהִי כַּאֲשֶׁר קָרַב אֶל־הַמַּחֲנֶה וַיַּרְא אֶת־
הָעֵגֶל וּמְחֹלֹת וַיִּחַר־אַף מֹשֶׁה וַיַּשְׁלֵךְ מידו
מִיָּדָיו אֶת־הַלֻּחֹת וַיְשַׁבֵּר אֹתָם תַּחַת הָהָר׃
20 וַיִּקַּח אֶת־הָעֵגֶל אֲשֶׁר עָשׂוּ וַיִּשְׂרֹף בָּאֵשׁ
וַיִּטְחַן עַד אֲשֶׁר־דָּק וַיִּזֶר עַל־פְּנֵי הַמַּיִם
וַיַּשְׁקְ אֶת־בְּנֵי יִשְׂרָאֵל׃
21 וַיֹּאמֶר מֹשֶׁה אֶל־אַהֲרֹן מֶה־עָשָׂה לְךָ
הָעָם הַזֶּה כִּי־הֵבֵאתָ עָלָיו חֲטָאָה גְדֹלָה׃

### MOSES' ANGER AT THE PEOPLE AND AARON (32:15–29)

Moses descends from the mountain with two tablets—which he furiously hurls to the ground. The detailed description of the tablets and their identification as "God's work" (v. 16) highlight their sacrality and underscore the drama of their destruction.

*19. dancing.* The term here for dancing (*m'cholot*) probably refers to women's circle dancing rather than men's leaping dances, indicating women's participation in the transgressive acts. In all eight instances where the Bible specifies the performers of this activity, they are women (Exodus 15:20; Judges 11:34, 21:21, 23; I Samuel 18:6, 21:12; Jeremiah 31:4, 13).

*20. He took the calf... and so made the Israelites drink it.* This punishment resembles the ordeal of the suspected adulteress in Numbers 5:11–31, in which the woman suspected of adultery is forced to swallow a potion made with ink from a ritual scroll and with dirt from the Tabernacle floor. While it is doubtful that there is a historical connection between the two cases, the similarities between these texts form the basis of midrashic comments that understand the construction of the Golden Calf to be a form of theological adultery (see further the Post-biblical Interpretations at 32:19, p. 515).

upon them?" 22 Aaron said, "Let not my lord be enraged. You know that this people is bent on evil. 23 They said to me, 'Make us a god to lead us; for that fellow Moses—the leader who brought us from the land of Egypt—we do not know what has happened to him.' 24 So I said to them, 'Whoever has gold, take it off!' They gave it to me and I hurled it into the fire and out came this calf!"

25 Moses saw that the people were out of control—since Aaron had let them get out of control—so that they were a menace to any who might oppose them. 26 Moses stood up in the gate of the camp and said, "Whoever is for יהוה, come here!" And all the men of Levi rallied to him. 27 He said to them, "Thus says יהוה, the God of Israel: Each of you put sword on thigh, go back and forth from gate to gate throughout the camp, and slay sibling, neighbor, and kin." 28 The men of Levi did as Moses had bidden; and some three thousand of the people fell that day. 29 And Moses said, "Dedicate yourselves to יהוה this day—for each of you has been against blood relations—that [God] may bestow a blessing upon you today."

22 וַיֹּאמֶר אַהֲרֹן אַל־יִחַר אַף אֲדֹנִי אַתָּה
יָדַעְתָּ אֶת־הָעָם כִּי בְרָע הוּא׃ 23 וַיֹּאמְרוּ
לִי עֲשֵׂה־לָנוּ אֱלֹהִים אֲשֶׁר יֵלְכוּ לְפָנֵינוּ
כִּי־זֶה ׀ מֹשֶׁה הָאִישׁ אֲשֶׁר הֶעֱלָנוּ מֵאֶרֶץ
מִצְרַיִם לֹא יָדַעְנוּ מֶה־הָיָה לוֹ׃ 24 וָאֹמַר
לָהֶם לְמִי זָהָב הִתְפָּרָקוּ וַיִּתְּנוּ־לִי
וָאַשְׁלִכֵהוּ בָאֵשׁ וַיֵּצֵא הָעֵגֶל הַזֶּה׃
25 וַיַּרְא מֹשֶׁה אֶת־הָעָם כִּי פָרֻעַ הוּא כִּי־
פְרָעֹה אַהֲרֹן לְשִׁמְצָה בְּקָמֵיהֶם׃ 26 וַיַּעֲמֹד
מֹשֶׁה בְּשַׁעַר הַמַּחֲנֶה וַיֹּאמֶר מִי לַיהוָֹה
אֵלָי וַיֵּאָסְפוּ אֵלָיו כָּל־בְּנֵי לֵוִי׃ 27 וַיֹּאמֶר
לָהֶם כֹּה־אָמַר יְהוָֹה אֱלֹהֵי יִשְׂרָאֵל שִׂימוּ
אִישׁ־חַרְבּוֹ עַל־יְרֵכוֹ עִבְרוּ וָשׁוּבוּ מִשַּׁעַר
לָשַׁעַר בַּמַּחֲנֶה וְהִרְגוּ אִישׁ־אֶת־אָחִיו וְאִישׁ
אֶת־רֵעֵהוּ וְאִישׁ אֶת־קְרֹבוֹ׃ 28 וַיַּעֲשׂוּ בְנֵי־
לֵוִי כִּדְבַר מֹשֶׁה וַיִּפֹּל מִן־הָעָם בַּיּוֹם הַהוּא
כִּשְׁלֹשֶׁת אַלְפֵי אִישׁ׃ 29 וַיֹּאמֶר מֹשֶׁה
מִלְאוּ יֶדְכֶם הַיּוֹם לַיהוָֹה כִּי אִישׁ בִּבְנוֹ
וּבְאָחִיו וְלָתֵת עֲלֵיכֶם הַיּוֹם בְּרָכָה׃

***22–24. Aaron said.*** Aaron shifts the blame away from himself by identifying Moses' prolonged absence as the root of the problem and limiting his involvement to the hurling of the gold into the fire (compare v. 8). Ironically, in his attempt to absolve himself, Aaron ascribes supernatural power to the calf.

***27. "Each of you put sword on thigh."*** The violence perpetrated by the Levites—which contemporary readers may find disturbing—resonates interestingly with the violence perpetrated by their ancestor Levi following the violation of his sister Dinah (Genesis 34). There, Levi and his brother Simeon massacre the residents of Shechem. In Genesis 49:5–7, Levi is also portrayed as violent. While the earlier acts of violence are condemned, this one is praised. (See also *Vayikra*, Contemporary Reflection, p. 589.)

***29. "Dedicate yourselves."*** Literally, "fill your hands"—a term that is usually used for the ordination of priests. According to some interpreters, this verse means that by killing their kin, the Levites consecrated themselves to God and earned God's blessing. Others conclude the opposite: because of their actions, the Levites must dedicate themselves in atonement in order to receive God's blessing. Note that the massacre does not suffice as punishment or atonement for the people's transgression, for Moses still needs to beg for the people's forgiveness and God still sends a plague as punishment (see 32:30–35).

***"blood relations."*** [Literally, "his son and his brother." Grammatically speaking, the reference is indefinite and nonspecific; hence the language does not specify social gender. The present translation presumes that the expression refers to fellow Israelite victims, women or men, to whom the Levites had felt personal devotion. —*Ed.*]

[30]The next day Moses said to the people, "You have been guilty of a great sin. Yet I will now go up to יהוה; perhaps I may win forgiveness for your sin." [31]Moses went back to יהוה and said, "Alas, this people is guilty of a great sin in making for themselves a god of gold. [32]Now, if You will forgive their sin [well and good]; but if not, erase me from the record which You have written!" [33]But יהוה said to Moses, "Only one who has sinned against Me will I erase from My record. [34]Go now, lead the people where I told you. See, My angel shall go before you. But when I make an accounting, I will bring them to account for their sins."

[35]Then יהוה sent a plague upon the people, for what they did with the calf that Aaron made.

33 Then יהוה said to Moses, "Set out from here, you and the people that you have brought up from the land of Egypt, to the land of which I swore to Abraham, Isaac, and Jacob, saying, 'To your offspring will I give it'—[2]I will send an angel before you, and I will drive out the Canaanites, the Amorites, the Hittites, the Perizzites, the Hivites, and the Jebusites—[3]a land flowing with milk and honey. But I will not go in your midst, since you are a stiffnecked people, lest I destroy you on the way."

30 וַיְהִי֙ מִֽמָּחֳרָ֔ת וַיֹּ֥אמֶר מֹשֶׁ֖ה אֶל־הָעָ֑ם
אַתֶּ֥ם חֲטָאתֶ֖ם חֲטָאָ֣ה גְדֹלָ֑ה וְעַתָּה֙ אֶעֱלֶ֣ה
אֶל־יְהֹוָ֔ה אוּלַ֥י אֲכַפְּרָ֖ה בְּעַ֥ד חַטַּאתְכֶֽם׃
31 וַיָּ֧שָׁב מֹשֶׁ֛ה אֶל־יְהֹוָ֖ה וַיֹּאמַ֑ר אָ֣נָּ֗א חָטָ֞א
הָעָ֤ם הַזֶּה֙ חֲטָאָ֣ה גְדֹלָ֔ה וַיַּעֲשׂ֥וּ לָהֶ֖ם אֱלֹהֵ֥י
זָהָֽב׃ 32 וְעַתָּ֖ה אִם־תִּשָּׂ֣א חַטָּאתָ֑ם וְאִם־אַ֕יִן
מְחֵ֣נִי נָ֔א מִֽסִּפְרְךָ֖ אֲשֶׁ֥ר כָּתָֽבְתָּ׃ 33 וַיֹּ֥אמֶר
יְהֹוָ֖ה אֶל־מֹשֶׁ֑ה מִ֚י אֲשֶׁ֣ר חָטָא־לִ֔י אֶמְחֶ֖נּוּ
מִסִּפְרִֽי׃ 34 וְעַתָּ֞ה לֵ֣ךְ ׀ נְחֵ֣ה אֶת־הָעָ֗ם אֶ֤ל
אֲשֶׁר־דִּבַּ֙רְתִּי֙ לָ֔ךְ הִנֵּ֥ה מַלְאָכִ֖י יֵלֵ֣ךְ לְפָנֶ֑יךָ
וּבְי֣וֹם פָּקְדִ֔י וּפָקַדְתִּ֥י עֲלֵהֶ֖ם חַטָּאתָֽם׃
35 וַיִּגֹּ֥ף יְהֹוָ֖ה אֶת־הָעָ֑ם עַ֚ל אֲשֶׁ֣ר עָשׂ֣וּ אֶת־
הָעֵ֔גֶל אֲשֶׁ֥ר עָשָׂ֖ה אַהֲרֹֽן׃ ס

לג וַיְדַבֵּ֨ר יְהֹוָ֤ה אֶל־מֹשֶׁה֙ לֵ֣ךְ עֲלֵ֣ה מִזֶּ֔ה
אַתָּ֣ה וְהָעָ֔ם אֲשֶׁ֥ר הֶעֱלִ֖יתָ מֵאֶ֣רֶץ מִצְרָ֑יִם
אֶל־הָאָ֗רֶץ אֲשֶׁ֣ר נִ֠שְׁבַּ֠עְתִּי לְאַבְרָהָ֨ם לְיִצְחָ֤ק
וּֽלְיַעֲקֹב֙ לֵאמֹ֔ר לְזַרְעֲךָ֖ אֶתְּנֶֽנָּה׃ 2 וְשָׁלַחְתִּ֥י
לְפָנֶ֖יךָ מַלְאָ֑ךְ וְגֵֽרַשְׁתִּ֗י אֶת־הַֽכְּנַעֲנִי֙ הָֽאֱמֹרִ֔י
וְהַֽחִתִּי֙ וְהַפְּרִזִּ֔י הַחִוִּ֖י וְהַיְבוּסִֽי׃ 3 אֶל־אֶ֛רֶץ
זָבַ֥ת חָלָ֖ב וּדְבָ֑שׁ כִּי֩ לֹ֨א אֶֽעֱלֶ֜ה בְּקִרְבְּךָ֗ כִּ֤י
עַם־קְשֵׁה־עֹ֙רֶף֙ אַ֔תָּה פֶּן־אֲכֶלְךָ֖ בַּדָּֽרֶךְ׃

### MOSES' INTERCESSION AND GOD'S RESPONSE (32:30–35)

Moses again intercedes on behalf of the people, pleading with God to forgive them. In response, God grants a suspended sentence, but not complete atonement. In the context of the parashah, this "atonement" forms a stark contrast with the expiation of 30:11–16 with which the parashah began.

*31. "Alas, this people."* Compare the way that blame is assigned in 32:4–5, 8, 24.

*35. **Then יהוה sent a plague.*** This verse is in tension both with the preceding one, which indicates that God will reserve punishment until a later time, and with v. 14, which reported God's decision not to annihilate the people.

## *Aftermath* (33:1–23)

This unit describes the reconciliation between God and Israel that takes into account the lessons learned during the Golden Calf episode.

### GOD'S REFUSAL TO ACCOMPANY THE ISRAELITES (33:1–6)

God reaffirms the promise of land made to the ancestors. However, God refuses to accompany the

[4]When the people heard this harsh word, they went into mourning, and none put on finery.

[5]יהוה said to Moses, "Say to the Israelite people, 'You are a stiffnecked people. If I were to go in your midst for one moment, I would destroy you. Now, then, leave off your finery, and I will consider what to do to you.'" [6]So the Israelites remained stripped of the finery from Mount Horeb on.

4 וַיִּשְׁמַע הָעָם אֶת־הַדָּבָר הָרָע הַזֶּה
וַיִּתְאַבָּלוּ וְלֹא־שָׁתוּ אִישׁ עֶדְיוֹ עָלָיו׃
5 וַיֹּאמֶר יְהֹוָה אֶל־מֹשֶׁה אֱמֹר אֶל־בְּנֵי־
יִשְׂרָאֵל אַתֶּם עַם־קְשֵׁה־עֹרֶף רֶגַע אֶחָד
אֶעֱלֶה בְקִרְבְּךָ וְכִלִּיתִיךָ וְעַתָּה הוֹרֵד עֶדְיְךָ
מֵעָלֶיךָ וְאֵדְעָה מָה אֶעֱשֶׂה־לָּךְ׃ 6 וַיִּתְנַצְּלוּ
בְנֵי־יִשְׂרָאֵל אֶת־עֶדְיָם מֵהַר חוֹרֵב׃

[7]Now Moses would take the Tent and pitch it outside the camp, at some distance from the camp. It was called the Tent of Meeting, and whoever sought יהוה would go out to the Tent of Meeting that was outside the camp. [8]Whenever Moses went out to the Tent, all the people would rise and stand, at the entrance of each tent, and gaze after Moses until he had entered the Tent. [9]And when Moses entered the Tent, the pillar of cloud would descend and stand at the entrance of the Tent, while [God] spoke with Moses. [10]When all the people saw the

7 וּמֹשֶׁה יִקַּח אֶת־הָאֹהֶל וְנָטָה־לוֹ ׀ מִחוּץ
לַמַּחֲנֶה הַרְחֵק מִן־הַמַּחֲנֶה וְקָרָא לוֹ אֹהֶל
מוֹעֵד וְהָיָה כָּל־מְבַקֵּשׁ יְהֹוָה יֵצֵא אֶל־אֹהֶל
מוֹעֵד אֲשֶׁר מִחוּץ לַמַּחֲנֶה׃ 8 וְהָיָה כְּצֵאת
מֹשֶׁה אֶל־הָאֹהֶל יָקוּמוּ כָּל־הָעָם וְנִצְּבוּ
אִישׁ פֶּתַח אָהֳלוֹ וְהִבִּיטוּ אַחֲרֵי מֹשֶׁה עַד־
בֹּאוֹ הָאֹהֱלָה׃ 9 וְהָיָה כְּבֹא מֹשֶׁה הָאֹהֱלָה
יֵרֵד עַמּוּד הֶעָנָן וְעָמַד פֶּתַח הָאֹהֶל וְדִבֶּר
עִם־מֹשֶׁה׃ 10 וְרָאָה כָל־הָעָם אֶת־עַמּוּד

current generation, lest their wayward actions prompt divine retribution.

*4–6. finery.* Adornment is a prominent motif in the parashah. Jewelry is misused in the construction of the calf (32:2–3), and here "finery" is removed as a sign of penance.

*6. from Mount Horeb.* The Golden Calf episode transpired at Horeb (3:1, 12), also called Sinai (31:18), the very site of the formation of the covenant (Exodus 19 and 24). See also at 18:5.

### GOD'S CONCESSIONS AND FORMS OF REVELATION (33:7–23)

The focus now shifts to the question of how God will continue to become manifest to Israel and Moses. Several forms of divine revelation are presented, options that span a range of theological thinking, from the abstract—such as God's name or goodness—to the highly anthropomorphic—like God's back.

#### *Tent of Meeting* (33:7–11)

In the Torah, two different terms are used to refer to Israel's portable wilderness sanctuary: Tabernacle and Tent of Meeting. The tent described here represents an alternate tradition that differs significantly from the Tabernacle tradition that dominates Exodus 25–31 and 35–40 (see also at 27:21; *Vayak'heil*, Another View, p. 538). In the texts that refer to the sanctuary as "Tabernacle," God's presence is very powerful and potentially very dangerous; nevertheless, by rigorously maintaining the purity of the shrine, the Israelites can safely preserve the vital presence of God in their midst. Here, the Tent tradition—which is perhaps much older than the Tabernacle one—expresses a different perspective, one in which the stiffnecked nature of the Israelites is incompatible with the divine presence. Therefore, the Tent of Meeting stands outside the camp and only Moses and Joshua can enter it. While this view distances God further from the people, it imagines

pillar of cloud poised at the entrance of the Tent, all the people would rise and bow low, at the entrance of each tent. [11]יהוה would speak to Moses face to face, as one person speaks to another. And he would then return to the camp; but his attendant, Joshua son of Nun, [serving as] deputy, would not stir out of the Tent.

[12]Moses said to יהוה, "See, You say to me, 'Lead this people forward,' but You have not made known to me whom You will send with me. Further, You have said, 'I have singled you out by name, and you have, indeed, gained My favor.' [13]Now, if I have truly gained Your favor, pray let me know Your ways, that I may know You and continue in Your favor. Consider, too, that this nation is Your people." [14]And [God] said, "I will go in the lead and will lighten your burden." [15]And he replied, "Unless You go in the lead, do not make us leave this place. [16]For how shall it be known that Your people have gained Your favor unless You go with us, so that we may be distinguished, Your people and I, from every people on the face of the earth?"

[17]And יהוה said to Moses, "I will also do this thing that you have asked; for you have truly gained My favor and I have singled you out by name." [18]He said, "Oh, let me behold Your Presence!" [19]And [God] answered, "I will make all My good-

הֶעָנָן עֹמֵד פֶּתַח הָאֹהֶל וְקָם כָּל־הָעָם
וְהִשְׁתַּחֲווּ אִישׁ פֶּתַח אָהֳלוֹ׃ 11 וְדִבֶּר יְהֹוָה
אֶל־מֹשֶׁה פָּנִים אֶל־פָּנִים כַּאֲשֶׁר יְדַבֵּר אִישׁ
אֶל־רֵעֵהוּ וְשָׁב אֶל־הַמַּחֲנֶה וּמְשָׁרְתוֹ
יְהוֹשֻׁעַ בִּן־נוּן נַעַר לֹא יָמִישׁ מִתּוֹךְ
הָאֹהֶל׃ פ

12 וַיֹּאמֶר מֹשֶׁה אֶל־יְהֹוָה רְאֵה אַתָּה אֹמֵר
אֵלַי הַעַל אֶת־הָעָם הַזֶּה וְאַתָּה לֹא
הוֹדַעְתַּנִי אֵת אֲשֶׁר־תִּשְׁלַח עִמִּי וְאַתָּה
אָמַרְתָּ יְדַעְתִּיךָ בְשֵׁם וְגַם־מָצָאתָ חֵן
בְּעֵינָי׃ 13 וְעַתָּה אִם־נָא מָצָאתִי חֵן בְּעֵינֶיךָ
הוֹדִעֵנִי נָא אֶת־דְּרָכֶךָ וְאֵדָעֲךָ לְמַעַן
אֶמְצָא־חֵן בְּעֵינֶיךָ וּרְאֵה כִּי עַמְּךָ הַגּוֹי
הַזֶּה׃ 14 וַיֹּאמַר פָּנַי יֵלֵכוּ וַהֲנִחֹתִי לָךְ׃
15 וַיֹּאמֶר אֵלָיו אִם־אֵין פָּנֶיךָ הֹלְכִים אַל־
תַּעֲלֵנוּ מִזֶּה׃ 16 וּבַמֶּה ׀ יִוָּדַע אֵפוֹא כִּי־
מָצָאתִי חֵן בְּעֵינֶיךָ אֲנִי וְעַמֶּךָ הֲלוֹא
בְּלֶכְתְּךָ עִמָּנוּ וְנִפְלֵינוּ אֲנִי וְעַמְּךָ מִכָּל־
הָעָם אֲשֶׁר עַל־פְּנֵי הָאֲדָמָה׃ פ
17 וַיֹּאמֶר יְהֹוָה אֶל־מֹשֶׁה גַּם אֶת־הַדָּבָר
הַזֶּה אֲשֶׁר דִּבַּרְתָּ אֶעֱשֶׂה כִּי־מָצָאתָ חֵן
בְּעֵינַי וָאֵדָעֲךָ בְּשֵׁם׃ 18 וַיֹּאמַר הַרְאֵנִי נָא
אֶת־כְּבֹדֶךָ׃ 19 וַיֹּאמֶר אֲנִי אַעֲבִיר כָּל־טוּבִי

a far more direct relationship between God and Moses.

*11. face to face.* The word *panim* (face) is a key term in Exodus 33 (vv. 11, 14–16, 20, 23), appearing seven times. Here it signals a deeply intimate relationship between God and Moses.

### *Moses' Request for Revelation and God's Response* (33:12–23)

This passage resumes the action from v. 6, as Moses challenges God's refusal to accompany the people. In his continued persistence in seeking God's support for the people (see also 32:11–13, 31–32), Moses leverages God's acknowledged special affection for him in order to benefit the people as a whole. God agrees to once again personally lead the people.

*14. "I will go in the lead."* Literally, "My face (*panai*) will lead." Here and in v. 15, *panim* is used to signal a degree of divine presence.

*18. "Presence."* Heb. *kavod*, which refers here (as in 16:7; 24:17; 40:34–38) to a visible manifestation of God, usually in the form of cloud or fire.

*19.* Here God offers to reveal four aspects of the divine presence: goodness, the name יהוה, grace, and compassion. These terms represent at-

ness pass before you, and I will proclaim before you
the name Eternal, and the grace that I grant and the
compassion that I show," 20 continuing, "But you
cannot see My face, for a human being may not see
Me and live." 21 And יהוה said, "See, there is a place
near Me. Station yourself on the rock 22 and, as My
Presence passes by, I will put you in a cleft of the
rock and shield you with My hand until I have
passed by. 23 Then I will take My hand away and
you will see My back; but My face must not be
seen."
34 יהוה said to Moses: "Carve two tablets of
stone like the first, and I will inscribe upon the tablets the words that were on the first tablets, which
you shattered. 2 Be ready by morning, and in the
morning come up to Mount Sinai and present
yourself there to Me, on the top of the mountain.
3 No one else shall come up with you, and no one
else shall be seen anywhere on the mountain; nei-

עַל־פָּנֶיךָ וְקָרָאתִי בְשֵׁם יְהֹוָה לְפָנֶיךָ
וְחַנֹּתִי אֶת־אֲשֶׁר אָחֹן וְרִחַמְתִּי אֶת־אֲשֶׁר
אֲרַחֵם׃ 20 וַיֹּאמֶר לֹא תוּכַל לִרְאֹת אֶת־
פָּנָי כִּי לֹא־יִרְאַנִי הָאָדָם וָחָי׃ 21 וַיֹּאמֶר
יְהֹוָה הִנֵּה מָקוֹם אִתִּי וְנִצַּבְתָּ עַל־הַצּוּר׃
22 וְהָיָה בַּעֲבֹר כְּבֹדִי וְשַׂמְתִּיךָ בְּנִקְרַת
הַצּוּר וְשַׂכֹּתִי כַפִּי עָלֶיךָ עַד־עָבְרִי׃
23 וַהֲסִרֹתִי אֶת־כַּפִּי וְרָאִיתָ אֶת־אֲחֹרָי
וּפָנַי לֹא יֵרָאוּ׃ פ
לד וַיֹּאמֶר יְהֹוָה אֶל־מֹשֶׁה פְּסָל־לְךָ שְׁנֵי־
לֻחֹת אֲבָנִים כָּרִאשֹׁנִים וְכָתַבְתִּי עַל־
הַלֻּחֹת אֶת־הַדְּבָרִים אֲשֶׁר הָיוּ עַל־הַלֻּחֹת
הָרִאשֹׁנִים אֲשֶׁר שִׁבַּרְתָּ׃ 2 וֶהְיֵה נָכוֹן לַבֹּקֶר
וְעָלִיתָ בַבֹּקֶר אֶל־הַר סִינַי וְנִצַּבְתָּ לִי שָׁם
עַל־רֹאשׁ הָהָר׃ 3 וְאִישׁ לֹא־יַעֲלֶה עִמָּךְ

tributes of God that seem to be more abstract manifestations of the Divine than the *kavod* that Moses asked for.

***20. "But you cannot see My face."*** Here *panim* ("face") refers to a manifestation of the Divine that is too intense for a human to experience safely. This verse seems to contradict the earlier account of Moses' encounters with God "face to face" in the Tent of Meeting (33:11), although that phrase may not be meant literally but rather may denote intense intimacy.

***23. "My hand . . . My back . . . My face."*** Verses 21–23 present one of the most rigorously anthropomorphic representations of God in the Torah. The references to God's face, hand, and back must be understood in literal terms. The radical anthropomorphism communicates a vision of God that is simultaneously dangerously transcendent and intimately protective: God's body shields Moses from God's face (*panim*), which is portrayed as so intense that viewing it would be fatal.

## *Restoration of the Covenant* (34:1–35)

In the final unit of the parashah, God restores the covenant with Israel, thus affirming that reconciliation is possible, even after a dramatic violation of their relationship. Unlike in Exodus 32, when Moses descends the mountain in fury and breaks the two tablets inscribed by God, this time Moses comes down from Mount Sinai with the new tablets he wrote himself and with his face radiant with his encounter with the Divine.

### REVELATION OF GOD'S NAME (34:1–9)

The preparations for this divine encounter resemble the first Sinaitic revelation in Exodus 19–20, but now only Moses can set foot anywhere on the mountain. After exploring various means of divine revelation in Exodus 33, the text reverts to the revelation of the divine name as a central means of divine revelation. (On God's name, see at 3:14 and 6:2.)

ther shall the flocks and the herds graze at the foot of this mountain."

[4]So Moses carved two tablets of stone, like the first, and early in the morning he went up on Mount Sinai, as יהוה had commanded him, taking the two stone tablets with him. [5]יהוה came down in a cloud—and stood with him there, proclaiming the name Eternal. [6]יהוה passed before him and proclaimed: "יהוה! יהוה! a God compassionate and gracious, slow to anger, abounding in kindness and faithfulness, [7]extending kindness to the thousandth generation, forgiving iniquity, transgression, and sin—yet not remitting all punishment, but visiting the iniquity of parents upon children and children's children, upon the third and fourth generations."

[8]Moses hastened to bow low to the ground in homage, [9]and said, "If I have gained Your favor, O my lord, pray, let my lord go in our midst, even though this is a stiffnecked people. Pardon our iniquity and our sin, and take us for Your own!"

[10][God] said: I hereby make a covenant. Before all your people I will work such wonders as have not been wrought on all the earth or in any nation; and all the people who are with you shall see how awesome are יהוה's deeds which I will perform for you. [11]Mark well what I command you this day. I will drive out before you the Amorites, the Canaanites,

וְגַם־אִישׁ אַל־יֵרָא בְּכָל־הָהָר גַּם־הַצֹּאן
וְהַבָּקָר אַל־יִרְעוּ אֶל־מוּל הָהָר הַהוּא׃
4 וַיִּפְסֹל שְׁנֵי־לֻחֹת אֲבָנִים כָּרִאשֹׁנִים
וַיַּשְׁכֵּם מֹשֶׁה בַבֹּקֶר וַיַּעַל אֶל־הַר סִינַי
כַּאֲשֶׁר צִוָּה יְהֹוָה אֹתוֹ וַיִּקַּח בְּיָדוֹ שְׁנֵי לֻחֹת
אֲבָנִים׃ 5 וַיֵּרֶד יְהֹוָה בֶּעָנָן וַיִּתְיַצֵּב עִמּוֹ
שָׁם וַיִּקְרָא בְשֵׁם יְהֹוָה׃ 6 וַיַּעֲבֹר יְהֹוָה ׀ עַל־
פָּנָיו וַיִּקְרָא יְהֹוָה ׀ יְהֹוָה אֵל רַחוּם וְחַנּוּן
אֶרֶךְ אַפַּיִם וְרַב־חֶסֶד וֶאֱמֶת׃ 7 נֹצֵר חֶסֶד
לָאֲלָפִים נֹשֵׂא עָוֺן וָפֶשַׁע וְחַטָּאָה וְנַקֵּה לֹא
יְנַקֶּה פֹּקֵד ׀ עֲוֺן אָבוֹת עַל־בָּנִים וְעַל־בְּנֵי
בָנִים עַל־שִׁלֵּשִׁים וְעַל־רִבֵּעִים׃
8 וַיְמַהֵר מֹשֶׁה וַיִּקֹּד אַרְצָה וַיִּשְׁתָּחוּ׃
9 וַיֹּאמֶר אִם־נָא מָצָאתִי חֵן בְּעֵינֶיךָ אֲדֹנָי
יֵלֶךְ־נָא אֲדֹנָי בְּקִרְבֵּנוּ כִּי עַם־קְשֵׁה־
עֹרֶף הוּא וְסָלַחְתָּ לַעֲוֺנֵנוּ וּלְחַטָּאתֵנוּ
וּנְחַלְתָּנוּ׃
10 וַיֹּאמֶר הִנֵּה אָנֹכִי כֹּרֵת בְּרִית נֶגֶד כָּל־
עַמְּךָ אֶעֱשֶׂה נִפְלָאֹת אֲשֶׁר לֹא־נִבְרְאוּ
בְכָל־הָאָרֶץ וּבְכָל־הַגּוֹיִם וְרָאָה כָל־הָעָם
אֲשֶׁר־אַתָּה בְקִרְבּוֹ אֶת־מַעֲשֵׂה יְהֹוָה כִּי־
נוֹרָא הוּא אֲשֶׁר אֲנִי עֹשֶׂה עִמָּךְ׃ 11 שְׁמָר־
לְךָ אֵת אֲשֶׁר אָנֹכִי מְצַוְּךָ הַיּוֹם הִנְנִי גֹרֵשׁ

*6–7.* This divine self-description, referred to in the post-biblical period as the "Thirteen Attributes," becomes a core part of the Jewish penitential liturgy for the High Holy Days, festivals, and fast days. This declaration asserts that God grants abundant mercy to the faithful and also inflicts trans-generational punishment for transgressors. (This last point is omitted from the liturgical uses of this passage.)

### TERMS OF THE COVENANT (34:10–28)

God responds to Moses' request to accompany and pardon the people by restoring the covenant. This passage begins with God's promise to drive out the current inhabitants of Canaan. In exchange, the Israelites are to refrain from forming alliances with these inhabitants and to commit to a set of commandments similar, but not identical, to those in Exodus 24.

*11–12.* ***I will drive out . . . Beware of making a covenant.*** If God drives out all the inhabitants, how can the Israelites make covenants with them? The conflict in this promise and admonition reflects a tension between two accounts of the settlement of the Promised Land in Joshua and Judges. In one version, the indigenous people are utterly displaced or destroyed; in the other, the Israelites live alongside them in the land.

the Hittites, the Perizzites, the Hivites, and the Jebusites. [12]Beware of making a covenant with the inhabitants of the land against which you are advancing, lest they be a snare in your midst. [13]No, you must tear down their altars, smash their pillars, and cut down their sacred posts; [14]for you must not worship any other god, because יהוה, whose name is Impassioned, is an impassioned God. [15]You must not make a covenant with the inhabitants of the land, for they will lust after their gods and sacrifice to their gods and invite you, and you will eat of their sacrifices. [16]And when you take wives from among their daughters for your sons, their daughters will lust after their gods and will cause your sons to lust after their gods.

[17]You shall not make molten gods for yourselves.

[18]You shall observe the Feast of Unleavened Bread—eating unleavened bread for seven days, as I have commanded you—at the set time of the month of Abib, for in the month of Abib you went forth from Egypt.

[19]Every first issue of the womb is Mine, from all

מִפָּנֶיךָ אֶת־הָאֱמֹרִי וְהַכְּנַעֲנִי וְהַחִתִּי וְהַפְּרִזִּי
וְהַחִוִּי וְהַיְבוּסִי׃ 12 הִשָּׁמֶר לְךָ פֶּן־תִּכְרֹת
בְּרִית לְיוֹשֵׁב הָאָרֶץ אֲשֶׁר אַתָּה בָּא
עָלֶיהָ פֶּן־יִהְיֶה לְמוֹקֵשׁ בְּקִרְבֶּךָ׃ 13 כִּי אֶת־
מִזְבְּחֹתָם תִּתֹּצוּן וְאֶת־מַצֵּבֹתָם תְּשַׁבֵּרוּן
וְאֶת־אֲשֵׁרָיו תִּכְרֹתוּן׃ 14 כִּי לֹא תִשְׁתַּחֲוֶה
לְאֵל אַחֵר כִּי יְהוָה קַנָּא שְׁמוֹ אֵל קַנָּא
הוּא׃ 15 פֶּן־תִּכְרֹת בְּרִית לְיוֹשֵׁב הָאָרֶץ וְזָנוּ
אַחֲרֵי אֱלֹהֵיהֶם וְזָבְחוּ לֵאלֹהֵיהֶם וְקָרָא
לְךָ וְאָכַלְתָּ מִזִּבְחוֹ׃ 16 וְלָקַחְתָּ מִבְּנֹתָיו
לְבָנֶיךָ וְזָנוּ בְנֹתָיו אַחֲרֵי אֱלֹהֵיהֶן וְהִזְנוּ
אֶת־בָּנֶיךָ אַחֲרֵי אֱלֹהֵיהֶן׃
17 אֱלֹהֵי מַסֵּכָה לֹא תַעֲשֶׂה־לָּךְ׃
18 אֶת־חַג הַמַּצּוֹת תִּשְׁמֹר שִׁבְעַת יָמִים
תֹּאכַל מַצּוֹת אֲשֶׁר צִוִּיתִךָ לְמוֹעֵד חֹדֶשׁ
הָאָבִיב כִּי בְּחֹדֶשׁ הָאָבִיב יָצָאתָ
מִמִּצְרָיִם׃
19 כָּל־פֶּטֶר רֶחֶם לִי וְכָל־מִקְנְךָ תִּזָּכָר פֶּטֶר

*12–15.* Covenants with the indigenous people are viewed as dangerous because they will lead to the worship of foreign gods.

*13. sacred posts.* Heb. *asherim* (which appears in the Bible also with a feminine plural, *asherot*; singular *asherah*). These ritual objects were probably associated with the goddess Asherah, a goddess who is identified in 14th-century-B.C.E. Ugaritic (northern Canaanite) texts as the consort of the high god El, and who is mentioned in the Bible in conjunction with the Canaanite god Baal. In addition, inscriptions from ancient Israel identify Asherah apparently as the companion of the God of Israel. These inscriptions, and the repeated polemics against the *asherim* in the Bible, suggest that worship of Asherah through prayers and ritual objects was once a common part of Israelite worship. The rise of strict monotheism in ancient Israel and its insistence on the legitimacy of only one God mandated Asherah's elimination.

*16. And when you take wives.* The Bible expresses a range of views about marriage between Israelites and non-Israelites, from the prohibition of all marriages between Israelites and non-Israelites, to the ban on marriages between Israelite men and indigenous women of Canaan as seen here. Such marriages are viewed as risky because the women might lure their husbands into the worship of other gods. (See also Another View, p. 514.)

*19. Every first issue.* In ancient Israel, as similarly in many ancient cultures, the "first-born" of select animals and humans—males only—were perceived as belonging to God and were returned to the deity either through sacrifice or a redemptive substitution. (See also at 13:2, 15; Leviticus 27:26–27; Deuteronomy 15:19–23.)

your livestock that drop a male as firstling, whether cattle or sheep. [20]But the firstling of an ass you shall redeem with a sheep; if you do not redeem it, you must break its neck. And you must redeem every male first-born among your children.

None shall appear before Me empty-handed.

[21]Six days you shall work, but on the seventh day you shall cease from labor; you shall cease from labor even at plowing time and harvest time.

[22]You shall observe the Feast of Weeks, of the first fruits of the wheat harvest; and the Feast of Ingathering at the turn of the year. [23]Three times a year all your males shall appear before the Sovereign יהוה, the God of Israel. [24]I will drive out nations from your path and enlarge your territory; no one will covet your land when you go up to appear before your God יהוה three times a year.

[25]You shall not offer the blood of My sacrifice with anything leavened; and the sacrifice of the Feast of Passover shall not be left lying until morning.

[26]The choice first fruits of your soil you shall bring to the house of your God יהוה.

You shall not boil a kid in its mother's milk.

[27]And יהוה said to Moses: Write down these commandments, for in accordance with these commandments I make a covenant with you and with Israel.

[28]And he was there with יהוה forty days and forty nights; he ate no bread and drank no water; and he wrote down on the tablets the terms of the covenant, the Ten Commandments.

[29]So Moses came down from Mount Sinai. And as Moses came down from the mountain bearing

שׁוֹר וָשֶׂה׃ 20 וּפֶטֶר חֲמוֹר תִּפְדֶּה בְשֶׂה
וְאִם־לֹא תִפְדֶּה וַעֲרַפְתּוֹ כֹּל בְּכוֹר בָּנֶיךָ
תִּפְדֶּה
וְלֹא־יֵרָאוּ פָנַי רֵיקָם׃
21 שֵׁשֶׁת יָמִים תַּעֲבֹד וּבַיּוֹם הַשְּׁבִיעִי
תִּשְׁבֹּת בֶּחָרִישׁ וּבַקָּצִיר תִּשְׁבֹּת׃
22 וְחַג שָׁבֻעֹת תַּעֲשֶׂה לְךָ בִּכּוּרֵי קְצִיר
חִטִּים וְחַג הָאָסִיף תְּקוּפַת הַשָּׁנָה׃ 23 שָׁלֹשׁ
פְּעָמִים בַּשָּׁנָה יֵרָאֶה כָּל־זְכוּרְךָ אֶת־פְּנֵי
הָאָדֹן ׀ יְהוָה אֱלֹהֵי יִשְׂרָאֵל׃ 24 כִּי־אוֹרִישׁ
גּוֹיִם מִפָּנֶיךָ וְהִרְחַבְתִּי אֶת־גְּבֻלֶךָ וְלֹא־
יַחְמֹד אִישׁ אֶת־אַרְצְךָ בַּעֲלֹתְךָ לֵרָאוֹת
אֶת־פְּנֵי יְהוָה אֱלֹהֶיךָ שָׁלֹשׁ פְּעָמִים
בַּשָּׁנָה׃
25 לֹא־תִשְׁחַט עַל־חָמֵץ דַּם־זִבְחִי וְלֹא־יָלִין
לַבֹּקֶר זֶבַח חַג הַפָּסַח׃
26 רֵאשִׁית בִּכּוּרֵי אַדְמָתְךָ תָּבִיא בֵּית יְהוָה
אֱלֹהֶיךָ
לֹא־תְבַשֵּׁל גְּדִי בַּחֲלֵב אִמּוֹ׃ פ
27 וַיֹּאמֶר יְהוָה אֶל־מֹשֶׁה כְּתָב־לְךָ אֶת־
הַדְּבָרִים הָאֵלֶּה כִּי עַל־פִּי ׀ הַדְּבָרִים הָאֵלֶּה
כָּרַתִּי אִתְּךָ בְּרִית וְאֶת־יִשְׂרָאֵל׃
28 וַיְהִי־שָׁם עִם־יְהוָה אַרְבָּעִים יוֹם
וְאַרְבָּעִים לַיְלָה לֶחֶם לֹא אָכַל וּמַיִם לֹא
שָׁתָה וַיִּכְתֹּב עַל־הַלֻּחֹת אֵת דִּבְרֵי הַבְּרִית
עֲשֶׂרֶת הַדְּבָרִים׃
29 וַיְהִי בְּרֶדֶת מֹשֶׁה מֵהַר סִינַי וּשְׁנֵי לֻחֹת
הָעֵדֻת בְּיַד־מֹשֶׁה בְּרִדְתּוֹ מִן־הָהָר וּמֹשֶׁה

*23. all your males shall appear.* The requirement to celebrate these three festivals is limited to men here and in 23:17. In contrast, Deuteronomy 16:11–16 requires women to participate in the festivals, although only men are required to make pilgrimage to Jerusalem.

A VISIBLE CHANGE IN MOSES (34:29–35)

Moses is physically transformed by his intimate encounter with God. The rays of light radiating from his face provide evidence of his relationship with God; and they inspire fear and, at least tempo-

the two tablets of the Pact, Moses was not aware that the skin of his face was radiant, since he had spoken with God. [30]Aaron and all the Israelites saw that the skin of Moses' face was radiant; and they shrank from coming near him. [31]But Moses called to them, and Aaron and all the chieftains in the assembly returned to him, and Moses spoke to them. [32]Afterward all the Israelites came near, and he instructed them concerning all that יהוה had imparted to him on Mount Sinai. [33]And when Moses had finished speaking with them, he put a veil over his face.

[34]Whenever Moses went in before יהוה to converse, he would leave the veil off until he came out; and when he came out and told the Israelites what he had been commanded, [35]the Israelites would see how radiant the skin of Moses' face was. Moses would then put the veil back over his face until he went in to speak with God.

לֹא־יָדַ֗ע כִּ֣י קָרַ֛ן ע֥וֹר פָּנָ֖יו בְּדַבְּר֥וֹ אִתּֽוֹ׃
30 וַיַּ֨רְא אַהֲרֹ֜ן וְכׇל־בְּנֵ֤י יִשְׂרָאֵל֙ אֶת־מֹשֶׁ֔ה וְהִנֵּ֥ה קָרַ֖ן ע֣וֹר פָּנָ֑יו וַיִּֽירְא֖וּ מִגֶּ֥שֶׁת אֵלָֽיו׃
31 וַיִּקְרָ֤א אֲלֵהֶם֙ מֹשֶׁ֔ה וַיָּשֻׁ֧בוּ אֵלָ֛יו אַהֲרֹ֥ן וְכׇל־הַנְּשִׂאִ֖ים בָּעֵדָ֑ה וַיְדַבֵּ֥ר מֹשֶׁ֖ה אֲלֵהֶֽם׃
32 וְאַֽחֲרֵי־כֵ֥ן נִגְּשׁ֖וּ כׇּל־בְּנֵ֣י יִשְׂרָאֵ֑ל וַיְצַוֵּ֕ם אֵת֩ כׇּל־אֲשֶׁ֨ר דִּבֶּ֧ר יְהֹוָ֛ה אִתּ֖וֹ בְּהַ֥ר סִינָֽי׃
33 וַיְכַ֣ל מֹשֶׁ֔ה מִדַּבֵּ֖ר אִתָּ֑ם וַיִּתֵּ֥ן עַל־פָּנָ֖יו מַסְוֶֽה׃
34 וּבְבֹ֨א מֹשֶׁ֜ה לִפְנֵ֤י יְהֹוָה֙ לְדַבֵּ֣ר אִתּ֔וֹ יָסִ֥יר אֶת־הַמַּסְוֶ֖ה עַד־צֵאת֑וֹ וְיָצָ֗א וְדִבֶּר֙ אֶל־בְּנֵ֣י יִשְׂרָאֵ֔ל אֵ֖ת אֲשֶׁ֥ר יְצֻוֶּֽה׃ 35 וְרָא֤וּ בְנֵֽי־ יִשְׂרָאֵל֙ אֶת־פְּנֵ֣י מֹשֶׁ֔ה כִּ֣י קָרַ֔ן ע֖וֹר פְּנֵ֣י מֹשֶׁ֑ה וְהֵשִׁ֨יב מֹשֶׁ֤ה אֶת־הַמַּסְוֶה֙ עַל־פָּנָ֔יו עַד־בֹּא֖וֹ לְדַבֵּ֥ר אִתּֽוֹ׃ ס

---

rarily, respectful obedience from the Israelites. This supernatural transformation validates Moses' role as a legitimate mediator between God and Israel, the third strategy for maintaining a relationship with God.

**29.** *the skin of his face was radiant.* Heb. *karan or panav*, literally probably "the skin of his face radiated." The words *karan or* were understood by Christian interpreters to mean "horns of light," which led to the depiction of Moses with horns

by many Christian Renaissance artists. Other scholars have argued that "horns" is in fact the correct translation. According to such a reading, as a result of his intimate encounter with God, Moses is supernaturally marked with the sacred symbol of Israel's God.

**30.** *they shrank from coming near him.* In 33:12–23, concern was expressed about the revelation of God's face; here it is Moses' face that bears the fearsome mark of his intimacy with God.

—*Elsie R. Stern*

## *Another View*

The verse in this parashah forbidding Israelite "sons" to marry non-Israelite "daughters" (34:16) has troubled many readers, both because of its negative view of outsiders and because of the way it denigrates the religious beliefs of foreign women. On each count, however, closer scrutiny provides a more nuanced, less problematic understanding.

The one-sided nature of this mandate—forbidding men but not women from marrying out (exogamy)—differs from other biblical texts (like Deuteronomy 7:3) that proscribe exogamy for both women and men. Such gender-inclusive prohibitions express larger concerns for setting ethnic boundaries. Forbidding only non-Israelite *wives* may represent a different practice or tradition, one sensitive to the family dynamics of agrarian societies.

The justification for prohibiting foreign wives in Exodus 34:16 is that it will prevent the worship of foreign gods. This religious reason should be understood in broader terms, with foreign religion standing for the cultural patterns of another people. Endogamous marriages—in which wives shared the same culture as their husbands—perhaps better served community needs. Such brides would be well versed in the particular social customs and technologies necessary for household life, an important consideration in the precarious environment of the farming communities of the biblical period. Thus, marrying an Israelite woman was likely a strategy for survival, not an expression of cultural disdain.

In this respect, note that none of the biblical statements against intermarriage (like Genesis 24:3 or Nehemiah 13:25–27) are absolute prohibitions; they are concerned only with marrying members of local populations. After all, several prominent biblical figures—both women (such as Bathsheba and Esther) and men (such as Moses, David, and Solomon)—have foreign spouses.

> *In Israelite households, it was women who dominated religious praxis.*

Although the religious motivation given in 34:16 for eschewing foreign brides may represent an aversion to foreign culture more generally, it is nonetheless instructive to note that the verse depicts the religious (cultural) practices of women as being more powerful than those of their husbands. Such a view is consonant with what is known about the dynamics of Israelite households: women dominated household religious praxis and exercised considerable managerial control over household life. —*Carol Meyers*

## *Post-biblical Interpretations*

***See, I have singled out by name Bezalel . . . I have endowed him with . . . skill, ability, and knowledge*** (31:2–3). According to rabbinic midrash, Miriam's husband was Caleb (*Sh'mot Rabbah* 1.17; *Sifrei B'midbar* 78; BT *Sotah* 12a); given that Bezalel—the craftsman who designed the Tabernacle and supervised its construction—was Caleb's great-grandson (I Chronicles 2:18–20), this means that he was also Miriam's great-grandson. In *Sh'mot Rabbah* 48:3–4, the Rabbis connected Exodus 31:2–3 with Job 28:28, "See! Fear of Adonai is wisdom (*chochmah*); / To shun evil is understanding (*binah*)." They explained that "fear of Adonai" referred to Jochebed and Miriam, whom the Rabbis identified with the God-fearing midwives of Exodus 1:21. Since the reward for fearing God is Torah, Jochebed gave birth to Moses, through whom the Torah was revealed. As for Miriam, because she "shunned evil" she became the great-grandmother of Bezalel, known for his "skill (*chochmah*), ability (*t'vunah*—a noun related to *binah*), and knowledge" (31:3).

***Upon finishing speaking with him . . . ,*** [***God***] ***gave Moses the two tablets*** (31:18). The Hebrew expression rendered here as "upon finishing" (*k'chaloto*) is almost identical to a term that means "as his bride." (The two words differ by one vowel.) Based on that wordplay, the Rabbis sometimes understood part of this verse as: [*God*] *gave Moses, as his bride, the two tablets.* The feminine personification of the Torah as the bride of Israel is an ancient tradition. In *Sh'mot Rabbah* 41.5, the Rabbis declared that when God "gave the Torah to Israel, it was then as dear to them as a bride is to her spouse."

*The Israelite women refused to surrender their earrings for the Golden Calf.*

***all the people took off the gold rings that were in their ears*** (32:2–3). According to Midrash *Pirkei D'Rabbi Eliezer* 45, only the men contributed jewelry; the Israelite women refused to surrender their earrings for the forging of the Golden Calf, rejecting it as "a graven and molten image without any power." In recognition of their faithfulness, God rewarded the women both in this world and the world-to-come. In this world, they received special privileges on Rosh Chodesh (the New Moon), traditionally a day on which Jewish women abstained from work. And in the world-to-come, "women are destined to be renewed like the new moons." (For more on women and Rosh Chodesh, see *P'kudei*, Post-biblical Interpretations, p. 560.)

***As soon as Moses came near the camp . . . he hurled the tablets from his hands*** (32:19). The Rabbis repeatedly compared Israel's rejection of God in favor of the Golden Calf to a woman's sexual betrayal of her fiancé or husband. In *Sh'mot Rabbah* 43.1, they likened Moses' decision to destroy the tablets to the act of a marriage broker, sent by a king to betroth a certain woman. While the broker was en route with the marriage document, the woman "corrupted herself with another man." The broker immediately destroyed the marriage document, saying it was better that she be judged as an unattached wanton woman than as a married woman who had been unfaithful. Similarly, Moses destroyed the tablets, saying it was better that Israel be judged as ignorant and foolish rather than as having deliberately disobeyed the commandments forbidding idolatry that they had just received.

***And*** יהוה ***said to Moses: Write down these commandments*** (34:27). Midrash *D'varim Rabbah* 3.17 asks why the first tablets were written by God and the second set were inscribed by a human being. The reply is another analogy: This is like a king who married a woman and gladly paid for all the expenses of preparing the marriage contract. When he saw his wife behaving in an inappropriate manner with one of his servants, he was enraged and sent her away. His groomsman pled on her behalf and explained that since she was brought up among servants, she did not know her actions were wrong. The king agreed to be reconciled with his wife, but he required the groomsman to pay the costs for a new marriage contract. Similarly, Moses beseeched God to remember that Israel had spent many years in "Egypt, the house of idolatry," and to forgive the lapse with the Golden Calf. Although God agreed to the reconciliation, God's ardor was now cooled and Moses was required to prepare and inscribe the tablets himself. (So also *Sh'mot Rabbah* 47.2.)

—*Judith R. Baskin*

# *Contemporary Reflection*

Years ago, my boyfriend and I climbed the alleged Mount Sinai, with the shower of Perseus streaking the Egyptian night sky with shooting stars. At the summit, as God pulled the sun up from the fragrant desert floor, Jonathan held up a ring and proposed. It is written in *Pirkei Avot*, "Every day a voice goes forth from Sinai" (6:2). That dawn, I heard the reverberation of a sacred voice in the words, "Would you be willing to spend your life with me?"

The revelation at Mount Sinai was a wedding—an eternal, loving joining between God and Israel. The story we read is but a veil covering a radiance we must allow ourselves to know.

This Torah portion, *Ki Tisa*, begins with Moses taking a census. God then chooses Bezalel to be the artisan of the Tabernacle. Moses climbs Mount Sinai, shrouded in mist and mystery, while the Israelites below build their golden idol. When Moses sees this, he breaks the stone tablets, grinds up the golden calf, and makes the Israelites drink it. Moses ascends the mountain a second time. When he descends, his face is so radiant that he must wear a veil.

But a light *ruach* (wind) blows from the west, disturbing the mist, and we see the radiant face just beneath the veil of text.

Moses is the master alchemist. He climbs the mountain, hides in the cleft of the *tzur* (rock). He speaks with the philosopher's stone face to face. He holds the two tablets of prime matter in his hands. When he grinds up the calf into a fine powder, stirs it into water, holds it up into the air, a brilliant liquid shimmering with flakes of gold, he creates a dizzyingly potent potion, a love potion, an elixir of life. A toast!

We drink of it. Our eyes are opened to see beneath the veil. *Ki Tisa* is not about frenzied idol worship, but the detailed description of a spectacular wedding feast between God and the people Israel. God-the-Lover and Moses-the-beloved take a census of who shall be invited, and they make the long guest list: 600,000 and growing. Bezalel is singled out to decorate the Tent, arrange the flowers, and adorn the feast.

Time passes, and we find ourselves in the whirl of the banquet festivity. There is dancing and singing, and in the very center, what seems to be a golden calf. But blink your eyes! It is the glittering pile of precious wedding gifts.

High on the *bimah* (platform), under a *chuppah* (wedding canopy) of cloud, God presents Moses with the marriage contract, our *ketubah*. One commentator points out that 31:18, which is translated "Upon finishing (*ke-challoto*) speaking with him... [God] gave Moses the two tablets," could also be read, with the slight change of one vowel: "And [God] gave Moses as [God's] bride (*ke-challato*)... the two tablets." Moses, our symbolic bride, turns around in the *chuppah* and faces the guests. He lifts the contract for all to see—and then smashes the glass beneath his foot.

> *"Would you be willing to spend your life with me?"*

Now it is time for *yichud*, when husband and wife are alone together for the first time. In 33:12–23, we read excerpts from a conversation between God and Moses that sound particularly romantic: "Pray let me know Your ways, that I may know You and continue in Your favor" (v. 13). "You have truly gained My favor and I have singled you out by name" (v. 17). "Oh, let me behold Your Presence!" (v. 18). "I will make all My goodness pass before you," (v. 19). And, at the end, God's hand reaches out for Moses (v. 22).

Moses comes down from the mountain blushing, a crimson glow in his cheeks. Earlier, when he went into the Tent to meet our Love, he removed his veil, so only God should see his glowing face; but when he leaves the Tent, he lowers the veil.

But this is only one way to imagine this mythic wedding. Instead of seeing *Moses* (representing all the Israelites) as the bride and *God* as the groom, some commentators understand *Israel* to be the groom and *Torah* the bride. In *Midrash HaGadol*, for example, it is written:

> *In the third month... they entered the wilderness of Sinai* (19:1).... [This may be compared] to a king who betrothed a woman, and set a time [for the marriage]. When the time arrived they said: "It is time for the woman to enter the *chuppah*." Similarly, when the time arrived for the Torah to be given, they said, "It is time for the Torah to be given to Israel" (Elliot R. Wolfson, *Circle in the Square*, 1995, p. 4).

Here, Torah is the bride and Israel is the groom.

On the summit of the mountain, within the curtain of cloud, the question of who is marrying whom is enveloped in dreamlike fog. We might even wonder if the true union taking place upon Mount Sinai is perhaps the revelatory union of heavenly *Adonai* with earthbound *Shechinah*: God's masculine and feminine Presence united through Israel, in love.

When the potion wears off, the children of Israel look around them. Once again they are in the desert, long dragged-out footsteps stretching behind them. And they say one to the other, "Love is in this place, and we did not know it! What have we been doing all of this time? Where have we been? Is this the desert, or is it *gan eiden* (Garden of Eden)? Are we lost and alone, or are we this moment caught up in a fierce union with God? Are we wandering with sandals filled with dust, or are we soaring on eagles' wings?"

We look from one to the other—and wonder what is the face beneath the face beneath the face we wear every day. Sometimes the beauty of the other is as allusive as a sunray on the water. We seek the radiant face beneath the veil.

Messy world. Angry, idolatrous world. Tired, hungry, sick, and sorry world. But if we could lift the sooty, splattered veil... we might see...

This thing between God and Israel—it is not that we are in *covenant*. It is that we are in *love*. Every day a voice comes forth from Sinai and begs your answer, "Would you be willing to spend your life with Me?"

*Yes.*

—*Zoë Klein*

# *Voices*

## *We reach for You, our God*

Priscilla Stern

*Exodus 31:12–17*

We reach for You, our God
from our quiet places.
May we stand still,
for a brief moment, and
listen to the rain—
Stand still, for a brief
moment, and watch the
play of sunlight and
shadow on the leaves.
For a brief moment—
listen to the world.

Let us stop the wheels
of every day to be aware of
Shabbat. Find the stillness
of the sanctuary
which the soul cherishes.
Renew the covenant
of an ancient people.

We need a quiet
space to test the balance
of our days. The weight
of our own needs
against the heaviness
of the world's demands.
The balance is
precarious—steady
us with faith.

Quiet places and
stillness—where we will
hear our own best
impulses speak.
Quiet places and
stillness—from which
we will reach out to
each other.

We will find
strength in silence
and with this
strength we will
turn again to Your
service.

## *Will*

Marcia Falk

*Exodus 31:12–17*

Three generations back
my family had only

to light a candle
and the world parted.

Today, Friday afternoon,
I disconnect clocks and phones.

When night fills my house
with passages,

I begin saving
my life.

## *A Song of Descent*

Sue Levi Elwell

*Exodus 32:1–6*

Remembering Egyptian nights
of seductive scents and throbbing drums,
we rubbed the sand from our feet and prepared
to celebrate Your presence among us.

Adorned in jewelry long hidden away,
we claimed beauty again.
Slaves no more,
we stepped into the circle
and began a chant
to glorify You.

Drunk with the first taste of freedom
we thought we saw
the gold in our ears
reflected in Your bovine eyes.

## *Somewhere in Samaria*

Lea Goldberg (transl. Rachel Tzvia Back)

*Exodus 33*

I picked a wildflower and tossed it away.
      I waited
two days in the rain at a forgotten station.
My God, you'll never believe in me again!
      I passed by
so close and didn't recognize you.

## *Sinai Again*

Merle Feld

*Exodus 33*

I'm coming back to this mountain now
alone.
It's quiet,
the barren brush,
the stillness,
match my mood.

I haven't seen you in a long time God,
where've you been keeping yourself?

Me, I've had two kids,
work has its ups and downs,
I'm still married to the same man.

I don't know if you noticed,
but I stopped talking to you.
I called to you,
I called and called,
but you didn't answer,

you pushed me far away,
so far that even I
who has so little pride after all,
even I couldn't bring myself
to come crawling back—
I don't know if you noticed.

I only returned now to walk around,
kick the brush across the sand,
to walk around and think
about us.

This could be a holy place again
if you would just give me a sign—
a thrush or a hare
or a mountain goat
gracefully coming toward me.

## *In Your Image*

Shulamis Yelin

*Exodus 34:6–7*

In your image,
in your image, God,
You made me in your image,
and I reach upward, seeking—
to be like You, God.

Just? Like You I'm vengeful.
Merciful? Like You I seek an understanding
heart.
Jealous? Yes, I'm jealous
and iniquitous
and long suffering—
and like You
I dream to make a world,
(in miniature, God),
to do my bidding.

And loving I can be, yes, loving,
to a penitent punished child.

Yet clearly, God, most clearly,
do I see in me your oneness,
your all-oneness,
your aloneness—
in my heart.

## *To God*

Else Lasker-Schüler (transl. Janine Canan)

*Exodus 33:13; 34:9*

You restrain neither the good, nor the evil stars;
all their moods stream forth.
In my brow the furrow aches,
this deep crown of dusky light.

And my world is silent—
You have not restrained my mood.
God, where are You?

I'd like to lean upon your heart and listen,
immerse myself in your vast presence,
when gold-transfigured in your Realm
of infinitely blissful Light
all the good and the evil fountains roar.

## *Elul*

Rivka Miriam (transl. Linda Stern Zisquit)

*Exodus 34:9*

Here the rocks came to be forgiven
because they couldn't move
and the heights came to receive compassion
for being so distant from earth.
The sea swallowed its waves, embarrassed
for being restless.
Only forgiveness itself, weak-finned
pure as lightning that doesn't burn,
didn't know from whom to beg forgiveness.
Only forgiveness itself
blurred as the line between dusk and sunset
fell on its knees before itself.

# ויקהל ✦ *Vayak'heil*

## EXODUS 35:1–38:20

## *Making a Place for God: The Tabernacle's Components*

PARASHAT VAYAK'HEIL ("he convoked") begins the portion of Exodus known as the *descriptive* Tabernacle texts (Exodus 35–40) because they describe the implementation of the earlier instructions. God gives detailed instructions to Moses about the Tabernacle, its materials, and its personnel in Exodus 25–30, known as the *prescriptive* Tabernacle texts because they prescribe what is to be done. While the Golden Calf episode in *Ki Tisa* seems to interrupt the Tabernacle account, its overall message—that the people can sin and still have their covenant with God affirmed—may be an integral part of the Tabernacle concept. The Golden Calf incident indicates that the people seem to doubt God's presence among them and God's commitment to them. Only after that incident is resolved, with God and the people reconciled, can they proceed to build the shrine. The people now feel sure that God will be with them even if they do disobey God's word.

The disobedience that marks the preceding parashah now contrasts sharply with the people's willing complicity in carrying out the directives for building the Tabernacle. An introductory unit (35:1–36:7) reviews the Sabbath precept, describes the collection of donations, and designates the artisans who are to collect and use the materials. The next three units report the implementation of God's commands to build the Tabernacle: the tent (36:8–38), its furnishings (37:1–29), and the courtyard with its installations (38:1–20).

Much of the information presented in the elaborate instructions for making the Tabernacle and priestly vestments (the prescriptive texts in Exodus 25–31) is repeated, at times word-for-word, in this parashah and the next. While the content of the accounts is almost identical, the order is significantly different. Instead of presenting the components in order of degree of sanctity—starting with the Ark and the other golden furnishings—the description of their fabrication proceeds according to technological logic: first the structure itself is erected (36:8–38), then the interior furnishings are made (37:1–29), and finally the courtyard and its installations are constructed (38:1–20). The descriptive texts are somewhat briefer because they omit information about how items are to be used, indicating an interest in fabrication rather than function. Another major difference is that in the descriptive texts Moses is much more prominent than Aaron—the dominant figure in the prescriptive passages. It is fitting that Aaron is less important following the

*The willingness to build the Tabernacle contrasts with the earlier disobedience.*

Golden Calf episode, since he was considered complicit in the people's sinfulness.

Although the priestly personnel apparently are all men, as are the chief artisans, women appear in this parashah as significant contributors of materials. They also are the ones who turn the raw materials of textile production into the requisite fabrics. Because woven fabrics are key components of the tent shrine, the skilled labor of female artisans (35:25–26) is integral to the construction of the Tabernacle (see also *T'rumah,* Another View, p. 467; *P'kudei,* Another View, p. 560). In addition, the surprising mention of "women who performed tasks at the entrance of the Tent of Meeting" (38:8) hints at roles performed by women at the sanctuary.

—*Carol Meyers*

## *Outline*

*I.* Introductory Procedures (35:1–36:7)

- *A.* Sabbath observance (35:1–3)
- *B.* Donations for the Tabernacle (35:4–29)
- *C.* Appointment of artisans (35:30–36:7)

*II.* Building the Tabernacle Structure as a Place of God (36:8–38)

- *A.* Coverings (vv. 8–19)
- *B.* Frames (vv. 20–34)
- *C.* Textile partitions (vv. 35–38)

*III.* Constructing the Interior Furnishings (37:1–29)

- *A.* Ark and its cover (vv. 1–9)
- *B.* Table and menorah (vv. 10–24)
- *C.* Incense altar (vv. 25–28)
- *D.* Anointing oil and incense (v. 29)

*IV.* Completing the Courtyard (38:1–20)

- *A.* Altar and laver (vv. 1–8)
- *B.* Enclosure (vv. 9–20)

35:1

Moses then convoked the whole Israelite community and said to them:

These are the things that יהוה has commanded

לה וַיַּקְהֵ֣ל מֹשֶׁ֗ה אֶֽת־כׇּל־עֲדַ֛ת בְּנֵ֥י
יִשְׂרָאֵ֖ל וַיֹּ֣אמֶר אֲלֵהֶ֑ם
אֵ֚לֶּה הַדְּבָרִ֔ים אֲשֶׁר־צִוָּ֥ה יְהֹוָ֖ה לַעֲשֹׂ֥ת

## *Introductory Procedures* (35:1–36:7)

Before the Israelites begin carrying out the instructions for constructing the Tabernacle, several introductory steps must be taken. The first part of this parashah begins with two directives, the first concerning the Sabbath (35:1–3) and the second concerning materials (35:4–19). Next comes an account of the people's response to this call for contributions (35:20–29). Finally, the appointment of artisans to work with the materials that begin pouring in is announced (35:30–36:7).

### SABBATH OBSERVANCE (35:1–3)

The prescriptive texts containing the instructions for the Tabernacle (Exodus 25–31) concluded with a passage about the Sabbath (31:12–17); the descriptive texts now begin with a somewhat briefer passage on the same subject. The prominence of the day of rest after six days of labor, a contrast to the intensity of the work on the Tabernacle, may relate to the importance of the Sabbath as part of Israelite identity at the time—during or after the exile—when these texts were being collected and redacted. (For the prescriptive text earlier in Exodus that parallels this descriptive section, see 31:12–17.)

*1. **Moses.*** It is fitting that Moses' name appears at the beginning of *Vayak'heil*, for he is mentioned often in this parashah and the next, whereas Aaron's name appears infrequently in these last two *parashot* of Exodus. Here, Mosaic (that is, prophetic) leadership dominates rather than priestly leadership.

***the whole Israelite community.*** The word for community (*edah*) sometimes refers narrowly to adult males or to officers (as in Numbers 1:2; 27:21); in other instances the term signifies the entire people (see at Exodus 12:3). That the broader sense operates here is indicated by the fact that the Sabbath observance, about which Moses is to speak, includes everyone. Furthermore, when the "whole community" is enjoined to bring materials in v. 4, both women and men explicitly do so (vv. 20, 22). Although (male) priests largely will carry out the cultic activities (see *T'tzaveh*, Another View, p. 489), the sacred shrine itself will belong to the entire community; and the resultant presence of God will benefit everyone.

***things.*** Heb. *d'varim*, which is the same term used for the stipulations ("words") of the Decalogue ("Ten Commandments"; see 20:1 and 34:1). Thus, the Sabbath and Tabernacle directives that follow are conceptually linked to the most significant of all divine commands, the Decalogue, as emblematic of the covenant between God and Israel.


➤ Scholars debate the relationship between the Tabernacle and the Jerusalem Temple.

ANOTHER VIEW ➤ *538*

➤ The *Menorah* is yet a different sort of tree. Who ever heard of a tree perpetually on fire?

CONTEMPORARY REFLECTION ➤ *539*

➤ The Israelite women had used those mirrors for a most holy purpose.

POST-BIBLICAL INTERPRETATIONS ➤ *538*

➤ Those who worship carry away with them / more than they bring.

VOICES ➤ *542*

you to do: [2]On six days work may be done, but on
the seventh day you shall have a sabbath of complete rest, holy to יהוה; whoever does any work on
it shall be put to death. [3]You shall kindle no fire
throughout your settlements on the sabbath day.

[4]Moses said further to the whole community of
Israelites:

This is what יהוה has commanded: [5]Take from
among you gifts to יהוה; everyone whose heart is so
moved shall bring them—gifts for יהוה: gold, silver,
and copper; [6]blue, purple, and crimson yarns, fine
linen, and goats' hair; [7]tanned ram skins, dolphin
skins, and acacia wood; [8]oil for lighting, spices for
the anointing oil and for the aromatic incense;

אֹתָם׃ 2 שֵׁשֶׁת יָמִים תֵּעָשֶׂה מְלָאכָה וּבַיּוֹם
הַשְּׁבִיעִי יִהְיֶה לָכֶם קֹדֶשׁ שַׁבַּת שַׁבָּתוֹן
לַיהוָֹה כָּל־הָעֹשֶׂה בוֹ מְלָאכָה יוּמָת׃
3 לֹא־תְבַעֲרוּ אֵשׁ בְּכֹל מֹשְׁבֹתֵיכֶם בְּיוֹם
הַשַּׁבָּת׃ פ
4 וַיֹּאמֶר מֹשֶׁה אֶל־כָּל־עֲדַת בְּנֵי־יִשְׂרָאֵל
לֵאמֹר
זֶה הַדָּבָר אֲשֶׁר־צִוָּה יְהוָֹה לֵאמֹר׃ 5 קְחוּ
מֵאִתְּכֶם תְּרוּמָה לַיהוָֹה כֹּל נְדִיב לִבּוֹ
יְבִיאֶהָ אֵת תְּרוּמַת יְהוָֹה זָהָב וָכֶסֶף
וּנְחֹשֶׁת׃ 6 וּתְכֵלֶת וְאַרְגָּמָן וְתוֹלַעַת שָׁנִי
וְשֵׁשׁ וְעִזִּים׃ 7 וְעֹרֹת אֵילִם מְאָדָּמִים וְעֹרֹת
תְּחָשִׁים וַעֲצֵי שִׁטִּים׃ 8 וְשֶׁמֶן לַמָּאוֹר
וּבְשָׂמִים לְשֶׁמֶן הַמִּשְׁחָה וְלִקְטֹרֶת הַסַּמִּים׃

## DONATIONS FOR THE TABERNACLE (35:4–29)

This unit, which elicits the donation of materials for the Tabernacle, is longer and also more systematic than the parallel prescriptive passage in 25:1–9. It specifies not only the materials that are to be collected but also the purposes for which they are to be used. It anticipates the somewhat fuller listing that comes at the completion of the project (39:33–43; compare 31:7–11).

4. ***whole community of Israelites . . . יהוה has commanded.*** The language here again indicates that both women and men are included, and it underscores God's role in this project.

5. ***heart is so moved.*** When the root *n-d-b* ("to be willing, be moved") is used with "heart," it treats the heart as the source of human motivation. In biblical antiquity, people believed the heart to be the identity or essence of a person (see also at 28:29).

***for יהוה.*** The notion that the gifts are for God, which appears twice in this verse and again in v. 24, emphasizes the purpose for which they will be used, namely, to construct God's dwelling place.

***gold, silver, and copper.*** These three metals will be used for the components of the Tabernacle according to their proximity to the Holy of Holies. The most sacred objects will be made of gold.

***copper.*** The Hebrew term also designates bronze (a copper-based alloy), which, given its strength and hardness, is more likely the intended meaning with regard to the Tabernacle.

6. ***blue, purple, and crimson yarns.*** These were the most desirable and expensive yarns in ancient Israel and the wider Near East. (On the manufacture of these yarns and on women's role in this process, see at 25:4; at 35:25–26; *T'rumah*, Another View, p. 467; *P'kudei*, Another View, p. 560.)

7. ***dolphin.*** This meaning of this Hebrew term is uncertain; perhaps it represents a specific color—probably rust—of tanned and dyed sheep- or goat-skin, rather than a sea animal.

8. ***oil.*** Along with its many other vital uses in daily life, olive oil served as a clean-burning lamp fuel, and it was used to consecrate objects and individuals (see at 29:7). Like blood and water, oil was a liquid associated with transformation and holiness. The preparation of olive oil—at least in village settings in the Land of Israel—was likely a woman's task. See further at 27:20.

9 lapis lazuli and other stones for setting, for the ephod and the breastpiece.

10 And let all among you who are skilled come and make all that יהוה has commanded: 11 the Tabernacle, its tent and its covering, its clasps and its planks, its bars, its posts, and its sockets; 12 the ark and its poles, the cover, and the curtain for the screen; 13 the table, and its poles and all its utensils; and the bread of display; 14 the lampstand for lighting, its furnishings and its lamps, and the oil for lighting; 15 the altar of incense and its poles; the anointing oil and the aromatic incense; and the entrance screen for the entrance of the Tabernacle; 16 the altar of burnt offering, its copper grating, its poles, and all its furnishings; the laver and its stand; 17 the hangings of the enclosure, its posts and its sockets, and the screen for the gate of the court; 18 the pegs for the Tabernacle, the pegs for the enclosure, and their cords; 19 the service vestments for officiating in the sanctuary, the sacral vestments of Aaron the priest and the vestments of his sons for priestly service.

20 So the whole community of the Israelites left Moses' presence. 21 And everyone who excelled in

9 וְאַבְנֵי־שֹׁהַם וְאַבְנֵי מִלֻּאִים לָאֵפוֹד
וְלַחֹשֶׁן׃
10 וְכָל־חֲכַם־לֵב בָּכֶם יָבֹאוּ וְיַעֲשׂוּ אֵת כָּל־
אֲשֶׁר צִוָּה יְהֹוָה׃ 11 אֶת־הַמִּשְׁכָּן אֶת־אָהֳלוֹ
וְאֶת־מִכְסֵהוּ אֶת־קְרָסָיו וְאֶת־קְרָשָׁיו אֶת־
בריחו בְּרִיחָיו אֶת־עַמֻּדָיו וְאֶת־אֲדָנָיו׃
12 אֶת־הָאָרֹן וְאֶת־בַּדָּיו אֶת־הַכַּפֹּרֶת וְאֵת
פָּרֹכֶת הַמָּסָךְ׃ 13 אֶת־הַשֻּׁלְחָן וְאֶת־בַּדָּיו
וְאֶת־כָּל־כֵּלָיו וְאֵת לֶחֶם הַפָּנִים׃ 14 וְאֶת־
מְנֹרַת הַמָּאוֹר וְאֶת־כֵּלֶיהָ וְאֶת־נֵרֹתֶיהָ וְאֵת
שֶׁמֶן הַמָּאוֹר׃ 15 וְאֶת־מִזְבַּח הַקְּטֹרֶת וְאֶת־
בַּדָּיו וְאֵת שֶׁמֶן הַמִּשְׁחָה וְאֵת קְטֹרֶת
הַסַּמִּים וְאֶת־מָסַךְ הַפֶּתַח לְפֶתַח הַמִּשְׁכָּן׃
16 אֵת ׀ מִזְבַּח הָעֹלָה וְאֶת־מִכְבַּר הַנְּחֹשֶׁת
אֲשֶׁר־לוֹ אֶת־בַּדָּיו וְאֶת־כָּל־כֵּלָיו אֶת־הַכִּיֹּר
וְאֶת־כַּנּוֹ׃ 17 אֵת קַלְעֵי הֶחָצֵר אֶת־עַמֻּדָיו
וְאֶת־אֲדָנֶיהָ וְאֵת מָסַךְ שַׁעַר הֶחָצֵר׃
18 אֶת־יִתְדֹת הַמִּשְׁכָּן וְאֶת־יִתְדֹת הֶחָצֵר
וְאֶת־מֵיתְרֵיהֶם׃ 19 אֶת־בִּגְדֵי הַשְּׂרָד לְשָׁרֵת
בַּקֹּדֶשׁ אֶת־בִּגְדֵי הַקֹּדֶשׁ לְאַהֲרֹן הַכֹּהֵן
וְאֶת־בִּגְדֵי בָנָיו לְכַהֵן׃
20 וַיֵּצְאוּ כָּל־עֲדַת בְּנֵי־יִשְׂרָאֵל מִלִּפְנֵי
מֹשֶׁה׃ 21 וַיָּבֹאוּ כָּל־אִישׁ אֲשֶׁר־נְשָׂאוֹ לִבּוֹ

*9. lapis lazuli.* More likely onyx or possibly carnelian.

*10. skilled.* Although the commissioning of the artisans does not appear until the end of this parashah, their work is anticipated here. The word "skilled" translates the expression *chacham lev* (literally "wisdom of heart"), a phrase that treats the heart as the source of technical expertise and of wisdom more generally (compare at v. 5).

*11. Tabernacle, its tent and its covering.* The term Tabernacle ("dwelling"; see at 25:8 and 9) here has two components: the tent and its coverings.

*12–15.* The internal furnishings—the ark, table, lampstand, and altar—are listed in the same order as in Exodus 25, with the exception of the gilded incense altar, which in the prescriptive texts is not mentioned until 30:1–10.

*19. service vestments.* Even though the ceremonial priestly garments are not structural items, they are appended to the list of its components because they are considered part of the shrine.

*20. whole community.* As in vv. 1 and 4, this phrase includes women and men. Here, this designation for the people introduces the response to the call for contributions.

*21. everyone.* Heb. *ish,* which sometimes means "man" but here is used generically, as is confirmed in 35:22, 29, and 36:6.

ability and everyone whose spirit was moved came,
bringing to יהוה an offering for the work of the
Tent of Meeting and for all its service and for the
sacral vestments. 22 Men and women, all whose
hearts moved them, all who would make an elevation offering of gold to יהוה, came bringing
brooches, earrings, rings, and pendants—gold objects of all kinds. 23 And everyone who possessed
blue, purple, and crimson yarns, fine linen, goats'
hair, tanned ram skins, and dolphin skins, brought
them; 24 everyone who would make gifts of silver or
copper brought them as gifts for יהוה; and everyone
who possessed acacia wood for any work of the

וְכֹל אֲשֶׁר נָדְבָה רוּחוֹ אֹתוֹ הֵבִיאוּ אֶת־
תְּרוּמַת יְהֹוָה לִמְלֶאכֶת אֹהֶל מוֹעֵד וּלְכָל־
עֲבֹדָתוֹ וּלְבִגְדֵי הַקֹּדֶשׁ׃ 22 וַיָּבֹאוּ הָאֲנָשִׁים
עַל־הַנָּשִׁים כֹּל ׀ נְדִיב לֵב הֵבִיאוּ חָח וָנֶזֶם
וְטַבַּעַת וְכוּמָז כָּל־כְּלִי זָהָב וְכָל־אִישׁ אֲשֶׁר
הֵנִיף תְּנוּפַת זָהָב לַיהֹוָה׃ 23 וְכָל־אִישׁ
אֲשֶׁר־נִמְצָא אִתּוֹ תְּכֵלֶת וְאַרְגָּמָן וְתוֹלַעַת
שָׁנִי וְשֵׁשׁ וְעִזִּים וְעֹרֹת אֵילִם מְאָדָּמִים
וְעֹרֹת תְּחָשִׁים הֵבִיאוּ׃ 24 כָּל־מֵרִים
תְּרוּמַת כֶּסֶף וּנְחֹשֶׁת הֵבִיאוּ אֵת תְּרוּמַת
יְהֹוָה וְכֹל אֲשֶׁר נִמְצָא אִתּוֹ עֲצֵי שִׁטִּים

***who excelled in ability.*** The Hebrew expression (literally "whose heart was lifted") is similar to "skilled" (literally "wise of heart") in v. 10.

***spirit.*** Heb. *ruach*, which refers to the vitalizing force given by God, the "divine spirit" mentioned in 31:3 and 35:31—and manifest in human mental abilities, talents, and emotions.

***Tent of Meeting.*** The term *ohel mo'ed* is an alternate, perhaps more ancient, name for the tent shrine usually called the Tabernacle (see at 27:21 and at 33:7–11).

22. ***Men and women.*** The plural Hebrew word for "women" (*nashim*) appears rarely in Exodus, only six times: in 1:19 in reference to Egyptian women giving birth; in 15:20 to denote the women who performed with Miriam after crossing the sea; in 22:23 (translated "wives") to indicate those who will become widows if their husbands disobey God; in 32:2 to signify the female donors of gold used to make the Golden Calf; here, to designate the female contributors of materials for the Tabernacle (note the singular used in 35:29 and 36:6); and in 35:26 to point out female artisans. More often, women are subsumed under collective "masculine" terminology that is employed inclusively, such as *ish* (in this book often translated generically as "everyone," as in vv. 21, 23, 24) and *b'nei yisrael* ("Israelites"—literally "sons of Israel"). Nevertheless, female terms sometimes are essential, as is the case here because of the gender-specific ownership of the costly items to be donated. That is, women owned valuables and could make decisions, independently of their husbands or fathers, about using them as donations (see also at 25:2). The English translation "men and women" obscures the Hebrew (*ha-anashim al ha-nashim*), which seems to say that the men came "in addition to" the women, perhaps indicating primacy of women as donors.

***whose hearts moved them.*** The narrative underscores that women were motivated to contribute their resources to this sacred endeavor (see at 35:5).

***elevation offering.*** Heb. *t'nufah*, which denotes food offerings in 29:24–27, refers to a special sanctification ritual employed when dedicating something to God. Here, it indicates the special status of the objects to be used for God's dwelling.

***brooches, earrings, rings, and pendants.*** Textual and archeological evidence shows that men as well as women wore various kinds of jewelry in the ancient world. The impulse for self-decoration transcended gender, whether to connote status, to offer protection (because shiny jewelry was believed to keep harmful spirits at bay), to indicate a social or political position, to function in economic transactions, or to indicate piety. Note that in 3:22 both sons and daughters wear the precious metal objects taken from the Egyptians.

23–24. ***possessed . . . possessed.*** The verb (*m-tz-a*,

service brought that. [25]And all the skilled women spun with their own hands, and brought what they had spun, in blue, purple, and crimson yarns, and in fine linen. [26]And all the women who excelled in that skill spun the goats' hair. [27]And the chieftains brought lapis lazuli and other stones for setting, for the ephod and for the breastpiece; [28]and spices and oil for lighting, for the anointing oil, and for the

לְכָל־מְלֶאכֶת הָעֲבֹדָה הֵבִיאוּ׃ 25 וְכָל־
אִשָּׁה חַכְמַת־לֵב בְּיָדֶיהָ טָווּ וַיָּבִיאוּ מַטְוֶה
אֶת־הַתְּכֵלֶת וְאֶת־הָאַרְגָּמָן אֶת־תּוֹלַעַת
הַשָּׁנִי וְאֶת־הַשֵּׁשׁ׃ 26 וְכָל־הַנָּשִׁים אֲשֶׁר
נָשָׂא לִבָּן אֹתָנָה בְּחָכְמָה טָווּ אֶת־הָעִזִּים׃
27 וְהַנְּשִׂאִם הֵבִיאוּ אֵת אַבְנֵי הַשֹּׁהַם וְאֵת
אַבְנֵי הַמִּלֻּאִים לָאֵפוֹד וְלַחֹשֶׁן׃ 28 וְאֶת־
הַבֹּשֶׂם וְאֶת־הַשָּׁמֶן לְמָאוֹר וּלְשֶׁמֶן

"to find") is used here in a passive form to indicate something that "is found" in a given place or with a given person. As shown by the way this verb is used in the legal prescriptions of Exodus (such as 21:16; 22:3), it indicates possession and is tantamount to ownership. Thus, women and men each owned and had the right to dispose of the items listed here.

*25.* This verse and the next one confirm the vital role of women in textile production in the ancient world, a fact confirmed by archeological evidence (see *T'rumah*, Another View, p. 467; *P'kudei*, Another View, p. 560).

***skilled women.*** Literally, "every woman [with] wisdom of the heart," thus indicating technological know-how, as in v. 10. Like other female professionals in ancient Israel (such as midwives and musicians), women who were experts in textile production made important contributions to community life and would have experienced the respect of others for their work and concomitant self-esteem.

***spun with their own hands . . . spun.*** The word for "spin" occurs in the Bible only here and in the next verse, although references to spindles are found in Proverbs 31:19 and elsewhere. Plant and animal fibers, usually no more than a few inches long, cannot be used directly to make textiles; they must first be twisted tightly, by spinning them on a wooden stick (spindle), to form string or yarn. Spinning techniques, developed and carried out almost exclusively by women, were highly developed in ancient Israel and the wider Near East. Because it is such a time-consuming task, women typically gathered together to spin; such gender-specific group activities likely contributed to female bonding and networks. Proverbs 31 presents an idealized but accurate depiction of an adult woman (*eishet chayil*) in a settled community who produces textiles for domestic use and market.

***with their own hands.*** Spinning requires the use of both hands—one to hold the spindle and the other to feed fibers onto it—and even then it is difficult to maintain the separate actions of each hand.

***brought . . . linen.*** The text is elliptical, in that it has mentioned spinning and now specifies the colored woolen and the linen fabrics; it omits the elaborate dying process required to produce the colored yarns. (For more details on this process, see *T'rumah*, Another View, p. 467.)

***26. excelled.*** As in v. 21, a higher level of expertise is indicated for the female spinners.

***spun the goats' hair.*** Extra skill was needed for spinning goats' hair, perhaps because the hairs tend to be shorter than those of sheep and thus more difficult to pull onto a spindle.

***27. chieftains.*** The term for these officials (*nasi* in the singular) is used throughout the priestly literature of the Torah to designate tribal leaders (as in Numbers 1:16). As in any society with different socio-political ranks, gifts and tribute collected by leaders make them more affluent and thus able to provide the costly gemstones mentioned in this verse.

***28. spices and oil.*** These substances for different parts of the ritual are mentioned together here. Although the chieftains bring these items, they likely were prepared by women, who were typically

aromatic incense. 29 Thus the Israelites, all the men and women whose hearts moved them to bring anything for the work that יהוה, through Moses, had commanded to be done, brought it as a freewill offering to יהוה.

30 And Moses said to the Israelites: See, יהוה has singled out by name Bezalel, son of Uri son of Hur, of the tribe of Judah, 31 endowing him with a divine spirit of skill, ability, and knowledge in every kind of craft, 32 and inspiring him to make designs for work in gold, silver, and copper, 33 to cut stones for setting and to carve wood—to work in every kind of designer's craft—34 and to give directions. He and Oholiab son of Ahisamach of the tribe of Dan 35 have been endowed with the skill to do any work—of the carver, the designer, the embroiderer in blue, purple, crimson yarns, and in fine linen, and of the weaver—as workers in all crafts and as

הַמִּשְׁחָה וְלִקְטֹרֶת הַסַּמִּים׃ 29 כָּל־אִישׁ
וְאִשָּׁה אֲשֶׁר נָדַב לִבָּם אֹתָם לְהָבִיא
לְכָל־הַמְּלָאכָה אֲשֶׁר צִוָּה יְהֹוָה לַעֲשׂוֹת
בְּיַד־מֹשֶׁה הֵבִיאוּ בְנֵי־יִשְׂרָאֵל נְדָבָה
לַיהֹוָה׃ פ
30 וַיֹּאמֶר מֹשֶׁה אֶל־בְּנֵי יִשְׂרָאֵל רְאוּ קָרָא
יְהֹוָה בְּשֵׁם בְּצַלְאֵל בֶּן־אוּרִי בֶן־חוּר לְמַטֵּה
יְהוּדָה׃ 31 וַיְמַלֵּא אֹתוֹ רוּחַ אֱלֹהִים
בְּחָכְמָה בִּתְבוּנָה וּבְדַעַת וּבְכָל־מְלָאכָה׃
32 וְלַחְשֹׁב מַחֲשָׁבֹת לַעֲשֹׂת בַּזָּהָב וּבַכֶּסֶף
וּבַנְּחֹשֶׁת׃ 33 וּבַחֲרֹשֶׁת אֶבֶן לְמַלֹּאת
וּבַחֲרֹשֶׁת עֵץ לַעֲשׂוֹת בְּכָל־מְלֶאכֶת
מַחֲשָׁבֶת׃ 34 וּלְהוֹרֹת נָתַן בְּלִבּוֹ הוּא
וְאָהֳלִיאָב בֶּן־אֲחִיסָמָךְ לְמַטֵּה־דָן׃ 35 מִלֵּא
אֹתָם חָכְמַת־לֵב לַעֲשׂוֹת כָּל־מְלֶאכֶת
חָרָשׁ ׀ וְחֹשֵׁב וְרֹקֵם בַּתְּכֵלֶת וּבָאַרְגָּמָן
בְּתוֹלַעַת הַשָּׁנִי וּבַשֵּׁשׁ וְאֹרֵג עֹשֵׂי כָּל־

the "perfumers" in ancient Israel (see I Samuel 8:13). Women's skills in food preparation probably suited them to be the keepers of the special formulas used to produce aromatic substances and fine oils (but see I Chronicles 9:30).

*29. men and women.* This summary of the donation of materials again emphasizes that everyone—women as well as men—participated (see at v. 22 and 36:6).

*freewill offering.* Heb. *n'davah*, which refers to private and voluntary offerings to God. Although Moses has called for contributions, the gifts are considered voluntary.

## APPOINTMENT OF ARTISANS (35:30–36:7)

With an abundance of materials in hand, the commissioning of the artisans is the last step before the actual construction of the Tabernacle can begin. The designation of these workers, given to Moses prescriptively in 31:1–11, is now announced to the community; and the materials are handed over to the artisans so that they can begin their task.

*32. inspiring him.* The Hebrew here consists of a verb-noun pair from the root *ch-sh-b* ("to think"), thus emphasizing the creativity and brilliance of Bezalel's designs, artisanship, and leadership.

*34. give directions.* Although the translation says "directions," the term generally means basic instruction, which is relevant here. The other workers will owe their artisanship to the teaching abilities of Bezalel and perhaps to those of Bezalel's second-in-command, Oholiab (36:1), who are not only skilled artisans themselves but also skilled teachers.

*35. as workers in all crafts and as makers of designs.* This phrase divides the procedures into execution and planning. Four procedures have been mentioned: carving, designing, embroidering, and weaving.

makers of designs. **36** Let, then, Bezalel and Oholiab and all the skilled persons whom יהוה has endowed with skill and ability to perform expertly all the tasks connected with the service of the sanctuary carry out all that יהוה has commanded.

2 Moses then called Bezalel and Oholiab, and every skilled person whom יהוה had endowed with skill, everyone who excelled in ability, to undertake the task and carry it out. 3 They took over from Moses all the gifts that the Israelites had brought, to carry out the tasks connected with the service of the sanctuary. But when these continued to bring freewill offerings to him morning after morning, 4 all the artisans who were engaged in the tasks of the sanctuary came, from the task upon which each one was engaged, 5 and said to Moses, "The people are bringing more than is needed for the tasks entailed in the work that יהוה has commanded to be done." 6 Moses thereupon had this proclamation made throughout the camp: "Let no man or woman make further effort toward gifts for the sanctuary!" So the people stopped bringing: 7 their efforts had been more than enough for all the tasks to be done.

מְלָאכָה וְחֹשְׁבֵי מַחֲשָׁבֹת׃ **לו** וְעָשָׂה
בְצַלְאֵל וְאָהֳלִיאָב וְכֹל ׀ אִישׁ חֲכַם־לֵב
אֲשֶׁר נָתַן יְהֹוָה חָכְמָה וּתְבוּנָה בָּהֵמָּה
לָדַעַת לַעֲשֹׂת אֶת־כָּל־מְלֶאכֶת עֲבֹדַת
הַקֹּדֶשׁ לְכֹל אֲשֶׁר־צִוָּה יְהֹוָה׃
2 וַיִּקְרָא מֹשֶׁה אֶל־בְּצַלְאֵל וְאֶל־אָהֳלִיאָב
וְאֶל כָּל־אִישׁ חֲכַם־לֵב אֲשֶׁר נָתַן יְהֹוָה
חָכְמָה בְּלִבּוֹ כֹּל אֲשֶׁר נְשָׂאוֹ לִבּוֹ לְקָרְבָה
אֶל־הַמְּלָאכָה לַעֲשֹׂת אֹתָהּ׃ 3 וַיִּקְחוּ
מִלִּפְנֵי מֹשֶׁה אֵת כָּל־הַתְּרוּמָה אֲשֶׁר
הֵבִיאוּ בְּנֵי יִשְׂרָאֵל לִמְלֶאכֶת עֲבֹדַת הַקֹּדֶשׁ
לַעֲשֹׂת אֹתָהּ וְהֵם הֵבִיאוּ אֵלָיו עוֹד
נְדָבָה בַּבֹּקֶר בַּבֹּקֶר׃ 4 וַיָּבֹאוּ כָּל־הַחֲכָמִים
הָעֹשִׂים אֵת כָּל־מְלֶאכֶת הַקֹּדֶשׁ אִישׁ־אִישׁ
מִמְּלַאכְתּוֹ אֲשֶׁר־הֵמָּה עֹשִׂים׃ 5 וַיֹּאמְרוּ
אֶל־מֹשֶׁה לֵּאמֹר מַרְבִּים הָעָם לְהָבִיא מִדֵּי
הָעֲבֹדָה לַמְּלָאכָה אֲשֶׁר־צִוָּה יְהֹוָה לַעֲשֹׂת
אֹתָהּ׃ 6 וַיְצַו מֹשֶׁה וַיַּעֲבִירוּ קוֹל בַּמַּחֲנֶה
לֵאמֹר אִישׁ וְאִשָּׁה אַל־יַעֲשׂוּ־עוֹד מְלָאכָה
לִתְרוּמַת הַקֹּדֶשׁ וַיִּכָּלֵא הָעָם מֵהָבִיא׃
7 וְהַמְּלָאכָה הָיְתָה דַיָּם לְכָל־הַמְּלָאכָה
לַעֲשׂוֹת אֹתָהּ וְהוֹתֵר׃ ס

*36:1. all the skilled persons.* Literally, "every *ish* [with] wisdom of heart." The word *ish* sometimes means "man" but is often used generically when it refers to a category of persons (see at 35:21), as it does here. Because of the mention of "the weaver" in the previous verse, and because the quality of being "wise of heart" was associated specifically with women in 35:25, the present translation presumes that women were among the artisans discussed here.

*2. Moses then called.* God has proclaimed who the artisans will be and has given them the requisite abilities, but it is up to Moses to assemble them.

*3. continued to bring.* Contributions arrive even after construction begins. It seems likely that they are going directly to the artisans, for the builders need to make Moses aware of this overabundance.

*6. proclamation.* Only an official decree from Moses can stop the flow of donations.

*"no man or woman."* Instead of using a generic term for those receiving the injunction to cease bringing materials, for the third time the genders are mentioned separately, probably because of the prominence of women in contributing items for the Tabernacle (see also at 35:22, 29).

[8]Then all the skilled among those engaged in the work made the tabernacle of ten strips of cloth, which they made of fine twisted linen, blue, purple, and crimson yarns; into these they worked a design of cherubim. [9]The length of each cloth was twenty-eight cubits, and the width of each cloth was four cubits, all cloths having the same measurements. [10]They joined five of the cloths to one another, and they joined the other five cloths to one another. [11]They made loops of blue wool on the edge of the outermost cloth of the one set, and did the same on the edge of the outermost cloth of the other set: [12]they made fifty loops on the one cloth, and they made fifty loops on the edge of the end cloth of the other set, the loops being opposite one another. [13]And they made fifty gold clasps and coupled the units to one another with the clasps, so that the tabernacle became one whole.

[14]They made cloths of goats' hair for a tent over the tabernacle; they made the cloths eleven in number. [15]The length of each cloth was thirty cubits, and the width of each cloth was four cubits, the eleven cloths having the same measurements. [16]They joined five of the cloths by themselves, and

8 וַיַּעֲשׂוּ כָל־חֲכַם־לֵב בְּעֹשֵׂי הַמְּלָאכָה אֶת־
הַמִּשְׁכָּן עֶשֶׂר יְרִיעֹת שֵׁשׁ מָשְׁזָר וּתְכֵלֶת
וְאַרְגָּמָן וְתוֹלַעַת שָׁנִי כְּרֻבִים מַעֲשֵׂה חֹשֵׁב
עָשָׂה אֹתָם׃ 9 אֹרֶךְ הַיְרִיעָה הָאַחַת שְׁמֹנֶה
וְעֶשְׂרִים בָּאַמָּה וְרֹחַב אַרְבַּע בָּאַמָּה
הַיְרִיעָה הָאֶחָת מִדָּה אַחַת לְכָל־הַיְרִיעֹת׃
10 וַיְחַבֵּר אֶת־חֲמֵשׁ הַיְרִיעֹת אַחַת אֶל־
אֶחָת וְחָמֵשׁ יְרִיעֹת חִבַּר אַחַת אֶל־אֶחָת׃
11 וַיַּעַשׂ לֻלְאֹת תְּכֵלֶת עַל שְׂפַת הַיְרִיעָה
הָאֶחָת מִקָּצָה בַּמַּחְבָּרֶת כֵּן עָשָׂה בִּשְׂפַת
הַיְרִיעָה הַקִּיצוֹנָה בַּמַּחְבֶּרֶת הַשֵּׁנִית׃
12 חֲמִשִּׁים לֻלָאֹת עָשָׂה בַּיְרִיעָה הָאֶחָת
וַחֲמִשִּׁים לֻלָאֹת עָשָׂה בִּקְצֵה הַיְרִיעָה אֲשֶׁר
בַּמַּחְבֶּרֶת הַשֵּׁנִית מַקְבִּילֹת הַלֻּלָאֹת אַחַת
אֶל־אֶחָת׃ 13 וַיַּעַשׂ חֲמִשִּׁים קַרְסֵי זָהָב
וַיְחַבֵּר אֶת־הַיְרִיעֹת אַחַת אֶל־אַחַת
בַּקְּרָסִים וַיְהִי הַמִּשְׁכָּן אֶחָד׃ פ
14 וַיַּעַשׂ יְרִיעֹת עִזִּים לְאֹהֶל עַל־הַמִּשְׁכָּן
עַשְׁתֵּי־עֶשְׂרֵה יְרִיעֹת עָשָׂה אֹתָם׃ 15 אֹרֶךְ
הַיְרִיעָה הָאַחַת שְׁלֹשִׁים בָּאַמָּה וְאַרְבַּע
אַמּוֹת רֹחַב הַיְרִיעָה הָאֶחָת מִדָּה אַחַת
לְעַשְׁתֵּי עֶשְׂרֵה יְרִיעֹת׃ 16 וַיְחַבֵּר אֶת־חֲמֵשׁ
הַיְרִיעֹת לְבָד וְאֶת־שֵׁשׁ הַיְרִיעֹת לְבָד׃

## *Building the Tabernacle Structure as a Place of God*

(36:8–38)

With materials and artisans assembled, construction work can begin. The narrative proceeds in a fashion that makes sense technologically: here, the components for the structure are fabricated before its furnishings are crafted, whereas in the earlier, prescriptive texts the furnishings come first. However, the internal order of this unit is the same as in the corresponding unit in Exodus 26: first the coverings (36:8–19), then the frames (36:20–34), and finally the textile partitions (36:35–38).

### COVERINGS (36:8–19)

The Tabernacle is a tent. Its major components are two layers of woven textiles (one of a linen-wool mix, the other of goats' hair) covered by two layers (one of ram skins, the other of "dolphin" skins). The various fastening devices are also enumerated. (See further at the prescriptive text that parallels this descriptive section, 26:1–14. On women's roles as textile artisans, see at 35:25.)

***8. tabernacle.*** The translation does not capitalize this word in this passage (vv. 8–19), to indicate that here the Hebrew noun *mishkan* denotes only the dwelling's inner fabric component, which is made of decorated linen.

the other six cloths by themselves. 17 They made
fifty loops on the edge of the outermost cloth of the
one set, and they made fifty loops on the edge of
the end cloth of the other set. 18 They made fifty
copper clasps to couple the Tent together so that
it might become one whole. 19 And they made
a covering of tanned ram skins for the tent, and a
covering of dolphin skins above.

20 They made the planks for the Tabernacle of
acacia wood, upright. 21 The length of each plank
was ten cubits, the width of each plank a cubit and
a half. 22 Each plank had two tenons, parallel to each
other; they did the same with all the planks of
the Tabernacle. 23 Of the planks of the Tabernacle,
they made twenty planks for the south side, 24 making forty silver sockets under the twenty planks,
two sockets under one plank for its two tenons and
two sockets under each following plank for its two
tenons; 25 and for the other side wall of the Tabernacle, the north side, twenty planks, 26 with their
forty silver sockets, two sockets under one plank
and two sockets under each following plank. 27 And
for the rear of the Tabernacle, to the west, they
made six planks; 28 and they made two planks for
the corners of the Tabernacle at the rear. 29 They
matched at the bottom, but terminated as one at
the top into one ring; they did so with both of them
at the two corners. 30 Thus there were eight planks
with their sockets of silver: sixteen sockets, two
under each plank.

17 וַיַּעַשׂ לֻלָאֹת חֲמִשִּׁים עַל שְׂפַת הַיְרִיעָה
הַקִּיצֹנָה בַּמַּחְבָּרֶת וַחֲמִשִּׁים לֻלָאֹת עָשָׂה
עַל־שְׂפַת הַיְרִיעָה הַחֹבֶרֶת הַשֵּׁנִית׃
18 וַיַּעַשׂ קַרְסֵי נְחֹשֶׁת חֲמִשִּׁים לְחַבֵּר אֶת־
הָאֹהֶל לִהְיֹת אֶחָד׃ 19 וַיַּעַשׂ מִכְסֶה לָאֹהֶל
עֹרֹת אֵילִם מְאָדָּמִים וּמִכְסֵה עֹרֹת תְּחָשִׁים
מִלְמָעְלָה׃ ס

20 וַיַּעַשׂ אֶת־הַקְּרָשִׁים לַמִּשְׁכָּן עֲצֵי שִׁטִּים
עֹמְדִים׃ 21 עֶשֶׂר אַמֹּת אֹרֶךְ הַקָּרֶשׁ וְאַמָּה
וַחֲצִי הָאַמָּה רֹחַב הַקֶּרֶשׁ הָאֶחָד׃ 22 שְׁתֵּי
יָדֹת לַקֶּרֶשׁ הָאֶחָד מְשֻׁלָּבֹת אַחַת אֶל־
אֶחָת כֵּן עָשָׂה לְכֹל קַרְשֵׁי הַמִּשְׁכָּן׃ 23 וַיַּעַשׂ
אֶת־הַקְּרָשִׁים לַמִּשְׁכָּן עֶשְׂרִים קְרָשִׁים
לִפְאַת נֶגֶב תֵּימָנָה׃ 24 וְאַרְבָּעִים אַדְנֵי־
כֶסֶף עָשָׂה תַּחַת עֶשְׂרִים הַקְּרָשִׁים שְׁנֵי
אֲדָנִים תַּחַת־הַקֶּרֶשׁ הָאֶחָד לִשְׁתֵּי יְדֹתָיו
וּשְׁנֵי אֲדָנִים תַּחַת־הַקֶּרֶשׁ הָאֶחָד לִשְׁתֵּי
יְדֹתָיו׃ 25 וּלְצֶלַע הַמִּשְׁכָּן הַשֵּׁנִית לִפְאַת
צָפוֹן עָשָׂה עֶשְׂרִים קְרָשִׁים׃ 26 וְאַרְבָּעִים
אַדְנֵיהֶם כָּסֶף שְׁנֵי אֲדָנִים תַּחַת הַקֶּרֶשׁ
הָאֶחָד וּשְׁנֵי אֲדָנִים תַּחַת הַקֶּרֶשׁ הָאֶחָד׃
27 וּלְיַרְכְּתֵי הַמִּשְׁכָּן יָמָּה עָשָׂה שִׁשָּׁה
קְרָשִׁים׃ 28 וּשְׁנֵי קְרָשִׁים עָשָׂה לִמְקֻצְעֹת
הַמִּשְׁכָּן בַּיַּרְכָתָיִם׃ 29 וְהָיוּ תוֹאֲמִם
מִלְּמַטָּה וְיַחְדָּו יִהְיוּ תַמִּים אֶל־רֹאשׁוֹ
אֶל־הַטַּבַּעַת הָאֶחָת כֵּן עָשָׂה לִשְׁנֵיהֶם
לִשְׁנֵי הַמִּקְצֹעֹת׃ 30 וְהָיוּ שְׁמֹנָה קְרָשִׁים
וְאַדְנֵיהֶם כֶּסֶף שִׁשָּׁה עָשָׂר אֲדָנִים שְׁנֵי
אֲדָנִים שְׁנֵי אֲדָנִים תַּחַת הַקֶּרֶשׁ הָאֶחָד׃

### FRAMES (36:20–34)

The structure's frame is to be constructed of a complex system of gilded boards and bars with metal fastenings; the frame is to be set into bases (see at 26:15–30).

[31]They made bars of acacia wood, five for the planks of the one side wall of the Tabernacle, [32]five bars for the planks of the other side wall of the Tabernacle, and five bars for the planks of the wall of the Tabernacle at the rear, to the west; [33]they made the center bar to run, halfway up the planks, from end to end. [34]They overlaid the planks with gold, and made their rings of gold, as holders for the bars; and they overlaid the bars with gold.

[35]They made the curtain of blue, purple, and crimson yarns, and fine twisted linen, working into it a design of cherubim. [36]They made for it four posts of acacia wood and overlaid them with gold, with their hooks of gold; and they cast for them four silver sockets.

[37]They made the screen for the entrance of the Tent, of blue, purple, and crimson yarns, and fine twisted linen, done in embroidery; [38]and five posts for it with their hooks. They overlaid their tops and their bands with gold; but the five sockets were of copper.

**37** Bezalel made the ark of acacia wood, two and a half cubits long, a cubit and a half wide, and a cubit and a half high. [2]He overlaid it with pure gold, inside and out; and he made a gold molding for it round about. [3]He cast four gold rings for it, for its four feet: two rings on one of its side walls

31 וַיַּעַשׂ בְּרִיחֵי עֲצֵי שִׁטִּים חֲמִשָּׁה לְקַרְשֵׁי
צֶלַע־הַמִּשְׁכָּן הָאֶחָת׃ 32 וַחֲמִשָּׁה בְרִיחִם
לְקַרְשֵׁי צֶלַע־הַמִּשְׁכָּן הַשֵּׁנִית וַחֲמִשָּׁה
בְרִיחִם לְקַרְשֵׁי הַמִּשְׁכָּן לַיַּרְכָתַיִם יָמָּה׃
33 וַיַּעַשׂ אֶת־הַבְּרִיחַ הַתִּיכֹן לִבְרֹחַ בְּתוֹךְ
הַקְּרָשִׁים מִן־הַקָּצֶה אֶל־הַקָּצֶה׃ 34 וְאֶת־
הַקְּרָשִׁים צִפָּה זָהָב וְאֶת־טַבְּעֹתָם עָשָׂה
זָהָב בָּתִּים לַבְּרִיחִם וַיְצַף אֶת־הַבְּרִיחִם
זָהָב׃
35 וַיַּעַשׂ אֶת־הַפָּרֹכֶת תְּכֵלֶת וְאַרְגָּמָן
וְתוֹלַעַת שָׁנִי וְשֵׁשׁ מָשְׁזָר מַעֲשֵׂה חֹשֵׁב
עָשָׂה אֹתָהּ כְּרֻבִים׃ 36 וַיַּעַשׂ לָהּ אַרְבָּעָה
עַמּוּדֵי שִׁטִּים וַיְצַפֵּם זָהָב וָוֵיהֶם זָהָב וַיִּצֹק
לָהֶם אַרְבָּעָה אַדְנֵי־כָסֶף׃
37 וַיַּעַשׂ מָסָךְ לְפֶתַח הָאֹהֶל תְּכֵלֶת וְאַרְגָּמָן
וְתוֹלַעַת שָׁנִי וְשֵׁשׁ מָשְׁזָר מַעֲשֵׂה רֹקֵם׃
38 וְאֶת־עַמּוּדָיו חֲמִשָּׁה וְאֶת־וָוֵיהֶם וְצִפָּה
רָאשֵׁיהֶם וַחֲשֻׁקֵיהֶם זָהָב וְאַדְנֵיהֶם חֲמִשָּׁה
נְחֹשֶׁת׃ פ
לז וַיַּעַשׂ בְּצַלְאֵל אֶת־הָאָרֹן עֲצֵי שִׁטִּים
אַמָּתַיִם וָחֵצִי אָרְכּוֹ וְאַמָּה וָחֵצִי רָחְבּוֹ
וְאַמָּה וָחֵצִי קֹמָתוֹ׃ 2 וַיְצַפֵּהוּ זָהָב טָהוֹר
מִבַּיִת וּמִחוּץ וַיַּעַשׂ לוֹ זֵר זָהָב סָבִיב׃
3 וַיִּצֹק לוֹ אַרְבַּע טַבְּעֹת זָהָב עַל אַרְבַּע
פַּעֲמֹתָיו וּשְׁתֵּי טַבָּעֹת עַל־צַלְעוֹ הָאֶחָת

### TEXTILE PARTITIONS (36:35–38)

This passage describes the construction of the fabric divider ("curtain" or *parochet*) that will separate the large interior space into two main sections: the Holy of Holies, and the Holy space—where the daily and weekly rituals of light, incense, and bread are to take place. The other divider ("screen") will separate the interior space from the surrounding courtyard. (See further at the prescriptive text that parallels this descriptive section, 26:31–37.)

## *Constructing the Interior Furnishings* (37:1–29)

Once the directions for making the tent's components have been obeyed, the narrative turns to the furnishings for its interior. The furnishings are made in the order for which instructions have been given in Exodus 25: first the Ark and its cover, followed by the offering table, and then the menorah. However, this unit differs from the prescriptive texts in that it includes the golden incense altar,

and two rings on the other. 4He made poles of
acacia wood, overlaid them with gold, 5and inserted
the poles into the rings on the side walls of the ark
for carrying the ark.
6He made a cover of pure gold, two and a half
cubits long and a cubit and a half wide. 7He made
two cherubim of gold; he made them of hammered
work, at the two ends of the cover: 8one cherub at
one end and the other cherub at the other end; he
made the cherubim of one piece with the cover, at
its two ends. 9The cherubim had their wings spread
out above, shielding the cover with their wings.
They faced each other; the faces of the cherubim
were turned toward the cover.
10He made the table of acacia wood, two cubits
long, one cubit wide, and a cubit and a half high;
11he overlaid it with pure gold and made a gold
molding around it. 12He made a rim of a hand's
breadth around it and made a gold molding for its
rim round about. 13He cast four gold rings for it
and attached the rings to the four corners at its four
legs. 14The rings were next to the rim, as holders for
the poles to carry the table. 15He made the poles of
acacia wood for carrying the table, and overlaid
them with gold. 16The utensils that were to be upon

וּשְׁתֵּי טַבָּעֹת עַל־צַלְעוֹ הַשֵּׁנִית׃ 4 וַיַּעַשׂ
בַּדֵּי עֲצֵי שִׁטִּים וַיְצַף אֹתָם זָהָב׃ 5 וַיָּבֵא
אֶת־הַבַּדִּים בַּטַּבָּעֹת עַל צַלְעֹת הָאָרֹן
לָשֵׂאת אֶת־הָאָרֹן׃
6 וַיַּעַשׂ כַּפֹּרֶת זָהָב טָהוֹר אַמָּתַיִם וָחֵצִי
אָרְכָּהּ וְאַמָּה וָחֵצִי רָחְבָּהּ׃ 7 וַיַּעַשׂ שְׁנֵי
כְרֻבִים זָהָב מִקְשָׁה עָשָׂה אֹתָם מִשְּׁנֵי
קְצוֹת הַכַּפֹּרֶת׃ 8 כְּרוּב־אֶחָד מִקָּצָה מִזֶּה
וּכְרוּב־אֶחָד מִקָּצָה מִזֶּה מִן־הַכַּפֹּרֶת עָשָׂה
אֶת־הַכְּרֻבִים מִשְּׁנֵי קצוותו קְצוֹתָיו׃ 9 וַיִּהְיוּ
הַכְּרֻבִים פֹּרְשֵׂי כְנָפַיִם לְמַעְלָה סֹכְכִים
בְּכַנְפֵיהֶם עַל־הַכַּפֹּרֶת וּפְנֵיהֶם אִישׁ אֶל־
אָחִיו אֶל־הַכַּפֹּרֶת הָיוּ פְּנֵי הַכְּרֻבִים׃ פ
10 וַיַּעַשׂ אֶת־הַשֻּׁלְחָן עֲצֵי שִׁטִּים אַמָּתַיִם
אָרְכּוֹ וְאַמָּה רָחְבּוֹ וְאַמָּה וָחֵצִי קֹמָתוֹ׃
11 וַיְצַף אֹתוֹ זָהָב טָהוֹר וַיַּעַשׂ לוֹ זֵר זָהָב
סָבִיב׃ 12 וַיַּעַשׂ לוֹ מִסְגֶּרֶת טֹפַח סָבִיב וַיַּעַשׂ
זֵר־זָהָב לְמִסְגַּרְתּוֹ סָבִיב׃ 13 וַיִּצֹק לוֹ אַרְבַּע
טַבְּעֹת זָהָב וַיִּתֵּן אֶת־הַטַּבָּעֹת עַל אַרְבַּע
הַפֵּאֹת אֲשֶׁר לְאַרְבַּע רַגְלָיו׃ 14 לְעֻמַּת
הַמִּסְגֶּרֶת הָיוּ הַטַּבָּעֹת בָּתִּים לַבַּדִּים
לָשֵׂאת אֶת־הַשֻּׁלְחָן׃ 15 וַיַּעַשׂ אֶת־הַבַּדִּים
עֲצֵי שִׁטִּים וַיְצַף אֹתָם זָהָב לָשֵׂאת אֶת־
הַשֻּׁלְחָן׃ 16 וַיַּעַשׂ אֶת־הַכֵּלִים ׀ אֲשֶׁר עַל־

which is to be placed between the table and the menorah, and also the oil and incense.

### ARK AND ITS COVER (37:1–9)

The first item, the Ark, is the holiest. It will be placed in the most sacred space in the Tabernacle—the Holy of Holies—and it will serve as the repository for the covenant document, referred to as the "tablets of the Pact" (31:18). For a people generally reluctant to use anthropomorphic images of a deity, the Ark serves as a symbol of God's presence. The Ark and its cover (*kaporet*) also seem to represent a footrest for the invisible God enthroned above it. (See further at the prescriptive text that parallels this descriptive section, 25:10–22.)

### TABLE AND MENORAH (37:10–24)

The table and the lampstand are to be placed in the second most holy zone, the main room of the tent shrine, along with the incense altar. These items provide two essential needs of a residence: food and drink, and light. (See further at the prescriptive text that parallels this descriptive section, 25:23–40.)

the table—its bowls, ladles, jugs, and jars with
which to offer libations—he made of pure gold.
17 He made the lampstand of pure gold. He
made the lampstand—its base and its shaft—of
hammered work; its cups, calyxes, and petals were
of one piece with it. 18 Six branches issued from its
sides: three branches from one side of the lampstand, and three branches from the other side of the
lampstand. 19 There were three cups shaped like
almond-blossoms, each with calyx and petals, on
one branch; and there were three cups shaped like
almond-blossoms, each with calyx and petals, on
the next branch; so for all six branches issuing from
the lampstand. 20 On the lampstand itself there
were four cups shaped like almond-blossoms, each
with calyx and petals: 21 a calyx, of one piece with it,
under a pair of branches; and a calyx, of one piece
with it, under the second pair of branches; and a
calyx, of one piece with it, under the last pair of
branches; so for all six branches issuing from it.
22 Their calyxes and their stems were of one piece
with it, the whole of it a single hammered piece of
pure gold. 23 He made its seven lamps, its tongs, and
its fire pans of pure gold. 24 He made it and all its
furnishings out of a talent of pure gold.
25 He made the incense altar of acacia wood, a
cubit long and a cubit wide—square—and two
cubits high; its horns were of one piece with it.
26 He overlaid it with pure gold: its top, its sides
round about, and its horns; and he made a gold
molding for it round about. 27 He made two gold
rings for it under its molding, on its two walls—on
opposite sides—as holders for the poles with which

הַשֻּׁלְחָן אֶת־קְעָרֹתָיו וְאֶת־כַּפֹּתָיו וְאֵת
מְנַקִּיֹּתָיו וְאֶת־הַקְּשָׂוֹת אֲשֶׁר יֻסַּךְ בָּהֵן
זָהָב טָהוֹר׃ פ
17 וַיַּעַשׂ אֶת־הַמְּנֹרָה זָהָב טָהוֹר מִקְשָׁה
עָשָׂה אֶת־הַמְּנֹרָה יְרֵכָהּ וְקָנָהּ גְּבִיעֶיהָ
כַּפְתֹּרֶיהָ וּפְרָחֶיהָ מִמֶּנָּה הָיוּ׃ 18 וְשִׁשָּׁה
קָנִים יֹצְאִים מִצִּדֶּיהָ שְׁלֹשָׁה ׀ קְנֵי מְנֹרָה
מִצִּדָּהּ הָאֶחָד וּשְׁלֹשָׁה קְנֵי מְנֹרָה מִצִּדָּהּ
הַשֵּׁנִי׃ 19 שְׁלֹשָׁה גְבִעִים מְשֻׁקָּדִים בַּקָּנֶה
הָאֶחָד כַּפְתֹּר וָפֶרַח וּשְׁלֹשָׁה גְבִעִים
מְשֻׁקָּדִים בְּקָנֶה אֶחָד כַּפְתֹּר וָפָרַח כֵּן
לְשֵׁשֶׁת הַקָּנִים הַיֹּצְאִים מִן־הַמְּנֹרָה׃
20 וּבַמְּנֹרָה אַרְבָּעָה גְבִעִים מְשֻׁקָּדִים
כַּפְתֹּרֶיהָ וּפְרָחֶיהָ׃ 21 וְכַפְתֹּר תַּחַת שְׁנֵי
הַקָּנִים מִמֶּנָּה וְכַפְתֹּר תַּחַת שְׁנֵי
הַקָּנִים מִמֶּנָּה וְכַפְתֹּר תַּחַת־שְׁנֵי הַקָּנִים
מִמֶּנָּה לְשֵׁשֶׁת הַקָּנִים הַיֹּצְאִים מִמֶּנָּה׃
22 כַּפְתֹּרֵיהֶם וּקְנֹתָם מִמֶּנָּה הָיוּ כֻּלָּהּ
מִקְשָׁה אַחַת זָהָב טָהוֹר׃ 23 וַיַּעַשׂ אֶת־
נֵרֹתֶיהָ שִׁבְעָה וּמַלְקָחֶיהָ וּמַחְתֹּתֶיהָ זָהָב
טָהוֹר׃ 24 כִּכָּר זָהָב טָהוֹר עָשָׂה אֹתָהּ וְאֵת
כָּל־כֵּלֶיהָ׃ פ
25 וַיַּעַשׂ אֶת־מִזְבַּח הַקְּטֹרֶת עֲצֵי שִׁטִּים
אַמָּה אָרְכּוֹ וְאַמָּה רָחְבּוֹ רָבוּעַ וְאַמָּתַיִם
קֹמָתוֹ מִמֶּנּוּ הָיוּ קַרְנֹתָיו׃ 26 וַיְצַף אֹתוֹ זָהָב
טָהוֹר אֶת־גַּגּוֹ וְאֶת־קִירֹתָיו סָבִיב וְאֶת־
קַרְנֹתָיו וַיַּעַשׂ לוֹ זֵר זָהָב סָבִיב׃ 27 וּשְׁתֵּי
טַבְּעֹת זָהָב עָשָׂה־לוֹ ׀ מִתַּחַת לְזֵרוֹ עַל שְׁתֵּי
צַלְעֹתָיו עַל שְׁנֵי צִדָּיו לְבָתִּים לְבַדִּים

INCENSE ALTAR (37:25–28)

Incense altars were standard items in shrines in the ancient Near East, just as some mechanism for freshening the air was part of every household. (See further at the prescriptive text that parallels this descriptive section, 30:1–10.)

to carry it. 28 He made the poles of acacia wood, and
overlaid them with gold. 29 He prepared the sacred
anointing oil and the pure aromatic incense, expertly blended.

38 He made the altar for burnt offering of
acacia wood, five cubits long and five cubits wide—
square—and three cubits high. 2 He made horns for
it on its four corners, the horns being of one piece
with it; and he overlaid it with copper. 3 He made all
the utensils of the altar—the pails, the scrapers, the
basins, the flesh hooks, and the fire pans; he made
all these utensils of copper. 4 He made for the altar a
grating of meshwork in copper, extending below,

לָשֵׂאת אֹתוֹ בָּהֶם׃ 28 וַיַּעַשׂ אֶת־הַבַּדִּים
עֲצֵי שִׁטִּים וַיְצַף אֹתָם זָהָב׃ 29 וַיַּעַשׂ אֶת־
שֶׁמֶן הַמִּשְׁחָה קֹדֶשׁ וְאֶת־קְטֹרֶת הַסַּמִּים
טָהוֹר מַעֲשֵׂה רֹקֵחַ׃ ס
לח וַיַּעַשׂ אֶת־מִזְבַּח הָעֹלָה עֲצֵי שִׁטִּים
חָמֵשׁ אַמּוֹת אָרְכּוֹ וְחָמֵשׁ־אַמּוֹת רָחְבּוֹ
רָבוּעַ וְשָׁלֹשׁ אַמּוֹת קֹמָתוֹ׃ 2 וַיַּעַשׂ קַרְנֹתָיו
עַל אַרְבַּע פִּנֹּתָיו מִמֶּנּוּ הָיוּ קַרְנֹתָיו וַיְצַף
אֹתוֹ נְחֹשֶׁת׃ 3 וַיַּעַשׂ אֶת־כָּל־כְּלֵי הַמִּזְבֵּחַ
אֶת־הַסִּירֹת וְאֶת־הַיָּעִים וְאֶת־הַמִּזְרָקֹת
אֶת־הַמִּזְלָגֹת וְאֶת־הַמַּחְתֹּת כָּל־כֵּלָיו
עָשָׂה נְחֹשֶׁת׃ 4 וַיַּעַשׂ לַמִּזְבֵּחַ מִכְבָּר
מַעֲשֵׂה רֶשֶׁת נְחֹשֶׁת תַּחַת כַּרְכֻּבּוֹ

### ANOINTING OIL AND INCENSE (37:29)

The section on the furnishings concludes with a single verse concerning two of the substances to be used in the Tabernacle: the anointing oil and the incense. Perhaps the anointing oil is paired with the incense because the two items are similarly associated in the prescriptive text of 30:22–38 and because anointing oil is blended with aromatic substances similar to those used in compounding incense. (See further at 30:22–28.) How the anointing oil is to be used is described in 40:9–15 (see also at 27:20–21); and the burning of incense is mentioned in 40:27 (see also at 30:7).

## *Completing the Courtyard* (38:1–20)

With the components of the tent prepared and the furnishings constructed, the narrative now turns to the one remaining part of the sacred precinct, the courtyard. Like most households and palaces in the ancient Near East, the Tabernacle is to have an unroofed outdoor space, a courtyard. Whereas the other parts of the Tabernacle were reserved for the priests, the courtyard was a place where the rest of the people, including women, could enter and offer sacrifices.

### ALTAR AND LAVER (38:1–8)

The altar and laver are to be placed in the courtyard, the third and least holy zone of the Tabernacle. (For the parallel prescriptive texts earlier in Exodus, see 27:1–8 and 30:17–21.)

*1. altar for burnt offering.* The horned altar is made of acacia wood and overlaid with bronze. It is described in 27:1 as being about 7½ feet (more than 2 meters) square and 4½ feet (almost 1½ meters) high. Such a massive wooden altar, even one covered with metal, is unlikely to have been functional; it is possible that altars familiar from a later period have been retrojected onto the image of the Tabernacle altar.

under its ledge, to its middle. 5 He cast four rings, at
the four corners of the copper grating, as holders for
the poles. 6 He made the poles of acacia wood and
overlaid them with copper; 7 and he inserted the
poles into the rings on the side walls of the altar, to
carry it by them. He made it hollow, of boards.

8 He made the laver of copper and its stand of
copper, from the mirrors of the women who performed tasks at the entrance of the Tent of Meeting.

מִלְמַטָּה עַד־חֶצְיוֹ׃ 5 וַיִּצֹק אַרְבַּע טַבָּעֹת
בְּאַרְבַּע הַקְּצָוֹת לְמִכְבַּר הַנְּחֹשֶׁת בָּתִּים
לַבַּדִּים׃ 6 וַיַּעַשׂ אֶת־הַבַּדִּים עֲצֵי שִׁטִּים
וַיְצַף אֹתָם נְחֹשֶׁת׃ 7 וַיָּבֵא אֶת־הַבַּדִּים
בַּטַּבָּעֹת עַל צַלְעֹת הַמִּזְבֵּחַ לָשֵׂאת אֹתוֹ
בָּהֶם נְבוּב לֻחֹת עָשָׂה אֹתוֹ׃ ס
8 וַיַּעַשׂ אֵת הַכִּיּוֹר נְחֹשֶׁת וְאֵת כַּנּוֹ נְחֹשֶׁת
בְּמַרְאֹת הַצֹּבְאֹת אֲשֶׁר צָבְאוּ פֶּתַח אֹהֶל
מוֹעֵד׃ ס

*8. laver.* Placed between the altar and the entrance to the tent, the bronze ("copper") laver would be filled with water so that priests entering the tent or serving at the altar could perform the purifying and protective measure of washing their hands and feet.

***mirrors.*** Handheld mirrors made of highly polished metal such as copper were highly valued in the biblical world. That these women owned them indicates they were persons of means.

***women who performed tasks.*** The word "women" does not actually appear in the Hebrew, for these English words translate *ha-tzovot asher tzavu*, meaning "those who were doing service." Because *tzovot* is grammatically feminine, these persons—sometimes called "servitors" or "women who serve"—are clearly female. (The word "women" actually appears in a similar passage in I Samuel 2:22.) The unusual Hebrew phrase, using a root that otherwise indicates military service, is used in a Tabernacle context both here and for the work of some (male) Levites in Numbers 4. The term seems to indicate the work of a support staff (rather than of officiating priests) that performed menial labor to maintain the sanctuary. This verse thus challenges the prevailing assumption that only men worked in the tent shrine. Moreover, the fact that these women are mentioned in an aside in relation to their mirrors, rather than in a listing of Tabernacle jobs, raises the possibility that there were other female workers in the sacred complex.

***at the entrance.*** The fact that the narrator felt the need to identify these women on the basis of where they did their job suggests that there may have been other women working elsewhere in the holy precinct. This particular location, most likely in front of the tent and visible to the community, was an important part of the sacred space; certain rituals are carried out there (see, for instance, 29:4, 32, 42), and it is where the pillar of cloud rests when Moses enters the tent to meet with God (33:9–10). This location, at the entrance of the Tent of Meeting, was not off-limits to women (see Numbers 27:1–2).

[9]He made the enclosure:

On the south side, a hundred cubits of hangings of fine twisted linen for the enclosure—[10]with their twenty posts and their twenty sockets of copper, the hooks and bands of the posts being silver.

[11]On the north side, a hundred cubits—with their twenty posts and their twenty sockets of copper, the hooks and bands of the posts being silver.

[12]On the west side, fifty cubits of hangings—with their ten posts and their ten sockets, the hooks and bands of the posts being silver.

[13]And on the front side, to the east, fifty cubits: [14]fifteen cubits of hangings on the one flank, with their three posts and their three sockets, [15]and fifteen cubits of hangings on the other flank—on each side of the gate of the enclosure—with their three posts and their three sockets.

[16]All the hangings around the enclosure were of fine twisted linen. [17]The sockets for the posts were of copper, the hooks and bands of the posts were of silver, the overlay of their tops was of silver; all the posts of the enclosure were banded with silver.—[18]The screen of the gate of the enclosure, done in embroidery, was of blue, purple, and crimson yarns, and fine twisted linen. It was twenty cubits long. Its height—or width—was five cubits, like that of the hangings of the enclosure. [19]The posts were four; their four sockets were of copper, their hooks of silver; and the overlay of their tops was of silver, as were also their bands.—[20]All the pegs of the Tabernacle and of the enclosure round about were of copper.

9 וַיַּעַשׂ אֶת־הֶחָצֵר
לִפְאַת ׀ נֶגֶב תֵּימָנָה קַלְעֵי הֶחָצֵר שֵׁשׁ
מָשְׁזָר מֵאָה בָּאַמָּה׃ 10 עַמּוּדֵיהֶם עֶשְׂרִים
וְאַדְנֵיהֶם עֶשְׂרִים נְחֹשֶׁת וָוֵי הָעַמּוּדִים
וַחֲשֻׁקֵיהֶם כָּסֶף׃
11 וְלִפְאַת צָפוֹן מֵאָה בָאַמָּה עַמּוּדֵיהֶם
עֶשְׂרִים וְאַדְנֵיהֶם עֶשְׂרִים נְחֹשֶׁת וָוֵי
הָעַמּוּדִים וַחֲשֻׁקֵיהֶם כָּסֶף׃
12 וְלִפְאַת־יָם קְלָעִים חֲמִשִּׁים בָּאַמָּה
עַמּוּדֵיהֶם עֲשָׂרָה וְאַדְנֵיהֶם עֲשָׂרָה וָוֵי
הָעַמֻּדִים וַחֲשׁוּקֵיהֶם כָּסֶף׃
13 וְלִפְאַת קֵדְמָה מִזְרָחָה חֲמִשִּׁים אַמָּה׃
14 קְלָעִים חֲמֵשׁ־עֶשְׂרֵה אַמָּה אֶל־הַכָּתֵף
עַמּוּדֵיהֶם שְׁלֹשָׁה וְאַדְנֵיהֶם שְׁלֹשָׁה׃
15 וְלַכָּתֵף הַשֵּׁנִית מִזֶּה וּמִזֶּה לְשַׁעַר הֶחָצֵר
קְלָעִים חֲמֵשׁ עֶשְׂרֵה אַמָּה עַמֻּדֵיהֶם
שְׁלֹשָׁה וְאַדְנֵיהֶם שְׁלֹשָׁה׃
16 כָּל־קַלְעֵי הֶחָצֵר סָבִיב שֵׁשׁ מָשְׁזָר׃
17 וְהָאֲדָנִים לָעַמֻּדִים נְחֹשֶׁת וָוֵי הָעַמּוּדִים
וַחֲשׁוּקֵיהֶם כֶּסֶף וְצִפּוּי רָאשֵׁיהֶם כֶּסֶף וְהֵם
מְחֻשָּׁקִים כֶּסֶף כֹּל עַמֻּדֵי הֶחָצֵר׃ 18 וּמָסַךְ
שַׁעַר הֶחָצֵר מַעֲשֵׂה רֹקֵם תְּכֵלֶת וְאַרְגָּמָן
וְתוֹלַעַת שָׁנִי וְשֵׁשׁ מָשְׁזָר וְעֶשְׂרִים אַמָּה
אֹרֶךְ וְקוֹמָה בְרֹחַב חָמֵשׁ אַמּוֹת לְעֻמַּת
קַלְעֵי הֶחָצֵר׃ 19 וְעַמֻּדֵיהֶם אַרְבָּעָה
וְאַדְנֵיהֶם אַרְבָּעָה נְחֹשֶׁת וָוֵיהֶם כֶּסֶף וְצִפּוּי
רָאשֵׁיהֶם וַחֲשֻׁקֵיהֶם כָּסֶף׃ 20 וְכָל־הַיְתֵדֹת
לַמִּשְׁכָּן וְלֶחָצֵר סָבִיב נְחֹשֶׁת׃ ס

### ENCLOSURE (38:9–20)

This parashah concludes with the fabrication of the enclosure, made of fabric panels attached to wooden posts set into metal bases, that surrounds the Tabernacle courtyard and serves as the boundary between the holy space within and the profane space outside. (For the prescriptive text earlier in Exodus that parallels this descriptive section, see 27:9–19.)

—*Carol Meyers*

## Another View

THERE IS MUCH DEBATE among scholars about the relationship between the Tabernacle and the Jerusalem Temple. Some scholars think that the Tabernacle is a completely mythic structure whose description is based on the Temple constructed early in the 1st millennium B.C.E. These scholars argue that the Tabernacle tradition evolved to justify and provide a pedigree for the Temple. Other scholars argue that there existed a portable Tabernacle that pre-dated the Temple. Although it would not have been as elaborate as the Tabernacle described in the Torah, this structure must have formed the basis for the portable divine dwelling recounted in Exodus 25–40.

While it is currently impossible to determine the historicity of the Tabernacle texts, it is clear that within the Bible, the Tabernacle and the Temple provide two models of sacred space. The Temple model was particularly resonant when Israel/Judea was a sovereign kingdom (10th–6th centuries B.C.E.). The Temple was a symbol of God's sanction of the Davidic monarchy, and it functioned as a key element in the Judean monarchy's attempts to centralize national and religious authority (II Samuel 7:11–16; I Kings 8; 12:26–27).

The Tabernacle model was particularly resonant in the absence of Judean—and later, Jewish—sovereignty (after the Babylonian conquest in 587 B.C.E.). According to the Tabernacle model, God is manifest in the community no matter where the community resides. In order to come into contact with God, the people do not need to make pilgrimages to a fixed location. Instead, they need only maintain a set of behaviors that will allow God to reside in their midst no matter where they are. According to the Rabbis, when the Jews went into exile, God's presence (*Shechinah*) went with them and continues to manifest itself wherever Jews pray or study Torah. The medieval Kabbalists understood the *Shechinah* to be a feminine aspect of God. The idea of the *Shechinah* as an immanent and feminine divine presence has been a source of reflection and inspiration for feminist theologians like Judith Plaskow and Lynn Gottlieb.

*According to the Tabernacle model, God is manifest wherever the community resides.*

—*Elsie R. Stern*

## Post-biblical Interpretations

***Men and women... came bringing... gold objects of all kinds*** (35:22). Because the Hebrew wording is unusual, literally "the men on [or: over] the women came...," many medieval commentators understood it as referring to relations between men and women. Rashi and Ibn Ezra understood the passage simply as "the men came *with* the women." Nachmanides explained that the men followed the women's example and donated jewelry only *after* the latter had already done so. Chizz'kuni said that the men collected the jewelry from the women in order to then donate it for the building effort. And Sforno interpreted the words to mean that husbands accompanied wives who were bringing gift offerings in order to indicate their approval. (Two other verses in this parashah, 35:25 and 38:8, also mention women bringing gifts for the building of the Tabernacle.)

***all the skilled women spun with their own hands*** (35:25). "Skilled" in this verse is literally "wise-hearted." This beautiful tribute to the work of women's hands provides the proof text for Rabbi Eliezer's infamous statement: "A woman's wisdom is only in (connection with) the spindle" (BT *Yoma* 66b). Rabbi Eliezer believed that women were unfit for Torah study, declaring that "anyone who teaches his daughter Torah, it is as if he taught her *tiflut* (licentiousness)" (BT *Sotah* 21b). His opinion expressed the dominant rabbinic attitude which limited Jewish women's access to traditional Jewish learning for centuries. The sage Ben Azzai expressed the opposite point of view, "A man is obligated to teach his daughter Torah" (BT *Sotah* 20a); however, this remained a minority view.

*The men donated jewelry only after the women had already done so.*

***He made the laver of copper and its stand of copper, from the mirrors of the women who performed tasks at the entrance of the Tent of Meeting*** (38:8). Who were these women and what were they doing? Ibn Ezra, Chizz'kuni, and Sforno all agreed that this verse refers to women who had cast away their jewelry in order to devote themselves to God. They came to the Tent of Meeting to pray and hear either "words of the living God" (Sforno), the praises of God pronounced by the priests (Chizz'kuni), or words of *mitzvot* (commandments) (Ibn Ezra). By donating their mirrors they also renounced personal vanity. Ibn Ezra explained that the reference to their gathering at the entrance of the Tent of Meeting indicated that there was a large group of such women.

Rashi explained the significance of the mirrors through a midrashic tradition, in which Moses first rejected the mirrors, angry that objects associated with vanity and the Evil Inclination would be used in constructing something holy. But God told Moses to accept the mirrors because the Israelite women had used them for a most holy purpose during their enslavement in Egypt: When Pharaoh decreed that the men could not return home from the fields at the end of the day, the women went out to the fields, bringing their husbands hot food and drink. After their husbands had eaten, each woman pulled out her mirror and held it up to catch the image of her husband's face together with her own. "I am more beautiful than you," she flirted with him. In this way, God explained, the women awakened desire in their exhausted husbands and ensured the Israelites a future generation of children. BT *Sotah* 11b cites this midrash along with other examples of women's contributions to Israel's survival and redemption, stating that it was on account of the righteousness of the women during the generations of slavery that the Israelites were taken out of Egypt.

*—Ruth H. Sohn*

# Contemporary Reflection

PARASHAT VAYAK'HEIL GIVES US a detailed description of the construction and furnishings of the Tabernacle; in fact, more than most of us wish to hear. Why include this data? Why does it matter? It matters because in the ancient world, a temple was a model of the cosmos (Mircea Eliade, *The Myth of the Eternal Return*, 1954). How the temple is designed and furnished and where objects are positioned express symbolically what its builders believe about the nature of the cosmos. *Vayak'heil* gives us the specifications for these symbols, but it cannot tell us all that they mean. Symbols and metaphors exist precisely because they point toward what cannot be entirely expressed. Moreover, symbols and rituals are not static. They grow and change along with the people who use them, acquiring new layers of meaning along the way.

As an example, let's look at a symbolic object from the Tabernacle that we recognize, the *Menorah* (lampstand). What does it mean? The *Menorah's* function is to give light, and light is an important element in our own ritual acts as well. We kindle lights for *Shabbat, Havdalah, Yom Tov* (holiday), *yortsayt* (or *yahrzeit*, memorial occasion). The philosopher Ernst Cassirer says that the creation of light, which begins many creation myths, represents the creation of consciousness (*Language and Myth*, 1946). Perhaps, when we ritually kindle light, we reenact the dawning of consciousness that enables us both to know God and to be aware of ourselves. Is the *Menorah* a lamp representing the light-giving or knowledge-giving aspect of the cosmos?

The *Menorah* is not just any lamp, however. It is a giant lamp of unusual design, so tall that a priest must ascend a ramp to light it. Twice, in 25:31–40 and then in our parashah (37:17–24), the *Menorah* is painstakingly described: a golden base, a tall shaft, six golden branches issuing from the sides, each branch bearing cups shaped like almond blossoms, detailed with calyx and petals, plus more blossom-cups on the shaft itself. Atop these branches are seven golden lamps.

Clearly the *Menorah* embodies some kind of metaphor. But metaphor has rules, just like tennis or Scrabble®. One rule is that there has to be some link between the *tenor* (the topic under discussion) and the *vehicle* (the concrete object to which it is being compared). What, then, is tall, has a *kaneh* (stem), with *kanim* (branches) extending from it, and *p'rachim* (flowers) intermixed with bud-like swellings (*kaftorim*)? The *Menorah* is a representation of a flowering almond tree!

The almond tree is distinctive not only in that it blossoms early, but also in that it then rapidly buds leaves, develops new branches, and forms its sustaining fruit—all before the flowers' calyx drops off (Nogah Hareuveni, *Nature in Our Biblical Heritage*, 1980, p. 130). Its Hebrew name, *shaked*, means "the early waker," and it may symbolize God's watchfulness or the speed with which God responds (see Jeremiah 1:11). It is also the legitimating emblem of the Aaronite priesthood. At the end of Korah's rebellion in Numbers 17,

### *Why does the Torah include a detailed description of the Tabernacle?*

Moses deposits the staffs of all the Israelite chieftains in the Tent of Meeting, "and there the staff of Aaron . . . had sprouted: it had brought forth sprouts, produced blossoms and borne almonds" (17:23).

Trees, as well as light, are associated with consciousness for Jews. Our moral consciousness comes from having eaten the fruit of a tree (Genesis 3). The Torah is "a tree of life to all who hold fast to her" (Proverbs 3:18). Trees are elders of the living earth. Their rootedness, endurance, and capacity for renewal is a blessing extended to the righteous: "The righteous shall flourish like the date palm" (Psalm 92:13). The righteous too shall be trees of life.

But the *Menorah* is yet a different sort of tree, because its branches are crowned with bowls filled with oil that are lit regularly by the priests. Who ever heard of a tree perpetually on fire?

> He gazed and there was a bush all aflame, yet the bush was not consumed. . . . God called to him out of the bush: "Moses! Moses!" He answered, "Here I am." And [God] said, "Do not come closer! Remove your sandals from your feet, for the place on which you stand is holy ground!" (3:2–5).

In his book *Sinai and Zion* (1985), Jon Levenson describes how the religion of Sinai was transformed into the religion of Zion. In the *Tanach*'s account of the settlement of the Land of Israel, Sinai—the wilderness mountain of the *s'neh* (thornbush), the site of Israel's revelation and covenant—was refashioned as Zion, the holy mountain of the Jerusalem temple. The Burning Bush itself was reproduced as a golden tree lit by priests. Levenson speculates that the emblem of the deity of Sinai was some sort of tree. He points out that the blessing in Deuteronomy 33:16 identifies God as *shochni s'neh*, "the Presence in the Bush."

The feminist theologian Nelle Morton describes metaphor as an explosive process with a trajectory, like a meteor (*The Journey is Home*, 1985). The tree on fire that is not consumed—this is an image on an immense journey. The metaphor has traveled from Sinai to Zion, to Exile and beyond, and we have not even begun to exhaust its resonances.

A tree on fire embraces what we misperceive as antitheses: earth and heaven, matter and energy. What we are accustomed to polarize is revealed to us in blazing union. A tree on fire unconsumed proclaims that what is material, temporal, perishable, can sustain what the Christian theologian Rudolf Otto calls the "fearsome and fascinating mystery" of the presence of God (*The Idea of the Holy*, 1923). If we were only able to see, the whole earth would appear to us like a tree on fire, and we would see a tree on fire in every human frame.

We cannot relive the moment when a startled shepherd sees a terrible and wonderful sight: a tree on fire, unconsumed. We can only make a memory-tree to remind us of that moment, an artifice that we ourselves ceremoniously set afire amidst song and liturgy. The memory tree is a tree of wonder only and not a tree of terror. We take our chances, stubbornly continuing to set our memory-tree on fire—real fire, with all its potential for enlightenment and danger, reproducing the encounter with that fiery presence we seek and yet fear: the revealer of mysteries, the dweller in the bush.

—*Rachel Adler*

# Voices

## Delight

Dahlia Ravikovitch
(transl. Chana Bloch and Chana Kronfeld)

*Exodus 35:1–3*

There did I know a delight beyond all delight,
And it came to pass upon the Sabbath day
As tree boughs reached for the sky with all
their might.

Round and round like a river streamed the light,
And the wheel of the eye craved the sunwheel
that day.
Then did I know a delight beyond all delight.

The heads of the bushes blazed, insatiable bright
Sunlight striking the waves, igniting the spray.
It would swallow my head like a golden orange,
that light.

Water lilies were gaping their yellow bright
Mouths to swallow the ripples and reeds in
their way.
And indeed it came to pass on the Sabbath day
As tree boughs lusted for the sky with all their
might,
And then did I know a delight beyond all
delight.

## First a Spark

Sandy Eisenberg Sasso

*Exodus 35:1–3*

First a spark
then candle glow.

I watched you at sunset time
eyes sparkling in Shabbat light.

Circling above the flames,
my hands pulled
the warmth of Shabbat peace inside.

Praying for a good week and for blessing.

Take time—the lights beckon
for dreams and wonder,
for the candles grow smaller,
the children taller,
even as we pray.

Hold this sunset moment and let it go
into morning light.

Another generation's candlesticks
receive the next generation's lights.

And somewhere in the middle
we stand, holding hands
with yesterday and tomorrow,
linking echoes of ancient melodies
with the breath of our children.

Finding God and hope in their embrace,
renewing days of creation.

In ordinary time—remember—
First a spark
and then candle glow.

## *They Build the Tabernacle*

Ruth Brin

*Exodus 35:4–29*

To devotion God set no limits,
and to dedication of the spirit
God set not bounds;

But great quantities of tribute God did not
    demand,
and the people were restrained from bringing
too much gold for the Tabernacle.

Though the Temples of Solomon and Herod
were far more costly,
it is written that the Divine Presence was found
more constantly in the humbler structure.

To dedicate the spirit to God is more difficult
than to give money,
to devote the whole heart to God
is more difficult than bringing gifts.

Not because of the gold on the walls
does the light of the sanctuary shine forth,
but because of the spirit within.

Those who worship carry away with them
more than they bring
for they find there the light to illumine
their lives.

## *Earrings*

Annette Bialik Harchik

*Exodus 35:22*

A Bialik tradition back home was
for a woman to wear earrings
from birth to death.

Ears pierced in infancy were
adorned with string;
golden hoops for girlhood;
diamond studs for marriage.

When the trains pulled up
at Auschwitz
my mother was stripped, shorn, tattooed,
and commanded to leave her earrings
in a huge glitter pile of jewelry.

Under her wavy white hair
her lobes hang heavy,
the empty holes
grown shut.

## *Prescience*

Ruth Fainlight

*Exodus 38:8*

Long ago, when I was a girl,
constantly, obsessively, I drew
faces of uncertain gender:
philosophers who'd lost conviction,
blocked, bitter artists, or ageing
women with the deep eye-sockets
and bony structures I aspired to,
strong vertical lines marking each
side of a mouth that once was softer,

a face which only now (flinching from
the prospect of what's still to come)
I recognize reflected back
from the mirror—and must acknowledge
the prescience of that young girl
whose hand, as though it held a wicked
fairy's wand or Clotho's spindle and
not a brush or pen, unerringly
created this face, that future.

## *From My Mother's Home*

Lea Goldberg (transl. Ezra Spicehandler)

*Exodus 38:8*

My mother's mother died
In the spring of her days.
And her daughter
Did not remember her face.
Her portrait, engraved
Upon my grandfather's heart,
Was erased from the world of images
After his death.
Only her mirror remained in the home,
Sunken with age into the silver frame.
And I, her pale granddaughter, who does not
 resemble her,
Look into it today as into
A pool which conceals its treasures
Beneath the waters.
Very deep down, behind my face,
I see a young woman
Pink-cheeked, smiling.
And a wig on her head.
She puts
An elongated earring on her ear-lobe,
 threading it
Through a tiny hole in the dainty flesh
Of her ear.
Very deep down, behind my face, the bright
 goldness
of her eyes sends out rays,
And the mirror carries on the tradition of
The family: That she was very beautiful.

## *The Mirror*

Rachel Hadas

*Exodus 38:8*

Paradise: first the world within the mirror
and then the knowledge that the mirror mother
and father faithfully
would render back the world and never waver
or crack. So that the lesson
of the broken world
needs to be taught remedially to us
big oafs who saw ourselves
in surfaces that never seemed to tremble.
Visions from which they scrupulously shaded
our infant eyes light up
belatedly. The atmosphere
we bathed our little kids in
dries; unfamiliar absences take shape
and death's black hole. But wait,
absence is the other side of love.
All of us, confronting—sooner, later—
some version of the mirror
recognize our faces cracked with age
suspended in solution for our children
to find themselves within our steady gaze.

# פְּקוּדֵי ✦ P'kudei

## EXODUS 38:21–40:38

## *Completing and Consecrating the Tabernacle*

PARASHAT P'KUDEI ("records [of]") brings to a conclusion the long Tabernacle narrative and the book of Exodus. In this book, the Israelites have been transformed from slaves building store cities for Pharaoh (1:11–14) into a free people building a "home" for the God who will now dwell among them (25:8). Once the Tabernacle is completed, God's presence fills the sacred space. Just as God's cloud and fire led the Israelites from the Sea of Reeds to Sinai and then hovered over the holy mountain, God will now be with them when the wilderness journey resumes, as recounted in the book of Numbers.

As the parashah begins, the Israelites have fabricated all the components of the tent and its enclosure, interior, and courtyard furnishings (see *parashat Vayak'heil*); now they inventory the collected materials (38:21–31). Only the instructions for the priestly vestments given in *parashat T'tzaveh* (28:1–43) have not yet been fulfilled. Thus, before the Israelites erect and dedicate the Tabernacle, they must make the garments for Aaron and his descendants (39:1–31). The description of the vestments here is quite similar to that of the earlier instructions. However, there are some differences, most notably the virtual absence of Aaron's name, even though he serves as the chief priestly official (the "high priest"). Instead, the final part of Exodus returns to highlighting Aaron's brother, Moses, and his special relationship with God.

After reporting that the vestments are completed, the text presents a final summation of the construction work (39:33–43), after which the actual assembly of the shrine can begin. God gives Moses the orders to set up the Tabernacle and install its furnishings (40:1–8) and then to consecrate them and also the priests (40:9–16). All the pieces now come together under the leadership of Moses, who carries out God's commandments to erect the shrine and place its furnishings in the proper place (40:17–33). With the Tabernacle complete, God's presence enters this sumptuous earthly abode (40:34–38). Some of the language here evokes the creation of the world in Genesis 1, reflecting the momentous significance that the text bestows upon this event.

*Once the Tabernacle is completed, God's presence fills the sacred space.*

Once everything is complete, Moses reviews the work and blesses the Israelites (39:43). Finally, God's invisible presence fills the *Mishkan* (40:34–35). In contrast to the prior Torah portion, where women (and men) are mentioned explicitly as contributors to the Tabernacle and as participants in essential aspects of its construction and service, here neither women nor men are directly visible as such, apart from three specified leaders. Rather, those women (and men) remain in view while their gender recedes into the background. Indirectly—as previously mentioned donors, fabricators, and members of the collective Israelite community—they are included in the final account of the sacred portable structure erected so that God "may dwell among them" (25:8; 29:46).

*—Carol Meyers*

## *Outline*

*I.* Inventory of Donated Metals and Their Use (38:21–31)

*II.* Priestly Vestments (39:1–31)

- *A.* Introduction (v. 1)
- *B.* Ritual items (vv. 2–21)
- *C.* Apparel (vv. 22–31)

*III.* Summary of the Completed Components (39:32–43)

- *A.* Announcement of completion (v. 32)
- *B.* General inventory of completed components (vv. 33–43)

*IV.* Erection and Consecration of the Tabernacle (40:1–38)

- *A.* Directions for erecting the Tabernacle complex (vv. 1–8)
- *B.* Directions for anointing the Tabernacle complex and personnel (vv. 9–16)
- *C.* Execution of the directions (vv. 17–33)
- *D.* Entry of God's presence (vv. 34–38)

These are the records of the Tabernacle, the Tabernacle of the Pact, which were drawn up at Moses' bidding—the work of the Levites under the direction of Ithamar son of Aaron the priest.
22Now Bezalel, son of Uri son of Hur, of the tribe

לח 21 אֵלֶּה פְקוּדֵי הַמִּשְׁכָּן מִשְׁכַּן הָעֵדֻת
אֲשֶׁר פֻּקַּד עַל־פִּי מֹשֶׁה עֲבֹדַת הַלְוִיִּם בְּיַד
אִיתָמָר בֶּן־אַהֲרֹן הַכֹּהֵן׃ 22 וּבְצַלְאֵל בֶּן־
אוּרִי בֶן־חוּר לְמַטֵּה יְהוּדָה עָשָׂה אֵת

## *Inventory of Donated Metals and Their Use* (38:21–31)

This section, which takes the form of archival data recorded by levitical priests, is an inventory of the metals—gold, silver, and "copper" (see at v. 29)—used for the Tabernacle. The kind of information provided about each metal varies. Prior to the tally, vv. 21–23 reiterate that specially designated artisans used these materials.

*21. records.* More precisely, this term probably refers to a record of things that are counted up, as in a tally. The verbal root of this noun (*p-k-d*), which gives this parashah its name, also is used in Numbers in reference to the census count (as in Numbers 1:3).

*Tabernacle of the Pact.* This is the only verse in Exodus in which the words *mishkan* (Tabernacle) and *edut* (Pact) are used together (see at 25:9 and 25:16); and the combination is found only three times elsewhere in the Torah (Numbers 1:50, 53; 10:11). The phrase emphasizes that the Tabernacle is the repository for God's covenant with Israel as well as the place for God's presence to abide. With this statement, the meaning of Sinai is transferred to the Tabernacle, ready to accompany the Israelites on their journey.

*at Moses' bidding.* This emphasizes Moses' involvement in administrative concerns, as well as in priestly and prophetic matters.

*work.* This refers to the job of producing the tally.

*Levites.* The Levites are entrusted with record-keeping for the Tabernacle, perhaps in anticipation of the role they will be given in Numbers 3:6–10.

*Ithamar.* One of Aaron's four sons, he appears first in the genealogical passage in 6:23 and again in 28:1, at the beginning of the instructions for the priestly vestments.

*Aaron the priest.* This designation for Aaron rarely appears in Exodus. Aaron's responsibilities as "the priest" are said to include various matters of ritual (for example, 27:21, 28:35, 30:7–8), judicial proceedings (28:29–30), and instruction (Leviticus 10:11). The Bible never refers to Aaron by the title "high priest"—a term that seems to refer to an office that developed over time so that its responsibilities included also finance and management.

▶ What kind of staff maintained the Tabernacle, and later the Jerusalem Temple?

ANOTHER VIEW ➤ *560*

▶ The source of Bezalel's inspiration was none other than his great-grandmother, Miriam.

POST-BIBLICAL INTERPRETATIONS ➤ *560*

▶ What would happen if we started looking for God's presence in fire and clouds once more?

CONTEMPORARY REFLECTION ➤ *562*

▶ By the well they're sitting, spinning, / . . . Whispering the story, never-ending.

VOICES ➤ *564*

of Judah, had made all that יהוה had commanded
Moses; [23]at his side was Oholiab son of Ahisamach,
of the tribe of Dan, carver and designer, and embroiderer in blue, purple, and crimson yarns and in
fine linen.

[24]All the gold that was used for the work, in all
the work of the sanctuary—the elevation offering
of gold—came to 29 talents and 730 shekels by the
sanctuary weight. [25]The silver of those of the community who were recorded came to 100 talents and
1,775 shekels by the sanctuary weight: [26]a half-
shekel a head, half a shekel by the sanctuary weight,
for each one who was entered in the records, from
the age of twenty years up, 603,550 men. [27]The 100

כָּל־אֲשֶׁר־צִוָּה יְהֹוָה אֶת־מֹשֶׁה׃ 23 וְאִתּוֹ
אָהֳלִיאָב בֶּן־אֲחִיסָמָךְ לְמַטֵּה־דָן חָרָשׁ
וְחֹשֵׁב וְרֹקֵם בַּתְּכֵלֶת וּבָאַרְגָּמָן וּבְתוֹלַעַת
הַשָּׁנִי וּבַשֵּׁשׁ׃ ס
24 כָּל־הַזָּהָב הֶעָשׂוּי לַמְּלָאכָה בְּכֹל
מְלֶאכֶת הַקֹּדֶשׁ וַיְהִי ׀ זְהַב הַתְּנוּפָה תֵּשַׁע
וְעֶשְׂרִים כִּכָּר וּשְׁבַע מֵאוֹת וּשְׁלֹשִׁים שֶׁקֶל
בְּשֶׁקֶל הַקֹּדֶשׁ׃ 25 וְכֶסֶף פְּקוּדֵי הָעֵדָה מְאַת
כִּכָּר וְאֶלֶף וּשְׁבַע מֵאוֹת וַחֲמִשָּׁה וְשִׁבְעִים
שֶׁקֶל בְּשֶׁקֶל הַקֹּדֶשׁ׃ 26 בֶּקַע לַגֻּלְגֹּלֶת
מַחֲצִית הַשֶּׁקֶל בְּשֶׁקֶל הַקֹּדֶשׁ לְכֹל הָעֹבֵר
עַל־הַפְּקֻדִים מִבֶּן עֶשְׂרִים שָׁנָה וָמַעְלָה
לְשֵׁשׁ־מֵאוֹת אֶלֶף וּשְׁלֹשֶׁת אֲלָפִים וַחֲמֵשׁ
מֵאוֹת וַחֲמִשִּׁים׃ 27 וַיְהִי מְאַת כִּכַּר הַכֶּסֶף

*22. **all that יהוה had commanded Moses.*** This clause appears only a few times in Exodus up to this point. Now it recurs in rapid-fire succession, fourteen times in this parashah, especially in Exodus 39–40. The phrase emphasizes that the Tabernacle project is the result of Moses' unique role as intermediary between God and the people.

*24. **elevation offering.*** Heb. *t'nufah* ("elevation offering"), which refers to a ritual used to dedicate something to God. Elevation offerings of food appear in 29:24–27 and of gold here and in 35:22. This phrase is also used for "copper" (bronze) donations in this inventory (v. 29), but silver is inexplicably omitted.

***29 talents and 730 shekels.*** Calculating the modern equivalents of biblical weights is imprecise; but it is estimated that a talent, which in the ancient Near East equaled three thousand shekels, would have weighed about seventy-five pounds (33 kilograms). The amassed gold would have weighed more than two thousand pounds (roughly a thousand kilograms), an unlikely amount. Thus, this inventory apparently deals in symbolic numbers, although the nature of the symbolism is no longer clear.

***sanctuary weight.*** This may be different than the normal weight, but it may also be asserting that the priestly officials were the ones who set weights (see 30:13).

*25. **100 talents and 1,775 shekels.*** Another unlikely large and presumably symbolic amount—more than three times the quantity in the previous verse—is given for the quantity of donated silver.

*26. **a half-shekel a head.*** The military census that involved individual men's contributions to the Tabernacle, mandated in 30:11–16, accounts here for all of the silver collected. For some reason, the free-will contributions of silver that presumably came from both women and men (35:24; compare 11:2) are not tallied.

***603,550.*** This figure is equivalent to that of the military census in Numbers 1:46; both count only males above the age of twenty. This impossibly large and thus symbolic number, perhaps meant to include all Israelites in times to come, is slightly larger than the number of men who left Egypt: 600,000 men (Exodus 12:37).

***men.*** Specification of gender does not appear explicitly in the Hebrew here, but it is implied by the act of a military census (see at 30:11–16).

talents of silver were for casting the sockets of the sanctuary and the sockets for the curtain, 100 sockets to the 100 talents, a talent a socket. [28]And of the 1,775 shekels he made hooks for the posts, overlay for their tops, and bands around them.

[29]The copper from the elevation offering came to 70 talents and 2,400 shekels. [30]Of it he made the sockets for the entrance of the Tent of Meeting; the copper altar and its copper grating and all the utensils of the altar; [31]the sockets of the enclosure round about and the sockets of the gate of the enclosure; and all the pegs of the Tabernacle and all the pegs of the enclosure round about.

39 Of the blue, purple, and crimson yarns

לָצֶ֗קֶת אֵ֚ת אַדְנֵ֣י הַקֹּ֔דֶשׁ וְאֵ֖ת אַדְנֵ֣י הַפָּרֹ֑כֶת
מְאַ֧ת אֲדָנִ֛ים לִמְאַ֥ת הַכִּכָּ֖ר כִּכָּ֥ר לָאָֽדֶן׃
28 וְאֶת־הָאֶ֜לֶף וּשְׁבַ֤ע הַמֵּאוֹת֙ וַחֲמִשָּׁ֣ה
וְשִׁבְעִ֔ים עָשָׂ֥ה וָוִ֖ים לָעַמּוּדִ֑ים וְצִפָּ֥ה
רָאשֵׁיהֶ֖ם וְחִשַּׁ֥ק אֹתָֽם׃
29 וּנְחֹ֥שֶׁת הַתְּנוּפָ֖ה שִׁבְעִ֣ים כִּכָּ֑ר וְאַלְפַּ֥יִם
וְאַרְבַּע־מֵא֖וֹת שָֽׁקֶל׃ 30 וַיַּ֣עַשׂ בָּ֗הּ אֶת־
אַדְנֵי֙ פֶּ֚תַח אֹ֣הֶל מוֹעֵ֔ד וְאֵת֙ מִזְבַּ֣ח הַנְּחֹ֔שֶׁת
וְאֶת־מִכְבַּ֥ר הַנְּחֹ֖שֶׁת אֲשֶׁר־ל֑וֹ וְאֵ֖ת כָּל־כְּלֵ֥י
הַמִּזְבֵּֽחַ׃ 31 וְאֶת־אַדְנֵ֤י הֶֽחָצֵר֙ סָבִ֔יב וְאֶת־
אַדְנֵ֖י שַׁ֣עַר הֶחָצֵ֑ר וְאֵ֨ת כָּל־יִתְדֹ֧ת הַמִּשְׁכָּ֛ן
וְאֶת־כָּל־יִתְדֹ֥ת הֶחָצֵ֖ר סָבִֽיב׃
לט וּמִן־הַתְּכֵ֤לֶת וְהָֽאַרְגָּמָן֙ וְתוֹלַ֣עַת

***29. copper.*** The Hebrew term probably refers more precisely to bronze; see at 25:3.

***elevation offering.*** Like gold (v. 24), the "copper" (or bronze) is dedicated through the ritual of the wave offering. The "copper" (or bronze) from the mirrors of the women serving "at the entrance of the Tent of Meeting" (38:8) is not mentioned, perhaps because the laver for which they donated their mirrors is omitted in the list of uses for the "copper" in the next two verses.

***70 talents and 2,400 shekels.*** The quantity of "copper" (bronze) is more than double the amount of gold; on the import of this quantity, see at v. 24.

# *Priestly Vestments*

(39:1–31)

The catalogue of priestly vestments is similar to that of the earlier prescriptive texts that provide instructions for making these items (28:1–43). Apparently because of the focus in this parashah on construction rather than use, this unit adds technical details but omits some information about function. The most remarkable difference between the two accounts is the almost complete absence of any mention of Aaron, whose name appears some sixteen times in the equivalent unit in *parashat T'tzaveh* but only twice here (vv. 1, 27). In contrast, Moses' name, which is absent from the earlier account of the vestments, appears repeatedly here.

## INTRODUCTION (39:1)

The introductory verse mentions only the apparel of the chief priestly officer, whose elaborate vestments are described in considerable detail in the next section. (For the parallel prescriptive text earlier in Exodus, see 28:1–5.)

***1. yarns.*** Although other materials are involved in making the priestly apparel, only the dyed woolen yarns, and not even the gold or the linen threads (which appear in subsequent verses), are mentioned.

they also made the service vestments for officiating in the sanctuary; they made Aaron's sacral vestments—as יהוה had commanded Moses.

[2]The ephod was made of gold, blue, purple, and crimson yarns, and fine twisted linen. [3]They hammered out sheets of gold and cut threads to be worked into designs among the blue, the purple, and the crimson yarns, and the fine linen. [4]They made for it attaching shoulder-pieces; they were attached at its two ends. [5]The decorated band that was upon it was made like it, of one piece with it; of gold, blue, purple, and crimson yarns, and fine twisted linen—as יהוה had commanded Moses.

[6]They bordered the lazuli stones with frames of gold, engraved with seal engravings of the names of the sons of Israel. [7]They were set on the shoulder-

הַשָּׁנִי עָשׂוּ בִגְדֵי־שְׂרָד לְשָׁרֵת בַּקֹּדֶשׁ וַיַּעֲשׂוּ
אֶת־בִּגְדֵי הַקֹּדֶשׁ אֲשֶׁר לְאַהֲרֹן כַּאֲשֶׁר צִוָּה
יְהוָה אֶת־מֹשֶׁה׃ פ
2 וַיַּעַשׂ אֶת־הָאֵפֹד זָהָב תְּכֵלֶת וְאַרְגָּמָן
וְתוֹלַעַת שָׁנִי וְשֵׁשׁ מָשְׁזָר׃ 3 וַיְרַקְּעוּ אֶת־
פַּחֵי הַזָּהָב וְקִצֵּץ פְּתִילִם לַעֲשׂוֹת בְּתוֹךְ
הַתְּכֵלֶת וּבְתוֹךְ הָאַרְגָּמָן וּבְתוֹךְ תּוֹלַעַת
הַשָּׁנִי וּבְתוֹךְ הַשֵּׁשׁ מַעֲשֵׂה חֹשֵׁב׃ 4 כְּתֵפֹת
עָשׂוּ־לוֹ חֹבְרֹת עַל־שְׁנֵי קצוותו קְצוֹתָיו
חֻבָּר׃ 5 וְחֵשֶׁב אֲפֻדָּתוֹ אֲשֶׁר עָלָיו מִמֶּנּוּ
הוּא כְּמַעֲשֵׂהוּ זָהָב תְּכֵלֶת וְאַרְגָּמָן וְתוֹלַעַת
שָׁנִי וְשֵׁשׁ מָשְׁזָר כַּאֲשֶׁר צִוָּה יְהוָה אֶת־
מֹשֶׁה׃ ס
6 וַיַּעֲשׂוּ אֶת־אַבְנֵי הַשֹּׁהַם מֻסַבֹּת מִשְׁבְּצֹת
זָהָב מְפֻתָּחֹת פִּתּוּחֵי חוֹתָם עַל־שְׁמוֹת בְּנֵי
יִשְׂרָאֵל׃ 7 וַיָּשֶׂם אֹתָם עַל כִּתְפֹת הָאֵפֹד

***they . . . made the service vestments.*** Although women are not explicitly mentioned, they are likely in view here, given that women were typically the textile workers in ancient Israel (see at 35:25), just as Hannah is said to have made her son Samuel's robe when he served as a priest at Shiloh (I Samuel 2:19).

***Aaron.*** This is one of only two places where Aaron's name is used in this narrative (Exodus 39), in contrast to his prominence in the equivalent prescriptive texts. His complicity in the Golden Calf incident may account for his near absence here. In effect, the text emphasizes the enduring office, not one particular officeholder. It does, however, give Moses a relatively exalted place.

***as יהוה had commanded Moses.*** This clause appears seven times in this unit (see at 38:22). With seven denoting totality or completeness in Semitic parlance, such repetition gives prominence to the role of Moses, not Aaron, as the authoritative conduit of God's will, even for making the priestly garments.

## RITUAL ITEMS (39:2–21)

The vestments of the chief priestly official are not simply items of clothing; rather, they have ritual functions. This description differs from that of the earlier, prescriptive instructions (28:6–30) in adjusting to the different context and in being somewhat less detailed, especially by omitting information about the use of these items.

*2.* ***The ephod.*** The biblical sources that mention the ephod (such as Judges 8:24–27, I Samuel 30:7, and Hosea 3:4) contain such disparate information that it is difficult to understand what an ephod looked like or how it was used. Although the appearance and use of the ephod varied over time, what is constant is that the ephod always is related to ritual matters—sometime as a ritual garment, sometimes as a divinatory device, and sometimes as both. In Exodus, its details and its association with the breastpiece of decision make it likely that the ephod was worn by the priest and used for oracular (divinatory) purposes.

*3.* Costly garments embroidered with gold

pieces of the ephod, as stones of remembrance for the Israelites—as יהוה had commanded Moses.

[8]The breastpiece was made in the style of the ephod: of gold, blue, purple, and crimson yarns, and fine twisted linen. [9]It was square; they made the breastpiece doubled—a span in length and a span in width, doubled. [10]They set in it four rows of stones. The first row was a row of carnelian, chrysolite, and emerald; [11]the second row: a turquoise, a sapphire, and an amethyst; [12]the third row: a jacinth, an agate, and a crystal; [13]and the fourth row: a beryl, a lapis lazuli, and a jasper. They were encircled in their mountings with frames of gold. [14]The stones corresponded [in number] to the names of the sons of Israel: twelve, corresponding to their names; engraved like seals, each with its name, for the twelve tribes.

[15]On the breastpiece they made braided chains of corded work in pure gold. [16]They made two frames of gold and two rings of gold, and fastened the two rings at the two ends of the breastpiece, [17]attaching the two golden cords to the two rings at the ends of the breastpiece. [18]They then fastened the two ends of the cords to the two frames, attaching them to the shoulder-pieces of the ephod, at the front. [19]They made two rings of gold and attached them to the two ends of the breastpiece, at

אַבְנֵי זִכָּרוֹן לִבְנֵי יִשְׂרָאֵל כַּאֲשֶׁר צִוָּה יְהֹוָה
אֶת־מֹשֶׁה׃ פ
8 וַיַּעַשׂ אֶת־הַחֹשֶׁן מַעֲשֵׂה חֹשֵׁב כְּמַעֲשֵׂה
אֵפֹד זָהָב תְּכֵלֶת וְאַרְגָּמָן וְתוֹלַעַת שָׁנִי
וְשֵׁשׁ מָשְׁזָר׃ 9 רָבוּעַ הָיָה כָּפוּל עָשׂוּ אֶת־
הַחֹשֶׁן זֶרֶת אָרְכּוֹ וְזֶרֶת רָחְבּוֹ כָּפוּל׃
10 וַיְמַלְאוּ־בוֹ אַרְבָּעָה טוּרֵי אָבֶן טוּר אֹדֶם
פִּטְדָה וּבָרֶקֶת הַטּוּר הָאֶחָד׃ 11 וְהַטּוּר
הַשֵּׁנִי נֹפֶךְ סַפִּיר וְיָהֲלֹם׃ 12 וְהַטּוּר
הַשְּׁלִישִׁי לֶשֶׁם שְׁבוֹ וְאַחְלָמָה׃ 13 וְהַטּוּר
הָרְבִיעִי תַּרְשִׁישׁ שֹׁהַם וְיָשְׁפֵה מוּסַבֹּת
מִשְׁבְּצֹת זָהָב בְּמִלֻּאֹתָם׃ 14 וְהָאֲבָנִים עַל־
שְׁמֹת בְּנֵי־יִשְׂרָאֵל הֵנָּה שְׁתֵּים עֶשְׂרֵה עַל־
שְׁמֹתָם פִּתּוּחֵי חֹתָם אִישׁ עַל־שְׁמוֹ לִשְׁנֵים
עָשָׂר שָׁבֶט׃
15 וַיַּעֲשׂוּ עַל־הַחֹשֶׁן שַׁרְשְׁרֹת גַּבְלֻת מַעֲשֵׂה
עֲבֹת זָהָב טָהוֹר׃ 16 וַיַּעֲשׂוּ שְׁתֵּי מִשְׁבְּצֹת
זָהָב וּשְׁתֵּי טַבְּעֹת זָהָב וַיִּתְּנוּ אֶת־שְׁתֵּי
הַטַּבָּעֹת עַל־שְׁנֵי קְצוֹת הַחֹשֶׁן׃ 17 וַיִּתְּנוּ
שְׁתֵּי הָעֲבֹתֹת הַזָּהָב עַל־שְׁתֵּי הַטַּבָּעֹת עַל־
קְצוֹת הַחֹשֶׁן׃ 18 וְאֵת שְׁתֵּי קְצוֹת שְׁתֵּי
הָעֲבֹתֹת נָתְנוּ עַל־שְׁתֵּי הַמִּשְׁבְּצֹת וַיִּתְּנֻם
עַל־כִּתְפֹת הָאֵפֹד אֶל־מוּל פָּנָיו׃ 19 וַיַּעֲשׂוּ
שְׁתֵּי טַבְּעֹת זָהָב וַיָּשִׂימוּ עַל־שְׁנֵי קְצוֹת
הַחֹשֶׁן עַל־שְׂפָתוֹ אֲשֶׁר אֶל־עֵבֶר הָאֵפֹד

threads, which other ancient Near Eastern cultures used to clothe the statues of deities, were considered to have special sanctity.

*7. **stones of remembrance.*** According to the earlier, prescriptive text, God had specified that both the ephod and breastpiece be adorned with gemstones engraved for "remembrance" (28:12, 29) with the names of the Israelite tribes. This feature has commemorative symbolic value, bringing all Israel into the Tabernacle with the chief priestly officer as he carries out the rituals thought to help secure the well-being of the people or to adjudicate their conflicts.

*8. **The breastpiece was made.*** The description of the breastpiece's manufacture does not use the longer phrase "breastpiece of decision" (28:15, 29, 30), which indicates that the breastpiece plays a role in the judicial functions of the priesthood. Also missing from this passage is any mention of two associated items, the Urim and Thummim (see at 28:30), used by the priest to discern God's will.

בִּיתָה׃ 20 וַיַּעֲשׂוּ שְׁתֵּי טַבְּעֹת זָהָב וַיִּתְּנֻם
עַל־שְׁתֵּי כִתְפֹת הָאֵפֹד מִלְמַטָּה מִמּוּל פָּנָיו
לְעֻמַּת מַחְבַּרְתּוֹ מִמַּעַל לְחֵשֶׁב הָאֵפֹד׃
21 וַיִּרְכְּסוּ אֶת־הַחֹשֶׁן מִטַּבְּעֹתָיו אֶל־טַבְּעֹת
הָאֵפֹד בִּפְתִיל תְּכֵלֶת לִהְיֹת עַל־חֵשֶׁב
הָאֵפֹד וְלֹא־יִזַּח הַחֹשֶׁן מֵעַל הָאֵפֹד כַּאֲשֶׁר
צִוָּה יְהֹוָה אֶת־מֹשֶׁה׃ פ
22 וַיַּעַשׂ אֶת־מְעִיל הָאֵפֹד מַעֲשֵׂה אֹרֵג
כְּלִיל תְּכֵלֶת׃ 23 וּפִי־הַמְּעִיל בְּתוֹכוֹ כְּפִי
תַחְרָא שָׂפָה לְפִיו סָבִיב לֹא יִקָּרֵעַ׃
24 וַיַּעֲשׂוּ עַל־שׁוּלֵי הַמְּעִיל רִמּוֹנֵי תְּכֵלֶת
וְאַרְגָּמָן וְתוֹלַעַת שָׁנִי מָשְׁזָר׃ 25 וַיַּעֲשׂוּ
פַעֲמֹנֵי זָהָב טָהוֹר וַיִּתְּנוּ אֶת־הַפַּעֲמֹנִים
בְּתוֹךְ הָרִמֹּנִים עַל־שׁוּלֵי הַמְּעִיל סָבִיב
בְּתוֹךְ הָרִמֹּנִים׃ 26 פַּעֲמֹן וְרִמֹּן פַּעֲמֹן וְרִמֹּן
עַל־שׁוּלֵי הַמְּעִיל סָבִיב לְשָׁרֵת כַּאֲשֶׁר צִוָּה
יְהֹוָה אֶת־מֹשֶׁה׃ ס
27 וַיַּעֲשׂוּ אֶת־הַכָּתְנֹת שֵׁשׁ מַעֲשֵׂה אֹרֵג
לְאַהֲרֹן וּלְבָנָיו׃ 28 וְאֵת הַמִּצְנֶפֶת שֵׁשׁ
וְאֶת־פַּאֲרֵי הַמִּגְבָּעֹת שֵׁשׁ וְאֶת־מִכְנְסֵי

its inner edge, which faced the ephod. 20They made
two other rings of gold and fastened them on the
front of the ephod, low on the two shoulder-pieces,
close to its seam above the decorated band. 21The
breastpiece was held in place by a cord of blue from
its rings to the rings of the ephod, so that the
breastpiece rested on the decorated band and did
not come loose from the ephod—as יהוה had commanded Moses.

22The robe for the ephod was made of woven
work, of pure blue. 23The opening of the robe, in
the middle of it, was like the opening of a coat of
mail, with a binding around the opening, so that it
would not tear. 24On the hem of the robe they
made pomegranates of blue, purple, and crimson
yarns, twisted. 25They also made bells of pure gold,
and attached the bells between the pomegranates,
all around the hem of the robe, between the pomegranates: 26a bell and a pomegranate, a bell and a
pomegranate, all around the hem of the robe for officiating in—as יהוה had commanded Moses.

27They made the tunics of fine linen, of woven
work, for Aaron and his sons; 28and the headdress
of fine linen, and the decorated turbans of fine

APPAREL (39:22–31)

In addition to the ritual items, Aaron and the other priests wear special garments. The description of these garments in this section includes somewhat more detail than in the earlier, prescriptive account (28:31–43), but it abbreviates the information about when these garments are worn (28:34, 41–43). These items of clothing may not have a direct role in what the priests do, but they contribute to the overall sanctity of the Tabernacle and its rituals.

22. *The robe.* The artisans make the special robe for the chief priestly officer. The full-length robe was blue, with bells and multicolored tassels in the shape of pomegranates on the skirt (see at 28:31–35).

24. *pomegranates.* The pomegranate was a symbol of fertility and a well-known decorative element in ancient Near Eastern art.

25. *bells.* The sound of the bells apparently was intended to ward off danger. In this case, the danger would have been the intense holiness emanating from the presence of God as the chief priestly official enters the holy zone of the Tabernacle (28:35).

27. *tunics of fine linen.* A tunic was the standard garment for both women and men in the eastern Mediterranean region for about a thousand years (in the Late Bronze and Iron Ages, from the mid-2nd to the mid-1st millennia B.C.E.).

28. *headdress... decorated turbans.* The headdress of Aaron's sons is actually more of a cap than a

linen, and the linen breeches of fine twisted linen; [29]and sashes of fine twisted linen, blue, purple, and crimson yarns, done in embroidery—as יהוה had commanded Moses.

[30]They made the frontlet for the holy diadem of pure gold, and incised upon it the seal inscription: "Holy to יהוה." [31]They attached to it a cord of blue to fix it upon the headdress above—as יהוה had commanded Moses.

[32]Thus was completed all the work of the Tabernacle of the Tent of Meeting. The Israelites did so; just as יהוה had commanded Moses, so they did.

הַבָּד שֵׁשׁ מָשְׁזָר׃ 29 וְאֶת־הָאַבְנֵט שֵׁשׁ
מָשְׁזָר וּתְכֵלֶת וְאַרְגָּמָן וְתוֹלַעַת שָׁנִי
מַעֲשֵׂה רֹקֵם כַּאֲשֶׁר צִוָּה יְהוָה אֶת־
מֹשֶׁה׃ ס
30 וַיַּעֲשׂוּ אֶת־צִיץ נֵזֶר־הַקֹּדֶשׁ זָהָב טָהוֹר
וַיִּכְתְּבוּ עָלָיו מִכְתַּב פִּתּוּחֵי חוֹתָם קֹדֶשׁ
לַיהוָה׃ 31 וַיִּתְּנוּ עָלָיו פְּתִיל תְּכֵלֶת לָתֵת
עַל־הַמִּצְנֶפֶת מִלְמָעְלָה כַּאֲשֶׁר צִוָּה יְהוָה
אֶת־מֹשֶׁה׃ ס
32 וַתֵּכֶל כָּל־עֲבֹדַת מִשְׁכַּן אֹהֶל מוֹעֵד
וַיַּעֲשׂוּ בְּנֵי יִשְׂרָאֵל כְּכֹל אֲשֶׁר צִוָּה יְהוָה
אֶת־מֹשֶׁה כֵּן עָשׂוּ׃ פ

turban. The headgear of the chief priestly official is more elaborate and includes a crown or diadem (29:6); see also at 28:36.

***linen breeches.*** Earlier in the text, God mandated these breeches to function as an undergarment worn by all priestly ranks, perhaps for reasons of modesty (28:42–43). Undergarments were not part of ordinary apparel in biblical times, nor were they sacral garments.

## *Summary of the Completed Components* (39:32–43)

The completion of the vestments brings to an end the task of making all the components of the Tabernacle. The narrative proclaims this fact (39:32) and then describes how all the constituent parts are brought to Moses for him to see and bless (39:33–43).

### ANNOUNCEMENT OF COMPLETION (39:32)

Although some consider this verse a concluding observation to the preceding unit on the vestments, the language seems to be quite general, referring to the completion of the components of the entire project.

*32. completed.* The term for completing the work is the same as that used in Genesis 2:1, 2 for the completion of God's creation of the world. This allusion to divine creation, in which the construction of God's earthly abode reflects aspects of the creation of the world, anticipates the profusion of such allusions in Exodus 40.

***Tabernacle of the Tent of Meeting.*** These two designations, *Mishkan* and *Ohel Mo'ed*, are juxtaposed only here and in 40:2, 6, 29, thus bringing together the sacred shrine's two functions: the Tabernacle (*Mishkan*) as dwelling-palace for God (see at 25:8), and the Tent of Meeting (*Ohel Mo'ed*) as the place where God will "meet" with priestly and prophetic leaders to communicate the divine will (see at 27:21).

***The Israelites did so.*** Artisans have actually done the work, yet they represent the Israelites. All the people—women and men—contributed materials; and the edifice will serve them all.

***as יהוה had commanded Moses.*** This clause is used to attribute the making of the Tabernacle's components to Moses' role as mediator of God's commands.

[33]Then they brought the Tabernacle to Moses,
with the Tent and all its furnishings: its clasps, its
planks, its bars, its posts, and its sockets; [34]the covering of tanned ram skins, the covering of dolphin
skins, and the curtain for the screen; [35]the Ark of
the Pact and its poles, and the cover; [36]the table and
all its utensils, and the bread of display; [37]the pure
lampstand, its lamps—lamps in due order—and all
its fittings, and the oil for lighting; [38]the altar of
gold, the oil for anointing, the aromatic incense,
and the screen for the entrance of the Tent; [39]the
copper altar with its copper grating, its poles and all
its utensils, and the laver and its stand; [40]the hangings of the enclosure, its posts and its sockets, the
screen for the gate of the enclosure, its cords and its
pegs—all the furnishings for the service of the Tabernacle, the Tent of Meeting; [41]the service vestments for officiating in the sanctuary, the sacral
vestments of Aaron the priest, and the vestments of
his sons for priestly service. [42]Just as יהוה had commanded Moses, so the Israelites had done all the
work. [43]And when Moses saw that they had performed all the tasks—as יהוה had commanded, so
they had done—Moses blessed them.

33 וַיָּבִ֣יאוּ אֶת־הַמִּשְׁכָּן֮ אֶל־מֹשֶׁה֒ אֶת־
הָאֹ֖הֶל וְאֶת־כָּל־כֵּלָ֑יו קְרָסָ֣יו קְרָשָׁ֔יו בריחו
בְּרִיחָ֖יו וְעַמֻּדָ֥יו וַאֲדָנָֽיו׃ 34 וְאֶת־מִכְסֵ֞ה
עוֹרֹ֤ת הָֽאֵילִם֙ הַמְאָדָּמִ֔ים וְאֶת־מִכְסֵ֖ה עֹרֹ֣ת
הַתְּחָשִׁ֑ים וְאֵ֖ת פָּרֹ֥כֶת הַמָּסָֽךְ׃ 35 אֶת־אֲר֥וֹן
הָעֵדֻ֖ת וְאֶת־בַּדָּ֑יו וְאֵ֖ת הַכַּפֹּֽרֶת׃ 36 אֶת־
הַשֻּׁלְחָן֙ אֶת־כָּל־כֵּלָ֔יו וְאֵ֖ת לֶ֥חֶם הַפָּנִֽים׃
37 אֶת־הַמְּנֹרָ֨ה הַטְּהֹרָ֜ה אֶת־נֵרֹתֶ֗יהָ נֵרֹ֛ת
הַמַּעֲרָכָ֖ה וְאֶת־כָּל־כֵּלֶ֑יהָ וְאֵ֖ת שֶׁ֥מֶן
הַמָּאֽוֹר׃ 38 וְאֵ֗ת מִזְבַּ֣ח הַזָּהָ֔ב וְאֵת֙ שֶׁ֣מֶן
הַמִּשְׁחָ֔ה וְאֵ֖ת קְטֹ֣רֶת הַסַּמִּ֑ים וְאֵ֕ת מָסַ֖ךְ
פֶּ֥תַח הָאֹֽהֶל׃ 39 אֵ֣ת ׀ מִזְבַּ֣ח הַנְּחֹ֗שֶׁת וְאֶת־
מִכְבַּ֤ר הַנְּחֹ֙שֶׁת֙ אֲשֶׁר־ל֔וֹ אֶת־בַּדָּ֖יו וְאֶת־
כָּל־כֵּלָ֑יו אֶת־הַכִּיֹּ֖ר וְאֶת־כַּנּֽוֹ׃ 40 אֵת֩ קַלְעֵ֨י
הֶחָצֵ֜ר אֶת־עַמֻּדֶ֣יהָ וְאֶת־אֲדָנֶ֗יהָ וְאֶת־
הַמָּסָךְ֙ לְשַׁ֣עַר הֶחָצֵ֔ר אֶת־מֵיתָרָ֖יו וִיתֵדֹתֶ֑יהָ
וְאֵ֗ת כָּל־כְּלֵ֛י עֲבֹדַ֥ת הַמִּשְׁכָּ֖ן לְאֹ֥הֶל מוֹעֵֽד׃
41 אֶת־בִּגְדֵ֥י הַשְּׂרָ֖ד לְשָׁרֵ֣ת בַּקֹּ֑דֶשׁ אֶת־בִּגְדֵ֤י
הַקֹּ֙דֶשׁ֙ לְאַהֲרֹ֣ן הַכֹּהֵ֔ן וְאֶת־בִּגְדֵ֥י בָנָ֖יו
לְכַהֵֽן׃ 42 כְּכֹ֛ל אֲשֶׁר־צִוָּ֥ה יְהוָ֖ה אֶת־מֹשֶׁ֑ה
כֵּ֤ן עָשׂוּ֙ בְּנֵ֣י יִשְׂרָאֵ֔ל אֵ֖ת כָּל־הָעֲבֹדָֽה׃
43 וַיַּ֨רְא מֹשֶׁ֜ה אֶת־כָּל־הַמְּלָאכָ֗ה וְהִנֵּה֙
עָשׂ֣וּ אֹתָ֔הּ כַּאֲשֶׁ֛ר צִוָּ֥ה יְהוָ֖ה כֵּ֣ן עָשׂ֑וּ
וַיְבָ֥רֶךְ אֹתָ֖ם מֹשֶֽׁה׃ פ

### GENERAL INVENTORY OF COMPLETED COMPONENTS (39:33–43)

Moses has commissioned all the components of the Tabernacle, which now are brought to him. The items are listed in the order in which they have been made.

*33. Tabernacle.* Here the term *mishkan* designates the entire complex, with its furnishings and installations, in contrast to 26:1–14 and 36:8–19, where the term denotes just the tent itself.

*42. Just as* יהוה *had commanded Moses.* In somewhat abbreviated and rearranged fashion, this verse repeats v. 32, which began this inventory passage.

*43. when Moses saw . . . Moses blessed them.* This verse contains another echo of the first creation account of Genesis. Just as God saw all the created components of the universe in Genesis 1, so Moses sees all the components of the Tabernacle. And just as God offers a blessing at the end of creation (Genesis 2:3; see also 1:22, 28), so Moses blesses the people who have completed their creative tasks.

**40** And יהוה spoke to Moses, saying:
[2]On the first day of the first month you shall set
up the Tabernacle of the Tent of Meeting. [3]Place
there the Ark of the Pact, and screen off the ark
with the curtain. [4]Bring in the table and lay out its
due setting; bring in the lampstand and light its
lamps; [5]and place the gold altar of incense before
the Ark of the Pact. Then put up the screen for the
entrance of the Tabernacle.
[6]You shall place the altar of burnt offering
before the entrance of the Tabernacle of the Tent
of Meeting. [7]Place the laver between the Tent of

מ וַיְדַבֵּ֥ר יְהֹוָ֖ה אֶל־מֹשֶׁ֥ה לֵּאמֹֽר׃
2 בְּיוֹם־הַחֹ֥דֶשׁ הָרִאשׁ֖וֹן בְּאֶחָ֣ד לַחֹ֑דֶשׁ
תָּקִ֕ים אֶת־מִשְׁכַּ֖ן אֹ֥הֶל מוֹעֵֽד׃ 3 וְשַׂמְתָּ֣
שָׁ֔ם אֵ֖ת אֲר֣וֹן הָעֵד֑וּת וְסַכֹּתָ֥ עַל־הָאָרֹ֖ן אֶת־
הַפָּרֹֽכֶת׃ 4 וְהֵבֵאתָ֙ אֶת־הַשֻּׁלְחָ֔ן וְעָרַכְתָּ֖
אֶת־עֶרְכּ֑וֹ וְהֵבֵאתָ֙ אֶת־הַמְּנֹרָ֔ה וְהַעֲלֵיתָ֖
אֶת־נֵרֹתֶֽיהָ׃ 5 וְנָתַתָּ֞ה אֶת־מִזְבַּ֤ח הַזָּהָב֙
לִקְטֹ֔רֶת לִפְנֵ֖י אֲר֣וֹן הָעֵדֻ֑ת וְשַׂמְתָּ֛ אֶת־
מָסַ֥ךְ הַפֶּ֖תַח לַמִּשְׁכָּֽן׃
6 וְנָ֣תַתָּ֔ה אֵ֖ת מִזְבַּ֣ח הָעֹלָ֑ה לִפְנֵ֕י פֶּ֖תַח
מִשְׁכַּ֥ן אֹֽהֶל־מוֹעֵֽד׃ 7 וְנָתַתָּ֙ אֶת־הַכִּיֹּ֔ר בֵּֽין־

## *Erection and Consecration of the Tabernacle* (40:1–38)

The last unit of this parashah mirrors Genesis 1, in which God's creative acts are first stated ("Let there be…") and then carried out ("…and so it was"). The first half of Exodus 40 is the equivalent of "Let there be…," in which God gives Moses a final set of instructions for erecting the sacred shrine (vv. 1–16). The next part of the unit reflects the "…and so it was" aspect of the Tabernacle (vv. 17–33). Thus the erection of God's earthly abode is tantamount to the creation of the world; indeed, as was the case for temple buildings in the ancient Near East, the Tabernacle is conceptually a microcosm of the universe. (See also *Vayak'heil*, Contemporary Reflection, p. 539.)

The last few verses of Exodus describe God's entry into the Tabernacle (vv. 34–38).

### DIRECTIONS FOR ERECTING THE TABERNACLE COMPLEX (40:1–8)

The order of God's succinct instructions fits the logic of building construction.

*2. first day of the first month.* This refers to New Year's Day. Thus, the beginning of the existence of the shrine, which is a microcosm of the cosmos, is keyed to the creation of the world. It is as if God's role as omnipotent creator is mirrored in and signified by God's earthly abode. But the Tabernacle's existence is also keyed to the beginning of Israel's existence as a free people: it comes nine months after the people arrive at Sinai (19:1) and virtually on the first anniversary of the beginning of freedom, which was on the "fourteenth day of the first month" (12:6, 18). The month is not named, but it is probably Nisan. Thus the Tabernacle would be completed in time for the first celebration of Pesach (see Numbers 9:1–14).

*set up.* The priestly narrator frequently, as here, uses a causative form of the Hebrew verb (*k-w-m*, "to stand, rise") to indicate the establishment of the *Mishkan.* (On the "priestly" voice in the Torah, see p. 566.) In priestly texts, the root also occurs as part of the expression "to establish the covenant" with God (see 6:4). Using the same verb for the Tabernacle and the covenant provides a connection between these two foundational aspects of Israelite national life.

*Tabernacle of the Tent of Meeting.* This phrase is an inclusive term for the portable wilderness edifice (see at 39:32).

*3–8.* This is the briefest of all the listings of the fixed components of the sacred shrine, and it excludes the vestments.

Meeting and the altar, and put water in it. 8 Set up
the enclosure round about, and put in place the
screen for the gate of the enclosure.

9 You shall take the anointing oil and anoint the
Tabernacle and all that is in it to consecrate it and
all its furnishings, so that it shall be holy. 10 Then
anoint the altar of burnt offering and all its utensils
to consecrate the altar, so that the altar shall be
most holy. 11 And anoint the laver and its stand to
consecrate it.

12 You shall bring Aaron and his sons forward
to the entrance of the Tent of Meeting and wash
them with the water. 13 Put the sacral vestments on
Aaron, and anoint him and consecrate him, that he
may serve Me as priest. 14 Then bring his sons forward, put tunics on them, 15 and anoint them as you
have anointed their father, that they may serve Me
as priests. This their anointing shall serve them for
everlasting priesthood throughout the ages.

16 This Moses did; just as יהוה had commanded
him, so he did.

אֹהֶל מוֹעֵד וּבֵין הַמִּזְבֵּחַ וְנָתַתָּ שָׁם מָיִם׃
8 וְשַׂמְתָּ אֶת־הֶחָצֵר סָבִיב וְנָתַתָּ אֶת־מָסַךְ
שַׁעַר הֶחָצֵר׃
9 וְלָקַחְתָּ אֶת־שֶׁמֶן הַמִּשְׁחָה וּמָשַׁחְתָּ אֶת־
הַמִּשְׁכָּן וְאֶת־כָּל־אֲשֶׁר־בּוֹ וְקִדַּשְׁתָּ אֹתוֹ
וְאֶת־כָּל־כֵּלָיו וְהָיָה קֹדֶשׁ׃ 10 וּמָשַׁחְתָּ
אֶת־מִזְבַּח הָעֹלָה וְאֶת־כָּל־כֵּלָיו וְקִדַּשְׁתָּ
אֶת־הַמִּזְבֵּחַ וְהָיָה הַמִּזְבֵּחַ קֹדֶשׁ קָדָשִׁים׃
11 וּמָשַׁחְתָּ אֶת־הַכִּיֹּר וְאֶת־כַּנּוֹ וְקִדַּשְׁתָּ
אֹתוֹ׃
12 וְהִקְרַבְתָּ אֶת־אַהֲרֹן וְאֶת־בָּנָיו אֶל־פֶּתַח
אֹהֶל מוֹעֵד וְרָחַצְתָּ אֹתָם בַּמָּיִם׃
13 וְהִלְבַּשְׁתָּ אֶת־אַהֲרֹן אֵת בִּגְדֵי הַקֹּדֶשׁ
וּמָשַׁחְתָּ אֹתוֹ וְקִדַּשְׁתָּ אֹתוֹ וְכִהֵן לִי׃
14 וְאֶת־בָּנָיו תַּקְרִיב וְהִלְבַּשְׁתָּ אֹתָם
כֻּתֳּנֹת׃ 15 וּמָשַׁחְתָּ אֹתָם כַּאֲשֶׁר מָשַׁחְתָּ
אֶת־אֲבִיהֶם וְכִהֲנוּ לִי וְהָיְתָה לִהְיֹת לָהֶם
מָשְׁחָתָם לִכְהֻנַּת עוֹלָם לְדֹרֹתָם׃
16 וַיַּעַשׂ מֹשֶׁה כְּכֹל אֲשֶׁר צִוָּה יְהוָה אֹתוֹ
כֵּן עָשָׂה׃ ס

### DIRECTIONS FOR ANOINTING THE TABERNACLE COMPLEX AND PERSONNEL (40:9–16)

Erecting the shrine does not in and of itself make it sacred. A special ceremony of consecration—in which all the components (including the vestments), as well as the priests themselves are anointed—will change the status of the entire complex from profane to holy.

*9.* ***anointing oil.*** Anointing brings about an elevation of status in the ancient Near East and in ancient Israel (see at 29:7).

***consecrate.*** The allusions to creation continue, for the Hebrew here echoes the language of Genesis 2:3, when God blesses and consecrates the seventh day (in the present translation, "made it holy").

*12–15.* This section discusses the same three procedures—washing, enrobing, anointing—as prescribed in Exodus 29. However, there is no hint of the elaborate sacrificial offerings detailed in that unit. Perhaps the Aaron-centered nature of the sacrifices would have been out of place in this Moses-centered conclusion.

*15.* ***throughout the ages.*** This is language typically used to justify a status or practice at the time of the narrator on the basis of its authoritative origin (as in 12:14).

*16.* Since Moses appears here and in 40:1, he frames the two sets of directives, thus intensifying his involvement with all these final tasks assigned by God.

[17]In the first month of the second year, on the first of the month, the Tabernacle was set up. [18]Moses set up the Tabernacle, placing its sockets, setting up its planks, inserting its bars, and erecting its posts. [19]He spread the tent over the Tabernacle, placing the covering of the tent on top of it—just as יהוה had commanded Moses.

[20]He took the Pact and placed it in the ark; he fixed the poles to the ark, placed the cover on top of the ark, [21]and brought the ark inside the Tabernacle. Then he put up the curtain for screening, and screened off the Ark of the Pact—just as יהוה had commanded Moses.

[22]He placed the table in the Tent of Meeting, outside the curtain, on the north side of the Tabernacle. [23]Upon it he laid out the setting of bread before יהוה—as יהוה had commanded Moses. [24]He placed the lampstand in the Tent of Meeting opposite the table, on the south side of the Tabernacle. [25]And he lit the lamps before יהוה—as יהוה had commanded Moses. [26]He placed the altar of gold in the Tent of Meeting, before the curtain. [27]On it he burned aromatic incense—as יהוה had commanded Moses.

17 וַיְהִ֞י בַּחֹ֧דֶשׁ הָרִאשׁ֛וֹן בַּשָּׁנָ֥ה הַשֵּׁנִ֖ית
בְּאֶחָ֣ד לַחֹ֑דֶשׁ הוּקַ֖ם הַמִּשְׁכָּֽן׃ 18 וַיָּ֨קֶם
מֹשֶׁ֜ה אֶת־הַמִּשְׁכָּ֗ן וַיִּתֵּן֙ אֶת־אֲדָנָ֔יו וַיָּ֨שֶׂם֙
אֶת־קְרָשָׁ֔יו וַיִּתֵּ֖ן אֶת־בְּרִיחָ֑יו וַיָּ֖קֶם אֶת־
עַמּוּדָֽיו׃ 19 וַיִּפְרֹ֤שׂ אֶת־הָאֹ֙הֶל֙ עַל־הַמִּשְׁכָּ֔ן
וַיָּ֜שֶׂם אֶת־מִכְסֵ֥ה הָאֹ֛הֶל עָלָ֖יו מִלְמָ֑עְלָה
כַּאֲשֶׁ֛ר צִוָּ֥ה יְהֹוָ֖ה אֶת־מֹשֶֽׁה׃ ס
20 וַיִּקַּ֞ח וַיִּתֵּ֤ן אֶת־הָֽעֵדֻת֙ אֶל־הָ֣אָרֹ֔ן וַיָּ֥שֶׂם
אֶת־הַבַּדִּ֖ים עַל־הָאָרֹ֑ן וַיִּתֵּ֧ן אֶת־הַכַּפֹּ֛רֶת
עַל־הָאָרֹ֖ן מִלְמָֽעְלָה׃ 21 וַיָּבֵ֣א אֶת־הָאָרֹן֮
אֶל־הַמִּשְׁכָּן֒ וַיָּ֗שֶׂם אֵ֚ת פָּרֹ֣כֶת הַמָּסָ֔ךְ וַיָּ֕סֶךְ
עַ֖ל אֲר֣וֹן הָעֵד֑וּת כַּאֲשֶׁ֛ר צִוָּ֥ה יְהֹוָ֖ה אֶת־
מֹשֶֽׁה׃ ס
22 וַיִּתֵּ֤ן אֶת־הַשֻּׁלְחָן֙ בְּאֹ֣הֶל מוֹעֵ֔ד עַ֛ל יֶ֥רֶךְ
הַמִּשְׁכָּ֖ן צָפֹ֑נָה מִח֖וּץ לַפָּרֹֽכֶת׃ 23 וַיַּעֲרֹ֥ךְ
עָלָ֛יו עֵ֥רֶךְ לֶ֖חֶם לִפְנֵ֣י יְהֹוָ֑ה כַּאֲשֶׁ֛ר צִוָּ֥ה
יְהֹוָ֖ה אֶת־מֹשֶֽׁה׃ ס 24 וַיָּ֤שֶׂם אֶת־
הַמְּנֹרָה֙ בְּאֹ֣הֶל מוֹעֵ֔ד נֹ֖כַח הַשֻּׁלְחָ֑ן עַ֛ל
יֶ֥רֶךְ הַמִּשְׁכָּ֖ן נֶֽגְבָּה׃ 25 וַיַּ֥עַל הַנֵּרֹ֖ת לִפְנֵ֣י
יְהֹוָ֑ה כַּאֲשֶׁ֛ר צִוָּ֥ה יְהֹוָ֖ה אֶת־מֹשֶֽׁה׃ ס
26 וַיָּ֛שֶׂם אֶת־מִזְבַּ֥ח הַזָּהָ֖ב בְּאֹ֣הֶל מוֹעֵ֑ד
לִפְנֵ֖י הַפָּרֹֽכֶת׃ 27 וַיַּקְטֵ֥ר עָלָ֖יו קְטֹ֣רֶת סַמִּ֑ים
כַּאֲשֶׁ֛ר צִוָּ֥ה יְהֹוָ֖ה אֶת־מֹשֶֽׁה׃ ס

## EXECUTION OF THE DIRECTIONS (40:17–33)

Moses now carries out God's commands to erect the Tabernacle and all its components. There is no mention, however, of the vestments or the consecration of the priests (see Leviticus 8). The clause "as יהוה commanded Moses" appears seven times in this passage (vv. 19, 21, 23, 25, 27, 29, and 32), echoing the seven units of time in the creation account of Genesis 1–2:4. As the world was created in seven days, so the Tabernacle—the microcosm of the world—is erected in seven stages. The exalted God-like role of Moses is reflected in the attribution to him alone of all the elaborate construction work, inconceivable without a team of workers.

*17. first month of the second year, on the first of the month.* The same information was given in 40:2, although here the year is added—presumably "the second year" after the departure from Egypt.

*18–33.* This passage presents a final listing of the components of the sacred shrine, including the initial use of all the ritual components. Moses eclipses Aaron once more in this parashah by initiating what are otherwise considered priestly assignments. Moses already possesses sanctity, which the priests do not gain until they have been sanctified by being washed, clothed, anointed, and daubed with ritual fluids—procedures not mentioned until Leviticus 8.

[28]Then he put up the screen for the entrance of
the Tabernacle. [29]At the entrance of the Tabernacle
of the Tent of Meeting he placed the altar of burnt
offering. On it he offered up the burnt offering and
the meal offering—as יהוה had commanded Moses.
[30]He placed the laver between the Tent of Meeting
and the altar, and put water in it for washing.
[31]From it Moses and Aaron and his sons would
wash their hands and feet; [32]they washed when they
entered the Tent of Meeting and when they approached the altar—as יהוה had commanded Moses. [33]And he set up the enclosure around the Tabernacle and the altar, and put up the screen for the
gate of the enclosure.

When Moses had finished the work, [34]the cloud
covered the Tent of Meeting, and the Presence of
יהוה filled the Tabernacle. [35]Moses could not enter
the Tent of Meeting, because the cloud had settled

28 וַיָּ֥שֶׂם אֶת־מָסַ֛ךְ הַפֶּ֖תַח לַמִּשְׁכָּֽן׃ 29 וְאֵת֙
מִזְבַּ֣ח הָעֹלָ֔ה שָׂ֕ם פֶּ֖תַח מִשְׁכַּ֣ן אֹֽהֶל־מוֹעֵ֑ד
וַיַּ֣עַל עָלָ֗יו אֶת־הָֽעֹלָה֙ וְאֶת־הַמִּנְחָ֔ה כַּאֲשֶׁ֛ר
צִוָּ֥ה יְהֹוָ֖ה אֶת־מֹשֶֽׁה׃ ס 30 וַיָּ֙שֶׂם֙ אֶת־
הַכִּיֹּ֔ר בֵּֽין־אֹ֥הֶל מוֹעֵ֖ד וּבֵ֣ין הַמִּזְבֵּ֑חַ וַיִּתֵּ֥ן
שָׁ֛מָּה מַ֖יִם לְרָחְצָֽה׃ 31 וְרָחֲצ֣וּ מִמֶּ֔נּוּ מֹשֶׁ֖ה
וְאַהֲרֹ֣ן וּבָנָ֑יו אֶת־יְדֵיהֶ֖ם וְאֶת־רַגְלֵיהֶֽם׃
32 בְּבֹאָ֞ם אֶל־אֹ֣הֶל מוֹעֵ֗ד וּבְקָֽרְבָתָ֛ם אֶל־
הַמִּזְבֵּ֖חַ יִרְחָ֑צוּ כַּאֲשֶׁ֛ר צִוָּ֥ה יְהֹוָ֖ה אֶת־
מֹשֶֽׁה׃ ס 33 וַיָּ֣קֶם אֶת־הֶחָצֵ֗ר סָבִיב֙
לַמִּשְׁכָּ֣ן וְלַמִּזְבֵּ֔חַ וַיִּתֵּ֕ן אֶת־מָסַ֖ךְ שַׁ֣עַר
הֶחָצֵ֑ר
וַיְכַ֥ל מֹשֶׁ֖ה אֶת־הַמְּלָאכָֽה׃ פ 34 וַיְכַ֥ס
הֶעָנָ֖ן אֶת־אֹ֣הֶל מוֹעֵ֑ד וּכְב֣וֹד יְהֹוָ֔ה מָלֵ֖א
אֶת־הַמִּשְׁכָּֽן׃ 35 וְלֹֽא־יָכֹ֣ל מֹשֶׁ֗ה לָבוֹא֙ אֶל־
אֹ֣הֶל מוֹעֵ֔ד כִּֽי־שָׁכַ֥ן עָלָ֖יו הֶעָנָ֑ן וּכְב֣וֹד יְהֹוָ֔ה

*30. He placed the laver between the Tent of Meeting and the altar.* The laver, or wash basin, was made from mirrors donated by women (see at 38:8). Washing from it symbolized or effected the purification of the priests before they performed sacral rites.

*33. When Moses had finished the work.* In this edition of the Torah, this clause is considered the beginning of a new unit of thought. However, it could also be translated "and Moses finished his work," thus completing the account of Moses erecting the shrine. Either way, the language echoes Genesis 2:2, "God finished the work" of Creation.

## ENTRY OF GOD'S PRESENCE (40:34–38)

Moses has completed the creation of God's earthy abode; now the divine presence can enter the sacred shrine. This passage is the climax of this parashah, and indeed of the entire book of Exodus. The promise that God would dwell among the people and be their God can now be realized (see at 25:8; 29:45). What an enormous contrast: the homeless people who departed Egypt now have a glorious home for their deity!

*34. cloud.* The narratives of the wilderness, Sinai, and the Golden Calf all associate the cloud with the divine presence (see at 13:21). Its appearance here links these major elements of the book of Exodus with the Tabernacle project.

*35.* At first glance it seems surprising that Moses and God's presence could not be in the tent at the same time—especially in light of 33:9–11, where God spoke directly to Moses inside the Tent of Meeting (outside the camp) while the cloud hovered at the entrance. However, the present passage concerns the function of the cloud (and fire) in the journey to the Promised Land that is about to start up again, not the oracular function of the tent as expressed in Exodus 33.

*settled.* The verb comes from the root *sh-k-n*, which means "to dwell" as well as "to settle" (see at 25:8); it is the root for the noun *mishkan* (Tabernacle) as well as *Shechinah* (see *T'rumah*, Post-biblical Interpretations, p. 468).

upon it and the Presence of יהוה filled the Tabernacle. 36When the cloud lifted from the Tabernacle,
the Israelites would set out, on their various journeys; 37but if the cloud did not lift, they would not set out until such time as it did lift. 38For over the Tabernacle a cloud of יהוה rested by day, and fire would appear in it by night, in the view of all the house of Israel throughout their journeys.

מָלֵ֥א אֶת־הַמִּשְׁכָּֽן׃ 36 וּבְהֵעָל֤וֹת הֶֽעָנָן֙ מֵעַ֣ל
הַמִּשְׁכָּ֔ן יִסְע֖וּ בְּנֵ֣י יִשְׂרָאֵ֑ל בְּכֹ֖ל מַסְעֵיהֶֽם׃
37 וְאִם־לֹ֥א יֵעָלֶ֖ה הֶעָנָ֑ן וְלֹ֣א יִסְע֔וּ עַד־י֖וֹם
הֵעָלֹתֽוֹ׃ 38 כִּ֣י עֲנַ֨ן יְהוָ֤ה עַל־הַמִּשְׁכָּן֙ יוֹמָ֔ם
וְאֵ֕שׁ תִּהְיֶ֥ה לַ֖יְלָה בּ֑וֹ לְעֵינֵ֥י כָל־בֵּֽית־
יִשְׂרָאֵ֖ל בְּכָל־מַסְעֵיהֶֽם׃

*36. When the cloud lifted.* God does not permanently fill the shrine. When the cloud lifts, the people dismantle and pack up the Tabernacle and then travel onward. God is not confined to a single place or space, although God's imminence is more likely in the sacred space—Tabernacle or Temple—that the people construct according to divine specifications.

*38. journeys.* Heb. *masa.* It is fitting that Exodus ends with this word; its verbal root (*n-s-e*) was used frequently in Genesis for the movements of the ancestors, including their descent to Egypt (Genesis 46:1). The same root then appeared in Exodus to indicate the stages of travel of the Israelites from Egypt to Sinai (12:37; 13:20; 16:1; 17:1; and 19:2). It is also found frequently in Numbers, in reference to the wilderness wanderings (as in Numbers 10:12). Thus, the word "journeys" situates the entire Exodus narrative within the larger story of the Torah. Just as important, the concluding verse of Exodus proclaims that the Israelites will not be alone on their long and difficult journey to the Promised Land. Rather, they are to be guided night and day by the luminous cloud of God's presence.

—*Carol Meyers*

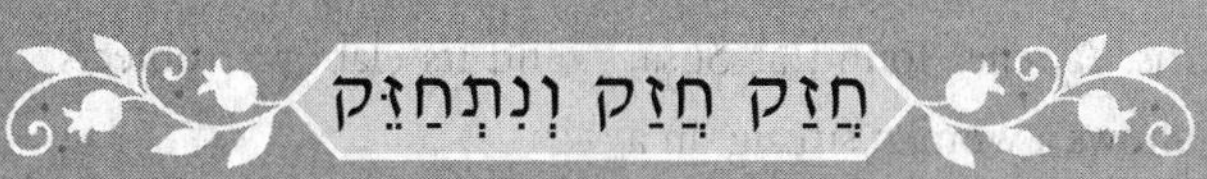

## Another View

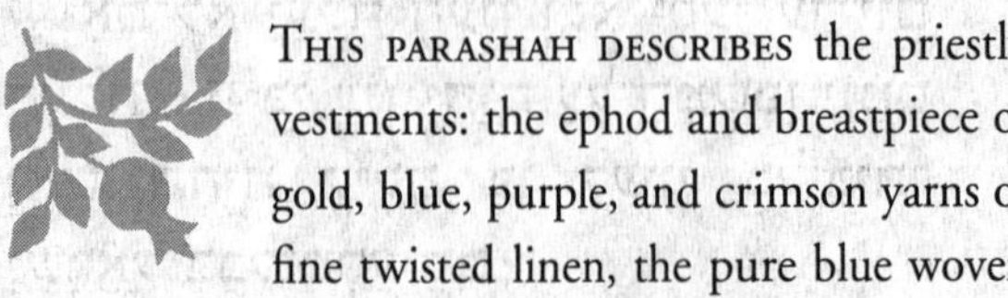

THIS PARASHAH DESCRIBES the priestly vestments: the ephod and breastpiece of gold, blue, purple, and crimson yarns of fine twisted linen, the pure blue woven robe with its pomegranates of blue, purple, and twisted crimson yarns on the hem, the tunics of fine linen woven work to be worn by Aaron and his sons, their headdress and decorated turbans of fine linen, and their sashes of fine embroidered blue, purple, and crimson linen yarns. Besides the priests' vestments, the text also mentions the hangings and curtains used to decorate the Tabernacle and to separate the rooms.

Producing textiles like these required a series of steps—carding, spinning, dyeing, and weaving the cotton, linen, or wool—tasks typically performed by women in the ancient Near East. Graves of women and girls often include weaving equipment such as bobbins and loom weights, whereas men's and boy's graves lack such equipment. Likewise, 4000-year-old graves of women in Turkmenia include specialized knives similar to those used by carpet weavers who live there today. An ancient Egyptian wooden model of a weaver's house shows women at work weaving, spinning, and winding the yarns. A relief found at Susa, dated to circa 1000 B.C.E., shows a woman sitting on a stool as she spins.

The objects described in this parashah were for use in the Tabernacle and later in the Jerusalem Temple. What kind of staff maintained those facilities? Consider that Mesopotamian and Egyptian temples were large estates that employed thousands of workers. Female workers associated with these large temples cared for the sick and served as midwives, cooks and pastry chefs, menial cleaners, and janitors, as well as spinners and weavers.

According to Exodus, women performed the skilled work involved in preparing the yarn and weaving the fabrics for the Tabernacle (35:25–26). Although women are not mentioned explicitly in this parashah, archeological evidence and biblical references to women spinning and weaving (Proverbs 31:19; II Kings 23:7; compare Isaiah 19:9) allow us to reconstruct the vital role that Exodus presumes that women played in the construction of the Tabernacle and its elaborate objects.

*Women played a vital role in the construction of the Tabernacle.*

*—Lisbeth S. Fried*

## Post-biblical Interpretations

***Now Bezalel, son of Uri son of Hur, of the tribe of Judah, had made all that* יהוה *had commanded Moses*** (38:22). Although no women are mentioned in Bezalel's genealogy, rabbinic tradition connected him with Moses' sister Miriam. Hur's father was Caleb, and Caleb's wife was Ephrath (I Chronicles 2:19). But Midrash *Sh'mot Rabbah* 1.13 and 1.17 suggested that Ephrath was, in fact, another name for Miriam—who was also identified with Puah, one of the heroic midwives of Exodus 1. All of these conflated identities combined to make Miriam the great-grandmother of Bezalel. According to *Sh'mot Rabbah* 48.4, Miriam was not only Bezalel's great-grandmother; she was also the source of his inspiration. As one of the two midwives who saved the Israelite infants, Miriam was rewarded with special access to wisdom. This midrashic tradition is based on the biblical statement that God "established households [literally: houses]" for the midwives (1:21); according to the Rabbis, Miriam's house was the house of wisdom. Since Bezalel, too, is associated with wisdom (35:31), the Rabbis assumed that the source of his special knowledge must have been Miriam. Thus, women played key roles at both the beginning and the conclusion of the book of Exodus: Moses could not have been saved without the ingenuity and bravery of women—including the midwives, his mother and sister, and Pharaoh's daughter—nor could the Tabernacle have been built without the wisdom that Miriam bequeathed to Bezalel.

*Women are able to discern when a cause is worthy of their generosity.*

***Then they brought the Tabernacle to Moses*** (39:33). For the Rabbis, the establishment of the Tabernacle represented the culmination of Israel's relationship with God. In a metaphor often found in rabbinic literature, *Sh'mot Rabbah* 52.5 invokes the relationship between a man and a woman to reflect upon the bond between God and Israel. However, while most such interpretations envisioned a marital relationship in which God was imagined as the husband and Israel as the wife, here we see something different. Based on Song of Songs 3:11, "O maidens of Zion, go forth / And gaze upon King Solomon / Wearing the crown that his mother / Gave him on his wedding day, / On his day of bliss," Rabbi Eleazar ben Rabbi Yose suggested that God first loved Israel like a father loves his daughter, and then, as God's love increased, like a man loves his sister. Finally, God's love for Israel reached the point where it was like the love a man has for his mother. Thus, each successive example represented a more intense love, including this striking idealization of the relationship between mother and son. Rabbi Eleazar then offered an interpretation based on the marital relationship; he concluded with a reflection on the destruction of the Temple and the promise that God would rebuild Jerusalem. Here, the proof text is Isaiah 51:3, and the image is of God comforting Zion in a time when "joy and gladness are found, thanksgiving and the strains of song." Ultimately, we learn from this midrash that when we read about the Tabernacle, we are to imagine both its destruction and its ultimate rebuilding. Above all, we are to remember that the loving and intimate relationship between God and Israel—whichever relational imagery we use—remains intact.

***In the first month . . . on the first of the month, the Tabernacle was set up*** (40:17). The rabbinic association of women with Rosh Chodesh, the celebration of the New Moon and the beginning of a month, has become well known. The usual explanation is that Rosh Chodesh was a reward for the Israelite women's refusal to contribute their jewelry to the making of the Golden Calf (Midrash *Pirkei D'Rabbi Eliezer* 45). However, another rabbinic tradition also links women with Rosh Chodesh via the erection of the Tabernacle. As we read in this verse, the Tabernacle was erected on the first day of the first month, namely, Rosh Chodesh Nisan. According to the *Shulchan Aruch* and its commentaries (*Orach Chaim* 417.1), this day was the original women's holiday, from which the idea of Rosh Chodesh arose. Women were connected with the erection of the Tabernacle because they were the first to contribute when the Tabernacle was being built (Nachmanides on 35:22). Women's support of the Tabernacle strengthens the significance of their earlier refusal to contribute to the Golden Calf: it indicates that women are able to discern when a cause is worthy of their generosity.

*—Lisa J. Grushcow*

# Contemporary Reflection

For the first time in the Torah, with the completion of the *Mishkan*, the presence of God has a regular home, an earthly residence. And this home is not only for God; it is a "Tent of Meeting" for Israel as well. When God's presence enters the *Mishkan*, it is clear that Israel's work in building this sacred structure has been blessed. For the first time, by learning from past mistakes, Israel—all Israel—has a place to experience God.

In other words, the same Israelites who once sought to contain power and divinity within the idol of the Golden Calf (Exodus 32) now create the *Mishkan* (Exodus 35–40), which, while made of the same materials and by some of the very same processes, emphatically does not attempt to contain God. Having been given an explicit opportunity to fall again into the trap of deifying something material, having been handed the opportunity to make a cage for God, the people instead create the *Mishkan* and regard it only as a space, not as a stand-in or a container for God (Avivah Gottlieb Zornberg, *The Particulars of Rapture*, 2001, pp. 480–481, 330–333). Once this purpose is established, God's presence dwells in the *Mishkan*, in their midst; the process of *t'shuvah* (repentance) is complete.

Given the prohibitions against making images of God, the disaster of the Golden Calf, and the lesson the Israelites have begun to learn that God cannot be represented physically, we might expect the presence of God in the *Mishkan* to be without form altogether, invisible. Wouldn't God's complete lack of form at this moment make perfect sense in light of the Israelites' newfound awareness and understanding?

However, God's presence is manifested in the *Mishkan* in not one but two different ways: as a cloud by day and fire by night. Why does God come to the Israelites (and to us, as we read) in these very common forms? Wouldn't the lesson of the Golden Calf be more clearly enforced if now God's presence remained untainted by any physical form?

Perhaps these manifestations exist precisely in order to teach the Israelites that an experience of God can exist within the visual and tangible realms. That is, the problem with worshipping the Golden Calf was not that the calf could be seen; it was that the Golden Calf was worshipped as if it contained God entirely, as if God was nowhere else. Here, the Israelites learn that an encounter with God does not have to be so abstract, so removed from their sensory experience that they are left without any means of comprehending or describing it. In other words, the divine experience can include things seen. However, it must also transform our grasp of the seen object, our understanding of God, and, by extension, the act of seeing and the seer.

*We look for visual evidence of God's presence in the world around us.*

Remember the narrative of the Burning Bush that was on fire but not consumed (3:1–4). This phenomenon is contrary to our understanding of what happens when a bush catches on fire. For Moses, the very existence of the Burning Bush not consumed awakens the possibility that there is something divine in that fire. God could just have easily come to Moses without a Burning Bush; however, this is what enables Moses to find evidence of God's presence. Before God even addresses Moses, he sees the fire acting differently and realizes that there is more to the world than what he knows.

Later, we read about two pillars that accompany the Israelites as they leave Egypt: a pillar of cloud by day and a pillar of fire by night (13:20–22). The cloud is a signpost and the fire an illuminated guide in the darkness; both show Israel the path to follow on their journey through the wilderness. But note that neither object acts naturally. The cloud does not blanket and obscure, as we expect clouds to do; instead, it is contained in a pillar and provides direction for the Israelites. Similarly, the fire does not spread and destroy whatever is in its path, as we expect fire to do; like the cloud, the fire is contained, a giant torch. In both of these manifestations, the Israelites began to see, just as Moses saw in the bush, the possibility of natural things, things of-this-earth, being bent and shaped in unnatural, divine ways.

Focusing on our parashah (40:34–38), God's presence now dwells in the completed *Mishkan,* not as something invisible to Israel, but as something very familiar. Just as before, God's presence is manifested as a cloud by day and fire by night. Here, too, the familiar acts in an unusual way. The cloud remains in the *Mishkan*; it does not drift or dissipate. Even more remarkably, the fire burns night after night and does not consume anything; each morning, the *Mishkan* remains intact (Zornberg, p. 492). These manifestations—these miracles—allow Israel to find and perceive God's presence but still remain aware that their perceptions cannot begin to encompass the totality of that presence.

Had God dwelt invisibly in the *Mishkan,* had the Israelites never seen God's presence there, they might have assumed that seeking visual encounters with God is a form of idolatry. By appearing "in the view of all the house of Israel" (40:38), God teaches that the problem with worshipping idols is not the visual experience itself; the problem occurs when the act merely confirms our preconceptions about God (Zornberg, p. 482). The Israelites see God's presence in natural, familiar forms that then transcend and undermine those forms. This seeing, and this dissonance, tests their understanding of the world and leads to a more complex relationship with God.

So it is for us: We need not be wary of looking for visual evidence of God's presence in the world around us. Seeking God's presence with our eyes is not idolatrous; it is only idolatry when we "know" in advance what we will see, when our expectations restrain us. Unfortunately, we may have been so afraid of making idols that we have limited ourselves to divine experiences that are abstract and often detached, expecting ourselves to develop a relationship with God without using our eyes. What would happen if we started looking for God's presence in fire and clouds once more? How much do our relationships with God stand to gain from our actually seeing what may have been there all along? At the very least, we will benefit from the search alone, from our looking day and night. And at best, it is possible that if we look, we will see. And then, we will never see the same way again, for we ourselves will have changed.

*—Noa Kushner*

# *Voices*

## *from* Bezalel

Amy Blank

*Exodus 38:22*

It was almost a disaster.

Moses knew only my skill,
my fingers fashioned by God.
The great dreamer placed his dream
into my hands—
the given Word that should become the given
form.

True, my fingers tingle
on fine grain of wood,
cool metals and thin-spun thread—
but Moses knew only the artisan.
I was silent before his fervor,
silent before the glowing pile of copper,
gold and silver from the mines;
sweet-scented wood freshly cut from forests;
the palette of scarlet, blue and purple threads;
linens—woven and embroidered,
wool and goatskins newly dressed,
even porpoise hides bright from the sea.
Was craftsman ever so endowed?

I heard his words:
"Create," he said, "the Tent of Meeting,
House of God." Words of command.
Moses forgot I was an artist
sudden in perception,
proud in fulfillment.
Even from Moses,
even from him
I would not take dictation.
Overwhelmed by the riches (legacy of Egypt)
and all the detail of the master-plan
I stood there speechless.
And it seemed that in the hollow of my hand
I held the image of a simple cup
clay-rounded to the palm—
a cup to drink from;
And I dreamed a perfect pitcher.

Moses, the artist of the Word,
had instant intuition—
"Then teach," he cried.
"Summon the artisans,
make live to them the Word
and let their fingers
drag the dream into reality."

So I did.
I need not wallow in the gold,
nor be entangled in the rainbow web
nor fall prey to jewels.
Each day brought quiet after-glow of sunsets
and in my palm the perfect cup
is fashioned, and in my hand,
I hold the perfect pitcher.

Glory to God! The Tent is done.

## *At Blue Dawn IX*

Kadya Molodowsky (transl. Kathryn Hellerstein)

*Exodus 39:1*

By the well they're sitting, spinning,
Seven women, seven women,
Ten threads, white on white, they're spinning,
Whispering the story, never-ending.
Says the first:
White goats are what I raise and keep
For rocking children fast asleep.
Says the second:
I plant the trees and sow the flowers
For children in the coming hours.
Says the third:
I sharpen arrows and bend bows
For amusement and repose.
Says the fourth:
I make chains, link part to part
For the binding of young hearts.
The fifth says nothing:
Red as sparks, the thread she pulls
And dips into the wells and cools.
Says the sixth:
I determine the weight
And measure
To measure fortune and weigh treasure.
Says the last:
This thread of mine
Is white, short-spun—
And with this thread, the story's done!

## *from* In Place of Belief

Grace Schulman

*Exodus 40:3–5*

Tradition threatens. Far off, I heard bells,
those pebbly ones that top scrolls in the ark.
Up ahead, gargoyles with toothy snarls
glared from a synagogue on Central Park.

I'd read the place grew from a wooden house.
When razed, its holy innards were sent on
to other temples: lamps, goblets for wine,
pointers, and floorboards that soak up prayers.

Once, turning thirteen, called to the ark,
I touched a scroll whose black letters blurred
like scuff marks on sand the sea had washed.
I listened for God's bass and heard instead

chatter, a squeaky platform. Shuddering,
how could I even mumble sacred songs.
Only now, through doors of a massive building
whose ark is curtained shut, silver bells ring.

## *At the Tent of Meeting*

Sherry Blumberg

*Exodus 40:33–34*

Finally, after long work, physical and mental,
I come to the opening of the tent.
I know, God—but do You know—
what this work means?

You have always been in my thoughts
always in my mind
and even sometimes in my aching back
as I worked and struggled on Your behalf.

Let the opening of the tent,
encourage the opening of the text
and let me, Your humble daughter,
enter and not hold back.

## *Psalm 32: A Song of Endings and Beginnings*

Debbie Perlman

*Exodus 40:33–38*

Let us sing of our completions, smooth, round,
Silvered voices to praise Your Name.

Every season holds starts and stops,
Years of trees and spirits and souls,
Days ripe with harmony and turning,
Circled, cycled, to order our lives.

Inside each completion,
We hear Your creation;
Inside our creations,
We resound with Your voice.

Let us mold a new shape for our completions,
Fluid and longing, subtle limbs
That lead us onward to praise Your Name.

Every season casts away its jagged edges.
Rubs away the torn moments
To rejoice in the realignment
Of old ways made straight.

Inside each refitting,
We renew again Your creation,
Pulling it taut against us,
A firm bound shield of Your affection.

Let us sing of our completions.
Your hand hovers, blesses,
Bids us move to new beginnings.
Your hand moves us forward,
Toward unimagined completions.

# ויקרא ✦ *Vayikra*

# LEVITICUS

LEVITICUS AIMS TO shape the Israelites into a holy people and to safeguard the purity that it considers essential for contact with the holy. The Hebrew name, *Vayikra* ("and [God] called"), refers to God's summoning Moses and giving him the instructions that constitute most of the book. The English name "Leviticus" refers to Levi, a son of Leah and Jacob and the ancestor of the priests.

Leviticus reflects the perception that God's created world is fundamentally harmonious, good, and orderly (as in Genesis 1). To preserve God's orderly world, where everything has an assigned place, Leviticus specifies what must be done whenever boundaries are wrongfully crossed, be they boundaries of the body, time, or space—such as between sacred and non-sacred, or between life and death. In this book's worldview, anyone who breaks God's ordained harmony can—and must—repair it. Rituals, including sacrifices, serve to cancel or neutralize damage done to the created order and thereby restore the equilibrium.

In Leviticus, a person's body, the sanctuary, and the community each constitute a microcosm of the universe in its sacred aspect.

*This book shows how women contribute to Israel's quest for a holy life.*

Each reflects and has an impact upon the larger, integrated whole. Consequently, holiness and purity are relevant to all aspects of Israelite life; they apply not merely to the sanctuary, but also to the body and the home. Therefore, the book legislates laws about food (Leviticus 11), sexual relations (Leviticus 18 and 20), and ethics (Leviticus 19), in addition to providing extensive instructions about sacrificial offerings (Leviticus 1–7). Although the priests have a unique role, all Israelites must be holy, for God is holy (see at 19:2).

Contemporary scholars ascribe Leviticus to priestly circles also responsible for other portions of the Torah (such as Genesis 1, the Tabernacle accounts in Exodus 25–40, and most of Numbers). Such scholars often differentiate between two priestly writings: the Priestly collection (Leviticus 1–16) that they call "P," and the Holiness Code (Leviticus 17–26) that they call "H," with Leviticus 27 as an appendix. While P emphasizes the unique privileges and responsibilities of the priests (defined as Aaron and his sons), H widens the notion of holiness to apply to all Israelites. For P, the priests (*kohanim*) and the Tabernacle are the exclusive intermediaries (and guardians) with regard to God's holiness; H, however, focuses on the people themselves as the vehicle for God's holiness.

Although Leviticus mentions only one woman by name (the otherwise unknown Shelomith; see at 24:11), many of its teachings clearly apply to women as members of the Israelite community. Like the men, women are bound by the book's various laws and must refrain from actions that may contaminate God's sanctuary or the community. In addition, Leviticus includes three types of laws uniquely relevant to women:

1. *Regulations about the processes by which women regain access to the sanctuary after childbirth and menstruation.* These conditions, like other conditions that pertain to the nexus between life and death (such as seminal emission for men), require ritual purification before normal life patterns may be resumed (see at Leviticus 12 and 15).

2. *Laws about sexual relations.* Regulations about prohibited sexual relationships demarcate for an Israelite male those women whose sexuality belongs to another man and are therefore forbidden to him; they also identify kinship structures that help locate women in the family constellation (see at Leviticus 18 and 20). Laws like these indicate that typically a woman's sexuality is only partly under her control. For example, as Judith Wegner notes, "an unmarried girl's biological function belongs legally to her father." According to Wegner, this does not mean a man could do with his daughter as he pleased. Rather, "the Torah certainly expects a father to protect his daughter's chastity until she reaches puberty and is married off" ("Leviticus," 1992, p. 45; but see *Acharei Mot*, Another View, p. 694, as well as at 18:10–17 and 20:17).

3. *Laws specifically concerning women in priestly families.* These include regulations as to whom a priest may marry (see at Leviticus 21), as well as when women may partake of the special holy portions designated for the priests.

Through all of these regulations, Leviticus shows, even when not addressing women, how women contribute to Israel's quest for a holy life.

—*Tamara Cohn Eskenazi*

# ויקרא ◆ *Vayikra*

LEVITICUS 1:1–5:26

## *A Call to Approach God*

PARASHAT VAYIKRA ("and [God] called") introduces one of the most challenging texts for contemporary readers. This portion begins the instructions on how to approach God by means of sacrificial offerings. Animal sacrifices are foreign to most modern readers and offensive to many. They were, however, integral to most recorded worship practices in the ancient Near Eastern and Mediterranean regions. Sacrifice continued well into the Common Era as the major way to approach the gods and to thank or appease them. Provisions for animal sacrifice are also included in the Koran, the sacred text of Islam.

Scholars of religion, attempting to understand the practice of animal sacrifice in the ancient world, suggest a number of possible explanations for why the practice endured. The rationale most frequently expressed in extra-biblical sources is that gods need to be fed as well as propitiated. Furthermore, life and fertility are gifts from the gods—gifts for which humans must show appreciation by offering something precious in return. In agricultural societies, the intimate connection between livestock and persons fostered an understanding that certain domestic animals could substitute for a human life. While these suggested explanations pertain to explicit reasons, some scholars link the pervasiveness of sacrifices in antiquity with a community's unacknowledged desire to reduce violence. Ritual slaughtering of animals as opposed to random killings, the explanation goes, would channel people's aggression into a socially constructive function and away from other forms of violence.

Israelite religion officially rejected an older idea that God requires sustenance like human beings. Nevertheless, it kept the *practice* of offering sacrifices as a way of serving God. The

*The legislation in this parashah applies equally to Israelite women and men.*

Hebrew word usually translated as "sacrifice," *korban*, implies coming close to God (the root *k-r-b* that forms *korban* also means "to come near") and is better translated as "near-offering." One underlying rationale for many biblical sacrifices is to express gratitude for one's good fortune; another rationale is that it is a means of returning the best to God—much like the payment of rent to a venerable landowner. In addition, certain sacrifices are aimed at helping people deal with the guilt of wrongdoing and with the impurity of sin, so that Israel would be on good terms with their Deity.

Sociologically speaking, sacrificial rites in antiquity served to bind community by providing a common meal that made scarce and costly meat available to many. Certain sacrifices functioned like a neighborhood barbecue celebrating a modern holiday: an opportunity to socialize and to eat well. Leviticus, however, seems to sanction killing an animal and eating its meat only as part of a sacrificial offering.

Although sacrifices form the major focus of this parashah, the concluding section expresses a deep concern with social and economic justice (see 5:20–26). Defrauding another person constitutes a sin against God; yet one must make amends to the injured party before offering a sacrifice to God.

The legislation in this parashah applies equally to Israelite women and men. Its terminology is pointedly gender inclusive, implying that women are expected to bring offerings. A later passage, Leviticus 12:6–8, explicitly addresses a situation in which a woman must bring two of the sacrifices mentioned in this parashah. Other biblical texts also describe women's participation in sanctuary-centered activities. In I Samuel 1, Elkanah's wives—Hannah and Peninnah—regularly visit the sanctuary with him, as do his daughters. Moreover, he and Hannah present and slaughter the offering that she has brought there, as payment for a vow. Many scholars hold that women's religious activities were even more extensive than can be garnered from these texts (see Another View, p. 587; "Women in Ancient Israel—An Overview," p. xli). Nevertheless, Leviticus authorizes only men from the family of Aaron to serve as priests in the sanctuary (see in the next parashah at 6:2).

—*Tamara Cohn Eskenazi*

## Outline

*I.* PROCEDURES FOR THREE TYPES OF BASIC OFFERINGS (1:1–3:17)

- *A.* Burnt offering—*olah* (1:1–17)
- *B.* Meal offering—*minchah* (2:1–16)
- *C.* Well-being offering—*sh'lamim* (3:1–17)

*II.* PROCEDURES FOR OFFERINGS TO RESTORE ORDER (4:1–5:26)

- *A.* Purgation offering—*chatat* (4:1–5:13)
  - *1.* Introduction (4:1–2)
  - *2.* When the priest incurs guilt (4:3–12)
  - *3.* When the congregation incurs guilt (4:13–21)
  - *4.* When a leader incurs guilt (4:22–26)
  - *5.* When anyone else incurs guilt (4:27–35)
  - *6.* Specific cases that require offerings (5:1–13)
- *B.* Reparation offering—*asham* (5:14–26)

יהוה called to Moses and spoke to him from the Tent of Meeting, saying: ²Speak to the Israelite people, and say to them:

א וַיִּקְרָ֖א אֶל־מֹשֶׁ֑ה וַיְדַבֵּ֤ר יְהֹוָה֙ אֵלָ֔יו מֵאֹ֥הֶל מוֹעֵ֖ד לֵאמֹֽר׃ 2 דַּבֵּ֞ר אֶל־בְּנֵ֤י יִשְׂרָאֵל֙ וְאָמַרְתָּ֖ אֲלֵהֶ֑ם

## Procedures for Three Basic Offerings
### (1:1–3:17)

The first unit of Leviticus functions as an overview and describes the "what" and "how" of the most common sacrifices that Israelites must bring. The emphasis falls on the types of offerings and the procedures for conducting the sacrifices, rather than on the occasions calling for sacrifices.

This unit reads like an instruction manual, which it may have been. But note that these instructions are to be disclosed to all Israel, whereas in other cultures priests typically guard the knowledge about their professional rites of worship. Although Leviticus preserves the priests' privileged monopoly regarding the service at the altar and its sacrifices, these instructions demystify the priests' role by making knowledge about their activities known to every Israelite.

The anthropologist Mary Douglas observes that the arrangement of the offerings on the altar re-creates a movement from the outside (of the animal's body) to the center and toward greater holiness. A similar journey takes place as a person enters the Tabernacle, or as Moses ascends Mount Sinai (*Leviticus as Literature*, 1999, ch. 4). Douglas also notes the relationship between what is offered on the altar and what a person may eat (Leviticus 11):

The meat that one may offer God is the same as that which one may eat. The parallels make the human body an analogue to the Tabernacle: a holy place designated for serving God.

Sacrifice takes place at the altar located at the entrance of the Tent of Meeting. The procedure for most types of sacrifices is similar: First, someone brings a sacrificial offering either on their own behalf or on behalf of their household (some or all of whom may be present); that person presents the sacrificial offering to a priest. When the offering is an animal, the person lays a hand on it. Next, the animal is slaughtered, possibly by the person who provides the offering. (Most likely over time, the priests as experts assumed the task of slaughtering on the offerer's behalf.) The priest collects the animal's blood and dashes it on the four corners of the altar—apparently as a purifying substance. Afterward, the animal is skinned and sectioned (probably by the priest and his assistants), and its entrails and skin are washed. Finally, the priest prepares the fire and then lays down the appropriate pieces of the animal on the altar for the sacrifice. Burnt offerings are burned completely, while other offerings provide meat for the priests or the community as a whole. Eating the appropriate portions of the offering constitutes the final step of the ritual.

▶ Religious activities carried out *only* by women were part of Israelite household life.

ANOTHER VIEW ➤ *587*

▶ The priests become feminized men—cooking and cleaning in God's holy dwelling.

CONTEMPORARY REFLECTION ➤ *589*

▶ We realize our full potential through our bonds to the community of Israel.

POST-BIBLICAL INTERPRETATIONS ➤ *587*

▶ But how to make one's daily life maintain / a balance between plenitude and pain...?

VOICES ➤ *591*

When any of you presents an offering of cattle to יהוה: You shall choose your offering from the herd or from the flock.

אָדָ֗ם כִּֽי־יַקְרִ֥יב מִכֶּ֛ם קׇרְבָּ֖ן לַֽיהֹוָ֑ה מִן־
הַבְּהֵמָ֗ה מִן־הַבָּקָר֙ וּמִן־הַצֹּ֔אן תַּקְרִ֖יבוּ אֶת־
קׇרְבַּנְכֶֽם׃

BURNT OFFERING—*olah* (1:1–17)

The Hebrew name of this offering, *olah*, comes from the root *e-l-h*, meaning "to go up," and expresses the idea that the entire offering "goes up" to God as smoke, the substance into which the animal has been transformed by fire. The burnt offering is unique because all of it must be burned, except for the skin. The English term "holocaust" originally referred to this specific sacrifice. The text makes no mention of the purpose of the ritual. The idea seems to be that this gift of life belongs completely to God—who gives life. It may express a recognition that a part of what one has received from God must return completely to God. God demands of Abraham a burnt offering, namely, Isaac (Genesis 22). Leviticus 23 is one of several passages that describe occasions that require a burnt offering.

The fact that the burnt offering usually appears first in a series of sacrifices suggests that its purpose may be to open up communication with the Divine; if so, then that goal would be accomplished by manifesting generosity—giving part of one's wealth to God (David Stein, personal communication).

*1.* ***יהוה called to Moses.*** This opening of Leviticus follows the conclusion of the book of Exodus (40:38), which describes the completion of the Tabernacle. Now that God's abode is complete, Leviticus provides instructions for its proper use. The only other place in the Torah where God "calls," rather than speaks, to Moses is when summoning him to the top of Mount Sinai (Exodus 24:16).

***from the Tent of Meeting.*** The portable Tent, which will accompany the Israelites through the wilderness, symbolically replaces Mount Sinai as the source from which divine messages come.

*2.* ***Speak to the Israelite people.*** Leviticus begins with an address that is intended for the people as a whole, not only for an elite group of priests. In so doing, the book establishes the principle that priestly activities are open to scrutiny by the people as a whole. Just as this "manual" for priestly activities is to be taught to all Israel, so the legal precepts of the Torah are to be taught to all the Israelites (for example, Exodus 21:1).

***When any of you.*** The Hebrew has "when an *adam* from among you." Because the word *adam* refers to a human being in a generic sense (see at Genesis 1:26; 5:2), the language of this verse makes clear that the laws apply to both women and men. The subsequent verbs and pronouns appear in a masculine form only for the sake of agreement with *adam* as a grammatically masculine noun. (Hebrew has no neutral "it"; all verbs take a masculine or feminine form that matches the grammatical gender of the subject; in this case, as in many others, the noun's grammatical gender has nothing to do with social gender. For example, "a table" is grammatically masculine and "a door" is feminine.)

***presents an offering.*** English has no good way of reproducing the important wordplay embedded in this phrase. The two Hebrew words translated as "presents" and "offering" (*yakriv*... *korban*) are derived from the same root, *k-r-b*, meaning "to come near." Thus, the language of sacrifice carries a sense of coming close to the Divine, describing a safe way to interact with the supreme power. The precautions taken by ancient worshippers and priests (such as approaching only in specified ways and times) are analogous to those taken by modern technicians when handling radioactive material: potent energy that can heal and kill must be approached with maximum attention to protective procedures.

3If your offering is a burnt offering from the herd, you shall make your offering a male without blemish. You shall bring it to the entrance of the Tent of Meeting, for acceptance in your behalf before יהוה. 4You shall lay a hand upon the head of the burnt offering, that it may be acceptable in your behalf, in expiation for you. 5The bull shall be slaughtered before יהוה; and Aaron's sons, the priests, shall offer the blood, dashing the blood against all sides of the altar which is at the entrance of the Tent of Meeting. 6The burnt offering shall be flayed and cut up into sections. 7The sons of Aaron the priest shall put fire on the altar and lay out wood upon the fire; 8and Aaron's sons, the priests, shall lay out the sections, with the head and the suet, on the wood that is on the fire upon the altar. 9Its entrails and legs shall be washed with water, and the priest shall turn the whole into smoke on the altar as a burnt offering, an offering by fire of pleasing odor to יהוה.

3 אִם־עֹלָה קָרְבָּנוֹ מִן־הַבָּקָר זָכָר תָּמִים
יַקְרִיבֶנּוּ אֶל־פֶּתַח אֹהֶל מוֹעֵד יַקְרִיב אֹתוֹ
לִרְצֹנוֹ לִפְנֵי יְהוָה׃ 4 וְסָמַךְ יָדוֹ עַל רֹאשׁ
הָעֹלָה וְנִרְצָה לוֹ לְכַפֵּר עָלָיו׃ 5 וְשָׁחַט
אֶת־בֶּן הַבָּקָר לִפְנֵי יְהוָה וְהִקְרִיבוּ בְּנֵי
אַהֲרֹן הַכֹּהֲנִים אֶת־הַדָּם וְזָרְקוּ אֶת־הַדָּם
עַל־הַמִּזְבֵּחַ סָבִיב אֲשֶׁר־פֶּתַח אֹהֶל מוֹעֵד׃
6 וְהִפְשִׁיט אֶת־הָעֹלָה וְנִתַּח אֹתָהּ לִנְתָחֶיהָ׃
7 וְנָתְנוּ בְּנֵי אַהֲרֹן הַכֹּהֵן אֵשׁ עַל־הַמִּזְבֵּחַ
וְעָרְכוּ עֵצִים עַל־הָאֵשׁ׃ 8 וְעָרְכוּ בְּנֵי אַהֲרֹן
הַכֹּהֲנִים אֵת הַנְּתָחִים אֶת־הָרֹאשׁ וְאֶת־
הַפָּדֶר עַל־הָעֵצִים אֲשֶׁר עַל־הָאֵשׁ אֲשֶׁר
עַל־הַמִּזְבֵּחַ׃ 9 וְקִרְבּוֹ וּכְרָעָיו יִרְחַץ בַּמָּיִם
וְהִקְטִיר הַכֹּהֵן אֶת־הַכֹּל הַמִּזְבֵּחָה עֹלָה
אִשֵּׁה רֵיחַ־נִיחוֹחַ לַיהוָה׃ ס

3. ***If your offering is . . . from the herd.*** Different types of animals can be used as a burnt offering: cattle, sheep, or goats (1:10–13), or birds (1:14–17). The procedure is essentially the same for each one.

***your.*** In Hebrew, a masculine third-person pronoun refers back to *adam* (see at v. 2). In this passage, the present translation conveys the gender-inclusive sense by rendering such pronouns in the second person.

***male without blemish.*** It is not clear what the animal's sex symbolizes. Nicole Ruane, who examines the sacrificial system with regard to the sex of its victims, concludes that the highest level of holiness is symbolized in Leviticus by perfect masculinity. Femininity can express various gradations away from the ideal (*Sacrifice, Purity and Gender in Priestly Law*, forthcoming).

5. ***The bull shall be slaughtered.*** The Torah does not specify who slaughters the animal—the one who has brought the offering (hence either a woman or a man) or the priest. As Mayer Gruber points out, ancient Near Eastern texts and pictures portray sacrificial slaughter by women as well as by men ("Women in the Cult," 1992, n. 37). The story of the woman in En-dor, who slaughters a stall-fed calf in her home to feed King Saul, suggests that it was considered unremarkable that a woman slaughtered large animals (I Samuel 28:24).

***blood.*** Blood represents life. Thus, Leviticus 17:11 states: "For the life of the flesh is in the blood. . . . It is the blood, as life, that effects expiation." In Leviticus, the blood of ritually slaughtered animals functions as the element that erases impurities, much like a disinfectant is used in the modern world to remove unwelcome bacteria.

9. In contrast to other sacrifices, the burnt offering is to burn completely. This feature may express a belief that all that one owns belongs to God, and thus a part of one's belongings must return completely to God.

***turn the whole into smoke.*** The transformation of substance into smoke that rises into heaven seems also to convey the worshipper's communica-

[10]If your offering for a burnt offering is from the flock, of sheep or of goats, you shall make your offering a male without blemish. [11]It shall be slaughtered before יהוה on the north side of the altar, and Aaron's sons, the priests, shall dash its blood against all sides of the altar. [12]When it has been cut up into sections, the priest shall lay them out, with the head and the suet, on the wood that is on the fire upon the altar. [13]The entrails and the legs shall be washed with water; the priest shall offer up and turn the whole into smoke on the altar. It is a burnt offering, an offering by fire, of pleasing odor to יהוה.

[14]If your offering to יהוה is a burnt offering of birds, you shall choose your offering from turtledoves or pigeons. [15]The priest shall bring it to the altar, pinch off its head, and turn it into smoke on the altar; and its blood shall be drained out against the side of the altar. [16]He shall remove its crop with its contents, and cast it into the place of the ashes, at the east side of the altar. [17]The priest shall tear it open by its wings, without severing it, and turn it into smoke on the altar, upon the wood that is on the fire. It is a burnt offering, an offering by fire, of pleasing odor to יהוה.

10 וְאִם־מִן־הַצֹּ֨אן קָרְבָּנ֧וֹ מִן־הַכְּשָׂבִ֛ים א֥וֹ
מִן־הָֽעִזִּ֖ים לְעֹלָ֑ה זָכָ֥ר תָּמִ֖ים יַקְרִיבֶֽנּוּ׃
11 וְשָׁחַ֨ט אֹת֜וֹ עַ֣ל יֶ֧רֶךְ הַמִּזְבֵּ֛חַ צָפֹ֖נָה
לִפְנֵ֣י יְהֹוָ֑ה וְזָרְק֡וּ בְּנֵי֩ אַהֲרֹ֨ן הַכֹּהֲנִ֧ים
אֶת־דָּמ֛וֹ עַל־הַמִּזְבֵּ֖חַ סָבִֽיב׃ 12 וְנִתַּ֤ח אֹתוֹ֙
לִנְתָחָ֔יו וְאֶת־רֹאשׁ֖וֹ וְאֶת־פִּדְר֑וֹ וְעָרַ֤ךְ הַכֹּהֵן֙
אֹתָ֔ם עַל־הָעֵצִים֙ אֲשֶׁ֣ר עַל־הָאֵ֔שׁ אֲשֶׁ֖ר
עַל־הַמִּזְבֵּֽחַ׃ 13 וְהַקֶּ֥רֶב וְהַכְּרָעַ֖יִם יִרְחַ֣ץ
בַּמָּ֑יִם וְהִקְרִ֨יב הַכֹּהֵ֤ן אֶת־הַכֹּל֙ וְהִקְטִ֣יר
הַמִּזְבֵּ֔חָה עֹלָ֣ה ה֗וּא אִשֵּׁ֛ה רֵ֥יחַ נִיחֹ֖חַ
לַיהֹוָֽה׃ פ
14 וְאִ֧ם מִן־הָע֛וֹף עֹלָ֥ה קָרְבָּנ֖וֹ לַיהֹוָ֑ה
וְהִקְרִ֣יב מִן־הַתֹּרִ֗ים א֛וֹ מִן־בְּנֵ֥י הַיּוֹנָ֖ה
אֶת־קָרְבָּנֽוֹ׃ 15 וְהִקְרִיב֤וֹ הַכֹּהֵן֙ אֶל־הַמִּזְבֵּ֔חַ
וּמָלַק֙ אֶת־רֹאשׁ֔וֹ וְהִקְטִ֖יר הַמִּזְבֵּ֑חָה וְנִמְצָ֣ה
דָמ֔וֹ עַ֖ל קִ֥יר הַמִּזְבֵּֽחַ׃ 16 וְהֵסִ֥יר אֶת־מֻרְאָת֖וֹ
בְּנֹצָתָ֑הּ וְהִשְׁלִ֨יךְ אֹתָ֜הּ אֵ֤צֶל הַמִּזְבֵּ֙חַ֙ קֵ֔דְמָה
אֶל־מְק֖וֹם הַדָּֽשֶׁן׃ 17 וְשִׁסַּ֨ע אֹת֣וֹ בִכְנָפָיו֮
לֹ֣א יַבְדִּיל֒ וְהִקְטִ֨יר אֹת֤וֹ הַכֹּהֵן֙ הַמִּזְבֵּ֔חָה
עַל־הָעֵצִ֖ים אֲשֶׁ֣ר עַל־הָאֵ֑שׁ עֹלָ֣ה ה֗וּא
אִשֵּׁ֛ה רֵ֥יחַ נִיחֹ֖חַ לַיהֹוָֽה׃ ס

2 When a person presents an offering of meal to יהוה: The offering shall be of choice flour; the offerer shall pour oil upon it, lay frankincense on

ב וְנֶ֗פֶשׁ כִּֽי־תַקְרִ֞יב קָרְבַּ֤ן מִנְחָה֙ לַיהֹוָ֔ה
סֹ֖לֶת יִהְיֶ֣ה קָרְבָּנ֑וֹ וְיָצַ֤ק עָלֶ֙יהָ֙ שֶׁ֔מֶן

---

tion to an invisible God. This ephemeral substance visibly travels heavenward, the space often associated with God's abode.

*10. If...from the flock.* See at 1:3.

*14. birds.* Offering a bird provides an alternative to livestock, no doubt to make the ritual more affordable to persons with meager means (compare 12:8).

*17. pleasing odor to* **יהוה**. This refrain concludes the descriptions of other offerings as well. It signals the belief that the smoke reaches God, who welcomes this offering. This anthropomorphism (representation of God as possessing human characteristics) reflects a level of comfort with references to God's physicality despite the theoretical rejection of God's corporeal nature.

### MEAL OFFERING—*minchah* (2:1–16)

This section contains two parts. The first passage (vv. 1–13) discusses wheat offerings that can be made throughout the year. The second part (vv. 14–16) concerns a special offering at the start of the wheat harvest. The word *minchah* means "gift" and expresses the idea that an offering is a gift to God (compare Genesis 32:14).

it, 2 and present it to Aaron's sons, the priests. The
priest shall scoop out of it a handful of its choice
flour and oil, as well as all of its frankincense; and
this token portion he shall turn into smoke on the
altar, as an offering by fire, of pleasing odor to יהוה.
3 And the remainder of the meal offering shall be for
Aaron and his sons, a most holy portion from יהוה's
offerings by fire.

4 When you present an offering of meal baked in
the oven, [it shall be of] choice flour: unleavened
cakes with oil mixed in, or unleavened wafers
spread with oil.

5 If your offering is a meal offering on a griddle,
it shall be of choice flour with oil mixed in, unleavened. 6 Break it into bits and pour oil on it; it is a
meal offering.

7 If your offering is a meal offering in a pan, it
shall be made of choice flour in oil.

8 When you present to יהוה a meal offering that
is made in any of these ways, it shall be brought to
the priest who shall take it up to the altar. 9 The
priest shall remove the token portion from the meal
offering and turn it into smoke on the altar as an
offering by fire, of pleasing odor to יהוה. 10 And the
remainder of the meal offering shall be for Aaron
and his sons, a most holy portion from יהוה's offerings by fire.

וְנָתַן עָלֶיהָ לְבֹנָה׃ 2 וֶהֱבִיאָהּ אֶל־בְּנֵי
אַהֲרֹן הַכֹּהֲנִים וְקָמַץ מִשָּׁם מְלֹא קֻמְצוֹ
מִסָּלְתָּהּ וּמִשַּׁמְנָהּ עַל כָּל־לְבֹנָתָהּ וְהִקְטִיר
הַכֹּהֵן אֶת־אַזְכָּרָתָהּ הַמִּזְבֵּחָה אִשֵּׁה רֵיחַ
נִיחֹחַ לַיהוָה׃ 3 וְהַנּוֹתֶרֶת מִן־הַמִּנְחָה
לְאַהֲרֹן וּלְבָנָיו קֹדֶשׁ קָדָשִׁים מֵאִשֵּׁי
יְהוָה׃ ס

4 וְכִי תַקְרִב קָרְבַּן מִנְחָה מַאֲפֵה תַנּוּר סֹלֶת
חַלּוֹת מַצֹּת בְּלוּלֹת בַּשֶּׁמֶן וּרְקִיקֵי מַצּוֹת
מְשֻׁחִים בַּשָּׁמֶן׃ ס

5 וְאִם־מִנְחָה עַל־הַמַּחֲבַת קָרְבָּנֶךָ סֹלֶת
בְּלוּלָה בַשֶּׁמֶן מַצָּה תִהְיֶה׃ 6 פָּתוֹת
אֹתָהּ פִּתִּים וְיָצַקְתָּ עָלֶיהָ שָׁמֶן מִנְחָה
הִוא׃ ס

7 וְאִם־מִנְחַת מַרְחֶשֶׁת קָרְבָּנֶךָ סֹלֶת בַּשֶּׁמֶן
תֵּעָשֶׂה׃

8 וְהֵבֵאתָ אֶת־הַמִּנְחָה אֲשֶׁר יֵעָשֶׂה מֵאֵלֶּה
לַיהוָה וְהִקְרִיבָהּ אֶל־הַכֹּהֵן וְהִגִּישָׁהּ אֶל־
הַמִּזְבֵּחַ׃ 9 וְהֵרִים הַכֹּהֵן מִן־הַמִּנְחָה אֶת־
אַזְכָּרָתָהּ וְהִקְטִיר הַמִּזְבֵּחָה אִשֵּׁה רֵיחַ נִיחֹחַ
לַיהוָה׃ 10 וְהַנּוֹתֶרֶת מִן־הַמִּנְחָה לְאַהֲרֹן
וּלְבָנָיו קֹדֶשׁ קָדָשִׁים מֵאִשֵּׁי יְהוָה׃

*1–13.* This passage describes a type of offering that can accompany animal sacrifices or be an independent offering. The ingredients for this *minchah* ("meal offering") are semolina (the choice sifted granules from ground wheat kernels), olive oil, and frankincense. The offerer can prepare it in one of three ways: griddle, pan, or oven. According to Leviticus 5:11, a poor person can substitute this offering for more costly offerings in certain situations. This section does not specify the purpose of the offering or prescribe words to recite.

*1. **person.*** Heb. *nefesh*; like the word *adam* (see at 1:2), it is an inclusive term for a human being.

*3. **the remainder . . . shall be for Aaron and his sons.*** Unlike the burnt offering that is completely consumed by fire, the *minchah* offering is shared by the priests and their families. Priests were not to own land and thus were unable to grow crops or keep livestock. Their allocations from the sacrifices thus constituted their livelihood. (On the distinction between a priest's sons and his daughters, see *Tzav*, Another View, p. 608, and at Leviticus 22:12–13.)

***a most holy portion.*** Heb. *kodesh kodashim*, which applies here to the remainder of the offering for the priests' use. Elsewhere, it also designates the holiest part of the Tabernacle (*kodesh hakodashim*, the Holy of Holies; for example, Exodus 26:34) and later of the Temple. The language creates an analogy between sacred space and food offerings.

<sup>11</sup>No meal offering that you offer to יהוה shall be made with leaven, for no leaven or honey may be turned into smoke as an offering by fire to יהוה. <sup>12</sup>You may bring them to יהוה as an offering of choice products; but they shall not be offered up on the altar for a pleasing odor. <sup>13</sup>You shall season your every offering of meal with salt; you shall not omit from your meal offering the salt of your covenant with God; with all your offerings you must offer salt.

<sup>14</sup>If you bring a meal offering of first fruits to יהוה, you shall bring new ears parched with fire, grits of the fresh grain, as your meal offering of first fruits. <sup>15</sup>You shall add oil to it and lay frankincense on it; it is a meal offering. <sup>16</sup>And the priest shall turn a token portion of it into smoke: some of the grits and oil, with all of the frankincense, as an offering by fire to יהוה.

3   If your offering is a sacrifice of well-being—
    If you offer of the herd, whether a male or a fe-

11 כָּל־הַמִּנְחָ֗ה אֲשֶׁ֤ר תַּקְרִ֙יבוּ֙ לַֽיהֹוָ֔ה לֹ֥א תֵעָשֶׂ֖ה חָמֵ֑ץ כִּ֤י כָל־שְׂאֹר֙ וְכָל־דְּבַ֔שׁ לֹֽא־תַקְטִ֧ירוּ מִמֶּ֛נּוּ אִשֶּׁ֖ה לַֽיהֹוָֽה: 12 קָרְבַּ֥ן רֵאשִׁ֛ית תַּקְרִ֥יבוּ אֹתָ֖ם לַֽיהֹוָ֑ה וְאֶל־הַמִּזְבֵּ֥חַ לֹא־יַֽעֲל֖וּ לְרֵ֥יחַ נִיחֹֽחַ: 13 וְכָל־קָרְבַּ֣ן מִנְחָֽתְךָ֮ בַּמֶּ֣לַח תִּמְלָח֒ וְלֹ֣א תַשְׁבִּ֗ית מֶ֚לַח בְּרִ֣ית אֱלֹהֶ֔יךָ מֵעַ֖ל מִנְחָתֶ֑ךָ עַ֥ל כָּל־קָרְבָּֽנְךָ֖ תַּקְרִ֥יב מֶֽלַח: ס

14 וְאִם־תַּקְרִ֛יב מִנְחַ֥ת בִּכּוּרִ֖ים לַֽיהֹוָ֑ה אָבִ֞יב קָל֤וּי בָּאֵשׁ֙ גֶּ֣רֶשׂ כַּרְמֶ֔ל תַּקְרִ֕יב אֵ֖ת מִנְחַ֥ת בִּכּוּרֶֽיךָ: 15 וְנָֽתַתָּ֤ עָלֶ֙יהָ֙ שֶׁ֔מֶן וְשַׂמְתָּ֥ עָלֶ֖יהָ לְבֹנָ֑ה מִנְחָ֖ה הִֽוא: 16 וְהִקְטִ֙יר הַכֹּהֵ֜ן אֶת־אַזְכָּ֣רָתָ֗הּ מִגִּרְשָׂהּ֙ וּמִשַּׁמְנָ֔הּ עַ֖ל כָּל־לְבֹֽנָתָ֑הּ אִשֶּׁ֖ה לַֽיהֹוָֽה: פ

ג   וְאִם־זֶ֥בַח שְׁלָמִ֖ים קָרְבָּנ֑וֹ אִ֤ם מִן־הַבָּקָר֙ ה֣וּא מַקְרִ֔יב אִם־זָכָר֙ אִם־

---

*14–16.* The second type of *minchah* refers to ripe grain from the new crop that is roasted and then made into grits. The priest offers a token portion of the roasted grain mixture to God. This offering may represent the produce of the earth returned, in gratitude, to the God responsible for the fertility of the land.

### WELL-BEING OFFERING—*sh'lamim* (3:1–17)

The offering of *sh'lamim*, translated here as "sacrifice of well-being," resembles the burnt offering but with one main difference: only a portion of it "turns into smoke" (see below for details). The largest part of the sacrifice is distributed between priests and offerers, thus providing food for the Israelites. This passage does not mention a specific occasion, but subsequent instructions link the *sh'lamim* with celebrations and show that often this offering was to be brought after a burnt offering. It constitutes the basic form of sacrifice for feast days

(Deuteronomy 12:11–12). This means that when Israelites brought sacrifices, some offerings were solely for God, as it were, and some to be eaten by community members.

This practice turns the eating of meat into a sacred act (17:1–7) and reflects the concern for taking life for human consumption; the sacrifice has nothing to do with atonement. As Jacob Milgrom observes, this ritual allowed the Israelites to acknowledge the miracles of their lives and express gratitude for them (*Leviticus: A Book of Ritual and Ethics*, 2004, p. 28).

*1.   your.*  See at 1:2.

*well-being.*  Heb. *sh'lamim*, a word related to *shalom* or *shalem*, and which therefore means "wholeness," "well-being," or "peace." Baruch Levine renders it as "a sacred gift of greeting," an expression that enriches one's awareness of the function of this offering.

*of the herd.*  A variety of animals qualify for this sacrifice. (See at 1:3.)

male, you shall bring before יהוה one without blemish. [2]You shall lay a hand upon the head of your offering and slaughter it at the entrance of the Tent of Meeting; and Aaron's sons, the priests, shall dash the blood against all sides of the altar. [3]Then present from the sacrifice of well-being, as an offering by fire to יהוה, the fat that covers the entrails and all the fat that is about the entrails; [4]the two kidneys and the fat that is on them, that is at the loins; and the protuberance on the liver, which you shall remove with the kidneys. [5]Aaron's sons shall turn these into smoke on the altar, with the burnt offering which is upon the wood that is on the fire, as an offering by fire, of pleasing odor to יהוה.

[6]And if your offering for a sacrifice of well-being to יהוה is from the flock, whether a male or a female, you shall offer one without blemish. [7]If you present a sheep as your offering, you shall bring it before יהוה [8]and lay a hand upon the head of your offering. It shall be slaughtered before the Tent of Meeting, and Aaron's sons shall dash its blood against all sides of the altar. [9]Then present, as an offering by fire to יהוה, the fat from the sacrifice of well-being: the whole broad tail, which you shall remove close to the backbone; the fat that covers the entrails and all the fat that is about the entrails; [10]the two kidneys and the fat that is on them, that is at the loins; and the protuberance on the liver, which you shall remove with the kidneys. [11]The priest shall turn these into smoke on the altar as food, an offering by fire to יהוה.

[12]And if your offering is a goat, you shall bring it before יהוה [13]and lay a hand upon its head. It

נְקֵבָה תָּמִים יַקְרִיבֶנּוּ לִפְנֵי יְהֹוָה׃ 2 וְסָמַךְ
יָדוֹ עַל־רֹאשׁ קָרְבָּנוֹ וּשְׁחָטוֹ פֶּתַח אֹהֶל
מוֹעֵד וְזָרְקוּ בְּנֵי אַהֲרֹן הַכֹּהֲנִים אֶת־
הַדָּם עַל־הַמִּזְבֵּחַ סָבִיב׃ 3 וְהִקְרִיב מִזֶּבַח
הַשְּׁלָמִים אִשֶּׁה לַיהֹוָה אֶת־הַחֵלֶב הַמְכַסֶּה
אֶת־הַקֶּרֶב וְאֵת כָּל־הַחֵלֶב אֲשֶׁר עַל־
הַקֶּרֶב׃ 4 וְאֵת שְׁתֵּי הַכְּלָיֹת וְאֶת־הַחֵלֶב
אֲשֶׁר עֲלֵהֶן אֲשֶׁר עַל־הַכְּסָלִים וְאֶת־
הַיֹּתֶרֶת עַל־הַכָּבֵד עַל־הַכְּלָיוֹת יְסִירֶנָּה׃
5 וְהִקְטִירוּ אֹתוֹ בְנֵי־אַהֲרֹן הַמִּזְבֵּחָה עַל־
הָעֹלָה אֲשֶׁר עַל־הָעֵצִים אֲשֶׁר עַל־הָאֵשׁ
אִשֵּׁה רֵיחַ נִיחֹחַ לַיהֹוָה׃ פ
6 וְאִם־מִן־הַצֹּאן קָרְבָּנוֹ לְזֶבַח שְׁלָמִים
לַיהֹוָה זָכָר אוֹ נְקֵבָה תָּמִים יַקְרִיבֶנּוּ׃
7 אִם־כֶּשֶׂב הוּא־מַקְרִיב אֶת־קָרְבָּנוֹ וְהִקְרִיב
אֹתוֹ לִפְנֵי יְהֹוָה׃ 8 וְסָמַךְ אֶת־יָדוֹ עַל־רֹאשׁ
קָרְבָּנוֹ וְשָׁחַט אֹתוֹ לִפְנֵי אֹהֶל מוֹעֵד וְזָרְקוּ
בְּנֵי אַהֲרֹן אֶת־דָּמוֹ עַל־הַמִּזְבֵּחַ סָבִיב׃
9 וְהִקְרִיב מִזֶּבַח הַשְּׁלָמִים אִשֶּׁה לַיהֹוָה
חֶלְבּוֹ הָאַלְיָה תְמִימָה לְעֻמַּת הֶעָצֶה
יְסִירֶנָּה וְאֶת־הַחֵלֶב הַמְכַסֶּה אֶת־הַקֶּרֶב
וְאֵת כָּל־הַחֵלֶב אֲשֶׁר עַל־הַקֶּרֶב׃ 10 וְאֵת
שְׁתֵּי הַכְּלָיֹת וְאֶת־הַחֵלֶב אֲשֶׁר עֲלֵהֶן
אֲשֶׁר עַל־הַכְּסָלִים וְאֶת־הַיֹּתֶרֶת עַל־הַכָּבֵד
עַל־הַכְּלָיֹת יְסִירֶנָּה׃ 11 וְהִקְטִירוֹ הַכֹּהֵן
הַמִּזְבֵּחָה לֶחֶם אִשֶּׁה לַיהֹוָה׃ פ
12 וְאִם עֵז קָרְבָּנוֹ וְהִקְרִיבוֹ לִפְנֵי יְהֹוָה׃
13 וְסָמַךְ אֶת־יָדוֹ עַל־רֹאשׁוֹ וְשָׁחַט אֹתוֹ

*a male or a female.* It is not clear why either male or female animals may be used in this case.

*bring.* The Hebrew root is *k-r-b,* which also forms the words for both "sacrifice" and "nearness" (see at 1:2).

*3–5.* These verses describe the parts of the animal that are consumed in their entirety. The procedures are similar to the burnt offering, except that only specified portions of the animal are placed on the altar to be burnt: certain fatty portions, including the fat that covers the entrails and the kidneys and is on the loins, as well as an appendage on the liver, and the two kidneys. The rest is divided between the priest and the one making the offering.

shall be slaughtered before the Tent of Meeting,
and Aaron's sons shall dash its blood against all
sides of the altar. [14]Then present as your offering
from it, as an offering by fire to יהוה, the fat that
covers the entrails and all the fat that is about the
entrails; [15]the two kidneys and the fat that is on
them, that is at the loins; and the protuberance on
the liver, which you shall remove with the kidneys.
[16]The priest shall turn these into smoke on the altar
as food, an offering by fire, of pleasing odor.

All fat is יהוה's. [17]It is a law for all time throughout the ages, in all your settlements: you must not
eat any fat or any blood.

לִפְנֵי אֹהֶל מוֹעֵד וְזָרְקוּ בְּנֵי אַהֲרֹן אֶת־דָּמוֹ
עַל־הַמִּזְבֵּחַ סָבִיב׃ 14 וְהִקְרִיב מִמֶּנּוּ קָרְבָּנוֹ
אִשֶּׁה לַיהוָה אֶת־הַחֵלֶב הַמְכַסֶּה אֶת־
הַקֶּרֶב וְאֵת כָּל־הַחֵלֶב אֲשֶׁר עַל־הַקֶּרֶב׃
15 וְאֵת שְׁתֵּי הַכְּלָיֹת וְאֶת־הַחֵלֶב אֲשֶׁר
עֲלֵהֶן אֲשֶׁר עַל־הַכְּסָלִים וְאֶת־הַיֹּתֶרֶת עַל־
הַכָּבֵד עַל־הַכְּלָיֹת יְסִירֶנָּה׃ 16 וְהִקְטִירָם
הַכֹּהֵן הַמִּזְבֵּחָה לֶחֶם אִשֶּׁה לְרֵיחַ נִיחֹחַ
כָּל־חֵלֶב לַיהוָה׃ 17 חֻקַּת עוֹלָם לְדֹרֹתֵיכֶם
בְּכֹל מוֹשְׁבֹתֵיכֶם כָּל־חֵלֶב וְכָל־דָּם לֹא
תֹאכֵלוּ׃ פ

4 יהוה spoke to Moses, saying: [2]Speak to the
Israelite people thus:

ד וַיְדַבֵּר יְהוָה אֶל־מֹשֶׁה לֵּאמֹר׃ 2 דַּבֵּר
אֶל־בְּנֵי יִשְׂרָאֵל לֵאמֹר

*17. you must not eat any fat or any blood.* The prohibition against eating blood is explicitly linked elsewhere with the conviction that blood represents life (see at 1:5 and 17:11). However, it is not obvious why the fat is prohibited. Perhaps this is another way of offering the best to God, since fat is considered valuable in a number of passages (see, for example, the expression "the fat of the land" in Genesis 45:18).

## Procedures for Offerings to Restore Order
(4:1–5:26)

Leviticus 4 and 5 link two major types of offerings to offenses that undermine the balance of the created order. The book of Leviticus maintains that God has created a harmonious world and that persons must—and can—restore that harmony even when they have transgressed and thereby damaged such harmony. The earlier, conventional English terms for the two offerings in this unit are "sin offering" and "guilt offering" (based on the root meanings of the Hebrew names of these sacrifices; see below). But the more current terminology, which replaces "sin" with "purgation," and "guilt" with "reparation," better captures the function of these offerings: the purgation offering clears away the damaging substance; and the reparation offering reconstructs or restores the system to its normative, harmonious wholeness.

These offerings take place in a world in which the spiritual was perceived as integral to the physical—and thus directly affecting the physical. Israel's neighbors (and no doubt many Israelites) believed in demons, a view that Leviticus rejects by ignoring it (see the lone, obscure mention of *se'irim* in 17:7).

Nonetheless, Leviticus regards (invisible) spiritual and moral transgressions as causes of physical (visible and invisible) harm that can be "managed" by proper rituals. At the most immediate level of priestly concern, the impurity of transgressions is considered capable of becoming airborne and contaminating the sanctuary. Thus, the purgation offering aims to cleanse the sanctuary of such contamination, much like a disinfectant purges a hospital room from harmful bacteria.

When a person unwittingly incurs guilt in regard to any of יהוה's commandments about things not to be done, and does one of them—

[3]If it is the anointed priest who has incurred guilt, so that blame falls upon the people, he shall offer for the sin of which he is guilty a bull of the herd without blemish as a purgation offering to יהוה. [4]He shall bring the bull to the entrance of the Tent of Meeting, before יהוה, and lay a hand upon the head of the bull. The bull shall be slaughtered before יהוה, [5]and the anointed priest shall take some of the bull's blood and bring it into the Tent of Meeting. [6]The priest shall dip his finger in the blood, and sprinkle of the blood seven times before יהוה, in front of the curtain of the Shrine. [7]The priest shall put some of the blood on the horns of the altar of aromatic incense, which is in the Tent of Meeting, before יהוה; and all the rest of the bull's

נֶ֣פֶשׁ כִּֽי־תֶחֱטָ֣א בִשְׁגָגָ֗ה מִכֹּל֙ מִצְוֺ֣ת יְהֹוָ֔ה
אֲשֶׁ֖ר לֹ֣א תֵעָשֶׂ֑ינָה וְעָשָׂ֕ה מֵאַחַ֖ת מֵהֵֽנָּה׃ [3] אִ֣ם הַכֹּהֵ֧ן הַמָּשִׁ֛יחַ יֶחֱטָ֖א לְאַשְׁמַ֣ת הָעָ֑ם
וְהִקְרִ֡יב עַ֣ל חַטָּאתוֹ֩ אֲשֶׁ֨ר חָטָ֜א פַּ֣ר בֶּן־בָּקָ֥ר
תָּמִ֛ים לַֽיהֹוָ֖ה לְחַטָּֽאת׃ [4] וְהֵבִ֣יא אֶת־הַפָּ֗ר
אֶל־פֶּ֛תַח אֹ֥הֶל מוֹעֵ֖ד לִפְנֵ֣י יְהֹוָ֑ה וְסָמַ֤ךְ
אֶת־יָדוֹ֙ עַל־רֹ֣אשׁ הַפָּ֔ר וְשָׁחַ֥ט אֶת־הַפָּ֖ר
לִפְנֵ֥י יְהֹוָֽה׃ [5] וְלָקַ֛ח הַכֹּהֵ֥ן הַמָּשִׁ֖יחַ מִדַּ֣ם
הַפָּ֑ר וְהֵבִ֥יא אֹת֖וֹ אֶל־אֹ֥הֶל מוֹעֵֽד׃ [6] וְטָבַ֧ל
הַכֹּהֵ֛ן אֶת־אֶצְבָּע֖וֹ בַּדָּ֑ם וְהִזָּ֨ה מִן־הַדָּ֜ם
שֶׁ֤בַע פְּעָמִים֙ לִפְנֵ֣י יְהֹוָ֔ה אֶת־פְּנֵ֖י פָּרֹ֥כֶת
הַקֹּֽדֶשׁ׃ [7] וְנָתַן֩ הַכֹּהֵ֨ן מִן־הַדָּ֜ם עַל־קַרְנ֨וֹת
מִזְבַּ֜ח קְטֹ֤רֶת הַסַּמִּים֙ לִפְנֵ֣י יְהֹוָ֔ה אֲשֶׁ֖ר
בְּאֹ֣הֶל מוֹעֵ֑ד וְאֵ֣ת ׀ כׇּל־דַּ֣ם הַפָּ֗ר יִשְׁפֹּךְ֙

. . . . . . . . . . . . . . . . . . . . . . . . . . . . . . . . . . . . . . .

**PURGATION OFFERING**—*chatat* (4:1–5:13)

### Introduction (4:1–2)

The name of this sacrifice, *chatat*, is derived from the same root as the word *chet* (sin); it means "that which cancels out sin." The English term "purgation" (purification or decontamination) succinctly captures the ritual's function. The analogy between the Tabernacle and the larger world—microcosm and macrocosm—means that such acts have even wider ramifications. In a symbolic sense, one is restoring order to the world as a whole.

The *chatat* follows upon any accidental—not deliberate—violation of certain ethical and ritual prohibitions, of things "not to be done" (4:2, 13, 22, 27). The person who brings the *chatat* then "shall be forgiven" (4:20, 26, 31, 35).

This offering takes different forms depending on the social status of the transgressor. The different steps indicate greater degrees of responsibility and culpability, with infractions by priests being subject to the most stringent procedures. The rules thus emphasize accountability rather than privilege.

*2. person.* Heb. *nefesh*, which indicates that the law applies equally to women and men (see at 1:2).

*unwittingly incurs guilt.* The concern is with inadvertent moral or physical violations.

### When the Priest Incurs Guilt (4:3–12)

Impurity of the priest in charge of sacrificial rituals (see 6:15) puts everyone at the greatest risk because his impurity infects the sanctuary most directly. The procedure for this offering resembles that of the well-being offering, with one telling exception: the priest, who in other instances benefits from animal sacrifices (see Leviticus 3), is not permitted such gain in this case.

The priest's purification ritual is more extensive than that of a layperson who transgresses (see below, vv. 27–31). In addition to offering a sacrifice, the priest must also purify the inner altar and other parts of the sanctuary, especially just in front of the Holy of Holies (see Exodus 25–26 for the arrangement of the Tabernacle and its furnishings).

*5. the bull's blood.* See at 1:6.

blood he shall pour out at the base of the altar of
burnt offering, which is at the entrance of the Tent
of Meeting. [8]He shall remove all the fat from the
bull of purgation offering: the fat that covers the
entrails and all the fat that is about the entrails;
[9]the two kidneys and the fat that is on them, that is
at the loins; and the protuberance on the liver,
which he shall remove with the kidneys—[10]just
as it is removed from the ox of the sacrifice of well-
being. The priest shall turn them into smoke on the
altar of burnt offering. [11]But the hide of the bull,
and all its flesh, as well as its head and legs, its entrails and its dung—[12]all the rest of the bull—he
shall carry to a pure place outside the camp, to the
ash heap, and burn it up in a wood fire; it shall be
burned on the ash heap.

[13]If it is the community leadership of Israel that
has erred and the matter escapes the notice of the
congregation, so that they do any of the things
which by יהוה's commandments ought not to be
done, and they realize guilt—[14]when the sin through
which they incurred guilt becomes known, the congregation shall offer a bull of the herd as a purgation offering, and bring it before the Tent of
Meeting. [15]The elders of the community shall lay
their hands upon the head of the bull before יהוה,

אֶל־יְסוֹד מִזְבַּח הָעֹלָה אֲשֶׁר־פֶּתַח אֹהֶל
מוֹעֵד׃ 8 וְאֶת־כָּל־חֵלֶב פַּר הַחַטָּאת יָרִים
מִמֶּנּוּ אֶת־הַחֵלֶב הַמְכַסֶּה עַל־הַקֶּרֶב וְאֵת
כָּל־הַחֵלֶב אֲשֶׁר עַל־הַקֶּרֶב׃ 9 וְאֵת שְׁתֵּי
הַכְּלָיֹת וְאֶת־הַחֵלֶב אֲשֶׁר עֲלֵיהֶן אֲשֶׁר עַל־
הַכְּסָלִים וְאֶת־הַיֹּתֶרֶת עַל־הַכָּבֵד עַל־
הַכְּלָיוֹת יְסִירֶנָּה׃ 10 כַּאֲשֶׁר יוּרַם מִשּׁוֹר
זֶבַח הַשְּׁלָמִים וְהִקְטִירָם הַכֹּהֵן עַל מִזְבַּח
הָעֹלָה׃ 11 וְאֶת־עוֹר הַפָּר וְאֶת־כָּל־בְּשָׂרוֹ
עַל־רֹאשׁוֹ וְעַל־כְּרָעָיו וְקִרְבּוֹ וּפִרְשׁוֹ׃
12 וְהוֹצִיא אֶת־כָּל־הַפָּר אֶל־מִחוּץ לַמַּחֲנֶה
אֶל־מָקוֹם טָהוֹר אֶל־שֶׁפֶךְ הַדֶּשֶׁן וְשָׂרַף
אֹתוֹ עַל־עֵצִים בָּאֵשׁ עַל־שֶׁפֶךְ הַדֶּשֶׁן
יִשָּׂרֵף׃ פ
13 וְאִם כָּל־עֲדַת יִשְׂרָאֵל יִשְׁגּוּ וְנֶעְלַם דָּבָר
מֵעֵינֵי הַקָּהָל וְעָשׂוּ אַחַת מִכָּל־מִצְוֺת יְהוָה
אֲשֶׁר לֹא־תֵעָשֶׂינָה וְאָשֵׁמוּ׃ 14 וְנוֹדְעָה
הַחַטָּאת אֲשֶׁר חָטְאוּ עָלֶיהָ וְהִקְרִיבוּ
הַקָּהָל פַּר בֶּן־בָּקָר לְחַטָּאת וְהֵבִיאוּ אֹתוֹ
לִפְנֵי אֹהֶל מוֹעֵד׃ 15 וְסָמְכוּ זִקְנֵי הָעֵדָה
אֶת־יְדֵיהֶם עַל־רֹאשׁ הַפָּר לִפְנֵי יְהוָה

*12. **the rest . . . outside the camp.*** The priest who unwittingly transgresses does not benefit from the offering. (Ordinarily, a portion of the well-being offering is not placed on the altar but rather is available to the priest and layperson for their consumption. Here, the entire animal is eventually burned; parts are placed on the altar, but the rest is burned away from the altar.)

*When the Congregation Incurs Guilt* (4:13–21)

This ritual of purification is essentially identical to the procedure for the offending priest: a bull is brought for sacrifice and the Tabernacle is purified, particularly the inner altar and the space separating the Holy from the Holy of Holies. On behalf of the community, the elders (persons who achieved distinction either due to age, experience, or wealth) place their hands on the bull at the beginning of the ritual. At the end, no one benefits from the animal's meat.

*13. **the community leadership.*** Literally, "the entire community"; this translation aims to clarify that the word for community, *edah* (which is related to the word *eid,* "witness"), refers more precisely here to a representative body of some kind, most likely made up of adult males.

***congregation.*** Ezra 10:1 defines a congregation as "men, women, and children." The same meaning most likely applies here.

and the bull shall be slaughtered before יהוה. [16]The anointed priest shall bring some of the blood of the bull into the Tent of Meeting, [17]and the priest shall dip his finger in the blood and sprinkle of it seven times before יהוה, in front of the curtain. [18]Some of the blood he shall put on the horns of the altar which is before יהוה in the Tent of Meeting, and all the rest of the blood he shall pour out at the base of the altar of burnt offering, which is at the entrance of the Tent of Meeting. [19]He shall remove all its fat from it and turn it into smoke on the altar. [20]He shall do with this bull just as is done with the [priest's] bull of purgation offering; he shall do the same with it. The priest shall thus make expiation for them, and they shall be forgiven. [21]He shall carry the bull outside the camp and burn it as he burned the first bull; it is the purgation offering of the congregation.

[22]In case it is a chieftain who incurs guilt by doing unwittingly any of the things which by the commandment of his God יהוה ought not to be done, and he realizes guilt—[23]or the sin of which he is guilty is made known—he shall bring as his offering a male goat without blemish. [24]He shall lay a hand upon the goat's head, and it shall be slaughtered at the spot where the burnt offering is slaughtered before יהוה; it is a purgation offering. [25]The priest shall take with his finger some of the blood of the purgation offering and put it on the horns of the altar of burnt offering; and the rest of its blood he shall pour out at the base of the altar of burnt offering. [26]All its fat he shall turn into smoke on the altar, like the fat of the sacrifice of well-being. The priest shall thus make expiation on his behalf for his sin, and he shall be forgiven.

וְשָׁחַט אֶת־הַפָּר לִפְנֵי יְהוָה׃ 16 וְהֵבִיא
הַכֹּהֵן הַמָּשִׁיחַ מִדַּם הַפָּר אֶל־אֹהֶל מוֹעֵד׃
17 וְטָבַל הַכֹּהֵן אֶצְבָּעוֹ מִן־הַדָּם וְהִזָּה שֶׁבַע
פְּעָמִים לִפְנֵי יְהוָה אֵת פְּנֵי הַפָּרֹכֶת׃
18 וּמִן־הַדָּם יִתֵּן ׀ עַל־קַרְנֹת הַמִּזְבֵּחַ אֲשֶׁר
לִפְנֵי יְהוָה אֲשֶׁר בְּאֹהֶל מוֹעֵד וְאֵת כָּל־
הַדָּם יִשְׁפֹּךְ אֶל־יְסוֹד מִזְבַּח הָעֹלָה אֲשֶׁר־
פֶּתַח אֹהֶל מוֹעֵד׃ 19 וְאֵת כָּל־חֶלְבּוֹ יָרִים
מִמֶּנּוּ וְהִקְטִיר הַמִּזְבֵּחָה׃ 20 וְעָשָׂה לַפָּר
כַּאֲשֶׁר עָשָׂה לְפַר הַחַטָּאת כֵּן יַעֲשֶׂה־לּוֹ
וְכִפֶּר עֲלֵהֶם הַכֹּהֵן וְנִסְלַח לָהֶם׃ 21 וְהוֹצִיא
אֶת־הַפָּר אֶל־מִחוּץ לַמַּחֲנֶה וְשָׂרַף אֹתוֹ
כַּאֲשֶׁר שָׂרַף אֵת הַפָּר הָרִאשׁוֹן חַטַּאת
הַקָּהָל הוּא׃ פ

22 אֲשֶׁר נָשִׂיא יֶחֱטָא וְעָשָׂה אַחַת מִכָּל־
מִצְוֺת יְהוָה אֱלֹהָיו אֲשֶׁר לֹא־תֵעָשֶׂינָה
בִּשְׁגָגָה וְאָשֵׁם׃ 23 אוֹ־הוֹדַע אֵלָיו חַטָּאתוֹ
אֲשֶׁר חָטָא בָּהּ וְהֵבִיא אֶת־קָרְבָּנוֹ שְׂעִיר
עִזִּים זָכָר תָּמִים׃ 24 וְסָמַךְ יָדוֹ עַל־רֹאשׁ
הַשָּׂעִיר וְשָׁחַט אֹתוֹ בִּמְקוֹם אֲשֶׁר־יִשְׁחַט
אֶת־הָעֹלָה לִפְנֵי יְהוָה חַטָּאת הוּא׃
25 וְלָקַח הַכֹּהֵן מִדַּם הַחַטָּאת בְּאֶצְבָּעוֹ
וְנָתַן עַל־קַרְנֹת מִזְבַּח הָעֹלָה וְאֶת־דָּמוֹ
יִשְׁפֹּךְ אֶל־יְסוֹד מִזְבַּח הָעֹלָה׃ 26 וְאֶת־כָּל־
חֶלְבּוֹ יַקְטִיר הַמִּזְבֵּחָה כְּחֵלֶב זֶבַח
הַשְּׁלָמִים וְכִפֶּר עָלָיו הַכֹּהֵן מֵחַטָּאתוֹ
וְנִסְלַח לוֹ׃ פ

### *When a Leader Incurs Guilt*
(4:22–26)

*22. chieftain.* Heb. *nasi,* which in Numbers refers to a tribal leader (for example, 2:3) and in Ezekiel to a king (for example, 34:24); both meanings probably apply here, signifying a high—or the highest—political leader.

*23. or the sin . . . is made known.* The chieftain is responsible even when initially unaware of the violation and is only informed about it later by others. Ignorance does not absolve the offender.

<sup>27</sup>If any person from among the populace unwittingly incurs guilt by doing any of the things which by יהוה's commandments ought not to be done, and realizes guilt—<sup>28</sup>or the sin of which one is guilty is made known—that person shall bring a female goat without blemish as an offering for the sin of which that one is guilty. <sup>29</sup>The offerer shall lay a hand upon the head of the purgation offering. The purgation offering shall be slaughtered at the place of the burnt offering. <sup>30</sup>The priest shall take with his finger some of its blood and put it on the horns of the altar of burnt offering; and all the rest of its blood he shall pour out at the base of the altar. <sup>31</sup>The offerer shall remove all its fat, just as the fat is removed from the sacrifice of well-being; and the priest shall turn it into smoke on the altar, for a pleasing odor to יהוה. The priest shall thus make expiation for that person, who shall be forgiven.

<sup>32</sup>If the offering one brings as a purgation offering is a sheep, that person shall bring a female without blemish. <sup>33</sup>The offerer shall lay a hand upon the head of the purgation offering, and it shall be slaughtered as a purgation offering at the spot where the burnt offering is slaughtered. <sup>34</sup>The priest shall take with his finger some of the blood of the purgation offering and put it on the horns of the altar of burnt offering, and all the rest of its blood he shall pour out at the base of the altar. <sup>35</sup>And all its fat the offerer shall remove, just as the fat of the sheep of the sacrifice of well-being is removed; and this the priest shall turn into smoke on the altar, over יהוה's offering by fire. For the sin of

27 וְאִם־נֶ֣פֶשׁ אַחַ֡ת תֶּחֱטָא֩ בִשְׁגָגָ֨ה מֵעַ֣ם הָאָ֗רֶץ בַּ֠עֲשֹׂתָ֠הּ אַחַ֨ת מִמִּצְוֺ֧ת יְהֹוָ֛ה אֲשֶׁ֥ר לֹא־תֵעָשֶׂ֖ינָה וְאָשֵֽׁם: 28 א֚וֹ הוֹדַ֣ע אֵלָ֔יו חַטָּאת֖וֹ אֲשֶׁ֣ר חָטָ֑א וְהֵבִ֨יא קָרְבָּנ֜וֹ שְׂעִירַ֤ת עִזִּים֙ תְּמִימָ֣ה נְקֵבָ֔ה עַל־חַטָּאת֖וֹ אֲשֶׁ֥ר חָטָֽא: 29 וְסָמַךְ֙ אֶת־יָד֔וֹ עַ֖ל רֹ֣אשׁ הַֽחַטָּ֑את וְשָׁחַט֙ אֶת־הַ֣חַטָּ֔את בִּמְק֖וֹם הָֽעֹלָֽה: 30 וְלָקַ֨ח הַכֹּהֵ֤ן מִדָּמָהּ֙ בְּאֶצְבָּע֔וֹ וְנָתַ֕ן עַל־קַרְנֹ֖ת מִזְבַּ֣ח הָֽעֹלָ֑ה וְאֶת־כָּל־דָּמָ֣הּ יִשְׁפֹּ֔ךְ אֶל־יְס֖וֹד הַמִּזְבֵּֽחַ: 31 וְאֶת־כָּל־חֶלְבָּ֣הּ יָסִ֗יר כַּאֲשֶׁ֨ר הוּסַ֣ר חֵ֘לֶב֮ מֵעַ֣ל זֶ֣בַח הַשְּׁלָמִים֒ וְהִקְטִ֤יר הַכֹּהֵן֙ הַמִּזְבֵּ֔חָה לְרֵ֥יחַ נִיחֹ֖חַ לַֽיהֹוָ֑ה וְכִפֶּ֥ר עָלָ֛יו הַכֹּהֵ֖ן וְנִסְלַ֥ח לֽוֹ: פ

32 וְאִם־כֶּ֛בֶשׂ יָבִ֥יא קָרְבָּנ֖וֹ לְחַטָּ֑את נְקֵבָ֥ה תְמִימָ֖ה יְבִיאֶֽנָּה: 33 וְסָמַךְ֙ אֶת־יָד֔וֹ עַ֖ל רֹ֣אשׁ הַֽחַטָּ֑את וְשָׁחַ֤ט אֹתָהּ֙ לְחַטָּ֔את בִּמְק֕וֹם אֲשֶׁ֥ר יִשְׁחַ֖ט אֶת־הָֽעֹלָֽה: 34 וְלָקַ֨ח הַכֹּהֵ֜ן מִדַּ֤ם הַֽחַטָּאת֙ בְּאֶצְבָּע֔וֹ וְנָתַ֕ן עַל־קַרְנֹ֖ת מִזְבַּ֣ח הָֽעֹלָ֑ה וְאֶת־כָּל־דָּמָ֣הּ יִשְׁפֹּ֔ךְ אֶל־יְס֖וֹד הַמִּזְבֵּֽחַ: 35 וְאֶת־כָּל־חֶלְבָּ֣הּ יָסִ֗יר כַּאֲשֶׁ֨ר יוּסַ֥ר חֵֽלֶב־הַכֶּ֘שֶׂב֮ מִזֶּ֣בַח הַשְּׁלָמִים֒ וְהִקְטִ֨יר הַכֹּהֵ֤ן אֹתָם֙ הַמִּזְבֵּ֔חָה עַ֖ל אִשֵּׁ֣י

. . . . . . . . . . . . . . . . . . . . . . . . . .

### When Anyone Else Incurs Guilt (4:27–35)

The ritual for any ordinary individual resembles that of the *chatat* offering for a chieftain (see 4:22–26); however, the offerer may choose to bring either a female goat (v. 28) or female sheep (v. 32). No self-evident rationale accounts for the specified sex of the sacrificial animals. One could conclude that a female might represent a greater loss in terms of

long-term investment (because more females than males are necessary for reproduction, and because females also produce milk). There is no mention as to what is to be done with the parts of the animal that are not burned on the altar. Usually, the remainder is shared by the priest and the offerer in the case of a well-being offering.

*27. person.* Heb. *nefesh*, an inclusive noun that refers to a woman or man. (See at 2:1.)

which one is guilty, the priest shall thus make expiation on behalf of that person, who shall be forgiven.

5 If a person incurs guilt—

When one has heard a public imprecation but (although able to testify as having either seen or learned of the matter) has not given information and thus is subject to punishment;

[2]Or when a person touches any impure thing (be it the carcass of an impure beast or the carcass of impure cattle or the carcass of an impure creeping thing) and the fact has escaped notice, and then, being impure, that person realizes guilt;

[3]Or when one touches human impurity (any such impurity whereby someone becomes impure) and, though having known about it, the fact has escaped notice, but later that person realizes guilt;

[4]Or when a person utters an oath to bad or good purpose (whatever a human being may utter in an oath) and, though having known about

יְהוָ֑ה וְכִפֶּ֨ר עָלָ֧יו הַכֹּהֵ֛ן עַל־חַטָּאת֥וֹ אֲשֶׁר־
חָטָ֖א וְנִסְלַ֥ח לֽוֹ׃ פ

ה וְנֶ֣פֶשׁ כִּֽי־תֶחֱטָ֗א
וְשָֽׁמְעָה֙ ק֣וֹל אָלָ֔ה וְה֣וּא עֵ֔ד א֥וֹ רָאָ֖ה א֣וֹ
יָדָ֑ע אִם־ל֥וֹא יַגִּ֖יד וְנָשָׂ֥א עֲוֺנֽוֹ׃
2 א֣וֹ נֶ֗פֶשׁ אֲשֶׁ֣ר תִּגַּע֮ בְּכָל־דָּבָ֣ר טָמֵא֒ א֡וֹ
בְנִבְלַת֩ חַיָּ֨ה טְמֵאָ֜ה א֗וֹ בְּנִבְלַת֙ בְּהֵמָ֣ה
טְמֵאָ֔ה א֕וֹ בְּנִבְלַ֖ת שֶׁ֣רֶץ טָמֵ֑א וְנֶעְלַ֣ם
מִמֶּ֔נּוּ וְה֥וּא טָמֵ֖א וְאָשֵֽׁם׃
3 א֣וֹ כִ֤י יִגַּע֙ בְּטֻמְאַ֣ת אָדָ֔ם לְכֹל֙ טֻמְאָת֔וֹ
אֲשֶׁ֥ר יִטְמָ֖א בָּ֑הּ וְנֶעְלַ֣ם מִמֶּ֔נּוּ וְה֥וּא יָדַ֖ע
וְאָשֵֽׁם׃
4 א֣וֹ נֶ֡פֶשׁ כִּ֣י תִשָּׁבַע֩ לְבַטֵּ֨א בִשְׂפָתַ֜יִם
לְהָרַ֣ע ׀ א֣וֹ לְהֵיטִ֗יב לְכֹל֩ אֲשֶׁ֨ר יְבַטֵּ֧א

*Specific Cases That Require Offerings* (5:1–13)

This passage includes types of violations of which only the offender would be aware. These constitute what we might call ethical offenses, like withholding information in legal situations (v. 1), or ritual violations, like touching something considered impure (v. 2). The word *yada* ("have known" or "have learned of") appears in Hebrew with each of these transgressions (vv. 1, 3, 4) and the ritual includes making the transgression known, *hitvada* (a form of *yada*, translated in v. 5 as "confess"). This section also describes three options for the purgation offering, depending on a person's economic resources. The placement of more affordable options at the conclusion of the section on purgation offerings (4:1–5:13) could imply that these options also apply to the earlier cases that require purgation offerings, not only to those in 5:1–4. (However, this is not how the Rabbis understand it.)

*1. **has not given information.*** This is the first specific transgression that the book of Leviticus mentions. It refers to a person who has refused to disclose information that is needed to establish the facts of a legal case. Such an offense might seem minor, but in fact it compromises a person's integrity and also undermines the legal system. An after-the-fact ritual cannot change the external circumstances of the case, but it provides the transgressor with a means to amend symbolically a wrongdoing that has damaged the fabric of society and self.

*2–3.* Realizing later that one has touched a corpse does not undo the original damage of defilement, practically speaking; nonetheless, Leviticus offers a restoration of balance by means of a belated ritual.

*4.* This passage acknowledges the importance

it, the fact has escaped notice, but later that person realizes guilt in any of these matters—
[5]upon realizing guilt in any of these matters, one shall confess having sinned in that way. [6]And one shall bring as a penalty to יהוה, for the sin of which one is guilty, a female from the flock, sheep or goat, as a purgation offering; and the priest shall make expiation for the sin, on that person's behalf.

[7]But if one's means do not suffice for a sheep, that person shall bring to יהוה, as the penalty for that of which one is guilty, two turtledoves or two pigeons—one for a purgation offering and the other for a burnt offering. [8]The offerer shall bring them to the priest, who shall offer first the bird for the purgation offering, pinching its head at the nape without severing it. [9]He shall sprinkle some of the blood of the purgation offering on the side of the altar, and what remains of the blood shall be drained out at the base of the altar; it is a purgation offering. [10]And the second bird he shall prepare as a burnt offering, according to regulation. For the sin of which one is guilty, the priest shall thus make expiation on behalf of that person, who shall be forgiven.

[11]And if one's means do not suffice for two turtledoves or two pigeons, that person shall bring as an offering for that of which one is guilty a tenth of an *eifah* of choice flour for a purgation offering; one shall not add oil to it or lay frankincense on it, for it is a purgation offering. [12]The offerer shall bring it to the priest, and the priest shall scoop out of it a handful as a token portion and turn it into smoke on the altar, with יהוה's offerings by fire; it is a pur-

הָאָדָם בִּשְׁבֻעָה וְנֶעְלַם מִמֶּנּוּ וְהוּא־יָדַע
וְאָשֵׁם לְאַחַת מֵאֵלֶּה׃
5 וְהָיָה כִי־יֶאְשַׁם לְאַחַת מֵאֵלֶּה וְהִתְוַדָּה
אֲשֶׁר חָטָא עָלֶיהָ׃ 6 וְהֵבִיא אֶת־אֲשָׁמוֹ
לַיהוָה עַל חַטָּאתוֹ אֲשֶׁר חָטָא נְקֵבָה מִן־
הַצֹּאן כִּשְׂבָּה אוֹ־שְׂעִירַת עִזִּים לְחַטָּאת
וְכִפֶּר עָלָיו הַכֹּהֵן מֵחַטָּאתוֹ׃
7 וְאִם־לֹא תַגִּיעַ יָדוֹ דֵּי שֶׂה וְהֵבִיא אֶת־
אֲשָׁמוֹ אֲשֶׁר חָטָא שְׁתֵּי תֹרִים אוֹ־שְׁנֵי בְנֵי־
יוֹנָה לַיהוָה אֶחָד לְחַטָּאת וְאֶחָד לְעֹלָה׃
8 וְהֵבִיא אֹתָם אֶל־הַכֹּהֵן וְהִקְרִיב אֶת־
אֲשֶׁר לַחַטָּאת רִאשׁוֹנָה וּמָלַק אֶת־רֹאשׁוֹ
מִמּוּל עָרְפּוֹ וְלֹא יַבְדִּיל׃ 9 וְהִזָּה מִדַּם
הַחַטָּאת עַל־קִיר הַמִּזְבֵּחַ וְהַנִּשְׁאָר בַּדָּם
יִמָּצֵה אֶל־יְסוֹד הַמִּזְבֵּחַ חַטָּאת הוּא׃
10 וְאֶת־הַשֵּׁנִי יַעֲשֶׂה עֹלָה כַּמִּשְׁפָּט וְכִפֶּר
עָלָיו הַכֹּהֵן מֵחַטָּאתוֹ אֲשֶׁר־חָטָא וְנִסְלַח
לוֹ׃ ס
11 וְאִם־לֹא תַשִּׂיג יָדוֹ לִשְׁתֵּי תֹרִים אוֹ
לִשְׁנֵי בְנֵי־יוֹנָה וְהֵבִיא אֶת־קָרְבָּנוֹ אֲשֶׁר
חָטָא עֲשִׂירִת הָאֵפָה סֹלֶת לְחַטָּאת לֹא־
יָשִׂים עָלֶיהָ שֶׁמֶן וְלֹא־יִתֵּן עָלֶיהָ לְבֹנָה כִּי
חַטָּאת הִוא׃ 12 וֶהֱבִיאָהּ אֶל־הַכֹּהֵן וְקָמַץ
הַכֹּהֵן ׀ מִמֶּנָּה מְלוֹא קֻמְצוֹ אֶת־אַזְכָּרָתָהּ
וְהִקְטִיר הַמִּזְבֵּחָה עַל אִשֵּׁי יְהוָה חַטָּאת

of treating promises to oneself (when expressed as an oath) as seriously as promises to another.

*6.* This verse first states the usual offering for persons in one of the foregoing situations: an animal from the flock. However, two more options will follow for persons in certain circumstances.

*7.* ***But if one's means do not suffice.*** Like 1:14–17, this passage lists a more affordable offering—this time, however, stating a rationale that was only implicit in the case of the burnt offering. This second option uses two birds, one of which is entirely consumed, as in a burnt offering (1:17).

*11.* ***And if one's means do not suffice.*** A third option for a poor person is limited to a grain offering, which resembles the meal offering (see 2:1–16).

gation offering. [13]For whichever of these sins one is guilty, the priest shall thus make expiation on behalf of that person, who shall be forgiven. It shall belong to the priest, like the meal offering.

[14]And יהוה spoke to Moses, saying:

[15]When a person commits a trespass, being unwittingly remiss about any of יהוה's sacred things: One shall bring as a penalty to יהוה a ram without blemish from the flock, convertible into payment in silver by the sanctuary weight, as a reparation offering. [16]That person shall make restitution for the remission regarding the sacred things, adding a fifth part to it and giving it to the priest. The priest shall make expiation with the ram of the reparation offering on behalf of that person, who shall be forgiven.

[17]And a person who, without knowing it, sins in regard to any of יהוה's commandments about things not to be done, and then realizes guilt: Such a person shall be subject to punishment. [18]That person shall bring to the priest a ram without blemish from the flock, or the equivalent, as a reparation offering. For the error committed unwittingly, the

הוּא: 13 וְכִפֶּ֨ר עָלָ֤יו הַכֹּהֵן֙ עַל־חַטָּאת֣וֹ אֲשֶׁר־חָטָ֖א מֵאַחַ֣ת מֵאֵ֑לֶּה וְנִסְלַ֣ח ל֑וֹ וְהָיְתָ֥ה לַכֹּהֵ֖ן כַּמִּנְחָֽה: ס

14 וַיְדַבֵּ֥ר יְהֹוָ֖ה אֶל־מֹשֶׁ֥ה לֵּאמֹֽר: 15 נֶ֣פֶשׁ כִּֽי־תִמְעֹ֣ל מַ֔עַל וְחָֽטְאָה֙ בִּשְׁגָגָ֔ה מִקׇּדְשֵׁ֖י יְהֹוָ֑ה וְהֵבִ֣יא אֶת־אֲשָׁמ֣וֹ לַֽיהֹוָ֗ה אַ֧יִל תָּמִ֛ים מִן־הַצֹּ֖אן בְּעֶרְכְּךָ֣ כֶּֽסֶף־שְׁקָלִ֞ים בְּשֶֽׁקֶל־הַקֹּ֖דֶשׁ לְאָשָֽׁם: 16 וְאֵ֣ת אֲשֶׁר֩ חָטָ֨א מִן־הַקֹּ֜דֶשׁ יְשַׁלֵּ֗ם וְאֶת־חֲמִֽישִׁתוֹ֙ יוֹסֵ֣ף עָלָ֔יו וְנָתַ֥ן אֹת֖וֹ לַכֹּהֵ֑ן וְהַכֹּהֵ֗ן יְכַפֵּ֥ר עָלָ֛יו בְּאֵ֥יל הָֽאָשָׁ֖ם וְנִסְלַ֥ח לֽוֹ: פ

17 וְאִם־נֶ֙פֶשׁ֙ כִּ֣י תֶֽחֱטָ֔א וְעָֽשְׂתָ֗ה אַחַת֙ מִכׇּל־מִצְוֺ֣ת יְהֹוָ֔ה אֲשֶׁ֖ר לֹ֣א תֵעָשֶׂ֑ינָה וְלֹֽא־יָדַ֥ע וְאָשֵׁ֖ם וְנָשָׂ֥א עֲוֺנֽוֹ: 18 וְהֵבִ֡יא אַ֩יִל֩ תָּמִ֨ים מִן־הַצֹּ֤אן בְּעֶרְכְּךָ֙ לְאָשָׁם֙ אֶל־הַכֹּהֵ֔ן וְכִפֶּר֩ עָלָ֨יו הַכֹּהֵ֜ן עַ֣ל שִׁגְגָת֧וֹ אֲשֶׁר־

- - - - - - - - - - - - - - -

REPARATION OFFERING—*asham* (5:14–26)

The name for this offering, *asham*, elsewhere means "guilt," which is why in English it is sometimes called a "guilt offering." The more recent term, "reparation offering," more accurately reflects the purpose of the ritual, which is to repair the damage done in specified cases. In contrast to the earlier instructions in this parashah, the section on the reparation offering focuses on the nature of the transgression and on payment of reparations, not on the presentation and disposition of the sacrificial offering. Restoration involves directly compensating those who have been harmed by the act.

The section begins with reparation of damage done to sacred items and concludes with damage to persons. These laws echo the Decalogue (Exodus 20:2–14; Deuteronomy 5:6–18) in that crimes against another person are considered a crime against God and thus require similar reparation. The assertion that crimes against persons are also crimes against God also stands out as the central message of biblical prophets like Amos or Isaiah, and it constitutes a distinctive contribution of the Bible to Western ethics. Leviticus presents this idea, radical for its own time, as the final point in this parashah.

*14–16.* Mishandling items that belong to the sanctuary, considered to be an overt crime against God, requires a sacrificial animal (a ram) or its substitution rendered in silver. The person must make restitution for the damaged item, plus twenty percent interest.

*17–19.* It is not obvious why a reparation offering rather than purgation offering applies in the case of an inadvertent transgression of a prohibition.

priest shall make expiation on behalf of that person, who shall be forgiven. [19]It is a reparation offering; guilt has been incurred before יהוה.

[20]יהוה spoke to Moses, saying: [21]When a person sins and commits a trespass against יהוה—by dealing deceitfully with another in the matter of a deposit or a pledge, or through robbery, or by defrauding another, [22]or by finding something lost and lying about it; if one swears falsely regarding any one of the various things that someone may do and sin thereby—[23]when one has thus sinned and, realizing guilt, would restore either that which was gotten through robbery or fraud, or the entrusted deposit, or the lost thing that was found, [24]or anything else about which one swore falsely, that person shall repay the principal amount and add a fifth part to it. One shall pay it to its owner upon realizing guilt. [25]Then that person shall bring to the priest, as a penalty to יהוה, a ram without blemish from the flock, or the equivalent, as a reparation offering. [26]The priest shall make expiation before יהוה on behalf of that person, who shall be forgiven for whatever was done to draw blame thereby.

שָׁגָג וְהוּא לֹא־יָדַע וְנִסְלַח לוֹ׃ 19 אָשָׁם
הוּא אָשֹׁם אָשַׁם לַיהוָה׃ פ
20 וַיְדַבֵּר יְהוָה אֶל־מֹשֶׁה לֵּאמֹר׃ 21 נֶפֶשׁ
כִּי תֶחֱטָא וּמָעֲלָה מַעַל בַּיהוָה וְכִחֵשׁ
בַּעֲמִיתוֹ בְּפִקָּדוֹן אוֹ־בִתְשׂוּמֶת יָד אוֹ בְגָזֵל
אוֹ עָשַׁק אֶת־עֲמִיתוֹ׃ 22 אוֹ־מָצָא אֲבֵדָה
וְכִחֶשׁ בָּהּ וְנִשְׁבַּע עַל־שָׁקֶר עַל־אַחַת מִכֹּל
אֲשֶׁר־יַעֲשֶׂה הָאָדָם לַחֲטֹא בָהֵנָּה׃ 23 וְהָיָה
כִּי־יֶחֱטָא וְאָשֵׁם וְהֵשִׁיב אֶת־הַגְּזֵלָה אֲשֶׁר
גָּזָל אוֹ אֶת־הָעֹשֶׁק אֲשֶׁר עָשָׁק אוֹ אֶת־
הַפִּקָּדוֹן אֲשֶׁר הָפְקַד אִתּוֹ אוֹ אֶת־הָאֲבֵדָה
אֲשֶׁר מָצָא׃ 24 אוֹ מִכֹּל אֲשֶׁר־יִשָּׁבַע עָלָיו
לַשֶּׁקֶר וְשִׁלַּם אֹתוֹ בְּרֹאשׁוֹ וַחֲמִשִׁתָיו יֹסֵף
עָלָיו לַאֲשֶׁר הוּא לוֹ יִתְּנֶנּוּ בְּיוֹם אַשְׁמָתוֹ׃
25 וְאֶת־אֲשָׁמוֹ יָבִיא לַיהוָה אַיִל תָּמִים מִן־
הַצֹּאן בְּעֶרְכְּךָ לְאָשָׁם אֶל־הַכֹּהֵן׃ 26 וְכִפֶּר
עָלָיו הַכֹּהֵן לִפְנֵי יְהוָה וְנִסְלַח לוֹ עַל־אַחַת
מִכֹּל אֲשֶׁר־יַעֲשֶׂה לְאַשְׁמָה בָהּ׃ פ

*20–26. **When a person sins and commits a trespass against יהוה—by dealing deceitfully with another.*** This parashah, which lingers so long on rites in the sanctuary, concludes with a list of offenses against another person, what we might call ethical and social or economic violations. Each of these wrongs requires first and foremost a restitution of the damage done to the other person. This section introduces the deep concern in Leviticus for social justice and equity, a concern often overlooked as a result of the book's detailed information about ritual.

*21. trespass.* Heb. *maal*; it can also be translated as "sacrilege," a term that rightly highlights the religious component of what might otherwise be considered a civil matter.

*against יהוה.* Here Leviticus expresses the idea that crimes against another person are also crimes against God. This message, radical for its own time, also characterizes the message of Leviticus 19 and of prophets like Amos and Isaiah.

*22. swears falsely.* False testimony undermines the judicial system and makes a mockery of attempts at securing justice (see also Exodus 20:13 and Deuteronomy 5:17).

*24. shall repay.* These instructions insist on the equitable restoration of any ill-gained possessions, with an additional twenty percent compensation. Only after such recompense can a person approach the altar and offer a sacrifice.

*25. **Then that person shall bring.*** Only after restoring justice in the human realm should a person bring an offering to God. This emphasis on justice stands as the culmination of the parashah.

—*Tamara Cohn Eskenazi*

# *Another View*

All of this parashah and most of the next one contain instructions for sacrifices, offered by individuals (either women or men) and by households at the central shrine. Yet the extensive focus on communal rites of worship in this part of the Torah may create the impression that other religious practices were either non-existent or discouraged. However, that impression would be erroneous, for—as in traditional societies everywhere—religious activities carried out *only* by women were part of Israelite household life. Such practices are virtually invisible in the Bible. Nevertheless, archeological evidence, interpreted in light of ethnographic data and anthropological models, allows us to recognize this aspect of women's lives in the biblical period.

The gender-specific religious behaviors of women centered on the reproductive process. Women faced the possibility of infertility, complications of pregnancy, and insufficient lactation; they were also aware of high infant mortality. Today we deal with these reproductive problems medically. But in antiquity women carried out procedures—which we might view as superstitious—that were fundamentally religious in nature. That is, women performed rituals both to avert the evil forces (like Lilith) believed to be the cause of problems and also to attract benevolent spirits in order to achieve reproductive success.

Such practices were generally apotropaic (protective). Women might wear shiny jewelry or amulets to keep the "evil eye" away. They would tie a red thread around an infant's limb for similar reasons, a practice that continues to this day among certain Jewish groups. They might keep a lamp burning in or near a birthing room, and they would salt and swaddle a newborn (see Ezekiel 16:4). Other practices, involving

*Women were ritual experts no less than the priests.*

votive figurines and fertility symbols known from other ancient cultures, can also be identified. Such religious behaviors focus on the welfare of childbearing women and their offspring. No doubt women considered them necessary for the creation and safeguarding of new life. Carrying out such practices, which they believed could be effective, would have given women a sense of agency in dealing with considerable reproductive risk. This also means that they were ritual experts no less than the priests in charge of the official sacrificial regimen set forth in *Vayikra*. (See also "Women in Ancient Israel—An Overview," p. xli.)

—*Carol Meyers*

# *Post-biblical Interpretations*

**יהוה** ***called to Moses*** (1:1). Midrash *Vayikra Rabbah* 7.3 addresses the custom of beginning children's education with the book of Leviticus, asking why study commences with Leviticus instead of Genesis. The response is that "children are pure and the sacrifices [described in Leviticus] are pure; let those who are pure study that which is pure."

**יהוה** ***called to Moses*** (1:1). "*Vayikra*," the opening word of Leviticus, ends with an *alef* that in Torah scrolls is inscribed smaller than the other letters in the word. A number of commentators seek a reason for this. One argues that the small *alef* recalls the word *adam* (human being), and reminds individuals to "make themselves small," that is, to avoid arrogance. Another sees a play on the word *aluf* (leader), spelled using the same letters as the word *alef*: Moses, who was extremely close to God, maintained his humility. A third commentator explains that the Torah does not include an exhortation to be humble because were humility to be commanded, it would no longer be humility. Rather, the commentator concludes, every person should cultivate true humility (*Itturei Torah* on Leviticus 1:1, IV, 1998, pp. 7–8).

Several commentators note that this is the only time in the Torah that the verb "to call" precedes the verb "to speak." They point out that at the end of Exodus, Moses was unable to enter the Tent of Meeting when the cloud symbolizing God's presence descended (40:35). *Vayikra* begins with God's call to Moses, indicating that Moses had achieved permission to come before the divine Presence (Rashi and Rashbam on 1:1).

***from the Tent of Meeting*** (1:1). One rabbi notes that until now, God had spoken to Moses in open places—such as the burning bush in the wilderness, Midian, and Sinai, where God's presence was public and without bounds. Thus "a (lowly) maidservant saw at the Sea of Reeds what even the prophet Ezekiel was not privileged to see." However, once the Tent of Meeting was erected, God chose concealment over openness. This is a sign of divine modesty, since what is private is seen by God as more precious (*Itturei Torah* on 1:1, IV, p. 8). According to Midrash *Tanchuma, Vayikra* 4 (ed. Buber, II, p. 475), God chose to leave the high heavens and descend to the earth, to the Tent of Meeting, for love of Israel.

***When any of you presents an offering... to יהוה*** (1:2). This portion discusses a variety of ritual sacrifices. A number of interpreters take this opportunity to consider "sacrifice" in a broader, less material sense. Remarking on the Hebrew word for "presents an offering" (*yakriv*), one commentator says, "When we want to draw close (*l'hitkarev*) to God, we must offer something of our own, that is, our 'evil inclination.'" Another suggests that this verse calls upon individuals to offer God their innermost strength and will, to submit to God, and to dedicate all of their acts to the service of God (*Itturei Torah* on Leviticus 1:2, IV, p. 10).

One commentator on this verse cites BT *Kiddushin* 40b, "Those individuals who perform a single mitzvah draw themselves and the entire world toward righteousness." Responding to the mixing of the singular

*To draw close to God, bring a sacrifice: offer up your "evil inclination."*

and the plural verb forms in Leviticus 1:2, another interpretation urges that we each acknowledge that we realize our full potential through our bonds to the community of Israel (*Itturei Torah* on 1:2, IV, p. 11).

***You shall lay a hand upon the head of the burnt offering*** (1:4). While the Rabbis exempted women from the legal obligation to lay hands upon one's burnt offering, some rabbis permitted them to participate in this mitzvah "if they choose" (BT *Rosh HaShanah* 33a; *Vayikra Rabbah* 1.7). This view is one of those cited within the contemporary halachic community in support of expanding women's roles in ritual.

***The bull shall be slaughtered... and Aaron's sons, the priests, shall offer the blood*** (1:5). The first verb of this verse is impersonal, and it mentions the priests only after the animal has been killed. Citing these details of wording, the Rabbis validated animal slaughter by any lay person—male or female—whether for a sacrificial offering or for purely human consumption (Midrash *Sifra*; BT *Z'vachim* 32a; see also Mishnah *Z'vachim* 3:1, *Chulin* 1:1). Late medieval historical sources document that Jewish women were slaughtering animals for kosher meat (*sh'chitah*) in various parts of Europe as a matter of course; in Italy, they did so from at least the Renaissance into the 20th century.

***When a person presents an offering of meal to* יהוה** (2:1). Midrash *Tanchuma, Vayikra* 5 (ed. Buber, p. 475) notes that this is the only instance in the prolonged discussion of sacrifices in which the word for "person" is *nefesh* instead of *ish* (man) or *adam* (human being). The midrash says that the meal offering is a poor person's donation, brought by an individual who cannot afford to present an animal or bird sacrifice. According to this view, God responds to the offering of the poor "as if that individual had offered his or her own life (*nefesh*)."

—*Dvora E. Weisberg*

# Contemporary Reflection

"AND AARON'S SONS, the priests, shall offer the blood" (1:5). That is pretty much how *parashat Vayikra* introduces Leviticus, a book that sits smack in the center of the Torah like a tough vein of gristle that runs through a tender, juicy steak. Most of Leviticus is hard to digest. *Vayikra* is an instruction manual, and technical writing rarely yields compelling drama or inspiring ethical teachings. The language of our portion is formal, stylized, repetitive, precise. Yet the dryness of language cannot quite disguise the essential problem with what transpires here: the portion is slippery with blood. Rising up from the page are the screams of dying animals, the pungent stink of smoke and burning flesh.

The priestly passages in the Torah not only arouse anxiety in the squeamish—they often seem to be among the most irrelevant we encounter in our sacred text. After all, the major skills of Levites and *kohanim* (the priests), technicians of the sacred, became obsolete almost two thousand years ago when the Temple went up in flames. While Jews with the status of *kohanim* survive in our own day, their role is marginal even in traditional synagogues, and Reform Jews have virtually eliminated their special status. Yet the Torah promises that Israelites who are faithful to the covenant will become *mamlechet kohanim*—a kingdom of priests; it envisions an entire people which serves in a priestly role (Exodus 19:6).

No doubt many of us would have preferred that the Torah command us to become "a kingdom of prophets," collectively denouncing the world's inequities, speaking out for justice and defending the downtrodden. But it is to the priesthood that we Jews are taught to aspire, and the priesthood from which we must seek instruction in *parashat Vayikra*. What can we learn from the role of the priests—and from these methodical instructions for the slaughter and dismemberment of animals for ritual offering on the altar?

If human beings were gentle and benevolent by nature we might not need the stern, disciplinary teachings of the priesthood. The Torah's insight is that priestly service is what our homicidal proclivities demand and deserve. So the descendants of Phinehas, a family whose origins are murderous and full of rage (see Numbers 25:1–14), are taught to (re)direct their zealous energies to the service of God. They turn from uncontrolled aggression to the discipline of ritual slaughter, hedged about with myriad laws and regulations. As officiants at the altar, their killing is tamed and domesticated, their dangerous proclivities neutralized. Stripped of the normal male prerogatives of land ownership and military service, they become, as my teacher Melila Hellner-Eshed suggests, "God's housewives"—feminized men who dress in skirts and busy themselves with the domestic work of cooking and cleaning in God's holy dwelling.

Sublimation of aggression may, in fact, underlie

the entire sacrificial system of worship. A *korban*, an offering to God, is more than an act of violence. It is violence transmuted into something higher; it is God re-shaping a destructive human drive into productive, creative energy. Through bringing offerings to the altar, the fierce passions of the ego are not indulged but controlled and transcended. Animals, valued possessions and markers of wealth, are given selflessly to God—and thus the worshiper learns gradually to overcome narcissism and greed. Animal blood is dashed on the altar, but human blood may not be shed; substitution trains the worshipers to restrain their own innate savagery.

The opening of our parashah reads: *Adam ki yakriv mikem korban l'Adonai*—"When any of you presents an offering of cattle to יהוה" (1:2). A Hasidic commentator offers an interpretive reading: "One who wants to become *karov*—close to God—must bring an offering *mikem*—that is, from oneself." And what is the offering? It is the beast within ourselves—the part of ourselves that is capable of cruelty and brutality, even to those we love (*Itturei Torah*, IV, 1998, p. 10). The ritual of animal sacrifice, understood symbolically, conveys the struggle of flawed human beings to become more humane.

The Israelites approached the altar in order to attain closeness to the Divine—to experience what we today would call spiritual elevation, a consciousness of being lifted up to something higher than themselves. They drew nearer to God not by denying the body and its drives but by raising the physical to a sacred purpose. From the rituals of worship set forth in *Vayikra* we learn that aggression need not be extinguished in the personality in order to lead a holy life; it may instead be channeled in constructive directions and employed for the good.

A Talmudic passage reminds us that certain traits may be inborn, but character is never determined by fate. All human energies are ours to activate as we wish, in accordance with our freedom. Rav Nachman bar Yitzchak observed: "One who is born under the

*As a kingdom of priests, we can sanctify even the darkest forces within the psyche.*

sign of Mars will be a shedder of blood." Rav Ashi did not see such a prediction as necessarily bad, for as he pointed out, one could "shed blood" for a good cause—by becoming "either a surgeon, ... a ritual slaughterer (*shochet*), or a circumciser (*mohel*)" (BT *Shabbat* 156a).

So we may aspire, even today, to be a kingdom of priests—a people committed to elevating and sanctifying even the darkest forces within the psyche. If we closely read the seemingly dry instructions and bloody details of *parashat Vayikra*, we learn that through the discipline of our faith we can redeem what is broken and flawed within ourselves, transforming barbaric urges into opportunities for blessing.

—*Janet Marder*

# *Voices*

## *Psalm 50*

Debbie Perlman

You are the Open Door
That beckons me in;
Peeking around the door frame,
I begin to enter into Your glory.

You move me forward, O Eternal,
To step beyond self-made boundaries;
Lift my foot over the threshold
That I might abide with You.

In the house of the Eternal,
I found my questions;
Waiting to be posed,
They filled me with wonder.

Through the doorway of the Eternal
Come jumbled sounds and mingled scents;
Warm sunlight falls across my lap:
All this, all this, Your creation.

Sit with me, Eternal Teacher,
Encourage my seeking;
As I fill my hours with Your *mitzvot*,
So shall I be filled.

Then send me through Your door
Stretching up to honor Your Name,
Sharing out this wonder,
Enriching myself in the giving.

## *A Mother's Morning Prayer*

Hava Pincas-Cohen
(transl. Jules Harlow and Rochelle Furstenberg)

At this time as I stand cooking oatmeal,
Remove all sorts of alien thoughts from me
And when I touch the baby's back and take his temperature
May all sorts of problems disappear,
May they not confuse my thoughts.
And give me the strength to scrub my face
So that each one of my children
Can see his face in mine
As in a mirror washed for a festival.

And the darkness sunk within
My face—cover it with light
So that I don't lose my patience, and I won't be hoarse
From coarse, insistent screaming.
May I not experience weakness
Before the unknowable
And may it never end, even for a moment,
The touch of flesh upon flesh, my children's and mine.

Give me so much of Your love
That I can stand at the door and hand it out
With the simplicity of someone slicing bread
And smearing butter every morning.
Renew the sweet offering of boiling milk bubbling over
and the smell of coffee hovering above
The thanksgiving sacrifice and the daily sacrifice
That I never learned how to give.

## *Coda*

Rachel Hadas

The future's where we place our hope and fear.
What's done is done. The past cannot recur.
Anecdote, dream, and memory all refer
to experience no longer there.
Yet look at what is rising through the air!
Fox fur, ginger, melting lemon ice
successively appear. Can we live twice?
Is nothing lost? I reach a new conclusion:
leave the future to its own confusion.
My business is with what I find I know
through story, memory, dream. Since this is so,
I am a vessel full beyond the brim
even as life leaks out, a steady stream
of losses running toward oblivion.
But how to make one's daily life maintain
a balance between plenitude and pain,
such fullness and such unremitting waste?
Ginger offered in an outstretched hand.
A blond recorder resting in its stand.
Kippers. Pastries. A remembered taste.

## *How divine is forgiving?*

Marge Piercy

*Leviticus 5:10–26*

It's a nice concept
but what's under the sculptured draperies?
We forgive when we don't really care
because what was done to us brought
    unexpected
harvest, as I always try to explain
to the peach trees as I prune them hard,
to the cats when I shove pills against
the Gothic vaults of their mouths.

We forgive those who betrayed us
years later because memory has rotted
through like something left out in the weather
battered clean then littered dirty
in the rain, chewed by mice and beetles,
frozen and baked and stripped by the wind
till it is unrecognizable, corpse
or broken machine, something long useless.

We forgive those whom their own machinations
have sufficiently tangled, enshrouded,
the fly who bit us to draw blood and who
hangs now a gutted trophy in a spider's
airy larder; more exactly, the friend
whose habit of lying has immobilized him
at last like a dog trapped in a cocoon
of fishing line and barbed hooks.

We forgive those we firmly love
because anger hurts, a coal that burns
and smoulders still scorching the tissues
inside, blistering wherever it touches
so that finally it is to ease our own pain
that we bury the hot clinkers in a mound
of caring, suffocate the sparks with promises,
drown them in tears, reconciling.

We forgive mostly not from strength
but through imperfections, for memory
wears transparent as a glass with the pattern
washed off, till we stare past what injured us.
We forgive because we too have done
the same to others easy as a mudslide;
or because anger is a fire that must be fed
and we are too tired to rise and haul a log.

# צו ◆ *Tzav*

LEVITICUS 6:1–8:36

## *The Priestly Torah and the Priests' Ordination*

PARASHAT TZAV ("issue a command") continues with instructions about sacrificial offerings that began in Leviticus 1–5. However, whereas 1:1–2 began with instructions to all the people of Israel, 6:1 starts with a command specifically addressed to the priests. The first section of the parashah (Leviticus 6–7) contains instructions about the priests' portions from the sacrificial rituals. The second section (Leviticus 8) records the ordination of the priests.

In establishing a sacrificial system and a professional priesthood, biblical Israel resembled other ancient cultures. One notes, however, two differences. First, priests in most cultures in the ancient world kept the secrets of their profession away from the public eye and transmitted them privately from generation to generation. In contrast, Leviticus reflects a commitment to keep the rules of the trade, as it were, in public view.

A second difference is that neighboring cultures such as Mesopotamia included women priests (even though they did not perform the same rituals as male priests), whereas the Bible recognizes only male priests. Scholars concur, however, that women played an important role in many facets of popular religion in ancient Israel (as did men), even though the priestly teachings in Leviticus do not acknowledge or discuss such roles.

Although *parashat Tzav* does not mention women explicitly, it treats three areas that do involve women. The first pertains to the roles and possible privileges of women as members of priests' families. Such women apparently benefit from the priests' share of sacrificial foods. There is a question, however, whether they may eat the part of the offering designated as "most holy" (see Another View, p. 608).

The second area concerning women pertains to the highly valued, formal priestly garments (see Exodus 28 and Leviticus 8). Archeological and biblical evidence shows that women excelled in weaving, spinning, and sewing (see at Exodus 35:25; *T'tzaveh*, Another View, p. 489; *P'kudei*, Another View, p. 560). Therefore, we may assume that women made the priestly garments. According to the book of Samuel, each year Hannah made and brought a special garment for her son Samuel who served at the sanctuary at Shiloh (I Samuel 2:19). Plausibly priests' mothers and wives likewise made clothing for their family members.

*The Bible stands out by placing the priestly trade in public view and restricting it to men.*

The third area to consider is whether women were among those who offered the sacrifices that these passages discuss. Biblical references elsewhere do suggest that Israelite women, like Israelite men, worshipped and sacrificed in the shrines—often as part of their households. For example, according to Leviticus 12:6 and 15:29, women are obligated to offer sacrifices after childbirth and irregular bleeding. Proverbs 7:14 presents a female persona who mentions her need to offer the well-being offerings. And in I Samuel 1, Hannah and her husband present and slaughter the offering that she has brought—together with a portion of flour and a jar of wine—to the shrine in Shiloh as payment for a vow.

(On the widespread ancient practice of offering sacrifices and its rationale, and on the role of sacrifices in ancient Israel, see the introduction to the previous parashah, pp. 569–71.)

—*Tamara Cohn Eskenazi*

## *Outline*

*I.* Supplemental Instructions to the Priests Regarding Sacrifices (6:1–7:38)

- *A.* Instructions for the burnt offering (6:1–6)
- *B.* Instructions for the meal offering (6:7–16)
- *C.* Instructions for the purgation offering (6:17–23)
- *D.* Instructions for the reparation offering (7:1–6)
- *E.* Concluding instructions for the preceding offerings (7:7–10)
- *F.* Instructions for the well-being sacrifice (7:11–21)
- *G.* Prohibitions regarding the fat and the blood (7:22–27)
- *H.* Further details regarding the well-being sacrifice (7:28–36)
- *I.* Affirmation of the Sinaitic origin of the sacrificial practices (7:37–38)

*II.* The Ordination of the Priests (8:1–36)

- *A.* God's instructions regarding the ordination of the priests (vv. 1–3)
- *B.* Moses' ordination of the priests (vv. 4–30)
- *C.* Final preparatory steps: seven days of priests' isolation (vv. 31–36)

יהוה spoke to Moses, saying: [2]Command
Aaron and his sons thus:
This is the ritual of the burnt offering: The
burnt offering itself shall remain where it is burned
upon the altar all night until morning, while the fire
on the altar is kept going on it. [3]The priest shall
dress in linen raiment, with linen breeches next to
his body; and he shall take up the ashes to which
the fire has reduced the burnt offering on the altar
and place them beside the altar. [4]He shall then take

ו וַיְדַבֵּר יְהֹוָה אֶל־מֹשֶׁה לֵּאמֹר׃ 2 צַו אֶת־
אַהֲרֹן וְאֶת־בָּנָיו לֵאמֹר
זֹאת תּוֹרַת הָעֹלָה הִוא הָעֹלָה עַל מוֹקְדָה
עַל־הַמִּזְבֵּחַ כָּל־הַלַּיְלָה עַד־הַבֹּקֶר וְאֵשׁ
הַמִּזְבֵּחַ תּוּקַד בּוֹ׃ 3 וְלָבַשׁ הַכֹּהֵן מִדּוֹ בַד
וּמִכְנְסֵי־בַד יִלְבַּשׁ עַל־בְּשָׂרוֹ וְהֵרִים אֶת־
הַדֶּשֶׁן אֲשֶׁר תֹּאכַל הָאֵשׁ אֶת־הָעֹלָה עַל־
הַמִּזְבֵּחַ וְשָׂמוֹ אֵצֶל הַמִּזְבֵּחַ׃ 4 וּפָשַׁט אֶת־

## *Supplemental Instructions to the Priests Regarding Sacrifices*

(6:1–7:38)

### INSTRUCTIONS FOR THE BURNT OFFERING (6:1–6)

Detailed instructions about this offering appeared in Leviticus 1, indicating that the entire animal is to be "turned into smoke" (see 1:9). The additional details here focus on the activity of the priests, instructing them concerning the permanent fire that must burn on the altar, and concerning the clothing the officiating priest must wear at different stages when disposing of the offering's remains.

*2. Command Aaron and his sons.* Whereas Moses is charged with communicating most other laws to the people, here God directs Moses to convey these laws specifically to Aaron and his sons. (Because the laws apply to the priests themselves, it is reasonable to translate the plural noun *banim* here as "sons" rather than as "children.")

***ritual.*** Heb. *torah*, which more widely means an "instruction" or "teaching" (see the introduction to Deuteronomy 6:20–25). Rendered as "Torah" (capitalized), this term comes to represent the entire first five books of the Bible (see at Deuteronomy 31:9). This is the first time that this term is employed in Leviticus.

*3. The priest shall dress in linen raiment.* The fabrics that the "skilled women" wove for the Tabernacle (Exodus 35:25) were nearly identical to the material specified for the priestly garments (Exodus 28:5). Thus women probably also wove the fabrics for the priestly garments such as those mentioned here. Weaving is one of the household crafts or tasks typically carried out by women in traditional cultures (see *T'rumah*, Another View, p. 467; *P'kudei*, Another View, p. 560).

*4.* The change of clothing allows the priest to leave the sacred precinct of the altar and dispose of the remains of the offering.

◗ Why can the females in Aaron's line not partake of these offerings?

ANOTHER VIEW ➤ *608*

◗ Women became the ritual specialists for temple sacrifice in its domestic transformation.

CONTEMPORARY REFLECTION ➤ *610*

◗ The Midrash lists examples where the value of peace is deemed higher than the value of truth.

POST-BIBLICAL INTERPRETATIONS ➤ *608*

◗ Modest, I know, the offerings / of your daughter: / Only an outburst of song…

VOICES ➤ *612*

off his vestments and put on other vestments, and carry the ashes outside the camp to a pure place. [5]The fire on the altar shall be kept burning, not to go out: every morning the priest shall feed wood to it, lay out the burnt offering on it, and turn into smoke the fat parts of the offerings of well-being. [6]A perpetual fire shall be kept burning on the altar, not to go out.

[7]And this is the ritual of the meal offering: Aaron's sons shall present it before יהוה, in front of the altar. [8]A handful of the choice flour and oil of the meal offering shall be taken from it, with all the frankincense that is on the meal offering, and this token portion shall be turned into smoke on the altar as a pleasing odor to יהוה. [9]What is left of it shall be eaten by Aaron and his sons; it shall be eaten as unleavened cakes, in the sacred precinct; they shall eat it in the enclosure of the Tent of Meeting. [10]It shall not be baked with leaven; I have given it as their portion from My offerings by fire; it is most holy, like the purgation offering and the reparation offering. [11]Only the males among Aaron's

בְּגָדָיו וְלָבַשׁ בְּגָדִים אֲחֵרִים וְהוֹצִיא אֶת־
הַדֶּשֶׁן אֶל־מִחוּץ לַמַּחֲנֶה אֶל־מָקוֹם טָהוֹר׃
5 וְהָאֵשׁ עַל־הַמִּזְבֵּחַ תּוּקַד־בּוֹ לֹא תִכְבֶּה
וּבִעֵר עָלֶיהָ הַכֹּהֵן עֵצִים בַּבֹּקֶר בַּבֹּקֶר
וְעָרַךְ עָלֶיהָ הָעֹלָה וְהִקְטִיר עָלֶיהָ חֶלְבֵי
הַשְּׁלָמִים׃ 6 אֵשׁ תָּמִיד תּוּקַד עַל־הַמִּזְבֵּחַ
לֹא תִכְבֶּה׃ ס
7 וְזֹאת תּוֹרַת הַמִּנְחָה הַקְרֵב אֹתָהּ בְּנֵי־
אַהֲרֹן לִפְנֵי יְהֹוָה אֶל־פְּנֵי הַמִּזְבֵּחַ׃ 8 וְהֵרִים
מִמֶּנּוּ בְּקֻמְצוֹ מִסֹּלֶת הַמִּנְחָה וּמִשַּׁמְנָהּ וְאֵת
כָּל־הַלְּבֹנָה אֲשֶׁר עַל־הַמִּנְחָה וְהִקְטִיר
הַמִּזְבֵּחַ רֵיחַ נִיחֹחַ אַזְכָּרָתָהּ לַיהֹוָה׃
9 וְהַנּוֹתֶרֶת מִמֶּנָּה יֹאכְלוּ אַהֲרֹן וּבָנָיו
מַצּוֹת תֵּאָכֵל בְּמָקוֹם קָדֹשׁ בַּחֲצַר אֹהֶל־
מוֹעֵד יֹאכְלוּהָ׃ 10 לֹא תֵאָפֶה חָמֵץ חֶלְקָם
נָתַתִּי אֹתָהּ מֵאִשָּׁי קֹדֶשׁ קָדָשִׁים הִוא
כַּחַטָּאת וְכָאָשָׁם׃ 11 כָּל־זָכָר בִּבְנֵי אַהֲרֹן

*5.* ***The fire on the altar shall be kept burning.*** The fire both consumes the offerings and cleanses the altar from any leftover meat.

*6.* ***perpetual fire.*** The priest keeps the sanctuary's fire going. He takes care of the altar in the ways that homemakers—typically women—take care of the home. On the priests as "God's housewives," see *Vayikra*, Contemporary Reflection, p. 589.

INSTRUCTIONS FOR THE MEAL OFFERING (6:7–16)

This section repeats some of the information from Leviticus 2 but adds a few details, namely who can eat the offering and what to do with it when a priest is being ordained. On this type of offering, see Leviticus 2.

*7.* ***ritual.*** Heb. *torah*; see at 6:2.

*10.* ***most holy.*** This term, also translated "holy of holies," typically designates the innermost sacred section of the Tabernacle (see Exodus 26:34). The sacred status of food consumed in the Tabernacle highlights the analogy between the Tabernacle and the body (see the introduction to *Vayikra*, p. 569).

*11.* ***Only the males.*** The translation here restricts eating of this sacrifice to Aaron and his sons. However, if one construes the Hebrew words as "every male" or "all males" (which is how this same translation understands the phrase in 24 out of 27 cases; see, for example, Numbers 1:20), the statement would permit all priests—not only the officiating priests—to partake in the offering. The purpose of the instruction may be to clarify that priests who are otherwise disqualified from officiating in the sacrificial ritual (because of characteristics described

descendants may eat of it, as their due for all time throughout the ages from יהוה's offerings by fire. Anything that touches these shall become holy.

<sup>12</sup>יהוה spoke to Moses, saying: <sup>13</sup>This is the offering that Aaron and his sons shall offer to יהוה on the occasion of his anointment: a tenth of an *eifah* of choice flour as a regular meal offering, half of it in the morning and half of it in the evening, <sup>14</sup>shall be prepared with oil on a griddle. You shall bring it well soaked, and offer it as a meal offering of baked slices, of pleasing odor to יהוה. <sup>15</sup>And so shall the priest, anointed from among his sons to succeed him, prepare it; it is יהוה's—a law for all time—to be turned entirely into smoke. <sup>16</sup>So, too, every meal offering of a priest shall be a whole offering: it shall not be eaten.

<sup>17</sup>יהוה spoke to Moses, saying: <sup>18</sup>Speak to Aaron and his sons thus: This is the ritual of the purgation offering: the purgation offering shall be slaughtered before יהוה, at the spot where the burnt offering is slaughtered: it is most holy. <sup>19</sup>The priest who offers

יֹאכְלֶ֑נָּה חָק־עוֹלָ֤ם לְדֹרֹֽתֵיכֶם֙ מֵאִשֵּׁ֣י יְהֹוָ֔ה
כֹּ֛ל אֲשֶׁר־יִגַּ֥ע בָּהֶ֖ם יִקְדָּֽשׁ׃ פ

<sup>12</sup> וַיְדַבֵּ֥ר יְהֹוָ֖ה אֶל־מֹשֶׁ֥ה לֵּאמֹֽר׃ <sup>13</sup> זֶ֡ה קׇרְבַּן֩ אַהֲרֹ֨ן וּבָנָ֜יו אֲשֶׁר־יַקְרִ֣יבוּ לַֽיהֹוָ֗ה בְּיוֹם֙ הִמָּשַׁ֣ח אֹת֔וֹ עֲשִׂירִ֨ת הָאֵפָ֥ה סֹ֛לֶת מִנְחָ֖ה תָּמִ֑יד מַחֲצִיתָ֣הּ בַּבֹּ֔קֶר וּמַחֲצִיתָ֖הּ בָּעָֽרֶב׃ <sup>14</sup> עַל־מַֽחֲבַ֗ת בַּשֶּׁ֛מֶן תֵּעָשֶׂ֖ה מֻרְבֶּ֣כֶת תְּבִיאֶ֑נָּה תֻּפִינֵי֙ מִנְחַ֣ת פִּתִּ֔ים תַּקְרִ֥יב רֵֽיחַ־נִיחֹ֖חַ לַֽיהֹוָֽה׃ <sup>15</sup> וְהַכֹּהֵ֨ן הַמָּשִׁ֧יחַ תַּחְתָּ֛יו מִבָּנָ֖יו יַעֲשֶׂ֣ה אֹתָ֑הּ חׇק־עוֹלָ֕ם לַֽיהֹוָ֖ה כָּלִ֥יל תׇּקְטָֽר׃ <sup>16</sup> וְכׇל־מִנְחַ֥ת כֹּהֵ֛ן כָּלִ֥יל תִּהְיֶ֖ה לֹ֥א תֵאָכֵֽל׃ פ

<sup>17</sup> וַיְדַבֵּ֥ר יְהֹוָ֖ה אֶל־מֹשֶׁ֥ה לֵּאמֹֽר׃ <sup>18</sup> דַּבֵּ֤ר אֶֽל־אַהֲרֹן֙ וְאֶל־בָּנָ֣יו לֵאמֹ֔ר זֹ֖את תּוֹרַ֣ת הַֽחַטָּ֑את בִּמְק֡וֹם אֲשֶׁר֩ תִּשָּׁחֵ֨ט הָעֹלָ֜ה תִּשָּׁחֵ֤ט הַֽחַטָּאת֙ לִפְנֵ֣י יְהֹוָ֔ה קֹ֥דֶשׁ קׇֽדָשִׁ֖ים הִֽוא׃ <sup>19</sup> הַכֹּהֵ֛ן הַֽמְחַטֵּ֥א אֹתָ֖הּ יֹאכְלֶ֑נָּה

* * *

in 21:16–23; compare 22:1–7) nonetheless may eat of these portions. See also Another View, p. 608, and at 10:12–14.

**Anything that touches these shall become holy.** "These" refers to the *kodesh kodashim* ("most holy"), which in this context means the portion of the offering designated for the priests. This statement conflicts with Haggai 2:12–13, which claims that only impurity, not holiness, is contagious when touched. In either case, the notion of holiness in the Bible can be likened in modern terms to electric energy or radiation, either of which has the power to heal or to kill, depending on how it is handled. Jacob Milgrom uses the analogy of "high voltage" (*Leviticus: A Book of Ritual and Ethics*, 2004, p. 64). It is also possible that the statement means that a person must be in a state of purity before touching this offering.

*12–16.* These verses essentially constitute a recipe

for preparing the grain for the special meal offering on the occasion of a priest's ordination. The priest offers it on his own behalf.

*16.* Ordinarily the priest eats the meal offerings; however, at ordination, the priest does not eat this special offering.

### INSTRUCTIONS FOR THE PURGATION OFFERING (6:17–23)

These verses amplify the laws in Leviticus 4 by focusing on the different procedures regarding contact with the offering. They describe which portion of the sacrificial animal belongs to the priest and how priests must handle the dedicated food. While sometimes translated as "sin offering," this sacrifice aims to cleanse the sanctuary from visible and invisible impurities that contaminate it. See further at Leviticus 4.

it as a purgation offering shall eat of it; it shall be eaten in the sacred precinct, in the enclosure of the Tent of Meeting. ²⁰Anything that touches its flesh shall become holy; and if any of its blood is spattered upon a garment, you shall wash the bespattered part in the sacred precinct. ²¹An earthen vessel in which it was boiled shall be broken; if it was boiled in a copper vessel, [the vessel] shall be scoured and rinsed with water. ²²Only the males in the priestly line may eat of it: it is most holy. ²³But no purgation offering may be eaten from which any blood is brought into the Tent of Meeting for expiation in the sanctuary; any such shall be consumed in fire.

7 This is the ritual of the reparation offering: it is most holy. ²The reparation offering shall be slaughtered at the spot where the burnt offering is slaughtered, and the blood shall be dashed on all sides of the altar. ³All its fat shall be offered: the broad tail; the fat that covers the entrails; ⁴the two kidneys and the fat that is on them at the loins; and the protuberance on the liver, which shall be removed with the kidneys. ⁵The priest shall turn them into smoke on the altar as an offering by fire

בְּמָק֤וֹם קָדֹשׁ֙ תֵּֽאָכֵ֔ל בַּחֲצַ֖ר אֹ֥הֶל מוֹעֵֽד׃
20 כֹּ֛ל אֲשֶׁר־יִגַּ֥ע בִּבְשָׂרָ֖הּ יִקְדָּ֑שׁ וַאֲשֶׁ֨ר יִזֶּ֤ה מִדָּמָהּ֙ עַל־הַבֶּ֔גֶד אֲשֶׁר֙ יִזֶּ֣ה עָלֶ֔יהָ תְּכַבֵּ֖ס בְּמָק֥וֹם קָדֹֽשׁ׃ 21 וּכְלִי־חֶ֛רֶשׂ אֲשֶׁ֥ר תְּבֻשַּׁל־בּ֖וֹ יִשָּׁבֵ֑ר וְאִם־בִּכְלִ֤י נְחֹ֙שֶׁת֙ בֻּשָּׁ֔לָה וּמֹרַ֥ק וְשֻׁטַּ֖ף בַּמָּֽיִם׃ 22 כָּל־זָכָ֥ר בַּכֹּהֲנִ֖ים יֹאכַ֣ל אֹתָ֑הּ קֹ֥דֶשׁ קָֽדָשִׁ֖ים הִֽוא׃ 23 וְכָל־חַטָּ֡את אֲשֶׁר֩ יוּבָ֨א מִדָּמָ֜הּ אֶל־אֹ֧הֶל מוֹעֵ֛ד לְכַפֵּ֥ר בַּקֹּ֖דֶשׁ לֹ֣א תֵאָכֵ֑ל בָּאֵ֖שׁ תִּשָּׂרֵֽף׃ פ

7 וְזֹ֖את תּוֹרַ֣ת הָאָשָׁ֑ם קֹ֥דֶשׁ קָֽדָשִׁ֖ים הֽוּא׃ 2 בִּמְק֗וֹם אֲשֶׁ֤ר יִשְׁחֲטוּ֙ אֶת־הָ֣עֹלָ֔ה יִשְׁחֲט֖וּ אֶת־הָאָשָׁ֑ם וְאֶת־דָּמ֛וֹ יִזְרֹ֥ק עַל־הַמִּזְבֵּ֖חַ סָבִֽיב׃ 3 וְאֵ֥ת כָּל־חֶלְבּ֖וֹ יַקְרִ֣יב מִמֶּ֑נּוּ אֵ֚ת הָֽאַלְיָ֔ה וְאֶת־הַחֵ֖לֶב הַֽמְכַסֶּ֥ה אֶת־הַקֶּֽרֶב׃ 4 וְאֵת֙ שְׁתֵּ֣י הַכְּלָיֹ֔ת וְאֶת־הַחֵ֙לֶב֙ אֲשֶׁ֣ר עֲלֵיהֶ֔ן אֲשֶׁ֖ר עַל־הַכְּסָלִ֑ים וְאֶת־הַיֹּתֶ֙רֶת֙ עַל־הַכָּבֵ֔ד עַל־הַכְּלָיֹ֖ת יְסִירֶֽנָּה׃ 5 וְהִקְטִ֨יר אֹתָ֤ם הַכֹּהֵן֙ הַמִּזְבֵּ֔חָה אִשֶּׁ֖ה לַיהֹוָ֑ה אָשָׁ֖ם

20. *Anything that touches its flesh shall become holy.* See at v. 11.

21. *An earthen vessel...a copper vessel.* Vessels in which the meat is prepared must be purified. Since earthenware is porous, it cannot be completely "disinfected" and therefore has to be destroyed; metal vessels, however, can be washed. While these rules may correspond to safety measures intended to remove bacterial contamination, the official basis for these precautions in Leviticus is religious, not medical.

22. *Only the males.* Or "every male." See at v. 11.

## INSTRUCTIONS FOR THE REPARATION OFFERING (7:1–6)

The instructions about reparation offerings in Leviticus 5 focused in large measure on who needs to bring it, and on the alternate offerings that depend on the circumstances of the transgressor. The present section supplements those earlier instructions by focusing on the priest's role and on his share of the offering. While sometimes translated as "guilt offering," this type of sacrifice aims to restore the system to a normative wholeness (see at 5:14–26).

1. *ritual.* Heb. *torah*; see at 6:2.

הוּא׃ 6 כָּל־זָכָר בַּכֹּהֲנִים יֹאכְלֶנּוּ בְּמָקוֹם
קָדוֹשׁ יֵאָכֵל קֹדֶשׁ קָדָשִׁים הוּא׃
7 כַּחַטָּאת כָּאָשָׁם תּוֹרָה אַחַת לָהֶם הַכֹּהֵן
אֲשֶׁר יְכַפֶּר־בּוֹ לוֹ יִהְיֶה׃ 8 וְהַכֹּהֵן הַמַּקְרִיב
אֶת־עֹלַת אִישׁ עוֹר הָעֹלָה אֲשֶׁר הִקְרִיב
לַכֹּהֵן לוֹ יִהְיֶה׃ 9 וְכָל־מִנְחָה אֲשֶׁר תֵּאָפֶה
בַּתַּנּוּר וְכָל־נַעֲשָׂה בַמַּרְחֶשֶׁת וְעַל־מַחֲבַת
לַכֹּהֵן הַמַּקְרִיב אֹתָהּ לוֹ תִהְיֶה׃ 10 וְכָל־
מִנְחָה בְלוּלָה־בַשֶּׁמֶן וַחֲרֵבָה לְכָל־בְּנֵי
אַהֲרֹן תִּהְיֶה אִישׁ כְּאָחִיו׃ פ

11 וְזֹאת תּוֹרַת זֶבַח הַשְּׁלָמִים אֲשֶׁר יַקְרִיב
לַיהוָה׃
12 אִם עַל־תּוֹדָה יַקְרִיבֶנּוּ וְהִקְרִיב ׀ עַל־זֶבַח
הַתּוֹדָה חַלּוֹת מַצּוֹת בְּלוּלֹת בַּשֶּׁמֶן וּרְקִיקֵי

to יהוה; it is a reparation offering. [6]Only the males
in the priestly line may eat of it; it shall be eaten in
the sacred precinct: it is most holy.

[7]The reparation offering is like the purgation
offering. The same rule applies to both: it shall
belong to the priest who makes expiation thereby.
[8]So, too, the priest who offers a person's burnt offering shall keep the skin of the burnt offering that
was offered. [9]Further, any meal offering that is
baked in an oven, and any that is prepared in a pan
or on a griddle, shall belong to the priest who offers
it. [10]But every other meal offering, with oil mixed
in or dry, shall go to the sons of Aaron all alike.

[11]This is the ritual of the sacrifice of well-being
that one may offer to יהוה:

[12]One who offers it for thanksgiving shall offer,
together with the sacrifice of thanksgiving, unleavened cakes with oil mixed in—unleavened wafers

---

*6. most holy.* Heb. *kodesh kodashim*, which also means "holy of holies"; see at 6:10.

### CONCLUDING INSTRUCTIONS FOR THE PRECEDING OFFERINGS (7:7–10)

This section completes the earlier discussion of these sacrifices by designating explicitly what the priests are to receive in these cases. The officiating priest is to receive the benefit from both purgation and reparation offerings (7:7). The animal's skin goes to the officiating priest in the case of the burnt offering (7:8). Presumably that skin would be made into leather used for clothing, footwear, and possibly writing material. One type of meal offering goes only to the officiating priest (7:9), whereas the other kind (7:10) goes to all priests. For more about these sacrifices, see Leviticus 1–5.

### INSTRUCTIONS FOR THE WELL-BEING SACRIFICE (7:11–21)

Leviticus 3 described the sacrifice of well-being in great detail, focusing on the types of animal to be offered. This section supplements those instructions by discussing the occasions and different types of well-being sacrifices, as well as the manner in which they are to be distributed and eaten. Well-being offerings include thanksgiving offerings, votive offerings, and freewill offerings. The Bible elsewhere presumes that women are among those who bring these types of offerings (Numbers 30:4; I Samuel 1:3–4, 21, 24–28; Proverbs 7:14.)

*11. ritual.* Heb. *torah*; see at 6:2.

*12. thanksgiving.* Heb. *todah* ("thanks") designates the first type of well-being sacrifice. Whereas Leviticus 3 described the procedures regarding the sacrificial meat, this section describes the grain portion that accompanies the eating of the sacrifice.

*unleavened wafers.* Heb. *challot matzot*, combining the terms for two types of "breads": the *challah* and the *matzah*. (Subsequently, both terms come to be associated specifically with rituals for the Jewish home: *matzah* for Passover, and *challah* for Shabbat.) Women in the ancient world were the ones typically responsible for household baking. In

spread with oil—and cakes of choice flour with oil
mixed in, well soaked. 13 This offering, with cakes of
leavened bread added, shall be offered along with
one's thanksgiving sacrifice of well-being. 14 Out of
this the person shall offer one of each kind as a gift
to יהוה; it shall go to the priest who dashes the
blood of the offering of well-being. 15 And the flesh
of the thanksgiving sacrifice of well-being shall be
eaten on the day that it is offered; none of it shall
be set aside until morning.

16 If, however, the sacrifice offered is a votive or a
freewill offering, it shall be eaten on the day that
one offers the sacrifice, and what is left of it shall be
eaten on the morrow. 17 What is then left of the
flesh of the sacrifice shall be consumed in fire on the
third day. 18 If any of the flesh of the sacrifice of
well-being is eaten on the third day, it shall not be
acceptable; it shall not count for the one who offered it. It is an offensive thing, and the person who
eats of it shall bear the guilt.

19 Flesh that touches anything impure shall not
be eaten; it shall be consumed in fire. As for other

מַצּוֹת מְשֻׁחִים בַּשָּׁמֶן וְסֹלֶת מֻרְבֶּכֶת חַלֹּת
בְּלוּלֹת בַּשָּׁמֶן׃ 13 עַל־חַלֹּת לֶחֶם חָמֵץ
יַקְרִיב קָרְבָּנוֹ עַל־זֶבַח תּוֹדַת שְׁלָמָיו׃
14 וְהִקְרִיב מִמֶּנּוּ אֶחָד מִכָּל־קָרְבָּן תְּרוּמָה
לַיהוָה לַכֹּהֵן הַזֹּרֵק אֶת־דַּם הַשְּׁלָמִים לוֹ
יִהְיֶה׃ 15 וּבְשַׂר זֶבַח תּוֹדַת שְׁלָמָיו בְּיוֹם
קָרְבָּנוֹ יֵאָכֵל לֹא־יַנִּיחַ מִמֶּנּוּ עַד־בֹּקֶר׃
16 וְאִם־נֶדֶר ׀ אוֹ נְדָבָה זֶבַח קָרְבָּנוֹ בְּיוֹם
הַקְרִיבוֹ אֶת־זִבְחוֹ יֵאָכֵל וּמִמָּחֳרָת וְהַנּוֹתָר
מִמֶּנּוּ יֵאָכֵל׃ 17 וְהַנּוֹתָר מִבְּשַׂר הַזָּבַח בַּיּוֹם
הַשְּׁלִישִׁי בָּאֵשׁ יִשָּׂרֵף׃ 18 וְאִם הֵאָכֹל יֵאָכֵל
מִבְּשַׂר־זֶבַח שְׁלָמָיו בַּיּוֹם הַשְּׁלִישִׁי לֹא
יֵרָצֶה הַמַּקְרִיב אֹתוֹ לֹא יֵחָשֵׁב לוֹ פִּגּוּל
יִהְיֶה וְהַנֶּפֶשׁ הָאֹכֶלֶת מִמֶּנּוּ עֲוֺנָהּ תִּשָּׂא׃
19 וְהַבָּשָׂר אֲשֶׁר־יִגַּע בְּכָל־טָמֵא לֹא יֵאָכֵל
בָּאֵשׁ יִשָּׂרֵף וְהַבָּשָׂר כָּל־טָהוֹר יֹאכַל

Genesis 18:6–7 Abraham instructs Sarah to bake cakes for the unexpected guests while a male servant prepares meat. Jeremiah 7:18 condemns women for kneading dough to make cakes for the worship of the "Queen of Heaven," whom they presumably viewed as the female consort of Israel's (male) God. See at Exodus 16:3 and 25:30 and at Leviticus 26:26 for more details about women and baking.

*13.* ***cakes.*** Heb. *challot*, the plural form of *challah*; in the Bible, this term does not refer to the braided bread associated with today's use of this term.

*14.* A portion of this offering goes to the priest. Another goes to the party who is offering the sacrifice. This sacrifice thus enables the entire community to share a meal with each other and—symbolically—also with God.

*15.* There is no explanation as to why certain offerings (like thanksgiving or well-being offerings) must be eaten entirely on the first day, while others (like votive and freewill offerings, see next verse) can be kept for a couple of days. Health factors do not account for the difference.

*16.* ***votive or a freewill offering.*** These types of well-being sacrifices are also shared between the priest and the offering party. Their meat may be eaten for two days.

*18.* Leftover sacrificial meat must be destroyed by fire when not consumed within the designated time period. Keeping meat for three days in the climactic conditions of Israel would have been a health hazard and may underlie the concern in this case. However, this reason alone cannot explain why the other well-being sacrifice—the one for thanksgiving—cannot be kept even for one day.

*19.* ***Flesh that touches anything impure.*** Because the meat of this sacrifice is eaten in a public place, it is not necessarily subject to the carefully

flesh, only one who is pure may eat such flesh. [20]But the person who, in a state of impurity, eats flesh from יהוה's sacrifices of well-being, that person shall be cut off from kin. [21]When a person touches anything impure, be it human impurity or an impure animal or any impure creature, and eats flesh from יהוה's sacrifices of well-being, that person shall be cut off from kin.

[22]And יהוה spoke to Moses, saying: [23]Speak to the Israelite people thus: You shall eat no fat of ox or sheep or goat. [24]Fat from animals that died or were torn by beasts may be put to any use, but you must not eat it. [25]If anyone eats the fat of animals from which offerings by fire may be made to יהוה, the person who eats it shall be cut off from kin. [26]And you must not consume any blood, either of

בָּשָׂר׃ 20 וְהַנֶּפֶשׁ אֲשֶׁר־תֹּאכַל בָּשָׂר מִזֶּבַח
הַשְּׁלָמִים אֲשֶׁר לַיהֹוָה וְטֻמְאָתוֹ עָלָיו
וְנִכְרְתָה הַנֶּפֶשׁ הַהִוא מֵעַמֶּיהָ׃ 21 וְנֶפֶשׁ
כִּי־תִגַּע בְּכָל־טָמֵא בְּטֻמְאַת אָדָם אוֹ ׀
בִּבְהֵמָה טְמֵאָה אוֹ בְּכָל־שֶׁקֶץ טָמֵא וְאָכַל
מִבְּשַׂר־זֶבַח הַשְּׁלָמִים אֲשֶׁר לַיהֹוָה
וְנִכְרְתָה הַנֶּפֶשׁ הַהִוא מֵעַמֶּיהָ׃ פ

22 וַיְדַבֵּר יְהֹוָה אֶל־מֹשֶׁה לֵּאמֹר׃ 23 דַּבֵּר
אֶל־בְּנֵי יִשְׂרָאֵל לֵאמֹר כָּל־חֵלֶב שׁוֹר
וְכֶשֶׂב וָעֵז לֹא תֹאכֵלוּ׃ 24 וְחֵלֶב נְבֵלָה
וְחֵלֶב טְרֵפָה יֵעָשֶׂה לְכָל־מְלָאכָה וְאָכֹל
לֹא תֹאכְלֻהוּ׃ 25 כִּי כָּל־אֹכֵל חֵלֶב מִן־
הַבְּהֵמָה אֲשֶׁר יַקְרִיב מִמֶּנָּה אִשֶּׁה לַיהֹוָה
וְנִכְרְתָה הַנֶּפֶשׁ הָאֹכֶלֶת מֵעַמֶּיהָ׃ 26 וְכָל־
דָּם לֹא תֹאכְלוּ בְּכֹל מוֹשְׁבֹתֵיכֶם לָעוֹף

monitored conditions of the Tabernacle; therefore, the Torah specifies the care that a person must take when eating this offering.

***only one who is pure.*** The requirement of ritual purity (see Leviticus 15) means that a woman may not bring this sacrifice or eat from it during her term of menstrual impurity (*niddah*), nor for several weeks following childbirth (40 days after the birth of a son, and 80 days after the birth of a daughter; see at Leviticus 12). Likewise, a man who has an emission of semen or other discharges cannot offer the sacrifice or eat from it until he regains a state of ritual purity.

***20. cut off from kin.*** This punishment of being "cut off" (Heb. *kareit*) can be understood in a number of ways. The expression could mean that the individual should be ostracized, that is, deliberately excluded from the community. The term could also refer to divinely inflicted childlessness, a condition that in time will "cut" that person's bloodline from the community (a consequence that does not entail communal punishment). Jacob Milgrom suggests in addition that *kareit* could mean that such a person will not be buried with the ancestors—and thus be denied the kind of reunification that marks a full life (*Leviticus*, 2004, p. 66). There are eighteen cases in the Torah that prescribe *kareit* (see Milgrom, p. 65). The verb form of the root *k-r-t* also appears as the term for making a covenant, such as when God makes a covenant with Abram (*karat . . . b'rit*) in Genesis 15:18.

***kin.*** Heb. *ammim*, which in this expression the text's intended audience would have understood in a gender-inclusive sense, as the translation reflects. Despite the Bible's penchant for patrilineal genealogies and patronyms, female relatives also counted as kin. See at Genesis 10:1. (See also "predecessors" in *The Contemporary Torah*, 2006, p. 408.)

## PROHIBITIONS REGARDING THE FAT AND THE BLOOD (7:22–27)

Leviticus 3:17 prohibits eating the blood and certain types of fat of the sacrificed animal. The present section adds a punishment for violating this command. The rationale for not consuming blood (according to 17:10–12) is that the life of a living being is in the blood. No explanation is given for

bird or of animal, in any of your settlements. 27Any-
one who eats blood shall be cut off from kin.

28And יהוה spoke to Moses, saying: 29Speak to
the Israelite people thus: The offering to יהוה from
a sacrifice of well-being must be presented by the
one who offers that sacrifice of well-being to יהוה:
30one's own hands shall present יהוה's offerings by
fire. The offerer shall present the fat with the breast,
the breast to be elevated as an elevation offering before יהוה; 31the priest shall turn the fat into smoke
on the altar, and the breast shall go to Aaron and his
sons. 32And the right thigh from your sacrifices of
well-being you shall present to the priest as a gift;
33he from among Aaron's sons who offers the blood
and the fat of the offering of well-being shall get
the right thigh as his portion. 34For I have taken the
breast of elevation offering and the thigh of gift
offering from the Israelites, from their sacrifices of
well-being, and given them to Aaron the priest and
to his sons as their due from the Israelites for all
time.

35Those shall be the perquisites of Aaron and
the perquisites of his sons from יהוה's offerings by
fire, once they have been inducted to serve יהוה as
priests; 36these יהוה commanded to be given them,

וְלַבְּהֵמָה׃ 27 כָּל־נֶפֶשׁ אֲשֶׁר־תֹּאכַל כָּל־דָּם
וְנִכְרְתָה הַנֶּפֶשׁ הַהִוא מֵעַמֶּיהָ׃ פ

28 וַיְדַבֵּר יְהֹוָה אֶל־מֹשֶׁה לֵּאמֹר׃ 29 דַּבֵּר
אֶל־בְּנֵי יִשְׂרָאֵל לֵאמֹר הַמַּקְרִיב אֶת־זֶבַח
שְׁלָמָיו לַיהֹוָה יָבִיא אֶת־קָרְבָּנוֹ לַיהֹוָה
מִזֶּבַח שְׁלָמָיו׃ 30 יָדָיו תְּבִיאֶינָה אֵת אִשֵּׁי
יְהֹוָה אֶת־הַחֵלֶב עַל־הֶחָזֶה יְבִיאֶנּוּ אֵת
הֶחָזֶה לְהָנִיף אֹתוֹ תְּנוּפָה לִפְנֵי יְהֹוָה׃
31 וְהִקְטִיר הַכֹּהֵן אֶת־הַחֵלֶב הַמִּזְבֵּחָה
וְהָיָה הֶחָזֶה לְאַהֲרֹן וּלְבָנָיו׃ 32 וְאֵת שׁוֹק
הַיָּמִין תִּתְּנוּ תְרוּמָה לַכֹּהֵן מִזִּבְחֵי
שַׁלְמֵיכֶם׃ 33 הַמַּקְרִיב אֶת־דַּם הַשְּׁלָמִים
וְאֶת־הַחֵלֶב מִבְּנֵי אַהֲרֹן לוֹ תִהְיֶה שׁוֹק
הַיָּמִין לְמָנָה׃ 34 כִּי אֶת־חֲזֵה הַתְּנוּפָה וְאֵת ׀
שׁוֹק הַתְּרוּמָה לָקַחְתִּי מֵאֵת בְּנֵי־יִשְׂרָאֵל
מִזִּבְחֵי שַׁלְמֵיהֶם וָאֶתֵּן אֹתָם לְאַהֲרֹן הַכֹּהֵן
וּלְבָנָיו לְחָק־עוֹלָם מֵאֵת בְּנֵי יִשְׂרָאֵל׃
35 זֹאת מִשְׁחַת אַהֲרֹן וּמִשְׁחַת בָּנָיו מֵאִשֵּׁי
יְהֹוָה בְּיוֹם הִקְרִיב אֹתָם לְכַהֵן לַיהֹוָה׃
36 אֲשֶׁר צִוָּה יְהֹוָה לָתֵת לָהֶם בְּיוֹם מָשְׁחוֹ

not eating the fat. However, references to "fat" elsewhere as especially valuable (for example, Genesis 45:18), suggest that burning fat completely might represent offering a precious gift to God. Here end the instructions to the priests.

### FURTHER DETAILS REGARDING THE WELL-BEING SACRIFICE (7:28–36)

This section, addressed to all, describes a division of labor between those who bring the offering and the officiating priest. It specifies which portion of the sacrifice goes to the officiating priest (the breast and the right thigh) and which to the party making the offering (the rest of the offering).

*30. one's own hands shall present.* Those making a sacrifice physically bring the offering to the altar. We learn from Numbers 30 that women make vows, and we learn from Leviticus 7:16 that vows often entailed making an offering. The present law implies that Israelite women, like Israelite men, would have access to the altar on these occasions if they were in a state of ritual purity. Note the story of Hannah: she vows to dedicate her son; then she brings him to the sanctuary where she also slaughters a sacrifice (I Samuel 1:11, 24–25).

*34. the breast . . . and the thigh.* These large portions of the animal provide economic compensation to the priests, who did not usually own land and therefore could not produce their own food like other Israelites (Numbers 18:20; but see Joshua 21, where priests do seem to get some pasture land).

once they had been anointed, as a due from the Israelites for all time throughout the ages.

[37]Such are the rituals of the burnt offering, the meal offering, the purgation offering, the reparation offering, the offering of ordination, and the sacrifice of well-being, [38]with which יהוה charged Moses on Mount Sinai, when commanding that the Israelites present their offerings to יהוה, in the wilderness of Sinai.

*8* יהוה spoke to Moses, saying: [2]Take Aaron along with his sons, and the vestments, the anoint-

אֹתָם מֵאֵת בְּנֵי יִשְׂרָאֵל חֻקַּת עוֹלָם
לְדֹרֹתָם׃

37 זֹאת הַתּוֹרָה לָעֹלָה לַמִּנְחָה וְלַחַטָּאת
וְלָאָשָׁם וְלַמִּלּוּאִים וּלְזֶבַח הַשְּׁלָמִים׃
38 אֲשֶׁר צִוָּה יְהֹוָה אֶת־מֹשֶׁה בְּהַר סִינָי
בְּיוֹם צַוֺּתוֹ אֶת־בְּנֵי יִשְׂרָאֵל לְהַקְרִיב אֶת־
קָרְבְּנֵיהֶם לַיהֹוָה בְּמִדְבַּר סִינָי׃ פ

ח וַיְדַבֵּר יְהֹוָה אֶל־מֹשֶׁה לֵּאמֹר׃ 2 קַח
אֶת־אַהֲרֹן וְאֶת־בָּנָיו אִתּוֹ וְאֵת הַבְּגָדִים

AFFIRMATION OF THE SINAITIC ORIGIN OF THE SACRIFICIAL PRACTICES (7:37–38)

This concluding section brings to a close the extensive instructions about sacrifices that began in Leviticus 1:2. These verses specify that the anointed priests must come from the line of Aaron.

*37. **rituals.*** Heb. *torah*; see at 6:2.

*38. **on Mount Sinai . . . in the wilderness of Sinai.*** The opening of Leviticus specified that God spoke to Moses from the Tent of Meeting (1:1) when commanding these sacrifices. The reference to Mount Sinai here stands in tension with that earlier mention of the Tent of Meeting. Contemporary critical scholars acknowledge the probability that various laws were assembled at different historical periods before reaching their final form. The attribution to Sinai aims to unify such traditions and communicate their antiquity and authority.

## *The Ordination of the Priests* (8:1–36)

Detailed instructions for the ordination of the priests appeared in Exodus 28. The present passage describes the execution of these instructions. The account of the ordination, like that of building the Tabernacle itself, emphasizes that the instructions were carried out precisely (even if some of the details vary slightly). The ceremony entails the formal dressing of Aaron and his four sons. In English, the words "investment" and "investiture" refer (among other things) to the ritual of placing clothing—vestments—upon the priest. (Nowadays the term "invested" also applies to the official status conferred on a cantor, analogous to an "ordained" rabbi.)

Two issues in this section pertain indirectly to women. First, the priesthood in Leviticus is bestowed exclusively upon Aaron and his sons. Although it is common for priests in the ancient world to come from specifically designated families, it is unusual to have only a single family serve exclusively for generations. Moreover, whereas women in ancient Mesopotamia could be priests, the Torah authorizes only males from the line of Aaron to supervise and formally officiate at the communal sanctuary. The reason for this difference is not clear; see *Vayikra*, Another View, p. 587. As for the women in priestly families—wives, daughters, and sisters—Leviticus 21–22 indicate that women are beneficiaries of certain privileges and also accountable to special standards (see especially at 22:12–13).

Second, the emphasis on the priests' garments raises the question as to who made (and also who repaired) them. Did women in the priests' household participate by spinning the yarn, weaving the fabric, and fashioning the garments? The Torah

ing oil, the bull of purgation offering, the two rams, and the basket of unleavened bread; [3]and assemble the community leadership at the entrance of the Tent of Meeting. [4]Moses did as יהוה commanded him. And when the leadership was assembled at the entrance of the Tent of Meeting, [5]Moses said to the leadership, "This is what יהוה has commanded to be done."

[6]Then Moses brought Aaron and his sons forward and washed them with water. [7]He put the tunic on him, girded him with the sash, clothed him with the robe, and put the ephod on him, girding

וְאֵת שֶׁמֶן הַמִּשְׁחָה וְאֵת ׀ פַּר הַחַטָּאת
וְאֵת שְׁנֵי הָאֵילִים וְאֵת סַל הַמַּצּוֹת: 3 וְאֵת
כׇּל־הָעֵדָה הַקְהֵל אֶל־פֶּתַח אֹהֶל מוֹעֵד:
4 וַיַּעַשׂ מֹשֶׁה כַּאֲשֶׁר צִוָּה יְהֹוָה אֹתוֹ
וַתִּקָּהֵל הָעֵדָה אֶל־פֶּתַח אֹהֶל מוֹעֵד:
5 וַיֹּאמֶר מֹשֶׁה אֶל־הָעֵדָה זֶה הַדָּבָר אֲשֶׁר־
צִוָּה יְהֹוָה לַעֲשׂוֹת:
6 וַיַּקְרֵב מֹשֶׁה אֶת־אַהֲרֹן וְאֶת־בָּנָיו וַיִּרְחַץ
אֹתָם בַּמָּיִם: 7 וַיִּתֵּן עָלָיו אֶת־הַכֻּתֹּנֶת
וַיַּחְגֹּר אֹתוֹ בָּאַבְנֵט וַיַּלְבֵּשׁ אֹתוֹ אֶת־

does not provide this information here, but see at 6:3. What does appear to be important to the writer of these accounts is that the ordination of the priests—rather than other communal events—constitutes a turning point that deserves close attention.

The ordination ceremony includes sacrifices delineated in Leviticus 1–7. One of the most unusual aspects of the ceremony is the smearing of certain parts of the priest's body with oil and blood (8:22–24). Such a ritual also marks the purification of a *m'tzora*—a person afflicted with certain types of skin disease (see 14:9–20 and 23–29).

## GOD'S INSTRUCTIONS REGARDING THE ORDINATION OF THE PRIESTS (8:1–3)

The ordination of the priests begins when Moses places upon them their special accoutrements. Only priestly garments, not other clothes, receive an extensive description in the Bible. (Even the book of Esther, with its emphasis on the role of clothing, does not include detailed descriptions of clothes.) On the likelihood that women wove the fabric, see at 6:3.

2. ***Take Aaron along with his sons, and the vestments.*** A central feature of the ordination of the priests entails the formal dressing of the priests in "vestments," an act that is reflected in English by the terms "vesting" and "investiture." Exodus 28 describes these garments in detail, listing six items that are adorned with expensive material: a breastpiece, an ephod, a robe, a fringed tunic, a headdress, and a sash.

3. ***community leadership.*** Literally, "the whole community," but the term can also refer to representative adult males, which better fits the present context. See at 4:13.

## MOSES' ORDINATION OF THE PRIESTS (8:4–30)

Moses, who himself is not a priest but only a member of the tribe that claims descent from Levi, has the authority to sanctify and ordain the priests.

6. ***brought...forward.*** The Hebrew word is the same one used for offering a sacrifice (the root *k-r-b*). The priests in this ritual are, in a sense, an offering to God.

***washed them.*** Ritual washing accompanies virtually all acts of purification. See, for example, 14:9.

7. ***robe.*** According to the book of Samuel, in the years after Hannah brings her young son to serve in God's sanctuary, she makes for him "a little robe" (I Samuel 2:19) to go with his linen ephod (2:18).

***ephod.*** This priestly outer garment was made of a variety of materials, including fabric most likely woven by women (see Exodus 28:5–12 for details and at Leviticus 6:3, above).

him with the decorated band with which he tied it to him. 8 He put the breastpiece on him, and put into the breastpiece the Urim and Thummim. 9 And he set the headdress on his head; and on the headdress, in front, he put the gold frontlet, the holy diadem—as יהוה had commanded Moses.

10 Moses took the anointing oil and anointed the Tabernacle and all that was in it, thus consecrating them. 11 He sprinkled some of it on the altar seven times, anointing the altar, all its utensils, and the laver with its stand, to consecrate them. 12 He poured some of the anointing oil upon Aaron's head and anointed him, to consecrate him. 13 Moses then brought Aaron's sons forward, clothed them in tunics, girded them with sashes, and wound turbans upon them, as יהוה had commanded Moses.

14 He led forward the bull of purgation offering. Aaron and his sons laid their hands upon the head of the bull of purgation offering, 15 and it was slaughtered. Moses took the blood and with his finger put some on each of the horns of the altar, purifying the altar; then he poured out the blood at the base of the altar. Thus he consecrated it in order to make expiation upon it.

16 Moses then took all the fat that was about the entrails, and the protuberance of the liver, and the two kidneys and their fat, and turned them into smoke on the altar. 17 The rest of the bull, its hide,

הַמְּעִיל וַיִּתֵּן עָלָיו אֶת־הָאֵפֹד וַיַּחְגֹּר אֹתוֹ
בְּחֵשֶׁב הָאֵפֹד וַיֶּאְפֹּד לוֹ בּוֹ׃ 8 וַיָּשֶׂם עָלָיו
אֶת־הַחֹשֶׁן וַיִּתֵּן אֶל־הַחֹשֶׁן אֶת־הָאוּרִים
וְאֶת־הַתֻּמִּים׃ 9 וַיָּשֶׂם אֶת־הַמִּצְנֶפֶת עַל־
רֹאשׁוֹ וַיָּשֶׂם עַל־הַמִּצְנֶפֶת אֶל־מוּל פָּנָיו
אֵת צִיץ הַזָּהָב נֵזֶר הַקֹּדֶשׁ כַּאֲשֶׁר צִוָּה
יְהֹוָה אֶת־מֹשֶׁה׃
10 וַיִּקַּח מֹשֶׁה אֶת־שֶׁמֶן הַמִּשְׁחָה וַיִּמְשַׁח
אֶת־הַמִּשְׁכָּן וְאֶת־כָּל־אֲשֶׁר־בּוֹ וַיְקַדֵּשׁ
אֹתָם׃ 11 וַיַּז מִמֶּנּוּ עַל־הַמִּזְבֵּחַ שֶׁבַע
פְּעָמִים וַיִּמְשַׁח אֶת־הַמִּזְבֵּחַ וְאֶת־כָּל־כֵּלָיו
וְאֶת־הַכִּיֹּר וְאֶת־כַּנּוֹ לְקַדְּשָׁם׃ 12 וַיִּצֹק
מִשֶּׁמֶן הַמִּשְׁחָה עַל רֹאשׁ אַהֲרֹן וַיִּמְשַׁח
אֹתוֹ לְקַדְּשׁוֹ׃ 13 וַיַּקְרֵב מֹשֶׁה אֶת־בְּנֵי
אַהֲרֹן וַיַּלְבִּשֵׁם כֻּתֳּנֹת וַיַּחְגֹּר אֹתָם אַבְנֵט
וַיַּחֲבֹשׁ לָהֶם מִגְבָּעוֹת כַּאֲשֶׁר צִוָּה יְהֹוָה
אֶת־מֹשֶׁה׃
14 וַיַּגֵּשׁ אֵת פַּר הַחַטָּאת וַיִּסְמֹךְ אַהֲרֹן
וּבָנָיו אֶת־יְדֵיהֶם עַל־רֹאשׁ פַּר הַחַטָּאת׃
15 וַיִּשְׁחָט וַיִּקַּח מֹשֶׁה אֶת־הַדָּם וַיִּתֵּן עַל־
קַרְנוֹת הַמִּזְבֵּחַ סָבִיב בְּאֶצְבָּעוֹ וַיְחַטֵּא אֶת־
הַמִּזְבֵּחַ וְאֶת־הַדָּם יָצַק אֶל־יְסוֹד הַמִּזְבֵּחַ
וַיְקַדְּשֵׁהוּ לְכַפֵּר עָלָיו׃
16 וַיִּקַּח אֶת־כָּל־הַחֵלֶב אֲשֶׁר עַל־הַקֶּרֶב
וְאֵת יֹתֶרֶת הַכָּבֵד וְאֶת־שְׁתֵּי הַכְּלָיֹת וְאֶת־
חֶלְבְּהֶן וַיַּקְטֵר מֹשֶׁה הַמִּזְבֵּחָה׃ 17 וְאֶת־
הַפָּר וְאֶת־עֹרוֹ וְאֶת־בְּשָׂרוֹ וְאֶת־פִּרְשׁוֹ שָׂרַף

---

*8. **breastpiece.*** This is a jeweled metal plate that the priest wears, which lists the tribes of Israel—whom the priest symbolically carries when he officiates; see at Exodus 28:15–30. (Nowadays the metal breastplate or breastpiece on Torah scrolls in many synagogues represents an attempt to reproduce or symbolize this item.)

***Urim and Thummim.*** The reference is to some physical object that priests used for consulting with God. It is unclear what the name means and what the object or objects looked like, although scholars have suggested that it was somewhat like a pair of dice that, when tossed, gave a "yes" or "no" answer to questions posed by the priest. See also at Exodus 28:30. The names suggest the meanings "light" (*urim*) and "right" or "whole" (*tumim*).

***10–12.*** As these verses indicate, the act of anointing sanctifies the Tabernacle and its furnishing, as well as the priests.

its flesh, and its dung, he put to the fire outside the camp—as יהוה had commanded Moses.

18 Then he brought forward the ram of burnt offering. Aaron and his sons laid their hands upon the ram's head, 19 and it was slaughtered. Moses dashed the blood against all sides of the altar. 20 The ram was cut up into sections and Moses turned the head, the sections, and the suet into smoke on the altar; 21 Moses washed the entrails and the legs with water and turned all of the ram into smoke. That was a burnt offering for a pleasing odor, an offering by fire to יהוה—as יהוה had commanded Moses.

22 He brought forward the second ram, the ram of ordination. Aaron and his sons laid their hands upon the ram's head, 23 and it was slaughtered. Moses took some of its blood and put it on the ridge of Aaron's right ear, and on the thumb of his right hand, and on the big toe of his right foot. 24 Moses then brought forward the sons of Aaron, and put some of the blood on the ridges of their right ears, and on the thumbs of their right hands, and on the big toes of their right feet; and the rest of the blood Moses dashed against every side of the altar. 25 He took the fat—the broad tail, all the fat about the entrails, the protuberance of the liver, and the two kidneys and their fat—and the right thigh. 26 From the basket of unleavened bread that was before יהוה, he took one cake of unleavened bread, one cake of oil bread, and one wafer, and placed them on the fat parts and on the right thigh. 27 He placed all these on the palms of Aaron and on the palms of

בָּאֵ֔שׁ מִח֖וּץ לַֽמַּחֲנֶ֑ה כַּאֲשֶׁ֛ר צִוָּ֥ה יְהֹוָ֖ה
אֶת־מֹשֶֽׁה׃
18 וַיַּקְרֵ֕ב אֵ֖ת אֵ֣יל הָעֹלָ֑ה וַֽיִּסְמְכ֞וּ אַהֲרֹ֧ן
וּבָנָ֛יו אֶת־יְדֵיהֶ֖ם עַל־רֹ֥אשׁ הָאָֽיִל׃
19 וַיִּשְׁחָ֑ט וַיִּזְרֹ֨ק מֹשֶׁ֧ה אֶת־הַדָּ֛ם עַל־
הַמִּזְבֵּ֖חַ סָבִֽיב׃ 20 וְאֶת־הָאַ֕יִל נִתַּ֖ח לִנְתָחָ֑יו
וַיַּקְטֵ֤ר מֹשֶׁה֙ אֶת־הָרֹ֔אשׁ וְאֶת־הַנְּתָחִ֖ים
וְאֶת־הַפָּֽדֶר׃ 21 וְאֶת־הַקֶּ֥רֶב וְאֶת־הַכְּרָעַ֖יִם
רָחַ֣ץ בַּמָּ֑יִם וַיַּקְטֵר֩ מֹשֶׁ֨ה אֶת־כָּל־
הָאַ֜יִל הַמִּזְבֵּ֗חָה עֹלָ֨ה ה֤וּא לְרֵֽיחַ־נִיחֹ֙חַ֙
אִשֶּׁ֥ה הוּא֙ לַֽיהֹוָ֔ה כַּאֲשֶׁ֛ר צִוָּ֥ה יְהֹוָ֖ה אֶת־
מֹשֶֽׁה׃
22 וַיַּקְרֵב֙ אֶת־הָאַ֣יִל הַשֵּׁנִ֔י אֵ֖יל הַמִּלֻּאִ֑ים
וַֽיִּסְמְכ֞וּ אַהֲרֹ֧ן וּבָנָ֛יו אֶת־יְדֵיהֶ֖ם עַל־רֹ֥אשׁ
הָאָֽיִל׃ 23 וַיִּשְׁחָ֓ט ׀ וַיִּקַּ֤ח מֹשֶׁה֙ מִדָּמ֔וֹ וַיִּתֵּ֛ן
עַל־תְּנ֥וּךְ אֹֽזֶן־אַהֲרֹ֖ן הַיְמָנִ֑ית וְעַל־בֹּ֤הֶן יָדוֹ֙
הַיְמָנִ֔ית וְעַל־בֹּ֖הֶן רַגְל֥וֹ הַיְמָנִֽית׃ 24 וַיַּקְרֵ֞ב
אֶת־בְּנֵ֣י אַהֲרֹ֗ן וַיִּתֵּ֨ן מֹשֶׁ֥ה מִן־הַדָּם֮ עַל־
תְּנ֤וּךְ אָזְנָם֙ הַיְמָנִ֔ית וְעַל־בֹּ֤הֶן יָדָם֙ הַיְמָנִ֔ית
וְעַל־בֹּ֥הֶן רַגְלָ֖ם הַיְמָנִ֑ית וַיִּזְרֹ֨ק מֹשֶׁ֧ה אֶת־
הַדָּ֛ם עַל־הַמִּזְבֵּ֖חַ סָבִֽיב׃ 25 וַיִּקַּ֞ח אֶת־
הַחֵ֣לֶב וְאֶת־הָֽאַלְיָ֗ה וְאֶת־כָּל־הַחֵ֘לֶב֮ אֲשֶׁ֣ר
עַל־הַקֶּרֶב֒ וְאֵ֨ת יֹתֶ֤רֶת הַכָּבֵד֙ וְאֶת־שְׁתֵּ֥י
הַכְּלָיֹ֖ת וְאֶת־חֶלְבְּהֶ֑ן וְאֵ֖ת שׁ֥וֹק הַיָּמִֽין׃
26 וּמִסַּ֨ל הַמַּצּ֜וֹת אֲשֶׁ֣ר ׀ לִפְנֵ֣י יְהֹוָ֗ה לָ֠קַח
חַלַּ֨ת מַצָּ֤ה אַחַת֙ וְחַלַּ֨ת לֶ֥חֶם שֶׁ֛מֶן אַחַ֖ת
וְרָקִ֣יק אֶחָ֑ד וַיָּ֙שֶׂם֙ עַל־הַ֣חֲלָבִ֔ים וְעַ֖ל שׁ֥וֹק
הַיָּמִֽין׃ 27 וַיִּתֵּן֙ אֶת־הַכֹּ֔ל עַ֚ל כַּפֵּ֣י אַהֲרֹ֔ן

*22–24.* The ordination ritual includes the peculiar act of smearing some of the animal's blood and some oil upon the priest's head, right ear, right thumb, and right toe—parts of the body that seem to represent the circumference of the whole. Leviticus does not explain the meaning of this act. Most likely it symbolizes the dedication and purification of the entire body or person. An identical ritual signals the purification of the *m'tzora*, the person stricken with a particular skin disease (on account of which he or she has been previously isolated from the community). This ritual is unique to these two occasions. It implies an analogy between the transition that the priest undergoes and that of the healed *m'tzora*. See Leviticus 14:9–20 and the comments there.

his sons, and elevated them as an elevation offering before יהוה. [28]Then Moses took them from their hands and turned them into smoke on the altar with the burnt offering. This was an ordination offering for a pleasing odor; it was an offering by fire to יהוה. [29]Moses took the breast and elevated it as an elevation offering before יהוה; it was Moses' portion of the ram of ordination—as יהוה had commanded Moses.

[30]And Moses took some of the anointing oil and some of the blood that was on the altar and sprinkled it upon Aaron and upon his vestments, and also upon his sons and upon their vestments. Thus he consecrated Aaron and his vestments, and also his sons and their vestments.

[31]Moses said to Aaron and his sons: Boil the flesh at the entrance of the Tent of Meeting and eat it there with the bread that is in the basket of ordination—as I commanded: Aaron and his sons shall eat it; [32]and what is left over of the flesh and the bread you shall consume in fire. [33]You shall not go outside the entrance of the Tent of Meeting for seven days, until the day that your period of ordination is completed. For your ordination will require seven days. [34]Everything done today, יהוה has commanded to be done [seven days], to make expiation for you. [35]You shall remain at the entrance of the Tent of Meeting day and night for seven days, keeping יהוה's charge—that you may not die—for so I have been commanded.

[36]And Aaron and his sons did all the things that יהוה had commanded through Moses.

וְעַל כַּפֵּי בָנָיו וַיָּנֶף אֹתָם תְּנוּפָה לִפְנֵי
יְהוָה: 28 וַיִּקַּח מֹשֶׁה אֹתָם מֵעַל כַּפֵּיהֶם
וַיַּקְטֵר הַמִּזְבֵּחָה עַל־הָעֹלָה מִלֻּאִים הֵם
לְרֵיחַ נִיחֹחַ אִשֶּׁה הוּא לַיהוָה: 29 וַיִּקַּח
מֹשֶׁה אֶת־הֶחָזֶה וַיְנִיפֵהוּ תְנוּפָה לִפְנֵי
יְהוָה מֵאֵיל הַמִּלֻּאִים לְמֹשֶׁה הָיָה לְמָנָה
כַּאֲשֶׁר צִוָּה יְהוָה אֶת־מֹשֶׁה:
30 וַיִּקַּח מֹשֶׁה מִשֶּׁמֶן הַמִּשְׁחָה וּמִן־הַדָּם
אֲשֶׁר עַל־הַמִּזְבֵּחַ וַיַּז עַל־אַהֲרֹן עַל־בְּגָדָיו
וְעַל־בָּנָיו וְעַל־בִּגְדֵי בָנָיו אִתּוֹ וַיְקַדֵּשׁ אֶת־
אַהֲרֹן אֶת־בְּגָדָיו וְאֶת־בָּנָיו וְאֶת־בִּגְדֵי בָנָיו
אִתּוֹ:
31 וַיֹּאמֶר מֹשֶׁה אֶל־אַהֲרֹן וְאֶל־בָּנָיו בַּשְּׁלוּ
אֶת־הַבָּשָׂר פֶּתַח אֹהֶל מוֹעֵד וְשָׁם תֹּאכְלוּ
אֹתוֹ וְאֶת־הַלֶּחֶם אֲשֶׁר בְּסַל הַמִּלֻּאִים
כַּאֲשֶׁר צִוֵּיתִי לֵאמֹר אַהֲרֹן וּבָנָיו יֹאכְלֻהוּ:
32 וְהַנּוֹתָר בַּבָּשָׂר וּבַלָּחֶם בָּאֵשׁ תִּשְׂרֹפוּ:
33 וּמִפֶּתַח אֹהֶל מוֹעֵד לֹא תֵצְאוּ שִׁבְעַת
יָמִים עַד יוֹם מְלֹאת יְמֵי מִלֻּאֵיכֶם כִּי
שִׁבְעַת יָמִים יְמַלֵּא אֶת־יֶדְכֶם: 34 כַּאֲשֶׁר
עָשָׂה בַּיּוֹם הַזֶּה צִוָּה יְהוָה לַעֲשֹׂת לְכַפֵּר
עֲלֵיכֶם: 35 וּפֶתַח אֹהֶל מוֹעֵד תֵּשְׁבוּ יוֹמָם
וָלַיְלָה שִׁבְעַת יָמִים וּשְׁמַרְתֶּם אֶת־מִשְׁמֶרֶת
יְהוָה וְלֹא תָמוּתוּ כִּי־כֵן צֻוֵּיתִי:
36 וַיַּעַשׂ אַהֲרֹן וּבָנָיו אֵת כָּל־הַדְּבָרִים
אֲשֶׁר־צִוָּה יְהוָה בְּיַד־מֹשֶׁה: ס

### FINAL PREPARATORY STEPS: SEVEN DAYS OF THE PRIESTS' ISOLATION (8:31–36)

The ordination ritual bestows holiness on the priests. Their isolation, which echoes that of menstruating women or persons isolated for skin disease in Leviticus 13–15, emphasizes the power and danger of the holy. Only after these seven days can the priests officiate in sacrificial service. With the completion of this ritual, all is ready for initiating the sacrificial system of the Tabernacle for the benefit of the community. The next parashah begins by describing that event as taking place on the eighth day.

—*Tamara Cohn Eskenazi*

# Another View

Most likely, Leviticus 6:11 specifies that "only the males" among Aaron's descendants may eat of certain sacrifices (rather than "every male"). Why can the females in Aaron's line not partake of these offerings? What determines which priestly portions are restricted to the sons of Aaron, and which may be shared by his daughters as well?

The answer lies in the degree of holiness of the offering. The biblical text distinguishes between sacrifices considered to be "most sacred" (*kodesh kodashim*) and those considered to be "sacred" (*kodesh*). Three types of offerings fall under the rubric of "most sacred": the meal offering (6:10), the purgation offering (6:18) and the reparation offering (7:6). The three most sacred offerings are considered most holy, which means that anyone who touches them—much less partakes of them—must have been previously consecrated, that is, made holy. For this reason, these three sacrifices may be eaten only by Aaron and his sons, that is, the male descendants of the priestly line. Any male of Aaron's line who has been consecrated—even the blemished priests who are not permitted to officiate—may partake of the most sacred portions within the sanctuary precinct.

In contrast, the priestly portions of offerings labeled simply as "sacred," rather than "most sacred," such as the sacrifice of well-being and the first fruits offerings, are not restricted to those who have been consecrated. These offerings can be consumed by all members of the priestly family and household, including both the sons and the daughters of the line of Aaron, as long as they are not in a state of ritual impurity (see Numbers 18:11–19 and Leviticus 22:1–16).

### *Which sacrificial portions may a priest share with his daughters?*

It is interesting to note, however, that the daughter of a priest may eat of the portion of the sacred donations assigned to priests only while she is a member of a priestly household. According to Leviticus 22:12–14, if the daughter of a priest marries a layman, she may no longer eat of the sacred gifts. However, if she is widowed or divorced and without offspring, and she rejoins her father's household, she can once again partake of the portion of sacred offerings allocated to the priests' families.

*—Hilary Lipka*

# Post-biblical Interpretations

***This is the ritual of the burnt offering*** (6:2). The Rabbis understood the burnt offering as a sacrifice brought for sins of the heart or mind, *hirhur halev.* According to *Vayikra Rabbah* 7.3, this notion was derived from Job's explanation of his burnt offerings on behalf of his children, when he said, "Perhaps my children have sinned and blasphemed God in their thoughts" (Job 1:5). In an ongoing midrashic discussion as to which sacrifice is divinely preferred, *Vayikra Rabbah* 7.4 maintains that God favors the burnt offering because it is the only sacrifice that remains on the altar at night as well as during the day. A parable compares the situation to that of a king traveling in the desert. He stops first at one inn and eats and drinks, and then at another inn where he not only eats and drinks but also stays overnight, showing that he favors the latter. Conversely, *Vayikra Rabbah* 3 argues that God most esteems the meal offering because of its association with poverty.

***He shall then take off his vestments*** (6:4). The medieval commentator Rashi explains that this verse is a lesson in etiquette (*derech eretz*), teaching that a servant should change clothes between preparing food and serving it.

***One who offers it for thanksgiving*** (7:12). *Vayikra Rabbah* 9.4 asserts that God favors the thanksgiving offering because it is a freewill offering, rather than

*The thanksgiving offering is an appropriate response to recovery from a serious illness.*

an obligatory one brought for the expiation of a sin. According to the Rabbis, the thanksgiving offering is the only sacrifice that will remain in the world-to-come (*Vayikra Rabbah* 9.7). Rashi comments on this verse (based on BT *B'rachot* 54b) that the thanksgiving offering is an appropriate response to the following "miraculous" deliverances: a safe journey across an ocean or desert, release from imprisonment, and recovery from a serious illness.

***Such are the rituals of the burnt offering... and the sacrifice of well-being*** (7:37). *Vayikra Rabbah* 9.9 suggests that the sacrifice of well-being, the *sh'lamim*, is last in this list of sacrifices because of the importance of *shalom*, peace, a theme which also appears at the end of many prayers. The Midrash lists a number of examples where the value of peace is deemed higher than the value of truth. Many of these situations involve women and endorse the value of peace in marriage. The most famous biblical example is that of Sarah and Abraham: When Sarah laughs at the possibility of conceiving a child, she says that it is impossible because of her husband's age. However, when God repeats Sarah's words to Abraham, God reports only that she complained of her own age (Genesis 18). This "lie" is understood by the Rabbis as a sign of the greater importance of marital harmony over truth. A story is also told about Rabbi Meir and a woman who came to hear him preach one Friday night and ended up staying so late that she angered her husband. When her husband swore that she must spit in Rabbi Meir's face, Rabbi Meir miraculously understood this and pretended that he needed her to spit in his face for medical reasons, thereby restoring marital harmony (also *Sifrei B'midbar* 42; *B'reishit Rabbah* 48).

***Take Aaron*** (8:2). The Rabbis connect this "taking" of Aaron for his priestly duties with another biblical use of the word "taking" with respect to Aaron—his taking of the people's gold and silver to make the Golden Calf in Exodus 32:4. As *Vayikra Rabbah* 10.4 puts it, "Let this 'taking' come and atone for that 'taking.'"

***anointing oil.*** *Vayikra Rabbah* 10.8 relates that the original 12 *logs* of oil (72 rabbinic "eggs'" worth) prepared by Moses miraculously sufficed not only to anoint the sanctuary and its vessels, and Aaron and his sons on each of the seven days of the sanctuary's consecration, but also to anoint future generations of high priests and kings.

***You shall remain at the entrance of the Tent of Meeting day and night for seven days, keeping יהוה's charge*** (8:35). Midrash *Tanchuma* connects this seven-day seclusion of the priests to the customary seven days of mourning after a family member's death: Aaron was unknowingly in mourning for the future death of his two oldest sons on the eighth day—the day of the final consecration of the Tabernacle (see the next parashah). Aaron's period of pre-mourning is compared to the pre-mourning that God is said to have done for seven days prior to the Flood (*Tanchuma*, ed. Buber II, 21–22).

—*Rachel Anisfeld*

# Contemporary Reflection

Elizabeth Ehrlich was once a comfortable "cultural Jew." The practice of Jewish religion held little attraction for her. *Miriam's Kitchen: A Memoir* (1997) is Ehrlich's report on a year spent learning from her mother-in-law, Miriam, a Polish Holocaust survivor, the details of domestic religion—the laws and the lore. As the year passed, Ehrlich grew increasingly interested in becoming a ritual specialist in her home. She wanted to "infuse the minutiae of everyday life with something more." She recognized that someone would have to make this a "priority mission," and that that someone would be her.

We can draw an arc from Elizabeth Ehrlich's kitchen back to the Torah portion before us. Many contemporary Jews find this portion among those that make their eyes glaze over. Reform theologian Rachel Adler reports that when she was growing up she never heard the word "ritual" without it being prefaced by the word "meaningless." Likewise, Arnold Eisen, a scholar of contemporary Judaism, for many years kept his sights on so-called higher things (like faith and covenant) in lieu of studying the sacrificial system (*Taking Hold of Torah*, 1997, p. 71). If the rituals of sacrifice in the sanctuary (6:1–7:48) seem to be of little interest, the elaborate rites for ordaining priests (8:1–36) appear to be both archaic and problematic in their exclusion of women from spiritual leadership.

Over the years Adler, Eisen, and many others have come to appreciate the power of the rituals described in this parashah. As we learn about ritual as a human phenomenon, we come to understand it as a language of its own, uniquely meaningful. To do justice to the sacrificial system, we need to contextualize Israelite sacrifice with the help of anthropology, sociology, comparative religion, and even neurobiology. We can ask also how this ritual of sacrifice was transformed in Christianity and in Judaism. When we consider the Jewish transformation of the sacrificial system, the question of gender, power, spirituality, and leadership can emerge in a more nuanced light.

Anthropologist Mary Douglas, who has been called "the mother of ritual studies," shows that Leviticus has a specific way to approach the subject of spirituality and the body in relation to sacrifices (see the introduction to 1:1–3:7, p. 571).

Christianity transformed sacrifices by bringing sacrifices' symbolism right into the heart of its worship service. Priests prepared and congregants ate and drank the Eucharist, the body and blood of the ultimate "lamb" of God. Carolyn Walker Bynum documents that although women were marginalized, in the Middle Ages nuns and upper-class lay women found their way into this system of sacralized food through rituals of fasting and in ecstatic feasting (*Holy Feast and Holy Fast*, 1987).

*We can draw an arc from our kitchen of today back to the Torah portion before us.*

After the destruction of Jerusalem's Temple, the Rabbis replaced the sacrificial system in two ways. The first was to commune with God through prayer and study. The second was via a system that maintained sacrifices in a new form, hinted at in 7:22–27: The whole complex of laws and rituals around preparing and eating food became another way in which the sacrificial system lived on. With this change, women became the ritual specialists for what was once temple sacrifice in its domestic transformation—because women in traditional Jewish society, as in many cultures, control food resources.

The Talmud says that the table upon which we eat is like the altar of the Temple (BT *B'rachot* 55a). We are bidden to wash our hands before breaking bread not simply to cleanse them, but because the priests washed their hands before they offered a sacrifice. When making bread, the baker takes a small piece of the dough (*challah*) and burns it to represent the sacrifice. On the Sabbath, the *challot* represent the showbreads sacrificed at the Temple.

Guarding the traditional food taboos, taking *challah*, preparing the home for holidays and for the Sabbath (literally "making Sabbath"), and distributing food to the poor—all of these are areas in which women have controlled and executed significant ritual functions. There is an old saying quoted by Hayim Soloveitchik: "A *yidishe bale-boste* (Jewish home-maker) takes instruction from her mother only."

Susan Starr Sered, an anthropologist of religion, conducted a study of illiterate Kurdish Jewish women who were living in Jerusalem. That research led her to challenge preconceptions about the nature of spirituality and the holy. In her book *Women as Ritual Experts* (1992), she reports that these women developed religious culture alongside the Judaism of text and synagogue practiced by the men. As she notes, what anthropologist Robert Redfield calls the "little tradition" was based in the home, where women were the ritual experts. The domestic religion used many of the same symbols and ideas of the "male" Judaism but applied them to sanctify the daily tasks of the women, in the domain that they controlled. In Sered's study, food preparation loomed large, from maintaining the laws of kashrut in the home to distributing cookies at the graves of ancestors after prayers had been answered. These women had developed what she called a "devotional autonomy."

During the Holocaust, some Jewish women who were interned in Terezin compiled a cookbook from memory. The Terezin prisoners recalled and wrote down their recipes for chocolate torte, breast of goose, plum strudel, and other traditional dishes while surviving on potato scraps. Their effort was a kind of spiritual revolt, an act of resistance against brutality, calling to mind the everyday world they had known and presided over. These half-forgotten recipes, scribbled on scraps of paper, became the texts that helped them to transcend their situation. Decades later, their book found its way to the daughter of one of the authors who had died in the camps. The book was published as *In Memory's Kitchen* in 1996 by Cara de Silva.

Elizabeth Ehrlich—the kitchen apprentice to her mother-in-law—learned something surprising about spiritual leadership. This is not to say that women today should accept exclusion from the realms of study or politics and retreat back to home and hearth. Rather, as we seek lives of spiritual integrity, we would do well to widen our gaze beyond the so-called higher things, to recall the power of the home through which Jewish women—against great odds—have powerfully continued connection to God and community across generations.

*—Nancy Fuchs Kreimer*

# *Voices*

## *from* *To My Country*

Rahel (transl. Robert Friend)

*Leviticus 6:12–16*

Modest are the gifts I bring you.
I know this, mother.
Modest, I know, the offerings
of your daughter:
Only an outburst of song
on a day when the light flares up,
only a silent tear
for your poverty.

## *Eating the Bones*

Ellen Bass

*Leviticus 7:15–18*

The women in my family
strip the succulent
flesh from broiled chicken,
scrape the drumstick clean;
bite off the cartilage, chew the gristle,
crush the porous swellings
at the ends of each slender baton.
With strong molars
they split the tibia, sucking out
the dense marrow.
They use up love, they swallow
every dark grain,
so at the end there's nothing left,
a scant pile of splinters
on the empty white plate.

## *No Sign*

Linda Stern Zisquit

*Leviticus 7:37*

My body moves
through the flame of yours

without a trace of carbon
on my skin, no sign

I burn, no evidence
how flammable

how charred
these sinewy parts are.

## *When I Melt Down*

Naomi Replansky

*Leviticus 7:37*

When I melt down in your furnace
I want to take shape in your mold.
Blast me, cast me, change me,
Before the wind turns cold.

Look, from the red-hot center
I lift up my white-hot face.
My nose finds its bridge as always,
My eyes flow back into place.

Neither destroyed nor diamond
I walk from the core of your flame,
The rain does not hiss when it hits me,
And I answer to my old name.

## *Celebrating Courage and Vision: An Appreciation of Rabbi Sally Priesand*

Jennifer Clayman

*Leviticus 8*

Because of you, Sally, and those who came after you, I was never told that a woman can't be a rabbi. Because of you and those who came after you, my rabbi was able to stand up on the bimah at my Bat Mitzvah and tell me that he thought I should be a rabbi. And because of you and those who came after you, my colleagues and I have been blessed by the presence of rabbinic mentors, both female and male.

Today, celebrating your retirement, 35 years since you were the first woman ever to be ordained by a rabbinical seminary, I wouldn't say that I take women rabbis for granted, because I don't. And I won't say that we're accepted everywhere, because we're not. But we're not so unusual, either. I was the fourth woman rabbi hired by my congregation, and we've since been joined by the fifth. The congregation is accustomed to women's voices from the pulpit, women's ideas about God, Torah and Israel, and women's authority in difficult times.

We owe you a great deal. Your *chesed* has changed our lives and changed a world that has missed women rabbis for far too long.

## *Tzav*

Laurie Patton

*Leviticus 8:10–12*

This was no sprinkling.

It was more majestic,
and thorough.
The desert world
stood solemn
as Aaron's whole head
was oiled;
and then it gleamed,
pink and comforting,
while the sand and stone
cooled in the evening.

But however dignified
Aaron was that day,
he must also have thought
of a child's bath,
and a woman's hands
tracing white rivers of soap
down his head.

At once priest and infant,
he must have known
the strong, safe palms
of a mother,
and of Moses,
and of God
had become one.

## *from* Clothes My Mother Made

Hanna Zacks

*Leviticus 8:7*

In the drawer of the bedroom chest
Two dresses and several sweaters
Some crocheted, some knit,
Are carefully folded.
Over thirty years ago my mother made them.
In the evenings, sitting in her armchair,
Tirelessly, with needles or crocheting hooks,
She would interlace loop after loop of yarn,
To create the material for the clothes
She would then send me.

A pleasure, doing this work was,
Not a hardship.
She wrote in answer to my question,
It made her feel closer to me.
Her love, her longing,
The very essence of her soul,
She wove into every stitch.
Permeated by her energy,
Soft and warm like tender caresses,
Like the comforting touch of her hand,
The things she made felt on my skin.

## *from* The Tapestry of Jewish Time

Nina Beth Cardin

*Leviticus 8:7*

We Jews are a union of weavers. Interlacing our traditions and languages, our rituals and laws, with fibers gathered from the cultures around us, we each weave a personal shawl of Judaism. Some shawls are open and loose, allowing the currents of other cultures to flow in and out easily. Others are fine and tight, holding much of Jewish culture in and foreign cultures out.

The world of Judaism is filled with shawls of different weaves, from loose to fine.... Each adds its flair, its strength, and its warmth to the sacred garment of the Jewish people.... And every now and then we add a thread or two of a new hue and a new texture that serves to enrich and extend our wardrobe.

## At the Loom

Linda Pastan

*Leviticus 8:7*

You sit at the loom,
your hands raised
like silhouetted birds,
or like a harpist poised
at the strings of an instrument
whose chords are colors,
their slow accumulation,
thread by thread—
a kind of bleeding upward
the way the sky bleeds
from the horizon up
after certain sunsets.
Monk's belt and rosepath...
plainweave and twill...
The shuttle moves back
and forth, trailing
its wake of yarn
as if by accident,
and patterns that seem
random at first multiply
into beauty.
No wonder Penelope burned
with patience.
Somewhere a sheep bleats
in the night, a silkworm
stirs in its cocoon.
You weave a spell,
I wear it on my back,
and though the chilly stars
go bone naked
we are clothed.

# שְׁמִינִי ✦ *Sh'mini*

LEVITICUS 9:1–11:47

## *Purity and Danger in the Sanctuary and the Home*

PARASHAT SH'MINI ("eighth," referring to the eighth day of ordination) describes the ritual on the day after Aaron's ordination ceremony. In the previous two parashot, Leviticus 1–7 presented rules for the sacrificial service, while Leviticus 8 described the priestly ordination of Aaron and his sons. In this parashah, Aaron begins to officiate as chief priest.

This parashah includes a strange story of the fire from God which kills Nadab and Abihu, Aaron's oldest sons (10:1–7). It concludes with dietary laws and with the demand that Israel be holy—for God is holy (11:45). In this parashah, the theme of holiness expands from the sanctuary to the priests and to the people.

Contemporary readers are often troubled by the descriptions of the sacrificial service. Nevertheless, sacrifice was an integral part of society in the ancient Near East. Every major city in antiquity had its temple where specially ordained priests conducted animal sacrifices. As elsewhere in antiquity, Leviticus also demands that no one can eat meat unless a portion of it is offered first as a sacrifice to God. The sacrificial altar is God's dining table.

This parashah says practically nothing about women. Many temples in the ancient world included women as priests, but ancient Israel seems to have recognized only males in this role (see *T'tzaveh*, Another View, p. 489; and at 9:1). Although the priestly laws in the Bible mostly concern men, priests' daughters—and presumably wives—were able to partake of some of the offerings, as 10:14 indicates (see also 22:12–13).

*Women were responsible for applying the dietary laws.*

Of special relevance to women are the dietary laws in Leviticus. These apply to all Israelites. However, because women were responsible for food preparation, they were responsible for applying these laws (see at Leviticus 11).

*—Lisbeth S. Fried*

## *Outline*

*I.* Ritual Offerings Begin (9:1–24)

- *A.* Ritual of purgation for Aaron the priest and his household (vv. 1–14)
- *B.* Ritual of purgation for the people (vv. 15–21)
- *C.* Conclusion: appearance of the presence of God (vv. 22–24)

*II.* The Strange Fire of Nadab and Abihu (10:1–7)

*III.* Laws for Aaron the Priest and his Household (10:8–20)

*IV.* Dietary Laws for the Israelite People (11:1–47)

- *A.* Laws regarding animals that walk on land (vv. 1–8)
- *B.* Laws regarding animals that live in water (vv. 9–12)
- *C.* Laws regarding animals that fly in the air (vv. 13–19)
- *D.* Laws regarding animals that swarm in the air (vv. 20–23)
- *E.* Laws regarding carcasses of non-edible animals (vv. 24–28)
- *F.* More laws regarding forbidden foods (vv. 29–43)
- *G.* Summary statement and rationale: you shall be holy (vv. 44–47)

On the eighth day Moses called Aaron and his sons, and the elders of Israel. [2]He said to Aaron: "Take a calf of the herd for a purgation offering and a ram for a burnt offering, without blemish, and bring them before יהוה. [3]And speak to the Israelites, saying: Take a he-goat for a purgation offering; a calf and a lamb, yearlings without blemish, for a burnt offering; [4]and an ox and a ram for an offering of well-being to sacrifice before יהוה;

ט וַיְהִי֙ בַּיּ֣וֹם הַשְּׁמִינִ֔י קָרָ֣א מֹשֶׁ֔ה לְאַהֲרֹ֖ן וּלְבָנָ֑יו וּלְזִקְנֵ֖י יִשְׂרָאֵֽל: 2 וַיֹּ֣אמֶר אֶֽל־אַהֲרֹ֗ן קַח־לְ֠ךָ עֵ֣גֶל בֶּן־בָּקָ֧ר לְחַטָּ֛את וְאַ֥יִל לְעֹלָ֖ה תְּמִימִ֑ם וְהַקְרֵ֖ב לִפְנֵ֥י יְהֹוָֽה: 3 וְאֶל־בְּנֵ֥י יִשְׂרָאֵ֖ל תְּדַבֵּ֣ר לֵאמֹ֑ר קְחֽוּ שְׂעִיר־עִזִּים֙ לְחַטָּ֔את וְעֵ֨גֶל וָכֶ֧בֶשׂ בְּנֵֽי־שָׁנָ֛ה תְּמִימִ֖ם לְעֹלָֽה: 4 וְשׁ֨וֹר וָאַ֜יִל לִשְׁלָמִ֗ים לִזְבֹּ֙חַ֙ לִפְנֵ֣י

· · · · · · · · · · · · · · · · · · · · · · · · · · · · · · · · · · · · · · · · · · · · · · · · · · · ·

## Ritual Offerings Begin  (9:1–24)

The parashah begins on the eighth day (hence its name), the day after the seven-day ordination ceremony of the priests. Aaron now begins his priestly duties and the Tabernacle's activities commence. The first part of Leviticus provided the rules for the sacrificial system, but only now that the priests have been ordained can the worship itself be inaugurated.

### RITUAL OF PURGATION FOR AARON THE PRIEST AND HIS HOUSEHOLD (9:1–14)

Prior to officiating, the priests themselves must undergo a ritual of purification in order to protect both the sanctuary and the people from contaminating elements.

*1. Aaron and his sons.* Aaron's sons begin now to function as priests, and they will lead the congregation upon his death. According to 10:14, Aaron also has (unnamed) daughters. Do they also participate in running the Tabernacle along with his sons? According to Exodus 38:8, women "perform tasks (*tzovot*) at the entrance of the Tent of Meeting." As noted in the comment there, the verb *tzovot* seems to indicate the work of a support staff. Perhaps that reference to women alludes to, or at least includes, Aaron's daughters. They might prepare the basins, the knives, the water, and other materials needed for the Tabernacle.

*2–4.* The inauguration involves four different types of sacrifice: a purgation offering (see Leviticus 4); a burnt offering (see Leviticus 1); an offering of well-being (see Leviticus 3); and a meal offering (see Leviticus 2). Every type of offering is brought except the *asham*, the reparation offering (see 5:15–26). There is no implication that the priests or the people had deliberately trespassed; therefore, perhaps, there is no need for the *asham*.

▶ Food prohibitions fit into the historical and sociological realities of the Jews.

ANOTHER VIEW ➤ 630

▶ How did the Israelites conduct the purifying washings that are mentioned in Leviticus?

POST-BIBLICAL INTERPRETATIONS ➤ 630

▶ Aaron's silence is the profoundest response to the reality that good people die tragically.

CONTEMPORARY REFLECTION ➤ 632

▶ Mourning my son has similarities to labor. …I feel the pain of him in my belly.

VOICES ➤ 634

and a meal offering with oil mixed in. For today יהוה will appear to you."

⁵They brought to the front of the Tent of Meeting the things that Moses had commanded, and the community leadership came forward and stood before יהוה. ⁶Moses said: "This is what יהוה has commanded that you do, that the Presence of יהוה may appear to you." ⁷Then Moses said to Aaron: "Come forward to the altar and sacrifice your purgation offering and your burnt offering, making expiation for yourself and for the people; and sacrifice the people's offering and make expiation for them, as יהוה has commanded."

⁸Aaron came forward to the altar and slaughtered his calf of purgation offering. ⁹Aaron's sons brought the blood to him; he dipped his finger in the blood and put it on the horns of the altar; and he poured out the rest of the blood at the base of the altar. ¹⁰The fat, the kidneys, and the protuberance of the liver from the purgation offering he turned into smoke on the altar—as יהוה had commanded Moses; ¹¹and the flesh and the skin were consumed in fire outside the camp. ¹²Then he slaughtered the burnt offering. Aaron's sons passed the blood to him, and he dashed it against all sides of the altar. ¹³They passed the burnt offering to him in sections, as well as the head, and he turned it into smoke on the altar. ¹⁴He washed the entrails and the legs, and turned them into smoke on the altar with the burnt offering.

יְהֹוָ֖ה וּמִנְחָ֥ה בְלוּלָ֖ה בַשָּׁ֑מֶן כִּ֣י הַיּ֔וֹם יְהֹוָ֖ה נִרְאָ֥ה אֲלֵיכֶֽם: ⁵וַיִּקְח֗וּ אֵ֚ת אֲשֶׁ֣ר צִוָּ֣ה מֹשֶׁ֔ה אֶל־פְּנֵ֖י אֹ֣הֶל מוֹעֵ֑ד וַיִּקְרְבוּ֙ כָּל־הָ֣עֵדָ֔ה וַיַּֽעַמְד֖וּ לִפְנֵ֥י יְהֹוָֽה: ⁶וַיֹּ֣אמֶר מֹשֶׁ֔ה זֶ֧ה הַדָּבָ֛ר אֲשֶׁר־צִוָּ֥ה יְהֹוָ֖ה תַּֽעֲשׂ֑וּ וְיֵרָ֥א אֲלֵיכֶ֖ם כְּב֥וֹד יְהֹוָֽה: ⁷וַיֹּ֨אמֶר מֹשֶׁ֜ה אֶל־אַֽהֲרֹ֗ן קְרַ֤ב אֶל־הַמִּזְבֵּ֨חַ֙ וַֽעֲשֵׂ֞ה אֶת־חַטָּֽאתְךָ֙ וְאֶת־עֹ֣לָתֶ֔ךָ וְכַפֵּ֥ר בַּֽעַדְךָ֖ וּבְעַ֣ד הָעָ֑ם וַֽעֲשֵׂ֞ה אֶת־קָרְבַּ֤ן הָעָם֙ וְכַפֵּ֣ר בַּֽעֲדָ֔ם כַּֽאֲשֶׁ֖ר צִוָּ֥ה יְהֹוָֽה: ⁸וַיִּקְרַ֥ב אַֽהֲרֹ֖ן אֶל־הַמִּזְבֵּ֑חַ וַיִּשְׁחַ֛ט אֶת־עֵ֥גֶל הַֽחַטָּ֖את אֲשֶׁר־לֽוֹ: ⁹וַ֠יַּקְרִ֠בוּ בְּנֵ֨י אַֽהֲרֹ֣ן אֶת־הַדָּם֮ אֵלָיו֒ וַיִּטְבֹּ֤ל אֶצְבָּעוֹ֙ בַּדָּ֔ם וַיִּתֵּ֖ן עַל־קַרְנ֣וֹת הַמִּזְבֵּ֑חַ וְאֶת־הַדָּ֣ם יָצַ֔ק אֶל־יְס֖וֹד הַמִּזְבֵּֽחַ: ¹⁰וְאֶת־הַחֵ֨לֶב וְאֶת־הַכְּלָיֹ֜ת וְאֶת־הַיֹּתֶ֤רֶת מִן־הַכָּבֵד֙ מִן־הַ֣חַטָּ֔את הִקְטִ֖יר הַמִּזְבֵּ֑חָה כַּֽאֲשֶׁ֛ר צִוָּ֥ה יְהֹוָ֖ה אֶת־מֹשֶֽׁה: ¹¹וְאֶת־הַבָּשָׂ֖ר וְאֶת־הָע֑וֹר שָׂרַ֣ף בָּאֵ֔שׁ מִח֖וּץ לַֽמַּֽחֲנֶֽה: ¹²וַיִּשְׁחַ֖ט אֶת־הָֽעֹלָ֑ה וַ֠יַּמְצִ֠אוּ בְּנֵ֨י אַֽהֲרֹ֤ן אֵלָיו֙ אֶת־הַדָּ֔ם וַיִּזְרְקֵ֥הוּ עַל־הַמִּזְבֵּ֖חַ סָבִֽיב: ¹³וְאֶת־הָֽעֹלָ֗ה הִמְצִ֤יאוּ אֵלָיו֙ לִנְתָחֶ֔יהָ וְאֶת־הָרֹ֑אשׁ וַיַּקְטֵ֖ר עַל־הַמִּזְבֵּֽחַ: ¹⁴וַיִּרְחַ֥ץ אֶת־הַקֶּ֖רֶב וְאֶת־הַכְּרָעָ֑יִם וַיַּקְטֵ֧ר עַל־הָֽעֹלָ֛ה הַמִּזְבֵּֽחָה:

* * * * * * * * * * * * * * * * * * * * *

*"today יהוה will appear to you."* The plural "you" in the Hebrew means that God is to appear to everyone present—men, women, and children.

*5. the community leadership.* Literally, "the entire congregation," as in 8:3. [Because the whole community could not fit in the courtyard area in front of the Tent of Meeting, the present translation understands the term in its more restricted sense as representative leaders—presumably referring to the (male) elders mentioned in v. 1. —*Ed.*]

*9. Aaron's sons.* The word "sons" can sometimes be translated "children," but here—despite the fact that Aaron also has daughters (see 10:14)—the word "sons" must be retained.

*brought the blood.* Leviticus 4 describes how blood is used in the procedure to be followed when an anointed priest incurs guilt. This sacrifice is in case a sin is committed unintentionally and without the knowledge of either the priest or the congregation (Numbers 15:24).

[15]Next he brought forward the people's offering. He took the goat for the people's purgation offering, and slaughtered it, and presented it as a purgation offering like the previous one. [16]He brought forward the burnt offering and sacrificed it according to regulation. [17]He then brought forward the meal offering and, taking a handful of it, he turned it into smoke on the altar—in addition to the burnt offering of the morning. [18]He slaughtered the ox and the ram, the people's sacrifice of well-being. Aaron's sons passed the blood to him—which he dashed against every side of the altar—[19]and the fat parts of the ox and the ram: the broad tail, the covering [fat], the kidneys, and the protuberances of the livers. [20]They laid these fat parts over the breasts; and Aaron turned the fat parts into smoke on the altar, [21]and elevated the breasts and the right thighs as an elevation offering before יהוה—as Moses had commanded.

[22]Aaron lifted his hands toward the people and blessed them; and he stepped down after offering the purgation offering, the burnt offering, and the offering of well-being. [23]Moses and Aaron then went inside the Tent of Meeting. When they came out, they blessed the people; and the Presence of יהוה appeared to all the people. [24]Fire came forth from before יהוה and consumed the burnt offering and the fat parts on the altar. And all the people saw, and shouted, and fell on their faces.

15 וַיַּקְרֵ֕ב אֵ֖ת קָרְבַּ֣ן הָעָ֑ם וַיִּקַּ֞ח אֶת־שְׂעִ֤יר
הַֽחַטָּאת֙ אֲשֶׁ֣ר לָעָ֔ם וַיִּשְׁחָטֵ֥הוּ וַֽיְחַטְּאֵ֖הוּ
כָּרִאשֽׁוֹן׃ 16 וַיַּקְרֵ֖ב אֶת־הָעֹלָ֑ה וַֽיַּעֲשֶׂ֖הָ
כַּמִּשְׁפָּֽט׃ 17 וַיַּקְרֵב֮ אֶת־הַמִּנְחָה֒ וַיְמַלֵּ֤א
כַפּוֹ֙ מִמֶּ֔נָּה וַיַּקְטֵ֖ר עַל־הַמִּזְבֵּ֑חַ מִלְּבַ֖ד עֹלַ֥ת
הַבֹּֽקֶר׃ 18 וַיִּשְׁחַ֤ט אֶת־הַשּׁוֹר֙ וְאֶת־הָאַ֔יִל
זֶ֥בַח הַשְּׁלָמִ֖ים אֲשֶׁ֣ר לָעָ֑ם וַ֠יַּמְצִאוּ בְּנֵ֨י
אַהֲרֹ֤ן אֶת־הַדָּם֙ אֵלָ֔יו וַיִּזְרְקֵ֥הוּ עַל־הַמִּזְבֵּ֖חַ
סָבִֽיב׃ 19 וְאֶת־הַחֲלָבִ֖ים מִן־הַשּׁ֑וֹר וּמִֽן־
הָאַ֔יִל הָֽאַלְיָ֤ה וְהַֽמְכַסֶּה֙ וְהַכְּלָיֹ֔ת וְיֹתֶ֖רֶת
הַכָּבֵֽד׃ 20 וַיָּשִׂ֥ימוּ אֶת־הַחֲלָבִ֖ים עַל־הֶחָז֑וֹת
וַיַּקְטֵ֥ר הַחֲלָבִ֖ים הַמִּזְבֵּֽחָה׃ 21 וְאֵ֣ת הֶחָז֗וֹת
וְאֵת֙ שׁ֣וֹק הַיָּמִ֔ין הֵנִ֧יף אַהֲרֹ֛ן תְּנוּפָ֖ה לִפְנֵ֣י
יְהוָ֑ה כַּאֲשֶׁ֖ר צִוָּ֥ה מֹשֶֽׁה׃
22 וַיִּשָּׂ֨א אַהֲרֹ֧ן אֶת־ידו יָדָ֛יו אֶל־הָעָ֖ם
וַֽיְבָרְכֵ֑ם וַיֵּ֗רֶד מֵעֲשֹׂ֧ת הַֽחַטָּ֛את וְהָעֹלָ֖ה
וְהַשְּׁלָמִֽים׃ 23 וַיָּבֹ֨א מֹשֶׁ֤ה וְאַהֲרֹן֙ אֶל־
אֹ֣הֶל מוֹעֵ֔ד וַיֵּ֣צְא֔וּ וַֽיְבָרְכ֖וּ אֶת־הָעָ֑ם וַיֵּרָ֥א
כְבוֹד־יְהוָ֖ה אֶל־כָּל־הָעָֽם׃ 24 וַתֵּ֤צֵא אֵשׁ֙
מִלִּפְנֵ֣י יְהוָ֔ה וַתֹּ֙אכַל֙ עַל־הַמִּזְבֵּ֔חַ אֶת־
הָעֹלָ֖ה וְאֶת־הַחֲלָבִ֑ים וַיַּ֤רְא כָּל־הָעָם֙ וַיָּרֹ֔נּוּ
וַֽיִּפְּל֖וּ עַל־פְּנֵיהֶֽם׃

### RITUAL OF PURGATION FOR THE PEOPLE (9:15–21)

The people's purgation offering is like Aaron's own purgation offering (vv. 8–11) that he incinerated outside the camp.

### CONCLUSION: APPEARANCE OF THE PRESENCE OF GOD (9:22–24)

Witnessing God's presence culminates the week-long ceremony of ordination and the inauguration of the Tabernacle and its personnel; it shows that God has accepted both the priesthood as officiants and the Tent of Meeting as an earthly abode.

*22. **Aaron lifted his hands.*** In the Bible, one hand is raised in oath-taking; but two hands are always raised for prayer and blessings.

*23. **Presence.*** Heb. *kavod*, often translated as God's "glory."

*24. **Fire came forth from before*** **יהוה**. The fire is not God, but it came forth from God.

**10** Now Aaron's sons Nadab and Abihu each
took his fire pan, put fire in it, and laid incense on
it; and they offered before יהוה alien fire, which had
not been enjoined upon them. 2 And fire came forth
from יהוה and consumed them; thus they died at
the instance of יהוה. 3 Then Moses said to Aaron,
"This is what יהוה meant by saying:

Through those near to Me I show Myself holy,
And gain glory before all the people."

And Aaron was silent.

1 וַיִּקְח֣וּ בְנֵי־אַ֠הֲרֹן נָדָ֨ב וַאֲבִיה֜וּא אִ֣ישׁ
מַחְתָּת֗וֹ וַיִּתְּנ֤וּ בָהֵן֙ אֵ֔שׁ וַיָּשִׂ֥ימוּ עָלֶ֖יהָ
קְטֹ֑רֶת וַיַּקְרִ֜בוּ לִפְנֵ֤י יְהוָה֙ אֵ֣שׁ זָרָ֔ה אֲשֶׁ֛ר
לֹ֥א צִוָּ֖ה אֹתָֽם׃ 2 וַתֵּ֥צֵא אֵ֛שׁ מִלִּפְנֵ֥י יְהוָ֖ה
וַתֹּ֣אכַל אוֹתָ֑ם וַיָּמֻ֖תוּ לִפְנֵ֥י יְהוָֽה׃ 3 וַיֹּ֨אמֶר
מֹשֶׁ֜ה אֶֽל־אַהֲרֹ֗ן הוּא֩ אֲשֶׁר־דִּבֶּ֨ר יְהוָ֤ה ׀
לֵאמֹר֙

בִּקְרֹבַ֣י אֶקָּדֵ֔שׁ
וְעַל־פְּנֵ֥י כָל־הָעָ֖ם אֶכָּבֵ֑ד
וַיִּדֹּ֖ם אַהֲרֹֽן׃

## *The Strange Fire of Nadab and Abihu* (10:1–7)

In the tragic story that follows, Nadab and Abihu, Aaron's two oldest sons, offer a ritual fire that God did not command. As a result, fire comes from God and kills them. Like good tragedy everywhere, the story is intended to elicit pity and fear—pity for Nadab, Abihu, their father, mother, and siblings; and fear that God's terrifying power may burst forth again. The world is perceived as a dangerous place, and God can protect but also create harm (Isaiah 45:7). The ancient world's protection is the sacrificial ritual correctly performed according to the prescribed rules. However, contact with the holy must be rigorously safeguarded from illegitimate incursion. If the procedures are performed incorrectly, the sanctuary becomes defiled, with disastrous consequences (15:31). This story, however, leaves the reader uncertain as to what precisely constitutes the sons' transgression.

*1. **alien fire.*** Literally, strange or foreign fire. What makes the fire strange is unclear.

***which had not been enjoined upon them.*** The verse implies that the offering might have been fine if it had been ordered by a proper authority. This episode underscores what everyone in the ancient Near East apparently believed: the deity must be worshipped precisely as specified or catastrophe occurs.

*2. **And fire came forth from יהוה and... they died.*** The exact reasons for this punishment are unclear. The Bible records another story where God destroys a person for touching the ark in an unauthorized manner: King David decides to bring the ark of God to Jerusalem. En route the ark begins to slip off the ox-cart. Unbidden, a man reaches out his hand to steady the ark and God kills him (II Samuel 6:6–7). Both that story and the present one illustrate the danger ascribed to the holy. Indeed, ritual aims to contain and protect against the danger inherent in the holy.

*3. **"This is what יהוה meant by saying."*** There is no record of God's having said these words earlier.

***"Through those near to Me I show Myself holy."*** Or, "I sanctify myself by means of those near to me." That is, I reveal my holiness among those near to me. The ones "nearest" to God were Nadab and Abihu: when they offered the incense they literally "came near" (10:1; see 16:1); and as priests, they are "nearer" to God than non-priests. These deaths evince God's power as awesome and the Tabernacle's status as holy. According to this reading, then, God uses the deaths of Nadab and Abihu to magnify Godself. The story of Nadab and Abihu may aim, among other things, to illustrate that priestly privilege may not be abused.

***"And gain glory before all the people."*** All the people saw the fire and the deaths of Nadab and

[4]Moses called Mishael and Elzaphan, sons of Uzziel the uncle of Aaron, and said to them, "Come forward and carry your kinsmen away from the front of the sanctuary to a place outside the camp." [5]They came forward and carried them out of the camp by their tunics, as Moses had ordered. [6]And Moses said to Aaron and to his sons Eleazar and Ithamar, "Do not bare your heads and do not rend your clothes, lest you die and anger strike the whole community. But your kin, all the house of Israel, shall bewail the burning that יהוה has wrought. [7]And so do not go outside the entrance of the Tent of Meeting, lest you die, for יהוה's anointing oil is upon you." And they did as Moses had bidden.

[8]And יהוה spoke to Aaron, saying: [9]Drink no wine or other intoxicant, you or your sons, when

4 וַיִּקְרָא מֹשֶׁה אֶל־מִישָׁאֵל וְאֶל אֶלְצָפָן בְּנֵי
עֻזִּיאֵל דֹּד אַהֲרֹן וַיֹּאמֶר אֲלֵהֶם קִרְבוּ שְׂאוּ
אֶת־אֲחֵיכֶם מֵאֵת פְּנֵי־הַקֹּדֶשׁ אֶל־מִחוּץ
לַמַּחֲנֶה׃ 5 וַיִּקְרְבוּ וַיִּשָּׂאֻם בְּכֻתֳּנֹתָם אֶל־
מִחוּץ לַמַּחֲנֶה כַּאֲשֶׁר דִּבֶּר מֹשֶׁה׃ 6 וַיֹּאמֶר
מֹשֶׁה אֶל־אַהֲרֹן וּלְאֶלְעָזָר וּלְאִיתָמָר ׀ בָּנָיו
רָאשֵׁיכֶם אַל־תִּפְרָעוּ ׀ וּבִגְדֵיכֶם לֹא־תִפְרֹמוּ
וְלֹא תָמֻתוּ וְעַל כָּל־הָעֵדָה יִקְצֹף וַאֲחֵיכֶם
כָּל־בֵּית יִשְׂרָאֵל יִבְכּוּ אֶת־הַשְּׂרֵפָה אֲשֶׁר
שָׂרַף יְהוָה׃ 7 וּמִפֶּתַח אֹהֶל מוֹעֵד לֹא
תֵצְאוּ פֶּן־תָּמֻתוּ כִּי־שֶׁמֶן מִשְׁחַת יְהוָה
עֲלֵיכֶם וַיַּעֲשׂוּ כִּדְבַר מֹשֶׁה׃ פ
8 וַיְדַבֵּר יְהוָה אֶל־אַהֲרֹן לֵאמֹר׃ 9 יַיִן וְשֵׁכָר
אַל־תֵּשְׁתְּ ׀ אַתָּה ׀ וּבָנֶיךָ אִתָּךְ בְּבֹאֲכֶם

Abihu. God's awesome power is revealed in God's acts.

***Aaron was silent.*** There is not much that one can say when confronted with the awesome power of God. But what was the reaction of Nadab and Abihu's mother, Elisheba (see Exodus 6:23)? The text does not record her response to this tragedy. On Aaron's silence, see Contemporary Reflection, p. 632.

*6.* ***"bare your heads . . . rend your clothes."*** Moses describes two of the actions associated elsewhere in the Bible with mourning.

***"kin."*** Heb. *achim*, literally "brothers," has a gender-inclusive sense here. The Bible takes for granted that ancient Israelite women feature in the public bewailing of communal tragedies such as the death of leaders (Jeremiah 9:16–19; II Chronicles 35:25; Exodus 33:4; see *Chayei Sarah*, Contemporary Reflection, p. 129).

*7.* ***"do not go outside."*** Aaron must not go out to bury his sons.

***"for יהוה's anointing oil is upon you."*** The anointing oil is holy and must be used in the manner prescribed, that is, by the high priest when he conducts the sacrificial rites (Exodus 30:30–33). If Aaron is outside the tent or in the presence of the dead, he defiles the oil and also the sanctuary (21:10–12). If the sanctuary becomes defiled, the entire community could perish (15:31). An ordinary priest may defile himself through burial of his son and other members of his immediate family (Leviticus 21:1), but not the chief priest (21:10–12).

## *Laws for Aaron the Priest and His Household* (10:8–20)

The Tent of Meeting must be purged of the contamination of the corpse defilement that occurred with the deaths of Nadab and Abihu, but that report appears only later, in Leviticus 16. Here, following additional instructions to the priests (vv. 8–15), comes an odd story about the purgation offering. Moses suddenly chastises Aaron and his remaining sons for erroneously burning the goat rather than eating it (see 9:1–4 for relevant laws). Aaron obliquely asks: if they had eaten it, would his sons have been spared? Moses has no answer.

*9.* ***Drink no wine or other intoxicant.*** The mention of wine and strong drink here leads some

you enter the Tent of Meeting, that you may not
die. This is a law for all time throughout the ages,
10 for you must distinguish between the sacred and
the profane, and between the impure and the pure;
11 and you must teach the Israelites all the laws
which יהוה has imparted to them through Moses.

12 Moses spoke to Aaron and to his remaining
sons, Eleazar and Ithamar: Take the meal offering
that is left over from יהוה's offerings by fire and eat
it unleavened beside the altar, for it is most holy.
13 You shall eat it in the sacred precinct, inasmuch as
it is your due, and that of your sons, from יהוה's
offerings by fire; for so I have been commanded.
14 But the breast of elevation offering and the thigh
of gift offering you [and your wife], and your sons
and daughters with you, may eat in any pure place,
for they have been assigned as a due to you and
your sons from the Israelites' sacrifices of well-

אֶל־אֹ֥הֶל מוֹעֵ֖ד וְלֹ֣א תָמֻ֑תוּ חֻקַּ֥ת עוֹלָ֖ם
לְדֹרֹתֵיכֶֽם׃ 10 וּֽלְהַבְדִּ֔יל בֵּ֥ין הַקֹּ֖דֶשׁ וּבֵ֣ין
הַחֹ֑ל וּבֵ֥ין הַטָּמֵ֖א וּבֵ֥ין הַטָּהֽוֹר׃ 11 וּלְהוֹרֹ֖ת
אֶת־בְּנֵ֣י יִשְׂרָאֵ֑ל אֵ֚ת כָּל־הַ֣חֻקִּ֔ים אֲשֶׁ֨ר דִּבֶּ֧ר
יְהוָ֛ה אֲלֵיהֶ֖ם בְּיַד־מֹשֶֽׁה׃ פ

12 וַיְדַבֵּ֨ר מֹשֶׁ֜ה אֶֽל־אַהֲרֹ֗ן וְאֶ֣ל אֶ֠לְעָזָ֠ר וְאֶל־
אִ֨יתָמָ֥ר ׀ בָּנָיו֮ הַנּֽוֹתָרִים֒ קְח֣וּ אֶת־הַמִּנְחָ֗ה
הַנּוֹתֶ֙רֶת֙ מֵאִשֵּׁ֣י יְהוָ֔ה וְאִכְל֥וּהָ מַצּ֖וֹת אֵ֣צֶל
הַמִּזְבֵּ֑חַ כִּ֛י קֹ֥דֶשׁ קָֽדָשִׁ֖ים הִֽוא׃ 13 וַאֲכַלְתֶּ֤ם
אֹתָהּ֙ בְּמָק֣וֹם קָד֔וֹשׁ כִּ֣י חָקְךָ֤ וְחָק־בָּנֶ֙יךָ֙ הִ֔וא
מֵאִשֵּׁ֖י יְהוָ֑ה כִּי־כֵ֖ן צֻוֵּֽיתִי׃ 14 וְאֵ֣ת חֲזֵ֣ה
הַתְּנוּפָ֡ה וְאֵ֣ת ׀ שׁ֣וֹק הַתְּרוּמָ֗ה תֹּֽאכְלוּ֙
בְּמָק֣וֹם טָה֔וֹר אַתָּ֕ה וּבָנֶ֥יךָ וּבְנֹתֶ֖יךָ אִתָּ֑ךְ כִּֽי־
חָקְךָ֤ וְחָק־בָּנֶ֙יךָ֙ נִתְּנ֔וּ מִזִּבְחֵ֥י שַׁלְמֵ֖י בְּנֵ֥י

to suggest that the placement of this verse implies that strong drink caused Nadab and Abihu to act precipitously. More likely, however, this placement is coincidental.

*10. you must distinguish.* That is, you must make a separation.

*11. and you must teach.* The priests are also to teach the people to make a separation themselves between the pure and the impure, the holy and the profane (see Ezekiel 22:26; 42:20; 44:23).

*12–13.* Two verses describe laws regarding the meal offering (see Leviticus 2).

*Eleazar and Ithamar.* Citing Aaron's sons specifically by name may indicate that only the chief priest and his male heirs are entitled to the "most holy" offerings—daughters being excluded. As indicated by v. 14 (compare 23:20) and by 22:12–13, a priest's daughter may eat "holy" food, if not the "most holy," so long as she is part of her father's household. (See further at 6:11; *Tzav*, Another View, p. 608.)

*13. your due.* The priest's food comes partly from these offerings.

*sons.* Heb. *banim*, which can also signify offspring of both genders ("children"). Here, the word refers specifically to "sons" if the injunction regarding this offering in 6:11 means that "only the males . . . may eat of it"; see the discussion there. See also at v. 12.

*14.* The rules for the elevation offerings appear in Exodus 29:22–27 and Leviticus 7:29–34.

*you [and your wife].* [This is one of several passages in the Torah where syntax and context together indicate that the Hebrew's second-person masculine singular language implicitly addresses a conjugal pair: the head of household and his wife. See the introduction to the Decalogue, p. 416; *Mishpatim*, Another View, p. 445. —*Ed.*]

*your sons and daughters.* Designated parts of the meal and gift offering may be eaten by women as well as by anyone belonging to the priest's household (22:10–13).

*a due to . . . your sons.* Here, as in v. 13, the word *banim* does not include daughters. These donations primarily compensate the (male) priests for their ritual role; only secondarily do they serve

being. [15]Together with the fat of fire offering, they must present the thigh of gift offering and the breast of elevation offering, which are to be elevated as an elevation offering before יהוה, and which are to be your due and that of your sons with you for all time—as יהוה has commanded.

[16]Then Moses inquired about the goat of purgation offering, and it had already been burned! He was angry with Eleazar and Ithamar, Aaron's remaining sons, and said, [17]"Why did you not eat the purgation offering in the sacred area? For it is most holy, and it is what was given to you to remove the guilt of the community and to make expiation for them before יהוה. [18]Since its blood was not brought inside the sanctuary, you should certainly have eaten it in the sanctuary, as I commanded." [19]And Aaron spoke to Moses, "See, this day they brought their purgation offering and their burnt offering before יהוה, and such things have befallen me! Had I eaten purgation offering today, would יהוה have approved?" [20]And when Moses heard this, he approved.

*11* יהוה spoke to Moses and Aaron, saying to them: [2]Speak to the Israelite people thus:

יִשְׂרָאֵֽל: 15 שׁ֣וֹק הַתְּרוּמָ֗ה וַחֲזֵ֣ה הַתְּנוּפָ֔ה עַ֣ל אִשֵּׁ֣י הַחֲלָבִ֔ים יָבִ֕יאוּ לְהָנִ֥יף תְּנוּפָ֖ה לִפְנֵ֣י יְהֹוָ֑ה וְהָיָ֨ה לְךָ֜ וּלְבָנֶ֤יךָ אִתְּךָ֙ לְחׇק־עוֹלָ֔ם כַּאֲשֶׁ֖ר צִוָּ֥ה יְהֹוָֽה:

16 וְאֵ֣ת | שְׂעִ֣יר הַֽחַטָּ֗את דָּרֹ֥שׁ דָּרַ֛שׁ מֹשֶׁ֖ה וְהִנֵּ֣ה שֹׂרָ֑ף וַ֠יִּקְצֹ֠ף עַל־אֶלְעָזָ֤ר וְעַל־אִֽיתָמָר֙ בְּנֵ֣י אַהֲרֹ֔ן הַנּֽוֹתָרִ֖ם לֵאמֹֽר: 17 מַדּ֗וּעַ לֹֽא־אֲכַלְתֶּ֤ם אֶת־הַֽחַטָּאת֙ בִּמְק֣וֹם הַקֹּ֔דֶשׁ כִּ֛י קֹ֥דֶשׁ קׇֽדָשִׁ֖ים הִ֑וא וְאֹתָ֣הּ | נָתַ֣ן לָכֶ֗ם לָשֵׂ֙את֙ אֶת־עֲוֺ֣ן הָֽעֵדָ֔ה לְכַפֵּ֥ר עֲלֵיהֶ֖ם לִפְנֵ֥י יְהֹוָֽה: 18 הֵ֚ן לֹא־הוּבָ֣א אֶת־דָּמָ֔הּ אֶל־הַקֹּ֖דֶשׁ פְּנִ֑ימָה אָכ֨וֹל תֹּאכְל֥וּ אֹתָ֛הּ בַּקֹּ֖דֶשׁ כַּאֲשֶׁ֥ר צִוֵּֽיתִי: 19 וַיְדַבֵּ֨ר אַהֲרֹ֜ן אֶל־מֹשֶׁ֗ה הֵ֣ן הַ֠יּ֠וֹם הִקְרִ֨יבוּ אֶת־חַטָּאתָ֤ם וְאֶת־עֹֽלָתָם֙ לִפְנֵ֣י יְהֹוָ֔ה וַתִּקְרֶ֥אנָה אֹתִ֖י כָּאֵ֑לֶּה וְאָכַ֤לְתִּי חַטָּאת֙ הַיּ֔וֹם הַיִּיטַ֖ב בְּעֵינֵ֥י יְהֹוָֽה: 20 וַיִּשְׁמַ֣ע מֹשֶׁ֔ה וַיִּיטַ֖ב בְּעֵינָֽיו: פ

יא וַיְדַבֵּ֧ר יְהֹוָ֛ה אֶל־מֹשֶׁ֥ה וְאֶֽל־אַהֲרֹ֖ן לֵאמֹ֥ר אֲלֵהֶֽם: 2 דַּבְּר֞וּ אֶל־בְּנֵ֤י יִשְׂרָאֵל֙ לֵאמֹ֔ר

- - - - - - - - - - - - - - - - - - - - - - - - - - - - - -

to feed members of the family who are not serving as priests.

*16.* Moses' anger regarding the sacrifice of the goat is puzzling. Was he not there when they burned it? Moses chastises Aaron and his remaining sons for further lack of scrupulousness in carrying out their responsibilities, but perhaps he is passing off his own derelication of duties onto them.

*17–18.* Moses' point is that a purgation offering is not complete until the priests have eaten their share of the meat from it. The law requires that it be eaten in a pure place ("in the sacred precinct," 6:19).

*19.* *"would יהוה have approved?"* Aaron's rhetorical question implies that God would not have approved. Aaron apparently has reasoned that the death of Nadab and Abihu has polluted the area

(compare Numbers 19:14)—and yet Aaron and his sons cannot leave the vicinity (above, v. 7). Thus the priests have no place available where they can eat the meat.

*20.* Moses is forced to agree.

## Dietary Laws for the Israelite People (11:1–47)

At this point in the narrative, the Israelites have set up the Tabernacle (Exodus 40), received specifications for the sacrifices (Leviticus 1–7), ordained the priesthood (Leviticus 8), and initiated formal worship (Leviticus 9–10). God has assigned the priests their task of teaching Israel to distin-

These are the creatures that you may eat from among all the land animals: [3]any animal that has

זֹאת הַחַיָּה אֲשֶׁר תֹּאכְלוּ מִכׇּל־הַבְּהֵמָה אֲשֶׁר עַל־הָאָרֶץ׃ 3 כֹּל ׀ מַפְרֶסֶת פַּרְסָה

guish between the ritually pure and the impure (10:10–11). This task includes being able to differentiate between pure and impure foods, to which the text now turns. The people must make such distinctions in their daily, household life, not merely in relation to the sanctuary. The practice of differentiating between the pure and the impure in one's eating creates a relationship between the priests' work in the sanctuary and ordinary Israelites at home.

No explanation is offered for what makes these items unfit as food, and none is needed. These specific food prohibitions likely reflect ancient cultural dislikes ("taboos" is too strong a word) that eventually become solidified into law (see also at Deuteronomy 14:3–21). They later become explicit indicators of identity, however. That is, loyalty to one's Judaism and to Judaism's God came to be expressed via resistance to violating the dietary laws. For example, according to II Maccabees 7, a mother instructs her sons to die rather than eat pork publicly. [Some food prohibitions may also have had functional economic reasons behind them (such as an attempt to avoid economic dependence on other groups). Others may have been symbolic, such as avoiding predatory animals (possibly with a rationale that "you are what you eat"). *—Ed.*]

This unit has special relevance for women. The ancient Israelite diet consisted mostly of grains—supplemented with milk curds, cheese, yogurt, wine, olive oil, legumes, and fruits and vegetables. In ancient Israel preparing those foodstuffs was the domain of women; it was they who typically supervised or performed tasks such as building the fire, drawing water from the well, grinding the grain, kneading the dough, forming the cakes, milking the sheep and goats, making the cheese and yogurt, gathering the olives and dates, and treading the grapes. As a result, we can assume that women were responsible for maintaining the dietary laws.

Meat was reserved for special occasions. Scholars debate the role of women in slaughtering animals for meat in ancient Israel. Some suggest, on the basis of ancient reliefs, that during certain periods, animals were slaughtered domestically. In those periods, women may have participated in the task. (In I Samuel 28:24, the woman of En-dor slaughters a calf on her own initiative and prepares a meal with it.) However, other evidence suggests that women did not slaughter animals. If slaughtering was restricted to the sanctuary—even a local sanctuary—it would have been unlikely that women would perform the actual sacrifice. If women went at all, they would have been accompanied by a man who would have performed the sacrifice rite. (For a different opinion, see at 1:5.).

It has been suggested that women also controlled food distribution in the household. However, it is perhaps more likely that the customs in present-day traditional Arabic and Afghani societies are relevant in this regard. In these societies women do prepare the food, but the men and boys get the lion's share; the women and girls wait in the back room until the men are done eating. The food is not allocated, but simply laid on the floor on platters in front of the men and boys, who eat with their hands from the common pot until they are done. Then the women eat. These customs go back into antiquity; they may also reflect the customs of ancient Israel. (A similar picture may be implicit in Genesis 18.) [It is also possible that the overall role of women in Islamic cultures today is significantly different from that of ancient Israel and thus may not provide a reliable analogy. Some ethnographic evidence indicates that in ancient Palestine the whole family ordinarily ate together, gathered around common dishes. *—Ed.*]

true hoofs, with clefts through the hoofs, and that chews the cud—such you may eat. [4]The following, however, of those that either chew the cud or have true hoofs, you shall not eat: the camel—although it chews the cud, it has no true hoofs: it is impure for you; [5]the daman—although it chews the cud, it has no true hoofs: it is impure for you; [6]the hare—although it chews the cud, it has no true hoofs: it is impure for you; [7]and the swine—although it has true hoofs, with the hoofs cleft through, it does not chew the cud: it is impure for you. [8]You shall not eat of their flesh nor touch their carcasses; they are impure for you.

[9]These you may eat of all that live in water: anything in water, whether in the seas or in the streams, that has fins and scales—these you may

וְשֹׁסַעַת שֶׁסַע פְּרָסֹת מַעֲלַת גֵּרָה בַּבְּהֵמָה
אֹתָהּ תֹּאכֵלוּ׃ 4 אַךְ אֶת־זֶה לֹא תֹאכְלוּ
מִמַּעֲלֵי הַגֵּרָה וּמִמַּפְרִסֵי הַפַּרְסָה אֶת־
הַגָּמָל כִּי־מַעֲלֵה גֵרָה הוּא וּפַרְסָה אֵינֶנּוּ
מַפְרִיס טָמֵא הוּא לָכֶם׃ 5 וְאֶת־הַשָּׁפָן כִּי־
מַעֲלֵה גֵרָה הוּא וּפַרְסָה לֹא יַפְרִיס טָמֵא
הוּא לָכֶם׃ 6 וְאֶת־הָאַרְנֶבֶת כִּי־מַעֲלַת גֵּרָה
הִוא וּפַרְסָה לֹא הִפְרִיסָה טְמֵאָה הִוא
לָכֶם׃ 7 וְאֶת־הַחֲזִיר כִּי־מַפְרִיס פַּרְסָה הוּא
וְשֹׁסַע שֶׁסַע פַּרְסָה וְהוּא גֵּרָה לֹא־יִגָּר
טָמֵא הוּא לָכֶם׃ 8 מִבְּשָׂרָם לֹא תֹאכֵלוּ
וּבְנִבְלָתָם לֹא תִגָּעוּ טְמֵאִים הֵם לָכֶם׃
9 אֶת־זֶה תֹּאכְלוּ מִכֹּל אֲשֶׁר בַּמָּיִם כֹּל
אֲשֶׁר־לוֹ סְנַפִּיר וְקַשְׂקֶשֶׂת בַּמַּיִם בַּיַּמִּים

### LAWS REGARDING ANIMALS THAT WALK ON LAND (11:1–8)

*3. any animal that has true hooves . . . and that chews the cud.* The text could simply restrict the permitted animals to those that chew (literally "bring up") the cud, since every true ruminant has cloven hooves.

*4. impure for you.* That is, not impure intrinsically.

*5. the daman.* If this identification is correct, then this creature is a member of the hyrax family, which is native to Africa and southwest Asia, including Israel. A hyrax is a brownish-gray mammal that is rabbit-sized and resembles a guinea pig.

*6. hare.* The species that lives in Israel is a larger relative of the common rabbit. Neither the rabbit nor the hare chews cud, but like ruminants they digest their food more than once.

*7. the swine.* Pigs were raised in Syria and the Levant in antiquity prior to the advent of the Israelite presence in the Judean highlands. Iron Age Israelite settlements show only very few pig bones, in contrast to earlier settlements there, and in contrast to neighboring areas (of the Philistines, Moabites, and Ammonites) where pig bones are well attested during the same time period. It is thus likely that the prohibition against eating pig among the Israelites is very ancient.

*8. touch their carcasses.* Anthropologist Mary Douglas suggests that the prohibition of touching the carcass of the inedible mammals protects these animals in their lifetime. Since they cannot be skinned, dismembered, or exploited after death, they need not be hunted or killed. Thus elephants would not be killed for their tusks, alligators for their hides, mink or ermine for their fur, nor turtles for their shells. However, the Rabbis may be right in interpreting this prohibition as applying only to priests serving in the sanctuary (22:8) and not to the laity. The prohibition has meaning only for members of a priestly household: One who touches such a carcass is ritually impure. In order to eat of the sacred donations, he or she must bathe and remain impure until evening. (See further at v. 24.)

### LAWS REGARDING ANIMALS THAT LIVE IN WATER (11:9–12)

*9. fins and scales.* Ancient Israelites would not have known many fish. There were few varieties or numbers of fish in the Sea of Galilee, and the

eat. [10]But anything in the seas or in the streams that has no fins and scales, among all the swarming things of the water and among all the other living creatures that are in the water—they are an abomination for you [11]and an abomination for you they shall remain: you shall not eat of their flesh and you shall abominate their carcasses. [12]Everything in water that has no fins and scales shall be an abomination for you.

[13]The following you shall abominate among the birds—they shall not be eaten, they are an abomination: the eagle, the vulture, and the black vulture; [14]the kite, falcons of every variety; [15]all varieties of raven; [16]the ostrich, the nighthawk, the sea gull; hawks of every variety; [17]the little owl, the cormorant, and the great owl; [18]the white owl, the pelican, and the bustard; [19]the stork; herons of every variety; the hoopoe, and the bat.

[20]All winged swarming things that walk on fours shall be an abomination for you. [21]But these you may eat among all the winged swarming things that walk on fours: all that have, above their feet,

וּבַנְּחָלִים אֹתָם תֹּאכֵלוּ׃ 10 וְכֹל אֲשֶׁר אֵין־
לוֹ סְנַפִּיר וְקַשְׂקֶשֶׂת בַּיַּמִּים וּבַנְּחָלִים מִכֹּל
שֶׁרֶץ הַמַּיִם וּמִכֹּל נֶפֶשׁ הַחַיָּה אֲשֶׁר בַּמָּיִם
שֶׁקֶץ הֵם לָכֶם׃ 11 וְשֶׁקֶץ יִהְיוּ לָכֶם
מִבְּשָׂרָם לֹא תֹאכֵלוּ וְאֶת־נִבְלָתָם תְּשַׁקֵּצוּ׃
12 כֹּל אֲשֶׁר אֵין־לוֹ סְנַפִּיר וְקַשְׂקֶשֶׂת בַּמָּיִם
שֶׁקֶץ הוּא לָכֶם׃
13 וְאֶת־אֵלֶּה תְּשַׁקְּצוּ מִן־הָעוֹף לֹא יֵאָכְלוּ
שֶׁקֶץ הֵם אֶת־הַנֶּשֶׁר וְאֶת־הַפֶּרֶס וְאֵת
הָעָזְנִיָּה׃ 14 וְאֶת־הַדָּאָה וְאֶת־הָאַיָּה
לְמִינָהּ׃ 15 אֵת כָּל־עֹרֵב לְמִינוֹ׃ 16 וְאֵת בַּת
הַיַּעֲנָה וְאֶת־הַתַּחְמָס וְאֶת־הַשָּׁחַף וְאֶת־הַנֵּץ
לְמִינֵהוּ׃ 17 וְאֶת־הַכּוֹס וְאֶת־הַשָּׁלָךְ וְאֶת־
הַיַּנְשׁוּף׃ 18 וְאֶת־הַתִּנְשֶׁמֶת וְאֶת־הַקָּאָת
וְאֶת־הָרָחָם׃ 19 וְאֵת הַחֲסִידָה הָאֲנָפָה
לְמִינָהּ וְאֶת־הַדּוּכִיפַת וְאֶת־הָעֲטַלֵּף׃
20 כֹּל שֶׁרֶץ הָעוֹף הַהֹלֵךְ עַל־אַרְבַּע שֶׁקֶץ
הוּא לָכֶם׃ 21 אַךְ אֶת־זֶה תֹּאכְלוּ מִכֹּל
שֶׁרֶץ הָעוֹף הַהֹלֵךְ עַל־אַרְבַּע אֲשֶׁר־לא לוֹ
כְרָעַיִם מִמַּעַל לְרַגְלָיו לְנַתֵּר בָּהֵן עַל־

southeastern Mediterranean was practically devoid of fish before the Persian king Darius dug his canal between the Red Sea and the Nile during the 6th century B.C.E. Most fish were purchased from the Phoenicians (Nehemiah 13:16). (Some later rabbinic opinions permit fish that have scales at one point in their life even though they lose them later, such as the swordfish.)

*11. abomination.* Heb. *sheketz* (disgusting), not *tamei* ("impure").

## LAWS REGARDING ANIMALS THAT FLY IN THE AIR (11:13–19)

Birds not listed in this section are permitted.

*13–15.* These prohibited birds (with the possible exception of the *bat yaanah,* typically translated as "ostrich" but probably a type of owl) either eat carrion or grasp their prey and eat it alive.

*19. the bat.* This is a mammal, not a bird; but it is classed here because it flies.

## LAWS REGARDING ANIMALS THAT SWARM IN THE AIR (11:20–23)

*21. above their feet, jointed legs.* The locust is the migratory phase of the grasshopper. When conditions become sufficiently crowded, the usually solitary grasshopper undergoes a morphological and behavioral transformation during which it flies in huge swarms. The palace reliefs of Sennacherib at Nineveh (now in the British Museum) show that grasshoppers were delicacies fit for a king. A scene depicting a line of attendants carrying food items includes at least one figure with rows of grasshoppers skewered on two sticks (somewhat like corn dogs).

jointed legs to leap with on the ground—[22]of these you may eat the following: locusts of every variety; all varieties of bald locust; crickets of every variety; and all varieties of grasshopper. [23]But all other winged swarming things that have four legs shall be an abomination for you.

הָאָרֶץ׃ 22 אֶת־אֵלֶּה מֵהֶם תֹּאכֵלוּ אֶת־
הָאַרְבֶּה לְמִינוֹ וְאֶת־הַסָּלְעָם לְמִינֵהוּ וְאֶת־
הַחַרְגֹּל לְמִינֵהוּ וְאֶת־הֶחָגָב לְמִינֵהוּ׃
23 וְכֹל שֶׁרֶץ הָעוֹף אֲשֶׁר־לוֹ אַרְבַּע רַגְלָיִם
שֶׁקֶץ הוּא לָכֶם׃

[24]And the following shall make you impure—whoever touches their carcasses shall be impure until evening, [25]and whoever carries the carcasses of any of them shall wash those clothes and be impure until evening—[26]every animal that has true hoofs but without clefts through the hoofs, or that does not chew the cud. They are impure for you; whoever touches them shall be impure. [27]Also all animals that walk on paws, among those that walk on fours, are impure for you; whoever touches their carcasses shall be impure until evening. [28]And anyone who carries their carcasses shall wash those clothes and remain impure until evening. They are impure for you.

[29]The following shall be impure for you from among the things that swarm on the earth: the mole, the mouse, and great lizards of every variety; [30]the gecko, the land crocodile, the lizard, the sand lizard, and the chameleon. [31]Those are for you the impure among all the swarming things; whoever touches them when they are dead shall be impure

24 וּלְאֵלֶּה תִּטַּמָּאוּ כָּל־הַנֹּגֵעַ בְּנִבְלָתָם
יִטְמָא עַד־הָעָרֶב׃ 25 וְכָל־הַנֹּשֵׂא מִנִּבְלָתָם
יְכַבֵּס בְּגָדָיו וְטָמֵא עַד־הָעָרֶב׃ 26 לְכָל־
הַבְּהֵמָה אֲשֶׁר הִוא מַפְרֶסֶת פַּרְסָה וְשֶׁסַע ׀
אֵינֶנָּה שֹׁסַעַת וְגֵרָה אֵינֶנָּה מַעֲלָה טְמֵאִים
הֵם לָכֶם כָּל־הַנֹּגֵעַ בָּהֶם יִטְמָא׃ 27 וְכֹל ׀
הוֹלֵךְ עַל־כַּפָּיו בְּכָל־הַחַיָּה הַהֹלֶכֶת עַל־
אַרְבַּע טְמֵאִים הֵם לָכֶם כָּל־הַנֹּגֵעַ בְּנִבְלָתָם
יִטְמָא עַד־הָעָרֶב׃ 28 וְהַנֹּשֵׂא אֶת־נִבְלָתָם
יְכַבֵּס בְּגָדָיו וְטָמֵא עַד־הָעָרֶב טְמֵאִים הֵמָּה
לָכֶם׃ ס
29 וְזֶה לָכֶם הַטָּמֵא בַּשֶּׁרֶץ הַשֹּׁרֵץ עַל־
הָאָרֶץ הַחֹלֶד וְהָעַכְבָּר וְהַצָּב לְמִינֵהוּ׃
30 וְהָאֲנָקָה וְהַכֹּחַ וְהַלְּטָאָה וְהַחֹמֶט
וְהַתִּנְשָׁמֶת׃ 31 אֵלֶּה הַטְּמֵאִים לָכֶם בְּכָל־
הַשָּׁרֶץ כָּל־הַנֹּגֵעַ בָּהֶם בְּמֹתָם יִטְמָא עַד־

### LAWS REGARDING CARCASSES OF NON-EDIBLE ANIMALS (11:24–28)

These verses explain the ramifications of v. 8, above. They seem out of place here.

*24. carcasses.* The term is not defined. In a later era, the Rabbis considered the carcass to be the flesh only and permitted use of the bones, skin, hair, and teeth; the Dead Sea sect took a different position and forbade the use of even these items.

*impure until evening.* In contrast to carcasses, live animals do not impart impurity.

### MORE LAWS REGARDING FORBIDDEN FOODS (11:29–43)

This section describes what happens after prohibited swarming animals come in contact with other household objects.

*29–31.* The reference is to creatures that enter a household on their own. The exact identifications are not certain.

*31. when they are dead.* See above at v. 24.

until evening. 32 And anything on which one of them falls when dead shall be impure: be it any article of wood, or a cloth, or a skin, or a sack—any such article that can be put to use shall be dipped in water, and it shall remain impure until evening; then it shall be pure. 33 And if any of those falls into an earthen vessel, everything inside it shall be impure and [the vessel] itself you shall break. 34 As to any food that may be eaten, it shall become impure if it came in contact with water; as to any liquid that may be drunk, it shall become impure if it was inside any vessel. 35 Everything on which the carcass of any of them falls shall be impure: an oven or stove shall be smashed. They are impure—and impure they shall remain for you. 36 However, a spring or cistern in which water is collected shall be pure, but whoever touches such a carcass in it shall be impure. 37 If such a carcass falls upon seed grain that is to be sown, it is pure; 38 but if water is put on the seed and any part of a carcass falls upon it, it shall be impure for you.

הָעָֽרֶב׃ 32 וְכֹל אֲשֶׁר־יִפֹּל־עָלָיו מֵהֶם ׀
בְּמֹתָם יִטְמָא מִכָּל־כְּלִי־עֵץ אוֹ בֶגֶד אוֹ־
עוֹר אוֹ שָׂק כָּל־כְּלִי אֲשֶׁר־יֵעָשֶׂה מְלָאכָה
בָּהֶם בַּמַּיִם יוּבָא וְטָמֵא עַד־הָעֶרֶב וְטָהֵר׃
33 וְכָל־כְּלִי־חֶרֶשׂ אֲשֶׁר־יִפֹּל מֵהֶם אֶל־תּוֹכוֹ
כֹּל אֲשֶׁר בְּתוֹכוֹ יִטְמָא וְאֹתוֹ תִשְׁבֹּרוּ׃
34 מִכָּל־הָאֹכֶל אֲשֶׁר יֵאָכֵל אֲשֶׁר יָבוֹא עָלָיו
מַיִם יִטְמָא וְכָל־מַשְׁקֶה אֲשֶׁר יִשָּׁתֶה בְּכָל־
כְּלִי יִטְמָא׃ 35 וְכֹל אֲשֶׁר־יִפֹּל מִנִּבְלָתָם ׀
עָלָיו יִטְמָא תַּנּוּר וְכִירַיִם יֻתָּץ טְמֵאִים הֵם
וּטְמֵאִים יִהְיוּ לָכֶם׃ 36 אַךְ מַעְיָן וּבוֹר
מִקְוֵה־מַיִם יִהְיֶה טָהוֹר וְנֹגֵעַ בְּנִבְלָתָם
יִטְמָא׃ 37 וְכִי יִפֹּל מִנִּבְלָתָם עַל־כָּל־זֶרַע
זֵרוּעַ אֲשֶׁר יִזָּרֵעַ טָהוֹר הוּא׃ 38 וְכִי יֻתַּן־
מַיִם עַל־זֶרַע וְנָפַל מִנִּבְלָתָם עָלָיו טָמֵא
הוּא לָכֶם׃ ס

*32.* Objects like containers, tools, and musical instruments that come into contact with the carcass of these animals must be washed. The prohibition does not apply to surfaces like floors or tables.

*33.* Because an earthenware vessel cannot be purified, it must be broken. Anything inside it must be discarded. But if the carcass touches only the outside, the vessel is not impure, a provision motivated perhaps by economic considerations.

*34.* ***any food... in contact with water.*** Wet food becomes impure if it comes into contact with the carcass of one of the animals named in vv. 29–30. Dry food and seeds that come into contact with such carcasses are not affected.

***any liquid . . . inside any vessel.*** A liquid that comes into contact with a carcass of one of the animals listed in vv. 29–30 is impure only if the liquid is inside a vessel. Liquids in a lake, stream, or well are not rendered impure.

*35.* ***oven or stove.*** These items were made of earthenware, like the vessels mentioned in v. 33.

*36.* ***cistern.*** A cistern was usually cut into bedrock and used for collecting and storing runoff. It was kept covered with a stone when not in use. If the rock was porous, the cistern was waterproofed by being plastered with lime. Cisterns, in which water could be stored for the dry season, made settled living possible in the Land of Israel, with its dry climate and its few year-round sources of water. A 9th-century-B.C.E. king of Moab boasts on his victory monument that he built a cistern for every house—using the labor of Israelite prisoners of war. [Cisterns near the household would have made women's lives considerably easier, since drawing water was typically the work of women, often girls. (See Genesis 24:11, 13 and I Samuel 9:11.) *—Ed.*]

*37–38.* ***seed grain.*** Seed to be planted is pure even if it touched a carcass of the forbidden animals. Seed to be eaten is impure if it touches the carcass and it is wet.

[39]If an animal that you may eat has died, anyone who touches its carcass shall be impure until evening; [40]anyone who eats of its carcass shall wash those clothes and remain impure until evening; and anyone who carries its carcass shall wash those clothes and remain impure until evening.

[41]All the things that swarm upon the earth are an abomination; they shall not be eaten. [42]You shall not eat, among all things that swarm upon the earth, anything that crawls on its belly, or anything that walks on fours, or anything that has many legs; for they are an abomination. [43]You shall not draw abomination upon yourselves through anything that swarms; you shall not make yourselves impure therewith and thus become impure. [44]For I יהוה am your God: you shall sanctify yourselves and be holy, for I am holy. You shall not make yourselves impure through any swarming thing that moves upon the earth. [45]For I יהוה am the One who brought you up from the land of Egypt to be your God: you shall be holy, for I am holy.

[46]These are the instructions concerning animals, birds, all living creatures that move in water, and all creatures that swarm on earth, [47]for distinguishing between the impure and the pure, between the living things that may be eaten and the living things that may not be eaten.

39 וְכִ֤י יָמוּת֙ מִן־הַבְּהֵמָ֔ה אֲשֶׁר־הִ֥יא לָכֶ֖ם
לְאָכְלָ֑ה הַנֹּגֵ֥עַ בְּנִבְלָתָ֖הּ יִטְמָ֥א עַד־הָעָֽרֶב׃
40 וְהָֽאֹכֵל֙ מִנִּבְלָתָ֔הּ יְכַבֵּ֥ס בְּגָדָ֖יו וְטָמֵ֣א עַד־
הָעָ֑רֶב וְהַנֹּשֵׂא֙ אֶת־נִבְלָתָ֔הּ יְכַבֵּ֥ס בְּגָדָ֖יו
וְטָמֵ֥א עַד־הָעָֽרֶב׃
41 וְכָל־הַשֶּׁ֖רֶץ הַשֹּׁרֵ֣ץ עַל־הָאָ֑רֶץ שֶׁ֥קֶץ ה֖וּא
לֹ֥א יֵאָכֵֽל׃ 42 כֹּל֩ הוֹלֵ֨ךְ עַל־גָּח֜וֹן וְכֹ֣ל ׀
הוֹלֵ֣ךְ עַל־אַרְבַּ֗ע עַ֚ד כָּל־מַרְבֵּ֣ה רַגְלַ֔יִם
לְכָל־הַשֶּׁ֖רֶץ הַשֹּׁרֵ֣ץ עַל־הָאָ֑רֶץ לֹ֥א
תֹאכְל֖וּם כִּי־שֶׁ֥קֶץ הֵֽם׃ 43 אַל־תְּשַׁקְּצוּ֙
אֶת־נַפְשֹׁ֣תֵיכֶ֔ם בְּכָל־הַשֶּׁ֖רֶץ הַשֹּׁרֵ֑ץ וְלֹ֤א
תִֽטַּמְּאוּ֙ בָּהֶ֔ם וְנִטְמֵתֶ֖ם בָּֽם׃ 44 כִּ֣י אֲנִ֣י יְהוָה֮
אֱלֹֽהֵיכֶם֒ וְהִתְקַדִּשְׁתֶּם֙ וִהְיִיתֶ֣ם קְדֹשִׁ֔ים כִּ֥י
קָד֖וֹשׁ אָ֑נִי וְלֹ֤א תְטַמְּאוּ֙ אֶת־נַפְשֹׁ֣תֵיכֶ֔ם
בְּכָל־הַשֶּׁ֖רֶץ הָרֹמֵ֥שׂ עַל־הָאָֽרֶץ׃ 45 כִּ֣י ׀
אֲנִ֣י יְהוָ֗ה הַמַּעֲלֶ֤ה אֶתְכֶם֙ מֵאֶ֣רֶץ מִצְרַ֔יִם
לִהְיֹ֥ת לָכֶ֖ם לֵאלֹהִ֑ים וִהְיִיתֶ֣ם קְדֹשִׁ֔ים כִּ֥י
קָד֖וֹשׁ אָֽנִי׃
46 זֹ֣את תּוֹרַ֤ת הַבְּהֵמָה֙ וְהָע֔וֹף וְכֹל֙ נֶ֣פֶשׁ
הַֽחַיָּ֔ה הָֽרֹמֶ֖שֶׂת בַּמָּ֑יִם וּלְכָל־נֶ֖פֶשׁ הַשֹּׁרֶ֥צֶת
עַל־הָאָֽרֶץ׃ 47 לְהַבְדִּ֕יל בֵּ֥ין הַטָּמֵ֖א וּבֵ֣ין
הַטָּהֹ֑ר וּבֵ֤ין הַֽחַיָּה֙ הַֽנֶּאֱכֶ֔לֶת וּבֵין֙ הַֽחַיָּ֔ה
אֲשֶׁ֖ר לֹ֥א תֵאָכֵֽל׃ פ

***39. has died.*** That is, without being ritually slaughtered.

***41–43. things that swarm upon the earth.*** That is, the animals discussed in vv. 29–30.

### SUMMARY STATEMENT AND RATIONALE: YOU SHALL BE HOLY (11:44–47)

God's holiness is given as the reason for all the dietary restrictions.

The statement in v. 45 suggests that there are parallels between what is offered to God and what Israelites have to do when striving toward holiness. To sanctify oneself is to keep apart from impurities as well as transgressions.

That verse, together with v. 44, are the first clear statements in which Israelites are commanded to emulate God's holiness, an idea that is developed at length beginning with Leviticus 19.

*—Lisbeth S. Fried*

# *Another View*

Parashat Sh'mini challenges the notion of a rational religion, yet we still seek a logical basis for the food laws in Leviticus 11. Mary Douglas, who examines the food prohibitions in Leviticus from an anthropological perspective, looks for the underlying rationale. In her influential work *Purity and Danger* (1966), she concludes that the distinctions between pure and impure animals are based on the principle that pure animals are those that stay well within the bounds of their habitat. The qualities of impure animals are seen as unsuitable for their habitat, thereby threatening to blur the boundaries established by pure animals, who possess qualities seen as suitable for that habitat. Douglas's categories rely largely on the means of locomotion appropriate to each sphere: wings for air, cleft hooves for earth, fins and scales for water. Everything that blurs these boundaries is segregated and put into a category of defilement.

Less well known is a brilliant and complex later essay, "Self Evidence" (in her book *Implicit Meanings*, 1975), in which Douglas suggests how biblical food prohibitions fit into the wider historical and sociological realities of the Israelites and later of the Jews, throughout their history. This preoccupation with distinguishing what is inside bounds from what is outside bounds is a reflection, according to Douglas, of Israelite history and sociology. Inside Israel's frail boundaries is a small political unit surrounded by powerful enemies. Douglas concludes that here is a people who cherish their boundaries and want nothing better than to keep them strong and high; any attempt to cross them is seen as a hostile intrusion.

The mysteries of the parashah and the rational connection between religion and culture come together here. For biblical Israel, being holy means being set apart. Food prohibitions reflect Israel's preoccupation with clearly defined categories. This preoccupation continues to be expressed when Jews differentiate between the holy and profane, between light and darkness, between Israel and other nations, between Shabbat and the rest of the week. What Douglas illustrates, in both her earlier and later works, is how such religious practices and systems are shaped by sociopolitical circumstances, and, in turn, shape the norms of the community.

*Food prohibitions reflect Israel's preoccupation with clearly defined categories.*

*—Diane M. Sharon*

# *Post-biblical Interpretations*

***a spring or cistern in which water is collected shall be pure*** (11:35–36). The biblical phrase "a cistern in which water is collected" (*mikvei-mayim*) provides the foundation for rabbinic justifications for required immersion in the *mikveh*, the ritual bathing pool. This phrase, *mikvei-mayim*, referring to an accumulation of water, also appears in Genesis 1:10 and Exodus 7:19. The Bible does not use the word *mikveh* by itself except in the form of a variant (*mikvah*) in Isaiah 22:11. There is no biblical reference to the legislated use of such pools or cisterns for ritual immersion. Since no ritual baths from the time of the First Temple have been found, scholars do not know how the earliest Israelites conducted the purifying washings that are mentioned in such places as Leviticus 15.

The Rabbis inherited from the Torah a ritual purity system that had involved both priests and laity, and both women and men; those sages assumed that the biblical commandments for ritual purification required full immersion in a *mikveh* (plural, *mikva'ot*). In biblical times, however, ritual washing could have been achieved instead by splashing, pouring (affusion), or rinsing. The range of available strategies is illustrated in Greek red- and black-figure pottery from the 6th century B.C.E. onward, where scenes depict men or women showering from spigots in a slightly stooped but standing position, using tubs and basins, or having water from large jugs poured upon them while in a crouched position. Neighboring Near Eastern cultures also had a variety of forms of purification, and there is no reason to think that uniformity was the rule in ancient Israel as well. When rabbinic Judaism eventually emerged as the dominant form of Jewish practice, however, the *mikveh* would become the only acceptable type of installation for ritual immersion.

*The mikveh has been used most frequently by women.*

Archeologists have found numerous ritual bathing pools that Jews constructed during the Second Temple period (some two thousand years ago), indicating their practice of full bodily immersion. Since stored rainwater was always a scarce commodity, Jews utilized water diverted from caves, springs, and rivers whenever possible in building ritual baths. The most common use of such *mikva'ot* during this era was purification prior to entering the area of the Temple. Rabbinic sources indicate that the Jewish court (*beit din*) supervised the construction, validity, measurements, and cleanliness of these *mikva'ot*. During Second Temple times, however, it appears that Jews had not achieved uniformity of opinion as to *mikveh* requirements: the pools found do not all adhere to the same configurations, and surviving texts reveal doctrinal differences.

*Mikva'ot* is the sixth tractate in the order *T'harot* (Purities) of the Mishnah. It discusses the characteristics of a valid *mikveh*, various ways of constructing a *mikveh*, and the nature and sources of the water necessary for a valid *mikveh*. This tractate also explains what constitutes valid immersion.

According to tractate *Mikva'ot* and other rabbinic sources, a *mikveh* must be hewn out of rock or built into the ground; it must also be made watertight, usually with plaster, since any leakage invalidates it. A ritual bath must contain a minimum of forty *se'ah*s (at least two hundred gallons, or more than 750 liters) of free-flowing clean water, sufficient for full immersion either vertically or horizontally. Rain or spring water is valid, as is water diverted from a river, lake, or ocean. Once a *mikveh* contains the minimum quantity of valid water, drawn water of any amount may be added.

Most biblical laws of ritual purity lapsed with the destruction of the Second Temple in 70 C.E. Since that time, the *mikveh* has been used most frequently by women. They immerse on a variety of occasions: prior to marriage, at a specified time in each menstrual cycle, and following the birth of children. Traditionally, *mikveh* immersion is part of conversion to Judaism. Some authorities have encouraged men to immerse in a *mikveh* on the eve of the Sabbath and festivals. In accordance with Numbers 31:22–23, some Jews also immerse in the *mikveh* their new metal and glass vessels and vessels purchased from non-Jews.

Rabbinic efforts to justify immersion indicate that the rationale was secondary to the practice. Midrash *Sifra* connects the ritual immersion of a vessel to another requirement for purification, namely, waiting for the sun to set. The midrash states that just as purification is linked to the *simultaneous* setting of the entire sun, so purification should be understood to refer to *simultaneous* immersion of the entire vessel (*Sh'mini* 8). —*Carol Selkin Wise*

# Contemporary Reflection

All Israel is a kingdom of priests (Exodus 19:6). Some among them are priests of priests. At the top of the priestly pyramid stands Aaron, the *kohein gadol* (high priest). The *kohein gadol* is vested with considerable power and responsibility. Though everything is new—and no models exist for him to follow—Aaron carries out his role with great competency and dignity as he offers up the first sacrifices to God.

In *parashat Sh'mini*, we find ourselves with Aaron and his family at an exhilarating moment. It is the climactic eighth day of dedication of the Tabernacle. Exultant and joyful, Aaron and his sons bless the people—and the glory of God appears before all. A fire of heavenly origin consumes the sacrifices in their entirety; the people fall on their faces in awe and love of God. Aaron's joy must surely be overflowing.

Suddenly, the scene turns into heartbreak. Though not commanded to do so, Nadab and Abihu, Aaron's elder sons, put incense into pans and bring it as an offering. Instantly, a fire of God leaps out and consumes them. Aaron is devastated. These two sons were outstanding young men: they were deemed worthy of ascending Mt. Sinai in a most prestigious order—after Moses and Aaron, and before the 70 elders—and worthy of participating in the festive meal at which God's face was shown (Exodus 24:1, 9–11).

What could have happened? We struggle to understand. Was this a punishment from God, or a random accident? What crime could they have committed that was so heinous as to warrant death by flash fire? Perhaps they were acting out of enthusiasm and desire to serve. Perhaps they were overcome simply by the pure joy of being in the presence of God—and wished only to increase awe in the hearts of the people. And even if they were guilty of not following God's word to the last, did not their father Aaron have credit in the storehouse of good deeds? Was there not some milder punishment that could have been meted out on the scale, such as that meted out to other miscreants in the Torah?

Yet despite the fact that they performed everything else properly and created a glorious Tabernacle celebration, despite their father's merit or their own, they are swiftly cut down.

When I was growing up, my high school Torah teacher, Mar Yerushalmi, communicated unequivocally to his students that Nadab and Abihu were punished for the grave sin of eating in the place where they should not have. Whenever a student would be caught chewing gum in class as we studied Torah with Rashi's commentary, Yerushalmi would remind her of Nadab and Abihu. On the one hand, this devout teacher was implying that the sons were guilty and deserved what they got; on the other, likening their crime to a teenager's act of chewing gum in the wrong setting was his way of subtly suggesting to a class of impressionable teenagers that he, too, felt the punishment did not fit the crime.

> *Why is there a halachah enjoining the comforting visitor to hold back in silence?*

The Torah narrative teaches us that Moses struggles with the same issue, trying to find an explanation. He wants to offer consolation to his beloved brother and closest friend, yet he takes care not to betray his responsibility as the leader who must teach the people to follow God's law. "This is what יהוה meant by saying, 'Through those near to Me I show Myself holy'" (10:3). Moses' delicate message to the people—and his only consolation to Aaron—is that this was not a random act but a sentence decreed on those closest to God, who are thus held to a higher standard.

What was Aaron's response? Two simple words:

*vayidom Aharon* ("And Aaron was silent"). The word *vayidom* means more than he kept quiet—*vayishtok*. Aaron responded with a profound, shattering silence, a stunning silence, a shocked silence. He does not justify the cruel decree by blaming his sons and accepting their fate as punishment for their sins. Yet, neither does he revolt or protest God's action. Total silence.

Aaron's response is the profoundest human and religious response to the reality that there are times when good people die unjustly or are consumed in tragedies that seem to be arbitrary, shocking, without justification, and with nothing to ameliorate the pain and loss of those who love them.

A few years ago, in 2002, my beloved son JJ, age 36, was killed while riding a bicycle in Israel. He had arrived the night before to celebrate the holidays with the whole family and was bicycling with his brother to visit his sister in Zichron Yaakov, when a young driver ran a yellow light with great speed—and took JJ's life in an instant. JJ loved Israel, family, Judaism, athletics, God, nature, and life; and he was celebrating all of these loves when his life was snuffed out.

When my husband and I sat *shiva*, most people came with no forethought agenda or explanation, though a few—out of good intention and compassion—tried to justify God or soften the loss by giving it some meaning. "He was so good that God needed him by His side" was one such attempt, to which on one occasion—unable to hold back my words—I responded, "But we on Earth need him more!" Most people understood at the deepest level that there was nothing that could justify, nothing that could offset the pain or soften the blow, and they wisely remained silent. And we ourselves were silent, as there were no words we could speak that would make any sense of it.

At times, devout members of religions that affirm an afterlife are tempted to say that the deceased is "in a better place—living a better life in a better world"; or they are tempted to suggest that there must be some sin or error or judgment that has brought this fate upon the victim. Such persons cannot tolerate the thought that what has happened is unjustified, for it violates their deepest principles about good and evil, reward and punishment. They need somehow to internally rationalize and justify a reality in order to bring the world back to proper equilibrium.

The Jewish laws of bereavement, so exquisitely tuned to the needs of the mourners, stipulate that the *shiva* visitor should not speak until the mourner speaks. I had always thought that the point of that precept was to ensure that the conversation would flow to the place the mourner needs it to reach. But I now understand that the halachah enjoining the comforting visitor to hold back in silence serves a different function: to caution against offering a rationale for the decree of death. The deeper human religious response is to be silent, to live with the contradiction, and to affirm that we need not force meaning into tragedy. Sometimes, the deepest response of love is to be silent.

—*Blu Greenberg*

# *Voices*

## *My Dead*

Rahel (transl. Robert Friend)

*Leviticus 10:1–3*

*"Only the dead don't die"*

Only they are left me, they are faithful still
whom death's sharpest knife can no longer kill.

At the turn of the highway, at the close of day
they silently surround me, they quietly go my
way.

A true pact is ours, a tie time cannot dissever.
Only what I have lost is what I possess forever.

## *from* Contractions of Death

Sherri Mandell

*Leviticus 10:1–3*

Mourning my son has similarities to labor. The contractions of pain rush through my body like a knot that is tied tighter and tighter so that I am unable to breathe, dead along with my son. My womb becomes a grave. I feel the pain of him in my belly, a pressure bearing down on me. It will always be inside of me. And though I hope and pray that one day I will not be as great with pain as I am now, the pain will never leave me.

## *If I Only Knew*

Nelly Sachs (transl. Ruth and Matthew Mead)

*Leviticus 10:1–3*

If I only knew
On what your last look rested.
Was it a stone that had drunk
So many last looks that they fell
Blindly upon its blindness?

Or was it earth
Enough to fill a shoe,
And black already
With so much parting
And with so much killing?

Or was it your last road
That brought you a farewell from all the roads
You had walked?

A puddle, a bit of shining metal,
Perhaps the buckle of your enemy's belt,
Or some other small augury
Of heaven?

Or did this earth,
Which lets no one depart unloved,
Send you a bird-sign through the air,
Reminding your soul that it quivered
In the torment of its burnt body?

## *A Pure Whole Memory*

Dahlia Ravikovitch
(transl. Chana Bloch and Chana Kronfeld)

*Leviticus 10:1–3*

Only when the face is erased
can anything here be remembered whole,
only when the face is erased.
Then the lights go wild,
the colors start from their frames.
Stars plunge from their height like epileptics.
Grasses groan up out of the earth
(their growing pains greater than wilting pangs).

All those things that blind our eyes
draw back to the shadows.
So too the face.
Something begins to stir in the depths.

How many days,
how many years of wind and weather,
have we waited for it to erupt
from the depths of the earth,
one pure whole memory
like a lily,
pale red.

## *For the Last Time*

Robin Fox

*Leviticus 10:1–3*

How do you know
when it's the last time?
The last time to ask
"How are you?
How was your day?"
The last time to say
"I love you.
Good night . . . sweet dreams."

You don't.
And so you must reach out
with love and compassion
at every opportunity
to show those who love you
that you care
you love
and need to be needed . . .
in a world where you suddenly find yourself
alone once again
in an achingly painful way
because someone you love
has left you behind
to seek your own paths
and truths
in an uncertain place.

The only thing certain
is that you're not truly alone
because of those who do love you
and for that be thankful
and grateful
and feel blessed
that you were able to say
"Good night . . . I love you"
one last time.

## *Inheritance*

Sue Hubbard

*Leviticus 11*

Childhood Sundays: the dread,
and the polished patina of oak
with crimson claret, the snowy
linen in initialed silver rings
and hexagrams of cutlery on
tablemats of hunting scenes—
pink coats and fox-hounds braying
for the kill and my father skilfully
carving the strained lacunae
thin as slices of rare beef.
Days when grandma came, the air
was sharp as English mustard
—she wouldn't eat the meat,
instead brought pots of pickled
cucumber, chopped liver, balls
of *gefilte* fish in waxy paper-bags
which made my mother sigh.
"It's not kosher" grandma said
when I asked *why?* unlocking
clouded memories, three generations'
climb from East End tenement
to this wooden Surrey Hill.
This was a house of tea cups,
of cupboards layered with mounds
of my father's crisp starched shirts,
of rose beds and clipped lawns,
where I learned to stitch on
that elastic tennis-club smile
to cover the slow dawning
that I was a Jew.

# תזריע ✦ *Tazria*

## LEVITICUS 12:1–13:59

## *Purity, Birth, and Illness*

PARASHAT TAZRIA continues the theme of ritual purity that extends also to *parashat M'tzora* (Leviticus 14–15). While Leviticus 12 deals with the impurity of the woman who suffers from bleeding after childbirth, Leviticus 15 will concern women and men who experience other kinds of genital discharge, both normal and abnormal. The intervening passage, Leviticus 13–14, concerns *tzaraat*—certain growths on skin, fabric, or leather. Traditionally the term has been translated as "leprosy," but in English "leprosy" nowadays refers to something other than the conditions that the Torah describes.

*Parashat Tazria* thus includes two different subjects: (*1*) the impurity from childbirth (Leviticus 12); and (*2*) the diagnosis of and regulations concerning skin, garments, and leather goods with certain kinds of surface eruptions (Leviticus 13). Common to both, however, is the Israelite notion that physical conditions can produce a pollution that affects not only the party afflicted but also the sanctuary—the abode of the divine Presence. Therefore, the individuals affected must not "touch any consecrated thing, nor enter the sanctuary" during prescribed periods (12:4). Being denied access to holiness extends to all whom the Torah considers impure (*tamei*). Certain sins also result in the pollution of Israel's holy place (see, for example, 16:16, 18:24–25, 20:3).

The common denominator regarding all the physical conditions that produce impurity is their association with the nexus of life and death. Numbers 12 shows that the Israelites associated *tzaraat* with death: when Miriam is stricken with it, Aaron pleads, "Let her not be as a stillbirth [literally "a dead person"] which emerges from its mother's womb with half its flesh eaten away!" (12:12). In the Torah, blood is synonymous with life (Genesis 9:4; Leviticus 17:14). Vaginal blood had an even greater significance for some of the ancients, who thought that it contained the seed that united with the male seed (semen) to produce a human being (Jacob Milgrom, *Leviticus 1–16*, 1991, pp. 744, 767, 950). As menstrual fluid, it signified a lost opportunity to create life, thus linked with the process of death. This applied as well to the person who suffered from scale disease.

*This legislation has had an enormous impact upon the lives of Jewish women.*

The legislation in Leviticus 12 and its focus upon the menstruating woman have had an enormous impact upon the lives of Jewish women. (For the practical consequences of impurity for women in ancient Israel, see the introduction to *parashat M'tzora*, p. 657.) The view that women—via their normal, recurring bodily functions—generate a pollution antagonistic to holiness served as a justification for women's distance from the sacred throughout Jewish history. Women were disqualified from the Israelite priesthood perhaps because of fear that the sudden onset of menstruation would result in the clash of impurity and holiness, with presumed dire consequences. (For a different perspective, see *T'tzaveh*, Another View, p. 489.) After the destruction of the Temple, which was the focus for the laws of ritual purity, women were often prevented from having contact with a Torah scroll, for example, because of the fear of giving affront to God by approaching in an impure state. The basis for many of the restrictions imposed upon the menstruant and the woman who gave birth was found not in Jewish law but rather in popular custom, which triumphed despite the objections of some rabbis. In addition to her participation in public religious life, the private life of the Jewish woman was affected: she and her husband were not allowed to engage in sexual relations during extensive periods of time, which greatly impacted her fertility and married life in general.

—*Elaine Goodfriend*

## *Outline*

I. Laws for the Impurity of a Woman after Giving Birth (12:1–8)
- A. Impurity after the birth of a male (vv. 1–4)
- B. Impurity after the birth of a female (vv. 5)
- C. Sacrifices by a woman who gave birth (vv. 6–8)

II. Laws for Diagnosing and Containing Skin Diseases (13:1–59)
- A. Skin diseases and procedures for diagnosing and containing them (vv. 1–44)
  1. Shiny marks (vv. 1–8)
  2. Discolorations (vv. 9–17)
  3. Boils (vv. 18–23)
  4. Burns (vv. 24–28)
  5. Infection of the scalp or beard (vv. 29–37)
  6. Vitiligo (vv. 38–39)
  7. Baldness (vv. 40–44)
- B. Restrictions for the person with scale disease (vv. 45–46)
- C. Infection of fabrics and of articles made of skin (vv. 47–59)

יהוה spoke to Moses, saying: [2]Speak to the Israelite people thus: When a woman at childbirth bears a male, she shall be impure seven

יב וַיְדַבֵּר יְהֹוָה אֶל־מֹשֶׁה לֵּאמֹר׃ 2 דַּבֵּר
אֶל־בְּנֵי יִשְׂרָאֵל לֵאמֹר אִשָּׁה כִּי תַזְרִיעַ
וְיָלְדָה זָכָר וְטָמְאָה שִׁבְעַת יָמִים כִּימֵי נִדַּת

## *Laws for the Impurity of a Woman after Giving Birth* (12:1–8)

The section that delineates purification rituals for women after childbirth differentiates between the birth of a son and that of a daughter. For the first 7 days after the birth of a son, and for 14 days after that of a daughter, the woman is in a ritual state equivalent to that of a menstruating woman (see Leviticus 15). Afterward she must still abstain from contact with the sacred items or the sanctuary for another 33 days in the case of a son and 66 days in the case of a daughter. Leviticus offers no explanation for the differences in duration.

Despite the fact that Leviticus 12 does not mention bathing, most commentators assume that the act of ritual bathing or immersion marks the end of a woman's period of impurity. Bathing signifies the termination of impurity from other causes (see 14:8, 9). On bathing in a ritual bath (*mikveh*), which became mandatory for women in subsequent periods, see *Sh'mini*, Post-biblical Interpretations, p. 630; *M'tzora,* Contemporary Reflection, p. 674.

### IMPURITY AFTER THE BIRTH OF A MALE (12:1–4)

The notion that the woman who gave birth bears impurity is characteristic of many ancient cultures. Among Israel's neighbors, it was common for the parturient (a woman about to give birth) to be quarantined and taboo, and special purification rituals were performed for the woman and her newborn among some groups. In Leviticus, this period of severe impurity (as opposed to the lesser degree described in v. 4) terminates after seven days when the newborn is male and after fourteen days when the newborn is female; compare v. 5.

2. ***at childbirth.*** [Heb. *tazria* (which becomes the name of the parashah). The verb refers to a woman producing an offspring. In Genesis 1:11–12, it means "produce seed" or "bring forth seed" (regarding trees). The collective noun *zera* from the same root refers to offspring when used for persons, and to seed when used in agricultural contexts. Several texts mention a woman's own offspring. See, for example, when an angel promises Hagar that her *zera* will be numerous ("descendants," Genesis 16:10; see also the blessing of Rebekah in 24:60). More often the references are to a man's offspring (as when God makes the covenant with Abraham in Genesis 17:7). Baruch Levine translates the clause with *tazria* as "when a woman is inseminated" (*Leviticus*, 1989, p. 72). That rendering, however, does not sufficiently highlight the active role of the woman in this parashah. —*Ed.*]

Why must a woman spend twice as long in a state of impurity following the birth of a girl?

ANOTHER VIEW ➤ *650*

To enter the *mikveh* is to plunge into fresh connections with Creation and spirituality.

CONTEMPORARY REFLECTION ➤ *652*

"There are three partners in procreation: the Holy One, the father, and the mother."

POST-BIBLICAL INTERPRETATIONS ➤ *650*

She was the essence of beauty . . . when the child was placed on her belly.

VOICES ➤ *654*

days; she shall be impure as at the time of her condition of menstrual separation.—3On the eighth
day the flesh of his foreskin shall be circumcised.—
4She shall remain in a state of blood purification for
thirty-three days: she shall not touch any consecrated thing, nor enter the sanctuary until her

דְּוֺתָ֖הּ תִּטְמָֽא׃ 3 וּבַיּ֖וֹם הַשְּׁמִינִ֑י יִמּ֖וֹל בְּשַׂ֥ר
עׇרְלָתֽוֹ׃ 4 וּשְׁלֹשִׁ֥ים יוֹם֙ וּשְׁלֹ֣שֶׁת יָמִ֔ים
תֵּשֵׁ֖ב בִּדְמֵ֣י טׇהֳרָ֑ה בְּכׇל־קֹ֣דֶשׁ לֹֽא־תִגָּ֗ע
וְאֶל־הַמִּקְדָּשׁ֙ לֹ֣א תָבֹ֔א עַד־מְלֹ֖את יְמֵ֥י

***as at the time of her condition of menstrual separation.*** Menstruation creates impurity and requires seven days of separation followed by a purification ritual. According to 15:19–24, those who have contact with a menstruating woman, or with any object upon which she lies or sits, become impure and must bathe, launder their garments, and wait till evening before having contact with the sanctuary or items earmarked for it.

***condition of.*** Heb. *davah* could be associated with the idea of flowing (so Rashi) but also illness (for this sense, see Deuteronomy 7:15, 28:60; Isaiah 1:5).

***menstrual separation.*** Heb. *niddah*, which designates menstruation. In later Jewish texts, this word expresses the supposedly repulsive state of women with a genital discharge. Here, however, the term designates a kind of impurity that requires attention yet without apparent stigma (see further at Leviticus 15, especially 15:1–24).

*3.* While this verse could be viewed as a sort of parenthetical reminder, a few commentators have suggested that the timing of a boy's circumcision is coordinated with the diminishing of his mother's impure status. It may be that the removal of the foreskin was viewed as a sort of purification ritual, so that both mother and son can achieve purity on consecutive days. Perhaps circumcision is delayed until the eighth day, when mother and (consequently) infant are in a less severe state of impurity, in order to prevent the contamination of the person who performs the circumcision. Therefore, circumcision may have been seen as a postpartum ritual associated with the separation of a male child from the impurity of his mother.

The renowned anthropologist Mary Douglas offers another interpretation of the role of circumcision in the context of postpartum impurity. She writes that circumcision played a protective role for mother and son, so that they were perceived as safer than a mother and daughter. This enhanced protection allowed the new mother and her son to venture out sooner, whereas a mother and her daughter had to lie low to avoid danger. Impurity was viewed as having a protective function. One might ask, "Protection from what?" Douglas's theory assumes that the people of ancient Israel retained a strong fear of demons (for a possible allusion to such demonic forces, see Exodus 4:24–26). The Torah, however, makes no obvious allusions to such a fear, nor does it make an obvious link between impurity and protection with regard to individuals who become *tamei* for other reasons.

A baby boy who had completed his first week of life is ready for entrance into the covenant, similar to the acceptability of an animal for sacrifice after it had completed its first week of life (Exodus 22:29, Leviticus 22:27).

*4.* ***a state of blood purification for thirty-three days.*** This period differs from the initial seven-day period in that the woman now has access to the common sphere, including her husband. She remains impure only in regard to the sanctuary and holy objects. Thus, this section prescribes a total of forty days for the purification period following the birth of a boy.

***consecrated thing.*** Heb. *kodesh*, a reference to items earmarked for donation to the sanctuary and its priesthood: these include first-fruits, tithes, and animals designated for sacrifice.

period of purification is completed. 5If she bears a
female, she shall be impure two weeks as during her
menstruation, and she shall remain in a state of
blood purification for sixty-six days.
6On the completion of her period of purification, for either son or daughter, she shall bring
to the priest, at the entrance of the Tent of Meeting, a lamb in its first year for a burnt offering, and
a pigeon or a turtledove for a purgation offering.

טָהֳרָהּ׃ 5 וְאִם־נְקֵבָה תֵלֵד וְטָמְאָה שְׁבֻעַיִם
כְּנִדָּתָהּ וְשִׁשִּׁים יוֹם וְשֵׁשֶׁת יָמִים תֵּשֵׁב עַל־
דְּמֵי טָהֳרָה׃
6 וּבִמְלֹאת ׀ יְמֵי טָהֳרָהּ לְבֵן אוֹ לְבַת תָּבִיא
כֶּבֶשׂ בֶּן־שְׁנָתוֹ לְעֹלָה וּבֶן־יוֹנָה אוֹ־תֹר
לְחַטָּאת אֶל־פֶּתַח אֹהֶל־מוֹעֵד אֶל־הַכֹּהֵן׃

## IMPURITY AFTER THE BIRTH OF A FEMALE (12:5)

The purification period for a woman after giving birth to a female child is 80 days, twice as long as after a male child. But the provisions follow the same two-step pattern: for the first two weeks, she is in a state of impurity comparable to a menstruating woman; and for sixty-six days she remains impure in regard to the sanctuary and items consecrated to it. The reason for the longer state of impurity after the birth of a girl is unclear. One proposed explanation is that the baby girl is a potential menstruant and mother, and so a future source of impurity. [Nicole Ruane challenges this view in her recent dissertation ("Male without Blemish: Sacrifice and Gender Ideologies in Priestly Ritual Law," 2005). Instead, she argues that the text presumes the following worldview: "While it is imperfect that women give birth to boys, it is even less perfect when a woman bears a girl" (p. 164). Thus a woman who bears a boy is "rewarded" by having the time of her impurity halved. This possible understanding of birth and of gender would apply to certain priestly writings for which patrilineal continuity is a central concern; we have no information as to how widespread this idea might have been, nor how widely practiced this regulation was. —*Ed.*] See also Another View, p. 650.

Other less likely proposals attribute the longer time following the birth of a girl to the ancients' notion that male embryos were completely formed in forty-one days and females in eighty-two, or posit that the Torah is accounting to the mother the occasional vaginal bleeding which afflicts newborn females (Jonathan Magonet, "... The Riddle of Leviticus 12:5," in *Reading Leviticus*, 1996, pp. 144–52), or ascribe a protective function to the state of impurity (see at v. 3).

Some have suggested that the prolonged impurity of the baby girl's mother reflects the social inferiority of females (a judgment not stated in the biblical text). Others counter that the greater potential for defilement does not indicate social status; after all, the handling of a human corpse defiles to a far greater degree than touching a dead lizard (compare 11:29–31 and Numbers 19), yet the status of the human is higher than that of a reptile.

## SACRIFICES BY A WOMAN WHO GAVE BIRTH (12:6–8)

*6.* When the mother reaches either the fortieth or eightieth day post-partum, she must take the necessary ritual steps to regain access to the holy sphere. Leviticus does not prescribe immersion for the woman's post-partum purification (although the Rabbis assume a second immersion at this point, in addition to the ritual bathing at the end of seven or fourteen days). Rather, two sacrifices mark the end of the period of impurity.

***burnt offering.*** Heb. *olah*, which elsewhere has one of several functions: to atone for sin, to offer thanksgiving, or to pay homage to God (see Leviticus 1).

***purgation offering.*** Heb. *chatat*, which cleanses

[7]He shall offer it before יהוה and make expiation on her behalf; she shall then be pure from her flow of blood. Such are the rituals concerning her who bears a child, male or female. [8]If, however, her means do not suffice for a sheep, she shall take two turtledoves or two pigeons, one for a burnt offering and the other for a purgation offering. The priest shall make expiation on her behalf, and she shall be pure.

13 יהוה spoke to Moses and Aaron, saying: [2]When a person has on the skin of the body a

7 וְהִקְרִיבוֹ לִפְנֵי יְהוָה וְכִפֶּר עָלֶיהָ וְטָהֲרָה
מִמְּקֹר דָּמֶיהָ זֹאת תּוֹרַת הַיֹּלֶדֶת לַזָּכָר אוֹ
לַנְּקֵבָה׃ 8 וְאִם־לֹא תִמְצָא יָדָהּ דֵּי שֶׂה
וְלָקְחָה שְׁתֵּי־תֹרִים אוֹ שְׁנֵי בְּנֵי יוֹנָה אֶחָד
לְעֹלָה וְאֶחָד לְחַטָּאת וְכִפֶּר עָלֶיהָ הַכֹּהֵן
וְטָהֵרָה׃ פ

יג וַיְדַבֵּר יְהוָה אֶל־מֹשֶׁה וְאֶל־אַהֲרֹן
לֵאמֹר׃
2 אָדָם כִּי־יִהְיֶה בְעוֹר־בְּשָׂרוֹ שְׂאֵת אוֹ־

the sanctuary of the impurity generated by the mother's severe discharge; blood from the sacrifice serves as a ritual detergent (see Leviticus 4). Thus, while human blood or discharge is a source of impurity, the blood of an animal sacrifice is what counteracts its effect on the sphere of holiness.

7. ***she shall then be pure from her flow of blood.*** The passage of time, the offering of sacrifices, and perhaps a ritual bathing (unwritten but apparently assumed) all contribute to her renewed ability to touch and eat sacred food and enter holy space. [To generalize, Leviticus presumes that women have access to sacred space whenever they are ritually pure. —*Ed.*]

***8.*** Provisions for a reduction in the cost of the sacrifice for the poor are found elsewhere in the Torah as well (5:7, 11; 14:21). Otherwise, poor Israelites would have had no means to eliminate impurity.

## *Laws for Diagnosing and Containing Skin Diseases* (13:1–59)

For a long time, biblical *tzaraat* has been equated with leprosy (also called Hansen's Disease), but such a view is mistaken. This unit expects the skin eruptions that it describes to change in appearance or disappear at the end of seven or fourteen days (13:6–8, 27, 35–36), unlike what is known as leprosy today. The Torah appears to group together under the term *tzaraat* at least three different diseases that cause scaly or discolored skin: probably psoriasis, favus (a fungus infection), and vitiligo. These three conditions, however, do not change appreciably or disappear over the course of a week or two, which leads some scholars to hesitate in making a certain identification with *tzaraat*.

Modern translations use various terms for *tzaraat* (sometimes inconsistently), including "scaly affection," "affection," "eruption," "scale disease," and "leprosy." Leviticus focuses on the appearance of the disease, not only upon the human body, but also upon fabrics, leather, and houses (13:47–59, 14:33–53). That is, Leviticus is primarily concerned not with the disease but with its manifestation.

Numbers 12 helps explain why the appearance of *tzaraat* causes its inclusion in the Torah's system of impurities. There, Miriam and Aaron, Moses' older siblings, criticize Moses on account of his Cushite wife and dispute Moses' preeminence as a prophet. God punishes Miriam; and she becomes stricken with *tzaraat* that is "as snow," a reference to its whiteness or its flaky nature. Aaron then pleads with Moses on her behalf: "Let her not be as a stillbirth, who emerges from its mother's womb with its flesh half-eaten away!" (12:12). Thus, the person afflicted with *tzaraat* seems like a decomposing corpse, as the skin has the appearance of wasting away. This accords with the suggestion (see the introduction, p. 637) that the common feature

swelling, a rash, or a discoloration, and it develops into a scaly affection on the skin of the body, it shall be reported to Aaron the priest or to one of his sons, the priests. [3]The priest shall examine the affection on the skin of the body: if hair in the affected patch has turned white and the affection appears to be deeper than the skin of the body, it is a leprous affection; when the priest sees it, he shall pronounce the person impure. [4]But if it is a white discoloration on the skin of the body which does not appear to be deeper than the skin and the hair

סַפַּ֫חַת א֤וֹ בַהֶ֔רֶת וְהָיָ֥ה בְעוֹר־בְּשָׂר֖וֹ לְנֶ֣גַע
צָרָ֑עַת וְהוּבָא֙ אֶל־אַהֲרֹ֣ן הַכֹּהֵ֔ן א֛וֹ אֶל־
אַחַ֥ד מִבָּנָ֖יו הַכֹּהֲנִֽים׃ 3 וְרָאָ֣ה הַכֹּהֵ֣ן אֶת־
הַנֶּ֣גַע בְּעוֹר־הַ֠בָּשָׂר וְשֵׂעָ֨ר בַּנֶּ֜גַע הָפַ֣ךְ ׀ לָבָ֗ן
וּמַרְאֵ֤ה הַנֶּ֙גַע֙ עָמֹק֙ מֵע֣וֹר בְּשָׂר֔וֹ נֶ֥גַע צָרַ֖עַת
ה֑וּא וְרָאָ֥הוּ הַכֹּהֵ֖ן וְטִמֵּ֥א אֹתֽוֹ׃ 4 וְאִם־
בַּהֶ֣רֶת לְבָנָ֜ה הִ֗וא בְּע֣וֹר בְּשָׂר֔וֹ וְעָמֹק֙ אֵין־
מַרְאֶ֣הָ מִן־הָע֔וֹר וּשְׂעָרָ֖ה לֹא־הָפַ֣ךְ לָבָ֑ן

---

of all of the physical conditions that generate impurity is their association with death, a force antithetical to holiness.

The religions of the ancient Near East and ancient Greece regarded scale disease, like most maladies, as divine punishment, often for the violation of treaties. Numbers 12, along with II Kings 5 and II Kings 15 (II Chronicles 26), depicts *tzaraat* as a condition visited by God upon the sinner. In the case of Miriam, the Rabbis deduce that her sin is maligning Moses; they perceive the disease as the punishment for slander, among other sins. However, Leviticus never implies that the disease is a punishment from God. Rather, it refrains from imputing guilt to the affected individual and describes only the affliction and procedures for coping with its effect.

## SKIN DISEASES AND PROCEDURES FOR DIAGNOSING AND CONTAINING THEM (13:1–44)

*1.* Only Moses and Aaron initially receive the information concerning the diagnosis of scale disease. This contrasts with other legislation, which is to be conveyed to the people of Israel (compare 12:1 or 15:1–2). The priests descended from Aaron will be experts in the diagnosis and ritual treatment of *tzaraat* but not of other diseases, thus confirming the ritual—not medical—nature of the Torah's concern.

### *Shiny Marks* (13:1–8)

*2.* ***person.*** Heb. *adam,* which refers to both men and women (see Genesis 5:2, where God identifies both woman and man as *adam*). Miriam's case in Numbers 12 demonstrates that women can be afflicted (see also below, vv. 29, 38).

***and it develops into a scaly affection.*** If the initial eruptions grow, they may qualify as a "scaly affection" (*nega tzaraat*). In Hebrew *nega,* "affection" (literally "touch") always refers to a divine punishment in other biblical books (Genesis 12:17; Exodus 11:1; II Kings 15:5), but Leviticus never presents the affliction as punishment.

*3.* For a positive diagnosis of the disease, the hair in the affected patch of skin must also appear white, while the area must appear sunken compared to the skin around it.

***leprous.*** [Here the original JPS translators note: "Where a human being is declared impure by reason of *tzaraat,* the traditional translation 'leprosy' has been retained without regard to modern medical terminology." The reason for doing so, according to a member of the translation committee, was "to convey the horror that the Bible attaches to this affliction." —*Ed.*]

in it has not turned white, the priest shall isolate the affected person for seven days. [5]On the seventh day the priest shall conduct an examination, and if the affection has remained unchanged in color and the disease has not spread on the skin, the priest shall isolate that person for another seven days. [6]On the seventh day the priest shall again conduct an examination: if the affection has faded and has not spread on the skin, the priest shall pronounce the person pure. It is a rash; after washing those clothes, that person shall be pure. [7]But if the rash should spread on the skin after the person has been seen by the priest and pronounced pure, that person shall again report to the priest. [8]And if the priest sees that the rash has spread on the skin, the priest shall pronounce that person impure; it is leprosy.

[9]When a person has a scaly affection, it shall be reported to the priest. [10]If the priest finds on the skin a white swelling which has turned some hair white, with a patch of undiscolored flesh in the swelling, [11]it is chronic leprosy on the skin of the body, and the priest shall pronounce the person impure; being impure, that person need not be isolated. [12]If the eruption spreads out over the skin so that it covers all the skin of the affected person from head to foot, wherever the priest can see—[13]if the priest sees that the eruption has covered the whole body—he shall pronounce as pure the affected person, who is pure from having turned all white. [14]But as soon as undiscolored flesh appears in it,

וְהִסְגִּיר הַכֹּהֵן אֶת־הַנֶּגַע שִׁבְעַת יָמִים׃
5 וְרָאָהוּ הַכֹּהֵן בַּיּוֹם הַשְּׁבִיעִי וְהִנֵּה הַנֶּגַע
עָמַד בְּעֵינָיו לֹא־פָשָׂה הַנֶּגַע בָּעוֹר וְהִסְגִּירוֹ
הַכֹּהֵן שִׁבְעַת יָמִים שֵׁנִית׃ 6 וְרָאָה הַכֹּהֵן
אֹתוֹ בַּיּוֹם הַשְּׁבִיעִי שֵׁנִית וְהִנֵּה כֵּהָה הַנֶּגַע
וְלֹא־פָשָׂה הַנֶּגַע בָּעוֹר וְטִהֲרוֹ הַכֹּהֵן
מִסְפַּחַת הִוא וְכִבֶּס בְּגָדָיו וְטָהֵר׃ 7 וְאִם־
פָּשֹׂה תִפְשֶׂה הַמִּסְפַּחַת בָּעוֹר אַחֲרֵי
הֵרָאֹתוֹ אֶל־הַכֹּהֵן לְטָהֳרָתוֹ וְנִרְאָה שֵׁנִית
אֶל־הַכֹּהֵן׃ 8 וְרָאָה הַכֹּהֵן וְהִנֵּה פָּשְׂתָה
הַמִּסְפַּחַת בָּעוֹר וְטִמְּאוֹ הַכֹּהֵן צָרַעַת
הִוא׃ פ
9 נֶגַע צָרַעַת כִּי תִהְיֶה בְּאָדָם וְהוּבָא אֶל־
הַכֹּהֵן׃ 10 וְרָאָה הַכֹּהֵן וְהִנֵּה שְׂאֵת־לְבָנָה
בָּעוֹר וְהִיא הָפְכָה שֵׂעָר לָבָן וּמִחְיַת בָּשָׂר
חַי בַּשְׂאֵת׃ 11 צָרַעַת נוֹשֶׁנֶת הִוא בְּעוֹר
בְּשָׂרוֹ וְטִמְּאוֹ הַכֹּהֵן לֹא יַסְגִּרֶנּוּ כִּי טָמֵא
הוּא׃ 12 וְאִם־פָּרוֹחַ תִּפְרַח הַצָּרַעַת בָּעוֹר
וְכִסְּתָה הַצָּרַעַת אֵת כָּל־עוֹר הַנֶּגַע מֵרֹאשׁוֹ
וְעַד־רַגְלָיו לְכָל־מַרְאֵה עֵינֵי הַכֹּהֵן׃
13 וְרָאָה הַכֹּהֵן וְהִנֵּה כִסְּתָה הַצָּרַעַת אֶת־
כָּל־בְּשָׂרוֹ וְטִהַר אֶת־הַנֶּגַע כֻּלּוֹ הָפַךְ לָבָן
טָהוֹר הוּא׃ 14 וּבְיוֹם הֵרָאוֹת בּוֹ בָּשָׂר חַי

*4. the priest shall isolate the affected person for seven days.* If the diagnosis is uncertain, the individual is quarantined. The priestly writers seem to advocate special quarters for the afflicted, probably outside the camp for the wilderness period and other quarters, after Israel's settlement in the land of Canaan.

*6.* If the infection has not increased, the priest will declare the person ritually pure. Seclusion ends after the laundering of clothes and perhaps immersion.

*8. the priest shall pronounce that person impure; it is leprosy.* Alternatively, if the infection has spread after the initial examination, the diagnosis is certain; so when the infection ceases, the individual must undergo the complex ritual described in 14:1–32.

### *Discolorations* (13:9–17)

This passage expands the previous criteria for diagnosis but adds a new element, the appearance of a "patch of undiscolored flesh" (v. 10).

that person shall be impure; 15when the priest sees
the undiscolored flesh, he shall pronounce the person impure. The undiscolored flesh is impure; it is
leprosy. 16But if the undiscolored flesh again turns
white, that person shall come to the priest, 17and
the priest shall conduct an examination: if the affection has turned white, the priest shall pronounce
as pure the affected person, who is then pure.

18When an inflammation appears on the skin of
one's body and it heals, 19and a white swelling or
a white discoloration streaked with red develops
where the inflammation was, that person shall report to the priest. 20If the priest finds that it appears
lower than the rest of the skin and that the hair
in it has turned white, the priest shall pronounce
the person impure; it is a leprous affection that has
broken out in the inflammation. 21But if the priest
finds that there is no white hair in it and it is not
lower than the rest of the skin, and it is faded, the
priest shall isolate that person for seven days. 22If
it should spread in the skin, the priest shall pronounce the person impure; it is an affection. 23But
if the discoloration remains stationary, not having
spread, it is the scar of the inflammation; the priest
shall pronounce that person pure.

24When the skin of one's body sustains a burn
by fire, and the patch from the burn is a discoloration, either white streaked with red, or white, 25the
priest shall examine it. If some hair has turned
white in the discoloration, which itself appears to
go deeper than the skin, it is leprosy that has
broken out in the burn. The priest shall pronounce
the person impure; it is a leprous affection. 26But if
the priest finds that there is no white hair in the
discoloration, and that it is not lower than the rest

יִטְמָא׃ 15 וְרָאָה הַכֹּהֵן אֶת־הַבָּשָׂר הַחַי
וְטִמְּאוֹ הַבָּשָׂר הַחַי טָמֵא הוּא צָרַעַת הוּא׃
16 אוֹ כִי יָשׁוּב הַבָּשָׂר הַחַי וְנֶהְפַּךְ לְלָבָן
וּבָא אֶל־הַכֹּהֵן׃ 17 וְרָאָהוּ הַכֹּהֵן וְהִנֵּה
נֶהְפַּךְ הַנֶּגַע לְלָבָן וְטִהַר הַכֹּהֵן אֶת־הַנֶּגַע
טָהוֹר הוּא׃ פ

18 וּבָשָׂר כִּי־יִהְיֶה בוֹ־בְעֹרוֹ שְׁחִין וְנִרְפָּא׃
19 וְהָיָה בִּמְקוֹם הַשְּׁחִין שְׂאֵת לְבָנָה אוֹ
בַהֶרֶת לְבָנָה אֲדַמְדָּמֶת וְנִרְאָה אֶל־הַכֹּהֵן׃
20 וְרָאָה הַכֹּהֵן וְהִנֵּה מַרְאֶהָ שָׁפָל מִן־הָעוֹר
וּשְׂעָרָהּ הָפַךְ לָבָן וְטִמְּאוֹ הַכֹּהֵן נֶגַע־צָרַעַת
הִוא בַּשְּׁחִין פָּרָחָה׃ 21 וְאִם ׀ יִרְאֶנָּה הַכֹּהֵן
וְהִנֵּה אֵין־בָּהּ שֵׂעָר לָבָן וּשְׁפָלָה אֵינֶנָּה מִן־
הָעוֹר וְהִיא כֵהָה וְהִסְגִּירוֹ הַכֹּהֵן שִׁבְעַת
יָמִים׃ 22 וְאִם־פָּשֹׂה תִפְשֶׂה בָּעוֹר וְטִמֵּא
הַכֹּהֵן אֹתוֹ נֶגַע הִוא׃ 23 וְאִם־תַּחְתֶּיהָ
תַּעֲמֹד הַבַּהֶרֶת לֹא פָשָׂתָה צָרֶבֶת הַשְּׁחִין
הִוא וְטִהֲרוֹ הַכֹּהֵן׃ ס

24 אוֹ בָשָׂר כִּי־יִהְיֶה בְעֹרוֹ מִכְוַת־אֵשׁ
וְהָיְתָה מִחְיַת הַמִּכְוָה בַּהֶרֶת לְבָנָה
אֲדַמְדֶּמֶת אוֹ לְבָנָה׃ 25 וְרָאָה אֹתָהּ הַכֹּהֵן
וְהִנֵּה נֶהְפַּךְ שֵׂעָר לָבָן בַּבַּהֶרֶת וּמַרְאֶהָ עָמֹק
מִן־הָעוֹר צָרַעַת הִוא בַּמִּכְוָה פָּרָחָה וְטִמֵּא
אֹתוֹ הַכֹּהֵן נֶגַע צָרַעַת הִוא׃ 26 וְאִם ׀
יִרְאֶנָּה הַכֹּהֵן וְהִנֵּה אֵין־בַּבַּהֶרֶת שֵׂעָר לָבָן

*Boils* (13:18–23)

In this passage, *tzaraat* appears as a complication of a boil that has already healed; again, the priest uses criteria similar to the above cases in order to declare the infected individual pure or impure.

*Burns* (13:24–28)

In this passage, scale disease appears as a secondary development in a burn.

*24. patch from the burn.* The Hebrew here is uncertain.

of the skin, and it is faded, the priest shall isolate that person for seven days. 27 On the seventh day the priest shall conduct an examination: if it has spread in the skin, the priest shall pronounce the person impure; it is a leprous affection. 28 But if the discoloration has remained stationary, not having spread on the skin, and it is faded, it is the swelling from the burn. The priest shall pronounce that person pure, for it is the scar of the burn.

29 If a man or a woman has an affection on the head or in the beard, 30 the priest shall examine the affection. If it appears to go deeper than the skin and there is thin yellow hair in it, the priest shall pronounce the person impure; it is a scall, a scaly eruption in the hair or beard. 31 But if the priest finds that the scall affection does not appear to go deeper than the skin, yet there is no black hair in it, the priest shall isolate the person with the scall affection for seven days. 32 On the seventh day the priest shall examine the affection. If the scall has not spread and no yellow hair has appeared in it, and the scall does not appear to go deeper than the skin, 33 the person with the scall shall shave—but without shaving the scall; the priest shall isolate that person for another seven days. 34 On the seventh day the priest shall examine the scall. If the scall has not spread on the skin, and does not appear to go deeper than the skin, the priest shall pronounce the person pure; after washing those clothes, that person shall be pure. 35 If, however, the scall should spread on the skin after the person has been pronounced pure, 36 the priest shall conduct an exami-

וּשְׁפָלָה אֵינֶנָּה מִן־הָעוֹר וְהִוא כֵהָה
וְהִסְגִּירוֹ הַכֹּהֵן שִׁבְעַת יָמִים׃ 27 וְרָאָהוּ
הַכֹּהֵן בַּיּוֹם הַשְּׁבִיעִי אִם־פָּשֹׂה תִפְשֶׂה
בָּעוֹר וְטִמֵּא הַכֹּהֵן אֹתוֹ נֶגַע צָרַעַת הִוא׃
28 וְאִם־תַּחְתֶּיהָ תַעֲמֹד הַבַּהֶרֶת לֹא־פָשְׂתָה
בָעוֹר וְהִוא כֵהָה שְׂאֵת הַמִּכְוָה הִוא וְטִהֲרוֹ
הַכֹּהֵן כִּי־צָרֶבֶת הַמִּכְוָה הִוא׃ פ
29 וְאִישׁ אוֹ אִשָּׁה כִּי־יִהְיֶה בוֹ נָגַע בְּרֹאשׁ
אוֹ בְזָקָן׃ 30 וְרָאָה הַכֹּהֵן אֶת־הַנֶּגַע וְהִנֵּה
מַרְאֵהוּ עָמֹק מִן־הָעוֹר וּבוֹ שֵׂעָר צָהֹב דָּק
וְטִמֵּא אֹתוֹ הַכֹּהֵן נֶתֶק הוּא צָרַעַת הָרֹאשׁ
אוֹ הַזָּקָן הוּא׃ 31 וְכִי־יִרְאֶה הַכֹּהֵן אֶת־נֶגַע
הַנֶּתֶק וְהִנֵּה אֵין־מַרְאֵהוּ עָמֹק מִן־הָעוֹר
וְשֵׂעָר שָׁחֹר אֵין בּוֹ וְהִסְגִּיר הַכֹּהֵן אֶת־נֶגַע
הַנֶּתֶק שִׁבְעַת יָמִים׃ 32 וְרָאָה הַכֹּהֵן אֶת־
הַנֶּגַע בַּיּוֹם הַשְּׁבִיעִי וְהִנֵּה לֹא־פָשָׂה הַנֶּתֶק
וְלֹא־הָיָה בוֹ שֵׂעָר צָהֹב וּמַרְאֵה הַנֶּתֶק
אֵין עָמֹק מִן־הָעוֹר׃ 33 וְהִתְגַּלָּח וְאֶת־
הַנֶּתֶק לֹא יְגַלֵּחַ וְהִסְגִּיר הַכֹּהֵן אֶת־הַנֶּתֶק
שִׁבְעַת יָמִים שֵׁנִית׃ 34 וְרָאָה הַכֹּהֵן אֶת־
הַנֶּתֶק בַּיּוֹם הַשְּׁבִיעִי וְהִנֵּה לֹא־פָשָׂה
הַנֶּתֶק בָּעוֹר וּמַרְאֵהוּ אֵינֶנּוּ עָמֹק מִן־הָעוֹר
וְטִהַר אֹתוֹ הַכֹּהֵן וְכִבֶּס בְּגָדָיו וְטָהֵר׃
35 וְאִם־פָּשֹׂה יִפְשֶׂה הַנֶּתֶק בָּעוֹר אַחֲרֵי
טָהֳרָתוֹ׃ 36 וְרָאָהוּ הַכֹּהֵן וְהִנֵּה פָּשָׂה הַנֶּתֶק

*Infection of the Scalp or Beard* (13:29–37)

Some moderns identify the condition with favus, a contagious skin disease caused by a fungus. Another possibility is that chronic protein deficiency has turned the normal hair color to a lighter shade.

*31.* If there were black hair growing in the suspect patch of skin, the priest would have declared the individual pure, as yellow hair is characteristic of the disease. Thus, the priest isolates the person for seven days. Perhaps one can derive from the mention of black hair as the healthy norm that there were few or no blonds or redheads among the ancient Israelites, a possibility suggested by ancient Egyptian wall paintings that depict visiting Semites as black-haired.

nation. If the scall has spread on the skin, the priest need not look for yellow hair: the person is impure. [37]But if the scall has remained unchanged in color, and black hair has grown in it, the scall is healed; the person is pure. The priest shall pronounce that person pure.

[38]If a man or a woman has the skin of the body streaked with white discolorations, [39]and the priest sees that the discolorations on the skin of the body are of a dull white, it is a tetter broken out on the skin; that person is pure.

[40]If a man loses the hair of his head and becomes bald, he is pure. [41]If he loses the hair on the front part of his head and becomes bald at the forehead, he is pure. [42]But if a white affection streaked with red appears on the bald part in the front or at the back of the head, it is a scaly eruption that is spreading over the bald part in the front or at the back of the head. [43]The priest shall examine him: if the swollen affection on the bald part in the front or at the back of his head is white streaked with red, like the leprosy of body skin in appearance, [44]he is among the leprous; he is impure. The priest shall pronounce him impure; he has the affection on his head.

[45]As for the person with a leprous affection: the clothes shall be rent, the head shall be left bare, and

בָּעוֹר לֹא־יְבַקֵּר הַכֹּהֵן לַשֵּׂעָר הַצָּהֹב טָמֵא
הוּא׃ 37 וְאִם־בְּעֵינָיו עָמַד הַנֶּתֶק וְשֵׂעָר
שָׁחֹר צָמַח־בּוֹ נִרְפָּא הַנֶּתֶק טָהוֹר הוּא
וְטִהֲרוֹ הַכֹּהֵן׃ ס
38 וְאִישׁ אוֹ־אִשָּׁה כִּי־יִהְיֶה בְעוֹר־בְּשָׂרָם
בֶּהָרֹת בֶּהָרֹת לְבָנֹת׃ 39 וְרָאָה הַכֹּהֵן וְהִנֵּה
בְעוֹר־בְּשָׂרָם בֶּהָרֹת כֵּהוֹת לְבָנֹת בֹּהַק הוּא
פָּרַח בָּעוֹר טָהוֹר הוּא׃ ס
40 וְאִישׁ כִּי יִמָּרֵט רֹאשׁוֹ קֵרֵחַ הוּא טָהוֹר
הוּא׃ 41 וְאִם מִפְּאַת פָּנָיו יִמָּרֵט רֹאשׁוֹ גִּבֵּחַ
הוּא טָהוֹר הוּא׃ 42 וְכִי־יִהְיֶה בַקָּרַחַת אוֹ
בַגַּבַּחַת נֶגַע לָבָן אֲדַמְדָּם צָרַעַת פֹּרַחַת
הִוא בְּקָרַחְתּוֹ אוֹ בְגַבַּחְתּוֹ׃ 43 וְרָאָה אֹתוֹ
הַכֹּהֵן וְהִנֵּה שְׂאֵת־הַנֶּגַע לְבָנָה אֲדַמְדֶּמֶת
בְּקָרַחְתּוֹ אוֹ בְגַבַּחְתּוֹ כְּמַרְאֵה צָרַעַת עוֹר
בָּשָׂר׃ 44 אִישׁ־צָרוּעַ הוּא טָמֵא הוּא טַמֵּא
יְטַמְּאֶנּוּ הַכֹּהֵן בְּרֹאשׁוֹ נִגְעוֹ׃
45 וְהַצָּרוּעַ אֲשֶׁר־בּוֹ הַנֶּגַע בְּגָדָיו יִהְיוּ
פְרֻמִים וְרֹאשׁוֹ יִהְיֶה פָרוּעַ וְעַל־שָׂפָם

### *Vitiligo* (13:38–39)

Some moderns identify this condition with vitiligo or leukoderma, which involves a deficiency in pigment. The Torah cautions the priest, however, that this condition should not be mistaken for *tzaraat*; and so the individual is declared pure.

### *Baldness* (13:40–44)

Biblical Hebrew has two terms for baldness. One refers to baldness at the top and back of the head, while the other refers to baldness at the front of the head or forehead.

### RESTRICTIONS FOR THE PERSON WITH SCALE DISEASE (13:45–46)

We learned above that the person with a suspected case of scale disease is confined or excluded from normal social relations, but now we see additional restrictions placed upon the woman or man judged by the priest to be impure.

***45. the clothes shall be rent, the head shall be left bare.*** The first restriction is that the afflicted person should go about in ripped clothes. The second restriction means that the person's hair shall be *parua*, that is, disheveled. Both of these are indica-

the upper lip shall be covered over; and that person shall call out, "Impure! Impure!" [46]The person shall be impure as long as the disease is present. Being impure, that person shall dwell apart—in a dwelling outside the camp.

[47]When an eruptive affection occurs in a cloth of wool or linen fabric, [48]in the warp or in the woof of the linen or the wool, or in a skin or in anything made of skin; [49]if the affection in the cloth or the skin, in the warp or the woof, or in any article of skin, is streaky green or red, it is an eruptive affection. It shall be shown to the priest; [50]and the priest, after examining the affection, shall isolate the affected article for seven days. [51]On the seventh day he shall examine the affection: if the affection has spread in the cloth—whether in the warp or the

יַעְטֶ֖ה וְטָמֵ֥א ׀ טָמֵ֖א יִקְרָֽא׃ 46 כָּל־יְמֵ֞י אֲשֶׁ֨ר הַנֶּ֥גַע בּ֛וֹ יִטְמָ֖א טָמֵ֣א ה֑וּא בָּדָ֣ד יֵשֵׁ֔ב מִח֥וּץ לַֽמַּחֲנֶ֖ה מוֹשָׁבֽוֹ׃ ס

47 וְהַבֶּ֕גֶד כִּֽי־יִהְיֶ֥ה ב֖וֹ נֶ֣גַע צָרָ֑עַת בְּבֶ֣גֶד צֶ֔מֶר א֖וֹ בְּבֶ֥גֶד פִּשְׁתִּֽים׃ 48 א֤וֹ בִֽשְׁתִי֙ א֣וֹ בְעֵ֔רֶב לַפִּשְׁתִּ֖ים וְלַצָּ֑מֶר א֣וֹ בְע֔וֹר א֖וֹ בְּכָל־ מְלֶ֥אכֶת עֽוֹר׃ 49 וְהָיָ֨ה הַנֶּ֜גַע יְרַקְרַ֣ק ׀ א֣וֹ אֲדַמְדָּ֗ם בַּבֶּ֩גֶד֩ א֨וֹ בָע֜וֹר אֽוֹ־בַשְּׁתִ֤י אֽוֹ־ בָעֵ֙רֶב֙ א֣וֹ בְכָל־כְּלִי־ע֔וֹר נֶ֥גַע צָרַ֖עַת ה֑וּא וְהָרְאָ֖ה אֶת־הַכֹּהֵֽן׃ 50 וְרָאָ֥ה הַכֹּהֵ֖ן אֶת־ הַנָּ֑גַע וְהִסְגִּ֥יר אֶת־הַנֶּ֖גַע שִׁבְעַ֥ת יָמִֽים׃ 51 וְרָאָ֨ה אֶת־הַנֶּ֜גַע בַּיּ֣וֹם הַשְּׁבִיעִ֗י כִּֽי־ פָשָׂ֤ה הַנֶּ֙גַע֙ בַּבֶּ֔גֶד אֽוֹ־בַשְּׁתִ֥י אֽוֹ־בָעֵ֖רֶב א֥וֹ

tors of a person in mourning (see 10:6). Compare Numbers 5:18, where a priest dishevels the hair of a woman accused (without evidence) of adultery.

*the upper lip shall be covered.* This requirement may reflect the belief that the person afflicted with scale disease is able to contaminate others with her or his breath, an indicator of the power attributed to the impurity of *tzaraat.*

*"Impure! Impure!"* A warning for people to avoid the afflicted person, presumably so that they will not be rendered impure by touch or breath.

*46.* The individual's isolation is not simply because scaly disease is deemed contagious, but also because of the fear that impurity would spread from the afflicted party to pure persons in the same structure. The impurity of scale disease and of corpses share the ability to pollute others under the same roof (see Numbers 19:14). If the afflicted party remains in the community, others unaware of the impurity might enter the same structure. If that second individual then enters the sanctuary or eats sacred food, this would bring ritual impurity into a sacred context, leading to potentially disastrous consequences.

## INFECTION OF FABRICS AND OF ARTICLES MADE OF SKIN (13:47–59)

The Torah juxtaposes people with fabric or leather because *tzaraat* can afflict both. While *tzaraat* refers to scale disease when it afflicts persons, in the present context it seems appropriate to understand *tzaraat* as mold or fungus. The Torah nowhere indicates that the infection of the garment is the by-product of its owner's *tzaraat.*

*47.* Wool and linen fabrics are the only types mentioned because these were by far the most common in ancient Israel; cotton and silk were still extremely rare. (The mention of fabric calls women to mind, for typically it was women who produced fabrics; see *T'rumah,* Another View, p. 467; at Exodus 35:25–26; and *P'kudei,* Another View, p. 560.)

*48. in a skin or in anything made of skin.* The Israelites used leather for sandals and belts, an occasional loincloth (II Kings 1:8), vessels for liquids (Genesis 21:14), a writing surface (perhaps Jeremiah 36), and a covering for tents (Exodus 26:14).

woof, or in the skin, for whatever purpose the skin may be used—the affection is a malignant eruption; it is impure. 52 The cloth—whether warp or woof in wool or linen, or any article of skin—in which the affection is found, shall be burned, for it is a malignant eruption; it shall be consumed in fire. 53 But if the priest sees that the affection in the cloth—whether in warp or in woof, or in any article of skin—has not spread, 54 the priest shall order the affected article washed, and he shall isolate it for another seven days. 55 And if, after the affected article has been washed, the priest sees that the affection has not changed color and that it has not spread, it is impure. It shall be consumed in fire; it is a fret, whether on its inner side or on its outer side. 56 But if the priest sees that the affected part, after it has been washed, is faded, he shall tear it out from the cloth or skin, whether in the warp or in the woof; 57 and if it occurs again in the cloth—whether in warp or in woof—or in any article of skin, it is a wild growth; the affected article shall be consumed in fire. 58 If, however, the affection disappears from the cloth—warp or woof—or from any article of skin that has been washed, it shall be washed again, and it shall be pure.

59 Such is the procedure for eruptive affections of cloth, woolen or linen, in warp or in woof, or of any article of skin, for pronouncing it pure or impure.

בָּע֔וֹר לְכֹ֛ל אֲשֶׁר־יֵעָשֶׂ֥ה הָע֖וֹר לִמְלָאכָ֑ה
צָרַ֧עַת מַמְאֶ֛רֶת הַנֶּ֖גַע טָמֵ֥א הֽוּא׃ 52 וְשָׂרַ֨ף
אֶת־הַבֶּ֜גֶד א֣וֹ אֶת־הַשְּׁתִ֣י ׀ א֣וֹ אֶת־הָעֵ֗רֶב
בַּצֶּ֙מֶר֙ א֣וֹ בַפִּשְׁתִּ֔ים א֚וֹ אֶת־כׇּל־כְּלִ֣י הָע֔וֹר
אֲשֶׁר־יִהְיֶ֥ה ב֖וֹ הַנָּ֑גַע כִּֽי־צָרַ֤עַת מַמְאֶ֙רֶת֙
הִ֔וא בָּאֵ֖שׁ תִּשָּׂרֵֽף׃ 53 וְאִם֙ יִרְאֶ֣ה הַכֹּהֵ֔ן
וְהִנֵּה֙ לֹא־פָשָׂ֣ה הַנֶּ֔גַע בַּבֶּ֑גֶד א֥וֹ בַשְּׁתִ֖י א֥וֹ
בָעֵ֑רֶב א֖וֹ בְּכׇל־כְּלִי־עֽוֹר׃ 54 וְצִוָּה֙ הַכֹּהֵ֔ן
וְכִ֨בְּס֔וּ אֵ֥ת אֲשֶׁר־בּ֖וֹ הַנָּ֑גַע וְהִסְגִּיר֥וֹ שִׁבְעַֽת־
יָמִ֖ים שֵׁנִֽית׃ 55 וְרָאָ֨ה הַכֹּהֵ֜ן אַחֲרֵ֣י ׀ הֻכַּבֵּ֣ס
אֶת־הַנֶּ֗גַע וְ֠הִנֵּה לֹא־הָפַ֨ךְ הַנֶּ֤גַע אֶת־עֵינוֹ֙
וְהַנֶּ֣גַע לֹא־פָשָׂ֔ה טָמֵ֣א ה֔וּא בָּאֵ֖שׁ תִּשְׂרְפֶ֑נּוּ
פְּחֶ֣תֶת הִ֔וא בְּקָרַחְתּ֖וֹ א֥וֹ בְגַבַּחְתּֽוֹ׃ 56 וְאִם֙
רָאָ֣ה הַכֹּהֵ֔ן וְהִנֵּה֙ כֵּהָ֣ה הַנֶּ֔גַע אַחֲרֵ֖י הֻכַּבֵּ֣ס
אֹת֑וֹ וְקָרַ֣ע אֹת֗וֹ מִן־הַבֶּ֙גֶד֙ א֣וֹ מִן־הָע֔וֹר א֥וֹ
מִן־הַשְּׁתִ֖י א֥וֹ מִן־הָעֵֽרֶב׃ 57 וְאִם־תֵּרָאֶ֨ה
ע֜וֹד בַּבֶּ֗גֶד אֽוֹ־בַשְּׁתִ֤י אֽוֹ־בָעֵ֙רֶב֙ א֣וֹ בְכׇל־
כְּלִי־ע֔וֹר פֹּרַ֖חַת הִ֑וא בָּאֵ֣שׁ תִּשְׂרְפֶ֔נּוּ אֵ֥ת
אֲשֶׁר־בּ֖וֹ הַנָּֽגַע׃ 58 וְהַבֶּ֡גֶד אֽוֹ־הַשְּׁתִ֨י אֽוֹ־
הָעֵ֜רֶב אֽוֹ־כׇל־כְּלִ֤י הָעוֹר֙ אֲשֶׁ֣ר תְּכַבֵּ֔ס וְסָ֥ר
מֵהֶ֖ם הַנָּ֑גַע וְכֻבַּ֥ס שֵׁנִ֖ית וְטָהֵֽר׃
59 זֹ֡את תּוֹרַ֣ת נֶֽגַע־צָרַ֩עַת֩ בֶּ֨גֶד הַצֶּ֜מֶר ׀ א֣וֹ
הַפִּשְׁתִּ֗ים א֤וֹ הַשְּׁתִי֙ א֣וֹ הָעֵ֔רֶב א֖וֹ כׇּל־כְּלִי־
ע֑וֹר לְטַהֲר֖וֹ א֥וֹ לְטַמְּאֽוֹ׃ פ

*52.* If the mold eruption has spread, it is considered an acute or malignant case, and so the article's owner must destroy it by burning.

*56.* ***he shall tear it out from the cloth or skin.*** If, after laundering, the affected section is faded, this part alone may be torn away and the rest of the article retained. Clearly, economic considerations play a role in this injunction, for there are poor individuals who own only one garment or cloak, which also serves as a blanket for sleep (see Exodus 22:26, Deuteronomy 24:12–13).

*—Elaine Goodfriend*

# Another View

PARASHAT TAZRIA CONTAINS one of the most puzzling, even disturbing, passages in Leviticus, a book concerned with holiness. *Tazria* challenges us, for it places childbirth among the sources of ritual impurity—from which one then needs purification (12:1–8)—and it reckons the birth of a daughter at twice the length of impurity as the birth of a son (12:2, 4–5). In Leviticus, the commandment of purification after childbirth is consistent with the priestly insistence that blood contains or represents the life force. The priestly authors of Leviticus believe that blood, whether menstrual or post-partum, is so powerful as a source of life that only purification rituals can allow those who come into contact with it to rejoin their community. These rituals serve to contain the life force that places contaminated people outside the normative community, by returning them to a state of purity in which they can reenter God's holy community.

Regardless of whether a woman bears a son or a daughter, the rituals of purification are the same. Why, then must a woman spend twice as long in a state of impurity following the birth of a girl than following the birth of a boy? Traditional interpreters have assumed that this is because the birth of a girl creates a kind of double impurity, possibly because newborn girls contain the latent capacity for menstruation and reproduction. But another point is also important here: in ancient Israel, baby girls arguably faced lives filled with more risks than did baby boys. Israel was a society in which economic value accrued primarily to sons. They remained part of their fathers' households even when they married, inherited their families' ancestral lands, and cared for their aging parents. In contrast, there is evidence to suggest that girls were sometimes thought of as expendable. In times of need, famine, and war, baby girls might suffer hunger and neglect, or even be abandoned and left to die.

*This troubling passage can be understood as a way to promote God's loving community.*

The priestly authors seem to be concerned about this situation and try to avert such tragedies by ensuring that baby girls stay in their mothers' protective care for an extended period of time. This not only allows mother and daughter to bond tightly, but also ensures that the child is nursed and cared for. Thus, this troubling passage can be understood not as discrimination against women but as a way to promote God's loving community—and to guarantee that women and men, both created in the divine image, are nurtured and protected.

—*Beth Alpert Nakhai*

# Post-biblical Interpretations

***a woman at childbirth*** (12:2). The literal meaning of the word *tazria*, translated here as "at childbirth," is that the woman "produces seed." The talmudic rabbis—who had much to say about matters of conception, pregnancy, the formation of the embryo, and birth—played upon such a reading when some of them held that both woman and man can emit "seed." A statement in the Talmud, frequently repeated in medieval biblical commentaries, asserts that "if the woman emits her 'seed' first, she bears a male child; if the man emits his seed [semen] first, she bears a female child" (BT *Niddah* 25b, 28a, 31a; BT *B'rachot* 60a). Presumably this comment models female genital secretions after the male seminal emission. Among other proofs, the Rabbis cite the language in this verse (BT *Niddah* 31a). Based on this theory, some rabbis speculated on how men should conduct their sexual lives in order to produce offspring of the desired gender. These suggestions were later anthologized in the mystically inspired medieval sex manual *The Holy Letter*. Another area of rabbinic interest was the genetic material from which the embryo is made. One opinion in the Talmud suggests that "there are three partners in [the procreation of] a person: the blessed Holy One, the father, and the mother" (BT *Niddah* 31a). The father is said to supply the seed (*mazria*) of the body's white substances, such as bones, sinews, nails, the brain, and the white of the eye. The mother supplies the seed (*mazraat*) of what the Rabbis consider to be the red substances, such as skin, flesh, blood, and the pupil of the eye. And God gives the child its breath, along with beauty of feature, eyesight, the powers of hearing and speaking, the ability to walk, and intellectual capabilities.

*If the woman emits her "seed" first, she bears a male child.*

***If she bears a female, she shall be impure two weeks*** (12:5). Like modern commentators, the talmudic rabbis were puzzled by the doubling of the mother's status of ritual impurity following the birth of a daughter. Mishnah *Niddah* 3:7 touches on this question in a rabbinic disagreement about embryology. According to the opinion of Rabbi Ishmael, the male embryo is fully fashioned after forty-one days, while the female embryo requires eighty-one days. The Talmud suggests that Rabbi Ishmael deduces these numbers from our verse: 7 plus 33 days for a male embryo, completed on the forty-first day; and 14 plus 66 days for a female embryo, completed on the eighty-first day. (Early Greek scholars, such as Aristotle and Hippocrates, also assumed a slower development of the female embryo.) However, a majority of rabbis in this debate disagree and affirm the equal development of male and female embryos at forty-one days. Elsewhere, the Talmud (BT *B'rachot* 60a) considers whether, if the sex of the child is already determined at conception, it would be useful during the first forty days of a woman's pregnancy to pray that the child be male. According to Mishnah *B'rachot* 9:3, a prayer for a male baby at any point during pregnancy is to be considered "a vain prayer"; the Talmud, however, suggests that it may avail in certain circumstances if it is made in the first forty days of pregnancy.

***she shall bring . . . a purgation offering*** (12:6). Again, the rabbis of the Talmud wondered why the postpartum woman should have to bring a *chatat*-offering to the priest and why he would need to make expiation on her behalf. While modern translations and commentaries usually construe this particular *chatat*-offering as unrelated to prior sin, the Rabbis did not easily dismiss the usual connection of the *chatat*-offering with sin (see 4:1–5:13), even in the context of birth. As one tradition has it: "Rabbi Simeon ben Yohai was asked by his disciples: Why did the Torah ordain that a woman after childbirth should bring a sacrifice? He replied: When she kneels in bearing she swears spontaneously that she will have no more sex with her husband. The Torah, therefore ordained that she should bring a sacrifice" (BT *Niddah* 31b). This prompts some talmudic rabbis to a somewhat far-fetched explanation for the double length of the mother's impurity following the birth of a female child (see 12:5), based on the social attitudes of Jewish antiquity: They suggest that since everyone is happy about the birth of the boy, the mother quickly regrets her oath made while she was suffering the pains of labor; however, for a girl, whose birth prompts little celebration, regret at the oath does not set in for fourteen days (BT *Niddah* 31b). Elsewhere, however, the Talmud (BT *K'ritot* 26a) denies that the *chatat*-offering expiates the mother's supposed sin of an unintended oath, and instead emphasizes its purifying function, thus anticipating contemporary commentators.

—*Charlotte Elisheva Fonrobert*

# *Contemporary Reflection*

To PLUNGE INTO the *mikveh* (Jewish ritual bath) is to plunge into fresh connections with Creation and with our spirituality.

The Rabbis derived their laws that require an immersion in the *mikveh* in large measure from Leviticus (see at 12:1–8, 15:16, and 11:36). They rooted the laws in a need to purify oneself ritually after certain conditions such as menstruation, male seminal emission, certain skin diseases, or contact with the dead. Removing impurities was a precondition for coming into contact with the holy, such as in approaching the sanctuary. With the destruction of the Temple, these laws remained mandatory for women and optional for men (see *Sh'mini*, Post-biblical Interpretations, p. 630). While traditional Jews continue to use the *mikveh* for "family purity," most liberal Jews rarely enter the *mikveh*. When they do, they often enter the *mikveh* for different reasons. What might prompt liberal Jews to immerse in the *mikveh*'s waters?

*Creation.* The *mikveh* takes us back in time, as we immerse ourselves in the world of Creation. The root *k-v-h* that forms the word *mikveh* appears for the first time in Genesis (1:9): "Let the waters beneath the sky be collected [*yikavu*] in one place." Further, in the next verse emerges the expression *mikveh hamayim*, the name given to the seas, where *k-v-h* connotes "the gathering." This first *mikveh* is filled with *mayim* (water).

In the most archaic Hebrew script, the letter *mem* is a zigzagging line, drawn like waves that recall water. It is interesting to note that in many languages, the phoneme *"m"* is associated with "mother" (*ima, umm, mutter, mère, madre, mama*, etc.). The person who plunges into the ritual bath of the *mikveh*—entirely surrounded by water, nude, without any barriers, and without touching its sides—resembles the fetus in the mother's womb. The immersion in the *mikveh* becomes a return to the sensations of the uterus, a return to our source and an act of renewal.

You cannot know who you are without knowing whence you came. This return to what happened before is sometimes a way of softening the traumas of the past, to start anew after a difficult life experience. Conversely, sometimes it is a way to celebrate something precious in one's life or something new. The word *kav* means "to be strong" or "strength" in Aramaic. The return to our source reinforces us.

*The mikveh takes us back in time, as we immerse in the world of Creation.*

*Spirituality.* Water appears first in the second verse of the story of Creation: "God's spirit (*ruach*) glided over the face of the waters" (1:2). Thus, from the very beginning, water is forever linked to the divine, to the spiritual. Spirituality in relation to water is not necessarily about "purity." Purity was originally attached to the mission of the Temple; since the Temple exists no more, purification need not apply to contemporary immersion in the *mikveh*. Going to a *mikveh* is not only a means of washing away the past, of removing the legacy of some "sin," but also of preparing for the future. This is how the *mikveh* functions when used to prepare for Shabbat and holidays or important moments in life. In this case, *mikveh* is practiced by both women and men.

Traditional Jewish law requires that only women go to the *mikveh*. However, when the immersion in a *mikveh* is part of a couple's sexual life, if both partners go to the *mikveh*, they together assert that they are taking charge of their sex life. Making a visit to the *mikveh* a regular part of the cycle of a couple's sexual life does not imply a denial of sexuality, but rather a couple's decision to set temporal boundaries to their sexuality. Jewish tradition honors sexual impulses. The Talmud (BT *Yoma* 69b) tells us that without passion the world would cease to exist. However, sexuality, like water, must be channeled in order for life to flourish fully. Passion is exhilarating, but it is not a permanent condition. Moreover, it may gain in intensity when limits are set, as is true with music—where the silent notes underscore the melody. So it goes with sexuality: the downtime (which could be confined to menstruation in the case of women), punctuated by the *mikveh* utilized by both partners, is a form of suspension—a Sabbath—of sexuality. It can leave the space necessary to discover a different face of the other, in a more disciplined tension.

In Genesis 1, God creates the world by separating the waters and then withdrawing them to make space for earth and life to appear. The Akkadian root *ku'û* (one of the possible antecedents of the Hebrew word *kav*) means "to wait for, to stretch, to underscore the tension of enduring or waiting." Oscar Wilde said: "In this world there are only two tragedies; one is not getting what one wants, the other is getting it." Expectation is the romantic framework of love and desire. The *mikveh* reintroduces the other as a friend; the lover becomes a friend again—and the friend, a lover.

The *mikveh* likewise reintroduces spirituality into our lives in a habitual manner. The rabbinic sages capture the power of habits in their determination that frequently occurring rituals take precedence over infrequently occurring rituals (BT *Sukkah* 54b, 56a; *P'sachim* 114a; *M'gillah* 29b; and elsewhere). We are called upon not to build life upon the exceptional but rather to renew the ordinary; such is perhaps one of the secrets of one's being together with another in partnership.

When one plunges into the *mikveh*, the links with Creation and with our spirituality extend even further. When we remember that we are created in the image of God, *mikveh* becomes a reminder of the infinite within the finite, the immortal within the human, the limitless options offered to humanity. It is not surprising then that the Torah is compared to water in rabbinic literature. To immerse in water is also to plunge into the "Universe of the Torah," the infinite source of transformation of the world.

—*Pauline Bebe*

# Voices

## We Mothers

Nelly Sachs (transl. Ruth and Matthew Mead)

*Leviticus 12*

We mothers,
we gather seeds of desire
from oceanic night,
we are gatherers
of scattered goods,

We mothers,
pacing dreamily
with the constellations,
the floods
of past and future,
leave us alone
with our birth
like an island.

We mothers
who say to death:
blossom in our blood,
We who impel sand to love and bring
a mirroring world to the stars—

We mothers,
who rock in the cradles
the shadowy memories
of creation's day—
the to and fro of each breath
is the melody of our love song.

We mothers
rock into the heart of the world
the melody of peace.

## Women-Poems VII

Kadya Molodowsky (transl. Kathryn Hellerstein)

*Leviticus 12*

These are the spring nights
When up from under a stone, a grass blade
pushes forth from the earth,
And fresh moss makes a green cushion
Under the skull of a dead horse,
And all of a woman's limbs beg for the hurt
of childbirth.
And women come and lie down like sick sheep
By wells to heal their bodies,
And their faces are dark
From the long years of thirsting for the cry of
a child.
These are the spring nights
When lightning splits the black earth
With silver slaughtering knives,
And pregnant women approach
White tables in the hospital with quiet steps
And smile at the yet-unborn child
And perhaps even at death.
These are the spring nights
When up from under a stone, a grass blade
pushes forth from the earth.

## *Believe Me*

Esther Ettinger (transl. Mariana Barr)

*Leviticus 12*

Believe me, she grew more beautiful from
    moment to moment
her face poised, calm
from contraction to contraction, peaks of
    pleasure and pain
known in love.
The air was full and thick
and the spotlight upsetting the peace piercing
but she was so beautiful, rose of a perfect rose
till the child's head broke forth from within her,
    his shoulders, his body
and the umbilical cord wriggled and shone with
    light bluer
than the bottom of the sea.
I don't want to ease over the agony and the blood
only to tell you she was the essence of beauty
becoming elation when the child was placed on
    her belly.
And I who stood there cried with him, a first cry
clean of joy, clean of pain,
the purity of crying.
How is it that she went from beauty to beauty
like memory to memory
to the place of love where you say
you grow more beautiful as you go, more
    beautiful as you go
just as it is written
"weeping as he goes, weeping..."

NOTE
*"weeping..."* From Psalms 126:6.

## *[This child inside me]*

Galit Hasan-Rokem (transl. Kathryn Hellerstein)

*Leviticus 12*

This child inside me
sorts my existence into elements:
blood and urine
calcium and iron.
In my sleep I am a quarry
where rare treasures are suddenly found.

## *To a Nursling before Dawn*

Lynn Levin

*Leviticus 12*

My son, you rise before dawn, cat-yowling
at the milky moon,
and you thrash with an anger only food can
    appease.
I tumble from bed, sleepwalk to your room,
put you to my breast. Your little head
rests in the crook of my arm,
your eyes close in contentment.
Only your jaw works overtime. You snuffle and
    sigh.
Let me stroke the pleasing roundness of your face.
How it comforts a hand that time's begun to etch.
Nodding, I cradle your tiny hand in mine.
Hunger fades. Its tight bud unfolds
as the rarest flower.
Child, in the life before life we dreamed
    together.
Hand in hand, we dream again.
The sweet milk of love flows from me to you,
and it gladdens us. Whitening sky
blue as milk, moon awash in the early haze—
you look at me, drunk and happy.
A stray drop clings to your cheek like dew.
Let us laze. We wake too soon.

## *The Blood of Birth*

Tikva Frymer-Kensky

In the blood of the mother you come,
blood washing over you,
purifying you,
cleansing you,
anointing you—
tabernacle of God—
at the moment of your consecration.

In the blood of life you come,
essence of life,
purest of the pure.
The flowing of blood carries us between worlds.
The blood on the child
is the blood of the mother.
The mother's blood flows, you come to our
land of life.
Her blood stops flowing, she will stay with
you here.
Only an instant separates life from death,
only a breath and the flow of blood.

O my child, you are marked with the substance
of life itself.
Blood of the covenant,
which bonds us to God,
blood of the lamb,
the blood of delivery.
Blood of redemption,
blood of life.

O Child, my blood of life surrounds you,
*b'damai chayee*: through my blood, may you
live.
Today your blood of life flows through your
own body,
*b'damayich chayee, b'damayich chayee,*
through your blood, live!
With your blood, live!

## *My Friends Baked Cake and We Ordered Lox and Whitefish from the Deli*

Merle Feld

*Leviticus 12:3*

I stood there shoulder to shoulder with the men
when they hacked a piece off your little thing—
could I really sit in the room next door
and let my fantasies run wild when I heard
you cry?

And yet, at the crucial moment, I wasn't
watching.
I was staring off into space at some invisible
focal point.
The same one I'd stared at through the hours
of labor?
Maybe.
Maybe the same one Sarah stared at
when Abraham took her baby up to the
mountain.

I'm not angry, but you know,
you're a little weird, you male Jewish God.
What do you need with all those foreskins
anyway?

# מצרע ✦ *M'tzora*

LEVITICUS 14:1–15:33

## *Restoring Ritual Purity*

PARASHAT M'TZORA ("a person with *tzaraat*," that is, a skin affliction) completes the laws in Leviticus about impurity. Along with the preceding parashah, *Tazria* (Leviticus 12–13), this parashah deals with laws about individuals afflicted with *nega tzaraat*, sometimes translated as "scaly disease" (the traditional translation as "leprosy" is somewhat misleading; see below) and with genital discharges.

Reflected in this passage is the Torah's notion that certain actions and physical conditions produce an invisible, airborne pollution that invades the Sanctuary, the dwelling place of the divine Presence. (The Torah's theology, like that in the extant literature of Israel's ancient neighbors, imagines that the Deity can simultaneously dwell in a temple and in heaven, and that the earthly sanctuary is a smaller replica of its heavenly counterpart.) If the impurity is not disposed of, the accumulated pollution could cause Israel's God to abandon the Sanctuary, an event thought to bring about national disaster.

It should be emphasized, however, that in Leviticus *tzaraat* does not imply any sin on the part of the individual and that God is not depicted as the cause of *tzaraat* (except when it strikes the house; see at 14:34). For a rationale for Israel's impurity laws, see the introduction to Leviticus 14.

Leviticus 15 is one among several biblical texts that have played a role in forming the Israelite and Jewish attitudes to menstruation. The perspective in this parashah lacks the stigma attached to menstruation in other biblical passages (see at 15:24). In Leviticus 15, the woman and man are equally impure if they have sexual relations while the woman is menstruating; the purification period and process for each is identical (15:24).

The Hebrew term *niddah* refers to a menstruant woman or menstruation. *Niddah* renders a woman impure, just as a man's seminal ejection renders a man impure, and their impurity contaminates whatever they touch or sit on. The major difference, however, between a male's ejaculation and female menstruation is the duration of impurity: since menstruation lasts longer, the woman is in the impure state considerably longer than the man.

*This is one of the texts that has formed Jewish attitudes to menstruation.*

According to Leviticus, what are the practical consequences for the person who is deemed ritually impure? The impure person may not "touch any consecrated thing, nor enter the sanctuary" (12:4). *Parashat M'tzora* offers us a detailed account of restrictions placed upon the menstruant as well, but it does not provide a complete picture of the ways that menstruation was viewed in ancient Israel. On the practical impact of menstruation on a woman's life, see at 15:20.

—*Elaine Goodfriend*

## *Outline*

*I.* Purification Ritual for a Person with *nega tzaraat* (14:1–32)

- *A.* Purification ritual for the afflicted person: days 1–7 (vv. 1–9)
- *B.* Sacrifice by the afflicted person: day 8 (vv. 10–20)
- *C.* Sacrifice by the afflicted person of lesser means: day 8 (vv. 21–32)

*II.* Diagnosis and Purification of a House with *nega tzaraat* (14:33–53)

*III.* Purification Laws for Persons with Genital Discharge (15:1–33)

- *A.* The Israelite male (vv. 1–18)
  - *1.* Laws about abnormal discharges from the penis (vv. 1–15)
  - *2.* Laws about normal seminal emissions (vv. 16–18)
- *B.* The Israelite female (vv. 19–30)
  - *1.* Laws about menstruation (vv. 19–24)
  - *2.* Laws about abnormal discharge of blood (vv. 25–30)
- *C.* Conclusion (vv. 31–33)

יד וַיְדַבֵּר יְהֹוָה אֶל־מֹשֶׁה לֵּאמֹר׃ 2 זֹאת
תִּהְיֶה תּוֹרַת הַמְּצֹרָע בְּיוֹם טׇהׇרָתוֹ

יהוה spoke to Moses, saying: [2]This shall be
the ritual for a leper at the time of
being purified.

## *Purification Ritual for a Person with nega tzaraat*

(14:1–32)

The word *tzaraat* refers to a skin disease sometimes translated as "scale disease," "scaly disease," "eruption," and (erroneously) "leprosy." The diagnosis of *tzaraat* was the concern of the preceding passage at the end of *parashat Tazria*. There, we were told that the person whom a priest diagnoses as having *tzaraat* "shall dwell apart—in a dwelling outside the camp" (13:46). The present unit commences with the priest's exiting the camp to initiate the ritual that will remove the afflicted person's impurity. The process of rehabilitating the *m'tzora* (the afflicted person) has three stages: the first phase when the priest verifies that the individual is cured; the second, on the seventh day, when the afflicted person shaves, washes, and launders her or his garments; and the third stage, on the eighth day, when the afflicted brings a combination of sacrifices to the Sanctuary.

Of all the types of persons who become ritually impure, only the *m'tzora* undergoes such extensive ritual, preceded by exclusion from the community. Numbers 5:2 demands the removal of other categories of impure people from the camp of Israel, but their situation does not apply to the later period, after settlement in the Land of Israel.

The Bible's ideas about purity are linked to the association of Israel's God with life—as the Creator of life, whose life is eternal and whose laws give life. Thus the prophet Ezekiel calls the Torah's legislation "laws of life" (33:15), while according to Psalm 116:9, one who walks with Israel's God journeys in the "lands of the living." Impurity, or estrangement from God, results from certain physical states that were associated with death. For example, a human corpse is a potent source of impurity that infects a house and the living people within it (Numbers 19). The association of *tzaraat* with death is evident from Numbers 12:12, when—after Miriam has been "stricken with snow-white scales"—Aaron implores, "Let her not be as a stillbirth [literally: a dead person], which emerges from its mother's womb with half its flesh eaten away!" This suggests that the appearance of the person afflicted with *tzaraat* was—at least in one form of the disease—akin to that of a disintegrating corpse (see at 14:4). The priest in Leviticus is charged with diagnosing no other disease except for *tzaraat*, which also indicates the symbolic nature of this condition.

▶ The ability to become pure underlies the prophetic notion of reversing sinful acts.

ANOTHER VIEW ➤ 672

▶ Throughout Jewish history, women have used the laws of *niddah* for empowerment.

POST-BIBLICAL INTERPRETATIONS ➤ 672

▶ "Women's bodies may be the hardest place for women to find sacredness."

CONTEMPORARY REFLECTION ➤ 674

▶ what is one open sore / when the moment has come / to close the wounds / of the world?

VOICES ➤ 676

When it has been reported to the priest, [3]the
priest shall go outside the camp. If the priest sees
that the leper has been healed of the scaly affection,
[4]the priest shall order two live pure birds, cedar
wood, crimson stuff, and hyssop to be brought for
the one to be purified. [5]The priest shall order one of
the birds slaughtered over fresh water in an earthen
vessel; [6]and he shall take the live bird, along with
the cedar wood, the crimson stuff, and the hyssop,
and dip them together with the live bird in the
blood of the bird that was slaughtered over the fresh
water. [7]He shall then sprinkle it seven times on
the one to be purified of the eruption and effect the
purification; and he shall set the live bird free in

וְהוּבָ֖א אֶל־הַכֹּהֵֽן׃ 3 וְיָצָא֙ הַכֹּהֵ֔ן אֶל־מִח֖וּץ
לַֽמַּחֲנֶ֑ה וְרָאָה֙ הַכֹּהֵ֔ן וְהִנֵּ֛ה נִרְפָּ֥א נֶֽגַע־
הַצָּרַ֖עַת מִן־הַצָּרֽוּעַ׃ 4 וְצִוָּה֙ הַכֹּהֵ֔ן וְלָקַ֧ח
לַמִּטַּהֵ֛ר שְׁתֵּֽי־צִפֳּרִ֥ים חַיּ֖וֹת טְהֹר֑וֹת וְעֵ֣ץ
אֶ֔רֶז וּשְׁנִ֥י תוֹלַ֖עַת וְאֵזֹֽב׃ 5 וְצִוָּה֙ הַכֹּהֵ֔ן
וְשָׁחַ֖ט אֶת־הַצִּפּ֣וֹר הָאֶחָ֑ת אֶל־כְּלִי־חֶ֖רֶשׂ
עַל־מַ֥יִם חַיִּֽים׃ 6 אֶת־הַצִּפֹּ֤ר הַֽחַיָּה֙ יִקַּ֣ח
אֹתָ֔הּ וְאֶת־עֵ֥ץ הָאֶ֖רֶז וְאֶת־שְׁנִ֣י הַתּוֹלַ֑עַת
וְאֶת־הָאֵזֹ֑ב וְטָבַ֨ל אוֹתָ֜ם וְאֵ֣ת ׀ הַצִּפֹּ֣ר הַֽחַיָּ֗ה
בְּדַם֙ הַצִּפֹּ֣ר הַשְּׁחֻטָ֔ה עַ֖ל הַמַּ֥יִם הַֽחַיִּֽים׃
7 וְהִזָּ֗ה עַ֧ל הַמִּטַּהֵ֛ר מִן־הַצָּרַ֖עַת שֶׁ֣בַע
פְּעָמִ֑ים וְטִ֣הֲר֔וֹ וְשִׁלַּ֛ח אֶת־הַצִּפֹּ֥ר הַֽחַיָּ֖ה

### PURIFICATION RITUAL FOR THE AFFLICTED PERSON: DAYS 1–7 (14:1–9)

As noted above, scale disease renders the afflicted impure because of its association with death. The purpose of the ritual in vv. 1–9 is to rid the individual of impurity and perhaps symbolically restore the person to life; thus the Hebrew *chai* or *chayim* ("alive" or "live") is a repeated element. As a result of this phase of the ritual, the *m'tzora* (the afflicted person) may enter the camp but may not yet return home (v. 8).

*1. **leper.*** Heb. *m'tzora* refers to the person suffering from one of several skin diseases. Traditionally the term for those diseases, *tzaraat*, has been translated as "leprosy," but in English that word nowadays refers to something other than the conditions that the Torah describes; these are now called "scale disease," "scaly disease," or (in this translation) also simply "affection" or "eruption." [The JPS translators note: "Where a human being is declared impure by reason of *tzaraat*, the traditional translation 'leprosy' has been retained without regard to modern medical terminology." The reason for doing so, according to a member of the translation committee, was "to convey the horror that the Bible attaches to this affliction." —*Ed.*]

*3. **If the priest sees that the leper has been healed.*** The priest is not a healer; rather, he facilitates the removing of ritual impurity once the person is healed.

*4. **the priest shall order two live pure birds.*** One of the two birds is intended to carry the impurity out into open country (v. 7). Thus it must be a wild bird, or else it would bring that impurity back to the community. The Rabbis identify the bird as an untamed sparrow. (Note the similarity between the function of the bird here and the scapegoat that in the Day of Atonement ritual bears the accumulated sin of the people; see 16:21.)

***cedar wood, crimson stuff, and hyssop.*** In Numbers 19, the ritual for the person rendered impure by a corpse specifies these same three substances. The similarity of ritual ingredients reinforces the link of *tzaraat* with death.

*5. **fresh.*** Heb. *chayim* (literally "living"), which refers to perpetually flowing water, such as from a spring or river.

*7. **He shall then sprinkle it seven times on the one to be purified.*** The purpose of the process seems to be purification: the effects of the disease are transferred to the bloodied water, then the live bird that is dipped in it seems to carry away the person's defilement. Why the person is sprinkled with the bloodied water is unclear, but this act is akin to

the open country. 8The one to be purified shall
wash those clothes, shave off all hair, and bathe in
water—and then shall be pure. After that, the camp
may be entered but one must remain outside one's
tent seven days. 9On the seventh day all hair shall be
shaved off—of head, beard [if any], and eyebrows.
Having shaved off all hair, the person shall wash
those clothes and bathe the body in water—and
then shall be pure. 10On the eighth day that person
shall take two male lambs without blemish, one
ewe lamb in its first year without blemish, three-
tenths of a measure of choice flour with oil mixed
in for a meal offering, and one *log* of oil. 11These
shall be presented before יהוה, with the person to be
purified, at the entrance of the Tent of Meeting, by
the priest who performs the purification.

12The priest shall take one of the male lambs
and offer it with the *log* of oil as a reparation offering, and he shall elevate them as an elevation offering before יהוה. 13The lamb shall be slaughtered
at the spot in the sacred area where the purgation
offering and the burnt offering are slaughtered. For
the reparation offering, like the purgation offering,

עַל־פְּנֵי הַשָּׂדֶה׃ 8 וְכִבֶּס הַמִּטַּהֵר אֶת־בְּגָדָיו
וְגִלַּח אֶת־כׇּל־שְׂעָרוֹ וְרָחַץ בַּמַּיִם וְטָהֵר
וְאַחַר יָבוֹא אֶל־הַמַּחֲנֶה וְיָשַׁב מִחוּץ
לְאׇהֳלוֹ שִׁבְעַת יָמִים׃ 9 וְהָיָה בַיּוֹם
הַשְּׁבִיעִי יְגַלַּח אֶת־כׇּל־שְׂעָרוֹ אֶת־רֹאשׁוֹ
וְאֶת־זְקָנוֹ וְאֵת גַּבֹּת עֵינָיו וְאֶת־כׇּל־שְׂעָרוֹ
יְגַלֵּחַ וְכִבֶּס אֶת־בְּגָדָיו וְרָחַץ אֶת־בְּשָׂרוֹ
בַּמַּיִם וְטָהֵר׃ 10 וּבַיּוֹם הַשְּׁמִינִי יִקַּח שְׁנֵי־
כְבָשִׂים תְּמִימִם וְכַבְשָׂה אַחַת בַּת־שְׁנָתָהּ
תְּמִימָה וּשְׁלֹשָׁה עֶשְׂרֹנִים סֹלֶת מִנְחָה
בְּלוּלָה בַשֶּׁמֶן וְלֹג אֶחָד שָׁמֶן׃ 11 וְהֶעֱמִיד
הַכֹּהֵן הַמְטַהֵר אֵת הָאִישׁ הַמִּטַּהֵר וְאֹתָם
לִפְנֵי יְהֹוָה פֶּתַח אֹהֶל מוֹעֵד׃
12 וְלָקַח הַכֹּהֵן אֶת־הַכֶּבֶשׂ הָאֶחָד וְהִקְרִיב
אֹתוֹ לְאָשָׁם וְאֶת־לֹג הַשָּׁמֶן וְהֵנִיף אֹתָם
תְּנוּפָה לִפְנֵי יְהֹוָה׃ 13 וְשָׁחַט אֶת־הַכֶּבֶשׂ
בִּמְקוֹם אֲשֶׁר יִשְׁחַט אֶת־הַחַטָּאת וְאֶת־
הָעֹלָה בִּמְקוֹם הַקֹּדֶשׁ כִּי כַּחַטָּאת הָאָשָׁם

the sprinkling ritual performed on the individual made impure via contact with a corpse (see Numbers 19). In the latter case, the water is mixed with another reddish material, the ashes of a red (or brown) cow. Elsewhere in Leviticus the sprinkling of the blood of a purgation sacrifice removes impurity (4:6, 17).

*8.* Laundering the garments worn during periods of impurity is a necessary element in rehabilitation (11:25, 40; Leviticus 15; Numbers 19). The person afflicted with *tzaraat* has to shave all body and head hair before bathing, which reflects the severity of the defilement.

***After that, the camp may be entered.*** The individual may enter the camp—but not her or his tent, as impurity can still be communicated to those in the same dwelling.

*9.* ***then shall be pure.*** After seven days of waiting, and a second round of laundering, shaving, and washing, the individual can now go home.

### SACRIFICE BY THE AFFLICTED PERSON: DAY 8 (14:10–20)

The last phase of the process involves the decontamination of the Sanctuary and the complete rehabilitation of the individual. The ceremony of the final stage includes a procedure (v. 14) similar to the ordination of the priests in Leviticus 8 (see also Exodus 29), the only other case where such a ritual is required. This correspondence of the *m'tzora* with the initiated priest elevates the formerly excluded person.

goes to the priest; it is most holy. [14]The priest shall take some of the blood of the reparation offering, and the priest shall put it on the ridge of the right ear of the one who is being purified, and on the thumb of the right hand, and on the big toe of the right foot. [15]The priest shall then take some of the *log* of oil and pour it into the palm of his own left hand. [16]And the priest shall dip his right finger in the oil that is in the palm of his left hand and sprinkle some of the oil with his finger seven times before יהוה. [17]Some of the oil left in his palm shall be put by the priest on the ridge of the right ear of the one being purified, on the thumb of the right hand, and on the big toe of the right foot—over the blood of the reparation offering. [18]The rest of the oil in his palm the priest shall put on the head of the one being purified. Thus the priest shall make expiation for that person before יהוה. [19]The priest shall then offer the purgation offering and make expiation for the one being purified of defilement. Last, the burnt offering shall be slaughtered, [20]and the priest shall offer the burnt offering and the meal offering on the altar; the priest shall make expiation for that person, who shall then be pure.

[21]If, however, one is poor and without sufficient means, that person shall take one male lamb for a reparation offering, to be elevated in expiation, one-tenth of a measure of choice flour with oil mixed in for a meal offering, and a *log* of oil; [22]and two turtledoves or two pigeons—depending on that person's means—the one to be the purgation offering and the other the burnt offering. [23]On the

הוּא לַכֹּהֵן קֹדֶשׁ קָדָשִׁים הוּא׃ 14 וְלָקַח
הַכֹּהֵן מִדַּם הָאָשָׁם וְנָתַן הַכֹּהֵן עַל־
תְּנוּךְ אֹזֶן הַמִּטַּהֵר הַיְמָנִית וְעַל־בֹּהֶן
יָדוֹ הַיְמָנִית וְעַל־בֹּהֶן רַגְלוֹ הַיְמָנִית׃
15 וְלָקַח הַכֹּהֵן מִלֹּג הַשָּׁמֶן וְיָצַק עַל־כַּף
הַכֹּהֵן הַשְּׂמָאלִית׃ 16 וְטָבַל הַכֹּהֵן אֶת־
אֶצְבָּעוֹ הַיְמָנִית מִן־הַשֶּׁמֶן אֲשֶׁר עַל־כַּפּוֹ
הַשְּׂמָאלִית וְהִזָּה מִן־הַשֶּׁמֶן בְּאֶצְבָּעוֹ שֶׁבַע
פְּעָמִים לִפְנֵי יְהוָה׃ 17 וּמִיֶּתֶר הַשֶּׁמֶן אֲשֶׁר
עַל־כַּפּוֹ יִתֵּן הַכֹּהֵן עַל־תְּנוּךְ אֹזֶן הַמִּטַּהֵר
הַיְמָנִית וְעַל־בֹּהֶן יָדוֹ הַיְמָנִית וְעַל־בֹּהֶן
רַגְלוֹ הַיְמָנִית עַל דַּם הָאָשָׁם׃ 18 וְהַנּוֹתָר
בַּשֶּׁמֶן אֲשֶׁר עַל־כַּף הַכֹּהֵן יִתֵּן עַל־רֹאשׁ
הַמִּטַּהֵר וְכִפֶּר עָלָיו הַכֹּהֵן לִפְנֵי יְהוָה׃
19 וְעָשָׂה הַכֹּהֵן אֶת־הַחַטָּאת וְכִפֶּר עַל־
הַמִּטַּהֵר מִטֻּמְאָתוֹ וְאַחַר יִשְׁחַט אֶת־
הָעֹלָה׃ 20 וְהֶעֱלָה הַכֹּהֵן אֶת־הָעֹלָה
וְאֶת־הַמִּנְחָה הַמִּזְבֵּחָה וְכִפֶּר עָלָיו הַכֹּהֵן
וְטָהֵר׃ ס
21 וְאִם־דַּל הוּא וְאֵין יָדוֹ מַשֶּׂגֶת וְלָקַח כֶּבֶשׂ
אֶחָד אָשָׁם לִתְנוּפָה לְכַפֵּר עָלָיו וְעִשָּׂרוֹן
סֹלֶת אֶחָד בָּלוּל בַּשֶּׁמֶן לְמִנְחָה וְלֹג שָׁמֶן׃
22 וּשְׁתֵּי תֹרִים אוֹ שְׁנֵי בְּנֵי יוֹנָה אֲשֶׁר תַּשִּׂיג
יָדוֹ וְהָיָה אֶחָד חַטָּאת וְהָאֶחָד עֹלָה׃
23 וְהֵבִיא אֹתָם בַּיּוֹם הַשְּׁמִינִי לְטָהֳרָתוֹ

*14. on the ridge of the right ear . . . on the thumb of the right hand, and on the big toe of the right foot.* In the Bible and the cultures that surrounded ancient Israel, the right is the preferred side (see Genesis 48:17–19). The extremities, from head to toe, symbolize the entire individual, whom the ritual both purifies and reintegrates into the community.

*19–20. purgation offering.* To cleanse the sanctuary of any residual impurity (see Leviticus 4).

*burnt offering . . . meal offering.* These have the general function of atonement (see Leviticus 1–2).

### SACRIFICE BY THE AFFLICTED PERSON OF LESSER MEANS: DAY 8 (14:21–32)

A concession is made for those who cannot afford flock animals (see also 5:11).

eighth day of purification, the person shall bring
them to the priest at the entrance of the Tent of
Meeting, before יהוה. 24The priest shall take the
lamb of reparation offering and the *log* of oil, and
elevate them as an elevation offering before יהוה.
25When the lamb of reparation offering has been
slaughtered, the priest shall take some of the blood
of the reparation offering and put it on the ridge
of the right ear of the one being purified, on the
thumb of the right hand, and on the big toe of
the right foot. 26The priest shall then pour some
of the oil into the palm of his own left hand, 27and
with the finger of his right hand the priest shall
sprinkle some of the oil that is in the palm of his
left hand seven times before יהוה. 28Some of the oil
in his palm shall be put by the priest on the ridge
of the right ear of the one being purified, on the
thumb of the right hand, and on the big toe of
the right foot, over the same places as the blood
of the reparation offering; 29and what is left of the
oil in his palm the priest shall put on the head of
the one being purified, to make expiation for that
person before יהוה. 30That person shall then offer
one of the turtledoves or pigeons, depending on the
person's means—31whichever that person can afford—the one as a purgation offering and the other
as a burnt offering, together with the meal offering.
Thus the priest shall make expiation before יהוה for
the one being purified. 32Such is the ritual for one
who has a scaly affection and whose means for purification are limited.

אֶל־הַכֹּהֵן אֶל־פֶּתַח אֹהֶל־מוֹעֵד לִפְנֵי
יְהוָה׃ 24 וְלָקַח הַכֹּהֵן אֶת־כֶּבֶשׂ הָאָשָׁם
וְאֶת־לֹג הַשָּׁמֶן וְהֵנִיף אֹתָם הַכֹּהֵן תְּנוּפָה
לִפְנֵי יְהוָה׃ 25 וְשָׁחַט אֶת־כֶּבֶשׂ הָאָשָׁם
וְלָקַח הַכֹּהֵן מִדַּם הָאָשָׁם וְנָתַן עַל־תְּנוּךְ
אֹזֶן־הַמִּטַּהֵר הַיְמָנִית וְעַל־בֹּהֶן יָדוֹ הַיְמָנִית
וְעַל־בֹּהֶן רַגְלוֹ הַיְמָנִית׃ 26 וּמִן־הַשֶּׁמֶן יִצֹק
הַכֹּהֵן עַל־כַּף הַכֹּהֵן הַשְּׂמָאלִית׃ 27 וְהִזָּה
הַכֹּהֵן בְּאֶצְבָּעוֹ הַיְמָנִית מִן־הַשֶּׁמֶן אֲשֶׁר
עַל־כַּפּוֹ הַשְּׂמָאלִית שֶׁבַע פְּעָמִים לִפְנֵי
יְהוָה׃ 28 וְנָתַן הַכֹּהֵן מִן־הַשֶּׁמֶן ׀ אֲשֶׁר עַל־
כַּפּוֹ עַל־תְּנוּךְ אֹזֶן הַמִּטַּהֵר הַיְמָנִית וְעַל־
בֹּהֶן יָדוֹ הַיְמָנִית וְעַל־בֹּהֶן רַגְלוֹ הַיְמָנִית
עַל־מְקוֹם דַּם הָאָשָׁם׃ 29 וְהַנּוֹתָר מִן־
הַשֶּׁמֶן אֲשֶׁר עַל־כַּף הַכֹּהֵן יִתֵּן עַל־רֹאשׁ
הַמִּטַּהֵר לְכַפֵּר עָלָיו לִפְנֵי יְהוָה׃ 30 וְעָשָׂה
אֶת־הָאֶחָד מִן־הַתֹּרִים אוֹ מִן־בְּנֵי הַיּוֹנָה
מֵאֲשֶׁר תַּשִּׂיג יָדוֹ׃ 31 אֵת אֲשֶׁר־תַּשִּׂיג יָדוֹ
אֶת־הָאֶחָד חַטָּאת וְאֶת־הָאֶחָד עֹלָה עַל־
הַמִּנְחָה וְכִפֶּר הַכֹּהֵן עַל הַמִּטַּהֵר לִפְנֵי
יְהוָה׃ 32 זֹאת תּוֹרַת אֲשֶׁר־בּוֹ נֶגַע צָרָעַת
אֲשֶׁר לֹא־תַשִּׂיג יָדוֹ בְּטָהֳרָתוֹ׃ פ

33יהוה spoke to Moses and Aaron, saying:

33 וַיְדַבֵּר יְהוָה אֶל־מֹשֶׁה וְאֶל־אַהֲרֹן
לֵאמֹר׃

## *Diagnosis and Purification of a House with nega tzaraat* (14:33–53)

Leviticus 13 detailed the diagnosis of *tzaraat* in people, fabric, and leather garments. The same symptoms could also characterize the interior walls of houses (see 13:47–59). *Tzaraat* in a house seems to be a kind of mold or fungus that attaches itself to building stones. After a seven-day quarantine, if the fungus has spread, the affected stones and all interior plaster have to be removed and transferred to a dump for impure waste, surely outside the city limits. The house is then repaired, unless the mold returns. If, after the initial seven-day quarantine, the infection has not spread, the priest conducts a purification rite (vv. 49–53) similar to that for an

³⁴When you enter the land of Canaan that I give you as a possession, and I inflict an eruptive plague upon a house in the land you possess, ³⁵the owner of the house shall come and tell the priest, saying, "Something like a plague has appeared upon my house." ³⁶The priest shall order the house cleared before the priest enters to examine the plague, so that nothing in the house may become impure; after that the priest shall enter to examine the house. ³⁷If, when he examines the plague, the plague in the walls of the house is found to consist of greenish or reddish streaks that appear to go deep into the wall, ³⁸the priest shall come out of the house to the entrance of the house, and close up the house for seven days. ³⁹On the seventh day the priest shall return. If he sees that the plague has spread on the walls of the house, ⁴⁰the priest shall order the stones with the plague in them to be pulled out and cast outside the city into an impure place. ⁴¹The house shall be scraped inside all around, and the coating that is scraped off shall be dumped outside the city in an impure place. ⁴²They shall take other stones and replace those stones with them, and take other coating and plaster the house.

⁴³If the plague again breaks out in the house, after the stones have been pulled out and after the house has been scraped and replastered, ⁴⁴the priest shall come to examine: if the plague has spread in the house, it is a malignant eruption in the house; it is impure. ⁴⁵The house shall be torn down—its stones and timber and all the coating on the house—and taken to an impure place outside the city.

³⁴ כִּי תָבֹאוּ אֶל־אֶרֶץ כְּנַעַן אֲשֶׁר אֲנִי נֹתֵן לָכֶם לַאֲחֻזָּה וְנָתַתִּי נֶגַע צָרַעַת בְּבֵית אֶרֶץ אֲחֻזַּתְכֶם: ³⁵ וּבָא אֲשֶׁר־לוֹ הַבַּיִת וְהִגִּיד לַכֹּהֵן לֵאמֹר כְּנֶגַע נִרְאָה לִי בַּבָּיִת: ³⁶ וְצִוָּה הַכֹּהֵן וּפִנּוּ אֶת־הַבַּיִת בְּטֶרֶם יָבֹא הַכֹּהֵן לִרְאוֹת אֶת־הַנֶּגַע וְלֹא יִטְמָא כָּל־אֲשֶׁר בַּבָּיִת וְאַחַר כֵּן יָבֹא הַכֹּהֵן לִרְאוֹת אֶת־הַבָּיִת: ³⁷ וְרָאָה אֶת־הַנֶּגַע וְהִנֵּה הַנֶּגַע בְּקִירֹת הַבַּיִת שְׁקַעֲרוּרֹת יְרַקְרַקֹּת אוֹ אֲדַמְדַּמֹּת וּמַרְאֵיהֶן שָׁפָל מִן־הַקִּיר: ³⁸ וְיָצָא הַכֹּהֵן מִן־הַבַּיִת אֶל־פֶּתַח הַבָּיִת וְהִסְגִּיר אֶת־הַבַּיִת שִׁבְעַת יָמִים: ³⁹ וְשָׁב הַכֹּהֵן בַּיּוֹם הַשְּׁבִיעִי וְרָאָה וְהִנֵּה פָּשָׂה הַנֶּגַע בְּקִירֹת הַבָּיִת: ⁴⁰ וְצִוָּה הַכֹּהֵן וְחִלְּצוּ אֶת־הָאֲבָנִים אֲשֶׁר בָּהֵן הַנָּגַע וְהִשְׁלִיכוּ אֶתְהֶן אֶל־מִחוּץ לָעִיר אֶל־מָקוֹם טָמֵא: ⁴¹ וְאֶת־הַבַּיִת יַקְצִעַ מִבַּיִת סָבִיב וְשָׁפְכוּ אֶת־הֶעָפָר אֲשֶׁר הִקְצוּ אֶל־מִחוּץ לָעִיר אֶל־מָקוֹם טָמֵא: ⁴² וְלָקְחוּ אֲבָנִים אֲחֵרוֹת וְהֵבִיאוּ אֶל־תַּחַת הָאֲבָנִים וְעָפָר אַחֵר יִקַּח וְטָח אֶת־הַבָּיִת: ⁴³ וְאִם־יָשׁוּב הַנֶּגַע וּפָרַח בַּבַּיִת אַחַר חִלֵּץ אֶת־הָאֲבָנִים וְאַחֲרֵי הִקְצוֹת אֶת־הַבַּיִת וְאַחֲרֵי הִטּוֹחַ: ⁴⁴ וּבָא הַכֹּהֵן וְרָאָה וְהִנֵּה פָּשָׂה הַנֶּגַע בַּבָּיִת צָרַעַת מַמְאֶרֶת הִוא בַּבַּיִת טָמֵא הוּא: ⁴⁵ וְנָתַץ אֶת־הַבַּיִת אֶת־אֲבָנָיו וְאֶת־עֵצָיו וְאֵת כָּל־עֲפַר הַבָּיִת וְהוֹצִיא אֶל־מִחוּץ לָעִיר אֶל־מָקוֹם טָמֵא:

- - - - - - - - - - - - - - - - - - - -

afflicted person on the first day after she or he has been declared healed (vv. 1–7).

**34. When … I inflict an eruptive plague upon a house.** This is the only case in Leviticus claiming that God causes a form of *tzaraat*. Even here, the text does not present illness and disease as being divine retribution. Leviticus offers no explanation for the cause of disease. Instead, it focuses only on pro-

tecting persons and the sanctuary from contamination once the disease appears.

**36. The priest shall order the house cleared.** The house is emptied prior to its inspection so that the owner incurs no financial loss from the priest's diagnosis. According to vv. 46–47, only those who may have entered the house during the quarantine are considered impure.

46 Whoever enters the house while it is closed up shall be impure until evening. 47 Whoever sleeps in the house must wash those clothes, and whoever eats in the house must wash those clothes.

48 If, however, the priest comes and sees that the plague has not spread in the house after the house was replastered, the priest shall pronounce the house pure, for the plague has healed. 49 To purge the house, he shall take two birds, cedar wood, crimson stuff, and hyssop. 50 He shall slaughter the one bird over fresh water in an earthen vessel. 51 He shall take the cedar wood, the hyssop, the crimson stuff, and the live bird, and dip them in the blood of the slaughtered bird and the fresh water, and sprinkle on the house seven times. 52 Having purged the house with the blood of the bird, the fresh water, the live bird, the cedar wood, the hyssop, and the crimson stuff, 53 he shall set the live bird free outside the city in the open country. Thus he shall make expiation for the house, and it shall be pure.

54 Such is the ritual for every eruptive affection—for scalls, 55 for an eruption on a cloth or a house, 56 for swellings, for rashes, or for discolorations— 57 to determine when they are impure and when they are pure.

Such is the ritual concerning eruptions.

*15* יהוה spoke to Moses and Aaron, saying: 2 Speak to the Israelite people and say to them:

46 וְהַבָּא֙ אֶל־הַבַּ֔יִת כׇּל־יְמֵ֖י הִסְגִּ֣יר אֹת֑וֹ
יִטְמָ֖א עַד־הָעָֽרֶב׃ 47 וְהַשֹּׁכֵ֣ב בַּבַּ֔יִת יְכַבֵּ֖ס
אֶת־בְּגָדָ֑יו וְהָאֹכֵ֣ל בַּבַּ֔יִת יְכַבֵּ֖ס אֶת־
בְּגָדָֽיו׃
48 וְאִם־בֹּ֨א יָבֹ֜א הַכֹּהֵ֗ן וְרָאָה֙ וְהִנֵּ֨ה לֹֽא־
פָשָׂ֤ה הַנֶּ֙גַע֙ בַּבַּ֔יִת אַחֲרֵ֖י הִטֹּ֣חַ אֶת־הַבָּ֑יִת
וְטִהַ֤ר הַכֹּהֵן֙ אֶת־הַבַּ֔יִת כִּ֥י נִרְפָּ֖א הַנָּֽגַע׃
49 וְלָקַ֛ח לְחַטֵּ֥א אֶת־הַבַּ֖יִת שְׁתֵּ֣י צִפֳּרִ֑ים
וְעֵ֣ץ אֶ֔רֶז וּשְׁנִ֥י תוֹלַ֖עַת וְאֵזֹֽב׃ 50 וְשָׁחַ֖ט אֶת־
הַצִּפֹּ֣ר הָאֶחָ֑ת אֶל־כְּלִי־חֶ֖רֶשׂ עַל־מַ֥יִם
חַיִּֽים׃ 51 וְלָקַ֣ח אֶת־עֵֽץ־הָ֠אֶרֶז וְאֶת־הָ֨אֵזֹ֜ב
וְאֵ֣ת ׀ שְׁנִ֣י הַתּוֹלַ֗עַת וְאֵת֮ הַצִּפֹּ֣ר הַֽחַיָּה֒
וְטָבַ֣ל אֹתָ֗ם בְּדַם֙ הַצִּפֹּ֣ר הַשְּׁחוּטָ֔ה וּבַמַּ֖יִם
הַחַיִּ֑ים וְהִזָּ֥ה אֶל־הַבַּ֖יִת שֶׁ֥בַע פְּעָמִֽים׃
52 וְחִטֵּ֣א אֶת־הַבַּ֔יִת בְּדַם֙ הַצִּפּ֔וֹר וּבַמַּ֖יִם
הַחַיִּ֑ים וּבַצִּפֹּ֣ר הַחַיָּ֗ה וּבְעֵ֥ץ הָאֶ֛רֶז וּבָאֵזֹ֖ב
וּבִשְׁנִ֥י הַתּוֹלָֽעַת׃ 53 וְשִׁלַּ֞ח אֶת־הַצִּפֹּ֧ר
הַֽחַיָּ֛ה אֶל־מִח֥וּץ לָעִ֖יר אֶל־פְּנֵ֣י הַשָּׂדֶ֑ה
וְכִפֶּ֥ר עַל־הַבַּ֖יִת וְטָהֵֽר׃

54 זֹ֖את הַתּוֹרָ֑ה לְכׇל־נֶ֥גַע הַצָּרַ֖עַת וְלַנָּֽתֶק׃
55 וּלְצָרַ֥עַת הַבֶּ֖גֶד וְלַבָּֽיִת׃ 56 וְלַשְׂאֵ֥ת
וְלַסַּפַּ֖חַת וְלַבֶּהָֽרֶת׃ 57 לְהוֹרֹ֕ת בְּי֥וֹם הַטָּמֵ֖א
וּבְי֣וֹם הַטָּהֹ֑ר
זֹ֥את תּוֹרַ֖ת הַצָּרָֽעַת׃ פ

טו וַיְדַבֵּ֣ר יְהֹוָ֔ה אֶל־מֹשֶׁ֥ה וְאֶֽל־אַהֲרֹ֖ן
לֵאמֹֽר׃ 2 דַּבְּרוּ֙ אֶל־בְּנֵ֣י יִשְׂרָאֵ֔ל וַאֲמַרְתֶּ֖ם
אֲלֵהֶ֑ם

## *Purification Laws for Persons with Genital Discharge* (15:1–33)

The arrangement of Leviticus 15 is chiastic, meaning that each section of the first half of this unit parallels a passage in the second half, but in reverse order:

Male: abnormal discharge (vv. 1–15)
Male: normal discharge (vv. 16–17)
Concerning male–female intercourse (v. 18)
Female: normal menstruation (vv. 19–24)
Female: abnormal vaginal bleeding (vv. 25–30)

Normal genital discharges (semen or blood) render the individual impure and necessitate laundering,

When any man has a discharge issuing from his
member, he is impure. [3]The impurity from his discharge shall mean the following—whether his
member runs with the discharge or is stopped up
so that there is no discharge, his impurity means
this: [4]Any bedding on which the one with the discharge lies shall be impure, and every object on
which he sits shall be impure. [5]All those who touch
his bedding shall wash their clothes, bathe in water,
and remain impure until evening. [6]All those who sit
on an object on which the one with the discharge
has sat shall wash their clothes, bathe in water, and
remain impure until evening. [7]All those who touch
the body of the one with the discharge shall wash
their clothes, bathe in water, and remain impure
until evening. [8]If the one with a discharge spits on
someone who is pure, the latter shall wash those
clothes, bathe in water, and remain impure until
evening. [9]Any means for riding that the one with a
discharge has mounted shall be impure; [10]all those
who touch anything that was under him shall be
impure until evening; and all those who carry such

אִ֣ישׁ אִ֔ישׁ כִּ֥י יִהְיֶה֙ זָ֣ב מִבְּשָׂר֔וֹ זוֹב֖וֹ טָמֵ֥א
הֽוּא׃ 3 וְזֹ֛את תִּהְיֶ֥ה טֻמְאָת֖וֹ בְּזוֹב֑וֹ רָ֨ר
בְּשָׂר֜וֹ אֶת־זוֹב֗וֹ אֽוֹ־הֶחְתִּ֤ים בְּשָׂרוֹ֙ מִזּוֹב֔וֹ
טֻמְאָת֖וֹ הִֽוא׃ 4 כָּל־הַמִּשְׁכָּ֗ב אֲשֶׁ֨ר יִשְׁכַּ֥ב
עָלָ֛יו הַזָּ֖ב יִטְמָ֑א וְכָֽל־הַכְּלִ֛י אֲשֶׁר־יֵשֵׁ֥ב עָלָ֖יו
יִטְמָֽא׃ 5 וְאִ֕ישׁ אֲשֶׁ֥ר יִגַּ֖ע בְּמִשְׁכָּב֑וֹ יְכַבֵּ֧ס
בְּגָדָ֛יו וְרָחַ֥ץ בַּמַּ֖יִם וְטָמֵ֥א עַד־הָעָֽרֶב׃
6 וְהַיֹּשֵׁב֙ עַֽל־הַכְּלִ֔י אֲשֶׁר־יֵשֵׁ֥ב עָלָ֖יו הַזָּ֑ב
יְכַבֵּ֧ס בְּגָדָ֛יו וְרָחַ֥ץ בַּמַּ֖יִם וְטָמֵ֥א עַד־הָעָֽרֶב׃
7 וְהַנֹּגֵ֖עַ בִּבְשַׂ֣ר הַזָּ֑ב יְכַבֵּ֧ס בְּגָדָ֛יו וְרָחַ֥ץ
בַּמַּ֖יִם וְטָמֵ֥א עַד־הָעָֽרֶב׃ 8 וְכִֽי־יָרֹ֥ק הַזָּ֖ב
בַּטָּה֑וֹר וְכִבֶּ֧ס בְּגָדָ֛יו וְרָחַ֥ץ בַּמַּ֖יִם וְטָמֵ֥א
עַד־הָעָֽרֶב׃ 9 וְכָל־הַמֶּרְכָּ֗ב אֲשֶׁ֨ר יִרְכַּ֥ב
עָלָ֛יו הַזָּ֖ב יִטְמָֽא׃ 10 וְכָל־הַנֹּגֵ֗עַ בְּכֹל֙ אֲשֶׁ֣ר
יִהְיֶ֣ה תַחְתָּ֔יו יִטְמָ֖א עַד־הָעָ֑רֶב וְהַנּוֹשֵׂ֣א

bathing, and waiting till nightfall in order to regain the state of ritual purity; for the male, this means the nightfall after the ejaculation, and for the female, since it involves blood, the evening of the seventh day. No sacrifice need be offered for normal discharges. No sin is imputed to the man with a seminal discharge. In fact, the commandment to "be fruitful and multiply" (Genesis 1:28) necessitates seminal emissions. When a man comes in contact with menstrual blood through intercourse with a menstruating woman, he too must wait seven days before he is ritually pure. Abnormal discharges (those described in vv. 2–15 and vv. 25–30) involve a longer waiting period and necessitate a purgation offering to eliminate the resulting impurity that accumulated in the sanctuary. Leviticus imputes no wrongdoing to the individual who suffers from those maladies.

### THE ISRAELITE MALE (15:1–18)

#### *Laws about Abnormal Discharges from the Penis* (15:1–15)

*3. **runs.*** Heb. *zav*; when this term applies to a male, it refers only to one with abnormal discharge. The underlying condition might be a form of gonorrhea or an infection of the urinary tract or other organs. The term conveys the idea of "oozing" or "exuding greatly"; the same verb appears in the expression "a land flowing with milk and honey" (see, for example, Exodus 3:8). For the term's specific application to females, see below (vv. 19, 25).

*4–10.* The basic principle that emerges is that all articles under a man with abnormal discharge are impure; as such, they in turn disseminate a one-day impurity to all who touch them. This principle also applies to the menstruating woman (v. 21).

*5. **those.*** [The Hebrew term is singular but

things shall wash their clothes, bathe in water, and remain impure until evening. [11]All those whom the one with a discharge touches, without having rinsed his hands in water, shall wash their clothes, bathe in water, and remain impure until evening. [12]An earthen vessel that the one with a discharge touches shall be broken; and any wooden implement shall be rinsed with water.

[13]When the one with a discharge becomes purified of his discharge, he shall count off seven days for his purification, wash those clothes, and bathe his body in fresh water; then he shall be pure. [14]On the eighth day he shall take two turtledoves or two pigeons and come before יהוה at the entrance of the Tent of Meeting and give them to the priest. [15]The priest shall offer them, the one as a purgation offering and the other as a burnt offering. Thus the priest shall make expiation on his behalf, for his discharge, before יהוה.

[16]When a man has an emission of semen, he shall bathe his whole body in water and remain impure until evening. [17]All cloth or leather on which semen falls shall be washed in water and remain impure until evening.

אוֹתָם יְכַבֵּס בְּגָדָיו וְרָחַץ בַּמַּיִם וְטָמֵא
עַד־הָעָרֶב׃ 11 וְכֹל אֲשֶׁר יִגַּע־בּוֹ הַזָּב
וְיָדָיו לֹא־שָׁטַף בַּמָּיִם וְכִבֶּס בְּגָדָיו וְרָחַץ
בַּמַּיִם וְטָמֵא עַד־הָעָרֶב׃ 12 וּכְלִי־חֶרֶשׂ
אֲשֶׁר־יִגַּע־בּוֹ הַזָּב יִשָּׁבֵר וְכָל־כְּלִי־עֵץ
יִשָּׁטֵף בַּמָּיִם׃
13 וְכִי־יִטְהַר הַזָּב מִזּוֹבוֹ וְסָפַר לוֹ שִׁבְעַת
יָמִים לְטָהֳרָתוֹ וְכִבֶּס בְּגָדָיו וְרָחַץ בְּשָׂרוֹ
בְּמַיִם חַיִּים וְטָהֵר׃ 14 וּבַיּוֹם הַשְּׁמִינִי יִקַּח־
לוֹ שְׁתֵּי תֹרִים אוֹ שְׁנֵי בְּנֵי יוֹנָה וּבָא ׀ לִפְנֵי
יְהֹוָה אֶל־פֶּתַח אֹהֶל מוֹעֵד וּנְתָנָם אֶל־
הַכֹּהֵן׃ 15 וְעָשָׂה אֹתָם הַכֹּהֵן אֶחָד חַטָּאת
וְהָאֶחָד עֹלָה וְכִפֶּר עָלָיו הַכֹּהֵן לִפְנֵי יְהֹוָה
מִזּוֹבוֹ׃ ס
16 וְאִישׁ כִּי־תֵצֵא מִמֶּנּוּ שִׁכְבַת־זָרַע וְרָחַץ
בַּמַּיִם אֶת־כׇּל־בְּשָׂרוֹ וְטָמֵא עַד־הָעָרֶב׃
17 וְכׇל־בֶּגֶד וְכׇל־עוֹר אֲשֶׁר־יִהְיֶה עָלָיו
שִׁכְבַת־זָרַע וְכֻבַּס בַּמַּיִם וְטָמֵא עַד־הָעָרֶב׃

---

used collectively. Here and elsewhere in Leviticus 15, the present translation renders such language in the plural, in order to convey the gender-neutral sense. —*Ed.*]

*11.* This verse has puzzled commentators since ancient times, because it states that if the *zav* rinses his hands in water, the person whom he touches will not contract impurity. Most likely this is a concession to allow the person suffering from a chronic discharge to retain somewhat normal social relationships: as long as he rinses his hands on a regular basis, he may have contact with family and community. These rules would seem to apply as well to women with genital discharges, even though such is not stated in the text (see at v. 20).

*13.* ***fresh.*** See at 14:5.

*14.* ***On the eighth day he shall take two turtledoves.*** Severe impurities necessitate sacrificial offerings. The sacrifice of two birds corresponds to the offering given by the person of insufficient means in 12:8 and 14:21. The reason a *zav* makes a donation of lesser value is probably due to the correspondence of his title to the *zavah* (the woman who suffers from irregular bleeding); the Torah tries to minimize the economic burden for her (see at v. 29), and consequently, for him.

### *Laws about Normal Seminal Emissions* (15:16–18)

This section here probably refers to an involuntary ejaculation or nocturnal emission. Deuteronomy 23:11 bars the man who has had a nocturnal emission from remaining in an Israelite military encampment until he has washed and waited till evening.

pure until evening. [18]Likewise for a woman: when a man has carnal relations with her, both shall bathe in water and remain impure until evening.

[19]When a woman has a discharge, her discharge

18 וְאִשָּׁה אֲשֶׁר יִשְׁכַּב אִישׁ אֹתָהּ שִׁכְבַת־
זָרַע וְרָחֲצוּ בַמַּיִם וְטָמְאוּ עַד־הָעָרֶב׃ פ
19 וְאִשָּׁה כִּי־תִהְיֶה זָבָה דָּם יִהְיֶה זֹבָהּ

*18.* Just as seminal emissions render objects impure (vv. 16–17), so they also make a man's sexual partner impure. The key term in each verse is *shichvat zera* ("emission of semen," literally "a laying down of [what can become] offspring"). Many cultures in the ancient world share the idea that sexual intercourse and participation in religious ritual must be separated by washing and waiting. Earlier in the Torah, Moses anticipated God's descent upon Mount Sinai by prohibiting the Israelites from sexual relations for three days (see at Exodus 19:10, 15).

## THE ISRAELITE FEMALE (15:19–30)

### *Laws about Menstruation* (15:19–24)

Frequent menstruation is the product of various factors of modern life that were not relevant to our foremothers. Women in ancient Israel (and the ancient world in general) probably menstruated less frequently than modern women, for several reasons. Due to sparser diet, females in pre-modern times began to menstruate on average at age 14, as opposed to an average of age 12 today. Women married soon after they began to menstruate, and generally they experienced more pregnancies in their lifetime than their average modern Jewish counterparts (see *B'reishit*, Another View, p. 27). Breast-feeding typically for three years (see at Exodus 2:10) would have further reduced the number of menstrual cycles they experienced. Therefore, the regulations in this passage probably had a smaller practical impact than we might at first imagine.

The original meaning of the key term for menstruation in the Bible, *niddah*, is unclear, but several Hebrew roots with the letter combination *n-d* have the general sense of "expel" or "throw." It is possible that the word was used for the expulsion or elimination of the menstrual blood (see also at 12:2). In Leviticus 15, the term is neutral and without any stigma. In contrast to the pragmatic attitude in this parashah, some later biblical texts use the term *niddah* as a term of abomination and revulsion, including Leviticus 20:21; Lamentations 1:8, 17; Ezra 9:11; and II Chronicles 29:5. Ezekiel, a 6th-century-B.C.E. prophet, justifies the destruction of Jerusalem by saying: "Their ways were in My sight like the impurity of a menstruous woman" (36:17). Note that there and in Ezekiel 18:6 and 22:10, the prophet uses the term *niddah* for the menstruating woman herself. At the same time, however, the expression *mei niddah* ("water of lustration") refers to a potion that *removes* impurity generated by a corpse; it could be translated "water for *the elimination of* impurity" (Numbers 19:9, 13, 20, 21; see also Zechariah 13:1). On *niddah*, see also at Numbers 19:9.

[In Leviticus, the menstruant is separated from the sancta (the sacred). The social and ritual isolation of menstruating women is found in many cultures around the world ("Introduction," Thomas Buckley and Alma Gottlieb, eds., *Blood Magic*, 1988, p. 12). However, the social functions of menstrual taboos are culturally variable and specific. In one society, these taboos function to subordinate women; in another, they give women exclusive ritual powers; and yet another culture views menstruation ambivalently, as both containing and enhancing women's power (Buckley and Gottlieb, p. 14). The legislation in Leviticus can be seen as moderate in that the menstruating woman remains at home and has somewhat normal family and social relationships; see above at v. 11, and below at v. 20. —*Ed.*]

*19. discharge.* Heb. *zavah*, the feminine equiv-

being blood from her body, she shall remain in her menstrual separation seven days; whoever touches her shall be impure until evening. [20]Anything that she lies on during her menstrual separation shall be impure; and anything that she sits on shall be impure. [21]All those who touch her bedding shall wash their clothes, bathe in water, and remain impure until evening; [22]and all those who touch any object on which she has sat shall wash their clothes, bathe in water, and remain impure until evening. [23]Be it the bedding or be it the object on which she has sat, on touching it one shall be impure until evening. [24]And if a man lies with her, her menstrual separation applies to him; he shall be impure seven days, and any bedding on which he lies shall become impure.

בִּבְשָׂרָ֑הּ שִׁבְעַ֤ת יָמִים֙ תִּהְיֶ֣ה בְנִדָּתָ֔הּ וְכׇל־
הַנֹּגֵ֥עַ בָּ֖הּ יִטְמָ֥א עַד־הָעָֽרֶב׃ 20 וְכֹל֩ אֲשֶׁ֨ר
תִּשְׁכַּ֥ב עָלָ֛יו בְּנִדָּתָ֖הּ יִטְמָ֑א וְכֹ֛ל אֲשֶׁר־תֵּשֵׁ֥ב
עָלָ֖יו יִטְמָֽא׃ 21 וְכׇל־הַנֹּגֵ֖עַ בְּמִשְׁכָּבָ֑הּ יְכַבֵּ֧ס
בְּגָדָ֛יו וְרָחַ֥ץ בַּמַּ֖יִם וְטָמֵ֥א עַד־הָעָֽרֶב׃
22 וְכׇל־הַנֹּגֵ֔עַ בְּכׇל־כְּלִ֖י אֲשֶׁר־תֵּשֵׁ֣ב עָלָ֑יו
יְכַבֵּ֧ס בְּגָדָ֛יו וְרָחַ֥ץ בַּמַּ֖יִם וְטָמֵ֥א עַד־הָעָֽרֶב׃
23 וְאִ֨ם עַֽל־הַמִּשְׁכָּ֜ב ה֗וּא א֧וֹ עַֽל־הַכְּלִ֛י
אֲשֶׁר־הִ֥וא יֹשֶֽׁבֶת־עָלָ֖יו בְּנׇגְעוֹ־ב֑וֹ יִטְמָ֖א
עַד־הָעָֽרֶב׃ 24 וְאִ֡ם שָׁכֹב֩ יִשְׁכַּ֨ב אִ֜ישׁ אֹתָ֗הּ
וּתְהִ֤י נִדָּתָהּ֙ עָלָ֔יו וְטָמֵ֖א שִׁבְעַ֣ת יָמִ֑ים וְכׇל־
הַמִּשְׁכָּ֛ב אֲשֶׁר־יִשְׁכַּ֥ב עָלָ֖יו יִטְמָֽא׃ ס

alent of the term that in v. 2 referred to the man with an abnormal emission. In women, however, this passage uses the word to refer to both normal and abnormal bleeding. (It is difficult to explain the omission of this term in Leviticus 12, which indirectly discusses postpartum bleeding.) The only identified difference between normal and abnormal female bleeding is timing (v. 25). See further below at v. 33.

***seven days.*** The Torah limits the impurity of the menstruating woman to seven days, as opposed to rabbinic practice, which extends her taboo status seven days beyond the end of her period.

***20.*** What are the practical implications of the regulations in this passage? Leviticus 15 nowhere requires the isolation of the menstruant or her removal from her normal context to some other space. The rules concerning her are similar to those of the (male) *zav*. Objects under her are impure and impart a one-day impurity to all those who touch them (15:4–6, 20–22). The person who touches her becomes impure (15:7, 19). Two additional rules for the woman in *niddah* are absent for the *zav*: anyone who has sexual relations with her is impure for seven days (v. 24), and the person who touches an object on the same bedding or chair where she is sitting becomes ritually polluted (v. 23; the Hebrew is difficult). Thus, the menstruant has to be careful regarding where she lies and sits, and she must avoid the touch of others (although the laws are addressed to others, not the woman herself). According to v. 11, the *zav* may touch another person without consequence but only if he has rinsed his hands; the text does not say whether this applies to the menstruant, but logic suggests that it does. After all, menstruation, a "normal" cause of impurity, does not require a purgation offering as does the "abnormal" case of the man with a chronic discharge. Further, if the priestly regulations mean to imply that anyone whom she touches would become impure, then all the people for whom she cares in the course of her duties would be affected, whether they be her children or the elders of her household. It therefore seems likely that Leviticus intends that the frequent rinsing of her hands would allow the woman to function in her usual capacity.

***21.*** ***All those.*** See above at v. 5.

***24.*** The central concern of Leviticus 15 is couched in this verse: the violation of purity rules when a man has sexual contact with a menstruating woman (see the outline in the unit introduction,

25 When a woman has had a discharge of blood for many days, not at the time of her menstrual separation, or when she has a discharge beyond her period of menstrual separation, she shall be impure, as though at the time of her menstrual separation, as long as her discharge lasts. 26 Any bedding on which she lies while her discharge lasts shall be for her like bedding during her menstrual separation; and any object on which she sits shall become impure, as it does during her menstrual separation: 27 All those who touch them shall be impure—and shall wash their clothes, bathe in water, and remain impure until evening.

28 When she becomes purified of her discharge, she shall count off seven days, and after that she shall be pure. 29 On the eighth day she shall take two turtledoves or two pigeons, and bring them to

25 וְאִשָּׁ֡ה כִּֽי־יָז֩וּב ז֨וֹב דָּמָ֜הּ יָמִ֣ים רַבִּ֗ים
בְּלֹא֙ עֶת־נִדָּתָ֔הּ א֥וֹ כִֽי־תָז֖וּב עַל־נִדָּתָ֑הּ
כָּל־יְמֵ֞י ז֣וֹב טֻמְאָתָ֗הּ כִּימֵ֧י נִדָּתָ֛הּ תִּהְיֶ֖ה
טְמֵאָ֥ה הִֽוא׃ 26 כָּל־הַמִּשְׁכָּ֞ב אֲשֶׁר־תִּשְׁכַּ֤ב
עָלָיו֙ כָּל־יְמֵ֣י זוֹבָ֔הּ כְּמִשְׁכַּ֥ב נִדָּתָ֖הּ יִֽהְיֶה־
לָּ֑הּ וְכָֽל־הַכְּלִי֙ אֲשֶׁ֣ר תֵּשֵׁ֣ב עָלָ֔יו טָמֵ֣א
יִהְיֶ֔ה כְּטֻמְאַ֖ת נִדָּתָֽהּ׃ 27 וְכָל־הַנּוֹגֵ֥עַ בָּ֖ם
יִטְמָ֑א וְכִבֶּ֧ס בְּגָדָ֛יו וְרָחַ֥ץ בַּמַּ֖יִם וְטָמֵ֥א
עַד־הָעָֽרֶב׃
28 וְאִֽם־טָהֲרָ֖ה מִזּוֹבָ֑הּ וְסָ֥פְרָה לָּ֛הּ שִׁבְעַ֥ת
יָמִ֖ים וְאַחַ֥ר תִּטְהָֽר׃ 29 וּבַיּ֣וֹם הַשְּׁמִינִ֗י
תִּֽקַּֽח־לָהּ֙ שְׁתֵּ֣י תֹרִ֔ים א֥וֹ שְׁנֵ֖י בְּנֵ֣י יוֹנָ֑ה

p. 665). Of all the various kinds of contact with a woman in *niddah* or her belongings, only sexual contact results in a period of impurity equal to that of the woman herself—seven days. Perhaps this is because the male comes into direct contact with her menstrual fluid. Leviticus 20:18 twice denounces both sexual partners as guilty for revealing "her source [or: flow] (of blood)," so it is the intimate nature of their contact that explains his extended period of pollution.

Elsewhere we find more severe consequences for sex with a menstruating woman than simply becoming ritually impure. Leviticus 20:18 decrees that "both of them shall be cut off from among their people." Both that verse and Leviticus 18:19 place this act in the context of violations of the Covenant that imperil Israel's tenancy in the land of Canaan. (On *niddah*, see also Ezekiel 18:6; 22:10.)

### *Laws about Abnormal Discharge of Blood* (15:25–30)

*25.* This verse defines the *zavah* as a woman who experiences either genital bleeding that is not consistent with her normal menstrual cycle, or a menstrual period that is prolonged beyond the Torah's norm of seven days (v. 18). In both these cases, the rules that apply to the normally menstruating woman apply to the *zavah* here during the time of her bleeding and for seven additional days after the bleeding stops (v. 28). The Christians' New Testament mentions a woman who experienced bleeding such as this for twelve years (Matthew 9:20; Mark 5:25; Luke 8:43).

*26–27.* These rules for the woman with abnormal bleeding correspond to those that apply to the woman in *niddah* in vv. 20–22. Although the additional strictures for the woman in *niddah* of vv. 23–24 are not repeated in this passage, it is logical to assume that they apply to the *zavah* as well: anyone who touches an object that is resting on the bed or chair upon which she sits is polluted; and the man who has intercourse with her is impure for seven days.

*29. **On the eighth day.*** Because of her prolonged period of impurity, she must bring a sacrifice, similar to that of the *zav* of vv. 3–15. Her donation is akin to that of a person of lesser means (12:8, 14:21), probably because of the frequent occurrence of such "abnormal" bleeding.

the priest at the entrance of the Tent of Meeting.
30 The priest shall offer the one as a purgation offering and the other as a burnt offering; and the
priest shall make expiation on her behalf, for her
impure discharge, before יהוה.
31 You shall put the Israelites on guard against
their impurity, lest they die through their impurity
by defiling My Tabernacle which is among them.
32 Such is the ritual concerning one who has a
discharge: concerning him who has an emission of
semen and becomes impure thereby; 33 and concerning her whose condition is that of menstrual
separation; and concerning anyone, male or female,
who has a discharge; and concerning a man who lies
with an impure woman.

וְהֵבִיאָה אוֹתָם֙ אֶל־הַכֹּהֵ֔ן אֶל־פֶּ֖תַח אֹ֥הֶל
מוֹעֵֽד׃ 30 וְעָשָׂ֤ה הַכֹּהֵן֙ אֶת־הָאֶחָ֣ד חַטָּ֔את
וְאֶת־הָאֶחָ֖ד עֹלָ֑ה וְכִפֶּ֨ר עָלֶ֜יהָ הַכֹּהֵ֗ן לִפְנֵ֣י
יְהֹוָ֔ה מִזּ֖וֹב טֻמְאָתָֽהּ׃
31 וְהִזַּרְתֶּ֥ם אֶת־בְּנֵֽי־יִשְׂרָאֵ֖ל מִטֻּמְאָתָ֑ם וְלֹ֤א
יָמֻ֙תוּ֙ בְּטֻמְאָתָ֔ם בְּטַמְּאָ֥ם אֶת־מִשְׁכָּנִ֖י אֲשֶׁ֥ר
בְּתוֹכָֽם׃
32 זֹ֛את תּוֹרַ֥ת הַזָּ֖ב וַאֲשֶׁ֨ר תֵּצֵ֥א מִמֶּ֛נּוּ
שִׁכְבַת־זֶ֖רַע לְטָמְאָה־בָֽהּ׃ 33 וְהַדָּוָה֙ בְּנִדָּתָ֔הּ
וְהַזָּב֙ אֶת־זוֹב֔וֹ לַזָּכָ֖ר וְלַנְּקֵבָ֑ה וּלְאִ֕ישׁ אֲשֶׁ֥ר
יִשְׁכַּ֖ב עִם־טְמֵאָֽה׃ פ

### CONCLUSION (15:31–33)

*31. **You shall put the Israelites on guard.*** The exact force of the rare Hebrew verb here is disputed. The verbal root refers to separation. Thus this clause may well be telling Aaron (see v. 1) and his descendants—whose priestly function it is to "distinguish between . . . the impure and the pure" (10:10)—to "separate" the people of Israel from their impurity.

***lest they die.*** That is, the consequence of allowing impurity to accumulate without taking the necessary remedial steps is national suicide. The "death" threatened here is not the death of the impure individual, but the collective existence of the people among whom God resides.

*32. **Such is the ritual concerning.*** Literally, "this is the *torah* of . . . ," one of several places where the word *torah* (teaching) has a specific, limited sense (so also 14:2; see at 6:2, Deuteronomy 31:9).

*33. **condition.*** Heb. *davah*; see at 12:2.

*—Elaine Goodfriend*

## Another View

BY MOVING FROM a state of ritual impurity to one of ritual purity, the ever-changing human body serves as the index for the transformation of identity. The person departing from the state of *m'tzora* (a person with *tzaraat*, conventionally translated as a "leper") follows about ten steps that separate the ritually pure from the ritually impure state. The spectrum between the pure and the impure becomes apparent in the gradations of being outside the camp, then inside the camp but outside one's tent, and finally inside the community and inside the home. That the ritually impure state is transitional becomes apparent in the time-bound nature of each stage. The body passes through the various stages and is likely to cross several borders between ritually pure and impure over the course of its existence.

As the body undergoes the permutations of ritual purity and impurity, the impure body is sometimes exiled—but not abandoned to its exile. The appearance of a priest outside the camp (14:3) signals that exile is ephemeral and that restoration will begin. No particular priestly category fixes the body, but rather it moves through a full range of categories. This sense of the body as changeable and the potential reversibility of its status are what underlie prophetic notions that sinful actions can be retracted and a dire fate averted.

Focus on the body emphasizes the changes undergone by the self in the process of becoming another self. Signs on the body gauge identity and mark transformation. When the sick are healed, their bodies bear

*The human body is both an indicator of change and a vessel of memory.*

the proof. Yet one's body is not only an indicator of change but also a vessel of memory. Illness and trauma are remembered by nerves, muscles, and scars. The body that gives birth will forever maintain a link with its offspring. The body attests to change as well as to the indelibility of experience. Therefore descriptions of identity, predicated as they are on the language of body, convey the tension between the possibility of change and the integrity of forms.

—*Rachel Havrelock*

## Post-biblical Interpretations

***This shall be the ritual for a leper*** (14:2). In BT *Arachin* 15b the Rabbis interpreted this biblical word for "leper" (*m'tzora*, the person afflicted with *tzaraat*) as an acronym for the Hebrew term for slander (*motzi shem ra*). Thus, they insisted that *tzaraat* is a divine punishment for defaming others, a grave transgression in a culture that highly valued oral communication (BT *Bava M'tzia* 58a). The connection between slander and *tzaraat* already appears in Numbers 12 when Miriam is afflicted for complaining about her brother Moses. In Midrash *Sifra, M'tzora* 5.7, the Rabbis emphasize that Miriam's contraction of *tzaraat* (Numbers 12:10) was the result of her denunciation of Moses, particularly because she slandered him behind his back.

***When . . . I inflict an eruptive plague upon a house*** (14:34). From early on, the Rabbis held that the house afflicted by this strange plague never existed and never will exist—and that the only reason that this law exists is for the purpose of theoretical study (Tosefta *N'gaim* 6:1). The Talmud does not develop the Mishnah tractate devoted to the topic.

***he shall . . . bathe his body in fresh water*** (15:13). Heb. *mayim chayim* ("fresh water," literally "living water") is required as a means of purification not only for the man with a discharge but also in the case of *tzaraat* for both people and houses (14:5–6, 50–52), and in the case of corpse impurity (Numbers 19:8). All of these cases of ritual impurity last for at least seven days. However, the Torah notably does not mention the requirement of immersion in water for cases of impurity of similar duration that are specific to women, such as those resulting from birth, menstruation, or irregular genital bleeding. The Mishnah assumes that immersion in fresh water applies to women's impurities as well (*Mikvaot* 1:8).

*The Talmud institutes the rabbinic sage as a sort of gynecological expert.*

***When a woman has a discharge*** (15:19). This passage establishes the rules of purification concerning a woman's menstrual period. The Rabbis developed these regulations into an entire tractate called *Niddah*, the "menstruating woman," which is part of the mishnaic order called *Purities*. Much like the priestly writers of Leviticus, the Rabbis did not consider purity and impurity a matter of morality, but rather a matter of ritual status with regard to access to the Temple in Jerusalem. Thus, many of the rules of purity and impurity detailed in the biblical passage here and in Mishnah *Niddah* had no application in a post-Temple reality. However, the rules of sexual abstinence during the wife's menstrual period, which the Rabbis derived from Leviticus 18:19 and 20:18, are not dependent on the historical existence of the Temple and continue to regulate the sex life of married couples in traditional Jewish communities to this day. Indeed, many of the rabbinic discussions in BT *Niddah* focus on the workings of menstruation and on women's physiology in general, instituting the rabbinic sage as a sort of gynecological expert to be consulted when problems arise.

***a discharge of blood for many days*** (15:25). The Torah assumes a menstrual calendar of seven days of bleeding. It considers any bleeding beyond seven days or outside of the seven regular days to be abnormal. It categorizes a woman with an irregular discharge as a *zavah*, parallel to the male category of *zav* (15:13). In a tractate called *Zavim*, the Mishnah discusses both men and women with irregular genital discharges. In biblical law, the rules of purification for the *zavah* differ from the rules for menstruation. Notably, the afflicted woman must count seven days after the irregular discharge has ceased before purification can take place. The Talmud, however, merges the two categories of regular and irregular bleeding. Accordingly, a woman is to count seven "white" days without discharge after her menses before she immerses in a *mikveh* and resumes marital intimacy. The Talmud famously attributes this more stringent practice to women: "Rabbi Zera said: The daughters of Israel (*b'not Yisrael*) have imposed upon themselves the stringency that even where they observe only a drop of blood the size of a mustard seed, they wait on account of it seven clean days" (BT *Niddah* 66a). One should not dismiss Rabbi Zera's attribution of this legal stringency to women too readily, considering that throughout Jewish history women have used the laws of *niddah* toward their own spiritual empowerment, as well as for practical purposes, including control over their sex lives.

—*Charlotte Elisheva Fonrobert*

# Contemporary Reflection

THEOLOGIAN ELIZABETH DODSON GRAY notes: "Women's bodies may be the hardest place for women to find sacredness" (*Sacred Dimensions of Women's Experience*, 1988, p. 197). Our society sends negative messages to women from earliest childhood about the expected perfection of their physiques and the disappointments of any flaws in the female form. *Parashat M'tzora*, then, with its focus on menstrual impurity (15:19–24), seems to impart the same kind of unfavorable sense. Rejecting our own received biases and patriarchal assumptions about menstruation, however, can help us form a contemporary view of these so-called taboos.

What the Torah deems as *tamei* ("impure") or *tahor* ("pure") is not actually attached to cleanliness, even though they are often translated as "unclean" and "clean." These Hebrew words are ritual terms, meant to designate those in a physical and spiritual state unable to enter the *Mishkan* (Tabernacle; and in later times, the Temple), or those able to do so. Those who are considered *tamei* are taboo (which is not what we think of as "bad"), meaning that they cannot enter the sacred space; and the thing that causes them to be ineligible to enter is also understood to be taboo. Anthropologists note that taboos are the system by which a culture sets aside certain objects or persons as either sacred or accursed. Such objects or persons inspire both fear and respect. Penelope Washbourn writes: "Menstruation symbolizes the advent of a new power that is *mana* . . . 'sacred.' . . . A taboo expresses this feeling that something special, some holy power, is involved, and our response to it must be very careful" (in *WomanSpirit Rising*, 1989, p. 251). This mixed message of fear and power, contact and avoidance, actually dominates all the Torah's passages around blood. Blood, which is to be avoided in the realm of eating and sex, is the same substance that atones for the community in the sacrificial system, and it binds the individual male child to the Israelite covenant through circumcision. Blood both sustains and endangers; it is the medium of plague or deliverance. Thus blood—like every potent symbol—has the double quality and the twin potential of birth and decay, purity and impurity.

So too with menstrual blood. We who are often uninspired and unaffected by our bodies should reject the negative connotation of taboo—and explore, instead, the positive and sacred aspect. Surely a religion

*We should recite a blessing for the coming and going of menstruation.*

that has a blessing for an activity as mundane as going to the bathroom should have a blessing for the coming and going of menstruation. Since the male composers of the liturgy, living in a world where modesty was central and women's bodies were a mystery at best, were not able—or more likely, not willing—to imagine such a blessing, we must be the first generation to do so.

More than thirty years ago, I did just this: I wrote a blessing for menstruation and have been writing about it and teaching it ever since. When I crafted my *b'rachah*, I reappropriated the difficult and offensive morning blessing in the traditional prayer book, which reads: "Blessed are You, Adonai our God, Ruler of the Universe, who has not made me a woman." (Traditionally, women say instead, "who has made me according to Your will.") Each month, when I get my period, I say: "*Baruch atah Adonai, eloheinu melech haolam, she'asani ishah*: Blessed are You, Adonai our God, Ruler of the Universe, who has made me a woman." Saying the blessing becomes a revolutionary moment, for this slight change in wording—changing the negative "who has not made me a woman" into the positive "who has made me a woman"—affirms my holiness and sanctity within the context of menstruation, not despite it.

I believe it is possible to rescue the aspects of mystery inherent in menstruation. While we reject menstrual huts, a separation from the sancta, and antiquated notions of cleanliness, we can still emerge with a sense of the overwhelming mystery of life and death that is embodied in our corporeal female selves. While many women associate menstruation with physical pain and discomfort, the experience nonetheless involves a degree of power. We should reject the notion that menstruation makes a woman "unclean" and instead think of this time as a period of intense electrical charges—the charge of life and death—pulsing through our bodies. Blu Greenberg urges us to focus more on the positive, "to restore that element of holiness to our bodies, our selves" (*On Women and Judaism*, 1981, pp. 118–120).

We can also consider a connection between menstruation and covenant. The prophet Zechariah speaks to "daughter Jerusalem" and "daughter Zion" about "your covenant of blood" as that which releases prisoners from the dry pit (9:9–11). It does not say "the covenant of blood," as most translations render it, but rather emphasizes that blood is the focus of the covenant. The address to the feminine persona suggests that all "daughters of Zion" have that covenant of blood. It is through menstruation—from puberty when we accept our responsibilities as Jews, through the elder years when bleeding stops and deep wisdom starts—that the entire world is saved from the dry pit of death, in which there is no water, no womb, no regeneration, no rebirth.

See menstrual blood, then, as women's covenantal blood—just as the blood of *b'rit milah* (ritual circumcision) is men's. The possibilities for rituals around this abound. For women too have a *b'rit* (covenant) inscribed in our flesh as an "everlasting covenant" (Genesis 17:19): not just once, at eight days old, but every single month. And *M'tzora,* in its ancient and perhaps awkward way, attempts to remind us.

—*Elyse Goldstein*

# Voices

## M'tzora

Laurie Patton

*Leviticus 14:2*

It takes time
to clean
and wrap
leprous bandages.

Elijah told the rabbi
that the Messiah
was a leper
sitting at the gates
of the city,
bandaging his wounds
one at a time.

"Ah," said the rabbi,
"he is being thorough.
He is taking his time."

"No," said Elijah.
"This way,
the Messiah can come
any time he is called,
and he will not be delayed."

He would rush out—
no time for cover
or cleaning—
what is one open sore
when the moment has come
to close the wounds
of the world?

## Otwock II

Kadya Molodowsky (transl. Kathryn Hellerstein)

*Leviticus 14:1–32*

We are sick here—a multitude of locusts
Fallen suddenly upon the whiteness
Of the wintry wood.
With mouths open in putrid breathing,
We draw out a word like hoarse fiddles.
Who still needs us,
Wrapped up in shawls, with feverish eyes?
And what use are we?
Pines raise their branches high
In order not to touch us,
In order to shun us, shun us.
We scream to the woods
And spit blood into their fragrant roots.
That's why the trees stir at night and tell
How big is the cemetery here,
And mock the dying
To the last shadow of memory
With their tall growth, with their fat trunks
And millennial lives.
I am here, too, solitary,
Sick, wrapped in a shawl,
And I step slowly in the snow among the trees,
And no one knows
That I am still myself.

## *Blood*

Alicia Suskin Ostriker

*Leviticus 15:19–24*

Of all bodily fluids, blood is the one most often named, the bravest and most dramatic, the fluid of heroes and of atonement. The fluid of crime. Of shame, when its river floods from a woman's body. It is vivid red, and soon becomes clotted, sticky, stale. The tangy scent of it is a stimulant. Simple people know this. Children dare each other to taste it.

we are connected to earth by our menstrual
  blood
and the blood of warriors flowing from open
  wounds
like open lips, gratifying the soil
moistening dry bones—
without these things, can the earth yield?

## *from Transforming the Meaning of Purity*

Rachel Adler

*Leviticus 15*

We must keep asking the Torah to speak to us in human language, this crude jargon studded with constraints and distortions, silences and brutalities, that is our only vessel for holiness and truth and peace. We must keep teaching each other, we and our study partner the Torah, all that it means to be human. Human is not whole. Human is full of holes. Human bleeds. Human births its worlds in agonies of blood and bellyaches. Human owns no perfect, timeless texts because human inhabits no perfect, timeless contexts.

## *The Ritual Bath*

Sarah Antine

*Leviticus 15:19–30*

It takes a tree a year
to do what I do in a month;
The moon unfolding its pearl—

At the edge of the night
I peel off
layers of myself.

Maple leaves redden and drop,
limbs shedding their temporary hands.

Full of rainwater, I go to the ritual bath,
a room between I am alone
and I am together
with you.

May no part of me stay up when I go under—
Water closes its ceiling above me.
I am no longer a container for sadness.

## *from* Jewish Feminism: Go to Yourself

Laura Geller

*Leviticus 15:19–24*

When I was a rabbinical student there were no other women in my class. In Talmud class as we learned about the tradition of occasional blessings, the teacher explained that there is no important moment in the lifetime of a Jew for which there is no blessing. And I thought to myself, this is wonderful, the idea that all of life is holy. Then I thought to myself, wait a second, that is not true. There were moments in my life that weren't sanctified by a blessing. And I remembered, while sitting with my male colleagues and male professors, the moment when I got my period for the first time and what it was like not to have a blessing to sanctify that. I learned then one of the unanticipated consequences of admitting women to rabbinical school. And I began to understand that my experience as a woman begins with the experience of my body, and that I must listen to that experience and respond by creating new rituals to celebrate powerful events in women's lives: menarche, birth, lactation, weaning, menopause, abortion, miscarriage and more. Once we begin to experience and sanctify moments that start with our bodies, we can begin to sanctify other moments in our lives.

## The Curse

Sue Hubbard

*Leviticus 15:19–24*

She is all woman now
daughter become sister
spindle-prick of peony
smearing her whites.

A butterfly wing of bright
crimson surprises her waking,
shyly she comes to me bringing her
ring-o-roses, her scarlet bouquet.

We are joined in blood
by the slow pull of the moon's
waning and the small secrets
of darkened bathroom shelves.

How the past echoes. My mother's
silent mouthing of those witch-craft
words. The Curse, as she taught me
to name that first staining.

Have we forgotten those cackle
voices; conspiratorial whispers
echoing among unguents and tinctures
in white-tiled rooms?

And I who was mute, spineless
as a sea-horse, wish you brave
and beautiful. Feel your roots, deep
and damp, as rusty beets smelling of earth.

# אחרי מות ✦ *Acharei Mot*

## LEVITICUS 16:1–18:30

### *Boundaries of Rituals: The Sanctuary and the Body*

At the root of *parashat Acharei Mot* ("after the death [of]") is the question of change. How is it that a person undergoes a transformation? What does it mean and how does it change her orientation to the Divine? The priestly writers also wonder how the people of Israel can undergo a collective change. The answer they provide is that change comes about through properly performed ritual. The priestly writers credited with much of Leviticus (see p. 567) advocate constant change. According to them, the body itself is an ongoing process of flux.

Fascinated with the body and the body politic, the priests speculate that both have the potential to reach purity and optimal holiness. The converse is also true—the body can become impure and the community tainted by transgression. Neither the state of impurity nor the state of purity is eternal. Both are time-bound and set within a spectrum of gradations between purity and impurity. Priestly ritual mediates between these states, and it demarcates them so that individual and community alike can know where they stand in relation to God and to others.

The body is not at fault for entering the state of impurity, which can be reversed through time and water. As it develops, priestly thought comes to consider the states of purity and impurity as larger than the physical body and affected by moral transgressions as well. This parashah combines two strata of priestly thought that modern critical scholars label as "P" for the Priestly School (Leviticus 16) and "H" for the Holiness School (Leviticus 17–18). The holiness of the sanctuary most concerns the P source, whereas the sacred nature of the land most concerns the H source. Both sources grant contaminating and purifying power to blood. Whereas Leviticus 16 attends to transformation, Leviticus 17 stipulates how people should introduce holiness into their diet.

*This portion mentions women only in terms of the dangers posed by their sexuality.*

Women must read and write themselves into the holy community presented in the H source. When Leviticus 18 specifically mentions women, it is in terms of the dangerous and potentially contaminating force of their sexuality. They are figures in the household whose bodies require policing. Leviticus 18 circumscribes the bodies of female relatives as forbidden, thus setting up a system of protection within the domestic domain. At the same time, these safeguards designate women as extensions of their husbands, brothers, and grandfathers and thereby restrict them. Such techniques are classic means of limiting women's freedom.

—*Rachel Havrelock*

## *Outline*

*I.* Steps to Ensure Safety in Approaching the Divine (16:1–34)

- *A.* The expiation and purification of the Shrine (vv. 1–19)
- *B.* The scapegoat ritual (vv. 20–22)
- *C.* Post-ritual purification of priest and people (vv. 23–28)
- *D.* The establishment of the ritual as an annual day of atonement (vv. 29–34)

*II.* Laws about Eating Meat (17:1–16)

- *A.* Eating sacrificial meat (vv. 1–9)
- *B.* Eating non-sacrificial meat (vv. 10–16)

*III.* Laws About Sexual Limits (18:1–30)

- *A.* The basic principle and the reason: Don't do as the Canaanites do (vv. 1–5)
- *B.* Forbidden relations (vv. 6–23)
- *C.* Reasons and consequences: Don't do as the Canaanites did (vv. 24–30)

יהוה spoke to Moses after the death of the two sons of Aaron who died when they drew too close to the presence of יהוה. [2] יהוה said to Moses:

Tell your brother Aaron that he is not to come at will into the Shrine behind the curtain, in front

טז וַיְדַבֵּ֤ר יְהֹוָה֙ אֶל־מֹשֶׁ֔ה אַחֲרֵ֣י מ֔וֹת שְׁנֵ֖י בְּנֵ֣י אַהֲרֹ֑ן בְּקׇרְבָתָ֥ם לִפְנֵי־יְהֹוָ֖ה וַיָּמֻֽתוּ׃ [2] וַיֹּ֤אמֶר יְהֹוָה֙ אֶל־מֹשֶׁ֔ה דַּבֵּר֙ אֶל־אַהֲרֹ֣ן אָחִ֔יךָ וְאַל־יָבֹ֤א בְכׇל־עֵת֙ אֶל־הַקֹּ֔דֶשׁ מִבֵּ֖ית לַפָּרֹ֑כֶת אֶל־פְּנֵ֨י הַכַּפֹּ֜רֶת

## Steps to Ensure Safety in Approaching the Divine (16:1–34)

The parashah begins with a reminder about the penalty for the improper execution of ritual and for encroaching on the sanctuary. Aaron's sons, Nadab and Abihu, deviated from sacrificial protocol by offering "alien fire" (10:1) that prompted their deaths. Leviticus 10 pointed to an incorrect way to approach the Divine; Leviticus 16 now details a correct one. Together the two passages function as an envelope enclosing the laws of purity. The priests who execute the purity rituals are themselves subject to the fluctuating states of purity and impurity. The system is upheld on every level.

The key to understanding the often arcane priestly rituals is the notion of boundaries. The priests are invested in maintaining distinctions: Divine and human, Israel and Other, priests and people of Israel. As anthropologist Mary Douglas has shown, those distinctions function as homologies in the interlocking system of priestly boundaries: enforcing one boundary in this tight system simultaneously upholds the others. The conceptual boundaries become real in the social sphere when the people of Israel abide by the laws and perform the rituals.

### THE EXPIATION AND PURIFICATION OF THE SHRINE (16:1–19)

The demarcation of a specific area as the dwelling place of the Divine maintains the distinction between the holy and the profane. Other means of upholding this distinction include offering sacrifices at a precise time, and ensuring that all bodies involved in a ritual are in a state of purity—with no life-giving fluids seeping out.

*1. after the death of the two sons.* See discussion in 10:1–3 for the disturbing story of the death of Aaron's sons.

*2.* In order to avoid the death of more priests, a spatial boundary is established between the holy shrine and the Holy of Holies behind the curtain. Aaron, as well as his successors as chief priest, must not cross this line except on the Day of Atonement (16:29–33). Crossing at any other time will result in death, since God's Presence is tangible beyond the curtain.

*the Shrine.* Heb. *ha-kodesh;* this most interior

▸ When listing "off-limits" females, why does the Torah not explicitly identify the daughter?

ANOTHER VIEW ➤ *694*

▸ Rabbi Yehudah suggests that a "back-up" wife must be prepared for the high priest.

POST-BIBLICAL INTERPRETATIONS ➤ *694*

▸ We can use these laws as a starting point for questioning our own sexual values.

CONTEMPORARY REFLECTION ➤ *696*

▸ I tread gently on the alpine meadow, / ...Do I deal as gently with those I love...?

VOICES ➤ *698*

of the cover that is upon the ark, lest he die; for I appear in the cloud over the cover. 3Thus only shall Aaron enter the Shrine: with a bull of the herd for a purgation offering and a ram for a burnt offering.—4He shall be dressed in a sacral linen tunic, with linen breeches next to his flesh, and be girt with a linen sash, and he shall wear a linen turban. They are sacral vestments; he shall bathe his body in water and then put them on.—5And from the Israelite community he shall take two he-goats for a purgation offering and a ram for a burnt offering.

6Aaron is to offer his own bull of purgation offering, to make expiation for himself and for his household. 7Aaron shall take the two he-goats and let them stand before יהוה at the entrance of the Tent of Meeting; 8and he shall place lots upon the two goats, one marked for יהוה and the other marked for Azazel. 9Aaron shall bring forward the goat designated by lot for יהוה, which he is to offer as a purgation offering; 10while the goat designated by lot for Azazel shall be left standing alive before יהוה, to make expiation with it and to send it off to the wilderness for Azazel.

אֲשֶׁר עַל־הָאָרֹן וְלֹא יָמוּת כִּי בֶּעָנָן אֵרָאֶה
עַל־הַכַּפֹּרֶת׃ 3 בְּזֹאת יָבֹא אַהֲרֹן אֶל־
הַקֹּדֶשׁ בְּפַר בֶּן־בָּקָר לְחַטָּאת וְאַיִל
לְעֹלָה׃ 4 כְּתֹנֶת־בַּד קֹדֶשׁ יִלְבָּשׁ וּמִכְנְסֵי־
בַד יִהְיוּ עַל־בְּשָׂרוֹ וּבְאַבְנֵט בַּד יַחְגֹּר
וּבְמִצְנֶפֶת בַּד יִצְנֹף בִּגְדֵי־קֹדֶשׁ הֵם וְרָחַץ
בַּמַּיִם אֶת־בְּשָׂרוֹ וּלְבֵשָׁם׃ 5 וּמֵאֵת עֲדַת
בְּנֵי יִשְׂרָאֵל יִקַּח שְׁנֵי־שְׂעִירֵי עִזִּים לְחַטָּאת
וְאַיִל אֶחָד לְעֹלָה׃
6 וְהִקְרִיב אַהֲרֹן אֶת־פַּר הַחַטָּאת אֲשֶׁר־לוֹ
וְכִפֶּר בַּעֲדוֹ וּבְעַד בֵּיתוֹ׃ 7 וְלָקַח אֶת־שְׁנֵי
הַשְּׂעִירִם וְהֶעֱמִיד אֹתָם לִפְנֵי יְהוָה פֶּתַח
אֹהֶל מוֹעֵד׃ 8 וְנָתַן אַהֲרֹן עַל־שְׁנֵי הַשְּׂעִירִם
גֹּרָלוֹת גּוֹרָל אֶחָד לַיהוָה וְגוֹרָל אֶחָד
לַעֲזָאזֵל׃ 9 וְהִקְרִיב אַהֲרֹן אֶת־הַשָּׂעִיר
אֲשֶׁר עָלָה עָלָיו הַגּוֹרָל לַיהוָה וְעָשָׂהוּ
חַטָּאת׃ 10 וְהַשָּׂעִיר אֲשֶׁר עָלָה עָלָיו הַגּוֹרָל
לַעֲזָאזֵל יָעֳמַד־חַי לִפְנֵי יְהוָה לְכַפֵּר עָלָיו
לְשַׁלַּח אֹתוֹ לַעֲזָאזֵל הַמִּדְבָּרָה׃

of sacred spaces that contains the Ark is elsewhere called *kodesh ha-kodashim*, "the Holy of Holies" (Exodus 26:33–34).

4. ***sacral linen tunic, with linen breeches.*** This simple raiment serves as a marker of the body's purity while also demarcating the boundaries of the body. Similarly, clothing conveys that the body is in a state of ritual purity in the contemporary practices of wearing a white robe on Yom Kippur, and of the Muslim practice of *Ihram* (wearing white clothing) during the *Hajj* (pilgrimage to Mecca).

***he shall bathe his body in water.*** Water in the priestly view is a powerful agent—it has the ability to dissolve impurity and usher a body into the state of purity. As he affects the transformation of all the people, the priest himself enters a different state bounded by a ritual bath before and after the rite.

6. ***to make expiation for himself and for his household.*** The premise here is that the chief priest can externalize misdeeds and transfer them to a sacrificial animal. As he sacrifices the animal, he removes the transgressions from an individual or from the community. (After the destruction of the Temple and the end of the sacrificial system, individuals became responsible for articulating their mistakes and separating from them through the language of repentance and prayer.)

8. ***Azazel.*** This is the name of the wilderness beyond the boundaries of settled life; most likely it originated as the name of a demon. Azazel in this case is best imagined as the antithesis of the Tabernacle/sanctuary, a place of disorder devoid of the relevant priestly distinctions. By carrying Israel's impurities to such a wilderness, the scapegoat effectively conveys the chaotic aspects of human life back to a place of origin.

11 Aaron shall then offer his bull of purgation offering, to make expiation for himself and his household. He shall slaughter his bull of purgation offering, 12 and he shall take a panful of glowing coals scooped from the altar before יהוה, and two handfuls of finely ground aromatic incense, and bring this behind the curtain. 13 He shall put the incense on the fire before יהוה, so that the cloud from the incense screens the cover that is over [the Ark of] the Pact, lest he die. 14 He shall take some of the blood of the bull and sprinkle it with his finger over the cover on the east side; and in front of the cover he shall sprinkle some of the blood with his finger seven times. 15 He shall then slaughter the people's goat of purgation offering, bring its blood behind the curtain, and do with its blood as he has done with the blood of the bull: he shall sprinkle it over the cover and in front of the cover.

16 Thus he shall purge the Shrine of the impurity and transgression of the Israelites, whatever their sins; and he shall do the same for the Tent of Meeting, which abides with them in the midst of their impurity. 17 When he goes in to make expiation in the Shrine, nobody else shall be in the Tent of Meeting until he comes out.

When he has made expiation for himself and his household, and for the whole congregation of Israel, 18 he shall go out to the altar that is before יהוה and purge it: he shall take some of the blood of the bull and of the goat and apply it to each of

11 וְהִקְרִיב אַהֲרֹן אֶת־פַּר הַחַטָּאת אֲשֶׁר־לוֹ
וְכִפֶּר בַּעֲדוֹ וּבְעַד בֵּיתוֹ וְשָׁחַט אֶת־פַּר
הַחַטָּאת אֲשֶׁר־לוֹ׃ 12 וְלָקַח מְלֹא־הַמַּחְתָּה
גַּחֲלֵי־אֵשׁ מֵעַל הַמִּזְבֵּחַ מִלִּפְנֵי יְהוָה וּמְלֹא
חָפְנָיו קְטֹרֶת סַמִּים דַּקָּה וְהֵבִיא מִבֵּית
לַפָּרֹכֶת׃ 13 וְנָתַן אֶת־הַקְּטֹרֶת עַל־הָאֵשׁ
לִפְנֵי יְהוָה וְכִסָּה ׀ עֲנַן הַקְּטֹרֶת אֶת־הַכַּפֹּרֶת
אֲשֶׁר עַל־הָעֵדוּת וְלֹא יָמוּת׃ 14 וְלָקַח מִדַּם
הַפָּר וְהִזָּה בְאֶצְבָּעוֹ עַל־פְּנֵי הַכַּפֹּרֶת קֵדְמָה
וְלִפְנֵי הַכַּפֹּרֶת יַזֶּה שֶׁבַע־פְּעָמִים מִן־הַדָּם
בְּאֶצְבָּעוֹ׃ 15 וְשָׁחַט אֶת־שְׂעִיר הַחַטָּאת
אֲשֶׁר לָעָם וְהֵבִיא אֶת־דָּמוֹ אֶל־מִבֵּית
לַפָּרֹכֶת וְעָשָׂה אֶת־דָּמוֹ כַּאֲשֶׁר עָשָׂה לְדַם
הַפָּר וְהִזָּה אֹתוֹ עַל־הַכַּפֹּרֶת וְלִפְנֵי
הַכַּפֹּרֶת׃

16 וְכִפֶּר עַל־הַקֹּדֶשׁ מִטֻּמְאֹת בְּנֵי יִשְׂרָאֵל
וּמִפִּשְׁעֵיהֶם לְכָל־חַטֹּאתָם וְכֵן יַעֲשֶׂה
לְאֹהֶל מוֹעֵד הַשֹּׁכֵן אִתָּם בְּתוֹךְ טֻמְאֹתָם׃
17 וְכָל־אָדָם לֹא־יִהְיֶה ׀ בְּאֹהֶל מוֹעֵד בְּבֹאוֹ
לְכַפֵּר בַּקֹּדֶשׁ עַד־צֵאתוֹ

וְכִפֶּר בַּעֲדוֹ וּבְעַד בֵּיתוֹ וּבְעַד כָּל־קְהַל
יִשְׂרָאֵל׃ 18 וְיָצָא אֶל־הַמִּזְבֵּחַ אֲשֶׁר לִפְנֵי־
יְהוָה וְכִפֶּר עָלָיו וְלָקַח מִדַּם הַפָּר וּמִדַּם
הַשָּׂעִיר וְנָתַן עַל־קַרְנוֹת הַמִּזְבֵּחַ סָבִיב׃

*14.* As the sacrifice of the animals dispenses with the people's transgressions, the sacrificial blood serves as a purifying agent that transforms the inner sanctum.

***seven times.*** The number seven alludes to the restoration of order and wholeness by recalling the seven days of Creation.

*16.* ***the Tent of Meeting, which abides with them in the midst of their impurity.*** In the priestly view, the body exists in a constant state of flux, moving in and out of various states. On one end of the spectrum rests the state of impurity. Although specific practices dissolve physical impurities, the residue of impurity accumulates at the central ritual site. Misdeeds also cause a kind of moral impurity that individuals must purge through acts of atonement. Since Israel's actions impact its sacred space, the Tent of Meeting—like the body—must undergo a period of purification and subsequent transformation. In this sense, the body and sacred space are parallel domains.

the horns of the altar; [19]and the rest of the blood he shall sprinkle on it with his finger seven times. Thus he shall purify it of the defilement of the Israelites and consecrate it.

[20]When he has finished purging the Shrine, the Tent of Meeting, and the altar, the live goat shall be brought forward. [21]Aaron shall lay both his hands upon the head of the live goat and confess over it all the iniquities and transgressions of the Israelites, whatever their sins, putting them on the head of the goat; and it shall be sent off to the wilderness through a designated agent. [22]Thus the goat shall carry on it all their iniquities to an inaccessible region; and the goat shall be set free in the wilderness.

[23]And Aaron shall go into the Tent of Meeting, take off the linen vestments that he put on when he entered the Shrine, and leave them there. [24]He shall bathe his body in water in the holy precinct and put on his vestments; then he shall come out and offer his burnt offering and the burnt offering of the people, making expiation for himself and for the people. [25]The fat of the purgation offering he shall turn into smoke on the altar.

19 וְהִזָּה עָלָיו מִן־הַדָּם בְּאֶצְבָּעוֹ שֶׁבַע
פְּעָמִים וְטִהֲרוֹ וְקִדְּשׁוֹ מִטֻּמְאֹת בְּנֵי
יִשְׂרָאֵל:
20 וְכִלָּה מִכַּפֵּר אֶת־הַקֹּדֶשׁ וְאֶת־אֹהֶל
מוֹעֵד וְאֶת־הַמִּזְבֵּחַ וְהִקְרִיב אֶת־הַשָּׂעִיר
הֶחָי: 21 וְסָמַךְ אַהֲרֹן אֶת־שְׁתֵּי ידו יָדָיו עַל
רֹאשׁ הַשָּׂעִיר הַחַי וְהִתְוַדָּה עָלָיו אֶת־כָּל־
עֲוֹנֹת בְּנֵי יִשְׂרָאֵל וְאֶת־כָּל־פִּשְׁעֵיהֶם לְכָל־
חַטֹּאתָם וְנָתַן אֹתָם עַל־רֹאשׁ הַשָּׂעִיר
וְשִׁלַּח בְּיַד־אִישׁ עִתִּי הַמִּדְבָּרָה: 22 וְנָשָׂא
הַשָּׂעִיר עָלָיו אֶת־כָּל־עֲוֹנֹתָם אֶל־אֶרֶץ
גְּזֵרָה וְשִׁלַּח אֶת־הַשָּׂעִיר בַּמִּדְבָּר:
23 וּבָא אַהֲרֹן אֶל־אֹהֶל מוֹעֵד וּפָשַׁט אֶת־
בִּגְדֵי הַבָּד אֲשֶׁר לָבַשׁ בְּבֹאוֹ אֶל־הַקֹּדֶשׁ
וְהִנִּיחָם שָׁם: 24 וְרָחַץ אֶת־בְּשָׂרוֹ בַמַּיִם
בְּמָקוֹם קָדוֹשׁ וְלָבַשׁ אֶת־בְּגָדָיו וְיָצָא וְעָשָׂה
אֶת־עֹלָתוֹ וְאֶת־עֹלַת הָעָם וְכִפֶּר בַּעֲדוֹ
וּבְעַד הָעָם: 25 וְאֵת חֵלֶב הַחַטָּאת יַקְטִיר
הַמִּזְבֵּחָה:

*19.* The priest brings the sanctuary into a state of purity and consecration. It is possible to see these two states as a result of all the actions performed by the priest (sacrifice, sprinkling of blood, and smearing blood on the horns of the altar). Jacob Milgrom sees the daubing of the altar horns as enacting purification, and the sprinkling as an act of consecration (*Leviticus 1–16*, 1991, p. 1040). Another perspective is that the sprinkling of blood absorbs the taint of the people's misdeeds from the Shrine and thereby purifies it.

### THE SCAPEGOAT RITUAL (16:20–22)

Removed from the corporate body of the community and from the space of the Shrine, the people's transgressions must be transferred elsewhere. The scapegoat is the vehicle of this transference. First the chief priest conveys the transgressions to the goat by laying his hands upon it; then, through the priest's speech-act of confession, the goat carries this load into a distant wilderness.

### POST-RITUAL PURIFICATION OF PRIEST AND PEOPLE (16:23–28)

As discussed above at v. 4, the priests perceived water as a powerful annulling agent with the ability to dissolve physical states and usher the body into a new state of being. In priestly ritual, contact with water marks the place between the states of impurity and purity. Its cleansing power removes visible dirt as well as invisible impurities.

In prophetic thought, water has the ability to transform not only physical states, but also a moral state of impurity. The prophet Isaiah says: "Your

26 The one who set the Azazel-goat free shall wash those clothes and bathe the body in water—and after that may reenter the camp.

27 The bull of purgation offering and the goat of purgation offering whose blood was brought in to purge the Shrine shall be taken outside the camp; and their hides, flesh, and dung shall be consumed in fire. 28 The one who burned them shall wash those clothes and bathe the body in water—and after that may re-enter the camp.

29 And this shall be to you a law for all time: In the seventh month, on the tenth day of the month, you shall practice self-denial; and you shall do no manner of work, neither the citizen nor the alien who resides among you. 30 For on this day atonement shall be made for you to purify you of all your sins; you shall be pure before יהוה. 31 It shall be a sabbath of complete rest for you, and you shall practice self-denial; it is a law for all time. 32 The priest who has been anointed and ordained to serve as priest in place of his father shall make expiation. He shall put on the linen vestments, the sacral vestments. 33 He shall purge the innermost Shrine; he

26 וְהַֽמְשַׁלֵּחַ אֶת־הַשָּׂעִיר לַֽעֲזָאזֵל יְכַבֵּס
בְּגָדָיו וְרָחַץ אֶת־בְּשָׂרוֹ בַּמָּיִם וְאַחֲרֵי־כֵן
יָבוֹא אֶל־הַֽמַּחֲנֶה׃
27 וְאֵת פַּר הַֽחַטָּאת וְאֵת ׀ שְׂעִיר הַֽחַטָּאת
אֲשֶׁר הוּבָא אֶת־דָּמָם לְכַפֵּר בַּקֹּדֶשׁ יוֹצִיא
אֶל־מִחוּץ לַמַּחֲנֶה וְשָׂרְפוּ בָאֵשׁ אֶת־עֹרֹתָם
וְאֶת־בְּשָׂרָם וְאֶת־פִּרְשָׁם׃ 28 וְהַשֹּׂרֵף אֹתָם
יְכַבֵּס בְּגָדָיו וְרָחַץ אֶת־בְּשָׂרוֹ בַּמָּיִם וְאַחֲרֵי־
כֵן יָבוֹא אֶל־הַֽמַּחֲנֶה׃
29 וְהָיְתָה לָכֶם לְחֻקַּת עוֹלָם בַּחֹדֶשׁ
הַשְּׁבִיעִי בֶּעָשׂוֹר לַחֹדֶשׁ תְּעַנּוּ אֶת־
נַפְשֹׁתֵיכֶם וְכָל־מְלָאכָה לֹא תַעֲשׂוּ הָֽאֶזְרָח
וְהַגֵּר הַגָּר בְּתוֹכְכֶם׃ 30 כִּֽי־בַיּוֹם הַזֶּה יְכַפֵּר
עֲלֵיכֶם לְטַהֵר אֶתְכֶם מִכֹּל חַטֹּאתֵיכֶם לִפְנֵי
יְהוָה תִּטְהָרוּ׃ 31 שַׁבַּת שַׁבָּתוֹן הִיא לָכֶם
וְעִנִּיתֶם אֶת־נַפְשֹׁתֵיכֶם חֻקַּת עוֹלָם׃
32 וְכִפֶּר הַכֹּהֵן אֲשֶׁר־יִמְשַׁח אֹתוֹ וַאֲשֶׁר
יְמַלֵּא אֶת־יָדוֹ לְכַהֵן תַּחַת אָבִיו וְלָבַשׁ אֶת־
בִּגְדֵי הַבָּד בִּגְדֵי הַקֹּדֶשׁ׃ 33 וְכִפֶּר אֶת־מִקְדַּשׁ

---

hands are filled with blood / Wash yourselves; cleanse yourselves" (Isaiah 1:15–16). A combination of priestly and prophetic perceptions of the transforming power of water rests in the background of the immersion ritual that effects conversion in Judaism as well as the Christian ritual of baptism (see *Sh'mini*, Post-biblical Interpretations, p. 630).

***27. consumed in fire.*** Burning the remnants of the offerings beyond the boundaries of the community disposes of the remnants of human iniquities.

## THE ESTABLISHMENT OF THE RITUAL AS AN ANNUAL DAY OF ATONEMENT (16:29–34)

***29. in the seventh month.*** The seventh month ushers the people into an annual period of renewal and redemption, much as the seventh day does in the weekly cycle.

***practice self-denial.*** Self-denial pertains to the abstention from food. As water cleanses the surface of the body from transgression, so fasting cleanses the internal organs.

***30. you shall be pure before* יהוה.** The cleansing transforms the people in the eyes of God. It also maintains a good relationship between Israel and the Divine by restoring the people and the Shrine to a state of purity. Whereas an impure community exists in a precarious relationship to the Divine, a pure community can enjoy a proximate, reciprocal relationship.

***33. He shall purge the innermost Shrine.*** After the priest removes past taint and transgression from Israel's sacred sites, the priests and people alike enjoy safety and a new standing before the divine Presence in their midst. This tenth day serves as a day of collective transformation when all enter a

shall purge the Tent of Meeting and the altar; and he shall make expiation for the priests and for all the people of the congregation.

[34]This shall be to you a law for all time: to make atonement for the Israelites for all their sins once a year.

And Moses did as יהוה had commanded him.

*17* יהוה spoke to Moses, saying: [2]Speak to Aaron and his sons and to all the Israelite people and say to them:

This is what יהוה has commanded: [3]if anyone of the house of Israel slaughters an ox or sheep or goat in the camp, or does so outside the camp, [4]and does not bring it to the entrance of the Tent of Meeting to present it as an offering to יהוה, before יהוה's Tabernacle, bloodguilt shall be imputed to that person: having shed blood, that person shall be cut off from among this people. [5]This is in order that the Israelites may bring the sacrifices which they have been making in the open—that they may bring them before יהוה, to the priest, at the entrance of the Tent of Meeting, and offer them as sacrifices of well-being to יהוה; [6]that the priest may dash the blood against the altar of יהוה at the entrance of the Tent of Meeting, and turn the fat into smoke as a

הַקֹּדֶשׁ וְאֶת־אֹהֶל מוֹעֵד וְאֶת־הַמִּזְבֵּחַ יְכַפֵּר
וְעַל הַכֹּהֲנִים וְעַל־כׇּל־עַם הַקָּהָל יְכַפֵּר׃
34 וְהָיְתָה־זֹּאת לָכֶם לְחֻקַּת עוֹלָם לְכַפֵּר
עַל־בְּנֵי יִשְׂרָאֵל מִכׇּל־חַטֹּאתָם אַחַת
בַּשָּׁנָה
וַיַּעַשׂ כַּאֲשֶׁר צִוָּה יְהֹוָה אֶת־מֹשֶׁה׃ פ

יז וַיְדַבֵּר יְהֹוָה אֶל־מֹשֶׁה לֵּאמֹר׃ 2 דַּבֵּר
אֶל־אַהֲרֹן וְאֶל־בָּנָיו וְאֶל כׇּל־בְּנֵי יִשְׂרָאֵל
וְאָמַרְתָּ אֲלֵיהֶם
זֶה הַדָּבָר אֲשֶׁר־צִוָּה יְהֹוָה לֵאמֹר׃ 3 אִישׁ
אִישׁ מִבֵּית יִשְׂרָאֵל אֲשֶׁר יִשְׁחַט שׁוֹר אוֹ־
כֶשֶׂב אוֹ־עֵז בַּמַּחֲנֶה אוֹ אֲשֶׁר יִשְׁחַט מִחוּץ
לַמַּחֲנֶה׃ 4 וְאֶל־פֶּתַח אֹהֶל מוֹעֵד לֹא
הֱבִיאוֹ לְהַקְרִיב קׇרְבָּן לַיהֹוָה לִפְנֵי מִשְׁכַּן
יְהֹוָה דָּם יֵחָשֵׁב לָאִישׁ הַהוּא דָּם שָׁפָךְ
וְנִכְרַת הָאִישׁ הַהוּא מִקֶּרֶב עַמּוֹ׃ 5 לְמַעַן
אֲשֶׁר יָבִיאוּ בְּנֵי יִשְׂרָאֵל אֶת־זִבְחֵיהֶם אֲשֶׁר
הֵם זֹבְחִים עַל־פְּנֵי הַשָּׂדֶה וֶהֱבִיאֻם לַיהֹוָה
אֶל־פֶּתַח אֹהֶל מוֹעֵד אֶל־הַכֹּהֵן וְזָבְחוּ
זִבְחֵי שְׁלָמִים לַיהֹוָה אוֹתָם׃ 6 וְזָרַק הַכֹּהֵן
אֶת־הַדָּם עַל־מִזְבַּח יְהֹוָה פֶּתַח אֹהֶל מוֹעֵד

renewed state of purity. All assume some responsibility for tainting the shrine and the community, and they release themselves from the consequences through the chief priest's confessions and the symbolic rites of sacrifice.

## *Laws about Eating Meat* (17:1–16)

According to Leviticus, one must acknowledge and sanctify at all occasions the life-giving force of blood through precise adherence to the laws of sacrifice and of eating meat.

### EATING SACRIFICIAL MEAT (17:1–9)

This section opens the Holiness Code (Leviticus 17–26), a biblical source concerned with defining the proper conduct for all Israelites as a holy people. (See at 19:2.)

*5. sacrifices which they have been making in the open.* In terms of the history of religion, a timeline becomes evident. In an early period of Israelite religion, people slaughtered animals in the fields or at local religious sites as part of regional festivals where the offering and eating of meat had ritual significance. As the priests began to assert

pleasing odor to יהוה; [7]and that they may offer their sacrifices no more to the goat-demons after whom they stray. This shall be to them a law for all time, throughout the ages.

[8]Say to them further: If anyone of the house of Israel or of the strangers who reside among them offers a burnt offering or a sacrifice, [9]and does not bring it to the entrance of the Tent of Meeting to offer it to יהוה, that person shall be cut off from this people.

[10]And if anyone of the house of Israel or of the strangers who reside among them partakes of any blood, I will set My face against the person who partakes of the blood; I will cut that person off from among kin. [11]For the life of the flesh is in the blood, and I have assigned it to you for making expiation for your lives upon the altar; it is the blood, as life, that effects expiation. [12]Therefore I say to the Israelite people: No person among you shall partake of blood, nor shall the stranger who resides among you partake of blood.

[13]And if any Israelite or any stranger who resides among them hunts down an animal or a bird that may be eaten, that person shall pour out its blood and cover it with earth. [14]For the life of all flesh—its blood is its life. Therefore I say to the Israelite people: You shall not partake of the blood of any

וְהִקְטִיר הַחֵלֶב לְרֵיחַ נִיחֹחַ לַיהוָה׃ 7 וְלֹא־
יִזְבְּחוּ עוֹד אֶת־זִבְחֵיהֶם לַשְּׂעִירִם אֲשֶׁר הֵם
זֹנִים אַחֲרֵיהֶם חֻקַּת עוֹלָם תִּהְיֶה־זֹּאת
לָהֶם לְדֹרֹתָם׃
8 וַאֲלֵהֶם תֹּאמַר אִישׁ אִישׁ מִבֵּית יִשְׂרָאֵל
וּמִן־הַגֵּר אֲשֶׁר־יָגוּר בְּתוֹכָם אֲשֶׁר־יַעֲלֶה
עֹלָה אוֹ־זָבַח׃ 9 וְאֶל־פֶּתַח אֹהֶל מוֹעֵד לֹא
יְבִיאֶנּוּ לַעֲשׂוֹת אֹתוֹ לַיהוָה וְנִכְרַת הָאִישׁ
הַהוּא מֵעַמָּיו׃
10 וְאִישׁ אִישׁ מִבֵּית יִשְׂרָאֵל וּמִן־הַגֵּר הַגָּר
בְּתוֹכָם אֲשֶׁר יֹאכַל כָּל־דָּם וְנָתַתִּי פָנַי
בַּנֶּפֶשׁ הָאֹכֶלֶת אֶת־הַדָּם וְהִכְרַתִּי אֹתָהּ
מִקֶּרֶב עַמָּהּ׃ 11 כִּי נֶפֶשׁ הַבָּשָׂר בַּדָּם הִוא
וַאֲנִי נְתַתִּיו לָכֶם עַל־הַמִּזְבֵּחַ לְכַפֵּר עַל־
נַפְשֹׁתֵיכֶם כִּי־הַדָּם הוּא בַּנֶּפֶשׁ יְכַפֵּר׃
12 עַל־כֵּן אָמַרְתִּי לִבְנֵי יִשְׂרָאֵל כָּל־נֶפֶשׁ
מִכֶּם לֹא־תֹאכַל דָּם וְהַגֵּר הַגָּר בְּתוֹכְכֶם
לֹא־יֹאכַל דָּם׃ ס
13 וְאִישׁ אִישׁ מִבְּנֵי יִשְׂרָאֵל וּמִן־הַגֵּר הַגָּר
בְּתוֹכָם אֲשֶׁר יָצוּד צֵיד חַיָּה אוֹ־עוֹף אֲשֶׁר
יֵאָכֵל וְשָׁפַךְ אֶת־דָּמוֹ וְכִסָּהוּ בֶּעָפָר׃ 14 כִּי־
נֶפֶשׁ כָּל־בָּשָׂר דָּמוֹ בְנַפְשׁוֹ הוּא וָאֹמַר לִבְנֵי

centralized power, they outlawed such offerings and mandated sacrifice officiated by a priest at a specific site. (Compare to Deuteronomy 12:20–25.)

*7. the goat-demons after whom they stray.* Eating, sex, and worship are interrelated aspects of life in the biblical imagination. In the ancient world, meals and feasts alike were dedicated to deities. Thus the book of Numbers recounts an episode when the Israelite men go astray in the wilderness by eating contraband food, having sex with Moabite women, and thus drawing close to the god Baal-peor (25:1–3). Likewise, according to the present verse, eating meat whose blood does not come into contact with the altar of Israel's God counts as an illicit tryst with goat-demons.

## EATING NON-SACRIFICIAL MEAT (17:10–16)

*11. For the life of the flesh is in the blood.* The ingestion of blood crosses the boundary between life and death and thus mixes two discrete forces. When spilled, blood—the very force of life—represents death. Thus by consuming blood, a person eats death while also ingesting the life force of another being.

*13.* After hunting an animal or bird, a person

flesh, for the life of all flesh is its blood. Anyone
who partakes of it shall be cut off.
15Any person, whether citizen or stranger, who
eats what has died or has been torn by beasts shall
wash those clothes, bathe in water, remain impure
until evening—and shall then be pure. 16But if the
clothes are not washed and the body is not bathed,
that person shall bear the guilt.

18 יהוה spoke to Moses, saying: 2Speak to the
Israelite people and say to them:
I יהוה am your God. 3You shall not copy the
practices of the land of Egypt where you dwelt, or
of the land of Canaan to which I am taking you;

יִשְׂרָאֵל דַּם כָּל־בָּשָׂר לֹא תֹאכֵלוּ כִּי נֶפֶשׁ
כָּל־בָּשָׂר דָּמוֹ הִוא כָּל־אֹכְלָיו יִכָּרֵת׃
15 וְכָל־נֶפֶשׁ אֲשֶׁר תֹּאכַל נְבֵלָה וּטְרֵפָה
בָּאֶזְרָח וּבַגֵּר וְכִבֶּס בְּגָדָיו וְרָחַץ בַּמַּיִם
וְטָמֵא עַד־הָעֶרֶב וְטָהֵר׃ 16 וְאִם לֹא יְכַבֵּס
וּבְשָׂרוֹ לֹא יִרְחָץ וְנָשָׂא עֲוֺנוֹ׃ פ

יח וַיְדַבֵּר יְהֹוָה אֶל־מֹשֶׁה לֵּאמֹר׃ 2 דַּבֵּר
אֶל־בְּנֵי יִשְׂרָאֵל וְאָמַרְתָּ אֲלֵהֶם
אֲנִי יְהֹוָה אֱלֹהֵיכֶם׃ 3 כְּמַעֲשֵׂה אֶרֶץ־
מִצְרַיִם אֲשֶׁר יְשַׁבְתֶּם־בָּהּ לֹא תַעֲשׂוּ
וּכְמַעֲשֵׂה אֶרֶץ־כְּנַעַן אֲשֶׁר אֲנִי מֵבִיא
אֶתְכֶם שָׁמָּה לֹא תַעֲשׂוּ וּבְחֻקֹּתֵיהֶם לֹא

must drain and bury the prey's blood before enjoying the yield.

*15.* Ingestion of the flesh of an animal found dead will render a person impure. Dissolving the impurity then requires the washing, bathing, and time restraints of the basic purification ritual.

## *Laws about Sexual Limits*

(18:1–30)

The book of Leviticus maps an elaborate terrain of states and objects both pure and impure, placing clear borders between them. As leading scholars of Leviticus emphasize, the states of "ritually pure" or "ritually impure" are not moral categories, but rather indices of how close a particular body can draw to the spaces demarcated as repositories of the holy. As the holy is bounded and separated from the profane, so must the body adhere to boundaries when approaching the holy. Leviticus defines geography and physicality by corresponding conceptions of boundaries. As collective recognition of limits uphold sacred space, so individuals maintain the sanctity of the body by policing what goes into and comes out of it.

### THE BASIC PRINCIPLE AND THE REASON: DON'T DO AS THE CANAANITES DO (18:1–5)

The distinction that concerns the writers in Leviticus 18 is that of Israel versus other nations: the people of Israel are not to behave like Egyptians or Canaanites. Although the unit distinctly deals with prohibited sexual couplings, the issue here is one of geography and identity more than physicality. In this respect, the laws establish geographic and cultural borders between the people of Israel and the Egyptian empire, as well between Israel and the Canaanites among whom they live. Israel is different, according to Leviticus, in not allowing the perverse couplings permitted among the other peoples. This does not prove that the sexual practices forbidden to the Israelites were ones actually practiced by the Egyptians or Canaanites; rather, these laws help to produce the categories of Israel and Other. Geography is at stake because Israel's most powerful memory is the exodus from Egypt. As for Canaan, in addition to divine promise, Israel's land claim derives from the Canaanites' having made the land odious by their practice, which requires the redemptive purification of Israelite settlement. By

nor shall you follow their laws. 4My rules alone shall you observe, and faithfully follow My laws: I יהוה am your God.

5You shall keep My laws and My rules, by the pursuit of which human beings shall live: I am יהוה.

6None of you men shall come near anyone of his own flesh to uncover nakedness: I am יהוה.

7Your father's nakedness, that is, the nakedness of your mother, you shall not uncover; she is your mother—you shall not uncover her nakedness.

תֵלֵכוּ׃ 4 אֶת־מִשְׁפָּטַי תַּעֲשׂוּ וְאֶת־חֻקֹּתַי
תִּשְׁמְרוּ לָלֶכֶת בָּהֶם אֲנִי יְהֹוָה אֱלֹהֵיכֶם׃
5 וּשְׁמַרְתֶּם אֶת־חֻקֹּתַי וְאֶת־מִשְׁפָּטַי אֲשֶׁר
יַעֲשֶׂה אֹתָם הָאָדָם וָחַי בָּהֶם אֲנִי
יְהֹוָה׃ ס
6 אִישׁ אִישׁ אֶל־כׇּל־שְׁאֵר בְּשָׂרוֹ לֹא תִקְרְבוּ
לְגַלּוֹת עֶרְוָה אֲנִי יְהֹוָה׃ ס
7 עֶרְוַת אָבִיךָ וְעֶרְוַת אִמְּךָ לֹא תְגַלֵּה אִמְּךָ
הִוא לֹא תְגַלֶּה עֶרְוָתָהּ׃ ס

outlining the forbidden limits of Israelite sexuality, the priestly writers symbolically establish an ideal set of "geographic" borders that definitively separate Israel from other nations.

*5. **human beings shall live.*** The common thread through Leviticus 16–18 concerns how to live and stay alive alongside the powerful Presence of the Divine. The priests prescribe a lifestyle in which upholding distinctions maintains purity while ritual practice sheds impurity.

## FORBIDDEN RELATIONS (18:6–23)

The sexual laws, addressed to men as normative, begin with the prohibition of incest and sexual relations among close kin relations. Anthropologists maintain that prohibitions to establish distinctions in the familial realm are the very basis of culture. The prohibitions against incest—an act that effaces the difference between family members—are consistent with the priestly agenda of maintaining categories. This section outlines who an Israelite man cannot have sexual relations with because they are too close, while at the same time it points out bodies that are forbidden because they are too far from being Israelite. The nuclear family, even step and half-members, is too close, while members of nations such as Egypt and Canaan are too far. Setting such internal and external borders carves out a sexual identity for Israel in the space between.

With the exception of the law forbidding coupling with animals (18:23), this litany of sexual laws does not address women. Rather than subjects, women are objects to be or not be "uncovered." One wonders how the laws might be different had they been addressed to women and men as equal sexual partners and also what unwritten codes determined the sexual practices of Israelite women.

*6. None of you men.* The overriding principle is that no man should pursue intimate relations with his family members. The family is thus defined in relation to a virile man positioned at the center.

*7. Your father's nakedness.* The "uncovering" of nakedness refers to different types of sexual interactions. According to a story early in Genesis, Noah "exposed himself" in a drunken stupor after the Flood; his son Ham saw his "father's nakedness" and related the observation to his brothers (Genesis 9:21–22). Noah cursed Ham's Canaanite descendents as a result.

*your mother.* As in the commandment to honor one's parents (Exodus 20:12; Deuteronomy 5:16), mother and father are grouped together in the law forbidding incest. A mother's status is emphasized through repetition. The law prohibits the maternal body because it belongs to the father and because it is the site of birth. [It is noteworthy, however, that the mother's nakedness is not explicitly tied to the father, unlike the case of the father's wife (v. 8). —*Ed.*]

⁸Do not uncover the nakedness of your father's wife; it is the nakedness of your father.

⁹The nakedness of your sister—your father's daughter or your mother's, whether born into the household or outside—do not uncover their nakedness.

¹⁰The nakedness of your son's daughter, or of your daughter's daughter—do not uncover their nakedness; for their nakedness is yours.

¹¹The nakedness of your father's wife's daughter, who was born into your father's household—she is your sister; do not uncover her nakedness.

¹²Do not uncover the nakedness of your father's sister; she is your father's flesh.

¹³Do not uncover the nakedness of your mother's sister; for she is your mother's flesh.

¹⁴Do not uncover the nakedness of your father's brother: do not approach his wife; she is your aunt.

¹⁵Do not uncover the nakedness of your daughter-in-law: she is your son's wife; you shall not uncover her nakedness.

8 עֶרְוַ֤ת אֵֽשֶׁת־אָבִ֙יךָ֙ לֹ֣א תְגַלֵּ֔ה עֶרְוַ֥ת אָבִ֖יךָ הִֽוא׃ ס

9 עֶרְוַ֨ת אֲחֽוֹתְךָ֤ בַת־אָבִ֙יךָ֙ א֣וֹ בַת־אִמֶּ֔ךָ מוֹלֶ֣דֶת בַּ֔יִת א֖וֹ מוֹלֶ֣דֶת ח֑וּץ לֹ֥א תְגַלֶּ֖ה עֶרְוָתָֽן׃ ס

10 עֶרְוַ֤ת בַּת־בִּנְךָ֙ א֣וֹ בַֽת־בִּתְּךָ֔ לֹ֥א תְגַלֶּ֖ה עֶרְוָתָ֑ן כִּ֥י עֶרְוָתְךָ֖ הֵֽנָּה׃ ס

11 עֶרְוַ֨ת בַּת־אֵ֤שֶׁת אָבִ֙יךָ֙ מוֹלֶ֣דֶת אָבִ֔יךָ אֲחֽוֹתְךָ֖ הִ֑וא לֹ֥א תְגַלֶּ֖ה עֶרְוָתָֽהּ׃ ס

12 עֶרְוַ֥ת אֲחֽוֹת־אָבִ֖יךָ לֹ֣א תְגַלֵּ֑ה שְׁאֵ֥ר אָבִ֖יךָ הִֽוא׃ ס

13 עֶרְוַ֥ת אֲחֽוֹת־אִמְּךָ֖ לֹ֣א תְגַלֵּ֑ה כִּֽי־שְׁאֵ֥ר אִמְּךָ֖ הִֽוא׃ ס

14 עֶרְוַ֥ת אֲחִֽי־אָבִ֖יךָ לֹ֣א תְגַלֵּ֑ה אֶל־אִשְׁתּוֹ֙ לֹ֣א תִקְרָ֔ב דֹּדָֽתְךָ֖ הִֽוא׃ ס

15 עֶרְוַ֣ת כַּלָּֽתְךָ֖ לֹ֣א תְגַלֵּ֑ה אֵ֤שֶׁת בִּנְךָ֙ הִ֔וא לֹ֥א תְגַלֶּ֖ה עֶרְוָתָֽהּ׃ ס

- - - - - - - - - - - - - - - - - - - - - - - - - - - -

8. *your father's wife.* As noted earlier, in this section's litany of sexual laws, women are objects to be or not be "uncovered." Here, the prohibition against intimacy with a stepmother follows that of parental incest because a stepmother is seen as an extension of the father. Marriage, in the biblical view, conjoins two bodies as one flesh (Genesis 2:24).

In contrast to the sexual prohibitions enumerated in Leviticus 20, here there are no attendant penalties for perpetrating such acts. In Leviticus 20:11 a man who lies with his father's wife is put to death along with the woman; here, it is simply forbidden. Reuben, who slept with his father's concubine, Bilhah, is cursed by Jacob on his deathbed (Genesis 49:4).

9. *your sister.* A polygamous family in antiquity likely hosted siblings close in age born to different mothers. The verse makes clear that a sister, even a half-sister or one raised elsewhere, is always off-limits. The destructive effects of sibling incest and rape emerge in full force in the story of Amnon's rape of his half-sister Tamar, both the offspring of King David (II Samuel 13).

10. *your son's daughter.* The palpable absence here is the prohibition of intercourse with one's own daughter. Although some scholars claim such a ban to be implicit, it is unsettling not to find it expressly stated. (See also Another View, p. 694.) The nakedness of grandchildren is classified as "your" nakedness, perhaps conveying the sense that they are a man's lineage and bearers of his name.

*your daughter's daughter.* [This phrase reminds us that in the Bible, patrilineal relationships are not the only ones that count. Here, close kinship is defined via a woman, namely, the man's daughter. On women and kinship, see further at Genesis 10:1. —*Ed.*]

15. *your daughter-in-law.* In Genesis 38, Judah transgresses this law by unknowingly having sex

<sup>16</sup>Do not uncover the nakedness of your brother's wife; it is the nakedness of your brother.

<sup>17</sup>Do not uncover the nakedness of a woman and her daughter; nor shall you marry her son's daughter or her daughter's daughter and uncover her nakedness: they are kindred; it is depravity.

<sup>18</sup>Do not marry a woman as a rival to her sister and uncover her nakedness in the other's lifetime.

<sup>19</sup>Do not come near a woman during her menstrual period of impurity to uncover her nakedness.

<sup>20</sup>Do not have carnal relations with your neighbor's wife and defile yourself with her.

<sup>21</sup>Do not allow any of your offspring to be offered up to Molech, and do not profane the name of your God: I am יהוה.

16 עֶרְוַ֞ת אֵֽשֶׁת־אָחִ֖יךָ לֹ֣א תְגַלֵּ֑ה עֶרְוַ֥ת אָחִ֖יךָ הִֽוא׃ ס

17 עֶרְוַ֨ת אִשָּׁ֤ה וּבִתָּהּ֙ לֹ֣א תְגַלֵּ֔ה אֶת־בַּת־בְּנָ֞הּ וְאֶת־בַּת־בִּתָּ֗הּ לֹ֤א תִקַּח֙ לְגַלּ֣וֹת עֶרְוָתָ֔הּ שַֽׁאֲרָ֥ה הֵ֖נָּה זִמָּ֥ה הִֽוא׃

18 וְאִשָּׁ֥ה אֶל־אֲחֹתָ֖הּ לֹ֣א תִקָּ֑ח לִצְרֹ֗ר לְגַלּ֧וֹת עֶרְוָתָ֛הּ עָלֶ֖יהָ בְּחַיֶּֽיהָ׃

19 וְאֶל־אִשָּׁ֖ה בְּנִדַּ֣ת טֻמְאָתָ֑הּ לֹ֣א תִקְרַ֔ב לְגַלּ֖וֹת עֶרְוָתָֽהּ׃

20 וְאֶל־אֵ֙שֶׁת֙ עֲמִֽיתְךָ֔ לֹא־תִתֵּ֥ן שְׁכׇבְתְּךָ֖ לְזָ֑רַע לְטׇמְאָה־בָֽהּ׃

21 וּמִֽזַּרְעֲךָ֥ לֹא־תִתֵּ֖ן לְהַעֲבִ֣יר לַמֹּ֑לֶךְ וְלֹ֧א תְחַלֵּ֛ל אֶת־שֵׁ֥ם אֱלֹהֶ֖יךָ אֲנִ֥י יְהֹוָֽה׃

. . . . . . . . . . . . . . . . . . . . . . . . . . . . . . . . . . . . .

with his daughter-in-law, Tamar. Instead of punishment, Tamar's action results in the birth of twins who are part of the Davidic line. A fascinating tension that arises from the combination of law and narrative in the *Tanach* is that characters in the stories sometimes violate the dictates of the laws. Many commentators claim that the laws are later than the narratives and seek to clarify some of the ambiguously ethical decisions made by biblical characters. However, it is best to view the tension between law and narrative as that which arises between principles and their execution in family and social life.

*16. your brother's wife.* To a certain extent, this law contradicts the procedure of levirate marriage as stipulated in Deuteronomy 25:5–10.

*17. a woman and her daughter.* This prohibition alone emphasizes that it outlaws depraved actions. While having relations with a woman as well as with her daughter or granddaughter does not seem worse than the other forms of incest, perhaps the writers call it depravity since it injures two parties: the woman herself and her descendant.

*18.* According to Genesis, Jacob marries two sisters, Leah and Rachel, who at an early point in the narrative engage in a fierce rivalry (Genesis 29)—although Jacob does not knowingly marry Leah or

intend for her to be a rival to Rachel. On the tension between law and narrative, see at v. 15.

*19.* The topic shifts in this verse from incest to other kinds of forbidden sexual acts. In Leviticus, the body in its pure state is discrete and bounded, with no internal fluids seeping out. In the creation story of Genesis 1, God orders the primordial chaos into distinct categories with boundaries between the elements. The blending of categories on the cosmic or the human level is a movement out of order and into chaos—or, in other words, from life to death. The impure body has sores or oozes fluids that transgress physical boundaries (Leviticus 14–15). That which the body should contain flows out and mixes with the external world. Priestly authorities disqualify such a body from participation in ritual. This, as well as an interest that sex result in procreation, lies behind the interdiction against approaching a menstruating woman in order to "uncover her nakedness." Sex with a menstruating woman becomes an increasingly grave transgression in the sequence of Leviticus: In 15:24 the man who thus has sex with a menstruating woman enters a parallel state of impurity that lasts for seven days; in our verse, such a mingling is expressly forbidden; and in 20:18, the offense is grounds enough for the expulsion of both partners.

22 Do not lie with a male as one lies with a
woman; it is an abhorrence.
23 Do not have carnal relations with any beast
and defile yourself thereby. Likewise for a woman:
she shall not lend herself to a beast to mate with it;
it is perversion.
24 Do not defile yourselves in any of those ways,
for it is by such that the nations that I am casting
out before you defiled themselves. 25 Thus the land

22 וְאֶת־זָכָר לֹא תִשְׁכַּב מִשְׁכְּבֵי אִשָּׁה
תּוֹעֵבָה הִוא׃
23 וּבְכָל־בְּהֵמָה לֹא־תִתֵּן שְׁכָבְתְּךָ לְטָמְאָה־
בָהּ וְאִשָּׁה לֹא־תַעֲמֹד לִפְנֵי בְהֵמָה לְרִבְעָהּ
תֶּבֶל הוּא׃
24 אַל־תִּטַּמְּאוּ בְּכָל־אֵלֶּה כִּי בְכָל־אֵלֶּה
נִטְמְאוּ הַגּוֹיִם אֲשֶׁר־אֲנִי מְשַׁלֵּחַ מִפְּנֵיכֶם׃
25 וַתִּטְמָא הָאָרֶץ וָאֶפְקֹד עֲוֺנָהּ עָלֶיהָ וַתָּקִא

*22.* In the early 21st century, this is one of the most misinterpreted, abused, and decontextualized verses in the Torah. This verse, ripped from its place in the system of levitical laws, is often mobilized to justify discriminatory legislation and behavior against homosexuals and their families. While the act of anal intercourse would present a problem to the person who organized his life according to the levitical laws, it has no place in judicial systems not governed by the total system of Leviticus—and does not cohere with contemporary sexual notions of mutual consent and sexual preference.

In Leviticus, the priestly writers want to prevent the mixture of different types of fluid, as well as uphold distinctions. In terms of blending fluids, anal intercourse is problematic for the same reason as is intercourse with a menstruating woman: semen, an agent of life, potentially mixes with feces, a substance that symbolizes decay and death. This is similar to the mixture of semen and menstrual blood that indicates the absence of conception. In addition, the priestly writers want to avoid the blending of gender categories, as evident in their choice of language. They do not command "do not lie with a male," but rather "do not lie with a male as one lies with a woman." The problem arises when someone treats a male body like a female one. Indeed, such distinctions between the male and the female body define women as those who are penetrated during sexual intercourse and dominated during social intercourse. While treating a man in this manner is odious behavior, it is construed as the natural way to engage women. (See also at 20:13.)

***it is an abhorrence.*** That is, homosexual sex transgresses the boundary between male and female by penetrating the male body as one does the female body. The priestly writers speak of it as an act of mixture that confused categories in the same way that combining certain foods, seeds, or fabrics confuse categories (see 19:19).

*23.* ***Likewise for a woman.*** Where the previous verse speaks of lying with a woman, this verse speaks of a woman directly. Unlike the male subject addressed as "you," the female subject appears in the third person. Curiously, the only law directed to women is that forbidding bestiality. Perhaps this expresses a chain of sexual command in the priestly imagination, in which a man always has power over a woman and a woman is only more powerful than animals. (In the more severe context of Leviticus 20, woman and man alike who have carnal relations with a beast are slated for death.) However, this law also places a woman in charge of her own sexuality. Rather than holding men responsible for women who engage in bestiality, this law depicts women as commanding their own sexual actions in this instance.

## REASONS AND CONSEQUENCES: DON'T DO AS THE CANAANITES DID (18:24–30)

The writers justify Israelite penetration into the land because the other inhabitants have defiled it. The issue of which bodies can be penetrated (the topic of vv. 6–23) now finds its corollary in why

became defiled; and I called it to account for its iniquity, and the land spewed out its inhabitants.
26 But you must keep My laws and My rules, and
you must not do any of those abhorrent things,
neither the citizen nor the stranger who resides
among you; 27 for all those abhorrent things were
done by the people who were in the land before
you, and the land became defiled. 28 So let not the
land spew you out for defiling it, as it spewed out
the nation that came before you. 29 All who do any
of those abhorrent things—such persons shall be
cut off from their people. 30 You shall keep My
charge not to engage in any of the abhorrent
practices that were carried on before you, and you
shall not defile yourselves through them: I יהוה am
your God.

הָאָ֖רֶץ אֶת־יֹשְׁבֶֽיהָ׃ 26 וּשְׁמַרְתֶּ֣ם אַתֶּ֗ם אֶת־
חֻקֹּתַי֙ וְאֶת־מִשְׁפָּטַ֔י וְלֹ֣א תַעֲשׂ֔וּ מִכֹּ֥ל
הַתּוֹעֵבֹ֖ת הָאֵ֑לֶּה הָֽאֶזְרָ֔ח וְהַגֵּ֖ר הַגָּ֥ר
בְּתוֹכְכֶֽם׃ 27 כִּ֚י אֶת־כָּל־הַתּוֹעֵבֹ֣ת הָאֵ֔ל
עָשׂ֥וּ אַנְשֵׁי־הָאָ֖רֶץ אֲשֶׁ֣ר לִפְנֵיכֶ֑ם וַתִּטְמָ֖א
הָאָֽרֶץ׃ 28 וְלֹֽא־תָקִ֤יא הָאָ֙רֶץ֙ אֶתְכֶ֔ם
בְּטַֽמַּאֲכֶ֖ם אֹתָ֑הּ כַּאֲשֶׁ֥ר קָאָ֛ה אֶת־הַגּ֖וֹי
אֲשֶׁ֥ר לִפְנֵיכֶֽם׃ 29 כִּ֚י כָּל־אֲשֶׁ֣ר יַעֲשֶׂ֔ה מִכֹּ֥ל
הַתּוֹעֵבֹ֖ת הָאֵ֑לֶּה וְנִכְרְת֛וּ הַנְּפָשׁ֥וֹת הָעֹשֹׂ֖ת
מִקֶּ֥רֶב עַמָּֽם׃ 30 וּשְׁמַרְתֶּ֣ם אֶת־מִשְׁמַרְתִּ֗י
לְבִלְתִּ֨י עֲשׂ֜וֹת מֵֽחֻקּ֤וֹת הַתּֽוֹעֵבֹת֙ אֲשֶׁ֣ר
נַעֲשׂ֣וּ לִפְנֵיכֶ֔ם וְלֹ֥א תִֽטַּמְּא֖וּ בָּהֶ֑ם אֲנִ֖י יְהוָ֥ה
אֱלֹהֵיכֶֽם׃ פ

---

the Israelites must penetrate and conquer the land. The land appears as a kind of geographic female body that rejects the practitioners of impure acts by spewing them out.

***28. So let not the land spew you out.*** Adherence to the laws is the safeguard against rejection by the land. While Israel elsewhere figures as the bride in its relationship to God (see, for example, Hosea 2), it figures here as the groom in its relationship to the land. If Israel contaminates the land with non-sanctioned mixtures and couplings, then she will throw him out as she has earlier partners.

—*Rachel Havrelock*

# Another View

Leviticus 18 lists twelve categories of females who are sexually off-limits to men, based on blood and marital connection. Strikingly, a man's natural daughter is absent from the list (and from the parallel list in Leviticus 20). Interpreters have approached this glaring omission in a variety of ways. For example:

1. Some readers argue that she is in fact included in the list. Leviticus 18:17 prohibits a man from sexual intercourse with a woman and her daughter; the rabbinic sages extended this to apply to all daughters. Others have argued that Leviticus 18:6, the introductory statement banning men from sexually approaching *sh'er b'saro*, one's own flesh, naturally implies daughters. This explanation is unsatisfactory because the other relations are enumerated; the author does not explicitly identify the daughter, as he does the sister.
2. Some argue that it was not necessary to write about the daughter, either because the taboo against father-daughter sexual contact was so ingrained in society that it did not need to be listed, or because fathers supposedly would never approach their daughters sexually. Some interpreters have suggested that a father would not have sex with his daughter because he would lose the ability to garner a generous bride-price for a non-virgin.
3. Finally, some argue that the Torah does not legislate what one does with one's personal property, and a daughter was considered the property of her father (until transferred to another man).

However, each of these attempts at explanation is problematic. The omission of the daughter is even more troublesome when we note that Israel's neighbors did explicitly ban father-daughter sexual relations in their law collections; in fact, the Laws of Hammurabi (¶ 154) goes so far as to banish a man who lies with his daughter.

*Our task today is to take seriously the daughter's absence from the list.*

To this date, nobody has made a convincing argument to demonstrate that the daughter is implicitly included in the list. Our task today is to take her absence seriously. We know all too well the startling number of fathers who sexually abuse their daughters in our society. Even if we do not know the real situation for daughters in the biblical period, we must be sensitive to the current message that the daughter's omission may have for today's survivors and perpetrators.

—*S. Tamar Kamionkowski*

# Post-biblical Interpretations

***Thus only shall Aaron enter the Shrine*** (16:3). According to Midrash *Vayikra Rabbah* 21.11, the three animals sacrificed on the Day of Atonement together evoke the merits of the patriarchs who will intercede on Israel's behalf. Thus, the bull represents Abraham, who prepared a calf for his visitors (Genesis 18:7), while the ram stands for Isaac, in whose place a ram was sacrificed (22:13). The two goats recall Jacob, who deceived Isaac into giving him Esau's blessing with goat meat and skins (27:9–29). According to the Rabbis, the high priest also calls upon the merit of the matriarchs in 16:4, when he replaces his usual ornate vestments with four linen garments (tunic, breeches, sash, and turban), one for each Mother of Israel.

***Aaron is... to make expiation for himself and for his household*** (16:6). According to rabbinic law, the high priest who officiates on the Day of Atonement must be married. The Hebrew word *beito* ("his household," literally "his house") is said to mean "his wife." In Mishnah *Yoma* 1:1, Rabbi Yehudah suggests that a "back-up" wife must be prepared for the high priest—lest something happen to the first and the priest be disqualified. Other Rabbis respond, however, "If so, there would be no end to the matter!" JT *Yoma* 1:1 and BT *Yoma* 13a–b (also Midrash *Sifra, Acharei Mot* 8.6), consider the possibility that the high priest is *forbidden* to have more than one wife, noting that the verse demands that he atone for his "house," in the singular.

*The high priest's Yom Kippur garments evoke the merit of the four matriarchs.*

***For the life of all flesh—its blood is its life*** (17:14). Discussing this verse, the 13th-century commentator Nachmanides notes that the relationship between life (*nefesh*) and blood (*dam*) is referred to three times in this unit. According to 17:11, the life is "in" the blood (*ki nefesh habasar b̲'dam hi*) while the beginning of 17:14 teaches that the blood is "in" the life (*ki nefesh kol basar damo b̲'nafsho hu*). Using the analogy of wine mixed with water, Nachmanides suggests that one can equally say that the water is "in" the wine or the wine is "in" the water. Thus, the end of v. 14 states that the life "is" the blood (*ki nefesh kol-basar damo hu*). Ultimately, he claims, the two are inseparable; one cannot be found without the other.

***None of you men shall come near anyone of his own flesh to uncover nakedness*** (18:6). Translated hyperliterally, this verse reads, "A man, a man (*ish ish*), to any of his near flesh, you (plural) shall not come near (*lo tikr'vu*)." Although one might think that these incest prohibitions are directed only at men, the *Sifra* (*Acharei Mot* 13.1) explains that the verse applies to everyone: the repetition of "man" (*ish*) is said to include non-Jews, while the second-person plural (*tikr'vu*) includes women.

***Do not uncover the nakedness of a woman and her daughter; nor shall you marry her son's daughter or her daughter's daughter*** (18:17). Mishnah *Sanhedrin* 9:1 makes clear that although the Torah in this passage does not explicitly mention incestuous relations with a daughter or step-daughter, it prohibits such relations as well, and deems them punishable by death. The Talmud points to this verse as the source for these prohibitions (JT *Sanhedrin* 9:1, BT *Sanhedrin* 76a). The Rabbis understood this verse to prohibit a man from sexual relations with a woman when he is *married* to her daughter or to her mother (based on the parallel verse in Leviticus 20:14, which forbids a man from *marrying* a mother and daughter). Thus, a man's sexual connection with his own daughter by his wife or with his wife's daughter by another man also means that he has violated this prohibition. As for incest between a man and his daughter by a woman to whom he was not married, the Rabbis derived the prohibition by logical inference: since this verse (and similarly in v. 10) forbids relations with a granddaughter, then all the more so it must forbid relations with a daughter.

***Do not marry a woman as a rival to her sister*** (18:18). In his commentary on this verse, Nachmanides observes that sisters should not be rivals since they are meant to love each other. In their interpretations, Rashi and Sforno both note that following his wife's death, a husband may marry her surviving sister. According to BT *P'sachim* 119b, at the end of days God will reward the righteous with a great banquet. The patriarch Jacob will decline the honor of leading the blessings after the meal, because his marriages to Leah and Rachel violated this prohibition.

—*Gail Labovitz*

# Contemporary Reflection

LEVITICUS 18 IS one of two passages in the Torah (the other being Leviticus 20) that consists of sexual regulations meant to distinguish Israel from the surrounding nations and make it a holy people. Although the prohibitions in our passage have had a profound impact on Western sexual morality, its assumptions are remote from—and in some cases even abhorrent to—contemporary sensibilities.

First of all, Leviticus evaluates sexual behaviors not in terms of the emotional and relational dimensions of sexual experience that are so central to judgments about sexual morality today, but in terms of the categories of purity and pollution. The purpose of anti-pollution laws is to impose structure on the chaos of experience by ensuring that social and symbolic boundaries are respected and that things conform to their proper class. Leviticus 18 forbids a series of discrete behaviors that supposedly cause defilement and thus disrupt the social/religious world, but it offers no *positive* understanding of holy sexuality.

Second, if we look at the social order that the Levitical anti-pollution laws protect, it seems to consist of extended patriarchal families in which the honor and authority of male heads of household is the primary social value. Verses 7 and 8 do not forbid the father to sexually violate his child but rather *forbid the son to violate the sexuality of his father* by committing incestuous adultery with the father's wife. The verses instruct the less powerful party not to dishonor the powerful by treating the wife's sexuality simply as her husband's possession. Some of the incest prohibitions, such as the outlawing of marriage with two sisters (v. 18), work to the benefit of women, but it is not women's concerns and interests that animate the text. The striking absence of the most prevalent incest violation, namely that between father and daughter, makes clear that it is not the purpose of Leviticus in this case to protect the weak and defenseless.

Third, the marginalization of women within the social world presupposed by Leviticus 18 is underscored by the prohibition of sex with a menstruant in v. 19. On one level, this prohibition fits quite seamlessly into the purity-related concerns of Leviticus. The book earlier defines many bodily emissions as defiling, placing menstrual blood in a similar category with semen and other discharges from the penis, as well as nonmenstrual discharges from the vagina (Leviticus 15). On another level, however, the proscription of sex with a menstruating woman is part of a larger symbolic complex in which menstrual blood has particularly negative associations. The prophets liken adultery, idolatry, and murder to menstrual impurity (see Ezekiel 36:17, for example), while the book of Lamentations describes conquered Jerusalem as a menstruating woman whose "impurity clings to her skirts" (1:9).

*A contemporary response to Leviticus 18 requires both criticism and transformation.*

Fourth, the passage in Leviticus 18 most often cited today, namely the prohibition of male anal intercourse in v. 22, serves as a major justification for homophobia in current religious and political debates and also helps to maintain gender hierarchy. A man who penetrates another man "as one lies with a woman" is guilty of mixing or confusing kinds. He treats another man as one should treat only a woman, thereby moving a male body into the category of female. In the world of Leviticus, doing so both unmans the particular man who is the penetrated partner and threatens the notion of penetrative intercourse as a defining aspect of gender difference.

It seems then that, despite its attempts to promote holiness, Leviticus 18, far from fostering holiness in sexual relations, reflects and reinforces many of the structures of domination that support sexual and family violence. The passage contains important insights that contemporary Jews can affirm: we need some boundaries in sexual relationships; sexual behavior is not simply a private matter; individual behavior is connected with the ethical character of our social world. Leviticus 18 seeks to implement these ideas in its own time and place. But we need to find ways to express these insights in the context of an ethic of sexual holiness appropriate for the 21st century.

We can see Leviticus 18 not as a static document that we must either accept or reject but as a part of Jewish tradition that grapples problematically with ongoing human problems. If so, we can also use it as a starting point for raising hard questions about our own sexual values. What should be included on a list of forbidden and permitted relationships today? Are there certain "bottom lines" that we would want to be part of any statement of sexual norms? How do we balance the need to safeguard those with less power in sexual relationships with the desire to lay out a constructive vision of holy sexuality? How might we articulate a person-centered ethic that focuses on qualities of human connection rather than on the intrinsic nature of particular sexual behaviors? How do we ensure that our sexual values reflect fundamental ethical values such as honesty and justice that ought to guide all human interactions? What place do we give to feelings as a dimension of holy sex? How should pleasure figure into our ethic, for example? How do we attend to the social structures that undergird and make possible holy and sustainable relationships? What social rights and obligations might we see as fundamentally connected to the ability to create satisfying relationships?

A contemporary response to Leviticus 18, in other words, requires both criticism and transformation. It requires careful examination and rejection of those presuppositions of Leviticus that produce and support sexual injustice. But it also involves imagining an alternative ethic that brings in the concerns and questions of those whose perspectives are erased or marginalized by Leviticus itself—as well as by our culture today. Such a response seeks to create the foundation for a sexuality and sensuality that is life-giving for all.

—*Judith Plaskow*

# Voices

## *from* yom kippur

Alicia Suskin Ostriker

*Leviticus 16*

we destroy we break we are broken
and this is the fast you have chosen
*on rosh hashanah it is written*
*on yom kippur it is sealed*

who shall live and who shall die
which goat will have his throat cut
like an unlucky isaac

spitting a red thread and which goat
will be sent alive to the pit where the crazies are
thread tied lightly around its neck

who will possess diamonds and pearls
and who will be killed
by an addicted lover

who shall voyage the web of the world
like an eagle, and who shall curl to sleep
over a steam grate like a worm

who shall be photographed and whose
face will disappear like smoke

this is the fast you have chosen, *turn return*
how to turn like leaves like a page like
a corner
*what is our knowledge, what is our strength*

## In Everything

Lea Goldberg (transl. Rachel Tzvia Back)

*Leviticus 16:1*

In everything there is at least an eighth part
that is death. Its weight is not great.
With what secret and carefree grace
we carry it everywhere we go.
On lovely awakenings, on journeys,
in lovers' words, in our distraction
forgotten at the edges of our affairs
it is always with us. Weighing
hardly anything at all.

## Yom Kippur Prayer

Shirley Blumberg

*Leviticus 16*

I tread gently on the alpine meadow,
and the blue lake does not suffer from my
presence.
Do I deal as gently with those I love
and who love me?
I scorn those who leave rutted scars
on tender mountain earth.
Have I left scars on the souls of those
who put their trust in me?
I hope not, oh how I hope not,
but what I meant to be justice
may have been felt as harshness,
and all my warm interest as unwelcome
intrusion,
and my kind helpful guidance
as unpleasant nagging,
as perhaps it really was.

## *For the Sin . . .*

Shirley Kaufman

*Leviticus 16*

Day of Atonement and the long walk
at sundown to the Wall.
What the sun does to itself,
beating its chest all day,
is already forgotten,
and the goat has gone out
of the Dung Gate with our sins.

The old man lifts his *shofar*
toward the gates of heaven,
blowing the notes to swing them wide
for the last time
before they are bolted for another year.

Now all our days
are measured in the book
against our repentance.

That's a small comfort.
A prayer is not a bird.

## *Elul*

Linda Stern Zisquit

*Leviticus 16*

Welts across my chest
are a sign. I who so wantonly
clamored anarchic

against you, bare myself
repentant, resplendent
this time. Turning

toward you and blemished
in these days set aside
for a body's climb.

## *Acharei Mot*

Laurie Patton

*Leviticus 16:21*

*Ish iti*,
the rabbis say, is
"outside of time,"
walking with all our sins
into a swathe
of beetles and branches–
no past, no present, no future.

*Are sins outside of time?*
Consider the stain
on my great-great-
grandmother's tablecloth.
It congealed in a moment.
I don't know
whose moment it was.

No one got divorced then.
Before the decree,
Mr. Grandmother was jailed
for disorderly conduct.
She walked with a limp.

The stain I see
every sweet Sabbath
is the same
as the sadness
still falling
from her picture,

like some stray
warning light
from the street
that awakes us
from an uneasy dream.

NOTE

*Ish iti.* This obscure Hebrew phrase in 16:21 is translated in this commentary as "designated agent." The word *iti* seems to be related to the word for "time."

## *White Petticoats*

Chana Bloch

*Leviticus 18:6–22*

If the egg had one spot of blood on it
the rabbis said, Throw it away!
As if they could legislate
perfection.
Dress the bride in white
petticoats! Let there be

no stain
on your ceremony! As if
we could keep our lives
from spilling
onto our new clothes. That night
we came home

strangers, too tired
for words,
fog in the high trees
and a trunk full of shiny boxes
we didn't unwrap.
There's a bravery

in being naked.
We left our clothes
on the doorknob, the floor, the bed,
and a live moon opened its arms
around the dark.

## *Annunciation*

Karen Alkalay-Gut

*Leviticus 18:6–22*

Through the open window
the desert breeze
pauses at naked bodies on the bed,
promises
new beginnings.

## *Whatever In Me Is of Heaven*

Deborah Ascarelli

*Leviticus 18:6–22*

Whatever in me is of heaven
Is born because from your blossoms
I collect the gentle honeydew
And I find delight and satisfaction
In feasting eagerly on your Ambrosia.
From you comes the sweet liquid
From you issues the true Love
And your thoughts and your words
Awaken the soul to the Creator of the Sun.

## *[When this old body]*

Grace Paley

*Leviticus 18:6–22*

When this old body
finds that old body
what a nice day it is

when that old body
loves this old body
it's dreamless to sleep
and busy to wake up

when this old body says
you're a little lumpy here and there
but you're the same old body after all

old body    old body    in which somewhere
between crooked toe and forgetful head
the flesh encounters soul
and whispers    you

# קדשים ✦ *K'doshim*

## LEVITICUS 19:1–20:27

## *A Call to Holiness*

PARASHAT K'DOSHIM ("holy") stands at the physical center of the Torah, coming roughly at the midway point between Genesis 1 and Deuteronomy 34. We move into this Torah portion on the heels of a series of sexual taboos (Leviticus 18), and we will end the parashah with a parallel list of taboos (Leviticus 20). Between these two sections, we encounter one of the most beautiful and inspiring passages in the Torah, Leviticus 19. This passage contains a series of seemingly disparate laws covering the gamut from ritual, criminal, and civil legislation to commandments addressing attitudes. The laws touch upon what people do in the privacy of their own homes, how they conduct their business, what they are thinking, and how they worship together. The modern distinctions between criminal, civil, and religious law have absolutely no application in this text.

The primary theme that emerges time and again in Leviticus 19 is the preservation of holiness. "You shall be holy, for I, your God יהוה, am holy." All the commandments are set within the context that God is holy and that we ought to strive toward holiness in every aspect of our lives.

Holiness here differs radically from what we have encountered in previous Torah texts. Leviticus 19 offers a fundamentally new vision of holiness, one that has the potential to bring women and other disenfranchised populations within Israel into the realm of holiness. No longer limited to the male, hereditary priesthood, *parashat K'doshim* democratizes access to and relationship with the Divine in a new way.

Within the particular laws of this parashah, women figure rather prominently as we hear about mothers, daughters, wives, and slaves. The tendency is to protect the rights of women in particularly vulnerable positions. We might wish for equality, and thus a complete dismantling of the practice of categorizing women only in relation to men in the biblical period. The Holiness Code (Leviticus 17–26) does not go that far; however, it is somewhat progressive given its ancient context.

*This portion contains one of the Torah's most beautiful and inspiring passages.*

—*S. Tamar Kamionkowski*

## *Outline*

*I.* A Compendium of Paths to Holiness (19:1–37)

- *A.* The holiness formula (vv. 1–2)
- *B.* On parents and idols (vv. 3–4)
- *C.* Democratization of sacrifice (vv. 5–8)
- *D.* Rights of the poor (vv. 9–10)
- *E.* Theft, deceit and fair courts of law (vv. 11–16)
- *F.* Handling anger in action and thought (vv. 17–18)
- *G.* Maintaining distinct categories (v. 19)
- *H.* Ambiguous status of the slave woman (vv. 20–22)
- *I.* First fruits (vv. 23–25)
- *J.* What we do with our bodies (vv. 26–28)
- *K.* The sacred status of daughters (vv. 29–30)
- *L.* Consulting ghosts and spirits (v. 31)
- *M.* Respect for elders (v. 32)
- *N.* Care for the stranger (vv. 33–34)
- *O.* Fair commerce practices (vv. 35–36a)
- *P.* Conclusion (vv. 36b–37)

*II.* Danger to Holiness and the Dynamics of Holiness (20:1–8)

- *A.* Desecrating God's name through Molech worship (vv. 1–5)
- *B.* Consulting ghosts and spirits (v. 6)
- *C.* The dynamics of holiness (vv. 7–8)

*III.* Family and Sex Ethics (20:9–21)

*IV.* Holiness of the Land (20:22–27)

19:1

יהוה spoke to Moses, saying: [2]Speak to the whole Israelite community and say to them:

You shall be holy, for I, your God יהוה, am holy.

יט וַיְדַבֵּר יְהֹוָה אֶל־מֹשֶׁה לֵּאמֹר׃ 2 דַּבֵּר
אֶל־כׇּל־עֲדַת בְּנֵי־יִשְׂרָאֵל וְאָמַרְתָּ אֲלֵהֶם
קְדֹשִׁים תִּהְיוּ כִּי קָדוֹשׁ אֲנִי יְהֹוָה אֱלֹהֵיכֶם׃

## *A Compendium of Paths to Holiness*

(19:1–37)

Within the framework of holiness, *parashat K'doshim* groups together laws that, in the main, appear elsewhere in the Torah. Why do the biblical writers repeat and enumerate these particular laws at this point in Leviticus? A number of Jewish biblical scholars recently have argued that these units were written by priests who were influenced by the work of the prophet Isaiah. If this is correct, then Leviticus 17–26 can be read as a response by reform-minded priests (a group of anonymous writers) to an earlier group of priests whose writings are preserved in Leviticus 1–16 and elsewhere in the Torah. (Modern critical scholars refer to Leviticus 17–26 as "H," which stands for the Holiness Code, in contrast to "P," which stands for the earlier priestly writings.) *Parashat K'doshim* expresses, clearly and beautifully, the theological position of these presumed religious reformers.

*Parashat K'doshim* begins with echoes of three of the Ten Commandments, in laws that address respect for one's parents, observance of Shabbat, and a prohibition against the worship of other gods. There may be further traces of the Decalogue elsewhere in this unit: the prohibition against murder has been likened to v. 16; the commandment against adultery, to v. 29; the law against stealing, to v. 11; the admonition against bearing false witness, to v. 11 or v. 16; and the commandment concerning coveting, to v. 18. But note a significant difference in the order of the commandments: the laws in this collection start with an emphasis on the relationships between human beings (in rabbinic parlance, *bein adam lachavero*), whereas the Decalogue begins with a focus on laws between people and God (*bein adam lamakom*). This arrangement suggests that Israel brings holiness into its communities with attention to the realm of everyday life, particularly the family.

### THE HOLINESS FORMULA (19:1–2)

2. ***Speak to the whole Israelite community.*** The entire community is addressed, women and men.

***You shall be holy, for I . . . am holy.*** The call to holiness and the identification of this deity as Israel's God frame Leviticus 19, and these elements are intended to impact our understanding of our obligations in following these laws. The term *k'doshim* (holy), although familiar, is a difficult term

In *parashat K'doshim*, holiness comes from cultivating relationships.

ANOTHER VIEW ➤ *716*

Confrontation can clear up misunderstandings and obviate resentment or even hatred.

POST-BIBLICAL INTERPRETATIONS ➤ *716*

How do women experience holiness?

CONTEMPORARY REFLECTION ➤ *718*

When my father died, my mother would not permit others to take her daughters' place in saying the *Kaddish*.

VOICES ➤ *720*

[3]You shall each revere your mother and your
father, and keep My sabbaths: I יהוה am your God.
[4]Do not turn to idols or make molten gods for
yourselves: I יהוה am your God.
[5]When you sacrifice an offering of well-being to
יהוה, sacrifice it so that it may be accepted on your
behalf. [6]It shall be eaten on the day you sacrifice it,

3 אִ֣ישׁ אִמּ֤וֹ וְאָבִיו֙ תִּירָ֔אוּ וְאֶת־שַׁבְּתֹתַ֖י
תִּשְׁמֹ֑רוּ אֲנִ֖י יְהוָ֥ה אֱלֹהֵיכֶֽם׃
4 אַל־תִּפְנוּ֙ אֶל־הָ֣אֱלִילִ֔ם וֵֽאלֹהֵי֙ מַסֵּכָ֔ה לֹ֥א
תַעֲשׂ֖וּ לָכֶ֑ם אֲנִ֖י יְהוָ֥ה אֱלֹהֵיכֶֽם׃
5 וְכִ֧י תִזְבְּח֛וּ זֶ֥בַח שְׁלָמִ֖ים לַֽיהוָ֑ה לִֽרְצֹנְכֶ֖ם
תִּזְבָּחֻֽהוּ׃ 6 בְּי֧וֹם זִבְחֲכֶ֛ם יֵאָכֵ֖ל וּמִֽמָּחֳרָ֑ת

to define. The basic word, in its varying formulations, appears fifty-nine times in the Holiness Code (Leviticus 17–26).

Our ancestors understood this notion of holiness in varying ways. The Holiness Code offers a distinct (and complex) understanding of holiness. In the book of Deuteronomy (see 7:6), all of Israel is considered holy by the fact of its covenantal relationship with God. Yet in most priestly writings (for example, in Leviticus 1–16), holiness is defined in cultic terms: the priestly writers ascribed holiness to God's sancta (the sanctuary and its contents), to time—namely, *Shabbat* and holy days—and to the priests from the family line of Aaron. The priestly writers viewed holiness as a primary attribute of God; they believed, however, that certain people, places, and times could share the condition or status of holiness. Israel is commanded to follow God's laws in order to maintain the boundaries between the holy and the not-holy, which thus assures God's presence (*kavod*) in the sanctuary. Whereas the notion of holiness in the earlier priestly writings is highly static, the Holiness Code offers a radically new view of holiness that is dynamic and constantly shifting according to our actions in the world. Holiness is also democratized; it extends beyond the priesthood and the sanctuary to the entire community and the whole Land of Israel. Anyone in Israel can strive toward the holy through right action.

### ON PARENTS AND IDOLS (19:3–4)

These two verses together echo three of the Decalogue's precepts.

*3. **your mother and your father.*** In other biblical passages that mention both of these parental roles, the father is listed before the mother (for example, Exodus 20:12; 21:15, 17; Deuteronomy 5:16; 21:18; Proverbs 1:8; 20:20). The inverted order here gives special honor to the mother.

*4. **to idols or . . . molten gods.*** Both *elilim* ("idols") and *elohei maseichah* ("molten gods") refer specifically to tangible, human-made representations of gods.

### DEMOCRATIZATION OF SACRIFICE (19:5–8)

Modern critical scholars believe that most of Leviticus 1–16 was originally intended as a priestly manual regarding procedures for communal sanctuaries. Leviticus 19:5–8 is an excerpt from that priestly manual, with modifications introduced for the laity. This passage conveys the message that holiness must attend to all aspects of life. By now applying the material that already appeared in Leviticus 7 to a wider audience, this writer communicates to the Israelites in general that they have a larger role in the complex system of sacrifice. They cannot rely completely on the priests but must themselves be invested in the rituals.

*5. **offering of well-being.*** Leviticus 7:11–21 breaks down the offering of well-being into different sub-categories. The Holiness Code writers are not concerned with expounding the details of each type of sacrifice. They are interested in the broad category of the well-being offering because it is the only holy object that a lay person may handle and even consume.

***be accepted on your behalf.*** The writers of the Holiness Code added this phrase to the earlier for-

or on the day following; but what is left by the third
day must be consumed in fire. [7]If it should be eaten
on the third day, it is an offensive thing, it will not
be acceptable. [8]And one who eats of it shall bear the
guilt for having profaned what is sacred to יהוה;
that person shall be cut off from kin.

[9]When you reap the harvest of your land, you
shall not reap all the way to the edges of your field,
or gather the gleanings of your harvest. [10]You shall
not pick your vineyard bare, or gather the fallen
fruit of your vineyard; you shall leave them for the
poor and the stranger: I יהוה am your God.

[11]You shall not steal; you shall not deal deceit-

וְהַנּוֹתָר֙ עַד־י֣וֹם הַשְּׁלִישִׁ֔י בָּאֵ֖שׁ יִשָּׂרֵֽף׃
7 וְאִ֛ם הֵאָכֹ֥ל יֵאָכֵ֖ל בַּיּ֣וֹם הַשְּׁלִישִׁ֑י פִּגּ֥וּל
ה֖וּא לֹ֥א יֵרָצֶֽה׃ 8 וְאֹֽכְלָיו֙ עֲוֺנ֣וֹ יִשָּׂ֔א כִּֽי־
אֶת־קֹ֥דֶשׁ יְהוָ֖ה חִלֵּ֑ל וְנִכְרְתָ֛ה הַנֶּ֥פֶשׁ הַהִ֖וא
מֵעַמֶּֽיהָ׃
9 וּֽבְקֻצְרְכֶם֙ אֶת־קְצִ֣יר אַרְצְכֶ֔ם לֹ֧א תְכַלֶּ֛ה
פְּאַ֥ת שָׂדְךָ֖ לִקְצֹ֑ר וְלֶ֥קֶט קְצִֽירְךָ֖ לֹ֥א תְלַקֵּֽט׃
10 וְכַרְמְךָ֙ לֹ֣א תְעוֹלֵ֔ל וּפֶ֥רֶט כַּרְמְךָ֖ לֹ֣א
תְלַקֵּ֑ט לֶֽעָנִ֤י וְלַגֵּר֙ תַּעֲזֹ֣ב אֹתָ֔ם אֲנִ֖י יְהוָ֥ה
אֱלֹהֵיכֶֽם׃
11 לֹ֖א תִּגְנֹ֑בוּ וְלֹא־תְכַחֲשׁ֥וּ וְלֹֽא־תְשַׁקְּר֖וּ

mulation of the well-being offering, and they apparently did so for a specific theological purpose. By its form, the Hebrew word *lirtzonchem* is ambiguous; it means both "be sure that the offering is acceptable (to God) on your behalf" and "be sure that the sacrifice is offered by you willingly and with full heart." The usage of the plural emphasizes that the writer addresses all Israel, not just the priests. This seemingly minor addition actually demands that the entire population become invested in what had become the domain of the priests alone.

*8. that person shall be cut off from kin.* This formulaic expression (which appears frequently in the Torah) probably indicates that the offender will suffer an untimely death, not excommunication (but see at 7:20).

## RIGHTS OF THE POOR (19:9–10)

This section moves from ritual duty to the domain of economic justice. The writers of the text acknowledge the uneven distribution of wealth, and they put measures into place to ensure that these inequalities are addressed, even if only in some small measure. The rationale for the precepts is neither mercy nor pity, but rather duty and justice. Deuteronomy 24:19–20 adds to this teaching, emphasizing that whatever falls to the ground during the reaping season cannot be picked up again in a second sweep. The book of Ruth describes the practice mandated in our passage. In Ruth 2 we find an example of women participating in this program. Ruth stands behind the reapers as they cut and gather the sheaves. Whatever they do not grab by hand is left on the ground for Ruth and others to pick up. Ruth 2 also mentions that Boaz, the property owner, orders his workers not to touch Ruth.

*10. pick... bare.* Although the meaning of the Hebrew verb *t'olel* is not entirely clear, the sense is that some grapes were to be left on the vine, in parallel to leaving a furrow of the field for the poor to harvest. In both cases, the poor were to have the opportunity to pick what had been dropped or left by regular workers.

## THEFT, DECEIT, AND FAIR COURTS OF LAW (19:11–16)

This collection of laws addresses potential opportunities for exploitation between neighbors and within courts of law. Justice is the central theme, whether the justice is to be carried out in courts of law or only in the eyes of God.

*11. steal.* Heb. *ganav*, a term that refers to kidnapping and not only to theft of property. There are only two cases in the Bible of women stealing: the matriarch Rachel stealing her father's *t'rafim* (the household religious figurines) when she leaves

fully or falsely with one another. 12 You shall not swear falsely by My name, profaning the name of your God: I am יהוה.

13 You shall not defraud your fellow [Israelite]. You shall not commit robbery. The wages of a laborer shall not remain with you until morning.

14 You shall not insult the deaf, or place a stumbling block before the blind. You shall fear your God: I am יהוה.

15 You shall not render an unfair decision: do not favor the poor or show deference to the rich; judge your kin fairly. 16 Do not deal basely with members of your people. Do not profit by the blood of your fellow [Israelite]: I am יהוה.

17 You shall not hate your kinsfolk in your heart. Reprove your kin but incur no guilt on their ac-

אִישׁ בַּעֲמִיתוֹ׃ 12 וְלֹא־תִשָּׁבְעוּ בִשְׁמִי
לַשָּׁקֶר וְחִלַּלְתָּ אֶת־שֵׁם אֱלֹהֶיךָ אֲנִי
יְהֹוָה׃
13 לֹא־תַעֲשֹׁק אֶת־רֵעֲךָ וְלֹא תִגְזֹל לֹא־
תָלִין פְּעֻלַּת שָׂכִיר אִתְּךָ עַד־בֹּקֶר׃
14 לֹא־תְקַלֵּל חֵרֵשׁ וְלִפְנֵי עִוֵּר לֹא תִתֵּן
מִכְשֹׁל וְיָרֵאתָ מֵּאֱלֹהֶיךָ אֲנִי יְהֹוָה׃
15 לֹא־תַעֲשׂוּ עָוֶל בַּמִּשְׁפָּט לֹא־תִשָּׂא פְנֵי־
דָל וְלֹא תֶהְדַּר פְּנֵי גָדוֹל בְּצֶדֶק תִּשְׁפֹּט
עֲמִיתֶךָ׃ 16 לֹא־תֵלֵךְ רָכִיל בְּעַמֶּיךָ לֹא
תַעֲמֹד עַל־דַּם רֵעֶךָ אֲנִי יְהֹוָה׃
17 לֹא־תִשְׂנָא אֶת־אָחִיךָ בִּלְבָבֶךָ הוֹכֵחַ
תּוֹכִיחַ אֶת־עֲמִיתֶךָ וְלֹא־תִשָּׂא עָלָיו חֵטְא׃

her father's household (see at Genesis 31:19), and the princess Jehoshabeath, who steals away the young prince Joash to protect him from a military coup and slaughter (II Chronicles 22:11; she is named Jehosheba in II Kings 11:2). In both cases, the act of theft is motivated by a desire to protect the continuity of the family line.

*14. insult.* Literally, "utter a curse." Just as the blind cannot see a physical obstacle in their path, so the deaf cannot hear a curse and take precautions against it.

*You shall fear your God.* This phrase serves as a warning against haughtiness, reminding each individual that there is a force far beyond one's understanding. Proper perspective helps persons to treat others with compassion.

*16. basely.* The corresponding Hebrew word is also associated with gossip, the misuse of speech. In this particular context, the Torah teaches that unfair accusations and rumors may have dire consequences. (Nowhere does the Bible explicitly associate women with gossip. It is only in rabbinic literature that gossip, *l'shon hara*, comes to be connected with women, through a midrash on Numbers 12 and Miriam.)

*Do not profit by the blood of your fellow.* Two other translations for this clause are "do not stand by idly" and "do not conspire against" your fellow.

## HANDLING ANGER IN ACTION AND THOUGHT (19:17–18)

The commandments in these two verses are particularly striking insofar as they command what one ought to feel. These laws deal with intentions and emotions. The biblical writers make no distinction between those laws that other people could monitor and enforce, and those that only God could watch, so to speak.

*17. hate.* The corresponding Hebrew term denotes both an emotion and a cognitive state of being. Our ancestors recognized that it is difficult to separate one's emotions from one's attitudes and actions.

*incur no guilt on their account.* There are a multitude of interpretations for this clause. Some suggest that if you do not reprove the offending individuals, you become an accomplice in their wrongdoing. Others believe that if you do not face the source of your disquiet, it may grow into rage and possibly result in injury.

count. <sup>18</sup>You shall not take vengeance or bear a grudge against members of your people. Love your fellow [Israelite] as yourself: I am יהוה.

<sup>19</sup>You shall observe My laws.

You shall not let your cattle mate with a different kind; you shall not sow your field with two kinds of seed; you shall not put on cloth from a mixture of two kinds of material.

<sup>20</sup>If a man has carnal relations with a woman who is a slave and has been designated for another

18 לֹא־תִקֹּם וְלֹא־תִטֹּר אֶת־בְּנֵי עַמֶּ֔ךָ וְאָהַבְתָּ לְרֵעֲךָ כָּמ֑וֹךָ אֲנִי יְהוָֽה:

19 אֶת־חֻקֹּתַי תִּשְׁמֹ֒רוּ֒ בְּהֶמְתְּךָ֙ לֹא־תַרְבִּ֣יעַ כִּלְאַ֔יִם שָׂדְךָ֖ לֹא־תִזְרַ֣ע כִּלְאָ֑יִם וּבֶ֤גֶד כִּלְאַ֙יִם֙ שַֽׁעַטְנֵ֔ז לֹ֥א יַעֲלֶ֖ה עָלֶֽיךָ:

20 וְ֠אִישׁ כִּֽי־יִשְׁכַּ֨ב אֶת־אִשָּׁ֜ה שִׁכְבַת־זֶ֗רַע וְהִ֤וא שִׁפְחָה֙ נֶחֱרֶ֣פֶת לְאִ֔ישׁ וְהָפְדֵּה֙ לֹ֣א

- - - - - - - - - - - - - - - - - - - - - - - - - - - - - - - - - - -

*18.* *not take vengeance or bear a grudge.* Taking vengeance means a deed, and bearing a grudge reflects thought. Again, deed and thought—act and intention—are interwoven.

*Love your fellow.* The verb for love, *ahav*, is here followed by the preposition using the letter *lamed* ("l" in English). This form is found in only four cases in the Bible; Abraham Malamat notes that in all four cases, there is an implication of action, not just feeling ("You Shall Love . . . ," 1990). See, for example, Leviticus 19:34, where Israelites are commanded to love the foreigner in their midst, which implies merciful and kind action.

### MAINTAINING DISTINCT CATEGORIES (19:19)

This verse forbids the breeding or mixing of animals, seeds, or cloths of different species or categories (see also Deuteronomy 22:9–11). The rationale behind this prohibition is connected to the rationale behind the dietary laws (Leviticus 11, Deuteronomy 14), the law that forbids crossdressing (Deuteronomy 22:5), and the law requiring that animals die for killing human beings (Exodus 21:29). Our ancestors believed that species and gender were set out at creation and were to be maintained as distinct categories. Genesis 1:20–30 describes the creation of trees according to their kind, and animals according to their place in the world; Genesis 1:27 states that God created human beings, male and female. Mary Douglas has shown

that the dietary laws are an attempt to maintain these clear categories and differentiations. It is this kind of thinking, in sharp categories and distinctions, that leads to the banning of same-sex sexual relations in the Bible (see at Leviticus 20:13) and in other ancient texts—and that assigns different dress, behavior, and social roles for women and men.

*19.* *mixture.* Heb. *shaatnez*; the word's precise meaning is unclear. It appears in the Bible only here and in Deuteronomy 22:11 (which clarifies that this term refers to a combination of wool and linen). Languages related to Hebrew seem to lack a similar word.

### AMBIGUOUS STATUS OF THE SLAVE WOMAN (19:20–22)

The transition to this topic is rooted in the idea that it is problematic to mix categories. In this case, the "mixing" involves sexual relations, and the complication concerns a woman who is both a slave and an intended wife. The slave woman has been designated for a man (who is not her owner) when another man has sexual relations with her. This passage portrays the woman as an object: the man performs the sexual act upon her (on this idiom, see at Exodus 19:15); and the guilty party is the man who has offended both her current owner and God, to whom the offender must make amends through a ritual sacrifice. The fate of the woman is not the primary concern of the writers of this text. They do not address whether she is likely to remain a slave

נִפְדָּתָה אוֹ חֻפְשָׁה לֹא נִתַּן־לָהּ בִּקֹּרֶת
תִּהְיֶה לֹא יוּמְתוּ כִּי־לֹא חֻפָּשָׁה׃ 21 וְהֵבִיא
אֶת־אֲשָׁמוֹ לַיהוָה אֶל־פֶּתַח אֹהֶל מוֹעֵד
אֵיל אָשָׁם׃ 22 וְכִפֶּר עָלָיו הַכֹּהֵן בְּאֵיל
הָאָשָׁם לִפְנֵי יְהוָה עַל־חַטָּאתוֹ אֲשֶׁר חָטָא
וְנִסְלַח לוֹ מֵחַטָּאתוֹ אֲשֶׁר חָטָא׃ פ
23 וְכִי־תָבֹאוּ אֶל־הָאָרֶץ וּנְטַעְתֶּם כָּל־עֵץ
מַאֲכָל וַעֲרַלְתֶּם עָרְלָתוֹ אֶת־פִּרְיוֹ שָׁלֹשׁ
שָׁנִים יִהְיֶה לָכֶם עֲרֵלִים לֹא יֵאָכֵל׃

man, but has not been redeemed or given her freedom, there shall be an indemnity; they shall not,
however, be put to death, since she has not been
freed. 21 But he must bring to the entrance of the
Tent of Meeting, as his reparation offering to יהוה,
a ram of reparation offering. 22 With the ram of reparation offering the priest shall make expiation for
him before יהוה for the sin that he committed; and
the sin that he committed will be forgiven him.
23 When you enter the land and plant any tree
for food, you shall regard its fruit as forbidden.
Three years it shall be forbidden for you, not to be

or to become the wife of the prospective husband. (See also Exodus 21:7–11 for laws about women sold into slavery.)

*20. has carnal relations.* The verb *shachav*, "to lie down" or "to engage in sexual intercourse," can take either the direct-object marker *et* or the preposition *im* ("with"). In this case, the writer has used the former. This grammatical form—in which the object is relatively passive—may be a linguistic convention, or it may be a clue to the priestly understanding of the relationship between the sexes in this case.

*slave.* In Leviticus 25, also part of the Holiness Code, the writers abolish slavery completely for all Israelites. This contradiction suggests that Leviticus 19 is a compilation of laws from various sources whose purpose was to express the specific concerns of this particular school of ancient Israel (see at 19:2). If the woman in this case had not been a slave, Deuteronomy 22:23–27 would have applied, prescribing the death penalty for the woman and man. But the woman here is in an ambiguous state, for she is both a slave woman and a nearly betrothed woman. As seen in v. 19, the Holiness Code writers are particularly interested in liminal states and concerned about confusion caused by overlapping categories.

*indemnity.* The corresponding Hebrew word appears only here in the Bible; others translate it as "inquisition." The question is whether an investigation to clarify her status is required or whether the offender is required simply to pay a fine to the man who owns the woman (either the current master or the future husband).

*21. reparation offering.* Since this illicit sexual act is not subject to the death penalty (v. 20), the offender must appease God through a sacrificial offering.

### FIRST FRUITS (19:23–25)

The Holiness Code writers believed that the community of Israel maintains holiness not only by the way it treats its members and the sancta (the sacred things), but also by the way it cares for the fruit of the land. One was not to pick fruit from new fruit-bearing trees for three years. In the fourth year, Israelites would dedicate the first fruits to God.

*23. you shall regard its fruit as forbidden.* Literally, "you shall treat as foreskin its foreskin with its fruit." As Jacob Milgrom has argued, the foreskin refers to the fruit while it is still in its bud; therefore the text commands the removal of the buds—with the incipient fruit inside—from juvenile trees during their first few years (*Leviticus 17–22*, 2000, p. 1679). Thus, the term *arel* ("foreskin" or "uncircumcised") here has both a literal meaning (referring to the bud) and a metaphoric meaning (referring to its forbidden nature).

24 וּבַשָּׁנָה הָרְבִיעִת יִהְיֶה כָּל־פִּרְיוֹ קֹדֶשׁ
הִלּוּלִים לַיהוָה׃ 25 וּבַשָּׁנָה הַחֲמִישִׁת
תֹּאכְלוּ אֶת־פִּרְיוֹ לְהוֹסִיף לָכֶם תְּבוּאָתוֹ
אֲנִי יְהוָה אֱלֹהֵיכֶם׃
26 לֹא תֹאכְלוּ עַל־הַדָּם לֹא תְנַחֲשׁוּ וְלֹא
תְעוֹנֵנוּ׃ 27 לֹא תַקִּפוּ פְּאַת רֹאשְׁכֶם וְלֹא
תַשְׁחִית אֵת פְּאַת זְקָנֶךָ׃ 28 וְשֶׂרֶט לָנֶפֶשׁ
לֹא תִתְּנוּ בִּבְשַׂרְכֶם וּכְתֹבֶת קַעֲקַע לֹא
תִתְּנוּ בָּכֶם אֲנִי יְהוָה׃
29 אַל־תְּחַלֵּל אֶת־בִּתְּךָ לְהַזְנוֹתָהּ וְלֹא־
תִזְנֶה הָאָרֶץ וּמָלְאָה הָאָרֶץ זִמָּה׃ 30 אֶת־
שַׁבְּתֹתַי תִּשְׁמֹרוּ וּמִקְדָּשִׁי תִּירָאוּ אֲנִי
יְהוָה׃

eaten. [24]In the fourth year all its fruit shall be set
aside for jubilation before יהוה; [25]and only in the
fifth year may you use its fruit—that its yield to you
may be increased: I יהוה am your God.
[26]You shall not eat anything with its blood. You
shall not practice divination or soothsaying. [27]You
[men] shall not round off the side-growth on your
head, or destroy the side-growth of your beard.
[28]You shall not make gashes in your flesh for the
dead, or incise any marks on yourselves: I am יהוה.
[29]Do not degrade your daughter and make her a
harlot, lest the land fall into harlotry and the land
be filled with depravity. [30]You shall keep My sabbaths and venerate My sanctuary: I am יהוה.

*24. set aside.* Heb. *kodesh*; that is, the fruit is to be considered *kadosh* (holy). This designation is no coincidence; biblical literature commonly distinguishes between "the uncircumcised" (see at v. 23) as foreign to God and "the holy" as a part of God.

### WHAT WE DO WITH OUR BODIES (19:26–28)

These prohibitions refer to practices that the writers associated with non-Israelite worship.

*26. You shall not eat . . . blood.* In Leviticus, meat may not be consumed until the blood has been drained and offered to God. The biblical writers understood blood as being the life-source of a being (as in 17:11; Deuteronomy 12:23).

*27–28.* These prohibitions refer to certain acts of mourning in the ancient Near East (see also at Deuteronomy 14:1–2). Mourning acts that the Bible considers appropriate include wearing sackcloth and ashes, and fasting.

*28. incise any marks.* The corresponding Hebrew term appears nowhere else and, in this context, is assumed to refer to tattoos.

### THE SACRED STATUS OF DAUGHTERS (19:29–30)

These verses reflect one of the central themes in the Holiness Code as a whole: the Israelite role in the maintenance and expansion of holiness. On the surface, v. 29 simply seems to prohibit the use of daughters as prostitutes. The key word in this verse is "degrade," which should be rendered more accurately as "desecrate." The verb *ch-l-l* is a technical term in the Holiness Code indicating a decrease in the level of holiness. The use of this verb implies that the daughter is not only a member of society, but also bears the responsibility for aspects of holiness in the community. If a father puts his daughter in a position that diminishes her holiness, that action affects the entire land negatively. This point is made even more strongly by coupling this teaching with a reminder to observe Shabbat and to keep watch over God's holy space. To some degree, the holiness of a daughter is akin to the holiness of the sanctuary.

31Do not turn to ghosts and do not inquire of
familiar spirits, to be defiled by them: I יהוה am
your God.
32You shall rise before the aged and show deference to the old; you shall fear your God: I am יהוה.
33When strangers reside with you in your land,
you shall not wrong them. 34The strangers who reside with you shall be to you as your citizens; you
shall love each one as yourself, for you were strangers in the land of Egypt: I יהוה am your God.
35You shall not falsify measures of length,
weight, or capacity. 36You shall have an honest balance, honest weights, an honest *eifah*, and an honest *hin*.
I יהוה am your God who freed you from the

31 אַל־תִּפְנוּ אֶל־הָאֹבֹת וְאֶל־הַיִּדְּעֹנִים
אַל־תְּבַקְשׁוּ לְטָמְאָה בָהֶם אֲנִי יְהוָה
אֱלֹהֵיכֶם׃
32 מִפְּנֵי שֵׂיבָה תָּקוּם וְהָדַרְתָּ פְּנֵי זָקֵן
וְיָרֵאתָ מֵּאֱלֹהֶיךָ אֲנִי יְהוָה׃ ס
33 וְכִי־יָגוּר אִתְּךָ גֵּר בְּאַרְצְכֶם לֹא תוֹנוּ
אֹתוֹ׃ 34 כְּאֶזְרָח מִכֶּם יִהְיֶה לָכֶם הַגֵּר ׀ הַגָּר
אִתְּכֶם וְאָהַבְתָּ לוֹ כָּמוֹךָ כִּי־גֵרִים הֱיִיתֶם
בְּאֶרֶץ מִצְרָיִם אֲנִי יְהוָה אֱלֹהֵיכֶם׃
35 לֹא־תַעֲשׂוּ עָוֶל בַּמִּשְׁפָּט בַּמִּדָּה בַּמִּשְׁקָל
וּבַמְּשׂוּרָה׃ 36 מֹאזְנֵי צֶדֶק אַבְנֵי־צֶדֶק אֵיפַת
צֶדֶק וְהִין צֶדֶק יִהְיֶה לָכֶם
אֲנִי יְהוָה אֱלֹהֵיכֶם אֲשֶׁר־הוֹצֵאתִי אֶתְכֶם

### CONSULTING GHOSTS AND SPIRITS (19:31)

Some scholars argue that consulting ghosts and using divination was problematic because of their inherent magical tendencies, that is, the attempt to manipulate the divine realm. Others assert that there were bans on such practices because they were considered too pagan-like. These conclusions fail, however, given the use of Urim and Thummim by the biblical priests (see Exodus 28:30), for this was a pagan-like device that arguably manipulates the divine. Therefore, one might conclude that the prohibition was motivated in part by the desire to curtail women's access to the divine. (See further at 20:6.)

### RESPECT FOR ELDERS (19:32)

The biblical tradition is consistent in its call for respect and care for the elderly.

### CARE FOR THE STRANGER (19:33–34)

Every law collection in the Bible advocates care for the foreigner who resides in the land of Israel (for example, Exodus 22:20; 23:9; Deuteronomy 14:29; 24:14, 17). These admonitions frequently remind the reader that our ancestors were once strangers in the land of Egypt and that we should remember the vulnerability of the outsider. Elsewhere in the Bible, the stranger is mentioned alongside the widow and orphan.

*33. strangers.* The *ger* was the non-Israelite who lived either temporarily or long-term in the Land of Israel but did not belong to the ethnic (later political) body of Israel. [Because the *ger*'s situation and responsibilities do not require that only a male could have such a status, the present translation construes the Hebrew term as gender inclusive and renders the Hebrew masculine form in the plural. —*Ed.*]

### FAIR COMMERCE PRACTICES (19:35–36a)

The use of fair weights and measures is also discussed in Deuteronomy 25:13–16.

### CONCLUSION (19:36b–37)

*36. I* יהוה *am your God who freed you from the land of Egypt.* The formula *ani* יהוה ("I יהוה" or "I am יהוה"), which appears fifteen times in Leviticus 19, is an abbreviation for the full text that is now provided as a conclusion. This clause encourages the reader to remember that one must emulate

land of Egypt. [37]You shall faithfully observe all My laws and all My rules: I am יהוה.

מֵאֶרֶץ מִצְרָיִם׃ 37 וּשְׁמַרְתֶּם אֶת־כָּל־חֻקֹּתַי
וְאֶת־כָּל־מִשְׁפָּטַי וַעֲשִׂיתֶם אֹתָם אֲנִי
יְהוָה׃ פ

**20** And יהוה spoke to Moses: [2]Say further to the Israelite people:

Anyone among the Israelites, or among the strangers residing in Israel, who gives any offspring to Molech, shall be put to death; the people of the land shall pelt the person with stones. [3]And I will set My face against that person, whom I will cut off from among the people for having given offspring to Molech and so defiled My sanctuary and profaned My holy name. [4]And if the people of the land should shut their eyes to that person's giving offspring to Molech, and should not put the person to death, [5]I Myself will set My face against that person's kin as well; and I will cut off from among

כ וַיְדַבֵּר יְהוָה אֶל־מֹשֶׁה לֵּאמֹר׃ 2 וְאֶל־
בְּנֵי יִשְׂרָאֵל תֹּאמַר
אִישׁ אִישׁ מִבְּנֵי יִשְׂרָאֵל וּמִן־הַגֵּר ׀ הַגָּר
בְּיִשְׂרָאֵל אֲשֶׁר יִתֵּן מִזַּרְעוֹ לַמֹּלֶךְ מוֹת יוּמָת
עַם הָאָרֶץ יִרְגְּמֻהוּ בָאָבֶן׃ 3 וַאֲנִי אֶתֵּן אֶת־
פָּנַי בָּאִישׁ הַהוּא וְהִכְרַתִּי אֹתוֹ מִקֶּרֶב עַמּוֹ
כִּי מִזַּרְעוֹ נָתַן לַמֹּלֶךְ לְמַעַן טַמֵּא אֶת־
מִקְדָּשִׁי וּלְחַלֵּל אֶת־שֵׁם קָדְשִׁי׃ 4 וְאִם
הַעְלֵם יַעְלִימוּ עַם הָאָרֶץ אֶת־עֵינֵיהֶם
מִן־הָאִישׁ הַהוּא בְּתִתּוֹ מִזַּרְעוֹ לַמֹּלֶךְ
לְבִלְתִּי הָמִית אֹתוֹ׃ 5 וְשַׂמְתִּי אֲנִי אֶת־
פָּנַי בָּאִישׁ הַהוּא וּבְמִשְׁפַּחְתּוֹ וְהִכְרַתִּי אֹתוֹ

God and seek to become holy because God saved Israel in the past.

## *Danger to Holiness and the Dynamics of Holiness* (20:1–8)

This unit warns against the practices that desecrate God's sanctity.

### DESECRATING GOD'S NAME THROUGH MOLECH WORSHIP (20:1–5)

The book of Kings mentions a practice wherein individuals (including kings) would sacrifice their children by putting them to the fire for the worship of Molech, the god of the Ammonites, who are Israel's neighbors to the east (I Kings 11:7; II Kings 23:10). Although some extra-biblical evidence suggests that such practices did take place, the biblical writers—as anti-pagan polemic—probably exaggerate their extent (see also Leviticus 18:21 and Jeremiah 7:31 on child sacrifice).

*3. **profaned My holy name.*** Traditional Jewish commentators have interpreted this phrase to mean that one can damage God's reputation among the nations of the world through wrong actions. The concept is still current today in describing public acts that can bring shame upon the people Israel and its God as acts of *chillul haShem.* However, in the context of the Holiness Code, the teaching is much more profound, for the message is that wrong human actions can actually have an impact upon that aspect of God known as *shem*, name. One can increase God's holiness through right actions, and one can diminish God's presence in the world through wrong actions. Holiness, being pliable and malleable (see 19:2), is the arena in which persons are in relationship with the Divine. God is affected by human actions—both the good and the bad. According to the Holiness Code, God does not remove the divine Presence (*kavod*) from Israel's midst, nor does God act out of great wrath. God may detach an individual from the covenantal promises ("I will set My face against X . . . whom I will cut off from among the people," 17:10; 20:3; 20:6); but more often, wrongdoing simply diminishes God's *shem*.

their people both that person and all who follow in going astray after Molech. [6]And if any person turns to ghosts and familiar spirits and goes astray after them, I will set My face against that person, whom I will cut off from among the people.

[7]You shall sanctify yourselves and be holy, for I יהוה am your God. [8]You shall faithfully observe My laws: I יהוה make you holy.

[9]If anyone insults either father or mother, that person shall be put to death; that person has insulted father and mother—and retains the bloodguilt.

[10]If a man commits adultery with another's wife

וְאֵת ׀ כָּל־הַזֹּנִים אַחֲרָיו לִזְנוֹת אַחֲרֵי הַמֹּלֶךְ
מִקֶּרֶב עַמָּם׃ 6 וְהַנֶּפֶשׁ אֲשֶׁר תִּפְנֶה אֶל־
הָאֹבֹת וְאֶל־הַיִּדְּעֹנִים לִזְנֹת אַחֲרֵיהֶם
וְנָתַתִּי אֶת־פָּנַי בַּנֶּפֶשׁ הַהִוא וְהִכְרַתִּי אֹתוֹ
מִקֶּרֶב עַמּוֹ׃
7 וְהִתְקַדִּשְׁתֶּם וִהְיִיתֶם קְדֹשִׁים כִּי אֲנִי
יְהֹוָה אֱלֹהֵיכֶם׃ 8 וּשְׁמַרְתֶּם אֶת־חֻקֹּתַי
וַעֲשִׂיתֶם אֹתָם אֲנִי יְהֹוָה מְקַדִּשְׁכֶם׃
9 כִּי־אִישׁ אִישׁ אֲשֶׁר יְקַלֵּל אֶת־אָבִיו וְאֶת־
אִמּוֹ מוֹת יוּמָת אָבִיו וְאִמּוֹ קִלֵּל דָּמָיו
בּוֹ׃
10 וְאִישׁ אֲשֶׁר יִנְאַף אֶת־אֵשֶׁת אִישׁ אֲשֶׁר

CONSULTING GHOSTS AND SPIRITS (20:6)

The ban on practicing necromancy and certain types of divination appears three times in this parashah (19:31; here; and 20:27). With every prohibition against divination, the punishment becomes more severe, moving from impurity, to being cut off from one's people, to the death penalty. See also at 19:31, 20:27, and Exodus 22:17.

THE DYNAMICS OF HOLINESS (20:7–8)

These two verses express the heart of the Holiness Code. The ultimate goal is for the community to sanctify itself by observing the precepts outlined in the Code and to strive for holiness at all times. The reason behind this goal is that God is holy and that the proper medium for a connection between God and Israel is holy action. Through proper action, the people come closer to God, and God reaches out toward the community.

## *Family and Sex Ethics* (20:9–21)

This unit closely parallels the material found in Leviticus 18. Both units list incest taboos, laws against male anal penetration, and prohibitions against adultery, bestiality, and Molech worship. The present unit adds prohibitions against cursing parents and the use of seers. Leviticus 20 organizes these laws by the severity of the punishment, whereas Leviticus 18 orders its material according to family relationships. The wording of some of the specific laws differs, but the basic sense of the prohibitions is similar in the two units.

*9.* This verse introduces the new unit on sexual taboos; see further at Leviticus 18. Illicit sexual relationships, especially incest, are understood to be destructive to the family and clan.

***shall be put to death.*** Heb. *mot yumat*, the technical term for the death penalty as prescribed by a court of law. In most cases within Torah, capital punishment was to be carried out by stoning.

*10.* The parallel passage in Leviticus 18:20 indicates that when a man has sexual relations with his neighbor's wife, it makes both parties impure. In contrast, this verse and Deuteronomy 22:22 specify that both the man and the woman are to be put to death. These passages focus on the man as the subject and provide no information about the woman's complicity in the illicit sexual act. Some have argued that killing the woman makes the woman accountable for her own actions and therefore grants her a level of personhood that is absent from the text in Leviticus. It is also possible that the

—committing adultery with the wife of his fellow [Israelite]—the adulterer and the adulteress shall be put to death. [11]If a man lies with his father's wife, it is the nakedness of his father that he has uncovered; the two shall be put to death—and they retain the bloodguilt. [12]If a man lies with his daughter-in-law, both of them shall be put to death; they have committed incest—and they retain the bloodguilt. [13]If a man lies with a male as one lies with a woman, the two of them have done an abhorrent thing; they shall be put to death—and they retain the bloodguilt. [14]If a man marries a woman and her mother, it is depravity; both he and they shall be put to the fire, that there be no depravity among you. [15]If a man has carnal relations with a beast, he shall be put to death; and you shall kill the beast. [16]If a woman approaches any beast to mate with it, you shall kill the woman and the beast; they shall be put to death—and they retain the bloodguilt.

[17]If a man marries his sister, the daughter of either his father or his mother, so that he sees her nakedness and she sees his nakedness, it is a disgrace; they shall be excommunicated in the sight of their kinsfolk. He has uncovered the nakedness of his sister, he shall bear the guilt. [18]If a man lies with a woman during her menstrual condition and un-

יִנְאַף אֶת־אֵשֶׁת רֵעֵהוּ מוֹת־יוּמַת הַנֹּאֵף
וְהַנֹּאָפֶת׃ 11 וְאִישׁ אֲשֶׁר יִשְׁכַּב אֶת־אֵשֶׁת
אָבִיו עֶרְוַת אָבִיו גִּלָּה מוֹת־יוּמְתוּ שְׁנֵיהֶם
דְּמֵיהֶם בָּם׃ 12 וְאִישׁ אֲשֶׁר יִשְׁכַּב אֶת־
כַּלָּתוֹ מוֹת יוּמְתוּ שְׁנֵיהֶם תֶּבֶל עָשׂוּ
דְּמֵיהֶם בָּם׃ 13 וְאִישׁ אֲשֶׁר יִשְׁכַּב אֶת־
זָכָר מִשְׁכְּבֵי אִשָּׁה תּוֹעֵבָה עָשׂוּ שְׁנֵיהֶם
מוֹת יוּמָתוּ דְּמֵיהֶם בָּם׃ 14 וְאִישׁ אֲשֶׁר יִקַּח
אֶת־אִשָּׁה וְאֶת־אִמָּהּ זִמָּה הִוא בָּאֵשׁ
יִשְׂרְפוּ אֹתוֹ וְאֶתְהֶן וְלֹא־תִהְיֶה זִמָּה
בְּתוֹכְכֶם׃ 15 וְאִישׁ אֲשֶׁר יִתֵּן שְׁכָבְתּוֹ
בִּבְהֵמָה מוֹת יוּמָת וְאֶת־הַבְּהֵמָה תַּהֲרֹגוּ׃
16 וְאִשָּׁה אֲשֶׁר תִּקְרַב אֶל־כָּל־בְּהֵמָה
לְרִבְעָה אֹתָהּ וְהָרַגְתָּ אֶת־הָאִשָּׁה וְאֶת־
הַבְּהֵמָה מוֹת יוּמָתוּ דְּמֵיהֶם בָּם׃
17 וְאִישׁ אֲשֶׁר־יִקַּח אֶת־אֲחֹתוֹ בַּת־אָבִיו אוֹ
בַת־אִמּוֹ וְרָאָה אֶת־עֶרְוָתָהּ וְהִיא־תִרְאֶה
אֶת־עֶרְוָתוֹ חֶסֶד הוּא וְנִכְרְתוּ לְעֵינֵי בְּנֵי
עַמָּם עֶרְוַת אֲחֹתוֹ גִּלָּה עֲוֺנוֹ יִשָּׂא׃ 18 וְאִישׁ
אֲשֶׁר־יִשְׁכַּב אֶת־אִשָּׁה דָּוָה וְגִלָּה אֶת־

woman is to be put to death to avoid paternity confusion.

***If a man commits adultery.*** Adultery in the Bible pertains to a sex act between a man and a married or betrothed woman; sex between a married man and a woman not designated to another man is not considered adultery.

*12.* ***If a man lies with his daughter-in-law.*** Both here and in Leviticus 18, there is no prohibition against a man having sexual relations with his own blood daughter, which is highly problematic. See *Acharei Mot*, Another View, p. 694.

*13.* ***If a man lies with a male.*** Penile penetration with emission of semen defines the sexual act, so it is not surprising that there is no prohibition against female-with-female sex acts. What we today might define as sexual or erotic activity between two women was not a category of thought in the biblical mind-set. The "problem" with male-with-male sex acts apparently was that it put one man in the receptive position, thus emasculating him and confusing sex roles (see at 19:19 regarding the importance of maintaining category distinctions). (See also at 18:22.)

*16.* ***If a woman approaches any beast.*** This is the only verse in the unit in which the woman is the subject and agent of the action.

*18.* ***menstrual condition.*** Heb. *davah,* a relatively rare term that elsewhere conveys a sense of physical and emotional vulnerability (see also at

covers her nakedness, he has laid bare her flow and
she has exposed her blood flow; both of them shall
be cut off from among their people. 19 You [males]
shall not uncover the nakedness of your mother's
sister or of your father's sister, for that is laying bare
one's own flesh; they shall bear their guilt. 20 If a
man lies with his uncle's wife, it is his uncle's
nakedness that he has uncovered. They shall bear
their guilt: they shall die childless. 21 If a man marries the wife of his brother, it is indecency. It is the
nakedness of his brother that he has uncovered;
they shall remain childless.

22 You shall faithfully observe all My laws and all
My regulations, lest the land to which I bring you
to settle in spew you out. 23 You shall not follow the
practices of the nation that I am driving out before
you. For it is because they did all these things that
I abhorred them 24 and said to you: You shall possess
their land, for I will give it to you to possess, a land
flowing with milk and honey. I יהוה am your God
who has set you apart from other peoples. 25 So you
shall set apart the pure beast from the impure, the
impure bird from the pure. You shall not draw
abomination upon yourselves through beast or bird
or anything with which the ground is alive, which I
have set apart for you to treat as impure. 26 You shall

עֶרְוָתָהּ אֶת־מְקֹרָהּ הֶעֱרָה וְהִוא גִּלְּתָה
אֶת־מְקוֹר דָּמֶיהָ וְנִכְרְתוּ שְׁנֵיהֶם מִקֶּרֶב
עַמָּם׃ 19 וְעֶרְוַת אֲחוֹת אִמְּךָ וַאֲחוֹת אָבִיךָ
לֹא תְגַלֵּה כִּי אֶת־שְׁאֵרוֹ הֶעֱרָה עֲוֺנָם
יִשָּׂאוּ׃ 20 וְאִישׁ אֲשֶׁר יִשְׁכַּב אֶת־דֹּדָתוֹ
עֶרְוַת דֹּדוֹ גִּלָּה חֶטְאָם יִשָּׂאוּ עֲרִירִים
יָמֻתוּ׃ 21 וְאִישׁ אֲשֶׁר יִקַּח אֶת־אֵשֶׁת אָחִיו
נִדָּה הִוא עֶרְוַת אָחִיו גִּלָּה עֲרִירִים יִהְיוּ׃
22 וּשְׁמַרְתֶּם אֶת־כָּל־חֻקֹּתַי וְאֶת־כָּל־
מִשְׁפָּטַי וַעֲשִׂיתֶם אֹתָם וְלֹא־תָקִיא אֶתְכֶם
הָאָרֶץ אֲשֶׁר אֲנִי מֵבִיא אֶתְכֶם שָׁמָּה
לָשֶׁבֶת בָּהּ׃ 23 וְלֹא תֵלְכוּ בְּחֻקֹּת הַגּוֹי
אֲשֶׁר־אֲנִי מְשַׁלֵּחַ מִפְּנֵיכֶם כִּי אֶת־כָּל־
אֵלֶּה עָשׂוּ וָאָקֻץ בָּם׃ 24 וָאֹמַר לָכֶם אַתֶּם
תִּירְשׁוּ אֶת־אַדְמָתָם וַאֲנִי אֶתְּנֶנָּה לָכֶם
לָרֶשֶׁת אֹתָהּ אֶרֶץ זָבַת חָלָב וּדְבָשׁ אֲנִי
יְהֹוָה אֱלֹהֵיכֶם אֲשֶׁר־הִבְדַּלְתִּי אֶתְכֶם
מִן־הָעַמִּים׃ 25 וְהִבְדַּלְתֶּם בֵּין־הַבְּהֵמָה
הַטְּהֹרָה לַטְּמֵאָה וּבֵין־הָעוֹף הַטָּמֵא לַטָּהֹר
וְלֹא־תְשַׁקְּצוּ אֶת־נַפְשֹׁתֵיכֶם בַּבְּהֵמָה וּבָעוֹף
וּבְכֹל אֲשֶׁר תִּרְמֹשׂ הָאֲדָמָה אֲשֶׁר־הִבְדַּלְתִּי
לָכֶם לְטַמֵּא׃ 26 וִהְיִיתֶם לִי קְדֹשִׁים כִּי

12:2 and 15:33). Possibly the primary concern behind this verse's prohibition is not sexual intercourse with a menstruant (since it does not say *niddah*, "menstruant"), but sexual intercourse with a woman who is not well. This may include a woman's discomfort during menstruation and other conditions in which there is a genital flow due to illness. Leviticus 15:24 establishes a period of seven days of impurity for a man who lies with a menstruant. Our passage prescribes *kareit*, a cutting off from the community—either as an untimely death or some other form of exclusion (see at 7:20). Leviticus 15 is concerned with impurities and their contagion, while the present unit attempts to curtail certain sexual acts. In other words, the same act is viewed differently through two different social (or theological) lenses.

## *Holiness of the Land* (20:22–27)

The parashah concludes with a theme that appears many times in the Torah: inheritance of the land. However, this passage offers an interesting and unique angle on the divine promise: if the people fail to observe the teachings of God, the land itself will spew them out. For the Holiness Code writers, the entire Land of Israel is God's holy sanc-

be holy to Me, for I יהוה am holy, and I have set you apart from other peoples to be Mine.

27 A man or a woman who has a ghost or a familiar spirit shall be put to death; they shall be pelted with stones—and they shall retain the bloodguilt.

קָד֖וֹשׁ אֲנִ֣י יְהֹוָ֑ה וָאַבְדִּ֥ל אֶתְכֶ֛ם מִן־הָֽעַמִּ֖ים
לִהְי֥וֹת לִֽי׃
27 וְאִ֣ישׁ אֽוֹ־אִשָּׁ֗ה כִּֽי־יִהְיֶ֨ה בָהֶ֥ם א֛וֹב א֥וֹ
יִדְּעֹנִ֖י מ֣וֹת יוּמָ֑תוּ בָּאֶ֛בֶן יִרְגְּמ֥וּ אֹתָ֖ם
דְּמֵיהֶ֥ם בָּֽם׃ פ

tuary. As such, all of the people throughout the land must maintain holiness and purity in order to allow for the holy community and the holy land to co-exist.

*27.* The placement of this rule here appears to connect necromancy with the holiness of the land.

***a man or a woman.*** In contrast to the Covenant Collection in Exodus (*parashat Mishpatim*), the Holiness Code rarely includes women explicitly. Such mention here suggests that one of the priestly writers' concerns is with women's accessing the divine realm. I Samuel 28 tells the story of King Saul's consultation with the woman of En-dor, who provides him with access to the ghost of the prophet Samuel. The woman fears for her life because she knows that necromancy is banned, yet Saul has recognized that some Israelites must nevertheless be practicing it and that he needs the woman's assistance. In a world in which only men could enter into the priesthood and in which men dominated the prophetic guilds, it is likely that women used other forms of divination to access the divine realm. (See also at 19:31 and 20:6.)

*—S. Tamar Kamionkowski*

# Another View

Parashat K'doshim articulates more comprehensively than any other portion of the Torah what it means for persons and community to be holy. Dictionary definitions of the Bible's concept of holiness emphasize the notion of separation. In *parashat K'doshim*, however, holiness comes from cultivating relationships. Connections—not only separations—define the holy community: the connection to parents whom one must honor, to the poor and the disadvantaged whom one must protect, to the neighbor and stranger whom one must love, and of course to God.

God commands Israel to "love" three times in the Torah. One case is in the text that follows the *Sh'ma* ("You shall love your God יהוה with all your heart," Deuteronomy 6:5), known as the *V'ahavta*. Our parashah mentions the other two commands: to love the one who is a member of one's group ("Love your fellow [Israelite] as yourself," 19:18); and finally, to love the stranger (19:34). Loving the stranger is a unique notion in the ancient world. The verse's rationale for loving the stranger—"for you were strangers in the land of Egypt"—has continuing ramifications that are often overlooked: the proper response to having suffered abuse is not vengeance or special entitlement, but rather sensitivity and determination to prevent such an abuse of others, including strangers. The three commandments are three dimensions of a single, deep connection: to love God is to love others, those like us and those who are not.

Ruth the Moabite stands as the exemplar of what it means to love, including loving the stranger. While still in the land of Moab, Ruth vows an undying loyalty to Naomi, Naomi's people, and Naomi's God (Ruth 1:16–17). After she arrives in Bethlehem, Ruth's behavior and commitment become a model for others: Boaz acknowledges that his kindness to Ruth is prompted by her prior generosity to Naomi (2:11); and the women of the town proclaim that Naomi's eventual reversal of fortune came about because of "your daughter-in-law, who loves you" (4:15). Even without using the word *kadosh* ("holy"), the story of Ruth points to the transformation that the "love commandments" in this parashah can bring about—and to the ways that these precepts serve to sanctify life and community.

*Ruth the Moabite stands as the exemplar of what it means to love.*

—*Tamara Cohn Eskenazi*

# Post-biblical Interpretations

***You shall be holy*** (19:1). Commentators have been challenged by the interweaving of ritual and civil commandments in *parashat K'doshim*. Observing that both Leviticus 18 and 20 list prohibited sexual partners, Rashi suggests that 19:1 teaches that separating ourselves from forbidden sexual relations and transgressions is the path to holiness, "for every place (in the Torah) you find instruction to fence yourself in against such relations, you also find mention of holiness." Nachmanides views this verse as commanding moderation in satisfying physical urges such as eating, drinking, and sexual relations.

***Do not deal basely with members of your people***

(19:16). The Rabbis identify these words as the source for the prohibition against *l'shon hara* (evil speech or gossip). Even if what we are saying is true, if it is negative and the person is not present to defend herself, it is prohibited (Maimonides, *Mishneh Torah, Hilchot De'ot* 7.2). The Talmud teaches that *l'shon hara* kills three parties: the person speaking, the person listening, and the person against whom the comment is being made (BT *Arachin* 15b–16a).

***Reprove your kin... incur no guilt on their account*** (19:17). The double verb in the command *hochei-ach tochi-ach* (whose plain sense is: "you shall [*surely*] reprove") has inspired much commentary. According to BT *Arachin* 16b, the first part of this verse teaches that when someone has done something offensive, confrontation is essential. While many people might hesitate out of fear of stirring up conflict and resentment, Midrash *B'reishit Rabbah* 54.3 urges confrontation as a way to improve understanding and increase caring. BT *Arachin* 16b also suggests that the command to rebuke is doubled in order to teach us that when we do confront the offending individuals, if they do not correct their behavior we must go back and confront them again. But—the Talmud continues—we must not embarrass such persons, making sure that we "incur no guilt on their account." Rashi advises that we avoid causing embarrassment by making sure not to confront others in public.

*Confrontation can be a way to improve understanding and increase caring.*

In BT *Bava M'tzia* 31a, Rava teaches that the Torah's double verb in the command means that we must rebuke even an authority figure, such as a teacher, parent, or employer. Ibn Ezra comments that confrontation can clear up misunderstandings and obviate resentment or even hatred. BT *Shabbat* 54b insists that we speak out to prevent wrongdoing; failing to do so leaves us partly responsible for injustice, whether in our family, our community, or even the world at large. Our sources are divided on what to do about the person who will not listen. BT *Shabbat* 55a suggests that only God really knows how a person will respond, and so we are *always* obligated to confront the person who is doing something wrong.

***Love your fellow** [**Israelite**] **as yourself*** (19:18). Rabbi Akiba said that this is the most important teaching in the Torah. For Ibn Ezra, this verse teaches us to treat others the way we want to be treated (so also Midrash *Sifra, K'doshim* 2.4). Other rabbis suggest we should express this love by being a good friend and neighbor, and by accepting the rebuke of others in a loving way.

***If a man lies with a male as one lies with a woman ... they retain the bloodguilt*** (20:13). While Rashi and others understood this verse as specifically prohibiting anal intercourse, BT *Sanhedrin* 54a–b saw it (along with 18:22) as prohibiting male homosexual acts in general. While Rabbi Judah forbade two bachelors to sleep under the same blanket, a majority of the Rabbis of the Talmud permit it (BT *Kiddushin* 82a). Maimonides agreed, stating that "Jews are not suspected of engaging in homosexual relations" (*Mishneh Torah, Laws of Forbidden Intercourse* 22.2). This disagreement persists in later codes, with some, like the *Shulchan Aruch*, counseling against two men sleeping under the same blanket.

The Rabbis limited their reading of this verse to male homosexual acts, noting that the Torah nowhere explicitly prohibits sex between two women. However, in BT *Y'vamot* 76a, Rav Huna argued that women who engage in lesbian sex cannot marry priests. Rabbi Eliezer urged leniency, on the grounds that sex between women does not involve penetration and therefore is "mere indecency." *Sifra, Acharei Mot* 9.8, prohibits marriage between women as something done by the Egyptians that, based on Leviticus 18:3, we must not imitate. Maimonides combined these two teachings in his *Mishneh Torah* (*Laws of Forbidden Intercourse* 21.8), noting that sexual relations between women are prohibited because they are among the "ways of the Egyptians," but that such acts are not punished with stoning or even lashes, as there is no act of penetration and the women violate no explicit biblical prohibition. A woman who has engaged in lesbian sex would be permitted to marry or stay married, even to a priest. Still, Maimonides says that such a woman should be punished with lashes for breaking a rabbinic law, and he advises husbands not to allow their wives to spend time with women known as lesbians, to avoid their being tempted to engage in sexual relations with another woman. —*Ruth H. Sohn*

# *Contemporary Reflection*

PARASHAT K'DOSHIM PLACES before us one of the most difficult commandments in the whole Torah—not kashrut or Shabbat, nor even the rules of sexual conduct, but rather the admonition and expectation to "be holy." Throughout the Torah, we are given rules and statutes that tell us what to do. Here we are told what to be. We find a similar statement in Exodus 19:6, commanding us to be a "kingdom of priests and a holy people." But what does it mean to be holy? *K'doshim* does not tell us. The guidance that the parashah gives us is in the specifics: the "who, when, why, and how" of the injunction.

First, *who* is to be holy? The entire people is addressed: *kol adat b'nei yisrael*; all Israel is told: "You shall be holy, for I, your God יהוה, am holy" (19:2). Not just the priests or Levites, not only the women or men, but everyone is part of this command to be holy. The 16th-century commentator Rabbi Moshe Alshech asks why such important rules as the ones that follow upon this verse are not taught person by person, group by group, rather than to one large assembly. He suggests that the opening of *K'doshim* emphasizes the ability of any Jew to attain even the highest and noblest principles of Judaism; thus these laws, and the paradigm of "holiness," are not only for a select few, but for everyone.

*When* are we to be holy? The verb *tih'yu* in verse 2 can be read—and is often read—as a command ("be holy!"). But it is grammatically a future form ("you shall be holy"). The implications are: "Be holy—now! And you shall be holy—in the future." Thus holiness is a daily struggle, in the here and now, as well as a future yearning.

*Why* are we to be holy? Because God is holy. The 16th-century commentator Rabbi Obadiah Sforno notes that this verse teaches us that we are to remember and act "in the image of our Creator," as much as that is possible. Philosophers refer to this concept via the Latin term *imitatio dei*. We try and "imitate" the Divine. As God cares for the widow and orphan, so do we. As God rests on the seventh day, so do we. In imitating God we can achieve a higher sense of purpose and our actions will reflect the ongoing concern of the Divine for the world. In imitating God's holiness we make holiness our behavioral ideal.

*What does it mean to be holy?*
*Is the answer different for women?*

In much of the Torah, it is God who sanctifies—as we read in Genesis 2:3: "Then God blessed the seventh day and made it holy." But in *K'doshim*, the command to make things holy is addressed to humanity. The task of sanctifying our lives is placed upon us, as an act of partnership between human beings and God. This is one way that we strive to act in God's image.

The *how* to be holy is what follows—as the parashah lists a wide-ranging series of ethical laws, including honoring one's parents, respecting the elderly, justice for the stranger, love of one's fellow human, and more. But note that even though the parashah enumerates the specifics of holy behavior, it never defines what it means by the word *kadosh* ("holy"). Many commentators have tried to understand the term *kadosh* as indicating a state of being. Rashi (11th century) and Ramban (13th century) both interpret "you shall be holy" as meaning "you shall be separate." For them, holiness requires standing apart as Jews, with a firm set of boundaries. The end of *K'doshim* underscores their point: "You shall be holy to Me, for I יהוה am holy, and I have set you apart from other peoples to be Mine" (20:26).

This concept of separation is critical to understanding Jewish spirituality. For example, in the classic Jewish marriage formula, the phrase *harei at m'kudeshet li* means "you are set apart for me from others." (Wedding officiants are fond of claiming that it means "you are sanctified to me," which is a more midrashic derivation.) In the Talmud, *hekdesh* is money or goods set aside or separated for tithing or donation. Holiness seems intrinsically linked in Judaism to separation (*havdalah*), making distinctions: milk or meat, Shabbat or weekday, Jew or gentile, female or male.

But does this concept of spirituality ring true for women? Would there be a different kind of *imitatio dei* for women? Do women experience holiness differently? For those women who carry life inside, attached to another being who is—at the same time—part of them, separateness does not equal spirituality. For those women who breastfeed—who nurture and sustain from their very own bodies—connection is more at the root of holiness. For those women who form bonded friendships from earliest memory, or who bring the family together, who are the cohesive force in a group, a definition of holiness is needed that does not imply building fences. Thus, though *parashat K'doshim* demands holiness, it is up to us to define holiness in a way that is truthful for both women and men.

As is apparent, then, Rashi's definition of *kadosh* as "separate" presents a fundamental feminist challenge. The challenge is evident as well throughout rabbinic Judaism where authorities have portrayed the mitzvot as drawing lines between "us" and "them," lines that demarcate who is *in* (for example, circumcision marking a Jewish boy) and who is *out* (for example, the halachah of not counting women in a minyan). While feminists have challenged specific mitzvot, finding a way "in" through creative rereading and even reinventing, we have not yet sufficiently challenged the very notion of mitzvot that rest upon the "spirituality of separation." This notion is at the heart of much that Jews do—including kashrut, Shabbat, and the marriage ceremony, just to name a few. Redefining the mitzvot as connectors rather than as boundaries, as dialogue rather than as answers, is a first step toward addressing the question of how we as women will be *kadosh*. Although we are still at the beginning of exploring what a fully developed feminist notion of being holy might look like, the opening words of this parashah—*k'doshim tih'yu*—carry both a command for now and promise for the future: we can and we will find ways to be holy.

*—Elyse Goldstein*

# *Voices*

## *Weathering*

Rachel Hadas

*Leviticus 19:3, 32*

My mother had, I thought,
when I was growing up,
a uniform smooth surface like a rock
polished by waves. Or like
a flight of steps worn concave
at the center of each tread
she had been hollowed out.
This weathering, it took me years to see,
was neither luck nor personality.
Motherhood and years wear women down.
Either can alone;
but motherhood, although it saves no one,
mitigates the wear and tear somehow
with kindness—or with blindness. Take my
hand
before we both are ground back into sand.

## *Gravity, Death*

Agi Mishol (transl. Lisa Katz)

*Leviticus 19:3, 32*

How resistance to the force of gravity has
weakened:
hair falls out, jaws drop, and legs don't step
off the earth anymore.
The spent body stoops over the ground,
only a walking stick separates them like a kind
of extension.

He sits opposite me in a cloud of unraveling
sentences,
his skin like clothing hastily left behind
on a chair.

For a moment I sit with my father, for a
moment with my death
fraternizing with me through my crumbling
father who begins
to return spirit unto spirit
and dust unto dust.

## *Letter to Haym Peretz*

Henrietta Szold

*Leviticus 19:3*

It is impossible for me to find words in which to tell you how deeply I was touched by your offer to act as *"Kaddish"* for my dear mother. I cannot even thank you—it is something that goes beyond thanks. It is beautiful, what you have offered to do—and I shall never forget it.

You will wonder, then, that I cannot accept your offer. Perhaps it would be best for me not to try to explain to you in writing, but to wait until I see you to tell you why it is so. I know well, and appreciate what you say about, the Jewish custom; and Jewish custom is very dear and sacred to me. And yet I cannot ask you to say *Kaddish* after my mother. The *Kaddish* means to me that the survivor publicly and markedly manifests his wish and intention to assume the relation to the Jewish community which his parent had, and that so the chain of tradition remains unbroken from generation to generation, each adding its own link. You can do that for the generations of your family, I must do that for the generations of my family.

I believe that the elimination of women from such duties was never intended by our law and custom—women were freed from positive duties when they could not perform them, but not when they could. It was never intended that, if they could perform them, their performance of them should not be considered as valuable and valid as when one of the male sex performed them. And of the *Kaddish* I feel sure this is particularly true.

My mother had eight daughters and no son; and yet never did I hear a word of regret pass the lips of either my mother or my father that one of us was not a son. When my father died, my mother would not permit others to take her daughters' place in saying the *Kaddish*, and so I am sure I am acting in her spirit when I am moved to decline your offer. But beautiful your offer remains nevertheless, and, I repeat, I know full well that it is much more in consonance with the generally accepted Jewish tradition than is my or my family's conception. You understand, don't you?

NOTE

***Jewish custom.*** After a parent's death, Jewish law obliges a male child to recite *Kaddish* at synagogue services. The usual duration of this practice is one year less thirty days. A female child is exempt from this mourning practice, and in traditional communities women have customarily not recited *Kaddish*. When no child survives the deceased and in the absence of another male relative to take on the obligation, occasionally a male friend will recite *Kaddish* out of love or loyalty.

## *Gray Hairs*

Naomi Replansky

*Leviticus 19:32*

Gray hairs
crowd out the black.
Not one of them
brings me wisdom.

Wrinkles
provide no armor.
I still quiver
to anyone's dart.

## *Age*

Esther Raab

*Leviticus 19:32*

The old lady in the mirror—
who is she?
Seventy-one
years old—
whose?
She plucks
wild daffodil
in the mud,
gathers mushrooms
after rain,
in the fat black
slit of the wadi-slope
leaps on "Hans"—
at sundown,
for a last gallop
before nightfall;
catches leaves
in flight
crushes them
to release their fragrance

a thousand pranks
and one
lurk in her eyes,
in her heart:
scorn, fury, affection—
and now she falls asleep
in crests of pine
clasped in their perfumed
arms.
Seventy-one – – –

## *Turning to Rest in Sappho's Poems*

Agi Mishol (transl. Tsipi Keller)

*Leviticus 20:10–21*

We're sprawled across the cool stone
under glittering stars
bite into an apple
honoring all the loved ones
women and men
who came to rest
between our thighs

We talk about love
its smallest detail

talk about life that makes us thirsty
about the tree that is
a green fountain

her beautiful head is next to mine
her curls in mine

she says
I say
and our giggles escape
into the vine whose scent
spreads out from us

# אֱמֹר ✦ *Emor*

## LEVITICUS 21:1–24:23

### *Preserving the Holiness of Priests, Times, and Spaces*

PARASHAT EMOR ("say") continues the holiness-centered legislation of the previous parashah. It, too, is part of the Holiness Code—the collection of laws in Leviticus 17–26, which modern critical scholars refer to as "H" and attribute to a specific group of reform-minded priests.

This parashah contains instructions concerning the sanctity of the priests and the sacrificial offerings, the weekly Sabbath and annual festivals, and the maintenance of the Tabernacle lamp and showbread. The parashah ends with a story about the crime and punishment of a blasphemer. It also includes brief legal conclusions about damages governed by the retaliation principle (Latin: *lex talionis;* sometimes referred to via the biblical expression "eye for an eye"). In discussing the priests, the writers distinguish between three types: the chief priest, other priests who may officiate, and those who may receive some of the benefits but cannot carry out public roles because of disqualifying circumstances.

Several issues related to women arise in *parashat Emor.* Leviticus 21 provides strict guidelines for priests regarding various areas of family life, including which women in their family they can bury, which women they can marry, and how they must respond to a daughter's sexual misbehavior. Leviticus 22, discussing who may partake of the priest's portion of the sacred donations, addresses the question of when a priest's daughter is considered a part of his household and would thus be entitled to part of her father's share. Additionally, 24:10–14 mentions Shelomith, daughter of Dibri of the tribe of Dan, one of the few named individuals in all of Leviticus, and the only named woman. Shelomith's unnamed son, whose father is an unnamed Egyptian, commits an act of blasphemy, and the Israelite judicial system must determine how to respond to this crime. This episode raises the question of who in the community must comply with the divine commandments.

*Shelomith daughter of Dibri is the only named woman in all of Leviticus.*

—*Hilary Lipka*

## *Outline*

*I.* Holiness and Worship
*Regulations for the Priests' Holiness and for the Offerings* (21:1–22:33)

*A.* Regulations for priests' families (21:1–9)
*B.* Regulations for the chief priest, including choice of a wife (21:10–15)
*C.* Regulations for disqualified priests (21:16–24)
*D.* Regulations for sacred food (22:1–16)
*E.* Regulations for blemished sacrificial animals (22:17–25)
*F.* Additional criteria for sacrificial animals (22:26–30)
*G.* Concluding exhortation (22:31–33)

*II.* Sacred Times
*Regulations for the Sabbath and Festivals* (23:1–44)

*A.* Introduction (vv. 1–2)
*B.* The Sabbath and festivals, and conclusion (vv. 3–44)

*III.* The Tabernacle (24:1–9)

*IV.* The Case of the Blasphemer (24:10–23)

*A.* The story of the blasphemer (vv. 10–16)
*B.* The retaliation laws (*lex talionis*) (vv. 17–22)
*C.* The punishment of the blasphemer (v. 23)

יהוה said to Moses: Speak to the priests,
the sons of Aaron, and say to them:
None shall defile himself for any [dead] person
among his kin, [2]except for the relatives that are
closest to him: his mother, his father, his son, his

כא וַיֹּאמֶר יְהוָה אֶל־מֹשֶׁה אֱמֹר אֶל־
הַכֹּהֲנִים בְּנֵי אַהֲרֹן וְאָמַרְתָּ אֲלֵהֶם
לְנֶפֶשׁ לֹא־יִטַּמָּא בְּעַמָּיו׃ 2 כִּי אִם־לִשְׁאֵרוֹ
הַקָּרֹב אֵלָיו לְאִמּוֹ וּלְאָבִיו וְלִבְנוֹ וּלְבִתּוֹ

## *Holiness and Worship*

### REGULATIONS FOR THE PRIESTS' HOLINESS AND FOR THE OFFERINGS (21:1–22:33)

*Parashat Emor* opens with guidelines regarding the holiness of priests (Leviticus 21) and sacrificial offerings (Leviticus 22). Unlike *parashat K'doshim* (Leviticus 19–20), which addressed the entire people, Leviticus 21 and 22 primarily address the priests. The text places emphasis on avoiding desecration of the sanctuary by keeping the holy from coming into contact with impurity or with disqualifying imperfections.

### REGULATIONS FOR PRIESTS' FAMILIES (21:1–9)

Because the priests are charged with the performance of sacred rites, they must observe strict codes of purity, lest any sort of impurity profane the sanctuary or its sacred objects and thus drive out God's Presence. This section addresses two primary issues regarding priests: defilement by corpses and the purity of their wives and daughters. In both instances there are obvious ramifications concerning women.

*1. **None shall defile himself for any** [**dead**] **person.*** While lay people may come into contact with corpses, priests must restrict such contact, since dead bodies are considered highly defiling. Although priests are generally prohibited from such exposure, a concession allows them to defile themselves for their closest blood relatives—but not for kinfolk related by marriage. The list of exemptions does not mention the wife. This raises the question: is a priest allowed to participate in the burial of his own wife? Although the topic is not addressed explicitly, this passage seems to preclude a priest from touching his dead wife and attending her burial. Presumably, he can supervise the burial from a certain distance. (See further at v. 4.)

*2. **relatives.*** Heb. *sh'eir* (literally "flesh") is a kinship term that denotes what in English are known as "blood" ties. [The present translation renders the term literally in 18:12–13, which prohibit a man from sexual relations with his aunt because she is his parent's "flesh." —*Ed.*] The priest may defile himself only for certain "flesh and blood" relatives.

***his mother, his father.*** The mother precedes the father in the list of blood relatives. Later, in

◗ If a priest may not bury his wife, who then buries her?

ANOTHER VIEW ➤ *741*

◗ The Bible and much of Western culture frequently equate beauty with goodness.

CONTEMPORARY REFLECTION ➤ *743*

◗ Women are considered responsible for obeying most of Judaism's positive commandments.

POST-BIBLICAL INTERPRETATIONS ➤ *741*

◗ The *yahrzeit* flame / is beating its wings in a cup / on the edge of my kitchen sink.

VOICES ➤ *745*

daughter, and his brother; [3]also for a virgin sister, close to him because she has not married, for her he may defile himself. [4]But he shall not defile himself as a kinsman by marriage, and so profane himself. [5]They shall not shave smooth any part of their heads, or cut the side-growth of their beards, or make gashes in their flesh. [6]They shall be holy to their God and not profane the name of their God;

וּלְאָחִֽיו׃ 3 וְלַאֲחֹת֤וֹ הַבְּתוּלָה֙ הַקְּרוֹבָ֣ה
אֵלָ֔יו אֲשֶׁ֥ר לֹא־הָיְתָ֖ה לְאִ֑ישׁ לָ֖הּ יִטַּמָּֽא׃
4 לֹ֥א יִטַּמָּ֖א בַּ֣עַל בְּעַמָּ֑יו לְהֵ֖חַלּֽוֹ׃
5 לֹא־יקרחה יִקְרְח֤וּ קָרְחָה֙ בְּרֹאשָׁ֔ם וּפְאַ֥ת
זְקָנָ֖ם לֹ֣א יְגַלֵּ֑חוּ וּבִ֨בְשָׂרָ֔ם לֹ֥א יִשְׂרְט֖וּ
שָׂרָֽטֶת׃ 6 קְדֹשִׁ֤ים יִהְיוּ֙ לֵֽאלֹהֵיהֶ֔ם וְלֹ֥א

v. 11, the father precedes the mother in a similar list. The inversion is most likely a literary device.

*3. virgin.* Heb. *b'tulah* is better understood here in a more general sense to refer to a stage in a woman's life characterized by youth and nubility. A more accurate translation might be "adolescent," since there are contexts in which a *b'tulah* evidently is not a virgin (Esther 2:17–19). Moreover, sometimes the term *b'tulah* is qualified by the clause "whom no man had yet known [sexually]" or its variant, "who had not [sexually] known a man" (as in Judges 11:37–39; 21:12; Genesis 24:16), further indicating that *b'tulah* is not always synonymous with what we mean by "virgin." An adolescent girl who was not yet married in ancient Israel would have been presumed to be a virgin, since girls were married very young and bridal virginity was the expected norm. In certain cases (including vv. 13–14, below), the context dictates that the translation "virgin" is most appropriate. In the present verse, however, as in the great majority of cases, such a specific translation would be inappropriate.

*close to him because she has not married.* A sister is considered "close" until she marries and leaves the household to live with her husband's family. Once she is living with her husband's family, the concession that permits the priest to attend a sister's burial no longer applies in her case because the wording presumes that her husband's family will attend to her. However, if his sister is still living within the priest's household when she dies, the priest is responsible for attending to her burial.

*4. as a kinsman by marriage.* Literally, "as a husband among his kin." This obscure wording appears to prohibit a priest from attending to the burial of his wife or coming close to her place of burial, since she is kin by marriage, not by blood. In ancient Israel a husband normally would have been responsible for the burial of his wife; since priests were prohibited from burying anyone other than blood kin (v. 1), presumably they were expected to arrange for others—members of the household or designated agents—to bury her. (At a later period, the Rabbis, reading *sh'eiro* in v. 2 as "his wife," found a way to interpret the law so as to include the priest's wife among those members of the family that he could personally bury.)

*5. They shall not shave smooth . . . or make gashes in their flesh.* The law does not prohibit priests from all displays of mourning. However, this verse outlaws these particular mourning rites, perhaps because they were associated with Canaanite funerary practices (see at Deuteronomy 14:1–2).

*6. They shall . . . not profane the name of their God.* What does it mean to profane the name of God? In the Holiness Code (see the parashah introduction), God's name stands for God's reality and therefore has the power to sanctify the people and the priests, bringing the lay population closer to their aspired level of holiness. The concern with profaning God's name runs throughout the parashah (for example, 21:6; 22:32; 24:10–16). Profaning the divine name takes away its power to sanctify and thus nullifies whatever holiness has been achieved through the observance of God's laws and regulations. Why does the concern about desecration focus on God's name, rather than on God? The Holiness Code carefully avoids anthropomor-

for they offer יהוה's offerings by fire, the food of their God, and so must be holy.

7They shall not marry a woman defiled by harlotry, nor shall they marry one divorced from her husband. For they are holy to their God 8and you must treat them as holy, since they offer the food of your God; they shall be holy to you, for I יהוה who sanctify you am holy.

יְחַלְּלוּ שֵׁם אֱלֹהֵיהֶם כִּי אֶת־אִשֵּׁי יְהוָֹה
לֶחֶם אֱלֹהֵיהֶם הֵם מַקְרִיבִם וְהָיוּ קֹדֶשׁ׃
7 אִשָּׁה זֹנָה וַחֲלָלָה לֹא יִקָּחוּ וְאִשָּׁה גְּרוּשָׁה
מֵאִישָׁהּ לֹא יִקָּחוּ כִּי־קָדֹשׁ הוּא לֵאלֹהָיו׃
8 וְקִדַּשְׁתּוֹ כִּי־אֶת־לֶחֶם אֱלֹהֶיךָ הוּא
מַקְרִיב קָדֹשׁ יִהְיֶה־לָּךְ כִּי קָדוֹשׁ אֲנִי יְהוָֹה
מְקַדִּשְׁכֶם׃

phic images of God (compare Deuteronomy 32). The priests responsible for this material hold that God cannot possibly be contaminated, desecrated, or directly affected in a way that diminishes God's own holiness. Therefore it speaks in terms of the desecration of God's name—rather than God's self.

*7–8.* The restrictions concerning whom priests may marry reflect a concern with protecting both the priests' lineage and their reputation. On the one hand, the priesthood passes down from father to son, and thus the marriage restrictions can assure priests that their sons are of their own line. On the other hand, priests—who are charged with the care and maintenance of the sanctuary—are most likely expected to behave in a way appropriate to their esteemed station. Since the members of a priest's family partake of his portion of the holy sacrifices and live in his household, the Holiness Code (see the parashah introduction) likewise expects them to conduct themselves with a certain level of propriety; thus, only women of good repute are considered appropriate wives. For the same reason, a priest's daughter comes under close scrutiny, and her father should take action if her behavior is inappropriate for one of her station.

*7. **a woman defiled by harlotry.*** This phrase, literally "a harlot woman and one defiled," is a hendiadys (the use of two words to express a single concept). Here the term "defiled" is probably intended in a figurative rather than a literal sense, and thus we should understand it as "degraded by harlotry." According to the Holiness Code (see the parashah introduction), a man who makes his daughter into a prostitute "defiles" (that is, degrades) her; moreover, his action results in the land's being filled with depravity—since other fathers, following his example, will prostitute their daughters (19:29). The reason for the disqualification of a harlot as an appropriate wife for a priest is two-fold. First, pragmatically speaking, the priest would never be sure that the harlot's offspring would be his own. Second, given that the Holiness Code considers prostitution to be a form of depravity, having a harlot for a wife would be highly inappropriate. The very existence of this prohibition raises the possibility that the Holiness Code does not object to lay members of the community marrying prostitutes.

***nor... one divorced from her husband.*** There are only a few references to men divorcing their wives in biblical texts. Deuteronomy 22:13–14 presents the case of a man, apparently seeking to divorce his wife after taking an aversion to her, who makes up charges of sexual misconduct against her (claiming that she was not a virgin when they married). In Deuteronomy 24:1, a man divorces his wife because he finds in her *ervat davar*, literally "the nakedness of the thing," a term whose meaning is unclear, but could refer to some type of behavioral impropriety, possibly sexual in nature. (Deuteronomy 23:15, the only other place where this expression appears, seems to support this interpretation.) In Hosea 2:4–7, God's metaphoric wife Israel is threatened with divorce because of her infidelities. Each of these cases involves either improper behavior or false charges of improper behavior on the part of the wife, mainly of a sexual nature. This pattern or assumption might explain

9When the daughter of a priest defiles herself
through harlotry, it is her father whom she defiles;
she shall be put to the fire.
10The priest who is exalted above his fellows,
on whose head the anointing oil has been poured
and who has been ordained to wear the vestments,
shall not bare his head or rend his vestments.
11He shall not go in where there is any dead body;

9 וּבַת֙ אִ֣ישׁ כֹּהֵ֔ן כִּ֥י תֵחֵ֖ל לִזְנ֑וֹת אֶת־אָבִ֙יהָ֙
הִ֣יא מְחַלֶּ֔לֶת בָּאֵ֖שׁ תִּשָּׂרֵֽף׃ ס
10 וְהַכֹּהֵן֩ הַגָּד֨וֹל מֵאֶחָ֜יו אֲֽשֶׁר־יוּצַ֥ק עַל־
רֹאשׁ֣וֹ ׀ שֶׁ֤מֶן הַמִּשְׁחָה֙ וּמִלֵּ֣א אֶת־יָד֔וֹ לִלְבֹּ֖שׁ
אֶת־הַבְּגָדִ֑ים אֶת־רֹאשׁוֹ֙ לֹ֣א יִפְרָ֔ע וּבְגָדָ֖יו
לֹ֥א יִפְרֹֽם׃ 11 וְעַ֛ל כָּל־נַפְשֹׁ֥ת מֵ֖ת לֹ֣א יָבֹ֑א

why the present verse prohibits a priest from marrying a divorcée. Marriage to a woman possibly prone to sexual promiscuity is problematic for priests, who must be sure that their progeny is their own, and whose family must maintain a certain level of propriety. Note that widows, who generally were above such suspicions, are acceptable marital candidates for priests, except for the chief priest (see v. 14). [As for divorce, Jewish documents from Elephantine, Egypt, dating to the 5th century B.C.E., show that a woman could divorce her husband. Either partner could initiate a "no-fault" divorce, indicating that moral failing was not necessarily an integral part of divorce for either party. —*Ed.*]

***9. harlotry.*** There are two possible interpretations of the verbal root *z-n-h* ("harlotry") in this passage. The term could refer to the actual practice of prostitution, as it does in Genesis 38:15 and Leviticus 19:29; or it could be used in a metaphoric sense to denote illicit sexual activity by a woman (premarital sex or adultery), as it does in Genesis 38:24 and Deuteronomy 22:21. Both interpretations would work equally well in this context. A priest's daughter, like his wife, is expected to maintain a high level of propriety, since her behavior reflects upon her father. As noted above (v. 7), although the Holiness Code does not prohibit prostitution outright, it considers the practice to be degrading and thus inappropriate for the daughter of a priest. Either prostitution or promiscuity would have brought shame and disgrace to the woman's family.

***it is her father whom she defiles.*** The unity of the household means that a daughter's action is not an independent action but an extension of the father. Impropriety on her part profanes the father and interferes with his ability to carry out his priestly duties.

***she shall be put to the fire.*** There are only three other cases in the Bible in which we read of such a punishment, and two of them involve sexual offenses. In Genesis 38:24, Judah demands that his daughter-in-law, Tamar, be put to death by fire for committing adultery while awaiting levirate marriage, although in the end she avoids punishment. Leviticus 20:14 states that if a man marries both a woman and her mother, all three are to be put to the fire. In Joshua 7:25, the Israelites stone and burn Achan (a certain member of the tribe of Judah) and his household for his violating the sacred ban (*cherem*), a prohibition against taking enemy property that was dedicated to God. Since fire is often regarded as a purifying substance, it may have been reserved for offenses where a form of purgation was deemed necessary due to the level of pollution incurred by the offender.

## REGULATIONS FOR THE CHIEF PRIEST, INCLUDING CHOICE OF A WIFE (21:10–15)

Even stricter regulations follow for the chief priest concerning matters of defilement by corpses, mourning practices, and whom he may marry. (On the more common English designation "high priest," see at Exodus 28:1.)

he shall not defile himself even for his father or mother. [12]He shall not go outside the sanctuary and profane the sanctuary of his God, for upon him is the distinction of the anointing oil of his God, Mine יהוה's. [13]He may marry only a woman who is a virgin. [14]A widow, or a divorced woman, or one who is degraded by harlotry—such he may not marry. Only a virgin of his own kin may he take to wife—[15]that he may not profane his offspring among his kin, for I יהוה have sanctified him.

[16]יהוה spoke further to Moses: [17]Speak to Aaron and say: No man of your offspring throughout the ages who has a defect shall be qualified to offer the food of his God. [18]No one at all who has a defect shall be qualified: no man who is blind, or lame, or has a limb too short or too long; [19]no man who has a broken leg or a broken arm; [20]or who is a hunchback, or a dwarf, or who has a growth in his eye, or

לְאָבִ֥יו וּלְאִמּ֖וֹ לֹ֥א יִטַּמָּֽא׃ 12 וּמִן־הַמִּקְדָּשׁ֙
לֹ֣א יֵצֵ֔א וְלֹ֣א יְחַלֵּ֔ל אֵ֖ת מִקְדַּ֣שׁ אֱלֹהָ֑יו
כִּ֡י נֵ֠זֶר שֶׁ֣מֶן מִשְׁחַ֧ת אֱלֹהָ֛יו עָלָ֖יו אֲנִ֥י יְהוָֽה׃
13 וְה֕וּא אִשָּׁ֥ה בִבְתוּלֶ֖יהָ יִקָּֽח׃ 14 אַלְמָנָ֤ה
וּגְרוּשָׁה֙ וַחֲלָלָ֣ה זֹנָ֔ה אֶת־אֵ֖לֶּה לֹ֣א יִקָּ֑ח
כִּ֛י אִם־בְּתוּלָ֥ה מֵעַמָּ֖יו יִקַּ֥ח אִשָּֽׁה׃
15 וְלֹֽא־יְחַלֵּ֥ל זַרְע֖וֹ בְּעַמָּ֑יו כִּ֛י אֲנִ֥י יְהוָ֖ה
מְקַדְּשֽׁוֹ׃ ס
16 וַיְדַבֵּ֥ר יְהוָ֖ה אֶל־מֹשֶׁ֥ה לֵּאמֹֽר׃ 17 דַּבֵּ֥ר
אֶֽל־אַהֲרֹ֖ן לֵאמֹ֑ר אִ֣ישׁ מִֽזַּרְעֲךָ֞ לְדֹרֹתָ֗ם
אֲשֶׁ֨ר יִהְיֶ֥ה בוֹ֙ מ֔וּם לֹ֣א יִקְרַ֔ב לְהַקְרִ֖יב לֶ֥חֶם
אֱלֹהָֽיו׃ 18 כִּ֥י כָל־אִ֛ישׁ אֲשֶׁר־בּ֥וֹ מ֖וּם לֹ֣א
יִקְרָ֑ב אִ֤ישׁ עִוֵּר֙ א֣וֹ פִסֵּ֔חַ א֥וֹ חָרֻ֖ם א֥וֹ שָׂרֽוּעַ׃
19 א֣וֹ אִ֔ישׁ אֲשֶׁר־יִהְיֶ֥ה ב֖וֹ שֶׁ֣בֶר רָ֑גֶל א֖וֹ
שֶׁ֥בֶר יָֽד׃ 20 אֽוֹ־גִבֵּ֣ן אוֹ־דַ֔ק א֖וֹ תְּבַלֻּ֣ל בְּעֵינ֑וֹ

*11. he shall not defile himself even for his father or mother.* While a concession allows ordinary priests to defile themselves for their immediate blood relatives (vv. 1–3), no such concession is made for the chief priest. Note the order of father and mother here: a reversal of the reference to mother and father in v. 2.

*13. virgin.* Heb. *b'tulim* is an abstract noun derived from *b'tulah* (see at v. 3). In some biblical passages such as the reference to Jephthah's daughter in Judges 11:37–38, the word seems to simply refer to a young woman's adolescence, that is, the stage of her life characterized by youth and nubility. Other passages, such as Deuteronomy 22:13–21 and the verse at hand, appear to use the noun as a technical term for virginity.

*14. A widow...he may not marry.* In contrast to ordinary priests, the chief priest is not permitted to marry a widow.

*virgin.* Heb. *b'tulah* in this context is best translated as "virgin" (see at v. 3), since it appears that the chief priest cannot marry any woman who has had prior sexual relations. Since the chief priest must maintain the highest level of purity, it is logical that the purest possible woman is required for his wife. A virgin has not been "defiled" by sex with another man.

*of his own kin.* This added restriction is probably out of concern for the purity of his line by assurance of paternity. That is, it seeks to ensure that the chief priest will unquestionably be descended from Aaron.

## REGULATIONS FOR DISQUALIFIED PRIESTS (21:16–24)

This section stipulates that only priests with no physical defects are able to approach the altar and make sacrifices. Priests with physical impairments, whether as a result of a birth defect or accident, are ineligible to approach the altar to make offerings because they are not considered whole. Although they may not officiate, disqualified priests still are considered priests—and thus entitled to eat the priestly portions of the sacrifices.

who has a boil-scar, or scurvy, or crushed testes.
21 No man among the offspring of Aaron the priest
who has a defect shall be qualified to offer יהוה's offering by fire; having a defect, he shall not be qualified to offer the food of his God. 22 He may eat of
the food of his God, of the most holy as well as
of the holy; 23 but he shall not enter behind the curtain or come near the altar, for he has a defect. He
shall not profane these places sacred to Me, for I
יהוה have sanctified them.

24 Thus Moses spoke to Aaron and his sons and
to all the Israelites.

**22** יהוה spoke to Moses, saying: 2 Instruct
Aaron and his sons to be scrupulous about the
sacred donations that the Israelite people consecrate
to Me, lest they profane My holy name, Mine
יהוה's. 3 Say to them:

Throughout the ages, if any man among your
offspring, while in a state of impurity, partakes of
any sacred donation that the Israelite people may
consecrate to יהוה, that person shall be cut off from
before Me: I am יהוה. 4 No man of Aaron's offspring
who has an eruption or a discharge shall eat of the
sacred donations until he is pure. If one touches
anything made impure by a corpse, or if a man has
an emission of semen, 5 or if a man touches any
swarming thing by which he is made impure or any
human being by whom he is made impure—whatever his impurity— 6 the person who touches such
shall be impure until evening and shall not eat of
the sacred donations unless he has washed his body

אוֹ גָרָב אוֹ יַלֶּפֶת אוֹ מְרוֹחַ אָשֶׁךְ׃ 21 כָּל־
אִישׁ אֲשֶׁר־בּוֹ מוּם מִזֶּרַע אַהֲרֹן הַכֹּהֵן לֹא
יִגַּשׁ לְהַקְרִיב אֶת־אִשֵּׁי יְהֹוָה מוּם בּוֹ אֵת
לֶחֶם אֱלֹהָיו לֹא יִגַּשׁ לְהַקְרִיב׃ 22 לֶחֶם
אֱלֹהָיו מִקָּדְשֵׁי הַקֳּדָשִׁים וּמִן־הַקֳּדָשִׁים
יֹאכֵל׃ 23 אַךְ אֶל־הַפָּרֹכֶת לֹא יָבֹא וְאֶל־
הַמִּזְבֵּחַ לֹא יִגַּשׁ כִּי־מוּם בּוֹ וְלֹא יְחַלֵּל
אֶת־מִקְדָּשַׁי כִּי אֲנִי יְהֹוָה מְקַדְּשָׁם׃

24 וַיְדַבֵּר מֹשֶׁה אֶל־אַהֲרֹן וְאֶל־בָּנָיו וְאֶל־
כָּל־בְּנֵי יִשְׂרָאֵל׃ פ

כב וַיְדַבֵּר יְהֹוָה אֶל־מֹשֶׁה לֵּאמֹר׃ 2 דַּבֵּר
אֶל־אַהֲרֹן וְאֶל־בָּנָיו וְיִנָּזְרוּ מִקָּדְשֵׁי בְנֵי־
יִשְׂרָאֵל וְלֹא יְחַלְּלוּ אֶת־שֵׁם קָדְשִׁי אֲשֶׁר
הֵם מַקְדִּשִׁים לִי אֲנִי יְהֹוָה׃ 3 אֱמֹר
אֲלֵהֶם

לְדֹרֹתֵיכֶם כָּל־אִישׁ ׀ אֲשֶׁר־יִקְרַב מִכָּל־
זַרְעֲכֶם אֶל־הַקֳּדָשִׁים אֲשֶׁר יַקְדִּישׁוּ בְנֵי־
יִשְׂרָאֵל לַיהֹוָה וְטֻמְאָתוֹ עָלָיו וְנִכְרְתָה
הַנֶּפֶשׁ הַהִוא מִלְּפָנַי אֲנִי יְהֹוָה׃ 4 אִישׁ
אִישׁ מִזֶּרַע אַהֲרֹן וְהוּא צָרוּעַ אוֹ זָב
בַּקֳּדָשִׁים לֹא יֹאכַל עַד אֲשֶׁר יִטְהָר וְהַנֹּגֵעַ
בְּכָל־טְמֵא־נֶפֶשׁ אוֹ אִישׁ אֲשֶׁר־תֵּצֵא מִמֶּנּוּ
שִׁכְבַת־זָרַע׃ 5 אוֹ־אִישׁ אֲשֶׁר יִגַּע בְּכָל־
שֶׁרֶץ אֲשֶׁר יִטְמָא־לוֹ אוֹ בְאָדָם אֲשֶׁר
יִטְמָא־לוֹ לְכֹל טֻמְאָתוֹ׃ 6 נֶפֶשׁ אֲשֶׁר
תִּגַּע־בּוֹ וְטָמְאָה עַד־הָעָרֶב וְלֹא יֹאכַל מִן־

## REGULATIONS FOR SACRED FOOD (22:1–16)

This section addresses questions regarding who may partake of the sacred donations, which portions of the sacrifices are assigned to the priests, and who among the lay population may share in these portions. The passage ends with a discussion of what to do if a lay person accidentally partakes of the sacred donation.

2. ***sacred donations.*** This phrase refers to the portions of sacrifices assigned to the priests. Some sacred donations only the priests may eat, while others, such as gift offerings, they may share with their household. See Leviticus 6–7; regarding women's access to this food, see *Tzav*, Another View, p. 608.

3. ***cut off from before Me.*** See at 7:20 for a similar expression and its implications.

in water. 7 As soon as the sun sets, he shall be pure; and afterward he may eat of the sacred donations, for they are his food. 8 He shall not eat anything that died or was torn by beasts, thereby becoming impure: I am יהוה. 9 They shall keep My charge, lest they incur guilt thereby and die for it, having committed profanation: I יהוה consecrate them.

10 No lay person shall eat of the sacred donations. No bound or hired laborer of a priest shall eat of the sacred donations; 11 but a person who is a priest's property by purchase may eat of them; and those that are born into his household may eat of his food. 12 If a priest's daughter marries a layman, she may not eat of the sacred gifts; 13 but if the priest's daughter is widowed or divorced and without offspring, and is back in her father's house as in her youth, she may eat of her father's food. No lay person may eat of it: 14 but if a person eats of a sacred donation unwittingly, the priest shall be paid for the sacred donation, adding one-fifth of its value. 15 But [the priests] must not allow the Israelites to profane the sacred donations that they set aside for יהוה, 16 or to incur guilt requiring a penalty

הַקֳּדָשִׁ֔ים כִּ֛י אִם־רָחַ֥ץ בְּשָׂר֖וֹ בַּמָּֽיִם׃ 7 וּבָ֥א
הַשֶּׁ֖מֶשׁ וְטָהֵ֑ר וְאַחַר֙ יֹאכַ֣ל מִן־הַקֳּדָשִׁ֔ים כִּ֥י
לַחְמ֖וֹ הֽוּא׃ 8 נְבֵלָ֧ה וּטְרֵפָ֛ה לֹ֥א יֹאכַ֖ל
לְטָמְאָה־בָ֑הּ אֲנִ֖י יְהֹוָֽה׃ 9 וְשָׁמְר֣וּ אֶת־
מִשְׁמַרְתִּ֗י וְלֹֽא־יִשְׂא֤וּ עָלָיו֙ חֵ֔טְא וּמֵ֥תוּ ב֖וֹ
כִּ֣י יְחַלְּלֻ֑הוּ אֲנִ֥י יְהֹוָ֖ה מְקַדְּשָֽׁם׃
10 וְכָל־זָ֖ר לֹא־יֹ֣אכַל קֹ֑דֶשׁ תּוֹשַׁ֥ב כֹּהֵ֛ן
וְשָׂכִ֖יר לֹא־יֹ֥אכַל קֹֽדֶשׁ׃ 11 וְכֹהֵ֗ן כִּֽי־יִקְנֶ֥ה
נֶ֙פֶשׁ֙ קִנְיַ֣ן כַּסְפּ֔וֹ ה֖וּא יֹ֣אכַל בּ֑וֹ וִילִ֣יד בֵּית֔וֹ
הֵ֖ם יֹאכְל֥וּ בְלַחְמֽוֹ׃ 12 וּבַת־כֹּהֵ֔ן כִּ֥י תִהְיֶ֖ה
לְאִ֣ישׁ זָ֑ר הִ֕וא בִּתְרוּמַ֥ת הַקֳּדָשִׁ֖ים לֹ֥א
תֹאכֵֽל׃ 13 וּבַת־כֹּהֵ֡ן כִּי֩ תִהְיֶ֨ה אַלְמָנָ֜ה
וּגְרוּשָׁ֗ה וְזֶ֘רַע֮ אֵ֣ין לָהּ֒ וְשָׁבָ֞ה אֶל־בֵּ֣ית
אָבִ֗יהָ כִּנְעוּרֶ֔יהָ מִלֶּ֥חֶם אָבִ֖יהָ תֹּאכֵ֑ל וְכָל־
זָ֖ר לֹא־יֹ֥אכַל בּֽוֹ׃ 14 וְאִ֕ישׁ כִּֽי־יֹאכַ֥ל קֹ֖דֶשׁ
בִּשְׁגָגָ֑ה וְיָסַ֤ף חֲמִשִׁיתוֹ֙ עָלָ֔יו וְנָתַ֥ן לַכֹּהֵ֖ן
אֶת־הַקֹּֽדֶשׁ׃ 15 וְלֹ֣א יְחַלְּל֔וּ אֶת־קָדְשֵׁ֖י בְּנֵ֣י
יִשְׂרָאֵ֑ל אֵ֥ת אֲשֶׁר־יָרִ֖ימוּ לַיהֹוָֽה׃ 16 וְהִשִּׂ֤יאוּ

*12–13.* These verses give special attention to the question of when a priest's daughter may partake of the sacred offerings. A priest's daughter is entitled to partake of her father's portion of the sacred donations so long as she is part of his household. If she marries a member of the priesthood, her entitlement then derives from her husband. If she marries outside the priesthood, she becomes a part of the lay community and thus loses her entitlement to partake of the sacred donations. This passage indirectly sheds light on the status of daughters and is consistent with intimations elsewhere (see v. 9).

*13. **without offspring, and is back in her father's house as in her youth.*** It is not clear under what conditions a widow in ancient Israel would inherit her husband's estate. A widow or divorcée without children might well have no claim to that estate, in which case she would likely have to go back to her father's household, since she would have no other means of support (see the story of Tamar in Genesis 38). Here, when a priest's daughter who has married a lay person re-enters her father's household under such circumstances, she regains her entitlement to partake of her father's portion of the sacred donations.

Some widows or divorcées may have had independent means of support. According to biblical law, when a householder dies without making a will, his sons inherit his estate; if he has no sons, his daughters inherit—as in the case of the daughters of Zelophehad, Numbers 27:7–9. If he has no children, the estate stays within his family. Furthermore, a householder apparently could either will his property to his wife or gift it to his daughter, as with Achsah in Joshua 15:16–19.

payment, by eating such sacred donations: for it is I יהוה who make them sacred.

17 יהוה spoke to Moses, saying: 18 Speak to Aaron and his sons, and to all the Israelite people, and say to them:

When any person of the house of Israel or of the strangers in Israel presents a burnt offering as the offering for any of the votive or any of the freewill offerings that they offer to יהוה, 19 it must, to be acceptable in your favor, be a male without blemish, from cattle or sheep or goats. 20 You shall not offer any that has a defect, for it will not be accepted in your favor.

21 And when a person offers, from the herd or the flock, a sacrifice of well-being to יהוה for an explicit vow or as a freewill offering, it must, to be acceptable, be without blemish; there must be no defect in it. 22 Anything blind, or injured, or maimed, or with a wen, boil-scar, or scurvy—such you shall not offer to יהוה; you shall not put any of them on the altar as offerings by fire to יהוה. 23 You may, however, present as a freewill offering an ox or a sheep with a limb extended or contracted; but it will not be accepted for a vow. 24 You shall not offer to יהוה anything [with its testes] bruised or crushed or torn or cut. You shall have no such practices in your own land, 25 nor shall you accept such [animals] from a foreigner for offering as food for your God, for they are mutilated, they have a defect; they shall not be accepted in your favor.

26 יהוה spoke to Moses, saying: 27 When an ox or a sheep or a goat is born, it shall stay seven days

אוֹתָם֙ עֲוֺ֣ן אַשְׁמָ֔ה בְּאָכְלָ֖ם אֶת־קָדְשֵׁיהֶ֑ם
כִּ֛י אֲנִ֥י יְהוָ֖ה מְקַדְּשָֽׁם׃ פ
17 וַיְדַבֵּ֥ר יְהוָ֖ה אֶל־מֹשֶׁ֥ה לֵּאמֹֽר׃ 18 דַּבֵּ֨ר
אֶֽל־אַהֲרֹ֜ן וְאֶל־בָּנָ֗יו וְאֶל֙ כָּל־בְּנֵ֣י יִשְׂרָאֵ֔ל
וְאָמַרְתָּ֖ אֲלֵהֶ֑ם
אִ֣ישׁ אִ֣ישׁ מִבֵּ֣ית יִשְׂרָאֵ֡ל וּמִן־הַגֵּ֣ר בְּיִשְׂרָאֵ֗ל
אֲשֶׁ֨ר יַקְרִ֤יב קָרְבָּנוֹ֙ לְכָל־נִדְרֵיהֶם֙ וּלְכָל־
נִדְבוֹתָ֔ם אֲשֶׁר־יַקְרִ֥יבוּ לַיהוָ֖ה לְעֹלָֽה׃
19 לִרְצֹנְכֶ֑ם תָּמִ֣ים זָכָ֔ר בַּבָּקָ֕ר בַּכְּשָׂבִ֖ים
וּבָעִזִּֽים׃ 20 כֹּ֛ל אֲשֶׁר־בּ֥וֹ מ֖וּם לֹ֣א תַקְרִ֑יבוּ
כִּי־לֹ֥א לְרָצ֖וֹן יִהְיֶ֥ה לָכֶֽם׃
21 וְאִ֗ישׁ כִּֽי־יַקְרִ֤יב זֶֽבַח־שְׁלָמִים֙ לַֽיהוָ֔ה
לְפַלֵּא־נֶ֙דֶר֙ א֣וֹ לִנְדָבָ֔ה בַּבָּקָ֖ר א֣וֹ בַצֹּ֑אן
תָּמִ֤ים יִהְיֶה֙ לְרָצ֔וֹן כָּל־מ֖וּם לֹ֥א יִהְיֶה־בּֽוֹ׃
22 עַוֶּ֩רֶת֩ א֨וֹ שָׁב֜וּר אֽוֹ־חָר֣וּץ אֽוֹ־יַבֶּ֗לֶת א֤וֹ
גָרָב֙ א֣וֹ יַלֶּ֔פֶת לֹא־תַקְרִ֥יבוּ אֵ֖לֶּה לַֽיהוָ֑ה
וְאִשֶּׁ֗ה לֹא־תִתְּנ֥וּ מֵהֶ֛ם עַל־הַמִּזְבֵּ֖חַ לַיהוָֽה׃
23 וְשׁ֣וֹר וָשֶׂ֔ה שָׂר֖וּעַ וְקָל֑וּט נְדָבָה֙ תַּעֲשֶׂ֣ה
אֹת֔וֹ וּלְנֵ֖דֶר לֹ֥א יֵרָצֶֽה׃ 24 וּמָע֤וּךְ וְכָתוּת֙
וְנָת֣וּק וְכָר֔וּת לֹ֥א תַקְרִ֖יבוּ לַיהוָ֑ה וּבְאַרְצְכֶ֖ם
לֹ֥א תַעֲשֽׂוּ׃ 25 וּמִיַּ֣ד בֶּן־נֵכָ֗ר לֹ֥א תַקְרִ֛יבוּ
אֶת־לֶ֥חֶם אֱלֹהֵיכֶ֖ם מִכָּל־אֵ֑לֶּה כִּ֣י מָשְׁחָתָ֤ם
בָּהֶם֙ מ֣וּם בָּ֔ם לֹ֥א יֵרָצ֖וּ לָכֶֽם׃ ס
26 וַיְדַבֵּ֥ר יְהוָ֖ה אֶל־מֹשֶׁ֥ה לֵּאמֹֽר׃ 27 שׁ֣וֹר
אוֹ־כֶ֤שֶׂב אוֹ־עֵז֙ כִּ֣י יִוָּלֵ֔ד וְהָיָ֛ה שִׁבְעַ֥ת יָמִ֖ים

## REGULATIONS FOR BLEMISHED SACRIFICIAL ANIMALS (22:17–25)

The instructions shift to identifying acceptable animals for two types of sacrifices: the burnt offering and the sacrifice of well-being. The list of disqualifying defects for sacrificial offerings has twelve items, just like the list of disqualifying defects of a priest in Leviticus 21:18–20; there is a close correspondence between the two passages.

## ADDITIONAL CRITERIA FOR SACRIFICIAL ANIMALS (22:26–30)

This section gives three additional regulations concerning sacrificial animals.

with its mother, and from the eighth day on it shall be acceptable as an offering by fire to יהוה. <sup>28</sup>However, no animal from the herd or from the flock shall be slaughtered on the same day with its young.

<sup>29</sup>When you sacrifice a thanksgiving offering to יהוה, sacrifice it so that it may be acceptable in your favor. <sup>30</sup>It shall be eaten on the same day; you shall not leave any of it until morning: I am יהוה.

<sup>31</sup>You shall faithfully observe My commandments: I am יהוה. <sup>32</sup>You shall not profane My holy name, that I may be sanctified in the midst of the Israelite people—I יהוה who sanctify you, <sup>33</sup>I who brought you out of the land of Egypt to be your God, I יהוה.

23 יהוה spoke to Moses, saying: <sup>2</sup>Speak to the Israelite people and say to them:

These are My fixed times, the fixed times of יהוה, which you shall proclaim as sacred occasions.

תַּ֣חַת אִמּ֔וֹ וּמִיּ֤וֹם הַשְּׁמִינִי֙ וָהָ֔לְאָה יֵרָצֶ֕ה לְקׇרְבַּ֥ן אִשֶּׁ֖ה לַֽיהֹוָֽה׃ 28 וְשׁ֖וֹר אוֹ־שֶׂ֑ה אֹת֣וֹ וְאֶת־בְּנ֔וֹ לֹ֥א תִשְׁחֲט֖וּ בְּי֥וֹם אֶחָֽד׃ 29 וְכִֽי־תִזְבְּח֥וּ זֶֽבַח־תּוֹדָ֖ה לַֽיהֹוָ֑ה לִֽרְצֹנְכֶ֖ם תִּזְבָּֽחוּ׃ 30 בַּיּ֤וֹם הַהוּא֙ יֵֽאָכֵ֔ל לֹֽא־תוֹתִ֥ירוּ מִמֶּ֖נּוּ עַד־בֹּ֑קֶר אֲנִ֖י יְהֹוָֽה׃ 31 וּשְׁמַרְתֶּם֙ מִצְוֺתַ֔י וַעֲשִׂיתֶ֖ם אֹתָ֑ם אֲנִ֖י יְהֹוָֽה׃ 32 וְלֹ֤א תְחַלְּלוּ֙ אֶת־שֵׁ֣ם קׇדְשִׁ֔י וְנִ֨קְדַּשְׁתִּ֔י בְּת֖וֹךְ בְּנֵ֣י יִשְׂרָאֵ֑ל אֲנִ֥י יְהֹוָ֖ה מְקַדִּשְׁכֶֽם׃ 33 הַמּוֹצִ֤יא אֶתְכֶם֙ מֵאֶ֣רֶץ מִצְרַ֔יִם לִהְי֥וֹת לָכֶ֖ם לֵֽאלֹהִ֑ים אֲנִ֖י יְהֹוָֽה׃ פ

כג וַיְדַבֵּ֥ר יְהֹוָ֖ה אֶל־מֹשֶׁ֥ה לֵּאמֹֽר׃ 2 דַּבֵּ֞ר אֶל־בְּנֵ֤י יִשְׂרָאֵל֙ וְאָמַרְתָּ֣ אֲלֵהֶ֔ם מֽוֹעֲדֵ֣י יְהֹוָ֔ה אֲשֶׁר־תִּקְרְא֥וּ אֹתָ֖ם מִקְרָאֵ֣י קֹ֑דֶשׁ אֵ֥לֶּה הֵ֖ם מֽוֹעֲדָֽי׃

• • • • • • • • • • • • • • • • • • • • • • •

**28.** This verse's restriction is similar to the teaching about the mother bird in Deuteronomy 22:6–7. Such laws appear to stem from a perception that animals have an emotional attachment to their young, and from a humane concern to limit their distress.

### CONCLUDING EXHORTATION (22:31–33)

The reminder that Israel's God brought the people out of Egypt serves as the basis of the demand for obedience to God's commandments.

## Sacred Times
### REGULATIONS FOR THE SABBATH AND FESTIVALS (23:1–44)

Leviticus 23 presents a calendar of sacred occasions—dates set apart and designated as belonging to God. This calendar includes the weekly Sabbath, as well as the annual festivals, beginning in the spring with the paschal offering and ending in the fall with Sukkot and Sh'mini Atzeret. The parallel calendar in Numbers 28–29 focuses on the required sacrificial offerings for each sacred occasion, information provided in some of the instructions here. The present passage focuses mainly on explicating the times of the sacred occasions and prohibiting work on certain days. For a discussion of women's roles in these sacred times, see "Women in Ancient Israel—An Overview," p. xli.

### INTRODUCTION (23:1–2)

Leviticus 21–22 largely addressed the priests and dealt with priestly matters. But the regulations for sacred times concern the community at large and thus are addressed to the entire people. Women are not specifically mentioned in these laws, yet there is no reason to presume that they are excluded from this legislation.

[3]On six days work may be done, but on the seventh day there shall be a sabbath of complete rest, a sacred occasion. You shall do no work; it shall be a sabbath of יהוה throughout your settlements.

[4]These are the set times of יהוה, the sacred occasions, which you shall celebrate each at its appointed time: [5]In the first month, on the fourteenth day of the month, at twilight, there shall be a passover offering to יהוה, [6]and on the fifteenth day of that month יהוה's Feast of Unleavened Bread. You shall eat unleavened bread for seven days. [7]On the first day you shall celebrate a sacred occasion: you shall not work at your occupations. [8]Seven days you shall make offerings by fire to יהוה. The seventh day shall be a sacred occasion: you shall not work at your occupations.

[9]יהוה spoke to Moses, saying: [10]Speak to the Israelite people and say to them:

When you enter the land that I am giving to you and you reap its harvest, you shall bring the first sheaf of your harvest to the priest. [11]He shall elevate the sheaf before יהוה for acceptance in your behalf; the priest shall elevate it on the day after the sabbath. [12]On the day that you elevate the sheaf,

3 שֵׁ֣שֶׁת יָמִים֮ תֵּעָשֶׂ֣ה מְלָאכָה֒ וּבַיּ֣וֹם
הַשְּׁבִיעִ֗י שַׁבַּ֤ת שַׁבָּתוֹן֙ מִקְרָא־קֹ֔דֶשׁ כׇּל־
מְלָאכָ֖ה לֹ֣א תַעֲשׂ֑וּ שַׁבָּ֥ת הִוא֙ לַיהֹוָ֔ה בְּכֹ֖ל
מוֹשְׁבֹתֵיכֶֽם׃ פ
4 אֵ֚לֶּה מוֹעֲדֵ֣י יְהֹוָ֔ה מִקְרָאֵ֖י קֹ֑דֶשׁ אֲשֶׁר־
תִּקְרְא֥וּ אֹתָ֖ם בְּמוֹעֲדָֽם׃ 5 בַּחֹ֣דֶשׁ הָרִאשׁ֗וֹן
בְּאַרְבָּעָ֥ה עָשָׂ֛ר לַחֹ֖דֶשׁ בֵּ֣ין הָֽעַרְבָּ֑יִם פֶּ֖סַח
לַיהֹוָֽה׃ 6 וּבַחֲמִשָּׁ֨ה עָשָׂ֥ר יוֹם֙ לַחֹ֣דֶשׁ הַזֶּ֔ה
חַ֥ג הַמַּצּ֖וֹת לַיהֹוָ֑ה שִׁבְעַ֥ת יָמִ֖ים מַצּ֥וֹת
תֹּאכֵֽלוּ׃ 7 בַּיּוֹם֙ הָֽרִאשׁ֔וֹן מִקְרָא־קֹ֖דֶשׁ יִהְיֶ֣ה
לָכֶ֑ם כׇּל־מְלֶ֥אכֶת עֲבֹדָ֖ה לֹ֥א תַעֲשֽׂוּ׃
8 וְהִקְרַבְתֶּ֥ם אִשֶּׁ֛ה לַיהֹוָ֖ה שִׁבְעַ֣ת יָמִ֑ים
בַּיּ֤וֹם הַשְּׁבִיעִי֙ מִקְרָא־קֹ֔דֶשׁ כׇּל־מְלֶ֥אכֶת
עֲבֹדָ֖ה לֹ֥א תַעֲשֽׂוּ׃ פ

9 וַיְדַבֵּ֥ר יְהֹוָ֖ה אֶל־מֹשֶׁ֥ה לֵּאמֹֽר׃ 10 דַּבֵּ֞ר
אֶל־בְּנֵ֤י יִשְׂרָאֵל֙ וְאָמַרְתָּ֣ אֲלֵהֶ֔ם
כִּֽי־תָבֹ֣אוּ אֶל־הָאָ֗רֶץ אֲשֶׁ֤ר אֲנִי֙ נֹתֵ֣ן לָכֶ֔ם
וּקְצַרְתֶּ֖ם אֶת־קְצִירָ֑הּ וַהֲבֵאתֶ֥ם אֶת־עֹ֛מֶר
רֵאשִׁ֥ית קְצִירְכֶ֖ם אֶל־הַכֹּהֵֽן׃ 11 וְהֵנִ֧יף אֶת־
הָעֹ֛מֶר לִפְנֵ֥י יְהֹוָ֖ה לִֽרְצֹנְכֶ֑ם מִֽמׇּחֳרַת֙
הַשַּׁבָּ֔ת יְנִיפֶ֖נּוּ הַכֹּהֵֽן׃ 12 וַעֲשִׂיתֶ֗ם בְּי֛וֹם

### THE SABBATH AND FESTIVALS, AND CONCLUSION (23:3–44)

The sequence in this section is as follows: the Sabbath (v. 3); the Passover Offering and the Feast of Unleavened Bread (vv. 5–8); the First Barley Offering (vv. 9–14); the First Wheat Offering (Shavuot) (vv. 15–22); the Festival of Alarm Blasts (Rosh HaShanah) (vv. 23–25); the Day of Atonement (Yom Kippur) (vv. 26–32); the Festival of Booths (Sukkot) (vv. 33–35); the Solemn Gathering (Sh'mini Atzeret) (v. 36); conclusion (vv. 37–38); and further laws for the Festival of Booths (vv. 39–43).

*3.* The Sabbath is described as a day without work. In contrast to Numbers 28:9–10, there is no reference to sacrifices here. The passage does not specify what counts as "work," although other passages do supply some details (see Exodus 35:1–3 and Numbers 15:32–36). On the meaning of the Sabbath, see Exodus 31:12–17.

*7. you shall not work at your occupations.* This clause, which is also used in vv. 8, 21, 25, 35, and 36, is apparently distinct from "you shall do no work," which is commanded for the Sabbath and Day of Atonement (vv. 3 and 28). Rabbinic law accordingly holds that work required for the preparation of food is permissible on festival days, but not on the Sabbath or Day of Atonement; see also Exodus 12:16 (Mishnah *Beitzah* 5:2; *M'gillah* 1:5).

you shall offer as a burnt offering to יהוה a lamb of
the first year without blemish. [13]The meal offering
with it shall be two-tenths of a measure of choice
flour with oil mixed in, an offering by fire of pleasing odor to יהוה; and the libation with it shall be of
wine, a quarter of a *hin*. [14]Until that very day, until
you have brought the offering of your God, you
shall eat no bread or parched grain or fresh ears; it is
a law for all time throughout the ages in all your
settlements.

[15]And from the day on which you bring the
sheaf of elevation offering—the day after the sabbath—you shall count off seven weeks. They must
be complete: [16]you must count until the day after
the seventh week—fifty days; then you shall bring
an offering of new grain to יהוה. [17]You shall bring
from your settlements two loaves of bread as an
elevation offering; each shall be made of two-tenths
of a measure of choice flour, baked after leavening,
as first fruits to יהוה. [18]With the bread you shall
present, as burnt offerings to יהוה, seven yearling
lambs without blemish, one bull of the herd, and
two rams, with their meal offerings and libations,
an offering by fire of pleasing odor to יהוה. [19]You
shall also offer one he-goat as a purgation offering
and two yearling lambs as a sacrifice of well-being.
[20]The priest shall elevate these—the two lambs—
together with the bread of first fruits as an elevation
offering before יהוה; they shall be holy to יהוה, for
the priest. [21]On that same day you shall hold a
celebration; it shall be a sacred occasion for you;
you shall not work at your occupations. This is a
law for all time in all your settlements, throughout
the ages.

[22]And when you reap the harvest of your land,
you shall not reap all the way to the edges of your
field, or gather the gleanings of your harvest; you
shall leave them for the poor and the stranger: I
יהוה am your God.

[23]יהוה spoke to Moses, saying: [24]Speak to the Israelite people thus: In the seventh month, on the
first day of the month, you shall observe complete

הֲנִיפְכֶם אֶת־הָעֹמֶר כֶּבֶשׂ תָּמִים בֶּן־שְׁנָתוֹ
לְעֹלָה לַיהֹוָה׃ 13 וּמִנְחָתוֹ שְׁנֵי עֶשְׂרֹנִים
סֹלֶת בְּלוּלָה בַשֶּׁמֶן אִשֶּׁה לַיהֹוָה רֵיחַ נִיחֹחַ
ונסכה וְנִסְכּוֹ יַיִן רְבִיעִת הַהִין׃ 14 וְלֶחֶם
וְקָלִי וְכַרְמֶל לֹא תֹאכְלוּ עַד־עֶצֶם הַיּוֹם
הַזֶּה עַד הֲבִיאֲכֶם אֶת־קָרְבַּן אֱלֹהֵיכֶם חֻקַּת
עוֹלָם לְדֹרֹתֵיכֶם בְּכֹל מֹשְׁבֹתֵיכֶם׃ ס
15 וּסְפַרְתֶּם לָכֶם מִמָּחֳרַת הַשַּׁבָּת מִיּוֹם
הֲבִיאֲכֶם אֶת־עֹמֶר הַתְּנוּפָה שֶׁבַע שַׁבָּתוֹת
תְּמִימֹת תִּהְיֶינָה׃ 16 עַד מִמָּחֳרַת הַשַּׁבָּת
הַשְּׁבִיעִת תִּסְפְּרוּ חֲמִשִּׁים יוֹם וְהִקְרַבְתֶּם
מִנְחָה חֲדָשָׁה לַיהֹוָה׃ 17 מִמּוֹשְׁבֹתֵיכֶם
תָּבִיאוּ ׀ לֶחֶם תְּנוּפָה שְׁתַּיִם שְׁנֵי עֶשְׂרֹנִים
סֹלֶת תִּהְיֶינָה חָמֵץ תֵּאָפֶינָה בִּכּוּרִים
לַיהֹוָה׃ 18 וְהִקְרַבְתֶּם עַל־הַלֶּחֶם שִׁבְעַת
כְּבָשִׂים תְּמִימִם בְּנֵי שָׁנָה וּפַר בֶּן־בָּקָר אֶחָד
וְאֵילִם שְׁנָיִם יִהְיוּ עֹלָה לַיהֹוָה וּמִנְחָתָם
וְנִסְכֵּיהֶם אִשֵּׁה רֵיחַ־נִיחֹחַ לַיהֹוָה׃
19 וַעֲשִׂיתֶם שְׂעִיר־עִזִּים אֶחָד לְחַטָּאת
וּשְׁנֵי כְבָשִׂים בְּנֵי שָׁנָה לְזֶבַח שְׁלָמִים׃
20 וְהֵנִיף הַכֹּהֵן ׀ אֹתָם עַל לֶחֶם הַבִּכֻּרִים
תְּנוּפָה לִפְנֵי יְהֹוָה עַל־שְׁנֵי כְּבָשִׂים קֹדֶשׁ
יִהְיוּ לַיהֹוָה לַכֹּהֵן׃ 21 וּקְרָאתֶם בְּעֶצֶם ׀
הַיּוֹם הַזֶּה מִקְרָא־קֹדֶשׁ יִהְיֶה לָכֶם כָּל־
מְלֶאכֶת עֲבֹדָה לֹא תַעֲשׂוּ חֻקַּת עוֹלָם
בְּכָל־מוֹשְׁבֹתֵיכֶם לְדֹרֹתֵיכֶם׃
22 וּבְקֻצְרְכֶם אֶת־קְצִיר אַרְצְכֶם לֹא־תְכַלֶּה
פְּאַת שָׂדְךָ בְּקֻצְרֶךָ וְלֶקֶט קְצִירְךָ לֹא
תְלַקֵּט לֶעָנִי וְלַגֵּר תַּעֲזֹב אֹתָם אֲנִי יְהֹוָה
אֱלֹהֵיכֶם׃ פ
23 וַיְדַבֵּר יְהֹוָה אֶל־מֹשֶׁה לֵּאמֹר׃ 24 דַּבֵּר
אֶל־בְּנֵי יִשְׂרָאֵל לֵאמֹר בַּחֹדֶשׁ הַשְּׁבִיעִי
בְּאֶחָד לַחֹדֶשׁ יִהְיֶה לָכֶם שַׁבָּתוֹן זִכְרוֹן

rest, a sacred occasion commemorated with loud blasts. [25]You shall not work at your occupations; and you shall bring an offering by fire to יהוה.

[26]יהוה spoke to Moses, saying: [27]Mark, the tenth day of this seventh month is the Day of Atonement. It shall be a sacred occasion for you: you shall practice self-denial, and you shall bring an offering by fire to יהוה; [28]you shall do no work throughout that day. For it is a Day of Atonement, on which expiation is made on your behalf before your God יהוה. [29]Indeed, any person who does not practice self-denial throughout that day shall be cut off from kin; [30]and whoever does any work throughout that day, I will cause that person to perish from among the people. [31]Do no work whatever; it is a law for all time, throughout the ages in all your settlements. [32]It shall be a sabbath of complete rest for you, and you shall practice self-denial; on the ninth day of the month at evening, from evening to evening, you shall observe this your sabbath.

[33]יהוה spoke to Moses, saying: [34]Say to the Israelite people:

On the fifteenth day of this seventh month there shall be the Feast of Booths to יהוה, [to last] seven days. [35]The first day shall be a sacred occasion: you shall not work at your occupations; [36]seven days you shall bring offerings by fire to יהוה. On the eighth day you shall observe a sacred occasion and bring an offering by fire to יהוה; it is a solemn gathering: you shall not work at your occupations.

[37]Those are the set times of יהוה that you shall celebrate as sacred occasions, bringing offerings by fire to יהוה—burnt offerings, meal offerings, sacrifices, and libations, on each day what is proper to

תְּרוּעָה מִקְרָא־קֹדֶשׁ׃ 25 כָּל־מְלֶאכֶת עֲבֹדָה
לֹא תַעֲשׂוּ וְהִקְרַבְתֶּם אִשֶּׁה לַיהוָה׃ ס
26 וַיְדַבֵּר יְהוָה אֶל־מֹשֶׁה לֵּאמֹר׃ 27 אַךְ
בֶּעָשׂוֹר לַחֹדֶשׁ הַשְּׁבִיעִי הַזֶּה יוֹם הַכִּפֻּרִים
הוּא מִקְרָא־קֹדֶשׁ יִהְיֶה לָכֶם וְעִנִּיתֶם
אֶת־נַפְשֹׁתֵיכֶם וְהִקְרַבְתֶּם אִשֶּׁה לַיהוָה׃
28 וְכָל־מְלָאכָה לֹא תַעֲשׂוּ בְּעֶצֶם הַיּוֹם
הַזֶּה כִּי יוֹם כִּפֻּרִים הוּא לְכַפֵּר עֲלֵיכֶם
לִפְנֵי יְהוָה אֱלֹהֵיכֶם׃ 29 כִּי כָל־הַנֶּפֶשׁ אֲשֶׁר
לֹא־תְעֻנֶּה בְּעֶצֶם הַיּוֹם הַזֶּה וְנִכְרְתָה
מֵעַמֶּיהָ׃ 30 וְכָל־הַנֶּפֶשׁ אֲשֶׁר תַּעֲשֶׂה כָּל־
מְלָאכָה בְּעֶצֶם הַיּוֹם הַזֶּה וְהַאֲבַדְתִּי
אֶת־הַנֶּפֶשׁ הַהִוא מִקֶּרֶב עַמָּהּ׃ 31 כָּל־
מְלָאכָה לֹא תַעֲשׂוּ חֻקַּת עוֹלָם לְדֹרֹתֵיכֶם
בְּכֹל מֹשְׁבֹתֵיכֶם׃ 32 שַׁבַּת שַׁבָּתוֹן הוּא
לָכֶם וְעִנִּיתֶם אֶת־נַפְשֹׁתֵיכֶם בְּתִשְׁעָה
לַחֹדֶשׁ בָּעֶרֶב מֵעֶרֶב עַד־עֶרֶב תִּשְׁבְּתוּ
שַׁבַּתְּכֶם׃ פ

33 וַיְדַבֵּר יְהוָה אֶל־מֹשֶׁה לֵּאמֹר׃ 34 דַּבֵּר
אֶל־בְּנֵי יִשְׂרָאֵל לֵאמֹר
בַּחֲמִשָּׁה עָשָׂר יוֹם לַחֹדֶשׁ הַשְּׁבִיעִי הַזֶּה חַג
הַסֻּכּוֹת שִׁבְעַת יָמִים לַיהוָה׃ 35 בַּיּוֹם
הָרִאשׁוֹן מִקְרָא־קֹדֶשׁ כָּל־מְלֶאכֶת עֲבֹדָה
לֹא תַעֲשׂוּ׃ 36 שִׁבְעַת יָמִים תַּקְרִיבוּ אִשֶּׁה
לַיהוָה בַּיּוֹם הַשְּׁמִינִי מִקְרָא־קֹדֶשׁ יִהְיֶה
לָכֶם וְהִקְרַבְתֶּם אִשֶּׁה לַיהוָה עֲצֶרֶת הִוא
כָּל־מְלֶאכֶת עֲבֹדָה לֹא תַעֲשׂוּ׃

37 אֵלֶּה מוֹעֲדֵי יְהוָה אֲשֶׁר־תִּקְרְאוּ אֹתָם
מִקְרָאֵי קֹדֶשׁ לְהַקְרִיב אִשֶּׁה לַיהוָה עֹלָה
וּמִנְחָה זֶבַח וּנְסָכִים דְּבַר־יוֹם בְּיוֹמוֹ׃

27. *Day of Atonement.* Leviticus 16 gives further detailed instructions for the chief priest on this occasion.

29. *practice self-denial.* See at Numbers 30 for regulations about women who individually undertake vows of self-denial.

it—38apart from the sabbaths of יהוה, and apart
from your gifts and from all your votive offerings
and from all your freewill offerings that you give to
יהוה.
39Mark, on the fifteenth day of the seventh
month, when you have gathered in the yield of
your land, you shall observe the festival of יהוה
[to last] seven days: a complete rest on the first day,
and a complete rest on the eighth day. 40On the
first day you shall take the product of *hadar* trees,
branches of palm trees, boughs of leafy trees, and
willows of the brook, and you shall rejoice before
your God יהוה seven days. 41You shall observe it as
a festival of יהוה for seven days in the year; you shall
observe it in the seventh month as a law for all time,
throughout the ages. 42You shall live in booths
seven days; all citizens in Israel shall live in booths,
43in order that future generations may know that
I made the Israelite people live in booths when I
brought them out of the land of Egypt, I your God
יהוה.
44So Moses declared to the Israelites the set
times of יהוה.

24 יהוה spoke to Moses, saying:
2Command the Israelite people to bring you
clear oil of beaten olives for lighting, for kindling
lamps regularly. 3Aaron shall set them up in the
Tent of Meeting outside the curtain of the Pact [to
burn] from evening to morning before יהוה regularly; it is a law for all time throughout the ages. 4He

38 מִלְּבַד שַׁבְּתֹת יְהֹוָה וּמִלְּבַד מַתְּנוֹתֵיכֶם
וּמִלְּבַד כׇּל־נִדְרֵיכֶם וּמִלְּבַד כׇּל־נִדְבֹתֵיכֶם
אֲשֶׁר תִּתְּנוּ לַיהֹוָה׃
39 אַךְ בַּחֲמִשָּׁה עָשָׂר יוֹם לַחֹדֶשׁ הַשְּׁבִיעִי
בְּאׇסְפְּכֶם אֶת־תְּבוּאַת הָאָרֶץ תָּחֹגּוּ אֶת־
חַג־יְהֹוָה שִׁבְעַת יָמִים בַּיּוֹם הָרִאשׁוֹן
שַׁבָּתוֹן וּבַיּוֹם הַשְּׁמִינִי שַׁבָּתוֹן׃ 40 וּלְקַחְתֶּם
לָכֶם בַּיּוֹם הָרִאשׁוֹן פְּרִי עֵץ הָדָר
כַּפֹּת תְּמָרִים וַעֲנַף עֵץ־עָבֹת וְעַרְבֵי־נָחַל
וּשְׂמַחְתֶּם לִפְנֵי יְהֹוָה אֱלֹהֵיכֶם שִׁבְעַת
יָמִים׃ 41 וְחַגֹּתֶם אֹתוֹ חַג לַיהֹוָה שִׁבְעַת
יָמִים בַּשָּׁנָה חֻקַּת עוֹלָם לְדֹרֹתֵיכֶם בַּחֹדֶשׁ
הַשְּׁבִיעִי תָּחֹגּוּ אֹתוֹ׃ 42 בַּסֻּכֹּת תֵּשְׁבוּ
שִׁבְעַת יָמִים כׇּל־הָאֶזְרָח בְּיִשְׂרָאֵל יֵשְׁבוּ
בַּסֻּכֹּת׃ 43 לְמַעַן יֵדְעוּ דֹרֹתֵיכֶם כִּי בַסֻּכּוֹת
הוֹשַׁבְתִּי אֶת־בְּנֵי יִשְׂרָאֵל בְּהוֹצִיאִי אוֹתָם
מֵאֶרֶץ מִצְרָיִם אֲנִי יְהֹוָה אֱלֹהֵיכֶם׃
44 וַיְדַבֵּר מֹשֶׁה אֶת־מֹעֲדֵי יְהֹוָה אֶל־בְּנֵי
יִשְׂרָאֵל׃ פ

כד וַיְדַבֵּר יְהֹוָה אֶל־מֹשֶׁה לֵּאמֹר׃
2 צַו אֶת־בְּנֵי יִשְׂרָאֵל וְיִקְחוּ אֵלֶיךָ שֶׁמֶן זַיִת
זָךְ כָּתִית לַמָּאוֹר לְהַעֲלֹת נֵר תָּמִיד׃
3 מִחוּץ לְפָרֹכֶת הָעֵדֻת בְּאֹהֶל מוֹעֵד יַעֲרֹךְ
אֹתוֹ אַהֲרֹן מֵעֶרֶב עַד־בֹּקֶר לִפְנֵי יְהֹוָה
תָּמִיד חֻקַּת עוֹלָם לְדֹרֹתֵיכֶם׃ 4 עַל הַמְּנֹרָה

*40. hadar trees.* Heb. *hadar* may have been a general descriptive term denoting majesty or stateliness, in which case the identification of the tree's fruit as the citron may date to rabbinic times.

*43. that future generations may know.* This commemorative explanation for the requirement to dwell in booths during the festival is unique to Leviticus in the Torah. Numbers 29:12–34 and Deuteronomy 16:13–15 also deal with Sukkot.

## *The Tabernacle* (24:1–9)

Much of the book of Exodus focused on aspects of the Tabernacle, the portable sanctuary that the Israelites construct while encamped at Mount Sinai. The present unit contains further regulations concerning the Tabernacle's lamp and bread of display, focusing on their maintenance. Perhaps these instructions appear here because the

shall set up the lamps on the pure lampstand before יהוה [to burn] regularly.

[5]You shall take choice flour and bake of it twelve loaves, two-tenths of a measure for each loaf. [6]Place them on the pure table before יהוה in two rows, six to a row. [7]With each row you shall place pure frankincense, which is to be a token offering for the bread, as an offering by fire to יהוה. [8]He shall arrange them before יהוה regularly every sabbath day—it is a commitment for all time on the part of the Israelites. [9]They shall belong to Aaron and his sons, who shall eat them in the sacred precinct; for they are his as most holy things from יהוה's offerings by fire, a due for all time.

[10]There came out among the Israelites a man whose mother was Israelite and whose father was Egyptian. And a fight broke out in the camp be-

הַטְּהֹרָה יַעֲרֹךְ אֶת־הַנֵּרוֹת לִפְנֵי יְהוָה
תָּמִיד׃ פ
5 וְלָקַחְתָּ סֹלֶת וְאָפִיתָ אֹתָהּ שְׁתֵּים עֶשְׂרֵה
חַלּוֹת שְׁנֵי עֶשְׂרֹנִים יִהְיֶה הַחַלָּה הָאֶחָת׃
6 וְשַׂמְתָּ אוֹתָם שְׁתַּיִם מַעֲרָכוֹת שֵׁשׁ
הַמַּעֲרָכֶת עַל הַשֻּׁלְחָן הַטָּהֹר לִפְנֵי יְהוָה׃
7 וְנָתַתָּ עַל־הַמַּעֲרֶכֶת לְבֹנָה זַכָּה וְהָיְתָה
לַלֶּחֶם לְאַזְכָּרָה אִשֶּׁה לַיהוָה׃ 8 בְּיוֹם
הַשַּׁבָּת בְּיוֹם הַשַּׁבָּת יַעַרְכֶנּוּ לִפְנֵי יְהוָה
תָּמִיד מֵאֵת בְּנֵי־יִשְׂרָאֵל בְּרִית עוֹלָם׃
9 וְהָיְתָה לְאַהֲרֹן וּלְבָנָיו וַאֲכָלֻהוּ בְּמָקוֹם
קָדֹשׁ כִּי קֹדֶשׁ קָדָשִׁים הוּא לוֹ מֵאִשֵּׁי יְהוָה
חָק־עוֹלָם׃ ס
10 וַיֵּצֵא בֶּן־אִשָּׁה יִשְׂרְאֵלִית וְהוּא בֶּן־אִישׁ
מִצְרִי בְּתוֹךְ בְּנֵי יִשְׂרָאֵל וַיִּנָּצוּ בַּמַּחֲנֶה בֶּן

daily maintenance of the Tabernacle objects was considered supplementary to the observation of sacred times addressed in the previous unit.

*1–4.* Similar instructions regarding oil for the Tabernacle lamps, which must remain lit throughout the night, appear in Exodus 27:20–21.

*5–9.* The instructions regarding the displaying of the twelve loaves, known as the "bread of display" or "bread of the Presence" (Exodus 25:30), do not mention who bakes the loaves. Possibly women were responsible for making this bread; see at Leviticus 7:12.

## *The Case of the Blasphemer*
(24:10–23)

The parashah closes with the second of two narratives in Leviticus that interrupt laws (the first being the story of Nadab and Abihu in Leviticus 10). This passage recounts the crime of the blasphemer and its resolution. A man whose mother is Israelite and whose father is Egyptian utters God's name in blasphemy, meaning that he may have done something such as curse God, saying, for example, "May such and such befall יהוה!" An unusual facet of this story is that it records the name of the mother, Shelomith (an Israelite), along with her tribal ancestry, information not provided for the father (see v. 11).

### THE STORY OF THE BLASPHEMER (24:10–16)

The story of the blasphemer touches on a number of issues in addition to the desecration of God's name: What is the status of a person from a "mixed marriage" of an Israelite woman and an Egyptian man? To what extent do Israelite laws apply to such a person?

***10. a man whose mother was Israelite and whose father was Egyptian.*** The Hebrew identifies the offender first as "a son of an Israelite woman," then adds, "and he is a son of an Egyptian man." The blasphemer's mixed ancestry seems central to this

tween that half-Israelite and a certain Israelite man. ¹¹The son of the Israelite woman pronounced the Name in blasphemy, and he was brought to Moses —now his mother's name was Shelomith daughter of Dibri of the tribe of Dan—¹²and he was placed in custody, until the decision of יהוה should be made clear to them.

¹³And יהוה spoke to Moses, saying: ¹⁴Take the blasphemer outside the camp; and let all who were within hearing lay their hands upon his head, and let the community leadership stone him.

¹⁵And to the Israelite people speak thus: Anyone who blasphemes God shall bear the guilt; ¹⁶and one who also pronounces the name Eternal shall be put to death. The community leadership shall stone that person; stranger or citizen—having thus pronounced the Name—shall be put to death.

הַיִּשְׂרְאֵלִ֗ית וְאִ֛ישׁ הַיִּשְׂרְאֵלִֽי: ¹¹ וַיִּקֹּ֣ב בֶּן־
הָאִשָּׁ֤ה הַיִּשְׂרְאֵלִית֙ אֶת־הַשֵּׁ֣ם וַיְקַלֵּ֔ל
וַיָּבִ֥יאוּ אֹת֖וֹ אֶל־מֹשֶׁ֑ה וְשֵׁ֥ם אִמּ֛וֹ שְׁלֹמִ֥ית
בַּת־דִּבְרִ֖י לְמַטֵּה־דָֽן: ¹² וַיַּנִּיחֻ֖הוּ בַּמִּשְׁמָ֑ר
לִפְרֹ֥שׁ לָהֶ֖ם עַל־פִּ֥י יְהוָֽה: פ
¹³ וַיְדַבֵּ֥ר יְהוָ֖ה אֶל־מֹשֶׁ֥ה לֵּאמֹֽר: ¹⁴ הוֹצֵ֣א
אֶת־הַֽמְקַלֵּ֗ל אֶל־מִחוּץ֙ לַֽמַּחֲנֶ֔ה וְסָמְכ֧וּ כָֽל־
הַשֹּׁמְעִ֛ים אֶת־יְדֵיהֶ֖ם עַל־רֹאשׁ֑וֹ וְרָגְמ֥וּ
אֹת֖וֹ כָּל־הָעֵדָֽה:
¹⁵ וְאֶל־בְּנֵ֥י יִשְׂרָאֵ֖ל תְּדַבֵּ֣ר לֵאמֹ֑ר אִ֥ישׁ אִ֛ישׁ
כִּֽי־יְקַלֵּ֥ל אֱלֹהָ֖יו וְנָשָׂ֥א חֶטְאֽוֹ: ¹⁶ וְנֹקֵ֤ב שֵׁם־
יְהוָה֙ מ֣וֹת יוּמָ֔ת רָג֥וֹם יִרְגְּמוּ־ב֖וֹ כָּל־הָעֵדָ֑ה
כַּגֵּר֙ כָּֽאֶזְרָ֔ח בְּנׇקְבוֹ־שֵׁ֖ם יוּמָֽת:

· · · · · · · · · · · · · · · · · · · · · · · · · · ·

episode. Since his mother is Israelite but not his father, he has become a member of the clan but is not considered a full-fledged Israelite (Deuteronomy 23:8–9). The man's mixed ancestry raises the question of whether those not considered full-fledged Israelites can be held liable for blasphemy as Israelite citizens. It is noteworthy that no overt criticism is made about the marriage itself.

**11.  *pronounced the Name in blasphemy.*** Blasphemy consists of pronouncing the divine name in a curse against God, that is, uttering an imprecation against the Deity that includes God's name (see Exodus 22:27, which prohibits it). In I Kings 21:1–16, Queen Jezebel frames a landowner named Naboth for the crime of blasphemy in order to have him stoned to death so that her husband can obtain Naboth's land.

***his mother's name was Shelomith daughter of Dibri of the tribe of Dan.*** The author takes great care to note the name, lineage, and tribe of the blasphemer's mother—the only place in the Bible where her name appears. This unusual attention to the lineage of the blasphemer's mother may be part of a subtle condemnation of the tribe of Dan and their

northern Israelite temple, which the Jerusalemite priesthood considered illegitimate. The mention of her lineage could also indicate Shelomith's prominence in the community.

**14.  *lay their hands upon his head.*** By laying their hands on the blasphemer's head, those who heard the blasphemous words transfer onto the blasphemer the guilt they incurred from hearing God's name desecrated.

***community leadership.*** On this translation, see at 8:3 and compare at 4:13.

**16.** This verse establishes the principle that the desecration of the divine name is a capital offense, whether committed by an Israelite or a resident alien (*ger*).

***community leadership.*** See at v. 14.

***stone that person.*** The public, communal, and visually arresting nature of stoning aims to discourage others from engaging in such activities and also serves to unify the community in a common stance against such behavior. In addition, this form of punishment, reserved for especially serious offenses, allows people to express their outrage as a unified group.

[17]If anyone kills any human being, that person shall be put to death. [18]One who kills a beast shall make restitution for it: life for life. [19]If anyone maims another [person]: what was done shall be done in return—[20]fracture for fracture, eye for eye, tooth for tooth. The injury inflicted on a human being shall be inflicted in return. [21]One who kills a beast shall make restitution for it; but one who kills a human being shall be put to death. [22]You shall have one standard for stranger and citizen alike: for I יהוה am your God.

[23]Moses spoke thus to the Israelites. And they took the blasphemer outside the camp and pelted him with stones. The Israelites did as יהוה had commanded Moses.

17 וְאִ֕ישׁ כִּ֥י יַכֶּ֖ה כׇּל־נֶ֣פֶשׁ אָדָ֑ם מ֖וֹת יוּמָֽת׃
18 וּמַכֵּ֥ה נֶֽפֶשׁ־בְּהֵמָ֖ה יְשַׁלְּמֶ֑נָּה נֶ֖פֶשׁ תַּ֥חַת
נָֽפֶשׁ׃ 19 וְאִ֕ישׁ כִּֽי־יִתֵּ֥ן מ֖וּם בַּעֲמִית֑וֹ כַּאֲשֶׁ֣ר
עָשָׂ֔ה כֵּ֖ן יֵעָ֥שֶׂה לּֽוֹ׃ 20 שֶׁ֚בֶר תַּ֣חַת שֶׁ֔בֶר עַ֚יִן
תַּ֣חַת עַ֔יִן שֵׁ֖ן תַּ֣חַת שֵׁ֑ן כַּאֲשֶׁ֨ר יִתֵּ֥ן מוּם֙
בָּֽאָדָ֔ם כֵּ֖ן יִנָּ֥תֶן בּֽוֹ׃ 21 וּמַכֵּ֥ה בְהֵמָ֖ה
יְשַׁלְּמֶ֑נָּה וּמַכֵּ֥ה אָדָ֖ם יוּמָֽת׃ 22 מִשְׁפַּ֤ט אֶחָד֙
יִהְיֶ֣ה לָכֶ֔ם כַּגֵּ֥ר כָּאֶזְרָ֖ח יִהְיֶ֑ה כִּ֛י אֲנִ֥י יְהֹוָ֖ה
אֱלֹהֵיכֶֽם׃
23 וַיְדַבֵּ֣ר מֹשֶׁה֮ אֶל־בְּנֵ֣י יִשְׂרָאֵל֒ וַיּוֹצִ֣יאוּ
אֶת־הַֽמְקַלֵּ֗ל אֶל־מִחוּץ֙ לַֽמַּחֲנֶ֔ה וַיִּרְגְּמ֥וּ
אֹת֖וֹ אָ֑בֶן וּבְנֵֽי־יִשְׂרָאֵ֣ל עָשׂ֔וּ כַּאֲשֶׁ֛ר צִוָּ֥ה
יְהֹוָ֖ה אֶת־מֹשֶֽׁה׃ פ

### THE RETALIATION LAWS (*lex talionis*) (24:17–22)

The message of this parenthetical collection of laws is simply that with regard to retaliation (eye-for-an-eye) laws, the resident alien is under the same obligations as the citizen.

***20. eye for eye.*** See at Exodus 21:24 for the same law and its elaboration.

### THE PUNISHMENT OF THE BLASPHEMER (24:23)

The parashah concludes with the communal stoning of the blasphemer.

*—Hilary Lipka*

# Another View

A PRIEST MAY NOT come in contact with a corpse except when the deceased is a close relative (21:1–3). The list of relatives does not mention the wife.

How do we account for the text's silence concerning the wife? The Torah gives two examples of a husband's burying a wife: Abraham buries Sarah (Genesis 23), and Jacob buries Rachel (Genesis 35). But these cases do not pertain to priests and thus do not shed light on this law.

One could claim that the wife's absence from the list of relatives reflects her more marginal status. As Katarzyna Grosz observes after studying documents from the 14th century B.C.E., "women do not become members of their husband's lineage—only their children do. . . . [The women] could be termed as a 'foreign element' in their husbands' families" ("Some Aspects of the Position of Women in Nuzi," in *Women's Earliest Records*, ed. B. S. Lesko, 1989, p. 178).

Yet one could also argue the reverse: no mention is made because none is necessary—because the wife is included ipso facto. Three lines of evidence support this interpretation. First is the idea that Leviticus 20:11 expresses about a unity between husband and wife. According to this verse, the nakedness of the mother is equivalent to that of the father, implying that the two are as one. Second, Genesis 2:24 expresses the unity of the couple by stating that the two become one flesh. Third, the Torah in several places includes a wife without mentioning her (see at Leviticus 10:14); in other words, the writer expects readers to keep wives in mind.

*How do we account for the text's silence concerning the wife?*

While both interpretations remain plausible in *parashat Emor*, neither can be confirmed.

If a priest may not bury his wife, who then buries her? The law in *parashat Emor* permits the priest to bury his mother, and thus a priest's wife can definitely be buried by her son. If there is no son, then the female members of the household, or members of her family of origin (if they are not priests) can still come in contact with her corpse and bury her.

—*Tamara Cohn Eskenazi*

# Post-biblical Interpretations

***None shall defile himself*** (21:1–2). These verses stipulate that *kohanim* (priests) may not come into contact with a corpse, with the exception of close relations. The Rabbis of the Talmud later applied this list of close relatives to all mourners. That is, the relatives for whom a Jew sits shivah are those enumerated in *Emor*, with the Rabbis' additions of wives and married sisters (BT *Mo'ed Katan* 20b). The Rabbis interpreted the clause "except for the relatives that are closest (literally 'flesh') to him . . . he may defile himself" as a veiled reference to a wife (Midrash *Sifra, Emor* 1.4).

In spelling out the rabbinic definition of marriage, the Mishnah obliges a husband to bury his deceased wife—and then raises the issue of what constitutes a proper burial. One rabbi's answer takes for granted the vital role of women professionals in public mourning:

"Even the poorest husband in Israel must hire at least two flute-players and one wailing woman" (*K'tubot* 4:4).

In general, the laws of mourning treat men and women with parity. Women mourn, and are mourned, with only minor differences from men.

***A widow . . . such he may not marry*** (21:14). The Rabbis preserved these biblical prohibitions limiting which women a man of priestly origin could marry. In fact, they went so far as to say that *kohanim* are hot-headed and sometimes divorce their wives without good reason; upon calming down, they then discover they cannot take their divorced wives back. To save *kohanim* from this predicament, the Rabbis instituted a special bill of divorce for *kohanim* that takes longer to prepare and would not be completed until the *kohein* has regained his composure. This would give him an opportunity to call off the divorce proceedings before it is too late (BT *Bava Batra* 160b).

***These are My fixed times*** (23:2). Leviticus 23 provides information about the Sabbath, the New Moon, Pesach, Shavuot, New Year, Yom Kippur, and Sukkot. These verses address the people in the second person masculine plural and nowhere is there any reference to women. Thus, one must inquire: were women, too, expected to offer a paschal lamb, blow the shofar, dwell in a sukkah, refrain from work on the Sabbath and holy days, and afflict themselves on Yom Kippur?

The Rabbis answered these questions in different ways and they also discussed women's obligations for Purim and Chanukah, two festivals that are not mentioned in the Torah. The basic premise is that women are considered responsible for obeying all of Judaism's negative commandments and for observing most of the positive commandments, including celebrating Shabbat and the festivals. A man should cause his children and household to rejoice on a festival (BT *P'sachim* 109a). However, the Rabbis explicitly exempted women from hearing the shofar on Rosh HaShanah; dwelling in a sukkah during the Sukkot festival; waving the *lulav* on Sukkot; and counting the *Omer* between Pesach and Shavuot. Since these are all commandments to be performed at fixed times of the year, they conform to the exemption of women from time-bound commandments prescribed in Mishnah *Kiddushin* 1:7.

However, the Talmud specifically obligated women to other time-bound festival observances. These included *Kiddush* (sanctification of wine) on the Sabbath (BT *B'rachot* 20b) and, according to most authorities, on the festivals as well; kindling Sabbath and festival lights and the Chanukah lamp (BT *Shabbat* 23a); listening to *M'gillat Esther* on Purim (BT *M'gillah* 4a); and eating matzah (BT *P'sachim* 43b) and drinking four cups of wine at the Passover seder. Rabbi Joshua ben Levi justified women's inclusion in these Chanukah (BT *Shabbat* 23a), Pesach, and Purim rituals (BT *M'gillah* 4a), on the grounds that women, too, were included in these miracles. Women, like men, are required to fast and afflict themselves in various ways on the Day of Atonement and to refrain from doing any work (BT *Sukkah* 28b); they are also obligated to observe all other mandated fast days. [In the course of the 20th century, liberal movements in Judaism fostered women's equal participation in all aspects of festival and holiday observance and introduced a number of new rituals, some of which focus specifically on women and female experience. —*Ed.*]

*Women must obey all of the negative commandments regarding sacred times.*

***There came out . . . a man whose mother*** (24:10). This narrative, by noting the Egyptian lineage of the father of the man who cursed God, implies that his mother was responsible for her son's horrendous behavior because she had married an Egyptian. Some of the Rabbis disagreed and exempted her from wrongdoing, suggesting that the Egyptian man slipped into her bed unbeknownst to her, and this was why her offspring was tainted (*Tanchuma, Sh'mot* 9). Others said the Torah recorded her name in full because she alone behaved in a promiscuous manner, whereas the other Israelite women acted modestly and did not consort with foreign men (Midrash *B'midbar Rabbah* 20).

—*Judith Hauptman*

# Contemporary Reflection

ALTHOUGH THE DESTRUCTION of the Temple (70 C.E.) eliminated the conditions that required priests to preserve certain laws of purity, the influence of such laws nevertheless continues. According to *Emor*, a priest (*kohein*) has to guard against possible defilement at all times. A movie produced by several religiously observant students at the Ma'ale School of Television, Film, and the Arts in Jerusalem illustrates some consequences of these laws for their contemporary circles.

Entitled "Cohen's Wife," this film concerns Rivki Cohen, a young ultra-orthodox woman who opens the door slightly for a strange man who has come asking for *tzedakah* (charity). The stranger then forces his way in and rapes her. This crime renders Rivki ritually impure to her husband. The film deals with how the husband approaches the rabbinical court as to whether he—a *kohein*—must divorce his wife because she is now defiled.

This deeply moving film depicts a loving couple that desperately wants to remain married, while at the same time wanting to observe Jewish law. The wife turns out to have the key to saving the marriage—by not saying the words "I was raped," and certainly not to her husband. Thus, since there was no witness, the husband could seek a sympathetic set of rabbis who simply would pretend that the rape had not taken place, thus allowing the couple to remain intact.

The problem, of course, is the guilt and confusion that both the wife and husband feel after the rabbinic decision; have they themselves resolved the problem or not? Will they be able to live their lives in peace with their guilty secret? This movie, like most made at Ma'ale, exposes viewers to the human conflicts, tragedies, and even comic situations that arise when people wish to live both according to Jewish law and to their honest feelings.

While we can expect the laws of Leviticus to have a strong impact primarily in certain religious circles, other ideas in *Emor* continue to have subtle ramifications for general society. One example is the stress found in *Emor* on the ideal of physical "perfection."

*Some of the ideas behind priestly laws of ritual purity still influence our lives.*

Leviticus 21:17–20 disqualifies a descendant of Aaron from carrying out the rituals of the priesthood if he is subject to certain physical deficiencies or disfigurations. Physical imperfection, it seems, impairs holiness.

While the priest's bodily perfection may no longer be a Jewish necessity, the idea and expectation of bodily perfection have become a cultural goal of the wider American Jewish population, with terrible consequences—particularly for women, regardless of age. By now most people are aware that many American Jewish girls starve themselves or over-exercise to become thin, or they have surgery on their noses and elsewhere to be more beautiful. So too, older Jewish women undergo a wide range of plastic surgery to remain attractive. On this drive among young girls to be pretty at all costs—and to be intolerant of those who are not—see *The JGirl's Guide: The Young Jewish Woman's Handbook for Coming of Age* (co-authored by me, Penina Adelman, and Ali Feldman, 2005). Mothers pass the goal of beauty on to their daughters, and men reinforce it. By manipulating women's self-confidence about their appearance, the beauty industry has become a highly lucrative business. The point is that each girl or woman considers herself to be defective or imperfect, no matter what she does. This idea derives from the notion that there *is* such a thing as bodily perfection, a concept presented in *Emor*.

The motivation to be beautiful by any means should not be dismissed out of hand as misguided, however. After all, the Bible and much of Western culture frequently equate beauty with goodness.

Several admired matriarchs—Sarah and Rebekah, for example—are beautiful, even "very beautiful." In fact, one term for beauty in the Bible actually uses forms of the word *tov* (good), further promoting such associations. Thus, kindly Rebekah is *tovat mar'eh* ("exceedingly beautiful," Genesis 24:16). And Esther is touted for her beauty, which enables her to carry out later virtuous deeds. Based on these cases and many others, I suggest that the Torah's preference for beauty is a clear theme that appears in many places, including the *Emor* section on the necessity for physical perfection among priests.

By and large it is not only the preference for beauty that has spilled into Western culture, but also the equation between beauty and goodness. Children's fairy tales typically feature the beautiful princess who is good, the handsome prince who is also good, and the ugly witch who is evil. Psychologists have found that people who are attractive are trusted more than those who are not; handsome people are likely to rise in the ranks of their organizations and be elected to office. Physically attractive individuals, research shows, are perceived as more intelligent, sociable, talented, and moral. There is even a term for this prejudice: beautyism—the idea that what is beautiful is good, and what is not beautiful is bad. Beautyism is a danger to the self-esteem of those who are not physically attractive and can lead to arrogance among those who are. While efforts to urge children to look beyond physical appearance may address race and disability, they almost never deal with beauty. This silent prejudice is thus able to persist and be reinforced throughout popular culture, religious instruction, and the education system.

Some passages in the Bible, however, do not equate beauty with goodness, possibly in an attempt to counteract the heavy emphasis on the subtle equation elsewhere. Ruth, for example, is a model of goodness but is never called beautiful. More notable is the description of the "woman of valor" (*eshet chayil*) in Proverbs 31, which explicitly repudiates beauty as a criterion for virtue: "Grace is deceptive, and beauty is illusory; it is for her fear of יהוה that a woman is to be praised" (31:30). Yet the negation can be also read as an admission that the cultural norm is otherwise.

*Emor*'s implication that a priest must not remain married to his wife if she is raped is a case of punishing the victim. So, too, *Emor*'s exclusion of a blind descendant of Aaron from priestly activities punishes the handicapped. Contemporary society tries not to punish rape victims or disabled individuals. While it is true that we have tried to distance ourselves from these two ancient ideas, we have made hardly any progress with regard to the obverse, that is, unfairly rewarding those who are physically beautiful and punishing those who are not.

—*Shulamit Reinharz*

# Voices

## *from* The Kohain's Wife

Shulamith Surnamer

*Leviticus 21:1–4*

*In the month of Av*
*month of mourning*
*my rabbi-father yet alive*
*but my mother*
*newly-gone . . .*

It is lonely to be
the wife
of a kohain
at funeral time
by myself I sit
in the front row
at the funeral chapel
listening to the eulogy
over my nearest flesh and blood
knowing that my husband
and sons
are standing in the parking lot
of the funeral home
listening
to the same eulogy
piped over a loudspeaker
outside
just for them
who may not be in the same room
with death

## Yahrzeit

Enid Dame

*Leviticus 21:1–3*

The *yahrzeit* flame
is beating its wings in a cup
on the edge of my kitchen sink.
Its stealthy gold shadow
breathing along the wall
suddenly terrifies me:
like finding a bird in my bedroom
still alive pulsating nervous,
changing the shape of the day.

No intruder is ever harmless.
And, Mother, I've got you cornered,
fierce memory pacing your glass cage,
houseguest with nowhere to go.
I'll lock myself in alongside you.
Today, we'll remind each other
of old connections, old journeys,
from muddy, sincere Indiana
to ragged-edged Brooklyn
with all its stray cats, its ecstatic
vegetable stands.

## *from* A Prayer for Parents of Babies with Disabilities

Debra Orenstein

*Leviticus 21:16–23*

Our fantasy of birth is that all goes well, . . . that mother and child emerge healthy and "perfect." For parents who have a child with disabilities, many of the standard phrases and clichés—the counting of toes and fingers, the wish for a future filled with Torah learning—ring hollow, or even sound cruel. Yet the exceptional child is created in God's image, and tradition teaches that God's *chesed* (steadfast love) for us has nothing to do with physical prowess or mental agility, and everything to do with the simple fact that we are.

## *Looking toward Shabbat*

Shelly Goldman, Lara Laufer, Shari Lore

*Leviticus 23:3*

The week is done...
I washed 7 loads of laundry,
I filed 15 briefs with the courts,
I prepared 21 meals,
I listened to 30 customer complaints,
I carried 60 pounds of groceries,
I graded 100 spelling tests,
I drove 200 miles in carpools,
I dried buckets of tears.

All my hours have been
Used up by others' needs,
others' demands,
others' priorities.

When the week is done, and
I light the Shabbat candles,
my time begins.
I take a deep breath and
let go.
I embrace the peace of Shabbat,
Standing with the women
who came before me and
those who will follow.

The candles' flames draw me in,
Allowing me to lay down
the burdens of the week,
In order to restore and
refresh my soul.

This is my time to take in Shabbat,
and keep it with me
for the rest of the week—
Giving me strength to
Wash 7 loads of laundry
File 15 briefs with the courts
Prepare 21 meals...

## *The Sabbath Song*

Kadya Molodowsky (transl. Kathryn Hellerstein)

*Leviticus 23:3*

I fought until Sabbath eve
With the six emperors
Of the six days of the week.
Sunday they confiscated my sleep.
Monday they scattered my salt.
And on the third day, my God,
They flung away my bread
And, above my face, they fenced with knights.
They caught my flying dove
And slaughtered her.
And so forth, until Friday dawn.
And this, you see, ends my whole week,
With the dying of my dove-flying.

At dusk, I kindled four candles
And the Sabbath Queen came to me.
Her countenance shone
And the whole world became Sabbath.
My scattered salt
Glittered in the saltshaker,
And my dove, my flying dove,
Flapped her wings
And groomed her throat.

The Sabbath Queen blessed my candles.
They shone with a clear flame.
The light covered the days of the week
And the battle with the six emperors.
The greenness of mountains—
Is the greenness of Sabbath.
The silver of a river—
Is the silver of Sabbath.
The song of the wind—
Is the singing of Sabbath.
And the song of my heart
Is the eternal Sabbath.

# בהר ✦ *B'har*

## LEVITICUS 25:1–26:2

## *Proclaiming and Protecting Liberty*

PARASHAT B'HAR ("at the mountain [of]") contains laws that aim to protect economically disadvantaged members of the community from permanently losing their freedom and means of livelihood. In Israel, as in other parts of the ancient Near East, those households that fell into economically precarious situations risked losing their land; moreover, their members might become indentured servants or slaves. Israel, like its neighbors, developed legislation to prevent the rich from exploiting the poor. This parashah highlights economic and social concerns through a theological lens. In the process, it expresses what it means for the Israelites to be both a holy people and God's freed servants. Ethics and social justice do not constitute a separate sphere from ritual in the book of Leviticus but are integral to it. See, for example, the laws at the end of *parashat Vayikra* (5:20–26). *Parashat B'har* illustrates how the demand for holiness needs to be implemented in socioeconomic practices, making it possible for economically disadvantaged Israelites to "come back home" to family and land.

Leviticus 25, like Exodus 21 and Deuteronomy 15, seeks to provide a safety net to preserve and protect land-holdings and economic stability. In other parts of the ancient Near East, kings issued royal edicts in an attempt to restore economic balance by canceling certain debts, especially when the rulers ascended to the throne. The jubilee legislation envisions a permanently regulated system for adjusting economic imbalance every 50 years, independently of the goodwill of rulers. The legislation also serves to protect the land itself from exploitation. The rationale for land protection is theological: the land belongs to God; moreover, the destiny of the land and of the people are intertwined.

The laws include the following: (*1*) land must lie fallow every seventh year and in the fiftieth (jubilee) year; (*2*) land holdings must return to their original owners at the jubilee year or be redeemed earlier; (*3*) indentured servants or slaves must be released at the jubilee year or be redeemed earlier. Leviticus 25 is the only place in the Torah that describes the jubilee laws. Its laws, however, stand in tension with those in Exodus and Deuteronomy that institute release in the seventh year.

*In the book of Leviticus, ethics and social justice are integrated with ritual.*

The only women explicitly mentioned in this parashah are slaves or servants (the Hebrew *amah* could mean either; see at v. 44). Leviticus 25:6–7 states that female slaves or servants, like male ones, are to benefit from the land's Sabbath; vv. 44–46 state that foreign slaves, including women, are to remain slaves in perpetuity (unlike Israelite slaves).

The language of release and redemption in the parashah takes the masculine form but functions inclusively to refer to both women and men. Other biblical texts illuminate how such laws would apply to women. Narratives such as Numbers 27 and 36 describe women inheriting land; II Kings 4, 6, and Nehemiah 5 depict situations in which women are subject to loss of freedom and land due to destitution; Jeremiah 34 refers to the release of female slaves; and Ruth 4 describes the redemption of land sold by Naomi. Clearly, conditions that drive persons into servitude—and the resolutions of those conditions that Leviticus requires—apply to women as well as to men.

*—Tamara Cohn Eskenazi*
*Jocelyn Hudson*

## Outline

I. Introduction
*Additional Teachings from Sinai* (25:1)

II. Laws Regarding the Land's Sabbath (25:2–7)

III. The Fiftieth-Year Jubilee (25:8–54)

- A. Jubilee laws for the land (vv. 8–22)
- B. Reasons for the jubilee: proclamation of liberty (vv. 23–24)
- C. Laws protecting Israelites from permanent poverty and servitude (vv. 25–54)
  1. Laws to protect land holdings (vv. 25–28)
  2. Laws to protect homes (vv. 29–34)
  3. Laws to protect Israelites from debt-slavery (vv. 35–54)

IV. Conclusion
*God's Ownership of the Israelites as Basis for Jubilee Laws* (25:55–26:2)

25:1

יהוה spoke to Moses on Mount Sinai:
[2]Speak to the Israelite people and
say to them:

When you enter the land that I assign to you,
the land shall observe a sabbath of יהוה. [3]Six years
you may sow your field and six years you may
prune your vineyard and gather in the yield. [4]But
in the seventh year the land shall have a sabbath of

כה וַיְדַבֵּר יְהֹוָה אֶל־מֹשֶׁה בְּהַר סִינַי
לֵאמֹר׃ 2 דַּבֵּר אֶל־בְּנֵי יִשְׂרָאֵל וְאָמַרְתָּ
אֲלֵהֶם
כִּי תָבֹאוּ אֶל־הָאָרֶץ אֲשֶׁר אֲנִי נֹתֵן לָכֶם
וְשָׁבְתָה הָאָרֶץ שַׁבָּת לַיהֹוָה׃ 3 שֵׁשׁ שָׁנִים
תִּזְרַע שָׂדֶךָ וְשֵׁשׁ שָׁנִים תִּזְמֹר כַּרְמֶךָ
וְאָסַפְתָּ אֶת־תְּבוּאָתָהּ׃ 4 וּבַשָּׁנָה הַשְּׁבִיעִת

## *Introduction*

### ADDITIONAL TEACHINGS FROM SINAI (25:1)

Leviticus 1:1 states that God spoke to Moses "from the Tent of Meeting"; but here, God speaks to Moses "on Mount Sinai." According to many scholars, Leviticus 25 represents an independent tradition that concludes in 26:46. The attribution to Sinai emphasizes the critical importance of ensuring freedom and combating social and economic injustice: breaking these rules constitutes breaking the Sinai covenant.

## *Laws Regarding the Land's Sabbath* (25:2–7)

The land, like the people, must have a sabbath rest, and therefore it must lie fallow every seventh year. The idea may seem like a utopian fantasy, but Baruch Levine points out that letting the land lie fallow was a practical aspect of ancient agriculture, especially where extensive irrigation was utilized. He explains that it "served to reduce the quantity of alkalines, sodium and calcium deposited in the soil" (*Leviticus*, 1989, p. 272) and thus helped preserve the land's fertility. Practical considerations aside, for Leviticus this law expresses the supremacy of God, to whom Israel and the land ultimately belong.

2. ***When you enter the land.*** Unlike the weekly Shabbat that the Israelites are to observe in all places and at all times, the land's *shabbat* is to be observed only in the Land of Israel.

4. ***in the seventh year.*** Exodus 23:10–11 also mandates letting the land lie fallow every seventh year. Scholars suggest that Exodus refers to a rotating fallow year; each Israelite farmer would calculate every seventh year individually for his or her own parcel of land. Our parashah, however, describes a uniform calendar in which every farmer must observe the fallow year at the same seventh year, as part of a fiftieth-year jubilee. Josephus, the 1st-century Jewish historian, reports that the Jews

The text does not appear to address many questions regarding the status of women.

ANOTHER VIEW ➤ *760*

What regulations do we require today to help us nurture ourselves and the planet?

CONTEMPORARY REFLECTION ➤ *762*

We learn that a husband should honor his wife more than he honors himself.

POST-BIBLICAL INTERPRETATIONS ➤ *760*

Gruel was a great luxury in our home, and I bitterly resented having to share any of it.

VOICES ➤ *764*

complete rest, a sabbath of יהוה: you shall not sow
your field or prune your vineyard. 5You shall not
reap the aftergrowth of your harvest or gather the
grapes of your untrimmed vines; it shall be a year of
complete rest for the land. 6But you may eat whatever the land during its sabbath will produce—you,
your male and female slaves, the hired and bound
laborers who live with you, 7and your cattle and the
beasts in your land may eat all its yield.

8You shall count off seven weeks of years—
seven times seven years—so that the period of
seven weeks of years gives you a total of forty-nine

שַׁבַּ֤ת שַׁבָּתוֹן֙ יִהְיֶ֣ה לָאָ֔רֶץ שַׁבָּ֖ת לַֽיהוָ֑ה
שָֽׂדְךָ֙ לֹ֣א תִזְרָ֔ע וְכַרְמְךָ֖ לֹ֥א תִזְמֹֽר׃ 5 אֵ֣ת
סְפִ֤יחַ קְצִֽירְךָ֙ לֹ֣א תִקְצ֔וֹר וְאֶת־עִנְּבֵ֥י נְזִירֶ֖ךָ
לֹ֣א תִבְצֹ֑ר שְׁנַ֥ת שַׁבָּת֖וֹן יִהְיֶ֥ה לָאָֽרֶץ׃
6 וְֽהָיְתָ֞ה שַׁבַּ֨ת הָאָ֤רֶץ לָכֶם֙ לְאָכְלָ֔ה לְךָ֖
וּלְעַבְדְּךָ֣ וְלַאֲמָתֶ֑ךָ וְלִשְׂכִֽירְךָ֙ וּלְתוֹשָׁ֣בְךָ֔
הַגָּרִ֖ים עִמָּֽךְ׃ 7 וְלִ֨בְהֶמְתְּךָ֔ וְלַֽחַיָּ֖ה אֲשֶׁ֣ר
בְּאַרְצֶ֑ךָ תִּהְיֶ֥ה כָל־תְּבוּאָתָ֖הּ לֶאֱכֹֽל׃ ס
8 וְסָפַרְתָּ֣ לְךָ֗ שֶׁ֚בַע שַׁבְּתֹ֣ת שָׁנִ֔ים שֶׁ֥בַע
שָׁנִ֖ים שֶׁ֣בַע פְּעָמִ֑ים וְהָי֣וּ לְךָ֗ יְמֵי֙ שֶׁ֚בַע
שַׁבְּתֹ֣ת הַשָּׁנִ֔ים תֵּ֥שַׁע וְאַרְבָּעִ֖ים שָׁנָֽה׃

were exempt from a certain imperial tax on the seventh year "which they call the Sabbatical Year, because thereon they neither receive the fruits of their trees, nor do they sow their land" (*Antiquities of the Jews* 14.10.6).

*5–6.* Israelite farmers and their households may eat from the aftergrowth of their fields—making it possible for families to live off the land. With a fixed seventh-year land rest, only fallow land would be available every seven years. Because this system would not provide a social network for the poor, Leviticus 19:9–10 and 23:22 state that one must leave the edges of one's field and the gleanings of one's harvest for the poor and the stranger, and not pick one's vineyards bare or gather fallen fruit. (Exodus 23 does not specify these provisions but implies a rotation of fallow land; see the previous comment.)

***you, your male and female slaves, the hired and bound laborers.*** Here the Hebrew term for "you" is masculine singular, yet it clearly includes the entire extended family. This usage confirms that elsewhere the text's second-person masculine language does not necessarily exclude women from its audience.

This phrase contains one of only two explicit references to females in the parashah (see also vv. 44–46). The language echoes the Sabbath ruling in Deuteronomy 5:14 in which the entire household is to rest. Here the goal is to provide food for these otherwise vulnerable members of the household.

Landowners are responsible for feeding those individuals directly under their control, but not the poor or disenfranchised at large, perhaps because the predictable aftergrowth was not abundant (see Jacob Milgrom, *Leviticus 23–27*, 2001, p. 2162).

## *The Fiftieth-Year Jubilee*
(25:8–54)

Jubilee laws demand the release of land and persons every fifty years. The purpose of the laws is to ensure the economic and social freedom of the Israelites, whom God collectively redeemed from slavery in Egypt. These statutes attempt to preserve land tenure. (In Numbers 36, clan leaders—concerned about land transfer to another tribe—invoke the laws of the jubilee when they raise questions about the land granted to Zelophehad's daughters, Mahlah, Noah, Hoglah, Milcah, and Tirzah.) The laws also aim to guarantee that no Israelite will be permanently destitute. Land and people constitute the most basic resources necessary to ensure livelihood. Therefore, the jubilee laws address these issues together—and in doing so, solidify the claim that only God can own Israelite people and land.

years. 9Then you shall sound the horn loud; in the
seventh month, on the tenth day of the month—
the Day of Atonement—you shall have the horn
sounded throughout your land 10and you shall
hallow the fiftieth year. You shall proclaim release
throughout the land for all its inhabitants. It shall
be a jubilee for you: each of you shall return to your
holding and each of you shall return to your family.
11That fiftieth year shall be a jubilee for you: you
shall not sow, neither shall you reap the aftergrowth
or harvest the untrimmed vines, 12for it is a jubilee.
It shall be holy to you: you may only eat the growth
direct from the field.

13In this year of jubilee, each of you shall return
to your holding. 14When you sell property to your

9 וְהַעֲבַרְתָּ֞ שׁוֹפַ֤ר תְּרוּעָה֙ בַּחֹ֣דֶשׁ הַשְּׁבִעִ֔י
בֶּעָשׂ֖וֹר לַחֹ֑דֶשׁ בְּיוֹם֙ הַכִּפֻּרִ֔ים תַּעֲבִ֥ירוּ
שׁוֹפָ֖ר בְּכָל־אַרְצְכֶֽם׃ 10 וְקִדַּשְׁתֶּ֗ם אֵ֣ת שְׁנַ֤ת
הַחֲמִשִּׁים֙ שָׁנָ֔ה וּקְרָאתֶ֥ם דְּר֛וֹר בָּאָ֖רֶץ
לְכָל־יֹשְׁבֶ֑יהָ יוֹבֵ֥ל הִוא֙ תִּהְיֶ֣ה לָכֶ֔ם וְשַׁבְתֶּ֗ם
אִ֚ישׁ אֶל־אֲחֻזָּת֔וֹ וְאִ֥ישׁ אֶל־מִשְׁפַּחְתּ֖וֹ
תָּשֻֽׁבוּ׃ 11 יוֹבֵ֣ל הִ֗וא שְׁנַ֛ת הַחֲמִשִּׁ֥ים שָׁנָ֖ה
תִּהְיֶ֣ה לָכֶ֑ם לֹ֣א תִזְרָ֔עוּ וְלֹ֤א תִקְצְרוּ֙ אֶת־
סְפִיחֶ֔יהָ וְלֹ֥א תִבְצְר֖וּ אֶת־נְזִרֶֽיהָ׃ 12 כִּ֚י
יוֹבֵ֣ל הִ֔וא קֹ֖דֶשׁ תִּהְיֶ֣ה לָכֶ֑ם מִ֨ן־הַשָּׂדֶ֔ה
תֹּאכְל֖וּ אֶת־תְּבוּאָתָֽהּ׃
13 בִּשְׁנַ֥ת הַיּוֹבֵ֖ל הַזֹּ֑את תָּשֻׁ֕בוּ אִ֖ישׁ אֶל־
אֲחֻזָּתֽוֹ׃ 14 וְכִֽי־תִמְכְּר֤וּ מִמְכָּר֙ לַעֲמִיתֶ֔ךָ א֥וֹ

JUBILEE LAWS FOR THE LAND
(25:8–22)

Leviticus 25 demands that the land, like the people, have a Shabbat in the fiftieth year (in addition to every seventh year). Such legislation symbolizes the intimate bond between the Land of Israel, the people, and God. Some scholars question whether Jews actually observed these laws in ancient times—and if so, to what extent. Josephus, when discussing the jubilee year, does not mention any land lying fallow (*Antiquities of the Jews* 3.12.3).

***9. seventh month.*** The jubilee and sabbatical years begin in the month of Tishrei. (Nisan remains the first month, commemorating the exodus from Egypt.)

***10. hallow.*** The Hebrew verbal root is *k-d-sh.* Just like the seventh day (see for example, Genesis 2:3), so too the jubilee year is sanctified. See also v. 12.

***proclaim release throughout the land for all its inhabitants.*** This verse sums up the goal of the laws in the parashah: to ensure the fundamental freedom from economic oppression. Heb. *dror* ("release") has often been translated as "freedom" or "liberty." In 1751, the Pennsylvania Assembly ordered a bronze bell to be cast with an English translation of this clause inscribed on it, to commemorate the fiftieth anniversary of that American colony's constitution; the inscription on that bell, now known as the Liberty Bell, is: "Proclaim Liberty throughout all the land unto all the inhabitants thereof."

***jubilee.*** Heb. *yovel,* a word that in the Torah is confined to Leviticus 25 and 27 (seventeen times), with one exception (Numbers 36:4; see the introduction to this unit on p. 750, above). The word also means "a ram" or "a ram's horn."

***return to your holding... return to your family.*** The jubilee system aims principally at reuniting families and allowing them to live on their land.

***13. your holding.*** Land holdings are inalienable, meaning that persons who sell such holdings regain them automatically and freely at the time of the jubilee. Holdings that have been sold can be redeemed prior to the jubilee by paying for them.

Several biblical texts take for granted that Israelite women sometimes own land. In Numbers 27, five sisters—Mahlah, Noah, Hoglah, Milcah, and Tirzah—demand and inherit their father's land. From Joshua 15:16–19 and Judges 1:12–15, it seems that a certain Achsah requested and received land from her father after she had married. In addition, II Kings 4:8–37 and 8:1–6 describe a wealthy woman who owns land.

neighbor, or buy any from your neighbor, you shall not wrong one another. 15 In buying from your neighbor, you shall deduct only for the number of years since the jubilee; and in selling to you, that person shall charge you only for the remaining crop years: 16 the more such years, the higher the price you pay; the fewer such years, the lower the price; for what is being sold to you is a number of harvests. 17 Do not wrong one another, but fear your God; for I יהוה am your God.

18 You shall observe My laws and faithfully keep My rules, that you may live upon the land in security; 19 the land shall yield its fruit and you shall eat your fill, and you shall live upon it in security. 20 And should you ask, "What are we to eat in the seventh year, if we may neither sow nor gather in our crops?" 21 I will ordain My blessing for you in the sixth year, so that it shall yield a crop sufficient for three years. 22 When you sow in the eighth year, you will still be eating old grain of that crop; you will be eating the old until the ninth year, until its crops come in.

קֹנֶה מִיַּד עֲמִיתֶךָ אַל־תּוֹנוּ אִישׁ אֶת־אָחִיו׃
15 בְּמִסְפַּר שָׁנִים אַחַר הַיּוֹבֵל תִּקְנֶה מֵאֵת
עֲמִיתֶךָ בְּמִסְפַּר שְׁנֵי־תְבוּאֹת יִמְכָּר־לָךְ׃
16 לְפִי | רֹב הַשָּׁנִים תַּרְבֶּה מִקְנָתוֹ וּלְפִי
מְעֹט הַשָּׁנִים תַּמְעִיט מִקְנָתוֹ כִּי מִסְפַּר
תְּבוּאֹת הוּא מֹכֵר לָךְ׃ 17 וְלֹא תוֹנוּ אִישׁ
אֶת־עֲמִיתוֹ וְיָרֵאתָ מֵאֱלֹהֶיךָ כִּי אֲנִי יְהוָה
אֱלֹהֵיכֶם׃
18 וַעֲשִׂיתֶם אֶת־חֻקֹּתַי וְאֶת־מִשְׁפָּטַי
תִּשְׁמְרוּ וַעֲשִׂיתֶם אֹתָם וִישַׁבְתֶּם עַל־
הָאָרֶץ לָבֶטַח׃ 19 וְנָתְנָה הָאָרֶץ פִּרְיָהּ
וַאֲכַלְתֶּם לָשֹׂבַע וִישַׁבְתֶּם לָבֶטַח עָלֶיהָ׃
20 וְכִי תֹאמְרוּ מַה־נֹּאכַל בַּשָּׁנָה הַשְּׁבִיעִת
הֵן לֹא נִזְרָע וְלֹא נֶאֱסֹף אֶת־תְּבוּאָתֵנוּ׃
21 וְצִוִּיתִי אֶת־בִּרְכָתִי לָכֶם בַּשָּׁנָה הַשִּׁשִּׁית
וְעָשָׂת אֶת־הַתְּבוּאָה לִשְׁלֹשׁ הַשָּׁנִים׃
22 וּזְרַעְתֶּם אֵת הַשָּׁנָה הַשְּׁמִינִת וַאֲכַלְתֶּם
מִן־הַתְּבוּאָה יָשָׁן עַד | הַשָּׁנָה הַתְּשִׁיעִת עַד־
בּוֹא תְּבוּאָתָהּ תֹּאכְלוּ יָשָׁן׃

*14–22.* Persons with little or no reserve food sources become especially vulnerable when they cannot raise crops. Leviticus repeatedly warns against exploiting these vulnerable Israelites, and it promises sufficient produce for all if the society follows these laws and reveres God.

*14. **neighbor.*** Heb. *amit*, which refers to a fellow Israelite.

***you shall not wrong one another.*** In this verse, the assumed relationship is between one Israelite and another—a relationship of equals. Elsewhere, the Torah commands the Israelites not to wrong a stranger, a foreigner (Exodus 22:20, Leviticus 19:33), or a runaway slave (Deuteronomy 23:17).

*15–16.* The number of years to the jubilee's release determines the price of redemption.

*17. **Do not wrong one another.*** This repeated prohibition (see v. 14) links ethical behavior between Israelites with their relationship to the Divine.

***but fear your God.*** Fearing God stands in direct contrast to wronging another person.

*18–19.* These verses promise security to the people if they follow God's rules. Security includes having ample food—enough to satisfy (*sova*). It also includes living securely in the land—being safe from enemies.

*20–22.* These verses address pragmatic concerns regarding the economic viability of the jubilee system. God promises agricultural surplus and instructs the Israelites how to prepare for it and use it. This passage underscores the convictions that the land belongs solely to God and that God controls its productivity. Assurance is given that God will provide for those who observe the jubilee laws.

[23]But the land must not be sold beyond reclaim, for the land is Mine; you are but strangers resident with Me. [24]Throughout the land that you hold, you must provide for the redemption of the land.

[25]If one of your kin is in straits and has to sell part of a holding, the nearest redeemer shall come and redeem what that relative has sold. [26]If a person has no one to be redeemer but prospers and

23 וְהָאָרֶץ לֹא תִמָּכֵר לִצְמִתֻת כִּי־לִי
הָאָרֶץ כִּי־גֵרִים וְתוֹשָׁבִים אַתֶּם עִמָּדִי׃
24 וּבְכֹל אֶרֶץ אֲחֻזַּתְכֶם גְּאֻלָּה תִּתְּנוּ
לָאָרֶץ׃ ס
25 כִּי־יָמוּךְ אָחִיךָ וּמָכַר מֵאֲחֻזָּתוֹ וּבָא גֹאֲלוֹ
הַקָּרֹב אֵלָיו וְגָאַל אֵת מִמְכַּר אָחִיו׃
26 וְאִישׁ כִּי לֹא יִהְיֶה־לּוֹ גֹּאֵל וְהִשִּׂיגָה

### REASONS FOR THE JUBILEE: PROCLAMATION OF LIBERTY (25:23–24)

These verses articulate the rationale for the jubilee laws that preceded, and they set the stage for the ones that are to follow: The land, like the people (see also v. 55), belongs exclusively to God. People's claim to the land and to each other cannot supersede God's claim. The jubilee's laws of redemption are an expression of God's ultimate ownership of the land (and of the people).

### LAWS PROTECTING ISRAELITES FROM PERMANENT POVERTY AND SERVITUDE (25:25–54)

Jubilee regulations stipulate both the return of land and the release of Israelites who were indentured on account of insolvency. The laws in this section apply to persons compelled to sell their land, home, and persons—three related stages of decline into poverty. Initial responsibility to help falls on relatives of the impoverished seller. If they do not do so, chances are that the seller will fall victim to further stages of destitution. The laws that follow aim to prevent the decline from becoming irreversible.

#### *Laws to Protect Land Holdings* (25:25–28)

Once the ancient Israelites are established in the Land of Israel, they live in an agricultural society—in which land equals life. Selling a portion of one's inherited holding would mean giving up a vital source of livelihood, because most Israelites are members of farm families that depend on the land's produce. Such a sale would be a first step in the slippery slope toward potential destitution. Jubilee laws presume that agricultural land holdings are inalienable: they belong to God, who gave each one to a particular Israelite clan in perpetuity.

*25. **If one of your kin.*** Verses 48–49 list genealogical relationships from nearest to the more distant. Generally speaking, kinship ties in the Bible include female as well as male relations. For example, Jacob goes to the family of his mother Rebekah to escape his brother's wrath (Genesis 28; see further at Genesis 10:1). Leviticus 25, however, seems to extend the notion of kinship to embrace the entire Israelite community.

***redeemer.*** Heb. *goel,* meaning a family member with means, who is obligated to "bail out" destitute relatives. Since Leviticus 25 extends the notion of kinship, it fundamentally makes all members of the Israelite community responsible for the economic welfare of the disadvantaged. The book of Ruth illustrates a redemption process: Boaz, a relative of impoverished Naomi, informs a closer relative that Naomi had sold or is selling land. Boaz invites the other man to redeem the land, though he proposes to redeem it himself if this potential redeemer does not (4:1–12). The land is presumably expected to revert back to Naomi's (or Ruth's) heir, which may explain why the less affluent relative lets wealthy Boaz acquire the land. It is noteworthy that Naomi sells the land but that Boaz negotiates on her behalf.

acquires enough to redeem with, 27 the years since its sale shall be computed and the difference shall be refunded to the person to whom it was sold, so that the person returns to that holding. 28 If that person lacks sufficient means to recover it, what was sold shall remain with the purchaser until the jubilee; in the jubilee year it shall be released, so that the person returns to that holding.

29 If someone sells a dwelling house in a walled city, it may be redeemed until a year has elapsed since its sale; the redemption period shall be a year. 30 If it is not redeemed before a full year has elapsed, the house in the walled city shall pass to the purchaser beyond reclaim throughout the ages; it shall not be released in the jubilee. 31 But houses in villages that have no encircling walls shall be classed as open country: they may be redeemed, and they shall be released through the jubilee. 32 As for the cities of Levi, the houses in the cities it holds: Levi shall forever have the right of redemption. 33 Such property as may be redeemed from Levi—houses sold in a city it holds—shall be released through the jubilee; for the houses in the cities of Levi are its holding among the Israelites. 34 But the unenclosed land about its cities cannot be sold, for that is its holding for all time.

יָדוֹ וּמָצָא כְּדֵי גְאֻלָּתוֹ׃ 27 וְחִשַּׁב אֶת־שְׁנֵי
מִמְכָּרוֹ וְהֵשִׁיב אֶת־הָעֹדֵף לָאִישׁ אֲשֶׁר
מָכַר־לוֹ וְשָׁב לַאֲחֻזָּתוֹ׃ 28 וְאִם לֹא־מָצְאָה
יָדוֹ דֵּי הָשִׁיב לוֹ וְהָיָה מִמְכָּרוֹ בְּיַד הַקֹּנֶה
אֹתוֹ עַד שְׁנַת הַיּוֹבֵל וְיָצָא בַּיֹּבֵל וְשָׁב
לַאֲחֻזָּתוֹ׃
29 וְאִישׁ כִּי־יִמְכֹּר בֵּית־מוֹשַׁב עִיר חוֹמָה
וְהָיְתָה גְּאֻלָּתוֹ עַד־תֹּם שְׁנַת מִמְכָּרוֹ יָמִים
תִּהְיֶה גְאֻלָּתוֹ׃ 30 וְאִם לֹא־יִגָּאֵל עַד־
מְלֹאת לוֹ שָׁנָה תְמִימָה וְקָם הַבַּיִת אֲשֶׁר־
בָּעִיר אֲשֶׁר־לא לוֹ חֹמָה לַצְּמִיתֻת לַקֹּנֶה
אֹתוֹ לְדֹרֹתָיו לֹא יֵצֵא בַּיֹּבֵל׃ 31 וּבָתֵּי
הַחֲצֵרִים אֲשֶׁר אֵין־לָהֶם חֹמָה סָבִיב עַל־
שְׂדֵה הָאָרֶץ יֵחָשֵׁב גְּאֻלָּה תִּהְיֶה־לּוֹ וּבַיֹּבֵל
יֵצֵא׃ 32 וְעָרֵי הַלְוִיִּם בָּתֵּי עָרֵי אֲחֻזָּתָם
גְּאֻלַּת עוֹלָם תִּהְיֶה לַלְוִיִּם׃ 33 וַאֲשֶׁר יִגְאַל
מִן־הַלְוִיִּם וְיָצָא מִמְכַּר־בַּיִת וְעִיר אֲחֻזָּתוֹ
בַּיֹּבֵל כִּי בָתֵּי עָרֵי הַלְוִיִּם הִוא אֲחֻזָּתָם
בְּתוֹךְ בְּנֵי יִשְׂרָאֵל׃ 34 וּשְׂדֵה מִגְרַשׁ עָרֵיהֶם
לֹא יִמָּכֵר כִּי־אֲחֻזַּת עוֹלָם הוּא לָהֶם׃ ס

*27–28.* The original owner has the right to redeem the holding at any point. If that does not happen, the holding reverts back to the original owner in the jubilee year. The price for redeeming the land early must be computed fairly, taking into account the value that the buyer already received and the number of harvests (years) to the next jubilee.

*Laws to Protect Homes* (25:29–34)

Loss of a home through foreclosure or sale represents the next step in the economic decline. Nehemiah 5:1–5 describes persons mortgaging their fields and homes in order to get food—and even losing them due to insolvency. The laws of jubilee seek to enable persons to repossess their homes.

*29–31.* Leviticus 25 reflects the different economic realities of urban and rural communities. Urban dwellings are not as protected by jubilee laws and do not revert back to the owner. They can, however, be redeemed within a year. Possibly these dwellings were not perceived as integral to a person's work.

*32–34.* This is the only mention of Levites in the book of Leviticus. The Levites function as sanctuary personnel for all Israelites and therefore do not have their own tribal land. Instead, they receive 48 towns scattered among other tribe's portions (see Numbers 35:1–18). Their urban holdings are therefore inalienable (like farm holdings), remaining theirs in perpetuity.

[35]If your kin, being in straits, come under your
authority, and are held by you as though resident
aliens, let them live by your side: [36]do not exact
advance or accrued interest, but fear your God. Let

35 וְכִֽי־יָמ֣וּךְ אָחִ֔יךָ וּמָ֥טָה יָד֖וֹ עִמָּ֑ךְ וְהֶחֱזַ֣קְתָּ
בּ֔וֹ גֵּ֧ר וְתוֹשָׁ֛ב וָחַ֖י עִמָּֽךְ׃ 36 אַל־תִּקַּ֤ח מֵֽאִתּוֹ֙
נֶ֣שֶׁךְ וְתַרְבִּ֔ית וְיָרֵ֖אתָ מֵֽאֱלֹהֶ֑יךָ וְחֵ֥י אָחִ֖יךָ

## *Laws to Protect Israelites from Debt-Slavery* (25:35–54)

Debt-slavery represents the most severe consequence of insolvency. Some biblical evidence suggests that daughters may have been especially vulnerable to being used as indentured labor for the household's debts (see at Exodus 21:7–11). Thus indenture may have been particularly unfortunate for nubile females, whose virginity (and thus marriageability) may have been at risk in an indentured context. At the same time, it is possible that children benefited from access to food in the more affluent household to which they were indentured.

Several laws in the Torah seek to regulate and ameliorate the conditions of Israelite debt-slaves. Exodus 21:2–11 and Deuteronomy 15:12–18 demand the release of slaves in the seventh year, and Deuteronomy 15:1–3 requires canceling debts in the seventh year. These laws stand in tension with Leviticus 25, which mentions mandatory release only in the fiftieth year.

Some scholars attempt to account for the inconsistency by claiming that Exodus and Deuteronomy refer to selling a *dependent* member of the household, whereas Leviticus 25 pertains to the head of the household (so Gregory C. Chirichigno, *Debt-Slavery in Israel and the Ancient Near East*, 1993, pp. 352–54). More likely, however, the tradition preserves diverse perspectives in the attempt to cope with complex issues and changing circumstances.

*35–46.* The Hebrew that refers to impoverished kin is couched mostly in the singular. To reflect the gender-inclusive sense here, the present translation extends the plural language of the summary statement in v. 42 to the rest of the passage, as needed.

*35–38.* These laws attempt to protect Israelites from irreversible poverty by prohibiting Israelites from charging interest on loans to other Israelites in distress.

*35. If your kin.* Scholars debate whether the reference pertains only to a blood relative or extends to any member of the Israelite community.

***let them live by your side.*** Immediate relatives are urged to support the poor member of the family. A 21st-century analogy might be finding the person a job in one's own business so as to prevent homelessness and starvation.

*36.* A drought, a bad harvest, or an illness might force a farmer to seek loans. To help prevent decline into irreversible poverty, these verses permit only interest-free loans to fellow Israelites (a practice that is still maintained today through the "Hebrew Free Loan" associations). Ancient Mesopotamian documents show interest rates for loans of money, seed, or food as high as 60 percent. Such rates would make repayment impossible and push the debtor deeper into destitution.

***do not exact.*** Israelite lenders may not take advantage of the economically vulnerable members of the community when misfortune strikes.

***advance . . . interest.*** That is, taking a "bite"—a discount—from the loan. (The Hebrew for "advance" relates to the verb for "bite.") See also Deuteronomy 23:20–21 (but unlike Deuteronomy 15, Leviticus does not mention cancellation of debt). The prohibition also applies to confiscating a pledge (person or property) when the loan is delinquent. The book of Kings mentions a widow who begs the prophet Elisha to help her: "a creditor is coming to take away my two sons to be his slaves" (II Kings 4:1; Elisha provides a miraculous source of oil, which enables her to pay off the creditor and keep her family intact, 4:7).

your kin live by your side as such. 37 Do not lend
your money at advance interest, nor give your food
at accrued interest. 38 I יהוה am your God, who
brought you out of the land of Egypt, to give you
the land of Canaan, to be your God.

39 If your kin under you continue in straits and
must be given over to you, do not subject them to
the treatment of a slave. 40 Remaining with you as a
hired or bound laborer, they shall serve with you
only until the jubilee year. 41 Then they, along with
any children, shall be free of your authority; they
shall go back to their family and return to the ancestral holding.—42 For they are My servants, whom I
freed from the land of Egypt; they may not give

עִמָּֽךְ׃ 37 אֶת־כַּסְפְּךָ לֹא־תִתֵּן לוֹ בְּנֶשֶׁךְ
וּבְמַרְבִּית לֹא־תִתֵּן אָכְלֶךָ׃ 38 אֲנִי יְהוָה
אֱלֹהֵיכֶם אֲשֶׁר־הוֹצֵאתִי אֶתְכֶם מֵאֶרֶץ
מִצְרָיִם לָתֵת לָכֶם אֶת־אֶרֶץ כְּנַעַן לִהְיוֹת
לָכֶם לֵאלֹהִים׃ ס

39 וְכִי־יָמוּךְ אָחִיךָ עִמָּךְ וְנִמְכַּר־לָךְ לֹא־
תַעֲבֹד בּוֹ עֲבֹדַת עָבֶד׃ 40 כְּשָׂכִיר כְּתוֹשָׁב
יִהְיֶה עִמָּךְ עַד־שְׁנַת הַיֹּבֵל יַעֲבֹד עִמָּךְ׃
41 וְיָצָא מֵעִמָּךְ הוּא וּבָנָיו עִמּוֹ וְשָׁב אֶל־
מִשְׁפַּחְתּוֹ וְאֶל־אֲחֻזַּת אֲבֹתָיו יָשׁוּב׃ 42 כִּי־
עֲבָדַי הֵם אֲשֶׁר־הוֹצֵאתִי אֹתָם מֵאֶרֶץ

*39–43.* These verses address the next stage of economic decline: insolvency that forces persons into debt-servitude. The children of the widow in II Kings 4:1 (see previous comment) are subject to such servitude. Likewise, Nehemiah 5 describes the predicament of Judeans in the 5th century B.C.E.: "There was a great outcry by the common people and their wives against their fellow Jews. Some said, 'Our sons and daughters are numerous; we must get grain to eat in order that we may live!' Others said, 'We must pawn our fields, our vineyards, and our homes to get grain to stave off hunger.' Yet others said, 'We have borrowed money against our fields . . . we are subjecting our sons and daughters to slavery—some of our daughters are already subjected—and we are powerless'" (Nehemiah 5:1–5). For insight into the complex circumstances of women slaves, see also at Leviticus 19:20–22 and Exodus 21:7–11.

Indentured Israelites must be treated as day laborers or hired hands, not as slaves. Chirichigno, basing his view on Mesopotamian laws, suggests that this includes providing them with housing and fair allowances (*Debt-Slavery*, p. 343).

***40. until the jubilee year.*** Unlike Exodus 21 and Deuteronomy 15, Leviticus does not mention slaves' release in the seventh year but only in the jubilee year. The fiftieth year is part of the national calendar. According to this law, one who begins service in the forty-sixth year of the jubilee's cycle would be released less than four years later.

***41. they, along with any children.*** The Hebrew uses masculine language (which, in its most restricted sense, means "he and his sons with him"), raising the question whether wives and other female members of the family are to receive their freedom (see Another View, p. 760). Presumably a daughter, if she became sexually attached to a man in the "owner's" house, did not have the option of release; however, she might have other legal protections (see at Exodus 21:7–11). In Jeremiah 34:12–16, a law about slavery formulated in masculine language explicitly applies to women as well as men. (That passage describes the release of slave women and men in a time of siege. Jeremiah also notes, however, that these released slaves are repossessed shortly after, and he condemns the repossession as profaning God's name.) Here, too, there is no reason to exclude women from view; war, famine, plague, and the like could easily put women in the position of becoming debt-slaves if they (or their husbands) suddenly found themselves without the normal protection of a household or clan and its access to land. To convey the gender-inclusive sense of the Hebrew wording, the translation here uses plural language.

themselves over into servitude.—43You shall not
rule over them ruthlessly; you shall fear your God.
44Such male and female slaves as you may have—it
is from the nations round about you that you may
acquire male and female slaves. 45You may also buy
them from among the children of aliens resident
among you, or from their families that are among
you, whom they begot in your land. These shall become your property: 46you may keep them as a possession for your children after you, for them to inherit as property for all time. Such you may treat as
slaves. But as for your Israelite kin, no one shall rule
ruthlessly over another.

47If a resident alien among you has prospered,
and your kin, being in straits, comes under that
one's authority and is given over to the resident
alien among you, or to an offshoot of an alien's

מִצְרָ֑יִם לֹ֥א יִמָּכְר֖וּ מִמְכֶּ֥רֶת עָֽבֶד׃ 43 לֹא־
תִרְדֶּ֥ה ב֖וֹ בְּפָ֑רֶךְ וְיָרֵ֖אתָ מֵאֱלֹהֶֽיךָ׃ 44 וְעַבְדְּךָ֥
וַאֲמָתְךָ֖ אֲשֶׁ֣ר יִהְיוּ־לָ֑ךְ מֵאֵ֣ת הַגּוֹיִ֗ם אֲשֶׁר֙
סְבִיבֹ֣תֵיכֶ֔ם מֵהֶ֥ם תִּקְנ֖וּ עֶ֥בֶד וְאָמָֽה׃ 45 וְגַ֡ם
מִבְּנֵי֩ הַתּוֹשָׁבִ֨ים הַגָּרִ֤ים עִמָּכֶם֙ מֵהֶ֣ם
תִּקְנ֔וּ וּמִמִּשְׁפַּחְתָּם֙ אֲשֶׁ֣ר עִמָּכֶ֔ם אֲשֶׁ֥ר
הוֹלִ֖ידוּ בְּאַרְצְכֶ֑ם וְהָי֥וּ לָכֶ֖ם לַאֲחֻזָּֽה׃
46 וְהִתְנַחַלְתֶּ֨ם אֹתָ֜ם לִבְנֵיכֶ֤ם אַחֲרֵיכֶם֙
לָרֶ֣שֶׁת אֲחֻזָּ֔ה לְעֹלָ֖ם בָּהֶ֣ם תַּעֲבֹ֑דוּ
וּבְאַ֨חֵיכֶ֤ם בְּנֵֽי־יִשְׂרָאֵל֙ אִ֣ישׁ בְּאָחִ֔יו לֹֽא־
תִרְדֶּ֥ה ב֖וֹ בְּפָֽרֶךְ׃ ס
47 וְכִ֣י תַשִּׂ֗יג יַ֣ד גֵּ֤ר וְתוֹשָׁב֙ עִמָּ֔ךְ וּמָ֥ךְ אָחִ֖יךָ
עִמּ֑וֹ וְנִמְכַּ֗ר לְגֵ֤ר תּוֹשָׁב֙ עִמָּ֔ךְ א֥וֹ לְעֵ֖קֶר

*43.* ***ruthlessly.*** The same Hebrew word describes the abuse that the Israelites suffered in Egypt (Exodus 1:13). They are not to perpetuate such oppression.

*44–46.* Indentured foreign females and males do not go free. When sold into slavery, foreigners become the Israelites' possession "for all time" (v. 46). This harsh ruling contradicts other laws in Leviticus that specify an identical law for the Israelite, the foreigner, and the resident alien (as 24:22 states: "you shall have one standard for stranger and citizen alike"; see also Exodus 12:49 and Numbers 15:16). Later rabbinic traditions attempt to ameliorate this legislation by interpreting "for all time" to mean "until the jubilee year," but such a generous reading contradicts the plain sense of this passage.

*44.* ***male and female slaves.*** This is the second place in this parashah that mentions women explicitly (see also females slaves in vv. 6–7). The specification of females at this juncture may serve to emphasize that there is no special treatment for women slaves when they are foreign (whereas other biblical laws such as Exodus 21:2–11 do distinguish between the fate of female and male slaves). Verse 46 makes it clear that a foreign female (or male) slave was to have no automatic chance of regaining freedom. | The term for "female slave," *amah*, is best translated as "handmaid" because *amah* also refers to the forearm (and, like "foot" in English, also functions as a measuring unit—namely, in this case, the cubit). Sarah refers to Hagar the Egyptian as *amah* when she demands her expulsion (Genesis 21:10), and both Bilhah and Zilpah receive this title on occasion (see Genesis 30:3), although the more common term for all three women is *shifchah*. Free women can use *amah* to express deference, as when Ruth the Moabite calls herself an *amah* when addressing Boaz in Ruth 3:9.

*47–54.* A family member must redeem an Israelite whom a resident alien purchases or seizes to cover a debt. The price of redemption is to be determined fairly on the basis of expected years of servitude until the year of the jubilee. These laws apply only within Israelite settlements in the Land of Israel. The Bible meanwhile includes some stories about Israelite slaves in non-Israelite households outside the land. One such anecdote in II Kings 5:1–4 mentions a young Israelite slave girl (a war

family, [48][your kin] shall have the right of redemption even after having been given over. [Typically,] a brother shall do the redeeming, [49]or an uncle or an uncle's son shall do the redeeming—anyone in the family who is of the same flesh shall do the redeeming; or, having prospered, [your formerly impoverished kin] may do the redeeming. [50]The total shall be computed with the purchaser as from the year of being given over to the other until the jubilee year; the price of sale shall be applied to the number of years, as though it were for a term as a hired laborer under the other's authority. [51]If many years remain, [your kin] shall pay back for the redemption in proportion to the purchase price; [52]and if few years remain until the jubilee year, so shall it be computed: payment shall be made for the redemption according to the years involved. [53]One shall be under the other's authority as a laborer hired by the year; the other shall not rule ruthlessly in your sight. [54]If not redeemed in any of those ways, that person, along with any children, shall go free in the jubilee year. [55]For it is to Me that the

מִשְׁפַּחַת גֵּר׃ 48 אַחֲרֵי נִמְכַּר גְּאֻלָּה תִּהְיֶה־
לּוֹ אֶחָד מֵאֶחָיו יִגְאָלֶנּוּ׃ 49 אוֹ־דֹדוֹ אוֹ בֶן־
דֹּדוֹ יִגְאָלֶנּוּ אוֹ־מִשְּׁאֵר בְּשָׂרוֹ מִמִּשְׁפַּחְתּוֹ
יִגְאָלֶנּוּ אוֹ־הִשִּׂיגָה יָדוֹ וְנִגְאָל׃ 50 וְחִשַּׁב
עִם־קֹנֵהוּ מִשְּׁנַת הִמָּכְרוֹ לוֹ עַד שְׁנַת
הַיֹּבֵל וְהָיָה כֶּסֶף מִמְכָּרוֹ בְּמִסְפַּר שָׁנִים
כִּימֵי שָׂכִיר יִהְיֶה עִמּוֹ׃ 51 אִם־עוֹד רַבּוֹת
בַּשָּׁנִים לְפִיהֶן יָשִׁיב גְּאֻלָּתוֹ מִכֶּסֶף
מִקְנָתוֹ׃ 52 וְאִם־מְעַט נִשְׁאַר בַּשָּׁנִים עַד־
שְׁנַת הַיֹּבֵל וְחִשַּׁב־לוֹ כְּפִי שָׁנָיו יָשִׁיב
אֶת־גְּאֻלָּתוֹ׃ 53 כִּשְׂכִיר שָׁנָה בְּשָׁנָה יִהְיֶה
עִמּוֹ לֹא־יִרְדֶּנּוּ בְּפֶרֶךְ לְעֵינֶיךָ׃ 54 וְאִם־לֹא
יִגָּאֵל בְּאֵלֶּה וְיָצָא בִּשְׁנַת הַיֹּבֵל הוּא
וּבָנָיו עִמּוֹ׃ 55 כִּי־לִי בְנֵי־יִשְׂרָאֵל עֲבָדִים

captive) serving a household in a neighboring country. Seeing that her mistress's husband—the general Naaman—had contracted a skin disease (*tzaraat*), the Israelite slave girl informs the wife that a prophet in Israel could cure the husband. Grace Aguilar, the English Jewish poet, novelist, and theologian (1817–1847), claimed that this story was proof that even a young slave girl in biblical times knew about her "Jewish" tradition and resources. Aguilar used this story to campaign for extending Jewish education to women in her own time.

*48. right of redemption.* Implicitly, the foreign owner cannot reject an offer of redemption.

*48–49. [Typically,] a brother . . . or an uncle . . . anyone in the family.* The line of kinship bond of those who must redeem an indentured Israelite extends to all blood relatives.

*49. same flesh.* From how Leviticus 21:2–4 defines this term, we can suppose that the line of potential redeemers here includes mothers, sisters, and daughters.

*50–51.* The redeemer must offer a fair price. The redeemed is obligated to repay the redeemer and can do so by working for the redeemer as a hired hand until the year of the jubilee.

*53. ruthlessly.* See at v. 43.

## *Conclusion*

### GOD'S OWNERSHIP OF THE ISRAELITES AS BASIS FOR JUBILEE LAWS (25:55–26:2)

The conclusion of the parashah expresses the theological or religious underpinning of the jubilee and slavery legislation: Israelites are God's servants and therefore may not belong to others. In keeping God's sabbaths, both people and land experience the freedom that service to God entails.

Israelites are servants: they are My servants, whom I freed from the land of Egypt, I your God יהוה.

עֲבָדַי הֵם אֲשֶׁר־הוֹצֵאתִי אוֹתָם מֵאֶרֶץ
מִצְרָיִם אֲנִי יְהוָה אֱלֹהֵיכֶם׃

26 You shall not make idols for yourselves, or
set up for yourselves carved images or pillars, or
place figured stones in your land to worship upon,
for I יהוה am your God. [2]You shall keep My sabbaths and venerate My sanctuary, Mine, יהוה's.

כו לֹא־תַעֲשׂוּ לָכֶם אֱלִילִם וּפֶסֶל וּמַצֵּבָה
לֹא־תָקִימוּ לָכֶם וְאֶבֶן מַשְׂכִּית לֹא תִתְּנוּ
בְּאַרְצְכֶם לְהִשְׁתַּחֲוֺת עָלֶיהָ כִּי אֲנִי יְהוָה
אֱלֹהֵיכֶם׃ 2 אֶת־שַׁבְּתֹתַי תִּשְׁמֹרוּ וּמִקְדָּשִׁי
תִּירָאוּ אֲנִי יְהוָה׃ פ

*55. My servants.* Heb. *avadim* (*eved* in the singular) can refer variously to servants, slaves, and worshippers. In the Torah, the difference between servitude and freedom depends on whom one serves. God instructed Moses to tell Pharaoh not merely "Let My people go!" but "Let My people go so that they may *serve* Me!" (Exodus 7:16). Significantly, many editions translate the verb *e-v-d* in Exodus 7:16 and elsewhere as "worship," which highlights the nuanced ways in which that verb functions.

*26:2. My sabbaths.* In Deuteronomy 5:15, the purpose of the Sabbath is to enable female and male slaves to rest because "you were a slave in the land of Egypt." The entire jubilee system is rooted in the multiple ways in which the observance of the Sabbath is to be implemented.

***venerate My sanctuary.*** In the context of this parashah, the sanctuary appears to include not only the Tabernacle but also the Land of Israel and the people of Israel. (See also at 26:11.)

—*Tamara Cohn Eskenazi*
*Jocelyn Hudson*

# Another View

THE BIBLICAL SYSTEM of a jubilee year has been described as utopian in its vision, promoting a system whereby lands sold under financial distress would be returned to the original owners every fifty years. Under this system, there are checks and balances ensuring a redistribution of wealth at set intervals. This is indeed a utopian vision, grounded both in the religious belief that only God owns the land and people are but tenants on it, and in the socio-economic vision of a remission of debts at set periods.

One would like to think that if this legislation had been in force during some period in history, it would have had a beneficial impact on women and other vulnerable members of society. However, the text does not seem to address many questions regarding the status of women under this system. For example, Leviticus 25:41 uses only grammatically masculine language and male terms to refer to an Israelite who becomes the debt-slave of a fellow Israelite. The text forbids that individual from being treated as a (non-Israelite) slave. The text literally reads that at the year of the jubilee, "he and his children with him shall be free" (25:41). Where is the wife? Commentators often argue that she must be included here, but it is striking that she is missing. According to Exodus 21:2–6, a male Hebrew slave is released after six years of service, but a female slave apparently remains with her master forever—presumably, according to some interpreters, because she has become the sexual property of the owner (21:7–11). The law in Exodus 21, in conjunction with the absence of women in the jubilee laws, prompts disturbing questions.

Similarly, Leviticus 25:47–49 spells out the order of kinsfolk who are required to redeem relatives sold

> *Would this legislation have had a beneficial impact on women?*

to non-Israelites. The order begins with brothers, uncles, and then male cousins. Again the text is silent on women, suggesting that only men were active participants in this utopian vision of release from servitude and reclamation of ancestral lands.

However, a close reading of the text, along with a study of other sources, demonstrates that despite the seeming omission of women in this account, women were in fact recognized as active participants in all these cases. Jeremiah 34 mentions the release of women slaves; and Numbers 27 and 36 show that women could own land and thus have resources to redeem relatives.

—*S. Tamar Kamionkowski*

# Post-biblical Interpretations

***you shall not wrong one another… Do not wrong one another, but fear your God*** (25:14, 17). The discussion of this passage in the midrash collection *Sifra* leads us to one of the most important passages in rabbinic literature, one in which women play central roles. The Rabbis explain the apparent repetition of the command not to oppress one's neighbor as follows: Each verse speaks of a different kind of oppression; the oppression of v. 14 is economic oppression, while that in v. 17 is inflicted psychologically. The Tosefta repeats this interpretation in *Bava M'tzia* 3:25–29, and the Talmud deeply explores the issues in BT *Bava M'tzia* 58b–60b. There we learn how important feelings are, and how critical it is for us not to hurt them. According to the Rabbis, the archetypal example of someone who preferred death to hurting another person's feelings is Tamar (Genesis 38). The Rabbis maintain that rather than shame her father-in-law in public, she was willing to be burned to death. We then learn that it is especially important not to distress one's wife (BT *Bava M'tzia* 59a and subsequently in *Shulchan Aruch, Choshen Mishpat* 228:3). A husband can easily wound his wife's feelings because she is close to him, and he also has many opportunities to hurt her. He must therefore take proportionately more care not to do so. We learn, too, of the counter-example of Rav's difficult marriage. Rav asserted that anyone who followed his wife's advice would descend into *Geihinom* (the place of eternal punishment). When we examine a description of his married life, we can see why he might say this. His wife is said to have constantly tormented him and contradicted his smallest wish (BT *Y'vamot* 63a). Of course, this androcentric text does not consider how Rav's treatment of his spouse may have contributed to such behavior.

*This discussion leads to one of the most important passages in rabbinic literature.*

Rav Pappa seems to have had a good marriage, since he quotes the folk saying that if one's wife is short, one should bend down and listen to her opinion. Other teachings are likewise designed to increase marital harmony. One such teaching urges that grain always be available in the home, as lack of food is often the cause of marital strife. We learn, too, that a husband should be careful to honor his wife more than he honors himself. He should show this by dressing her in better clothes than he himself wears (BT *Bava M'tzia* 59a and subsequently in *Mishneh Torah, Sefer Nashim, Hilchot Ishut* 15:19). In the same passage, Rav Helbo asserts that blessings are found in a man's house only on account of his wife; and Rava opines that honoring one's wife is the road to wealth.

What follows is one of the most famous legends in all of rabbinic literature. It appears in BT *Bava M'tzia* 59b and concerns Rabbi Eliezer and his wife, Imma Shalom (which means "Mother of Peace"). Imma Shalom came from a distinguished family of Davidic heritage. Her brother was Rabban Gamliel, who, at that time, presided over the academy in which her husband, Rabbi Eliezer, was one of the greatest sages. Her husband had a strong disagreement of opinion with the rest of the academy. When they would not accept his opinion he brought all sorts of supernatural proofs that his was the correct view. Even a voice out of heaven was summoned, which duly testified that he was, in fact, right. At this, Rabbi Yehoshua, Rabbi Eliezer's study partner, stood up and said, "The Torah is no longer in heaven" (Deuteronomy 30:12). In other words, we decide law and practice here on earth and do not take heavenly voices into account. Finally, Rabban Gamliel expelled Rabbi Eliezer from the academy, and he was excommunicated. Imma Shalom, knowing what harm her husband could do out of the pain of his humiliation, kept watch on Rabbi Eliezer day and night, so that he would not have the opportunity to pray for Rabban Gamliel's death. One day her attention was diverted, and she saw afterward that Rabbi Eliezer was prostrated on the ground, supplicating God for succor from his hurt feelings. Seeing this, she said, "Rise. You have killed my brother!" At that moment a shofar blast was heard, signaling that Rabban Gamliel had died. Rabbi Eliezer then asked his wife, "How did you know my prayer worked, and I had killed him?" She replied, quoting learning as easily and with as much authority as her husband, "I learned it from my grandfather's house: All the gates of heaven are locked except for the gates of hurt feelings."

—*Judith Z. Abrams*

# Contemporary Reflection

In parashat B'har, God declares to Moses that the land is a sacred trust and commands the people to observe periods of comprehensive release. This parashah invites us to consider how, in each generation, we can best serve as guarantors of this trust, respect the duty to rest ourselves and our natural resources, and experience "release." The legislation in *B'har* presumes the value of balance and regulates a balance among productivity, rest, and relinquishment. Inasmuch as punctuating productivity with long pauses lends perspective to life and encourages us to express gratitude for the earth's bounty, we may wonder what regulations we require today to help us nurture ourselves, one another, and the planet. As women join men in leadership positions and in the work force, it is becoming a Jewish communal priority to effect social and institutional adjustments that allow for a healthy balance between people's needs and obligations.

*B'har* affirms that the land belongs to God, and it must be permitted to observe its Sabbaths. The sensibility that the Land of Israel has a responsibility all its own to the Creator recognizes nature's independence from humanity. The land must be permitted, just like human servants, to praise creation through Shabbat. In the psalmist's words: *kol han'shamah t'halel Yah*, "All that breathes praises God" (Psalm 150). The earth must speak its own gratitude.

In the Torah, the earth is an expressive organism. We read that when Miriam died, "the community was without water" (Numbers 20:2). Observing, as it were, its mourning for a heroine whose miracles were all associated with water, the earth dries up. To hear the speech of the earth is a blessing; but if we do not listen, the consequences of our deafness to the planet are traumatic. The ecology movement reminds us of what our biblical forebears understood: the independent consciousness of nature.

Nature's independence is trumpeted on Yom Kippur after a fifty-year countdown. This is when we must (as the Liberty Bell translates the verse) "proclaim Liberty throughout all the land unto all the inhabitants thereof" (Leviticus 25:10). We more closely translate *dror* ("Liberty") as a proclamation of "release," a letting go. Counting toward release, we can celebrate release—or we can live in fear of it. And so the liturgy tells us *limnot yameinu*, to count our days (Psalm 90:12), by which we are meant to understand that since our days are numbered, the trick is to make them count. Our duty is not to scramble tirelessly, but to be grateful and generous, to assume our small place in creation, and to join the trees in praise. Underlying the laws of *B'har* is an obligation to take care of each other, to leave no one homeless: "Do not wrong one another, but fear your God" (Leviticus 25:17).

*We must seek a balanced definition of adulthood, with sabbatical and jubilation.*

The laws of the sabbatical year echo biblical Creation. The rhythm of the work week undergoes a cosmic magnification: people, imitating the Creator, are productive for six days and then rest. Nature is productive for six years and rests; and then geometrically, after the land has maintained this rhythm for seven cycles of seven: jubilee. The *yovel*, the jubilee, is a call to restore primal order: indentured servants are freed, debts are forgiven, and property is restored to its original owners. Here is a caution against struggling to amass more, and against warring over real estate—reminding us that all things are, eventually, released (one way or another) from our possession and control. After the divine promise to Noah that humanity would never again be destroyed by flood, God devises the jubilee as a peaceful strategy for restoring the world to its original state.

Appreciating that freedom must be learned, a midrash teaches that the Israelites wandered in desert circles for forty years to make the short trip from Egypt to Canaan because it took that long for the slave population to learn how to manage its freedom. Today, it behooves us to reflect on the substantial gains of the women's movement and admit that, as *B'har* teaches, we suffer the consequences of depletion if we do not adequately regulate our hard-won freedoms. Not only do many of us live unbalanced lives, but schools and charities have not corrected for the absence of an earlier generation of volunteer women, to the detriment of children and the poor. Society needs to effect adjustments so as to make two-career families more viable; and we risk perpetuating conditions of stress at work and home if we do not emphasize to rising generations the need to change existing institutional structures and correct continued gender inequities. One wonders whether, in the years since the onset of the contemporary women's movement, we have been panting from exertion without having paused often enough to ask about the meaning of life. High-achieving adolescents too often suffer from depression, and teenage girls suffer from diminished self-worth. Perhaps we have been communicating an unbalanced definition of adulthood—adulthood without sabbatical and jubilation.

The land, our possessions, our bodies, our children, and we ourselves are a sacred trust, and it is not our right to be infinitely demanding on them. We are commanded to rest, not when we are exhausted or having a breakdown, but regularly, as we count the days to *Shabbat*, to the seven years to the land's sabbatical, and to the forty-nine years to the releases of jubilee.

Organizations such as Ma'yan: The Jewish Women's Project (at the JCC in Manhattan) and Advancing Women Professionals and the Jewish Community (AWP, founded by Shifra Bronznick) are addressing unhealthy patterns by exploring how to create humane workplaces that foster living balanced lives. Projects like these articulate demands for institutional change and new regulations that honor the spirit that informs *parashat B'har.*

*—Lori Lefkovitz*

# Voices

## Childhood in the Shtetl

Golda Meir

*Leviticus 25:25–28*

There was never enough of anything, not food, not warm clothing, not heat at home. I was always a little too cold outside and a little too empty inside. Even now, from that very distant past, I can summon up with no effort at all, almost intact, the picture of myself sitting in tears in the kitchen, watching my mother feed some of the gruel that rightfully belonged to me to my younger sister, Zipke. Gruel was a great luxury in our home in those days, and I bitterly resented having to share any of it, even with the baby. Years later I was to experience the dread of my own children's hunger and to learn for myself what it is like to have to decide which child is to receive more food, but, of course, in that kitchen in Kiev, I knew only that life was hard and that there was no justice anywhere. I am glad that no one told me then that my older sister, Sheyna, often fainted from hunger in school.

## The First Wriggle

Elaine Feinstein

*Leviticus 25:10*

Going to buy milk from the corner shop
on a Tuesday in August with the warm rain
tasting of roses, I suddenly felt an illicit
moment of good fortune: a freedom

in which poems could happen.
It's rather like the grander forms of creation.
Worms on Mars should surprise nobody;
life will form, wherever there's opportunity.

## At Blue Dawn II

Kadya Molodowsky (transl. Kathryn Hellerstein)

*Leviticus 25:25–28*

For what I own there is no weight or measure.
Strewn on streets, unburied treasure,
It hides in all the crevices, in every crack.
Caresses by the thousands on my neck,
Kisses as hot as sunlight on my cheeks.
Bound up with fraying strings
And concealed at the corners of streets
Lie my tender heartbeats.
And dreams floating up from all
The beds at night in cities and towns
Beat their white and fragile wings
Against the hard brick wall.
For what I own there's no weight
Or measure.

## All the Winds

Rachel Korn (transl. Marcia Falk)

*Leviticus 25:25–55*

All the winds have grown still
as though someone rocked them softly to sleep
between naked branches of the trees
on a rainy autumn night.

All the sorrows have made their home
at my doorstep, as though—in all the world—
they had no other harbor
but my eyes, my hands, my smile, my word.

# בחקתי ✦ B'chukotai

## LEVITICUS 26:3–27:34

### *Ensuring Obedience to God, and the Sanctuary's Welfare*

PARASHAT B'CHUKOTAI ("my laws") concludes Leviticus, a book devoted to instructing the people of Israel how to conduct their lives in keeping with their status as God's people. The first part of the parashah seeks to ensure obedience to these instructions by providing strong motivation in the form of a series of blessings and curses. God, through Moses, promises the people prosperity and peace if they follow the path laid out by God; and God threatens them with famine, war, and eventually exile, if they choose to spurn God's laws and commandments (26:3–46). The second part of the parashah (27:1–34) is an appendix that addresses issues related to communal funding, especially of the priesthood and of the sanctuary.

Explicit information about women in these passages, while scant, does shed some additional light on their status and the nature of their household responsibilities in ancient Israel. Especially significant for our understanding of the status of women in this culture is the material in 27:3–7, which lists monetary equivalents for the worth of individuals whose services are vowed to the temple. Leviticus, we learn, bases these assessments and values on a combination of the factors of age and gender (see also Another View, p. 780).

In addition, the content of 27:1–25, which deals with vows and gifts of property to the temple, touches upon several other issues that relate to the lives of women in ancient Israel, such as whose vows were binding and under what conditions, who could partake in the priests' portion of sacrificial animals (a major source of food for priests and their households), and who could inherit and possess property. While Leviticus 27 does not directly deal with these issues, all of them are crucial for those wishing to understand the significance of the instruction in this text for women in ancient Israel.

*This parashah sheds light on women's status and responsibilities in ancient Israel.*

The explicit reference in 26:26 to women who bake bread further highlights the lives of women.

—*Hilary Lipka*

# *Outline*

*I.* Epilogue

*Ensuring Obedience to God* (26:3–46)

- *A.* Blessings for obedience (vv. 3–13)
- *B.* Curses for disobedience (vv. 14–45)
- *C.* Conclusion (v. 46)

*II.* Appendix

*The Sanctuary: Funding, Gifts, and Dues* (27:1–34)

- *A.* Votary pledges of people (vv. 1–8)
- *B.* Votary pledges of animals (vv. 9–13)
- *C.* Consecrations of property (vv. 14–25)
- *D.* Firstlings (vv. 26–27)
- *E.* Proscriptions (vv. 28–29)
- *F.* Tithes (vv. 30–33)
- *G.* Conclusion (v. 34)

26:3
If you follow My laws and faithfully observe My
commandments, 4 I will grant your rains in their
season, so that the earth shall yield its produce and
the trees of the field their fruit. 5 Your threshing
shall overtake the vintage, and your vintage shall
overtake the sowing; you shall eat your fill of bread
and dwell securely in your land.

כו 3 אִם־בְּחֻקֹּתַי תֵּלֵכוּ וְאֶת־מִצְוֺתַי
תִּשְׁמְרוּ וַעֲשִׂיתֶם אֹתָם׃ 4 וְנָתַתִּי גִשְׁמֵיכֶם
בְּעִתָּם וְנָתְנָה הָאָרֶץ יְבוּלָהּ וְעֵץ הַשָּׂדֶה
יִתֵּן פִּרְיוֹ׃ 5 וְהִשִּׂיג לָכֶם דַּיִשׁ אֶת־בָּצִיר
וּבָצִיר יַשִּׂיג אֶת־זָרַע וַאֲכַלְתֶּם לַחְמְכֶם
לָשֹׂבַע וִישַׁבְתֶּם לָבֶטַח בְּאַרְצְכֶם׃

## *Epilogue*

### ENSURING OBEDIENCE TO GOD (26:3–46)

The opening unit of the parashah presents an epilogue to the book of Leviticus as a whole. God addresses the Israelites who are about to enter the Promised Land, assuring them of great rewards if they follow God's instructions, and threatening them with a series of increasingly severe punishments if they disobey. The laws pertain to women and men together as a community. The rewards and the punishments are symmetrical: the punishments reverse each of the promised rewards via a contrasting threat. For example, a promise of fertility of the land (vv. 4–5 and 10) contrasts with the threat of a barren and fruitless land (vv. 16, 19–20). The symmetry, among other things, expresses a balanced and ordered universe, a theme that is important in priestly writings (see Genesis 1). These blessings and curses resemble those that conclude Deuteronomy's laws (Deuteronomy 28–30) and many ancient Near Eastern treaties. In all of these instances, the curses section tends to be much longer and more detailed than the blessings section, most likely to frighten the hearers into obedience through the threat of divine enforcement.

### BLESSINGS FOR OBEDIENCE (26:3–13)

The blessings that will be bestowed upon Israel if the people follow God's laws include: peace, prosperity, safety from wild beasts, fertility of both the people and the land, and victory over their enemies. God will uphold the covenant and reside in Israel's midst, ensuring that the people will flourish and prosper and be free from all oppression.

*4. **rains in their season.*** Survival in this agricultural economy depended on timely rain. Too much at the wrong time or too little devastated crops and resulted in famine. (See also Deuteronomy 11:11, 33:13.)

*5.* The blessing will consist of having such bountiful harvests that the harvesting season will last until the next planting season.

◗ The table of valuations in 27:2–8 provides evidence of a positive estimation of women.

ANOTHER VIEW ➤ *780*

◗ Our ancestors regarded the litany of blessings and curses as a prayer for justice.

CONTEMPORARY REFLECTION ➤ *782*

◗ Rabbinic literature records the names of women who made vows of various kinds.

POST-BIBLICAL INTERPRETATIONS ➤ *780*

◗ My greatest challenge in ballroom dance has been learning to follow.

VOICES ➤ *784*

6 וְנָתַתִּי שָׁלוֹם בָּאָרֶץ וּשְׁכַבְתֶּם וְאֵין
מַחֲרִיד וְהִשְׁבַּתִּי חַיָּה רָעָה מִן־הָאָרֶץ וְחֶרֶב
לֹא־תַעֲבֹר בְּאַרְצְכֶם׃ 7 וּרְדַפְתֶּם אֶת־
אֹיְבֵיכֶם וְנָפְלוּ לִפְנֵיכֶם לֶחָרֶב׃ 8 וְרָדְפוּ
מִכֶּם חֲמִשָּׁה מֵאָה וּמֵאָה מִכֶּם רְבָבָה
יִרְדֹּפוּ וְנָפְלוּ אֹיְבֵיכֶם לִפְנֵיכֶם לֶחָרֶב׃
9 וּפָנִיתִי אֲלֵיכֶם וְהִפְרֵיתִי אֶתְכֶם וְהִרְבֵּיתִי
אֶתְכֶם וַהֲקִימֹתִי אֶת־בְּרִיתִי אִתְּכֶם׃
10 וַאֲכַלְתֶּם יָשָׁן נוֹשָׁן וְיָשָׁן מִפְּנֵי חָדָשׁ
תּוֹצִיאוּ׃
11 וְנָתַתִּי מִשְׁכָּנִי בְּתוֹכְכֶם וְלֹא־תִגְעַל נַפְשִׁי
אֶתְכֶם׃ 12 וְהִתְהַלַּכְתִּי בְּתוֹכְכֶם וְהָיִיתִי
לָכֶם לֵאלֹהִים וְאַתֶּם תִּהְיוּ־לִי לְעָם׃
13 אֲנִי יְהֹוָה אֱלֹהֵיכֶם אֲשֶׁר הוֹצֵאתִי
אֶתְכֶם מֵאֶרֶץ מִצְרַיִם מִהְיֹת לָהֶם עֲבָדִים
וָאֶשְׁבֹּר מֹטֹת עֻלְּכֶם וָאוֹלֵךְ אֶתְכֶם
קוֹמְמִיּוּת׃ פ

6 I will grant peace in the land, and you shall lie down untroubled by anyone; I will give the land respite from vicious beasts, and no sword shall cross your land. 7 [Your army] shall give chase to your enemies, and they shall fall before you by the sword. 8 Five of you shall give chase to a hundred, and a hundred of you shall give chase to ten thousand; your enemies shall fall before you by the sword.

9 I will look with favor upon you, and make you fertile and multiply you; and I will maintain My covenant with you. 10 You shall eat old grain long stored, and you shall have to clear out the old to make room for the new.

11 I will establish My abode in your midst, and I will not spurn you. 12 I will be ever present in your midst: I will be your God, and you shall be My people. 13 I יהוה am your God who brought you out from the land of the Egyptians to be their slaves no more, who broke the bars of your yoke and made you walk erect.

*9. I will . . . make you fertile.* On God's role in fertility, see the introduction to Genesis 16:1–6 and at Deuteronomy 33:13.

***I will maintain My covenant with you.*** God's covenantal faithfulness serves as guarantee that these promises will come true.

*11. abode.* Heb. *mishkan* is translated elsewhere as "Tabernacle" (as in Exodus 25:9 and Leviticus 8:10); here, however, the term carries a much broader sense. God assures the people that the Deity will reside with Israel in the land. The text emphasizes the presence of God with the people as a whole, not confined to the sanctuary.

***I will not spurn you.*** Spurning (or rejecting) is something of a leitmotif in this unit. First, God promises never to spurn Israel if the people follow the laws and commandments (v. 11). Next, if the people choose to spurn these laws and commandments (v. 15), the punishments will begin. Finally, God will spurn Israel temporarily should the people fail to return to God after a series of increasingly severe punishments (v. 30; but see v. 44, when God relents nonetheless).

*12. I will be ever present in your midst.* Literally, "I will walk about in your midst." This description might refer back to the story of the Garden of Eden when God is depicted as walking about the Garden (see Genesis 3:8). The establishment of God's abode in Israel's midst will ensure a period of prosperity and peace—as well as a palpable relationship with God.

***I will be your God, and you shall be My people.*** This expression refers back to the covenantal promise made at Sinai (Exodus 6:2–8) and reiterates mutual commitment.

*13.* The blessings' section concludes by reminding Israel of their special relationship to God, and of what God has done for them in the past, thereby also alluding to what God is capable of doing for them in the future.

[14]But if you do not obey Me and do not observe all these commandments, [15]if you reject My laws and spurn My rules, so that you do not observe all My commandments and you break My covenant, [16]I in turn will do this to you: I will wreak misery upon you—consumption and fever, which cause the eyes to pine and the body to languish; you shall sow your seed to no purpose, for your enemies shall eat it. [17]I will set My face against you: you shall be routed by your enemies, and your foes shall dominate you. You shall flee though none pursues.

[18]And if, for all that, you do not obey Me, I will go on to discipline you sevenfold for your sins, [19]and I will break your proud glory. I will make your skies like iron and your earth like copper, [20]so that your strength shall be spent to no purpose. Your land shall not yield its produce, nor shall the trees of the land yield their fruit.

[21]And if you remain hostile toward Me and refuse to obey Me, I will go on smiting you sevenfold for your sins. [22]I will loose wild beasts against you, and they shall bereave you of your children and wipe out your cattle. They shall decimate you, and your roads shall be deserted.

[23]And if these things fail to discipline you for Me, and you remain hostile to Me, [24]I too will remain hostile to you: I in turn will smite you seven-

14 וְאִם־לֹא תִשְׁמְעוּ לִי וְלֹא תַעֲשׂוּ אֵת כָּל־
הַמִּצְוֺת הָאֵלֶּה׃ 15 וְאִם־בְּחֻקֹּתַי תִּמְאָסוּ
וְאִם אֶת־מִשְׁפָּטַי תִּגְעַל נַפְשְׁכֶם לְבִלְתִּי
עֲשׂוֹת אֶת־כָּל־מִצְוֺתַי לְהַפְרְכֶם אֶת־
בְּרִיתִי׃ 16 אַף־אֲנִי אֶעֱשֶׂה־זֹּאת לָכֶם
וְהִפְקַדְתִּי עֲלֵיכֶם בֶּהָלָה אֶת־הַשַּׁחֶפֶת
וְאֶת־הַקַּדַּחַת מְכַלּוֹת עֵינַיִם וּמְדִיבֹת נָפֶשׁ
וּזְרַעְתֶּם לָרִיק זַרְעֲכֶם וַאֲכָלֻהוּ אֹיְבֵיכֶם׃
17 וְנָתַתִּי פָנַי בָּכֶם וְנִגַּפְתֶּם לִפְנֵי אֹיְבֵיכֶם
וְרָדוּ בָכֶם שֹׂנְאֵיכֶם וְנַסְתֶּם וְאֵין־רֹדֵף
אֶתְכֶם׃
18 וְאִם־עַד־אֵלֶּה לֹא תִשְׁמְעוּ לִי וְיָסַפְתִּי
לְיַסְּרָה אֶתְכֶם שֶׁבַע עַל־חַטֹּאתֵיכֶם׃
19 וְשָׁבַרְתִּי אֶת־גְּאוֹן עֻזְּכֶם וְנָתַתִּי אֶת־
שְׁמֵיכֶם כַּבַּרְזֶל וְאֶת־אַרְצְכֶם כַּנְּחֻשָׁה׃
20 וְתַם לָרִיק כֹּחֲכֶם וְלֹא־תִתֵּן אַרְצְכֶם
אֶת־יְבוּלָהּ וְעֵץ הָאָרֶץ לֹא יִתֵּן פִּרְיוֹ׃
21 וְאִם־תֵּלְכוּ עִמִּי קֶרִי וְלֹא תֹאבוּ לִשְׁמֹעַ
לִי וְיָסַפְתִּי עֲלֵיכֶם מַכָּה שֶׁבַע כְּחַטֹּאתֵיכֶם׃
22 וְהִשְׁלַחְתִּי בָכֶם אֶת־חַיַּת הַשָּׂדֶה וְשִׁכְּלָה
אֶתְכֶם וְהִכְרִיתָה אֶת־בְּהֶמְתְּכֶם וְהִמְעִיטָה
אֶתְכֶם וְנָשַׁמּוּ דַּרְכֵיכֶם׃
23 וְאִם־בְּאֵלֶּה לֹא תִוָּסְרוּ לִי וַהֲלַכְתֶּם עִמִּי
קֶרִי׃ 24 וְהָלַכְתִּי אַף־אֲנִי עִמָּכֶם בְּקֶרִי
וְהִכֵּיתִי אֶתְכֶם גַּם־אָנִי שֶׁבַע עַל־

## CURSES FOR DISOBEDIENCE (26:14–45)

In contrast to the rather brief section of blessings, the list of curses is longer and more detailed. It threatens Israel with the consequences that will follow if the people spurn God's rules and fail to observe God's laws. The curses in Leviticus 26:14–45 largely mirror the blessings in the previous section and also have many similarities to the curses in Deuteronomy 28:15–68. However, in Deuteronomy the curses appear as punishment, while here they are presented also as God's attempt to influence the people to return to the right path (see vv. 18, 21, 23, and 27). With each increasingly severe measure, God hopes that Israel will have learned its lesson. The punishments will stop at any point when the Israelites relent and turn back to God.

These writings probably gave hope to the people of Israel after the Babylonian Exile (597/587–538 B.C.E.) because they provide an explanation for how God could have allowed the downfall of Jerusalem and the Exile to come about; Leviticus 26 also emphasizes the promise of restoration once the people repent.

fold for your sins. 25I will bring a sword against you
to wreak vengeance for the covenant; and if you
withdraw into your cities, I will send pestilence
among you, and you shall be delivered into enemy
hands. 26When I break your staff of bread, ten
women shall bake your bread in a single oven; they
shall dole out your bread by weight, and though
you eat, you shall not be satisfied.

27But if, despite this, you disobey Me and remain hostile to Me, 28I will act against you in
wrathful hostility; I, for My part, will discipline
you sevenfold for your sins. 29You shall eat the flesh

חַטֹּאתֵיכֶם׃ 25 וְהֵבֵאתִי עֲלֵיכֶם חֶרֶב נֹקֶמֶת
נְקַם־בְּרִית וְנֶאֱסַפְתֶּם אֶל־עָרֵיכֶם וְשִׁלַּחְתִּי
דֶבֶר בְּתוֹכְכֶם וְנִתַּתֶּם בְּיַד־אוֹיֵב׃ 26 בְּשִׁבְרִי
לָכֶם מַטֵּה־לֶחֶם וְאָפוּ עֶשֶׂר נָשִׁים לַחְמְכֶם
בְּתַנּוּר אֶחָד וְהֵשִׁיבוּ לַחְמְכֶם בַּמִּשְׁקָל
וַאֲכַלְתֶּם וְלֹא תִשְׂבָּעוּ׃ ס

27 וְאִם־בְּזֹאת לֹא תִשְׁמְעוּ לִי וַהֲלַכְתֶּם
עִמִּי בְּקֶרִי׃ 28 וְהָלַכְתִּי עִמָּכֶם בַּחֲמַת־
קֶרִי וְיִסַּרְתִּי אֶתְכֶם אַף־אָנִי שֶׁבַע עַל־
חַטֹּאתֵיכֶם׃ 29 וַאֲכַלְתֶּם בְּשַׂר בְּנֵיכֶם וּבְשַׂר

*26.* ***ten women shall bake your bread in a single oven.*** Many women will all share one oven, whether for lack of dough or for lack of wood to fuel the oven. Either way, the threat is that of famine. Variations on this theme are common in ancient Near Eastern curses. For example, a curse in the Aramaic Sefire inscription (mid–8th century B.C.E.) reads: "And may his seven daughters bake bread in an oven but not fill it"; and a curse in the bilingual Assyrian-Aramaic Tell Fekheriyeh inscription (9th century B.C.E.) reads, "May a hundred women bake bread in an oven and not fill it."

[It appears that ovens were beehive-shaped forms, made of a mixture of chopped clay and straw, sometimes with broken shards pressed onto the oven. They could be slightly recessed into the ground. (See P. King and L. Stager, *Life in Biblical Israel*, 2001, p. 67.) They were generally in the courtyard and probably served several adjacent dwellings. But they could also be in interior space; a baker would more likely fire up an interior oven in cold rainy weather. The bread could be baked on a baking tray, set over the fire inside the oven. —*Ed.*] Oven fuel consisted of branches or dung (see Malachi 3:19; Jacob Milgrom, *Leviticus 23–27*, 2001, p. 2314).

Here the text specifies women as the ones who bake the bread. This provides some insight into the division of labor in the ancient Israelite household. While women were the ones responsible for childbearing and childrearing, they also divided with men the other duties necessary to sustain and support the household. This text, then, provides evidence that women were predominantly responsible for tasks related to food production, that is, the transformation of raw foodstuffs into consumable goods. In the ancient world this was a very important and time-consuming task. Other biblical texts, through their association of women and food production in various forms, support this conclusion. For example, in I Samuel 28:24, the medium of En-dor prepares a calf and makes bread for King Saul. In Jeremiah 7:17–18, women are described as kneading dough for cakes to offer to the Queen of Heaven. In I Samuel 8:13, the prophet Samuel warns the people that monarchy will make many demands of them, including that the king "will take your daughters as perfumers, cooks, and bakers." This last text implies that women indeed served those functions at the royal palace, as well as in ordinary households. See further at Exodus 16:3.

*29.* ***You shall eat the flesh of your sons and the flesh of your daughters.*** The horrific prospect of cannibalism as a result of siege, extreme famine, or both is a recurrent theme in Israelite and other ancient Near Eastern curses. An extreme version of this theme appears in II Kings 6:28–29, when a king in besieged and famine-struck Samaria must decide between two women who had agreed to eat their respective children, first one and then the other, to stave off starvation. A conflict erupts when, after

of your sons and the flesh of your daughters. [30]I will destroy your cult places and cut down your incense stands, and I will heap your carcasses upon your lifeless fetishes.

I will spurn you. [31]I will lay your cities in ruin and make your sanctuaries desolate, and I will not savor your pleasing odors. [32]I will make the land desolate, so that your enemies who settle in it shall

בְּנֹתֵיכֶם תֹּאכֵלוּ׃ 30 וְהִשְׁמַדְתִּי אֶת־
בָּמֹתֵיכֶם וְהִכְרַתִּי אֶת־חַמָּנֵיכֶם וְנָתַתִּי
אֶת־פִּגְרֵיכֶם עַל־פִּגְרֵי גִּלּוּלֵיכֶם
וְגָעֲלָה נַפְשִׁי אֶתְכֶם׃ 31 וְנָתַתִּי אֶת־עָרֵיכֶם
חָרְבָּה וַהֲשִׁמּוֹתִי אֶת־מִקְדְּשֵׁיכֶם וְלֹא
אָרִיחַ בְּרֵיחַ נִיחֹחֲכֶם׃ 32 וַהֲשִׁמֹּתִי אֲנִי
אֶת־הָאָרֶץ וְשָׁמְמוּ עָלֶיהָ אֹיְבֵיכֶם הַיֹּשְׁבִים

having shared in eating the first woman's child, the second mother hides her son. (The story is an ironic twist on the episode in which King Solomon demonstrates his superb wisdom by determining which harlot is the rightful mother of a baby; see I Kings 3:16–28.) In Lamentations 2:20 and 4:10, references to women desperate enough to eat their own children show how terrible the situation for the people of Judah has become. In both of these texts, the image of women eating their children exemplifies a crisis so severe that it reverses even the maternal instinct: instead of being willing to sacrifice everything—even themselves—for their children, these mothers sacrifice their children in the most horrific way possible, so that they may live. The image is that of a world turned tragically upside down by the horrors of wartime siege and famine.

*30.* ***I will destroy your cult places and cut down your incense stands.*** Biblical references use neutral terms for cult places (sometimes translated as "high places") or local shrines in early stages of Israelite life but criticize these for the period after the building of the temple in Jerusalem (in the 10th or 9th century B.C.E.). For example, I Kings 22:44 and II Kings 15:35 mention people worshiping God at such high places; that author does not approve of the practice yet apparently tolerates it. More so than men, women most likely depended on local shrines to enable them to participate in communal events. (They probably also had home shrines.) The Bible—and probably the Israelites in general—apparently considered worship of God at these local shrines to be a legitimate religious outlet until centralization of worship at the Temple began to be enforced (see at Deuteronomy 12:2–14). The Bible suggests that this centralization began around the 7th century B.C.E., in the reigns of King Hezekiah and, later, Josiah. The Bible associates worship at local shrines after that time with idolatry, regardless of who was worshiped there.

Centralization of worship probably had a huge impact on women, who would have been less able than men were to leave their families and their domestic and reproductive responsibilities in order to travel to Jerusalem. Once the worship of God at local shrines ceased to be legitimate, women lost important communal religious practices. When the Bible mentions women's worship from the period of the monarchy on, it mostly categorizes it as worship of false deities, probably considered noteworthy because such practices undermined the central sanctuary. See, for example, the association of women with the worship of Asherah (I Kings 15:13 = II Chronicles 15:16; I Kings 18:19; and II Kings 23:4); references to female worship of the Queen of Heaven (Jeremiah 7:18 and 44:15–25); and women weeping for Tammuz (Ezekiel 8:14). From an Israelite woman's perspective, many of these practices were probably traditional and legitimate (see women's defense of the worship in Jeremiah 44).

*32.* Those who will replace the deported or destroyed Israelites will be so horrified by the level of desolation and destruction of the land that they will wonder what the inhabitants had done to incur such divine wrath against them (see also Deuteronomy 29:21–23).

בָּהּ׃ 33 וְאֶתְכֶם֙ אֱזָרֶ֣ה בַגּוֹיִ֔ם וַהֲרִיקֹתִ֥י
אַחֲרֵיכֶ֖ם חָ֑רֶב וְהָיְתָ֤ה אַרְצְכֶם֙ שְׁמָמָ֔ה
וְעָרֵיכֶ֖ם יִהְי֥וּ חָרְבָּֽה׃
34 אָז֩ תִּרְצֶ֨ה הָאָ֜רֶץ אֶת־שַׁבְּתֹתֶ֗יהָ כֹּ֚ל
יְמֵ֣י הָשַּׁמָּ֔ה וְאַתֶּ֖ם בְּאֶ֣רֶץ אֹיְבֵיכֶ֑ם אָ֚ז
תִּשְׁבַּ֣ת הָאָ֔רֶץ וְהִרְצָ֖ת אֶת־שַׁבְּתֹתֶֽיהָ׃
35 כָּל־יְמֵ֥י הָשַּׁמָּ֖ה תִּשְׁבֹּ֑ת אֵ֣ת אֲשֶׁ֧ר לֹא־
שָׁבְתָ֛ה בְּשַׁבְּתֹתֵיכֶ֖ם בְּשִׁבְתְּכֶ֥ם עָלֶֽיהָ׃
36 וְהַנִּשְׁאָרִ֣ים בָּכֶ֔ם וְהֵבֵ֤אתִי מֹ֙רֶךְ֙ בִּלְבָבָ֔ם
בְּאַרְצֹ֖ת אֹיְבֵיהֶ֑ם וְרָדַ֣ף אֹתָ֗ם ק֚וֹל עָלֶ֣ה נִדָּ֔ף
וְנָס֧וּ מְנֻֽסַת־חֶ֛רֶב וְנָפְל֖וּ וְאֵ֥ין רֹדֵֽף׃ 37 וְכָשְׁל֧וּ
אִישׁ־בְּאָחִ֛יו כְּמִפְּנֵי־חֶ֖רֶב וְרֹדֵ֣ף אָ֑יִן וְלֹא־
תִהְיֶ֤ה לָכֶם֙ תְּקוּמָ֔ה לִפְנֵ֖י אֹיְבֵיכֶֽם׃
38 וַאֲבַדְתֶּ֖ם בַּגּוֹיִ֑ם וְאָכְלָ֣ה אֶתְכֶ֔ם אֶ֖רֶץ
אֹיְבֵיכֶֽם׃
39 וְהַנִּשְׁאָרִ֣ים בָּכֶ֗ם יִמַּ֙קּוּ֙ בַּעֲוֺנָ֔ם בְּאַרְצֹ֖ת
אֹיְבֵיכֶ֑ם וְאַ֛ף בַּעֲוֺנֹ֥ת אֲבֹתָ֖ם אִתָּ֥ם יִמָּֽקּוּ׃
40 וְהִתְוַדּ֤וּ אֶת־עֲוֺנָם֙ וְאֶת־עֲוֺ֣ן אֲבֹתָ֔ם
בְּמַעֲלָ֖ם אֲשֶׁ֣ר מָֽעֲלוּ־בִ֑י וְאַ֕ף אֲשֶׁר־הָלְכ֥וּ
עִמִּ֖י בְּקֶֽרִי׃ 41 אַף־אֲנִ֗י אֵלֵ֤ךְ עִמָּם֙ בְּקֶ֔רִי
וְהֵבֵאתִ֣י אֹתָ֔ם בְּאֶ֖רֶץ אֹיְבֵיהֶ֑ם אוֹ־אָ֣ז
יִכָּנַ֗ע לְבָבָם֙ הֶֽעָרֵ֔ל וְאָ֖ז יִרְצ֥וּ אֶת־עֲוֺנָֽם׃
42 וְזָכַרְתִּ֖י אֶת־בְּרִיתִ֣י יַעֲק֑וֹב וְאַ֨ף אֶת־

be appalled by it. [33]And you I will scatter among the nations, and I will unsheath the sword against you. Your land shall become a desolation and your cities a ruin.

[34]Then shall the land make up for its sabbath years throughout the time that it is desolate and you are in the land of your enemies; then shall the land rest and make up for its sabbath years. [35]Throughout the time that it is desolate, it shall observe the rest that it did not observe in your sabbath years while you were dwelling upon it. [36]As for those of you who survive, I will cast a faintness into their hearts in the land of their enemies. The sound of a driven leaf shall put them to flight. Fleeing as though from the sword, they shall fall though none pursues. [37]With no one pursuing, they shall stumble over one another as before the sword. You shall not be able to stand your ground before your enemies, [38]but shall perish among the nations; and the land of your enemies shall consume you.

[39]Those of you who survive shall be heartsick over their iniquity in the land of your enemies; more, they shall be heartsick over the iniquities of their forebears; [40]and they shall confess their iniquity and the iniquity of their forebears, in that they trespassed against Me, yea, were hostile to Me. [41]When I, in turn, have been hostile to them and have removed them into the land of their enemies, then at last shall their obdurate heart humble itself, and they shall atone for their iniquity. [42]Then will I remember My covenant with Jacob; I will remem-

---

*34.* ***Then shall the land make up for its sabbath years.*** In a case of poetic justice, the land in its desolation will at last lie fallow. This will make up for all of the years that the Israelites abused it by continuous cultivation, contravening laws such as Leviticus 25.

*41.* ***obdurate heart.*** Literally, "uncircumcised heart." The metaphor implies that their heart is covered as if by uncircumcised foreskin: it is unresponsive and unfeeling.

*42.* ***Then will I remember My covenant.*** This theme of God recalling the covenant and responding in compassion appears in Exodus 6:5 (in the context of the liberation from Egypt) and throughout the Bible. Especially interesting is Isaiah 54:1–10, where God addresses Israel as a wife and promises "her" eternal covenant faithfulness (in the context of restoration).

***Jacob . . . Isaac . . . Abraham.*** The reversed order of the patriarchs may reflect God's looking

ber also My covenant with Isaac, and also My covenant with Abraham; and I will remember the land. [43]For the land shall be forsaken of them, making up for its sabbath years by being desolate of them, while they atone for their iniquity; for the abundant reason that they rejected My rules and spurned My laws. [44]Yet, even then, when they are in the land of their enemies, I will not reject them or spurn them so as to destroy them, annulling My covenant with them: for I יהוה am their God. [45]I will remember in their favor the covenant with the ancients, whom I freed from the land of Egypt in the sight of the nations to be their God: I, יהוה.

[46]These are the laws, rules, and instructions that יהוה established, through Moses on Mount Sinai, with the Israelite people.

27  יהוה spoke to Moses, saying: [2]Speak to the Israelite people and say to them:

בְּרִיתִ֣י יִצְחָ֗ק וְאַ֧ף אֶת־בְּרִיתִ֛י אַבְרָהָ֖ם אֶזְכֹּ֑ר וְהָאָ֖רֶץ אֶזְכֹּֽר׃

43 וְהָאָ֩רֶץ֩ תֵּעָזֵ֨ב מֵהֶ֜ם וְתִ֣רֶץ אֶת־שַׁבְּתֹתֶ֗יהָ בׇּהְשַׁמָּה֙ מֵהֶ֔ם וְהֵ֖ם יִרְצ֣וּ אֶת־עֲוֺנָ֑ם יַ֣עַן וּבְיַ֗עַן בְּמִשְׁפָּטַ֣י מָאָ֔סוּ וְאֶת־חֻקֹּתַ֖י גָּעֲלָ֥ה נַפְשָֽׁם׃ 44 וְאַף־גַּם־זֹ֡את בִּֽהְיוֹתָם֩ בְּאֶ֨רֶץ אֹֽיְבֵיהֶ֜ם לֹֽא־מְאַסְתִּ֤ים וְלֹֽא־גְעַלְתִּים֙ לְכַלֹּתָ֔ם לְהָפֵ֥ר בְּרִיתִ֖י אִתָּ֑ם כִּ֛י אֲנִ֥י יְהֹוָ֖ה אֱלֹהֵיהֶֽם׃ 45 וְזָכַרְתִּ֥י לָהֶ֖ם בְּרִ֣ית רִֽאשֹׁנִ֑ים אֲשֶׁ֣ר הוֹצֵֽאתִי־אֹתָ֩ם מֵאֶ֨רֶץ מִצְרַ֜יִם לְעֵינֵ֣י הַגּוֹיִ֗ם לִהְיֹ֥ות לָהֶ֛ם לֵאלֹהִ֖ים אֲנִ֥י יְהֹוָֽה׃

46 אֵ֠לֶּה הַֽחֻקִּ֣ים וְהַמִּשְׁפָּטִים֮ וְהַתּוֹרֹת֒ אֲשֶׁר֩ נָתַ֨ן יְהֹוָ֜ה בֵּינ֣וֹ וּבֵ֗ין בְּנֵ֣י יִשְׂרָאֵ֑ל בְּהַ֥ר סִינַ֖י בְּיַד־מֹשֶֽׁה׃ פ

כז וַיְדַבֵּ֥ר יְהֹוָ֖ה אֶל־מֹשֶׁ֥ה לֵּאמֹֽר׃ 2 דַּבֵּ֞ר אֶל־בְּנֵ֤י יִשְׂרָאֵל֙ וְאָמַרְתָּ֣ אֲלֵהֶ֔ם אִ֕ישׁ כִּ֣י

backward in time to the very first commitment to this people.

**44.   I will not reject them or spurn them.**   That is, even though Israel spurned God, God will never spurn Israel completely by annulling the covenant.

**45.   the covenant with the ancients, whom I freed from the land of Egypt.**   Reference to the generation of the Exodus includes those who took part in the Sinai covenant.

CONCLUSION
(26:46)

The book of Leviticus probably ended with this verse at one point. The reference to Sinai aims to emphasize the authority of these laws (see also at 25:1). The subsequent unit most likely is a later addition to this earlier conclusion.

## Appendix

THE SANCTUARY:
FUNDING, GIFTS, AND DUES   (27:1–34)

This last unit of Leviticus specifies how to make various dedications to the sanctuary, how their value is determined, and whether they can be redeemed (that is, whether a monetary substitute is acceptable). These details supplement the laws about sacrifices with which the book began (Leviticus 1–7). [Monetary valuation may also be related to the redemption laws of Leviticus 25 in that, like "actuary tables," they help estimate what redemption costs might entail. —*Ed.*]

Vows are essentially conditional promises to God, to be fulfilled if and when the requested conditions come to pass. According to biblical portrayals, one

When anyone explicitly vows to יהוה the equivalent for a human being, [3]the following scale shall apply: If it is a male from twenty to sixty years of age, the equivalent is fifty shekels of silver by the sanctuary

יַפְלִא נֶדֶר בְּעֶרְכְּךָ נְפָשֹׁת לַיהוָה׃ 3 וְהָיָה
עֶרְכְּךָ הַזָּכָר מִבֶּן עֶשְׂרִים שָׁנָה וְעַד בֶּן־
שִׁשִּׁים שָׁנָה וְהָיָה עֶרְכְּךָ חֲמִשִּׁים שֶׁקֶל כֶּסֶף

is most likely to utter a vow at a time of great distress, when direct appeal to God seems the only option left. A person often promises to dedicate or sacrifice an animal; but sometimes one offers service to the shrine, either by oneself or one's child, such as in the case of Hannah (I Samuel 1:1–11), who promises God that if granted a son, she will dedicate his service to the sanctuary at Shiloh. The warrior Jephthah vows to sacrifice what comes from his house; it turns out to be his daughter (Judges 11:29–40; see at Numbers 30:10). As an act of individual piety or desperation, one could utter a vow anywhere; therefore, vows were a popular form of religious devotion, one in which women could participate freely. (See additional references to women making vows in Numbers 6:2, 30:4–17; Jeremiah 44:15–25; and Proverbs 31:2.)

VOTARY PLEDGES OF PEOPLE (27:1–8)

Leviticus 27 opens with instructions concerning the fulfillment of vows. There is evidence that at certain periods vows could be fulfilled at any sanctuary. In I Samuel 1–2, Hannah appeals to God at the sanctuary at Shiloh, and that is where she brings her son Samuel for the vowed service. However, at some point the priesthood set limitations regarding whose vows were binding, what one could promise, and where payment could be made. Often these regulations limited the ability of women to make and keep vows. According to Numbers 30:10, vows made by independent women, whether divorcées or widows, are binding. However, the vow of a woman who is under a male's authority can be annulled by that father or husband upon first hearing of it (Numbers 30:4–9; see further at Numbers 30:2–17). The centralization of worship further limited the ability of women to partake fully in this form of religious devotion by restricting the payment of vows to a central location (Deuteronomy 12:5–6, 11, 17, and 26).

Leviticus 27 lists fixed monetary equivalents for pledges to the sanctuary according to age and gender. Noteworthy is the lower value assigned to females in each age group. Carol Meyers suggests that the Leviticus valuation may accurately reflect the relative potential for economic productivity of each gender at various stages of life (see below) and does not reflect a notion that men are inherently more valuable than women. A high mortality rate is also no doubt a factor. Carol Meyers reports that skeletal remains in some ancient tombs help to determine mortality rates among different age and gender groups in ancient Israel. These remains indicate that the death rate was highest among the pre-adult population. In one tomb group, for example, nearly half the population did not survive to the age of 18 ("The Roots of Restriction: Women in Early Israel," 1978, p. 95).

2. ***When anyone explicitly vows to* יהוה.** The practice of vowing the value of a person to the sanctuary presumably has its roots in the earlier practice of dedicating people for lifelong service to the sanctuary (such as the vow made by Hannah in I Samuel 1:1–11). The monetary value in Leviticus 27 represents the amount of money that a vowed person's service to the sanctuary would be worth. Thus, instead of using the services of the vowed person, the priests can use the money, presumably for the maintenance of the sanctuary. The option of dedicating materials to the sanctuary not only seeks to fill a vower's personal need but also provides resources for maintaining the national sanctuary—including its personnel, especially priests (see also Numbers 6:2–21 and 30:3–15).

3. ***If it is a male from twenty to sixty.*** There

weight; [4]if it is a female, the equivalent is thirty shekels. [5]If the age is from five years to twenty years, the equivalent is twenty shekels for a male and ten shekels for a female. [6]If the age is from one month to five years, the equivalent for a male is five shekels of silver, and the equivalent for a female is three shekels of silver. [7]If the age is sixty years or over, the equivalent is fifteen shekels in the case of a male and ten shekels for a female. [8]But if one cannot afford the equivalent, that person shall be presented before the priest, and the priest shall make an assessment; the priest shall make the assessment according to what the vower can afford.

בְּשֶׁ֥קֶל הַקֹּֽדֶשׁ׃ 4 וְאִם־נְקֵבָ֖ה הִ֑וא וְהָיָ֥ה
עֶרְכְּךָ֖ שְׁלֹשִׁ֥ים שָֽׁקֶל׃ 5 וְאִ֨ם מִבֶּן־חָמֵ֜שׁ
שָׁנִ֗ים וְעַד֙ בֶּן־עֶשְׂרִ֣ים שָׁנָ֔ה וְהָיָ֧ה עֶרְכְּךָ֛
הַזָּכָ֖ר עֶשְׂרִ֣ים שְׁקָלִ֑ים וְלַנְּקֵבָ֖ה עֲשֶׂ֥רֶת
שְׁקָלִֽים׃ 6 וְאִ֣ם מִבֶּן־חֹ֗דֶשׁ וְעַד֙ בֶּן־חָמֵ֣שׁ
שָׁנִ֔ים וְהָיָ֣ה עֶרְכְּךָ֣ הַזָּכָ֔ר חֲמִשָּׁ֥ה שְׁקָלִ֖ים
כָּ֑סֶף וְלַנְּקֵבָ֣ה עֶרְכְּךָ֔ שְׁלֹ֥שֶׁת שְׁקָלִ֖ים כָּֽסֶף׃
7 וְאִ֡ם מִבֶּן־שִׁשִּׁ֨ים שָׁנָ֤ה וָמַ֙עְלָה֙ אִם־זָכָ֔ר
וְהָיָ֣ה עֶרְכְּךָ֔ חֲמִשָּׁ֥ה עָשָׂ֖ר שָׁ֑קֶל וְלַנְּקֵבָ֖ה
עֲשָׂרָ֥ה שְׁקָלִֽים׃ 8 וְאִם־מָ֥ךְ הוּא֙ מֵֽעֶרְכֶּ֔ךָ
וְהֶֽעֱמִידוֹ֙ לִפְנֵ֣י הַכֹּהֵ֔ן וְהֶעֱרִ֥יךְ אֹת֖וֹ הַכֹּהֵ֑ן
עַל־פִּ֗י אֲשֶׁ֤ר תַּשִּׂיג֙ יַ֣ד הַנֹּדֵ֔ר יַעֲרִיכֶ֖נּוּ
הַכֹּהֵֽן׃ ס

is some biblical evidence that men, at least, were considered to be most productive between twenty to sixty years of age. The book of Numbers legislates military conscription at twenty (Numbers 1:3) and service in the Tabernacle to between twenty and fifty (4:3, 23).

*4. if it is a female.* The calculated 30 shekels for a woman in this category, when compared with 50 shekels for the male, places the woman's relative economic worth in this age category at 38% of the total contribution of both genders. As Meyers notes, sociological studies show that when women contribute 40% to the economy's productive labor, their status is at its highest. Their status diminishes if their contribution is higher ("Procreation, Production, and Protection: Male-Female Balance in Early Israel," 1983, pp. 569–93, especially p. 575). See further Another View, p. 780.

*5. If the age is from five years to twenty.* The relative valuation of females in comparison with males is lowest in the five to twenty age group (for the female, 33% of the total contribution of both genders). Meyers observes that this period coincides with peak childbearing years, when women, occupied with childbearing and childrearing, could not provide as much in the way of other economic productivity. In addition, the fact that many women died in childbirth would also explain a devaluation of women's economic worth relative to men in this age group.

*6. If the age is from one month to five years.* A child could not be dedicated before it was one month old, most likely reflecting a high newborn mortality rate. This also accounts for the relatively low monetary value. Only at one month was a child considered viable and more likely to survive.

*7. If the age is sixty years or over.* The woman's relative economic worth is highest in the over sixty category (40% of the total contribution of both genders), when male efficiency declines, while females are able to continue their domestic responsibilities with only a minimal decrease in productivity ("Procreation, Production, and Protection," pp. 584–93).

*8. But if one cannot afford the equivalent.* This flexibility allows poor people who wish to make dedications of this kind to the sanctuary even if they cannot afford the listed amounts. The sacrificial system incorporates similar concessions to the poor (see 12:6–8).

9 If [the vow concerns] any animal that may be brought as an offering to יהוה, any such that may be given to יהוה shall be holy. 10 One may not exchange or substitute another for it, either good for bad, or bad for good; if one does substitute one animal for another, the thing vowed and its substitute shall both be holy. 11 If [the vow concerns] any impure animal that may not be brought as an offering to יהוה, the animal shall be presented before the priest, 12 and the priest shall assess it. Whether high or low, whatever assessment is set by the priest shall stand; 13 and if one wishes to redeem it, one-fifth must be added to its assessment.

14 If anyone consecrates a house to יהוה, the

9 וְאִם־בְּהֵמָה אֲשֶׁר יַקְרִיבוּ מִמֶּנָּה קָרְבָּן
לַיהֹוָה כֹּל אֲשֶׁר יִתֵּן מִמֶּנּוּ לַיהֹוָה יִהְיֶה־
קֹּדֶשׁ׃ 10 לֹא יַחֲלִיפֶנּוּ וְלֹא־יָמִיר אֹתוֹ טוֹב
בְּרָע אוֹ־רַע בְּטוֹב וְאִם־הָמֵר יָמִיר בְּהֵמָה
בִּבְהֵמָה וְהָיָה־הוּא וּתְמוּרָתוֹ יִהְיֶה־קֹּדֶשׁ׃
11 וְאִם כָּל־בְּהֵמָה טְמֵאָה אֲשֶׁר לֹא־יַקְרִיבוּ
מִמֶּנָּה קָרְבָּן לַיהֹוָה וְהֶעֱמִיד אֶת־הַבְּהֵמָה
לִפְנֵי הַכֹּהֵן׃ 12 וְהֶעֱרִיךְ הַכֹּהֵן אֹתָהּ בֵּין
טוֹב וּבֵין רָע כְּעֶרְכְּךָ הַכֹּהֵן כֵּן יִהְיֶה׃
13 וְאִם־גָּאֹל יִגְאָלֶנָּה וְיָסַף חֲמִישִׁתוֹ עַל־
עֶרְכֶּךָ׃
14 וְאִישׁ כִּי־יַקְדִּשׁ אֶת־בֵּיתוֹ קֹדֶשׁ לַיהֹוָה

## VOTARY PLEDGES OF ANIMALS (27:9–13)

The next section concerns two categories of animal offerings: those that are fit for sacrifice (vv. 9–10) and those that are not (vv. 11–13). Once a sacrificable animal is pledged, it must be brought in to fulfill the vow and cannot be replaced by another animal. However, a pledged animal that is unfit for sacrifice because it is ritually impure (see Leviticus 11 for a list of animals) is brought to the priest, who assigns it a value, for which the Tabernacle's staff will sell it to raise money for the sanctuary. The owner can also choose to redeem the animal, for twenty percent more than the value assessed by the priest.

The ritually pure sacrificial animals that are vowed are eaten by the priests and their households (after certain parts are burned entirely as God's portion). Leviticus 22:1–16 indicates who may partake of the priest's portion of the sacred donations. Of special interest is the question of when a priest's daughter is entitled to part of her father's share. Verses 12–13 of that passage determine that she is entitled to partake of her father's portion of the sacred donations so long as she is part of his household. If she marries a member of the priesthood, her entitlement then derives from her husband. If she marries outside the priesthood, she becomes part of the lay community and thus loses her entitlement to partake of the sacred donations. However, if she is then widowed or divorced without children, and thus has no claim to her husband's estate, she can go back to her father's household and regain her entitlement to partake of her father's portion of the sacred donations.

## CONSECRATIONS OF PROPERTY (27:14–25)

This section treats three types of property pledges: dwellings (vv. 14–15), personal land holdings (vv. 16–20), and acquired land (vv. 22–25). Personal landholdings, that is, parcels of farmland, are assessed at a fixed rate according to how much seed it takes to plant them, which probably measures their size rather than how much the land has produced. The assessed value also depends on the timing of the jubilee (see 25:29–34), decreasing every year as the jubilee approaches. Several biblical texts mention women's holding land, including Zelophehad's daughters, Mahlah, Noah, Hoglah, Milcah, and Tirzah (see at Numbers 27:1–11 and 36:1–12); the wealthy woman from Shunem (II Kings 4:8–37 and 8:1–6); Achsah, whose father apparently gave her land as a dowry (Joshua 15:16–19 = Judges 1:12–15); and Naomi (Ruth 4:3–11), who is selling

priest shall assess it. Whether high or low, as the priest assesses it, so it shall stand; 15and if the one who has consecrated the house wishes to redeem it, one-fifth must be added to the sum at which it was assessed, and then it shall be returned.

16If anyone consecrates to יהוה any land-holding, its assessment shall be in accordance with its seed requirement: fifty shekels of silver to a *chomer* of barley seed. 17If the land is consecrated as of the jubilee year, its assessment stands. 18But if the land is consecrated after the jubilee, the priest shall compute the price according to the years that are left until the jubilee year, and its assessment shall be so reduced; 19and if the one who consecrated the land wishes to redeem it, one-fifth must be added to the sum at which it was assessed, and it shall be passed back. 20But if the one [who consecrated it] does not redeem the land, and the land is sold to another, it shall no longer be redeemable: 21when it is released in the jubilee, the land shall be holy to יהוה, as land proscribed; it becomes the priest's holding.

22If one consecrates to יהוה land that was purchased, which is not one's land-holding, 23the priest shall compute the proportionate assessment up to the jubilee year, and the assessment shall be paid as of that day, a sacred donation to יהוה. 24In the jubilee year the land shall revert to the one from whom it was bought, whose holding the land is. 25All assessments shall be by the sanctuary weight, the shekel being twenty *gerah*s.

26A firstling of animals, however, which—as a

וְהֶעֱרִיכוֹ הַכֹּהֵן בֵּין טוֹב וּבֵין רָע כַּאֲשֶׁר
יַעֲרִיךְ אֹתוֹ הַכֹּהֵן כֵּן יָקוּם׃ 15 וְאִם־
הַמַּקְדִּישׁ יִגְאַל אֶת־בֵּיתוֹ וְיָסַף חֲמִישִׁית
כֶּסֶף־עֶרְכְּךָ עָלָיו וְהָיָה לוֹ׃
16 וְאִם ׀ מִשְּׂדֵה אֲחֻזָּתוֹ יַקְדִּישׁ אִישׁ לַיהֹוָה
וְהָיָה עֶרְכְּךָ לְפִי זַרְעוֹ זֶרַע חֹמֶר שְׂעֹרִים
בַּחֲמִשִּׁים שֶׁקֶל כָּסֶף׃ 17 אִם־מִשְּׁנַת הַיֹּבֵל
יַקְדִּישׁ שָׂדֵהוּ כְּעֶרְכְּךָ יָקוּם׃ 18 וְאִם־אַחַר
הַיֹּבֵל יַקְדִּישׁ שָׂדֵהוּ וְחִשַּׁב־לוֹ הַכֹּהֵן אֶת־
הַכֶּסֶף עַל־פִּי הַשָּׁנִים הַנּוֹתָרֹת עַד שְׁנַת
הַיֹּבֵל וְנִגְרַע מֵעֶרְכֶּךָ׃ 19 וְאִם־גָּאֹל יִגְאַל
אֶת־הַשָּׂדֶה הַמַּקְדִּישׁ אֹתוֹ וְיָסַף חֲמִשִׁית
כֶּסֶף־עֶרְכְּךָ עָלָיו וְקָם לוֹ׃ 20 וְאִם־לֹא יִגְאַל
אֶת־הַשָּׂדֶה וְאִם־מָכַר אֶת־הַשָּׂדֶה לְאִישׁ
אַחֵר לֹא יִגָּאֵל עוֹד׃ 21 וְהָיָה הַשָּׂדֶה
בְּצֵאתוֹ בַיֹּבֵל קֹדֶשׁ לַיהֹוָה כִּשְׂדֵה הַחֵרֶם
לַכֹּהֵן תִּהְיֶה אֲחֻזָּתוֹ׃
22 וְאִם אֶת־שְׂדֵה מִקְנָתוֹ אֲשֶׁר לֹא מִשְּׂדֵה
אֲחֻזָּתוֹ יַקְדִּישׁ לַיהֹוָה׃ 23 וְחִשַּׁב־לוֹ הַכֹּהֵן
אֵת מִכְסַת הָעֶרְכְּךָ עַד שְׁנַת הַיֹּבֵל וְנָתַן
אֶת־הָעֶרְכְּךָ בַּיּוֹם הַהוּא קֹדֶשׁ לַיהֹוָה׃
24 בִּשְׁנַת הַיּוֹבֵל יָשׁוּב הַשָּׂדֶה לַאֲשֶׁר
קָנָהוּ מֵאִתּוֹ לַאֲשֶׁר־לוֹ אֲחֻזַּת הָאָרֶץ׃
25 וְכָל־עֶרְכְּךָ יִהְיֶה בְּשֶׁקֶל הַקֹּדֶשׁ עֶשְׂרִים
גֵּרָה יִהְיֶה הַשָּׁקֶל׃
26 אַךְ־בְּכוֹר אֲשֶׁר־יְבֻכַּר לַיהֹוָה בִּבְהֵמָה

her dead husband's land, which seems to indicate that under certain circumstances widows could inherit and sell their husband's property. Presumably a female landholder could consecrate land to the sanctuary.

***14. consecrates.*** The verbal root is *k-d-sh* ("holy" or "set apart"). Here the verb means dedicating something to God, thus making it holy.

***house.*** This probably refers to urban dwellings, for houses located elsewhere are subject to being returned to their owner in the jubilee year (see 25:29–31).

### FIRSTLINGS (27:26–27)

The Torah's legislation views all firstlings as automatically consecrated to God; their owners cannot dedicate them to the sanctuary, since they are

firstling—is יהוה's, cannot be consecrated by anybody; whether ox or sheep, it is יהוה's. 27 But if it is of impure animals, it may be ransomed as its assessment, with one-fifth added; if it is not redeemed, it shall be sold at its assessment.

28 But of all that anyone owns, be it human or beast or land-holding, nothing that has been proscribed for יהוה may be sold or redeemed; every proscribed thing is totally consecrated to יהוה. 29 No human being who has been proscribed can be ransomed: that person shall be put to death.

30 All tithes from the land, whether seed from the ground or fruit from the tree, are יהוה's; they are holy to יהוה. 31 If anyone wishes to redeem any tithes, one-fifth must be added to them. 32 All tithes of the herd or flock—of all that passes under the shepherd's staff, every tenth one—shall be holy to יהוה. 33 One must not look out for good as against bad, or make substitution for it. If one does make substitution for it, then it and its substitute shall both be holy: it cannot be redeemed.

לֹא־יַקְדִּישׁ אִישׁ אֹתוֹ אִם־שׁוֹר אִם־שֶׂה
לַיהֹוָה הוּא׃ 27 וְאִם בַּבְּהֵמָה הַטְּמֵאָה
וּפָדָה בְעֶרְכֶּךָ וְיָסַף חֲמִשִׁתוֹ עָלָיו וְאִם־לֹא
יִגָּאֵל וְנִמְכַּר בְּעֶרְכֶּךָ׃
28 אַךְ־כׇּל־חֵרֶם אֲשֶׁר יַחֲרִם אִישׁ לַיהֹוָה
מִכׇּל־אֲשֶׁר־לוֹ מֵאָדָם וּבְהֵמָה וּמִשְּׂדֵה
אֲחֻזָּתוֹ לֹא יִמָּכֵר וְלֹא יִגָּאֵל כׇּל־חֵרֶם
קֹדֶשׁ־קׇדָשִׁים הוּא לַיהֹוָה׃ 29 כׇּל־חֵרֶם
אֲשֶׁר יׇחֳרַם מִן־הָאָדָם לֹא יִפָּדֶה מוֹת
יוּמָת׃
30 וְכׇל־מַעְשַׂר הָאָרֶץ מִזֶּרַע הָאָרֶץ מִפְּרִי
הָעֵץ לַיהֹוָה הוּא קֹדֶשׁ לַיהֹוָה׃ 31 וְאִם־
גָּאֹל יִגְאַל אִישׁ מִמַּעַשְׂרוֹ חֲמִשִׁיתוֹ יֹסֵף
עָלָיו׃ 32 וְכׇל־מַעְשַׂר בָּקָר וָצֹאן כֹּל אֲשֶׁר־
יַעֲבֹר תַּחַת הַשָּׁבֶט הָעֲשִׂירִי יִהְיֶה־קֹּדֶשׁ
לַיהֹוָה׃ 33 לֹא יְבַקֵּר בֵּין־טוֹב לָרַע וְלֹא
יְמִירֶנּוּ וְאִם־הָמֵר יְמִירֶנּוּ וְהָיָה־הוּא
וּתְמוּרָתוֹ יִהְיֶה־קֹּדֶשׁ לֹא יִגָּאֵל׃

already God's property (see, for example, Exodus 13:2). Animals that are not fit for sacrifice can be redeemed by the owner. Otherwise, the sanctuary may sell them as a source of income.

## PROSCRIPTIONS (27:28–29)

While most references to *cherem* (proscription) in the Bible deal with the proscription of Israel's enemies and their property at times of war (for example, Numbers 21:2–3), Leviticus 27 seems to be addressing cases within the Israelite community. Proscribed property becomes the permanent property of the sanctuary.

These verses seem to presume a distinction between two types of persons. Verse 28 treats non-Israelite slaves who are proscribed as part of an owner's property and then become the permanent property of the sanctuary. Verse 29 applies to individuals whom some authorized communal body (probably a court) has proscribed, and who are thus under a death sentence.

***28. totally consecrated.*** Heb. *kodesh kodashim.* Objects permanently dedicated to God have the status of most holy; they are immutably sacred.

## TITHES (27:30–33)

These laws about two categories of tithes, agricultural and livestock, diverge from other biblical sources on tithes (see, for example, Numbers 18:21–24). As such, this section may represent either a very old tradition or a radical attempt at reform.

*33.* The tenth animal, whatever its condition, is designated for the tithe. It is unclear how in practice the status of tenth animal was to be assigned.

³⁴These are the commandments that יהוה gave Moses for the Israelite people on Mount Sinai.

³⁴ אֵ֣לֶּה הַמִּצְוֹ֗ת אֲשֶׁ֨ר צִוָּ֧ה יְהֹוָ֛ה אֶת־מֹשֶׁ֖ה אֶל־בְּנֵ֣י יִשְׂרָאֵ֑ל בְּהַ֖ר סִינָֽי׃

---

## CONCLUSION (27:34)

The final verse functions as a new conclusion to the book of Leviticus, complementing and completing the one in 26:46, which it closely resembles.

Leviticus concludes by claiming that God gave these commandments to Moses on Mount Sinai. That is, even the material that seems to be appended has its origin in the original revelation and is essential to the covenant at Sinai.

—*Hilary Lipka*



חֲזַק חֲזַק וְנִתְחַזֵּק

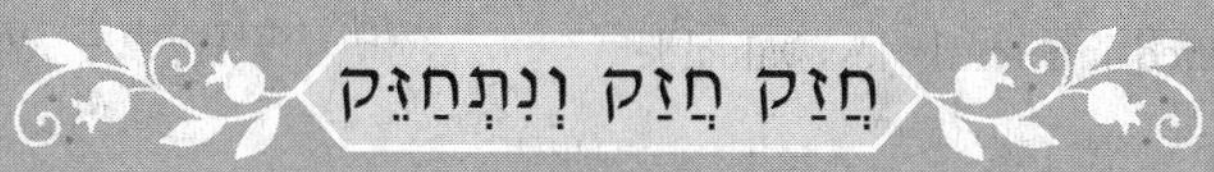

# Another View

The concluding unit of Leviticus concerns the economic support base, in the form of vowed resources, for ancient Israel's central shrine. The first set of such votary pledges, Leviticus 27:2–8, involves the equivalence in silver of persons according to categories of gender and age, with separate assessments listed for females and males in four age groups. Because of the greater monetary values assigned to males in each age category, scholars have sometimes understood this table of valuations as an expression of gender bias, with females considered inherently less valuable than males.

However, many commentators now understand that this table relates mainly to labor potential rather than to intrinsic worth. The highest monetary values appear for persons of ages twenty to sixty; such people would be considered mature adults, given the fact that biblical census texts list males of age twenty and above (namely, those who might be conscripted into military service; see Numbers 1:3). That the youngest age category is that of one- to five-year-olds can be explained by presuming that ancient Israel was like many premodern agrarian societies in expecting children of very young ages to perform simple household tasks. Perhaps because of average differences in physical strength, women or girls were deemed to have a lower productive capacity than males of the same age, and thus Leviticus 27 assigns them a somewhat lower valuation in all categories.

The differential shekel values attached to females and males provide an insight into the labor patterns in Israelite households and the associated status of women. The best way to view the table is to sum the value of the two genders in each age bracket, thus obtaining the combined labor value of a female-male

*This ratio of labor contribution correlates with maximum prestige for women.*

pair of workers in each category; then we can compare the contribution of each gender to this total amount. Except for the five to twenty category, in which childbearing (presumably beginning at puberty) might reduce the labor potential of females, the female percentage of that combined female-male amount is at or near 40 percent. Social scientists who study the relative contributions of women and men to household labor in various cultures have noted that a 2 : 3 female-to-male ratio, with women supplying 40 percent of the subsistence labor, correlates with the maximum prestige for women. Thus the table of valuations in Leviticus 27 is hardly a reflection of female inferiority but rather provides evidence of a positive estimation of women.

—*Carol Meyers*

# Post-biblical Interpretations

***When anyone explicitly vows to* יהוה** (27:2). The Hebrew noun translated here as "anyone" is *ish*, which in some contexts refers only to males. This verse's formulation contrasts with the nazirite vow in Numbers 6:2 and with the general vows and oaths in Numbers 30:3–4, which both specify also the female counterpart noun, *ishah*, as a potential oath taker (see commentaries there). Nonetheless, the Rabbis (Mishnah *Arachin* 1:1) explicate that both men and women can make the type of vow presumed by this biblical unit, implying that *ish* as used here is to be read inclusively.

In several different places, Mishnah *Arachin* records the names of women who made vows of various kinds, mostly related to their children. In the current context, it mentions the mother of a girl by the name of Yirmatia (or Domitia in a manuscript version) who vowed her daughter's weight, although it is unclear to what purpose (5:1). Elsewhere in the Mishnah, Helena—the queen of Adiabene, a convert to Judaism

*Both women and men can make the type of vow presumed by Leviticus 27.*

who is also mentioned by the 1st-century-C.E. historian Josephus—is said to have vowed to become a nazirite for seven years if her son returned "in safety from the war" (Mishnah *Nazir* 3:6). Also a certain Miriam of Palmyra brings offerings to fulfill a vow related to her dying daughter (*Nazir* 6:11). Josephus further mentions that his contemporary Berenice—sister of the Jewish Herodian ruler Agrippa II, and lover of Titus (the Roman general and later emperor)—made a vow of abstention.

Nonetheless, even though women appear prominently as autonomous oath takers in rabbinic aggadic literature, halachically a woman's oaths were subject to a father's or husband's annulment, much as specified already in biblical law (Numbers 30:4–17). Only widows, divorcées, or unmarried women above the age of 12½ could make vows as freely as any adult male.

***the equivalent for a human being*** (27:2). Although the vows of dedication to the Temple lost their relevance after its destruction in 70 C.E., the Rabbis developed the regulations outlined in Leviticus 27 into a special mishnaic tractate called *Arachin* (Valuations), derived from the biblical word translated here as "equivalent" (*erech*). Indeed, the subject of vows and oaths occupied the Rabbis greatly as they set about organizing their formulation of Jewish law. Indeed, the Mishnah devoted three additional tractates to this topic—*N'darim* (Vows), *Nazir* (Nazirite), and *Sh'vuot* (Oaths)—all of which received extensive talmudic discussion. Perhaps this indicates the popularity of oaths and vows as an expression of religiosity, extending into rabbinic times. Other evidence of this propensity is found in the words of the 4th-century Christian leader John Chrysostom of Antioch and Constantinople, known for his anti-Jewish sermons, who chastised his audience for flocking to the synagogues to take oaths.

***if it is a female, the equivalent is thirty shekels*** (27:4). The scale of fixed human value established here remains uncontested and unchanged in rabbinic tradition and does not receive much further commentary. The Rabbis devoted much more attention to regulating individualized vows such as vowing someone's weight, or even the weight of a particular body part (Mishnah *Arachin* 5:1–2). Interestingly, the Rabbis take note that the Torah differentiates between the weight of male (*zachar*) and female (*n'kevah*), and they therefore insist that this refers to those who are "definitely male" and "definitely female." This is one of the many contexts in Jewish law where the Rabbis introduce the concept of indeterminable sexual identity, namely the hermaphrodite (*androginos*) and the nonsexed person (*tumtum*), only to exclude such people from the scale of human valuation. However, the Mishnah considers both the *androginos* and the *tumtum* fully human and therefore able to make vows of valuation on someone who is of unambiguous sexual identity (*Arachin* 1:1).

***If the age is from one month to five years, the equivalent for a male is five shekels of silver*** (27:6). Numbers 18:15–16 likewise prescribe five shekels for the redemption of a month-old first-born son from the priest. Since this practice persisted in Jewish communities beyond Temple times (*pidyon haben*), the

Rabbis in Mishnah *B'chorot* 8:7 attempted to determine the contemporary coinage that contained the equivalent amount of silver. The talmudic Rabbis emphasize that women are exempt from the commandment of redeeming the first-born son, just as they are not obligated to circumcise their infant sons (BT *Kiddushin* 29a).

—*Charlotte Elisheva Fonrobert*

# Contemporary Reflection

THERE IS SOMETHING profoundly unsettling about *B'chukotai*. It seems to posit a world that we know, empirically, does not exist. It claims that there is a direct correlation between our actions and the natural order of the universe. Leviticus 26:3–5 promises unambiguously: "If you follow My laws and faithfully observe My commandments, I will grant you rains in their season . . . you shall eat your fill of bread. . . ." Verses 14–16 warn just as clearly: "But if you do not obey Me and do not observe all these commandments . . . I will wreak misery upon you. . . ." The seeming system of reward and punishment that these biblical passages proclaim appears to contradict the troubling reality that we witness, in which good people suffer, and evil people often prosper.

Passages like these seem to provide justification for those who reject both faith and God. How often do we hear, in the face of personal trauma or tragedy, "I can no longer believe in God" or "I can't believe in a God who would do this"? How are we to understand God's threats and promises?

According to the biblical scholar Nehama Leibowitz, our ancestors regarded blessings and curses, such as those in *B'chukotai*, as forms of prayer: these are the things that people hoped for, even willed to happen, in their longing for a world in which justice would visibly prevail. Perhaps this parashah is telling us, in its own theological language, that there is a moral order to the universe that is intrinsically connected to the natural order of the universe—and that the two orders are mutually dependent. In these teachings, it is as if God gives humankind every opportunity to discern that human action is intrinsic, and essential, to the proper functioning of the cosmos. Over and over again, the Torah enjoins us to act, to do, and to be because we "were slaves to Pharaoh in Egypt" (Deuteronomy 6:21), because we "know the feelings of the stranger" (Exodus 23:9), and through these experiences have been given the opportunity to glimpse this truth. This is why we were chosen to bear witness to God's revelation that "I, your God יהוה, am holy" (Leviticus 19:2). We are created in God's image and we, as God's partners, were chosen for a sacred task. This is our heritage and our responsibility; this is what it means to complete the work of Creation. But what if we forget, neglect, or ignore our sacred task of following the commandments?

*The physical and ethical dimensions of Creation are dependent upon each other.*

The catalogue of threats and promises is a biblical way to explain how intimate the connection of the natural realm of the universe is to the moral realm. The two realms do not function independently of each other. There is a moral order to the universe as surely as there is a more easily observable natural order of "rains in their season."

And it is in the moral realm where God cannot function alone. God never could—and so kept looking for partners. What did we expect of a God who created the natural universe? That the moral dimension was an afterthought? Our sages believed it pre-existed. God did not neglect the moral realm. On the contrary, humankind did. God kept expecting humankind to behave morally and was constantly disappointed—with Adam, with Noah, with the generations after the Flood. Finally, God found Abraham, the person who engaged God as an equal on ethical ground: "Must not the Judge of all the earth do justly?" (Genesis 18:25), and the process of Revelation began.

The essential unity of all aspects of God's Creation appears as well in Lurianic Kabbalah's formulation of the universe. Isaac Luria's theory of *Sh'virat Hakeilim* (Shattering of the Vessels) seeks to explain the brokenness of our world, and to advance the means to restore it to its original unity. For Luria in the 16th century, it was the great cosmic shattering that had brought about our exile from God and from God's Creation. Luria not only understood the primordial unity of God's intention but also yearned for a return to it. In God's promise of "rains in their season [and presence] in your midst," Luria could see the opportunity for humankind to repair the world, to release the sparks, to play a role in the restoration of the universe through the performance of mitzvot.

In Judaism, the mystic does not seek to transcend or deny the material world. Rather, the mystic's goal is the objective of this Torah portion: to restore the world, materially and spiritually, to a "single divine reality." As Lawrence Fine describes that goal in his study of Luria, *Physician of the Soul, Healer of the Cosmos* (2003), it is the "dream that collective human effort can mend a broken world." This is the vision of *B'chukotai.*

In these final verses of the book of Leviticus, God describes—in the most tactile, physical, understandable terms possible—the relationship between God's Creation and humankind's responsibility. It is simultaneously bribe and promise, exhortation and encouragement. At the foundation of it all is the essential understanding of Torah: the physical and ethical dimensions of God's Creation are wholly dependent upon each other, and we ignore that relationship at our peril. There is no quid pro quo for individuals in the world—God's scheme is far grander and more subtle than that. The issue is not one of personal reward and punishment. It is the unity of God, the unity of the prophetic vision as rendered in the Reform liturgy: "On that day, all the world shall be One and God's name shall be One" (Zechariah 14:9). It is the ultimate fulfillment of Torah—as expressed in Leviticus 26:46: "These are the laws, rules, and *torot* that יהוה established *beino uvein b'nei Yisrael* (in relationship with the Children of Israel)." This is the partnership that must one day bring about the fulfillment of our hopes, dreams, and strivings—the sparks released as heaven and earth, heart and mind and soul are united at last.

—*Sarah Sager*

# *Voices*

## *from* You are Wondrous

Lea Goldberg (transl. Rachel Tzvia Back)

*Leviticus 26:4–10*

By law I am not entitled
to this joy. I know, by law
I do not deserve the splendor of bridal clothes
but the sackcloth of the penitent.

But I am guilty that at my journey's end,
my eyes toward the wasteland,
happiness caught me like a downpour
and I had no time to cover my head.

Ever since I have been like a tree in the heart
of the desert
on which a thousand birds have descended,
its dry branches filling with song.

Ever since I have been a pool in the heart of
night—
in their randomness, generous skies
have scattered in it all the stars.

## The Dance of the Reform Jew

Myra Soifer

*Leviticus 26:3*

Though the translation renders the word *teileichu* as "follow," the usual meaning of its root, *h-l-ch*, is actually "to walk." Jewish law is known as *halachah*, "the walking path." As a Reform Jew, walking in God's laws is not for me. I'd rather dance them. Lately, I've become a passionate dancer. I tap dance for fun, but ballroom dance is my unbridled joy. And on the dance floor, I've learned quite a bit about God and mitzvot. Dancing is a whole new way of being in the world. While I live pretty rationally, I dance best when I'm least cerebral. I'm not too bad at learning Torah and Talmud, but learning dance steps uses a whole different sort of memory. It's muscle memory, body memory—a kind of memory that goes deeper and far beyond the scope of my intellect. My greatest challenge in ballroom dance has been learning to follow. I am used to being in control and trust my own abilities more easily than I trust my partners. It took me a long time to understand that following is a real blessing; trusting someone else to lead when I can anticipate and know the steps to come has become an important part of my joy as I whirl around the dance floor. Is God the supreme dance partner who invites me to join the dance of life, and to follow a rhythm that engages my body and my spirit?

## *Broken Prayer*

Yerra Sugarman

*Leviticus 26:14–45*

Dear God of Israel, my heart is a ship
on high swells, a reed

cradle. Lapis
lit with affliction.

You, who made the heart whole, why
do you unfasten from it

the soul—so glass—
so broken—

## *That Very Night*

Rivka Miriam (transl. Linda Stern Zisquit)

*Leviticus 27:1–8*

*1*
That very night it became clear to him that
I'm a man
a heavy man with strict countenance
whose talk is mixed with strange dialects
and until now when he was touching me
otherwise
he was wrong.
I'm a man.
So he saw.
"She's a man," he said,
for he was used to calling me "she"
all those years.
Together we'll go to the store
and buy matching hats
and speak to each other
in thick voices.

*2*
Now that it is clear that I'm a man
it turns out that I'm the father of my children
and their growth was in a father's womb
warm and hairy and tearless.
Children, call me mother
and when I speak to you I'll try
my thinnest voice
bonnets and aprons I'll continue to embroider
with my large fingers.
Children, call me mother
even if the milk froze at the tip of my nipples.

*3*
All the words I've written till now—
a man wrote.
Once I thought they were like a woman
swelling and shrinking with the seasons, like
her.
It's not so.
They were straight and set, void of curves.
When a girl approaches them
with a confident arm, they'll embrace her
and she'll open up wide.

## *Packing Slip*

Jessica Greenbaum

*Leviticus 27:3–4*

White, Jewish female, 5′ 4½″, 112 lbs, brown eyes, brown hair, from hirsute tribes in Poland and Russia, Tay-Sachs positive, HIV negative, anemia prevents selling blood for pocket money when traveling in Greece or other countries, Raynaud's disease causes numbness in digits when cold, often followed by sense of home-sickness for some place as yet unnamed; fallen arches from thirty years of running the streets of Roslyn, Manhattan, Houston, Brooklyn, and wherever she woke up; aversion to cilantro, and violent response to tickling; wide scar down belly from amateurish removal of ovarian cyst ("who did that, a butcher?" asked the gynecologist); slight knife-fight scar on shoulder from lung surgery, with side-effect of permanent tenderness in left breast; pregnancies to term: 2; abortions for medical reasons: 2; for non-medical: 1; miscarriage followed by d&c's: 3; able to swim a mile without shortness of breath and lift heavy packages in single heave; fine sense of smell though Semitic nose reflects, through complexion, emotional climate, intake of hot drinks, alcohol, spices and chocolate; can sit cross-legged and touch toes (separate times), stalled lifelong at 11 push-ups; legally blind without specs, sensitivity to sunlight has bred the wearing of sunglasses indoors in such places as rude brightness requires; no fear of bats, snakes or spiders, but scurrying rodents evoke generic screech. In general, however, heart seems unafraid: shows buds, rings, and other surprising signs of new growth and heartiness for winter months; flowers and fruit collected last spring still out for analysis; lab technicians have reported falling into dream-like faint upon attempt to decode spell and provide explanations. Contents, which may have settled during living, contain live cultures.

Inspector # 9

## *Nearing 80*

Bracha Kopstein

*Leviticus 27:7*

I look into the mirror and smile,
Laugh not at myself, but at the calendar—
Have never been eighty before.

I was frightened at the thought of eighty,
Here I am, the calendar says—
Reaching the shore.

I am a living book, a pageless book
That I could never re-read
Within eighty years.

I need more years.
I am so busy with life and with words
That I cannot pronounce, like a newborn baby.

I want to understand myself,
Neighbors, family, country—
I desire a great number of years.

Will I ever learn at all?
Never!
I want to feel, as I do:
Numberless, young old, I am I.

I can see, I can hear, I can cry,
I can smile
The same as yesterday, a century ago
With all the pages of the book unopened,
I have new ones yet to write.

What a delight
Nearing eighty,
To say to the calendar:
Forgive me, But I doubt your power—
I feel, and I am.

# במדבר ✦ *B'midbar*

# NUMBERS

The book of Numbers records the Israelites' forty years' journey from Sinai to the plains (or steppes) of Moab, their last stop before entering the Promised Land. The book begins with a census that numbers the eligible fighting men among the people who left Egypt—hence the English name "Numbers." Yet it is the Hebrew name of the book, *B'midbar* ("in the wilderness [of]"), that aptly captures the challenges the book describes. Wilderness is a place—or time—without orienting landmarks or structure. Numbers charts the journey through a wilderness and attempts to create new structures in this intermediary space for future life in the land.

The book is itself a kind of wilderness, a seemingly chaotic combination of narratives, laws, and lists that can be roughly divided into three parts. Numbers' narrative begins where Exodus 40 left off. The first part describes orderly preparations and departure from Sinai, where the Israelites had camped for two years (Numbers 1–10). The second part describes descent into chaos, with the Israelites' (mis)-adventures during the journey. This section is

*This book treats women as a force to contend with, and as a source of Torah.*

marked by "murmurings" and rebellions, and their dire consequences (Numbers 11–25), including God's decision to doom the generation of the Exodus to die in the wilderness. The third part describes the preparation of the new generation for life in the Promised Land (Numbers 26–37).

The book's major themes include: conflicts and decisions over leadership, worship and sanctuary, and land inheritance. Numbers reflects competition over legitimate priesthood between the line of Aaron and other members from the tribe of Levi, to which Moses and Miriam also belong. The book grants the priesthood solely to men of the line of Aaron and only secondary responsibilities for the sanctuary to the rest of the men of Levi, known as Levites. Like Leviticus, Numbers is also concerned with ritual purity and thus it likewise prescribes steps to guard the sanctity of the sanctuary as well as the purity of all who approach it. Critical scholars typically question the book's historical accuracy as a depiction of life in the wilderness; they conclude that Israel's memory of this period was shaped over a long period of time, and that the laws and narratives in Numbers come primarily from priestly sources (see Women and Interpretation of the Torah, p. xxxvi).

Women appear more prominently in Numbers than in Leviticus—both as those to whom laws apply and as active figures in narratives; they play a significant role in nine out of thirty-six chapters.

Although most of the laws in Numbers pertain to women and men alike, some specifically concern women. These include the case of the wife suspected of adultery (Numbers 5:11–31), which describes the ordeal she must undergo in such a situation; the laws about vows (Numbers 30) that delineate who determines what vows a woman must honor; and laws of inheritance for when a man dies without a will and has daughters but no sons (Numbers 27 and 36).

Whereas the case of the suspected wife and that of vows have women as their object of concern, the stories about inheritance present women as subjects: women who take action and initiate a new ruling that enables them as well as future women to inherit their ancestral land if their father has no sons. Here, five sisters named Mahlah, Noah, Hoglah, Milcah, and Tirzah (also known as Zelophehad's daughters) argue their case before Israel's leaders and the larger community, thereby effecting change. Perhaps most astonishing, their story also depicts a situation in which a Torah law emerges not from Sinai but from the women themselves (for details, see at Numbers 27 and 36).

Other stories include Miriam's (and Aaron's) challenge to Moses in Numbers 12 and the stories about dangerous women, especially foreign women (see the case of the Moabite/Midianite women in Numbers 25 and 33 who are depicted as luring Israel away from God). Ultimately, little can be determined from Numbers about the actual lives of women in ancient Israel. Yet one can conclude from this book that women were perceived as a force to contend with, as well as a source for Torah.

—*Tamara Cohn Eskenazi*

# במדבר ✦ *B'midbar*

## NUMBERS 1:1–4:20

## *The Architecture of a Count and the Architecture of Account*

THE SACRED SPACE described in *parashat B'midbar* bridges the end of Exodus and the beginning of Numbers. Exodus concludes with a magisterial description of the Tabernacle and the priests—both resplendent in the colorful handiwork of Israelite women. Once God's presence fills the Tabernacle and not even Moses can enter, a distinction between Divine and human becomes clear. Leviticus follows, with laws concerning how to negotiate this boundary between Divine and human. Numbers then returns to the topic with which Exodus ends. In Numbers the perspective is widened to include the formation in which Israel camps with the Tabernacle at its center. The Tabernacle complex, with its collapsible boundaries and open spaces, creates a sense of order in the unfamiliar chaos of the wilderness. The Tabernacle also helps orient the Israelites in the vast expanse of that wilderness, since they stay or go based on the ascent and descent of the cloud of God's Presence. In this sense, God lives amidst the Israelites throughout their journey to the Promised Land.

"Numbers," the English name of the book, alludes to the social organization of the Israelites and the two censuses that frame the book (Numbers 1 and 26); the Hebrew title, *B'midbar* (from the first distinctive word, meaning "in the wilderness [of]"), highlights the transitory setting of the narrative. The contrast between these two titles reflects a tension between order and chaos, culture and nature, obedience and rebellion that characterizes the book and drives its plot. This type of tension also suffuses the concept of holiness that operates in this book, in which one recognizes both the creative and the destructive power of God.

---

*Ordering the community creates the space for encounters with the Divine.*

---

While contact with God makes Israel holy, encountering God without preparation is potentially lethal.

Although the scrupulous detail of this parashah and other parts of the book may not immediately grip the reader, the underlying idea is that the ordering of the community—and by extension, one's life—creates the space for encounters with the Divine. The power of this book emerges from the image of the encampment's concentric rectangles radiating inward to a core of supreme holiness. In this geometry of moving from the periphery to the center, the tribes encamp around the Levites, who encircle the high priestly family, who surround the Tabernacle's curtained walls that enclose the court that buffers the Holy of Holies. This symmetry—constructed on the ground as well as in prose—is a collective act of ordering chaos that emulates the creation of the world in Genesis 1:1–2:4.

*Parashat B'midbar* illustrates how hierarchies in a given society are "spatialized," meaning that its power structures are evident in the physical spaces of the society, such as city plans or religious architecture. In Numbers, for example, the arrangement of the camp favors the sons of Aaron as *kohanim* (priests), whereas the marching order gives prominence to the sons of Judah. Military language and concepts infuse the description of the camp's arrangement. It is not surprising, therefore, that women do not appear in this parashah; counting conceals the female presence in the community. (For a somewhat different perspective on women's apparent absence, see Another View, p. 808.)

—*Rachel Havrelock*

## Outline

*I.* NAMES AND NUMBERS
*The Israelites in the Wilderness* (1:1–54)

- *A.* The tribes (vv. 1–19)
- *B.* The census (vv. 20–46)
- *C.* The Levites (vv. 47–54)

*II.* THE GEOMETRY OF THE HOLY (2:1–34)

- *A.* The east (vv. 1–9)
- *B.* The south (vv. 10–16)
- *C.* The center (v. 17)
- *D.* The west (vv. 18–24)
- *E.* The north (vv. 25–31)
- *F.* Conclusion (vv. 32–34)

*III.* THE LEVITES (3:1–4:20)

- *A.* The election of the priests (3:1–10)
- *B.* The election of the Levites (3:11–22)
- *C.* The organization of the Levites (3:23–39)
- *D.* The price of redemption (3:40–51)
- *E.* The service of the Levites (4:1–20)

On the first day of the second month, in the second year following the exodus from the land of Egypt, יהוה spoke to Moses in the wilderness of Sinai, in the Tent of Meeting, saying:
[2]Take a census of the whole Israelite company

א וַיְדַבֵּר יְהֹוָה אֶל־מֹשֶׁה בְּמִדְבַּר סִינַי
בְּאֹהֶל מוֹעֵד בְּאֶחָד לַחֹדֶשׁ הַשֵּׁנִי בַּשָּׁנָה
הַשֵּׁנִית לְצֵאתָם מֵאֶרֶץ מִצְרַיִם לֵאמֹר׃
2 שְׂאוּ אֶת־רֹאשׁ כׇּל־עֲדַת בְּנֵי־יִשְׂרָאֵל

## *Names and Numbers*

### THE ISRAELITES IN THE WILDERNESS (1:1–54)

*B'midbar* opens by setting the date of the census: *Rosh Chodesh Iyar*, the start of the second month of the second year since Israel departed from Egypt. Although the Israelites are more than a year deep in their journey, this date marks something of a new beginning since they are now in possession of laws as well as the Tabernacle. A central theme of the book of Numbers is transition; the census relates to this theme by depicting the transition of the tribes into a national body.

How are we to understand the litany of names that fill this parashah? The ordering of the camp is akin to the necessary preparations that precede any expedition or long trip, as departure requires taking stock of what one brings along. The dominant motivation of this census is to organize Israel into battalions in order to begin the march toward Canaan. As the Torah reminds us, other nations inhabit the Promised Land; so before Israel claims the destination as home, it will have to reconstitute itself as a nation of warriors.

But the census also represents a point reached in every community when the group takes stock of who stands in its ranks. This, then, is a moment of Israel's self-assessment, where the generation previously numbered only as slaves in Egypt perceives itself as a unified nation. However, in an important sense, the opening of Numbers is utopian; as the rest of the book demonstrates, the generation that once knew slavery in Egypt proves incapable of remaking itself into a nation of warriors and reaching the Promised Land. Their fate instead will be to perish in the wilderness and find consolation in the fact that their children will achieve what they could not.

### THE TRIBES (1:1–19)

2. ***Take a census.*** A census is a practical tool but also a mode of enforcing power. Who does the recording and who is recorded are not incidental issues; rather, the answers provide a form of centralizing authority and of creating a definitive hierarchy. The *Tanach* records several censuses and (in its characteristic way) includes examples that express ambivalence about this practice. While there is something rousing about the emergence of organized troops from the newly liberated and still somewhat

The Israelite encampment is structured according to four important women.

ANOTHER VIEW ➤ *808*

The question is not whether everyone is counted, but whether everyone matters.

CONTEMPORARY REFLECTION ➤ *810*

One reason for the deaths of Aaron's sons was their arrogance in refusing to marry.

POST-BIBLICAL INTERPRETATIONS ➤ *809*

I am a wandering girl. / My heart is practiced in longing. . . .

VOICES ➤ *812*

[of fighters] by the clans of its ancestral houses, listing the names, every male, head by head. 3You and Aaron shall record them by their groups, from the age of twenty years up, all those in Israel who are able to bear arms. 4Associated with you shall be a representative of each tribe, each one the head of his ancestral house.

5These are the names of the representatives who shall assist you:

From Reuben, Elizur son of Shedeur.

6From Simeon, Shelumiel son of Zurishaddai.

לְמִשְׁפְּחֹתָם לְבֵית אֲבֹתָם בְּמִסְפַּר שֵׁמוֹת
כָּל־זָכָר לְגֻלְגְּלֹתָם׃ 3 מִבֶּן עֶשְׂרִים שָׁנָה
וָמַעְלָה כָּל־יֹצֵא צָבָא בְּיִשְׂרָאֵל תִּפְקְדוּ
אֹתָם לְצִבְאֹתָם אַתָּה וְאַהֲרֹן׃ 4 וְאִתְּכֶם
יִהְיוּ אִישׁ אִישׁ לַמַּטֶּה אִישׁ רֹאשׁ לְבֵית־
אֲבֹתָיו הוּא׃
5 וְאֵלֶּה שְׁמוֹת הָאֲנָשִׁים אֲשֶׁר יַעַמְדוּ
אִתְּכֶם
לִרְאוּבֵן אֱלִיצוּר בֶּן־שְׁדֵיאוּר׃
6 לְשִׁמְעוֹן שְׁלֻמִיאֵל בֶּן־צוּרִישַׁדָּי׃

beleaguered people of Israel, other occasions of census taking unleash chaos on the Israelites (II Samuel 24:1–10; I Chronicles 21:1–8; 27:23–24). There is thematic tension between the idea that Israel should be numberless (Genesis 15:5; I Kings 3:8) and the occasions of census taking.

***ancestral houses.*** Heb. *beit avot.* The tribes are made up of clans comprised of families, and the family unit in turn includes a cluster of households. The "ancestral house" (extended family) is the core institution of the agricultural and tribal system of ancient Israel. This unit claims a specific tract of land as well as its yield and workers. The *beit avot* (also called *beit av,* as when Rachel and Leah speak in Genesis 31:14) is an extended-family structure made up of all the descendants of a living ancestor, whereas the larger clan and tribal units rally around the memory of a more distant patriarchal figure. When a female member of the *beit avot* marries, she generally departs from her *beit avot* and joins that of her husband. At no level in this parashah are women recorded, but the very notion of a family or a household as a basis of society demands recognition of female power and agency.

***every male.*** The hierarchy at work becomes apparent as only men are counted as Israelites at this juncture, and as priests and Levites secure exemptions. The census regroups Israel along military lines, yet we note that all of the potential fighting men of Israel comprise less than half of the community, not the whole.

*3.* ***groups . . . bear arms.*** Heb. *tz'vaot . . . tzava.* These terms refer here to military roles fulfilled by men. However, the same root (*tz-v-a*) is used elsewhere to describe the women who served at the entrance of the Tent of Meeting (see at Exodus 38:8; I Samuel 2:22). In Isaiah 40:2 the same term, referring to conscript service, is ascribed to Jerusalem personified as a woman. When the prophet Deborah commands the Israelites to go to war, she appoints a man, Barak, to lead the troops. (Upon Barak's insistence, however, Deborah accompanies him in battle; see Judges 4:1–10.)

*4.* ***representative of each tribe.*** At certain junctures in the wilderness, it becomes apparent that Israel comprises twelve tribes. Each tribe adheres to an internal order while participating in the larger community. Maintaining tribal boundaries with respect to land inheritance will later prompt one group to challenge the unqualified grant of land to the daughters of Zelophehad: Mahlah, Tirzah, Hoglah, Milcah, and Noah. See at 36:1–13.

*5.* ***These are the names.*** The list of tribal chieftains groups the tribes according to their ancestral mothers (Genesis 35:22–26). The Leah tribes appear first, followed by the Rachel tribes; the Bilhah and Zilpah tribes are then interspersed.

7 From Judah, Nahshon son of Amminadab.
8 From Issachar, Nethanel son of Zuar.
9 From Zebulun, Eliab son of Helon.
10 From the sons of Joseph:
from Ephraim, Elishama son of Ammihud;
from Manasseh, Gamaliel son of Pedahzur.
11 From Benjamin, Abidan son of Gideoni.
12 From Dan, Ahiezer son of Ammishaddai.
13 From Asher, Pagiel son of Ochran.
14 From Gad, Eliasaph son of Deuel.
15 From Naphtali, Ahira son of Enan.
16 Those are the elected of the assembly, the chieftains of their ancestral tribes: they are the heads of the contingents of Israel.

17 So Moses and Aaron took those representatives, who were designated by name,
18 and on the first day of the second month they convoked the whole company [of fighters], who were registered by the clans of their ancestral houses—the names of those aged twenty years and over being listed head by head.
19 As יהוה had commanded Moses, so he recorded them in the wilderness of Sinai.

7 לִיהוּדָ֕ה נַחְשׁ֖וֹן בֶּן־עַמִּינָדָֽב׃
8 לישׂשכר לְיִ֨שָּׂשכָ֔ר נְתַנְאֵ֖ל בֶּן־צוּעָֽר׃
9 לִזְבוּלֻ֕ן אֱלִיאָ֖ב בֶּן־חֵלֹֽן׃
10 לִבְנֵ֣י יוֹסֵ֔ף לְאֶפְרַ֕יִם אֱלִישָׁמָ֖ע בֶּן־
עַמִּיה֑וּד
לִמְנַשֶּׁ֕ה גַּמְלִיאֵ֖ל בֶּן־פְּדָהצֽוּר׃
11 לְבִ֨נְיָמִ֔ן אֲבִידָ֖ן בֶּן־גִּדְעֹנִֽי׃
12 לְדָ֕ן אֲחִיעֶ֖זֶר בֶּן־עַמִּישַׁדָּֽי׃
13 לְאָשֵׁ֕ר פַּגְעִיאֵ֖ל בֶּן־עָכְרָֽן׃
14 לְגָ֕ד אֶלְיָסָ֖ף בֶּן־דְּעוּאֵֽל׃
15 לְנַ֨פְתָּלִ֔י אֲחִירַ֖ע בֶּן־עֵינָֽן׃
16 אֵ֚לֶּה קריאי קְרוּאֵ֣י הָעֵדָ֔ה נְשִׂיאֵ֖י מַטּ֣וֹת
אֲבוֹתָ֑ם רָאשֵׁ֛י אַלְפֵ֥י יִשְׂרָאֵ֖ל הֵֽם׃
17 וַיִּקַּ֥ח מֹשֶׁ֖ה וְאַהֲרֹ֑ן אֵ֚ת הָאֲנָשִׁ֣ים הָאֵ֔לֶּה
אֲשֶׁ֥ר נִקְּב֖וּ בְּשֵׁמֽוֹת׃ 18 וְאֵ֨ת כָּל־הָעֵדָ֜ה
הִקְהִ֗ילוּ בְּאֶחָד֙ לַחֹ֣דֶשׁ הַשֵּׁנִ֔י וַיִּתְיַֽלְד֥וּ עַל־
מִשְׁפְּחֹתָ֖ם לְבֵ֣ית אֲבֹתָ֑ם בְּמִסְפַּ֣ר שֵׁמ֗וֹת
מִבֶּ֨ן עֶשְׂרִ֥ים שָׁנָ֛ה וָמַ֖עְלָה לְגֻלְגְּלֹתָֽם׃
19 כַּאֲשֶׁ֛ר צִוָּ֥ה יְהֹוָ֖ה אֶת־מֹשֶׁ֑ה וַֽיִּפְקְדֵ֖ם
בְּמִדְבַּ֥ר סִינָֽי׃

*7. Nahshon son of Amminadab.* The tribal representative from Judah is the nephew of Elisheba, wife to Aaron the chief priest and mother of the priests Nadab, Abihu, Eleazar, and Ithamar (Exodus 6:23). The tribes of Judah and Levi were thus allied when a prominent woman of Judah married Aaron. This foreshadows the fact that the Temple will be built in the territory of Judah. The book of Ruth also enumerates Nahshon in its genealogy (Ruth 4:20).

*16. the heads of the contingents of Israel.* The tribal heads simultaneously command military contingents.

*18. they convoked the whole company [of fighters].* Following the census, those listed in the ranks gather under the banner or "standard" of their tribes and stand proud as the army of Israel. The army that here appears well poised for battle will not prove psychologically ready, so invasion is postponed for a generation (see Deuteronomy 2:14–16). The representation of the people Israel as an army renders women invisible.

*who were registered.* [The Hebrew word that is uniquely translated here as "registered" is a form of the verbal root *y-l-d*, which elsewhere means "to give birth." The self-reflexive nature of the verb here almost suggests that this army gave birth to itself. —*Ed.*]

*19. As* יהוה *had commanded Moses, so he recorded them in the wilderness of Sinai.* This summation of the command closes this section, which began, "God spoke to Moses in the wilderness of Sinai" (1:1). Divine speech frames this section and legitimizes the subsequent census by marking it as a reflection of divine will. This emphasis is important in light of God's reported opposition elsewhere

20 They totaled as follows:
The descendants of Reuben, Israel's first-born,
the registration of the clans of their ancestral house,
as listed by name, head by head, all males aged
twenty years and over, all who were able to bear
arms— 21 those enrolled from the tribe of Reuben:
46,500.
22 Of the descendants of Simeon, the registration of the clans of their ancestral house, their enrollment as listed by name, head by head, all males
aged twenty years and over, all who were able to
bear arms— 23 those enrolled from the tribe of
Simeon: 59,300.
24 Of the descendants of Gad, the registration of
the clans of their ancestral house, as listed by name,
aged twenty years and over, all who were able to
bear arms— 25 those enrolled from the tribe of Gad:
45,650.
26 Of the descendants of Judah, the registration
of the clans of their ancestral house, as listed by
name, aged twenty years and over, all who were
able to bear arms— 27 those enrolled from the tribe
of Judah: 74,600.
28 Of the descendants of Issachar, the registration of the clans of their ancestral house, as listed
by name, aged twenty years and over, all who were

20 וַיִּהְי֤וּ
בְנֵֽי־רְאוּבֵן֙ בְּכֹ֣ר יִשְׂרָאֵ֔ל תּוֹלְדֹתָ֥ם
לְמִשְׁפְּחֹתָ֖ם לְבֵ֣ית אֲבֹתָ֑ם בְּמִסְפַּ֤ר שֵׁמוֹת֙
לְגֻלְגְּלֹתָ֔ם כָּל־זָכָ֗ר מִבֶּ֨ן עֶשְׂרִ֤ים שָׁנָה֙
וָמַ֔עְלָה כֹּ֖ל יֹצֵ֥א צָבָֽא׃ 21 פְּקֻדֵיהֶ֖ם לְמַטֵּ֣ה
רְאוּבֵ֑ן שִׁשָּׁ֧ה וְאַרְבָּעִ֛ים אֶ֖לֶף וַחֲמֵ֥שׁ
מֵאֽוֹת׃ פ
22 לִבְנֵ֣י שִׁמְע֔וֹן תּוֹלְדֹתָ֥ם לְמִשְׁפְּחֹתָ֖ם לְבֵ֣ית
אֲבֹתָ֑ם פְּקֻדָ֗יו בְּמִסְפַּ֤ר שֵׁמוֹת֙ לְגֻלְגְּלֹתָ֔ם
כָּל־זָכָ֗ר מִבֶּ֨ן עֶשְׂרִ֤ים שָׁנָה֙ וָמַ֔עְלָה כֹּ֖ל יֹצֵ֥א
צָבָֽא׃ 23 פְּקֻדֵיהֶ֖ם לְמַטֵּ֣ה שִׁמְע֑וֹן תִּשְׁעָ֧ה
וַחֲמִשִּׁ֛ים אֶ֖לֶף וּשְׁלֹ֥שׁ מֵאֽוֹת׃ פ
24 לִבְנֵ֣י גָ֔ד תּוֹלְדֹתָ֥ם לְמִשְׁפְּחֹתָ֖ם לְבֵ֣ית
אֲבֹתָ֑ם בְּמִסְפַּ֣ר שֵׁמ֗וֹת מִבֶּ֨ן עֶשְׂרִ֤ים שָׁנָה֙
וָמַ֔עְלָה כֹּ֖ל יֹצֵ֥א צָבָֽא׃ 25 פְּקֻדֵיהֶ֖ם לְמַטֵּ֣ה
גָ֑ד חֲמִשָּׁ֤ה וְאַרְבָּעִים֙ אֶ֔לֶף וְשֵׁ֥שׁ מֵא֖וֹת
וַחֲמִשִּֽׁים׃ פ
26 לִבְנֵ֣י יְהוּדָ֔ה תּוֹלְדֹתָ֥ם לְמִשְׁפְּחֹתָ֖ם לְבֵ֣ית
אֲבֹתָ֑ם בְּמִסְפַּ֣ר שֵׁמֹ֗ת מִבֶּ֨ן עֶשְׂרִ֤ים שָׁנָה֙
וָמַ֔עְלָה כֹּ֖ל יֹצֵ֥א צָבָֽא׃ 27 פְּקֻדֵיהֶ֖ם לְמַטֵּ֣ה
יְהוּדָ֑ה אַרְבָּעָ֧ה וְשִׁבְעִ֛ים אֶ֖לֶף וְשֵׁ֥שׁ
מֵאֽוֹת׃ פ
28 לִבְנֵ֣י יששכר יִשָּׂשכָ֔ר תּוֹלְדֹתָ֥ם לְמִשְׁפְּחֹתָ֖ם
לְבֵ֣ית אֲבֹתָ֑ם בְּמִסְפַּ֣ר שֵׁמֹ֗ת מִבֶּ֨ן עֶשְׂרִ֤ים

to taking a census (see, for example, II Samuel 24:1–10, where God punishes Israel for King David's decision to take a census).

THE CENSUS (1:20–46)

In military formation, the twelve tribes of Israel are Reuben, Simon, Gad, Judah, Issachar, Zebulun, Ephraim, Manasseh, Benjamin, Dan, Asher, and Naphtali. (The tribe of Levi is counted separately; see below at 1:47–54.) Rachel's son Joseph is represented in terms of his and Asenath's two sons, Ephraim and Manasseh. According to this parashah, the men of Israel over twenty years of age number 603,550; but the sum is more impressive when one thinks of more than double the number of women and children. Exodus 12:37 counts the number of men who leave Egypt as roughly six hundred thousand. Jacob Milgrom suggests that the tribal numbers may symbolize astronomical calculations intended to present Israel as God's battalions (Exodus 7:4; 12:41) corresponding to the astral bodies metaphorically understood as God's celestial troops (*Numbers*, 1990, p. 338).

able to bear arms—29those enrolled from the tribe
of Issachar: 54,400.

30Of the descendants of Zebulun, the registration of the clans of their ancestral house, as listed
by name, aged twenty years and over, all who were
able to bear arms—31those enrolled from the tribe
of Zebulun: 57,400.

32Of the descendants of Joseph:

Of the descendants of Ephraim, the registration
of the clans of their ancestral house, as listed by
name, aged twenty years and over, all who were
able to bear arms—33those enrolled from the tribe
of Ephraim: 40,500.

34Of the descendants of Manasseh, the registration of the clans of their ancestral house, as listed
by name, aged twenty years and over, all who were
able to bear arms—35those enrolled from the tribe
of Manasseh: 32,200.

36Of the descendants of Benjamin, the registration of the clans of their ancestral house, as listed
by name, aged twenty years and over, all who were
able to bear arms—37those enrolled from the tribe
of Benjamin: 35,400.

38Of the descendants of Dan, the registration of
the clans of their ancestral house, as listed by name,
aged twenty years and over, all who were able to
bear arms—39those enrolled from the tribe of Dan:
62,700.

40Of the descendants of Asher, the registration
of the clans of their ancestral house, as listed by
name, aged twenty years and over, all who were
able to bear arms—41those enrolled from the tribe
of Asher: 41,500.

42[Of] the descendants of Naphtali, the registration of the clans of their ancestral house as listed
by name, aged twenty years and over, all who were

שָׁנָה֙ וָמַ֔עְלָה כֹּ֖ל יֹצֵ֥א צָבָֽא׃ 29 פְּקֻדֵיהֶ֖ם
לְמַטֵּ֣ה יששכר יִשָּׂשכָ֑ר אַרְבָּעָ֧ה וַחֲמִשִּׁ֛ים אֶ֖לֶף
וְאַרְבַּ֥ע מֵאֽוֹת׃ פ
30 לִבְנֵ֣י זְבוּלֻ֔ן תּוֹלְדֹתָ֥ם לְמִשְׁפְּחֹתָ֖ם לְבֵ֣ית
אֲבֹתָ֑ם בְּמִסְפַּ֣ר שֵׁמֹ֗ת מִבֶּ֨ן עֶשְׂרִ֤ים שָׁנָה֙
וָמַ֔עְלָה כֹּ֖ל יֹצֵ֥א צָבָֽא׃ 31 פְּקֻדֵיהֶ֖ם לְמַטֵּ֣ה
זְבוּלֻ֑ן שִׁבְעָ֧ה וַחֲמִשִּׁ֛ים אֶ֖לֶף וְאַרְבַּ֥ע
מֵאֽוֹת׃ פ
32 לִבְנֵ֤י יוֹסֵף֙
לִבְנֵ֣י אֶפְרַ֔יִם תּוֹלְדֹתָ֥ם לְמִשְׁפְּחֹתָ֖ם לְבֵ֣ית
אֲבֹתָ֑ם בְּמִסְפַּ֣ר שֵׁמֹ֗ת מִבֶּ֨ן עֶשְׂרִ֤ים שָׁנָה֙
וָמַ֔עְלָה כֹּ֖ל יֹצֵ֥א צָבָֽא׃ 33 פְּקֻדֵיהֶ֖ם
לְמַטֵּ֣ה אֶפְרָ֑יִם אַרְבָּעִ֥ים אֶ֖לֶף וַחֲמֵ֥שׁ
מֵאֽוֹת׃ פ
34 לִבְנֵ֣י מְנַשֶּׁ֔ה תּוֹלְדֹתָ֥ם לְמִשְׁפְּחֹתָ֖ם לְבֵ֣ית
אֲבֹתָ֑ם בְּמִסְפַּ֣ר שֵׁמ֗וֹת מִבֶּ֨ן עֶשְׂרִ֤ים שָׁנָה֙
וָמַ֔עְלָה כֹּ֖ל יֹצֵ֥א צָבָֽא׃ 35 פְּקֻדֵיהֶ֖ם
לְמַטֵּ֣ה מְנַשֶּׁ֑ה שְׁנַ֧יִם וּשְׁלֹשִׁ֛ים אֶ֖לֶף
וּמָאתָֽיִם׃ פ
36 לִבְנֵ֣י בִנְיָמִ֔ן תּוֹלְדֹתָ֥ם לְמִשְׁפְּחֹתָ֖ם לְבֵ֣ית
אֲבֹתָ֑ם בְּמִסְפַּ֣ר שֵׁמֹ֗ת מִבֶּ֨ן עֶשְׂרִ֤ים שָׁנָה֙
וָמַ֔עְלָה כֹּ֖ל יֹצֵ֥א צָבָֽא׃ 37 פְּקֻדֵיהֶ֖ם לְמַטֵּ֣ה
בִנְיָמִ֑ן חֲמִשָּׁ֧ה וּשְׁלֹשִׁ֛ים אֶ֖לֶף וְאַרְבַּ֥ע
מֵאֽוֹת׃ פ
38 לִבְנֵ֣י דָ֔ן תּוֹלְדֹתָ֥ם לְמִשְׁפְּחֹתָ֖ם לְבֵ֣ית
אֲבֹתָ֑ם בְּמִסְפַּ֣ר שֵׁמֹ֗ת מִבֶּ֨ן עֶשְׂרִ֤ים שָׁנָה֙
וָמַ֔עְלָה כֹּ֖ל יֹצֵ֥א צָבָֽא׃ 39 פְּקֻדֵיהֶ֖ם
לְמַטֵּ֣ה דָ֑ן שְׁנַ֧יִם וְשִׁשִּׁ֛ים אֶ֖לֶף וּשְׁבַ֥ע
מֵאֽוֹת׃ פ
40 לִבְנֵ֣י אָשֵׁ֔ר תּוֹלְדֹתָ֥ם לְמִשְׁפְּחֹתָ֖ם לְבֵ֣ית
אֲבֹתָ֑ם בְּמִסְפַּ֣ר שֵׁמֹ֗ת מִבֶּ֨ן עֶשְׂרִ֤ים שָׁנָה֙
וָמַ֔עְלָה כֹּ֖ל יֹצֵ֥א צָבָֽא׃ 41 פְּקֻדֵיהֶ֖ם
לְמַטֵּ֣ה אָשֵׁ֑ר אֶחָ֧ד וְאַרְבָּעִ֛ים אֶ֖לֶף וַחֲמֵ֥שׁ
מֵאֽוֹת׃ פ
42 בְּנֵ֣י נַפְתָּלִ֔י תּוֹלְדֹתָ֥ם לְמִשְׁפְּחֹתָ֖ם לְבֵ֣ית
אֲבֹתָ֑ם בְּמִסְפַּ֣ר שֵׁמֹ֗ת מִבֶּ֨ן עֶשְׂרִ֤ים שָׁנָה֙

able to bear arms—[43]those enrolled from the tribe of Naphtali: 53,400.

[44]Those are the enrollments recorded by Moses and Aaron and by the chieftains of Israel, who were twelve in number, one representative of each ancestral house. [45]All the Israelite males, aged twenty years and over, enrolled by ancestral houses, all those in Israel who were able to bear arms—[46]all who were enrolled came to 603,550.

[47]The Levites, however, were not recorded among them by their ancestral tribe. [48]For יהוה had spoken to Moses, saying: [49]Do not on any account enroll the tribe of Levi or take a census of them with the Israelites. [50]You shall put the Levites in charge of the Tabernacle of the Pact, all its furnishings, and everything that pertains to it: they shall carry the Tabernacle and all its furnishings, and they shall tend it; and they shall camp around the Tabernacle. [51]When the Tabernacle is to set out, the Levites shall take it down, and when the Tabernacle is to be pitched, the Levites shall set it up; any outsider who encroaches shall be put to death.

וָמַעְלָה כֹּל יֹצֵא צָבָא׃ 43 פְּקֻדֵיהֶם לְמַטֵּה
נַפְתָּלִי שְׁלֹשָׁה וַחֲמִשִּׁים אֶלֶף וְאַרְבַּע
מֵאוֹת׃ פ
44 אֵלֶּה הַפְּקֻדִים אֲשֶׁר פָּקַד מֹשֶׁה וְאַהֲרֹן
וּנְשִׂיאֵי יִשְׂרָאֵל שְׁנֵים עָשָׂר אִישׁ אִישׁ־אֶחָד
לְבֵית־אֲבֹתָיו הָיוּ׃ 45 וַיִּהְיוּ כָּל־פְּקוּדֵי בְנֵי־
יִשְׂרָאֵל לְבֵית אֲבֹתָם מִבֶּן עֶשְׂרִים שָׁנָה
וָמַעְלָה כָּל־יֹצֵא צָבָא בְּיִשְׂרָאֵל׃ 46 וַיִּהְיוּ
כָּל־הַפְּקֻדִים שֵׁשׁ־מֵאוֹת אֶלֶף וּשְׁלֹשֶׁת
אֲלָפִים וַחֲמֵשׁ מֵאוֹת וַחֲמִשִּׁים׃
47 וְהַלְוִיִּם לְמַטֵּה אֲבֹתָם לֹא הָתְפָּקְדוּ
בְּתוֹכָם׃ פ 48 וַיְדַבֵּר יְהוָה אֶל־מֹשֶׁה
לֵּאמֹר׃ 49 אַךְ אֶת־מַטֵּה לֵוִי לֹא תִפְקֹד
וְאֶת־רֹאשָׁם לֹא תִשָּׂא בְּתוֹךְ בְּנֵי יִשְׂרָאֵל׃
50 וְאַתָּה הַפְקֵד אֶת־הַלְוִיִּם עַל־מִשְׁכַּן
הָעֵדֻת וְעַל כָּל־כֵּלָיו וְעַל כָּל־אֲשֶׁר־לוֹ
הֵמָּה יִשְׂאוּ אֶת־הַמִּשְׁכָּן וְאֶת־כָּל־כֵּלָיו
וְהֵם יְשָׁרְתֻהוּ וְסָבִיב לַמִּשְׁכָּן יַחֲנוּ׃
51 וּבִנְסֹעַ הַמִּשְׁכָּן יוֹרִידוּ אֹתוֹ הַלְוִיִּם
וּבַחֲנֹת הַמִּשְׁכָּן יָקִימוּ אֹתוֹ הַלְוִיִּם וְהַזָּר

## THE LEVITES (1:47–54)

The book of Numbers divides the men of the tribe of Levi into subordinate Levites and superior priests (the latter being of direct descent from Aaron). The Levites were not listed among the other tribes previously counted since they are exempt from military service. The Levites will not inherit territory in the land, claiming their patrimony instead in the sphere of Tabernacle service (see Numbers 3–4 and 8). Although Levites will not face the dangers of war, they must contend with the dangers of the holy, for if they do not maintain optimal holiness, they risk being destroyed by proximity to the Divine.

*50. the Levites in charge of the Tabernacle.* Levites set up the portable shrine, maintain its various components, dismantle it when it is time for Israel to journey forward, and carry it to the next encampment. After they set up the Tabernacle at a certain place, the Levites camp around it, in order to buffer divine power.

*Tabernacle.* See at Exodus 25:9.

*Pact.* See at Exodus 25:16.

*51. any outsider who encroaches shall be put to death.* This severe prohibition aims to maintain boundaries. The Levites buffer and protect the Tabernacle from outside encroachment. The severe penalty of death is meant less as an assurance of inevitable violence and more as a means of maintaining the definitive boundaries between the holy and the profane, as well as between Levites and Israelites. An analogue is at work between the Israelite body and the Tabernacle. As the body undergoes purification rituals when interior fluids seep out, so the priests sanctify the Tabernacle interiors. As the

52The Israelites shall encamp troop by troop, each
man with his division and each under his standard.
53The Levites, however, shall camp around the
Tabernacle of the Pact, that wrath may not strike
the Israelite community; the Levites shall stand
guard around the Tabernacle of the Pact.
54The Israelites did accordingly; just as יהוה had
commanded Moses, so they did.

2 יהוה spoke to Moses and Aaron, saying:
2The Israelites shall camp each man with his stan-

הַקָּרֵב יוּמָת׃ 52 וְחָנוּ בְּנֵי יִשְׂרָאֵל אִישׁ
עַל־מַחֲנֵהוּ וְאִישׁ עַל־דִּגְלוֹ לְצִבְאֹתָם׃
53 וְהַלְוִיִּם יַחֲנוּ סָבִיב לְמִשְׁכַּן הָעֵדֻת וְלֹא־
יִהְיֶה קֶצֶף עַל־עֲדַת בְּנֵי יִשְׂרָאֵל וְשָׁמְרוּ
הַלְוִיִּם אֶת־מִשְׁמֶרֶת מִשְׁכַּן הָעֵדוּת׃
54 וַיַּעֲשׂוּ בְּנֵי יִשְׂרָאֵל כְּכֹל אֲשֶׁר צִוָּה יְהוָה
אֶת־מֹשֶׁה כֵּן עָשׂוּ׃ פ

ב וַיְדַבֵּר יְהוָה אֶל־מֹשֶׁה וְאֶל־אַהֲרֹן
לֵאמֹר׃ 2 אִישׁ עַל־דִּגְלוֹ בְאֹתֹת לְבֵית

body must be protected from foreign organisms, so the Levites shield the Tabernacle margins.

*52. each man with his division.* [The translator notes: Or "each [household] with its division." (Similarly in 2:2, 34.) —*Ed.*]

*standard.* Heb. *degel.* This military term can be translated as "banner." We know that in the ancient Jewish colony at Elephantine, Egypt, *degel* designated a military unit. So the term means not only a standard but also the force that marches beneath the standard. (In modern Hebrew it refers to a flag.) The twelve tribes will be organized under four such standards or banners.

*53. around the Tabernacle.* This literary unit ends with an image of the Tabernacle encircled by the Levites, who are surrounded by a perimeter of Israelite tribes unified under their banners.

## *The Geometry of the Holy* (2:1–34)

The sacred structure houses a Tent of Meeting or Tabernacle (the terms appear to be used interchangeably in this parashah) at its center. Priests sacrifice in the court and offer incense inside as a way of communicating with God. Four groups of Levites surround the Tent, one group on each side, with Moses and Aaron's family in the most privileged position (see below). The tribes of Israel appear around the Levites' camp in four groups, each composed of three tribes united under a single standard or division. When Israel marches through the wilderness, the eastern (Judah) and southern (Reuben) divisions lead, followed by the Levites transporting the Tabernacle and backed up by the western (Ephraim) and northern (Dan) divisions.

It is most likely that such a configuration never actually existed in the historical past. Instead, the Tabernacle is the mythic structure behind Israelite—and later, Jewish—sacred space. According to the book of Kings, it is this structure—with concentric spheres of increasing holiness—that King Solomon employs when building the Temple in Jerusalem. The synagogue, which after the Temple's destruction (70 C.E.) would stand at the center of Jewish life, realizes this myth by placing the Ark that holds the Torah in a prominent place in the sanctuary. The biblical Ark of the Torah signifies the Ark of the Covenant, and the shared contents bind contemporary Jews to their ancient ancestors. (For more on the Tabernacle, see the introduction to *T'rumah*, p. 451; and *Vayak'heil*, Another View, p. 538.)

### THE EAST (2:1–9)

The notion that the cardinal directions provide orientation assumes a double meaning here. Not only do the directions augment a geographic sensibility, but they also determine the marching order of the Israelite tribes.

The Judah tribe leads the eastern division, which includes Issachar and Zebulun, all offspring of Leah.

dard, under the banners of their ancestral house; they shall camp around the Tent of Meeting at a distance.

3 Camped on the front, or east side: the standard of the division of Judah, troop by troop.

Chieftain of the Judites: Nahshon son of Amminadab. 4 His troop, as enrolled: 74,600.

5 Camping next to it:

The tribe of Issachar.

Chieftain of the Issacharites: Nethanel son of Zuar. 6 His troop, as enrolled: 54,400.

7 The tribe of Zebulun.

Chieftain of the Zebulunites: Eliab son of Helon. 8 His troop, as enrolled: 57,400.

9 The total enrolled in the division of Judah: 186,400, for all troops. These shall march first.

10 On the south: the standard of the division of Reuben, troop by troop.

Chieftain of the Reubenites: Elizur son of Shedeur. 11 His troop, as enrolled: 46,500.

12 Camping next to it:

The tribe of Simeon.

Chieftain of the Simeonites: Shelumiel son of Zurishaddai.

אֲבֹתָם יַחֲנוּ בְּנֵי יִשְׂרָאֵל מִנֶּגֶד סָבִיב
לְאֹהֶל־מוֹעֵד יַחֲנוּ׃
3 וְהַחֹנִים קֵדְמָה מִזְרָחָה דֶּגֶל מַחֲנֵה יְהוּדָה
לְצִבְאֹתָם
וְנָשִׂיא לִבְנֵי יְהוּדָה נַחְשׁוֹן בֶּן־עַמִּינָדָב׃
4 וּצְבָאוֹ וּפְקֻדֵיהֶם אַרְבָּעָה וְשִׁבְעִים אֶלֶף
וְשֵׁשׁ מֵאוֹת׃ 5 וְהַחֹנִים עָלָיו מַטֵּה יששכר
יִשָּׂשכָר וְנָשִׂיא לִבְנֵי יששכר יִשָּׂשכָר נְתַנְאֵל בֶּן־
צוּעָר׃ 6 וּצְבָאוֹ וּפְקֻדָיו אַרְבָּעָה וַחֲמִשִּׁים
אֶלֶף וְאַרְבַּע מֵאוֹת׃ 7 מַטֵּה זְבוּלֻן וְנָשִׂיא
לִבְנֵי זְבוּלֻן אֱלִיאָב בֶּן־חֵלֹן׃ 8 וּצְבָאוֹ
וּפְקֻדָיו שִׁבְעָה וַחֲמִשִּׁים אֶלֶף וְאַרְבַּע
מֵאוֹת׃
9 כָּל־הַפְּקֻדִים לְמַחֲנֵה יְהוּדָה מְאַת אֶלֶף
וּשְׁמֹנִים אֶלֶף וְשֵׁשֶׁת־אֲלָפִים וְאַרְבַּע־מֵאוֹת
לְצִבְאֹתָם רִאשֹׁנָה יִסָּעוּ׃ ס
10 דֶּגֶל מַחֲנֵה רְאוּבֵן תֵּימָנָה לְצִבְאֹתָם
וְנָשִׂיא לִבְנֵי רְאוּבֵן אֱלִיצוּר בֶּן־שְׁדֵיאוּר׃
11 וּצְבָאוֹ וּפְקֻדָיו שִׁשָּׁה וְאַרְבָּעִים אֶלֶף
וַחֲמֵשׁ מֵאוֹת׃ 12 וְהַחוֹנִם עָלָיו מַטֵּה
שִׁמְעוֹן וְנָשִׂיא לִבְנֵי שִׁמְעוֹן שְׁלֻמִיאֵל בֶּן־

*2. camp around the Tent of Meeting at a distance.* The God who spoke to the Israelites from atop Mount Sinai now dwells in their midst and travels with them. The distance between the divine dwelling and the rest of Israel's camp is determined and mediated by the Levites and priests.

*Tent of Meeting.* See at Exodus 27:21.

*3. Camped on the . . . east side.* The east side is favored. The Tabernacle's entrance is located on this side. This is where Aaron and the Judah tribes are positioned.

*9. These shall march first.* When the camp marches forward, the tribes who hold the position of the rising sun (the east) move first. The configuration of the camp has both ritual and military implications. During periods of encampment, the band of tribes surrounding the Tabernacle serves as a line of defense protecting the sanctuary; and during the march, the infantry tribes are reinforced by God's presence hovering over the sacred items of the Tent.

### THE SOUTH (2:10–16)

The Reuben tribe leads the southern division, which includes two Leah tribes, Reuben and Simeon, and one Zilpah tribe, Gad. In the formation, the tribes that predominate are the descendants of the less-loved sister, Leah, whose sons were not as beloved by Jacob as Rachel's. (See also Another View, p. 808.)

¹³His troop, as enrolled: 59,300.

¹⁴And the tribe of Gad.

Chieftain of the Gadites: Eliasaph son of Reuel. ¹⁵His troop, as enrolled: 45,650.

¹⁶The total enrolled in the division of Reuben: 151,450, for all troops. These shall march second.

¹⁷Then, midway between the divisions, the Tent of Meeting, the division of the Levites, shall move. As they camp, so they shall march, each in position, by their standards.

¹⁸On the west: the standard of the division of Ephraim, troop by troop.

Chieftain of the Ephraimites: Elishama son of Ammihud. ¹⁹His troop, as enrolled: 40,500.

²⁰Next to it:

The tribe of Manasseh.

Chieftain of the Manassites: Gamaliel son of Pedahzur. ²¹His troop, as enrolled: 32,200.

²²And the tribe of Benjamin.

Chieftain of the Benjaminites: Abidan son of Gideoni. ²³His troop, as enrolled: 35,400.

²⁴The total enrolled in the division of Ephraim: 108,100 for all troops. These shall march third.

²⁵On the north: the standard of the division of Dan, troop by troop.

13 וּצְבָא֖וֹ וּפְקֻדֵיהֶ֑ם תִּשְׁעָ֧ה וַחֲמִשִּׁ֛ים אֶ֖לֶף וּשְׁלֹ֥שׁ מֵאֽוֹת: 14 וּמַטֵּ֖ה גָּ֑ד וְנָשִׂיא֙ לִבְנֵ֣י גָ֔ד אֶלְיָסָ֖ף בֶּן־רְעוּאֵֽל: 15 וּצְבָא֖וֹ וּפְקֻדֵיהֶ֑ם חֲמִשָּׁ֧ה וְאַרְבָּעִ֛ים אֶ֖לֶף וְשֵׁ֥שׁ מֵא֖וֹת וַחֲמִשִּֽׁים: 16 כָּל־הַפְּקֻדִ֞ים לְמַחֲנֵ֣ה רְאוּבֵ֗ן מְאַ֪ת אֶ֟לֶף וְאֶחָ֨ד וַחֲמִשִּׁ֥ים אֶ֛לֶף וְאַרְבַּע־מֵא֖וֹת וַחֲמִשִּׁ֑ים לְצִבְאֹתָ֑ם וּשְׁנִיָּ֖ם יִסָּֽעוּ: ס 17 וְנָסַ֧ע אֹֽהֶל־מוֹעֵ֛ד מַחֲנֵ֥ה הַלְוִיִּ֖ם בְּת֣וֹךְ הַֽמַּחֲנֹ֑ת כַּאֲשֶׁ֤ר יַחֲנוּ֙ כֵּ֣ן יִסָּ֔עוּ אִ֥ישׁ עַל־יָד֖וֹ לְדִגְלֵיהֶֽם: ס 18 דֶּ֣גֶל מַחֲנֵ֥ה אֶפְרַ֛יִם לְצִבְאֹתָ֖ם יָ֑מָּה וְנָשִׂיא֙ לִבְנֵ֣י אֶפְרַ֔יִם אֱלִישָׁמָ֖ע בֶּן־עַמִּיהֽוּד: 19 וּצְבָא֖וֹ וּפְקֻדֵיהֶ֑ם אַרְבָּעִ֥ים אֶ֖לֶף וַחֲמֵ֥שׁ מֵאֽוֹת: 20 וְעָלָ֖יו מַטֵּ֣ה מְנַשֶּׁ֑ה וְנָשִׂיא֙ לִבְנֵ֣י מְנַשֶּׁ֔ה גַּמְלִיאֵ֖ל בֶּן־פְּדָהצֽוּר: 21 וּצְבָא֖וֹ וּפְקֻדֵיהֶ֑ם שְׁנַ֧יִם וּשְׁלֹשִׁ֛ים אֶ֖לֶף וּמָאתָֽיִם: 22 וּמַטֵּ֖ה בִּנְיָמִ֑ן וְנָשִׂיא֙ לִבְנֵ֣י בִנְיָמִ֔ן אֲבִידָ֖ן בֶּן־גִּדְעֹנִֽי: 23 וּצְבָא֖וֹ וּפְקֻדֵיהֶ֑ם חֲמִשָּׁ֧ה וּשְׁלֹשִׁ֛ים אֶ֖לֶף וְאַרְבַּ֥ע מֵאֽוֹת: 24 כָּל־הַפְּקֻדִ֞ים לְמַחֲנֵ֣ה אֶפְרַ֗יִם מְאַ֥ת אֶ֛לֶף וּשְׁמֹנַת־אֲלָפִ֥ים וּמֵאָ֖ה לְצִבְאֹתָ֑ם וּשְׁלִשִׁ֖ים יִסָּֽעוּ: ס 25 דֶּ֣גֶל מַחֲנֵ֥ה דָ֛ן צָפֹ֖נָה לְצִבְאֹתָֽם

## THE CENTER (2:17)

When the people of Israel travel, the levitical Merari and Gershon clans carry the Tent of Meeting. They buffer the privileged Kohath clan that transports the sanctuary furnishings. The sacred center is maintained in transit and well as in encampment.

## THE WEST (2:18–24)

The western, or "seaward" (*yamah*), tribes include Benjamin, Ephraim, and Manasseh. All three

are Rachel tribes, as Ephraim and Manasseh are the two tribal divisions stemming from Joseph and his Egyptian wife, Asenath. The tribes descended from Rachel are stationed farthest from the Tabernacle entrance, perhaps referencing Rachel's untimely death outside the entrance of the town of Ephrath (Genesis 35:16).

## THE NORTH (2:25–31)

The Dan tribe leads the northern division, which includes Asher, an offspring of Zilpah (Leah's hand-

Chieftain of the Danites: Ahiezer son of Ammishaddai. 26His troop, as enrolled: 62,700.
27Camping next to it:
The tribe of Asher.
Chieftain of the Asherites: Pagiel son of Ochran. 28His troop, as enrolled: 41,500.
29And the tribe of Naphtali.
Chieftain of the Naphtalites: Ahira son of Enan. 30His troop, as enrolled: 53,400.
31The total enrolled in the division of Dan: 157,600. These shall march last, by their standards.

32Those are the enrollments of the Israelites by ancestral houses. The total enrolled in the divisions, for all troops: 603,550. 33The Levites, however, were not recorded among the Israelites, as יהוה had commanded Moses.

34The Israelites did accordingly; just as יהוה had commanded Moses, so they camped by their standards, and so they marched, each man with his clan according to his ancestral house.

**3** This is the line of Aaron and Moses at the time that יהוה spoke with Moses on Mount Sinai. 2These were the names of Aaron's sons: Nadab, the

וּנְשִׂיא לִבְנֵי דָן אֲחִיעֶזֶר בֶּן־עַמִּישַׁדָּי׃
26 וּצְבָאוֹ וּפְקֻדֵיהֶם שְׁנַיִם וְשִׁשִּׁים אֶלֶף
וּשְׁבַע מֵאוֹת׃ 27 וְהַחֹנִים עָלָיו מַטֵּה אָשֵׁר
וְנָשִׂיא לִבְנֵי אָשֵׁר פַּגְעִיאֵל בֶּן־עָכְרָן׃
28 וּצְבָאוֹ וּפְקֻדֵיהֶם אֶחָד וְאַרְבָּעִים אֶלֶף
וַחֲמֵשׁ מֵאוֹת׃ 29 וּמַטֵּה נַפְתָּלִי וְנָשִׂיא לִבְנֵי
נַפְתָּלִי אֲחִירַע בֶּן־עֵינָן׃ 30 וּצְבָאוֹ וּפְקֻדֵיהֶם
שְׁלֹשָׁה וַחֲמִשִּׁים אֶלֶף וְאַרְבַּע מֵאוֹת׃
31 כָּל־הַפְּקֻדִים לְמַחֲנֵה דָן מְאַת אֶלֶף
וְשִׁבְעָה וַחֲמִשִּׁים אֶלֶף וְשֵׁשׁ מֵאוֹת
לָאַחֲרֹנָה יִסְעוּ לְדִגְלֵיהֶם׃ פ
32 אֵלֶּה פְּקוּדֵי בְנֵי־יִשְׂרָאֵל לְבֵית אֲבֹתָם
כָּל־פְּקוּדֵי הַמַּחֲנֹת לְצִבְאֹתָם שֵׁשׁ־מֵאוֹת
אֶלֶף וּשְׁלֹשֶׁת אֲלָפִים וַחֲמֵשׁ מֵאוֹת
וַחֲמִשִּׁים׃ 33 וְהַלְוִיִּם לֹא הָתְפָּקְדוּ בְּתוֹךְ
בְּנֵי יִשְׂרָאֵל כַּאֲשֶׁר צִוָּה יְהֹוָה אֶת־מֹשֶׁה׃
34 וַיַּעֲשׂוּ בְּנֵי יִשְׂרָאֵל כְּכֹל אֲשֶׁר־צִוָּה יְהֹוָה
אֶת־מֹשֶׁה כֵּן־חָנוּ לְדִגְלֵיהֶם וְכֵן נָסָעוּ אִישׁ
לְמִשְׁפְּחֹתָיו עַל־בֵּית אֲבֹתָיו׃ פ

ג וְאֵלֶּה תּוֹלְדֹת אַהֲרֹן וּמֹשֶׁה בְּיוֹם דִּבֶּר
יְהֹוָה אֶת־מֹשֶׁה בְּהַר סִינָי׃ 2 וְאֵלֶּה שְׁמוֹת

maid), as well as Naphtali and Dan, the two offspring of Bilhah (Rachel's handmaid).

### CONCLUSION (2:32–34)

The concluding summary reports that Israel carries out God's instructions, maintaining this tribal order and sacred geometry when they camp and when they march.

## *The Levites*

(3:1–4:20)

The tribe of the Levites, to which both Moses and Aaron belong, was barely mentioned in Leviticus, which focuses on the priests. In Numbers, however, the Levites receive privileges that set them apart from other tribes. This step enlarges the structure of those who officiate at the Tabernacle. This broader circle of official personnel does not seem to include women. On women and Israel's priesthood, see *T'tzaveh*, Another View, p. 489.

The tribe of Levi is favored in this parashah. For example, the priests and Levites who camp around the Tabernacle are also elected to maintain it. In addition, the Levites stand in for Israel's first-born sons, who belong to God as an eternal ransom for the first-born sons who were not killed during the tenth plague on Egypt (see vv. 12–13). Such features suggest that it was priests who edited or authored the first part of the book of Numbers.

first-born, and Abihu, Eleazar and Ithamar; 3 those
were the names of Aaron's sons, the anointed
priests who were ordained for priesthood. 4 But
Nadab and Abihu died by the will of יהוה, when
they offered alien fire before יהוה in the wilderness
of Sinai; and they left no sons. So it was Eleazar and
Ithamar who served as priests in the lifetime of
their father Aaron.

5 יהוה spoke to Moses, saying: 6 Advance the
tribe of Levi and place its [men] in attendance
upon Aaron the priest to serve him. 7 They shall
perform duties for him and for the whole community before the Tent of Meeting, doing the work of
the Tabernacle. 8 They shall take charge of all the

בְּנֵי־אַהֲרֹן הַבְּכֹר ׀ נָדָב וַאֲבִיהוּא אֶלְעָזָר
וְאִיתָמָר׃ 3 אֵלֶּה שְׁמוֹת בְּנֵי אַהֲרֹן הַכֹּהֲנִים
הַמְּשֻׁחִים אֲשֶׁר־מִלֵּא יָדָם לְכַהֵן׃ 4 וַיָּמָת
נָדָב וַאֲבִיהוּא לִפְנֵי יְהוָה בְּהַקְרִבָם אֵשׁ
זָרָה לִפְנֵי יְהוָה בְּמִדְבַּר סִינַי וּבָנִים לֹא־הָיוּ
לָהֶם וַיְכַהֵן אֶלְעָזָר וְאִיתָמָר עַל־פְּנֵי אַהֲרֹן
אֲבִיהֶם׃ פ

5 וַיְדַבֵּר יְהוָה אֶל־מֹשֶׁה לֵּאמֹר׃ 6 הַקְרֵב
אֶת־מַטֵּה לֵוִי וְהַעֲמַדְתָּ אֹתוֹ לִפְנֵי אַהֲרֹן
הַכֹּהֵן וְשֵׁרְתוּ אֹתוֹ׃ 7 וְשָׁמְרוּ אֶת־מִשְׁמַרְתּוֹ
וְאֶת־מִשְׁמֶרֶת כָּל־הָעֵדָה לִפְנֵי אֹהֶל מוֹעֵד
לַעֲבֹד אֶת־עֲבֹדַת הַמִּשְׁכָּן׃ 8 וְשָׁמְרוּ אֶת־

THE ELECTION OF THE PRIESTS (3:1–10)

In this section, the text's composers—presumably Aaron's descendants—give first priority to the authority of the priests. However, they are not apologists. Their honored ancestor, Aaron, is recorded later in Numbers as transgressing (20:1–13) and dies far from the Promised Land (20:22–29).

*1. This is the line of Aaron and Moses.* The priestly writers are invested in a kind of deterministic genealogy. In other words, they see social position as arising from one's station at birth. Such a hereditary principle supports the idea of priestly distinction. Although they are brothers, only Aaron, not Moses, transmits the priesthood. Aaron's sons become the religious elite.

*2. These were the names of Aaron's sons.* The book of Numbers distinguishes Aaron's family as the only legitimate priests among the tribe of Levi.

*3. anointed.* As a standard of hygiene and often as a form of luxury, people in the ancient Near East—including women—used to anoint themselves and their children with oil (I Samuel 14:2; Ezekiel 16:9; Ruth 3:3). But here the Hebrew uses a special verb that, when applied to persons, refers to pouring oil on the head in order to signal the assumption of an office, usually the kingship or the priesthood. That verbal root (*m-sh-ch*) also forms the noun *mashiach*, which later becomes the title "Messiah." (See also at Exodus 27:20 and 29:7.)

*4. Nadab and Abihu.* These two sons of Aaron and Elisheba (Exodus 6:23) were instantly annihilated when they encroached upon the Holy with the wrong sort of offering (see at Leviticus 10:1–2). Since they had no sons, no trace of them remains except in their substitution by their younger brothers Eleazar and Ithamar.

*6. the tribe of Levi... Aaron the priest.* Just as the Levites have a distinct position within Israel, so the *kohanim* (priests) of the family of Aaron have a preferred position within the tribe of Levi. This social configuration parallels that of the Tabernacle by recognizing a particularly holy family within a holy tribe that is within a holy people.

*7. before the Tent of Meeting.* The priestly hierarchy is realized in the system of access to the various interiors of the Tent of Meeting. As the priests perform their sacred duties inside it, the Levites stand watch around the perimeter; all other members of Israel may approach the Divine at the threshold at specified times when they are in the correct state of purity. The priests supervise Israel's access to the Tent of Meeting.

furnishings of the Tent of Meeting—a duty on behalf of the Israelites—doing the work of the Tabernacle. 9You shall assign the Levites to Aaron and
to his sons: they are formally assigned to him from
among the Israelites. 10You shall make Aaron and
his sons responsible for observing their priestly
duties; and any outsider who encroaches shall be
put to death.

11יהוה spoke to Moses, saying: 12I hereby take
the Levites from among the Israelites in place of all
the male first-born, the first issue of the womb
among the Israelites: the Levites shall be Mine.
13For every male first-born is Mine: at the time
that I smote every [male] first-born in the land of
Egypt, I consecrated every male first-born in Israel,
human and beast, to Myself, to be Mine, יהוה's.

14יהוה spoke to Moses in the wilderness of Sinai,
saying: 15Record the descendants of Levi by ancestral house and by clan; record every male among
them from the age of one month up. 16So Moses
recorded them at the command of יהוה, as he was

כָּל־כְּלֵי אֹהֶל מוֹעֵד וְאֶת־מִשְׁמֶרֶת בְּנֵי
יִשְׂרָאֵל לַעֲבֹד אֶת־עֲבֹדַת הַמִּשְׁכָּן׃
9 וְנָתַתָּה אֶת־הַלְוִיִּם לְאַהֲרֹן וּלְבָנָיו נְתוּנִם
נְתוּנִם הֵמָּה לוֹ מֵאֵת בְּנֵי יִשְׂרָאֵל׃ 10 וְאֶת־
אַהֲרֹן וְאֶת־בָּנָיו תִּפְקֹד וְשָׁמְרוּ אֶת־כְּהֻנָּתָם
וְהַזָּר הַקָּרֵב יוּמָת׃ פ
11 וַיְדַבֵּר יְהֹוָה אֶל־מֹשֶׁה לֵּאמֹר׃ 12 וַאֲנִי
הִנֵּה לָקַחְתִּי אֶת־הַלְוִיִּם מִתּוֹךְ בְּנֵי יִשְׂרָאֵל
תַּחַת כָּל־בְּכוֹר פֶּטֶר רֶחֶם מִבְּנֵי יִשְׂרָאֵל
וְהָיוּ לִי הַלְוִיִּם׃ 13 כִּי לִי כָּל־בְּכוֹר בְּיוֹם
הַכֹּתִי כָל־בְּכוֹר בְּאֶרֶץ מִצְרַיִם הִקְדַּשְׁתִּי לִי
כָל־בְּכוֹר בְּיִשְׂרָאֵל מֵאָדָם עַד־בְּהֵמָה לִי
יִהְיוּ אֲנִי יְהֹוָה׃ פ
14 וַיְדַבֵּר יְהֹוָה אֶל־מֹשֶׁה בְּמִדְבַּר סִינַי
לֵאמֹר׃ 15 פְּקֹד אֶת־בְּנֵי לֵוִי לְבֵית אֲבֹתָם
לְמִשְׁפְּחֹתָם כָּל־זָכָר מִבֶּן־חֹדֶשׁ וָמַעְלָה
תִּפְקְדֵם׃ 16 וַיִּפְקֹד אֹתָם מֹשֶׁה עַל־פִּי

*10. any outsider who encroaches shall be put to death.* The border lines of the holy are not to be breached; the severe penalty associates these borders with the boundary that separates life and death.

### THE ELECTION OF THE LEVITES (3:11–22)

The Levites replace first-born Israelites who would otherwise belong to God (according to Exodus 13:12–13). The male members of the tribe of Levi now function as a hereditary caste of personnel dedicated to God's service but serving under the priests.

*12. the first issue of the womb.* This verse defines who exactly counts as first-born for the purpose of this legislation. The definition refers specifically to a woman's first-born (not a man's first-born). By speaking of the womb rather than the woman, the fertile womb is disassociated from the mother. The image is of a womb magically yielding offspring in the absence of female reproductive agency. (See also at Exodus 13:2.)

*13. For every male first-born is Mine.* This verse explains that all first-born males belong to God as an eternal ransom for the sparing of Israel's first-born males at the tenth plague (Exodus 11:1–10; 12:29–36). According to this passage, God is willing to accept the substitution of the Levites for all of Israel's first-born males. The status of the first-born male is unstable in the *Tanach*; although first-born sons have the right of predominant inheritance, they are constantly being supplanted (see Jacob's supplanting of Esau in Genesis 25–27).

*15. from the age of one month up.* A Levite is recognized after one month of life. However, scholars dispute at what age a Levite is to actually begin his service.

bidden. [17]These were the sons of Levi by name: Gershon, Kohath, and Merari. [18]These were the names of the sons of Gershon by clan: Libni and Shimei. [19]The sons of Kohath by clan: Amram and Izhar, Hebron and Uzziel. [20]The sons of Merari by clan: Mahli and Mushi.

These were the clans of the Levites within their ancestral houses:

[21]To Gershon belonged the clan of the Libnites and the clan of the Shimeites; those were the clans of the Gershonites. [22]The recorded entries of all their males from the age of one month up, as recorded, came to 7,500. [23]The clans of the Gershonites were to camp behind the Tabernacle, to the west. [24]The chieftain of the ancestral house of the Gershonites was Eliasaph son of Lael. [25]The duties of the Gershonites in the Tent of Meeting comprised: the tabernacle, the tent, its covering, and the screen for the entrance of the Tent of Meeting; [26]the hangings of the enclosure, the screen for the entrance of the enclosure which surrounds the Tabernacle, the cords thereof, and the altar—all the service connected with these.

[27]To Kohath belonged the clan of the Amramites, the clan of the Izharites, the clan of the Hebronites, and the clan of the Uzzielites; those were the clans of the Kohathites. [28]All the listed males from the age of one month up came to 8,600, attending to the duties of the sanctuary. [29]The clans of the Kohathites were to camp along the

יְהוָה כַּאֲשֶׁר צֻוָּה׃ 17 וַיִּהְיוּ־אֵלֶּה בְנֵי־לֵוִי
בִּשְׁמֹתָם גֵּרְשׁוֹן וּקְהָת וּמְרָרִי׃ 18 וְאֵלֶּה
שְׁמוֹת בְּנֵי־גֵרְשׁוֹן לְמִשְׁפְּחֹתָם לִבְנִי
וְשִׁמְעִי׃ 19 וּבְנֵי קְהָת לְמִשְׁפְּחֹתָם עַמְרָם
וְיִצְהָר חֶבְרוֹן וְעֻזִּיאֵל׃ 20 וּבְנֵי מְרָרִי
לְמִשְׁפְּחֹתָם מַחְלִי וּמוּשִׁי
אֵלֶּה הֵם מִשְׁפְּחֹת הַלֵּוִי לְבֵית אֲבֹתָם׃
21 לְגֵרְשׁוֹן מִשְׁפַּחַת הַלִּבְנִי וּמִשְׁפַּחַת
הַשִּׁמְעִי אֵלֶּה הֵם מִשְׁפְּחֹת הַגֵּרְשֻׁנִּי׃
22 פְּקֻדֵיהֶם בְּמִסְפַּר כָּל־זָכָר מִבֶּן־חֹדֶשׁ
וָמָעְלָה פְּקֻדֵיהֶם שִׁבְעַת אֲלָפִים וַחֲמֵשׁ
מֵאוֹת׃ 23 מִשְׁפְּחֹת הַגֵּרְשֻׁנִּי אַחֲרֵי הַמִּשְׁכָּן
יַחֲנוּ יָמָּה׃ 24 וּנְשִׂיא בֵית־אָב לַגֵּרְשֻׁנִּי
אֶלְיָסָף בֶּן־לָאֵל׃ 25 וּמִשְׁמֶרֶת בְּנֵי־גֵרְשׁוֹן
בְּאֹהֶל מוֹעֵד הַמִּשְׁכָּן וְהָאֹהֶל מִכְסֵהוּ וּמָסַךְ
פֶּתַח אֹהֶל מוֹעֵד׃ 26 וְקַלְעֵי הֶחָצֵר וְאֶת־
מָסַךְ פֶּתַח הֶחָצֵר אֲשֶׁר עַל־הַמִּשְׁכָּן
וְעַל־הַמִּזְבֵּחַ סָבִיב וְאֵת מֵיתָרָיו לְכֹל
עֲבֹדָתוֹ׃ ס
27 וְלִקְהָת מִשְׁפַּחַת הָעַמְרָמִי וּמִשְׁפַּחַת
הַיִּצְהָרִי וּמִשְׁפַּחַת הַחֶבְרֹנִי וּמִשְׁפַּחַת
הָעָזִּיאֵלִי אֵלֶּה הֵם מִשְׁפְּחֹת הַקְּהָתִי׃
28 בְּמִסְפַּר כָּל־זָכָר מִבֶּן־חֹדֶשׁ וָמָעְלָה
שְׁמֹנַת אֲלָפִים וְשֵׁשׁ מֵאוֹת שֹׁמְרֵי מִשְׁמֶרֶת
הַקֹּדֶשׁ׃ 29 מִשְׁפְּחֹת בְּנֵי־קְהָת יַחֲנוּ עַל

## THE ORGANIZATION OF THE LEVITES (3:23–39)

As the outer ring of the encampment follows a hierarchy, so does the inner ring of levitical families.

*23. The clans of the Gershonites.* The Gershon clan represents the first-born of Levi, who was the third son of Jacob.

*25–26.* The Gershonites not only guard the western side of the Tabernacle but also transport its curtains, fabrics, and screens. In other words, the Gershonites carry and set up the flexible boundaries that define the sacred space. Numbers 4:21–49 delineates their duties more fully.

*29.* The Kohath clan carries the most holy objects on the journey—including the Ark, the table, the menorah, the altars, and the sacred utensils. They set up their own camp on the south side. The Kohath clan represents the second-born of Levi. According to Exodus 6:17–21 and Numbers 3:19,

south side of the Tabernacle. ³⁰The chieftain of the ancestral house of the Kohathite clans was Elizaphan son of Uzziel. ³¹Their duties comprised: the ark, the table, the lampstand, the altars, and the sacred utensils that were used with them, and the screen—all the service connected with these. ³²The head chieftain of the Levites was Eleazar son of Aaron the priest, in charge of those attending to the duties of the sanctuary.

³³To Merari belonged the clan of the Mahlites and the clan of the Mushites; those were the clans of Merari. ³⁴The recorded entries of all their males from the age of one month up came to 6,200. ³⁵The chieftain of the ancestral house of the clans of Merari was Zuriel son of Abihail. They were to camp along the north side of the Tabernacle. ³⁶The assigned duties of the Merarites comprised: the planks of the Tabernacle, its bars, posts, and sockets, and all its furnishings—all the service connected with these; ³⁷also the posts around the enclosure and their sockets, pegs, and cords.

³⁸Those who were to camp before the Tabernacle, in front—before the Tent of Meeting, on the east—were Moses and Aaron and his sons, attending to the duties of the sanctuary, as a duty on behalf of the Israelites; and any outsider who encroached was to be put to death. ³⁹All the Levites who were recorded, whom at יהוה's command Moses and Aaron recorded by their clans, all the males from the age of one month up, came to 22,000.

יֶ֥רֶךְ הַמִּשְׁכָּ֖ן תֵּימָ֑נָה: ³⁰ וּנְשִׂ֥יא בֵֽית־אָ֛ב לְמִשְׁפְּחֹ֥ת הַקְּהָתִ֖י אֱלִיצָפָ֥ן בֶּן־עֻזִּיאֵֽל: ³¹ וּמִשְׁמַרְתָּ֗ם הָאָרֹ֤ן וְהַשֻּׁלְחָן֙ וְהַמְּנֹרָ֣ה וְהַֽמִּזְבְּחֹ֔ת וּכְלֵ֣י הַקֹּ֔דֶשׁ אֲשֶׁ֥ר יְשָׁרְת֖וּ בָּהֶ֑ם וְהַ֨מָּסָ֔ךְ וְכֹ֖ל עֲבֹדָתֽוֹ: ³² וּנְשִׂיא֙ נְשִׂיאֵ֣י הַלֵּוִ֔י אֶלְעָזָ֖ר בֶּן־אַהֲרֹ֣ן הַכֹּהֵ֑ן פְּקֻדַּ֕ת שֹׁמְרֵ֖י מִשְׁמֶ֥רֶת הַקֹּֽדֶשׁ:

³³ לִמְרָרִ֕י מִשְׁפַּ֣חַת הַמַּחְלִ֔י וּמִשְׁפַּ֖חַת הַמּוּשִׁ֑י אֵ֥לֶּה הֵ֖ם מִשְׁפְּחֹ֥ת מְרָרִֽי: ³⁴ וּפְקֻדֵיהֶם֙ בְּמִסְפַּ֣ר כָּל־זָכָ֔ר מִבֶּן־חֹ֖דֶשׁ וָמָ֑עְלָה שֵׁ֥שֶׁת אֲלָפִ֖ים וּמָאתָֽיִם: ³⁵ וּנְשִׂ֞יא בֵֽית־אָ֨ב לְמִשְׁפְּחֹ֤ת מְרָרִי֙ צֽוּרִיאֵ֣ל בֶּן־אֲבִיחָ֔יִל עַ֣ל יֶ֧רֶךְ הַמִּשְׁכָּ֛ן יַחֲנ֖וּ צָפֹֽנָה: ³⁶ וּפְקֻדַּ֣ת מִשְׁמֶ֗רֶת בְּנֵ֣י מְרָרִ֔י קַרְשֵׁי֙ הַמִּשְׁכָּ֔ן וּבְרִיחָ֖יו וְעַמֻּדָ֣יו וַאֲדָנָ֑יו וְכָ֨ל־כֵּלָ֔יו וְכֹ֖ל עֲבֹדָתֽוֹ: ³⁷ וְעַמֻּדֵ֧י הֶחָצֵ֛ר סָבִ֖יב וְאַדְנֵיהֶ֑ם וִיתֵדֹתָ֖ם וּמֵיתְרֵיהֶֽם:

³⁸ וְהַחֹנִ֣ים לִפְנֵ֣י הַמִּשְׁכָּ֡ן קֵ֣דְמָה לִפְנֵי֩ אֹֽהֶל־מוֹעֵ֨ד ׀ מִזְרָ֜חָה מֹשֶׁ֣ה ׀ וְאַהֲרֹ֣ן וּבָנָ֗יו שֹֽׁמְרִים֙ מִשְׁמֶ֣רֶת הַמִּקְדָּ֔שׁ לְמִשְׁמֶ֖רֶת בְּנֵ֣י יִשְׂרָאֵ֑ל וְהַזָּ֥ר הַקָּרֵ֖ב יוּמָֽת: ³⁹ כָּל־פְּקוּדֵ֨י הַלְוִיִּ֜ם אֲשֶׁר֩ פָּקַ֨ד מֹשֶׁ֧ה וְֽאַהֲרֹ֛ן עַל־פִּ֥י יְהֹוָ֖ה לְמִשְׁפְּחֹתָ֑ם כָּל־זָכָר֙ מִבֶּן־חֹ֣דֶשׁ וָמַ֔עְלָה שְׁנַ֥יִם וְעֶשְׂרִ֖ים אָֽלֶף: ס

this clan includes Aaron and Moses, who are Kohath's grandsons.

*33–37.* The Merari clan carries the structure of the Tabernacle, including bars, posts, sockets, and planks. While they carry the tent poles, their cousins—the Gershonites—carry the coverings. The Merari clan represents the third son of Levi.

*38.* ***before the Tent of Meeting, on the east.*** While all sides of the Tabernacle are recognized as holy, nothing tops the elite east—opposite the Tabernacle entrance where Moses, Aaron, and Aaron's offspring dwell. The administration of the Tabernacle as well as the entire camp is in their hands, and anyone who approaches without invitation can be put to death. Prohibition as well as position maintain the status of the Aaronide family. We are left to wonder about the role of women on the east, as well as on the other sides of the Tabernacle complex.

40יהוה said to Moses: Record every first-born
male of the Israelite people from the age of one
month up, and make a list of their names; 41and
take the Levites for Me, יהוה, in place of every male
first-born among the Israelite people, and the cattle
of the Levites in place of every male first-born
among the cattle of the Israelites. 42So Moses recorded all the male first-born among the Israelites,
as יהוה had commanded him. 43All the first-born
males as listed by name, recorded from the age of
one month up, came to 22,273.

44יהוה spoke to Moses, saying: 45Take the Levites in place of all the male first-born among the
Israelite people, and the cattle of the Levites in
place of their cattle; and the Levites shall be Mine,
יהוה's. 46And as the redemption price of the 273
Israelite male first-born over and above the number
of the Levites, 47take five shekels per head—take
this by the sanctuary weight, twenty *gerah*s to the
shekel—48and give the money to Aaron and his
sons as the redemption price for those who are in
excess. 49So Moses took the redemption money
from those over and above the ones redeemed by
the Levites; 50he took the money from the male
first-born of the Israelites, 1,365 sanctuary shekels.
51And Moses gave the redemption money to Aaron
and his sons at יהוה's bidding, as יהוה had commanded Moses.

40 וַיֹּאמֶר יְהֹוָה אֶל־מֹשֶׁה פְּקֹד כָּל־בְּכֹר
זָכָר לִבְנֵי יִשְׂרָאֵל מִבֶּן־חֹדֶשׁ וָמָעְלָה וְשָׂא
אֵת מִסְפַּר שְׁמֹתָם׃ 41 וְלָקַחְתָּ אֶת־הַלְוִיִּם
לִי אֲנִי יְהֹוָה תַּחַת כָּל־בְּכֹר בִּבְנֵי יִשְׂרָאֵל
וְאֵת בֶּהֱמַת הַלְוִיִּם תַּחַת כָּל־בְּכוֹר בְּבֶהֱמַת
בְּנֵי יִשְׂרָאֵל׃ 42 וַיִּפְקֹד מֹשֶׁה כַּאֲשֶׁר צִוָּה
יְהֹוָה אֹתוֹ אֶת־כָּל־בְּכוֹר בִּבְנֵי יִשְׂרָאֵל׃
43 וַיְהִי כָל־בְּכוֹר זָכָר בְּמִסְפַּר שֵׁמֹת מִבֶּן־
חֹדֶשׁ וָמַעְלָה לִפְקֻדֵיהֶם שְׁנַיִם וְעֶשְׂרִים
אֶלֶף שְׁלֹשָׁה וְשִׁבְעִים וּמָאתָיִם׃ פ
44 וַיְדַבֵּר יְהֹוָה אֶל־מֹשֶׁה לֵּאמֹר׃ 45 קַח
אֶת־הַלְוִיִּם תַּחַת כָּל־בְּכוֹר בִּבְנֵי יִשְׂרָאֵל
וְאֶת־בֶּהֱמַת הַלְוִיִּם תַּחַת בְּהֶמְתָּם וְהָיוּ־לִי
הַלְוִיִּם אֲנִי יְהֹוָה׃ 46 וְאֵת פְּדוּיֵי הַשְּׁלֹשָׁה
וְהַשִּׁבְעִים וְהַמָּאתַיִם הָעֹדְפִים עַל־הַלְוִיִּם
מִבְּכוֹר בְּנֵי יִשְׂרָאֵל׃ 47 וְלָקַחְתָּ חֲמֵשֶׁת
חֲמֵשֶׁת שְׁקָלִים לַגֻּלְגֹּלֶת בְּשֶׁקֶל הַקֹּדֶשׁ
תִּקָּח עֶשְׂרִים גֵּרָה הַשָּׁקֶל׃ 48 וְנָתַתָּה
הַכֶּסֶף לְאַהֲרֹן וּלְבָנָיו פְּדוּיֵי הָעֹדְפִים
בָּהֶם׃ 49 וַיִּקַּח מֹשֶׁה אֵת כֶּסֶף הַפִּדְיוֹם
מֵאֵת הָעֹדְפִים עַל פְּדוּיֵי הַלְוִיִּם׃ 50 מֵאֵת
בְּכוֹר בְּנֵי יִשְׂרָאֵל לָקַח אֶת־הַכָּסֶף חֲמִשָּׁה
וְשִׁשִּׁים וּשְׁלֹשׁ מֵאוֹת וָאֶלֶף בְּשֶׁקֶל הַקֹּדֶשׁ׃
51 וַיִּתֵּן מֹשֶׁה אֶת־כֶּסֶף הַפְּדֻיִם לְאַהֲרֹן
וּלְבָנָיו עַל־פִּי יְהֹוָה כַּאֲשֶׁר צִוָּה יְהֹוָה אֶת־
מֹשֶׁה׃ פ

## THE PRICE OF REDEMPTION (3:40–51)

In this parashah, the title of "first-born" applies to a woman's first-born male alone. Genesis 29–30 provides glimpses of how an Israelite mother celebrated his birth—and that of her other children as well. There, mothers Leah and Rachel named their children in ways that reflected their experiences of fertility, conception, pregnancy, and birth. One wonders whether women had specific rituals to celebrate the birth of a first child, and also about what roles levitical mothers played in rearing and raising the clerical class.

***48. give the money to Aaron and his sons as the redemption price.*** The practice of redemption in this section grants special benefits to the priests who receive money. It also exempts Israelites from special service at the sanctuary. This exchange confers 1,365 shekels on Aaron and his sons. On redemption, see also at Exodus 13:15.

4 יהוה spoke to Moses and Aaron, saying: [2]Take a [separate] census of the Kohathites among the Levites, by the clans of their ancestral house, [3]from the age of thirty years up to the age of fifty, all who are subject to service, to perform tasks for the Tent of Meeting. [4]This is the responsibility of the Kohathites in the Tent of Meeting: the most sacred objects.

[5]At the breaking of camp, Aaron and his sons shall go in and take down the screening curtain and cover the Ark of the Pact with it. [6]They shall lay a covering of dolphin skin over it and spread a cloth of pure blue on top; and they shall put its poles in place.

[7]Over the table of display they shall spread a blue cloth; they shall place upon it the bowls, the ladles, the jars, and the libation jugs; and the regular bread shall rest upon it. [8]They shall spread over these a crimson cloth which they shall cover with a covering of dolphin skin; and they shall put the poles in place.

[9]Then they shall take a blue cloth and cover the lampstand for lighting, with its lamps, its tongs, and its fire pans, as well as all the oil vessels that are used in its service. [10]They shall put it and all its

ד וַיְדַבֵּר יְהֹוָה אֶל־מֹשֶׁה וְאֶל־אַהֲרֹן
לֵאמֹר׃
2 נָשֹׂא אֶת־רֹאשׁ בְּנֵי קְהָת מִתּוֹךְ בְּנֵי לֵוִי
לְמִשְׁפְּחֹתָם לְבֵית אֲבֹתָם׃ 3 מִבֶּן שְׁלֹשִׁים
שָׁנָה וָמַעְלָה וְעַד בֶּן־חֲמִשִּׁים שָׁנָה כָּל־בָּא
לַצָּבָא לַעֲשׂוֹת מְלָאכָה בְּאֹהֶל מוֹעֵד׃
4 זֹאת עֲבֹדַת בְּנֵי־קְהָת בְּאֹהֶל מוֹעֵד קֹדֶשׁ
הַקֳּדָשִׁים׃

5 וּבָא אַהֲרֹן וּבָנָיו בִּנְסֹעַ הַמַּחֲנֶה וְהוֹרִדוּ
אֵת פָּרֹכֶת הַמָּסָךְ וְכִסּוּ־בָהּ אֵת אֲרֹן
הָעֵדֻת׃ 6 וְנָתְנוּ עָלָיו כְּסוּי עוֹר תַּחַשׁ
וּפָרְשׂוּ בֶגֶד־כְּלִיל תְּכֵלֶת מִלְמָעְלָה וְשָׂמוּ
בַּדָּיו׃
7 וְעַל ׀ שֻׁלְחַן הַפָּנִים יִפְרְשׂוּ בֶּגֶד תְּכֵלֶת
וְנָתְנוּ עָלָיו אֶת־הַקְּעָרֹת וְאֶת־הַכַּפֹּת וְאֶת־
הַמְּנַקִּיֹּת וְאֵת קְשׂוֹת הַנָּסֶךְ וְלֶחֶם הַתָּמִיד
עָלָיו יִהְיֶה׃ 8 וּפָרְשׂוּ עֲלֵיהֶם בֶּגֶד תּוֹלַעַת
שָׁנִי וְכִסּוּ אֹתוֹ בְּמִכְסֵה עוֹר תָּחַשׁ וְשָׂמוּ
אֶת־בַּדָּיו׃
9 וְלָקְחוּ ׀ בֶּגֶד תְּכֵלֶת וְכִסּוּ אֶת־מְנֹרַת
הַמָּאוֹר וְאֶת־נֵרֹתֶיהָ וְאֶת־מַלְקָחֶיהָ וְאֶת־
מַחְתֹּתֶיהָ וְאֵת כָּל־כְּלֵי שַׁמְנָהּ אֲשֶׁר
יְשָׁרְתוּ־לָהּ בָּהֶם׃ 10 וְנָתְנוּ אֹתָהּ וְאֶת־כָּל־

THE SERVICE OF THE LEVITES (4:1–20)

This section describes the work of the Levites as caretakers of the Tabernacle—"housekeepers," as it were—in contrast to the priests, who officiate and conduct the sacrifices (see also *Vayikra*, Contemporary Reflection, p. 589).

2. ***Kohathites.*** When the people of Israel travel, the Kohath clan is to carry the sacred Ark. In addition, they are to transport the table on which the bread of display is laid, the menorah, the lamps and oils for Tabernacle lighting, and the altar (see Exodus 25:10–40 for descriptions of these objects). Because Aaron and his sons wrap each instrument of worship in blue or purple cloths and skins, the Kohathites never touch them. Should a Kohathite come into direct contact with any of the items, then he is to be killed (v. 15, below).

4. ***the most sacred objects.*** Heb. *kodesh ha-kodashim* usually designates either the innermost room of the Tabernacle or the status of certain sacrificial offerings, but in this section the term refers to the objects inside the Tent.

5. ***cover the Ark of the Pact.*** Only Aaronite hands ever touch the Ark when they wrap it for transport, and no one ever looks at it.

7–8. ***cloth.*** On women as spinners and weavers of the Tabernacle's furnishing, see at Exodus 35:25–26; *T'rumah*, Another View, p. 467; and *P'kudei*, Another View, p. 560.

furnishings into a covering of dolphin skin, which they shall then place on a carrying frame.

[11]Next they shall spread a blue cloth over the altar of gold and cover it with a covering of dolphin skin; and they shall put its poles in place. [12]They shall take all the service vessels with which the service in the sanctuary is performed, put them into a blue cloth and cover them with a covering of dolphin skin, which they shall then place on a carrying frame. [13]They shall remove the ashes from the [copper] altar and spread a purple cloth over it. [14]Upon it they shall place all the vessels that are used in its service: the fire pans, the flesh hooks, the scrapers, and the basins—all the vessels of the altar—and over it they shall spread a covering of dolphin skin; and they shall put its poles in place.

[15]When Aaron and his sons have finished covering the sacred objects and all the furnishings of the sacred objects at the breaking of camp, only then shall the Kohathites come and lift them, so that they do not come in contact with the sacred objects and die. These things in the Tent of Meeting shall be the porterage of the Kohathites.

[16]Responsibility shall rest with Eleazar son of Aaron the priest for the lighting oil, the aromatic incense, the regular meal offering, and the anointing oil—responsibility for the whole Tabernacle and for everything consecrated that is in it or in its vessels.

[17]יהוה spoke to Moses and Aaron, saying: [18]Do not let the group of Kohathite clans be cut off from the Levites. [19]Do this with them, that they may live and not die when they approach the most sacred objects: let Aaron and his sons go in and assign each of them to his duties and to his porterage. [20]But let not [the Kohathites] go inside and witness the dismantling of the sanctuary, lest they die.

כֵּלָ֔יהָ אֶל־מִכְסֵ֖ה ע֣וֹר תָּ֑חַשׁ וְנָתְנ֖וּ עַל־הַמּֽוֹט׃

[11] וְעַ֣ל ׀ מִזְבַּ֣ח הַזָּהָ֗ב יִפְרְשׂוּ֙ בֶּ֣גֶד תְּכֵ֔לֶת וְכִסּ֣וּ אֹת֔וֹ בְּמִכְסֵ֖ה ע֣וֹר תָּ֑חַשׁ וְשָׂמ֖וּ אֶת־בַּדָּֽיו׃ [12] וְלָקְחוּ֩ אֶת־כׇּל־כְּלֵ֨י הַשָּׁרֵ֜ת אֲשֶׁ֧ר יְשָֽׁרְתוּ־בָ֣ם בַּקֹּ֗דֶשׁ וְנָֽתְנוּ֙ אֶל־בֶּ֣גֶד תְּכֵ֔לֶת וְכִסּ֣וּ אוֹתָ֔ם בְּמִכְסֵ֖ה ע֣וֹר תָּ֑חַשׁ וְנָתְנ֖וּ עַל־הַמּֽוֹט׃ [13] וְדִשְּׁנ֖וּ אֶת־הַמִּזְבֵּ֑חַ וּפָרְשׂ֣וּ עָלָ֔יו בֶּ֖גֶד אַרְגָּמָֽן׃ [14] וְנָתְנ֣וּ עָ֠לָ֠יו אֶֽת־כׇּל־כֵּלָ֞יו אֲשֶׁ֣ר יְשָֽׁרְת֧וּ עָלָ֣יו בָּהֶ֗ם אֶת־הַמַּחְתֹּ֤ת אֶת־הַמִּזְלָגֹת֙ וְאֶת־הַיָּעִ֣ים וְאֶת־הַמִּזְרָקֹ֔ת כֹּ֖ל כְּלֵ֣י הַמִּזְבֵּ֑חַ וּפָרְשׂ֣וּ עָלָ֗יו כְּס֛וּי ע֥וֹר תַּ֖חַשׁ וְשָׂמ֥וּ בַדָּֽיו׃

[15] וְכִלָּ֣ה אַֽהֲרֹן־וּבָנָ֡יו לְכַסֹּ֣ת אֶת־הַקֹּ֩דֶשׁ֩ וְאֶת־כׇּל־כְּלֵ֨י הַקֹּ֜דֶשׁ בִּנְסֹ֣עַ הַֽמַּחֲנֶ֗ה וְאַֽחֲרֵי־כֵ֞ן יָבֹ֤אוּ בְנֵֽי־קְהָת֙ לָשֵׂ֔את וְלֹֽא־יִגְּע֥וּ אֶל־הַקֹּ֖דֶשׁ וָמֵ֑תוּ אֵ֛לֶּה מַשָּׂ֥א בְנֵֽי־קְהָ֖ת בְּאֹ֥הֶל מוֹעֵֽד׃

[16] וּפְקֻדַּ֞ת אֶלְעָזָ֣ר ׀ בֶּן־אַֽהֲרֹ֣ן הַכֹּהֵ֗ן שֶׁ֤מֶן הַמָּאוֹר֙ וּקְטֹ֣רֶת הַסַּמִּ֔ים וּמִנְחַ֥ת הַתָּמִ֖יד וְשֶׁ֣מֶן הַמִּשְׁחָ֑ה פְּקֻדַּ֗ת כׇּל־הַמִּשְׁכָּן֙ וְכׇל־אֲשֶׁר־בּ֔וֹ בְּקֹ֖דֶשׁ וּבְכֵלָֽיו׃ פ

[17] וַיְדַבֵּ֣ר יְהֹוָ֔ה אֶל־מֹשֶׁ֥ה וְאֶֽל־אַהֲרֹ֖ן לֵאמֹֽר׃ [18] אַל־תַּכְרִ֕יתוּ אֶת־שֵׁ֖בֶט מִשְׁפְּחֹ֣ת הַקְּהָתִ֑י מִתּ֖וֹךְ הַֽלְוִיִּֽם׃ [19] וְזֹ֣את ׀ עֲשׂ֣וּ לָהֶ֗ם וְחָיוּ֙ וְלֹ֣א יָמֻ֔תוּ בְּגִשְׁתָּ֖ם אֶת־קֹ֣דֶשׁ הַקֳּדָשִׁ֑ים אַֽהֲרֹ֤ן וּבָנָיו֙ יָבֹ֔אוּ וְשָׂמ֣וּ אוֹתָ֗ם אִ֥ישׁ אִ֛ישׁ עַל־עֲבֹדָת֖וֹ וְאֶל־מַשָּׂאֽוֹ׃ [20] וְלֹא־יָבֹ֧אוּ לִרְא֛וֹת כְּבַלַּ֥ע אֶת־הַקֹּ֖דֶשׁ וָמֵֽתוּ׃ פ

· · · · · · · · · · · · · · · · · · · · · · · · · · · ·

**20.** The Tent of Meeting retains its sanctity even when dismantled, and therefore it endangers all but Aaron and his descendants. As each Tabernacle piece remains part of the whole even when wrapped in its own cover, so are Kohathites and priests part of the tribe of Levi even when distinguished by individual roles. The boundaries of the holy reverberate on every level.
—*Rachel Havrelock*

# *Another View*

As the Israelites prepare to resume their journey, Moses leads the community in organizational activities: census-taking and the placement of tribal units in preparation for the march. The principles of organization are value-laden; they count only able-bodied men of fighting age in the initial census, and they divide the Levites into units with unequal privileges concerning the holy sanctuary. Though all of the members of the community are traveling to the same place, they do so in a structured fashion in which the boundaries of tribal units are carefully maintained, and in which some groups have more responsibility—and more access to the divine sphere—than others. The overarching tone of the parashah is subsequently patriarchal and hierarchical.

Patriarchy as a cultural system is based on power differentials; able-bodied men are defined as the powerful and active members of the community. (See, for example, bell hooks, *Feminist Theory from Margin to Center*, 1984.) This is evident in the notable absence of women and other marginal figures from this parashah. What is the place allotted in the Israelite encampment for women, children, or the infirm? Even when the men of Levi are assigned to be Tabernacle functionaries, God states that they are taken for this role as redemption for the Israelite first-born males (3:12). Again, it is men who are the focus of the narrative, and all important tasks in this parashah are done by men.

It is possible, however, to glean from this text a lesson about a handful of important women: Jacob's wives and the wives' handmaids. The structure of the Israelite encampment is not random; rather, it groups together certain tribes while separating others. Leah's descendants—Judah, Issachar, and Zebulun—have pride of place within the Israelite encampment, on the east side closest to the entrance to the Tabernacle. Her other descendants—Reuben, Simeon, and Gad—

*This parashah makes a strong statement about the matriarchs of Israel.*

are located on the south side of the Tabernacle. Their placement can be explained by Genesis 49: all three of these tribal ancestors committed acts that drew harsh criticism from Jacob, and subsequently they are held in lower esteem than their full brothers. The children of the handmaids Bilhah and Zilpah are represented on the northern side of the encampment, and Rachel's offspring are located on the western side, farthest from the Tabernacle entrance. Hence the descendants of Jacob's most beloved wife are in a position of less honor than the children of the long-suffering Leah. Even while ignoring the roles of women in defining the community, this parashah still makes a strong statement about the matriarchs of Israel. (See further Mary Douglas, *In the Wilderness*, 1993, pp. 172–95.)

—*Beatrice Lawrence*

# Post-biblical Interpretations

***יהוה*** ***spoke to Moses in the wilderness of Sinai*** (1:1). Midrash *B'midbar Rabbah* 1.2 connects this verse with Jeremiah 2:31: "O generation, behold the word of יהוה! Have I been like a wilderness to Israel?" and explains that compared to slavery in Egypt, the wilderness experience was luxurious. Furthermore, according to this midrash, God assigned three mentors to sustain Israel in the wilderness: Moses, Aaron, and Miriam. Due to the merits of Moses, the people ate manna; due to the merits of Aaron, God encircled Israel with clouds of glory; and due to the merits of Miriam, a miraculous well accompanied them. The passage continues, "How was the well constructed? It was rock-shaped like a kind of beehive, and wherever they journeyed it rolled along and came with them." When the Israelites stopped and the portable Tabernacle was erected, the well would establish itself in the Tent of Meeting. "Then the leaders of the tribes would come and stand upon it and say, 'Spring up, O well!' (21:17) and it would rise."

***The Israelites shall camp each man with his standard, under the banners of their ancestral house*** (2:2). *B'midbar Rabbah* 2.7 relates that each tribe had a different colored flag, corresponding to the precious stones on Aaron's breastplate. For example, "Reuben's stone was ruby and the color of his flag was red, and embroidered on it were mandrakes." (On mandrakes, see Genesis 30:14–15.) "Judah's stone was a carbuncle and the color of his flag was something like the heavens; embroidered on it was a lion." This midrash adds that the nations of the world provided themselves with distinctive flags based on Israel's example.

***But Nadab and Abihu died by the will of*** **יהוה*...* *and they left no sons*** (3:4). Midrash *P'sikta D'Rav Kahana* 26.9 explains that one of the reasons for the mysterious deaths of Aaron's sons was their arrogance in refusing to marry, even though the chief priest was commanded to make atonement for himself and "his household" (Leviticus 16:6). The midrash explains that "his household" (literally "his house") signifies "his wife" and relates that "many young women sat grieving, waiting in vain to be asked in marriage by Nadab or Abihu." But the young men said, "Our father's brother [Moses] is king (Deuteronomy 33:5), our mother's brother [Nahshon] is prince (Exodus 6:23; Numbers 2:3), our father is chief priest; we are adjutants of the chief priest. What women are worthy of us?"

> *Due to the merits of Miriam, a miraculous well accompanied the Israelites.*

***So it was Eleazar and Ithamar who served as priests in the lifetime of their father Aaron*** (3:4). The Rabbis were interested in how Aaron, Eleazar, and Ithamar shared their duties as priests. *B'midbar Rabbah* 2.26 reports that when one of those men was incapacitated, one of the others took on the role of chief priest in his stead. This text goes on to discuss a woman named Kimhith who lived many centuries later: she had seven sons and each of them served in the office of chief priest. On one occasion, two sons served as chief priest on the same day. The Rabbis paid her a visit and asked her, "What good deeds have you performed to merit such an honor?" She responded, "So help me Heaven! In all my life the rafters of my house have never looked upon the hair of my head." Rabbinic society, like many surrounding cultures, believed that married women should cover their heads when they went out in public. Kimhith's modesty was such that she did not uncover her hair, even in the privacy of her own home. Punning on her name, the Rabbis observed, "All flours (*kimha*) are flour; but the flour of Kimhith is fine flour," and they applied to her Psalm 45:14, "All glorious is the king's daughter within the palace," as an indication that the domestic domain is the best place for a praiseworthy and virtuous woman.

***record every male among them*** (3:15). The Rabbis asked, "Why every male, without mentioning every female?" and they responded, "Because the glory of the blessed Holy One is derived from the males." This is proven by Psalm 127:3, "Sons are the provision of יהוה; the fruit of the womb, [God's] reward." The midrash explains that "provision of יהוה" refers to males, while if females come, they are also "a reward" (*B'midbar Rabbah* 3.8). Rabbinic Judaism valued males over females but recognized that women, too, have multiple virtues and are essential for human society and human continuity. —*Judith R. Baskin*

## Contemporary Reflection

THERE IS POWER in taking a census. When God commands Moses to do so at the beginning of *parashat B'midbar*, only male Israelites over the age of 20 who are able to bear arms are considered. In the text, Moses is told to tally up *kol adat b'nei yisrael*, literally "the whole community of the Children of Israel." But do able-bodied males over 20 years old represent the *whole* community? While *adat* is often translated as "community," it can also refer to an "assembly, band, company, or faction," hence only one segment of the larger population. This nuance allows us to recognize all who are *not* counted: women, minors, the elderly, and the physically, mentally, or emotionally challenged. In Torah, these people are usually missing from numerations as well as narrations. Those who are counted have a special worth to the society, while those who are not may be considered less valuable and are, therefore, less visible.

There is also danger in taking a census. This parashah is all about enumerating people, as the English name of the book, "Numbers," suggests. However, the Talmud asserts that "it is forbidden to count [the nation of] Israel even for the sake of a commandment . . . [because] whoever counts Israel transgresses a prohibition, as it is written, 'The number of the children of Israel shall be like the sands of the sea, not to be measured' (Hosea 2:1)" (BT *Yoma* 22b). Rashi explains that we must count something each person gives (like the half-shekel) rather than count actual people, because then "there will not be a plague among them, for the evil eye can affect that which is counted—and a plague may come upon them as we found in the days of David" (Rashi on Exodus 30:1). Is Rashi merely superstitious, or is he suggesting that it is dangerous to trivialize a person's essence? His comment teaches us that we must value each human as one who is made *b'tzelem Elohim*, in God's image (Genesis 1:27). A number can measure whether an army has enough people, but it can never measure the worth of the individual people in that army.

*Is being counted what makes us count?*

Today, American society is obsessed with numbers, censuses, and demographic studies. Now when we calculate our Temple membership, for instance, we include everybody: the women and the men, the young and the old, the "typical" and the challenged. We can look at sum totals, categories, and sub-categories of these studies; and while they provide valuable information, they still may not show us who or what really counts. Can we say that all people matter when our

Jewish institutions are not accessible to every individual? Taking the synagogue as an example, do we value each person when a member in a wheelchair cannot come up to the Ark to take the Torah? Do we include everyone in worship services when we do not offer large-print prayer books or when we do not provide hearing aids to those who need them? Do we validate those with different learning styles and abilities when we hire inexperienced educators for our Religious School classes? If we compare our raw data with the facts within the synagogue walls, who really matters—the ones who are counted, or the ones for whom we take extra measures? While numbers may be essential, they do not represent the sum total of what is truly important. But what does?

In *B'midbar*, one could argue that the number of troops is what really counts, since they are the ones included in the census. But when we read between the lines, when we ask who is not included, we can see how the untold stories of the unmentioned people matter too. For instance, what about the woman who might have wished to fight? Or how about the 19-year-old man, just months short of his 20th birthday, eager to serve God and his people? And how about the 23-year-old male Israelite who can count the right number of years but not the right number of limbs since one of his was lost in a childhood accident? And the pregnant soldier's wife who calculates the number of weeks until her baby arrives, knowing that the baby's father's days may be numbered? There may be contextually legitimate reasons why these people are omitted from the census, and, ultimately, from the Torah text, but their exclusion means we miss the opportunity to see what they can offer the community.

We all hear stories about those who lose one thing and gain something even greater through their loss. There is an urban legend about violin virtuoso Itzhak Perlman, who taught that lesson by happenstance when he played a concerto at Avery Fisher Hall in New York City with a broken string. One might think it impossible to play with just three strings a concerto written for violin, but Perlman did it and did so with great fervor. Upon completing his dazzling performance, he (so the story goes) said humbly to the audience, "You know, sometimes it is the artist's task to find out how much music you can still make with what you have left." Perhaps this is true for all of us, not only artists. Losses can lead to inner strengths and life changes that we did not dream were possible. We are more than the sum total of our parts.

The Israelites may have needed parameters for whom to include and whom to exclude from the census described in *B'midbar*, but we must remember why even those not tallied do, in fact, matter. Today we may count every individual in our community, but may still discount how much they have to offer. The missing members in this parashah can teach us to reconsider what it means to count. As the numerous stories in the Bible and in our lives remind us, even those not included are important, and all those we now seek to include genuinely are individuals with much to gain from and offer to our communities.

—*Rachel Stock Spilker*

# *Voices*

## *Otwock VI*

Kadya Molodowsky (transl. Kathryn Hellerstein)

I am a wandering girl.
My heart is practiced in longing.
And when the day eats up the dew of the night,
I tuck up the small white curtain from my
window pane,
And look upon a new street.
There lies coiled up
In a little corner of my heart
Such a singular, trembling idea:
Maybe no one here will love me.
Maybe no one here will want to know me!
But God forbid!
Like the threat of rain always hanging in the air
And falling in unexpected abundance on the
earth,
That's how each new city is for me,
Each new place.
And I don't know how manifold my flesh is.
Every year a new ring
Grows in me, as on a tree,
I am mazily woven of rising and setting.
I am a wandering girl,
My heart is practiced in longing.

## *I Say*

Malka Heifetz Tussman (transl. Marcia Falk)

I say to the Almighty:

Ever-homeless Wanderer,
I would—
if but my heart were pure—
invite
you in, to spend the night.

## *The Window*

Irena Klepfisz

She looks out the window.
All is present.
The shadows of the past
fall elsewhere.

This is the wilderness
she thinks.

And our tongues have become
dry    the wilderness has
dried out our tongues    and
we have forgotten speech.

She looks out the window.
All is present.

## *from Every City Has a Soul*

Jill Hammer

. . . wilderness is not a place
it is a time
longing to mend
what cannot be mended
longing to break
what cannot be broken
wilderness is a name
you call in the ear of a lover
but you are speaking to someone else

## *Forgotten*

Lisa Levine

*Numbers 1:2*

I wondered
On the day of the counting
Why my husband
And his brothers
And their sons
Were numbered among
The stars of heaven
But my daughters and I
Were not even noticed
Doing the washing
Baking the bread
Raising our children
I wondered
Why I
The womb that held them
Was
Forgotten.

## *A Prayer for the Journey*

Sheila Peltz Weinberg

A prayer for the journey
We could say it every day
When we first leave the soft warmth of our beds
And don't know for sure if we'll return at night
When we get in the trains, planes and
automobiles
And put our lives in the hands of many
strangers.
Or when we leave our homes for a day, a week,
a month or more—
Will we return to a peaceful home? Untouched
by fire, flood or crime?
How will our travels change us?
What gives us the courage to go through that
door?

A prayer for the journey
For the journey we take in this fragile vessel
of flesh.
A finite number of years and we will reach
The unknown, where it all began.
Every life, every day, every hour is a journey.
In the travel is the discovery,
the wisdom, the joy.
Every life, every day, every hour is a journey.
In the travel is the reward,
the peace, the blessing.

## *They Had Names*

Susan Glickman

*Numbers 1:5*

They had names like Auntie Bea and Aunt Laura and wore tight corsets.
When you put your arms around them you could feel the wires.

They had papery skins; cheeks like moths' wings that trembled when you kissed them. Their husbands were dead, or they were called Sam, or Arthur, and wore hats even in summer.

They smoked cigars that always went out and they let them go out.
The old people had candies in their pockets, and Kleenex; they carried pictures of grandchildren and knew all the stories about who was related to whom, and why, and remembered them.

When I was a child I was told all the stories again and again, who was related to whom, and why, and who died and why but I always forgot.
Years later, I have no one to tell me the stories. I remember the ladies' perfumes: lilac, carnation and rose; they smelled like sachets.

And I remember arthritic fingers, wedding bands sunk in the flesh; I always imagined they'd have to cut them off.

They kept trying to decide whose eyes I had, whose nose, and what were my talents. I didn't listen.

Now I want to know, I want to know where I fit in that long line of descendants from the country of the old.

## *Each of Us Has a Name*

Zelda (transl. Marcia Falk)

*Numbers 1:5*

Each of us has a name
given by God
and given by our parents

Each of us has a name
given by our stature and our smile
and given by what we wear

Each of us has a name
given by the mountains
and given by our walls

Each of us has a name
given by the stars
and given by our neighbors

Each of us has a name
given by our sins
and given by our longing

Each of us has a name
given by our enemies
and given by our love

Each of us has a name
given by our celebrations
and given by our work

Each of us has a name
given by the seasons
and given by our blindness

Each of us has a name
given by the sea
and given by
our death.

# נשא ✦ Naso

## NUMBERS 4:21–7:89

### *Suspicion and Sanctity*

IN THE OPENING UNITS of the book of Numbers, the Israelites organize themselves for their trek to the Promised Land. Not only must they navigate through the wilderness a group that the Torah claims to include more than two million individuals (600,000 fighting men—plus women, children, and other males), but also they must maintain the proper worship of God throughout their journey.

*Parashat Naso* ("lift up") focuses on the Israelite cultic structures throughout the journey. Two detailed administrative accounts frame this parashah: the Levite census (4:21–49) and the record of the tribal chiefs' gifts for the dedication of the altar (7:1–88). Whereas Leviticus typically focuses on the ritual purity of the sanctuary, Numbers is concerned with maintaining the purity of the camp as a whole.

The Israelites can protect this purity through the service of sanctified individuals like the *nazir* (6:1–21) or the priests (6:22–27), as well as through responses to threats of perversion, exemplified by the ritual of the wife accused by her husband of adultery (5:11–31). (Rabbinic literature uses the term *sotah* to refer to aspects of this case, although the word itself —meaning "a woman who strayed"—does not actually appear in the Bible. This commentary will employ the rabbinic term, which has come to be used widely when discussing this passage.)

The structure of this parashah reflects well the role of women within the Israelite community. Women, like most men, could not be cultic officials—neither priests, Levites, nor tribal chiefs—and therefore they remain absent from the administrative framework of the parashah. Yet they occupy a central place within the religion, either as cause for concern, such as the *sotah*, or, more surprisingly, as devotional exemplars such as the *nazir*—the individual who dedicates herself or himself to God. (The specifically feminine form is *n'zirah*, although only the generic form *nazir* appears in the Bible.)

*Women remain absent from administration, yet their place in the religion is central.*

At first glance, the *sotah* and the *nazir* seem to represent mutually exclusive ends of the spectrum for a woman's place within Israelite society. A woman could either find herself tottering on the margins of society—accused, vulnerable, and at the mercy of her husband or priest—or she could establish her place among the elite of society by dedicating her life to God. Yet the juxtaposition of these figures within the parashah, and the linguistic links between the passages describing them, together suggest an intrinsic relationship between the *sotah* and the *nazir*. Read together, these figures inform, challenge, and broaden our perceptions of women's roles within the religion and society of ancient Israel. —*Amy Kalmanofsky*

## Outline

*I.* Cultic Administration
*Census of the Levites* (4:21–49)

*II.* Maintaining Community Sanctity by Countering Threats of Impurity (5:1–31)

A. Procedure for the physically impure (vv. 1–4)
B. Procedure for a person who betrays another (vv. 5–10)
C. Procedure for a wife accused of adultery (vv. 11–31)

*III.* Maintaining Community Sanctity through Religious Leaders (6:1–27)

A. Laws of the *nazir* (vv. 1–21)
B. Priestly blessing (vv. 22–27)

*IV.* Record of the Tribal Chiefs' Gifts (7:1–89)

A. Gifts for the Levites (vv. 1–9)
B. Gifts for the dedication of the altar (vv. 10–88)
C. Conclusion (v. 89)

יהוה spoke to Moses: [22]Take a census of the Gershonites also, by their ancestral house and by their clans. [23]Record them from the age of thirty years up to the age of fifty, all who are subject to service in the performance of tasks for the Tent of Meeting. [24]These are the duties of the Gershonite clans as to labor and porterage: [25]they shall carry the cloths of the Tabernacle, the Tent of Meeting with its covering, the covering of dolphin skin that is on top of it, and the screen for the entrance of the Tent of Meeting; [26]the hangings of the enclosure, the screen at the entrance of the gate of the enclosure that surrounds the Tabernacle, the cords thereof, and the altar, and all their service equipment and all their accessories; and they shall perform the service. [27]All the duties of the Ger-

ד 21 וַיְדַבֵּ֥ר יְהוָ֖ה אֶל־מֹשֶׁ֥ה לֵּאמֹֽר׃
22 נָשֹׂ֗א אֶת־רֹ֛אשׁ בְּנֵ֥י גֵרְשׁ֖וֹן גַּם־הֵ֑ם
לְבֵ֥ית אֲבֹתָ֖ם לְמִשְׁפְּחֹתָֽם׃ 23 מִבֶּן֩ שְׁלֹשִׁ֨ים
שָׁנָ֜ה וָמַ֗עְלָה עַ֚ד בֶּן־חֲמִשִּׁ֣ים שָׁנָ֔ה תִּפְקֹ֖ד
אוֹתָ֑ם כָּל־הַבָּא֙ לִצְבֹ֣א צָבָ֔א לַעֲבֹ֥ד עֲבֹדָ֖ה
בְּאֹ֥הֶל מוֹעֵֽד׃ 24 זֹ֣את עֲבֹדַ֔ת מִשְׁפְּחֹ֖ת
הַגֵּרְשֻׁנִּ֑י לַעֲבֹ֖ד וּלְמַשָּֽׂא׃ 25 וְנָ֨שְׂא֜וּ אֶת־
יְרִיעֹ֤ת הַמִּשְׁכָּן֙ וְאֶת־אֹ֣הֶל מוֹעֵ֔ד מִכְסֵ֕הוּ
וּמִכְסֵ֛ה הַתַּ֥חַשׁ אֲשֶׁר־עָלָ֖יו מִלְמָ֑עְלָה
וְאֶ֨ת־מָסַ֔ךְ פֶּ֖תַח אֹ֥הֶל מוֹעֵֽד׃ 26 וְאֵת֩
קַלְעֵ֨י הֶחָצֵ֜ר וְאֶת־מָסַ֣ךְ ׀ פֶּ֣תַח ׀ שַׁ֣עַר
הֶחָצֵ֗ר אֲשֶׁ֨ר עַל־הַמִּשְׁכָּ֤ן וְעַל־הַמִּזְבֵּ֙חַ֙
סָבִ֔יב וְאֵת֙ מֵיתְרֵיהֶ֔ם וְאֶת־כָּל־כְּלֵ֖י עֲבֹדָתָ֑ם
וְאֵ֨ת כָּל־אֲשֶׁ֧ר יֵעָשֶׂ֛ה לָהֶ֖ם וְעָבָֽדוּ׃
27 עַל־פִּי֩ אַהֲרֹ֨ן וּבָנָ֜יו תִּהְיֶ֗ה כָּל־עֲבֹדַת֙

## *Cultic Administration*

### CENSUS OF THE LEVITES (4:21–49)

According to Numbers 1:48–49, the tribe of Levi is subject to a census separate from the greater Israelite community. Although the Torah does not provide a clear reason for this, one explanation is that the men of this tribe are exempt from regular military service and assigned to protect the Tabernacle. The Torah records two levitical censuses: one counts males older than one month (3:15), and the other counts men aged 30 to 50, presumably, the work force (see 4:1–3). The Torah does not explain why Levites could not begin service before the age of 30 nor work past 50. The mandated retirement age makes sense given the physical demands.

*22. **Gershonites.*** Gershon was Levi's eldest son (Exodus 6:16). His descendants comprise one of the three levitical clans who care for the Tabernacle and its associated sacred objects (Numbers 18).

*23. **from the age of thirty years up to the age of fifty.*** This census is concerned only with those eligible for the work force. The starting age for a Levite's service is given as 30 years (Numbers 4:3, 23, and 30), and as 25 years (Numbers 8:23–24).

▶ The case involves a pregnant woman whose husband suspects that he is not the father.

ANOTHER VIEW ➤ *836*

▶ The *sotah* ritual's history teaches us that change is a way to be true to Jewish tradition.

CONTEMPORARY REFLECTION ➤ *838*

▶ The Rabbis viewed the "errant wife" as a metaphor for the entire Jewish people.

POST-BIBLICAL INTERPRETATIONS ➤ *836*

▶ Daughters of the tribe of Dinah . . . brought a silver bowl, / to hold the flow of birth. . . .

VOICES ➤ *840*

shonites, all their porterage and all their service, shall be performed on orders from Aaron and his sons; you shall make them responsible for attending to all their porterage. [28]Those are the duties of the Gershonite clans for the Tent of Meeting; they shall attend to them under the direction of Ithamar son of Aaron the priest.

[29]As for the Merarites, you shall record them by the clans of their ancestral house; [30]you shall record them from the age of thirty years up to the age of fifty, all who are subject to service in the performance of the duties for the Tent of Meeting. [31]These are their porterage tasks in connection with their various duties for the Tent of Meeting: the planks, the bars, the posts, and the sockets of the Tabernacle; [32]the posts around the enclosure and their sockets, pegs, and cords—all these furnishings and their service: you shall list by name the objects that are their porterage tasks. [33]Those are the duties of the Merarite clans, pertaining to their various duties in the Tent of Meeting under the direction of Ithamar son of Aaron the priest.

[34]So Moses, Aaron, and the chieftains of the community recorded the Kohathites by the clans of their ancestral house, [35]from the age of thirty years up to the age of fifty, all who were subject to service for work relating to the Tent of Meeting. [36]Those recorded by their clans came to 2,750. [37]That was the enrollment of the Kohathite clans, all those who performed duties relating to the Tent of Meeting, whom Moses and Aaron recorded at the command of יהוה through Moses.

[38]The Gershonites who were recorded by the clans of their ancestral house, [39]from the age of

בְּנֵ֣י הַגֵּֽרְשֻׁנִּ֔י לְכָל־מַשָּׂאָ֖ם וּלְכֹ֣ל עֲבֹדָתָ֑ם
וּפְקַדְתֶּ֤ם עֲלֵהֶם֙ בְּמִשְׁמֶ֔רֶת אֵ֖ת כָּל־מַשָּׂאָֽם׃
28 זֹ֣את עֲבֹדַ֗ת מִשְׁפְּחֹ֛ת בְּנֵ֥י הַגֵּרְשֻׁנִּ֖י בְּאֹ֣הֶל
מוֹעֵ֑ד וּמִ֨שְׁמַרְתָּ֔ם בְּיַד֙ אִֽיתָמָ֔ר בֶּֽן־אַהֲרֹ֖ן
הַכֹּהֵֽן׃ ס
29 בְּנֵ֖י מְרָרִ֑י לְמִשְׁפְּחֹתָ֥ם לְבֵית־אֲבֹתָ֖ם
תִּפְקֹ֥ד אֹתָֽם׃ 30 מִבֶּן֩ שְׁלֹשִׁ֨ים שָׁנָ֜ה וָמַ֗עְלָה
וְעַ֛ד בֶּן־חֲמִשִּׁ֥ים שָׁנָ֖ה תִּפְקְדֵ֑ם כָּל־הַבָּא֙
לַצָּבָ֔א לַעֲבֹ֕ד אֶת־עֲבֹדַ֖ת אֹ֥הֶל מוֹעֵֽד׃
31 וְזֹאת֙ מִשְׁמֶ֣רֶת מַשָּׂאָ֔ם לְכָל־עֲבֹדָתָ֖ם
בְּאֹ֣הֶל מוֹעֵ֑ד קַרְשֵׁי֙ הַמִּשְׁכָּ֔ן וּבְרִיחָ֖יו
וְעַמּוּדָ֥יו וַאֲדָנָֽיו׃ 32 וְעַמּוּדֵ֨י הֶחָצֵ֜ר סָבִ֗יב
וְאַדְנֵיהֶם֙ וִיתֵדֹתָ֣ם וּמֵֽיתְרֵיהֶ֔ם לְכָל־כְּלֵיהֶ֖ם
וּלְכֹ֣ל עֲבֹדָתָ֑ם וּבְשֵׁמֹ֣ת תִּפְקְד֔וּ אֶת־כְּלֵ֖י
מִשְׁמֶ֥רֶת מַשָּׂאָֽם׃ 33 זֹ֣את עֲבֹדַ֗ת מִשְׁפְּחֹת֙
בְּנֵ֣י מְרָרִ֔י לְכָל־עֲבֹדָתָ֖ם בְּאֹ֣הֶל מוֹעֵ֑ד בְּיַד֙
אִֽיתָמָ֔ר בֶּֽן־אַהֲרֹ֖ן הַכֹּהֵֽן׃
34 וַיִּפְקֹ֨ד מֹשֶׁ֧ה וְאַהֲרֹ֛ן וּנְשִׂיאֵ֥י הָעֵדָ֖ה אֶת־
בְּנֵ֣י הַקְּהָתִ֑י לְמִשְׁפְּחֹתָ֖ם וּלְבֵ֥ית אֲבֹתָֽם׃
35 מִבֶּ֨ן שְׁלֹשִׁ֤ים שָׁנָה֙ וָמַ֔עְלָה וְעַ֖ד בֶּן־
חֲמִשִּׁ֣ים שָׁנָ֑ה כָּל־הַבָּא֙ לַצָּבָ֔א לַעֲבֹדָ֖ה
בְּאֹ֥הֶל מוֹעֵֽד׃ 36 וַיִּהְי֥וּ פְקֻדֵיהֶ֖ם
לְמִשְׁפְּחֹתָ֑ם אַלְפַּ֕יִם שְׁבַ֥ע מֵא֖וֹת וַחֲמִשִּֽׁים׃
37 אֵ֣לֶּה פְקוּדֵי֙ מִשְׁפְּחֹ֣ת הַקְּהָתִ֔י כָּל־הָעֹבֵ֖ד
בְּאֹ֣הֶל מוֹעֵ֑ד אֲשֶׁ֨ר פָּקַ֤ד מֹשֶׁה֙ וְאַהֲרֹ֔ן עַל־
פִּ֥י יְהוָ֖ה בְּיַד־מֹשֶֽׁה׃ ס
38 וּפְקוּדֵ֖י בְּנֵ֣י גֵרְשׁ֑וֹן לְמִשְׁפְּחוֹתָ֖ם וּלְבֵ֥ית
אֲבֹתָֽם׃ 39 מִבֶּ֨ן שְׁלֹשִׁ֤ים שָׁנָה֙ וָמַ֔עְלָה

*27. on orders from Aaron and his sons.* That is, Levites are subordinate to priests—the direct descendants of Aaron. Whereas Numbers 8 portrays a harmonious relationship between Levites and priests, tension is evident in the story of Korah (Numbers 16). Deuteronomy 18:1–8 portrays the status of the Levites as more on a par with that of the priests.

*29. Merarites.* Merari was Levi's third son (Exodus 6:16).

*34. Kohathites.* Kohath was Levi's second son (Exodus 6:16) and an ancestor of Aaron. The Kohathites are designated to care for the Tabernacle's most sacred objects (4:4–15).

thirty years up to the age of fifty, all who were subject to service for work relating to the Tent of Meeting—[40]those recorded by the clans of their ancestral house came to 2,630. [41]That was the enrollment of the Gershonite clans, all those performing duties relating to the Tent of Meeting whom Moses and Aaron recorded at the command of יהוה.

[42]The enrollment of the Merarite clans by the clans of their ancestral house, [43]from the age of thirty years up to the age of fifty, all who were subject to service for work relating to the Tent of Meeting—[44]those recorded by their clans came to 3,200. [45]That was the enrollment of the Merarite clans which Moses and Aaron recorded at the command of יהוה through Moses.

[46]All the Levites whom Moses, Aaron, and the chieftains of Israel recorded by the clans of their ancestral houses, [47]from the age of thirty years up to the age of fifty, all who were subject to duties of service and porterage relating to the Tent of Meeting—[48]those recorded came to 8,580. [49]Each one was given responsibility for his service and porterage at the command of יהוה through Moses, and each was recorded as יהוה had commanded Moses.

*5* יהוה spoke to Moses, saying: [2]Instruct the Israelites to remove from camp anyone with an

וְעַד בֶּן־חֲמִשִּׁים שָׁנָה כָּל־הַבָּא לַצָּבָא
לַעֲבֹדָה בְּאֹהֶל מוֹעֵד׃ 40 וַיִּהְיוּ פְּקֻדֵיהֶם
לְמִשְׁפְּחֹתָם לְבֵית אֲבֹתָם אַלְפַּיִם וְשֵׁשׁ
מֵאוֹת וּשְׁלֹשִׁים׃ 41 אֵלֶּה פְּקוּדֵי מִשְׁפְּחֹת
בְּנֵי גֵרְשׁוֹן כָּל־הָעֹבֵד בְּאֹהֶל מוֹעֵד אֲשֶׁר
פָּקַד מֹשֶׁה וְאַהֲרֹן עַל־פִּי יְהֹוָה׃
42 וּפְקוּדֵי מִשְׁפְּחֹת בְּנֵי מְרָרִי לְמִשְׁפְּחֹתָם
לְבֵית אֲבֹתָם׃ 43 מִבֶּן שְׁלֹשִׁים שָׁנָה וָמַעְלָה
וְעַד בֶּן־חֲמִשִּׁים שָׁנָה כָּל־הַבָּא לַצָּבָא
לַעֲבֹדָה בְּאֹהֶל מוֹעֵד׃ 44 וַיִּהְיוּ פְקֻדֵיהֶם
לְמִשְׁפְּחֹתָם שְׁלֹשֶׁת אֲלָפִים וּמָאתָיִם׃
45 אֵלֶּה פְקוּדֵי מִשְׁפְּחֹת בְּנֵי מְרָרִי אֲשֶׁר
פָּקַד מֹשֶׁה וְאַהֲרֹן עַל־פִּי יְהֹוָה בְּיַד־
מֹשֶׁה׃
46 כָּל־הַפְּקֻדִים אֲשֶׁר פָּקַד מֹשֶׁה וְאַהֲרֹן
וּנְשִׂיאֵי יִשְׂרָאֵל אֶת־הַלְוִיִּם לְמִשְׁפְּחֹתָם
וּלְבֵית אֲבֹתָם׃ 47 מִבֶּן שְׁלֹשִׁים שָׁנָה
וָמַעְלָה וְעַד בֶּן־חֲמִשִּׁים שָׁנָה כָּל־הַבָּא
לַעֲבֹד עֲבֹדַת עֲבֹדָה וַעֲבֹדַת מַשָּׂא בְּאֹהֶל
מוֹעֵד׃ 48 וַיִּהְיוּ פְּקֻדֵיהֶם שְׁמֹנַת אֲלָפִים
וַחֲמֵשׁ מֵאוֹת וּשְׁמֹנִים׃ 49 עַל־פִּי יְהֹוָה פָּקַד
אוֹתָם בְּיַד־מֹשֶׁה אִישׁ אִישׁ עַל־עֲבֹדָתוֹ
וְעַל־מַשָּׂאוֹ וּפְקֻדָיו אֲשֶׁר־צִוָּה יְהֹוָה אֶת־
מֹשֶׁה׃ פ

ה וַיְדַבֵּר יְהֹוָה אֶל־מֹשֶׁה לֵּאמֹר׃ 2 צַו
אֶת־בְּנֵי יִשְׂרָאֵל וִישַׁלְּחוּ מִן־הַמַּחֲנֶה כָּל־

## *Maintaining Community Sanctity by Countering Threats of Impurity*

(5:1–31)

No matter how well organized the Tabernacle and surrounding camp may be, the community remains vulnerable to physical and spiritual impurities. In Leviticus and Numbers, women often figure prominently in discussions of impurity. Therefore, it is no surprise that women are mentioned in each of the cases described in Numbers 5. Although the situations appear unrelated, they all reflect a concern for communal purity.

### PROCEDURE FOR THE PHYSICALLY IMPURE (5:1–4)

The first threat addressed is that of accidental impurity: individuals who are blameless—perhaps

eruption or a discharge and anyone defiled by a corpse. [3]Remove male and female alike; put them outside the camp so that they do not defile the camp of those in whose midst I dwell.

[4]The Israelites did so, putting them outside the camp; as יהוה had spoken to Moses, so the Israelites did.

[5]יהוה spoke to Moses, saying: [6]Speak to the Israelites: When men or women individually commit any wrong toward a fellow human being, thus breaking faith with יהוה, and they realize their

צָר֛וּעַ וְכָל־זָ֖ב וְכֹ֣ל טָמֵ֣א לָנָ֑פֶשׁ׃ [3] מִזָּכָ֤ר עַד־נְקֵבָה֙ תְּשַׁלֵּ֔חוּ אֶל־מִח֥וּץ לַֽמַּחֲנֶ֖ה תְּשַׁלְּח֑וּם וְלֹ֤א יְטַמְּאוּ֙ אֶת־מַ֣חֲנֵיהֶ֔ם אֲשֶׁ֥ר אֲנִ֖י שֹׁכֵ֥ן בְּתוֹכָֽם׃

[4] וַיַּֽעֲשׂוּ־כֵן֙ בְּנֵ֣י יִשְׂרָאֵ֔ל וַיְשַׁלְּח֣וּ אוֹתָ֔ם אֶל־מִח֖וּץ לַֽמַּחֲנֶ֑ה כַּֽאֲשֶׁ֨ר דִּבֶּ֤ר יְהוָה֙ אֶל־מֹשֶׁ֔ה כֵּ֥ן עָשׂ֖וּ בְּנֵ֥י יִשְׂרָאֵֽל׃ פ

[5] וַיְדַבֵּ֥ר יְהוָ֖ה אֶל־מֹשֶׁ֥ה לֵּאמֹֽר׃ [6] דַּבֵּר֙ אֶל־בְּנֵ֣י יִשְׂרָאֵ֔ל אִ֣ישׁ אֽוֹ־אִשָּׁ֗ה כִּ֤י יַֽעֲשׂוּ֙ מִכָּל־חַטֹּ֣את הָֽאָדָ֔ם לִמְעֹ֥ל מַ֖עַל בַּֽיהוָ֑ה וְאָֽשְׁמָ֖ה

- - - - - - - - - - - - - - - - - - - - - - - - - - - - - - - - - - - - - - - -

even passive—recipients of physical impurity resulting from disease, or from contact with the dead. Such individuals must be expelled physically before their impurity penetrates and thus defiles the sacred camp; and they must remain outside the camp until purification takes place.

*2. eruption.* This refers to the ailment detailed in Leviticus 13–14. It is translated there as "scaly affection" and as "leprosy" (to convey the horror attached to the condition in question), but the actual disease remains unknown.

*discharge.* This refers to an abnormal genital discharge, not a typical menstrual flow. The laws relating to this condition are found in Leviticus 15, though that passage does not mandate expulsion from the camp. Note that neither the impurity resulting from menstruation (Leviticus 15:19–24) nor from giving birth (Leviticus 12) is mentioned here. The absence of these more common impurities emphasizes the unexpected and irregular nature of the conditions that the text does mention.

*anyone defiled by a corpse.* Numbers 19 details the purification ritual for someone who comes in contact with a dead body.

*3. male and female alike.* Heb. *mi-zachar ad n'kevah.* Everyone is subject to these temporary impurities. What is the difference between this expression and the expression *ish o ishah* ("men or women," literally "man or woman") in Numbers 5:6 and 6:2? The first expression is applied to animals more often (Genesis 6:19; 7:3, 9, 16; Leviticus 3:1) and seems to identify sexuality as opposed to gender. The primordial humans were created as "male and female" (biological categories) in the image of God in Genesis 1:27, but become gendered as "man and woman" (social categories) in the Garden of Eden in Genesis 2:23–24.

*in whose midst I dwell.* This rationale for the expulsion of these individuals from the camp makes it clear that the goal of removing the infected individuals is to protect the sanctity of the Israelite camp and maintain the divine Presence there.

## PROCEDURE FOR A PERSON WHO BETRAYS ANOTHER (5:5–10)

The crime of betrayal that here is called *maal* is illuminated by Leviticus 5:14–16 and 5:20–26, where the term *maal* refers to the inadvertent and intentional misappropriation of property. According to Leviticus, the penalty for this crime is a form of economic restitution.

*6. When men or women.* Having moved away from the clinical language used in the preceding section to describe impure bodies, the inclusive phrase "male and female" becomes "men or women" (see at v. 3). The specific mention of "women" presumes that women could commit this type of crime, and some probably did.

*breaking faith.* Heb. *maal,* which has both the

guilt, 7they shall confess the wrong that they have
done. They shall make restitution in the principal
amount and add one-fifth to it, giving it to the one
who was wronged. 8If that party [is deceased and]
has no kin to whom restitution can be made, the
amount repaid shall go to יהוה for the priest—in
addition to the ram of expiation with which expiation is made on their behalf. 9So, too, any gift
among the sacred donations that the Israelites offer
shall be the priest's. 10And each shall retain his
sacred donations: each priest shall keep what is
given to him.

11יהוה spoke to Moses, saying: 12Speak to the
Israelite people and say to them:

הַנֶּפֶשׁ הַהִוא׃ 7 וְהִתְוַדּוּ אֶת־חַטָּאתָם אֲשֶׁר
עָשׂוּ וְהֵשִׁיב אֶת־אֲשָׁמוֹ בְּרֹאשׁוֹ וַחֲמִישִׁתוֹ
יֹסֵף עָלָיו וְנָתַן לַאֲשֶׁר אָשַׁם לוֹ׃ 8 וְאִם־אֵין
לָאִישׁ גֹּאֵל לְהָשִׁיב הָאָשָׁם אֵלָיו הָאָשָׁם
הַמּוּשָׁב לַיהֹוָה לַכֹּהֵן מִלְּבַד אֵיל הַכִּפֻּרִים
אֲשֶׁר יְכַפֶּר־בּוֹ עָלָיו׃ 9 וְכָל־תְּרוּמָה לְכָל־
קָדְשֵׁי בְנֵי־יִשְׂרָאֵל אֲשֶׁר־יַקְרִיבוּ לַכֹּהֵן לוֹ
יִהְיֶה׃ 10 וְאִישׁ אֶת־קֳדָשָׁיו לוֹ יִהְיוּ אִישׁ
אֲשֶׁר־יִתֵּן לַכֹּהֵן לוֹ יִהְיֶה׃ פ

11 וַיְדַבֵּר יְהֹוָה אֶל־מֹשֶׁה לֵּאמֹר׃ 12 דַּבֵּר
אֶל־בְּנֵי יִשְׂרָאֵל וְאָמַרְתָּ אֲלֵהֶם

technical or legal meaning of misappropriation of property as well as a broader idiomatic meaning of betrayal. The next section in this parashah will apply the idiomatic meaning of *maal* to a faithless wife. This use of the identical term for crimes against both God and other people (5:6) indicates that both varieties of *maal* may have been considered acts of betrayal against God.

*7. they shall confess.* Unlike the Leviticus passages describing *maal* (Leviticus 5:14–16, 20–26), this verse demands that the guilty party confess before making restitution. As in the case of the *sotah* (5:22), *maal* ("breaking faith") requires a potent ritual including a verbal expression and a physical action.

## PROCEDURE FOR A WIFE ACCUSED OF ADULTERY (5:11–31)

One of the most enigmatic passages in the Torah, this description of the ritual inflicted upon a suspected wayward wife (whom rabbinic literature refers to as a *sotah*; see at v. 12) has elicited a wide range of reactions. It has inspired enormous efforts at interpretation extending from rabbinic to contemporary times. Some readers consider the ritual to be unforgivably misogynistic, demonstrating the vulnerability of women and the privileged position of men in Israelite society. Others believe this ritual works to protect accused women.

The ritual of the *sotah* is unique in the *Tanach*. Perhaps the closest analogue is the ritual used in response to an unsolved murder (Deuteronomy 21:1–9). Both rituals are to be performed when the community faces the possibility of a capital crime without the necessary evidence to determine innocence or guilt. The *sotah* ritual may be a biblical example of a "trial by ordeal." Used throughout the ancient Near East, such trials helped to decide cases in which witnesses were conflicted or lacking. The Laws of Hammurabi (see ¶ 132) provide a relevant example in which a woman is accused of adultery without evidence and must undergo a trial by ordeal in a river to determine her fate. The *sotah* ritual is likewise administered to a woman accused by her husband of adultery (5:13–15).

If found innocent, the vindicated woman will remain fertile. If guilty, her body will swell grotesquely; and she will presumably be rendered infertile (5:19–22). [Note that there is no mention of, or procedure for, the man who is a necessary suspect along with the woman; he is never formally confronted or tested. —*Ed.*]

In biblical law, the crime of adultery warranted

If any wife has gone astray and broken faith
with her husband, [13]in that a man has had carnal
relations with her unbeknown to her husband, and
she keeps secret the fact that she has defiled herself without being forced, and there is no witness
against her—[14]but a fit of jealousy comes over him

אִישׁ אִישׁ כִּי־תִשְׂטֶה אִשְׁתּוֹ וּמָעֲלָה בוֹ
מָעַל׃ 13 וְשָׁכַב אִישׁ אֹתָהּ שִׁכְבַת־זֶרַע
וְנֶעְלַם מֵעֵינֵי אִישָׁהּ וְנִסְתְּרָה וְהִיא
נִטְמָאָה וְעֵד אֵין בָּהּ וְהִוא לֹא נִתְפָּשָׂה׃
14 וְעָבַר עָלָיו רוּחַ־קִנְאָה וְקִנֵּא אֶת־אִשְׁתּוֹ

death (Leviticus 20:10; Deuteronomy 22:22). Therefore this ritual, which does not result in death even of the guilty woman, may reflect a more compassionate form of punishment. The question "Whom does the ritual protect, the suspicious husband or the accused wife?" receives no easy answer. Because of linguistic difficulties that riddle this passage, an accurate understanding of the details of the ritual and the motivation behind them may forever elude readers. Yet the ambiguity of the passage, if not intentional, is a gift for interpreters who value indeterminate meaning in a text. Particularly for feminist readers, the ritual of the *sotah* reflects the ambiguity of women's roles in the Bible and the vulnerability of women within ancient Israelite society.

*12. gone astray.* Heb. *tisteh.* The verbal root *s-t-h* appears four times in this passage (5:12, 19, 20, 29), but only twice more in the rest of the *Tanach,* when Proverbs 4:15 and 7:25 warn young men to remain righteous and resist the seductions of dangerous women. In both Numbers and Proverbs, the verb connotes illicit sex. Yet it is interesting to note that the more explicit term used for adultery, *naaf,* is missing in this passage. Perhaps the vagueness of the accusation due to the lack of concrete evidence explains the use of a less exacting, more suggestive term for the alleged crime. (From this verbal root the Rabbis derived their term for the woman in question, *sotah.*)

*broken faith.* Heb. *maal.* The repetition of this word links the *sotah* with the preceding passage (see at v. 6).

One might imagine that the Torah would say that a man who has sexual relations with a married woman has, in effect, taken what belongs to another man. In this passage, however, it is the woman, and not her lover, who is accused of the crime of *maal,* misappropriation of property. Certainly, an act of adultery would be an act of betrayal. Yet the use of this term may also carry its legal meaning and suggest that the errant wife has taken something belonging to her husband—perhaps his honor, her fidelity, or the exclusive right to her sexuality.

*13. a man has had carnal relations with her.* When referring to sexual intercourse, the subject switches from the wife to the adulterous man; grammatically, the woman thus assumes a passive position. On this idiom, see at Exodus 19:15.

*she keeps secret.* The accused woman again becomes the subject of the verse. Her silence perpetuates his ignorance of the crime.

*she has defiled herself.* The mention of her defilement reflects one of the central concerns of this parashah: the purity of the camp depends on the purity of its members. A woman's self-defilement suggests ethical, not ritual defilement. It was not the semen that rendered her impure, but rather her unethical betrayal of her husband.

*without being forced.* There are two possible readings of this phrase. One interpretation is that the phrase refers to the woman's sexual consent, meaning that she was not raped (see how this verb is used in Deuteronomy 22:28). Another reading understands the verb *tapas* as meaning "caught," which would indicate that she escaped detection.

*there is no witness against her.* The lack of a witness is what necessitates the ritual. According to Deuteronomy 22:22, if there is a witness, the court is to execute the woman and her lover.

*14. fit of jealousy.* The husband's suspicions trigger the ordeal, in order to determine whether

and he is wrought up about the wife who has defiled herself; or if a fit of jealousy comes over one and he is wrought up about his wife although she has not defiled herself—[15]the husband shall bring his wife to the priest. And he shall bring as an offering for her one-tenth of an *eifah* of barley flour. No oil shall be poured upon it and no frankincense shall be laid on it, for it is a meal offering of jealousy, a meal offering of remembrance which recalls wrongdoing.

[16]The priest shall bring her forward and have her stand before יהוה. [17]The priest shall take sacral water in an earthen vessel and, taking some of the earth that is on the floor of the Tabernacle, the priest shall put it into the water. [18]After he has made the wife stand before יהוה, the priest shall bare the wife's head and place upon her hands the meal offering of remembrance, which is a meal offering of jealousy. And in the priest's hands shall be the water of bitterness that induces the spell.

וְהִוא נִטְמָאָה אוֹ־עָבַר עָלָיו רוּחַ־קִנְאָה
וְקִנֵּא אֶת־אִשְׁתּוֹ וְהִיא לֹא נִטְמָאָה׃
15 וְהֵבִיא הָאִישׁ אֶת־אִשְׁתּוֹ אֶל־הַכֹּהֵן
וְהֵבִיא אֶת־קָרְבָּנָהּ עָלֶיהָ עֲשִׂירִת הָאֵיפָה
קֶמַח שְׂעֹרִים לֹא־יִצֹק עָלָיו שֶׁמֶן וְלֹא־יִתֵּן
עָלָיו לְבֹנָה כִּי־מִנְחַת קְנָאֹת הוּא מִנְחַת
זִכָּרוֹן מַזְכֶּרֶת עָוֺן׃
16 וְהִקְרִיב אֹתָהּ הַכֹּהֵן וְהֶעֱמִדָהּ לִפְנֵי
יְהוָה׃ 17 וְלָקַח הַכֹּהֵן מַיִם קְדֹשִׁים בִּכְלִי־
חָרֶשׂ וּמִן־הֶעָפָר אֲשֶׁר יִהְיֶה בְּקַרְקַע
הַמִּשְׁכָּן יִקַּח הַכֹּהֵן וְנָתַן אֶל־הַמָּיִם׃
18 וְהֶעֱמִיד הַכֹּהֵן אֶת־הָאִשָּׁה לִפְנֵי יְהוָה
וּפָרַע אֶת־רֹאשׁ הָאִשָּׁה וְנָתַן עַל־כַּפֶּיהָ
אֵת מִנְחַת הַזִּכָּרוֹן מִנְחַת קְנָאֹת הִוא
וּבְיַד הַכֹּהֵן יִהְיוּ מֵי הַמָּרִים הַמְאָרְרִים׃

the woman is guilty or not. Perhaps the *sotah* trial serves mainly to allay the husband's jealousy, in which case he, not she, is the true focus of this ritual, as some scholars suggest. Proverbs 6:34–35 describes a husband's jealousy, *kinah,* as a powerful and violent force.

***although she has not defiled herself.*** The text does not assume that the woman is guilty. The stated possibility that the woman is innocent supports the interpretation that the ritual works to protect her from her husband's unfounded jealousy and restore some semblance of emotional stability to the household.

***15. the husband shall bring his wife to the priest.*** From this point on, the narration of the ritual depicts the woman as a passive participant. The husband brings her and her "meal offering of jealousy" (v. 15) to the priest. The priest loosens her hair (v. 18) and offers her a liquid that enters her body and apparently affects her fertility (v. 22).

***16. before יהוה.*** The ritual must take place in front of the Tabernacle, the place where adjudication usually takes place (see 12:5). The public location adds to the woman's humiliation.

***18. the priest shall bare the wife's head.*** Baring her head further humiliates the woman. The *sotah*'s bare head links this passage with the subsequent section describing the *nazir* (see at 6:1–21).

***the water of bitterness.*** Heb. *mei ha-marim.* The precise meaning of this expression eludes translators, who contend that a little earth does not make water bitter. Alternative translations based on different or cognate roots are "water of blessing," "water of contention," and "water of revelation." Tikva Frymer-Kensky translates the phrase in vv. 18, 19, and 24, as "the 'spell-effecting revelation waters,' indicating that the 'spell-effecting waters' would enter the woman to effect the revelation of guilt or innocence" ("The Strange Case of the Suspected Sotah: Numbers V 11–31" in A. Bach, ed., *Women in the Hebrew Bible: A Reader,* 1999, p. 472). The potion mixes sanctified water and earth from

[19]The priest shall adjure the wife, saying to her, "If
no man has lain with you, if you have not gone
astray in defilement while married to your husband,
be immune to harm from this water of bitterness
that induces the spell. [20]But if you have gone astray
while married to your husband and have defiled
yourself, if a man other than your husband has had
carnal relations with you"—[21]here the priest shall
administer the curse of adjuration to the wife, as the
priest goes on to say to the wife—"may יהוה make
you a curse and an imprecation among your people,
as יהוה causes your thigh to sag and your belly to
distend; [22]may this water that induces the spell
enter your body, causing the belly to distend and
the thigh to sag." And the wife shall say, "Amen,
amen!"
[23]The priest shall put these curses down in writing and rub it off into the water of bitterness. [24]He
is to make the wife drink the water of bitterness

19 וְהִשְׁבִּיעַ אֹתָהּ הַכֹּהֵן וְאָמַר אֶל־הָאִשָּׁה
אִם־לֹא שָׁכַב אִישׁ אֹתָךְ וְאִם־לֹא שָׂטִית
טֻמְאָה תַּחַת אִישֵׁךְ הִנָּקִי מִמֵּי הַמָּרִים
הַמְאָרְרִים הָאֵלֶּה׃ 20 וְאַתְּ כִּי שָׂטִית תַּחַת
אִישֵׁךְ וְכִי נִטְמֵאת וַיִּתֵּן אִישׁ בָּךְ אֶת־
שְׁכָבְתּוֹ מִבַּלְעֲדֵי אִישֵׁךְ׃ 21 וְהִשְׁבִּיעַ הַכֹּהֵן
אֶת־הָאִשָּׁה בִּשְׁבֻעַת הָאָלָה וְאָמַר הַכֹּהֵן
לָאִשָּׁה יִתֵּן יְהוָה אוֹתָךְ לְאָלָה וְלִשְׁבֻעָה
בְּתוֹךְ עַמֵּךְ בְּתֵת יְהוָה אֶת־יְרֵכֵךְ נֹפֶלֶת
וְאֶת־בִּטְנֵךְ צָבָה׃ 22 וּבָאוּ הַמַּיִם הַמְאָרְרִים
הָאֵלֶּה בְּמֵעַיִךְ לַצְבּוֹת בֶּטֶן וְלַנְפִּל יָרֵךְ
וְאָמְרָה הָאִשָּׁה אָמֵן ׀ אָמֵן׃
23 וְכָתַב אֶת־הָאָלֹת הָאֵלֶּה הַכֹּהֵן בַּסֵּפֶר
וּמָחָה אֶל־מֵי הַמָּרִים׃ 24 וְהִשְׁקָה אֶת־
הָאִשָּׁה אֶת־מֵי הַמָּרִים הַמְאָרְרִים וּבָאוּ

---

the Tabernacle floor inside a clay vessel (5:17). The symbolism of combining holy water with holy earth is clear: the possibly impure woman ingests a pure and holy liquid to see if her body rejects it. Yet the potion's purported physical impact on the body remains unclear.

*19. The priest shall adjure the wife.* The priest presents two possible outcomes, indicating that the woman is presumed neither innocent nor guilty.

*be immune.* This verb, literally "be cleansed," appears elsewhere as a legal term for innocence (Exodus 21:19; 23:7).

*22. causing the belly to distend and the thigh to sag.* Although the exact nature of the potential affliction remains unclear, the damage appears to relate to the woman's fertility. Most likely the thigh, used frequently as a euphemism for male genitalia (Genesis 24:2, 9; 46:26; Exodus 1:5), is here a euphemism for female genitalia. Since an innocent woman will be able to conceive (5:28), the implied contrast suggests that a guilty woman will be rendered infertile. There is no reason to restrict this ritual to cases where the guilty woman is already pregnant and promptly miscarries. (For a different interpretation, see Another View, p. 836.) Identifying an apt illness seems beside the point; what matters more is recognizing that the ritual targets the woman's reproductive system—the part of her that belongs to her husband, nurtures his heirs, and secures her value within her community.

*22. "Amen, amen!"* When the woman finally speaks, her simple acceptance of the oath contrasts with the passage's repetitiousness and the priest's verbosity. Though her verbal consenting to the oath is formulaic (see Deuteronomy 27:15–26), her voice momentarily draws attention to herself as a flesh-and-blood human being who is suffering an ordeal.

*23. rub it off into the water of bitterness.* After the priest dissolves the writing in the "bitter" waters, the *sotah* must ingest the oath to release its magic potency within her body (compare Jeremiah 51:59–64).

*24. He is to make the wife drink.* As the verbs in this passage demonstrate, the priest is the central actor in the ritual.

that induces the spell, so that the spell-inducing water may enter into her to bring on bitterness. 25Then the priest shall take from the wife's hand the meal offering of jealousy, elevate the meal offering before יהוה, and present it on the altar. 26The priest shall scoop out of the meal offering a token part of it and turn it into smoke on the altar. Last, he shall make the wife drink the water.

27Once he has made her drink the water—if she has defiled herself by breaking faith with her husband, the spell-inducing water shall enter into her to bring on bitterness, so that her belly shall distend and her thigh shall sag; and the wife shall become a curse among her people. 28But if the wife has not defiled herself and is pure, she shall be unharmed and able to retain seed.

29This is the ritual in cases of jealousy, when a wife goes astray while married to her husband and defiles herself, 30or when a fit of jealousy comes over a husband and he is wrought up over his wife: the wife shall be made to stand before יהוה and the priest shall carry out all this ritual with her. 31The husband shall be clear of guilt; but that wife shall suffer for her guilt.

*6* יהוה spoke to Moses, saying: 2Speak to the Israelites and say to them: If any men or women

בָּ֖הּ הַמַּ֥יִם הַמְאָרְרִ֖ים לְמָרִֽים׃ 25 וְלָקַ֣ח
הַכֹּהֵ֗ן מִיַּ֣ד הָֽאִשָּׁ֔ה אֵ֖ת מִנְחַ֣ת הַקְּנָאֹ֑ת
וְהֵנִ֤יף אֶת־הַמִּנְחָה֙ לִפְנֵ֣י יְהֹוָ֔ה וְהִקְרִ֥יב
אֹתָ֖הּ אֶל־הַמִּזְבֵּֽחַ׃ 26 וְקָמַ֨ץ הַכֹּהֵ֤ן מִן־
הַמִּנְחָה֙ אֶת־אַזְכָּ֣רָתָ֔הּ וְהִקְטִ֖יר הַמִּזְבֵּ֑חָה
וְאַחַ֛ר יַשְׁקֶ֥ה אֶת־הָאִשָּׁ֖ה אֶת־הַמָּֽיִם׃
27 וְהִשְׁקָ֣הּ אֶת־הַמַּ֗יִם וְהָיְתָ֣ה אִֽם־נִטְמְאָה֮
וַתִּמְעֹ֣ל מַ֣עַל בְּאִישָׁהּ֒ וּבָ֨אוּ בָ֜הּ הַמַּ֤יִם
הַמְאָֽרְרִים֙ לְמָרִ֔ים וְצָבְתָ֥ה בִטְנָ֖הּ וְנָפְלָ֣ה
יְרֵכָ֑הּ וְהָיְתָ֧ה הָאִשָּׁ֛ה לְאָלָ֖ה בְּקֶ֥רֶב עַמָּֽהּ׃
28 וְאִם־לֹ֤א נִטְמְאָה֙ הָֽאִשָּׁ֔ה וּטְהֹרָ֖ה הִ֑וא
וְנִקְּתָ֖ה וְנִזְרְעָ֥ה זָֽרַע׃
29 זֹ֥את תּוֹרַ֖ת הַקְּנָאֹ֑ת אֲשֶׁ֨ר תִּשְׂטֶ֥ה אִשָּׁ֛ה
תַּ֥חַת אִישָׁ֖הּ וְנִטְמָֽאָה׃ 30 א֣וֹ אִ֗ישׁ אֲשֶׁ֨ר
תַּעֲבֹ֥ר עָלָ֛יו ר֥וּחַ קִנְאָ֖ה וְקִנֵּ֣א אֶת־אִשְׁתּ֑וֹ
וְהֶעֱמִ֤יד אֶת־הָֽאִשָּׁה֙ לִפְנֵ֣י יְהֹוָ֔ה וְעָ֤שָׂה לָהּ֙
הַכֹּהֵ֔ן אֵ֖ת כׇּל־הַתּוֹרָ֥ה הַזֹּֽאת׃ 31 וְנִקָּ֥ה
הָאִ֖ישׁ מֵעָוֺ֑ן וְהָאִשָּׁ֣ה הַהִ֔וא תִּשָּׂ֖א אֶת־
עֲוֺנָֽהּ׃ פ

ו וַיְדַבֵּ֥ר יְהֹוָ֖ה אֶל־מֹשֶׁ֥ה לֵּאמֹֽר׃ 2 דַּבֵּר֙
אֶל־בְּנֵ֣י יִשְׂרָאֵ֔ל וְאָמַרְתָּ֖ אֲלֵהֶ֑ם אִ֣ישׁ אֽוֹ־

*28. able to retain seed.* This expression refers to her ability to conceive.

*31. The husband shall be clear of guilt.* If the husband's accusations prove false, he suffers no punishment. Yet the lack of repercussions for the wrongly suspicious husband also may protect his wife by convincing him to initiate the ritual. Assuming the "bitter" waters are humiliating but harmless, it may be better for the wife to undergo the trial than to live with a jealous husband.

*but that wife shall suffer for her guilt.* If the woman is guilty, she is not executed, as an adulteress would be. Without a witness to the crime, the woman cannot be put to death. The expression "suffer for her guilt" indicates that God, not the court, determines the punishment (Leviticus 5:1, 17; 20:17; Numbers 9:13).

## *Maintaining Community Sanctity through Religious Leaders* (6:1–27)

Moving beyond concerns with threats to the sanctity of the Israelite community, the parashah now focuses upon individuals who enhance and maintain that sanctity. Strikingly, women are

explicitly utter a nazirite's vow, to set themselves apart for יהוה, [3]they shall abstain from wine and any other intoxicant; they shall not drink vinegar of wine or of any other intoxicant, neither shall they drink anything in which grapes have been steeped, nor eat grapes fresh or dried. [4]Throughout their term as nazirite, they may not eat anything that is obtained from the grapevine, even seeds or skin.

[5]Throughout the term of their vow as nazirite, no razor shall touch their head; it shall remain consecrated until the completion of their term as nazirite of יהוה, the hair of their head being left

אִשָּׁ֗ה כִּ֤י יַפְלִא֙ לִנְדֹּר֙ נֶ֣דֶר נָזִ֔יר לְהַזִּ֖יר
לַֽיהוָֽה׃ 3 מִיַּ֤יִן וְשֵׁכָר֙ יַזִּ֔יר חֹ֥מֶץ יַ֛יִן וְחֹ֥מֶץ
שֵׁכָ֖ר לֹ֣א יִשְׁתֶּ֑ה וְכָל־מִשְׁרַ֤ת עֲנָבִים֙ לֹ֣א
יִשְׁתֶּ֔ה וַעֲנָבִ֛ים לַחִ֥ים וִיבֵשִׁ֖ים לֹ֥א יֹאכֵֽל׃
4 כֹּ֖ל יְמֵ֣י נִזְר֑וֹ מִכֹּל֩ אֲשֶׁ֨ר יֵעָשֶׂ֜ה מִגֶּ֣פֶן הַיַּ֗יִן
מֵחַרְצַנִּ֛ים וְעַד־זָ֖ג לֹ֥א יֹאכֵֽל׃
5 כָּל־יְמֵי֙ נֶ֣דֶר נִזְר֔וֹ תַּ֖עַר לֹא־יַעֲבֹ֣ר עַל־
רֹאשׁ֑וֹ עַד־מְלֹ֨את הַיָּמִ֜ם אֲשֶׁר־יַזִּ֤יר לַֽיהוָה֙

included among those individuals. By dedicating themselves as nazirites, women are able to contribute to the holiness of Israel.

### LAWS OF THE NAZIR (6:1–21)

With the introduction of the *nazir*, an individual who dedicates herself or himself to God, the parashah shifts its focus from a problematic woman to a respectable, if not honored, woman or man. Yet, the shared mention of bare or untrimmed hair (5:18, 6:5) suggests an implicit relationship between the *sotah* and the *nazir*. Both are marginal, set apart from the community-at-large. However, while the *nazir* chooses to distinguish herself or himself, the *sotah* is at the mercy of her husband. Placed together, these figures represent a typology, albeit extreme, of women within Israelite society that issues a message. A disciplined woman who controls her wildness and dedicates herself (and her wildness) to God may become a *n'zirah* (the specifically feminine form of *nazir*). One who does not discipline her wildness may become a *sotah*.

The Bible distinguishes between the life-long *nazir*, such as Samson (Judges 13–16) and Samuel (I Samuel 1), and the temporary *nazir* of this passage. Because the laws of the *nazir* pertain to prohibitions, they reveal little about whether or how the *nazir* functioned within the community. Although nazirites behaved similarly to priests in certain ways, there is no indication that they served alongside them in the sanctuary. Still, the existence of female nazirites illustrates that women, like men, could and did dedicate themselves to God.

*2. **If any men or women explicitly utter a nazirite's vow.*** The word *nazir* comes from the root *n-z-r*, meaning to "dedicate" or "to set aside," and may be related to the root *n-d-r*, meaning "vow." Women can make binding vows; according to Numbers 30, either their fathers or their husbands can annul them, but only upon first hearing of them (30:4–16). Thus, a married woman or a daughter in her father's house—unlike a widow or a divorcée living on her own—depends on the consent of a man in order to become a *nazir*. The two biblical nazirites, Samuel and Samson, are designated as nazirites by their mothers. During her pregnancy, Samson's unnamed mother follows the prohibitions for the *nazir* in Numbers and effectively becomes a temporary nazirite herself (Judges 13:3–5, 13–14).

*3.* All intoxicants and grape products are forbidden to the *nazir*. This prohibition resembles a less severe version imposed on priests, who are forbidden intoxicants when they enter the sanctuary (Leviticus 10:9; Ezekiel 44:21), but otherwise are allowed to drink (Isaiah 28:7).

*5.* Untrimmed hair is the defining physical characteristic of the *nazir* and reflects the vitality of an individual dedicated to God. In ancient cultures, hair—which grows throughout life and appears to

to grow untrimmed. 6Throughout the term that
they have set apart for יהוה, they shall not go in
where there is a dead person. 7Even if their father or
mother, or their brother or sister should die, they
must not become defiled for any of them, since
hair set apart for their God is upon their head:
8throughout their term as nazirite they are consecrated to יהוה.

9If someone dies suddenly nearby, defiling the
consecrated hair, [the nazirite] shall shave the head
at the time of becoming pure, shaving it on the
seventh day. 10On the eighth day the person shall
bring two turtledoves or two pigeons to the priest,
at the entrance of the Tent of Meeting. 11The priest
shall offer one as a purgation offering and the other
as a burnt offering, and make expiation on the person's behalf for the guilt incurred through the
corpse. That same day the head shall be reconse-
crated; 12and the person shall rededicate to יהוה the
term as nazirite, bringing a lamb in its first year as a
penalty offering. The previous period shall be void,
since the consecrated hair was defiled.

13This is the ritual for the nazirite: On the day
that the term as nazirite is completed, the person
shall be brought to the entrance of the Tent of

קָדֹשׁ יִהְיֶה גַּדֵּל פֶּרַע שְׂעַר רֹאשׁוֹ׃ 6 כָּל־יְמֵי
הַזִּרוֹ לַיהוָה עַל־נֶפֶשׁ מֵת לֹא יָבֹא׃
7 לְאָבִיו וּלְאִמּוֹ לְאָחִיו וּלְאַחֹתוֹ לֹא־
יִטַּמָּא לָהֶם בְּמֹתָם כִּי נֵזֶר אֱלֹהָיו עַל־
רֹאשׁוֹ׃ 8 כֹּל יְמֵי נִזְרוֹ קָדֹשׁ הוּא לַיהוָה׃
9 וְכִי־יָמוּת מֵת עָלָיו בְּפֶתַע פִּתְאֹם וְטִמֵּא
רֹאשׁ נִזְרוֹ וְגִלַּח רֹאשׁוֹ בְּיוֹם טָהֳרָתוֹ בַּיּוֹם
הַשְּׁבִיעִי יְגַלְּחֶנּוּ׃ 10 וּבַיּוֹם הַשְּׁמִינִי יָבִא
שְׁתֵּי תֹרִים אוֹ שְׁנֵי בְּנֵי יוֹנָה אֶל־הַכֹּהֵן אֶל־
פֶּתַח אֹהֶל מוֹעֵד׃ 11 וְעָשָׂה הַכֹּהֵן אֶחָד
לְחַטָּאת וְאֶחָד לְעֹלָה וְכִפֶּר עָלָיו מֵאֲשֶׁר
חָטָא עַל־הַנָּפֶשׁ וְקִדַּשׁ אֶת־רֹאשׁוֹ בַּיּוֹם
הַהוּא׃ 12 וְהִזִּיר לַיהוָה אֶת־יְמֵי נִזְרוֹ
וְהֵבִיא כֶּבֶשׂ בֶּן־שְׁנָתוֹ לְאָשָׁם וְהַיָּמִים
הָרִאשֹׁנִים יִפְּלוּ כִּי טָמֵא נִזְרוֹ׃
13 וְזֹאת תּוֹרַת הַנָּזִיר בְּיוֹם מְלֹאת יְמֵי
נִזְרוֹ יָבִיא אֹתוֹ אֶל־פֶּתַח אֹהֶל מוֹעֵד׃

grow even in death—represented vitality and was often offered as a gift to one's deity. In the Bible, hair also reflects a character's strength. A haircut renders mighty Samson impotent (Judges 16:17); the hair of a captive woman must be shaved at first as a sign of mourning (Deuteronomy 21:12).

*7.* The *nazir* is forbidden to bury even immediate family members; in this respect a nazirite is like only the chief priest (compare Leviticus 21:1–4, 11). Contact with a corpse contaminates anyone temporarily (Numbers 5:2; 19:11), but such contact in addition disrupts the status of *nazir* (below, vv. 9–12), just as it can ruin a priest's ability to function. (Note that the list of deceased family members does not mention a spouse. Regarding spousal death, see the analogous case of a priest at Leviticus 21:1–4.)

*8. they are consecrated to* יהוה. Priests are also described as "consecrated to יהוה" (Leviticus 21:7).

*9. shall shave the head.* If the *nazir* becomes contaminated by unexpected exposure to a corpse, she or he must first observe the rite of purification (Numbers 19) before shaving the hair. The requirement to shave after purification suggests that hair cannot be purified and so it must be removed.

*12. since the consecrated hair was defiled.* Although one should be cautious about drawing conclusions from silence, it must be observed that other sources of contamination are not mentioned, particularly those incurred via menstruation or the emission of bodily fluids. It is interesting to consider what may have happened to female nazirites when they menstruated.

Meeting. 14As an offering to יהוה the person shall
present: one male lamb in its first year, without
blemish, for a burnt offering; one ewe lamb in its
first year, without blemish, for a purgation offering;
one ram without blemish for an offering of well-
being; 15a basket of unleavened cakes of choice
flour with oil mixed in, and unleavened wafers
spread with oil; and the proper meal offerings and
libations.

16The priest shall present them before יהוה and
offer the purgation offering and the burnt offering.
17He shall offer the ram as a sacrifice of well-being
to יהוה, together with the basket of unleavened
cakes; the priest shall also offer the meal offerings
and the libations. 18The nazirite shall then shave
the consecrated hair, at the entrance of the Tent of
Meeting, and take those locks of consecrated hair
and put them on the fire that is under the sacrifice
of well-being.

19The priest shall take the shoulder of the ram
when it has been boiled, one unleavened cake from
the basket, and one unleavened wafer, and place
them on the hands of the nazirite after the consecrated hair has been shaved. 20The priest shall
elevate them as an elevation offering before יהוה;
and this shall be a sacred donation for the priest, in
addition to the breast of the elevation offering and
the thigh of gift offering. After that the nazirite may
drink wine.

21Such is the obligation of a nazirite; except that
those who vow an offering to יהוה of what they can
afford, beyond their nazirite requirements, must do
exactly according to the vow that they have made
beyond their obligation as nazirites.

14 וְהִקְרִיב אֶת־קָרְבָּנוֹ לַיהֹוָה כֶּבֶשׂ בֶּן־
שְׁנָתוֹ תָמִים אֶחָד לְעֹלָה וְכַבְשָׂה אַחַת
בַּת־שְׁנָתָהּ תְּמִימָה לְחַטָּאת וְאַיִל־אֶחָד
תָּמִים לִשְׁלָמִים׃ 15 וְסַל מַצּוֹת סֹלֶת חַלֹּת
בְּלוּלֹת בַּשֶּׁמֶן וּרְקִיקֵי מַצּוֹת מְשֻׁחִים בַּשָּׁמֶן
וּמִנְחָתָם וְנִסְכֵּיהֶם׃

16 וְהִקְרִיב הַכֹּהֵן לִפְנֵי יְהֹוָה וְעָשָׂה אֶת־
חַטָּאתוֹ וְאֶת־עֹלָתוֹ׃ 17 וְאֶת־הָאַיִל יַעֲשֶׂה
זֶבַח שְׁלָמִים לַיהֹוָה עַל סַל הַמַּצּוֹת וְעָשָׂה
הַכֹּהֵן אֶת־מִנְחָתוֹ וְאֶת־נִסְכּוֹ׃ 18 וְגִלַּח
הַנָּזִיר פֶּתַח אֹהֶל מוֹעֵד אֶת־רֹאשׁ נִזְרוֹ
וְלָקַח אֶת־שְׂעַר רֹאשׁ נִזְרוֹ וְנָתַן עַל־הָאֵשׁ
אֲשֶׁר־תַּחַת זֶבַח הַשְּׁלָמִים׃

19 וְלָקַח הַכֹּהֵן אֶת־הַזְּרֹעַ בְּשֵׁלָה מִן־הָאַיִל
וְחַלַּת מַצָּה אַחַת מִן־הַסַּל וּרְקִיק מַצָּה
אֶחָד וְנָתַן עַל־כַּפֵּי הַנָּזִיר אַחַר הִתְגַּלְּחוֹ
אֶת־נִזְרוֹ׃ 20 וְהֵנִיף אוֹתָם הַכֹּהֵן ׀ תְּנוּפָה
לִפְנֵי יְהֹוָה קֹדֶשׁ הוּא לַכֹּהֵן עַל חֲזֵה
הַתְּנוּפָה וְעַל שׁוֹק הַתְּרוּמָה וְאַחַר יִשְׁתֶּה
הַנָּזִיר יָיִן׃

21 זֹאת תּוֹרַת הַנָּזִיר אֲשֶׁר יִדֹּר קָרְבָּנוֹ
לַיהֹוָה עַל־נִזְרוֹ מִלְּבַד אֲשֶׁר־תַּשִּׂיג יָדוֹ
כְּפִי נִדְרוֹ אֲשֶׁר יִדֹּר כֵּן יַעֲשֶׂה עַל תּוֹרַת
נִזְרוֹ׃ פ

*16.* ***The priest shall present them.*** Just as the priest brings the *sotah* before God (5:16), the priest assumes the active role and presents the *nazir* and the offering before God. Despite a seemingly common passivity of these two figures (in contrast to the active priest), their differences stand out. Through an act of dedication and religious desire, the *nazir* comes willingly before God. Charged with deception and sexual desire, the *sotah* is forcibly brought before God.

*18.* ***put them on the fire that is under the sacrifice.*** The placement of the nazirite's consecrated locks directly *under* the ram suggests that the *nazir*'s hair is considered one of the offerings.

[22]יהוה spoke to Moses: [23]Speak to Aaron and his sons: Thus shall you bless the people of Israel. Say to them:

[24]יהוה bless you and protect you!

[25]יהוה deal kindly and graciously with you!

[26]יהוה bestow [divine] favor upon you and grant you peace!

[27]Thus they shall link My name with the people of Israel, and I will bless them.

22 וַיְדַבֵּר יְהֹוָה אֶל־מֹשֶׁה לֵּאמֹר׃ 23 דַּבֵּר
אֶל־אַהֲרֹן וְאֶל־בָּנָיו לֵאמֹר כֹּה תְבָרְכוּ אֶת־
בְּנֵי יִשְׂרָאֵל אָמוֹר לָהֶם׃ ס
24 יְבָרֶכְךָ יְהֹוָה וְיִשְׁמְרֶךָ׃ ס
25 יָאֵר יְהֹוָה ׀ פָּנָיו אֵלֶיךָ וִיחֻנֶּךָּ׃ ס
26 יִשָּׂא יְהֹוָה ׀ פָּנָיו אֵלֶיךָ וְיָשֵׂם לְךָ
שָׁלוֹם׃ ס
27 וְשָׂמוּ אֶת־שְׁמִי עַל־בְּנֵי יִשְׂרָאֵל וַאֲנִי
אֲבָרְכֵם׃ ס

7 On the day that Moses finished setting up the Tabernacle, he anointed and consecrated it and all its furnishings, as well as the altar and its utensils. When he had anointed and consecrated them,

ז וַיְהִי בְּיוֹם כַּלּוֹת מֹשֶׁה לְהָקִים אֶת־
הַמִּשְׁכָּן וַיִּמְשַׁח אֹתוֹ וַיְקַדֵּשׁ אֹתוֹ וְאֶת־כָּל־
כֵּלָיו וְאֶת־הַמִּזְבֵּחַ וְאֶת־כָּל־כֵּלָיו וַיִּמְשָׁחֵם

PRIESTLY BLESSING (6:22–27)

According to Leviticus 9:22, at the conclusion of the ceremony consecrating the priests and the Tabernacle, Aaron raises his hands and blesses the community of Israel. Although the text does not report Aaron's words, rabbinic commentators suggest that he recites Numbers 6:24–27, which has become known as the "Priestly Blessing." Its words affirm that God blesses and protects, deals kindly and graciously, bestows favor, and grants peace. Each of its three verses contains two blessings, yet the verses expand in length from three to five to seven words, suggesting that God's blessing expands. Verse 27 echoes both the form and content of v. 23, creating an envelope structure for the blessing.

In 1979, archaeologists discovered in Jerusalem two small silver scrolls dated to the late 7th or early 6th century B.C.E., inscribed with a text nearly identical to the Priestly Blessing. Although their function remains unknown, these silver scrolls provide the earliest known parallel to a biblical text and probably served as protective amulets. The blessing as found in the Torah remains an integral part of Jewish liturgy and is recited as part of the *Amidah* prayer.

*25.* **יהוה** ***deal kindly.*** Literally, "may the face of יהוה shine upon you." The next verse also mentions God's face (translated as "favor"). The desire for God's face to be "directed toward" the people is best understood in contrast to the "hiding" of God's face, which is a painful—often punitive—consequence of sin that appears throughout the Bible (see at Deuteronomy 31:17; 32:20; Isaiah 54:8; Psalm 13:2). Though the mention of God's face may be a metaphor for divine grace, it also carries a sense of intimacy. God's presence and personal engagement bring blessing.

*27.* ***Thus they shall link My name with.*** Literally, "they shall place my name on," which perhaps refers to amulets hung on one's body—as with the silver scrolls mentioned above, which were designed to be worn.

## *Record of the Tribal Chiefs' Gifts*

(7:1–89)

Having addressed matters related to the sanctity of the camp, the parashah concludes as it began—with administrative records.

[2]the chieftains of Israel, the heads of ancestral houses, namely, the chieftains of the tribes, those who were in charge of enrollment, drew near [3]and brought their offering before יהוה: six draught carts and twelve oxen, a cart for every two chieftains and an ox for each one.

When they had brought them before the Tabernacle, [4]יהוה said to Moses: [5]Accept these from them for use in the service of the Tent of Meeting, and give them to the Levites according to their respective services.

[6]Moses took the carts and the oxen and gave them to the Levites. [7]Two carts and four oxen he gave to the Gershonites, as required for their service, [8]and four carts and eight oxen he gave to the Merarites, as required for their service—under the direction of Ithamar son of Aaron the priest. [9]But to the Kohathites he did not give any; since theirs was the service of the [most] sacred objects, their porterage was by shoulder.

[10]The chieftains also brought the dedication offering for the altar upon its being anointed. As the chieftains were presenting their offerings before the altar, [11]יהוה said to Moses: Let them present their offerings for the dedication of the altar, one chieftain each day.

[12]The one who presented his offering on the first day was Nahshon son of Amminadab of the tribe of Judah. [13]His offering: one silver bowl weighing 130 shekels and one silver basin of 70 shekels by the sanctuary weight, both filled with

וַיְקַדֵּשׁ אֹתָם׃ 2 וַיַּקְרִיבוּ נְשִׂיאֵי יִשְׂרָאֵל
רָאשֵׁי בֵּית אֲבֹתָם הֵם נְשִׂיאֵי הַמַּטֹּת הֵם
הָעֹמְדִים עַל־הַפְּקֻדִים׃ 3 וַיָּבִיאוּ אֶת־
קָרְבָּנָם לִפְנֵי יְהֹוָה שֵׁשׁ־עֶגְלֹת צָב וּשְׁנֵי
עָשָׂר בָּקָר עֲגָלָה עַל־שְׁנֵי הַנְּשִׂאִים וְשׁוֹר
לְאֶחָד
וַיַּקְרִיבוּ אוֹתָם לִפְנֵי הַמִּשְׁכָּן׃ 4 וַיֹּאמֶר
יְהֹוָה אֶל־מֹשֶׁה לֵּאמֹר׃ 5 קַח מֵאִתָּם וְהָיוּ
לַעֲבֹד אֶת־עֲבֹדַת אֹהֶל מוֹעֵד וְנָתַתָּה
אוֹתָם אֶל־הַלְוִיִּם אִישׁ כְּפִי עֲבֹדָתוֹ׃
6 וַיִּקַּח מֹשֶׁה אֶת־הָעֲגָלֹת וְאֶת־הַבָּקָר וַיִּתֵּן
אוֹתָם אֶל־הַלְוִיִּם׃ 7 אֵת ׀ שְׁתֵּי הָעֲגָלוֹת
וְאֵת אַרְבַּעַת הַבָּקָר נָתַן לִבְנֵי גֵרְשׁוֹן כְּפִי
עֲבֹדָתָם׃ 8 וְאֵת ׀ אַרְבַּע הָעֲגָלֹת וְאֵת
שְׁמֹנַת הַבָּקָר נָתַן לִבְנֵי מְרָרִי כְּפִי
עֲבֹדָתָם בְּיַד אִיתָמָר בֶּן־אַהֲרֹן הַכֹּהֵן׃
9 וְלִבְנֵי קְהָת לֹא נָתָן כִּי־עֲבֹדַת הַקֹּדֶשׁ
עֲלֵהֶם בַּכָּתֵף יִשָּׂאוּ׃
10 וַיַּקְרִיבוּ הַנְּשִׂאִים אֵת חֲנֻכַּת הַמִּזְבֵּחַ
בְּיוֹם הִמָּשַׁח אֹתוֹ וַיַּקְרִיבוּ הַנְּשִׂיאִם
אֶת־קָרְבָּנָם לִפְנֵי הַמִּזְבֵּחַ׃ 11 וַיֹּאמֶר יְהֹוָה
אֶל־מֹשֶׁה נָשִׂיא אֶחָד לַיּוֹם נָשִׂיא
אֶחָד לַיּוֹם יַקְרִיבוּ אֶת־קָרְבָּנָם לַחֲנֻכַּת
הַמִּזְבֵּחַ׃ ס
12 וַיְהִי הַמַּקְרִיב בַּיּוֹם הָרִאשׁוֹן אֶת־
קָרְבָּנוֹ נַחְשׁוֹן בֶּן־עַמִּינָדָב לְמַטֵּה יְהוּדָה׃
13 וְקָרְבָּנוֹ קַעֲרַת־כֶּסֶף אַחַת שְׁלֹשִׁים וּמֵאָה
מִשְׁקָלָהּ מִזְרָק אֶחָד כֶּסֶף שִׁבְעִים שֶׁקֶל

### GIFTS FOR THE LEVITES (7:1–9)

From the tribal chiefs' gifts in honor of the consecration of the Tabernacle, Moses allocates carts and oxen to be used by the Gershonites and the Merarites. (The Kohathites, who are responsible for the most sacred objects, carry them on their shoulders.)

### GIFTS FOR THE DEDICATION OF THE ALTAR (7:10–88)

The lengthy, repetitive record of the tribal chiefs' gifts appears to reflect a form of ancient Near Eastern accounting, in which items were listed horizontally according to genre. This record's style is that of an administrative as opposed to a cultic account.

choice flour with oil mixed in, for a meal offering; [14]one gold ladle of 10 shekels, filled with incense; [15]one bull of the herd, one ram, and one lamb in its first year, for a burnt offering; [16]one goat for a purgation offering; [17]and for his sacrifice of well-being: two oxen, five rams, five he-goats, and five yearling lambs. That was the offering of Nahshon son of Amminadab.

[18]On the second day, Nethanel son of Zuar, chieftain of Issachar, made his offering. [19]He presented as his offering: one silver bowl weighing 130 shekels and one silver basin of 70 shekels by the sanctuary weight, both filled with choice flour with oil mixed in, for a meal offering; [20]one gold ladle of 10 shekels, filled with incense; [21]one bull of the herd, one ram, and one lamb in its first year, for a burnt offering; [22]one goat for a purgation offering; [23]and for his sacrifice of well-being: two oxen, five rams, five he-goats, and five yearling lambs. That was the offering of Nethanel son of Zuar.

[24]On the third day, it was the chieftain of the Zebulunites, Eliab son of Helon. [25]His offering: one silver bowl weighing 130 shekels and one silver basin of 70 shekels by the sanctuary weight, both filled with choice flour with oil mixed in, for a meal offering; [26]one gold ladle of 10 shekels, filled with incense; [27]one bull of the herd, one ram, and one lamb in its first year, for a burnt offering; [28]one goat for a purgation offering; [29]and for his sacrifice of well-being: two oxen, five rams, five he-goats, and five yearling lambs. That was the offering of Eliab son of Helon.

[30]On the fourth day, it was the chieftain of the Reubenites, Elizur son of Shedeur. [31]His offering: one silver bowl weighing 130 shekels and one silver basin of 70 shekels by the sanctuary weight, both filled with choice flour with oil mixed in, for a meal

בְּשֶׁ֣קֶל הַקֹּ֑דֶשׁ שְׁנֵיהֶ֣ם ׀ מְלֵאִ֗ים סֹ֛לֶת
בְּלוּלָ֥ה בַשֶּׁ֖מֶן לְמִנְחָֽה׃ 14 כַּ֥ף אַחַ֛ת
עֲשָׂרָ֥ה זָהָ֖ב מְלֵאָ֥ה קְטֹֽרֶת׃ 15 פַּ֣ר אֶחָ֞ד
בֶּן־בָּקָ֗ר אַ֧יִל אֶחָ֛ד כֶּֽבֶשׂ־אֶחָ֥ד בֶּן־שְׁנָת֖וֹ
לְעֹלָֽה׃ 16 שְׂעִיר־עִזִּ֥ים אֶחָ֖ד לְחַטָּֽאת׃
17 וּלְזֶ֣בַח הַשְּׁלָמִים֮ בָּקָ֣ר שְׁנַ֒יִם֒ אֵילִ֤ם
חֲמִשָּׁה֙ עַתּוּדִ֣ים חֲמִשָּׁ֔ה כְּבָשִׂ֥ים בְּנֵי־שָׁנָ֖ה
חֲמִשָּׁ֑ה זֶ֛ה קָרְבַּ֥ן נַחְשׁ֖וֹן בֶּן־עַמִּינָדָֽב׃ פ
18 בַּיּוֹם֙ הַשֵּׁנִ֔י הִקְרִ֖יב נְתַנְאֵ֣ל בֶּן־צוּעָ֑ר
נְשִׂ֖יא ישׂשכר יִשָּׂשכָֽר׃ 19 הִקְרִ֨ב אֶת־קָרְבָּנ֜וֹ
קַֽעֲרַת־כֶּ֣סֶף אַחַ֗ת שְׁלֹשִׁ֣ים וּמֵאָה֮ מִשְׁקָלָהּ֒
מִזְרָ֤ק אֶחָד֙ כֶּ֔סֶף שִׁבְעִ֥ים שֶׁ֖קֶל בְּשֶׁ֣קֶל
הַקֹּ֑דֶשׁ שְׁנֵיהֶ֣ם ׀ מְלֵאִ֗ים סֹ֛לֶת בְּלוּלָ֥ה בַשֶּׁ֖מֶן
לְמִנְחָֽה׃ 20 כַּ֥ף אַחַ֛ת עֲשָׂרָ֥ה זָהָ֖ב מְלֵאָ֥ה
קְטֹֽרֶת׃ 21 פַּ֣ר אֶחָ֞ד בֶּן־בָּקָ֗ר אַ֧יִל אֶחָ֛ד
כֶּֽבֶשׂ־אֶחָ֥ד בֶּן־שְׁנָת֖וֹ לְעֹלָֽה׃ 22 שְׂעִיר־עִזִּ֥ים
אֶחָ֖ד לְחַטָּֽאת׃ 23 וּלְזֶ֣בַח הַשְּׁלָמִים֮ בָּקָ֣ר
שְׁנַ֒יִם֒ אֵילִ֤ם חֲמִשָּׁה֙ עַתֻּדִ֣ים חֲמִשָּׁ֔ה
כְּבָשִׂ֥ים בְּנֵי־שָׁנָ֖ה חֲמִשָּׁ֑ה זֶ֛ה קָרְבַּ֥ן נְתַנְאֵ֖ל
בֶּן־צוּעָֽר׃ פ
24 בַּיּוֹם֙ הַשְּׁלִישִׁ֔י נָשִׂ֖יא לִבְנֵ֣י זְבוּלֻ֑ן אֱלִיאָ֖ב
בֶּן־חֵלֹֽן׃ 25 קָרְבָּנ֞וֹ קַעֲרַת־כֶּ֣סֶף אַחַ֗ת
שְׁלֹשִׁ֣ים וּמֵאָה֮ מִשְׁקָלָהּ֒ מִזְרָ֤ק אֶחָד֙ כֶּ֔סֶף
שִׁבְעִ֥ים שֶׁ֖קֶל בְּשֶׁ֣קֶל הַקֹּ֑דֶשׁ שְׁנֵיהֶ֣ם ׀
מְלֵאִ֗ים סֹ֛לֶת בְּלוּלָ֥ה בַשֶּׁ֖מֶן לְמִנְחָֽה׃
26 כַּ֥ף אַחַ֛ת עֲשָׂרָ֥ה זָהָ֖ב מְלֵאָ֥ה קְטֹֽרֶת׃
27 פַּ֣ר אֶחָ֞ד בֶּן־בָּקָ֗ר אַ֧יִל אֶחָ֛ד כֶּֽבֶשׂ־אֶחָ֥ד
בֶּן־שְׁנָת֖וֹ לְעֹלָֽה׃ 28 שְׂעִיר־עִזִּ֥ים אֶחָ֖ד
לְחַטָּֽאת׃ 29 וּלְזֶ֣בַח הַשְּׁלָמִים֮ בָּקָ֣ר שְׁנַ֒יִם֒
אֵילִ֤ם חֲמִשָּׁה֙ עַתֻּדִ֣ים חֲמִשָּׁ֔ה כְּבָשִׂ֥ים
בְּנֵי־שָׁנָ֖ה חֲמִשָּׁ֑ה זֶ֛ה קָרְבַּ֥ן אֱלִיאָ֖ב בֶּן־
חֵלֹֽן׃ פ
30 בַּיּוֹם֙ הָרְבִיעִ֔י נָשִׂ֖יא לִבְנֵ֣י רְאוּבֵ֑ן אֱלִיצ֖וּר
בֶּן־שְׁדֵיאֽוּר׃ 31 קָרְבָּנ֞וֹ קַֽעֲרַת־כֶּ֣סֶף אַחַ֗ת
שְׁלֹשִׁ֣ים וּמֵאָה֮ מִשְׁקָלָהּ֒ מִזְרָ֤ק אֶחָד֙ כֶּ֔סֶף
שִׁבְעִ֥ים שֶׁ֖קֶל בְּשֶׁ֣קֶל הַקֹּ֑דֶשׁ שְׁנֵיהֶ֣ם ׀

offering; [32]one gold ladle of 10 shekels, filled with
incense; [33]one bull of the herd, one ram, and one
lamb in its first year, for a burnt offering; [34]one goat
for a purgation offering; [35]and for his sacrifice of
well-being: two oxen, five rams, five he-goats, and
five yearling lambs. That was the offering of Elizur
son of Shedeur.

[36]On the fifth day, it was the chieftain of the
Simeonites, Shelumiel son of Zurishaddai. [37]His
offering: one silver bowl weighing 130 shekels and
one silver basin of 70 shekels by the sanctuary
weight, both filled with choice flour with oil mixed
in, for a meal offering; [38]one gold ladle of 10
shekels, filled with incense; [39]one bull of the herd,
one ram, and one lamb in its first year, for a burnt
offering; [40]one goat for a purgation offering; [41]and
for his sacrifice of well-being: two oxen, five rams,
five he-goats, and five yearling lambs. That was the
offering of Shelumiel son of Zurishaddai.

[42]On the sixth day, it was the chieftain of the
Gadites, Eliasaph son of Deuel. [43]His offering: one
silver bowl weighing 130 shekels and one silver
basin of 70 shekels by the sanctuary weight, both
filled with choice flour with oil mixed in, for a meal
offering; [44]one gold ladle of 10 shekels, filled with
incense; [45]one bull of the herd, one ram, and one
lamb in its first year, for a burnt offering; [46]one goat
for a purgation offering; [47]and for his sacrifice of
well-being: two oxen, five rams, five he-goats, and
five yearling lambs. That was the offering of Eliasaph son of Deuel.

[48]On the seventh day, it was the chieftain of the
Ephraimites, Elishama son of Ammihud. [49]His
offering: one silver bowl weighing 130 shekels and
one silver basin of 70 shekels by the sanctuary

מְלֵאִים סֹלֶת בְּלוּלָה בַשֶּׁמֶן לְמִנְחָה׃ 32 כַּף
אַחַת עֲשָׂרָה זָהָב מְלֵאָה קְטֹרֶת׃ 33 פַּר
אֶחָד בֶּן־בָּקָר אַיִל אֶחָד כֶּבֶשׂ־אֶחָד בֶּן־
שְׁנָתוֹ לְעֹלָה׃ 34 שְׂעִיר־עִזִּים אֶחָד
לְחַטָּאת׃ 35 וּלְזֶבַח הַשְּׁלָמִים בָּקָר שְׁנַיִם
אֵילִם חֲמִשָּׁה עַתֻּדִים חֲמִשָּׁה כְּבָשִׂים
בְּנֵי־שָׁנָה חֲמִשָּׁה זֶה קָרְבַּן אֱלִיצוּר בֶּן־
שְׁדֵיאוּר׃ פ

36 בַּיּוֹם הַחֲמִישִׁי נָשִׂיא לִבְנֵי שִׁמְעוֹן
שְׁלֻמִיאֵל בֶּן־צוּרִישַׁדָּי׃ 37 קָרְבָּנוֹ קַעֲרַת־
כֶּסֶף אַחַת שְׁלֹשִׁים וּמֵאָה מִשְׁקָלָהּ מִזְרָק
אֶחָד כֶּסֶף שִׁבְעִים שֶׁקֶל בְּשֶׁקֶל הַקֹּדֶשׁ
שְׁנֵיהֶם ׀ מְלֵאִים סֹלֶת בְּלוּלָה בַשֶּׁמֶן
לְמִנְחָה׃ 38 כַּף אַחַת עֲשָׂרָה זָהָב מְלֵאָה
קְטֹרֶת׃ 39 פַּר אֶחָד בֶּן־בָּקָר אַיִל אֶחָד
כֶּבֶשׂ־אֶחָד בֶּן־שְׁנָתוֹ לְעֹלָה׃ 40 שְׂעִיר־עִזִּים
אֶחָד לְחַטָּאת׃ 41 וּלְזֶבַח הַשְּׁלָמִים בָּקָר
שְׁנַיִם אֵילִם חֲמִשָּׁה עַתֻּדִים חֲמִשָּׁה
כְּבָשִׂים בְּנֵי־שָׁנָה חֲמִשָּׁה זֶה קָרְבַּן
שְׁלֻמִיאֵל בֶּן־צוּרִישַׁדָּי׃ פ

42 בַּיּוֹם הַשִּׁשִּׁי נָשִׂיא לִבְנֵי גָד אֶלְיָסָף
בֶּן־דְּעוּאֵל׃ 43 קָרְבָּנוֹ קַעֲרַת־כֶּסֶף אַחַת
שְׁלֹשִׁים וּמֵאָה מִשְׁקָלָהּ מִזְרָק אֶחָד כֶּסֶף
שִׁבְעִים שֶׁקֶל בְּשֶׁקֶל הַקֹּדֶשׁ שְׁנֵיהֶם ׀
מְלֵאִים סֹלֶת בְּלוּלָה בַשֶּׁמֶן לְמִנְחָה׃
44 כַּף אַחַת עֲשָׂרָה זָהָב מְלֵאָה קְטֹרֶת׃
45 פַּר אֶחָד בֶּן־בָּקָר אַיִל אֶחָד כֶּבֶשׂ־אֶחָד
בֶּן־שְׁנָתוֹ לְעֹלָה׃ 46 שְׂעִיר־עִזִּים אֶחָד
לְחַטָּאת׃ 47 וּלְזֶבַח הַשְּׁלָמִים בָּקָר שְׁנַיִם
אֵילִם חֲמִשָּׁה עַתֻּדִים חֲמִשָּׁה כְּבָשִׂים
בְּנֵי־שָׁנָה חֲמִשָּׁה זֶה קָרְבַּן אֶלְיָסָף בֶּן־
דְּעוּאֵל׃ פ

48 בַּיּוֹם הַשְּׁבִיעִי נָשִׂיא לִבְנֵי אֶפְרָיִם
אֱלִישָׁמָע בֶּן־עַמִּיהוּד׃ 49 קָרְבָּנוֹ קַעֲרַת־
כֶּסֶף אַחַת שְׁלֹשִׁים וּמֵאָה מִשְׁקָלָהּ מִזְרָק
אֶחָד כֶּסֶף שִׁבְעִים שֶׁקֶל בְּשֶׁקֶל הַקֹּדֶשׁ

weight, both filled with choice flour with oil mixed in, for a meal offering; [50]one gold ladle of 10 shekels, filled with incense; [51]one bull of the herd, one ram, and one lamb in its first year, for a burnt offering; [52]one goat for a purgation offering; [53]and for his sacrifice of well-being: two oxen, five rams, five he-goats, and five yearling lambs. That was the offering of Elishama son of Ammihud.

[54]On the eighth day, it was the chieftain of the Manassites, Gamaliel son of Pedahzur. [55]His offering: one silver bowl weighing 130 shekels and one silver basin of 70 shekels by the sanctuary weight, both filled with choice flour with oil mixed in, for a meal offering; [56] one gold ladle of 10 shekels, filled with incense; [57]one bull of the herd, one ram, and one lamb in its first year, for a burnt offering; [58]one goat for a purgation offering; [59]and for his sacrifice of well-being: two oxen, five rams, five he-goats, and five yearling lambs. That was the offering of Gamaliel son of Pedahzur.

[60]On the ninth day, it was the chieftain of the Benjaminites, Abidan son of Gideoni. [61]His offering: one silver bowl weighing 130 shekels and one silver basin of 70 shekels by the sanctuary weight, both filled with choice flour with oil mixed in, for a meal offering; [62]one gold ladle of 10 shekels, filled with incense; [63]one bull of the herd, one ram, and one lamb in its first year, for a burnt offering; [64]one goat for a purgation offering; [65]and for his sacrifice of well-being: two oxen, five rams, five he-goats, and five yearling lambs. That was the offering of Abidan son of Gideoni.

[66]On the tenth day, it was the chieftain of the Danites, Ahiezer son of Ammishaddai. [67]His offering: one silver bowl weighing 130 shekels and one silver basin of 70 shekels by the sanctuary weight,

שְׁנֵיהֶ֗ם ׀ מְלֵאִ֤ים סֹ֨לֶת֙ בְּלוּלָ֣ה בַשֶּׁ֔מֶן לְמִנְחָֽה: 50 כַּ֤ף אַחַת֙ עֲשָׂרָ֣ה זָהָ֔ב מְלֵאָ֖ה קְטֹֽרֶת: 51 פַּ֣ר אֶחָ֞ד בֶּן־בָּקָ֗ר אַ֧יִל אֶחָ֛ד כֶּֽבֶשׂ־אֶחָ֥ד בֶּן־שְׁנָת֖וֹ לְעֹלָֽה: 52 שְׂעִיר־עִזִּ֥ים אֶחָ֖ד לְחַטָּֽאת: 53 וּלְזֶ֣בַח הַשְּׁלָמִים֮ בָּקָ֣ר שְׁנַ֒יִם֒ אֵילִ֤ם חֲמִשָּׁה֙ עַתֻּדִ֣ים חֲמִשָּׁ֔ה כְּבָשִׂ֥ים בְּנֵֽי־שָׁנָ֖ה חֲמִשָּׁ֑ה זֶ֛ה קָרְבַּ֥ן אֱלִישָׁמָ֖ע בֶּן־עַמִּיהֽוּד: פ

54 בַּיּוֹם֙ הַשְּׁמִינִ֔י נָשִׂ֖יא לִבְנֵ֣י מְנַשֶּׁ֑ה גַּמְלִיאֵ֖ל בֶּן־פְּדָהצֽוּר: 55 קָרְבָּנ֞וֹ קַֽעֲרַת־ כֶּ֣סֶף אַחַ֗ת שְׁלֹשִׁ֣ים וּמֵאָה֮ מִשְׁקָלָהּ֒ מִזְרָ֤ק אֶחָד֙ כֶּ֣סֶף שִׁבְעִ֣ים שֶׁ֔קֶל בְּשֶׁ֖קֶל הַקֹּ֑דֶשׁ שְׁנֵיהֶ֣ם ׀ מְלֵאִ֗ים סֹ֛לֶת בְּלוּלָ֥ה בַשֶּׁ֖מֶן לְמִנְחָֽה: 56 כַּ֤ף אַחַת֙ עֲשָׂרָ֣ה זָהָ֔ב מְלֵאָ֖ה קְטֹֽרֶת: 57 פַּ֣ר אֶחָ֞ד בֶּן־בָּקָ֗ר אַ֧יִל אֶחָ֛ד כֶּֽבֶשׂ־אֶחָ֥ד בֶּן־שְׁנָת֖וֹ לְעֹלָֽה: 58 שְׂעִיר־עִזִּ֥ים אֶחָ֖ד לְחַטָּֽאת: 59 וּלְזֶ֣בַח הַשְּׁלָמִים֮ בָּקָ֣ר שְׁנַ֒יִם֒ אֵילִ֤ם חֲמִשָּׁה֙ עַתֻּדִ֣ים חֲמִשָּׁ֔ה כְּבָשִׂ֥ים בְּנֵֽי־שָׁנָ֖ה חֲמִשָּׁ֑ה זֶ֛ה קָרְבַּ֥ן גַּמְלִיאֵ֖ל בֶּן־פְּדָהצֽוּר: פ

60 בַּיּוֹם֙ הַתְּשִׁיעִ֔י נָשִׂ֖יא לִבְנֵ֣י בִנְיָמִ֑ן אֲבִידָ֖ן בֶּן־גִּדְעֹנִֽי: 61 קָרְבָּנ֞וֹ קַֽעֲרַת־כֶּ֣סֶף אַחַ֗ת שְׁלֹשִׁ֣ים וּמֵאָה֮ מִשְׁקָלָהּ֒ מִזְרָ֤ק אֶחָד֙ כֶּ֣סֶף שִׁבְעִ֣ים שֶׁ֔קֶל בְּשֶׁ֖קֶל הַקֹּ֑דֶשׁ שְׁנֵיהֶ֣ם ׀ מְלֵאִ֗ים סֹ֛לֶת בְּלוּלָ֥ה בַשֶּׁ֖מֶן לְמִנְחָֽה: 62 כַּ֤ף אַחַת֙ עֲשָׂרָ֣ה זָהָ֔ב מְלֵאָ֖ה קְטֹֽרֶת: 63 פַּ֣ר אֶחָ֞ד בֶּן־בָּקָ֗ר אַ֧יִל אֶחָ֛ד כֶּֽבֶשׂ־אֶחָ֥ד בֶּן־שְׁנָת֖וֹ לְעֹלָֽה: 64 שְׂעִיר־עִזִּ֥ים אֶחָ֖ד לְחַטָּֽאת: 65 וּלְזֶ֣בַח הַשְּׁלָמִים֮ בָּקָ֣ר שְׁנַ֒יִם֒ אֵילִ֤ם חֲמִשָּׁה֙ עַתֻּדִ֣ים חֲמִשָּׁ֔ה כְּבָשִׂ֥ים בְּנֵֽי־שָׁנָ֖ה חֲמִשָּׁ֑ה זֶ֛ה קָרְבַּ֥ן אֲבִידָ֖ן בֶּן־ גִּדְעֹנִֽי: פ

66 בַּיּוֹם֙ הָֽעֲשִׂירִ֔י נָשִׂ֖יא לִבְנֵ֣י דָ֑ן אֲחִיעֶ֖זֶר בֶּן־עַמִּֽישַׁדָּֽי: 67 קָרְבָּנ֞וֹ קַֽעֲרַת־כֶּ֣סֶף אַחַ֗ת שְׁלֹשִׁ֣ים וּמֵאָה֮ מִשְׁקָלָהּ֒ מִזְרָ֤ק אֶחָד֙ כֶּ֣סֶף שִׁבְעִ֣ים שֶׁ֔קֶל בְּשֶׁ֖קֶל הַקֹּ֑דֶשׁ שְׁנֵיהֶ֣ם ׀

both filled with choice flour with oil mixed in, for a
meal offering; 68one gold ladle of 10 shekels, filled
with incense; 69one bull of the herd, one ram, and
one lamb in its first year, for a burnt offering; 70one
goat for a purgation offering; 71and for his sacrifice
of well-being: two oxen, five rams, five he-goats,
and five yearling lambs. That was the offering of
Ahiezer son of Ammishaddai.

72On the eleventh day, it was the chieftain of
the Asherites, Pagiel son of Ochran. 73His offering:
one silver bowl weighing 130 shekels and one silver
basin of 70 shekels by the sanctuary weight, both
filled with choice flour with oil mixed in, for a meal
offering; 74one gold ladle of 10 shekels, filled with
incense; 75one bull of the herd, one ram, and one
lamb in its first year, for a burnt offering; 76one goat
for a purgation offering; 77and for his sacrifice of
well-being: two oxen, five rams, five he-goats, and
five yearling lambs. That was the offering of Pagiel
son of Ochran.

78On the twelfth day, it was the chieftain of the
Naphtalites, Ahira son of Enan. 79His offering: one
silver bowl weighing 130 shekels and one silver
basin of 70 shekels by the sanctuary weight, both
filled with choice flour with oil mixed in, for a meal
offering; 80one gold ladle of 10 shekels, filled with
incense; 81one bull of the herd, one ram, and one
lamb in its first year, for a burnt offering; 82one goat
for a purgation offering; 83and for his sacrifice of
well-being: two oxen, five rams, five he-goats, and
five yearling lambs. That was the offering of Ahira
son of Enan.

84This was the dedication offering for the altar
from the chieftains of Israel upon its being
anointed: silver bowls, 12; silver basins, 12; gold

מְלֵאִ֗ים סֹ֛לֶת בְּלוּלָ֥ה בַשֶּׁ֖מֶן לְמִנְחָֽה׃ 68 כַּ֥ף
אַחַ֛ת עֲשָׂרָ֥ה זָהָ֖ב מְלֵאָ֥ה קְטֹֽרֶת׃ 69 פַּ֣ר
אֶחָ֞ד בֶּן־בָּקָ֗ר אַ֧יִל אֶחָ֛ד כֶּֽבֶשׂ־אֶחָ֥ד בֶּן־
שְׁנָת֖וֹ לְעֹלָֽה׃ 70 שְׂעִיר־עִזִּ֥ים אֶחָ֖ד
לְחַטָּֽאת׃ 71 וּלְזֶ֣בַח הַשְּׁלָמִים֮ בָּקָ֣ר שְׁנַ֒יִם֒
אֵילִ֤ם חֲמִשָּׁה֙ עַתֻּדִ֣ים חֲמִשָּׁ֔ה כְּבָשִׂ֥ים בְּנֵֽי־
שָׁנָ֖ה חֲמִשָּׁ֑ה זֶ֛ה קָרְבַּ֥ן אֲחִיעֶ֖זֶר בֶּן־
עַמִּֽישַׁדָּֽי׃ פ

72 בְּיוֹם֙ עַשְׁתֵּ֣י עָשָׂ֣ר י֔וֹם נָשִׂ֖יא לִבְנֵ֣י אָשֵׁ֑ר
פַּגְעִיאֵ֖ל בֶּן־עָכְרָֽן׃ 73 קָרְבָּנ֞וֹ קַֽעֲרַת־כֶּ֣סֶף
אַחַ֗ת שְׁלֹשִׁ֣ים וּמֵאָה֮ מִשְׁקָלָהּ֒ מִזְרָ֤ק אֶחָד֙
כֶּ֔סֶף שִׁבְעִ֥ים שֶׁ֖קֶל בְּשֶׁ֣קֶל הַקֹּ֑דֶשׁ שְׁנֵיהֶ֣ם ׀
מְלֵאִ֗ים סֹ֛לֶת בְּלוּלָ֥ה בַשֶּׁ֖מֶן לְמִנְחָֽה׃
74 כַּ֥ף אַחַ֛ת עֲשָׂרָ֥ה זָהָ֖ב מְלֵאָ֥ה קְטֹֽרֶת׃
75 פַּ֣ר אֶחָ֞ד בֶּן־בָּקָ֗ר אַ֧יִל אֶחָ֛ד כֶּֽבֶשׂ־אֶחָ֥ד
בֶּן־שְׁנָת֖וֹ לְעֹלָֽה׃ 76 שְׂעִיר־עִזִּ֥ים אֶחָ֖ד
לְחַטָּֽאת׃ 77 וּלְזֶ֣בַח הַשְּׁלָמִים֮ בָּקָ֣ר שְׁנַ֒יִם֒
אֵילִ֤ם חֲמִשָּׁה֙ עַתֻּדִ֣ים חֲמִשָּׁ֔ה כְּבָשִׂ֥ים
בְּנֵֽי־שָׁנָ֖ה חֲמִשָּׁ֑ה זֶ֛ה קָרְבַּ֥ן פַּגְעִיאֵ֖ל בֶּן־
עָכְרָֽן׃ פ

78 בְּיוֹם֙ שְׁנֵ֣ים עָשָׂ֣ר י֔וֹם נָשִׂ֖יא לִבְנֵ֣י נַפְתָּלִ֑י
אֲחִירַ֖ע בֶּן־עֵינָֽן׃ 79 קָרְבָּנ֞וֹ קַֽעֲרַת־כֶּ֣סֶף
אַחַ֗ת שְׁלֹשִׁ֣ים וּמֵאָה֮ מִשְׁקָלָהּ֒ מִזְרָ֤ק אֶחָד֙
כֶּ֔סֶף שִׁבְעִ֥ים שֶׁ֖קֶל בְּשֶׁ֣קֶל הַקֹּ֑דֶשׁ שְׁנֵיהֶ֣ם ׀
מְלֵאִ֗ים סֹ֛לֶת בְּלוּלָ֥ה בַשֶּׁ֖מֶן לְמִנְחָֽה׃
80 כַּ֥ף אַחַ֛ת עֲשָׂרָ֥ה זָהָ֖ב מְלֵאָ֥ה קְטֹֽרֶת׃
81 פַּ֣ר אֶחָ֞ד בֶּן־בָּקָ֗ר אַ֧יִל אֶחָ֛ד כֶּֽבֶשׂ־אֶחָ֥ד
בֶּן־שְׁנָת֖וֹ לְעֹלָֽה׃ 82 שְׂעִיר־עִזִּ֥ים אֶחָ֖ד
לְחַטָּֽאת׃ 83 וּלְזֶ֣בַח הַשְּׁלָמִים֮ בָּקָ֣ר שְׁנַ֒יִם֒
אֵילִ֤ם חֲמִשָּׁה֙ עַתֻּדִ֣ים חֲמִשָּׁ֔ה כְּבָשִׂ֥ים
בְּנֵֽי־שָׁנָ֖ה חֲמִשָּׁ֑ה זֶ֛ה קָרְבַּ֥ן אֲחִירַ֖ע בֶּן־
עֵינָֽן׃ פ

84 זֹ֣את ׀ חֲנֻכַּ֣ת הַמִּזְבֵּ֗חַ בְּיוֹם֙ הִמָּשַׁ֣ח אֹת֔וֹ
מֵאֵ֖ת נְשִׂיאֵ֣י יִשְׂרָאֵ֑ל קַעֲרֹ֨ת כֶּ֜סֶף שְׁתֵּ֣ים
עֶשְׂרֵ֗ה מִֽזְרְקֵי־כֶ֙סֶף֙ שְׁנֵ֣ים עָשָׂ֔ר כַּפּ֥וֹת זָהָ֖ב

ladles, 12. 85 Silver per bowl, 130; per basin, 70. Total silver of vessels, 2,400 sanctuary shekels. 86 The 12 gold ladles filled with incense—10 sanctuary shekels per ladle—total gold of the ladles, 120.

87 Total of herd animals for burnt offerings, 12 bulls; of rams, 12; of yearling lambs, 12—with their proper meal offerings; of goats for purgation offerings, 12. 88 Total of herd animals for sacrifices of well-being, 24 bulls; of rams, 60; of he-goats, 60; of yearling lambs, 60. That was the dedication offering for the altar after its anointing.

89 When Moses went into the Tent of Meeting to speak with [God], he would hear the Voice addressing him from above the cover that was on top of the Ark of the Pact between the two cherubim; thus [God] spoke to him.

שְׁתֵּים עֶשְׂרֵה׃ 85 שְׁלֹשִׁים וּמֵאָה הַקְּעָרָה
הָאַחַת כֶּסֶף וְשִׁבְעִים הַמִּזְרָק הָאֶחָד כֹּל
כֶּסֶף הַכֵּלִים אַלְפַּיִם וְאַרְבַּע־מֵאוֹת בְּשֶׁקֶל
הַקֹּדֶשׁ׃ 86 כַּפּוֹת זָהָב שְׁתֵּים־עֶשְׂרֵה מְלֵאֹת
קְטֹרֶת עֲשָׂרָה עֲשָׂרָה הַכַּף בְּשֶׁקֶל הַקֹּדֶשׁ
כָּל־זְהַב הַכַּפּוֹת עֶשְׂרִים וּמֵאָה׃

87 כָּל־הַבָּקָר לָעֹלָה שְׁנֵים עָשָׂר פָּרִים
אֵילִם שְׁנֵים־עָשָׂר כְּבָשִׂים בְּנֵי־שָׁנָה שְׁנֵים
עָשָׂר וּמִנְחָתָם וּשְׂעִירֵי עִזִּים שְׁנֵים עָשָׂר
לְחַטָּאת׃ 88 וְכֹל בְּקַר ׀ זֶבַח הַשְּׁלָמִים
עֶשְׂרִים וְאַרְבָּעָה פָּרִים אֵילִם שִׁשִּׁים
עַתֻּדִים שִׁשִּׁים כְּבָשִׂים בְּנֵי־שָׁנָה שִׁשִּׁים
זֹאת חֲנֻכַּת הַמִּזְבֵּחַ אַחֲרֵי הִמָּשַׁח אֹתוֹ׃

89 וּבְבֹא מֹשֶׁה אֶל־אֹהֶל מוֹעֵד לְדַבֵּר אִתּוֹ
וַיִּשְׁמַע אֶת־הַקּוֹל מִדַּבֵּר אֵלָיו מֵעַל
הַכַּפֹּרֶת אֲשֶׁר עַל־אֲרֹן הָעֵדֻת מִבֵּין שְׁנֵי
הַכְּרֻבִים וַיְדַבֵּר אֵלָיו׃ פ

## CONCLUSION (7:89)

Although the parashah is concerned mostly with the sanctity of the community at large and with the individuals responsible for that sanctity, it concludes by describing a private moment between God and Moses. Whereas the moment appears intimate, the verse makes clear that even Moses stands at an appropriate distance from the Divine when he enters the Tabernacle's interior. Despite the promise in the Priestly Blessing that God's "face" will shine down upon Israel (see at 6:25), Moses' experience of revelation is purely auditory. Even Israel's greatest leader, the only one who elsewhere speaks to God face-to-face or mouth-to-mouth (Exodus 33:11; Numbers 12:8; Deuteronomy 34:10), listens in the Tent of Meeting to a disembodied voice emanating from above the cover of the Ark.

—*Amy Kalmanofsky*

## *Another View*

NUMBERS 5:12–31 DESCRIBES the ordeal of the *sotah*, the so-called errant wife or "woman accused of adultery." If a man suspects that his wife has been unfaithful but lacks proof, she is brought to the priest, who puts her through a magical trial or ordeal to ascertain her innocence or guilt. We are not told what brings about the husband's "fit of jealousy" (v. 14) nor is the spell-induced outcome for the guilty wife plainly described. The text simply states: "if she has defiled herself by breaking faith with her husband... her belly shall distend and her thigh shall sag; and the wife shall become a curse among her people" (v. 27). However, if the woman is innocent, she will be "unharmed and able to retain seed" (v. 28). This verse provides the clue to the entire passage; it helps us understand why the husband suspects his wife in the first place, and how to interpret the symptoms that the guilty woman will suffer.

Verse 28 is best understood to mean that the innocent wife will be able to maintain her pregnancy. If so, then the context of the *sotah* ritual can be seen as involving a pregnant woman whose husband suspects that he is not the father. It is the husband's distrust of the origin of his wife's pregnancy that causes the "fit of jealousy." Therefore, the central issue is paternity: if the wife is innocent and the husband is truly the unborn child's father, then the fetus will grow to term. It follows, therefore, that if the wife is guilty and the husband is not the father, then the wife will not be able "to retain seed." That is, the spell of the ordeal will induce a miscarriage: "if she has defiled herself by breaking faith with her husband... her belly shall distend and her thigh shall sag" (v. 27). Ultimately, regardless of how we today might assess paternity, in the biblical context an intact pregnancy after this ritual is sufficient proof that the husband had indeed fathered this child.

*If the wife is guilty, then the fetus inside her will not grow to term.*

—*Sharon Keller*

## *Post-biblical Interpretations*

***When men or women individually commit any wrong*** (5:6). This is one of only a few places in the Torah where a woman is mentioned as committing a wrong and being punished for it. The Rabbis of the Talmud derive from this passage the principle that men and women are to be treated alike with regard to punishment for all kinds of misbehavior (BT *Bava Kama* 15a).

***If any wife has gone astray*** (5:12). This passage speaks of a woman whom her husband accuses of adultery, even though he has insufficient evidence to convict her. The Rabbis later developed Numbers 5:11–31 into an entire tractate in the Talmud, called *Sotah*, "the errant wife." It describes in detail the ordeal that she will endure, filling in much that the Torah does not mention, but also encasing this ritual in a set of rules that transform it into an unusual and infrequent event. According to Mishnah *Sotah* 1:1, only if a husband warns his wife in advance not to seclude herself with a particular man, and only if there are witnesses to the warning and to the act of seclusion, only then may he force her to go with him to the Temple. Since such a complex sequence of events is unlikely to happen, the chances of administering this degrading ritual decrease dramatically. The Rabbis also stipulate, based on close readings of the biblical verses, that the waters would test not only the woman suspected of infidelity but also her supposed partner. They add that if a jealous husband had himself committed adultery in the past, then the waters would not be able to harm his wife (BT *Sotah* 47b).

According to Mishnah *Sotah* 9:9, this ritual was abolished toward the end of the Second Temple period. [That mishnah attributes the suspension of the ritual to Rabbi Yohanan ben Zakkai, who acted in light of a proliferation in adultery during that era. He cited the prophet Hosea to explain why it was no longer meaningful to accuse wives of unfaithfulness in an atmosphere of widespread dissipation: "I will not punish their daughters for fornicating / Nor their daughters-in-law for committing adultery; / For they themselves turn aside with whores / And sacrifice with prostitutes, / And a people that is without sense must stumble" (4:14). —*Ed.*] The Rabbis viewed the errant wife as a metaphor for the entire Jewish people, whose betrayal of God and divine commandments was understood to have led to the destruction of the Second Temple in 70 C.E.

*Men and women are to be treated alike with regard to punishments.*

***If any... women explicitly utter a nazirite's vow*** (6:2). Since a female nazirite was required to bring the sacrifice, just like a male, the Torah implies that women owned and controlled property. Mishnah *Nazir* refers to two women who took nazirite vows: Miriam of Tadmor became a nazirite to pray for her sick daughter (6:11), and Queen Helena of Adiabene, a 1st-century-C.E. convert to Judaism, vowed to become a nazirite for seven years if her son returned safely from war (3:6). Josephus mentions the nazirite vow of Berenice of the Herodian royal family (*Wars of the Jews* 2, 15:1). Thus, we learn that becoming a nazirite in the rabbinic period was viewed as a way of prompting God to answer one's prayers, often on behalf of family members in difficult circumstances. Clearly, these traditions presume that women chose this option when they found themselves in situations of personal duress.

***Thus shall you bless the people of Israel*** (6:23). The three-fold priestly blessing appears immediately after a number of other topics, such as the *sotah* and the nazirite, that require the involvement of priests. Women could not serve as priests and hence did not utter this blessing. Although the verses that frame the blessing appear in the plural (6:23, 27), the words of the blessing themselves are all in the singular. The priest does not himself bless the people but serves as a vehicle for transmitting God's blessing to them. According to the talmudic sources, the main venue for the recitation of the priestly blessing was the Temple in Jerusalem, until it was destroyed in 70 C.E. If recited in a communal context, the blessing is addressed to the entire congregation, men and women alike.

—*Judith Hauptman*

# Contemporary Reflection

THE SOTAH RITUAL (5:11–31), in which a man suspects his wife of adultery and subjects her to an ordeal, has been notoriously difficult for contemporary readers, especially from a feminist perspective. The unequal application of the ritual to women and not men, the lack of due process, the physical and emotional humiliation—all of these combine to make this passage a challenging place in which to find meaning.

As such, this passage keeps company with a number of other biblical texts that are problematic, even painful, to read. Rabbi Rebecca Alpert offers a valuable model for confronting such troubling teachings. In her book *Like Bread on a Seder Plate: Jewish Lesbians and the Transformation of Tradition* (1997), Alpert presents a number of approaches for dealing with traditional texts on homosexuality. She suggests that we can understand these texts by interpreting them in the context of their own time and place. We also can try to wrest new meaning from them, or we can simply acknowledge the pain that they have caused—and continue to cause. These approaches are not, of course, mutually exclusive, and they can apply also to this parashah.

Certainly in the case of the *sotah*, we can analyze it in light of its historical context. Comparing this passage with other ancient Near Eastern texts reveals it to be in keeping with other laws contemporary to Torah times.

In terms of the pain the passage has caused, we can easily imagine its effect on women thousands of years ago, but we ourselves are spared direct impact. Modern readers have long taken solace in the fact that this practice is no longer in force—and thus is far from the purview of synagogue ritual committees. In fact, it is unclear whether this ritual ever took place. Even in the Torah, the law is given without a connection to any particular incident. The Mishnah states that an early rabbinic leader discontinued the ritual of the *sotah* (*Sotah* 9:9). The entire body of rabbinic literature cites only one example of its implementation. Regarding the medieval period, a little-known fragment from the Cairo Geniza still gives instructions as to how to perform the ritual in one's neighborhood synagogue; but there too, no record has been found of anyone actually doing so. (For details, see Lisa Grushcow, *Writing the Wayward Wife: Rabbinic Interpretations of Sotah*, 2006, pp. 297–300.)

When we try to understand the *sotah* ritual in context, we can be relieved that it has not been implemented for at least two thousand years. But how can we wrest meaning from this difficult text? Interestingly, the very discontinuation of the ritual—and the rabbinic explanation of its abandonment—may give us a way to find meaning. The official suspension of the *sotah* ritual provides an example of how religious and legal change happens, and how such change is explained. For those of us who are committed to the Torah and also see Judaism as a path that embraces change, this is a crucial issue.

## *How does religious change happen, and how is it explained?*

Some modern scholars assume that the ritual of the *sotah* disappeared because of the destruction of the Temple. Others argue that the ritual was abolished as a bold rabbinic move, to remove a practice that was seen to be unfair. But when one looks closely at the rabbinic texts, neither of these reasons is found. Rather, the explanation given is that things were getting worse—either more people were openly committing adultery, or more husbands were sinning in such a way that the *sotah* ritual did not then work on their wives. The Rabbis account for these and other examples of decline by claiming that the deaths of certain sages led to the disappearance of certain qualities from the world (see for example, Mishnah *Sotah* 9:9).

Thus, in these rabbinic texts, *change results from a world that is getting worse.* It is also worth noting that we find a similar outlook in the Greco-Roman world that surrounded the ancient rabbis. From that perspective, religious and legal changes were a response to moral, sexual, intellectual, or political collapse.

Coming back to the *sotah* ritual, then, it seems that our ancestors did not abolish the ritual because they found it morally objectionable. Instead, they used the best conceptual tools of their time to make sense of why change had happened, and those tools explained change as the product of decline.

Our modern paradigm, in contrast, is fundamentally based on the assumptions of science, the Enlightenment, and Emancipation: *we believe that it is possible for humanity to make changes based on progress*, not decline. The optimism of the Enlightenment has been tempered by the Holocaust and other tragedies of modern times, but the fundamental shift remains. For us, change can be positive, even holy. We believe that God continues to speak to us. Living in accordance with our new understandings of gender and sexual identity has enriched our clergy and communities. Living in a world more openly diverse has taught us the importance of outreach and inreach for our communities, in all their diversity. Scientific insights spur us to find new ethical and spiritual answers to questions of life and death. The existence of the modern state of Israel challenges us to live richer Jewish lives, wherever we are in the world. These changes and others are celebrated, not lamented as evidence of decline.

Ultimately, then, the *sotah* ritual is most powerful as a teacher of change: how we understood change in the past, and how we might understand it now. Just as the Rabbis of the Mishnah and Talmud used the best conceptual tools of their time to understand change, so must we—with the tools of our own time. Such an approach is not abandoning our tradition; it is being true to it.

The end of the Babylonian Talmud's tractate on *sotah* gives us a glimmer of possibility: some of our ancestors might also have had a different perspective on change and decline. Mishnah *Sotah* 9:9 ends with the statement that with the death of Rabbi Judah haNasi, humility and the fear of sin disappeared. In the Talmud's commentary, this statement is challenged. "Do not teach that humility is gone," says Rav Joseph, "for I am still here!" "Do not teach that the fear of sin is gone," says Rav Nachman, "for I am still here!" (BT *Sotah* 49b). Rav Nachman's self-proclaimed fear of sin—not to mention Rav Joseph's self-proclaimed humility—suggests that our ancestors, like ourselves, thought that they still had something to add.

*—Lisa J. Grushcow*

# *Voices*

## *Precious Gifts*

Anne Ebersman

*Numbers 4:22*

God tells Moses to take a census, literally, to raise the heads of the Levites. But aren't the Levites already weighed down? After all, their job is to carry the Tabernacle through the wilderness. From this we learn that the things that we carry—the things that weigh us down—actually raise us up. These are our most precious gifts.

## *How to Resist Temptation*

Linda Stern Zisquit

*Numbers 5:11–31*

Read the notes from the morning's class
on the *Sota*
and the winds of folly that blow through
the secret place
where God is asked to vacate
and no witness sees.
Don't mention it to a soul.
Try to imagine the ink in which all of
his names
are erased
and the swallowing
and the fumes that rise
through the mouth of flesh.
Then take a human step
back.

## *I Am Accursed*

Lisa Levine

*Numbers 5:11–31*

Accused out of jealousy
Humiliated and tormented
By the Priest of my people
What is this curse
Brought on by my husband?
I have done nothing
Nothing
Have I not always
Served him well?
What is this bitter spell
Forced upon me in rage?
I drink of the potion
Hoping for death
Instead, I live,
To be tormented
Again

## *While Three Men Sit in the Next Room Discussing the Talmudic Tractate on How to Prove a Woman Adulterous*

Linda Stern Zisquit

*Numbers 5:11–31*

Before the poison works its fever
before the regrets
begin
and I melt in the
shadow of their presence,
I'll treat them to a taste
of sweet division
and lock the remains
in a vial
just as green.

## *Naso*

Laurie Patton

*Numbers 5:15–16*

The rite is forgotten—
reviled and left behind
like a dusty wrapping
of a simpler antiquity—

Yet there are still
those words:
offering
and
jealousy
set against each other

*jealousy*—
the dark colors
of bitter water,
hands holding grain
without the joys of incense—

*offering*—
an altar-like embrace,
or Aaron's measured cubits—
the breastplates of ancestors
loved and imagined
as simple and sincere—

we have wondered
for millennia
how the exactitude of hate
so closely mirrors
the exactitude of love:

And Your offering
of jealousy—
Your gift
of remembered wrongs—
only makes us wonder this
with more precision

## *The Butcher's Wife*

Shelley Savren

*Numbers 5:15–31*

The year was round with zeros, 1900,
and they lived in a Lithuanian *shtetl*
where her garden smelled like roses and mint
and she collected eggs each day
from fifteen chickens
to sell at the market stand.

Her husband was a butcher,
a *moyl* really, but who could make a living
doing circumcisions?
He had a shop and knives, lots of knives.

A peddler came to the farm one day
and showed her how to open her mouth
and kiss. When he left,
she ran her tongue along the surface
of her teeth and smiled.

It took three days for her husband
to spill her confession.
Why else would a peddler spend
a sunny afternoon at one farm?
So she fasted, a full week, as he ordered,
and scrubbed her mouth with soap.

She had no words that week.
Nothing passed between her lips.
But when she stepped into her garden
her whole mouth blossomed
like roses, like the taste of mint.

## *A Blessing*

Leila Gal Berner

*Numbers 6:22–27*

May the *Shechinah*, the Holy Presence,
that brings forth the female in the Divine,
spread Her wings over you and protect you.
May Her light shine upon you with
compassion,
And may Her countenance illumine your lives
With wholeness and peace.

## *Gifts*

Jill Hammer

*Numbers 7:10–11*

Each of the twelve princes brought one silver
bowl:
twelve shining moons for the months of the
year,
twelve mirrors to reflect the spirit of each tribe.
The tribe of Judah brought, and Naftali and
Zebulun,
and Issachar and Dan and all the rest,

and the thirteenth gift,
brought to complete the thirteen moons of
the seasons,
was brought by three daughters of the tribe
of Dinah,
Chushim, Woman-of-the-Senses, who married
a son of Benjamin,
and her sister-wives Baara, Woman of Fire,
and Chodesh, Woman of the New Moon.

They brought a silver bowl,
to hold the flow of birth in its deep curve,
and a silver basin
to cradle life's end in its embrace.
They brought a cow of the herd, and a ewe,
and a lamb
for an offering of community and kindness,
and a she-goat for wiliness and persistence,
and as a sacrifice to give thanks for their
well-being,
they brought small shoes of children who had
grown out of them.
They brought small gifts from all the men and
women who were not princes
and had no silver bowls, and piled them on the
cow's back
for her to carry proudly.
They brought water, and fire, and breath: the
warmth of their bodies.

They presented their offering at night, when all
the princes had gone home,
but a heavenly scribe took note of them,
and in the Torah, where the thirteenth offering
should have appeared,
wrote: "This was the dedication of the altar."

Chushim, Baara, and Chodesh never knew
these words were written.
But they were the mothers of the world,
and generations later, the secrets of the universe
were taught in their honor.

NOTE

***Chushim . . . Baara . . . Chodesh.*** Women who are mentioned in I Chronicles 8:8–9. Their names mean "feelings" (or "senses"), "fire," and "moon" (or "renewal"), respectively. The final letters of Baara, Chushim, and Chodesh are *alef*, *mem*, and *shin*. The *Sefer Y'tzirah*, an ancient work of Jewish mysticism, calls these letters the "three mothers of the universe."

# בהעלתך ◆ *B'haalot'cha*

## NUMBERS 8:1–12:16

### *The Journey from Sinai Begins*

PARASHAT B'HAALOT'CHA ("when you bring up") chronicles, in three major units, the start of the Israelites' journey from Mount Sinai toward the Promised Land. The first unit (8:1–9:14) concerns the Tabernacle: its rituals, special laws regarding the Levites who serve in it, and the laws concerning the passover offering. It includes the purification and consecration of the Levites. It also addresses the situation of those who, because of being ritually impure, are unable to observe the passover offering at the right time; it institutes a substitute "second Passover" (*pesach sheni*), observed a month after the original due time of the passover offering (9:9–13).

The second unit (9:15–10:36) concentrates on the instructions for the traveling of the Israelites: the signals for moving ahead in the right direction and for making camp (the cloud and the trumpets). It concludes with the description of the first stage of the journey after leaving Sinai.

The third unit (Numbers 11–12) dramatically illustrates the discontent of certain Israelites who begin to challenge Moses (and, less directly, God) by their complaints on this first leg of the journey, and the divine punishments that follow as a consequence. An outstanding example is when, nostalgic for the plentitude left behind in Egypt, the people complain harshly about the lack of meat. Moses reacts with deep despair—to the point of asking to die rather than bear the burden of leadership. In response to his petition concerning the burden of bearing the people all by himself, God instructs him to gather representative elders of Israel and bestow some of his spirit upon them. This approach both shares the burden and demonstrates Moses' spiritual superiority. Paradoxically, however, Moses' authority is challenged by two of those elders (11:26–29) and then by his own siblings, Miriam and Aaron (12:1–2). In each of these episodes, Moses appears as a patient, caring, and extremely modest leader. While the narrator emphasizes his greatness and nobility, the people are presented as rebellious and ungrateful.

*This parashah features an enigmatic and disturbing story about Miriam.*

With regard to women, the parashah includes the enigmatic and disturbing story about Miriam. Moses' sibling complains against Moses' and his (new?) marriage to a "dark-skinned" (or "Cushite") woman (12:1). In her challenge, Miriam—together with her brother Aaron—attempts to claim equal footing with Moses as a prophet (12:2). God punishes Miriam—not Aaron—with a skin disease because of her complaints, and she recovers only due to Moses' intercessory prayer. Feminist interpreters often understand this story as an intended rebuke of a woman who aspires to a leadership role equal to a man's, reading it as prejudicial to women on a number of levels. As we will see below, it is also possible to read this account more sympathetically, as a case in which God sides with one maligned woman (Moses' wife) against a more powerful one (Miriam).

—*Masha Turner*

## *Outline*

*I.* FINAL RITUAL PREPARATIONS (8:1–9:14)

- *A.* Lighting the lamps of the lampstand (8:1–4)
- *B.* Purifying, consecrating, and appointing the Levites (8:5–26)
- *C.* Celebrating the passover offering and adding a "Second Passover" (9:1–14)

*II.* THE ISRAELITES' TRAVEL PROTOCOL (9:15–10:36)

- *A.* Planning the travel protocol (9:15–10:10)
- *B.* Leaving Sinai (10:11–28)
- *C.* Inviting Hobab to accompany Israel (10:29–32)
- *D.* Beginning the journey with the Ark (10:33–36)

*III.* ISRAELITE CHALLENGES TO MOSES AND GOD (11:1–12:16)

- *A.* Complaining (11:1–3)
- *B.* Craving meat (11:4–35)
- *C.* Criticizing Moses: Miriam, Aaron, and the Cushite woman (12:1–16)

8:1

יהוה spoke to Moses, saying: [2]Speak to
Aaron and say to him, "When you
mount the lamps, let the seven lamps give light at
the front of the lampstand." [3]Aaron did so; he
mounted the lamps at the front of the lampstand,
as יהוה had commanded Moses.—[4]Now this is how
the lampstand was made: it was hammered work of
gold, hammered from base to petal. According to
the pattern that יהוה had shown Moses, so was the
lampstand made.

[5]יהוה spoke to Moses, saying: [6]Take the Levites

ח וַיְדַבֵּר יְהֹוָה אֶל־מֹשֶׁה לֵּאמֹר׃ 2 דַּבֵּר
אֶל־אַהֲרֹן וְאָמַרְתָּ אֵלָיו בְּהַעֲלֹתְךָ אֶת־
הַנֵּרֹת אֶל־מוּל פְּנֵי הַמְּנוֹרָה יָאִירוּ שִׁבְעַת
הַנֵּרוֹת׃ 3 וַיַּעַשׂ כֵּן אַהֲרֹן אֶל־מוּל פְּנֵי
הַמְּנוֹרָה הֶעֱלָה נֵרֹתֶיהָ כַּאֲשֶׁר צִוָּה יְהֹוָה
אֶת־מֹשֶׁה׃ 4 וְזֶה מַעֲשֵׂה הַמְּנֹרָה מִקְשָׁה
זָהָב עַד־יְרֵכָהּ עַד־פִּרְחָהּ מִקְשָׁה הִוא
כַּמַּרְאֶה אֲשֶׁר הֶרְאָה יְהֹוָה אֶת־מֹשֶׁה כֵּן
עָשָׂה אֶת־הַמְּנֹרָה׃ פ

5 וַיְדַבֵּר יְהֹוָה אֶל־מֹשֶׁה לֵּאמֹר׃ 6 קַח אֶת־

## *Final Ritual Preparations* (8:1–9:14)

The parashah opens with the final commands for the Israelites before they begin their journey away from Sinai. It includes rituals regarding the kindling of the menorah's lamps, the purification of the Levites, and the passover sacrifice.

### LIGHTING THE LAMPS OF THE LAMPSTAND (8:1–4)

Aaron is charged with lighting the menorah (see Exodus 27:21) and now does so. This completes the story of the Tabernacle's erection and dedication and also concludes the story of the dedication offerings brought by Israelite chieftains at the conclusion of the previous parashah (Numbers 7), pointing out the unique "offering" that was presented by Aaron, the chieftain of Levi's tribe. For descriptions of the lampstand and its function, see Exodus 25:31–40 and 37:17–24.

### PURIFYING, CONSECRATING, AND APPOINTING THE LEVITES (8:5–26)

Even before this parashah, a number of passages have singled out the tribe of Levi (to which Moses and Aaron belong). In Exodus, the men of Levi zealously side with Moses following the incident of the Golden Calf, wreaking vengeance on the guilty parties (Exodus 32:26). Numbers 1:46–49, 2:33, and 3:15 make clear that the men of Levi are counted separately from the other tribes in the census since they have to be dedicated to God's service by being appointed over the holy work in the Tabernacle (1:50–54).

*6. **Take the Levites from among the Israelites and purify them.*** Now the Levites are singled out


◗ At first, the story of snow-white Miriam seems a perfect example of a double standard.

ANOTHER VIEW ➤ *862*

◗ For the caregiver, there is time only for truncated and hurried prayer.

CONTEMPORARY REFLECTION ➤ *864*

◗ Zipporah remarked that she felt pity for the wives of the prophesying elders.

POST-BIBLICAL INTERPRETATIONS ➤ *862*

◗ Today I'm a hill, / Tomorrow a sea. / Wandering all day / Like Miriam's well. . . .

VOICES ➤ *866*

from among the Israelites and purify them. 7This is what you shall do to them to purify them: sprinkle on them water of purification, and let them go over their whole body with a razor, and wash their clothes; thus they shall be purified. 8Let them take a bull of the herd, and with it a meal offering of choice flour with oil mixed in, and you take a second bull of the herd for a purgation offering. 9You shall bring the Levites forward before the Tent of Meeting. Assemble the Israelite community leadership, 10and bring the Levites forward before יהוה. Let the Israelites lay their hands upon the Levites, 11and let Aaron designate the Levites before יהוה as an elevation offering from the Israelites, that they may perform the service of יהוה. 12The Levites shall now lay their hands upon the heads of the bulls; one shall be offered to יהוה as a purgation offering and the other as a burnt offering, to make expiation for the Levites.

13You shall place the Levites in attendance upon Aaron and his sons, and designate them as an elevation offering to יהוה. 14Thus you shall set the Levites apart from the Israelites, and the Levites shall be Mine. 15Thereafter the Levites shall be qualified for the service of the Tent of Meeting, once you have purified them and designated them as an elevation offering. 16For they are formally assigned to Me from among the Israelites: I have taken them

הַלְוִיִּם מִתּוֹךְ בְּנֵי יִשְׂרָאֵל וְטִהַרְתָּ אֹתָם׃
7 וְכֹה־תַעֲשֶׂה לָהֶם לְטַהֲרָם הַזֵּה עֲלֵיהֶם
מֵי חַטָּאת וְהֶעֱבִירוּ תַעַר עַל־כׇּל־בְּשָׂרָם
וְכִבְּסוּ בִגְדֵיהֶם וְהִטֶּהָרוּ׃ 8 וְלָקְחוּ פַּר בֶּן־
בָּקָר וּמִנְחָתוֹ סֹלֶת בְּלוּלָה בַשָּׁמֶן וּפַר־שֵׁנִי
בֶן־בָּקָר תִּקַּח לְחַטָּאת׃ 9 וְהִקְרַבְתָּ אֶת־
הַלְוִיִּם לִפְנֵי אֹהֶל מוֹעֵד וְהִקְהַלְתָּ אֶת־כׇּל־
עֲדַת בְּנֵי יִשְׂרָאֵל׃ 10 וְהִקְרַבְתָּ אֶת־הַלְוִיִּם
לִפְנֵי יְהֹוָה וְסָמְכוּ בְנֵי־יִשְׂרָאֵל אֶת־יְדֵיהֶם
עַל־הַלְוִיִּם׃ 11 וְהֵנִיף אַהֲרֹן אֶת־הַלְוִיִּם
תְּנוּפָה לִפְנֵי יְהֹוָה מֵאֵת בְּנֵי יִשְׂרָאֵל וְהָיוּ
לַעֲבֹד אֶת־עֲבֹדַת יְהֹוָה׃ 12 וְהַלְוִיִּם יִסְמְכוּ
אֶת־יְדֵיהֶם עַל רֹאשׁ הַפָּרִים וַעֲשֵׂה אֶת־
הָאֶחָד חַטָּאת וְאֶת־הָאֶחָד עֹלָה לַיהֹוָה
לְכַפֵּר עַל־הַלְוִיִּם׃
13 וְהַעֲמַדְתָּ אֶת־הַלְוִיִּם לִפְנֵי אַהֲרֹן וְלִפְנֵי
בָנָיו וְהֵנַפְתָּ אֹתָם תְּנוּפָה לַיהֹוָה׃
14 וְהִבְדַּלְתָּ אֶת־הַלְוִיִּם מִתּוֹךְ בְּנֵי יִשְׂרָאֵל
וְהָיוּ לִי הַלְוִיִּם׃ 15 וְאַחֲרֵי־כֵן יָבֹאוּ הַלְוִיִּם
לַעֲבֹד אֶת־אֹהֶל מוֹעֵד וְטִהַרְתָּ אֹתָם
וְהֵנַפְתָּ אֹתָם תְּנוּפָה׃ 16 כִּי נְתֻנִים נְתֻנִים
הֵמָּה לִי מִתּוֹךְ בְּנֵי יִשְׂרָאֵל תַּחַת פִּטְרַת

further, this time formally dedicated to God's service, such as by assisting the priests, the sons of Aaron. (For the purifying, consecrating, and appointing of Aaron and his sons as priests, see Exodus 28–29 and Leviticus 8.)

*7–12.* Moses is instructed to purify the Levites through a special ceremony.

*9. **community leadership.*** Literally, "the entire community"; this translation construes the word for community, *edah*, as referring here to a representative body made up of adult males. However the terms are parsed, the entire community is to formally bestow its agreement to accept the Levites as representing it before God; but practically speaking, only a part of the Israelites will lay their hands (v. 10) on the Levites.

*13–20.* The Levites are "set apart" as attendants to Aaron and his sons (the priests), and are *themselves* dedicated as an elevation offering before God. The Levites are further set apart as dedicated to God's service, in lieu of the male first-born of each Israelite woman outside of the Levite tribe (8:16–17; see also at 3:12–13). As the parashah continues, it reiterates that each of the three levitical familial groupings—Gershonites, Kohathites, and Merarites (named for the grandfather and great-

for Myself in place of all the first issue of the womb, of all the male first-born of the Israelites. [17]For every male first-born among the Israelites, human as well as beast, is Mine; I consecrated them to Myself at the time that I smote every [male] first-born in the land of Egypt. [18]Now I take the Levites instead of every male first-born of the Israelites; [19]and from among the Israelites I formally assign the Levites to Aaron and his sons, to perform the service for the Israelites in the Tent of Meeting and to make expiation for the Israelites, so that no plague may afflict the Israelites for coming too near the sanctuary.

[20]Moses, Aaron, and the Israelite community leadership did with the Levites accordingly; just as יהוה had commanded Moses in regard to the Levites, so the Israelites did with them. [21]The Levites purified themselves and washed their clothes; and Aaron designated them as an elevation offering before יהוה, and Aaron made expiation for them to purify them. [22]Thereafter the Levites were qualified to perform their service in the Tent of Meeting, under Aaron and his sons. As יהוה had commanded Moses in regard to the Levites, so they did to them.

[23]יהוה spoke to Moses, saying: [24]This is the rule for the Levites. From twenty-five years of age up they shall participate in the work force in the service of the Tent of Meeting; [25]but at the age of fifty they shall retire from the work force and shall serve no more. [26]They may assist their brother Levites at the Tent of Meeting by standing guard, but they

כָּל־רֶ֫חֶם בְּכ֥וֹר כֹּל֙ מִבְּנֵ֣י יִשְׂרָאֵ֔ל לָקַ֥חְתִּי אֹתָ֖ם לִֽי: 17 כִּ֣י לִ֤י כָל־בְּכוֹר֙ בִּבְנֵ֣י יִשְׂרָאֵ֔ל בָּאָדָ֖ם וּבַבְּהֵמָ֑ה בְּי֗וֹם הַכֹּתִ֤י כָל־בְּכוֹר֙ בְּאֶ֣רֶץ מִצְרַ֔יִם הִקְדַּ֥שְׁתִּי אֹתָ֖ם לִֽי: 18 וָאֶקַּח֙ אֶת־הַלְוִיִּ֔ם תַּ֖חַת כָּל־בְּכ֥וֹר בִּבְנֵ֥י יִשְׂרָאֵֽל: 19 וָאֶתְּנָ֨ה אֶת־הַלְוִיִּ֜ם נְתֻנִ֣ים ׀ לְאַהֲרֹ֣ן וּלְבָנָ֗יו מִתּוֹךְ֮ בְּנֵ֣י יִשְׂרָאֵל֒ לַעֲבֹ֞ד אֶת־עֲבֹדַ֤ת בְּנֵֽי־יִשְׂרָאֵל֙ בְּאֹ֣הֶל מוֹעֵ֔ד וּלְכַפֵּ֖ר עַל־בְּנֵ֣י יִשְׂרָאֵ֑ל וְלֹ֨א יִהְיֶ֜ה בִּבְנֵ֤י יִשְׂרָאֵל֙ נֶ֔גֶף בְּגֶ֥שֶׁת בְּנֵֽי־יִשְׂרָאֵ֖ל אֶל־הַקֹּֽדֶשׁ: 20 וַיַּ֨עַשׂ מֹשֶׁ֧ה וְאַהֲרֹ֛ן וְכָל־עֲדַ֥ת בְּנֵֽי־יִשְׂרָאֵ֖ל לַלְוִיִּ֑ם כְּ֠כֹל אֲשֶׁר־צִוָּ֨ה יְהֹוָ֤ה אֶת־מֹשֶׁה֙ לַלְוִיִּ֔ם כֵּן־עָשׂ֥וּ לָהֶ֖ם בְּנֵ֥י יִשְׂרָאֵֽל: 21 וַיִּֽתְחַטְּא֣וּ הַלְוִיִּ֗ם וַֽיְכַבְּסוּ֙ בִּגְדֵיהֶ֔ם וַיָּ֨נֶף אַהֲרֹ֥ן אֹתָ֛ם תְּנוּפָ֖ה לִפְנֵ֣י יְהֹוָ֑ה וַיְכַפֵּ֧ר עֲלֵיהֶ֛ם אַהֲרֹ֖ן לְטַהֲרָֽם: 22 וְאַחֲרֵי־כֵ֞ן בָּ֣אוּ הַלְוִיִּ֗ם לַעֲבֹ֤ד אֶת־עֲבֹֽדָתָם֙ בְּאֹ֣הֶל מוֹעֵ֔ד לִפְנֵ֥י אַהֲרֹ֖ן וְלִפְנֵ֣י בָנָ֑יו כַּאֲשֶׁר֩ צִוָּ֨ה יְהֹוָ֤ה אֶת־מֹשֶׁה֙ עַל־הַלְוִיִּ֔ם כֵּ֥ן עָשׂ֖וּ לָהֶֽם: ס

23 וַיְדַבֵּ֥ר יְהֹוָ֖ה אֶל־מֹשֶׁ֥ה לֵּאמֹֽר: 24 זֹ֖את אֲשֶׁ֣ר לַלְוִיִּ֑ם מִבֶּן֩ חָמֵ֨שׁ וְעֶשְׂרִ֤ים שָׁנָה֙ וָמַ֔עְלָה יָבוֹא֙ לִצְבֹ֣א צָבָ֔א בַּעֲבֹדַ֖ת אֹ֥הֶל מוֹעֵֽד: 25 וּמִבֶּן֙ חֲמִשִּׁ֣ים שָׁנָ֔ה יָשׁ֖וּב מִצְּבָ֣א הָעֲבֹדָ֑ה וְלֹ֥א יַעֲבֹ֖ד עֽוֹד: 26 וְשֵׁרֵ֨ת אֶת־אֶחָ֜יו בְּאֹ֣הֶל מוֹעֵ֗ד לִשְׁמֹ֣ר מִשְׁמֶ֔רֶת

- - - - - - - - - - - - - - - - - - - - - - - - - - -

uncles of Moses, Miriam, and Aaron) has its own task in the Tabernacle service and its own Tabernacle components to carry (10:17, 21; compare 3:23–39).

**24.** *twenty-five years of age.* The levitical service in Numbers 4:3, 23, and 30 begins at age 30. One way to reconcile the two versions is to consider that between the ages of 25 to 30, the Levites are to be trained and educated for their holy service.

*8:24. participate … work force.* Forms of the Hebrew word *tzava* appear twice in this verse (and again once in the next verse). In the context of the Levites, *tzava* means to fulfill a duty or to undertake a task. [Similar forms of the word also appear twice in Exodus when referring to women "who performed tasks at the entrance of the Tent of Meeting"; see at Exodus 38:8. —*Ed.*]

shall perform no labor. Thus you shall deal with the
Levites in regard to their duties.

9 יהוה spoke to Moses in the wilderness of
Sinai, on the first new moon of the second year
following the exodus from the land of Egypt, saying: 2Let the Israelite people offer the passover sacrifice at its set time: 3you shall offer it on the fourteenth day of this month, at twilight, at its set time;
you shall offer it in accordance with all its rules and
rites.
4Moses instructed the Israelites to offer the passover sacrifice; 5and they offered the passover sacrifice in the first month, on the fourteenth day of the
month, at twilight, in the wilderness of Sinai. Just
as יהוה had commanded Moses, so the Israelites
did.
6But there were some householders who were
impure by reason of a corpse and could not offer
the passover sacrifice on that day. Appearing that
same day before Moses and Aaron, 7those householders said to them, "Impure though we are by

וַעֲבֹדָה לֹא יַעֲבֹד כָּכָה תַּעֲשֶׂה לַלְוִיִּם
בְּמִשְׁמְרֹתָם׃ פ

ט וַיְדַבֵּר יְהוָה אֶל־מֹשֶׁה בְמִדְבַּר־סִינַי
בַּשָּׁנָה הַשֵּׁנִית לְצֵאתָם מֵאֶרֶץ מִצְרַיִם
בַּחֹדֶשׁ הָרִאשׁוֹן לֵאמֹר׃ 2 וְיַעֲשׂוּ בְנֵי־
יִשְׂרָאֵל אֶת־הַפָּסַח בְּמוֹעֲדוֹ׃ 3 בְּאַרְבָּעָה
עָשָׂר־יוֹם בַּחֹדֶשׁ הַזֶּה בֵּין הָעַרְבַּיִם תַּעֲשׂוּ
אֹתוֹ בְּמֹעֲדוֹ כְּכָל־חֻקֹּתָיו וּכְכָל־מִשְׁפָּטָיו
תַּעֲשׂוּ אֹתוֹ׃
4 וַיְדַבֵּר מֹשֶׁה אֶל־בְּנֵי יִשְׂרָאֵל לַעֲשֹׂת
הַפָּסַח׃ 5 וַיַּעֲשׂוּ אֶת־הַפֶּסַח בָּרִאשׁוֹן
בְּאַרְבָּעָה עָשָׂר יוֹם לַחֹדֶשׁ בֵּין הָעַרְבַּיִם
בְּמִדְבַּר סִינָי כְּכֹל אֲשֶׁר צִוָּה יְהוָה אֶת־
מֹשֶׁה כֵּן עָשׂוּ בְּנֵי יִשְׂרָאֵל׃
6 וַיְהִי אֲנָשִׁים אֲשֶׁר הָיוּ טְמֵאִים לְנֶפֶשׁ
אָדָם וְלֹא־יָכְלוּ לַעֲשֹׂת־הַפֶּסַח בַּיּוֹם הַהוּא
וַיִּקְרְבוּ לִפְנֵי מֹשֶׁה וְלִפְנֵי אַהֲרֹן בַּיּוֹם
הַהוּא׃ 7 וַיֹּאמְרוּ הָאֲנָשִׁים הָהֵמָּה אֵלָיו

## CELEBRATING THE PASSOVER OFFERING AND ADDING A "SECOND PASSOVER" (9:1–14)

This section records an existential problem addressed to Moses, namely, the fact that it is impossible for some Israelites to be ritually pure in time for the passover sacrifice. The section concludes with a legal mandate from God, instituting a second opportunity for the people to observe the passover offering a month later. This legal mandate widens to include also Israelite householders (and perhaps others) who happen to be distant from the Tabernacle and are unable to perform the passover offering at the right time. We find four other cases in the Torah when a query prompts a new law: the case of the blasphemer (Leviticus 24:10–16); the case of the man gathering sticks on the Sabbath (Numbers 15:32–36); and twice, the case of the daughters of Zelophehad, namely Mahlah, Milcah, Noah, Hoglah, and Tirzah (see at 27:1–11 and 36:1–12).

*6. householders.* The original passover offering was arranged by household (Exodus 12:3), which is the basic unit of Israelite society. This translation presumes that it is a household's head who would normally "present" the passover sacrifice (v. 7) on behalf of the household, before sharing it with all of its members. (Presumably householders were males, a fact that would go without saying.) It is also possible that the group in question was composed of other impure individuals, women and men, not specifically householders.

*7–8.* Moses brings the problem before God: what to do when ritual impurity bars an Israelite (who is commanded to carry out a passover sacrifice) from making the sacrifice at the designated time?

reason of a corpse, why must we be debarred from presenting יהוה's offering at its set time with the rest of the Israelites?" [8]Moses said to them, "Stand by, and let me hear what instructions יהוה gives about you."

[9]And יהוה spoke to Moses, saying: [10]Speak to the Israelite people, saying: When any of you or of your posterity who are defiled by a corpse or are on a long journey would offer a passover sacrifice to יהוה—[11]they shall offer it in the second month, on the fourteenth day of the month, at twilight. They shall eat it with unleavened bread and bitter herbs, [12]and they shall not leave any of it over until morning. They shall not break a bone of it. They shall offer it in strict accord with the law of the passover sacrifice. [13]But if a householder who is pure and not on a journey refrains from offering the passover sacrifice, that person shall be cut off from kin, for יהוה's offering was not presented at its set time; that householder shall bear the guilt.

[14]And when a stranger who resides with you would offer a passover sacrifice to יהוה, it must be offered in accordance with the rules and rites of the passover sacrifice. There shall be one law for you, whether stranger or citizen of the country.

[15]On the day that the Tabernacle was set up, the cloud covered the Tabernacle, the Tent of the Pact;

אֲנַחְנוּ טְמֵאִים לְנֶפֶשׁ אָדָם לָמָּה נִגָּרַע
לְבִלְתִּי הַקְרִיב אֶת־קָרְבַּן יְהֹוָה בְּמֹעֲדוֹ
בְּתוֹךְ בְּנֵי יִשְׂרָאֵל׃ 8 וַיֹּאמֶר אֲלֵהֶם
מֹשֶׁה עִמְדוּ וְאֶשְׁמְעָה מַה־יְצַוֶּה יְהֹוָה
לָכֶם׃ פ
9 וַיְדַבֵּר יְהֹוָה אֶל־מֹשֶׁה לֵּאמֹר׃ 10 דַּבֵּר
אֶל־בְּנֵי יִשְׂרָאֵל לֵאמֹר אִישׁ אִישׁ כִּי־יִהְיֶה־
טָמֵא ׀ לָנֶפֶשׁ אוֹ בְדֶרֶךְ רְחֹקָה לָכֶם אוֹ
לְדֹרֹתֵיכֶם וְעָשָׂה פֶסַח לַיהֹוָה׃ 11 בַּחֹדֶשׁ
הַשֵּׁנִי בְּאַרְבָּעָה עָשָׂר יוֹם בֵּין הָעַרְבַּיִם
יַעֲשׂוּ אֹתוֹ עַל־מַצּוֹת וּמְרֹרִים יֹאכְלֻהוּ׃
12 לֹא־יַשְׁאִירוּ מִמֶּנּוּ עַד־בֹּקֶר וְעֶצֶם לֹא
יִשְׁבְּרוּ־בוֹ כְּכָל־חֻקַּת הַפֶּסַח יַעֲשׂוּ אֹתוֹ׃
13 וְהָאִישׁ אֲשֶׁר־הוּא טָהוֹר וּבְדֶרֶךְ לֹא־הָיָה
וְחָדַל לַעֲשׂוֹת הַפֶּסַח וְנִכְרְתָה הַנֶּפֶשׁ הַהִוא
מֵעַמֶּיהָ כִּי ׀ קָרְבַּן יְהֹוָה לֹא הִקְרִיב בְּמֹעֲדוֹ
חֶטְאוֹ יִשָּׂא הָאִישׁ הַהוּא׃
14 וְכִי־יָגוּר אִתְּכֶם גֵּר וְעָשָׂה פֶסַח
לַיהֹוָה כְּחֻקַּת הַפֶּסַח וּכְמִשְׁפָּטוֹ כֵּן יַעֲשֶׂה
חֻקָּה אַחַת יִהְיֶה לָכֶם וְלַגֵּר וּלְאֶזְרַח
הָאָרֶץ׃ ס
15 וּבְיוֹם הָקִים אֶת־הַמִּשְׁכָּן כִּסָּה הֶעָנָן
אֶת־הַמִּשְׁכָּן לְאֹהֶל הָעֵדֻת וּבָעֶרֶב יִהְיֶה

*11.* God mandates that those unable to observe the Passover ritual at the designated time, on the fourteenth day of the first month, offer their sacrifice a month later, on the fourteenth of the following month.

[This option of an alternative passover offering a month later (what the Rabbis called "Second Passover" or *pesach sheni*) illustrates a capacity to modify time-bound obligations on account of certain circumstances. One wonders whether this precedence and flexibility could also apply when women were ritually impure because of childbirth or menstruation. However, there is no mention of such modifications regarding women. —*Ed.*]

*14. There shall be one law for you, whether stranger or citizen of the country.* This rule applies specifically to observing Passover but can be interpreted as a general principle that applies in other cases as well.

## *The Israelites' Travel Protocol*

(9:15–10:36)

The Israelites' long journey from Egypt to Canaan is full of starts and stops (see 33:1–49). Unlike conventional journeys, in which travel is dictated by constraints of geography, climate, and

and in the evening it rested over the Tabernacle in the likeness of fire until morning. [16]It was always so: the cloud covered it, appearing as fire by night. [17]And whenever the cloud lifted from the Tent, the Israelites would set out accordingly; and at the spot where the cloud settled, there the Israelites would make camp. [18]At a command of יהוה the Israelites broke camp, and at a command of יהוה they made camp: they remained encamped as long as the cloud stayed over the Tabernacle. [19]When the cloud lingered over the Tabernacle many days, the Israelites observed יהוה's mandate and did not journey on. [20]At such times as the cloud rested over the Tabernacle for but a few days, they remained encamped at a command of יהוה, and broke camp at a command of יהוה. [21]And at such times as the cloud stayed from evening until morning, they broke camp as soon as the cloud lifted in the morning. Day or night, whenever the cloud lifted, they would break camp. [22]Whether it was two days or a month or a year—however long the cloud lingered over the Tabernacle—the Israelites remained encamped and did not set out; only when it lifted did they break camp. [23]On a sign from יהוה they made camp and on a sign from יהוה they broke camp; they observed יהוה's mandate at יהוה's bidding through Moses.

*10* יהוה spoke to Moses, saying: [2]Have two silver trumpets made; make them of hammered work. They shall serve you to summon [military bodies of] the community and to set the divisions in motion. [3]When both are blown in long blasts,

עַל־הַמִּשְׁכָּן כְּמַרְאֵה־אֵשׁ עַד־בֹּקֶר׃ 16 כֵּן
יִהְיֶה תָמִיד הֶעָנָן יְכַסֶּנּוּ וּמַרְאֵה־אֵשׁ
לָיְלָה׃ 17 וּלְפִי הֵעָלוֹת הֶעָנָן מֵעַל הָאֹהֶל
וְאַחֲרֵי כֵן יִסְעוּ בְּנֵי יִשְׂרָאֵל וּבִמְקוֹם אֲשֶׁר
יִשְׁכָּן־שָׁם הֶעָנָן שָׁם יַחֲנוּ בְּנֵי יִשְׂרָאֵל׃
18 עַל־פִּי יְהוָה יִסְעוּ בְּנֵי יִשְׂרָאֵל וְעַל־פִּי
יְהוָה יַחֲנוּ כָּל־יְמֵי אֲשֶׁר יִשְׁכֹּן הֶעָנָן עַל־
הַמִּשְׁכָּן יַחֲנוּ׃ 19 וּבְהַאֲרִיךְ הֶעָנָן עַל־
הַמִּשְׁכָּן יָמִים רַבִּים וְשָׁמְרוּ בְנֵי־יִשְׂרָאֵל
אֶת־מִשְׁמֶרֶת יְהוָה וְלֹא יִסָּעוּ׃ 20 וְיֵשׁ אֲשֶׁר
יִהְיֶה הֶעָנָן יָמִים מִסְפָּר עַל־הַמִּשְׁכָּן עַל־פִּי
יְהוָה יַחֲנוּ וְעַל־פִּי יְהוָה יִסָּעוּ׃ 21 וְיֵשׁ
אֲשֶׁר־יִהְיֶה הֶעָנָן מֵעֶרֶב עַד־בֹּקֶר וְנַעֲלָה
הֶעָנָן בַּבֹּקֶר וְנָסָעוּ אוֹ יוֹמָם וָלַיְלָה וְנַעֲלָה
הֶעָנָן וְנָסָעוּ׃ 22 אוֹ־יֹמַיִם אוֹ־חֹדֶשׁ אוֹ־יָמִים
בְּהַאֲרִיךְ הֶעָנָן עַל־הַמִּשְׁכָּן לִשְׁכֹּן עָלָיו
יַחֲנוּ בְנֵי־יִשְׂרָאֵל וְלֹא יִסָּעוּ וּבְהֵעָלֹתוֹ
יִסָּעוּ׃ 23 עַל־פִּי יְהוָה יַחֲנוּ וְעַל־פִּי יְהוָה
יִסָּעוּ אֶת־מִשְׁמֶרֶת יְהוָה שָׁמָרוּ עַל־פִּי
יְהוָה בְּיַד־מֹשֶׁה׃ פ

י וַיְדַבֵּר יְהוָה אֶל־מֹשֶׁה לֵּאמֹר׃ 2 עֲשֵׂה
לְךָ שְׁתֵּי חֲצוֹצְרֹת כֶּסֶף מִקְשָׁה תַּעֲשֶׂה
אֹתָם וְהָיוּ לְךָ לְמִקְרָא הָעֵדָה וּלְמַסַּע אֶת־
הַמַּחֲנוֹת׃ 3 וְתָקְעוּ בָּהֵן וְנוֹעֲדוּ אֵלֶיךָ כָּל־

security, the Israelites' journey is directed supernaturally. This unit provides instructions for the journey.

### PLANNING THE TRAVEL PROTOCOL (9:15–10:10)

God has led the people by means of a cloud by day and a pillar of fire by night, both of which traveled before the camp (Exodus 13:21–22). Here we learn that the cloud's coming to a halt and resting over the Tabernacle signals that they must encamp (9:17–23).

***18. At a command of* יהוה.** God alone determines the duration of their travel and encampment, as well as the direction of their travel.

הָֽעֵדָ֔ה אֶל־פֶּ֖תַח אֹ֥הֶל מוֹעֵֽד׃ 4 וְאִם־בְּאַחַ֖ת
יִתְקָ֑עוּ וְנוֹעֲד֤וּ אֵלֶ֙יךָ֙ הַנְּשִׂיאִ֔ים רָאשֵׁ֖י אַלְפֵ֥י
יִשְׂרָאֵֽל׃ 5 וּתְקַעְתֶּ֖ם תְּרוּעָ֑ה וְנָֽסְעוּ֙ הַֽמַּחֲנ֔וֹת
הַחֹנִ֖ים קֵֽדְמָה׃ 6 וּתְקַעְתֶּ֤ם תְּרוּעָה֙ שֵׁנִ֔ית
וְנָֽסְעוּ֙ הַמַּחֲנ֔וֹת הַחֹנִ֖ים תֵּימָ֑נָה תְּרוּעָ֥ה
יִתְקְע֖וּ לְמַסְעֵיהֶֽם׃ 7 וּבְהַקְהִ֖יל אֶת־הַקָּהָ֑ל
תִּתְקְע֖וּ וְלֹ֥א תָרִֽיעוּ׃ 8 וּבְנֵ֤י אַהֲרֹן֙ הַכֹּ֣הֲנִ֔ים
יִתְקְע֖וּ בַּחֲצֹצְר֑וֹת וְהָי֥וּ לָכֶ֛ם לְחֻקַּ֥ת עוֹלָ֖ם
לְדֹרֹתֵיכֶֽם׃
9 וְכִֽי־תָבֹ֨אוּ מִלְחָמָ֜ה בְּאַרְצְכֶ֗ם עַל־הַצַּר֙
הַצֹּרֵ֣ר אֶתְכֶ֔ם וַהֲרֵעֹתֶ֖ם בַּחֲצֹצְרֹ֑ת וְנִזְכַּרְתֶּ֗ם
לִפְנֵי֙ יְהוָ֣ה אֱלֹהֵיכֶ֔ם וְנוֹשַׁעְתֶּ֖ם מֵאֹיְבֵיכֶֽם׃
10 וּבְי֨וֹם שִׂמְחַתְכֶ֥ם וּֽבְמוֹעֲדֵיכֶם֮ וּבְרָאשֵׁ֣י
חָדְשֵׁיכֶם֒ וּתְקַעְתֶּ֣ם בַּחֲצֹצְרֹ֗ת עַ֚ל עֹלֹ֣תֵיכֶ֔ם
וְעַ֖ל זִבְחֵ֣י שַׁלְמֵיכֶ֑ם וְהָי֨וּ לָכֶ֤ם לְזִכָּרוֹן֙ לִפְנֵ֣י
אֱלֹהֵיכֶ֔ם אֲנִ֖י יְהוָ֥ה אֱלֹהֵיכֶֽם׃ פ

11 וַיְהִ֞י בַּשָּׁנָ֧ה הַשֵּׁנִ֛ית בַּחֹ֥דֶשׁ הַשֵּׁנִ֖י
בְּעֶשְׂרִ֣ים בַּחֹ֑דֶשׁ נַעֲלָה֙ הֶֽעָנָ֔ן מֵעַ֖ל מִשְׁכַּ֥ן
הָעֵדֻֽת׃ 12 וַיִּסְע֧וּ בְנֵֽי־יִשְׂרָאֵ֛ל לְמַסְעֵיהֶ֖ם
מִמִּדְבַּ֣ר סִינָ֑י וַיִּשְׁכֹּ֥ן הֶֽעָנָ֖ן בְּמִדְבַּ֥ר פָּארָֽן׃
13 וַיִּסְע֖וּ בָּרִאשֹׁנָ֑ה עַל־פִּ֥י יְהוָ֖ה בְּיַד־מֹשֶֽׁה׃
14 וַיִּסַּ֞ע דֶּ֣גֶל מַחֲנֵ֧ה בְנֵי־יְהוּדָ֛ה בָּרִאשֹׁנָ֖ה

the whole company [of fighters] shall assemble before you at the entrance of the Tent of Meeting;
[4]and if only one is blown, the chieftains, heads of Israel's contingents, shall assemble before you. [5]But
when you sound short blasts, the divisions encamped on the east shall move forward; [6]and when
you sound short blasts a second time, those encamped on the south shall move forward. Thus short blasts shall be blown for setting them in
motion, [7]while to convoke [military bodies of] the congregation you shall blow long blasts, not short
ones. [8]The trumpets shall be blown by Aaron's sons, the priests; they shall be for you an institution for all time throughout the ages.

[9]When you are at war in your land against an aggressor who attacks you, you shall sound short blasts on the trumpets, that you may be remembered before your God יהוה and be delivered from
your enemies. [10]And on your joyous occasions—your fixed festivals and new moon days—you shall sound the trumpets over your burnt offerings and your sacrifices of well-being. They shall be a reminder of you before your God: I, יהוה, am your God.

[11]In the second year, on the twentieth day of the second month, the cloud lifted from the Tabernacle of the Pact
[12]and the Israelites set out on their journeys from the wilderness of Sinai. The cloud came to rest in the wilderness of Paran.

[13]When the march was to begin, at יהוה's command through Moses,
[14]the first standard to set out, troop by troop, was the division of Judah. In com-

LEAVING SINAI (10:11–28)

Previously, all the details of the travel protocol were theoretical; now, they are going to be applied. The Torah recounts this first journey from Sinai with great pomp by describing the rank and file of the tribes and the transportation of the Tabernacle. The arrangement of the tribes reflects the status of the tribal ancestors' mothers, namely Leah, Rachel, Bilhah, and Zilpah. (See also *B'midbar*, Another View, p. 808.)

*12.* Finally, after all the detailed preparations, the Israelites embark from Sinai for the first time.

*14.* The first three tribes to embark on the journey are descended from three of the sons of Leah: Judah, Issachar, and Zebulun.

mand of its troops was Nahshon son of Amminadab; 15 in command of the tribal troop of Issachar, Nethanel son of Zuar; 16 and in command of
the tribal troop of Zebulun, Eliab son of Helon.

17 Then the Tabernacle would be taken apart;
and the Gershonites and the Merarites, who carried
the Tabernacle, would set out.

18 The next standard to set out, troop by troop,
was the division of Reuben. In command of its
troop was Elizur son of Shedeur; 19 in command of
the tribal troop of Simeon, Shelumiel son of Zurishaddai; 20 and in command of the tribal troop of
Gad, Eliasaph son of Deuel.

21 Then the Kohathites, who carried the sacred
objects, would set out; and by the time they arrived,
the Tabernacle would be set up again.

22 The next standard to set out, troop by troop,
was the division of Ephraim. In command of its
troop was Elishama son of Ammihud; 23 in command of the tribal troop of Manasseh, Gamaliel son
of Pedahzur; 24 and in command of the tribal troop
of Benjamin, Abidan son of Gideoni.

25 Then, as the rear guard of all the divisions, the
standard of the division of Dan would set out,
troop by troop. In command of its troop was
Ahiezer son of Ammishaddai; 26 in command of
the tribal troop of Asher, Pagiel son of Ochran;
27 and in command of the tribal troop of Naphtali,
Ahira son of Enan.

28 Such was the order of march of the Israelites,
as they marched troop by troop.

לְצִבְאֹתָם וְעַל־צְבָאוֹ נַחְשׁוֹן בֶּן־עַמִּינָדָב׃
15 וְעַל־צְבָא מַטֵּה בְּנֵי יששכר יִשָּׂשכָר נְתַנְאֵל
בֶּן־צוּעָר׃ 16 וְעַל־צְבָא מַטֵּה בְּנֵי זְבוּלֻן
אֱלִיאָב בֶּן־חֵלֹן׃
17 וְהוּרַד הַמִּשְׁכָּן וְנָסְעוּ בְנֵי־גֵרְשׁוֹן וּבְנֵי
מְרָרִי נֹשְׂאֵי הַמִּשְׁכָּן׃
18 וְנָסַע דֶּגֶל מַחֲנֵה רְאוּבֵן לְצִבְאֹתָם וְעַל־
צְבָאוֹ אֱלִיצוּר בֶּן־שְׁדֵיאוּר׃ 19 וְעַל־צְבָא
מַטֵּה בְּנֵי שִׁמְעוֹן שְׁלֻמִיאֵל בֶּן־צוּרִישַׁדָּי׃
20 וְעַל־צְבָא מַטֵּה בְנֵי־גָד אֶלְיָסָף בֶּן־
דְּעוּאֵל׃
21 וְנָסְעוּ הַקְּהָתִים נֹשְׂאֵי הַמִּקְדָּשׁ וְהֵקִימוּ
אֶת־הַמִּשְׁכָּן עַד־בֹּאָם׃
22 וְנָסַע דֶּגֶל מַחֲנֵה בְנֵי־אֶפְרַיִם לְצִבְאֹתָם
וְעַל־צְבָאוֹ אֱלִישָׁמָע בֶּן־עַמִּיהוּד׃ 23 וְעַל־
צְבָא מַטֵּה בְּנֵי מְנַשֶּׁה גַּמְלִיאֵל בֶּן־
פְּדָהצוּר׃ 24 וְעַל־צְבָא מַטֵּה בְּנֵי בִנְיָמִן
אֲבִידָן בֶּן־גִּדְעוֹנִי׃
25 וְנָסַע דֶּגֶל מַחֲנֵה בְנֵי־דָן מְאַסֵּף לְכָל־
הַמַּחֲנֹת לְצִבְאֹתָם וְעַל־צְבָאוֹ אֲחִיעֶזֶר בֶּן־
עַמִּישַׁדָּי׃ 26 וְעַל־צְבָא מַטֵּה בְּנֵי אָשֵׁר
פַּגְעִיאֵל בֶּן־עָכְרָן׃ 27 וְעַל־צְבָא מַטֵּה בְּנֵי
נַפְתָּלִי אֲחִירַע בֶּן־עֵינָן׃
28 אֵלֶּה מַסְעֵי בְנֵי־יִשְׂרָאֵל לְצִבְאֹתָם
וַיִּסָּעוּ׃ ס

*17.* The first group is followed by the dismantled Tabernacle, borne by the levitical clans of Gershon and Merari.

*18.* The next group that sets out are the tribes of Reuben, Simeon, and Gad, who are descendants of Leah and her maid Zilpah.

*21.* The sons of the levitical clan of Kohath follow with the well-covered Tabernacle vessels. Since they travel behind the Gershonites and Merarites, who carry the dismantled Tabernacle, the latter can fully set up the Tabernacle at each site by the time the Kohathites arrive to place the holy vessels inside it.

*22.* After the Kohathites, the group that sets out are the tribes of Rachel: Ephraim, Manasseh, and Benjamin.

*25–27.* The tribes of Dan, Asher, and Naphtali—the offspring of Bilhah and Zilpah—are last.

²⁹Moses said to Hobab son of Reuel the Midianite, Moses' father-in-law, "We are setting out for the place of which יהוה has said, 'I will give it to you.' Come with us and we will be generous with you; for יהוה has promised to be generous to Israel."

³⁰"I will not go," he replied to him, "but will return to my native land." ³¹He said, "Please do not leave us, inasmuch as you know where we should camp in the wilderness and can be our guide. ³²So if you come with us, we will extend to you the same bounty that יהוה grants us."

³³They marched from the mountain of יהוה a distance of three days. The Ark of the Covenant of יהוה traveled in front of them on that three days' journey to seek out a resting place for them; ³⁴and יהוה's cloud kept above them by day, as they moved on from camp.

³⁵When the Ark was to set out, Moses would say:

29 וַיֹּ֣אמֶר מֹשֶׁ֗ה לְ֠חֹבָ֠ב בֶּן־רְעוּאֵ֣ל הַמִּדְיָנִי֮ חֹתֵ֣ן מֹשֶׁה֒ נֹסְעִ֣ים ׀ אֲנַ֗חְנוּ אֶל־הַמָּקוֹם֙ אֲשֶׁ֣ר אָמַ֣ר יְהֹוָ֔ה אֹת֖וֹ אֶתֵּ֣ן לָכֶ֑ם לְכָ֤ה אִתָּ֙נוּ֙ וְהֵטַ֣בְנוּ לָ֔ךְ כִּֽי־יְהֹוָ֥ה דִּבֶּר־ט֖וֹב עַל־יִשְׂרָאֵֽל:

30 וַיֹּ֥אמֶר אֵלָ֖יו לֹ֣א אֵלֵ֑ךְ כִּ֧י אִם־אֶל־אַרְצִ֛י וְאֶל־מוֹלַדְתִּ֖י אֵלֵֽךְ: 31 וַיֹּ֕אמֶר אַל־נָ֖א תַּעֲזֹ֣ב אֹתָ֑נוּ כִּ֣י ׀ עַל־כֵּ֣ן יָדַ֗עְתָּ חֲנֹתֵ֙נוּ֙ בַּמִּדְבָּ֔ר וְהָיִ֥יתָ לָּ֖נוּ לְעֵינָֽיִם: 32 וְהָיָ֖ה כִּי־תֵלֵ֣ךְ עִמָּ֑נוּ וְהָיָ֣ה ׀ הַטּ֣וֹב הַה֗וּא אֲשֶׁ֨ר יֵיטִ֧יב יְהֹוָ֛ה עִמָּ֖נוּ וְהֵטַ֥בְנוּ לָֽךְ:

33 וַיִּסְעוּ֙ מֵהַ֣ר יְהֹוָ֔ה דֶּ֖רֶךְ שְׁלֹ֣שֶׁת יָמִ֑ים וַאֲר֨וֹן בְּרִית־יְהֹוָ֜ה נֹסֵ֣עַ לִפְנֵיהֶ֗ם דֶּ֚רֶךְ שְׁלֹ֣שֶׁת יָמִ֔ים לָת֥וּר לָהֶ֖ם מְנוּחָֽה: 34 וַעֲנַ֧ן יְהֹוָ֛ה עֲלֵיהֶ֖ם יוֹמָ֑ם בְּנָסְעָ֖ם מִן־הַֽמַּחֲנֶֽה: ס 35 וַיְהִ֛י בִּנְסֹ֥עַ הָאָרֹ֖ן וַיֹּ֥אמֶר מֹשֶׁ֑ה

• • • • • • • • • • • • • • • • • • • • • • • • • • • • • • • • • • • • • • •

### INVITING HOBAB TO ACCOMPANY ISRAEL (10:29–32)

Amid all the details of the journey, the Torah weaves in a human interest story. Here, Moses addresses Hobab the Midianite, who until now has been staying with the Israelites in the Sinai wilderness—asking him to accompany them on their continuing journey to the Land of Israel.

**29.** *Hobab son of Reuel the Midianite, Moses' father-in-law.* Hobab is either another name for Moses' father-in-law, Jethro (father of Zipporah), or perhaps Moses' brother-in-law. [Either way, it remains unclear what happens to Zipporah, Moses' wife. In Exodus 18, Jethro brings his daughter back to Moses, along with "her two sons" (see Exodus 18:6); presumably these are also Moses' children. The soon-to-be-mentioned controversy about Moses' wife (Numbers 12) makes this question all the more pressing. —*Ed.*]

**32.** Though the dialogue between them seems incomplete, we can learn from Moses' request how

strongly he wishes Hobab to accompany Israel, and how convinced he is of the great goodness promised by God that await the Israelites upon their arrival in the land.

### BEGINNING THE JOURNEY WITH THE ARK (10:33–36)

While the cloud leads the way before the people, thereby giving expression to God's constant accompaniment of Israel, the Ark symbolizes God's intimate presence among the people (see also Exodus 25:22), as well as God's role in protecting and defending them.

**33.** *traveled in front of them.* Whereas vv. 17–21 describe the Tabernacle as traveling *with* the camp, this passage depicts the Ark as traveling ahead of the camp.

**35–36.** Jewish tradition has woven these verses containing Moses' two prayers into the liturgy of the Torah service, often before and after the Torah reading.

Advance, O יהוה!

May Your enemies be scattered,

And may Your foes flee before You!

<sup>36</sup>And when it halted, he would say:

Return, O יהוה,

You who are Israel's myriads of thousands!

**11** The people took to complaining bitterly before יהוה. יהוה heard and was incensed: a fire of יהוה broke out against them, ravaging the outskirts of the camp. <sup>2</sup>The people cried out to Moses. Moses prayed to יהוה, and the fire died down. <sup>3</sup>That place was named Taberah, because a fire of יהוה had broken out against them.

<sup>4</sup>The riffraff in their midst felt a gluttonous craving; and then the Israelites wept and said, "If only we had meat to eat! <sup>5</sup>We remember the fish

קוּמָ֣ה ׀ יְהֹוָ֗ה

וְיָפֻ֙צוּ֙ אֹ֣יְבֶ֔יךָ

וְיָנֻ֥סוּ מְשַׂנְאֶ֖יךָ מִפָּנֶֽיךָ:

36 וּבְנֻחֹ֖ה יֹאמַ֑ר

שׁוּבָ֣ה יְהֹוָ֔ה

רִֽבְב֖וֹת אַלְפֵ֥י יִשְׂרָאֵֽל: ‪ ‬ פ

יא וַיְהִ֤י הָעָם֙ כְּמִתְאֹ֣נְנִ֔ים רַ֖ע בְּאָזְנֵ֣י יְהֹוָ֑ה וַיִּשְׁמַ֤ע יְהֹוָה֙ וַיִּ֣חַר אַפּ֔וֹ וַתִּבְעַר־בָּם֙ אֵ֣שׁ יְהֹוָ֔ה וַתֹּ֖אכַל בִּקְצֵ֥ה הַֽמַּחֲנֶֽה: 2 וַיִּצְעַ֥ק הָעָ֖ם אֶל־מֹשֶׁ֑ה וַיִּתְפַּלֵּ֤ל מֹשֶׁה֙ אֶל־יְהֹוָ֔ה וַתִּשְׁקַ֖ע הָאֵֽשׁ: 3 וַיִּקְרָ֛א שֵֽׁם־הַמָּק֥וֹם הַה֖וּא תַּבְעֵרָ֑ה כִּֽי־בָעֲרָ֥ה בָ֖ם אֵ֥שׁ יְהֹוָֽה:

4 וְהָֽאסַפְסֻף֙ אֲשֶׁ֣ר בְּקִרְבּ֔וֹ הִתְאַוּ֖וּ תַּֽאֲוָ֑ה וַיָּשֻׁ֣בוּ וַיִּבְכּ֗וּ גַּ֚ם בְּנֵ֣י יִשְׂרָאֵ֔ל וַיֹּ֣אמְר֔וּ מִ֥י יַֽאֲכִלֵ֖נוּ בָּשָֽׂר: 5 זָכַ֙רְנוּ֙ אֶת־הַדָּגָ֔ה אֲשֶׁר־

- - - - - - - - - - - - - - - - - - - - - - -

## Israelite Challenges to Moses and God (11:1–12:16)

This unit describes three major challenges to Moses and God. In all three cases, fixed elements appear in a similar order: the sin of the people (or a group among the people); God's punishment; a petition to Moses requesting that the punishment be removed; Moses' prayer; the punishment's termination; and the naming of the site after the episode that occurred there.

### COMPLAINING (11:1–3)

This first tale of woe—the incident at Taberah—is exceedingly concise (three verses), yet it comprises an entire story. Despite its brevity, this episode is instructive in its content and can serve as a good introduction to all three challenges in this parashah; it contains all of the fixed elements described above.

*1. The people took to complaining.* This passage does not indicate what the people complained about. By not making the content of the complaint clear within these verses, the story of the incident

at Taberah suggests that their sin was in the very act of complaining.

*3. Taberah.* Heb. "fire." The site receives its name because of the divine wrathful fire that burns there as a consequence of the people's complaint.

### CRAVING MEAT (11:4–35)

This story is more complex and developed than the tale of the complainers (11:1–3), and its plot has more twists. In contrast to the previous episode, here the people's sin is specified: they crave meat. Moses, in anguish, places his two problems before God. How is he to carry all these people whom he did not produce? Where will he get meat to feed them? These two questions shape the structure and development of the story. God responds by commissioning seventy representative elders to help Moses and by providing meat.

*4. "If only we had meat to eat!"* This statement—literally "*Who* shall give us meat to eat?"—alludes to the people's lack of faith in God's will and ability to provide them with meat (compare Exodus 17:7).

that we used to eat free in Egypt, the cucumbers,
the melons, the leeks, the onions, and the garlic.
6 Now our gullets are shriveled. There is nothing at
all! Nothing but this manna to look to!"
7 Now the manna was like coriander seed, and in
color it was like bdellium. 8 The people would go
about and gather it, grind it between millstones or
pound it in a mortar, boil it in a pot, and make it
into cakes. It tasted like rich cream. 9 When the dew
fell on the camp at night, the manna would fall
upon it.

10 Moses heard the people weeping, every clan
apart, at the entrance of each tent. יהוה was very
angry, and Moses was distressed. 11 And Moses said
to יהוה, "Why have You dealt ill with Your servant,
and why have I not enjoyed Your favor, that You
have laid the burden of all this people upon me?
12 Did I produce all this people, did I engender
them, that You should say to me, 'Carry them in
your bosom as a caretaker carries an infant,' to the
land that You have promised on oath to their fa-

נֹאכַל בְּמִצְרַיִם חִנָּם אֵת הַקִּשֻּׁאִים וְאֵת
הָאֲבַטִּחִים וְאֶת־הֶחָצִיר וְאֶת־הַבְּצָלִים
וְאֶת־הַשּׁוּמִים׃ 6 וְעַתָּה נַפְשֵׁנוּ יְבֵשָׁה אֵין
כֹּל בִּלְתִּי אֶל־הַמָּן עֵינֵינוּ׃
7 וְהַמָּן כִּזְרַע־גַּד הוּא וְעֵינוֹ כְּעֵין הַבְּדֹלַח׃
8 שָׁטוּ הָעָם וְלָקְטוּ וְטָחֲנוּ בָרֵחַיִם אוֹ דָכוּ
בַּמְּדֹכָה וּבִשְּׁלוּ בַּפָּרוּר וְעָשׂוּ אֹתוֹ עֻגוֹת
וְהָיָה טַעְמוֹ כְּטַעַם לְשַׁד הַשָּׁמֶן׃ 9 וּבְרֶדֶת
הַטַּל עַל־הַמַּחֲנֶה לָיְלָה יֵרֵד הַמָּן עָלָיו׃
10 וַיִּשְׁמַע מֹשֶׁה אֶת־הָעָם בֹּכֶה
לְמִשְׁפְּחֹתָיו אִישׁ לְפֶתַח אָהֳלוֹ וַיִּחַר־
אַף יְהֹוָה מְאֹד וּבְעֵינֵי מֹשֶׁה רָע׃ 11 וַיֹּאמֶר
מֹשֶׁה אֶל־יְהֹוָה לָמָה הֲרֵעֹתָ לְעַבְדֶּךָ וְלָמָּה
לֹא־מָצָתִי חֵן בְּעֵינֶיךָ לָשׂוּם אֶת־מַשָּׂא
כָּל־הָעָם הַזֶּה עָלָי׃ 12 הֶאָנֹכִי הָרִיתִי אֵת
כָּל־הָעָם הַזֶּה אִם־אָנֹכִי יְלִדְתִּיהוּ כִּי־
תֹאמַר אֵלַי שָׂאֵהוּ בְחֵיקֶךָ כַּאֲשֶׁר יִשָּׂא
הָאֹמֵן אֶת־הַיֹּנֵק עַל הָאֲדָמָה אֲשֶׁר נִשְׁבַּעְתָּ

*5. "We remember the fish."* Their great craving leads them to fantasize nostalgically about the food they enjoyed in Egypt.

*6. "Nothing but this manna."* They express contempt for the manna, the gift of heaven, that descends from heaven each morning (see Exodus 16:21). They argue that it is unvarying and boring.

*7. Now the manna was like coriander seed.* The details about manna's virtues refute each of the arguments that the people raise, especially their claim that the manna is dry. Their complaints, together with this report of the manna's merits, reflect the people's gluttony and ingratitude. Their nostalgia for Egypt, which was known as their house of bondage (as in Exodus 13:3), shows their ingratitude for all the bounty that God showered and continues to shower upon them.

*11. Moses said to* **יהוה**. Moses turns to God before the punishment that befalls the people. Rather than praying that God's punishment be lifted from the people (as in the story of the complainers, 11:1–3), Moses here bares his soul regarding his own bitter fate and complains about the difficulty of leadership.

*12.* Moses' questions are rhetorical and the simple meaning of the verse is: "I did not produce all these people, so why do you put all this burden on me?" As he attempts to illustrate the absurdity of his situation, Moses uses motherhood as the ultimate symbol of devotion. He cites a mother's enormous love and compassion, concern for all of her children's needs, and boundless dedication. One way to read Moses' questions is that he is comparing himself to that ideal mother. [The rhetorical questions also suggest that it was not Moses who was Israel's mother, but rather God. The verbs that Moses uses specifically refer to pregnancy (*hariti*, here rendered as "produce") and birthing (*yalad'ti*,

thers? [13]Where am I to get meat to give to all this people, when they whine before me and say, 'Give us meat to eat!' [14]I cannot carry all this people by myself, for it is too much for me. [15]If You would deal thus with me, kill me rather, I beg You, and let me see no more of my wretchedness!"

[16]Then יהוה said to Moses, "Gather for Me seventy of Israel's elders of whom you have experience as elders and officers of the people, and bring them to the Tent of Meeting and let them take their place there with you. [17]I will come down and speak with you there, and I will draw upon the spirit that is on you and put it upon them; they shall share the burden of the people with you, and you shall not bear it alone. [18]And say to the people: Purify yourselves for tomorrow and you shall eat meat, for you have kept whining before יהוה and saying, 'If only we had meat to eat! Indeed, we were better off in Egypt!' יהוה will give you meat and you shall eat. [19]You shall eat not one day, not two, not even five days or ten or twenty, [20]but a whole month, until it comes out of your nostrils and becomes loathsome to you. For you have rejected

לַאֲבֹתָיו: 13 מֵאַ֫יִן לִ֣י בָּשָׂ֔ר לָתֵ֖ת לְכׇל־הָעָ֣ם הַזֶּ֑ה כִּֽי־יִבְכּ֤וּ עָלַי֙ לֵאמֹ֔ר תְּנָה־לָּ֥נוּ בָשָׂ֖ר וְנֹאכֵֽלָה: 14 לֹֽא־אוּכַ֤ל אָֽנֹכִי֙ לְבַדִּ֔י לָשֵׂ֖את אֶת־כׇּל־הָעָ֣ם הַזֶּ֑ה כִּ֥י כָבֵ֖ד מִמֶּֽנִּי: 15 וְאִם־כָּ֣כָה ׀ אַתְּ־עֹ֣שֶׂה לִּ֗י הׇרְגֵ֤נִי נָא֙ הָרֹ֔ג אִם־מָצָ֥אתִי חֵ֖ן בְּעֵינֶ֑יךָ וְאַל־אֶרְאֶ֖ה בְּרָעָתִֽי: פ

16 וַיֹּ֨אמֶר יְהֹוָ֜ה אֶל־מֹשֶׁ֗ה אֶסְפָה־לִּ֞י שִׁבְעִ֣ים אִישׁ֮ מִזִּקְנֵ֣י יִשְׂרָאֵל֒ אֲשֶׁ֣ר יָדַ֔עְתָּ כִּי־הֵ֛ם זִקְנֵ֥י הָעָ֖ם וְשֹׁטְרָ֑יו וְלָקַחְתָּ֤ אֹתָם֙ אֶל־אֹ֣הֶל מוֹעֵ֔ד וְהִֽתְיַצְּב֥וּ שָׁ֖ם עִמָּֽךְ: 17 וְיָרַדְתִּ֗י וְדִבַּרְתִּ֣י עִמְּךָ֮ שָׁם֒ וְאָצַלְתִּ֗י מִן־הָר֛וּחַ אֲשֶׁ֥ר עָלֶ֖יךָ וְשַׂמְתִּ֣י עֲלֵיהֶ֑ם וְנָשְׂא֤וּ אִתְּךָ֙ בְּמַשָּׂ֣א הָעָ֔ם וְלֹא־תִשָּׂ֥א אַתָּ֖ה לְבַדֶּֽךָ: 18 וְאֶל־הָעָ֣ם תֹּאמַ֗ר הִתְקַדְּשׁ֣וּ לְמָחָר֮ וַאֲכַלְתֶּ֣ם בָּשָׂר֒ כִּ֡י בְּכִיתֶם֩ בְּאׇזְנֵ֨י יְהֹוָ֜ה לֵאמֹ֗ר מִ֤י יַאֲכִלֵ֙נוּ֙ בָּשָׂ֔ר כִּי־ט֥וֹב לָ֖נוּ בְּמִצְרָ֑יִם וְנָתַ֨ן יְהֹוָ֥ה לָכֶ֛ם בָּשָׂ֖ר וַאֲכַלְתֶּֽם: 19 לֹ֣א י֥וֹם אֶחָ֛ד תֹּאכְל֖וּן וְלֹ֣א יוֹמָ֑יִם וְלֹ֣א ׀ חֲמִשָּׁ֣ה יָמִ֗ים וְלֹא֙ עֲשָׂרָ֣ה יָמִ֔ים וְלֹ֖א עֶשְׂרִ֥ים יֽוֹם: 20 עַ֣ד ׀ חֹ֣דֶשׁ יָמִ֗ים עַ֤ד אֲשֶׁר־יֵצֵא֙ מֵֽאַפְּכֶ֔ם וְהָיָ֥ה לָכֶ֖ם לְזָרָ֑א

here translated as "engender"). By implication Moses asserts that God is the one who—as it were—conceived Israel, was pregnant, gave birth to Israel, and now should carry Israel. Although Israel's God transcends gender, the Bible contains gendered images of the Divine: male imagery is more common (see at Exodus 15:3 and Deuteronomy 32:6), but we do find female imagery for God (see the introduction to Exodus 15:22–17:16, and see at Deuteronomy 32:13, 18). Here in Numbers we have a striking depiction of God that refers to women's activities such as giving birth. Moses uses such strong maternal language to characterize God's unique relationship with the people. —*Ed*.]

13. *"Where am I to get meat."* Before focusing on his own needs, Moses asks a question on behalf of the people.

16. *"Gather for Me seventy of Israel's elders."* God offers to divide the burden of leadership between Moses and seventy representative assistants.

17. *"I will draw upon the spirit that is on you."* In Exodus 19, Moses' father-in-law, Jethro, advised Moses to appoint judges in order to reduce his administrative burden. Here, the seventy elders, upon whom God bestows some of Moses' spirit, are to be selected to fill a prophetic-spiritual role.

18. *"tomorrow . . . you shall eat meat."* God's promise to provide meat in response to the people's craving is also a threat, as v. 20 makes unmistakably clear.

יהוה who is among you, by whining before [God] and saying, 'Oh, why did we ever leave Egypt!'"

21 But Moses said, "The people who are with me number six hundred thousand foot soldiers; yet You say, 'I will give them enough meat to eat for a whole month.' 22 Could enough flocks and herds be slaughtered to suffice them? Or could all the fish of the sea be gathered for them to suffice them?" 23 And יהוה answered Moses, "Is there a limit to יהוה's power? You shall soon see whether what I have said happens to you or not!"

24 Moses went out and reported the words of יהוה to the people. He gathered seventy of the people's elders and stationed them around the Tent. 25 Then, after coming down in a cloud and speaking to him, יהוה drew upon the spirit that was on him and put it upon the seventy representative elders. And when the spirit rested upon them, they spoke in ecstasy, but did not continue.

26 Two of the representatives, one named Eldad and the other Medad, had remained in camp; yet the spirit rested upon them—they were among those recorded, but they had not gone out to the Tent—and they spoke in ecstasy in the camp. 27 An assistant ran out and told Moses, saying, "Eldad and Medad are acting the prophet in the camp!" 28 And Joshua son of Nun, Moses' attendant from his youth, spoke up and said, "My lord Moses, restrain them!" 29 But Moses said to him, "Are you wrought up on my account? Would that all יהוה's people were prophets, that יהוה put [the divine]

יַ֗עַן כִּֽי־מְאַסְתֶּ֤ם אֶת־יְהוָה֙ אֲשֶׁ֣ר בְּקִרְבְּכֶ֔ם
וַתִּבְכּ֤וּ לְפָנָיו֙ לֵאמֹ֔ר לָ֥מָּה זֶּ֖ה יָצָ֥אנוּ
מִמִּצְרָֽיִם׃
21 וַיֹּ֘אמֶר֮ מֹשֶׁה֒ שֵׁשׁ־מֵא֤וֹת אֶ֙לֶף֙ רַגְלִ֔י הָעָ֕ם
אֲשֶׁ֥ר אָנֹכִ֖י בְּקִרְבּ֑וֹ וְאַתָּ֣ה אָמַ֗רְתָּ בָּשָׂר֙ אֶתֵּ֣ן
לָהֶ֔ם וְאָכְל֖וּ חֹ֥דֶשׁ יָמִֽים׃ 22 הֲצֹ֧אן וּבָקָ֛ר
יִשָּׁחֵ֥ט לָהֶ֖ם וּמָצָ֣א לָהֶ֑ם אִ֣ם אֶת־כָּל־
דְּגֵ֥י הַיָּ֛ם יֵאָסֵ֥ף לָהֶ֖ם וּמָצָ֥א לָהֶֽם׃ פ
23 וַיֹּ֤אמֶר יְהוָה֙ אֶל־מֹשֶׁ֔ה הֲיַ֥ד יְהוָ֖ה תִּקְצָ֑ר
עַתָּ֥ה תִרְאֶ֛ה הֲיִקְרְךָ֥ דְבָרִ֖י אִם־לֹֽא׃
24 וַיֵּצֵ֣א מֹשֶׁ֗ה וַיְדַבֵּר֙ אֶל־הָעָ֔ם אֵ֖ת דִּבְרֵ֣י
יְהוָ֑ה וַיֶּאֱסֹ֞ף שִׁבְעִ֥ים אִישׁ֙ מִזִּקְנֵ֣י הָעָ֔ם
וַיַּעֲמֵ֥ד אֹתָ֖ם סְבִיבֹ֥ת הָאֹֽהֶל׃ 25 וַיֵּ֨רֶד יְהוָ֥ה ׀
בֶּֽעָנָן֮ וַיְדַבֵּ֣ר אֵלָיו֒ וַיָּ֗אצֶל מִן־הָר֙וּחַ֙ אֲשֶׁ֣ר
עָלָ֔יו וַיִּתֵּ֕ן עַל־שִׁבְעִ֥ים אִ֖ישׁ הַזְּקֵנִ֑ים וַיְהִ֗י
כְּנ֤וֹחַ עֲלֵיהֶם֙ הָר֔וּחַ וַיִּֽתְנַבְּא֖וּ וְלֹ֥א יָסָֽפוּ׃
26 וַיִּשָּׁאֲר֣וּ שְׁנֵֽי־אֲנָשִׁ֣ים ׀ בַּֽמַּחֲנֶ֡ה שֵׁ֣ם
הָאֶחָ֣ד ׀ אֶלְדָּ֡ד וְשֵׁם֩ הַשֵּׁנִ֨י מֵידָ֜ד וַתָּ֧נַח
עֲלֵהֶ֣ם הָר֗וּחַ וְהֵ֙מָּה֙ בַּכְּתֻבִ֔ים וְלֹ֥א יָצְא֖וּ
הָאֹ֑הֱלָה וַיִּֽתְנַבְּא֖וּ בַּֽמַּחֲנֶה׃ 27 וַיָּ֣רָץ הַנַּ֔עַר
וַיַּגֵּ֥ד לְמֹשֶׁ֖ה וַיֹּאמַ֑ר אֶלְדָּ֣ד וּמֵידָ֔ד מִֽתְנַבְּאִ֖ים
בַּֽמַּחֲנֶֽה׃ 28 וַיַּ֜עַן יְהוֹשֻׁ֣עַ בִּן־נ֗וּן מְשָׁרֵ֥ת
מֹשֶׁ֛ה מִבְּחֻרָ֖יו וַיֹּאמַ֑ר אֲדֹנִ֥י מֹשֶׁ֖ה כְּלָאֵֽם׃
29 וַיֹּ֤אמֶר לוֹ֙ מֹשֶׁ֔ה הַֽמְקַנֵּ֥א אַתָּ֖ה לִ֑י וּמִ֨י
יִתֵּ֜ן כָּל־עַ֤ם יְהוָה֙ נְבִיאִ֔ים כִּֽי־יִתֵּ֧ן יְהוָ֛ה

***26. they spoke in ecstasy in the camp.*** Eldad and Medad stir up a tempest by prophesying in the camp without having Moses' spirit bestowed upon them among the seventy elders (vv. 24–25).

***27–28.*** First, a young assistant runs to Moses, in excitement and alarm, to inform him about this irregular behavior. Next comes Joshua, who suggests that the offenders be restrained, either as a punishment or to prevent further illegitimate prophecy.

***29. "Would that all יהוה's people were prophets."*** Only Moses, with enormous generosity of spirit, reacts with happiness and acceptance. He is neither threatened nor jealous but, instead, expresses a desire that there be more, rather than fewer, prophets among God's people. (His response is all the more striking given God's reaction to Miriam and Aaron's boast of their prophetic gifts; see at Numbers 12.)

spirit upon them!" [30]Moses then reentered the camp together with the elders of Israel.

[31]A wind from יהוה started up, swept quail from the sea and strewed them over the camp, about a day's journey on this side and about a day's journey on that side, all around the camp, and some two cubits deep on the ground. [32]The people set to gathering quail all that day and night and all the next day—even the one who gathered least had ten *chomers*—and they spread them out all around the camp. [33]The meat was still between their teeth, not yet chewed, when the anger of יהוה blazed forth against the people and יהוה struck the people with a very severe plague. [34]That place was named Kibroth-hattaavah, because the people who had the craving were buried there.

[35]Then the people set out from Kibroth-hattaavah for Hazeroth.

אֶת־רוּחוֹ עֲלֵיהֶֽם: 30 וַיֵּאָסֵף מֹשֶׁה אֶל־הַֽמַּחֲנֶה הוּא וְזִקְנֵי יִשְׂרָאֵֽל: 31 וְרוּחַ נָסַע ׀ מֵאֵת יְהוָה וַיָּגָז שַׂלְוִים מִן־הַיָּם וַיִּטֹּשׁ עַל־הַֽמַּחֲנֶה כְּדֶרֶךְ יוֹם כֹּה וּכְדֶרֶךְ יוֹם כֹּה סְבִיבוֹת הַֽמַּחֲנֶה וּכְאַמָּתַיִם עַל־פְּנֵי הָאָֽרֶץ: 32 וַיָּקָם הָעָם כָּל־הַיּוֹם הַהוּא וְכָל־הַלַּיְלָה וְכֹל ׀ יוֹם הַֽמָּחֳרָת וַיַּֽאַסְפוּ אֶת־הַשְּׂלָו הַמַּמְעִיט אָסַף עֲשָׂרָה חֳמָרִים וַיִּשְׁטְחוּ לָהֶם שָׁטוֹחַ סְבִיבוֹת הַֽמַּחֲנֶֽה: 33 הַבָּשָׂר עוֹדֶנּוּ בֵּין שִׁנֵּיהֶם טֶרֶם יִכָּרֵת וְאַף יְהוָה חָרָה בָעָם וַיַּךְ יְהוָה בָּעָם מַכָּה רַבָּה מְאֹֽד: 34 וַיִּקְרָא אֶת־שֵׁם־הַמָּקוֹם הַהוּא קִבְרוֹת הַֽתַּאֲוָה כִּי־שָׁם קָֽבְרוּ אֶת־הָעָם הַמִּתְאַוִּֽים: 35 מִקִּבְרוֹת הַֽתַּאֲוָה נָסְעוּ הָעָם חֲצֵרוֹת

* * * * * * * * * * * * * * * * * * *

*31–33.* In response to Moses' petition in v. 13— "Where am I to get meat?"—God supplies meat from an unexpected source: a flock of quail blown in by sea wind, which arrives at the Israelite camp. The plentiful quantity suffices for the entire people. However, the people's craving and hunger are so great that they fall upon the birds without restraint or embarrassment, filling their mouths and bellies. Their frenzied consumption of the quails causes a plague that spreads among those who consume them.

*34. Kibroth-hattaavah.* The people bury the many victims at a site whose name translates as "Graves of Craving." This name indicates that the people's sin is in craving for meat when God has already provided sufficient manna to sustain them. The Torah blames the people for not making do with manna as their food.

Generally speaking, the Torah displays a multi-faceted relationship to meat consumption. Genesis

1:29 seems to advocate vegetarianism; Genesis 9:4 and Deuteronomy 12:16 allow eating meat but prohibit the consumption of blood; Leviticus 11 and Deuteronomy 14 limit the consumption of meat to specific animals. Only in reference to meat consumption does the Torah use the verb "crave" (also Deuteronomy 12:15, 20, 21). [At the same time, priests and other Israelites are expected to eat the meat that they have together consecrated as sacrifices (see Leviticus 1–7). —*Ed.*]

If cravings for meat so angered God, then why does God supply the people with what they ask, and in such great quantities? The story indicates that God's intent in bringing the quails is chiefly "educational," to prove God's unlimited powers to the people. On the one hand, God has power complete enough to satisfy all creatures' needs, if God so desires. On the other hand, God is liable, where needed, to punish them as well.

When they were in Hazeroth, 12 Miriam
and Aaron spoke against Moses because of the
Cushite woman he had married: "He married a
Cushite woman!"
2They said, "Has יהוה spoken only through
Moses? Has [God] not spoken through us as well?"
יהוה heard it. 3Now Moses was a very humble
leader, more so than any other human being on

וַיִּהְיוּ בַּחֲצֵרוֹת׃ פ יב וַתְּדַבֵּר מִרְיָם
וְאַהֲרֹן בְּמֹשֶׁה עַל־אֹדוֹת הָאִשָּׁה הַכֻּשִׁית
אֲשֶׁר לָקָח כִּי־אִשָּׁה כֻשִׁית לָקָח׃
2 וַיֹּאמְרוּ הֲרַק אַךְ־בְּמֹשֶׁה דִּבֶּר יְהֹוָה הֲלֹא
גַּם־בָּנוּ דִבֵּר וַיִּשְׁמַע יְהֹוָה׃ 3 וְהָאִישׁ מֹשֶׁה
ענו עָנָיו מְאֹד מִכֹּל הָאָדָם אֲשֶׁר עַל־פְּנֵי

## CRITICIZING MOSES: MIRIAM, AARON, AND THE CUSHITE WOMAN (12:1–16)

The presence of two female characters stands out in this story. One, Miriam, is active and central; she constitutes the story's axis. The other, Moses' unnamed wife, called the "dark-skinned" or "Cushite" woman, is unseen and silent; though from her behind-the-scenes position, she is the story's catalyst. The story constitutes a family drama of siblings who speak out against their brother and his wife.

This section contains numerous gaps, making it difficult to bridge from one verse to the next (particularly in the first three verses) and provoking a variety of questions—as discussed in turn, below.

*1. Miriam and Aaron spoke against Moses.* The verb "spoke" is in the feminine singular form, indicating that Miriam is the chief spokesperson.

*Cushite woman.* Heb. *cushit*, which may have been understood either to mean "Cushite" (that is, from Cush) or "dark-skinned." In the Bible, Cush seems to be located in the south of Egypt, east of Sudan. However, references to *cushim* (Cushites, plural) pertain to tribes who lived in different places in Africa and Asia, as well as in the southern part of ancient Israel. The Bible refers to Cushites with awareness of their dark skin (Jeremiah 13:23). In Jeremiah 38:7–13, a Cushite saves Jeremiah's life. In Amos 9:7, Cushites are presented as equal to Israelites in God's view.

*he had married.* Who is this woman? Have we encountered her before? Is she Zipporah, the wife of Moses and the daughter of the Midianite priest (Exodus 2:21)? If so, she may well have been "dark-skinned" (Ibn Ezra). Or, is this another wife—unnamed and mentioned in the Bible only here—a native of Ethiopia, whom Moses married in addition to Zipporah, or after Moses sent Zipporah home (see Exodus 18:2)?

*"He married a Cushite woman!"* What is Miriam and Aaron's complaint against their brother and his marriage? Are they attacking Moses for marrying a woman with dark skin? Is it a diatribe against marriage outside of the Israelite tribal structure?

*2. "Has* יהוה *spoken only through Moses?"* What connection does the previously mentioned woman bear to this complaint about Moses in relation to his siblings' prophetic roles? The statement highlights one of several crucial gaps in this story. As prophets themselves, the siblings may think that they are entitled to the same privileged status accorded Moses. Indeed, if status is Miriam and Aaron's primary concern, then perhaps they oppose Moses' marriage because his wife is of the "wrong" status. Alternatively, this complaint may parallel what will be expressed by Korah and his assembly when they accuse Moses and Aaron of exalting themselves "above" God's congregation (16:1–3).

*3.* The Torah insists that Moses, far from raising himself above others, is more modest than any other human being on earth. Moses, in his great humility, does not react or protest Miriam and Aaron's words. That is why God now proceeds to intervene on behalf of Moses, reproaching Miriam and Aaron.

earth. [4]Suddenly יהוה called to Moses, Aaron, and Miriam, "Come out, you three, to the Tent of Meeting." So the three of them went out. [5]יהוה came down in a pillar of cloud, stopped at the entrance of the Tent, and called out, "Aaron and Miriam!" The two of them came forward; [6]and [God] said, "Hear these My words: When prophets of יהוה arise among you, I make Myself known to them in a vision, I speak with them in a dream. [7]Not so with My servant Moses; he is trusted throughout My household. [8]With him I speak mouth to mouth, plainly and not in riddles, and he beholds the likeness of יהוה. How then did you not shrink from speaking against My servant Moses!" [9]Still incensed with them, יהוה departed.

[10]As the cloud withdrew from the Tent, there was Miriam stricken with snow-white scales! When Aaron turned toward Miriam, he saw that she was

הָאֲדָמָה׃ ס 4 וַיֹּאמֶר יְהֹוָה פִּתְאֹם
אֶל־מֹשֶׁה וְאֶל־אַהֲרֹן וְאֶל־מִרְיָם צְאוּ
שְׁלָשְׁתְּכֶם אֶל־אֹהֶל מוֹעֵד וַיֵּצְאוּ שְׁלָשְׁתָּם׃
5 וַיֵּרֶד יְהֹוָה בְּעַמּוּד עָנָן וַיַּעֲמֹד פֶּתַח
הָאֹהֶל וַיִּקְרָא אַהֲרֹן וּמִרְיָם וַיֵּצְאוּ שְׁנֵיהֶם׃
6 וַיֹּאמֶר שִׁמְעוּ־נָא דְבָרָי אִם־יִהְיֶה נְבִיאֲכֶם
יְהֹוָה בַּמַּרְאָה אֵלָיו אֶתְוַדָּע בַּחֲלוֹם אֲדַבֶּר־
בּוֹ׃ 7 לֹא־כֵן עַבְדִּי מֹשֶׁה בְּכָל־בֵּיתִי נֶאֱמָן
הוּא׃ 8 פֶּה אֶל־פֶּה אֲדַבֶּר־בּוֹ וּמַרְאֶה וְלֹא
בְחִידֹת וּתְמֻנַת יְהֹוָה יַבִּיט וּמַדּוּעַ לֹא
יְרֵאתֶם לְדַבֵּר בְּעַבְדִּי בְמֹשֶׁה׃ 9 וַיִּחַר־אַף
יְהֹוָה בָּם וַיֵּלַךְ׃
10 וְהֶעָנָן סָר מֵעַל הָאֹהֶל וְהִנֵּה מִרְיָם
מְצֹרַעַת כַּשָּׁלֶג וַיִּפֶן אַהֲרֹן אֶל־מִרְיָם וְהִנֵּה

*4.* **יהוה** ***called to Moses, Aaron, and Miriam.*** All three siblings are summoned, with Miriam in the third position—as in the words of the prophet Micah (Micah 6:4).

*6.* ***"Hear these My words."*** God speaks in the second person *plural*, censuring both Miriam and Aaron; but only Miriam will be punished (below). God's verbal castigation of the siblings only addresses the issue of Moses' prophetic leadership and not the issue of Moses' marriage.

*7.* ***"Not so with My servant Moses."*** God asserts that Moses' prophetic status is unique. This undermines both of the siblings' demand that their prophetic status be honored.

*8.* ***"mouth to mouth."*** God describes the great and unique intimacy between Moses and God, as well as the unique authority of Moses as God's spokesperson. Only Moses receives words directly from God, whereas all other prophets have access to the Divine through other means, like dreams and visions.

*10.* ***there was Miriam.*** Why is Miriam alone punished for the siblings' complaint? Is it because she is a woman who demands a leading position? Many commentaries hold that she—and not Aaron—is punished because she is the primary speaker against Moses. Whereas both of them complain about Moses' prophetic status (v. 2 uses the plural verb *vayomru*), it is possible that only Miriam criticizes Moses' marriage (v. 1 uses the feminine singular *va-t'daber*); and thus only Miriam receives God's punishment for that criticism. Some contemporary commentators, who consider the text here to be sexist, also argue that Miriam alone is punished because she is a woman who dares challenge authority. However, if we understand the word *cushit* ("Cushite" in our translation) to mean "dark-skinned," then Miriam may be punished for insulting a dark-skinned woman. She alone turns white (in an ironic twist) because she alone spoke out on that particular subject.

***stricken with snow-white scales.*** [The same words describe the temporary condition of Moses' hand in Exodus 4:6 when God prepares him to face Pharaoh. There the condition implies an example, not a punishment. In II Kings 5:27, the only other

stricken with scales. [11]And Aaron said to Moses, "O my lord, account not to us the sin which we committed in our folly. [12]Let her not be as a stillbirth which emerges from its mother's womb with half its flesh eaten away!" [13]So Moses cried out to יהוה, saying, "O God, pray heal her!"

[14]But יהוה said to Moses, "If her father spat in her face, would she not bear her shame for seven days? Let her be shut out of camp for seven days, and then let her be readmitted." [15]So Miriam was shut out of camp seven days; and the people did not march on until Miriam was readmitted. [16]After that the people set out from Hazeroth and encamped in the wilderness of Paran.

מְצֹרָעַת׃ 11 וַיֹּאמֶר אַהֲרֹן אֶל־מֹשֶׁה בִּי
אֲדֹנִי אַל־נָא תָשֵׁת עָלֵינוּ חַטָּאת אֲשֶׁר
נוֹאַלְנוּ וַאֲשֶׁר חָטָאנוּ׃ 12 אַל־נָא תְהִי כַּמֵּת
אֲשֶׁר בְּצֵאתוֹ מֵרֶחֶם אִמּוֹ וַיֵּאָכֵל חֲצִי
בְשָׂרוֹ׃ 13 וַיִּצְעַק מֹשֶׁה אֶל־יְהֹוָה לֵאמֹר אֵל
נָא רְפָא נָא לָהּ׃
14 וַיֹּאמֶר יְהֹוָה אֶל־מֹשֶׁה וְאָבִיהָ יָרֹק יָרַק
בְּפָנֶיהָ הֲלֹא תִכָּלֵם שִׁבְעַת יָמִים תִּסָּגֵר
שִׁבְעַת יָמִים מִחוּץ לַמַּחֲנֶה וְאַחַר תֵּאָסֵף׃
15 וַתִּסָּגֵר מִרְיָם מִחוּץ לַמַּחֲנֶה שִׁבְעַת
יָמִים וְהָעָם לֹא נָסַע עַד־הֵאָסֵף מִרְיָם׃
16 וְאַחַר נָסְעוּ הָעָם מֵחֲצֵרוֹת וַיַּחֲנוּ בְּמִדְבַּר
פָּארָן׃ פ

use of these words, the expression refers to a punishment. —*Ed.*]

*11.* ***"the sin which we committed."*** Aaron confesses both his and Miriam's sin and asks for forgiveness for Miriam.

*12.* ***"Let her not be as a stillbirth."*** As her partner in crime, Aaron intervenes on Miriam's behalf; this is fitting since all the burden of punishment has fallen upon her.

***"half its flesh eaten away."*** This description conveys an association with death. Commentators suggest that this is why *tzaraat* (scale disease) is subject to special strictures (see *parashat M'tzora*).

*13.* ***"O God, pray heal her!"*** Moses reacts immediately to Aaron's words, without any grudge or hesitation. The words of his succinct prayer seeking his sister's cure have since become part of Jewish healing services (see Contemporary Reflection, p. 864).

*14.* ***"If her father spat in her face, would she not bear her shame for seven days?"*** God's response includes a symbolic punishment after Moses' intercession. The full ramifications of God's explanation remain obscure. Three points, however, are clear. First, God's words imply that the reason for the seven days' seclusion is shame—like the shame that befalls a daughter who was insulted by her father. This is not like the usual seclusion of the *m'tzora* (the person stricken with scale disease; see at Leviticus 13). Second, the statement (that a daughter is shamed for seven days when her father spits on her) discloses something of an assumed and accepted practice in the community. Third, the father-daughter analogy seems to soften the harshness of the incident by referring to God as father and Miriam as God's daughter: she is still a member of God's household, as it were (compare v. 7).

***"Let her be shut out of camp for seven days."*** Miriam is to be quarantined outside the camp. Leviticus 13 prescribes a seven-day seclusion for a person stricken with *tzaraat* (a scale disease). But here God uses a different rationale for Miriam's seclusion (see previous comment). On the relative leniency of this punishment, see the introduction to Numbers 16:1–35. Miriam's affliction and quarantine are referred to again in Deuteronomy 24:8–9.

*15.* ***the people did not march on until Miriam was readmitted.*** Without necessarily taking sides in Miriam's dispute with Moses, the people demonstrate their solidarity with her by waiting until she can rejoin the camp.

—*Masha Turner*

# Another View

IT IS HARD TO KNOW what to make of the story of Miriam: she is afflicted with snow-white scales for daring to challenge Moses—and by implication, God (12:1–16). First of all, this reader is outraged. Why is Miriam punished, but not her brother Aaron? And why is she punished at all, given the legitimacy of their complaint against Moses? Like so many passages in the Torah, *B'haalot'cha* seems to express values that are difficult to accept. Upon reflection, though, this reader's outrage is softened—for there is much here that speaks to the power of women, even as it reflects unease about their authoritative voice.

Moses has married a foreign woman and his siblings complain, perhaps upset that Moses continues to lead Israel despite violating the law while they, leaders who are guilty of no such wrong, remain subject to his authority. Imagine their surprise when God responds directly to their complaint—and their dismay when God chastises them and supports Moses. Aaron seems not to suffer for his insubordination, but Miriam's punishment is described in detail. She is afflicted with a horrible skin ailment that threatens to place her in a state of ritual impurity and block her access to God's holiness. As if this were not enough, she must remain outside the Israelite encampment for a full week, like a disobedient daughter shamed by her father.

At first, the story of snow-white Miriam seems a perfect example of a double standard, for God permits the brother independent thought but punishes the sister for the very same ideas and words. Still, the story is more than that, for it shows us how much all of Israel valued Miriam. Her brothers plead for her, as Aaron beseeches Moses and then Moses prays to God to reverse their sister's punishment. And the people do not respond by abandoning this victim of God's great anger. Rather, they "did not march on until Miriam was readmitted" seven days later (v. 15), thus expressing their solidarity with the woman who in happier times led them in victory song and celebration (Exodus 15:20–21). —*Beth Alpert Nakhai*

*This reader finds the story of snow-white Miriam to be outrageous—at least at first.*

# Post-biblical Interpretations

***Miriam and Aaron spoke against Moses*** (12:1). This episode raises several concerns. God nominates male priests, male Levites, and male elders to run the enterprise of Israel, whereas women are all but absent. The only women we meet are Moses' sister Miriam, who speaks (out of turn), and his Ethiopian wife, who is silent. In Exodus 15:20, Miriam had been designated as a prophet, and she now claims a prophetic role for herself. Yet, although Miriam and Aaron both discuss Moses' wife, it is only Miriam who is punished for her words.

The question of God's partial administration of justice is the only one of these issues that is explored in the Rabbis' discourse on this parashah. The tannaitic Midrash *Sifrei B'midbar* 99 raises the inequity of Miriam's treatment and answers with the words: "This shows that it was Miriam who first raised the issue." That is, Miriam was responsible for initiating the critical conversation about Moses' wife and thus was the person punished. Yet, not all the Rabbis were happy with this superficial solution. In BT *Shabbat* 97a, Rabbi Akiva argues that Aaron too was afflicted with leprosy, based on the notice in v. 9 that God was "incensed with *them*" (plural). However, this is a minority view; the general opinion in that talmudic passage is that Aaron was not similarly stricken. Another halachic midrash, *Sifra, M'tzora* 5.7, identifies *tzaraat* as the quintessential punishment for slander,

*Women are subordinate to men—say various midrashim—and it should stay that way.*

and it emphasizes that Miriam's contraction of *tzaraat* (Numbers 12:10) was the result of her denunciation of Moses, essentially because she slandered him behind his back.

The sages were also interested in solving the apparent contradiction between what we hear about Moses' marrying an Ethiopian woman and what we know about his marriage to the Midianite woman, Zipporah (Exodus 2:21). Earlier Jewish Hellenistic literature suggested that young Moses—while still an Egyptian prince—had carried out a campaign against Ethiopia and there married an Ethiopian princess (Josephus, *Antiquities* 252–3). Yet the Rabbis do not adopt this solution. In their opinion, the Ethiopian woman is none other than Zipporah herself, and thus they need to explain why she is called Ethiopian—and why Miriam and Aaron found it necessary to speak about her. Already in *Sifrei B'midbar* 99, we learn that Miriam spoke against Moses because he had refrained from having sexual intercourse with Zipporah ever since God had begun speaking to him face to face. The Rabbis tell us that Miriam and Zipporah had been standing together when the news came that Eldad and Medad were prophesying. Zipporah remarked that she felt pity for their wives, for they would now suffer her fate, meaning that their husbands would no longer sleep with them. Miriam then said to Aaron, "Why does Moses have to behave this way? Has not God also spoken to us, and we have not refrained from sex with our spouses?" (*Sifrei B'midbar* 99). Obviously the question that bothers the Rabbis here is a contrived one, not actually found in the Bible: namely, the connection between holiness and refraining from sexual activity. It is likely that this discussion originates in rabbinic knowledge of contemporaneous non-Jewish practices that advocated celibacy of religious leaders.

If the wife that Moses took, and about whom Miriam and Aaron spoke, was actually Zipporah, the Rabbis still needed to explain why she was designated as Ethiopian. They explained that the term *kushit*, usually translated as Ethiopian or Cushite, in fact refers to exceptional beauty. Just as Ethiopians are unusual in their skin color, so was Zipporah unusual to behold (*Sifrei B'midbar* 99). This interpretation removes from the biblical text any hint of bigotry, but leaves one with the lingering feeling that Ethiopian skin color is at some level an issue.

Much of rabbinic interpretation on this episode is concerned with correct hierarchy and gender ordering. The same midrash that states that it was Miriam who initiated this conversation about Moses' wife comments that it was unusual for her to speak to her brother Aaron before she was spoken to (*Sifrei B'midbar* 99). Another early midrash teaches that if Miriam was punished for speaking against her younger brother, one should all the more so refrain from speaking against one's superiors (*Sifrei D'varim* 1). Midrash *D'varim Rabbah* 6.12 notices the absence of the title "prophet" here in connection with Miriam and suggests that this is a warning that slanderous talk brings about loss of status. Midrash *B'reishit Rabbah* 45.5 cites this episode to denigrate women in general as overly talkative. The import of all these texts is that women are viewed as subordinate to men and that society should endeavor to maintain men's gender-based prerogatives.

Yet the Rabbis too are aware of Miriam's unique status. In Mishnah *Sotah* 1:9, the notice that "the people did not march on until Miriam was readmitted" (12:15) is interpreted as proof that "a human being is treated according to how that person treats others" (Mishnah *Sotah* 1:7). Miriam herself had many years earlier waited for her infant brother Moses after his mother had set him afloat in the Nile (Exodus 2:4). For this, according to the Rabbis, she was rewarded at the end of Numbers 12, when the Israelites did not continue their march without her.

*—Tal Ilan*

• • •

# Contemporary Reflection

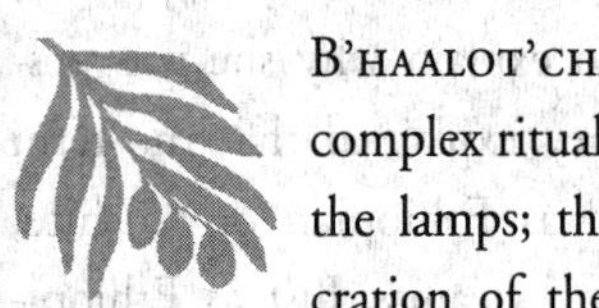

B'HAALOT'CHA IS OVERFLOWING with complex ritual and detail: the lighting of the lamps; the purification and consecration of the Levites; the elaboration of the *pesach* sacrifice; the carefully choreographed journey through the wilderness; the mutiny of meat, manna, and quail precipitating a plague for those who were led by their appetites; the challenge of Moses' siblings to his leadership; and finally, the sudden onset of his sister Miriam's disease. Yet amidst these richly detailed stories, we find one contrasting, stark, parsimonious prayer: "*El na r'fa na lah*" ("O God, pray heal her!").

Five words—eleven Hebrew letters—are all that Moses speaks (12:13). Except for God's name, each word ends in a vowel, as if each word were an unending cry. It is as if each word is punctuated with an exclamation point, the brevity of the syllables giving voice to the tortured helplessness of the supplicant: "God! Please! Heal! Please! Her!" In the midst of catastrophe, the verb of consequence—the bull's-eye of the prayer—is the central plea: heal! Indeed, the prayer is nearly a palindrome—reading the same forwards as it does backwards—homing in with laser precision on that most urgent desire: heal!

This prayer has few words but much resonance. It is a primal cry, capturing fear, powerlessness, and incomprehensibility in the face of sudden illness, accident, or injury. It is not the entreaty of the one beset by the catastrophe, but rather that of the witness, the powerless onlooker, the potential caregiver absorbing the shock, the one who is overwhelmed and stymied about how to help.

When illness, accident, or injury comes to those we love, it is up to us—those who are comparatively healthy and able—not only to beseech but also to provide hope and healing. For the caregiver, there is time only for truncated and hurried prayer, time only for stolen moments of naked cries and yearnings of hope. For the caregiver shouldering the burdens of action—making the loved one comfortable, researching treatment, running interference with physicians, reporting news, calming fears—prayer is a blessed moment of calm in an otherwise turbulent time.

*The essence of what we seek is still found in Moses' direct and eternal prayer.*

When one whom we love is in danger, not only our loved one but also we ourselves face darkness. According to Jewish tradition, the first person who prayed in darkness was young Jacob, on the eve of his exile from home. The Midrash describes the confluence of physical and metaphorical darkness this way: "In order to speak to Jacob in private, God caused the sun to go down—like a king who calls for the light to be extinguished, as he wishes to speak to his friend in private" (*B'reishit Rabbah* 68.10). So, too, the prayer of the caregiver is private, conspiratorial, hidden from the one who is the object of supplication, yet revealed to the One who can respond. We want to protect the one who is suffering from the compounded weight of the caregiver's distress. But in the darkness, it is safe to give voice to our fear of dreadful scenarios and of the unknown. In the darkness, it is a relief to relinquish the weight of trying to hold up another's spirits, and to acknowledge that Someone with far more power than we possess is the ultimate caregiver. In the darkness, it is possible to renew courage, to find new paths, to discover the equanimity essential to living with the terror of catastrophe.

Medical sociologist Alexandra Dundas Todd begins *Double Vision*, a memoir of her son's treatment and recovery from brain cancer, with this reflection:

> "The Chinese word for crisis consists of two characters: danger and opportunity. When my son, Drew, a senior in college, was diagnosed with a rare form of cancer bordering his brain, the danger was clear; the opportunity was less apparent. Danger flashed through our lives daily, while opportunities lay waiting in murky waters, to emerge only tentatively. Family closeness, the ability to savor each moment, to find strength and courage where we didn't know they existed, to discover new methods of treatment that complemented all the surgeries and radiation and eased both body and mind, all contributed to making the unbearable bearable, turning an assault into a challenge" (*Double Vision: An East-West Collaboration for Coping with Cancer*, 1994, p. xiii).

It does, indeed, take "double vision" to see both blessing and curse, to picture opportunity amidst danger. Courage grows through hope, through the willingness to look for unknown possibilities and to grasp them, through refusing to see only *danger* in darkness when its counterpart, *opportunity*, may be waiting in the shadows. The prayer of the caregiver, the cry of the distraught parent, the reassuring whisper of the loving spouse, can help to wrest some measure of opportunity out of danger.

*El na r'fa na la.* In its simplicity and raw clarity, this prayer of healing recognizes that more than double vision, the vision of the Divine is immeasurable, and the capacity of the Healer is limitless. In response to Moses' prayer, God reveals the duration of Miriam's exile to the wilderness of disease. Her fortunate loved ones have only to wait out a time of disequilibrium and uncertainty; they have received Sacred reassurance that all will be well. Yet in anticipating her return, the Torah conveys a truth well known to the loved ones of someone contending with affliction and crisis—*v'haam lo nasa ad heasef miryam* ("and the people did not march on until Miriam was readmitted," 12:15). Life does not go on with any sense of normalcy or progression while one whom we love is endangered; the caregiver's attention and effort revolves around the one who is stricken. Time and space are altered. The yearning for healing expands to fill both.

Our present rituals may not be as formulaic as those described in *B'haalot'cha*; our contemporary prayers of healing may have become longer and more specific; our modern understanding of treatment may be more nuanced and comprehensive; but Moses' wisdom abides. The essence of what we seek is still found in his direct and eternal prayer. *El na r'fa na la*: God! Please! Heal! Please! Her!

*—Patricia Karlin-Neumann*

# Voices

## *from* An Opening Ceremony

Vicki Hollander

*Numbers 10:10*

Like the moon,
we shed our layers.
Leave them at the door.
We who caretake life.
We who are healers.
We who are doers.
We who mother
the world....

The moon now glides toward darkness,
toward rest.
She retreats
in order to emerge
whole.
She quiets
in order to
fill night
with light.

So too shall we
make a space for ourselves.
A space of renewal.
So we who nourish life
can emerge as the moon,
bearing
our light
our touch
to aid in repairing our world.

## Mother to Mother

Tikva Frymer-Kensky

*Numbers 11:12*

When you were pregnant with Israel, Lord
—did your ankles swell?
—did your fingers tingle and droop?
Did you spend your time waiting, marking time,
and doing infinite chores?

After you announced the birth of the nation
knowing it would be long, three generations long,
till the birth of the people on its land—
After you announced the birth, Lord—
did you sit counting the days and the years?
Did you plan on how you would raise Ephraim,
your darling child?
how you would call him from Egypt,
draw him with cords of love?
Did you count the days
till you could teach him to walk?
till you could bend down and feed him each morsel?
When you carried Israel in your womb,
O Lord,
did you think how you would nurture forever,
how you would carry him till old-age?
Did you plan every moment of his upbringing,
dreaming of the perfect child?
Or were you very busy, Lord,
planning universes,
setting up laws,
organizing history?

## *Miriam*

Yocheved Bat-Miriam (transl. Ilana Pardes)

*Numbers 12*

She stood facing the reeds and papyrus
and breathed in stars and desert.
The round sleeping eye of Apis
flooded its glimmered blue

on the sand, on its golden rustle,
on the smile of a hidden princess,
on a dialogue between hieroglyphs on stone
and a marched palace song.

At a distance, in the fertile soil of memory,
like a horned viper in everlasting desire,
trampled Goshen adopted
a dim tribal imagination.

—With you, with you in the storm
your body twisting like a timbrel,
with you in your dance facing fervor
smell of dunes and infinity.

—I will speak jealous and leprous,
I will speak complaining of myself.
I adjure you in your unsurrendered
monasticism
in your resplendent isolation—do live!

She stood rocked by the spell
as by the white of the wave's beats.
She bent over the baby as a vow,
as decree,
as redemption,
as fate.

## *Autumn Measure*

Robin Becker

*Numbers 12:13*

Violence done to the body
to save the body: tomorrow
my friend will leave the hospital
without her breasts. We say *at least*
*she has her life, her work, her legs.*
Fate's impersonal face looks back
at me from every burning bush.
The crack I hear isn't a bullet
but another apple falling
hard on the tin roof overhead.

## *Untitled*

Drora Setel

*Numbers 12*

The girl's name is forgotten
but we know of her skill.
Assisting the midwives,
she carried water from the river
in preparation for the birth.
It was she who circled the bed and sang,
her voice a liturgy
of guidance for the woman in labor,
of celebration for a safe delivery,
of delight in a healthy baby,
of mourning for those who died in the process.

The woman's name is known
but its meaning was forgotten.
Some said "bitter"—
bitter with jealousy
bitter with sorrow
bitter with barrenness
bitter with shame
Because her power was forgotten.

## *For Days Miriam Sat Outside*

Wendy Zierler

*Numbers 12*

Before she could utter another word, a dark cloud appeared and rumbled above Miriam and Aaron like a rebuke. When the cloud lifted, as suddenly as it appeared, the skin on Miriam's arm was covered with snow-white scales. In panic and confusion, Aaron banished her from the camp. For days, Miriam sat in exile, her arm a scaly blaze of white fire. Late on the seventh day, alone and looking uneasy, Moses appeared. Miriam remained silent, her eyes glaring. Halting, Moses began to speak: "You know, sister, I never wanted this post. I tried to tell the voice in the burning bush that I was not suited for this. But God insisted and told me to make snakes out of sticks. The voice in the bush said, 'If you want to see My powers as expressed in you, put your hand into your bosom and then pull it out.' And there it was before me: covered with snowy scales! Don't you see? God has now spoken to you, too, from a cloud. Beware of what you ask for, my sister. God has answered you and etched the power of prophecy onto your skin. Now you too must bear the burden of this people, whom I have neither fathered nor mothered, but nevertheless, I carry on my back." Miriam looked at her arm, and behold, the scales were healed. Her arm tingling, she followed her brother Moses back to the camp. Reverently, the people waited as she gathered her things, and took her place at the head of the line.

## *Magic Spells*

Dahlia Ravikovitch
(transl. Chana Bloch and Chana Kronfeld)

*Numbers 12*

Today I'm a hill,
Tomorrow a sea.
Wandering all day
Like Miriam's well,
A bubble astray
In a crannied wall.

At night in my bed
I dreamt horses red,
Purple and green,

In the morning I heard
A babble of water,
The parrots' yatter.

Today I'm a snail,
Tomorrow a tall
Palm tree.

A cleft yesterday,
A seashell today.
Tomorrow I'm tomorrow.

## *After Fighting All Night We Watch the Sun Rise*

Anna Ziegler

*Numbers 12:15*

It isn't slow, or drawn out;
it simply appears, a ribbon of pink
rising like smoke and on its heels,
the event, as though this is
what we've been waiting for,
as though it's never happened
like this before.

# שלח לך ✦ *Sh'lach L'cha*

## NUMBERS 13:1–15:41

### *Sending Scouts and Challenging Leaders*

Parashat Sh'lach L'cha ("Send for yourself") continues the theme in Numbers of challenges to Moses' leadership. In the previous parashah, Miriam and Aaron challenge Moses' leadership (Numbers 12); here, several tribal leaders—and ultimately the populace—do so. The parashah opens with the Israelites apparently nearing the end of their wilderness trek as they prepare to enter Canaan from the south. In anticipation of the invasion, Moses chooses scouts to reconnoiter Canaan. The goal of the expedition is twofold: to assess the strength of the indigenous populations and the strongholds in which they reside, and also to investigate the productivity of the land. One could argue that the venture is superfluous, since God has already ordained the conquest of Canaan by Israel. Seemingly, the objective is to test the faithfulness of the scouts and the Israelites as a whole.

The theme of rebellion at the heart of this parashah centers on the events in Numbers 13–14: the reconnaissance of Canaan, the scouts' report, the Israelites' response, and God's reaction. The keys to the story and subsequent wilderness accounts are the negativity expressed about the mission by ten of the twelve scouts as well as by the populace, and the consequences of that attitude. Only two scouts, Caleb and Joshua, remain enthusiastic about entering the Promised Land, thereby demonstrating trust in God. The sin of faithlessness, exemplified by the majority, threatens the extermination of all Israel. Only Moses' intercession, coupled with God's mercy, saves the people, but not without a heavy price: condemnation to forty years of wandering and certain death for the entire wilderness generation.

The remaining portion of the parashah (15:1–41) focuses on a variety of laws, mostly relating to the sacrificial system. The delineation of laws is interrupted by a case study involving the willful breaking of the law: the desecration of Shabbat. The parashah then ends with the commandment to wear "fringes" (*tzitzit*) on one's garment as a reminder to obey God's laws. Notably, all these laws, even that of the *tzitzit*, are designated for all Israel—and apparently are inclusive of women. Otherwise, there is no explicit attention to women or to issues specifically relating to them. For implicit issues concerning women, see the comments on the sacrificial food such as the *challah* (bread dough offering, 15:19–21). Another indirect way to consider the roles of women in this parashah is to compare the story of the scouts in this parashah with the narrative involving Rahab the prostitute and the scouts in Joshua 2 (see introduction to Numbers 13, below).

*The theme of rebellion is at the heart of this parashah.*

—*Nili Sacher Fox*

## *Outline*

*I.* The Scouts' Expedition and Report
*Fear and Faithlessness* (13:1–33)

*A.* Moses chooses and instructs the scouts (vv. 1–20)
*B.* The scouts reconnoiter Canaan (vv. 21–24)
*C.* The scouts give their report and evaluation (vv. 25–33)

*II.* Aftermath of the Scouting Expedition
*The People's Rebellion and Divine Retribution* (14:1–45)

*A.* The scouts discourage the people with their report (vv. 1–5)
*B.* Joshua and Caleb contradict the report (vv. 6–9)
*C.* God punishes the community for its lack of faith (vv. 10–38)
*D.* The people attempt a military expedition (vv. 39–45)

*III.* An Insertion of a Miscellany of Laws (15:1–41)

*A.* Sacrifices and their accompaniments (vv. 1–16)
*B.* Challah: offering of the first dough (vv. 17–21)
*C.* Inadvertent communal and individual wrongs (vv. 22–31)
*D.* A case of willful Shabbat violation (vv. 32–36)
*E.* The law of *tzitzit* (vv. 37–41)

יהוה spoke to Moses, saying, 2"Send emissaries to scout the land of Canaan,
which I am giving to the Israelite people; send one

יג וַיְדַבֵּר יְהוָה אֶל־מֹשֶׁה לֵּאמֹר׃ 2 שְׁלַח־
לְךָ אֲנָשִׁים וְיָתֻרוּ אֶת־אֶרֶץ כְּנַעַן אֲשֶׁר־אֲנִי
נֹתֵן לִבְנֵי יִשְׂרָאֵל אִישׁ אֶחָד אִישׁ אֶחָד

## *The Scouts' Expedition and Report*

### FEAR AND FAITHLESSNESS (13:1–33)

The opening of this Torah portion is set in the Israelite encampment in the wilderness. At God's command, Moses appoints twelve chieftains, one from each tribe, for a scouting expedition to Canaan to spy out the land and its inhabitants. During their reconnaissance, the scouts cut down a huge cluster of grapes, as well as pomegranates and figs, to bring back to camp as samples of the land's produce. As they make their report, the scouts claim to have encountered populations of giants, inhabitants that dwarf their own size, convincing ten of the scouts that any conquest attempt is doomed to failure. Notably, subsequent scouting expeditions mentioned in the Bible produce the opposite effect, frightening the enemy rather than the Israelites (see Joshua 2; Judges 18). Most significant is the story about Rahab, the harlot in Jericho who risks her life by hiding the two Israelite spies sent by Joshua. In that account, a woman of Canaanite origin is depicted as a God-fearing individual who trusts in Israel's victory. In essence, she becomes the hero of the story, the conduit to Israel's military success.

The narrative in Numbers is a conflation of at least two traditions that reflect different written sources and result in discrepancies. (On J, E, and P as the scholarly names for those sources, see Women and Interpretation of the Torah, page xxxvi.) The differences revolve around two issues: the geographical area of Canaan that is scouted, and the number of scouts who bring a positive report. In the earlier version (JE), the scouts reconnoiter the southern portion of Canaan (13:17), and Caleb alone recommends that Israel proceed with the conquest (13:30). The later priestly account (P) expands the scouting expedition so that they traverse the entire land of Canaan (13:21), plus it adds Joshua as a spokesman for undertaking the conquest (14:6–9).

### MOSES CHOOSES AND INSTRUCTS THE SCOUTS (13:1–20)

The scouts represent the twelve tribes of Israel. The text reiterates their leadership status, probably to underscore their ultimate failure as leaders and to highlight their faithlessness. Moses instructs them to assess the strength of Canaan's inhabitants, both the size of their population and the settlements in which they reside. The scouts are also to evaluate the productivity of the land and return with samples of the fruit of the season (summer).

**2.** ***emissaries.*** Heb. *anashim,* whose basic meaning is "representative members of a group";

▸ The scouts' story is the anti-myth of the Promised Land.

ANOTHER VIEW ➤ *886*

▸ This parashah challenges us to perceive the world in all its nuanced complexity.

CONTEMPORARY REFLECTION ➤ *888*

▸ Separating *challah* is one of three commandments specifically associated with women.

POST-BIBLICAL INTERPRETATIONS ➤ *886*

▸ I fill up my *tallit.* No matter my size, I always will.

VOICES ➤ *890*

representative from each of their ancestral tribes, each one a chieftain among them." 3So Moses, by יהוה's command, sent them out from the wilderness of Paran, all of them being notables, leaders of the Israelites. 4And these were their names:

From the tribe of Reuben, Shammua son of Zaccur.

5From the tribe of Simeon, Shaphat son of Hori.

6From the tribe of Judah, Caleb son of Jephunneh.

7From the tribe of Issachar, Igal son of Joseph.

8From the tribe of Ephraim, Hosea son of Nun.

9From the tribe of Benjamin, Palti son of Rafu.

10From the tribe of Zebulun, Gaddiel son of Sodi.

11From the tribe of Joseph, namely, the tribe of Manasseh, Gaddi son of Susi.

12From the tribe of Dan, Ammiel son of Gemalli.

13From the tribe of Asher, Sethur son of Michael.

14From the tribe of Naphtali, Nahbi son of Vophsi.

15From the tribe of Gad, Geuel son of Machi.

16Those were the names of the emissaries whom Moses sent to scout the land; but Moses changed the name of Hosea son of Nun to Joshua.

17When Moses sent them to scout the land of Canaan, he said to them, "Go up there into the

לְמַטֵּ֤ה אֲבֹתָיו֙ תִּשְׁלָ֔חוּ כֹּ֖ל נָשִׂ֥יא בָהֶֽם׃
3 וַיִּשְׁלַ֨ח אֹתָ֥ם מֹשֶׁ֛ה מִמִּדְבַּ֥ר פָּארָ֖ן עַל־פִּ֣י
יְהֹוָ֑ה כֻּלָּ֣ם אֲנָשִׁ֔ים רָאשֵׁ֥י בְנֵֽי־יִשְׂרָאֵ֖ל
הֵֽמָּה׃ 4 וְאֵ֖לֶּה שְׁמוֹתָ֑ם
לְמַטֵּ֣ה רְאוּבֵ֔ן שַׁמּ֖וּעַ בֶּן־זַכּֽוּר׃
5 לְמַטֵּ֣ה שִׁמְע֔וֹן שָׁפָ֖ט בֶּן־חוֹרִֽי׃
6 לְמַטֵּ֣ה יְהוּדָ֔ה כָּלֵ֖ב בֶּן־יְפֻנֶּֽה׃
7 לְמַטֵּ֣ה ישׂשכר יִשָּׂכָ֔ר יִגְאָ֖ל בֶּן־יוֹסֵֽף׃
8 לְמַטֵּ֥ה אֶפְרָ֖יִם הוֹשֵׁ֥עַ בִּן־נֽוּן׃
9 לְמַטֵּ֣ה בִנְיָמִ֔ן פַּלְטִ֖י בֶּן־רָפֽוּא׃
10 לְמַטֵּ֣ה זְבוּלֻ֔ן גַּדִּיאֵ֖ל בֶּן־סוֹדִֽי׃
11 לְמַטֵּ֥ה יוֹסֵ֖ף לְמַטֵּ֣ה מְנַשֶּׁ֑ה גַּדִּ֖י בֶּן־
סוּסִֽי׃
12 לְמַטֵּ֣ה דָ֔ן עַמִּיאֵ֖ל בֶּן־גְּמַלִּֽי׃
13 לְמַטֵּ֣ה אָשֵׁ֔ר סְת֖וּר בֶּן־מִיכָאֵֽל׃
14 לְמַטֵּ֣ה נַפְתָּלִ֔י נַחְבִּ֖י בֶּן־וָפְסִֽי׃
15 לְמַטֵּ֣ה גָ֔ד גְּאוּאֵ֖ל בֶּן־מָכִֽי׃
16 אֵ֚לֶּה שְׁמ֣וֹת הָֽאֲנָשִׁ֔ים אֲשֶׁר־שָׁלַ֥ח מֹשֶׁ֖ה
לָת֣וּר אֶת־הָאָ֑רֶץ וַיִּקְרָ֥א מֹשֶׁ֛ה לְהוֹשֵׁ֥עַ בִּן־
נ֖וּן יְהוֹשֻֽׁעַ׃
17 וַיִּשְׁלַ֤ח אֹתָם֙ מֹשֶׁ֔ה לָת֖וּר אֶת־אֶ֣רֶץ כְּנָ֑עַן
וַיֹּ֣אמֶר אֲלֵהֶ֗ם עֲל֥וּ זֶה֙ בַּנֶּ֔גֶב וַעֲלִיתֶ֖ם אֶת־

traditionally it has often been translated as "men" or, more inclusively, "people." Throughout this commentary, these individuals are referred to as "scouts," not "spies" (as the Rabbis and later commentators often call them), since according to the present account, their mandate is to survey the land, not engage in espionage.

***16. son of Nun.*** It is noteworthy that Joshua's genealogy does not include a mother's name ("matronymic"), like that of Moses (Exodus 6:20) and of notable Israelite kings, such as Amaziah, whose mother's name is Jehoaddan (II Kings 14:2), and Hezekiah, whose mother's name is Abi (II Kings 18:2).

***Joshua.*** Moses emends this chieftain's name, which originally appears as *Hoshe'a* (Hosea, v. 8), to *Y'hoshua* (Joshua). The new first syllable *y'ho* may signify the deity name ("theophoric element") associated with Israel's God (as in the names of the Israelite kings Jehoshaphat, Jehoahaz, Jehoram, and others).

Negeb and on into the hill country, [18]and see what
kind of country it is. Are the people who dwell in it
strong or weak, few or many? [19]Is the country in
which they dwell good or bad? Are the towns they
live in open or fortified? [20]Is the soil rich or poor? Is
it wooded or not? And take pains to bring back
some of the fruit of the land."—Now it happened
to be the season of the first ripe grapes.

[21]They went up and scouted the land, from the
wilderness of Zin to Rehob, at Lebo-hamath.
[22]They went up into the Negeb and came to
Hebron, where lived Ahiman, Sheshai, and Talmai,
the Anakites.—Now Hebron was founded seven
years before Zoan of Egypt.—[23]They reached the
wadi Eshcol, and there they cut down a branch with
a single cluster of grapes—it had to be borne on a
carrying frame by two of them—and some pomegranates and figs. [24]That place was named the wadi
Eshcol because of the cluster that the Israelites cut
down there.

הָהָר׃ 18 וּרְאִיתֶם אֶת־הָאָרֶץ מַה־הִוא
וְאֶת־הָעָם הַיֹּשֵׁב עָלֶיהָ הֶחָזָק הוּא הֲרָפֶה
הַמְעַט הוּא אִם־רָב׃ 19 וּמָה הָאָרֶץ אֲשֶׁר־
הוּא יֹשֵׁב בָּהּ הֲטוֹבָה הִוא אִם־רָעָה וּמָה
הֶעָרִים אֲשֶׁר־הוּא יוֹשֵׁב בָּהֵנָּה הַבְּמַחֲנִים
אִם בְּמִבְצָרִים׃ 20 וּמָה הָאָרֶץ הַשְּׁמֵנָה
הִוא אִם־רָזָה הֲיֵשׁ־בָּהּ עֵץ אִם־אַיִן
וְהִתְחַזַּקְתֶּם וּלְקַחְתֶּם מִפְּרִי הָאָרֶץ וְהַיָּמִים
יְמֵי בִּכּוּרֵי עֲנָבִים׃
21 וַיַּעֲלוּ וַיָּתֻרוּ אֶת־הָאָרֶץ מִמִּדְבַּר־צִן עַד־
רְחֹב לְבֹא חֲמָת׃ 22 וַיַּעֲלוּ בַנֶּגֶב וַיָּבֹא עַד־
חֶבְרוֹן וְשָׁם אֲחִימַן שֵׁשַׁי וְתַלְמַי יְלִידֵי
הָעֲנָק וְחֶבְרוֹן שֶׁבַע שָׁנִים נִבְנְתָה לִפְנֵי צֹעַן
מִצְרָיִם׃ 23 וַיָּבֹאוּ עַד־נַחַל אֶשְׁכֹּל וַיִּכְרְתוּ
מִשָּׁם זְמוֹרָה וְאֶשְׁכּוֹל עֲנָבִים אֶחָד וַיִּשָּׂאֻהוּ
בַמּוֹט בִּשְׁנָיִם וּמִן־הָרִמֹּנִים וּמִן־הַתְּאֵנִים׃
24 לַמָּקוֹם הַהוּא קָרָא נַחַל אֶשְׁכּוֹל עַל
אֹדוֹת הָאֶשְׁכּוֹל אֲשֶׁר־כָּרְתוּ מִשָּׁם בְּנֵי
יִשְׂרָאֵל׃

***19. open or fortified.*** Canaanite settlements in the Bronze and Iron Ages consisted both of unwalled villages and of walled cities with fortified gates. The latter were constructed to withstand attacks and sieges; they required more advanced military machinery to penetrate. This information would have been strategically vital to a conquest plan.

### THE SCOUTS RECONNOITER CANAAN (13:21–24)

The expedition outlined in these verses reflects a conflation of two traditions: the scouting of the entire land (v. 21) and the scouting of only the area of the city of Hebron and south (vv. 22–24). In the region of Hebron, the scouts encounter clans of aboriginal giants.

The grapes, pomegranates, and figs that they bring back—all late summer fruit—suggest the season of the expedition. But since in the Bible these fruits commonly symbolize the productivity of the Promised Land, they may also be simply a literary device.

### THE SCOUTS GIVE THEIR REPORT AND EVALUATION (13:25–33)

Upon their return, the scouts begin by highlighting the positive aspects of the land. Yet, they quickly change their tone and dwell on its negative features, mainly its formidable population and cities.

At first, Caleb is the only scout who speaks favorably of an Israelite conquest of Canaan. Joshua's role as a faithful leader does not appear until later in the narrative (14:6), which is a section clearly derived from an alternate tradition. (Caleb, the chieftain who represents Judah, will continue to play a key role in the conquest of Canaan, particularly in the tribal territory of Judah. In Joshua

25 At the end of forty days they returned from scouting the land. 26 They went straight to Moses and Aaron and the whole Israelite community at Kadesh in the wilderness of Paran, and they made their report to them and to the whole community, as they showed them the fruit of the land. 27 This is what they told him: "We came to the land you sent us to; it does indeed flow with milk and honey, and this is its fruit. 28 However, the people who inhabit the country are powerful, and the cities are fortified and very large; moreover, we saw the Anakites there. 29 Amalekites dwell in the Negeb region; Hittites, Jebusites, and Amorites inhabit the hill country; and Canaanites dwell by the Sea and along the Jordan."

25 וַיָּשֻׁבוּ מִתּוּר הָאָרֶץ מִקֵּץ אַרְבָּעִים יוֹם׃
26 וַיֵּלְכוּ וַיָּבֹאוּ אֶל־מֹשֶׁה וְאֶל־אַהֲרֹן וְאֶל־
כָּל־עֲדַת בְּנֵי־יִשְׂרָאֵל אֶל־מִדְבַּר פָּארָן
קָדֵשָׁה וַיָּשִׁיבוּ אֹתָם דָּבָר וְאֶת־כָּל־הָעֵדָה
וַיַּרְאוּם אֶת־פְּרִי הָאָרֶץ׃ 27 וַיְסַפְּרוּ־לוֹ
וַיֹּאמְרוּ בָּאנוּ אֶל־הָאָרֶץ אֲשֶׁר שְׁלַחְתָּנוּ
וְגַם זָבַת חָלָב וּדְבַשׁ הִוא וְזֶה־פִּרְיָהּ׃
28 אֶפֶס כִּי־עַז הָעָם הַיֹּשֵׁב בָּאָרֶץ וְהֶעָרִים
בְּצֻרוֹת גְּדֹלֹת מְאֹד וְגַם־יְלִדֵי הָעֲנָק רָאִינוּ
שָׁם׃ 29 עֲמָלֵק יוֹשֵׁב בְּאֶרֶץ הַנֶּגֶב וְהַחִתִּי
וְהַיְבוּסִי וְהָאֱמֹרִי יוֹשֵׁב בָּהָר וְהַכְּנַעֲנִי יֹשֵׁב
עַל־הַיָּם וְעַל יַד הַיַּרְדֵּן׃

15:13–19 and Judges 1:12–15, he promises his daughter Achsah in marriage to the conqueror of the city of Kiriath-Sepher, also known as Debir. The narrative then gives voice to Achsah as she cleverly appeals to Caleb's sense of honor as a father, prompting him to bestow property with water springs in the Negeb to her and her new husband, Othniel.)

*25. forty days.* The duration of the scouting expedition is formulaic and reminiscent of other significant events, such as the length of the Flood (Genesis 7:17) and the amount of time Moses spent on Mount Sinai (Exodus 24:18).

*27. **flow with milk and honey.*** As an epithet for the Promised Land, this biblical phrase (also Exodus 3:8, 17) has been used through the ages, even in modern times.

Heb. *d'vash* can refer either to a sweet syrup made from mashed dates or to bees' honey. A recent archeological discovery in the Beit She'an Valley of a large beehive colony dated to the 10th–9th century B.C.E. now proves that beekeeping for production of honey was an industry in biblical Israel.

*28. Anakites.* They and the Nephilim (v. 33) are giants or super-humans mentioned also in other biblical texts. Genesis 6:1–4 recounts the origin of the Nephilim. David's Philistine adversary, Goliath, is depicted as a giant (I Samuel 17:4) descended from another group of giants, the Rephaim (I Chronicles 20:5–6).

It is difficult to interpret the meaning of "giants" in the scouts' report. In the case of the Philistines, it may be that their tall headdresses (pictured in Egyptian art) contributed to their gigantic image. More importantly, the report of giants in the land makes the Canaanites more intimidating and their eventual defeat by the Israelites more spectacular. Notably, Anakites are also mentioned in Egyptian literature (Papyrus Anastasi I, *Context of Scripture*, 2002, 3:13) where they are identified as Shasu (a nomadic group) about 6′8″–8′6″ (2–2.6 meters) tall. The Shasu were enemies of the Egyptians and their depiction as giants functions as a literary device similar to that in the biblical story. Some scholars actually connect the Shasu with proto-Israelites.

*29. **Amalekites . . . Hittites, Jebusites, and Amorites.*** For the indigenous population of Canaan, see the table of nations in Genesis 10:15–20. Deuteronomy 7:1–3 includes most of these among the people who must be destroyed upon Israel's entering the land; that passage (as well as Exodus 34:11–16) also forbids giving daughters in marriage to these groups or taking daughters from them.

30Caleb hushed the people before Moses and
said, "Let us by all means go up, and we shall gain
possession of it, for we shall surely overcome it."
31But the emissaries who had gone up with
him said, "We cannot attack that people, for it is
stronger than we." 32Thus they spread calumnies
among the Israelites about the land they had
scouted, saying, "The country that we traversed
and scouted is one that devours its settlers. All the
people that we saw in it are of great size; 33we saw
the Nephilim there—the Anakites are part of the
Nephilim—and we looked like grasshoppers to
ourselves, and so we must have looked to them."

14 The whole community broke into loud
cries, and the people wept that night. 2All the Israelites railed against Moses and Aaron. "If only we
had died in the land of Egypt," the whole community shouted at them, "or if only we might die in

30 וַיַּ֧הַס כָּלֵ֛ב אֶת־הָעָ֖ם אֶל־מֹשֶׁ֑ה וַיֹּ֗אמֶר
עָלֹ֤ה נַעֲלֶה֙ וְיָרַ֣שְׁנוּ אֹתָ֔הּ כִּֽי־יָכ֥וֹל נוּכַ֖ל
לָֽהּ׃
31 וְהָאֲנָשִׁ֗ים אֲשֶׁר־עָל֤וּ עִמּוֹ֙ אָֽמְר֔וּ לֹ֥א נוּכַ֖ל
לַעֲל֣וֹת אֶל־הָעָ֑ם כִּֽי־חָזָ֥ק ה֖וּא מִמֶּֽנּוּ׃
32 וַיֹּצִ֜יאוּ דִּבַּ֤ת הָאָ֙רֶץ֙ אֲשֶׁ֣ר תָּר֣וּ אֹתָ֔הּ
אֶל־בְּנֵ֖י יִשְׂרָאֵ֣ל לֵאמֹ֑ר הָאָ֡רֶץ אֲשֶׁר֩ עָבַ֨רְנוּ
בָ֜הּ לָת֣וּר אֹתָ֗הּ אֶ֣רֶץ אֹכֶ֤לֶת יוֹשְׁבֶ֙יהָ֙ הִ֔וא
וְכָל־הָעָ֛ם אֲשֶׁר־רָאִ֥ינוּ בְתוֹכָ֖הּ אַנְשֵׁ֥י
מִדּֽוֹת׃ 33 וְשָׁ֣ם רָאִ֗ינוּ אֶת־הַנְּפִילִ֛ים בְּנֵ֥י
עֲנָ֖ק מִן־הַנְּפִלִ֑ים וַנְּהִ֤י בְעֵינֵ֙ינוּ֙ כַּחֲגָבִ֔ים וְכֵ֥ן
הָיִ֖ינוּ בְּעֵינֵיהֶֽם׃

יד וַתִּשָּׂא֙ כָּל־הָ֣עֵדָ֔ה וַֽיִּתְּנ֖וּ אֶת־קוֹלָ֑ם
וַיִּבְכּ֥וּ הָעָ֖ם בַּלַּ֥יְלָה הַהֽוּא׃ 2 וַיִּלֹּ֙נוּ֙ עַל־
מֹשֶׁ֣ה וְעַֽל־אַהֲרֹ֔ן כֹּ֖ל בְּנֵ֣י יִשְׂרָאֵ֑ל וַיֹּאמְר֨וּ
אֲלֵהֶ֜ם כָּל־הָעֵדָ֗ה לוּ־מַ֙תְנוּ֙ בְּאֶ֣רֶץ מִצְרַ֔יִם

*32.* ***devours its settlers.*** Most likely, this phrase alludes to the results of frequent warfare, which ravaged Canaan (see Ezekiel 36:13–14). An alternate explanation is that the expression refers to the infertility of the land, but this would contradict the scouts' earlier report and hence is less likely.

*33.* ***we looked like grasshoppers.*** The scouts underscore the enormous size of the giants of Canaan by depicting their own stature in comparison.

## *Aftermath of the Scouting Expedition*

### THE PEOPLE'S REBELLION AND DIVINE RETRIBUTION (14:1–45)

In the continuous cycle of rebellions by the Israelites in the wilderness, this one is the most egregious. The ten scouts who incite the populace advocate abandoning Israel's ultimate goal of settling the Promised Land. This extreme display of faithlessness before God, similar to that in the Golden Calf episode (Exodus 32), provokes God's fiery anger—which threatens to annihilate the whole nation. As before, Moses becomes an intercessor, a part he has learned to play well. Still, here the punishment is most severe and far-reaching.

### THE SCOUTS DISCOURAGE THE PEOPLE WITH THEIR REPORT (14:1–5)

Reacting to the scouts' frightening description of the fierce inhabitants of Canaan, the Israelites cry out in fear. Clearly, they have accepted the veracity of the scouts' military analysis and expect to be defeated. They are ready to return to Egypt rather than face the enemy in Canaan, apparently having forgotten the wrath of the Egyptian army that pursued them when they escaped from Egypt. It appears that the series of murmurings and rebellions in the wilderness has reached a climax at the gates of the Promised Land.

*1.* ***The whole community.*** This phrase indicates the widespread nature of the rebellion. Presumably the women are included.

this wilderness!” 3 “Why is יהוה taking us to that land to fall by the sword?” “Our wives and children will be carried off! It would be better for us to go back to Egypt!” 4 And they said to one another, “Let us head back for Egypt.”

5 Then Moses and Aaron fell on their faces before all the assembled congregation of Israelites. 6 And Joshua son of Nun and Caleb son of Jephunneh, of those who had scouted the land, rent their clothes 7 and exhorted the whole Israelite community: “The land that we traversed and scouted is an exceedingly good land. 8 If pleased with us, יהוה will bring us into that land, a land that flows with milk and honey, and give it to us; 9 only you must not rebel against יהוה. Have no fear then of the people of the country, for they are our prey: their protection has departed from them, but יהוה is with us. Have no fear of them!” 10 As the whole community threatened to pelt them with stones, the

אֽוֹ בַּמִּדְבָּ֥ר הַזֶּ֖ה לוּ־מָֽתְנוּ׃ 3 וְלָמָ֣ה יְהֹוָ֗ה
מֵבִ֨יא אֹתָ֜נוּ אֶל־הָאָ֤רֶץ הַזֹּאת֙ לִנְפֹּ֣ל בַּחֶ֔רֶב
נָשֵׁ֥ינוּ וְטַפֵּ֖נוּ יִהְי֣וּ לָבַ֑ז הֲל֧וֹא ט֛וֹב לָ֖נוּ שׁ֥וּב
מִצְרָֽיְמָה׃ 4 וַיֹּאמְר֖וּ אִ֣ישׁ אֶל־אָחִ֑יו נִתְּנָ֥ה
רֹ֖אשׁ וְנָשׁ֥וּבָה מִצְרָֽיְמָה׃
5 וַיִּפֹּ֥ל מֹשֶׁ֛ה וְאַהֲרֹ֖ן עַל־פְּנֵיהֶ֑ם לִפְנֵ֕י כָּל־
קְהַ֖ל עֲדַ֥ת בְּנֵ֥י יִשְׂרָאֵֽל׃ 6 וִיהוֹשֻׁ֣עַ בִּן־נ֗וּן
וְכָלֵב֙ בֶּן־יְפֻנֶּ֔ה מִן־הַתָּרִ֖ים אֶת־הָאָ֑רֶץ קָרְע֖וּ
בִּגְדֵיהֶֽם׃ 7 וַיֹּ֣אמְר֔וּ אֶל־כָּל־עֲדַ֥ת בְּנֵֽי־
יִשְׂרָאֵ֖ל לֵאמֹ֑ר הָאָ֗רֶץ אֲשֶׁ֨ר עָבַ֤רְנוּ בָהּ֙
לָת֣וּר אֹתָ֔הּ טוֹבָ֥ה הָאָ֖רֶץ מְאֹ֥ד מְאֹֽד׃
8 אִם־חָפֵ֥ץ בָּ֙נוּ֙ יְהֹוָ֔ה וְהֵבִ֤יא אֹתָ֙נוּ֙ אֶל־
הָאָ֣רֶץ הַזֹּ֔את וּנְתָנָ֖הּ לָ֑נוּ אֶ֕רֶץ אֲשֶׁר־הִ֛וא
זָבַ֥ת חָלָ֖ב וּדְבָֽשׁ׃ 9 אַ֣ךְ בַּיהֹוָה֮ אַל־תִּמְרֹ֒דוּ֒
וְאַתֶּ֗ם אַל־תִּֽירְאוּ֙ אֶת־עַ֣ם הָאָ֔רֶץ כִּ֥י לַחְמֵ֖נוּ
הֵ֑ם סָ֣ר צִלָּ֧ם מֵעֲלֵיהֶ֛ם וַיהֹוָ֥ה אִתָּ֖נוּ אַל־
תִּירָאֻֽם׃ 10 וַיֹּֽאמְרוּ֙ כָּל־הָ֣עֵדָ֔ה לִרְגּ֥וֹם אֹתָ֖ם

*3. “Our wives and children will be carried off!”* Several biblical texts describe situations in which women and children are carried off as booty. In one case, I Samuel 30, David rescues the wives and children of his men (and his own family as well). Commonly, the attackers kill the captive wives but keep alive the virgins, “women who have not known a man” (see Judges 21). Deuteronomic law regulates the treatment of women taken captive by Israelite men (Deuteronomy 21:10–14).

*4. “Let us head back.”* The Hebrew phrase can also mean “let us appoint a leader,” indicating that the Israelites are ready to replace Moses and return to Egypt under new leadership.

*5.* Desperate, Moses and Aaron prostrate themselves before the people. They seem helpless in the face of a national rebellion that questions not only the Israelites' allegiance to God but also their human leadership.

### JOSHUA AND CALEB CONTRADICT THE REPORT (14:6–9)

In the face of Moses and Aaron's temporary abdication of leadership, Joshua and Caleb assume responsibility. They staunchly articulate that the outcome of the mission will be determined by Israel's God, not by military fortitude. The extent of the people's rebellion is evident by their readiness to stone Joshua and Caleb. It is only the sudden appearance of God's Presence before the people that saves them.

*6. rent their clothes.* This act, a sign of grief and mourning, probably took the place of mutilating oneself with gashes and the like (a biblical prohibition, Leviticus 19:28). Tearing one's garment is an ancient custom that has survived to the present day. In the Bible, for example, King David's daughter Tamar rends her garments, puts dust

Presence of יהוה appeared in the Tent of Meeting
to all the Israelites.
11 And יהוה said to Moses, "How long will this
people spurn Me, and how long will they have no
faith in Me despite all the signs that I have performed in their midst? 12 I will strike them with
pestilence and disown them, and I will make of you
a nation far more numerous than they!" 13 But
Moses said to יהוה, "When the Egyptians, from
whose midst You brought up this people in Your
might, hear the news, 14 they will tell it to the inhabitants of that land. Now they have heard that
You, יהוה, are in the midst of this people; that You,
יהוה, appear in plain sight when Your cloud rests
over them and when You go before them in a pillar
of cloud by day and in a pillar of fire by night. 15 If
then You slay this people wholesale, the nations
who have heard Your fame will say, 16 "It must be
because יהוה was powerless to bring that people

בָּאֲבָנִים וּכְבוֹד יְהוָֹה נִרְאָה בְּאֹהֶל מוֹעֵד
אֶל־כָּל־בְּנֵי יִשְׂרָאֵל׃ פ
11 וַיֹּאמֶר יְהוָֹה אֶל־מֹשֶׁה עַד־אָנָה יְנַאֲצֻנִי
הָעָם הַזֶּה וְעַד־אָנָה לֹא־יַאֲמִינוּ בִי בְּכֹל
הָאֹתוֹת אֲשֶׁר עָשִׂיתִי בְּקִרְבּוֹ׃ 12 אַכֶּנּוּ
בַדֶּבֶר וְאוֹרִשֶׁנּוּ וְאֶעֱשֶׂה אֹתְךָ לְגוֹי־גָּדוֹל
וְעָצוּם מִמֶּנּוּ׃ 13 וַיֹּאמֶר מֹשֶׁה אֶל־יְהוָֹה
וְשָׁמְעוּ מִצְרַיִם כִּי־הֶעֱלִיתָ בְכֹחֲךָ אֶת־הָעָם
הַזֶּה מִקִּרְבּוֹ׃ 14 וְאָמְרוּ אֶל־יוֹשֵׁב הָאָרֶץ
הַזֹּאת שָׁמְעוּ כִּי־אַתָּה יְהוָֹה בְּקֶרֶב הָעָם
הַזֶּה אֲשֶׁר־עַיִן בְּעַיִן נִרְאָה ׀ אַתָּה יְהוָֹה
וַעֲנָנְךָ עֹמֵד עֲלֵהֶם וּבְעַמֻּד עָנָן אַתָּה
הֹלֵךְ לִפְנֵיהֶם יוֹמָם וּבְעַמּוּד אֵשׁ לָיְלָה׃
15 וְהֵמַתָּה אֶת־הָעָם הַזֶּה כְּאִישׁ אֶחָד
וְאָמְרוּ הַגּוֹיִם אֲשֶׁר־שָׁמְעוּ אֶת־שִׁמְעֲךָ
לֵאמֹר׃ 16 מִבִּלְתִּי יְכֹלֶת יְהוָֹה לְהָבִיא

on her head, and cries loudly, grieving after her half-brother Amnon rapes her (II Samuel 13; compare also Genesis 44:13).

### GOD PUNISHES THE COMMUNITY FOR ITS LACK OF FAITH (14:10–38)

God is prepared to eradicate all Israel in a plague—with the exception of Moses, from whose descendants God proposes to create a new nation. Since the sins surrounding the scouting expedition and the Golden Calf (Exodus 32) are the only two events eliciting such severe divine retribution, it seems that their gravity is comparable. As in the past, Moses intercedes on behalf of the people. He argues first that God's reputation among the nations as a most powerful deity must be preserved; his second argument appeals to God's attribute of mercy (see Exodus 34:6–7). Moses' lengthy prayer for the nation contrasts sharply with his very brief prayer on behalf of his sister Miriam (12:13), who was stricken with a skin disease for challenging Moses' position.

As is often the case in the Torah, God responds favorably to Moses' plea, promising to spare the nation. The Israelites are condemned to wander in the wilderness until nearly all the adults have died, presumably of natural causes (vv. 22–23, 28–33); but the ten faithless scouts are struck down on the spot (vv. 36–37). The tribe of Levi is not among those who are doomed to die in the wilderness, apparently because it had not been represented among the scouts. Of the remaining Israelites, only Joshua and Caleb and the children "born in the wilderness" will enter the Promised Land.

God's decree in this passage is woven from two sources or traditions, JE (vv. 20–24) and a priestly source (vv. 26–38). (On these sources, see Women and Interpretation of the Torah, page xxxvi.) In the former, only Caleb is singled out to be spared (v. 24) because he alone among the scouts was faithful; in the latter, both Caleb and Joshua are listed as those who will settle Canaan (v. 30).

***10. Presence.*** Heb. *kavod*, the typical term for describing God's manifestation in a cloud in priestly writings.

into the land promised them on oath that [that god] slaughtered them in the wilderness.' [17]Therefore, I pray, let my lord's forbearance be great, as You have declared, saying, [18]'יהוה! slow to anger and abounding in kindness; forgiving iniquity and transgression; yet not remitting all punishment, but visiting the iniquity of parents upon children, upon the third and fourth generations.' [19]Pardon, I pray, the iniquity of this people according to Your great kindness, as You have forgiven this people ever since Egypt."

[20]And יהוה said, "I pardon, as you have asked. [21]Nevertheless, as I live and as יהוה's Presence fills the whole world, [22]none of the adults who have seen My Presence and the signs that I have performed in Egypt and in the wilderness, and who have tried Me these many times and have disobeyed Me, [23]shall see the land that I promised on oath to their fathers; none of those who spurn Me shall see it. [24]But My servant Caleb, because he was imbued with a different spirit and remained loyal to Me—him will I bring into the land that he entered, and his offspring shall hold it as a possession. [25]Now the Amalekites and the Canaanites occupy the valleys. Start out, then, tomorrow and march into the wilderness by way of the Sea of Reeds."

אֶת־הָעָם הַזֶּה אֶל־הָאָרֶץ אֲשֶׁר־נִשְׁבַּע
לָהֶם וַיִּשְׁחָטֵם בַּמִּדְבָּר׃ 17 וְעַתָּה יִגְדַּל־נָא
כֹּחַ אֲדֹנָי כַּאֲשֶׁר דִּבַּרְתָּ לֵאמֹר׃ 18 יְהֹוָה
אֶרֶךְ אַפַּיִם וְרַב־חֶסֶד נֹשֵׂא עָוֺן וָפָשַׁע
וְנַקֵּה לֹא יְנַקֶּה פֹּקֵד עֲוֺן אָבוֹת עַל־בָּנִים
עַל־שִׁלֵּשִׁים וְעַל־רִבֵּעִים׃ 19 סְלַח־נָא לַעֲוֺן
הָעָם הַזֶּה כְּגֹדֶל חַסְדֶּךָ וְכַאֲשֶׁר נָשָׂאתָה
לָעָם הַזֶּה מִמִּצְרַיִם וְעַד־הֵנָּה׃
20 וַיֹּאמֶר יְהֹוָה סָלַחְתִּי כִּדְבָרֶךָ׃ 21 וְאוּלָם
חַי־אָנִי וְיִמָּלֵא כְבוֹד־יְהֹוָה אֶת־כָּל־הָאָרֶץ׃
22 כִּי כָל־הָאֲנָשִׁים הָרֹאִים אֶת־כְּבֹדִי וְאֶת־
אֹתֹתַי אֲשֶׁר־עָשִׂיתִי בְמִצְרַיִם וּבַמִּדְבָּר
וַיְנַסּוּ אֹתִי זֶה עֶשֶׂר פְּעָמִים וְלֹא שָׁמְעוּ
בְּקוֹלִי׃ 23 אִם־יִרְאוּ אֶת־הָאָרֶץ אֲשֶׁר
נִשְׁבַּעְתִּי לַאֲבֹתָם וְכָל־מְנַאֲצַי לֹא יִרְאוּהָ׃
24 וְעַבְדִּי כָלֵב עֵקֶב הָיְתָה רוּחַ אַחֶרֶת עִמּוֹ
וַיְמַלֵּא אַחֲרָי וַהֲבִיאֹתִיו אֶל־הָאָרֶץ אֲשֶׁר־
בָּא שָׁמָּה וְזַרְעוֹ יוֹרִשֶׁנָּה׃ 25 וְהָעֲמָלֵקִי
וְהַכְּנַעֲנִי יוֹשֵׁב בָּעֵמֶק מָחָר פְּנוּ וּסְעוּ לָכֶם
הַמִּדְבָּר דֶּרֶךְ יַם־סוּף׃ פ

*18. "יהוה! slow to anger . . . visiting the iniquity of parents upon children."* The entire formula of God's attributes is found in Exodus 34:6–7; portions are quoted here as well as in the Decalogue (Exodus 20:5–6; Deuteronomy 5:9–10). Moses is clearly appealing to God's merciful nature, which should prevent God from carrying out the threat to slaughter the entire nation. Simultaneously, Moses notes that God does not remit full punishment; in fact, future generations share the punishment of their guilty ancestors. Deuteronomy offers a different perspective on this matter, arguing that subsequent generations are punished only if they persist in those sins (Deuteronomy 5:9–10).

*21. "as I live."* This expression, also found in v. 28, is an oath formula. God vows to mitigate the people's punishment so as to not wipe out the entire nation.

*22. "none of the adults."* Except for Joshua, Caleb, and the tribe of Levi (see above), the current adult generation will not inherit Canaan; instead, they will perish in the wilderness according to their wish expressed earlier (v. 2). In essence, the wilderness becomes a vehicle for cleansing the sin of the older generation and preparing the younger Israelites to become the new inheritors of the Promised Land.

*25.* After having prepared them to enter the Promised Land, God now orders the Israelites to retreat from the border of Canaan back into the wilderness.

26 יהוה spoke further to Moses and Aaron,
27 "How much longer shall that wicked community
keep muttering against Me? Very well, I have
heeded the incessant muttering of the Israelites
against Me. 28 Say to them: 'As I live,' says יהוה, 'I
will do to you just as you have urged Me. 29 In this
very wilderness shall your carcasses drop. Of all of
you [men] who were recorded in your various lists
from the age of twenty years up, you who have
muttered against Me, 30 not one shall enter the land
in which I swore to settle you—save Caleb son of
Jephunneh and Joshua son of Nun. 31 Your children
who, you said, would be carried off—these will I
allow to enter; they shall know the land that you
have rejected. 32 But your carcasses shall drop in this
wilderness, 33 while your children roam the wilderness for forty years, suffering for your faithlessness,
until the last of your carcasses is down in the wilderness. 34 You shall bear your punishment for forty
years, corresponding to the number of days—forty
days—that you scouted the land: a year for each
day. Thus you shall know what it means to thwart
Me. 35 I יהוה have spoken: Thus will I do to all that
wicked band that has banded together against Me:
in this very wilderness they shall die and so be finished off.'"

36 As for the emissaries whom Moses sent to
scout the land, those who came back and caused the
whole community to mutter against him by spreading calumnies about the land— 37 those who spread
such calumnies about the land died of plague, by

26 וַיְדַבֵּר יְהוָה אֶל־מֹשֶׁה וְאֶל־אַהֲרֹן
לֵאמֹר׃ 27 עַד־מָתַי לָעֵדָה הָרָעָה הַזֹּאת
אֲשֶׁר הֵמָּה מַלִּינִים עָלָי אֶת־תְּלֻנּוֹת בְּנֵי
יִשְׂרָאֵל אֲשֶׁר הֵמָּה מַלִּינִים עָלַי שָׁמָעְתִּי׃
28 אֱמֹר אֲלֵהֶם חַי־אָנִי נְאֻם־יְהוָה אִם־לֹא
כַּאֲשֶׁר דִּבַּרְתֶּם בְּאָזְנָי כֵּן אֶעֱשֶׂה לָכֶם׃
29 בַּמִּדְבָּר הַזֶּה יִפְּלוּ פִגְרֵיכֶם וְכָל־פְּקֻדֵיכֶם
לְכָל־מִסְפַּרְכֶם מִבֶּן עֶשְׂרִים שָׁנָה וָמָעְלָה
אֲשֶׁר הֲלִינֹתֶם עָלָי׃ 30 אִם־אַתֶּם תָּבֹאוּ
אֶל־הָאָרֶץ אֲשֶׁר נָשָׂאתִי אֶת־יָדִי לְשַׁכֵּן
אֶתְכֶם בָּהּ כִּי אִם־כָּלֵב בֶּן־יְפֻנֶּה וִיהוֹשֻׁעַ
בִּן־נוּן׃ 31 וְטַפְּכֶם אֲשֶׁר אֲמַרְתֶּם לָבַז יִהְיֶה
וְהֵבֵיאתִי אֹתָם וְיָדְעוּ אֶת־הָאָרֶץ אֲשֶׁר
מְאַסְתֶּם בָּהּ׃ 32 וּפִגְרֵיכֶם אַתֶּם יִפְּלוּ
בַּמִּדְבָּר הַזֶּה׃ 33 וּבְנֵיכֶם יִהְיוּ רֹעִים בַּמִּדְבָּר
אַרְבָּעִים שָׁנָה וְנָשְׂאוּ אֶת־זְנוּתֵיכֶם עַד־תֹּם
פִּגְרֵיכֶם בַּמִּדְבָּר׃ 34 בְּמִסְפַּר הַיָּמִים אֲשֶׁר־
תַּרְתֶּם אֶת־הָאָרֶץ אַרְבָּעִים יוֹם יוֹם לַשָּׁנָה
יוֹם לַשָּׁנָה תִּשְׂאוּ אֶת־עֲוֺנֹתֵיכֶם אַרְבָּעִים
שָׁנָה וִידַעְתֶּם אֶת־תְּנוּאָתִי׃ 35 אֲנִי יְהוָה
דִּבַּרְתִּי אִם־לֹא ׀ זֹאת אֶעֱשֶׂה לְכָל־הָעֵדָה
הָרָעָה הַזֹּאת הַנּוֹעָדִים עָלָי בַּמִּדְבָּר הַזֶּה
יִתַּמּוּ וְשָׁם יָמֻתוּ׃
36 וְהָאֲנָשִׁים אֲשֶׁר־שָׁלַח מֹשֶׁה לָתוּר אֶת־
הָאָרֶץ וַיָּשֻׁבוּ וילונו וַיַּלִּינוּ עָלָיו אֶת־כָּל־
הָעֵדָה לְהוֹצִיא דִבָּה עַל־הָאָרֶץ׃ 37 וַיָּמֻתוּ
הָאֲנָשִׁים מוֹצִאֵי דִבַּת־הָאָרֶץ רָעָה בַּמַּגֵּפָה

*29. "you [men]."* Here an insertion reminds the reader that the census in question had counted only battle-worthy men (1:2–3).

*33. "suffering for your faithlessness."* Literally, "bearing your harlotry," indicating the infidelity of the older generation to God. The Bible often uses the term "harlotry" metaphorically to refer to Israelite idolatrous practices, a manifestation of their infidelity to God (see especially Hosea 1–3). This pejorative image is underscored in some of the biblical depictions of the harlot (as in Proverbs 23:27).

*37.* The ten scouts who incited the rebellion with their negative report die in a plague sent by God. Their sin is too grave to mitigate. That they get no second chance is a reflection of just how seriously the Bible treats the responsibilities of leadership; indeed, these scouts demonstrated the huge impact that a leader can have.

the will of יהוה. ³⁸Of those emissaries who had gone to scout the land, only Joshua son of Nun and Caleb son of Jephunneh survived.

³⁹When Moses repeated these words to all the Israelites, the people were overcome by grief. ⁴⁰Early next morning [their fighting force] set out toward the crest of the hill country, saying, "We are prepared to go up to the place that יהוה has spoken of, for we were wrong." ⁴¹But Moses said, "Why do you transgress יהוה's command? This will not succeed. ⁴²Do not go up, lest you be routed by your enemies, for יהוה is not in your midst. ⁴³For the Amalekites and the Canaanites will be there to face you, and you will fall by the sword, inasmuch as you have turned from following יהוה and יהוה will not be with you."

⁴⁴Yet defiantly they marched toward the crest of the hill country, though neither יהוה's Ark of the Covenant nor Moses stirred from the camp. ⁴⁵And the Amalekites and the Canaanites who dwelt in that hill country came down and dealt them a shattering blow at Hormah.

15 יהוה spoke to Moses, saying: ²Speak to the Israelite people and say to them:

לִפְנֵי יְהוָה: ³⁸ וִיהוֹשֻׁעַ בִּן־נ֔וּן וְכָלֵ֖ב בֶּן־יְפֻנֶּ֑ה חָי֗וּ מִן־הָאֲנָשִׁים֙ הָהֵ֔ם הַהֹלְכִ֖ים לָת֥וּר אֶת־הָאָֽרֶץ: ³⁹ וַיְדַבֵּ֤ר מֹשֶׁה֙ אֶת־הַדְּבָרִ֣ים הָאֵ֔לֶּה אֶל־כׇּל־בְּנֵ֖י יִשְׂרָאֵ֑ל וַיִּתְאַבְּל֥וּ הָעָ֖ם מְאֹֽד: ⁴⁰ וַיַּשְׁכִּ֣מוּ בַבֹּ֔קֶר וַיַּעֲל֥וּ אֶל־רֹאשׁ־הָהָ֖ר לֵאמֹ֑ר הִנֶּ֗נּוּ וְעָלִ֛ינוּ אֶל־הַמָּק֛וֹם אֲשֶׁר־אָמַ֥ר יְהוָ֖ה כִּ֥י חָטָֽאנוּ: ⁴¹ וַיֹּ֣אמֶר מֹשֶׁ֔ה לָ֥מָּה זֶּ֛ה אַתֶּ֥ם עֹבְרִ֖ים אֶת־פִּ֣י יְהוָ֑ה וְהִ֖וא לֹ֥א תִצְלָֽח: ⁴² אַֽל־תַּעֲל֔וּ כִּ֣י אֵ֤ין יְהוָה֙ בְּקִרְבְּכֶ֔ם וְלֹא֙ תִּנָּ֣גְפ֔וּ לִפְנֵ֖י אֹיְבֵיכֶֽם: ⁴³ כִּי֩ הָעֲמָלֵקִ֨י וְהַכְּנַעֲנִ֥י שָׁם֙ לִפְנֵיכֶ֔ם וּנְפַלְתֶּ֖ם בֶּחָ֑רֶב כִּֽי־עַל־כֵּ֤ן שַׁבְתֶּם֙ מֵאַחֲרֵ֣י יְהוָ֔ה וְלֹא־יִהְיֶ֥ה יְהוָ֖ה עִמָּכֶֽם: ⁴⁴ וַיַּעְפִּ֕לוּ לַעֲל֖וֹת אֶל־רֹ֣אשׁ הָהָ֑ר וַאֲר֤וֹן בְּרִית־יְהוָה֙ וּמֹשֶׁ֔ה לֹא־מָ֖שׁוּ מִקֶּ֥רֶב הַֽמַּחֲנֶֽה: ⁴⁵ וַיֵּ֤רֶד הָעֲמָלֵקִי֙ וְהַֽכְּנַעֲנִ֔י הַיֹּשֵׁ֖ב בָּהָ֣ר הַה֑וּא וַיַּכּ֥וּם וַֽיַּכְּת֖וּם עַד־הַֽחׇרְמָֽה: פ

טו וַיְדַבֵּ֥ר יְהוָ֖ה אֶל־מֹשֶׁ֥ה לֵּאמֹֽר: ² דַּבֵּ֗ר אֶל־בְּנֵ֤י יִשְׂרָאֵל֙ וְאָמַרְתָּ֣ אֲלֵהֶ֔ם

---

### THE PEOPLE ATTEMPT A MILITARY EXPEDITION (14:39–45)

A group of Israelites attempts to invade Canaan despite a warning to the contrary. Their motivation is either regret for their previous open lack of trust in God or a hope to reverse God's decree. In any case, the invasion fails, and they are defeated. The message here is clear: without God's blessing and presence in battle (marked by the accompanying Ark), conquest is impossible. The function of the Ark in the military camp is also emphasized in this section.

*45. Hormah.* This place name, meaning "destruction," also indicates that the Amalekites and Canaanites utterly defeated the invading Israelites.

### An Insertion of a Miscellany of Laws (15:1–41)

Legal material interrupts the narrative of the wandering in the wilderness. Its purpose, immediately following God's punishment of the faithless Israelites, may be to reiterate the promise that eventually they will indeed inherit Canaan—as signaled by the introduction to the first two sets of laws: "When you enter the land" (vv. 2, 18). The laws in this unit, with the exception of the last, deal with the sacrificial system. The last law, about *tzitzit* (fringes), is preceded by a case study of a wood-gatherer who violates Shabbat and is stoned to death by the community. The placement of the

When you enter the land that I am giving you to settle in, [3]and would present an offering by fire to יהוה from the herd or from the flock, be it burnt offering or sacrifice, in fulfillment of a vow explicitly uttered, or as a freewill offering, or at your fixed occasions, producing an odor pleasing to יהוה:

[4]The person who presents the offering to יהוה shall bring as a meal offering: a tenth of a measure of choice flour with a quarter of a *hin* of oil mixed in. [5]You shall also offer, with the burnt offering or the sacrifice, a quarter of a *hin* of wine as a libation for each sheep.

[6]In the case of a ram, you shall present as a meal offering: two-tenths of a measure of choice flour with a third of a *hin* of oil mixed in; [7]and a third of a *hin* of wine as a libation—as an offering of pleasing odor to יהוה.

[8]And if it is an animal from the herd that you offer to יהוה as a burnt offering or as a sacrifice, in fulfillment of a vow explicitly uttered or as an offering of well-being, [9]there shall be offered a meal offering along with the animal: three-tenths of a measure of choice flour with half a *hin* of oil mixed in; [10]and as libation you shall offer half a *hin* of wine—these being offerings by fire of pleasing odor to יהוה.

[11]Thus shall be done with each ox, with each ram, and with any sheep or goat, [12]as many as you offer; you shall do thus with each one, as many as

כִּי תָבֹאוּ אֶל־אֶרֶץ מוֹשְׁבֹתֵיכֶם אֲשֶׁר
אֲנִי נֹתֵן לָכֶם׃ 3 וַעֲשִׂיתֶם אִשֶּׁה לַיהוָה
עֹלָה אוֹ־זֶבַח לְפַלֵּא־נֶדֶר אוֹ בִנְדָבָה אוֹ
בְּמֹעֲדֵיכֶם לַעֲשׂוֹת רֵיחַ נִיחֹחַ לַיהוָה מִן־
הַבָּקָר אוֹ מִן־הַצֹּאן׃
4 וְהִקְרִיב הַמַּקְרִיב קָרְבָּנוֹ לַיהוָה מִנְחָה
סֹלֶת עִשָּׂרוֹן בָּלוּל בִּרְבִעִית הַהִין שָׁמֶן׃
5 וְיַיִן לַנֶּסֶךְ רְבִיעִית הַהִין תַּעֲשֶׂה עַל־
הָעֹלָה אוֹ לַזָּבַח לַכֶּבֶשׂ הָאֶחָד׃
6 אוֹ לָאַיִל תַּעֲשֶׂה מִנְחָה סֹלֶת שְׁנֵי
עֶשְׂרֹנִים בְּלוּלָה בַשֶּׁמֶן שְׁלִשִׁית הַהִין׃
7 וְיַיִן לַנֶּסֶךְ שְׁלִשִׁית הַהִין תַּקְרִיב רֵיחַ־
נִיחֹחַ לַיהוָה׃
8 וְכִי־תַעֲשֶׂה בֶן־בָּקָר עֹלָה אוֹ־זָבַח לְפַלֵּא־
נֶדֶר אוֹ־שְׁלָמִים לַיהוָה׃ 9 וְהִקְרִיב עַל־בֶּן־
הַבָּקָר מִנְחָה סֹלֶת שְׁלֹשָׁה עֶשְׂרֹנִים בָּלוּל
בַּשֶּׁמֶן חֲצִי הַהִין׃ 10 וְיַיִן תַּקְרִיב לַנֶּסֶךְ חֲצִי
הַהִין אִשֵּׁה רֵיחַ־נִיחֹחַ לַיהוָה׃
11 כָּכָה יֵעָשֶׂה לַשּׁוֹר הָאֶחָד אוֹ לָאַיִל
הָאֶחָד אוֹ־לַשֶּׂה בַכְּבָשִׂים אוֹ בָעִזִּים׃
12 כַּמִּסְפָּר אֲשֶׁר תַּעֲשׂוּ כָּכָה תַּעֲשׂוּ לָאֶחָד

law of *tzitzit* after that case is probably designed to illustrate how to prevent such violations of the commandments in the first place.

Many scholars maintain that the laws in Numbers 15 are late (post-exilic), serving to complement and supplement earlier laws in other parts of the Torah.

### SACRIFICES AND THEIR ACCOMPANIMENTS (15:1–16)

This section of laws addresses the individual Israelite regarding the correct combination of ingredients for the various sacrifices. The rituals outlined here call for animal burnt offerings (*olah*) and offerings of well-being (*zevach*) to be accompanied by a grain and oil mixture and wine (see Leviticus 1–3; 6–7), the combination being reminiscent of a complete meal. In the case of sacrifices, the meal is for the Deity. Although the Bible describes these offerings as "producing an odor pleasing to יהוה," it never states that God actually eats them.

*4. hin.* An Egyptian liquid measure equal to approximately six liters ($1\frac{1}{2}$ gallons).

*mixed in.* Or possibly "poured over."

there are. [13]Every citizen, when presenting an offering by fire of pleasing odor to יהוה, shall do so with them.

[14]And when, throughout the ages, a stranger who has taken up residence with you, or one who lives among you, would present an offering by fire of pleasing odor to יהוה—as you do, so shall it be done by [15]the rest of the congregation. There shall be one law for you and for the resident stranger; it shall be a law for all time throughout the ages. You and the stranger shall be alike before יהוה; [16]the same ritual and the same rule shall apply to you and to the stranger who resides among you.

[17]יהוה spoke to Moses, saying: [18]Speak to the Israelite people and say to them:

When you enter the land to which I am taking you [19]and you eat of the bread of the land, you shall set some aside as a gift to יהוה: [20]as the first yield of your baking, you shall set aside a loaf as a gift; you shall set it aside as a gift like the gift from the

כְּמִסְפָּרָם׃ 13 כָּל־הָאֶזְרָח יַעֲשֶׂה־כָּכָה אֶת־
אֵלֶּה לְהַקְרִיב אִשֵּׁה רֵיחַ־נִיחֹחַ לַיהֹוָה׃
14 וְכִי־יָגוּר אִתְּכֶם גֵּר אוֹ אֲשֶׁר־בְּתוֹכְכֶם
לְדֹרֹתֵיכֶם וְעָשָׂה אִשֵּׁה רֵיחַ־נִיחֹחַ לַיהֹוָה
כַּאֲשֶׁר תַּעֲשׂוּ כֵּן יַעֲשֶׂה׃ 15 הַקָּהָל חֻקָּה
אַחַת לָכֶם וְלַגֵּר הַגָּר חֻקַּת עוֹלָם
לְדֹרֹתֵיכֶם כָּכֶם כַּגֵּר יִהְיֶה לִפְנֵי יְהֹוָה׃
16 תּוֹרָה אַחַת וּמִשְׁפָּט אֶחָד יִהְיֶה לָכֶם
וְלַגֵּר הַגָּר אִתְּכֶם׃ פ

17 וַיְדַבֵּר יְהֹוָה אֶל־מֹשֶׁה לֵּאמֹר׃ 18 דַּבֵּר
אֶל־בְּנֵי יִשְׂרָאֵל וְאָמַרְתָּ אֲלֵהֶם
בְּבֹאֲכֶם אֶל־הָאָרֶץ אֲשֶׁר אֲנִי מֵבִיא
אֶתְכֶם שָׁמָּה׃ 19 וְהָיָה בַּאֲכָלְכֶם מִלֶּחֶם
הָאָרֶץ תָּרִימוּ תְרוּמָה לַיהֹוָה׃ 20 רֵאשִׁית
עֲרִסֹתֵכֶם חַלָּה תָּרִימוּ תְרוּמָה כִּתְרוּמַת גֹּרֶן

*15. one law for you and for the resident stranger.* In most matters, including sacrifices (except for the paschal lamb; see Exodus 12:48), the resident alien must be treated as the native Israelite.

## CHALLAH: OFFERING OF THE FIRST DOUGH (15:17–21)

The *challah* (dough offering) is the first part of dough made from grains prepared in the kneading basin. While somewhat analogous to the first fruits offering (Deuteronomy 26:1–11) and the tithes (Deuteronomy 14:22–29), the dough offering seems to be an additional levy, in this case for a product manufactured from already tithed grain. The dough, a gift dedicated to the sanctuary, is given to the priest; in turn, the homes of the Israelites are blessed (see Ezekiel 44:30). Women played an important role in food production in ancient Israel (see also at Exodus 16:3; 25:30). Not only did they perform agricultural tasks, but also they prepared the family meals. Making bread would have been a woman's daily chore. Tabuns ("ovens," from the Arabic) are often uncovered in excavations of residential courtyards. The Bible describes several women as kneading bread or cakes (Sarah in Genesis 18:6; the unnamed medium of En-dor in I Samuel 28:24; Tamar in II Samuel 13:8; see also at Leviticus 26:26). According to Jeremiah, women kneaded dough for cakes offered to the Queen of Heaven, a local goddess (Jeremiah 7:18).

*20. the first yield of your baking.* Literally, "the first of your baking vessel." The "baking vessel" (*arisah*) is evidently the term for a type of vessel used for kneading dough, possibly shaped like a crib (*eres*).

*20. loaf.* Heb. *challah*, a noun that seems to derive from the verbal root *ch-w-l*, "to be round." This type of raised loaf differs from the flat pita-like bread (so common in the region from antiquity to the present day) that the Bible likewise associates with offerings (like matzot in Leviticus 2:4).

threshing floor. [21]You shall make a gift to יהוה from
the first yield of your baking, throughout the ages.
[22]If you unwittingly fail to observe any one of
the commandments that יהוה has declared to Moses—[23]anything that יהוה has enjoined upon you
through Moses—from the day that יהוה gave the
commandment and on through the ages:
[24]If this was done unwittingly, through the in-
advertence of the community, the community
leaders shall present one bull of the herd as a burnt
offering of pleasing odor to יהוה, with its proper
meal offering and libation, and one he-goat as a
purgation offering. [25]The priest shall make expiation for the whole Israelite community and they
shall be forgiven; for it was an error, and for their
error they have brought their offering, an offering
by fire to יהוה and their purgation offering before
יהוה. [26]The whole Israelite community and the
stranger residing among them shall be forgiven, for
it happened to the entire people through error.
[27]In case it is an individual who has sinned unwittingly, that person shall offer a she-goat in its
first year as a purgation offering. [28]The priest shall
make expiation before יהוה on behalf of the person
who erred, for having sinned unwittingly, making
such expiation that the person may be forgiven.
[29]For the citizen among the Israelites and for the
stranger who resides among them—you shall have
one ritual for anyone who acts in error.

כֵּן תָּרִימוּ אֹתָהּ׃ 21 מֵרֵאשִׁית עֲרִסֹתֵיכֶם
תִּתְּנוּ לַיהוָה תְּרוּמָה לְדֹרֹתֵיכֶם׃
22 וְכִי תִשְׁגּוּ וְלֹא תַעֲשׂוּ אֵת כָּל־ ס
הַמִּצְוֺת הָאֵלֶּה אֲשֶׁר־דִּבֶּר יְהוָה אֶל־מֹשֶׁה׃
23 אֵת כָּל־אֲשֶׁר צִוָּה יְהוָה אֲלֵיכֶם בְּיַד־
מֹשֶׁה מִן־הַיּוֹם אֲשֶׁר צִוָּה יְהוָה וָהָלְאָה
לְדֹרֹתֵיכֶם׃
24 וְהָיָה אִם מֵעֵינֵי הָעֵדָה נֶעֶשְׂתָה לִשְׁגָגָה
וְעָשׂוּ כָל־הָעֵדָה פַּר בֶּן־בָּקָר אֶחָד לְעֹלָה
לְרֵיחַ נִיחֹחַ לַיהוָה וּמִנְחָתוֹ וְנִסְכּוֹ כַּמִּשְׁפָּט
וּשְׂעִיר־עִזִּים אֶחָד לְחַטָּת׃ 25 וְכִפֶּר הַכֹּהֵן
עַל־כָּל־עֲדַת בְּנֵי יִשְׂרָאֵל וְנִסְלַח לָהֶם כִּי־
שְׁגָגָה הִוא וְהֵם הֵבִיאוּ אֶת־קָרְבָּנָם אִשֶּׁה
לַיהוָה וְחַטָּאתָם לִפְנֵי יְהוָה עַל־שִׁגְגָתָם׃
26 וְנִסְלַח לְכָל־עֲדַת בְּנֵי יִשְׂרָאֵל וְלַגֵּר הַגָּר
בְּתוֹכָם כִּי לְכָל־הָעָם בִּשְׁגָגָה׃ ס
27 וְאִם־נֶפֶשׁ אַחַת תֶּחֱטָא בִשְׁגָגָה
וְהִקְרִיבָה עֵז בַּת־שְׁנָתָהּ לְחַטָּאת׃ 28 וְכִפֶּר
הַכֹּהֵן עַל־הַנֶּפֶשׁ הַשֹּׁגֶגֶת בְּחֶטְאָה בִשְׁגָגָה
לִפְנֵי יְהוָה לְכַפֵּר עָלָיו וְנִסְלַח לוֹ׃
29 הָאֶזְרָח בִּבְנֵי יִשְׂרָאֵל וְלַגֵּר הַגָּר בְּתוֹכָם
תּוֹרָה אַחַת יִהְיֶה לָכֶם לָעֹשֶׂה בִּשְׁגָגָה׃

*Challah* may be related to a type of Egyptian bread that was baked in pans to produce rounded dome-shaped loafs (Tomb painting of Ti, 5th Dynasty—Sakkara). Egyptians considered flat-bread undesirable (as in *lechem oni* or "bread of distress" in Deuteronomy 16:3).

## INADVERTENT COMMUNAL AND INDIVIDUAL WRONGS (15:22–31)

This section deals specifically with sacrificial offerings that function as expiation for inadvertent violations of the commandments. As prescribed for other sacrifices (vv. 1–16), these too require the proper accompaniments. This section ends with a warning.

***24. community leaders.*** Literally, "the entire community"; this translation aims to clarify that the word for community, *edah*, refers more precisely here to a representative body of some kind (most likely made up of adult males).

***29. one ritual.*** More correctly, "one law (*torah*)" applies to both Israelites and alien residents. Breaking a law has a negative effect on the Land of Israel's

<sup>30</sup>But the person, whether citizen or stranger, who acts defiantly reviles יהוה; that person shall be cut off from among the people. <sup>31</sup>Because it was the word of יהוה that was spurned and [God's] commandment that was violated, that person shall be cut off—and bears the guilt.

<sup>32</sup>Once, when the Israelites were in the wilderness, one of their fellows was found gathering wood on the sabbath day. <sup>33</sup>Those who found him as he was gathering wood brought him before Moses, Aaron, and the community leadership. <sup>34</sup>He was placed in custody, for it had not been specified what should be done to him. <sup>35</sup>Then יהוה said to Moses, "This fellow shall be put to death: the community leadership shall pelt him with stones outside the camp." <sup>36</sup>So the community leadership took him outside the camp and stoned him to death—as יהוה had commanded Moses.

<sup>37</sup>יהוה said to Moses as follows: <sup>38</sup>Speak to the Israelite people and instruct them to make for

30 וְהַנֶּ֣פֶשׁ אֲשֶֽׁר־תַּעֲשֶׂ֣ה ׀ בְּיָ֣ד רָמָ֗ה מִן־הָֽאֶזְרָח֙ וּמִן־הַגֵּ֔ר אֶת־יְהֹוָ֖ה ה֣וּא מְגַדֵּ֑ף וְנִכְרְתָ֛ה הַנֶּ֥פֶשׁ הַהִ֖וא מִקֶּ֥רֶב עַמָּֽהּ: 31 כִּ֤י דְבַר־יְהֹוָה֙ בָּזָ֔ה וְאֶת־מִצְוָת֖וֹ הֵפַ֑ר הִכָּרֵ֧ת ׀ תִּכָּרֵ֛ת הַנֶּ֥פֶשׁ הַהִ֖וא עֲוֺנָ֥ה בָֽהּ: פ

32 וַיִּהְי֥וּ בְנֵֽי־יִשְׂרָאֵ֖ל בַּמִּדְבָּ֑ר וַיִּמְצְא֗וּ אִ֛ישׁ מְקֹשֵׁ֥שׁ עֵצִ֖ים בְּי֥וֹם הַשַּׁבָּֽת: 33 וַיַּקְרִ֣יבוּ אֹת֔וֹ הַמֹּצְאִ֥ים אֹת֖וֹ מְקֹשֵׁ֣שׁ עֵצִ֑ים אֶל־מֹשֶׁה֙ וְאֶֽל־אַהֲרֹ֔ן וְאֶ֖ל כׇּל־הָעֵדָֽה: 34 וַיַּנִּ֥יחוּ אֹת֖וֹ בַּמִּשְׁמָ֑ר כִּ֚י לֹ֣א פֹרַ֔שׁ מַה־יֵּעָשֶׂ֖ה לֽוֹ: ס 35 וַיֹּ֤אמֶר יְהֹוָה֙ אֶל־מֹשֶׁ֔ה מ֥וֹת יוּמַ֖ת הָאִ֑ישׁ רָג֨וֹם אֹת֤וֹ בָֽאֲבָנִים֙ כׇּל־הָ֣עֵדָ֔ה מִח֖וּץ לַֽמַּחֲנֶֽה: 36 וַיֹּצִ֨יאוּ אֹת֜וֹ כׇּל־הָעֵדָ֗ה אֶל־מִחוּץ֙ לַֽמַּחֲנֶ֔ה וַיִּרְגְּמ֥וּ אֹת֛וֹ בָּאֲבָנִ֖ים וַיָּמֹ֑ת כַּאֲשֶׁ֛ר צִוָּ֥ה יְהֹוָ֖ה אֶת־מֹשֶֽׁה: פ

37 וַיֹּ֥אמֶר יְהֹוָ֖ה אֶל־מֹשֶׁ֥ה לֵּאמֹֽר: 38 דַּבֵּ֞ר אֶל־בְּנֵ֤י יִשְׂרָאֵל֙ וְאָמַרְתָּ֣ אֲלֵהֶ֔ם וְעָשׂ֨וּ לָהֶ֥ם

- - - - - - - - - - - - - - - - - - - - - - - - -

ability to retain God's Presence, therefore any lawbreaking inhabitant must make expiation.

**30. *that person shall be cut off.*** Defiant, willful violation of ritual law cannot be expiated in the manner of an inadvertent sin. *Kareit*, the "cutting off" of a person, is a punishment enacted by the Divine. What exactly constitutes the punishment is not defined here but can be gleaned from other biblical passages that indicate punishments affecting both sinners and their progeny (for example, Malachi 2:12, "To the one who does this, may יהוה leave no descendants...").

### A CASE OF
### WILLFUL SHABBAT VIOLATION (15:32–36)

The case of the wood-gatherer illustrates a most severe violation of the law, the willful desecration of Shabbat, which is a capital offense. It is not totally

clear why Moses consults God regarding the offender's punishment. Possibly, the reason is that earlier legislative texts that prescribe the death penalty are unclear as to whether punishment is to be exacted by a human court or by God (Exodus 31:14–15). So that no doubt remains, God sentences the violator to stoning at the hands of the community. This serious offense apparently is an affront to the entire community.

### THE LAW OF TZITZIT (15:37–41)

In antiquity, tassels and fringes were common on Canaanite and Mesopotamian clothing, and they held special significance. For example, prophets from the Babylonian city of Mari (second millennium) legitimated their oracles to the king by sending a fringe from their garment. Symbolically, the fringe was like a signature. The imprinting of

themselves fringes on the corners of their garments throughout the ages; let them attach a cord of blue to the fringe at each corner. 39That shall be your fringe; look at it and recall all the commandments of יהוה and observe them, so that you do not follow your heart and eyes in your lustful urge. 40Thus you shall be reminded to observe all My commandments and to be holy to your God. 41I יהוה am your God, who brought you out of the land of Egypt to be your God: I, your God יהוה.

צִיצִת עַל־כַּנְפֵי בִגְדֵיהֶם לְדֹרֹתָם וְנָתְנוּ
עַל־צִיצִת הַכָּנָף פְּתִיל תְּכֵלֶת׃ 39 וְהָיָה
לָכֶם לְצִיצִת וּרְאִיתֶם אֹתוֹ וּזְכַרְתֶּם אֶת־
כָּל־מִצְוֺת יְהוָה וַעֲשִׂיתֶם אֹתָם וְלֹא־
תָתוּרוּ אַחֲרֵי לְבַבְכֶם וְאַחֲרֵי עֵינֵיכֶם
אֲשֶׁר־אַתֶּם זֹנִים אַחֲרֵיהֶם׃ 40 לְמַעַן תִּזְכְּרוּ
וַעֲשִׂיתֶם אֶת־כָּל־מִצְוֺתָי וִהְיִיתֶם קְדֹשִׁים
לֵאלֹהֵיכֶם׃ 41 אֲנִי יְהוָה אֱלֹהֵיכֶם אֲשֶׁר
הוֹצֵאתִי אֶתְכֶם מֵאֶרֶץ מִצְרַיִם לִהְיוֹת
לָכֶם לֵאלֹהִים אֲנִי יְהוָה אֱלֹהֵיכֶם׃ פ

fringes on clay tablets was also a way of endorsing or verifying a written document. Like garments and hair, fringes were considered part of the individual's identity; thus, for example, giving one's fringe to another person signified a pledge of loyalty. Artistic depictions from these cultures show women wearing tasseled garments, especially women of high status.

Since in the ancient Near East both genders customarily wore fringed garments, and since biblical laws are commonly prescribed for the people as a whole, we can assume that the law of *tzitzit* was ordained for all Israelites, females and males. According to this text, the purpose of the tassels on the corners of the outer garments was to call the Israelites to action regarding the fulfillment of the commandments. What seems to distinguish these tassels from the more popular garment fringes is the addition of a colored cord that is to stand out in contrast to the other tassel fibers and remind the wearer of the commandments. It is probably not accidental that this cord is identical to the one that hangs from the high priest's headdress (Exodus 28:37). The *tzitzit* on the garments of Israelites identified them as being holy to God and symbolically may have connected them to the priests. Israelites who pledged loyalty to God also would have been loyal to the priests who oversaw God's laws.

***38. fringes.*** Heb. *tzitzit* probably means "ornament," something that draws attention to itself. In Exodus 28:36, the related noun *tzitz* describes the gold frontlet suspended on a blue chord that dangled from the priest's headdress.

***cord of blue.*** Deuteronomy 22:12 refers to nonspecific garment tassels as *g'dilim* ("twisted threads"), making no mention of any colored cords.

***blue.*** Heb. *t'cheilet*, a violet blue. On the dyeing of this color and on its social significance, see *T'rumah*, Another View, p. 476.

***39. recall.*** Heb. *zachor*, meaning "to remember," is often in the Bible a verb of action rather than thought (see Exodus 12:14).

***40. Thus you shall be reminded.*** [Verses 40 and 41 are the concluding part of the Jewish prayer known as Recitation of the *Sh'ma*. The Rabbis considered this prayer, which begins with "Hear, O Israel!" and continues with "You shall love your God יהוה with all your heart . . . ," to be central to the liturgy (see at Deuteronomy 6:4–9). —*Ed.*]

***be holy.*** On the call to holiness, see at Leviticus 19.

***41. I יהוה am your God, who brought you out of the land of Egypt.*** The parashah ends with reference to the redemption from Egyptian slavery, a theme often employed as grounds for Israelite allegiance to God (as in Exodus 6:7; 20:2–5; Leviticus 11:45).

—*Nili Sacher Fox*

# Another View

THE SCOUTS DISPATCHED to investigate the nature of the Promised Land have suffered from a bad reputation. The Torah and the commentators blame them for one generation's loss of the land, for forty years of wandering through the wilderness, and for Moses' untimely demise just beyond the border of the land. The ten scouts, however, can be seen in a different light.

When they commence their reconnaissance mission, all that the scouts and the people of Israel have heard of their destination is that God promised it to their ancestors, that it flows with milk and honey, and that it is populated by other peoples. The scouts' uncertainty as to whether Israel really belongs in its Promised Land results from their lack of knowledge and familiarity with this place. They experience Canaan through the filter of God's description and probe its veracity more than they investigate the landscape. Because they are unable to find evidence that legitimates God's promise of the land, the scouts reject promise and land alike.

The scouts begin by corroborating God's description: "it does indeed flow with milk and honey" (13:27), and it is inhabited by other people; but they go on to invert the elements of God's version. The land flowing with milk and honey becomes the land that eats its inhabitants; it is not like a nourishing mother offering sweet milk, but a cannibalistic mother not to be trusted (13:32). The peoples of Canaan are no ordinary nations, but Nephilim—a race of demigods born from the union of the sons of God and the daughters of humans (13:33; see also at Genesis 6:2–4). Next to their "enormous stature" the Israelites seem like "grasshoppers." In the land of primordial giants, Israel's ancestors are nowhere to be seen.

At this juncture, the majority of the scouts and the people have no will to wage war against giants or the land's inhabitants; better they should have no homeland than engage in what seem to be fruitless wars. The scouts' report fuels a narrative of opposition to the Promised Land—the place is a curse and not a blessing! It also opens up the possibility of a new identity: being an Israelite resistant to the notion that the people belong within a circumscribed territory. Instead of an inaugural vision, what the scouts report makes Israel want to go back to Egypt (Numbers 14:3–4). The scouts' story is the anti-myth of the Promised Land.

*The ten scouts have suffered from a bad reputation, yet their role was vital.*

—*Rachel Havrelock*

# Post-biblical Interpretations

***Send emissaries*** (13:2). A hyperliteral translation of the first three words of this verse reads, "Send for yourself men." In his 1602 commentary, the *Kli Yakar* (Rabbi Efraim Shlomo of Luntshits, Poland) claims that while the Israelite men of the wilderness generation hated the Land of Israel, the Israelite women loved it. His proof is based on the argument that the demand of the discontented Israelites, "Let us head back for Egypt" (14:4), represents the feelings of all the men, while "Give us a holding [in the Land of Israel] among our father's kinsmen!" (27:4)—although formally attributed only to the daughters of Zelophehad—actually represents the feelings of all of the women.

Based on these generalizations, the *Kli Yakar* claims that if God had chosen the scouts, God would have selected female scouts who loved the land, in order to ensure a positive report. Instead, when Moses was given permission to choose the scouts ("for yourself"), he made the tactical error of sending men instead.

***From the tribe of Judah, Caleb son of Jephunneh*** (13:6). Caleb, introduced for the first time in this verse, is identified by the names of his father and of his tribe. His wife's name, not surprisingly, is not included here, but she is identified in the Midrash. In fact, two wives are mentioned—each in a different midrashic text—and it is unclear if the Rabbis believed that he was married to both women at the same time, or to one after the other, or whether the two teachings existed independently. The wife more commonly connected with Caleb is Miriam, the sister of Moses (*Sh'mot Rabbah* 1.17). Meanwhile, Pharaoh's daughter, who had adopted Moses and whom rabbinic literature identifies as Bitya, is also described as Caleb's wife (BT *M'gillah* 13a). Neither of these marriages is mentioned in the Bible, and each is derived from a complex rabbinic interpretation of different genealogical lists in the book of Chronicles (I Chronicles 2:18–19 for Miriam; I Chronicles 4:18 for Bitya).

*If God had chosen the scouts, they would have been women—not men.*

***and you eat of the bread of the land, you shall set some aside*** (15:19). This verse describes the commandment of *challah*. This commandment does not mandate the eating of special loaves of bread on Shabbat (known later in Judaism also as "challah") but applies instead to the baking process. To perform the mitzvah of *challah*, the baker ritually removes a tiny portion of the raw dough and recites a specific blessing. When the Temple stood in Jerusalem, this consecrated portion was to be eaten by the priests. Since the destruction of the Temple in 70 C.E., the piece of separated dough is to be burned in the oven and thrown away. Separating *challah* is one of three commandments that are traditionally and specifically associated with—and performed by—women. (The other two are candle lighting for Shabbat and the rituals concerning menstrual purity.)

Bread baking is usually regarded as a female activity, but it may also be seen as the exemplar of the many mundane tasks needed to provide physical nourishment for one's family. The anonymous author of the 13th-century *Sefer haChinuch* (385:1) emphasized this latter aspect of bread baking when he suggested that the commandment of *challah* allows women to take an ordinary act and elevate it to the spiritual. While eating the bread feeds the body, the ritual aspect of making the bread feeds the soul.

Midrash *B'reishit Rabbah* 17.8, which connects the idea of *challah* with the creation of humankind, takes a less positive view of women's fulfillment of this commandment. This midrash imagines that at the moment of human creation God removed a small portion of the newly formed earth for a special purpose, the creation of Adam. Thus, Adam became the *challah* of the world. Eve, the first woman, corrupted Adam by encouraging him to eat from the forbidden Tree of Knowledge. According to this rabbinic view, the commandment of *challah* was specifically given to women as a reminder of Eve's sin and as a means of spiritual atonement.

[Some of the extant early modern supplicatory prayers in Yiddish (*tkhines*) were intended for women to recite while separating *challah*. These prayers refer to the ancient bringing of tithes and recall female participation in ancient Temple worship. They also invoke the messianic era when the Temple's rites will be restored. One such supplication requests that an angel guard the baking and prevent the bread from burning, just as angels had guarded the *challah* of the biblical matriarchs (Chava Weissler, *Voices of the Matriarchs*, 1998, pp. 29–35, 68–75). —*Ed.*]

—*Anna Urowitz-Freudenstein*

# Contemporary Reflection

WHEN MOSES SENDS the scouts to survey the land of Canaan, he gives them a list of very specific things to investigate. He charges them: "Go up there into the Negeb and on into the hill country, and see what kind of country it is. Are the people who dwell in it strong or weak, few or many? Is the country in which they dwell good or bad? Are the towns they live in open or fortified? Is the soil rich or poor? Is it wooded or not?" (13:17–20). Twelve emissaries go out and return after forty days, reporting on what they saw in this exotic new land. All but two of the scouts are punished later; victims of a plague, they die in the wilderness.

What is their sin? According to our tradition, they sin by not trusting God's vision and not having faith: "How long will this people spurn Me, and how long will they have no faith in Me despite all the signs that I have performed in their midst?" (14:11). Furthermore, they sin because they "caused the whole community to mutter against him [Moses] by spreading calumnies about the land" (14:36).

I question not only the nature of their sin, but also Moses' approach to their mission. Moses' instructions divide the world into either/or categories that ignore the nuances within a complex reality. Instead of asking such specific questions, what if he had said to them, "When you return, tell us what you see. How did you experience this new place? What was the land like? How were the people?" Perhaps these kinds of open-ended questions would have led the scouts to bring back a different report. At least these sorts of instructions might have given them more room to develop their own stories in a less dualistic fashion; the scouts might have been inspired to bring back a different description of what they saw.

Or is it simply a matter of perspective? After all, the twelve emissaries all observe and experience the same things, and yet two of them return with an account that is entirely different from that of the other ten. What is it that enables Joshua and Caleb to see the Promised Land through different eyes?

In his book *The Courage to Create* (1975), Rollo May writes, "We are called upon to do something new, to confront a no-man's-land, to push into a forest where there are no well-worn paths and from which no one has returned to guide us. This is what existentialists call the anxiety of nothingness. . . . To live into the future means to leap into the unknown, and this requires a degree of courage for which there is no immediate precedent and which few people realize." He asserts that "if you do not express your own original ideas, if you do not listen to your own being, you will have betrayed yourself. Also you will have betrayed our community in failing to make your contribution to the whole" (pp. 12–13).

*What enables Joshua and Caleb to see the Promised Land through different eyes?*

The ten emissaries start their report with a positive statement about the land overflowing with milk and honey; they then switch to the negatively colored description of the fortified cities and powerful people (13:27–29). The Rabbis describe this as the way slanderers speak: "They begin with flattering and end with evil" (BT *Sotah* 35a). Or, in more modern terms: the pessimist observes a situation, generalizes about the bad aspects, and interprets them as a permanent and constant feature. In contrast, the optimist observes the same situation and sees the bad aspects, but particularizes them and interprets them as a temporary obstacle that can be overcome.

This then is the sin of the scouts: their failure to contribute to their community because of their negative attitude and narrow perspective. They seemingly lack the courage to leap into the unknown and confront "no-man's-land." Where the ten see potential failure and defeat, Joshua and Caleb see potential success and possibility. They had the courage to leap into the unknown and envision a new reality. While they acknowledge the challenges that lie ahead, they are able to "listen to their own being" and trust in the people's ability to overcome those challenges with God's promised help and protection: "The land that we traversed and scouted is an exceedingly good land. If pleased with us, יהוה will bring us into that land, a land that flows with milk and honey, and give it to us; only you must not rebel against יהוה. Have no fear then of the people of the country, for they are our prey: their protection has departed from them, but יהוה is with us" (14:7–9).

As Harvey Fields wrote, we too can "conquer 'Promised Lands' when we have regard for our talents and believe in our creative powers. The sin of the spies grows from their failure of self-love and self-respect. . . . Only Joshua and Caleb, who refuse to see themselves as 'grasshoppers,' are worthy of entering the Promised Land" (*A Torah Commentary for Our Times*, 1993, p. 42).

These, to me, are the challenges of *Sh'lach L'cha*: First, the challenge to perceive the world in all its nuanced complexity—and not reduce it to simplistic either/or, black/white categories. Second, and more central to the parashah, the challenge of really loving ourselves and trusting our instincts, the challenge of not making ourselves into anything less than we truly are (since this would diminish the One in whose image we are created), and the challenge of living with the "anxiety of nothingness" in order to create a new reality.

As long as we see ourselves merely as grasshoppers up against giants, we will set ourselves up for failure. If we want to create anything new and to enter into the Promised Land, then we have no choice but to leap into the unknown, to believe in ourselves, and to trust in God's faith in us. This voice of optimism and hope is what separates Joshua and Caleb from the other scouts. This is what—in spite of a long history filled with good reasons to see ourselves as grasshoppers and to give up—has enabled the Jewish people to continue and to thrive.

—*Josee Wolff*

# Voices

## At Light's Border

Lea Goldberg (transl. Rachel Tzvia Back)

*Numbers 13:27–33*

*1*
Here heavy birds alight to rest
on trees dark in the day's decline,
and in reaped fields the wind wanders
toward the firmament's red trail.

A gust of salt air from across the sea,
a crescent moon painting itself on the sky,
a flickering white, cautious, unsure
it is all vacillation between day and night.

This is the hour of transition wherein we
stand mute
at light's border—
where will our hearts turn?
Will we return, my brother,
will we cross over?

*2*
All the riddles time has posed
skies like these awaken anew,
the innocent will tell their dreams
and the clever their answers conceal.

And again our hearts will bathe in blood
as empty regrets guard every step,
and again you unknowingly ask
all the riddles time has kept.

My brother, my brother, how can we stand
mute
at light's border—
what path is before us?
Will we return, my brother,
will we cross over?

## Sh'lach L'cha

Laurie Patton

*Numbers 13:27–33*

When one visits a Vision,
one must always
struggle with scale:

Their visit
was like watching
the shoes and skirts
and deep voices
at a parents' reception—
watching, overwhelmed
and hiding, under the stair

or the coding
and decoding
of the signals of elm trees
and broken twigs—
the ciphers of sparrows
and their forgotten eggs
in the immense forests
of an aunt's small garden

or the daily memory
of a schoolyard
filled with light—
wet, and covered with apples—
a huge space,
with windows beckoning
to the soul

Visions are so wide,
they require the courage
of painters, trying out
a new and startling scale;

and they require an answer
to the question:
Shall I belong here?

## *from* A Poem to the Paper Bridge

Kadya Molodowsky (transl. Kathryn Hellerstein)

*Numbers 13:27–33*

Oh, paper bridge, lead me into your land,
White and constant and mild.
I am tired of the desert where manna was
strewn
Made of milk and honey and bread.

A simple people, with their earthen jugs,
With children, with cattle, with tears,
Constructed a paper bridge of such strength
It withstands the destruction of years.

## Prayer for Burning the End Piece of the Challah

Lynn Gottlieb

*Numbers 15:18–21*

With this challah, I honor my mothers,
Who enticed wisdom from grain.
I honor the fire,
Which transforms again and again.
I honor the love which flows through my hands,
And I honor the Spirit
That brings forth this bread from the earth.
Amen.

## *from* Dakota Diaspora: Memoirs of a Jewish Homesteader

Sophie Trupin

*Numbers 15:18–21*

I remember my mother arising on Fridays while it was still dark to begin the added tasks of preparing for the Sabbath. Dough was kneaded the night before and lay in a large basin which was nestled in the hollow of a huge feather pillow. The pillow kept the dough warm all night so it would rise. A white tablecloth was placed over the basin, and in the morning the dough would look like an enormous mushroom extending over the rim of the basin. My mother would press her fist into the center of the mound, which would collapse in a wrinkled heap. She would continue to knead it for a few minutes, then replace the white tablecloth and allow it to rise once more. After a few hours the tablecloth would again be lifted into a mound; it was then ready to make the Sabbath loaf, or *challah.* While my mother braided the long ropes of dough into a huge oval, I would have a piece of dough to make a miniature *challah.* At first I could only manipulate three strands, braiding them into something like my own braided hair; but then, as I watched my mother working with four strands of dough, I practiced until I could do it too.

Before baking the loaves, which had risen and been glossed over with beaten egg applied with a goose feather, my mother would take a small piece of dough and throw it into the flame of the kitchen range, reciting a special prayer. It was some relic of the old days of sacrifice—some part of an ancient ritual.

## *My Entitlement and My Obligation*

Riv-Ellen Prell

*Numbers 15:37–41*

The transforming moment of my life as a Jewish feminist came when I began wearing a *tallit*. . . . I don't remember putting the *tallit* on for the first time; it wasn't a moment I ritualized. I simply became a Jew who prayed in a *tallit*, experiencing my entitlement to its sensuous beauty as part of my obligation to wear this garment. My public and unambiguous violation of normative Judaism was linked to my growing private life as a Jew. My *tallit* left me nowhere to hide.

## *from The Tapestry of Jewish Time*

Nina Beth Cardin

*Numbers 15:37–41*

When I put on a *tallit*, even when I am alone, I place myself in the folds of my people. Donning the *tallit* is a daily, visual symbol of my identity, reminding me to whom I belong as I begin my day's journey. It protects me, shields me and defines me. Falling around my shoulders and arms, the *tallit* provides me with a secure awareness of my body and its boundaries. I am not lost there, but found. Others are outside, I am inside, but we are one. I fill up my *tallit*. No matter my size, I always will. And it is in that fullness that I am counted as a member of the congregation.

## *Fringes in My Heart*

Nancy Abraham

*Numbers 15:37–41*

There are fringes in my heart  
knotted with love for You  
They hang from the four chambers  
sway gently as tides within  
rise      recede rise      recede  
Sometimes when still  
I can even hear You  
brushing against them  
these fringes composed of all  
You ask us to be  
woven of your essence  
they are bound in me  
I in them  
a sign of sacred servitude

With this knotting  
swaying  
brushing  
weaving,  
Your presence hangs  
pulling me, like water,  
to the surety of freedom exacted  
for such blessed binding  
between my heart and Yours.

# קרח ✦ *Korach*

## NUMBERS 16:1–18:32

### *Leadership, Rebellions, and Punishments*

MOSES' LEADERSHIP is challenged repeatedly throughout the book of Numbers (see, for example, Numbers 12, 14, and 21). In this parashah, rebels challenge not only Moses' guidance, but also Aaron's religious authority. Scholars have long recognized that Numbers 16 combines at least two stories of insurrection: Korah and his company challenge Aaron's exclusive right to make ritual offerings to God; Dathan and Abiram question Moses' abilities and authority. Each story has a separate focus and outcome; nevertheless, they share important features in common. Both of them turn on questions of the legitimacy of the current leadership, both demonstrate that the current leadership is divinely ordained, and both are resolved by divine wrath in a way in which the punishment fits the crime.

In these two episodes, the people fail to see that God—not Moses or Aaron—is the one responsible for electing the civil and religious authorities. When the challengers continue to speak against Moses and Aaron, God sends a plague (17:6–15). To demonstrate that Aaron's post as chief priest is due to divine preference and not human election, God commands each of the tribes to present a staff at the Tabernacle (17:16–26). The miraculous fruit-bearing of only Aaron's staff proves that God has chosen only the House of Aaron for the priesthood. The different duties, responsibilities, and restrictions associated with Levites and priests then are further specified and detailed at the end of the parashah (18:1–32).

Women do not play much of a role in *parashat Korach*, with good reason: there is little place for women in a contest for either religious or political leadership. Aside from Miriam, Deborah (Judges 4–5), and Queen Athaliah (II Kings 11), there are hardly any female Israelite leaders recorded as such in the Bible. Miriam is a notable exception to the near absence of female

*Dathan's and Abiram's wives suffer God's wrath; those of Korah's company do not.*

leaders, for she is included in the inner circle of power along with Moses and Aaron. The prophet Micah (8th century B.C.E.) reflects this view when he proclaims in God's name, "I redeemed you from the house of bondage, and I sent before you Moses, Aaron, and Miriam" (Micah 6:4). Thus, the possibility of a female leader alongside male leaders certainly existed.

It is true that, as Tikva Frymer-Kensky has noted, the book of Samuel depicts an *ishah* of special status who claimed the authority to represent her town in emergency negotiations with a hostile general who recognized her authority as a matter of course (II Samuel 20:15–22). Apparently it went without saying that she was an elder, because that presumption best accounts for the city elders' otherwise striking absence in the negotiations (compare Judges 8, 9, 11; *Reading the Women of the Bible*, 2002, pp. 58–61). And Susan Ackerman has argued that it may have gone without saying that the role of queen mother was an acknowledged position of political and religious leadership (*Warrior, Dancer, Seductress, Queen*, 1998, pp. 133–141). However, while female leadership may be occasionally discernible in Israelite historical memory, the Bible itself highlights very few women in leadership roles.

Even though the rebels' wives are not involved in the uprising, they pay the price for their husbands' actions, as the families of Dathan and Abiram also suffer the fate of God's wrath. In contrast, the women related to Korah's company are not punished for their challenge to the priesthood. Perhaps this is because women cannot serve as priests; hence, they may not have been present when their husbands offered incense to God. Unlike in Numbers 12, where both Miriam and Aaron spoke against Moses yet only Miriam bore the punishment, in *parashat Korach*, Dathan's and Abiram's families are included in the punishment for political insurrection. This suggests that the punishment would have served as a warning to any contender for power, female or male.

—*Shawna Dolansky*

## *Outline*

*I.* The Rebellions (16:1–35)

- A. Korah's challenge to the Aaronite priesthood (vv. 1–11)
- B. Dathan and Abiram's mutiny against Mosaic leadership (vv. 12–15)
- C. Korah's test (vv. 16–24)
- D. Dathan and Abiram's punishment (vv. 25–31)
- E. Korah's punishment (vv. 32–35)

*II.* The Aftermath (17:1–28)

- A. Transformation of the fire pans (vv. 1–5)
- B. More rebellion (vv. 6–7)
- C. Plague and expiation (vv. 8–15)
- D. Aaron's budding rod (vv. 16–28)

*III.* Priestly Responsibilities (18:1–32)

- A. Priests and Levites (vv. 1–7)
- B. Gifts (vv. 8–20)
- C. Tithes (vv. 21–32)

Now Korah, son of Izhar son of Kohath son of Levi, betook himself, along with Dathan and Abiram sons of Eliab, and On son of Peleth—descendants of Reuben—2to rise up against Moses,

טז וַיִּקַּח קֹרַח בֶּן־יִצְהָר בֶּן־קְהָת בֶּן־לֵוִי
וְדָתָן וַאֲבִירָם בְּנֵי אֱלִיאָב וְאוֹן בֶּן־פֶּלֶת בְּנֵי
רְאוּבֵן׃ 2 וַיָּקֻמוּ לִפְנֵי מֹשֶׁה וַאֲנָשִׁים מִבְּנֵי־

## *The Rebellions* (16:1–35)

Two distinct groups, from two separate tribes, rise up together against Moses and Aaron. Moses addresses them in parallel fashion in two incidents that culminate in the destruction of each group. Because of the separate nature of the two rebellions and their ensuing punishments, scholars suspect that these were originally independent, unconnected stories. This theory is strengthened by Deuteronomy 11:6, which refers to Dathan and Abiram without, however, mentioning Korah or any Levites.

Korah, a first cousin of Moses and Aaron (Exodus 6:18–21), and certain Levite representatives challenge Aaron's exclusive right to the priesthood, whereas Dathan and Abiram question Moses' leadership abilities. That incident resembles Miriam and Aaron's challenge of Moses' role as prophet (Numbers 12), though the contrast in God's retaliation may suggest a leniency with respect to Miriam—and even more so, Aaron—in Numbers 12. The Korah rebellion frames the separate confrontation by Dathan and Abiram, who challenge Moses.

### KORAH'S CHALLENGE TO THE AARONITE PRIESTHOOD (16:1–11)

Korah's challenge to the Aaronite priesthood can be explained by his own Levite lineage, which the narrator pointedly notes (v. 1). Korah protests to Moses that all Levites should be considered holy enough for the priesthood. (In 8:5–22, God had uniquely consecrated the Levites, providing some grounds for Korah's presumption.)

[When the daughters of Zelophehad (from the tribe of Manasseh) later confront the leadership, they find it politic to contrast their challenge with Korah's rebellion. When they demand their father's land, they cleverly distance their dead father from Korah by hastening to say: "Our father . . . was not one of the faction, Korah's faction, which banded together against יהוה" (27:3). —*Ed.*]

*1. Korah . . . son of Levi . . . along with Dathan and Abiram . . . descendants of Reuben.* Korah is identified by his father, grandfather, and tribal affiliation. This partly accounts for his claim to the priesthood: he is Aaron's patrilineal first cousin. But Dathan and Abiram's rebellion against Mosaic leadership is not readily explicable by lineage. Perhaps

▶ The story's focus shifts authority away from the family's head and toward the priests.

ANOTHER VIEW ➤ *909*

▶ How do I recognize Korah in my own thoughts and actions?

CONTEMPORARY REFLECTION ➤ *911*

▶ Why was that rebel On not punished? —His wife got him drunk and kept him home.

POST-BIBLICAL INTERPRETATIONS ➤ *909*

▶ a fist of life / thrusts up through sand / and opens its palm. . . .

VOICES ➤ *913*

together with two hundred and fifty representatives of the Israelites: chieftains of the community, chosen in the assembly, with fine reputations. 3They combined against Moses and Aaron and said to them, "You have gone too far! For all the community are holy, all of them, and יהוה is in their midst. Why then do you raise yourselves above יהוה's congregation?"

4When Moses heard this, he fell on his face. 5Then he spoke to Korah and all his company, saying, "Come morning, יהוה will make known who is [God's] and who is holy, and will grant him direct access; the one whom [God] has chosen will be granted access. 6Do this: You, Korah and all your band, take fire pans, 7and tomorrow put fire in

יִשְׂרָאֵל חֲמִשִּׁים וּמָאתָיִם נְשִׂיאֵי עֵדָה
קְרִאֵי מוֹעֵד אַנְשֵׁי־שֵׁם׃ 3 וַיִּקָּהֲלוּ עַל־מֹשֶׁה
וְעַל־אַהֲרֹן וַיֹּאמְרוּ אֲלֵהֶם רַב־לָכֶם כִּי כׇל־
הָעֵדָה כֻּלָּם קְדֹשִׁים וּבְתוֹכָם יְהֹוָה וּמַדּוּעַ
תִּתְנַשְּׂאוּ עַל־קְהַל יְהֹוָה׃
4 וַיִּשְׁמַע מֹשֶׁה וַיִּפֹּל עַל־פָּנָיו׃ 5 וַיְדַבֵּר אֶל־
קֹרַח וְאֶל־כׇּל־עֲדָתוֹ לֵאמֹר בֹּקֶר וְיֹדַע יְהֹוָה
אֶת־אֲשֶׁר־לוֹ וְאֶת־הַקָּדוֹשׁ וְהִקְרִיב אֵלָיו
וְאֵת אֲשֶׁר יִבְחַר־בּוֹ יַקְרִיב אֵלָיו׃ 6 זֹאת
עֲשׂוּ קְחוּ־לָכֶם מַחְתּוֹת קֹרַח וְכׇל־עֲדָתוֹ׃
7 וּתְנוּ בָהֵן ׀ אֵשׁ וְשִׂימוּ עֲלֵיהֶן ׀ קְטֹרֶת לִפְנֵי

Dathan and Abiram are simply representative of the general Israelite unhappiness with the wilderness experience and Moses' leadership, an unhappiness that forms a theme throughout Exodus and Numbers. [Reuben was Jacob's first-born son; Reubenites may have seen themselves as rightful leaders. —*Ed.*]

2. ***together with two hundred and fifty representatives of the Israelites: chieftains of the community.*** Later in the narrative, these chieftains who join the mutiny against Moses are connected with the Levites who challenge Aaron (v. 35), providing a good example of the redactional activity that links these originally separate texts.

3. ***"You have gone too far!"*** Heb. *rav lachem*, an idiom that more literally means: "It is more than enough for you."

***"For all the community are holy."*** This statement is the focus of Korah's challenge to Aaron's exclusive right to the priesthood, but the language is abstract enough that it works for Dathan and Abiram's rebellion against Moses' civic leadership as well. That they are two separate rebellions, with distinct foci, is evidenced instead from Moses' different responses to each party. One thing that they share in common, however, is that they address their complaints about leadership choices to Moses.

***"and יהוה is in their midst."*** The rebels state that the entire congregation is holy because God dwells within it, and this appears to be consonant with priestly literature in which God promises to live in Israel's midst (see Exodus 29:45) and where the people are called to be holy (see Exodus 19:6). This ideal of a holy nation recurs throughout the priestly texts, including the ending of the previous story, which again calls Israel to be holy (Numbers 15:40). But the challengers miss the point of these divine injunctions toward holiness: the congregation is not holy by virtue of God's presence, but in fact they must maintain holiness in order to ensure God's continued residence among them. Korah challenges the need for a priestly hierarchy if all are holy. The lesson to be derived from his fiery death is that the priestly hierarchy is necessary in order to maintain the congregation's holiness.

5. ***"will grant him . . . access."*** Literally, God "will bring him closer." The verb *hikriv* (from the root *k-r-b*) means "to bring near" and is related to the noun for "sacrifice" (*korban*). The priests possess a higher degree of holiness by virtue of their closeness to God. The test that Moses poses will separate those who are closest to God from the rest of the congregation.

6–7. ***"take fire pans . . . and lay incense on them."*** It was precisely a misuse of incense that

them and lay incense on them before יהוה. Then the candidate whom יהוה chooses, he shall be the holy one. You have gone too far, sons of Levi!"

[8]Moses said further to Korah, "Hear me, sons of Levi. [9]Is it not enough for you that the God of Israel has set you apart from the community of Israel and given you direct access, to perform the duties of יהוה's Tabernacle and to minister to the community and serve them? [10]Now that [God] has advanced you and all your fellow Levites with you, do you seek the priesthood too? [11]Truly, it is against יהוה that you and all your company have banded together. For who is Aaron that you should rail against him?"

[12]Moses sent for Dathan and Abiram, sons of Eliab; but they said, "We will not come! [13]Is it not

יְהוָה מָחָר וְהָיָה הָאִישׁ אֲשֶׁר־יִבְחַר יְהוָה
הוּא הַקָּדוֹשׁ רַב־לָכֶם בְּנֵי לֵוִי׃
8 וַיֹּאמֶר מֹשֶׁה אֶל־קֹרַח שִׁמְעוּ־נָא בְּנֵי לֵוִי׃
9 הַמְעַט מִכֶּם כִּי־הִבְדִּיל אֱלֹהֵי יִשְׂרָאֵל
אֶתְכֶם מֵעֲדַת יִשְׂרָאֵל לְהַקְרִיב אֶתְכֶם
אֵלָיו לַעֲבֹד אֶת־עֲבֹדַת מִשְׁכַּן יְהוָה וְלַעֲמֹד
לִפְנֵי הָעֵדָה לְשָׁרְתָם׃ 10 וַיַּקְרֵב אֹתְךָ וְאֶת־
כָּל־אַחֶיךָ בְנֵי־לֵוִי אִתָּךְ וּבִקַּשְׁתֶּם גַּם־
כְּהֻנָּה׃ 11 לָכֵן אַתָּה וְכָל־עֲדָתְךָ הַנֹּעָדִים
עַל־יְהוָה וְאַהֲרֹן מַה־הוּא כִּי תלונו תַלִּינוּ
עָלָיו׃
12 וַיִּשְׁלַח מֹשֶׁה לִקְרֹא לְדָתָן וְלַאֲבִירָם בְּנֵי
אֱלִיאָב וַיֹּאמְרוּ לֹא נַעֲלֶה׃ 13 הַמְעַט כִּי

had resulted in the deaths of Aaron's sons Nadab and Abihu (Leviticus 10:1–2). Korah is making a claim on the priesthood, so Moses challenges Korah to demonstrate that he can perform a priestly task. Moses' test does not aim to show who can *best* perform priestly services for the community. Rather, it is designed to demonstrate that God is the one who has chosen Aaron for the priesthood.

*10. "Levites . . . priesthood."* General holiness is demanded of a congregation in which God dwells (see at 16:3). Moses here refers to two higher levels of holiness. Above the general congregation is the additional holiness of the Levites (*b'nei Levi*) who are "close to" God (*k-r-b* again; see at v. 5) and can therefore minister on behalf of the congregation at the Tabernacle. The third and the highest level of holiness is demonstrated by the additional closeness to God enjoyed exclusively by Aaron and his descendants, the priests (*kohanim*). Note that since only Aaron and his descendants are priests, Moses himself implicitly belongs among the Levites, like the rest of the house of Levi apart from his brother's line.

*11. "it is against* **יהוה** *that you and all your company have banded together."* God is the one who elevated Aaron's status beyond the other Levites; neither Aaron's appointment as chief priest, nor the punishment that Korah receives for attempting to replace him, result from choices that Moses has made. By deferring judgment and punishment to God in the test-by-incense, Moses demonstrates that Korah's complaint to Moses should have been addressed to God in the first place.

### DATHAN AND ABIRAM'S MUTINY AGAINST MOSAIC LEADERSHIP (16:12–15)

Dathan and Abiram criticize Moses' leadership, blaming him for the poor conditions of the people in the wilderness and accusing him of not fulfilling his promises to them of land and possessions. As with Korah, the accusations are misplaced. Moses is responsible for neither the wilderness situation nor the choice of Aaron as high priest. The second story of rebellion begins when Moses sends for Dathan and Abiram, but they refuse to come—complaining bitterly about Moses' leadership of the people in the wilderness.

*12. "We will not come!"* This translation of Dathan and Abiram's response does not convey the subtle irony inherent in the use of the verb *alah* ("to go up"). Here they declare, "We will not come

enough that you brought us from a land flowing with milk and honey to have us die in the wilderness, that you would also lord it over us? [14]Even if you had brought us to a land flowing with milk and honey, and given us possession of fields and vineyards, should you gouge out those subordinates' eyes? We will not come!" [15]Moses was much aggrieved and he said to יהוה, "Pay no regard to their oblation. I have not taken the ass of any one of them, nor have I wronged any one of them."

[16]And Moses said to Korah, "Tomorrow, you and all your company appear before יהוה, you and they and Aaron. [17]Each of you take his fire pan and lay incense on it, and each of you bring his fire pan

הֶעֱלִיתָ֙נוּ֙ מֵאֶ֣רֶץ זָבַ֤ת חָלָב֙ וּדְבַ֔שׁ לַהֲמִיתֵ֖נוּ בַּמִּדְבָּ֑ר כִּֽי־תִשְׂתָּרֵ֥ר עָלֵ֖ינוּ גַּם־הִשְׂתָּרֵֽר׃
14 אַ֡ף לֹ֣א אֶל־אֶ֩רֶץ֩ זָבַ֨ת חָלָ֤ב וּדְבַשׁ֙ הֲבִ֣יאֹתָ֔נוּ וַתִּ֨תֶּן־לָ֔נוּ נַחֲלַ֖ת שָׂדֶ֣ה וָכָ֑רֶם הַעֵינֵ֞י הָאֲנָשִׁ֥ים הָהֵ֛ם תְּנַקֵּ֖ר לֹ֥א נַעֲלֶֽה׃
15 וַיִּ֤חַר לְמֹשֶׁה֙ מְאֹ֔ד וַיֹּ֙אמֶר֙ אֶל־יְהֹוָ֔ה אַל־תֵּ֖פֶן אֶל־מִנְחָתָ֑ם לֹ֠א חֲמ֨וֹר אֶחָ֤ד מֵהֶם֙ נָשָׂ֔אתִי וְלֹ֥א הֲרֵעֹ֖תִי אֶת־אַחַ֥ד מֵהֶֽם׃
16 וַיֹּ֤אמֶר מֹשֶׁה֙ אֶל־קֹ֔רַח אַתָּה֙ וְכׇל־עֲדָ֣תְךָ֔ הֱי֖וּ לִפְנֵ֣י יְהֹוָ֑ה אַתָּ֥ה וָהֵ֛ם וְאַהֲרֹ֖ן מָחָֽר׃
17 וּקְח֣וּ ׀ אִ֣ישׁ מַחְתָּת֗וֹ וּנְתַתֶּ֤ם עֲלֵיהֶם֙ קְטֹ֔רֶת וְהִקְרַבְתֶּ֞ם לִפְנֵ֣י יְהֹוָ֗ה אִ֚ישׁ מַחְתָּת֔וֹ

---

up"; later, they will indeed be punished by being brought *down* into the depths of the earth (vv. 31–33), never to "come up" again.

*13.    "a land flowing with milk and honey."*    The rebels' sarcastic remarks invert Moses' promises to bring the Israelites from Egypt to a land flowing with milk and honey (Exodus 13:5; Numbers 14:8). They use the expression instead to describe Egypt as a paradise (see also Exodus 16:3).

*"to have us die."*    Literally, "to kill us." Dathan and Abiram imply that Moses aims to cause their deaths through the harsh conditions in the wilderness (see also Exodus 16:3). Ironically, the reason for the delay in reaching the Promised Land is a similar protest in Numbers 14. There, when the people complained that God had brought them out of Egypt only to die in the wilderness (14:2), God threatened to destroy the entire congregation (14:12). Moses pleaded with God on their behalf, and God relented (14:23). Again, it is clear that the present complaint against Moses is misdirected, as Moses points out to God in the following verse, and as he will further inform the people in v. 28.

*"you would also lord it over us."*    More precisely, "you continue to act as a prince over us." The Heb. *tistarer* is a verbal form of the noun "prince" (*sar*). This is a direct challenge to Moses' continued leadership, based on his perceived failure to deliver on his promise of fields and vineyards in a land flowing with milk and honey (Exodus 3:8, 17; 13:5; 33:3). These words echo an earlier accusation against Moses in Exodus 2:14, when one of the Hebrews asks Moses, "Who made you a prince (*sar*) and judge over us?"

*15.    "Pay no regard to their oblation."*    Moses asks God not to accept the rebels' sacrificial offering, protesting that he has done nothing to deserve their accusations. This type of plea to a god or gods was common in ancient Near Eastern treaty curses and execrations, which implore the deity not to accept the offerings of anyone who either violates the terms of the treaty or who acts disrespectfully toward the king (see Malachi 2:13).

## KORAH'S TEST (16:16–24)

Having set forth the two types of challenges, one about priestly authority and the other about civic leadership, the narrative turns from Dathan and Abiram back to Korah. Korah's entire company will undergo the test, including the 250 chieftains mentioned in 16:2, as they all attempt to offer incense alongside Moses and Aaron in front of the divine Presence at the Tent of Meeting.

before יהוה, two hundred and fifty fire pans; you and Aaron also [bring] your fire pans." [18]Each of them took his fire pan, put fire in it, laid incense on it, and took his place at the entrance of the Tent of Meeting, as did Moses and Aaron. [19]Korah gathered the whole community against them at the entrance of the Tent of Meeting.

Then the Presence of יהוה appeared to the whole community, [20]and יהוה spoke to Moses and Aaron, saying, [21]"Stand back from this community that I may annihilate them in an instant!" [22]But they fell on their faces and said, "O God, Source of the breath of all flesh! When one member sins, will You be wrathful with the whole community?"

[23]יהוה spoke to Moses, saying, [24]"Speak to the community and say: Withdraw from about the abodes of Korah, Dathan, and Abiram."

[25]Moses rose and went to Dathan and Abiram, the elders of Israel following him. [26]He addressed the community, saying, "Move away from the tents of these wicked fellows and touch nothing that belongs to them, lest you be wiped out for all their

חֲמִשִּׁים וּמָאתַיִם מַחְתֹּת וְאַתָּה וְאַהֲרֹן
אִישׁ מַחְתָּתוֹ׃ 18 וַיִּקְחוּ אִישׁ מַחְתָּתוֹ וַיִּתְּנוּ
עֲלֵיהֶם אֵשׁ וַיָּשִׂימוּ עֲלֵיהֶם קְטֹרֶת וַיַּעַמְדוּ
פֶּתַח אֹהֶל מוֹעֵד וּמֹשֶׁה וְאַהֲרֹן׃ 19 וַיַּקְהֵל
עֲלֵיהֶם קֹרַח אֶת־כָּל־הָעֵדָה אֶל־פֶּתַח
אֹהֶל מוֹעֵד
וַיֵּרָא כְבוֹד־יְהֹוָה אֶל־כָּל־הָעֵדָה׃ ס
20 וַיְדַבֵּר יְהֹוָה אֶל־מֹשֶׁה וְאֶל־אַהֲרֹן
לֵאמֹר׃ 21 הִבָּדְלוּ מִתּוֹךְ הָעֵדָה הַזֹּאת
וַאֲכַלֶּה אֹתָם כְּרָגַע׃ 22 וַיִּפְּלוּ עַל־פְּנֵיהֶם
וַיֹּאמְרוּ אֵל אֱלֹהֵי הָרוּחֹת לְכָל־בָּשָׂר הָאִישׁ
אֶחָד יֶחֱטָא וְעַל כָּל־הָעֵדָה תִּקְצֹף׃ ס
23 וַיְדַבֵּר יְהֹוָה אֶל־מֹשֶׁה לֵּאמֹר׃ 24 דַּבֵּר
אֶל־הָעֵדָה לֵאמֹר הֵעָלוּ מִסָּבִיב לְמִשְׁכַּן־
קֹרַח דָּתָן וַאֲבִירָם׃
25 וַיָּקָם מֹשֶׁה וַיֵּלֶךְ אֶל־דָּתָן וַאֲבִירָם וַיֵּלְכוּ
אַחֲרָיו זִקְנֵי יִשְׂרָאֵל׃ 26 וַיְדַבֵּר אֶל־הָעֵדָה
לֵאמֹר סוּרוּ נָא מֵעַל אָהֳלֵי הָאֲנָשִׁים
הָרְשָׁעִים הָאֵלֶּה וְאַל־תִּגְּעוּ בְּכָל־אֲשֶׁר

*21.* *"Stand back from this community."* Moses and Aaron are instructed to move away from the congregation, all of whom, it appears, are to be punished for the sins of the rebels (see 16:26 and 17:10).

*22.* ***But they fell on their faces.*** Moses had the same reaction in v. 4 when he first heard the rebels' complaint. Earlier, it was an act of grief (see also 14:5); here, Moses and Aaron are bowing before divine authority, appealing to God for assistance, and attempting to appease God's wrath against the innocent members of the community.

***"When one member sins, will You be wrathful with the whole community?"*** Korah has included the entire community in his challenge (v. 19), and God has threatened to destroy all of them (v. 21); but Moses and Aaron ask that only the sinners be punished. This key question about theodicy, that is, God's justice, recurs throughout the Bible. Abraham appeals to God's justice when he asks God to not destroy the righteous along with the wicked (Genesis 18:23–25). Ezekiel articulates this concept most strongly when he asserts, "The person who commits an offense—he shall die" (Ezekiel 18:4).

*23–24.* God responds to Moses by now instructing the community at large to withdraw from the tents of Korah, Dathan, and Abiram; only they—and their families—will be destroyed (see at v. 27).

### DATHAN AND ABIRAM'S PUNISHMENT (16:25–31)

The names of Dathan and Abiram were likely inserted in v. 24 by a later hand when linking their mutiny with Korah's. The story of Dathan and Abiram resumes in v. 25, in which Korah is not mentioned (but note the insertion of his name in v. 27, with nothing following it up).

sins." [27]So they withdrew from about the abodes of Korah, Dathan, and Abiram.

Now Dathan and Abiram had come out and they stood at the entrance of their tents, with their wives, their children, and their little ones. [28]And Moses said, "By this you shall know that it was יהוה who sent me to do all these things; that they are not of my own devising: [29]if these people's death is that of all humankind, if their lot is humankind's common fate, it was not יהוה who sent me. [30]But if יהוה brings about something unheard-of, so that the ground opens its mouth and swallows them up with all that belongs to them, and they go down alive into Sheol, you shall know that these fellows have spurned יהוה." [31]Scarcely had he finished speaking all these words when the ground under them burst asunder, [32]and the earth opened its mouth and swallowed them up with their households, all

לָהֶם פֶּן־תִּסָּפוּ בְּכָל־חַטֹּאתָם׃ 27 וַיֵּעָלוּ
מֵעַל מִשְׁכַּן־קֹרַח דָּתָן וַאֲבִירָם מִסָּבִיב
וְדָתָן וַאֲבִירָם יָצְאוּ נִצָּבִים פֶּתַח אָהֳלֵיהֶם
וּנְשֵׁיהֶם וּבְנֵיהֶם וְטַפָּם׃ 28 וַיֹּאמֶר מֹשֶׁה
בְּזֹאת תֵּדְעוּן כִּי־יְהוָה שְׁלָחַנִי לַעֲשׂוֹת אֵת
כָּל־הַמַּעֲשִׂים הָאֵלֶּה כִּי־לֹא מִלִּבִּי׃ 29 אִם־
כְּמוֹת כָּל־הָאָדָם יְמֻתוּן אֵלֶּה וּפְקֻדַּת כָּל־
הָאָדָם יִפָּקֵד עֲלֵיהֶם לֹא יְהוָה שְׁלָחָנִי׃
30 וְאִם־בְּרִיאָה יִבְרָא יְהוָה וּפָצְתָה
הָאֲדָמָה אֶת־פִּיהָ וּבָלְעָה אֹתָם וְאֶת־כָּל־
אֲשֶׁר לָהֶם וְיָרְדוּ חַיִּים שְׁאֹלָה וִידַעְתֶּם
כִּי נִאֲצוּ הָאֲנָשִׁים הָאֵלֶּה אֶת־יְהוָה׃
31 וַיְהִי כְּכַלֹּתוֹ לְדַבֵּר אֵת כָּל־הַדְּבָרִים
הָאֵלֶּה וַתִּבָּקַע הָאֲדָמָה אֲשֶׁר תַּחְתֵּיהֶם׃
32 וַתִּפְתַּח הָאָרֶץ אֶת־פִּיהָ וַתִּבְלַע אֹתָם
וְאֶת־בָּתֵּיהֶם וְאֵת כָּל־הָאָדָם אֲשֶׁר לְקֹרַח

27. ***with their wives, their children, and their little ones.*** Not only Dathan and Abiram are to be punished, but also the family as a whole. This seems to contradict Deuteronomy 24:16, which states that children are not to suffer for their parents' actions; in addition, Ezekiel 18:4 tells us that each person is responsible for his or her own crimes. But it seems from the current passage, and a parallel passage in Joshua 7:24, that this principle applies only to laws that do not concern sacred items or places. When there has been a violation of ritual law, anyone who comes into contact with the source of the offense is tainted by it, even to the third and fourth generations (Exodus 20:5). Thus, the fact that the punishment is enacted against the entire household of each of the rebels further demonstrates that the offense is understood to be against God, and not against God's human representatives—even though Korah, Dathan, and Abiram perceive themselves to be challenging only the authority of Moses and Aaron.

30. ***"if יהוה brings about something unheard-of."*** Moses' ability to dictate the terms of Dathan's and Abiram's deaths is interesting. His point is, "By this you shall know that it was יהוה who sent me to do all these things; that they are not of my own devising" (v. 28). And yet, without prompting from God, Moses announces the terms of the rebels' deaths, bringing about a sudden earthquake that swallows up Dathan, Abiram, and their families. To the onlooking Israelites, this presumably would have appeared to be a result of Moses' own power; and perhaps that is intended to serve the purpose of quashing potential future challenges to his authority. In fact, however, it will have the opposite effect (see 17:6–7).

### KORAH'S PUNISHMENT (16:32–35)

In this section the interweaving of the two stories of insurrection is particularly confusing. Later, at 17:5, Korah's death by fire will be confirmed, but here in v. 32 it appears that "Korah's people," the 250 incense-offerers described in vv. 18–19, are consumed in the earthquake along with Dathan and

Korah's people and all their possessions. [33]They
went down alive into Sheol, with all that belonged
to them; the earth closed over them and they van-
ished from the midst of the congregation. [34]All Israel around them fled at their shrieks, for they said,
"The earth might swallow us!"

[35]And a fire went forth from יהוה and consumed the two hundred and fifty representatives
offering the incense.

**17** יהוה spoke to Moses, saying: [2]Order Eleazar
son of Aaron the priest to remove the fire pans—for
they have become sacred—from among the charred

וְאֵת כׇּל־הָרְכוּשׁ׃ 33 וַיֵּרְדוּ הֵם וְכׇל־אֲשֶׁר
לָהֶם חַיִּים שְׁאֹלָה וַתְּכַס עֲלֵיהֶם הָאָרֶץ
וַיֹּאבְדוּ מִתּוֹךְ הַקָּהָל׃ 34 וְכׇל־יִשְׂרָאֵל אֲשֶׁר
סְבִיבֹתֵיהֶם נָסוּ לְקֹלָם כִּי אָמְרוּ פֶּן־
תִּבְלָעֵנוּ הָאָרֶץ׃
35 וְאֵשׁ יָצְאָה מֵאֵת יְהֹוָה וַתֹּאכַל
אֵת הַחֲמִשִּׁים וּמָאתַיִם אִישׁ מַקְרִיבֵי
הַקְּטֹרֶת׃ ס

יז וַיְדַבֵּר יְהֹוָה אֶל־מֹשֶׁה לֵּאמֹר׃ 2 אֱמֹר
אֶל־אֶלְעָזָר בֶּן־אַהֲרֹן הַכֹּהֵן וְיָרֵם אֶת־
הַמַּחְתֹּת מִבֵּין הַשְּׂרֵפָה וְאֶת־הָאֵשׁ זְרֵה־

Abiram. Reading the Hebrew closely, however, reveals the editor's cleverness in tying together the different endings for each rebel group. In v. 35 we are told literally that "fire had gone forth" (a past perfect verb). According to the final, redacted version, the incident described in this verse, namely the burning of Korah's incense-offering group, occurred before the earthquake swallowed them along with Dathan's and Abiram's households.

Thus, in vv. 18–19, Korah and his 250 companions attempted to offer incense with their fire pans at the entrance of the Tent of Meeting. God's immediate annihilation of them is described now in v. 35. Note that Moses does not act at all here. God's Presence appears in view of the entire community (v. 19), and a fire issues forth directly from God to consume the offenders.

The difference in the enactment of each punishment highlights the difference between the two types of rebellion. The challenge to Moses' leadership is punished by Moses with God's backing. This pattern reflects the overarching model in which the leader—Moses, whom God has chosen—acts on God's behalf and behest in order to take care of the people. Conversely, God handles the challenge to priestly authority directly.

*33.* ***Sheol.*** This term for the underworld appears 65 times in the *Tanach.* The ancient Israelites believed in a shadowy post-mortem existence for all—regardless of moral virtue—in Sheol. Dathan, Abiram, and their households are brought down alive to the land of the dead.

## *The Aftermath* (17:1–28)

Further accusations against Moses and Aaron follow, as the community holds them responsible for the deaths of the rebels. Clearly, the people have missed the point of the earlier punishments, and God acts immediately by sending a plague. Moses instructs Aaron to quickly make an expiation offering on behalf of the people to avert further destruction by God, and the plague is stopped after 14,700 deaths.

God decides to further establish Aaron's supremacy, and his divine backing, by demanding that the staff of each tribal leader be placed in the Tent of Meeting. Aaron's staff bears fruit, proving that God has chosen the house of Aaron alone as priests.

### TRANSFORMATION OF THE FIRE PANS (17:1–5)

Paradoxically and inexplicably, the copper fire pans that Korah and his companions used are rendered holy, either by the act of having been offered to God improperly or by the holy fire that consumed

remains; and scatter the coals abroad. 3[Remove]
the fire pans of those who have sinned at the cost of
their lives, and let them be made into hammered
sheets as plating for the altar—for once they have
been used for offering to יהוה, they have become
sacred—and let them serve as a warning to the people of Israel. 4Eleazar the priest took the copper fire
pans which had been used for offering by those who
died in the fire; and they were hammered into plating for the altar, 5as יהוה had ordered him through
Moses. It was to be a reminder to the Israelites, so
that no outsider—one not of Aaron's offspring—
should presume to offer incense before יהוה and
suffer the fate of Korah and his band.

6Next day the whole Israelite community railed
against Moses and Aaron, saying, "You two have
brought death upon יהוה's people!" 7But as the community gathered against them, Moses and Aaron
turned toward the Tent of Meeting; the cloud had
covered it and the Presence of יהוה appeared.

8When Moses and Aaron reached the Tent of
Meeting, 9יהוה spoke to Moses, saying, 10"Remove

הַלְאָה כִּי קָדֵשׁוּ׃ 3 אֵת מַחְתּוֹת הַחַטָּאִים
הָאֵלֶּה בְּנַפְשֹׁתָם וְעָשׂוּ אֹתָם רִקֻּעֵי פַחִים
צִפּוּי לַמִּזְבֵּחַ כִּי־הִקְרִיבֻם לִפְנֵי־יְהֹוָה
וַיִּקְדָּשׁוּ וְיִהְיוּ לְאוֹת לִבְנֵי יִשְׂרָאֵל׃ 4 וַיִּקַּח
אֶלְעָזָר הַכֹּהֵן אֵת מַחְתּוֹת הַנְּחֹשֶׁת אֲשֶׁר
הִקְרִיבוּ הַשְּׂרֻפִים וַיְרַקְּעוּם צִפּוּי לַמִּזְבֵּחַ׃
5 זִכָּרוֹן לִבְנֵי יִשְׂרָאֵל לְמַעַן אֲשֶׁר לֹא־יִקְרַב
אִישׁ זָר אֲשֶׁר לֹא מִזֶּרַע אַהֲרֹן הוּא לְהַקְטִיר
קְטֹרֶת לִפְנֵי יְהֹוָה וְלֹא־יִהְיֶה כְקֹרַח וְכַעֲדָתוֹ
כַּאֲשֶׁר דִּבֶּר יְהֹוָה בְּיַד־מֹשֶׁה לוֹ׃ פ
6 וַיִּלֹּנוּ כָּל־עֲדַת בְּנֵי־יִשְׂרָאֵל מִמָּחֳרָת עַל־
מֹשֶׁה וְעַל־אַהֲרֹן לֵאמֹר אַתֶּם הֲמִתֶּם אֶת־
עַם יְהֹוָה׃ 7 וַיְהִי בְּהִקָּהֵל הָעֵדָה עַל־מֹשֶׁה
וְעַל־אַהֲרֹן וַיִּפְנוּ אֶל־אֹהֶל מוֹעֵד וְהִנֵּה
כִסָּהוּ הֶעָנָן וַיֵּרָא כְּבוֹד יְהֹוָה׃
8 וַיָּבֹא מֹשֶׁה וְאַהֲרֹן אֶל־פְּנֵי אֹהֶל
מוֹעֵד׃ ס 9 וַיְדַבֵּר יְהֹוָה אֶל־מֹשֶׁה
לֵאמֹר׃ 10 הֵרֹמּוּ מִתּוֹךְ הָעֵדָה הַזֹּאת

---

their bearers. The fire pans are to become a visible warning intended to stop those who would presume the powers of the priesthood and the ability to approach God at the Tabernacle.

*5. It was to be a reminder to the Israelites.* The same Hebrew terms are used to describe the function of the *t'fillin* (Exodus 13:9) and the rainbow at the end of the flood story (Genesis 9:12–17). They refer to an action or an object that is symbolically, rather than intrinsically, significant.

### MORE REBELLION (17:6–7)

Once again, the congregation misses the point. Not only do they focus on Moses and Aaron instead of on God, but also they blame their human leaders for causing the deaths of the rebels, although Moses had taken pains to demonstrate that both his authority, and the punishments wrought, came from God.

*6. "יהוה's people."* In referring to the human leaders in this way, the community claims them as their own—while ironically placing them in opposition to God.

### PLAGUE AND EXPIATION (17:8–15)

As in the incineration of Korah and his company (16:35), this punishment comes directly from God. As proof, the human leaders intervene on behalf of the community to save them from God's wrath, demonstrating both that God is the one who has determined the punishment and enacted it, and that they are God's legitimate human representatives.

*9–10.* God's response compounds the bitter irony: the congregation accuses Moses and Aaron of

yourselves from this community, that I may annihilate them in an instant." They fell on their faces. [11]Then Moses said to Aaron, "Take the fire pan, and put on it fire from the altar. Add incense and take it quickly to the community and make expiation for them. For wrath has gone forth from יהוה: the plague has begun!" [12]Aaron took it, as Moses had ordered, and ran to the midst of the congregation, where the plague had begun among the people. He put on the incense and made expiation for the people; [13]he stood between the dead and the living until the plague was checked. [14]Those who died of the plague came to fourteen thousand and seven hundred, aside from those who died on account of Korah. [15]Aaron then returned to Moses at the entrance of the Tent of Meeting, since the plague was checked.

וַאֲכַלֶּה אֹתָם כְּרָגַע וַיִּפְּלוּ עַל־פְּנֵיהֶם׃
11 וַיֹּאמֶר מֹשֶׁה אֶל־אַהֲרֹן קַח אֶת־
הַמַּחְתָּה וְתֶן־עָלֶיהָ אֵשׁ מֵעַל הַמִּזְבֵּחַ
וְשִׂים קְטֹרֶת וְהוֹלֵךְ מְהֵרָה אֶל־הָעֵדָה
וְכַפֵּר עֲלֵיהֶם כִּי־יָצָא הַקֶּצֶף מִלִּפְנֵי יְהוָה
הֵחֵל הַנָּגֶף׃ 12 וַיִּקַּח אַהֲרֹן כַּאֲשֶׁר ׀ דִּבֶּר
מֹשֶׁה וַיָּרָץ אֶל־תּוֹךְ הַקָּהָל וְהִנֵּה הֵחֵל
הַנֶּגֶף בָּעָם וַיִּתֵּן אֶת־הַקְּטֹרֶת וַיְכַפֵּר עַל־
הָעָם׃ 13 וַיַּעֲמֹד בֵּין־הַמֵּתִים וּבֵין הַחַיִּים
וַתֵּעָצַר הַמַּגֵּפָה׃ 14 וַיִּהְיוּ הַמֵּתִים בַּמַּגֵּפָה
אַרְבָּעָה עָשָׂר אֶלֶף וּשְׁבַע מֵאוֹת מִלְּבַד
הַמֵּתִים עַל־דְּבַר־קֹרַח׃ 15 וַיָּשָׁב אַהֲרֹן
אֶל־מֹשֶׁה אֶל־פֶּתַח אֹהֶל מוֹעֵד וְהַמַּגֵּפָה
נֶעֱצָרָה׃ פ

[16]יהוה spoke to Moses, saying: [17]Speak to the Israelite people and take from them—from the chieftains of their ancestral houses—one staff for each chieftain of an ancestral house: twelve staffs in all. Inscribe each one's name on his staff, [18]there being one staff for each head of an ancestral house; also inscribe Aaron's name on the staff of Levi. [19]Deposit them in the Tent of Meeting before the Pact, where I meet with you. [20]The staff of the candidate whom I choose shall sprout, and I will rid Myself of the incessant mutterings of the Israelites against you.

[21]Moses spoke thus to the Israelites. Their chieftains gave him a staff for each chieftain of an ancestral house, twelve staffs in all; among these staffs

16 וַיְדַבֵּר יְהוָה אֶל־מֹשֶׁה לֵּאמֹר׃ 17 דַּבֵּר ׀
אֶל־בְּנֵי יִשְׂרָאֵל וְקַח מֵאִתָּם מַטֶּה מַטֶּה
לְבֵית אָב מֵאֵת כָּל־נְשִׂיאֵהֶם לְבֵית אֲבֹתָם
שְׁנֵים עָשָׂר מַטּוֹת אִישׁ אֶת־שְׁמוֹ תִּכְתֹּב
עַל־מַטֵּהוּ׃ 18 וְאֵת שֵׁם אַהֲרֹן תִּכְתֹּב עַל־
מַטֵּה לֵוִי כִּי מַטֶּה אֶחָד לְרֹאשׁ בֵּית
אֲבוֹתָם׃ 19 וְהִנַּחְתָּם בְּאֹהֶל מוֹעֵד לִפְנֵי
הָעֵדוּת אֲשֶׁר אִוָּעֵד לָכֶם שָׁמָּה׃ 20 וְהָיָה
הָאִישׁ אֲשֶׁר אֶבְחַר־בּוֹ מַטֵּהוּ יִפְרָח
וַהֲשִׁכֹּתִי מֵעָלַי אֶת־תְּלֻנּוֹת בְּנֵי יִשְׂרָאֵל
אֲשֶׁר הֵם מַלִּינִם עֲלֵיכֶם׃
21 וַיְדַבֵּר מֹשֶׁה אֶל־בְּנֵי יִשְׂרָאֵל וַיִּתְּנוּ אֵלָיו ׀
כָּל־נְשִׂיאֵיהֶם מַטֶּה לְנָשִׂיא אֶחָד מַטֶּה
לְנָשִׂיא אֶחָד לְבֵית אֲבֹתָם שְׁנֵים עָשָׂר

killing God's people (see at v. 6), so now God threatens to kill the people for their accusations of Moses and Aaron.

*11–13.* The irony culminates when Moses and Aaron save the people from God's wrath and the plague that follows—and they do so through the proper and sanctioned burning of incense to God.

### AARON'S BUDDING ROD (17:16–28)

God establishes another test to demonstrate the election of the House of Aaron to the priesthood. This time the miracle requires no human intercession and thus the people should perceive it as wholly divine in nature—in order, God says, to "rid Myself

was that of Aaron. 22Moses deposited the staffs before יהוה, in the Tent of the Pact. 23The next day
Moses entered the Tent of the Pact, and there the
staff of Aaron of the house of Levi had sprouted: it
had brought forth sprouts, produced blossoms, and
borne almonds. 24Moses then brought out all the
staffs from before יהוה to all the Israelites; each
identified and recovered his staff.

25יהוה said to Moses, "Put Aaron's staff back
before the Pact, to be kept as a lesson to rebels, so
that their mutterings against Me may cease, lest
they die." 26This Moses did; just as יהוה had commanded him, so he did.

27But the Israelites said to Moses, "Lo, we
perish! We are lost, all of us lost! 28Everyone who
so much as ventures near יהוה's Tabernacle must
die. Alas, we are doomed to perish!"

18 יהוה said to Aaron: You and your sons and
the ancestral house under your charge shall bear any
guilt connected with the sanctuary; you and your
sons alone shall bear any guilt connected with your

מַטּוֹת וּמַטֵּה אַהֲרֹן בְּתוֹךְ מַטּוֹתָם׃ 22 וַיַּנַּח
מֹשֶׁה אֶת־הַמַּטֹּת לִפְנֵי יְהֹוָה בְּאֹהֶל
הָעֵדֻת׃ 23 וַיְהִי מִמָּחֳרָת וַיָּבֹא מֹשֶׁה אֶל־
אֹהֶל הָעֵדוּת וְהִנֵּה פָּרַח מַטֵּה־אַהֲרֹן לְבֵית
לֵוִי וַיֹּצֵא פֶרַח וַיָּצֵץ צִיץ וַיִּגְמֹל שְׁקֵדִים׃
24 וַיֹּצֵא מֹשֶׁה אֶת־כׇּל־הַמַּטֹּת מִלִּפְנֵי יְהֹוָה
אֶל־כׇּל־בְּנֵי יִשְׂרָאֵל וַיִּרְאוּ וַיִּקְחוּ אִישׁ
מַטֵּהוּ׃ פ

25 וַיֹּאמֶר יְהֹוָה אֶל־מֹשֶׁה הָשֵׁב אֶת־מַטֵּה
אַהֲרֹן לִפְנֵי הָעֵדוּת לְמִשְׁמֶרֶת לְאוֹת לִבְנֵי־
מֶרִי וּתְכַל תְּלוּנֹּתָם מֵעָלַי וְלֹא יָמֻתוּ׃
26 וַיַּעַשׂ מֹשֶׁה כַּאֲשֶׁר צִוָּה יְהֹוָה אֹתוֹ כֵּן
עָשָׂה׃ פ

27 וַיֹּאמְרוּ בְּנֵי יִשְׂרָאֵל אֶל־מֹשֶׁה לֵאמֹר הֵן
גָּוַעְנוּ אָבַדְנוּ כֻּלָּנוּ אָבָדְנוּ׃ 28 כֹּל הַקָּרֵב ׀
הַקָּרֵב אֶל־מִשְׁכַּן יְהֹוָה יָמוּת הַאִם תַּמְנוּ
לִגְוֺעַ׃

יח וַיֹּאמֶר יְהֹוָה אֶל־אַהֲרֹן אַתָּה וּבָנֶיךָ
וּבֵית־אָבִיךָ אִתָּךְ תִּשְׂאוּ אֶת־עֲוֺן הַמִּקְדָּשׁ
וְאַתָּה וּבָנֶיךָ אִתָּךְ תִּשְׂאוּ אֶת־עֲוֺן

of the incessant mutterings . . . against [Moses and Aaron]" (v. 20). On the earlier role of Aaron's rod in Egypt and its import, see at Exodus 7:9; on almonds, see *Vayak'heil*, Contemporary Reflection, p. 540.

## *Priestly Responsibilities* (18:1–32)

Like 8:5–26, this unit discusses the special duties of the Aaronite priests relative to the Levites. Having addressed challenges to the priesthood and its hierarchy, the narrative turns to rules that illustrate and sustain the correct ritual system. This text makes it clear that with duties come privileges. For their services to God on behalf of the people, the priests and Levites are to be supported by the community via a system of gifts and tithes.

### PRIESTS AND LEVITES (18:1–7)

The priests, that is, the men from the family of Aaron, are responsible for preserving the purity of the sanctuary and its contents. The Levites are to have access only to the outer areas of the sanctuary. (Exodus 38:8 mentions women who are serving at the entrance of the Tent of Meeting. It is not clear whether that fleeting depiction conflicts with the current instructions.)

*1. to Aaron.* God speaks directly to him, rather than through Moses. This occurs in only one other place in the Torah: Leviticus 10:8.

***you . . . shall bear any guilt.*** God's introduction to the instructions here emphasizes that it is on Aaron and his descendants that God is placing the burden of responsibility for maintaining the sanctity of the Tabernacle.

priesthood. <sup>2</sup>You shall also associate with yourself your kinsmen the tribe of Levi, your ancestral tribe, to be attached to you and to minister to you, while you and your sons under your charge are before the Tent of the Pact. <sup>3</sup>They shall discharge their duties to you and to the Tent as a whole, but they must not have any contact with the furnishings of the Shrine or with the altar, lest both they and you die. <sup>4</sup>They shall be attached to you and discharge the duties of the Tent of Meeting, all the service of the Tent; but no outsider shall intrude upon you <sup>5</sup>as you discharge the duties connected with the Shrine and the altar, that wrath may not again strike the Israelites.

<sup>6</sup>I hereby take your fellow Levites from among the Israelites; they are assigned to you in dedication to יהוה, to do the work of the Tent of Meeting; <sup>7</sup>while you and your sons shall be careful to perform your priestly duties in everything pertaining to the altar and to what is behind the curtain. I make your priesthood a service of dedication; any outsider who encroaches shall be put to death.

<sup>8</sup>יהוה spoke further to Aaron: I hereby give you charge of My gifts, all the sacred donations of the Israelites; I grant them to you and to your sons as a perquisite, a due for all time. <sup>9</sup>This shall be yours from the most holy sacrifices, the offerings by fire: every such offering that they render to Me as most holy sacrifices, namely, every meal offering,

כְּהֻנַּתְכֶם: 2 וְגַם אֶת־אַחֶ֫יךָ מַטֵּה לֵוִי שֵׁבֶט אָבִ֫יךָ הַקְרֵב אִתָּ֫ךְ וְיִלָּו֫וּ עָלֶ֫יךָ וִישָׁרְת֫וּךָ וְאַתָּה וּבָנֶ֫יךָ אִתָּ֫ךְ לִפְנֵי אֹ֫הֶל הָעֵדֻת: 3 וְשָׁמְרוּ֙ מִֽשְׁמַרְתְּךָ֔ וּמִשְׁמֶ֫רֶת כׇּל־הָאֹ֫הֶל אַ֣ךְ אֶל־כְּלֵ֤י הַקֹּ֫דֶשׁ וְאֶל־הַמִּזְבֵּ֫חַ לֹ֣א יִקְרָ֔בוּ וְלֹֽא־יָמֻ֫תוּ גַם־הֵ֫ם גַּם־אַתֶּ֑ם: 4 וְנִלְו֣וּ עָלֶ֔יךָ וְשָֽׁמְרוּ֙ אֶת־מִשְׁמֶ֫רֶת אֹ֫הֶל מוֹעֵ֔ד לְכֹ֖ל עֲבֹדַ֣ת הָאֹ֑הֶל וְזָ֖ר לֹא־יִקְרַ֥ב אֲלֵיכֶֽם: 5 וּשְׁמַרְתֶּ֗ם אֵ֚ת מִשְׁמֶ֣רֶת הַקֹּ֔דֶשׁ וְאֵ֖ת מִשְׁמֶ֣רֶת הַמִּזְבֵּ֑חַ וְלֹֽא־יִהְיֶ֥ה ע֛וֹד קֶ֖צֶף עַל־בְּנֵ֥י יִשְׂרָאֵֽל:

6 וַאֲנִ֗י הִנֵּ֤ה לָקַ֫חְתִּי֙ אֶת־אֲחֵיכֶ֣ם הַלְוִיִּ֔ם מִתּ֖וֹךְ בְּנֵ֣י יִשְׂרָאֵ֑ל לָכֶ֞ם מַתָּנָ֤ה נְתֻנִים֙ לַֽיהֹוָ֔ה לַעֲבֹ֕ד אֶת־עֲבֹדַ֖ת אֹ֥הֶל מוֹעֵֽד: 7 וְאַתָּ֣ה וּבָנֶ֣יךָ אִ֠תְּךָ֠ תִּשְׁמְר֨וּ אֶת־כְּהֻנַּתְכֶ֜ם לְכׇל־דְּבַ֧ר הַמִּזְבֵּ֛חַ וּלְמִבֵּ֥ית לַפָּרֹ֖כֶת וַעֲבַדְתֶּ֑ם עֲבֹדַ֣ת מַתָּנָ֗ה אֶתֵּן֙ אֶת־כְּהֻנַּתְכֶ֔ם וְהַזָּ֥ר הַקָּרֵ֖ב יוּמָֽת: פ

8 וַיְדַבֵּ֣ר יְהֹוָה֮ אֶֽל־אַהֲרֹן֒ וַאֲנִי֙ הִנֵּ֣ה נָתַ֣תִּי לְךָ֗ אֶת־מִשְׁמֶ֫רֶת תְּרֽוּמֹתָ֑י לְכׇל־קׇדְשֵׁ֣י בְנֵֽי־יִשְׂרָאֵ֗ל לְךָ֣ נְתַתִּ֧ים לְמׇשְׁחָ֛ה וּלְבָנֶ֖יךָ לְחׇק־עוֹלָֽם: 9 זֶֽה־יִהְיֶ֥ה לְךָ֛ מִקֹּ֥דֶשׁ הַקֳּדָשִׁ֖ים מִן־הָאֵ֑שׁ כׇּל־קׇרְבָּנָ֡ם לְֽכׇל־מִנְחָתָ֡ם וּלְכׇל־חַטָּאתָ֩ם וּלְכׇל־אֲשָׁמָ֨ם אֲשֶׁ֤ר יָשִׁ֫יבוּ לִ֫י

- - - - - - - - - - - - - - - - - - - - - - - - - - - - - - - - - - - - - - - - - -

**2.** *to be attached to you.* Heb. *yillavu*, which is a verbal form of the noun "Levite." Originally, the term "Levite" may have referred to someone attached to the sacred in order to perform rituals—that is, a priest. However, here the term refers to those who are attached to the priests in order to serve them. The book of Numbers, with its privileging of priests, thus designates Levites as secondary clergy whose duties are to assist the priestly descendants of Aaron. (Deuteronomy presents a different understanding; see at Deuteronomy 18:1.)

GIFTS (18:8–20)

**9.** *from the most holy sacrifices.* The Bible's sacrificial laws divide priestly portions into two types, "most holy" and "holy," which are designated for consumption accordingly, by males in the sacred precinct and by their female relatives at home (see Ezekiel 44:29–30). "Most holy" includes the parts of the purgation and reparation offerings that are not burnt (see Leviticus 6:1–7:10).

purgation offering, and reparation offering of theirs, shall belong to you and your sons. [10]You shall partake of them as most sacred donations: only males may eat them; you shall treat them as consecrated.

[11]This, too, shall be yours: the gift offerings of their contributions, all the elevation offerings of the Israelites, I give to you [and your wives], to your sons, and to the daughters that are with you, as a due for all time; everyone of your household who is pure may eat it.

[12]All the best of the new oil, wine, and grain—the choice parts that they present to יהוה—I give to you. [13]The first fruits of everything in their land, that they bring to יהוה, shall be yours; everyone of your household who is pure may eat them. [14]Everything that has been proscribed in Israel shall be yours. [15]The first [male] issue of the womb of every being, human or beast, that is offered to יהוה, shall be yours; but you shall have the male first-born of human beings redeemed, and you shall also have the firstling of impure animals redeemed. [16]Take as their redemption price, from the age of one month up, the money equivalent of five shekels by the sanctuary weight, which is twenty *gerah*s. [17]But the firstlings of cattle, sheep, or goats may not be redeemed; they are consecrated. You shall dash their blood against the altar, and turn their fat into smoke as an offering by fire for a pleasing odor to יהוה. [18]But their meat shall be yours: it shall be yours like the breast of elevation offering and like the right thigh.

קֹ֣דֶשׁ קׇֽדָשִׁ֛ים לְךָ֥ ה֖וּא וּלְבָנֶֽיךָ׃ 10 בְּקֹ֥דֶשׁ
הַקֳּדָשִׁ֖ים תֹּאכְלֶ֑נּוּ כׇּל־זָכָר֙ יֹאכַ֣ל אֹת֔וֹ קֹ֖דֶשׁ
יִֽהְיֶה־לָּֽךְ׃
11 וְזֶה־לְּךָ֞ תְּרוּמַ֣ת מַתָּנָ֗ם לְכׇל־תְּנוּפֹת֮
בְּנֵ֣י יִשְׂרָאֵל֒ לְךָ֣ נְתַתִּ֗ים וּלְבָנֶ֧יךָ וְלִבְנֹתֶ֛יךָ
אִתְּךָ֖ לְחׇק־עוֹלָ֑ם כׇּל־טָה֥וֹר בְּבֵיתְךָ֖ יֹאכַ֥ל
אֹתֽוֹ׃
12 כֹּ֚ל חֵ֣לֶב יִצְהָ֔ר וְכׇל־חֵ֖לֶב תִּיר֣וֹשׁ וְדָגָ֑ן
רֵאשִׁיתָ֛ם אֲשֶׁר־יִתְּנ֥וּ לַיהֹוָ֖ה לְךָ֥ נְתַתִּֽים׃
13 בִּכּוּרֵ֞י כׇּל־אֲשֶׁ֧ר בְּאַרְצָ֛ם אֲשֶׁר־יָבִ֥יאוּ
לַיהֹוָ֖ה לְךָ֣ יִהְיֶ֑ה כׇּל־טָה֥וֹר בְּבֵיתְךָ֖ יֹאכְלֶֽנּוּ׃
14 כׇּל־חֵ֥רֶם בְּיִשְׂרָאֵ֖ל לְךָ֥ יִהְיֶֽה׃ 15 כׇּל־
פֶּ֣טֶר רֶ֠חֶם לְכׇל־בָּשָׂ֞ר אֲשֶׁר־יַקְרִ֧יבוּ לַיהֹוָ֛ה
בָּאָדָ֥ם וּבַבְּהֵמָ֖ה יִֽהְיֶה־לָּ֑ךְ אַ֣ךְ ׀ פָּדֹ֣ה תִפְדֶּ֗ה
אֵ֚ת בְּכ֣וֹר הָֽאָדָ֔ם וְאֵ֛ת בְּכֽוֹר־הַבְּהֵמָ֥ה
הַטְּמֵאָ֖ה תִּפְדֶּֽה׃ 16 וּפְדוּיָו֙ מִבֶּן־חֹ֣דֶשׁ
תִּפְדֶּ֔ה בְּעֶ֨רְכְּךָ֔ כֶּ֖סֶף חֲמֵ֣שֶׁת שְׁקָלִ֑ים
בְּשֶׁ֥קֶל הַקֹּ֖דֶשׁ עֶשְׂרִ֥ים גֵּרָ֖ה הֽוּא׃ 17 אַ֣ךְ
בְּכוֹר־שׁ֡וֹר אֽוֹ־בְכ֨וֹר כֶּ֜שֶׂב אֽוֹ־בְכ֥וֹר עֵ֛ז לֹ֥א
תִפְדֶּ֖ה קֹ֣דֶשׁ הֵ֑ם אֶת־דָּמָ֞ם תִּזְרֹ֤ק עַל־
הַמִּזְבֵּ֙חַ֙ וְאֶת־חֶלְבָּ֣ם תַּקְטִ֔יר אִשֶּׁ֛ה לְרֵ֥יחַ
נִיחֹ֖חַ לַיהֹוָֽה׃ 18 וּבְשָׂרָ֖ם יִֽהְיֶה־לָּ֑ךְ כַּחֲזֵ֧ה
הַתְּנוּפָ֛ה וּכְשׁ֥וֹק הַיָּמִ֖ין לְךָ֥ יִהְיֶֽה׃

*10. only males may eat them.* The "most holy" portions from the meal, purgation, and reparation offerings are to be consumed only by the male priests. See also at Leviticus 6:11 for a discussion of such a phrase and its implications.

*11. to you* [*and your wives*] *. . . and to the daughters that are with you.* Women in priestly families could share heave offerings and first fruits. The explicit mention of daughters, rather than wives or women, may be necessary in light of the shifting position of a daughter within a household, after she marries. (See *Tzav*, Another View, p. 608; and at Leviticus 21:12–13 for rules concerning a priest's daughter.) The mention of wives in this translation reflects the understanding that the "you" here refers to the household's primary couple, who runs the household (see *Mishpatim*, Another View, p. 445).

19 All the sacred gifts that the Israelites set aside for יהוה I give to you, to your sons, and to the daughters that are with you, as a due for all time. It shall be an everlasting covenant of salt before יהוה for you and for your offspring as well. 20 And יהוה said to Aaron: You shall, however, have no territorial share among them or own any portion in their midst; I am your portion and your share among the Israelites.

21 And to the Levites I hereby give all the tithes in Israel as their share in return for the services that they perform, the services of the Tent of Meeting. 22 Henceforth, Israelites shall not trespass on the Tent of Meeting, and thus incur guilt and die: 23 only Levites shall perform the services of the Tent of Meeting; others would incur guilt. It is the law for all time throughout the ages. But they shall have no territorial share among the Israelites; 24 for it is the tithes set aside by the Israelites as a gift to יהוה that I give to the Levites as their share. Therefore I have said concerning them: They shall have no territorial share among the Israelites.

25 יהוה spoke to Moses, saying: 26 Speak to the Levites and say to them: When you receive from the Israelites their tithes, which I have assigned to you as your share, you shall set aside from them one-tenth of the tithe as a gift to יהוה. 27 This shall be accounted to you as your gift. As with the new grain from the threshing floor or the flow from the vat, 28 so shall you on your part set aside a gift for יהוה from all the tithes that you receive from the

19 כֹּל | תְּרוּמֹת הַקֳּדָשִׁים אֲשֶׁר יָרִימוּ בְנֵי־
יִשְׂרָאֵל לַיהוָה נָתַתִּי לְךָ וּלְבָנֶיךָ וְלִבְנֹתֶיךָ
אִתְּךָ לְחָק־עוֹלָם בְּרִית מֶלַח עוֹלָם הִוא
לִפְנֵי יְהוָה לְךָ וּלְזַרְעֲךָ אִתָּךְ׃ 20 וַיֹּאמֶר
יְהוָה אֶל־אַהֲרֹן בְּאַרְצָם לֹא תִנְחָל וְחֵלֶק
לֹא־יִהְיֶה לְךָ בְּתוֹכָם אֲנִי חֶלְקְךָ וְנַחֲלָתְךָ
בְּתוֹךְ בְּנֵי יִשְׂרָאֵל׃ ס
21 וְלִבְנֵי לֵוִי הִנֵּה נָתַתִּי כָּל־מַעֲשֵׂר
בְּיִשְׂרָאֵל לְנַחֲלָה חֵלֶף עֲבֹדָתָם אֲשֶׁר־הֵם
עֹבְדִים אֶת־עֲבֹדַת אֹהֶל מוֹעֵד׃ 22 וְלֹא־
יִקְרְבוּ עוֹד בְּנֵי יִשְׂרָאֵל אֶל־אֹהֶל מוֹעֵד
לָשֵׂאת חֵטְא לָמוּת׃ 23 וְעָבַד הַלֵּוִי הוּא
אֶת־עֲבֹדַת אֹהֶל מוֹעֵד וְהֵם יִשְׂאוּ עֲוֺנָם
חֻקַּת עוֹלָם לְדֹרֹתֵיכֶם וּבְתוֹךְ בְּנֵי יִשְׂרָאֵל
לֹא יִנְחֲלוּ נַחֲלָה׃ 24 כִּי אֶת־מַעְשַׂר בְּנֵי־
יִשְׂרָאֵל אֲשֶׁר יָרִימוּ לַיהוָה תְּרוּמָה נָתַתִּי
לַלְוִיִּם לְנַחֲלָה עַל־כֵּן אָמַרְתִּי לָהֶם בְּתוֹךְ
בְּנֵי יִשְׂרָאֵל לֹא יִנְחֲלוּ נַחֲלָה׃ פ
25 וַיְדַבֵּר יְהוָה אֶל־מֹשֶׁה לֵּאמֹר׃ 26 וְאֶל־
הַלְוִיִּם תְּדַבֵּר וְאָמַרְתָּ אֲלֵהֶם כִּי־תִקְחוּ
מֵאֵת בְּנֵי־יִשְׂרָאֵל אֶת־הַמַּעֲשֵׂר אֲשֶׁר נָתַתִּי
לָכֶם מֵאִתָּם בְּנַחֲלַתְכֶם וַהֲרֵמֹתֶם מִמֶּנּוּ
תְּרוּמַת יְהוָה מַעֲשֵׂר מִן־הַמַּעֲשֵׂר׃
27 וְנֶחְשַׁב לָכֶם תְּרוּמַתְכֶם כַּדָּגָן מִן־הַגֹּרֶן
וְכַמְלֵאָה מִן־הַיָּקֶב׃ 28 כֵּן תָּרִימוּ גַם־אַתֶּם
תְּרוּמַת יְהוָה מִכֹּל מַעְשְׂרֹתֵיכֶם אֲשֶׁר

*19. everlasting covenant of salt.* The expression "covenant of salt" occurs in the Bible only here and in II Chronicles 13:5. Due to salt's preservative qualities, many interpreters (including Rashi) construe its mention here as a symbol of permanence. Perhaps this is why Leviticus 2:13 commands that the Israelites season every grain offering with salt. To commemorate this practice in the absence of sacrificial offerings, it is a custom to this day to sprinkle salt on the bread of the Sabbath meal.

### TITHES (18:21–32)

Laws concerning tithes are also detailed in Leviticus 27:30–32 and Deuteronomy 12:17–19; 14:22–29. For their service, Levites are to be compensated with tithes, although they in turn have to donate one-tenth of the tithes they collect to the priests. This addition to the law in Leviticus 27 further distinguishes the status of Levites from that of priests; like other Israelites, the Levites also must themselves pay tithes, while priests are exempt.

Israelites; and from them you shall bring the gift for יהוה to Aaron the priest. 29You shall set aside all gifts due to יהוה from everything that is donated to you, from each thing its best portion, the part thereof that is to be consecrated.

30Say to them further: When you have removed the best part from it, you Levites may consider it the same as the yield of threshing floor or vat. 31You and your households may eat it anywhere, for it is your recompense for your services in the Tent of Meeting. 32You will incur no guilt through it, once you have removed the best part from it; but you must not profane the sacred donations of the Israelites, lest you die.

תִּקְחוּ מֵאֵת בְּנֵי יִשְׂרָאֵל וּנְתַתֶּם מִמֶּנּוּ אֶת־
תְּרוּמַת יְהוָה לְאַהֲרֹן הַכֹּהֵן׃ 29 מִכֹּל
מַתְּנֹתֵיכֶם תָּרִימוּ אֵת כָּל־תְּרוּמַת יְהוָה
מִכָּל־חֶלְבּוֹ אֶת־מִקְדְּשׁוֹ מִמֶּנּוּ׃
30 וְאָמַרְתָּ אֲלֵהֶם בַּהֲרִימְכֶם אֶת־חֶלְבּוֹ
מִמֶּנּוּ וְנֶחְשַׁב לַלְוִיִּם כִּתְבוּאַת גֹּרֶן
וְכִתְבוּאַת יָקֶב׃ 31 וַאֲכַלְתֶּם אֹתוֹ בְּכָל־
מָקוֹם אַתֶּם וּבֵיתְכֶם כִּי־שָׂכָר הוּא לָכֶם
חֵלֶף עֲבֹדַתְכֶם בְּאֹהֶל מוֹעֵד׃ 32 וְלֹא־
תִשְׂאוּ עָלָיו חֵטְא בַּהֲרִימְכֶם אֶת־חֶלְבּוֹ
מִמֶּנּוּ וְאֶת־קָדְשֵׁי בְנֵי־יִשְׂרָאֵל לֹא תְחַלְּלוּ
וְלֹא תָמוּתוּ׃ פ

*31. You and your households.* In contrast to the hierarchy within the priestly family, all members of the Levite household, presumably including women, share the food offered as tithes. Thus, donations to "the Levite" are for his whole family.

*32. You will incur no guilt.* [This concluding message to the Levites assures them of their safety when they follow God's instructions. This message is especially apt after the death of Korah, the rebellious Levite. —*Ed.*]

—*Shawna Dolansky*

# Another View

PARASHAT KORACH DESCRIBES the punishment that befalls two groups of challengers. In the case of Dathan and Abiram, the rebels' wives die along with their husbands. Yet in the Korah episode, only the men are punished. The story as a whole reflects a central biblical theme: the tension between a clan-based system of authority and a centralized system of priestly authority.

Dathan and Abiram represent what can be called clan heads or household heads. (The biblical terminology is not always consistent.) Early in Israel's history, male heads of families had authority and jurisdiction over their families. For example, in Genesis 38 the patriarch Judah decides whether his pregnant, seemingly adulterous daughter-in-law Tamar should live or die. In contrast, the priest administers the ritual to determine whether a woman is an adulteress in Numbers 5.

According to the Bible, women within the clan system of authority played a significant role and exercised power as well as some authority. Although subject to the authority of the male head of the household, women clearly influenced the family head. For instance, unable to tolerate her rival, Sarah demands that Abraham expel Hagar. Despite Abraham's reluctance, God tells him to obey Sarah (Genesis 21:12).

Texts that focus on the priesthood shift authority away from the family's head toward the central sanctuary and its priests. Women, in particular, are affected by this shift (see at Leviticus 26:30). Whereas in Genesis 38 Tamar actively works to secure her fate, in Numbers 5 the suspected woman is a passive figure. The inclusion of the wives of Dathan and Abiram reflects the role that women played within the clan system.

Thus, Numbers 16 is not only a story of infighting among families, ultimately championing Aaron and his descendants; it also tells a story about the seeming demise of an important notion of the "biblical family." The deaths of Dathan, Abiram, and their wives at the doorway to their tents (16:27) make the point painfully clear: after all, the entrance to the tent is a place associated with theophany and judgment in the clan system, and hence also a symbol of authority (Genesis 18:1; Deuteronomy 22:21). Together, Dathan, Abiram, *and* their wives represent the clan system that must be erased—swallowed whole—in order to establish the authority of the priesthood. —*Amy Kalmanofsky*

*Numbers 16 tells of the metaphoric demise of patriarchal authority within the family.*

# Post-biblical Interpretations

***Now Korah . . . betook himself*** (16:1). Literally, "and Korah took" (*va-yikach Korach*), which presents a dilemma for translators and commentators since the verb lacks a direct object. What did Korah take? Midrash *B'midbar Rabbah* 18.4 explains that Korah "took" his *tallit*—and went to get advice from his wife. BT *Sanhedrin* 110a goes further and portrays Korah's wife as playing an active role in the development of his resentment. She complains that Moses has become a king, his brother Aaron is chief priest, and Aaron's sons are priests, while Levites such as Korah are disadvantaged in a number of ways. Moreover, she continues, Moses humiliated the Levites by ordering them to shave their entire bodies (8:7). Finally, Korah's wife ridicules the commandment of *tzitzit* (15:37–41), which requires the presence in the fringes of *t'cheilet* (a blue thread). If blue thread is so important, she asks rhetorically, why not wear a cloak made entirely of blue thread?

Why does the Babylonian Talmud—and, by implication, *B'midbar Rabbah*—portray Korah's wife in this negative way? Rabbi Hanokh Zundel (author of the *Etz Yosef* commentary on *B'midbar Rabbah*) hypothesized that because Dathan's and Abiram's wives and children were with the rebels at the fateful moment of being swallowed up (16:27), their wives must have shared their husbands' rebellious sentiments. Presumably, Korah's wife also agreed with Korah's anger. Of course, in a patriarchal society, women would have had little choice but to "agree" with their husbands. Korah's wife, however, may have had a more specific motivation: given that Korah was a first cousin of Moses and Aaron, his rebellion was a family affair—at least in part. Korah's wife may have zealously pursued what she saw as her husband's legitimate interests against her powerful cousins-in-law. It is also possible that the Rabbis, who often impute the worst possible motives to women, are portraying Korah's wife as another Eve who (in rabbinic lore) is leading her innocent husband into temptation and disaster.

***On son of Peleth*** (16:1). The Rabbis give us a different model of a rebel's spouse in their construction of the wife of On son of Peleth. The Rabbis assume that On did not see the rebellion through to the end, and thus he was spared the collective punishment. This is because he is listed among the rebels in 16:1, but there is no specific mention of his death in 16:23–35 when the rebels are destroyed. In a story found in two versions (*B'midbar Rabbah* 18.20 and BT *Sanhedrin* 109b–110a), the Rabbis attribute On's rescue to his wife. In both versions, On's wife points out to him that the rebellion will leave him no better off: he is currently subordinate to Aaron; if the rebellion is successful, he will be subordinate to Korah. She observes to herself, "I know that all of the congregation is holy," citing as proof Korah's own words in 16:3. She then gets her husband drunk, puts him to bed, and sits at their front door with her hair undone and exposed. The holiness of the congregation is made manifest when the rebels approach the house to summon her husband—and withdraw immediately upon seeing her immodest appearance. By the time On awakens from his drunken sleep, the rebellion has been put down and the rebels destroyed.

*Korah's wife played an active role in the development of his resentment.*

In the version of this story in the Midrash (*B'midbar Rabbah*), On never speaks; we do not know if he agrees with his wife or not. We may reasonably infer that he does not; otherwise, why would she have to get him drunk to put an end to his participation in the rebellion? In the version in the Talmud, however, On appears to agree with his spouse's assessment of his status after the rebellion. When he asks her, "What should I do?" she makes her observation about communal holiness and executes her plan to save her family from destruction.

The possible appeal to women—especially poor women—of Korah's overall critique of the Mosaic order is illustrated differently in *Midrash T'hillim* 1:15. Korah is represented there as showing the injustice of Torah laws by pointing out their adverse impact on a widow with two daughters. Whether the poor widow wishes to plow, sow, harvest, or raise animals—Korah notes—Moses and Aaron are there to regulate how she should plow and sow, and to insist that she gives portions of her harvest and her herds to the priests. The widow, frustrated at all these restraints and exactions, ends up bereft and weeping together with her children. —*Alyssa M. Gray*

# *Contemporary Reflection*

What a dramatic power struggle we have just witnessed in this parashah! A cabal of influential rebels tries to take power from Moses, daring to risk their lives to promote their own self-interest over the sacred destiny of their people. Their downfall is stark and dreadful.

Yet, the Torah teaches, even though Korah dies, his descendants live on (Numbers 26:11). We certainly see them today: cynical political, religious, and communal leaders cloaking self-interest in the language of democracy, nationalism, or God. In wielding power in such shortsighted ways, these modern-day rebels present an even greater threat to God's creation than Korah did to Moses' leadership. This Torah portion urges us to be vigilant, lest such persons undermine the communities that we are called to create and sustain.

But it is not only public leaders who play Korah's role today. We, too, live with an ongoing conflict between an "inner Moses" and an "inner Korah"—between humility and arrogance, between selflessness and selfishness. And until we can hear the difference between those two voices, our actions will not be effective in countering the power of the Korahs at large in the world. We need to be clear when it is the voice of our needy, small-minded self that advises us to act, or when it is the wise voice that speaks from our deepest and best values and truth. We need a practice of reflection to discern which voice is guiding us. Happily, we can also find some guidance in this parashah.

In our tradition Moses is seen as humility embodied—the true servant of God. The *S'fas Emes*, a 19th-century Hasidic master, understood Moses as being so far from pride in his bearing that people could not fathom his modesty. In *parashat Korach*, we see Moses in that place of humility, able to lead because he loves God and the Israelites with every fiber of his being, despite his constant frustration with both of them. Twice he falls on his face—before Korah and before God—trying to stop the rebellion and to prevent God from destroying the persistently disobedient Israelites. Moses acts from the deep understanding that Korah's challenge has nothing to do with him; it is a challenge to God. He knows himself to be the vessel through which God's vision for the Israelites could become manifest, not the man who has to prove himself superior to an insolent competitor. Throughout the journeys of the Israelites, we see Moses grow as a spiritual leader: from a reluctant young man who struggles with anger and lack of self-confidence to become the quintessential leader—one who is able to overcome his own ego in order to serve a much greater cause. Finally, he becomes one who accepts God's decision that he will die—and that he will die outside the land of Israel.

> *We live with an ongoing conflict between an "inner Moses" and an "inner Korah."*

Korah is different. His challenge to Moses is rooted in personal ambition, not love of God or of the Israelites. Unlike Moses, who hesitated to take the leadership that God offered, Korah seeks to grab it for himself. Tradition interprets the opening of the parashah—literally "And Korah took"—to mean that he took himself *apart from the people* (Tzvi Hirsch Kalischer; *Torah Gems*, 1998, p. 77). Korah would have done nothing to stop God from destroying the Israelites, for he would have loved to be the sire of a whole new people. Unlike Moses, Korah sees the whole story as being about himself and the role he wants to play as a powerful chief priest.

Reading this parashah, I ask: how do I recognize Korah in my own thoughts and actions, and how do I liberate the consciousness that Moses had? In my job as the director of a wonderful non-profit institute, I find that Korah seems to pop up most frequently when I am afraid. What if I don't succeed at raising enough money? What if I don't succeed at making our work known? What if I am not good enough? What if this work fails because of my incompetence? In such moments of doubt, I make myself the central actor on stage, starring in the "The Tragedy of Rachel." In that place of fear, I separate myself from the community doing the work, and I clutch for some way to feel in control. I can't see the whole. There is no way to make wise decisions.

But if I make time, like Moses, to fall on my face—to breathe and reflect—I can hear the "I" shouting out in all its grandiosity. I reply, "*Rav l'kha* (Enough of this), Korah!"—acknowledging that once again I have made the story about me and my fears. In that space, Moses can emerge and call me back to humility—to the recognition that I, like everybody else, am but a bit player on this stage. I can rekindle the trust that I have in the wisdom of the unfolding of the work and in the wisdom of my colleagues to figure out what will flow from this moment.

The Korah in all of us gets triggered by different emotions: fear, anger, anxiety, greed or doubt. When this happens, we lose sight of the whole and become caught up in our own inner dramas. Our needs eclipse the needs of others.

Moses' path—and ours—is to move from the narrow place of doubt, fear, anger, and jealousy to an expansive covenanted life in a community of mutual care and responsibility. In such a community, all people are holy. They—we—can remind each other that what matters is not the ambition of the self, but the work of helping to make the soul, the home, the office, and the world a safer, wiser, more compassionate place for all. Such a perspective helps each of us to come closer to being a humble servant of God.

—*Rachel Cowan*

# Voices

## Korach

Laurie Patton

*Numbers 16:3–5*

Moses gave Korach one night.

The origins of insomnia
must be in those hours,
as each man wondered
about the lands
of milk and honey,
and his rights
to hoist banners
for the crowds who loved him.

Moses sure of God's voice,
and Korach sure of his own—
each trying to tell
the difference
between arrogance
and righteous anger—
a line so thin—
thin as a flame
in a fire pan

Their sleepless night
is our own,
echoing restlessly
as we sort spices
in our dark kitchens
and arrange furniture
by moonlight

Sweating in starlight,
we remember arrogance
and mutter righteous anger,
and then quietly beg
to hear God—

for when the dawn comes,
we do not know
which of our sacrifices
will be the right ones

## From Day to Night

Dahlia Ravikovitch
(transl. Chana Bloch and Chana Kronfeld)

*Numbers 17:6*

Every day I rise from sleep again
as if for the last time.
I don't know what awaits me,
perhaps it follows logically, then,
that nothing awaits me.
The spring that's on its way
is like the spring that's gone.
I know about the month of May
but pay it no mind.
I don't mark the border between night and day,
just that night is colder
though silence is equal to them both.
At dawn I hear the voices of birds.
I fall asleep easily
out of affection for them.
The one who is dear to me is not here,
perhaps he simply is not.
I cross over from day to night
from day to day
like a feather
the bird doesn't feel as it falls away.

## *Poem 21*

Ruth Whitman

*Numbers 18:12*

a fist of life
thrusts up through sand
and opens its palm:

a rainbow of vegetables:
black olives, seas of oranges,
eggplants, shiny purple,
artichokes, small
scarlet tomatoes,
parsley
curled in bushes
raisins garlic cumin

seeds fall through the air:
the sun is a cauldron
of hot oil.

## *Turning the Garden in Middle Age*

Maxine Kumin

*Numbers 18:12–13*

They have lain a long time, these two:
parsnip with his beard on his foot
pudding stone with fool's gold in her ear
until, under the thrust of my fork,
earthlock lets go. Mineral
and marrow are flung loose in May
still clinging together as if
they had intended this embrace.

I think then of skulls picked clean
underground, and the long bones
of animals overturned in the woods
and the gorgeous insurgency
of these smart green weeds
erect now in every furrow
that lure me once more
to set seeds in the loam.

## *A Box of Clementines in the Maternity Ward*

Jessica Greenbaum

*Numbers 18:12–15*

You couldn't sleep and you cried
unless I nursed you while I walked
around the room. On the oval table
in their small wooden crate
sat the clementines, packed neatly
and glowing like embers
beneath their red netting. Rounding
the dark room, singing a song
that came with you and is lost
with those early days (half of life,
my love, is disappearance) I stopped
at the table and peeled one clementine
every few laps, the skin falling
off the globe with completion and ease,
a yellowed veil barely clinging,
the little smoke rising to your initiating
dream, the whole fruit punctuating
my thirst and hunger. My body
was an enormous land you just left,
my belly so soft after your departure
it seemed to ripple like a lake.
Into that darkness
dropped the clementines,
both you and I lifting to our lips
something we tasted
for the first time, in an orbit we followed
without haste or destination.

# חקת ✦ Chukat

## NUMBERS 19:1–22:1

### *Leadership and Loss in the Wilderness*

PARASHAT CHUKAT ("law [that]") acknowledges the grim reality of death in the wilderness, a necessary succession in leadership, and the approach of the journey's end. Repeatedly in this parashah, healing and new life follow death. In the face of the chaos and unpredictability of death and its contaminating powers, Numbers 19 responds with a priestly ritual, recording instructions that contain a great deal of regulatory detail, delivered in an orderly, precise tone. Numbers 20 focuses on two significant deaths in the community of Israel, that of Miriam and her brother Aaron. Numbers 21 focuses on new opportunities in spite of deep disappointment, as successful battles mark a positive change in Israel's fortune. After the loss of his siblings, Moses remains, leading Israel ever closer to the edges of the Promised Land, a land that he himself will never enter.

The deaths of Miriam and Aaron are central to this parashah, providing us an opportunity to consider the role of each within the Israelite camp. Gender politics can be detected in the more elaborate details concerning the punishment and death of Aaron in comparison to the report of Miriam's death. Nevertheless, the mere fact that the time and place of Miriam's death are recorded is highly unusual and therefore quite striking. One intriguing detail even

*Repeatedly in this parashah, healing and new life follow death.*

places her on a par with Moses: he too is condemned to death in the same literary unit in which Miriam and Aaron die. Could it be mere coincidence that these three siblings are grouped together in this fashion? Indeed, the prophet Micah places Miriam on a par with her brothers: "I brought you up from the land of Egypt, redeemed you from the house of bondage, and sent Moses, Aaron, and Miriam to lead you" (Micah 6:4). Miriam's death provides an opportunity to reflect on her life and to appreciate the unique features of this biblical leader (see at 20:1).

*—Adriane Leveen*

## Outline

*I.* The "Red Cow" Ritual after Contact with a Corpse (19:1–22)

- *A.* Instructions for handling the red cow (vv. 1–10)
- *B.* Rituals after contact with a corpse, human bones, or a grave (vv. 11–22)

*II.* The Deaths of Miriam and Aaron (20:1–29)

- *A.* Miriam's death (v. 1)
- *B.* Moses and Aaron punished: Fateful incident at Meribah (vv. 2–13)
- *C.* Failed negotiations with the king of Edom (vv. 14–21)
- *D.* Aaron's death and Eleazar's succession as chief priest (vv. 22–29)

*III.* Toward the Journey's End
*Itineraries and Songs, Negotiations and Battles* (21:1–22:1)

- *A.* Successful battle against the king of Arad (21:1–3)
- *B.* Further complaints (21:4–9)
- *C.* Itinerary of travels and Israel's song (21:10–20)
- *D.* Successful political negotiations and military victories (21:21–22:1)

יט וַיְדַבֵּר יְהֹוָה אֶל־מֹשֶׁה וְאֶל־אַהֲרֹן
לֵאמֹר׃ 2 זֹאת חֻקַּת הַתּוֹרָה אֲשֶׁר־צִוָּה
יְהֹוָה לֵאמֹר
דַּבֵּר ׀ אֶל־בְּנֵי יִשְׂרָאֵל וְיִקְחוּ אֵלֶיךָ פָרָה
אֲדֻמָּה תְּמִימָה אֲשֶׁר אֵין־בָּהּ מוּם אֲשֶׁר
לֹא־עָלָה עָלֶיהָ עֹל׃ 3 וּנְתַתֶּם אֹתָהּ אֶל־
אֶלְעָזָר הַכֹּהֵן וְהוֹצִיא אֹתָהּ אֶל־מִחוּץ
לַמַּחֲנֶה וְשָׁחַט אֹתָהּ לְפָנָיו׃ 4 וְלָקַח אֶלְעָזָר
הַכֹּהֵן מִדָּמָהּ בְּאֶצְבָּעוֹ וְהִזָּה אֶל־נֹכַח פְּנֵי

יהוה spoke to Moses and Aaron, saying:
2This is the ritual law that יהוה has commanded:

Instruct the Israelite people to bring you a red cow without blemish, in which there is no defect and on which no yoke has been laid.
3You shall give it to Eleazar the priest. It shall be taken outside the camp and slaughtered in his presence.
4Eleazar the priest shall take some of its blood with his finger and sprinkle it seven times toward the front of the

## *The "Red Cow" Ritual after Contact with a Corpse* (19:1–22)

The parashah begins with God's instructions for creating a water-based mixture called "water of *niddah* (lustration)." The reader learns only in v. 9 that the mixture is an antidote for specific contaminations that trigger the need for purification. These include a corpse, human bones, or a grave. Contamination may occur inside a tent or out in the open field. Such contact is presented as a real and present danger, requiring an immediate antidote.

*2. **red.*** This color reinforces the use of blood in aid of purification (see at Leviticus 1:6).

***cow.*** The present offering, which is intended for individual use, calls for a female of the herd (Jacob Milgrom, *Numbers*, 1990, pp. 437–47).

***without blemish.*** Heb. *t'mimah*, which could also be translated as "faultless," signals that the animal is suitable for sacrifice (see Leviticus 14:10) and is "whole or complete" (Leviticus 3:9).

### INSTRUCTIONS FOR HANDLING THE RED COW (19:1–10)

The preparations of the "water of lustration" begin with a series of steps performed by Eleazar, Aaron's son. The officiant takes the red cow outside the camp, slaughters it, and then purifies those involved. The entire procedure is considered highly impure (*tamei*).

*3. **outside the camp.*** Priestly texts are vigilant concerning boundaries. This unit deals repeatedly with such delineations: outside and inside the camp, as well as inside a tent, and out in an open field. The Israelite priestly outlook emphasizes containment and order in the face of the chaos and unpredictability of death.

*4. **take some of its blood.*** In this case, the

▶ The public silence about Miriam's death apparently did not go unnoticed.

ANOTHER VIEW ➤ *931*

▶ Moses grasped that something vital might have died with Miriam.

CONTEMPORARY REFLECTION ➤ *933*

▶ Miriam's Well traveled with the nation in the wilderness and had healing powers.

POST-BIBLICAL INTERPRETATIONS ➤ *931*

▶ I told you, when rocks crack, it happens by surprise. / Not to mention people.

VOICES ➤ *935*

Tent of Meeting. 5 The cow shall be burned in his
sight—its hide, flesh, and blood shall be burned, its
dung included—6 and the priest shall take cedar
wood, hyssop, and crimson stuff, and throw them
into the fire consuming the cow. 7 The priest shall
wash his garments and bathe his body in water;
after that the priest may reenter the camp, but he
shall be impure until evening. 8 He who performed
the burning shall also wash his garments in water,
bathe his body in water, and be impure until evening. 9 A man who is pure shall gather up the ashes

אֹהֶל־מוֹעֵד מִדָּמָהּ שֶׁבַע פְּעָמִים׃ 5 וְשָׂרַף
אֶת־הַפָּרָה לְעֵינָיו אֶת־עֹרָהּ וְאֶת־בְּשָׂרָהּ
וְאֶת־דָּמָהּ עַל־פִּרְשָׁהּ יִשְׂרֹף׃ 6 וְלָקַח הַכֹּהֵן
עֵץ אֶרֶז וְאֵזוֹב וּשְׁנִי תוֹלָעַת וְהִשְׁלִיךְ אֶל־
תּוֹךְ שְׂרֵפַת הַפָּרָה׃ 7 וְכִבֶּס בְּגָדָיו הַכֹּהֵן
וְרָחַץ בְּשָׂרוֹ בַּמַּיִם וְאַחַר יָבֹא אֶל־הַמַּחֲנֶה
וְטָמֵא הַכֹּהֵן עַד־הָעָרֶב׃ 8 וְהַשֹּׂרֵף אֹתָהּ
יְכַבֵּס בְּגָדָיו בַּמַּיִם וְרָחַץ בְּשָׂרוֹ בַּמָּיִם וְטָמֵא
עַד־הָעָרֶב׃ 9 וְאָסַף ׀ אִישׁ טָהוֹר אֵת אֵפֶר

priest sprinkles the blood at the front of the Tent of Meeting. At other times, the priest sprinkles blood directly on the altar. Jacob Milgrom draws an analogy between sacrificial blood and a cleansing agent such as detergent (*Numbers*, 1990, p. 439; see also at Leviticus 1:6).

Stephen Geller offers a trenchant summation of blood's use both as a sign of sinfulness and its opposite—an agent of creative purification ("Blood Cult," 1992, pp. 97–124). As he points out, blood signals loss of life, including murder; for instance, the blood of Abel testifies that Cain murdered him (Genesis 4:10). But blood also symbolizes life itself; therefore, according to the Bible, God has forbidden humans to eat flesh without first draining its blood (Genesis 9:4–6). Blood saves Israel from death in Exodus 12:13. Paradoxically, in Leviticus 12, after the woman gives birth she remains in a state of "blood purification" that marks the arrival of new life; but in Leviticus 15, blood of the menstruating woman represents the missed opportunity of conception. Both conditions make a woman temporarily impure.

These symbolic dimensions of blood are captured in the ritual of the red cow. An actual encounter with death requires that one be washed with a watery mixture containing the ashes of incinerated blood. The mixture is acquired through an animal's death in a ceremony of purifying renewal that allows one to return to the community of the living.

*5. its hide, flesh, and blood.* Every part of the animal is to be used. While the present ritual is unusual in adding the blood of the sacrifice to the mixture, in other respects it follows priestly precedent (as in Leviticus 4:12).

*6. cedar wood, hyssop, and crimson stuff.* In Exodus 12:22, God ordered the Israelites to dip hyssop into blood to smear on their doorposts, thus associating hyssop with the life-saving dimension of blood. "Crimson stuff" (dyed yarn) is used in Exodus 36:8, 35, 37 as part of the material in the Tabernacle, and in Exodus 39:1–2 as part of the sacred vestments of the high priest. Thus these materials are already connected with the saving of life, a sacred site, and a religious leader, marking them as powerful and efficacious—which also explains their present use. All three materials are also used in the purification rituals for *tzaraat* (see Leviticus 14).

*8. He who performed the burning.* [Both here and in the next verse, the probable reference is to a (male) priest or Levite; on the other hand, these may have been the kinds of tasks in which an Israelite sanctuary's female staff could be expected to take part, if there were indeed such workers. (On women's working at the sanctuary, see at Exodus 38:8.) Possibly gender is not an issue in the text at this point; if so, then the translation should be in gender-neutral terms. —*Ed.*]

*9. A man who is pure.* Those involved in burning the cow and in collecting the ashes, including

of the cow and deposit them outside the camp in a pure place, to be kept for water of lustration for the

הַפָּרָ֔ה וְהִנִּ֛יחַ מִח֥וּץ לַֽמַּחֲנֶ֖ה בְּמָק֣וֹם טָה֑וֹר וְהָיְתָה֩ לַעֲדַ֨ת בְּנֵי־יִשְׂרָאֵ֧ל לְמִשְׁמֶ֛רֶת לְמֵ֥י

the priest, become impure (*tamei*) until evening. A person who is pure (*tahor*) deposits the ashes in a pure site. The terms *tamei* and *tahor*, which priestly texts almost always juxtapose to each other, make their appearance together in Numbers 19. Their frequent use in this passage suggests their importance as the focus of the discussion.

The priestly system functions through a series of opposites—purity and impurity, holiness and unholiness, life and death—that mimic God's creation of the world in Genesis 1 through the imposition of an orderly plan for the earth based on distinct categories. In the face of disorder and death, the priestly legislation strives to restore such a state of order.

***water of lustration . . . for purgation.*** The term for lustration, *niddah*, illustrates the way in which a word may take on contradictory meanings in different biblical traditions. Later commentary has conflated those meanings and woefully misunderstood them.

The noun *niddah* derives from the root *n-d-d* "to depart, flee, wander"; the causative use of the root means "to chase away, put aside," related to the Akkadian cognate, "to throw, cast down." Jacob Milgrom understands *niddah* as having originally referred to the menstrual blood, which was discharged or eliminated. *Niddah* came to refer to the menstruant herself, "for she too was 'discharged' and 'excluded' from her society not by being kept at arm's length from others but, in many communities, by being banished to and quarantined in separate quarters" (*Leviticus 1–16*, 1991, p. 745). *Niddah* occurs 29 times in the *Tanach*, conveying at least three possible meanings: menstrual impurity (the most frequent meaning), indecency, and purification (the present case).

*Niddah* is used in Leviticus 12 and 15 matter-of-factly, in the midst of details concerning states of impurity for males as well as females, to designate the flow of blood during menstruation. It does not convey a negative attitude toward a menstruating woman. In Leviticus 20:21, however, the term takes on a more negative meaning as "indecency" when used in reference to when a man marries his brother's wife. Milgrom captures the distinction between these texts, explaining that in Leviticus 12 and 15 "the word *niddah* is a technical term for menstrual discharge"; yet in Leviticus 20 and derivative literature, "it becomes a metaphor for impurity, indecency or disgrace that stems from moral rather than physical causes" (*Leviticus 1–16*, p. 744).

A prime example of the derivative literature is Ezekiel 36:17, where the prophet uses the term in an explicitly degrading sense, comparing Israel's defilement of the land to a menstruating woman. Reading the continuation of this passage, Jonathan Klawans suggests that the menstruating woman in Ezekiel is an apt image since she "can cleanse herself quickly and easily from her ritual impurity, so too will God purify the people from the defiling force of their sins" (*Impurity and Sin in Ancient Judaism*, 2000, p. 31). However, one can read it in a more blatantly pejorative way, and legitimately conclude that Ezekiel resorts to the image in order to impugn Israel severely (see also Ezekiel 7:19;18:6; 22:10).

Similarly, Ezra 9:11 borrows the analogy of the menstruating woman to emphasize that the land had been defiled by its inhabitants' abominations. In II Chronicles 29:5, *niddah* is used in contradistinction to holiness. Nevertheless, none of these increasingly negative uses of *niddah* explains its use in Numbers 19.

In the present verse, *niddah* conveys the nuance found in the term's original meaning—being set apart—since the watery mixture is to remain *outside* the camp. Yet through purification it restores the individual to her or his proper place *within* the camp. Zechariah 13:1 highlights that sense of restoration. The prophet envisions the day on which God will vindicate Jerusalem: "On that day a foun-

Israelite community. It is for purgation. [10]He who gathers up the ashes of the cow shall also wash his clothes and be impure until evening.

This shall be a permanent law for the Israelites and for the strangers who reside among you.

[11]Those who touch the corpse of any human being shall be impure for seven days. [12]They shall purify themselves with [the ashes] on the third day and on the seventh day, and then be pure; if they fail to purify themselves on the third and seventh days, they shall not be pure. [13]Those who touch a corpse, the body of a person who has died, and do not purify themselves, defile יהוה's Tabernacle; those persons shall be cut off from Israel. Since the water of lustration was not dashed on them, they remain impure; their impurity is still upon them.

[14]This is the ritual: When a person dies in a tent, whoever enters the tent and whoever is in the

נִדָּ֖ה חַטָּ֥את הִֽוא׃ 10 וְ֠כִבֶּס הָאֹסֵ֨ף אֶת־אֵ֤פֶר
הַפָּרָה֙ אֶת־בְּגָדָ֔יו וְטָמֵ֖א עַד־הָעָ֑רֶב
וְהָ֨יְתָ֜ה לִבְנֵ֣י יִשְׂרָאֵ֗ל וְלַגֵּ֛ר הַגָּ֥ר בְּתוֹכָ֖ם
לְחֻקַּ֥ת עוֹלָֽם׃
11 הַנֹּגֵ֥עַ בְּמֵ֖ת לְכָל־נֶ֣פֶשׁ אָדָ֑ם וְטָמֵ֖א
שִׁבְעַ֥ת יָמִֽים׃ 12 ה֣וּא יִתְחַטָּא־ב֞וֹ בַּיּ֧וֹם
הַשְּׁלִישִׁ֛י וּבַיּ֥וֹם הַשְּׁבִיעִ֖י יִטְהָ֑ר וְאִם־לֹ֨א
יִתְחַטָּ֜א בַּיּ֧וֹם הַשְּׁלִישִׁ֛י וּבַיּ֥וֹם הַשְּׁבִיעִ֖י לֹ֥א
יִטְהָֽר׃ 13 כָּל־הַנֹּגֵ֡עַ בְּמֵ֣ת בְּנֶפֶשׁ֩ הָאָדָ֨ם
אֲשֶׁר־יָמ֜וּת וְלֹ֣א יִתְחַטָּ֗א אֶת־מִשְׁכַּ֤ן יְהוָה֙
טִמֵּ֔א וְנִכְרְתָ֛ה הַנֶּ֥פֶשׁ הַהִ֖וא מִיִּשְׂרָאֵ֑ל כִּי֩
מֵ֨י נִדָּ֜ה לֹא־זֹרַ֤ק עָלָיו֙ טָמֵ֣א יִהְיֶ֔ה ע֖וֹד
טֻמְאָת֥וֹ בֽוֹ׃
14 זֹ֚את הַתּוֹרָ֔ה אָדָ֖ם כִּֽי־יָמ֣וּת בְּאֹ֑הֶל כָּל־
הַבָּ֤א אֶל־הָאֹ֙הֶל֙ וְכָל־אֲשֶׁ֣ר בָּאֹ֔הֶל יִטְמָ֖א

tain opened to the . . . inhabitants of Jerusalem for cleansing [*chatat*] and for sprinkling [*niddah*]." Thus, both that oracle and the present verse use *niddah* in close connection to *chatat*. In both texts *niddah* is understood not as defiling or abhorrent, but as its opposite, ensuring purification. Both passages suggest a moment of restoration and joyous relief.

*11. Those.* [In this paragraph, the Hebrew is couched in the singular but is impersonal. The translator found nothing in the Bible or ancient Near Eastern cultures to imply that women would be excluded from consideration in this ritual law. So that the gender-neutral sense is clear in translation, the English is phrased in the plural. —*Ed.*]

## RITUALS AFTER CONTACT WITH A CORPSE, HUMAN BONES, OR A GRAVE (19:11–22)

A person who touches or is exposed to the dead becomes contaminated (ritually impure). Verses 11–13 set up the general principle: the contaminated individual remains so for seven days. The individual must undergo purification on the third day and then becomes pure on the seventh. Although the individual is referred to as male, v. 14 states that whoever enters a tent in which someone has died faces contamination. Surely a woman runs the same risk of encountering the dead as a man. Yet, as in many other ritual procedures, the woman goes unmentioned. Given the inclusive use of the masculine pronoun elsewhere in priestly writings, one can conclude that these laws apply to women as well.

A contaminated individual who fails to purify herself or himself remains impure and will defile the Tabernacle. To discourage such an outcome, the negligent individual is threatened with one of the most severe penalties possible in ancient Israelite law: *kareit* or excommunication. The prominence and intermingling of the words for purity (twice) and impurity (four times) along with purification (three times) urgently draw attention to maintaining the Tabernacle in its required state of purity—so that God remains in the midst of Israel.

tent shall be impure seven days; 15 and every open vessel, with no lid fastened down, shall be impure. 16 And in the open, anyone who touches a person who was killed or who died naturally, or human bone, or a grave, shall be impure seven days. 17 Some of the ashes from the fire of purgation shall be taken for the impure person, and fresh water shall be added to them in a vessel. 18 A person who is pure shall take hyssop, dip it in the water, and sprinkle on the tent and on all the vessels and people who were there, or on the one who touched the bones or the person who was killed or died naturally or the grave. 19 The pure person shall sprinkle it upon the impure person on the third day and on the seventh day, thus purifying that person by the seventh day. [The one being purified] shall then wash those clothes and bathe in water—and at nightfall shall be pure. 20 If anyone who has become impure fails to undergo purification, that person shall be cut off from the congregation for having defiled יהוה's sanctuary. The water of lustration was not dashed on that person, who is impure.

21 That shall be for them a law for all time. Further, the one who sprinkled the water of lustration shall wash those clothes; and whoever touches the water of lustration shall be impure until evening. 22 Whatever that impure person touches shall be impure; and the person who touches the impure one shall be impure until evening.

שִׁבְעַ֥ת יָמִֽים׃ 15 וְכֹל֙ כְּלִ֣י פָת֔וּחַ אֲשֶׁ֛ר אֵין־
צָמִ֥יד פָּתִ֖יל עָלָ֑יו טָמֵ֖א הֽוּא׃ 16 וְכֹ֨ל אֲשֶׁר־
יִגַּ֜ע עַל־פְּנֵ֣י הַשָּׂדֶ֗ה בַּֽחֲלַל־חֶ֙רֶב֙ א֣וֹ בְמֵ֔ת
אֽוֹ־בְעֶ֥צֶם אָדָ֖ם א֣וֹ בְקָ֑בֶר יִטְמָ֖א שִׁבְעַ֥ת
יָמִֽים׃ 17 וְלָֽקְחוּ֙ לַטָּמֵ֔א מֵֽעֲפַ֖ר שְׂרֵפַ֣ת
הַֽחַטָּ֑את וְנָתַ֥ן עָלָ֛יו מַ֥יִם חַיִּ֖ים אֶל־כֶּֽלִי׃
18 וְלָקַ֨ח אֵז֜וֹב וְטָבַ֣ל בַּמַּ֘יִם֮ אִ֣ישׁ טָהוֹר֒ וְהִזָּ֤ה
עַל־הָאֹ֙הֶל֙ וְעַל־כָּל־הַכֵּלִ֔ים וְעַל־הַנְּפָשׁ֖וֹת
אֲשֶׁ֣ר הָֽיוּ־שָׁ֑ם וְעַל־הַנֹּגֵ֗עַ בַּעֶ֙צֶם֙ א֣וֹ בֶֽחָלָ֔ל
א֥וֹ בַמֵּ֖ת א֥וֹ בַקָּֽבֶר׃ 19 וְהִזָּ֤ה הַטָּהֹר֙ עַל־
הַטָּמֵ֔א בַּיּ֥וֹם הַשְּׁלִישִׁ֖י וּבַיּ֣וֹם הַשְּׁבִיעִ֑י
וְחִטְּאוֹ֙ בַּיּ֣וֹם הַשְּׁבִיעִ֔י וְכִבֶּ֧ס בְּגָדָ֛יו וְרָחַ֥ץ
בַּמַּ֖יִם וְטָהֵ֥ר בָּעָֽרֶב׃ 20 וְאִ֤ישׁ אֲשֶׁר־יִטְמָא֙
וְלֹ֣א יִתְחַטָּ֔א וְנִכְרְתָ֛ה הַנֶּ֥פֶשׁ הַהִ֖וא מִתּ֣וֹךְ
הַקָּהָ֑ל כִּי֩ אֶת־מִקְדַּ֨שׁ יְהֹוָ֜ה טִמֵּ֗א מֵ֥י נִדָּ֛ה
לֹא־זֹרַ֥ק עָלָ֖יו טָמֵ֥א הֽוּא׃
21 וְהָיְתָ֥ה לָהֶ֖ם לְחֻקַּ֣ת עוֹלָ֑ם וּמַזֵּ֤ה מֵֽי־
הַנִּדָּה֙ יְכַבֵּ֣ס בְּגָדָ֔יו וְהַנֹּגֵ֙עַ֙ בְּמֵ֣י הַנִּדָּ֔ה
יִטְמָ֖א עַד־הָעָֽרֶב׃ 22 וְכֹ֧ל אֲשֶׁר־יִגַּע־בּ֛וֹ
הַטָּמֵ֖א יִטְמָ֑א וְהַנֶּ֥פֶשׁ הַנֹּגַ֖עַת תִּטְמָ֥א עַד־
הָעָֽרֶב׃ פ

*17. fresh water.* In this procedure of purification, "living water" (as in Genesis 26:19) is added to the ashes, mixed together, and sprinkled on the contaminated tent, vessels, and person. Leviticus 14:5 and 50 cite "living water" as part of the rituals to purify a *m'tzora* (the so-called leper, that is, a person afflicted with *tzaraat*) or a similarly afflicted house (along with the three substances cited in 19:6). Close connections exist between the present ritual of purification and that found in Leviticus, strengthening the claims that both texts are priestly, and that death and *tzaraat* are intertwined in the priestly imagination. (See further the introduction to Leviticus 14.)

*20. cut off from the congregation.* The instructions repeat the warning declared in v. 13, highlighting the threat to Israel: the possible defilement of the sanctuary and the banishment of God from their midst. (On being "cut off," see at Numbers 15:30.)

20 The Israelites arrived in a body at the wilderness of Zin on the first new moon, and the people stayed at Kadesh. Miriam died there and was buried there.

כ וַיָּבֹ֣אוּ בְנֵֽי־יִ֠שְׂרָאֵל כָּל־הָ֨עֵדָ֜ה מִדְבַּר־צִ֗ן בַּחֹ֙דֶשׁ֙ הָֽרִאשׁ֔וֹן וַיֵּ֥שֶׁב הָעָ֖ם בְּקָדֵ֑שׁ וַתָּ֤מָת שָׁם֙ מִרְיָ֔ם וַתִּקָּבֵ֖ר שָֽׁם׃

## *The Deaths of Miriam and Aaron*
(20:1–29)

The ritual of purification is immediately relevant since Miriam now dies. Perhaps as a result of her death, Moses and Aaron behave at Meribah in such a way as to be denied entry into the Promised Land. Aaron dies at the end of the unit, so the deaths of Moses' siblings bracket a unit that also recounts unsuccessful negotiations with the King of Edom.

Death reports in the Bible are highly political. Here, the politics of gender appear to play a role in the greater length and quantity of details reported of Aaron's death versus that of his sister, Miriam. Through the shaping of their deaths in Numbers 20, the biblical writer reinforces and strengthens the status of Aaron at the expense of his sister. However, we readers are free to revise that opinion.

### MIRIAM'S DEATH (20:1)

In one brief verse—astonishing in its terseness—we learn of the death of Miriam.

Miriam remains an enigmatic figure. Unlike the majority of other women in the *Tanach* (the Hebrew Bible), her reputation does not rest on being someone's mother or wife. She has an independent existence. The *Tanach* even accords her the title of "prophet" (Exodus 15:20). That she is mentioned as late as the book of Chronicles testifies to "the tenacity of her place in Israel's memory" (Rita J. Burns, *Has the Lord Indeed Spoken Only Through Moses?*, 1987, pp. 92, 129). Rita Burns suggests that Miriam's name derives from the Egyptian *mry*, meaning "beloved" (Burns, p. 10).

In spite of tantalizing hints like these, we see her fleetingly in powerful and contradictory images: joyously leading the women in song at God's deliverance of Israel from the Sea (Exodus 15), or punished by God with "snow-white *tzaraat*" after challenging Moses' exclusive leadership (Numbers 12). These fragmented views of Miriam suggest a more elaborate tradition that has not been preserved. Perhaps she held such an established reputation as a leader of Israel that she threatened the interests represented by the Torah's later editors, and therefore Numbers 12 extinguishes her voice. Unlike Moses and Aaron, Miriam has no successor.

Nonetheless, the details of Miriam's death in this verse—the first new moon, the place of her burial, especially the notice that she is buried—suggest that she is a leader of significant import in the Torah. After all, the death of most characters in the Bible receives no notice. This is true especially of women; elsewhere the Torah records the deaths only of Sarah (Genesis 23:2), Rachel (Genesis 35:19), and Rachel's nurse, Deborah (Genesis 35:8). In addition, Miriam's death is to be followed by that of her brothers, which cannot be coincidence. The three die, each in turn, on the last three stops of the journey.

In her extensive study of Miriam, Burns draws the following conclusion: "Six of the seven . . . texts which mention her represent her as a leader. In her initial [named] appearance in the narratives (Exodus 15:20–21), Miriam officiates at a celebration of the foundational event of Hebrew religion. . . . In designating Miriam as 'sister' of Aaron (Exodus 15:20) and of Aaron and Moses (26:59; I Chronicles 5:29) the biblical writers use kinship terminology to express Miriam's parallel status in religious leadership vis-à-vis that of the two other leading figures in the wilderness. . . . Micah 6:4 . . . [says] that Miriam (along with Moses and Aaron) was divinely commissioned as a leader in the wilderness" (Burns, p. 121).

[2]The community was without water, and they joined against Moses and Aaron. [3]The people quarreled with Moses, saying, "If only we had perished when our brothers perished at the instance of יהוה! [4]Why have you brought יהוה's congregation into this wilderness for us and our beasts to die there? [5]Why did you make us leave Egypt to bring us to this wretched place, a place with no grain or figs or vines or pomegranates? There is not even water to drink!"

[6]Moses and Aaron came away from the congregation to the entrance of the Tent of Meeting, and fell on their faces. The Presence of יהוה appeared to them, [7]and יהוה spoke to Moses, saying, [8]"You and your brother Aaron take the rod and assemble the community, and before their very eyes order the rock to yield its water. Thus you shall produce water for them from the rock and provide drink for the congregation and their beasts."

2 וְלֹא־הָ֥יָה מַ֖יִם לָֽעֵדָ֑ה וַיִּקָּ֣הֲל֔וּ עַל־מֹשֶׁ֖ה
וְעַֽל־אַהֲרֹֽן׃ 3 וַיָּ֥רֶב הָעָ֖ם עִם־מֹשֶׁ֑ה וַיֹּאמְר֣וּ
לֵאמֹ֔ר וְל֥וּ גָוַ֛עְנוּ בִּגְוַ֥ע אַחֵ֖ינוּ לִפְנֵ֥י יְהֹוָֽה׃
4 וְלָמָ֤ה הֲבֵאתֶם֙ אֶת־קְהַ֣ל יְהֹוָ֔ה אֶל־
הַמִּדְבָּ֖ר הַזֶּ֑ה לָמ֣וּת שָׁ֔ם אֲנַ֖חְנוּ וּבְעִירֵֽנוּ׃
5 וְלָמָ֤ה הֶֽעֱלִיתֻ֙נוּ֙ מִמִּצְרַ֔יִם לְהָבִ֣יא אֹתָ֔נוּ
אֶל־הַמָּק֥וֹם הָרָ֖ע הַזֶּ֑ה לֹ֣א ׀ מְק֣וֹם זֶ֗רַע
וּתְאֵנָ֤ה וְגֶ֙פֶן֙ וְרִמּ֔וֹן וּמַ֥יִם אַ֖יִן לִשְׁתּֽוֹת׃
6 וַיָּבֹא֩ מֹשֶׁ֨ה וְאַהֲרֹ֜ן מִפְּנֵ֣י הַקָּהָ֗ל אֶל־פֶּ֙תַח֙
אֹ֣הֶל מוֹעֵ֔ד וַֽיִּפְּל֖וּ עַל־פְּנֵיהֶ֑ם וַיֵּרָ֥א כְבוֹד־
יְהֹוָ֖ה אֲלֵיהֶֽם׃ פ 7 וַיְדַבֵּ֥ר יְהֹוָ֖ה אֶל־
מֹשֶׁ֥ה לֵּאמֹֽר׃ 8 קַ֣ח אֶת־הַמַּטֶּ֗ה וְהַקְהֵ֤ל
אֶת־הָֽעֵדָה֙ אַתָּה֙ וְאַהֲרֹ֣ן אָחִ֔יךָ וְדִבַּרְתֶּ֧ם
אֶל־הַסֶּ֛לַע לְעֵינֵיהֶ֖ם וְנָתַ֣ן מֵימָ֑יו וְהוֹצֵאתָ֨
לָהֶ֥ם מַ֙יִם֙ מִן־הַסֶּ֔לַע וְהִשְׁקִיתָ֥ אֶת־הָעֵדָ֖ה
וְאֶת־בְּעִירָֽם׃

## MOSES AND AARON PUNISHED: FATEFUL INCIDENT AT MERIBAH (20:2–13)

Following closely on the heels of Miriam's death, God now informs Aaron and Moses of their impending deaths. In contrast to Miriam's death, the deaths of the brothers are explicitly considered a punishment.

*2. The community.* Verses 1 and 2 mention "the Israelites," "the people," and a verbal form of "joined" which also appears in the unit as "community." The interweaving of these terms focuses on Israel as a collective in all its manifestations. Everyone is implicated in the events of the journey; we learn that even the fates of Moses and Aaron connect irretrievably to that of Israel.

***without water.*** Is the timing of the present complaint for water significant? Miriam is closely associated with water: she observes the deliverance of Moses from drowning in the Nile (Exodus 2:1–9), and she celebrates with him at the sea (Exodus 15:20–21). Right before she dies, new ritual instructions require "water of lustration" that is made from "living water" (Numbers 19). And now, immediately after Miriam's death, the people desperately cry for water. Because the two episodes follow each other sequentially, the Rabbis explicitly connect Miriam's death to the lack of water. The linkage suggested to the midrashic imagination that she was the source of the water now gone.

*3–5.* Israel's complaint resembles that of Numbers 14, in which the people bitterly complain about leaving Egypt only to die in the wilderness (see also Exodus 16:3). Denied entry to Canaan due to their lack of belief in God's power to ensure its conquest, they now pine after the food of that promised land: grain, figs, vines, and pomegranates.

*8. "order the rock to yield its water."* In a parallel episode in Exodus 17:5–6, God instructs Moses to use his rod *to strike* the rock to release its water. This time, God tells Moses *to speak* to the rock before their eyes (so that the people see him do so and not just hear the words) to release its water.

⁹Moses took the rod from before יהוה, as he had been commanded. ¹⁰Moses and Aaron assembled the congregation in front of the rock; and he said to them, "Listen, you rebels, shall we get water for you out of this rock?" ¹¹And Moses raised his hand and struck the rock twice with his rod. Out came copious water, and the community and their beasts drank.

¹²But יהוה said to Moses and Aaron, "Because you did not trust Me enough to affirm My sanctity in the sight of the Israelite people, therefore you shall not lead this congregation into the land that I have given them." ¹³Those are the Waters of Meribah—meaning that the Israelites quarrelled with יהוה—whose sanctity was affirmed through them.

9 וַיִּקַּ֤ח מֹשֶׁה֙ אֶת־הַמַּטֶּ֔ה מִלִּפְנֵ֖י יְהֹוָ֑ה כַּאֲשֶׁ֖ר צִוָּֽהוּ׃ 10 וַיַּקְהִ֜לוּ מֹשֶׁ֧ה וְאַהֲרֹ֛ן אֶת־הַקָּהָ֖ל אֶל־פְּנֵ֣י הַסָּ֑לַע וַיֹּ֣אמֶר לָהֶ֗ם שִׁמְעוּ־נָא֙ הַמֹּרִ֔ים הֲמִן־הַסֶּ֣לַע הַזֶּ֔ה נוֹצִ֥יא לָכֶ֖ם מָֽיִם׃ 11 וַיָּ֨רֶם מֹשֶׁ֜ה אֶת־יָד֗וֹ וַיַּ֨ךְ אֶת־הַסֶּ֤לַע בְּמַטֵּ֙הוּ֙ פַּעֲמָ֔יִם וַיֵּצְאוּ֙ מַ֣יִם רַבִּ֔ים וַתֵּ֥שְׁתְּ הָעֵדָ֖ה וּבְעִירָֽם׃ ס 12 וַיֹּ֣אמֶר יְהֹוָה֮ אֶל־מֹשֶׁ֣ה וְאֶֽל־אַהֲרֹן֒ יַ֚עַן לֹא־הֶאֱמַנְתֶּ֣ם בִּ֔י לְהַ֨קְדִּישֵׁ֔נִי לְעֵינֵ֖י בְּנֵ֣י יִשְׂרָאֵ֑ל לָכֵ֗ן לֹ֤א תָבִ֙יאוּ֙ אֶת־הַקָּהָ֣ל הַזֶּ֔ה אֶל־הָאָ֖רֶץ אֲשֶׁר־נָתַ֥תִּי לָהֶֽם׃ 13 הֵ֚מָּה מֵ֣י מְרִיבָ֔ה אֲשֶׁר־רָב֥וּ בְנֵֽי־יִשְׂרָאֵ֖ל אֶת־יְהֹוָ֑ה וַיִּקָּדֵ֖שׁ בָּֽם׃ ס

· · · · · · · · · · · · · · · · · · · · · · · · · · · · · ·

*10. "rebels."* Heb. *morim.* In frustration, Moses addresses the Israelites with a term that echoes Miriam's name (see Another View, p. 931).

*11. struck the rock twice.* Instead of speaking to it (v. 8).

*12–13.* These verses describe God's punishment of Moses and Aaron. What wrong could Moses and Aaron have committed severe enough to warrant God's punishment after years of loyal service? The laconic quality of the narrative has provoked thousands of years of interpretation in an attempt to identify their misdeed. [Because Moses' and Aaron's "crime" here is not self-evident, contemporary scholars, like early rabbinic interpreters, have offered a wide range of possible explanations in addition to the one proposed here. Some suggest that the "crime" concerns striking the rock: Moses struck the rock instead of speaking to it, or perhaps he violated God's instructions by striking it twice instead of once. Others suggest that God is angry because the incident discloses problematic aspects of Moses' character as a leader: Moses lost his temper in an inappropriate manner. Still others suggest that Moses' language was wrong: By phrasing his words as a question (v. 10), he could have been misunderstood as doubting God; by saying "shall we get water

for you" (v. 10), he positioned himself and Aaron—instead of God—as the chief actors; or by calling the people "rebels" he denigrated them. —*Ed.*]

*12. "affirm... sanctity."* The verbal root *k-d-sh* echoes the place name Kadesh, returning the audience to v. 1 and the death of Miriam. Her death haunts this literary unit.

*"in the sight of the Israelite people."* The emphasis on sight—as in v. 8, God mentions literally the "eyes" of Israel—suggests that by not following the letter of God's instructions in the sight of Israel, Moses provides an example that would be fatal to Israel if they followed him.

*"the land that I have given them."* To "them"—and not to "you." God's ultimate concern is a divine relationship with the people Israel, not with any one leader.

*13. Waters of Meribah.* Heb. *mei m'rivah,* which echoes the "water of lustration" and "fresh water" (both terms being plural in the literal Hebrew) in Numbers 19. In contrast to the hopefulness of the ritual of purification and the renewal offered by it, Israel is again plunged into a dark moment in its journey. The term also picks up on the verb "quarreled" (*vayarev*) in 20:3.

[14]From Kadesh, Moses sent messengers to the king of Edom: "Thus says your brother, Israel: You know all the hardships that have befallen us; [15]that our ancestors went down to Egypt, that we dwelt in Egypt a long time, and that the Egyptians dealt harshly with us and our ancestors. [16]We cried to יהוה who heard our plea, sending a messenger who freed us from Egypt. Now we are in Kadesh, the town on the border of your territory. [17]Allow us, then, to cross your country. We will not pass through fields or vineyards, and we will not drink water from wells. We will follow the king's highway, turning off neither to the right nor to the left until we have crossed your territory."

[18]But Edom answered him, "You shall not pass through us, else we will go out against you with the sword." [19]"We will keep to the beaten track," the Israelites said to them, "and if we or our cattle drink your water, we will pay for it. We ask only for passage on foot—it is but a small matter." [20]But they replied, "You shall not pass through!" And Edom went out against them in heavy force, strongly armed. [21]So Edom would not let Israel cross their territory, and Israel turned away from them.

[22]Setting out from Kadesh, the Israelites arrived in a body at Mount Hor. [23]At Mount Hor, on the boundary of the land of Edom, יהוה said to Moses and Aaron, [24]"Let Aaron be gathered to his kin: he

14 וַיִּשְׁלַח מֹשֶׁה מַלְאָכִים מִקָּדֵשׁ אֶל־מֶלֶךְ
אֱדוֹם כֹּה אָמַר אָחִיךָ יִשְׂרָאֵל אַתָּה יָדַעְתָּ
אֵת כָּל־הַתְּלָאָה אֲשֶׁר מְצָאָתְנוּ׃ 15 וַיֵּרְדוּ
אֲבֹתֵינוּ מִצְרַיְמָה וַנֵּשֶׁב בְּמִצְרַיִם יָמִים
רַבִּים וַיָּרֵעוּ לָנוּ מִצְרַיִם וְלַאֲבֹתֵינוּ׃
16 וַנִּצְעַק אֶל־יְהוָה וַיִּשְׁמַע קֹלֵנוּ וַיִּשְׁלַח
מַלְאָךְ וַיֹּצִאֵנוּ מִמִּצְרָיִם וְהִנֵּה אֲנַחְנוּ בְקָדֵשׁ
עִיר קְצֵה גְבוּלֶךָ׃ 17 נַעְבְּרָה־נָּא בְאַרְצֶךָ לֹא
נַעֲבֹר בְּשָׂדֶה וּבְכֶרֶם וְלֹא נִשְׁתֶּה מֵי בְאֵר
דֶּרֶךְ הַמֶּלֶךְ נֵלֵךְ לֹא נִטֶּה יָמִין וּשְׂמֹאול עַד
אֲשֶׁר־נַעֲבֹר גְּבֻלֶךָ׃
18 וַיֹּאמֶר אֵלָיו אֱדוֹם לֹא תַעֲבֹר בִּי פֶּן־
בַּחֶרֶב אֵצֵא לִקְרָאתֶךָ׃ 19 וַיֹּאמְרוּ אֵלָיו
בְּנֵי־יִשְׂרָאֵל בַּמְסִלָּה נַעֲלֶה וְאִם־מֵימֶיךָ
נִשְׁתֶּה אֲנִי וּמִקְנַי וְנָתַתִּי מִכְרָם רַק אֵין־
דָּבָר בְּרַגְלַי אֶעֱבֹרָה׃ 20 וַיֹּאמֶר לֹא תַעֲבֹר
וַיֵּצֵא אֱדוֹם לִקְרָאתוֹ בְּעַם כָּבֵד וּבְיָד חֲזָקָה׃
21 וַיְמָאֵן ׀ אֱדוֹם נְתֹן אֶת־יִשְׂרָאֵל עֲבֹר
בִּגְבֻלוֹ וַיֵּט יִשְׂרָאֵל מֵעָלָיו׃ פ
22 וַיִּסְעוּ מִקָּדֵשׁ וַיָּבֹאוּ בְנֵי־יִשְׂרָאֵל כָּל־
הָעֵדָה הֹר הָהָר׃ 23 וַיֹּאמֶר יְהוָה אֶל־מֹשֶׁה
וְאֶל־אַהֲרֹן בְּהֹר הָהָר עַל־גְּבוּל אֶרֶץ־אֱדוֹם
לֵאמֹר׃ 24 יֵאָסֵף אַהֲרֹן אֶל־עַמָּיו כִּי לֹא

### FAILED NEGOTIATIONS WITH THE KING OF EDOM (20:14–21)

Seemingly undeterred, Moses faces the next challenge of the journey as he attempts to negotiate safe passage through Edom. Not succeeding, Moses turns away without a fight.

### AARON'S DEATH AND ELEAZAR'S SUCCESSION AS CHIEF PRIEST (20:22–29)

The two deaths bookend the unit: Miriam in v. 1, and Aaron here.

*22. the Israelites arrived in a body at Mount Hor.* The phrase is identical to the description of Israel just moments before Miriam's death in v. 1.

*24. "Let Aaron be gathered to his kin."* This phrase is found in the Torah only in connection with the deaths of six characters, all of whom are male leaders: Abraham, Ishmael, Isaac, Jacob, Moses, and Aaron. This verb, however, is also used in 12:14–15 when Miriam is "readmitted" to the camp: she is "gathered in" by the people before they continue their march.

is not to enter the land that I have assigned to the Israelite people, because you disobeyed my command about the waters of Meribah. 25 Take Aaron and his son Eleazar and bring them up on Mount Hor. 26 Strip Aaron of his vestments and put them on his son Eleazar. There Aaron shall be gathered unto the dead."

27 Moses did as יהוה had commanded. They ascended Mount Hor in the sight of the whole community. 28 Moses stripped Aaron of his vestments and put them on his son Eleazar, and Aaron died there on the summit of the mountain. When Moses and Eleazar came down from the mountain, 29 the whole community knew that Aaron had breathed his last. All the house of Israel bewailed Aaron thirty days.

*21* When the Canaanite, king of Arad, who dwelt in the Negeb, learned that Israel was coming by the way of Atharim, he engaged Israel in battle and took some of them captive. 2 Then Israel made a vow to יהוה and said, "If You deliver this people

יָבֹא אֶל־הָאָרֶץ אֲשֶׁר נָתַתִּי לִבְנֵי יִשְׂרָאֵל
עַל אֲשֶׁר־מְרִיתֶם אֶת־פִּי לְמֵי מְרִיבָה׃
25 קַח אֶת־אַהֲרֹן וְאֶת־אֶלְעָזָר בְּנוֹ וְהַעַל
אֹתָם הֹר הָהָר׃ 26 וְהַפְשֵׁט אֶת־אַהֲרֹן אֶת־
בְּגָדָיו וְהִלְבַּשְׁתָּם אֶת־אֶלְעָזָר בְּנוֹ וְאַהֲרֹן
יֵאָסֵף וּמֵת שָׁם׃
27 וַיַּעַשׂ מֹשֶׁה כַּאֲשֶׁר צִוָּה יְהוָה וַיַּעֲלוּ אֶל־
הֹר הָהָר לְעֵינֵי כָּל־הָעֵדָה׃ 28 וַיַּפְשֵׁט מֹשֶׁה
אֶת־אַהֲרֹן אֶת־בְּגָדָיו וַיַּלְבֵּשׁ אֹתָם אֶת־
אֶלְעָזָר בְּנוֹ וַיָּמָת אַהֲרֹן שָׁם בְּרֹאשׁ הָהָר
וַיֵּרֶד מֹשֶׁה וְאֶלְעָזָר מִן־הָהָר׃ 29 וַיִּרְאוּ כָּל־
הָעֵדָה כִּי גָוַע אַהֲרֹן וַיִּבְכּוּ אֶת־אַהֲרֹן
שְׁלֹשִׁים יוֹם כֹּל בֵּית יִשְׂרָאֵל׃ ס

כא וַיִּשְׁמַע הַכְּנַעֲנִי מֶלֶךְ־עֲרָד יֹשֵׁב הַנֶּגֶב
כִּי בָּא יִשְׂרָאֵל דֶּרֶךְ הָאֲתָרִים וַיִּלָּחֶם
בְּיִשְׂרָאֵל וַיִּשְׁבְּ ׀ מִמֶּנּוּ שֶׁבִי׃ 2 וַיִּדַּר יִשְׂרָאֵל
נֶדֶר לַיהוָה וַיֹּאמַר אִם־נָתֹן תִּתֵּן אֶת־הָעָם

**29. *thirty days.*** Moses too will be mourned for this period of time at his death (Deuteronomy 34:8).

## *Toward the Journey's End*

### ITINERARIES AND SONGS, NEGOTIATIONS AND BATTLES (21:1–22:1)

This unit begins by reporting on a successful battle (vv. 1–3), and in so doing introduces the unit's most important topic: the positive change in Israel's fortune. After yet another episode of complaint (vv. 4–9), a set of itineraries in vv. 10–20 bracket obscure materials: the "Book of the Wars of יהוה" (v. 14) and a poem celebrating the discovery of water (v. 17). An account of two successful battles follows (21:21–22:1), including an apparently ancient victory song (vv. 27–30).

Several topics link Numbers 20 and 21, including parallel episodes of complaint, the motif of water, and negotiations with foreign kings. Yet the discovery of water and the successful battles of Numbers 21 serve to underline a crucial difference: the fortunes of Israel have now decidedly improved for the new generation.

#### SUCCESSFUL BATTLE AGAINST THE KING OF ARAD (21:1–3)

Israel will be victorious in all subsequent battles on the way to the Promised Land. The use of the name Hormah cleverly signals the change in their fortunes. Earlier, Israel received a "shattering blow" at Hormah (14:45); here, after the deaths of almost all of the earlier generation, Israel emerges victorious.

into our hand, we will proscribe their towns." [3]יהוה
heeded Israel's plea and delivered up the Canaanites; and they and their cities were proscribed. So
that place was named Hormah.

[4]They set out from Mount Hor by way of the
Sea of Reeds to skirt the land of Edom. But the
people grew restive on the journey, [5]and the people
spoke against God and against Moses, "Why did
you make us leave Egypt to die in the wilderness?
There is no bread and no water, and we have come
to loathe this miserable food." [6]יהוה sent *seraph*
serpents against the people. They bit the people and
many of the Israelites died. [7]The people came to
Moses and said, "We sinned by speaking against
יהוה and against you. Intercede with יהוה to take
away the serpents from us!" And Moses interceded
for the people. [8]Then יהוה said to Moses, "Make a
*seraph* figure and mount it on a standard. And
anyone who was bitten who then looks at it shall
recover." [9]Moses made a copper serpent and
mounted it on a standard; and when bitten by a
serpent, anyone who looked at the copper serpent
would recover.

הַזֶּה בְּיָדִי וְהַחֲרַמְתִּי אֶת־עָרֵיהֶם׃ 3 וַיִּשְׁמַע
יְהֹוָה בְּקוֹל יִשְׂרָאֵל וַיִּתֵּן אֶת־הַכְּנַעֲנִי
וַיַּחֲרֵם אֶתְהֶם וְאֶת־עָרֵיהֶם וַיִּקְרָא שֵׁם־
הַמָּקוֹם חָרְמָה׃ פ

4 וַיִּסְעוּ מֵהֹר הָהָר דֶּרֶךְ יַם־סוּף לִסְבֹב אֶת־
אֶרֶץ אֱדוֹם וַתִּקְצַר נֶפֶשׁ־הָעָם בַּדָּרֶךְ׃
5 וַיְדַבֵּר הָעָם בֵּאלֹהִים וּבְמֹשֶׁה לָמָה
הֶעֱלִיתֻנוּ מִמִּצְרַיִם לָמוּת בַּמִּדְבָּר כִּי אֵין
לֶחֶם וְאֵין מַיִם וְנַפְשֵׁנוּ קָצָה בַּלֶּחֶם
הַקְּלֹקֵל׃ 6 וַיְשַׁלַּח יְהֹוָה בָּעָם אֵת הַנְּחָשִׁים
הַשְּׂרָפִים וַיְנַשְּׁכוּ אֶת־הָעָם וַיָּמָת עַם־רָב
מִיִּשְׂרָאֵל׃ 7 וַיָּבֹא הָעָם אֶל־מֹשֶׁה וַיֹּאמְרוּ
חָטָאנוּ כִּי־דִבַּרְנוּ בַיהֹוָה וָבָךְ הִתְפַּלֵּל אֶל־
יְהֹוָה וְיָסֵר מֵעָלֵינוּ אֶת־הַנָּחָשׁ וַיִּתְפַּלֵּל
מֹשֶׁה בְּעַד הָעָם׃ 8 וַיֹּאמֶר יְהֹוָה אֶל־מֹשֶׁה
עֲשֵׂה לְךָ שָׂרָף וְשִׂים אֹתוֹ עַל־נֵס וְהָיָה
כׇּל־הַנָּשׁוּךְ וְרָאָה אֹתוֹ וָחָי׃ 9 וַיַּעַשׂ מֹשֶׁה
נְחַשׁ נְחֹשֶׁת וַיְשִׂמֵהוּ עַל־הַנֵּס וְהָיָה אִם־
נָשַׁךְ הַנָּחָשׁ אֶת־אִישׁ וְהִבִּיט אֶל־נְחַשׁ
הַנְּחֹשֶׁת וָחָי׃

### FURTHER COMPLAINTS (21:4–9)

After mourning Aaron at Mt. Hor (20:29), the Israelites complain again, precisely as they behaved after Miriam's death.

*6. seraph serpents.* In the ancient world, snakes often symbolized fertility and healing, since they shed their skins only to grow new ones repeatedly in a cycle of destruction and rebirth. In the *Tanach*, the combination of *seraph* and "serpent" also occurs in Deuteronomy 8:15; in both cases, the creatures signal terror and cruelty as part of the wilderness setting. Since they are deadly, only God's interventions allow the people to survive.

*7. "We sinned by speaking."* For the first time, the people acknowledge the effects of their speech and its contaminating influence on their collective fate.

*And Moses interceded for the people.* In spite of their repeated failures, Moses advocates to God on behalf of the people, as he does following the Golden Calf and the incident with the scouts (Exodus 32:31–32; Numbers 14:5–19).

*9. anyone who looked at the copper serpent would recover.* Healing and new life follow death yet again in this parashah, much as the ritual of the healing water in Numbers 19 responds to the pervasiveness of death with purifying restoration. The snake as a symbol of both destruction and rebirth brilliantly represents the movement between death and life so prevalent in the narrative of the wilderness journey.

<sup>10</sup>The Israelites marched on and encamped at Oboth. <sup>11</sup>They set out from Oboth and encamped at Iye-abarim, in the wilderness bordering on Moab to the east. <sup>12</sup>From there they set out and encamped at the wadi Zered. <sup>13</sup>From there they set out and encamped beyond the Arnon, that is, in the wilderness that extends from the territory of the Amorites. For the Arnon is the boundary of Moab, between Moab and the Amorites. <sup>14</sup>Therefore the Book of the Wars of יהוה speaks of "... Waheb in Suphah, and the wadis: the Arnon <sup>15</sup>with its tributary wadis, stretched along the settled country of Ar, hugging the territory of Moab ..."

<sup>16</sup>And from there to Beer, which is the well where יהוה said to Moses, "Assemble the people that I may give them water." <sup>17</sup>Then Israel sang this song:

Spring up, O well—sing to it—
<sup>18</sup>The well which the chieftains dug,
Which the nobles of the people started
With maces, with their own staffs.

And from Midbar to Mattanah, <sup>19</sup>and from Mattanah to Nahaliel, and from Nahaliel to Bamoth, <sup>20</sup>and from Bamoth to the valley that is in the country of Moab, at the peak of Pisgah, overlooking the wasteland.

<sup>21</sup>Israel now sent messengers to Sihon king of the Amorites, saying, <sup>22</sup>"Let me pass through your

10 וַיִּסְע֖וּ בְּנֵ֣י יִשְׂרָאֵ֑ל וַֽיַּחֲנ֖וּ בְּאֹבֹֽת׃ 11 וַיִּסְע֖וּ מֵאֹבֹ֑ת וַֽיַּחֲנ֞וּ בְּעִיֵּ֣י הָֽעֲבָרִ֗ים בַּמִּדְבָּר֙ אֲשֶׁר֙ עַל־פְּנֵ֣י מוֹאָ֔ב מִמִּזְרַ֖ח הַשָּֽׁמֶשׁ׃ 12 מִשָּׁ֖ם נָסָ֑עוּ וַֽיַּחֲנ֖וּ בְּנַ֥חַל זָֽרֶד׃ 13 מִשָּׁם֮ נָסָ֒עוּ֒ וַֽיַּחֲנ֗וּ מֵעֵ֤בֶר אַרְנוֹן֙ אֲשֶׁ֣ר בַּמִּדְבָּ֔ר הַיֹּצֵ֖א מִגְּבֻ֣ל הָֽאֱמֹרִ֑י כִּ֣י אַרְנ֗וֹן גְּב֤וּל מוֹאָב֙ בֵּ֣ין מוֹאָ֔ב וּבֵ֖ין הָֽאֱמֹרִֽי׃ 14 עַל־כֵּן֙ יֵֽאָמַ֔ר בְּסֵ֖פֶר מִלְחֲמֹ֣ת יְהוָ֑ה אֶת־וָהֵ֣ב בְּסוּפָ֔ה וְאֶת־הַנְּחָלִ֖ים אַרְנֽוֹן׃ 15 וְאֶ֙שֶׁד֙ הַנְּחָלִ֔ים אֲשֶׁ֥ר נָטָ֖ה לְשֶׁ֣בֶת עָ֑ר וְנִשְׁעַ֖ן לִגְב֥וּל מוֹאָֽב׃ 16 וּמִשָּׁ֖ם בְּאֵ֑רָה הִ֣וא הַבְּאֵ֗ר אֲשֶׁ֨ר אָמַ֤ר יְהוָה֙ לְמֹשֶׁ֔ה אֱסֹף֙ אֶת־הָעָ֔ם וְאֶתְּנָ֥ה לָהֶ֖ם מָֽיִם׃ ס 17 אָ֚ז יָשִׁ֣יר יִשְׂרָאֵ֔ל אֶת־הַשִּׁירָ֖ה הַזֹּ֑את

עֲלִ֥י בְאֵ֖ר עֱנוּ־לָֽהּ׃
18 בְּאֵ֞ר חֲפָר֣וּהָ שָׂרִ֗ים
כָּר֙וּהָ֙ נְדִיבֵ֣י הָעָ֔ם
בִּמְחֹקֵ֖ק בְּמִשְׁעֲנֹתָ֑ם

וּמִמִּדְבָּ֖ר מַתָּנָֽה׃ 19 וּמִמַּתָּנָ֖ה נַחֲלִיאֵ֑ל וּמִנַּחֲלִיאֵ֖ל בָּמֽוֹת׃ 20 וּמִבָּמ֗וֹת הַגַּיְא֙ אֲשֶׁר֙ בִּשְׂדֵ֣ה מוֹאָ֔ב רֹ֖אשׁ הַפִּסְגָּ֑ה וְנִשְׁקָ֖פָה עַל־פְּנֵ֥י הַיְשִׁימֹֽן׃ פ

21 וַיִּשְׁלַ֤ח יִשְׂרָאֵל֙ מַלְאָכִ֔ים אֶל־סִיחֹ֥ן מֶֽלֶךְ־הָֽאֱמֹרִ֖י לֵאמֹֽר׃ 22 אֶעְבְּרָ֣ה בְאַרְצֶ֔ךָ לֹ֤א

---

### ITINERARY OF TRAVELS AND ISRAEL'S SONG (21:10–20)

Itineraries locate the journey along specific stops, lending an air of authenticity to the wilderness wanderings. Reference to an outside source long lost to Israel, "the Book of the Wars of יהוה," further suggests a documented past.

*17–18.* This fragment, an ancient poem, functions as a corrective to the grievous complaints for water in Numbers 20. Now, as part of the positive tone of Numbers 21, the well assuages the people's thirst, leading to an outpouring of grateful and cele-

bratory song. The Rabbis later trace both the well and the song back to Miriam, which is fitting since v. 17 begins with a phrase that parallels the lead-in to the Song at the Sea in Exodus 15:1. (For the suggestion that the Song at the Sea should be attributed to Miriam, see at Exodus 15:1–19.)

### SUCCESSFUL POLITICAL NEGOTIATIONS AND MILITARY VICTORIES (21:21–22:1)

The unsuccessful petition made by Moses to cross the territory of Edom in 20:14–21 is now followed in 21:21–25 by the successful possession by

country. We will not turn off into fields or vineyards, and we will not drink water from wells. We
will follow the king's highway until we have crossed
your territory." 23But Sihon would not let Israel
pass through his territory. Sihon gathered all his
people and went out against Israel in the wilderness. He came to Jahaz and engaged Israel in battle.
24But Israel put them to the sword, and took possession of their land, from the Arnon to the Jabbok,
as far as [Az] of the Ammonites, for Az marked the
boundary of the Ammonites. 25Israel took all those
towns. And Israel settled in all the towns of the
Amorites, in Heshbon and all its dependencies.
26Now Heshbon was the city of Sihon king of
the Amorites, who had fought against a former king
of Moab and taken all his land from him as far as
the Arnon. 27Therefore the bards would recite:

"Come to Heshbon; firmly built
And well founded is Sihon's city.
28For fire went forth from Heshbon,
Flame from Sihon's city,
Consuming Ar of Moab,
The lords of Bamoth by the Arnon.
29Woe to you, O Moab!
You are undone, O people of Chemosh!
His sons are rendered fugitive
And his daughters captive
By an Amorite king, Sihon."

נִטֶּה בְּשָׂדֶה וּבְכֶרֶם לֹא נִשְׁתֶּה מֵי בְאֵר
בְּדֶרֶךְ הַמֶּלֶךְ נֵלֵךְ עַד אֲשֶׁר־נַעֲבֹר גְּבֻלֶךָ׃
23 וְלֹא־נָתַן סִיחֹן אֶת־יִשְׂרָאֵל עֲבֹר בִּגְבֻלוֹ
וַיֶּאֱסֹף סִיחֹן אֶת־כָּל־עַמּוֹ וַיֵּצֵא לִקְרַאת
יִשְׂרָאֵל הַמִּדְבָּרָה וַיָּבֹא יָהְצָה וַיִּלָּחֶם
בְּיִשְׂרָאֵל׃ 24 וַיַּכֵּהוּ יִשְׂרָאֵל לְפִי־חָרֶב
וַיִּירַשׁ אֶת־אַרְצוֹ מֵאַרְנֹן עַד־יַבֹּק עַד־בְּנֵי
עַמּוֹן כִּי עַז גְּבוּל בְּנֵי עַמּוֹן׃ 25 וַיִּקַּח יִשְׂרָאֵל
אֵת כָּל־הֶעָרִים הָאֵלֶּה וַיֵּשֶׁב יִשְׂרָאֵל בְּכָל־
עָרֵי הָאֱמֹרִי בְּחֶשְׁבּוֹן וּבְכָל־בְּנֹתֶיהָ׃
26 כִּי חֶשְׁבּוֹן עִיר סִיחֹן מֶלֶךְ הָאֱמֹרִי הִוא
וְהוּא נִלְחַם בְּמֶלֶךְ מוֹאָב הָרִאשׁוֹן וַיִּקַּח
אֶת־כָּל־אַרְצוֹ מִיָּדוֹ עַד־אַרְנֹן׃ 27 עַל־כֵּן
יֹאמְרוּ הַמֹּשְׁלִים
בֹּאוּ חֶשְׁבּוֹן תִּבָּנֶה
וְתִכּוֹנֵן עִיר סִיחוֹן׃
28 כִּי־אֵשׁ יָצְאָה מֵחֶשְׁבּוֹן
לֶהָבָה מִקִּרְיַת סִיחֹן
אָכְלָה עָר מוֹאָב
בַּעֲלֵי בָּמוֹת אַרְנֹן׃
29 אוֹי־לְךָ מוֹאָב
אָבַדְתָּ עַם־כְּמוֹשׁ
נָתַן בָּנָיו פְּלֵיטִם
וּבְנֹתָיו בַּשְּׁבִית
לְמֶלֶךְ אֱמֹרִי סִיחוֹן׃

---

the Israelites of the land of the Amorites. Previously Moses, who was near to his own death, failed; now Israel succeeds.

*25. and all its dependencies.* Literally, "all its daughters." The *Tanach* uses terms of female relations to describe a walled city as a "mother" and an open village as a "daughter." The "mother" city (since walled) is better protected than her daughter from attack. As F. S. Frick observes, these female terms reflect and reinforce a pattern of domestic relations as well as societal conceptions of the strengths and weaknesses of a female at different points in her life: "Mothers had considerable authority over their daughters—hence the analogy of a walled mother-city exerting control of the unwalled. Just as a mother had major responsibilities in caring for her children, so the city provided protection for its people.... The fundamental awareness of maternal care permeates the concept of cities as female" ("Mother/Daughter as Territory," in *Women in Scripture*, 2000, pp. 532–33).

[30]Yet we have cast them down utterly,
Heshbon along with Dibon;
We have wrought desolation at Nophah,
Which is hard by Medeba.
[31]So Israel occupied the land of the Amorites.
[32]Then Moses sent to spy out Jazer, and they captured its dependencies and dispossessed the Amorites who were there.

[33]They marched on and went up the road to Bashan, and King Og of Bashan, with all his troops, came out to Edrei to engage them in battle. [34]But יהוה said to Moses, "Do not fear him, for I give him and all his troops and his land into your hand. You shall do to him as you did to Sihon king of the Amorites who dwelt in Heshbon." [35]They defeated him and his sons and all his troops, until no remnant was left him; and they took possession of his country. 22 The Israelites then marched on and encamped in the steppes of Moab, across the Jordan from Jericho.

30 וַנִּירָ֛ם אָבַ֥ד
חֶשְׁבּ֖וֹן עַד־דִּיבֹ֑ן
וַנַּשִּׁ֣ים עַד־נֹ֔פַח
אֲשֶׁ֖ר עַד־מֵֽידְבָֽא׃
31 וַיֵּ֙שֶׁב֙ יִשְׂרָאֵ֔ל בְּאֶ֖רֶץ הָֽאֱמֹרִֽי׃ 32 וַיִּשְׁלַ֤ח
מֹשֶׁה֙ לְרַגֵּ֣ל אֶת־יַעְזֵ֔ר וַֽיִּלְכְּד֖וּ בְּנֹתֶ֑יהָ ויירש
וַיּ֖וֹרֶשׁ אֶת־הָאֱמֹרִ֥י אֲשֶׁר־שָֽׁם׃
33 וַיִּפְנוּ֙ וַֽיַּעֲל֔וּ דֶּ֖רֶךְ הַבָּשָׁ֑ן וַיֵּצֵ֣א עוֹג֩ מֶֽלֶךְ־
הַבָּשָׁ֨ן לִקְרָאתָ֜ם ה֧וּא וְכָל־עַמּ֛וֹ לַמִּלְחָמָ֖ה
אֶדְרֶֽעִי׃ 34 וַיֹּ֨אמֶר יְהוָ֤ה אֶל־מֹשֶׁה֙ אַל־
תִּירָ֣א אֹת֔וֹ כִּ֣י בְיָדְךָ֞ נָתַ֧תִּי אֹת֛וֹ וְאֶת־
כָּל־עַמּ֖וֹ וְאֶת־אַרְצ֑וֹ וְעָשִׂ֣יתָ לּ֔וֹ כַּאֲשֶׁ֣ר
עָשִׂ֗יתָ לְסִיחֹן֙ מֶ֣לֶךְ הָֽאֱמֹרִ֔י אֲשֶׁ֥ר יוֹשֵׁ֖ב
בְּחֶשְׁבּֽוֹן׃ 35 וַיַּכּ֨וּ אֹת֤וֹ וְאֶת־בָּנָיו֙ וְאֶת־כָּל־
עַמּ֔וֹ עַד־בִּלְתִּ֥י הִשְׁאִֽיר־ל֖וֹ שָׂרִ֑יד וַיִּֽירְשׁ֖וּ
אֶת־אַרְצֽוֹ׃ כב וַיִּסְע֖וּ בְּנֵ֣י יִשְׂרָאֵ֑ל
וַֽיַּחֲנוּ֙ בְּעַֽרְב֣וֹת מוֹאָ֔ב מֵעֵ֖בֶר לְיַרְדֵּ֥ן
יְרֵחֽוֹ׃ ס

***21:33–22:1.*** After the successful battle against Og of Bashan, Israel arrives at the steppes of Moab. The deaths and discord, complaints and failure in Numbers 20 have been followed in Numbers 21 by steady progress along the path, accompanied by songs of gratitude and victory, punctuated by successful battles.

—*Adriane Leveen*

# Another View

MIRIAM, WHO HAS PLAYED both a vital and a subdued role in the story of the Exodus and the wilderness wanderings, dies in this parashah. Her death is reported briefly: "Miriam died there, and was buried there" (20:1). There is no mention of people mourning her death or feeling the loss of her contribution to the Israelite people. Not long afterward, when Aaron is about to die, Moses in an elaborate ceremony publicly passes on Aaron's ritual clothing, signs of his exalted position, to Aaron's son Eleazar. Then, the people mourn him for thirty days (20:22–29). This contrast between Miriam's and Aaron's deaths is striking and troubling.

How does Moses respond to Miriam's death? While the text does not record his reaction, we can glean important insights from the way he handles (or mishandles) the subsequent crisis over water and from the way her name appears obliquely in this episode.

In the debacle that immediately follows Miriam's death, when the Israelites clamor for water (20:2–5), Moses hits the rock instead of speaking to it as instructed (v. 8). God punishes both Moses and Aaron for this failure by having them die in the wilderness instead of permitting them to enter the Promised Land. The telling clue to Moses' attitude is suggested by his words. Before hitting the rock, Moses cries out "Listen, you rebels!" (v. 10). The word for "rebels" is *morim*, and it appears nowhere else in the Bible in this form. Remarkably, in their unvocalized form the words, *morim* (rebels) and *miryam* (Miriam) are identical; both words are made up of the same four Hebrew consonants: *m-r-y-m*.

This verbal coincidence may intimate that Moses' behavior has as much to do with losing Miriam as with his frustration with the Israelite people. It suggests that when faced with the task of producing water, Moses recalls Miriam as his older sister, his co-leader, and perhaps most of all, the clever caretaker who guarded him at the Nile.

*How does Moses respond to Miriam's death?*

Moses may have learned the hard way that the public silence about Miriam's loss was a mistake. Perhaps, then, the elaborate mourning for Aaron reflects what Moses gleaned from that lesson.

—*Ora Horn Prouser*

# Post-biblical Interpretations

***Miriam died*** (20:1). Midrash *Kohelet Rabbah* 7:4 uses this occasion to reflect upon the lives of righteous people in general, noting that when the righteous are born nobody feels the difference, but when they die, many are affected. Following Miriam's death, for example, her well—which had provided water for the Israelites in the wilderness—ceased to exist, and everybody felt her loss (also Tosefta *Sotah* 11:10). The Bible does not mention the marvel known as Miriam's Well. However, the earliest forms of rabbinic literature discuss how the death of each of the three leaders in the wilderness resulted in the end of a beneficial supernatural phenomenon that had assisted the Children of Israel. The supernatural qualities of Miriam's Well include that it traveled with the nation in the wilderness

(BT *Shabbat* 35a) and that it later had healing powers (Midrash *Vayikra Rabbah* 22.4). The medieval commentator Rashi explains the connection between Miriam's death and the disappearance of the well (on BT *Shabbat* 35a) by pointing out that the subsequent verse states, "The community was without water" (20:2).

***Miriam died*** (20:1). The Talmud (*Mo'ed Katan* 28a) asks, "Why is the death of Miriam juxtaposed to the portion of the *parah adumah* (the red heifer of Numbers 19)?" It then provides the answer that the ritual of the *parah adumah*, which according to the Rabbis was performed until the destruction of the Second Temple in Jerusalem (70 C.E.), was intended to provide atonement for specific types of sin. Therefore, the Talmud explains, the deaths of righteous people, including Miriam, have an atoning effect. This emphasis on atonement seems to stray from the biblical presentation of the *parah adumah* as a ritual purification sacrifice and ceremony. The talmudic linkage to the idea of atonement is clarified by the *Tosafot* to that passage; it states that the *parah adumah*, as described in Numbers 19, provided atonement for the sin of the Golden Calf (Exodus 32).

The theological idea that the death of Miriam, or any righteous person, enables atonement is a difficult concept for modern Jews to accept. Ours is evidently not the first generation to grapple with the notion of vicarious atonement, since it was already discussed in the 13th-century commentary of Rabbi Menachem ben Solomon Meiri. He stated that it is not the act of the righteous dying that atones for sins; rather, these deaths often move the living toward introspection and private acknowledgement of wrongdoing, which then results in personal prayer for repentance.

***Miriam died there*** (20:1). A rabbinic tradition (BT *Baba Batra* 27a) states that six people did not die as ordinary mortals do. By the conventional method, as explained by the Rabbis, it is the Angel of Death who takes individuals from this world. The six who did not die in this manner experienced their deaths by God's "kiss"—that is, their lives were taken by God directly. These six were Abraham, Isaac, Jacob, Moses, Aaron, and Miriam. The Talmud discusses the last three individuals in this list, noting that the Torah text can be said to describe Moses and Aaron's demise explicitly as "by the kiss of" God (translated in this book as "at the command of," but literally "by the mouth of," Deuteronomy 34:5; Numbers 33:38). Miriam's death "by the kiss of" God, however, is derived via a midrashic method that compares the technical language used in describing her death to the technical language used for the deaths

*Miriam's death was unconventional: she died via a kiss from God.*

of her brothers. The language is similar enough to imply that the details of their deaths were similar as well. After comparing these deaths, the Talmud then goes on to explain that Miriam's death by God's "kiss" is implicit rather than explicit, because it would be considered indelicate for her—the only woman on this list—to have been described in such a manner (BT *Mo'ed Katan* 28a).

***Spring up, O well—sing to it*** (21:17). This is the beginning of the song of thanksgiving that was recited by the Israelites after God gave them water from a well in the region of Beer (sometime after Miriam's death). Although the Torah does not mention Miriam in connection with this biblical incident, rabbinic traditions did link her to it later. One of the ancient Aramaic translations of the Torah, the *Targum Yerushalmi*, incorporates an elaboration of this verse, explaining that this well was brought forth due to the merit of Miriam. It also links her to a tradition of wells associated with other biblical figures, namely, Abraham, Isaac, Jacob, Moses, Aaron, as well as other unnamed leaders.

*—Anna Urowitz-Freudenstein*

# Contemporary Reflection

MIRIAM, LIKE MOSES AND AARON, was a child of Amram and Jochebed, both of the tribe of Levi. The prophet Micah recognizes all three siblings as Israel's leaders when he proclaims in God's name: "I redeemed you from the house of bondage, and sent Moses, Aaron, and Miriam to lead you" (Micah 6:4). Although the Bible preserves only a few direct references to Miriam, her importance to the Israelites' story shines through even this leanest of biographical sketches. First, Miriam is called a prophet (in Exodus 15:20), although her prophetic teachings are not recorded. Second, she sings and leads the women in song to God following her people's safe passage across the Sea of Reeds (Exodus 15:21). Third, she (along with Aaron) speaks out against Moses about his wife and his authority (12:1–2). Fourth, she is shut out of the camp when she is stricken with skin disease; tellingly, the Israelites refuse to move on until she returns (12:10–15). Finally, she dies and is buried in Kadesh (20:1), a place name that evokes the holy (*kadosh*). These few references to Miriam are but clues to the larger story of her life and importance.

Let us imagine that larger story by creating a midrash. Picture Moses as he climbed Mount Nebo to see the Promised Land he would never enter and to experience God's drawing out his soul as gently as a kiss draws out the breath (Deuteronomy 34; on God's kiss, see Post-biblical Interpretations, p. 932, at "Miriam died there"). What was he thinking at that moment? In the midrash we are creating we may imagine that this inspiring leader thought about the future of his people and about who would preserve the Covenant for future generations. First, he considered Aaron's son Eleazar, who would carry on the priestly functions; he could reassure himself that the priests would preserve the teachings of the Torah. Indeed, for a time, the priests did maintain their role. However, following the destruction of the Second Temple, the priests no longer played a central role in the people's observance of the Covenant. Moses then thought of Joshua, who was chosen to lead the Israelites into the Promised Land. He could reassure himself that through the land, the faith would be preserved. Yet for nearly two millennia, the people of Israel would live in exile from the Promised Land. Finally, Moses then thought of Miriam. But failing to recognize earlier what she had contributed to preserving the faith, he realized that he had made no effort to ensure that her function be taken up by someone else.

Was there a leadership role that was lost with the death of Miriam? If the Israelites were to remain true to their religion in the generations to come, it would be because the women passed their faith and traditions on to their children. Moses' efforts had gone into legislating primarily for the Israelite men and had largely neglected to consider the roles of women, who were often invisible in the legal codes. In our midrash, however, Miriam had seen to the women and the education of the children. What qualifications would there be for Miriam's successor? Eleazar was destined for his priestly role by virtue of his lineage. Joshua had been chosen because he was judged to be a capable military commander. But whoever was to succeed Miriam would have to qualify directly through God's gift, because no one had thought to name a successor. Moses, in that one prescient moment, understood that a vital piece of the community might have died with Miriam.

### *How can we best understand what Miriam's Well represented?*

But it did not die, although it became obscured. Miriam's legacy, which we are just beginning to retrieve, models our capacity to care for those more vulnerable than ourselves (as she did for her infant brother), to intervene in history regardless of our position (as she did when she approached the princess and when she challenged Moses' conduct and leadership), and to dance as well as to sing publicly as a form of worship.

In our parashah, we learn something else as well: "The Israelites arrived in a body at the wilderness of Zin on the first new moon, and the people stayed at Kadesh. Miriam died there and was buried there. The community was without water, and they joined against Moses and Aaron" (20:1–2). Rabbinic tradition, recognizing that something of major import was lost with the death of Miriam, found in the juxtaposition of Miriam's death with the peoples' crying out for water a powerful symbol for this loss. A midrash tells us that throughout the Israelites' sojourn in the wilderness, a well followed them. With the death of Miriam, the well dried up. How can we best understand what Miriam's Well represented?

Israel in the Bible had two main centers of practice: the Tent of Meeting (or Tabernacle, later replaced by the Temple) and the home. The rules governing the Tent of Meeting take up much of Leviticus, but the life that is to be conducted in the home receives relatively little mention. Moses, we might say, had focused on institutional religion. But in our midrashic rendering of the story, Miriam's gift was to raise up the personal practices of the Israelites and to help the women of Israel recognize and claim their homes as a sacred place. Each woman's own Sabbath table became like an altar. While Moses showed the Israelites the God who spoke to them from the top of Sinai, Miriam enabled the women to see that God could also be found around the cooking fires in their own tents.

Miriam also helped the women change their idea of holy space (from the set-apart Tent of Meeting to their own homes). In a time when the male leaders were focusing on all that was separate and distinct, Miriam taught the women to find the holy wherever they were open to it, whenever they could be responsive.

And just as her imagined teachings sought to move beyond separation, her own tradition is not to be found in a separate text but in the words that mothers have told their daughters and sons since then: God is found in and through all that we remember, all that we experience, all that we hope for. Miriam's Well stands for what is nourishing and life-giving—it stands for the dining table, the cradle, and the welcoming embrace of our loved ones.

—*Carol Ochs*

# Voices

## Ritual
Ellen Bass

*Numbers 19*

A curved bar of soap floated,
a child's boat in the basin of water
as I touched her ruched lids,
then washed her face, the smooth
muzzle like the pale center
of the faces of apes.
I sponged her swollen ankles,
their thin red veins cracks in raku,
the crease down her back a seam
drawn in dough.
I washed under her arms,
spare hairs hanging limp and colorless,
lifted her slack breasts
and soaped her belly, quilt of scars.

Like setting the Passover table
with matzoh and marror, bitter herbs,
like casting crumbs into the sea
this too had its precise commands
and I had done everything wrong:

Too late I learned the purification
of Taharah requires windows
be opened, the deceased lowered
to a white sheet on straw,
cleansed right side before left, then lifted,
twenty-four quarts of water flowing
over the crown and down the body,
cascading in one continuous stream,
rinsing away all sin. The shroud
must be linen, hand-sewn, no buttons,
each tie twined with four knots,
the head of each knot facing the heart,
no pockets for worldly goods.

But how could my mother care?
She spent her Sabbaths with the god
of commerce, the god of feeding her children
and sending them off to college.
At precisely nine she'd unlock the glass door,
the phone coming to life, customers entering.
Her hands were not yet smudged with newsprint,
her lipstick was still a clear strong red.
Greeting each by name, she'd bag
cold six-packs of Rolling Rock, a pint of Old Crow,
pressing coins into their open palms,
making sure to touch them.

## Pride
Dahlia Ravikovitch
(transl. Chana Bloch and Chana Kronfeld)

*Numbers 20*

Even rocks crack, I tell you,
and not on account of age.
For years they lie on their backs
in the cold and the heat,
so many years,
it almost creates the impression of calm.
They don't move, so the cracks can hide.
A kind of pride.
Years pass over them as they wait.
Whoever is going to shatter them
hasn't come yet.
And so the moss flourishes, the seaweed is
cast about,
the sea bursts out and slides back—
and it seems the rocks are perfectly still.
Till a little seal comes to rub against them,
comes and goes—
and suddenly the stone has an open wound.
I told you, when rocks crack, it happens by
surprise.
Not to mention people.

## *Moses Leans Over the Stone*

Jill Hammer

*Numbers 20:1–13*

*The Torah is a door to the deep.*

I know this stone.
Its hidden textures
hold water for my people.
If I stroke it,
caress,
it will give forth its
liquid gifts.
But the squeezing of it is hard,
and I tire,
While all around me the people cry
"Water, water!"

Once, in Egypt,
after I fought with my brother and sister,
my mother showed me a stone,
a gray triangle in her earth-rubbed hand.
"Here are you, Aaron, and Miriam."
Each of you holds a side of the truth.
"Where are you, Mother?" I asked.
She turned the stone over
to show me its wet bottom.

All my life,
I have looked for the underside of things:
the scorchless base of the bush,
the cave inside the mountain,
the back of God.
If I turn over this stone,
will an old love wait there for me,
secrete its silver words,
or will I find another mystery?

The crowd, impatient, growls.
The sand and sun reflect each other's faces.
Within me, anger at the silence.

I strike the stone.

## *The Hard Rock*

Rivka Miriam (transl. Linda Stern Zisquit)

*Numbers 20:10–11*

Consolation is found in the hard rock
that won't come into the house
won't sit on a chair
and will eat no bread.
When the rock passes at evening on the path
in front of the house
it won't turn when its name is called.
If a hand holding a rod would strike it
water would not pour out.
Sometimes suddenly the rock spreads out on
one of the slopes
and from the open window the sound of its
flute is heard.

## *Miriam's Well*

Rivka Miriam (transl. Linda Stern Zisquit)

*Numbers 21:17–18*

Miriam's well was rolling in the desert
made of the mouths of fish.
The nation drinking from it
turned to water
and rolled after her in the desert
and the desert rolled after them like a carpet.
Rise up, well, sang the people
their voices a density of cloud
and the dryness quenched their voices.

# בלק ✦ *Balak*

## NUMBERS 22:2–25:9

### *Dangerous Foreigners*

PARASHAT BALAK centers on the actions of the Moabite king Balak and the prophet Balaam son of Beor, whom he hires to curse Israel into oblivion (22:2–24:25). It concludes with a dangerous encounter and worship of Baal-peor, a Canaanite god.

At the close of the previous parashah, the people of Israel were making final preparations to enter Canaan. The story of Balaam is inserted at this juncture because its outcome determines whether Israel will indeed inherit the Promised Land. Actually, it is a contest in the divine realm between the God of Israel and those supernatural elements available to Balak. At times amusing and somewhat mocking of the non-Israelite prophet, the message of the story is quite serious: God's intent reigns supreme and cannot be superseded. Israel's deity ultimately controls even the powers of a well-known foreign seer. In the end, Balaam's four oracles reverse Balak's goal—by blessing Israel and cursing her enemies. Notably, Balaam's talking donkey, who is portrayed as the wiser of the pair, is a jenny (a female donkey)—perhaps reminiscent of the biblical personification of *chochmah*, "wisdom," as female (see, for example, Proverbs 1:20).

Importantly, a visionary named Balaam son of Beor is mentioned outside the Bible; he is featured on an ancient but fragmentary plaster wall inscription, located not far from where the biblical story is set (see further below).

The final portion of the parashah (25:1–9) resumes the narrative begun in the first verse of Numbers 22 but interrupted by the story of Balak and Balaam. It recounts the misadventure of a group of Israelite men who have sexual encounters with local Moabite women—and end up worshipping the local deity, Baal-peor. The account focuses on one particular couple: an Israelite man and his partner, a Midianite woman. The priest Phinehas impales the two in a fit of religious zeal. The Baal-peor incident results in the death of 24,000 Israelites who are struck down by a divinely sent plague.

> *In this episode, the Moabite women are depicted as dangerous enticers.*

In this episode the Moabite women are depicted as dangerous enticers who lead the Israelite men to idolatry. The account serves to highlight the biblical portrait of the dangerous foreign woman, a motif prevalent in the book of Proverbs, where young men are repeatedly warned to avoid her (Proverbs 2:16; 5:3, 20; 7:5; 23:27; 27:13). A similar theme is found in other biblical passages as well (see Exodus 34:16).

—*Nili Sacher Fox*

## *Outline*

*I.* Balak Hires Balaam to Curse Israel (22:2–41)

- *A.* Balak's invitation to Balaam (vv. 2–21)
- *B.* The story of the talking she-donkey (vv. 22–35)
- *C.* Balaam's arrival in Moab (vv. 36–41)

*II.* Balaam's Oracles and Balak's Responses (23:1–24:25)

- *A.* Balaam's first oracle and Balak's response (23:1–12)
- *B.* Balaam's second oracle and Balak's response (23:13–26)
- *C.* Balaam's third oracle and Balak's response (23:27–24:11)
- *D.* Balaam's fourth oracle (24:12–25)

*III.* Apostasy at Baal-peor (25:1–9)

- *A.* Israel's flirtation with foreign women and idolatry (vv. 1–5)
- *B.* Phinehas's vengeance (vv. 6–9)

Balak son of Zippor saw all that Israel had done to the Amorites.

כב 2 וַיַּ֥רְא בָּלָ֖ק בֶּן־צִפּ֑וֹר אֵ֛ת כָּל־אֲשֶׁר־
עָשָׂ֥ה יִשְׂרָאֵ֖ל לָאֱמֹרִֽי׃

## *Balak Hires Balaam to Curse Israel*

(22:2–41)

The main part of this Torah portion consists of the pericope about Balak and Balaam. The story fits well with other events of the wilderness experience in the sense that it recounts another link in what seems to be an endless chain of obstacles to Israel's entrance into Canaan. It begins when the Moabite king, Balak, seeks to hire the seer Balaam to curse Israel to oblivion. The notion that cursing is an efficacious means of subduing one's enemy was well accepted in antiquity. Certain Egyptian texts composed in the early 2nd millennium B.C.E. exemplify that practice; these "Execration Texts" are smashed ceramic vessels and figurines inscribed with curses directed at Egypt's enemies, including the rulers of Canaanite cities. Balaam's role as a prophet and diviner likewise fits with other known examples from Mesopotamia, also from the early second millennium.

The material about Balak and Balaam seems to be an independent composition. Its narrative and poetry probably originated in a different scribal circle than those associated with other portions of Numbers.

Evidence indicates that the biblical composition is related to the non-biblical tradition attested in a wall inscription found at Deir Alla, a site east of the Jordan River. The inscription, written in a language close to Aramaic and dated to the early 8th century B.C.E., records the night visions of a seer named Balaam son of Beor. That Balaam is credited with saving his people and the land from perpetual darkness by his use of oracles and exorcism. Apparently, his powers reversed the edict of a group of trouble-making deities and freed the goddess Shagar-and-Ishtar (a local version of the Mesopotamian high goddess Ishtar), whom those deities had imprisoned and forced to comply with their evil directives. It is unclear whether Balaam was a legendary character of antiquity, or a real person of some fame in the region. At any rate, the talents of that Balaam are precisely what the Moabite king, Balak, is looking for in the biblical account.

Whether legendary or historical, the Balaam story was clearly known in the 8th century (the date of the Deir Alla texts). An unanswered question is: were these traditions already circulating in Israel's early settlement period (12th century), or did a later biblical writer cast them into the historical memory of that period?

### BALAK'S INVITATION TO BALAAM (22:2–21)

Having witnessed Israel's destructive power in her recent encounter with the Amorites (21:21–32), Balak seeks to engage the prophet Balaam, appar-

Numbers 25:6–9 seems to reflect an unusually hostile attitude toward intermarriage.

ANOTHER VIEW ➤ *954*

She would refuse to have sex with him until he bowed down to the local idol.

POST-BIBLICAL INTERPRETATIONS ➤ *954*

Are we ready to open our tents and our hearts to those who wish to dream?

CONTEMPORARY REFLECTION ➤ *956*

On your journey you will come to a time of waking. / The others may be asleep. . . .

VOICES ➤ *958*

3 Moab was alarmed because that people was so
numerous. Moab dreaded the Israelites, 4 and Moab
said to the elders of Midian, "Now this horde will
lick clean all that is about us as an ox licks up the
grass of the field."
Balak son of Zippor, who was king of Moab at
that time, 5 sent messengers to Balaam son of Beor
in Pethor, which is by the Euphrates, in the land of
his kinsfolk, to invite him, saying, "There is a people that came out of Egypt; it hides the earth from
view, and it is settled next to me. 6 Come then, put
a curse upon this people for me, since they are too
numerous for me; perhaps I can thus defeat them
and drive them out of the land. For I know that he
whom you bless is blessed indeed, and he whom
you curse is cursed."
7 The elders of Moab and the elders of Midian,
versed in divination, set out. They came to Balaam

3 וַיָּ֨גָר מוֹאָ֜ב מִפְּנֵ֥י הָעָ֛ם מְאֹ֖ד כִּ֣י רַב־ה֑וּא
וַיָּ֣קָץ מוֹאָ֔ב מִפְּנֵ֖י בְּנֵ֥י יִשְׂרָאֵֽל׃ 4 וַיֹּ֨אמֶר
מוֹאָ֜ב אֶל־זִקְנֵ֣י מִדְיָ֗ן עַתָּ֞ה יְלַחֲכ֤וּ הַקָּהָל֙
אֶת־כָּל־סְבִ֣יבֹתֵ֔ינוּ כִּלְחֹ֣ךְ הַשּׁ֔וֹר אֵ֖ת יֶ֣רֶק
הַשָּׂדֶ֑ה
וּבָלָ֧ק בֶּן־צִפּ֛וֹר מֶ֥לֶךְ לְמוֹאָ֖ב בָּעֵ֥ת הַהִֽוא׃
5 וַיִּשְׁלַ֨ח מַלְאָכִ֜ים אֶל־בִּלְעָ֣ם בֶּן־בְּעֹ֗ר
פְּ֠תוֹרָה אֲשֶׁ֧ר עַל־הַנָּהָ֛ר אֶ֥רֶץ בְּנֵֽי־עַמּ֖וֹ
לִקְרֹא־ל֑וֹ לֵאמֹ֗ר הִ֠נֵּה עַ֨ם יָצָ֤א מִמִּצְרַ֙יִם֙
הִנֵּ֤ה כִסָּה֙ אֶת־עֵ֣ין הָאָ֔רֶץ וְה֥וּא יֹשֵׁ֖ב
מִמֻּלִֽי׃ 6 וְעַתָּה֩ לְכָה־נָּ֨א אָֽרָה־לִּ֜י אֶת־הָעָ֣ם
הַזֶּ֗ה כִּֽי־עָצ֥וּם הוּא֙ מִמֶּ֔נִּי אוּלַ֤י אוּכַל֙ נַכֶּה־
בּ֔וֹ וַאֲגָרְשֶׁ֖נּוּ מִן־הָאָ֑רֶץ כִּ֣י יָדַ֗עְתִּי אֵ֤ת
אֲשֶׁר־תְּבָרֵךְ֙ מְבֹרָ֔ךְ וַאֲשֶׁ֥ר תָּאֹ֖ר יוּאָֽר׃
7 וַיֵּ֨לְכ֜וּ זִקְנֵ֤י מוֹאָב֙ וְזִקְנֵ֣י מִדְיָ֔ן וּקְסָמִ֖ים
בְּיָדָ֑ם וַיָּבֹ֙אוּ֙ אֶל־בִּלְעָ֔ם וַיְדַבְּר֥וּ אֵלָ֖יו דִּבְרֵ֥י

---

ently because of Balaam's reputation as a seer who can effectuate curses. Balaam refuses to come, after having consulted with the Israelite God and been warned not to curse the people that God has blessed. Balak ignores Balaam's initial refusal and sends additional dignitaries tempting Balaam with promises of riches. With God's approval, Balaam agrees to go, but only to prophesy God's message.

The Bible gives conflicting reports of Balaam's intentions, apparently due to inconsistent pre-biblical traditions. The account here presents Balaam in a positive light. His words and actions are bound to the will of Israel's God. Likewise, the 8th-century prophet Micah views Balaam favorably (Micah 6:5). In contrast, in Deuteronomy (23:4–7) and Joshua (24:9–10), it is God who reverses Balaam's actual intent; and another narrative in Numbers (31:16) blames Balaam for Israel's apostasy at Baal-peor.

*5. **Balaam son of Beor.*** The seer of the Deir Alla inscription (see the unit introduction, above) bears the same name and patronymic.

*7. **elders.*** [Heb. *z'kenim*, a plural noun that refers to social status. Given what we know about the ancient Near East, the presence of women among a given group of elders is unlikely, yet it cannot be entirely excluded. For instance, II Samuel 20:15–22 depicts an Israelite woman of apparently special status who fills the role that we would expect an elder to play: she represents her town in emergency negotiations with a hostile army commander. Described as an *ishah chachamah* (literally "wise woman") and unnamed, she says of herself, "I am one of those who seek the welfare of the faithful in Israel." The commander then treats her as having an elder's authority. Claudia Camp suggests that the story "attests to what must have been a regularized public role for women, at least through the early period of the Israelite monarchy" (*Women in Scripture*, 2000, p. 267; see also Tikva Frymer-Kensky, *Reading the Women of the Bible*, 2002, pp. 58–61). *—Ed.*]

***divination.*** Heb. *kesem* (plural in this verse) refers to the taking of omens, a practice popular in the ancient Near East. Most likely these elders were professional diviners. Professional diviners who served at court are widely known from the ancient

and gave him Balak's message. [8]He said to them, "Spend the night here, and I shall reply to you as יהוה may instruct me." So the Moabite dignitaries stayed with Balaam.

[9]God came to Balaam and said, "What do these envoys want of you?" [10]Balaam said to God, "Balak son of Zippor, king of Moab, sent me this message: [11]Here is a people that came out from Egypt and hides the earth from view. Come now and curse them for me; perhaps I can engage them in battle and drive them off." [12]But God said to Balaam, "Do not go with them. You must not curse that people, for they are blessed."

[13]Balaam arose in the morning and said to Balak's dignitaries, "Go back to your own country, for יהוה will not let me go with you." [14]The Moabite dignitaries left, and they came to Balak and said, "Balaam refused to come with us."

[15]Then Balak sent other dignitaries, more numerous and distinguished than the first. [16]They came to Balaam and said to him, "Thus says Balak son of Zippor: Please do not refuse to come to me. [17]I will reward you richly and I will do anything you ask of me. Only come and damn this people for me." [18]Balaam replied to Balak's officials, "Though Balak were to give me his house full of silver and gold, I could not do anything, big or little, contrary to the command of my God יהוה. [19]So you, too, stay here overnight, and let me find out what else יהוה may say to me." [20]That night God came to Balaam and said to him, "If these envoys have come to invite you, you may go with them. But whatever I command you, that you shall do."

בָּלָק׃ 8 וַיֹּאמֶר אֲלֵיהֶם לִינוּ פֹה הַלַּיְלָה
וַהֲשִׁבֹתִי אֶתְכֶם דָּבָר כַּאֲשֶׁר יְדַבֵּר יְהֹוָה
אֵלָי וַיֵּשְׁבוּ שָׂרֵי־מוֹאָב עִם־בִּלְעָם׃
9 וַיָּבֹא אֱלֹהִים אֶל־בִּלְעָם וַיֹּאמֶר מִי
הָאֲנָשִׁים הָאֵלֶּה עִמָּךְ׃ 10 וַיֹּאמֶר בִּלְעָם
אֶל־הָאֱלֹהִים בָּלָק בֶּן־צִפֹּר מֶלֶךְ מוֹאָב
שָׁלַח אֵלָי׃ 11 הִנֵּה הָעָם הַיֹּצֵא מִמִּצְרַיִם
וַיְכַס אֶת־עֵין הָאָרֶץ עַתָּה לְכָה קָבָה־לִּי
אֹתוֹ אוּלַי אוּכַל לְהִלָּחֶם בּוֹ וְגֵרַשְׁתִּיו׃
12 וַיֹּאמֶר אֱלֹהִים אֶל־בִּלְעָם לֹא תֵלֵךְ
עִמָּהֶם לֹא תָאֹר אֶת־הָעָם כִּי בָרוּךְ הוּא׃
13 וַיָּקָם בִּלְעָם בַּבֹּקֶר וַיֹּאמֶר אֶל־שָׂרֵי בָלָק
לְכוּ אֶל־אַרְצְכֶם כִּי מֵאֵן יְהֹוָה לְתִתִּי
לַהֲלֹךְ עִמָּכֶם׃ 14 וַיָּקוּמוּ שָׂרֵי מוֹאָב וַיָּבֹאוּ
אֶל־בָּלָק וַיֹּאמְרוּ מֵאֵן בִּלְעָם הֲלֹךְ עִמָּנוּ׃
15 וַיֹּסֶף עוֹד בָּלָק שְׁלֹחַ שָׂרִים רַבִּים
וְנִכְבָּדִים מֵאֵלֶּה׃ 16 וַיָּבֹאוּ אֶל־בִּלְעָם
וַיֹּאמְרוּ לוֹ כֹּה אָמַר בָּלָק בֶּן־צִפּוֹר אַל־
נָא תִמָּנַע מֵהֲלֹךְ אֵלָי׃ 17 כִּי־כַבֵּד אֲכַבֶּדְךָ
מְאֹד וְכֹל אֲשֶׁר־תֹּאמַר אֵלַי אֶעֱשֶׂה וּלְכָה־
נָּא קָבָה־לִּי אֵת הָעָם הַזֶּה׃ 18 וַיַּעַן בִּלְעָם
וַיֹּאמֶר אֶל־עַבְדֵי בָלָק אִם־יִתֶּן־לִי בָלָק
מְלֹא בֵיתוֹ כֶּסֶף וְזָהָב לֹא אוּכַל לַעֲבֹר אֶת־
פִּי יְהֹוָה אֱלֹהָי לַעֲשׂוֹת קְטַנָּה אוֹ גְדוֹלָה׃
19 וְעַתָּה שְׁבוּ נָא בָזֶה גַּם־אַתֶּם הַלָּיְלָה
וְאֵדְעָה מַה־יֹּסֵף יְהֹוָה דַּבֵּר עִמִּי׃ 20 וַיָּבֹא
אֱלֹהִים ׀ אֶל־בִּלְעָם לַיְלָה וַיֹּאמֶר לוֹ
אִם־לִקְרֹא לְךָ בָּאוּ הָאֲנָשִׁים קוּם לֵךְ
אִתָּם וְאַךְ אֶת־הַדָּבָר אֲשֶׁר־אֲדַבֵּר אֵלֶיךָ
אֹתוֹ תַעֲשֶׂה׃

Near East. Divination was regarded as a legitimate "science" in antiquity. The Bible condemns it as abhorrent to God (see Deuteronomy 18:10–11, 14), implying that control of natural forces and events are God's dominion. On Israel's practice of certain types of divination and women's role in it, see further at Leviticus 19:31, 20:6, and 20:27.

*11. "hides the earth from view."* The Israelites are pictured as so numerous that they obscure one's view of the ground on which they have encamped.

²¹When he arose in the morning, Balaam saddled his ass and departed with the Moabite dignitaries. ²²But God was incensed at his going; so an angel of יהוה took a position in his way as an adversary.

He was riding on his she-ass, with his two servants alongside, ²³when the ass caught sight of the angel of יהוה standing in the way, with his drawn sword in his hand. The ass swerved from the road and went into the fields; and Balaam beat the ass to turn her back onto the road. ²⁴The angel of יהוה then stationed himself in a lane between the vineyards, with a fence on either side. ²⁵The ass, seeing the angel of יהוה, pressed herself against the wall and squeezed Balaam's foot against the wall; so he

21 וַיָּ֤קָם בִּלְעָם֙ בַּבֹּ֔קֶר וַֽיַּחֲבֹ֖שׁ אֶת־אֲתֹנ֑וֹ
וַיֵּ֖לֶךְ עִם־שָׂרֵ֥י מוֹאָֽב: 22 וַיִּֽחַר־אַ֣ף אֱלֹהִים֮
כִּֽי־הוֹלֵ֣ךְ הוּא֒ וַיִּתְיַצֵּ֞ב מַלְאַ֧ךְ יְהוָ֛ה בַּדֶּ֖רֶךְ
לְשָׂטָ֣ן ל֑וֹ
וְהוּא֙ רֹכֵ֣ב עַל־אֲתֹנ֔וֹ וּשְׁנֵ֥י נְעָרָ֖יו עִמּֽוֹ:
23 וַתֵּ֣רֶא הָאָתוֹן֩ אֶת־מַלְאַ֨ךְ יְהוָ֜ה נִצָּ֣ב
בַּדֶּ֗רֶךְ וְחַרְבּ֤וֹ שְׁלוּפָה֙ בְּיָד֔וֹ וַתֵּ֤ט הָֽאָתוֹן֙
מִן־הַדֶּ֔רֶךְ וַתֵּ֖לֶךְ בַּשָּׂדֶ֑ה וַיַּ֤ךְ בִּלְעָם֙ אֶת־
הָ֣אָת֔וֹן לְהַטֹּתָ֖הּ הַדָּֽרֶךְ: 24 וַֽיַּעֲמֹד֙ מַלְאַ֣ךְ
יְהוָ֔ה בְּמִשְׁע֖וֹל הַכְּרָמִ֑ים גָּדֵ֥ר מִזֶּ֖ה וְגָדֵ֥ר
מִזֶּֽה: 25 וַתֵּ֨רֶא הָאָת֜וֹן אֶת־מַלְאַ֣ךְ יְהוָ֗ה
וַתִּלָּחֵץ֙ אֶל־הַקִּ֔יר וַתִּלְחַ֥ץ אֶת־רֶ֖גֶל בִּלְעָם֙

---

**21. ass.** Heb. *aton* refers specifically to a jenny (she-donkey). [The Bible mentions three women of means as riding on donkeys. The wealthy woman of Shunem rides a jenny when she hurries to get help for her son (II Kings 4:22–24). The text is not sex-specific with regard to the other women's mounts (Achsah in Joshua 15:18 and Judges 1:14; Abigail in I Samuel 25:20, 42). —*Ed.*]

### THE STORY OF THE
### TALKING SHE-DONKEY (22:22–35)

This tale of Balaam and the jenny—which breaks the action of the main narrative—contradicts the more favorable view of Balaam expressed by the main story; this episode apparently derives from a different tradition. In this fable, in which an animal speaks, God is angry with the seer and depicts the donkey as the actual visionary. Balaam becomes the object of mockery, being blind to the divine will that only the jenny sees. Thus the usual biblical roles of humans and animals are reversed.

Speaking animals of various kinds, including equids (horses and donkeys), are known from other ancient Near Eastern literary sources.

Perhaps significant is the fact that the donkey is female (see above at v. 21). Her role as the insightful one of the pair is reminiscent of the biblical notion of Lady Wisdom (especially in Proverbs 8–9). Perhaps, however, the story is merely suggesting that even a female donkey, the lowliest of the low animals, is more perceptive than Balaam.

**22. angel.** The Hebrew word for "angel" and "messenger" is the same.

**as an adversary.** Heb. *satan*, a term that is used here attributively (as in I Samuel 29:4, where Philistines worry that David "may become our *satan* [adversary] in battle"). When personified (Job 1:6–12; I Chronicles 21:1), *satan* refers to a divine being who answers to God. In Job, the adversary functions as a kind of prosecutor in God's court. (The concept of Satan as God's adversary is a post-biblical development.)

**23. when the ass caught sight.** The jenny, not the seer, is the one who sees their obstacle. Balaam is unaware of the danger.

**25. The ass, seeing the angel.** Apparently, God's angel is revealed only to the animal. The seer, who is clearly blind to the ongoing events, is being mocked, perhaps in keeping with his doomed mission.

beat her again. [26]Once more the angel of יהוה moved forward and stationed himself on a spot so narrow that there was no room to swerve right or left. [27]When the ass now saw the angel of יהוה, she lay down under Balaam; and Balaam was furious and beat the ass with his stick.

[28]Then יהוה opened the ass's mouth, and she said to Balaam, "What have I done to you that you have beaten me these three times?" [29]Balaam said to the ass, "You have made a mockery of me! If I had a sword with me, I'd kill you." [30]The ass said to Balaam, "Look, I am the ass that you have been riding all along until this day! Have I been in the habit of doing thus to you?" And he answered, "No."

[31]Then יהוה uncovered Balaam's eyes, and he saw the angel of יהוה standing in the way, his drawn sword in his hand; thereupon he bowed right down to the ground. [32]The angel of יהוה said to him, "Why have you beaten your ass these three times? It is I who came out as an adversary, for the errand is obnoxious to me. [33]And when the ass saw me, she shied away because of me those three times. If she had not shied away from me, you are the one I should have killed, while sparing her." [34]Balaam said to the angel of יהוה, "I erred because I did not know that you were standing in my way. If you still disapprove, I will turn back." [35]But the angel of יהוה said to Balaam, "Go with those envoys. But

אֶל־הַקִּ֑יר וַיֹּ֖סֶף לְהַכֹּתָֽהּ׃ 26 וַיּ֥וֹסֶף מַלְאַךְ־
יְהוָ֖ה עֲב֑וֹר וַֽיַּעֲמֹד֙ בְּמָק֣וֹם צָ֔ר אֲשֶׁ֥ר אֵין־
דֶּ֛רֶךְ לִנְט֖וֹת יָמִ֥ין וּשְׂמֹֽאול׃ 27 וַתֵּ֤רֶא הָֽאָתוֹן֙
אֶת־מַלְאַ֣ךְ יְהוָ֔ה וַתִּרְבַּ֖ץ תַּ֣חַת בִּלְעָ֑ם
וַיִּֽחַר־אַ֣ף בִּלְעָ֔ם וַיַּ֥ךְ אֶת־הָאָת֖וֹן בַּמַּקֵּֽל׃
28 וַיִּפְתַּ֥ח יְהוָ֖ה אֶת־פִּ֣י הָאָת֑וֹן וַתֹּ֤אמֶר
לְבִלְעָם֙ מֶה־עָשִׂ֣יתִֽי לְךָ֔ כִּ֣י הִכִּיתַ֔נִי זֶ֖ה
שָׁלֹ֥שׁ רְגָלִֽים׃ 29 וַיֹּ֤אמֶר בִּלְעָם֙ לָֽאָת֔וֹן כִּ֥י
הִתְעַלַּ֖לְתְּ בִּ֑י ל֤וּ יֶשׁ־חֶ֙רֶב֙ בְּיָדִ֔י כִּ֥י עַתָּ֖ה
הֲרַגְתִּֽיךְ׃ 30 וַתֹּ֨אמֶר הָאָת֜וֹן אֶל־בִּלְעָ֗ם
הֲלוֹא֩ אָנֹכִ֨י אֲתֹֽנְךָ֜ אֲשֶׁר־רָכַ֣בְתָּ עָלַ֗י מֵעֽוֹדְךָ֙
עַד־הַיּ֣וֹם הַזֶּ֔ה הַהַסְכֵּ֣ן הִסְכַּ֔נְתִּי לַעֲשׂ֥וֹת לְךָ֖
כֹּ֑ה וַיֹּ֖אמֶר לֹֽא׃
31 וַיְגַ֣ל יְהוָה֮ אֶת־עֵינֵ֣י בִלְעָם֒ וַיַּ֞רְא אֶת־
מַלְאַ֣ךְ יְהוָ֗ה נִצָּ֤ב בַּדֶּ֙רֶךְ֙ וְחַרְבּ֥וֹ שְׁלֻפָ֖ה בְּיָד֑וֹ
וַיִּקֹּ֥ד וַיִּשְׁתַּ֖חוּ לְאַפָּֽיו׃ 32 וַיֹּ֤אמֶר אֵלָיו֙
מַלְאַ֣ךְ יְהוָ֔ה עַל־מָ֗ה הִכִּ֙יתָ֙ אֶת־אֲתֹ֣נְךָ֔ זֶ֖ה
שָׁל֣וֹשׁ רְגָלִ֑ים הִנֵּ֤ה אָנֹכִי֙ יָצָ֣אתִי לְשָׂטָ֔ן כִּֽי־
יָרַ֥ט הַדֶּ֖רֶךְ לְנֶגְדִּֽי׃ 33 וַתִּרְאַ֙נִי֙ הָֽאָת֔וֹן וַתֵּ֣ט
לְפָנַ֔י זֶ֖ה שָׁלֹ֣שׁ רְגָלִ֑ים אוּלַי֙ נָטְתָ֣ה מִפָּנַ֔י כִּ֥י
עַתָּ֛ה גַּם־אֹתְכָ֥ה הָרַ֖גְתִּי וְאוֹתָ֥הּ הֶחֱיֵֽיתִי׃
34 וַיֹּ֨אמֶר בִּלְעָ֜ם אֶל־מַלְאַ֤ךְ יְהוָה֙ חָטָ֔אתִי
כִּ֚י לֹ֣א יָדַ֔עְתִּי כִּ֥י אַתָּ֛ה נִצָּ֥ב לִקְרָאתִ֖י
בַּדָּ֑רֶךְ וְעַתָּ֛ה אִם־רַ֥ע בְּעֵינֶ֖יךָ אָשׁ֥וּבָה לִּֽי׃
35 וַיֹּאמֶר֩ מַלְאַ֨ךְ יְהוָ֜ה אֶל־בִּלְעָ֗ם לֵ֚ךְ עִם־
הָֽאֲנָשִׁ֔ים וְאֶ֗פֶס אֶת־הַדָּבָ֛ר אֲשֶׁר־אֲדַבֵּ֥ר

*27.* Balaam, totally unaware of the situation, beats the ass for being insubordinate. He is about to learn that God's will can be realized even through the meekest of creatures, and that his status and reputation do not guarantee success if Israel's God opposes it.

*28.* ***יהוה opened the ass's mouth.*** God is clearly in control, giving speech even to a donkey in order to make the divine will known. This jenny, however, does more than speak. In a comic twist, she sees what Balaam the seer cannot. She is perceptive, a gift attributed to the wise woman (see the Woman of Valor in Proverbs 31) and more generally to Lady Wisdom (Proverbs 8 and 9).

*33.* ***"you . . . I should have killed, while sparing her."*** It is unclear whether the anger is actually a reaction to Balaam's ill treatment of his she-donkey or to Balaam's refusal in this episode to heed God's warning.

you must say nothing except what I tell you." So Balaam went on with Balak's dignitaries.

<sup>36</sup>When Balak heard that Balaam was coming, he went out to meet him at Ir-moab, which is on the Arnon border, at its farthest point. <sup>37</sup>Balak said to Balaam, "When I first sent to invite you, why didn't you come to me? Am I really unable to reward you?" <sup>38</sup>But Balaam said to Balak, "And now that I have come to you, have I the power to speak freely? I can utter only the word that God puts into my mouth."

<sup>39</sup>Balaam went with Balak and they came to Kiriath-huzoth.

<sup>40</sup>Balak sacrificed oxen and sheep, and had them served to Balaam and the dignitaries with him. <sup>41</sup>In the morning Balak took Balaam up to Bamoth-baal. From there he could see a portion of the people.

23 Balaam said to Balak, "Build me seven altars here and have seven bulls and seven rams

אֵלֶ֙יךָ֙ אֹת֣וֹ תְדַבֵּ֔ר וַיֵּ֥לֶךְ בִּלְעָ֖ם עִם־שָׂרֵ֥י בָלָֽק׃

<sup>36</sup> וַיִּשְׁמַ֥ע בָּלָ֖ק כִּ֣י בָ֣א בִלְעָ֑ם וַיֵּצֵ֣א לִקְרָאת֡וֹ אֶל־עִ֣יר מוֹאָב֩ אֲשֶׁ֨ר עַל־גְּב֤וּל אַרְנֹן֙ אֲשֶׁ֖ר בִּקְצֵ֥ה הַגְּבֽוּל׃ <sup>37</sup> וַיֹּ֤אמֶר בָּלָק֙ אֶל־בִּלְעָ֔ם הֲלֹא֩ שָׁלֹ֨חַ שָׁלַ֤חְתִּי אֵלֶ֙יךָ֙ לִקְרֹא־לָ֔ךְ לָ֥מָּה לֹא־הָלַ֖כְתָּ אֵלָ֑י הַֽאֻמְנָ֔ם לֹ֥א אוּכַ֖ל כַּבְּדֶֽךָ׃ <sup>38</sup> וַיֹּ֨אמֶר בִּלְעָ֜ם אֶל־בָּלָ֗ק הִֽנֵּה־בָ֙אתִי֙ אֵלֶ֔יךָ עַתָּ֕ה הֲיָכֹ֥ל אוּכַ֖ל דַּבֵּ֣ר מְא֑וּמָה הַדָּבָ֗ר אֲשֶׁ֨ר יָשִׂ֧ים אֱלֹהִ֛ים בְּפִ֖י אֹת֥וֹ אֲדַבֵּֽר׃ <sup>39</sup> וַיֵּ֥לֶךְ בִּלְעָ֖ם עִם־בָּלָ֑ק וַיָּבֹ֖אוּ קִרְיַ֥ת חֻצֽוֹת׃ <sup>40</sup> וַיִּזְבַּ֥ח בָּלָ֖ק בָּקָ֣ר וָצֹ֑אן וַיְשַׁלַּ֣ח לְבִלְעָ֔ם וְלַשָּׂרִ֖ים אֲשֶׁ֥ר אִתּֽוֹ׃ <sup>41</sup> וַיְהִ֣י בַבֹּ֔קֶר וַיִּקַּ֤ח בָּלָק֙ אֶת־בִּלְעָ֔ם וַֽיַּעֲלֵ֖הוּ בָּמ֣וֹת בָּ֑עַל וַיַּ֥רְא מִשָּׁ֖ם קְצֵ֥ה הָעָֽם׃

כג וַיֹּ֤אמֶר בִּלְעָם֙ אֶל־בָּלָ֔ק בְּנֵה־לִ֥י בָזֶ֖ה שִׁבְעָ֣ה מִזְבְּחֹ֑ת וְהָכֵ֥ן לִי֙ בָּזֶ֔ה שִׁבְעָ֥ה פָרִ֖ים

## BALAAM'S ARRIVAL IN MOAB (22:36–41)

The account interrupted by the tale of the jenny continues here. After arriving in Moab, Balak, playing the proper host, offers a sacrifice of well-being as a gesture of welcome; it is eaten by Balaam and his entourage.

*41. Bamoth-baal.* This place name indicates that there was an altar at that site, dedicated to the deity Baal. Apparently it was also at a high elevation, from where Balaam could view the Israelite camp.

## Balaam's Oracles and Balak's Responses (23:1–24:25)

This unit features the reports about four oracles uttered by Balaam. It repeatedly reminds the reader that Balaam's words are God's message, not his own. The first three reports follow the same

pattern: Balaam prepares to divine; this is followed by the oracle itself (in poetic form), concluding with Balak's (frustrated) reaction to the oracle. The fourth oracle breaks the pattern and ends with Balaam's returning home. The first oracle contains a brief summary of the introductory narrative (Numbers 22), hinting that originally the poems may have existed independently of the story. The poetic form of Balaam's oracles contrasts with the surrounding narratives. The poetry seems to lend authority to the narrative, and its composition may actually be older in time than the narrative.

## BALAAM'S FIRST ORACLE AND BALAK'S RESPONSE (23:1–12)

Before seeking omens and revelation, Balaam instructs Balak to sacrifice seven bulls and seven rams. In the biblical world, the number seven often signals completeness or perfection (see Genesis 1:1–2:4).

ready here for me." ²Balak did as Balaam directed; and Balak and Balaam offered up a bull and a ram on each altar. ³Then Balaam said to Balak, "Stay here beside your offerings while I am gone. Perhaps יהוה will grant me a manifestation, and whatever is revealed to me I will tell you." And he went off alone.

⁴God became manifest to Balaam, who stated, "I have set up the seven altars and offered up a bull and a ram on each altar." ⁵And יהוה put a word in Balaam's mouth and said, "Return to Balak and speak thus."

⁶So he returned to him and found him standing beside his offerings, and all the Moabite dignitaries with him. ⁷He took up his theme, and said:

From Aram has Balak brought me,
Moab's king from the hills of the East:
Come, curse me Jacob,
Come, tell Israel's doom!
⁸How can I damn whom God has not damned,
How doom when יהוה has not doomed?
⁹As I see them from the mountain tops,
Gaze on them from the heights,
There is a people that dwells apart,
Not reckoned among the nations,
¹⁰Who can count the dust of Jacob,
Number the dust-cloud of Israel?
May I die the death of the upright,
May my fate be like theirs!

וְשִׁבְעָה אֵילִֽים: ² וַיַּעַשׂ בָּלָק כַּאֲשֶׁר דִּבֶּר
בִּלְעָם וַיַּעַל בָּלָק וּבִלְעָם פָּר וָאַיִל בַּמִּזְבֵּֽחַ:
³ וַיֹּאמֶר בִּלְעָם לְבָלָק הִתְיַצֵּב עַל־עֹלָתֶךָ
וְאֵלְכָה אוּלַי יִקָּרֵה יְהוָה לִקְרָאתִי וּדְבַר
מַה־יַּרְאֵנִי וְהִגַּדְתִּי לָךְ וַיֵּלֶךְ שֶׁפִי:
⁴ וַיִּקָּר אֱלֹהִים אֶל־בִּלְעָם וַיֹּאמֶר אֵלָיו אֶת־
שִׁבְעַת הַמִּזְבְּחֹת עָרַכְתִּי וָאַעַל פָּר וָאַיִל
בַּמִּזְבֵּֽחַ: ⁵ וַיָּשֶׂם יְהוָה דָּבָר בְּפִי בִלְעָם
וַיֹּאמֶר שׁוּב אֶל־בָּלָק וְכֹה תְדַבֵּֽר:
⁶ וַיָּשָׁב אֵלָיו וְהִנֵּה נִצָּב עַל־עֹלָתוֹ הוּא
וְכָל־שָׂרֵי מוֹאָֽב: ⁷ וַיִּשָּׂא מְשָׁלוֹ וַיֹּאמַר

מִן־אֲרָם יַנְחֵנִי בָלָק
מֶֽלֶךְ־מוֹאָב מֵהַֽרְרֵי־קֶדֶם
לְכָה אָֽרָה־לִּי יַעֲקֹב
וּלְכָה זֹעֲמָה יִשְׂרָאֵֽל:
⁸ מָה אֶקֹּב לֹא קַבֹּה אֵל
וּמָה אֶזְעֹם לֹא זָעַם יְהוָֽה:
⁹ כִּֽי־מֵרֹאשׁ צֻרִים אֶרְאֶנּוּ
וּמִגְּבָעוֹת אֲשׁוּרֶנּוּ
הֶן־עָם לְבָדָד יִשְׁכֹּן
וּבַגּוֹיִם לֹא יִתְחַשָּֽׁב:
¹⁰ מִי מָנָה עֲפַר יַעֲקֹב
וּמִסְפָּר אֶת־רֹבַע יִשְׂרָאֵל
תָּמֹת נַפְשִׁי מוֹת יְשָׁרִים
וּתְהִי אַחֲרִיתִי כָּמֹֽהוּ:

⁘ ⁘ ⁘ ⁘ ⁘ ⁘ ⁘ ⁘ ⁘ ⁘ ⁘ ⁘

Balak's offerings indeed elicit the Deity's message. But instead of curses from Balaam, blessings for Israel come forth.

**3.** *"grant me a manifestation."* The verbal root k-r-h means "to encounter occasionally," and its use here and in v. 4 may reflect the unusual, occasional circumstance in which Israel's God communicates with a non-Israelite prophet.

The book of Ruth uses the same root when Ruth ends up gleaning in her kinsman Boaz's field (Ruth 2:3). In both instances the language may imply that these are *not* happenstance occurrences.

**7.** *theme.* Heb. *mashal*, indicative of wisdom sayings that have a particular message.

**8.** *God.* Heb. *el*, which here may be short for *elohim*, the noun usually translated as "God," or it may refer to the Canaanite god El, which at one time was apparently also worshipped by Israel. In the Deir Alla inscription (see the introduction to the previous unit, p. 939), Balaam's mission is charged by the deity El.

**10.** *Who can count the dust of Jacob.* This expression reverberates in the ancestral blessing (Genesis 13:16).

[11]Then Balak said to Balaam, "What have you
done to me? Here I brought you to damn my enemies, and instead you have blessed them!" [12]He
replied, "I can only repeat faithfully what יהוה puts
in my mouth." [13]Then Balak said to him, "Come
with me to another place from which you can see
them—you will see only a portion of them; you will
not see all of them—and damn them for me from
there." [14]With that, he took him to Sedehzophim,
on the summit of Pisgah. He built seven altars
and offered a bull and a ram on each altar. [15]And
[Balaam] said to Balak, "Stay here beside your offerings, while I seek a manifestation yonder."

[16]יהוה became manifest to Balaam and put a
word in his mouth, saying, "Return to Balak and
speak thus." [17]He went to him and found him
standing beside his offerings, and the Moabite
dignitaries with him. Balak asked him, "What did
יהוה say?" [18]And he took up his theme, and said:

Up, Balak, attend,
Give ear unto me, son of Zippor!
[19]God is not human to be capricious,
Or mortal to have a change of heart.
Would [God] speak and not act,
Promise and not fulfill?

11 וַיֹּאמֶר בָּלָק אֶל־בִּלְעָם מֶה עָשִׂיתָ לִי
לָקֹב אֹיְבַי לְקַחְתִּיךְ וְהִנֵּה בֵּרַכְתָּ בָרֵךְ׃
12 וַיַּעַן וַיֹּאמַר הֲלֹא אֵת אֲשֶׁר יָשִׂים יְהוָה
בְּפִי אֹתוֹ אֶשְׁמֹר לְדַבֵּר׃ 13 וַיֹּאמֶר אֵלָיו
בָּלָק לך נא לְכָה־נָּא אִתִּי אֶל־מָקוֹם אַחֵר
אֲשֶׁר תִּרְאֶנּוּ מִשָּׁם אֶפֶס קָצֵהוּ תִרְאֶה וְכֻלּוֹ
לֹא תִרְאֶה וְקָבְנוֹ־לִי מִשָּׁם׃ 14 וַיִּקָּחֵהוּ
שְׂדֵה צֹפִים אֶל־רֹאשׁ הַפִּסְגָּה וַיִּבֶן שִׁבְעָה
מִזְבְּחֹת וַיַּעַל פָּר וָאַיִל בַּמִּזְבֵּחַ׃ 15 וַיֹּאמֶר
אֶל־בָּלָק הִתְיַצֵּב כֹּה עַל־עֹלָתֶךָ וְאָנֹכִי
אִקָּרֶה כֹּה׃
16 וַיִּקָּר יְהוָה אֶל־בִּלְעָם וַיָּשֶׂם דָּבָר בְּפִיו
וַיֹּאמֶר שׁוּב אֶל־בָּלָק וְכֹה תְדַבֵּר׃ 17 וַיָּבֹא
אֵלָיו וְהִנּוֹ נִצָּב עַל־עֹלָתוֹ וְשָׂרֵי מוֹאָב אִתּוֹ
וַיֹּאמֶר לוֹ בָּלָק מַה־דִּבֶּר יְהוָה׃ 18 וַיִּשָּׂא
מְשָׁלוֹ וַיֹּאמַר

קוּם בָּלָק וּשְׁמָע
הַאֲזִינָה עָדַי בְּנוֹ צִפֹּר׃
19 לֹא אִישׁ אֵל וִיכַזֵּב
וּבֶן־אָדָם וְיִתְנֶחָם
הַהוּא אָמַר וְלֹא יַעֲשֶׂה
וְדִבֶּר וְלֹא יְקִימֶנָּה׃

### BALAAM'S SECOND ORACLE AND BALAK'S RESPONSE (23:13–26)

Balaam's second oracle (vv. 18–24) expands on the themes of the initial message. It focuses on God's attributes of faithfulness vis-à-vis Israel and acknowledges Balaam's task to actually bless Israel. The poem closes with a statement of Israel's great power. Balak, however, is unwilling to accept the inevitable and persists in resisting the finality of the prophecy.

*13–17.* After the initial blessing of Israel, Balak attempts to elicit a curse from Balaam by having the prophet view the Israelite camp from a less awesome angle. The narrator mocks Balak, who fails to understand that God's desire may not be contravened in this manner.

*13.* ***"a portion of them."*** Literally, "its edge," indicating that Balaam would only see a small segment of the Israelite camp. Apparently Balak believes that Balaam might actually curse them if they did not appear so overwhelming to him.

*18–24.* The message of the second oracle underscores that of the first. Balaam emphasizes God's constancy in general—and specifically a devotion to Israel's welfare. Balaam cites the redemption from Egypt as evidence of God's power and allegiance to Israel.

[20]My message was to bless:
When [God] blesses, I cannot reverse it.
[21]No harm is in sight for Jacob,
No woe in view for Israel.
Their God יהוה is with them,
And their King's acclaim in their midst.
[22]God who freed them from Egypt
Is for them like the horns of the wild ox.
[23]Lo, there is no augury in Jacob,
No divining in Israel:
Jacob is told at once,
Yea Israel, what God has planned.
[24]Lo, a people that rises like a lioness,
Leaps up like a lion,
Rests not till it has feasted on prey
And drunk the blood of the slain.

[25]Thereupon Balak said to Balaam, "Don't curse them and don't bless them!" [26]In reply, Balaam said to Balak, "But I told you: Whatever יהוה says, that I must do." [27]Then Balak said to Balaam, "Come now, I will take you to another place. Perhaps God will deem it right that you

20 הִנֵּה בָרֵךְ לָקָחְתִּי
וּבֵרֵךְ וְלֹא אֲשִׁיבֶנָּה׃
21 לֹא־הִבִּיט אָוֶן בְּיַעֲקֹב
וְלֹא־רָאָה עָמָל בְּיִשְׂרָאֵל
יְהוָה אֱלֹהָיו עִמּוֹ
וּתְרוּעַת מֶלֶךְ בּוֹ׃
22 אֵל מוֹצִיאָם מִמִּצְרָיִם
כְּתוֹעֲפֹת רְאֵם לוֹ׃
23 כִּי לֹא־נַחַשׁ בְּיַעֲקֹב
וְלֹא־קֶסֶם בְּיִשְׂרָאֵל
כָּעֵת יֵאָמֵר לְיַעֲקֹב
וּלְיִשְׂרָאֵל מַה־פָּעַל אֵל׃
24 הֶן־עָם כְּלָבִיא יָקוּם
וְכַאֲרִי יִתְנַשָּׂא
לֹא יִשְׁכַּב עַד־יֹאכַל טֶרֶף
וְדַם־חֲלָלִים יִשְׁתֶּה׃
25 וַיֹּאמֶר בָּלָק אֶל־בִּלְעָם גַּם־קֹב לֹא
תִקֳּבֶנּוּ גַּם־בָּרֵךְ לֹא תְבָרְכֶנּוּ׃ 26 וַיַּעַן
בִּלְעָם וַיֹּאמֶר אֶל־בָּלָק הֲלֹא דִּבַּרְתִּי
אֵלֶיךָ לֵאמֹר כֹּל אֲשֶׁר־יְדַבֵּר יְהוָה אֹתוֹ
אֶעֱשֶׂה׃ 27 וַיֹּאמֶר בָּלָק אֶל־בִּלְעָם לְכָה־נָּא
אֶקָּחֲךָ אֶל־מָקוֹם אַחֵר אוּלַי יִישַׁר בְּעֵינֵי

*23. no augury.* Heb. *nachash*, like *kesem* ("divining," see at 22:7), refers to the taking of omens, a practice popular in the ancient Near East but prohibited in the Bible (see Deuteronomy 18:10–12).

*24. like a lioness . . . like a lion.* These similes preview Israel's military victories and kingdom in Canaan (see Genesis 49:9–10).

*25–26.* The distressed and foolish Moabite king, in contrast to the seer, is not resigned to accept God's expressed will as the last word.

*25. "Don't curse them and don't bless them!"* The implication is that Balaam's attempted curse translates into a blessing; therefore, it is better to abandon the entire enterprise.

## BALAAM'S THIRD ORACLE AND BALAK'S RESPONSE (23:27–24:11)

The section begins with Balak's acknowledgment that Israel's God is the one who controls Balaam's ability to curse Israel. This time, when Balaam utters his prophecy, he is apparently imbued with the divine spirit common to Israel's prophets. It seems that his role has changed from that of pagan seer to a prophet of God. The third oracle sings the praises of a triumphant Israel and concludes by cursing her enemies.

*23:27–24:2.* This time the narrator states that Balaam does not search for omens in the process of

damn them for me there." [28]Balak took Balaam to
the peak of Peor, which overlooks the wasteland.
[29]Balaam said to Balak, "Build me here seven altars,
and have seven bulls and seven rams ready for me
here." [30]Balak did as Balaam said: he offered up a
bull and a ram on each altar.

24 Now Balaam, seeing that it pleased יהוה
to bless Israel, did not, as on previous occasions, go
in search of omens, but turned his face toward the
wilderness. [2]As Balaam looked up and saw Israel
encamped tribe by tribe, the spirit of God came
upon him. [3]Taking up his theme, he said:

Word of Balaam son of Beor,
Word of the man whose eye is true,
[4]Word of one who hears God's speech,
Who beholds visions from the Almighty,
Prostrate, but with eyes unveiled:
[5]How fair are your tents, O Jacob,
Your dwellings, O Israel!
[6]Like palm-groves that stretch out,

הָאֱלֹהִים וְקַבֹּתוֹ לִי מִשָּׁם׃ 28 וַיִּקַּח בָּלָק
אֶת־בִּלְעָם רֹאשׁ הַפְּעוֹר הַנִּשְׁקָף עַל־פְּנֵי
הַיְשִׁימֹן׃ 29 וַיֹּאמֶר בִּלְעָם אֶל־בָּלָק בְּנֵה־לִי
בָזֶה שִׁבְעָה מִזְבְּחֹת וְהָכֵן לִי בָּזֶה שִׁבְעָה
פָרִים וְשִׁבְעָה אֵילִם׃ 30 וַיַּעַשׂ בָּלָק כַּאֲשֶׁר
אָמַר בִּלְעָם וַיַּעַל פָּר וָאַיִל בַּמִּזְבֵּחַ׃
כד וַיַּרְא בִּלְעָם כִּי טוֹב בְּעֵינֵי יְהוָה
לְבָרֵךְ אֶת־יִשְׂרָאֵל וְלֹא־הָלַךְ כְּפַעַם־בְּפַעַם
לִקְרַאת נְחָשִׁים וַיָּשֶׁת אֶל־הַמִּדְבָּר פָּנָיו׃
2 וַיִּשָּׂא בִלְעָם אֶת־עֵינָיו וַיַּרְא אֶת־יִשְׂרָאֵל
שֹׁכֵן לִשְׁבָטָיו וַתְּהִי עָלָיו רוּחַ אֱלֹהִים׃
3 וַיִּשָּׂא מְשָׁלוֹ וַיֹּאמַר

נְאֻם בִּלְעָם בְּנוֹ בְעֹר
וּנְאֻם הַגֶּבֶר שְׁתֻם הָעָיִן׃
4 נְאֻם שֹׁמֵעַ אִמְרֵי־אֵל
אֲשֶׁר מַחֲזֵה שַׁדַּי יֶחֱזֶה
נֹפֵל וּגְלוּי עֵינָיִם׃
5 מַה־טֹּבוּ אֹהָלֶיךָ יַעֲקֹב
מִשְׁכְּנֹתֶיךָ יִשְׂרָאֵל׃
6 כִּנְחָלִים נִטָּיוּ

seeking the divine spirit, implying that he did so previously. For the first time, Balaam views the entire Israelite camp (compare 22:41; 23:13).

*28. the peak of Peor.* The site, high on a hill, is not only ideal for viewing the Israelite camp, but also would have housed a sanctuary to the god Baal-peor, a site that will soon become infamous when Israelite men consort there with local women (see below at 25:1–18).

*24:3–9.* This third vision describes the Israelite encampment as a lush oasis (vv. 6–7), which stands in stark contrast to the wilderness background of Balaam's actual view of that encampment (24:1). The oracle ends by reiterating the promise to Israel's ancestors (Genesis 12:3; 27:29) that anyone who blesses Israel will be blessed in turn, but that anyone who curses Israel is cursed in return. Verse 5 from this oracle has become a part of Jewish liturgy.

*4. the Almighty.* Heb. *shaddai* is an epithet of God common in the stories of the patriarchs and matriarchs (Genesis 17:1; 28:3; 35:11). Its likely meaning, "high," is related to the Akkadian term for mountain. (See further at Genesis 17:1 and Exodus 6:2.) In contrast to the biblical *shaddai*, in the Deir Alla inscription (see the introduction to the previous unit, p. 939), the *shdyn* ("Shadday-gods") are independent deities with powers to challenge those of the head god El.

*5. How fair are your tents, O Jacob.* Heb. *mah tovu ohalecha yaakov*. This verse from Balaam's blessing of Israel is preserved in modern times in the opening of the morning liturgy. The picture of Israel residing securely in its tents provides an idyllic image.

Like gardens beside a river,
Like aloes planted by יהוה,
Like cedars beside the water;
7Their boughs drip with moisture,
Their roots have abundant water.
Their ruler shall rise above Agag,
Their sovereignty shall be exalted.
8God who freed them from Egypt
Is for them like the horns of the wild ox.
They shall devour enemy nations,
Crush their bones,
And smash their arrows.
9They crouch, they lie down like a lion,
Like a lioness; who dares rouse them?
Blessed are they who bless you,
Accursed they who curse you!

10Enraged at Balaam, Balak struck his hands
together. "I called you," Balak said to Balaam, "to
damn my enemies, and instead you have blessed
them these three times! 11Back with you at once to
your own place! I was going to reward you richly,
but יהוה has denied you the reward." 12Balaam replied to Balak, "But I even told the messengers you

כְּגַנֹּת עֲלֵי נָהָר
כַּאֲהָלִים נָטַע יְהֹוָה
כַּאֲרָזִים עֲלֵי־מָיִם׃
7 יִזַּל־מַיִם מִדָּלְיָו
וְזַרְעוֹ בְּמַיִם רַבִּים
וְיָרֹם מֵאֲגַג מַלְכּוֹ
וְתִנַּשֵּׂא מַלְכֻתוֹ׃
8 אֵל מוֹצִיאוֹ מִמִּצְרַיִם
כְּתוֹעֲפֹת רְאֵם לוֹ
יֹאכַל גּוֹיִם צָרָיו
וְעַצְמֹתֵיהֶם יְגָרֵם
וְחִצָּיו יִמְחָץ׃
9 כָּרַע שָׁכַב כַּאֲרִי
וּכְלָבִיא מִי יְקִימֶנּוּ
מְבָרְכֶיךָ בָרוּךְ
וְאֹרְרֶיךָ אָרוּר׃

10 וַיִּחַר־אַף בָּלָק אֶל־בִּלְעָם וַיִּסְפֹּק אֶת־
כַּפָּיו וַיֹּאמֶר בָּלָק אֶל־בִּלְעָם לָקֹב אֹיְבַי
קְרָאתִיךָ וְהִנֵּה בֵּרַכְתָּ בָרֵךְ זֶה שָׁלֹשׁ
פְּעָמִים׃ 11 וְעַתָּה בְּרַח־לְךָ אֶל־מְקוֹמֶךָ
אָמַרְתִּי כַּבֵּד אֲכַבֶּדְךָ וְהִנֵּה מְנָעֲךָ יְהֹוָה
מִכָּבוֹד׃ 12 וַיֹּאמֶר בִּלְעָם אֶל־בָּלָק הֲלֹא גַּם
אֶל־מַלְאָכֶיךָ אֲשֶׁר־שָׁלַחְתָּ אֵלַי דִּבַּרְתִּי

*7. Agag.* Agag is the king of Amalek at the time of Saul's reign (I Samuel 15:8). Saul's victory is in effect foretold here. Critical scholars take this as evidence that this text dates from after that event, that is, after approximately 1000 B.C.E.

*10. Enraged at Balaam.* Balak's reaction to Balaam's third oracle is no doubt exacerbated by the pronouncement that he who curses Israel will be cursed in turn.

*struck his hands together.* A gesture of anguish and anger attested elsewhere in the Bible. The book of Lamentations depicts Jerusalem as a disgraced woman, whom passersby jeer as they strike their hands in derision (Lamentations 2:15).

*11.* Balak sends Balaam home without payment for his services.

BALAAM'S FOURTH ORACLE (24:12–25)

Balaam makes it clear to Balak that even great riches cannot entice him if Israel's God does not will it. In the power struggle between earthly king and the kingship of God, the victor is clearly the God of Israel. In that sense, the encounters between Balak and Balaam are comparable to those between Moses and Pharaoh prior to the Exodus.

Balaam utters a fourth oracle on his own accord following his dismissal by the angry Moabite king.

sent to me, [13]'Though Balak were to give me his house full of silver and gold, I could not of my own accord do anything good or bad contrary to יהוה's command. What יהוה says, that I must say.' [14]And now, as I go back to my people, let me inform you of what this people will do to your people in days to come." [15]He took up his theme, and said:

Word of Balaam son of Beor,
Word of the man whose eye is true,
[16]Word of one who hears God's speech,
Who obtains knowledge from the Most High,
And beholds visions from the Almighty,
Prostrate, but with eyes unveiled:
[17]What I see for them is not yet,
What I behold will not be soon:
A star rises from Jacob,
A scepter comes forth from Israel;
It smashes the brow of Moab,
The foundation of all children of Seth.
[18]Edom becomes a possession,
Yea, Seir a possession of its enemies;
But Israel is triumphant.

לֵאמֹ֑ר׃ 13 אִם־יִתֶּן־לִ֨י בָלָ֜ק מְלֹ֣א בֵיתוֹ֮ כֶּ֣סֶף
וְזָהָב֒ לֹ֣א אוּכַ֗ל לַעֲבֹר֙ אֶת־פִּ֣י יְהֹוָ֔ה לַעֲשׂ֥וֹת
טוֹבָ֛ה א֥וֹ רָעָ֖ה מִלִּבִּ֑י אֲשֶׁר־יְדַבֵּ֥ר יְהֹוָ֖ה אֹת֥וֹ
אֲדַבֵּֽר׃ 14 וְעַתָּ֕ה הִנְנִ֥י הוֹלֵ֖ךְ לְעַמִּ֑י לְכָה֙
אִיעָ֣צְךָ֔ אֲשֶׁ֨ר יַעֲשֶׂ֜ה הָעָ֥ם הַזֶּ֛ה לְעַמְּךָ֖
בְּאַחֲרִ֥ית הַיָּמִֽים׃ 15 וַיִּשָּׂ֥א מְשָׁל֖וֹ וַיֹּאמַ֑ר

נְאֻ֤ם בִּלְעָם֙ בְּנ֣וֹ בְעֹ֔ר
וּנְאֻ֥ם הַגֶּ֖בֶר שְׁתֻ֥ם הָעָֽיִן׃
16 נְאֻ֕ם שֹׁמֵ֖עַ אִמְרֵי־אֵ֑ל
וְיֹדֵ֖עַ דַּ֣עַת עֶלְי֑וֹן
מַחֲזֵ֤ה שַׁדַּי֙ יֶֽחֱזֶ֔ה
נֹפֵ֖ל וּגְל֥וּי עֵינָֽיִם׃
17 אֶרְאֶ֙נּוּ֙ וְלֹ֣א עַתָּ֔ה
אֲשׁוּרֶ֖נּוּ וְלֹ֣א קָר֑וֹב
דָּרַ֨ךְ כּוֹכָ֜ב מִֽיַּעֲקֹ֗ב
וְקָ֥ם שֵׁ֙בֶט֙ מִיִּשְׂרָאֵ֔ל
וּמָחַץ֙ פַּאֲתֵ֣י מוֹאָ֔ב
וְקַרְקַ֖ר כָּל־בְּנֵי־שֵֽׁת׃
18 וְהָיָ֨ה אֱד֜וֹם יְרֵשָׁ֗ה
וְהָיָ֥ה יְרֵשָׁ֛ה שֵׂעִ֖יר אֹיְבָ֑יו
וְיִשְׂרָאֵ֖ל עֹ֥שֶׂה חָֽיִל׃

- - - - - - - - - - - - - - - - - - - - - - - - - -

This last speech not only prophesies Israel's ultimate triumph over the other nations, but it assumes the rise of kingship and an Israelite empire.

This fourth oracle refers to several ethnic groups in the context of Israel's future victories. Balaam predicts the destruction of Moab at the hands of an unnamed Israelite king. Judging by other biblical accounts, either David or Ahab qualifies as that king (II Samuel 8:2; II Kings 3:4–5). Indeed, the Mesha Stele—a Moabite inscription of the 9th century B.C.E.—commemorates the independence of Moab after years of subservience to Israel. Overall, the fourth oracle is the climax of Balaam's prophecies, predicting a more distant but bright future awaiting Israel. As Balaam relates each of the first three oracles, his status rises; with the fourth and

final oracle he becomes a universal prophet in the sense that his visions encompass future events for the entire region. A very common pattern in biblical literature is followed here: the 3+1 pattern, where the fourth element is climactic.

The narrative ends with Balaam and Balak returning home, the latter's mission having failed. No additional words are exchanged between the Moabite king and the seer.

*14. "in days to come."* This expression denotes a future time but not in a messianic sense.

*17. A star rises from Jacob.* The epithet "star" refers to a divinely chosen king, in later periods identified with a messiah (for example, Bar Kochba, literally "Son of the Star," the leader of the second Jewish revolt against Rome in the 2nd century C.E.).

19 A victor issues from Jacob
To wipe out what is left of Ir.
20 He saw Amalek and, taking up his theme, he said:
A leading nation is Amalek;
But its fate is to perish forever.
21 He saw the Kenites and, taking up his theme, he said:
Though your abode be secure,
And your nest be set among cliffs,
22 Yet shall Kain be consumed,
When Asshur takes you captive.
23 He took up his theme and said:
Alas, who can survive except God has willed it!
24 Ships come from the quarter of Kittim;
They subject Asshur, subject Eber.
They, too, shall perish forever.
25 Then Balaam set out on his journey back home; and Balak also went his way.

**25** While Israel was staying at Shittim, the menfolk profaned themselves by whoring with the

19 וְיֵרְדְּ מִיַּעֲקֹב
וְהֶאֱבִיד שָׂרִיד מֵעִיר׃
20 וַיַּרְא אֶת־עֲמָלֵק וַיִּשָּׂא מְשָׁלוֹ וַיֹּאמַר
רֵאשִׁית גּוֹיִם עֲמָלֵק
וְאַחֲרִיתוֹ עֲדֵי אֹבֵד׃
21 וַיַּרְא אֶת־הַקֵּינִי וַיִּשָּׂא מְשָׁלוֹ וַיֹּאמַר
אֵיתָן מוֹשָׁבֶךָ
וְשִׂים בַּסֶּלַע קִנֶּךָ׃
22 כִּי אִם־יִהְיֶה לְבָעֵר קָיִן
עַד־מָה אַשּׁוּר תִּשְׁבֶּךָּ׃
23 וַיִּשָּׂא מְשָׁלוֹ וַיֹּאמַר
אוֹי מִי יִחְיֶה מִשֻּׂמוֹ אֵל׃
24 וְצִים מִיַּד כִּתִּים
וְעִנּוּ אַשּׁוּר וְעִנּוּ־עֵבֶר
וְגַם־הוּא עֲדֵי אֹבֵד׃
25 וַיָּקָם בִּלְעָם וַיֵּלֶךְ וַיָּשָׁב לִמְקֹמוֹ וְגַם־בָּלָק
הָלַךְ לְדַרְכּוֹ׃ פ

כה וַיֵּשֶׁב יִשְׂרָאֵל בַּשִּׁטִּים וַיָּחֶל הָעָם

*24. Kittim.* Invaders from Cyprus, who infiltrated the region of Syria and Mesopotamia. The historical setting for this prophecy is unclear.

## *Apostasy at Baal-peor* (25:1–9)

Numbers 25 continues the narrative begun in 22:1 that was interrupted by the insertion of the story of Balaam and Balak. It recounts a specific event that occurs while Israel is still encamped on the plains of Moab, awaiting the crossing into Canaan. According to the account, which is apparently woven from different traditions, a group of Israelite men mingle with local non-Israelite women; the resulting sexual relationships lead to idolatrous worship of the local god, Baal-peor, and ultimately to the slaughter of thousands of people.

Three smaller segments comprise the story: vv. 1–5; 6–9; and 10–19 (which appears in the next parashah, *Pinchas*). In the latter two segments Phinehas, Aaron's grandson, is central to the expiation of the sin, his role superseding even that of Moses. Clearly, that rendition's objective is to support the claim that the Aaronite priesthood was divinely appointed.

Memory of Israel's apostasy at Baal-peor and subsequent punishment is preserved in several biblical accounts outside the book of Numbers (see Deuteronomy 4:3; Joshua 22:17; Hosea 9:10; Psalm 106:28). But it is the account in Numbers that specifically develops the theme of the dangerous for-

Moabite women, [2]who invited the menfolk to the sacrifices for their god. The menfolk partook of them and worshiped that god. [3]Thus Israel attached itself to Baal-peor, and יהוה was incensed with Israel. [4]יהוה said to Moses, "Take all the ringleaders and have them publicly impaled before יהוה, so that יהוה's wrath may turn away from Israel." [5]So Moses said to Israel's officials, "Each of you slay those of his men who attached themselves to Baal-peor."

לִזְנוֹת אֶל־בְּנוֹת מוֹאָב׃ 2 וַתִּקְרֶאןָ לָעָם
לְזִבְחֵי אֱלֹהֵיהֶן וַיֹּאכַל הָעָם וַיִּשְׁתַּחֲווּ
לֵאלֹהֵיהֶן׃ 3 וַיִּצָּמֶד יִשְׂרָאֵל לְבַעַל פְּעוֹר
וַיִּחַר־אַף יְהֹוָה בְּיִשְׂרָאֵל׃ 4 וַיֹּאמֶר יְהֹוָה
אֶל־מֹשֶׁה קַח אֶת־כׇּל־רָאשֵׁי הָעָם וְהוֹקַע
אוֹתָם לַיהֹוָה נֶגֶד הַשָּׁמֶשׁ וְיָשֹׁב חֲרוֹן אַף־
יְהֹוָה מִיִּשְׂרָאֵל׃ 5 וַיֹּאמֶר מֹשֶׁה אֶל־שֹׁפְטֵי
יִשְׂרָאֵל הִרְגוּ אִישׁ אֲנָשָׁיו הַנִּצְמָדִים לְבַעַל
פְּעוֹר׃

eign woman who entices the men to sin (as in Proverbs 2:16; 5:3, 20; 7:5; 23:27; 27:13). Except for Hosea 9:10, all other references to the sin of Baal-peor focus solely on the idolatrous worship.

## ISRAEL'S FLIRTATION WITH FOREIGN WOMEN AND IDOLATRY (25:1–5)

The setting of this episode is the last Israelite encampment outside Canaan, at Shittim—just east of the Jordan River. Israel's apostasy, actually involving only males, centers around their contact with Moabite women, whom the writer clearly condemns in keeping with a strand of biblical ideology that prohibits marriage with foreign women (see Deuteronomy 7:3). King Solomon himself is condemned for marrying foreign women, among them a Moabite, because they ostensibly enticed him to worship foreign gods (I Kings 11:1–6). A contrasting tradition, which welcomes a foreign woman, is the story of Ruth the Moabite. The brief story of Israel's apostasy in Numbers 25 moves swiftly from a sexual encounter to idolatrous worship and God's reprisal.

*1. **Moabite women.*** The Moabite women in this account are viewed as dangerous enticers. Unlike Ruth, who is accepted into Israelite society and even identified as the ancestor of King David (Ruth 4:17), Moabite women in this parashah are considered totally unacceptable partners for the Israelite men. Undoubtedly, Ruth's complete break with her own family and religion and total adoption of Israelite culture differentiates her case.

*2. **invited the menfolk.*** The text makes it clear that it is the Moabite women who entice the Israelite men to join their ritual feast. In that way this sin differs from the one of the Golden Calf, whose construction and worship was initiated by Israel (Exodus 32:1–6). [While the case of the Golden Calf implicates women and men alike, the present story singles out women as enticers to sin, while it labels men as sinners. —*Ed.*]

***partook of them.*** Heb. *vayochal*, literally "ate," seems to refer to a ritual sacrificial feast, possibly connected with a funerary cult. (See *Va-y'chi*, Another View, p. 297.)

*3. **Baal-peor.*** Baal-peor is the local manifestation of the storm-god Baal of the Canaanite religion. Peor is a geographical name previously mentioned in the Balaam saga (23:28; also Deuteronomy 3:29).

*4. **"Take all the ringleaders and have them publicly impaled."*** The ringleaders, in Hebrew "heads of the people," are to be put to death; perhaps included are those who did not take part in the apostasy but were liable for the people's actions nonetheless. Their execution and subsequent public impalement serves as expiation for Israel's violation of the Sinai covenant, which prohibits foreign worship. The extreme measure is needed to control divine wrath.

*5. **"slay those . . . who attached themselves to Baal-peor."*** Moses apparently intervenes, instructing Israel's officials to slay only the guilty.

<sup>6</sup>Just then one of the Israelite notables came and brought a Midianite woman over to his companions, in the sight of Moses and of the whole Israelite community who were weeping at the entrance of the Tent of Meeting. <sup>7</sup>When Phinehas, son of Eleazar son of Aaron the priest, saw this, he left the assembly and, taking a spear in his hand, <sup>8</sup>he followed the Israelite notable into the chamber and stabbed both of them, the Israelite notable and the woman, through the belly. Then the plague against the Israelites was checked. <sup>9</sup>Those who died of the plague numbered twenty-four thousand.

6 וְהִנֵּ֡ה אִישׁ֩ מִבְּנֵ֨י יִשְׂרָאֵ֜ל בָּ֗א וַיַּקְרֵ֤ב אֶל־אֶחָיו֙ אֶת־הַמִּדְיָנִ֔ית לְעֵינֵ֣י מֹשֶׁ֔ה וּלְעֵינֵ֖י כָּל־עֲדַ֣ת בְּנֵֽי־יִשְׂרָאֵ֑ל וְהֵ֣מָּה בֹכִ֔ים פֶּ֖תַח אֹ֥הֶל מוֹעֵֽד׃ 7 וַיַּ֗רְא פִּֽינְחָס֙ בֶּן־אֶלְעָזָ֔ר בֶּֽן־אַהֲרֹ֖ן הַכֹּהֵ֑ן וַיָּ֙קָם֙ מִתּ֣וֹךְ הָֽעֵדָ֔ה וַיִּקַּ֥ח רֹ֖מַח בְּיָדֽוֹ׃ 8 וַ֠יָּבֹא אַחַ֨ר אִֽישׁ־יִשְׂרָאֵ֜ל אֶל־הַקֻּבָּ֗ה וַיִּדְקֹר֙ אֶת־שְׁנֵיהֶ֔ם אֵ֚ת אִ֣ישׁ יִשְׂרָאֵ֔ל וְאֶת־הָאִשָּׁ֖ה אֶל־קֳבָתָ֑הּ וַתֵּֽעָצַר֙ הַמַּגֵּפָ֔ה מֵעַ֖ל בְּנֵ֥י יִשְׂרָאֵֽל׃ 9 וַיִּהְי֕וּ הַמֵּתִ֖ים בַּמַּגֵּפָ֑ה אַרְבָּעָ֥ה וְעֶשְׂרִ֖ים אָֽלֶף׃ פ

— — — — — — — — — — — — — — — — — — — — — —

### PHINEHAS'S VENGEANCE (25:6–9)

This passage focuses on one particular couple guilty of apostasy. Interestingly, the man and woman are not identified by name or status until after Phinehas kills them and expiates their sin (25:14–15). Clearly, the emphasis in this portion of the account is on the brave, redeeming act of Phinehas, the priest who preserves the community's sanctity. The couple is identified in the next parashah, where we learn that they come from leading families. Their actions as leaders and role models render them even more culpable.

**6. *Midianite woman.*** Verse 1 identified the women in question as Moabite. According to the Torah, Moses had married Zipporah, a Midianite, the daughter of a priest, more than forty years earlier (Exodus 2:21 and 18:1–12). The Midianites are said to be descended from Abraham and his wife Keturah (Genesis 25:1–4). The Bible preserves conflicting traditions about relations with Midianites.

**8. *the chamber.*** Heb. *hakubbah*, which probably refers to a tent (as in Arabic) that is part of the cultic area. Thus the transgression involves worship of a foreign deity.

**9. *Those who died of the plague.*** Punishing offenders by a divinely sent plague is known from elsewhere in the Bible. (Presumably any remaining members of the Exodus generation are among the victims of this plague, since the census that will follow shortly in Numbers 26 indicates that by that point they have all been wiped out.) The sin of the Golden Calf, especially, is a comparable example (Exodus 32:35). Possibly, the reference at the end of that account to future divine reprisal (32:34) is fulfilled by the punishment exacted now at Baal-peor.

—*Nili Sacher Fox*

## Another View

IN THE BRIEF and gruesome episode at the conclusion of *parashat Balak* (25:6–9), what do the Israelite man and the Midianite woman do to provoke Phinehas's wrath? Apparently it is the brazenness of an Israelite leader engaging in idolatrous worship with the daughter of a Midianite chieftain within the sight of the whole community that causes Phinehas's immediate, violent reaction. But the text raises a number of questions and gives a few hints that something else may have incited his brutal response as well.

First, the priestly author mentions that the man brought the woman (identified in the next parashah respectively as Zimri and Cozbi), to *echav*, translated here as "his companions" (v. 6). The term *ach* is a kinship term, often translated as "brother" or more loosely as "kin." If, following Ibn Ezra, we translate *echav* as "kinsmen," then it appears that Zimri is introducing Cozbi to his family. Then they step into the *kubbah*, a word that appears nowhere else in the Bible, here translated as "chamber" (v. 8). If they are simply going there to engage in idolatry, why would he have introduced her to his family? Second, why does Phinehas kill both Zimri and Cozbi, when Moses commanded to kill only the Israelites who were engaging in idolatry (v. 4)? Third, why does the author include the detail that Phinehas stabs both Zimri and Cozbi in the belly (v. 8) if their crime is worshipping foreign gods?

One explanation that answers all of these questions is that the author conveys through these details that Zimri has married Cozbi, and that they come to the Israelite camp so that he can introduce his bride to his family. Thus, the *kubbah* is a marriage canopy where the couple goes to consummate the marriage. Therefore, the issue is also intermarriage, not only idolatry.

If this interpretation is correct, then the recounting of this incident reflects an attitude toward intermarriage that conflicts with other biblical stories. Possibly the report about Moses' own wife Zipporah, which states that she was a Midianite woman and a priest's daughter, aims specifically to illustrate a different perspective toward foreign women (Exodus 2:16–21; see also how Zipporah rescues Moses from death in Exodus 4:24–26). The book of Ruth, where a Moabite woman becomes the progenitor of King David, likewise challenges an exclusionary perspective.

*Why do the Israelite notable and the Midianite woman provoke Phinehas's wrath?*

—*Hilary Lipka*

## Post-biblical Interpretations

***Balaam son of Beor*** (22:5). For the Rabbis, the biblical soothsayer Balaam personified the perceived gentile evils of immorality, idolatry, and sorcery. Rabbinic literature consistently portrays the wicked Balaam as advising other nations' kings on how to destroy Israel, iniquity noted already in Numbers 31:16 (not in this parashah). The Rabbis affirm that Balaam had great prophetic powers and the facility to bless and curse effectively. According to Midrash *B'midbar Rabbah* 14.20, God bestowed these special abilities on Balaam so that the nations of the world should not say: "Had we possessed a prophet like Moses we [too] would have worshipped the blessed Holy One." Thus, the nations wasted their opportunity to find a way to the worship of God and could not claim that Israel had special privileges.

***While Israel was staying at Shittim*** (25:1). *B'midbar Rabbah* 20.22 recounts that during all the years in the wilderness, the Israelites acted virtuously; they did not commit any sexual sins until they came to Shittim. The reason for their lapse, according to the midrash, was the waters of the local spring: "Some fountains produce strong men and some weaklings, some handsome men and some ugly men, some chaste men and some men who are steeped in lewdness." According to the Sages, this fountain of Shittim, which promoted immoral sexual behavior, was also the fountain that provided the water for Sodom. They predicted that at some future time God would cause this cursed spring to dry up and then renew it in purity, as the prophet Joel predicted, "A spring shall issue from the House of יהוה, and shall water the valley of Shittim" (Joel 4:18).

> *"Cast a staff into the air, and it will fall back to its place of origin."*

***whoring with the Moabite women*** (25:1). The Rabbis recall that the Moabites were descended from the incestuous union of Lot and his older daughter (Genesis 19:33–35), following the destruction of Sodom and Gomorrah. The Sages usually treat this event positively, since the two daughters believed that the rest of the world had been destroyed and they were trying to reconstitute humanity by sleeping with their father. In *B'midbar Rabbah* 20.23, however, this act of incest is cited as the beginning of a history of debauchery by the women of Moab: "Cast a staff into the air, and it will fall back to its place of origin. The one who began the harlotry in the beginning [Lot's older daughter], finally committed it again [the Moabite women]."

***who invited the menfolk to the sacrifices for their god*** (25:2). According to a number of rabbinic sources, including BT *Sanhedrin* 106a, the plot to seduce the Israelite men, which led to the deaths of 24,000 people (25:9), was concocted by the villainous Balaam, in accordance with what Numbers 31:16 states in the next parashah. In order to ensnare Israel, Balaam advised Balak to erect stalls where old women would offer linen garments to the Israelite men. However, inside the stalls, young women offered to sell the same items for less. Having established a relationship with a particular man, the young woman would say to him: "You are now like one of the family.... Why is it that though we love you, you hate us?... Are we not all the children of one man, Terah the father of Abraham?" She would then encourage him to drink wine, and he would desire her—as it says in the Prophets, "Harlotry, wine, and new wine destroy the mind of My people" (Hosea 4:11). At that point, the young woman would refuse to have sexual relations with the Israelite man until he had sacrificed an animal and bowed down to the local idol, Baal-peor.

***who were weeping at the entrance of the Tent of Meeting*** (25:6). *B'midbar Rabbah* 20.24 suggests that Moses and the Israelite leaders were weeping because they were so shocked and disappointed at the behavior of the Israelite men who were worshiping Baal-peor. The midrash offers a parable: "It is like a king's daughter, adorned for her wedding and sitting in her bridal litter, who was discovered in a compromising position with a stranger, and so the king and her relatives lost faith in her. It was the same with Israel. At the end of forty years they camped by the Jordan to cross over into the Land of Israel... and there they gave way to harlotry. [At this betrayal] the courage of Moses failed him, as did that of the righteous with him."

*—Judith R. Baskin*

# Contemporary Reflection

In the midst of our book of wandering, we read of how a Moabite sovereign engages a seer from a distant land in the hopes of cursing and thus defeating the Israelites. In the central irony of a fanciful tale that opens with "[he] saw" (22:2), neither King Balak nor his hireling Balaam are able to "see" the Israelites. Balaam and Balak position and re-position themselves in an attempt to assess the multitude that "hides the earth from view" (22:5). The two travel from point to point without gaining the perspective they seek.

Only when the Holy One opens his eyes can Balaam see more than a portion of the people he has been sent to curse. He sees the tents that are the homes and the gathering places of the women, children, and men who live as a community marked by care and mutual respect. Seemingly stunned by his newfound perspective on the Israelite compound, Balaam describes the people in language that evokes Eden: "Like palm-groves that stretch out, / Like gardens beside a river, / Like aloes planted by יהוה, / Like cedars beside the water; / Their boughs drip with moisture, / Their roots have abundant water" (24:6–7). Have the eyes of the desert diviner cleared sufficiently so that he can see a people who one day would have the power to make the desert bloom? Do his words reflect dreams of cities with palm-lined boulevards and garden neighborhoods that would, in the future, challenge and transform the arid landscape?

For a moment, Balaam sees a community as it can be: a society of mutual dependence and trust, a community where each person is treated with dignity, and he exclaims: *Mah tovu ohalecha, Yaakov / mishk'notecha, Yisrael* ("How fair are your tents, O Jacob, / Your dwellings, O Israel"; 24:5). But when Balaam extends his description, the utopian vision fades, and the people become just like any other who seek domination over their foes. He concludes, "Blessed are they who bless you, / Accursed they who curse you!" (24:9). As in the beginning of this portion, the world is divided into two: those who seek to maintain power, and those who attempt to usurp it—the victors and the vanquished, the blessed and the cursed.

The concluding story of this portion (25:1–9) illustrates the tragedy of seeing the world dichotomized in this way. Exhausted from a journey that seems to have no end, the Israelite men forget who they are. They forget their privileged relationship with the One who brought them out of slavery.

*Let's move beyond the dichotomous thinking that blinded Balaam in this portion.*

Balaam's recognition of Israel's goodness has become part of our liturgy known as the *Mah tovu* (literally "how good are"): *Mah tovu ohalecha, Yaakov / mishk'notecha, Yisrael* ("How fair are your tents, O Jacob, / Your dwellings, O Israel!"). The Rabbis who created our liturgy recognized the power of this sentence, and so they intentionally positioned it as the opening of a daily prayer sequence that fixes the individual in the context of the community of Israel. They expand Balaam's blessing with four verses from Psalms written in the first person. In so doing, they enable each worshipper to claim a place as a member of the collective.

I, through Your abundant love, enter Your house;
I bow down in awe at Your holy temple (Psalm 5:8).
יהוה, I love Your temple abode,

The dwelling-place of Your glory (Psalm 26:8).
Let me bow down and kneel before God my maker (Psalm 95:6).
As for me, may my prayer come to You, O יהוה,
At a favorable moment;
O God, in Your abundant faithfulness,
Answer me with Your sure deliverance (Psalm 69:14).

With these phrases, the Rabbis transform Balaam's God of war into a God of *chesed* (loving-kindness), and each Jew who utters these words becomes the prayer. In the parashah, Balaam follows his original utterance of the verse with two descriptions of Israel: an Israel that lives in a lush and verdant world, and a nation that is victorious against enemies. But Balaam's utterance is also incomplete, which is why our liturgy expands it—and also shifts the focus to the relationship of the individual with God.

I propose a third reading, one that returns to the evocation of the community as a source of power and that extends it, connecting the people with God and with their unique challenge.

Consider the following combination of 24:5 with the words from the book of Isaiah:

How fair are your tents, O Jacob,
Your dwelling places, O Israel! (24:5)
I, the Holy One, have called you in righteousness,
and taken you by the hand.
I am the One who created you
and made you a covenant people,
a light to the nations:
to open eyes that are blind,
to bring the captive out of confinement (Isaiah 42:6–7).

This clear challenge invites us to move beyond the narrow, dichotomous thinking that blinded Balak and Balaam in this portion. These verses from Isaiah anticipate—and fulfill—the subsequent prophetic call about tents and dwellings: "Enlarge the space for your tent (*oholech*); / do not spare the canvas for your dwelling-place (*mishk'notayich*)" (Isaiah 54:2). Here the prophet urges Jerusalem—personified as a woman—to widen her tent with joy and make room for the multitudes who will enter the capital city. An expanded tent in a gracious and open city reflects the utopian and achievable goal of moving beyond oppositional concepts of native/stranger, friend/foe, chosen/rejected, male/female.

Are we ready to open our tents and our hearts to those who wish to dream—and then to build sacred communities that not only tolerate diversity and difference but also celebrate them? Can we move beyond narrow, divisive definitions and descriptions that are no longer useful? Might we transform our communities by welcoming those who come into our houses of worship with words that describe what our community can be? When our dwelling places become sanctuaries for all seekers of peace and justice, when our homes welcome all who no longer objectify the other, then we can truthfully declare, *Mah tovu*—how good, how fair, are our tents. —*Sue Levi Elwell*

## *Voices*

### *Balak*

Laurie Patton

*Numbers 22:21–35*

At eleven forty five
in the dark,
the dog whose eyes
are so fixed and steady
that I am daily convinced
of his next, human life

walked to the bottom shelf
of the back library,
and slowly pulled
at a small book
with his teeth—
Ted Hughes,
"Poetry in the Making,"
the chapter on writing
about animals.

With his paws,
he held down page fourteen,
"The Thought Fox":
a poem about a fox
who suddenly climbs
into the poet's head
at midnight.

I read between his paws:

*Till with the sudden sharp hot stink of fox*
*It enters the dark hole of the head*
*The window is starless still; the clock ticks,*
*The page is printed.*

And the dog looked up
amidst the snowy crumbs
of chewed paper

and that curtain—
that frustrating scrim
between animals like me
and the ones like him—
was lifted
in our startled gaze

"Yes, you *are*
the thought fox!"
I said to him,
"and yes, it is time
for you to be
inside my head!"

"And by the way,"
I went on,
"What other angels
have you been
falling in front of...

And what else
do I need to know
from their presence
in my road?"

He kept chewing
but did not answer.

## *from* Hidden Treasures

Yocheved Bat-Miriam (transl. Bernhard Frank)

*Numbers 23:11*

Just as you see me, that's how I am:
no eye-shadow, rouge; neither makeup nor
charm,
but barbaric, perverse, and extremely rude—
that's how I want to stand before you.

So and so many feet is the sum of my height,
so and so many years my lease on this earth.
An extra measure for my spirit's flight
when it bursts from its cage and wanders
without word.

And my chatter won't transport me to heaven,
a chatter turned stammer with sudden dismay.
I don't know how to address you, even,
I who am dying with each passing day.

With each passing day, like a dream's illusion
both land and sea still rise and shine,
as whitewashed highways from nought to
nothing
will tug at the azure of the sky and the brine.

## Fastening the Light of the Sabbath Candles

Rivka Miriam (transl. Linda Stern Zisquit)

*Numbers 24:5*

Fastening the light of the Sabbath candles
to my eyes, my palms are tents
where my fathers rested in the desert.
The light wraps itself to my eyes.
The light gathers into me.
When they wandered in the desert
the openings of their tents
were turned away from each other.
While they wandered in the desert their
openings
covered clouds. Sand and light mixed.
My fingers are brittle.
My hair is veiled.

## Untitled

Muriel Rukeyser

*Numbers 24:1–9*

On your journey you will come to a time of
waking.
The others may be asleep. Or you may be alone.

Immediacy of song moving the titled
Visions of children and the linking stars.

You will begin then to remember. You
Hear the voice relating after late listening.

You remember even falling asleep, or a dream
of sleep.
For now the song is given and you remember.

At every clear waking you have known this song,
The cities of this music identified

By the white springs of singing, and their
fountains
Reflected in windows, in all the human eyes.

The wishes, the need growing. The song growing.

## *Desolate Valley*

Rachel Luzzatto Morpurgo (transl. Nina Davis Salaman)

*Numbers 24:1–9*

From a distance, I look upon the eternal hills,
Their face covered with glorious flowers.
I rise high, as if on eagle's wings, to cast a
glance,
Raising my head to view the sun.
Heaven! How beautiful you stream forth,
Winds sweeping across your stage,
Revealing the place where freedom ever lives.
Who, who can express its sweetness!

## *from* Thistles

Esther Raab (transl. Harold Schimmel)

*Numbers 24:1–9*

My heart, homeland, is with your dews,
at night on fields of bramble,
and to the cypress's scent, and moist thistle,
I will extend a hidden wing.
Your paths are soft cradles of sand
atretching between acacia hedges,
as though on a surface of pure silk
I'll move forever upon them
held by some unfathomable charm,
and transparent skies whisper over
the dark—a frozen sea of trees.

## *Holy Quiet*

Malka Heifetz Tussman (transl. Marcia Falk)

*Numbers 24:1–7*

Quietly you utter
the word "quiet"
and already you have marred
the quiet.

I was in a holy quiet
only once.

Once—
Once I had an orchard—
apples, pears, cherries, plums,
and at the fringes, by the fences,
raspberries, gooseberries, currants,
and all kinds of flowers.

Summer dusk. Alone in my orchard.
A moment, an eternity:
the owl held back its poo-hoo,
the cuckoo forgot its cuckoo—
a wild berry by the path in the weeds
fixed in its gaze.
And I—
quiet multiplied by quiet—
did not interrupt my quiet prayer
with even a quiver
when the Shekhinah
kissed a leaf down from a pear tree,
carried it away,
and let it fall onto the brook
at the orchard's edge.

# פִּינְחָס ✦ *Pinchas*

NUMBERS 25:10–30:1

## *Legacy of Law, Leadership, and Land*

As their forty years' journey in the wilderness is coming to an end, the Israelites' focus shifts to final preparations for entering the Promised Land. It is a time of uncertainty in the face of transition. *Parashat Pinchas* (named after the priest known in English as Phinehas) describes actions and instructions for securing stability and continuity, with special attention to division of the land among the Israelite tribes. The setting is the plains of Moab, on the eastern side of the Jordan near Jericho (25:43), within view of the Promised Land. The opening verses conclude the disturbing incident of Baal-peor (25:1–9). After a census and the appointment of Moses' successor, the parashah ends with a lengthy account of the sacrificial offerings for various sacred occasions. The final words of the Torah portion affirm that Moses instructed Israel according to God's commands (30:1).

Five daring sisters—Mahlah, Noah, Hoglah, Milcah, and Tirzah, also known as Zelophehad's daughters—loom large in this Torah portion, and again later in Numbers 36 (and also Joshua 17). They brilliantly challenge the inheritance system (which has disenfranchised them) when they request a share in the land (27:1–11). They are so important that each of their names appears in every episode about them. In this episode these sisters succeed in securing a legacy for themselves, so that they, rather than their father's male relatives, will inherit his portion. But they do even more than that, something unique and extraordinary: they initiate a Torah law, a legal precept that becomes a legacy for future generations because what they ask for themselves becomes a law sanctioned by God. This case is important in showing (among other things) women who challenge community practices and who thereby bring significant modifications to existing legislation in order to meet changing social needs.

> *Five daring sisters loom large in this Torah portion.*

The resolution of their case is that brotherless daughters can inherit parental property. Thus, this new law preserves the integrity of family property in case only daughters are born to an Israelite couple. It also provides economic security to daughters who otherwise would depend on male relatives for sustenance.

A striking aspect of these stories about Mahlah, Noah, Hoglah, Milcah, and Tirzah concerns archeological information about territorial holdings in Israel during the monarchy. Two of these names—Noah and Hoglah—appear on ostraca (ancient clay fragments). The names seem to refer to areas of considerable size in northern Israel (see at 27:1–2).

Other fascinating women make cameo appearances as mother (Jochebed, 26:59), sister (Miriam, 26:59), or daughter; yet they are remembered mainly in relation to an important man. We find also the "dangerous" foreign woman (Cozbi; 25:15–18) and the mysterious Serah, who is named only to disappear without a story (26:46).

—*Tamara Cohn Eskenazi*

## Outline

*I.* THE LEGACY OF PRIESTLY LEADERSHIP
*Phinehas and the Covenant of Perpetual Priesthood* (25:10–18)

A. Phinehas's reward: permanent priestly leadership (vv. 10–13)

B. The culprits and their crime (vv. 14–18)

*II.* LEGACY OF LAND
*Census of a New Generation* (25:19–26:65)

A. The census of the Israelites (25:19–26:51)

B. Instructions about dividing the land (26:52–56)

C. The census of the Levites (26:57–62)

D. Conclusion of the census (26:63–65)

*III.* LEGACY AND LAND
*Mahlah, Noah, Hoglah, Milcah, and Tirzah* (27:1–11)

A. The setting (vv. 1–2)

B. The sisters' request: to inherit their father's land (vv. 3–4)

C. The results: the sisters receive the promise of land (vv. 5–11)

*IV.* LEGACY OF MOSAIC LEADERSHIP AND AUTHORITY
*Joshua Appointed as Successor* (27:12–23)

A. God prepares Moses for death (vv. 12–14)

B. Moses asks God to appoint a successor (vv. 15–17)

C. God selects Joshua as successor (vv. 18–21)

D. Conclusion: Moses commissions Joshua (vv. 22–23)

*V.* COMMUNAL LEGACY FOR CONTINUING RELATIONS WITH GOD
*Sacrificial Offerings* (28:1–30:1)

A. Introduction (28:1–3a)

B. List of occasions and offerings (28:3b–29:38)

C. Conclusion (29:39–30:1)

**יהוה** spoke to Moses, saying, [11]"Phinehas,
son of Eleazar son of Aaron the priest,
has turned back My wrath from the Israelites by
displaying among them his passion for Me, so that I
did not wipe out the Israelite people in My passion.
[12]Say, therefore, 'I grant him My pact of friendship.
[13]It shall be for him and his descendants after him a

כה 10 וַיְדַבֵּר יְהֹוָה אֶל־מֹשֶׁה לֵּאמֹר׃
11 פִּינְחָס בֶּן־אֶלְעָזָר בֶּן־אַהֲרֹן הַכֹּהֵן
הֵשִׁיב אֶת־חֲמָתִי מֵעַל בְּנֵי־יִשְׂרָאֵל בְּקַנְאוֹ
אֶת־קִנְאָתִי בְּתוֹכָם וְלֹא־כִלִּיתִי אֶת־בְּנֵי־
יִשְׂרָאֵל בְּקִנְאָתִי׃ 12 לָכֵן אֱמֹר הִנְנִי נֹתֵן לוֹ
אֶת־בְּרִיתִי שָׁלוֹם׃ 13 וְהָיְתָה לּוֹ וּלְזַרְעוֹ

## *The Legacy of Priestly Leadership*

### PHINEHAS AND THE COVENANT OF PERPETUAL PRIESTHOOD (25:10–18)

Although the five sisters Mahlah, Noah, Hoglah, Milcah, and Tirzah will feature prominently in this Torah portion, it begins with Phinehas (in Hebrew, *Pinchas*). It concludes the gruesome episode that took place in the previous parashah: Israel succumbed to the sin of idolatry, and Phinehas the priest—Aaron's grandson—responded by slaying a couple who had committed idolatry in front of the community. Now God rewards Phinehas. (For a different interpretation, see *Balak*, Another View, p. 954.)

This opening scene is disturbing for a number of reasons: first, because the new generation of Israelites falls prey to idolatry—and does so within view of the Promised Land; second, because Phinehas is rewarded for acting violently and without recourse to due process; and third, because women (albeit foreign) receive a disproportionate blame for the people's downfall.

### PHINEHAS'S REWARD: PERMANENT PRIESTLY LEADERSHIP (25:10–13)

God rewards Phinehas with hereditary priesthood, elevating him above other descendants of Aaron. Why? The reason seems to be Phinehas's swift and ruthless response to idolatry. Unlike his grandfather Aaron, who collaborated with idolators in the infamous case of the Golden Calf (see Exodus 32, especially vv. 5 and 21–25), Phinehas demonstrates unflinching loyalty to God. He thus restores the stature of priests as deserving mediators between Israel and God.

Although God had ordered death for all the ringleaders (25:4), Phinehas satisfies God's demand for punishment by the single act of slaying two leaders. He thereby causes less rather than more bloodshed.

*12. My pact of friendship.* Literally, "covenant of peace." In Numbers 6, God requires that the priests transmit blessings of peace. (See "And grant you peace" in the conclusion of the Priestly Benediction, 6:22–26.)

***13. for him and his descendants after him a pact of priesthood.*** According to later narratives,


▸ She lives among her kin and her land belongs to her—what a difference this makes!

ANOTHER VIEW ➤ *982*

▸ Serah bat Asher is among the nine persons who are said to have entered heaven alive.

POST-BIBLICAL INTERPRETATIONS ➤ *983*

▸ The sisters insist on change by engaging Israelite traditions effectively.

CONTEMPORARY REFLECTION ➤ *985*

▸ I know about the woman / who sits and waits . . . for her life / to begin. . . .

VOICES ➤ *987*

pact of priesthood for all time, because he took impassioned action for his God, thus making expiation for the Israelites.'"

[14]The name of the Israelite notable who was killed, the one who was killed with the Midianite woman, was Zimri son of Salu, chieftain of a Simeonite ancestral house. [15]The name of the Midianite woman who was killed was Cozbi daughter of Zur; he was the tribal head of an ancestral house in Midian.

[16]יהוה spoke to Moses, saying, [17]"Assail the Midianites and defeat them—[18]for they assailed you by the trickery they practiced against you—

אַחֲרָ֗יו בְּרִ֛ית כְּהֻנַּ֥ת עוֹלָ֖ם תַּ֣חַת אֲשֶׁ֣ר קִנֵּ֣א לֵֽאלֹהָ֔יו וַיְכַפֵּ֖ר עַל־בְּנֵ֥י יִשְׂרָאֵֽל׃

14 וְשֵׁם֩ אִ֨ישׁ יִשְׂרָאֵ֜ל הַמֻּכֶּ֗ה אֲשֶׁ֤ר הֻכָּה֙ אֶת־הַמִּדְיָנִ֔ית זִמְרִ֖י בֶּן־סָל֑וּא נְשִׂ֥יא בֵית־אָ֖ב לַשִּׁמְעֹנִֽי׃ 15 וְשֵׁ֨ם הָֽאִשָּׁ֧ה הַמֻּכָּ֛ה הַמִּדְיָנִ֖ית כׇּזְבִּ֣י בַת־צ֑וּר רֹ֣אשׁ אֻמּ֥וֹת בֵּֽית־אָ֛ב בְּמִדְיָ֖ן הֽוּא׃ פ

16 וַיְדַבֵּ֥ר יְהֹוָ֖ה אֶל־מֹשֶׁ֥ה לֵּאמֹֽר׃ 17 צָר֖וֹר אֶת־הַמִּדְיָנִ֑ים וְהִכִּיתֶ֖ם אוֹתָֽם׃ 18 כִּ֣י צֹרְרִ֥ים הֵ֛ם לָכֶ֖ם בְּנִכְלֵיהֶ֑ם אֲשֶׁר־נִכְּל֣וּ

---

Israel's chief priests descended from Phinehas rather than from Aaron's other descendants.

### THE CULPRITS AND THEIR CRIME (25:14–18)

For the first time, the narrator discloses the name and rank of Phinehas's victims: Zimri the Israelite man and Cozbi the Midianite woman. Their story articulates a theme that recurs in several biblical books: the potentially dangerous influence of foreign women.

In some cases, foreign women play a positive role, helping to ensure survival. The daughter of Pharaoh saves Moses (Exodus 2:5–10). Zipporah, Moses' Midianite wife, averts God's wrath by circumcising their son (Exodus 4:24–26). Rahab the harlot helps Israelite spies (Joshua 2). Jael saves the nation by killing its arch-enemy Sisera (Judges 4). Ruth the Moabite sustains Naomi and becomes an ancestress of King David (Ruth 4:17–22).

Elsewhere, however, women are blamed for leading Israelite men to idolatry. Thus the warning in Exodus 34:16: "And when you take wives from among their daughters for your sons, their daughters will lust after their gods and will cause your sons to lust after their gods." (See also Deuteronomy 7:4, which adds that God's anger will blaze, "promptly wiping you out.") In addition, I Kings

11:1–13 blames Solomon's fall from grace on his foreign wives, and I Kings 18 portrays Queen Jezebel, a Phoenician princess married to an Israelite king, as a major proponent of idolatry. Recognizing women's powerful influence on cultural and religious life, the Bible at certain junctures expresses anxiety over foreign women. The standard charge is idolatry, often cast in sexual terms. Women who keep their own religious traditions instead of Israel's seem to threaten the entire fabric of the nation. They possess the potential to lure their husbands and future generations away from fidelity to Israelite traditions. The danger is deemed acute in times of transition, when Israel's boundaries—social as well as political—are not clearly established, as here, when entering the land.

*14–15. Zimri ... Cozbi daughter of Zur ... tribal head.* Cozbi's name derives from a Hebrew root *k-z-b*, meaning "a lie" or "falsehood." Both Cozbi and Zimri come from leading families. In the previous Torah portion, responsibility for initiating this crisis had already been placed on women: "they," specifically the women (the verb is in feminine plural form), invited the people to offer sacrifices to "their" (again, feminine form) god (for details, see at 25:1–2). Here Cozbi receives the greater share of the blame. She is mentioned twice (see below); Zimri is mentioned only once.

because of the affair of Peor and because of the affair of their kinswoman Cozbi, daughter of the Midianite chieftain, who was killed at the time of the plague on account of Peor."

19 When the plague was over, 26 יהוה said to
Moses and to Eleazar son of Aaron the priest,
2 "Take a census of the whole Israelite company
[of fighters] from the age of twenty years up, by
their ancestral houses, all Israelite males able to bear
arms." 3 So Moses and Eleazar the priest, on the
steppes of Moab, at the Jordan near Jericho, gave

לָכֶם עַל־דְּבַר־פְּעוֹר וְעַל־דְּבַר כׇּזְבִּי בַת־
נְשִׂיא מִדְיָן אֲחֹתָם הַמֻּכָּה בְיוֹם־הַמַּגֵּפָה
עַל־דְּבַר־פְּעוֹר׃

19 וַיְהִי אַחֲרֵי הַמַּגֵּפָה פ כו וַיֹּאמֶר
יְהֹוָה אֶל־מֹשֶׁה וְאֶל אֶלְעָזָר בֶּן־אַהֲרֹן
הַכֹּהֵן לֵאמֹר׃ 2 שְׂאוּ אֶת־רֹאשׁ | כׇּל־עֲדַת
בְּנֵי־יִשְׂרָאֵל מִבֶּן עֶשְׂרִים שָׁנָה וָמַעְלָה
לְבֵית אֲבֹתָם כׇּל־יֹצֵא צָבָא בְּיִשְׂרָאֵל׃
3 וַיְדַבֵּר מֹשֶׁה וְאֶלְעָזָר הַכֹּהֵן אֹתָם

*18. because of the affair of . . . Cozbi.* She alone now represents the entire episode. This scandal becomes known as "the affair of Cozbi," not "the affair of Zimri," the Israelite man. The repetition of her name here, this time with no reference to Zimri, singles her out as the dominant symbol of this sinful event that will mar Israel's relations with the Midianites (see also 31:1–54).

***Peor.*** The site in Moab where these events took place, identified as Shittim in 25:1.

***their kinswoman.*** Literally, "their sister." In the census that follows, Miriam will be identified by the same Hebrew phrase (26:59; see there). The foreign woman as sister appears here as a source of death, whereas the Israelite sister remains a preserver of life.

***daughter of the Midianite chieftain.*** For Rashi, her pedigree teaches "the extent of the Midianites' hatred, who went so far as to prostitute a king's daughter in order to bring Israel into sin." His interpretation thus shifts some blame away from Cozbi to her family.

## *Legacy of Land*

### CENSUS OF A NEW GENERATION (25:19–26:65)

The list of the men reared in the wilderness and those destined to inherit the Promised Land links the past with the future to establish continuity. The census identifies those who survived the journey (and the recent debacle at Peor), as well as the men whose households will receive land. The order follows the earlier list of those who began the journey in Numbers 1. One generation is passing; its children now stand ready to carry on. If Numbers 1 is an "exit poll," this census is an "entrance poll."

### THE CENSUS OF THE ISRAELITES (25:19–26:51)

The tribes bear the names of Jacob's twelve sons by different mothers, though none of the matriarchs is mentioned. Most of the individual heads of households named here are otherwise unknown. The significance of the order of the list is not self-evident beyond its parallel to Numbers 1. About the names of the tribes as given by Leah and Rachel to their sons, see at Genesis 29–30.

The list of men is interrupted only rarely. The mention of Serah, daughter of Asher (26:46) and of Jochebed and Miriam (26:59) are two such occasions.

***26:3. steppes of Moab.*** This is the last stop before entering Canaan; this area, also called the plains of Moab, is located on the eastern side of the Jordan River.

instructions about them, namely, 4 those from twenty years up, as יהוה had commanded Moses.

The [eligible male] descendants of the Israelites who came out of the land of Egypt were:

5 Reuben, Israel's first-born. Descendants of Reuben: [Of] Enoch, the clan of the Enochites; of Pallu, the clan of the Palluites; 6 of Hezron, the clan of the Hezronites; of Carmi, the clan of the Carmites. 7 Those are the clans of the Reubenites. The men enrolled came to 43,730.

8 Born to Pallu: Eliab. 9 The sons of Eliab were Nemuel, and Dathan and Abiram. These are the same Dathan and Abiram, chosen in the assembly, who agitated against Moses and Aaron as part of Korah's band when they agitated against יהוה. 10 Whereupon the earth opened its mouth and swallowed them up with Korah—when that band died, when the fire consumed the two hundred and fifty representatives—and they became an example. 11 The sons of Korah, however, did not die.

12 Descendants of Simeon by their clans: Of Nemuel, the clan of the Nemuelites; of Jamin, the clan of the Jaminites; of Jachin, the clan of the Jachinites; 13 of Zerah, the clan of the Zerahites; of Saul, the clan of the Saulites. 14 Those are the clans of the Simeonites; [men enrolled:] 22,200.

15 Descendants of Gad by their clans: Of Zephon, the clan of the Zephonites; of Haggi, the clan of the Haggites; of Shuni, the clan of the Shunites; 16 of Ozni, the clan of the Oznites; of Eri, the clan of the Erites; 17 of Arod, the clan of the Arodites; of Areli, the clan of the Arelites. 18 Those are the clans of Gad's descendants; men enrolled: 40,500.

בְּעַרְבֹת מוֹאָב עַל־יַרְדֵּן יְרֵחוֹ לֵאמֹר׃ 4 מִבֶּן
עֶשְׂרִים שָׁנָה וָמָעְלָה כַּאֲשֶׁר צִוָּה יְהֹוָה
אֶת־מֹשֶׁה
וּבְנֵי יִשְׂרָאֵל הַיֹּצְאִים מֵאֶרֶץ מִצְרָיִם׃
5 רְאוּבֵן בְּכוֹר יִשְׂרָאֵל בְּנֵי רְאוּבֵן חֲנוֹךְ
מִשְׁפַּחַת הַחֲנֹכִי לְפַלּוּא מִשְׁפַּחַת הַפַּלֻּאִי׃
6 לְחֶצְרֹן מִשְׁפַּחַת הַחֶצְרוֹנִי לְכַרְמִי
מִשְׁפַּחַת הַכַּרְמִי׃ 7 אֵלֶּה מִשְׁפְּחֹת
הָראוּבֵנִי וַיִּהְיוּ פְקֻדֵיהֶם שְׁלֹשָׁה וְאַרְבָּעִים
אֶלֶף וּשְׁבַע מֵאוֹת וּשְׁלֹשִׁים׃
8 וּבְנֵי פַלּוּא אֱלִיאָב׃ 9 וּבְנֵי אֱלִיאָב נְמוּאֵל
וְדָתָן וַאֲבִירָם הוּא־דָתָן וַאֲבִירָם קרואי
קְרִיאֵי הָעֵדָה אֲשֶׁר הִצּוּ עַל־מֹשֶׁה וְעַל־
אַהֲרֹן בַּעֲדַת־קֹרַח בְּהַצֹּתָם עַל־יְהֹוָה׃
10 וַתִּפְתַּח הָאָרֶץ אֶת־פִּיהָ וַתִּבְלַע אֹתָם
וְאֶת־קֹרַח בְּמוֹת הָעֵדָה בַּאֲכֹל הָאֵשׁ אֵת
חֲמִשִּׁים וּמָאתַיִם אִישׁ וַיִּהְיוּ לְנֵס׃ 11 וּבְנֵי־
קֹרַח לֹא־מֵתוּ׃ ס
12 בְּנֵי שִׁמְעוֹן לְמִשְׁפְּחֹתָם לִנְמוּאֵל
מִשְׁפַּחַת הַנְּמוּאֵלִי לְיָמִין מִשְׁפַּחַת הַיָּמִינִי
לְיָכִין מִשְׁפַּחַת הַיָּכִינִי׃ 13 לְזֶרַח מִשְׁפַּחַת
הַזַּרְחִי לְשָׁאוּל מִשְׁפַּחַת הַשָּׁאוּלִי׃ 14 אֵלֶּה
מִשְׁפְּחֹת הַשִּׁמְעֹנִי שְׁנַיִם וְעֶשְׂרִים אֶלֶף
וּמָאתָיִם׃ ס
15 בְּנֵי גָד לְמִשְׁפְּחֹתָם לִצְפוֹן מִשְׁפַּחַת
הַצְּפוֹנִי לְחַגִּי מִשְׁפַּחַת הַחַגִּי לְשׁוּנִי
מִשְׁפַּחַת הַשּׁוּנִי׃ 16 לְאָזְנִי מִשְׁפַּחַת הָאָזְנִי
לְעֵרִי מִשְׁפַּחַת הָעֵרִי׃ 17 לַאֲרוֹד מִשְׁפַּחַת
הָאֲרוֹדִי לְאַרְאֵלִי מִשְׁפַּחַת הָאַרְאֵלִי׃
18 אֵלֶּה מִשְׁפְּחֹת בְּנֵי־גָד לִפְקֻדֵיהֶם
אַרְבָּעִים אֶלֶף וַחֲמֵשׁ מֵאוֹת׃ ס

*5.* ***Reuben.*** Leah's first-born (Genesis 29:32).

*9.* For the revolt of Korach, Dathan, and Abiram, see Numbers 16.

*11.* ***sons of Korah.*** Presumably they did not participate in the rebellion, which indicates that punishment is limited to actual offenders, not to the entire family.

*12.* ***Simeon.*** Leah's second son (Genesis 29:33).

*15.* ***Gad.*** Zilpah's (Leah's handmaid's) first-born (Genesis 30:10–11).

19Born to Judah: Er and Onan. Er and Onan
died in the land of Canaan.

20Descendants of Judah by their clans: Of
Shelah, the clan of the Shelanites; of Perez, the clan
of the Perezites; of Zerah, the clan of the Zerahites.
21Descendants of Perez: of Hezron, the clan of the
Hezronites; of Hamul, the clan of the Hamulites.
22Those are the clans of Judah; men enrolled:
76,500.

23Descendants of Issachar by their clans: [Of]
Tola, the clan of the Tolaites; of Puvah, the clan of
the Punites; 24of Jashub, the clan of the Jashubites;
of Shimron, the clan of the Shimronites. 25Those
are the clans of Issachar; men enrolled: 64,300.

26Descendants of Zebulun by their clans: Of
Sered, the clan of the Seredites; of Elon, the clan of
the Elonites; of Jahleel, the clan of the Jahleelites.
27Those are the clans of the Zebulunites; men enrolled: 60,500.

28The sons of Joseph were Manasseh and
Ephraim—by their clans.

29Descendants of Manasseh: Of Machir, the
clan of the Machirites.—Machir begot Gilead.—
Of Gilead, the clan of the Gileadites. 30These were
the descendants of Gilead: [Of] Iezer, the clan of
the Iezerites; of Helek, the clan of the Helekites;
31[of] Asriel, the clan of the Asrielites; [of]
Shechem, the clan of the Shechemites; 32[of]
Shemida, the clan of the Shemidaites; [of] Hepher,

19 בְּנֵי יְהוּדָה עֵר וְאוֹנָן וַיָּמָת עֵר וְאוֹנָן
בְּאֶרֶץ כְּנָעַן׃
20 וַיִּהְיוּ בְנֵי־יְהוּדָה לְמִשְׁפְּחֹתָם לְשֵׁלָה
מִשְׁפַּחַת הַשֵּׁלָנִי לְפֶרֶץ מִשְׁפַּחַת הַפַּרְצִי
לְזֶרַח מִשְׁפַּחַת הַזַּרְחִי׃ 21 וַיִּהְיוּ בְנֵי־פֶרֶץ
לְחֶצְרֹן מִשְׁפַּחַת הַחֶצְרֹנִי לְחָמוּל מִשְׁפַּחַת
הֶחָמוּלִי׃ 22 אֵלֶּה מִשְׁפְּחֹת יְהוּדָה
לִפְקֻדֵיהֶם שִׁשָּׁה וְשִׁבְעִים אֶלֶף וַחֲמֵשׁ
מֵאוֹת׃ ס
23 בְּנֵי ישׂשכר יִשָּׂשכָר לְמִשְׁפְּחֹתָם תּוֹלָע
מִשְׁפַּחַת הַתּוֹלָעִי לְפֻוָּה מִשְׁפַּחַת הַפּוּנִי׃
24 לְיָשׁוּב מִשְׁפַּחַת הַיָּשֻׁבִי לְשִׁמְרֹן
מִשְׁפַּחַת הַשִּׁמְרֹנִי׃ 25 אֵלֶּה מִשְׁפְּחֹת
ישׂשכר יִשָּׂשכָר לִפְקֻדֵיהֶם אַרְבָּעָה וְשִׁשִּׁים
אֶלֶף וּשְׁלֹשׁ מֵאוֹת׃ ס
26 בְּנֵי זְבוּלֻן לְמִשְׁפְּחֹתָם לְסֶרֶד מִשְׁפַּחַת
הַסַּרְדִּי לְאֵלוֹן מִשְׁפַּחַת הָאֵלֹנִי לְיַחְלְאֵל
מִשְׁפַּחַת הַיַּחְלְאֵלִי׃ 27 אֵלֶּה מִשְׁפְּחֹת
הַזְּבוּלֹנִי לִפְקֻדֵיהֶם שִׁשִּׁים אֶלֶף וַחֲמֵשׁ
מֵאוֹת׃ ס
28 בְּנֵי יוֹסֵף לְמִשְׁפְּחֹתָם מְנַשֶּׁה וְאֶפְרָיִם׃
29 בְּנֵי מְנַשֶּׁה לְמָכִיר מִשְׁפַּחַת הַמָּכִירִי
וּמָכִיר הוֹלִיד אֶת־גִּלְעָד לְגִלְעָד מִשְׁפַּחַת
הַגִּלְעָדִי׃ 30 אֵלֶּה בְּנֵי גִלְעָד אִיעֶזֶר
מִשְׁפַּחַת הָאִיעֶזְרִי לְחֵלֶק מִשְׁפַּחַת
הַחֶלְקִי׃ 31 וְאַשְׂרִיאֵל מִשְׁפַּחַת הָאַשְׂרִאֵלִי
וְשֶׁכֶם מִשְׁפַּחַת הַשִּׁכְמִי׃ 32 וּשְׁמִידָע
מִשְׁפַּחַת הַשְּׁמִידָעִי וְחֵפֶר מִשְׁפַּחַת

*19. Judah.* Leah's fourth son (Genesis 29:35). His son Er died while married to Tamar. His son Onan was killed by God because he violated his familial responsibilities toward Tamar (see Genesis 38).

*20. Perez... Zerah.* Judah and Tamar's twin sons (see Genesis 38).

*23. Issachar.* Leah's fifth son (Genesis 30:18).

*26. Zebulun.* Leah's sixth son (Genesis 30:19–20).

*28. Joseph.* Rachel's first-born (Genesis 30:22–24). His two sons with Asenath, an Egyptian woman, are privileged to become heads of individual tribes, presumably because of Jacob's love for Rachel (Genesis 41:50–52; 48:12–21).

the clan of the Hepherites.—[33]Now Zelophehad
son of Hepher had no sons, only daughters. The
names of Zelophehad's daughters were Mahlah,
Noah, Hoglah, Milcah, and Tirzah.—[34]Those are
the clans of Manasseh; men enrolled: 52,700.
[35]These are the descendants of Ephraim by their
clans: Of Shuthelah, the clan of the Shuthelahites;
of Becher, the clan of the Becherites; of Tahan, the
clan of the Tahanites. [36]These are the descendants
of Shuthelah: Of Eran, the clan of the Eranites.
[37]Those are the clans of Ephraim's descendants;
men enrolled: 32,500.

Those are the descendants of Joseph by their
clans.

[38]The descendants of Benjamin by their clans:
Of Bela, the clan of the Belaites; of Ashbel, the clan
of the Ashbelites; of Ahiram, the clan of the Ahi-
ramites; [39]of Shephupham, the clan of the Shupha-
mites; of Hupham, the clan of the Huphamites.
[40]The sons of Bela were Ard and Naaman: [Of
Ard,] the clan of the Ardites; of Naaman, the clan
of the Naamanites. [41]Those are the descendants of
Benjamin by their clans; men enrolled: 45,600.
[42]These are the descendants of Dan by their
clans: Of Shuham, the clan of the Shuhamites.
Those are the clans of Dan, by their clans. [43]All the
clans of the Shuhamites; men enrolled: 64,400.
[44]Descendants of Asher by their clans: Of
Imnah, the clan of the Imnites; of Ishvi, the clan
of the Ishvites; of Beriah, the clan of the Beriites.
[45]Of the descendants of Beriah: Of Heber, the clan
of the Heberites; of Malchiel, the clan of the

הַֽחֶפְרִֽי׃ 33 וּצְלָפְחָד֙ בֶּן־חֵ֔פֶר לֹא־הָ֥יוּ ל֛וֹ
בָּנִ֖ים כִּ֣י אִם־בָּנ֑וֹת וְשֵׁם֙ בְּנ֣וֹת צְלָפְחָ֔ד
מַחְלָ֣ה וְנֹעָ֔ה חָגְלָ֥ה מִלְכָּ֖ה וְתִרְצָֽה׃ 34 אֵ֖לֶּה
מִשְׁפְּחֹ֣ת מְנַשֶּׁ֑ה וּפְקֻדֵיהֶ֕ם שְׁנַ֧יִם וַחֲמִשִּׁ֛ים
אֶ֖לֶף וּשְׁבַ֥ע מֵאֽוֹת׃ ס
35 אֵ֣לֶּה בְנֵֽי־אֶפְרַיִם֮ לְמִשְׁפְּחֹתָם֒ לְשׁוּתֶ֗לַח
מִשְׁפַּ֙חַת֙ הַשֻּׁ֣תַלְחִ֔י לְבֶ֕כֶר מִשְׁפַּ֖חַת הַבַּכְרִ֑י
לְתַ֕חַן מִשְׁפַּ֖חַת הַתַּחֲנִֽי׃ 36 וְאֵ֖לֶּה בְּנֵ֣י
שׁוּתָ֑לַח לְעֵרָ֕ן מִשְׁפַּ֖חַת הָעֵרָנִֽי׃ 37 אֵ֣לֶּה
מִשְׁפְּחֹ֤ת בְּנֵֽי־אֶפְרַ֙יִם֙ לִפְקֻדֵיהֶ֔ם שְׁנַ֛יִם
וּשְׁלֹשִׁ֥ים אֶ֖לֶף וַחֲמֵ֣שׁ מֵא֑וֹת
אֵ֥לֶּה בְנֵֽי־יוֹסֵ֖ף לְמִשְׁפְּחֹתָֽם׃ ס
38 בְּנֵ֣י בִנְיָמִן֮ לְמִשְׁפְּחֹתָם֒ לְבֶ֗לַע מִשְׁפַּ֙חַת֙
הַבַּלְעִ֔י לְאַשְׁבֵּ֕ל מִשְׁפַּ֖חַת הָאַשְׁבֵּלִ֑י
לַאֲחִירָ֕ם מִשְׁפַּ֖חַת הָאֲחִירָמִֽי׃ 39 לִשְׁפוּפָ֕ם
מִשְׁפַּ֖חַת הַשּֽׁוּפָמִ֑י לְחוּפָ֕ם מִשְׁפַּ֖חַת
הַחוּפָמִֽי׃ 40 וַיִּהְי֥וּ בְנֵי־בֶ֖לַע אַ֣רְדְּ וְנַעֲמָ֑ן
מִשְׁפַּ֙חַת֙ הָֽאַרְדִּ֔י לְנַעֲמָ֕ן מִשְׁפַּ֖חַת הַנַּעֲמִֽי׃
41 אֵ֥לֶּה בְנֵֽי־בִנְיָמִ֖ן לְמִשְׁפְּחֹתָ֑ם וּפְקֻדֵיהֶ֗ם
חֲמִשָּׁ֧ה וְאַרְבָּעִ֛ים אֶ֖לֶף וְשֵׁ֥שׁ מֵאֽוֹת׃ ס
42 אֵ֤לֶּה בְנֵי־דָן֙ לְמִשְׁפְּחֹתָ֔ם לְשׁוּחָ֕ם
מִשְׁפַּ֖חַת הַשּׁוּחָמִ֑י אֵ֛לֶּה מִשְׁפְּחֹ֥ת דָּ֖ן
לְמִשְׁפְּחֹתָֽם׃ 43 כָּל־מִשְׁפְּחֹ֥ת הַשּׁוּחָמִ֖י
לִפְקֻדֵיהֶ֑ם אַרְבָּעָ֧ה וְשִׁשִּׁ֛ים אֶ֖לֶף וְאַרְבַּ֥ע
מֵאֽוֹת׃ ס
44 בְּנֵ֣י אָשֵׁר֮ לְמִשְׁפְּחֹתָם֒ לְיִמְנָ֗ה מִשְׁפַּ֙חַת֙
הַיִּמְנָ֔ה לְיִשְׁוִ֕י מִשְׁפַּ֖חַת הַיִּשְׁוִ֑י לִבְרִיעָ֕ה
מִשְׁפַּ֖חַת הַבְּרִיעִֽי׃ 45 לִבְנֵ֣י בְרִיעָ֔ה לְחֶ֕בֶר
מִשְׁפַּ֖חַת הַֽחֶבְרִ֑י לְמַ֨לְכִּיאֵ֔ל מִשְׁפַּ֖חַת

*33. The names of Zelophehad's daughters were Mahlah, Noah, Hoglah, Milcah, and Tirzah.* These influential five daughters are named four times in the Bible (see Numbers 27:1, 36:11; Joshua 17:3). For their important story, see at 27:1–11.

*38. Benjamin.* Rachel's second and last son. She dies in childbirth (Genesis 35:16–20).

*42. Dan.* Bilhah's (Rachel's handmaid's) first-born (Genesis 30:6).

*44. Asher.* Zilpah's second son (Genesis 30:13).

Malchielites.—[46]The name of Asher's daughter was Serah.—[47]These are the clans of Asher's descendants; men enrolled: 53,400.

[48]Descendants of Naphtali by their clans: Of Jahzeel, the clan of the Jahzeelites; of Guni, the clan of the Gunites; [49]of Jezer, the clan of the Jezerites; of Shillem, the clan of the Shillemites. [50]Those are the clans of the Naphtalites, clan by clan; men enrolled: 45,400.

[51]This is the enrollment of the Israelite men: 601,730.

[52]יהוה spoke to Moses, saying, [53]"Among these shall the land be apportioned as shares, according to the listed names: [54]with larger groups increase the share, with smaller groups reduce the share. Each is to be assigned its share according to its enrollment. [55]The land, moreover, is to be apportioned by lot; and the allotment shall be made according to the listings of their ancestral tribes. [56]Each portion shall be assigned by lot, whether for larger or smaller groups."

[57]This is the enrollment of the Levites by their clans: Of Gershon, the clan of the Gershonites; of Kohath, the clan of the Kohathites; of Merari, the clan of the Merarites. [58]These are the clans of Levi: The clan of the Libnites, the clan of the Hebron-

הַמַּלְכִּיאֵלִֽי׃ 46 וְשֵׁ֥ם בַּת־אָשֵׁ֖ר שָֽׂרַח׃
47 אֵ֛לֶּה מִשְׁפְּחֹ֥ת בְּנֵֽי־אָשֵׁ֖ר לִפְקֻדֵיהֶ֑ם
שְׁלֹשָׁ֧ה וַחֲמִשִּׁ֛ים אֶ֖לֶף וְאַרְבַּ֥ע מֵאֽוֹת׃ ס
48 בְּנֵ֤י נַפְתָּלִי֙ לְמִשְׁפְּחֹתָ֔ם לְיַ֨חְצְאֵ֔ל
מִשְׁפַּ֖חַת הַיַּחְצְאֵלִ֑י לְגוּנִ֕י מִשְׁפַּ֖חַת הַגּוּנִֽי׃
49 לְיֵ֕צֶר מִשְׁפַּ֖חַת הַיִּצְרִ֑י לְשִׁלֵּ֕ם מִשְׁפַּ֖חַת
הַשִּׁלֵּמִֽי׃ 50 אֵ֛לֶּה מִשְׁפְּחֹ֥ת נַפְתָּלִ֖י
לְמִשְׁפְּחֹתָ֑ם וּפְקֻדֵיהֶ֗ם חֲמִשָּׁ֤ה וְאַרְבָּעִים֙
אֶ֔לֶף וְאַרְבַּ֖ע מֵאֽוֹת׃
51 אֵ֗לֶּה פְּקוּדֵי֙ בְּנֵ֣י יִשְׂרָאֵ֔ל שֵׁשׁ־מֵא֥וֹת אֶ֖לֶף
וָאָ֑לֶף שְׁבַ֥ע מֵא֖וֹת וּשְׁלֹשִֽׁים׃ פ
52 וַיְדַבֵּ֥ר יְהוָ֖ה אֶל־מֹשֶׁ֥ה לֵּאמֹֽר׃ 53 לָאֵ֗לֶּה
תֵּחָלֵ֥ק הָאָ֛רֶץ בְּנַחֲלָ֖ה בְּמִסְפַּ֥ר שֵׁמֽוֹת׃
54 לָרַ֗ב תַּרְבֶּה֙ נַחֲלָת֔וֹ וְלַמְעַ֖ט תַּמְעִ֣יט
נַחֲלָת֑וֹ אִ֚ישׁ לְפִ֣י פְקֻדָ֔יו יֻתַּ֖ן נַחֲלָתֽוֹ׃
55 אַךְ־בְּגוֹרָ֕ל יֵחָלֵ֖ק אֶת־הָאָ֑רֶץ לִשְׁמ֥וֹת
מַטּוֹת־אֲבֹתָ֖ם יִנְחָֽלוּ׃ 56 עַל־פִּי֙ הַגּוֹרָ֔ל
תֵּחָלֵ֖ק נַחֲלָת֑וֹ בֵּ֥ין רַ֖ב לִמְעָֽט׃ ס
57 וְאֵ֨לֶּה פְקוּדֵ֣י הַלֵּוִי֮ לְמִשְׁפְּחֹתָם֒ לְגֵרְשׁ֕וֹן
מִשְׁפַּ֙חַת֙ הַגֵּ֣רְשֻׁנִּ֔י לִקְהָ֕ת מִשְׁפַּ֖חַת הַקְּהָתִ֑י
לִמְרָרִ֕י מִשְׁפַּ֖חַת הַמְּרָרִֽי׃ 58 אֵ֣לֶּה ׀ מִשְׁפְּחֹ֣ת
לֵוִ֗י מִשְׁפַּ֨חַת הַלִּבְנִ֜י מִשְׁפַּ֤חַת הַחֶבְרֹנִי֙

*46. Asher's daughter was Serah.* The inexplicable mention of Serah here (and in Genesis 46:17 and I Chronicles 7:30) implies that she played an important role in Israel's memory. However, the Torah does not preserve her story. Rabbinic traditions elaborate on her importance (see Post-biblical Interpretations, p. 983).

*48. Naphtali.* Bilhah's second son (Genesis 30:8).

*51. Israelite men: 601,730.* The number of able-bodied men who enter the land is slightly larger than the number who left Egypt. Compare with the traditional 600,000 for the generation that stood at Sinai (on the symbolic nature of these numbers, see at Exodus 12:37).

## INSTRUCTIONS ABOUT DIVIDING THE LAND (26:52–56)

Two sets of criteria determine the distribution of land: the size of apportioned land depends on tribal size; the location depends on casting lots.

## THE CENSUS OF THE LEVITES (26:57–62)

Since Levites do not inherit land (26:62) but instead live in the midst of the other tribes (see at 3:1–46), their list is separate and forms the conclusion of the census. The family of Moses—though not Moses himself—receives special attention, highlighting Jochebed and Miriam.

ites, the clan of the Mahlites, the clan of the Mushites, the clan of the Korahites.—Kohath begot Amram. <sup>59</sup>The name of Amram's wife was Jochebed daughter of Levi, who was born to Levi in Egypt; she bore to Amram Aaron and Moses and their sister Miriam. <sup>60</sup>To Aaron were born Nadab and Abihu, Eleazar and Ithamar. <sup>61</sup>Nadab and Abihu died when they offered alien fire before יהוה.—<sup>62</sup>Their enrollment of 23,000 comprised all males from a month up. They were not part of the regular enrollment of the Israelites, since no share was assigned to them among the Israelites.

<sup>63</sup>These are the males enrolled by Moses and Eleazar the priest who registered the Israelites on the steppes of Moab, at the Jordan near Jericho. <sup>64</sup>Among these there was not one of those enrolled by Moses and Aaron the priest when they recorded the Israelites in the wilderness of Sinai. <sup>65</sup>For יהוה had said of them, "They shall die in the wilder-

מִשְׁפַּ֣חַת הַמַּחְלִ֔י מִשְׁפַּ֖חַת הַמּוּשִׁ֑י מִשְׁפַּ֖חַת הַקָּרְחִ֑י וּקְהָ֖ת הוֹלִ֥ד אֶת־עַמְרָֽם׃ 59 וְשֵׁ֣ם ׀ אֵ֣שֶׁת עַמְרָ֗ם יוֹכֶ֙בֶד֙ בַּת־לֵוִ֔י אֲשֶׁ֨ר יָלְדָ֥ה אֹתָ֛הּ לְלֵוִ֖י בְּמִצְרָ֑יִם וַתֵּ֣לֶד לְעַמְרָ֗ם אֶֽת־אַהֲרֹן֙ וְאֶת־מֹשֶׁ֔ה וְאֵ֖ת מִרְיָ֥ם אֲחֹתָֽם׃ 60 וַיִּוָּלֵ֣ד לְאַהֲרֹ֔ן אֶת־נָדָ֖ב וְאֶת־אֲבִיה֑וּא אֶת־אֶלְעָזָ֖ר וְאֶת־אִיתָמָֽר׃ 61 וַיָּ֥מׇת נָדָ֖ב וַאֲבִיה֑וּא בְּהַקְרִיבָ֥ם אֵשׁ־זָרָ֖ה לִפְנֵ֥י יְהֹוָֽה׃ 62 וַיִּהְי֣וּ פְקֻדֵיהֶ֗ם שְׁלֹשָׁ֤ה וְעֶשְׂרִים֙ אֶ֔לֶף כׇּל־זָכָ֖ר מִבֶּן־חֹ֣דֶשׁ וָמָ֑עְלָה כִּ֣י ׀ לֹ֣א הׇתְפָּ֗קְדוּ בְּתוֹךְ֙ בְּנֵ֣י יִשְׂרָאֵ֔ל כִּ֠י לֹא־נִתַּ֤ן לָהֶם֙ נַחֲלָ֔ה בְּת֖וֹךְ בְּנֵ֥י יִשְׂרָאֵֽל׃

63 אֵ֚לֶּה פְּקוּדֵ֣י מֹשֶׁ֔ה וְאֶלְעָזָ֖ר הַכֹּהֵ֑ן אֲשֶׁ֨ר פָּ֣קְד֜וּ אֶת־בְּנֵ֤י יִשְׂרָאֵל֙ בְּעַֽרְבֹ֣ת מוֹאָ֔ב עַ֖ל יַרְדֵּ֥ן יְרֵחֽוֹ׃ 64 וּבְאֵ֙לֶּה֙ לֹא־הָ֣יָה אִ֔ישׁ מִפְּקוּדֵ֣י מֹשֶׁ֔ה וְאַהֲרֹ֖ן הַכֹּהֵ֑ן אֲשֶׁ֥ר פָּקְד֛וּ אֶת־בְּנֵ֥י יִשְׂרָאֵ֖ל בְּמִדְבַּ֥ר סִינָֽי׃ 65 כִּֽי־אָמַ֤ר יְהֹוָה֙ לָהֶ֔ם מ֥וֹת יָמֻ֖תוּ בַּמִּדְבָּ֑ר וְלֹא־נוֹתַ֤ר

---

*59.* In this verse, emphasis falls on the women's family positions: Jochebed as wife and mother, and Miriam as a daughter as well as "their sister." In this census, the constellation of birth references is unique. The text records Jochebed's own birth, itself an unusual detail. Obviously all the persons named in the census list have mothers, but the reference here emphasizes that these particular family events are not merely personal but of national consequence. The brief references suggest, in telegraphic fashion, that it is precisely their actions as mother and sister that matter for the life of Israel. One thereby remembers the wife, Jochebed, who not only bore a child but took exceptional risks to protect him, and Miriam the sister who supervised his rescue and reconnected him with his mother (Exodus 2).

*their sister Miriam.* For the first time Miriam is explicitly named as Moses' sister. Exodus 2 referred only to an unnamed sister of Moses; but the genealogy of Moses and Aaron in Exodus 6 did not include her. While Exodus 15:20 identified her as "Miriam the prophet, Aaron's sister," her relation to either man is not noted in Numbers 12—where she and Aaron challenge Moses—nor in her death notice in Numbers 20:1. Only here, perhaps as a way of tying up loose ends, is she specifically identified as the sister of both men. Indeed, the list departs from standard form to provide this information. In contrast to Cozbi (see at 25:18), who appears as an agent of danger and death, Miriam is an instrument of life. (See further at Numbers 20:1.)

## CONCLUSION OF THE CENSUS (26:63–65)

God has condemned the generation of the Exodus to die in the wilderness because of disobedience but has spared Caleb and Joshua.

ness." Not one of them survived, except Caleb son of Jephunneh and Joshua son of Nun.

27 The daughters of Zelophehad, of Manassite family—son of Hepher son of Gilead son of Machir son of Manasseh son of Joseph—came for-

מֵהֶם֙ אִ֔ישׁ כִּ֚י אִם־כָּלֵ֣ב בֶּן־יְפֻנֶּ֔ה וִיהוֹשֻׁ֖עַ
בִּן־נֽוּן׃ ס

כז וַתִּקְרַ֜בְנָה בְּנ֣וֹת צְלָפְחָ֗ד בֶּן־חֵ֙פֶר֙ בֶּן־
גִּלְעָ֔ד בֶּן־מָכִ֣יר בֶּן־מְנַשֶּׁ֔ה לְמִשְׁפְּחֹ֖ת מְנַשֶּׁ֣ה

## *Legacy and Land*

### MAHLAH, NOAH, HOGLAH, MILCAH, AND TIRZAH (27:1–11)

The story of Zelophehad's daughters appears in three different places in the Bible (Numbers 27 and 36; Joshua 17) and concerns itself with providing land for five remarkable daughters who, as sisters, always appear together. So important are they that their names are repeated in full in each episode. The fact that they receive so much "press" in the Bible is itself proof of their significance. But it takes attention to details to appreciate fully their accomplishments.

In the Torah, the story of Zelophehad's daughters depicts a two-part reformulation of a law, enabling daughters to inherit land (Numbers 27 and 36). In the first part, the daughters receive a promise of land; in the second, the law concerning the land is amended (see at Numbers 36). Finally, Joshua and other leaders then implement the law (at the sisters' request) in Joshua 17, and the women take possession of their land.

One notes two striking features of the story. First, disenfranchised women successfully confront an unjust system and propose a more equitable law. Second, God approves of their proposal and formulates it as a new law, one that enables other women as well to inherit land in certain circumstances. As unmarried women whose father had died, the five daughters represent the least powerful members of the community. Yet they dare challenge the tradition and call for change when the tradition is unjust. In the end, their proposal becomes God's Torah. Rashi notes this dramatic development when he explicitly attributes this new Torah to the women. Their law, he says, "deserved to have been written by Moses"; but the women were worthy and hence "it was written by them."

The story matters for other weighty reasons as well: it offers crucial information about land rights and kinship structures, as well as about the roles and status of women; it provides a rare opportunity for seeing how the legal process was perceived in biblical Israel. Thus the implications of the story extend beyond concern with the women in question. But the fact that the women in the Torah initiate this particular process and even the law itself, makes their story extraordinary.

Only three other cases in the entire Torah describe a legislative process in action: the cases of (*1*) the blasphemer (Leviticus 24:10–22); (*2*) those impure for the passover sacrifice (Numbers 9:6–14); and (*3*) the Shabbat violator (15:32–36). These three narratives describe procedural debates about applying already existing laws. But only the case of the five sisters shows a law actually being created, not merely applied. Moreover, this law is first proposed by people and only then confirmed, approved and extended by God as Torah. What perhaps makes this story most extraordinary and crucially important is that the people who create this Torah teaching are five women: Mahlah, Noah, Hoglah, Milcah, and Tirzah.

### THE SETTING (27:1–2)

The event takes place at the entrance of the Tent of Meeting, Israel's holy shrine. The sisters confront

ward. The names of the daughters were Mahlah,
Noah, Hoglah, Milcah, and Tirzah. 2They stood
before Moses, Eleazar the priest, the chieftains, and
the whole assembly, at the entrance of the Tent of
Meeting, and they said, 3"Our father died in the
wilderness. He was not one of the faction, Korah's
faction, which banded together against יהוה, but
died for his own sin; and he has left no sons. 4Let
not our father's name be lost to his clan just because
he had no son! Give us a holding among our father's kinsmen!"

בֶּן־יוֹסֵף וְאֵלֶּה שְׁמוֹת בְּנֹתָיו מַחְלָה נֹעָה
וְחָגְלָה וּמִלְכָּה וְתִרְצָה׃ 2 וַתַּעֲמֹדְנָה לִפְנֵי
מֹשֶׁה וְלִפְנֵי אֶלְעָזָר הַכֹּהֵן וְלִפְנֵי הַנְּשִׂיאִם
וְכָל־הָעֵדָה פֶּתַח אֹהֶל־מוֹעֵד לֵאמֹר׃
3 אָבִינוּ מֵת בַּמִּדְבָּר וְהוּא לֹא־הָיָה בְּתוֹךְ
הָעֵדָה הַנּוֹעָדִים עַל־יְהֹוָה בַּעֲדַת־קֹרַח כִּי־
בְחֶטְאוֹ מֵת וּבָנִים לֹא־הָיוּ לוֹ׃ 4 לָמָּה יִגָּרַע
שֵׁם־אָבִינוּ מִתּוֹךְ מִשְׁפַּחְתּוֹ כִּי אֵין לוֹ בֵּן
תְּנָה־לָּנוּ אֲחֻזָּה בְּתוֹךְ אֲחֵי אָבִינוּ׃

a full house: Moses, the chief priest, the leaders and the entire congregation. Their demand is as public as possible.

*1. The names of the daughters.* Each one's name appears in every episode about them.

***Mahlah, Noah, Hoglah, Milcah, and Tirzah.*** The sisters are introduced by name, not merely as Zelophehad's daughters. Their names recur in each episode (though the order varies for no apparent reason). The meanings of their names remain uncertain but the impact of their actions in the Bible is clear. In addition, archeologists have discovered two of these names, Noah and Hoglah, listed as town names on clay fragments from the 8th century B.C.E., known as the Samaria Ostraca (see at 27:5–11). Similarly, Tirzah, Milcah, and Mahlah appear as names of towns or regions in Israelite territory in various biblical texts (see below at 27:5–11).

***Mahlah.*** A version of this name also appears as a place name in I Kings 19:16.

***Noah.*** This name appears on three different fragments (ostraca 50, 52, and 64) as "of Noah." The fragments appear to record delivery of wine or oil.

***Hoglah.*** This name also appears on three different fragments (ostraca 45, 47 and 66).

***Milcah.*** Scholars maintain that the name also refers to the region between Noah and Hoglah. The name appears in Genesis as well, as the name of Rebekah's grandmother (see at Genesis 24:24).

***Tirzah.*** This name refers also to the well-known royal city of the northern kingdom (see, for example, I Kings 14:17). The man in Song of Songs describes the woman as "beautiful . . . as Tirzah" (6:4).

## THE SISTERS' REQUEST: TO INHERIT THEIR FATHER'S LAND (27:3–4)

The women first challenge an unfair system but then immediately propose a solution. Their choice of words is astute. They use the language of loyalty to family, making a claim on behalf of their dead father. By emphasizing the desire to perpetuate their father's name, they speak to a timely communal and familial concern in an era of transition.

*3. "Our father died in the wilderness."* As such, he is unable to claim the land to which he is entitled.

***"not one of . . . Korah's faction."*** By distancing their father from Korah, who had rebelled against Aaron (see Numbers 16), the daughters legitimate themselves in at least two ways. First, they explain that their father did not forfeit his inheritance (see 26:11 above). Second, they distance themselves from suspicion of illegitimate challenge to authority.

*4. "Let not our father's name be lost."* Preserving a man's name—that is, his property and legacy—stands out as a venerable obligation in the Bible (see the levirate laws of Deuteronomy 25:5–10). The women thus cleverly frame their request in the shared language of communal, especially male, concern.

***"Give us a holding."*** The language is bold. Note the absence of any polite petitionary language

5 Moses brought their case before יהוה.
6 And יהוה said to Moses, 7 "The plea of Zelophehad's daughters is just: you should give them a
hereditary holding among their father's kinsmen;
transfer their father's share to them.
8 "Further, speak to the Israelite people as follows: 'If a householder dies without leaving a son,

5 וַיַּקְרֵב מֹשֶׁה אֶת־מִשְׁפָּטָן לִפְנֵי יְהֹוָה׃ פ
6 וַיֹּאמֶר יְהֹוָה אֶל־מֹשֶׁה לֵּאמֹר׃ 7 כֵּן בְּנוֹת
צְלָפְחָד דֹּבְרֹת נָתֹן תִּתֵּן לָהֶם אֲחֻזַּת נַחֲלָה
בְּתוֹךְ אֲחֵי אֲבִיהֶם וְהַעֲבַרְתָּ אֶת־נַחֲלַת
אֲבִיהֶן לָהֶן׃
8 וְאֶל־בְּנֵי יִשְׂרָאֵל תְּדַבֵּר לֵאמֹר אִישׁ כִּי־
יָמוּת וּבֵן אֵין לוֹ וְהַעֲבַרְתֶּם אֶת־נַחֲלָתוֹ

equivalent to "please." Instead, the women use the commanding imperative "give."

***"among our father's kinsmen."*** As some rabbinic sages note, the women make clear their desire to remain connected to community and family. This statement adds moral force to their request.

### THE RESULTS: THE SISTERS RECEIVE THE PROMISE OF LAND (27:5–11)

The women's request launches a process that leads to a new law. Furthermore, this episode may reflect the historical reality that some women were inheritors of territory. A significant discovery early in the 20th century brought to light dozens of ostraca dating to the mid–8th century B.C.E. These ostraca come from Samaria, the capital of the Northern Kingdom. (Ostraca are shards of pottery inscribed with ink; they were often used for short notes or for administrative records.) Some sixty-six ostraca record the delivery of fine oil and wine, perhaps as taxes, from the surrounding towns in the territory of Manasseh to the capital. The names of two of the five daughters of Zelophehad appear in these fragments, each in three different inscriptions: Hoglah and Noah. The appearance of those names on the ostraca, together with the fact that Joshua 17:3–6 lists all five daughters as receivers of land in the northern region of Manasseh, suggests that these women were significant figures in early Israel. It is conceivable that the five sisters are among the ancestors whose names became toponyms (place names). This conclusion is strengthened by the fact that many of the other fragments from Samaria also mention other names from Joshua 17, referring to individuals who appear elsewhere as clan names as well as territory names. [Carol Meyers contributed to the discussion of these ostraca in this commentary. —*Ed.*]

*5.* ***Moses brought their case.*** This translation (like most translations of this verse) does not adequately capture the force of this sentence. What is translated as "case" is the Hebrew word *mishpat*, a noun that is often rendered elsewhere as "law" or "rule"; see, for example, Exodus 21:1 when it categorizes the laws given at Sinai. What must be stressed, therefore, is that *their* (namely, the daughters') rule or law now goes before God.

*7.* ***"The plea of Zelophehad's daughters is just."*** God responds with emphatic approval—literally, "Rightly the daughters of Zelophehad speak."

***"give them a hereditary holding among their father's kinsmen."*** God issues two related demands. First, here God decrees that the leaders grant the women's request. God's language practically repeats that of the daughters, emphasizing that their petition be fulfilled in accordance with their request.

The one difference strengthens their claim: in an astonishing move, God adds that this land be given to them as "hereditary." They not only get a holding (*achuzah*) but receive land that they can bestow as an inheritance on others (*nachalah*). The women who sought to ensure that their father's name not be written out of history now enter history themselves by gaining a legacy of land and law.

*8–11.* Second, God extends this decree as a law for all generations. God issues a general law to accommodate the five daughters. What these daugh-

you shall transfer his property to his daughter. 9 If
he has no daughter, you shall assign his property to
his brothers. 10 If he has no brothers, you shall assign his property to his father's brothers. 11 If his
father had no brothers, you shall assign his property
to his nearest relative in his own clan, who shall
inherit it.' This shall be the law of procedure for the
Israelites, in accordance with יהוה's command to
Moses."

12 יהוה said to Moses, "Ascend these heights of
Abarim and view the land that I have given to the
Israelite people. 13 When you have seen it, you too
shall be gathered to your kin, just as your brother
Aaron was. 14 For, in the wilderness of Zin, when
the community was contentious, you disobeyed
My command to uphold My sanctity in their sight
by means of the water." Those are the Waters of
Meribath-kadesh, in the wilderness of Zin.
15 Moses spoke to יהוה, saying, 16 "Let יהוה,
Source of the breath of all flesh, appoint a leader
for the community 17 who shall go out before them
and come in before them, and who shall take them
out and bring them in, so that יהוה's community
may not be like sheep that have no shepherd."

לְבִתּֽוֹ׃ 9 וְאִם־אֵ֥ין ל֖וֹ בַּ֑ת וּנְתַתֶּ֥ם אֶת־
נַחֲלָת֖וֹ לְאֶחָֽיו׃ 10 וְאִם־אֵ֥ין ל֖וֹ אַחִ֑ים
וּנְתַתֶּ֥ם אֶת־נַחֲלָת֖וֹ לַאֲחֵ֥י אָבִֽיו׃ 11 וְאִם־
אֵ֣ין אַחִים֮ לְאָבִיו֒ וּנְתַתֶּ֣ם אֶת־נַחֲלָת֗וֹ
לִשְׁאֵר֞וֹ הַקָּרֹ֥ב אֵלָ֛יו מִמִּשְׁפַּחְתּ֖וֹ וְיָרַ֣שׁ
אֹתָ֑הּ וְהָֽיְתָה֩ לִבְנֵ֨י יִשְׂרָאֵ֜ל לְחֻקַּ֣ת מִשְׁפָּ֔ט
כַּאֲשֶׁ֛ר צִוָּ֥ה יְהֹוָ֖ה אֶת־מֹשֶֽׁה׃ פ

12 וַיֹּ֤אמֶר יְהֹוָה֙ אֶל־מֹשֶׁ֔ה עֲלֵ֛ה אֶל־הַ֥ר
הָעֲבָרִ֖ים הַזֶּ֑ה וּרְאֵה֙ אֶת־הָאָ֔רֶץ אֲשֶׁ֥ר נָתַ֖תִּי
לִבְנֵ֥י יִשְׂרָאֵֽל׃ 13 וְרָאִ֣יתָה אֹתָ֔הּ וְנֶאֱסַפְתָּ֥
אֶל־עַמֶּ֖יךָ גַּם־אָ֑תָּה כַּאֲשֶׁ֥ר נֶאֱסַ֖ף אַהֲרֹ֥ן
אָחִֽיךָ׃ 14 כַּאֲשֶׁ֨ר מְרִיתֶ֜ם פִּ֗י בְּמִדְבַּר־צִ֗ן
בִּמְרִיבַת֙ הָֽעֵדָ֔ה לְהַקְדִּישֵׁ֥נִי בַמַּ֖יִם לְעֵינֵיהֶ֑ם
הֵ֛ם מֵֽי־מְרִיבַ֥ת קָדֵ֖שׁ מִדְבַּר־צִֽן׃ ס
15 וַיְדַבֵּ֣ר מֹשֶׁ֔ה אֶל־יְהֹוָ֖ה לֵאמֹֽר׃ 16 יִפְקֹ֣ד
יְהֹוָ֔ה אֱלֹהֵ֥י הָרוּחֹ֖ת לְכָל־בָּשָׂ֑ר אִ֖ישׁ עַל־
הָעֵדָֽה׃ 17 אֲשֶׁר־יֵצֵ֣א לִפְנֵיהֶ֗ם וַאֲשֶׁ֤ר יָבֹא֙
לִפְנֵיהֶ֔ם וַאֲשֶׁ֥ר יוֹצִיאֵ֖ם וַאֲשֶׁ֣ר יְבִיאֵ֑ם וְלֹ֤א
תִהְיֶה֙ עֲדַ֣ת יְהֹוָ֔ה כַּצֹּ֕אן אֲשֶׁ֥ר אֵין־לָהֶ֖ם

ters request will benefit other women in the same situation. Daughters now take precedence over other family members when there are no sons. (See further at 36:11.)

## *Legacy of Mosaic Leadership and Authority*

### JOSHUA APPOINTED AS SUCCESSOR (27:12–23)

God guides Moses as he appoints a successor to lead the Israelites into the Promised Land, since Moses himself will not enter the Land. The narrative of these events resumes in Deuteronomy 31–34.

### GOD PREPARES MOSES FOR DEATH (27:12–14)

The problematic incident at Meribah (see at Numbers 20) led God to punish Moses and Aaron for disobedience. Now God invites Moses to view the land in preparation for his impending death.

### MOSES ASKS GOD TO APPOINT A SUCCESSOR (27:15–17)

The scene is filled with pathos, especially since Moses' foremost concern does not focus on his personal loss but on the fate of the people bereft of a leader.

[18]And יהוה answered Moses, "Single out Joshua son
of Nun, an inspired leader, and lay your hand upon
him. [19]Have him stand before Eleazar the priest
and before the whole community, and commission
him in their sight. [20]Invest him with some of your
authority, so that the whole Israelite community
may obey. [21]But he shall present himself to Eleazar
the priest, who shall on his behalf seek the decision
of the Urim before יהוה. By such instruction they
shall go out and by such instruction they shall come
in, he and all the Israelite [militia], and the whole
community."

[22]Moses did as יהוה commanded him. He took
Joshua and had him stand before Eleazar the priest
and before the whole community. [23]He laid his
hands upon him and commissioned him—as יהוה
had spoken through Moses.

28 יהוה spoke to Moses, saying: [2]Command
the Israelite people and say to them: Be punctilious

רֹעֶה׃ 18 וַיֹּ֨אמֶר יְהֹוָ֤ה אֶל־מֹשֶׁה֙ קַח־לְךָ֙
אֶת־יְהוֹשֻׁ֣עַ בִּן־נ֔וּן אִ֖ישׁ אֲשֶׁר־ר֣וּחַ בּ֑וֹ
וְסָמַכְתָּ֥ אֶת־יָדְךָ֖ עָלָֽיו׃ 19 וְהַֽעֲמַדְתָּ֣ אֹת֗וֹ
לִפְנֵי֙ אֶלְעָזָ֣ר הַכֹּהֵ֔ן וְלִפְנֵ֖י כָּל־הָֽעֵדָ֑ה
וְצִוִּיתָ֥ה אֹת֖וֹ לְעֵינֵיהֶֽם׃ 20 וְנָתַתָּ֥ה מֵהֽוֹדְךָ֖
עָלָ֑יו לְמַ֣עַן יִשְׁמְע֔וּ כָּל־עֲדַ֖ת בְּנֵ֥י יִשְׂרָאֵֽל׃
21 וְלִפְנֵ֨י אֶלְעָזָ֤ר הַכֹּהֵן֙ יַֽעֲמֹ֔ד וְשָׁ֥אַל ל֛וֹ
בְּמִשְׁפַּ֥ט הָֽאוּרִ֖ים לִפְנֵ֣י יְהֹוָ֑ה עַל־פִּ֨יו יֵ֜צְא֗וּ
וְעַל־פִּ֤יו יָבֹ֙אוּ֙ ה֛וּא וְכָל־בְּנֵֽי־יִשְׂרָאֵ֥ל אִתּ֖וֹ
וְכָל־הָֽעֵדָֽה׃
22 וַיַּ֣עַשׂ מֹשֶׁ֔ה כַּאֲשֶׁ֛ר צִוָּ֥ה יְהֹוָ֖ה אֹת֑וֹ
וַיִּקַּ֣ח אֶת־יְהוֹשֻׁ֗עַ וַיַּֽעֲמִדֵ֙הוּ֙ לִפְנֵי֙ אֶלְעָזָ֣ר
הַכֹּהֵ֔ן וְלִפְנֵ֖י כָּל־הָֽעֵדָֽה׃ 23 וַיִּסְמֹ֥ךְ אֶת־
יָדָ֛יו עָלָ֖יו וַיְצַוֵּ֑הוּ כַּאֲשֶׁ֛ר דִּבֶּ֥ר יְהֹוָ֖ה בְּיַד־
מֹשֶֽׁה׃ פ

כח וַיְדַבֵּ֥ר יְהֹוָ֖ה אֶל־מֹשֶׁ֥ה לֵּאמֹֽר׃ 2 צַ֚ו
אֶת־בְּנֵ֣י יִשְׂרָאֵ֔ל וְאָמַרְתָּ֖ אֲלֵהֶ֑ם אֶת־קָרְבָּנִ֨י

### GOD SELECTS JOSHUA AS SUCCESSOR (27:18–21)

Joshua is one of the only two Israelites from the adult generation of the Exodus who may enter the land. Although Joshua will be expected to lead Israel in war, the only quality that God singles out in choosing him is spiritual.

*18. "lay your hand."* The practice of ordaining someone by means of laying hands is modeled on this first investiture of authority by Moses. The word *s'michah* (as "rabbinic ordination") comes from the term used here for "lay."

*19.* Although he emerges as Moses' successor, Joshua nevertheless must work in partnership with the priest and consult him.

*20. "Invest him."* Literally, "give of your glory to him."

*21. "decision of the Urim."* The Urim and Thummim are divination devices that priests use to consult with God (see at Exodus 28:30; Leviticus 8:8).

*"By such instruction."* Literally, "by his mouth," most likely that of Eleazar the priest.

### CONCLUSION: MOSES COMMISSIONS JOSHUA (27:22–23)

The text emphasizes through repetition that Moses' investiture of Joshua takes place in accordance with God's instructions.

## Communal Legacy for Continuing Relations with God

### SACRIFICIAL OFFERINGS (28:1–30:1)

The sacrificial system entails sharing the benefits of the land with God as well as providing support for the landless priests. The prospect of the death of Moses the mediator leads to greater em-

לַחְמִ֜י לְאִשַּׁ֗י רֵ֚יחַ נִֽיחֹחִ֔י תִּשְׁמְר֕וּ לְהַקְרִ֥יב
לִ֖י בְּמוֹעֲדֽוֹ׃
3 וְאָמַרְתָּ֣ לָהֶ֔ם זֶ֚ה הָֽאִשֶּׁ֔ה אֲשֶׁ֥ר תַּקְרִ֖יבוּ
לַיהֹוָ֑ה
כְּבָשִׂ֨ים בְּנֵֽי־שָׁנָ֧ה תְמִימִ֛ם שְׁנַ֥יִם לַיּ֖וֹם עֹלָ֥ה
תָמִֽיד׃ 4 אֶת־הַכֶּ֥בֶשׂ אֶחָ֖ד תַּעֲשֶׂ֣ה בַבֹּ֑קֶר

in presenting to Me at stated times the offerings of
food due Me, as offerings by fire of pleasing odor
to Me.
3 Say to them: These are the offerings by fire that
you are to present to יהוה:
As a regular burnt offering every day, two yearling lambs without blemish. 4 You shall offer one

phasis on laws that will bind God and Israel more closely together. The word "offerings," also translated as "sacrifices," comes from the root *k-r-b*, meaning "bring near." Integral to the biblical notion of sacrifice is the understanding that offerings bring God and humanity closer. These offerings thus serve to ensure continuity of the relationship between God and Israel when Israel possesses the land. The feasts also bring Israelites together as a community.

Extensive regulations for holy occasions appear also in Leviticus 23, though some of the details vary. For this reason, the instructions in Numbers are interpreted as "additional" sacrifices or *musaf.* After the destruction of the Second Temple, the *musaf* as additional offerings was replaced by the *Musaf* as an additional service in the synagogue. (On sacrificial offerings, see also the introduction to *parashat Vayikra*, p. 569, and at Leviticus 1–7.)

Most of the sacrifices follow a similar pattern: two bulls, one ram, seven lambs, and a goat for a purgation offering. The Shabbat requires only two lambs and no other animal offerings. The Feast of Booths (or Sukkot) differs considerably. The number of sacrificial animals is much larger: fourteen lambs and two rams daily. In addition, the number of bulls changes daily, decreasing from fourteen to seven, adding up to a total of seventy bulls. Because the number seventy represents the nations of the world (see Genesis 10), the rabbinic sages concluded that these offerings include an invocation for protection of the gentile nations (Rashi and BT *Sukkah* 55b). Presumably women were expected to bring offerings to the shrine and to participate in at least a number of communal religious practices. Deuteronomy 16:11 and 14 specify that women are to celebrate certain feasts with the rest of the household. Also, several biblical texts (see Leviticus 12:6 and I Samuel 1:25) as well as ancient Near Eastern depictions portray women as offering sacrifices (see at Leviticus 1:5). On women's participation in Israelite celebrations, see also *R'eih*, Another View, p. 1134; "Women in Ancient Israel—An Overview," p. xli.

### INTRODUCTION (28:1–3a)

This section specifies that Moses must announce these laws to all the Israelites, not to a select group of leaders.

### LIST OF OCCASIONS AND OFFERINGS (28:3b–29:38)

The list of special occasions follows from the most common (daily offering) to the annual cycle. The order largely resembles that of Leviticus 23 (see the commentary there for details). The sequence is as follows:

| | |
|---|---|
| 28:3–8 | Daily offerings |
| 9–10 | Sabbath |
| 11–15 | New moon—Rosh Chodesh |
| 16 | Passover |
| 17–25 | Unleavened bread |
| 26–31 | Feast of Weeks (Shavuot) |
| 29:1–6 | First of the 7th month (Rosh Hashanah) |
| 7–11 | Tenth of the 7th month (Yom Kippur) |
| 12–34 | "The Feast" (Feast of Booths, or Sukkot) |
| 35–38 | Solemn gathering (Sh'mini Atzeret) |

lamb in the morning, and the other lamb you shall offer at twilight. [5]And as a meal offering, there shall be a tenth of an *eifah* of choice flour with a quarter of a *hin* of beaten oil mixed in—[6]the regular burnt offering instituted at Mount Sinai—an offering by fire of pleasing odor to יהוה.

[7]The libation with it shall be a quarter of a *hin* for each lamb, to be poured in the sacred precinct as an offering of fermented drink to יהוה. [8]The other lamb you shall offer at twilight, preparing the same meal offering and libation as in the morning—an offering by fire of pleasing odor to יהוה.

[9]On the sabbath day: two yearling lambs without blemish, together with two-tenths of a measure of choice flour with oil mixed in as a meal offering, and with the proper libation—[10]a burnt offering for every sabbath, in addition to the regular burnt offering and its libation.

[11]On your new moons you shall present a burnt offering to יהוה: two bulls of the herd, one ram, and seven yearling lambs, without blemish. [12]As meal offering for each bull: three-tenths of a measure of choice flour with oil mixed in. As meal offering for each ram: two-tenths of a measure of choice flour with oil mixed in. [13]As meal offering for each lamb: a tenth of a measure of fine flour with oil mixed in. Such shall be the burnt offering of pleasing odor, an offering by fire to יהוה. [14]Their libations shall be: half a *hin* of wine for a bull, a third of a *hin* for a ram, and a quarter of a *hin* for a lamb. That shall be

וְאֵת֙ הַכֶּ֣בֶשׂ הַשֵּׁנִ֔י תַּעֲשֶׂ֖ה בֵּ֥ין הָעַרְבָּֽיִם׃
[5] וַעֲשִׂירִ֧ית הָאֵיפָ֛ה סֹ֖לֶת לְמִנְחָ֑ה בְּלוּלָ֕ה בְּשֶׁ֥מֶן כָּתִ֖ית רְבִיעִ֥ת הַהִֽין׃ [6] עֹלַ֤ת תָּמִיד֙ הָעֲשֻׂיָ֔ה בְּהַ֖ר סִינַ֑י לְרֵ֣יחַ נִיחֹ֔חַ אִשֶּׁ֖ה לַיהוָֽה׃
[7] וְנִסְכּוֹ֙ רְבִיעִ֣ת הַהִ֔ין לַכֶּ֖בֶשׂ הָאֶחָ֑ד בַּקֹּ֗דֶשׁ הַסֵּ֛ךְ נֶ֥סֶךְ שֵׁכָ֖ר לַיהוָֽה׃ [8] וְאֵת֙ הַכֶּ֣בֶשׂ הַשֵּׁנִ֔י תַּעֲשֶׂ֖ה בֵּ֣ין הָעַרְבָּ֑יִם כְּמִנְחַ֨ת הַבֹּ֤קֶר וּכְנִסְכּוֹ֙ תַּעֲשֶׂ֔ה אִשֵּׁ֛ה רֵ֥יחַ נִיחֹ֖חַ לַיהוָֽה׃ פ
[9] וּבְיוֹם֙ הַשַּׁבָּ֔ת שְׁנֵֽי־כְבָשִׂ֥ים בְּנֵֽי־שָׁנָ֖ה תְּמִימִ֑ם וּשְׁנֵ֣י עֶשְׂרֹנִ֗ים סֹ֤לֶת מִנְחָה֙ בְּלוּלָ֣ה בַשֶּׁ֔מֶן וְנִסְכּֽוֹ׃ [10] עֹלַ֥ת שַׁבַּ֖ת בְּשַׁבַּתּ֑וֹ עַל־עֹלַ֥ת הַתָּמִ֖יד וְנִסְכָּֽהּ׃ פ
[11] וּבְרָאשֵׁי֙ חָדְשֵׁיכֶ֔ם תַּקְרִ֥יבוּ עֹלָ֖ה לַיהוָ֑ה פָּרִ֨ים בְּנֵֽי־בָקָ֤ר שְׁנַ֙יִם֙ וְאַ֣יִל אֶחָ֔ד כְּבָשִׂ֧ים בְּנֵֽי־שָׁנָ֛ה שִׁבְעָ֖ה תְּמִימִֽם׃ [12] וּשְׁלֹשָׁ֣ה עֶשְׂרֹנִ֗ים סֹ֤לֶת מִנְחָה֙ בְּלוּלָ֣ה בַשֶּׁ֔מֶן לַפָּ֖ר הָאֶחָ֑ד וּשְׁנֵ֣י עֶשְׂרֹנִ֗ים סֹ֤לֶת מִנְחָה֙ בְּלוּלָ֣ה בַשֶּׁ֔מֶן לָאַ֖יִל הָאֶחָֽד׃ [13] וְעִשָּׂרֹ֣ן עִשָּׂר֗וֹן סֹ֤לֶת מִנְחָה֙ בְּלוּלָ֣ה בַשֶּׁ֔מֶן לַכֶּ֖בֶשׂ הָאֶחָ֑ד עֹלָה֙ רֵ֣יחַ נִיחֹ֔חַ אִשֶּׁ֖ה לַיהוָֽה׃ [14] וְנִסְכֵּיהֶ֗ם חֲצִ֤י הַהִין֙ יִהְיֶ֣ה לַפָּ֔ר וּשְׁלִישִׁ֧ת הַהִ֛ין לָאַ֖יִל

- - - - - - - - - - - - - - - - - - - - - - - - - - - - -

*5. eifah . . . hin.* Hebrew terms for dry and liquid measures, respectively.

*6. instituted at Mount Sinai.* This mention that daily offering was commanded at Sinai (Exodus 29:38–42) implies that these offerings represent a daily connection to that encounter between God and Israel.

*9–10.* The parallel in Leviticus 23:3 prohibits work on the Sabbath but makes no reference to sacrifices. Numbers adds a doubling of daily sacrifices

for the Sabbath. In traditional liturgy, this passage is incorporated into the Sabbath Amidah prayer.

*11. new moons.* Heb. *rosh chodesh.* The beginning of the month was a sacred occasion in biblical Israel. The elaborate offerings in this passage of Numbers indicate that Rosh Chodesh constituted an important event. (According to rabbinic traditions, it should have been annulled after the Temple was destroyed in 70 C.E., but the persistence of women preserved it.) With the emergence

the monthly burnt offering for each new moon of the year. 15And there shall be one goat as a purgation offering to יהוה, to be offered in addition to the regular burnt offering and its libation.

16In the first month, on the fourteenth day of the month, there shall be a passover sacrifice to יהוה, 17and on the fifteenth day of that month a festival. Unleavened bread shall be eaten for seven days. 18The first day shall be a sacred occasion: you shall not work at your occupations. 19You shall present an offering by fire, a burnt offering, to יהוה: two bulls of the herd, one ram, and seven yearling lambs—see that they are without blemish. 20The meal offering with them shall be of choice flour with oil mixed in: prepare three-tenths of a measure for a bull, two-tenths for a ram; 21and for each of the seven lambs prepare one-tenth of a measure. 22And there shall be one goat for a purgation offering, to make expiation in your behalf. 23You shall present these in addition to the morning portion of the regular burnt offering. 24You shall offer the like daily for seven days as food, an offering by fire of pleasing odor to יהוה; they shall be offered, with their libations, in addition to the regular burnt offering. 25And the seventh day shall be a sacred occasion for you: you shall not work at your occupations.

26On the day of the first fruits, your Feast of Weeks, when you bring an offering of new grain to יהוה, you shall observe a sacred occasion: you shall not work at your occupations. 27You shall present a burnt offering of pleasing odor to יהוה: two bulls of the herd, one ram, seven yearling lambs. 28The meal offering with them shall be of choice flour

וּרְבִיעִת הַהִין לַכֶּבֶשׂ יָיִן זֹאת עֹלַת חֹדֶשׁ
בְּחָדְשׁוֹ לְחָדְשֵׁי הַשָּׁנָה: 15 וּשְׂעִיר עִזִּים
אֶחָד לְחַטָּאת לַיהוָה עַל־עֹלַת הַתָּמִיד
יֵעָשֶׂה וְנִסְכּוֹ: ס
16 וּבַחֹדֶשׁ הָרִאשׁוֹן בְּאַרְבָּעָה עָשָׂר יוֹם
לַחֹדֶשׁ פֶּסַח לַיהוָה: 17 וּבַחֲמִשָּׁה עָשָׂר יוֹם
לַחֹדֶשׁ הַזֶּה חָג שִׁבְעַת יָמִים מַצּוֹת יֵאָכֵל:
18 בַּיּוֹם הָרִאשׁוֹן מִקְרָא־קֹדֶשׁ כָּל־מְלֶאכֶת
עֲבֹדָה לֹא תַעֲשׂוּ: 19 וְהִקְרַבְתֶּם אִשֶּׁה עֹלָה
לַיהוָה פָּרִים בְּנֵי־בָקָר שְׁנַיִם וְאַיִל אֶחָד
וְשִׁבְעָה כְבָשִׂים בְּנֵי שָׁנָה תְּמִימִם יִהְיוּ
לָכֶם: 20 וּמִנְחָתָם סֹלֶת בְּלוּלָה בַשָּׁמֶן
שְׁלֹשָׁה עֶשְׂרֹנִים לַפָּר וּשְׁנֵי עֶשְׂרֹנִים
לָאַיִל תַּעֲשׂוּ: 21 עִשָּׂרוֹן עִשָּׂרוֹן תַּעֲשֶׂה
לַכֶּבֶשׂ הָאֶחָד לְשִׁבְעַת הַכְּבָשִׂים: 22 וּשְׂעִיר
חַטָּאת אֶחָד לְכַפֵּר עֲלֵיכֶם: 23 מִלְּבַד עֹלַת
הַבֹּקֶר אֲשֶׁר לְעֹלַת הַתָּמִיד תַּעֲשׂוּ אֶת־
אֵלֶּה: 24 כָּאֵלֶּה תַּעֲשׂוּ לַיּוֹם שִׁבְעַת יָמִים
לֶחֶם אִשֵּׁה רֵיחַ־נִיחֹחַ לַיהוָה עַל־עוֹלַת
הַתָּמִיד יֵעָשֶׂה וְנִסְכּוֹ: 25 וּבַיּוֹם הַשְּׁבִיעִי
מִקְרָא־קֹדֶשׁ יִהְיֶה לָכֶם כָּל־מְלֶאכֶת עֲבֹדָה
לֹא תַעֲשׂוּ: ס
26 וּבְיוֹם הַבִּכּוּרִים בְּהַקְרִיבְכֶם מִנְחָה
חֲדָשָׁה לַיהוָה בְּשָׁבֻעֹתֵיכֶם מִקְרָא־קֹדֶשׁ
יִהְיֶה לָכֶם כָּל־מְלֶאכֶת עֲבֹדָה לֹא תַעֲשׂוּ:
27 וְהִקְרַבְתֶּם עוֹלָה לְרֵיחַ נִיחֹחַ לַיהוָה
פָּרִים בְּנֵי־בָקָר שְׁנַיִם אַיִל אֶחָד שִׁבְעָה
כְבָשִׂים בְּנֵי שָׁנָה: 28 וּמִנְחָתָם סֹלֶת בְּלוּלָה

of women's movements in the 20th century, Rosh Chodesh has come to occupy a special place in women's rituals.

*15. goat as a purgation offering.* This is a regular atonement offering for inadvertent transgressions.

*16.* This verse mentions but does not describe the passover sacrifice; detailed instructions appear in Exodus 12.

*26–31. day of the first fruits.* The Torah refers to the third major festival also as Shavuot, or Feast of Weeks, coming seven weeks after Passover (see Deuteronomy 16:10–11).

with oil mixed in, three-tenths of a measure for a
bull, two-tenths for a ram, 29and one-tenth for each
of the seven lambs. 30And there shall be one goat
for expiation in your behalf. 31You shall present
them—see that they are without blemish—with
their libations, in addition to the regular burnt offering and its meal offering.

*29* In the seventh month, on the first day of
the month, you shall observe a sacred occasion: you
shall not work at your occupations. You shall observe it as a day when the horn is sounded. 2You
shall present a burnt offering of pleasing odor to
יהוה: one bull of the herd, one ram, and seven yearling lambs, without blemish. 3The meal offering
with them—choice flour with oil mixed in—shall
be: three-tenths of a measure for a bull, two-tenths
for a ram, 4and one-tenth for each of the seven
lambs. 5And there shall be one goat for a purgation
offering, to make expiation in your behalf—6in addition to the burnt offering of the new moon with
its meal offering and the regular burnt offering with
its meal offering, each with its libation as prescribed, offerings by fire of pleasing odor to יהוה.

7On the tenth day of the same seventh month
you shall observe a sacred occasion when you shall
practice self-denial. You shall do no work. 8You
shall present to יהוה a burnt offering of pleasing
odor: one bull of the herd, one ram, seven yearling
lambs; see that they are without blemish. 9The meal
offering with them—of choice flour with oil mixed
in—shall be: three-tenths of a measure for a bull,
two-tenths for the one ram, 10one-tenth for each of
the seven lambs. 11And there shall be one goat for a
purgation offering, in addition to the purgation
offering of expiation and the regular burnt offering
with its meal offering, each with its libation.

12On the fifteenth day of the seventh month,
you shall observe a sacred occasion: you shall not

בַּשָּׁמֶן שְׁלֹשָׁה עֶשְׂרֹנִים לַפָּר הָאֶחָד שְׁנֵי
עֶשְׂרֹנִים לָאַיִל הָאֶחָד׃ 29 עִשָּׂרוֹן עִשָּׂרוֹן
לַכֶּבֶשׂ הָאֶחָד לְשִׁבְעַת הַכְּבָשִׂים׃ 30 שְׂעִיר
עִזִּים אֶחָד לְכַפֵּר עֲלֵיכֶם׃ 31 מִלְּבַד עֹלַת
הַתָּמִיד וּמִנְחָתוֹ תַּעֲשׂוּ תְּמִימִם יִהְיוּ־לָכֶם
וְנִסְכֵּיהֶם׃ פ

כט וּבַחֹדֶשׁ הַשְּׁבִיעִי בְּאֶחָד לַחֹדֶשׁ
מִקְרָא־קֹדֶשׁ יִהְיֶה לָכֶם כָּל־מְלֶאכֶת
עֲבֹדָה לֹא תַעֲשׂוּ יוֹם תְּרוּעָה יִהְיֶה לָכֶם׃
2 וַעֲשִׂיתֶם עֹלָה לְרֵיחַ נִיחֹחַ לַיהוָה פַּר בֶּן־
בָּקָר אֶחָד אַיִל אֶחָד כְּבָשִׂים בְּנֵי־שָׁנָה
שִׁבְעָה תְּמִימִם׃ 3 וּמִנְחָתָם סֹלֶת בְּלוּלָה
בַשָּׁמֶן שְׁלֹשָׁה עֶשְׂרֹנִים לַפָּר שְׁנֵי עֶשְׂרֹנִים
לָאָיִל׃ 4 וְעִשָּׂרוֹן אֶחָד לַכֶּבֶשׂ הָאֶחָד
לְשִׁבְעַת הַכְּבָשִׂים׃ 5 וּשְׂעִיר־עִזִּים אֶחָד
חַטָּאת לְכַפֵּר עֲלֵיכֶם׃ 6 מִלְּבַד עֹלַת הַחֹדֶשׁ
וּמִנְחָתָהּ וְעֹלַת הַתָּמִיד וּמִנְחָתָהּ וְנִסְכֵּיהֶם
כְּמִשְׁפָּטָם לְרֵיחַ נִיחֹחַ אִשֶּׁה לַיהוָה׃ ס
7 וּבֶעָשׂוֹר לַחֹדֶשׁ הַשְּׁבִיעִי הַזֶּה מִקְרָא־
קֹדֶשׁ יִהְיֶה לָכֶם וְעִנִּיתֶם אֶת־נַפְשֹׁתֵיכֶם
כָּל־מְלָאכָה לֹא תַעֲשׂוּ׃ 8 וְהִקְרַבְתֶּם עֹלָה
לַיהוָה רֵיחַ נִיחֹחַ פַּר בֶּן־בָּקָר אֶחָד אַיִל
אֶחָד כְּבָשִׂים בְּנֵי־שָׁנָה שִׁבְעָה תְּמִימִם יִהְיוּ
לָכֶם׃ 9 וּמִנְחָתָם סֹלֶת בְּלוּלָה בַּשָּׁמֶן
שְׁלֹשָׁה עֶשְׂרֹנִים לַפָּר שְׁנֵי עֶשְׂרֹנִים לָאַיִל
הָאֶחָד׃ 10 עִשָּׂרוֹן עִשָּׂרוֹן לַכֶּבֶשׂ הָאֶחָד
לְשִׁבְעַת הַכְּבָשִׂים׃ 11 שְׂעִיר־עִזִּים אֶחָד
חַטָּאת מִלְּבַד חַטַּאת הַכִּפֻּרִים וְעֹלַת
הַתָּמִיד וּמִנְחָתָהּ וְנִסְכֵּיהֶם׃ ס
12 וּבַחֲמִשָּׁה עָשָׂר יוֹם לַחֹדֶשׁ הַשְּׁבִיעִי
מִקְרָא־קֹדֶשׁ יִהְיֶה לָכֶם כָּל־מְלֶאכֶת עֲבֹדָה

*29:12–34.* The Feast of Booths receives much attention. Numbers 29 prohibits work on the first and last days, but an elaborate system of sacrifices marks every day of the festival. (For more on Sukkot, see Deuteronomy 16:13–15.)

work at your occupations.—Seven days you shall observe a festival of יהוה.—[13]You shall present a burnt offering, an offering by fire of pleasing odor to יהוה: Thirteen bulls of the herd, two rams, fourteen yearling lambs; they shall be without blemish. [14]The meal offerings with them—of choice flour with oil mixed in—shall be: three-tenths of a measure for each of the thirteen bulls, two-tenths for each of the two rams, [15]and one-tenth for each of the fourteen lambs. [16]And there shall be one goat for a purgation offering—in addition to the regular burnt offering, its meal offering and libation.

[17]Second day: Twelve bulls of the herd, two rams, fourteen yearling lambs, without blemish; [18]the meal offerings and libations for the bulls, rams, and lambs, in the quantities prescribed; [19]and one goat for a purgation offering—in addition to the regular burnt offering, its meal offering and libations.

[20]Third day: Eleven bulls, two rams, fourteen yearling lambs, without blemish; [21]the meal offerings and libations for the bulls, rams, and lambs, in the quantities prescribed; [22]and one goat for a purgation offering—in addition to the regular burnt offering, its meal offering and libation.

[23]Fourth day: Ten bulls, two rams, fourteen yearling lambs, without blemish; [24]the meal offerings and libations for the bulls, rams, and lambs, in the quantities prescribed; [25]and one goat for a purgation offering—in addition to the regular burnt offering, its meal offering and libation.

[26]Fifth day: Nine bulls, two rams, fourteen yearling lambs, without blemish; [27]the meal offerings and libations for the bulls, rams, and lambs, in the quantities prescribed; [28]and one goat for a purgation offering—in addition to the regular burnt offering, its meal offering and libation.

לֹא תַעֲשׂוּ וְחַגֹּתֶם חַג לַיהוָה שִׁבְעַת יָמִים׃
13 וְהִקְרַבְתֶּם עֹלָה אִשֵּׁה רֵיחַ נִיחֹחַ לַיהוָה
פָּרִים בְּנֵי־בָקָר שְׁלֹשָׁה עָשָׂר אֵילִם שְׁנָיִם
כְּבָשִׂים בְּנֵי־שָׁנָה אַרְבָּעָה עָשָׂר תְּמִימִם
יִהְיוּ׃ 14 וּמִנְחָתָם סֹלֶת בְּלוּלָה בַשָּׁמֶן
שְׁלֹשָׁה עֶשְׂרֹנִים לַפָּר הָאֶחָד לִשְׁלֹשָׁה
עָשָׂר פָּרִים שְׁנֵי עֶשְׂרֹנִים לָאַיִל הָאֶחָד
לִשְׁנֵי הָאֵילִם׃ 15 וְעִשָּׂרוֹן עִשָּׂרוֹן לַכֶּבֶשׂ
הָאֶחָד לְאַרְבָּעָה עָשָׂר כְּבָשִׂים׃ 16 וּשְׂעִיר־
עִזִּים אֶחָד חַטָּאת מִלְּבַד עֹלַת הַתָּמִיד
מִנְחָתָהּ וְנִסְכָּהּ׃ ס
17 וּבַיּוֹם הַשֵּׁנִי פָּרִים בְּנֵי־בָקָר שְׁנֵים עָשָׂר
אֵילִם שְׁנָיִם כְּבָשִׂים בְּנֵי־שָׁנָה אַרְבָּעָה
עָשָׂר תְּמִימִם׃ 18 וּמִנְחָתָם וְנִסְכֵּיהֶם לַפָּרִים
לָאֵילִם וְלַכְּבָשִׂים בְּמִסְפָּרָם כַּמִּשְׁפָּט׃
19 וּשְׂעִיר־עִזִּים אֶחָד חַטָּאת מִלְּבַד עֹלַת
הַתָּמִיד וּמִנְחָתָהּ וְנִסְכֵּיהֶם׃ ס
20 וּבַיּוֹם הַשְּׁלִישִׁי פָּרִים עַשְׁתֵּי־עָשָׂר אֵילִם
שְׁנָיִם כְּבָשִׂים בְּנֵי־שָׁנָה אַרְבָּעָה עָשָׂר
תְּמִימִם׃ 21 וּמִנְחָתָם וְנִסְכֵּיהֶם לַפָּרִים
לָאֵילִם וְלַכְּבָשִׂים בְּמִסְפָּרָם כַּמִּשְׁפָּט׃
22 וּשְׂעִיר חַטָּאת אֶחָד מִלְּבַד עֹלַת הַתָּמִיד
וּמִנְחָתָהּ וְנִסְכָּהּ׃ ס
23 וּבַיּוֹם הָרְבִיעִי פָּרִים עֲשָׂרָה אֵילִם שְׁנָיִם
כְּבָשִׂים בְּנֵי־שָׁנָה אַרְבָּעָה עָשָׂר תְּמִימִם׃
24 מִנְחָתָם וְנִסְכֵּיהֶם לַפָּרִים לָאֵילִם
וְלַכְּבָשִׂים בְּמִסְפָּרָם כַּמִּשְׁפָּט׃ 25 וּשְׂעִיר־
עִזִּים אֶחָד חַטָּאת מִלְּבַד עֹלַת הַתָּמִיד
מִנְחָתָהּ וְנִסְכָּהּ׃ ס
26 וּבַיּוֹם הַחֲמִישִׁי פָּרִים תִּשְׁעָה אֵילִם
שְׁנָיִם כְּבָשִׂים בְּנֵי־שָׁנָה אַרְבָּעָה עָשָׂר
תְּמִימִם׃ 27 וּמִנְחָתָם וְנִסְכֵּיהֶם לַפָּרִים
לָאֵילִם וְלַכְּבָשִׂים בְּמִסְפָּרָם כַּמִּשְׁפָּט׃
28 וּשְׂעִיר חַטָּאת אֶחָד מִלְּבַד עֹלַת הַתָּמִיד
וּמִנְחָתָהּ וְנִסְכָּהּ׃ ס

[29]Sixth day: Eight bulls, two rams, fourteen yearling lambs, without blemish; [30]the meal offerings and libations for the bulls, rams, and lambs, in the quantities prescribed; [31]and one goat for a purgation offering—in addition to the regular burnt offering, its meal offering and libations.

[32]Seventh day: Seven bulls, two rams, fourteen yearling lambs, without blemish; [33]the meal offerings and libations for the bulls, rams, and lambs, in the quantities prescribed; [34]and one goat for a purgation offering—in addition to the regular burnt offering, its meal offering and libation.

[35]On the eighth day you shall hold a solemn gathering; you shall not work at your occupations. [36]You shall present a burnt offering, an offering by fire of pleasing odor to יהוה; one bull, one ram, seven yearling lambs, without blemish; [37]the meal offerings and libations for the bull, the ram, and the lambs, in the quantities prescribed; [38]and one goat for a purgation offering—in addition to the regular burnt offering, its meal offering and libation.

[39]All these you shall offer to יהוה at the stated times, in addition to your votive and freewill offerings, be they burnt offerings, meal offerings, libations, or offerings of well-being. **30** So Moses spoke to the Israelites just as יהוה had commanded Moses.

29 וּבַיּוֹם הַשִּׁשִּׁי פָּרִים שְׁמֹנָה אֵילִם שְׁנָיִם
כְּבָשִׂים בְּנֵי־שָׁנָה אַרְבָּעָה עָשָׂר תְּמִימִם׃
30 וּמִנְחָתָם וְנִסְכֵּיהֶם לַפָּרִים לָאֵילִם
וְלַכְּבָשִׂים בְּמִסְפָּרָם כַּמִּשְׁפָּט׃ 31 וּשְׂעִיר
חַטָּאת אֶחָד מִלְּבַד עֹלַת הַתָּמִיד מִנְחָתָהּ
וּנְסָכֶיהָ׃ ס
32 וּבַיּוֹם הַשְּׁבִיעִי פָּרִים שִׁבְעָה אֵילִם שְׁנָיִם
כְּבָשִׂים בְּנֵי־שָׁנָה אַרְבָּעָה עָשָׂר תְּמִימִם׃
33 וּמִנְחָתָם וְנִסְכֵּהֶם לַפָּרִים לָאֵילִם
וְלַכְּבָשִׂים בְּמִסְפָּרָם כְּמִשְׁפָּטָם׃ 34 וּשְׂעִיר
חַטָּאת אֶחָד מִלְּבַד עֹלַת הַתָּמִיד מִנְחָתָהּ
וְנִסְכָּהּ׃ ס
35 בַּיּוֹם הַשְּׁמִינִי עֲצֶרֶת תִּהְיֶה לָכֶם כָּל־
מְלֶאכֶת עֲבֹדָה לֹא תַעֲשׂוּ׃ 36 וְהִקְרַבְתֶּם
עֹלָה אִשֵּׁה רֵיחַ נִיחֹחַ לַיהֹוָה פַּר אֶחָד אַיִל
אֶחָד כְּבָשִׂים בְּנֵי־שָׁנָה שִׁבְעָה תְּמִימִם׃
37 מִנְחָתָם וְנִסְכֵּיהֶם לַפָּר לָאַיִל וְלַכְּבָשִׂים
בְּמִסְפָּרָם כַּמִּשְׁפָּט׃ 38 וּשְׂעִיר חַטָּאת אֶחָד
מִלְּבַד עֹלַת הַתָּמִיד וּמִנְחָתָהּ וְנִסְכָּהּ׃
39 אֵלֶּה תַּעֲשׂוּ לַיהֹוָה בְּמוֹעֲדֵיכֶם
לְבַד מִנִּדְרֵיכֶם וְנִדְבֹתֵיכֶם לְעֹלֹתֵיכֶם
וּלְמִנְחֹתֵיכֶם וּלְנִסְכֵּיכֶם וּלְשַׁלְמֵיכֶם׃
ל וַיֹּאמֶר מֹשֶׁה אֶל־בְּנֵי יִשְׂרָאֵל כְּכֹל
אֲשֶׁר־צִוָּה יְהֹוָה אֶת־מֹשֶׁה׃ פ

*35.* The Feast of Booths (Sukkot) lasts seven days but the eighth day is appended to it as a separate holy day.

*39.* ***votive.*** The word can be rendered as "vows." On women's vows, see especially at 30:4–17.

CONCLUSION (29:39–30:1)

The conclusion affirms that Moses faithfully transmitted all that God commanded, and that the preceding instructions were indeed God's own words for Israel.

*—Tamara Cohn Eskenazi*

# Another View

THIS PARASHAH STARTS in a significant place: in the aftermath of the momentous events at Peor. One would think that the reward of Phinehas should have concluded the last parashah instead of starting a new one. But this new parashah is about the future; specifically, changes God makes for the future, changes that affect the priesthood, the government, and the women of Israel.

*Concerning Phinehas.* A more literal translation of v. 11 may make it easier to understand why Phinehas is rewarded for his violent act. Phinehas "was zealous for יהוה's zeal." *Kinah* ("zeal" or "jealousy") is the furious sense of righteous indignation that one may feel when one has been betrayed by someone who owed one allegiance and fidelity.

A husband may feel "a fit of jealousy" (5:14), and Israel is warned many times that God is a "jealous God" (Exodus 20:5; 34:14; Deuteronomy 4:24; 5:9; Joshua 24:19) and that this "jealousy" may make God utterly destroy Israel if they abandon God (Deuteronomy 6:14–15). Now God's wrath has been kindled and a plague is raging within the Israelite camp when Phinehas steps in to prevent God from wiping out all of Israel. Like Elijah, who is also "zealous for יהוה" (I Kings 19:10), Phinehas empathizes with God's rage and acts it out. He acts with violence to stop violence, like setting a backfire to stop a wildfire.

Phinehas's action works. But in the new world that this parashah is setting up, God does not want to perpetuate the cycle of violence. And so, even in the act of rewarding Phinehas, God establishes a new order by granting him a "covenant of peace" (*shalom,* not "friendship") in 25:12. The eternal priesthood will create peace and reconciliation, not by killing evildoers but by the sacrificial system. Their violence is limited to killing an animal—the bloodshed confined to dashing the blood on the altar. Once again, a careful translation brings out the meaning: "he and his seed will have a covenant of eternal priesthood because he was zealous for his God, and he will make atonement for the Children of Israel" (25:13).

Phinehas has been much discussed in our tradition. Psalm 106:30 states only that Phinehas stood in prayer and thus stopped the plague. During the Maccabean period, Phinehas was the model for Mattathias, who also acted with zeal for God (I Maccabees 2:26, 50–64). Eventually, the Rabbis became uncomfortable

*This new parashah is about the future.*

with the idea of people taking the law into their own hands, and they transformed even the image of Phinehas into a calm presenter of legal argument. In their assessment of this parashah, although recognizing Phinehas's pure motives, they frame his act as part of the past—never to be repeated—but rather to be replaced by the ordinary actions of priests.

In this parashah the priests figure also in the new role for the leader. Moses appoints Joshua his successor, but with a difference: Joshua will not have all of Moses' powers. Instead, Joshua is a temporal ruler, neither priest nor prophet. But the priests, using the Urim and Thummim, will channel God's commands (27:21).

*Concerning the Daughters of Zelophehad.* Part of this new world order involves the right of brotherless women to inherit their father's land. This decision is similar to the ancient Greek rule of the *epi-klara,* who also inherits her father's land and must marry her kin. Often we assume that this makes the women just a "place marker," holding the empty place in the paternal succession; but the story of the Shunammite in

II Kings 4 and 8 shows how important it is to a woman to hold land. The wealthy Shunammite becomes the prophet Elisha's benefactor; when he offers a reward, she responds, "I live among my own kin" (II Kings 4:13). Unusually, she has not left her kin to live with her husband's family. Alone among the childless women of the Bible, she is not actively seeking a child. (However, once she gives birth, she is fiercely protective of her son.) Later, Elisha warns her of famine; she leaves the land and returns seven years later to petition the king to give her back her property. She comes to cry for "her land and her field," and the king instructs, "Return to her all that is hers." In a comparable situation elsewhere in the Bible, the land Naomi seeks to sell is carefully called "the portion of field that belonged to our brother Elimelech" (Ruth 4:3), and the property is called "all that was Elimelech's" (Ruth 4:8). The fact that the Shunammite's land is *hers* and that she lives among *her* people suggests that she is a latter-day daughter of Zelophehad: she lives among her own kin, and her land belongs to her. And what a difference this makes: she is independent in her actions and not worried about her lack of children. The economic security of owning her own land gives her independence from her husband; she neither asks his permission to be Elisha's patron nor to seek the prophet as a client. The Shunammite may be an example of how women act when the economic constraints of patriarchy are removed. This is why she is identified by place rather than by name or as "Mrs. Somebody." Shunem is her village—the village of her father's household and the village where she lives as an adult woman, the locale of the land that she owns. She is a woman of place and—by contrast—she shows how significant the lack of such place is to most women's history.

The limitation of women's property rights is the economic linchpin of patriarchal structure. The basic fact that women did not normally own land in ancient Israel made them economically dependent on men—first on their fathers, then on their husbands, and ultimately on their sons. But the daughters of Zelophehad—and the rule that they initiated—let some women escape this dependence. —*Tikva Frymer-Kensky*

• • • • •

## Post-biblical Interpretations

***Cozbi daughter of Zur; he was the tribal head of an ancestral house in Midian*** (25:15). As related at the end of the last parashah, Phinehas the priest killed Cozbi and her Israelite lover, Zimri, at Shittim (25:6–9). Some traditions portray the highly born Cozbi as the innocent victim of her father's hatred for Israel. According to Midrash *B'midbar Rabbah* 21.3, Zur was so eager to ensnare the Israelites in sin (Numbers 25:1–5) that he sacrificed his own daughter, a princess, to harlotry. *B'midbar Rabbah* 20.24 relates that Zur had instructed Cozbi to have relations with no one but Moses, but Zimri convinced her that he was even higher in rank.

BT *Sanhedrin* 82a, discussing consequences for men who have sexual relations with non-Jewish women, denigrates Cozbi, a reflection of the considerable sexual anxiety the Rabbis harbored about the attractions of foreign women. Cozbi's name is linked to *kazav*, the Hebrew word for "falsehood," and she is castigated in the coarsest terms as a common prostitute.

This passage about Cozbi also reveals the serious problems raised for rabbinic commentators by Moses' passivity in the face of the events at Shittim and by

Phinehas's extreme zealotry. The Rabbis explain that Zimri justified his relationship with Cozbi to Moses and the elders of Israel on the grounds that Moses had also taken a foreign consort, the Midianite Zipporah. Moses was rendered speechless by this challenge, and his great-nephew, the fervent Phinehas, had to remind him of the prohibition against cohabitation with foreign women, a law that Moses himself had taught the people when he descended from Mount Sinai. *B'midbar Rabbah* 20.24 describes how Moses' failure to act at this moment of crisis demoralized all the Israelites except Phinehas and concludes that it was in punishment for this public weakness that Moses was buried in an unknown location. The passage concludes, "This serves to teach you that we must each be as fierce as a leopard, swift as an eagle, fleet as a hart, and strong as a lion in the performance of our Maker's will."

***The name of Asher's daughter was Serah*** (26:46). This statement in the tribal genealogies of Numbers 26 is startling because Serah bat Asher was also mentioned among the seventy family members who accompanied Jacob to Egypt several centuries earlier (Genesis 46:17). The Rabbis transform Serah into the longest-lived individual in midrashic literature and praise her for her wisdom. They attribute her remarkable longevity to the potent blessing that her grandfather Jacob was said to have given her after she informed him through music that Joseph was still alive. BT *Sotah* 13a relates that it was Serah who later showed Moses where Joseph was buried at the time of the Exodus so that his coffin might be returned to the land of Israel. Midrash *B'reishit Rabbah* 94.9 identifies her also with the clever woman who negotiated on behalf of her city with David's general Joab (II Samuel 20:16–22). And Midrash *P'sikta D'Rav Kahana* 11:13 even imagines the venerable Serah resolving rabbinic disputes about events that she witnessed in biblical times. In medieval writings, Serah is among the nine human beings who are said to have entered heaven alive; according to the *Zohar* (3:167b), she lives in a heavenly palace and teaches Torah.

***The daughters of Zelophehad . . . came forward*** (27:1). The Rabbis taught: "When the daughters of Zelophehad heard that the land of Israel was being apportioned among the males of the tribes but not the females, they consulted together as to how to make their claim. They said: 'The compassion of God is not like human compassion. Human rulers are more concerned with males than with females—but the One who spoke and brought the world into being is not like that. Rather, God shows mercy to every living thing,

*By expanding the Torah, these women earned merit for themselves and for their forebears.*

as Scripture says, *Who gives food to all flesh / Whose steadfast love is eternal* (Psalm 136:25), and *The Sovereign is good to all / God's mercy is upon all God's works* (Psalm 145:9).'" This rabbinic midrash from *Sifrei B'midbar* 133 represents the daughters of Zelophehad as canny and competent women who trusted that divine mercy would transcend the mutable norms of a human society in which women were subordinate beings. According to the Rabbis, these admirable sisters epitomized the females of the wilderness generation who consistently outshone their male contemporaries in their faith in God and their personal courage. *B'midbar Rabbah* 21.10 relates that women refused to participate in making the Golden Calf; they also rejected the disheartening counsel of the scouts who warned of the dangers of invading Canaan. Similarly, the daughters of Zelophehad are understood to have demonstrated their complete confidence in the ultimate fulfillment of the divine promise when they petition Moses to secure their inheritance in the land of Israel.

BT *Bava Batra* 119b praises the daughters of Zelophehad in three ways: as intelligent women, since they spoke at an opportune moment; as scriptural exegetes knowledgeable in Jewish law, since they were aware of the legal issues involved in their situation; and as sexually chaste, since they did not marry until their inheritance status was resolved, despite their advanced ages. The rabbinic sages awarded the daughters of Zelophehad this exalted standing among biblical women because they prompted Moses to seek divine help in clarifying the laws of succession of property. Nor did it hurt that God supported the sisters' claim. According to *B'midbar Rabbah* 21.11, by expanding the Torah these women earned merit for themselves and for their forebears listed in 27:1—including Joseph, the founder of their tribe. So pious and self-sacrificing were these women that they are said to have humbled Moses himself.

The Rabbis, who sought meaning in every detail of the biblical text, noticed that the order in which the five daughters are named is not always the same. *Sifrei B'midbar* 133 says that this inconsistency is meant to show that all the women were equal in good qualities. BT *Bava Batra* 120a speculates that 27:1, where the daughters seek their inheritance, names them according to their wisdom, while 36:10, which describes their marriages, lists them by age—since age takes precedence at a festive gathering.

*—Judith R. Baskin*

# *Contemporary Reflection*

The story in *parashat Pinchas* about Zelophehad's five daughters—Mahlah, Noah, Hoglah, Milcah, and Tirzah (Numbers 27:1–11)—encapsulates the challenges that women faced and what they had to do in order to affirm their rights with dignity. Numbers 26 describes a census taken of all males over the age of 20 (v. 2). As part of the list of the various clans, we read that "Zelophehad... had no sons, only daughters" (v. 33). As the census was concluded, God instructs Moses: "Among these shall the land be apportioned as shares" (v. 53). "Among these" refers to the males listed in the census; hence, we can conclude that Zelophehad's daughters were not counted in the census and also were not to receive any land as inheritance.

We might expect that women, heirs to Egyptian slavery and then put under law that frequently favors men, might react by keeping silent, by accepting as natural the rule decreed for them to follow. We might expect women in those days to stay close to their tents, remain out of sight, and not go far from their families. So how and why did Zelophehad's daughters write a new chapter in history? First, they dared to "go out" from their living place, from their social space, from the destiny imposed on them. The text states: "The daughters of Zelophehad... came forward. The names of the daughters were Mahlah, Noah, Hoglah, Milcah, and Tirzah. They stood before Moses, Eleazar the priest, the chieftains, and the whole assembly, at the entrance of the Tent of Meeting" (27:1–2).

Let's imagine the scene: the Israelite camp is formed of tribes, each of whom has a determined place, with the Tabernacle in the middle; and in the center stand the main authority figures, all of them men: Moses, the priest Eleazar, and the chieftains. Imposing as this structure may have been, the five sisters decide to claim their rights. Together, they go out of their tents, without being called by anyone, to the place where only the high-ranking men congregate, to the place where the Tablets from Sinai rest in the Ark, to the place of holiness and authority, to a place where women did not have authority. These men must have been overwhelmed when they saw such a startling, unprecedented situation!

> *Zelophehad's daughters call to us to take hold of life with our own hands.*

But this is not all that the five sisters do. They not

only come forth, but also they speak with determination: "Our father died in the wilderness. He was not one of the faction, Korah's faction, which banded together against יהוה, but died for his own sin; and he has left no sons. Let not our father's name be lost to his clan just because he had no son! Give us a holding among our father's kinsmen!" (Numbers 27:3–4). Let's analyze what this text reflects about these women. First, note that these women know their law and history. They use the fact that their father was not involved in Korah's rebellion (Numbers 16) as evidence to support his—and their—claim to the land. They know that the continuity of family name depends on inheritance of the land; and they realize that the current law is not adequate, for it does not take into account the unusual circumstances of a man without sons. They possess the acumen to recognize this omission—in God's law! But because they consider God's law to be just, or to aim to be just, they show no hesitation in pointing out the unfair nature of the present situation with complete confidence and supporting their claim with compelling arguments.

How does Moses react? The following verse states: "Moses brought their case before יהוה" (27:5). Moses discloses his inability to assess the claims of these sisters. He takes the case to God, who responds by unequivocally supporting the sisters' demand and even by promulgating a new and permanent law to secure inheritance for any daughters in such circumstances (27:6–8). Thus, the sisters' claim leads to the law of inheritance's being changed forever.

As stated above, a key to the sisters' success is their full awareness of God's laws and the people's history and story. They insist on change by engaging Israelite traditions effectively, something the rabbinic sages recognized when they described the women. According to the Talmud (BT *Bava Batra* 119b), Zelophehad's daughters were wise (*chachamot*), astute interpreters (*darshanyiot*), and pious (*rachmanyiot*): "wise" because they spoke in the precise moment when the decision was issued; "interpreters" because they in essence said, "If our father had a son, we would not have spoken—because he would have the inheritance"; and "pious" because they did not want to marry men who were not worthy.

The achievement of Zelophehad's daughters was a landmark in women's rights regarding the inheritance of land, from those days up to now. In addition, however, the story of these five women offers a compelling lesson for all those who believe that their destiny is fixed or that divine justice has abandoned them. It encourages us to think differently—and provides a message of hope for all those faced with obstacles.

Perhaps the most important legacy of Zelophehad's daughters is their call to us to take hold of life with our own hands, to move from the place that the others have given us—or that we have decided to keep because we feel immobile—and to walk, even to the most holy center, to where nobody seems to be able to go. After all, nothing is more sacred than life itself and the fight for what we believe is worthy. Thus, this parashah inspires us to discover that we too have the ability to know what is right for ourselves and what our rights ought to be. When we believe in our capacity to shape our history, to the point of being able to change even a law that came from the Revelation at Sinai, then we pay a tribute to Zelophehad's daughters.

In our era, we can see this legacy in women such as Judith Eisenstein, who was the first to become a bat mitzvah in 1922, and in the first women ordained as rabbis: Regina Jonas (in 1935), Sally Priesand (Hebrew Union College–Jewish Institute of Religion in 1973), Sandy Sasso (Reconstructionist Rabbinical College in 1974), and Amy Eilberg (Jewish Theological Seminary in 1985). Like Mahlah, Noah, Hoglah, Milcah, and Tirzah, they and the many other courageous women who followed in their footsteps came forth and opened the future for all women seeking to reclaim their Jewish inheritance in new and powerful ways.

*—Silvina Chemen*

# Voices

## For My Daughter on Her Twenty-First Birthday

Ellen Bass

*Numbers 26:33; 27:1–11*

When they laid you in the crook
of my arms like a bouquet and I looked
into your eyes, dark bits of evening sky,
I thought, *of course this is you*,
like a person who has never seen the sea
can recognize it instantly.

They pulled you from me like a cork
and all the love flowed out. I adored you
with the squandering passion of spring
that shoots green from every pore.

You dug me out like a well. You lit
the deadwood of my heart. You pinned me
to the earth with the points of stars.

I was sure that kind of love would be
enough. I thought I was your mother.
How could I have known that over and over
you would crack the sky like lightning,
illuminating all my fears, my weaknesses,
    my sins.

Massive the burden this flesh
must learn to bear, like mules of love.

## *from* Look There

Agi Mishol

*Numbers 26:33, 27:3*

The ceremony was modest.
A government clerk handed me
your final papers. You
who never graduated anything
were suddenly entitled to a lovely
death certificate
with the symbol of the state
as if you had mastered something
and fulfilled all the requirements.

She asked me if I wanted to update
(that's what she said)
father's death certificate.
Then she placed them side by side
like a pair of matching gravestones
and pressed the electric buzzer.

I went down to the street
walking
like a little girl
holding the hands
of paper parents
flapping in the wind.

## *I Know About the Woman Who Sits and Waits*

Judith Rose

*Numbers 26:33; 27:1–11*

I know about the woman
who sits and waits
who sits and waits for her life
to begin:

I know about the young girl who sits with her mother
who sits and waits
for her father
to come

I know about the young woman who sits and waits
who sits and waits
for her lover
to come

I know about the woman who sits and waits
who sits and waits
for her husband
to come

I know about the woman who sits and waits
who sits and waits
for someone / something
to come

I know about the woman who sits and waits
who passes the waiting
onto her daughter

I know about the daughter who sits and frets
who frets about more than time
misplaced

I know about the daughter longing for change
who can/ no longer/ sit and wait
I know about the daughter longing for change
who gives her Self the gift of
meaning full spaces

I know about the daughter longing for change
who hopes for her daughter
not
to sit and wait

# מטות ✦ Matot

## NUMBERS 30:2–32:42

## *Vows and Vengeance*

PARASHAT MATOT ("tribes") presents final preparations for entering into the Promised Land and offers further guidelines to the Israelites for practices once they settle in the land. As the Israelites camp in the plains of Moab, their final stop before entering the land, God instructs Moses on matters that relate to the internal workings of the Israelite community and also to the community's relationship with its neighbors.

The parashah first supplements earlier laws about vows (Leviticus 27; Numbers 6), then picks up the story about the incident at Baal-peor, where Israelite men sinned by succumbing to idolatry (Numbers 25). In that earlier account at Baal-peor, the priest Phinehas appeased God's wrath by killing two chief offenders, an Israelite man and a Midianite woman. In this parashah, God demands that the Israelites fight against the Midianites and thereby avenge that earlier wrong.

After the successful war against the Midianites, two tribes request to remain east of the Jordan. Moses resolves this potential split among the tribes by granting the request on the condition that the fighting men from these tribes will cross the Jordan with the rest of the tribes while their families settle down in the eastern region, as requested.

Women are prominent in the discussions of both vows and the war against the Midianites. In the first case, the text delineates the rights of women who make vows (30:2–17). These instructions shed important light on the status of women within the family and illustrate the circumstances under which the male head of the household can overrule decisions made by the women within the household. At the same time, these detailed laws indicate that women could make independent vows to God and, under normal circumstances, would be held accountable for fulfilling them.

*Women are prominent in the discussions both of vows and of the Midianite war.*

The subsequent section on war against the Midianites (31:1–12) focuses on Midianite women as the chief culprits in Israel's earlier transgressions at Baal-peor (25:1–18). The structure of the parashah thus indirectly contrasts the Israelite women (who turn to God) with the foreign "perverse" women of Midian (who turn Israelite men away from God).

Finally, the mention of the "water of lustration" (*mei niddah*) in 31:23, the mixture that the warriors use to purify themselves after the battle, suggests a connection to women, since the word *niddah* is also used for menstruation or a menstruant (see at Leviticus 15:19–30).

—*Elizabeth Goldstein*

## Outline

*I.* Internal Life of the Israelites

*Instructions Regarding Vows and Oaths* (30:2–17)

- *A.* Introduction (v. 2)
- *B.* A man's vows and oaths (v. 3)
- *C.* A woman's vows and oaths (vv. 4–17)
  - *1.* A woman's vow or oath uttered in her father's house (vv. 4–6)
  - *2.* A married woman's vow or oath (vv. 7–9)
  - *3.* A widow's or a divorced woman's vow or oath (v. 10)
  - *4.* Further discussion of a married woman's vow or oath (vv. 11–17)

*II.* External Relationships

*Revenge against the Midianites* (31:1–54)

- *A.* The war against the Midianites (vv. 1–12)
- *B.* Specific revenge against Midianite women (vv. 13–18)
- *C.* Aftermath: purification rituals and distribution of spoils (vv. 19–54)

*III.* Negotiating Settlements

*Provisions for Tribal Territory East of the Jordan* (32:1–42)

Moses spoke to the heads of the Israelite tribes, saying: This is what יהוה has commanded:
3If a householder makes a vow to יהוה or takes

ל 2 וַיְדַבֵּר מֹשֶׁה אֶל־רָאשֵׁי הַמַּטּוֹת לִבְנֵי
יִשְׂרָאֵל לֵאמֹר זֶה הַדָּבָר אֲשֶׁר צִוָּה
יְהוָה׃
3 אִישׁ כִּי־יִדֹּר נֶדֶר לַיהוָה אוֹ־הִשָּׁבַע

## *Internal Life of the Israelites*

### INSTRUCTIONS REGARDING VOWS AND OATHS (30:2–17)

The instructions in this unit regarding vows focus primarily on women, unlike those that appear earlier, in Leviticus 27 and Numbers 6. Those biblical laws listed monetary valuation for the sanctuary in cases of vows (see at Leviticus 27) and delineated regulations for the vow of the nazirites, those women and men who dedicate themselves to God in specific ways (see at Numbers 6). Here the regulations pertain to the extent to which women are responsible for fulfilling their vows and oaths.

Scholars debate whether the legal scenarios depicted in this unit were ever applied before exile (587 B.C.E.), or whether they are the product of the later Persian period (539–330 B.C.E.). Either way, the parashah provides important information about the lives of women in ancient Israel, or at least on how women's lives and practices were understood by the authors or editors of the text.

In the Bible, the noun *neder* ("vow") denotes a promise to dedicate something to God only if and when the supplicant's request is fulfilled. Such conditional pledges are attested also in other ancient Near Eastern cultures, including Egypt, Mesopotamia, and Ugarit (a kingdom situated on the coast of what is now Lebanon during the 14th–12th centuries B.C.E.). All vows and oaths are sworn or taken in God's name.

### INTRODUCTION (30:2)

Moses prepares the Israelites by instructing the leaders. The word *matot,* translated here as "tribes" also means "staffs" and stands for a person's authority. In Genesis 38, when Judah negotiates with Tamar for her sexual favors, she demands—and receives—Judah's staff as a guarantee (see Genesis 38:18).

### A MAN'S VOWS AND OATHS (30:3)

The discussion of men's vows is very brief, stressing that a male householder—or a man in general, according to most interpreters—is not to go back on his word when he utters a vow to God. The story about Jephthah in Judges 11 illustrates the seriousness with which vows were regarded. Judges tells of a warrior named Jephthah who vows to sacrifice whoever or


This parashah's laws invite us to reflect on the (in)famous story of Jephthah's daughter.

ANOTHER VIEW ➤ *1006*

When we women give up our aspirations because of external pressures, we pay a price.

CONTEMPORARY REFLECTION ➤ *1008*

A husband should divorce his wife rather than make vows that cause her discomfort.

POST-BIBLICAL INTERPRETATIONS ➤ *1006*

All vows are cancelled now, / all words undone like chains / that snap. . . .

VOICES ➤ *1010*

an oath imposing an obligation on himself, he shall
not break his pledge; he must carry out all that has
crossed his lips.
4 If a woman makes a vow to יהוה or assumes an

שְׁבֻעָה לֶאְסֹר אִסָּר עַל־נַפְשׁוֹ לֹא יַחֵל דְּבָרוֹ
כְּכָל־הַיֹּצֵא מִפִּיו יַעֲשֶׂה׃
4 וְאִשָּׁה כִּי־תִדֹּר נֶדֶר לַיהוָה וְאָסְרָה אִסָּר

whatever first comes out from his house should he win a battle (Judges 11:30–31). Tragically, his only child—a daughter—comes out to meet him and thus becomes the promised victim. The daughter, whose name is never revealed, willingly capitulates to her father's obligation to fulfill his vow. She only requests two months with her women companions in order to lament the fact that she will die a virgin. Judges then reports that after her death, "it became a custom in Israel for the maidens of Israel to go every year, for four days in the year, and chant dirges for the daughter of Jephthah" (Judges 11:39–40). (See also Another View, p. 1006.)

*3. a vow to* **יהוה**. People typically make vows in times of great distress, as when ill or infertile. A vow can be made in private and does not need to be witnessed by a priest or a similar functionary, but apparently it is to be uttered aloud. Thus in I Samuel 1, when Hannah makes a vow in the presence of a priest, she does not need him to officiate or approve (I Samuel 1:9–14).

*an oath.* Two kinds of oaths exist in the Bible. First, an oath can establish innocence if a person has been charged with a crime. See, for example, the oath of the woman accused of adultery (in rabbinic parlance, a *sotah*) in Numbers 5:20–25. The second kind of oath, like the vow, is a binding promise to another party, as in the context of a covenant, with at least one member of the party invoking God (Baruch Levine, *Numbers 21–36*, 2000, p. 428).

*he shall not break his pledge.* Deuteronomy 23:22 specifies that a person sins if she or he does not make good on a promised pledge.

## A WOMAN'S VOWS AND OATHS (30:4–17)

Although we do not know how common it was for women to make vows or oaths, or what these typically entailed, the laws in this parashah establish, at the very least, that the biblical writers assumed that women were making vows and oaths, and that these situations required legal attention on the part of the writer. The discussion of vows in Numbers 29:39 already implicitly includes women. In this parashah, however, women's vows constitute a major subject. The chief concern seems to be to regulate the impact that a woman's vow might have upon the household (which is represented by the male head of the household: her father or husband). Vows and oaths grant women a sphere in which they can articulate certain needs and have them met (consider Hannah wishing for a son and promising that son to God, irrespective of her husband's views on the matter, I Samuel 1). The laws perhaps indicate men's concern that the vow of a woman in their household could lead to a destabilizing loss of property. As we will see, however, the power of some women to make vows or oaths is not cut off. Rather, male heads of households are given veto power in certain situations. Widows and divorcées are free from such constraints.

### *A Woman's Vow or Oath Uttered in Her Father's House* (30:4–6)

The first discussion of women and vows or oaths establishes the parameters of authority for women still in their father's household. The woman is not described as a child. Nonetheless, under certain conditions, her father can annul her vows and oaths. The text does not indicate the kinds of vows and oaths that women might have made or the kinds of materials they might have promised. In this passage, the lawmakers seem to accommodate both benevolent and anxious fathers, so a father is allowed to annul his daughter's vow or oath under certain conditions.

obligation while still in her father's household by reason of her youth, [5]and her father learns of her

בְּבֵית אָבִיהָ בִּנְעֻרֶיהָ׃ 5 וְשָׁמַע אָבִיהָ אֶת־
נִדְרָהּ וֶאֱסָרָהּ אֲשֶׁר אָסְרָה עַל־נַפְשָׁהּ

4. *If a woman makes a vow.* The Bible does not limit the kind of property that can be vowed, and it mentions several women who make vows. We deduce from such sources that vows included a wide variety of promised offerings. For example, Hannah vows to dedicate to the sanctuary the son whom she hopes to bear (I Samuel 1:11). Women can dedicate themselves as nazirites (Numbers 6:2). And in Proverbs 7:10–21, a married woman reports that she has fulfilled her vow by making a payment (7:14). The nature of Proverbs as wisdom literature makes it difficult to assess its value as reflecting ancient practices. Jacques Berlinerblau argues that the polemical purpose of the story in Proverbs is to warn men against seductive women, which makes the text an unreliable source for the lives of real women (*The Vow and the "Popular Religious Groups" of Ancient Israel: A Philological and Sociological Inquiry*, 1996, pp. 141–3). Nevertheless, the story suggests that readers are expected to find it credible that a married woman could make independent vows.

***assumes an obligation.*** [The Hebrew actually refers to prohibiting something to oneself, that is abstaining from something. This expression, like "vow," appears in every single verse from vv. 3–15. Together, the terms treat obligations that are positive (to do something) and negative (to not do something), both types operating under the same rules. Unlike the vows that pledge to give something to God (or the sanctuary) should one's request be fulfilled, the prohibition means denying something to oneself (possibly only for a stated period of time), like nazirite vows, which are largely about abstaining from certain foods. In her book *Holy Feast and Holy Fast: The Religious Significance of Food to Medieval Women* (1988), Carolyn Bynum illustrates how women, under the rubrics of piety, used food not merely for self-control but for control of circumstances. She also argues that through self-imposed food practices women managed to develop their own practices and social roles. It is conceivable that such considerations are at work with the preoccupation with women's vows and self-denials here. Other areas where self-denial may operate might concern specific household responsibilities, privileges, and marital relationships. In all these arenas, women who undertake an oath to forego certain things have an impact on the household in general and the authority of men in particular. This may account for the lengthy discussion of women's vows. —*Ed.*]

***while still in her father's household.*** That is, she is unmarried and most likely does not own property. By implication, anything she offers as a pledge belongs to the household, not to her, including a measure of control of her sexuality. A father typically sets the terms of his daughter's marriage, including the required bridal gift, and he may subject her to debt-slavery (see at Exodus 21:7–11). This verse shows that a vow is not contingent on a person's legal right to own property. A woman, even one who is young and unmarried, can still utter binding vows and oaths; she does not require her father's consent. However, he has the option of annulling the vow under certain conditions. This law affirms a woman's practice. In addition, there may be a practical, economic consideration: the priestly authors of this text, or their descendants, most likely would benefit from additional sanctuary dedications collected from women's vows.

***by reason of her youth.*** We are not privy to the woman's exact age. She could be on the cusp of eligibility for marriage or of marriageable age. We might expect that this woman is either a little younger or a little older than 12. The use of the term "woman" rather than "girl" or "daughter" suggests that the vows of children are not valid. The law does not explicitly account for an unmarried woman who is neither "youthful," widowed, nor divorced.

וְהֶחֱרִישׁ לָהּ אָבִיהָ וְקָמוּ כָּל־נְדָרֶיהָ וְכָל־
אִסָּר אֲשֶׁר־אָסְרָה עַל־נַפְשָׁהּ יָקוּם׃ 6 וְאִם־
הֵנִיא אָבִיהָ אֹתָהּ בְּיוֹם שָׁמְעוֹ כָּל־נְדָרֶיהָ
וֶאֱסָרֶיהָ אֲשֶׁר־אָסְרָה עַל־נַפְשָׁהּ לֹא יָקוּם
וַיהוָה יִסְלַח־לָהּ כִּי־הֵנִיא אָבִיהָ אֹתָהּ׃
7 וְאִם־הָיוֹ תִהְיֶה לְאִישׁ וּנְדָרֶיהָ עָלֶיהָ אוֹ
מִבְטָא שְׂפָתֶיהָ אֲשֶׁר אָסְרָה עַל־נַפְשָׁהּ׃
8 וְשָׁמַע אִישָׁהּ בְּיוֹם שָׁמְעוֹ וְהֶחֱרִישׁ לָהּ
וְקָמוּ נְדָרֶיהָ וֶאֱסָרֶהָ אֲשֶׁר־אָסְרָה עַל־
נַפְשָׁהּ יָקֻמוּ׃ 9 וְאִם בְּיוֹם שְׁמֹעַ אִישָׁהּ
יָנִיא אוֹתָהּ וְהֵפֵר אֶת־נִדְרָהּ אֲשֶׁר עָלֶיהָ
וְאֵת מִבְטָא שְׂפָתֶיהָ אֲשֶׁר אָסְרָה עַל־
נַפְשָׁהּ וַיהוָה יִסְלַח־לָהּ׃ 10 וְנֵדֶר אַלְמָנָה

vow or her self-imposed obligation and offers no
objection, all her vows shall stand and every self-
imposed obligation shall stand. 6 But if her father
restrains her on the day he finds out, none of her
vows or self-imposed obligations shall stand; and
יהוה will forgive her, since her father restrained her.
7 If she should marry while her vow or the commitment to which she bound herself is still in force,
8 and her husband learns of it and offers no objection on the day he finds out, her vows shall stand
and her self-imposed obligations shall stand. 9 But if
her husband restrains her on the day that he learns
of it, he thereby annuls her vow which was in force
or the commitment to which she bound herself;
and יהוה will forgive her.—10 The vow of a widow

*5. **self-imposed.*** Literally, "imposed upon her *nefesh*," that is, her life or being. *Nefesh*, sometimes (mis)translated as "soul," is a feminine noun that often means "a person." See also at v. 4, above.

***offers no objection.*** Thus he tacitly agrees.

*6. **But if her father restrains her.*** Since the woman is a member of her father's household and any property she vows to dedicate to God's sanctuary will come from the household's belongings, the Torah gives the man who is considered the head of the household the right to annul her vow.

***on the day he finds out.*** That is, only on that same day. He cannot change his mind the next day and annul the vow without penalty (see v. 16 and Deuteronomy 23:22).

**יהוה *will forgive her.*** Although her father may be angry that she vowed the household's property or her time to the sanctuary, there is no penalty imposed upon the woman for simply making the vow. Jacob Milgrom suggests that the woman ought not feel guilty on account of the canceled vow (*Numbers*, 1990, p. 252).

### *A Married Woman's Vow or Oath* (30:7–9)

According to certain passages of the Bible, married women live under the authority of their husbands; but, like the young woman living in her father's house, they can dedicate their husband's property (perhaps even their own) or some of their time to the sanctuary. When Hannah utters her vow in the Shiloh sanctuary (I Samuel 1), she dedicates her first-born son. According to this passage, her husband Elkanah could overturn Hannah's vow when he learns of it (see v. 12, below), but he does not.

*7.* The new husband is given the option to annul his bride's vow even though he was not present when she first made it. However, if he does not annul it on the day he hears of it, the vow stands as is.

### *A Widow's or a Divorced Woman's Vow or Oath* (30:10)

A woman who falls into either of these two categories is not beholden to a man with regard to vows and oaths. She can act autonomously; she alone is responsible for fulfilling her vow or oath. Because the Hebrew Bible typically perceives the widow as one of the most vulnerable members of its society, it legally provides for the needs of widows with regard to food, clothing, and other protections. (See at Exodus 22:21 and at Deuteronomy 10:18; 14:29; see also *Eikev*, Another View, p. 1108.) However,

וּגְרוּשָׁ֑ה כֹּ֛ל אֲשֶׁר־אָסְרָ֥ה עַל־נַפְשָׁ֖הּ יָק֥וּם
עָלֶֽיהָ׃ 11 וְאִם־בֵּ֥ית אִישָׁ֖הּ נָדָ֑רָה אוֹ־אָסְרָ֥ה
אִסָּ֛ר עַל־נַפְשָׁ֖הּ בִּשְׁבֻעָֽה׃ 12 וְשָׁמַ֤ע אִישָׁהּ֙
וְהֶחֱרִ֣שׁ לָ֔הּ לֹ֖א הֵנִ֣יא אֹתָ֑הּ וְקָ֙מוּ֙ כָּל־
נְדָרֶ֔יהָ וְכָל־אִסָּ֛ר אֲשֶׁר־אָסְרָ֥ה עַל־נַפְשָׁ֖הּ
יָקֽוּם׃ 13 וְאִם־הָפֵ֨ר יָפֵ֜ר אֹתָ֣ם ׀ אִישָׁהּ֮ בְּי֣וֹם
שָׁמְעוֹ֒ כָּל־מוֹצָ֨א שְׂפָתֶ֧יהָ לִנְדָרֶ֛יהָ וּלְאִסַּ֥ר
נַפְשָׁ֖הּ לֹ֣א יָק֑וּם אִישָׁ֣הּ הֲפֵרָ֔ם וַיהוָ֖ה
יִֽסְלַֽח־לָֽהּ׃ 14 כָּל־נֵ֛דֶר וְכָל־שְׁבֻ֥עַת אִסָּ֖ר
לְעַנֹּ֣ת נָ֑פֶשׁ אִישָׁ֥הּ יְקִימֶ֖נּוּ וְאִישָׁ֥הּ יְפֵרֶֽנּוּ׃
15 וְאִם־הַחֲרֵשׁ֩ יַחֲרִ֨ישׁ לָ֥הּ אִישָׁהּ֮ מִיּ֣וֹם
אֶל־יוֹם֒ וְהֵקִים֙ אֶת־כָּל־נְדָרֶ֔יהָ א֥וֹ אֶת־כָּל־
אֱסָרֶ֖יהָ אֲשֶׁ֣ר עָלֶ֑יהָ הֵקִ֣ים אֹתָ֔ם כִּי־הֶחֱרִ֥שׁ
לָ֖הּ בְּי֥וֹם שָׁמְעֽוֹ׃ 16 וְאִם־הָפֵ֥ר יָפֵ֛ר אֹתָ֖ם
אַחֲרֵ֣י שָׁמְע֑וֹ וְנָשָׂ֖א אֶת־עֲוֺנָֽהּ׃

or of a divorced woman, however, whatever she has imposed on herself, shall be binding upon her.—
[11]So, too, if, while in her husband's household, she makes a vow or imposes an obligation on herself by oath,
[12]and her husband learns of it, yet offers no objection—thus failing to restrain her—all her vows shall stand and all her self-imposed obligations shall stand.
[13]But if her husband does annul them on the day he finds out, then nothing that has crossed her lips shall stand, whether vows or self-imposed obligations. Her husband has annulled them, and יהוה will forgive her.
[14]Every vow and every sworn obligation of self-denial may be upheld by her husband or annulled by her husband.
[15]If her husband offers no objection from that day to the next, he has upheld all the vows or obligations she has assumed: he has upheld them by offering no objection on the day he found out.
[16]But if he annuls them after [the day] he finds out, he shall bear her guilt.

the Bible also mentions apparently wealthy widows such as Abigail, widow of Nabal, who marries David (I Samuel 25:42).

*Further Discussion of a Married Woman's Vow or Oath* (30:11–17)

The text returns to cases of married women, to situations such as that of Hannah, who vows her (and her husband's) hoped-for son before the child is conceived. We assume that Elkanah later acquiesces to the terms of his wife's vow, since Hannah simply tells him that she will not part with her son until he is weaned. Elkanah agrees, saying, "As long as God's word is fulfilled" (I Samuel 1:23). Young Samuel's parents deliver him to the Shiloh sanctuary without a recorded discussion.

*11. **if, while in her husband's household.*** The rules concerning a wife are identical to those concerning a daughter. The woman may make a vow, but her husband may annul it under certain circumstances.

*13. **crossed her lips.*** Although the vow or oath must be uttered, there is no rule as to how loudly it must be spoken. In I Samuel 1:11–13, the priest Eli thinks Hannah is drunk when she is offering her vow and prayers through tears.

*14. **self-denial.*** Heb. *l'anot nefesh,* more precisely, "to afflict the person." The text does not spell out the kinds of activities from which the woman might elect to abstain, but they might include, though not be limited to, abstentions observed by the nazirite. These include abstention from wine and grapes and refraining from contact with the dead (see Numbers 6). [The language implies that the woman's vow may include abstention from other activities as well, a behavior that might have repercussions for the husband, for example, if she takes a vow of celibacy. *—Ed.*]

[17]Those are the laws that יהוה enjoined upon Moses between a husband and his wife, and as between a father and his daughter while in her father's household by reason of her youth.

*31*    יהוה spoke to Moses, saying, [2]"Avenge the Israelite people on the Midianites; then you shall be gathered to your kin."

17 אֵ֣לֶּה הַֽחֻקִּ֗ים אֲשֶׁ֨ר צִוָּ֤ה יְהוָה֙ אֶת־מֹשֶׁ֔ה בֵּ֥ין אִ֖ישׁ לְאִשְׁתּ֑וֹ בֵּֽין־אָ֣ב לְבִתּ֔וֹ בִּנְעֻרֶ֖יהָ בֵּ֥ית אָבִֽיהָ׃ פ

לא וַיְדַבֵּ֥ר יְהוָ֖ה אֶל־מֹשֶׁ֥ה לֵּאמֹֽר׃ 2 נְקֹ֗ם נִקְמַת֙ בְּנֵ֣י יִשְׂרָאֵ֔ל מֵאֵ֖ת הַמִּדְיָנִ֑ים אַחַ֖ר תֵּאָסֵ֥ף אֶל־עַמֶּֽיךָ׃

---

*17. between a husband and his wife... between a father and his daughter.* The overarching purpose for these laws about vows is elucidated here. This passage is concerned with specifying the range of a woman's power as it relates to her own religious life and with ensuring that her independence does not conflict with the needs or preferences of the male head of the household. The laws illustrate that a woman who is not divorced or widowed is considered under the authority of either her father or her husband with respect to vows or oaths, yet only under certain conditions can he limit her decisions as an individual making a vow.

## External Relationships
### REVENGE AGAINST THE MIDIANITES
(31:1–54)

Numbers 25 described an episode of Baal-peor, in which Israelite men were "prostituting themselves" with Moabite women (Number 25:1). Such an allegation seemed to involve sexual acts in combination with foreign worship, not merely sex outside the boundaries of marriage (see also at Deuteronomy 31:16, as well as, for example, Ezekiel 16 and 22). God at that point cast a plague upon the community, but Phinehas the priest placated God by driving a spear through the copulating bodies of an Israelite man and a Midianite woman in front of the Tent of Meeting (25:7–8). He thus brought an end to the plague. In our para-

shah, God now commands Moses to punish the Midianites for that earlier incident at Baal-peor.

### THE WAR AGAINST THE MIDIANITES
(31:1–12)

The following episode of vengeance is not unique to the Bible, but it is one of the few in which women are particularly targeted. Moses holds Midianite women responsible for enticing Israelite men into foreign worship and specifically demands their deaths. The vengeance against the Midianites raises questions. First, what is the position of Moses' Midianite wife, Zipporah (Exodus 2:21), in this conflict? Second, Numbers 25 depicts Moabite, not Midianite, women as seducing Israelite men (25:1–2); why then is this a campaign against the Midianites? Finally, why is Balaam punished when in Numbers 24 he blesses, not curses, Israel? Contemporary scholars attribute the inconsistencies to the editors' choice to weave together different sources or traditions.

*2. "then you shall be gathered to your kin."* The idiom throughout the Bible indicates death, presuming the usual practice of interment in the family tomb. Thus Jacob buries Leah in the tomb of his ancestors where he too expects to be buried (see Genesis 49:29–32 and at 25:8). King David's aged supporter Barzillai the Gileadite expresses his preference to die "in my own town, near the graves of my father and mother" (II Samuel 19:38). In Moses' case the idiom is a metaphor. This will be Moses' final battle before he dies.

3Moses spoke to the militia, saying, "Let troops be picked out from among you for a campaign, and let them fall upon Midian to wreak יהוה's vengeance on Midian. 4You shall dispatch on the campaign a thousand from every one of the tribes of Israel."

5So a thousand from each tribe were furnished from the divisions of Israel, twelve thousand picked for the campaign. 6Moses dispatched them on the campaign, a thousand from each tribe, with Phinehas son of Eleazar serving as a priest on the campaign, equipped with the sacred utensils and the trumpets for sounding the blasts. 7They took the field against Midian, as יהוה had commanded Moses, and slew every male. 8Along with their other victims, they slew the kings of Midian: Evi, Rekem, Zur, Hur, and Reba, the five kings of Midian. They also put Balaam son of Beor to the sword.

9The Israelites took the women and other dependents of the Midianites captive, and seized as booty all their beasts, all their herds, and all their wealth. 10And they destroyed by fire all the towns in which they were settled, and their encampments. 11They gathered all the spoil and all the booty, human and beast, 12and they brought the captives, the booty, and the spoil to Moses, Eleazar the priest,

3 וַיְדַבֵּר מֹשֶׁה אֶל־הָעָם לֵאמֹר הֵחָלְצוּ
מֵאִתְּכֶם אֲנָשִׁים לַצָּבָא וְיִהְיוּ עַל־מִדְיָן
לָתֵת נִקְמַת־יְהוָה בְּמִדְיָן׃ 4 אֶלֶף לַמַּטֶּה
אֶלֶף לַמַּטֶּה לְכֹל מַטּוֹת יִשְׂרָאֵל תִּשְׁלְחוּ
לַצָּבָא׃
5 וַיִּמָּסְרוּ מֵאַלְפֵי יִשְׂרָאֵל אֶלֶף לַמַּטֶּה
שְׁנֵים־עָשָׂר אֶלֶף חֲלוּצֵי צָבָא׃ 6 וַיִּשְׁלַח
אֹתָם מֹשֶׁה אֶלֶף לַמַּטֶּה לַצָּבָא אֹתָם וְאֶת־
פִּינְחָס בֶּן־אֶלְעָזָר הַכֹּהֵן לַצָּבָא וּכְלֵי הַקֹּדֶשׁ
וַחֲצֹצְרוֹת הַתְּרוּעָה בְּיָדוֹ׃ 7 וַיִּצְבְּאוּ עַל־
מִדְיָן כַּאֲשֶׁר צִוָּה יְהוָה אֶת־מֹשֶׁה וַיַּהַרְגוּ
כָּל־זָכָר׃ 8 וְאֶת־מַלְכֵי מִדְיָן הָרְגוּ עַל־
חַלְלֵיהֶם אֶת־אֱוִי וְאֶת־רֶקֶם וְאֶת־צוּר
וְאֶת־חוּר וְאֶת־רֶבַע חֲמֵשֶׁת מַלְכֵי מִדְיָן
וְאֵת בִּלְעָם בֶּן־בְּעוֹר הָרְגוּ בֶּחָרֶב׃
9 וַיִּשְׁבּוּ בְנֵי־יִשְׂרָאֵל אֶת־נְשֵׁי מִדְיָן וְאֶת־
טַפָּם וְאֵת כָּל־בְּהֶמְתָּם וְאֶת־כָּל־מִקְנֵהֶם
וְאֶת־כָּל־חֵילָם בָּזָזוּ׃ 10 וְאֵת כָּל־עָרֵיהֶם
בְּמוֹשְׁבֹתָם וְאֵת כָּל־טִירֹתָם שָׂרְפוּ בָּאֵשׁ׃
11 וַיִּקְחוּ אֶת־כָּל־הַשָּׁלָל וְאֵת כָּל־הַמַּלְקוֹחַ
בָּאָדָם וּבַבְּהֵמָה׃ 12 וַיָּבִאוּ אֶל־מֹשֶׁה וְאֶל־
אֶלְעָזָר הַכֹּהֵן וְאֶל־עֲדַת בְּנֵי־יִשְׂרָאֵל אֶת־
הַשְּׁבִי וְאֶת־הַמַּלְקוֹחַ וְאֶת־הַשָּׁלָל אֶל־

3. ***"let them fall upon Midian."*** Numbers 25 mentions Moabite women who entice Israelite men (v. 1) but then focuses on one Midianite woman, Cozbi, who has sex with Zimri the Israelite (25:6–15). Why is revenge now directed only at Midian and not Moab? Many modern biblical scholars see the stories of the Moabites and the Midianites as distinct sagas that a later editor combined in order to honor both renditions of Israel's history.

6. ***Phinehas son of Eleazar.*** Phinehas is the zealous grandson of Moses' brother, Aaron; he kills an Israelite man and a Midianite woman copulating at the entrance of the Tent of Meeting (see at 25:8).

8. ***Balaam son of Beor.*** Why does the Israelite army kill Balaam, who blessed the Israelites even at considerable cost to himself (Numbers 22–24)? After all, he is responsible for the famous verse "How fair are your tents O Jacob, / Your dwellings, O Israel!" (24:5) and other poetic oracles. One explanation claims that since the text juxtaposes the story of apostasy in Numbers 25 with the mention of Balaam's return home, he must have been involved in that apostasy (so Rashi, who follows the Talmud). Contemporary scholars explain the incongruence as a result of the combination of two versions of the story (see at v. 3, above).

and the whole Israelite community, at the camp in the steppes of Moab, at the Jordan near Jericho.

13Moses, Eleazar the priest, and all the chieftains of the community came out to meet them outside the camp. 14Moses became angry with the commanders of the army, the officers of thousands and the officers of hundreds, who had come back from the military campaign. 15Moses said to them, "You have spared every female! 16Yet they are the very ones who, at the bidding of Balaam, induced the Israelites to trespass against יהוה in the matter of Peor, so that יהוה's community was struck by the plague. 17Now, therefore, slay every male among the dependents, and slay also every woman who has known a man carnally; 18but spare every female dependent who has not had carnal relations with a man.

הַֽמַּחֲנֶה אֶל־עַרְבֹת מוֹאָב אֲשֶׁר עַל־יַרְדֵּן
יְרֵחוֹ׃ ס
13 וַיֵּצְאוּ מֹשֶׁה וְאֶלְעָזָר הַכֹּהֵן וְכָל־נְשִׂיאֵי
הָעֵדָה לִקְרָאתָם אֶל־מִחוּץ לַמַּחֲנֶה׃
14 וַיִּקְצֹף מֹשֶׁה עַל פְּקוּדֵי הֶחָיִל שָׂרֵי
הָאֲלָפִים וְשָׂרֵי הַמֵּאוֹת הַבָּאִים מִצְּבָא
הַמִּלְחָמָה׃ 15 וַיֹּאמֶר אֲלֵיהֶם מֹשֶׁה
הַחִיִּיתֶם כָּל־נְקֵבָה׃ 16 הֵן הֵנָּה הָיוּ לִבְנֵי
יִשְׂרָאֵל בִּדְבַר בִּלְעָם לִמְסָר־מַעַל בַּיהוָה
עַל־דְּבַר־פְּעוֹר וַתְּהִי הַמַּגֵּפָה בַּעֲדַת יְהוָה׃
17 וְעַתָּה הִרְגוּ כָל־זָכָר בַּטָּף וְכָל־אִשָּׁה
יֹדַעַת אִישׁ לְמִשְׁכַּב זָכָר הֲרֹגוּ׃ 18 וְכֹל הַטַּף
בַּנָּשִׁים אֲשֶׁר לֹא־יָדְעוּ מִשְׁכַּב זָכָר הַחֲיוּ
לָכֶם׃

## SPECIFIC REVENGE AGAINST MIDIANITE WOMEN (31:13–18)

Moses becomes enraged when his troops do not kill the Midianite women since, in his opinion, they were the ones who caused the Israelite men to go astray from God. In effect he commands them to kill all but the young, virgin girls.

*15.* ***"You have spared every female!"*** Not only did God refrain from mentioning this command to Moses in v. 2, but Moses does not inform his troops of his wishes until after they return from the battle. No mention is made of Zipporah, Moses' Midianite wife, but it should be assumed that the battle targeted only people outside of the camp.

***"female."*** Note the use of biological description rather than the more common term, woman, elsewhere in this account.

*16.* ***"they are the very ones."*** The use of feminine pronouns makes it clear that the women are considered responsible for initiating what happened earlier at Baal-peor.

***"who, at the bidding of Balaam."*** Thus far there has been nothing in the biblical text about Balaam's involvement in the apostasy at Baal-peor. Numbers 24:25 merely reports that Balaam returned to his home after he finished relating the oracles. (See above at v. 8.)

*17.* ***"slay every male among the dependents."*** This command includes young male children. There may be a fear that the young boys will grow up and take revenge on those who attacked their families. Ironically, Moses himself is an escaped victim of a similar decree by Pharaoh (Exodus 1) in which infant girls were saved while infant boys were to be thrown into the river.

***"known a man carnally."*** [Moses' demand that all such women be killed is based on the women's presumed culpability in the incident at Baal-peor. However, such regulations that make a woman's sexual history essential to her destiny also imply that the intended role of women captured in war is sexual. This symbol of conquest may also help with the demographic problem, namely a shortage of women because of higher female mortality, usually from childbirth and ensuing complications. *—Ed.*]

*18.* ***"spare."*** Literally, "keep alive for yourselves," that is, the surviving captives are to be saved for the Israelite warriors.

***"has not had carnal relations with a man."***

[19]"You shall then stay outside the camp seven days; every one among you or among your captives who has slain a person or touched a corpse shall purify himself on the third and seventh days. [20]You shall also purify every cloth, every article of skin, everything made of goats' hair, and every object of wood."

[21]Eleazar the priest said to the troops who had taken part in the fighting, "This is the ritual law that יהוה has enjoined upon Moses: [22]Gold and silver, copper, iron, tin, and lead—[23]any article that can withstand fire—these you shall pass through fire and they shall be pure, except that they must be purified with water of lustration; and anything that cannot withstand fire you must pass through water.

19 וְאַתֶּם חֲנוּ מִחוּץ לַמַּחֲנֶה שִׁבְעַת יָמִים
כֹּל הֹרֵג נֶפֶשׁ וְכֹל ׀ נֹגֵעַ בֶּחָלָל תִּתְחַטְּאוּ
בַּיּוֹם הַשְּׁלִישִׁי וּבַיּוֹם הַשְּׁבִיעִי אַתֶּם
וּשְׁבִיכֶם׃ 20 וְכָל־בֶּגֶד וְכָל־כְּלִי־עוֹר וְכָל־
מַעֲשֵׂה עִזִּים וְכָל־כְּלִי־עֵץ תִּתְחַטָּאוּ׃ ס
21 וַיֹּאמֶר אֶלְעָזָר הַכֹּהֵן אֶל־אַנְשֵׁי הַצָּבָא
הַבָּאִים לַמִּלְחָמָה זֹאת חֻקַּת הַתּוֹרָה
אֲשֶׁר־צִוָּה יְהוָה אֶת־מֹשֶׁה׃ 22 אַךְ אֶת־
הַזָּהָב וְאֶת־הַכָּסֶף אֶת־הַנְּחֹשֶׁת אֶת־הַבַּרְזֶל
אֶת־הַבְּדִיל וְאֶת־הָעֹפָרֶת׃ 23 כָּל־דָּבָר
אֲשֶׁר־יָבֹא בָאֵשׁ תַּעֲבִירוּ בָאֵשׁ וְטָהֵר אַךְ
בְּמֵי נִדָּה יִתְחַטָּא וְכֹל אֲשֶׁר לֹא־יָבֹא בָּאֵשׁ

There is no way a virgin could have participated in the events at Baal-peor since the apostasy involved sexual relations.

### AFTERMATH: PURIFICATION RITUALS AND DISTRIBUTION OF SPOILS (31:19–54)

Since taking of human life renders persons impure by putting them in contact with dead bodies, those responsible for the killing must undergo the purification ritual prescribed in detail in Numbers 19. This entails being sprinkled with a special mixture called "water of lustration" ("water of *niddah*"; see at 19:9), a combination of ashes of the red heifer mixed with water. The demand for a cleansing ritual underscores the power the ancients attributed to coming into physical contact with the finality of human life. The biblical writers understood that the "life . . . is in the blood" (Leviticus 17:11). The red heifer is one of the very few female animals to be used in Israelite ritual sacrifice. Therefore, some scholars suggest a connection between the femaleness of the animal and the expression "water of *niddah*" (*niddah* usually means menstruation or menstruant), translated as "water of lustration" (see at v. 23).

*19.* As Numbers 19 indicates, a person impure by virtue of contact with death contaminates the sanctuary of God. This is a violation with severe consequences.

*23. "water of lustration."* Heb. *mei niddah.* The word *niddah* elsewhere refers to menstruation or a menstruating woman (see Leviticus 15). Many scholars argue that no real connection exists between the water and the woman, other than that both refer to matters in the purity system. However, Hyam Maccoby asserts that the term should be translated literally as "waters of menstruation." He claims that in a time predating the biblical period, menstrual blood was not only defiling but also maintained healing and purifying properties. Biblical examples of blood as a cleansing agent include the case of the *chatat* ("purgation offering"), in which blood is sprinkled on the altar in a purifying manner (see Exodus 29:36; Leviticus 4:25); but there the blood is that of a male animal sacrificed to God. Maccoby maintains that the red heifer is different from other biblical sacrifices in part because the heifer is a female sacrificial animal and in part because of its distinct coloring. The red cow is not just symbolic of blood in general, but of menstrual blood in particular, which has the

[24]On the seventh day you shall wash your clothes and be pure, and after that you may enter the camp."

[25]יהוה said to Moses: [26]"You and Eleazar the priest and the family heads of the community take an inventory of the booty that was captured, human and beast, [27]and divide the booty equally between the combatants who engaged in the campaign and the rest of the community. [28]You shall exact a levy for יהוה: in the case of the warriors who engaged in the campaign, one item in five hundred, of persons, oxen, asses, and sheep, [29]shall be taken from their half-share and given to Eleazar the priest as a contribution to יהוה; [30]and from the half-share of the other Israelites you shall withhold one in every fifty human beings as well as cattle, asses, and sheep—all the animals—and give them to the Levites, who attend to the duties of יהוה's Tabernacle."

[31]Moses and Eleazar the priest did as יהוה commanded Moses. [32]The amount of booty, other than the spoil that the troops had plundered, came to 675,000 sheep, [33]72,000 head of cattle, [34]61,000 asses, [35]and a total of 32,000 human beings, namely, the females who had not had carnal relations.

[36]Thus, the half-share of those who had engaged in the campaign [was as follows]: The number of sheep was 337,500, [37]and יהוה's levy from the sheep was 675; [38]the cattle came to 36,000, from which יהוה's levy was 72; [39]the asses came to 30,500, from

תַּעֲבִירוּ בַמָּיִם׃ 24 וְכִבַּסְתֶּם בִּגְדֵיכֶם בַּיּוֹם
הַשְּׁבִיעִי וּטְהַרְתֶּם וְאַחַר תָּבֹאוּ אֶל־
הַמַּחֲנֶה׃ ס
25 וַיֹּאמֶר יְהוָה אֶל־מֹשֶׁה לֵּאמֹר׃ 26 שָׂא
אֵת רֹאשׁ מַלְקוֹחַ הַשְּׁבִי בָּאָדָם וּבַבְּהֵמָה
אַתָּה וְאֶלְעָזָר הַכֹּהֵן וְרָאשֵׁי אֲבוֹת הָעֵדָה׃
27 וְחָצִיתָ אֶת־הַמַּלְקוֹחַ בֵּין תֹּפְשֵׂי
הַמִּלְחָמָה הַיֹּצְאִים לַצָּבָא וּבֵין כָּל־הָעֵדָה׃
28 וַהֲרֵמֹתָ מֶכֶס לַיהוָה מֵאֵת אַנְשֵׁי
הַמִּלְחָמָה הַיֹּצְאִים לַצָּבָא אֶחָד נֶפֶשׁ
מֵחֲמֵשׁ הַמֵּאוֹת מִן־הָאָדָם וּמִן־הַבָּקָר וּמִן־
הַחֲמֹרִים וּמִן־הַצֹּאן׃ 29 מִמַּחֲצִיתָם תִּקָּחוּ
וְנָתַתָּה לְאֶלְעָזָר הַכֹּהֵן תְּרוּמַת יְהוָה׃
30 וּמִמַּחֲצִת בְּנֵי־יִשְׂרָאֵל תִּקַּח ׀ אֶחָד ׀
אָחֻז מִן־הַחֲמִשִּׁים מִן־הָאָדָם מִן־הַבָּקָר
מִן־הַחֲמֹרִים וּמִן־הַצֹּאן מִכָּל־הַבְּהֵמָה
וְנָתַתָּה אֹתָם לַלְוִיִּם שֹׁמְרֵי מִשְׁמֶרֶת
מִשְׁכַּן יְהוָה׃
31 וַיַּעַשׂ מֹשֶׁה וְאֶלְעָזָר הַכֹּהֵן כַּאֲשֶׁר צִוָּה
יְהוָה אֶת־מֹשֶׁה׃ 32 וַיְהִי הַמַּלְקוֹחַ יֶתֶר
הַבָּז אֲשֶׁר בָּזְזוּ עַם הַצָּבָא צֹאן שֵׁשׁ־מֵאוֹת
אֶלֶף וְשִׁבְעִים אֶלֶף וַחֲמֵשֶׁת אֲלָפִים׃
33 וּבָקָר שְׁנַיִם וְשִׁבְעִים אָלֶף׃ 34 וַחֲמֹרִים
אֶחָד וְשִׁשִּׁים אָלֶף׃ 35 וְנֶפֶשׁ אָדָם מִן־
הַנָּשִׁים אֲשֶׁר לֹא־יָדְעוּ מִשְׁכַּב זָכָר כָּל־נֶפֶשׁ
שְׁנַיִם וּשְׁלֹשִׁים אָלֶף׃
36 וַתְּהִי הַמֶּחֱצָה חֵלֶק הַיֹּצְאִים בַּצָּבָא
מִסְפַּר הַצֹּאן שְׁלֹשׁ־מֵאוֹת אֶלֶף וּשְׁלֹשִׁים
אֶלֶף וְשִׁבְעַת אֲלָפִים וַחֲמֵשׁ מֵאוֹת׃ 37 וַיְהִי
הַמֶּכֶס לַיהוָה מִן־הַצֹּאן שֵׁשׁ מֵאוֹת חָמֵשׁ
וְשִׁבְעִים׃ 38 וְהַבָּקָר שִׁשָּׁה וּשְׁלֹשִׁים אָלֶף
וּמִכְסָם לַיהוָה שְׁנַיִם וְשִׁבְעִים׃ 39 וַחֲמֹרִים

symbolic power of life, death, and fertility (*Ritual and Morality: The Ritual Purity System and its Place in Judaism*, 1999, pp. 105–17).

For additional discussion of *mei niddah* ("water of lustration"), see at Numbers 19:9.

which יהוה's levy was 61. ⁴⁰And the number of human beings was 16,000, from which יהוה's levy was 32. ⁴¹Moses gave the contributions levied for יהוה to Eleazar the priest, as יהוה had commanded Moses.

⁴²As for the half-share of the other Israelites, which Moses withdrew from the troops who had taken the field, ⁴³that half-share of the community consisted of 337,500 sheep, ⁴⁴36,000 head of cattle, ⁴⁵30,500 asses, ⁴⁶and 16,000 human beings. ⁴⁷From this half-share of the Israelites, Moses withheld one in every fifty humans and animals; and he gave them to the Levites, who attended to the duties of יהוה's Tabernacle, as יהוה had commanded Moses.

⁴⁸The commanders of the troop divisions, the officers of thousands and the officers of hundreds, approached Moses. ⁴⁹They said to Moses, "Your servants have made a check of the warriors in our charge, and not one of us is missing. ⁵⁰So we have brought as an offering to יהוה such articles of gold as each of us came upon: armlets, bracelets, signet rings, earrings, and pendants, that expiation may be made for our persons before יהוה." ⁵¹Moses and Eleazar the priest accepted the gold from them, all kinds of wrought articles. ⁵²All the gold that was offered by the officers of thousands and the officers of hundreds as a contribution to יהוה came to 16,750 shekels.—⁵³But in the ranks, everyone kept his booty for himself.—⁵⁴So Moses and Eleazar the priest accepted the gold from the officers of thousands and the officers of hundreds and brought it to the Tent of Meeting, as a reminder in behalf of the Israelites before יהוה.

שְׁלֹשִׁים אֶלֶף וַחֲמֵשׁ מֵאוֹת וּמִכְסָם לַיהֹוָה אֶחָד וְשִׁשִּׁים: 40 וְנֶפֶשׁ אָדָם שִׁשָּׁה עָשָׂר אָלֶף וּמִכְסָם לַיהֹוָה שְׁנַיִם וּשְׁלֹשִׁים נָפֶשׁ: 41 וַיִּתֵּן מֹשֶׁה אֶת־מֶכֶס תְּרוּמַת יְהֹוָה לְאֶלְעָזָר הַכֹּהֵן כַּאֲשֶׁר צִוָּה יְהֹוָה אֶת־מֹשֶׁה: 42 וּמִמַּחֲצִית בְּנֵי יִשְׂרָאֵל אֲשֶׁר חָצָה מֹשֶׁה מִן־הָאֲנָשִׁים הַצֹּבְאִים: 43 וַתְּהִי מֶחֱצַת הָעֵדָה מִן־הַצֹּאן שְׁלֹשׁ־מֵאוֹת אֶלֶף וּשְׁלֹשִׁים אֶלֶף שִׁבְעַת אֲלָפִים וַחֲמֵשׁ מֵאוֹת: 44 וּבָקָר שִׁשָּׁה וּשְׁלֹשִׁים אָלֶף: 45 וַחֲמֹרִים שְׁלֹשִׁים אֶלֶף וַחֲמֵשׁ מֵאוֹת: 46 וְנֶפֶשׁ אָדָם שִׁשָּׁה עָשָׂר אָלֶף: 47 וַיִּקַּח מֹשֶׁה מִמַּחֲצִת בְּנֵי־יִשְׂרָאֵל אֶת־הָאָחֻז אֶחָד מִן־הַחֲמִשִּׁים מִן־הָאָדָם וּמִן־הַבְּהֵמָה וַיִּתֵּן אֹתָם לַלְוִיִּם שֹׁמְרֵי מִשְׁמֶרֶת מִשְׁכַּן יְהֹוָה כַּאֲשֶׁר צִוָּה יְהֹוָה אֶת־מֹשֶׁה: 48 וַיִּקְרְבוּ אֶל־מֹשֶׁה הַפְּקֻדִים אֲשֶׁר לְאַלְפֵי הַצָּבָא שָׂרֵי הָאֲלָפִים וְשָׂרֵי הַמֵּאוֹת: 49 וַיֹּאמְרוּ אֶל־מֹשֶׁה עֲבָדֶיךָ נָשְׂאוּ אֶת־רֹאשׁ אַנְשֵׁי הַמִּלְחָמָה אֲשֶׁר בְּיָדֵנוּ וְלֹא־נִפְקַד מִמֶּנּוּ אִישׁ: 50 וַנַּקְרֵב אֶת־קָרְבַּן יְהֹוָה אִישׁ אֲשֶׁר מָצָא כְלִי־זָהָב אֶצְעָדָה וְצָמִיד טַבַּעַת עָגִיל וְכוּמָז לְכַפֵּר עַל־נַפְשֹׁתֵינוּ לִפְנֵי יְהֹוָה: 51 וַיִּקַּח מֹשֶׁה וְאֶלְעָזָר הַכֹּהֵן אֶת־הַזָּהָב מֵאִתָּם כֹּל כְּלִי מַעֲשֶׂה: 52 וַיְהִי כָּל־זְהַב הַתְּרוּמָה אֲשֶׁר הֵרִימוּ לַיהֹוָה שִׁשָּׁה עָשָׂר אֶלֶף שְׁבַע־מֵאוֹת וַחֲמִשִּׁים שָׁקֶל מֵאֵת שָׂרֵי הָאֲלָפִים וּמֵאֵת שָׂרֵי הַמֵּאוֹת: 53 אַנְשֵׁי הַצָּבָא בָּזְזוּ אִישׁ לוֹ: 54 וַיִּקַּח מֹשֶׁה וְאֶלְעָזָר הַכֹּהֵן אֶת־הַזָּהָב מֵאֵת שָׂרֵי הָאֲלָפִים וְהַמֵּאוֹת וַיָּבִאוּ אֹתוֹ אֶל־אֹהֶל מוֹעֵד זִכָּרוֹן לִבְנֵי־יִשְׂרָאֵל לִפְנֵי יְהֹוָה: פ

32 The Reubenites and the Gadites owned cattle in very great numbers. Noting that the lands of Jazer and Gilead were a region suitable for cattle, [2]the Gadite and Reubenite [leaders] came to Moses, Eleazar the priest, and the chieftains of the community, and said, [3]"Ataroth, Dibon, Jazer, Nimrah, Heshbon, Elealeh, Sebam, Nebo, and Beon—[4]the land that יהוה has conquered for the community of Israel—is cattle country, and your servants have cattle. [5]It would be a favor to us," they continued, "if this land were given to your servants as a holding; do not move us across the Jordan."

[6]Moses replied to the Gadites and the Reubenites, "Are your brothers to go to war while you stay here? [7]Why will you turn the minds of the Israelites from crossing into the land that יהוה has given them? [8]That is what your fathers did when I sent them from Kadesh-barnea to survey the land. [9]After going up to the wadi Eshcol and surveying the land, they turned the minds of the Israelites from invading the land that יהוה had given them. [10]Thereupon יהוה was incensed and swore, [11]'None of the men from twenty years up who came out of

לב וּמִקְנֶה ׀ רַב הָיָה לִבְנֵי רְאוּבֵן וְלִבְנֵי־
גָד עָצוּם מְאֹד וַיִּרְאוּ אֶת־אֶרֶץ יַעְזֵר וְאֶת־
אֶרֶץ גִּלְעָד וְהִנֵּה הַמָּקוֹם מְקוֹם מִקְנֶה׃
2 וַיָּבֹאוּ בְנֵי־גָד וּבְנֵי רְאוּבֵן וַיֹּאמְרוּ אֶל־
מֹשֶׁה וְאֶל־אֶלְעָזָר הַכֹּהֵן וְאֶל־נְשִׂיאֵי
הָעֵדָה לֵאמֹר׃ 3 עֲטָרוֹת וְדִיבֹן וְיַעְזֵר
וְנִמְרָה וְחֶשְׁבּוֹן וְאֶלְעָלֵה וּשְׂבָם וּנְבוֹ
וּבְעֹן׃ 4 הָאָרֶץ אֲשֶׁר הִכָּה יְהוָה לִפְנֵי
עֲדַת יִשְׂרָאֵל אֶרֶץ מִקְנֶה הִוא וְלַעֲבָדֶיךָ
מִקְנֶה׃ ס 5 וַיֹּאמְרוּ אִם־מָצָאנוּ חֵן
בְּעֵינֶיךָ יֻתַּן אֶת־הָאָרֶץ הַזֹּאת לַעֲבָדֶיךָ
לַאֲחֻזָּה אַל־תַּעֲבִרֵנוּ אֶת־הַיַּרְדֵּן׃
6 וַיֹּאמֶר מֹשֶׁה לִבְנֵי־גָד וְלִבְנֵי רְאוּבֵן
הַאַחֵיכֶם יָבֹאוּ לַמִּלְחָמָה וְאַתֶּם תֵּשְׁבוּ
פֹה׃ 7 וְלָמָּה תנואון תְנִיאוּן אֶת־לֵב בְּנֵי
יִשְׂרָאֵל מֵעֲבֹר אֶל־הָאָרֶץ אֲשֶׁר־נָתַן לָהֶם
יְהוָה׃ 8 כֹּה עָשׂוּ אֲבֹתֵיכֶם בְּשָׁלְחִי אֹתָם
מִקָּדֵשׁ בַּרְנֵעַ לִרְאוֹת אֶת־הָאָרֶץ׃ 9 וַיַּעֲלוּ
עַד־נַחַל אֶשְׁכּוֹל וַיִּרְאוּ אֶת־הָאָרֶץ וַיָּנִיאוּ
אֶת־לֵב בְּנֵי יִשְׂרָאֵל לְבִלְתִּי־בֹא אֶל־הָאָרֶץ
אֲשֶׁר־נָתַן לָהֶם יְהוָה׃ 10 וַיִּחַר־אַף יְהוָה
בַּיּוֹם הַהוּא וַיִּשָּׁבַע לֵאמֹר׃ 11 אִם־יִרְאוּ
הָאֲנָשִׁים הָעֹלִים מִמִּצְרַיִם מִבֶּן עֶשְׂרִים

## *Negotiating Settlements*

### PROVISIONS FOR TRIBAL TERRITORY EAST OF THE JORDAN (32:1–42)

Earlier, in Numbers 21, the Israelites conquered the territory east of the Jordan River. Here, two and half tribes (Reuben, Gad, and half of Manasseh) request to settle there. As in prior incidents, Moses is portrayed as one who must help his people deal with difficult transitions. In this case, a sub-group of Israelites successfully makes the transition from wanderers to settlers; but they do so prematurely. Moses reminds them of their obligations to the Israelite people as a whole: he demands that even if they are given the dispensation to remain occupants of Transjordan, they must continue to help their brothers in battle.

*3. "Nebo."* This is the location of the mountain on top of which a dying Moses will view the Promised Land (see Deuteronomy 34:1–5). Tradition identifies this location with a mountain in Jordan with an expansive vista overlooking the land of Israel.

*8. "That is what your fathers did."* Moses compares the stance of Reuben and Gad to that of the scouts who were sent to survey the land and who then discouraged the people (Numbers 13).

Egypt shall see the land that I promised on oath to Abraham, Isaac, and Jacob, for they did not remain loyal to Me—[12]none except Caleb son of Jephunneh the Kenizzite and Joshua son of Nun, for they remained loyal to יהוה.' [13]יהוה, incensed at Israel, made them wander in the wilderness for forty years, until the whole generation that had provoked יהוה's displeasure was gone. [14]And now you, a breed of sinful men, have replaced your fathers, to add still further to יהוה's wrath against Israel. [15]If you turn away from [God], who then abandons them once more in the wilderness, you will bring calamity upon all this people."

[16]Then they stepped up to him and said, "We will build here sheepfolds for our flocks and towns for our children. [17]And we will hasten as shock-troops in the van of the Israelites until we have established them in their home, while our children stay in the fortified towns because of the inhabitants of the land. [18]We will not return to our homes until the Israelites—every one of them—are in possession of their portion. [19]But we will not have a share with them in the territory beyond the Jordan, for we have received our share on the east side of the Jordan."

[20]Moses said to them, "If you do this, if you go to battle as shock-troops, at the instance of יהוה, [21]and every shock-fighter among you crosses the Jordan, at the instance of יהוה, until [God] has personally dispossessed the enemies, [22]and the land has been subdued, at the instance of יהוה, and then you return—you shall be clear before יהוה and before Israel; and this land shall be your holding under יהוה. [23]But if you do not do so, you will have sinned against יהוה; and know that your sin will overtake you. [24]Build towns for your children and sheepfolds for your flocks, but do what you have promised."

[25]The Gadites and the Reubenites answered Moses, "Your servants will do as my lord commands. [26]Our children, our wives, our flocks, and all our other livestock will stay behind in the towns

שָׁנָה וָמַעְלָה אֵת הָאֲדָמָה אֲשֶׁר נִשְׁבַּעְתִּי
לְאַבְרָהָם לְיִצְחָק וּלְיַעֲקֹב כִּי לֹא־מִלְאוּ
אַחֲרָי׃ 12 בִּלְתִּי כָּלֵב בֶּן־יְפֻנֶּה הַקְּנִזִּי
וִיהוֹשֻׁעַ בִּן־נוּן כִּי מִלְאוּ אַחֲרֵי יְהוָה׃
13 וַיִּחַר־אַף יְהוָה בְּיִשְׂרָאֵל וַיְנִעֵם בַּמִּדְבָּר
אַרְבָּעִים שָׁנָה עַד־תֹּם כָּל־הַדּוֹר הָעֹשֶׂה
הָרַע בְּעֵינֵי יְהוָה׃ 14 וְהִנֵּה קַמְתֶּם תַּחַת
אֲבֹתֵיכֶם תַּרְבּוּת אֲנָשִׁים חַטָּאִים לִסְפּוֹת
עוֹד עַל חֲרוֹן אַף־יְהוָה אֶל־יִשְׂרָאֵל׃ 15 כִּי
תְשׁוּבֻן מֵאַחֲרָיו וְיָסַף עוֹד לְהַנִּיחוֹ בַּמִּדְבָּר
וְשִׁחַתֶּם לְכָל־הָעָם הַזֶּה׃ ס
16 וַיִּגְּשׁוּ אֵלָיו וַיֹּאמְרוּ גִּדְרֹת צֹאן נִבְנֶה
לְמִקְנֵנוּ פֹּה וְעָרִים לְטַפֵּנוּ׃ 17 וַאֲנַחְנוּ נֵחָלֵץ
חֻשִׁים לִפְנֵי בְּנֵי יִשְׂרָאֵל עַד אֲשֶׁר אִם־
הֲבִיאֹנֻם אֶל־מְקוֹמָם וְיָשַׁב טַפֵּנוּ בְּעָרֵי
הַמִּבְצָר מִפְּנֵי יֹשְׁבֵי הָאָרֶץ׃ 18 לֹא נָשׁוּב
אֶל־בָּתֵּינוּ עַד הִתְנַחֵל בְּנֵי יִשְׂרָאֵל אִישׁ
נַחֲלָתוֹ׃ 19 כִּי לֹא נִנְחַל אִתָּם מֵעֵבֶר לַיַּרְדֵּן
וָהָלְאָה כִּי בָאָה נַחֲלָתֵנוּ אֵלֵינוּ מֵעֵבֶר
הַיַּרְדֵּן מִזְרָחָה׃ פ
20 וַיֹּאמֶר אֲלֵיהֶם מֹשֶׁה אִם־תַּעֲשׂוּן אֶת־
הַדָּבָר הַזֶּה אִם־תֵּחָלְצוּ לִפְנֵי יְהוָה
לַמִּלְחָמָה׃ 21 וְעָבַר לָכֶם כָּל־חָלוּץ אֶת־
הַיַּרְדֵּן לִפְנֵי יְהוָה עַד הוֹרִישׁוֹ אֶת־אֹיְבָיו
מִפָּנָיו׃ 22 וְנִכְבְּשָׁה הָאָרֶץ לִפְנֵי יְהוָה וְאַחַר
תָּשֻׁבוּ וִהְיִיתֶם נְקִיִּם מֵיְהוָה וּמִיִּשְׂרָאֵל
וְהָיְתָה הָאָרֶץ הַזֹּאת לָכֶם לַאֲחֻזָּה לִפְנֵי
יְהוָה׃ 23 וְאִם־לֹא תַעֲשׂוּן כֵּן הִנֵּה חֲטָאתֶם
לַיהוָה וּדְעוּ חַטַּאתְכֶם אֲשֶׁר תִּמְצָא
אֶתְכֶם׃ 24 בְּנוּ־לָכֶם עָרִים לְטַפְּכֶם וּגְדֵרֹת
לְצֹנַאֲכֶם וְהַיֹּצֵא מִפִּיכֶם תַּעֲשׂוּ׃
25 וַיֹּאמֶר בְּנֵי־גָד וּבְנֵי רְאוּבֵן אֶל־מֹשֶׁה
לֵאמֹר עֲבָדֶיךָ יַעֲשׂוּ כַּאֲשֶׁר אֲדֹנִי מְצַוֶּה׃
26 טַפֵּנוּ נָשֵׁינוּ מִקְנֵנוּ וְכָל־בְּהֶמְתֵּנוּ יִהְיוּ־

of Gilead; 27while your servants, all those recruited for war, cross over, at the instance of יהוה, to engage in battle—as my lord orders."

28Then Moses gave instructions concerning them to Eleazar the priest, Joshua son of Nun, and the family heads of the Israelite tribes. 29Moses said to them, "If every shock-fighter among the Gadites and the Reubenites crosses the Jordan with you to do battle, at the instance of יהוה, and the land is subdued before you, you shall give them the land of Gilead as a holding. 30But if they do not cross over with you as shock-troops, they shall receive holdings among you in the land of Canaan."

31The Gadites and the Reubenites said in reply, "Whatever יהוה has spoken concerning your servants, that we will do. 32We ourselves will cross over as shock-troops, at the instance of יהוה, into the land of Canaan; and we shall keep our hereditary holding across the Jordan."

33So Moses assigned to them—to the Gadites, the Reubenites, and the half-tribe of Manasseh son of Joseph—the kingdom of Sihon king of the Amorites and the kingdom of King Og of Bashan, the land with its various cities and the territories of their surrounding towns. 34The Gadites rebuilt Dibon, Ataroth, Aroer, 35Atroth-shophan, Jazer, Jogbehah, 36Beth-nimrah, and Beth-haran as fortified towns or as enclosures for flocks. 37The Reubenites rebuilt Heshbon, Elealeh, Kiriathaim, 38Nebo, Baal-meon—some names being changed—and Sibmah; they gave [their own] names to towns that they rebuilt. 39The descendants of Machir son of Manasseh went to Gilead and captured it, dispossessing the Amorites who were there;

שָׁם בְּעָרֵי הַגִּלְעָד׃ 27 וַעֲבָדֶיךָ יַעַבְרוּ כָּל־
חֲלוּץ צָבָא לִפְנֵי יְהוָה לַמִּלְחָמָה כַּאֲשֶׁר
אֲדֹנִי דֹּבֵר׃
28 וַיְצַו לָהֶם מֹשֶׁה אֵת אֶלְעָזָר הַכֹּהֵן וְאֵת
יְהוֹשֻׁעַ בִּן־נוּן וְאֶת־רָאשֵׁי אֲבוֹת הַמַּטּוֹת
לִבְנֵי יִשְׂרָאֵל׃ 29 וַיֹּאמֶר מֹשֶׁה אֲלֵהֶם אִם־
יַעַבְרוּ בְנֵי־גָד וּבְנֵי־רְאוּבֵן ׀ אִתְּכֶם אֶת־
הַיַּרְדֵּן כָּל־חָלוּץ לַמִּלְחָמָה לִפְנֵי יְהוָה
וְנִכְבְּשָׁה הָאָרֶץ לִפְנֵיכֶם וּנְתַתֶּם לָהֶם
אֶת־אֶרֶץ הַגִּלְעָד לַאֲחֻזָּה׃ 30 וְאִם־לֹא
יַעַבְרוּ חֲלוּצִים אִתְּכֶם וְנֹאחֲזוּ בְתֹכְכֶם
בְּאֶרֶץ כְּנָעַן׃
31 וַיַּעֲנוּ בְנֵי־גָד וּבְנֵי רְאוּבֵן לֵאמֹר אֵת
אֲשֶׁר דִּבֶּר יְהוָה אֶל־עֲבָדֶיךָ כֵּן נַעֲשֶׂה׃
32 נַחְנוּ נַעֲבֹר חֲלוּצִים לִפְנֵי יְהוָה אֶרֶץ
כְּנָעַן וְאִתָּנוּ אֲחֻזַּת נַחֲלָתֵנוּ מֵעֵבֶר
לַיַּרְדֵּן׃
33 וַיִּתֵּן לָהֶם ׀ מֹשֶׁה לִבְנֵי־גָד וְלִבְנֵי רְאוּבֵן
וְלַחֲצִי ׀ שֵׁבֶט ׀ מְנַשֶּׁה בֶן־יוֹסֵף אֶת־מַמְלֶכֶת
סִיחֹן מֶלֶךְ הָאֱמֹרִי וְאֶת־מַמְלֶכֶת עוֹג מֶלֶךְ
הַבָּשָׁן הָאָרֶץ לְעָרֶיהָ בִּגְבֻלֹת עָרֵי הָאָרֶץ
סָבִיב׃ 34 וַיִּבְנוּ בְנֵי־גָד אֶת־דִּיבֹן וְאֶת־
עֲטָרֹת וְאֵת עֲרֹעֵר׃ 35 וְאֶת־עַטְרֹת שׁוֹפָן
וְאֶת־יַעְזֵר וְיָגְבְּהָה׃ 36 וְאֶת־בֵּית נִמְרָה
וְאֶת־בֵּית הָרָן עָרֵי מִבְצָר וְגִדְרֹת צֹאן׃
37 וּבְנֵי רְאוּבֵן בָּנוּ אֶת־חֶשְׁבּוֹן וְאֶת־
אֶלְעָלֵא וְאֵת קִרְיָתָיִם׃ 38 וְאֶת־נְבוֹ וְאֶת־
בַּעַל מְעוֹן מוּסַבֹּת שֵׁם וְאֶת־שִׂבְמָה וַיִּקְרְאוּ
בְשֵׁמֹת אֶת־שְׁמוֹת הֶעָרִים אֲשֶׁר בָּנוּ׃
39 וַיֵּלְכוּ בְּנֵי מָכִיר בֶּן־מְנַשֶּׁה גִּלְעָדָה
וַיִּלְכְּדֻהָ וַיּוֹרֶשׁ אֶת־הָאֱמֹרִי אֲשֶׁר־בָּהּ׃

*38. some names being changed.* Remarks like these often go unnoticed, yet they provide interesting clues in determining when and by whom biblical texts were composed. An internal comment like this one reveals the hand of a later historiographer trying to make these places familiar to his audience.

[40]so Moses gave Gilead to Machir son of Manasseh,
and he settled there. [41]Jair son of Manasseh went
and captured their villages, which he renamed
Havvoth-jair. [42]And Nobah went and captured
Kenath and its dependencies, renaming it Nobah
after himself.

40 וַיִּתֵּ֤ן מֹשֶׁה֙ אֶת־הַגִּלְעָ֔ד לְמָכִ֖יר בֶּן־מְנַשֶּׁ֑ה
וַיֵּ֖שֶׁב בָּֽהּ׃ 41 וְיָאִ֤יר בֶּן־מְנַשֶּׁה֙ הָלַ֔ךְ וַיִּלְכֹּ֖ד
אֶת־חַוֺּתֵיהֶ֑ם וַיִּקְרָ֥א אֶתְהֶ֖ן חַוֺּ֥ת יָאִֽיר׃
42 וְנֹ֣בַח הָלַ֔ךְ וַיִּלְכֹּ֥ד אֶת־קְנָ֖ת וְאֶת־בְּנֹתֶ֑יהָ
וַיִּקְרָ֥א לָ֛ה נֹ֖בַח בִּשְׁמֽוֹ׃ פ

*40. so Moses gave Gilead to Machir son of Manasseh.* This statement contradicts vv. 1–4 and 29, where Reuben and Gad petition for Gilead. Some scholars explain that vv. 39–42 come from a different source, for not only does Moses give permission to the Manassites to take what has already been given to the Gadites, but also a battle of occupation ensues. This is the only war mentioned in this literary unit.

*Gilead…Machir son of Manasseh.* This part of the verse evokes the family line of Zelophehad's daughters—Mahlah, Tirzah, Hoglah, Milcah, and Noah—whose land was granted to them according to Numbers 27 and who are a subject of discussion again in Numbers 36.

—*Elizabeth Goldstein*

# Another View

Laws about vows in this parashah invite readers to reflect on the most (in)famous story about vows in the Bible: that of Jephthah's daughter. Her father, the warrior Jephthah, vows to sacrifice as a burnt offering the first thing to come out of his house should he win a particular battle (Judges 11:30–31). When his only child, his daughter, comes out dancing to greet him after his victory, Jephthah bemoans his (!) predicament. But far from challenging his rash vow, Jephthah's unnamed daughter encourages him to fulfill it (Judges 11:36). Her only request is that she be allowed to spend two months alone with her female companions in order to "bewail [her] maidenhood" (Judges 11:38). Afterward, "he did to her as he had vowed" (Judges 11:39). The narrator concludes by noting that it became a custom for young Israelite women to gather annually for four days to chant dirges in the daughter's memory (11:39–40). Tikva Frymer-Kensky suggests that no one in Israel would have viewed this death lightly. "Jephthah's daughter is a pious and faithful woman who is remembered in cult and story" ("The Bible and Women's Studies," *Studies in the Bible and Feminist Criticism*, 2006, p. 172). But what messages does her memory convey?

A story about a rash oath by another father, King Saul, suggests a comparison. Saul takes an oath that whoever eats or drinks during a particular battle will be put to death (I Samuel 14:24). His son Jonathan inadvertently violates the oath (even ridiculing it when he learns of it afterward), and Saul commands that Jonathan be executed. Jonathan expresses his readiness to die (v. 44). The troops, however, protest and instead ransom Jonathan (v. 45). Although we do not know what such "ransom" entails, Jonathan's life is spared.

*What messages does her memory convey?*

The two stories come from different settings and function as a critique within their context. Taken together, the stories of Jephthah's daughter and of Jonathan also convey messages about community and protest. Jonathan's story illustrates the power in community to discover ways to overturn rash pronouncements when it would cost a human life. Perhaps the legacy of Jephthah's daughter resides in the formation of community that can protest. It begins with the women who gather annually and chant, making their voices heard. —*Tamara Cohn Eskenazi*

# Post-biblical Interpretations

***Moses spoke to the heads of the Israelite tribes*** (30:2). Rabbi Moses Sofer, a Hungarian communal leader of the early 19th century, suggests that the Torah's discussion of vows and oaths is addressed to the "heads of the Israelite tribes" because it is leaders who most often fail to fulfill their promises and commitments (cited in A.Y. Greenberg, *Itturei Torah*, 1985).

***If a woman makes a vow*** (30:4). The Rabbis imagined that women made vows denying themselves certain foods, bathing, the use of cosmetics and jewelry, and sexual intercourse (BT *N'darim* 79a–b, 81b–82a), perhaps because these were things over which women had some control and which also gave them pleasure.

***in her father's household*** (30:4). According to Midrash *Sifrei B'midbar* on this verse, a young woman was still under her father's authority, even if she was not literally in her father's home when she made the vow. The medieval French commentator Rashi comments that the phrase "by reason of her youth" excludes both a very young girl, whose vows have no legal force, and a young woman who has reached the age of majority. An adult woman is not under her father's legal control, even if she is still living at home, and her father cannot annul her vows.

***But if her husband restrains her*** (30:9). BT *N'darim* 79a–b restricts a husband's power to annul his wife's vows to those of self-denial or that have an impact on the marital relationship. Depending on the interpreter, the husband's power of cancellation could be limited to vows that interfere with the couple's sexual relationship or could include any vow that might cause contention in the marriage (Adin Steinsaltz on *N'darim* 79b, citing R. Isaac DeTrani and R. Menachem Meiri). A vow to abstain from sexual intercourse could certainly be annulled by the husband.

*If an adult woman is living at home, her father cannot annul her vows.*

***The vow of a widow or of a divorced woman . . . shall be binding upon her*** (30:10). Since widows and divorcées are independent entities, no one is in a position to annul their vows. According to BT *Gittin* 79b, if a husband had annulled his wife's vows that had a negative impact on the marital relationship, the woman is obligated to fulfill those vows should she become a divorcée or widow. Once vows purely of self-denial have been annulled, however, they are cancelled permanently.

***But if he annuls them after [the day] he finds out, he shall bear her guilt*** (30:16). The Rabbis were concerned that a woman's ability to make vows could harm her marriage. Mishnah *Gittin* 4:7 discusses a husband's decision to divorce his wife due to her vows, while BT *Gittin* 46a indicates that a husband may simply not want to be married to a woman who makes vows.

The discussion of women's vows in Numbers 30 indicates that women are, in principle, capable of making and fulfilling vows. The restrictions on the vows of a minor daughter or wife in no way negate this ability. Rather, the laws recognize a certain understanding of the father-daughter and husband-wife relationship, one in which the man has a significant amount of power over the woman. This power is tempered, at least in a marital relationship, by rabbinic legislation. Mishnah *K'tubot* 7:1–5 teaches that a husband who makes vows that compromise his wife's ability to eat certain foods or wear jewelry, to visit her family or attend social functions, or who upholds his wife's own vows of self-denial for a lengthy period of time should divorce her, since his actions make her life uncomfortable.

***The Reubenites and the Gadites*** (32:1). Midrashic commentaries, such as *Tanchuma, Matot* 7, criticize the request of the Reubenites and the Gadites. They note that the tribes speak of providing shelter for their flocks before mentioning their children, an indication that they loved their possessions more than their families. Moses hints at their need to rethink their priorities; in his reply, he reverses the order, instructing them to "build towns for your children and [then] sheepfolds for your flocks" (32:24). According to *Tanchuma, Matot* 5, their inordinate love of possessions is what led these tribes to live outside of the land of Israel; as a result, they were exiled from their land before the other tribes (I Chronicles 5:26).

*—Dvora E. Weisberg*

# Contemporary Reflection

I HAVE ALWAYS been amazed by the power of Kol Nidrei, the prayer that introduces the evening service on Yom Kippur. Each year, I marvel at the sheer number of people who put aside all other commitments in order to be in synagogue, to be present to hear these ancient words. What brings us in the doors? Is it the haunting melody? Is it the threefold repetition of the prayer that moves us toward an emotional crescendo? Or is it the message of this prayer, which promises to absolve us of our responsibility for any vows that we may make in the coming year?

When we make vows, we put into speech our deepest fears and most profound hopes. Like Hannah who vows to dedicate her son to the sanctuary if God grants her a son (I Samuel 1:11), many of us make various commitments to do certain things or give up certain things that we cherish, in order to avert danger or bring about a hoped-for future. Yet some vows are rash, regrettable, or unrealizable; some are made under duress. Kol Nidrei reminds us that we have the choice to keep or annul our vows, thus affirming our most basic rights to self-expression and self-determination. This is part of what gives both the prayer and its recitation its profound power.

*Parashat Matot* enumerates various regulations concerning the status of women's vows (30:3–17). It also describes the circumstances under which a woman's vow may be annulled. We read that if her father or husband hears the vow on the day that she makes it, the vow can be nullified. The woman's personal status—whether she is a child, married, or divorced—will determine the status and power of the vow and whether she may fulfill it. Although she possesses the ability to make a vow, she may have to abandon her oaths and vows if the male authority figure in her life hears them. Given that fact, what are her options? She could take her chances with vowing and being heard. Or, to avoid her vow being annulled, she might either choose not to take on the responsibility involved in making an oath or a vow, or she might opt to make her vow but without anyone hearing her; in both of these options, she would be forced to follow, and be complicit in maintaining, the culture's attitude toward her desire for personal expression. She herself thus participates in her own silencing, because only by vowing without being heard, will she fulfill the mandate that her vow establishes. She acts by pretending that she has not acted. She can transgress the restrictions only by forcing herself to take part in them at the same time. She must betray herself to be true to herself.

*How can we stimulate and support women who long to fulfill their dreams?*

While we think we are free from these kinds of constraints, this is often not quite true. As mothers, when we chose to take emotional and physical care of our children, we voluntarily relinquish the freedom we might have enjoyed at an earlier time. Similarly, we may accept professional positions that do not sufficiently reflect our capabilities, in order to be available to support a beloved spouse, partner, or aging parent. We may not explicitly associate such situations with vow making or breaking, but in a certain important way, the relationship to vows exists. Like vow-making in the Bible, women's aspirations, spoken or not, are promises we make, even if only to ourselves. When we give them up because of external pressures, we pay a price.

On the one hand, we live in a time when, as women, we are blessedly free from the kind of controls that Numbers prescribes. On the other hand, we find ourselves within a web of relationships where we often give up what we had promised to ourselves, or we redirect our abilities. The stereotype of the Jewish mother may represent, in some ways, a woman's efforts to take power through the very vehicles that entrap her—by making a nice home, cooking gourmet meals, and having successful children.

Some may see these concessions as choices; others may see them as abandonment of self. We want to fulfill our responsibilities and live up to our expectations as spouses, mothers, and daughters; but we also want to be heard, to play an active role in our communities, to see ourselves and to be seen as powerful. We are aware that our culture could not survive if we sometimes did not voluntarily place our own needs as secondary. Yet, we are not always aware of the price some of us pay for that choice.

We see in our society rising rates of depression, eating disorders, premature sexuality, and self-destructive behaviors. A 2002 report of the American Psychological Association indicates that of the 17 million Americans who suffer from depression yearly, "women are twice as likely as men to experience a major depressive episode. Depression may occur at any age during a woman's life with certain events like puberty, pregnancy, perimenopause, trauma, substance abuse and quality of relationships." The report also notes that current research shows that women typically "place their needs secondary to those of others." One cannot simplistically attribute depression to a single cause, but it is difficult not to wonder to what extent the thwarting of one's longings and hopes, either by implicit social pressures or explicit ones, plays a role.

How can we can stimulate and support, rather than stifle, women who long to fulfill their ambitions and dreams, so that their vows to themselves—and others—can become a reality? As a Jewish community we are still working on answers to such questions, both in the personal and institutional realms. We no longer need to be complicit in the denial and abandonment of self that pervades our culture. Instead, we can speak honestly and openly about our lives and our choices. No longer must we voice our desires in an undertone, hoping that no one will hear. Instead, we can search to find—whether in studying the Torah or participating in the world—the truth of our lives that will help us to find the truth in God's teachings, so that we can live in a more just relationship with our loved ones and with our God.

*—Jacqueline Koch Ellenson*

# Voices

## Kol Nidrei, September 2001

Grace Schulman

*Numbers 30*

All vows are cancelled now,
all words undone like chains
that snap, their lockets smashed.
All sentences cut short,

main clauses powerless
to govern their dependents
or lead the voice in prayer.
All syllables annulled.

Verbs lag. All images
envisioned by blind eyes.
All penciled lines erased
that trembling hands composed.

My court, a grove at sundown:
sun rays pour through stiff branches,
unearthly yet of earth;
stump of a fallen oak

whose mate once flourished green
and now looms red and yellow
like towers burst into flame.
No ark with scrolls, no benches,

no prayer shawls, holy books,
or ram's horn. Only trees
stand witness in this silence,
and autumn's humid air

blurs a bark's crevices.
As this cloud turns to vapor,
all forms circle in smoke,
all promises unravel,

all pages torn to shreds
and blown to drift in wind
whose words cannot reveal
the truth of what I've seen.

## I'll Drop My Plea

Rivka Miriam (transl. Linda Stern Zisquit)

*Numbers 30:4–16*

I'll drop my plea
For I can no longer carry it.
Where will I drop it?
My plea sticks to me with dread.
My plea becomes mute out of fear.
Many years it clung to me.
Where should I drop it?
I whisper it a secret.
Out of fear it seals itself up.
Many years I carried my plea—
How can I drop it?

## *from* In the Sudan

Mary Loving Blanchard

*Numbers 30:4–16*

The women
reveal themselves
only at darkest moonless mid-night—
where they learn
some things, where they teach
some things

where they watch
from their homes, steal glances
through keyholes, inside
where they season soup with prayer

and interpret nothing
fearing prophecy

## *Dissolve in Slow Motion*

Alicia Suskin Ostriker

*Numbers 30:10*

When you watch a marriage
Dissolve, in slow motion,
Like a film, there is a point
Early on when the astute
Observer understands nothing
Can prevent the undesired
End, not shrinks, or friends,
Or how-to-love books,
Or the decency or the will
Of the two protagonists
Who struggle gamely like lab
Mice dropped in a jar
Of something viscous: the
Observer would rather snap
The marriage like a twig,
Speed the suffering up, but
The rules of the lab forbid.
Other rules govern decay
From within; so she just watches.

The little paws claw
Then cease, the furred
Bubbles of lungs stop.
The creatures get rigid.
Has something been measured?
It all gets thrown away.

## *from Songs of a Foreign Woman*

Lea Goldberg (transl. Rachel Tzvia Back)

*Numbers 31:13–18*

I am green and replete like a song that has
passed through the grass
I am soft and deep like a bird's nest.
I am from long ago,
from a forest that taught me to breathe
from the languor of lovers asleep in the grass
locked in each other's arms.

I am from there—
from the village of small winds.
On the last hilltop there stood a windmill
and the sky hung on its wings clouds mixed
with smoke.
And the wind came and the wind went.
I am from a village beating a rhythm on wooden
spoons
I am from there.

## *Mother Earth, Well Worn, Sun Washed*

Anna Margolin (transl. Adrienne Cooper)

*Numbers 32:1–5*

Mother earth, well worn, sun washed
Both slave and mistress am I beloved
Out of me, the humble and dejected
You grow, you push your roots through me
And like the blazing stars, like the flame of
    the sun
In long blind silences I run
Through your roots, in your branches
And half awake, and half in dream
I seek the sky through you.

## *Listen to the Bird*

Laya Firestone Seghi

*Numbers 32:1–27*

Listen to the bird
Flying
Singing
Signaling with sound
Or song
Traveling from one heart
To another.

After many miles of silence
A sound
One small signal
Starts circulation
On the desert of the soul.

The wagons have been dismembered
Wheels rolled into sand
Bones unburied
And what was once owned
Strewn about, no longer
Part of household or home.
Dried wood lies bleached in the sun
And there are no words
To leap like birds
With messages of how the world turns.

What is the sound?
Simple beyond recognition
It persists
Like water hitting the stone
And wherever the sound rings
The shape of the land
Takes form.

# מסעי ✦ *Mas'ei*

NUMBERS 33:1–36:13

## *The Journey's End*

PARASHAT MAS'EI ("marches") begins with exactly that: a review of Israel's travels through the wilderness. Numbers 33 presents a step-by-step itinerary describing the journey of the Israelites from the time they left Egypt to their arrival in the plains of Moab. A number of places serve as markers not merely of a geographical itinerary but also of experiences that shaped, and at times transformed, the Israelites from slaves to a people ready to possess the Promised Land.

After Numbers 33 recounts the travels of the past, Numbers 34–36 turn to the future; these units provide details about how Israel should function as a nation in its own land. As Hara E. Person notes, the parashah is about boundaries, both geographic and social (*The Women's Torah Commentary*, ed. Elyse Goldstein, 2000, p. 321). Specifically, God delineates the borders of the land and then appoints leaders from each tribe to oversee the distribution of each tribal portion.

After God and Moses assign the tribes their territories, the focus falls on the one tribe that is noticeably absent from the list: the Levites. Instead of possessing their own portion of land, the Levites will receive forty-eight cities in which to dwell. Since six of these cities will be set aside as cities of refuge for those guilty of unintentional homicide, God's speech turns to a definition of murder, the requirements for witnesses in capital cases, and other relevant rules to ensure safety and equity.

The book of Numbers concludes by revisiting the case of the daughters of Zelophehad, with a stipulation added to ensure that the ancestral territories they inherit will always belong to their tribe, Manasseh.

At the conclusion of the book of Numbers, the people stand at the plains of Moab, poised to enter the Promised Land. Here, the story of Israel's journey ends. (The book of Deuteronomy—which is composed almost entirely of Moses' speeches—does not carry the story further except in its final scene, the death of Moses.)

> *Two sets of five women form the bookends of Israel's journey from slavery.*

Although not visible in the travel accounts recorded in this parashah, women come to the fore at the end of the book, with the story about Mahlah, Tirzah, Hoglah, Milcah, and Noah, the five daughters of Zelophehad who are entitled to inherit his land (Numbers 27). In Numbers 36, leaders of their clan raise a concern: the land might be lost to the tribe if the women marry men from another tribe. Moses solves the problem by restricting the group from which the daughters may choose a spouse. Even though Numbers 36 restricts their marriage options to those of their tribe, it also guarantees that the five women will have what they demanded in 27:4—an inheritance among their kin. In addition, and as a result, their names are perpetuated in Israel's story.

The appearance of these five women at the conclusion of Numbers mirrors the reference to five women at the beginning of Exodus: Shiphrah and Puah, Moses' unnamed mother and sister (later identified as Jochebed and Miriam), and Pharaoh's daughter (Exodus 1–2), all of whom engaged in saving children's lives, Moses' life in particular. These two sets of five courageous and resourceful women thus form the bookends of Israel's journey from slavery.

—*Tamara Cohn Eskenazi*
*Elizabeth Goldstein*

## *Outline*

I. Remembering the Journey (33:1–56)
- A. The journey from Egypt (vv. 1–37)
- B. The death of Aaron (vv. 38–40)
- C. The journey to Moab (vv. 41–49)
- D. Directives for the future (vv. 50–56)

II. Preparing for the Future (34:1–35:34)
- A. Setting the boundaries of the Promised Land (34:1–15)
- B. Appointing leaders to oversee land allotment (34:16–29)
- C. Building a just infrastructure: cities of refuge (35:1–34)

III. Securing Land and Limits for Zelophehad's Daughters (36:1–12)
- A. The problem: land might transfer to another tribe (vv. 1–4)
- B. The solution: heiresses must marry within the tribe (vv. 5–9)
- C. The resolution: the daughters marry within their tribe (vv. 10–12)

IV. Conclusion (36:13)

These were the marches of the Israelites who
started out from the land of Egypt, troop by
troop, in the charge of Moses and Aaron. 2 Moses recorded the starting points of their various marches
as directed by יהוה. Their marches, by starting
points, were as follows:
3 They set out from Rameses in the first month,
on the fifteenth day of the first month. It was on
the morrow of the passover offering that the Israelites started out defiantly, in plain view of all the

לג אֵלֶּה מַסְעֵי בְנֵי־יִשְׂרָאֵל אֲשֶׁר יָצְאוּ
מֵאֶרֶץ מִצְרַיִם לְצִבְאֹתָם בְּיַד־מֹשֶׁה
וְאַהֲרֹן׃ 2 וַיִּכְתֹּב מֹשֶׁה אֶת־מוֹצָאֵיהֶם
לְמַסְעֵיהֶם עַל־פִּי יְהוָה וְאֵלֶּה מַסְעֵיהֶם
לְמוֹצָאֵיהֶם׃
3 וַיִּסְעוּ מֵרַעְמְסֵס בַּחֹדֶשׁ הָרִאשׁוֹן בַּחֲמִשָּׁה
עָשָׂר יוֹם לַחֹדֶשׁ הָרִאשׁוֹן מִמָּחֳרַת הַפֶּסַח
יָצְאוּ בְנֵי־יִשְׂרָאֵל בְּיָד רָמָה לְעֵינֵי כָּל־

## *Remembering the Journey*
(33:1–56)

This unit reviews the Israelites' journey from Egypt to their arrival in the plains of Moab. After listing the forty-two places that Israel stopped during their journey, the unit concludes with God's instructions about the future: once they possess the Promised Land, the Israelites must destroy the objects associated with foreign worship and apportion the land according to the size of the individual tribes or clans.

### THE JOURNEY FROM EGYPT (33:1–37)

This section contains the Torah's longest continuous list of the places where the Israelites encamped. To this day, the location of many of these places eludes biblical scholars and archeologists; the list is in tension with other accounts of the journey and may include symbolic elements no longer detectable. The narratives of Exodus, Numbers, and Deuteronomy also mention many of the places recounted in this section, but sometimes in a different order. Many scholars think that the editors of the Torah used this ancient list in Numbers 33 as a guide by which to arrange the individual episodes of Exodus and Numbers. Certain places evoke incidents recounted in other biblical narratives, whereas some remain otherwise unknown.

*2. **Moses recorded the starting points.*** This is one of very few places where Moses is actually credited with writing parts of what becomes the Torah.

*3. **They set out.*** Heb. *vayis'u,* which is a verb form of *mas'ei*, the name of this parashah, and means "they traveled." This verb punctuates the itinerary with its persistent repetition.

***in the first month, on the fifteenth day of the first month.*** The day that they left Egypt, the 15th of Nisan, corresponds to the first day of Passover, when Jews commemorate that exodus (see also Exodus 12).

◗ This parashah constitutes the philosophical basis for ongoing authoritative interpretation.

ANOTHER VIEW ➤ *1030*

◗ This law shows compassion for a person who accidentally kills another human being.

POST-BIBLICAL INTERPRETATIONS ➤ *1030*

◗ This amendment shows how an idea may require fine-tuning even after it becomes law.

CONTEMPORARY REFLECTION ➤ *1032*

◗ Oh God, . . . / Finally, for the first time in my life, / you gave me something I wanted.

VOICES ➤ *1034*

Egyptians. 4 The Egyptians meanwhile were burying those among them whom יהוה had struck down, every [male] first-born—whereby יהוה executed judgment on their gods.

5 The Israelites set out from Rameses and encamped at Succoth. 6 They set out from Succoth and encamped at Etham, which is on the edge of the wilderness. 7 They set out from Etham and turned about toward Pi-hahiroth, which faces Baal-zephon, and they encamped before Migdol. 8 They set out from Pene-hahiroth and passed through the sea into the wilderness; and they made a three-days' journey in the wilderness of Etham and encamped at Marah. 9 They set out from Marah and came to Elim. There were twelve springs in Elim and seventy palm trees, so they encamped there. 10 They set out from Elim and encamped by the Sea of Reeds. 11 They set out from the Sea of Reeds and encamped in the wilderness of Sin. 12 They set out from the wilderness of Sin and encamped at Dophkah. 13 They set out from Dophkah and encamped at Alush. 14 They set out from Alush and encamped at Rephidim; it was there that the people had no water to drink. 15 They set out from Rephidim and encamped in the wilderness of Sinai. 16 They set out from the wilderness of Sinai and encamped at Kibroth-hattaavah. 17 They set out from Kibroth-hattaavah and encamped at Hazeroth. 18 They set out from Hazeroth and encamped at Rithmah. 19 They set out from Rithmah and encamped at Rimmon-perez. 20 They set out from Rimmon-perez and encamped at

מִצְרָֽיִם׃ 4 וּמִצְרַ֣יִם מְקַבְּרִ֗ים אֵת֩ אֲשֶׁ֨ר
הִכָּ֧ה יְהוָ֛ה בָּהֶ֖ם כָּל־בְּכ֑וֹר וּבֵאלֹ֣הֵיהֶ֔ם
עָשָׂ֥ה יְהוָ֖ה שְׁפָטִֽים׃
5 וַיִּסְע֥וּ בְנֵֽי־יִשְׂרָאֵ֖ל מֵֽרַעְמְסֵ֑ס וַֽיַּחֲנ֖וּ
בְּסֻכֹּֽת׃ 6 וַיִּסְע֖וּ מִסֻּכֹּ֑ת וַיַּחֲנ֣וּ בְאֵתָ֔ם אֲשֶׁ֖ר
בִּקְצֵ֥ה הַמִּדְבָּֽר׃ 7 וַיִּסְעוּ֙ מֵֽאֵתָ֔ם וַיָּ֙שָׁב֙
עַל־פִּ֣י הַֽחִירֹ֔ת אֲשֶׁ֥ר עַל־פְּנֵ֖י בַּ֣עַל צְפ֑וֹן
וַֽיַּחֲנ֖וּ לִפְנֵ֥י מִגְדֹּֽל׃ 8 וַיִּסְעוּ֙ מִפְּנֵ֣י הַֽחִירֹ֔ת
וַיַּעַבְר֥וּ בְתוֹךְ־הַיָּ֖ם הַמִּדְבָּ֑רָה וַיֵּ֨לְכ֜וּ דֶּ֣רֶךְ
שְׁלֹ֤שֶׁת יָמִים֙ בְּמִדְבַּ֣ר אֵתָ֔ם וַֽיַּחֲנ֖וּ בְּמָרָֽה׃
9 וַיִּסְעוּ֙ מִמָּרָ֔ה וַיָּבֹ֖אוּ אֵילִ֑מָה וּ֠בְאֵילִ֠ם
שְׁתֵּ֞ים עֶשְׂרֵ֛ה עֵינֹ֥ת מַ֛יִם וְשִׁבְעִ֥ים תְּמָרִ֖ים
וַיַּחֲנוּ־שָֽׁם׃ 10 וַיִּסְע֖וּ מֵאֵילִ֑ם וַֽיַּחֲנ֖וּ עַל־יַם־
סֽוּף׃ 11 וַיִּסְע֖וּ מִיַּם־ס֑וּף וַֽיַּחֲנ֖וּ בְּמִדְבַּר־סִֽין׃
12 וַיִּסְע֖וּ מִמִּדְבַּר־סִ֑ין וַֽיַּחֲנ֖וּ בְּדָפְקָֽה׃
13 וַיִּסְע֖וּ מִדָּפְקָ֑ה וַֽיַּחֲנ֖וּ בְּאָלֽוּשׁ׃ 14 וַיִּסְע֖וּ
מֵאָל֑וּשׁ וַֽיַּחֲנוּ֙ בִּרְפִידִ֔ם וְלֹא־הָ֨יָה שָׁ֥ם מַ֛יִם
לָעָ֖ם לִשְׁתּֽוֹת׃ 15 וַיִּסְע֖וּ מֵרְפִידִ֑ם וַֽיַּחֲנ֖וּ
בְּמִדְבַּ֥ר סִינָֽי׃ 16 וַיִּסְע֖וּ מִמִּדְבַּ֣ר סִינָ֑י וַֽיַּחֲנ֖וּ
בְּקִבְרֹ֥ת הַֽתַּאֲוָֽה׃ 17 וַיִּסְע֖וּ מִקִּבְרֹ֣ת הַֽתַּאֲוָ֑ה
וַֽיַּחֲנ֖וּ בַּחֲצֵרֹֽת׃ 18 וַיִּסְע֖וּ מֵחֲצֵרֹ֑ת וַֽיַּחֲנ֖וּ
בְּרִתְמָֽה׃ 19 וַיִּסְע֖וּ מֵרִתְמָ֑ה וַֽיַּחֲנ֖וּ בְּרִמֹּ֥ן
פָּֽרֶץ׃ 20 וַיִּסְע֖וּ מֵרִמֹּ֣ן פָּ֑רֶץ וַֽיַּחֲנ֖וּ בְּלִבְנָֽה׃

*5. **Rameses.*** Rameses is one of the cities that the Israelites are said to have built when they were slaves (Exodus 1:11) and also the place where they observed the passover sacrifice and experienced the deliverance that the annual Passover festival commemorates (see above, v. 3).

*8–9.* Marah is noteworthy for its bitter water, which Moses sweetens with God's help; the name is also memorable as the place where the Israelites rebelled against God for the first time (see Exodus 15:22–25; Numbers 20 reflects a similar episode about the waters of Meribah).

*14–15. **Rephidim.*** This is where the Israelites fought against Amalek (see Exodus 17).

Libnah. 21 They set out from Libnah and encamped
at Rissah. 22 They set out from Rissah and encamped at Kehelath. 23 They set out from Kehelath
and encamped at Mount Shepher. 24 They set out
from Mount Shepher and encamped at Haradah.
25 They set out from Haradah and encamped at
Makheloth. 26 They set out from Makheloth and
encamped at Tahath. 27 They set out from Tahath
and encamped at Terah. 28 They set out from Terah
and encamped at Mithkah. 29 They set out from
Mithkah and encamped at Hashmonah. 30 They set
out from Hashmonah and encamped at Moseroth.
31 They set out from Moseroth and encamped at
Bene-jaakan. 32 They set out from Bene-jaakan and
encamped at Hor-haggidgad. 33 They set out from
Hor-haggidgad and encamped at Jotbath. 34 They
set out from Jotbath and encamped at Abronah.
35 They set out from Abronah and encamped at
Ezion-geber. 36 They set out from Ezion-geber and
encamped in the wilderness of Zin, that is, Kadesh.
37 They set out from Kadesh and encamped at
Mount Hor, on the edge of the land of Edom.

38 Aaron the priest ascended Mount Hor at the
command of יהוה and died there, in the fortieth
year after the Israelites had left the land of Egypt,
on the first day of the fifth month. 39 Aaron was a
hundred and twenty-three years old when he died
on Mount Hor. 40 And the Canaanite, king of Arad,
who dwelt in the Negeb, in the land of Canaan,
learned of the coming of the Israelites.

21 וַיִּסְעוּ מִלִּבְנָה וַיַּחֲנוּ בְּרִסָּה: 22 וַיִּסְעוּ
מֵרִסָּה וַיַּחֲנוּ בִּקְהֵלָתָה: 23 וַיִּסְעוּ מִקְּהֵלָתָה
וַיַּחֲנוּ בְּהַר־שָׁפֶר: 24 וַיִּסְעוּ מֵהַר־שָׁפֶר וַיַּחֲנוּ
בַּחֲרָדָה: 25 וַיִּסְעוּ מֵחֲרָדָה וַיַּחֲנוּ בְּמַקְהֵלֹת:
26 וַיִּסְעוּ מִמַּקְהֵלֹת וַיַּחֲנוּ בְּתָחַת: 27 וַיִּסְעוּ
מִתָּחַת וַיַּחֲנוּ בְּתָרַח: 28 וַיִּסְעוּ מִתָּרַח
וַיַּחֲנוּ בְּמִתְקָה: 29 וַיִּסְעוּ מִמִּתְקָה וַיַּחֲנוּ
בְּחַשְׁמֹנָה: 30 וַיִּסְעוּ מֵחַשְׁמֹנָה וַיַּחֲנוּ
בְּמֹסֵרוֹת: 31 וַיִּסְעוּ מִמֹּסֵרוֹת וַיַּחֲנוּ בִּבְנֵי
יַעֲקָן: 32 וַיִּסְעוּ מִבְּנֵי יַעֲקָן וַיַּחֲנוּ בְּחֹר
הַגִּדְגָּד: 33 וַיִּסְעוּ מֵחֹר הַגִּדְגָּד וַיַּחֲנוּ
בְּיָטְבָתָה: 34 וַיִּסְעוּ מִיָּטְבָתָה וַיַּחֲנוּ
בְּעַבְרֹנָה: 35 וַיִּסְעוּ מֵעַבְרֹנָה וַיַּחֲנוּ בְּעֶצְיֹן
גָּבֶר: 36 וַיִּסְעוּ מֵעֶצְיֹן גָּבֶר וַיַּחֲנוּ בְמִדְבַּר־צִן
הִוא קָדֵשׁ: 37 וַיִּסְעוּ מִקָּדֵשׁ וַיַּחֲנוּ בְּהֹר
הָהָר בִּקְצֵה אֶרֶץ אֱדוֹם:
38 וַיַּעַל אַהֲרֹן הַכֹּהֵן אֶל־הֹר הָהָר עַל־פִּי
יְהֹוָה וַיָּמָת שָׁם בִּשְׁנַת הָאַרְבָּעִים לְצֵאת
בְּנֵי־יִשְׂרָאֵל מֵאֶרֶץ מִצְרַיִם בַּחֹדֶשׁ הַחֲמִישִׁי
בְּאֶחָד לַחֹדֶשׁ: 39 וְאַהֲרֹן בֶּן־שָׁלֹשׁ וְעֶשְׂרִים
וּמְאַת שָׁנָה בְּמֹתוֹ בְּהֹר הָהָר: ס
40 וַיִּשְׁמַע הַכְּנַעֲנִי מֶלֶךְ עֲרָד וְהוּא־יֹשֵׁב
בַּנֶּגֶב בְּאֶרֶץ כְּנָעַן בְּבֹא בְּנֵי יִשְׂרָאֵל:

***36.*** The wilderness of Zin, also known as Kadesh, is where Miriam died (20:1); however, the itinerary notice here does not mention this event. (Contrast that silence with the mention of her brother Aaron's death in vv. 38–39.)

### THE DEATH OF AARON (33:38–40)

This account provides Aaron's age as well as the day and month of his death. He died at age 123, which is less than Sarah's age (127 years) but more than Moses' (120 years). This is one of three death notices for Aaron (see also 20:24–26, which includes more details, and Deuteronomy 10:6, which reports that he died in Moserah and not on Mount Hor). According to a non-biblical tradition, Aaron's tomb is located on an isolated peak in the southern Jordanian desert of Petra. Jewish pilgrims have ascended this mountain for centuries and left their names in inscriptions and registers at the tomb.

[41]They set out from Mount Hor and encamped
at Zalmonah. [42]They set out from Zalmonah and
encamped at Punon. [43]They set out from Punon
and encamped at Oboth. [44]They set out from
Oboth and encamped at Iye-abarim, in the territory of Moab. [45]They set out from Iyim and encamped at Dibon-gad. [46]They set out from Dibon-
gad and encamped at Almon-diblathaim. [47]They
set out from Almon-diblathaim and encamped in
the hills of Abarim, before Nebo. [48]They set out
from the hills of Abarim and encamped in the
steppes of Moab, at the Jordan near Jericho; [49]they
encamped by the Jordan from Beth-jeshimoth as
far as Abel-shittim, in the steppes of Moab.

[50]In the steppes of Moab, at the Jordan near
Jericho, יהוה spoke to Moses, saying: [51]Speak to the
Israelite people and say to them: When you cross
the Jordan into the land of Canaan, [52]you shall dispossess all the inhabitants of the land; you shall
destroy all their figured objects; you shall destroy
all their molten images, and you shall demolish all
their cult places. [53]And you shall take possession of

41 וַיִּסְעוּ מֵהֹר הָהָר וַיַּחֲנוּ בְּצַלְמֹנָה׃
42 וַיִּסְעוּ מִצַּלְמֹנָה וַיַּחֲנוּ בְּפוּנֹן׃ 43 וַיִּסְעוּ
מִפּוּנֹן וַיַּחֲנוּ בְּאֹבֹת׃ 44 וַיִּסְעוּ מֵאֹבֹת וַיַּחֲנוּ
בְּעִיֵּי הָעֲבָרִים בִּגְבוּל מוֹאָב׃ 45 וַיִּסְעוּ
מֵעִיִּים וַיַּחֲנוּ בְּדִיבֹן גָּד׃ 46 וַיִּסְעוּ מִדִּיבֹן
גָּד וַיַּחֲנוּ בְּעַלְמֹן דִּבְלָתָיְמָה׃ 47 וַיִּסְעוּ
מֵעַלְמֹן דִּבְלָתָיְמָה וַיַּחֲנוּ בְּהָרֵי הָעֲבָרִים
לִפְנֵי נְבוֹ׃ 48 וַיִּסְעוּ מֵהָרֵי הָעֲבָרִים וַיַּחֲנוּ
בְּעַרְבֹת מוֹאָב עַל יַרְדֵּן יְרֵחוֹ׃ 49 וַיַּחֲנוּ עַל־
הַיַּרְדֵּן מִבֵּית הַיְשִׁמֹת עַד אָבֵל הַשִּׁטִּים
בְּעַרְבֹת מוֹאָב׃ ס

50 וַיְדַבֵּר יְהֹוָה אֶל־מֹשֶׁה בְּעַרְבֹת מוֹאָב
עַל־יַרְדֵּן יְרֵחוֹ לֵאמֹר׃ 51 דַּבֵּר אֶל־בְּנֵי
יִשְׂרָאֵל וְאָמַרְתָּ אֲלֵהֶם כִּי אַתֶּם עֹבְרִים
אֶת־הַיַּרְדֵּן אֶל־אֶרֶץ כְּנָעַן׃ 52 וְהוֹרַשְׁתֶּם
אֶת־כׇּל־יֹשְׁבֵי הָאָרֶץ מִפְּנֵיכֶם וְאִבַּדְתֶּם
אֵת כׇּל־מַשְׂכִּיֹּתָם וְאֵת כׇּל־צַלְמֵי מַסֵּכֹתָם
תְּאַבֵּדוּ וְאֵת כׇּל־בָּמוֹתָם תַּשְׁמִידוּ׃
53 וְהוֹרַשְׁתֶּם אֶת־הָאָרֶץ וִישַׁבְתֶּם־בָּהּ

## THE JOURNEY TO MOAB (33:41–49)

The last stations mentioned in this list are those that lead to the steppes (plains) of Moab, the final stop for Moses. Some of these stopping places appear also in the description of the Israelites' travels in Numbers 21. Jacob Milgrom suggests that the list in Numbers 21, describing the journey, was edited to conform to this list (*Numbers*, 1990, p. 175). The compilation in this parashah mentions neither the rebellious words of the Israelites in Numbers 21 nor the deadly snakes that God sent to punish the people.

***49. steppes of Moab.*** This area east of the Jordan River, also sometimes known as the plains of Moab, marks the Israelites' final stop before entering the land. According to Deuteronomy, Moses speaks his final words to the people in this location. He will die here, atop Mount Nebo.

## DIRECTIVES FOR THE FUTURE (33:50–56)

God instructs Moses to proclaim an entrance strategy, describing the protocol concerning the inhabitants of Canaan. The instructions are concise and severe, calling upon the Israelites to dispossess the inhabitants completely; to destroy figured objects, molten images, and all worship places; and then to settle in the land. They are instructed to divide the land in proportion to the size of the tribes (or perhaps of the clans) once they enter the land. They are warned that God would destroy them should they neglect to destroy all the inhabitants. The rationale for complete destruction of the inhabitants is the danger that their presence would pose for Israel's future. According to Numbers' ideology, as well as Deuteronomy's, Israel cannot survive if it is subject to the influence and presence of Canaanites. The perspective of this disturbing

the land and settle in it, for I have assigned the land to you to possess. 54 You shall apportion the land among yourselves by lot, clan by clan: with larger groups increase the share, with smaller groups reduce the share. Wherever the lot falls for it, that shall be its location. You shall have your portions according to your ancestral tribes. 55 But if you do not dispossess the inhabitants of the land, those whom you allow to remain shall be stings in your eyes and thorns in your sides, and they shall harass you in the land in which you live; 56 so that I will do to you what I planned to do to them.

*34* יהוה spoke to Moses, saying: 2 Instruct the Israelite people and say to them: When you enter the land of Canaan, this is the land that shall fall to you as your portion, the land of Canaan with its various boundaries:

3 Your southern sector shall extend from the wilderness of Zin alongside Edom. Your southern boundary shall start on the east from the tip of the Dead Sea. 4 Your boundary shall then turn to pass south of the ascent of Akrabbim and continue to Zin, and its limits shall be south of Kadesh-barnea, reaching Hazar-addar and continuing to Azmon. 5 From Azmon the boundary shall turn toward the Wadi of Egypt and terminate at the Sea.

כִּי לָכֶם נָתַתִּי אֶת־הָאָרֶץ לָרֶשֶׁת
אֹתָהּ׃ 54 וְהִתְנַחַלְתֶּם אֶת־הָאָרֶץ בְּגוֹרָל
לְמִשְׁפְּחֹתֵיכֶם לָרַב תַּרְבּוּ אֶת־נַחֲלָתוֹ
וְלַמְעַט תַּמְעִיט אֶת־נַחֲלָתוֹ אֶל אֲשֶׁר־יֵצֵא
לוֹ שָׁמָּה הַגּוֹרָל לוֹ יִהְיֶה לְמַטּוֹת אֲבֹתֵיכֶם
תִּתְנֶחָלוּ׃ 55 וְאִם־לֹא תוֹרִישׁוּ אֶת־יֹשְׁבֵי
הָאָרֶץ מִפְּנֵיכֶם וְהָיָה אֲשֶׁר תּוֹתִירוּ מֵהֶם
לְשִׂכִּים בְּעֵינֵיכֶם וְלִצְנִינִם בְּצִדֵּיכֶם וְצָרְרוּ
אֶתְכֶם עַל־הָאָרֶץ אֲשֶׁר אַתֶּם יֹשְׁבִים בָּהּ׃
56 וְהָיָה כַּאֲשֶׁר דִּמִּיתִי לַעֲשׂוֹת לָהֶם
אֶעֱשֶׂה לָכֶם׃ פ
לד וַיְדַבֵּר יְהוָה אֶל־מֹשֶׁה לֵּאמֹר׃ 2 צַו
אֶת־בְּנֵי יִשְׂרָאֵל וְאָמַרְתָּ אֲלֵהֶם כִּי־אַתֶּם
בָּאִים אֶל־הָאָרֶץ כְּנָעַן זֹאת הָאָרֶץ אֲשֶׁר
תִּפֹּל לָכֶם בְּנַחֲלָה אֶרֶץ כְּנַעַן לִגְבֻלֹתֶיהָ׃
3 וְהָיָה לָכֶם פְּאַת־נֶגֶב מִמִּדְבַּר־צִן עַל־יְדֵי
אֱדוֹם וְהָיָה לָכֶם גְּבוּל נֶגֶב מִקְצֵה יָם־
הַמֶּלַח קֵדְמָה׃ 4 וְנָסַב לָכֶם הַגְּבוּל מִנֶּגֶב
לְמַעֲלֵה עַקְרַבִּים וְעָבַר צִנָה והיה וְהָיוּ
תּוֹצְאֹתָיו מִנֶּגֶב לְקָדֵשׁ בַּרְנֵעַ וְיָצָא חֲצַר־
אַדָּר וְעָבַר עַצְמֹנָה׃ 5 וְנָסַב הַגְּבוּל מֵעַצְמוֹן
נַחְלָה מִצְרָיִם וְהָיוּ תוֹצְאֹתָיו הַיָּמָּה׃

mandate reflects an understanding of Israel as small, inhabiting a landscape surrounded by (and infiltrated by) a stronger and more numerous people, the Canaanites. Historically speaking, the Canaanites and the Israelites were closely related. For example, what we know of contemporaneous Canaanite languages is that (like Phoenician to the north, and Moabite to the east) they were very close to Hebrew. Indeed, historians argue that the separation of Israelites from other Canaanites was a slow process. Some scholars maintain that the Bible is most severe with regard to Canaanites because Canaanite culture is most easily confused with that of Israel, as it attempts to establish a distinct identity. (See also at Deuteronomy 7:1–5, 24; 12:29–31.)

## *Preparing for the Future* (34:1–35:34)

In this unit, composed entirely of God's words to Moses, God marks the specific borders of Canaan, so that the people will learn the extent of the territory that they will inherit. Since Moses will not be accompanying the people across the Jordan, Joshua and Eleazar will lead the appointed tribal leaders in the division of lands. Discussion of external boundaries and tribal chiefs quickly moves to laws concerning the internal workings of the community. Numbers 35 addresses the practical and ritual issues of homicide that will unfortunately, yet inevitably, arise when the people establish new societies in Canaan.

[6]For the western boundary you shall have the coast of the Great Sea; that shall serve as your western boundary.

[7]This shall be your northern boundary: Draw a line from the Great Sea to Mount Hor; [8]from Mount Hor draw a line to Lebo-hamath, and let the boundary reach Zedad. [9]The boundary shall then run to Ziphron and terminate at Hazar-enan. That shall be your northern boundary.

[10]For your eastern boundary you shall draw a line from Hazar-enan to Shepham. [11]From Shepham the boundary shall descend to Riblah on the east side of Ain; from there the boundary shall continue downward and abut on the eastern slopes of the Sea of Chinnereth. [12]The boundary shall then descend along the Jordan and terminate at the Dead Sea.

That shall be your land as defined by its boundaries on all sides.

[13]Moses instructed the Israelites, saying: This is the land you are to receive by lot as your hereditary portion, which יהוה has commanded to be given to the nine and a half tribes. [14]For the Reubenite tribe by its ancestral houses, the Gadite tribe by its ancestral houses, and the half-tribe of Manasseh have already received their portions: [15]those two and a half tribes have received their portions across the Jordan, opposite Jericho, on the east, the orient side.

[16]יהוה spoke to Moses, saying: [17]These are the names of the commissioners through whom the land shall be apportioned for you: Eleazar the priest and Joshua son of Nun. [18]And you shall also take a chieftain from each tribe through whom the land

6 וּגְב֣וּל יָ֔ם וְהָיָ֥ה לָכֶ֛ם הַיָּ֥ם הַגָּד֖וֹל וּגְב֑וּל
זֶה־יִהְיֶ֥ה לָכֶ֖ם גְּב֥וּל יָֽם׃
7 וְזֶה־יִהְיֶ֥ה לָכֶ֖ם גְּב֣וּל צָפ֑וֹן מִן־הַיָּם֙ הַגָּדֹ֔ל
תְּתָא֥וּ לָכֶ֖ם הֹ֥ר הָהָֽר׃ 8 מֵהֹ֣ר הָהָ֔ר תְּתָא֖וּ
לְבֹ֣א חֲמָ֑ת וְהָי֛וּ תּוֹצְאֹ֥ת הַגְּבֻ֖ל צְדָֽדָה׃
9 וְיָצָ֤א הַגְּבֻל֙ זִפְרֹ֔נָה וְהָי֥וּ תוֹצְאֹתָ֖יו חֲצַ֣ר
עֵינָ֑ן זֶה־יִהְיֶ֥ה לָכֶ֖ם גְּב֥וּל צָפֽוֹן׃
10 וְהִתְאַוִּיתֶ֥ם לָכֶ֖ם לִגְב֣וּל קֵ֑דְמָה מֵחֲצַ֥ר
עֵינָ֖ן שְׁפָֽמָה׃ 11 וְיָרַ֨ד הַגְּבֻ֧ל מִשְּׁפָ֛ם הָרִבְלָ֖ה
מִקֶּ֣דֶם לָעָ֑יִן וְיָרַ֣ד הַגְּבֻ֔ל וּמָחָ֛ה עַל־כֶּ֥תֶף יָֽם־
כִּנֶּ֖רֶת קֵֽדְמָה׃ 12 וְיָרַ֤ד הַגְּבוּל֙ הַיַּרְדֵּ֔נָה וְהָי֥וּ
תוֹצְאֹתָ֖יו יָ֣ם הַמֶּ֑לַח
זֹאת֩ תִּהְיֶ֨ה לָכֶ֥ם הָאָ֛רֶץ לִגְבֻלֹתֶ֖יהָ סָבִֽיב׃
13 וַיְצַ֣ו מֹשֶׁ֔ה אֶת־בְּנֵ֥י יִשְׂרָאֵ֖ל לֵאמֹ֑ר זֹ֣את
הָאָ֗רֶץ אֲשֶׁ֨ר תִּתְנַחֲל֤וּ אֹתָהּ֙ בְּגוֹרָ֔ל אֲשֶׁר֙
צִוָּ֣ה יְהֹוָ֔ה לָתֵ֛ת לְתִשְׁעַ֥ת הַמַּטּ֖וֹת וַחֲצִ֥י
הַמַּטֶּֽה׃ 14 כִּ֣י לָֽקְח֞וּ מַטֵּ֨ה בְנֵ֤י הָרְאוּבֵנִי֙
לְבֵ֣ית אֲבֹתָ֔ם וּמַטֵּ֥ה בְנֵי־הַגָּדִ֖י לְבֵ֣ית אֲבֹתָ֑ם
וַחֲצִי֙ מַטֵּ֣ה מְנַשֶּׁ֔ה לָקְח֖וּ נַחֲלָתָֽם׃ 15 שְׁנֵ֥י
הַמַּטּ֖וֹת וַחֲצִ֣י הַמַּטֶּ֑ה לָֽקְח֣וּ נַחֲלָתָ֗ם מֵעֵ֛בֶר
לְיַרְדֵּ֥ן יְרֵח֖וֹ קֵ֥דְמָה מִזְרָֽחָה׃ פ
16 וַיְדַבֵּ֥ר יְהֹוָ֖ה אֶל־מֹשֶׁ֥ה לֵּאמֹֽר׃ 17 אֵ֚לֶּה
שְׁמ֣וֹת הָֽאֲנָשִׁ֔ים אֲשֶׁר־יִנְחֲל֥וּ לָכֶ֖ם אֶת־
הָאָ֑רֶץ אֶלְעָזָר֙ הַכֹּהֵ֔ן וִיהוֹשֻׁ֖עַ בִּן־נֽוּן׃
18 וְנָשִׂ֥יא אֶחָ֛ד נָשִׂ֥יא אֶחָ֖ד מִמַּטֶּ֑ה תִּקְח֖וּ

SETTING THE BOUNDARIES OF THE PROMISED LAND (34:1–15)

The borders of Canaan that this section outlines correspond approximately to the borders listed in Joshua 15 and Ezekiel 47, although the Ezekiel description utilizes place names that were probably more familiar to a post-exilic audience.

APPOINTING LEADERS TO OVERSEE LAND ALLOTMENT (34:16–29)

God commands Moses to appoint Joshua and Eleazar to oversee the tribal leaders in the apportioning of land. Why not select Caleb to work with Joshua? After all, Joshua and Caleb had been partners previously, as when they brought back a favor-

shall be apportioned. [19]These are the names of the commissioners: from the tribe of Judah: Caleb son of Jephunneh. [20]From the Simeonite tribe: Samuel son of Ammihud. [21]From the tribe of Benjamin: Elidad son of Chislon. [22]From the Danite tribe: a chieftain, Bukki son of Jogli. [23]For the descendants of Joseph: from the Manassite tribe: a chieftain, Hanniel son of Ephod; [24]and from the Ephraimite tribe: a chieftain, Kemuel son of Shiphtan. [25]From the Zebulunite tribe: a chieftain, Elizaphan son of Parnach. [26]From the Issacharite tribe: a chieftain, Paltiel son of Azzan. [27]From the Asherite tribe: a chieftain, Ahihud son of Shelomi. [28]From the Naphtalite tribe: a chieftain, Pedahel son of Ammihud.

[29]It was these whom יהוה designated to allot portions to the Israelites in the land of Canaan.

לִנְחֹ֖ל אֶת־הָאָֽרֶץ׃ 19 וְאֵ֖לֶּה שְׁמ֣וֹת
הָֽאֲנָשִׁ֑ים לְמַטֵּ֣ה יְהוּדָ֔ה כָּלֵ֖ב בֶּן־יְפֻנֶּֽה׃
20 וּלְמַטֵּה֙ בְּנֵ֣י שִׁמְע֔וֹן שְׁמוּאֵ֖ל בֶּן־
עַמִּיהֽוּד׃ 21 לְמַטֵּ֣ה בִנְיָמִ֔ן אֱלִידָ֖ד בֶּן־
כִּסְלֽוֹן׃ 22 וּלְמַטֵּ֥ה בְנֵי־דָ֖ן נָשִׂ֑יא בֻּקִּ֖י בֶּן־
יׇגְלִֽי׃ 23 לִבְנֵ֣י יוֹסֵ֔ף לְמַטֵּ֥ה בְנֵֽי־מְנַשֶּׁ֖ה נָשִׂ֑יא
חַנִּיאֵ֖ל בֶּן־אֵפֹֽד׃ 24 וּלְמַטֵּ֥ה בְנֵֽי־אֶפְרַ֖יִם
נָשִׂ֑יא קְמוּאֵ֖ל בֶּן־שִׁפְטָֽן׃ 25 וּלְמַטֵּ֥ה בְנֵֽי־
זְבוּלֻ֖ן נָשִׂ֑יא אֱלִיצָפָ֖ן בֶּן־פַּרְנָֽךְ׃ 26 וּלְמַטֵּ֥ה
בְנֵֽי־יששכר יִשָּׂשכָ֖ר נָשִׂ֑יא פַּלְטִיאֵ֖ל בֶּן־
עַזָּֽן׃ 27 וּלְמַטֵּ֥ה בְנֵֽי־אָשֵׁ֖ר נָשִׂ֑יא אֲחִיה֖וּד
בֶּן־שְׁלֹמִֽי׃ 28 וּלְמַטֵּ֥ה בְנֵֽי־נַפְתָּלִ֖י נָשִׂ֑יא
פְּדַהְאֵ֖ל בֶּן־עַמִּיהֽוּד׃
29 אֵ֕לֶּה אֲשֶׁ֖ר צִוָּ֣ה יְהֹוָ֑ה לְנַחֵ֥ל אֶת־בְּנֵֽי־
יִשְׂרָאֵ֖ל בְּאֶ֥רֶץ כְּנָֽעַן׃ פ

**35** יהוה spoke to Moses in the steppes of Moab at the Jordan near Jericho, saying: [2]Instruct the Israelite people to assign, out of the holdings apportioned to them, towns for the Levites to dwell in; you shall also assign to the Levites pasture land around their towns. [3]The towns shall be theirs to dwell in, and the pasture shall be for the cattle they

לה וַיְדַבֵּ֧ר יְהֹוָ֛ה אֶל־מֹשֶׁ֖ה בְּעַרְבֹ֣ת מוֹאָ֑ב
עַל־יַרְדֵּ֥ן יְרֵחֽוֹ לֵאמֹֽר׃ 2 צַו֮ אֶת־בְּנֵ֣י יִשְׂרָאֵל֒
וְנָתְנ֣וּ לַלְוִיִּ֗ם מִנַּחֲלַ֛ת אֲחֻזָּתָ֖ם עָרִ֣ים לָשָׁ֑בֶת
וּמִגְרָ֗שׁ לֶֽעָרִים֙ סְבִיבֹ֣תֵיהֶ֔ם תִּתְּנ֖וּ לַלְוִיִּֽם׃
3 וְהָי֧וּ הֶעָרִ֛ים לָהֶ֖ם לָשָׁ֑בֶת וּמִגְרְשֵׁיהֶ֗ם
יִהְי֤וּ לִבְהֶמְתָּם֙ וְלִרְכֻשָׁ֔ם וּלְכֹ֖ל חַיָּתָֽם׃

able report after the scouting expedition; hence they are the only non-Levites in the Exodus generation who will live to enter the Promised Land (Numbers 14). Here, God chooses a priest, not another military leader, to help in the delicate process of dividing territory. As a priest, Eleazar will not inherit land; thus his leadership is both logical and invaluable.

## BUILDING A JUST INFRASTRUCTURE: CITIES OF REFUGE (35:1–34)

Having delineated the land's boundaries, the Torah turns to guidelines for living within those boundaries. Any emerging social group must incorporate explicit directions for dealing with homicide, both intentional and unintentional. The Bible carefully predicts different situations with varying degrees of conflict in order to protect the rights of both the victim's family and the one who is responsible for an accidental homicide. (See also at Deuteronomy 19:1–13.)

*1–15.* According to Numbers 18:21–24, the tribe of the Levites is not to receive its own land like the other tribes but to serve as special personnel dedicated to God's service, for which they are due to receive a share of tithes from Israelite produce. Now we learn that the Levites will receive, in addition, forty-two towns in which their families can live. The pastureland that they are to receive with their cities is not official farmland—what the Bible

own and all their other beasts. [4]The town pasture that you are to assign to the Levites shall extend a thousand cubits outside the town wall all around. [5]You shall measure off two thousand cubits outside the town on the east side, two thousand on the south side, two thousand on the west side, and two thousand on the north side, with the town in the center. That shall be the pasture for their towns.

[6]The towns that you assign to the Levites shall comprise the six cities of refuge that you are to designate for a [male] killer to flee to, to which you shall add forty-two towns. [7]Thus the total of the towns that you assign to the Levites shall be forty-eight towns, with their pasture. [8]In assigning towns from the holdings of the Israelites, take more from the larger groups and less from the smaller, so that each assigns towns to the Levites in proportion to the share it receives.

[9]יהוה spoke further to Moses: [10]Speak to the Israelite people and say to them: When you cross the Jordan into the land of Canaan, [11]you shall provide yourselves with places to serve you as cities of refuge to which a [male] killer who has slain a person unintentionally may flee. [12]The cities shall serve you as a refuge from the avenger, so that the killer may not die unless he has stood trial before the assembly.

4 וּמִגְרְשֵׁי הֶעָרִים אֲשֶׁר תִּתְּנוּ לַלְוִיִּם מִקִּיר
הָעִיר וָחוּצָה אֶלֶף אַמָּה סָבִיב׃ 5 וּמַדֹּתֶם
מִחוּץ לָעִיר אֶת־פְּאַת־קֵדְמָה אַלְפַּיִם
בָּאַמָּה וְאֶת־פְּאַת־נֶגֶב אַלְפַּיִם בָּאַמָּה
וְאֶת־פְּאַת־יָם ׀ אַלְפַּיִם בָּאַמָּה וְאֵת
פְּאַת צָפוֹן אַלְפַּיִם בָּאַמָּה וְהָעִיר בַּתָּוֶךְ זֶה
יִהְיֶה לָהֶם מִגְרְשֵׁי הֶעָרִים׃
6 וְאֵת הֶעָרִים אֲשֶׁר תִּתְּנוּ לַלְוִיִּם אֵת שֵׁשׁ־
עָרֵי הַמִּקְלָט אֲשֶׁר תִּתְּנוּ לָנֻס שָׁמָּה הָרֹצֵחַ
וַעֲלֵיהֶם תִּתְּנוּ אַרְבָּעִים וּשְׁתַּיִם עִיר׃
7 כָּל־הֶעָרִים אֲשֶׁר תִּתְּנוּ לַלְוִיִּם אַרְבָּעִים
וּשְׁמֹנֶה עִיר אֶתְהֶן וְאֶת־מִגְרְשֵׁיהֶן׃
8 וְהֶעָרִים אֲשֶׁר תִּתְּנוּ מֵאֲחֻזַּת בְּנֵי־יִשְׂרָאֵל
מֵאֵת הָרַב תַּרְבּוּ וּמֵאֵת הַמְעַט תַּמְעִיטוּ
אִישׁ כְּפִי נַחֲלָתוֹ אֲשֶׁר יִנְחָלוּ יִתֵּן מֵעָרָיו
לַלְוִיִּם׃ פ
9 וַיְדַבֵּר יְהוָה אֶל־מֹשֶׁה לֵּאמֹר׃ 10 דַּבֵּר
אֶל־בְּנֵי יִשְׂרָאֵל וְאָמַרְתָּ אֲלֵהֶם כִּי
אַתֶּם עֹבְרִים אֶת־הַיַּרְדֵּן אַרְצָה כְּנָעַן׃
11 וְהִקְרִיתֶם לָכֶם עָרִים עָרֵי מִקְלָט
תִּהְיֶינָה לָכֶם וְנָס שָׁמָּה רֹצֵחַ מַכֵּה־נֶפֶשׁ
בִּשְׁגָגָה׃ 12 וְהָיוּ לָכֶם הֶעָרִים לְמִקְלָט
מִגֹּאֵל וְלֹא יָמוּת הָרֹצֵחַ עַד־עָמְדוֹ לִפְנֵי
הָעֵדָה לַמִּשְׁפָּט׃

---

calls *nachalah*. Rather, the land is to serve as pasture areas for their respective cities. The difference between these levitical city pastures and the farmland inheritances of other tribes is in the size and in the nature of the inheritance. The Levites are also to receive six cities of refuge for those guilty of unintentional homicide.

*6. [male].* The present translation presumes that the case of a female killer would be more complicated than the case that the Torah outlines. (See also at Exodus 21:13; Deuteronomy 19:3.)

***11. person.*** Heb. *nefesh*, a gender-neutral term (compare Leviticus 2:1). The blood-avenger is expected to protect the clan's women as well as its men.

***12. avenger.*** Although the Hebrew wording is not gender-specific, the translation presumes that this role was a man's job. In the ancient Near East, using weapons to defend the family honor was typically the responsibility of men. According to David Stein, women apparently were not expected to undertake an active hunt for the killer of their kin, but if an opportunity for vengeance presented itself to a woman in the victim's family, she might choose to seize that opportunity (*The Torah: Documentation for the Revised Edition*, 2005, at this verse).

***so that the killer may not die.*** The Torah offers

13 The towns that you thus assign shall be six cities of refuge in all. 14 Three cities shall be designated beyond the Jordan, and the other three shall be designated in the land of Canaan: they shall serve as cities of refuge. 15 These six cities shall serve the Israelites and the resident aliens among them for refuge, so that any man who slays a person unintentionally may flee there.

16 Anyone, however, who strikes another with an iron object so that death results is a murderer; the murderer must be put to death. 17 If one struck another with a stone tool that could cause death, and death resulted, that person is a murderer; the murderer must be put to death. 18 Similarly, if one struck another with a wooden tool that could cause death, and death resulted, that person is a murderer; the murderer must be put to death. 19 The blood-avenger himself shall put the murderer to death; it is he who shall put that person to death upon encounter. 20 So, too, if one pushed another in hate or hurled something at [the victim] on purpose and death resulted, 21 or if one struck another with the hand in enmity and death resulted, the assailant shall be put to death; that person is a murderer. The blood-avenger shall put the murderer to death upon encounter.

22 But if [a man] pushed without malice aforethought or hurled any object at [the victim] unintentionally, 23 or inadvertently dropped upon [the victim] any deadly object of stone, and death resulted—though not being an enemy and not seeking to harm—24 in such cases the assembly shall

13 וְהֶעָרִ֖ים אֲשֶׁ֣ר תִּתֵּ֑נוּ שֵׁשׁ־עָרֵ֥י מִקְלָ֖ט
תִּהְיֶ֥ינָה לָכֶֽם׃ 14 אֵ֣ת ׀ שְׁלֹ֣שׁ הֶעָרִ֗ים תִּתְּנוּ֙
מֵעֵ֣בֶר לַיַּרְדֵּ֔ן וְאֵת֙ שְׁלֹ֣שׁ הֶעָרִ֔ים תִּתְּנ֖וּ
בְּאֶ֣רֶץ כְּנָ֑עַן עָרֵ֥י מִקְלָ֖ט תִּהְיֶֽינָה׃ 15 לִבְנֵ֨י
יִשְׂרָאֵ֜ל וְלַגֵּ֣ר וְלַתּוֹשָׁב֙ בְּתוֹכָ֔ם תִּהְיֶ֛ינָה
שֵׁשׁ־הֶעָרִ֥ים הָאֵ֖לֶּה לְמִקְלָ֑ט לָנ֣וּס שָׁ֔מָּה
כָּל־מַכֵּה־נֶ֖פֶשׁ בִּשְׁגָגָֽה׃
16 וְאִם־בִּכְלִ֨י בַרְזֶ֧ל ׀ הִכָּ֛הוּ וַיָּמֹ֖ת רֹצֵ֣חַ ה֑וּא
מ֥וֹת יוּמַ֖ת הָרֹצֵֽחַ׃ 17 וְאִ֨ם בְּאֶ֧בֶן יָ֛ד אֲשֶׁר־
יָמ֥וּת בָּ֛הּ הִכָּ֖הוּ וַיָּמֹ֑ת רֹצֵ֣חַ ה֔וּא מ֥וֹת יוּמַ֖ת
הָרֹצֵֽחַ׃ 18 א֨וֹ בִּכְלִ֤י עֵץ־יָד֙ אֲשֶׁר־יָמ֣וּת בּ֔וֹ
הִכָּ֖הוּ וַיָּמֹ֑ת רֹצֵ֣חַ ה֔וּא מ֥וֹת יוּמַ֖ת הָרֹצֵֽחַ׃
19 גֹּאֵ֣ל הַדָּ֔ם ה֥וּא יָמִ֖ית אֶת־הָרֹצֵ֑חַ בְּפִגְעוֹ־
ב֖וֹ ה֥וּא יְמִתֶֽנּוּ׃ 20 וְאִם־בְּשִׂנְאָ֖ה יֶהְדֳּפֶ֑נּוּ
אוֹ־הִשְׁלִ֥יךְ עָלָ֛יו בִּצְדִיָּ֖ה וַיָּמֹֽת׃ 21 א֣וֹ
בְאֵיבָ֞ה הִכָּ֤הוּ בְיָדוֹ֙ וַיָּמֹ֔ת מֽוֹת־יוּמַ֥ת
הַמַּכֶּ֖ה רֹצֵ֣חַ ה֑וּא גֹּאֵ֣ל הַדָּ֗ם יָמִ֛ית אֶת־
הָרֹצֵ֖חַ בְּפִגְעוֹ־בֽוֹ׃
22 וְאִם־בְּפֶ֥תַע בְּלֹֽא־אֵיבָ֖ה הֲדָפ֑וֹ אֽוֹ־
הִשְׁלִ֥יךְ עָלָ֛יו כָּל־כְּלִ֖י בְּלֹ֥א צְדִיָּֽה׃ 23 א֣וֹ
בְכָל־אֶ֜בֶן אֲשֶׁר־יָמ֥וּת בָּהּ֙ בְּלֹ֣א רְא֔וֹת וַיַּפֵּ֥ל
עָלָ֖יו וַיָּמֹ֑ת וְהוּא֙ לֹא־אוֹיֵ֣ב ל֔וֹ וְלֹ֥א מְבַקֵּ֖שׁ
רָעָתֽוֹ׃ 24 וְשָֽׁפְטוּ֙ הָֽעֵדָ֔ה בֵּ֚ין הַמַּכֶּ֔ה וּבֵ֖ין

those who kill accidentally a safe haven from angry and grief-stricken relatives, discouraging both those who may wish to take the law into their own hands and those who may otherwise feel obliged to avenge out of a sense of duty. In addition to the physical protection afforded by a walled city, this institution protects the killer by making the victim's relatives liable for bloodguilt if they choose to disregard the law.

***16–28.*** These verses describe various cases of homicide. Verses 16–18 discuss acts unequivocally deemed intentional homicide, so the offender is expected to die by none other than the avenging relative. Only this formula can complete the Torah's particular ordained cycle of blood vengeance.

***24. assembly shall decide.*** Even seemingly obvious cases of unintentional homicide must be heard before an officially assembled group of leaders.

גֹּאֵל הַדָּם עַל הַמִּשְׁפָּטִים הָאֵלֶּה׃
25 וְהִצִּילוּ הָעֵדָה אֶת־הָרֹצֵחַ מִיַּד גֹּאֵל
הַדָּם וְהֵשִׁיבוּ אֹתוֹ הָעֵדָה אֶל־עִיר מִקְלָטוֹ
אֲשֶׁר־נָס שָׁמָּה וְיָשַׁב בָּהּ עַד־מוֹת הַכֹּהֵן
הַגָּדֹל אֲשֶׁר־מָשַׁח אֹתוֹ בְּשֶׁמֶן הַקֹּדֶשׁ׃
26 וְאִם־יָצֹא יֵצֵא הָרֹצֵחַ אֶת־גְּבוּל עִיר
מִקְלָטוֹ אֲשֶׁר יָנוּס שָׁמָּה׃ 27 וּמָצָא אֹתוֹ
גֹּאֵל הַדָּם מִחוּץ לִגְבוּל עִיר מִקְלָטוֹ וְרָצַח
גֹּאֵל הַדָּם אֶת־הָרֹצֵחַ אֵין לוֹ דָּם׃ 28 כִּי
בְעִיר מִקְלָטוֹ יֵשֵׁב עַד־מוֹת הַכֹּהֵן הַגָּדֹל
וְאַחֲרֵי מוֹת הַכֹּהֵן הַגָּדֹל יָשׁוּב הָרֹצֵחַ אֶל־
אֶרֶץ אֲחֻזָּתוֹ׃
29 וְהָיוּ אֵלֶּה לָכֶם לְחֻקַּת מִשְׁפָּט לְדֹרֹתֵיכֶם
בְּכֹל מוֹשְׁבֹתֵיכֶם׃
30 כָּל־מַכֵּה־נֶפֶשׁ לְפִי עֵדִים יִרְצַח אֶת־
הָרֹצֵחַ וְעֵד אֶחָד לֹא־יַעֲנֶה בְנֶפֶשׁ לָמוּת׃
31 וְלֹא־תִקְחוּ כֹפֶר לְנֶפֶשׁ רֹצֵחַ אֲשֶׁר־הוּא
רָשָׁע לָמוּת כִּי־מוֹת יוּמָת׃ 32 וְלֹא־תִקְחוּ
כֹפֶר לָנוּס אֶל־עִיר מִקְלָטוֹ לָשׁוּב לָשֶׁבֶת
בָּאָרֶץ עַד־מוֹת הַכֹּהֵן׃ 33 וְלֹא־תַחֲנִיפוּ
אֶת־הָאָרֶץ אֲשֶׁר אַתֶּם בָּהּ כִּי הַדָּם הוּא
יַחֲנִיף אֶת־הָאָרֶץ וְלָאָרֶץ לֹא־יְכֻפַּר לַדָּם

decide between the slayer and the blood-avenger.
25The assembly shall protect the killer from the blood-avenger, and the assembly shall restore him to the city of refuge to which he fled, and there he shall remain until the death of the high priest who was anointed with the sacred oil.
26But if the killer ever goes outside the limits of the city of refuge to which he has fled,
27and the blood-avenger comes upon him outside the limits of his city of refuge, and the blood-avenger kills the killer, there is no bloodguilt on his account.
28For he must remain inside his city of refuge until the death of the high priest; after the death of the high priest, the killer may return to his land holding.

29Such shall be your law of procedure throughout the ages in all your settlements.

30If anyone slays a person, the killer may be executed only on the evidence of witnesses; the testimony of a single witness against a person shall not suffice for a sentence of death.
31You may not accept a ransom for the life of a murderer who is guilty of a capital crime; [a murderer] must be put to death.
32Nor may you accept ransom in lieu of flight to a city of refuge, enabling a man to return to live on his land before the death of the priest.
33You shall not pollute the land in which you live; for blood pollutes the land, and the land can have no expiation for blood that is shed on it, except by

---

*25.* The (presumably natural) death of the chief priest marks the end period of the killer's culpability. Although the Hebrew Bible generally frowns on regarding a person's death as atonement for another's sin, the death of the chief priest seems to function that way symbolically. Although no one is killed, the priest's death benefits the life of another. The killer can return home, thus ending the exile.

*30. evidence of witnesses.* A single witness cannot convict a suspected killer in cases of capital offense. It is not only the gravity of the situation for the suspect that demands verifiable testimony but also the risk to the community, lest it mistakenly condemn itself to death for permitting the shedding of more innocent blood. (See also at Deuteronomy 17:16; 19:15–16.)

*31–34.* The biblical principle of bloodguilt, in which the spilled blood of murder must be avenged by causing the murderer's own blood to flow, was implicit in vv. 18–19, and is implicit again in vv. 31–32. Finally, vv. 33–34 explain the root of this principle: If a victim's blood is not avenged, the land becomes polluted. Examples of this concept can be found throughout the Hebrew Bible. For example,

the blood of the one who shed it. 34You shall not
defile the land in which you live, in which I Myself
abide, for I יהוה abide among the Israelite people.

36 The family heads in the clan of the descendants of Gilead son of Machir son of Manasseh, one of the Josephite clans, came forward and
appealed to Moses and the chieftains, family heads
of the Israelites. 2They said, "יהוה commanded my

אֲשֶׁר שֻׁפַּךְ־בָּהּ כִּי־אִם בְּדַם שֹׁפְכוֹ׃ 34 וְלֹא
תְטַמֵּא אֶת־הָאָרֶץ אֲשֶׁר אַתֶּם יֹשְׁבִים בָּהּ
אֲשֶׁר אֲנִי שֹׁכֵן בְּתוֹכָהּ כִּי אֲנִי יְהוָה שֹׁכֵן
בְּתוֹךְ בְּנֵי יִשְׂרָאֵל׃ פ

לו וַיִּקְרְבוּ רָאשֵׁי הָאָבוֹת לְמִשְׁפַּחַת בְּנֵי־
גִלְעָד בֶּן־מָכִיר בֶּן־מְנַשֶּׁה מִמִּשְׁפְּחֹת בְּנֵי
יוֹסֵף וַיְדַבְּרוּ לִפְנֵי מֹשֶׁה וְלִפְנֵי הַנְּשִׂאִים
רָאשֵׁי אָבוֹת לִבְנֵי יִשְׂרָאֵל׃ 2 וַיֹּאמְרוּ אֶת־

in Genesis 4:10, God reproaches Cain saying, "What have you done? Your brother's blood is shrieking to Me from the ground." This passage of Numbers teaches that no bloodguilt is required from someone who kills unintentionally.

## *Securing Land and Limits for Zelophehad's Daughters* (36:1–12)

The last episode in the book of Numbers is devoted entirely to the case of Mahlah, Tirzah, Hoglah, Milcah, and Noah. In one sense, their story seeks to resolve a potential crossing of boundaries in a book particularly concerned with setting boundaries (because the daughters' land risks being transferred to another tribe). In another sense, the story of these five sisters forms a counterpoint to stories about the five women in Exodus 1 and 2 who rescued Israelite children: the midwives Shiphrah and Puah, Moses' unnamed mother (later identified as Jochebed), Moses' unnamed sister (later identified as Miriam), and Pharaoh's unnamed daughter. Although there is no more than a literary connection between these two groups of women, the framing of Israel's journey as a whole with stories of women creates a symbolic symmetry.

In Numbers 27, the five daughters were granted the right to inherit their dead father's land, with no strings attached. In this parashah, at the urging of leaders of the clan and in order to protect it from losing the land permanently, Moses proclaims a new law that requires the women to marry only within their clan or tribe (v. 6; the instructions are not clear as to whether the husband must come from the clan or can be anyone in the larger tribe).

Whereas the legal resolution concludes the book of Numbers, it does not conclude the story of Mahlah, Tirzah, Hoglah, Milcah, and Noah (see below at v. 12).

### THE PROBLEM: LAND MIGHT TRANSFER TO ANOTHER TRIBE (36:1–4)

The clan leaders of the five sisters point out a potential problem: granting land to the sisters might mean loss of land to the Manasseh tribe if the women marry men from other tribes and their shares become parts of their husbands' tribes. The transfer of land from one tribe to another would then violate the divine command that prescribes that each tribe possesses its land permanently (Leviticus 25).

*1. Gilead.* According to the genealogies in Numbers 26:29–33, Gilead is the great-grandfather of the sisters.

*came forward.* As did the daughters of Zelophehad (27:1). Here the location is not stated—in contrast with 27:2, where the daughters approached the leaders and "the entire community" at "the entrance of the Tent of Meeting."

*2. "**יהוה** commanded . . . was further commanded by **יהוה**."* God has issued two commands that in some way conflict with each other.

lord to assign the land to the Israelites as shares by lot, and my lord was further commanded by יהוה to assign the share of our kinsman Zelophehad to his daughters. [3]Now, if they marry persons from another Israelite tribe, their share will be cut off from our ancestral portion and be added to the portion of the tribe into which they marry; thus our allotted portion will be diminished. [4]And even when the Israelites observe the jubilee, their share will be added to that of the tribe into which they marry, and their share will be cut off from the ancestral portion of our tribe."

[5]So Moses, at יהוה's bidding, instructed the Israelites, saying: "The plea of the Josephite tribe is just. [6]This is what יהוה has commanded concerning the daughters of Zelophehad: They may marry any-

אֲדֹנִי צִוָּה יְהֹוָה לָתֵת אֶת־הָאָרֶץ בְּנַחֲלָה
בְּגוֹרָל לִבְנֵי יִשְׂרָאֵל וַאדֹנִי צֻוָּה בַיהֹוָה
לָתֵת אֶת־נַחֲלַת צְלָפְחָד אָחִינוּ לִבְנֹתָיו׃
3 וְהָיוּ לְאֶחָד מִבְּנֵי שִׁבְטֵי בְנֵי־יִשְׂרָאֵל
לְנָשִׁים וְנִגְרְעָה נַחֲלָתָן מִנַּחֲלַת אֲבֹתֵינוּ
וְנוֹסַף עַל נַחֲלַת הַמַּטֶּה אֲשֶׁר תִּהְיֶינָה לָהֶם
וּמִגֹּרַל נַחֲלָתֵנוּ יִגָּרֵעַ׃ 4 וְאִם־יִהְיֶה הַיֹּבֵל
לִבְנֵי יִשְׂרָאֵל וְנוֹסְפָה נַחֲלָתָן עַל נַחֲלַת
הַמַּטֶּה אֲשֶׁר תִּהְיֶינָה לָהֶם וּמִנַּחֲלַת מַטֵּה
אֲבֹתֵינוּ יִגָּרַע נַחֲלָתָן׃
5 וַיְצַו מֹשֶׁה אֶת־בְּנֵי יִשְׂרָאֵל עַל־פִּי יְהֹוָה
לֵאמֹר כֵּן מַטֵּה בְנֵי־יוֹסֵף דֹּבְרִים׃ 6 זֶה
הַדָּבָר אֲשֶׁר־צִוָּה יְהֹוָה לִבְנוֹת צְלָפְחָד

*"assign the land . . . as shares."* At the heart of the issue stand two related laws. First, the requirement that the land allotted to each tribe should belong to that group permanently. Second, that at the fifty-year jubilee, land that has been transferred or sold returns to the permanent owner (see at Leviticus 25:10–28).

*"assign the share . . . to his daughters."* The relatives do not question the legitimacy of the daughters' claim or the divine origin of the allotment of land to them.

*3. "if they marry . . . our ancestral portion . . . be added to . . . the tribe into which they marry."* There are three ways to explain the concern about the loss of the clan's land. Most likely the complaint anticipates that the inherited land will eventually belong to the women's sons and thus (if the husband is from another tribe) no longer be part of the Gilead/Manasseh tribe. It is also possible that the complaint implies that the women belong to the clan of their husband when they marry and therefore their land also belongs to that tribe. A third, but least likely, possibility is that the complaint implies that, in marriage, the land will become the husband's property.

*4.* According to jubilee laws, sold or mortgaged ancestral land returns to its original owner every 50 years (see Leviticus 25). The land of the daughters would remain permanently with them and their heirs, and thus potentially a part of the clan into which they marry.

## THE SOLUTION: HEIRESSES MUST MARRY WITHIN THE TRIBE (36:5–9)

Moses resolves the conflict by limiting the women's marriage options. This solution is only necessary should the women marry. The possibility that the women might not marry is not addressed.

*5. Moses, at יהוה's bidding, instructed.* In the first episode of the three scenes about Zelophehad's daughters, Moses had brought their case before God (27:5). There is no mention here that Moses sought divine guidance for this new complication. He does, however, speak in God's name.

*6. "They may marry anyone they wish."* The free choice of spouses granted to the five sisters is especially significant in the context of the ancient world, because it excludes any male relative who wishes to claim the more typical role of a guardian

one they wish, provided they marry into a clan of their father's tribe. ⁷No inheritance of the Israelites may pass over from one tribe to another, but the Israelite [heirs]—each of them—must remain bound to the ancestral portion of their tribe. ⁸Every daughter among the Israelite tribes who inherits a share must marry someone from a clan of her father's tribe, in order that every Israelite [heir] may keep an ancestral share. ⁹Thus no inheritance shall pass over from one tribe to another, but the Israelite tribes shall remain bound each to its portion."

¹⁰The daughters of Zelophehad did as יהוה had commanded Moses: ¹¹Mahlah, Tirzah, Hoglah, Milcah, and Noah, Zelophehad's daughters, were

לֵאמֹ֣ר לַטּ֣וֹב בְּעֵינֵיהֶ֖ם תִּהְיֶ֣ינָה לְנָשִׁ֑ים אַ֗ךְ לְמִשְׁפַּ֛חַת מַטֵּ֥ה אֲבִיהֶ֖ם תִּהְיֶ֥ינָה לְנָשִֽׁים: ⁷ וְלֹֽא־תִסֹּ֤ב נַחֲלָה֙ לִבְנֵ֣י יִשְׂרָאֵ֔ל מִמַּטֶּ֖ה אֶל־מַטֶּ֑ה כִּ֣י אִ֗ישׁ בְּנַחֲלַת֙ מַטֵּ֣ה אֲבֹתָ֔יו יִדְבְּק֖וּ בְּנֵ֥י יִשְׂרָאֵֽל: ⁸ וְכׇל־בַּ֞ת יֹרֶ֣שֶׁת נַחֲלָ֗ה מִמַּטּוֹת֮ בְּנֵ֣י יִשְׂרָאֵל֒ לְאֶחָ֗ד מִמִּשְׁפַּ֛חַת מַטֵּ֥ה אָבִ֖יהָ תִּהְיֶ֣ה לְאִשָּׁ֑ה לְמַ֗עַן יִֽירְשׁוּ֙ בְּנֵ֣י יִשְׂרָאֵ֔ל אִ֖ישׁ נַחֲלַ֥ת אֲבֹתָֽיו: ⁹ וְלֹֽא־תִסֹּ֧ב נַחֲלָ֛ה מִמַּטֶּ֖ה לְמַטֶּ֣ה אַחֵ֑ר כִּי־אִ֗ישׁ בְּנַ֣חֲלָת֔וֹ יִדְבְּק֖וּ מַטּ֥וֹת בְּנֵ֥י יִשְׂרָאֵֽל: ¹⁰ כַּאֲשֶׁ֛ר צִוָּ֥ה יְהֹוָ֖ה אֶת־מֹשֶׁ֑ה כֵּ֣ן עָשׂ֔וּ בְּנ֖וֹת צְלׇפְחָֽד: ¹¹ וַתִּהְיֶ֜ינָה מַחְלָ֣ה תִרְצָ֗ה וְחׇגְלָ֧ה וּמִלְכָּ֛ה וְנֹעָ֖ה בְּנ֣וֹת צְלׇפְחָ֑ד לִבְנֵ֖י

for the unmarried daughters. Contrast this with the status of the heiress in classical Athens who is subject to the automatic control by a male relative in regard to marriage, as the way of protecting and preserving family property.

*"provided they marry into a clan of their father's tribe."* From a modern perspective, this restriction might appear as a step back after the forward steps in Numbers 27, since God's law granted the land to the sisters in Numbers 27 with no strings attached. Practically speaking, however, the freedom to choose a spouse from their clan is less constricting than it might seem, given the size of this tribe (one of the largest among the Israelites).

*7.* *"No inheritance of the Israelites may pass over from one tribe to another."* An attempt to secure the greater good of protecting tribal ownership of the land, rather than a gender-specific goal, stands as the basis for restricting the marriage choices of the sisters. In other words, the issue of who inherits land is not depicted as an objection to women's owning land but rather as a concern for preserving tribal ownership of allotted land.

*8.* *"Every daughter . . . who inherits."* Like the ruling that allows all daughters to inherit land when there are no sons (27:8), this modification clause also applies to all comparable situations. All daugh

ters who inherit land must marry members of their tribe.

*"in order that every Israelite [heir] may keep an ancestral share."* The goal of the compromise is unambiguous.

*9.* Moses once more reiterates the underlying principle of the law, an emphasis that is particularly significant coming at the last stop of the journey and at the end of the book.

### THE RESOLUTION: THE DAUGHTERS MARRY WITHIN THEIR TRIBE (36:10–12)

The narrator confirms that the daughters followed God's and Moses' command, albeit without naming the daughters' mates.

*11.* *Mahlah, Tirzah, Hoglah, Milcah, and Noah.* The sister's names appear for the first time in this parashah. Whereas the speakers thus far (the relatives and Moses) refer to the five sisters as "Zelophehad's daughters" (vv. 2, 6), the narrator now calls them by their names. The sisters' own names appear in all three episodes about them. The order here, however, differs from that of Numbers 27 and Joshua 17, and there is no obvious explanation for the sequence. On the names and their connection to places, see at 27:1–11.

married to sons of their uncles, [12]marrying into clans of descendants of Manasseh son of Joseph; and so their share remained in the tribe of their father's clan.

דֹדֵיהֶ֖ן לְנָשִֽׁים׃ 12 מִֽמִּשְׁפְּחֹ֛ת בְּנֵֽי־מְנַשֶּׁ֥ה
בֶן־יוֹסֵ֖ף הָי֣וּ לְנָשִׁ֑ים וַתְּהִי֙ נַחֲלָתָ֔ן עַל־מַטֵּ֖ה
מִשְׁפַּ֥חַת אֲבִיהֶֽן׃

***were married to sons of their uncles.*** Although they can marry any man from the very large tribe of Manasseh, the sisters choose their cousins. There is no reason to suppose (as Jacob Milgrom does) that the land was transferred to the husbands once the women married (*Numbers*, 1990, p. 298). The Bible does not prohibit wives from owning property.

Furthermore, the earliest Jewish contracts that we have illustrate that women continued to own property after marriage and that parents bequeathed property to both sons and daughters. Documents from the Jewish community in Elephantine, Egypt, include several marriage contracts and sale contracts. In several documents (dated around 460–447 B.C.E.), the father of Mibtahiah transfers property to her even though he has sons. The property remains hers at marriage. In one case, her husband, who apparently improved one of the several properties in question, or is expected to, is assured that he will have power over half of that particular property "for the improvement which you made" (Cowley 9:11–12). He cannot sell that half, and it goes to their children after him (Cowley 9). In another contract dated 434 B.C.E., a husband transfers ownership of half of a newly purchased property to his wife irreversibly and makes their children (a boy and a girl) equal heirs of his portion (Kraeling 4).

It is difficult to assess the relationships between practices of this particular Jewish community and those in the Bible and ancient Israel in earlier periods. But evidence that women retained their property after marriage and were also able to inherit should caution us against concluding otherwise in this case without evidence. Moreover, the appearance of some of the women's names as place names on early clay fragments suggest that they were recognized as primary owners (see below at v. 12 and at 27:1–2).

*12.* To underscore the perfect execution of divine command, the narrator adds that the women's marriages indeed preserve the inherited land within their father's tribe. The story of Mahlah, Tirzah, Hoglah, Milcah, and Noah will conclude in Joshua 17, in the report about apportioning the land among the tribes. There, we read that "Mahlah, Noah, Hoglah, Milcah, and Tirzah . . . appeared before the priest Eleazar, Joshua son of Nun, and the chieftains, saying: 'יהוה commanded Moses to grant us a portion among our male kinsmen.' So, in accordance with יהוה's instructions, they were granted a portion among their father's kinsmen" (17:3–4). This passage makes no mention of their husbands. Furthermore, "Manasseh's daughters inherited a portion in these together with his sons, while the land of Gilead was assigned to the rest of Manasseh's descendants" (17:6; note that in Joshua the women are also called "Manasseh's daughters"!). Although the historical reliability of the material in Joshua is subject to debate, it is safe to say that the book of Joshua portrays the inheritance of Mahlah, Noah, Hoglah, Milcah, and Tirzah as a large one. The 8th-century-B.C.E. clay fragments that bear names of towns, including Noah and Hoglah, illustrate the persistence of these names in Israelite tradition (see the introduction to Numbers 27:1–2). Tirzah is also the name of the royal city in the Northern Kingdom in the 10th century (see I Kings 14). (For more on the daughters' names, see at 27:1–11.)

[13]These are the commandments and regulations that יהוה enjoined upon the Israelites, through Moses, on the steppes of Moab, at the Jordan near Jericho.

13 אֵ֧לֶּה הַמִּצְוֹ֣ת וְהַמִּשְׁפָּטִ֗ים אֲשֶׁ֨ר צִוָּ֧ה
יְהֹוָ֛ה בְּיַד־מֹשֶׁ֖ה אֶל־בְּנֵ֣י יִשְׂרָאֵ֑ל בְּעַרְבֹ֣ת
מוֹאָ֔ב עַ֖ל יַרְדֵּ֥ן יְרֵחֽוֹ׃

## *Conclusion* (36:13)

The conclusion to the book of Numbers marks the conclusion of the journey to the Promised Land. The plains (or steppes) of Moab will be the setting for the book of Deuteronomy, the place where Moses will pronounce his last teachings before he dies. The concluding statement specifies that God is the source of the last group of laws that Moses teaches.

—*Tamara Cohn Eskenazi*
*Elizabeth Goldstein*

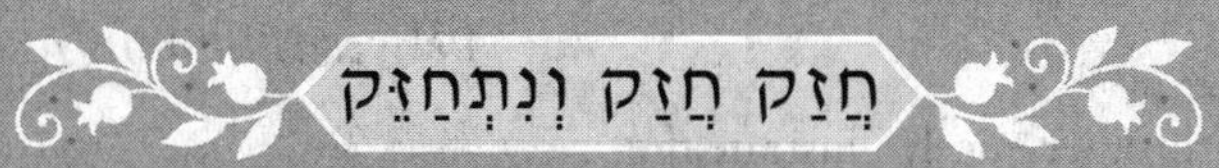

# Another View

NUMBERS 27 DESCRIBED the amending of a law regarding who may inherit land: Zelophehad's daughters—Mahlah, Noah, Hoglah, Milcah, and Tirzah—brought their case before Moses; after they demanded their share of the land, the law was amended to enable them to inherit their father's land. However, in this parashah (Numbers 36), the clan heads of their tribe approach Moses and ask him to prevent the discrimination stemming from the previously amended law. Apparently, correcting the earlier inequity created a new one, this time for the tribe to which they belong. As before, Moses amends the legislation, under God's guidance.

The two stories, taken together, nicely illustrate the fact that some laws in the Torah are the outcome of cooperation between God and human beings. This raises the question concerning the nature of the Torah's laws. Most of the commandments in the Torah appear as if written a priori and seem sealed and unchangeable. Nevertheless, five commandments happen to be the outcome of certain circumstances that called for God's intervention and resulted in new legislation and amendments. (The other three cases are: the stories of the blasphemer in Leviticus 24:10–16; the man gathering sticks in Numbers 15:32–36; and the ritually impure individuals prevented from bringing the paschal offering on time in 9:1–14.)

The Torah could have preserved only the final laws, without the narratives that describe their emergence. But it seems that the Torah intentionally highlights a principle of dialogue between human groups and divine legislation. The purpose of the laws is that "one shall live by them" (Leviticus 18:5), meaning that the laws of the Torah must fit life. Such a goal is achieved by an openness to change, albeit with God's explicit consent and command. As a result, this parashah constitutes the philosophical basis for the Oral Torah—that is, the ongoing, authoritative interpretations of Scripture. The presupposition is that its legal kernel and principles are embedded within the Written Torah, and that through different sorts of exegesis of the Torah (that is, through its explanation and interpretation), the Oral Torah is fleshed out. By way of constant searching, responses are revealed to never-ending questions.

*The Torah highlights a principle of dialogue between humans and divine legislation.*

—*Masha Turner*

# Post-biblical Interpretations

***These were the marches of the Israelites*** (33:1). Why does the Torah recount all of the steps of Israel's forty-year wanderings? Midrash *Tanchuma, Mas'ei* 11 draws a parallel to a king who takes his child on a journey to seek a cure for the child's sickness. On the return trip, the doting father recalls each leg of the original trip, remembering how they traveled together and how he worried about his child's condition. So the Torah in recalling the journey calls to mind the struggle God had with the Israelites in the wilderness.

***The towns that you assign to the Levites*** (35:6). *Tanchuma, Mas'ei* 11 draws a parallel between God's punishment of Adam and the law of the individual who commits homicide. God had told Adam that eating the fruit of the tree of knowledge would result in his death; nevertheless, God was merciful and exiled Adam from the Garden of Eden as a punishment for bringing death into the world. So too this law shows compassion for a person who accidentally kills another human being, exiling the killer to a city of refuge rather than mandating the killer's death.

***The blood-avenger himself shall put the murderer to death*** (35:19). The Torah recognizes that homicide can easily lead to a blood feud between families, with one act of vengeance leading to another and then another. JT *Makot* 2:5 even considers the possibility that the killer and his victim might be relatives, leading to a situation where to avenge one family member, a person might seek vengeance on another relative.

*Do not mention a woman's age while she is single, for it is irrelevant after marriage.*

***the assembly shall decide*** (35:24). Since the assembly that decides between the killer and the blood-avenger must be impartial, relatives of the accused and his victim are excluded from the assembly (JT *Sanhedrin* 3:9).

***This is what*** (36:6). Rabbinic sources (BT *Taanit* 30b; *Bava Batra* 120a) indicate that this law, requiring daughters who inherit from their father to marry within the clan, applied only to the generation of the wilderness, or to a time in which land was held by the tribes (Baruch HaLevi Epstein, *Torah T'mimah* on 36:6).

***They may marry anyone they wish, provided they marry into a clan of their father's tribe*** (36:6). This statement seems contradictory. A tradition in BT *Bava Batra* 120a explains that the daughters of Zelophehad were permitted to marry into any of the tribes, but the Torah advised them to make "suitable" marriages that would please both themselves and their father's clan members.

***Mahlah, Tirzah, Hoglah, Milcah, and Noah*** (36:11). Zelophehad's daughters are listed in a different order here than in Numbers 27. According to BT *Bava Batra* 120a, this indicates that each of them was equal to the other. This text also suggests that Numbers 36 lists the women in the order in which they were born, while Numbers 27 mentions them in order of wisdom.

These different orders are cited in several 19th-century anecdotes that discuss women's experiences and characteristics (cited in A. I. Greenberg, *Itturei Torah* on 36:11). A disciple of Rabbi Elijah ben Solomon Zalman ("the Vilna Gaon") was approached by a man who complained that after marrying his son to the daughter of an important man, he discovered that his daughter-in-law, a woman whom he described as both intelligent and pious, was ten years older than her new husband. The rabbi responded with humor, pointing out that the daughters of Zelophehad were listed in chronological order only after they were married, to teach that a woman's age should not be mentioned while she is single since it becomes irrelevant after marriage.

In another story, the wife of Rabbi Saul of Amsterdam, known in her youth as a brilliant woman, was asked why she had abandoned her studies after marrying and having children. She replied by noting that before their marriage, the daughters of Zelophehad were listed by (that is, known for) their wisdom, but "after they married and accepted the millstone [of household duties and childrearing] around their necks, their wisdom was forgotten and they were thereafter listed by their ages." This story acknowledges the challenges that intelligent and learned women faced in continuing their studies in a society that expected married women to devote themselves to their husbands and children.

—*Dvora E. Weisberg*

# Contemporary Reflection

THE LAST PARASHAH in the book of Numbers ends with a second story about the five daughters of Zelophehad—Mahlah, Noah, Hoglah, Milcah, and Tirzah. The first story, in Numbers 27, shows how the sisters demanded and received a promise—from God, no less—that they will inherit their family's ancestral land (since their father died without leaving a son). Here in *parashat Mas'ei*, the daughters' male relatives challenge the women's inheritance right in order to protect ownership of tribal land. Moses responds *al pi Adonai*—"at God's bidding" (36:5), by amending the new law. The change requires women who inherit ancestral land to marry into a family of their father's tribe (36:6), thereby limiting these women's choice of spouses, but keeping the property within the tribe. The parashah and the book end by confirming that the sisters did marry accordingly.

This sequel in Numbers 36 appears to be a setback after the daughters' startling triumph in *parashat Pinchas* (Numbers 27), where they won significant inheritance rights for themselves and for their "sisters" in the future. The five sisters in particular, and Israelite women in general, walk away from *parashat Mas'ei* with less than they had before. As some scholars observe, when the sisters marry their first cousins, they essentially hand over their inheritance to the same men who would otherwise have inherited the land had the women never stood up for themselves (Hara E. Person, "Masa'ei: Boundaries and Limits," in *The Women's Torah Commentary*, 2000, p. 327; and Jacob Milgrom, *Numbers*, 1990, p. 298). Moreover, in giving up some of their gains for the sake of larger familial and communal needs, they seem to perpetuate the all-too-familiar situation of women foregoing their own needs for the sake of others in the family.

Nevertheless, while the decree in this parashah certainly is a step back from the full rights given to the daughters previously, it is not a full retreat; they still end up with more than they had in the first place. To begin with, the sisters marry from a position of strength, not dependency. What would have happened to the sisters had they not stepped forward to ask for their inheritance? Given the frequency with which the Torah reminds us of our societal obligation to care for widows and orphans, we can guess what might have happened to Zelophehad's daughters had they remained landless. Furthermore, the daughters' actions and triumph eliminate a whole category of dependent orphans (the girls and women who until then did not inherit).

The story of Zelophehad's daughters invites us to reflect on the roles that family members and community play in one's life. Our freedom as women to make choices and demands stems in part from our Jewish heritage in which women such as Mahlah, Noah, Hoglah, Milcah, and Tirzah stood together to argue for equal rights, convincing leadership—human and divine—of the justness of their cause.

*The most effective and enduring changes create justice for all members of society.*

Today our individual commitments and decisions from the everyday to the profound (taking a class at night, accepting a board position, making a career change) affect our partners and our children, regardless of who makes them. Likewise, our seemingly private decisions launch a whole range of new communal developments. For example, working and studying mothers and their partners require, and therefore initiate, new structures for childcare that were not available to the previous generation. Such choices compel (or inspire) others to "think outside the box" to accommodate new challenges.

Especially in egalitarian relationships, each person's words and visions, choices and decisions, actions and reactions, construct an unfolding dialogue, ever-growing and often life-changing in much wider circles than one would have envisioned. What began as a seemingly private demand by five sisters for their share of land became a new law to protect all women in unforeseen circumstances.

In *parashat Mas'ei*, at the end of the Israelites' journey in the wilderness, the amending of the ruling for Zelophehad's daughters (along with the concomitant change in inheritance laws in perpetuity for all Israelites, 36:8–9) teaches modern lessons for intertwined lives: in a society, community, or family, one person's needs and desires must be weighed against those of others. Final authority should not belong to one member only, nor should laws be made based on the interests of only one party.

The amendments in Numbers 36 also emphasize the need for lawmakers to look always at the rights of *all* citizens, and not just at the issues brought by lobbyists. The women's movement, like all movements of liberation, discovered long ago that the most effective and enduring changes are those that create justice for *all* members of society.

This observation does not negate the need to speak out for special interests. Just as the prayer of our matriarch Hannah became for the rabbis of the Talmud the model of how to pray (I Samuel 1:10–11; BT *B'rachot* 31a–b), so in their own time, the daughters of Zelophehad model how to be an advocate for one's own rights. Had Hannah not prayed or the sisters not spoken up, no change would have taken place. Speaking out opens up a public space where the diverse needs of community members can be examined in order to negotiate for equitable resolutions. Because the original ruling given in *parashat Pinchas* benefited the daughters but not the tribe, the amendment here in *parashat Mas'ei* demonstrates how an idea may require fine-tuning even after it becomes law.

The ending of the book of Numbers sets the stage for processes of change, showing us that even within the Torah itself, lawmaking is an inexact science requiring flexibility to change as issues arise and society evolves. We honor the sisters' ability to speak up, and their grace to concede when their gain is shown to be against community interests. We are the inheritors of their chutzpah and their quest for equal rights.

*—Lisa Edwards*
*Jill Berkson Zimmerman*

# *Voices*

## *from* *Poems of the Journey's End*

Lea Goldberg (transl. Rachel Tzvia Back)

*Numbers 33*

*1*

The path is so lovely—said the boy.
The path is so hard—said the lad.
The path is so long—said the man.
The grandfather sat on the side of the path
to rest.

Sunset paints his grey head gold and red,
the grass glows at his feet in the evening dew,
above him the day's last bird sings:
—Will you remember how lovely, how hard,
how long was the path?

*2*

You said: Day chases day and night—night.
In your heart you said: Now the time has come.
You see evenings and mornings visit your
window,
and you say: There is nothing new under
the sun.

Now, with the days, you have whitened and
aged
your days numbered and tenfold dearer,
and you know: Every day is the last under
the sun,
and you know: Every day is new under the sun.

## *The Sorrow of Night*

Dahlia Ravikovitch
(transl. Chana Bloch and Chana Kronfeld)

*Numbers 33*

The road so remote and steep,
The crescent moon like hammered tin,
And who can tell gold
From a bit of tin
No man would ever keep.

Clouds float steaming in the skies,
Dolorous roofs and towers rise,
And soaring on high, the foxes' cries
As their bodies writhe in the hedge.

Stars and planets, swarming bright,
Night falls into the Sea of Nights,
And leaping about like a doe, the light,
Like a spring gushing from a ledge.

A breaker claws the breasting waves,
Piercing the dread abyss headlong.
Lo, the sheaves stand upright in praise
And the reeds lift their voices in song:
*Return, O my soul, and rest thee*
*For the Lord thy God hath blest thee.*

The road so remote and steep,
The crescent moon like hammered tin,
And above it a light
All milky-white
Streams like deliverance deep.

## *from* The Way Out

Muriel Rukeyser

*Numbers 33*

Into that journey where all things speak to
all things
refusing to accept the curse, and taking
for signs the signs of all things, the world,
the body
which is part of the soul, and speaks to the
world,
all creation being created in one image, creation.
This is not the past walking into the future,
the walk is painful, into the present, the dance
not visible as dance until much later.
These dancers are discoverers of God.

## Not Every Day

Shifra Alon

*Numbers 33*

Not every day does one encounter God,
And not at every moment can one give
oneself to prayer;
Nor can every hour be an hour of
loving-kindness.
A person wanders and strays before reaching the
journey's end.
We start over again, and again we lose our way,
Groping and searching for our forgotten path.
But they—those who search and wander—
God seeks them out with candles.

## The New Egypt

Robin Becker

*Numbers 36*

I think of my father who believes
a Jew can outwit fate by owning land.
Slave to property now, I mow
and mow, my destiny the new Egypt.
From his father, the tailor, he learned not
to rent but to own; to borrow to buy.
To conform, I disguise myself and drag
the mower into the drive, where I ponder
the silky oil, the plastic casing, the choke.
From my father, I learned the dignity
of exile and the fire of acquisition,
not to live in places lightly, but to plant
the self like an orange tree in the desert
and irrigate, irrigate, irrigate.

## *The first time we made Shabbos together*

Merle Feld

*Numbers 36:10–12*

The first time we made Shabbos together
in our own home—
it wasn't really "our home"
it was your third floor walk-up
and we weren't even engaged yet—
I had cooked chicken,
my first chicken,
with a whole bulb of garlic—
my mother never used garlic—
and we sat down at that second-hand chrome
table
in the kitchen.
It was all so ugly that we turned out the lights.
Only the Shabbos candles flickered.

And then you made kiddush.

I sat there and wept—
Oh God, you have been so good to me!
Finally, for the first time in my life,
you gave me something I wanted.
This man, whose soul is the soul of Ein Gedi.
We will be silent together,
we will open our flowers in each other's
presence.

And indeed we have bloomed through the
years.

## *The Girls That Are Wanted*

Marie Odlum

*Numbers 36*

The girls that are wanted are good girls—
Good from the hearts to the lips;
Pure, as the lily is white and pure
From its heart to its sweet leaf tips.
The girls that are wanted are home girls—
Girls that are mother's right hand;
That father and brothers can trust too,
And the little ones understand.

Girls that are fair on the hearthstone,
And pleasant when nobody sees;
Kind and sweet to their own folks.
Ready and anxious to please.
The girls that are wanted are wise girls,
That know what to do and say;
That drive with a smile and soft word
The wrath of the household away.

The girls that are wanted are girls with hearts;
They are wanted for mothers and wives;
Wanted to cradle in loving arms
The strongest and frailest lives.

The clever, the witty, the brilliant girl
There are few who can understand;
But, Oh! for the wise, loving home girls
There's constant and steady demand.

# דברים ◆ *D'varim*

# DEUTERONOMY

MOST OF DEUTERONOMY is cast as Moses' final words to Israel while the people stand in the plains of Moab, poised to part from their long-suffering leader and at last enter the Promised Land. The book's Hebrew title, *D'varim* ("words"), reflects the book's presentation as a series of first-person speeches. The English name comes from the Greek translation of the Hebrew expression *mishnei ha-torah* (17:18); in its biblical context, the phrase means "copy of the Teaching," but as the book's title, it takes on the sense of a "second [or: repeated] law." This meaning also fits the nature of the book, which retells and reinterprets Israel's history and laws for a new generation, often with marked differences from other versions. Deuteronomy recalls past experiences—particularly the divine wonders witnessed firsthand while fleeing from Egypt and traveling through the wilderness—as lessons for future behavior. It also includes legal material distinctive for its attention to political, social, and economic issues. The book

*The book depicts God as a loving mother who gives birth to and nurses Israel.*

emphasizes that security and prosperity in the Promised Land depend on adherence to these laws and lessons.

The notion of a covenant between God and Israel pervades Deuteronomy, influencing its form and content. Like political treaties found in other parts of the ancient Near East, the book begins with a historical prologue (1:1–4:43) that establishes the foundation of the covenantal relationship. Then, after a preamble to the laws (6:1–11:32), it spells out the terms of the covenant (12:1–26:15). Blessings and curses follow (28:1–68), detailing the consequences of adhering to or disobeying the covenant. Echoes of ancient Near Eastern treaties also can be heard in certain formulaic phrases that mark the book, like the charge to "love your God יהוה with all your heart, with all your soul, and with all your might" (6:5).

Deuteronomy envisions a society structured around absolute loyalty to the one God and one sanctuary. At the same time, it decentralizes political power and empowers broader segments of society. In Deuteronomy, the community as a whole is responsible for maintaining justice and economic stability, protecting the rights of every member, even animals. Deuteronomy repeatedly instructs the Israelites to care for the vulnerable and needy, particularly the stranger, widow, fatherless, and Levite (and his family). The inclusion of the Levites is a hallmark of Deuteronomy, a result of one of its defining features: the centralization of sacrificial worship in "the site that your God יהוה will choose" (12:5), which the Bible considers to be Jerusalem.

Most scholars date the core of the book (the legal collection in Deuteronomy 12–26 or the laws and surrounding sections in 4:44–28:68) to the 7th century B.C.E.; yet they recognize that various stipulations originated earlier and other parts of the book were added to and revised during the exilic or post-exilic periods (6th century). Many link Deuteronomy to the discovery of a "book of the *torah*" during renovations of the Temple (II Kings 22; II Chronicles 34). The female prophet Huldah is a central figure in that episode, for she authenticates the scroll as God's teachings. (See *V'zot Hab'rachah*, Another View, p. 1284.)

The only woman named in Deuteronomy is Miriam (24:9). However, women are addressed in many parts of the book, even though the grammatically masculine language of the Hebrew often keeps their presence only implicit. Notably, 29:10 and 31:12 explicitly include women among those who take part in the covenant and are obligated to learn and follow the *torah*. Women figure prominently in the legal collection (particularly in *parashat Ki Teitzei*), as it addresses issues like the treatment of a captive woman, inheritance by the son of an unloved wife, adultery, forced and consensual sex, divorce, and levirate marriage.

Deuteronomy persistently warns of the divine wrath that will follow if either women or men disobey the covenant. Yet toward the end of the book, *parashat Haazinu* depicts God as a loving mother who labors to give birth to Israel and nurses Israel with honey and other delicacies of the Promised Land (32:13, 18), a striking image of the culmination of the saga that unfolds in the five books of the Torah.

—*Andrea L. Weiss*

# דברים ✦ *D'varim*

## DEUTERONOMY 1:1–3:22

## *At the Threshold of Canaan*

EVENTS IN PARASHAT D'VARIM ("words") take place on the plains of Moab in the lower Jordan valley, at the moment when Israel is poised to enter the land of Canaan. The parashah contains the beginning of Moses' first farewell address, in which he reminds the people of their history: the journey from Mount Sinai (called Horeb in Deuteronomy), the scouts' debacle, and encounters with foreign nations. Moses' speech is not a neutral rehearsal of Israel's history; rather, it underscores and supports central theological and ideological arguments found throughout Deuteronomy.

The words presented as Moses' farewell address are directed toward a double audience. The first audience is one within the biblical text, the people of Israel about to enter the Promised Land. This imagined audience is standing at a pivotal moment: its members can either follow God's commands or they can repeat the mistakes of the prior generation, presumably with disastrous consequences. Moses' account is designed to encourage the people to make the right choice.

The second intended audience consists of Israelites who were contemporaries of the authors of this opening part of Deuteronomy. Most scholars believe that the material in this parashah, through 4:43 in the following parashah, was written during the Babylonian exile (586–538 B.C.E.) as an introduction to the laws that form the core of the book (Deuteronomy 12–26) and the prologue to these laws (Deuteronomy 4:44–11:32). The exilic authors of our parashah present a version of the past that accomplishes three goals. First, this account of past events emphasizes God's role in Israel's history. Second, it justifies Israel's territory in theological terms. Third, it underscores obedience to God, as defined by Deuteronomy, as the key to Israel's ongoing political and military success.

*How do we assess the relationship between texts and a community's social reality?*

This parashah does not deal specifically with women. The seeming absence of women in this version of Israel's narrative, however, raises an issue that has concerned biblical scholars in general and feminist scholars in particular, namely, how to assess the relationship between texts and a community's social reality. Contemporary scholars, women and men alike, have shown how an account of the past is nearly always colored by an author's own subjective position and ideological stance. These scholars train readers to guard against taking historical accounts as mirror representations of historical events; they encourage us instead to explore what historical accounts disclose about their authors' historical and social situations. These methodological insights are particularly relevant to this opening part of Deuteronomy. In several places in this parashah, Moses' accounts of events differ from those in Exodus or Numbers. A comparison of the different versions provides insight into not only the variety of historical traditions that flourished in ancient Israel, but also the variety of theological and ideological viewpoints that shaped them.

—*Elsie R. Stern*

## Outline

*I.* Setting and Introduction to Moses' Address (1:1–5)

*II.* Moses' Review of the Journey from Horeb (Sinai) (1:6–3:11)

- *A.* Appointment of tribal leaders (1:6–18)
- *B.* Episode of the scouts (1:19–46)
  - *1.* The sending of scouts (1:19–33)
  - *2.* The consequences (1:34–46)
- *C.* Encounters with foreign nations (2:1–3:11)
  - *1.* Peaceful encounters with Edom, Moab, and Ammon (2:1–23)
  - *2.* Battles against Amorite kings (2:24–3:11)

*III.* Moses' Allotment of Land East of the Jordan (3:12–20)

*IV.* Moses' Charge to Joshua (3:21–22)

These are the words that Moses addressed to all Israel on the other side of the Jordan.—Through the wilderness, in the Arabah near Suph, between Paran and Tophel, Laban, Hazeroth, and Di-zahab,
2 it is eleven days from Horeb to Kadesh-barnea by the Mount Seir route.—
3 It was in the fortieth year, on the first day of the eleventh month, that Moses addressed the Israelites in ac-

א אֵ֣לֶּה הַדְּבָרִ֗ים אֲשֶׁ֨ר דִּבֶּ֤ר מֹשֶׁה֙ אֶל־
כׇּל־יִשְׂרָאֵ֔ל בְּעֵ֖בֶר הַיַּרְדֵּ֑ן בַּמִּדְבָּ֡ר בָּעֲרָבָה֩
מ֨וֹל ס֜וּף בֵּין־פָּארָ֧ן וּבֵֽין־תֹּ֛פֶל וְלָבָ֥ן וַחֲצֵרֹ֖ת
וְדִ֥י זָהָֽב׃ 2 אַחַ֨ד עָשָׂ֥ר יוֹם֙ מֵֽחֹרֵ֔ב דֶּ֖רֶךְ הַר־
שֵׂעִ֑יר עַ֖ד קָדֵ֥שׁ בַּרְנֵֽעַ׃ 3 וַֽיְהִי֙ בְּאַרְבָּעִ֣ים
שָׁנָ֔ה בְּעַשְׁתֵּֽי־עָשָׂ֥ר חֹ֖דֶשׁ בְּאֶחָ֣ד לַחֹ֑דֶשׁ
דִּבֶּ֤ר מֹשֶׁה֙ אֶל־בְּנֵ֣י יִשְׂרָאֵ֔ל כְּ֠כֹ֠ל אֲשֶׁ֨ר

## *Setting and Introduction to Moses' Address* (1:1–5)

When read as straightforward itineraries or markers of time and place, these verses are perplexing. Some place names do not appear in the Torah's primary accounts of Israel's wandering in the wilderness. Plus, there is a contradiction between v. 1, which states that Moses delivered these words at various points during the course of Israel's journey through the wilderness, and vv. 3–5, which state that he spoke them at the end of the journey, when the Israelites reached the plains of Moab. Despite such ambiguities, these verses possess a strong rhetorical logic, for they juxtapose sites of Israelite misbehavior and consequent circuitous wandering with sites of Israelite obedience and consequent success and progress toward the land of Canaan.

*1. **on the other side of the Jordan.*** While most of Deuteronomy is presented as Moses' speech to the Israelites before entering the land, the phrase "other side" here indicates that the entire book is addressed to the second intended audience, contemporaneous with the authors of the book as a whole, who were already looking back on the wilderness wandering and the entrance into the land as past events.

***Suph.*** Place names are arranged in a reverse order of the Israelites' journey from Horeb (Sinai) to Moab. The Israelites first doubted God's saving power near Suph, a reference to the Sea of Reeds (Exodus 14:10–12).

***Paran.*** The Israelites complained about wanting meat in the wilderness of Paran (Numbers 11); the episode of the scouts also occurred there (Numbers 13–14).

***Hazeroth.*** This is where Miriam and Aaron spoke against Moses (Numbers 12:1–2).

*3. **It was in the fortieth year.*** This verse emphasizes that Moses delivered the following words at the end of the forty years of wandering. Forty represents a symbolic time span, signifying a generation.


▸ The commentaries in this book echo Deuteronomy's own interpretive process.

ANOTHER VIEW ➤ *1056*

▸ As he reflects on what has transpired, Moses engages in a kind of counter-transference.

CONTEMPORARY REFLECTION ➤ *1058*

▸ The Israelites' ingratitude reminds God of Adam, who blamed Eve for his disobedience.

POST-BIBLICAL INTERPRETATIONS ➤ *1056*

▸ I dream with pain in the foreign land / of the flowering camps of Israel. . . .

VOICES ➤ *1060*

cordance with the instructions that יהוה had given him for them, [4]after he had defeated Sihon king of the Amorites, who dwelt in Heshbon, and King Og of Bashan, who dwelt at Ashtaroth [and] Edrei. [5]On the other side of the Jordan, in the land of Moab, Moses undertook to expound this Teaching. He said:

צִוָּה יְהוָה אֹתוֹ אֲלֵהֶם׃ 4 אַחֲרֵי הַכֹּתוֹ אֵת
סִיחֹן מֶלֶךְ הָאֱמֹרִי אֲשֶׁר יוֹשֵׁב בְּחֶשְׁבּוֹן
וְאֵת עוֹג מֶלֶךְ הַבָּשָׁן אֲשֶׁר־יוֹשֵׁב בְּעַשְׁתָּרֹת
בְּאֶדְרֶעִי׃ 5 בְּעֵבֶר הַיַּרְדֵּן בְּאֶרֶץ מוֹאָב
הוֹאִיל מֹשֶׁה בֵּאֵר אֶת־הַתּוֹרָה הַזֹּאת
לֵאמֹר׃

[6]Our God יהוה spoke to us at Horeb, saying: You have stayed long enough at this mountain. [7]Start out and make your way to the hill country of the Amorites and to all their neighbors in the Arabah, the hill country, the Shephelah, the Negeb, the seacoast, the land of the Canaanites, and the Lebanon, as far as the Great River, the river Euphrates. [8]See, I place the land at your disposal. Go, take possession of the land that יהוה swore to your fathers Abraham, Isaac, and Jacob, to assign to them and to their heirs after them.

6 יְהוָה אֱלֹהֵינוּ דִּבֶּר אֵלֵינוּ בְּחֹרֵב לֵאמֹר
רַב־לָכֶם שֶׁבֶת בָּהָר הַזֶּה׃ 7 פְּנוּ ׀ וּסְעוּ לָכֶם
וּבֹאוּ הַר הָאֱמֹרִי וְאֶל־כָּל־שְׁכֵנָיו בָּעֲרָבָה
בָהָר וּבַשְּׁפֵלָה וּבַנֶּגֶב וּבְחוֹף הַיָּם אֶרֶץ
הַכְּנַעֲנִי וְהַלְּבָנוֹן עַד־הַנָּהָר הַגָּדֹל נְהַר־
פְּרָת׃ 8 רְאֵה נָתַתִּי לִפְנֵיכֶם אֶת־הָאָרֶץ
בֹּאוּ וּרְשׁוּ אֶת־הָאָרֶץ אֲשֶׁר נִשְׁבַּע יְהוָה
לַאֲבֹתֵיכֶם לְאַבְרָהָם לְיִצְחָק וּלְיַעֲקֹב לָתֵת
לָהֶם וּלְזַרְעָם אַחֲרֵיהֶם׃

*5. Teaching.* Heb. *torah.* This term most likely refers here to Moses' speeches in Deuteronomy, not to the whole Pentateuch or so-called Five Books of Moses (see also at 31:9).

## *Moses' Review of the Journey from Horeb (Sinai)* (1:6–3:11)

Horeb (the name for Sinai used in Deuteronomy) and Kadesh-barnea represent the poles of Israelite behavior. These two sites become emblematic of the choice that confronts the Israelites: obey God and prosper in the Promised Land or disobey and be condemned to wandering circuitously outside the land. For Deuteronomy's exilic audience, Moses' speech argues for the ongoing importance of heeding God by obeying the laws that follow in Deuteronomy 12–26.

### APPOINTMENT OF TRIBAL LEADERS (1:6–18)

Moses begins his address by recounting God's charge to the Israelites to set out from Horeb and journey to the Promised Land (vv. 6–8). Then, Moses recalls how he created an administrative infrastructure by appointing additional leaders (vv. 9–18).

*6. Horeb.* Deuteronomy refers to Mount Sinai as Horeb (see at Exodus 18:5).

*7. the hill country of the Amorites . . . as far as . . . the river Euphrates.* The Torah includes different understandings of the exact parameters of the land that it says God promised to the patriarchs. Some passages envision it as including only the land of Canaan, with its northern border at Lebo-hamath (in the Bekaa Valley of modern-day Lebanon, north of Damascus; see Numbers 13:21; 34:8). In contrast, the present verse understands the divine land grant more expansively to include both sides of the

⁹Thereupon I said to you, "I cannot bear the burden of you by myself. ¹⁰Your God יהוה has multiplied you until you are today as numerous as the stars in the sky.—¹¹May יהוה, the God of your ancestors, increase your numbers a thousandfold, and bless you as promised.—¹²How can I bear unaided the trouble of you, and the burden, and the bickering! ¹³Pick from each of your tribes representatives who are wise, discerning, and experienced, and I will appoint them as your heads." ¹⁴You answered me and said, "What you propose to do is good." ¹⁵So I took your tribal leaders, wise

9 וָאֹמַ֥ר אֲלֵכֶ֖ם בָּעֵ֣ת הַהִ֑וא לֵאמֹ֔ר לֹא־
אוּכַ֥ל לְבַדִּ֖י שְׂאֵ֥ת אֶתְכֶֽם: 10 יְהֹוָ֣ה
אֱלֹהֵיכֶ֗ם הִרְבָּ֣ה אֶתְכֶ֔ם וְהִנְּכֶ֣ם הַיּ֔וֹם
כְּכוֹכְבֵ֥י הַשָּׁמַ֖יִם לָרֹֽב: 11 יְהֹוָ֞ה אֱלֹהֵ֣י
אֲבֽוֹתֵכֶ֗ם יֹסֵ֣ף עֲלֵיכֶ֛ם כָּכֶ֖ם אֶ֣לֶף פְּעָמִ֑ים
וִיבָרֵ֣ךְ אֶתְכֶ֔ם כַּאֲשֶׁ֖ר דִּבֶּ֥ר לָכֶֽם: 12 אֵיכָ֥ה
אֶשָּׂ֖א לְבַדִּ֑י טׇרְחֲכֶ֥ם וּמַֽשַּׂאֲכֶ֖ם וְרִֽיבְכֶֽם:
13 הָב֣וּ לָכֶ֗ם אֲנָשִׁ֤ים חֲכָמִים֙ וּנְבֹנִ֔ים
וִידֻעִ֖ים לְשִׁבְטֵיכֶ֑ם וַאֲשִׂימֵ֖ם בְּרָאשֵׁיכֶֽם:
14 וַתַּעֲנ֖וּ אֹתִ֑י וַתֹּ֣אמְר֔וּ טֽוֹב־הַדָּבָ֥ר אֲשֶׁר־
דִּבַּ֖רְתָּ לַעֲשֽׂוֹת: 15 וָאֶקַּ֞ח אֶת־רָאשֵׁ֣י

· · · · · · · · · · · · · · · · · · · · · · · · · ·

Jordan River, as far north as the Euphrates River (in today's Iraq; see also 11:24). The variations remind us that the idea of the Promised Land does not correlate with a single historical reality. Rather, the phrase reflects ongoing attempts by different generations of Israelite writers to understand their people's geopolitical aspirations and realities.

**9–18.** Moses recalls how he announced that the responsibility of leading the people, and especially of mediating their disputes, was too big for him to bear alone. He thus directs the people to choose wise and respected representatives from each of the tribes to serve as their leaders and judges.

This account conflates two earlier versions. In Exodus 18:13–27, Moses' Midianite father-in-law, Jethro, sees that Moses is exhausting himself in judging all the Israelites' disputes and advises Moses to delegate routine legal matters to others. In Numbers 11:10–17, the exasperated Moses complains to God about the burden of carrying the people singlehandedly. God then tells him to appoint seventy representative elders upon whom God will bestow God's holy spirit so that they can share the burden of leadership. In Deuteronomy's version, Moses complains of the burden, as he does in Numbers, but the solution is closer to that proffered by Jethro in Exodus.

**10–11.** *Your God יהוה has multiplied . . . stars in the sky.* This statement echoes and confirms

the fulfillment of God's promise to Abraham in Genesis 15:5 and 22:17; likewise, Genesis 24:60 predicts that Rebekah will "become thousands of myriads."

**12.** *the trouble of you, and the burden, and the bickering!* In the previous verses, Moses declared that he cannot lead the people alone because of their divinely granted magnitude. Here, he claims that he needs help because of their negative behavior. The juxtaposition of these two reasons reinforces two paradoxical themes in this parashah: God's loyalty to previous promises, and Israel's chronic misbehavior.

**13.** *Pick from each of your tribes.* This crucial moment of autonomy and self-determination for the people contrasts with the earlier versions (Exodus 18; Numbers 11) in which Moses picks the leaders himself. The criteria for leadership here also differ from those in the prior episodes. In Exodus 18, judges must fear God, be trustworthy, and lack greed. In Numbers 11, participation in the divine spirit qualifies the leaders. Here, the leaders' authority stems from their wisdom and experience, and the righteousness of their ruling derives from their ability to follow Moses' directives regarding fairness and justice. This contrast among the three criteria for leadership underscores Deuteronomy's respect for human wisdom and experience, and its faith in the guiding power of law.

and experienced representatives, and appointed them heads over you: chiefs of thousands, chiefs of hundreds, chiefs of fifties, and chiefs of tens, and officials for your tribes. [16]I charged your magistrates at that time as follows, "Hear out your fellow Israelites, and decide justly between anyone and a fellow Israelite or a stranger. [17]You shall not be partial in judgment: hear out low and high alike. Fear no one, for judgment is God's. And any matter that is too difficult for you, you shall bring to me and I will hear it." [18]Thus I instructed you, at that time, about the various things that you should do.

[19]We set out from Horeb and traveled the great and terrible wilderness that you saw, along the road to the hill country of the Amorites, as our God יהוה had commanded us. When we reached Kadesh-

שִׁבְטֵיכֶם אֲנָשִׁים חֲכָמִים וִידֻעִים וָאֶתֵּן
אֹתָם רָאשִׁים עֲלֵיכֶם שָׂרֵי אֲלָפִים וְשָׂרֵי
מֵאוֹת וְשָׂרֵי חֲמִשִּׁים וְשָׂרֵי עֲשָׂרֹת וְשֹׁטְרִים
לְשִׁבְטֵיכֶם׃ 16 וָאֲצַוֶּה אֶת־שֹׁפְטֵיכֶם בָּעֵת
הַהִוא לֵאמֹר שָׁמֹעַ בֵּין־אֲחֵיכֶם וּשְׁפַטְתֶּם
צֶדֶק בֵּין־אִישׁ וּבֵין־אָחִיו וּבֵין גֵּרוֹ׃ 17 לֹא־
תַכִּירוּ פָנִים בַּמִּשְׁפָּט כַּקָּטֹן כַּגָּדֹל תִּשְׁמָעוּן
לֹא תָגוּרוּ מִפְּנֵי־אִישׁ כִּי הַמִּשְׁפָּט לֵאלֹהִים
הוּא וְהַדָּבָר אֲשֶׁר יִקְשֶׁה מִכֶּם תַּקְרִבוּן אֵלַי
וּשְׁמַעְתִּיו׃ 18 וָאֲצַוֶּה אֶתְכֶם בָּעֵת הַהִוא
אֵת כָּל־הַדְּבָרִים אֲשֶׁר תַּעֲשׂוּן׃
19 וַנִּסַּע מֵחֹרֵב וַנֵּלֶךְ אֵת כָּל־הַמִּדְבָּר
הַגָּדוֹל וְהַנּוֹרָא הַהוּא אֲשֶׁר רְאִיתֶם דֶּרֶךְ
הַר הָאֱמֹרִי כַּאֲשֶׁר צִוָּה יְהוָה אֱלֹהֵינוּ

*16. stranger.* Heb. *ger* is more precisely translated as "resident alien," for it refers to those who live within the Israelite community but cannot own land and therefore are vulnerable economically.

## EPISODE OF THE SCOUTS (1:19–46)

This section recounts the events described in Numbers 13–14. Both versions tell of a reconnaissance mission by twelve scouts that results in the Israelites' terrified refusal to attempt the conquest of the land of Canaan. After God vows to punish them for their lack of faith, the Israelites invade the land without God's support and are defeated. As a result of this incident, God condemns the Israelites to linger in the wilderness until the current generation of adults dies off.

While the versions concur on major contours of the plot, there are significant differences between them. In Numbers 13:1–2, God requests the reconnaissance mission; in Deuteronomy 1:22, the people do. In Numbers 13:27–29, the scouts offer a mixed report: the land is bounteous and fertile, but its current inhabitants are terrifying. In Deuteronomy 1:25, they offer only a positive report. In Numbers 14:7–9, Joshua and Caleb encourage the Israelites to have faith in God's ability to grant them victory. In Deuteronomy 1:29–33, Moses plays this role. In Numbers 14:24, 30, God says that only Caleb and Joshua may enter the land of Canaan, with no mention of whether Moses is included with the people or exempted. In Deuteronomy 1:37, Moses is prohibited from entering the land as a consequence of the people's behavior in this episode.

These discrepancies underscore Deuteronomy's particular point of view. In Numbers 14:1–4, the people respond to the fearsome account of the land's inhabitants. Deuteronomy makes the people appear more cowardly: in 1:26–28, the people are too afraid to enter even though they have heard only a positive report. In this parashah, Moses states that he cannot enter the Promised Land as a result of the people's misdeeds, not his own (as Numbers 20:12 claims).

Retelling events with new—even conflicting—data and perspectives illustrates the ongoing nature of interpretation, already taking place in the Torah itself. Deuteronomy's retelling of the episode of the scouts demonstrates the effect of the experience of exile on the authors' self-perception. For the exilic

barnea, [20]I said to you, "You have come to the hill country of the Amorites which our God יהוה is giving to us. [21]See, your God יהוה has placed the land at your disposal. Go up, take possession, as יהוה, the God of your fathers, promised you. Fear not and be not dismayed."

[22]Then all of you came to me and said, "Let us send emissaries ahead to reconnoiter the land for us and bring back word on the route we shall follow and the cities we shall come to." [23]I approved of the plan, and so I selected from among you twelve representatives, one from each tribe. [24]They made for the hill country, came to the wadi Eshcol, and spied it out. [25]They took some of the fruit of the land with them and brought it down to us. And they gave us this report: "It is a good land that our God יהוה is giving to us."

[26]Yet you refused to go up, and flouted the command of your God יהוה. [27]You sulked in your tents and said, "It is out of hatred for us that יהוה brought us out of the land of Egypt, to hand us

עָד קָדֵשׁ בַּרְנֵעַ ‪:‬ ‪20‬ וָאֹמַ֣ר אֲלֵכֶ֔ם בָּאתֶם֙ עַד־הַ֣ר הָאֱמֹרִ֔י אֲשֶׁר־יְהוָ֥ה אֱלֹהֵ֖ינוּ נֹתֵ֣ן לָ֑נוּ ‪:‬ ‪21‬ רְאֵ֠ה נָתַ֨ן יְהוָ֧ה אֱלֹהֶ֛יךָ לְפָנֶ֖יךָ אֶת־הָאָ֑רֶץ עֲלֵ֣ה רֵ֗שׁ כַּאֲשֶׁר֩ דִּבֶּ֨ר יְהוָ֜ה אֱלֹהֵ֤י אֲבֹתֶ֙יךָ֙ לָ֔ךְ אַל־תִּירָ֖א וְאַל־תֵּחָֽת ‪:‬

‪22‬ וַתִּקְרְב֣וּן אֵלַי֮ כֻּלְּכֶם֒ וַתֹּאמְר֗וּ נִשְׁלְחָ֤ה אֲנָשִׁים֙ לְפָנֵ֔ינוּ וְיַחְפְּרוּ־לָ֖נוּ אֶת־הָאָ֑רֶץ וְיָשִׁ֤בוּ אֹתָ֙נוּ֙ דָּבָ֔ר אֶת־הַדֶּ֙רֶךְ֙ אֲשֶׁ֣ר נַֽעֲלֶה־בָּ֔הּ וְאֵת֙ הֶֽעָרִ֔ים אֲשֶׁ֥ר נָבֹ֖א אֲלֵיהֶֽן ‪:‬ ‪23‬ וַיִּיטַ֥ב בְּעֵינַ֖י הַדָּבָ֑ר וָאֶקַּ֤ח מִכֶּם֙ שְׁנֵ֣ים עָשָׂ֣ר אֲנָשִׁ֔ים אִ֥ישׁ אֶחָ֖ד לַשָּֽׁבֶט ‪:‬ ‪24‬ וַיִּפְנוּ֙ וַיַּֽעֲל֣וּ הָהָ֔רָה וַיָּבֹ֖אוּ עַד־נַ֣חַל אֶשְׁכֹּ֑ל וַֽיְרַגְּל֖וּ אֹתָֽהּ ‪:‬ ‪25‬ וַיִּקְח֤וּ בְיָדָם֙ מִפְּרִ֣י הָאָ֔רֶץ וַיּוֹרִ֖דוּ אֵלֵ֑ינוּ וַיָּשִׁ֨בוּ אֹתָ֤נוּ דָבָר֙ וַיֹּ֣אמְר֔וּ טוֹבָ֣ה הָאָ֔רֶץ אֲשֶׁר־יְהוָ֥ה אֱלֹהֵ֖ינוּ נֹתֵ֥ן לָֽנוּ ‪:‬

‪26‬ וְלֹ֥א אֲבִיתֶ֖ם לַֽעֲלֹ֑ת וַתַּמְר֕וּ אֶת־פִּ֥י יְהוָ֖ה אֱלֹהֵיכֶֽם ‪:‬ ‪27‬ וַתֵּרָֽגְנ֤וּ בְאָֽהֳלֵיכֶם֙ וַתֹּ֣אמְר֔וּ בְּשִׂנְאַ֤ת יְהוָה֙ אֹתָ֔נוּ הֽוֹצִיאָ֖נוּ מֵאֶ֣רֶץ מִצְרָ֑יִם לָתֵ֥ת אֹתָ֖נוּ בְּיַ֥ד הָֽאֱמֹרִ֖י

---

authors of this text, Israel's history is tragically marked by the people's inability to sustain their faith in God. For these authors, a primary goal is to encourage their contemporary audience to resist this pattern and abide by the covenant.

### The Sending of Scouts (1:19–33)

In Numbers 13:2, God begins the campaign for the Promised Land by telling Moses to send scouts into the land of Canaan. Here, that episode opens with Moses' charge to conquer the land and his assurance that God will guarantee the Israelites' victory. The people respond by asking Moses to send out scouts. By having the people ask for the reconnaissance mission *after* Moses has told them that God has guaranteed victory, the authors suggest that the request itself is symptomatic of the people's lack of faith.

*21.　take possession.* The root *y-r-sh* has a wide

range of meanings, including "to take possession by force" and "to inherit." Those quite different nuances of the root point to the complicated status of the acquisition of the territories identified as the Promised Land. The Bible depicts the entry into the land both as a violent (dis)possession and as a legitimate inheritance of what rightfully belongs to Israel through divine grant (see Joshua 1–Judges 1; see also at Deuteronomy 7:1–5, 24; 12:29–31; 31:16).

*21.*　Confidence in God's advocacy provides grounds for courage here and in other moments of military conquest and encounter.

*25.　"It is a good land that our God יהוה is giving to us."*　This concise report about the positive nature of the land contrasts sharply with the report in Numbers 13:27–29, which emphasizes both the quality of the land and the challenges it presents to conquest.

over to the Amorites to wipe us out. 28 What kind of place are we going to? Our brothers have taken the heart out of us, saying, 'We saw there a people stronger and taller than we, large cities with walls sky-high, and even Anakites.'"

29 I said to you, "Have no dread or fear of them. 30 None other than your God יהוה, who goes before you, will fight for you, just as [God] did for you in Egypt before your very eyes, 31 and in the wilderness, where you saw how your God יהוה carried you, as a householder carries his son, all the way that you traveled until you came to this place. 32 Yet for all that, you have no faith in your God יהוה, 33 who goes before you on your journeys—to scout the place where you are to encamp—in fire by night and in cloud by day, in order to guide you on the route you are to follow."

לְהַשְׁמִידֵנוּ׃ 28 אָנָה ׀ אֲנַחְנוּ עֹלִים אַחֵינוּ
הֵמַסּוּ אֶת־לְבָבֵנוּ לֵאמֹר עַם גָּדוֹל וָרָם
מִמֶּנּוּ עָרִים גְּדֹלֹת וּבְצוּרֹת בַּשָּׁמָיִם וְגַם־בְּנֵי
עֲנָקִים רָאִינוּ שָׁם׃
29 וָאֹמַר אֲלֵכֶם לֹא־תַעַרְצוּן וְלֹא־תִירְאוּן
מֵהֶם׃ 30 יְהוָה אֱלֹהֵיכֶם הַהֹלֵךְ לִפְנֵיכֶם
הוּא יִלָּחֵם לָכֶם כְּכֹל אֲשֶׁר עָשָׂה אִתְּכֶם
בְּמִצְרַיִם לְעֵינֵיכֶם׃ 31 וּבַמִּדְבָּר אֲשֶׁר רָאִיתָ
אֲשֶׁר נְשָׂאֲךָ יְהוָה אֱלֹהֶיךָ כַּאֲשֶׁר יִשָּׂא־
אִישׁ אֶת־בְּנוֹ בְּכָל־הַדֶּרֶךְ אֲשֶׁר הֲלַכְתֶּם
עַד־בֹּאֲכֶם עַד־הַמָּקוֹם הַזֶּה׃ 32 וּבַדָּבָר
הַזֶּה אֵינְכֶם מַאֲמִינִם בַּיהוָה אֱלֹהֵיכֶם׃
33 הַהֹלֵךְ לִפְנֵיכֶם בַּדֶּרֶךְ לָתוּר לָכֶם מָקוֹם
לַחֲנֹתְכֶם בָּאֵשׁ ׀ לַיְלָה לַרְאֹתְכֶם בַּדֶּרֶךְ
אֲשֶׁר תֵּלְכוּ־בָהּ וּבֶעָנָן יוֹמָם׃

*28. Anakites.* A people renowned for their mythic size (see at Numbers 13:28).

*29–33.* Moses tries to reassure the people by reminding them that they have been witnesses to God's miraculous power on their behalf. This testimony serves to show how cowardly the earlier generation was and to remind the later generation of God's past miraculous support of their ancestors.

*31. householder . . . son.* [Heb. *ish . . . ben.* This translation understands the noun *ish* (traditionally "a man") as referring to one who represents a group; here, the group is by default a household, the basic social and economic unit in the ancient Near East; and the head of a household, in turn, was presumably male. Responsible for his corporate household's continuity, a householder was expected to invest time and attention on raising his heir (*The Contemporary Torah*, 2006, pp. 385, 402). Certain biblical texts formally ascribe to the father the parental role as a child's protector and guide, as in Psalm 103:13 and Job 29:16.

Alternatively, one can translate this verse's simile in a gender-neutral sense: "as a parent carries a child." In ancient Israel, both women and men cared for children. A notable example of a mother physically carrying her child is when Abraham places Ishmael on Hagar's shoulder as he sends them away (Genesis 21:14).

Since this simile aims to describe God's actions on Israel's behalf, it is worthwhile to keep in mind that while a number of passages depict God metaphorically as a father (see at Deuteronomy 32:6), others avoid gender specification for parents. For instance, the metaphoric parent who gently nurtures Israel in Hosea 11 could be read either as mother or father. However, a few verses in the Bible clearly depict God in a maternal role. For example, the maternal imagery in the prophecies of consolation in Isaiah 40–66 describe both God's power (Isaiah 42:14) and God's unending devotion to Israel (Isaiah 49:14; 66:13). Likewise, Numbers 11:12 alludes to God as the one who gave birth to and cares for Israel (see also at Deuteronomy 32:13, 18). At its core, the imagery here conveys God's solicitous care for Israel, without necessarily reflecting on God's perceived gender. —*Ed.*]

³⁴יהוה heard your loud complaint and, becoming angry, vowed: ³⁵Not one of the men [counted in the census], this evil generation, shall see the good land that I swore to give to your fathers—³⁶none except Caleb son of Jephunneh; he shall see it, and to him and his descendants will I give the land on which he set foot, because he remained loyal to יהוה.—³⁷Because of you יהוה was incensed with me too, saying: You shall not enter it either. ³⁸Joshua son of Nun, who attends you, he shall enter it. Imbue him with strength, for he shall allot it to Israel. ³⁹Moreover, your little ones who you said would be carried off, your children who do not yet know good from bad, they shall enter it; to them will I give it and they shall possess it. ⁴⁰As for you, turn about and march into the wilderness by the way of the Sea of Reeds.

⁴¹You replied to me, saying, "We stand guilty before יהוה. We will go up now and fight, just as our God יהוה commanded us." And [the men among] you each girded yourselves with war gear and recklessly started for the hill country. ⁴²But יהוה said to me, "Warn them: Do not go up and do not fight, since I am not in your midst; else you will be routed by your enemies." ⁴³I spoke to you, but

³⁴ וַיִּשְׁמַ֥ע יְהֹוָ֖ה אֶת־ק֣וֹל דִּבְרֵיכֶ֑ם וַיִּקְצֹ֖ף וַיִּשָּׁבַ֥ע לֵאמֹֽר: ³⁵ אִם־יִרְאֶ֥ה אִישׁ֙ בָּאֲנָשִׁ֣ים הָאֵ֔לֶּה הַדּ֥וֹר הָרָ֖ע הַזֶּ֑ה אֵ֚ת הָאָ֣רֶץ הַטּוֹבָ֔ה אֲשֶׁ֣ר נִשְׁבַּ֔עְתִּי לָתֵ֖ת לַאֲבֹתֵיכֶֽם: ³⁶ זוּלָתִ֞י כָּלֵ֤ב בֶּן־יְפֻנֶּה֙ ה֣וּא יִרְאֶ֔נָּה וְלֽוֹ־אֶתֵּ֧ן אֶת־הָאָ֛רֶץ אֲשֶׁ֥ר דָּֽרַךְ־בָּ֖הּ וּלְבָנָ֑יו יַ֕עַן אֲשֶׁ֥ר מִלֵּ֖א אַחֲרֵ֥י יְהֹוָֽה: ³⁷ גַּם־בִּי֙ הִתְאַנַּ֣ף יְהֹוָ֔ה בִּגְלַלְכֶ֖ם לֵאמֹ֑ר גַּם־אַתָּ֖ה לֹא־תָבֹ֥א שָֽׁם: ³⁸ יְהוֹשֻׁ֤עַ בִּן־נוּן֙ הָעֹמֵ֣ד לְפָנֶ֔יךָ ה֖וּא יָ֣בֹא שָׁ֑מָּה אֹת֣וֹ חַזֵּ֔ק כִּי־ה֖וּא יַנְחִלֶ֥נָּה אֶת־יִשְׂרָאֵֽל: ³⁹ וְטַפְּכֶם֩ אֲשֶׁ֨ר אֲמַרְתֶּ֜ם לָבַ֣ז יִֽהְיֶ֗ה וּבְנֵיכֶ֡ם אֲשֶׁ֣ר לֹא־יָֽדְעוּ֩ הַיּ֨וֹם ט֜וֹב וָרָ֗ע הֵ֚מָּה יָבֹ֣אוּ שָׁ֔מָּה וְלָהֶ֣ם אֶתְּנֶ֔נָּה וְהֵ֖ם יִֽירָשֽׁוּהָ: ⁴⁰ וְאַתֶּ֖ם פְּנ֣וּ לָכֶ֑ם וּסְע֥וּ הַמִּדְבָּ֖רָה דֶּ֥רֶךְ יַם־סֽוּף:

⁴¹ וַתַּֽעֲנ֣וּ ׀ וַתֹּאמְר֣וּ אֵלַ֗י חָטָ֘אנוּ֘ לַֽיהֹוָה֒ אֲנַ֤חְנוּ נַעֲלֶה֙ וְנִלְחַ֔מְנוּ כְּכֹ֥ל אֲשֶׁר־צִוָּ֖נוּ יְהֹוָ֣ה אֱלֹהֵ֑ינוּ וַֽתַּחְגְּר֗וּ אִ֚ישׁ אֶת־כְּלֵ֣י מִלְחַמְתּ֔וֹ וַתָּהִ֖ינוּ לַעֲלֹ֥ת הָהָֽרָה: ⁴² וַיֹּ֨אמֶר יְהֹוָ֜ה אֵלַ֗י אֱמֹ֤ר לָהֶם֙ לֹ֤א תַֽעֲלוּ֙ וְלֹֽא־תִלָּ֣חֲמ֔וּ כִּ֥י אֵינֶ֖נִּי בְּקִרְבְּכֶ֑ם וְלֹא֙ תִּנָּ֣גְפ֔וּ לִפְנֵ֖י אֹיְבֵיכֶֽם: ⁴³ וָאֲדַבֵּ֥ר אֲלֵיכֶ֖ם וְלֹ֣א

- - - - - - - - - - - - - - - - - - - - - - - - - - - - - - - - - - - - - - - - - -

### The Consequences (1:34–46)

In Numbers, God responds angrily to the Israelites' fear and resistance and decides that none of the adult generation will live to enter the Promised Land except for Caleb and Joshua (see further at Numbers 14:10–38, especially at v. 21). In Moses' retelling here, even Moses will be prohibited from entering the land on account of the people's actions. When the Israelites hear God's decree, they repent of their fearfulness and prepare themselves to obey God's command to conquer the land. God, however, warns Moses that God will not support this mission and it will fail.

**36.** *Caleb.* A chieftain from the tribe of Judah

(Numbers 13:6). According to Numbers 14:6–9, Caleb and Joshua were the two scouts who assured the people that with God's help they could conquer the land of Canaan. According to Judges 1:12–15, Caleb and his tribe will lead the Israelites' campaign when entering the land. He will then offer his daughter Achsah as a prize to the warrior who captures the town of Kiriath-sepher.

**37.** *Because of you.* Deuteronomy conforms to the tradition that Moses was not allowed to enter the Promised Land but blames God's prohibition on the people's actions. In contrast, Numbers 20:12 implies that Moses himself is responsible for this punishment.

**38.** *Joshua.* See at 1:36.

you would not listen; you flouted יהוה's command and willfully marched into the hill country. ⁴⁴Then the Amorites who lived in those hills came out against you like so many bees and chased you, and they crushed you at Hormah in Seir. ⁴⁵Again you wept before יהוה; but יהוה would not heed your cry or give ear to you.

⁴⁶Thus, after you had remained at Kadesh all that long time, 2 we marched back into the wilderness by the way of the Sea of Reeds, as יהוה had spoken to me, and skirted the hill country of Seir a long time.

שְׁמַעְתֶּם וַתַּמְר֖וּ אֶת־פִּ֣י יְהֹוָ֑ה וַתָּזִ֙דוּ֙ וַתַּעֲל֖וּ הָהָֽרָה: ⁴⁴ וַיֵּצֵ֣א הָאֱמֹרִ֗י הַיֹּשֵׁב֙ בָּהָ֣ר הַה֔וּא לִקְרַאתְכֶ֖ם וַיִּרְדְּפ֣וּ אֶתְכֶ֔ם כַּאֲשֶׁ֥ר תַּעֲשֶׂ֖ינָה הַדְּבֹרִ֑ים וַֽיַּכְּת֥וּ אֶתְכֶ֛ם בְּשֵׂעִ֖יר עַד־חָרְמָֽה: ⁴⁵ וַתָּשֻׁ֥בוּ וַתִּבְכּ֖וּ לִפְנֵ֣י יְהֹוָ֑ה וְלֹא־שָׁמַ֤ע יְהֹוָה֙ בְּקֹ֣לְכֶ֔ם וְלֹ֥א הֶאֱזִ֖ין אֲלֵיכֶֽם:

⁴⁶ וַתֵּשְׁב֥וּ בְקָדֵ֖שׁ יָמִ֣ים רַבִּ֑ים כַּיָּמִ֖ים אֲשֶׁ֥ר יְשַׁבְתֶּֽם: ב וַנֵּ֜פֶן וַנִּסַּ֤ע הַמִּדְבָּ֙רָה֙ דֶּ֣רֶךְ יַם־ס֔וּף כַּאֲשֶׁ֛ר דִּבֶּ֥ר יְהֹוָ֖ה אֵלָ֑י וַנָּ֥סָב אֶת־ הַר־שֵׂעִ֖יר יָמִ֥ים רַבִּֽים: ס

. . . . . . . . . . . . . . . . . . . . . . . . . . . .

## ENCOUNTERS WITH FOREIGN NATIONS
### (2:1–3:11)

This section recounts Israel's encounters with five nations in the area nowadays known as Transjordan. In the first three episodes, God commands Israel not to militarily confront Edom (2:2–7), Moab (2:8–12), and Ammon (2:16–23) because they are Israel's kin. Rather, the Israelites are instructed to ask permission to pass peaceably through these foreign lands and to purchase food and water. In the latter two episodes, God commands Israel to wage war against Heshbon (2:24–37) and Bashan (3:1–7) and to conquer their lands. In contrast to the rebelliousness seen in the prior section, Israel here follows God's commands exactly and emerges unscathed from the first three encounters and victorious in the last two.

### Peaceful Encounters with Edom, Moab, and Ammon (2:1–23)

The parashah offers two reasons for God's command to behave peaceably toward these nations, all three of which are located in modern-day Jordan. First, they are described as Israel's kin: the Edomites are the descendants of Esau; Moab and Ammon are the descendants of Lot. (On the origin of Moab and Ammon from the sexual union between Lot and his unnamed daughters, see at Genesis 19:30–38.)

Secondly, as members of the Abrahamic family tree, these nations also are recipients of divinely granted territory (2:5, 9, 19), which they gained by dispossessing earlier residents of the land (just as Israel is about to dispossess the Canaanites). This assertion communicates several cultural and theological messages: it emphasizes that the Israelites have a privileged relationship with nations that are considered their "kin"; and it argues that God controls the history and territory of all the nations in Israel's purview, not just Israel itself.

The events recounted in this passage are found elsewhere in the Torah (Numbers 20–22 and Deuteronomy 23). Each of these traditions agrees that Israel never had a military conflict with Ammon, Moab, or Edom during their journey from Egypt to Canaan. However, they differ in their explanations why. In Numbers 20–22 the Edomites do not grant permission to pass through the land; Israel then turns away and takes another route. Numbers 21:24, which is difficult to decipher, suggests that Israel did not cross over into Ammonite territory because the Ammonites were strong. Deuteronomy 23:4–5 states that the Ammonites and Moabites are to be forever excluded from membership in Israel because "they did not meet you with food and water on your journey after you left Egypt," which then becomes a rationale for the exclusion of foreign wives (see at 2:13). In this section of Deuteronomy, Israel

<sup>2</sup>Then יהוה said to me: <sup>3</sup>You have been skirting this hill country long enough; now turn north. <sup>4</sup>And charge the people as follows: You will be passing through the territory of your kin, the descendants of Esau, who live in Seir. Though they will be afraid of you, be very careful <sup>5</sup>not to provoke them. For I will not give you of their land so much as a foot can tread on; I have given the hill country of Seir as a possession to Esau. <sup>6</sup>What food you eat you shall obtain from them for money; even the water you drink you shall procure from them for money. <sup>7</sup>Indeed, your God יהוה has blessed you in all your undertakings. [God] has watched over your wanderings through this great wilderness; your God יהוה has been with you these past forty years: you have lacked nothing.

<sup>8</sup>We then moved on, away from our kin, the descendants of Esau, who live in Seir, away from the road of the Arabah, away from Elath and Eziongeber; and we marched on in the direction of the wilderness of Moab. <sup>9</sup>And יהוה said to me: Do not harass the Moabites or provoke them to war. For I will not give you any of their land as a possession; I have assigned Ar as a possession to the descendants of Lot.—

2 וַיֹּ֥אמֶר יְהֹוָ֖ה אֵלַ֥י לֵאמֹֽר׃ 3 רַב־לָכֶ֕ם סֹ֖ב אֶת־הָהָ֣ר הַזֶּ֑ה פְּנ֥וּ לָכֶ֖ם צָפֹֽנָה׃ 4 וְאֶת־הָעָם֮ צַ֣ו לֵאמֹר֒ אַתֶּ֣ם עֹֽבְרִ֗ים בִּגְבוּל֙ אֲחֵיכֶ֣ם בְּנֵֽי־עֵשָׂ֔ו הַיֹּֽשְׁבִ֖ים בְּשֵׂעִ֑יר וְיִֽירְא֣וּ מִכֶּ֔ם וְנִשְׁמַרְתֶּ֖ם מְאֹֽד׃ 5 אַל־תִּתְגָּר֣וּ בָ֔ם כִּ֠י לֹֽא־אֶתֵּ֨ן לָכֶ֜ם מֵֽאַרְצָ֗ם עַ֚ד מִדְרַ֣ךְ כַּף־רָ֔גֶל כִּֽי־יְרֻשָּׁ֣ה לְעֵשָׂ֔ו נָתַ֖תִּי אֶת־הַ֥ר שֵׂעִֽיר׃ 6 אֹ֣כֶל תִּשְׁבְּר֧וּ מֵֽאִתָּ֛ם בַּכֶּ֖סֶף וַֽאֲכַלְתֶּ֑ם וְגַם־מַ֜יִם תִּכְר֧וּ מֵֽאִתָּ֛ם בַּכֶּ֖סֶף וּשְׁתִיתֶֽם׃ 7 כִּי֩ יְהֹוָ֨ה אֱלֹהֶ֜יךָ בֵּֽרַכְךָ֗ בְּכֹל֙ מַֽעֲשֵׂ֣ה יָדֶ֔ךָ יָדַ֣ע לֶכְתְּךָ֔ אֶת־הַמִּדְבָּ֥ר הַגָּדֹ֖ל הַזֶּ֑ה זֶ֣ה ׀ אַרְבָּעִ֣ים שָׁנָ֗ה יְהֹוָ֤ה אֱלֹהֶ֨יךָ֙ עִמָּ֔ךְ לֹ֥א חָסַ֖רְתָּ דָּבָֽר׃ 8 וַֽנַּֽעֲבֹ֞ר מֵאֵ֣ת אַחֵ֣ינוּ בְנֵי־עֵשָׂ֗ו הַיֹּֽשְׁבִים֙ בְּשֵׂעִ֔יר מִדֶּ֨רֶךְ֙ הָֽעֲרָבָ֔ה מֵֽאֵילַ֖ת וּמֵֽעֶצְיֹ֣ן גָּ֑בֶר ס וַנֵּ֨פֶן֙ וַֽנַּֽעֲבֹ֔ר דֶּ֖רֶךְ מִדְבַּ֥ר מוֹאָֽב׃ 9 וַיֹּ֨אמֶר יְהֹוָ֜ה אֵלַ֗י אַל־תָּ֨צַר֙ אֶת־מוֹאָ֔ב וְאַל־תִּתְגָּ֥ר בָּ֖ם מִלְחָמָ֑ה כִּ֠י לֹֽא־אֶתֵּ֨ן לְךָ֤ מֵֽאַרְצוֹ֙ יְרֻשָּׁ֔ה כִּ֣י לִבְנֵי־ל֔וֹט נָתַ֥תִּי אֶת־עָ֖ר יְרֻשָּֽׁה׃

. . . . . . . . . . . . . . . . . . . . . . . . . . . . . . . . . . . . . . . .

is portrayed not as weak, but rather as obedient to God's command and respectful of both kinship relationships and God's geopolitical plans and decisions (compare 7:7).

**4. your kin, the descendants of Esau.** "Kin" is a key concept in the laws of Deuteronomy, where it signifies those toward whom each individual Israelite has a heightened relationship of responsibility. By identifying the Edomites as "kin," this text suggests that they too, have a privileged relationship with the Israelites and that their rights, especially their property rights, are to be respected. (See 23:8–9, which permits their inclusion with Israel in the third generation.)

**9–13.** These comments about Moab closely parallel the previous section about Edom, with the addition of a digression regarding the occupation history of the lands of Moab and Edom. Both territories were formerly inhabited by strong peoples who were dispossessed as part of God's plan of conquest and land distribution. The territory of Moab carries the name given by Lot's eldest daughter to her son born of the incestuous relations with her father (see Genesis 19:30–38). This myth of origin reveals the Israelites' complicated attitude toward the Moabites: while they are kin, they are also the product of a deeply transgressive sexual union. The book of Ruth, about a Moabite woman who becomes the wife of a Judahite man and great-grandmother of King David, illustrates another facet of the complicated attitude.

[10]It was formerly inhabited by the Emim, a people great and numerous, and as tall as the Anakites. [11]Like the Anakites, they are counted as Rephaim; but the Moabites call them Emim. [12]Similarly, Seir was formerly inhabited by the Horites; but the descendants of Esau dispossessed them, wiping them out and settling in their place, just as Israel did in the land they were to possess, which יהוה had given to them.—

[13]Up now! Cross the wadi Zered!

So we crossed the wadi Zered. [14]The time that we spent in travel from Kadesh-barnea until we crossed the wadi Zered was thirty-eight years, until that whole generation of warriors had perished from the camp, as יהוה had sworn concerning them. [15]Indeed, the hand of יהוה struck them, to root them out from the camp until they were finished off.

[16]When all the warriors among the people had died off, [17]יהוה spoke to me, saying: [18]You are now passing through the territory of Moab, through Ar. [19]You will then be close to the Ammonites; do not

10 הָאֵמִ֥ים לְפָנִ֖ים יָ֣שְׁבוּ בָ֑הּ עַ֣ם גָּד֥וֹל וְרַ֛ב
וָרָ֖ם כַּעֲנָקִֽים׃ 11 רְפָאִ֛ים יֵחָשְׁב֥וּ אַף־הֵ֖ם
כַּעֲנָקִ֑ים וְהַמֹּ֣אָבִ֔ים יִקְרְא֥וּ לָהֶ֖ם אֵמִֽים׃
12 וּבְשֵׂעִ֞יר יָשְׁב֣וּ הַחֹרִים֮ לְפָנִים֒ וּבְנֵ֧י
עֵשָׂ֣ו יִירָשׁ֗וּם וַיַּשְׁמִידוּם֙ מִפְּנֵיהֶ֔ם וַיֵּשְׁב֖וּ
תַּחְתָּ֑ם כַּאֲשֶׁ֧ר עָשָׂ֣ה יִשְׂרָאֵ֗ל לְאֶ֙רֶץ֙
יְרֻשָּׁת֔וֹ אֲשֶׁר־נָתַ֥ן יְהֹוָ֖ה לָהֶֽם׃
13 עַתָּ֗ה קֻ֛מוּ וְעִבְר֥וּ לָכֶ֖ם אֶת־נַ֣חַל זָ֑רֶד
וַנַּעֲבֹ֖ר אֶת־נַ֥חַל זָֽרֶד׃ 14 וְהַיָּמִ֞ים אֲשֶׁר־
הָלַ֣כְנוּ ׀ מִקָּדֵ֣שׁ בַּרְנֵ֗עַ עַ֤ד אֲשֶׁר־עָבַ֙רְנוּ֙ אֶת־
נַ֣חַל זֶ֔רֶד שְׁלֹשִׁ֥ים וּשְׁמֹנֶ֖ה שָׁנָ֑ה עַד־תֹּ֨ם כָּל־
הַדּ֜וֹר אַנְשֵׁ֤י הַמִּלְחָמָה֙ מִקֶּ֣רֶב הַֽמַּחֲנֶ֔ה
כַּאֲשֶׁ֛ר נִשְׁבַּ֥ע יְהֹוָ֖ה לָהֶֽם׃ 15 וְגַ֤ם יַד־יְהֹוָה֙
הָ֣יְתָה בָּ֔ם לְהֻמָּ֖ם מִקֶּ֣רֶב הַֽמַּחֲנֶ֑ה עַ֖ד
תֻּמָּֽם׃
16 וַיְהִ֨י כַאֲשֶׁר־תַּ֜מּוּ כָּל־אַנְשֵׁ֧י הַמִּלְחָמָ֛ה
לָמ֖וּת מִקֶּ֥רֶב הָעָֽם׃ ס 17 וַיְדַבֵּ֥ר יְהֹוָ֖ה
אֵלַ֥י לֵאמֹֽר׃ 18 אַתָּ֨ה עֹבֵ֥ר הַיּ֛וֹם אֶת־גְּב֥וּל
מוֹאָ֖ב אֶת־עָֽר׃ 19 וְקָרַבְתָּ֗ מ֚וּל בְּנֵ֣י עַמּ֔וֹן

*10. as tall as the Anakites.* See at 1:28.

*12. just as Israel did in the land they were to possess.* The use of the past tense is anachronistic in the context of Moses' speech since the conquest has not yet occurred. This discrepancy reminds readers that Deuteronomy as a whole is addressed to a later, post-conquest audience.

*13.* The peaceful crossing that is recounted here contrasts somewhat with descriptions in Nehemiah 13:1–3, which imply some hostility from Moab. This hostility justifies the later exclusion of the Moabites, along with the Ammonites, from the Israelite community (23:4–7). Marriage with Ammonite and Moabite women is presented as a problem in Ezra 9–10 and Nehemiah 13, books dealing with the postexilic restructuring of Jewish life in Judah in the 5th century B.C.E.; but the book of Ruth offers a different perspective.

*14–15.* These verses mark the transition between the generation of the exodus and the generation of the conquest, as well as the transition between the wandering in the wilderness and the beginning of the acquisition of the Promised Land.

*15. Indeed, the hand of* ***יהוה***. This verse emphasizes that the deaths of the warriors were ordained and executed by God—and were not a natural part of the cycle of generations.

*16–23.* This passage describes encounters with Ammon in a way that parallels the two previous passages (vv. 2–7, 8–12); and like the one concerning Moab, it includes a digression about the occupation history of the land in question. The territory of Ammon, north of Moab, bears the name given by Lot's younger daughter to her son from the incestuous relations with her father (see at 2:9–13 and Genesis 19:37).

harass them or start a fight with them. For I will not give any part of the land of the Ammonites to you as a possession; I have assigned it as a possession to the descendants of Lot.—

²⁰It, too, is counted as Rephaim country. It was formerly inhabited by Rephaim, whom the Ammonites call Zamzummim, ²¹a people great and numerous and as tall as the Anakites. יהוה wiped them out, so that [the Ammonites] dispossessed them and settled in their place, ²²as [God] did for the descendants of Esau who live in Seir, by wiping out the Horites before them, so that they dispossessed them and settled in their place, as is still the case. ²³So, too, with the Avvim who dwelt in villages in the vicinity of Gaza: the Caphtorim, who came from Crete, wiped them out and settled in their place.—

²⁴Up! Set out across the wadi Arnon! See, I give into your power Sihon the Amorite, king of Heshbon, and his land. Begin the occupation: engage him in battle. ²⁵This day I begin to put the dread and fear of you upon the peoples everywhere under heaven,

אַל־תְּצֻרֵם וְאַל־תִּתְגָּ֣ר בָּ֑ם כִּ֠י לֹֽא־אֶתֵּ֨ן מֵאֶ֜רֶץ בְּנֵֽי־עַמּ֤וֹן לְךָ֙ יְרֻשָּׁ֔ה כִּ֥י לִבְנֵי־ל֖וֹט נְתַתִּ֥יהָ יְרֻשָּֽׁה׃

²⁰ אֶֽרֶץ־רְפָאִ֥ים תֵּחָשֵׁ֖ב אַף־הִ֑וא רְפָאִ֤ים יָֽשְׁבוּ־בָהּ֙ לְפָנִ֔ים וְהָֽעַמֹּנִ֔ים יִקְרְא֥וּ לָהֶ֖ם זַמְזֻמִּֽים׃ ²¹ עַ֣ם גָּד֥וֹל וְרַ֛ב וָרָ֖ם כָּעֲנָקִ֑ים וַיַּשְׁמִידֵ֤ם יְהוָה֙ מִפְּנֵיהֶ֔ם וַיִּֽירָשֻׁ֖ם וַיֵּשְׁב֥וּ תַחְתָּֽם׃ ²² כַּאֲשֶׁ֤ר עָשָׂה֙ לִבְנֵ֣י עֵשָׂ֔ו הַיֹּשְׁבִ֖ים בְּשֵׂעִ֑יר אֲשֶׁ֨ר הִשְׁמִ֤יד אֶת־הַחֹרִי֙ מִפְּנֵיהֶ֔ם וַיִּֽירָשֻׁם֙ וַיֵּשְׁב֣וּ תַחְתָּ֔ם עַ֖ד הַיּ֥וֹם הַזֶּֽה׃ ²³ וְהָֽעַוִּ֛ים הַיֹּשְׁבִ֥ים בַּחֲצֵרִ֖ים עַד־עַזָּ֑ה כַּפְתֹּרִים֙ הַיֹּצְאִ֣ים מִכַּפְתֹּ֔ר הִשְׁמִידֻ֖ם וַיֵּשְׁב֥וּ תַחְתָּֽם׃ ²⁴ ק֣וּמוּ סְּע֗וּ וְעִבְרוּ֙ אֶת־נַ֣חַל אַרְנֹ֔ן רְאֵ֣ה נָתַ֣תִּי בְ֠יָדְךָ אֶת־סִיחֹ֨ן מֶֽלֶךְ־חֶשְׁבּ֤וֹן הָֽאֱמֹרִי֙ וְאֶת־אַרְצ֔וֹ הָחֵ֣ל רָ֑שׁ וְהִתְגָּ֥ר בּ֖וֹ מִלְחָמָֽה׃ ²⁵ הַיּ֣וֹם הַזֶּ֗ה אָחֵל֙ תֵּ֤ת פַּחְדְּךָ֙ וְיִרְאָ֣תְךָ֔ עַל־

---

### Battles against Amorite Kings (2:24–3:11)

This passage tells of the first of Israel's conquests east of the Jordan and marks a transition from the peaceful encounters with Israel's kin to the military conquest of the Promised Land. The text justifies the occupation of the Amorites' land in three ways. First, in contrast to the prior sections dealing with Edom, Moab, and Ammon, this section omits any reference to a divine land grant to the Amorites, which suggests that the Amorites' sovereignty is not expressly authorized by God and thus is invalid. Second, the text offers a belated moral justification for the conquest, for vv. 26–31 recall how Moses asks Sihon, the Amorite king, to allow the Israelites to pass freely through his land; but God hardens Sihon's heart, and the king refuses to grant them passage. Third, the conquest of the Amorites serves

as evidence for the idea that if the Israelites obey God's commands, they will be rewarded with military victory.

This passage raises questions for contemporary readers, as it reveals the Bible's own ambivalence about what qualifies as proper justification for conquest. Does one people's moral transgressions justify military aggression by another people? Is any land not explicitly granted by God fair game for God's chosen people? What is, or should be, the role of moral and theological considerations in political and military action?

**24.** *Up! Set out across the wadi Arnon.* This verse echoes God's initial charge to the Israelites in 1:7, thus impressing upon the reader that this moment is a fresh beginning. It is a chance to correct the earlier mistakes that tragically derailed Israel's initial approach to the Promised Land.

so that they shall tremble and quake because of you whenever they hear you mentioned.

[26]Then I sent messengers from the wilderness of Kedemoth to King Sihon of Heshbon with an offer of peace, as follows, [27]"Let me pass through your country. I will keep strictly to the highway, turning off neither to the right nor to the left. [28]What food I eat you will supply for money, and what water I drink you will furnish for money; just let me pass through—[29]as the descendants of Esau who dwell in Seir did for me, and the Moabites who dwell in Ar—that I may cross the Jordan into the land that our God יהוה is giving us."

[30]But King Sihon of Heshbon refused to let us pass through, because יהוה had stiffened his will and hardened his heart in order to deliver him into your power—as is now the case. [31]And יהוה said to me: See, I begin by placing Sihon and his land at your disposal. Begin the occupation; take possession of his land.

[32]Sihon with all his troops took the field against us at Jahaz, [33]and our God יהוה delivered him to us and we defeated him and his sons and all his troops. [34]At that time we captured all his towns, and we doomed every town—men, women, and children—leaving no survivor. [35]We retained as booty only the cattle and the spoil of the cities that we captured. [36]From Aroer on the edge of the Arnon

פְּנֵי֙ הָֽעַמִּ֔ים תַּ֖חַת כָּל־הַשָּׁמָ֑יִם אֲשֶׁר֙
יִשְׁמְעוּן֙ שִׁמְעֲךָ֔ וְרָגְז֥וּ וְחָל֖וּ מִפָּנֶֽיךָ׃
26 וָאֶשְׁלַ֤ח מַלְאָכִים֙ מִמִּדְבַּ֣ר קְדֵמ֔וֹת אֶל־
סִיח֖וֹן מֶ֣לֶךְ חֶשְׁבּ֑וֹן דִּבְרֵ֥י שָׁל֖וֹם לֵאמֹֽר׃
27 אֶעְבְּרָ֣ה בְאַרְצֶ֔ךָ בַּדֶּ֥רֶךְ בַּדֶּ֖רֶךְ אֵלֵ֑ךְ לֹ֥א
אָס֖וּר יָמִ֥ין וּשְׂמֹֽאול׃ 28 אֹ֣כֶל בַּכֶּ֤סֶף
תַּשְׁבִּרֵ֙נִי֙ וְאָכַ֔לְתִּי וּמַ֛יִם בַּכֶּ֥סֶף תִּתֶּן־לִ֖י
וְשָׁתִ֑יתִי רַ֖ק אֶעְבְּרָ֥ה בְרַגְלָֽי׃ 29 כַּאֲשֶׁ֨ר
עָֽשׂוּ־לִ֜י בְּנֵ֣י עֵשָׂ֗ו הַיֹּֽשְׁבִים֙ בְּשֵׂעִ֔יר
וְהַמּ֣וֹאָבִ֔ים הַיֹּֽשְׁבִ֖ים בְּעָ֑ר עַ֤ד אֲשֶׁר־אֶֽעֱבֹר֙
אֶת־הַיַּרְדֵּ֔ן אֶל־הָאָ֕רֶץ אֲשֶׁר־יְהוָ֥ה אֱלֹהֵ֖ינוּ
נֹתֵ֥ן לָֽנוּ׃
30 וְלֹ֣א אָבָ֗ה סִיחֹן֙ מֶ֣לֶךְ חֶשְׁבּ֔וֹן הַעֲבִרֵ֖נוּ
בּ֑וֹ כִּֽי־הִקְשָׁה֩ יְהוָ֨ה אֱלֹהֶ֜יךָ אֶת־רוּח֗וֹ
וְאִמֵּץ֙ אֶת־לְבָב֔וֹ לְמַ֛עַן תִּתּ֥וֹ בְיָדְךָ֖ כַּיּ֥וֹם
הַזֶּֽה׃ ס 31 וַיֹּ֤אמֶר יְהוָה֙ אֵלַ֔י רְאֵ֗ה
הַחִלֹּ֙תִי֙ תֵּ֣ת לְפָנֶ֔יךָ אֶת־סִיחֹ֖ן וְאֶת־אַרְצ֑וֹ
הָחֵ֣ל רָ֔שׁ לָרֶ֖שֶׁת אֶת־אַרְצֽוֹ׃
32 וַיֵּצֵא֩ סִיחֹ֨ן לִקְרָאתֵ֜נוּ ה֧וּא וְכָל־עַמּ֛וֹ
לַמִּלְחָמָ֖ה יָֽהְצָה׃ 33 וַֽיִּתְּנֵ֛הוּ יְהוָ֥ה אֱלֹהֵ֖ינוּ
לְפָנֵ֑ינוּ וַנַּ֥ךְ אֹת֛וֹ וְאֶת־בנו בָּנָ֖יו וְאֶת־כָּל־
עַמּֽוֹ׃ 34 וַנִּלְכֹּ֤ד אֶת־כָּל־עָרָיו֙ בָּעֵ֣ת הַהִ֔וא
וַֽנַּחֲרֵם֙ אֶת־כָּל־עִ֣יר מְתִ֔ם וְהַנָּשִׁ֖ים וְהַטָּ֑ף
לֹ֥א הִשְׁאַ֖רְנוּ שָׂרִֽיד׃ 35 רַ֥ק הַבְּהֵמָ֖ה בָּזַ֣זְנוּ
לָ֑נוּ וּשְׁלַ֥ל הֶעָרִ֖ים אֲשֶׁ֥ר לָכָֽדְנוּ׃ 36 מֵעֲרֹעֵ֞ר
אֲשֶׁר֩ עַל־שְׂפַת־נַ֨חַל אַרְנֹ֜ן וְהָעִ֨יר אֲשֶׁ֤ר

*26–29.* King Sihon's refusal of the offer of peace justifies the Israelite conquest of his lands.

*30. because יהוה had . . . hardened his heart.* This verse recalls God's hardening of Pharaoh's heart (see Exodus 9:12; 10:20, 27; 11:10). In both stories, God causes a foreign leader to oppose Israel so that God will have the opportunity to demonstrate God's power and allegiance to Israel in response.

*31–37. See, I begin by placing Sihon . . . just as our God יהוה had commanded.* This is an example of a case in which God commands the Israelites to fight a war whose outcome God has already guaranteed.

*34. we doomed every town—men, women, and children.* The high degree of destruction depicted in this passage demonstrates that the Israelites are not fighting for mercenary reasons. Here, they take no prisoners but do retain booty. Other stories of wars describe how they destroy all property in order to demonstrate the purity of their motives (see I Samuel 15:3).

valley, including the town in the valley itself, to Gilead, not a city was too mighty for us; our God יהוה delivered everything to us. ³⁷But you did not encroach upon the land of the Ammonites, all along the wadi Jabbok and the towns of the hill country, just as our God יהוה had commanded.

3 We made our way up the road toward Bashan, and King Og of Bashan with all his troops took the field against us at Edrei. ²But יהוה said to me: Do not fear him, for I am delivering him and all his troops and his country into your power, and you will do to him as you did to Sihon king of the Amorites, who lived in Heshbon.

³So our God יהוה also delivered into our power King Og of Bashan, with all his troops, and we dealt them such a blow that no survivor was left. ⁴At that time we captured all his towns; there was not a town that we did not take from them: sixty towns, the whole district of Argob, the kingdom of Og in Bashan—⁵all those towns were fortified with high walls, gates, and bars—apart from a great number of unwalled towns. ⁶We doomed them as we had done in the case of King Sihon of Heshbon; we doomed every town—men, women, and children—⁷and retained as booty all the cattle and the spoil of the towns.

⁸Thus we seized, at that time, from the two Amorite kings, the country beyond the Jordan, from the wadi Arnon to Mount Hermon—⁹Sidonians called Hermon Sirion, and the Amorites call it Senir—¹⁰all the towns of the Tableland and the whole of Gilead and Bashan as far as Salcah and Edrei, the towns of Og's kingdom in Bashan.

בַּנַּ֫חַל֒ וְעַד־הַגִּלְעָד֙ לֹ֤א הָֽיְתָה֙ קִרְיָ֔ה אֲשֶׁ֥ר שָׂגְבָ֖ה מִמֶּ֑נּוּ אֶת־הַכֹּ֕ל נָתַ֛ן יְהֹוָ֥ה אֱלֹהֵ֖ינוּ לְפָנֵֽינוּ׃ ³⁷ רַ֛ק אֶל־אֶ֥רֶץ בְּנֵֽי־עַמּ֖וֹן לֹ֣א קָרָ֑בְתָּ כׇּל־יַ֞ד נַ֤חַל יַבֹּק֙ וְעָרֵ֣י הָהָ֔ר וְכֹ֥ל אֲשֶׁר־צִוָּ֖ה יְהֹוָ֥ה אֱלֹהֵֽינוּ׃

ג וַנֵּ֣פֶן וַנַּ֔עַל דֶּ֖רֶךְ הַבָּשָׁ֑ן וַיֵּצֵ֣א עוֹג֩ מֶֽלֶךְ־הַבָּשָׁ֨ן לִקְרָאתֵ֜נוּ ה֧וּא וְכׇל־עַמּ֛וֹ לַמִּלְחָמָ֖ה אֶדְרֶֽעִי׃ ² וַיֹּ֨אמֶר יְהֹוָ֤ה אֵלַי֙ אַל־תִּירָ֣א אֹת֔וֹ כִּ֣י בְיָדְךָ֞ נָתַ֧תִּי אֹת֛וֹ וְאֶת־כׇּל־עַמּ֖וֹ וְאֶת־אַרְצ֑וֹ וְעָשִׂ֣יתָ לּ֔וֹ כַּאֲשֶׁ֣ר עָשִׂ֗יתָ לְסִיחֹן֙ מֶ֣לֶךְ הָֽאֱמֹרִ֔י אֲשֶׁ֥ר יוֹשֵׁ֖ב בְּחֶשְׁבּֽוֹן׃ ³ וַיִּתֵּן֩ יְהֹוָ֨ה אֱלֹהֵ֤ינוּ בְּיָדֵ֙נוּ֙ גַּ֔ם אֶת־ע֖וֹג מֶֽלֶךְ־הַבָּשָׁ֑ן וְאֶת־כׇּל־עַמּ֑וֹ וַנַּכֵּ֕הוּ עַד־בִּלְתִּ֥י הִשְׁאִֽיר־ל֖וֹ שָׂרִֽיד׃ ⁴ וַנִּלְכֹּ֤ד אֶת־כׇּל־עָרָיו֙ בָּעֵ֣ת הַהִ֔וא לֹ֤א הָֽיְתָה֙ קִרְיָ֔ה אֲשֶׁ֥ר לֹֽא־לָקַ֖חְנוּ מֵֽאִתָּ֑ם שִׁשִּׁ֥ים עִיר֙ כׇּל־חֶ֣בֶל אַרְגֹּ֔ב מַמְלֶ֥כֶת ע֖וֹג בַּבָּשָֽׁן׃ ⁵ כׇּל־אֵ֜לֶּה עָרִ֧ים בְּצֻרֹ֛ת חוֹמָ֥ה גְבֹהָ֖ה דְּלָתַ֣יִם וּבְרִ֑יחַ לְבַ֛ד מֵעָרֵ֥י הַפְּרָזִ֖י הַרְבֵּ֥ה מְאֹֽד׃ ⁶ וַנַּחֲרֵ֣ם אוֹתָ֔ם כַּאֲשֶׁ֣ר עָשִׂ֔ינוּ לְסִיחֹ֖ן מֶ֣לֶךְ חֶשְׁבּ֑וֹן הַֽחֲרֵם֙ כׇּל־עִ֣יר מְתִ֔ם הַנָּשִׁ֖ים וְהַטָּֽף׃ ⁷ וְכׇל־הַבְּהֵמָ֛ה וּשְׁלַ֥ל הֶעָרִ֖ים בַּזּ֥וֹנוּ לָֽנוּ׃ ⁸ וַנִּקַּ֞ח בָּעֵ֤ת הַהִוא֙ אֶת־הָאָ֔רֶץ מִיַּ֗ד שְׁנֵי֙ מַלְכֵ֣י הָֽאֱמֹרִ֔י אֲשֶׁ֖ר בְּעֵ֣בֶר הַיַּרְדֵּ֑ן מִנַּ֥חַל אַרְנֹ֖ן עַד־הַ֥ר חֶרְמֽוֹן׃ ⁹ צִֽידֹנִ֛ים יִקְרְא֥וּ לְחֶרְמ֖וֹן שִׂרְיֹ֑ן וְהָ֣אֱמֹרִ֔י יִקְרְאוּ־ל֖וֹ שְׂנִֽיר׃ ¹⁰ כֹּ֣ל ׀ עָרֵ֣י הַמִּישֹׁ֗ר וְכׇל־הַגִּלְעָד֙ וְכׇל־הַבָּשָׁ֔ן עַד־סַלְכָ֖ה וְאֶדְרֶ֑עִי עָרֵ֖י מַמְלֶ֥כֶת ע֖וֹג בַּבָּשָֽׁן׃

---

**37. our God יהוה had commanded.** Along with the prior verse, this one emphasizes the convergence of God's will and Israel's obedience to both God's active and restrictive commands. They fought their designated enemy but did not encroach on the neighboring lands that were forbidden to them.

**3:1–7.** This retelling of the conquest of the

Bashan resembles the account of the victory over Sihon, king of Heshbon, and reinforces its messages.

**8–11.** These verses summarize the conquest of lands bordering Canaan across the Jordan. Israel's actions bring an end to a semi-mythic group of people called the Rephaim. Others were wiped out by the Moabites and Ammonites (2:10–11, 20–21).

11Only King Og of Bashan was left of the remaining Rephaim. His bedstead, an iron bedstead, is now in Rabbah of the Ammonites; it is nine cubits long and four cubits wide, by the standard cubit!

12And this is the land which we apportioned at that time: The part from Aroer along the wadi Arnon, with part of the hill country of Gilead and its towns, I assigned to the Reubenites and the Gadites. 13The rest of Gilead, and all of Bashan under Og's rule—the whole Argob district, all that part of Bashan which is called Rephaim country—I assigned to the half-tribe of Manasseh. 14Jair son of Manasseh received the whole Argob district (that is, Bashan) as far as the boundary of the Geshurites and the Maacathites, and named it after himself: Havvoth-jair—as is still the case. 15To Machir I assigned Gilead. 16And to the Reubenites and the Gadites I assigned the part from Gilead down to the wadi Arnon, the middle of the wadi being the boundary, and up to the wadi Jabbok, the boundary of the Ammonites.

17[We also seized] the Arabah, from the foot of the slopes of Pisgah on the east, to the edge of the Jordan, and from Chinnereth down to the sea of the Arabah, the Dead Sea.

18At that time I charged you [men of Reuben,

11 כִּ֣י רַק־ע֞וֹג מֶ֣לֶךְ הַבָּשָׁ֗ן נִשְׁאַר֮ מִיֶּ֣תֶר
הָרְפָאִים֒ הִנֵּ֤ה עַרְשׂוֹ֙ עֶ֣רֶשׂ בַּרְזֶ֔ל הֲלֹ֣ה הִ֔וא
בְּרַבַּ֖ת בְּנֵ֣י עַמּ֑וֹן תֵּ֨שַׁע אַמּ֤וֹת אָרְכָּהּ֙ וְאַרְבַּ֣ע
אַמּ֣וֹת רָחְבָּ֔הּ בְּאַמַּת־אִֽישׁ׃
12 וְאֶת־הָאָ֧רֶץ הַזֹּ֛את יָרַ֖שְׁנוּ בָּעֵ֣ת הַהִ֑וא
מֵעֲרֹעֵ֞ר אֲשֶׁר־עַל־נַ֣חַל אַרְנֹ֗ן וַחֲצִ֤י הַר־
הַגִּלְעָד֙ וְעָרָ֔יו נָתַ֕תִּי לָרֽאוּבֵנִ֖י וְלַגָּדִֽי׃
13 וְיֶ֨תֶר הַגִּלְעָ֤ד וְכָל־הַבָּשָׁן֙ מַמְלֶ֣כֶת ע֔וֹג
נָתַ֕תִּי לַחֲצִ֖י שֵׁ֣בֶט הַֽמְנַשֶּׁ֑ה כֹּ֣ל חֶ֤בֶל הָֽאַרְגֹּב֙
לְכָל־הַבָּשָׁ֔ן הַה֥וּא יִקָּרֵ֖א אֶ֥רֶץ רְפָאִֽים׃
14 יָאִ֣יר בֶּן־מְנַשֶּׁ֗ה לָקַח֙ אֶת־כָּל־חֶ֣בֶל אַרְגֹּ֔ב
עַד־גְּב֥וּל הַגְּשׁוּרִ֖י וְהַמַּעֲכָתִ֑י וַיִּקְרָא֩ אֹתָ֨ם
עַל־שְׁמ֤וֹ אֶת־הַבָּשָׁן֙ חַוֺּ֣ת יָאִ֔יר עַ֖ד הַיּ֥וֹם
הַזֶּֽה׃ 15 וּלְמָכִ֖יר נָתַ֥תִּי אֶת־הַגִּלְעָֽד׃
16 וְלָרֽאוּבֵנִ֨י וְלַגָּדִ֜י נָתַ֤תִּי מִן־הַגִּלְעָד֙ וְעַד־
נַ֣חַל אַרְנֹ֔ן תּ֥וֹךְ הַנַּ֖חַל וּגְבֻ֑ל וְעַד֙ יַבֹּ֣ק הַנַּ֔חַל
גְּב֖וּל בְּנֵ֥י עַמּֽוֹן׃
17 וְהָעֲרָבָ֖ה וְהַיַּרְדֵּ֣ן וּגְבֻ֑ל מִכִּנֶּ֗רֶת וְעַ֨ד יָ֤ם
הָעֲרָבָה֙ יָ֣ם הַמֶּ֔לַח תַּ֛חַת אַשְׁדֹּ֥ת הַפִּסְגָּ֖ה
מִזְרָֽחָה׃
18 וָאֲצַ֣ו אֶתְכֶ֔ם בָּעֵ֥ת הַהִ֖וא לֵאמֹ֑ר יְהוָ֣ה

*11. His bedstead . . . nine cubits long.* Og's bed would have been about $13\frac{1}{2}$ feet (more than 4 meters) long, demonstrating that he was a giant.

## *Moses' Allotment of Land East of the Jordan* (3:12–20)

In Numbers 32, the cattle-rearing tribes of Reuben and Gad ask Moses to take possession of these territories because they provide good grazing land. The half-tribe of Manasseh is also granted part of this East Jordanian territory. In the present text, the high concentration of the words "land," "take possession," and "I am giving to you" underscores a central concern: to show that the occupation of the land of Canaan and the lands across the Jordan are the results of God's "giving" of the territory to Israel as a possession or inheritance.

*13. Manasseh.* Numbers 27 and 36 mention the five daughters of Zelophehad (Mahlah, Noah, Hoglah, Tirzah, and Milcah) among the heirs of the Manasseh clans. Joshua 17 describes how these women receive their land.

*18–20.* Even though their land allotment has already been conquered, Moses requires the fighting men of these tribes to join with the rest of the Israelite forces when they invade and conquer the land of Canaan.

Gad, and Manasseh], saying, "Your God יהוה has given you this country to possess. You must go as shock-troops, warriors all, at the head of your Israelite kin. ¹⁹Only your wives, children, and livestock—I know that you have much livestock—shall be left in the towns I have assigned to you, ²⁰until יהוה has granted your kin a haven such as you have, and they too have taken possession of the land that your God יהוה is assigning them, beyond the Jordan. Then you may return each to the homestead that I have assigned to him."

²¹I also charged Joshua at that time, saying, "You have seen with your own eyes all that your God יהוה has done to these two kings; so shall יהוה do to all the kingdoms into which you shall cross over. ²²Do not fear them, for it is your God יהוה who will battle for you."

אֱלֹֽהֵיכֶ֗ם נָתַ֤ן לָכֶם֙ אֶת־הָאָ֣רֶץ הַזֹּ֔את לְרִשְׁתָּ֑הּ חֲלוּצִ֣ים תַּֽעַבְר֗וּ לִפְנֵ֛י אֲחֵיכֶ֥ם בְּנֵֽי־יִשְׂרָאֵ֖ל כָּל־בְּנֵי־חָֽיִל: ¹⁹ רַ֤ק נְשֵׁיכֶם֙ וְטַפְּכֶ֣ם וּמִקְנֵכֶ֔ם יָדַ֕עְתִּי כִּֽי־מִקְנֶ֥ה רַ֖ב לָכֶ֑ם יֵֽשְׁבוּ֙ בְּעָ֣רֵיכֶ֔ם אֲשֶׁ֥ר נָתַ֖תִּי לָכֶֽם: ²⁰ עַ֠ד אֲשֶׁר־יָנִ֨יחַ יְהֹוָ֥ה ׀ לַֽאֲחֵיכֶם֮ כָּכֶם֒ וְיָרְשׁ֣וּ גַם־הֵ֔ם אֶת־הָאָ֕רֶץ אֲשֶׁ֨ר יְהֹוָ֧ה אֱלֹֽהֵיכֶ֛ם נֹתֵ֥ן לָהֶ֖ם בְּעֵ֣בֶר הַיַּרְדֵּ֑ן וְשַׁבְתֶּ֗ם אִ֚ישׁ לִֽירֻשָּׁת֔וֹ אֲשֶׁ֥ר נָתַ֖תִּי לָכֶֽם:

²¹ וְאֶת־יְהוֹשׁ֣וּעַ צִוֵּ֔יתִי בָּעֵ֥ת הַהִ֖וא לֵאמֹ֑ר עֵינֶ֣יךָ הָֽרֹאֹ֗ת אֵת֩ כָּל־אֲשֶׁ֨ר עָשָׂ֜ה יְהֹוָ֤ה אֱלֹֽהֵיכֶם֙ לִשְׁנֵי֙ הַמְּלָכִ֣ים הָאֵ֔לֶּה כֵּֽן־יַעֲשֶׂ֤ה יְהֹוָה֙ לְכָל־הַמַּמְלָכ֔וֹת אֲשֶׁ֥ר אַתָּ֖ה עֹבֵ֥ר שָֽׁמָּה: ²² לֹ֖א תִּֽירָא֑וּם כִּ֚י יְהֹוָ֣ה אֱלֹֽהֵיכֶ֔ם ה֖וּא הַנִּלְחָ֥ם לָכֶֽם: ס

. . . . . . . . . . . . . . . . . . . . . . . . . . . . .

## Moses' Charge to Joshua   (3:21–22)

Moses charges Joshua to understand the victories over the kingdoms of Bashan and Sihon as evidence of God's allegiance to Israel and as foreshadowing and precedent for the imminent conquest of the land of Canaan.

—*Elsie R. Stern*

# Another View

Deuteronomy commences with a review of several prior moments in Israel's history. This parashah contains a theme relevant for women and all modern Jews, especially those interested in interpreting the text differently than has been done previously—for Moses, the great prophet and lawgiver, provides his own interpretation of Israel's history and even law.

The book begins by claiming that what follows are Moses' words, addressed to the Israelites (1:1), meaning that they are presented as his words, not those of the unidentified narrator. The text legitimates Moses' comments, noting that they are "in accordance with the instructions that יהוה had given him" (1:3).

Before the start of Moses' speech, we read, "Moses undertook to expound this Teaching" (*torah*; 1:5). The word translated as "undertook" expresses a decision connected with a new initiative or a bold action. The implication is that Moses initiates what becomes a long Jewish tradition: constant reinterpretation of the text. In an ironic and Jewish way, the Torah has already begun to be interpreted within the text.

A quick overview reveals that Moses' address agrees with in general, but is not identical to, the way that these events are described in previous books. In some of these instances, the differences actually put more power in the hands of the people for things like choosing judges (Deuteronomy 1:13 versus Exodus 18:25) or sending out the scouts (Deuteronomy 1:22 versus Numbers 13:1). The book's later portions even present some of the laws differently than in the prior books (see, for example, 12:2–28), indicating an early process of adaptation and interpretation, not just of history but of legal material as well.

*In an ironic and Jewish way, the Torah has already begun to interpret itself.*

Thus, the opening parashah of Deuteronomy, one of the most important books in the Hebrew Bible, teaches us an important lesson about the way traditions change over time, even within this most sacred text. This lesson is particularly relevant to women and liberal Jews, who at times have been criticized for engaging in what happens to be the very interpretive process witnessed in Deuteronomy—and exemplified in the work of the scholars who have contributed to this *Commentary*.

—*Tammi J. Schneider*

# Post-biblical Interpretations

***These are the words*** (1:1). This parashah is read in the synagogue on the Sabbath immediately preceding Tishah B'Av, the annual commemoration of the destructions of the First and Second Temples. Therefore, the haftarah reading (from Isaiah 1:1–27) and many of the rabbinic commentaries focus on images and themes of rebuke, in which Israel is called upon to repent and embrace a higher level of moral and ethical conduct.

Midrash *Sifrei D'varim* 1 is devoted almost entirely to the subject of rebuke. The midrash explains that Moses wrote the entire Torah, not just "these... words." If so, the midrash responds, then "these words" must be words of reproof as similarly seen in Amos, Jeremiah, and in reference to King David,

"These are the last words of David" (I Samuel 23:1). However, according to *Sifrei D'varim* 1, in some cases it is God, rather than Moses, who voices criticism. For example, God rebukes the Israelites for complaining about the manna they ate during their trek in the wilderness (Numbers 21:5), asserting that kings would willingly choose to eat such a food for its apparent health benefits. The Israelites' ingratitude reminds God of another ancestor, Adam, who was given Eve as a helper and mate—but then blamed her for his disobedience in eating the fruit (Genesis 3:12). In this unusual interpretation of Genesis 2–3, the Israelites' behavior is explained through a comparison with Adam, whom the Rabbis deem cowardly and unjust in attributing his own sin to Eve.

Elsewhere, the Rabbis view rebuke as a vehicle for repentance. In *P'sikta D'Rav Kahana* 15:5 (Mandelbaum edn.), a late midrashic compilation based on the liturgical cycle of holy days, the midrash for the Shabbat before Tishah B'Av focuses on Israel's abandonment of the study of Torah and its subsequent disastrous results: the destructions of the First and Second Temples. The Rabbis observe that a person who forsakes God but continues to study Torah will return to God by means of the power of the Torah itself.

***It was in the fortieth year*** (1:3). The Sages understood this phrase to mean that Moses did not rebuke the Israelites until he was about to die. A midrash found in *Sifrei D'varim* 2 and *B'reishit Rabbah* 54.3 cites a number of other cases of deathbed rebuke (including Abraham, Isaac, and Joshua), and then explains why one should not reprove another person until one's death is near. The reasons include avoiding reproaching another person repeatedly, preserving the chastised person from shame in the presence of the rebuker, preventing the individual from holding a grudge against the rebuker, and permitting the rebuked one to leave in peace, "for rebuke should bring about peace."

***Do not harass the Moabites . . . You will then be close to the Ammonites*** (2:9, 19). The Rabbis often interpret these verses about Moab and Ammon in relation to Ruth and Naamah, two foreign women who influenced Israelite history. According to the Bible, Ruth, a Moabite, remained faithful to her mother-in-law Naomi after both were widowed, and she adopted Naomi's people and their way of life. With Naomi's help, Ruth married Boaz, and became King David's great-grandmother. Naamah, an Ammonite, was King Solomon's wife and the mother of Rehoboam, the king of Judah after Solomon (I Kings 14:21). On their behalf, according to BT *Bava Kama* 38b, God instructed Moses not to wage war against the Moabites or Ammonites: "The idea you have in your mind is not the idea I have in My mind. In the future I will bring forth two doves from them: Ruth the Moabite and Naamah the Ammonite" (also BT *Nazir* 23b, BT *Horayot* 10b–11a).

*"In the future I will bring forth two doves from those peoples: Ruth and Naamah."*

These talmudic passages also note that Lot's two daughters were the matriarchs of Moab and Ammon through incestuous relations with their father (Genesis 19:37–38). The exegetical etymologies of the names of the offspring, and therefore of the tribes, are significant to the Rabbis. They view the name of the elder daughter's son (Moab, or "my father") as a reference to the sinful incestuous act, which explains for them why God forbade war with Moab but did not restrict Israel from harassing this potential enemy. The Rabbis use a Greek word, no doubt familiar from Roman rule, to describe this harassment as the seizure or subjugation of Moab for forced labor, particularly for public works projects. In the case of the younger daughter's son (Ben-ammi, meaning "son of my people," and rendered as Ammon), no reference is made to incest. As a result, the Sages explain, God forbade Israel from either warring with or harassing the Ammonites.

—*Deborah Green*

# *Contemporary Reflection*

THE BOOK OF DEUTERONOMY, dramatically set just outside the land of Canaan, is comprised of a series of farewell addresses delivered by Moses as he prepares to die, forever barred from the Promised Land. Unlike the previous four books of the Torah, which are narrated in the third person, Deuteronomy is narrated almost entirely in the first person, the "I" of Moses persistently addressing a "you." However, the "you" that Moses addresses is not always the same: sometimes it refers to all the Israelites who left Egypt, none of whom is still alive to hear these final words; other times it refers to their children, the generation of the wilderness, those now listening to Moses; still other times, it refers to a small group of Israelites, such as the twelve scouts, the two-and-a-half tribes who have chosen to settle on the east bank of the Jordan, or just Joshua and Caleb.

In fact, the word "you" punctuates this parashah like a drumbeat, appearing more than 100 times in slightly more than 100 verses, plus many other instances if the imperative verb form is included. Throughout, Moses primarily focuses on his I-You relationship with the people; yet the relationship is characterized more by conflict and alienation than by intimacy. As he recalls their journey, trying to make sense of the past forty years, he rewrites history, blaming the people for proposing that he send scouts to the land (an action commanded by God in Numbers 13:2) and for provoking him into delegating judicial authority (an idea suggested by his father-in-law Jethro in Exodus 18:17–23). Worst of all, Moses blames the children for the sins of their parents. Although it is the slave generation who has disappointed him, it is the next generation who now suffers Moses' rancor and regret.

Despite the fact that Deuteronomy is an ancient book, the insights revealed in this parashah resonate with our modern ideas about human psychology. Contemporary psychologists describe a process known as counter-transference, whereby a therapist projects onto her patients certain conflicts still unresolved within her own life story. Parents, too, can be guilty of such unconscious projection, ascribing to their children their own youthful errors and defeats.

Therefore, we can read this first farewell speech as the presentation of a leader who engages in a kind of counter-transference when he reflects back to the people what has transpired between him and them over the past four decades. Standing before them now on the threshold of death, he wonders: What has happened to this people that I led out of slavery? What has happened to our shared resolve? What has happened to me, who was to serve as God's emissary and representative? Why have the people doomed me—through their lack of faith, their ingratitude, their waywardness—to die without enjoying God's promise? We can see in Moses' flawed recollections and chastisement of the people a final attempt to reshape his life story so as to justify the past actions of this metaphoric parent.

> *As Moses tries to make sense of the past forty years, he rewrites history.*

Each year at the Passover seder, we Jews re-enact a similar drama, warning the next generation not to act the part of the *rasha*, the wicked child, in the haggadah's parable of the Four Children. If we look closely at this exchange between the parent and the wicked child, we can hear in the former's rebuke of the latter echoes of what we hear in this parashah. As some versions of the haggadah phrase the dialogue: "The wicked child asks: 'What is this service to *you*?' . . . And because these children exclude themselves from the community, you should chastise them, saying: 'Because of what God did for *me* when *I* came out of Egypt.' 'For me' and not 'for them,' for had they been there, they would not have been redeemed." This is a painful text for many Jews. Who among us does not know a contrary child, perhaps our own, who feels so alienated from Judaism that she is willing to be excluded from the community?

In order to truly understand what this vignette in fact conveys, we need to probe further. When we look up the original context of the *rasha*'s question (Exodus 12:26), we discover that the Rabbis have twisted words out of context. In their original setting, these words were intended to reinforce the tradition, not disparage it; indeed, the Torah instructs *all* Jewish children to pose this question. Why then did rabbinic tradition put this question only in the mouth of the *rasha*? Weren't they living proof that it is precisely this kind of personality—skeptical, provocative, contrary—that would best guarantee Jewish survival?

Like the parent of the *rasha*, Moses (as *parashat D'varim* presents him) seems ambivalent about his contrary people, and perhaps about himself. During much of his speech, he separates himself from the Israelites, addressing them as "you"; but on occasion he uses "we," as when reminiscing about battles they fought together (3:12). For that brief moment, he regards them as equals who have shared important decisions about the distribution of land. But before he even finishes the verse, he pulls back, telling them four times how "I [that is, Moses] assigned" the regions of that apportioned land.

The parashah invites us to see that, like most parents, Moses has loved his children even when they have acted the part of the *rasha.* And like most parents, he has sometimes felt rejected and betrayed when his children have asserted their autonomy. As he now prepares to let them go into the new land, he must decide what his final message to them should be. Tellingly, the parashah concludes with his encouraging words to Joshua, "Do not fear... for it is your God יהוה who will battle for you" (3:22). In the end, Moses recognizes that this is a new generation about to enter the land, and they need his blessing as well as God's.

—*Ellen Frankel*

# Voices

## God: Desert

Feiga Izrailevna Kogan (transl. Carole B. Balin)

I dream with pain in the foreign land
of the flowering camps of Israel;
copper horizons of the desert,
and golden waters of the Jordan;
Carmel sun-filled vine,
and sapphire of the Dead Sea,
and sacred roses of Sharon,
And banquets of fragrant lilies.

I remember the moment
when the Great one
split the Red Sea for us,

And all the people tread on the precious shore
and Miriam sang,
and in the distance
the beauty of the songs sounded,
and the air responded with reverberations
the prophetic lips quivered:

You allowed me to take part in these songs
in this prophetic exile
and gave me uncertain knowledge
and the ardor of my righteous heart.
So now with earthly sounds and my mortal
  music
let me glorify Your regal Name
beyond the seas of the sun.

## *from* The Generations Upon Me

Barbara Reisner

I walk through the tired city
carrying my satchels.

Behind the face of each building
I see my grandmother
carry her potato sacks
from village to village
and return each Sabbath to Azrian.

I smell the old *Sefer D'varim*
she brought with her to America.
I see her reading
"These are the words,"
believing them,
and I am haunted
by her face.

I build nothing.
I blush at Moses' command.
"Start out and make your way."

As mercy drifts through justice,
the sun drifts through the wind,
refreshing the city.

The hour turns. I continue walking
as if I were a guardian,
the generations upon me.

## *from* Nomad Land

Corie Feiner

You have it wrong.
We nomads are always
home.

Our search is not like the search
for a child who has fallen inside of the
toothless earth.

Our search is like
a smell. It pulls itself
up from the ground
lingers, and becomes
memory.

## *from* Home Again

Yerra Sugarman

Here each leaf
is a memory
crisply fallen
to land.
The land is an ocean
of leaves gone crimson;
the tips of branches
the color of pomegranates.

Here my thoughts are
burning the land in me

only speech rebuilds.

## Move

Alicia Suskin Ostriker

Whether it's a turtle who drags herself
Slowly to the sandlot where she digs
The sandy nest she was born to dig

And lay leathery eggs in, or whether it's salmon
Rocketing upstream
Towards pools that call: *Bring your eggs here*

*And nowhere else in the world,* whether it is
turtle-green
Ugliness and awkwardness, or the seething
Grace and gild of silky salmon, we

Are envious, our wishes speak out right here
Thirsty for a destiny like theirs,
And absolute right choice

To end all choices. Is it memory,
We ask, is it a smell
They remember

Or just what is it, some kind of blueprint
That makes them move, hot grain by grain,
Cold cascade above icy cascade,

Slipping through
Water's fingers
A hundred miles

Inland from the easy shiny sea—
And we also, in the company
Of our tribe

Or perhaps alone, like the turtle
On her wrinkled feet with the tapping nails,
We also are going to travel, we say let's be

Oblivious to all, save
That we travel, and we say
When we reach the place we'll know

We are in the right spot, somehow, like a breath
Entering a singer's chest, that shapes itself
For the song that is to follow.

## *They've Rolled the Parchment*

Shirley Kaufman

They've rolled the parchment
again
to its beginning

I want
to feel a rolling
under my feet
as if I am walking
in sand

*each point of arrival*
*a stepping-stone*

to the next oasis

what if
there were a shorter way
through the wilderness
would we
have arrived sooner
and to
what

Hittites
Canaanites
Shiites
Pre-Raphaelites
anchorites
plebiscites

would they have
opened
their arms to us and said
sister/brother

have some water
(and some oil)
make yourselves
at home

I strip myself
of the past year
enter the hum
of prayer

warm
as an old sweater
pulled over my head

# ואתחנן ✦ Va-et'chanan

## DEUTERONOMY 3:23–7:11

### *The Call to Loyalty and Love*

PARASHAT VA-ET'CHANAN ("I pleaded") begins with Moses' recollection of how he longingly prayed to God to be allowed to enter the Promised Land. This speech is part of a larger address to the Israelites in which Moses recounts for them all that occurred in the wilderness and the lessons they should derive from these experiences. Moses exhorts them to use the past as the basis for future behavior, making their first-hand knowledge of God and their national memory of the Sinai experience (here called Horeb) the basis for their relationship to God when they begin their lives in the new land without him.

Throughout this parashah, Moses plays the role of teacher. First, he spells out various reasons as to *why* the Israelites should obey God's teachings (4:1–40). Next, he reminds them of *what* God commanded at Horeb (Sinai) (4:44–5:30), including the Decalogue ("Ten Commandments") (5:6–18). Then, he teaches them *how* to fulfill the commandments by specifying the proper attitude to approach the Divine (6:1–7:5). Finally, he concludes by explaining the nature of God's love for them, the basis for the relationship between Israel and God (7:6–11). Throughout, Moses reiterates that while the people will be rewarded for their obedience and commitment to God, they will be punished severely if they stray from God's path. In particular, he emphasizes monotheism, a central theme in Deuteronomy as a whole. God's uniqueness and the demand for Israel's absolute loyalty find expression in the passages known as the *Sh'ma* and *V'ahavta* (6:4–9)—prayers that stand at the center of the Jewish proclamation of faith.

This parashah seems to include women as a matter of course when Moses addresses the Israelites in the second-person masculine singular or plural, as is typical elsewhere. In addition, women are mentioned specifically in the Decalogue as daughters, slaves, mothers, and wives (5:14, 16, 18), as well as in the prohibition of intermarriage, in which Canaanite women appear to possess the power to lead Israelites astray (7:3–4). More indirectly, the parashah's emphasis on education (6:20–25) invites readers to assess women's role in ancient Israel with respect to raising the next generation.

*This parashah invites us to assess women's role in raising the next generation.*

*—Ora Horn Prouser*

## Outline

*I.* Moses' Plea to Enter the Land (3:23–29)

*II.* Exhortations to Keep God's Commandments
*Why Follow the Laws* (4:1–40)

A. Exhortations to keep God's commandments as communicated (vv. 1–8)
B. Exhortations to remember the revelation at Horeb (Sinai) (vv. 9–14)
C. Exhortations regarding God's unique nature (vv. 15–40)

*III.* Interlude
*Cities of Refuge* (4:41–43)

*IV.* Review of Horeb (Sinai)
*What Laws to Follow* (4:44–5:30)

A. Introduction and setting the scene (4:44–5:5)
B. The Decalogue ("Ten Commandments") (5:6–18)
C. The people's fearful response and call for Moses' intercession (5:19–24)
D. God's response to the people's request (5:25–30)

*V.* Additional Teachings
*How to Follow the Laws* (6:1–7:5)

A. The call to love the one and only God (6:1–9)
B. The call to absolute loyalty to Israel's God (6:10–19)
C. The demand to teach future generations about the laws (6:20–25)
D. Prohibitions regarding the inhabitants of the land (7:1–5)

*VI.* Conclusion
*God's Love as Reason for the Laws* (7:6–11)

I pleaded with יהוה at that time, saying, ²⁴"O lord יהוה, You who let Your servant see the first works of Your greatness and Your mighty hand, You whose powerful deeds no god in heaven or on earth can equal! ²⁵Let me, I pray, cross over and see the good land on the other side of the Jordan, that good hill country, and the Lebanon." ²⁶But יהוה was wrathful with me on your account and would not listen to me. יהוה said to me, "Enough! Never speak to Me of this matter again! ²⁷Go up to the summit of Pisgah and gaze about, to the west, the north, the south, and the east. Look at it well, for you shall not go across yonder Jordan. ²⁸Give Joshua his instructions, and imbue him with strength and courage, for he shall go across at the

ג 23 וָאֶתְחַנַּ֖ן אֶל־יְהֹוָ֑ה בָּעֵ֥ת הַהִ֖וא לֵאמֹֽר: 24 אֲדֹנָ֣י יֱהֹוִ֗ה אַתָּ֤ה הַֽחִלּ֙וֹתָ֙ לְהַרְא֣וֹת אֶֽת־עַבְדְּךָ֔ אֶ֨ת־גׇּדְלְךָ֔ וְאֶת־יָדְךָ֖ הַֽחֲזָקָ֑ה אֲשֶׁ֤ר מִי־אֵל֙ בַּשָּׁמַ֣יִם וּבָאָ֔רֶץ אֲשֶׁר־יַעֲשֶׂ֥ה כְמַעֲשֶׂ֖יךָ וְכִגְבוּרֹתֶֽךָ: 25 אֶעְבְּרָה־נָּ֗א וְאֶרְאֶה֙ אֶת־הָאָ֣רֶץ הַטּוֹבָ֔ה אֲשֶׁ֖ר בְּעֵ֣בֶר הַיַּרְדֵּ֑ן הָהָ֥ר הַטּ֛וֹב הַזֶּ֖ה וְהַלְּבָנֹֽן: 26 וַיִּתְעַבֵּ֨ר יְהֹוָ֥ה בִּי֙ לְמַ֣עַנְכֶ֔ם וְלֹ֥א שָׁמַ֖ע אֵלָ֑י וַיֹּ֨אמֶר יְהֹוָ֤ה אֵלַי֙ רַב־לָ֔ךְ אַל־תּ֗וֹסֶף דַּבֵּ֥ר אֵלַ֛י ע֖וֹד בַּדָּבָ֥ר הַזֶּֽה: 27 עֲלֵ֣ה | רֹ֣אשׁ הַפִּסְגָּ֗ה וְשָׂ֥א עֵינֶ֛יךָ יָ֧מָּה וְצָפֹ֛נָה וְתֵימָ֖נָה וּמִזְרָ֑חָה וּרְאֵ֣ה בְעֵינֶ֑יךָ כִּי־לֹ֥א תַעֲבֹ֖ר אֶת־הַיַּרְדֵּ֥ן הַזֶּֽה: 28 וְצַ֥ו אֶת־יְהוֹשֻׁ֖עַ וְחַזְּקֵ֣הוּ וְאַמְּצֵ֑הוּ כִּֽי־

---

## Moses' Plea to Enter the Land
### (3:23–29)

This unit continues Moses' review of the Israelites' journey to the plains of Moab, in the lower Jordan valley. In preparing the people to enter the land, Moses explains why he cannot go forth with them. Earlier he blamed the people for his not being allowed to enter the land (1:37); here he discloses how he unsuccessfully beseeched God to reconsider.

**26. was wrathful.** Heb. *vayitaber.* There is a word play between this word and *eb'rah-na,* "let me cross over" in the previous verse. The root *e-b-r* is repeated numerous times in the previous parashah

(for example, 2:14; 3:21), highlighting the theme of "crossing over" at the beginning of Deuteronomy.

**on your account.** Moses again blames the Israelites for his punishment, as in 1:37. In contrast, Numbers 20 (where Moses strikes the rock to produce water) depicts the punishment as Moses' fault. This inconsistency exemplifies one of several contradictions between Deuteronomy's account of the wilderness journey and that of Exodus and Numbers (see at 1:9–18, 1:19–46). While Moses interprets God's response and behavior as anger (see also 4:21), one might also see a nurturing hand in God's allowing Moses to see the land and assuring him of an integral role in passing on leadership to Joshua.

---

▶ Biblical monotheism makes human beings the initiators of change within the universe.

ANOTHER VIEW ➤ *1082*

▶ How has the Israelites' understanding of the Decalogue grown since the original Revelation?

CONTEMPORARY REFLECTION ➤ *1084*

▶ This verse is cited as a proof text for determining Jewish descent by the mother's status.

POST-BIBLICAL INTERPRETATIONS ➤ *1083*

▶ We ascend to the Torah . . . to risk being known and seen, / to risk being at Sinai again.

VOICES ➤ *1086*

head of this people, and he shall allot to them the
land that you may only see."
29Meanwhile we stayed on in the valley near
Beth-peor.

הוּא יַעֲבֹר לִפְנֵי הָעָם הַזֶּה וְהוּא יַנְחִיל
אוֹתָם אֶת־הָאָרֶץ אֲשֶׁר תִּרְאֶה׃
29 וַנֵּשֶׁב בַּגָּיְא מוּל בֵּית פְּעוֹר׃ פ

4 And now, O Israel, give heed to the laws
and rules that I am instructing you to observe, so
that you may live to enter and occupy the land that
יהוה, the God of your fathers, is giving you. 2You
shall not add anything to what I command you nor
take anything away from it, but keep the commandments of your God יהוה that I enjoin upon
you. 3You saw with your own eyes what יהוה did in
the matter of Baal-peor, that your God יהוה wiped
out from among you every person who followed
Baal-peor; 4while you, who held fast to your God
יהוה, are all alive today.

ד וְעַתָּה יִשְׂרָאֵל שְׁמַע אֶל־הַחֻקִּים וְאֶל־
הַמִּשְׁפָּטִים אֲשֶׁר אָנֹכִי מְלַמֵּד אֶתְכֶם
לַעֲשׂוֹת לְמַעַן תִּחְיוּ וּבָאתֶם וִירִשְׁתֶּם
אֶת־הָאָרֶץ אֲשֶׁר יְהֹוָה אֱלֹהֵי אֲבֹתֵיכֶם
נֹתֵן לָכֶם׃ 2 לֹא תֹסִפוּ עַל־הַדָּבָר אֲשֶׁר
אָנֹכִי מְצַוֶּה אֶתְכֶם וְלֹא תִגְרְעוּ מִמֶּנּוּ
לִשְׁמֹר אֶת־מִצְוֺת יְהֹוָה אֱלֹהֵיכֶם אֲשֶׁר
אָנֹכִי מְצַוֶּה אֶתְכֶם׃ 3 עֵינֵיכֶם הָרֹאוֹת אֵת
אֲשֶׁר־עָשָׂה יְהֹוָה בְּבַעַל פְּעוֹר כִּי כָל־
הָאִישׁ אֲשֶׁר הָלַךְ אַחֲרֵי בַעַל־פְּעוֹר
הִשְׁמִידוֹ יְהֹוָה אֱלֹהֶיךָ מִקִּרְבֶּךָ׃ 4 וְאַתֶּם
הַדְּבֵקִים בַּיהֹוָה אֱלֹהֵיכֶם חַיִּים כֻּלְּכֶם
הַיּוֹם׃

## *Exhortations to Keep God's Commandments*

### WHY FOLLOW THE LAWS (4:1–40)

Moses' speeches at the start of Deuteronomy retell—and reinterpret—the formative events in Israel's journey as a way of exhorting his audience to obey the instructions. He argues that God's teachings must be followed strictly since there are dire consequences for disobeying them. At the same time, he emphasizes that these precepts should be obeyed because they provide Israel wisdom and discernment that will make this nation honored by other nations. Moses uses a combination of threats and promises to stress the need to follow these teachings even when he is no longer present as an intermediary and interpreter.

Here, as elsewhere, Deuteronomy speaks to multiple audiences: those who are described in the text as standing in Moab listening to Moses' words; the contemporaries of the exilic writers who composed the literary framework of the book (1:1–4:40; 31:1–34:12); and subsequent generations of readers. (See also the introduction to *parashat D'varim*, p. 1039.)

### EXHORTATIONS TO KEEP GOD'S COMMANDMENTS AS COMMUNICATED (4:1–8)

One way that Moses teaches the importance of obeying God's commandments is by emphasizing the lessons learned from personal experience. Here, he calls attention to what the people saw with their "own eyes" (v. 3) at Baal-peor.

*3. **Baal-peor.*** This refers to the incident in which some Israelite men lusted after foreign women who lured them into worship of their deity, Baal-peor (Numbers 25). In Numbers 31:14–18, Moses blames God's anger on the women, who are presented as seductive and dangerous; here, he makes no mention of the women.

[5]See, I have imparted to you laws and rules, as my God יהוה has commanded me, for you to abide by in the land that you are about to enter and occupy. [6]Observe them faithfully, for that will be proof of your wisdom and discernment to other peoples, who on hearing of all these laws will say, "Surely, that great nation is a wise and discerning people." [7]For what great nation is there that has a god so close at hand as is our God יהוה whenever we call? [8]Or what great nation has laws and rules as perfect as all this Teaching that I set before you this day?

[9]But take utmost care and watch yourselves scrupulously, so that you do not forget the things that you saw with your own eyes and so that they do not fade from your mind as long as you live. And make them known to your children and to your children's children: [10]The day you stood before your God יהוה at Horeb, when יהוה said to Me, "Gather the people to Me that I may let them hear My words, in order that they may learn to revere Me as long as they live on earth, and may so teach their children." [11]You came forward and stood at the foot of the mountain. The mountain was ablaze with flames to the very skies, dark with densest clouds. [12]יהוה spoke to you out of the fire;

5 רְאֵה | לִמַּדְתִּי אֶתְכֶם חֻקִּים וּמִשְׁפָּטִים
כַּאֲשֶׁר צִוַּנִי יְהֹוָה אֱלֹהָי לַעֲשׂוֹת כֵּן בְּקֶרֶב
הָאָרֶץ אֲשֶׁר אַתֶּם בָּאִים שָׁמָּה לְרִשְׁתָּהּ׃
6 וּשְׁמַרְתֶּם וַעֲשִׂיתֶם כִּי הִוא חָכְמַתְכֶם
וּבִינַתְכֶם לְעֵינֵי הָעַמִּים אֲשֶׁר יִשְׁמְעוּן אֵת
כָּל־הַחֻקִּים הָאֵלֶּה וְאָמְרוּ רַק עַם־חָכָם
וְנָבוֹן הַגּוֹי הַגָּדוֹל הַזֶּה׃ 7 כִּי מִי־גוֹי גָּדוֹל
אֲשֶׁר־לוֹ אֱלֹהִים קְרֹבִים אֵלָיו כַּיהֹוָה
אֱלֹהֵינוּ בְּכָל־קָרְאֵנוּ אֵלָיו׃ 8 וּמִי גּוֹי גָּדוֹל
אֲשֶׁר־לוֹ חֻקִּים וּמִשְׁפָּטִים צַדִּיקִם כְּכֹל
הַתּוֹרָה הַזֹּאת אֲשֶׁר אָנֹכִי נֹתֵן לִפְנֵיכֶם
הַיּוֹם׃
9 רַק הִשָּׁמֶר לְךָ וּשְׁמֹר נַפְשְׁךָ מְאֹד פֶּן־
תִּשְׁכַּח אֶת־הַדְּבָרִים אֲשֶׁר־רָאוּ עֵינֶיךָ וּפֶן־
יָסוּרוּ מִלְּבָבְךָ כֹּל יְמֵי חַיֶּיךָ וְהוֹדַעְתָּם
לְבָנֶיךָ וְלִבְנֵי בָנֶיךָ׃ 10 יוֹם אֲשֶׁר עָמַדְתָּ
לִפְנֵי יְהֹוָה אֱלֹהֶיךָ בְּחֹרֵב בֶּאֱמֹר יְהֹוָה
אֵלַי הַקְהֶל־לִי אֶת־הָעָם וְאַשְׁמִעֵם אֶת־
דְּבָרָי אֲשֶׁר יִלְמְדוּן לְיִרְאָה אֹתִי כָּל־הַיָּמִים
אֲשֶׁר הֵם חַיִּים עַל־הָאֲדָמָה וְאֶת־בְּנֵיהֶם
יְלַמֵּדוּן׃ 11 וַתִּקְרְבוּן וַתַּעַמְדוּן תַּחַת הָהָר
וְהָהָר בֹּעֵר בָּאֵשׁ עַד־לֵב הַשָּׁמַיִם חֹשֶׁךְ עָנָן
וַעֲרָפֶל׃ 12 וַיְדַבֵּר יְהֹוָה אֲלֵיכֶם מִתּוֹךְ הָאֵשׁ

*5–8.* One reason for observing the laws is that other nations will admire the Israelites for being wise enough to follow a responsive God who has established good and right precepts.

*8. Teaching.* Heb. *torah*. This term refers to the written teachings contained in the book of Deuteronomy. Later tradition enlarges the notion of *torah* to include Genesis through Deuteronomy. (See also at 31:9.)

### EXHORTATIONS TO REMEMBER THE REVELATION AT HOREB (SINAI) (4:9–14)

Moses calls upon the people to remember something that they supposedly witnessed with their "own eyes" (v. 9; also vv. 3, 34). Here the memory of a past event—the revelation at Horeb—is intended to motivate future observance of the covenant. Note, however, that almost none of the presumed audience would have been physically present at that historic moment, except perhaps as children (see at Numbers 14:10–38).

*10.* The text places a tremendous emphasis on memory and the need to pass information to the next generation. Shared memories of the past also shape and contribute to a community's identity as a people.

*Horeb.* The book of Deuteronomy refers to Mount Sinai as Horeb (see at Exodus 18:5).

you heard the sound of words but perceived no
shape—nothing but a voice. [13][God] declared to
you the covenant that you were commanded to observe, the Ten Commandments, inscribing them
on two tablets of stone. [14]At the same time יהוה
commanded me to impart to you laws and rules for
you to observe in the land that you are about to
cross into and occupy.

[15]For your own sake, therefore, be most careful—since you saw no shape when your God יהוה
spoke to you at Horeb out of the fire—[16]not to act
wickedly and make for yourselves a sculptured image in any likeness whatever: the form of a man or a
woman, [17]the form of any beast on earth, the form
of any winged bird that flies in the sky, [18]the form
of anything that creeps on the ground, the form of
any fish that is in the waters below the earth. [19]And
when you look up to the sky and behold the sun
and the moon and the stars, the whole heavenly
host, you must not be lured into bowing down to
them or serving them. These your God יהוה allotted to other peoples everywhere under heaven;
[20]but you יהוה took and brought out of Egypt, that
iron blast furnace, to be God's very own people, as
is now the case.

[21]Now יהוה was angry with me on your account
and swore that I should not cross the Jordan and

קוֹל דְּבָרִים אַתֶּם שֹׁמְעִים וּתְמוּנָה אֵינְכֶם
רֹאִים זוּלָתִי קוֹל׃ 13 וַיַּגֵּד לָכֶם אֶת־בְּרִיתוֹ
אֲשֶׁר צִוָּה אֶתְכֶם לַעֲשׂוֹת עֲשֶׂרֶת הַדְּבָרִים
וַיִּכְתְּבֵם עַל־שְׁנֵי לֻחוֹת אֲבָנִים׃ 14 וְאֹתִי
צִוָּה יְהֹוָה בָּעֵת הַהִוא לְלַמֵּד אֶתְכֶם חֻקִּים
וּמִשְׁפָּטִים לַעֲשֹׂתְכֶם אֹתָם בָּאָרֶץ אֲשֶׁר
אַתֶּם עֹבְרִים שָׁמָּה לְרִשְׁתָּהּ׃

15 וְנִשְׁמַרְתֶּם מְאֹד לְנַפְשֹׁתֵיכֶם כִּי לֹא
רְאִיתֶם כָּל־תְּמוּנָה בְּיוֹם דִּבֶּר יְהֹוָה
אֲלֵיכֶם בְּחֹרֵב מִתּוֹךְ הָאֵשׁ׃ 16 פֶּן־
תַּשְׁחִתוּן וַעֲשִׂיתֶם לָכֶם פֶּסֶל תְּמוּנַת
כָּל־סָמֶל תַּבְנִית זָכָר אוֹ נְקֵבָה׃ 17 תַּבְנִית
כָּל־בְּהֵמָה אֲשֶׁר בָּאָרֶץ תַּבְנִית כָּל־צִפּוֹר
כָּנָף אֲשֶׁר תָּעוּף בַּשָּׁמָיִם׃ 18 תַּבְנִית
כָּל־רֹמֵשׂ בָּאֲדָמָה תַּבְנִית כָּל־דָּגָה אֲשֶׁר־
בַּמַּיִם מִתַּחַת לָאָרֶץ׃ 19 וּפֶן־תִּשָּׂא עֵינֶיךָ
הַשָּׁמַיְמָה וְרָאִיתָ אֶת־הַשֶּׁמֶשׁ וְאֶת־הַיָּרֵחַ
וְאֶת־הַכּוֹכָבִים כֹּל צְבָא הַשָּׁמַיִם וְנִדַּחְתָּ
וְהִשְׁתַּחֲוִיתָ לָהֶם וַעֲבַדְתָּם אֲשֶׁר חָלַק
יְהֹוָה אֱלֹהֶיךָ אֹתָם לְכֹל הָעַמִּים תַּחַת
כָּל־הַשָּׁמָיִם׃ 20 וְאֶתְכֶם לָקַח יְהֹוָה וַיּוֹצִא
אֶתְכֶם מִכּוּר הַבַּרְזֶל מִמִּצְרָיִם לִהְיוֹת לוֹ
לְעַם נַחֲלָה כַּיּוֹם הַזֶּה׃

21 וַיהֹוָה הִתְאַנַּף־בִּי עַל־דִּבְרֵיכֶם וַיִּשָּׁבַע
לְבִלְתִּי עָבְרִי אֶת־הַיַּרְדֵּן וּלְבִלְתִּי־בֹא אֶל־

### EXHORTATIONS REGARDING GOD'S UNIQUE NATURE (4:15–40)

Israel's absolute loyalty to their one God is a key concern in this parashah and elsewhere in Deuteronomy.

*16.* One lesson to be learned from God's formless revelation at Horeb (Sinai) is that Israel must not make any sculptured images of God.

***form of a man or a woman.*** Literally, "... a male or a female." The wording of this verse's prohibition suggests that some Israelites conceived of their God in both female and male terms.

*19–20.* As part of his warning against idolatry, Moses forbids the worship of the celestial bodies. The passage states that God divided the heavenly beings among the other nations but selected Israel as God's own possession. In other words, God sanctioned the non-Israelites to worship lesser divine entities but restricted the Israelites to worship God alone. Verse 19 plays a central role in debates about the development of monotheism; for more on this subject, see at 4:35; 6:4; 32:8; Exodus 15:11; and Another View, p. 1082.

enter the good land that your God יהוה is assigning you as a heritage. <sup>22</sup>For I must die in this land; I shall not cross the Jordan. But you will cross and take possession of that good land. <sup>23</sup>Take care, then, not to forget the covenant that your God יהוה concluded with you, and not to make for yourselves a sculptured image in any likeness, against which your God יהוה has enjoined you. <sup>24</sup>For your God יהוה is a consuming fire, an impassioned God.

<sup>25</sup>When you have begotten children and children's children and are long established in the land, should you act wickedly and make for yourselves a sculptured image in any likeness, causing your God יהוה displeasure and vexation, <sup>26</sup>I call heaven and earth this day to witness against you that you shall soon perish from the land that you are crossing the Jordan to possess; you shall not long endure in it, but shall be utterly wiped out. <sup>27</sup>יהוה will scatter you among the peoples, and only a scant few of you shall be left among the nations to which יהוה will drive you. <sup>28</sup>There you will serve gods of wood and stone, made by human hands, that cannot see or hear or eat or smell.

<sup>29</sup>But if you search there, you will find your God יהוה, if only you seek with all your heart and soul—<sup>30</sup>when you are in distress because all these things have befallen you and, in the end, return to and obey your God יהוה. <sup>31</sup>For your God יהוה is a compassionate God, who will not fail you nor let

הָאָ֫רֶץ הַטּוֹבָ֔ה אֲשֶׁ֥ר יְהֹוָ֖ה אֱלֹהֶ֖יךָ נֹתֵ֥ן לְךָ֖ נַחֲלָֽה: 22 כִּ֣י אָנֹכִ֣י מֵת֮ בָּאָ֣רֶץ הַזֹּאת֒ אֵינֶ֕נִּי עֹבֵ֖ר אֶת־הַיַּרְדֵּ֑ן וְאַתֶּם֙ עֹֽבְרִ֔ים וִֽירִשְׁתֶּ֔ם אֶת־הָאָ֥רֶץ הַטּוֹבָ֖ה הַזֹּֽאת: 23 הִשָּׁמְר֣וּ לָכֶ֗ם פֶּֽן־תִּשְׁכְּחוּ֙ אֶת־בְּרִ֤ית יְהֹוָה֙ אֱלֹֽהֵיכֶ֔ם אֲשֶׁ֥ר כָּרַ֖ת עִמָּכֶ֑ם וַעֲשִׂיתֶ֨ם לָכֶ֥ם פֶּ֨סֶל֙ תְּמ֣וּנַת כֹּ֔ל אֲשֶׁ֥ר צִוְּךָ֖ יְהֹוָ֥ה אֱלֹהֶֽיךָ: 24 כִּ֚י יְהֹוָ֣ה אֱלֹהֶ֔יךָ אֵ֥שׁ אֹכְלָ֖ה ה֑וּא אֵ֖ל קַנָּֽא: פ

25 כִּֽי־תוֹלִ֤יד בָּנִים֙ וּבְנֵ֣י בָנִ֔ים וְנֽוֹשַׁנְתֶּ֖ם בָּאָ֑רֶץ וְהִשְׁחַתֶּ֗ם וַעֲשִׂ֤יתֶם פֶּ֨סֶל֙ תְּמ֣וּנַת כֹּ֔ל וַעֲשִׂיתֶ֥ם הָרַ֛ע בְּעֵינֵ֥י יְהֹוָֽה־אֱלֹהֶ֖יךָ לְהַכְעִיסֽוֹ: 26 הַעִידֹ֩תִי֩ בָכֶ֨ם הַיּ֜וֹם אֶת־הַשָּׁמַ֣יִם וְאֶת־הָאָ֗רֶץ כִּֽי־אָבֹ֣ד תֹּֽאבֵדוּן֮ מַהֵ֒ר֒ מֵעַ֣ל הָאָ֔רֶץ אֲשֶׁ֨ר אַתֶּ֜ם עֹבְרִ֧ים אֶת־הַיַּרְדֵּ֛ן שָׁ֖מָּה לְרִשְׁתָּ֑הּ לֹֽא־תַאֲרִיכֻ֤ן יָמִים֙ עָלֶ֔יהָ כִּ֥י הִשָּׁמֵ֖ד תִּשָּׁמֵדֽוּן: 27 וְהֵפִ֧יץ יְהֹוָ֛ה אֶתְכֶ֖ם בָּֽעַמִּ֑ים וְנִשְׁאַרְתֶּם֙ מְתֵ֣י מִסְפָּ֔ר בַּגּוֹיִ֕ם אֲשֶׁ֨ר יְנַהֵ֧ג יְהֹוָ֛ה אֶתְכֶ֖ם שָֽׁמָּה: 28 וַעֲבַדְתֶּם־שָׁ֣ם אֱלֹהִ֔ים מַעֲשֵׂ֖ה יְדֵ֣י אָדָ֑ם עֵ֣ץ וָאֶ֔בֶן אֲשֶׁ֤ר לֹֽא־יִרְאוּן֙ וְלֹ֣א יִשְׁמְע֔וּן וְלֹ֥א יֹֽאכְל֖וּן וְלֹ֥א יְרִיחֻֽן:

29 וּבִקַּשְׁתֶּ֥ם מִשָּׁ֛ם אֶת־יְהֹוָ֥ה אֱלֹהֶ֖יךָ וּמָצָ֑אתָ כִּ֣י תִדְרְשֶׁ֔נּוּ בְּכָל־לְבָבְךָ֖ וּבְכָל־נַפְשֶֽׁךָ: 30 בַּצַּ֣ר לְךָ֗ וּמְצָא֕וּךָ כֹּ֖ל הַדְּבָרִ֣ים הָאֵ֑לֶּה בְּאַחֲרִית֙ הַיָּמִ֔ים וְשַׁבְתָּ֙ עַד־יְהֹוָ֣ה אֱלֹהֶ֔יךָ וְשָׁמַעְתָּ֖ בְּקֹלֽוֹ: 31 כִּ֣י אֵ֤ל רַחוּם֙ יְהֹוָ֣ה אֱלֹהֶ֔יךָ לֹ֥א יַרְפְּךָ֖ וְלֹ֣א יַשְׁחִיתֶ֑ךָ וְלֹ֣א

---

**24. God is a consuming fire.** It is significant that as Moses delivers his farewell address, he refers to God as a consuming fire; he first met God in a fire that did not consume the bush (Exodus 3:2).

***impassioned God.*** See at 5:9.

**25–31.** Demanding absolute loyalty to the one God, Moses warns the Israelites that if they make idols they will be exiled from the land they currently wait to enter. According to some who date much of Deuteronomy to the 7th century B.C.E.,

this passage addresses an audience in Judah that fears imminent exile, having witnessed the exile of the Northern Kingdom of Israel in 722 B.C.E. Others who date Deuteronomy 4 even later, to the Babylonian exile, see this warning as an explanation after the fact, indicating why exile happened and offering comfort that restoration is possible.

**26. I call heaven and earth . . . as witnesses.** See at 32:1.

you perish; [God] will not forget the covenant made on oath with your fathers.

[32]You have but to inquire about bygone ages that came before you, ever since God created humankind on earth, from one end of heaven to the other: has anything as grand as this ever happened, or has its like ever been known? [33]Has any people heard the voice of a god speaking out of a fire, as you have, and survived? [34]Or has any deity ventured to go and take one nation from the midst of another by prodigious acts, by signs and portents, by war, by a mighty and an outstretched arm and awesome power, as your God יהוה did for you in Egypt before your very eyes? [35]It has been clearly demonstrated to you that יהוה alone is God; there is none else. [36]From the heavens [God] let you hear the divine voice to discipline you; on earth [God] let you see the great divine fire; and from amidst that fire you heard God's words. [37]And having loved your ancestors, [God] chose their heirs after them; [God] personally—in great, divine might—led you out of Egypt, [38]to drive from your path nations greater and more populous than you, to take you into their land and assign it to you as a

יִשְׁכַּח אֶת־בְּרִית אֲבֹתֶיךָ אֲשֶׁר נִשְׁבַּע
לָהֶם׃
32 כִּי שְׁאַל־נָא לְיָמִים רִאשֹׁנִים אֲשֶׁר־הָיוּ
לְפָנֶיךָ לְמִן־הַיּוֹם אֲשֶׁר בָּרָא אֱלֹהִים ׀ אָדָם
עַל־הָאָרֶץ וּלְמִקְצֵה הַשָּׁמַיִם וְעַד־קְצֵה
הַשָּׁמָיִם הֲנִהְיָה כַּדָּבָר הַגָּדוֹל הַזֶּה אוֹ
הֲנִשְׁמַע כָּמֹהוּ׃ 33 הֲשָׁמַע עָם קוֹל אֱלֹהִים
מְדַבֵּר מִתּוֹךְ־הָאֵשׁ כַּאֲשֶׁר־שָׁמַעְתָּ אַתָּה
וַיֶּחִי׃ 34 אוֹ ׀ הֲנִסָּה אֱלֹהִים לָבוֹא לָקַחַת לוֹ
גוֹי מִקֶּרֶב גּוֹי בְּמַסֹּת בְּאֹתֹת וּבְמוֹפְתִים
וּבְמִלְחָמָה וּבְיָד חֲזָקָה וּבִזְרוֹעַ נְטוּיָה
וּבְמוֹרָאִים גְּדֹלִים כְּכֹל אֲשֶׁר־עָשָׂה לָכֶם
יְהוָה אֱלֹהֵיכֶם בְּמִצְרַיִם לְעֵינֶיךָ׃ 35 אַתָּה
הָרְאֵתָ לָדַעַת כִּי יְהוָה הוּא הָאֱלֹהִים אֵין
עוֹד מִלְבַדּוֹ׃ 36 מִן־הַשָּׁמַיִם הִשְׁמִיעֲךָ אֶת־
קֹלוֹ לְיַסְּרֶךָּ וְעַל־הָאָרֶץ הֶרְאֲךָ אֶת־אִשּׁוֹ
הַגְּדוֹלָה וּדְבָרָיו שָׁמַעְתָּ מִתּוֹךְ הָאֵשׁ׃
37 וְתַחַת כִּי אָהַב אֶת־אֲבֹתֶיךָ וַיִּבְחַר
בְּזַרְעוֹ אַחֲרָיו וַיּוֹצִאֲךָ בְּפָנָיו בְּכֹחוֹ הַגָּדֹל
מִמִּצְרָיִם׃ 38 לְהוֹרִישׁ גּוֹיִם גְּדֹלִים וַעֲצֻמִים
מִמְּךָ מִפָּנֶיךָ לַהֲבִיאֲךָ לָתֶת־לְךָ אֶת־

*31.* ***[God] will not forget the covenant.*** Moses gives the Israelites this assurance as he admonishes them not to forget the events of the past (v. 9) and the lessons imparted from those experiences.

***fathers.*** Heb. *avot.* According to translator David Stein, this term can have either a male-only or an inclusive sense, depending on context. He argues that here the term refers specifically to the patriarchs (Abraham, Isaac, and Jacob), those with whom God formed a covenant in their capacity as (male) heads of their corporate households. It goes without saying that each patriarch represents the entire household, and that God's covenant applies to all its members—women and men alike ("Methodology," *The Torah: Documentation for the Revised Edition*, 2005, p. 6).

*32–40.* Starting with a series of rhetorical questions, this passage illustrates the uniqueness of God's relationship with Israel—perhaps the most important reason for observing God's laws—by retelling a sequence of spectacular and seemingly impossible events, including the redemption from Egypt and revelation of God's words.

*35.* **יהוה *alone is God; there is none else.*** This verse and v. 39 clearly and directly affirm the monotheistic belief in a single deity. In contrast, other passages in Deuteronomy reflect an acceptance that other gods existed, even though Israel was commanded to worship the one God exclusively; scholars refer to this belief as monolatry (see 5:7 in the Decalogue, as well as at 4:19–20; 6:4; 32:8; Exodus 15:11; and Another View, p. 1082).

heritage, as is still the case. 39Know therefore this
day and keep in mind that יהוה alone is God in
heaven above and on earth below; there is no other.
40Observe God's laws and commandments, which I
enjoin upon you this day, that it may go well with
you and your children after you, and that you may
long remain in the land that your God יהוה is
assigning to you for all time.

41Then Moses set aside three cities on the east
side of the Jordan 42to which a [male] killer could
escape, one who unwittingly slew another without
having been an enemy in the past; he could flee to
one of these cities and live: 43Bezer, in the wilderness in the Tableland, belonging to the Reubenites;
Ramoth, in Gilead, belonging to the Gadites; and
Golan, in Bashan, belonging to the Manassites.

44This is the Teaching that Moses set before the

אַרְצָם נַחֲלָה כַּיּוֹם הַזֶּה׃ 39 וְיָדַעְתָּ הַיּוֹם
וַהֲשֵׁבֹתָ אֶל־לְבָבֶךָ כִּי יְהוָה הוּא הָאֱלֹהִים
בַּשָּׁמַיִם מִמַּעַל וְעַל־הָאָרֶץ מִתָּחַת אֵין
עוֹד׃ 40 וְשָׁמַרְתָּ אֶת־חֻקָּיו וְאֶת־מִצְוֺתָיו
אֲשֶׁר אָנֹכִי מְצַוְּךָ הַיּוֹם אֲשֶׁר יִיטַב לְךָ
וּלְבָנֶיךָ אַחֲרֶיךָ וּלְמַעַן תַּאֲרִיךְ יָמִים עַל־
הָאֲדָמָה אֲשֶׁר יְהוָה אֱלֹהֶיךָ נֹתֵן לְךָ כָּל־
הַיָּמִים׃ פ

41 אָז יַבְדִּיל מֹשֶׁה שָׁלֹשׁ עָרִים בְּעֵבֶר
הַיַּרְדֵּן מִזְרְחָה שָׁמֶשׁ׃ 42 לָנֻס שָׁמָּה רוֹצֵחַ
אֲשֶׁר יִרְצַח אֶת־רֵעֵהוּ בִּבְלִי־דַעַת וְהוּא
לֹא־שֹׂנֵא לוֹ מִתְּמֹל שִׁלְשֹׁם וְנָס אֶל־אַחַת
מִן־הֶעָרִים הָאֵל וָחָי׃ 43 אֶת־בֶּצֶר בַּמִּדְבָּר
בְּאֶרֶץ הַמִּישֹׁר לָראוּבֵנִי וְאֶת־רָאמֹת
בַּגִּלְעָד לַגָּדִי וְאֶת־גּוֹלָן בַּבָּשָׁן לַמְנַשִּׁי׃

44 וְזֹאת הַתּוֹרָה אֲשֶׁר־שָׂם מֹשֶׁה לִפְנֵי

## *Interlude*

### CITIES OF REFUGE (4:41–43)

Moses sets aside three cities of refuge on the eastern side of the Jordan for people who kill inadvertently, in addition to the three cities already set aside elsewhere in the country (see at Numbers 35:1–34). Perhaps this way of dealing with sins committed by accident can be seen as a comfort to the Israelites who feared Moses' description of God's passionate, demanding nature (see at 5:9).

On the gender of the killer, of the victim, and of the blood-avenger, see at Numbers 35:6, 11, and 12, respectively.

## *Review of Horeb (Sinai)*

### WHAT LAWS TO FOLLOW (4:44–5:30)

The Decalogue ("Ten Commandments") first appears in Exodus 20. Here Moses restates these precepts, framing them with a recollection of how the people stood at the mountain in awe and fear and asked him to be their intermediary. This retelling aims to connect the new generation with its past.

### INTRODUCTION AND SETTING THE SCENE (4:44–5:5)

In line with Deuteronomy's emphasis on transmitting tradition, this section addresses the audience as if these events are part of its remembered experience. In so doing, the text makes the past a present experience as well.

*44. This is the Teaching that Moses set before the Israelites.* In many if not most synagogues,

Israelites: <sup>45</sup>these are the decrees, laws, and rules that Moses addressed to the people of Israel, after they had left Egypt, <sup>46</sup>beyond the Jordan, in the valley at Beth-peor, in the land of King Sihon of the Amorites, who dwelt in Heshbon, whom Moses and the Israelites defeated after they had left Egypt. <sup>47</sup>They had taken possession of his country and that of King Og of Bashan—the two kings of the Amorites—which were on the east side of the Jordan <sup>48</sup>from Aroer on the banks of the wadi Arnon, as far as Mount Sion, that is, Hermon; <sup>49</sup>also the whole Arabah on the east side of the Jordan, as far as the Sea of the Arabah, at the foot of the slopes of Pisgah.

5 Moses summoned all the Israelites and said to them: Hear, O Israel, the laws and rules that I proclaim to you this day! Study them and observe them faithfully!

<sup>2</sup>Our God יהוה made a covenant with us at Horeb. <sup>3</sup>It was not with our ancestors that יהוה made this covenant, but with us, the living, every one of us who is here today. <sup>4</sup>Face to face יהוה spoke to you on the mountain out of the fire— <sup>5</sup>I stood between יהוה and you at that time to convey יהוה's words to you, for you were afraid of the fire and did not go up the mountain—saying:

בְּנֵ֣י יִשְׂרָאֵ֑ל: 45 אֵ֚לֶּה הָעֵדֹ֔ת וְהַֽחֻקִּ֖ים וְהַמִּשְׁפָּטִ֑ים אֲשֶׁ֨ר דִּבֶּ֤ר מֹשֶׁה֙ אֶל־בְּנֵ֣י יִשְׂרָאֵ֔ל בְּצֵאתָ֖ם מִמִּצְרָֽיִם: 46 בְּעֵ֨בֶר הַיַּרְדֵּ֜ן בַּגַּ֗יְא מ֚וּל בֵּ֣ית פְּע֔וֹר בְּאֶ֗רֶץ סִיחֹן֙ מֶ֣לֶךְ הָֽאֱמֹרִ֔י אֲשֶׁ֥ר יוֹשֵׁ֖ב בְּחֶשְׁבּ֑וֹן אֲשֶׁ֨ר הִכָּ֤ה מֹשֶׁה֙ וּבְנֵ֣י יִשְׂרָאֵ֔ל בְּצֵאתָ֖ם מִמִּצְרָֽיִם: 47 וַיִּֽירְשׁ֣וּ אֶת־אַרְצ֗וֹ וְאֶת־אֶ֤רֶץ ׀ ע֚וֹג מֶֽלֶךְ־הַבָּשָׁ֔ן שְׁנֵי֙ מַלְכֵ֣י הָֽאֱמֹרִ֔י אֲשֶׁ֖ר בְּעֵ֣בֶר הַיַּרְדֵּ֑ן מִזְרַ֖ח שָֽׁמֶשׁ: 48 מֵֽעֲרֹעֵ֡ר אֲשֶׁ֨ר עַל־שְׂפַת־נַ֤חַל אַרְנֹן֙ וְעַד־הַ֣ר שִׂיאֹ֔ן ה֖וּא חֶרְמֽוֹן: 49 וְכָל־הָ֨עֲרָבָ֜ה עֵ֤בֶר הַיַּרְדֵּן֙ מִזְרָ֔חָה וְעַ֖ד יָ֣ם הָֽעֲרָבָ֑ה תַּ֖חַת אַשְׁדֹּ֥ת הַפִּסְגָּֽה: פ

ה וַיִּקְרָ֣א מֹשֶׁה֮ אֶל־כָּל־יִשְׂרָאֵל֒ וַיֹּ֣אמֶר אֲלֵהֶ֗ם שְׁמַ֤ע יִשְׂרָאֵל֙ אֶת־הַֽחֻקִּ֣ים וְאֶת־הַמִּשְׁפָּטִ֔ים אֲשֶׁ֧ר אָֽנֹכִ֛י דֹּבֵ֥ר בְּאָזְנֵיכֶ֖ם הַיּ֑וֹם וּלְמַדְתֶּ֣ם אֹתָ֔ם וּשְׁמַרְתֶּ֖ם לַֽעֲשֹׂתָֽם: 2 יְהֹוָ֣ה אֱלֹהֵ֗ינוּ כָּרַ֥ת עִמָּ֛נוּ בְּרִ֖ית בְּחֹרֵֽב: 3 לֹ֣א אֶת־אֲבֹתֵ֔ינוּ כָּרַ֥ת יְהֹוָ֖ה אֶת־הַבְּרִ֣ית הַזֹּ֑את כִּ֣י אִתָּ֗נוּ אֲנַ֨חְנוּ אֵ֥לֶּה פֹ֛ה הַיּ֖וֹם כֻּלָּ֥נוּ חַיִּֽים: 4 פָּנִ֣ים ׀ בְּפָנִ֗ים דִּבֶּ֨ר יְהֹוָ֧ה עִמָּכֶ֛ם בָּהָ֖ר מִתּ֥וֹךְ הָאֵֽשׁ: 5 אָֽנֹכִ֞י עֹמֵ֨ד בֵּֽין־יְהֹוָ֤ה וּבֵֽינֵיכֶם֙ בָּעֵ֣ת הַהִ֔וא לְהַגִּ֥יד לָכֶ֖ם אֶת־דְּבַ֣ר יְהֹוָ֑ה כִּ֤י יְרֵאתֶם֙ מִפְּנֵ֣י הָאֵ֔שׁ וְלֹֽא־עֲלִיתֶ֥ם בָּהָ֖ר לֵאמֹֽר: ס

this verse (*v'zot hatorah*...) is recited liturgically when the Torah is lifted for reading in public.

*45–49.* This passage tracks the Israelites from the exodus from Egypt through wilderness wanderings and military victories (see also 1:1–5).

*5:1–5.* As Moses expresses the importance of studying and observing the terms of God's teaching (see also 4:1), he emphasizes the inclusiveness of all Israelites in the covenant.

*4. Face to face.* Even though Moses is the only one who speaks with God "face to face" (Exodus 33:11; compare "mouth to mouth" in Numbers 12:8), he now claims that at Horeb all the people were privy to this same intimate relationship with God. This "revision" presents Moses as one who avoids claiming a privileged relationship with God and instead transfers it to the people as a whole.

[6]I יהוה am your God who brought you out of the land of Egypt, the house of bondage: [7]You shall have no other gods beside Me.

[8]You shall not make for yourself a sculptured image, any likeness of what is in the heavens above, or on the earth below, or in the waters below the earth. [9]You shall not bow down to them or serve them. For I your God יהוה am an impassioned God, visiting the guilt of the parents upon the children, upon the third and upon the fourth generations of those who reject Me, [10]but showing kindness to the thousandth generation of those who love Me and keep My commandments.

[11]You shall not swear falsely by the name of your God יהוה; for יהוה will not clear one who swears falsely by God's name.

[12]Observe the sabbath day and keep it holy, as your God יהוה has commanded you. [13]Six days you

6* אָנֹכִי יְהוָה אֱלֹהֶיךָ אֲשֶׁר הוֹצֵאתִיךָ
מֵאֶרֶץ מִצְרַיִם מִבֵּית עֲבָדִים 7 לֹא־יִהְיֶה
לְךָ אֱלֹהִים אֲחֵרִים עַל־פָּנָי:
8 לֹא־תַעֲשֶׂה לְךָ פֶסֶל כָּל־תְּמוּנָה אֲשֶׁר
בַּשָּׁמַיִם מִמַּעַל וַאֲשֶׁר בָּאָרֶץ מִתָּחַת וַאֲשֶׁר
בַּמַּיִם מִתַּחַת לָאָרֶץ: 9 לֹא־תִשְׁתַּחֲוֶה לָהֶם
וְלֹא תָעָבְדֵם כִּי אָנֹכִי יְהוָה אֱלֹהֶיךָ אֵל
קַנָּא פֹּקֵד עֲוֺן אָבוֹת עַל־בָּנִים וְעַל־שִׁלֵּשִׁים
וְעַל־רִבֵּעִים לְשֹׂנְאָי: 10 וְעֹשֶׂה חֶסֶד לַאֲלָפִים
לְאֹהֲבַי וּלְשֹׁמְרֵי מצותו מִצְוֺתָי: ס
11 לֹא תִשָּׂא אֶת־שֵׁם־יְהוָה אֱלֹהֶיךָ לַשָּׁוְא
כִּי לֹא יְנַקֶּה יְהוָה אֵת אֲשֶׁר־יִשָּׂא אֶת־שְׁמוֹ
לַשָּׁוְא: ס
12 שָׁמוֹר אֶת־יוֹם הַשַּׁבָּת לְקַדְּשׁוֹ כַּאֲשֶׁר
צִוְּךָ יְהוָה אֱלֹהֶיךָ: 13 שֵׁשֶׁת יָמִים תַּעֲבֹד

*This accent pattern for the Decalogue is the one that is customarily used for private study. (Masoretic tradition also includes an accent pattern that is used for public reading.) Verses are numbered according to a modern convention.

## THE DECALOGUE ("TEN COMMANDMENTS") (5:6–18)

The Decalogue emphasizes the family unit, including men, women, and children. Three separate commandments in vv. 16–18 deal solely with issues protecting the family. The commandments refer to women repeatedly, making it clear that these laws are considered an obligation for all Israel. For more on the (non)gendered language in the Decalogue and details concerning the structure of these commandments and their ancient Near East context, see at Exodus 20:2–14.

*6. who brought you out.* This verse, which is a statement and not a command per se, establishes the reason why the Israelites should observe God's laws. While some consider the historical prologue in this verse to be the first "commandment," others interpret both vv. 6–7 as the first precept (see also at Exodus 20:2); in Torah scrolls, vv. 6–10 are grouped together as one "command."

*7. You shall have no other gods.* Verses 7–10 establish the preeminent place of God in the world. (See also at Exodus 20:3–5.)

*9. impassioned.* Jeffrey Tigay explains that in the Bible the root *k-n-a*, meaning "to become dark red," is often associated with fire (as in 4:24) and is used to describe "fiery passions" like love, anger, and jealousy. He writes: "The term reflects the emotional tie between God and Israel that was described metaphorically by the prophets as a marital bond in which [God] is like the husband and Israel a wife" (*Deuteronomy*, 1996, p. 65). This metaphor captures the expected exclusive nature of the relationship between God and Israel, as well as the jealousy and anger sparked when Israel unfaithfully turns to other gods (see also at 31:16).

*11. You shall not swear falsely.* See at Exodus 20:7.

*12–15.* This commandment is explained differently here than in Exodus 20:8–11. Exodus exhorts the Israelites to "remember" the Sabbath,

shall labor and do all your work, [14]but the seventh day is a sabbath of your God יהוה; you shall not do any work—you, your son or your daughter, your male or female slave, your ox or your ass, or any of your cattle, or the stranger in your settlements, so that your male and female slave may rest as you do. [15]Remember that you were a slave in the land of Egypt and your God יהוה freed you from there with a mighty hand and an outstretched arm; therefore your God יהוה has commanded you to observe the sabbath day.

[16]Honor your father and your mother, as your God יהוה has commanded you, that you may long endure, and that you may fare well, in the land that your God יהוה is assigning to you.

[17]You shall not murder. You shall not commit adultery. You shall not steal. You shall not bear false witness against your neighbor.

וְעָשִׂ֖יתָ כָּל־מְלַאכְתֶּֽךָ׃ 14 וְי֙וֹם֙ הַשְּׁבִיעִ֔י שַׁבָּ֣ת ׀ לַיהֹוָ֣ה אֱלֹהֶ֗יךָ לֹ֣א תַעֲשֶׂ֣ה כָל־מְלָאכָ֡ה אַתָּ֣ה וּבִנְךָֽ־וּבִתֶּ֣ךָ וְעַבְדְּךָֽ־וַ֠אֲמָתֶ֠ךָ וְשׁוֹרְךָ֨ וַחֲמֹֽרְךָ֜ וְכָל־בְּהֶמְתֶּ֗ךָ וְגֵֽרְךָ֙ אֲשֶׁ֣ר בִּשְׁעָרֶ֔יךָ לְמַ֗עַן יָנ֛וּחַ עַבְדְּךָ֥ וַאֲמָתְךָ֖ כָּמֽוֹךָ׃ 15 וְזָ֣כַרְתָּ֗ כִּ֣י עֶ֤בֶד הָיִ֙יתָ֙ בְּאֶ֣רֶץ מִצְרַ֔יִם וַיֹּצִ֨אֲךָ֜ יְהֹוָ֤ה אֱלֹהֶ֙יךָ֙ מִשָּׁ֔ם בְּיָ֥ד חֲזָקָ֖ה וּבִזְרֹ֣עַ נְטוּיָ֑ה עַל־כֵּ֗ן צִוְּךָ֙ יְהֹוָ֣ה אֱלֹהֶ֔יךָ לַעֲשׂ֖וֹת אֶת־י֥וֹם הַשַּׁבָּֽת׃ ס 16 כַּבֵּ֤ד אֶת־אָבִ֙יךָ֙ וְאֶת־אִמֶּ֔ךָ כַּאֲשֶׁ֥ר צִוְּךָ֖ יְהֹוָ֣ה אֱלֹהֶ֑יךָ לְמַ֣עַן ׀ יַאֲרִיכֻ֣ן יָמֶ֗יךָ וּלְמַ֙עַן֙ יִ֣יטַב לָ֔ךְ עַ֚ל הָֽאֲדָמָ֔ה אֲשֶׁר־יְהֹוָ֥ה אֱלֹהֶ֖יךָ נֹתֵ֥ן לָֽךְ׃ ס 17 לֹ֥֖א תִּרְצָֽ֖ח ס וְלֹ֣֖א תִּנְאָֽ֑ף ס וְלֹ֣֖א תִּגְנֹֽ֔ב ס וְלֹֽא־תַעֲנֶ֥ה בְרֵעֲךָ֖ עֵ֥ד שָֽׁוְא׃ ס

* * *

while Deuteronomy commands the Israelites to "observe" the Sabbath. Exodus focuses on God's resting on the seventh day of creation as the reason for the observance, whereas Deuteronomy connects it to God's saving of the Israelites from Egypt. Exodus explains how the Sabbath came to be: it portrays God and Moses as proclaiming to newly liberated Israelites that they, like God, must rest on the Sabbath. Deuteronomy, addressed ostensibly to a generation of wilderness-born Israelites who have not experienced slavery, commands them to observe the Sabbath for the sake of their own slaves, lest they forget the historical experiences of their ancestors. [These differences have ramifications for how one understands the Torah as a continuous tradition. The revision reflected in Deuteronomy underscores the fluidity of even the Decalogue, as precepts are revised or reapplied for the circumstances of a new generation. (See further *D'varim*, Another View, p. 1056.) —*Ed.*]

16. *Honor your father and your mother.* The commandment to honor one's parents comes at the center of the Decalogue, and it is one of the few that promises a reward (see also v. 10). This com-

mandment reflects the need to preserve the family structure across generations in order to have a viable community; it helps to maintain parental authority and to ensure for the care of elderly parents. (See also at Exodus 20:12.)

*mother.* This is one of several biblical texts that emphasize the mother's importance (see also at Leviticus 19:3 and at Numbers 11:12). For instance, Genesis emphasizes a mother's role in the family structure (see Rebekah in Genesis 27–28); Proverbs 1:8 and 6:20 exhort children to be faithful to their mother's teachings.

*17. You shall not commit adultery.* In the Bible, adultery is defined as sex between a man and a married woman who is not his wife (see also at 22:22 and Exodus 20:13). Thus two commandments preserving the family unit frame the commandment against murder.

*You shall not bear false witness.* While this verse has been applied to lying in general, it refers here only to the act of lying as a witness in a legal situation. This prohibition does not apply to many cases in which biblical characters, including women,

[18]You [men] shall not covet your neighbor's wife. Likewise, none of you shall crave your neighbor's house, or field, or male or female slave, or ox, or ass, or anything that is your neighbor's.

[19]יהוה spoke those words—those and no more—to your whole congregation at the mountain, with a mighty voice out of the fire and the dense clouds. [God] inscribed them on two tablets of stone and gave them to me. [20]When you heard the voice out of the darkness, while the mountain was ablaze with fire, you came up to me, all your tribal heads and elders, [21]and said, "Our God יהוה has just shown us a majestic Presence, and we have heard God's voice out of the fire; we have seen this day that humankind may live though addressed by God. [22]Let us not die, then, for this fearsome fire will consume us; if we hear the voice of our God יהוה any longer, we shall die. [23]For what mortal ever heard the voice of the living God speak out of the fire, as we did, and lived? [24]You go closer and hear all that our God יהוה says, and then you tell us

18 וְלֹא תַחְמֹד אֵשֶׁת רֵעֶךָ ס וְלֹא
תִתְאַוֶּה בֵּית רֵעֶךָ שָׂדֵהוּ וְעַבְדּוֹ וַאֲמָתוֹ
שׁוֹרוֹ וַחֲמֹרוֹ וְכֹל אֲשֶׁר לְרֵעֶךָ׃ ס
19 אֶת־הַדְּבָרִים הָאֵלֶּה דִּבֶּר יְהוָה אֶל־כָּל־
קְהַלְכֶם בָּהָר מִתּוֹךְ הָאֵשׁ הֶעָנָן וְהָעֲרָפֶל
קוֹל גָּדוֹל וְלֹא יָסָף וַיִּכְתְּבֵם עַל־שְׁנֵי לֻחֹת
אֲבָנִים וַיִּתְּנֵם אֵלָי׃ 20 וַיְהִי כְּשָׁמְעֲכֶם אֶת־
הַקּוֹל מִתּוֹךְ הַחֹשֶׁךְ וְהָהָר בֹּעֵר בָּאֵשׁ
וַתִּקְרְבוּן אֵלַי כָּל־רָאשֵׁי שִׁבְטֵיכֶם וְזִקְנֵיכֶם׃
21 וַתֹּאמְרוּ הֵן הֶרְאָנוּ יְהוָה אֱלֹהֵינוּ אֶת־
כְּבֹדוֹ וְאֶת־גָּדְלוֹ וְאֶת־קֹלוֹ שָׁמַעְנוּ מִתּוֹךְ
הָאֵשׁ הַיּוֹם הַזֶּה רָאִינוּ כִּי־יְדַבֵּר אֱלֹהִים
אֶת־הָאָדָם וָחָי׃ 22 וְעַתָּה לָמָּה נָמוּת כִּי
תֹאכְלֵנוּ הָאֵשׁ הַגְּדֹלָה הַזֹּאת אִם־יֹסְפִים ׀
אֲנַחְנוּ לִשְׁמֹעַ אֶת־קוֹל יְהוָה אֱלֹהֵינוּ עוֹד
וָמָתְנוּ׃ 23 כִּי מִי כָל־בָּשָׂר אֲשֶׁר שָׁמַע קוֹל
אֱלֹהִים חַיִּים מְדַבֵּר מִתּוֹךְ־הָאֵשׁ כָּמֹנוּ
וַיֶּחִי׃ 24 קְרַב אַתָּה וּשְׁמָע אֵת כָּל־אֲשֶׁר
יֹאמַר יְהוָה אֱלֹהֵינוּ וְאַתְּ ׀ תְּדַבֵּר אֵלֵינוּ

use deception to subvert those in power and to achieve what, from the biblical perspective, can be considered legitimate ends (as does Rebekah in Genesis 27; see also Abraham at Genesis 12:10–20).

*18. You [men] shall not covet your neighbor's wife.* The Decalogue ends with another directive to protect the family. The term "covet" implies a more inward emotion. While many have questioned how an emotion can be legislated, others point out that some thoughts can be harmful; thus it is in a person's best interest to attempt to control ideas in their seedling states. This is one of the places where a commandment implicitly applies only to men; the reverse, a woman coveting her neighbor's husband, may also be implicit but unacknowledged. (For a different interpretation, see at Exodus 20:14 and *Mishpatim*, Another View, p. 445.)

***house.*** In Exodus 20:14, the order of the words in this commandment is different; there, the mention of a neighbor's house precedes the mention of his wife. Each version of the Decalogue thus evokes a different meaning of Heb. *bayit* ("household, house"). In effect, Exodus counts a wife as an element of the household, while Deuteronomy treats her apart from the household's assets.

## THE PEOPLE'S FEARFUL RESPONSE AND CALL FOR MOSES' INTERCESSION (5:19–24)

Moses reminds the people that it was their fear of encountering God directly that placed him in the role of intermediary. In this case, experiencing God did not lead the Israelites to desire a closer, more direct relationship with the Divine. This section may aim to remind the people, in anticipation of Moses' death, that his role was temporary.

everything that our God יהוה tells you, and we will willingly do it."

25יהוה heard the plea that you made to me, and יהוה said to me, "I have heard the plea that this people made to you; they did well to speak thus. 26May they always be of such mind, to revere Me and follow all My commandments, that it may go well with them and with their children forever! 27Go, say to them, 'Return to your tents.' 28But you remain here with Me, and I will give you the whole Instruction—the laws and the rules—that you shall impart to them, for them to observe in the land that I am giving them to possess."

29Be careful, then, to do as your God יהוה has commanded you. Do not turn aside to the right or to the left: 30follow only the path that your God יהוה has enjoined upon you, so that you may thrive and that it may go well with you, and that you may long endure in the land you are to possess.

אֵת כָּל־אֲשֶׁר יְדַבֵּר יְהֹוָה אֱלֹהֵינוּ אֵלֶיךָ
וְשָׁמַעְנוּ וְעָשִׂינוּ׃
25 וַיִּשְׁמַע יְהֹוָה אֶת־קוֹל דִּבְרֵיכֶם בְּדַבֶּרְכֶם
אֵלָי וַיֹּאמֶר יְהֹוָה אֵלַי שָׁמַעְתִּי אֶת־קוֹל
דִּבְרֵי הָעָם הַזֶּה אֲשֶׁר דִּבְּרוּ אֵלֶיךָ הֵיטִיבוּ
כָּל־אֲשֶׁר דִּבֵּרוּ׃ 26 מִי־יִתֵּן וְהָיָה לְבָבָם זֶה
לָהֶם לְיִרְאָה אֹתִי וְלִשְׁמֹר אֶת־כָּל־מִצְוֺתַי
כָּל־הַיָּמִים לְמַעַן יִיטַב לָהֶם וְלִבְנֵיהֶם
לְעֹלָם׃ 27 לֵךְ אֱמֹר לָהֶם שׁוּבוּ לָכֶם
לְאָהֳלֵיכֶם׃ 28 וְאַתָּה פֹּה עֲמֹד עִמָּדִי
וַאֲדַבְּרָה אֵלֶיךָ אֵת כָּל־הַמִּצְוָה וְהַחֻקִּים
וְהַמִּשְׁפָּטִים אֲשֶׁר תְּלַמְּדֵם וְעָשׂוּ בָאָרֶץ
אֲשֶׁר אָנֹכִי נֹתֵן לָהֶם לְרִשְׁתָּהּ׃
29 וּשְׁמַרְתֶּם לַעֲשׂוֹת כַּאֲשֶׁר צִוָּה יְהֹוָה
אֱלֹהֵיכֶם אֶתְכֶם לֹא תָסֻרוּ יָמִין וּשְׂמֹאל׃
30 בְּכָל־הַדֶּרֶךְ אֲשֶׁר צִוָּה יְהֹוָה אֱלֹהֵיכֶם
אֶתְכֶם תֵּלֵכוּ לְמַעַן תִּחְיוּן וְטוֹב לָכֶם
וְהַאֲרַכְתֶּם יָמִים בָּאָרֶץ אֲשֶׁר תִּירָשׁוּן׃

*6* And this is the Instruction—the laws and the rules—that your God יהוה has commanded [me] to impart to you, to be observed in the land that you are about to cross into and occupy, 2so that you, your children, and your children's children may revere your God יהוה and follow, as long as you live, all the divine laws and commandments that I enjoin upon you, to the end that you may

ו וְזֹאת הַמִּצְוָה הַחֻקִּים וְהַמִּשְׁפָּטִים אֲשֶׁר
צִוָּה יְהֹוָה אֱלֹהֵיכֶם לְלַמֵּד אֶתְכֶם לַעֲשׂוֹת
בָּאָרֶץ אֲשֶׁר אַתֶּם עֹבְרִים שָׁמָּה לְרִשְׁתָּהּ׃
2 לְמַעַן תִּירָא אֶת־יְהֹוָה אֱלֹהֶיךָ לִשְׁמֹר
אֶת־כָּל־חֻקֹּתָיו וּמִצְוֺתָיו אֲשֶׁר אָנֹכִי מְצַוֶּךָ
אַתָּה וּבִנְךָ וּבֶן־בִּנְךָ כֹּל יְמֵי חַיֶּיךָ וּלְמַעַן

### GOD'S RESPONSE TO THE PEOPLE'S REQUEST (5:25–30)

Moses adds that God was pleased with the Israelites' response to the revelation, appreciating the people's awe and need for an intermediary. Moses promises that if the people and their offspring revere God and obey the commandments, they will flourish in the land, a repeated message in Deuteronomy (see, for example, 7:12–15).

## *Additional Teachings*

### HOW TO FOLLOW THE LAWS (6:1–7:5)

As Moses' speech turns more to the future, he explains how one must carry out God's laws. Transmission of the teachings across generations remains a high priority; therefore the emphasis falls on remembering, teaching, and learning, with the love of God as an underlying attitude.

long endure. 3Obey, O Israel, willingly and faithfully, that it may go well with you and that you may
increase greatly [in] a land flowing with milk and
honey, as יהוה, the God of your ancestors, spoke
to you.
4Hear, O Israel! יהוה is our God, יהוה alone.
5You shall love your God יהוה with all your heart,
with all your soul, and with all your might. 6Take to
heart these instructions with which I charge you
this day. 7Impress them upon your children. Recite
them when you stay at home and when you are
away, when you lie down and when you get up.

יַאֲרִכֻן יָמֶיךָ׃ 3 וְשָׁמַעְתָּ יִשְׂרָאֵל וְשָׁמַרְתָּ
לַעֲשׂוֹת אֲשֶׁר יִיטַב לְךָ וַאֲשֶׁר תִּרְבּוּן מְאֹד
כַּאֲשֶׁר דִּבֶּר יְהוָה אֱלֹהֵי אֲבֹתֶיךָ לָךְ אֶרֶץ
זָבַת חָלָב וּדְבָשׁ׃ פ
4 שְׁמַע יִשְׂרָאֵל יְהוָה אֱלֹהֵינוּ יְהוָה | אֶחָד׃
5 וְאָהַבְתָּ אֵת יְהוָה אֱלֹהֶיךָ בְּכָל־לְבָבְךָ
וּבְכָל־נַפְשְׁךָ וּבְכָל־מְאֹדֶךָ׃ 6 וְהָיוּ הַדְּבָרִים
הָאֵלֶּה אֲשֶׁר אָנֹכִי מְצַוְּךָ הַיּוֹם עַל־לְבָבֶךָ׃
7 וְשִׁנַּנְתָּם לְבָנֶיךָ וְדִבַּרְתָּ בָּם בְּשִׁבְתְּךָ
בְּבֵיתֶךָ וּבְלֶכְתְּךָ בַדֶּרֶךְ וּבְשָׁכְבְּךָ וּבְקוּמֶךָ׃

## THE CALL TO LOVE THE ONE AND ONLY GOD (6:1–9)

This section includes two central passages in Jewish liturgy: the *Sh'ma* (6:4) and *V'ahavta* (6:4–9). The *Sh'ma* ("Hear") reminds the Israelites of God's essence and their relationship with the One God. The *V'ahavta* ("You shall love") describes how the people are to internalize the teachings and impart them to future generations.

The *Sh'ma* and *V'ahavta* hold special meaning when understood as directives to the Israelites about to cross the Jordan into Israel. At a time so central to the formation of the people, they are told about love and the importance of preserving family, educating one's children, and maintaining one's relationship to the Divine. These ideas have helped to sustain the people Israel throughout many years of waiting to "cross the Jordan."

*3. **Obey, O Israel, willingly.*** This charge refers to both listening and obeying, with alliteration linking the two words (*v'shamata* and *v'shamarta*).

*4.* Given the centrality of the *Sh'ma* as the "watchword of the Jewish faith," its meaning is surprisingly uncertain. Because of its grammatical construction and the various nuances of the word *echad* (translated here as "alone"), this declaration can be construed in different ways. Some translations have rendered it as: "The LORD our God, the LORD is one" (see the 1917 Jewish Publication Society translation, which is similar to the 1611 King James Version). Such a translation implies that the *Sh'ma* is a statement about God's essence, a reflection of the monotheistic belief in the existence of only one God.

Other translations resemble the one incorporated in this book. This version makes a claim about God's unique relationship to Israel, without necessarily denying the existence of other divine beings. Bernard Levinson points out: "The verse makes not a quantitative argument (about the number of deities) but a qualitative one about the nature of the relationship between God and Israel" ("Deuteronomy," *Jewish Study Bible*, 2004, p. 380). This understanding reflects what many scholars have concluded is a pre-monotheistic Israelite belief called monolatry: the allegiance to one god, while recognizing the existence of other deities. (See also at 4:19–20; 4:35; 32:8; Exodus 15:11; and Another View, p. 1082.)

*5. **You shall love יהוה.*** This language is rooted in ancient Near Eastern political treaties, where "love" implies a sense of loyalty to a greater power. The verb conveys not just an emotion, but a statement with implications for one's actions. God demands intellectual, emotional, and physical commitment. (See also at 7:13.)

*8–9.* This passage provides the basis for the laws of *t'fillin* (phylacteries) and of mezuzah. The idea is that at any time or place, engaged in any

8Bind them as a sign on your hand and let them serve as a symbol on your forehead; 9inscribe them on the doorposts of your house and on your gates.

10When your God יהוה brings you into the land that was sworn to your fathers Abraham, Isaac, and Jacob, to be assigned to you—great and flourishing cities that you did not build, 11houses full of all good things that you did not fill, hewn cisterns that you did not hew, vineyards and olive groves that you did not plant—and you eat your fill, 12take heed that you do not forget יהוה who freed you from the land of Egypt, the house of bondage. 13Revere only your God יהוה and worship [God] alone, and swear only by God's name. 14Do not follow other gods, any gods of the peoples about

8 וּקְשַׁרְתָּם לְאוֹת עַל־יָדֶךָ וְהָיוּ לְטֹטָפֹת
בֵּין עֵינֶיךָ׃ 9 וּכְתַבְתָּם עַל־מְזֻזוֹת בֵּיתֶךָ
וּבִשְׁעָרֶיךָ׃ ס
10 וְהָיָה כִּי יְבִיאֲךָ ׀ יְהוָה אֱלֹהֶיךָ אֶל־הָאָרֶץ
אֲשֶׁר נִשְׁבַּע לַאֲבֹתֶיךָ לְאַבְרָהָם לְיִצְחָק
וּלְיַעֲקֹב לָתֶת לָךְ עָרִים גְּדֹלֹת וְטֹבֹת אֲשֶׁר
לֹא־בָנִיתָ׃ 11 וּבָתִּים מְלֵאִים כָּל־טוּב אֲשֶׁר
לֹא־מִלֵּאתָ וּבֹרֹת חֲצוּבִים אֲשֶׁר לֹא־חָצַבְתָּ
כְּרָמִים וְזֵיתִים אֲשֶׁר לֹא־נָטָעְתָּ וְאָכַלְתָּ
וְשָׂבָעְתָּ׃ 12 הִשָּׁמֶר לְךָ פֶּן־תִּשְׁכַּח אֶת־
יְהוָה אֲשֶׁר הוֹצִיאֲךָ מֵאֶרֶץ מִצְרַיִם מִבֵּית
עֲבָדִים׃ 13 אֶת־יְהוָה אֱלֹהֶיךָ תִּירָא וְאֹתוֹ
תַעֲבֹד וּבִשְׁמוֹ תִּשָּׁבֵעַ׃ 14 לֹא תֵלְכוּן אַחֲרֵי
אֱלֹהִים אֲחֵרִים מֵאֱלֹהֵי הָעַמִּים אֲשֶׁר

activity, one should remain ever mindful of these teachings.

*8. sign.* While this language was probably originally understood figuratively, the practice developed of Jews' interpreting this verse literally as referring to the physical strapping of specified texts in small boxes called *t'fillin* onto the arm and head (see at Exodus 13:9).

*symbol.* See at Exodus 13:16.

*9. inscribe them on the doorposts.* In the ancient Near East, sacred words were literally written on doorposts and on plaques placed near entranceways; this practice had an apotropaic function, meaning that it was believed to help ward off evil. This evolved into the Jewish practice of writing selections from the Torah on a piece of parchment and affixing it to the doorpost, usually encased in a slender box (called a mezuzah).

### THE CALL TO ABSOLUTE LOYALTY TO ISRAEL'S GOD (6:10–19)

Moses now discloses the ramifications for how Israel must live in the land. He reminds the Israelites of what God has done in taking them out of Egypt and what this means in terms of God's relationship to them. Again, he emphasizes the need to transmit the teachings to future generations.

*10–15.* Remembering what God has done in the past is a starting point and guide to the future. Memory plays a crucial role in Deuteronomy as a whole and in this parashah in particular. It serves as a basis for gratitude to God and a precondition for keeping the commandments appropriately; it also functions to create and maintain community identity.

*10. sworn to your fathers.* Moses makes connections to the covenant with the patriarchs as a reminder that the relationship between God and Israel did not start at Horeb (Sinai). (On the translation "fathers," see at 4:31.)

*12–13. bondage . . . worship.* Heb. *avadim* . . . *taavod.* The repetition of the root *e-v-d* creates a word play that emphasizes the connection between Israel's obligations to serve ("worship") God and one of the reasons that they have this obligation.

you—[15]for your God יהוה in your midst is an impassioned God—lest the anger of your God יהוה blaze forth against you, wiping you off the face of the earth.

[16]Do not try your God יהוה, as you did at Massah. [17]Be sure to keep the commandments, decrees, and laws that your God יהוה has enjoined upon you. [18]Do what is right and good in the sight of יהוה, that it may go well with you and that you may be able to possess the good land that your God יהוה promised on oath to your fathers, [19]and that all your enemies may be driven out before you, as יהוה has spoken.

[20]When, in time to come, your children ask you, "What mean the decrees, laws, and rules that our God יהוה has enjoined upon you?" [21]you shall say to your children, "We were slaves to Pharaoh in Egypt and יהוה freed us from Egypt with a mighty hand. [22]יהוה wrought before our eyes marvelous and destructive signs and portents in Egypt, against Pharaoh and all his household; [23]and us [God] freed from there, in order to take us and give us the land promised on oath to our fathers. [24]Then יהוה commanded us to observe all these laws, to revere our God יהוה, for our lasting good and for our survival, as is now the case. [25]It will be therefore to our merit before our God יהוה to observe faithfully this whole Instruction, as [God] has commanded us."

סְבִיבוֹתֵיכֶם: 15 כִּי אֵל קַנָּא יְהֹוָה אֱלֹהֶיךָ בְּקִרְבֶּךָ פֶּן־יֶחֱרֶה אַף־יְהֹוָה אֱלֹהֶיךָ בָּךְ וְהִשְׁמִידְךָ מֵעַל פְּנֵי הָאֲדָמָה: ס 16 לֹא תְנַסּוּ אֶת־יְהֹוָה אֱלֹהֵיכֶם כַּאֲשֶׁר נִסִּיתֶם בַּמַּסָּה: 17 שָׁמוֹר תִּשְׁמְרוּן אֶת־מִצְוֹת יְהֹוָה אֱלֹהֵיכֶם וְעֵדֹתָיו וְחֻקָּיו אֲשֶׁר צִוָּךְ: 18 וְעָשִׂיתָ הַיָּשָׁר וְהַטּוֹב בְּעֵינֵי יְהֹוָה לְמַעַן יִיטַב לָךְ וּבָאתָ וְיָרַשְׁתָּ אֶת־הָאָרֶץ הַטֹּבָה אֲשֶׁר־נִשְׁבַּע יְהֹוָה לַאֲבֹתֶיךָ: 19 לַהֲדֹף אֶת־כָּל־אֹיְבֶיךָ מִפָּנֶיךָ כַּאֲשֶׁר דִּבֶּר יְהֹוָה: ס

20 כִּי־יִשְׁאָלְךָ בִנְךָ מָחָר לֵאמֹר מָה הָעֵדֹת וְהַחֻקִּים וְהַמִּשְׁפָּטִים אֲשֶׁר צִוָּה יְהֹוָה אֱלֹהֵינוּ אֶתְכֶם: 21 וְאָמַרְתָּ לְבִנְךָ עֲבָדִים הָיִינוּ לְפַרְעֹה בְּמִצְרָיִם וַיֹּצִיאֵנוּ יְהֹוָה מִמִּצְרַיִם בְּיָד חֲזָקָה: 22 וַיִּתֵּן יְהֹוָה אוֹתֹת וּמֹפְתִים גְּדֹלִים וְרָעִים | בְּמִצְרַיִם בְּפַרְעֹה וּבְכָל־בֵּיתוֹ לְעֵינֵינוּ: 23 וְאוֹתָנוּ הוֹצִיא מִשָּׁם לְמַעַן הָבִיא אֹתָנוּ לָתֶת לָנוּ אֶת־הָאָרֶץ אֲשֶׁר נִשְׁבַּע לַאֲבֹתֵינוּ: 24 וַיְצַוֵּנוּ יְהֹוָה לַעֲשׂוֹת אֶת־כָּל־הַחֻקִּים הָאֵלֶּה לְיִרְאָה אֶת־יְהֹוָה אֱלֹהֵינוּ לְטוֹב לָנוּ כָּל־הַיָּמִים לְחַיֹּתֵנוּ כְּהַיּוֹם הַזֶּה: 25 וּצְדָקָה תִּהְיֶה־לָּנוּ כִּי־נִשְׁמֹר לַעֲשׂוֹת אֶת־כָּל־הַמִּצְוָה הַזֹּאת לִפְנֵי יְהֹוָה אֱלֹהֵינוּ כַּאֲשֶׁר צִוָּנוּ: ס

---

15. *impassioned.* See at 5:9.

16. *Massah.* See Exodus 17:1–7.

### THE DEMAND TO TEACH FUTURE GENERATIONS ABOUT THE LAWS (6:20–25)

Moses emphasizes that education is central to Is-

rael's survival. Proverbs 1:8 and 6:20 recognize the role of women in teaching future generations, exhorting the child to focus on the father's instruction and the mother's teaching (*torah*).

20. *"What mean the decrees?"* This verse has been incorporated into the Four Children of the Passover Haggadah as the question of the wise child.

7 When your God יהוה brings you to the
land that you are about to enter and possess,
and [God] dislodges many nations before you—
the Hittites, Girgashites, Amorites, Canaanites,
Perizzites, Hivites, and Jebusites, seven nations
much larger than you—2and your God יהוה delivers them to you and you defeat them, you must
doom them to destruction: grant them no terms
and give them no quarter. 3You shall not intermarry
with them: do not give your daughters to their sons
or take their daughters for your sons. 4For they will
turn your children away from Me to worship other
gods, and יהוה's anger will blaze forth against you,
promptly wiping you out. 5Instead, this is what you
shall do to them: you shall tear down their altars,
smash their pillars, cut down their sacred posts, and
consign their images to the fire.

ז כִּי יְבִיאֲךָ יְהוָה אֱלֹהֶיךָ אֶל־הָאָרֶץ
אֲשֶׁר־אַתָּה בָא־שָׁמָּה לְרִשְׁתָּהּ וְנָשַׁל גּוֹיִם־
רַבִּים | מִפָּנֶיךָ הַחִתִּי וְהַגִּרְגָּשִׁי וְהָאֱמֹרִי
וְהַכְּנַעֲנִי וְהַפְּרִזִּי וְהַחִוִּי וְהַיְבוּסִי שִׁבְעָה
גוֹיִם רַבִּים וַעֲצוּמִים מִמֶּךָּ׃ 2 וּנְתָנָם יְהוָה
אֱלֹהֶיךָ לְפָנֶיךָ וְהִכִּיתָם הַחֲרֵם תַּחֲרִים
אֹתָם לֹא־תִכְרֹת לָהֶם בְּרִית וְלֹא תְחָנֵּם׃
3 וְלֹא תִתְחַתֵּן בָּם בִּתְּךָ לֹא־תִתֵּן לִבְנוֹ
וּבִתּוֹ לֹא־תִקַּח לִבְנֶךָ׃ 4 כִּי־יָסִיר אֶת־בִּנְךָ
מֵאַחֲרַי וְעָבְדוּ אֱלֹהִים אֲחֵרִים וְחָרָה אַף־
יְהוָה בָּכֶם וְהִשְׁמִידְךָ מַהֵר׃ 5 כִּי־אִם־כֹּה
תַעֲשׂוּ לָהֶם מִזְבְּחֹתֵיהֶם תִּתֹּצוּ וּמַצֵּבֹתָם
תְּשַׁבֵּרוּ וַאֲשֵׁירֵהֶם תְּגַדֵּעוּן וּפְסִילֵיהֶם
תִּשְׂרְפוּן בָּאֵשׁ׃

### PROHIBITIONS REGARDING THE INHABITANTS OF THE LAND (7:1–5)

The call to absolute loyalty to God and the memory of the past become the basis for the demand for complete separation from Israel's neighbors. Many later readers have struggled with the problematic concept that God charges the Israelites to destroy all the inhabitants when they enter the land. We must confront the fact that this is what the Torah says and be willing to disapprove of it. While we may attempt to understand this rhetoric in its historical context, we can still reject it as something we would not endorse today. In this parashah, the demand to destroy all the Canaanites is presented within a specific understanding of who Israel is at this point in its history: because the Israelites are weak and have demonstrated their inability to resist foreign worship in the past, they are instructed to isolate themselves in order to maintain their identity and remain loyal to their God. (See also at 7:24; 12:29–31; 31:16.) [Some scholars make the point that such calls for destruction most likely reflect the retrojected rhetoric of victory, a claim by later generations that the previous inhabitants were annihilated completely. However, had all the seven nations listed in v. 1 been destroyed, then the command not to intermarry (v. 3) would be irrelevant (see also Exodus 23:32–33 and 34:15–16, which imply the existence of other inhabitants of the land). While conquest certainly involves killing, Deuteronomy's representation of the wholesale slaughter of every living person (the proclamation of *cherem*) is unlikely to have been a historical actuality. —*Ed.*]

*1.* The forbidden nations are only those in the land; the Torah does not advocate hostility to other nations as a general principle.

*3.* The Israelites are directed not to intermarry with the offspring of the neighboring nations. Other biblical texts do not reflect an opposition to unions with non-Israelites (see *Mikeitz*, Another Contemporary Reflection, p. 256).

[6]For you are a people consecrated to your God יהוה: of all the peoples on earth your God יהוה chose you to be God's treasured people. [7]It is not because you are the most numerous of peoples that יהוה grew attached to you and chose you—indeed, you are the smallest of peoples; [8]but it was because יהוה favored you and kept the oath made to your fathers that יהוה freed you with a mighty hand and rescued you from the house of bondage, from the power of Pharaoh king of Egypt.

[9]Know, therefore, that only your God יהוה is God, the steadfast God who keeps the divine covenant faithfully to the thousandth generation of those who love [God] and keep the divine commandments, [10]but who instantly requites with destruction those who reject [God]—never slow with those who reject, but requiting them instantly. [11]Therefore, observe faithfully the Instruction—the laws and the rules—with which I charge you today.

6 כִּ֣י עַ֤ם קָדוֹשׁ֙ אַתָּ֔ה לַיהֹוָ֖ה אֱלֹהֶ֑יךָ בְּךָ֞ בָּחַ֣ר ׀ יְהֹוָ֣ה אֱלֹהֶ֗יךָ לִהְי֥וֹת לוֹ֙ לְעַ֣ם סְגֻלָּ֔ה מִכֹּל֙ הָֽעַמִּ֔ים אֲשֶׁ֖ר עַל־פְּנֵ֥י הָֽאֲדָמָֽה׃ 7 לֹ֣א מֵֽרֻבְּכֶ֞ם מִכָּל־הָֽעַמִּ֗ים חָשַׁ֧ק יְהֹוָ֛ה בָּכֶ֖ם וַיִּבְחַ֣ר בָּכֶ֑ם כִּֽי־אַתֶּ֥ם הַמְעַ֖ט מִכָּל־הָֽעַמִּֽים׃ 8 כִּי֩ מֵֽאַהֲבַ֨ת יְהֹוָ֜ה אֶתְכֶ֗ם וּמִשָּׁמְר֤וֹ אֶת־הַשְּׁבֻעָה֙ אֲשֶׁ֤ר נִשְׁבַּע֙ לַאֲבֹ֣תֵיכֶ֔ם הוֹצִ֧יא יְהֹוָ֛ה אֶתְכֶ֖ם בְּיָ֣ד חֲזָקָ֑ה וַֽיִּפְדְּךָ֙ מִבֵּ֣ית עֲבָדִ֔ים מִיַּ֖ד פַּרְעֹ֥ה מֶֽלֶךְ־מִצְרָֽיִם׃ 9 וְיָ֣דַעְתָּ֔ כִּֽי־יְהֹוָ֥ה אֱלֹהֶ֖יךָ ה֣וּא הָֽאֱלֹהִ֑ים הָאֵל֙ הַֽנֶּאֱמָ֔ן שֹׁמֵ֧ר הַבְּרִ֣ית וְהַחֶ֗סֶד לְאֹהֲבָ֛יו וּלְשֹׁמְרֵ֥י מצותו מִצְוֺתָ֖יו לְאֶ֥לֶף דּֽוֹר׃ 10 וּמְשַׁלֵּ֧ם לְשֹׂנְאָ֛יו אֶל־פָּנָ֖יו לְהַאֲבִיד֑וֹ לֹ֤א יְאַחֵר֙ לְשֹׂ֣נְא֔וֹ אֶל־פָּנָ֖יו יְשַׁלֶּם־לֽוֹ׃ 11 וְשָׁמַרְתָּ֣ אֶת־הַמִּצְוָ֗ה וְאֶת־הַֽחֻקִּ֤ים וְאֶת־הַמִּשְׁפָּטִים֙ אֲשֶׁ֨ר אָֽנֹכִ֧י מְצַוְּךָ֛ הַיּ֖וֹם לַעֲשׂוֹתָֽם׃ פ

- - - - - - - - - - - - - - - - - - - - - -

## Conclusion

### GOD'S LOVE AS REASON FOR THE LAWS
(7:6–11)

This is one of the Bible's strongest statements of God's special relationship with Israel. God has actively chosen this people and separated them from all others to be God's people. Therefore, they have the responsibility to maintain a separate identity, to keep themselves holy, and to live up to their side of the covenant with God.

6. *a people consecrated.* Heb. *am kadosh*, which Jeffrey Tigay connects to its cognate in talmudic Hebrew, *m'kudeshet* ("betrothed"). He claims that the term invokes a marital metaphor, as in 5:9, implying that the bride Israel commits to an exclusive relationship with her groom, God (*Deuteronomy*, 1996, p. 68). In contrast to Leviticus 19, which speaks of individual Israelites becoming holy, here Moses declares that the people already are holy.

7. *It is not because you are the most numerous.* In the Bible, God often chooses unlikely heroes (such as Jacob in Genesis 25) and works through the weaker party. This provides reassurance that Israel will not fail because of its small size and signals that success is achievable because of God's help, not through the work of powerful individuals alone. Women are among those who achieve success, as seen in their successful resistance to Pharaoh's rule in Exodus 1–2.

8. *favored.* Heb. *ahav*, literally "loved." Love serves as a basis for the covenantal relationship between God and Israel (see also at 6:5 and 7:13).

9–11. The parashah ends by reminding the people that their fulfillment of God's commandments will determine their destiny. They have the possibility of a long and successful life in their new land, depending upon their actions.

—*Ora Horn Prouser*

# Another View

[Tikva Frymer-Kensky ז״ל was an early contributor to this project (see *Pinchas*, Another View, p. 982) and served as a member of the Editorial Board. Because her illness and recent death prevented her from completing her planned contributions, here one of her students instead summarizes an important aspect of Frymer-Kensky's published work. —*Ed.*]

Parashat Va-et'chanan figures prominently in debates about the development of monotheism, the belief in God's oneness. While certain passages reflect Deuteronomy's mandate that a single God must be worshipped at one shrine by one people (see 4:35; 6:4), others suggest a belief in the existence in multiple deities (see 4:19–20). Despite the Bible's claim that Moses introduced monotheism to the world, many scholars recognize that Israel's commitment to monotheism developed over time. Texts such as 4:19–20 or Exodus 15:11 ("Who is like you, יהוה, among the celestials [literally: gods]?") likely represent an earlier stage in Israel's theological development. Furthermore, prophetic diatribes against idolatry (see, for instance, Jeremiah 2 or Hosea 2) suggest that monotheism may have been the ideal, but it may not have been the practice of the average Israelite until the 6th century B.C.E.

Tikva Frymer-Kensky shed enormous light on the process through which monotheism took root within Israelite culture and thus revolutionized biblical religion. In her influential 1992 book *In the Wake of the Goddesses*, she described the transition to monotheism as a process in which the image of Israel's God expanded to include all the functions previously attributed to various gods and goddesses—the multiple divine personalities thought to determine the natural world. Israel's God became the rainmaker, healer, warrior, and, as the many tales of barren women attest, controller of human reproduction.

However, this perception of one God as master of the universe creates a theological challenge. The polytheistic universe, observed Frymer-Kensky, is defined by change and flux in which humanity is at the mercy of the gods. Divine whims destroy cities; divine squabbles cause deluge or drought. Now, with one God in control, what accounts for destruction and tragedy? Frymer-Kensky asserted that biblical monotheism makes human beings the initiators of change within the universe. Human behavior becomes the variable that determines the course of history and the natural world. When Israel behaves, there is rain and abundance; when Israel sins, there is drought and death (Deuteronomy 11:13–17). Frymer-Kensky noted that biblical monotheism thus comes with a mandate: as God's partners, it becomes humanity's responsibility to maintain God's universe through right behavior and social justice.

*Now, with one God in control, what accounts for destruction and tragedy?*

—*Amy Kalmanofsky*

# Post-biblical Interpretations

***I pleaded with* יהוה *at that time*** (3:23). Midrash *D'varim Rabbah* 2.1 poses four rhetorical questions on the halachah of prayer. For the answers, it looks to the behavior of four biblical figures—Hannah, Daniel, David, and Solomon. The first question is whether a person should pray in a loud voice, as Moses apparently does in this passage. Based on the actions of Hannah, who prayed silently, with only her lips moving (I Samuel 1:13), the answer is no.

***Honor your father and your mother*** (5:16). The Rabbis (JT *Kiddushin* 1:7, 61b) illustrated this commandment with two exaggerated tales designed to emphasize the seriousness of the mitzvah. Rabbi Tarfon's mother was walking in her courtyard on Shabbat when her shoe broke, exposing her foot to the ground. Her son placed his hands under her feet step by step until she returned to her room. When she later complained to other Rabbis that her son had shown her too much honor, they disagreed. Even if he repeated that act thousands of times, he would still not have shown her even half the honor the Torah requires. Conversely, Rabbi Ishmael's mother complained to the Rabbis that her son did not honor her sufficiently when he refused to allow her to wash his feet and drink the wash water. The Rabbis insisted that if this was the honor she desired, then he must allow her to do it.

At BT *Kiddushin* 39b, the Rabbis compared the mitzvah of honoring parents with the commandment in Deuteronomy 22:6–7 to send away a mother bird before gathering up her eggs. In each case, the Torah promises long life to those who keep these mitzvot. And the comparison goes deeper: by sending away the mother bird, the egg gatherer shows sensitivity to a mother, albeit a non-human one. Broadly speaking, sending away the mother bird is "honoring a mother," or honoring motherhood.

***Hear, O Israel!* יהוה *is our God*** (6:4–9). The Rabbis saw the recitation of the *Sh'ma* as a Jew's acceptance of the "yoke of the Kingdom of Heaven"—that is, the acceptance of God's sovereignty, including acceptance of God's legitimate authority to require obedience to the Torah (for instance, Mishnah *B'rachot* 2:2, 5). The martyr Rabbi Akiva died while saying these words (BT *B'rachot* 61b). This entire passage, known as "recitation of the *Sh'ma*," became part of the standard prayer liturgy that men are required to recite twice daily. However, the Rabbis ruled that women are not required to recite the daily *Sh'ma* (Mishnah *B'rachot* 3:3) since it is a positive, time-bound commandment from which women are generally exempt in rabbinic law (BT *B'rachot* 20b). The Talmud raises the possibility that women should also be obligated in the recitation of *Sh'ma* because of its proclamation of God's sovereignty, but then dismisses this option. The insistence on women's exemption from time-bound commandments, even in the service of God, is a powerful talmudic statement of gender hierarchy and female spiritual marginalization. As Rabbi David Abudraham (14th-century Spain) explained, women are exempt from time-bound commandments so that they will not be occupied in divine service when their husbands need them for domestic service.

*The Rabbis ruled that women are not required to recite the twice-daily Sh'ma.*

***You shall not intermarry with them . . . For they will turn your children away from Me*** (7:3–4). The Torah forbids intermarriage with the seven Canaanite nations on the grounds that the Canaanite spouse could turn the Israelite spouse away from the worship of God. In their biblical context, these verses depict an equal-opportunity danger: whether the intermarrying Israelite is the bride or the groom, the fear is that the Canaanite spouse will lead the Israelite partner astray. Partly because the Canaanite concern was nonexistent in their time, and partly because rabbinic legal interpretation of Scripture generally tends to focus closely on words and phrases, the Rabbis read the grammatically masculine Hebrew of 7:4 with extreme literalness: "For *he* will turn *your son* away." In the Talmud this reading is used to justify the determination of Jewish descent according to whether one's mother is Jewish (BT *Kiddushin* 68b). The argument is that "he" (the Israelite daughter's Canaanite spouse) will turn away "your son" (the Israelite father-in-law's grandson from that union). This proves that the child of a Canaanite father and Israelite mother is considered "your son" (an Israelite), while the child of an Israelite father and Canaanite mother is, by implication, considered "her child" (a Canaanite). Thus, according to rabbinic halachah, in cases of intermarriage the children of an Israelite mother married to a non-Jew are considered part of the Jewish people, but the children of an Israelite father and a non-Israelite mother are not. (For the Reform Movement perspective, see *Mikeitz*, Another Contemporary Reflection, p. 256.)

*—Alyssa M. Gray*

# *Contemporary Reflection*

THE SECOND ACCOUNT of the Decalogue ("Ten Commandments") described in this portion has long been scrutinized for how it differs from the first version in *parashat Yitro*. One obvious difference is the reason given for observing the Sabbath. Exodus 20:11 states that we should rest on the seventh day in imitation of God at Creation, but Deuteronomy 5:15 focuses on our need as humans to rest. Another discrepancy is that Exodus 19 situates the revelation at Sinai, while 5:2 refers to this sacred site as Horeb. But the most significant difference between these two texts lies in the Israelites' own state of mind.

When the Israelites stand at Mount Sinai in Exodus 19–20, they have successfully fled the Egyptians, crossed the Sea of Reeds, and been fed in the wilderness on manna; the danger is behind them. When they hear the first of the "Ten Words"—"I יהוה am your God who brought you out of the land of Egypt"—each of them has a personal understanding of the God they have known and experienced.

In Deuteronomy, however, the danger lies ahead. Of those hearing Moses' recitation of the commandments this time, almost none actually fled Egypt themselves. Earlier, they may have witnessed their rebellious parents' refusal to fight for the Promised Land (Numbers 13–14); but now, precious few of them still has a living parent. The giants of their youth—Moses, Aaron, and Miriam—are either dead or soon will be. The Israelites themselves, untested, will have to battle their way into the Promised Land in order to settle there. In Exodus, the Israelites are preoccupied with the present; in Deuteronomy, they are focused on the future.

Religion promises us a meaningful world. If we are not free, whether because of physical or psychological enslavement, then life may not be meaningful. But death also threatens meaning, so one of religion's major tasks is to reconcile us to the losses we experience and, ultimately, to our own mortality. Our religion must convince us that although death exits, meaning abides. We are finite not only because we die, but also because we have chosen the particular life we live. A people's story spreads over a large canvas and lifts up everyone who participates in its story. When we identify with those who came before us and when we are invested in those who will come after us, then we are part of something much larger than our individual lives and efforts.

While religion can help us find meaning in the face of death, the experience of bereavement transcends our cognitive experience. In particular, with the death of one's parents comes a feeling of loss and, subsequently, a quest for enduring values. During the final

*With the death of one's parents comes a quest for enduring values.*

years in the wilderness, after their parents have died, the members of the generation about to enter into the Promised Land go through a gradual reassessment of their parents' identities, trying to figure out who their ancestors were and who they are themselves. As Moses recounts all that has transpired since the Israelites escaped from Egypt, he emphasizes that the prior generation died because they lacked faith: disillusioned, they had doubted God's plan to fulfill the covenant of the ancestors and settle them in the Promised Land. Now, standing in Moab, poised to complete the forty-year journey, the current generation comes to admire and appreciate the stark honesty of their parents, who had passed on the history of their own inadequacies so that their children would not "be like their ancestors, a wayward and defiant generation, a generation whose heart was inconstant, whose spirit was not true to God" (Psalm 78:8).

How much deeper their understanding of their parents must have become when they themselves became adults and assumed the formidable task of raising the next generation! Now they face the awesome but voluntary task of carrying on the chain of tradition. After all, if they do not do so, no one else will. Their parents' passing likely led them to understand that they are part of something larger than themselves, as well as to realize that they are merely a brief but significant moment in the life of the Jewish people. It is said that we become fully human and adult when we touch death. The loss of our parents makes us aware that we, too, are part of a generation that will die.

As the Israelites listen to Moses repeat the Decalogue, their biological parents are gone and their parent figure, Moses, will soon die. How can they find the invincible parent? Somehow, the people must internalize their ideal parent—in other words, they must parent themselves—and then raise the next generation. Their focus must shift to the next generation, the one without grandparents. The experience makes us better appreciate why the concept of *l'dor vador* ("from generation to generation") is so central in our tradition.

Since mourning is a creative process, we can ask what new growth there is in the Israelites' understanding of the Decalogue. Its commandments initially were addressed to those who had directly experienced the exodus from Egypt. If these words were to have the same force for subsequent generations, they must understand the word "Egypt" to represent all the ways in which they are constricted, degraded, and enslaved. And so, as those about to enter the Promised Land hear Moses repeat these words, they think of the "Egypt" of loss and the long "hard labor" of mourning. The God who had brought them out of Egypt becomes the God who comforts them, dries their tears, and encourages them to continue on their way after their parents have been buried in the wilderness. The God of comfort becomes a crucial addition to the ways in which the Israelites understand the One who freed them "from Egypt with a mighty hand" (6:21). As they prepare to settle in the Promised Land and face the vicissitudes of the next part of their formation as the Jewish people, this revelation of the Divine will prove to be particularly important.

—*Carol Ochs*

# Voices

## *Sinai*

Jill Hammer

*Deuteronomy 4:12, 6:4*

The sound of God's voice. The sound
Of nothing running to greet something.
Of a shocked laugh. Of one

who came again to this place,
searching. Who came to this place
and never left, like a broken wagon wheel.
Who came to this place once, and never again.

The sound of one
who almost spoke to us, as thunder
almost speaks to lightning
but misses by a few seconds. The sound of one
who was wiped free of sound.

The sound of one who knows and wants us
to know.
The sound of one who knows and wants us
to find out
but not yet. The sound of one who does not
know.

The sound of God's voice. The sound
of questions dropped into the mind
like stones into water. Yes, that sound.

## *Somewhere Out of Time*

Nancy Lee Gossels

*Deuteronomy 5:1–24*

Somewhere out of time
In the mystery of time
Somewhere between memory and forgetfulness,
Dimly though
I remember how once I stood
At Your mountain trembling
Amid the fire and the thunder.
How I stood there, out of bondage
In a strange land and afraid.
And You loved me and You fed me
And I feasted on Your words.
And yes, I can remember
How the thunder was my heart
And the fire was my soul.
O, God, I do remember.
The fire burns in me anew.
And here I am, once more
A witness to that timeless moment.
Present now in the light of Your Torah
I am reborn.

## *Aliyah is Ascent*

Sheila Peltz Weinberg

*Deuteronomy 5:1–24*

*Aliyah* is ascent.
We ascend to the Torah to acknowledge that we
choose to live under its laws and principles.
We ascend to the Torah to affirm that we are
part of a people and a story that is much
greater than ourselves.
We ascend to the Torah to represent those who
remain below.
We ascend to the Torah to risk receiving an
honor, to risk being known and seen,
to risk being at Sinai again.
We ascend to the Torah with slow steps, or
in haste, with enthusiasm or reluctance,
in awe or in fear, in hope and in love.

## *Sinai*

Merle Feld

*Deuteronomy 5:1–24*

The men rushed ahead,
they always do—
in battle to defend us,
in eagerness, to get the best view,
to be there with each other
as a community.

We followed later—
some of us waited
till we were done nursing,
others waited to go together
with those who were still nursing.
Most of us were herding several children
carrying a heavy two year old
on one hip
(it's hard to move forward quickly
with a heavy two year old on one hip).
Last came the very pregnant ones—
when you're that far along
it's your instinct to be afraid of crowds
afraid of being jostled
you hang back
you feel safer being last.

Anyway, I was one of the ones
with a heavy two year old on one hip—
such a sweet body he had
warm soft delicious flesh.
He was afraid of the noise
he clung to me so tightly,
his fingers in my neck,
his face buried in my neck.
I showered him with little kisses,
not so much to comfort him
as out of habit
and my pleasure.

The earth shook, it vibrated
and so did I,
my chest, my legs
all vibrating.
I sank to my knees
all the while with this little boy attached to me,
trying to merge himself back into me.

I closed my eyes
to be there more intensely,
it all washed over me—
wave upon wave upon wave...

And afterwards, the stillness
of a nation, a people
who had been flattened, forever imprinted,
slowly raising themselves, rising again from
the earth.

How to hold onto that moment
washed clean
reborn
holy silence...

## *from* The Tapestry of Jewish Time

Nina Beth Cardin

*Deuteronomy 4:44*

The origins of the Torah remain a mystery. Although it would be satisfying to know, the authority of the Torah need not be diminished by the mystery, for its authority goes beyond the origins of the text. It is grounded in the millions of Jews over hundreds of generations who claimed it, cherished it, nurtured it, obeyed it, embellished it, and built out of it a tradition that enriches the world and illumines our lives. That history both confers and confirms its holiness. Where the Torah came from is not as critical as what it means to us, how it has built our people and helped us map our world and our destination.

## *And You Shall Love*

Lynn Levin

*Deuteronomy 6:5–9*

And you shall love
with all your heart,
with all your soul,
and with all your might,
not to have to think about it.
But for now
you shall diligently teach your children
to look out for the odd package.
And you shall think about it
when you're walking by the way
through the market
or down a busy street,
when you're lying down
on a beach,
or when you're rising up
from your seat on a bus
or sitting down at a café.
And although for now you always keep it
in the forefront of your mind,
you wonder
when you will not have to
post warnings about it
on your doors and on your gates.

## *V'ahavta*

Marge Piercy

*Deuteronomy 6:5–9*

So you shall love what is holy
with all your courage, with all your passion
with all your strength.
Let the words that have come down
shine in our words and our actions.
We must teach our children to know and
understand them.
We must speak about what is good
and holy within our homes
when we are working, when we are at play,
when we lie down and when we get up.
Let the work of our hands speak of goodness.
Let it run in our blood
and glow from our doors and windows.

We should love ourselves, for we are of G-d.
We should love our neighbors as ourselves.
We should love the stranger, for we
were once strangers in the land of Egypt
and have been strangers in all the lands of the
world since.
Let love fill our hearts with its clear precious
water.
Heaven and earth observe how we cherish or
spoil our world.
Heaven and earth watch whether we choose
life or choose death.
We must choose life so our children's children
may live.
Be quiet and listen to the still small
voice within that speaks in love.
Open to that voice, hear it, heed it and work
for life.
Let us remember and strive to be good.
Let us remember to find what is holy
within and without.

# עקב ✦ *Eikev*

## DEUTERONOMY 7:12–11:25

## *Conditions for Life in the Land*

PARASHAT EIKEV ("if" or "as a result of") contains three speeches (7:12–8:20; 9:1–10:22; 11:1–25), all of which highlight the central position of the Promised Land in the relationship between God and Israel. The "good land" is the object of the divine oath to the ancestors (7:12–13; 8:1; 9:5; 11:9) and the goal reached after forty years of wandering in the wilderness (8:1–20). For Israel's sake, God constantly keeps an eye on the land of "milk and honey," which is so different from the land of Egypt (11:12).

Whereas the prior parashah presents categorical demands of loyalty and obedience (as in the Decalogue in 5:6–18 and the *Sh'ma* in 6:4–9), *Eikev* opens with a conditional clause that emphasizes that obedience brings blessings ("And if you do obey these rules . . ."). Throughout the parashah, Moses emphasizes that existence in the land is conditioned upon obedience, observance, and love—all of which are manifestations of Israel's loyalty to God (8:1–20; 11:8–9, 13–25). This message remains central in Jewish life, as 11:21–31 are traditionally recited twice daily as the second paragraph of the *Sh'ma,* and the same passage is inserted in the mezuzah and in *t'fillin.*

This parashah mentions women explicitly only a few times. One of the blessings promised if the people follow God's teachings is the absence of infertile women and men (7:14). A later passage extolling God's merits mentions that God "upholds the cause of . . . the widow" (10:18). As divine ruler (see at 10:17), God's role is to defend and provide for the vulnerable members of society, including widows—a frequent topic of concern in Deuteronomy.

*The Promised Land has a central place in the relationship between God and Israel.*

With regard to this parashah's use of feminine imagery, one verse open to interpretation is the analogy comparing the way God disciplines Israel to the actions of a human parent (8:5). Does the masculine language of this verse refer specifically to a father and son, or, more inclusively, to the way that either parent treats a daughter or son? (See further at 8:5.)

—*Dalit Rom-Shiloni*

## *Outline*

*I.* Faithfulness to the Covenant by God and Israel (7:12–8:20)

- *A.* Blessings and possession of the land (7:12–26)
- *B.* Call to observe and remember, remember and observe (8:1–20)

*II.* Principles of Reverence
*What Does God Demand of You?* (9:1–10:22)

- *A.* Possession of the land by a stiff-necked people (9:1–6)
- *B.* Retrospective of wilderness sins (9:7–24)
- *C.* Reaffirmation that Israel is God's people (9:25–10:11)
- *D.* Call for reverence, obedience, love, and worship (10:12–22)

*III.* Occupation of the Land as Divine Reward or Punishment (11:1–25)

- *A.* Past lessons as motivations for future actions (vv. 1–9)
- *B.* Special qualities of the land and incentives to obey God (vv. 10–21)
- *C.* Victory and territory as rewards for obedience (vv. 22–25)

And if you do obey these rules and observe them carefully, your God יהוה will maintain faithfully for you the covenant made on oath with

ז 12 וְהָיָה ׀ עֵקֶב תִּשְׁמְעוּן אֵת הַמִּשְׁפָּטִים
הָאֵלֶּה וּשְׁמַרְתֶּם וַעֲשִׂיתֶם אֹתָם וְשָׁמַר
יְהֹוָה אֱלֹהֶיךָ לְךָ אֶת־הַבְּרִית וְאֶת־הַחֶסֶד

## *Faithfulness to the Covenant by God and Israel*
(7:12–8:20)

The first speech in this parashah binds together two distinct passages. The first (7:12–26) concentrates on God's loyalty to the covenant and blessings for Israel. The second (8:1–20) calls Israel to bless God and accentuates the importance of recognition, remembrance, and obedience to God. These two sections are linked through the repetition of the word *eikev* and of the verb *sh-m-a* ("obey" or "heed," literally "hear") in the unit's first and last verses, which also frames this unit within a literary structure known as an inclusio. In 7:12, *eikev tishm'un* ("if you do obey") introduces a list of blessings; in 8:20, *eikev lo tishm'un* ("because you did not heed") closes the speech with an exhortation about disobedience. Note that these two verses (and the start of the second section, 8:1) speak to the people in the second-person plural, whereas the body of the speech addresses the people overwhelmingly in the singular, thus particularizing its message to each individual.

### BLESSINGS AND POSSESSION OF THE LAND (7:12–26)

Verse 12 presents God's faithfulness to the covenant as a conditional response to the people's obedience. God's kindness manifests itself in the blessings elaborated on in this section, which concern the fertility of people, agricultural products, and animals, as well as political dominance over other peoples (see also 15:6; 26:19; Genesis 12:2–3).

***12. faithfully.*** Heb. *chesed.* In this verse, *chesed* and *b'rit* (covenant) form a hendiadys (a compound expression for one idea), thus demonstrating that God shows kindness through God's faithfulness to the covenant with the ancestors and to the Sinai covenant. The word *chesed,* when used for human relationships, connotes an exceptional good deed done by one toward another, usually with the explicit expectation of an equivalent act in return (for example, Genesis 20:13; 21:23; I Samuel 20:8; II Samuel 2:5). God's deeds of *chesed* include acts of strength, victory, salvation, justice, righteousness, and mercy. In all these ways, in fulfillment of the covenantal relationship, God intervenes

God seeks redress for widows, not out of sympathy but out of a concern for justice.
ANOTHER VIEW ➤ *1108*

The Rabbis record the seven tasks expected of a wife, including the accompanying rituals.
POST-BIBLICAL INTERPRETATIONS ➤ *1108*

The Torah's corporeal imagery hints at the potentiality of our bodies to experience God.
CONTEMPORARY REFLECTION ➤ *1110*

Nine stars / and not one moon / around me / empress / of imagined fertility.
VOICES ➤ *1112*

your fathers: 13[God] will favor you and bless you and multiply you—blessing your issue from the womb and your produce from the soil, your new grain and wine and oil, your calving from the herd and your lambing from the flock, in the land sworn to your fathers to be assigned to you. 14You shall be blessed above all other peoples: there shall be no sterile male or female among you or among your livestock. 15יהוה will ward off from you all sickness; [God] will not bring upon you any of the dreadful

אֲשֶׁר נִשְׁבַּע לַאֲבֹתֶיךָ׃ 13 וַאֲהֵבְךָ וּבֵרַכְךָ
וְהִרְבֶּךָ וּבֵרַךְ פְּרִי־בִטְנְךָ וּפְרִי־אַדְמָתֶךָ דְּגָנְךָ
וְתִירֹשְׁךָ וְיִצְהָרֶךָ שְׁגַר־אֲלָפֶיךָ וְעַשְׁתְּרֹת
צֹאנֶךָ עַל הָאֲדָמָה אֲשֶׁר־נִשְׁבַּע לַאֲבֹתֶיךָ
לָתֶת לָךְ׃ 14 בָּרוּךְ תִּהְיֶה מִכָּל־הָעַמִּים
לֹא־יִהְיֶה בְךָ עָקָר וַעֲקָרָה וּבִבְהֶמְתֶּךָ׃
15 וְהֵסִיר יְהוָה מִמְּךָ כָּל־חֹלִי וְכָל־מַדְוֵי

---

on behalf of individuals and of the people Israel, showing God's loyalty and loving-kindness. (See at 5:9 for a discussion of how Deuteronomy and other biblical passages use marriage as a metaphor for the covenantal relationship between God and Israel.)

*fathers.* Why is *avot* translated here as "fathers" (also 7:13; 8:1, 18; 9:5) but elsewhere as "ancestors" (8:3, 16; 10:15)? Translator David Stein explains that this term can have either a male-only or an inclusive meaning, depending on context. He argues that in a verse like this, the noun refers specifically to the patriarchs (Abraham, Isaac, and Jacob), those with whom God formed a covenant in their capacity as (male) heads of their corporate households. It goes without saying that each patriarch represents the entire household, and that God's covenant applies to all its members—women and men alike ("Methodology," *The Torah: Documentation for the Revised Edition*, 2005, p. 6). Elsewhere, as in 8:3, the surrounding context makes the gender-inclusive sense of the term clear.

*13. [God] will favor.* Heb. *ahav* (literally "love"). Usually, the people are commanded to "love" God (as in 6:5; 11:1); but here the verb designates God's response to Israel (also 4:37; 10:15; 23:6). The composer(s) of Deuteronomy have borrowed this term from the ancient Near Eastern political sphere of suzerain-vassal relationships, applying it to the Israelite theological sphere of the relationship between God and the people. The people illustrate their love through their loyalty as subjects (vassals) to God; and God (like a suzerain or ruler) demonstrates love to the people through benevolent acts of *chesed* (see at v. 12).

*issue from the womb.* Heb. *pri beten* (literally "fruit of the belly"), an expression that uses agricultural production as a metaphor for children (so also in reference to animal offspring; see 28:4, 51; 30:9). The noun *beten* alone commonly refers to the womb, and thus to female fertility and motherhood (as in Genesis 25:23–24; 30:2). Yet here, in the context of a list of agricultural products and possessions that in the biblical world were understood to be the economic responsibility of the male head of the household, the phrase "your *pri beten*" most likely designates his descendants (so also 28:4, 11, 18, 53; 30:9; see Micah 6:7; Psalm 132:11).

*14. no sterile male or female.* This stands out as the only reference to male infertility in the Bible, in contrast to the usual focus—female sterility (compare Exodus 23:26). The Bible repeatedly emphasizes the importance of human fertility, as seen in the plights of Sarah (Genesis 11–21), Rachel (Genesis 30), and Hannah (I Samuel 1), all of whom suffer because they are infertile or "barren." It appears that Ruth's first husband may be infertile, for they are married for ten years before he dies without having children (Ruth 1:4–5); yet when Ruth marries Boaz, she conceives and bears a son (4:13). (For more on ancient approaches to infertility, see *Noach*, Another View, p. 53.)

diseases of Egypt, about which you know, but will inflict them upon all your enemies. [16]You shall destroy all the peoples that your God יהוה delivers to you, showing them no pity. And you shall not worship their gods, for that would be a snare to you. [17]Should you say to yourselves, "These nations are more numerous than we; how can we dispossess them?" [18]You need have no fear of them. You have but to bear in mind what your God יהוה did to Pharaoh and all the Egyptians: [19]the wondrous acts that you saw with your own eyes, the signs and the portents, the mighty hand, and the outstretched arm by which your God יהוה liberated you. Thus will your God יהוה do to all the peoples you now fear. [20]Your God יהוה will also send a plague against them, until those who are left in hiding perish before you. [21]Do not stand in dread of them, for your God יהוה is in your midst, a great and awesome God.

[22]Your God יהוה will dislodge those peoples before you little by little; you will not be able to put an end to them at once, else the wild beasts would multiply to your hurt. [23]Your God יהוה will deliver them up to you, throwing them into utter panic until they are wiped out. [24][God] will deliver their kings into your hand, and you shall obliterate their name from under the heavens; no one shall stand up to you, until you have wiped them out.

מִצְרַ֙יִם֙ הָרָעִ֔ים אֲשֶׁ֣ר יָדַ֔עְתָּ לֹ֥א יְשִׂימָ֖ם בָּ֑ךְ וּנְתָנָ֖ם בְּכָל־שֹׂנְאֶֽיךָ׃

[16] וְאָכַלְתָּ֣ אֶת־כָּל־הָֽעַמִּ֗ים אֲשֶׁ֨ר יְהֹוָ֤ה אֱלֹהֶ֙יךָ֙ נֹתֵ֣ן לָ֔ךְ לֹא־תָח֥וֹס עֵֽינְךָ֖ עֲלֵיהֶ֑ם וְלֹ֤א תַֽעֲבֹד֙ אֶת־אֱלֹ֣הֵיהֶ֔ם כִּֽי־מוֹקֵ֥שׁ ה֖וּא לָֽךְ׃ ס [17] כִּ֤י תֹאמַר֙ בִּלְבָ֣בְךָ֔ רַבִּ֛ים הַגּוֹיִ֥ם הָאֵ֖לֶּה מִמֶּ֑נִּי אֵיכָ֥ה אוּכַ֖ל לְהֽוֹרִישָֽׁם׃ [18] לֹ֥א תִירָ֖א מֵהֶ֑ם זָכֹ֣ר תִּזְכֹּ֗ר אֵ֤ת אֲשֶׁר־עָשָׂה֙ יְהֹוָ֣ה אֱלֹהֶ֔יךָ לְפַרְעֹ֖ה וּלְכָל־מִצְרָֽיִם׃ [19] הַמַּסֹּ֣ת הַגְּדֹלֹ֗ת אֲשֶׁר־רָא֣וּ עֵינֶ֡יךָ וְהָאֹתֹ֣ת וְהַמֹּֽפְתִ֡ים וְהַיָּ֣ד הַֽחֲזָקָה֩ וְהַזְּרֹ֨עַ הַנְּטוּיָ֜ה אֲשֶׁ֣ר הוֹצִֽאֲךָ֗ יְהֹוָ֣ה אֱלֹהֶ֑יךָ כֵּֽן־יַעֲשֶׂ֞ה יְהֹוָ֤ה אֱלֹהֶ֙יךָ֙ לְכָל־הָ֣עַמִּ֔ים אֲשֶׁר־אַתָּ֥ה יָרֵ֖א מִפְּנֵיהֶֽם׃ [20] וְגַם֙ אֶת־הַצִּרְעָ֔ה יְשַׁלַּ֛ח יְהֹוָ֥ה אֱלֹהֶ֖יךָ בָּ֑ם עַד־אֲבֹ֗ד הַנִּשְׁאָרִ֛ים וְהַנִּסְתָּרִ֖ים מִפָּנֶֽיךָ׃ [21] לֹ֥א תַעֲרֹ֖ץ מִפְּנֵיהֶ֑ם כִּֽי־יְהֹוָ֤ה אֱלֹהֶ֙יךָ֙ בְּקִרְבֶּ֔ךָ אֵ֥ל גָּד֖וֹל וְנוֹרָֽא׃

[22] וְנָשַׁל֩ יְהֹוָ֨ה אֱלֹהֶ֜יךָ אֶת־הַגּוֹיִ֥ם הָאֵ֛ל מִפָּנֶ֖יךָ מְעַ֣ט מְעָ֑ט לֹ֤א תוּכַל֙ כַּלֹּתָ֣ם מַהֵ֔ר פֶּן־תִּרְבֶּ֥ה עָלֶ֖יךָ חַיַּ֥ת הַשָּׂדֶֽה׃ [23] וּנְתָנָ֛ם יְהֹוָ֥ה אֱלֹהֶ֖יךָ לְפָנֶ֑יךָ וְהָמָם֙ מְהוּמָ֣ה גְדֹלָ֔ה עַ֖ד הִשָּֽׁמְדָֽם׃ [24] וְנָתַ֤ן מַלְכֵיהֶם֙ בְּיָדֶ֔ךָ וְהַאֲבַדְתָּ֣ אֶת־שְׁמָ֔ם מִתַּ֖חַת הַשָּׁמָ֑יִם לֹֽא־יִתְיַצֵּ֥ב אִישׁ֙ בְּפָנֶ֔יךָ עַ֥ד הִשְׁמִֽדְךָ֖ אֹתָֽם׃

. . . . . . . . . . . . . . . . . . . . . .

*17–26.* This passage elaborates on the three clauses of v. 16 ("You shall destroy . . . showing them no pity. . . you shall not worship"). First, vv. 17–21 depict the projected destruction of the Canaanite peoples as a miraculous action, analogous to God's wondrous acts against the Egyptians. Second, vv. 22–24 assure the Israelites that the occupation will entail a series of military actions in which God will gradually enable the invaders to destroy the local peoples. Third, vv. 25–26 focus on the dangers of personal and cultural-religious connections between Israelites and Canaanites.

*24. you shall obliterate their name.* Elimination of the name serves as a repeated curse in the Bible and extra-biblical sources. Since a name constitutes a person's identity, not having a name signals non-existence. In a national context, obliteration of the name signifies total extinction of the enemy, beyond their physical termination. (See *machah shem*, "to blot out a name," in 9:14; 25:19; 29:19; and Psalm 83:5.)

*until you have wiped them out.* The various verbs used in vv. 20–24 (like "perish," "dislodge," "wiped out," "obliterated") represent Deuteron-

[25]You shall consign the images of their gods to the fire; you shall not covet the silver and gold on them and keep it for yourselves, lest you be ensnared thereby; for that is abhorrent to your God יהוה. [26]You must not bring an abhorrent thing into your house, or you will be proscribed like it; you must reject it as abominable and abhorrent, for it is proscribed.

*8* You shall faithfully observe all the Instruction that I enjoin upon you today, that you may thrive and increase and be able to possess the land that יהוה promised on oath to your fathers.

[2]Remember the long way that your God יהוה has made you travel in the wilderness these past forty years, in order to test you by hardships to learn what was in your hearts: whether you would keep the divine commandments or not. [3][God] subjected you to the hardship of hunger and then gave you manna to eat, which neither you nor your

25 פְּסִילֵי אֱלֹהֵיהֶם תִּשְׂרְפוּן בָּאֵשׁ לֹא־
תַחְמֹד כֶּסֶף וְזָהָב עֲלֵיהֶם וְלָקַחְתָּ לָךְ פֶּן
תִּוָּקֵשׁ בּוֹ כִּי תוֹעֲבַת יְהוָה אֱלֹהֶיךָ הוּא׃
26 וְלֹא־תָבִיא תוֹעֵבָה אֶל־בֵּיתֶךָ וְהָיִיתָ
חֵרֶם כָּמֹהוּ שַׁקֵּץ ׀ תְּשַׁקְּצֶנּוּ וְתַעֵב ׀ תְּתַעֲבֶנּוּ
כִּי־חֵרֶם הוּא׃ פ

ח כָּל־הַמִּצְוָה אֲשֶׁר אָנֹכִי מְצַוְּךָ הַיּוֹם
תִּשְׁמְרוּן לַעֲשׂוֹת לְמַעַן תִּחְיוּן וּרְבִיתֶם
וּבָאתֶם וִירִשְׁתֶּם אֶת־הָאָרֶץ אֲשֶׁר־נִשְׁבַּע
יְהוָה לַאֲבֹתֵיכֶם׃
2 וְזָכַרְתָּ אֶת־כָּל־הַדֶּרֶךְ אֲשֶׁר הוֹלִיכְךָ יְהוָה
אֱלֹהֶיךָ זֶה אַרְבָּעִים שָׁנָה בַּמִּדְבָּר לְמַעַן
עַנֹּתְךָ לְנַסֹּתְךָ לָדַעַת אֶת־אֲשֶׁר בִּלְבָבְךָ
הֲתִשְׁמֹר מצותו מִצְוֺתָיו אִם־לֹא׃ 3 וַיְעַנְּךָ
וַיַּרְעִבֶךָ וַיַּאֲכִלְךָ אֶת־הַמָּן אֲשֶׁר לֹא־יָדַעְתָּ

omy's concept of the ban or *cherem* (see v. 26), signifying the total annihilation of the Canaanite population. This language may reflect rhetoric about Israel's total possession of the land and not an actual policy or historical fact. Texts such as Judges 1:21–33 and I Kings 9:20–21, along with archeological evidence, indicate that such a ban was never in fact activated. (See also at 2:34; 7:1–5; 12:29–31; 31:16.)

***25. abhorrent to your God* יהוה.** Heb. *to'evat YHVH*, a phrase that occurs repeatedly in Deuteronomy. It uses this expression, or the word *to'evah* alone, to denote activities that God detests, usually in the religious sphere: idolatry (as here; 13:15; 17:4); certain sacrifices (17:1; 23:19); ritually impure foods (14:3); putting on the apparel of the other sex (22:5); and certain marriages (24:4; compare at Leviticus 18:22). In one instance, Deuteronomy applies the term in the social-moral sphere (namely, falsification of weights and measures, 25:13–16).

## CALL TO OBSERVE AND REMEMBER, REMEMBER AND OBSERVE (8:1–20)

This speech is built on two antonyms: remember (*z-ch-r*) and forget (*sh-ch-ch*). Verses 2–10 call upon the people to remember two of God's major gifts: guiding the people through the hardships of the wilderness (vv. 2–5), and giving them the good land (vv. 7–10). Then, vv. 11–20 warn the people that once they settle in the land, human arrogance and idol worship—the results of forgetting God—will lead to annihilation (see also 6:10–15; 11:13–17; 32:13–18).

***2–3. in order to test you . . . in order to teach you.*** This passage presents the hardships in the wilderness not as a punishment (compare Numbers 14:26–38) but as having two other purposes. The first reason was for God to gain definitive knowledge concerning Israel's faith and behavior under stressful circumstances (see also Exodus 15:25; 16:4);

וְלֹא יָדְעוּן אֲבֹתֶיךָ לְמַעַן הוֹדִיעֲךָ כִּי לֹא
עַל־הַלֶּחֶם לְבַדּוֹ יִחְיֶה הָאָדָם כִּי עַל־כָּל־
מוֹצָא פִי־יְהֹוָה יִחְיֶה הָאָדָם׃ 4 שִׂמְלָתְךָ
לֹא בָלְתָה מֵעָלֶיךָ וְרַגְלְךָ לֹא בָצֵקָה זֶה
אַרְבָּעִים שָׁנָה׃ 5 וְיָדַעְתָּ עִם־לְבָבֶךָ כִּי
כַּאֲשֶׁר יְיַסֵּר אִישׁ אֶת־בְּנוֹ יְהֹוָה אֱלֹהֶיךָ
מְיַסְּרֶךָּ׃ 6 וְשָׁמַרְתָּ אֶת־מִצְוֺת יְהֹוָה אֱלֹהֶיךָ
לָלֶכֶת בִּדְרָכָיו וּלְיִרְאָה אֹתוֹ׃
7 כִּי יְהֹוָה אֱלֹהֶיךָ מְבִיאֲךָ אֶל־אֶרֶץ טוֹבָה
אֶרֶץ נַחֲלֵי מָיִם עֲיָנֹת וּתְהֹמֹת יֹצְאִים
בַּבִּקְעָה וּבָהָר׃ 8 אֶרֶץ חִטָּה וּשְׂעֹרָה וְגֶפֶן
וּתְאֵנָה וְרִמּוֹן אֶרֶץ־זֵית שֶׁמֶן וּדְבָשׁ׃ 9 אֶרֶץ
אֲשֶׁר לֹא בְמִסְכֵּנֻת תֹּאכַל־בָּהּ לֶחֶם לֹא־

ancestors had ever known, in order to teach you
that a human being does not live on bread alone,
but that one may live on anything that יהוה decrees.
4 The clothes upon you did not wear out, nor did
your feet swell these forty years. 5 Bear in mind that
your God יהוה disciplines you just as a householder
disciplines his son. 6 Therefore keep the commandments of your God יהוה: walk in God's ways and
show reverence.
7 For your God יהוה is bringing you into a good
land, a land with streams and springs and fountains
issuing from plain and hill; 8 a land of wheat and
barley, of vines, figs, and pomegranates, a land of
olive trees and honey; 9 a land where you may eat
food without stint, where you will lack nothing; a

this notion of a trial implies that God is not omniscient (see also Genesis 22:1–12; Deuteronomy 13:4; Judges 2:22; 3:4; Job 1:8–12). The second reason is didactic in nature: having completed the journey, only in retrospect will the people acknowledge that the hunger and the manna signify their dependence on God.

***ancestors.*** See at 7:12.

*5.* ***householder . . . son.*** [Heb. *ish . . . ben*. This translation understands the noun *ish* (traditionally "a man") as referring to one who represents a group. Here, the group is by default a household, the basic social and economic unit in the ancient Near East; and the head of a household, in turn, was presumably male. Responsible for his corporate household's continuity, a householder characteristically groomed his heir—that is, his son—to take over his father's position of responsibility (*The Contemporary Torah*, 2006, pp. 385, 402).

Alternatively, one can translate this verse's simile in a gender-neutral sense: "as a parent disciplines a child." The book of Proverbs provides support for a gender-inclusive interpretation of the language in this verse. The role of both parents in educating a child is apparent in Proverbs 1:8, which urges the reader both to obey the father's *musar* (discipline) and not to forsake the mother's *torah* (instruction). (See also Proverbs 6:20).

Regardless of whether or not the imagery is read gender inclusively, God's perceived gender is not at issue. Drawing an analogy from parental discipline, this verse exalts divine chastisement coupled with care and affection (see Proverbs 19:18; 29:17). Compare at Deuteronomy 1:31. —*Ed.*]

*7–10.* In marked contrast to the wilderness (see Numbers 20:5), this passage depicts the Promised Land as a place of plenitude and prosperity—with water, abundant agricultural products, and natural resources. This description displays an elevated style: first, the phrase "good land" frames the passage (an inclusio), occurring at its beginning and end; and second, the symbolically complete number seven appears twice: the key word *eretz* (land) occurs seven times, and the list of agricultural species includes seven items (v. 8).

*8.* ***wheat and barley, of vines, figs, and pomegranates . . . olive trees and honey.*** Deuteronomy elsewhere (as in 7:13) categorizes the land's produce via a triplet of agricultural staples: *dagan* (grain), *tirosh* (juice of the grapevine), and *yitzhar* (olive

land whose rocks are iron and from whose hills you can mine copper. [10]When you have eaten your fill, give thanks to your God יהוה for the good land given to you.

[11]Take care lest you forget your God יהוה and fail to keep the divine commandments, rules, and laws which I enjoin upon you today. [12]When you have eaten your fill, and have built fine houses to live in, [13]and your herds and flocks have multiplied, and your silver and gold have increased, and everything you own has prospered, [14]beware lest your heart grow haughty and you forget your God יהוה—who freed you from the land of Egypt, the house of bondage; [15]who led you through the great and terrible wilderness with its *seraph* serpents and scorpions, a parched land with no water in it, who brought forth water for you from the flinty rock; [16]who fed you in the wilderness with manna, which your ancestors had never known, in order to test you by hardships only to benefit you in the end—[17]and you say to yourselves, "My own power and the might of my own hand have won this wealth for me." [18]Remember that it is your God יהוה who gives you the power to get wealth, in fulfillment of the covenant made on oath with your fathers, as is still the case.

[19]If you do forget your God יהוה and follow other gods to serve them or bow down to them, I warn you this day that you shall certainly perish; [20]like the nations that יהוה will cause to perish before you, so shall you perish—because you did not heed your God יהוה.

תֶחְסַר כֹּל בָּהּ אֶרֶץ אֲשֶׁר אֲבָנֶיהָ בַרְזֶל
וּמֵהֲרָרֶיהָ תַּחְצֹב נְחֹשֶׁת׃ 10 וְאָכַלְתָּ
וְשָׂבָעְתָּ וּבֵרַכְתָּ אֶת־יְהוָה אֱלֹהֶיךָ עַל־
הָאָרֶץ הַטֹּבָה אֲשֶׁר נָתַן־לָךְ׃
11 הִשָּׁמֶר לְךָ פֶּן־תִּשְׁכַּח אֶת־יְהוָה אֱלֹהֶיךָ
לְבִלְתִּי שְׁמֹר מִצְוֺתָיו וּמִשְׁפָּטָיו וְחֻקֹּתָיו
אֲשֶׁר אָנֹכִי מְצַוְּךָ הַיּוֹם׃ 12 פֶּן־תֹּאכַל
וְשָׂבָעְתָּ וּבָתִּים טֹבִים תִּבְנֶה וְיָשָׁבְתָּ׃
13 וּבְקָרְךָ וְצֹאנְךָ יִרְבְּיֻן וְכֶסֶף וְזָהָב יִרְבֶּה־
לָּךְ וְכֹל אֲשֶׁר־לְךָ יִרְבֶּה׃ 14 וְרָם לְבָבֶךָ
וְשָׁכַחְתָּ אֶת־יְהוָה אֱלֹהֶיךָ הַמּוֹצִיאֲךָ
מֵאֶרֶץ מִצְרַיִם מִבֵּית עֲבָדִים׃ 15 הַמּוֹלִיכֲךָ
בַּמִּדְבָּר ׀ הַגָּדֹל וְהַנּוֹרָא נָחָשׁ ׀ שָׂרָף וְעַקְרָב
וְצִמָּאוֹן אֲשֶׁר אֵין־מָיִם הַמּוֹצִיא לְךָ מַיִם
מִצּוּר הַחַלָּמִישׁ׃ 16 הַמַּאֲכִלְךָ מָן בַּמִּדְבָּר
אֲשֶׁר לֹא־יָדְעוּן אֲבֹתֶיךָ לְמַעַן עַנֹּתְךָ וּלְמַעַן
נַסֹּתֶךָ לְהֵיטִבְךָ בְּאַחֲרִיתֶךָ׃ 17 וְאָמַרְתָּ
בִּלְבָבֶךָ כֹּחִי וְעֹצֶם יָדִי עָשָׂה לִי אֶת־
הַחַיִל הַזֶּה׃ 18 וְזָכַרְתָּ אֶת־יְהוָה אֱלֹהֶיךָ כִּי
הוּא הַנֹּתֵן לְךָ כֹּחַ לַעֲשׂוֹת חָיִל לְמַעַן
הָקִים אֶת־בְּרִיתוֹ אֲשֶׁר־נִשְׁבַּע לַאֲבֹתֶיךָ
כַּיּוֹם הַזֶּה׃ פ

19 וְהָיָה אִם־שָׁכֹחַ תִּשְׁכַּח אֶת־יְהוָה
אֱלֹהֶיךָ וְהָלַכְתָּ אַחֲרֵי אֱלֹהִים אֲחֵרִים
וַעֲבַדְתָּם וְהִשְׁתַּחֲוִיתָ לָהֶם הַעִדֹתִי בָכֶם
הַיּוֹם כִּי אָבֹד תֹּאבֵדוּן׃ 20 כַּגּוֹיִם אֲשֶׁר
יְהוָה מַאֲבִיד מִפְּנֵיכֶם כֵּן תֹּאבֵדוּן עֵקֶב לֹא
תִשְׁמְעוּן בְּקוֹל יְהוָה אֱלֹהֵיכֶם׃ פ

oil). The chain of trees in this verse suggests that the last item refers not to bee honey but rather a similar food made from mashed palm-dates (see also at Numbers 13:27).

***16. in order to test you by hardships only to benefit you.*** In contrast to v. 2, this verse presents the trial as an experience that would ultimately benefit the obedient people (a common theme in wisdom literature, as seen in Psalm 37:37–38).

*17–18.* Because material success can bring pride and boastfulness, Moses reminds the people that God is the provider of power and success (see also Zechariah 4:6).

*19.* The Bible often connects human arrogance to idol worship, since idols are hand-made statues (as in 32:15–16; Isaiah 2:7–22; 44:9–20; Hosea 14:4).

**9** Hear, O Israel! You are about to cross the Jordan to go in and dispossess nations greater and more populous than you: great cities with walls sky-high; [2] a people great and tall, the Anakites, of whom you have knowledge; for you have heard it said, "Who can stand up to the children of Anak?" [3] Know then this day that none other than your God יהוה is crossing at your head, a devouring fire; it is [God] who will wipe them out—subduing them before you, that you may quickly dispossess and destroy them, as יהוה promised you. [4] And when your God יהוה has thrust them from your path, say not to yourselves, "יהוה has enabled us to possess this land because of our virtues"; it is rather because of the wickedness of those nations that יהוה is dispossessing them before you. [5] It is not because of your virtues and your rectitude that you will be able to possess their country; but it is because of their wickedness that your God יהוה is dispossessing those nations before you, and in order to fulfill the oath that יהוה made to your fathers Abraham, Isaac, and Jacob.

ט שְׁמַ֣ע יִשְׂרָאֵ֗ל אַתָּ֨ה עֹבֵ֤ר הַיּוֹם֙ אֶת־הַיַּרְדֵּ֔ן לָבֹא֙ לָרֶ֣שֶׁת גּוֹיִ֔ם גְּדֹלִ֥ים וַעֲצֻמִ֖ים מִמֶּ֑ךָּ עָרִ֛ים גְּדֹלֹ֥ת וּבְצֻרֹ֖ת בַּשָּׁמָֽיִם: 2 עַם־גָּד֥וֹל וָרָ֖ם בְּנֵ֣י עֲנָקִ֑ים אֲשֶׁ֨ר אַתָּ֤ה יָדַ֙עְתָּ֙ וְאַתָּ֣ה שָׁמַ֔עְתָּ מִ֣י יִתְיַצֵּ֔ב לִפְנֵ֖י בְּנֵ֥י עֲנָֽק: 3 וְיָדַעְתָּ֣ הַיּ֗וֹם כִּי֩ יְהֹוָ֨ה אֱלֹהֶ֜יךָ הֽוּא־הָעֹבֵ֤ר לְפָנֶ֙יךָ֙ אֵ֣שׁ אֹֽכְלָ֔ה ה֧וּא יַשְׁמִידֵ֛ם וְה֥וּא יַכְנִיעֵ֖ם לְפָנֶ֑יךָ וְהֽוֹרַשְׁתָּ֤ם וְהַֽאֲבַדְתָּם֙ מַהֵ֔ר כַּאֲשֶׁ֛ר דִּבֶּ֥ר יְהֹוָ֖ה לָֽךְ: 4 אַל־תֹּאמַ֣ר בִּלְבָבְךָ֗ בַּהֲדֹ֣ף יְהֹוָה֩ אֱלֹהֶ֨יךָ אֹתָ֥ם ׀ מִלְּפָנֶ֘יךָ֘ לֵאמֹר֒ בְּצִדְקָתִי֙ הֱבִיאַ֣נִי יְהֹוָ֔ה לָרֶ֖שֶׁת אֶת־הָאָ֣רֶץ הַזֹּ֑את וּבְרִשְׁעַת֙ הַגּוֹיִ֣ם הָאֵ֔לֶּה יְהֹוָ֖ה מוֹרִישָׁ֥ם מִפָּנֶֽיךָ: 5 לֹ֣א בְצִדְקָתְךָ֗ וּבְיֹ֙שֶׁר֙ לְבָ֣בְךָ֔ אַתָּ֥ה בָ֖א לָרֶ֣שֶׁת אֶת־אַרְצָ֑ם כִּ֞י בְּרִשְׁעַ֣ת ׀ הַגּוֹיִ֣ם הָאֵ֗לֶּה יְהֹוָ֤ה אֱלֹהֶ֙יךָ֙ מוֹרִישָׁ֣ם מִפָּנֶ֔יךָ וּלְמַ֜עַן הָקִ֣ים אֶת־הַדָּבָ֗ר אֲשֶׁ֨ר נִשְׁבַּ֤ע יְהֹוָה֙ לַאֲבֹתֶ֔יךָ לְאַבְרָהָ֥ם לְיִצְחָ֖ק וּֽלְיַעֲקֹֽב:

---

## *Principles of Reverence*
### WHAT DOES GOD DEMAND OF YOU?
(9:1–10:22)

Focusing on theological and ideological implications of dispossessing the Canaanite peoples, Moses' second speech repudiates thoughts of superiority—the idea that God gave Israel the land because of their righteousness. On the contrary, the Israelites have already proven their stubborn and rebellious behavior (9:6–24). Only because of Moses, who repeatedly prayed on the people's behalf (vv. 18, 25), did God forgo their annihilation and allow the journey to resume (10:10–11). In reply to the question "What does your God יהוה demand of you?" (10:12), this speech answers with four principles: reverence, obedience, love, and worship.

## POSSESSION OF THE LAND BY A STIFF-NECKED PEOPLE (9:1–6)

Moses emphasizes that while the Canaanites' forthcoming defeat can be explained as retaliation for their wickedness (see Genesis 15:16), this does not mean that Israel's victory is due to their own virtues, nor is it a reward for their merits (compare 6:25; 24:13). Instead, God's loyalty to the oath to the ancestors is what maintains Israel's title to the land.

*3. a devouring fire.* This phrase transforms the allusion to the pillar of fire that guides the people during the wilderness wanderings (Exodus 13:21–22; 40:38; compare at Deuteronomy 4:24). This verse depicts God as a Warrior who will lead the people in battle as they conquer the land. (On the warrior metaphor, see further at 32:23; Exodus 14:14, 15:3; and *Haazinu*, Another View, p. 1265.)

6 Know, then, that it is not for any virtue of yours that your God יהוה is giving you this good land to possess; for you are a stiffnecked people. 7 Remember, never forget, how you provoked your God יהוה to anger in the wilderness: from the day that you left the land of Egypt until you reached this place, you have continued defiant toward יהוה. 8 At Horeb you so provoked יהוה that יהוה was angry enough with you to have destroyed you. 9 I had ascended the mountain to receive the tablets of stone, the Tablets of the Covenant that יהוה had made with you, and I stayed on the mountain forty days and forty nights, eating no bread and drinking no water. 10 And יהוה gave me the two tablets of stone inscribed by the finger of God, with the exact words that יהוה had addressed to you on the mountain out of the fire on the day of the Assembly.

11 At the end of those forty days and forty nights, יהוה gave me the two tablets of stone, the Tablets of the Covenant. 12 And יהוה said to me, "Hurry, go down from here at once, for the people whom you brought out of Egypt have acted wickedly; they have been quick to stray from the path that I enjoined upon them; they have made themselves a molten image." 13 יהוה further said to me, "I see that this is a stiffnecked people. 14 Let Me alone and I will destroy them and blot out their name from under heaven, and I will make you a nation far more numerous than they."

6 וְיָדַעְתָּ֗ כִּי֩ לֹ֨א בְצִדְקָתְךָ֜ יְהֹוָ֣ה אֱלֹהֶ֗יךָ נֹתֵ֨ן
לְךָ֜ אֶת־הָאָ֧רֶץ הַטּוֹבָ֛ה הַזֹּ֖את לְרִשְׁתָּ֑הּ כִּ֥י
עַם־קְשֵׁה־עֹ֖רֶף אָֽתָּה׃ 7 זְכֹר֙ אַל־תִּשְׁכַּ֔ח
אֵ֧ת אֲשֶׁר־הִקְצַ֛פְתָּ אֶת־יְהֹוָ֥ה אֱלֹהֶ֖יךָ
בַּמִּדְבָּ֑ר לְמִן־הַיּ֞וֹם אֲשֶׁר־יָצָ֣אתָ ׀ מֵאֶ֣רֶץ
מִצְרַ֗יִם עַד־בֹּֽאֲכֶם֙ עַד־הַמָּק֣וֹם הַזֶּ֔ה מַמְרִ֥ים
הֱיִיתֶ֖ם עִם־יְהֹוָֽה׃
8 וּבְחֹרֵ֥ב הִקְצַפְתֶּ֖ם אֶת־יְהֹוָ֑ה וַיִּתְאַנַּ֧ף יְהֹוָ֛ה
בָּכֶ֖ם לְהַשְׁמִ֥יד אֶתְכֶֽם׃ 9 בַּעֲלֹתִ֣י הָהָ֗רָה
לָקַ֜חַת לוּחֹ֤ת הָאֲבָנִים֙ לוּחֹ֣ת הַבְּרִ֔ית אֲשֶׁר־
כָּרַ֥ת יְהֹוָ֖ה עִמָּכֶ֑ם וָאֵשֵׁ֣ב בָּהָ֗ר אַרְבָּעִ֥ים יוֹם֙
וְאַרְבָּעִ֣ים לַ֔יְלָה לֶ֚חֶם לֹ֣א אָכַ֔לְתִּי וּמַ֖יִם לֹ֥א
שָׁתִֽיתִי׃ 10 וַיִּתֵּ֨ן יְהֹוָ֜ה אֵלַ֗י אֶת־שְׁנֵי֙ לוּחֹ֣ת
הָאֲבָנִ֔ים כְּתֻבִ֖ים בְּאֶצְבַּ֣ע אֱלֹהִ֑ים וַעֲלֵיהֶ֗ם
כְּֽכָל־הַדְּבָרִ֡ים אֲשֶׁר֩ דִּבֶּ֨ר יְהֹוָ֧ה עִמָּכֶ֛ם בָּהָ֖ר
מִתּ֥וֹךְ הָאֵ֖שׁ בְּי֥וֹם הַקָּהָֽל׃
11 וַיְהִ֗י מִקֵּץ֙ אַרְבָּעִ֣ים י֔וֹם וְאַרְבָּעִ֖ים לָ֑יְלָה
נָתַ֨ן יְהֹוָ֜ה אֵלַ֗י אֶת־שְׁנֵ֛י לֻחֹ֥ת הָאֲבָנִ֖ים
לֻח֥וֹת הַבְּרִֽית׃ 12 וַיֹּ֨אמֶר יְהֹוָ֜ה אֵלַ֗י ק֣וּם רֵ֤ד
מַהֵר֙ מִזֶּ֔ה כִּ֚י שִׁחֵ֣ת עַמְּךָ֔ אֲשֶׁ֥ר הוֹצֵ֖אתָ
מִמִּצְרָ֑יִם סָ֣רוּ מַהֵ֗ר מִן־הַדֶּ֙רֶךְ֙ אֲשֶׁ֣ר צִוִּיתִ֔ם
עָשׂ֥וּ לָהֶ֖ם מַסֵּכָֽה׃ 13 וַיֹּ֥אמֶר יְהֹוָ֖ה אֵלַ֣י
לֵאמֹ֑ר רָאִ֙יתִי֙ אֶת־הָעָ֣ם הַזֶּ֔ה וְהִנֵּ֥ה עַם־
קְשֵׁה־עֹ֖רֶף הֽוּא׃ 14 הֶ֤רֶף מִמֶּ֙נִּי֙ וְאַשְׁמִידֵ֔ם
וְאֶמְחֶ֣ה אֶת־שְׁמָ֔ם מִתַּ֖חַת הַשָּׁמָ֑יִם וְאֶֽעֱשֶׂה֙
אוֹתְךָ֔ לְגוֹי־עָצ֥וּם וָרָ֖ב מִמֶּֽנּוּ׃

### RETROSPECTIVE OF WILDERNESS SINS (9:7–24)

The verbal roots *k-tz-f* ("to provoke anger") and *m-r-h* ("to be defiant") serve as key words in this section, which recalls five sins that occurred in the wilderness: the Golden Calf incident (Exodus 32) and the sins at Taberah (Numbers 11:1–3), at Massah (Exodus 17:1–7), at Kibroth-hattaavah (Numbers 11:4–34), and at Kadesh-barnea (Numbers 14). This retrospective follows the journey from the establishment of the covenant in Horeb (called Sinai in Deuteronomy) to Kadesh, which designates the arrival at the border of the land (1:2, 19).

*8.* The accounts of the Golden Calf episode in Exodus 32 and Deuteronomy 9 both treat the "molten calf" as a case of idol worship rather than as an attempt to create a physical sign of God's presence (on the nature of the sin, see at Exodus 32:1–6). However, the present retelling shows several differences in comparison to the Exodus version (see below).

15 I started down the mountain, a mountain ablaze with fire, the two Tablets of the Covenant in my two hands. 16 I saw how you had sinned against your God יהוה: you had made yourselves a molten calf; you had been quick to stray from the path that יהוה had enjoined upon you. 17 Thereupon I gripped the two tablets and flung them away with both my hands, smashing them before your eyes. 18 I threw myself down before יהוה—eating no bread and drinking no water forty days and forty nights, as before—because of the great wrong you had committed, doing what displeased and vexed יהוה. 19 For I was in dread of the fierce anger against you which moved יהוה to wipe you out. And that time, too, יהוה gave heed to me.—20 Moreover, יהוה was angry enough with Aaron to have destroyed him; so I also interceded for Aaron at that time.—21 As for that sinful thing you had made, the calf, I took it and put it to the fire; I broke it to bits and ground it thoroughly until it was fine as dust, and I threw its dust into the brook that comes down from the mountain.

22 Again you provoked יהוה at Taberah, and at Massah, and at Kibroth-hattaavah.

23 And when יהוה sent you on from Kadesh-barnea, saying, "Go up and take possession of the land that I am giving you," you flouted the command of your God יהוה—whom you did not put your trust in nor obey.

24 As long as I have known you, you have been defiant toward יהוה.

15 וָאֵפֶן וָאֵרֵד מִן־הָהָר וְהָהָר בֹּעֵר בָּאֵשׁ
וּשְׁנֵי לוּחֹת הַבְּרִית עַל שְׁתֵּי יָדָי׃ 16 וָאֵרֶא
וְהִנֵּה חֲטָאתֶם לַיהֹוָה אֱלֹהֵיכֶם עֲשִׂיתֶם
לָכֶם עֵגֶל מַסֵּכָה סַרְתֶּם מַהֵר מִן־הַדֶּרֶךְ
אֲשֶׁר־צִוָּה יְהֹוָה אֶתְכֶם׃ 17 וָאֶתְפֹּשׂ בִּשְׁנֵי
הַלֻּחֹת וָאַשְׁלִכֵם מֵעַל שְׁתֵּי יָדָי וָאֲשַׁבְּרֵם
לְעֵינֵיכֶם׃ 18 וָאֶתְנַפַּל לִפְנֵי יְהֹוָה כָּרִאשֹׁנָה
אַרְבָּעִים יוֹם וְאַרְבָּעִים לַיְלָה לֶחֶם לֹא
אָכַלְתִּי וּמַיִם לֹא שָׁתִיתִי עַל כָּל־חַטַּאתְכֶם
אֲשֶׁר חֲטָאתֶם לַעֲשׂוֹת הָרַע בְּעֵינֵי יְהֹוָה
לְהַכְעִיסוֹ׃ 19 כִּי יָגֹרְתִּי מִפְּנֵי הָאַף וְהַחֵמָה
אֲשֶׁר קָצַף יְהֹוָה עֲלֵיכֶם לְהַשְׁמִיד אֶתְכֶם
וַיִּשְׁמַע יְהֹוָה אֵלַי גַּם בַּפַּעַם הַהִוא׃
20 וּבְאַהֲרֹן הִתְאַנַּף יְהֹוָה מְאֹד לְהַשְׁמִידוֹ
וָאֶתְפַּלֵּל גַּם־בְּעַד אַהֲרֹן בָּעֵת הַהִוא׃
21 וְאֶת־חַטַּאתְכֶם אֲשֶׁר־עֲשִׂיתֶם אֶת־הָעֵגֶל
לָקַחְתִּי וָאֶשְׂרֹף אֹתוֹ ׀ בָּאֵשׁ וָאֶכֹּת אֹתוֹ
טָחוֹן הֵיטֵב עַד אֲשֶׁר־דַּק לְעָפָר וָאַשְׁלִךְ
אֶת־עֲפָרוֹ אֶל־הַנַּחַל הַיֹּרֵד מִן־הָהָר׃
22 וּבְתַבְעֵרָה וּבְמַסָּה וּבְקִבְרֹת הַתַּאֲוָה
מַקְצִפִים הֱיִיתֶם אֶת־יְהֹוָה׃
23 וּבִשְׁלֹחַ יְהֹוָה אֶתְכֶם מִקָּדֵשׁ בַּרְנֵעַ
לֵאמֹר עֲלוּ וּרְשׁוּ אֶת־הָאָרֶץ אֲשֶׁר נָתַתִּי
לָכֶם וַתַּמְרוּ אֶת־פִּי יְהֹוָה אֱלֹהֵיכֶם וְלֹא
הֶאֱמַנְתֶּם לוֹ וְלֹא שְׁמַעְתֶּם בְּקֹלוֹ׃
24 מַמְרִים הֱיִיתֶם עִם־יְהֹוָה מִיּוֹם דַּעְתִּי
אֶתְכֶם׃

*18. I threw myself down before* **יהוה**. Moses recalls three times in which he prayed on behalf of the people for forty days and nights (9:18, 25–29; 10:10–11). In contrast, Exodus mentions only one prayer (32:11–13) and connects the fasting only to the second tablets (34:28). In his prayers on the people's behalf, Moses establishes a model of the prophet as intercessor between God and the people.

*20.* **יהוה** *was angry enough with Aaron to have destroyed him.* In Exodus 32, Aaron takes center stage as the major character as well as the major culprit. In contrast, this passage minimizes Aaron's role to this one verse and focuses instead on God's anger and Moses' role as intercessor, this time for Aaron's benefit.

[25]When I lay prostrate before יהוה those forty days and forty nights, because יהוה was determined to destroy you, [26]I prayed to יהוה and said, "O lord יהוה, do not annihilate Your very own people, whom You redeemed in Your majesty and whom You freed from Egypt with a mighty hand. [27]Give thought to Your servants Abraham, Isaac, and Jacob, and pay no heed to the stubbornness of this people, its wickedness, and its sinfulness. [28]Else the country from which You freed us will say, 'It was because יהוה was powerless to bring them into the land promised to them, and because of having rejected them, that [their god] brought them out to have them die in the wilderness.' [29]Yet they are Your very own people, whom You freed with Your great might and Your outstretched arm."

**10** Thereupon יהוה said to me, "Carve out two tablets of stone like the first, and come up to Me on the mountain; and make an ark of wood. [2]I will inscribe on the tablets the commandments that were on the first tablets that you smashed, and you shall deposit them in the ark."

[3]I made an ark of acacia wood and carved out two tablets of stone like the first; I took the two tablets with me and went up the mountain. [4]After inscribing on the tablets the same text as on the first—the Ten Commandments that יהוה addressed to you on the mountain out of the fire on the day of the Assembly—יהוה gave them to me. [5]Then I left

25 וָאֶתְנַפַּל לִפְנֵי יְהֹוָה אֵת אַרְבָּעִים הַיּוֹם
וְאֶת־אַרְבָּעִים הַלַּיְלָה אֲשֶׁר הִתְנַפָּלְתִּי כִּי־
אָמַר יְהֹוָה לְהַשְׁמִיד אֶתְכֶם׃ 26 וָאֶתְפַּלֵּל
אֶל־יְהֹוָה וָאֹמַר אֲדֹנָי יהוה אֱלֹהִים אַל־
תַּשְׁחֵת עַמְּךָ וְנַחֲלָתְךָ אֲשֶׁר פָּדִיתָ בְּגָדְלֶךָ
אֲשֶׁר־הוֹצֵאתָ מִמִּצְרַיִם בְּיָד חֲזָקָה׃ 27 זְכֹר
לַעֲבָדֶיךָ לְאַבְרָהָם לְיִצְחָק וּלְיַעֲקֹב אַל־תֵּפֶן
אֶל־קְשִׁי הָעָם הַזֶּה וְאֶל־רִשְׁעוֹ וְאֶל־
חַטָּאתוֹ׃ 28 פֶּן־יֹאמְרוּ הָאָרֶץ אֲשֶׁר
הוֹצֵאתָנוּ מִשָּׁם מִבְּלִי יְכֹלֶת יְהֹוָה לַהֲבִיאָם
אֶל־הָאָרֶץ אֲשֶׁר־דִּבֶּר לָהֶם וּמִשִּׂנְאָתוֹ
אוֹתָם הוֹצִיאָם לַהֲמִתָם בַּמִּדְבָּר׃ 29 וְהֵם
עַמְּךָ וְנַחֲלָתֶךָ אֲשֶׁר הוֹצֵאתָ בְּכֹחֲךָ הַגָּדֹל
וּבִזְרֹעֲךָ הַנְּטוּיָה׃ פ

י בָּעֵת הַהִוא אָמַר יְהֹוָה אֵלַי פְּסָל־לְךָ
שְׁנֵי־לוּחֹת אֲבָנִים כָּרִאשֹׁנִים וַעֲלֵה אֵלַי
הָהָרָה וְעָשִׂיתָ לְּךָ אֲרוֹן עֵץ׃ 2 וְאֶכְתֹּב עַל־
הַלֻּחֹת אֶת־הַדְּבָרִים אֲשֶׁר הָיוּ עַל־הַלֻּחֹת
הָרִאשֹׁנִים אֲשֶׁר שִׁבַּרְתָּ וְשַׂמְתָּם בָּאָרוֹן׃
3 וָאַעַשׂ אֲרוֹן עֲצֵי שִׁטִּים וָאֶפְסֹל שְׁנֵי־לֻחֹת
אֲבָנִים כָּרִאשֹׁנִים וָאַעַל הָהָרָה וּשְׁנֵי
הַלֻּחֹת בְּיָדִי׃ 4 וַיִּכְתֹּב עַל־הַלֻּחֹת כַּמִּכְתָּב
הָרִאשׁוֹן אֵת עֲשֶׂרֶת הַדְּבָרִים אֲשֶׁר דִּבֶּר
יְהֹוָה אֲלֵיכֶם בָּהָר מִתּוֹךְ הָאֵשׁ בְּיוֹם
הַקָּהָל וַיִּתְּנֵם יְהֹוָה אֵלָי׃ 5 וָאֵפֶן וָאֵרֵד

### REAFFIRMATION THAT ISRAEL IS GOD'S PEOPLE (9:25–10:11)

In this section, Moses recounts the aftermath of the Golden Calf incident—how God refrained from the express intention to destroy Israel in the wilderness, restored the covenant through the second set of tablets, and continued to lead them to the Promised Land (10:6–11). In contrast to God's previous destructive intentions (9:11–14), this section reaffirms God's commitments to the people and recounts the deeds performed to fulfill those promises.

*26–29. I prayed to* **יהוה***.* Moses presents three main reasons to refrain from destroying Israel: God's own efforts (9:26, 29), God's people (9:27), and God's enemies—the Egyptians (9:28).

*27.* In Exodus 32:13, Moses invokes the patriarchs in order to call to mind God's loyalty to the earlier promises. Here, he likewise mentions Abraham, Isaac, and Jacob, but for a different purpose: to set up a contrast with their sinful descendants.

and went down from the mountain, and I deposited the tablets in the ark that I had made, where they still are, as יהוה had commanded me.

[6]From Beeroth-bene-jaakan the Israelites marched to Moserah. Aaron died there and was buried there; and his son Eleazar became priest in his stead. [7]From there they marched to Gudgod, and from Gudgod to Jotbath, a region of running brooks.

[8]At that time יהוה set apart the tribe of Levi to carry the Ark of יהוה's Covenant, to stand in attendance upon יהוה, and to bless in God's name, as is still the case. [9]That is why Levi has received no hereditary portion along with its kin: יהוה is its portion, as your God יהוה spoke concerning it.

[10]I had stayed on the mountain, as I did the first time, forty days and forty nights; and יהוה heeded me once again: יהוה agreed not to destroy you. [11]And יהוה said to me, "Up, resume the march at the head of the people, that they may go in and possess the land that I swore to their fathers to give them."

מִן־הָהָ֔ר וָֽאָשִׂם֙ אֶת־הַלֻּחֹ֔ת בָּאָר֖וֹן אֲשֶׁ֣ר
עָשִׂ֑יתִי וַיִּ֣הְיוּ שָׁ֔ם כַּאֲשֶׁ֥ר צִוַּ֖נִי יְהֹוָֽה׃
6 וּבְנֵ֣י יִשְׂרָאֵ֗ל נָֽסְע֛וּ מִבְּאֵרֹ֥ת בְּנֵי־יַעֲקָ֖ן
מוֹסֵרָ֑ה שָׁ֣ם מֵ֤ת אַהֲרֹן֙ וַיִּקָּבֵ֣ר שָׁ֔ם וַיְכַהֵ֛ן
אֶלְעָזָ֥ר בְּנ֖וֹ תַּחְתָּֽיו׃ 7 מִשָּׁ֥ם נָֽסְע֖וּ הַגֻּדְגֹּ֑דָה
וּמִן־הַגֻּדְגֹּ֣דָה יָטְבָ֔תָה אֶ֖רֶץ נַ֥חֲלֵי מָֽיִם׃
8 בָּעֵ֣ת הַהִ֗וא הִבְדִּ֤יל יְהֹוָה֙ אֶת־שֵׁ֣בֶט הַלֵּוִ֔י
לָשֵׂ֖את אֶת־אֲר֣וֹן בְּרִית־יְהֹוָ֑ה לַעֲמֹד֩ לִפְנֵ֨י
יְהֹוָ֤ה לְשָֽׁרְתוֹ֙ וּלְבָרֵ֣ךְ בִּשְׁמ֔וֹ עַ֖ד הַיּ֥וֹם הַזֶּֽה׃
9 עַל־כֵּ֞ן לֹא־הָיָ֧ה לְלֵוִ֛י חֵ֥לֶק וְנַחֲלָ֖ה עִם־
אֶחָ֑יו יְהֹוָה֙ ה֣וּא נַחֲלָת֔וֹ כַּאֲשֶׁ֥ר דִּבֶּ֛ר יְהֹוָ֥ה
אֱלֹהֶ֖יךָ לֽוֹ׃

10 וְאָנֹכִ֞י עָמַ֣דְתִּי בָהָ֗ר כַּיָּמִים֙ הָרִ֣אשֹׁנִ֔ים
אַרְבָּעִ֣ים י֔וֹם וְאַרְבָּעִ֖ים לָ֑יְלָה וַיִּשְׁמַ֨ע
יְהֹוָ֜ה אֵלַ֗י גַּ֚ם בַּפַּ֣עַם הַהִ֔וא לֹא־אָבָ֥ה
יְהֹוָ֖ה הַשְׁחִיתֶֽךָ׃ 11 וַיֹּ֤אמֶר יְהֹוָה֙ אֵלַ֔י ק֛וּם
לֵ֥ךְ לְמַסַּ֖ע לִפְנֵ֣י הָעָ֑ם וְיָבֹ֙אוּ֙ וְיִֽירְשׁ֣וּ אֶת־
הָאָ֔רֶץ אֲשֶׁר־נִשְׁבַּ֥עְתִּי לַאֲבֹתָ֖ם לָתֵ֥ת
לָהֶֽם׃ פ

*10:5. I deposited the tablets in the ark.* In Deuteronomy, the Ark serves as a container to protect the tablets, just as ancient Near Eastern officials deposited political treaties in their cities' temples. In contrast, Exodus conceives of the Ark as God's throne, a symbol of God's presence, as well as a container for the Tablets of the Pact (see at Exodus 25:10–22).

*8. יהוה set apart the tribe of Levi.* Choosing the Levites for certain religious responsibilities is presented as a further consequence of the Golden Calf incident, in recognition of when the men of Levi rallied to Moses' call and killed 3,000 perpetrators (Exodus 32:26–29). In specifying the roles of the tribe of Levi, Deuteronomy presents an inclusive approach to "the priests, sons of Levi" (21:5; see at 18:1), in contrast to the distinction in priestly texts between the descendants of Aaron, who serve as priests (*kohanim*), and the other descendants of Levi, who are referred to simply as "Levites" (Numbers 3–4).

*11. "Up, resume."* Heb. *kum lech*, which evokes God's previous command to Moses following the construction of the calf—*kum red*, "Hurry, go down" (9:12)—and signals the reconciliation in the relationship between God and Israel.

*possess the land.* Moses concludes the retelling of the covenant's restoration by returning to the main theme of this sermon: the possession of the Promised Land (9:1–6).

12And now, O Israel, what does your God יהוה
demand of you? Only this: to revere your God
יהוה, to walk only in divine paths, to love and to
serve your God יהוה with all your heart and soul,
13keeping יהוה's commandments and laws, which I
enjoin upon you today, for your good. 14Mark, the
heavens to their uttermost reaches belong to your
God יהוה, the earth and all that is on it! 15Yet it was
to your ancestors that יהוה was drawn out of love
for them, so that you, their lineal descendants, were
chosen from among all peoples—as is now the case.
16Cut away, therefore, the thickening about your
hearts and stiffen your necks no more. 17For your
God יהוה is God supreme and Lord supreme, the
great, the mighty, and the awesome God, who
shows no favor and takes no bribe, 18but upholds
the cause of the fatherless and the widow, and be-
friends the stranger, providing food and clothing.—

12 וְעַתָּה יִשְׂרָאֵל מָה יְהוָה אֱלֹהֶיךָ שֹׁאֵל
מֵעִמָּךְ כִּי אִם־לְיִרְאָה אֶת־יְהוָה אֱלֹהֶיךָ
לָלֶכֶת בְּכָל־דְּרָכָיו וּלְאַהֲבָה אֹתוֹ וְלַעֲבֹד
אֶת־יְהוָה אֱלֹהֶיךָ בְּכָל־לְבָבְךָ וּבְכָל־נַפְשֶׁךָ׃
13 לִשְׁמֹר אֶת־מִצְוֺת יְהוָה וְאֶת־חֻקֹּתָיו
אֲשֶׁר אָנֹכִי מְצַוְּךָ הַיּוֹם לְטוֹב לָךְ׃ 14 הֵן
לַיהוָה אֱלֹהֶיךָ הַשָּׁמַיִם וּשְׁמֵי הַשָּׁמָיִם
הָאָרֶץ וְכָל־אֲשֶׁר־בָּהּ׃ 15 רַק בַּאֲבֹתֶיךָ
חָשַׁק יְהוָה לְאַהֲבָה אוֹתָם וַיִּבְחַר בְּזַרְעָם
אַחֲרֵיהֶם בָּכֶם מִכָּל־הָעַמִּים כַּיּוֹם הַזֶּה׃
16 וּמַלְתֶּם אֵת עָרְלַת לְבַבְכֶם וְעָרְפְּכֶם לֹא
תַקְשׁוּ עוֹד׃ 17 כִּי יְהוָה אֱלֹהֵיכֶם הוּא
אֱלֹהֵי הָאֱלֹהִים וַאֲדֹנֵי הָאֲדֹנִים הָאֵל הַגָּדֹל
הַגִּבֹּר וְהַנּוֹרָא אֲשֶׁר לֹא־יִשָּׂא פָנִים וְלֹא
יִקַּח שֹׁחַד׃ 18 עֹשֶׂה מִשְׁפַּט יָתוֹם וְאַלְמָנָה
וְאֹהֵב גֵּר לָתֶת לוֹ לֶחֶם וְשִׂמְלָה׃

## CALL FOR REVERENCE, OBEDIENCE, LOVE, AND WORSHIP (10:12–22)

Based on this rebellious history, Moses outlines five principal demands for the people to follow in order to ensure that they thrive once they enter the land: to revere, to walk, to love, to serve, to keep (vv. 12–13). The force of these requirements lies in their inclusive, general character (compare the detailed commandments in Exodus 34:10–26).

*16. Cut away, therefore, the thickening about your hearts.* Literally, "circumcise the foreskin of your heart." This expression refers to the metaphoric removal of the emotional blocks that prevent the people from following God's teachings and that result in their rebellious behavior (see also at 30:6; Leviticus 26:41; Jeremiah 4:4).

*17. God supreme and Lord supreme.* Literally, "the god of gods, and the lord of lords." Ancient Near Eastern texts employ these two epithets as royal attributes. Here and elsewhere, Deuteronomy refers to the existence of other deities, in relation to which God proves incomparable in majesty and powers (see also at 4:19–20; 6:4; 32:8). [Calling God the "lord of lords" takes for granted the ancient Near Eastern hierarchies of status and gender, while proclaiming that God's authority transcends even male authority figures. —*Ed.*]

***who shows no favor and takes no bribe.*** Verses 17–18 depict God metaphorically as the ideal ruler. The first part of this verse reflects one of the king's major roles: to be a mighty warrior. This second part refers to the king's other key function: to be a judge who defends the poor and needy with justice and loving-kindness (as in Psalms 72; 146:5–10). [Recourse to male imagery does not necessarily mean that the composer(s) of Deuteronomy conceived of Israel's God as a male being. See further at 33:5. —*Ed.*]

*18. the fatherless and the widow... the stranger.* Heb. *yatom v'almanah... ger.* These are the three disadvantaged members of the society for whom Deuteronomy repeatedly demands legal protection (24:17–18; 27:19) and economic support

19 You too must befriend the stranger, for you were
strangers in the land of Egypt.
20 You must revere יהוה: only your God shall
you worship, to [God] shall you hold fast, and by
God's name shall you swear. 21 [יהוה] is your glory
and your God, who wrought for you those marvelous, awesome deeds that you saw with your own
eyes. 22 Your ancestors went down to Egypt seventy
persons; and now your God יהוה has made you as
numerous as the stars of heaven.
11 Love, therefore, your God יהוה, and always keep God's charge, God's laws, God's rules,
and God's commandments.
2 Take thought this day that it was not your
children, who neither experienced nor witnessed
the lesson of your God יהוה—

God's majesty, mighty hand, and outstretched arm; 3 the signs and the deeds that
[God] performed in Egypt against Pharaoh
king of Egypt and all his land; 4 what [God]
did to Egypt's army, its horses and chariots;
how יהוה rolled back upon them the waters of

19 וַאֲהַבְתֶּם אֶת־הַגֵּר כִּי־גֵרִים הֱיִיתֶם
בְּאֶרֶץ מִצְרָיִם׃
20 אֶת־יְהֹוָה אֱלֹהֶיךָ תִּירָא אֹתוֹ תַעֲבֹד וּבוֹ
תִדְבָּק וּבִשְׁמוֹ תִּשָּׁבֵעַ׃ 21 הוּא תְהִלָּתְךָ
וְהוּא אֱלֹהֶיךָ אֲשֶׁר־עָשָׂה אִתְּךָ אֶת־הַגְּדֹלֹת
וְאֶת־הַנּוֹרָאֹת הָאֵלֶּה אֲשֶׁר רָאוּ עֵינֶיךָ׃
22 בְּשִׁבְעִים נֶפֶשׁ יָרְדוּ אֲבֹתֶיךָ מִצְרָיְמָה
וְעַתָּה שָׂמְךָ יְהֹוָה אֱלֹהֶיךָ כְּכוֹכְבֵי הַשָּׁמַיִם
לָרֹב׃
יא וְאָהַבְתָּ אֵת יְהֹוָה אֱלֹהֶיךָ וְשָׁמַרְתָּ
מִשְׁמַרְתּוֹ וְחֻקֹּתָיו וּמִשְׁפָּטָיו וּמִצְוֺתָיו כָּל־
הַיָּמִים׃
2 וִידַעְתֶּם הַיּוֹם כִּי ׀ לֹא אֶת־בְּנֵיכֶם אֲשֶׁר
לֹא־יָדְעוּ וַאֲשֶׁר לֹא־רָאוּ אֶת־מוּסַר יְהֹוָה
אֱלֹהֵיכֶם

אֶת־גָּדְלוֹ אֶת־יָדוֹ הַחֲזָקָה וּזְרֹעוֹ הַנְּטוּיָה׃
3 וְאֶת־אֹתֹתָיו וְאֶת־מַעֲשָׂיו אֲשֶׁר עָשָׂה
בְּתוֹךְ מִצְרָיִם לְפַרְעֹה מֶלֶךְ־מִצְרַיִם
וּלְכָל־אַרְצוֹ׃ 4 וַאֲשֶׁר עָשָׂה לְחֵיל מִצְרַיִם
לְסוּסָיו וּלְרִכְבּוֹ אֲשֶׁר הֵצִיף אֶת־מֵי

(14:28–29; 16:11, 14; 24:19–21; 26:12–13; note that the landless Levite is included among the needy).

Our verse is unique in presenting God in two roles, both as their legal defender ("upholds the cause of") and as their provider ("providing food and clothing"); compare Exodus 22:20–23; Psalm 146:9. (See also Another View, p. 1108.)

*19. the stranger.* Heb. *ger* refers to those who are alien to their place of sojourn, like Abraham immigrating to Canaan (Genesis 23:4), Moses in Jethro's house (Exodus 2:22), and most of all, Israel as strangers in Egypt (Genesis 15:13), a key part of Israel's national consciousness. Based on the memory of this experience, all biblical legal collections empathetically demand the favorable treatment of strangers, including their legal and economic protection (see also Exodus 22:20; 23:9; Leviticus 19:34).

## *Occupation of the Land as Divine Reward or Punishment* (11:1–25)

The third speech of *Eikev* continues Deuteronomy's characteristic attitude toward time: the notion that historical observations provide central lessons for the present, and critical signs for the future. This sermon concentrates on the future possession and inheritance of the land, promising prosperity as the major reward for obedience, while threatening total annihilation in retaliation for disobedience.

### PAST LESSONS AS MOTIVATION FOR FUTURE ACTIONS (11:1–9)

In the middle of the demand to obey God's commandments (v. 1) and the promised reward of

the Sea of Reeds when they were pursuing
you, thus destroying them once and for all;
5what [God] did for you in the wilderness before you arrived in this place; 6and what
[God] did to Dathan and Abiram, sons of
Eliab son of Reuben, when the earth opened
her mouth and swallowed them, along with
their households, their tents, and every living
thing in their train, from amidst all Israel—
7but that it was you who saw with your own eyes all
the marvelous deeds that יהוה performed.

8Keep, therefore, all the Instruction that I enjoin upon you today, so that you may have the
strength to enter and take possession of the land
that you are about to cross into and possess, 9and
that you may long endure upon the soil that יהוה
swore to your fathers to assign to them and to their
heirs, a land flowing with milk and honey.

10For the land that you are about to enter and

יַם־סוּף עַל־פְּנֵיהֶם בְּרָדְפָם אַחֲרֵיכֶם
וַיְאַבְּדֵם יְהוָה עַד הַיּוֹם הַזֶּה׃ 5 וַאֲשֶׁר
עָשָׂה לָכֶם בַּמִּדְבָּר עַד־בֹּאֲכֶם עַד־
הַמָּקוֹם הַזֶּה׃ 6 וַאֲשֶׁר עָשָׂה לְדָתָן
וְלַאֲבִירָם בְּנֵי אֱלִיאָב בֶּן־רְאוּבֵן אֲשֶׁר
פָּצְתָה הָאָרֶץ אֶת־פִּיהָ וַתִּבְלָעֵם וְאֶת־
בָּתֵּיהֶם וְאֶת־אָהֳלֵיהֶם וְאֵת כָּל־הַיְקוּם
אֲשֶׁר בְּרַגְלֵיהֶם בְּקֶרֶב כָּל־יִשְׂרָאֵל׃
7 כִּי עֵינֵיכֶם הָרֹאֹת אֶת־כָּל־מַעֲשֵׂה יְהוָה
הַגָּדֹל אֲשֶׁר עָשָׂה׃
8 וּשְׁמַרְתֶּם אֶת־כָּל־הַמִּצְוָה אֲשֶׁר אָנֹכִי
מְצַוְּךָ הַיּוֹם לְמַעַן תֶּחֶזְקוּ וּבָאתֶם וִירִשְׁתֶּם
אֶת־הָאָרֶץ אֲשֶׁר אַתֶּם עֹבְרִים שָׁמָּה
לְרִשְׁתָּהּ׃ 9 וּלְמַעַן תַּאֲרִיכוּ יָמִים עַל־
הָאֲדָמָה אֲשֶׁר נִשְׁבַּע יְהוָה לַאֲבֹתֵיכֶם
לָתֵת לָהֶם וּלְזַרְעָם אֶרֶץ זָבַת חָלָב
וּדְבָשׁ׃ ס
10 כִּי הָאָרֶץ אֲשֶׁר אַתָּה בָא־שָׁמָּה לְרִשְׁתָּהּ

possessing and enduring upon the land (vv. 8–9), a long and complicated sentence (vv. 2–7) sets the present wilderness generation apart from their descendants (compare the distinction between the present generation and their ancestors in 5:2–5). The verb *raah* ("to see" or "to witness") recurs twice (vv. 2, 7), the first time in conjunction with the verb *yada* ("to know" or "to experience"), thus demonstrating that the major generational difference resides in the actual, first-hand witnessing of God's deeds. This cardinal concept of a direct experience of God's involvement in Israel's history governs the historical consciousness of Israel, as exemplified by the repeated command to retell the story of the exodus to one's children (Exodus 12:26–27; 13:14; Deuteronomy 6:20–21), as well as in the historical recitation at the first-fruit ceremony (26:5–10) and the ratification of the covenant on the Plains of Moab (28:69–30:20).

5. ***what** [God] **did for you.*** Rather, "what [God] did *to* you." In the Hebrew, Moses employs the expression "*asah l-*" four times in this passage; in v. 3, it is translated as "performed . . . against," and as "did to" in vv. 4 and 6. Although the Hebrew preposition can have either meaning, here it should be understood in line with the rest of this passage, in which the enumerated divine deeds are all punitive, aimed at the Egyptians (vv. 3–4) and Israelites alike (vv. 5–6).

## SPECIAL QUALITIES OF THE LAND AND INCENTIVES TO OBEY GOD (11:10–21)

In this part of his speech, Moses draws attention to geographical and climatic qualities of the Promised Land, resulting in the marked differences between agriculture in Israel and Egypt. The ability to enjoy the special features of the land will depend on the people's conduct.

possess is not like the land of Egypt from which you have come. There the grain you sowed had to be watered by your own labors, like a vegetable garden; [11]but the land you are about to cross into and possess, a land of hills and valleys, soaks up its water from the rains of heaven. [12]It is a land which your God יהוה looks after, on which your God יהוה always keeps an eye, from year's beginning to year's end.

[13]If, then, you obey the commandments that I enjoin upon you this day, loving your God יהוה and serving [God] with all your heart and soul, [14]I will grant the rain for your land in season, the early rain and the late. You shall gather in your new grain and wine and oil—[15]I will also provide grass in the fields for your cattle—and thus you shall eat your fill. [16]Take care not to be lured away to serve other gods and bow to them. [17]For יהוה's anger will flare up against you, shutting up the skies so that there will be no rain and the ground will not yield its produce; and you will soon perish from the good land that יהוה is assigning to you.

לֹא כְאֶרֶץ מִצְרַיִם הִוא אֲשֶׁר יְצָאתֶם מִשָּׁם
אֲשֶׁר תִּזְרַע אֶת־זַרְעֲךָ וְהִשְׁקִיתָ בְרַגְלְךָ כְּגַן
הַיָּרָק׃ 11 וְהָאָרֶץ אֲשֶׁר אַתֶּם עֹבְרִים שָׁמָּה
לְרִשְׁתָּהּ אֶרֶץ הָרִים וּבְקָעֹת לִמְטַר הַשָּׁמַיִם
תִּשְׁתֶּה־מָּיִם׃ 12 אֶרֶץ אֲשֶׁר־יְהֹוָה אֱלֹהֶיךָ
דֹּרֵשׁ אֹתָהּ תָּמִיד עֵינֵי יְהֹוָה אֱלֹהֶיךָ בָּהּ
מֵרֵשִׁית הַשָּׁנָה וְעַד אַחֲרִית שָׁנָה׃ ס
13 וְהָיָה אִם־שָׁמֹעַ תִּשְׁמְעוּ אֶל־מִצְוֺתַי
אֲשֶׁר אָנֹכִי מְצַוֶּה אֶתְכֶם הַיּוֹם לְאַהֲבָה
אֶת־יְהֹוָה אֱלֹהֵיכֶם וּלְעָבְדוֹ בְּכָל־לְבַבְכֶם
וּבְכָל־נַפְשְׁכֶם׃ 14 וְנָתַתִּי מְטַר־אַרְצְכֶם
בְּעִתּוֹ יוֹרֶה וּמַלְקוֹשׁ וְאָסַפְתָּ דְגָנֶךָ וְתִירֹשְׁךָ
וְיִצְהָרֶךָ׃ 15 וְנָתַתִּי עֵשֶׂב בְּשָׂדְךָ לִבְהֶמְתֶּךָ
וְאָכַלְתָּ וְשָׂבָעְתָּ׃ 16 הִשָּׁמְרוּ לָכֶם פֶּן יִפְתֶּה
לְבַבְכֶם וְסַרְתֶּם וַעֲבַדְתֶּם אֱלֹהִים אֲחֵרִים
וְהִשְׁתַּחֲוִיתֶם לָהֶם׃ 17 וְחָרָה אַף־יְהֹוָה
בָּכֶם וְעָצַר אֶת־הַשָּׁמַיִם וְלֹא־יִהְיֶה מָטָר
וְהָאֲדָמָה לֹא תִתֵּן אֶת־יְבוּלָהּ וַאֲבַדְתֶּם
מְהֵרָה מֵעַל הָאָרֶץ הַטֹּבָה אֲשֶׁר יְהֹוָה נֹתֵן
לָכֶם׃

***10. watered by your own labors.*** Literally, "watered by your foot." With the Nile as its main, year-round water source, Egypt's agriculture is based on an irrigation system of ditches, canals, and reservoirs constructed to lead the water from the river to the fields. Farmers control the water flow to each field by using the heels of their feet to easily open a channel in the simple dirt ridges of the irrigation system.

*11.* Since Israel depends on seasonal rains, its agriculture differs dramatically from that of Egypt. The water resources are never assured, for the number of rainy days and amount of rain from year to year change rapidly due to fluctuation in the winds and other climate conditions.

***12. a land which your God*** **יהוה** ***looks after.*** The instability of the water resources obliges God's careful attention. What may seem like the land's disadvantage turns out to be a measure of Israel's dependence on—and confidence in—God.

***13. If, then, you obey.*** This passage links the distinctive qualities of the land and its agricultural fertility to the concept of divine reward and retribution. God rewards obedience via timely rain that will assure plenitude of crops and success; God retaliates against disobedience with a lack of rain—and thus with a lack of produce that will result in famine and annihilation.

Having given these geographical and climatic conditions such theological importance, vv. 13–21 were incorporated by the Rabbis into the daily liturgy as the second paragraph of the *Sh'ma*, following the *V'ahavta* (6:5–9). The Rabbis further secured the prominence of this passage by having it placed in the mezuzah and in the *t'fillin*, along with other passages from the Torah.

[18]Therefore impress these My words upon your
very heart: bind them as a sign on your hand and let
them serve as a symbol on your forehead, [19]and
teach them to your children—reciting them when
you stay at home and when you are away, when you
lie down and when you get up; [20]and inscribe them
on the doorposts of your house and on your gates—
[21]to the end that you and your children may endure, in the land that יהוה swore to your fathers to
assign to them, as long as there is a heaven over the
earth.
[22]If, then, you faithfully keep all this Instruction
that I command you, loving your God יהוה, walking in all God's ways, and holding fast to [God],
[23]יהוה will dislodge before you all these nations: you
will dispossess nations greater and more numerous
than you. [24]Every spot on which your foot treads
shall be yours; your territory shall extend from the
wilderness to the Lebanon and from the River—the

18 וְשַׂמְתֶּם אֶת־דְּבָרַי אֵלֶּה עַל־לְבַבְכֶם
וְעַל־נַפְשְׁכֶם וּקְשַׁרְתֶּם אֹתָם לְאוֹת
עַל־יֶדְכֶם וְהָיוּ לְטוֹטָפֹת בֵּין עֵינֵיכֶם׃
19 וְלִמַּדְתֶּם אֹתָם אֶת־בְּנֵיכֶם לְדַבֵּר בָּם
בְּשִׁבְתְּךָ בְּבֵיתֶךָ וּבְלֶכְתְּךָ בַדֶּרֶךְ וּבְשָׁכְבְּךָ
וּבְקוּמֶךָ׃ 20 וּכְתַבְתָּם עַל־מְזוּזוֹת בֵּיתֶךָ
וּבִשְׁעָרֶיךָ׃ 21 לְמַעַן יִרְבּוּ יְמֵיכֶם וִימֵי
בְנֵיכֶם עַל הָאֲדָמָה אֲשֶׁר נִשְׁבַּע יְהֹוָה
לַאֲבֹתֵיכֶם לָתֵת לָהֶם כִּימֵי הַשָּׁמַיִם עַל־
הָאָרֶץ׃ ס
22 כִּי אִם־שָׁמֹר תִּשְׁמְרוּן אֶת־כָּל־הַמִּצְוָה
הַזֹּאת אֲשֶׁר אָנֹכִי מְצַוֶּה אֶתְכֶם לַעֲשֹׂתָהּ
לְאַהֲבָה אֶת־יְהֹוָה אֱלֹהֵיכֶם לָלֶכֶת בְּכָל־
דְּרָכָיו וּלְדָבְקָה־בוֹ׃ 23 וְהוֹרִישׁ יְהֹוָה אֶת־
כָּל־הַגּוֹיִם הָאֵלֶּה מִלִּפְנֵיכֶם וִירִשְׁתֶּם גּוֹיִם
גְּדֹלִים וַעֲצֻמִים מִכֶּם׃ 24 כָּל־הַמָּקוֹם אֲשֶׁר
תִּדְרֹךְ כַּף־רַגְלְכֶם בּוֹ לָכֶם יִהְיֶה מִן־
הַמִּדְבָּר וְהַלְּבָנוֹן מִן־הַנָּהָר נְהַר־פְּרָת וְעַד

*18. sign . . . symbol.* See at Exodus 13:9.

### VICTORY AND TERRITORY AS REWARDS FOR OBEDIENCE (11:22–25)

Obedience and love reoccur at the close of this speech, though in reverse order (v. 22 in comparison to v. 1). This section contains yet another conditional statement, promising that obedience will result in military success, victory, and possession of the land within wide borders (vv. 23–25). The wording underscores the claimed linkage between the demand and its reward through a symmetrical repetition of four phrases designating an entirety (*kol*): "all this Instruction" and "all God's ways" in the clause that expresses the condition (v. 22); "all these nations" and "every spot" in the clause that expresses the consequence (vv. 23–24).

*24. Every spot on which your foot treads shall be yours.* This promise here and in v. 25 reflects an ancient Near Eastern legal practice of establishing ownership of a land by walking through it. This notion gains a theological-ideological content in the biblical concept of the land (see Genesis 13:17; Joshua 1:3–4).

*from the wilderness to the Lebanon and from the River . . . to the Western Sea.* The present description is unique in its four poles. It starts with the earthly regions from south (the Sinai wilderness) to north (Lebanon, as in 1:7; Joshua 1:4), and then proceeds to the water resources from the northeast (the Euphrates) to the southwest extremes (the Mediterranean Sea). This language seems not to designate actual borders of the land, but instead to demonstrate divine promises of political sovereignty (see also at 1:7).

Euphrates—to the Western Sea. [25]No one shall stand up to you: your God יהוה will put the dread and the fear of you over the whole land in which you set foot, as promised.

הַיָּם הָאַחֲר֔וֹן יִהְיֶ֖ה גְּבֻלְכֶֽם׃ 25 לֹא־יִתְיַצֵּ֥ב
אִ֖ישׁ בִּפְנֵיכֶ֑ם פַּחְדְּכֶ֨ם וּמוֹרַאֲכֶ֜ם יִתֵּ֣ן ׀ יְהֹוָ֣ה
אֱלֹהֵיכֶ֗ם עַל־פְּנֵ֤י כָל־הָאָ֙רֶץ֙ אֲשֶׁ֣ר תִּדְרְכוּ־
בָ֔הּ כַּאֲשֶׁ֖ר דִּבֶּ֥ר לָכֶֽם׃ ס

*25. as promised.* This phrase evokes the promises with which the first and the second speeches of *parashat Eikev* open (see 7:17–24 and 9:1).

Although filled with chastisement and threats, along with promises, the Torah portion ends as it began, with an assurance. The prospect of blessings and success thus frames the entire parashah.

*—Dalit Rom-Shiloni*

## Another View

AMONG ALL THE BLESSINGS and exhortations of *parashat Eikev*, the social role of women is addressed most explicitly with reference to the widow (10:18). In a patriarchal world, the widow, like the fatherless child, lacks a man to defend her rights. According to the Bible, the *almanah* (widow) functions in an ill-defined but usually perilous role, for women are primarily defined by their relationships to men in positions of power, first as daughters and then as wives. When no grandfather, father, or adult son is living, an *almanah* has no man with authority over her—or responsibility for her. Although an *almanah* may be independent of male domination, she would probably have difficulty functioning as an autonomous individual in ancient Israel's kinship-based, agricultural society.

In this context, God appeals to justice: an *almanah* must be recognized as an independent agent in order to support herself; to do otherwise would be unjust. God seeks redress, not out of sympathy for the "pitiable" widow, but because the woman should rightly be allowed to function on her own authority. (See Numbers 30:10, which holds widows and divorcees solely responsible for their vows, in contrast to young-adult daughters and to wives.)

Deuteronomy is particularly concerned with the *almanah*; it employs the word eleven times (10:18; 14:29; 16:11, 14; 24:17, 19, 20, 21; 26:12, 13; 27:19), compared to six instances in the rest of the Torah. In Deuteronomy, she is always mentioned with the command that her welfare be guaranteed and protected. Significantly, the masculine form of the word appears only once in the Bible (Jeremiah 51:5), whereas *almanah* (singular or plural) appears fifty-five times with the sense of "widow." Several biblical narratives illustrate the problems that widows face and some of the areas where they experience autonomy. Judging by I Samuel 25, wealthy widows probably do well, for there Abigail seems to inherit her husband's property before she marries David. On the other hand, the story of Ruth and Naomi illustrates the peril of poor widows with no one to advocate or provide for them.

*Deuteronomy is particularly concerned with widows.*

*—Lillian Klein Abensohn*

## Post-biblical Interpretations

***who fed you in the wilderness with manna*** (8:16). Here God is portrayed in feminine terms as a provider of food. It is usually women who do the cooking and baking in the Bible, as illustrated by the "Woman of Valor," who rises early to cook and bake (Proverbs 31:15), and by Sarah, who prepares all manner of food for the visitors (Genesis 18:6–7). The Rabbis record the seven tasks expected of a wife, including grinding grain, baking bread, and cooking food (Mishnah *K'tubot* 5:5). Women were also expected to perform the accompanying religious rituals, such as separating a portion of dough for the priest (Numbers 15:20; Mishnah *Shabbat* 2:6).

***As for that sinful thing you had made, the calf, I . . . ground it thoroughly*** (9:21). In this passage,

Moses recounts how he put the Golden Calf to the fire, ground it thoroughly, and threw the dust into the brook. The version in Exodus 32:20 is a bit different, for it describes how Moses burned the calf, ground it into dust, sprinkled the dust on the water, and made the people drink. The latter's similarity to the *sotah* ritual in Numbers 5 is obvious. Just as the wife accused of adultery must be tested by drinking a potion, so the Israelites had to drink the dust of the idol for which they abandoned God. This parallel creates the impression, further developed by the biblical prophets, that Israel's relationship with God was like that of a wife and husband or a pair of lovers. In worshiping an idol, Israel betrayed an intimate partner; therefore, God's punishment was swift and severe. It is ironic that the Rabbis deduce from the phrase "and all the people took off the gold rings that were in their ears" (Exodus 32:3) that the women refused to hand their rings over to their husbands for inclusion in the Calf. God rewarded the women with a holiday of their own, Rosh Chodesh, the New Moon, a day on which they were to abstain from household chores (*Pirkei D'Rabbi Eliezer* 45).

*The Rabbis consider women to be better advocates before God than men are.*

***upholds the cause of the fatherless and the widow*** (10:18). In the rabbinic period, a principal purpose of the marriage contract (*k'tubah*) was to provide women with economic sustenance when widowed or divorced. Nevertheless, much like the Bible did, talmudic texts often portray widows as needing protection and financial support (see, for example, BT *Gittin* 35a).

***If, then, you obey the commandments*** (11:13–21). This passage constitutes the second paragraph of the *Sh'ma* (Mishnah *B'rachot* 2:2) that is traditionally recited twice daily, together with 6:4–9 (*Sh'ma*) and Numbers 15:37–41 (on *tzitzit*). Mishnah *B'rachot* 3:3 exempts women from the daily obligation to recite the *Sh'ma* and from donning *t'fillin* (11:18), but it obligates them to hang a mezuzah on the doorposts of their home (11:20), pray daily, and recite the blessing after meals (*Birkat HaMazon*). Most of these exemptions and obligations are consistent with the general rules enunciated in Mishnah *Kiddushin* 1:7, that women are exempt from positive time-dependent ritual acts but obligated to all others. Recitation of the *Sh'ma* and donning *t'fillin* must be done at specified times of the day, whereas hanging a mezuzah may be done at any time. But women are obligated to prayer at fixed times because the Rabbis consider them better advocates before God than men are (BT *B'rachot* 20b).

***loving your God*** יהוה ***and serving*** [*God*] ***with all your heart and soul*** (11:13). The Rabbis attach to these words one of their favorite ideas: that one must be engaged in study for its own sake (*Torah lishmah*). Should people say that they will learn in order to become rich, or to be called "Rabbi," or to receive a reward in the world-to-come, this verse teaches that such motivations are not acceptable. Instead, one should spend time in the study of Torah for its own sake—out of the love both of learning and of engagement with God's words (*Sifrei D'varim, Eikev* 41). Since women were not obligated to study sacred texts, any instance of women engaged in Torah study implies that it was for its own sake. A clear but chilling case of a woman studying Torah can be found in BT *Yoma* 66b: a woman came before Rabbi Eliezer and asked him a detailed question about the punishments meted out by God for worship of the Golden Calf; but he would not answer her. The reason for his reticence, according to another version of this tale (JT *Sotah* 3:3, 19a), was that "it is better to burn the words of Torah than turn them over to women."

—*Judith Hauptman*

# Contemporary Reflection

SCRIPTURE DESCENDS to speak to us, using metaphor to reveal the holy. In *parashat Eikev*, we find references to the "mighty hand and the outstretched arm" by which God liberated the Israelites from Egypt (7:19). When the Torah uses the human body as a code to decipher God, we glimpse through ourselves the presence of the One in whose image we are created. Knowing that God is incorporeal, some find such physical descriptions of God inadequate and turn to the natural world. Thus we may imagine God as a rock (*hatzur*, as in 32:4), as dew (Hosea 14:6), or as a spring of living water (Jeremiah 17:13). Nevertheless, if we look closely at the corporeal imagery in *parashat Eikev*, we discover that its imagery hints at the luminous potentiality of our bodies to experience God.

The portion begins, "And if (*eikev*) you do obey these rules and observe them carefully, your God יהוה will maintain faithfully for you the covenant" (7:12). Why is the term *eikev* (here translated as "if") used to introduce the conditional clause, instead of a word more commonly employed for that purpose (such as *im* or *ki*)? The unusual language that begins our parashah invites the early medieval commentator Rashi to engage in word play, linking *eikev* to the noun *akeiv* ("heel"). Rashi writes that if we heed even minor commandments that are easy to trample over with our heels (in other words, commandments that we are likely to treat lightly), then God will keep the promises given to our ancestors. Read in this manner, the portion opens with a warning about not allowing thick skin to divert us from the path on which we walk toward God. Like Moses who takes off his sandals to experience holiness emanating from the earth, so we too are called to remove all barriers between God and ourselves.

The next verse states, "[God] will favor you and bless you and multiply you—blessing your issue of the (literally: your) womb" (7:13). What is interesting here is that the Hebrew wording is all in the masculine singular. Are men imagined as having wombs, or more darkly, as owning women's wombs? Perhaps we can generously understand the verse as a suggestion that empathy can allow anyone to feel the blessing of a full womb. We know God first as the Creator, the womb of the world. The organ that nurtures potential life may be found in only half the population, yet the Torah suggests that both men and women celebrate pregnancy and birth.

If we accept this idea, then women can look at a later verse in our parashah that speaks in an unequivocally male metaphor and not feel excluded. Although

*Like Moses, we too are called to remove all barriers between God and ourselves.*

our translation reads, "Cut away... the thickening about your hearts" (10:16), a more literal translation of this verse is, "Circumcise... the foreskin of your heart." In other words, remove that which obstructs your heart and keeps you from following God's teachings; open yourself up to experiencing "the great, the mighty, and the awesome God" (10:17). The foreskin in this expression can be likened to the thick skin on our feet that keeps us from feeling our connection to the Holy most intimately. Women and men alike can have a heart that is tender, loving, and open to the Divine, not just those who have literally been circumcised.

The metaphor that calls for a naked heart may help us to understand a deeper reason for the mysterious—and frankly disturbing—ritual of *b'rit milah* (circumcision). Native American and Mayan beliefs align with Kabbalah in understanding the left side of the body as feminine and the right as masculine. Since the heart rests on the left side, circumcising the heart brings feminine energies into play. Would the addition of a circumcised heart bring into a balance the masculine and feminine energies? Perhaps the metaphor found in *parashat Eikev* hints that the purpose of the ritual is to remind both men and women to keep the heart tender, for this is not only a woman's quality.

The circumcised heart is not gender specific. All of us are called to bring forth creative and nurturing energy within ourselves and to act with an empathic heart. Some say that the reason girls do not have an equivalent physical ritual to *b'rit milah* is that they are born circumcised, the implication being that they are born with unveiled hearts. *B'rit milah*, then, becomes a spiritual catch-up for boys to approach the open-hearted potential of girls.

Being a mother of sons, I have trouble with this explanation, yet we know that women walk through the world with circumcised hearts by their very place in many cultures. They reveal themselves because they often have less power and therefore less to lose. When we think of the hardened, calloused heel that feels little under it, experience shows that women do not have the luxury of stepping without looking carefully. Every misstep becomes a reason for others to keep us back; it becomes an accusation of our iniquity or incompetence.

Rabbi David Mark sees *b'rit milah* in a broadened mythic context when he compares the phallus to the ancient symbol that the Greeks called *ouroboros*, the mystical snake that rolls through eternity with its tail in its mouth. He asserts that removing the foreskin from the phallus is like when the snake—a symbol of eternal life—sheds its skin. As a result, through the act of *b'rit milah*, we incorporate God's promise of eternal life for the Jewish people directly into the male organ of reproduction. When applied to *parashat Eikev*, this interpretation helps us to see that a circumcised heart, possible for all of us, allows for growth and expansion, and provides a model for sloughing off gratuitous, constraining defenses.

Torah gives us a language that speaks beyond the physical world and gender. Both women and men embody God in their ordinary lived experience. Just as when we are in danger or despair we reach for another person to lift us up, so we understand that God is reaching for us with an outstretched arm to free us from slavery. In our female and male bodies we find God, and in this discovery we know ourselves to be more than physical beings. All of us are called upon to be creative, transparent, and loving before God.

*—Malka Drucker*

# Voices

## The Empress of Imagined Fertility

Leah Aini (transl. Miriyam Glazer)

*Deuteronomy 7:14*

A baby carriage abandoned
in the stairwell
A colorful napkin staining
the strip of grass behind me.
In the yard
mothers on one leg
lighting butt from butt,
baby slings strapped
round their hips,
creatures kicking in their bellies.
And I, mad, on the roof
nestle in snowing laundry
pregnant with pain.
Nine stars
and not one moon
around me,
empress
of imagined
fertility.

## For a Child Not Yet Conceived

Pamela Melnikoff

*Deuteronomy 7:14*

Your room awaits you, and a cherry-tree
That never bloomed till now: and clematis
Purpling the kitchen wall; and ancestors
Whose faith and kindness reach out down
the years
To touch you with their light; and happy
friends;
And books and music, art and poetry
And all the precious and God-given things
That we have found and hoarded for your sake;
And aunts and cousins; and a squalling nest
Under the eaves; and daisies in the grass;
Laughter and love, legend and fantasy,
And such a welcome as the flowers of March
And every blessing sent to make men glad
And all the saints and prophets never had.

Why do you linger still, then, in that sad
Populous kingdom where our lost dreams are,
Ungathered fruit and every unborn thing?
The years are passing, and we pass likewise
And cannot wait forever on your whim.
You must come soon, or you may wait too long
And come too late, and find the hearth grown
cold,
The windows shuttered, and your parents old.

Sarah, they say, laughed when the angel told
How she, at ninety years of age, would bring
A shining son out of her shriveled womb,
And would my laughter, do you think, be less;
My miracle, and my sweet thankfulness?

## *Released*

Elaine Feinstein

*Deuteronomy 11:14*

In lovely rain now
this two weeks' tyranny of
sun is past and the trees

are dark          the air has
shed the dry pollens.
Now the garden follows me into

the house gently and every membrane
welcomes the soft presence.
The solar blast was a

dish of silence over me:
now I look for stars or blonde
lions in the wet undergrowth.

## *Covenant*

Sharon Kessler

*Deuteronomy 11:18*

In the desert
where old legends
conspire, we
are making fresh
tracks in the sand,
carrying our burden
to some resting place.

Above
the black crest
of rock,
an arc of slow fire
rises. Morning again.
We march forward,
a tribe of mute warriors,
daughters of a race
so lost
no legend tells of us.

We too heard voices in the wilderness
but we built
no tabernacle
to contain them.

The sign of the covenant
is not incised upon our flesh,

but deep in the one heart
of our body
the everlasting bush burns
and is not consumed.

## *Eikev*

Laurie Patton

*Deuteronomy 11:20–21*

There is a lightness
when we cross a threshold—
wood-frames sunk into soft soil,
steel-frames of old tenements
that have carried the weight
of slow, sad steps above them;
sometimes, even,
a mezuzah points upward
like a finger:

No matter the sorrow,
every door holds a hope
of difference, of newness—
the thought that
our days will multiply

And then:
anticipation splinters
into the past
of a room,
where
we have to come to terms
with objects—

Take, for instance, the kitchen:
the way my eye catches
the light on the grapes,
like the boat-shells
gathered in your hands
at that lowest of tides;

or the way the bowls tilt,
like the heads of the seals
who watched us, clapping,
on Barnacle Rock;

or the way the rims
of the wine-glasses
curve, like the ripples
off your paddle
dipping near Seaweed Island

In this doorway,
pieces of the summer
before you died
multiply like so many days
of a future—

a past hauled up
from the Zero
of forgetting
into the More-than-One
of surprised memory

Yes,
says the red and peeling paint
of the cheerful frame:

Our days will multiply,
and they do so
in both directions.

# ראה ✦ R'eih

## DEUTERONOMY 11:26–16:17

### *Laws and Loyalty*

PARASHAT R'EIH ("see") introduces the legal collection that extends from Deuteronomy 12 to 26. Like the two other major biblical collections of legal material (the Book of the Covenant in Exodus 21–24 and the priestly legislation in Exodus, Leviticus, and Numbers), these laws are conceived of as part of the covenantal relationship between Israel and God, with responsibilities incumbent upon both parties. The legal collection here offers a unifying vision of Israel: it insists on absolute loyalty to the one God—and to God's Chosen Place, the sole official shrine.

According to Deuteronomy 1:5, the location for the expounding of these laws is the land of Moab, east of the Jordan River, before Israel enters the land. This would be during the 2nd millennium B.C.E., according to the implied chronology and the imagined "original" audience (see introduction to *parashat D'varim*, p. 1039). But historians believe that these laws were actually compiled in the 7th century B.C.E. or later, and that they comprise part of the "book of the *torah* (Teaching)," the phrase used in Deuteronomy to refer to the exhortations and laws in this book (not to the so-called Five Books of Moses). According to II Kings 22 (and II Chronicles 34:14–28), a reportedly similar "book of the *torah*" is discovered during the reign of King Josiah, in the midst of renovations of the Temple. The King orders his scribes to consult with the female prophet Huldah, who authenticates the scroll. Its laws represent a reform of earlier traditions and of existing practice. The book of Kings further reports that King Josiah implemented some of those reforms in about 622 B.C.E. (On the economic aspects of this "reform," see at 12:2–3.)

The laws in this parashah (like those in the three portions that follow) contain various precepts designed to regulate activity in the Promised Land and to bind Israel to its God. The parashah includes rules about many aspects of life: the consumption of meat (12:15–28; 14:3–21; 15:21–23), avoidance of the local non-Israelite peoples' worship practices (12:30–31; 13:6–18; 14:1–2), true and false prophecy (13:1–5), tithing (14:28), remission of debts (15:1–6), care for the needy (15:7–11), debt-slavery (15:12–17), dedication of first-born male animals (15:19–20), and the pilgrimage festivals (16:1–17).

> *The legal collection here offers a unifying vision of Israel.*

While the legislation here applies to all Israel, several teachings at first glance seem to address only the presumably male heads of household (12:7–8, 12, 18; 13:7; 15:20; 16:11, 14). This raises the following questions: What about their wives, who are not mentioned? Furthermore, are all of these laws intended only for men and not for women? The answers are not always clear. However, some laws implicitly address everyone, such as those that regulate diet (14:3–21). Others explicitly include women, as when they are expected to attend festive celebrations at Israel's official sanctuary (12:12, 18; 16:11, 14).

A powerful theme in *parashat R'eih*, alongside the prominent concern for the loyal worship of Israel's God alone, is caring for the needy. It is possible that a concern for women's welfare lies behind certain economic legislation to protect the vulnerable (see at 14:29), since women were often at risk in ancient Israelite society.

*—Beth Alpert Nakhai*

## *Outline*

*I.* The Choice between Blessing and Curse (11:26–32)

*II.* Commencement of Deuteronomy's Legal Collection (12:1–16:17)

- A. Introduction (12:1)
- B. Demand for centralization of sacrifice in God's Chosen Place (12:2–14)
- C. Rules about the consumption of meat and tithes (12:15–28)
- D. Warnings against worshipping as other nations do (12:29–31)
- E. Warnings against false prophets or diviners (13:1–19)
- F. Warnings against illicit mourning practices (14:1–2)
- G. Dietary laws (14:3–21)
- H. Tithing regulations (14:22–29)
- I. Laws of release in the seventh year (15:1–18)
  - 1. Remission of debt (15:1–11)
  - 2. Release of debt-servants (15:12–18)
- J. Laws about the dedication of first-born male livestock (15:19–23)
- K. Laws about the pilgrimage festivals (16:1–17)

See, this day I set before you blessing and curse: [27]blessing, if you obey the commandments of your God יהוה that I enjoin upon you this day; [28]and curse, if you do not obey the commandments of your God יהוה, but turn away from the path that I enjoin upon you this day and follow other gods, whom you have not experienced. [29]When your God יהוה brings you into the land that you are about to enter and possess, you shall pronounce the blessing at Mount Gerizim and the curse at Mount Ebal.—[30]Both are on the other side of the Jordan, beyond the west road that is in the land of the Canaanites who dwell in the Arabah—near Gilgal, by the terebinths of Moreh.

[31]For you are about to cross the Jordan to enter and possess the land that your God יהוה is assigning to you. When you have occupied it and are settled in it, [32]take care to observe all the laws and rules that I have set before you this day.

יא 26 רְאֵ֗ה אָנֹכִ֛י נֹתֵ֥ן לִפְנֵיכֶ֖ם הַיּ֑וֹם בְּרָכָ֖ה וּקְלָלָֽה: 27 אֶֽת־הַבְּרָכָ֑ה אֲשֶׁ֣ר תִּשְׁמְע֗וּ אֶל־מִצְוֺת֙ יְהֹוָ֣ה אֱלֹֽהֵיכֶ֔ם אֲשֶׁ֧ר אָנֹכִ֛י מְצַוֶּ֥ה אֶתְכֶ֖ם הַיּֽוֹם: 28 וְהַקְּלָלָ֗ה אִם־לֹ֤א תִשְׁמְעוּ֙ אֶל־מִצְוֺת֙ יְהֹוָ֣ה אֱלֹֽהֵיכֶ֔ם וְסַרְתֶּ֣ם מִן־הַדֶּ֔רֶךְ אֲשֶׁ֧ר אָנֹכִ֛י מְצַוֶּ֥ה אֶתְכֶ֖ם הַיּ֑וֹם לָלֶ֗כֶת אַחֲרֵ֛י אֱלֹהִ֥ים אֲחֵרִ֖ים אֲשֶׁ֥ר לֹֽא־יְדַעְתֶּֽם: ס 29 וְהָיָ֗ה כִּ֤י יְבִֽיאֲךָ֙ יְהֹוָ֣ה אֱלֹהֶ֔יךָ אֶל־הָאָ֕רֶץ אֲשֶׁר־אַתָּ֥ה בָא־שָׁ֖מָּה לְרִשְׁתָּ֑הּ וְנָתַתָּ֤ה אֶת־הַבְּרָכָה֙ עַל־הַ֣ר גְּרִזִ֔ים וְאֶת־הַקְּלָלָ֖ה עַל־הַ֥ר עֵיבָֽל: 30 הֲלֹא־הֵ֜מָּה בְּעֵ֣בֶר הַיַּרְדֵּ֗ן אַֽחֲרֵי֙ דֶּ֚רֶךְ מְב֣וֹא הַשֶּׁ֔מֶשׁ בְּאֶ֙רֶץ֙ הַֽכְּנַעֲנִ֔י הַיֹּשֵׁ֖ב בָּֽעֲרָבָ֑ה מ֚וּל הַגִּלְגָּ֔ל אֵ֖צֶל אֵלוֹנֵ֥י מֹרֶֽה:

31 כִּ֤י אַתֶּם֙ עֹֽבְרִ֣ים אֶת־הַיַּרְדֵּ֔ן לָבֹא֙ לָרֶ֣שֶׁת אֶת־הָאָ֔רֶץ אֲשֶׁר־יְהֹוָ֥ה אֱלֹֽהֵיכֶ֖ם נֹתֵ֣ן לָכֶ֑ם וִֽירִשְׁתֶּ֥ם אֹתָ֖הּ וִֽישַׁבְתֶּם־בָּֽהּ: 32 וּשְׁמַרְתֶּ֣ם לַעֲשׂ֔וֹת אֵ֥ת כׇּל־הַֽחֻקִּ֖ים וְאֶת־הַמִּשְׁפָּטִ֑ים אֲשֶׁ֧ר אָנֹכִ֛י נֹתֵ֥ן לִפְנֵיכֶ֖ם הַיּֽוֹם:

## The Choice between Blessing and Curse (11:26–32)

The legal material in Deuteronomy is framed by two sets of blessings and curses (here and 28:1–68). Similarly, ancient Near Eastern political treaties and the Laws of Hammurabi contain curses warning of the calamities that will transpire if the treaty's stipulations or the laws are violated (see also at 28:1–68).

**29. *blessing at Mount Gerizim . . . curse at Mount Ebal.*** Two mountains west of the Jordan are the sites for the covenant affirmation ritual (see also at 27:11–13).

▶ Celebrations include daughters, female slaves, and widows; why are wives not mentioned?

ANOTHER VIEW ➤ 1134

▶ Kashrut reminds us that Jewish spirituality is inseparable from physical reality.

CONTEMPORARY REFLECTION ➤ 1136

▶ On festivals, a husband should provide his wife with new clothes, so that she rejoices.

POST-BIBLICAL INTERPRETATIONS ➤ 1134

▶ Instead of observing Passover this year, / I have a fight with my boyfriend...

VOICES ➤ 1138

*12* These are the laws and rules that you must carefully observe in the land that יהוה, God of your ancestors, is giving you to possess, as long as you live on earth.

²You must destroy all the sites at which the nations you are to dispossess worshiped their gods, whether on lofty mountains and on hills or under any luxuriant tree. ³Tear down their altars, smash their pillars, put their sacred posts to the fire, and cut down the images of their gods, obliterating their name from that site.

יב אֵ֣לֶּה הַֽחֻקִּ֤ים וְהַמִּשְׁפָּטִים֙ אֲשֶׁ֣ר תִּשְׁמְר֣וּן לַעֲשׂ֔וֹת בָּאָ֕רֶץ אֲשֶׁר֩ נָתַ֨ן יְהֹוָ֜ה אֱלֹהֵ֧י אֲבֹתֶ֛יךָ לְךָ֖ לְרִשְׁתָּ֑הּ כׇּל־הַ֨יָּמִ֔ים אֲשֶׁר־אַתֶּ֥ם חַיִּ֖ים עַל־הָאֲדָמָֽה׃ ² אַבֵּ֣ד תְּ֠אַבְּד֠וּן אֶֽת־כׇּל־הַמְּקֹמ֞וֹת אֲשֶׁ֧ר עָֽבְדוּ־שָׁ֣ם הַגּוֹיִ֗ם אֲשֶׁ֥ר אַתֶּ֛ם יֹרְשִׁ֥ים אֹתָ֖ם אֶת־אֱלֹהֵיהֶ֑ם עַל־הֶהָרִ֤ים הָֽרָמִים֙ וְעַל־הַגְּבָע֔וֹת וְתַ֖חַת כׇּל־עֵ֥ץ רַעֲנָֽן׃ ³ וְנִתַּצְתֶּ֣ם אֶת־מִזְבְּחֹתָ֗ם וְשִׁבַּרְתֶּם֙ אֶת־מַצֵּ֣בֹתָ֔ם וַאֲשֵֽׁרֵיהֶם֙ תִּשְׂרְפ֣וּן בָּאֵ֔שׁ וּפְסִילֵ֥י אֱלֹהֵיהֶ֖ם תְּגַדֵּע֑וּן וְאִבַּדְתֶּ֣ם אֶת־שְׁמָ֔ם מִן־הַמָּק֖וֹם הַהֽוּא׃

- - - - - - - - - - - - - - - - - - - - - - - -

## Commencement of Deuteronomy's Legal Collection (12:1–16:17)

The rules in *parashat R'eih* begin the extensive legal collection that continues through Deuteronomy 26. Most scholars agree that even though Deuteronomy presents this material as Moses' teachings, these precepts were compiled hundreds of years later. Evidence indicates that the compilers of the laws in Deuteronomy were an eclectic group—including scribes, priests, prophets, and other intellectuals—who formulated a notion of Israel as a nation guided by God. What makes their work unique is the powerful, unified vision that serves as the basis for their editorial work. Their distinctive perspective includes the idea that all Israel—kings and commoners alike—are to be judged by the degree to which they adhere to the laws of Deuteronomy. In particular, the laws considerably limit the roles of the king and priests and redistribute power to broader segments of the Israelite community (see at 17:14–20 and 18:1–8).

### INTRODUCTION (12:1)

This verse specifies that the laws that follow must be observed in the Promised Land.

## DEMAND FOR CENTRALIZATION OF SACRIFICE IN GOD'S CHOSEN PLACE (12:2–14)

The commands to destroy places where foreign gods are worshipped (vv. 2–3) and to worship by offering sacrifices to God only in one select location (vv. 4–14) express one of Deuteronomy's distinctive features: establishing the legitimacy of only one central shrine (which scholars often refer to as Deuteronomy's "centralization of the cult"). Although Deuteronomy does not name the location of the shrine, other books in the Bible make clear that the Chosen Place is Jerusalem.

*2–3.* The Israelites are charged to destroy places of worship and ritual objects that are sacred to the non-Israelite inhabitants of the land of Canaan, in order to prevent Israel from straying from God. Many modern scholars have concluded that in reality, this regulation targeted village sanctuaries where Israel's own deity was worshipped. Such sacred sites had been legitimate places of Israelite and Judean worship in the centuries before the centralization mandated in Deuteronomy. (Note, for example, Hannah's visits to the shrine in Shiloh in I Samuel 1.) Conducting sacrifices only in Jerusalem would have been a boon for that city's econ-

4 Do not worship your God יהוה in like manner, 5 but look only to the site that your God יהוה will choose amidst all your tribes as God's habitation, to establish the divine name there. There you are to go, 6 and there you are to bring your burnt offerings and other sacrifices, your tithes and contributions, your votive and freewill offerings, and the firstlings of your herds and flocks. 7 Together with your households, you shall feast there before your God יהוה, happy in all the undertakings in which your God יהוה has blessed you.

8 You shall not act at all as we now act here, each [householder] as he pleases, 9 because you have not yet come to the allotted haven that your God יהוה is giving you. 10 When you cross the Jordan and settle in the land that your God יהוה is allotting to you, and [God] grants you safety from all your enemies around you and you live in security, 11 then you must bring everything that I command you to the site where your God יהוה will choose to establish the divine name: your burnt offerings and other sacrifices, your tithes and contributions, and all the choice votive offerings that you vow to יהוה.

4 לֹא־תַעֲשׂוּן כֵּן לַיהֹוָה אֱלֹהֵיכֶם׃ 5 כִּי אִם־
אֶל־הַמָּקוֹם אֲשֶׁר־יִבְחַר יְהֹוָה אֱלֹהֵיכֶם
מִכׇּל־שִׁבְטֵיכֶם לָשׂוּם אֶת־שְׁמוֹ שָׁם לְשִׁכְנוֹ
תִדְרְשׁוּ וּבָאתָ שָׁמָּה׃ 6 וַהֲבֵאתֶם שָׁמָּה
עֹלֹתֵיכֶם וְזִבְחֵיכֶם וְאֵת מַעְשְׂרֹתֵיכֶם וְאֵת
תְּרוּמַת יֶדְכֶם וְנִדְרֵיכֶם וְנִדְבֹתֵיכֶם וּבְכֹרֹת
בְּקַרְכֶם וְצֹאנְכֶם׃ 7 וַאֲכַלְתֶּם־שָׁם לִפְנֵי
יְהֹוָה אֱלֹהֵיכֶם וּשְׂמַחְתֶּם בְּכֹל מִשְׁלַח
יֶדְכֶם אַתֶּם וּבָתֵּיכֶם אֲשֶׁר בֵּרַכְךָ יְהֹוָה
אֱלֹהֶיךָ׃
8 לֹא תַעֲשׂוּן כְּכֹל אֲשֶׁר אֲנַחְנוּ עֹשִׂים פֹּה
הַיּוֹם אִישׁ כׇּל־הַיָּשָׁר בְּעֵינָיו׃ 9 כִּי לֹא־
בָאתֶם עַד־עָתָּה אֶל־הַמְּנוּחָה וְאֶל־הַנַּחֲלָה
אֲשֶׁר־יְהֹוָה אֱלֹהֶיךָ נֹתֵן לָךְ׃ 10 וַעֲבַרְתֶּם
אֶת־הַיַּרְדֵּן וִישַׁבְתֶּם בָּאָרֶץ אֲשֶׁר־יְהֹוָה
אֱלֹהֵיכֶם מַנְחִיל אֶתְכֶם וְהֵנִיחַ לָכֶם
מִכׇּל־אֹיְבֵיכֶם מִסָּבִיב וִישַׁבְתֶּם־בֶּטַח׃
11 וְהָיָה הַמָּקוֹם אֲשֶׁר־יִבְחַר יְהֹוָה
אֱלֹהֵיכֶם בּוֹ לְשַׁכֵּן שְׁמוֹ שָׁם שָׁמָּה תָבִיאוּ
אֵת כׇּל־אֲשֶׁר אָנֹכִי מְצַוֶּה אֶתְכֶם עוֹלֹתֵיכֶם
וְזִבְחֵיכֶם מַעְשְׂרֹתֵיכֶם וּתְרֻמַת יֶדְכֶם וְכֹל
מִבְחַר נִדְרֵיכֶם אֲשֶׁר תִּדְּרוּ לַיהֹוָה׃

omy, strengthening the crown as it faced Assyrian imperialism, especially in the 7th century B.C.E.

*3. altars . . . pillars . . . sacred posts . . . images.* Archeologists have discovered these objects at sacred sites throughout the land of Israel. Ritual objects like these were earlier used by Canaanites and then adopted by the Israelites, thus indicating the debt they owed to their predecessors in the Promised Land.

***sacred posts.*** Heb. *asherim* (plural of *asherah*), ritual objects probably related to the worship of the goddess Asherah. According to II Kings 23, King Josiah removed the *asherah* from numerous sites, including the Temple itself and the place where "the women wove coverings for *asherah*" (II Kings 23:7). (See further at 16:21 and at Exodus 34:13.)

*5. **the site that your God יהוה will choose.*** Deuteronomy does not mention either Jerusalem or the Temple by name, since Jerusalem was not Israelite and the Temple not yet built during the time of Moses in which Deuteronomy is set.

*7. **households.*** Heb. *bayit* (literally "house"; plural, *batim*) here refers to the occupants of the household compound—the extended family, including slaves and other dependents. The inclusion of the household in feasting at the sanctuary suggests a venue in which women would play a role. Families would join together to experience the joy of partaking in a sacral meal in a sacred setting.

[12]And you shall rejoice before your God יהוה with your sons and daughters and with your male and female slaves, along with the [family of the] Levite in your settlements, for he has no territorial allotment among you.

[13]Take care not to sacrifice your burnt offerings in any place you like, [14]but only in the place that יהוה will choose in one of your tribal territories. There you shall sacrifice your burnt offerings and there you shall observe all that I enjoin upon you. [15]But whenever you desire, you may slaughter and eat meat in any of your settlements, according to the blessing that your God יהוה has granted you. The impure and the pure alike may partake of it,

12 וּשְׂמַחְתֶּ֗ם לִפְנֵי֮ יְהֹוָ֣ה אֱלֹהֵיכֶם֒ אַתֶּ֕ם
וּבְנֵיכֶם֙ וּבְנֹ֣תֵיכֶ֔ם וְעַבְדֵיכֶ֖ם וְאַמְהֹתֵיכֶ֑ם
וְהַלֵּוִי֙ אֲשֶׁ֣ר בְּשַׁעֲרֵיכֶ֔ם כִּ֣י אֵ֥ין ל֛וֹ חֵ֥לֶק
וְנַחֲלָ֖ה אִתְּכֶֽם׃
13 הִשָּׁ֣מֶר לְךָ֔ פֶּן־תַּעֲלֶ֖ה עֹלֹתֶ֑יךָ בְּכׇל־מָק֖וֹם
אֲשֶׁ֥ר תִּרְאֶֽה׃ 14 כִּ֣י אִם־בַּמָּק֞וֹם אֲשֶׁר־
יִבְחַ֤ר יְהֹוָה֙ בְּאַחַ֣ד שְׁבָטֶ֔יךָ שָׁ֖ם תַּעֲלֶ֣ה
עֹלֹתֶ֑יךָ וְשָׁ֣ם תַּעֲשֶׂ֔ה כֹּ֛ל אֲשֶׁ֥ר אָנֹכִ֖י מְצַוֶּֽךָּ׃
15 רַק֩ בְּכׇל־אַוַּ֨ת נַפְשְׁךָ֜ תִּזְבַּ֣ח ׀ וְאָכַלְתָּ֣ בָשָׂ֗ר
כְּבִרְכַּ֨ת יְהֹוָ֧ה אֱלֹהֶ֛יךָ אֲשֶׁ֥ר נָֽתַן־לְךָ֖ בְּכׇל־
שְׁעָרֶ֑יךָ הַטָּמֵ֤א וְהַטָּהוֹר֙ יֹאכְלֶ֔נּוּ כַּצְּבִ֖י

12. ***sons and daughters . . . male and female slaves.*** The specific mention of those with least access to resources is an important component of the laws in Deuteronomy. Free Israelite women are conspicuous by their absence from the list, which suggests that they were already included in the masculine plural command to rejoice before God (see also at 16:11 and Another View, p. 1134). The verse does not specify whether "slaves" refers to indentured servants, chattel slaves, or both; see further at 15:12–18; Exodus 21:2–11; Leviticus 25:35–54.

***Levite.*** According to Numbers 8, men from the tribe of Levi were not to receive land, but they were dedicated uniquely to God's service. A distinctive feature of Deuteronomy is that it adds Levites—and implicitly their families—to the list of those who need special consideration or protection (see at v. 19, below), a likely result of closing the local sanctuaries that were a major source of livelihood for Levites.

### RULES ABOUT THE CONSUMPTION OF MEAT AND TITHES (12:15–28)

For Israelites as for others in the ancient world, meat-eating was not part of the daily diet, since they valued animals most for what they could produce while they were alive, including milk, wool, dung (used for fuel and construction), and offspring. Also, meat from an entire animal would have to be consumed at once, given the lack of refrigeration. Thus, eating the meat not otherwise utilized for sacrifice in festive meals provided one way for people to partake of meat. Exodus 20:21 implies that sacrifices could take place anywhere; however, if centralization of sacrifice meant that there were no longer any local sanctuaries at which to sacrifice animals, then how would those who lived far from Jerusalem be able to eat meat? In order to ensure that the consumption of meat did not cease with the cessation of village sacrifice, Deuteronomy allows Israelites to slaughter and eat meat in their own settlements, as long as they follow these detailed regulations. Deuteronomy's laws in this case conflict with Leviticus 17:2–7, which permits eating meat only at a sanctuary.

15. ***The impure and the pure alike may partake of it.*** When animals for human consumption are no longer dedicated to God, everyone can partake of them, not only those who are ritually pure. This regulation makes it easier for women to consume meat because ritual impurity on account of menstruation and childbirth (see Leviticus 12; 15:19–30) no longer bars their participation.

as of the gazelle and the deer. ¹⁶But you must not partake of the blood; you shall pour it out on the ground like water.

¹⁷You may not partake in your settlements of the tithes of your new grain or wine or oil, or of the firstlings of your herds and flocks, or of any of the votive offerings that you vow, or of your freewill offerings, or of your contributions. ¹⁸These you must consume before your God יהוה in the place that your God יהוה will choose—you and your sons and your daughters, your male and female slaves, and the [family of the] Levite in your settlements—happy before your God יהוה in all your undertakings. ¹⁹Be sure not to neglect the [family of the] Levite as long as you live in your land.

²⁰When יהוה enlarges your territory, as promised, and you say, "I shall eat some meat," for you have the urge to eat meat, you may eat meat whenever you wish. ²¹If the place where יהוה has chosen to establish the divine name is too far from you, you may slaughter any of the cattle or sheep that יהוה gives you, as I have instructed you; and you may eat to your heart's content in your settlements. ²²Eat it, however, as the gazelle and the deer are eaten: the impure may eat it together with the pure. ²³But make sure that you do not partake of the blood; for the blood is the life, and you must not consume the life with the flesh. ²⁴You must not partake of it; you

וְכָאַיָּ֑ל : ¹⁶ רַ֣ק הַדָּ֗ם לֹ֤א תֹאכֵ֔לוּ עַל־הָאָ֖רֶץ תִּשְׁפְּכֶ֥נּוּ כַּמָּֽיִם :

¹⁷ לֹֽא־תוּכַ֞ל לֶאֱכֹ֣ל בִּשְׁעָרֶ֗יךָ מַעְשַׂ֤ר דְּגָֽנְךָ֙ וְתִירֹֽשְׁךָ֣ וְיִצְהָרֶ֔ךָ וּבְכֹרֹ֥ת בְּקָֽרְךָ֖ וְצֹאנֶ֑ךָ וְכָל־ נְדָרֶ֙יךָ֙ אֲשֶׁ֣ר תִּדֹּ֔ר וְנִדְבֹתֶ֖יךָ וּתְרוּמַ֥ת יָדֶֽךָ : ¹⁸ כִּ֡י אִם־לִפְנֵי֩ יְהֹוָ֨ה אֱלֹהֶ֜יךָ תֹּאכְלֶ֗נּוּ בַּמָּקוֹם֙ אֲשֶׁ֨ר יִבְחַ֜ר יְהֹוָ֣ה אֱלֹהֶ֘יךָ֘ בּוֹ֒ אַתָּ֨ה וּבִנְךָ֤ וּבִתֶּ֙ךָ֙ וְעַבְדְּךָ֣ וַאֲמָתֶ֔ךָ וְהַלֵּוִ֖י אֲשֶׁ֣ר בִּשְׁעָרֶ֑יךָ וְשָׂמַחְתָּ֗ לִפְנֵי֙ יְהֹוָ֣ה אֱלֹהֶ֔יךָ בְּכֹ֖ל מִשְׁלַ֥ח יָדֶֽךָ : ¹⁹ הִשָּׁ֣מֶר לְךָ֔ פֶּֽן־תַּעֲזֹ֖ב אֶת־הַלֵּוִ֑י כָּל־יָמֶ֖יךָ עַל־אַדְמָתֶֽךָ : ס

²⁰ כִּֽי־יַרְחִ֣יב יְהֹוָ֩ה אֱלֹהֶ֨יךָ אֶֽת־גְּבֻֽלְךָ֜ כַּאֲשֶׁ֣ר דִּבֶּר־לָ֗ךְ וְאָמַרְתָּ֙ אֹכְלָ֣ה בָשָׂ֔ר כִּֽי־ תְאַוֶּ֥ה נַפְשְׁךָ֖ לֶאֱכֹ֣ל בָּשָׂ֑ר בְּכָל־אַוַּ֥ת נַפְשְׁךָ֖ תֹּאכַ֥ל בָּשָֽׂר : ²¹ כִּֽי־יִרְחַ֨ק מִמְּךָ֜ הַמָּק֗וֹם אֲשֶׁ֨ר יִבְחַ֜ר יְהֹוָ֣ה אֱלֹהֶ֘יךָ֘ לָשׂ֣וּם שְׁמ֣וֹ שָׁם֒ וְזָבַחְתָּ֞ מִבְּקָֽרְךָ֣ וּמִצֹּֽאנְךָ֗ אֲשֶׁ֨ר נָתַ֤ן יְהֹוָה֙ לְךָ֔ כַּאֲשֶׁ֖ר צִוִּיתִ֑ךָ וְאָֽכַלְתָּ֙ בִּשְׁעָרֶ֔יךָ בְּכֹ֖ל אַוַּ֥ת נַפְשֶֽׁךָ : ²² אַ֗ךְ כַּאֲשֶׁ֨ר יֵאָכֵ֤ל אֶֽת־הַצְּבִי֙ וְאֶת־ הָ֣אַיָּ֔ל כֵּ֖ן תֹּאכְלֶ֑נּוּ הַטָּמֵא֙ וְהַטָּה֔וֹר יַחְדָּ֖ו יֹאכְלֶֽנּוּ : ²³ רַ֣ק חֲזַ֗ק לְבִלְתִּי֙ אֲכֹ֣ל הַדָּ֔ם כִּ֥י הַדָּ֖ם ה֣וּא הַנָּ֑פֶשׁ וְלֹא־תֹאכַ֥ל הַנֶּ֖פֶשׁ עִם־ הַבָּשָֽׂר : ²⁴ לֹ֖א תֹּאכְלֶ֑נּוּ עַל־הָאָ֛רֶץ תִּשְׁפְּכֶ֖נּוּ

---

**16.** *you must not partake of the blood.* Eating blood is prohibited because blood symbolizes life—and life belongs to God (see Genesis 9:4; Leviticus 17:11).

**17–18.** Common among other peoples in the ancient Near East, tithes were a kind of assessment that could be fulfilled by designating agricultural products or livestock, which would be consumed in sacred ceremonies (see also at 14:22–29). This passage establishes that tithes are no longer to be consumed within the towns or villages of Israel; rather, they are to be joyfully shared by all members of the

community, female and male alike, at God's Chosen Place.

**18.** *you.* In the singular; on who is being addressed, see at v. 12.

**19.** The centralization of sacrifice means that the landless Levites (see Numbers 8) who served local sanctuaries would have lost their means of livelihood. In an agrarian culture such as ancient Israel, those who did not own land were at risk of chronic starvation and even death. Therefore, the Levites would have become part of Israel's underclass, unable to provide for themselves and their families.

must pour it out on the ground like water: <sup>25</sup>you must not partake of it, in order that it may go well with you and with your descendants to come, for you will be doing what is right in the sight of יהוה.

<sup>26</sup>But such sacred and votive donations as you may have shall be taken by you to the site that יהוה will choose. <sup>27</sup>You shall offer your burnt offerings, both the flesh and the blood, on the altar of your God יהוה; and of your other sacrifices, the blood shall be poured out on the altar of your God יהוה, and you shall eat the flesh.

<sup>28</sup>Be careful to heed all these commandments that I enjoin upon you; thus it will go well with you and with your descendants after you forever, for you will be doing what is good and right in the sight of your God יהוה.

<sup>29</sup>When your God יהוה has cut down before you the nations that you are about to enter and dispossess, and you have dispossessed them and settled in their land, <sup>30</sup>beware of being lured into their ways after they have been wiped out before you! Do not inquire about their gods, saying, "How did those nations worship their gods? I too will follow those practices." <sup>31</sup>You shall not act thus toward your God יהוה, for they perform for their gods every abhorrent act that יהוה detests; they even offer up their sons and daughters in fire to their gods.

כַּמָּ֑יִם ׃ 25 לֹ֖א תֹּאכְלֶ֑נּוּ לְמַ֨עַן֙ יִיטַ֣ב לְךָ֔ וּלְבָנֶ֖יךָ אַחֲרֶ֑יךָ כִּי־תַעֲשֶׂ֥ה הַיָּשָׁ֖ר בְּעֵינֵ֥י יְהֹוָֽה ׃

26 רַ֧ק קָֽדָשֶׁ֛יךָ אֲשֶׁר־יִֽהְי֥וּ לְךָ֖ וּנְדָרֶ֑יךָ תִּשָּׂ֣א וּבָ֔אתָ אֶל־הַמָּק֖וֹם אֲשֶׁר־יִבְחַ֥ר יְהֹוָֽה ׃

27 וְעָשִׂ֤יתָ עֹֽלֹתֶ֨יךָ֙ הַבָּשָׂ֣ר וְהַדָּ֔ם עַל־מִזְבַּ֖ח יְהֹוָ֣ה אֱלֹהֶ֑יךָ וְדַם־זְבָחֶ֗יךָ יִשָּׁפֵךְ֙ עַל־מִזְבַּח֙ יְהֹוָ֣ה אֱלֹהֶ֔יךָ וְהַבָּשָׂ֖ר תֹּאכֵֽל ׃

28 שְׁמֹ֣ר וְשָׁמַעְתָּ֗ אֵ֚ת כָּל־הַדְּבָרִ֣ים הָאֵ֔לֶּה אֲשֶׁ֥ר אָֽנֹכִ֖י מְצַוֶּ֑ךָּ לְמַ֩עַן֩ יִיטַ֨ב לְךָ֜ וּלְבָנֶ֤יךָ אַחֲרֶ֨יךָ֙ עַד־עוֹלָ֔ם כִּ֤י תַעֲשֶׂה֙ הַטּ֣וֹב וְהַיָּשָׁ֔ר בְּעֵינֵ֖י יְהֹוָ֥ה אֱלֹהֶֽיךָ ׃ ס

29 כִּֽי־יַכְרִית֩ יְהֹוָ֨ה אֱלֹהֶ֜יךָ אֶת־הַגּוֹיִ֗ם אֲשֶׁ֨ר אַתָּ֥ה בָא־שָׁ֛מָּה לָרֶ֥שֶׁת אוֹתָ֖ם מִפָּנֶ֑יךָ וְיָרַשְׁתָּ֣ אֹתָ֔ם וְיָשַׁבְתָּ֖ בְּאַרְצָֽם ׃ 30 הִשָּׁ֣מֶר לְךָ֗ פֶּן־תִּנָּקֵשׁ֙ אַחֲרֵיהֶ֔ם אַחֲרֵ֖י הִשָּׁמְדָ֣ם מִפָּנֶ֑יךָ וּפֶן־תִּדְרֹ֨שׁ לֵאלֹֽהֵיהֶ֜ם לֵאמֹ֗ר אֵיכָ֨ה יַעַבְד֜וּ הַגּוֹיִ֤ם הָאֵ֨לֶּה֙ אֶת־אֱלֹ֣הֵיהֶ֔ם וְאֶעֱשֶׂה־כֵּ֖ן גַּם־אָֽנִי ׃ 31 לֹא־תַעֲשֶׂ֣ה כֵ֔ן לַיהֹוָ֖ה אֱלֹהֶ֑יךָ כִּי֩ כָל־תּוֹעֲבַ֨ת יְהֹוָ֜ה אֲשֶׁ֣ר שָׂנֵ֗א עָשׂוּ֙ לֵאלֹ֣הֵיהֶ֔ם כִּ֣י גַ֤ם אֶת־בְּנֵיהֶם֙ וְאֶת־בְּנֹ֣תֵיהֶ֔ם יִשְׂרְפ֥וּ בָאֵ֖שׁ לֵאלֹֽהֵיהֶֽם ׃

## WARNINGS AGAINST WORSHIPPING
## AS OTHER NATIONS DO (12:29–31)

The crucial injunction condemning the worship of any deity other than Israel's God is predicated upon the settlement of the land, after God will "cut down" the existing inhabitants. Certain biblical depictions of the conquest of the land (found especially in Joshua and Judges) claim that such destruction happened, whereas other passages portray a long period of Israelite coexistence with Canaanite and other ethnic communities in the very heartland of what would later become the Israel of the Monar-

chy. The results of decades of archeological research indicate that the latter version is the historically accurate one (see also at 2:34; 7:1–5, 24; 31:16).

*31. offer up their sons and daughters in fire.* While child sacrifice is condemned here as an abhorrent religious ritual, other passages reveal that at times even Israelites sacrificed their children (as implied by Genesis 22:1–19). According to II Kings 3:27, the Moabite king sacrifices his first-born son as a last resort. The Israelite child most renowned for having been sacrificed is Jephthah's daughter (Judges 11:29–40).

13 Be careful to observe only that which I enjoin
upon you: neither add to it nor take away from it.

[2]If there appears among you a prophet or a
dream-diviner, who gives you a sign or a portent,
[3]saying, "Let us follow and worship another god"—
whom you have not experienced—even if the sign
or portent named to you comes true, [4]do not heed
the words of that prophet or that dream-diviner.
For your God יהוה is testing you to see whether
you really love your God יהוה with all your heart
and soul. [5]It is your God יהוה alone whom you
should follow, whom you should revere, whose
commandments you should observe, whose orders
you should heed, whom you should worship, and
to whom you should hold fast. [6]As for that prophet
or dream-diviner, such a one shall be put to death
for having urged disloyalty to your God יהוה—who
freed you from the land of Egypt and who redeemed you from the house of bondage—to make
you stray from the path that your God יהוה commanded you to follow. Thus you will sweep out evil
from your midst.
[7]If your brother, your own mother's son, or

יג אֶת כׇּל־הַדָּבָר אֲשֶׁר אָנֹכִי מְצַוֶּה
אֶתְכֶם אֹתוֹ תִשְׁמְרוּ לַעֲשׂוֹת לֹא־תֹסֵף
עָלָיו וְלֹא תִגְרַע מִמֶּנּוּ׃ פ

2 כִּי־יָקוּם בְּקִרְבְּךָ נָבִיא אוֹ חֹלֵם חֲלוֹם
וְנָתַן אֵלֶיךָ אוֹת אוֹ מוֹפֵת׃ 3 וּבָא הָאוֹת
וְהַמּוֹפֵת אֲשֶׁר־דִּבֶּר אֵלֶיךָ לֵאמֹר נֵלְכָה
אַחֲרֵי אֱלֹהִים אֲחֵרִים אֲשֶׁר לֹא־יְדַעְתָּם
וְנׇעׇבְדֵם׃ 4 לֹא תִשְׁמַע אֶל־דִּבְרֵי הַנָּבִיא
הַהוּא אוֹ אֶל־חוֹלֵם הַחֲלוֹם הַהוּא כִּי
מְנַסֶּה יְהֹוָה אֱלֹהֵיכֶם אֶתְכֶם לָדַעַת
הֲיִשְׁכֶם אֹהֲבִים אֶת־יְהֹוָה אֱלֹהֵיכֶם בְּכׇל־
לְבַבְכֶם וּבְכׇל־נַפְשְׁכֶם׃ 5 אַחֲרֵי יְהֹוָה
אֱלֹהֵיכֶם תֵּלֵכוּ וְאֹתוֹ תִירָאוּ וְאֶת־מִצְוֺתָיו
תִּשְׁמֹרוּ וּבְקֹלוֹ תִשְׁמָעוּ וְאֹתוֹ תַעֲבֹדוּ וּבוֹ
תִדְבָּקוּן׃ 6 וְהַנָּבִיא הַהוּא אוֹ חֹלֵם הַחֲלוֹם
הַהוּא יוּמָת כִּי דִבֶּר־סָרָה עַל־יְהֹוָה
אֱלֹהֵיכֶם הַמּוֹצִיא אֶתְכֶם ׀ מֵאֶרֶץ מִצְרַיִם
וְהַפֹּדְךָ מִבֵּית עֲבָדִים לְהַדִּיחֲךָ מִן־הַדֶּרֶךְ
אֲשֶׁר צִוְּךָ יְהֹוָה אֱלֹהֶיךָ לָלֶכֶת בָּהּ וּבִעַרְתָּ
הָרָע מִקִּרְבֶּךָ׃ ס
7 כִּי יְסִיתְךָ אָחִיךָ בֶן־אִמֶּךָ אוֹ־בִנְךָ אוֹ־בִתְּךָ

## WARNINGS AGAINST FALSE PROPHETS OR DIVINERS (13:1–19)

This section warns against three capital offenses that might lead Israelites astray from absolute and exclusive allegiance to Israel's God.

*2. prophet.* The first situation involves what we might call "religious professionals," beginning with prophets. The problem of false prophecy was important because people needed to know which individuals truly spoke for God (see at 18:9–22). The *Tanach* includes stories about four female prophets: Miriam (Exodus 15), Deborah (Judges 4–5), Huldah (II Kings 22:14–20), and Noadiah (Nehemiah 6:14), as well as several unnamed female prophets (Isaiah 8:3; Ezekiel 13:17; Joel 3:1). Nehemiah, the governor of Judah in the 5th century B.C.E., implies that Noadiah is a false prophet. (On women prophets, see at 18:15 and *V'zot Hab'rachah*, Another View, p. 1284.)

***dream-diviner.*** Ancient peoples believed that their deities sometimes communicated through signs and dreams if properly interpreted by skilled practitioners. Deuteronomy considers any such practices illegitimate and dangerous; but compare Genesis 40–41, where Joseph interprets dreams without condemnation.

*7–12.* The second case underscores the danger of false worship by prescribing the death penalty for all those—even family members and close friends—

your son or daughter, or the wife of your bosom, or
your closest friend entices you in secret, saying,
"Come let us worship other gods"—whom neither
you nor your ancestors have experienced—8from
among the gods of the peoples around you, either
near to you or distant, anywhere from one end of
the earth to the other: 9do not assent or give heed to
any of them. Show no pity or compassion, and do
not cover up the matter; 10but take that person's
life. Let your hand be the first to put that person
to death, followed by the hand of the rest of the
people. 11Stone that person to death for having
sought to make you stray from your God יהוה,
who brought you out of the land of Egypt, out of
the house of bondage. 12Thus all Israel will hear
and be afraid, and such evil things will not be done
again in your midst.

13If you hear it said, of one of the towns that
your God יהוה is giving you to dwell in, 14that some
scoundrels from among you have gone and subverted the inhabitants of their town, saying,
"Come let us worship other gods"—whom you
have not experienced—15you shall investigate and
inquire and interrogate thoroughly. If it is true, the
fact is established—that abhorrent thing was perpetrated in your midst—16put the inhabitants of that
town to the sword and put its cattle to the sword.
Doom it and all that is in it to destruction: 17gather
all its spoil into the open square, and burn the town
and all its spoil as a holocaust to your God יהוה.
And it shall remain an everlasting ruin, never to be
rebuilt. 18Let nothing that has been doomed stick
to your hand, in order that יהוה may turn from a

אוֹ ׀ אֵשֶׁת חֵיקֶךָ אוֹ רֵעֲךָ אֲשֶׁר כְּנַפְשְׁךָ
בַּסֵּתֶר לֵאמֹר נֵלְכָה וְנַעַבְדָה אֱלֹהִים
אֲחֵרִים אֲשֶׁר לֹא יָדַעְתָּ אַתָּה וַאֲבֹתֶיךָ׃
8 מֵאֱלֹהֵי הָעַמִּים אֲשֶׁר סְבִיבֹתֵיכֶם
הַקְּרֹבִים אֵלֶיךָ אוֹ הָרְחֹקִים מִמֶּךָּ מִקְצֵה
הָאָרֶץ וְעַד־קְצֵה הָאָרֶץ׃ 9 לֹא־תֹאבֶה לוֹ
וְלֹא תִשְׁמַע אֵלָיו וְלֹא־תָחוֹס עֵינְךָ עָלָיו
וְלֹא־תַחְמֹל וְלֹא־תְכַסֶּה עָלָיו׃ 10 כִּי הָרֹג
תַּהַרְגֶנּוּ יָדְךָ תִּהְיֶה־בּוֹ בָרִאשׁוֹנָה לַהֲמִיתוֹ
וְיַד כָּל־הָעָם בָּאַחֲרֹנָה׃ 11 וּסְקַלְתּוֹ בָאֲבָנִים
וָמֵת כִּי בִקֵּשׁ לְהַדִּיחֲךָ מֵעַל יְהוָה אֱלֹהֶיךָ
הַמּוֹצִיאֲךָ מֵאֶרֶץ מִצְרַיִם מִבֵּית עֲבָדִים׃
12 וְכָל־יִשְׂרָאֵל יִשְׁמְעוּ וְיִרָאוּן וְלֹא־יוֹסִפוּ
לַעֲשׂוֹת כַּדָּבָר הָרָע הַזֶּה בְּקִרְבֶּךָ׃ ס
13 כִּי־תִשְׁמַע בְּאַחַת עָרֶיךָ אֲשֶׁר יְהוָה
אֱלֹהֶיךָ נֹתֵן לְךָ לָשֶׁבֶת שָׁם לֵאמֹר׃ 14 יָצְאוּ
אֲנָשִׁים בְּנֵי־בְלִיַּעַל מִקִּרְבֶּךָ וַיַּדִּיחוּ אֶת־
יֹשְׁבֵי עִירָם לֵאמֹר נֵלְכָה וְנַעַבְדָה אֱלֹהִים
אֲחֵרִים אֲשֶׁר לֹא־יְדַעְתֶּם׃ 15 וְדָרַשְׁתָּ
וְחָקַרְתָּ וְשָׁאַלְתָּ הֵיטֵב וְהִנֵּה אֱמֶת נָכוֹן
הַדָּבָר נֶעֶשְׂתָה הַתּוֹעֵבָה הַזֹּאת בְּקִרְבֶּךָ׃
16 הַכֵּה תַכֶּה אֶת־יֹשְׁבֵי הָעִיר הַהִוא לְפִי־
חָרֶב הַחֲרֵם אֹתָהּ וְאֶת־כָּל־אֲשֶׁר־בָּהּ וְאֶת־
בְּהֶמְתָּהּ לְפִי־חָרֶב׃ 17 וְאֶת־כָּל־שְׁלָלָהּ
תִּקְבֹּץ אֶל־תּוֹךְ רְחֹבָהּ וְשָׂרַפְתָּ בָאֵשׁ אֶת־
הָעִיר וְאֶת־כָּל־שְׁלָלָהּ כָּלִיל לַיהוָה אֱלֹהֶיךָ
וְהָיְתָה תֵּל עוֹלָם לֹא תִבָּנֶה עוֹד׃ 18 וְלֹא־
יִדְבַּק בְּיָדְךָ מְאוּמָה מִן־הַחֵרֶם לְמַעַן יָשׁוּב

who entice someone to secretly worship deities other than Israel's God. Wives and daughters are mentioned alongside brothers and sons as people who might entice one to false worship.

*7. wife of your bosom.* This phrase suggests the physical and emotional intimacy of the marital relationship. As it does so, it highlights the grievousness of the transgression and the mandated punishment. Even a loving wife who attempts to lead her husband astray must be stoned to death, with her husband the first person to throw the stone.

*13–19.* The third example moves from the personal to the general, as disloyalty to God condemns an entire town to death.

blazing anger and show you compassion, and in
compassion increase you as promised on oath to
your fathers—[19]for you will be heeding your God
יהוה, obeying all the divine commandments that
I enjoin upon you this day, doing what is right in
the sight of your God יהוה.

יְהֹוָה מֵחֲרוֹן אַפּוֹ וְנָתַן־לְךָ רַחֲמִים וְרִחַמְךָ
וְהִרְבֶּךָ כַּאֲשֶׁר נִשְׁבַּע לַאֲבֹתֶיךָ׃ 19 כִּי
תִשְׁמַע בְּקוֹל יְהֹוָה אֱלֹהֶיךָ לִשְׁמֹר אֶת־
כָּל־מִצְוֺתָיו אֲשֶׁר אָנֹכִי מְצַוְּךָ הַיּוֹם לַעֲשׂוֹת
הַיָּשָׁר בְּעֵינֵי יְהֹוָה אֱלֹהֶיךָ׃ ס

14 You are children of your God יהוה. You
shall not gash yourselves or shave the front of your
heads because of the dead. [2]For you are a people
consecrated to your God יהוה: your God יהוה chose
you from among all other peoples on earth to be a
treasured people.
[3]You shall not eat anything abhorrent. [4]These
are the animals that you may eat: the ox, the sheep,

יד בָּנִים אַתֶּם לַיהֹוָה אֱלֹהֵיכֶם לֹא
תִתְגֹּדְדוּ וְלֹא־תָשִׂימוּ קָרְחָה בֵּין עֵינֵיכֶם
לָמֵת׃ 2 כִּי עַם קָדוֹשׁ אַתָּה לַיהֹוָה אֱלֹהֶיךָ
וּבְךָ בָּחַר יְהֹוָה לִהְיוֹת לוֹ לְעַם סְגֻלָּה מִכֹּל
הָעַמִּים אֲשֶׁר עַל־פְּנֵי הָאֲדָמָה׃ ס
3 לֹא תֹאכַל כָּל־תּוֹעֵבָה׃ 4 זֹאת הַבְּהֵמָה
אֲשֶׁר תֹּאכֵלוּ שׁוֹר שֵׂה כְשָׂבִים וְשֵׂה

## WARNINGS AGAINST ILLICIT MOURNING PRACTICES (14:1–2)

Gashing the skin until it bleeds and shaving were mourning customs practiced by Israelites and some of their neighbors. The other biblical passages that mention gashing or shaving have the connotation of foreignness, even when done by Israelites. For instance, I Kings 18:28 portrays Baal's prophets mourning their god's absence in their time of need by gashing themselves (see also Jeremiah 16:6–7; 41:4–5; 47:5). The textual evidence is ambiguous as to whether women as well as men engaged in these public mourning rituals; yet we do know that certain women were trained to chant dirges that accompanied burial ceremonies (see Jeremiah 9:16–17 and *Chayei Sarah*, Contemporary Reflection, p. 129). Furthermore, iconographic evidence recovered by archeologists depicts women tearing their hair and beating their breasts as signs of mourning.

## DIETARY LAWS (14:3–21)

The dietary laws provide another venue in which Israel must demonstrate its allegiance to God. The regulations found here and in Leviticus 11 are straightforward: Israelites may consume only certain specified animals in order to remain within God's holy community. However, the rationale behind these rules is less transparent. Rabbis, biblical scholars, archeologists, and anthropologists have tried to go beyond the arcane lists of permitted and prohibited animals to understand the purpose for these regulations. While explanations vary, most agree that dietary laws, whatever their origins, were eventually meant to distinguish Israel from other nations and to allow them to demonstrate their loyalty to God. Whether all Israelites were aware of and adhered to the dietary laws is uncertain. However, the absence of pig bones at Israelite sites suggests obedience to at least that rule.

The degree to which dietary rules had an impact on women's lives is unclear. Both women and men worked in the fields, orchards, and gardens—the source of most Israelite food; and both genders tended livestock, while hunting was done mostly by men. [Food preparation was most often a woman's task, but the dietary laws do not directly concern that issue. Rather, they concern which animals are permitted and which are forbidden, and they also ban the consumption of blood. The responsibility for draining blood likely fell to those individuals,

and the goat; [5]the deer, the gazelle, the roebuck, the wild goat, the ibex, the antelope, the mountain sheep, [6]and any other animal that has true hoofs which are cleft in two and brings up the cud—such you may eat. [7]But the following, which do bring up the cud or have true hoofs which are cleft through, you may not eat: the camel, the hare, and the daman—for although they bring up the cud, they have no true hoofs—they are impure for you; [8]also the swine—for although it has true hoofs, it does not bring up the cud—is impure for you. You shall not eat of their flesh or touch their carcasses.

[9]These you may eat of all that live in water: you may eat anything that has fins and scales. [10]But you may not eat anything that has no fins and scales: it is impure for you.

[11]You may eat any pure bird. [12]The following you may not eat: the eagle, the vulture, and the black vulture; [13]the kite, the falcon, and the buzzard of any variety; [14]every variety of raven; [15]the ostrich, the nighthawk, the sea gull, and the hawk of any variety; [16]the little owl, the great owl, and the white owl; [17]the pelican, the bustard, and the cormorant; [18]the stork, any variety of heron, the hoopoe, and the bat.

עִזִּֽים׃ [5] אַיָּ֥ל וּצְבִ֖י וְיַחְמ֑וּר וְאַקּ֥וֹ וְדִישֹׁ֖ן
וּתְא֥וֹ וָזָֽמֶר׃ [6] וְכָל־בְּהֵמָ֞ה מַפְרֶ֣סֶת פַּרְסָ֗ה
וְשֹׁסַ֤עַת שֶׁ֙סַע֙ שְׁתֵּ֣י פְרָס֔וֹת מַעֲלַ֥ת גֵּרָ֖ה
בַּבְּהֵמָ֑ה אֹתָ֖הּ תֹּאכֵֽלוּ׃ [7] אַ֣ךְ אֶת־זֶ֞ה לֹ֤א
תֹֽאכְלוּ֙ מִמַּֽעֲלֵ֣י הַגֵּרָ֔ה וּמִמַּפְרִיסֵ֥י הַפַּרְסָ֖ה
הַשְּׁסוּעָ֑ה אֶֽת־הַגָּמָ֧ל וְאֶת־הָאַרְנֶ֣בֶת וְאֶת־
הַשָּׁפָ֗ן כִּֽי־מַעֲלֵ֧ה גֵרָ֣ה הֵ֗מָּה וּפַרְסָה֙ לֹ֣א
הִפְרִ֔יסוּ טְמֵאִ֥ים הֵ֖ם לָכֶֽם׃ [8] וְאֶת־הַ֠חֲזִ֠יר
כִּֽי־מַפְרִ֨יס פַּרְסָ֥ה הוּא֙ וְלֹ֣א גֵרָ֔ה טָמֵ֥א
ה֖וּא לָכֶ֑ם מִבְּשָׂרָם֙ לֹ֣א תֹאכֵ֔לוּ וּבְנִבְלָתָ֖ם
לֹ֥א תִגָּֽעוּ׃ ס

[9] אֶת־זֶה֙ תֹּֽאכְל֔וּ מִכֹּ֖ל אֲשֶׁ֣ר בַּמָּ֑יִם כֹּ֧ל
אֲשֶׁר־לוֹ֛ סְנַפִּ֥יר וְקַשְׂקֶ֖שֶׂת תֹּאכֵֽלוּ׃ [10] וְכֹ֣ל
אֲשֶׁ֣ר אֵֽין־ל֗וֹ סְנַפִּ֧יר וְקַשְׂקֶ֛שֶׂת לֹ֥א תֹאכֵ֖לוּ
טָמֵ֥א ה֖וּא לָכֶֽם׃ ס

[11] כָּל־צִפּ֥וֹר טְהֹרָ֖ה תֹּאכֵֽלוּ׃ [12] וְזֶ֕ה אֲשֶׁ֥ר
לֹֽא־תֹאכְל֖וּ מֵהֶ֑ם הַנֶּ֥שֶׁר וְהַפֶּ֖רֶס וְהָֽעָזְנִיָּֽה׃
[13] וְהָרָאָ֕ה וְאֶת־הָֽאַיָּ֖ה וְהַדַּיָּ֥ה לְמִינָֽהּ׃
[14] וְאֵ֥ת כָּל־עֹרֵ֖ב לְמִינֽוֹ׃ [15] וְאֵת֙ בַּ֣ת
הַֽיַּעֲנָ֔ה וְאֶת־הַתַּחְמָ֖ס וְאֶת־הַשָּׁ֑חַף וְאֶת־
הַנֵּ֖ץ לְמִינֵֽהוּ׃ [16] אֶת־הַכּ֥וֹס וְאֶת־הַיַּנְשׁ֖וּף
וְהַתִּנְשָֽׁמֶת׃ [17] וְהַקָּאָ֥ת וְאֶת־הָֽרָחָ֖מָה וְאֶת־
הַשָּׁלָֽךְ׃ [18] וְהַחֲסִידָ֞ה וְהָאֲנָפָ֖ה לְמִינָ֑הּ
וְהַדּֽוּכִיפַ֖ת וְהָעֲטַלֵּֽף׃

---

female or male, who slaughtered animals. Some scholars believe that slaughtering and butchering were men's tasks; but the narrative of the medium at En-dor reports that she slaughters a calf (I Samuel 28:24), perhaps indicating that both genders would have had responsibility for adhering to the dietary stipulations. —*Ed.*] (For more on the dietary laws and women's role in food preparation, see at Leviticus 11:1–46.)

*3–8.* These verses allow for the consumption of ruminants with cleft hooves. Such mammals include domestic livestock (sheep, goats, and cattle), those animals most accessible to the average Israelite.

*7. they are impure for you.* The use of the word "impure" (repeated in vv. 8, 10, 19) suggests that dietary laws have a spiritual component and should not be understood as deriving from concerns for health, taste, or aesthetics. (For a different perspective, see at Leviticus 11:1–46.)

*9–10.* For more on the restriction of consuming seafood only with scales and fins, see at Leviticus 11:9.

*11–18.* The list of forbidden birds focuses upon birds of prey. Since the carrion they eat contains blood, eating birds of prey would place Israelites in danger of consuming this prohibited substance.

[19]All winged swarming things are impure for you: they may not be eaten. [20]You may eat only pure winged creatures.

[21]You shall not eat anything that has died a natural death; give it to the stranger in your community to eat, or you may sell it to a foreigner. For you are a people consecrated to your God יהוה.

You shall not boil a kid in its mother's milk.

[22]You shall set aside every year a tenth part of all the yield of your sowing that is brought from the field. [23]You shall consume the tithes of your new grain and wine and oil, and the firstlings of your herds and flocks, in the presence of your God יהוה, in the place where [God] will choose to establish the divine name, so that you may learn to revere your God יהוה forever. [24]Should the distance be too

19 וְכֹל֙ שֶׁ֣רֶץ הָע֔וֹף טָמֵ֥א ה֖וּא לָכֶ֑ם לֹ֖א
יֵאָכֵֽלוּ׃ 20 כׇּל־ע֥וֹף טָה֖וֹר תֹּאכֵֽלוּ׃
21 לֹ֣א תֹאכְל֣וּ כׇל־נְ֠בֵלָ֠ה לַגֵּ֨ר אֲשֶׁר־
בִּשְׁעָרֶ֜יךָ תִּתְּנֶ֣נָּה וַאֲכָלָ֗הּ א֤וֹ מָכֹר֙ לְנׇכְרִ֔י
כִּ֣י עַ֤ם קָדוֹשׁ֙ אַתָּ֔ה לַיהֹוָ֖ה אֱלֹהֶ֑יךָ
לֹא־תְבַשֵּׁ֥ל גְּדִ֖י בַּחֲלֵ֥ב אִמּֽוֹ׃ פ

22 עַשֵּׂ֣ר תְּעַשֵּׂ֔ר אֵ֖ת כׇּל־תְּבוּאַ֣ת זַרְעֶ֑ךָ
הַיֹּצֵ֥א הַשָּׂדֶ֖ה שָׁנָ֥ה שָׁנָֽה׃ 23 וְאָכַלְתָּ֞
לִפְנֵ֣י ׀ יְהֹוָ֣ה אֱלֹהֶ֗יךָ בַּמָּק֣וֹם אֲשֶׁר־יִבְחַר֮
לְשַׁכֵּ֣ן שְׁמ֣וֹ שָׁם֒ מַעְשַׂ֤ר דְּגָֽנְךָ֙ תִּירֹשְׁךָ֣
וְיִצְהָרֶ֔ךָ וּבְכֹרֹ֥ת בְּקָרְךָ֖ וְצֹאנֶ֑ךָ לְמַ֣עַן
תִּלְמַ֗ד לְיִרְאָ֛ה אֶת־יְהֹוָ֥ה אֱלֹהֶ֖יךָ כׇּל־
הַיָּמִֽים׃ 24 וְכִֽי־יִרְבֶּ֨ה מִמְּךָ֜ הַדֶּ֗רֶךְ כִּ֣י לֹ֮א

*19–20.* In general, winged insects that swarm are forbidden as food; but some (a particular type of locust, as well as crickets and grasshoppers) are permitted (Leviticus 11:20–23).

*21.* This verse adds two other food regulations.

***anything that has died a natural death.*** Presumably such animals are prohibited as food for Israelites because they were not slaughtered and then drained of all their blood. In addition, contact with dead animals was a source of ritual contamination that removed people from God's holy community.

***you are a people consecrated.*** According to Deuteronomy, Israelites are God's holy people (see also at Leviticus 19:2); consequently, they must preserve that holiness in their daily lives.

***You shall not boil a kid in its mother's milk.*** The implications and reasons for the injunction against boiling a baby goat in its mother's milk are obscure. Scholars have not found parallels in other ancient Near Eastern legal material. While some see this as a polemic against a pagan rite, most likely this rule attests to biblical respect for the relationship between a mother and her offspring (see 22:6–7), as well as revulsion at the idea that mothers' milk could contribute to death rather than life. [Some contemporary scholars offer a different explanation, arguing that the consonants in the noun *chalav* (milk) can be read as *chelev* (fat); in that case, the verse would forbid cooking a young animal in "its mother's fat." This prohibition would avoid the economic loss involved in slaughtering two animals, one of whom could still bear more young. (See Carol Meyers' discussion of Jack Sasson's research in *Exodus*, 2005, p. 203.) —*Ed.*]

## TITHING REGULATIONS (14:22–29)

Like the dietary laws, obedience to the laws of tithing is considered another requisite for inclusion in God's holy community. Tithing is a type of taxation system, whereby a tenth of what one produced in the fields, vines, and orchards, together with the firstlings of one's herds, is to be consecrated to God. In Deuteronomy the injunction applies to the entire household, women and men alike, who are to rejoice together in God's presence as they consume these tithes at the central sanctuary. (See also Leviticus 27:30–33 and Numbers 18:21–32.)

*24–26.* The stipulation allowing for money to be substituted for agricultural products or animals

great for you, should you be unable to transport them, because the place where your God יהוה has chosen to establish the divine name is far from you and because your God יהוה has blessed you, 25 you may convert them into money. Wrap up the money and take it with you to the place that your God יהוה has chosen, 26 and spend the money on anything you want—cattle, sheep, wine, or other intoxicant, or anything you may desire. And you shall feast there, in the presence of your God יהוה, and rejoice with your household.

27 But do not neglect the [family of the] Levite in your community, for he has no hereditary portion as you have.

28 Every third year you shall bring out the full tithe of your yield of that year, but leave it within your settlements. 29 Then the [family of the] Levite, who has no hereditary portion as you have, and the stranger, the fatherless, and the widow in your settlements shall come and eat their fill, so that your God יהוה may bless you in all the enterprises you undertake.

תּוּכַל֮ שְׂאֵתוֹ֒ כִּֽי־יִרְחַ֤ק מִמְּךָ֙ הַמָּק֔וֹם אֲשֶׁ֤ר
יִבְחַר֙ יְהוָ֣ה אֱלֹהֶ֔יךָ לָשׂ֥וּם שְׁמ֖וֹ שָׁ֑ם כִּ֥י
יְבָרֶכְךָ֖ יְהוָ֥ה אֱלֹהֶֽיךָ׃ 25 וְנָתַתָּ֖ה בַּכָּ֑סֶף
וְצַרְתָּ֤ הַכֶּ֙סֶף֙ בְּיָ֣דְךָ֔ וְהָֽלַכְתָּ֙ אֶל־הַמָּק֔וֹם
אֲשֶׁ֥ר יִבְחַ֛ר יְהוָ֥ה אֱלֹהֶ֖יךָ בּֽוֹ׃ 26 וְנָתַתָּ֣ה
הַכֶּ֡סֶף בְּכֹל֩ אֲשֶׁר־תְּאַוֶּ֨ה נַפְשְׁךָ֜ בַּבָּקָ֣ר
וּבַצֹּ֗אן וּבַיַּ֙יִן֙ וּבַשֵּׁכָ֔ר וּבְכֹ֛ל אֲשֶׁ֥ר תִּֽשְׁאָלְךָ֖
נַפְשֶׁ֑ךָ וְאָכַ֣לְתָּ שָּׁ֗ם לִפְנֵי֙ יְהוָ֣ה אֱלֹהֶ֔יךָ
וְשָׂמַחְתָּ֖ אַתָּ֥ה וּבֵיתֶֽךָ׃
27 וְהַלֵּוִ֥י אֲשֶׁר־בִּשְׁעָרֶ֖יךָ לֹ֣א תַעַזְבֶ֑נּוּ כִּ֣י אֵ֥ין
ל֛וֹ חֵ֥לֶק וְנַחֲלָ֖ה עִמָּֽךְ׃ ס
28 מִקְצֵ֣ה ׀ שָׁלֹ֣שׁ שָׁנִ֗ים תּוֹצִיא֙ אֶת־כָּל־
מַעְשַׂר֙ תְּבוּאָ֣תְךָ֔ בַּשָּׁנָ֖ה הַהִ֑וא וְהִנַּחְתָּ֖
בִּשְׁעָרֶֽיךָ׃ 29 וּבָ֣א הַלֵּוִ֡י כִּ֣י אֵין־לוֹ֩ חֵ֨לֶק
וְנַחֲלָ֜ה עִמָּ֗ךְ וְ֠הַגֵּר וְהַיָּת֤וֹם וְהָֽאַלְמָנָה֙
אֲשֶׁ֣ר בִּשְׁעָרֶ֔יךָ וְאָכְל֖וּ וְשָׂבֵ֑עוּ לְמַ֤עַן יְבָרֶכְךָ֙
יְהוָ֣ה אֱלֹהֶ֔יךָ בְּכָל־מַעֲשֵׂ֥ה יָדְךָ֖ אֲשֶׁ֥ר
תַּעֲשֶֽׂה׃ ס

acknowledges the logistic difficulties encountered when traveling long distances burdened by heavy loads. As seen here and in rules regarding the consumption of meat (12:15–28), Deuteronomy seeks to address the hardships created by centralization of sacrifice, particularly for those living far from Jerusalem. This legislation strives to institute practices that will make it feasible for everyone to participate in the sacred life of the community.

*25. money.* Literally, "silver." Ancient Israel had no official currency system; rather, farmers exchanged standard quantities of grains, produce, and the like for fixed weights of silver. This silver might be in the form of jewelry, cast into ingots, or cut into pieces. Such currency would be easy to carry and could be exchanged for the requisite food and drink in the Chosen Place.

*27–29.* In the third and sixth years of the seven-year sabbatical cycle, Israelites are to give the tithe of their harvest to the needy in their own community, rather than consume it in the Chosen Place of worship.

*29. the [family of the] Levite.* See at 12:19.

*the fatherless, and the widow.* These two individuals lacked the protection of an adult male. Note that the Torah does not offer a systematic way to integrate them into alternate family settings so that they could be cared for and protected by clan elders; neither are they given resources that would enable them to fend for themselves. Rather, like the Levites and like strangers living within Israel's borders, they are placed at the mercy of others who are charged with the responsibility to provide for them. (See also at 10:18 and *Eikev*, Another View, p. 1108.)

**15** Every seventh year you shall practice remission of debts. [2]This shall be the nature of the remission: all creditors shall remit the due that they claim from their fellow [Israelites]; they shall not dun their fellow [Israelites] or kin, for the remission proclaimed is of יהוה. [3]You may dun the foreigner; but you must remit whatever is due you from your kin.

[4]There shall be no needy among you—since your God יהוה will bless you in the land that your God יהוה is giving you as a hereditary portion— [5]if only you heed your God יהוה and take care to keep all this Instruction that I enjoin upon you this day. [6]For your God יהוה will bless you as promised: you will extend loans to many nations, but require none yourself; you will dominate many nations, but they will not dominate you.

[7]If, however, there is a needy person among you, one of your kin in any of your settlements in the land that your God יהוה is giving you, do not harden your heart and shut your hand against your needy kin. [8]Rather, you must open your hand and lend whatever is sufficient to meet the need. [9]Beware lest you harbor the base thought, "The

טו מִקֵּץ שֶׁבַע־שָׁנִים תַּעֲשֶׂה שְׁמִטָּה: [2]וְזֶה֙ דְּבַ֣ר הַשְּׁמִטָּ֔ה שָׁמ֗וֹט כָּל־בַּ֙עַל֙ מַשֵּׁ֣ה יָד֔וֹ אֲשֶׁ֥ר יַשֶּׁ֖ה בְּרֵעֵ֑הוּ לֹֽא־יִגֹּ֤שׂ אֶת־רֵעֵ֙הוּ֙ וְאֶת־אָחִ֔יו כִּֽי־קָרָ֥א שְׁמִטָּ֖ה לַֽיהֹוָֽה: [3]אֶת־הַנָּכְרִ֖י תִּגֹּ֑שׂ וַאֲשֶׁ֨ר יִהְיֶ֥ה לְךָ֛ אֶת־אָחִ֖יךָ תַּשְׁמֵ֥ט יָדֶֽךָ: [4]אֶ֕פֶס כִּ֛י לֹ֥א יִֽהְיֶה־בְּךָ֖ אֶבְי֑וֹן כִּֽי־בָרֵ֤ךְ יְבָרֶכְךָ֙ יְהֹוָ֔ה בָּאָ֕רֶץ אֲשֶׁר֙ יְהֹוָ֣ה אֱלֹהֶ֔יךָ נֹֽתֵן־לְךָ֥ נַחֲלָ֖ה לְרִשְׁתָּֽהּ: [5]רַ֚ק אִם־שָׁמ֣וֹעַ תִּשְׁמַ֔ע בְּק֖וֹל יְהֹוָ֣ה אֱלֹהֶ֑יךָ לִשְׁמֹ֤ר לַעֲשׂוֹת֙ אֶת־כָּל־הַמִּצְוָ֣ה הַזֹּ֔את אֲשֶׁ֛ר אָנֹכִ֥י מְצַוְּךָ֖ הַיּֽוֹם: [6]כִּֽי־יְהֹוָ֤ה אֱלֹהֶ֙יךָ֙ בֵּֽרַכְךָ֔ כַּאֲשֶׁ֖ר דִּבֶּר־לָ֑ךְ וְהַֽעֲבַטְתָּ֞ גּוֹיִ֣ם רַבִּ֗ים וְאַתָּה֙ לֹ֣א תַעֲבֹ֔ט וּמָֽשַׁלְתָּ֙ בְּגוֹיִ֣ם רַבִּ֔ים וּבְךָ֖ לֹ֥א יִמְשֹֽׁלוּ: ס [7]כִּֽי־יִהְיֶה֩ בְךָ֨ אֶבְי֜וֹן מֵאַחַ֤ד אַחֶ֙יךָ֙ בְּאַחַ֣ד שְׁעָרֶ֔יךָ בְּאַ֨רְצְךָ֔ אֲשֶׁר־יְהֹוָ֥ה אֱלֹהֶ֖יךָ נֹתֵ֣ן לָ֑ךְ לֹ֧א תְאַמֵּ֣ץ אֶת־לְבָבְךָ֗ וְלֹ֤א תִקְפֹּץ֙ אֶת־יָ֣דְךָ֔ מֵאָחִ֖יךָ הָאֶבְיֽוֹן: [8]כִּֽי־פָתֹ֧חַ תִּפְתַּ֛ח אֶת־יָֽדְךָ֖ ל֑וֹ וְהַעֲבֵט֙ תַּעֲבִיטֶ֔נּוּ דֵּ֚י מַחְסֹר֔וֹ אֲשֶׁ֥ר יֶחְסַ֖ר לֽוֹ: [9]הִשָּׁ֣מֶר לְךָ֡ פֶּן־יִהְיֶ֣ה דָבָר֩

· · · · · · · · · · · · · · · · · · · · · · · · · · · · · · · · · · · ·

### LAWS OF RELEASE IN THE SEVENTH YEAR (15:1–18)

Similar to the Jubilee laws in Leviticus 25, Deuteronomy seeks to redress certain economic inequities at regular intervals. However, whereas Leviticus 25 prescribes release regulations for a fifty-year cycle, Deuteronomy requires a seven-year adjustment.

### *Remission of Debt* (15:1–11)

This passage articulates the ideal that there will be no needy requiring loans or other forms of assistance, since obeying God's teachings will bring blessing and avert poverty. Nevertheless, it acknowledges that needy individuals will always exist.

**4–5.** Deuteronomy repeatedly makes the point that plenty and well-being come not from hard work or good fortune but rather from God, who blesses those who follow God's instruction.

**4. *hereditary portion.*** In the Bible, the land is Israel's inheritance, promised by God to Israel's ancestors. Although women share in the blessing of its bounty, they generally do not seem to inherit land—the basis for survival. The Bible mentions several cases of women able to inherit land, such as Zelophehad's daughters (see at Numbers 27:1–11 and 36:1–12), the woman of Shunem (II Kings 4), and Job's daughters (Job 42:13–15); but these appear to be exceptions. See further at Numbers 36:11.

**7–11.** This passage enjoins Israelites to lend to their kin with a generous spirit even if they risk losing what they loaned in the seventh-year remission of debt.

seventh year, the year of remission, is approaching," so that you are mean and give nothing to your needy kin—who will cry out to יהוה against you, and you will incur guilt. 10 Give readily and have no regrets when you do so, for in return your God יהוה will bless you in all your efforts and in all your undertakings. 11 For there will never cease to be needy ones in your land, which is why I command you: open your hand to the poor and needy kin in your land.

12 If a fellow Hebrew man—or woman—is sold to you, he shall serve you six years, and in the seventh year you shall set him free. 13 When you set him free, do not let him go empty-handed: 14 Furnish him out of the flock, threshing floor, and vat, with which your God יהוה has blessed you. 15 Bear in mind that you were slaves in the land of Egypt and your God יהוה redeemed you; therefore I enjoin this commandment upon you today.

16 But should he say to you, "I do not want to leave you"—for he loves you and your household

עִם־לְבָבְךָ בְלִיַּעַל לֵאמֹר קָרְבָה שְׁנַת־
הַשֶּׁבַע שְׁנַת הַשְּׁמִטָּה וְרָעָה עֵינְךָ בְּאָחִיךָ
הָאֶבְיוֹן וְלֹא תִתֵּן לוֹ וְקָרָא עָלֶיךָ אֶל־יְהֹוָה
וְהָיָה בְךָ חֵטְא׃ 10 נָתוֹן תִּתֵּן לוֹ וְלֹא־יֵרַע
לְבָבְךָ בְּתִתְּךָ לוֹ כִּי בִּגְלַל ׀ הַדָּבָר הַזֶּה
יְבָרֶכְךָ יְהֹוָה אֱלֹהֶיךָ בְּכָל־מַעֲשֶׂךָ וּבְכֹל
מִשְׁלַח יָדֶךָ׃ 11 כִּי לֹא־יֶחְדַּל אֶבְיוֹן מִקֶּרֶב
הָאָרֶץ עַל־כֵּן אָנֹכִי מְצַוְּךָ לֵאמֹר פָּתֹחַ
תִּפְתַּח אֶת־יָדְךָ לְאָחִיךָ לַעֲנִיֶּךָ וּלְאֶבְיֹנְךָ
בְּאַרְצֶךָ׃ ס

12 כִּי־יִמָּכֵר לְךָ אָחִיךָ הָעִבְרִי אוֹ הָעִבְרִיָּה
וַעֲבָדְךָ שֵׁשׁ שָׁנִים וּבַשָּׁנָה הַשְּׁבִיעִת
תְּשַׁלְּחֶנּוּ חָפְשִׁי מֵעִמָּךְ׃ 13 וְכִי־תְשַׁלְּחֶנּוּ
חָפְשִׁי מֵעִמָּךְ לֹא תְשַׁלְּחֶנּוּ רֵיקָם׃ 14 הַעֲנֵיק
תַּעֲנִיק לוֹ מִצֹּאנְךָ וּמִגָּרְנְךָ וּמִיִּקְבֶךָ אֲשֶׁר
בֵּרַכְךָ יְהֹוָה אֱלֹהֶיךָ תִּתֶּן־לוֹ׃ 15 וְזָכַרְתָּ כִּי
עֶבֶד הָיִיתָ בְּאֶרֶץ מִצְרַיִם וַיִּפְדְּךָ יְהֹוָה
אֱלֹהֶיךָ עַל־כֵּן אָנֹכִי מְצַוְּךָ אֶת־הַדָּבָר הַזֶּה
הַיּוֹם׃

16 וְהָיָה כִּי־יֹאמַר אֵלֶיךָ לֹא אֵצֵא מֵעִמָּךְ כִּי
אֲהֵבְךָ וְאֶת־בֵּיתֶךָ כִּי־טוֹב לוֹ עִמָּךְ׃

*Release of Debt-Servants* (15:12–18)

This passage concerns the Israelite woman or man who becomes a servant as a consequence of financial problems or to fulfill a court judgment. The institution of indentured servitude was common throughout the ancient Near East.

Israelites risked becoming debt-servants when they could not repay loans, pay taxes, or meet other financial obligations. They might be forced to sell themselves or their children into debt-servitude in order to forestall financial ruin or starvation. Children could also become debt-servants after having been pledged as security on a loan that the parents were unable to repay. Because of the six-year limit on the term of servitude, the Hebrew debt-servant is in a position different from that of the foreigner taken as a prisoner of war or purchased from a foreign owner and kept as a slave for life. The Torah regulates the treatment of slaves and forbids the worst of abuses. (See also at Exodus 21:2–11 and Leviticus 25:39–54.)

*12. **Hebrew man—or woman.*** Women were more likely to be sold into servitude on account of the debts of their fathers or husbands, rather than because of debts they themselves incurred. Exodus 21:7–11 provides special rules for the daughter sold into servitude by her parents. In that case, the woman would have been treated as a wife for one of the men in the household; therefore, marital law applied to her, and she would not be expected to leave the household.

and is happy with you—<sup>17</sup>you shall take an awl and put it through his ear into the door, and he shall become your slave in perpetuity. Do the same with your female slave. <sup>18</sup>When you do set either one free, do not feel aggrieved; for in the six years you have been given double the service of a hired worker. Moreover, your God יהוה will bless you in all you do.

<sup>19</sup>You shall consecrate to your God יהוה all male firstlings that are born in your herd and in your flock: you must not work your firstling ox or shear your firstling sheep. <sup>20</sup>You and your household shall eat it annually before your God יהוה in the place that יהוה will choose. <sup>21</sup>But if it has a defect, lameness or blindness, any serious defect, you shall not sacrifice it to your God יהוה. <sup>22</sup>Eat it in your settlements, the impure among you no less than the pure, just like the gazelle and the deer. <sup>23</sup>Only you must not partake of its blood; you shall pour it out on the ground like water.

16 Observe the month of Abib and offer a passover sacrifice to your God יהוה, for it was in the

17 וְלָקַחְתָּ֣ אֶת־הַמַּרְצֵ֗עַ וְנָתַתָּ֤ה בְאָזְנוֹ֙ וּבַדֶּ֔לֶת וְהָיָ֥ה לְךָ֖ עֶ֣בֶד עוֹלָ֑ם וְאַ֥ף לַאֲמָתְךָ֖ תַּעֲשֶׂה־כֵּֽן: 18 לֹא־יִקְשֶׁ֣ה בְעֵינֶ֗ךָ בְּשַׁלֵּֽחֲךָ֙ אֹת֤וֹ חָפְשִׁי֙ מֵֽעִמָּ֔ךְ כִּ֗י מִשְׁנֶה֙ שְׂכַ֣ר שָׂכִ֔יר עֲבָֽדְךָ֖ שֵׁ֣שׁ שָׁנִ֑ים וּבֵֽרַכְךָ֙ יְהֹוָ֣ה אֱלֹהֶ֔יךָ בְּכֹ֖ל אֲשֶׁ֥ר תַּעֲשֶֽׂה: פ

19 כָּל־הַבְּכ֡וֹר אֲשֶׁר֩ יִוָּלֵ֨ד בִּבְקָרְךָ֤ וּבְצֹֽאנְךָ֙ הַזָּכָ֔ר תַּקְדִּ֖ישׁ לַיהֹוָ֣ה אֱלֹהֶ֑יךָ לֹ֤א תַעֲבֹד֙ בִּבְכֹ֣ר שׁוֹרֶ֔ךָ וְלֹ֥א תָגֹ֖ז בְּכ֥וֹר צֹאנֶֽךָ: 20 לִפְנֵי֩ יְהֹוָ֨ה אֱלֹהֶ֤יךָ תֹֽאכְלֶ֨נּוּ֙ שָׁנָ֣ה בְשָׁנָ֔ה בַּמָּק֖וֹם אֲשֶׁר־יִבְחַ֣ר יְהֹוָ֑ה אַתָּ֖ה וּבֵיתֶֽךָ: 21 וְכִי־יִֽהְיֶ֨ה ב֜וֹ מ֗וּם פִּסֵּ֨חַ֙ א֣וֹ עִוֵּ֔ר כֹּ֖ל מ֣וּם רָ֑ע לֹ֣א תִזְבָּחֶ֔נּוּ לַיהֹוָ֖ה אֱלֹהֶֽיךָ: 22 בִּשְׁעָרֶ֖יךָ תֹּֽאכְלֶ֑נּוּ הַטָּמֵ֤א וְהַטָּהוֹר֙ יַחְדָּ֔ו כַּצְּבִ֖י וְכָֽאַיָּֽל: 23 רַ֥ק אֶת־דָּמ֖וֹ לֹ֣א תֹאכֵ֑ל עַל־הָאָ֥רֶץ תִּשְׁפְּכֶ֖נּוּ כַּמָּֽיִם: פ

טז שָׁמוֹר֙ אֶת־חֹ֣דֶשׁ הָֽאָבִ֔יב וְעָשִׂ֣יתָ פֶּ֔סַח לַֽיהֹוָ֖ה אֱלֹהֶ֑יךָ כִּ֞י בְּחֹ֣דֶשׁ הָֽאָבִ֗יב הוֹצִ֨יאֲךָ֜

· · · · · · · · · · · · · · · · · · · · · · · ·

*17. Do the same with your female slave.* Here, in contrast to Exodus 21:7–11, male and female servants are treated equally.

*18. do not feel aggrieved.* As in vv. 9–10, the text anticipates the understandable reluctance by some individuals to follow these laws and offers reassurance.

### LAWS ABOUT THE DEDICATION OF FIRST-BORN MALE LIVESTOCK (15:19–23)

This section establishes that a family must sacrifice and consume unblemished firstlings annually in the Chosen Place (see also 12:17–18; 14:22–29). Similar legislation in Exodus 13:11–15, Leviticus 27:26–27, and Numbers 18:15 designates the firstlings instead for the priests.

### LAWS ABOUT THE PILGRIMAGE FESTIVALS (16:1–17)

These rules for the observance of the three major festivals account for the fact that Israelites are now to celebrate in the Chosen Place, rather than in their own local communities.

*1–8.* The Passover (Pesach) celebration commemorates God's freeing Israel from Egypt. The highlight of the pilgrimage to God's Chosen Place is the sacrifice and consumption of a domesticated animal, with unleavened bread eaten for the duration of the weeklong festival; a solemn gathering is to be held on the last day. Whereas other Passover regulations envision Israelites eating the sacrifice in their homes (see Exodus 12:46), Deuteronomy permits it only in the central sanctuary, a stipulation

month of Abib, at night, that your God יהוה freed you from Egypt. [2]You shall slaughter the passover sacrifice for your God יהוה, from the flock and the herd, in the place where יהוה will choose to establish the divine name. [3]You shall not eat anything leavened with it; for seven days thereafter you shall eat unleavened bread, bread of distress—for you departed from the land of Egypt hurriedly—so that you may remember the day of your departure from the land of Egypt as long as you live. [4]For seven days no leaven shall be found with you in all your territory, and none of the flesh of what you slaughter on the evening of the first day shall be left until morning.

[5]You are not permitted to slaughter the passover sacrifice in any of the settlements that your God יהוה is giving you; [6]but at the place where your God יהוה will choose to establish the divine name, there alone shall you slaughter the passover sacrifice, in the evening, at sundown, the time of day when you departed from Egypt. [7]You shall cook and eat it at the place that your God יהוה will choose; and in the morning you may start back on your journey home. [8]After eating unleavened bread six days, you shall hold a solemn gathering for your God יהוה on the seventh day: you shall do no work.

[9]You shall count off seven weeks; start to count the seven weeks when the sickle is first put to the standing grain. [10]Then you shall observe the Feast of Weeks for your God יהוה, offering your freewill contribution according as your God יהוה has blessed you. [11]You shall rejoice before your God

יְהוָ֨ה אֱלֹהֶ֛יךָ מִמִּצְרַ֖יִם לָֽיְלָה׃ 2 וְזָבַ֥חְתָּ
פֶּ֛סַח לַיהוָ֥ה אֱלֹהֶ֖יךָ צֹ֣אן וּבָקָ֑ר בַּמָּקוֹם֙
אֲשֶׁ֣ר יִבְחַ֣ר יְהוָ֔ה לְשַׁכֵּ֥ן שְׁמ֖וֹ שָֽׁם׃ 3 לֹא־
תֹאכַ֤ל עָלָיו֙ חָמֵ֔ץ שִׁבְעַ֥ת יָמִ֛ים תֹּֽאכַל־
עָלָ֥יו מַצּ֖וֹת לֶ֣חֶם עֹ֑נִי כִּ֣י בְחִפָּז֗וֹן יָצָ֙אתָ֙
מֵאֶ֣רֶץ מִצְרַ֔יִם לְמַ֣עַן תִּזְכֹּ֗ר אֶת־י֤וֹם צֵֽאתְךָ֙
מֵאֶ֣רֶץ מִצְרַ֔יִם כֹּ֖ל יְמֵ֥י חַיֶּֽיךָ׃ 4 וְלֹא־יֵרָאֶ֨ה
לְךָ֥ שְׂאֹ֛ר בְּכָל־גְּבֻלְךָ֖ שִׁבְעַ֣ת יָמִ֑ים וְלֹא־יָלִ֣ין
מִן־הַבָּשָׂ֗ר אֲשֶׁ֨ר תִּזְבַּ֥ח בָּעֶ֛רֶב בַּיּ֥וֹם
הָרִאשׁ֖וֹן לַבֹּֽקֶר׃
5 לֹ֥א תוּכַ֖ל לִזְבֹּ֣חַ אֶת־הַפָּ֑סַח בְּאַחַ֣ד
שְׁעָרֶ֔יךָ אֲשֶׁר־יְהוָ֥ה אֱלֹהֶ֖יךָ נֹתֵ֥ן לָֽךְ׃ 6 כִּ֣י
אִֽם־אֶל־הַמָּק֞וֹם אֲשֶׁר־יִבְחַ֨ר יְהוָ֤ה אֱלֹהֶ֙יךָ֙
לְשַׁכֵּ֣ן שְׁמ֔וֹ שָׁ֛ם תִּזְבַּ֥ח אֶת־הַפֶּ֖סַח בָּעָ֑רֶב
כְּב֣וֹא הַשֶּׁ֔מֶשׁ מוֹעֵ֖ד צֵאתְךָ֥ מִמִּצְרָֽיִם׃
7 וּבִשַּׁלְתָּ֙ וְאָ֣כַלְתָּ֔ בַּמָּק֕וֹם אֲשֶׁ֥ר יִבְחַ֛ר
יְהוָ֥ה אֱלֹהֶ֖יךָ בּ֑וֹ וּפָנִ֣יתָ בַבֹּ֔קֶר וְהָלַכְתָּ֖
לְאֹהָלֶֽיךָ׃ 8 שֵׁ֥שֶׁת יָמִ֖ים תֹּאכַ֣ל מַצּ֑וֹת
וּבַיּ֣וֹם הַשְּׁבִיעִ֗י עֲצֶ֙רֶת֙ לַיהוָ֣ה אֱלֹהֶ֔יךָ לֹ֥א
תַעֲשֶׂ֖ה מְלָאכָֽה׃ ס
9 שִׁבְעָ֥ה שָׁבֻעֹ֖ת תִּסְפָּר־לָ֑ךְ מֵהָחֵ֤ל חֶרְמֵשׁ֙
בַּקָּמָ֔ה תָּחֵ֣ל לִסְפֹּ֔ר שִׁבְעָ֖ה שָׁבֻעֽוֹת׃
10 וְעָשִׂ֜יתָ חַ֤ג שָׁבֻעוֹת֙ לַיהוָ֣ה אֱלֹהֶ֔יךָ
מִסַּ֛ת נִדְבַ֥ת יָדְךָ֖ אֲשֶׁ֣ר תִּתֵּ֑ן כַּאֲשֶׁ֥ר יְבָרֶכְךָ֖
יְהוָ֥ה אֱלֹהֶֽיךָ׃ 11 וְשָׂמַחְתָּ֞ לִפְנֵ֣י ׀ יְהוָ֣ה

that creates additional problems that the laws try to resolve. The language of the regulations uses male singular pronouns; but as 12:12 makes clear, women are expected to share in sacral meals. The problem for most women and many men would have been the distance to the Chosen Place.

*9–12.* The Feast of Weeks (that is, Shavuot) comes seven weeks after the beginning of the spring harvest. It, too, requires pilgrimage to the Chosen Place and is highlighted by a freewill offering that reflects the extent of God's blessing. As is typical of Deuteronomy, the joyous celebration is to be shared by a broad section of society.

*11.* The entire household, including the stranger, fatherless, and widow, is included in the injunction to rejoice before God. Although the Israel-

יהוה with your son and daughter, your male and female slave, the [family of the] Levite in your communities, and the stranger, the fatherless, and the widow in your midst, at the place where your God יהוה will choose to establish the divine name. ¹²Bear in mind that you were slaves in Egypt, and take care to obey these laws.

¹³After the ingathering from your threshing floor and your vat, you shall hold the Feast of Booths for seven days. ¹⁴You shall rejoice in your festival, with your son and daughter, your male and female slave, the [family of the] Levite, the stranger, the fatherless, and the widow in your communities. ¹⁵You shall hold a festival for your God יהוה seven days, in the place that יהוה will choose; for your God יהוה will bless all your crops and all your undertakings, and you shall have nothing but joy.

¹⁶Three times a year—on the Feast of Unleavened Bread, on the Feast of Weeks, and on the Feast of Booths—all your males shall appear before your God יהוה in the place that [God] will choose. They shall not appear before יהוה empty-handed, ¹⁷but each with his own gift, according to the blessing that your God יהוה has bestowed upon you.

אֱלֹהֶ֔יךָ אַתָּ֨ה וּבִנְךָ֤ וּבִתֶּ֙ךָ֙ וְעַבְדְּךָ֣ וַאֲמָתֶ֔ךָ וְהַלֵּוִ֞י אֲשֶׁ֣ר בִּשְׁעָרֶ֗יךָ וְהַגֵּ֤ר וְהַיָּתוֹם֙ וְהָֽאַלְמָנָ֔ה אֲשֶׁ֖ר בְּקִרְבֶּ֑ךָ בַּמָּק֔וֹם אֲשֶׁ֤ר יִבְחַר֙ יְהֹוָ֣ה אֱלֹהֶ֔יךָ לְשַׁכֵּ֥ן שְׁמ֖וֹ שָֽׁם׃ ¹²וְזָ֣כַרְתָּ֔ כִּי־עֶ֥בֶד הָיִ֖יתָ בְּמִצְרָ֑יִם וְשָׁמַרְתָּ֣ וְעָשִׂ֔יתָ אֶת־הַֽחֻקִּ֖ים הָאֵֽלֶּה׃ פ

¹³חַ֧ג הַסֻּכֹּ֛ת תַּעֲשֶׂ֥ה לְךָ֖ שִׁבְעַ֣ת יָמִ֑ים בְּאָ֨סְפְּךָ֔ מִֽגָּרְנְךָ֖ וּמִיִּקְבֶֽךָ׃ ¹⁴וְשָׂמַחְתָּ֖ בְּחַגֶּ֑ךָ אַתָּ֨ה וּבִנְךָ֤ וּבִתֶּ֙ךָ֙ וְעַבְדְּךָ֣ וַאֲמָתֶ֔ךָ וְהַלֵּוִ֗י וְהַגֵּ֤ר וְהַיָּתוֹם֙ וְהָֽאַלְמָנָ֔ה אֲשֶׁ֖ר בִּשְׁעָרֶֽיךָ׃ ¹⁵שִׁבְעַ֣ת יָמִ֗ים תָּחֹג֙ לַיהֹוָ֣ה אֱלֹהֶ֔יךָ בַּמָּק֖וֹם אֲשֶׁר־יִבְחַ֣ר יְהֹוָ֑ה כִּ֣י יְבָרֶכְךָ֞ יְהֹוָ֣ה אֱלֹהֶ֗יךָ בְּכֹ֤ל תְּבוּאָֽתְךָ֙ וּבְכֹל֙ מַעֲשֵׂ֣ה יָדֶ֔יךָ וְהָיִ֖יתָ אַ֥ךְ שָׂמֵֽחַ׃

¹⁶שָׁל֣וֹשׁ פְּעָמִ֣ים ׀ בַּשָּׁנָ֡ה יֵרָאֶ֨ה כׇל־זְכוּרְךָ֜ אֶת־פְּנֵ֣י ׀ יְהֹוָ֣ה אֱלֹהֶ֗יךָ בַּמָּק֛וֹם אֲשֶׁ֣ר יִבְחָ֑ר בְּחַ֧ג הַמַּצּ֛וֹת וּבְחַ֥ג הַשָּׁבֻע֖וֹת וּבְחַ֣ג הַסֻּכּ֑וֹת וְלֹ֧א יֵרָאֶ֛ה אֶת־פְּנֵ֥י יְהֹוָ֖ה רֵיקָֽם׃ ¹⁷אִ֖ישׁ כְּמַתְּנַ֣ת יָד֑וֹ כְּבִרְכַּ֛ת יְהֹוָ֥ה אֱלֹהֶ֖יךָ אֲשֶׁ֥ר נָֽתַן־לָֽךְ׃ ס

ite wife is not specifically mentioned, the inclusion of daughters, female slaves, and widows suggests that wives were included as well as a matter of fact. (See further at 12:12 and Another View, p. 1134.)

*13–15.* The Feast of Booths (Sukkot) also is to be celebrated with the entire community, including all female and male family members and the marginalized elements of society. Blessing and joy are the primary characteristics of this seven-day festival celebrated in the Chosen Place.

*14.* See at v. 11.

*16–17.* The final command, to celebrate the three major feasts in the Chosen Place, underscores gender inequality in Israelite community festivals. Each feast requires the offering of a gift, which reflects the blessing that God has bestowed upon the individual making the offering. Who is required to appear before God and bring a gift reflecting God's blessing? "All your males" (v. 16) are the ones who must see God's "face." [What this rule is meant to convey about females is not clear, especially given that 12:12 and other passages expect women to be present during festival celebrations as well. Assessing the relationship between obligations and exemptions is difficult. (See also Another View, p. 1134.) —*Ed.*]

—*Beth Alpert Nakhai*

# Another View

An important issue in this parashah is the centralization of religious life at the one chosen sanctuary. Yet the wording of several instructions raises at least two questions about the inclusion of women.

First, daughters and female slaves are commanded to celebrate two of the pilgrimage festivals—Shavuot (16:11) and Sukkot (16:14), but not Passover (16:5–8)—along with marginal individuals like widows and orphans. (See also 12:12.) But why are wives not mentioned? The command addressed to the head of household apparently includes the man's wife as the senior female of the household; the head of the household, when male, thus stands for both members of the conjugal pair (see also *Mishpatim*, Another View, p. 445). This implicit inclusion of the wife perhaps authorizes her to act on behalf of her husband should he be unable for any reason to make the pilgrimage trip. In fact, listing her separately would have precluded her status as "second-in-command."

The summary of the stipulations for the three pilgrim festivals presents a second problem, for it specifies that "all your males" shall come to the Chosen Place (16:16). Why are women not mentioned? Some have suggested that Deuteronomy exempts women because the journey might be too difficult for them, especially those with young children. But another possibility acknowledges that agrarian households included animals that could not be left untended for close to two weeks (the weeklong holiday plus travel time). As the chief household managers (see Proverbs 31:10–31), women were the natural ones to maintain the household at such times. Thus, the all-inclusive injunction for everyone to participate in the Sukkot festival every seventh year that is found elsewhere in Deuteronomy (31:10–12) may be idealistic. Alternatively, the insistence on women's participation on that

*The wording of several instructions raises questions about the inclusion of women.*

occasion may emphasize that they too should experience the special covenant renewal of the seventh-year celebration.

Twenty-first-century expectations for gender equality in the Torah are unrealistic. Because Israelite society was organized by lineage units, Deuteronomy addresses many of its instructions to the heads of households (usually male), who bear the main responsibility for fulfilling the Torah's cultic requirements. Yet, although women often are not addressed explicitly in the pilgrimage regulations, they are not forbidden to participate; in fact, several texts indicate their presence. In this respect, the festival commands of Deuteronomy seem more inclusive than comparable rules in Exodus (compare Exodus 23:14–17).

—*Carol Meyers*

# Post-biblical Interpretations

***Together with your households, you shall feast there before your God* יהוה** (12:7). The use of the phrase "your households" (literally "your houses") immediately raises questions about who is included in this designation. Subsequent verses in this parashah (12:12, 18; 16:11, 14) consistently omit wives from lists of participating household members, but they do include other women, such as daughters and female slaves. Thus, early rabbinic interpreters considered the expression for "house" here to mean "wife" (*Sifrei D'varim* 64); in fact, rabbinic texts often equate the two terms (Mishnah *Yoma* 1:1). Rabbinic sources frequently cite a statement to this effect attributed to Rabbi Yosi, who said, "All my life I never called my wife 'my wife' (*ishti*) and my ox 'my ox.' Instead, my wife I called 'my house' and my ox 'my field'" (BT *Shabbat* 118b; BT *Gittin* 52a, among others). Indeed,

*The responsibility to rejoice on festivals applies to everyone, both women and men.*

in talmudic Aramaic one of the words for "wife" is related to the word for "house." Thus, the Rabbis understood a wife to be the essence of a household, and they attached a great deal of significance to this fundamental conviction.

The metaphoric connection between woman and house in the rabbinic imagination led to further elaborations, such as references to the interior organs of the woman's body as various rooms. For example, "the sages made a simile (*mashal mash'lu*) with regard to the woman: the chamber, the antechamber, and the upper chamber" (Mishnah *Niddah* 2:5). At times, women's sexual organs are referred to as doors, hinges, and even keys (BT *B'chorot* 45a).

***You shall consecrate to your God יהוה all male firstlings*** (15:19). The repeated biblical insistence that the first-born be consecrated led to an entire mishnaic tractate, *B'chorot*, which is devoted to the legal aspects of this topic. Among many other concerns, Mishnah *B'chorot* inquires as to what constitutes the status of a first-born animal. Does this include, for instance, an animal that emerged from "its mother's side," presumably by Caesarean birth? The answer is that such a birth does not bestow first-born status on the animal since Numbers 18:15 defines the first-born as literally what "opens the womb." Moreover, biblical law explicitly requires a "male" first-born. Thus, any sexual ambiguity, whether a lack or a doubling of external sexual organs, constitutes a blemish that disqualifies an animal from sacrificial status as a first-born (Mishnah *B'chorot* 6:12).

***You shall rejoice in your festival*** (16:14). According to the Babylonian Talmud, this verse teaches that a husband is obligated to make his wife and children rejoice as part of the holiday observance. A Babylonian sage suggests that wives are made joyous with new clothes; he goes on to claim that in Babylonia women prefer colorful garments, while women in the Land of Israel prefer bleached clothes made from linen (BT *P'sachim* 109a). Another rabbinic tradition based on this verse prohibits weddings during the intermediary days of Passover or Sukkot, since "one should not mix up one joy with another" (BT *Mo'ed Katan* 8b).

***Three times a year... all your males shall appear before your God יהוה*** (16:16). The emphasis on "males" in the concluding verses of the parashah is noteworthy, especially since earlier statements imply that the entire extended household, including daughters and female slaves, was obligated to participate in festival observances. The exclusion of women in this verse appears to contradict the preceding passages. The Rabbis solved this contradiction by subdividing the responsibilities of rejoicing (v. 14) into various components. Accordingly, women and people with sexual ambiguities, such as the hermaphrodite and the non-sexed person, are said to be exempt from the commandment of appearing before God (Mishnah *Chagigah* 1:1), since the biblical verse specifies that males are to do this. "Appearance" (*r'iah*) entails both presence in the Temple and offering a sacrifice, since "they shall not appear before יהוה empty-handed" (16:16). Talmudic discussions (BT *Chagigah* 4b) suggest that the exemption of women from this particular obligation makes sense since bringing a sacrifice in this instance is a time-bound commandment (festival observances take place three times a year on specific days on the calendar). According to an early rabbinic principle, women are exempt from commandments that must be performed at fixed times (Mishnah *Kiddushin* 1:7). However, the responsibility to rejoice applies to everyone (Tosefta *Chagigah* 1:4 and BT *Chagigah* 6b); thus, in that aspect of the festival celebration, women and men are equally obligated.

—*Charlotte Elisheva Fonrobert*

# Contemporary Reflection

"YOU ARE WHAT YOU EAT," the common expression goes. I sometimes think of this saying in relation to kashrut (that is, keeping kosher). What do the choices that we make about what we eat reveal about who we really are? Many Jews today view kashrut as an outdated vestige of ancient Israelite practice, expanded upon by rabbinic Judaism, but no longer relevant to modern day life. However, the presentation of the prohibitions associated with kashrut in *parashat R'eih* challenges us to consider anew the purposes of kashrut.

Deuteronomy 14 tells us what animals, fish, and birds we can and cannot eat. It instructs us not to boil a kid (a young goat) in its mother's milk, an injunction that became the basis for the rabbinic separation between milk and meat (14:21; see also Exodus 23:19 and 34:26). While many Jews today believe the biblical prohibitions against certain meat and fish to be for health reasons, *parashat R'eih* makes no such claim. In fact, if this were the case, the explicit permission to give the stranger and the foreigner the foods we are forbidden to eat (14:21) would be frankly immoral. Rather, *parashat R'eih*, as the Torah does elsewhere, identifies the articulation of eating prohibitions strictly as part of the Israelites' particular path to holiness: "for you are a people consecrated to your God יהוה" (14:21). What is it about these prohibitions that can make us holy? Interestingly, the prohibited foods are identified as *tamei . . . lachem*—ritually impure "for you" (14:7, 8, 10). For this reason, it is perfectly acceptable for other people to eat them, just not for the people Israel.

Traditional and modern commentators have offered various explanations as to why particular fish, poultry, and animals are considered *tahor* ("ritually pure") and therefore acceptable to eat. But perhaps more important than the meaning of each of the details of the prohibitions is the simple fact that we are given a list of dos and don'ts that govern what we are to consume daily. According to the Torah, God asks that we abstain from eating certain foods, not because they are unhealthy or intrinsically problematic, but simply as an expression of our devotion. As with other *chukim* (laws that the rabbinic sages define as being without rational explanation), these prohibitions are like the requests of a beloved: we may not understand them, but we are, in essence, asked to follow them purely as an expression of our love. Daily, the observance of kashrut calls us back to a personal relationship with God.

The laws of kashrut offer a Jewish spiritual discipline that is rooted in the concrete choices and details of daily life—to be practiced in an area that seems most "mundane." In fact, part of the beauty of kashrut is that regardless of our age, personal interests, or geographic location, we all eat, and most of us do so several times a day. While we may sometimes choose to dine alone, eating is almost universally enjoyed as a social activity. A spiritual discipline around eating is one that carries the clear message that spirituality is about far more than what we do in synagogue and on holidays; it extends into every area of our lives, every single day.

Kashrut reminds us again and again that Jewish spirituality is inseparable from what one might term "physical." It teaches us that Jewish spiritual practice is about taking the most ordinary of experiences—in all aspects of our lives—and transforming them into moments of meaning, moments of connection. Kashrut provides a model for doing just that, around issues of food preparation and eating. It's time to cook dinner: What will we make, and how will we prepare it?

*What do our choices about eating reveal about who we really are?*

Will we be driven by an empty stomach or considerations that extend beyond it as well? In these moments, kashrut can connect us to Jewish tradition, to other Jews, and to God. We are hungry and sit down for a meal, but before digging in, we recall that Jewish tradition offers us the practice of pausing for a blessing and a moment of gratitude. We may take this a step further and decide to put aside *tzedakah* regularly at dinnertime, as some of us try to do. This can be seen as a practice similar to the tithing performed in ancient times, as outlined in the verses immediately following the rules of kashrut in our parashah (14:22–29). Instead of just wolfing down our food and moving on to the next activity, we can learn from Jewish rituals to pause and turn the act of eating into a moment of heightened spiritual awareness.

Increasing numbers of Jews today are expanding their kashrut practice to incorporate additional ethical and environmental considerations. Was the food produced under conditions that respect persons and the environment? Were the workers who picked or prepared the food paid a living wage? Did the processes of production treat animals humanely? In addition to allowing these questions to influence our choices about what to eat, we can direct our *tzedakah* money to organizations that address these issues, like environmental and farmworker advocacy groups.

From the time of the Torah onward, Jewish tradition teaches us that the spiritual realm encompasses all of life. Kashrut and the other Jewish practices related to eating exemplify this teaching and extend beyond themselves: they stand as daily reminders to look for additional ways to turn the ordinary into moments of deeper connection and intentionality. Every moment has the potential to be one of connection. Through other *mitzvot*, such as the laws governing proper speech and interpersonal ethics, as well as through the less well-known but rich Jewish tradition of cultivating *middot* (personal qualities such as patience and generosity in judgment), we can seek to deepen our connections with each other and with God. A Jewish spiritual discipline around eating, practiced with intention, can set us on this course every day. "You are what you eat." That is, what you choose to eat and how you choose to eat it says a lot about who you are and what kind of a life you are striving to achieve.

—*Ruth H. Sohn*

# Voices

## Merciful God

Kadya Molodowsky (transl. Kathryn Hellerstein)

*Deuteronomy 14:2*

Merciful God,
Choose another people,
Elect another.
We are tired of death and dying,
We have no more prayers.
Choose another people,
Elect another.
We have no more blood
To be a sacrifice.
Our house has become a desert.
The earth is insufficient for our graves,
No more laments for us,
No more dirges
In the old, holy books.

Merciful God,
Sanctify another country,
Another mountain.
We have strewn all the fields and every stone
With ash, with holy ash.
With the aged,
With the youthful,
And with babies, we have paid
for every letter of your Ten Commandments.

Merciful God,
Raise your fiery brow,
And see the peoples of the world—
Give them the prophecies and the Days of Awe.
Your word is babbled in every language—
Teach them the deeds,
The ways of temptation.

Merciful God,
Give us simple garments
Of shepherds with their sheep,
Blacksmiths at their hammers,
Laundry-washers, skin-flayers,
And even the more base.
And do us one more favor:
Merciful God,
Deprive us of the Divine Presence of genius.

## *from* The Primal Feast

Kim Chernin

*Deuteronomy 14:3–21*

"You'll sit there until you finish your meal," we say to the child who refuses to eat, without in the least realizing how potently we engage in this way a heated debate about identity. . . . Food is so charged, so significant, so informed with primal meaning and first impressions of life, mothering, and the world that we might well expect the communications that take place through food to carry even more weight than those that arise when a child totters about knocking into furniture or pushes a truck across the floor.

And so we come, stage by stage in this way, to adolescence, when the youth must struggle to form an image of what she is and may become. Is it a wonder, then, that she continues to express this struggle through her relationship to food?

## *Seder Eve*

Linda Rose Parkes

*Deuteronomy 16:1–8, 11*

"He who is hungry, come and eat.
He who is needy, come and join our *pesach*."

We have laid a place for the unknown guest.
On the table a bowl of ground almonds,
Boiled egg, fresh horseradish for the bitter herb,
black grapes. Wafting in from the kitchen
is the smell of cholent.

The children are red cheeked
dipping matzos into watered wine.
We stammer prayers from the Haggadah
in this first year of our mother's widowhood,
her grief's long journey.

As the youngest gets up
to open the door for the pilgrim
hope startles us—
Planted before you died,
are the climbing yellow roses;
rocked by the tide, their steady breathing.

## *Widows*

Rashelle Veprinski (transl. David Goldberg)

*Deuteronomy 14:29; 16:11, 14*

Widows—gray grass in autumn
bowed to the earth.
Eyes among shadows
seek buried summers.

Naked, their grief weeps, and they shame
to lift their eyes:
bowed
and bearing a dead name.

And the womb is difficult to bear
pinched to silence;
faces erased
are hid beneath lashes cast down.

They are lost on every path,
and God has quieted desire;
they pick, from life's abundant fields,
stalks of wheat left behind.

## *My Mother*

Celia Dropkin (transl. Kathryn Hellerstein)

*Deuteronomy 14:29, 16:11, 14*

Twenty-two years old,
A widow with two small children,
My mother modestly decided
Not to be anyone's wife again.
Her days and years continued quietly,
As if lit by a meager wax candle.
My mother became wife to no one,
But all the daily,
Yearly, nightly sighs
Of her young and affectionate being,
Of her longing blood
Seeped into me.
I knew them with my child's heart.
And like an underground spring,
My mother's seething, concealed longing
Flowed freely into me.
Now out of me, into the open
Spurts my mother's seething, holy,
Deeply hidden lust.

## *from* The Tapestry of Jewish Time

Nina Beth Cardin

*Deuteronomy 16:1–17*

If Pesach is about departures (for it recalls the Exodus from Egypt) and Shavuot is about arrivals (for it celebrates the giving of the Torah at Mount Sinai), Sukkot is about the journey. It is the holiday that best symbolizes where most of us are most of the time: somewhere in between, midway, sometimes moving, sometimes stuck, always heading—we hope—in the right direction. It reminds us that the way to get somewhere, what we do and learn along the way, where we detour and where we pause, whom we meet and whom we travel with, are as essential to the journey as is the arrival.

## The Journey

Anna Ziegler

*Deuteronomy 16:1–8*

Instead of observing Passover this year,
I have a fight with my boyfriend
outside of Krispy Kreme by the F train.
We can't decide whether or not
to move forward. The night's cool and
    I imagine everyone around me
has a beautiful family
and books on long shelves, candles.

Fast forward twenty years
and I sit at the head of a table
reading from the Haggadah.
There is nothing in me that
remembers wanting this; it feels
as though it's what I've always had.
And yet there was a journey—
desert and forty years
and starvation, the feeling of
being very far away
and not believing in home.

## Sukkot 2001

Julie Pelc

*Deuteronomy 16:13–15*

Beneath the wings of your shelter
I shudder.

You want so desperately to protect us
From the wind
Howling and blowing
Debris that hits
Our backs, our hands, our faces
We hide.

I watch as the four posts
Our stronghold
Sway lightly
And begin tipping, rocking
Leaving the ground
As the wind blows stronger,
Colder.

I look up,
Pray for the spaces
In the branched roof to
Grow smaller
Pray for reasons to stay here
Pray for calm.

But your shelter
Cannot shelter
Forever.

# שֹׁפְטִים ✦ *Shof'tim*

## DEUTERONOMY 16:18–21:9

### *Law and Order*

PARASHAT SHOF'TIM ("magistrates") continues Moses' speech in which he delineates various legal teachings for Israel. This portion focuses on the organization of the community and the promulgation of rules to promote justice within it. Although the logic behind the order of laws in the Bible is not always apparent, in this parashah we can see the relationship between many of the sections. These laws tend to be of a practical nature—for the Bible rarely theorizes or philosophizes. Yet taken together, they draw a picture of the type of ideal society that Deuteronomy envisions. In such a community, justice functions as the operative principle; and all individuals, even the king, come under its rules. Every member of society is entitled to the same justice, in both religious and civil matters. (These two areas of life were not distinguished in ancient times as they are today.) While mainly concerned with the internal workings of the community, justice also applies to the conduct of war. Along with the idea that people deserve a fair government, Deuteronomy expresses the even more important idea that the failure to perform justice constitutes a failure to heed God's commandments, which endangers the future of Israel.

Deuteronomy does not, for the most part, envision women serving as public officials and certainly not as priests or soldiers. However, women figure in a number of laws, especially in the following parashah (*Ki Teitzei*). Most of the laws are phrased in the grammatical masculine (the linguistically unmarked term that often includes both genders); but in some cases, to emphasize that the legislation concerns women and men, the text explicitly addresses both genders. For example, 17:2–5 stipulates that "the man or the woman" who engages in idolatrous worship will be put to death. Although the laws in Deuteronomy do not consider women to be the responsible party in their own right in all matters, they are protected when they might be victims and prosecuted when they are guilty of crimes.

*These laws protect women from victimization and prosecute them when they commit crimes.*

—*Adele Berlin*

## *Outline*

*I.* THE JUDICIAL SYSTEM AND PUBLIC OFFICIALS (16:18–18:22)

- *A.* The judicial system (16:18–17:13)
- *B.* Kings (17:14–20)
- *C.* Levitical priests (18:1–8)
- *D.* Prophets (18:9–22)

*II.* SAFEGUARDING THE JUDICIAL SYSTEM (19:1–21)

- *A.* Cities of refuge (vv. 1–13)
- *B.* Boundary markers (v. 14)
- *C.* Witnesses (vv. 15–21)

*III.* RULES FOR WAR (20:1–20)

*IV.* UNSOLVED MURDER (21:1–9)

*16:18*

You shall appoint magistrates and officials for
your tribes, in all the settlements that your God
יהוה is giving you, and they shall govern the people
with due justice. [19]You shall not judge unfairly: you
shall show no partiality; you shall not take bribes,

טז 18 שֹׁפְטִים וְשֹׁטְרִים תִּתֶּן־לְךָ בְּכָל־
שְׁעָרֶיךָ אֲשֶׁר יְהוָה אֱלֹהֶיךָ נֹתֵן לְךָ
לִשְׁבָטֶיךָ וְשָׁפְטוּ אֶת־הָעָם מִשְׁפַּט־צֶדֶק׃
19 לֹא־תַטֶּה מִשְׁפָּט לֹא תַכִּיר פָּנִים וְלֹא־

## *The Judicial System and Public Officials* (16:18–18:22)

For Deuteronomy, the so-called "civil" and "religious" authorities all fall under the constraints of the justice system. According to Bernard Levinson, this unit provides what appears to be "the first blueprint for a constitutional government" in which "no single branch of government and no single religious institution should have sole power" ("Deuteronomy," *Jewish Study Bible*, 2004, p. 403).

### THE JUDICIAL SYSTEM (16:18–17:13)

This section commands the community (not God) to appoint lay people (not priests or prophets) to serve as professional judges and judicial administrators. Such individuals appear to be selected from among the existing chiefs, military officers, or other types of officials (see 1:15). They are charged with the vital task of executing justice impartially. According to Nili Fox, in the monarchic period the king probably appointed these government officials, who often worked in conjunction with the elders in administering justice (*In the Service of the King*, 2000, pp. 165, 172). The text does not mention any qualifications or training for these "magistrates and officials," nor is their gender specified, for the language is couched in the default grammatical masculine. One may assume that in most cases they would be men, but the possibility of a woman serving as a judge (like Deborah) should not be excluded (see Judges 4–5).

*18. in all the settlements.* Although Deuteronomy centralizes sacrifice (see at 12:2–14), it makes no attempt to centralize the court system; people must be able to obtain justice locally. The Hebrew term translated here as "settlements" is literally "gates," the area at the entrance to a walled settlement where people would come together to conduct their commercial and legal affairs. For example, in Ruth 4:1, Boaz and the unnamed redeemer engage in the transfer of real estate and marriage rights at the gate, in the presence of ten representative elders. In Proverbs 31 (the "Woman of Valor" passage), the husband's position "in the gates" shows him to be a prominent citizen (v. 23); and the woman's works are publicly recognized "in the gates" (v. 31).

*19. you shall not take bribes.* Giving bribes or gifts was common in the ancient world and is often


▸ The military regulations in our parashah deal with the liminal aspects of war.

ANOTHER VIEW ➤ *1158*

▸ Where do we find out about the ways that women approach righteousness and justice?

CONTEMPORARY REFLECTION ➤ *1160*

▸ Apparently the interval between betrothal and marriage could be problematic.

POST-BIBLICAL INTERPRETATIONS ➤ *1158*

▸ War and détente will go on . . . / we can never break free from the dark and degrading past.

VOICES ➤ *1162*

for bribes blind the eyes of the discerning and upset the plea of the just. 20 Justice, justice shall you pursue, that you may thrive and occupy the land that your God יהוה is giving you.

21 You shall not set up a sacred post—any kind of pole beside the altar of your God יהוה that you may make— 22 or erect a stone pillar; for such your God יהוה detests.

17 You shall not sacrifice to your God יהוה an ox or a sheep that has any defect of a serious kind, for that is abhorrent to your God יהוה.

2 If there is found among you, in one of the settlements that your God יהוה is giving you, a man or woman who has affronted your God יהוה and transgressed the Covenant— 3 turning to the worship of other gods and bowing down to them, to the sun or the moon or any of the heavenly host,

תִּקַּח שֹׁחַד כִּי הַשֹּׁחַד יְעַוֵּר עֵינֵי חֲכָמִים
וִיסַלֵּף דִּבְרֵי צַדִּיקִם׃ 20 צֶדֶק צֶדֶק תִּרְדֹּף
לְמַעַן תִּחְיֶה וְיָרַשְׁתָּ אֶת־הָאָרֶץ אֲשֶׁר־יְהֹוָה
אֱלֹהֶיךָ נֹתֵן לָךְ׃ ס

21 לֹא־תִטַּע לְךָ אֲשֵׁרָה כָּל־עֵץ אֵצֶל מִזְבַּח
יְהֹוָה אֱלֹהֶיךָ אֲשֶׁר תַּעֲשֶׂה־לָּךְ׃ 22 וְלֹא־
תָקִים לְךָ מַצֵּבָה אֲשֶׁר שָׂנֵא יְהֹוָה
אֱלֹהֶיךָ׃ ס

יז לֹא־תִזְבַּח לַיהֹוָה אֱלֹהֶיךָ שׁוֹר וָשֶׂה
אֲשֶׁר יִהְיֶה בוֹ מוּם כֹּל דָּבָר רָע כִּי תוֹעֲבַת
יְהֹוָה אֱלֹהֶיךָ הוּא׃ ס

2 כִּי־יִמָּצֵא בְקִרְבְּךָ בְּאַחַד שְׁעָרֶיךָ אֲשֶׁר־
יְהֹוָה אֱלֹהֶיךָ נֹתֵן לָךְ אִישׁ אוֹ־אִשָּׁה אֲשֶׁר
יַעֲשֶׂה אֶת־הָרַע בְּעֵינֵי יְהֹוָה־אֱלֹהֶיךָ לַעֲבֹר
בְּרִיתוֹ׃ 3 וַיֵּלֶךְ וַיַּעֲבֹד אֱלֹהִים אֲחֵרִים
וַיִּשְׁתַּחוּ לָהֶם וְלַשֶּׁמֶשׁ ׀ אוֹ לַיָּרֵחַ אוֹ
לְכָל־צְבָא הַשָּׁמַיִם אֲשֶׁר לֹא־צִוִּיתִי׃

mentioned in the Bible (as in Exodus 23:8; I Samuel 8:3). A bribe may have been offered in order to secure a favorable decision or perhaps just to have the case heard in court.

*20. Justice, justice.* The repetition of the word *tzedek* emphasizes that the pursuit of justice is vital to Israelite society. This verse expresses a recurrent theme in Deuteronomy, that the failure to follow God's instructions will result in the loss of the Promised Land.

*16:21–17:1.* This passage condemns as affronts to God both Canaanite religious practices and wrongly performed Israelite religious practices. The juxtaposition of religious and civil laws here may emphasize that improprieties of civil justice are no less offensive to God than improper religious performance.

*21. sacred post.* Heb. *asherah*, also the name of a Canaanite goddess. Some contemporary scholars think that this goddess may have been popular among Israelites, who perhaps conceived of her as the consort of Israel's (male) God. The *asherah* here may refer to the symbol (a tree or wooden post), not to the goddess herself. (See also at 12:3 and Exodus 34:13.) Nevertheless, Deuteronomy is fiercely monotheistic and tolerates no hint of what it considers syncretism (the combination of Israelite and non-Israelite religious practices) or idolatry.

*17:2–7.* This passage applies to apostates the procedure for capital punishment. The case involves "a man or woman" (a phrase repeated three times in vv. 2, 5) who has transgressed the covenant by engaging in idolatrous practices, a severe transgression with a clear penalty (see 13:13–17). Notice that the text here considers women autonomous persons, responsible for their own actions (not under the control of fathers or husbands) and therefore potentially guilty of a capital offense. In contrast, the passage on prophets (18:15–22) is phrased solely in the masculine, although women prophets existed in the Bible and ancient Near East. (See *V'zot Hab'rachah*, Another View, p. 1284.)

something I never commanded—4and you have been informed or have learned of it, then you shall make a thorough inquiry. If it is true, the fact is established, that abhorrent thing was perpetrated in Israel, 5you shall take the man or the woman who did that wicked thing out to the public place, and you shall stone that man or woman to death.—6A person shall be put to death only on the testimony of two or more witnesses; no one shall be put to death on the testimony of a single witness.—7Let the hands of the witnesses be the first to put [the condemned] to death, followed by the hands of the rest of the people. Thus you will sweep out evil from your midst.

8If a case is too baffling for you to decide, be it a controversy over homicide, civil law, or as-

4 וְהֻגַּד־לְךָ וְשָׁמָעְתָּ וְדָרַשְׁתָּ הֵיטֵב וְהִנֵּה
אֱמֶת נָכוֹן הַדָּבָר נֶעֶשְׂתָה הַתּוֹעֵבָה הַזֹּאת
בְּיִשְׂרָאֵל׃ 5 וְהוֹצֵאתָ אֶת־הָאִישׁ הַהוּא אוֹ
אֶת־הָאִשָּׁה הַהִוא אֲשֶׁר עָשׂוּ אֶת־הַדָּבָר
הָרָע הַזֶּה אֶל־שְׁעָרֶיךָ אֶת־הָאִישׁ אוֹ אֶת־
הָאִשָּׁה וּסְקַלְתָּם בָּאֲבָנִים וָמֵתוּ׃ 6 עַל־פִּי ׀
שְׁנַיִם עֵדִים אוֹ שְׁלֹשָׁה עֵדִים יוּמַת הַמֵּת
לֹא יוּמַת עַל־פִּי עֵד אֶחָד׃ 7 יַד הָעֵדִים
תִּהְיֶה־בּוֹ בָרִאשֹׁנָה לַהֲמִיתוֹ וְיַד כָּל־הָעָם
בָּאַחֲרֹנָה וּבִעַרְתָּ הָרָע מִקִּרְבֶּךָ׃ פ
8 כִּי יִפָּלֵא מִמְּךָ דָבָר לַמִּשְׁפָּט בֵּין־דָּם ׀ לְדָם
בֵּין־דִּין לְדִין וּבֵין נֶגַע לָנֶגַע דִּבְרֵי רִיבֹת

*4. thorough inquiry.* The court establishes an apostate's guilt through physical evidence or, more likely, the testimony of at least two witnesses (v. 6).

*6. two or more witnesses.* The principle of a minimum of two witnesses is articulated again in 19:15 and Numbers 35:30. The Bible does not specify whether women could serve as witnesses. [In the Dead Sea Scrolls (2nd century B.C.E.), women are encouraged to testify as a witness against their husband in certain matters (see Tal Ilan, "Women," *Encyclopaedia Judaica*, 2nd edn., 2007, 21:164). This evidence suggests that women were able to serve as witnesses at certain early periods, perhaps also in the time of the Bible. —*Ed.*] A witness has a crucial role to play in the verdict, so giving false testimony constitutes a serious crime (19:15–21). In the story of Susanna (in the Apocrypha), two corrupt elders falsely accuse Susanna, a young and virtuous wife, of having an encounter with a young man other than her husband. They do so in an attempt to get even with Susanna for refusing their own advances; but when the wise Daniel interrogates the witnesses separately to see if their reports agree, he discovers the ruse.

*7. the hands of the rest of the people.* While public executions are not tasteful to many in contemporary Western societies, the participation of the entire community shows that everyone has a stake in "sweeping out evil" from the community. This practice does not delegate the "dirty work" to professional executioners, but instead holds all the people—or at least a body of their representatives—responsible for carrying out the sentence. (It remains unclear as to whether or not this includes women.)

*8–13.* This passage establishes that the priest or lay magistrate at the central sanctuary adjudicates cases that cannot be solved at the local level, a system similar to that described in Exodus 18:17–23.

*8. If a case is too baffling.* The baffling case involves a situation that lacks two witnesses or any other evidence upon which the local judges can ascertain the truth of the matter. When human beings cannot adjudicate, the case goes to the divine authority, so that God, through God's representatives, can determine the verdict (see 19:17; I Kings 8:31–32); ancient Near Eastern law collections have similar procedures. Before the centralization of sacrifice (the hallmark of Deuteronomy), people would have brought such a case to the local sanctuary.

בִּשְׁעָרֶיךָ וְקַמְתָּ וְעָלִיתָ אֶל־הַמָּקוֹם אֲשֶׁר
יִבְחַר יְהֹוָה אֱלֹהֶיךָ בּוֹ׃ 9 וּבָאתָ אֶל־
הַכֹּהֲנִים הַלְוִיִּם וְאֶל־הַשֹּׁפֵט אֲשֶׁר יִהְיֶה
בַּיָּמִים הָהֵם וְדָרַשְׁתָּ וְהִגִּידוּ לְךָ אֵת דְּבַר
הַמִּשְׁפָּט׃ 10 וְעָשִׂיתָ עַל־פִּי הַדָּבָר אֲשֶׁר
יַגִּידוּ לְךָ מִן־הַמָּקוֹם הַהוּא אֲשֶׁר יִבְחַר
יְהֹוָה וְשָׁמַרְתָּ לַעֲשׂוֹת כְּכֹל אֲשֶׁר יוֹרוּךָ׃
11 עַל־פִּי הַתּוֹרָה אֲשֶׁר יוֹרוּךָ וְעַל־הַמִּשְׁפָּט
אֲשֶׁר־יֹאמְרוּ לְךָ תַּעֲשֶׂה לֹא תָסוּר מִן־
הַדָּבָר אֲשֶׁר־יַגִּידוּ לְךָ יָמִין וּשְׂמֹאל׃
12 וְהָאִישׁ אֲשֶׁר־יַעֲשֶׂה בְזָדוֹן לְבִלְתִּי
שְׁמֹעַ אֶל־הַכֹּהֵן הָעֹמֵד לְשָׁרֶת שָׁם אֶת־
יְהֹוָה אֱלֹהֶיךָ אוֹ אֶל־הַשֹּׁפֵט וּמֵת הָאִישׁ
הַהוּא וּבִעַרְתָּ הָרָע מִיִּשְׂרָאֵל׃ 13 וְכָל־הָעָם
יִשְׁמְעוּ וְיִרָאוּ וְלֹא יְזִידוּן עוֹד׃ ס
14 כִּי־תָבֹא אֶל־הָאָרֶץ אֲשֶׁר יְהֹוָה אֱלֹהֶיךָ
נֹתֵן לָךְ וִירִשְׁתָּהּ וְיָשַׁבְתָּה בָּהּ וְאָמַרְתָּ

sault—matters of dispute in your courts—you shall
promptly repair to the place that your God יהוה
will have chosen, 9and appear before the levitical
priests, or the magistrate in charge at the time, and
present your problem. When they have announced
to you the verdict in the case, 10you shall carry out
the verdict that is announced to you from that place
that יהוה chose, observing scrupulously all their
instructions to you. 11You shall act in accordance
with the instructions given you and the ruling
handed down to you; you must not deviate from
the verdict that they announce to you either to the
right or to the left. 12Should either party act presumptuously and disregard the priest charged with
serving there your God יהוה, or the magistrate, that
party shall die. Thus you will sweep out evil from
Israel: 13all the people will hear and be afraid and
will not act presumptuously again.

14If, after you have entered the land that your
God יהוה has assigned to you, and taken possession

Now, with the absence of local sanctuaries, divine judgment can be rendered only at the central sanctuary (Bernard Levinson, "Deuteronomy," *Jewish Study Bible*, 2004, pp. 404–05).

*9. levitical priests.* This verse seems to refer to the Levites serving as priests at the central sanctuary (see at 18:1).

*or the magistrate.* Some interpreters think that the levitical priests rendered decisions on ritual matters, while the lay judges decided non-ritual cases. While this seems to be the view of II Chronicles 19:8, Deuteronomy 17:8 lists only non-ritual crimes.

*10–13.* The text emphasizes the need to adhere to the judgment rendered and to carry it out as prescribed. The fact that disregarding the verdict itself becomes a capital offense stresses the seriousness of the justice system and the safeguards Deuteronomy imposes to preserve it. At the same time, Deuteronomy limits the authority of human officials (see below).

### KINGS (17:14–20)

The Bible considers a king to be subordinate to God and the legal system; hence, in a remarkable move, it puts limitations on royal power. Unlike in the Laws of Hammurabi and other ancient Near Eastern texts, the king does not promulgate law but instead is subject to it. In Deuteronomy, the king does not explicitly figure in the local or central courts. Elsewhere in the Bible, kings function as the overall guardians of justice. Yet they serve as judges in only a few cases, as when Solomon decides the case of the prostitutes' two babies (I Kings 3:16–28) or when David deals with the "wise woman" of Tekoa, who presents a fabricated case calculated to make David bring his son Absalom back home (II Samuel 14). Perhaps even more surprising, he must continually read and obey the Teaching (*torah*). This section presents a picture here of a "constitutional monarchy" in which the king "will not act haughtily toward his fellows" (v. 20).

of it and settled in it, you decide, "I will set a king
over me, as do all the nations about me," 15 you shall
be free to set a king over yourself, one chosen by
your God יהוה. Be sure to set as king over yourself
one of your own people; you must not set a foreigner over you, one who is not your kin. 16 Moreover, he shall not keep many horses or send people
back to Egypt to add to his horses, since יהוה has
warned you, "You must not go back that way
again." 17 And he shall not have many wives, lest his
heart go astray; nor shall he amass silver and gold to
excess.

18 When he is seated on his royal throne, he shall
have a copy of this Teaching written for him on a

אָשִׂ֥ימָה עָלַי֙ מֶ֔לֶךְ כְּכָל־הַגּוֹיִ֖ם אֲשֶׁ֥ר
סְבִיבֹתָֽי׃ 15 שׂ֣וֹם תָּשִׂ֤ים עָלֶ֙יךָ֙ מֶ֔לֶךְ אֲשֶׁ֥ר
יִבְחַ֛ר יְהֹוָ֥ה אֱלֹהֶ֖יךָ בּ֑וֹ מִקֶּ֣רֶב אַחֶ֗יךָ תָּשִׂ֤ים
עָלֶ֙יךָ֙ מֶ֔לֶךְ לֹ֣א תוּכַ֗ל לָתֵ֤ת עָלֶ֙יךָ֙ אִ֣ישׁ נָכְרִ֔י
אֲשֶׁ֥ר לֹא־אָחִ֖יךָ הֽוּא׃ 16 רַק֮ לֹא־יַרְבֶּה־לּ֣וֹ
סוּסִים֒ וְלֹֽא־יָשִׁ֤יב אֶת־הָעָם֙ מִצְרַ֔יְמָה לְמַ֖עַן
הַרְבּ֣וֹת ס֑וּס וַֽיהֹוָה֙ אָמַ֣ר לָכֶ֔ם לֹ֣א תֹסִפ֗וּן
לָשׁ֛וּב בַּדֶּ֥רֶךְ הַזֶּ֖ה עֽוֹד׃ 17 וְלֹ֤א יַרְבֶּה־לּוֹ֙
נָשִׁ֔ים וְלֹ֥א יָס֖וּר לְבָב֑וֹ וְכֶ֣סֶף וְזָהָ֔ב לֹ֥א
יַרְבֶּה־לּ֖וֹ מְאֹֽד׃
18 וְהָיָ֣ה כְשִׁבְתּ֔וֹ עַ֖ל כִּסֵּ֣א מַמְלַכְתּ֑וֹ וְכָ֨תַב
ל֜וֹ אֶת־מִשְׁנֵ֨ה הַתּוֹרָ֤ה הַזֹּאת֙ עַל־סֵ֔פֶר

*14.* ***after you have entered the land.*** Although modern scholars date some parts of Deuteronomy to the time of Josiah (late 7th century B.C.E.) and other parts to the Babylonian exile (6th century B.C.E.), the book presents itself as reporting what took place just before the Israelites would cross the Jordan and enter Canaan.

***"as do all the nations about me."*** This statement, put into the mouths of the Israelites, anticipates the reason found in I Samuel 8:5 for requesting a king: because the other nations have kings. Such a request presumes that Israel must have this form of centralized government, rather than the decentralized tribal system, in order to be competitive with its neighbors, especially when it comes to military campaigns.

*16.* ***he shall not keep many horses.*** This and the following verse use the portrait of Solomon to criticize the dangers of excessive royal power. According to I Kings 5:6 and 10:26, Solomon had 40,000 stalls of horses, 12,000 horsemen, 1,400 chariots, and 12,000 horses, which he imported from Egypt and Kue. These large numbers function as a way to show Solomon's wealth and grandeur—precisely what Deuteronomy seeks to limit.

*17.* ***he shall not have many wives.*** This criticism also is built on the portrait of Solomon, who reportedly had a thousand wives (I Kings 11:1–5), many of them foreigners with whom he made political marriages. Such marriages were common in the ancient world for their diplomatic benefits, for they worked to assure peaceful relations between the royal families and thus their countries. The fact that Israelite kings had foreign wives of royal lineage shows they were players on the international scene. The Bible is concerned with the importation of foreign wives, because it believed these wives introduced their own forms of foreign worship into the royal court, thereby "leading the people astray" with idolatrous practices. Jezebel stands out as a prime example, for this Phoenician princess and wife of King Ahab worshipped Baal—and led her husband to do so as well (I Kings 16:31–33; 21:25–26).

***nor shall he amass silver and gold.*** The text also condemns accumulating large wealth, a danger in most monarchies. This, too, reflects the portrait of Solomon in I Kings 10.

*18.* ***a copy of this Teaching.*** Levitical priests will write a copy of the Teaching for the king, who must read it regularly. The word for "Teaching," *torah*, does not refer to the so-called Five Books of Moses, nor probably even to the book of Deuteronomy, but rather to this section pertaining to the king, or to other legal portions of Deuteronomy.

scroll by the levitical priests. [19]Let it remain with him and let him read in it all his life, so that he may learn to revere his God יהוה, to observe faithfully every word of this Teaching as well as these laws. [20]Thus he will not act haughtily toward his fellows or deviate from the Instruction to the right or to the left, to the end that he and his descendants may reign long in the midst of Israel.

*18* The levitical priests, the whole tribe of Levi, shall have no territorial portion with Israel. They shall live only off יהוה's offerings by fire as their portion, [2]and shall have no portion among their brother tribes: יהוה is their portion, as promised.

מִלִּפְנֵי הַכֹּהֲנִים הַלְוִיִּם׃ 19 וְהָיְתָה עִמּוֹ
וְקָרָא בוֹ כָּל־יְמֵי חַיָּיו לְמַעַן יִלְמַד לְיִרְאָה
אֶת־יְהֹוָה אֱלֹהָיו לִשְׁמֹר אֶת־כָּל־דִּבְרֵי
הַתּוֹרָה הַזֹּאת וְאֶת־הַחֻקִּים הָאֵלֶּה
לַעֲשֹׂתָם׃ 20 לְבִלְתִּי רוּם־לְבָבוֹ מֵאֶחָיו
וּלְבִלְתִּי סוּר מִן־הַמִּצְוָה יָמִין וּשְׂמֹאול
לְמַעַן יַאֲרִיךְ יָמִים עַל־מַמְלַכְתּוֹ הוּא וּבָנָיו
בְּקֶרֶב יִשְׂרָאֵל׃ ס

יח לֹא־יִהְיֶה לַכֹּהֲנִים הַלְוִיִּם כָּל־שֵׁבֶט
לֵוִי חֵלֶק וְנַחֲלָה עִם־יִשְׂרָאֵל אִשֵּׁי יְהֹוָה
וְנַחֲלָתוֹ יֹאכֵלוּן׃ 2 וְנַחֲלָה לֹא־יִהְיֶה־לּוֹ
בְּקֶרֶב אֶחָיו יְהֹוָה הוּא נַחֲלָתוֹ כַּאֲשֶׁר
דִּבֶּר־לוֹ׃ ס

This law aims to emphasize and remind the king constantly that he is subject to God's law. In Hebrew, the term *mishneh torah* ("copy of this Teaching," literally "a second *torah*") becomes one of the names for Deuteronomy in rabbinic literature, since the book reviews large parts of the earlier books of the Torah (*Sifrei D'varim* 160). The Greek translation of this term is "Deuteronomion," hence the English name of the book.

### LEVITICAL PRIESTS
(18:1–8)

Unlike the laws concerning the king, this section expresses no interest in limiting the power of the levitical priests, but rather in ensuring that they, as a disadvantaged class, obtain their due. Their disadvantage lies in the fact that they have no land holdings, the main source of income for non-levitical Israelites in an agricultural society (see at 12:19). Levites therefore depend for their livelihood on a "tax" levied on sacrifices and tithes. The Israelites, to whom these instructions are addressed, must see to it that the levitical priests receive their proper income.

*1.* ***The levitical priests, the whole tribe of Levi.*** Leviticus and Numbers typically distinguish between priests (*kohanim*, a special subset of Levites defined as the descendants of Aaron) and Levites; only the *kohanim* can officiate in the presentation of offerings to God and can eat certain portions of sacrificial foodstuffs (see Numbers 16 and 18). Deuteronomy uses the anomalous term "levitical priests" (literally "the priests the Levites"), suggesting that it does not see two distinct classes but rather one group of potential priests. Deuteronomy gives all Levites the same right to eat portions from the sacrifices (a privilege limited to the priests in the other sources), and permits all of them to serve at the central sanctuary if they choose.

*2.* **יהוה *is their portion.*** The Hebrew has a singular suffix, "his (or its) portion"; the translation understands the antecedent to be the tribe of Levi (as in 10:8–9). Any allotted portion would include the women in the families, hence the frequent insertion in our translation of the phrase "[family of the] Levite" (as in 12:12). This phrase occurs in *Yizkor*, the memorial prayers for the dead, who no longer have a stake in this world but are in God's care.

3 This then shall be the priests' due from the people: Everyone who offers a sacrifice, whether an ox or a sheep, must give the shoulder, the cheeks, and the stomach to the priest. 4 You shall also give him the first fruits of your new grain and wine and oil, and the first shearing of your sheep. 5 For your God יהוה has chosen him and his descendants, out of all your tribes, to be in attendance for service in the name of יהוה for all time.

6 If a Levite would go, from any of the settlements throughout Israel where he has been residing, to the place that יהוה has chosen, he may do so whenever he pleases. 7 He may serve in the name of his God יהוה like all his fellow Levites who are there in attendance before יהוה. 8 They shall receive equal shares of the dues, without regard to personal gifts or patrimonies.

9 When you enter the land that your God יהוה is giving you, you shall not learn to imitate the abhorrent practices of those nations. 10 Let no one be

3 וְזֶה יִהְיֶה מִשְׁפַּט הַכֹּהֲנִים מֵאֵת הָעָם
מֵאֵת זֹבְחֵי הַזֶּבַח אִם־שׁוֹר אִם־שֶׂה וְנָתַן
לַכֹּהֵן הַזְּרֹעַ וְהַלְּחָיַיִם וְהַקֵּבָה׃ 4 רֵאשִׁית
דְּגָנְךָ תִּירֹשְׁךָ וְיִצְהָרֶךָ וְרֵאשִׁית גֵּז צֹאנְךָ
תִּתֶּן־לּוֹ׃ 5 כִּי בוֹ בָּחַר יְהֹוָה אֱלֹהֶיךָ מִכָּל־
שְׁבָטֶיךָ לַעֲמֹד לְשָׁרֵת בְּשֵׁם־יְהֹוָה הוּא
וּבָנָיו כָּל־הַיָּמִים׃ ס

6 וְכִי־יָבֹא הַלֵּוִי מֵאַחַד שְׁעָרֶיךָ מִכָּל־
יִשְׂרָאֵל אֲשֶׁר־הוּא גָּר שָׁם וּבָא בְּכָל־
אַוַּת נַפְשׁוֹ אֶל־הַמָּקוֹם אֲשֶׁר־יִבְחַר יְהֹוָה׃
7 וְשֵׁרֵת בְּשֵׁם יְהֹוָה אֱלֹהָיו כְּכָל־אֶחָיו
הַלְוִיִּם הָעֹמְדִים שָׁם לִפְנֵי יְהֹוָה׃
8 חֵלֶק כְּחֵלֶק יֹאכֵלוּ לְבַד מִמְכָּרָיו עַל־
הָאָבוֹת׃ ס

9 כִּי אַתָּה בָּא אֶל־הָאָרֶץ אֲשֶׁר־יְהֹוָה
אֱלֹהֶיךָ נֹתֵן לָךְ לֹא־תִלְמַד לַעֲשׂוֹת
כְּתוֹעֲבֹת הַגּוֹיִם הָהֵם׃ 10 לֹא־יִמָּצֵא בְךָ

***6–8.*** Since Deuteronomy outlaws local sanctuaries, the Levites formerly serving at these sanctuaries can no longer earn a livelihood except at the central sanctuary. Those who do not serve there must depend on communal charity, along with the widow, the fatherless, and the stranger (see 14:27–29; 16:11, 14; 26:12). Our passage seems to try to avoid that situation by providing the option for the unemployed Levite to find employment and allotment from sacrifices at the central sanctuary.

***8.*** ***equal shares.*** The displaced Levites will share equally in the sacrificial portions enumerated in 18:3–4. In practice, the Jerusalem priesthood may have objected to this arrangement (see II Kings 23:9).

## PROPHETS (18:9–22)

After banning various types of foreign divination (18:9–14), Deuteronomy addresses the type of divine intermediary most common in the Bible, the prophet (18:15–22).

***9.*** ***When you enter the land.*** Like most of the laws in Deuteronomy, this one pertains to the settlement in the Promised Land. In this case, the danger concerns the negative religious influence of the Canaanites. Modern scholars note that by the time Deuteronomy was composed, the Canaanites were long gone. Thus, the Bible uses the term "Canaanite" anachronistically as a symbol for "the other," often defining what is Israelite in opposition to what it calls Canaanite. Our passage uses "those nations" to refer to the various nations living in Canaan (Canaanites, Perizzites, and so forth). The practices listed as abhorrent are attested widely throughout the ancient Near East.

***10–11.*** Deuteronomy takes for granted that either females or males might perform the types of divination listed here (compare Leviticus 20:27). These practices are abhorrent to God not because

מַעֲבִיר בְּנוֹ־וּבִתּוֹ בָּאֵשׁ קֹסֵם קְסָמִים מְעוֹנֵן
וּמְנַחֵשׁ וּמְכַשֵּׁף׃ 11 וְחֹבֵר חָבֶר וְשֹׁאֵל אוֹב
וְיִדְּעֹנִי וְדֹרֵשׁ אֶל־הַמֵּתִים׃ 12 כִּי־תוֹעֲבַת
יְהוָה כָּל־עֹשֵׂה אֵלֶּה וּבִגְלַל הַתּוֹעֵבֹת
הָאֵלֶּה יְהוָה אֱלֹהֶיךָ מוֹרִישׁ אוֹתָם מִפָּנֶיךָ׃
13 תָּמִים תִּהְיֶה עִם יְהוָה אֱלֹהֶיךָ׃ 14 כִּי ׀
הַגּוֹיִם הָאֵלֶּה אֲשֶׁר אַתָּה יוֹרֵשׁ אוֹתָם אֶל־
מְעֹנְנִים וְאֶל־קֹסְמִים יִשְׁמָעוּ וְאַתָּה לֹא כֵן
נָתַן לְךָ יְהוָה אֱלֹהֶיךָ׃
15 נָבִיא מִקִּרְבְּךָ מֵאַחֶיךָ כָּמֹנִי יָקִים לְךָ
יְהוָה אֱלֹהֶיךָ אֵלָיו תִּשְׁמָעוּן׃ 16 כְּכֹל

found among you who consigns a son or daughter
to the fire, or who is an augur, a soothsayer, a diviner, a sorcerer, 11 one who casts spells, or one who
consults ghosts or familiar spirits, or one who inquires of the dead. 12 For anyone who does such
things is abhorrent to יהוה, and it is because of
these abhorrent things that your God יהוה is dispossessing them before you. 13 You must be whole-
hearted with your God יהוה. 14 Those nations that
you are about to dispossess do indeed resort to
soothsayers and augurs; to you, however, your
God יהוה has not assigned the like.
15 From among your own people, your God יהוה
will raise up for you a prophet like myself; that is
whom you shall heed. 16 This is just what you asked

they are ineffective, but because they call upon powers other than God, thereby undermining monotheistic belief.

*10. consigns a son or daughter to the fire.* The nature of this practice remains unclear. Its link here with other types of divination suggests that it is not child sacrifice, but a form of divination no longer known to us.

*11. consults ghosts.* The story of the medium of En-dor (I Samuel 28) and Isaiah 29:4 both confirm that communicating with the dead, or necromancy, was practiced in Israel. King Saul consults the medium of En-dor, a female necromancer, when all other forms of communication with the Divine have failed; and she successfully enables Saul to communicate with the dead prophet Samuel. Many Israelites, like other peoples of the time and later, showed an abiding concern for the dead, especially dead ancestors (see also at 26:14).

*12. dispossessing them.* Genesis 15:16, Leviticus 18:24–30, and Deuteronomy 9:4 all note that Israel will be entitled to dispossess the indigenous nations of Canaan as a result of the abhorrent practices detailed there. Deuteronomy repeatedly reminds the people that Israel risks being dispossessed from the land for similar reasons.

*15–22.* Having banned various divinatory practices, Deuteronomy now explains the legitimate way for Israel to access God's will: through a prophet. The type of prophecy envisioned derives from the people's desire for professional intermediaries to whom they could pose questions and receive information that would help them make decisions. In addition, as part of the narrative of the revelation at Sinai, the people request an intermediary in order to avoid the dangers inherent when one has direct contact with God (see 5:19–24; Exodus 20:15–18).

*15. like myself.* Moses serves as the model for all later prophets, even though no prophet has as close contact with God as he did (see Deuteronomy 34:10). The Hebrew speaks of the prophet in the masculine, as this is the linguistic default; but that does not exclude female prophets. The Bible refers to four female prophets by name: Miriam (Exodus 15:20), Deborah (Judges 4:4), Huldah (II Kings 22:14–20), and Noadiah (Nehemiah 6:14); other passages mention unnamed female prophets (Isaiah 8:3; Ezekiel 13:17; Joel 3:1).

of your God יהוה at Horeb, on the day of the Assembly, saying, "Let me not hear the voice of my God יהוה any longer or see this wondrous fire any more, lest I die." [17]Whereupon יהוה said to me, "They have done well in speaking thus. [18]I will raise up for them from among their own people a prophet like yourself, in whose mouth I will put My words and who will speak to them all that I command; [19]and anybody who fails to heed the words [the prophet] speaks in My name, I Myself will call to account. [20]But any prophet who presumes to speak in My name an oracle that I did not command to be uttered, or who speaks in the name of other gods—that prophet shall die." [21]And should you ask yourselves, "How can we know that the oracle was not spoken by יהוה?"—[22]if the prophet speaks in the name of יהוה and the oracle does not come true, that oracle was not spoken by יהוה; the prophet has uttered it presumptuously: do not stand in dread of that person.

**19** When your God יהוה has cut down the nations whose land your God יהוה is assigning to you, and you have dispossessed them and settled in their towns and homes, [2]you shall set aside three

אֲשֶׁר־שָׁאַ֜לְתָּ מֵעִ֨ם יְהֹוָ֤ה אֱלֹהֶ֙יךָ֙ בְּחֹרֵ֔ב
בְּי֣וֹם הַקָּהָל֮ לֵאמֹר֒ לֹ֣א אֹסֵ֗ף לִשְׁמֹ֙עַ֙ אֶת־
ק֙וֹל֙ יְהֹוָ֣ה אֱלֹהָ֔י וְאֶת־הָאֵ֥שׁ הַגְּדֹלָ֛ה הַזֹּ֖את
לֹֽא־אֶרְאֶ֥ה ע֖וֹד וְלֹ֥א אָמֽוּת: [17]וַיֹּ֥אמֶר
יְהֹוָ֖ה אֵלָ֑י הֵיטִ֖יבוּ אֲשֶׁ֥ר דִּבֵּֽרוּ: [18]נָבִ֨יא
אָקִ֥ים לָהֶ֛ם מִקֶּ֥רֶב אֲחֵיהֶ֖ם כָּמ֑וֹךָ וְנָתַתִּ֤י
דְבָרַי֙ בְּפִ֔יו וְדִבֶּ֣ר אֲלֵיהֶ֔ם אֵ֖ת כָּל־אֲשֶׁ֥ר
אֲצַוֶּֽנּוּ: [19]וְהָיָ֣ה הָאִ֗ישׁ אֲשֶׁ֤ר לֹֽא־יִשְׁמַע֙
אֶל־דְּבָרַ֔י אֲשֶׁ֥ר יְדַבֵּ֖ר בִּשְׁמִ֑י אָנֹכִ֖י אֶדְרֹ֥שׁ
מֵעִמּֽוֹ: [20]אַ֣ךְ הַנָּבִ֡יא אֲשֶׁ֣ר יָזִיד֩ לְדַבֵּ֨ר דָּבָ֜ר
בִּשְׁמִ֗י אֵ֣ת אֲשֶׁ֤ר לֹֽא־צִוִּיתִיו֙ לְדַבֵּ֔ר וַאֲשֶׁ֣ר
יְדַבֵּ֔ר בְּשֵׁ֖ם אֱלֹהִ֣ים אֲחֵרִ֑ים וּמֵ֖ת הַנָּבִ֥יא
הַהֽוּא: [21]וְכִ֥י תֹאמַ֖ר בִּלְבָבֶ֑ךָ אֵיכָה֙ נֵדַ֣ע
אֶת־הַדָּבָ֔ר אֲשֶׁ֥ר לֹֽא־דִבְּר֖וֹ יְהֹוָֽה: [22]אֲשֶׁר֩
יְדַבֵּ֨ר הַנָּבִ֜יא בְּשֵׁ֣ם יְהֹוָ֗ה וְלֹֽא־יִהְיֶ֤ה הַדָּבָר֙
וְלֹ֣א יָבֹ֔א ה֣וּא הַדָּבָ֔ר אֲשֶׁ֥ר לֹֽא־דִבְּר֖וֹ יְהֹוָ֑ה
בְּזָדוֹן֙ דִּבְּר֣וֹ הַנָּבִ֔יא לֹ֥א תָג֖וּר מִמֶּֽנּוּ: ס

**יט** כִּֽי־יַכְרִ֞ית יְהֹוָ֤ה אֱלֹהֶ֙יךָ֙ אֶת־הַגּוֹיִ֔ם
אֲשֶׁר֙ יְהֹוָ֣ה אֱלֹהֶ֔יךָ נֹתֵ֥ן לְךָ֖ אֶת־אַרְצָ֑ם
וִֽירִשְׁתָּ֕ם וְיָשַׁבְתָּ֥ בְעָרֵיהֶ֖ם וּבְבָתֵּיהֶֽם:
[2]שָׁל֥וֹשׁ עָרִ֖ים תַּבְדִּ֣יל לָ֑ךְ בְּת֖וֹךְ אַרְצְךָ֙

---

**16.** *Horeb.* This is Deuteronomy's term for Sinai (see at Exodus 18:5). Moses explains that the people requested an intermediary lest direct contact with the Divine prove fatal.

**18–22.** The most crucial attribute of the true prophet is that he or she speaks in God's name. Since the prophet serves as the vehicle through whom God communicates, the true prophet must be taken seriously and heeded. Clearly, a prophet speaking in the name of a foreign god is false, but what about a prophet who claims to be speaking in God's name—how is the audience to know if the prophet truly speaks God's words? This passage establishes the criterion of whether or not those words come to pass, which means that the audience

must wait for the outcome of the prophecy. Jeremiah offers a slightly different test, suggesting that one need wait for the outcome only in prophecies of weal, whereas prophecies of doom should always be believed (Jeremiah 28:7–9).

## Safeguarding the Judicial System
### (19:1–21)

The three topics in this unit all involve guarding justice. The first two concern space or location pertaining to public officials; the third elaborates on the stipulations regarding witnesses introduced in 17:6.

cities in the land that your God יהוה is giving you to possess. ³You shall survey the distances, and divide into three parts the territory of the country that your God יהוה has allotted to you, so that any [male] killer may have a place to flee to.—⁴Now this is the case of the killer who may flee there and live: one who has slain a fellow [Israelite] unwittingly, without having been an enemy in the past. ⁵For instance, a man goes with another fellow into a grove to cut wood; as his hand swings the ax to cut down a tree, the ax-head flies off the handle and strikes the other so that he dies. That man shall flee to one of these cities and live.—⁶Otherwise, when the distance is great, the blood-avenger, pursuing the killer in hot anger, may overtake him and strike him down; yet he did not incur the death penalty, since he had never been the other's enemy. ⁷That is why I command you: set aside three cities.

⁸And when your God יהוה enlarges your territory, as was sworn to your fathers, and gives you all the land that was promised to be given to your fathers—⁹if you faithfully observe all this Instruction

אֲשֶׁר֩ יְהֹוָ֨ה אֱלֹהֶ֜יךָ נֹתֵ֥ן לְךָ֖ לְרִשְׁתָּֽהּ׃
3 תָּכִ֣ין לְךָ֮ הַדֶּ֒רֶךְ֒ וְשִׁלַּשְׁתָּ֙ אֶת־גְּב֣וּל אַרְצְךָ֔ אֲשֶׁ֥ר יַנְחִֽילְךָ֖ יְהֹוָ֣ה אֱלֹהֶ֑יךָ וְהָיָ֕ה לָנ֥וּס שָׁ֖מָּה כׇּל־רֹצֵֽחַ׃ 4 וְזֶה֙ דְּבַ֣ר הָרֹצֵ֔חַ אֲשֶׁר־יָנ֥וּס שָׁ֖מָּה וָחָ֑י אֲשֶׁ֨ר יַכֶּ֤ה אֶת־רֵעֵ֙הוּ֙ בִּבְלִי־דַ֔עַת וְה֛וּא לֹא־שֹׂנֵ֥א ל֖וֹ מִתְּמֹ֥ל שִׁלְשֹֽׁם׃ 5 וַאֲשֶׁר֩ יָבֹ֨א אֶת־רֵעֵ֥הוּ בַיַּ֘עַר֮ לַחְטֹ֣ב עֵצִים֒ וְנִדְּחָ֨ה יָד֤וֹ בַגַּרְזֶן֙ לִכְרֹ֣ת הָעֵ֔ץ וְנָשַׁ֤ל הַבַּרְזֶל֙ מִן־הָעֵ֔ץ וּמָצָ֥א אֶת־רֵעֵ֖הוּ וָמֵ֑ת ה֗וּא יָנ֛וּס אֶל־אַחַ֥ת הֶעָרִים־הָאֵ֖לֶּה וָחָֽי׃ 6 פֶּן־יִרְדֹּף֩ גֹּאֵ֨ל הַדָּ֜ם אַחֲרֵ֣י הָרֹצֵ֗חַ כִּי־יֵחַם֮ לְבָבוֹ֒ וְהִשִּׂיג֛וֹ כִּֽי־יִרְבֶּ֥ה הַדֶּ֖רֶךְ וְהִכָּ֣הוּ נָ֑פֶשׁ וְלוֹ֙ אֵ֣ין מִשְׁפַּט־מָ֔וֶת כִּ֠י לֹ֣א שֹׂנֵ֥א ה֛וּא ל֖וֹ מִתְּמ֥וֹל שִׁלְשֽׁוֹם׃ 7 עַל־כֵּ֛ן אָנֹכִ֥י מְצַוְּךָ֖ לֵאמֹ֑ר שָׁלֹ֥שׁ עָרִ֖ים תַּבְדִּ֥יל לָֽךְ׃ 8 וְאִם־יַרְחִ֞יב יְהֹוָ֤ה אֱלֹהֶ֙יךָ֙ אֶת־גְּבֻ֣לְךָ֔ כַּאֲשֶׁ֥ר נִשְׁבַּ֖ע לַאֲבֹתֶ֑יךָ וְנָ֤תַן לְךָ֙ אֶת־כׇּל־הָאָ֔רֶץ אֲשֶׁ֥ר דִּבֶּ֖ר לָתֵ֥ת לַאֲבֹתֶֽיךָ׃ 9 כִּֽי־תִשְׁמֹ֣ר אֶת־כׇּל־הַמִּצְוָ֣ה הַזֹּאת֮ לַעֲשֹׂתָהּ֒

- - - - - - - - - - - - - - - - - - - - - - - - - - - - - - - - -

## CITIES OF REFUGE (19:1–13)

This section mandates that the people should set aside three cities initially, with the addition of three more as needed, to provide refuge for persons guilty of unintentional homicide (see also 4:41–42; Exodus 21:13–14; Numbers 35:9–34). This law reflects an old practice that runs parallel to, and counter to, Deuteronomy's principle that the courts have jurisdiction over the sentencing of a person to capital punishment and the carrying out of that punishment if warranted; in this case, a relative avenges a killing. A person who commits manslaughter could, according to other texts, find refuge at an altar (see I Kings 2:28–34); but since Deuteronomy bans local sanctuaries, it must find a substitute site of refuge, which it does by establishing "secular" cities of refuge (not the same as the levitical cities mentioned

in Numbers 35). The principle inherent in this law fits with the Deuteronomic principles that innocent blood should not be spilled and that the guilty should receive just punishment.

*3. [male] killer.* Could women avail themselves of a city of refuge? This translation understands the person who commits manslaughter as being male. While certainly women were capable of committing murder or manslaughter, it seems reasonable to assume that the person fleeing to a city of refuge would more often be a male. One reason for this conclusion is that since women did not normally live independently, it would be problematic for a woman who commits manslaughter to leave her family and live in a city of refuge. (See also at 4:42, Exodus 21:13, and Numbers 35:6.)

*6. blood-avenger.* On the gender of this role, see at Numbers 35:12.

that I enjoin upon you this day, to love your God יהוה and to walk in God's ways at all times—then you shall add three more towns to those three. [10]Thus blood of the innocent will not be shed, bringing bloodguilt upon you in the land that your God יהוה is allotting to you.

[11]If, however, a man who is the enemy of another lies in wait and sets upon [the victim] and strikes a fatal blow and then flees to one of these towns, [12]the elders of his town shall have him brought back from there and shall hand him over to the blood-avenger to be put to death; [13]you must show him no pity. Thus you will purge Israel of the blood of the innocent, and it will go well with you.

[14]You shall not move your neighbor's landmarks, set up by previous generations, in the property that will be allotted to you in the land that your God יהוה is giving you to possess.

[15]A single witness may not validate against a person any guilt or blame for any offense that may be committed; a case can be valid only on the testimony of two witnesses or more. [16]If someone appears against another to testify maliciously and gives incriminating yet false testimony, [17]the two parties to the dispute shall appear before יהוה, before the priests or magistrates in authority at the time, [18]and the magistrates shall make a thorough investigation. If the one who testified is a false witness, having testified falsely against a fellow Israel-

אֲשֶׁ֨ר אָנֹכִ֣י מְצַוְּךָ֮ הַיּוֹם֒ לְאַהֲבָ֞ה אֶת־יְהֹוָ֣ה אֱלֹהֶ֗יךָ וְלָלֶ֧כֶת בִּדְרָכָ֛יו כָּל־הַיָּמִ֖ים וְיָסַפְתָּ֨ לְךָ֥ עוֹד֙ שָׁלֹ֣שׁ עָרִ֔ים עַ֖ל הַשָּׁלֹ֥שׁ הָאֵֽלֶּה: [10] וְלֹ֤א יִשָּׁפֵךְ֙ דָּ֣ם נָקִ֔י בְּקֶ֣רֶב אַרְצְךָ֔ אֲשֶׁר֙ יְהֹוָ֣ה אֱלֹהֶ֔יךָ נֹתֵ֥ן לְךָ֖ נַחֲלָ֑ה וְהָיָ֥ה עָלֶ֖יךָ דָּמִֽים: פ

[11] וְכִֽי־יִהְיֶ֥ה אִישׁ֙ שֹׂנֵ֣א לְרֵעֵ֔הוּ וְאָ֤רַב לוֹ֙ וְקָ֣ם עָלָ֔יו וְהִכָּ֥הוּ נֶ֖פֶשׁ וָמֵ֑ת וְנָ֕ס אֶל־אַחַ֖ת הֶעָרִ֥ים הָאֵֽל: [12] וְשָֽׁלְחוּ֙ זִקְנֵ֣י עִיר֔וֹ וְלָקְח֥וּ אֹת֖וֹ מִשָּׁ֑ם וְנָתְנ֣וּ אֹת֗וֹ בְּיַ֛ד גֹּאֵ֥ל הַדָּ֖ם וָמֵֽת: [13] לֹא־תָח֥וֹס עֵֽינְךָ֖ עָלָ֑יו וּבִֽעַרְתָּ֧ דַֽם־הַנָּקִ֛י מִיִּשְׂרָאֵ֖ל וְט֥וֹב לָֽךְ: ס

[14] לֹ֤א תַסִּיג֙ גְּב֣וּל רֵֽעֲךָ֔ אֲשֶׁ֥ר גָּבְל֖וּ רִֽאשֹׁנִ֑ים בְּנַחֲלָֽתְךָ֙ אֲשֶׁ֣ר תִּנְחַ֔ל בָּאָ֕רֶץ אֲשֶׁר֙ יְהֹוָ֣ה אֱלֹהֶ֔יךָ נֹתֵ֥ן לְךָ֖ לְרִשְׁתָּֽהּ: ס

[15] לֹֽא־יָקוּם֩ עֵ֨ד אֶחָ֜ד בְּאִ֗ישׁ לְכָל־עָוֺן֙ וּלְכָל־חַטָּ֔את בְּכָל־חֵ֖טְא אֲשֶׁ֣ר יֶֽחֱטָ֑א עַל־פִּ֣י ׀ שְׁנֵ֣י עֵדִ֗ים א֛וֹ עַל־פִּ֥י שְׁלֹשָֽׁה־עֵדִ֖ים יָק֥וּם דָּבָֽר: [16] כִּֽי־יָק֥וּם עֵד־חָמָ֖ס בְּאִ֑ישׁ לַעֲנ֥וֹת בּ֖וֹ סָרָֽה: [17] וְעָמְד֧וּ שְׁנֵֽי־הָאֲנָשִׁ֛ים אֲשֶׁר־לָהֶ֥ם הָרִ֖יב לִפְנֵ֣י יְהֹוָ֑ה לִפְנֵ֤י הַכֹּֽהֲנִים֙ וְהַשֹּׁ֣פְטִ֔ים אֲשֶׁ֥ר יִהְי֖וּ בַּיָּמִ֥ים הָהֵֽם: [18] וְדָרְשׁ֥וּ הַשֹּׁפְטִ֖ים הֵיטֵ֑ב וְהִנֵּ֤ה עֵֽד־שֶׁ֙קֶר֙

- - - - - - - - - - - - - - - - - - - - - -

## BOUNDARY MARKERS (19:14)

An important biblical principle holds that land should remain in the family to which it was originally allotted. Hence, moving a boundary marker is considered stealing property. The reason for the mention of this law here remains uncertain. This ancient law is known also from elsewhere in the Bible (see Hosea 5:10; Proverbs 22:28; 23:10–11; Job 24:2) and the ancient Near East.

## WITNESSES (19:15–21)

This section reiterates the principle of a minimum of two witnesses (see Deuteronomy 17:6). The Bible severely punishes false witnesses since they corrupt the legal system. The idea that a false witness deserves the punishment that would have been declared against the accused also appears in the Laws of Hammurabi (¶¶ 2–3).

ite, [19]you shall do to the one as the one schemed to do to the other. Thus you will sweep out evil from your midst; [20]others will hear and be afraid, and such evil things will not again be done in your midst. [21]Nor must you show pity: life for life, eye for eye, tooth for tooth, hand for hand, foot for foot.

*20* When you [an Israelite warrior] take the field against your enemies, and see horses and chariots—forces larger than yours—have no fear of them, for your God יהוה, who brought you from the land of Egypt, is with you. [2]Before you join battle, the priest shall come forward and address the troops. [3]He shall say to them, "Hear, O Israel! You are about to join battle with your enemy. Let not your courage falter. Do not be in fear, or in panic, or in dread of them. [4]For it is your God יהוה who marches with you to do battle for you against your enemy, to bring you victory."

[5]Then the officials shall address the troops, as follows: "Is there anyone who has built a new house but has not dedicated it? Let him go back to his home, lest he die in battle and another dedicate it. [6]Is there anyone who has planted a vineyard but has never harvested it? Let him go back to his home, lest he die in battle and another harvest it. [7]Is there

הָעֵד שֶׁקֶר עָנָה בְאָחִיו׃ 19 וַעֲשִׂיתֶם לוֹ
כַּאֲשֶׁר זָמַם לַעֲשׂוֹת לְאָחִיו וּבִעַרְתָּ הָרָע
מִקִּרְבֶּךָ׃ 20 וְהַנִּשְׁאָרִים יִשְׁמְעוּ וְיִרָאוּ וְלֹא־
יֹסִפוּ לַעֲשׂוֹת עוֹד כַּדָּבָר הָרָע הַזֶּה בְּקִרְבֶּךָ׃
21 וְלֹא תָחוֹס עֵינֶךָ נֶפֶשׁ בְּנֶפֶשׁ עַיִן בְּעַיִן שֵׁן
בְּשֵׁן יָד בְּיָד רֶגֶל בְּרָגֶל׃ ס

כ כִּי־תֵצֵא לַמִּלְחָמָה עַל־אֹיְבֶךָ וְרָאִיתָ
סוּס וָרֶכֶב עַם רַב מִמְּךָ לֹא תִירָא מֵהֶם כִּי־
יְהֹוָה אֱלֹהֶיךָ עִמָּךְ הַמַּעַלְךָ מֵאֶרֶץ מִצְרָיִם׃
2 וְהָיָה כְּקָרָבְכֶם אֶל־הַמִּלְחָמָה וְנִגַּשׁ הַכֹּהֵן
וְדִבֶּר אֶל־הָעָם׃ 3 וְאָמַר אֲלֵהֶם שְׁמַע
יִשְׂרָאֵל אַתֶּם קְרֵבִים הַיּוֹם לַמִּלְחָמָה עַל־
אֹיְבֵיכֶם אַל־יֵרַךְ לְבַבְכֶם אַל־תִּירְאוּ וְאַל־
תַּחְפְּזוּ וְאַל־תַּעַרְצוּ מִפְּנֵיהֶם׃ 4 כִּי יְהֹוָה
אֱלֹהֵיכֶם הַהֹלֵךְ עִמָּכֶם לְהִלָּחֵם לָכֶם עִם־
אֹיְבֵיכֶם לְהוֹשִׁיעַ אֶתְכֶם׃
5 וְדִבְּרוּ הַשֹּׁטְרִים אֶל־הָעָם לֵאמֹר מִי־
הָאִישׁ אֲשֶׁר בָּנָה בַיִת־חָדָשׁ וְלֹא חֲנָכוֹ יֵלֵךְ
וְיָשֹׁב לְבֵיתוֹ פֶּן־יָמוּת בַּמִּלְחָמָה וְאִישׁ
אַחֵר יַחְנְכֶנּוּ׃ 6 וּמִי־הָאִישׁ אֲשֶׁר־נָטַע
כֶּרֶם וְלֹא חִלְּלוֹ יֵלֵךְ וְיָשֹׁב לְבֵיתוֹ פֶּן־
יָמוּת בַּמִּלְחָמָה וְאִישׁ אַחֵר יְחַלְּלֶנּוּ׃ 7 וּמִי־

*19. sweep out evil from your midst.* This phrase recurs often in Deuteronomy (13:6; 17:7, 12; 21:21; 22:21, 22, 24; 24:7), as this book aims to create a just and moral society.

*21. life for life, eye for eye.* This verse invokes the law of talion, or precise retribution, in order to emphasize that justice must be meted out as required, "nor must you show pity." (See also at Exodus 21:24 and Leviticus 24:17–22.) A false witness must not get away with the crime, lest the justice system be undermined.

## *Rules for War* (20:1–20)

According to the narrative setting of Deuteronomy, Israel is on the brink of entering the Promised Land and will have to conduct a war of conquest. However, vv. 14–15 contain stipulations applying to foreign wars, not the conquest in Canaan. These rules aim to keep up morale by assuring the soldiers that God is with them.

*5–7.* These deferments or exemptions are designed to permit a young conscript to complete the

anyone who has paid the bride-price for a wife, but who has not yet married her? Let him go back to his home, lest he die in battle and another marry her." [8]The officials shall go on addressing the troops and say, "Is there anyone afraid and disheartened? Let him go back to his home, lest the courage of his comrades flag like his." [9]When the officials have finished addressing the troops, army commanders shall assume command of the troops.

[10]When you approach a town to attack it, you shall offer it terms of peace. [11]If it responds peaceably and lets you in, all the people present there shall serve you at forced labor. [12]If it does not surrender to you, but would join battle with you, you shall lay siege to it; [13]and when your God יהוה delivers it into your hand, you shall put all its males to the sword. [14]You may, however, take as your booty the women, the children, the livestock, and everything in the town—all its spoil—and enjoy the use of the spoil of your enemy, which your God יהוה gives you.

[15]Thus you shall deal with all towns that lie very far from you, towns that do not belong to nations

הָאִישׁ אֲשֶׁר־אֵרַשׂ אִשָּׁה וְלֹא לְקָחָהּ יֵלֵךְ
וְיָשֹׁב לְבֵיתוֹ פֶּן־יָמוּת בַּמִּלְחָמָה וְאִישׁ
אַחֵר יִקָּחֶנָּה׃ 8 וְיָסְפוּ הַשֹּׁטְרִים לְדַבֵּר
אֶל־הָעָם וְאָמְרוּ מִי־הָאִישׁ הַיָּרֵא וְרַךְ
הַלֵּבָב יֵלֵךְ וְיָשֹׁב לְבֵיתוֹ וְלֹא יִמַּס אֶת־
לְבַב אֶחָיו כִּלְבָבוֹ׃ 9 וְהָיָה כְּכַלֹּת הַשֹּׁטְרִים
לְדַבֵּר אֶל־הָעָם וּפָקְדוּ שָׂרֵי צְבָאוֹת בְּרֹאשׁ
הָעָם׃ ס
10 כִּי־תִקְרַב אֶל־עִיר לְהִלָּחֵם עָלֶיהָ וְקָרָאתָ
אֵלֶיהָ לְשָׁלוֹם׃ 11 וְהָיָה אִם־שָׁלוֹם תַּעַנְךָ
וּפָתְחָה לָךְ וְהָיָה כָּל־הָעָם הַנִּמְצָא־בָהּ
יִהְיוּ לְךָ לָמַס וַעֲבָדוּךָ׃ 12 וְאִם־לֹא תַשְׁלִים
עִמָּךְ וְעָשְׂתָה עִמְּךָ מִלְחָמָה וְצַרְתָּ עָלֶיהָ׃
13 וּנְתָנָהּ יְהֹוָה אֱלֹהֶיךָ בְּיָדֶךָ וְהִכִּיתָ אֶת־
כָּל־זְכוּרָהּ לְפִי־חָרֶב׃ 14 רַק הַנָּשִׁים וְהַטַּף
וְהַבְּהֵמָה וְכֹל אֲשֶׁר יִהְיֶה בָעִיר כָּל־שְׁלָלָהּ
תָּבֹז לָךְ וְאָכַלְתָּ אֶת־שְׁלַל אֹיְבֶיךָ אֲשֶׁר נָתַן
יְהֹוָה אֱלֹהֶיךָ לָךְ׃
15 כֵּן תַּעֲשֶׂה לְכָל־הֶעָרִים הָרְחֹקֹת מִמְּךָ
מְאֹד אֲשֶׁר לֹא־מֵעָרֵי הַגּוֹיִם־הָאֵלֶּה הֵנָּה׃

establishment of his home, agricultural livelihood, and family—the major anchors of society. The law is less concerned with the feelings of the individual soldier than with the formation of crucial social institutions. Establishing a house, farm, and family is the greater good, even in time of war; for without these there is no community (see also 24:5; 28:30; Jeremiah 29:5–6).

*7. bride-price.* Better, "betrothal gift." See further at Genesis 29:18, Exodus 22:15–16, and *Chayei Sarah*, Another View, p. 127. The marriage has been legally contracted but not consummated; the woman is considered married and cannot marry another man.

*8.* Because of the contagious nature of cowardliness, this verse instructs the officials to remove fearful soldiers lest they demoralize the rest of the troops.

*10–14.* These procedures are typical of ancient Near Eastern warfare. If a city capitulated by accepting the peace terms, it was spared a siege, which generally resulted in starvation and disease before capitulation. Peace terms would specify the payment of tribute, which included forced labor by the captives. The killing of the adult males and the taking of women, children, and livestock as booty are also typical (as seen in the case of the foreign woman taken in warfare in 21:10–14) and have the effect of further weakening—or even decimating—the losing side as well as providing human capital for the victors. In I Samuel 30, David's wives and the "wives and sons and daughters" of his six hundred men (30:3) are taken captive by a band of Amalekite raiders.

*15–16.* These verses distinguish wars outside Canaan, to which the stipulations listed above ap-

hereabout. [16]In the towns of the latter peoples, however, which your God יהוה is giving you as a heritage, you shall not let a soul remain alive. [17]No, you must proscribe them—the Hittites and the Amorites, the Canaanites and the Perizzites, the Hivites and the Jebusites—as your God יהוה has commanded you, [18]lest they lead you into doing all the abhorrent things that they have done for their gods and you stand guilty before your God יהוה.

[19]When in your war against a city you have to besiege it a long time in order to capture it, you must not destroy its trees, wielding the ax against them. You may eat of them, but you must not cut them down. Are trees of the field human to withdraw before you into the besieged city? [20]Only trees that you know do not yield food may be destroyed; you may cut them down for constructing siegeworks against the city that is waging war on you, until it has been reduced.

**21** If, in the land that your God יהוה is assigning you to possess, someone slain is found lying in the open, the identity of the slayer not being known, [2]your elders and magistrates shall go out and measure the distances from the corpse to the nearby towns. [3]The elders of the town nearest to the corpse shall then take a heifer which has never been worked, which has never pulled in a

16 רַק מֵעָרֵי הָעַמִּים הָאֵלֶּה אֲשֶׁר יְהוָה
אֱלֹהֶיךָ נֹתֵן לְךָ נַחֲלָה לֹא תְחַיֶּה כָּל־
נְשָׁמָה׃ 17 כִּי־הַחֲרֵם תַּחֲרִימֵם הַחִתִּי
וְהָאֱמֹרִי הַכְּנַעֲנִי וְהַפְּרִזִּי הַחִוִּי וְהַיְבוּסִי
כַּאֲשֶׁר צִוְּךָ יְהוָה אֱלֹהֶיךָ׃ 18 לְמַעַן אֲשֶׁר
לֹא־יְלַמְּדוּ אֶתְכֶם לַעֲשׂוֹת כְּכֹל תּוֹעֲבֹתָם
אֲשֶׁר עָשׂוּ לֵאלֹהֵיהֶם וַחֲטָאתֶם לַיהוָה
אֱלֹהֵיכֶם׃ ס
19 כִּי־תָצוּר אֶל־עִיר יָמִים רַבִּים לְהִלָּחֵם
עָלֶיהָ לְתָפְשָׂהּ לֹא־תַשְׁחִית אֶת־עֵצָהּ
לִנְדֹּחַ עָלָיו גַּרְזֶן כִּי מִמֶּנּוּ תֹאכֵל וְאֹתוֹ
לֹא תִכְרֹת כִּי הָאָדָם עֵץ הַשָּׂדֶה לָבֹא
מִפָּנֶיךָ בַּמָּצוֹר׃ 20 רַק עֵץ אֲשֶׁר־תֵּדַע כִּי־
לֹא־עֵץ מַאֲכָל הוּא אֹתוֹ תַשְׁחִית וְכָרָתָּ
וּבָנִיתָ מָצוֹר עַל־הָעִיר אֲשֶׁר־הִוא עֹשָׂה
עִמְּךָ מִלְחָמָה עַד רִדְתָּהּ׃ פ

כא כִּי־יִמָּצֵא חָלָל בָּאֲדָמָה אֲשֶׁר יְהוָה
אֱלֹהֶיךָ נֹתֵן לְךָ לְרִשְׁתָּהּ נֹפֵל בַּשָּׂדֶה לֹא
נוֹדַע מִי הִכָּהוּ׃ 2 וְיָצְאוּ זְקֵנֶיךָ וְשֹׁפְטֶיךָ
וּמָדְדוּ אֶל־הֶעָרִים אֲשֶׁר סְבִיבֹת הֶחָלָל׃
3 וְהָיָה הָעִיר הַקְּרֹבָה אֶל־הֶחָלָל וְלָקְחוּ
זִקְנֵי הָעִיר הַהִוא עֶגְלַת בָּקָר אֲשֶׁר לֹא־

ply, from wars within Canaan, which demand the complete eradication of all life, lest any survivors lead the Israelites into foreign worship practices.

*19–20.* This passage prohibits a "scorched-earth" policy. Only trees that do not provide food may be cut down, if necessary, to be used for constructing ramps and scaffolding to scale the city walls. To the contemporary reader this may sound like an ecologically minded policy; but the reason for it is unclear. Perhaps it was meant to ensure a food supply for the soldiers.

***Are trees of the field human.*** The Hebrew phrase is obscure; it may mean that trees are not the enemy, or that they cannot defend themselves and therefore should not be harmed, or both.

## *Unsolved Murder* (21:1–9)

Deuteronomy exhibits a concern not only with punishing the guilty, but also with ensuring that the community bears no responsibility for bloodshed, for the shedding of innocent blood makes the land impure (see also 19:10, 13). In this

yoke; [4]and the elders of that town shall bring the heifer down to an everflowing wadi, which is not tilled or sown. There, in the wadi, they shall break the heifer's neck. [5]The priests, sons of Levi, shall come forward; for your God יהוה has chosen them for divine service and to pronounce blessing in the name of יהוה, and every lawsuit and case of assault is subject to their ruling. [6]Then all the elders of the town nearest to the corpse shall wash their hands over the heifer whose neck was broken in the wadi. [7]And they shall make this declaration: "Our hands did not shed this blood, nor did our eyes see it done. [8]Absolve, יהוה, Your people Israel whom You redeemed, and do not let guilt for the blood of the innocent remain among Your people Israel." And they will be absolved of bloodguilt. [9]Thus you will remove from your midst guilt for the blood of the innocent, for you will be doing what is right in the sight of יהוה.

עֹבַ֖ד בָּ֑הּ אֲשֶׁ֛ר לֹא־מָשְׁכָ֥ה בְּעֹֽל׃ 4 וְהוֹרִ֡דוּ זִקְנֵי֩ הָעִ֨יר הַהִ֜וא אֶת־הָעֶגְלָ֗ה אֶל־נַ֙חַל֙ אֵיתָ֔ן אֲשֶׁ֛ר לֹא־יֵעָבֵ֥ד בּ֖וֹ וְלֹ֣א יִזָּרֵ֑עַ וְעָֽרְפוּ־ שָׁ֥ם אֶת־הָעֶגְלָ֖ה בַּנָּֽחַל׃ 5 וְנִגְּשׁ֣וּ הַכֹּהֲנִים֮ בְּנֵ֣י לֵוִי֒ כִּ֣י בָ֗ם בָּחַ֞ר יְהֹוָ֤ה אֱלֹהֶ֙יךָ֙ לְשָׁ֣רְת֔וֹ וּלְבָרֵ֖ךְ בְּשֵׁ֣ם יְהֹוָ֑ה וְעַל־פִּיהֶ֥ם יִהְיֶ֖ה כָּל־ רִ֥יב וְכָל־נָֽגַע׃ 6 וְכֹ֗ל זִקְנֵי֙ הָעִ֣יר הַהִ֔וא הַקְּרֹבִ֖ים אֶל־הֶחָלָ֑ל יִרְחֲצוּ֙ אֶת־יְדֵיהֶ֔ם עַל־ הָעֶגְלָ֖ה הָעֲרוּפָ֥ה בַנָּֽחַל׃ 7 וְעָנ֖וּ וְאָמְר֑וּ יָדֵ֗ינוּ לֹ֤א שפכה שָֽׁפְכוּ֙ אֶת־הַדָּ֣ם הַזֶּ֔ה וְעֵינֵ֖ינוּ לֹ֥א רָאֽוּ׃ 8 כַּפֵּר֩ לְעַמְּךָ֨ יִשְׂרָאֵ֤ל אֲשֶׁר־פָּדִ֙יתָ֙ יְהֹוָ֔ה וְאַל־תִּתֵּן֙ דָּ֣ם נָקִ֔י בְּקֶ֖רֶב עַמְּךָ֣ יִשְׂרָאֵ֑ל וְנִכַּפֵּ֥ר לָהֶ֖ם הַדָּֽם׃ 9 וְאַתָּ֗ה תְּבַעֵ֛ר הַדָּ֥ם הַנָּקִ֖י מִקִּרְבֶּ֑ךָ כִּֽי־תַעֲשֶׂ֥ה הַיָּשָׁ֖ר בְּעֵינֵ֥י יְהֹוָֽה׃ ס

case, there is no suspect to accuse of the killing, so the community is responsible. A ritual and a prayer will remove the bloodguilt from the town.

*7.* If no witnesses are found, the local elders must swear an oath declaring innocence of the action and lack of knowledge about the action.

*8.* A prayer that God will absolve the guilt follows the oath. Notice that it is no longer a matter of one town, but of "your people," that is, Israel as a whole. Even in the somewhat "secularized" laws of Deuteronomy, justice in human affairs is part of Israel's religious view.

—*Adele Berlin*

# Another View

DEUTERONOMY CONTAINS the only ancient Near Eastern legal corpus that extensively treats the question of correct wartime behavior. *Parashat Shof'tim* introduces the first group of regulations (20:1–9, 10–18, 19–20); the rest are scattered throughout the next parashah (21:10–14; 23:10–15; 24:5). Curiously, these regulations are not what one might expect from a collection of laws related to warfare. They are not concerned with strategic issues typical of warfare, like mustering the army, logistics, or battle tactics. Instead, the military regulations in our parashah deal with the peripheral aspects of war, particularly with those affected by it: women and children, cattle, trees, and even members of the attacking side.

The first, and therefore most prominent, rule defines those conscripts who are released from war (20:5–7): men who have built a new house, planted a vineyard, or given a betrothal gift, but they have not yet benefited from these three types of investments. The reason given is "lest he die in battle" and another person profit. This rationale echoes the curse familiar from ancient Near Eastern treaties: you will labor, but someone else will eat the fruit of your toil. It is noteworthy that in 28:30, precisely the three cases in our parashah are turned into curses. Thus, rather than glorify warfare, Deuteronomy views it as a curse that needs curbing, even for the attacking side.

Similar to the stipulations in our parashah pertaining to the establishment of a monarchy (17:14–20), these rules of war reflect a subversive criticism of a key element prevalent in ancient societies: in this case, wars of expansion inaugurated by the Neo-Assyrian empire in the 8th to 7th centuries B.C.E. Therefore, Deuteronomy's rules of warfare can be understood as an ideological polemic related to the military and political pressures that Israel and Judah experienced at the time.

*Deuteronomy views warfare as a curse that needs curbing.*

We see, then, that the attitude toward warfare in our parashah is a learned reaction to wars forced upon the small nations at that time. Criticizing military acts implicitly and indirectly reveals the viewpoint of the Israelite underdogs, the victims of such actions.

—*Nili Wazana*

# Post-biblical Interpretations

***A person shall be put to death only on the testimony of two or more witnesses*** (17:6). Despite the admirable exhortation in this parashah to pursue justice (16:20), post-biblical Judaism restricted women's participation in the judicial system. In response to the requirement of two witnesses for criminal cases in this verse and 19:15–17, *Sifrei D'varim* 190 asks, "Is a woman also qualified to give testimony?" Their answer is no, for they note that in 19:15 the Torah states "two witnesses" and further on, in 19:17, "two [men]." Reading these two biblical verses literally, the Rabbis reason: "As the meaning of 'two' in the one instance is men and not women, so the meaning of 'two' in the other instance is men and not women." Even earlier, the Jewish historian Josephus (1st century C.E.) asserted that "by Jewish law women are disqualified as witnesses" (*Jewish Antiquities* 4.219).

However, the Mishnah (*Y'vamot* 15:1–5 and 16:5) permits a woman to serve as a sole witness in establishing a man's death, thus allowing his widow to remarry. Since rabbinic courts accepted female testimony in this and some other situations, why were they excluded from most civil and criminal cases? The Rabbis did not give a reason for their general disqualification of women as legal witnesses. Perhaps women's dependence on their husbands or fathers was understood to compromise their ability to serve as independent witnesses. They could testify only when the two-witness paradigm did not hold. This proved especially important when women might have more access than men to necessary information.

*Rabbinic courts accepted female testimony only in certain situations.*

***Is there anyone who has paid the bride-price for a wife?*** (20:7). The groom becomes betrothed (*eiras*) after he gives a betrothal gift, which is referred to here as a "bride-price." This implies that the wife is an object acquired by her future husband. (For a different perspective on the institution of betrothal in the Bible, see at Genesis 29:18; Exodus 22:15–16; and *Chayei Sarah*, Another View, p. 127.) The Rabbis' use of the term *kiddushin* for "betrothal" might encourage us to think that women played a more active role in their own betrothals in rabbinic times. *Kiddushin* is connected to the Hebrew word for "holy," and "holy" in this context could indicate a relationship recognizing the betrothed woman as more than property. However, rabbinic writings (Tosefta *Kiddushin* 1:1 and BT *Kiddushin* 5b) make it clear that a betrothal is legitimate only if a man "acquires" a woman, whether he uses the term *m'oresset* or *m'kuddeshet* to assert his claim. Betrothal is not considered valid if a woman speaks or acts as the one changing the couple's status from single to betrothed.

Like the new house and newly planted vineyard (20:5–6), the betrothed woman (20:7) appears as a partially claimed property for whose full possession a man must take further action. Passages like this indicate that obligations accompanied betrothal (see also 22:23) and imply that some men may not have fulfilled them expeditiously. At any given time, significant numbers of betrothed women may have occupied a limbo state wherein they were already designated as "wife" but not entitled to that status. Although biblical sources are silent about mechanisms for canceling betrothals, the Rabbis insisted on divorce to terminate the betrothed couple's connection (Mishnah *Kiddushin* 1:1, 3:7).

Similar views that betrothal was tantamount to marriage are also found in Roman law. The 2nd-century historian Suetonius remarked, "[O]n finding that the spirit of the law was being evaded by betrothal with immature girls . . . [the Emperor Augustus] shortened the duration of betrothals" (*Augustus* 34.1–2). While Suetonius is discussing a binding betrothal that some elite men used to their advantage in order to avoid restrictions upon gifts and the higher taxes owed by unmarried men, the biblical example appears to establish the binding nature of betrothal intentionally. In both Jewish and Roman law and practice, a betrothal either led to a marriage or was terminated in some quiet manner.

In general, historians find references to betrothals only where problems have occurred or are envisioned. The present verse discusses one potential difficulty. A non-Jewish example appears in a legal ruling from Emperors Valerian and Gallienus (dated 259 C.E.) concerning a young woman who has been engaged for three years but her fiancé is abroad and unreachable. She would like to end the betrothal but cannot communicate this to him. This young woman's lawsuit expresses concern that she would be liable to charges of bigamy were she to marry someone else (Judith Evans Grubbs, *Law and Family in Late Antiquity*, 1995, pp. 167–8). That such cases required resolution suggests that the interval between betrothal and marriage could be problematic in both Jewish and Roman societies. However, the rarity of references to these cases raises more questions than answers about how betrothals really functioned in ancient Judaism.

*—Susan Marks*

## Contemporary Reflection

PARASHAT SHOF'TIM IS ONE OF our most neatly packaged Torah portions, beginning with commandments about the necessity for appointing "magistrates and officials" (16:18) and concluding with a procedure aimed to ensure that people do "what is right in the sight of יהוה" (21:9). From its opening words to its concluding phrases, this parashah is about righteousness and justice. Yet these concepts are meaningless unless rooted in concrete particulars so they can permeate the lives of those who wish to find meaning in the Torah. These are clearly universal values, but where do we find out about the ways women approach such values and concerns?

Among the commandments recounted in this portion are those about warfare. Can we retain humanity in time of war? The parashah asks us to attempt every other possible measure before war is undertaken, literally to "call her [that is, the city] to peace" (20:10), which indicates that war should be considered a last resort in resolving a conflict. All world leaders should familiarize themselves with this ethical teaching: negotiate before fighting by actively calling out in peace to one's opponent. This recalls the active language about Aaron the priest and his sons in *Pirkei Avot* 1:12, "Be like the disciples of Aaron: love peace and pursue it." Real peace needs strong verbs of "calling" and "pursuing"—and real attempts to forge it.

This concept of calling out in peace would seem to be a place where a value of negotiation rather than fighting has permeated the ways in which the society approaches war. In discussing 20:10, *Sefer HaChinuch* 503, a medieval compilation of mitzvot, states, "The quality of mercy (*rachmaniut*) is a good quality; and it is fitting for us, the holy seed, to behave thus in all matters even with our enemies, worshippers of idols." This notion that we should always behave with *rachamim* (mercy)—even to an enemy—is one that continues to apply to daily life, as well as to national crises. This would mean that we first would call to that person in peace, prior to arguing or becoming angry, difficult as it may be.

Are there any biblical examples of this mode of discourse? One example concerns a woman who saves an entire city from destruction (II Samuel 20:14–22). That passage tells how Joab, a warrior acting on the king's behalf, pursues Sheba son of Bichri, the leader of a group that has rebelled and fled to the town of Abel of Beth-maacah. When Joab besieges the city, a "wise woman" employs persuasive rhetoric and feminine imagery to avert war, warning Joab that he risks destroying a "mother city in Israel" (v. 19). Joab assures her that if the people hand over Sheba, he will not attack the city. The woman makes sure that this happens when she convinces the townspeople to cut off Sheba's head and toss it over the wall. In this case, the wise woman's sense of mercy and calling out in peace means that one life is sacrificed for the greater good, to avert large-scale bloodshed and ruin.

*Parashat Shof'tim* tells us that if war cannot be

avoided, there are humane ways to go about it: "When in your war against a city you have to besiege . . . you must not destroy its trees" (20:19). Why not? The verse continues, "*ki ha-adam etz ha-sadeh,*" which can be read either as "Are the trees of the field human?" or, alternatively, as "for a human is like a tree." Trees have the ability to draw water into themselves, and nourish themselves. What will sustain and nurture us? An answer may come from the end of the book of Deuteronomy, when Moses charges all the people—men, women, children, and strangers—to listen to and learn "every word of this Teaching (*torah*)" (31:12). Just as we may not cut down fruit trees so they may continue to bear fruit, so we must actively study and teach Torah, striving to incorporate it into our hearts and our minds. That way, the quality of mercy will envelop and permeate our individual lives and our society as a whole.

*When we incorporate Torah into our hearts, the quality of mercy will permeate society.*

Are there distinct ways that women strive to infuse our world with more mercy and peace? Professor Galia Golan, who has studied Israeli-Palestinian dialogue groups for twenty-five years, has found that dialogue groups composed of all women differ in certain respects from mixed-gender groups ("Reflections on Gender in Dialogue," *Nashim* 6, 2003). She has observed that women tend to start from their shared experiences, beginning the conversation not with an abstract, angry summation of the history of the conflict, but with emotional accounts of their personal experiences. According to Golan, women seem more invested in the ability to "dissolve the psychological barriers obstructing resolution of the conflict, by reversing the dehumanization of the enemy that takes place during a prolonged conflict; expanding understanding of the other's positions; creating empathy with the other side; and thus paving the way for eventual reconciliation." Dialogue shows unique ways that women call one another to peace, reminding us that through our words and our actions, we possess the potential to "love peace and pursue it."

It seems fitting that *parashat Shof'tim,* which is about justice, ends with a body. The crucial aspect of the perplexing ritual of the *eglah arufah* ("the broken-necked heifer") is to force the living to acknowledge their responsibility to the dead. This ritual provides a means to ascertain responsibility for the corpse. According to the Midrash, kindness to a dead person (*chesed shel emet*) is the truest kindness, for it cannot ever be repaid (*B'reishit Rabbah* 96.5; see also p. 297). Why do it? It is the right thing to do, both for the collective of society and for the dead individual.

It is only in this state of being a collective that a society can operate with justice. Through the totality of these laws, the parashah defines a just society—true kindness and mercy done to all—whether they are brothers, sisters, or enemies, living or dead, human or tree—so that all may find means of sustenance and peace. These values become societal values when they permeate all aspects of life.

*—Beth Kissileff*

# Voices

## Judgment

Eleanor Wilner

*Deuteronomy 16:18–20*

When they removed the bandages
from Justice's eyes, she had long since
gone blind. She had been too many days
in the dark, too long alone with
the scale in her numb hands; she could
no longer tell the true from the false.
She had stood so many years in the cold
outside the courts, as the law rushed
past, clinging to the sleeve
of power—until the chill
had turned her veins to marble,
her eyes to opalescent stone.

Yet those who tore the veil away
could swear they were being watched,
and though it must have been a bit of glass
that caught a ray of sun, it was not unlike
a bright, appraising eye. Whatever it was,
they felt caught out, ashamed,
and late at night, at home, they locked
their windows tight and slipped into the room
where the children slept, and looking down
on them—for what they couldn't say—they
wept.

## Sorcery

Marjorie Agosin (transl. Cola Franzen)

*Deuteronomy 18:10*

Because they taught her
to be silent,
to gather up the ashes of arrogant travelers,
because they taught her not to cry
during nights of high tide,
she wanted to be a sorceress,
free-wheeling, be able
to peddle destiny
with words.

## Military Washing

Karen Alkalay-Gut

*Deuteronomy 20*

On the opposite balcony Rochi hangs green
laundry.
She has pulled uniform after uniform from
the lines,
and now stretches out regulation long johns and
undershirts,
exhibiting for me the latest in foul-weather gear
for the troops up north.

Hanging on my line are enough white anklets
for an army of centipedes, olive sweaters and
skirts,
and the week's underwear. Newly shined boots
sit on the windowsill, next to a pair of black
oxfords
waiting their turn. "Parents really need
vacations from military chores," I say.

"Weekend furloughs are hell," she agrees.
"Let's meet in less fatiguing times."

## *Mobilization*

Karen Alkalay-Gut

*Deuteronomy 20*

*1.*
A month before mobilization
my daughter lies beside me and talks
the way she did at naptime
when she was three.

When I groan I need to sleep
she pats my stomach
and sings the tuneless lullaby
my mother sang to me.

Like blinds my eyes
flash open: How
does she know it? She laughs, chattering
in that tongue she never learned.

*2.*
The night before her mobilization
friends come to say goodbye
as if she were embarking on a long journey.

But there is only a kitbag, 3 pairs
of socks, long underwear
and a funny doll
God knows
where she will hide.

*3.*
"Women belong
in the same jobs as men,"
she retorts when the Rabbi on TV
calls for a demobilization of all women
from the army. Then, "Men belong
in the same jobs as women,
in their homes, in the kitchen,
in safe places
away from the borders."

## *Women and Horses*

Maxine Kumin

*Deuteronomy 20*

(*After Auschwitz, to write a poem is barbaric.*
—Theodor Adorno)

After Auschwitz: after ten of my father's kin—
the ones who stayed—starved, then were gassed
in the camps.
After Vietnam, after Korea, Kuwait, Somalia,
Haiti, Afghanistan.
After the Towers. This late in the life of our
haplessly orbiting world
let us celebrate whatever scraps the muse,
that naked child,
can pluck from the still-smoldering dumps.

If there's a lyre around, strike it! A body,
stand back, give it air!
Let us have sparrows laying their eggs in
bluebird boxes.
Let us have bluebirds insouciantly nesting
elsewhere.
Lend us navel-bared teens, eyebrow- and
nose-ringed prodigies
crumbling breakfast bagels over dogeared and
jelly-smeared texts.
Allow the able-bodied among us to have
steamy sex.

Let there be fat old ladies in flowery tent dresses
at bridge tables.
Howling babies in dirty diapers and babies
serenely at rest.
War and détente will go on, détente and
renewed tearings asunder,
we can never break free from the dark and
degrading past.
Let us see life again, nevertheless, in the words
of Isaac Babel
*as a meadow over which women and horses
wander.*

## *Olive Trees*

Lea Goldberg (transl. Rachel Tzvia Back)

*Deuteronomy 20:19–20*

They withstood the heat wave
and were confidants of the storm—
as though they had stationed themselves
for eternity
on the slope across from the ruined village,
where they silvered in the cool light of the
crescent moon.

Stand still, how abundant in this peace.
Here is ripe old age!
Listen, listen to the gusts
of wind through the landscape of olives.
What modest trees!
Can you hear? They are speaking now
wise and simple things.

## *Beheaded Heifer*

Dahlia Ravikovitch
(transl. Chana Bloch and Chana Kronfeld)

*Deuteronomy 21:1–9*

Took another step,
then a few steps more.
His glasses dropped,
his skullcap dropped.
He took another step
drenched in blood,
dragging his feet.
Ten steps more
and he's not a Jew
not an Arab anymore—
ethereal.

Godawful uproar; people shrieking, Why are
you murdering us?
Others hurrying about,
rushing to exact revenge.

He lies gasping on the ground: a death rattle,
a body torn open,
and the blood spilling out of the flesh,
the blood spilling out of the flesh.

He died here, or there—
some degree of uncertainty remains.
What do we know for a fact?
"One found slain in the field."

It is said, Suffering cleanseth sin,
man is like dust in the wind,
but who was that man
lying there lonely,
choking on his blood.
What did he see,
what did he hear
in the uproar that seethed
above him?
It is also said:
If thou seest even thine enemy's ass
lying under its burden,
thou shalt surely help.

If one be found slain in the field
if one be found slain on the ground,
let your elders go out and slaughter a heifer
and scatter its ashes in the stream.

NOTE

This poem is based on an actual incident in which a yeshiva student was shot in a Hebron marketplace and left to die because no one knew his identity; the Jews assumed that he was an Arab and the Arabs, a Jew.

# כי תצא ✦ *Ki Teitzei*

DEUTERONOMY 21:10–25:19

## *Relationships and Society*

PARASHAT KI TEITZEI ("when you go out") contains a wide range of criminal, civil, and family laws, featuring many of the humane precepts for which Deuteronomy is justly famous. The topics addressed include relationships within households (between men, women, and children), among neighbors, between the underprivileged and other members of society, and even between humans and animals. As elsewhere, notably in the preceding parashah, Deuteronomy is concerned with the formation of an ideal Israelite society. However, whereas *parashat Shof'tim* concentrates on public officials, most of the laws in *Ki Teitzei* are directed at ordinary individuals. What may have once been considered family matters—such as the rights of a lesser-loved wife, the punishment of wayward children, the finding of lost objects—here are matters of concern to the society at large that must be legislated publicly. The goal is to create a balanced society in which the poor and weak are legally protected from the rich and strong, in which both property and human lives are respected, and—most importantly—in which individuals are subject to the community and its laws.

While some laws in this parashah seem to follow a logical or topical order, others appear to have been inserted at random. Most of the laws offer no reason or justification for adhering to them; but some refer to events recounted earlier in the Torah, such as the skin affliction of Miriam (24:9). The repeated mention of God's approval or disapproval (as in 24:13 and 22:5) reminds us that no matter how secular the laws of Deuteronomy may appear to us, the book presents them as being on behalf of—and through—the will of God.

Issues pertaining to women are prominent in this parashah. They include the treatment of a captive woman, forced sex, accusations of non-virginity, divorce, and levirate marriage.

*Much in the ideal society that Deuteronomy envisions revolves around the status of women.*

Much in the ideal society that Deuteronomy envisions revolves around the status of women, generally their sexual status as wives or potential wives. Since the family unit is the basis of society, marriage and the women's position in the family unit are important. Deuteronomy advocates chastity before marriage but, at the same time, protects women in cases where premarital sex was forced upon them; however, the penalty for promiscuous sex is severe. Most of all, Deuteronomy seeks to ensure that women marry, for ancient Israelite society offered no good place for an adult unmarried woman.

*—Adele Berlin*

## *Outline*

*I.* Laws Regarding Family Relations (21:10–21)

- *A.* Marriage to a prisoner of war (vv. 10–14)
- *B.* Heir whose mother is an unloved wife (vv. 15–17)
- *C.* The incorrigible son (vv. 18–21)

*II.* Laws Regarding Neighbors, Nature, and Clothing (21:22–22:12)

*III.* Laws Regarding Sexual Misconduct (22:13–29)

- *A.* False and true accusations of unchastity (vv. 13–21)
- *B.* The penalty for adultery (v. 22)
- *C.* Forced and consensual sex with a betrothed woman (vv. 23–27)
- *D.* Forced sex with an unbetrothed woman (vv. 28–29)

*IV.* Laws Regarding Forbidden Relationships (23:1–9)

- *A.* Prohibition on marrying a father's former wife (v. 1)
- *B.* Restriction on who may enter God's congregation (vv. 2–9)

*V.* Miscellaneous Laws (23:10–24:9)

- *A.* Laws regarding soldiers, slaves, and prostitutes (23:10–19)
- *B.* Laws regarding commitments to God and neighbors (23:20–26)
- *C.* More laws regarding marriage (24:1–5)
- *D.* Miscellany: objects taken in pawn, kidnapping, skin affliction (24:6–9)

*VI.* Laws Protecting the Vulnerable (24:10–25:16)

- *A.* Obtaining pledges and paying wages (24:10–15)
- *B.* Prohibition on transgenerational punishment (24:16)
- *C.* Protecting the stranger, fatherless, and widow (24:17–20)
- *D.* Limits on flogging (25:1–3)
- *E.* Prohibition on muzzling an ox when it is threshing (25:4)
- *F.* Levirate marriage (25:5–10)
- *G.* Punishment of a woman who intervenes in her husband's fight (25:11–12)
- *H.* Honest weights and measures (25:13–16)

*VII.* Charge to Remember Amalek (25:17–19)

When you [an Israelite warrior] take the field against your enemies, and your God יהוה delivers them into your power and you take some of them captive, [11]and you see among the captives a beautiful woman and you desire her and would take her to wife, [12]you shall bring her into your house, and she shall trim her hair, pare her nails, [13]and discard her captive's garb. She shall spend a month's time in your house lamenting her father

כא 10 כִּי־תֵצֵא לַמִּלְחָמָה עַל־אֹיְבֶיךָ
וּנְתָנוֹ יְהוָה אֱלֹהֶיךָ בְּיָדֶךָ וְשָׁבִיתָ שִׁבְיוֹ׃
11 וְרָאִיתָ בַּשִּׁבְיָה אֵשֶׁת יְפַת־תֹּאַר וְחָשַׁקְתָּ
בָהּ וְלָקַחְתָּ לְךָ לְאִשָּׁה׃ 12 וַהֲבֵאתָהּ אֶל־
תּוֹךְ בֵּיתֶךָ וְגִלְּחָה אֶת־רֹאשָׁהּ וְעָשְׂתָה אֶת־
צִפָּרְנֶיהָ׃ 13 וְהֵסִירָה אֶת־שִׂמְלַת שִׁבְיָהּ
מֵעָלֶיהָ וְיָשְׁבָה בְּבֵיתֶךָ וּבָכְתָה אֶת־אָבִיהָ

## *Laws Regarding Family Relations*

(21:10–21)

This unit addresses three irregular family situations involving women and children.

### MARRIAGE TO A PRISONER OF WAR

(21:10–14)

This section on the captive wife continues the discussion of war in the preceding parashah (20:1–20). If an Israelite warrior wishes to marry a female captive, he is obligated to enable the woman to transition to her new status. The seeming conflict between this law and others that prohibit marrying women from the surrounding cultures (see especially 7:2–4) highlights the fact that the Torah does not unconditionally prohibit marrying foreign women. Rather, the prohibition pertains to those specific local Canaanite nations whose practices threaten Israel's identity and unconditional commitment to God. [The main purpose of this law is to protect the vulnerable (as is true of other laws in Deuteronomy) and to preserve the woman's position and dignity. That men legally had sexual access to women captured in war is evident in numerous texts from the ancient world; see, for example, the comments by the women who comfort the mother of Israel's enemy leader, Sisera, in the Song of Deborah (Judges 5:29–30). —*Ed.*]

*11. **beautiful woman.*** The Bible characterizes several women as beautiful, including Sarah, Rebekah, and Rachel (Genesis 12:11; 24:16; 29:17). Here, the woman's beauty is the source of the attraction. (For more on this topic, see *Emor*, Contemporary Reflection, p. 743.)

*12–13.* The captive woman enters the household, but only after she is given a month to mourn the loss of her parents can the Israelite marry her. The change in her status is signaled by trimming her hair and paring her nails (which may be signs of mourning or of the end of the mourning period), as well as by discarding her captive's clothing.

▶ Why would the male authors of this text legislate for female autonomy?

ANOTHER VIEW ➤ *1185*

▶ The parashah shows that memory can serve a wide variety of purposes.

CONTEMPORARY REFLECTION ➤ *1187*

▶ In antiquity, married Jewish women could and did initiate divorce.

POST-BIBLICAL INTERPRETATIONS ➤ *1185*

▶ If you should see me now / you would not recognize your yesterdays. . . .

VOICES ➤ *1189*

and mother; after that you may come to her and thus become her husband, and she shall be your wife. [14]Then, should you no longer want her, you must release her outright. You must not sell her for money: since you had your will of her, you must not enslave her.

[15]If a householder has two wives, one loved and the other unloved, and both the loved and the unloved have borne him sons, but the first-born is the son of the unloved one—[16]when he wills his property to his sons, he may not treat as first-born the son of the loved one in disregard of the son of the unloved one who is older. [17]Instead, he must accept the first-born, the son of the unloved one, and allot to him a double portion of all he possesses; since he is the first fruit of his vigor, the birthright is his due.

[18]If a householder has a wayward and defiant

וְאֶת־אִמָּהּ יֶ֣רַח יָמִים֒ וְאַחַ֣ר כֵּ֔ן תָּב֣וֹא אֵלֶ֔יהָ וּבְעַלְתָּ֖הּ וְהָיְתָ֥ה לְךָ֖ לְאִשָּֽׁה׃ 14 וְהָיָ֞ה אִם־ לֹ֧א חָפַ֣צְתָּ בָּ֗הּ וְשִׁלַּחְתָּהּ֙ לְנַפְשָׁ֔הּ וּמָכֹ֤ר לֹא־תִמְכְּרֶ֣נָּה בַּכָּ֑סֶף לֹא־תִתְעַמֵּ֣ר בָּ֔הּ תַּ֖חַת אֲשֶׁ֥ר עִנִּיתָֽהּ׃ ס

15 כִּֽי־תִהְיֶ֨יןָ לְאִ֜ישׁ שְׁתֵּ֣י נָשִׁ֗ים הָאַחַ֤ת אֲהוּבָה֙ וְהָאַחַ֣ת שְׂנוּאָ֔ה וְיָֽלְדוּ־ל֣וֹ בָנִ֔ים הָאֲהוּבָ֖ה וְהַשְּׂנוּאָ֑ה וְהָיָ֛ה הַבֵּ֥ן הַבְּכֹ֖ר לַשְּׂנִיאָֽה׃ 16 וְהָיָ֗ה בְּיוֹם֙ הַנְחִיל֣וֹ אֶת־בָּנָ֔יו אֵ֥ת אֲשֶׁר־יִהְיֶ֖ה ל֑וֹ לֹ֣א יוּכַ֗ל לְבַכֵּר֙ אֶת־בֶּן־ הָאֲהוּבָ֔ה עַל־פְּנֵ֥י בֶן־הַשְּׂנוּאָ֖ה הַבְּכֹֽר׃ 17 כִּי֩ אֶת־הַבְּכֹ֨ר בֶּן־הַשְּׂנוּאָ֜ה יַכִּ֗יר לָ֤תֶת לוֹ֙ פִּ֣י שְׁנַ֔יִם בְּכֹ֥ל אֲשֶׁר־יִמָּצֵ֖א ל֑וֹ כִּי־הוּא֙ רֵאשִׁ֣ית אֹנ֔וֹ ל֖וֹ מִשְׁפַּ֥ט הַבְּכֹרָֽה׃ ס

18 כִּֽי־יִהְיֶ֣ה לְאִ֗ישׁ בֵּ֚ן סוֹרֵ֣ר וּמוֹרֶ֔ה אֵינֶ֖נּוּ

- - - - - - - - - - - - - - - - - - - - - - - - - -

*14.* If the Israelite later rejects this foreign wife, he must free her outright. Her status as the wife of an Israelite forever protects her from becoming, or reverting to, the status of a foreign slave (compare Exodus 21:7–8).

***had your will of her.*** Heb. *innah*; this inflection of the verbal root *e-n-h* can mean to debase a woman by having sex with her outside of a regularly contracted marriage. (For more on this verb, see at Genesis 34:2.) This raises the possibility that the man had sex with the woman while she was still a captive, which would not have been unusual. Alternatively, this verb may indicate that the marriage, while recognized as legal, was not considered typical.

### HEIR WHOSE MOTHER IS AN
### UNLOVED WIFE (21:15–17)

The law concerns a man with two wives, although he presumably could have more. Indeed, several biblical narratives point to the two-wife family (plus concubines): Rachel and Leah (Genesis 29), Hannah and Peninnah (I Samuel 1), and the lesser-known wives of Lamech, Adah and Zillah (Genesis 4:19). The tension here over whose son has the rights of inheritance also informs the story of Sarah and Hagar (Genesis 16–21). This law is not intended to protect the unloved wife, rather, to protect the legal heir. As the husband's first-born son, the child must be designated as his heir and receive a double portion regardless of the man's feelings about the mother. Inheritance, which involved land, is extremely important in the Bible; thus, great pains are taken to identify the proper heirs and preserve the transmission of land holdings to them (see 25:5–10).

*15.* ***loved and the unloved.*** The same Hebrew words describe the situation of Leah and Rachel (see at Genesis 29:30–31), although there the subject of inheritance does not surface in the conflict.

### THE INCORRIGIBLE SON (21:18–21)

The law now moves to another type of child, the incorrigible son. This law probably does not apply to daughters, for the characteristics of being a glutton and a drunkard seem to be stereotypically male,

son, who does not heed his father or mother and does not obey them even after they discipline him, [19]his father and mother shall take hold of him and bring him out to the elders of his town at the public place of his community. [20]They shall say to the elders of his town, "This son of ours is disloyal and defiant; he does not heed us. He is a glutton and a drunkard." [21]Thereupon his town's council shall stone him to death. Thus you will sweep out evil from your midst: all Israel will hear and be afraid.

[22]If a party is guilty of a capital offense and is put to death, and you impale the body on a stake, [23]you must not let the corpse remain on the stake overnight, but must bury it the same day. For an impaled body is an affront to God: you shall not defile the land that your God יהוה is giving you to possess.

22 If you see your fellow Israelite's ox or sheep gone astray, do not ignore it; you must take it back to your peer. [2]If your fellow Israelite does not live near you or you do not know who [the owner] is, you shall bring it home and it shall remain with you until your peer claims it; then you shall give it back. [3]You shall do the same with that person's ass; you shall do the same with that person's garment; and so too shall you do with any-

שֹׁמֵעַ בְּקוֹל אָבִיו וּבְקוֹל אִמּוֹ וְיִסְּרוּ אֹתוֹ
וְלֹא יִשְׁמַע אֲלֵיהֶם׃ 19 וְתָפְשׂוּ בוֹ אָבִיו
וְאִמּוֹ וְהוֹצִיאוּ אֹתוֹ אֶל־זִקְנֵי עִירוֹ וְאֶל־
שַׁעַר מְקֹמוֹ׃ 20 וְאָמְרוּ אֶל־זִקְנֵי עִירוֹ בְּנֵנוּ
זֶה סוֹרֵר וּמֹרֶה אֵינֶנּוּ שֹׁמֵעַ בְּקֹלֵנוּ זוֹלֵל
וְסֹבֵא׃ 21 וּרְגָמֻהוּ כָּל־אַנְשֵׁי עִירוֹ בָאֲבָנִים
וָמֵת וּבִעַרְתָּ הָרָע מִקִּרְבֶּךָ וְכָל־יִשְׂרָאֵל
יִשְׁמְעוּ וְיִרָאוּ׃ ס

22 וְכִי־יִהְיֶה בְאִישׁ חֵטְא מִשְׁפַּט־מָוֶת
וְהוּמָת וְתָלִיתָ אֹתוֹ עַל־עֵץ׃ 23 לֹא־תָלִין
נִבְלָתוֹ עַל־הָעֵץ כִּי־קָבוֹר תִּקְבְּרֶנּוּ בַּיּוֹם
הַהוּא כִּי־קִלְלַת אֱלֹהִים תָּלוּי וְלֹא תְטַמֵּא
אֶת־אַדְמָתְךָ אֲשֶׁר יְהֹוָה אֱלֹהֶיךָ נֹתֵן לְךָ
נַחֲלָה׃ ס

כב לֹא־תִרְאֶה אֶת־שׁוֹר אָחִיךָ אוֹ אֶת־
שֵׂיוֹ נִדָּחִים וְהִתְעַלַּמְתָּ מֵהֶם הָשֵׁב תְּשִׁיבֵם
לְאָחִיךָ׃ 2 וְאִם־לֹא קָרוֹב אָחִיךָ אֵלֶיךָ וְלֹא
יְדַעְתּוֹ וַאֲסַפְתּוֹ אֶל־תּוֹךְ בֵּיתֶךָ וְהָיָה עִמְּךָ
עַד דְּרֹשׁ אָחִיךָ אֹתוֹ וַהֲשֵׁבֹתוֹ לוֹ׃ 3 וְכֵן
תַּעֲשֶׂה לַחֲמֹרוֹ וְכֵן תַּעֲשֶׂה לְשִׂמְלָתוֹ וְכֵן

whereas 22:20–21 does concern a rebellious daughter (see below). The text states explicitly that both mother and father are equally involved in multiple attempts to discipline the son. If they are unable to control him, it becomes the larger society's responsibility to deal with him. Insubordination to parents, a violation of "Honor your father and mother" (5:16; Exodus 20:12; also Leviticus 19:3), is considered a capital offense. Such behavior undermines the parents' authority and the function of families, which are the center of Israelite society.

***20. "disloyal and defiant."*** Here, disobedience is the crime; elsewhere, cursing and striking a parent are capital offenses (Exodus 21:15, 17; Leviticus 20:9; Deuteronomy 27:16).

## *Laws Regarding Neighbors, Nature, and Clothing* (21:22–22:12)

Generally speaking, the laws in this unit promote good citizenship by legislating areas of responsibility for what takes place outside of one's own household.

***22–23.*** This law limits the desecration of the corpse of an executed criminal by requiring relatively quick burial.

***22:1–4.*** By returning lost objects (vv. 1–3) and helping to raise a fallen animal (v. 4), individuals cooperate to form a stronger community. Compare Exodus 23:4–5, which demands the return of, or aid to, the animal of an enemy—not of a neighbor.

thing that your fellow Israelite loses and you find:
you must not remain indifferent.
4 If you see your fellow Israelite's ass or ox fallen
on the road, do not ignore it; you must raise it
together.
5 A woman must not put on man's apparel, nor
shall a man wear woman's clothing; for whoever
does these things is abhorrent to your God יהוה.
6 If, along the road, you chance upon a bird's
nest, in any tree or on the ground, with fledglings
or eggs and the mother sitting over the fledglings or
on the eggs, do not take the mother together with
her young. 7 Let the mother go, and take only the
young, in order that you may fare well and have a
long life.
8 When you build a new house, you shall make
a parapet for your roof, so that you do not bring
bloodguilt on your house if anyone should fall
from it.
9 You shall not sow your vineyard with a second
kind of seed, else the crop—from the seed you have
sown—and the yield of the vineyard may not be
used. 10 You shall not plow with an ox and an ass together. 11 You shall not wear cloth combining wool
and linen.
12 You shall make tassels on the four corners of
the garment with which you cover yourself.

תַּעֲשֶׂה לְכָל־אֲבֵדַת אָחִיךָ אֲשֶׁר־תֹּאבַד
מִמֶּנּוּ וּמְצָאתָהּ לֹא תוּכַל לְהִתְעַלֵּם׃ ס
4 לֹא־תִרְאֶה אֶת־חֲמוֹר אָחִיךָ אוֹ שׁוֹרוֹ
נֹפְלִים בַּדֶּרֶךְ וְהִתְעַלַּמְתָּ מֵהֶם הָקֵם תָּקִים
עִמּוֹ׃ פ
5 לֹא־יִהְיֶה כְלִי־גֶבֶר עַל־אִשָּׁה וְלֹא־יִלְבַּשׁ
גֶּבֶר שִׂמְלַת אִשָּׁה כִּי תוֹעֲבַת יְהֹוָה אֱלֹהֶיךָ
כָּל־עֹשֵׂה אֵלֶּה׃ פ
6 כִּי יִקָּרֵא קַן־צִפּוֹר ׀ לְפָנֶיךָ בַּדֶּרֶךְ בְּכָל־עֵץ ׀
אוֹ עַל־הָאָרֶץ אֶפְרֹחִים אוֹ בֵיצִים וְהָאֵם
רֹבֶצֶת עַל־הָאֶפְרֹחִים אוֹ עַל־הַבֵּיצִים לֹא־
תִקַּח הָאֵם עַל־הַבָּנִים׃ 7 שַׁלֵּחַ תְּשַׁלַּח
אֶת־הָאֵם וְאֶת־הַבָּנִים תִּקַּח־לָךְ לְמַעַן
יִיטַב לָךְ וְהַאֲרַכְתָּ יָמִים׃ ס
8 כִּי תִבְנֶה בַּיִת חָדָשׁ וְעָשִׂיתָ מַעֲקֶה לְגַגֶּךָ
וְלֹא־תָשִׂים דָּמִים בְּבֵיתֶךָ כִּי־יִפֹּל הַנֹּפֵל
מִמֶּנּוּ׃
9 לֹא־תִזְרַע כַּרְמְךָ כִּלְאָיִם פֶּן־תִּקְדַּשׁ
הַמְלֵאָה הַזֶּרַע אֲשֶׁר תִּזְרָע וּתְבוּאַת
הַכָּרֶם׃ ס 10 לֹא־תַחֲרֹשׁ בְּשׁוֹר־וּבַחֲמֹר
יַחְדָּו׃ 11 לֹא תִלְבַּשׁ שַׁעַטְנֵז צֶמֶר וּפִשְׁתִּים
יַחְדָּו׃ ס
12 גְּדִלִים תַּעֲשֶׂה־לָּךְ עַל־אַרְבַּע כַּנְפוֹת
כְּסוּתְךָ אֲשֶׁר תְּכַסֶּה־בָּהּ׃ ס

*5.* The prohibition on cross-dressing is not explained, except to note that it is abhorrent to God. This rule perhaps was intended to prevent unacceptable sexual practices or pagan cultic practices. More likely, it aims to maintain gender boundaries, analogous to the laws against forbidden mixtures in 22:9–11, thus preventing confusion about the public presentation of a person's gender identity.

*6–7.* This law deals with the humane treatment of a mother bird and her fledglings. Interpreters often compare it to the prohibition of cooking a kid (baby goat) in its mother's milk (see at 14:21; Exodus 23:19; 34:26), as well as with the prohibition against slaughtering an animal and its mother on the same day (Leviticus 22:28).

*8.* Since roofs were flat and rooftops were used as a living or work space, they needed a wall or fence around them so people would not fall off.

*9–11.* The list of forbidden mixtures covers plants, animals, and clothing. No reason for these prohibitions is provided. (See also at Leviticus 19:19.)

12. This verse does not explain why tassels (*g'dilim*) should be put on one's everyday clothes. However, Numbers 15:37–41 mandates *tzitzit* (there translated as "fringes") as reminders to obey God's commandments. The law appears to be gender neu-

[13]A householder marries a woman and cohabits
with her. Then he takes an aversion to her [14]and
makes up charges against her and defames her,
saying, "This is the party I married; but when I
approached her, I found that she was not a virgin."
[15]In such a case, the girl's father and mother shall
produce the evidence of the girl's virginity before
the elders of the town at the gate. [16]And the girl's
father shall say to the elders, "To this party I gave
my own daughter to wife, but he has taken an aver-

13 כִּֽי־יִקַּ֥ח אִ֖ישׁ אִשָּׁ֑ה וּבָ֥א אֵלֶ֖יהָ וּשְׂנֵאָֽהּ׃
14 וְשָׂ֥ם לָהּ֙ עֲלִילֹ֣ת דְּבָרִ֔ים וְהוֹצִ֥א עָלֶ֖יהָ
שֵׁ֣ם רָ֑ע וְאָמַ֗ר אֶת־הָאִשָּׁ֤ה הַזֹּאת֙ לָקַ֔חְתִּי
וָאֶקְרַ֣ב אֵלֶ֔יהָ וְלֹא־מָצָ֥אתִי לָ֖הּ בְּתוּלִֽים׃
15 וְלָקַ֛ח אֲבִ֥י הנער הַֽנַּעֲרָ֖ה וְאִמָּ֑הּ וְהוֹצִ֜יאוּ
אֶת־בְּתוּלֵ֧י הנער הַֽנַּעֲרָ֛ה אֶל־זִקְנֵ֥י הָעִ֖יר
הַשָּֽׁעְרָה׃ 16 וְאָמַ֛ר אֲבִ֥י הנער הַֽנַּעֲרָ֖ה אֶל־
הַזְּקֵנִ֑ים אֶת־בִּתִּ֗י נָתַ֛תִּי לָאִ֥ישׁ הַזֶּ֖ה לְאִשָּׁ֑ה

tral, in that women are not excluded from wearing tassels. (For more on tasseled garments, see at Numbers 15:37–41.)

## *Laws Regarding Sexual Misconduct*
(22:13–29)

In the Bible, women are expected to be chaste before marriage. This unit inquires into cases in which a woman's premarital chastity is either in doubt or known to have been violated. (For further discussion, see Tikva Frymer-Kensky, "Law and Philosophy: The Case of Sex in the Bible," reprinted in *Studies in Bible and Feminist Criticism*, 2006, pp. 239–54.)

### FALSE AND TRUE ACCUSATIONS OF UNCHASTITY (22:13–21)

This section focuses on false accusations of unchastity, which the law is intended to discourage, as well as the procedure if the accusation turns out to be true.

***13–19.*** This passage presents the case of a husband who falsely accuses his bride of having been unchaste before the marriage. Motivating this accusation is the husband's desire to get out of the marriage without incurring any financial costs. Under normal circumstances, if a man divorces his wife he must pay the support-money required by the marriage contract. However, if his accusation of unchastity succeeds, the husband will be able to rid himself of his wife without payment; and he might even benefit financially, for he is in essence accusing the bride's father of breach of contract. The husband claims that he contracted and gave the betrothal gift for a virgin but received a wife whose betrothal gift should have been less. If so, the contract would be declared invalid; as a result, the husband would recoup the betrothal gift he had paid and the father might have to pay additional money as damages to the husband.

***14–15.*** In this legal scenario, the husband makes public statements defaming the bride. Her parents sue the husband for defamation of character, of both the bride and her parents. According to this reading, the parents are the plaintiffs and the husband is the defendant. Alternatively, the husband is the plaintiff, bringing the legal claim of unchastity; and the parents are the defendants. Both mother and father bring evidence to the elders; but only the father utters the legal declaration, perhaps because the claim of breach of contract is directed at him. (Compare 21:20, where both parents make a legal declaration.)

***14. "party."*** [Heb. *ishah* (traditionally, "woman"). The present translation understands that the word *ishah* (and its corresponding male term, *ish*) has as its primary sense "a representative member of a group"; in legal settings, this sense translates to "a party (to the case at hand)." See *The Contemporary Torah*, 2006, pp. 394–5. —*Ed.*]

sion to her; 17 so he has made up charges, saying,
'I did not find your daughter a virgin.' But here is
the evidence of my daughter's virginity!" And they
shall spread out the cloth before the elders of the
town. 18 The elders of that town shall then take that
party and flog him, 19 and they shall fine him a
hundred [shekels of] silver and give it to the girl's
father; for [that householder] has defamed a virgin
in Israel. Moreover, she shall remain his wife; he
shall never have the right to divorce her.

20 But if the charge proves true, the girl was
found not to have been a virgin, 21 then the girl

וַיִּשְׂנָאֶהָ׃ 17 וְהִנֵּה־הוּא שָׂם עֲלִילֹת דְּבָרִים
לֵאמֹר לֹא־מָצָאתִי לְבִתְּךָ בְּתוּלִים וְאֵלֶּה
בְּתוּלֵי בִתִּי וּפָרְשׂוּ הַשִּׂמְלָה לִפְנֵי זִקְנֵי
הָעִיר׃ 18 וְלָקְחוּ זִקְנֵי הָעִיר־הַהִוא אֶת־
הָאִישׁ וְיִסְּרוּ אֹתוֹ׃ 19 וְעָנְשׁוּ אֹתוֹ מֵאָה
כֶסֶף וְנָתְנוּ לַאֲבִי הַנַּעֲרָה כִּי הוֹצִיא שֵׁם
רָע עַל בְּתוּלַת יִשְׂרָאֵל וְלוֹ־תִהְיֶה לְאִשָּׁה
לֹא־יוּכַל לְשַׁלְּחָהּ כָּל־יָמָיו׃ ס
20 וְאִם־אֱמֶת הָיָה הַדָּבָר הַזֶּה לֹא־נִמְצְאוּ
בְתוּלִים לנער לַנַּעֲרָה׃ 21 וְהוֹצִיאוּ אֶת־

*17. 'I did not find your daughter a virgin.'* The public statement by the husband in v. 14 did not say "your daughter" but rather "she." The father construes the case as an accusation against himself more than his daughter, for he is responsible for his daughter's chastity.

*the cloth.* Typically, readers assume this to be a blood-stained sheet from the wedding night. Many commentators, medieval and modern, have noted the flimsiness of this evidence and the impossibility of proving whether the bloodstain was faked or not, even assuming that the custom of saving the wedding sheet for such an occasion was indeed practiced in ancient Israel. On the other hand, it would have been difficult to prove that the evidence was faked. If the parents bring the lawsuit, with evidence that is hard to refute, then clearly the accusation is false. This action and the penalty that the elders impose upon the man aim at deterring such false accusations. Without such deterrence, husbands might all too easily accuse their unloved wives of premarital unchastity, to the detriment of a society in which marriage and family were the keystones.

*19. fine him a hundred* [*shekels*]. This is double the betrothal gift (v. 29) that the father would have returned had the accusation been true. Thus, the would-be "thief" pays double what he wishes to steal. The fine is paid to the father, not the wife, for he is considered the injured party in the lawsuit.

*he shall never have the right to divorce her.* The husband's aim from the start seems to have been to divorce his wife, and this option now is forever denied him. To a modern reader, this seems to be a punishment for the bride as well as for the husband. In ancient society, however, a woman was more secure economically when married than when divorced. (An individual could scarcely survive economically or socially unless she or he was a part of a family or similar group. This was especially true of women, who had few means of independent support and little chance for social standing or power outside the group. See at 22:29.) This law was probably intended to deter false accusations of unchastity, or perhaps to deter easy and baseless divorces.

*20–21.* If the accusation is true, the sentence is carried out at the entrance to the father's house, not at the town gate; the father is held responsible and thus is publicly dishonored. The penalty for the wife is death. Premarital sex in itself is not the problem (although it was certainly discouraged; see vv. 28–29); the problem here, from the husband's view, is misrepresentation—providing the husband with a wife whose due betrothal gift would have been lower than that of the virgin that he contracted for. Many scholars think that this section was added later for the sake of symmetry; clearly, the main emphasis is on the case of false, not true, accusation.

Modern scholars have understood this case as the female parallel to the incorrigible son. In both cases,

shall be brought out to the entrance of her father's house, and her town's council shall stone her to death; for she did a shameful thing in Israel, committing fornication while under her father's authority. Thus you will sweep away evil from your midst.
[22]If a man is found lying with another man's wife, both of them—the man and the woman with whom he lay—shall die. Thus you will sweep away evil from Israel.

[23]In the case of a virgin who is engaged to a man—if a man comes upon her in town and lies

הנער הַנַּעֲרָה אֶל־פֶּתַח בֵּית־אָבִיהָ וּסְקָלוּהָ
אַנְשֵׁי עִירָהּ בָּאֲבָנִים וָמֵתָה כִּי־עָשְׂתָה
נְבָלָה בְּיִשְׂרָאֵל לִזְנוֹת בֵּית אָבִיהָ וּבִעַרְתָּ
הָרָע מִקִּרְבֶּךָ׃ ס
22 כִּי־יִמָּצֵא אִישׁ שֹׁכֵב ׀ עִם־אִשָּׁה
בְעֻלַת־בַּעַל וּמֵתוּ גַּם־שְׁנֵיהֶם הָאִישׁ
הַשֹּׁכֵב עִם־הָאִשָּׁה וְהָאִשָּׁה וּבִעַרְתָּ הָרָע
מִיִּשְׂרָאֵל׃ ס
23 כִּי יִהְיֶה נער נַעֲרָה בְתוּלָה מְאֹרָשָׂה
לְאִישׁ וּמְצָאָהּ אִישׁ בָּעִיר וְשָׁכַב עִמָּהּ׃

the offspring fails to uphold the family standards and goes against parental authority. In both cases, the parents' testimony decides the outcome; and the penalty for disobeying parental authority is death by stoning. This parallel strongly suggests that in both cases, the issue is repeated, uncontrolled behavior—not a one-time occurrence. The "unchaste bride" is actually being accused of promiscuity and deception, not merely a pre-marital fling. These laws attempt to promote proper behavior by adolescent women and men who are at precisely the age when rebellion against parental authority is most likely. (See Adele Berlin, "Sex and the Single Girl in Deuteronomy 22," in Nili Fox et al., eds., *Mishneh Todah: Studies in Deuteronomy* . . . , 2008.)

***20. if the charge proves true.*** This refers to the husband's accusation (v. 14).

***the girl was found not to have been a virgin.*** Better, "no signs of virginity belonging to the girl were found." In other words, the parents could not or did not bring the cloth to the elders, so there was no way to disprove the husband's accusation.

### THE PENALTY FOR ADULTERY (22:22)

In the Bible, adultery is defined as sex between a married or betrothed woman and a man other than her husband or fiancé (see also Exodus 20:13). This verse is placed here to make clear that adultery is a capital offense and that both parties receive the death penalty. In the story of the adulterous encounter between King David and Bathsheba (II Samuel 11–12), God commutes David's death sentence; Bathsheba's guilt is not mentioned. While in that story it is David who initiates the sexual act, Proverbs 7 tells of a married woman who lures a young man into committing adultery.

### FORCED AND CONSENSUAL SEX WITH A BETROTHED WOMAN (22:23–27)

While Deuteronomy considers consensual pre-marital sex by a woman to be a capital offense (see below), it recognizes that in some cases women are victims of non-consensual sex and therefore seeks to protect them from a penalty in those cases. (A betrothed woman, meaning one whose marriage has been contracted, is for legal reasons considered like a married woman. If she engages in consensual sex with a man other than the one betrothed to her, both are committing adultery.) How does one determine if the sex was consensual or not? This section establishes that if the encounter took place in the town (vv. 23–24), where she could call for help if she needed it, then the sex is judged to be consensual and both are culpable. The supposition is that had she called for help, she would have been heard and rescued. However, in the country (vv. 25–27), where presumably no help is available, the sex is assumed to have been forced and the woman is not

with her, [24]you shall take the two of them out to the gate of that town and stone them to death: the girl because she did not cry for help in the town, and the man because he violated another man's wife. Thus you will sweep away evil from your midst. [25]But if the man comes upon the engaged girl in the open country, and the man lies with her by force, only the man who lay with her shall die, [26]but you shall do nothing to the girl. The girl did not incur the death penalty, for this case is like that of one party attacking and murdering another. [27]He came upon her in the open; though the engaged girl cried for help, there was no one to save her.

[28]If a man comes upon a virgin who is not engaged and he seizes her and lies with her, and they

24 וְהוֹצֵאתֶם אֶת־שְׁנֵיהֶם אֶל־שַׁעַר ׀ הָעִיר
הַהִוא וּסְקַלְתֶּם אֹתָם בָּאֲבָנִים וָמֵתוּ אֶת־
הַנַּעֲרָה עַל־דְּבַר אֲשֶׁר לֹא־צָעֲקָה הנער
בָעִיר וְאֶת־הָאִישׁ עַל־דְּבַר אֲשֶׁר־עִנָּה אֶת־
אֵשֶׁת רֵעֵהוּ וּבִעַרְתָּ הָרָע מִקִּרְבֶּךָ׃ ס
25 וְאִם־בַּשָּׂדֶה יִמְצָא הָאִישׁ אֶת־הנער
הַנַּעֲרָה הַמְאֹרָשָׂה וְהֶחֱזִיק־בָּהּ הָאִישׁ
וְשָׁכַב עִמָּהּ וּמֵת הָאִישׁ אֲשֶׁר־שָׁכַב עִמָּהּ
לְבַדּוֹ׃ 26 ולנער וְלַנַּעֲרָה לֹא־תַעֲשֶׂה דָבָר
אֵין לנער לַנַּעֲרָה חֵטְא מָוֶת כִּי כַּאֲשֶׁר יָקוּם
אִישׁ עַל־רֵעֵהוּ וּרְצָחוֹ נֶפֶשׁ כֵּן הַדָּבָר הַזֶּה׃
27 כִּי בַשָּׂדֶה מְצָאָהּ צָעֲקָה הנער הַנַּעֲרָה
הַמְאֹרָשָׂה וְאֵין מוֹשִׁיעַ לָהּ׃ ס
28 כִּי־יִמְצָא אִישׁ נער נַעֲרָה בְתוּלָה אֲשֶׁר
לֹא־אֹרָשָׂה וּתְפָשָׂהּ וְשָׁכַב עִמָּהּ וְנִמְצָאוּ׃

culpable. We may assume that the woman went on to marry her fiancé with no legal repercussions.

## FORCED SEX WITH AN UNBETROTHED WOMAN (22:28–29)

This case concerns a woman who is not married or betrothed, so engaging in sex with her does not constitute adultery. The law assumes that the man initiated the act and that there was some degree of coercion, as reflected in the statement, "he seizes her and lies with her" (v. 28; compare v. 23). The man is obligated to marry the woman and to pay the betrothal gift for virgins; he may never divorce her. (Compare Exodus 22:15–16, which does not include the no-divorce stipulation and provides for the father's refusal of the marriage.)

Some modern commentators wonder if this was a form of elopement, or a way for the woman to force her father to agree to her choice of a marriage partner. Others view the law as hard on the woman, who would have to remain married to her "rapist" (although this was not necessarily a rape). As in most cases, however, the law is not focused on the interests of women individually, but instead on families and society. The law assumes some initiative or even force on the man's part (on such language, see at Exodus 19:15); after all, voluntary sex on the woman's part that did not result in marriage to the sexual partner would leave her vulnerable to the true claim of unchastity by a subsequent husband (see vv. 20–21). This law seeks to prevent that situation. Sex by an unmarried or unbetrothed woman is, as it were, covered up by making it sound less-than-consensual and by quickly marrying off the woman to her sexual partner (who would hardly be in a position to later accuse her of unchastity). The man is obligated to remain married to her for much the same reason as the false accuser is (see at v. 19).

Permanent marriage without the possibility of divorce protects the woman (see at v. 19), who would find it difficult to contract another marriage if her past marital or sexual history were known. The law also protects the father's interest in that he receives the fullest betrothal gift. A never-married

are discovered, [29]the party who lay with her shall
pay the girl's father fifty [shekels of] silver, and she
shall be his wife. Because he has violated her, he can
never have the right to divorce her.

23 No householder shall marry his father's
former wife, so as to remove his father's garment.
[2]No man whose testes are crushed or whose
member is cut off shall be admitted into the congregation of יהוה.
[3]No one misbegotten shall be admitted into the
congregation of יהוה; no descendant of such, even
in the tenth generation, shall be admitted into the
congregation of יהוה.
[4]No Ammonite or Moabite shall be admitted
into the congregation of יהוה; no descendants of

29 וְנָתַן הָאִישׁ הַשֹּׁכֵב עִמָּהּ לַאֲבִי הנער
הַנַּעֲרָה חֲמִשִּׁים כָּסֶף וְלוֹ־תִהְיֶה לְאִשָּׁה
תַּחַת אֲשֶׁר עִנָּהּ לֹא־יוּכַל שַׁלְּחָהּ כָּל־
יָמָיו׃ ס

כג לֹא־יִקַּח אִישׁ אֶת־אֵשֶׁת אָבִיו וְלֹא
יְגַלֶּה כְּנַף אָבִיו׃ ס
2 לֹא־יָבֹא פְצוּעַ־דַּכָּה וּכְרוּת שָׁפְכָה בִּקְהַל
יְהוָה׃ ס
3 לֹא־יָבֹא מַמְזֵר בִּקְהַל יְהוָה גַּם דּוֹר
עֲשִׂירִי לֹא־יָבֹא לוֹ בִּקְהַל יְהוָה׃ ס
4 לֹא־יָבֹא עַמּוֹנִי וּמוֹאָבִי בִּקְהַל יְהוָה גַּם
דּוֹר עֲשִׂירִי לֹא־יָבֹא לָהֶם בִּקְהַל יְהוָה עַד־

---

non-virgin daughter would not be easy to marry off. Given that there must have been women of this description, Deuteronomy is at pains to protect them while still adhering to a high ideal standard for women's premarital sexual behavior.

## *Laws Regarding Forbidden Relationships* (23:1–9)

Following the prohibition of marrying one's father's former wife, this unit restricts membership in the community by sexual and ethnic characteristics.

### PROHIBITION ON MARRYING A FATHER'S FORMER WIFE (23:1)

This law appears in Leviticus 18:8 and 20:11 as part of a long list of prohibited incestuous relationships. The reference applies to a person's stepmother, not simply to his biological mother.

*1. to remove his father's garment.* That is, to lay claim to his father's wife (Leviticus 18:8, 20:11; Ezekiel 16:8; Ruth 3:9), whom it would be inappropriate to marry.

### RESTRICTION ON WHO MAY ENTER GOD'S CONGREGATION (23:2–9)

This section limits those included in the "congregation," which may mean the official members, or full citizens, of the Israelite community. (See also at Leviticus 21:16–24.)

*2.* Eunuchs are mentioned first. In the ancient world, young men captured in war were sometimes castrated and designated to serve in the court, a military unit, or a household.

*3. misbegotten.* Heb. *mamzer*, a status term whose precise meaning is uncertain because it appears only once more in the Bible, in an equally vague setting (Zechariah 9:6). (The Rabbis understood this term to refer to children of prohibited marriages.)

*4–7.* These verses exclude Ammonites and Moabites because they treated Israel poorly after the Exodus. According to Genesis 19:36–38, Ammon and Moab are the offspring of the incestuous unions between Lot and his daughters, which may explain why they are included just after the mention of the *mamzer*. Traditional commentators interpret this exclusion as applying only to male Ammonites and Moabites. This helps eliminate the contradic-

such, even in the tenth generation, shall ever be admitted into the congregation of יהוה, [5]because they did not meet you with food and water on your journey after you left Egypt, and because they hired Balaam son of Beor, from Pethor of Aram-naharaim, to curse you.—[6]But your God יהוה refused to heed Balaam; instead, your God יהוה turned the curse into a blessing for you, for your God יהוה loves you.—[7]You shall never concern yourself with their welfare or benefit as long as you live.

[8]You shall not abhor an Edomite, for such is your kin. You shall not abhor an Egyptian, for you were a stranger in that land. [9]Children born to them may be admitted into the congregation of יהוה in the third generation.

[10]When you [men] go out as a troop against your enemies, be on your guard against anything untoward. [11]If anyone among you has been rendered impure by a nocturnal emission, he must leave the camp, and he must not reenter the camp. [12]Toward evening he shall bathe in water, and at sundown he may reenter the camp. [13]Further, there shall be an area for you outside the camp, where you may relieve yourself. [14]With your gear you shall have a spike, and when you have squatted you shall dig a hole with it and cover up your excrement. [15]Since your God יהוה moves about in your camp

עוֹלָֽם׃ [5] עַל־דְּבַר֩ אֲשֶׁ֨ר לֹא־קִדְּמ֤וּ אֶתְכֶם֙ בַּלֶּ֣חֶם וּבַמַּ֔יִם בַּדֶּ֖רֶךְ בְּצֵאתְכֶ֣ם מִמִּצְרָ֑יִם וַאֲשֶׁר֩ שָׂכַ֨ר עָלֶ֜יךָ אֶת־בִּלְעָ֣ם בֶּן־בְּע֗וֹר מִפְּת֛וֹר אֲרַ֥ם נַהֲרַ֖יִם לְקַֽלְלֶֽךָּ׃ [6] וְלֹֽא־אָבָ֞ה יְהֹוָ֤ה אֱלֹהֶ֙יךָ֙ לִשְׁמֹ֣עַ אֶל־בִּלְעָ֔ם וַיַּהֲפֹךְ֩ יְהֹוָ֨ה אֱלֹהֶ֧יךָ לְּךָ֛ אֶת־הַקְּלָלָ֖ה לִבְרָכָ֑ה כִּ֥י אֲהֵֽבְךָ֖ יְהֹוָ֥ה אֱלֹהֶֽיךָ׃ [7] לֹא־תִדְרֹ֥שׁ שְׁלֹמָ֖ם וְטֹבָתָ֑ם כׇּל־יָמֶ֖יךָ לְעוֹלָֽם׃ ס

[8] לֹֽא־תְתַעֵ֣ב אֲדֹמִ֔י כִּ֥י אָחִ֖יךָ ה֑וּא לֹא־תְתַעֵ֣ב מִצְרִ֔י כִּי־גֵ֖ר הָיִ֥יתָ בְאַרְצֽוֹ׃ [9] בָּנִ֛ים אֲשֶׁר־יִוָּלְד֥וּ לָהֶ֖ם דּ֣וֹר שְׁלִישִׁ֑י יָבֹ֥א לָהֶ֖ם בִּקְהַ֥ל יְהֹוָֽה׃ ס

[10] כִּֽי־תֵצֵ֥א מַחֲנֶ֖ה עַל־אֹֽיְבֶ֑יךָ וְנִ֨שְׁמַרְתָּ֔ מִכֹּ֖ל דָּבָ֥ר רָֽע׃ [11] כִּֽי־יִהְיֶ֤ה בְךָ֙ אִ֔ישׁ אֲשֶׁ֛ר לֹא־יִהְיֶ֥ה טָה֖וֹר מִקְּרֵה־לָ֑יְלָה וְיָצָא֙ אֶל־מִח֣וּץ לַֽמַּחֲנֶ֔ה לֹ֥א יָבֹ֖א אֶל־תּ֥וֹךְ הַֽמַּחֲנֶֽה׃ [12] וְהָיָ֣ה לִפְנֽוֹת־עֶ֔רֶב יִרְחַ֖ץ בַּמָּ֑יִם וּכְבֹ֣א הַשֶּׁ֔מֶשׁ יָבֹ֖א אֶל־תּ֥וֹךְ הַֽמַּחֲנֶֽה׃ [13] וְיָד֙ תִּהְיֶ֣ה לְךָ֔ מִח֖וּץ לַֽמַּחֲנֶ֑ה וְיָצָ֥אתָ שָּׁ֖מָּה חֽוּץ׃ [14] וְיָתֵ֛ד תִּהְיֶ֥ה לְךָ֖ עַל־אֲזֵנֶ֑ךָ וְהָיָה֙ בְּשִׁבְתְּךָ֣ ח֔וּץ וְחָפַרְתָּ֣ה בָ֔הּ וְשַׁבְתָּ֖ וְכִסִּ֥יתָ אֶת־צֵאָתֶֽךָ׃ [15] כִּי֩ יְהֹוָ֨ה אֱלֹהֶ֜יךָ מִתְהַלֵּ֣ךְ ׀ בְּקֶ֣רֶב מַחֲנֶ֗ךָ

- - - - - - - - - - - - - - - - - - - - - - - - - - - - - - - - - - - - - - - -

tion between this verse and the book of Ruth, in which a Moabite woman (Ruth) is accepted into the Israelite community. The present translation understands the grammatically masculine language in this prohibition to refer to women as well, based on an allusion in I Kings 11:1–2 (*The Torah: A Modern Commentary*, revised edition, 2005, p. 1328). However the exclusion of Ammonites and Moabites is defined, its historical origin is not known, nor is it clear if Deuteronomy's denial of citizenship also included a ban on marrying them (although that may have been the result).

## Miscellaneous Laws  (23:10–24:9)

This unit contains a series of laws about purity in wartime, escaped slaves, prostitution, financial responsibilities, divorce, skin disease, and other assorted matters.

### LAWS REGARDING SOLDIERS, SLAVES, AND PROSTITUTES (23:10–19)

This passage concerns three seemingly unrelated groups of people: soldiers, slaves, and prostitutes.

to protect you and to deliver your enemies to you,
let your camp be holy; let [God] not find anything
unseemly among you and turn away from you.
16 You shall not turn over to the master a slave
who seeks refuge with you from that master. 17 Such
individuals shall live with you in any place they may
choose among the settlements in your midst, wherever they please; you must not ill-treat them.
18 No Israelite woman shall be a prostitute, nor
shall any Israelite man be a prostitute. 19 You shall
not bring the fee of a whore or the pay of a dog into
the house of your God יהוה in fulfillment of any
vow, for both are abhorrent to your God יהוה.

לְהַצִּילְךָ֙ וְלָתֵ֤ת אֹיְבֶ֙יךָ֙ לְפָנֶ֔יךָ וְהָיָ֥ה מַחֲנֶ֖יךָ
קָד֑וֹשׁ וְלֹֽא־יִרְאֶ֤ה בְךָ֙ עֶרְוַ֣ת דָּבָ֔ר וְשָׁ֖ב
מֵאַחֲרֶֽיךָ׃ ס
16 לֹא־תַסְגִּ֥יר עֶ֖בֶד אֶל־אֲדֹנָ֑יו אֲשֶׁר־יִנָּצֵ֥ל
אֵלֶ֖יךָ מֵעִ֥ם אֲדֹנָֽיו׃ 17 עִמְּךָ֞ יֵשֵׁ֣ב בְּקִרְבְּךָ֗
בַּמָּק֧וֹם אֲשֶׁר־יִבְחַ֛ר בְּאַחַ֥ד שְׁעָרֶ֖יךָ בַּטּ֣וֹב ל֑וֹ
לֹ֖א תּוֹנֶֽנּוּ׃ ס
18 לֹא־תִהְיֶ֥ה קְדֵשָׁ֖ה מִבְּנ֣וֹת יִשְׂרָאֵ֑ל וְלֹא־
יִהְיֶ֥ה קָדֵ֖שׁ מִבְּנֵ֥י יִשְׂרָאֵֽל׃ 19 לֹא־תָבִ֩יא
אֶתְנַ֨ן זוֹנָ֜ה וּמְחִ֣יר כֶּ֗לֶב בֵּ֛ית יְהוָ֥ה אֱלֹהֶ֖יךָ
לְכָל־נֶ֑דֶר כִּ֧י תוֹעֲבַ֛ת יְהוָ֥ה אֱלֹהֶ֖יךָ גַּם־
שְׁנֵיהֶֽם׃ ס

*10–15.* Ritual purity is required in the military camp, for God is thought to be present in it. Certain bodily functions render a man impure (see at Leviticus 15:1–18), but this should not be confused with uncleanliness.

*16–17.* Most commentators understand this asylum law to apply to foreign slaves, not Israelites. In contrast, ancient Near Eastern practice required the extradition of runaway slaves.

*18–19.* These verses seem to prohibit prostitution by females and males, though the meaning of v. 19 is obscure.

*18. prostitute.* Heb. *k'deishah* and *kadeish*. In the past, scholars understood these terms as a reference to male and female cult prostitution, which was associated with Canaanite and Mesopotamian fertility rites where ritual sexual union was believed to ensure agricultural fertility. The reason for this interpretation is that the term *k'deishah* derives from *k-d-sh* (meaning "holy" or "set apart") and the etymologically related Akkadian term *kadishtu* refers to a type of priestess. Recent scholarship, however, has questioned the existence of cult prostitution in the ancient Near East, although there may have been prostitutes in the vicinity of temples, and temples may have received funds from their activities. Many scholars now believe that *k'deishah* means a common prostitute (*zonah*), not a cult prostitute (see Genesis 38:15, 21, where both terms are used). [Others suggest different interpretations. Tikva Frymer-Kensky writes that *k'deishah* refers to "a public woman, who might be found along the roadway (as virgins or married women should not be). She could engage in sex, but might also be sought out for lactation, midwifery, and other female concerns" (*Women In Scripture*, 2000, p. 162). Phyllis A. Bird, who translates *k'deishah* as "hierodule" (from Greek, meaning "a sacred/holy servant") considers the term to refer to a variety of cult-related women (*Missing Persons and Mistaken Identities*, 1997, p. 199). —*Ed.*]

While the Bible certainly does not encourage prostitution, it acknowledges and accepts it as part of the social reality. Indeed, since prostitutes are among the socially inferior in that they do not belong to male-headed households, the Bible occasionally treats them with sympathy (see the depiction of Rahab in Joshua 2 and the two women who plead before Solomon in I Kings 3:16–27). Deuteronomy's strong stance against prostitution fits with the book's idealized picture of society.

[20]You shall not deduct interest from loans to your fellow Israelites, whether in money or food or anything else that can be deducted as interest; [21]but you may deduct interest from loans to foreigners. Do not deduct interest from loans to your fellow Israelites, so that your God יהוה may bless you in all your undertakings in the land that you are about to enter and possess.

[22]When you make a vow to your God יהוה, do not put off fulfilling it, for your God יהוה will require it of you, and you will have incurred guilt; [23]whereas you incur no guilt if you refrain from vowing. [24]You must fulfill what has crossed your lips and perform what you have voluntarily vowed to your God יהוה, having made the promise with your own mouth.

[25]When you enter a fellow [Israelite]'s vineyard, you may eat as many grapes as you want, until you are full, but you must not put any in your vessel. [26]When you enter a fellow [Israelite]'s field of standing grain, you may pluck ears with your hand; but you must not put a sickle to your neighbor's grain.

24 A householder takes a wife and becomes her husband. She fails to please him because he finds something obnoxious about her, and he writes

20 לֹא־תַשִּׁ֣יךְ לְאָחִ֗יךָ נֶ֥שֶׁךְ כֶּ֖סֶף נֶ֣שֶׁךְ אֹ֑כֶל
נֶ֕שֶׁךְ כָּל־דָּבָ֖ר אֲשֶׁ֥ר יִשָּֽׁךְ׃ 21 לַנָּכְרִ֣י תַשִּׁ֔יךְ
וּלְאָחִ֖יךָ לֹ֣א תַשִּׁ֑יךְ לְמַ֨עַן יְבָרֶכְךָ֜ יְהוָ֣ה
אֱלֹהֶ֗יךָ בְּכֹל֙ מִשְׁלַ֣ח יָדֶ֔ךָ עַל־הָאָ֕רֶץ אֲשֶׁר־
אַתָּ֥ה בָא־שָׁ֖מָּה לְרִשְׁתָּֽהּ׃ ס
22 כִּֽי־תִדֹּ֥ר נֶ֙דֶר֙ לַיהוָ֣ה אֱלֹהֶ֔יךָ לֹ֥א תְאַחֵ֖ר
לְשַׁלְּמ֑וֹ כִּֽי־דָרֹ֨שׁ יִדְרְשֶׁ֜נּוּ יְהוָ֤ה אֱלֹהֶ֙יךָ֙
מֵֽעִמָּ֔ךְ וְהָיָ֥ה בְךָ֖ חֵֽטְא׃ 23 וְכִ֥י תֶחְדַּ֖ל לִנְדֹּ֑ר
לֹא־יִהְיֶ֥ה בְךָ֖ חֵֽטְא׃ 24 מוֹצָ֥א שְׂפָתֶ֖יךָ
תִּשְׁמֹ֣ר וְעָשִׂ֑יתָ כַּאֲשֶׁ֨ר נָדַ֜רְתָּ לַיהוָ֤ה אֱלֹהֶ֙יךָ֙
נְדָבָ֔ה אֲשֶׁ֥ר דִּבַּ֖רְתָּ בְּפִֽיךָ׃ ס
25 כִּ֤י תָבֹא֙ בְּכֶ֣רֶם רֵעֶ֔ךָ וְאָכַלְתָּ֧ עֲנָבִ֛ים
כְּנַפְשְׁךָ֖ שָׂבְעֶ֑ךָ וְאֶל־כֶּלְיְךָ֖ לֹ֥א תִתֵּֽן׃ ס
26 כִּ֤י תָבֹא֙ בְּקָמַ֣ת רֵעֶ֔ךָ וְקָטַפְתָּ֥ מְלִילֹ֖ת
בְּיָדֶ֑ךָ וְחֶרְמֵשׁ֙ לֹ֣א תָנִ֔יף עַ֖ל קָמַ֥ת רֵעֶֽךָ׃ ס
כד כִּֽי־יִקַּ֥ח אִ֛ישׁ אִשָּׁ֖ה וּבְעָלָ֑הּ וְהָיָ֞ה אִם־
לֹ֧א תִמְצָא־חֵ֣ן בְּעֵינָ֗יו כִּֽי־מָ֤צָא בָהּ֙ עֶרְוַ֣ת

### LAWS REGARDING COMMITMENTS TO GOD AND NEIGHBORS (23:20–26)

Deuteronomy repeatedly expresses a concern with economic issues under the umbrella of divine law.

*20–21.* For more on laws protecting poor Israelites who depend on loans, see at Leviticus 25:36.

*22–24.* For more on vows, see at Numbers 6 and 30.

*25–26.* This law about eating unharvested crops applies to everyone, not only the poor. (See also Leviticus 19:9–10.)

### MORE LAWS REGARDING MARRIAGE (24:1–5)

The two laws in this section supplement material regarding marriage, first by setting conditions under which remarriage may be possible; and second, by prolonging a couple's "honeymoon," as it were.

*1–4.* This law about forbidden remarriage considers it indecent (akin to adultery) for a husband to remarry a woman he divorced who subsequently married another man. This may have been intended to deter quick divorce or to prevent promiscuity; concerns about paternity could also be an issue.

her a bill of divorcement, hands it to her, and sends her away from his house; ²she leaves his household and becomes the wife of another man; ³then this latter man rejects her, writes her a bill of divorcement, hands it to her, and sends her away from his house; or the man who married her last dies. ⁴Then the first husband who divorced her shall not take her to wife again, since she has been defiled—for that would be abhorrent to יהוה. You must not bring sin upon the land that your God יהוה is giving you as a heritage.

⁵When a householder has taken a bride, he shall not go out with the army or be assigned to it for any purpose; he shall be exempt one year for the sake of his household, to give happiness to the woman he has married.

⁶A handmill or an upper millstone shall not be taken in pawn, for that would be taking someone's life in pawn.

⁷If a party is found to have kidnapped—and then enslaved or sold—a fellow Israelite, that kid-

דָּבָר וְכָ֤תַב לָהּ֙ סֵ֣פֶר כְּרִיתֻת֙ וְנָתַ֣ן בְּיָדָ֔הּ וְשִׁלְּחָ֖הּ מִבֵּיתֽוֹ׃ ²וְיָצְאָ֖ה מִבֵּית֑וֹ וְהָלְכָ֖ה וְהָיְתָ֥ה לְאִישׁ־אַחֵֽר׃ ³וּשְׂנֵאָהּ֮ הָאִ֣ישׁ הָאַחֲרוֹן֒ וְכָ֤תַב לָהּ֙ סֵ֣פֶר כְּרִיתֻת֙ וְנָתַ֣ן בְּיָדָ֔הּ וְשִׁלְּחָ֖הּ מִבֵּית֑וֹ א֣וֹ כִ֤י יָמוּת֙ הָאִ֣ישׁ הָאַחֲר֔וֹן אֲשֶׁר־לְקָחָ֥הּ ל֖וֹ לְאִשָּֽׁה׃ ⁴לֹא־ יוּכַ֣ל בַּעְלָ֣הּ הָרִאשׁ֣וֹן אֲשֶֽׁר־שִׁלְּחָ֡הּ לָשׁ֣וּב לְקַחְתָּ֩הּ לִהְי֨וֹת ל֜וֹ לְאִשָּׁ֗ה אַחֲרֵי֙ אֲשֶׁ֣ר הֻטַּמָּ֔אָה כִּֽי־תוֹעֵבָ֥ה הִ֖וא לִפְנֵ֣י יְהֹוָ֑ה וְלֹ֣א תַחֲטִ֔יא אֶת־הָאָ֕רֶץ אֲשֶׁר֙ יְהֹוָ֣ה אֱלֹהֶ֔יךָ נֹתֵ֥ן לְךָ֖ נַחֲלָֽה׃ ס

⁵כִּֽי־יִקַּ֥ח אִישׁ֙ אִשָּׁ֣ה חֲדָשָׁ֔ה לֹ֤א יֵצֵא֙ בַּצָּבָ֔א וְלֹא־יַעֲבֹ֥ר עָלָ֖יו לְכׇל־דָּבָ֑ר נָקִ֞י יִהְיֶ֤ה לְבֵיתוֹ֙ שָׁנָ֣ה אֶחָ֔ת וְשִׂמַּ֖ח אֶת־אִשְׁתּ֥וֹ אֲשֶׁר־לָקָֽח׃

⁶לֹא־יַחֲבֹ֥ל רֵחַ֖יִם וָרָ֑כֶב כִּי־נֶ֖פֶשׁ ה֥וּא חֹבֵֽל׃ ס

⁷כִּֽי־יִמָּצֵ֣א אִ֗ישׁ גֹּנֵ֨ב נֶ֤פֶשׁ מֵאֶחָיו֙ מִבְּנֵ֣י

---

Note that David's wife Michal was given to another man, Paltiel, by her father King Saul, but David subsequently demanded her back as his wife (I Samuel 18:27; 25:44; II Samuel 3:13–16). (See also at Leviticus 21:7 and Another View, p. 1185.)

*1. something obnoxious about her.* The same idiom appears in 23:15, where the translation reads "anything unseemly." The verse does not specify the valid conditions for divorce.

*bill of divorcement.* This refers to some sort of legal divorce document.

*sends her away.* This technical language for divorce—the opposite of "takes her as a wife"— means that the woman is no longer part of the man's household. [This ruling was not always interpreted to mean that only husbands could initiate divorce. The oldest surviving Jewish marriage contracts (from a Jewish community in Elephantine, Egypt) show that in the 5th century B.C.E., wives could initiate a divorce. —*Ed.*]

*5.* This law concerning military deferments resembles 20:7, but here only the marital deferment is singled out, and the time of the deferment set at a year. To "give happiness" to his new wife presumably refers to conjugal pleasure. See also at 25:5–10.

### MISCELLANY: OBJECTS TAKEN IN PAWN, KIDNAPPING, SKIN AFFLICTION (24:6–9)

This section contains more laws tying everyday situations with divine law.

*6.* This law mandates that certain tools are not to be taken as pawns. If the millstones used to grind flour were accepted in pledge for a loan, the family would lack the tools needed to sustain itself. (On women's role in bread-making, see at Exodus 16:3 and 25:30, as well as at Leviticus 26:26.)

*7.* Kidnapping a fellow Israelite (female or male) for profit, either to get free labor or to sell the victim into slavery for money, is a capital offense.

napper shall die; thus you will sweep out evil from your midst.

8 In cases of a skin affection be most careful to do exactly as the levitical priests instruct you. Take care to do as I have commanded them. 9 Remember what your God יהוה did to Miriam on the journey after you left Egypt.

10 When you make a loan of any sort to your compatriot, you must not enter the house to seize the pledge. 11 You must remain outside, while the party to whom you made the loan brings the pledge out to you. 12 If the party is needy, you shall not go to sleep in that pledge; 13 you must return the pledge at sundown, that its owner may sleep in the cloth and bless you; and it will be to your merit before your God יהוה.

14 You shall not abuse a needy and destitute laborer, whether a fellow Israelite or a stranger in one of the communities of your land. 15 You must pay out the wages due on the same day, before the sun sets, for the worker is needy and urgently depends on it; else a cry to יהוה will be issued against you and you will incur guilt.

יִשְׂרָאֵל וְהִתְעַמֶּר־בּוֹ וּמְכָרוֹ וּמֵת הַגַּנָּב
הַהוּא וּבִעַרְתָּ הָרָע מִקִּרְבֶּךָ׃ ס
8 הִשָּׁמֶר בְּנֶגַע־הַצָּרַעַת לִשְׁמֹר מְאֹד
וְלַעֲשׂוֹת כְּכֹל אֲשֶׁר־יוֹרוּ אֶתְכֶם הַכֹּהֲנִים
הַלְוִיִּם כַּאֲשֶׁר צִוִּיתִם תִּשְׁמְרוּ לַעֲשׂוֹת׃
9 זָכוֹר אֵת אֲשֶׁר־עָשָׂה יְהוָה אֱלֹהֶיךָ
לְמִרְיָם בַּדֶּרֶךְ בְּצֵאתְכֶם מִמִּצְרָיִם׃ ס
10 כִּי־תַשֶּׁה בְרֵעֲךָ מַשַּׁאת מְאוּמָה לֹא־
תָבֹא אֶל־בֵּיתוֹ לַעֲבֹט עֲבֹטוֹ׃ 11 בַּחוּץ
תַּעֲמֹד וְהָאִישׁ אֲשֶׁר אַתָּה נֹשֶׁה בוֹ יוֹצִיא
אֵלֶיךָ אֶת־הַעֲבוֹט הַחוּצָה׃ 12 וְאִם־אִישׁ
עָנִי הוּא לֹא תִשְׁכַּב בַּעֲבֹטוֹ׃ 13 הָשֵׁב
תָּשִׁיב לוֹ אֶת־הַעֲבוֹט כְּבוֹא הַשֶּׁמֶשׁ וְשָׁכַב
בְּשַׂלְמָתוֹ וּבֵרֲכֶךָּ וּלְךָ תִּהְיֶה צְדָקָה לִפְנֵי
יְהוָה אֱלֹהֶיךָ׃ ס
14 לֹא־תַעֲשֹׁק שָׂכִיר עָנִי וְאֶבְיוֹן מֵאַחֶיךָ אוֹ
מִגֵּרְךָ אֲשֶׁר בְּאַרְצְךָ בִּשְׁעָרֶיךָ׃ 15 בְּיוֹמוֹ
תִתֵּן שְׂכָרוֹ וְלֹא־תָבוֹא עָלָיו הַשֶּׁמֶשׁ כִּי עָנִי
הוּא וְאֵלָיו הוּא נֹשֵׂא אֶת־נַפְשׁוֹ וְלֹא־יִקְרָא
עָלֶיךָ אֶל־יְהוָה וְהָיָה בְךָ חֵטְא׃ ס

---

*8–9.* For more on such skin conditions, see at Leviticus 13:1–59.

*9. **Miriam.*** This verse—the only verse in the Torah that mentions Miriam in words directly attributed to Moses—alludes to Numbers 12:10–15, where Miriam is stricken with skin disease for challenging Moses' authority. Here Moses holds her up as an example of the seriousness of skin disease and the need to heed God's instructions for dealing with it. (For more on Miriam, see at Numbers 20:1.)

## *Laws Protecting the Vulnerable*

(24:10–25:16)

This unit provides laws to protect various categories of economically disadvantaged persons, safeguarding, in particular, the welfare of the stranger, the orphan, and the widow.

### OBTAINING PLEDGES AND PAYING WAGES (24:10–15)

These rules aim to preserve a borrower's dignity and treat a worker justly.

*10–11.* The lender may not enter the borrower's home to obtain the pledge (an object taken to guarantee the repayment of a loan), for this might embarrass a borrower by showing her or his poverty.

*12–13.* A cloak or blanket given in pledge must be returned at night so that the borrower can use it as a covering at night (see also Exodus 22:25–26).

*15.* Since day-workers (not household servants) depend on their daily wages, they must be paid in a timely manner.

16 Parents shall not be put to death for children, nor children be put to death for parents: they shall each be put to death only for their own crime.

17 You shall not subvert the rights of the stranger or the fatherless; you shall not take a widow's garment in pawn. 18 Remember that you were a slave in Egypt and that your God יהוה redeemed you from there; therefore do I enjoin you to observe this commandment.

19 When you reap the harvest in your field and overlook a sheaf in the field, do not turn back to get it; it shall go to the stranger, the fatherless, and the widow—in order that your God יהוה may bless you in all your undertakings.

20 When you beat down the fruit of your olive trees, do not go over them again; that shall go to the stranger, the fatherless, and the widow. 21 When you gather the grapes of your vineyard, do not pick it over again; that shall go to the stranger, the fatherless, and the widow. 22 Always remember that you were a slave in the land of Egypt; therefore do I enjoin you to observe this commandment.

25 When there is a dispute between parties and they go to law, and a decision is rendered de-

16 לֹֽא־יוּמְת֤וּ אָבוֹת֙ עַל־בָּנִ֔ים וּבָנִ֕ים לֹא־
יוּמְת֖וּ עַל־אָב֑וֹת אִ֥ישׁ בְּחֶטְא֖וֹ יוּמָֽתוּ׃ ס
17 לֹ֣א תַטֶּ֔ה מִשְׁפַּ֖ט גֵּ֣ר יָת֑וֹם וְלֹ֣א תַחֲבֹ֔ל
בֶּ֖גֶד אַלְמָנָֽה׃ 18 וְזָכַרְתָּ֗ כִּ֣י עֶ֤בֶד הָיִ֙יתָ֙
בְּמִצְרַ֔יִם וַֽיִּפְדְּךָ֛ יְהוָ֥ה אֱלֹהֶ֖יךָ מִשָּׁ֑ם עַל־כֵּ֞ן
אָנֹכִ֤י מְצַוְּךָ֙ לַעֲשׂ֔וֹת אֶת־הַדָּבָ֖ר הַזֶּֽה׃ ס
19 כִּ֣י תִקְצֹר֩ קְצִֽירְךָ֨ בְשָׂדֶ֜ךָ וְשָֽׁכַחְתָּ֧ עֹ֣מֶר
בַּשָּׂדֶ֗ה לֹ֤א תָשׁוּב֙ לְקַחְתּ֔וֹ לַגֵּ֛ר לַיָּת֥וֹם
וְלָאַלְמָנָ֖ה יִהְיֶ֑ה לְמַ֤עַן יְבָרֶכְךָ֙ יְהוָ֣ה אֱלֹהֶ֔יךָ
בְּכֹ֖ל מַעֲשֵׂ֥ה יָדֶֽיךָ׃ ס
20 כִּ֤י תַחְבֹּט֙ זֵֽיתְךָ֔ לֹ֥א תְפַאֵ֖ר אַחֲרֶ֑יךָ לַגֵּ֛ר
לַיָּת֥וֹם וְלָאַלְמָנָ֖ה יִהְיֶֽה׃ 21 כִּ֤י תִבְצֹר֙ כַּרְמְךָ֔
לֹ֥א תְעוֹלֵ֖ל אַחֲרֶ֑יךָ לַגֵּ֛ר לַיָּת֥וֹם וְלָאַלְמָנָ֖ה
יִהְיֶֽה׃ 22 וְזָ֣כַרְתָּ֔ כִּי־עֶ֥בֶד הָיִ֖יתָ בְּאֶ֣רֶץ
מִצְרָ֑יִם עַל־כֵּ֞ן אָנֹכִ֤י מְצַוְּךָ֙ לַעֲשׂ֔וֹת אֶת־
הַדָּבָ֖ר הַזֶּֽה׃ ס

כה כִּֽי־יִהְיֶ֥ה רִיב֙ בֵּ֣ין אֲנָשִׁ֔ים וְנִגְּשׁ֥וּ אֶל־
הַמִּשְׁפָּ֖ט וּשְׁפָט֑וּם וְהִצְדִּ֙יקוּ֙ אֶת־הַצַּדִּ֔יק

### PROHIBITION ON TRANSGENERATIONAL PUNISHMENT (24:16)

Other ancient Near Eastern law collections consider children to be extensions of their parents; according to the principle of talion (exact retribution), if a person has caused the death of another person's son, the perpetrator's own son can be put to death (see, for example, Laws of Hammurabi ¶ 230). Deuteronomy forbids Israelites to inflict such punishment.

### PROTECTING THE STRANGER, FATHERLESS, AND WIDOW (24:17–20)

These three classes of people do not have a male head-of-household to protect them, support them, and look after their interests in public; therefore, society as a whole must watch out for and not take advantage of them.

*17. a widow's garment.* Special protection is granted to a widow, whose garment, unlike that of a day laborer, may not serve as a pledge for a loan. A sense of modesty also may inform this law.

*19.* The book of Ruth shows how reapers are expected to leave some produce for the needy to glean after the harvest (see also at Leviticus 19:9–10; 23:22).

### LIMITS ON FLOGGING (25:1–3)

Although flogging is a legal penalty, care must be taken to avoid beating the individual excessively in order to avoid dehumanizing the person.

וְהִרְשִׁיעוּ אֶת־הָרָשָׁע׃ 2 וְהָיָה אִם־בִּן הַכּוֹת
הָרָשָׁע וְהִפִּילוֹ הַשֹּׁפֵט וְהִכָּהוּ לְפָנָיו כְּדֵי
רִשְׁעָתוֹ בְּמִסְפָּר׃ 3 אַרְבָּעִים יַכֶּנּוּ לֹא יֹסִיף
פֶּן־יֹסִיף לְהַכֹּתוֹ עַל־אֵלֶּה מַכָּה רַבָּה
וְנִקְלָה אָחִיךָ לְעֵינֶיךָ׃
4 לֹא־תַחְסֹם שׁוֹר בְּדִישׁוֹ׃ ס
5 כִּי־יֵשְׁבוּ אַחִים יַחְדָּו וּמֵת אַחַד מֵהֶם וּבֵן
אֵין־לוֹ לֹא־תִהְיֶה אֵשֶׁת־הַמֵּת הַחוּצָה
לְאִישׁ זָר יְבָמָהּ יָבֹא עָלֶיהָ וּלְקָחָהּ לוֹ
לְאִשָּׁה וְיִבְּמָהּ׃ 6 וְהָיָה הַבְּכוֹר אֲשֶׁר תֵּלֵד
יָקוּם עַל־שֵׁם אָחִיו הַמֵּת וְלֹא־יִמָּחֶה שְׁמוֹ
מִיִּשְׂרָאֵל׃ 7 וְאִם־לֹא יַחְפֹּץ הָאִישׁ לָקַחַת
אֶת־יְבִמְתּוֹ וְעָלְתָה יְבִמְתּוֹ הַשַּׁעְרָה אֶל־
הַזְּקֵנִים וְאָמְרָה מֵאֵין יְבָמִי לְהָקִים לְאָחִיו

claring the one in the right and the other in the
wrong— 2 if the guilty one is to be flogged, the magistrate shall have the person lie down and shall supervise the giving of lashes, by count, as warranted
by the offense. 3 The guilty one may be given up to
forty lashes, but not more, lest being flogged further, to excess, your peer be degraded before your
eyes.

4 You shall not muzzle an ox while it is threshing.

5 When brothers dwell together and one of them
dies and leaves no offspring, the wife of the deceased shall not be married to a party outside the
family. Her husband's brother shall unite with her:
he shall take her as his wife and perform the levir's
duty. 6 The first child that she bears shall be accounted to the dead brother, that his name may not
be blotted out in Israel. 7 But if the [family] representative does not want to marry his brother's
widow, his brother's widow shall appear before
the elders in the gate and declare, "My husband's
brother refuses to establish a name in Israel for his

### PROHIBITION ON MUZZLING AN OX WHEN IT IS THRESHING (25:4)

This is another law that mandates kindness to animals (see also at 22:6–7), ensuring that the animal may eat some of the stalks being threshed.

### LEVIRATE MARRIAGE (25:5–10)

Levirate marriage is intended to secure the continuation of a deceased married man's lineage and land-inheritance if he has no children. This principle is operative in the story of Judah and Tamar (Genesis 38) and hinted at, although not in its normal form, in the book of Ruth. Deuteronomy provides a process for opting out of the levirate marriage, later called *chalitzah*, although in biblical times it seems that levirate marriage was preferred. The number of such marriages must have been relatively small, since most married couples would have produced a child within a few years of marriage, before the husband died. Military deferment for new husbands (24:5) helps to avoid the situation whereby a man is killed in war before he has sired a child.

*5. When brothers dwell together.* This means they live on their father's estate, which has not yet been legally subdivided among them.

*7. if the [family] representative does not want to marry his brother's widow.* There may be many reasons for his refusal, including that he would incur additional responsibilities for a family that is legally his brother's, not his. [An heir to the deceased brother would also prevent the living brother from gaining the dead brother's land. —*Ed.*]

***his brother's widow shall appear before the elders in the gate.*** The widow initiates the public proceedings after her brother-in-law denies her the

brother; he will not perform the duty of a levir." [8]The elders of his town shall then summon him and talk to him. If he insists, saying, "I do not want to marry her," [9]his brother's widow shall go up to him in the presence of the elders, pull the sandal off his foot, spit in his face, and make this declaration: Thus shall be done to the [family] representative who will not build up his brother's house! [10]And he shall go in Israel by the name of "the family of the unsandaled one."

[11]If two men get into a fight with each other, and the wife of one comes up to save her husband from his antagonist and puts out her hand and seizes him by his genitals, [12]you shall cut off her hand; show no pity.

[13]You shall not have in your pouch alternate weights, larger and smaller. [14]You shall not have in your house alternate measures, a larger and a smaller. [15]You must have completely honest weights and completely honest measures, if you are to endure long on the soil that your God יהוה is giving you. [16]For everyone who does those things, everyone who deals dishonestly, is abhorrent to your God יהוה.

שֵׁם בְּיִשְׂרָאֵל לֹא אָבָה יַבְּמִי׃ 8 וְקָרְאוּ־לוֹ
זִקְנֵי־עִירוֹ וְדִבְּרוּ אֵלָיו וְעָמַד וְאָמַר לֹא
חָפַצְתִּי לְקַחְתָּהּ׃ 9 וְנִגְּשָׁה יְבִמְתּוֹ אֵלָיו
לְעֵינֵי הַזְּקֵנִים וְחָלְצָה נַעֲלוֹ מֵעַל רַגְלוֹ
וְיָרְקָה בְּפָנָיו וְעָנְתָה וְאָמְרָה כָּכָה יֵעָשֶׂה
לָאִישׁ אֲשֶׁר לֹא־יִבְנֶה אֶת־בֵּית אָחִיו׃
10 וְנִקְרָא שְׁמוֹ בְּיִשְׂרָאֵל בֵּית חֲלוּץ
הַנָּעַל׃ ס

11 כִּי־יִנָּצוּ אֲנָשִׁים יַחְדָּו אִישׁ וְאָחִיו וְקָרְבָה
אֵשֶׁת הָאֶחָד לְהַצִּיל אֶת־אִישָׁהּ מִיַּד מַכֵּהוּ
וְשָׁלְחָה יָדָהּ וְהֶחֱזִיקָה בִּמְבֻשָׁיו׃ 12 וְקַצֹּתָה
אֶת־כַּפָּהּ לֹא תָחוֹס עֵינֶךָ׃ ס
13 לֹא־יִהְיֶה לְךָ בְּכִיסְךָ אֶבֶן וָאָבֶן גְּדוֹלָה
וּקְטַנָּה׃ 14 לֹא־יִהְיֶה לְךָ בְּבֵיתְךָ אֵיפָה
וְאֵיפָה גְּדוֹלָה וּקְטַנָּה׃ 15 אֶבֶן שְׁלֵמָה
וָצֶדֶק יִהְיֶה־לָּךְ אֵיפָה שְׁלֵמָה וָצֶדֶק יִהְיֶה־
לָּךְ לְמַעַן יַאֲרִיכוּ יָמֶיךָ עַל הָאֲדָמָה
אֲשֶׁר־יְהֹוָה אֱלֹהֶיךָ נֹתֵן לָךְ׃ 16 כִּי תוֹעֲבַת
יְהֹוָה אֱלֹהֶיךָ כָּל־עֹשֵׂה אֵלֶּה כֹּל עֹשֵׂה
עָוֶל׃ פ

protection and status that she would have as a wife and mother, and as the beneficiary of her husband's inheritance. The woman here clearly has legal standing and is entitled to bring a case to the court. Her words and actions, formalized by the law, are a performative way of publicly shaming the brother-in-law who refuses the levirate marriage.

The law does not envision a woman being able or desiring to reject a levirate marriage. After all, to become an unattached childless widow is a position most ancient women would have wished to avoid. Indeed, in the story of Judah and Tamar, Tamar resorts to extreme measures to avoid remaining a childless widow (see at Genesis 38).

### PUNISHMENT OF A WOMAN WHO INTERVENES IN HER HUSBAND'S FIGHT (25:11–12)

This law, which appears harsh and puzzling by modern standards, involves sexually shaming a man in public. While other ancient Near Eastern laws contain similar stipulations (see Middle Assyrian Laws A ¶ 8), the biblical law is relatively mild.

### HONEST WEIGHTS AND MEASURES (25:13–16)

The cheating of customers may have been a recurrent problem since it is mentioned often in an-

17 Remember what Amalek did to you on your journey, after you left Egypt—18 how, undeterred by fear of God, he surprised you on the march, when you were famished and weary, and cut down all the stragglers in your rear. 19 Therefore, when your God יהוה grants you safety from all your enemies around you, in the land that your God יהוה is giving you as a hereditary portion, you shall blot out the memory of Amalek from under heaven. Do not forget!

17 זָכ֕וֹר אֵ֛ת אֲשֶׁר־עָשָׂ֥ה לְךָ֖ עֲמָלֵ֑ק בַּדֶּ֖רֶךְ
בְּצֵאתְכֶ֥ם מִמִּצְרָֽיִם׃ 18 אֲשֶׁ֨ר קָֽרְךָ֜ בַּדֶּ֗רֶךְ
וַיְזַנֵּ֤ב בְּךָ֙ כָּל־הַנֶּחֱשָׁלִ֣ים אַֽחֲרֶ֔יךָ וְאַתָּ֖ה עָיֵ֣ף
וְיָגֵ֑עַ וְלֹ֥א יָרֵ֖א אֱלֹהִֽים׃ 19 וְהָיָ֡ה בְּהָנִ֣יחַ
יְהוָ֣ה אֱלֹהֶ֣יךָ ׀ לְ֠ךָ֠ מִכָּל־אֹ֨יְבֶ֜יךָ מִסָּבִ֗יב
בָּאָ֙רֶץ֙ אֲשֶׁ֣ר יְהוָֽה־אֱ֠לֹהֶ֠יךָ נֹתֵ֨ן לְךָ֤ נַחֲלָה֙
לְרִשְׁתָּ֔הּ תִּמְחֶה֙ אֶת־זֵ֣כֶר עֲמָלֵ֔ק מִתַּ֖חַת
הַשָּׁמָ֑יִם לֹ֖א תִּשְׁכָּֽח׃ פ

cient Near Eastern laws. Here, Deuteronomy presents proper business ethics as a religious principle that is crucial for the preservation of Israelite society.

## *Charge to Remember Amalek*

(25:17–19)

The parashah concludes with an injunction to remember the incident recounted in Exodus 17:8–16. Amalek is singled out for strong condemnation. The command to blot out the name of this enemy is emphasized by its being framed by "remember . . . do not forget." (There is an irony to the command to remember to blot out Amalek's name.) In synagogues, this passage is traditionally read aloud from the Torah on Shabbat Zachor, the sabbath before Purim. By calling Haman an Agagite, the book of Esther makes him an Amalekite, whose king in the time of Saul was Agag. Amalek became a symbol of later Jewish enemies as well.

*—Adele Berlin*

# Another View

THE LEGISLATION IN 24:1–4 deals not with divorce so much as with remarriage. The text mentions only in passing that grounds for divorce include *ervat davar*, translated here as "something obnoxious" in a woman (v. 1), and that a *sefer k'ritut*, a "bill of divorcement," changes hands (v. 3). The real concern of this section is to prohibit a man from *remarrying* a woman who had taken a new husband in the meantime, even if the subsequent marriage ended legitimately.

It remains unclear what, if anything, these verses signify about contractual relations between husbands and wives in ancient Israel; but what lessons can we draw from the text itself? Some commentators claim that this legislation is meant to guard against confusion over paternity; others posit that it discourages men from divorcing in haste and repenting at leisure. Yet these ends could be achieved without a new-husband clause, so why not simply prohibit remarriage to the same wife? One possible answer is that the new-husband clause might create a measure of autonomy for the woman, who is otherwise a passive party under biblical marriage law. She can put herself off limits to her first husband by agreeing to become another man's spouse, or she can signal her commitment to her first husband by remaining single.

But why would the male authors of this text legislate for female autonomy? Perhaps because of the intriguing theological implications as set forth in the book of Jeremiah. Along with some other prophets, Jeremiah envisages a metaphorical marriage in which God is the husband and Israel the wife who has done "something obnoxious" or "unseemly" (3:8). Israel has been unfaithful with many lovers (3:1), meaning that she has worshipped other gods. The prophet implies that even if God hands Israel a bill of divorce, she can refrain from taking a new husband (by no longer worshipping other gods) and can instead wait for her first husband, God, to take her back.

*The new-husband clause may have created some autonomy for the divorced woman.*

Like the wife in our parashah, Israel—as depicted by Jeremiah—can maintain some degree of autonomy by choosing to change her ways. With renewed commitment, she can reaffirm her sacred relationship with God.

—*Diana Lipton*

# Post-biblical Interpretations

***When you [an Israelite warrior] take the field*** (21:10–14). The Rabbis make no attempt to abrogate the law permitting Israelite men to bring home female war captives. However, they are not enthusiastic about the practice. Drawing upon an opinion in BT *Kiddushin* 21b, the 11th-century commentator Rashi claims (at 21:11) that the Torah is making a concession to the *yetzer hara* (often translated as the "evil impulse") when it permits the captive woman. Rashi indicates that were the Torah to forbid the women, men would take them anyway; instead, the Torah limits the practice.

***If a householder has a wayward and defiant son*** (21:18–20). The Rabbis restrict the law of the rebellious son, effectively legislating it out of existence.

One restriction involves requiring the consent of both parents to the punishment. The son cannot be subjected to the procedure unless he has both a father and a mother, and the parents' marriage must be a "suitable" one. If either parent has any one of a number of physical defects, the law does not apply (*Sifrei D'varim, Ki Teitzei, piska* 219).

***A woman must not put on man's apparel*** (22:5). The Sages argue that this verse prohibits wearing clothing associated with the opposite gender expressly for the purpose of passing oneself off as the opposite gender (*Sifrei D'varim, Ki Teitzei, piska* 226).

***A householder marries a woman and cohabits with her*** (22:13). *Sifrei D'varim, Ki Teitzei, piska* 235, comments that one sin leads to another. If a husband fails to love his wife, transgressing the command "You shall love your neighbor as yourself" (Leviticus 19:18), he is likely to transgress further. This formula suggests that the commentator sees a husband's claim against his wife's virginity as an expression of hatred rather than a legitimate use of law.

***he writes her a bill of divorcement . . . and sends her away*** (24:1). This passage (vv. 1–4) takes for granted a husband's right to initiate divorce. Citing this verse, some of the Rabbis allow a man to divorce his wife simply because he finds her housekeeping skills unsatisfactory or because he no longer finds her physically attractive (Mishnah *Gittin* 9:10).

The Torah does not mention a wife's right to initiate divorce, but Jews have nevertheless recognized it in various times and place (compare Exodus 21:10–11). Extant Jewish marriage contracts from the early Second Temple period stipulate either party's right to initiate divorce. Marriage contracts among rabbinic Jews of the early medieval Levant often contain similar stipulations.

Meanwhile, the Mishnah (*K'tubot* 5:7) mentions a different approach, wherein an unhappy wife can start a countdown for dissolution of the marriage by declaring herself to be a *moredet* (refusing or recalcitrant wife). After allowing time for reconciliation, the court would apparently compel her husband to divorce her, although she would not receive a divorcée's usual marriage settlement.

The Mishnah allows women to petition the court directly for release from an unsatisfactory marriage (*K'tubot* 7:10), and it describes instances in which a man's behavior would require that he divorce his wife (*K'tubot* 7:1–5). Yet according to another line of legal reasoning, a man cannot be divorced against his will (Mishnah *Gittin* 9:8; BT *Gittin* 88b). In Babylonia, most rabbinic authorities maintained that only a husband could initiate divorce, and this view prevailed in rabbinic Judaism by approximately the year 1300 C.E.

*If a husband fails to love his wife, he is likely to transgress further.*

***Remember what your God* יהוה *did to Miriam*** (24:9). Some rabbinic sources understand Moses as alluding to Miriam's being stricken with the skin disease *tzaraat* for speaking against him (Numbers 12:10–15). Rashi here echoes the words of *Sifrei D'varim*, "If you want to avoid being stricken with *tzaraat*, do not gossip, for Miriam gossiped about her brother and was stricken." The 13th-century commentator Nachmanides adds here that this exhortation should be understood as a positive commandment parallel to other verses that call on us to remember something in particular (such as Exodus 20:8; Deuteronomy 25:17). He notes that the gravity of this commandment is demonstrated by the affliction of Miriam, "a righteous woman, a prophet who spoke about her brother out of concern, loving him as she did herself." Although Miriam "did not speak directly to Moses so as not to embarrass him, nor did she speak in public, but only in private to her holy brother [Aaron]," nonetheless, and despite "all of her good deeds," she was punished. This demonstrates the enormity of gossip.

***When brothers dwell together*** (25:5–10). The Rabbis of the Mishnah limit the situations in which levirate marriage is required (for example, *Y'vamot* 1:1–3; 2:1–3). The Talmud recounts situations in which widows were reluctant to marry their brothers-in-law despite the men's eagerness to perform levirate marriage. These women confided their concerns to rabbis, who—convinced that the men's motives were selfish—tricked the men into releasing their sisters-in-law from their obligations (BT *Y'vamot* 106a).

Beginning already in the Talmud (BT *Y'vamot* 39a–b; 101b), rabbinic authorities differ as to whether a brother should fulfill his levirate obligation or undergo the ritual of vv. 7–10 (known as *chalitzah*). In the post-talmudic period, authorities disagreed as to whether levirate marriage or *chalitzah* was preferable. Today, all agree that *chalitzah* is mandatory. In liberal Judaism, neither levirate marriage nor *chalitzah* is employed.

—*Dvora E. Weisberg*

# *Contemporary Reflection*

The centrality of memory to Jewish self-understanding emerges with great vividness in *parashat Ki Teitzei*, which repeatedly enjoins us to remember events in ways that affect ongoing behavior and practice: "Always *remember* that you were a slave in the land of Egypt; therefore . . . observe this commandment" (24:22, 18). "In cases of a skin affection be most careful to do exactly as the levitical priests instruct you. . . . *Remember* what your God יהוה did to Miriam on the journey after you left Egypt" (24:8–9). "*Remember* what Amalek did to you on your journey, after you left Egypt . . . you shall blot out the memory of Amalek" (25:17, 19). Clearly, the major events of the Jewish past are not simply history but living, active memory that continues to shape Jewish identity in the present. Through telling the story of our past, we learn who we are and must become.

In insisting on the significance of memory for identity, the parashah shows that memory can serve a wide variety of purposes and can be used to support modes of being that seem to conflict with each other. The memory of enslavement in Egypt is repeatedly yoked with injunctions insisting upon justice and compassion: "You shall not subvert the rights of the stranger or the fatherless; you shall not take a widow's garment in pawn" (24:17). "When you reap the harvest in your field and overlook a sheaf in the field, do not turn back to get it; it shall go to the stranger, the fatherless, and the widow" (24:19). Because Jews once knew hunger and experienced what it was like to dwell as strangers on the margins of society, we are commanded to create a society in which the marginal are cared for and the hungry are provided with food.

Memories of the deeds of the Ammonites and Moabites and the perfidy of Amalek become the foundation for opposite injunctions, those concerning exclusion and vengeance. Because the Ammonites and Moabites did not provide Israel with food in the wilderness, the descendants of these nations should be excluded from God's congregation, even to the tenth generation (23:3–4). Because Amalek cut down stragglers in the line of march when Israel left Egypt hungry and tired, the memory of the Amalekites should be entirely obliterated (25:17–19).

The memory of Miriam's skin condition (*tzaraat*) is still another kind of memory, a highly truncated one. Already in the book of Exodus when Miriam is introduced, it seems clear that she is not being remembered fully. She appears suddenly, leading the women in song at a central moment of the people Israel's history (Exodus 15:20–21) as if she materialized out of the desert sands. Later, her death and burial are recorded in one verse (Numbers 20:1). There is no account of her passing or of the community's response; she vanishes, disappearing, as it were, into the desert sands. In this parashah, her *tzaraat* is remembered (24:8–9), but not her leadership; her punishment is recalled, but not the challenge to Moses' authority that she mounts with Aaron (Numbers 12:1–2).

If memory is foundational to Jewish community, then perhaps this one-sided memory of a very important woman in the Torah is part of what creates the preconditions for some of the sexual legislation in the parashah. It makes sense that a community that cannot remember its central female figures in all their roundedness will also have difficulty imagining women as agents of their own sexuality—and thus will repeatedly subordinate their interests to those of fathers and husbands. We read that if a woman is found not to be a virgin when she marries, she is stoned to death on her father's doorstep (22:13–21); that a virgin who is raped is then forced to marry her rapist (22:28–29); that a wife who ceases to please her husband can be given a bill of divorce (24:1–4); and that a woman who is widowed before she has children must marry her husband's brother (25:5–10). The Torah in this section offers no store of memories of women's perspectives and experiences that could provide the basis for an alternative ethic.

What do we do, then, when the demands of memory seem to be at odds with each other—when, for example, the partial and distorted memory of Miriam in this parashah collides with the notion of remembering the marginalized, including the marginalized within the Israelite community?

The process of remembering brings with it an obligation to ethical discernment: which memories do we want to affirm and further develop and which do we want to repudiate or transform? We cannot forget the commandments to exclude the Ammonites or blot out the memory of Amalek because their presence in the Torah reminds us of how easy it is to respond to vengeance with more vengeance, or injustice with more injustice. But we can also consciously cultivate memories that encourage us to stop the cycle of violence and domination. When we remember the courage and initiative of Miriam in helping to save her brother (Exodus 2:1–10), when we appreciate her importance to the Israelites who refused to move on without her

*Here the centrality of memory to Jewish self-understanding emerges vividly.*

(Numbers 12:15), when we honor her insistence that her own leadership be recognized (Numbers 12:2), then we lay the foundations for contemporary communities in which women and other "strangers" can take their full and rightful place.

Perhaps the process of sifting through memory also can help to make sense of the last, enigmatic verse of the parashah that enjoins us to "blot out" all memory of Amalek and yet "remember" at the same time. How is this possible? Having grown up in a Reform congregation in the 1950s in which women were on the *bimah* only to light candles, I am aware of how the enormous changes in women's roles over the last half century make such memories of prior injustices difficult to believe. We blot out the memory of Amalek when we create Jewish communities in which the perpetual exclusion of some group of people—or the denial of women's rights—are so contrary to current values as to be almost incredible. Yet, if we are to safeguard our achievements, we can also never forget to remember the history of inequality and the decisions and struggles that have made more equitable communities possible.

—*Judith Plaskow*

# Voices

## For My Daughter

Grace Paley

*Deuteronomy 22:15*

I wanted to bring her a chalice
or maybe a cup of love
or cool water    I wanted to sit
beside her as she rested
after the long day    I wanted to adjure
commend    admonish    saying don't
do that    of course    wonderful    try
I wanted to help her grow old    I wanted
to say last words    the words famous
for final enlightenment    I wanted
to say them now    in case I am in
calm sleep when the last sleep strikes
or aged into disorder    I wanted to
bring her a cup of cool water

I wanted to explain    tiredness is
expected    it is even appropriate
at the end of the day

## *from* Blessing of a Broken Heart

Sherri Mandell

*Deuteronomy 22:6–7*

[The Talmud] says that whoever thinks that the *mitzvah* of shooing away the mother bird shows God's compassion should be silenced. Because they don't understand. We can't say that the *mitzvah* of shooing away the mother bird (I am told later, also a charm for fertility) is a symbol of God's compassion. Because we can't understand God's compassion. If the *mitzvah* were a true symbol of God's compassion, then surely we wouldn't be allowed to take the baby bird at all.

## Toward Myself

Lea Goldberg (transl. Rachel Tzvia Back)

*Deuteronomy 24:1–4*

The years have made up my face
with memories of love
and have adorned my hair with light silver
    threads
making me most beautiful.

In my eyes
landscapes are reflected.
And the paths I have trod
have straightened my stride—
tired and lovely steps.

If you should see me now
you would not recognize your yesterdays—
I am walking toward myself
bearing the face you searched for in vain
when I was walking toward you.

## The Passage of Divorce: Paving One's Way

Vicki Hollander

*Deuteronomy 24:1–4*

To what does this compare?
To the earth
when it moves and quakes
and shifts beneath one's feet.
And when the movement stops,
one walks away transformed,
touched,
different.

## *Rape poem*

Marge Piercy

*Deuteronomy 22:25–27*

There is no difference between being raped
and being pushed down a flight of cement steps
except that the wounds also bleed inside.

There is no difference between being raped
and being run over by a truck
except that afterward men ask if you enjoyed it.

There is no difference between being raped
and being bit on the ankle by a rattlesnake
except that people ask if your skirt was short
and why you were out alone anyhow.

There is no difference between being raped
and going head first through a windshield
except that afterward you are afraid
not of cars
but half the human race.

The rapist is your boyfriend's brother.
He sits beside you in the movies eating
popcorn.
Rape fattens on the fantasies of the normal male
like a maggot in garbage.

Fear of rape is a cold wind blowing
all of the time on a woman's hunched back.
Never to stroll alone on a sand road through
pine woods,
never to climb a trail across a bald
without that aluminum in the mouth
when I see a man climbing toward me.

Never to open the door to a knock
without that razor just grazing the throat.
The fear of the dark side of hedges,
the back seat of the car, the empty house
rattling keys like a snake's warning.
The fear of the smiling man
in whose pocket is a knife.
The fear of the serious man
in whose fist is locked hatred.

All it takes to cast a rapist is seeing your body
as jackhammer, as blowtorch, as
adding-machine-gun.
All it takes is hating that body
your own, your self, your muscle that softens
to flab.

All it takes is to push what you hate,
what you fear onto the soft alien flesh.
To bucket out invincible as a tank
armored with treads without senses
to possess and punish in one act,
to rip up pleasure, to murder those who dare
live in the leafy flesh open to love.

## *At Blue Dawn VII*

Kadya Molodowsky (transl. Kathryn Hellerstein)

*Deuteronomy 25:13–16*

Pick up a stone and throw it
In the city
Or the countryside.
Wherever it may land,
Someone has told a lie.
And that's why clouds come over towns and
forests,
And that's why wild beasts devour sheep in the
fields,
And that's why small children cry out in the
nights,
and that's why the wind breaks down the roofs
of the poor.

# כי תבוא ✦ *Ki Tavo*

DEUTERONOMY 26:1–29:8

## *Entering the Land of Israel: Blessings and Curses*

PARASHAT KI TAVO ("when you enter") is concerned mostly with the Israelites' entrance into the Promised Land. There they must offer first fruits and tithes, according to the ceremonies outlined in 26:1–15; and there most of the laws in Deuteronomy 12–26 will take effect. These laws, outlined in the prior Torah portions and concluded here (26:16–19; 28:69), aim to regulate society when Israel settles in Canaan. Using language familiar from other parts of Deuteronomy, this parashah emphasizes that Israel should obey God's commandments faithfully, with all their heart and soul. Since the covenant between God and Israel establishes mutually binding obligations for both parties, God's commitments also are reaffirmed: the promise to make Israel a treasured, holy people. This parashah is directed to a dual audience: first, to Moses' imagined audience in Moab, the Israelites who listen to his words as he prepares them to enter the land of Canaan; and second, to the audience addressed by the authors of this part of Deuteronomy, who composed their work during the exile (586–538 B.C.E.) or even later, after the return from exile.

The parashah also details the ceremonies that the Israelites are to perform once they enter the land, as a way to reaffirm the covenant (27:1–26). As in the ancient Near Eastern treaties upon which Deuteronomy is modeled, the reiteration of the covenant concludes with a list of blessings for those who uphold it—and curses for those who do not (28:1–68). The last part of the parashah (29:1–8) begins Moses' final address to the people. He recounts the wondrous deeds that God performed on behalf of the people, the experiences that form the foundation of the covenantal relationship and that provide the inspiration for Israel to walk in God's ways.

The laws in the first part of this parashah mention women only as widows, who are counted among the underprivileged (26:12; 27:19), and as objects of impermissible sexual relations (27:20, 22–23). However, matters of gender take on more importance in the blessings and curses at the end of the covenant stipulations. Human fertility becomes a national issue that is linked to the fertility of livestock and the land, all of which are promised blessings if Israel obeys God's commands (28:4, 11, 18). In the subsequent section, one curse concerns a man who makes the arrangements to marry a woman, build a house, and plant a vineyard—all symbols of establishing a new family unit and household—but who will lose

> *Matters of gender take on more importance in the blessings and the curses.*

these things to another man before he has enjoyed their benefits (28:30–32). The horrors of siege, conquest, and exile—signaling the ultimate breakdown and destruction of Israel's society—affect women and men alike. Both sons and daughters will be taken into exile (28:32, 41); and in the famine of the siege, both women and men will become cannibals who horde their "food" from their loved ones (28:54–57). Such graphic curses depict what will transpire if Israel fails to obey God's commandments. Hence, in its strongest rhetoric, Deuteronomy urges its audience to follow the laws that form the heart of this book.

—*Adele Berlin*

## *Outline*

*I.* CEREMONIES FOR FIRST FRUITS AND TITHES (26:1–15)

- A. First fruits (vv. 1–11)
- B. Tithes (vv. 12–15)

*II.* CONCLUSION TO THE LAWS
*Obligations for Israel and God* (26:16–19)

*III.* CEREMONIES UPON ENTERING THE LAND (27:1–26)

- A. Erection of inscribed stones and a stone altar at Mount Ebal (vv. 1–8)
- B. Call to obey the covenant at Moab (vv. 9–10)
- C. Proclamation of blessings and curses at Mt. Gerizim and Mt. Ebal (vv. 11–26)

*IV.* CONSEQUENCES OF OBEYING OR DISOBEYING THE COVENANT (28:1–68)

- A. The blessings (vv. 1–14)
- B. The curses (vv. 15–68)

*V.* CONCLUDING STATEMENT TO THE COVENANT (28:69)

*VI.* COMMENCEMENT OF MOSES' LAST SPEECH (29:1–8)

When you enter the land that your God יהוה is giving you as a heritage, and you possess it and settle in it, 2you shall take some of every first fruit of the soil, which you harvest from the land that your God יהוה is giving you, put it in a basket and go to the place where your God יהוה will choose to establish the divine name. 3You shall go to the priest in charge at that time and say to him, "I acknowledge this day before your God יהוה that

כו וְהָיָה֙ כִּֽי־תָב֣וֹא אֶל־הָאָ֔רֶץ אֲשֶׁר֙ יְהֹוָ֣ה
אֱלֹהֶ֔יךָ נֹתֵ֥ן לְךָ֖ נַחֲלָ֑ה וִֽירִשְׁתָּ֖הּ וְיָשַׁ֥בְתָּ בָּֽהּ׃
2 וְלָקַחְתָּ֞ מֵרֵאשִׁ֣ית ׀ כׇּל־פְּרִ֣י הָאֲדָמָ֗ה אֲשֶׁ֨ר
תָּבִ֧יא מֵֽאַרְצְךָ֛ אֲשֶׁ֨ר יְהֹוָ֧ה אֱלֹהֶ֛יךָ נֹתֵ֥ן לָ֖ךְ
וְשַׂמְתָּ֣ בַטֶּ֑נֶא וְהָֽלַכְתָּ֙ אֶל־הַמָּק֔וֹם אֲשֶׁ֤ר
יִבְחַר֙ יְהֹוָ֣ה אֱלֹהֶ֔יךָ לְשַׁכֵּ֥ן שְׁמ֖וֹ שָֽׁם׃
3 וּבָאתָ֙ אֶל־הַכֹּהֵ֔ן אֲשֶׁ֥ר יִהְיֶ֖ה בַּיָּמִ֣ים
הָהֵ֑ם וְאָמַרְתָּ֣ אֵלָ֗יו הִגַּ֤דְתִּי הַיּוֹם֙ לַיהֹוָ֣ה

## *Ceremonies for First Fruits and Tithes* (26:1–15)

Both first fruits and tithes assume an agricultural society, which is to begin with the settlement in Canaan. (For information on women in agrarian society, see "Women in Ancient Israel—An Overview," p. xli.)

### FIRST FRUITS (26:1–11)

Generally, the Israelites are to dedicate first fruits to God in thanks for the fertility that yielded the produce—and with the hope that this fertility will continue (see at 15:19–23; Exodus 34:19; Leviticus 27:26–27). In this case, however, people are instructed to show gratitude for the possession of the land (mentioned three times in vv. 1–3) through a ceremony that celebrates the fulfillment of God's promise of land to the ancestors. After all, the offering of the first fruits is a direct outcome of, and a performative act in recognition of, God's giving the Promised Land to Israel. In keeping with Deuteronomy's principle of centralization of sacrificial worship, the first fruits are to be brought to God's Chosen Place (meaning the Temple in Jerusalem) on Shavuot, the late spring pilgrimage festival that celebrates the grain harvest (see at 16:9–12). The occasion includes a festive meal, to be shared with the Levites and resident aliens who would not have their own first fruits. Although there is no mention here of other family members participating in the ritual, 16:11 explicitly includes women in the Shavuot celebration.

*2. you.* Although the language in 26:1–15 is grammatically masculine singular, Moses addresses both the male head of the household and his wife or principal wife (see *R'eih*, Another View, p. 1134; *Mishpatim*, Another View, p. 445).


▶ Who are the enemies that the curses refer to? Deuteronomy blames the Israelites themselves.

ANOTHER VIEW ➤ *1210*

▶ Remembrance of things past is an essential part of developing a new identity.

CONTEMPORARY REFLECTION ➤ *1212*

▶ The tender mother who cares for her child stands for the world as it ought to be.

POST-BIBLICAL INTERPRETATIONS ➤ *1210*

▶ Nothing ever happens more than once. / The next time is never like before.

VOICES ➤ *1214*

I have entered the land that יהוה swore to our fathers to assign us."

⁴The priest shall take the basket from your hand and set it down in front of the altar of your God יהוה.

⁵You shall then recite as follows before your God יהוה: "My father was a fugitive Aramean. He went down to Egypt with meager numbers and sojourned there; but there he became a great and very populous nation. ⁶The Egyptians dealt harshly with us and oppressed us; they imposed heavy labor upon us. ⁷We cried to יהוה, the God of our ancestors, and יהוה heard our plea and saw our plight, our misery, and our oppression. ⁸יהוה freed us from Egypt by a mighty hand, by an outstretched arm and awesome power, and by signs and portents, ⁹bringing us to this place and giving us this land, a land flowing with milk and honey. ¹⁰Wherefore I now bring the first fruits of the soil which You, יהוה, have given me."

You shall leave it before your God יהוה and bow low before your God יהוה. ¹¹And you shall enjoy, together with the [family of the] Levite and the stranger in your midst, all the bounty that your God יהוה has bestowed upon you and your household.

¹²When you have set aside in full the tenth part of your yield—in the third year, the year of the

אֱלֹהֶיךָ כִּי־בָ֫אתִי אֶל־הָאָ֫רֶץ אֲשֶׁ֫ר נִשְׁבַּ֫ע יְהֹוָ֫ה לַאֲבֹתֵ֫ינוּ לָ֫תֶת לָֽנוּ:

⁴ וְלָקַ֫ח הַכֹּהֵ֫ן הַטֶּ֫נֶא מִיָּדֶ֑ךָ וְהִנִּיח֕וֹ לִפְנֵ֕י מִזְבַּ֫ח יְהֹוָ֫ה אֱלֹהֶֽיךָ:

⁵ וְעָנִ֫יתָ וְאָמַרְתָּ֫ לִפְנֵ֣י | יְהֹוָ֣ה אֱלֹהֶ֗יךָ אֲרַמִּי֙ אֹבֵ֣ד אָבִ֔י וַיֵּ֖רֶד מִצְרַ֙יְמָה֙ וַיָּ֣גָר שָׁ֔ם בִּמְתֵ֖י מְעָ֑ט וַֽיְהִי־שָׁ֕ם לְג֥וֹי גָּד֖וֹל עָצ֥וּם וָרָֽב:

⁶ וַיָּרֵ֫עוּ אֹתָ֫נוּ הַמִּצְרִ֑ים וַיְעַנּ֑וּנוּ וַיִּתְּנ֥וּ עָלֵ֖ינוּ עֲבֹדָ֥ה קָשָֽׁה: ⁷ וַנִּצְעַ֕ק אֶל־יְהֹוָ֕ה אֱלֹהֵ֣י אֲבֹתֵ֑ינוּ וַיִּשְׁמַ֤ע יְהֹוָה֙ אֶת־קֹלֵ֔נוּ וַיַּ֕רְא אֶת־עׇנְיֵ֫נוּ וְאֶת־עֲמָלֵ֖נוּ וְאֶת־לַחֲצֵֽנוּ: ⁸ וַיּֽוֹצִאֵ֫נוּ יְהֹוָה֙ מִמִּצְרַ֔יִם בְּיָ֤ד חֲזָקָה֙ וּבִזְרֹ֣עַ נְטוּיָ֔ה וּבְמֹרָ֖א גָּדֹ֑ל וּבְאֹת֖וֹת וּבְמֹפְתִֽים: ⁹ וַיְבִאֵ֕נוּ אֶל־הַמָּק֥וֹם הַזֶּ֑ה וַיִּתֶּן־לָ֙נוּ֙ אֶת־הָאָ֣רֶץ הַזֹּ֔את אֶ֛רֶץ זָבַ֥ת חָלָ֖ב וּדְבָֽשׁ: ¹⁰ וְעַתָּ֗ה הִנֵּ֤ה הֵבֵ֙אתִי֙ אֶת־רֵאשִׁית֙ פְּרִ֣י הָֽאֲדָמָ֔ה אֲשֶׁר־נָתַ֥תָּה לִּ֖י יְהֹוָ֑ה

וְהִנַּחְתּ֗וֹ לִפְנֵי֙ יְהֹוָ֣ה אֱלֹהֶ֔יךָ וְהִֽשְׁתַּחֲוִ֕יתָ לִפְנֵ֖י יְהֹוָ֥ה אֱלֹהֶֽיךָ: ¹¹ וְשָׂמַחְתָּ֣ בְכׇל־הַטּ֗וֹב אֲשֶׁ֫ר נָֽתַן־לְךָ֫ יְהֹוָ֫ה אֱלֹהֶ֑יךָ וּלְבֵיתֶ֑ךָ אַתָּה֙ וְהַלֵּוִ֔י וְהַגֵּ֕ר אֲשֶׁ֥ר בְּקִרְבֶּֽךָ: ס

¹² כִּ֣י תְכַלֶּ֗ה לַעְשֵׂ֫ר אֶת־כׇּל־מַעְשַׂ֫ר תְּבוּאָֽתְךָ֫ בַּשָּׁנָ֫ה הַשְּׁלִישִׁ֕ת שְׁנַ֥ת הַֽמַּעֲשֵׂ֑ר

⸻

3. *"our fathers."* In this translation, the term *avot* is understood to refer specifically to the patriarchs when they serve as representatives of their households (here and v. 15); elsewhere, it is rendered in a more inclusive sense as "ancestors" (as in v. 7). Although the forefathers alone are invoked in this verse, the covenantal promises are inclusive (see at Genesis 17).

5–11. The liturgy to be recited during this ceremony reviews Israel's history from the end of the descent to Egypt in the time of Jacob, through the Exodus, to the coming to the land; it omits the wilderness period and the revelation at Sinai. Instead, the text emphasizes the deeds that God performed for Israel. This passage, along with its midrashic explanation, has become a central part of the Passover Haggadah.

5. *"My father was a fugitive Aramean."* Or, "wandering Aramean." "My father" probably refers to Jacob, father of the twelve tribes. The patriarchs and matriarchs came from Aram Naharaim, which is where Jacob flees to and starts a family with Leah, Rachel, Zilpah, and Bilhah (Genesis 30).

TITHES (26:12–15)

The tithe of the third year is not to be taken to the central sanctuary like the tithes of the first and

וְנָתַתָּה לַלֵּוִי לַגֵּר לַיָּתוֹם וְלָאַלְמָנָה וְאָכְלוּ
בִשְׁעָרֶיךָ וְשָׂבֵעוּ׃ 13 וְאָמַרְתָּ לִפְנֵי יְהוָה
אֱלֹהֶיךָ בִּעַרְתִּי הַקֹּדֶשׁ מִן־הַבַּיִת וְגַם נְתַתִּיו
לַלֵּוִי וְלַגֵּר לַיָּתוֹם וְלָאַלְמָנָה כְּכָל־מִצְוָתְךָ
אֲשֶׁר צִוִּיתָנִי לֹא־עָבַרְתִּי מִמִּצְוֺתֶיךָ וְלֹא
שָׁכָחְתִּי׃ 14 לֹא־אָכַלְתִּי בְאֹנִי מִמֶּנּוּ וְלֹא־
בִעַרְתִּי מִמֶּנּוּ בְּטָמֵא וְלֹא־נָתַתִּי מִמֶּנּוּ
לְמֵת שָׁמַעְתִּי בְּקוֹל יְהוָה אֱלֹהָי עָשִׂיתִי
כְּכֹל אֲשֶׁר צִוִּיתָנִי׃ 15 הַשְׁקִיפָה מִמְּעוֹן
קָדְשְׁךָ מִן־הַשָּׁמַיִם וּבָרֵךְ אֶת־עַמְּךָ אֶת־
יִשְׂרָאֵל וְאֵת הָאֲדָמָה אֲשֶׁר נָתַתָּה לָנוּ
כַּאֲשֶׁר נִשְׁבַּעְתָּ לַאֲבֹתֵינוּ אֶרֶץ זָבַת חָלָב
וּדְבָשׁ׃ ס
16 הַיּוֹם הַזֶּה יְהוָה אֱלֹהֶיךָ מְצַוְּךָ לַעֲשׂוֹת
אֶת־הַחֻקִּים הָאֵלֶּה וְאֶת־הַמִּשְׁפָּטִים
וְשָׁמַרְתָּ וְעָשִׂיתָ אוֹתָם בְּכָל־לְבָבְךָ וּבְכָל־
נַפְשֶׁךָ׃ 17 אֶת־יְהוָה הֶאֱמַרְתָּ הַיּוֹם לִהְיוֹת
לְךָ לֵאלֹהִים וְלָלֶכֶת בִּדְרָכָיו וְלִשְׁמֹר חֻקָּיו

tithe—and have given it to the [family of the]
Levite, the stranger, the fatherless, and the widow,
that they may eat their fill in your settlements,
13you shall declare before your God יהוה: "I have
cleared out the consecrated portion from the house;
and I have given it to the [family of the] Levite, the
stranger, the fatherless, and the widow, just as You
commanded me; I have neither transgressed nor
neglected any of Your commandments: 14I have not
eaten of it while in mourning, I have not cleared
out any of it while I was impure, and I have not
deposited any of it with the dead. I have obeyed my
God יהוה; I have done just as You commanded me.
15Look down from Your holy abode, from heaven,
and bless Your people Israel and the soil You have
given us, a land flowing with milk and honey, as
You swore to our fathers."

16Your God יהוה commands you this day to
observe these laws and rules; observe them faithfully with all your heart and soul. 17You have
affirmed this day that יהוה is your God, in whose
ways you will walk, whose laws and commandments and rules you will observe, and whom you

second years (14:22–29); instead, it is distributed locally to those who are dependent on public assistance, including widows and Levites (see at 12:19).

*14. deposited any of it with the dead.* In ancient Israel, people believed that they could assist the spirits of the dead by providing food and drink for them to consume in Sheol, the place where all the dead resided. This verse does not prohibit this practice, though it does exclude the use of tithed foodstuff for this purpose. Contact with the dead is considered a source of ritual impurity (Jeffrey Tigay, *Deuteronomy*, 1996, p. 244).

*15. from Your holy abode, from heaven.* Elsewhere in the Bible, God's abode is conceived of as an earthly sacred space (as in Exodus 25:8); but in Deuteronomy, God is considered transcendent and not located in any place on earth. The book speaks of God's "name" dwelling in the Chosen Place (as in 12:5) to counter the impression that God literally dwells there. This verse shows how Deuteronomy uses a traditional idiom but modifies it to fit its distinctive theology.

## *Conclusion to the Laws*

### OBLIGATIONS FOR ISRAEL AND GOD (26:16–19)

The laws in Deuteronomy 12–26 now end with an exhortation calling upon Israel to obey the covenant between God and Israel. Both parties affirm their obligations: Israel is to follow the laws, while God is to maintain a special relationship with Israel.

will obey. [18]And יהוה has affirmed this day that you are, as promised, God's treasured people who shall observe all the divine commandments, [19]and that [God] will set you, in fame and renown and glory, high above all the nations that [God] has made; and that you shall be, as promised, a holy people to your God יהוה.

וּמִצְוֺתָיו וּמִשְׁפָּטָיו וְלִשְׁמֹעַ בְּקֹלוֹ׃ 18 וַיהוָה
הֶאֱמִירְךָ הַיּוֹם לִהְיוֹת לוֹ לְעַם סְגֻלָּה
כַּאֲשֶׁר דִּבֶּר־לָךְ וְלִשְׁמֹר כָּל־מִצְוֺתָיו׃
19 וּלְתִתְּךָ עֶלְיוֹן עַל כָּל־הַגּוֹיִם אֲשֶׁר עָשָׂה
לִתְהִלָּה וּלְשֵׁם וּלְתִפְאָרֶת וְלִהְיֹתְךָ עַם־
קָדֹשׁ לַיהוָה אֱלֹהֶיךָ כַּאֲשֶׁר דִּבֵּר׃ פ

27 Moses and the elders of Israel charged the people, saying: Observe all the Instruction that I enjoin upon you this day. [2]As soon as you have crossed the Jordan into the land that your God יהוה is giving you, you shall set up large stones. Coat them with plaster [3]and inscribe upon them all the words of this Teaching. When you cross over to enter the land that your God יהוה is giving you, a

כז וַיְצַו מֹשֶׁה וְזִקְנֵי יִשְׂרָאֵל אֶת־הָעָם
לֵאמֹר שָׁמֹר אֶת־כָּל־הַמִּצְוָה אֲשֶׁר אָנֹכִי
מְצַוֶּה אֶתְכֶם הַיּוֹם׃ 2 וְהָיָה בַּיּוֹם אֲשֶׁר
תַּעַבְרוּ אֶת־הַיַּרְדֵּן אֶל־הָאָרֶץ אֲשֶׁר־יְהוָה
אֱלֹהֶיךָ נֹתֵן לָךְ וַהֲקֵמֹתָ לְךָ אֲבָנִים גְּדֹלוֹת
וְשַׂדְתָּ אֹתָם בַּשִּׂיד׃ 3 וְכָתַבְתָּ עֲלֵיהֶן אֶת־
כָּל־דִּבְרֵי הַתּוֹרָה הַזֹּאת בְּעָבְרֶךָ לְמַעַן
אֲשֶׁר תָּבֹא אֶל־הָאָרֶץ אֲשֶׁר־יְהוָה אֱלֹהֶיךָ

*18. God's treasured people.* As in 7:6, this phrase means that God chooses Israel to be holy and set aside for God. This idea stems from the view that Israel's God assigned other gods to different nations (see at 4:19–20) while establishing a special relationship with the people of Israel. This does not mean that Israel views itself as innately superior to other peoples, although the God of Israel is considered more powerful than all other gods (see also at Exodus 19:5).

## *Ceremonies upon Entering the Land*

(27:1–26)

The laws in Deuteronomy 12–26 are framed by ceremonies to be performed once the people cross over into the Promised Land (see 11:29–32). Deuteronomy links the entrance into the land with obedience to the laws and repeatedly emphasizes that Israelite success and survival in the land depend upon their adherence to these laws. (One can best explain the several discontinuities or digressions in this unit as the result of later editorial activity.)

### ERECTION OF INSCRIBED STONES AND A STONE ALTAR AT MOUNT EBAL

(27:1–8)

This section instructs the Israelites to set up plaster-coated stones at Mount Ebal on which "this Teaching" will be written after they cross the Jordan. At the same location, they are to erect an altar of unhewn stone for offering sacrifices. Mount Ebal is located near the town of Shechem (modern day Nablus), about thirty miles from the site of the crossing of the Jordan and hence too far to reach on the same day. (Compare Joshua 4:19, which offers a different version of these events.)

*3. inscribe upon them.* Similarly, the law collection of the Babylonian king Hammurabi, including its prologue and epilogue, was inscribed on a stele and erected in a temple.

*this Teaching.* Heb. *ha-torah ha-zot,* which does not mean the entire Torah as we now have it, but instead the book of Deuteronomy, or perhaps only its legal portions (see also at 31:9).

land flowing with milk and honey, as יהוה, the God
of your ancestors, promised you—4 upon crossing
the Jordan, you shall set up these stones, about
which I charge you this day, on Mount Ebal, and
coat them with plaster. 5 There, too, you shall build
an altar to your God יהוה, an altar of stones. Do not
wield an iron tool over them; 6 you must build the
altar of your God יהוה of unhewn stones. You shall
offer on it burnt offerings to your God יהוה, 7 and
you shall sacrifice there offerings of well-being and
eat them, rejoicing before your God יהוה. 8 And on
those stones you shall inscribe every word of this
Teaching most distinctly.
9 Moses and the levitical priests spoke to all Israel, saying: Silence! Hear, O Israel! Today you
have become the people of your God יהוה: 10 Heed
your God יהוה and observe the divine commandments and laws, which I enjoin upon you this day.
11 Thereupon Moses charged the people, saying:
12 After you have crossed the Jordan, the following
shall stand on Mount Gerizim when the blessing
for the people is spoken: Simeon, Levi, Judah,

׀ נֹתֵן לָךְ אֶרֶץ זָבַת חָלָב וּדְבַשׁ כַּאֲשֶׁר דִּבֶּר
יְהוָה אֱלֹהֵי־אֲבֹתֶיךָ לָךְ׃ 4 וְהָיָה בְּעָבְרְכֶם
אֶת־הַיַּרְדֵּן תָּקִימוּ אֶת־הָאֲבָנִים הָאֵלֶּה
אֲשֶׁר אָנֹכִי מְצַוֶּה אֶתְכֶם הַיּוֹם בְּהַר
עֵיבָל וְשַׂדְתָּ אוֹתָם בַּשִּׂיד׃ 5 וּבָנִיתָ שָּׁם
מִזְבֵּחַ לַיהוָה אֱלֹהֶיךָ מִזְבַּח אֲבָנִים לֹא־
תָנִיף עֲלֵיהֶם בַּרְזֶל׃ 6 אֲבָנִים שְׁלֵמוֹת
תִּבְנֶה אֶת־מִזְבַּח יְהוָה אֱלֹהֶיךָ וְהַעֲלִיתָ
עָלָיו עוֹלֹת לַיהוָה אֱלֹהֶיךָ׃ 7 וְזָבַחְתָּ
שְׁלָמִים וְאָכַלְתָּ שָּׁם וְשָׂמַחְתָּ לִפְנֵי יְהוָה
אֱלֹהֶיךָ׃ 8 וְכָתַבְתָּ עַל־הָאֲבָנִים אֶת־כָּל־
דִּבְרֵי הַתּוֹרָה הַזֹּאת בַּאֵר הֵיטֵב׃ ס
9 וַיְדַבֵּר מֹשֶׁה וְהַכֹּהֲנִים הַלְוִיִּם אֶל כָּל־
יִשְׂרָאֵל לֵאמֹר הַסְכֵּת ׀ וּשְׁמַע יִשְׂרָאֵל
הַיּוֹם הַזֶּה נִהְיֵיתָ לְעָם לַיהוָה אֱלֹהֶיךָ׃
10 וְשָׁמַעְתָּ בְּקוֹל יְהוָה אֱלֹהֶיךָ וְעָשִׂיתָ אֶת־
מצותו מִצְוֹתָיו וְאֶת־חֻקָּיו אֲשֶׁר אָנֹכִי מְצַוְּךָ
הַיּוֹם׃ ס
11 וַיְצַו מֹשֶׁה אֶת־הָעָם בַּיּוֹם הַהוּא לֵאמֹר׃
12 אֵלֶּה יַעַמְדוּ לְבָרֵךְ אֶת־הָעָם עַל־הַר
גְּרִזִים בְּעָבְרְכֶם אֶת־הַיַּרְדֵּן שִׁמְעוֹן וְלֵוִי

## CALL TO OBEY THE COVENANT AT MOAB (27:9–10)

These verses declare that Israel is God's people and therefore obligated to obey God's laws. This section fits better with 26:17–18, the conclusion of the covenant at Moab.

## PROCLAMATION OF BLESSINGS AND CURSES AT MT. GERIZIM AND MT. EBAL (27:11–26)

Deuteronomy 11:26–30 first mentions a public ceremony to announce the consequences of keeping or neglecting the terms of the covenant (enacted in Joshua 8:33–35). Deuteronomy 28 contains the actual blessings and curses to be recited during the ceremony.

*11–13.* This passage adheres to 11:26–30, according to which the blessing for those who obey the commandments is to be proclaimed at Mount Gerizim and the curse for those who disobey at Mount Ebal. (Compare vv. 14–26, below.)

*12.* Six of the tribes, the descendants of Leah and Rachel, will utter the blessings on Mount Gerizim (north of Shechem); six others, the descendants of the handmaids Bilhah and Zilpah plus Reuben and Zebulun, will utter the curses on Mount Ebal (south of Shechem).

Issachar, Joseph, and Benjamin. 13 And for the curse, the following shall stand on Mount Ebal: Reuben, Gad, Asher, Zebulun, Dan, and Naphtali. 14 The Levites shall then proclaim in a loud voice to all the people of Israel:

15 Cursed be anyone who makes a sculptured or molten image, abhorred by יהוה, a craftsman's handiwork, and sets it up in secret.—And all the people shall respond, Amen.

16 Cursed be the one who insults father or mother.—And all the people shall say, Amen.

17 Cursed be the one who moves a neighbor's landmark.—And all the people shall say, Amen.

18 Cursed be the one who misdirects a blind person underway.—And all the people shall say, Amen.

19 Cursed be the one who subverts the rights of the stranger, the fatherless, and the widow.—And all the people shall say, Amen.

20 Cursed be the [man] who lies with his father's wife, for he has removed his father's garment.—And all the people shall say, Amen.

וִיהוּדָ֔ה ויששכר וְיִשָּׂשכָ֖ר וְיוֹסֵ֥ף וּבִנְיָמִֽן׃
13 וְאֵ֨לֶּה יַֽעַמְד֥וּ עַל־הַקְּלָלָ֖ה בְּהַ֣ר עֵיבָ֑ל
רְאוּבֵן֙ גָּ֣ד וְאָשֵׁ֔ר וּזְבוּלֻ֖ן דָּ֥ן וְנַפְתָּלִֽי׃ 14 וְעָנ֣וּ
הַלְוִיִּ֗ם וְאָֽמְר֛וּ אֶל־כׇּל־אִ֥ישׁ יִשְׂרָאֵ֖ל ק֥וֹל
רָֽם׃ ס
15 אָר֣וּר הָאִ֡ישׁ אֲשֶׁ֣ר יַֽעֲשֶׂה֩ פֶ֨סֶל וּמַסֵּכָ֜ה
תּוֹעֲבַ֣ת יְהֹוָ֗ה מַֽעֲשֵׂ֛ה יְדֵ֥י חָרָ֖שׁ וְשָׂ֣ם בַּסָּ֑תֶר
וְעָנ֧וּ כׇל־הָעָ֛ם וְאָמְר֖וּ אָמֵֽן׃ ס
16 אָר֕וּר מַקְלֶ֥ה אָבִ֖יו וְאִמּ֑וֹ וְאָמַ֥ר כׇּל־הָעָ֖ם
אָמֵֽן׃ ס
17 אָר֕וּר מַסִּ֖יג גְּב֣וּל רֵעֵ֑הוּ וְאָמַ֥ר כׇּל־הָעָ֖ם
אָמֵֽן׃ ס
18 אָר֕וּר מַשְׁגֶּ֥ה עִוֵּ֖ר בַּדָּ֑רֶךְ וְאָמַ֥ר כׇּל־הָעָ֖ם
אָמֵֽן׃ ס
19 אָר֗וּר מַטֶּ֛ה מִשְׁפַּ֥ט גֵּר־יָת֖וֹם וְאַלְמָנָ֑ה
וְאָמַ֥ר כׇּל־הָעָ֖ם אָמֵֽן׃
20 אָר֗וּר שֹׁכֵב֙ עִם־אֵ֣שֶׁת אָבִ֔יו כִּ֥י גִלָּ֖ה כְּנַ֣ף
אָבִ֑יו וְאָמַ֥ר כׇּל־הָעָ֖ם אָמֵֽן׃ ס

*14–26.* This passage seems to be an alternate version of the ceremony of vv. 11–13; here, the people all stand together and the Levites make the proclamation. And it is not a list of curses for disobeying the commandments, as in Deuteronomy 28; instead, this passage lists twelve sinful actions for which a person is declared deserving of being cursed, meaning that they warrant divine punishment. The list summarizes the larger body of Deuteronomic law, showing a concern for a just society, sexual mores, and protection of the vulnerable.

*15.* Deuteronomy is adamantly opposed to graven images or idols, be they of Israel's God (as in the episode of the molten calf in Exodus 32; Deuteronomy 9:12) or of foreign deities.

***Amen.*** To ratify their acceptance of each statement, people respond with "Amen," which means "true" or "I affirm the foregoing."

*16.* ***insults father or mother.*** This verse refers to one who treats a parent with disrespect (*m'kaleh*), as exemplified by the incorrigible son in 21:18–21. This statement is similar to, but broader than, Exodus 21:17 and Leviticus 20:9, which forbid "cursing" (*k-l-l*) one's parents. Our verse uses a similar sounding term, from the root *k-l-h,* meaning "to treat lightly." This is the opposite of honoring a parent (*k-b-d,* which derives from the root meaning "to be heavy"). Children are to treat both mothers and fathers with respect (see also at 5:16; Exodus 20:12).

*17.* See at 19:14.

*19.* ***widow.*** See *Eikev*, Another View, p. 1108.

*20.* ***father's wife.*** This refers to any wife of one's father, not just the mother of the man addressed by the law; the father's sexual rights are not to be impinged upon by "removing his garment." To "spread a garment" over a woman is to claim responsibility for her in marriage (Ezekiel 16:8;

²¹Cursed be the one who lies with any beast.—And all the people shall say, Amen.

²²Cursed be the [man] who lies with his sister, whether daughter of his father or of his mother.—And all the people shall say, Amen.

²³Cursed be the [man] who lies with his mother-in-law.—And all the people shall say, Amen.

²⁴Cursed be the one who strikes down a fellow [Israelite] in secret.—And all the people shall say, Amen.

²⁵Cursed be the one who accepts a bribe in the case of the murder of an innocent person.—And all the people shall say, Amen.

²⁶Cursed be whoever will not uphold the terms of this Teaching and observe them.—And all the people shall say, Amen.

28 Now, if you obey your God יהוה, to observe faithfully all the divine commandments which I enjoin upon you this day, your God יהוה will set you high above all the nations of the earth.

21 אָר֗וּר שֹׁכֵ֛ב עִם־כָּל־בְּהֵמָ֑ה וְאָמַ֥ר כָּל־הָעָ֖ם אָמֵֽן: ס

22 אָר֗וּר שֹׁכֵב֙ עִם־אֲחֹת֔וֹ בַּת־אָבִ֖יו א֣וֹ בַת־אִמּ֑וֹ וְאָמַ֥ר כָּל־הָעָ֖ם אָמֵֽן: ס

23 אָר֗וּר שֹׁכֵ֖ב עִם־חֹֽתַנְתּ֑וֹ וְאָמַ֥ר כָּל־הָעָ֖ם אָמֵֽן: ס

24 אָר֕וּר מַכֵּ֥ה רֵעֵ֖הוּ בַּסָּ֑תֶר וְאָמַ֥ר כָּל־הָעָ֖ם אָמֵֽן: ס

25 אָרוּר֙ לֹקֵ֣חַ שֹׁ֔חַד לְהַכּ֥וֹת נֶ֖פֶשׁ דָּ֣ם נָקִ֑י וְאָמַ֥ר כָּל־הָעָ֖ם אָמֵֽן: ס

26 אָר֗וּר אֲשֶׁ֧ר לֹֽא־יָקִ֛ים אֶת־דִּבְרֵ֥י הַתּוֹרָֽה־הַזֹּ֖את לַעֲשׂ֣וֹת אוֹתָ֑ם וְאָמַ֥ר כָּל־הָעָ֖ם אָמֵֽן: פ

כח וְהָיָ֗ה אִם־שָׁמ֤וֹעַ תִּשְׁמַע֙ בְּק֣וֹל יְהֹוָ֣ה אֱלֹהֶ֔יךָ לִשְׁמֹ֤ר לַעֲשׂוֹת֙ אֶת־כָּל־מִצְוֺתָ֔יו אֲשֶׁ֛ר אָנֹכִ֥י מְצַוְּךָ֖ הַיּ֑וֹם וּנְתָ֨נְךָ֜ יְהֹוָ֤ה אֱלֹהֶ֨יךָ֙

Ruth 3:9). (See also at Deuteronomy 23:1 and Leviticus 18:8.)

**22. his sister.** This verse forbids intercourse with one's sister or half-sister (see also at Leviticus 18:9). The book of Samuel tells of King David's son Amnon, who rapes his half-sister Tamar (II Samuel 13). In that story, the concern is more with forced sex outside of marriage that victimizes the woman than with the impropriety of sibling sex. Although the text remains ambiguous, it seems that Amnon could have married Tamar had he so wished, which would conflict with the law here.

**23.** One's mother-in-law is like one's father's wife in regard to impermissible sexual relations (compare Leviticus 18:17).

**25. accepts a bribe.** This statement probably condemns the acceptance of bribes by judges in a case that results in the death sentence for an innocent defendant. However, it may be directed to witnesses bribed to give false testimony.

## Consequences of Obeying or Disobeying the Covenant (28:1–68)

Unlike the proclamations in 27:11–26, the blessings and curses in this unit constitute promises or punishments that will befall Israel depending on whether the people obey or disobey God's commandments. Although the blessings and curses are formulated in second-person masculine singular language, they are addressed to the entire community and apply to the community as a whole, not to individuals. Similar examples of blessings and curses are found in Exodus 23:20–33 and Leviticus 26:3–45.

The Bible models the covenant between God and Israel on the model of a treaty between two human parties, one of whom is superior to the other: the superior promises protection, and the inferior promises loyalty. Ancient Near Eastern international treaties generally contain, near the end, warn-

[2]All these blessings shall come upon you and take effect, if you will but heed the word of your God יהוה:

[3]Blessed shall you be in the city and blessed shall you be in the country.

[4]Blessed shall be your issue from the womb, your produce from the soil, and your offspring from the cattle, your calving from the herd and your lambing from the flock.

[5]Blessed shall be your basket and your kneading bowl.

[6]Blessed shall you be in your comings and blessed shall you be in your goings.

[7]יהוה will put to rout before [your army] the enemies who attack you; they will march out against you by a single road, but flee from you by many roads. [8]יהוה will ordain blessings for you upon your barns and upon all your undertakings: you will be blessed in the land that your God יהוה is

עֶלְיוֹן עַל כׇּל־גּוֹיֵי הָאָרֶץ׃ 2 וּבָאוּ עָלֶיךָ כׇּל־
הַבְּרָכוֹת הָאֵלֶּה וְהִשִּׂיגֻךָ כִּי תִשְׁמַע בְּקוֹל
יְהֹוָה אֱלֹהֶיךָ׃
3 בָּרוּךְ אַתָּה בָּעִיר וּבָרוּךְ אַתָּה בַּשָּׂדֶה׃
4 בָּרוּךְ פְּרִי־בִטְנְךָ וּפְרִי אַדְמָתְךָ וּפְרִי
בְהֶמְתֶּךָ שְׁגַר אֲלָפֶיךָ וְעַשְׁתְּרוֹת צֹאנֶךָ׃
5 בָּרוּךְ טַנְאֲךָ וּמִשְׁאַרְתֶּךָ׃
6 בָּרוּךְ אַתָּה בְּבֹאֶךָ וּבָרוּךְ אַתָּה
בְּצֵאתֶךָ׃
7 יִתֵּן יְהֹוָה אֶת־אֹיְבֶיךָ הַקָּמִים עָלֶיךָ נִגָּפִים
לְפָנֶיךָ בְּדֶרֶךְ אֶחָד יֵצְאוּ אֵלֶיךָ וּבְשִׁבְעָה
דְרָכִים יָנוּסוּ לְפָנֶיךָ׃ 8 יְצַו יְהֹוָה אִתְּךָ אֶת־
הַבְּרָכָה בַּאֲסָמֶיךָ וּבְכֹל מִשְׁלַח יָדֶךָ וּבֵרַכְךָ

ings about the consequences of a breach of the treaty; such dire threats aim to motivate the inferior party to uphold the treaty and not rebel against the overlord. Deuteronomy 28 closely resembles one ancient treaty in particular, the Vassal Treaty of Esarhaddon, a Neo-Assyrian treaty dating from 672 B.C.E., the time when much of Deuteronomy is thought to have originated. The tradition of curses is also attested in legal texts going back at least as far as the Laws of Hammurabi (1792–1750 B.C.E.). The curses may reflect the actual experience of the Babylonian exile, assuming that this unit was one of those parts of Deuteronomy added or edited after the exile (586 B.C.E.).

### THE BLESSINGS (28:1–14)

The blessings are contingent on the people's obeying the divine laws (Deuteronomy 12–26). The totality of the blessings will lead to a strong, secure, and prosperous country, superior to its enemies and loyal to God.

*4. your issue from the womb.* Literally, "your fruit of the belly"; see at 7:13. The verse promises fertility for humans, soil, and domestic animals (see also vv. 11 and 18, below). Human fertility is often thought of as a woman's domain, but here it is clearly part of the community's blessing and of major concern to the men as well. Indeed, fertility—of humans, of the soil, and of domestic animals—is crucial to the existence of Israel (see also *Noach*, Another View, p. 53).

*5. your basket and your kneading bowl.* Women would have used these vessels for gathering grain and making bread (see at Exodus 16:3 and 25:30 for more on women's role in bread production). As in the previous verse, women's work is credited to the community as a whole.

*7–14.* These verses spell out applications of the foregoing verses, which were stated in general terms. They also express a common theme in Deuteronomy, emphasizing that the blessings depend on obedience to God.

giving you. 9 יהוה will establish you as God's holy
people, as was sworn to you, if you keep the commandments of your God יהוה and walk in God's
ways. 10 And all the peoples of the earth shall see
that יהוה's name is proclaimed over you, and they
shall stand in fear of you. 11 יהוה will give you
abounding prosperity in your issue from the womb,
your offspring from the cattle, and your produce
from the soil in the land that יהוה swore to your
fathers to assign to you. 12 יהוה will open for you
that bounteous store, the heavens, to provide rain
for your land in season and to bless all your undertakings. You will be creditor to many nations, but
debtor to none.

13 יהוה will make you the head, not the tail; you
will always be at the top and never at the bottom—
if only you obey and faithfully observe the commandments of your God יהוה that I enjoin upon
you this day, 14 and do not deviate to the right or to
the left from any of the commandments that I
enjoin upon you this day and turn to the worship
of other gods.

15 But if you do not obey your God יהוה to observe faithfully all the commandments and laws

בָּאָ֕רֶץ אֲשֶׁר־יְהֹוָ֥ה אֱלֹהֶ֖יךָ נֹתֵ֥ן לָֽךְ׃ 9 יְקִֽימְךָ֙
יְהֹוָ֥ה לוֹ֙ לְעַ֣ם קָד֔וֹשׁ כַּאֲשֶׁ֖ר נִֽשְׁבַּֽע־לָ֑ךְ כִּ֣י
תִשְׁמֹ֗ר אֶת־מִצְוֺת֙ יְהֹוָ֣ה אֱלֹהֶ֔יךָ וְהָלַכְתָּ֖
בִּדְרָכָֽיו׃ 10 וְרָאוּ֙ כׇּל־עַמֵּ֣י הָאָ֔רֶץ כִּ֛י שֵׁ֥ם
יְהֹוָ֖ה נִקְרָ֣א עָלֶ֑יךָ וְיָֽרְא֖וּ מִמֶּֽךָּ׃ 11 וְהוֹתִֽרְךָ֤
יְהֹוָה֙ לְטוֹבָ֔ה בִּפְרִ֧י בִטְנְךָ֛ וּבִפְרִ֥י בְהֶמְתְּךָ֖
וּבִפְרִ֣י אַדְמָתֶ֑ךָ עַ֚ל הָֽאֲדָמָ֔ה אֲשֶׁ֨ר נִשְׁבַּ֧ע
יְהֹוָ֛ה לַאֲבֹתֶ֖יךָ לָ֥תֶת לָֽךְ׃ 12 יִפְתַּ֣ח יְהֹוָ֣ה ׀
לְ֠ךָ֠ אֶת־אוֹצָר֨וֹ הַטּ֜וֹב אֶת־הַשָּׁמַ֗יִם לָתֵ֤ת
מְטַר־אַרְצְךָ֙ בְּעִתּ֔וֹ וּלְבָרֵ֕ךְ אֵ֖ת כׇּל־מַעֲשֵׂ֣ה
יָדֶ֑ךָ וְהִלְוִ֙יתָ֙ גּוֹיִ֣ם רַבִּ֔ים וְאַתָּ֖ה לֹ֥א
תִלְוֶֽה׃

13 וּנְתָנְךָ֨ יְהֹוָ֤ה לְרֹאשׁ֙ וְלֹ֣א לְזָנָ֔ב וְהָיִ֙יתָ֙ רַ֣ק
לְמַ֔עְלָה וְלֹ֥א תִהְיֶ֖ה לְמָ֑טָּה כִּֽי־תִשְׁמַ֞ע אֶל־
מִצְוֺ֣ת ׀ יְהֹוָ֣ה אֱלֹהֶ֗יךָ אֲשֶׁ֨ר אָנֹכִ֧י מְצַוְּךָ֛
הַיּ֖וֹם לִשְׁמֹ֥ר וְלַעֲשֽׂוֹת׃ 14 וְלֹ֣א תָס֗וּר מִכׇּל־
הַדְּבָרִ֡ים אֲשֶׁ֣ר אָנֹכִ֞י מְצַוֶּ֥ה אֶתְכֶ֛ם הַיּ֖וֹם
יָמִ֣ין וּשְׂמֹ֑אול לָלֶ֗כֶת אַחֲרֵ֛י אֱלֹהִ֥ים אֲחֵרִ֖ים
לְעׇבְדָֽם׃ פ

15 וְהָיָ֗ה אִם־לֹ֤א תִשְׁמַע֙ בְּק֙וֹל֙ יְהֹוָ֣ה
אֱלֹהֶ֔יךָ לִשְׁמֹ֤ר לַעֲשׂוֹת֙ אֶת־כׇּל־מִצְוֺתָ֣יו

---

*10.* ***יהוה's name is proclaimed over you.*** This expression means that God is the authority over Israel and that Israel is God's people.

*12.* This verse promises that God will provide the fertility by bringing the rain to water the crops. The importance of rain in Israel cannot be exaggerated (see also at 11:10–11). Human and animal fertility is dependent on agricultural fertility.

***that bounteous store.*** Literally, "[God's] bounteous store," which reflects the belief that rain was stored in the heavens and belonged to God. (See also at 33:13.)

***rain . . . in season.*** The proper timing of the rain is crucial. Rain must come in the right part of the growing season; rain during the harvest can ruin the crops.

***You will be creditor.*** As a result of the bounty described above, Israel will have a surplus to lend to other nations.

### THE CURSES (28:15–68)

The section on the curses is longer and more graphic than the depiction of the blessings, although they parallel each other in part. The curses warn that God will call upon nature and foreign enemies to bring ruin to Israel, which means that Israel will lose the land that God promised. Deuteronomy makes the continued settlement in the Promised Land contingent on obeying God (whereas the promise of the land to Abraham in Genesis was unconditional). The theology of Deu-

which I enjoin upon you this day, all these curses shall come upon you and take effect:

16Cursed shall you be in the city and cursed shall you be in the country.

17Cursed shall be your basket and your kneading bowl.

18Cursed shall be your issue from the womb and your produce from the soil, your calving from the herd and your lambing from the flock.

19Cursed shall you be in your comings and cursed shall you be in your goings.

20יהוה will let loose against you calamity, panic,
and frustration in all the enterprises you undertake,
so that you shall soon be utterly wiped out because
of your evildoing in forsaking Me. 21יהוה will make
pestilence cling to you, until putting an end to you
in the land that you are entering to possess. 22יהוה
will strike you with consumption, fever, and inflammation, with scorching heat and drought, with
blight and mildew; they shall hound you until you
perish. 23The skies above your head shall be copper
and the earth under you iron. 24יהוה will make the
rain of your land dust, and sand shall drop on you
from the sky, until you are wiped out.

25יהוה will put you to rout before your enemies;

וְחֻקֹּתָיו אֲשֶׁר אָנֹכִי מְצַוְּךָ הַיּוֹם וּבָאוּ עָלֶיךָ
כׇּל־הַקְּלָלוֹת הָאֵלֶּה וְהִשִּׂיגוּךָ׃
16 אָרוּר אַתָּה בָּעִיר וְאָרוּר אַתָּה בַּשָּׂדֶה׃
17 אָרוּר טַנְאֲךָ וּמִשְׁאַרְתֶּךָ׃
18 אָרוּר פְּרִי־בִטְנְךָ וּפְרִי אַדְמָתֶךָ שְׁגַר
אֲלָפֶיךָ וְעַשְׁתְּרֹת צֹאנֶךָ׃
19 אָרוּר אַתָּה בְּבֹאֶךָ וְאָרוּר אַתָּה
בְּצֵאתֶךָ׃
20 יְשַׁלַּח יְהֹוָה ׀ בְּךָ אֶת־הַמְּאֵרָה אֶת־
הַמְּהוּמָה וְאֶת־הַמִּגְעֶרֶת בְּכׇל־מִשְׁלַח יָדְךָ
אֲשֶׁר תַּעֲשֶׂה עַד הִשָּׁמֶדְךָ וְעַד־אֲבׇדְךָ מַהֵר
מִפְּנֵי רֹעַ מַעֲלָלֶיךָ אֲשֶׁר עֲזַבְתָּנִי׃ 21 יַדְבֵּק
יְהֹוָה בְּךָ אֶת־הַדָּבֶר עַד כַּלֹּתוֹ אֹתְךָ מֵעַל
הָאֲדָמָה אֲשֶׁר־אַתָּה בָא־שָׁמָּה לְרִשְׁתָּהּ׃
22 יַכְּכָה יְהֹוָה בַּשַּׁחֶפֶת וּבַקַּדַּחַת וּבַדַּלֶּקֶת
וּבַחַרְחֻר וּבַחֶרֶב וּבַשִּׁדָּפוֹן וּבַיֵּרָקוֹן וּרְדָפוּךָ
עַד אׇבְדֶךָ׃ 23 וְהָיוּ שָׁמֶיךָ אֲשֶׁר עַל־רֹאשְׁךָ
נְחֹשֶׁת וְהָאָרֶץ אֲשֶׁר־תַּחְתֶּיךָ בַּרְזֶל׃ 24 יִתֵּן
יְהֹוָה אֶת־מְטַר אַרְצְךָ אָבָק וְעָפָר מִן־
הַשָּׁמַיִם יֵרֵד עָלֶיךָ עַד הִשָּׁמְדָךְ׃
25 יִתֶּנְךָ יְהֹוָה ׀ נִגָּף לִפְנֵי אֹיְבֶיךָ בְּדֶרֶךְ אֶחָד

teronomy, which may be largely postexilic (after 586 B.C.E.), paves the way to explain the destruction of the Temple and the exile as resulting from Israel's sins and disobedience. This passage closely corresponds to the curses in Leviticus 26; both texts are considered so terrifying that the custom later arose to recite them in an undertone when reading the Torah aloud in the synagogue.

*15–19.* These verses parallel the opening of the section of blessings in vv. 1–6.

*20–44.* This passage elaborates on the general curses of vv. 16–19, in horrific detail.

*21–24.* These verses present a picture of a country wracked with heat, drought, pestilence, disease, and finally starvation and death, which is what will happen if God does not open the heavens and provide rain (v. 24). The description also correlates with conditions of a city under siege, as Jerusalem experienced before its destruction in 586 B.C.E., in which case disease and starvation would result not from lack of rain, but from the population's inability to obtain food.

*23. copper... iron.* "Copper" probably refers to bronze (the same Hebrew word denotes both); along with iron, these were the hardest metals known in ancient times. No rain can break through the bronzed (from the heat) sky, and no vegetation can break through the iron-hard soil.

*24. dust.* Dust and sand represent the antithesis of rain.

*25–26.* Instead of celebrating a victory over attacking enemies, as in vv. 7 and 10, Israel will be

you shall march out against them by a single road, but flee from them by many roads; and you shall become a horror to all the kingdoms of the earth. [26]Your carcasses shall become food for all the birds of the sky and all the beasts of the earth, with none to frighten them off.

[27]יהוה will strike you with the Egyptian inflammation, with hemorrhoids, boil-scars, and itch, from which you shall never recover.

[28]יהוה will strike you with madness, blindness, and dismay. [29]You shall grope at noon as the blind grope in the dark; you shall not prosper in your ventures, but shall be constantly abused and robbed, with none to give help.

[30]If you [a man] pay the bride-price for a wife, another man shall enjoy her.

If you build a house, you shall not live in it. If you plant a vineyard, you shall not harvest it. [31]Your ox shall be slaughtered before your eyes, but you shall not eat of it; your ass shall be seized in front of you, and it shall not be returned to you; your flock shall be delivered to your enemies, with

תֵּצֵ֣א אֵלָ֔יו וּבְשִׁבְעָ֥ה דְרָכִ֖ים תָּנ֣וּס לְפָנָ֑יו וְהָיִ֣יתָ לְזַעֲוָ֔ה לְכֹ֖ל מַמְלְכ֥וֹת הָאָֽרֶץ: [26]וְהָיְתָ֤ה נִבְלָֽתְךָ֙ לְמַאֲכָ֔ל לְכׇל־ע֥וֹף הַשָּׁמַ֖יִם וּלְבֶהֱמַ֣ת הָאָ֑רֶץ וְאֵ֖ין מַחֲרִֽיד: [27]יַכְּכָ֨ה יְהֹוָ֜ה בִּשְׁחִ֤ין מִצְרַ֙יִם֙ ובעפלים וּבַטְּחֹרִ֔ים וּבַגָּרָ֖ב וּבֶחָ֑רֶס אֲשֶׁ֥ר לֹא־תוּכַ֖ל לְהֵרָפֵֽא: [28]יַכְּכָ֣ה יְהֹוָ֔ה בְּשִׁגָּע֖וֹן וּבְעִוָּר֑וֹן וּבְתִמְה֖וֹן לֵבָֽב: [29]וְהָיִ֜יתָ מְמַשֵּׁ֣שׁ בַּֽצׇּהֳרַ֗יִם כַּאֲשֶׁ֨ר יְמַשֵּׁ֤שׁ הַֽעִוֵּר֙ בָּאֲפֵלָ֔ה וְלֹ֥א תַצְלִ֖יחַ אֶת־דְּרָכֶ֑יךָ וְהָיִ֜יתָ אַ֣ךְ עָשׁ֧וּק וְגָז֛וּל כׇּל־הַיָּמִ֖ים וְאֵ֥ין מוֹשִֽׁיעַ: [30]אִשָּׁ֣ה תְאָרֵ֗שׂ וְאִ֤ישׁ אַחֵר֙ ישגלנה יִשְׁכָּבֶ֔נָּה בַּ֤יִת תִּבְנֶה֙ וְלֹא־תֵשֵׁ֣ב בּ֔וֹ כֶּ֥רֶם תִּטַּ֖ע וְלֹ֥א תְחַלְּלֶֽנּוּ: [31]שֽׁוֹרְךָ֙ טָב֣וּחַ לְעֵינֶ֔יךָ וְלֹ֣א תֹאכַ֣ל מִמֶּ֔נּוּ חֲמֹֽרְךָ֙ גָּז֣וּל מִלְּפָנֶ֔יךָ וְלֹ֥א יָשׁ֖וּב לָ֑ךְ צֹֽאנְךָ֙ נְתֻנ֣וֹת לְאֹיְבֶ֔יךָ וְאֵ֥ין לְךָ֖

. . . . . . . . . . . . . . . . . . . . . . . . . . . . . . . . . . . .

powerless to defend itself and will become a disgusting sight to the other nations. Most dishonorably, the war-dead will lie unburied, with no one to care for them.

**27–29.** These verses describe various physical ailments and mental disabilities, subsumed under skin diseases and blindness, which were common ailments in the ancient world. The precise identification of these diseases is not known.

**30–35.** This passage warns that people will not benefit from their labors or enjoy their possessions.

**30.** This verse denies a man the benefits of the military deferment given in 20:5–7. Building a house, planting a vineyard, and taking a wife signify establishing a household.

*bride-price.* Better, "betrothal gift." (See at Exodus 22:15–16; *Chayei Sarah*, Another View,

p. 127; and "Women in Ancient Israel—An Overview," p. xli.)

*wife.* The payment of the betrothal gift by the groom to the bride's father constituted a legal marriage contract. Although the bride and groom thus were bound in marriage, the marriage was not consummated immediately.

*enjoy her.* The idiom means to have illegitimate sex with the woman, causing her to lose her virginity before the marriage has been consummated. The Hebrew term written unvocalized in the text (called the *k'tiv*) is vulgar, as seen in Isaiah 13:16 and Zechariah 14:2, where the same verb is used for the rape of women during war. Therefore, the tradition for public recitation (called the *k'rei*) has replaced the root *sh-g-l* with a euphemism that comes from the root *sh-k-b*, meaning "to lie with her."

none to help you. [32]Your sons and daughters shall be delivered to another people, while you look on; and your eyes shall strain for them constantly, but you shall be helpless. [33]A people you do not know shall eat up the produce of your soil and all your gains; you shall be abused and downtrodden continually, [34]until you are driven mad by what your eyes behold. [35]יהוה will afflict you at the knees and thighs with a severe inflammation, from which you shall never recover—from the sole of your foot to the crown of your head.

[36]יהוה will drive you, and the king you have set over you, to a nation unknown to you or your ancestors, where you shall serve other gods, of wood and stone. [37]You shall be a consternation, a proverb, and a byword among all the peoples to which יהוה will drive you.

[38]Though you take much seed out to the field, you shall gather in little, for the locust shall consume it. [39]Though you plant vineyards and till them, you shall have no wine to drink or store, for the worm shall devour them. [40]Though you have olive trees throughout your territory, you shall have no oil for anointment, for your olives shall drop off. [41]Though you beget sons and daughters, they shall not remain with you, for they shall go into captivity. [42]The cricket shall take over all the trees and produce of your land.

מוֹשִׁיעַ׃ 32 בָּנֶיךָ וּבְנֹתֶיךָ נְתֻנִים לְעַם אַחֵר
וְעֵינֶיךָ רֹאוֹת וְכָלוֹת אֲלֵיהֶם כָּל־הַיּוֹם וְאֵין
לְאֵל יָדֶךָ׃ 33 פְּרִי אַדְמָתְךָ וְכָל־יְגִיעֲךָ יֹאכַל
עַם אֲשֶׁר לֹא־יָדָעְתָּ וְהָיִיתָ רַק עָשׁוּק וְרָצוּץ
כָּל־הַיָּמִים׃ 34 וְהָיִיתָ מְשֻׁגָּע מִמַּרְאֵה עֵינֶיךָ
אֲשֶׁר תִּרְאֶה׃ 35 יַכְּכָה יְהוָה בִּשְׁחִין רָע
עַל־הַבִּרְכַּיִם וְעַל־הַשֹּׁקַיִם אֲשֶׁר לֹא־תוּכַל
לְהֵרָפֵא מִכַּף רַגְלְךָ וְעַד קָדְקֳדֶךָ׃
36 יוֹלֵךְ יְהוָה אֹתְךָ וְאֶת־מַלְכְּךָ אֲשֶׁר תָּקִים
עָלֶיךָ אֶל־גּוֹי אֲשֶׁר לֹא־יָדַעְתָּ אַתָּה
וַאֲבֹתֶיךָ וְעָבַדְתָּ שָּׁם אֱלֹהִים אֲחֵרִים עֵץ
וָאָבֶן׃ 37 וְהָיִיתָ לְשַׁמָּה לְמָשָׁל וְלִשְׁנִינָה
בְּכֹל הָעַמִּים אֲשֶׁר־יְנַהֶגְךָ יְהוָה שָׁמָּה׃
38 זֶרַע רַב תּוֹצִיא הַשָּׂדֶה וּמְעַט תֶּאֱסֹף כִּי
יַחְסְלֶנּוּ הָאַרְבֶּה׃ 39 כְּרָמִים תִּטַּע וְעָבָדְתָּ
וְיַיִן לֹא־תִשְׁתֶּה וְלֹא תֶאֱגֹר כִּי תֹאכְלֶנּוּ
הַתֹּלָעַת׃ 40 זֵיתִים יִהְיוּ לְךָ בְּכָל־גְּבוּלֶךָ
וְשֶׁמֶן לֹא תָסוּךְ כִּי יִשַּׁל זֵיתֶךָ׃ 41 בָּנִים
וּבָנוֹת תּוֹלִיד וְלֹא־יִהְיוּ לָךְ כִּי יֵלְכוּ בַּשֶּׁבִי׃
42 כָּל־עֵצְךָ וּפְרִי אַדְמָתֶךָ יְיָרֵשׁ הַצְּלָצַל׃

*32–33.* The threats that a person's children will be sold as slaves in a foreign land (see also 28:41) and that foreigners will eat someone's produce imply conquest by another country. Lamentations 5:2 speaks of the confiscation of land by foreigners in connection with the Babylonian exile, an experience perhaps in the author's mind.

*32. sons and daughters.* Four times this passage stresses that both female and male children will be affected by the threat (see also vv. 41, 53, 56).

*36–37.* These verses present an even stronger allusion to defeat and exile.

*a proverb, and a byword.* The foreign nations will taunt Israel by making up sayings about its defeat.

*38–40.* This passage refers to the non-fertility of the land, namely frustrating cases in which produce that has already grown will then be destroyed through natural causes.

*41.* As in vv. 4, 11, and 18, children are included among the agricultural items. Just as people will not enjoy the agricultural products that they plant and tend (vv. 38–40, 42), so they will not maintain possession of the children they raised. Isaiah 49:14–23 depicts Israel in exile as a bereaved woman who soon will watch her children return home to her.

43 The strangers in your midst shall rise above you higher and higher, while you sink lower and lower: 44 they shall be your creditors, but you shall not be theirs; they shall be the head and you the tail.

45 All these curses shall befall you; they shall pursue you and overtake you, until you are wiped out, because you did not heed your God יהוה and keep the commandments and laws that were enjoined upon you. 46 They shall serve as signs and proofs against you and your offspring for all time. 47 Because you would not serve your God יהוה in joy and gladness over the abundance of everything, 48 you shall have to serve—in hunger and thirst, naked and lacking everything—the enemies whom יהוה will let loose against you. [God] will put an iron yoke upon your neck until you are wiped out.

49 יהוה will bring a nation against you from afar, from the end of the earth, which will swoop down like the eagle—a nation whose language you do not understand, 50 a ruthless nation, that will show the influential no regard and the vulnerable no mercy. 51 It shall devour the offspring of your cattle and the produce of your soil, until you have been wiped out, leaving you nothing of new grain, wine, or oil, of the calving of your herds and the lambing of your flocks, until it has brought you to ruin. 52 It shall shut you up in all your towns throughout your land until every mighty, towering wall in which you trust has come down. And when you are shut up in all your towns throughout your land that your God יהוה has assigned to you, 53 you shall eat your own issue, the flesh of your sons and daughters that your God יהוה has assigned to you, because of the desperate straits to which your en-

43 הַגֵּר אֲשֶׁר בְּקִרְבְּךָ יַעֲלֶה עָלֶיךָ מַעְלָה
מָּעְלָה וְאַתָּה תֵרֵד מַטָּה מָּטָּה׃ 44 הוּא
יַלְוְךָ וְאַתָּה לֹא תַלְוֶנּוּ הוּא יִהְיֶה לְרֹאשׁ
וְאַתָּה תִּהְיֶה לְזָנָב׃
45 וּבָאוּ עָלֶיךָ כָּל־הַקְּלָלוֹת הָאֵלֶּה וּרְדָפוּךָ
וְהִשִּׂיגוּךָ עַד הִשָּׁמְדָךְ כִּי־לֹא שָׁמַעְתָּ בְּקוֹל
יְהֹוָה אֱלֹהֶיךָ לִשְׁמֹר מִצְוֺתָיו וְחֻקֹּתָיו אֲשֶׁר
צִוָּךְ׃ 46 וְהָיוּ בְךָ לְאוֹת וּלְמוֹפֵת וּבְזַרְעֲךָ
עַד־עוֹלָם׃ 47 תַּחַת אֲשֶׁר לֹא־עָבַדְתָּ אֶת־
יְהֹוָה אֱלֹהֶיךָ בְּשִׂמְחָה וּבְטוּב לֵבָב מֵרֹב
כֹּל׃ 48 וְעָבַדְתָּ אֶת־אֹיְבֶיךָ אֲשֶׁר יְשַׁלְּחֶנּוּ
יְהֹוָה בָּךְ בְּרָעָב וּבְצָמָא וּבְעֵירֹם וּבְחֹסֶר כֹּל
וְנָתַן עֹל בַּרְזֶל עַל־צַוָּארֶךָ עַד הִשְׁמִידוֹ
אֹתָךְ׃
49 יִשָּׂא יְהֹוָה עָלֶיךָ גּוֹי מֵרָחֹק מִקְצֵה
הָאָרֶץ כַּאֲשֶׁר יִדְאֶה הַנָּשֶׁר גּוֹי אֲשֶׁר לֹא־
תִשְׁמַע לְשֹׁנוֹ׃ 50 גּוֹי עַז פָּנִים אֲשֶׁר לֹא־
יִשָּׂא פָנִים לְזָקֵן וְנַעַר לֹא יָחֹן׃ 51 וְאָכַל פְּרִי
בְהֶמְתְּךָ וּפְרִי־אַדְמָתְךָ עַד הִשָּׁמְדָךְ אֲשֶׁר
לֹא־יַשְׁאִיר לְךָ דָּגָן תִּירוֹשׁ וְיִצְהָר שְׁגַר
אֲלָפֶיךָ וְעַשְׁתְּרֹת צֹאנֶךָ עַד הַאֲבִידוֹ אֹתָךְ׃
52 וְהֵצַר לְךָ בְּכָל־שְׁעָרֶיךָ עַד רֶדֶת חֹמֹתֶיךָ
הַגְּבֹהֹת וְהַבְּצֻרוֹת אֲשֶׁר אַתָּה בֹּטֵחַ בָּהֵן
בְּכָל־אַרְצֶךָ וְהֵצַר לְךָ בְּכָל־שְׁעָרֶיךָ בְּכָל־
אַרְצְךָ אֲשֶׁר נָתַן יְהֹוָה אֱלֹהֶיךָ לָךְ׃
53 וְאָכַלְתָּ פְרִי־בִטְנְךָ בְּשַׂר בָּנֶיךָ וּבְנֹתֶיךָ
אֲשֶׁר נָתַן־לְךָ יְהֹוָה אֱלֹהֶיךָ בְּמָצוֹר וּבְמָצוֹק

*43–44.* These verses threaten a reversal of the economic superiority promised in vv. 12–13.

*45–57.* After having suffered the losses and degradation mentioned so far, the people's ultimate end will be their annihilation. This moving description pictures the enemy's invasion and destruction of the agriculture of the land (partially, at least, to feed the invading army). Then come siege and starvation, which eventually lead to cannibalism. The unusually detailed descriptions of the selfish, secretive actions of the man and woman vividly convey the desperate and inhumane nature of the situation.

emy shall reduce you. [54]The householder who is most tender and fastidious among you shall be too mean to his brother and the wife of his bosom and the children he has spared [55]to share with any of them the flesh of the children that he eats, because he has nothing else left as a result of the desperate straits to which your enemy shall reduce you in all your towns. [56]And she who is most tender and dainty among you, so tender and dainty that she would never venture to set a foot on the ground, shall begrudge the husband of her bosom, and her son and her daughter, [57]the afterbirth that issues from between her legs and the babies she bears; she shall eat them secretly, because of utter want, in the desperate straits to which your enemy shall reduce you in your towns.

אֲשֶׁר־יָצִיק לְךָ אֹיְבֶךָ׃ 54 הָאִישׁ הָרַךְ בְּךָ
וְהֶעָנֹג מְאֹד תֵּרַע עֵינוֹ בְאָחִיו וּבְאֵשֶׁת חֵיקוֹ
וּבְיֶתֶר בָּנָיו אֲשֶׁר יוֹתִיר׃ 55 מִתֵּת | לְאַחַד
מֵהֶם מִבְּשַׂר בָּנָיו אֲשֶׁר יֹאכֵל מִבְּלִי
הִשְׁאִיר־לוֹ כֹּל בְּמָצוֹר וּבְמָצוֹק אֲשֶׁר יָצִיק
לְךָ אֹיִבְךָ בְּכָל־שְׁעָרֶיךָ׃ 56 הָרַכָּה בְךָ
וְהָעֲנֻגָּה אֲשֶׁר לֹא־נִסְּתָה כַף־רַגְלָהּ הַצֵּג
עַל־הָאָרֶץ מֵהִתְעַנֵּג וּמֵרֹךְ תֵּרַע עֵינָהּ
בְּאִישׁ חֵיקָהּ וּבִבְנָהּ וּבְבִתָּהּ׃ 57 וּבְשִׁלְיָתָהּ
הַיּוֹצֵת | מִבֵּין רַגְלֶיהָ וּבְבָנֶיהָ אֲשֶׁר תֵּלֵד כִּי־
תֹאכְלֵם בְּחֹסֶר־כֹּל בַּסָּתֶר בְּמָצוֹר וּבְמָצוֹק
אֲשֶׁר יָצִיק לְךָ אֹיִבְךָ בִּשְׁעָרֶיךָ׃

*54. **householder.*** Heb. *ish* (traditionally, "man"), which this translation understands here as the head of the household. The person normally responsible for the care and protection of its members now looks after only his own needs.

***wife of his bosom.*** The corresponding expression is used for the husband in v. 56 (see also at 13:7). In both cases, the phrase refers to one with whom someone has an intimate relationship, a person held dear and protected.

*55. **the children that he eats.*** As gruesome as this may seem, cannibalism is a common trope in descriptions of sieges (Leviticus 26:29; Lamentations 2:20; 4:10; II Kings 6:24–30; Jeremiah 19:9; Ezekiel 5:10; and in Assyria, the Vassal Treaties of Esarhaddon ¶¶ 47, 69, 71, 75). The verse refers not to killing the children, but to the eating of bodies that had already died from starvation.

*56. **most tender and dainty.*** This verse uses the same Hebrew terms to describe the woman as those found in v. 54 to characterize the man (translated there as "most tender and fastidious"). The attributes of softness and fastidiousness ascribed to both sexes, stemming from the high standard of living they previously enjoyed, will be undermined by the dire straits in which they find themselves. Then they will lose all traces of civilized behavior, even a sense of humanity.

***never venture to set a foot on the ground.*** The verse describes a woman who formerly lived in luxury, someone accustomed to riding in a sedan chair or carriage so that her feet did not come in contact with the ground. A modern equivalent would be "she never got her hands dirty."

***husband of her bosom.*** See above under "wife of his bosom" (v. 54).

*57.* Most difficult to read is the description of the mother eating her dead babies and even the afterbirth. Lamentations 2:20 and 4:10 also depict women as cannibals (see at v. 55 for additional references). The reversal of the woman's normal role nurturing children aims to illustrate just how gruesome the conditions might become. Likewise, in the account of a famine in Samaria (II Kings 6:24–30), what may look to some readers like the callous eating of children by the women illustrates the severity of the famine, not any fault in the women. Maternal cannibalism is considered the "end of the rope"; it convinces the king that all is lost. (See also Another View, p. 1210.)

58 If you fail to observe faithfully all the terms of
this Teaching that are written in this book, to
reverence this honored and awesome Name, your
God יהוה, 59 יהוה will inflict extraordinary plagues
upon you and your offspring, strange and lasting
plagues, malignant and chronic diseases—60 bringing back upon you all the sicknesses of Egypt that
you dreaded so, and they shall cling to you.
61 Moreover, יהוה will bring upon you all the
other diseases and plagues that are not mentioned
in this book of Teaching, until you are wiped out.
62 You shall be left a scant few, after having been
as numerous as the stars in the skies, because you
did not heed the command of your God יהוה.
63 And as יהוה once delighted in making you prosperous and many, so will יהוה now delight in causing you to perish and in wiping you out; you shall
be torn from the land that you are about to enter
and possess.

64 יהוה will scatter you among all the peoples
from one end of the earth to the other, and there
you shall serve other gods, wood and stone, whom
neither you nor your ancestors have experienced.
65 Yet even among those nations you shall find no
peace, nor shall your foot find a place to rest. יהוה
will give you there an anguished heart and eyes that
pine and a despondent spirit. 66 The life you face
shall be precarious; you shall be in terror, night and
day, with no assurance of survival. 67 In the morning
you shall say, "If only it were evening!" and in the
evening you shall say, "If only it were morning!"—
because of what your heart shall dread and your
eyes shall see. 68 יהוה will send you back to Egypt in
galleys, by a route which I told you you should not
see again. There you shall offer yourselves for sale to

58 אִם־לֹא תִשְׁמֹר לַעֲשׂוֹת אֶת־כָּל־דִּבְרֵי
הַתּוֹרָה הַזֹּאת הַכְּתוּבִים בַּסֵּפֶר הַזֶּה
לְיִרְאָה אֶת־הַשֵּׁם הַנִּכְבָּד וְהַנּוֹרָא הַזֶּה אֵת
יְהוָה אֱלֹהֶיךָ׃ 59 וְהִפְלָא יְהוָה אֶת־מַכֹּתְךָ
וְאֵת מַכּוֹת זַרְעֶךָ מַכּוֹת גְּדֹלֹת וְנֶאֱמָנוֹת
וָחֳלָיִם רָעִים וְנֶאֱמָנִים׃ 60 וְהֵשִׁיב בְּךָ אֵת
כָּל־מַדְוֵה מִצְרַיִם אֲשֶׁר יָגֹרְתָּ מִפְּנֵיהֶם
וְדָבְקוּ בָּךְ׃ 61 גַּם כָּל־חֳלִי וְכָל־מַכָּה אֲשֶׁר
לֹא כָתוּב בְּסֵפֶר הַתּוֹרָה הַזֹּאת יַעְלֵם יְהוָה
עָלֶיךָ עַד הִשָּׁמְדָךְ׃ 62 וְנִשְׁאַרְתֶּם בִּמְתֵי
מְעָט תַּחַת אֲשֶׁר הֱיִיתֶם כְּכוֹכְבֵי הַשָּׁמַיִם
לָרֹב כִּי־לֹא שָׁמַעְתָּ בְּקוֹל יְהוָה אֱלֹהֶיךָ׃
63 וְהָיָה כַּאֲשֶׁר־שָׂשׂ יְהוָה עֲלֵיכֶם לְהֵיטִיב
אֶתְכֶם וּלְהַרְבּוֹת אֶתְכֶם כֵּן יָשִׂישׂ יְהוָה
עֲלֵיכֶם לְהַאֲבִיד אֶתְכֶם וּלְהַשְׁמִיד אֶתְכֶם
וְנִסַּחְתֶּם מֵעַל הָאֲדָמָה אֲשֶׁר־אַתָּה בָא־
שָׁמָּה לְרִשְׁתָּהּ׃

64 וֶהֱפִיצְךָ יְהוָה בְּכָל־הָעַמִּים מִקְצֵה
הָאָרֶץ וְעַד־קְצֵה הָאָרֶץ וְעָבַדְתָּ שָּׁם
אֱלֹהִים אֲחֵרִים אֲשֶׁר לֹא־יָדַעְתָּ אַתָּה
וַאֲבֹתֶיךָ עֵץ וָאָבֶן׃ 65 וּבַגּוֹיִם הָהֵם לֹא
תַרְגִּיעַ וְלֹא־יִהְיֶה מָנוֹחַ לְכַף־רַגְלֶךָ וְנָתַן
יְהוָה לְךָ שָׁם לֵב רַגָּז וְכִלְיוֹן עֵינַיִם וְדַאֲבוֹן
נָפֶשׁ׃ 66 וְהָיוּ חַיֶּיךָ תְּלֻאִים לְךָ מִנֶּגֶד
וּפָחַדְתָּ לַיְלָה וְיוֹמָם וְלֹא תַאֲמִין בְּחַיֶּיךָ׃
67 בַּבֹּקֶר תֹּאמַר מִי־יִתֵּן עֶרֶב וּבָעֶרֶב תֹּאמַר
מִי־יִתֵּן בֹּקֶר מִפַּחַד לְבָבְךָ אֲשֶׁר תִּפְחָד
וּמִמַּרְאֵה עֵינֶיךָ אֲשֶׁר תִּרְאֶה׃ 68 וֶהֱשִׁיבְךָ
יְהוָה ׀ מִצְרַיִם בָּאֳנִיּוֹת בַּדֶּרֶךְ אֲשֶׁר אָמַרְתִּי
לְךָ לֹא־תֹסִיף עוֹד לִרְאֹתָהּ וְהִתְמַכַּרְתֶּם

*58–68.* After a warning about diseases that God will bring on Israel, this passage looks beyond the siege to the captivity and survival in a foreign land. Although a scattered remnant will remain, they will live in anguish and dread. Even worse, Israel's history will be reversed: the plagues that the Egyptians suffered will be visited upon Israel (v. 60); and the once numerous people will be reduced to a scant few (v. 62) as the exodus from Egypt is undone (v. 68).

your enemies as male and female slaves, but none will buy.

69These are the terms of the covenant which
יהוה commanded Moses to conclude with the Israelites in the land of Moab, in addition to the covenant which was made with them at Horeb.

29 Moses summoned all Israel and said to them:

You have seen all that יהוה did before your very eyes in the land of Egypt, to Pharaoh and to all his
courtiers and to his whole country: 2the wondrous
feats that you saw with your own eyes, those prodigious signs and marvels. 3Yet to this day יהוה has
not given you a mind to understand or eyes to see or ears to hear.

4I led you through the wilderness forty years; the clothes on your back did not wear out, nor did

שָׁם לְאֹיְבֶיךָ לַעֲבָדִים וְלִשְׁפָחוֹת וְאֵין
קֹנֶה׃ ס

69 אֵלֶּה דִבְרֵי הַבְּרִית אֲשֶׁר־צִוָּה יְהוָה
אֶת־מֹשֶׁה לִכְרֹת אֶת־בְּנֵי יִשְׂרָאֵל בְּאֶרֶץ
מוֹאָב מִלְּבַד הַבְּרִית אֲשֶׁר־כָּרַת אִתָּם
בְּחֹרֵב׃ פ

כט וַיִּקְרָא מֹשֶׁה אֶל־כָּל־יִשְׂרָאֵל וַיֹּאמֶר
אֲלֵהֶם
אַתֶּם רְאִיתֶם אֵת כָּל־אֲשֶׁר עָשָׂה יְהוָה
לְעֵינֵיכֶם בְּאֶרֶץ מִצְרַיִם לְפַרְעֹה וּלְכָל־
עֲבָדָיו וּלְכָל־אַרְצוֹ׃ 2 הַמַּסּוֹת הַגְּדֹלֹת אֲשֶׁר
רָאוּ עֵינֶיךָ הָאֹתֹת וְהַמֹּפְתִים הַגְּדֹלִים
הָהֵם׃ 3 וְלֹא־נָתַן יְהוָה לָכֶם לֵב לָדַעַת
וְעֵינַיִם לִרְאוֹת וְאָזְנַיִם לִשְׁמֹעַ עַד הַיּוֹם
הַזֶּה׃
4 וָאוֹלֵךְ אֶתְכֶם אַרְבָּעִים שָׁנָה בַּמִּדְבָּר לֹא־
בָלוּ שַׂלְמֹתֵיכֶם מֵעֲלֵיכֶם וְנַעַלְךָ לֹא־בָלְתָה

## *Concluding Statement to the Covenant* (28:69)

Deuteronomy here ties the covenant at Moab to the covenant at Horeb (Sinai). Up until this point, the laws of Deuteronomy 12–26 stood independently. According to 4:13 (and compare 10:4), only the Decalogue was revealed by God at Horeb; according to 4:14, Moses was commissioned at Horeb to provide the additional laws, which he does at Moab, just before the people enter the promised land where these laws will go into effect (Moshe Weinfeld, *Deuteronomy 1–11*, 1964, p. 205). The Deuteronomic view is that the laws delivered in Moab are now depicted as a supplement to the earlier Sinai covenant.

## *Commencement of Moses' Last Speech* (29:1–8)

According to Deuteronomy, Moses addresses the generation of Israelites who have experienced the exodus and wandering as they near the end of their journey. He reminds them of all that God did for them during the time of the exodus and wandering, which they are now in a better position to appreciate. These divine deeds form the reason why the people should obey the covenant.

*3. Yet to this day.* Moses announces that although the Israelites experienced these events, they were not able to understand their significance until they now prepare to enter the land, the culmination of and reason for all they have been through. Note,

the sandals on your feet; 5 you had no bread to eat
and no wine or other intoxicant to drink—that you
might know that I יהוה am your God.
6 When you reached this place, King Sihon of
Heshbon and King Og of Bashan came out to
engage us in battle, but we defeated them. 7 We
took their land and gave it to the Reubenites, the
Gadites, and the half-tribe of Manasseh as their
heritage. 8 Therefore observe faithfully all the terms
of this covenant, that you may succeed in all that
you undertake.

מֵעַ֥ל רַגְלֶֽךָ׃ 5 לֶ֚חֶם לֹ֣א אֲכַלְתֶּ֔ם וְיַ֥יִן וְשֵׁכָ֖ר
לֹ֣א שְׁתִיתֶ֑ם לְמַ֙עַן֙ תֵּֽדְע֔וּ כִּ֛י אֲנִ֥י יְהֹוָ֖ה
אֱלֹהֵיכֶֽם׃
6 וַתָּבֹ֖אוּ אֶל־הַמָּק֣וֹם הַזֶּ֑ה וַיֵּצֵ֣א סִיחֹ֣ן
מֶֽלֶךְ־חֶ֠שְׁבּוֹן וְע֨וֹג מֶֽלֶךְ־הַבָּשָׁ֧ן לִקְרָאתֵ֛נוּ
לַמִּלְחָמָ֖ה וַנַּכֵּֽם׃ 7 וַנִּקַּח֙ אֶת־אַרְצָ֔ם וַנִּתְּנָ֣הּ
לְנַחֲלָ֔ה לָרֽאוּבֵנִ֖י וְלַגָּדִ֑י וְלַחֲצִ֖י שֵׁ֥בֶט
הַֽמְנַשִּֽׁי׃ 8 וּשְׁמַרְתֶּ֗ם אֶת־דִּבְרֵי֙ הַבְּרִ֣ית
הַזֹּ֔את וַעֲשִׂיתֶ֖ם אֹתָ֑ם לְמַ֣עַן תַּשְׂכִּ֔ילוּ אֵ֖ת
כׇּל־אֲשֶׁ֥ר תַּעֲשֽׂוּן׃ פ

however, that the presumed audience may not have been physically present at those earlier historic moments, except perhaps as children.

*4. clothes . . . sandals.* [Whereas most of the past events that Moses has recalled thus far in Deuteronomy occurred some 40 years earlier, here Moses uses the pristine condition of the sojourners' clothing to demonstrate God's care in terms visible to the current generation. The rhetorical purpose here and throughout this parashah has been to impress upon the contemporary and future audiences just how generous and faithful God has been, and how and why the Israelites owe allegiance to their God. —*Ed.*]

*5. bread . . . wine or other intoxicant.* These staples of an agricultural society were not available in the wilderness, where the people survived on manna, quail, and water—unnatural foodstuffs divinely provided.

*8. terms of this covenant.* [Or "the words (*divrei*) of this covenant." The parashah concludes as it began, in the sense that it demands gratitude from the Israelites in light of all that God has done for them. It casts the people's obligation in terms of loyalty to the words of this covenant, that is, the comprehensive program for a just society that cares for all its members and is loyal to its one God. —*Ed.*]

—*Adele Berlin*

# *Another View*

Parashat Ki Tavo contrasts the blessings that reward those who keep the commandments with the curses that punish those who spurn them. Perhaps the most horrifying threat is that enemy invaders will devour the crops and cattle (28:51), causing even "tender" mothers to eat their own children (28:56–57). Here, as elsewhere, Deuteronomy presents a framework that we can fill out from other sources; the obvious intertext in this case is the book of Lamentations. Lamentations 4:5 depicts the upper class—"those who feasted on delicacies . . . those reared in crimson"—reduced to starvation and squalor. This helps us understand that in our parashah, the mother who "would never venture to set a foot on the ground" (28:56) is a member of the privileged elite, wearing the ancient equivalent of "taxi shoes" (those not for walking). One wonders if the adjective "tender" (v. 56) is ironic; not only does this mother eat her children, but according to Lamentations 4:10, she boils them first. These biblical passages remind us that enemies can reduce us to desperate measures and diminish us morally, causing us to perform formerly unimaginable acts in order to survive. Yet not all women eat their babies, even when in truly dire straits. How many actual mothers in Nazi concentration camps risked their own lives to preserve their children?

Who are the enemies that the curses of this parashah refer to? Deuteronomy blames the Israelites themselves: the enemy invasion and economic collapse are depicted as the self-induced consequences of failing to keep the commandments (28:15). People on the brink of death from starvation can face choices beyond their worst nightmares, but a reasoned choice was possible earlier on: the just society represented by Deuteronomy's laws versus the unjust society reflected by its curses.

*Perhaps the most horrifying threat is that mothers will eat their own children.*

For Deuteronomy, the measure of a just society is at the margins—the treatment of the stranger, fatherless, and widow (26:12). If a community does not respond to their needs, then it risks creating the very conditions in which, according to Deuteronomy, even the most privileged are bound to suffer. In such circumstances, how will we treat our babies and those in need?

*—Diana Lipton*

# *Post-biblical Interpretations*

***Now, if you obey*** (28:1). The Hebrew construction of this phrase gives double emphasis to the word "obey." Midrash *Sh'mot Rabbah* 7.1 suggests that this apparent repetition refers to the double reward that obedience to God's commandments in this world, such as synagogue worship and study, will merit in the world-to-come: "Whoever listens to the voice of the Torah in this world will be privileged to listen to the voice of which it is written, 'The voice of mirth and the voice of gladness, the voice of the bridegroom and the voice of the bride' (Jeremiah 16:9)." According to this midrash, "Moses said to Israel: 'Whoever listens to the words of the Torah is exalted in both worlds, so be diligent to listen to the words of the Torah.'"

***Blessed shall you be in the city*** (28:3). According to *Sh'mot Rabbah* 7.5, "in the city" refers to rewards for precepts performed in the city—including *challah* (dough offering; see Numbers 15:18–21), *tzitzit* (tassels), sukkah, and the kindling of the Sabbath lights. While only men must fulfill *tzitzit* and sukkah, rabbinic Judaism considered *challah* and the kindling of Sabbath lights (*hadlakat nerot*) to be specifically female ritual responsibilities. Together with observance of the laws connected with the *niddah* (menstruating woman), these three women's obligations were known in rabbinic parlance by the acronym *ChaNaH*, which spells the name "Hannah," alluding to Samuel's mother—whose supplication to God in I Samuel 2:1–10 is seen as the model of sincere prayer. According to Judith Hauptman, Mishnah *P'sachim* and its Tosefta both assume women's knowledge of key home rituals like separating challah or baking matzah. Rather than supervising the women, or assuming the duties themselves, men relied upon women's expertise in order to retain a state of sinlessness and ritual purity (*Women in the Rabbinic Kitchen*, forthcoming).

*The three women's obligations were known by the acronym ChaNaH ("Hannah").*

***And she who is most tender and dainty among you*** (28:56). Particularly horrific in this passage is the reference to the woman whose desperate hunger leads her to devour her own children. This image of the loving mother who turns deadly is a staple of folk literature; it appears in the Bible as a symbol of the world turned upside down by war and famine (II Kings 6:25–29; Lamentations 2:20). It also fits with the broader prophetic portrait of the nation as a formerly beautiful and prosperous woman now degraded and suffering (Amos 4:1–3; 5:1–3; Lamentations 1:1).

The Jewish historian Josephus underscores the depth of suffering during the war against Rome in 66–70 C.E. with the story of a wealthy woman of pedigree, Mary the daughter of Eleazar of Bethezuba, who roasts and eats half of her nursing baby: "She proceeded to an act of outrage on nature. Seizing her child, an infant at the breast, 'Poor babe,' she cried, 'amidst war, famine, and sedition, to what end should I preserve you?... Come, be food for me, to the rebels an avenging fury, and to the world a tale such as alone is wanting to the calamities of the Jews.' With these words she slew her son, and then, having roasted the body and devoured half of it, she covered up and stored the remainder. At once the rebels were upon her and, scenting the unholy odor, threatened her with instant death unless she produced what she had prepared. Replying that she had reserved a goodly portion for them also, she disclosed the remnants of her child" (*The Jewish War* 6.3.4 §§ 205–213). Even the Roman soldiers shrank away in horror from this sight, and the whole city shuddered at the abomination.

The same motifs appear in BT *Yoma* 38b and Midrash *Eichah Rabbah* 2.23 in a story about an infant named Doeg ben Joseph: "Every day his mother would measure him by handbreadths and would give his [added] weight in gold to the Temple. And when the enemy prevailed, she slaughtered him and ate him; and concerning her Jeremiah lamented, 'Shall the women eat their fruit, their new-born babes?' (Lamentations 2:20). Whereupon the Holy Spirit replied: 'Shall the priest and prophet be slain in the Sanctuary of יהוה?' (Lamentations 2:20)." For the Rabbis, the horror of the mother's actions parallels the divine outrage at the murder of Zechariah ben Jehoiada in the Temple, referred to in II Chronicles 24:20–22. Rabbinic attitudes toward women and their bodies are symbolic: the tender mother who cares for her child stands for the world as it ought to be, while the baby-devouring mother shows the world gone mad.

*—Claudia Setzer*

# Contemporary Reflection

THROUGHOUT OUR LIVES, we make numerous transitions and undergo various rites of passage, of both a formal and informal nature, consciously or unconsciously. Frequently these transitions are marked by ceremony and ritual of some kind: a *b'rit bat* or *b'rit milah*, a bat mitzvah or bar mitzvah, a *mikveh* immersion, a wedding. These are solemn moments, both for ourselves and for our closest relatives. Often they are accompanied by self-scrutiny, a vow, and a determination to improve, to "turn over a new leaf." The same is true of the beginning of each new year; indeed, this is the central theme of our prayers on both Rosh HaShanah and Yom Kippur. It also holds good when we move into a new home, freshly decorated, the walls clean and as yet unmarked by greasy fingers, the windows crystal-clear and gleaming, the empty rooms waiting to be filled with our lives. *Parashat Ki Tavo* begins with a ceremony that marks the entry into the Land of Israel (26:1–10): as an expression of gratitude, the people are to bring a basket filled with the first fruits of the land's bounty and to recount the events that led to the long-awaited settlement of the land.

When Benjamin Ze'ev (Theodor) Herzl gave expression to his extraordinary prophetic vision of a Jewish state in both *Der Judenstaat* (The Jews' State) and *Altneuland* (Old-New Land), he described a new community, one in which the land would be developed through science and technology, in which there would be tolerance in all spheres, and which would be organized socially on a cooperative ("mutualist") basis. The pioneers of the Second Aliyah, motivated by similar lofty ideals, developed precisely this kind of cooperative way of life when they founded the *kvutzot* and kibbutzim that became a hallmark of the new socialist communities—and eventually of the autonomous State of Israel. The Declaration of Independence drawn up by the founders of the state in 1948 also proclaimed equality of all citizens, irrespective of race, religion, or gender. Fundamental concepts of social justice, many of which are rooted in the precepts of Deuteronomy, ground much of the legislation passed by Israel's Knesset (Parliament) from its inception. Indeed, Israel was one of the first countries to pass a law stipulating equality between women and men. For most of the first fifty years of its existence, Israel was a welfare state. Underlying this new venture was not only divine promise but also the memory of past suffering, both recent and long gone by. When Herzl had presented his amazing plan to the Rothschild family, requesting their financial help in turning dream into reality, he wrote: "We are talking about a simple old matter—the exodus from Egypt."

*As a people, wherever we are, we have a remarkable and noble mission.*

Almost the entire book of Deuteronomy is a reprise, not only of the events of the forty years in the wilderness (which the people Moses is addressing have not witnessed themselves), but also of the commandments first encapsulated in the giving of the Decalogue at Sinai and later elaborated in the long, detailed catalogues of precepts and prohibitions. Now, in *Ki Tavo* and the passages that follow, the time has come to look toward the entry into the new home, to review the covenant, and to rededicate oneself—individually and as a people—by first acknowledging the fact that God has fulfilled the promise given to our forebears. This is to be immediately followed by an expression of awareness of past suffering—not necessarily one's own, but that of the collective. Remembrance of things past is an essential part of developing a new identity, beginning a new existence. The formulation of this memory in the First Fruits ceremony, with its reference to the "fugitive" or "wandering Aramean" (26:5), surely stirs within the modern reader recollections of the trials and tribulations of Jews in the Diaspora, which culminated in the unprecedented horrors of the Holocaust. The purpose of these recollections is to stimulate us to behave differently from those who oppressed us—to give to "the stranger, the fatherless, and the widow, that they may eat their fill" (26:12).

Being the favored of God entails duties and responsibilities. Failure to observe is to be cursed; obedience brings blessings, prosperity, fruitfulness. Above all, doing God's bidding means that Israel will be established as "God's holy people" (28:9) and will be "the head, not the tail" (28:13). In contrast, the detailed, terrifyingly graphic list of horrors that will be heaped upon the people if they fail to abide by God's laws ends with perhaps the direst of warnings: to be scattered among all the peoples "from one end of the earth to another" (28:64) and, worst of all, to become slaves once again (28:68).

The message of *parashat Ki Tavo* applies to us even now, whether we live in Israel or in the Diaspora. To justify Israel's existence as a Jewish state and homeland, it must forever strive to be a "light unto the nations" and not a state like any other. As a people, wherever we are, we have a remarkable and noble mission—to fulfill God's precepts, whether they deal with our relationship to the Divine or—more concretely—with our relationships with our fellow human beings, all of whom have been created in the divine image.

*—Alice Shalvi*

# Voices

## The Land of the Patriarchs

Hara E. Person

*Deuteronomy 26:1–15*

In the land of the patriarchs
stones leak the dust of dried tears
and walls hang heavy with photographs of
your ancestors
who in each generation picked up and moved
again
speaking to their children always in accents.

At dusk on the kibbutz windows open
houses begin to breathe once again
the night air carries conversations like scent
across distances
and the sweet-sour smell of the *refet* seeps
into our skin.
You burrow into me
one on either side,
like kittens you curl and unfurl
in this unfamiliar bed,
looking for just the right spot against my arm,
my hip, my chest, my neck.

In the day the white hot air sweeps into the
valley,
hanging like a curtain over bushes, trees,
tractors, buildings.
Fans whir and click,
trying to break up the thick heat
but the air is too heavy with memory
too laden with stories,
and instead it falls with a thud over the houses,
wisps of scorching air trying to enter the
shuttered windows
and curl under the shut doors.
It is a heat that slashes in its angry rage,
that suffocates with its jealous clasp.

The land of Abraham, Isaac, Jacob,
and your father,
a land so rich in layers of history,
so overburdened with purpose and destiny
that the very earth crumbles to pieces in
your fist
and swirls up in eddies as you run barefoot,
your feet slap slap slapping the ground
with your newly discovered un-Brooklyn
freedom.

Tonight I am your motherland.
For now, you belong here against me
entwined around each other,
in the twisted, too-small sheets
that wind around your soft bodies as you
dig into sleep.
For now I hold you tight and protected
safe and rooted in my embrace.

## Thankful

Ruth Fainlight

*Deuteronomy 26:4–11*

Nothing ever happens more than once.
The next time is never like before.
What you thought you learned doesn't apply.
Something is different. And just as real.
For which you might be thankful after all.

## *Still Dreaming of Home*

Merle Feld

*Deuteronomy 26:1–3*

And isn't that what nesting
is all about, that creative urge
when a new baby is on the way,
the urge men mock
or marvel at—

the drive to make a place
protected and pleasing—
we need that bit of fresh paint
and calico. As the body prepares
for the big day of crowning

and pushing, the heart and the hands
prepare a home, full of hope
that this time around
the human family
will not fail.

## *The Wild Heart*

Robin Becker

*Deuteronomy 28*

Taught, like all Jewish kids, to curse a boast,
or any declaration of good luck, I refuse!
I bless the day we ran smack into
each other on Sixth Avenue. I'll let you
*toi, toi, toi* with my old bubbe. OK, I can't—
it's true—stop thinking I'll pay for this:
renounce the gods of joy, betray my principles,
recant.
Oh darling, I'd like to surrender my one-
wrong-move philosophy, the slippery slope,
the fears of unwed motherhood, botulism,
poor expense records, impractical outer
garments.
Today I put my faith in our natural gifts—
good humor, good friends, the nick-of-time—
in your wild heart that inclines toward mine.

## *Requests*

Esther Raab (transl. Catherine Shaw and Moshe Dor)

*Deuteronomy 28:1–14*

I want beautiful trees—
and not wars!
and a coat of many colors
and not uniforms
for all my dear ones;
I want rain
and green furrows
and houses
full of babies;
a calendar of alliances
and a "brotherhood plaza"
and lightning and thunder—
in the sky;
and bountiful rains
on earth
and a pink crocus
in the ravines;
and pinecones
on a scented bed
of pine needles—
and bulbul birds rejoicing
among leafy orchards
and sails of peace
on the Mediterranean;
and white chrysanthemums
in the parks, their fall maneuvers;
and red balls rolling
along the paths
and the sleeves
of babies' garments signaling tranquility
on clotheslines.

## *Teach Me, O God, a Blessing*

Lea Goldberg (transl. Pnina Peli)

*Deuteronomy 28:1–14*

Teach me, O God, a blessing, a prayer
On the mystery of a withered leaf
On ripened fruit so fair,
On the freedom to see, to sense,
To breathe, to know, to hope, to despair.

Teach my lips a blessing, a hymn of praise,
As each morning and night
You renew Your days,
Lest my day be as the one before
Lest routine set my ways.

## *Prayers I*

Kadya Molodowsky (transl. Kathryn Hellerstein)

*Deuteronomy 28*

Don't let me fall
Like a stone that drops on the hard ground.
And don't let my hands become dry
As the twigs of a tree
When the wind beats down the last leaves.
And when the storm rips dust from the earth
Angry and howling,
Don't let me become the last fly
Trembling terrified on a windowpane.
Don't let me fall.
I have so much prayer,
But, as a blade of Your grass in a distant, wild
  field
Loses a seed in the lap of the earth
And dies away,
Sow in me Your living breath,
As You sow a seed in the earth.

## *Prayer for my Son*

Elaine Feinstein

*Deuteronomy 28:15–68*

Most things I worry over never happen,
but this, disguised in embarrassment,
turned risky in a day. Two years ago,
from the furthest edge of a blue sky,
an illness snatched his livelihood away.

Justice, Lord? How is this just? I
muttered, as if every generation must
learn the lesson again: there is
no special privilege protecting us.
He lay across his futon, white and thin

—the QEH sold out, his dep chosen—
in double torment. No one could comfort him.
I would have kissed the feet
of any holy man—as the Shumanite
woman did—to have the Lord relent.

But what since the miracle of his recovery?
Petty angers, like a girlish sulk. Forgive
me such ingratitude. Let him only live
with grace, unthreatened, on the sound of his
  flute
—and I'll stop clamouring for sweeter fruit.

# נִצָּבִים ✦ Nitzavim

## DEUTERONOMY 29:9–30:20

## Covenantal Choices

PARASHAT NITZAVIM ("stand") contains the bulk of Moses' third and final speech in the book of Deuteronomy, his last exhortation in Moab to observe the covenant. In this address, which began at the end of the previous parashah (29:1–8), Moses foreshadows the full sequence of iniquity, judgment, repentance, and deliverance that he predicts Israel will experience. He concludes his words with an impassioned plea to his audience to "choose life" (30:19) by adhering to the *torah* (Teaching), a choice that will guarantee peace and prosperity.

Each of the three units of *parashat Nitzavim* brings out its two governing themes—presence versus absence, and exposure versus concealment. The first part of the parashah (29:9–28) emphasizes the inclusion of every single member of the community in the covenant and their participation in the covenant ceremony. Women and men, officials and laborers, those standing before Moses in Moab and future generations—all commit themselves to uphold the terms of the covenant. This commitment leads to a warning against secret disobedient behavior, followed by a depiction of the fierce judgment God will unleash upon the land and the people if they turn away from God.

The second part of the parashah (30:1–10) opens with a promise of restoration once the people repent. Repeatedly, here and in the subsequent unit, Moses calls upon the people to love God with all their hearts and souls (vv. 6, 16, 20). This formulaic language is familiar from elsewhere in Deuteronomy (particularly 6:5), reminding the people that they must fulfill their part of the covenant through their fierce loyalty to God and God's teachings.

The third part of the parashah (30:11–20) returns to the subject of the covenant and the contrast between the overt and the covert. Moses assures the people that the "Instruction" (*mitzvah*) is not hidden or beyond reach, but is close and obtainable (30:11–14). He stresses that God gives each individual and the entire people two clear choices: "life and prosperity, death and adversity" (30:15). With heaven and earth as witnesses to the covenant, Moses implores the people to choose life instead of death, blessing instead of curse (v. 19).

*A hallmark of this parashah is its mention of women as present at the covenant ceremony.*

One of the hallmarks of this parashah is the inclusion of women in the list of social groups participating in the covenant ceremony. The explicit mention of women in 29:10 leaves no doubt that women are part of the people obliged to follow God's covenant. Nevertheless, their position in the list designates their lower status in ancient Israelite society (see at 29:9–10). The parashah refers to women again in 29:17 as part of a list of possible sinners. Thus, the text affirms that women and men alike, not only those preparing to enter the Promised Land but also the generations to follow, have the potential either to break or to maintain the covenant: it is "in your mouth and in your heart, to observe it" (30:14).

—*Dalit Rom-Shiloni*

## *Outline*

I. The Covenant Ceremony (29:9–28)

- A. Participation in the ceremony and commitment to the covenant (vv. 9–14)
- B. Concealed offense and overt judgment (vv. 15–20)
- C. Lesson learned from the destruction (vv. 21–27)
- D. Concealed and overt acts (v. 28)

II. Repentance and Restoration from Exile (30:1–10)

III. The Choice
*Life or Death, Blessing or Curse* (30:11–20)

- A. Encouragement that this instruction is not beyond reach (vv. 11–14)
- B. Charge: choose life and prosperity versus death and adversity (vv. 15–20)

You stand this day, all of you, before your God יהוה—you tribal heads, you elders, and you

כט 9 אַתֶּ֨ם נִצָּבִ֤ים הַיּוֹם֙ כֻּלְּכֶ֔ם לִפְנֵ֖י
יְהוָ֣ה אֱלֹהֵיכֶ֑ם רָאשֵׁיכֶ֣ם שִׁבְטֵיכֶ֗ם זִקְנֵיכֶ֙ם

## *The Covenant Ceremony* (29:9–28)

This unit emphasizes the full participation of all the people—women and men from all segments of the community—in the ceremony that establishes the covenant between God and Israel.

### PARTICIPATION IN THE CEREMONY AND COMMITMENT TO THE COVENANT (29:9–14)

The two phrases *avar bi-vrit* (entered into a covenant; v. 11) and *karat b'rit* (made a covenant; v. 13) designate ratifying a covenant by accepting its terms. In covenant rituals, *k-r-t* (whose basic meaning is "to cut") refers to the cutting of animals, and *e-b-r* (whose basic meaning is "to cross over") signifies the passing between the parts of the animal (see at Genesis 15:10; Jeremiah 34:18–19). Although this part of the parashah does not describe the covenant celebration, other biblical texts and ancient Near Eastern evidence indicate that sacrificial offerings were part of the acceptance of a covenant (see Genesis 31:44–54; Exodus 24:1–8; Deuteronomy 27:1–8). Furthermore, this section accentuates three conceptual angles of the covenant: its clear hierarchy of the parties, in that it is the people who "cross over" into God's covenant (v. 11); its content (v. 12); and the people's commitment to it, whether present in the ceremony or even absent from it (v. 14).

*9–10.* The inclusiveness described here is a unique feature of the Moab covenant. Compare the general term "the people" used to characterize the participation in the Sinai covenant (Exodus 19:9–13; 24:3, 7). Whereas the text in Exodus raises the question of whether or not women stood at Sinai (see *parashat Yitro*, pp. 407–424), here there is no doubt that both women and men are the recipients of God's teachings. The detailed list in this passage mentions various groups according to their social status. Verse 9 opens with leaders and concludes with "all the men of Israel"; v. 10 adds those dependent on the aforementioned men as heads of the household: children, women, and foreign workers. [While in some senses householders' senior wives were dependent, in other senses their status was complementary to that of their spouses and higher than that of other male members of the household. See further "Women in Ancient Israel—An Overview," p. xli. —*Ed.*]

*9. **You stand... before יהוה.*** This phrase designates one's presence in front of an authority (as in Exodus 7:15; 34:2).

***this day.*** The first part of Moses' speech (29:1–8, at the end of *parashat Ki Tavo*) looked back on key events in the past and the lessons to learn from

This articulation of free will has been central to Jewish self-understanding for centuries.

ANOTHER VIEW ➤ *1228*

The Torah belongs to every one of us, not just to experts—or to men alone.

CONTEMPORARY REFLECTION ➤ *1230*

All future generations of Israel, including all future converts, were at Sinai.

POST-BIBLICAL INTERPRETATIONS ➤ *1228*

I used to mumble many words in the prayerbook... until dear Clara was felled by a stroke.

VOICES ➤ *1232*

officials, all the men of Israel, [10]you children, you
women, even the stranger within your camp, from
woodchopper to water drawer—[11]to enter into the
covenant of your God יהוה, which your God יהוה is
concluding with you this day, with its sanctions;
[12]in order to establish you this day as God's people
and in order to be your God, as promised you and
as sworn to your fathers Abraham, Isaac, and Jacob.
[13]I make this covenant, with its sanctions, not with
you alone, [14]but both with those who are standing
here with us this day before our God יהוה and with
those who are not with us here this day.

[15]Well you know that we dwelt in the land of

וְשֹׁטְרֵיכֶם כֹּל אִישׁ יִשְׂרָאֵל׃ 10 טַפְּכֶם
נְשֵׁיכֶם וְגֵרְךָ אֲשֶׁר בְּקֶרֶב מַחֲנֶיךָ מֵחֹטֵב
עֵצֶיךָ עַד שֹׁאֵב מֵימֶיךָ׃ 11 לְעָבְרְךָ בִּבְרִית
יְהוָה אֱלֹהֶיךָ וּבְאָלָתוֹ אֲשֶׁר יְהוָה אֱלֹהֶיךָ
כֹּרֵת עִמְּךָ הַיּוֹם׃ 12 לְמַעַן הָקִים־אֹתְךָ
הַיּוֹם ׀ לוֹ לְעָם וְהוּא יִהְיֶה־לְּךָ לֵאלֹהִים
כַּאֲשֶׁר דִּבֶּר־לָךְ וְכַאֲשֶׁר נִשְׁבַּע לַאֲבֹתֶיךָ
לְאַבְרָהָם לְיִצְחָק וּלְיַעֲקֹב׃ 13 וְלֹא אִתְּכֶם
לְבַדְּכֶם אָנֹכִי כֹּרֵת אֶת־הַבְּרִית הַזֹּאת
וְאֶת־הָאָלָה הַזֹּאת׃ 14 כִּי אֶת־אֲשֶׁר יֶשְׁנוֹ
פֹּה עִמָּנוּ עֹמֵד הַיּוֹם לִפְנֵי יְהוָה אֱלֹהֵינוּ
וְאֵת אֲשֶׁר אֵינֶנּוּ פֹּה עִמָּנוּ הַיּוֹם׃
15 כִּי־אַתֶּם יְדַעְתֶּם אֵת אֲשֶׁר־יָשַׁבְנוּ בְּאֶרֶץ

them; now the focus shifts to the present moment and even to the future. The leitmotif "this day" (here and in v. 14) functions as a message to the double audience of Deuteronomy, namely, the implicit audience at the time of Moses and the audience contemporary with the author(s) of the book of Deuteronomy, centuries later. The ceremony validates the covenant's power to obligate the descendants to the treaty and to abide by its stipulations.

***you tribal heads.*** [The text identifies five of the subgroups listed in vv. 9–10 (tribal heads, elders, officials, children, women) via a second-person plural masculine suffix. In order to convey the understanding that each of these subgroups is part of the larger collective whom Moses addresses in this passage, the present translation has rendered the suffix "your" as "you." —*Ed.*]

***10. you children, you women.*** Within the groups enumerated in this verse, "children" appear prior to "women" (as in Numbers 32:26; but compare the opposite order in Deuteronomy 3:19; 20:14; 31:12). Women are likewise mentioned last in the common triplet of socially marginal people: stranger, fatherless, widow (see 14:29; 27:19).

***stranger.*** See at 10:19.

***from woodchopper to water drawer.*** These two types of laborers exemplify specific tasks performed by resident non-Israelites (the "stranger" included in the covenant) (see Joshua 9:21, 23, 27).

***12. as promised you and as sworn to your fathers.*** Verse 12 alludes to two separate covenant traditions. The first recalls the promise originally made to the Israelites in Egypt (Exodus 6:7; also Leviticus 26:12); the second refers to the covenant with Abraham (Genesis 17:7–8). The two traditions coalesce here as they each emphasize the institution of a mutual relationship between God and Israel. (On *avot* translated here as "fathers" instead of "ancestors" as in 30:9, see at 4:31.)

***14. those who are not with us here this day.*** That is, future generations. Binding the descendants to the covenant exemplifies its dynamic force, as it expects an everlasting renewal of this fundamental covenant.

## CONCEALED OFFENSE AND OVERT JUDGMENT (29:15–20)

Addressing the people in general, Moses raises another possible transgression of the covenant. He cautions the Israelites that individuals ("some man

Egypt and that we passed through the midst of various other nations through which you passed; [16]and you have seen the detestable things and the fetishes of wood and stone, silver and gold, that they keep. [17]Perchance there is among you some man or woman, or some clan or tribe, whose heart is even now turning away from our God יהוה to go and worship the gods of those nations—perchance there is among you a stock sprouting poison weed and wormwood. [18]When hearing the words of these sanctions, such a one may imagine a special immunity, thinking, "I shall be safe, though I fol-

מִצְרָ֑יִם וְאֵ֥ת אֲשֶׁר־עֲבַרְנוּ֛ בְּקֶ֥רֶב הַגּוֹיִ֖ם
אֲשֶׁ֥ר עֲבַרְתֶּֽם׃ 16 וַתִּרְאוּ֙ אֶת־שִׁקּ֣וּצֵיהֶ֔ם
וְאֵ֖ת גִּלֻּלֵיהֶ֑ם עֵ֣ץ וָאֶ֔בֶן כֶּ֥סֶף וְזָהָ֖ב אֲשֶׁ֥ר
עִמָּהֶֽם׃ 17 פֶּן־יֵ֣שׁ בָּ֠כֶם אִ֣ישׁ אוֹ־אִשָּׁ֞ה א֧וֹ
מִשְׁפָּחָ֣ה אוֹ־שֵׁ֗בֶט אֲשֶׁ֨ר לְבָב֜וֹ פֹנֶ֤ה הַיּוֹם֙
מֵעִם֙ יְהֹוָ֣ה אֱלֹהֵ֔ינוּ לָלֶ֣כֶת לַעֲבֹ֔ד אֶת־
אֱלֹהֵ֖י הַגּוֹיִ֣ם הָהֵ֑ם פֶּן־יֵ֣שׁ בָּכֶ֗ם שֹׁ֛רֶשׁ פֹּרֶ֥ה
רֹ֖אשׁ וְלַעֲנָֽה׃ 18 וְהָיָ֡ה בְּשָׁמְעוֹ֩ אֶת־דִּבְרֵ֨י
הָאָלָ֜ה הַזֹּ֗את וְהִתְבָּרֵ֨ךְ בִּלְבָב֤וֹ לֵאמֹר֙

or woman") or larger groups ("clan or tribe") might be tempted to worship other gods. While the offense is concealed, the divine wrath that follows as punishment is apparent and known.

In contrast to Deuteronomy 13 and 17:2–7, which concern cases where the community's fortune may be determined by the misconduct of but a few individuals, the present section focuses on a different aspect of the situation: singling out the persons who sin and threatening them with total annihilation. Deuteronomy's notion of communal responsibility and retribution still governs this passage; but this section also emphasizes the notion that the community is formed from its many individuals, each of whom is personally accountable for her or his own actions.

*15–16.* Idolatry is usually connected to Canaan and Canaanite influences. Yet this passage mentions worshipping other gods as a temptation to which the people were exposed earlier, in Egypt and on the journey to the Land (mostly by the nations of Transjordan, such as the Moabite women in Numbers 25:1–5). Nevertheless, these verses do not suggest that Israel as a nation was actually carried away to perform idolatrous practices prior to the settlement in the Land (compare the explicit accusations in Ezekiel 20:5–9; Joshua 24:14; Numbers 25:1–3).

*17. **man or woman.*** As in 17:2, 5, the text acknowledges the possibility that either women or men might lead the people astray. Cozbi and the Moabites in Numbers 25:1–18 illustrate this threat with regard to women.

***whose heart is even now turning away from our God יהוה.*** In contrast to Deuteronomy 13 and 17:2–7, which emphasize visible transgressions, our parashah focuses on the hidden thought and intention and on following the willful or the stiffened heart (*bishrirut lev*). The heart, which in Deuteronomy is often the innermost organ of intellectual acknowledgment and piety, serves frequently in the Bible as the secret place for self-reflection (as in Ecclesiastes 2:1, 15), personal or political evil-intent (as in Genesis 27:41; I Kings 12:26), or even for theologically illegitimate thoughts (as in 8:17; 9:4; Isaiah 14:13; 47:10). This last context seems to be the background of our passage's repeated usage of the heart as the organ where secret offense against God is concealed.

***poison weed and wormwood.*** These two plants appear together elsewhere in the Bible, where the poisonous nature of the one and the sharp bitterness of the other serve as metaphors to illustrate various points: social injustice (Hosea 10:4; Amos 5:7; 6:12); punishment for disobedience, particularly in worshipping other gods (Jeremiah 8:14; 9:14); and memories of distress and misery (Lamentations 3:19). Hence, this context is unique, as the plants express the danger that the sinner may cause to those around them.

low my own willful heart"—to the utter ruin of
moist and dry alike. [19]יהוה will never forgive such
individuals. Rather, יהוה's anger and passion will
rage against them, till every sanction recorded in
this book comes down upon them, and יהוה blots
out their name from under heaven.
[20][As for such a clan or tribe,] יהוה will single it
out from all the tribes of Israel for misfortune, in
accordance with all the sanctions of the covenant
recorded in this book of Teaching. [21]And later generations will ask—the children who succeed you,
and foreigners who come from distant lands and see
the plagues and diseases that יהוה has inflicted upon
that land, [22]all its soil devastated by sulfur and salt,
beyond sowing and producing, no grass growing in
it, just like the upheaval of Sodom and Gomorrah,

שָׁל֣וֹם יִֽהְיֶה־לִּ֔י כִּ֛י בִּשְׁרִר֥וּת לִבִּ֖י אֵלֵ֑ךְ
לְמַ֛עַן סְפ֥וֹת הָרָוָ֖ה אֶת־הַצְּמֵאָֽה׃ 19 לֹֽא־
יֹאבֶ֣ה יְהֹוָה֮ סְלֹ֣חַ לוֹ֒ כִּ֣י אָ֠ז יֶעְשַׁ֨ן אַף־יְהֹוָ֤ה
וְקִנְאָתוֹ֙ בָּאִ֣ישׁ הַה֔וּא וְרָ֤בְצָה בּוֹ֙ כָּל־הָ֣אָלָ֔ה
הַכְּתוּבָ֖ה בַּסֵּ֣פֶר הַזֶּ֑ה וּמָחָ֤ה יְהֹוָה֙ אֶת־שְׁמ֔וֹ
מִתַּ֖חַת הַשָּׁמָֽיִם׃
20 וְהִבְדִּיל֤וֹ יְהֹוָה֙ לְרָעָ֔ה מִכֹּ֖ל שִׁבְטֵ֣י
יִשְׂרָאֵ֑ל כְּכֹל֙ אָל֣וֹת הַבְּרִ֔ית הַכְּתוּבָ֕ה בְּסֵ֥פֶר
הַתּוֹרָ֖ה הַזֶּֽה׃ 21 וְאָמַ֞ר הַדּ֣וֹר הָאַחֲר֗וֹן
בְּנֵיכֶם֙ אֲשֶׁ֤ר יָק֙וּמוּ֙ מֵאַֽחֲרֵיכֶ֔ם וְהַנָּכְרִ֕י
אֲשֶׁ֥ר יָבֹ֖א מֵאֶ֣רֶץ רְחוֹקָ֑ה וְ֠רָאוּ אֶת־מַכּ֞וֹת
הָאָ֤רֶץ הַהִוא֙ וְאֶת־תַּ֣חֲלֻאֶ֔יהָ אֲשֶׁר־חִלָּ֥ה
יְהֹוָ֖ה בָּֽהּ׃ 22 גָּפְרִ֣ית וָמֶלַח֮ שְׂרֵפָ֣ה כָל־
אַרְצָהּ֒ לֹ֤א תִזָּרַע֙ וְלֹ֣א תַצְמִ֔חַ וְלֹא־יַעֲלֶ֥ה
בָ֖הּ כָּל־עֵ֑שֶׂב כְּמַהְפֵּכַ֞ת סְדֹ֣ם וַעֲמֹרָ֗ה

**18. *to the utter ruin of moist and dry alike.*** This idiom is puzzling. It seems to express the inevitable destructive consequences to the righteous as well as to the sinner.

***19–20.*** This passage describes the divine wrath and judgment on the transgressor as an implementation of the covenant's sanctions written in the book of Teaching (*torah*) (see 28:58). The language is in the third-person singular, thus suggesting the possibility of individual retribution (see at vv. 15–20 above), a concept that existed alongside the notion of collective retribution. While the entire community suffers as a result of the sins of the few, individual offenders still pay for their misdeeds, for they receive special punishments.

## LESSONS LEARNED FROM THE DESTRUCTION (29:21–27)

In a sharp change, the text moves from the individual judgment for a concealed sin (29:15–20) to the apparent destruction of both the land and people. In contrast to vv. 19–20, vv. 21–27 present a different concept of retribution: collective judgment and punishment for disobedience that affects even the land's ecological systems. The devastation becomes a lesson for later Israelite generations and foreigners who ask why God decimated the land (vv. 23–27). Destruction and exile are considered justifiable actions that God executes in reaction to Israel's sins. This perspective may reflect Israel and Judah's historical experience, like that of the entire region west of the Euphrates River, when they faced the aggressive Neo-Assyrian Empire (in the 9th–7th centuries, resulting in the destruction of the northern kingdom of Israel in 722 B.C.E.) and then the Neo-Babylonian regime (in the late 7th–6th centuries, resulting in the destruction of Jerusalem in 586 B.C.E.).

**22. *sulfur and salt . . . just like the upheaval of Sodom and Gomorrah.*** God rained sulfurous fire over Sodom and Gomorrah (Genesis 19:24). The well-remembered tradition of the fate of Sodom and Gomorrah (Genesis 18–19) is adapted here to describe the ecological consequences of destruction. The text posits no human enemy or human warfare; instead God, as divine Warrior, acts with great might against God's own people and land. This sort

Admah and Zeboiim, which יהוה overthrew in
fierce anger—23 all nations will ask, "Why did יהוה
do thus to this land? Wherefore that awful wrath?"
24 They will be told, "Because they forsook the
covenant that יהוה, God of their ancestors, made
with them upon freeing them from the land of
Egypt; 25 they turned to the service of other gods
and worshiped them, gods whom they had not
experienced and whom [God] had not allotted to
them. 26 So יהוה was incensed at that land and
brought upon it all the curses recorded in this book.
27 יהוה uprooted them from their soil in anger, fury,
and great wrath, and cast them into another land, as
is still the case."

אַדְמָה וצביים וּצְבוֹיִם אֲשֶׁר הָפַךְ יְהוָה
בְּאַפּוֹ וּבַחֲמָתוֹ׃ 23 וְאָמְרוּ כָּל־הַגּוֹיִם עַל־
מֶה עָשָׂה יְהוָה כָּכָה לָאָרֶץ הַזֹּאת מֶה חֳרִי
הָאַף הַגָּדוֹל הַזֶּה׃ 24 וְאָמְרוּ עַל אֲשֶׁר עָזְבוּ
אֶת־בְּרִית יְהוָה אֱלֹהֵי אֲבֹתָם אֲשֶׁר כָּרַת
עִמָּם בְּהוֹצִיאוֹ אֹתָם מֵאֶרֶץ מִצְרָיִם׃
25 וַיֵּלְכוּ וַיַּעַבְדוּ אֱלֹהִים אֲחֵרִים וַיִּשְׁתַּחֲווּ
לָהֶם אֱלֹהִים אֲשֶׁר לֹא־יְדָעוּם וְלֹא חָלַק
לָהֶם׃ 26 וַיִּחַר־אַף יְהוָה בָּאָרֶץ הַהִוא
לְהָבִיא עָלֶיהָ אֶת־כָּל־הַקְּלָלָה הַכְּתוּבָה
בַּסֵּפֶר הַזֶּה׃ 27 וַיִּתְּשֵׁם יְהוָה מֵעַל אַדְמָתָם
בְּאַף וּבְחֵמָה וּבְקֶצֶף גָּדוֹל וַיַּשְׁלִכֵם אֶל־
אֶרֶץ אַחֶרֶת כַּיּוֹם הַזֶּה׃

of ecological disaster stands in contrast to the divine oath after the deluge: "Never again will I bring doom upon the world on account of what people do" (Genesis 8:21).

*25. gods whom they had not experienced.* In contrast to relying on gods the people had not experienced, Deuteronomy repeatedly calls attention to the fact that the Israelites witnessed with their own eyes the many marvelous deeds that God performed on their behalf (for instance, 7:19; 11:7).

***and whom* [*God*] *had not allotted to them.*** The concept that God allocated other gods for the foreign nations to worship implies that Israel was not fully monotheistic at this stage. The statement reflects a belief called monolatry, which involves the allegiance to one god, but the recognition of the existence of other deities (see also at 4:19–20). Deuteronomy repeatedly makes the point that because Israel was chosen as God's people, they are forbidden from worshiping any other gods (as in 4:15–20; 5:7–9).

*27.* ***יהוה uprooted them from their soil in anger.*** This verse applies agricultural language to the concept of exile, which is treated as another divine action resulting from God's wrath.

***and cast them.*** Heb. *vayashlicheim.* Torah scribes write this verb with an enlarged letter *lamed* in the middle. While later interpreters have sought to derive meaning from this practice, the reason for this custom is unknown. (A midrashic explanation is that the large *lamed* designates the beginning of a new word, which leads one to read these letters with a different punctuation: *v'yesh lachem,* meaning, "But you [will] have [God in another land]" [David Zvi Hoffman, *Deuteronomy,* 1961, p. 516]. This midrashic reading provides a significant ideological comment for those in exile, reassuring them of God's presence among the people in a foreign land; compare Ezekiel 11:16.)

***"as is still the case."*** This phrase reveals the possible time of authorship of this section. Since the people presently experience exile (as in 4:29–31; 30:1–10), this suggests the text was written during the Babylonian exile. Another explanation is that these words were secondarily introduced into an earlier original pre-exilic passage that was later updated.

28 Concealed acts concern our God יהוה; but with overt acts, it is for us and our children ever to apply all the provisions of this Teaching.

30 When all these things befall you—the blessing and the curse that I have set before you—and you take them to heart amidst the various nations to which your God יהוה has banished

28 הַנִּסְתָּרֹת לַיהוָה אֱלֹהֵינוּ וְהַנִּגְלֹת לָנוּ
וּלְבָנֵינוּ עַד־עוֹלָם לַעֲשׂוֹת אֶת־כָּל־דִּבְרֵי
הַתּוֹרָה הַזֹּאת׃ ס

ל וְהָיָה כִי־יָבֹאוּ עָלֶיךָ כָּל־הַדְּבָרִים
הָאֵלֶּה הַבְּרָכָה וְהַקְּלָלָה אֲשֶׁר נָתַתִּי
לְפָנֶיךָ וַהֲשֵׁבֹתָ אֶל־לְבָבֶךָ בְּכָל־הַגּוֹיִם
אֲשֶׁר הִדִּיחֲךָ יְהוָה אֱלֹהֶיךָ שָׁמָּה׃

CONCEALED AND OVERT ACTS (29:28)

While this one enigmatic verse has accrued various interpretations over time, its possible plain meaning derives from context: the continuing opposition between the concealed and the overt in this parashah. One reading is that these are Moses' concluding words of assurance to the people. "Concealed acts" refer to sins committed by the individual in secret, thus only God can reveal and judge (following vv. 15–20), whereas "overt acts" refer to public sins of a group or of the whole collective, which human judges must punish according to "this Teaching" (*hatorah hazot*). Hence, the threat of destruction (vv. 21–27) stands as a punishment only if the people neglect their communal responsibility to punish individual sinners in order to save the innocent majority (so the medieval commentators Rashi and Nachmanides).

Another way to interpret this verse is to understand the concealed and the overt as time references. Hence, "concealed acts" are future events about which only God knows, such as the threatened destruction and exile (29:21–27) or the promised consolation and restoration (30:1–10). "Overt acts" are what God had revealed to the people concerning past divine deeds and the practical duties in God's Teaching (so Samuel R. Driver, *Deuteronomy*, 1902, p. 328, and others).

***28. it is for us and our children.*** Traditionally these two Hebrew words (*lanu ulvaneinu*) and the first letter following are written with extraordinary dots (*n'kudot*) over the letters, a scribal phenomenon that occurs in fifteen places throughout the Bible. In ancient manuscripts, such as the Qumran scrolls as well as Greek and Roman texts, dotted letters or words signify that they should be erased and clearly not pronounced. However, these biblical instances were exegetically reconsidered and the dots gained diverse symbolic values.

## *Repentance and Restoration from Exile* (30:1–10)

Following the blessings and curses in Deuteronomy 28, as well as the description of destruction and exile in 29:21–27, 30:1–10 functions to transition from judgment to salvation. Moses instructs the people on these future circumstances of national existence in exile, when reinstitution of the relationship with God will be a major issue. The theme of repentance stands out as a central topic, reflected in the fact that the verbal root *shuv* ("to turn or return") repeats as a key word in these verses. The sequence is clear: the initiative to repent should come from the people in exile, as individuals, and it will result in God's restoration of the people (vv. 2–3).

The root *shuv* holds several different meanings in its eight occurrences in this unit, all of which exemplify an internal process of change and transformation: return from the bad ways, regret, leaving the evil deeds behind, changing the way of life, and finally approaching God in a close relationship. The intertwining occurrences of the root *shuv*

2 וְשַׁבְתָּ֞ עַד־יְהֹוָ֤ה אֱלֹהֶ֙יךָ֙ וְשָׁמַעְתָּ֣ בְקֹל֔וֹ
כְּכֹ֛ל אֲשֶׁר־אָנֹכִ֥י מְצַוְּךָ֖ הַיּ֑וֹם אַתָּ֣ה וּבָנֶ֔יךָ
בְּכָל־לְבָבְךָ֖ וּבְכָל־נַפְשֶֽׁךָ׃ 3 וְשָׁ֨ב יְהֹוָ֧ה
אֱלֹהֶ֛יךָ אֶת־שְׁבוּתְךָ֖ וְרִחֲמֶ֑ךָ וְשָׁ֗ב וְקִבֶּצְךָ֙
מִכָּל־הָ֣עַמִּ֔ים אֲשֶׁ֧ר הֱפִיצְךָ֛ יְהֹוָ֥ה אֱלֹהֶ֖יךָ
שָֽׁמָּה׃ 4 אִם־יִהְיֶ֥ה נִֽדַּחֲךָ֖ בִּקְצֵ֣ה הַשָּׁמָ֑יִם
מִשָּׁ֗ם יְקַבֶּצְךָ֙ יְהֹוָ֣ה אֱלֹהֶ֔יךָ וּמִשָּׁ֖ם יִקָּחֶֽךָ׃
5 וֶהֱבִיאֲךָ֞ יְהֹוָ֣ה אֱלֹהֶ֗יךָ אֶל־הָאָ֛רֶץ אֲשֶׁר־
יָרְשׁ֥וּ אֲבֹתֶ֖יךָ וִֽירִשְׁתָּ֑הּ וְהֵיטִֽבְךָ֥ וְהִרְבְּךָ֖
מֵאֲבֹתֶֽיךָ׃
6 וּמָ֨ל יְהֹוָ֧ה אֱלֹהֶ֛יךָ אֶת־לְבָבְךָ֖ וְאֶת־לְבַ֣ב
זַרְעֶ֑ךָ לְאַהֲבָ֞ה אֶת־יְהֹוָ֧ה אֱלֹהֶ֛יךָ בְּכָל־
לְבָבְךָ֥ וּבְכָל־נַפְשְׁךָ֖ לְמַ֥עַן חַיֶּֽיךָ׃ 7 וְנָתַן֙
יְהֹוָ֣ה אֱלֹהֶ֔יךָ אֵ֚ת כָּל־הָאָל֣וֹת הָאֵ֔לֶּה עַל־
אֹיְבֶ֥יךָ וְעַל־שֹׂנְאֶ֖יךָ אֲשֶׁ֥ר רְדָפֽוּךָ׃ 8 וְאַתָּ֣ה
תָשׁ֔וּב וְשָׁמַעְתָּ֖ בְּק֣וֹל יְהֹוָ֑ה וְעָשִׂ֙יתָ֙ אֶת־כָּל־
מִצְוֺתָ֔יו אֲשֶׁ֛ר אָנֹכִ֥י מְצַוְּךָ֖ הַיּֽוֹם׃ 9 וְהוֹתִֽירְךָ֩
יְהֹוָ֨ה אֱלֹהֶ֜יךָ בְּכֹ֣ל ׀ מַעֲשֵׂ֣ה יָדֶ֗ךָ בִּפְרִ֨י בִטְנְךָ֜
וּבִפְרִ֧י בְהֶמְתְּךָ֛ וּבִפְרִ֥י אַדְמָתְךָ֖ לְטֹבָ֑ה כִּ֣י ׀
יָשׁ֣וּב יְהֹוָ֗ה לָשׂ֤וּשׂ עָלֶ֙יךָ֙ לְט֔וֹב כַּאֲשֶׁר־שָׂ֖שׂ

you, [2]and you return to your God יהוה, and you and your children heed God's command with all your heart and soul, just as I enjoin upon you this day, [3]then your God יהוה will restore your fortunes and take you back in love. [God] will bring you together again from all the peoples where your God יהוה has scattered you. [4]Even if your outcasts are at the ends of the world, from there your God יהוה will gather you, from there [God] will fetch you. [5]And your God יהוה will bring you to the land that your fathers possessed, and you shall possess it; and [God] will make you more prosperous and more numerous than your ancestors.

[6]Then your God יהוה will open up your heart and the hearts of your offspring—to love your God יהוה with all your heart and soul, in order that you may live. [7]Your God יהוה will inflict all those curses upon the enemies and foes who persecuted you. [8]You, however, will again heed יהוה and obey all the divine commandments that I enjoin upon you this day. [9]And your God יהוה will grant you abounding prosperity in all your undertakings, in your issue from the womb, your offspring from the cattle, and your produce from the soil. For יהוה will again delight in your well-being, as in that of your

emphasize the reciprocal nature of the God–human relationship. First, those in exile will "take to heart" (*vahasheivota*; literally, "your heart shall turn back") what has happened (v. 1), return (*v'shavta*) to God (v. 2), and obey God's teachings. In response, God will restore the people's fortune (*v'shav... et sh'vutcha*; literally, "return a return") and turn back (*v'shav*) to gather them to their land (v. 3). The people will again heed (*tashuv v'shamata*; literally, "turn back and heed") and be obedient to God (v. 8). As a result, God will again delight (*yashuv... lasus*; literally, "turn back and delight") in the people's well-being (v. 9), once they return (*tashuv*) to God with all their hearts and souls (v. 10).

*6. open up your heart.* Literally, "circumcise your heart." The metaphor of the circumcised heart exemplifies the profound internal transformation of each and every person. God needs to act upon the heart, where recognition of the sin develops (v. 2) and where full obedience and devotion reside (vv. 3, 10), in a circumcision-like procedure to ensure the permanency of this change. Deuteronomy previously mentioned circumcision of the heart ("cut away, therefore, the thickening about your hearts," 10:16) in its demand that the people not close their hearts and stiffen their necks. In contrast, the present circumcision of the heart is a divine action of grace (so Nachmanides), or maybe of compulsion (so according to the prophet Ezekiel, 11:19–20; 36:26–28).

*9. your issue from the womb.* See at 7:13; 28:4.

ancestors, 10 since you will be heeding your God יהוה and keeping the divine commandments and laws that are recorded in this book of the Teaching—once you return to your God יהוה with all your heart and soul.

11 Surely, this Instruction which I enjoin upon you this day is not too baffling for you, nor is it beyond reach. 12 It is not in the heavens, that you should say, "Who among us can go up to the heavens and get it for us and impart it to us, that we may observe it?" 13 Neither is it beyond the sea, that you should say, "Who among us can cross to the other side of the sea and get it for us and impart it to us, that we may observe it?" 14 No, the thing is very close to you, in your mouth and in your heart, to observe it.

עַל־אֲבֹתֶ֑יךָ׃ 10 כִּ֣י תִשְׁמַ֗ע בְּקוֹל֙ יְהֹוָ֣ה
אֱלֹהֶ֔יךָ לִשְׁמֹ֤ר מִצְוֺתָיו֙ וְחֻקֹּתָ֔יו הַכְּתוּבָ֕ה
בְּסֵ֥פֶר הַתּוֹרָ֖ה הַזֶּ֑ה כִּ֤י תָשׁוּב֙ אֶל־יְהֹוָ֣ה
אֱלֹהֶ֔יךָ בְּכׇל־לְבָבְךָ֖ וּבְכׇל־נַפְשֶֽׁךָ׃ ס
11 כִּ֚י הַמִּצְוָ֣ה הַזֹּ֔את אֲשֶׁ֛ר אָנֹכִ֥י מְצַוְּךָ֖
הַיּ֑וֹם לֹֽא־נִפְלֵ֥את הִוא֙ מִמְּךָ֔ וְלֹ֥א רְחֹקָ֖ה
הִֽוא׃ 12 לֹ֥א בַשָּׁמַ֖יִם הִ֑וא לֵאמֹ֗ר מִ֣י
יַעֲלֶה־לָּ֤נוּ הַשָּׁמַ֙יְמָה֙ וְיִקָּחֶ֣הָ לָּ֔נוּ וְיַשְׁמִעֵ֥נוּ
אֹתָ֖הּ וְנַעֲשֶֽׂנָּה׃ 13 וְלֹֽא־מֵעֵ֥בֶר לַיָּ֖ם הִ֑וא
לֵאמֹ֗ר מִ֣י יַעֲבׇר־לָ֜נוּ אֶל־עֵ֤בֶר הַיָּם֙ וְיִקָּחֶ֣הָ
לָּ֔נוּ וְיַשְׁמִעֵ֥נוּ אֹתָ֖הּ וְנַעֲשֶֽׂנָּה׃ 14 כִּֽי־
קָר֥וֹב אֵלֶ֛יךָ הַדָּבָ֖ר מְאֹ֑ד בְּפִ֥יךָ וּבִלְבָבְךָ֖
לַעֲשֹׂתֽוֹ׃ ס

## *The Choice*

### LIFE OR DEATH, BLESSING OR CURSE (30:11–20)

Moses' closing remarks in this unit resemble the concluding words of the book of Deuteronomy's prologue (the part that precedes the legal material): compare "See, this day I set before you..." (11:26) to "See, I set before you this day..." (30:15). Whereas in the earlier passage "blessing" and "curse" represent opposite alternatives, here Moses presents the people with a more detailed and radical choice, governed by the alternatives of life and death.

### ENCOURAGEMENT THAT THIS INSTRUCTION IS NOT BEYOND REACH (30:11–14)

This passage emphasizes that God's teaching ("the Instruction") is not unintelligible, but is within the realm of human comprehension. This is a polemic against the notion of wisdom as "hidden from the eyes of all living" (Job 28:21; also 42:2–3) or "elusive and deep" (Ecclesiastes 7:24; see also Proverbs 30:2–4, 18–20).

*11.* ***Instruction.*** Heb. *mitzvah*, a close parallel to *torah* ("Teaching," as in 29:28). Whereas the plural *mitzvot* is regularly translated as "commandments" (for instance, 4:2; 6:17), in the singular, *mitzvah* designates the legal corpus as a whole, the instruction which the people should follow in its entirety and by which they exemplify their devotion to God (as in 6:25; 8:1; 11:22; 15:5; 19:9). The noun holds this generic meaning also when it opens the tripartite cluster of *mitzvah*, *chukim*, and *mishpatim*, translated as "the Instruction—the laws and rules" (as in 6:1; 7:11).

*12.* ***It is not in the heavens.*** This verse accords with the general biblical perspective that emphasizes the human inability to reach heaven, the abode of God (Genesis 11; Proverbs 30:4), a theme profoundly anchored in Mesopotamian literature as well. The point is that this teaching is within reach, such that grasping it requires no supernatural help.

<sup>15</sup>See, I set before you this day life and prosperity, death and adversity. <sup>16</sup>For I command you this day, to love your God יהוה, to walk in God's ways, and to keep God's commandments, God's laws, and God's rules, that you may thrive and increase, and that your God יהוה may bless you in the land that you are about to enter and possess. <sup>17</sup>But if your heart turns away and you give no heed, and are lured into the worship and service of other gods, <sup>18</sup>I declare to you this day that you shall certainly perish; you shall not long endure on the soil that you are crossing the Jordan to enter and possess. <sup>19</sup>I call heaven and earth to witness against you this day: I have put before you life and death, blessing and curse. Choose life—if you and your offspring would live—<sup>20</sup>by loving your God יהוה, heeding God's commands, and holding fast to [God]. For thereby you shall have life and shall long endure upon the soil that יהוה swore to your fathers Abraham, Isaac, and Jacob, to give to them.

15 רְאֵ֨ה נָתַ֤תִּי לְפָנֶ֙יךָ֙ הַיּ֔וֹם אֶת־הַֽחַיִּ֖ים
וְאֶת־הַטּ֑וֹב וְאֶת־הַמָּ֖וֶת וְאֶת־הָרָֽע: 16 אֲשֶׁ֨ר
אָנֹכִ֣י מְצַוְּךָ֮ הַיּוֹם֒ לְאַהֲבָ֞ה אֶת־יְהֹוָ֤ה
אֱלֹהֶ֙יךָ֙ לָלֶ֣כֶת בִּדְרָכָ֔יו וְלִשְׁמֹ֛ר מִצְוֺתָ֥יו
וְחֻקֹּתָ֖יו וּמִשְׁפָּטָ֑יו וְחָיִ֣יתָ וְרָבִ֔יתָ וּבֵֽרַכְךָ֙
יְהֹוָ֣ה אֱלֹהֶ֔יךָ בָּאָ֕רֶץ אֲשֶׁר־אַתָּ֥ה בָֽא־שָׁ֖מָּה
לְרִשְׁתָּֽהּ: 17 וְאִם־יִפְנֶ֥ה לְבָֽבְךָ֖ וְלֹ֣א תִשְׁמָ֑ע
וְנִדַּחְתָּ֗ וְהִֽשְׁתַּחֲוִ֙יתָ֙ לֵֽאלֹהִ֣ים אֲחֵרִ֔ים
וַֽעֲבַדְתָּֽם: 18 הִגַּ֤דְתִּי לָכֶם֙ הַיּ֔וֹם כִּ֥י אָבֹ֖ד
תֹּאבֵד֑וּן לֹֽא־תַֽאֲרִיכֻ֤ן יָמִים֙ עַל־הָ֣אֲדָמָ֔ה
אֲשֶׁ֨ר אַתָּ֤ה עֹבֵר֙ אֶת־הַיַּרְדֵּ֔ן לָב֥וֹא שָׁ֖מָּה
לְרִשְׁתָּֽהּ: 19 הַעִדֹ֨תִי בָכֶ֣ם הַיּוֹם֮ אֶת־
הַשָּׁמַ֣יִם וְאֶת־הָאָרֶץ֒ הַֽחַיִּ֤ים וְהַמָּ֙וֶת֙ נָתַ֣תִּי
לְפָנֶ֔יךָ הַבְּרָכָ֖ה וְהַקְּלָלָ֑ה וּבָֽחַרְתָּ֙ בַּֽחַיִּ֔ים
לְמַ֥עַן תִּֽחְיֶ֖ה אַתָּ֥ה וְזַרְעֶֽךָ: 20 לְאַֽהֲבָה֙ אֶת־
יְהֹוָ֣ה אֱלֹהֶ֔יךָ לִשְׁמֹ֥עַ בְּקֹל֖וֹ וּלְדָבְקָה־ב֑וֹ כִּ֣י
ה֤וּא חַיֶּ֙יךָ֙ וְאֹ֣רֶךְ יָמֶ֔יךָ לָשֶׁ֣בֶת עַל־הָֽאֲדָמָ֗ה
אֲשֶׁר֩ נִשְׁבַּ֨ע יְהֹוָ֧ה לַֽאֲבֹתֶ֛יךָ לְאַבְרָהָ֛ם
לְיִצְחָ֥ק וּֽלְיַֽעֲקֹ֖ב לָתֵ֥ת לָהֶֽם: פ

• • • • • • • • • • • • • • • • • • • • • • • • • • • • • • •

## CHARGE: CHOOSE LIFE AND PROSPERITY VERSUS DEATH AND ADVERSITY (30:15–20)

Concluding his words on the covenant, obedience, the land, and blessing and curse, Moses offers a basic choice between two stark alternatives: life and death. He establishes a clear, logical connection between obedience to God and God's covenant on the one hand and the reward of life on the other, which entails prosperity and thriving upon the land (vv. 15–16). In contrast, disobedience will inevitably bring calamity in the land, adversity, and death (vv. 17–18). The passage moves from life to death to life, closing with a hopeful, positive perspective.

*19–20. Choose life . . . For thereby you shall have life.* Moses' last command to the people is not redundant. The two consecutive phrases present a close connection between an action and its reward. The verb "to live" and the noun "life" serve as key

words in this final passage, occurring interchangeably six times. In Deuteronomy, "life" refers to the reward for obeying specific laws (as in 16:20) or for obeying the Instruction (*torah*) in general (see 4:1; 30:6). In this passage, this language signifies the "path of life," the way that people choose to live their lives.

*20. by loving* יהוה. As is characteristic of Deuteronomy, love constitutes both the motive and the way to be in relation with God (see also at 7:13).

*holding fast.* The verbal root *d-b-k* first appears in Genesis 2:24, describing the close bond between the first man and woman. As this parashah comes to an end, Moses envisions the relationship between Israel and God as an equally intimate connection. (On marriage as a metaphor for the covenantal relationship between God and Israel, see at 5:9.)

—*Dalit Rom-Shiloni*

# Another View

The closing verses of *parashat Nitzavim* are frequently invoked as evidence of the Torah's insistence on human free will. According to Deuteronomy 30:15–21, God presents Israel with a clear-cut and seemingly obvious choice between obedience, which will lead to life, and disobedience, which will lead to death. This free-will paradigm argues that Israel is responsible for its fate and that national misfortune is caused by Israel's disobedience of the covenant. To modern historians, events like the conquest of the northern kingdom of Israel by the Assyrians (8th century B.C.E.) or the destruction of the southern kingdom of Judah by the Babylonians (6th century B.C.E.) would be evidence of Israel's essential powerlessness in the face of stronger nations. However, this parashah and other biblical texts insist that Israel is not a pawn at the mercy of foreign powers, but instead is wholly responsible for its own fate.

Although the articulation of free will in these verses has been central to Jewish self-understanding for centuries, in the parashah itself this notion was largely theoretical. When the exilic or post-exilic authors or redactors imagined the scene of covenant-making that occurred in the mythic past, they already knew the choice that Israel would make. If Israel experienced exile, Israel must, by definition, have made the wrong choice—namely, disobedience.

The pressing question then becomes not whether Israel has free will, but how Israel can achieve reconciliation after having made its self-destructive choice. This concern generates the other view of history articulated in this parashah: the notion that Israel's history is a repeated sequence of iniquity, judgment, repentance, and deliverance. The Bible reiterates this pattern in the book of Judges, which frames legends about Israel's past within statements regarding Israel's disobedience and punishment, followed by Israel's repentance and deliverance (as in Judges 3:5–15). Israel repeatedly disobeys the covenant and embarks on the journey of *t'shuvah* (repentance) that carries it from iniquity to deliverance. Thus, in Deuteronomy and other biblical texts, free will becomes operative not in moments of initial obedience or disobedience, but later, in the choice whether or not to repent, where the right decision ultimately leads to redemption.

*The pressing question then becomes: how can Israel achieve reconciliation?*

—*Elsie R. Stern*

# Post-biblical Interpretations

***You stand this day, all of you . . . from woodchopper to water drawer*** (29:9–10). Midrash *Kohelet Rabbah* 1.12 teaches that these verses should have been placed at the beginning of Deuteronomy, directly following the initial statement, "These are the words that Moses addressed to all Israel on the other side of the Jordan" (1:1). In this midrash, the Rabbis include Deuteronomy 29:9–10 among other biblical verses cited to substantiate the rabbinic dictum that the Torah does not follow a chronological order ("There is no before and after in Scripture"). With this suggestion, the Rabbis accomplish two things. First, 29:9–10 clarifies that "all Israel" in 1:1 includes tribal heads, elders and officials, children and women, as well as strangers within the camp. Second, they stress that 29:9–10 is a direct address to the people Israel. Juxtaposing these two verses emphasizes that Moses addressed all Israel, and that all Israel stood present "to enter into the covenant of your God יהוה" (29:11).

***with those who are standing here with us this day...and with those who are not with us here this day*** (29:14). This verse is part of Moses' speech to the Israelites in Moab, but the Rabbis connected it with the revelation at Sinai (Exodus 20), where all

*The Talmud teaches that although the Torah was given by God, it remains ours to interpret.*

Jews—present and future—are said to have participated in the revelation of Torah. According to Midrash *Sh'mot Rabbah* 28.6, the Rabbis wondered why the verb "standing" was not also used in the second part of the verse, which simply reads, "who are not with us." They suggested that the Torah was referring to future prophets and sages, whose words of wisdom appear in later parts of the Written and Oral Torah, respectively, but who were not physically present at Sinai because they had not yet been born: "Those are the souls who will one day be created.... Since there is not yet any substance in them, the word 'standing' is not used with them."

A similar tradition in BT *Sh'vuot* 39a uses 29:13–14 to teach that all future generations of Israel, including all future converts, were at Sinai. Although these traditions do not refer explicitly to women, *Sh'mot Rabbah* 28.2 affirms their presence. Noting an apparent redundancy in Exodus 19:3, "Thus shall you say to the house of Jacob and declare to the children of Israel," the midrash asks why the Torah mentions both the house of Jacob and the children of Israel. The answer is that "the house of Jacob" refers to the women and "the children of Israel" refers to the men. Indeed, the midrash further imagines that God addressed the women first in order to prevent a repetition of the catastrophe in the Garden of Eden when God initially commanded Adam, but Eve (who had not heard God's directive first-hand) transgressed "and spoiled the world." God, therefore, addressed the women first so they would not also "nullify the Torah."

***It is not in the heavens*** (30:12). Midrash *D'varim Rabbah* 8.6 imagines a dialogue based on 30:12–14 in which the Israelites ask Moses, "If the Torah is not in the heavens, nor beyond the sea, where is it?" Moses answers, "It is in a place very near, in your mouth and in your heart that you may do it." The emphasis on "doing" Torah, meaning living by it, is made clear by a rabbinic interpretation of Leviticus 26:3, "If you faithfully observe My commandments," literally "If you keep My commandments and do them." Midrash *Vayikra Rabbah* 35.7 teaches of those who learn Torah without "doing" Torah, that it would be better if they had not been born.

In a famous talmudic story known as the "Oven of Achnai" (JT *Mo'ed Katan* 3:1, 81c–d; BT *Bava M'tzia* 59a–b), in the midst of a legal dispute ostensibly about the ritual purity or impurity of an oven, Rabbi Yehoshua stands up and quotes this verse, proclaiming, "It [the Torah] is not in the heavens." Despite miraculous evidence supporting the oven's purity, Rabbi Yehoshua sides with the majority of the sages in declaring the oven impure. In doing so, he asserts that the Torah belongs to humanity (or at least to the Rabbis) here on earth—not "in the heavens." Miracles and even divine proclamations cannot overturn a community's ruling. Thus the Talmud teaches that although the Torah was given by God, it remains ours to interpret.

*—Gwynn Kessler*

# *Contemporary Reflection*

For the last four or five decades, feminist scholars have asserted that the Bible is an androcentric work reflecting a time when men controlled property, politics, and religious life, not to mention women themselves. Those insights de-legitimized the Torah as a source of meaning and authority for many women. How could a sacred text reflect the injustices of patriarchy? It did not seem possible.

However, the extent to which patriarchy de-legitimizes the Bible as a sacred book for women has become more nuanced in recent scholarship. While the Bible's male-centeredness generally goes undisputed, at least in academic circles, various scholars (such as Phyllis Trible, Tikva Frymer-Kensky, and Carol Meyers) have highlighted a number of potentially mitigating or even redemptive elements concerning women. First are the powerful and highly delineated female characters in the Bible, most notably Sarah, Rebekah, Tamar, Miriam, Rahab, Deborah, and Ruth, all of whom are leaders who transform the private or public realms in which they act. Second are the Bible's commandments that express a clear concern for the care of the marginal and/or impoverished in society: the stranger, the fatherless, and the widow. Third are the deep covenantal principles articulated in the Torah that can be used for feminist purposes. *Parashat Nitzavim* exemplifies this, with its rich, powerful—even revolutionary—concepts that can be used to further the creation of a feminist Judaism.

The parashah begins: "You stand this day, all of you, before your God יהוה—you tribal heads, you elders, and you officials, all the men of Israel, you children, you women, even the stranger within your camp, from woodchopper to water drawer—to enter into the covenant of your God יהוה" (29:9–11). Let's take a close look at the language surrounding women. First of all, from the nature of the list, one can pretty safely assume that the women were not tribal leaders, elders, woodchoppers, or water drawers. The crucial fact, however, is that they are included. They are standing before God as full members of the covenantal community. In many other instances in the Torah, only the men are addressed or female inclusion is ambiguous—eclipsed by the nature of the Hebrew language itself, which retains a grammatically masculine form whether addressing or referring to an all-male group or a mixed male and female group.

Secondly, the "women" listed belong to the "you" being addressed. (The word is often translated as "your wives," as if the women are not part of the "all of you" in v. 9.) But here "women" are not the only ones subject to belonging. Every individual belongs to a household, a clan, a tribe. In the Hebrew Bible, belonging *is* what constitutes a people. In this particular passage, leadership and power do not set one apart as an autonomous individual. No one, not even the most powerful male tribal leader, stands alone. For better or for worse, everyone is held in an inescapable web of interconnectedness and belonging.

> *It is time to do no less than to dress the Torah in the language of women.*

With all of that, one might still dismiss the applicability of the text to us as contemporary women. Yet I believe we should not overlook the value of this text for women "this day" (29:9). Perhaps the historical context can account for some of the dispiriting force of androcentrism. The biblical authors could not imagine women in roles other than daughters who then became wives (or widows, a state also defined by marriage). Women simply were not necessarily visible if they did not fulfill wifely or maternal duties. Here we can summon the traditional concept of "the Torah spoke in the language of human beings" (*dibrah torah kilshon b'nei adam*). An alternative translation of this saying would be: "The Torah spoke in the language of *men*." It is for us, as students of Torah and members of the covenantal people, to help construct our very lives in a way that takes text out of its historical context, out of its male dress or costume, and applies it to our own time. In this way, we redress Torah—and address it to ourselves and our own community, much as the Rabbis who authored the Midrash and Talmud did. It is time to do no less than to dress the Torah in the language of women.

The Torah itself is explicit about the fact that this covenant is not a thing of the past. As 29:13–14 makes clear, this covenant was intended for each one of us in our own time.

The covenant is made not only with those who stood in Moab listening to Moses' words, but also with future generations. Every Israelite since that day, and every Jew to come into this world in the future, is directly and personally included in this covenant. Thus are we—those reading the Torah now—empowered to forge our own relationship to the contents of the ongoing revelation. The tradition is not fixed; quite the contrary, it is our very active and receptive listening that gives this text its meaning and its very sanctity. The text gains its *k'dushah* ("holiness") from those in every generation who read it and add their voices to the endless, sacred conversation about what this all means. If women exclude themselves from that process, the full power, relevancy, and truth of the Torah are diminished.

To underline that point, the Torah itself adds words of encouragement further on in the parashah concerning our ability to apprehend this text: "Surely, this Instruction which I enjoin upon you this day is not too baffling for you, nor is it beyond reach . . . No, the thing is very close to you, in your mouth and in your heart, to observe it" (30:11, 14). The Torah belongs to every one of us, not just to experts or to certain segments of the community; it does not belong to men alone. As this parashah reminds us, the Torah is far more democratic, fluid, and subjective. We await revelation—and yet revelation is right here, precisely where we stand. "It is not in the heavens . . . No, the thing is very close to you" (30:12, 14)—exceedingly close.

*—Dianne Cohler-Esses*

# Voices

## In the Garden

Rahel (transl. Maurice Samuel)

*Deuteronomy 30:1–6*

Calm is the garden with blue and gray
 In the peace of dawn.
I will rise from the dust of yesterday
 To faith in the morn,
Accept with humble heart and free
The judgment that was given me.

A girl walks through the garden beds
 And scatters rain;
The withered leaves lift up their heads
 And live again.
The bitter things that God must do
I will forgive and start anew.

## *from* The Tapestry of Jewish Time

Nina Beth Cardin

*Deuteronomy 30:2–3*

Some people seek forgiveness face-to-face. Some find it easier to write a letter. Others may want to give the aggrieved a gift or do them a favor, all in the context of apologizing and making amends. Asking forgiveness may take many guises. But its one common element is that it must be intentional. Both parties must be aware of what is at stake. There is no such thing as accidental or casual forgiveness.

## This Place in the Ways

Muriel Rukeyser

*Deuteronomy 30:6*

Having come to this place
I set out once again
on the dark and marvelous way
from where I began:
belief in the love of the world,
woman, spirit, and man.

Having failed in all things
I enter a new age
seeing the old ways as toys,
the houses of a stage
painted and long forgot;
and I find love and rage.

Rage for the world as it is
but for what it may be
more love now than last year
and always less self-pity
since I know in a clearer light
the strength of the mystery.

And at this place in the ways
I wait for song.
My poem-hand still, on the paper,
all night long.
Poems in throat and hand, asleep,
and my storm beating strong!

## *Aphorism*

Sigrid Agocsi

*Deuteronomy 30:5*

I felt myself strange
in the country I grew up in.

Now having become a foreigner,
I have arrived at home.

## *from* *A Prayer When the Child Is Born*

Naomi Levy

*Deuteronomy 30:9*

Welcome, welcome to this breathtaking world. We have been waiting for you. Waiting to see your beautiful face, to hear the sound of your cry, to kiss you, hold you, rock you. You are the fruit of our love, of our hearts, of our souls.

We have prayed for this day, and now it is here. But no amount of anticipation could have prepared us for you. You are a miracle. You are a gift from God. You are ours.

May God watch over you in love and bless you with health. How can we express our gratitude to You, God? You have sent us a perfect blessing.

## *Sometimes while I am chanting*

Marge Piercy

*Deuteronomy 30:14*

Sometimes while I am chanting
the Hebrew words become liquid
as warm rain and I slip through
them as if they were water parting
to let me down to a clear place.

Sometimes when I am praying
the words stop and the darkness
rises like water in a basin
and I come into silence
rich as the heart of a rose.

Sometimes when I meditate
light swells along my limbs
and opens sweet as apple
blossoms from the hard wood
of my knobbly spine.

Light slides behind my eyes
light rises in my throat
light pulses in my chest.
There is no I   only you   only
light burning and unburnt.

## *I Do Not Ask*

Estelle Nachimoff Padawer

*Deuteronomy 30:19–20*

I used to mumble many words in the
 prayerbook
without much thought
even *all wise all good all powerful God*
until dear Clara was felled by a stroke
She who always did for others
now helpless  shorn of dignity

The contradiction of *those words*
struck me then
forced me to shake my head
over and over again

But saying no
and saying nothing are not for me

I need to say yes
—yes to a soap bubble afloat in sunshine
—to a newborn baby's perfect fingernails
—to a child reading a first sentence
—to the look of love that lights a face

I do not ask Who or How
I just say yes

## *Mikveh Mayim*

Ona Siporin

*Deuteronomy 30:15–20*

Where the island divides the river
you decide to forget to remember.
You dive into the glacial current

and, coming up,
lift your eyes, now unmarred,
to the clear heavens
mapped by the bare branches of spring.

When you dive deeply
and spread your fingers so far
no grasp is possible
you know what you own.

You waited all your life
for single moments
like this one
when you catch your breath,
shudder, when your body is
a trembling stalk, your mind
close, close
to the knowledge beyond you.

## *Torah*

Barbara D. Holender

*Deuteronomy 30:11–14*

Even when you hold it in your arms,
you have not grasped it.
Wrapped and turned it upon itself
the scroll says, Not yet.

Even when you take them into your eyes,
you have not seen them; elegant
in their crowns the letter stand aloof.

Even when you taste them in your mouth
and roll them on your tongue
or bite the sharp unyielding strokes
they say, Not yet.

And when the sounds pour from your throat
and reach deep into your lungs for breath,
even then the words say, Not quite.

But when your heart knows its own hunger
and your mind is seized and shaken,
and in the narrow space between the lines
your soul builds its nest,

Now, says Torah, now
you begin to understand.

# וילך ✦ Vayeilech

DEUTERONOMY 31:1–30

## *The Oral and the Written: Words of Encouragement and Warning*

PARASHAT VAYEILECH ("[he] went") is the shortest portion in the Torah, consisting of only thirty verses. It begins with Moses standing before the Israelites in the plains of Moab, just across the Jordan River from the Promised Land. He delivers an encouraging message to Israel (31:1–13), in which he assures the people that although he is about to die, God will lead them into the Land, wiping out any obstacles in their path. To reinforce Joshua's legitimacy as their new leader, Moses appoints him in front of all Israel.

Moses then writes down the Teaching (*torah*) and instructs the priests and elders regarding future public readings of the written text. As in 29:9–10, the text makes the inclusive nature of the covenant explicit, specifying that men, women, children, and strangers are to listen to and learn from God's Teaching (31:12).

In the second part of the parashah (vv. 14–23), God begins to speak, delivering a darkly pessimistic message. God anticipates that immediately after Moses' death, the people will go astray by worshiping other gods. As a result, Moses must write down the words of a poem as witness against the people.

Finally, Moses again speaks to the people (vv. 24–30); but now, as if infected by God's disappointment, Moses too predicts misfortune in Israel's future. In addition, repeatedly the parashah emphasizes the transmission of God's teaching as a written text.

Regarding the treatment of women in this parashah, they are mentioned explicitly only once (v. 12), although they are included implicitly as part of the "people." Nevertheless, readers might consider a number of questions sparked by the parashah:

*The parashah makes it clear: women and men must study Torah and apply it to their lives.*

- What are the repercussions of having the tale narrated by a single dominant male voice, that of Moses? The story as told is shaped by the teller and his particular interests; and, in turn, this story will shape the type of community that Israel will become. What if, instead, the story were to be told from the perspective of a female figure, such as Miriam? What might a female narrator have considered crucial if she were asked to retell the events of the wilderness journey? What vision of community might she propose?
- Moses passes the reins of communal leadership from himself to Joshua. Who would have been a fitting successor to his sister, Miriam—the prophet and leader who died not long beforehand (Numbers 20:1)?

- The depiction of Moses writing down the *torah* (which in this context refers to the teachings in Deuteronomy) prompts speculation: Could a female author have written a biblical book?

While answers to these questions remain largely conjectural, the parashah makes one thing quite clear: women as well as men must hear and study the Torah and apply it to their lives.

*—Adriane Leveen*

## Outline

*I.* Moses Assures Israel of Success (31:1–13)

*A.* Moses prepares the people for God and Joshua to take over (vv. 1–5)

*B.* Moses encourages the people and Joshua: "Be strong and resolute" (vv. 6–8)

*C.* Moses gives instructions for the public reading of the Torah (vv. 9–13)

*II.* God Rebukes Israel (31:14–23)

*A.* Moses and Joshua meet God in the Tent of Meeting (vv. 14–15)

*B.* God warns of Israel's future misbehavior and its consequences (vv. 16–21)

*C.* Moses writes down and teaches the poem (v. 22)

*D.* God encourages Joshua: "Be strong and resolute" (v. 23)

*III.* Moses Completes the Teaching (*torah*) and Recites the Poem (31:24–30)

*A.* Moses instructs the Levites to place the Teaching in the Ark (vv. 24–27)

*B.* Moses recites the poem as a warning (vv. 28–30)

Moses went and spoke these things to all Israel. 2He said to them:

I am now one hundred and twenty years old, I can no longer be active. Moreover, יהוה has said to me, "You shall not go across yonder Jordan." 3It is indeed your God יהוה who will cross over before you, and who will wipe out those nations from your path; and you shall dispossess them.—Joshua is the one who shall cross before you, as יהוה has

לא וַיֵּ֖לֶךְ מֹשֶׁ֑ה וַיְדַבֵּ֛ר אֶת־הַדְּבָרִ֥ים
הָאֵ֖לֶּה אֶל־כָּל־יִשְׂרָאֵֽל׃ 2 וַיֹּ֣אמֶר אֲלֵהֶ֗ם
בֶּן־מֵאָה֩ וְעֶשְׂרִ֨ים שָׁנָ֤ה אָנֹכִי֙ הַיּ֔וֹם לֹא־
אוּכַ֥ל ע֖וֹד לָצֵ֣את וְלָב֑וֹא וַֽיהֹוָה֙ אָמַ֣ר אֵלַ֔י
לֹ֥א תַעֲבֹ֖ר אֶת־הַיַּרְדֵּ֥ן הַזֶּֽה׃ 3 יְהֹוָ֨ה אֱלֹהֶ֜יךָ
ה֣וּא ׀ עֹבֵ֣ר לְפָנֶ֗יךָ הֽוּא־יַשְׁמִ֞יד אֶת־הַגּוֹיִ֥ם
הָאֵ֛לֶּה מִלְּפָנֶ֖יךָ וִירִשְׁתָּ֑ם יְהוֹשֻׁ֗עַ ה֚וּא עֹבֵ֣ר

## *Moses Assures Israel of Success*

(31:1–13)

Moses reminds the people of God's plans to take them across the Jordan into the Promised Land, accompanied by Joshua. Once there, the people are to gather and read the *torah* aloud every seventh year during the festival of Sukkot.

### MOSES PREPARES THE PEOPLE FOR GOD AND JOSHUA TO TAKE OVER (31:1–5)

Unable to enter the Promised Land, Moses reassures the people of success and appoints Joshua to take the lead.

*1. **Moses went.*** The verse suggests that Moses seeks out the people in order to deliver his message; time is of the essence since he knows that he is about to die.

***spoke . . . things.*** Heb. *va-ydaber . . . d'varim*, where both the verb and its object derive from the same root (*d-b-r*). This language echoes the opening verse of Deuteronomy, where the two forms of this root also appear together: "These are the words (*d'varim*) that Moses addressed (*dibber*) to all Israel" (1:1). Soon, at the end of his long series of speeches, Moses will write down these precious words as his legacy to Israel (v. 9). At Deuteronomy's end, the oral and the written become inextricably linked.

*2. **I can no longer be active.*** The Hebrew idiom for a lack of physical motion in an aged Moses is more suggestive—literally "I am no longer able to go out or come in." The image of movement is reinforced by God's next words, reminding Moses that he cannot cross over the Jordan and enter the land.

*3. **your God יהוה who will cross over before you.*** Moses turns from his own fate to the people's, who shortly will leave him behind. Poignantly he speaks of "your God," not including himself in the address. Since Moses will not cross the Jordan (v. 2), God and Joshua will cross before the Israelites (v. 3) to ensure victory as they settle the land.

***Joshua is the one who shall cross before you, as***

➤ Deuteronomy—via Moses—continually insists that no individual should be left out.

ANOTHER VIEW ➤ *1245*

➤ We women prepare ourselves for lives in which every possibility is open to us.

CONTEMPORARY REFLECTION ➤ *1247*

➤ Whereas the men were there to learn, the women were capable only of listening.

POST-BIBLICAL INTERPRETATIONS ➤ *1245*

➤ The keepers of my youth sit in wheelchairs / sunning themselves in the crisp autumn air.

VOICES ➤ *1249*

spoken.—[4]יהוה will do to them as was done to
Sihon and Og, kings of the Amorites, and to their
countries, when [God] wiped them out. [5]יהוה will
deliver them up to you, and you shall deal with
them in full accordance with the Instruction that
I have enjoined upon you. [6]Be strong and resolute,
be not in fear or in dread of them; for it is indeed
your God יהוה who marches with you: [God] will
not fail you or forsake you.

לְפָנֶ֔יךָ כַּאֲשֶׁ֖ר דִּבֶּ֥ר יְהוָֽה׃ 4 וְעָשָׂ֤ה יְהוָה֙
לָהֶ֔ם כַּאֲשֶׁ֣ר עָשָׂ֗ה לְסִיח֥וֹן וּלְע֛וֹג מַלְכֵ֥י
הָאֱמֹרִ֖י וּלְאַרְצָ֑ם אֲשֶׁ֥ר הִשְׁמִ֖יד אֹתָֽם׃
5 וּנְתָנָ֥ם יְהוָ֖ה לִפְנֵיכֶ֑ם וַעֲשִׂיתֶ֣ם לָהֶ֔ם
כְּכׇל־הַמִּצְוָ֔ה אֲשֶׁ֥ר צִוִּ֖יתִי אֶתְכֶֽם׃ 6 חִזְק֣וּ
וְאִמְצ֔וּ אַל־תִּֽירְא֥וּ וְאַל־תַּעַרְצ֖וּ מִפְּנֵיהֶ֑ם כִּ֣י
׀ יְהוָ֣ה אֱלֹהֶ֗יךָ ה֚וּא הַהֹלֵ֣ךְ עִמָּ֔ךְ לֹ֥א יַרְפְּךָ֖
וְלֹ֥א יַעַזְבֶֽךָּ׃ ס

**יהוה *has spoken.*** The syntax of this phrase is odd, forcing the English translation to add dashes to make sense of the sentence. The prior sentence states that God's destruction of the nations will end with Israel's dispossessing them. Then, almost as an afterthought, Joshua is introduced. This clearly tacked-on phrase suggests an editorial insertion to draw attention to the role that Joshua will assume. The verse reflects a tension between God's actions on our behalf and the human means by which those actions are accomplished.

*4.* About to die, Moses retells what happened in the past. As in *parashat D'varim,* he shapes Israel's memories of the wilderness journey in order to teach lessons pertinent to the present moment. (For speculation on how a female narrator might have reshaped the story, see the introduction to this parashah.)

## MOSES ENCOURAGES THE PEOPLE AND JOSHUA: "BE STRONG AND RESOLUTE" (31:6–8)

These three verses present the reader with an identifiable section that shows signs of careful editing through the use of repetition and inversion to make a highly political point to the Israelite audience. Verse 6 contains four clauses that claim a cause-and-effect relationship, stressing that the people Israel can be strong and free of fear because God is with them and will not let them down. Verses 7–8 include language nearly identical to that of Moses when he commissions Joshua. One noteworthy difference between vv. 7–8 and v. 6 is the insertion of Joshua's name as the one who will lead the people along with God. Because he assumes this role, Israel should accept his equally important function as the one who divides the land among the tribes. The politics of succession as well as the necessary persuasion to secure Joshua's legitimacy are in play here. The deft weaving together of similar language in each passage signals that God approves the arrangement.

***6. Be strong and resolute.*** This expression of encouragement, particularly used in the context of war, appears three times in this parashah (also vv. 7 and 23) and four times in Joshua 1 as the people prepare to enter the land (vv. 6, 7, 9, 18).

***forsake you.*** Here and in v. 8, Moses assures the people and Joshua that God will not forsake or abandon them. The same verbal root (*e-z-b*) is used later when God foreshadows that Israel will forsake God (v. 16), which in turn will result in God forsaking them (v. 17). In Isaiah 49:14–15, the identical verb is used when the people in exile express their anxiety that God has deserted them. In response, the prophet reassures them by means of a rhetorical question that compares God to a mother: "Can a mother forget her babe, or stop loving the child of her womb? Even these could forget, but I could not forget you."

7Then Moses called Joshua and said to him in
the sight of all Israel: "Be strong and resolute, for it
is you who shall go with this people into the land
that יהוה swore to their fathers to give them, and it
is you who shall apportion it to them. 8And it is
indeed יהוה who will go before you. [God] will be
with you—and will not fail you or forsake you. Fear
not and be not dismayed!"

9Moses wrote down this Teaching and gave it to

7 וַיִּקְרָא מֹשֶׁה לִיהוֹשֻׁעַ וַיֹּאמֶר אֵלָיו לְעֵינֵי
כָל־יִשְׂרָאֵל חֲזַק וֶאֱמָץ כִּי אַתָּה תָּבוֹא אֶת־
הָעָם הַזֶּה אֶל־הָאָרֶץ אֲשֶׁר נִשְׁבַּע יְהֹוָה
לַאֲבֹתָם לָתֵת לָהֶם וְאַתָּה תַּנְחִילֶנָּה
אוֹתָם׃ 8 וַיהֹוָה הוּא ׀ הַהֹלֵךְ לְפָנֶיךָ הוּא
יִהְיֶה עִמָּךְ לֹא יַרְפְּךָ וְלֹא יַעַזְבֶךָּ לֹא תִירָא
וְלֹא תֵחָת׃
9 וַיִּכְתֹּב מֹשֶׁה אֶת־הַתּוֹרָה הַזֹּאת וַיִּתְּנָהּ

*7. Then Moses called Joshua.* Just as Joshua prepares to take the lead after Moses' death, his brother Aaron also has a successor, Eleazar (Numbers 20:26). While no one is designated to succeed their sister Miriam, Deborah would be a fitting choice. Deborah, like Miriam (Exodus 15:20), is called a prophet (Judges 4:4); and she is praised as "Mother in Israel" (Judges 5:7), a title that most likely indicates her role as a leader during the period of the Judges. Also, just as Miriam sings a song of victory and praise after crossing the Sea of Reeds (Exodus 15:20–21), so too does Deborah sing a song of praise after the defeat of Sisera (Judges 5). It is intriguing that both of these two poems, which are thought to be among the oldest compositions in the Bible, are associated with women. (On women as singers of victory songs and other poetic compositions, see at Exodus 15:1–19 and Deuteronomy 32:1–43.)

*in the sight of all Israel.* That is, Joshua must be seen and accepted as the legitimate successor to Moses.

## MOSES GIVES INSTRUCTIONS FOR THE PUBLIC READING OF THE TORAH (31:9–13)

The text now shifts to a description of how Moses wrote down the Teaching and ensured its annual public reading.

*9. Moses wrote down this Teaching.* Here and in v. 24, we have explicit mention of Moses writing the Teaching (*torah*). Elsewhere in Deuteronomy, the written *torah* is discussed without attributing its writing to Moses (see 17:18; 27:8). Thus the later tradition that Moses wrote the entire Torah may begin with this parashah.

In certain passages in Exodus, the word *torah* refers to divine precepts authoritative for the community (for instance, see *torat YHVH* in Exodus 13:9). In Leviticus and Numbers, the term typically refers to priestly instructions, either oral or written on separate scrolls that priests keep to themselves; in such cases, the word often is translated as "ritual" (see at Leviticus 6:2). In Deuteronomy, *torah* generally refers to "this Teaching," meaning the book of Deuteronomy or perhaps its legal parts (see at 1:5; 17:18; 27:3); it designates a written text that becomes central to Israel's life as a community, for it contains God's rules for all of Israel. As many scholars note, Deuteronomy lays the foundation for Judaism's becoming a religion of the book.

Later biblical books speak of the *torah* of Moses (for instance, Joshua 8:31; 23:6; I Kings 2:3; II Kings 14:6; 23:25; Ezra 7:6; Nehemiah 8:1). These references to the Teaching of Moses appear in times of instability or crisis, including a transition in rule, a moment of religious or political reform, or the return of the exiles from Babylon. Thus the Teaching (*torah*) of Moses provides guidance and an anchor for Israel.

No such explicit association exists between a woman and a work of the Hebrew Bible. One possible comparison is Song of Songs. Although attributed to Solomon, this biblical book reproduces the

the priests, sons of Levi, who carried the Ark of יהוה's Covenant, and to all the elders of Israel.

[10]And Moses instructed them as follows: Every seventh year, the year set for remission, at the Feast of Booths, [11]when all Israel comes to appear before your God יהוה in the place that [God] will choose, you shall read this Teaching aloud in the presence of all Israel. [12]Gather the people—men, women, children, and the strangers in your communities—that they may hear and so learn to revere your God יהוה and to observe faithfully every word of this Teaching. [13]Their children, too, who have not had the experience, shall hear and learn to revere your God יהוה as long as they live in the land that you are about to cross the Jordan to possess.

אֶל־הַכֹּהֲנִים בְּנֵי לֵוִי הַנֹּשְׂאִים אֶת־אֲרוֹן
בְּרִית יְהוָה וְאֶל־כָּל־זִקְנֵי יִשְׂרָאֵל׃
10 וַיְצַו מֹשֶׁה אוֹתָם לֵאמֹר מִקֵּץ ׀ שֶׁבַע
שָׁנִים בְּמֹעֵד שְׁנַת הַשְּׁמִטָּה בְּחַג הַסֻּכּוֹת׃
11 בְּבוֹא כָל־יִשְׂרָאֵל לֵרָאוֹת אֶת־פְּנֵי יְהוָה
אֱלֹהֶיךָ בַּמָּקוֹם אֲשֶׁר יִבְחָר תִּקְרָא אֶת־
הַתּוֹרָה הַזֹּאת נֶגֶד כָּל־יִשְׂרָאֵל בְּאָזְנֵיהֶם׃
12 הַקְהֵל אֶת־הָעָם הָאֲנָשִׁים וְהַנָּשִׁים
וְהַטַּף וְגֵרְךָ אֲשֶׁר בִּשְׁעָרֶיךָ לְמַעַן יִשְׁמְעוּ
וּלְמַעַן יִלְמְדוּ וְיָרְאוּ אֶת־יְהוָה אֱלֹהֵיכֶם
וְשָׁמְרוּ לַעֲשׂוֹת אֶת־כָּל־דִּבְרֵי הַתּוֹרָה
הַזֹּאת׃ 13 וּבְנֵיהֶם אֲשֶׁר לֹא־יָדְעוּ יִשְׁמְעוּ
וְלָמְדוּ לְיִרְאָה אֶת־יְהוָה אֱלֹהֵיכֶם כָּל־
הַיָּמִים אֲשֶׁר אַתֶּם חַיִּים עַל־הָאֲדָמָה
אֲשֶׁר אַתֶּם עֹבְרִים אֶת־הַיַּרְדֵּן שָׁמָּה
לְרִשְׁתָּהּ׃ פ

voice of a woman as its chief speaker or singer. In addition, the book of Ruth could have been written by a woman, given the central relationship of the daughter-in-law to her mother-in-law and the dominance of female economic concerns.

***and gave it to the priests, sons of Levi.*** According to Deuteronomy, levitical priests are in charge of teaching the *torah* to the people.

*10.* ***at the Feast of Booths.*** Jeffrey Tigay suggests a practical reason for reading the Teaching at this time. Since Sukkot marks the end of the agricultural cycle, the people have some leisure and, depending on the harvest's success, a sense of security and gratitude. As a consequence, Sukkot in Jerusalem would have been the best-attended of the festivals, giving the Jerusalem priests both a large audience and ample time to read the Teaching publicly. He estimates that all of Deuteronomy could be read in three or four hours (*Deuteronomy*, 1996, pp. 291–92). Note the specific mention of women in 16:13–14 among those instructed to celebrate Sukkot.

*11.* ***in the place that*** [*God*] ***will choose.*** Deuteronomy is a book of religious vision and reform. An unnamed central site (presumably the Temple in Jerusalem) is to replace the many high places and cultic sites found in Judah at that time (see at 12:2–14). The public reading of the scroll would reinforce the centrality of the Temple in Jerusalem as God's Chosen Place.

***read this Teaching aloud.*** The *torah* is preserved and written down, but it is read aloud to the many who either do not have a copy or would not be able to read it. In narratives about the later periods in Israel's history, such a public reading is said to have occurred during the period of intense religious reform under Josiah (II Kings 23) and after the return from exile, when Ezra reads the Torah aloud (Nehemiah 8). Nehemiah 8:2 emphasizes that the audience is composed of "men and women and all who could listen with understanding" (also v. 3).

*12.* ***men, women, children, and the strangers.*** The list suggests as inclusive a group as possible; knowledge of God's teachings is open to everyone and expected of everyone.

14 יהוה said to Moses: The time is drawing near for you to die. Call Joshua and present yourselves in the Tent of Meeting, that I may instruct him. Moses and Joshua went and presented themselves in the Tent of Meeting. 15 יהוה appeared in the Tent, in a pillar of cloud, the pillar of cloud having come to rest at the entrance of the tent.

16 יהוה said to Moses: You are soon to lie with your ancestors. This people will thereupon go astray after the alien gods in their midst, in the

14 וַיֹּאמֶר יְהוָה אֶל־מֹשֶׁה הֵן קָרְבוּ יָמֶיךָ
לָמוּת קְרָא אֶת־יְהוֹשֻׁעַ וְהִתְיַצְּבוּ בְּאֹהֶל
מוֹעֵד וַאֲצַוֶּנּוּ וַיֵּלֶךְ מֹשֶׁה וִיהוֹשֻׁעַ וַיִּתְיַצְּבוּ
בְּאֹהֶל מוֹעֵד׃ 15 וַיֵּרָא יְהוָה בָּאֹהֶל בְּעַמּוּד
עָנָן וַיַּעֲמֹד עַמּוּד הֶעָנָן עַל־פֶּתַח הָאֹהֶל׃
16 וַיֹּאמֶר יְהוָה אֶל־מֹשֶׁה הִנְּךָ שֹׁכֵב עִם־
אֲבֹתֶיךָ וְקָם הָעָם הַזֶּה וְזָנָה ׀ אַחֲרֵי ׀ אֱלֹהֵי

## *God Rebukes Israel* (31:14–23)

In comparison to the foreboding message we are about to read, Deuteronomy 30 (in the prior parashah) exhibited a more compassionate tone and a more forgiving God. The contrast suggests the purposeful preservation of two different traditions concerning Moses' last speeches, the first offering a vision of God in harmony with Israel and the second presenting a warning of estrangement and disaster caused by the people's behavior.

### MOSES AND JOSHUA MEET GOD IN THE TENT OF MEETING (31:14–15)

God repeats what Moses announced to the people in v. 2, the fact of his impending death. In preparation for the change of leadership, God summons Moses and Joshua to the Tent of Meeting.

*14. Tent of Meeting.* Heb. *ohel mo'ed*, which refers to the tent located outside of the camp where God earlier appeared as a pillar of cloud in order to speak to Moses "face to face" and to Joshua as his attendant (see at Exodus 33:7–11). This is the same tent where God spoke directly to Miriam and to her brother Aaron (Numbers 12:4–9).

*that I may instruct him.* God now speaks directly to Joshua; Moses is not included.

*15. in a pillar of cloud.* God often appears to Moses, and at times to the people, behind a veil of some kind, shielding the observer from a direct view of God's manifestation. (See also at Exodus 13:21.)

### GOD WARNS OF ISRAEL'S FUTURE MISBEHAVIOR AND ITS CONSEQUENCES (31:16–21)

God's warning about the people's misbehavior that will follow Moses' death introduces an angry, melancholy note into the parashah. Just as earlier repentance and reconciliation are depicted as reciprocal (see at 30:1–10), so here are rebellion and rejection. The core message of this section is that since the people will abandon God, God will abandon the people (vv. 16–17; see at v. 6).

*16. go astray after.* Literally, "go whoring after." Here and in several prophetic books (see Hosea 2; Jeremiah 3:1; Ezekiel 16, 23), prostitution is used as a metaphor for adultery and apostasy. The betrayal involved in adultery forms the basis of an analogy to vividly express God's sense of betrayal when Israel worships other gods. This comparison fits with the broader conception of the relationship between God and Israel as a marriage, a metaphor that conveys both the love that binds the metaphoric husband and wife, as well as God's deep disappointment when Israel turns to "alien gods" (see also at 5:9).

*alien gods.* This expression refers to Canaanite gods. Yet in v. 3, Moses announces that God will destroy the nations (and presumably their idols) once they cross into the land of Canaan. This contradiction anticipates the tension found in the books of Joshua and Judges between the claim to have wiped out the local inhabitants and the fact

land that they are about to enter; they will forsake Me and break My covenant that I made with them. [17]Then My anger will flare up against them, and I will abandon them and hide My countenance from them. They shall be ready prey; and many evils and troubles shall befall them. And they shall say on that day, "Surely it is because our God is not in our midst that these evils have befallen us." [18]Yet I will keep My countenance hidden on that day, because of all the evil they have done in turning to other gods. [19]Therefore, write down this poem and teach it to the people of Israel; put it in their mouths, in order that this poem may be My witness against the people of Israel. [20]When I bring them into the land flowing with milk and honey that I promised on oath to their fathers, and they eat their fill and grow fat and turn to other gods and serve them, spurning Me and breaking My covenant, [21]and the many evils and troubles befall them—then this poem

נֵֽכַר־הָאָ֗רֶץ אֲשֶׁ֨ר ה֤וּא בָא־שָׁ֙מָּה֙ בְּקִרְבּ֔וֹ
וַעֲזָבַ֕נִי וְהֵפֵר֙ אֶת־בְּרִיתִ֔י אֲשֶׁ֥ר כָּרַ֖תִּי אִתּֽוֹ׃
17 וְחָרָ֣ה אַפִּ֣י ב֣וֹ בַיּוֹם־הַ֠הוּא וַעֲזַבְתִּ֞ים
וְהִסְתַּרְתִּ֨י פָנַ֤י מֵהֶם֙ וְהָיָ֣ה לֶֽאֱכֹ֔ל וּמְצָאֻ֛הוּ
רָע֥וֹת רַבּ֖וֹת וְצָר֑וֹת וְאָמַר֙ בַּיּ֣וֹם הַה֔וּא הֲלֹ֗א
עַ֣ל כִּי־אֵ֤ין אֱלֹהַי֙ בְּקִרְבִּ֔י מְצָא֖וּנִי הָרָע֥וֹת
הָאֵֽלֶּה׃ 18 וְאָנֹכִ֗י הַסְתֵּ֨ר אַסְתִּ֤יר פָּנַי֙ בַּיּ֣וֹם
הַה֔וּא עַ֥ל כָּל־הָרָעָ֖ה אֲשֶׁ֣ר עָשָׂ֑ה כִּ֣י פָנָ֔ה
אֶל־אֱלֹהִ֖ים אֲחֵרִֽים׃ 19 וְעַתָּ֗ה כִּתְב֤וּ לָכֶם֙
אֶת־הַשִּׁירָ֣ה הַזֹּ֔את וְלַמְּדָ֥הּ אֶת־בְּנֵֽי־
יִשְׂרָאֵ֖ל שִׂימָ֣הּ בְּפִיהֶ֑ם לְמַ֨עַן תִּֽהְיֶה־לִּ֜י
הַשִּׁירָ֥ה הַזֹּ֛את לְעֵ֖ד בִּבְנֵ֥י יִשְׂרָאֵֽל׃ 20 כִּֽי־
אֲבִיאֶ֜נּוּ אֶל־הָאֲדָמָ֣ה ׀ אֲשֶׁר־נִשְׁבַּ֣עְתִּי
לַאֲבֹתָ֗יו זָבַ֤ת חָלָב֙ וּדְבַ֔שׁ וְאָכַ֥ל וְשָׂבַ֖ע
וְדָשֵׁ֑ן וּפָנָ֞ה אֶל־אֱלֹהִ֤ים אֲחֵרִים֙ וַעֲבָד֔וּם
וְנִ֣אֲצ֔וּנִי וְהֵפֵ֖ר אֶת־בְּרִיתִֽי׃ 21 וְהָיָה֩ כִֽי־
תִמְצֶ֨אןָ אֹת֜וֹ רָע֣וֹת רַבּוֹת֮ וְצָרוֹת֒ וְעָנְתָ֨ה

that Israel repeatedly interacts with those already in the land. The contradiction seems to suggest that a widespread destruction of other peoples did not in fact occur (see also at 2:34; 7:1–5; 7:24; 12:29–31). Rather, Israel came into being in the midst of other cultures and widely and creatively adapted some of their practices and ideas into Israelite religious life.

*17. **hide My countenance from them.*** Here and in v. 18, this common biblical image (see, for instance, Isaiah 54:8; Psalm 30:8) depicts the remoteness of God's presence (literally "face"). The expression here suggests profound divine alienation from the people.

***"Surely it is because our God is not in our midst."*** The people will blame their troubles on God's absence, equated here with the denial of divine protection and sustenance.

*19. **Therefore, write down this poem.*** God's response to Moses' impending absence is to demand a written text. Some interpreters understand the poem to serve as an accusation against the people in the generations to come, preventing them from misconstruing the past. In other words, the poem will testify to the fact that God abandoned them for just cause (Jeffrey Tigay, *Deuteronomy*, 1996, p. 295). Others have reinterpreted this verse to understand the poem not as a witness *against* Israel, but as a witness *on behalf of* Israel, reminding God "not to judge the people Israel harshly in the future, for God was aware of their nature (v. 27) and chose them nonetheless" (attributed to Rabbi Meir "Malbim" in David Lieber, ed., *Etz Hayim*, 2001, p. 1177).

***20–21.*** These verses reiterate God's charge in vv. 16–19, but with an added accusation against Israel. After God fulfills the promise made to the ancestors—to settle their descendants in a land flowing with milk and honey—the people will partake of the land's abundance; but they will fail to connect their prosperity to the God who brought them there.

shall confront them as a witness, since it will never be lost from the mouth of their offspring. For I know what plans they are devising even now, before I bring them into the land that I promised on oath.

22That day, Moses wrote down this poem and taught it to the Israelites.

23And [God] charged Joshua son of Nun: "Be strong and resolute: for you shall bring the Israelites into the land that I promised them on oath, and I will be with you."

24When Moses had put down in writing the words of this Teaching to the very end, 25Moses charged the Levites who carried the Ark of the

הַשִּׁירָ֨ה הַזֹּ֤את לְפָנָיו֙ לְעֵ֔ד כִּ֛י לֹ֥א תִשָּׁכַ֖ח
מִפִּ֣י זַרְע֑וֹ כִּ֧י יָדַ֣עְתִּי אֶת־יִצְר֗וֹ אֲשֶׁ֨ר ה֤וּא
עֹשֶׂה֙ הַיּ֔וֹם בְּטֶ֣רֶם אֲבִיאֶ֔נּוּ אֶל־הָאָ֖רֶץ אֲשֶׁ֥ר
נִשְׁבָּֽעְתִּי׃
22 וַיִּכְתֹּ֥ב מֹשֶׁ֛ה אֶת־הַשִּׁירָ֥ה הַזֹּ֖את בַּיּ֣וֹם
הַה֑וּא וַֽיְלַמְּדָ֖הּ אֶת־בְּנֵ֥י יִשְׂרָאֵֽל׃
23 וַיְצַ֞ו אֶת־יְהוֹשֻׁ֣עַ בִּן־נ֗וּן וַיֹּאמֶר֮ חֲזַ֣ק
וֶֽאֱמָץ֒ כִּ֣י אַתָּ֗ה תָּבִיא֙ אֶת־בְּנֵ֣י יִשְׂרָאֵ֔ל
אֶל־הָאָ֖רֶץ אֲשֶׁר־נִשְׁבַּ֣עְתִּי לָהֶ֑ם וְאָנֹכִ֖י
אֶֽהְיֶ֥ה עִמָּֽךְ׃
24 וַיְהִ֣י ׀ כְּכַלּ֣וֹת מֹשֶׁ֗ה לִכְתֹּ֛ב אֶת־דִּבְרֵ֥י
הַתּוֹרָֽה־הַזֹּ֖את עַל־סֵ֑פֶר עַ֖ד תֻּמָּֽם׃ 25 וַיְצַ֣ו
מֹשֶׁ֗ה אֶת־הַלְוִיִּ֔ם נֹשְׂאֵ֛י אֲר֥וֹן בְּרִית־יְהֹוָ֖ה

**21. *it will never be lost from the mouth of their offspring.*** God now refers to the descendants who presumably will memorize the poem or talk about it.

#### MOSES WRITES DOWN AND TEACHES THE POEM (31:22)

This parashah centers on the writing and recitation of two texts: the Teaching (*torah*) (see at v. 9) and the poem (*shirah*), the text of which follows in Deuteronomy 32.

#### GOD ENCOURAGES JOSHUA: "BE STRONG AND RESOLUTE" (31:23)

Completing the preparations for the transition in leadership, God appoints Joshua, echoing the words Moses uttered in vv. 6–8.

## *Moses Completes the Teaching (torah) and Recites the Poem* (31:24–30)

Deuteronomy vacillates between the visionary rhetoric of promise-and-fulfillment and of its opposite, reproach-and-despair. So, too, does Moses. After his death, the people will remember him through his words and the written text.

#### MOSES INSTRUCTS THE LEVITES TO PLACE THE TEACHING IN THE ARK (31:24–27)

In v. 19, God instructs Moses to write down the poem, a task completed in v. 22. Now the focus reverts to the writing of the Teaching (*torah*). Verses 24–25 appear to be a resumption and repetition of v. 9, which describes how Moses finished writing the *torah* and gave it to the Levites. This section mentions only the Teaching—not the poem—which strongly suggests that vv. 16–22 (God's angry speech and the anticipation of the poem as a witness against Israel) were inserted into the account of Moses' completion of the writing of the Teaching.

Covenant of יהוה, saying: ²⁶Take this book of Teaching and place it beside the Ark of the Covenant of your God יהוה, and let it remain there as a witness against you. ²⁷Well I know how defiant and stiffnecked you are: even now, while I am still alive in your midst, you have been defiant toward יהוה; how much more, then, when I am dead! ²⁸Gather to me all the elders of your tribes and your officials, that I may speak all these words to them and that I may call heaven and earth to witness against them. ²⁹For I know that, when I am dead, you will act wickedly and turn away from the path that I enjoined upon you, and that in time to come misfortune will befall you for having done evil in the sight of יהוה, whom you vexed by your deeds.

³⁰Then Moses recited the words of the following poem to the very end, in the hearing of the whole congregation of Israel.

לֵאמֹ֑ר ²⁶ לָקֹ֗חַ אֵ֣ת סֵ֤פֶר הַתּוֹרָה֙ הַזֶּ֔ה וְשַׂמְתֶּ֣ם אֹת֔וֹ מִצַּ֕ד אֲר֖וֹן בְּרִית־יְהֹוָ֣ה אֱלֹהֵיכֶ֑ם וְהָֽיָה־שָׁ֥ם בְּךָ֖ לְעֵֽד׃ ²⁷ כִּ֣י אָנֹכִ֤י יָדַ֙עְתִּי֙ אֶֽת־מֶרְיְךָ֔ וְאֶֽת־עׇרְפְּךָ֖ הַקָּשֶׁ֑ה הֵ֣ן בְּעוֹדֶ֩נִּי֩ חַ֨י עִמָּכֶ֜ם הַיּ֗וֹם מַמְרִ֤ים הֱיִתֶם֙ עִם־יְהֹוָ֔ה וְאַ֖ף כִּֽי־אַחֲרֵ֥י מוֹתִֽי׃ ²⁸ הַקְהִ֧ילוּ אֵלַ֛י אֶת־כׇּל־זִקְנֵ֥י שִׁבְטֵיכֶ֖ם וְשֹׁטְרֵיכֶ֑ם וַאֲדַבְּרָ֣ה בְאׇזְנֵיהֶ֗ם אֵ֚ת הַדְּבָרִ֣ים הָאֵ֔לֶּה וְאָעִ֥ידָה בָּ֖ם אֶת־הַשָּׁמַ֥יִם וְאֶת־הָאָֽרֶץ׃ ²⁹ כִּ֣י יָדַ֗עְתִּי אַחֲרֵ֣י מוֹתִ֔י כִּֽי־הַשְׁחֵ֣ת תַּשְׁחִת֔וּן וְסַרְתֶּ֣ם מִן־הַדֶּ֔רֶךְ אֲשֶׁ֥ר צִוִּ֖יתִי אֶתְכֶ֑ם וְקָרָ֨את אֶתְכֶ֤ם הָֽרָעָה֙ בְּאַחֲרִ֣ית הַיָּמִ֔ים כִּֽי־תַעֲשׂ֤וּ אֶת־הָרַע֙ בְּעֵינֵ֣י יְהֹוָ֔ה לְהַכְעִיס֖וֹ בְּמַעֲשֵׂ֥ה יְדֵיכֶֽם׃ ³⁰ וַיְדַבֵּ֣ר מֹשֶׁ֗ה בְּאׇזְנֵ֛י כׇּל־קְהַ֥ל יִשְׂרָאֵ֖ל אֶת־דִּבְרֵ֥י הַשִּׁירָ֖ה הַזֹּ֑את עַ֖ד תֻּמָּֽם׃ פ

What links the two episodes is the importance and use of the written text. What separates them are their respective tones: optimistically hopeful versus starkly pessimistic.

**26. Take this book of Teaching and place it beside the Ark of the Covenant.** In contrast to the priestly description of the magnificent ark overlaid with gold found in Exodus and Leviticus (see at Exodus 25:10–22), Deuteronomy 31 values something else: an ark next to which is placed the written Teaching. Ancient Near Eastern political treaties were stored in containers and deposited in temples (see also at 10:5).

**let it remain there as a witness against you.** This clause forms another linkage between the two disparate passages of Deuteronomy 31. Just as the poem serves as a witness, so too does the Teaching.

**27. Well I know how defiant and stiffnecked you are . . . you have been defiant.** Moses now joins his wrathful voice to God's, seemingly on the point of despair. Could the repeated use of the verbal root m-r-h ("defiant") allude to the scene in Numbers 20:10 when a frustrated Moses calls the people by the same term after Miriam's death and just before his own punishment?

MOSES RECITES THE POEM
AS A WARNING (31:28–30)

The last verses of the parashah appear to return to the subject of the poem (Deuteronomy 32), not the Teaching. In v. 28, Moses gathers together the elders of the tribes and the officials; but v. 30 stresses that all of Israel must hear the words of the poem. While the writing down of texts is central to this parashah, it begins and ends with Moses speaking. Only after his death will the written word speak on his behalf.

—Adriane Leveen

# Another View

PARASHAT VAYEILECH DESCRIBES Moses' final preparations before taking leave of Israel. On the verge of his death, Moses appoints Joshua as military commander. He also sets the date on which the Torah should be read publicly; and, in an attempt to protect the people from God's wrath, he teaches the poem *Haazinu* (the content of Deuteronomy 32, in the next parashah). Knowing that he cannot enter the Promised Land and that he is about to die does not make Moses less committed to the nation. On the contrary, he carries out these preparations with great care and attention to detail, demonstrating his love and devotion to Israel.

One way that the parashah communicates this message is through the repetition of the word "all" (*kol*). Deuteronomy 31 begins with the statement that Moses addresses "all Israel" (31:1), and that "in the sight of all Israel" (31:7) he appoints Joshua as commander. The expression "all Israel" (*kol Yisrael*) is used frequently in Deuteronomy, reflecting the continued insistence that no individual should be left out. When Moses charges the priests and "all the elders of Israel" to impart God's Teaching (31:9), he repeats the command that this must be done when "all Israel" appears before God (31:11). Moses specifies that "men, women, children, and the strangers" must be gathered to learn "every word" of the Teaching (*kol divrei hatorah*) (31:12).

Moses demonstrates his concern and conscientiousness in other ways, too. In particular, he makes sure that women are included. Just as 29:10 makes it clear that women are part of the covenant ceremony, 31:12 states explicitly that women must study and faithfully observe the terms of the covenant. Similarly, Moses writes down the words of this Teaching "to the very end" (31:24), and he also recites the words of the poem "to the very end" (31:30).

The word *kol* also appears in an earlier passage, one that shows Moses at a rather different point in his life.

*Like a loving parent, Moses conscientiously prepares to bid his "children" farewell.*

During the course of the wilderness wanderings, Moses uses a striking maternal metaphor when, exasperated, he tries to distance himself from the people: "Did I produce [or: conceive] all this people (*kol haam*), did I engender [or: give birth to] them, that You should say to me, 'Carry them in your bosom as a caretaker carries an infant,' to the land that You have promised on oath to their fathers?" (Numbers 11:12). Now, at the end of the journey, Moses contemplates death, not birth. Like a loving parent, he conscientiously prepares to bid his "children" farewell as they enter the Promised Land without him.

—*Talia Sutskover*

# Post-biblical Interpretations

***He said to them: I am now one hundred and twenty years old, I can no longer be active*** (31:2). Some commentators could not imagine that Moses was deficient in any way. Ibn Ezra suggested that "I can no longer be active" meant that Moses could no longer wage war. A sage in BT *Sotah* 13b asserted that in his old age the "sources of wisdom" were stopped up for Moses to prevent his being troubled by the transfer of leadership to Joshua.

*Gather the people—men, women, children, and the strangers in your communities* (31:12). While the Rabbis apparently took for granted that the entire community of Israel was required to hear the divine "Teaching," medieval interpreters (not usually known for their egalitarianism) wondered why the women were included. Rashi emphasized the distinction between the men and women: whereas the men were there to learn, the women were capable only of listening. *Tanna D'Vei Eliyahu*, a book of midrashim collected in the 10th century C.E., uses this verse to prove that it is the man's responsibility to ensure that every member of his household follows the law faithfully (p. 112). The medieval commentator Nachmanides disagreed, emphasizing in his comments on this verse that the women who were present also learned to fear God.

*When Moses had put down in writing the words of this Teaching to the very end* (31:24). What does this "Teaching" constitute? Most of the Rabbis understood it to refer to the entire Torah, although they debated whether Moses actually wrote the last eight verses of Deuteronomy that recount his death (see BT *Bava Batra* 14b–15a). This understanding of Mosaic authorship is present in the Dead Sea Scrolls, where quotations from the Torah are often introduced by "Moses said," or "as written in the Book of Moses." However, *Tanna D'Vei Eliyahu* specifically designates God as the author, maintaining that the Torah was composed before the creation of the world (p. 160) (see Midrash *B'reishit Rabbah* 1.1). According to this midrash, the divinely revealed words are only called the "Torah of Moses" on account of God's great mercy toward Israel's greatest prophet. Several early interpretations of the Bible, such as the pseudepigraphical book of Jubilees, note that the purpose of the writing down of the Law was to remind future generations of the terms of the covenant and of Israel's obligations to fulfill it. The *Testament of Moses* 10:11, another pseudepigraphical book, emphasizes that it was now Joshua's responsibility to keep the words and the book.

*Take this book of Teaching and place it beside the Ark of the Covenant.... Then Moses recited the words of the following poem to the very end* (31:26, 30). Rabbinic and medieval commentators wondered about the relationship between the "Teaching" (*torah*; 31:9, 11–12, 24, 26) and the "poem" (*shirah*, often translated by others as "Song"; 31:19, 21–22, 30). According to Midrash *Sifrei D'varim*, this *shirah* (Deuteronomy 32), in which Moses calls upon heaven and earth as witnesses, is known as the "Song of Moses." Since 31:26 designates the Torah as witness against Israel, some of the Rabbis smoothed out the relationship between the "Teaching" and the "Song" by equating the two (see BT *Sanhedrin* 21b and BT *Chulin* 133a).

*Interpreters wondered why the women were required to hear the divine "Teaching."*

Although some commentaries interpret the poem as testimony by Moses *against* Israel, following the literal reading of 31:26, other rabbinic texts demonstrate that Moses frequently defended Israel to God. Thus, BT *B'rachot* 32a recalls that following the episode of the Golden Calf, God said, "Let Me alone and I will destroy them" (9:14); but Moses immediately "stood up, prayed vigorously, and begged for mercy" on Israel's behalf. According to Midrash *D'varim Rabbah* 3.11, "Moses left no corner in heaven upon which he did not prostrate himself in prayer" on Israel's behalf (also Midrash *Sh'mot Rabbah* 42.9). BT *Sanhedrin* 111a–b teaches that Moses continued to advocate for Israel, even after his death.

*Then Moses recited the words of the following poem* (31:30). The Rabbis speak of ten sublime "poems" (or "songs"; Heb. *shirah*) in the Hebrew Bible that mark central events in the history of the people of Israel; although they differ on the exact listing of the ten, they all include this poem (Midrash *M'chilta, B'shalach, Shirta* 1). Several of the other songs mentioned are specifically associated with women, including the Song of Miriam, in which she sang and led the women in dance (Exodus 15:20–21), and the Song of Deborah (Judges 5). Both celebrate Israel's victories over its enemies. According to the *M'chilta, B'shalach, Shirta* 1, the tenth song will be recited in the messianic era: "Sing a new song to יהוה; / sing God's praise, all the earth" (Isaiah 42:10). —*Meira Kensky*

## *Contemporary Reflection*

It was the moment for which Moses had prepared nearly all his life. Reared in Egyptian luxury, mothered by a princess, Moses might have lived out his 120 years in careless splendor, unconcerned with the fate of hordes of Israelite slaves who labored outside his palace. Yet, from the moment that Moses—still a young man—slays the Egyptian taskmaster, he chooses to cast his lot with the slaves. For their sake—and their God's—Moses spends forty years traversing the wilderness, leading a complaining and defiant people, interceding with an inscrutable and demanding Sovereign, and somehow transforming the despised and oppressed into witnesses of miracles and keepers of revelation. The work is almost finished. God and Moses have brought the people to the edge of the Promised Land, a place Moses will not reach. He will gaze upon it from the heights of Mount Nebo, but he will die before he enters it.

Why will Moses forgo the glorious completion of the task into which he has poured his very life? In *parashat Vayeilech*, Moses himself explains: "I am now one hundred and twenty years old, I can no longer be active" (31:2). Translated more literally, Moses says, "I can no longer go out and come in." Either way, the message seems clear: Moses is tired out; he is no longer feeling strong or vigorous. So he will remain on this side of the Jordan River, take a peek at the Promised Land, and then die a peaceful and contented death. It may seem strange that he is willing to miss this crowning achievement; but this appears to be his choice.

Except, of course, that he has not made such a choice. As the verse continues, Moses adds what might seem to be a secondary explanation, an afterthought—yet it contains some crucial information: "Moreover, יהוה has said to me, 'You shall not go across yonder Jordan'" (31:2).

After all, isn't this the real reason that Moses will not enter the Promised Land? The Torah itself is quite clear that what Moses had done at a certain point prompted God to forbid him from crossing the Jordan. We read the unequivocal divine decree first in Numbers 20:12. After devoting his life to serving God's chosen nation, Moses shall not set foot in God's chosen land.

Moses' fate is painful, even tragic. Standing before the people he has so steadfastly led, he prepares not to shepherd them triumphantly into the Promised Land, but to install a new leader who will bring them to their destiny. It is, for Moses, a moment of enormous loss. He may speak as if he has a choice—as if he could lead the Israelites into the Land if only he were a little younger, a little stronger—but truly there is no choice at all. He may act as if he has freely decided to stay behind, but it is clear that the choice was made for him.

Today, we like to make our own choices. We live in a time when almost every institution, every career, every level of leadership beckons us. We swell with pride and optimism as we see women serving in the highest echelons of government, in our universities and in our armed forces, as respected doctors, artists, scientists, teachers, philanthropists. We prepare ourselves and our daughters for lives in which every possibility is open to us. We can choose the life we want to live—except when we cannot.

Except when a 14-year-old girl falls prey to our society's unspoken message to young women—"You are not pretty enough. You are not popular enough. You are not thin enough"—and spends her adolescence battling hateful voices in her head. She may tell you that she chose to watch her weight and eat very little. But in many ways, that choice has been made for her.

Except when a wife endures an abusive relationship, convinced that she is worthless and unable to make her own way in the world. When her husband begins to threaten their children, she finally gathers her courage and flees. Without money or marketable skills, she earns only substandard wages. She may tell you that she chose to go it alone, to work for low pay because she needs a job, to do without health care for herself so that she could provide for her family. But in many ways, that choice has been made for her.

Except when a woman devotes countless eighty-hour workweeks to her career and so is only a year or two away from a prestigious promotion when she and her spouse have a baby. When she returns to the office, her appeals for flexible hours, the chance occasionally to work from home, even a private place to express breast milk, are refused. She may tell you that she chose to quit her job and not work in an unsupportive environment, chose the rewards of at-home motherhood over the rewards of professional life. But in many ways, that choice has been made for her.

We find women all around us submitting to pressures and expectations that undercut our right to choose the life we want to live. And yet, the pressures and the expectations that we encounter are not God's will. Whereas Moses' ability to choose his destiny ended when God made known the heavenly decree, our choices should not—must not—be bound by earthly decrees that dishonor and punish women, that teach young girls they are not good enough, that refuse to assist a persecuted victim in need, that force a mother to decide between her career and her child. Acknowledging the injustice of the choices women often face is surely the first step toward changing the pattern.

*She may tell you that it was her choice, but in many ways that choice was made for her.*

*—Elaine Rose Glickman*

# Voices

## The Keepers of My Youth

Karen Alkalay-Gut

*Deuteronomy 31:2*

At the Jewish Old Age Home in my home
town,
the keepers of my youth sit in wheelchairs
sunning themselves in the crisp autumn air.

Shriveled hands grasp at my clothes as I pass:
my third-grade teacher, the doctor who set
my arm
(broken from my first encounter with a
bicycle),
the smiling crossing guard, my Hebrew
school nurse.
Those who can speak and whose minds are clear
reminisce with tears in their eyes; others
look on and nod. "You played Haman in the
Purim Spiel,"
rasps the accompanist from the Folk Shule,
"and now you are a grown-up lady
with teenage children of your own."
"Look how tall she is—from all the lunches
she ate at my house," my old friend's mother
adds.

Here I am still in my flower. With a gentle hand
I smooth the shawls around their shoulders,
tuck the bright wool blankets into their chairs,
and whisper encouraging farewells to my troops
at the front.

## Moon Is Teaching Bible

Zelda (transl. Marcia Falk)

*Deuteronomy 31:10–13*

Moon is teaching Bible.
Cyclamen, Poppy, and Mountain
listen with joy.
Only the girl cries.
Poppy can't hear her crying—
Poppy is blazing in Torah,
Poppy is burning like the verse.
Cyclamen doesn't listen to the crying—
Cyclamen swoons
from the sweetness of the secret.
Mountain won't hear her crying—
Mountain is sunk
in thought.

But here comes Wind,
soft and fragrant,
to honor hope, to sing
the heart of each flying rider,
each ardent hunter
swept to the ends of the sea.

## Preparing for the Journey

Etty Hillesum

*Deuteronomy 31:2*

My heart failed a few times again today, but each time it came back to life. I say my goodbyes from minute to minute, shaking myself free of all outer things. I cut through the ropes that still hold me bound, I load up with everything I need to set out on my journey. I am sitting now by a quiet canal, my legs dangling over the stone wall, and I wonder whether one day my heart will be so weary and worn that it will no longer fly where it wants, free as a bird.

## *The Old Prayer Book*

Miriam Ulinover (transl. Kathryn Hellerstein)

*Deuteronomy 31:12*

In one hand the old prayer book, tuition fee
in her other,
And hanging from its string, the dangling
pointer,—
As a child, my grandmother used to run quickly
into the *kheder*
To repeat the alphabet, with the boys, in order.
Everything would have been fine; but the boys
would hit her—
A girls' voice yowling can carry high as heaven.
Once long ago she nearly fainted, nearly
perished
From the blows and benevolent slaps, what
a horror!
But therefore a young wife is put in an ample
chain,
With the same old prayer book, only now
without a pointer,
To lead the way through the entire *shtetl* to the
yard of the *shul.*
How the new wife proudly takes up marching!
Wives stay mute, bashfully, silently, the women
stare
At her mouth that does not rest from the
Sabbath prayer,
As she, together with the congregation and
the cantor,
Draws nearer the *Shekhine* praying, chanting.
In the *shul* an envious flurry, sweating,
and brow wiping,
As wives, poor things, can only turn the
pages . . .
She flares up and throws herself afresh into
the prayer:
For, of course, she is in her childhood home
in the old *siddur*!

## *What We Need*

Elaine Marcus Starkman

*Deuteronomy 31:19–22*

We women need poems—
leaping lines to store

for cold winter nights
when our tongues crave juice;

mirrors to the inside of our heads
when we cannot find our own reflections;

fancies that keep us
from meaningless work.

Depressions, holidays, lovers,
prayers, friends

won't do the trick alone;
the emptiness only snaps back,

but immersing minds,
losing our bodies

letting our poems
take on an enormity,

grace,
sanctity,

fill us with delicious
worth that feeds our hunger.

# האזינו ◆ *Haazinu*

DEUTERONOMY 32:1–52

## *The Song of Moses: A Foretelling of Future Events*

PARASHAT HAAZINU ("give ear") tells of a relationship gone awry. According to the poem at the heart of this parashah, God had established a special relationship with the people Israel and then lovingly watched over and cared for them, yet they rejected God and turned to other deities. Enraged at their betrayal, God resolves to decimate Israel. But God relents when realizing that the other nations might foolishly misinterpret Israel's demise as a result of their own power, not as a divinely inflicted punishment. Thus, with a change of heart, God decides instead to avenge the Israelites against their enemies.

In the prior parashah (*Vayeilech*), God predicted that after Moses' death, the people would go astray by worshiping other deities, which would prompt God to punish them (31:16–18). To prevent any misunderstanding of these future events, God instructed Moses to write down a particular poem and teach it to the people so that it would serve as a "witness," testifying to God's justice in the face of Israel's wayward behavior (31:19). That poem, which constitutes most of *parashat Haazinu* (32:1–43), is followed by a confirmation that Moses recites the poem to the people (32:44–47); then, the parashah looks ahead to Moses' imminent death (32:48–52).

Although the poem is not titled in the biblical text, people refer to it as "the Song of Moses" or "*Shirat Haazinu*" ("the Song [that begins with the word] *Haazinu*"). In light of various linguistic and grammatical features, most scholars agree that the Song originated earlier than the rest of the book, as an independent composition. While a precise date remains uncertain, scholars assume that the poem was written in response to some tragedy, in an attempt to make sense of the event and provide hope for the future. Later, Deuteronomy's creators appended this preexistent poem to the book in order to reinforce the consequences of breaking the Covenant, a central theme in Moses' parting words to the people.

*Women were responsible for crafting and reciting similar sorts of poetic compositions.*

While the name "Song of Moses" implies that Moses wrote this poem, authorship of the Song cannot be determined. Note, however, that a number of biblical passages indicate that women were responsible for crafting and reciting similar sorts of poetic compositions. Various women in the Bible perform songs to celebrate military victories (Miriam in Exodus 15:20–21; Deborah in Judges 5; Jephthah's daughter in Judges 11:34; and the women welcoming the heroes in I Samuel 18:6–7). Combining this textual evidence with other data, some scholars have concluded that another poem attributed to Moses, the Song at the Sea (Exodus 15:1–19), may have been authored by a woman (see pp. 386–87, 392). Other biblical texts indicate that women composed and chanted laments in times of national crisis or personal loss. For instance, God instructs the prophet Jeremiah to summon the "wailing women . . . the skillful ones" (Jeremiah 9:16). Jeremiah then calls all the women, not just the professional female mourners, to listen to God's word and then teach their daughters and friends a dirge (9:19).

As *Shirat Haazinu* recounts the troubled relationship between God and Israel, it specifies that both women and men alike will inflame God's anger (v. 19) and suffer God's wrath (v. 25).

The Song employs diverse metaphors to describe the Divine. In addition to the gender-neutral representations of God as a Rock (vv. 4, 15, 18, 30, 31, 37) and as an eagle (v. 11), God appears as a father (v. 6), warrior (vv. 23, 41–42), and, most remarkably, a mother who gave birth to and nursed her child, Israel (vv. 13, 18).

—*Andrea L. Weiss*

## *Outline*

*I.* The Song of Moses
*Shirat Haazinu* (32:1–43)

- *A.* Introductory invocation (vv. 1–3)
- *B.* Recollection of God's early relationship with Israel (vv. 4–14)
- *C.* Accusation of insubordination and idolatry (vv. 15–18)
- *D.* Punishment proposed (vv. 19–25)
- *E.* Punishment reconsidered (vv. 26–42)
- *F.* Concluding invocation (v. 43)

*II.* Final Instructions (32:44–52)

- *A.* Moses' charge to the people (vv. 44–47)
- *B.* God's instructions about Moses' imminent death (vv. 48–52)

32:1

Give ear, O heavens, let me speak;
Let the earth hear the words I utter!
2 May my discourse come down as the rain,
My speech distill as the dew,
Like showers on young growth,
Like droplets on the grass.

לב הַאֲזִינוּ הַשָּׁמַיִם וַאֲדַבֵּרָה
וְתִשְׁמַע הָאָרֶץ אִמְרֵי־פִי׃
2 יַעֲרֹף כַּמָּטָר לִקְחִי
תִּזַּל כַּטַּל אִמְרָתִי
כִּשְׂעִירִם עֲלֵי־דֶשֶׁא
וְכִרְבִיבִים עֲלֵי־עֵשֶׂב׃

## *The Song of Moses*

SHIRAT HAAZINU (32:1–43)

*Shirat Haazinu* exhibits the defining features of biblical poetry, such as poetic parallelism, terseness, elevated diction, and various forms of repetition and patterning. Biblical poetry typically contains two, sometimes three, lines (called a "bicolon" or "tricolon" in the singular, and "bicola" and "tricola" in the plural) that relate to one another in a variety of ways. Parallel lines often appear to mirror one another, with one colon seeming to echo the general sentiment of the other, as in v. 2: "Like showers on young growth, / Like droplets on the grass."

In other cases, while the lines as a whole may seem to be fairly synonymous, the individual word pairs within the parallel lines differ grammatically or semantically. For example, the two cola in v. 1 seem to be rather equivalent in terms of their overall meaning: "Give ear, O heavens, let me speak; / Let the earth hear the words I utter." However, "heaven" and "earth" represent two distinct and complementary entities asked to listen the poet's words. Plus, the end of the lines display a marked grammatical variance, for "let me speak" is a verbal phrase, whereas "the words I utter" (literally "the sayings of my mouth") is a nominal (noun) phrase.

Elsewhere, the lines may not echo one another with any degree of grammatical or semantic equivalence or variation, but together may express a continuous idea, as in v. 8: "[God] fixed the boundaries of peoples / In relation to Israel's numbers." Being attentive to the dynamics of poetic parallelism can help the reader better understand this challenging text.

### INTRODUCTORY INVOCATION (32:1–3)

Previously in Deuteronomy, Moses summoned heaven and earth as witnesses to the terms of the covenant (4:26; 30:19; 31:28), similar to the convention found in ancient Near Eastern political treaties. Here, the poet invites heaven and earth to listen to the words that follow. These two terms form a merism, which is an expression that uses two extremes to indicate a totality (see also at Exodus 10:9 and 11:5). By invoking these two contrasting


◗ Moses sings of God as faithful and nurturing, but also as violent and vengeful.

ANOTHER VIEW ➤ *1265*

◗ The God imagery of this parashah encourages us to create new images of the Deity.

CONTEMPORARY REFLECTION ➤ *1267*

◗ The Midrash imagines that Israel—personified as a woman—will implore God to listen.

POST-BIBLICAL INTERPRETATIONS ➤ *1265*

◗ The morning you wake to bury me, / you'll wonder what to wear.

VOICES ➤ *1269*

3For the name of יהוה I proclaim;
    Give glory to our God!

4The Rock!—whose deeds are perfect,
    Yea, all God's ways are just;
A faithful God, never false,
    True and upright indeed.
5Unworthy children—
    That crooked, perverse generation—
    Their baseness has played God false.
6Do you thus requite יהוה,
    O dull and witless people?
Is not this the Father who created you—
    Fashioned you and made you endure!

3 כִּי שֵׁם יְהוָה אֶקְרָא
הָבוּ גֹדֶל לֵאלֹהֵינוּ:
4 הַצּוּר תָּמִים פָּעֳלוֹ
כִּי כָל־דְּרָכָיו מִשְׁפָּט
אֵל אֱמוּנָה וְאֵין עָוֶל
צַדִּיק וְיָשָׁר הוּא:
5 שִׁחֵת לוֹ לֹא בָּנָיו מוּמָם
דּוֹר עִקֵּשׁ וּפְתַלְתֹּל:
6 הַ לְיהוָה תִּגְמְלוּ־זֹאת
עַם נָבָל וְלֹא חָכָם
הֲלוֹא־הוּא אָבִיךָ קָּנֶךָ
הוּא עָשְׂךָ וַיְכֹנְנֶךָ:

realms, the poet may also seek to call upon everything in between them, namely, the entire world. Four similes in v. 2 compare Moses' words to water. Just as water is essential for sustaining life, so Moses hopes that the recitation of this message will enable Israel to "long endure on the land" that they prepare to enter (32:47).

### RECOLLECTION OF GOD'S EARLY RELATIONSHIP WITH ISRAEL (32:4–14)

The first part of this section (vv. 4–6) establishes a stark contrast between God and Israel: God is "upright" (v. 4), but Israel is "crooked" (v. 5); God's deeds are "perfect" (v. 4), but Israel is "blemished" (rendered here as "unworthy," v. 5); God is Israel's "Father" (v. 6), but Israel is God's "non-children" (see at v. 5 below). The second part of the section (vv. 7–14) utilizes various metaphors to recount the beneficent acts God performed on Israel's behalf.

*4. The Rock!* The word "rock" (*tzur*) stands out as a key word in the Song, recurring eight times: once to designate a literal stone (v. 13), twice as an ironic reference to foreign gods (vv. 31, 37), and five times to depict the God of Israel (vv. 4, 15, 18, 30, 31).

The Bible portrays God metaphorically more than thirty times using the term *tzur*, which in such contexts conveys the image of a large rock formation or mountain. In the Psalms, *tzur* appears frequently as a divine name or epithet, as when a psalmist cries out to "my rock and my redeemer" (Psalm 19:15) or praises "my strength . . . my fortress, my rescuer, my God, my rock in whom I seek refuge" (Psalm 18:2–3). In the present verse, however, "the Rock" appears in conjunction with other words that highlight God's steadfast loyalty and righteousness.

*5.* Various proposals have been suggested for reconstructing this obscure verse, which literally reads: "He has dealt corruptly with him not his children their blemish." (For proposed solutions, see Jeffrey Tigay, *Deuteronomy*, 1996, p. 301.) The language in this verse reviles Israel by describing the people as having the opposite qualities as their God.

***children.*** The reference to Israel as God's children anticipates the subsequent metaphors of God as Father (see below at v. 6) and Mother (see at vv. 13, 18). Elsewhere in the Song, the people are envisioned as young eagles (v. 11), unruly animals (v. 15), and servants (v. 43).

*6. Father.* Far fewer biblical passages (about twelve) refer to God as a father (*av*) than speak of

7 Remember the days of old,
Consider the years of ages past;
Ask your parent, who will inform you,
Your elders, who will tell you:
8 When the Most High gave nations their homes
And set the divisions of humanity,
[God] fixed the boundaries of peoples
In relation to Israel's numbers.

7 זְכֹר֙ יְמ֣וֹת עוֹלָ֔ם
בִּ֖ינוּ שְׁנ֣וֹת דֹּר־וָדֹ֑ר
שְׁאַ֤ל אָבִ֙יךָ֙ וְיַגֵּ֔דְךָ
זְקֵנֶ֖יךָ וְיֹ֥אמְרוּ לָֽךְ׃
8 בְּהַנְחֵ֤ל עֶלְיוֹן֙ גּוֹיִ֔ם
בְּהַפְרִיד֖וֹ בְּנֵ֣י אָדָ֑ם
יַצֵּב֙ גְּבֻלֹ֣ת עַמִּ֔ים
לְמִסְפַּ֖ר בְּנֵ֥י יִשְׂרָאֵֽל׃

God metaphorically as a rock (see at v. 4). Here the paternal analogy focuses on God's role as creator (see also Malachi 2:10). Other passages speak of God as a father in order to portray God's love and compassion (Psalm 103:13; Isaiah 63:16) or God's disciplinary role (Proverbs 3:12). Elsewhere, the metaphor highlights the special bond between God and Israel, a relationship that brings with it often unmet expectations (see Jeremiah 3:4, 19; 31:9).

A number of texts speak of Israel metaphorically as God's child without identifying the gender of the parent (see Exodus 4:22; Deuteronomy 1:31; Isaiah 1:2; Jeremiah 31:20; Hosea 11:1–4). Tikva Frymer-Kensky observes that in contrast to metaphors of God as shepherd, king, or master that "emphasize the great gulf in power and wisdom between humans and [the] divine," the metaphor of God as parent in such passages "emphasizes the emotional aspect of the commitment between the partners." She notes that metaphors of God as both father and mother (see at vv. 13, 18) express God's "dependable love" and compassion, as well as the way God nurtures, teaches, punishes, and redeems Israel. Reflecting on how the parental analogy functions in the Song, Frymer-Kensky writes: "It offers hope for the people of Israel in the time of their greatest suffering, for it carries with it a sense of anticipatory forgiveness and the end of suffering, the promises of an eternal bond that remains unbroken even through difficult times" (*In the Wake of the Goddesses*, 1992, pp. 162–63).

***created you.*** This verb (from the root *k-n-h*) introduces a string of three verbs used to describe the way the divine Father begot Israel. Elsewhere, this verb is associated with the mother's reproductive capacity. After Eve gives birth to Cain (*kayin*), she explains the significance of his name: "Both I and יהוה have made (*kaniti*) a man" (Genesis 4:1). In Psalm 139:13, the speaker describes being created (*kanita*) by God "in my mother's womb."

*7.* ***your parent.*** Heb. *av* is used literally here, referring to biological parents, but figuratively in v. 6.

*8–9.* Tracing the relationship between God and Israel back to the "days of old," the poem refers to when God separated the human races into distinct nations (Genesis 10, 11:1–9) and selected Israel as God's "treasured people" (Deuteronomy 7:6).

*8.* ***In relation to Israel's numbers.*** As it stands, this verse implies that God divided all of humanity into a certain number of nations according to the number of Israelites. Many interpreters assume this means that God established 70 nations (Genesis 10) to match Jacob's 70 offspring (Exodus 1:5). However, variant readings preserved in the Qumran (Dead Sea) Scrolls and the ancient Jewish translation into Greek (Septuagint) suggest that this phrase originally read: "in relation to the number of divine beings" (*b'nei elim* instead of *b'nei Yisrael*). In that case, the verse asserts that God allotted lesser deities (such as those mentioned in Psalm 82) to the other nations to worship but set aside Israel as God's own

9 For יהוה's portion is this people;
Jacob, God's own allotment.

10 [God] found them in a desert region,
In an empty howling waste.
[God] engirded them, watched over them,
Guarded them as the pupil of God's eye.
11 Like an eagle who rouses its nestlings,
Gliding down to its young,
So did [God] spread wings and take them,
Bear them along on pinions;

9 כִּ֛י חֵ֥לֶק יְהֹוָ֖ה עַמּ֑וֹ
יַעֲקֹ֖ב חֶ֥בֶל נַחֲלָתֽוֹ׃
10 יִמְצָאֵ֙הוּ֙ בְּאֶ֣רֶץ מִדְבָּ֔ר
וּבְתֹ֖הוּ יְלֵ֣ל יְשִׁמֹ֑ן
יְסֹבְבֶ֙נְהוּ֙ יְב֣וֹנְנֵ֔הוּ
יִצְּרֶ֖נְהוּ כְּאִישׁ֥וֹן עֵינֽוֹ׃
11 כְּנֶ֙שֶׁר֙ יָעִ֣יר קִנּ֔וֹ
עַל־גּוֹזָלָ֖יו יְרַחֵ֑ף
יִפְרֹ֤שׂ כְּנָפָיו֙ יִקָּחֵ֔הוּ
יִשָּׂאֵ֖הוּ עַל־אֶבְרָתֽוֹ׃

people. As in Deuteronomy 4:19–20, such a reading would reflect a notion called monolatry, which refers to the allegiance to one God without denying the existence of other deities. Scholars assume that later scribes "corrected" the text (see also at v. 43) so that these words would conform to what became the monotheist standard: "I, I am the One; / There is no god beside Me" (v. 39).

*10.* ***[God] found them.*** By using this verb, the poet hints at several possible metaphors for the people Israel. What did God find in the wilderness? Hosea 9:10 employs the same verb when God reminisces: "Like grapes, in the wilderness I found Israel; like the first fig to ripen on a fig tree, I saw your ancestors." Ezekiel imagines God finding something different when he narrates how God discovered Israel as an abandoned baby girl. According to Ezekiel 16:3–6, Israel was rejected on the day of her birth and left to die in an open field. God passed by, saw Israel wallowing in her blood, and resolved to save the baby girl: "In your blood, live!" Thus, perhaps the language in this passage evokes images of Israel as an abandoned girl or succulent fruit.

***desert region.*** As in this verse, several prophetic passages look back nostalgically at the journey through the wilderness following the exodus from Egypt. For example, Jeremiah speaks of the time when Israel followed God in the wilderness with the devotion of a young bride (Jeremiah 2:2–3; see also 31:2–3; Hosea 2:16–17). Such depictions differ drastically from the way other parts of the Torah depict this time period (compare, for instance, 9:7 or Numbers 16–17).

***as the pupil of God's eye.*** This simile aims to illustrate how God guarded Israel in the wilderness like the blinking of the eyelid protects the vulnerable pupil. (Other translations employ an English idiom to render this expression as "the apple of His eye," but the Hebrew text does not literally mention an apple.) Psalm 17:8 pairs this simile with an image of protection found in the following verse of the Song: "Guard me like the pupil of your eye; hide me in the shadow of Your wings."

*11.* ***Like an eagle who rouses its nestlings.*** Many interpreters explain that this simile compares the way God cared for Israel in the wilderness to the way eagles train their young to fly. They assume the verb translated here as "rouse" implies that the mother or father eagle pushes the baby bird out of the nest and then hovers near by as the young bird tries to fly, ready to catch it should the need arise. Some scholars have questioned this interpretation, pointing out that observations by ornithologists do not confirm this type of behavior and that the verb in question might mean "protects." In that case, the simile would supplement the depiction of God's watchful care in the prior verse.

***spread wings.*** Similarly, Exodus 19:4 envisions

12 יהוה alone did guide them,
No alien god alongside.

13 [God] set them atop the highlands,
To feast on the yield of the earth;
Nursing them with honey from the crag,
And oil from the flinty rock,
14 Curd of kine and milk of flocks;
With the best of lambs,
And rams of Bashan, and he-goats;
With the very finest wheat—
And foaming grape-blood was your drink.

12 יְהוָה בָּדָד יַנְחֶנּוּ
וְאֵין עִמּוֹ אֵל נֵכָר׃
13 יַרְכִּבֵהוּ עַל־במותי בָּמֳתֵי אָרֶץ
וַיֹּאכַל תְּנוּבֹת שָׂדָי
וַיֵּנִקֵהוּ דְבַשׁ מִסֶּלַע
וְשֶׁמֶן מֵחַלְמִישׁ צוּר׃
14 חֶמְאַת בָּקָר וַחֲלֵב צֹאן
עִם־חֵלֶב כָּרִים
וְאֵילִים בְּנֵי־בָשָׁן וְעַתּוּדִים
עִם־חֵלֶב כִּלְיוֹת חִטָּה
וְדַם־עֵנָב תִּשְׁתֶּה־חָמֶר׃

God carrying Israel "on eagles' wings" (compare 1:31, which speaks of God carrying Israel through the wilderness as a parent). Several psalms speak of "the shadow of God's wing" as a place of protection (see Psalms 17:8; 36:8; 57:2). Boaz blesses Ruth with the acknowledgment that she has sought to come under God's sheltering wings (Ruth 2:12).

*13. set them.* Or "caused them to ride," which would continue the eagle imagery of v. 11.

*To feast.* The poet introduces a new metaphor to enhance the argument that God showered Israel with the utmost kindness and generosity, which makes Israel's subsequent defiance all the more astonishing. Carol Meyers argues that the general notion of God providing Israel with food likewise involves female divine imagery, for women prepared most of the food in ancient Israel (see the introduction to Exodus 15:22–17:16).

*Nursing them.* In applying to God the Hebrew verb *y-n-k* (which can be also translated as "suckling"), the poet adds an analogy to a mother with her newborn baby, an unmistakable maternal image. Thus, in describing how God nourished and sustained Israel, the poet juxtaposes the earlier image of God as father (v. 6) with a metaphor of God as mother. Although such specific female imagery for God is not common in the Bible, we do find other examples in which maternal metaphors depict God's love, devotion, and care for the people to whom God gave birth. For example, in Isaiah 49:15, best translated as "Can a woman forget her nursing child, or show no compassion for the child of her womb?" the prophet's rhetorical question reassures the people that God has not forgotten them (see also Isaiah 46:3–4 and at Numbers 11:12).

As Jeffrey Tigay observes, the verb *y-n-k* in this verse implies that "God fed Israel with virtually no effort on its part" by producing abundant food from unexpected sources: "honeycombs, found in the land's countless caves and fissures, and oil-producing olive trees that flourish in its rocky limestone soils" (*Deuteronomy*, 1996, p. 305). Whereas other texts tell about God providing water from rocks (Exodus 17:6; Numbers 20:8–11), here the provisions are more lavish, thus emphasizing how God, like a mother, lovingly indulged Israel.

*14. Curd . . . milk.* The foods listed in this verse represent the type of generous hospitality one would offer a special guest, as Sarah and Abraham do in Genesis 18:6–8. Jael uses these two dairy products to lure the enemy king Sisera to sleep before she kills him (Judges 5:25).

15 So Jeshurun grew fat and kicked—
You grew fat and gross and coarse—
They forsook the God who made them
And spurned the Rock of their support.
16 They incensed [God] with alien things,
Vexed [God] with abominations.
17 They sacrificed to demons, no-gods,
Gods they had never known,
New ones, who came but lately,
Who stirred not your forebears' fears.
18 You neglected the Rock who begot you,
Forgot the God who labored to bring you forth.

15 וַיִּשְׁמַן יְשֻׁרוּן וַיִּבְעָט
שָׁמַנְתָּ עָבִיתָ כָּשִׂיתָ
וַיִּטֹּשׁ אֱלוֹהַּ עָשָׂהוּ
וַיְנַבֵּל צוּר יְשֻׁעָתוֹ׃
16 יַקְנִאֻהוּ בְּזָרִים
בְּתוֹעֵבֹת יַכְעִיסֻהוּ׃
17 יִזְבְּחוּ לַשֵּׁדִים לֹא אֱלֹהַּ
אֱלֹהִים לֹא יְדָעוּם
חֲדָשִׁים מִקָּרֹב בָּאוּ
לֹא שְׂעָרוּם אֲבֹתֵיכֶם׃
18 צוּר יְלָדְךָ תֶּשִׁי
וַתִּשְׁכַּח אֵל מְחֹלְלֶךָ׃

## ACCUSATION OF INSUBORDINATION AND IDOLATRY (32:15–18)

The tone of the poem changes sharply as God's graciousness gives way to Israel's ingratitude and worship of foreign deities.

*15. grew fat.* Four verbs in the first half of this verse emphasize how Israel became bloated and gorged in response to God's sumptuous provisions. Moses repeatedly expresses the concern that once the people have settled in the land and "eaten their fill," they foolishly will attribute their success to their own actions and not acknowledge God's role in their success, which then will led them to forsake God and turn to other deities (6:10–13; 8:11–18; 11:15–16; 31:20). This sequence of events unfolds in the verses that follow.

*kicked.* This verb seems to introduce a new metaphor for Israel, who is envisioned as a fat, willful animal.

*who made them.* See at v. 18.

*Rock of their support.* This phrase invokes the more familiar characteristics associated with the rock analogy, namely, security and salvation (see at v. 4). However, the poet uses the metaphor ironically: the people have rejected God and sought support from alien gods.

*16. incensed...Vexed.* See at v. 21.

*17. demons.* Heb. *sheidim*, referring to protective spirits. Similar language appears in Psalm 106:37, which tells how the Israelites adopted the ways of their Canaanite neighbors and "sacrificed their sons and their daughters to the demons."

*18. the Rock.* See at vv. 4, 15. This time, the metaphor calls attention to God as Israel's creator.

*begot you.* Heb. *y'lad'cha.* This verb can signal a comparison between God and either a mother or father (as in Proverbs 23:22). However, nearly ten times as often, this root describes the mother's role in giving birth (as when Leah, Rachel, and their handmaids Bilhah and Zilpah give birth in Genesis 29–30). Given the ambiguity of the biological sex referred to by this verb, one also could translate this verb with a more gender-neutral locution like "gave birth to you."

*labored to bring you forth.* Whereas the previous verb in this verse ("begot") can be used with men or, more often, with women, the parallel verb (from the root *h-y-l*) specifically applies to women. Unambiguously, the poet casts God in the role of the Mother who labored to give birth to Israel. The identical verb appears in Isaiah 51:2 when the prophet charges the people: "Look back to Abraham your father, and to Sarah who labored to bring you forth (*h-y-l*)." (This is the only reference to Sarah outside of Genesis.) Several biblical passages

19יהוה saw and was vexed
And spurned these sons and daughters.
20[God] said: I will hide My countenance from them,
And see how they fare in the end.
For they are a treacherous breed,
Children with no loyalty in them.
21They incensed Me with no-gods,
Vexed Me with their futilities;
I'll incense them with a no-folk,
Vex them with a nation of fools.
22For a fire has flared in My wrath
And burned to the bottom of Sheol,
Has consumed the earth and its increase,
Eaten down to the base of the hills.

19 וַיַּ֥רְא יְהוָ֖ה וַיִּנְאָ֑ץ
מִכַּ֥עַס בָּנָ֖יו וּבְנֹתָֽיו׃
20 וַיֹּ֗אמֶר אַסְתִּ֤ירָה פָנַי֙ מֵהֶ֔ם
אֶרְאֶ֖ה מָ֣ה אַחֲרִיתָ֑ם
כִּ֣י ד֤וֹר תַּהְפֻּכֹת֙ הֵ֔מָּה
בָּנִ֖ים לֹא־אֵ֥מֻן בָּֽם׃
21 הֵ֚ם קִנְא֣וּנִי בְלֹא־אֵ֔ל
כִּעֲס֖וּנִי בְּהַבְלֵיהֶ֑ם
וַאֲנִי֙ אַקְנִיאֵ֣ם בְּלֹא־עָ֔ם
בְּג֥וֹי נָבָ֖ל אַכְעִיסֵֽם׃
22 כִּי־אֵשׁ֙ קָדְחָ֣ה בְאַפִּ֔י
וַתִּיקַ֖ד עַד־שְׁא֣וֹל תַּחְתִּ֑ית
וַתֹּ֤אכַל אֶ֙רֶץ֙ וִיבֻלָ֔הּ
וַתְּלַהֵ֖ט מוֹסְדֵ֥י הָרִֽים׃

use this root when they compare the trembling of people facing some desperate, dire situation to the writhing of a woman in labor (Isaiah 13:8; Jeremiah 4:31; 6:24; 22:23; Micah 4:9–10; Psalm 48:7; see also Jeremiah 30:6; 49:24). Isaiah 42:14, best translated as "Like a woman in labor I will scream, I will pant and I will gasp," dramatically transforms this simile when using it to describe the powerful way that God will bring about redemption. Reflecting on how this verb functions in *Shirat Haazinu*, Bernard Levinson observes: "That God had to suffer labor pains to bear Israel only increases the injustice of Israel's forgetting the divine parent." He adds that the maternal metaphors for God "provide an important alternative to the normal masculine imagery associated with God" ("Deuteronomy," *Jewish Study Bible*, 2004, p. 442).

## PUNISHMENT PROPOSED (32:19–25)

After indicting the Israelites with forsaking their God and worshipping beings whose divinity is denied, God announces the consequences: decimation of the population, famine, and other deadly scourges. The One whose "ways are just" (v. 4) ensures that the punishment fits the crime (see at v. 21).

*19. sons and daughters.* Several prior passages in Deuteronomy recognize the possibility that either women or men might lure the people to worship what the Bible presents as foreign gods (17:2; 29:17); others emphasize the role of women in such acts (7:3–4; see also Numbers 25:1–18 and Jeremiah 7:18).

*20. hide My countenance.* See at 31:17.

*Children.* See at v. 5.

*21. incensed...Vexed.* The repetition of these two verbs in both halves of the verse emphasizes that God intends to respond to Israel's apostasy with measure-for-measure punishment. (See at 5:9 for how the verb translated here as "incensed" relates to the metaphor of God as a jealous husband and Israel as an adulterous wife.)

*no-gods... no-folk.* Expressions with the word "no" recur throughout the poem (see at vv. 6, 17, 20); the linguistic repetition emphasizes the link between Israel's actions and God's reaction.

*22. Sheol.* This is the netherworld to which all the dead are believed to descend (see also at Genesis 42:38; I Samuel 2:6).

<sup>23</sup>I will sweep misfortunes on them,
Use up My arrows on them:
<sup>24</sup>Wasting famine, ravaging plague,
Deadly pestilence, and fanged beasts
Will I let loose against them,
With venomous creepers in dust.
<sup>25</sup>The sword shall deal death without,
As shall the terror within,
To youth and maiden alike,
The suckling as well as the aged.

<sup>26</sup>I might have reduced them to naught,
Made their memory cease among
humankind,
<sup>27</sup>But for fear of the taunts of the foe,
Their enemies who might misjudge
And say, "Our own hand has prevailed;
None of this was wrought by יהוה!"
<sup>28</sup>For they are a folk void of sense,
Lacking in all discernment.
<sup>29</sup>Were they wise, they would think upon this,
Gain insight into their future:

23 אַסְפֶּ֤ה עָלֵ֙ימוֹ֙ רָע֔וֹת
חִצַּ֖י אֲכַלֶּה־בָּֽם:
24 מְזֵ֥י רָעָ֛ב וּלְחֻ֥מֵי רֶ֖שֶׁף
וְקֶ֥טֶב מְרִירִ֑י וְשֶׁן־בְּהֵמֹת֙
אֲשַׁלַּח־בָּ֔ם
עִם־חֲמַ֖ת זֹחֲלֵ֥י עָפָֽר:
25 מִח֤וּץ תְּשַׁכֶּל־חֶ֙רֶב֙
וּמֵחֲדָרִ֣ים אֵימָ֔ה
גַּם־בָּחוּר֙ גַּם־בְּתוּלָ֔ה
יוֹנֵ֖ק עִם־אִ֥ישׁ שֵׂיבָֽה:
26 אָמַ֖רְתִּי אַפְאֵיהֶ֑ם
אַשְׁבִּ֥יתָה מֵאֱנ֖וֹשׁ זִכְרָֽם:
27 לוּלֵ֗י כַּ֤עַס אוֹיֵב֙ אָג֔וּר
פֶּֽן־יְנַכְּר֖וּ צָרֵ֑ימוֹ
פֶּן־יֹֽאמְרוּ֙ יָדֵ֣נוּ רָ֔מָה
וְלֹ֥א יְהֹוָ֖ה פָּעַ֥ל כָּל־זֹֽאת:
28 כִּי־ג֛וֹי אֹבַ֥ד עֵצ֖וֹת הֵ֑מָּה
וְאֵ֥ין בָּהֶ֖ם תְּבוּנָֽה:
29 ל֥וּ חָכְמ֖וּ יַשְׂכִּ֣ילוּ זֹ֑את
יָבִ֖ינוּ לְאַחֲרִיתָֽם:

• • • • • • • • • • • • • • • • • • • • • • • • • • • •

**23.** *My arrows.* Mention of weapons here and in vv. 25, 41–42 evokes the metaphor of God as a (male) warrior. This image figures prominently in the Song at the Sea, the victory song that the Israelites recite after fleeing from Egypt (Exodus 15). Carol Meyers emphasizes that depicting God in masculine imagery "does not mean that the Torah's composer(s) believed God to be a male being" (see at Exodus 14:14; 15:3); this observation also applies to the female divine imagery prominent in *Shirat Haazinu*. (For more on the warrior metaphor, see Another View, p. 1265.)

**25.** The poet employs a double merism (see at vv. 1–3), setting up an opposition between female and male, and young and old, to indicate that no one will escape God's punishing wrath. Commenting on the mention of women and men here and in v. 19, Marc Brettler writes: "The poem thus explicitly includes women within its intended audience; this fits the gender-inclusive tendency present elsewhere in Deuteronomy (for example, 31:12)" (*Women in Scripture*, 2000, p. 236).

### PUNISHMENT RECONSIDERED (32:26–42)

Having asserted that God would be justified in penalizing the people for their transgressions, the Song now takes an unexpected turn. Expressing concern that the foreign nations whom God wielded to punish Israel will attribute their victory to their own power, not to God's might, God resolves to defeat the enemies and deliver Israel.

<sup>30</sup>"How could one have routed a thousand,
　Or two put ten thousand to flight,
Unless their Rock had sold them,
　יהוה had given them up?"
<sup>31</sup>For their rock is not like our Rock,
　In our enemies' own estimation.

<sup>32</sup>Ah! The vine for them is from Sodom,
　From the vineyards of Gomorrah;
The grapes for them are poison,
　A bitter growth their clusters.
<sup>33</sup>Their wine is the venom of asps,
　The pitiless poison of vipers.
<sup>34</sup>Lo, I have it all put away,
　Sealed up in My storehouses,
<sup>35</sup>To be My vengeance and recompense,
　At the time that their foot falters.
Yea, their day of disaster is near,
　And destiny rushes upon them.
<sup>36</sup>For יהוה will vindicate God's people
　And take revenge for God's servants,
Upon seeing that their might is gone,
　And neither bond nor free is left.
<sup>37</sup>[God] will say: Where are their gods,
　The rock in whom they sought refuge,
<sup>38</sup>Who ate the fat of their offerings
　And drank their libation wine?

30 אֵיכָ֞ה יִרְדֹּ֤ף אֶחָד֙ אֶ֔לֶף
וּשְׁנַ֖יִם יָנִ֣יסוּ רְבָבָ֑ה
אִם־לֹא֙ כִּי־צוּרָ֣ם מְכָרָ֔ם
וַֽיהֹוָ֖ה הִסְגִּירָֽם׃

31 כִּ֛י לֹ֥א כְצוּרֵ֖נוּ צוּרָ֑ם
וְאֹיְבֵ֖ינוּ פְּלִילִֽים׃

32 כִּֽי־מִגֶּ֤פֶן סְדֹם֙ גַּפְנָ֔ם
וּמִשַּׁדְמֹ֖ת עֲמֹרָ֑ה
עֲנָבֵ֙מוֹ֙ עִנְּבֵי־ר֔וֹשׁ
אַשְׁכְּלֹ֥ת מְרֹרֹ֖ת לָֽמוֹ׃

33 חֲמַ֥ת תַּנִּינִ֖ם יֵינָ֑ם
וְרֹ֖אשׁ פְּתָנִ֥ים אַכְזָֽר׃

34 הֲלֹא־ה֖וּא כָּמֻ֣ס עִמָּדִ֑י
חָת֖וּם בְּאוֹצְרֹתָֽי׃

35 לִ֤י נָקָם֙ וְשִׁלֵּ֔ם
לְעֵ֖ת תָּמ֣וּט רַגְלָ֑ם
כִּ֤י קָרוֹב֙ י֣וֹם אֵידָ֔ם
וְחָ֖שׁ עֲתִדֹ֥ת לָֽמוֹ׃

36 כִּֽי־יָדִ֤ין יְהֹוָה֙ עַמּ֔וֹ
וְעַל־עֲבָדָ֖יו יִתְנֶחָ֑ם
כִּ֤י יִרְאֶה֙ כִּי־אָ֣זְלַת יָ֔ד
וְאֶ֖פֶס עָצ֥וּר וְעָזֽוּב׃

37 וְאָמַ֖ר אֵ֣י אֱלֹהֵ֑ימוֹ
צ֖וּר חָסָ֥יוּ בֽוֹ׃

38 אֲשֶׁ֨ר חֵ֤לֶב זְבָחֵ֙ימוֹ֙ יֹאכֵ֔לוּ
יִשְׁתּ֖וּ יֵ֣ין נְסִיכָ֑ם

• • • • •                                        • • • • •

**30. thousand ... ten thousand.** This word pair illustrates the type of intensification often involved in poetic parallelism, with the second line heightening the language of the first. For example, much to King Saul's chagrin, the women who come out singing and dancing to greet the victorious troops utter this same word pair, but they associate the higher number with the man who will soon become Saul's rival: "Saul has slain his thousands; David, his tens of thousands!" (I Samuel 18:7).

**31. their rock ... our Rock.** Here and in v. 37, the poet returns to the rock metaphor, but this time as a way to ridicule those who rely on false deities. The so-called gods of the foreign nations do not exhibit the strength nor provide the refuge typically associated with the rock metaphor (see at v. 4). The meaning of the second half of the verse is uncertain.

**32–33.** Whereas God nursed Israel on fine wine (v. 14), her enemies will drink poisonous wine and thus die like the people of Sodom and Gomorrah.

Let them rise up to your help,
    And let them be a shield unto you!
39See, then, that I, I am the One;
    There is no god beside Me.
I deal death and give life;
    I wounded and I will heal:
    None can deliver from My hand.
40Lo, I raise My hand to heaven
    And say: As I live forever,
41When I whet My flashing blade
    And My hand lays hold on judgment,
Vengeance will I wreak on My foes,
    Will I deal to those who reject Me.
42I will make My arrows drunk with blood—
    As My sword devours flesh—
Blood of the slain and the captive
    From the long-haired enemy chiefs.

43O nations, acclaim God's people!
    For He'll avenge the blood of His servants,
Wreak vengeance on His foes,
    And cleanse His people's land.

יָק֙וּמוּ֙ וְיַעְזְרֻכֶ֔ם
יְהִ֥י עֲלֵיכֶ֖ם סִתְרָֽה׃
39 רְא֣וּ ׀ עַתָּ֗ה כִּ֣י אֲנִ֤י אֲנִי֙ ה֔וּא
וְאֵ֥ין אֱלֹהִ֖ים עִמָּדִ֑י
אֲנִ֧י אָמִ֣ית וַאֲחַיֶּ֗ה
מָחַ֙צְתִּי֙ וַאֲנִ֣י אֶרְפָּ֔א
וְאֵ֥ין מִיָּדִ֖י מַצִּֽיל׃
40 כִּֽי־אֶשָּׂ֥א אֶל־שָׁמַ֖יִם יָדִ֑י
וְאָמַ֕רְתִּי חַ֥י אָנֹכִ֖י לְעֹלָֽם׃
41 אִם־שַׁנּוֹתִי֙ בְּרַ֣ק חַרְבִּ֔י
וְתֹאחֵ֥ז בְּמִשְׁפָּ֖ט יָדִ֑י
אָשִׁ֤יב נָקָם֙ לְצָרָ֔י
וְלִמְשַׂנְאַ֖י אֲשַׁלֵּֽם׃
42 אַשְׁכִּ֤יר חִצַּי֙ מִדָּ֔ם
וְחַרְבִּ֖י תֹּאכַ֣ל בָּשָׂ֑ר
מִדַּ֤ם חָלָל֙ וְשִׁבְיָ֔ה
מֵרֹ֖אשׁ פַּרְע֥וֹת אוֹיֵֽב׃
43 הַרְנִ֤ינוּ גוֹיִם֙ עַמּ֔וֹ
כִּ֥י דַם־עֲבָדָ֖יו יִקּ֑וֹם
וְנָקָם֙ יָשִׁ֣יב לְצָרָ֔יו
וְכִפֶּ֥ר אַדְמָת֖וֹ עַמּֽוֹ׃ פ

- - - - - - - - - - - - - - - - - - - - - - - - - - -

**39.** *no god beside Me.* See at 4:35.

*deal death and give life.* This verse encapsulates the seemingly contrasting facets of God's nature, a point communicated by the Song's diverse imagery. (See further Another View, p. 1265.)

*wounded and...heal.* Carol Meyers asserts that the depiction of God as healer may compare God to women as well as men, for both practiced folk medicine in ancient Israel (see at Exodus 15:26).

*41–42.* On the warrior imagery in these verses, see at v. 23.

### CONCLUDING INVOCATION (32:43)

As it stands now, the Song ends by calling upon the foreign nations, those whose bloody demise has just been foretold, to praise Israel. Given various problems with the logic and structure of the current text, as well as alternative readings preserved in the Qumran (Dead Sea) Scrolls and the ancient Jewish translation into Greek (Septuagint), many scholars have concluded that the original version of this verse was markedly different. The first colon likely summoned the heavens, not the nations, to rejoice with God, which would mirror the poem's introduction (v. 1). The current reference to God's servants likely spoke of God's children, which would recall v. 5 and the depictions of God as Father and Mother. More significantly, the first colon likely contained a parallel line that read: "Bow to [God] all divinities" (*elohim*), which would resemble the reconstructed reading of "divine beings" in v. 8. Later

44 Moses came, together with Hosea son of Nun, and recited all the words of this poem in the hearing of the people.

45 And when Moses finished reciting all these words to all Israel, 46 he said to them: Take to heart all the words with which I have warned you this day. Enjoin them upon your children, that they may observe faithfully all the terms of this Teaching. 47 For this is not a trifling thing for you: it is your very life; through it you shall long endure on the land that you are to possess upon crossing the Jordan.

48 That very day יהוה spoke to Moses: 49 Ascend these heights of Abarim to Mount Nebo, which is in the land of Moab facing Jericho, and view the land of Canaan, which I am giving the Israelites as

44 וַיָּבֹ֣א מֹשֶׁ֗ה וַיְדַבֵּ֛ר אֶֽת־כָּל־דִּבְרֵ֥י הַשִּׁירָֽה־
הַזֹּ֖את בְּאָזְנֵ֣י הָעָ֑ם ה֖וּא וְהוֹשֵׁ֥עַ בִּן־נֽוּן׃
45 וַיְכַ֣ל מֹשֶׁ֗ה לְדַבֵּ֛ר אֶת־כָּל־הַדְּבָרִ֥ים
הָאֵ֖לֶּה אֶל־כָּל־יִשְׂרָאֵֽל׃ 46 וַיֹּ֤אמֶר אֲלֵהֶם֙
שִׂ֣ימוּ לְבַבְכֶ֔ם לְכָל־הַדְּבָרִ֕ים אֲשֶׁ֧ר אָנֹכִ֛י
מֵעִ֥יד בָּכֶ֖ם הַיּ֑וֹם אֲשֶׁ֤ר תְּצַוֻּם֙ אֶת־בְּנֵיכֶ֔ם
לִשְׁמֹ֣ר לַעֲשׂ֔וֹת אֶֽת־כָּל־דִּבְרֵ֖י הַתּוֹרָ֥ה
הַזֹּֽאת׃ 47 כִּ֠י לֹֽא־דָבָ֨ר רֵ֥ק הוּא֙ מִכֶּ֔ם כִּי־
ה֖וּא חַיֵּיכֶ֑ם וּבַדָּבָ֣ר הַזֶּ֗ה תַּאֲרִ֤יכוּ יָמִים֙ עַל־
הָ֣אֲדָמָ֔ה אֲשֶׁ֨ר אַתֶּ֜ם עֹבְרִ֧ים אֶת־הַיַּרְדֵּ֛ן
שָׁ֖מָּה לְרִשְׁתָּֽהּ׃ פ
48 וַיְדַבֵּ֤ר יְהוָה֙ אֶל־מֹשֶׁ֔ה בְּעֶ֛צֶם הַיּ֥וֹם הַזֶּ֖ה
לֵאמֹֽר׃ 49 עֲלֵ֡ה אֶל־הַר֩ הָעֲבָרִ֨ים הַזֶּ֜ה
הַר־נְב֗וֹ אֲשֶׁר֙ בְּאֶ֣רֶץ מוֹאָ֔ב אֲשֶׁ֖ר עַל־פְּנֵ֣י
יְרֵח֑וֹ וּרְאֵה֙ אֶת־אֶ֣רֶץ כְּנַ֔עַן אֲשֶׁ֨ר אֲנִ֥י נֹתֵ֛ן

scribes then removed this line so that it would not conflict with what became the monotheistic norm. (For further details, see Jeffrey Tigay, *Deuteronomy*, 1996, pp. 516–18; see also at v. 8 and 6:4.)

## *Final Instructions* (32:44–52)

The prior parashah (*Vayeilech*) concerned the writing and teaching of both the *torah* (the "Teaching," meaning most of Deuteronomy) and the *shirah* (the poem in 32:1–43), as well as the transfer of leadership in light of Moses' imminent death. This prose unit touches upon these same topics.

### MOSES' CHARGE TO THE PEOPLE (32:44–47)

This section contains two parts. The first (v. 44) reiterates that Moses indeed taught the Song to the people, as God had instructed (31:19) and as reported earlier (31:22). The second (vv. 45–47) implores Israel to diligently follow the *torah* (see at 31:9), for their very existence in the land that they prepare to enter is said to hinge on their adherence to the laws and precepts preserved in the book of Deuteronomy.

***44. Hosea.*** A variant of the name Joshua; see Numbers 13:8, 16.

***the people.*** This verse and 31:30 form a prose frame around the poem.

### GOD'S INSTRUCTIONS ABOUT MOSES' IMMINENT DEATH (32:48–52)

According to 3:23–28, Moses had unsuccessfully pleaded with God to allow him to enter the Promised Land. As a concession, God instructed him to climb to the summit of Pisgah and survey the territory across the Jordan. This passage repeats those general instructions, but here God commands Moses to ascend "these heights of Abarim to Mount Nebo." Shortly, 34:1 will harmonize these two traditions by stating that Moses went up "to Mount Nebo, to the summit of Pisgah."

their holding. 50You shall die on the mountain that you are about to ascend, and shall be gathered to your kin, as your brother Aaron died on Mount Hor and was gathered to his kin; 51for you both broke faith with Me among the Israelite people, at the waters of Meribath-kadesh in the wilderness of Zin, by failing to uphold My sanctity among the Israelite people. 52You may view the land from a distance, but you shall not enter it—the land that I am giving to the Israelite people.

לִבְנֵי יִשְׂרָאֵל לַאֲחֻזָּה׃ 50 וּמֻת בָּהָר אֲשֶׁר
אַתָּה עֹלֶה שָׁמָּה וְהֵאָסֵף אֶל־עַמֶּיךָ כַּאֲשֶׁר־
מֵת אַהֲרֹן אָחִיךָ בְּהֹר הָהָר וַיֵּאָסֶף אֶל־
עַמָּיו׃ 51 עַל אֲשֶׁר מְעַלְתֶּם בִּי בְּתוֹךְ בְּנֵי
יִשְׂרָאֵל בְּמֵי־מְרִיבַת קָדֵשׁ מִדְבַּר־צִן עַל
אֲשֶׁר לֹא־קִדַּשְׁתֶּם אוֹתִי בְּתוֹךְ בְּנֵי יִשְׂרָאֵל׃
52 כִּי מִנֶּגֶד תִּרְאֶה אֶת־הָאָרֶץ וְשָׁמָּה לֹא
תָבוֹא אֶל־הָאָרֶץ אֲשֶׁר־אֲנִי נֹתֵן לִבְנֵי
יִשְׂרָאֵל׃ פ

*50. **You shall die . . . and shall be gathered to your kin.*** These two verbs are imperatives, as in the prior verse (literally, "Die . . . and be gathered").

***as your brother Aaron.*** This passage makes no mention of Miriam, the sister whose death and burial are briefly recorded shortly before Aaron's death (both in Numbers 20).

*51.* Here God blames Moses' (and Aaron's) inability to lead the people into the Promised Land on the incident at Kadesh when Moses aggressively strikes the rock to make it produce water (Numbers 20:1–13). In contrast, prior passages in Deuteronomy assert that Moses was punished as a result of the incident of the scouts (see at 1:35; also 3:26; 4:21). These inconsistencies probably reflect a merging of sources and a desire to preserve multiple perspectives on this most poignant moment.

*52.* With the very last words in the parashah, God offers Moses the small comfort of seeing the destination of his life's work from afar, while also reminding him that he will not be able to savor its rewards.

*—Andrea L. Weiss*

# Another View

PARASHAT HAAZINU PRESENTS us with startling contradictions: Moses sings of God as faithful and nurturing, but also as violent and vengeful. The images of God afflicting "the suckling as well as the aged" and firing arrows "drunk with blood" is disturbing at best. Where does this imagery come from, and how can it be reconciled with images of God as a tender caretaker?

Biblical portrayals of God as a warrior have deep roots in the traditions of the ancient Near East. As soon as warfare entered ancient Near Eastern culture (probably around 3000 B.C.E.), warrior gods rose to prominence throughout the region. Even a deity like Ishtar (sometimes referred to as Inanna), an ancient Mesopotamian goddess of love and fertility, took on a secondary role as a warrior. Likewise, epic poems related how Anat, the Canaanite goddess of love and war, rescues her brother Baal by killing the god Mot. According to the ancients, female and male warrior gods served as patrons to kings, who in turn carried out their warfare in the name of, and with assistance from, their patron deity. And Israel, by worshiping God as its divine ruler as well as the patron deity of its kings, affirmed that God was both willing and able to engage in bloody combat against all enemies.

Moses' Song in *Haazinu* demonstrates the violence that, in an ancient context, formed part of the image of God as warrior and king: when Israel rebelled against its divine ruler, honor demanded that the people be punished. God, however, carries out Israel's punishment by bringing foreign armies against the land—an event that could easily be interpreted as God's defeat at the hands of a foreign monarch and his deity. Therefore, God acts "for fear of the taunts of the foe" (v. 27) and destroys the foreign army as well.

*Violence, in an ancient context, formed part of the image of God.*

The biblical model of divine kingship affirms God's care, guidance, justice, and certainly God's power. But ancient kings were also expected to demonstrate their military prowess (hence God's title *Adonai Tz'vaot*, God of Armies). In *Shirat Haazinu*, this view of God as a warrior-king is tempered by images of the same God giving birth to and nurturing the people.

—*Julie Galambush*

# Post-biblical Interpretations

***Give ear, O heavens, let me speak*** (32:1). Midrash *Sifrei D'varim* 306 imagines that in the future, Israel—personified as a woman—will implore God to listen to her confession of sins. She will say, "Master of the universe, I now see the places that I corrupted, and I am ashamed"; but God will reply, "I shall cause them to pass away." She will continue, "Master of the universe, my name is linked with the *baalim* [foreign gods]"; but God will reply, "I shall cause it to pass away." Israel will then point out that if a man divorces a woman and she marries another man, he may never remarry her (24:1–4). However, the Almighty will respond, "Have you been divorced from Me, O house of Israel?" Thus, the Rabbis interpret the moment of divine judgment as a time of repentance (*t'shuvah*) and reconciliation, in which the unfaithful Israel confesses her misdeeds and a loving God forgives her offenses and reaffirms their intimate relationship.

***Like an eagle who rouses its nestlings*** (32:11). In *Sifrei D'varim* 314, the Rabbis expand on this biblical simile, comparing God to an eagle: "Just as the mother eagle does not enter her nest without first shaking her chicks with her wings, as she flies between one tree and another, between one bush and another, in order to rouse them so that they will be strong enough to receive her," so also when the Holy One revealed the divine Presence in order to give the Torah to Israel, God did so "not from only one direction but from all four directions," from Sinai, from Seir, from Mount Paran, and from Teman, to alert the people to the seriousness of the moment. Here the Sages evoke the *Shechinah*, the nurturing female aspect of the Divine, which is often described as drawing both converts and the faithful of Israel under her wings.

In this same midrashic passage, the Rabbis declare that 32:11 also alludes to other divine redemptions of Israel. In the second half of this verse, "So did [God] spread wings and take them" refers to Israel's emancipation from slavery, recalling "how I bore you on eagles' wings and brought you to Me" (Exodus 19:4). Similarly, the end of our verse, "Bear them along on pinions," speaks of the future redemption when the nations "shall cradle your sons in their arms, / and carry your daughters on their shoulders" (Isaiah 49:22).

***You neglected the Rock who begot you / Forgot the God who labored to bring you forth*** (32:18). Rabbinic interpreters were struck by the image of God—whose actions are generally described in male terms—as a woman in labor. They interpreted this verse as follows, "The Holy One... said to them, 'You caused Me to feel like a male trying to give birth.' If a woman about to give birth is sitting on the birth-stool, is she not anxious...? If she is in labor and giving birth for the first time, would she not be concerned...? If there are twins in her womb, would she not be uneasy...?" How much more so, "if it is a male, who does not ordinarily give birth but is trying to give birth, would not the pain be doubled and redoubled...?" Yet this is the extent to which God was prepared to labor and suffer out of love for Israel (*Sifrei D'varim* 319).

***The grapes for them are poison, / A bitter growth their clusters*** (32:32). In *P'sikta D'Rav Kahana* 20.6, this verse figures in a long debate over the correct identification of the forbidden fruit that Eve and Adam ate

*Rabbinic interpreters were struck by the Torah's image of God as a woman in labor.*

in the Garden of Eden (Genesis 3). According to one of the Rabbis, this verse proves that the fruit was grapes, since "those clusters that Adam ate brought bitterness into the world."

***through it you shall long endure*** (32:47). In its interpretation of this verse, *Sifrei D'varim* 336 observes that the study of Torah yields a double reward: one enjoys the fruit in this world and prolongs one's days in the world-to-come. The midrash goes on to teach that this concept of a twofold recompense also applies to those who honor their fathers and mothers, as well as to people who devote themselves to establishing peace. The midrashic passage concludes with a consolatory prophecy for the days to come: "All your children shall be taught by יהוה, and great shall be the happiness of your children" (Isaiah 54:13).

—*Judith R. Baskin*

# Contemporary Reflection

PARASHAT HAAZINU TROUBLES US with its extreme, opposing images of deity. Paradoxically, God is envisioned as comforting and frightening: the eternal guardian of Israel who eventually will redeem the people, and the jealous and judgmental deity who threatens to wreak vengeance on those who violate the covenant and turn to other gods. As Moses maintains, God is the giver of life and death, who heals as well as wounds (32:39–40). Thus, in his song to the Israelites contained in this parashah, Moses includes both a solemn warning that their lives as individuals and a people rest on their observing "faithfully all of the terms of this Teaching" (v. 46) and a final message of hope that God will one day deliver them from their enemies and they will "long endure on the land" given to them by God (v. 47).

As a contemporary reader I am prompted to ask numerous questions. For instance, why, in imagining God as comforter, does Moses use the image of an unmoving, unchanging rock (32:4, 15, 18, 30, 31)? Commentators view the metaphor of the rock as a vehicle for communicating the message that God's righteousness and loyalty to Israel never waver, or for highlighting the superior, incomparable nature of Israel's God. However, in spite of how the metaphor is used in the context of the Song, one could just as easily argue that this metaphor imagines God as a cold, unfeeling natural object, incapable of entering into a relationship with anyone or anything.

Moreover, why does Moses describe God anthropomorphically as a warrior whose "flashing blade / And . . . hand lays holds on judgment" (v. 41)? Where is God's compassion for God's people and for their enemies (who, after all, are also God's creations)? Is it not possible to influence and protect one's people without ruthless killing or threats of killing? Is the price of our deliverance the death of others?

Several feminists suggest that we respond to these questions by re-imagining our relationship with God. For example, in the place of God as rock or warrior, one might reclaim God as a parent who holds us in his or her arms, cares for us, and feels our pain. Some metaphors in the Song suggest such a perception, as when Moses speaks of God as a nursing mother (v. 13) who went through labor to bring forth Israel (v. 18; see also the indirectly maternal metaphor in Numbers 11:12). Jewish medieval mystics envisioned God as *Shechinah*, God's feminine presence who went into

## *Why does Moses describe God via the images of a rock and of a warrior?*

exile with the Jewish people, weeping with them and sheltering them in her wings (see *Va-eira*, Contemporary Reflection, p. 351). More recently, this image has been invoked by some Jewish feminists. Identifying *Shechinah* as "She Who Dwells Within," Rabbi Lynn Gottlieb envisions God as a Being who connects all of life, expresses our longing for wholeness, and like the God of Deuteronomy, ultimately calls us to justice (*She Who Dwells Within: A Feminist Vision of a Renewed Judaism*, 1995, pp. 25–48).

Some contemporary theologians have insisted that non-anthropomorphic images of God can also be images of intimacy, love, and creation. Marcia Falk, for example, draws on biblical phrases or concepts to "serve as fresh metaphors for Divinity." She has created new images drawn from traditional Jewish sources and composed of the basic elements of Creation (earth, water, wind, and fire), such as *ein hachayim*, "wellspring or source of life," *nishmat kol chai*, "breath of all living things," and *nitzotzot hanefesh*, "sparks of the inner, unseen self." Through these images, she hopes "to help construct a theology of immanence that will both affirm the sanctity of the world and shatter the idolatrous reign of the lord/God/king" ("Toward a Feminist Jewish Reconstruction of Monotheism," 1989, pp. 53, 56).

Judith Plaskow pursues a different path. While writing frequently about the importance of new, anthropomorphic images of deity, she maintains that "the traditional image of God as place (*makom*) evokes both the presence of the world in God and the extraordinary presence of God in particular places." She continues, "Lacking personal communal images to refer to God, we use this richly ambiguous term to point to community as a special place of God's self-manifestation" (*Standing Again at Sinai*, 1990, p. 165).

Viewed within its historical context, the God imagery of *parashat Haazinu* is understandable, even justifiable (see Another View, p. 1265). But its problematic vision for our time encourages us to create new images of the Deity that make the poem's underlying messages concerning the nature of God and the relationship between God and the Jewish people more compelling. This leads us to ask: What can we derive from *parashat Haazinu*? How else does it speak to us today? How can these images lead us to greater responsibility?

One clue may lie in the mention of Sodom and Gomorrah in v. 32. As part of the announcement of the punishment in store for Israel's enemies, this verse states: "Ah! The vine for them is from Sodom, / From the vineyards of Gomorrah." Through the metaphors in this verse, the Song maligns the nations as corrupt and foreshadows their fate. This calls to mind when God threatens to destroy those cities, prompting Abraham to protest: "Must not the Judge of all the earth do justly?" (Genesis 18:25). Perhaps *parashat Haazinu* can be seen as an invitation for us to act like Abraham and protest against what seems to be an indiscriminate, wholesale destruction. It is an opportunity to raise questions such as: Where is Your compassion, God, not only toward us but toward all of Your creation? Why frighten us with your threats? Will such threats make us abandon other deities or, just as likely, will they lead us to reject You? Such questions express what it means to be covenantal partners, willing to challenge God. Thus, beyond protesting against what we now deem unacceptable, this parashah can prompt us to examine who we mean by God. It also can remind us of what is required in order to create a just society and uphold a covenantal relationship.

—*Ellen M. Umansky*

# Voices

## My People

Else Lasker-Schüler (transl. Janine Canan)

*Deuteronomy 32:1–43*

The rock is crumbling
from which I arise
and sing my songs of God....
Suddenly I plunge from the path
and deep within stream
over wailing-stone
alone to the sea.

I have washed so far
from the ferment of my blood.
And still, within me, echoes the sound
when—shuddering eastward—
the crumbling rock-bones
of my People
cry out to God.

## The Messenger Came in the Night

Rahel (transl. Robert Friend)

*Deuteronomy 32:1–43*

The messenger came in the night
and sat on my bed,
his body all protruding bones,
the eye-holes deep in his head;

and I knew time's hands were dangling
(as though the words were unspoken),
that the bridge between future and past
had broken.

A bony fist now threatened,
and I heard aghast
sardonic laughter that said:
"This poem will be your last."

## Like a Poppy Borne by Wind

Esther Raab (transl. Harold Schimmel)

*Deuteronomy 32:50*

My God, when you come to pluck me,
scatter my leaves on wings of the wind
so I'll remain like a headless poppy
and bow down to the dust of my land
as parched clods gather me – – –
let a slate-blue sky
then gaze from above
with a forgotten cloud-end flung at its edge;
let a chain of hills listen
and Ebal and Gerizim of grave thoughts
blacken in shadow,
as dark cypresses sway in the wind
and fields burdened-with-green extend unto them;
let warblers rustle
in the acacia hedgerows
and bulbuls scissor orange grove lairs,
mustard and chamomile unfurl carpets
across expansive sands—
and my spirit hover above them
like a poor poppy borne by the wind – – –

## Journey's End

Linda Pastan

*Deuteronomy 32:50*

How hard we try to reach death safely,
luggage intact, each child accounted for,
the wounds of passage quickly bandaged up.
We treat the years like stops along the way
of a long flight from the catastrophe
we move to, thinking: home free all at last.
Wave, wave your hanky towards journey's end;
avert your eyes from windows grimed with
twilight
where landscapes rush by, terrible and lovely.

## *From a Mother to Her Girls*

Karyn Kedar

*Deuteronomy 32:50*

The morning you wake to bury me
you'll wonder what to wear.
The sun may be shining, or maybe it will rain;
it may be winter. Or not.
You'll say to your self, black, aren't you supposed to
wear black? Then you will remember all the times we went
together to buy clothes: the prom, homecoming,
just another pair of jeans,
another sweater, another pair of shoes.
I called you my Barbie dolls.
You will remember how I loved to dress you.
How beautiful you were in my eyes.

The morning you wake to bury me
you will look in the mirror in disbelief.
You'll reach for some makeup. Or not.
And you won't believe that
this is the morning you will bury your mother.
But it is. And as you gaze into that mirror you will
shed a tear. Or not. But look. Look carefully,
for hiding in your expression, you will find mine.
You will see me in your eyes, in the way you laugh.
You will feel me when you think of God,
and of love and struggle.

Look into the mirror and you will see me in a look, or in
the way you hold your mouth or stand, a little bent, or maybe straight.
But you will see me.

So let me tell you, one last time, before you dress,
what to wear. Put on any old thing. Black or red, skirt or pants.
Despite what I told you all these years, it doesn't really matter.
Because as I told you all these years, you are beautiful the way you are.
Dress yourself in honor and dignity.
Dress yourself in confidence and self-love.
Wear a sense of obligation to do for this world,
for you are one of the lucky ones and there is so much to do, to fix.
Take care of each other,
take care of your heart, of your soul.
Talk to God.
Wear humility and compassion.

When you wake to bury me,
put on a strong sense of self, courage, and understanding.
I am sorry. Forgive me. I am sorry.
Stand at my grave clothed in a gown of forgiveness,
dressed like an angel would be, showing compassion
and unconditional love.
For at that very moment, all that will be left of me to give is love.
Love.

# וזאת הברכה ✦ V'zot Hab'rachah

DEUTERONOMY 33:1–34:12

## Moses' Last Words: A Blessing for Israel

PARASHAT V'ZOT HAB'RACHAH ("this is the blessing") presents Moses' poetic blessing of the Israelites (33:1–29), which is followed by a brief record of Moses' death and a tribute to his unparalleled prophetic stature (34:1–12). As we come to the end of Moses' life, it seems fitting to reflect back on the epic story of Israel's unrivaled leader.

Moses' story begins in the book of Exodus (2:1–22), where we read that a Levite woman and a Levite man (later identified as Jochebed and Amram) give birth to a child whose life is imperiled by the Pharaoh's decree to kill all Israelite baby boys. Although Moses' mother initially defies the king and hides her son, after three months she is forced to abandon him, so she places him in a basket floating down the Nile. His sister, Miriam, then watches as Pharaoh's own daughter rescues and adopts the Hebrew child. At Miriam's suggestion, the princess hands Moses over to his mother, Jochebed, who nurses him for several years. Thus, it takes the courage, ingenuity, and collaboration of these three women to ensure the survival of Israel's future liberator and leader.

Although raised as Egyptian royalty, Moses eventually identifies with the plight of his enslaved kin. But when defending a beaten Israelite leads to manslaughter, Moses flees to Midian. There, he marries Zipporah, the daughter of the Midianite priest Yitro, and fathers two sons. Then, while shepherding his father-in-law's flocks on Mount Horeb (also known as Mount Sinai), he glimpses the Divine amidst a bush that burns yet remains unconsumed. Reluctantly, he accepts God's call to return to Egypt and rescue his people (Exodus 3–4). With the aid of his brother Aaron, Moses orchestrates God's signs and wonders and eventually persuades Pharaoh to let Israel go (Exodus 5–15).

The exodus from Egypt leads to a second encounter with God atop the same mountain,

*It seems fitting to reflect back on the epic story of Israel's unrivaled leader, Moses.*

where God communicates the precepts by which Israel is to live (Exodus 19–20). The rest of the Torah describes how Moses oversees the construction of the Tabernacle and the ordination of the priesthood and then leads the people on a forty-year trek through the wilderness. Once they reach the plains of Moab, Moses reaffirms the covenant and instructs the people how to live in order to thrive in the Promised Land. For Israel, the wilderness journey will culminate in the entry into the land of Canaan, as recounted in the book of Joshua. For Moses, as we read in this parashah, the journey will end atop another mountain, Mount Nebo, as he surveys the land and dies at God's command.

*Parashat V'zot Hab'rachah* is unique in that it is not designated as a weekly Torah portion. Instead, it is read on Simchat Torah, the holiday that marks the conclusion of the annual Torah reading cycle and the commencement of a new lectionary cycle of weekly Torah readings.

The focus of this parashah is on Moses and the tribes named for Jacob's sons; women are explicitly mentioned only once, in the reference to a mother in 33:9. However, 33:4 states, "Moses charged us with the Teaching [*torah*] as the heritage of the congregation of Jacob." Who is "us"? Prior passages in Deuteronomy specify that women were included in the covenant (29:10) and were taught the *torah* (31:12).

Finally, 34:8 mentions that "the Israelites bewailed Moses" for thirty days. Evidence shows that women were trained as singers of laments and likely would have played a main role in mourning Israel's most cherished leader.

—*Andrea L. Weiss*

## *Outline*

*I.* The Blessing of Moses (33:1–29)

- *A.* Prose introduction (v. 1)
- *B.* Prologue: God as warrior and king (vv. 2–5)
- *C.* Blessing of the tribes (vv. 6–25)
- *D.* Epilogue: God as refuge and warrior (vv. 26–29)

*II.* The Death of Moses (34:1–12)

- *A.* Survey of the Promised Land (vv. 1–4)
- *B.* Moses' death (vv. 5–7)
- *C.* Mourning for Moses, who is succeeded by Joshua (vv. 8–9)
- *D.* Tribute to Moses' unrivaled status (vv. 10–12)

This is the blessing with which Moses, God's envoy, bade the Israelites farewell before he died. 2He said:

יהוה came from Sinai,
And shone upon them from Seir;

לג וְזֹאת הַבְּרָכָה אֲשֶׁר בֵּרַךְ מֹשֶׁה אִישׁ הָאֱלֹהִים אֶת־בְּנֵי יִשְׂרָאֵל לִפְנֵי מוֹתוֹ׃
2 וַיֹּאמַר
יְהוָה מִסִּינַי בָּא
וְזָרַח מִשֵּׂעִיר לָמוֹ

## *The Blessing of Moses* (33:1–29)

Moses delivers his final words to the entire assembly of Israel—men, women, and children, everyone from the leaders of the tribes to those who chop wood and draw water (29:9–10)—just before the "Source of the breath of all flesh" (Numbers 27:16) takes his life. Like Jacob, who blessed his sons while he lay on his deathbed (Genesis 49), Moses blesses the tribes of Israel. But, whereas Jacob's words are often disparaging, Moses' message is decidedly positive: he looks ahead to a time when the tribes will enjoy prosperity and security. Here, the criticism voiced in Deuteronomy 32 gives way to assurances and praise.

Many scholars maintain that the Blessing of Moses, like the Song of Moses that precedes it (in *parashat Haazinu*), was originally a separate composition that later was inserted into the concluding section of the book. A number of words and even complete verses continue to baffle scholars, and opinions vary about the likely dating of this text. Some assert that the verses before and after the tribal blessings (vv. 2–5 and 26–29) at one time constituted a separate hymn or might have been written as a framework for the preexisting blessings. Although vv. 2–29 are not laid out in poetic form in Torah scrolls, they exhibit the typical features of biblical poetry (see the introduction to 32:1–43).

### PROSE INTRODUCTION (33:1)

This verse labels the poetic composition that follows as a "blessing." While it has the overall appearance of a father's last words to his offspring (as in Genesis 27:28–29, 39–40; 49:2–27), parts of the text display affinities to other genres, such as the hymn known as the Song of Deborah (Judges 5), and Balaam's blessings of Israel (Numbers 23–24).

*1. **bade . . . farewell.*** Literally, "blessed." See Genesis 27:10.

***God's envoy.*** Heb. *ish ha-elohim*, often translated as "man of God." Although this is the only time that this phrase appears in the Torah, it occurs frequently in the rest of the Bible to designate Moses, certain other prophets, and King David. (For instance, see how the widow uses the expression to refer to Elijah in I Kings 17:18, 24 and the Shunammite woman as a label for Elisha in II Kings 4:9, 16). The present translation takes *ish* as referring here to


▸ The Bible names four women prophets: Miriam, Deborah, Huldah, and Noadiah.
ANOTHER VIEW ➤ *1284*

▸ Jochebed heart-rendingly searches for her son, refusing to accept that he has died.
POST-BIBLICAL INTERPRETATIONS ➤ *1284*

▸ Moses' blessing involves the ability to dream of what he will not experience directly.
CONTEMPORARY REFLECTION ➤ *1286*

▸ I see you as you were, and as you never were . . . with the unrelenting mind of Spring . . .
VOICES ➤ *1288*

[God] appeared from Mount Paran,
And approached from Ribeboth-kodesh,
Lightning flashing at them from on the right.
[3]Lover, indeed, of the people,
Their hallowed are all in Your hand.
They followed in Your steps,
Accepting Your pronouncements,
[4]When Moses charged us with the Teaching
As the heritage of the congregation of Jacob.
[5]Then [God] became King in Jeshurun,
When the heads of the people assembled,
The tribes of Israel together.

הוֹפִ֙יעַ֙ מֵהַ֣ר פָּארָ֔ן
וְאָתָ֖ה מֵרִבְבֹ֣ת קֹ֑דֶשׁ
מִימִינ֕וֹ אשדת אֵ֥שׁ דָּ֖ת לָֽמוֹ:
3 אַ֚ף חֹבֵ֣ב עַמִּ֔ים
כָּל־קְדֹשָׁ֖יו בְּיָדֶ֑ךָ
וְהֵם֙ תֻּכּ֣וּ לְרַגְלֶ֔ךָ
יִשָּׂ֖א מִדַּבְּרֹתֶֽיךָ:
4 תּוֹרָ֥ה צִוָּה־לָ֖נוּ מֹשֶׁ֑ה
מוֹרָשָׁ֖ה קְהִלַּ֥ת יַעֲקֹֽב:
5 וַיְהִ֥י בִישֻׁר֖וּן מֶ֑לֶךְ
בְּהִתְאַסֵּף֙ רָ֣אשֵׁי עָ֔ם
יַ֖חַד שִׁבְטֵ֥י יִשְׂרָאֵֽל:

the role of representing another party on a mission (as in, for example, Genesis 24:21; Leviticus 16:21; Numbers 13:2; 22:9; Deuteronomy 1:22); in that sense, the expression *ish ha-elohim* neatly encapsulates Moses' forty-year career as God's agent, which began at the Burning Bush (Exodus 3:10; see also at v. 16, below). (See David Stein, "What Does It Mean to Be a 'Man'?" 2006–7, §§ II.B.1; III.B.8.)

## PROLOGUE: GOD AS WARRIOR AND KING (33:2–5)

This section (particularly v. 3) has baffled interpreters, ancient and modern, with its many difficulties. Nevertheless, the general message is that God came from the south to aid Israel (as in Judges 5:4; Habakkuk 3:3) and subsequently was considered Israel's king.

2. *Sinai.* This is the only time that this word appears in Deuteronomy; throughout the book, Horeb designates this mountain (see at Exodus 18:5).

*Lightning flashing at them.* Although the Hebrew here remains uncertain, the phrase seems to fit with the verse's underlying image of God as a (male) warrior who comes to Israel's salvation. (For more on the warrior metaphor, see at Exodus 14:14; 15:3; Deuteronomy 32:23; see also *Haazinu*, Another View, p. 1265.)

4. *Moses charged us.* Commentators have puzzled over the third-person reference to Moses in a text that he recites, as well as the relationship between this verse and its surrounding context. Some explain that God must have been the original subject; others view this as an acclamation of the people. Deuteronomy 31:12 emphasizes that the Levites are to teach the *torah* to all Israel—women and men, children and strangers.

*Teaching.* Heb. *torah*; see at 31:9.

5. *[God] became King.* Given the prominence of the image of God as king in Jewish liturgy, where most blessings contain the phrase *melech ha-olam* ("King of the universe"), it is surprising that the metaphor appears only three times in the Torah: here, Exodus 15:18, and Numbers 23:21. All three are poetic passages, which is where the king metaphor nearly always appears. It is found far more frequently elsewhere in the Bible (as in Isaiah 33:22; Psalm 24:7–10) and in ancient Near Eastern texts, where the notion of the divine king connotes not only power and authority, but also the execution of justice, compassion for the needy, and the maintenance of social order and prosperity (see Psalm 72).

Carol Meyers observes that the frequency and variety of andromorphic (male-shaped) images of God, such as divine king and warrior, "can produce

6May Reuben live and not die,
Though few be his numbers.

7And this he said of Judah:
Hear, יהוה, the voice of Judah
And restore him to his people.
Though his own hands strive for him,
Help him against his foes.

6 יְחִ֥י רְאוּבֵ֖ן וְאַל־יָמֹ֑ת
וִיהִ֥י מְתָ֖יו מִסְפָּֽר׃ ס
7 וְזֹ֣את לִֽיהוּדָה֮ וַיֹּאמַר֒
שְׁמַ֤ע יְהֹוָה֙ ק֣וֹל יְהוּדָ֔ה
וְאֶל־עַמּ֖וֹ תְּבִיאֶ֑נּוּ
יָדָיו֙ רָ֣ב ל֔וֹ
וְעֵ֥זֶר מִצָּרָ֖יו תִּהְיֶֽה׃ פ

the impression of God as exclusively male—the so-called patriarchal God of the Hebrew Bible." She adds that since Hebrew is a gendered language and the words for God generally are masculine, this further contributes to the sense of a male deity (*Women in Scripture*, 2000, p. 526). Yet as she and other scholars explain, one must look more closely in order to get an accurate picture. The male images actually convey things about God other than gender (see at 10:17). Apart from such imagery and from the linguistic necessity of using masculine wording, the Torah is conspicuously silent about God's gender, especially compared to ancient Near Eastern descriptions of other deities (see Tikva Frymer-Kensky, *In the Wake of the Goddesses*, 1992, pp. 83–99, 187–189). Meanwhile, female divine imagery, although less frequent, can in fact be found in the Bible (see at Exodus 15:22–17:16; 15:26; Numbers 11:12; Deuteronomy 32:13, 18). Biblical writers incorporated a range of female, male, and non-gendered metaphors for God as they attempted to articulate their understanding of who God is and how God operates in the world.

***Jeshurun.*** See at v. 26.

## BLESSING OF THE TRIBES (33:6–25)

Although Moses and his wife Zipporah have two sons, Gershom (Exodus 2:22; 18:3) and Eliezer (Exodus 18:4), as he approaches his death, Moses blesses not his biological heirs but the tribes, one by one. Usually, the tribes are listed in the birth order of their eponymous ancestors, grouped according to their mothers (see at Genesis 46:8–27 and at 49:1–27). Here, however, Moses addresses the tribes in geographical order, starting with Reuben, in whose territory the Israelites stand, and then moving across the River Jordan from Judah in the south to Asher in the north. Nevertheless, a maternal arrangement can be discerned, a likely reflection of existing geopolitical patterns: three of Leah's first four sons (Simeon is not mentioned; see at v. 7 below), followed by Rachel's two sons, then Leah's fifth and sixth sons, and then the four sons of the handmaids, Zilpah and Bilhah.

*6.* The blessing for Reuben constitutes a plea that the tribe not perish. Situated in the Transjordan (see Numbers 32), this tribe was cut off geographically from most of the other tribes by the Jordan river and likely would have been vulnerable to attacks by neighbors to the east and south.

*7.* The blessing for Judah calls upon God to rescue Judah from an unidentified enemy. The depiction of Judah's being in a precarious situation contrasts sharply with the characterization of Judah in Genesis 49:8–12. There, he is compared to a ferocious lion and described as being in a position of power and wealth. Some scholars posit that this verse originally may have contained a blessing for Simeon.

8 And of Levi he said:
Let Your Thummim and Urim
Be with Your faithful one,
Whom You tested at Massah,
Challenged at the waters of Meribah;
9 Who said of his father and mother,
"I consider them not."
His brothers he disregarded,
Ignored his own children.
Your precepts alone they observed,
And kept Your covenant.
10 They shall teach Your laws to Jacob
And Your instructions to Israel.
They shall offer You incense to savor
And whole-offerings on Your altar.
11 Bless, יהוה, his substance,
And favor his undertakings.

8 וּלְלֵוִ֣י אָמַ֔ר
תֻּמֶּ֥יךָ וְאוּרֶ֖יךָ
לְאִ֣ישׁ חֲסִידֶ֑ךָ
אֲשֶׁ֤ר נִסִּיתוֹ֙ בְּמַסָּ֔ה
תְּרִיבֵ֖הוּ עַל־מֵ֥י מְרִיבָֽה׃
9 הָאֹמֵ֞ר לְאָבִ֤יו וּלְאִמּוֹ֙
לֹ֣א רְאִיתִ֔יו
וְאֶת־אֶחָיו֙ לֹ֣א הִכִּ֔יר
וְאֶת־בנו בָּנָ֖יו לֹ֣א יָדָ֑ע
כִּ֤י שָֽׁמְרוּ֙ אִמְרָתֶ֔ךָ
וּבְרִֽיתְךָ֖ יִנְצֹֽרוּ׃
10 יוֹר֤וּ מִשְׁפָּטֶ֙יךָ֙ לְיַֽעֲקֹ֔ב
וְתוֹרָתְךָ֖ לְיִשְׂרָאֵ֑ל
יָשִׂ֤ימוּ קְטוֹרָה֙ בְּאַפֶּ֔ךָ
וְכָלִ֖יל עַל־מִזְבְּחֶֽךָ׃
11 בָּרֵ֤ךְ יְהֹוָה֙ חֵיל֔וֹ
וּפֹ֥עַל יָדָ֖יו תִּרְצֶ֑ה

*8–11.* The blessing for Levi emphasizes the tribe's loyalty to God. As a reward, they have merited the privilege of serving as priests, teaching God's precepts, and officiating at the sacrificial altar.

*8. Thummim and Urim.* These divinatory devices (usually listed in the reverse order) apparently consisted of some sort of lots kept in a pouch attached to the priest's breastplate (see at Exodus 28:30).

*Massah . . . Meribah.* The mention of these two place names seems to refer to the incident in Exodus 17:1–7, but there the thirsty Israelites test God and the Levites play no role in the episode. However, the Torah records two other incidents in which the Levites display their faithfulness to God at the expense of their fellow Israelites. In Exodus 32:26–29, following the construction of the Golden Calf, the Levites rally to Moses' call and kill 3,000 of their "kin." In Numbers 25, the priest (hence also Levite) Phinehas zealously stabs the Simeonite chieftain and the Midianite woman who are engaging in illicit activities at the entrance to the Tent of Meeting.

*9. father and mother.* This verse refers to an episode in which the Levites disregarded family ties in executing God's laws, possibly meaning the Golden Calf incident (Exodus 32:26–29). By implication, an Israelite man normally does—or at least should—consider the opinions of both his father and his mother. A number of biblical passage mention the mother alongside the father, most famously the command to honor one's father and mother (for example, see at Exodus 20:12 and at Leviticus 19:3, where the order is "mother and father"). In particular, Deuteronomy 13:7 warns against being lured into idolatrous practices by female or male relatives.

*10. They shall offer You incense . . . And whole-offerings.* While the priest officiates over the sacrificial system, those who bring the offerings—women and men alike—are to participate to some extent in the sacrificial ritual. (For details, see the Introduction to *parashat Vayikra*, p. 570.)

Smite the loins of his foes;
Let his enemies rise no more.

[12]Of Benjamin he said:
Beloved of יהוה,
He rests securely beside [God],
Who protects him always,
As he rests between God's shoulders.

[13]And of Joseph he said:
Blessed of יהוה be his land
With the bounty of dew from heaven,
And of the deep that couches below;
[14]With the bounteous yield of the sun,
And the bounteous crop of the moons;
[15]With the best from the ancient mountains,
And the bounty of hills immemorial;
[16]With the bounty of earth and its fullness,
And the favor of the Presence in the Bush.

מְחַ֨ץ מׇתְנַ֧יִם קָמָ֛יו
וּמְשַׂנְאָ֖יו מִן־יְקוּמֽוּן׃ ס

12 לְבִנְיָמִ֣ן אָמַ֔ר
יְדִ֣יד יְהֹוָ֔ה
יִשְׁכֹּ֥ן לָבֶ֖טַח עָלָ֑יו
חֹפֵ֤ף עָלָיו֙ כׇּל־הַיּ֔וֹם
וּבֵ֥ין כְּתֵפָ֖יו שָׁכֵֽן׃ ס

13 וּלְיוֹסֵ֣ף אָמַ֔ר
מְבֹרֶ֥כֶת יְהֹוָ֖ה אַרְצ֑וֹ
מִמֶּ֤גֶד שָׁמַ֙יִם֙ מִטָּ֔ל
וּמִתְּה֖וֹם רֹבֶ֥צֶת תָּֽחַת׃
14 וּמִמֶּ֖גֶד תְּבוּאֹ֣ת שָׁ֑מֶשׁ
וּמִמֶּ֖גֶד גֶּ֥רֶשׁ יְרָחִֽים׃
15 וּמֵרֹ֖אשׁ הַרְרֵי־קֶ֑דֶם
וּמִמֶּ֖גֶד גִּבְע֥וֹת עוֹלָֽם׃
16 וּמִמֶּ֗גֶד אֶ֚רֶץ וּמְלֹאָ֔הּ
וּרְצ֥וֹן שֹׁכְנִ֖י סְנֶ֑ה

*12.* The blessing for Benjamin expresses a hope for security for this relatively small tribe. The last line is ambiguous; alternatively, it could mean that Benjamin is carried on God's shoulders (see 1:31), or that God dwells amid Benjamin's "slopes."

*13–17.* Joseph receives the longest blessing, which covers the two tribes named after his sons, Ephraim and Manasseh. The blessing emphasizes the fertility of their territory and their prominence.

*13. the bounty.* Heb. *meged.* This key word repeats five times in vv. 13–16 as Moses elaborates on the fecundity of the land. In her book *In the Wake of the Goddesses* (1992), Tikva Frymer-Kensky argues that "the biblical understanding of fertility is radically different from that of ancient Near Eastern polytheism" (p. 92). She explains that in ancient Near Eastern polytheism "agricultural fertility is thought to result from the collective activity of male and female deities acting in concert (or consort)" (p. 89); yet in the Bible, God alone is responsible for the fertility of the land. Frymer-Kensky claims that a remarkable aspect of the creation account in Genesis 1 is that God makes the earth fertile, with seed-bearing plants able to reproduce if given the proper conditions. She writes: "To the Bible, God's fertility-bringing power lies in God's power over the rain. The natural state of the earth is fertile: it needs only the rain to activate this natural potential" (pp. 92–93).

*the deep.* Heb. *t'hom*, a noun that hints at a mythological link between the subterranean waters and the Mesopotamian goddess Tiamat (see at Genesis 1:2 and 7:11).

*16. Presence in the Bush.* Or "the One who Dwells in the Bush" (*shochni s'neh*); the later concept of God's Presence as the *Shechinah* comes from the same root as *shochni* (see *T'rumah,* Post-biblical Interpretations, p. 468). This unique epithet alludes to Moses' first encounter with God at the Burning Bush (Exodus 3:1–6).

May these rest on the head of Joseph,
On the crown of the elect of his brothers.
17 Like a firstling bull in his majesty,
He has horns like the horns of the wild-ox;
With them he gores the peoples,
The ends of the earth one and all.
These are the myriads of Ephraim,
Those are the thousands of Manasseh.

18 And of Zebulun he said:
Rejoice, O Zebulun, on your journeys,
And Issachar, in your tents.
19 They invite their kin to the mountain,
Where they offer sacrifices of success.
For they draw from the riches of the sea
And the hidden hoards of the sand.

20 And of Gad he said:
Blessed be the One who enlarges Gad!
Poised is he like a lion
To tear off arm and scalp.
21 He chose for himself the best,

תָּבוֹאתָה לְרֹאשׁ יוֹסֵף
וּלְקָדְקֹד נְזִיר אֶחָיו׃
17 בְּכוֹר שׁוֹרוֹ הָדָר לוֹ
וְקַרְנֵי רְאֵם קַרְנָיו
בָּהֶם עַמִּים יְנַגַּח
יַחְדָּו אַפְסֵי־אָרֶץ
וְהֵם רִבְבוֹת אֶפְרַיִם
וְהֵם אַלְפֵי מְנַשֶּׁה׃ ס

18 וְלִזְבוּלֻן אָמַר
שְׂמַח זְבוּלֻן בְּצֵאתֶךָ
וְיִשָּׂשכָר בְּאֹהָלֶיךָ׃ ויששכר
19 עַמִּים הַר־יִקְרָאוּ
שָׁם יִזְבְּחוּ זִבְחֵי־צֶדֶק
כִּי שֶׁפַע יַמִּים יִינָקוּ
וּשְׂפֻנֵי טְמוּנֵי חוֹל׃ ס

20 וּלְגָד אָמַר
בָּרוּךְ מַרְחִיב גָּד
כְּלָבִיא שָׁכֵן
וְטָרַף זְרוֹעַ אַף־קָדְקֹד׃
21 וַיַּרְא רֵאשִׁית לוֹ

*17. firstling.* Although Joseph was Jacob's eleventh son, not his first, he was Rachel's long-awaited first-born. According to I Chronicles 5:1–2, Reuben lost his status as first-born because he "defiled his father's bed" by sleeping with his father's concubine, Bilhah (Genesis 35:22); as a result, Joseph received the birthright, even though Judah became the most prominent.

***bull . . . wild-ox.*** These animals were common symbols of virility in the Bible and ancient Near Eastern texts.

*18–19.* This blessing speaks to the future fortune of both Zebulun and Issachar. It implies that the two tribes occupied the area from the Sea of Chinnereth (also called Lake Kinneret, or Sea of Galilee) as far as the Mediterranean, which allowed them to prosper due to their maritime ventures.

*19. they draw from the riches of the sea.* Literally, "they suckle," from the same root (*y-n-k*) used in the description of God nursing Israel with honey and oil (see at 32:13).

***riches of the sea . . . hoards of the sand.*** These phrases could refer to various goods, not only fish and shells, but also glass and murex snails—the treasured source of purple dye. (For more on the manufacture of dyed cloths and women's roles in these activities, see at Exodus 35:4 and *T'rumah*, Another View, p. 467.)

*20–21.* The blessing of Gad alludes to this tribe's military might and their request to settle in the choice pastureland east of the Jordan (Numbers 32).

For there is the portion of the revered chieftain,
Where the heads of the people come.
He executed יהוה's judgments
And God's decisions for Israel.

כִּי־שָׁם חֶלְקַת מְחֹקֵק סָפוּן
וַיֵּתֵא רָאשֵׁי עָם
צִדְקַת יְהוָה עָשָׂה
וּמִשְׁפָּטָיו עִם־יִשְׂרָאֵל׃ ס

22 And of Dan he said:
Dan is a lion's whelp
That leaps forth from Bashan.

22 וּלְדָן אָמַר
דָּן גּוּר אַרְיֵה
יְזַנֵּק מִן־הַבָּשָׁן׃

23 And of Naphtali he said:
O Naphtali, sated with favor
And full of יהוה's blessing,
Take possession on the west and south.

23 וּלְנַפְתָּלִי אָמַר
נַפְתָּלִי שְׂבַע רָצוֹן
וּמָלֵא בִּרְכַּת יְהוָה
יָם וְדָרוֹם יְרָשָׁה׃ ס

24 And of Asher he said:
Most blessed of sons be Asher;
May he be the favorite of his brothers,
May he dip his foot in oil.
25 May your doorbolts be iron and copper,
And your security last all your days.

24 וּלְאָשֵׁר אָמַר
בָּרוּךְ מִבָּנִים אָשֵׁר
יְהִי רְצוּי אֶחָיו
וְטֹבֵל בַּשֶּׁמֶן רַגְלוֹ׃
25 בַּרְזֶל וּנְחֹשֶׁת מִנְעָלֶךָ
וּכְיָמֶיךָ דָּבְאֶךָ׃

26 O Jeshurun, there is none like God,

26 אֵין כָּאֵל יְשֻׁרוּן

---

***22.*** The blessing of Dan uses a metaphor of a lion to depict their power and prowess (see also v. 20 and Genesis 49:9, where the image applies to Judah).

***leaps forth.*** Heb. *y'zanek*, from the rare root *z-n-k*. Jeffrey Tigay notes that some scholars suggest emending this verb to *yonek* (*y-n-k*), "to suckle," as in v. 19 (see also at 32:13). This would mean "that Dan is nourished effortlessly by the cattle and products of the fertile Bashan" (*Deuteronomy*, 1996, p. 411).

***23.*** The benevolent blessing of Naphtali reflects the tribe's location in the lush upper Galilee.

***24–25.*** The blessing for Asher revolves around the themes of agricultural fertility (see at v. 13) and security. The blessing seems fitting for the tribe's namesake, whom Leah named to capture her joy at giving birth to another son, through her handmaid Zilpah (Genesis 30:13).

***24.*** ***May he dip his foot in oil.*** This expression seems to reflect the abundance of olive trees in Asher's territory, in the highlands of the Galilee.

## EPILOGUE: GOD AS REFUGE AND WARRIOR (33:26–29)

In this concluding section, Moses turns his attention from the individual tribes to the people as a whole. As he extols God as Israel's source of security and prosperity, he makes it clear that the key blessings he hopes for the tribes—fertility of the land, military success, and tranquility—depend on God's unparalleled beneficence and power. These are Moses' last words in the Torah.

***26.*** ***Jeshurun.*** This fairly uncommon name for Israel also appeared in v. 5, thus forming a frame around the tribal blessings.

Riding through the heavens to help you,
Through the skies in His majesty.
27The ancient God is a refuge,
A support are the arms everlasting.
He drove out the enemy before you
By His command: Destroy!
28Thus Israel dwells in safety,
Untroubled is Jacob's abode,
In a land of grain and wine,
Under heavens dripping dew.
29O happy Israel! Who is like you,
A people delivered by יהוה,
Your protecting Shield, your Sword triumphant!
Your enemies shall come cringing before you,
And you shall tread on their backs.

רֹכֵב שָׁמַ֫יִם בְּעֶזְרֶ֔ךָ
וּבְגַאֲוָתוֹ שְׁחָקִים:
27 מְעֹנָה֙ אֱלֹ֣הֵי קֶ֔דֶם
וּמִתַּ֖חַת זְרֹעֹ֣ת עוֹלָ֑ם
וַיְגָ֧רֶשׁ מִפָּנֶ֛יךָ אוֹיֵ֖ב
וַיֹּ֥אמֶר הַשְׁמֵֽד:
28 וַיִּשְׁכֹּן֩ יִשְׂרָאֵ֨ל בֶּ֜טַח
בָּדָ֗ד עֵ֣ין יַעֲקֹ֔ב
אֶל־אֶ֖רֶץ דָּגָ֣ן וְתִיר֑וֹשׁ
אַף־שָׁמָ֖יו יַ֥עַרְפוּ טָֽל:
29 אַשְׁרֶ֨יךָ יִשְׂרָאֵ֜ל מִ֣י כָמ֗וֹךָ
עַ֚ם נוֹשַׁ֣ע בַּֽיהֹוָ֔ה
מָגֵ֣ן עֶזְרֶ֔ךָ וַאֲשֶׁר־חֶ֖רֶב גַּאֲוָתֶ֑ךָ
וְיִכָּחֲשׁ֤וּ אֹיְבֶ֙יךָ֙ לָ֔ךְ
וְאַתָּ֖ה עַל־בָּמוֹתֵ֥ימוֹ תִדְרֹֽךְ: ס

---

there is none like God. A hallmark of Deuteronomy is its insistence on God's unrivaled divinity. Certain passages express a clearly monotheistic perspective (see at 4:35); others herald God's uniqueness while allowing for the existence of other, minor deities—a notion referred to as monolatry (see at 4:19–20; 32:8, 43).

Riding through the heavens. In the Bible, God frequently appears as a (male) warrior riding through the skies in order to rescue Israel from her enemies. Various passages depict God descending to earth on a chariot (such as Habakkuk 3:8), clouds (such as Psalm 104:3), or cherub (such as Psalm 18:11). The image is also found in other ancient Near Eastern texts, particularly Ugaritic poems describing the storm god Baal.

27. arms everlasting. This expression of God's support for Israel seems to portray God embracing or carrying Israel. Similarly, Deuteronomy 1:31 compares God's treatment of Israel in the wilderness to a parent carrying a child. Isaiah 40:11 promises that when God redeems the Babylonian exiles,

God will be like a shepherd who gently gathers and carries the flock in his or her arms (for examples of female shepherds, see Genesis 29:9; Exodus 2:16). Isaiah 46:3–4 expresses a similar message using a maternal metaphor. God addresses the exiles—"who have been carried since birth, / Supported since leaving the womb"—and pledges to them: "Till you grow old, I will be the same; / When you turn gray, it is I who will carry; / I was the Maker, and I will be the Bearer; / And I will carry and rescue [you]."

drove out the enemy. This looks ahead to the defeat of the Canaanites when Israel enters the Promised Land (see at 7:24).

28. Under heavens dripping dew. On the importance of rain or other forms of moisture for the fertility of the land, see at v. 13.

29. Shield…Sword. See at v. 2.

you shall tread on their backs. In the Bible and ancient Near Eastern documents, placing one's foot on the enemy's back or neck symbolizes victory (see Joshua 10:24).

34 Moses went up from the steppes of Moab
to Mount Nebo, to the summit of Pisgah, opposite
Jericho, and יהוה showed him the whole land:
Gilead as far as Dan; 2 all Naphtali; the land of
Ephraim and Manasseh; the whole land of Judah
as far as the Western Sea; 3 the Negeb; and the
Plain—the Valley of Jericho, the city of palm
trees—as far as Zoar. 4 And יהוה said to him, "This
is the land of which I swore to Abraham, Isaac, and
Jacob, 'I will assign it to your offspring.' I have let

לד וַיַּעַל מֹשֶׁה מֵעַרְבֹת מוֹאָב אֶל־הַר
נְבוֹ רֹאשׁ הַפִּסְגָּה אֲשֶׁר עַל־פְּנֵי יְרֵחוֹ
וַיַּרְאֵהוּ יְהֹוָה אֶת־כָּל־הָאָרֶץ אֶת־הַגִּלְעָד
עַד־דָּן׃ 2 וְאֵת כָּל־נַפְתָּלִי וְאֶת־אֶרֶץ אֶפְרַיִם
וּמְנַשֶּׁה וְאֵת כָּל־אֶרֶץ יְהוּדָה עַד הַיָּם
הָאַחֲרוֹן׃ 3 וְאֶת־הַנֶּגֶב וְאֶת־הַכִּכָּר בִּקְעַת
יְרֵחוֹ עִיר הַתְּמָרִים עַד־צֹעַר׃ 4 וַיֹּאמֶר
יְהֹוָה אֵלָיו זֹאת הָאָרֶץ אֲשֶׁר נִשְׁבַּעְתִּי
לְאַבְרָהָם לְיִצְחָק וּלְיַעֲקֹב לֵאמֹר לְזַרְעֲךָ

## *The Death of Moses* (34:1–12)

The Torah preserves a number of narrative passages that record the deaths of select individuals: Sarah (Genesis 23:1–2), Abraham (Genesis 25:7–10), Ishmael (Genesis 25:17), Rebekah's nurse Deborah (Genesis 35:8), Rachel (Genesis 35:18–20), Isaac (Genesis 35:28–29), Jacob (Genesis 49:29–33), Joseph (Genesis 50:22–26), Miriam (Numbers 20:1), Aaron (Numbers 20:24–29), and Moses. These death reports show certain common elements, not all of which are mentioned for every character. Typical features include the person's age at the time of death, the location where the person died, the person's physical condition, a pronouncement of the death, typically with formulaic, euphemistic language (for example, "Isaac then breathed his last and died; he was gathered to his people old and full of years," Genesis 35:29), details about the burial, and a comment about the mourning that follows the death. Of all these reports, only Moses' contains every one of these elements. The length of this unit and the way that it characterizes Moses testify to the unparalleled stature of the leader who shepherded the Israelites from the house of bondage to the gateway to the Promised Land.

### SURVEY OF THE PROMISED LAND (34:1–4)

In 3:25, Moses recounted how he pleaded with God to reconsider his sentence: "Let me, I pray, cross over and see the good land on the other side of the Jordan." Although God rejected the first part of Moses' entreaty, God conceded to the second part and agreed to let Moses view the land someday from a mountaintop in Moab (3:27). Finally, that day has arrived.

Having spoken his last words, Moses now performs his two last acts: ascending Mount Nebo, and surveying the land. He first gazes northward along the eastern side of the Jordan and then north to south on the western side, all the way from Dan to the Negeb. It would not be humanly possible to see such a vast expanse of land from Moses' vantage point, but such a claim seems only fitting given the extraordinary nature of Moses' death and burial.

*1. **Moses went up.*** Two earlier verses record God's command to Moses to ascend a mountain to view the land (Numbers 27:12; Deuteronomy 32:49). In both cases, God reminds Moses that his inability to enter the land comes as a consequence of the incident at the waters of Meribath-kadesh when Moses "disobeyed" and "broke faith with" God (Numbers 27:14; Deuteronomy 32:51; contrast the explanation given in 1:37). Here, as is fitting for the laudatory nature of Moses' death report, neither God nor the narrator mentions anything about Moses' death atop Mount Nebo being a punishment.

***Mount Nebo, to the summit of Pisgah.*** This verse seems to combine two traditions about Moses' death: one associated with Pisgah (3:27) and the other with Mount Nebo (32:49).

you see it with your own eyes, but you shall not cross there."

[5]So Moses the servant of יהוה died there, in the
land of Moab, at the command of יהוה. [6][God]
buried him in the valley in the land of Moab, near Beth-peor; and no one knows his burial place to
this day. [7]Moses was a hundred and twenty years old when he died; his eyes were undimmed and his vigor unabated. [8]And the Israelites bewailed Moses in the steppes of Moab for thirty days.

The period of wailing and mourning for Moses
came to an end. [9]Now Joshua son of Nun was filled with the spirit of wisdom because Moses had laid his hands upon him; and the Israelites heeded him, doing as יהוה had commanded Moses.

אֶתְנֶנָּה הֶרְאִיתִיךָ בְעֵינֶיךָ וְשָׁמָּה לֹא
תַעֲבֹר׃
5 וַיָּמָת שָׁם מֹשֶׁה עֶבֶד־יְהֹוָה בְּאֶרֶץ מוֹאָב
עַל־פִּי יְהֹוָה׃ 6 וַיִּקְבֹּר אֹתוֹ בַגַּי בְּאֶרֶץ
מוֹאָב מוּל בֵּית פְּעוֹר וְלֹא־יָדַע אִישׁ אֶת־
קְבֻרָתוֹ עַד הַיּוֹם הַזֶּה׃ 7 וּמֹשֶׁה בֶּן־מֵאָה
וְעֶשְׂרִים שָׁנָה בְּמֹתוֹ לֹא־כָהֲתָה עֵינוֹ וְלֹא־
נָס לֵחֹה׃ 8 וַיִּבְכּוּ בְנֵי יִשְׂרָאֵל אֶת־מֹשֶׁה
בְּעַרְבֹת מוֹאָב שְׁלֹשִׁים יוֹם
וַיִּתְּמוּ יְמֵי בְכִי אֵבֶל מֹשֶׁה׃ 9 וִיהוֹשֻׁעַ בִּן־
נוּן מָלֵא רוּחַ חָכְמָה כִּי־סָמַךְ מֹשֶׁה אֶת־
יָדָיו עָלָיו וַיִּשְׁמְעוּ אֵלָיו בְּנֵי־יִשְׂרָאֵל וַיַּעֲשׂוּ
כַּאֲשֶׁר צִוָּה יְהֹוָה אֶת־מֹשֶׁה׃

*4. "see it with your own eyes."* Deuteronomy repeatedly uses this phrase to emphasize the importance of knowledge gained from firsthand experience (for instance, see 4:3, 9, 34).

### MOSES' DEATH (34:5–7)

The report of Moses' death emphasizes that he did not die of natural causes, but at God's behest.

*7. hundred and twenty years old.* Genesis 6:3 appears to establish 120 years as the ideal human lifespan, although thereafter some biblical figures live longer; Sarah, for example, dies at age 127 (Genesis 23:1). This typological number can be accounted for as being three times forty (a key number in the Bible, as in the length of time of the wilderness journey) or two times sixty (important in the Mesopotamian sexagesimal system). As W. Gunther Plaut points out, 120 is the multiple of the first five whole numbers (1 × 2 × 3 × 4 × 5) (*The Torah: A Modern Commentary*, revised edition, 2005, p. 1387).

*his vigor unabated.* Literally, "his moisture had not departed [or: dried up]." Earlier, Moses told the people that he "can no longer be active" (31:2). Jeffrey Tigay therefore argues that this clause should be understood instead as meaning "he had not become wrinkled" (*Deuteronomy*, 1996, p. 338). (Compare Sarah's description of herself as "withered" in Genesis 18:12.)

### MOURNING FOR MOSES, WHO IS SUCCEEDED BY JOSHUA (34:8–9)

As they did for Aaron (Numbers 20:29), the people mourn Moses for thirty days. Various sources of evidence indicate that throughout the ancient world, women typically were associated with mourning rituals, composing and performing laments in times of collective and personal grief (see *Chayei Sarah*, Contemporary Reflection, p. 129). This section also confirms the successful transition of leadership to Joshua. Although he is a qualified successor, the subsequent section stresses that no one can rival Moses.

<sup>10</sup>Never again did there arise in Israel a prophet like Moses—whom יהוה singled out, face to face, <sup>11</sup>for the various signs and portents that יהוה sent him to display in the land of Egypt, against Pharaoh and all his courtiers and his whole country, <sup>12</sup>and for all the great might and awesome power that Moses displayed before all Israel.

10 וְלֹא־קָ֨ם נָבִ֥יא ע֛וֹד בְּיִשְׂרָאֵ֖ל כְּמֹשֶׁ֑ה אֲשֶׁר֙ יְדָע֣וֹ יְהֹוָ֔ה פָּנִ֖ים אֶל־פָּנִֽים׃ 11 לְכָל־הָ֨אֹתֹ֜ת וְהַמּוֹפְתִ֗ים אֲשֶׁ֤ר שְׁלָחוֹ֙ יְהֹוָ֔ה לַעֲשׂ֖וֹת בְּאֶ֣רֶץ מִצְרָ֑יִם לְפַרְעֹ֥ה וּלְכָל־עֲבָדָ֖יו וּלְכָל־אַרְצֽוֹ׃ 12 וּלְכֹל֙ הַיָּ֣ד הַחֲזָקָ֔ה וּלְכֹ֖ל הַמּוֹרָ֣א הַגָּד֑וֹל אֲשֶׁר֙ עָשָׂ֣ה מֹשֶׁ֔ה לְעֵינֵ֖י כָּל־יִשְׂרָאֵֽל׃

⁕ ⁕ ⁕ ⁕ ⁕ ⁕ ⁕ ⁕ ⁕ ⁕ ⁕ ⁕ ⁕ ⁕ ⁕

### TRIBUTE TO MOSES' UNRIVALED STATUS (34:10–12)

These concluding verses function as a eulogy, acclaiming Moses' incomparable stature as the sole prophet who merited unmediated contact with the Divine. (On women prophets, see Another View, p. 1284.) Following the reference to the covenant with the ancestors in v. 4, the text now highlights another pivotal biblical event: the wondrous acts that Moses performed on God's behalf, resulting in Israel's deliverance from Egypt. Just as the Exodus forms the foundation of the covenantal relationship between God and Israel—as reflected in the first verse of the Decalogue (Exodus 20:2; Deuteronomy 5:6)—so it is appropriate that the book of Deuteronomy, and hence the entire Torah, ends with the recollection of this event. As befits someone who assiduously sought to have Israel recognize and faithfully worship its God, the last words about Moses' life reiterate his deep bond with, and loyal service to, the Divine. For Israel to thrive in the Promised Land, and beyond, they will need both God's "mighty hand" (34:12, translated here as "great might") and God's comforting embrace, the support of God's "arms everlasting" (33:27).

—*Andrea L. Weiss*



חֲזַק חֲזַק וְנִתְחַזֵּק

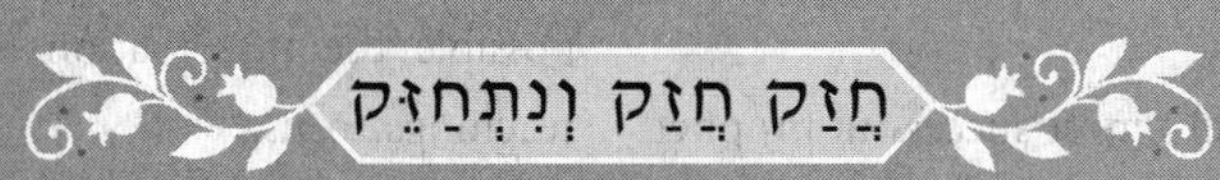

# Another View

DEUTERONOMY 34:10 CLAIMS THAT no other prophet ever matched Moses, whom God had "singled out, face to face." Albeit unique, Moses is only one of the many prophets who, as God's spokespersons, guided Israel. In the Bible, Miriam is the very first person to receive the title "prophet" (Exodus 15:20; Genesis 20:7 refers to Abraham's prophetic gifts, but he is not called "Abraham the prophet"). Along with several passages that mention unnamed female prophets (Isaiah 8:3; Ezekiel 13:17; Joel 3:1), the Bible names three other women prophets: Deborah, Huldah, and Noadiah.

Nothing is known about Noadiah (5th century B.C.E.) apart from Nehemiah's claim that she opposed him (Nehemiah 6:14); she must have been important enough to disturb Nehemiah, but it is her predecessors Deborah and Huldah who are praised as prominent and influential. Deborah leads the Israelites to victory and is the only chieftain in that period of Israelite history who is also a prophet (Judges 4:4). The poem attributed to Deborah refers to her as a "mother in Israel" (Judges 5:7), a title that probably designates her position as the people's protector rather than a biological maternity.

Huldah is perhaps Israel's most successful prophet. Whereas the messages of other prophets in the Bible often fall on deaf ears during their lifetime, Huldah's authority goes unquestioned and her words are heeded instantly. According to II Kings 22 and II Chronicles 34, a royal delegation in 622 B.C.E. consults Huldah about the "book of the *torah*" that was found at the Temple. When she authenticates it as God's teachings, the king immediately—and unquestioningly—implements the book's laws. Huldah is identified as a married woman, whose husband is the keeper of the king's wardrobe, while she herself holds "office" in a public area known as the Mishneh. Although the later rabbis express unease about the prominence of Huldah, the Bible presents her authority as a matter of fact. According to many modern scholars, the "book of the *torah*" that Huldah authenticates is Deuteronomy, or at least portions of it. If so, we owe the binding authority that Deuteronomy holds to none other than Huldah, whose own words confirmed and thus made possible the preservation and transmission of these teachings to us. —*Tamara Cohn Eskenazi*

*Huldah is perhaps Israel's most successful prophet: her words are heeded instantly.*

# Post-biblical Interpretations

***May Reuben live and not die*** (33:6). In his farewell blessing to the tribes of Israel, Moses first mentions the tribe of Reuben, descended from Jacob's eldest son. His benediction for Reuben is expressed in biblical poetic parallelism. To the modern reader this may seem redundant, since it expresses the same idea twice, albeit in different words. For the Rabbis, however, this apparent repetition was an opportunity for interpretation. They noticed that while the first half of the verse expresses the hope that Reuben would live, the second half states that he should not die. Both of these outcomes are positive for Reuben, but the former is phrased in upbeat language, whereas the latter uses negative terminology. Midrash *Sifrei D'varim* 347 finds different meanings in these linguistic nuances. Thus, the first phrase is said to refer to Reuben's reward for convincing his brothers not to treat Joseph as harshly as they would have liked (Genesis 37:22). The second half of the verse points to a death penalty decreed for Reuben that has been reversed ("not die"), referring to the punishment that Reuben deserved for having sexual relations with Bilhah, his father's concubine and the mother of some of his brothers (Genesis 35:22). However, a prominent rabbinic tradition

*Jochebed outlived her son Moses, entering the land of Israel at the age of 250.*

teaches that Reuben atoned for this sin and the decree of death was lifted. This midrash from *Sifrei D'varim* appears to link these two biblical incidents and implies that Reuben's good actions in one situation helped to atone for his bad actions in the other.

***So Moses the servant of* יהוה *died there*** (34:5). A medieval *piyut* (liturgical poem) begins with the words *Azlat Yocheved* ("Jochebed went out"), referring to Moses' mother (Exodus 6:20). This *piyut* is part of the Italian prayer tradition for the holiday of Simchat Torah, when the final Torah portion, including the account of the death of Moses, is read. (While there are no known midrashic parallels for the symbolic ideas in this *piyut*, it shares common motifs with rabbinic traditions, including a narrative about Moses' death found in *Avot D'Rabbi Natan* A 12, in which the angel of death, Samael, is the protagonist, rather than Jochebed.) In the *piyut*, Jochebed heart-rendingly searches for her son. She has heard of his death but refuses to accept that Moses has actually died. Understandably, a mother would not to want to learn that her son had preceded her in death. However, Jochebed's refusal to believe in Moses' demise is complicated by the fact that only God knows the circumstances of his death and his burial place. This *piyut* describes Jochebed traversing the world, including Egypt and various other pivotal places in Moses' life, searching for him. In her travels, she asks inanimate objects to tell her the whereabouts of her son. Her quest, of course, is unsuccessful, because he is, in fact already dead and buried.

The theme of the poem "*Azlat Yocheved*" is based on the rabbinic premise that Jochebed outlived her son Moses, who was 120 years old at his death (34:7). Jochebed's long life is discussed in a rabbinic midrash in *Seder Olam* 9, where she is described as surviving all of her children and entering the land of Israel at the age of 250.

*[God]* ***buried him in the valley in the land of Moab*** (34:6). A midrashic tradition physically connects the burial place of Moses, who was interred alone, to the graves of Abraham and Sarah in the Cave of Machpelah (Genesis 25:10). According to *Sifrei D'varim* 357, the two sites were linked by an underground tunnel.

Moses' grave is unknown to human beings but it is known to God. In fact, according to 34:6, Moses was buried by God. BT *Sotah* 14a explains that the Torah is framed by two divine demonstrations of loving-kindness. The charitable act in the beginning was "clothing the naked." This was fulfilled when God "made outfits out of skin for Adam and his wife, and clothed them" (Genesis 3:21). The loving-kindness at the end of the Torah was "burying the dead," God's final act of caring for Moses. According to rabbinic sources (BT *Shabbat* 127a), preparing the dead for burial is one of the ten ethical obligations for which there is no measure and whose reward is without measure.

*—Anna Urowitz-Freudenstein*

# *Contemporary Reflection*

Moses' final blessing to the tribes of Israel forms the coda for the five books of the Torah traditionally attributed to Moses. Often in Deuteronomy, Moses has admonished the people of Israel, sometimes threatening or even bullying them. Throughout the book, however, he also has offered the people blessings and a vision of God's love and potential rewards. Now, at the very end, Moses fills the people with hope and promise as he speaks to their best selves. As the greatest of teachers, Moses puts into words what they instinctively know what they long for but cannot quite articulate.

Moses and Israel began together as an erstwhile prince leading a band of slaves to freedom. Now, the people Israel are not only free, but also they are about to be responsible for their own lives in their own land. As they become a sovereign people, Moses (as it were) stitches them together, tribe after tribe, weaving a dramatic finale: "Thus Israel dwells in safety, / Untroubled is Jacob's abode" (33:28). This stunning statement confirms the Israelites' greatest hope, as well as ours today, envisioning a time even beyond the battles that lie ahead, when they finally will live in security and safety.

This parashah contains Moses' last blessing, indeed his last words to the entire people, one nation with many attributes and possibilities. Our Jewish religious tradition of blessings is not one of passive acceptance or recognition; instead, blessings demand action. This is why, for the most part, we recite a blessing before we carry out an action.

Some say that the Hebrew word for blessing (*b'rachah*) shares the same root as the word for knee (*berech*), as in "bend the knee." (Although there are scholars who dispute that theory, certainly our rabbis delighted in such wordplays.) When we recite a blessing, we bend ever so slightly, diminishing ourselves so as to affirm the Other and look deep into ourselves. Through prayer, we express our gratitude, ask for more blessings, and strive to reach beyond our present limitations. Acknowledging that which is not necessarily in our control, we hope for God's gifts of a healthy, secure, and bountiful life, a life of purpose and meaning. This is Moses' *b'rachah* to us, then and now: to gather the best within and around ourselves so as to fulfill the "promise" of the Promised Land.

After Moses blesses the tribes, he then stands atop Mount Nebo and surveys the entire land. Viewing the Negev and the valley of Jericho—city of date palms—south to Zoar, perhaps Moses is able to discard all the what if's, should have's, maybe's, and if only's. Perhaps he feels some sense of closure, an acceptance of what he could and could not accomplish in a lifetime. There is a certain humility in knowing our limits and recognizing when it is time to move on.

*Leadership is about affirming the future.*

Part of Moses' blessing involves the ability to dream of what he will not see or experience directly. Affirming the future is what leadership is all about: knowing and accepting that our best dreams may be realized by others who come after us. Moses' words remind us that we need to pray and work for the blessings of justice, equality, and peace in order to fulfill our promise as individuals and to build the best family, community, society, and country that we can. We learn from Moses that sometimes we have to scale mountains in order to come closer to these blessings.

The late Rev. Dr. Martin Luther King Jr. invoked the scene on Mount Nebo in the famous speech he delivered in Memphis the day before he was assassinated (1968). He said: "Well, I don't know what will happen now. We've got some difficult days ahead. But it doesn't matter with me now. Because I've been to the mountaintop. And I don't mind. Like anybody, I would like to live a long life. Longevity has its place. But I'm not concerned about that now. I just want to do God's will. And He's allowed me to go up to the mountain. And I've looked over. And I've seen the promised land. I may not get there with you. But I want you to know tonight, that we, as a people, will get to the promised land" ("I See the Promised Land," April 3, 1968). This speech turned out to be Dr. King's last. Like Moses, his final words were a blessing for justice and peace in the service of God. This legacy of hope and vision of who we can and must become urges us on, reminding us of the dreams that remain for us to actualize.

Whenever we finish a book of the Torah in the synagogue's cycle of readings, those who are present respond immediately with three words: *Chazak, chazak, v'nitchazek!* "Be strong, be strong [in the singular] and we will be strong [in the plural]." My late father, Rabbi Wolfe Kelman, taught: Why do we say *chazak* twice, when once would be enough? It is to tell us that if you and I each are strong, then together we are even stronger. In other words, this is a true "win/win" situation: I need you to be strong so I can be strong too.

My father's lesson is especially true for the Jewish people today. As Jewish women, we need to be strong so that we can experience and contribute to the fullness of our Jewish tradition. Women's entry into the leadership of Jewish life and their involvement in every aspect of communal, religious, and intellectual life is the blessing of the last 30 years. Women have opened new vistas, introduced innovations in every vital sphere of Jewish living, and empowered themselves and their daughters and granddaughters. The Jewish world has been profoundly reshaped; yet there is still a way to go. Future generations of women must continue to redefine family and work, renew ritual, scale new horizons of scholarship, write liturgy and poetry, and make music, all the while recreating the Jewish community and its structures. The Jewish people can only be strong when it embraces all of its members; it takes the involvement of both Jewish women and Jewish men to make our community fuller and more vibrant.

Thus, the reading of the Torah ends with blessings and the charge to strengthen ourselves and our community. Moses teaches us to reach for blessings for ourselves and others, to strive for the humility to know our task, and to dream of how to transform what *is* to what *can be.*

—*Naamah Kelman*

# Voices

## Last Prayer

Esther Raab (transl. Harold Schimmel)

*Deuteronomy 33*

Don't make me so good
so lean and impoverished,
so empty,
"and knowing before whom you stand"—
don't darken my final days
do not exalt me,
and don't make me
so modest,
and don't offer me
as nourishment
to any abject soul,
to any outcast;
straighten my back,
and strengthen my loins;
let me gather narcissus
in your forbidden
meadows
so I can toss them to the wind,
as if just once
the silo still brimmed over
with goodness;
let me take in
sacks of almonds
shedding a smell of mignonette
on the terrace;
a smell of new wine,
in wagons
loaded with grapes
in the yard.

## Unfulfilled Promise

Merle Feld

*Deuteronomy 34:5–9*

I guess I thought you'd lead me
to the promised land, but finally
I realize I never had a vision

of what that would look like,
or what it would feel like
to be free and whole at last.

All I had was confidence in you
as scout, trailblazer, trustworthy
and steady guide. I had faith

you'd take me the whole way
and deliver me safely
to the other side.

And now, we stand together
at the crossroads,
and you tell me,

*I've come as far as I can with you,*
*I've taught you whatever I know*
*about how to find water*

*in a wasteland, how to build*
*a temporary shelter, how to read*
*the sky, the stars, the trail and the winds.*

I look to the horizon
but all I see ahead of me
is more wasteland.

## *Anniversary*

Judy Katz

*Deuteronomy 34:5–8*

Everywhere I look I see you.
April again. The coffee sitting too long
in its white cup leaves a ring the color of your
straw hat,
the one you wore in the garden. In forsythia,
I see you.
The small diamond chip in a stranger's ear.
On the bus I see you, and in galleries and cafes.
Your red coat. I see you young and I see you
old.
Imagine, I see you old! Illumined by white hair,
you are
drinking juice. I see you in paintbrushes and
water towers.
On evening walks, in the broken sky
between buildings, I piece you
together.

It is Passover again.
I see you at the *seder*, your pink and white robe,
in sweet apples and salt water, in the blunt,
bitter root.
Tell me, exactly when is the moment
of passing?

I travel to the desert, and there you are—
the low airport buildings are yours; the sudden
mountains,
yours. I see you in the clear light, the thin air,
the fifty shades of green beside the road.
At midday,
the rutted hills are your hands. We drive
and I see them all day long.

I see you as you were, and as you never were.
In charcoal and in flesh, with the unrelenting
mind
of Spring, I see you. The petal of the crocus
that clings to my finger, the purple capillaries
sprouting in my leg. You are the pavement
under my feet,
the bucket of daffodils the grocer moves
to the front window.

## *from* In the Jerusalem Hills

Lea Goldberg (transl. Robert Friend)

*Deuteronomy 33:1–34:4*

All the things
outside love
come to me now:
this landscape with its old man's understanding
begging to live
one more year, one more year,
one generation more,
one more eternity.

To bring forth thorns endlessly,
to rock dead stones
like children in their cradles
before they sleep.
To silence ancient memories,
one more one more
one more.

How strong the lust for life
in those about to die.
How terrible the longing
and how vain:
to live, to live
one more year, one more year,
one generation more,
one more eternity.

## *The Death of Moses*

Jill Hammer

*Deuteronomy 34:1–8*

in the end it is we who come
the ones who birthed him into life
we come to bury him

called by the voices of birds
we come white-haired to the cave
of the kisses of God

we carry the burial shroud
we have woven together
in the dark of moonless nights
ever since he went up the mountain

we are the hands of the Shechinah
an old slave woman    a midwife
a princess    a stranger
our old feet have taken this journey
we have lost daughters and husbands

we began redemption together
on the banks of the Nile
weaving reeds    plots    baby clothes
now we are the ones who finish the circle
we do the last work of the wilderness

he has seen the whole land
but we, we have seen the universe
how a tiny child can become a river
how a salt sea can turn to earth

we bury him in the valley
in the land of Moab
where one day a mother and a daughter
will come to love one another
and redemption will be born

we bury him in the shifting sands
in a shroud white as the moon

"and no man knows his burial place
until this day"

## *Untitled*

Muriel Rukeyser

A tree of rivers flowing through our lives;
These lives moving through their starvation and
    greatness,
Masked away from each other, masked in lack.
Each woman seen as a river through whom
    lifetime
Gives, and feeds. Each man seen giving and
    feeding.
Under all the images, under all growth and
    form. The energy
        of each, which is relation,
A flare of linked fire which is the need to grow,
The human wish for meaning.
                        Roots of diversity
Each being witness to itself, entering to relate,
Bearing the flood, the food, the becoming of
    power,
Which is our eyes and our lives
Related, in bonds of flow.

## *There Are Stars*

Hannah Senesh (transl. Ziva Shapiro, adapted)

*Deuteronomy 34:10–12*

There are stars whose radiance is visible on earth though they have long been extinct. There are people whose brilliance continues to light the world though they are no longer among the living. These lights are particularly bright when the night is dark. They light the way for humankind.

# *Transliteration Guide*

This commentary has adopted the simplified transliteration proposed by Professor Werner Weinberg of HUC–JIR and brought it into consonance with URJ Press style. Rather than provide a character-for-character transcription of how the Hebrew is written, it reproduces how the Hebrew is sounded according to standard Israeli pronunciation. Its features include:

- No distinction for consonants that sound the same: שׂ/ס and ת/ט and ק/כ and ו/ב
- ח and כ both appear as "ch" (pronounced as in Scottish "loch" or German "buch")
- צ appears as "tz" (pronounced as in "blitz")
- Silent letters (and gutturals at the start of a word): omitted except when one separates two vowels inside a word, in which case a hyphen or an apostrophe is introduced (as in רֹאִי, *ro-i;* מוֹעֵד, *mo-eid;* רָקִיעַ, *raki'a*); in verbal roots, the letters *a* and *e* represent א and ע, respectively.
- Resting schwa is omitted; moving schwa is shown as an apostrophe (as in שְׁמַע, *sh'ma*)
- An apostrophe sometimes separates consonants to preclude their being misread
- Half vowels are transliterated as full vowels (as in אֱמֶת, *emet*)
- Other vowels appear as follows:

| | | |
|---|---|---|
| Xָ and Xַ | *kamatz gadol* and *patach* | *a* |
| Xָ | *kamatz katon* | *o* |
| Xֶ | *segol* | *e* |
| Xֵ | *tzerei* | *ei* or *e* |
| Xִ | *chirik* | *i* |
| וֹ Xֹ | *cholem-vav* and *cholem* | *o* |
| וּ and Xֻ | *shurek* and *kibbutz* | *u* |

- Pronunciation of transliterated vowels:

| | |
|---|---|
| *a* | as in "aha!" |
| *e* | as in "red" |
| *i* | as in "spin" or "police" |
| *o* | as in "hole" or "north" |
| *u* | as in "ruler" |
| *ai* | as in "Thailand" |
| *ei* | as in "eight" |
| *oi* | as in "join" |

- י as a vowel letter may be omitted
- Doubled consonants are usually transliterated with single consonants.
- Customary spelling has been maintained of a few Hebrew words that have become part of common usage, especially proper names (for example, Ishmael rather than Yishmael; *challah* rather than *chalah*; *niddah* rather than *nidah*)

# Bibliography


REFERENCE WORKS (cited by title)

*ANET* = *Ancient Near Eastern Texts Relating to the Old Testament*, 3rd edn., edited by James B. Pritchard. Princeton, NJ: Princeton University Press, 1969.

*The Contemporary Torah: A Gender-Sensitive Adaptation of the JPS Translation.* David E. S. Stein, revising ed.; Adele Berlin, Ellen Frankel, and Carol L. Meyers, consulting eds. Philadelphia: Jewish Publication Society, 2006.

*The Context of Scripture*, edited by William W. Hallo et al. 3 vols. Boston: Brill, 2003.

*The Torah: Documentation for the Revised Edition*, by David E. S. Stein. URJ Press. http://www.urjpress.com/torahrevision/documentation.html.

*The Torah: A Modern Commentary*, revised edn. W. Gunther Plaut, general editor; David E. S. Stein, general editor for rev. edn. New York: URJ Press, 2005.

*Women in Scripture: A Dictionary of Named and Unnamed Women in the Hebrew Bible*. . . . Edited by Carol Meyers et al. Boston: Houghton Mifflin, 2000.

OTHER WORKS (cited by author or editor)

Ackerman, Susan. *Warrior, Dancer, Seductress, Queen: Women in Judges and Biblical Israel.* New York: Doubleday, 1998.

Adelman, Penina V., Ali Feldman, and Shulamit Reinharz. *The JGirl's Guide: The Young Jewish Woman's Handbook for Coming of Age.* Woodstock, VT: Jewish Lights Publishing, 2005.

Adler, Rachel. *Engendering Judaism: An Inclusive Theology and Ethics.* Philadelphia: Jewish Publication Society, 1998.

Aguilar, Grace. *The Women of Israel or Characters and Sketches from the Holy Scriptures and Jewish History Illustrative of the Past History, Present Duty, and Future Destiny of the Hebrew Female, as Based on the Word of God* (1845). Reprinted London: G.S. Appleton, 1851.

Alexiou, Margaret. *The Ritual Lament in Greek Tradition.* Lanham, MD: Rowman & Littlefield, 2002.

Alpert, Rebecca T. *Like Bread on the Seder Plate: Jewish Lesbians and the Transformation of Tradition.* New York: Columbia University Press, 1997.

Alter, Robert. *The Art of Biblical Narrative.* New York: Basic Books, 1981.

Baskin, Judith. *Midrashic Women: Formations of the Feminine in Rabbinic Literature.* Hanover: Brandeis University Press, 2002.

Bellis, Alice Ogden. *Helpmates, Harlots, and Heroes: Women's Stories in the Hebrew Bible.* Louisville, KY: Westminster/John Knox Press, 1994; rev. edn. 2007.

Berlinerblau, Jacques. *The Vow and the "Popular Religious Groups" of Ancient Israel: A Philological and Sociological Inquiry.* Sheffield, England: Sheffield Academic Press, 1996.

Bird, Phyllis. "Bone of My Bone and Flesh of My Flesh." *Theology Today* 50 (January 1994): 573–84.

———. "The Harlot as Heroine." Chap. 9 in *Missing Persons and Mistaken Identities: Women and Gender in Ancient Israel.* Minneapolis: Fortress Press, 1997.

Brenner, Athalya, ed. *The Feminist Companion to the Bible.* Sheffield, England: Sheffield Academic Press, 1993–97 (10 vols.); second series, 1997–2001 (9 vols.).

Buckley, Thomas and Alma Gottlieb. "A Critical Appraisal of Theories of Menstrual Symbolism." In *Blood Magic: The Anthropology of Menstruation*, edited by Thomas Buckley and Alma Gottlieb, 1–44. Berkeley: University of California Press, 1988.

Burns, Rita J. *Has the Lord Indeed Spoken Only Through Moses?: A Study of the Biblical Portrait of Miriam.* Atlanta: Scholars Press, 1987.

Bynum, Caroline Walker. *Holy Feast and Holy Fast: The Religious Significance of Food to Medieval Women.* Berkeley: University of California Press, 1987.

Cardin, Nina Beth, ed. *Tears of Sorrow, Seeds of Hope: A Jewish Spiritual Companion for Infertility and Pregnancy Loss.* 2nd ed. Woodstock, VT: Jewish Lights, 2007.

Chirichigno, Gregory. *Debt-slavery in Israel and the Ancient Near East.* Sheffield: JSOT Press, 1993.

Cohen, Shaye J. D. *The Beginnings of Jewishness: Boundaries, Varieties, Uncertainties.* Berkeley: University of California Press, 1999.

Cohen, Tamara. *The Journey Continues: The Ma'yan Passover Haggadah.* New York: Ma'yan, 2002.

Cowley, A. *Aramaic Papyri of the Fifth Century B.C.* Oxford: Clarendon Press, 1923.

DeSilva, Cara, ed. *In Memory's Kitchen: A Legacy from the Women of Terezin.* Translated by Bianca Steiner Brown. Northvale, NJ: Jason Aronson, 1996.

Douglas, Mary. *Implicit Meanings: Essays in Anthropology.* Boston: Routledge & Paul, 1975.

———. *In the Wilderness: The Doctrine of Defilement in the Book of Numbers.* New York: Oxford University Press, 2001.

———. "Mountain, Tabernacle, Body in Leviticus 1–7." Chap. 4 in *Leviticus as Literature.* New York: Oxford University Press, 1999.

Ehrlich, Elizabeth. *Miriam's Kitchen: A Memoir.* New York: Viking, 1997.

Falk, Marcia. *The Book of Blessings: New Jewish Prayers for Daily Life, the Sabbath, and the New Moon Festival.* San Francisco: HarperSanFrancisco, 1996.

Fields, Harvey J. *A Torah Commentary for our Times.* New York: UAHC Press, 1990–1993.

Fine, Lawrence. *Physician of the Soul, Healer of the Cosmos: Isaac Luria and his Kabbalistic Fellowship.* Stanford, CA: Stanford University Press, 2003.

Fox, Nili Sacher. *In The Service of the King: Officialdom in Ancient Israel and Judah.* Cincinnati: Hebrew Union College, 2000.

Fromm, Erich. *You Shall Be As Gods: A Radical Interpretation of the Old Testament and Its Tradition.* New York: Holt, Rinehart and Winston, 1966.

Frymer-Kensky, Tikva. "The Atrahasis Epic and Its Significance for Our Understanding of Genesis 1–9," Chap. 4 in *Studies in Bible and Feminist Criticism.* Philadelphia: Jewish Publication Society, 2006.

———. "Deuteronomy." In Carol A. Newsom and Sharon H. Ringe, eds. *Women's Bible Commentary.* Louisville, KY: Westminster John Knox Press, 1992.

———. *In the Wake of the Goddesses: Women, Culture, and the Biblical Transformation of Pagan Myth.* New York: Free Press, 1992.

———. "Israelite Law: State and Judiciary Law," *Encyclopedia of Religion*, 2nd ed., New York: Macmillan Reference, 2005, 7:4741.

———. "Law and Philosophy: The Case of Sex in the Bible." Chap. 16 in *Studies in Bible and Feminist Criticism.* Philadelphia: Jewish Publication Society, 2006: 239–54.

———. *Reading the Women of the Bible.* New York: Schocken Books, 2002.

———. "The Strange Case of the Suspected Sotah: Numbers V 11–31." In *Women in the Hebrew Bible: A Reader*, edited by Alice Bach, 463–74. New York: Routledge, 1999.

———. *Studies in Bible and Feminist Criticism.* Philadelphia, PA: Jewish Publication Society, 2006.

Geller, Stephen A. "Blood Cult: Toward a Literary Theology of the Priestly Work of the Pentateuch." *Prooftexts* 12/2 (1992): 97–124.

Goldberg, Lea. *Selected Poetry and Drama.* Poetry selected and translated by Rachel Tzvia Back. New Milford, CT: Toby, 2005.

Goldstein, Elyse, ed. *The Women's Torah Commentary: New Insights from Women Rabbis on the 54 Weekly Torah Portions.* Woodstock, VT: Jewish Lights, 2000.

Grant, Alison M. "*'adam* and *'ish:* Man in the OT." *Australian Biblical Review* 25 (1977): 2–11.

Gray, Elizabeth Dodson. *Sacred Dimensions of Women's Experience.* Wellesley, MA: Roundtable Press, 1988.

Greenberg, Aharon Yaakov, ed. *Torah Gems.* Translated by Shmuel Himelstein. Brooklyn: Chemed Books and Co., 1992.

Greenberg, Blu. *On Women & Judaism: A View from Tradition.* Philadelphia: Jewish Publication Society of America, 1981.

Grosz, Katarzyna. "Some Aspects of the Position of Women in Nuzi." In *Women's Earliest Records from Ancient Egypt and Western Asia: Proceedings of the Conference on Women in the Ancient Near East, Brown University, . . . November 5–7, 1987,* edited by Barbara S. Lesko. Atlanta: Scholars Press, 1989.

Grubbs, Judith Evans. *Law and Family in Late Antiquity: The Emperor Constantine's Marriage Legislation.* New York: Oxford University Press, 1995.

Gruber, Mayer I. "Breast-Feeding Practices in Biblical Israel and in Old Babylonian Mesopotamia." *Journal of the Ancient Near Eastern Society* 19 (1989): 61–83. Reprinted in *The Motherhood of God and Other Studies,* 69–107. Atlanta: Scholars Press, 1992.

———. "Women in the Cult According to the Priestly Code." In *Judaic Perspectives on Ancient Israel,* edited by J. Neusner et al., 35–48. Philadelphia: Fortress, 1987. Reprinted in *The Motherhood of God and Other Studies,* 49–68. Atlanta: Scholars Press, 1992.

Grushcow, Lisa. *Writing the Wayward Wife: Rabbinic Interpretations of Sotah.* Boston: Brill, 2006.

Herzl, Theodor. *A Jewish State: An Attempt at a Modern Solution of the Jewish Question.* Translated by Sylvia d'Avigdor. New York: Federation of American Zionists, 1917.

———. *Old New Land.* Translated by Lotta Levensohn. New York: Bloch Publishing, 1941.

Hirt-Manheimer, Aron, ed. *The Jewish Condition: Essays on Contemporary Judaism Honoring Rabbi Alexander M. Schindler.* New York: UAHC Press, 1995.

hooks, bell. *Feminist Theory from Margin to Center.* Boston: South End Press, 1984.

Ilan, Tal. "Women and the Rabbis," section of larger article: "Woman." *Encyclopaedia Judaica,* 2nd ed. Detroit: Macmillan Reference USA, 2007, 21:164–65.

Kaufman, Shirley, Galit Hasan-Rokem, and Tamar S. Hess, eds. *Hebrew Feminist Poems from Antiquity to the Present: A Bilingual Anthology.* New York: Feminist Press at the City University of New York, 1999.

Keller, Catherine. *The Face of the Deep: A Theology of Becoming.* New York: Routledge, 2003.

King, Philip J. *Life in Biblical Israel.* Louisville, KY: Westminster John Knox Press, 2001.

Klawans, Jonathan. *Impurity and Sin in Ancient Judaism.* New York: Oxford University Press, 2000.

Koren, Sharon. "Shekhinah as a Female Symbol," section of larger article: "Shekhinah." *Encyclopaedia Judaica,* 2nd ed. Detroit: Macmillan Reference USA, 2007, 18:443–44.

Josephus, Flavius. *The Works of Flavius Josephus: Complete and Unabridged, New Updated Edition*, translated by William Whiston. Peabody, MA: Hendrickson Publishers, 1987.

*JPS Hebrew-English Tanakh: The Traditional Hebrew Text and the New JPS Translation—Second Edition.* Philadelphia: Jewish Publication Society, 1999.

Leibowitz, Nehama. *Studies in Bereshit (Genesis); Studies in Shemot (Exodus); Studies in Vayikra (Leviticus); Studies in Bamidbar (Numbers); Studies in Devarim (Deuteronomy).* 5 Vols. Translated and adapted from the Hebrew by Aryeh Newman. 4th ed. Jerusalem: World Zionist Organization, 1980.

Levine, Baruch A. *The JPS Torah Commentary: Leviticus.* Philadelphia: Jewish Publication Society, 1989.

Levinson, Bernard. "Deuteronomy." In *The Jewish Study Bible*, edited by Adele Berlin and Marc Zvi Brettler, 356–450. New York: Oxford University Press, 2004.

Levy, Richard. "Parashat Va-yechi." In *Learn Torah With... 5755 Torah Annual: A Collection of The Year's Best Torah*, edited by Joel Lurie Grishaver. Vol. 2, No. 12. Los Angeles: Alef Design Group, 1996.

Maccoby, Hyam. *Ritual and Morality: The Ritual Purity System and Its Place in Judaism.* New York: Cambridge University Press, 1999.

Magonet, Jonathan. "'But If It Is a Girl, She Is Unclean for Twice Seven Days': The Riddle of Leviticus 12:5." In *Reading Leviticus: A Conversation with Mary Douglas*, edited by John F. A. Sawyer, 144–52. Sheffield, England: Sheffield Academic Press, 1996.

Malamat, Abraham. "You Shall Love Your Neighbor as Yourself: A Case of Misinterpretation?" In *Die hebräische Bibel und ihre zweifache Nachgeschichte*, edited by E. Blum et al., 111–16. Neukirchen: Neukirchen Verlag, 1990.

May, Rollo. *The Courage to Create.* New York: Norton, 1975.

Meyers, Carol L. *Discovering Eve: Ancient Israelite Women in Context.* New York: Oxford University Press, 1988.

———. *Exodus.* The New Cambridge Bible Commentary. New York: Cambridge University Press, 2005.

———. "Procreation, Production, and Protection: Male-Female Balance in Early Israel." *Journal of the American Academy of Religion* 51/4 (Dec. 1983): 569–593.

———. "The Roots of Restriction: Women in Early Israel?" *The Biblical Archaeologist* 41/3 (1978): 91–103.

Milgrom, Jacob. *The JPS Torah Commentary: Numbers.* Philadelphia: Jewish Publication Society, 1990.

———. *Leviticus 1–16: A New Translation with Introduction and Commentary.* Anchor Bible. New York: Doubleday, 1991.

———. *Leviticus 23–27: A New Translation with Introduction and Commentary.* Anchor Bible. New York: Doubleday, 2001.

———. *Leviticus: A Book of Ritual and Ethics.* Minneapolis: Fortress Press, 2004.

Mintz, Alan, ed. *Reading Hebrew Literature.* Hanover, NH: Brandeis University Press, 2003.

Mirkin, Marsha Pravder. "Hearken to Her Voice: Empathy as *Teshuva*." In *Beginning Anew: A Woman's Companion to the High Holy Days*, edited by Gail Twersky Reimer and Judith A. Kates, 62–70. New York: Simon & Schuster, 1997.

Nizan, Tal, ed. *With an Iron Pen: Hebrew Protest Poems 1984–2004* [Hebrew]. Tel Aviv: Xargol Books, 2005.

Pardes, Ilana. *Countertraditions in the Bible: A Feminist Approach.* Cambridge, MA: Harvard University Press, 1992.

Person, Hara E. "Masa'ei (33:1–36:13): Boundaries and Limits." In *The Women's Torah Commentary: New Insights From Women Rabbis on the 54 Weekly Torah Portions*. Edited by Elyse Goldstein. 321–30. Woodstock, VT: Jewish Lights Publishing, 2000.

Plaskow, Judith. *Standing Again at Sinai: Judaism from a Feminist Perspective*. San Francisco: HarperCollins, 1990.

Rich, Adrienne Cecile. *An Atlas of the Difficult World: Poems, 1988–1991*. New York: W. W. Norton, 1991.

———. *Facts on a Doorframe: Poems 1950–2001*. New York: W. W. Norton, 2002.

———. *What is Found There: Notebooks on Poetry and Politics*. New York: W. W. Norton, 2003.

Scarry, Elaine. *The Body in Pain: The Making and Unmaking of the World*. New York: Oxford University Press, 1985.

Schiff, Daniel. *Abortion in Judaism*. New York: Cambridge University Press, 2002.

Schneider, Tammi. *Sarah: Mother of Nations*. New York: Continuum, 2004.

Sered, Susan Starr. *Women as Ritual Experts: The Religious Lives of Elderly Jewish Women in Jerusalem*. New York: Oxford University Press, 1992.

Stein, David E. S. "What Does It Mean to Be a 'Man'? The Noun *'ish* in Biblical Hebrew: A Reconsideration." Unpublished memorandum, 2006–7. http://home1.gte.net/res0z77f/'ish--Pt_1_of_7.Stein.7-30-06.pdf.

Suetonius Tranquillus, Gaius. *The Twelve Caesars*, translated by Robert Graves. Revised by Michael Grant. New York: Penguin, 2003.

Teubal, Savina. *Sarah the Priestess: The First Matriarch of Genesis*. Athens, Ohio: Swallow Press, 1984.

Tigay, Jeffrey. *The JPS Torah Commentary: Deuteronomy*. Philadelphia: Jewish Publication Society, 1996.

Trible, Phyllis. "Depatriarchalizing in Biblical Interpretation," *Journal of the American Academy of Religion* 41 (1973): 30–48.

Umansky, Ellen, and Dianne Ashton, eds. *Four Centuries of Jewish Women's Spirituality*. New York: Beacon Press, 1992.

Washbourn, Penelope. "Becoming Woman: Menstruation as Spiritual Experience." In *Womanspirit Rising: A Feminist Reader in Religion*, edited by Carol P. Christ and Judith Plaskow, 246–258. San Francisco: Harper & Row, 1979.

Weinfeld, Moshe. *Deuteronomy 1–11*. Anchor Bible. New York: Doubleday, 1991.

Weissler, Chava. *Voices of the Matriarchs: Listening to the Prayers of Early Modern Jewish Women*. Boston: Beacon Press, 1998.

Wolfson, Elliot R. *Circle in the Square: Studies in the Use of Gender in Kabbalistic Symbolism*. Albany: State University of New York Press, 1995.

Zornberg, Avivah Gottlieb. *The Particulars of Rapture: Reflections on Exodus*. New York: Doubleday, 2001.

# *Post-biblical Interpretation: About the Sources*

## MODERN SOURCES CITED AND REFERENCE WORKS


Baskin, Judith R. *Midrashic Women: Formations of the Feminine in Rabbinic Literature* (Hanover, NH: Brandeis University Press, 2002). Analyses of portrayals of women in rabbinic texts.

Berlin, Adele, and Marc Zvi Brettler, editors. *The Jewish Study Bible* (New York: Oxford University Press, 2004). See particularly the seven essays in the section "Jewish Interpretation of the Bible," pp. 1829–1919).

Brooten, Bernadette. *Women Leaders in the Ancient Synagogue* (Chico, CA: Scholars Press, 1982).

Ginzberg, Louis. *The Legends of the Jews.* 7 volumes (Philadelphia: Jewish Publication Society, 1909–1938; reprinted by Johns Hopkins University Press, 1988). Classic collection of *midrash aggadah*, translated, edited, and indexed by Henrietta Szold.

Holtz, Barry W. *Back to the Sources: Reading The Classic Jewish Texts* (New York: Touchstone, 1984). Excellent chapters on Talmud, midrash, and medieval biblical commentaries.

*Itturei Torah*, edited by Aharon Yaakov Greenberg (Tel Aviv: Yavneh, 1965–1991). 7 volumes; Hebrew. Selected comments on the Torah, featuring Chasidic and ethical materials. Available in a 3-vol. abridged English translation, *Torah Gems.*

Strack, H. L., and Günter Stemberger. *Introduction to the Talmud and Midrash.* 2nd Fortress Edition (Minneapolis: Fortress Press, 1996). Clear and inclusive introduction to the major works of rabbinic literature.

Weissler, Chava. *Voices of the Matriarchs: Listening to the Prayers of Early Modern Jewish Women* (Boston: Beacon Press, 1998). Pioneering study of early modern vernacular spiritual writings written for and by women.


## RABBINIC TEXTS

*Mishnah* Cited by tractate, chapter, and individual mishnah. Edited in the Land of Israel in the 3rd century C.E.

*Tosefta* Contemporaneous with the Mishnah

*Babylonian Talmud* Abbreviated as BT. Cited by tractate, page number, and front ("a") or back ("b") of page. Edited in the 6th century C.E.

*Talmud of the Land of Israel* Also known as the Jerusalem Talmud (and thus abbreviated as JT) or the Palestinian Talmud. Edited in the 5th century C.E.

## EARLY COMPILATIONS OF MIDRASH

*These date from the period of the Talmuds—no later than the 6th century C.E.*

*B'reishit Rabbah:* a commentary on Genesis

*M'chilta*: a commentary on Exodus; several versions

*Sifrei B'midbar*: a commentary on Numbers

*Sifrei Zuta*: a commentary on Numbers

*Sifra:* a commentary on Leviticus

*Sifrei D'varim:* a commentary on Deuteronomy

*Avot D'Rabbi Natan:* a commentary on Mishnah *Avot*; exists in two versions known as "A" and "B"

## SELECTED POST-TALMUDIC MIDRASH COLLECTIONS

*Most of these texts are extremely difficult to date since their contents evolved and were altered over time.*

*Midrash Kohelet:* a commentary on Ecclesiastes

*Midrash Ester:* a commentary on the book of Esther

*Pirkei D'Rabbi Eliezer:* a midrashic narrative of important events of the Torah

*P'sikta D'Rav Kahana:* commentaries on Torah and haftarah readings for festivals and other special occasions

*P'sikta Rabbati:* commentaries on Sabbath and holiday Torah and haftarah readings

*Tanchuma* or *Y'lamdeinu:* midrash collections on all five books of the Torah; several versions

*Midrash Sh'muel*: commentary on the two books of Samuel

*Midrash T'hillim:* commentary on Psalms

*Midrash Mishlei*: commentary on Proverbs

*Seder Olam Rabbah* (or simply *Seder Olam*): a midrashic history from Creation to the destruction of the Second Temple

*Yalkut Shimoni*: midrash collection on the entire Hebrew Scriptures

*Tanna D'Vei Eliyahu*: thematic midrash compilation on past and future eras of Jewish history

*Midrash Rabbah:* a large collection of separate commentaries on eight biblical books written in diverse times and places

*Midrash HaGadol:* a very large 14th-century compilation on the Torah; written in Yemen and preserved by Yemenite Jews

—*Judith R. Baskin*

# About the Authors

***Rabbi Judith Z. Abrams, Ph.D.***, directs Maqom, a school for adult Talmud study that she founded in 1995. She was ordained by Hebrew Union College–Jewish Institute of Religion in 1985 and received her Ph.D. from Baltimore Hebrew University in 1993. For ten years she served congregations as their rabbi. She received the Covenant Award for excellence in Jewish education (1999) and was named Senior Religious Advisor to the State of Texas in 2000. Her publications include numerous books on Talmud, as well as liturgies for children, and a wide variety of articles.

***Dr. Rachel Adler*** is Professor of Modern Jewish Thought and Judaism and Gender at Hebrew Union College–Jewish Institute of Religion, Los Angeles. She received her Ph.D. in Religion and Social Ethics from the University of Southern California with a concurrent certificate in Judaica from HUC–JIR. She also holds an M.A. in literature from Northwestern University and an M.S.W. from the University of Minnesota. She is the author of *Engendering Judaism* (1999), which won a National Jewish Book Award, as well as many articles on gender and Jewish theology and law. Her essay "The Jew Who Wasn't There" (1971) is often cited as the beginning of Jewish feminist thought.

***Dr. Yairah Amit*** is a full professor of Hebrew Bible in the Department of Hebrew Culture Studies at Tel Aviv University, and is head of the Training Program for Teachers of Hebrew Bible at the School of Education at Tel Aviv University. She holds an M.A. from the Hebrew University of Jerusalem and a Ph.D. from Tel Aviv University. She has authored books including *History and Ideology: An Introduction to Historiography in the Hebrew Bible* (1999), *Hidden Polemics in Biblical Narrative* (2000), and *Reading Biblical Narratives: Literary Criticism and the Hebrew Bible* (2001).

***Dr. Rachel Anisfeld*** is a Research Associate at the Center for Jewish Studies of the University at Albany. She holds a Ph.D. in Classical Midrash from the University of Pennsylvania and is working on a book about the historical development of amoraic homiletical midrash.

***Dr. Carol Bakhos*** is Associate Professor of Late Antique Judaism in the Department of Near Eastern Languages and Cultures at the University of California, Los Angeles. She earned her M.T.S. from Harvard and her Ph.D. from the Jewish Theological Seminary. She is the author of *Ishmael on the Border: Rabbinic Portrayals of the First Arab* (2007) and the editor of two volumes: *Ancient Judaism in its Hellenistic Context* (2004) and *Current Trends in the Study of Midrash* (2005).

***Rabbi Carole B. Balin, Ph.D.***, is Professor of Jewish History at Hebrew Union College–Jewish Institute of Religion, New York. She was educated at Wellesley College, ordained by HUC–JIR, and earned her Ph.D. at Columbia University. Her book *To Reveal Our Hearts: Jewish Women Writers in Tsarist Russia* (2000) won a Koret Publication Prize. She is currently working with Dr. Wendy Zierler on an anthology of the writings of Hava Shapiro, and with Dr. Eugene Borowitz on a revision of *Liberal Judaism*.

***Dr. Judith R. Baskin*** is Knight Professor of Humanities and Director of the Schnitzer Program in Judaic Studies at the University of Oregon. She holds a Ph.D. from Yale University. Her books include *Midrashic Women* (2002), *Pharaoh's Counsellors* (1982), and the edited collections *Jewish Women in Historical Perspective* (2nd ed., 1998) and *Women of the Word: Jewish Women and Jewish Writing* (1994).

***Rabbi Pauline Bebe*** was the first woman rabbi on Continental Europe since World War II and the only woman rabbi in France until 2007. She was ordained in 1990 by the Leo Baeck College of London. The founding rabbi of the Communauté Juive Libérale—Ile de France, Bebe is also author of *Le Judaïsme Libéral* (1993), *ISHA: Dictionnaire des Femmes et du Judaïsme* (2001), *Peut-on Faire le Bonheur de Ses Enfants* (2003), and *Qu'est-ce Que le Judaïsme Libéral?* (2006).

***Dr. Adele Berlin*** is the Robert H. Smith Professor of Biblical Studies at the University of Maryland and holds a Ph.D. from the University of Pennsylvania. Her main interests include biblical narrative and poetry and the interpretation of the Bible. She has written seven books and many articles. Most recently, she served as co-editor of *The Jewish Study Bible* (2004, with Marc Brettler), which received a National Jewish Book Award. She is currently working on a commentary on Psalms.

***Dr. Elizabeth Bloch-Smith*** has excavated for 35 years at sites in Israel, Cyprus, Tunisia, and Connecticut—the last 7 years at Tel Dor, Israel—and teaches courses in Bible and in archeology at universities in Philadelphia and New York. She holds a Ph.D. in Syro-Palestinian archeology at the University of Chicago. Her interests focus on the Iron Age and early Israel based on archeological remains together with biblical testimony, and she has written on sacred space and ritual practices, Solomon's temple, family life, and burial practices and beliefs about the dead.

***Dr. Athalya Brenner*** is Professor of the Hebrew Bible/Old Testament at the Universiteit van Amsterdam, The Netherlands. She holds a Ph.D. from the Department of Near Eastern Studies at the University of Manchester in England, and she is the editor of the 19-volume work, *Feminist Companion to the Bible* (first and second series; 1993–2001). Her most recent book is *I Am: Biblical Women Tell Their Own Stories* (2005). She lives in Amsterdam and in Haifa, Israel.

***Rabbi Silvina Chemen*** serves Kehilat Beth El, the first Conservative congregation in Latin America, and she is in charge of the Schlichei Tzibur School, a national program of the Argentine Jewish Communities Association. She was ordained at the Seminario Rabínico Latinoamericano, in Buenos Aires, Argentina, within the Conservative Movement, finishing her studies at Machon Schechter in Jerusalem. She is the first, and to date the only, woman rabbi in South America. Her publications include *Violence and School* (2001) and *Torah Umifgash* [Torah and Encounter] (2006).

***Rabbi Dianne Cohler-Esses*** serves as Scholar In Residence at UJA Federation in New York. She is the first woman from the Syrian Jewish community in Brooklyn to become a rabbi, ordained by the Jewish Theological Seminary (JTS) in 1995.

***Rabbi Rachel Cowan*** serves as Executive Director of the Institute for Jewish Spirituality. She was formerly the Director of Jewish Life at the Nathan Cummings Foundation. Rabbi Cowan earned her B.A. from Bryn Mawr College and Master's degrees from the University of Chicago School of Social Service Administration and was ordained by Hebrew Union College–Jewish Institute of Religion in 1989. She has written *Growing Up Yanqui* (1975) and *Mixed Blessings: Untangling the Knots in Interfaith Marriage* (1987, with Paul Cowan), as well as numerous articles.

***Dr. Shawn Lisa Dolansky*** is Assistant Professor of Religious Studies at Northeastern University and is a member of the advisory boards for Jewish Studies and Women's Studies at Northeastern. She earned her M.A. in Judaic Studies and her Ph.D. in History at the University of California, San Diego, where she subsequently taught as a Faculty Fellow. Her various publications in the field of biblical studies include the forthcoming book *Now You See It, Now You Don't: Biblical Perspectives on the Relationship Between Religion and Magic.*

***Rabbi Malka Drucker*** is the founding spiritual leader of HaMakom: The Place for Passionate and Progressive Judaism, in Santa Fe, New Mexico. She was ordained by the Academy for Jewish Religion. She is an award-winning author of more than twenty books for children and adults, including the Southwest PEN award winner *White Fire: A Portrait of Women Spiritual Leaders in America* (with photographer Gay Block), and *Rescuers: Portraits of Moral Courage in the Holocaust.* She is the Jewish volume editor for the forthcoming seven-volume set *Women and*

*Religion*, and her latest children's book *Portraits of Jewish-American Heroes* will be published in 2008.

***Rabbi Lisa A. Edwards, Ph.D.***, is rabbi of Beth Chayim Chadashim in Los Angeles, founded in 1972 as the world's first synagogue for gay and lesbian Jews. She received ordination from Hebrew Union College–Jewish Institute of Religion in 1994 and earned her Ph.D. in literature from the University of Iowa in 1984.

***Rabbi Denise L. Eger*** is the founding rabbi of Congregation Kol Ami in West Hollywood, California. She was ordained at HUC–JIR in 1988 and is active in the Board of Rabbis of Southern California and in the Pacific Association of Reform Rabbis. She has published numerous articles on human sexuality, in particular on gay and lesbian issues.

***Rabbi Jacqueline Koch Ellenson*** is currently the Director of the Women's Rabbinic Network. She also serves as the Chair of the Hadassah Foundation. Rabbi Ellenson is a graduate of Barnard College and was ordained at Hebrew Union College–Jewish Institute of Religion in 1983. For four years she has led a "Rosh Hodesh: It's a Girl Thing!" group at Congregation Rodeph Sholom in New York City.

***Rabbi Sue Levi Elwell, Ph.D.***, serves as Pennsylvania Regional Director, Union for Reform Judaism. The founding director of the Los Angeles Jewish Feminist Center, she served as the first rabbinic director of Ma'yan and also has taught at the University of Cincinnati; University of California, Los Angeles; and LaSalle University. A congregational rabbi for more than a decade, she was ordained by Hebrew Union College–Jewish Institute of Religion and received her doctorate from Indiana University. Her publications include: *The Jewish Women's Studies Guide* (1987); *The Open Door*, the CCAR Haggadah (2002); *Lesbian Rabbis: The First Generation* (2001); and she was one of the editors of *The Journey Continues: The Ma'yan Haggadah* (2002).

***Dr. Tamara Cohn Eskenazi*** is Professor of Bible at Hebrew Union College–Jewish Institute of Religion, Los Angeles. She was the first woman appointed to the rabbinical faculty of HUC–JIR. Previously she was on the faculty at the University of Denver and co-founded the Jewish Women's Resource Center in Denver, Colorado, in 1982. Her Ph.D. is from the University of Denver and the Iliff School of Theology. Her publications include *In an Age of Prose: A Literary Approach to Ezra-Nehemiah* (1988), *Telling the Queen Michal Story* (1991), and the forthcoming Anchor Bible Commentary on *Ezra-Nehemiah.*

***Dr. Charlotte Elisheva Fonrobert*** is Associate Professor of Religious Studies at Stanford University. Previously she taught Talmud at the University of Judaism in Los Angeles. She received her Ph.D. from the Graduate Theological Union. She has written a number of articles on gender in rabbinic Judaism, and her book *Menstrual Purity: Rabbinic and Christian Reconstructions of Biblical Gender* (2000) won the Baron Prize for a best first book in Jewish Studies. She is also a co-editor of *The Cambridge Companion to the Talmud and Rabbinic Literature* (2007).

***Dr. Nili Sacher Fox*** is Associate Professor of Bible and Director of the Archaeology Center at Hebrew Union College–Jewish Institute of Religion, Cincinnati, and co-director of the Tel Dan Excavations in Israel. She holds a Ph.D. in Biblical Studies from the University of Pennsylvania. She has written a number of articles and the book *In the Service of the King: Officialdom in Ancient Israel and Judah* (2001). She is currently researching aspects of identity formation in the ancient Near East, specifically phenomena involving costuming and body marking.

***Dr. Ellen Frankel*** is currently the CEO and Editor-in-Chief of the Jewish Publication Society. A scholar of Jewish folklore, she has published eight books, including *The Classic Tales: 4000 Years of Jewish Lore* (1994); *The Encyclopedia of Jewish Symbols* (1996, co-authored with artist Betsy Teutsch); *The Five Books of Miriam: A Woman's Commentary on the Torah* (1998); *The Jewish Spirit* (1997); and *The Illustrated Hebrew Bible* (2002). She has also been a regular contributor to the 10-volume series *My People's Prayerbook.*

***Dr. Lisbeth S. Fried*** serves as a Visiting Scholar at the Frankel Center for Judaic Studies and the Department of Near Eastern Studies at the University of Michigan in Ann Arbor. She received her Ph.D. in 2000 from New York University. She is the author of *The Priest and the Great King: Temple-Palace Relations in the Persian Empire* (2004) and has contributed articles and essays to numerous scholarly books and journals. She is working on a commentary of Ezra-Nehemiah for the Eerdmans Critical Commentary.

***Dr. Tikva Frymer-Kensky*** ז״ל was Professor of Hebrew Bible at the Divinity School at the University of Chicago until her death in 2006. Previously, she was Director of Biblical Studies at the Reconstructionist Rabbinical College, and Assistant Professor of Near Eastern Studies at Wayne State University. She earned bachelor's degrees from City College of New York and the Jewish Theological Seminary and her Ph.D. in Assyriology and Sumerology from Yale University. She was the author of many important works, including *In the Wake of the Goddesses: Women, Culture, and the Biblical Transformation of Pagan Myth* (1992); *Motherprayer: The Pregnant Woman's Spiritual Companion* (1996); and *Reading the Women of the Bible: A New Interpretation of Their Stories* (2004). Her essays were collected in *Studies in Bible and Feminist Criticism* (JPS Scholar of Distinction Series, 2006).

***Dr. Esther Fuchs*** is Professor of Near Eastern Studies and Judaic Studies at the University of Arizona in Tucson. She completed her B.A. at the Hebrew University and earned her M.A. and Ph.D. in Hebrew Literature from Brandeis University. She is the editor of *Women and the Holocaust: Narrative and Representation* (1999) and the author of *Israeli Women's Studies: A Reader* (2005) and *Sexual Politics in the Biblical Narrative: Reading the Hebrew Bible as a Woman* (2000). She co-edited *Wisdom on the Cutting Edge: The Study of Women in Biblical Worlds* (2003, with Alice Bach and Jane Schaberg). She is working on two volumes, *Feminist Theory and the Bible* and *Biblical Feminisms: An Anthology*.

***Rabbi Ruth Gais, Ph.D.***, is rabbi of Chavurat Lamdeinu in Madison, New Jersey. Previously she was the Director of the New York Kollel: The Center for Adult Jewish Studies. She was ordained by Hebrew Union College–Jewish Institute of Religion and received her doctorate from Princeton University in Classical Archaeology, and for many years she taught about the ancient world at a variety of institutions.

***Dr. Julie Galambush*** is Distinguished Associate Professor of Religious Studies at the College of William and Mary, in Williamsburg, Virginia. She holds an M.Div. from Yale and received her Ph.D. in Old Testament from Emory University. Raised an American Baptist, she was an ordained minister before her conversion to Judaism in 1994. Her most recent book, *The Reluctant Parting: How the New Testament's Jewish Authors Created a Christian Book* (2005), examines the Jewish origins of Christianity.

***Rabbi Laura Geller*** was the third woman to be ordained by Hebrew Union College–Jewish Institute of Religion, and the first to be the Senior Rabbi of a major metropolitan synagogue, Temple Emanuel of Beverly Hills, where she has been since 1994. She has been a trustee of the Corporation of Brown University and a member of the Board of Hebrew Union College–Jewish Institute of Religion, along with the boards of many other local and national Jewish and progressive organizations.

***Rabbi Miriyam Glazer, Ph.D.***, is Professor of Literature at the American Jewish University and a rabbi with the Conservative Movement. She received her Ph.D. from Brandeis University and holds a M.A. in Rabbinic Studies from the Ziegler School of Rabbinic Studies at the University of Judaism (now the American Jewish University). She writes and lectures frequently on Jewish spirituality and gender. Her books include *Dancing on the Edge of the World: Jewish Stories of Faith, Inspiration and Love* (2000) and *Dreaming the Actual: Contemporary Fiction and Poetry by Israeli Women Writers* (2000).

***Rabbi Elaine Rose Glickman*** was ordained by Hebrew Union College–Jewish Institute of Religion in 1998. She is the author of *Haman and the Jews* and the editor of *B'chol L'vavcha* (2002) and *Living Torah: Selections from Seven Years of Torat Chayim* (2005). Her work has appeared in *The Women's Haftarah Commentary*, *The Encyclopedia of Anti-Semitism*, *The CCAR Journal*, and *The American Rabbi*. Her newest book, on Jewish parenting, will be published in 2008.

***Rabbi Elizabeth Goldstein*** was ordained by Hebrew Union College–Jewish Institute of Religion, New York, in 2001. She is currently a Ph.D. candidate in Hebrew Bible at the University of California, San Diego. Her research interests include the intersection between anthropology and the Hebrew Bible, the evolution of the purity system in ancient Israelite religion, and biblical attitudes toward women.

***Rabbi Elyse Goldstein*** is the Rabbinic Director of Kolel: The Adult Centre for Liberal Jewish Learning in Toronto, Canada, and the 2005 Covenant Award Winner for Exceptional Jewish Educators. She is the author of *ReVisions: Seeing Torah through a Feminist Lens* (1998) and *Seek her Out* (2003), and the editor of *The Women's Torah Commentary* (2000) and *The Women's Haftarah Commentary* (2004).

***Dr. Elaine Adler Goodfriend*** teaches at California State University, Northridge, and at the American Jewish University. She earned her Ph.D. in Near Eastern Studies from the University of California, Berkeley. She has written entries for several books including the *Anchor Bible Dictionary* (1992) and *Women in Scripture: A Dictionary of Named and Unnamed Women in the Hebrew Bible, the Apocryphal/ Deuterocanonical Books and the New Testament* (2001).

***Dr. Lisa D. Grant*** is Associate Professor of Jewish Education at Hebrew Union College–Jewish Institute of Religion, New York. She earned her Ph.D. in Jewish Education from the Jewish Theological Seminary and holds an M.B.A. in public management from the University of Massachusetts. She is the lead author of *A Journey of Heart and Mind: Transformative Learning in Adulthood* (2004, with Diane Schuster, Meredith Woocher, and Steven M. Cohen), and she has written numerous articles on adult Jewish learning and on the role that Israel plays in American Jewish life.

***Dr. Alyssa Gray, J.D.***, is Associate Professor of Codes and Responsa Literature at Hebrew Union College–Jewish Institute of Religion, New York. She received her Ph.D. in Talmud and Rabbinics from the Jewish Theological Seminary, her LL.M. from the Hebrew University of Jerusalem, and her J.D. from Columbia University. She has written on poverty and charity, sexuality in Jewish tradition, and liturgy, and recently published a book on the editing and transmission of talmudic literature, *A Talmud in Exile: The Influence of Yerushalmi Avodah Zarah on the Formation of Bavli Avodah Zarah* (2005).

***Dr. Deborah Green*** is the Greenberg Assistant Professor of Hebrew Language and Literature, Department of Religious Studies, Harold Schnitzer Family Program of Judaic Studies, University of Oregon. She received her Ph.D. in the History of Judaism from the University of Chicago in 2003. She is co-editing two forthcoming works, *Commemorating the Dead: Texts and Artifacts in Context, Studies of Roman, Jewish and Christian Burials* and *Scriptural Exegesis: The Shapes of Culture and the Religious Imagination.*

***Blu Greenberg*** is the founding President of the Jewish Orthodox Feminist Alliance and has been active in Jewish feminism since the early 1970s. She chaired the Jewish Book Council, the National Jewish Family Center, and the Federation Commission on Synagogue Relations; and she was founding chair of the New York Federation Task Force on Jewish Women. Her writings include *On Women and Judaism: A View From Tradition* (1981) and *How to Run a Traditional Jewish Household* (1985).

***Rabbi Lisa J. Grushcow, D.Phil.***, serves as Associate Rabbi of Congregation Rodeph Sholom in New York City. She was ordained by Hebrew Union College–Jewish Institute of Religion and earned her master's and doctorate in Rabbinics at Oxford University, where she studied as a Rhodes Scholar. She is the author of *Writing the Wayward Wife: Rabbinic Interpretations of Sotah* (2005).

***Rabbi Judith Hauptman, Ph.D.***, is the E. Billi Ivry Professor of Talmud and Rabbinic Culture at the Jewish Theological Seminary, where she earned her doctorate in Talmud. She was ordained by the Academy for Jewish Religion. She is also the rabbi and founder of a free, walk-in High Holiday service, Ohel Ayalah, and she is a volunteer chaplain to the Jewish residents at the Cabrini Center for Nursing and Rehabilitation. Of her many publications, the best known is *Rereading the Rabbis, A Woman's Voice* (1998).

***Dr. Rachel Havrelock*** is an assistant professor of Jewish Studies and English at the University of Illinois at Chicago. She holds a B.A. from the University of California, Santa Cruz, and a Ph.D. in Bible and Rabbinics from the Joint Doctoral Program in Jewish Studies at the University of California, Berkeley, and the Graduate Theological Union. She co-authored *Women on the Biblical Road: Ruth, Naomi and the Female Journey* (1996), wrote and directed the play *From Tel Aviv to Ramallah*, and is the author of articles about gender in the Hebrew bible and borders in ancient and contemporary Judaisms. She is currently completing *River Jordan: The Mythic History of a Dividing Line.*

***Rabbi Jocee Hudson*** is the Director of Religious Education at Temple Beth Sholom in Santa Ana, California. She holds M.A. degrees in Jewish Education and Hebrew Letters and received her rabbinic ordination from Hebrew Union College–Jewish Institute of Religion, Los Angeles, in 2007. During her course of studies at HUC-JIR, Hudson received awards in Bible, liturgy, and Jewish education.

***Dr. Tal Ilan*** is Professor of Jewish Studies at the Freie Universität, Berlin, where she specializes in women and gender in post-biblical times. She received her Ph.D. from the Hebrew University of Jerusalem. Her publications include *Jewish Women in Greco-Roman Palestine* (1995); *Mine and Yours are Hers: Retrieving Women's History from Rabbinic Literature* (1997); *Integrating Women into Second Temple History* (1999), and *Silencing the Queen: The Literary Histories of Shelamzion and Other Jewish Women* (2006). She is currently the head of a project to produce a feminist commentary on the Babylonian Talmud.

***Rabbi Amy Kalmanofsky, Ph.D.***, is assistant professor of Bible at the Jewish Theological Seminary. She was ordained by the Reconstructionist Rabbinical College in 1995 and received her Ph.D. in Bible and Ancient Semitic Languages from JTS in 2003. Forthcoming publications include articles entitled "Israel's Baby: The Horror of Childbirth in the Biblical Prophets" and "Their Heart Cried Out to God: Gender and Prayer in the Book of Lamentations." She is working on a book, *Terror All Around: The Rhetoric of Horror in the Book of Jeremiah.*

***Dr. S. Tamar Kamionkowski*** is the Vice President for Academic Affairs and Associate Professor of Bible at the Reconstructionist Rabbinical College. She holds a bachelor's degree from Oberlin College, a master's degree from Harvard Divinity School, and a Ph.D. in Near Eastern and Judaic Studies from Brandeis University. She is the author of *Gender Reversal and Cosmic Chaos: Studies in the Book of Ezekiel* (2003) as well as numerous articles.

***Rabbi Patricia Karlin-Neumann*** is the Senior Associate Dean for Religious Life at Stanford. Ordained by Hebrew Union College–Jewish Institute of Religion in 1982, she has served as a Hillel Director, a congregational rabbi and a Regional Director for the Union for Reform Judaism. She teaches, writes and lectures on Jewish feminism, the nexus of education and religion, rabbinic ethics, and social justice.

***Dr. Sharon Keller*** is Assistant Professor of Bible at the Jewish Theological Seminary. She holds a bachelor's degree and a master's degree from New York University's Hebrew Culture and Education program. She graduated from the joint program between the Jewish Theological Seminary and Columbia University's School of Social Work, receiving master of arts and master of social work degrees. She received her doctorate in Hebrew and Judaic studies from New York University. She is a member of the Society of Biblical Literature Committee on Egyptology and Ancient Egypt, and has served for many years as a judge for the National Jewish Book Award. She is the author of *Jews: A Treasury of Art and Literature* (1992), awarded the National Jewish Book Award in 1993.

***Rabbi Naamah Kelman*** is the Director of the Year in Israel Program and Educational Initiatives at Hebrew Union College–Jewish Institute of Religion, Jerusalem. She is a descendent of ten generations of rabbis and the first woman to be ordained in Israel by Hebrew Union College–Jewish Institute of Religion (1992). Kelman has been intensely involved in the emerging education system of the Israeli Movement for Progressive (Reform) Judaism and is a board member of Rabbis for Human Rights, MELITZ, and the Tali Education Fund.

***Meira Kensky*** received a B.A. in Liberal Arts from Sarah Lawrence College and an M.A. from the University of Chicago. She is currently a Ph.D. candidate in Biblical Studies (New Testament) at the University of Chicago, where she is working on her dissertation, "Trying Man, Trying God: The Divine Courtroom in Jewish and Christian Literature."

***Dr. Gwynn Kessler*** is an Assistant Professor in the Department of Religion at the University of Florida in Gainesville and is affiliated with the university's Center for Jewish Studies and with the Center for Women's Studies and Gender. She received her Ph.D. in Rabbinics, with a specialization in Midrash, from the Jewish Theological Seminary. Her works include "Let's Cross That Body When We Get To It: Gender and Ethnicity in Rabbinic Literature" (2005) and "Bodies in Motion: Preliminary Notes on Queer Theory and Rabbinic Literature" (2007), both in the *Journal of the American Academy of Religion.*

***Dr. Beth Kissileff*** teaches in the English Department at the University of Minnesota and has taught English literature and Bible at Smith and Mount Holyoke Colleges. She holds a Ph.D. in comparative literature from the University of Pennsylvania and is completing a novel entitled *Questioning Return.*

***Rabbi Zoë Klein*** is the senior Rabbi of Temple Isaiah in Los Angeles. She was ordained by Hebrew Union College–Jewish Institute of Religion in 1998. In 2006–2007, Rabbi Klein was an ongoing contributor to *Reform Voices of Torah*, and her liturgy and poetry are used in houses of prayer around the country.

***Dr. Lillian Klein-Abensohn*** taught at American University in Washington, D.C., following twenty years teaching Literature and Bible in Munich, Germany. She received a Ph.D. in Literary Criticism from the University of California, Irvine. She is the author of *The Triumph of Irony in the Book of Judges* (1988) and *From Deborah to Esther: Sexual Politics in the Hebrew Bible* (2003) and a contributor to the *Feminist Companion to the Bible* series.

***Dr. Risa Levitt Kohn*** is Director of the Jewish Studies Program and Professor of Hebrew Bible and Judaism at San Diego State University. She was the first to earn a Ph.D. in ancient history and Hebrew Bible from the University of California, San Diego. She is the past-president of the Society of Biblical Literature (SBL), Pacific Coast Region, and serves as chair of the SBL Committee for the Status of Women in the Profession. Levitt Kohn's publications include *A New Heart and a New Soul: Ezekiel, the Exile and the Torah* (2002) and the forthcoming book, *A Portable God: The Origin of Judaism & Christianity.*

***Dr. Sharon Koren*** is an Assistant Professor of Medieval Jewish Culture at Hebrew Union College–Jewish Institute of Religion, New York, where she teaches courses in medieval history, biblical commentary, and Jewish Mysticism. Her research focuses on medieval religious history and Jewish women's spirituality. Her articles have appeared in *Nashim*, the *AJS Review*, and *Women and Water*, edited by Rahel Wasserfall. She is currently completing a book that explores the absence of female Jewish mystics during the Middle Ages.

***Rabbi Nancy Fuchs Kreimer, Ph.D.***, serves as the Director of the Religious Studies Program at the Reconstructionist Rabbinical College, where as Associate Professor she teaches courses in contemporary Jewish thought. She holds a bachelor's degree in Religion from Wesleyan University and a master's from Yale Divinity School. She received the title of rabbi from the Reconstructionist Rabbinical College, and her Ph.D. from Temple University Religion Department. She is the author of *Parenting as a Spiritual Journey* (1998) and co-author of *Judaism for Two* (2005, with Rabbi Nancy Wiener).

***Rabbi Noa Rachael Kushner*** serves Congregation Rodef Sholom in Marin, California, and previously was the Hillel Rabbi for Sarah Lawrence College and Stanford University. She holds a B.A. in Religious Studies from Brown University and was ordained by Hebrew Union College–Jewish Institute of Religion in 1998. Her poems and essays have been published in several books including, *Choosing a Jewish Life* (1998), and *The Women's Seder Sourcebook* (2006).

***Rabbi Gail Labovitz, Ph.D.***, is Assistant Professor of Rabbinics and chair of the Rabbinic Department at the Ziegler School of Rabbinic Studies of the American Jewish University. She was ordained by the Jewish Theological Seminary, where she also earned her Ph.D. in Talmud and Rabbinics. Her most recent article "The Scholarly Life—The Laboring Wife: Gender, Torah, and the Family Economy in Rabbinic Culture" was published in *Nashim* (Spring 2007).

***Beatrice Lawrence*** is Instructor of Bible at Hebrew Union College–Jewish Institute of Religion, Los Angeles. She received a B.A. from Carleton College and an M.A. from Emory University, and is also completing her Ph.D. in Hebrew Bible/Jewish Hermeneutics from Emory.

***Dr. Lori Hope Lefkovitz*** holds the Sadie Gottesman and Arlene Gottesman Reff chair in Gender and Judaism at Reconstructionist Rabbinical College, where she directs Kolot: the Center for Jewish Women's and Gender Studies and is executive editor of Ritualwell.org. She received a Ph.D. in English from Brown University and previously was associate professor of English literature at Kenyon College. She has published books and articles on literature, Bible, and feminist theory, including *Shaping Losses: Cultural Memory and the Holocaust* (2001, with Julia Epstein).

***Dr. Adriane Leveen*** teaches Bible at Hebrew Union College–Jewish Institute of Religion, New York, having previously taught at Stanford University and at HUC–JIR, Los Angeles. She received her Ph.D. from the University of California, Berkeley, in 2000. She has published articles in the *Journal for the Study of the Old Testament* and *Prooftexts* and co-edited an anthology of the poetry of Stanley Chyet. She is also a contributor to *Healing in the Jewish Imagination* (2007) and the forthcoming volume *Women Remaking American Judaism* (2007). Her book *Memory and Tradition in the Book of Numbers* will be published in 2008.

***Dr. Amy-Jill Levine*** is the E. Rhodes and Leona B. Carpenter Professor of New Testament Studies at Vanderbilt University Divinity School and Graduate Department of Religion. From 1995–2006 she was the Director of Vanderbilt's Carpenter Program in Religion, Gender, and Sexuality. She holds a B.A. from Smith College and an M.A. and Ph.D. from Duke University. Her publications include *The Misunderstood Jew: The Church and the Scandal of the Jewish Jesus* (2006), the 14-volume edited series *Feminist Companions to the New Testament and Early Christian Writings*, and the forthcoming *Jewish Backgrounds to the New Testament: An Essential Guide.*

***Rabbi Laura Lieber, Ph.D.***, is Assistant Professor of Classics and Religion at Middlebury College in Vermont. She received her rabbinic ordination from Hebrew Union College–Jewish Institute of Religion in 1999 and her Ph.D. in the History of Judaism from the University of Chicago in 2003. She is the author of *Study Guide to the JPS Bible Commentary: Haftarot* (2002).

***Rabbi Valerie Lieber*** has served as rabbi at Temple Israel of Jamaica in Queens, New York, since 2002 and will become Co-Rabbi in its consolidation with Temple Emanuel of New Hyde Park. She was ordained by Hebrew Union College–Jewish Institute of Religion, New York. She has published chapters in *The Women's Torah Commentary* (2000) and *The Women's Haftarah Commentary* (2004) and served as President of the New York Association of Reform Rabbis.

***Dr. Hilary Lipka*** is a Research Scholar at the Center for the Study of Women at the University of California, Los Angeles. She received her Ph.D. from Brandeis University in Near Eastern and Judaic Studies in 2004 and is the author of *Sexual Transgression in the Hebrew Bible* (2006).

***Dr. Diana Lipton*** is Lecturer in Hebrew Bible and Jewish Studies at King's College London. Previously, she was a Fellow of Newnham College, Cambridge, and taught Bible at Leo Baeck College–Centre for Jewish Education in London. She completed a Ph.D. at Cambridge University in 1996. Her publications include her book *Revisions of the Night: Politics and Promises in the Patriarchal Dreams of Genesis* (1999); the co-edited *Feminism and Theology*, a volume of Oxford Readings in Feminism (2003); and *Longing for Egypt and Other Unexpected Biblical Tales* (forthcoming). For many years, she ran the Hebrew School of Beth Shalom Reform Synagogue, Cambridge, where she continues to perform rabbinical functions.

**Rabbi Janet Marder** is the Senior Rabbi of Congregation Beth Am in Los Altos Hills, California. She graduated from the University of California, Santa Cruz, and was ordained in 1979 by Hebrew Union College–Jewish Institute of Religion, New York. She later pursued graduate studies in the Department of Comparative Literature at the University of California, Los Angeles, specializing in Modern Hebrew and Yiddish. Rabbi Marder was the first woman to serve as President of the Central Conference of American Rabbis. Her articles have appeared in *Reform Judaism* magazine, the *Reconstructionist*, *Sh'ma*, and several anthologies.

**Rabbi Susan Marks, Ph.D.**, is the Klingenstein Professor of Judaic Studies at New College of Florida, the Honors College of the State of Florida. While in rabbinic school she worked as an intern for what would later become Women of Reform Judaism. She was ordained by Hebrew Union College–Jewish Institute of Religion in 1988 and received her Ph.D. in Religious Studies from the University of Pennsylvania in 2003. Her article "Women in Early Judaism: Twenty-five Years of Research and Reenvisioning" in *Currents in Biblical Research* is forthcoming.

**Dr. Carol Meyers** is the Mary Grace Wilson Professor of Religion at Duke University, where she teaches biblical studies and archeology. An honors graduate of Wellesley College, she received her M.A. and Ph.D. in Near Eastern and Judaic Studies from Brandeis University. Among her hundreds of publications are several books relating to Israelite women, including *Discovering Eve: Ancient Israelite Women In Context* (1988); *Women In Scripture: A Dictionary of Named and Unnamed Women in the Hebrew Bible, the Apocryphal/Deuterocanonical Books and the New Testament* (2001), and *Households and Holiness: The Religious Culture of Israelite Women* (2005).

**Dr. Beth Alpert Nakhai** is an Associate Professor in the Arizona Center for Judaic Studies at the University of Arizona in Tucson. She received her M.T.S. from Harvard Divinity School and her M.A. and Ph.D. from the University of Arizona. She has written numerous publications reflecting her interests in Near Eastern archeology, biblical studies, women in ancient Israel, religion in antiquity, and terracotta figurines, including *Archaeology and the Religions of Canaan and Israel* (2001).

**Dr. Susan Niditch** is the Samuel Green Professor of Religion at Amherst College, where she has taught since 1978 after receiving her Ph.D. from Harvard University. Her scholarly interests and approaches are informed by a variety of fields including folklore studies, history of religion, religious ethics, and women's studies. Her books include *War in the Hebrew Bible* (1995), *Ancient Israelite Religion* (1998), and *Oral World and Written Word* (1996). She is currently working on a commentary on the book of Judges.

**Dr. Carol Ochs** is Director of Graduate Studies and Adjunct Professor of Jewish Religious Thought at Hebrew Union College–Jewish Institute of Religion, New York, where she teaches and provides spiritual guidance for rabbinic students and Doctor of Ministry candidates. She holds a Ph.D. in philosophy from Brandeis University and is professor emerita at Simmons College, Boston. She is the author of eight books, the most recent of which is *Reaching Godward: Voices from Spiritual Guidance* (2003). Among her other books are *Our Lives as Torah* (2001); *Jewish Spiritual Guidance* (1997, with Kerry Olitzky); and *Women and Spirituality* (1996).

**Rabbi Hara E. Person** is Editor in Chief of URJ Press. She holds a B.A. from Amherst College, an M.A. in Fine Arts from New York University, and was ordained by Hebrew Union College–Jewish Institute of Religion in 1998. Her publications include *That You May Live Long: Caring for Aging Parents, Caring for Ourselves* (2003, with Rabbi Richard Address), *Stories of Heaven and Earth: Bible Heroes in Contemporary Children's Literature* (2005, with her mother, Dr. Diane G. Person), and contributions to the forthcoming *Women and Religion in the World* and to *The Encyclopedia of Jewish American Popular Culture.*

**Dr. Judith Plaskow** is Professor of Religious Studies at Manhattan College in Riverdale, New York, and a Jewish feminist theologian. A graduate of Clark University (B.A., 1968) and Yale University (M.Phil., 1973, and Ph.D., 1975), she is author or editor of several groundbreaking works in feminist theology, including *Weaving the Visions: New Patterns in Feminist Spirituality* (1989); *Standing Again at Sinai: Judaism from a Feminist Perspective* (1991); and *The Coming of Lilith: Essays on Feminism, Judaism, and Sexual Ethics, 1972–2003* (2005).

***Dr. Ora Horn Prouser*** is Executive Vice President and Academic Dean at the Academy for Jewish Religion. She received her Ph.D. in Bible from the Jewish Theological Seminary, where she was an adjunct faculty member for twenty years. She served as an academic consultant with the Melton Center for Research in Jewish Education on its development of Bible curricula for day schools.

***Dr. Shulamit Reinharz*** is the Jacob Potofsky Professor of Sociology at Brandeis University. As director of the Women's Studies Program, she created the world's first Jewish Women's Studies M.A. program. She founded both the Hadassah-Brandeis Institute (HBI), whose mission is to develop fresh ways of thinking about Jews and gender, and the Women's Studies Research Center, including an art gallery. She is a founder of *Nashim: A Journal of Jewish Women's Studies and Gender Issues* and of the HBI Book Series on Jewish Women. Her numerous books include *Feminist Methods in Social Research* (1992), *The JGirls Guide* (2005, with Penina Adelman and Ali Feldman), and the edited collection of Manya Shohat's letters [Hebrew] (2005, with Jehuda Reinharz and Motti Golani).

***Dr. Dalit Rom-Shiloni*** teaches at Hebrew Union College–Jewish Institute of Religion, Jerusalem, as well as the Department of Hebrew Culture, Tel Aviv University. She has also taught at the Rothberg International School of the Hebrew University of Jerusalem. She holds a Ph.D. from the Hebrew University of Jerusalem, where she was trained in biblical studies and Ancient Semitic languages. She is preparing for publication her book *God in Times of Destruction and Exiles: Tanakh Theology*, which will appear in both Hebrew and English.

***Cantor Sarah Sager*** has served as Cantor of Anshe Chesed Fairmount Temple since 1980. She graduated from Brown University, holds a M.A. from the New England Conservatory of Music, and was invested by Hebrew Union College–Jewish Institute of Religion School of Sacred Music in 1978. Her keynote speech at the 1993 Women of Reform Judaism Assembly provided the original inspiration for this commentary.

***Dr. Tammi J. Schneider*** is Professor of Religion at Claremont Graduate University, and she currently co-directs the renewed excavations at Tel el-Far'ah (South) in Israel. She received her doctorate in Ancient History from the University of Pennsylvania. Her books include *Sarah: Mother of Nations* (2004) and *Judges* in the *Berit Olam* series (2000). She is the editor for the ancient Near East section of the journal *Religious Studies Review*.

***Dr. Claudia Setzer*** is Professor of Religious Studies at Manhattan College in Riverdale, New York. She received her M.A. from the Jewish Theological Seminary and her Ph.D. from Columbia University. She is the author of *Jewish Responses to Early Christians* and *Resurrection of the Body in Early Judaism and Early Christianity* (2004). She is active in Jewish/Christian relations at the scholarly and popular level and is a former chair of the early Jewish/Christian relations group of the Society of Biblical Literature. She is currently working on a book on the Bible and American culture.

***Dr. Alice Shalvi*** has most recently been Rector, President, and then Chair of the Executive of the Schechter Institute of Jewish Studies in Jerusalem, which is associated with the Jewish Theological Seminary. She obtained her Ph.D. at the Hebrew University of Jerusalem in 1962, where she taught in the English Department from 1950–1990. From 1975 to 1990 she headed the Pelech Experimental High School for Religious Girls and from 1984 to 2000 served as founding chairwoman of the Israel Women's Network. Her activities have won her many awards, including the 1978 President's Award for outstanding contribution to the quality of life in Israel, the 1991 Rothfield Education for Peace Prize, and the 1994 New Israel Fund's Israel Women's Leadership Award. In 2007 she was awarded the Israel Prize, Israel's highest honor, for lifetime achievement in education and women's rights.

***Dr. Diane M. Sharon*** is on the faculty in Bible at the

Academy for Jewish Religion. She has served as Director of Curriculum Development for Hadassah-WZOA, after serving as National Education Director of Young Judaea, the Jewish Zionist Youth Movement of Hadassah. Before that, she was Assistant Professor at the Jewish Theological Seminary and the first woman appointed to its Department of Bible and Ancient Semitic Languages. She received her Ph.D. from the Jewish Theological Seminary in 1995. She is the author of *Patterns of Destiny: Narrative Structures of Foundation and Doom in the Hebrew Bible* (2002), as well as articles on the Hebrew Bible in the context in the ancient Near East, comparative religion, and women's studies.

***Dr. Maeera Y. Shreiber*** is Assistant Professor of English at the University of Utah. She holds a Ph.D. from Brandeis University. She is the author of numerous articles on American poetry. She is the co-editor of *Dwelling in Possibility: Women Poets and Critics on Poetry* (1998) and *Mina Loy: Woman and Poet* (1998), as well as the forthcoming book *Singing in a Strange Land: Towards a Jewish American Poetics.*

***Rabbi Suzanne Singer*** was ordained by Hebrew Union College–Jewish Institute of Religion in 2003. She coordinates a leadership and social responsibility initiative for HUC–JIR, Los Angeles, meanwhile directing the Introduction to Judaism program for the URJ's Pacific Southwest Council, in addition to planning an interfaith social justice conference. She served for two years as a rabbi at Temple Sinai of Oakland, California. She holds three master's degrees and spent twenty years as a television producer and programming executive, primarily for public television, winning two Emmy Awards before becoming a rabbi.

***Rabbi Ruth H. Sohn*** teaches Jewish Studies at the Milken Community High School of Stephen S. Wise Temple and adult education in various settings in Los Angeles. She was ordained by Hebrew Union College–Jewish Institute of Religion in 1982. Her articles, biblical commentaries, and poetry have appeared in various periodicals, prayerbooks, and books including the anthology *Reading Ruth* (1996).

***Cantor Rachel Stock Spilker*** has served as Cantor at Mount Zion Temple in St. Paul, Minnesota, since 1997, following her position as Assistant Cantor at Congregation Rodeph Sholom in New York City. She holds a B.A. in Religious Studies from the University of Pittsburgh and a master's degree in Sacred Music and investiture as Cantor from Hebrew Union College–Jewish Institute of Religion.

***Dr. Naomi Steinberg*** is Associate Professor of Religious Studies at DePaul University, Chicago, Illinois. She holds a Ph.D. from Columbia University and is the author of *Kinship and Marriage in Genesis: A Household Economics Perspective* (1993) and numerous academic studies on family and gender in ancient Israel. Having worked as an advocate for children, her research is now moving into issues related to children in ancient Israel.

***Dr. Elsie R. Stern*** is Assistant Professor of Bible at the Reconstructionist Rabbinical College. She received her Ph.D. in Bible at the University of Chicago and served as Assistant Professor in the Department of Theology at Fordham University and as Assistant Director for Public Programs at the Center for Advanced Judaic Studies at the University of Pennsylvania. She is the author of *From Rebuke to Consolation: Exegesis and Theology in the Liturgical Anthology of the Ninth of Av Season* and is a contributor to *The Jewish Study Bible* (2004).

***Dr. Talia Sutskover*** teaches in the Department of Hebrew Culture at Tel Aviv University. She received her Ph.D. from Tel Aviv University in 2006. In addition to her scholarly interests in semantic fields, biblical narrative, and biblical Hebrew, she has written a book of short stories in Hebrew, *As a Woman Writes* (2005).

***Dr. Masha Turner*** taught Biblical Studies and Rabbinic Studies at Hebrew Union College–Jewish Institute of Religion, Jerusalem, for many years. She also taught at Beit Shmuel in Jerusalem and lectures in Maimonides and Medieval Jewish Philosophy at Bar-Ilan University, Ramat Gan, Israel, where she completed her Ph.D. She has published many biblical entries for the Curriculum Planning Department of Israel's Ministry of Education and has worked to bridge gaps between Israel's religious and secular groups.

***Dr. Ellen M. Umansky*** serves as the Carl and Dorothy Bennett Professor of Judaic Studies at Fairfield University in Fairfield, Connecticut. She received her Ph.D. from Columbia University and is the author of *From Christian Science to Jewish Science: Spiritual Healing and American Jews* (2005), and two books on Lily Montagu. She is working on a revised edition of *Four Centuries of Jewish Women's Spirituality: A Sourcebook* (originally published in 1992) and a book-length work of constructive feminist theology.

***Dr. Anna Urowitz-Freudenstein*** is Adjunct Professor of Jewish Studies at Gratz College, Melrose Park, Pennsylvania, and Department Head in Jewish Thought, Community Hebrew Academy of Toronto. From 1999–2006 she was the moderator for H-Judaic, an electronic scholarly forum for Judaic Studies. Previously, she has taught at the Jewish Theological Seminary and Rutgers University, as well as online for Hebrew College (Boston) and Gratz College. She holds an M.A. in Ancient Judaism and a Ph.D. in Midrash, both from the Jewish Theological Seminary. Her doctoral thesis was entitled "An Investigation of Exegetical Methods in the Tannaitic Midrashim: A Study of the Texts that Mention Individual Women."

***Dr. Nili Wazana*** chairs the Department of Bible at the Hebrew University of Jerusalem, where she received her Ph.D. in 1998. She is also a lecturer there in the Department of the History of the Jewish People. Her research deals with cultural, literary and historical contacts between biblical Israel and the ancient Near East. Her first book *The Extent of the Promised Land: Issues in Biblical Geography and Ideology in Light of the Ancient Near East* (in Hebrew) is forthcoming.

***Dr. Dvora E. Weisberg*** is Associate Professor of Rabbinics and Director of the Beit Midrash at Hebrew Union College–Jewish Institute of Religion, Los Angeles. She received her B.A. from Brandeis University and her M.A. and Ph.D. from the Jewish Theological Seminary. She is completing a book on levirate marriage and constructs of the family in rabbinic literature.

***Rabbi Andrea L. Weiss, Ph.D.***, is Assistant Professor of Bible at Hebrew Union College–Jewish Institute of Religion, New York. She was ordained by HUC–JIR and received her Ph.D. from the Department of Near Eastern Languages and Civilizations at the University of Pennsylvania. Her publications include *Figurative Language in Biblical Prose Narrative: Metaphor in the Book of Samuel* (2006) and articles on biblical poetry.

***Dr. Carol Selkin Wise*** has taught on a number of campuses, including California State University at Long Beach and Washington University in St. Louis. She holds a Ph.D. in Religion from Duke University. Her dissertation "Exegesis and Identity: The Hermeneutics of *Miqwa'ot* in the Greco-Roman Period" (1993) deals with ancient *mikvehs*.

***Cantor Josee Wolff*** is interim cantor of Temple Shaaray Tefilah in New York City as well as Director of Student Placement and an adjunct faculty member at the School of Sacred Music of Hebrew Union College–Jewish Institute of Religion, New York. A native of the Netherlands, Cantor Wolff loves teaching about synagogue music and worship throughout the Progressive Jewish world.

***Dr. Wendy Zierler*** is Associate Professor of Modern Jewish Literature and Feminist Studies at Hebrew Union College–Jewish Institute of Religion, New York. Before that, she was Research Fellow in the English Department of Hong Kong University. She received her Ph.D. from Princeton and is author of *And Rachel Stole the Idols: The Emergence of Modern Hebrew Women's Writing* (2004) and is co-editor, with Carole B. Balin, of a forthcoming collection of the selected writings of Hava Shapiro.

***Jill Zimmerman*** is a rabbinic student at Hebrew Union College–Jewish Institute of Religion, Los Angeles. Her first career was in organizational development, while also serving on the board and executive committee of Women of Reform Judaism. She holds M.Ed. and M.A.H.L. degrees from HUC–JIR.

NOTE: *The biographical information represents the diversity of talents among the contributors and their choice of how to identify themselves within the constraints of a brief entry.*

# *About the Voices Contributors*

Listed, where known and germane, are: the contributor's name (if it differs from her pen name), birthplace and birth year ("*b.*"), place of residence ("*r.*"), place and date of death ("*d.*"); and the language in which she writes.

***Nancy Satuloff Abraham***, *b.* New York, New York, 1956, *r.* Harrison, New York; English

***Rachel Adler***, *b.* Chicago, Illinois, *r.* Los Angeles, California; English

***Sigrid Agocsi***, *b.* Münster, Germany, 1961, *r.* London, England; English, German, and Hungarian

***Marjorie Agosin***, *b.* Bethesda, Maryland, 1955, *r.* Wellesley Hills, Massachusetts; Spanish/English

***Ada Aharoni***, *b.* Cairo, Egypt, *r.* Haifa, Israel; Hebrew

***Lea Aini***, *b.* Tel Aviv, Israel, 1962, *r.* Israel; Hebrew

***Karen Alkalay-Gut***, *b.* London, England, 1945, *r.* Tel Aviv, Israel; English

***Shifra Alon***, *b.* Vienna, Austria, *r.* Ramat Gan, Israel; Hebrew

***Sarah Antine***, *b.* Buffalo, New York, 1975, *r.* Potomac, Maryland; English

***Edna Aphek***, *r.* Jerusalem, Israel; Hebrew

***Deborah Ascarelli***, *b.* Rome, Italy, 16th century; Italian/Hebrew

***Ellen Bass***, *b.* Philadelphia, Pennsylvania, 1947, *r.* Santa Cruz, California; English

***Yocheved Bat-Miriam***, *b.* Keplits, Belorussia, 1901, *d.* Israel, 1980; Hebrew

***Robin Becker***, *b.* Philadelphia, Pennsylvania, 1951; English

***Leila Gal Berner***, *b.* San Francisco, California, 1950, *r.* Kensington, Maryland; English

***Mary Loving Blanchard***, *r.* Jersey City, New Jersey; English

***Amy Blank***, *b.* London, England, 1898, *d.* Cincinnati, Ohio, 1990; English

***Chana Bloch***, *b.* New York, New York, 1940, *r.* Berkeley, California; English

***Sherry Blumberg***, *b.* Tucson, Arizona, 1947, *r.* Milwaukee, Wisconsin; English

***Shirley Blumberg***, *b.* 1923, *r.* Mammoth Lakes, California; English

***Ruth Brin***, *b.* Saint Paul, Minnesota, 1921, *r.* Minneapolis, Minnesota, 1921; English

***Nina Beth Cardin***, *b.* Baltimore, Maryland, 1953, *r.* Baltimore; English

***Kim Chernin***, *b.* Bronx, New York, 1940, *r.* Berkeley, California; English

***Jennifer Clayman***, *b.* Silver Spring, Maryland, 1972, *r.* Westfield, New Jersey; English

***Enid Dame***, *b.* Beaver Falls, Pennsylvania, 1943, *d.* High Falls, New York, 2003; English

***Celia Dropkin***, *b.* Belorus, Russia, 1887, *d.* United States, 1956; Yiddish/Russian

***Anne Ebersman***, *b.* New York, New York, 1967, *r.* New York, New York; English

***Sue Levi Elwell***, *b.* Buffalo, New York, 1948, *r.* Philadelphia, Pennsylvania; English

***Esther Ettinger***, *b.* Jerusalem, Israel, 1941; Hebrew

***Ruth Fainlight***, *b.* New York, New York, 1931, *r.* London, England; English

***Marcia Falk***, *b.* New York, New York, *r.* Berkeley, California; English/Hebrew

***Corie Feiner***, *b.* Queens, New York, 1973; English

***Elaine Feinstein***, *b.* Liverpool, England, 1930, *r.* London, England; English

***Merle Feld***, *b.* Brooklyn, New York, 1947, *r.* Northampton, Massachusetts; English

***Nadell Fishman***, *r.* Vermont; English

***Robin Fox***, *b.* Los Angeles, California, 1950, *r.* Fresno, California; English

***Ellen Frankel***, *b.* New York, New York, 1951, *r.* Philadelphia, Pennsylvania; English

***Debbie Friedman***, *b.* Utica, New York, 1952, *r.* New York, New York; English/Hebrew

***Tikva Frymer-Kensky***, *b.* Chicago, Illinois, 1943, *d.* Wilmette, Illinois, 2006; English

***Laura Geller***, *b.* Boston, Massachusetts, 1950, *r.* Los Angeles, California.; English

***Elaine Rose Glickman***, *b.* El Paso, Texas, 1970, *r.* Sarasota, Florida; English

***Susan Glickman***, *b.* 1953; English

***Lea Goldberg***, *b.* East Prussia, 1911, *d.* Jerusalem, Israel, 1970; Hebrew

***Shelly Goldman***, *b.* Brookline, Massachusetts, 1942, *r.* Fairfax, Virginia; English

***Nancy Lee Gossels***, *b.* Norwich, Connecticut, 1934, *r.* Wayland, Massachusetts; English

***Lynn Gottlieb***, *b.* Bethlehem, Pennsylvania, 1945, *r.* Ojai, California; English

***Nechama Gottschalk***, *b.* Berkeley, California, 1951, *r.* Tallahassee, Florida; English

***Jessica Greenbaum***, *b.* Brooklyn, 1957, *r.* Brooklyn, New York; English

***Rachel Hadas***, *b.* New York, New York, 1948, *r.* New York, New York; English

***Jill Hammer***, *r.* New York, New York; English

***Ra'aya Harnik***, *b.* Berlin, Germany, 1933, *r.* Israel; Hebrew

***Galit Hasan-Rokem***, *b.* Helsinki, Finland, 1945; *r.* Israel; Hebrew

***Linda Hepner***, *b.* London, England, 1939, *r.* Los Angeles, California; English

***Etty Hillesum***, *b.* Middelburg, the Netherlands, 1914, *d.* Auschwitz, 1943; Dutch

***Linda Hirschhorn***, *b.* New York, New York, 1947, *r.* Oakland, California; English

***Barbara D. Holender***, *b.* Buffalo, New York, 1927, *r.* Buffalo, New York; English

***Vicki Hollander***, *b.* Cleveland, Ohio, 1952, *r.* Lubbock, Texas; English

***Lisa Hostein***, *b.* Queens, New York, 1961, *r.* Philadelphia, Pennsylvania; English

***Sue Hubbard***, *b.* London, England, *r.* London, England; English

***Beyle Hurvits***, circa 17th–18th century, Eastern Europe; Yiddish

***Regina Jonas***, *b.* Berlin, Germany, 1902, *d.* Auschwitz, 1944; German

***Judy Katz***, *b.* Memphis, Tennessee, 1959, *r.* New York, New York; English

***Shirley Kaufman***, *b.* Seattle, Washington, *r.* Jerusalem, Israel; English

***Karyn Kedar***, *b.* Washington, D.C., 1957, *r.* Deerfield, Illinois; English

***Sharon Kessler***, *r.* Pardes Chana, Israel

***Zoë Klein***, *b.* New York, New York, 1971, *r.* Los Angeles, California; English

***Irena Klepfisz***, *b.* Warsaw, 1941; *r.* New York, New York; English/Yiddish

***Feiga Izrailevna Kogan***, *b.* Moscow, Russia, 1891, *d.* Moscow, Russia, 1974; Russian

***Rachel Korn***, *b.* Podliszki, Galicia, 1898, *d.* Montreal, Canada, 1982; Polish/Yiddish

***Maxine Kumin***, *b.* Germantown, Pennsylvania, 1925; *r.* New Hampshire; English

***Else Lasker-Schüler***, *b.* Rhineland, Germany, 1869, *d.* Jerusalem, Israel, 1945; German

***Lara Laufer***, *b.* El Paso, Texas, 1970, *r.* Alexandria, Virginia; English

***Lynn Levin***, *b.* St. Louis, Missouri, 1953; *r.* Bucks County, Pennsylvania; English

***Lisa Levine***, *b.* Bakersfield, California, 1959, *r.* Stamford, Connecticut; English

***Naomi Levy***, *b.* Brooklyn, New York, *r.* Venice, California; English

***Shari Lore***, *b.* New Jersey, 1958, *r.* Fairfax, Virginia; English

***Bonnie Lyons***, *b.* Brooklyn, New York, 1944, *r.* San Antonio, Texas; English

***Sherri Mandell***, *b.* New York; *r.* Tekoa, Israel; English

***Anna Margolin***, *b.* Brest, Belarus, 1887, *d.* New York, New York, 1952; Yiddish

***Golda Meir***, *b.* Kiev, Russia, 1898, *d.* Jerusalem, Israel, 1978; Hebrew

***Pamela Melnikoff***, *r.* London, England; English

***Rivka Miriam***, *b.* Jerusalem, Israel, 1952, *r.* Jerusalem, Israel; Hebrew

***Marsha Pravder Mirkin***, *b.* Brooklyn, New York, 1953, *r.* Wellesley, Massachusetts; English

***Agi Mishol***, *b.* Hungary, 1947, *r.* Gedera, Israel; Hebrew

***Kadya Molodowsky***, *b.* Bereza Kartuska, White Russia, 1894, *d.* New York, New York, 1975; Yiddish

***Rachel Luzzatto Morpurgo***, *b.* Trieste, Italy, 1790, *d.* 1871; Hebrew

***Pamela S. Nadell***, *b.* Newark, New Jersey, 1951, *r.* Rockville, Maryland; English

***Clarisse Nicoïdski***, *b.* 1938, Lyons, France, *r.* Paris, France; French/Judezmo

***Vanessa Ochs***, *b.* Brooklyn, New York, 1937; *r.* Charlottesville, Virginia: English

***Debra Orenstein***, *b.* San Antonio, Texas, *r.* Los Angeles, California; English/Hebrew

***Alicia Suskin Ostriker***, *b.* Brooklyn, New York, 1937; *r.* Princeton, New Jersey; English

***Estelle Nachimoff Padawer***, *b.* Bronx, New York, 1927, *r.* Fort Lee, New Jersey: English

***Grace Paley***, *b.* Bronx, New York, 1922, *d.* Thetford, Vermont, 2007; English

***Helen Papell***, *b.* New York, New York, 1924, *r.* New York, New York; English

***Linda Rose Parkes***, *b.* Jersey, Channel Islands, United Kingdom, 1951, *r.* United Kingdom; English

***Linda Pastan***, *b.* Bronx, New York, 1932, *r.* Potomac, Maryland.; English

***Laurie Patton***, *b.* Boston, Massachusetts, 1961, *r.* Atlanta, Georgia; English

***Haviva Pedaya***, *b.* Jerusalem, Israel; Hebrew

***Julie Pelc***, *b.* Milwaukee, Wisconsin, 1976, *r.* Los Angeles, California; English

***Debbie Perlman***, *b.* Chicago, Illinois, 1951, *d.* Evanston, Illinois, 2002; English

***Hara E. Person***, *b.* New York, New York, 1964, *r.* Brooklyn, New York; English

***Marge Piercy***, *b.* Detroit, MI, 1936, *r.* Cape Cod, Massachusetts; English

***Hava Pincas-Cohen***, *b.* Jaffa, Israel, 1955, *r.* Rehovot, Israel; Hebrew

***Anda Pinkerfeld-Amir***, *b.* Rzesza, Galicia, 1902, *d.* Israel, 1981; Hebrew

***Riv-Ellen Prell***, *b.* Los Angeles, California, 1947, *r.* Minneapolis, Minnesota; English

***Esther Raab***, *b.* Petach Tikva, Israel, 1894, *d.* Tel Aviv, Israel, 1981; Hebrew

***Rahel***, Bluwstein, *b.* Vyatka, Russia, 1890, *d.* Israel, 1931; Hebrew

***Nessa Rapoport***, *b.* Canada, *r.* New York, New York; English

***Dahlia Ravikovitch***, *b.* Ramat Gan, Israel, 1936, *d.* Tel Aviv, Israel, 2005; Hebrew

***Barbara Reisner***, *b.* Pittsburgh, Pennsylvania, 1944, *r.* Allentown, Pennsylvania; English

***Naomi Replansky***, *b.* Bronx, New York, 1918, *r.* New York, New York; English

***Shira Rubenstein***, *b.* Glen Falls, New York, 1991, *r.* Saratoga Springs, New York; English

***Muriel Rukeyser***, *b.* New York, New York, 1913, *d.* New York, New York, 1980; English

***Nellie Sachs***, *b.* Berlin, Germany, 1891, *d.* Stockholm, Sweden, 1970; German

***Elizabeth Sarah***, *b.* South Shields, County Durham, England, 1955, *r.* Brighton, England; English

***Sandy Eisenberg Sasso***, *b.* 1947, *r.* Indianapolis, Indiana; English

***Shelley Savren***, *b.* Cleveland, Ohio, 1945; *r.* California; English

***Grace Schulman***, *r.* New York, New York; English

***Laya Firestone Seghi***, *b.* Missouri, *r.* Miami Beach, Florida; English

***Hannah Senesh***, *b.* Budapest, Hungary, 1921, *d.* Budapest, Hungary, 1944; Hungarian/Hebrew

***Drora Setel***, *b.* Lausanne, Switzerland, 1956, *r.* Buffalo, New York; English

***Ona Siporin***, *r.* Logan, Utah; English

***Ruth Sohn***, *b.* Pottsville, Pennsylvania, 1954, *r.* Los Angeles, California; English

***Myra Soifer***, *b.* Miami, Florida, 1950, *r.* Reno, Nevada; English

***Elaine Marcus Starkman***, *b.* Chicago, Illinois, *r.* Walnut Creek, California; English

***Priscilla Stern***, *b.* New York, New York, 1934, *d.* New York, New York, 2002; English

***Yerra Sugarman***, *b.* Toronto, Canada, 1955, *r.* New York, New York; English

***Shulamith Surnamer***, *b.* Brooklyn, New York, 1945, *r.* Long Beach, New York; English

***Anna Swanson***, *b.* Vancouver, Canada, 1974, *r.* Vancouver, Canada; English

***Henrietta Szold***, *b.* Baltimore, Maryland, 1860, *d.* Jerusalem, Israel, 1945; English

***Eva Tóth***, *b.* Hungary; *r.* Hungary; Hungarian

***Sophie Trupin***, *b.* Selz, Russia, 1903, *d.* United States, 1992; English

***Malka Heifetz Tussman***, *b.* Volhynia, Ukraine, 1893, *d.* Berkeley, California, 1987; Yiddish

***Miriam Ulinover***, *b.* Lodz, Poland, 1888, *d.* Auschwitz, 1944; Yiddish

***Sheila Peltz Weinberg***, *b.* New York, New York, 1946, *r.* Amherst, Massachusetts; English

***Andrea L. Weiss***, *b.* San Diego, California, 1965, *r.* Philadelphia, Pennsylvania; English, 2007.

***Ruth Whitman***, *b.* 1922, *d.* Middletown, Rhode Island, 1999; English

***Eleanor Wilner***, *b.* Ohio, 1937, *r.* Philadephia, Pennsylvania; English

***Shulamis Yelin***, *b.* Montreal, Canada, 1913, *d.* Montreal, Canada, 2002; English

***Hanna Zacks***, *b.* Haifa, Palestine, 1931, *r.* Binghamton, New York; English

***Nurit Zarchi***, *b.* Jerusalem, Israel, 1941, *r.* Jerusalem, Israel; Hebrew

***Zelda***, Shneurson Mishkowsky, *b.* Chernikoff, Ukraine, 1914, *d.* Jerusalem, Israel, 1984; Hebrew

***Anna Ziegler***, *b.* New York, New York, 1979, *r.* Brooklyn, New York; English

***Wendy Zierler***, *b.* Ontario, Canada, 1965, *r.* Riverdale, New York; English/Hebrew

***Linda Stern Zisquit***, *b.* Buffalo, New York, 1947, *r.* Jerusalem, Israel; English

# *Voices Publication Credits*

Extensive attempts have been made to obtain permission to reprint previously published material. Please inform us of any corrections or additions and we will be pleased to include them in the next printing of the book. The editors are grateful to those who have granted us permission to use their work, both previously published and original.

NANCY SATULOFF ABRAHAM: "Fringes in My Heart" by Nancy Satuloff Abraham. Copyright © Nancy Satuloff Abraham. Used by permission of the author.

RACHEL ADLER: Excerpt from *Lifecycles Vol. 1: Jewish Women on Life Passages & Personal Milestones* © 1994 Debra Orenstein (Woodstock, VT: Jewish Lights Publishing). $19.95 + $3.95 s/h. Order by mail or call 800-962-4544 or on-line at www.jewishlights.com. Permission granted by Jewish Lights Publishing, P.O. Box 237, Woodstock, VT 05091.

SIGRID AGOCSI: "Aphorism" originally published in *Dybbuk of Delight: An Anthology of Jewish Women's Poetry* edited by Sonja Lyndon and Sylvia Paskin, London, England: Five Leaves Publications, 1995. Copyright by Sigrid Agocsi. Used by permission of Sigrid Agocsi.

MARJORIE AGOSIN: "Sorcery," translated by Cola Franzen, from *Sargasso.* Copyright © 1993 by Marjorie Agosin. Translation copyright © 1993 by Cola Franzen. Reprinted with the permission of White Pine Press, www.whitepine.org.

ADA AHARONI: "Dear Descartes: Creativity" and "The Second Exodus" by Ada Aharoni. Used by permission of the author.

LEA AINI: "The Empress of Imagined Fertility" from *Dreaming the Actual: Contemporary Fiction and Poetry by Israeli Women Writers*, selected, edited and with an introduction by Miriyam Glazer (Albany, NY: SUNY Press, 2000). Copyright © by Miriyam Glazer. Used by permission of Miriyam Glazer.

KAREN ALKALAY-GUT: "Annunciation," "The Keepers of My Youth," "Mobilization," and "Military Washing" from *Ignorant Armies*, Copyright © 1994 by Cross-Cultural Communications and Karen Alkalay-Gut. Jewish Writers, Chapbook 4 (Merrick, NY: Cross-Cultural Communications, 1994). Series Editor: Stanley H. Barkan. Reprinted by permission of the publisher and on behalf of the author.

SHIFRA ALON: "Not Every Day" originally appeared in *P'tachim*, Tel Aviv.

SARAH ANTINE: "The Ritual Bath" from *Bridges: A Jewish Feminist Journal* Vol. 12 No. 1. Used by permission of Sarah Antine.

EDNA APHEK: "Sarah," "Enwombed," and "Jacob and Esau." Copyright © by Edna Aphek. Used by permission of Edna Aphek.

DEBORAH ASCARELLI: "Whatever in Me Is of Heaven" reprinted from *JPS Guide to Jewish Women: 600 B.C.E.–1900 C.E.*, edited by Sondra Henry, Emily Taitz, and Cheryl Tallen (Philadephia, PA: Jewish Publication Society, 2003). Copyright © 2003 by Sondra Henry, Emily Taitz, and Cheryl Tallen. Used by permission of The Jewish Publication Society.

ELLEN BASS: "Eating the Bones" and "Ritual" from *The Human Line.* Copyright © 2007 by Ellen Bass. Reprinted with the permission of Copper Canyon Press, www.coppercanyonpress.org. "For My Daughter on Her Twenty-First Birthday" from *Mules of Love.* Copyright © 2002 by Ellen Bass. Reprinted with permission of BOA Editions, Ltd., www.boaeditions.org.

YOCHEVED BAT-MIRIAM: "Before" reprinted from *And Rachel Stole the Idols: The Emergence of Modern Hebrew Women's Writing*, by Wendy Zierler (Detroit, MI: Wayne State University Press, 2004). Used with permission of Wayne State University Press. "Hagar" from *Shirim* (Tel Aviv: Sifriat Poalim Publishing House Ltd., 1963), translated by Zvi Jagendorf. Used by permission of Zvi Jagendorf. "From Hidden Treasures" from *Modern Hebrew Poetry* (Iowa City: University of Iowa Press, 1980), translated by Bernhard Frank. "Miriam" translated by Ilana Pardes, reprinted in revised form by translator from *Gender and Text in Modern Hebrew and Yiddish Literature,* edited by Naomi B. Sokoloff, Anne Lapidus Lerner, and Anita Norich (New York: The Jewish Theological Seminary of America, 1992). Used by permission of Ilana Pardes and JTS.

ROBIN BECKER: "The New Egypt," "Autumn Measure," and "The Wild Heart" from *Domain of Perfect Affection*, by Robin Becker, © 2006. Reprinted by permission of the University of Pittsburgh Press.

LEILA GAL BERNER: "A Blessing" by Rabbi Leila Gal Berner. Used by permission of Leila Gal Berner.

MARY LOVING BLANCHARD: "In the Sudan" originally published in *Bridges: A Jewish Feminist Journal*, vol. 9, no. 1, 2001. Used by permission of Mary Loving Blanchard.

AMY BLANK: "I Know Four" and "Rebecca" used by permission of the CCAR Press and Miriam Sachs. "And Jacob Blessed Pharoah," "Baruch Hu," and "Bezalel" used by permission of Miriam Sachs.

CHANA BLOCH: "The Flood," and "The Sacrifice" originally published in *Secrets of the Tribe*, Sheep Meadow Press, 1980. Used by permission of Chana Bloch. "Disquisition" originally published in *Women Speak to God: The Prayers and Poems of Jewish Women,* edited by Marcia Cohn Spiegel and Deborah L. Kremsdorf. Used by permission of Chana Bloch. "White Petticoats," from *The Past Keeps Changing,* Sheep Meadow Press, 1992. Used by permission of Chana Bloch.

SHERRY BLUMBERG: "Sarai," "From Leah to Her Sister," "Timna's Revenge," "Asenath's Plea to Her Husband Joseph," "Lea's Last Words," and "At the Tent of Meeting," used by permission of Sherry Blumberg.

SHIRLEY BLUMBERG: "Family Reunion" and "Yom Kippur Prayer" used by permission of Shirley Blumberg.

RUTH BRIN: "Joseph and Pharaoh" and "They Built the Tabernacle" reprinted from *Harvest: Collected Poems and Prayers.* Copyright © 1986, 1999 by Ruth Brin. Used by permission of The Reconstructionist Press.

NINA BETH CARDIN: Excerpts from *The Tapestry of Jewish Time*, by Nina Beth Cardin. © Behrman House, Inc., reprinted with permission www.behrmanhouse.com. Excerpt from *Tears of Sorrow, Seeds of Hope: A Jewish Spiritual Companion for Infertility and Pregnancy Loss* © 1999 by Nina Beth Cardin (Woodstock, VT: Jewish Lights Publishing) $18.95 + $3.95 s/h. Order by mail or call 800-962-4544 or on-line at www.jewishlights.com.

KIM CHERNIN: "Eve's Birth" by Kim Chernin. Used by permission of Kim Chernin. "The Primal Feast" from *The Hungry Self: Women, Eating, and Identity* (New York: Times Books, 1985). Copyright © 1985 by Kim Chernin.

JENNIFER CLAYMAN: "Celebrating Courage and Vision: An Appreciation of Rabbi Sally Priesand" used by permission of Rabbi Jennifer Clayman.

ENID DAME: "Yahrzeit" used by permission of Donald Lev.

CELIA DROPKIN: "My Mother" from *Jewish American Literature: A Norton Anthology* edited by Jules Chametzky, John Felstiner, Hilene Flanzbaum, and Kathryn Hellerstein, NY: Norton, 2001. Used by permission of Kathryn Hellerstein.

ANNE EBERSMAN: "Precious Gifts" used by permission of Rabbi Anne Ebersman.

SUE LEVI ELWELL: "Jacob Blesses Dinah," "Elisheba Speaks," and "A Song of Ascent" copyright © Sue Levi Elwell. Used by permission of Rabbi Sue Levi Elwell.

ESTHER ETTINGER: "Believe Me," translated by Marianna Barr, from *Dreaming the Actual: Contemporary Fiction and Poetry by Israeli Women Writers,* NY: SUNY Press, 2000. Copyright © Miriyam Glazer. Used by permission of Miriyam Glazer.

RUTH FAINLIGHT: "Dinah" from *Sugar-Paper Blue*, Bloodaxe Books (Northumberland, England, 1997). "Thankful" and "Prescience" from *Burning Wire*, Bloodaxe Books (Northumberland, 2002). Used by permission of Ruth Fainlight and Bloodaxe Books.

MARCIA FALK: "Will" from *The Book of Blessings: New Jewish Prayers for Daily Life, the Sabbath, and the New Moon Festival*, by Marcia Falk; Harper (1996), paperback edition, Beacon Press (1999); copyright © 1996 Marcia Lee Falk. Used by permission of the author.

CORIE FEINER: "Nomad Land" reprinted from *Zeek: A Jewish Journal of Thought and Culture*, May 2006, http://www.zeek.net/. Used by permission of Corie Feiner.

ELAINE FEINSTEIN: "A Prayer for my Son," "A Prayer for My Sons," "The First Wriggle," and "Released," from *Elaine Feinstein: Collected Poems and Translations*, Manchester, England: Carcanet Press Limited, © 2002. Used by permission of Carcanet Press.

MERLE FELD: "We All Stood Together," "Sinai," "Sinai Again," "My Friends Baked Cake and We Ordered Lox and Whitefish from the Deli," and "The First Time We Made Shabbos Together," reprinted from *A Spiritual Life: Exploring the Heart and Jewish Tradition,* Albany, NY: SUNY Press, 2007. Used by permission of Merle Feld. "Leaving Egypt," "Still Dreaming of Home," and "Unfulfilled Promise used by permission of Merle Feld.

ROBIN FOX: "For the Last Time" reprinted from *Covenant of the Soul: New Prayers, Poems, and Meditations*, NY: Women of Reform Judaism, 2000. Used by permission of Robin Fox.

ELLEN FRANKEL: from *The Five Books of Miriam: A Woman's Commentary on the Torah*, by Ellen Frankel, copyright © 1996 by Ellen Frankel, PhD. Used by permission of G.P. Putnam's Sons, a division of Penguin Group USA Inc.

DEBBIE FRIEDMAN: Courtesy of The Jewish Music Group, LLC www.jewishmusicgroup.com.

TIKVA FRYMER-KENSKY: "The Blood of Birth" and "Mother to Mother" reprinted from *Motherprayer: A Pregnant Woman's Spiritual Companion* by Tikva Frymer-Kensky, copyright © 1995 by Tikva Frymer-Kensky. Used by permission of Riverhead Books, an imprint of Penguin Group (USA) Inc.

LAURA GELLER: excerpted from "Jewish Feminism: Go to Yourself!" The Shalom Center, www.shalomctr.org. Used by permission of Rabbi Laura Geller.

ELAINE ROSE GLICKMAN: "Parashat Noach," "Zilpah Speaks to God," and "They Had Names," used by permission of Rabbi Elaine Rose Glickman.

SUSAN GLICKMAN: Reprinted from the siddur of Temple Mt. Sinai, El Paso, Texas.

LEA GOLDBERG: "A God Once Commanded Us," "In the Jerusalem Hills," and "Toward Myself," translation by Robert Friend, copyright © Jean Shapiro Cantu. "Somewhere in Samaria," "In Everything," "You Are Wondrous," "At Light's Border," "Songs of a Foreign Woman," "Poems of the Journey's End," and "Olive Trees" reprinted from *Selected Poetry and Drama of Lea Goldberg*, translated by Rachel Tzvia Back, New Milford, CT: Toby Press, 2005. Reprinted with permission of The Toby Press. "My Mother's House," translated by Ezra Spicehandler, reprinted from *The Modern Hebrew Poem Itself*, Detroit, MI: Wayne State University Press, 1965. Used by permission of Ezra Spicehandler. All poems used by permission of ACUM, Israel.

SHELLY GOLDMAN, LARA LAUFER, AND SHARI LORE: "Looking Toward Shabbat" reprinted from *Covenant of the Spirit: New Prayers, Poems, and Meditations from Women of Reform Judaism* (NY: Women of Reform Judaism, 2005). Used by permission of the authors.

NANCY LEE GOSSELS: "Somewhere Out of Time" by Nancy Lee Gossels. Copyright © Nancy Lee Gossels. Used by permission of the author.

LYNN GOTTLIEB: "Awakening" and "Prayer for Burning the End Piece of the Challah" from *She Who Dwells Within*, by Lynn Gottlieb. Copyright © 1995 by Lynn Gottlieb. Reprinted by permission of HarperCollins Publishers.

NECHAMA GOTTSCHALK: "Creation" by Nechama Gottschalk. Copyright © by Nechama Gottschalk. Used by permission of the author.

JESSICA GREENBAUM: "A Box of Clementines in the Maternity Ward" and "Under the Spell of Miscarriage" is reprinted from *Inventing Difficulty* by permission of Silverfish Review Press, © 2000 by Silverfish Review Press. "Packing Slip" originally appeared in *Salamander* Vol. II, No. 2, 2006. Used by permission of Jessica Greenbaum.

RACHEL HADAS: "Coda" in *The Empty Bed* © 1995 by Rachel Hadas and reprinted with permission of Wesleyan University Press. "Weathering" from *The River of Forgetfulness* by Rachel Hadas, © 2006 David Robert Brooks, Cincinnati, Ohio. "The Mirror" from *Mirrors of Astonishment* © 1992 by Rachel Hadas and reprinted by permission of Rutgers University Press.

JILL HAMMER: "Zilpah," "Menorah," "Every City Has a Soul," "Gifts," "Moses Leans Over the Stone," "Sinai," and "The Death of Moses" used by permission of Jill Hammer. "Every City Has a Soul" was previously published in *Zeek Magazine*, May 2004.

ANNETTE BIALIK HARCHIK: "Earrings" reprinted from *Ghosts of the Holocaust: An Anthology of Poetry by the Second Generation*, Stewart J. Florsheim, ed., 1989. Used by permission of Wayne State University Press.

RA'AYA HARNIK: "I Will Not Offer" reprinted from *Profane Scriptures: Reflections on the Dialogue with the Bible in Modern Hebrew Poetry* by Ruth Kartun-Blum and Menashe Kadishman. Copyright © 1999 by Hebrew Union College Press. Used by permission of Hebrew Union College Press.

GALIT HASAN-ROKEM: "[This child inside me]" translated by Kathryn Hellerstein. Reprinted from *The Defiant Muse: Hebrew Feminist Poems from Antiquity to the Present*, eds. Shirley Kaufman, Galit Hasan-Rokem, and Tamar S. Hess (New York: The Feminist Press of the City University of New York, 1999). Used by permission of Kathryn Hellerstein.

LINDA HEPNER: from "Potiphar's Wife," by Linda Hepner. Used by permission of the author.

ETTY HILLESUM: Excerpts from *An Interrupted Life: The Diaries, 1941–1943; and, Letters from Westerbork* by Etty Hillesum (New York: Henry Holt, 1996). Copyright © 1986 by Random House, Inc.

LINDA HIRSCHHORN: "Sarah and Hagar" © Linda Hirschhorn 1985, 2002 recorded on *Heartbeat* with Cantor Linda Hirschhorn and Volocot (http://www.lindahirschhorn.com). Used by permission of Linda Hirschhorn.

BARBARA D. HOLENDER: "Torah" excerpted from *Lifecycles Vol. 1: Jewish Women on Life Passages & Personal Milestones* © 1994 Debra Orenstein (Woodstock, VT: Jewish Lights Publishing). $19.95 + $3.95 s/h. Order by mail or call 800-962-4544 or on-line at www.jewishlights.com. Permission granted by Jewish Lights Publishing, P.O. Box 237, Woodstock, VT 0509, and by Barbara D. Holender.

VICKI HOLLANDER: Section from "After a Miscarriage: Hold Me Now" and "The Passage of Divorce: Paving One's Way" by Vicki Hollander excerpted from *Lifecycles Vol. 1: Jewish Women on Life Passages & Personal Milestones* © 1994 Debra Orenstein (Woodstock, VT: Jewish Lights Publishing). $19.95 + $3.95 s/h. Order by mail or call 800-962-4544 or on-line at www.jewishlights.com. Permission granted by Jewish Lights Publishing, P.O. Box 237, Woodstock, VT 05091. From "An Opening Ceremony" by Vicki Hollander, reprinted from *Four Centuries of Jewish Women's Spirituality: A Sourcebook*, edited by Ellen M. Umansky and Diane Ashton (Boston, MA: Beacon, 1992). Revised and used by permission of Vicki Hollander.

LISA HOSTEIN: "On Adoption" by Lisa Hostein. Used by permission of Lisa Hostein.

SUE HUBBARD: "Inheritance" and "The Curse" by Sue Hubbard, originally published in *The Dybbuk of Delight: An Anthology of Jewish Women's Poetry*, edited by Sonja Lyndon and Sylvia Paskin (Nottingham, England: Five Leaves Publication, 1995). Used by permission of the author.

BEYLE HURVITS: "This *Tkhine* Is Said before *Kedushe*" translated by Devra Kay. Reprinted from *Seyder Tkhines: The Forgotten Book of Common Prayer for Jewish Women*, by Devra Kay, Phila, PA: Jewish Publication Society, 2004. Used by permission of Jewish Publication Society.

REGINA JONAS: "Letter to Mala Laaser, 1938" reprinted from *Fraulein Rabbiner Jonas: The Story of the First Woman Rabbi*, by Elisa Klapheck and Toby Axelrod (NY: John Wiley and Sons, 2004). Copyright © 2004 by John Wiley and Sons.

JUDY KATZ: "Anniversary" used by permission of Judy Katz. Previously published in *Bellevue Literary Review*, Spring 2005 edition.

SHIRLEY KAUFMAN: "In the Beginning," "They've Rolled the Parchment" and "The Death of Rachel," reprinted from *Threshold*. Copyright © 2003 by Shirley Kaufman. Reprinted with the permission of Copper Canyon Press, www.coppercanyonpress.org. "The Wife of Moses" reprinted from *Rivers of Salt*. Copyright © 1993 by Shirley Kaufman. Reprinted with the permission of Copper Canyon Press, www.coppercanyonpress.org. "For the Sin..." reprinted from *Claims*. Copyright © 1984 by Shirley Kaufman. Used by permission of Shirley Kaufman. "His Wife," "Rebecca," "Leah," copyright © Shirley Kaufman. Used by permission of Shirley Kaufman.

KARYN KEDAR: "From a Mother to Her Girls" by Rabbi Karyn Kedar from *The Bridge to Forgiveness: Stories and Prayers for Finding God and Restoring Wholeness* © 2007 Karyn Kedar (Woodstock, VT: Jewish Lights Publishing). $19.95 + $3.95 s/h. Order by mail or call 800-962-4544 or on-line at www.jewishlights.com. Permission granted by Jewish Lights Publishing, P.O. Box 237, Woodstock, VT 05091.

SHARON KESSLER: "Covenant," in *Tikkun*, July/August 1989. Reprinted from *Tikkun: A Bimonthly Interfaith Critique of Politics, Culture & Society*. Used with permission of *Tikkun*.

ZOË KLEIN: "How Much Water Is Inside a Tear" by Rabbi Zoë Klein. Copyright © by Zoë Klein. Used by permission of the author. "Scatter Us in the Sea" originally published for Torat Chayim http://urj.org/torah/, a project of the Union for Reform Judaism. Used by permission of the author.

IRENA KLEPFISZ: "The Window" reprinted from *The Tribe of Dina: A Jewish Women's Anthology*, edited by Melanie Kaye/Kantrowitz and Irena Klepfisz (Boston: Beacon Press, 1989). Used by permission of Beacon Press.

FEIGA IZRAILEVNA KOGAN: "God: Desert" translated by Rabbi Carole B. Balin. Reprinted from *To Reveal Our Hearts: Jewish Women Writers in Tsarist Russia* (Cincinnati, OH: Hebrew Union College Press, 2000). Used by permission of Hebrew Union College Press.

BRACHA KOPSTEIN: "Nearing 80" reprinted from *P.E.N.: A Collection of Recent Writings in Israel*, edited by Chaim Shoham, Shin Shifra, et al. (Tirash Ltd). Used by permission of ACUM, Israel.

RACHEL KORN: "All the Winds" (Rachel Korn, translated by Marcia Falk) from *The Book of Blessings: New Jewish Prayers for Daily Life, the Sabbath, and the New Moon Festival*, Marcia Falk; Harper (1996), paperback edition, Beacon Press (1999); copyright © 1996 Marcia Lee Falk. Used by permission of the translator.

MAXINE KUMIN: "Turning the Garden in Middle Age" by Maxine Kumin, from *Selected Poems 1960–1990*. Copyright © 1996 by Maxine Kumin. "Women and Horses" by Maxine Kumin from *Jack and Other New Poems*. Copyright © 2005 by Maxine Kumin. Used by permission of W. W. Norton & Company, Inc.

ELSE LASKER-SCHÜLER: "I Know," "Pharaoh and Joseph," "To God," "My Freedom," and "My People" translated by Janine Canan. From *Star in My Forehead: Selected Poems of Else Lasker-Schüler*. Translation copyright © 2000 by Janine Canan. Reprinted with the permission of Holy Cow! Press, www.holycowpress.org.

LYNN LEVIN: "To a Nursling Before Dawn" reprinted from *A Few Questions About Paradise*. Originally published in *New Beginnings* January/February 1987 (La Leche League International). Used by permission of the author. "And You Shall Love" originally published in *Jewish Women's Literary Annual*, vol. 4, 2000–2001. Used by permission of the author.

LISA LEVINE: "Forgotten" and "I Am Accursed" used by permission of Cantor Lisa Levine. Copyright © Lisa Levine.

NAOMI LEVY: "A Prayer When the Child is Born" from *To Begin Again: The Journey Toward Comfort, Strength and Faith in Difficult Times* (NY: The Ballantine Publishing Group, 1998). Copyright © 1998 by Naomi Levy.

BONNIE LYONS: "Deliverance: Puah Explains" and "Zipporah's Return" by Bonnie Lyons, reprinted from *In Other Words* (San Antonio, TX: Pecan Grove Press, 2004). Copyright © 2004 by Bonnie Lyons. Used by permission of author.

SHERRI MANDELL: Excerpts from *The Blessing of a Broken Heart* by Sherri Mandell (New Milford, CT: Toby Press, 2003).

ANNA MARGOLIN: "Mother Earth, Well Worn, Sun Washed," translated by Adrienne Cooper. Originally published in *The Tribe of Dina: A Jewish Women's Anthology*, edited by Melanie Kaye/Kantrowitz and Irena Klepfisz (Boston: Beacon Press, 1989). Used by permission of Adrienne Cooper.

GOLDA MEIR: from *The Hungry Self: Women, Eating and Identity* by Kim Chernin (New York: Crown, 1985).

PAMELA MELNIKOFF: "For a Child Not Yet Conceived" originally published in *The Dybbuk of Delight: An Anthology of Jewish Women's Poetry*, edited by Sonja Lyndon and Sylvia Paskin (Nottingham, England: Five Leaves Publication, 1995). Used by permission of the author.

RIVKA MIRIAM: Translations © 2007 by Linda Stern Zisquit. Used by permission of Linda Stern Zisquit.

MARSHA PRAVDER MIRKIN: Excerpted from "Miriam," originally published in *Praise Her Works: Conversations with Biblical Women* edited by Penina Adelman (Philadelphia, PA:

Jewish Publication Society, 2005). Used by permission of The Jewish Publication Society.

AGI MISHOL: "Gravity, Death" and "Look There" originally published in *Look There: New and Selected Poems*, translated by Lisa Katz. © 2002 by Agi Mishol, reprinted with permission of Graywolf Press, Saint Paul, Minnesota. "Turning to Rest in Sappho's Poems," translation by Tsipi Keller, from *Contemporary Hebrew Poetry* (Albany, New York: SUNY Press, 2008). Used with permission of Tsipi Keller.

KADYA MOLODOWSKY: All poems originally published in *Paper Bridges: Selected Poems of Kadya Molodowsky*, translated and edited by Kathryn Hellerstein (Detroit: Wayne State University Press, 1999). Copyright © 1999 by Kathryn Hellerstein. Used by permission of Kathryn Hellerstein.

RACHEL LUZZATTO MORPURGO: "Desolate Valleys" reprinted from *JPS Guide to Jewish Women: 600 B.C.E.–1900 C.E.*, edited by Sondra Henry, Emily Taitz, and Cheryl Tallen (Philadephia, PA: Jewish Publication Society, 2003). Copyright © 2003 by Sondra Henry, Emily Taitz, and Cheryl Tallen. Used by permission of The Jewish Publication Society.

PAMELA S. NADELL: Excerpt from *Women Who Would Be Rabbis: A History of Women's Ordination 1889–1985* (Boston: Beacon Press, 1998). Copyright © 1998 by Pamela S. Nadell.

CLARISSE NICOÏDSKI: "Open Earth" translated by Stephen Levy. Reprinted from *Voices within the Ark: The Modern Jewish Poets*, edited by Howard Schwartz and Anthony Rudolf. New York: Avon Press, 1980. Copyright © by Stephen Levy.

VANESSA OCHS: "Dina's Own Story" and excerpt from "Yocheved's Own Story" reprinted from *Sarah Laughed: Modern Lessons from the Wisdom and Stories of Biblical Women* by Vanessa Ochs © 2004. Used by permission of The McGraw-Hill Companies.

MARIE ODLUM: "The Girls That Are Wanted" reprinted from *Sarah's Daughters Sing: A Sampler of Poems by Jewish Women*, edited by Henny Wenkart (Hoboken, NJ: KTAV, 1990).

DEBRA ORENSTEIN: "A Prayer for Parents of Babies with Disabilities" by Debra Orenstein excerpted from *Lifecycles Vol. 1: Jewish Women on Life Passages & Personal Milestones* © 1994 Debra Orenstein (Woodstock, VT: Jewish Lights Publishing) $19.95 + $3.95 s/h. Order by mail or call 800-962-4544 or online at www.jewishlights.com. Permission granted by Jewish Lights Publishing, P.O. Box 237, Woodstock, VT 05091.

ALICIA SUSKIN OSTRIKER: "A Meditation in Seven Days" and "Move" from *The Little Space: Poems Selected and New, 1968–1998*, by Alicia Suskin Ostriker, © 1998. Reprinted by permission of the University of Pittsburgh Press. "Dissolve in Slow Motion" from *The Imaginary Lover*, by Alicia Suskin Ostriker, © 1968. Reprinted by permission of the University of Pittsburgh Press. "Mother," "Blood" from the "Deaths, Transfigurations" poem cycle and "yom kippur" from the second section of "Days of Awe" from the "Turn and Return" poem cycle from *The Volcano Sequence*, by Alicia Suskin Ostriker, © 2002. Used by permission of the University of Pittsburgh Press and Alicia Suskin Ostriker. "The Nursing Father" and "Rachel Solo" from *The Nakedness of the Fathers: Biblical Visions and Revisions* copyright © 1994 by Alicia Suskin Ostriker (Piscataway, NJ: Rutgers University Press, 1997). Used by permission of Alicia Suskin Ostriker.

ESTELLE NACHIMOFF PADAWER: "I Do Not Ask." Used by permission of the author.

GRACE PALEY: "[When this old body]" and "For My Daughter" from *Begin Again: Collected Poems* by Grace Paley. Copyright © 2000 by Grace Paley. Used by permission of Farrar, Straus & Giroux, LLC.

HELEN PAPELL: "Prophet Miriam at Mount St. Helens, Washington, USA." Reprinted from *Jewish Women's Literary Annual*, Vol. 1, No. 1, 1994/1995. Used with permission of the author.

LINDA ROSE PARKES: "Seder Eve" reprinted from *The Dybbuk of Delight: An Anthology of Jewish Women's Poetry*, edited by Sonja Lyndon and Sylvia Paskin. Nottingham, England: Five Leaves Publications, 1995. Copyright © by Linda Rose Parkes. Reprinted by permission of the author.

LINDA PASTAN: "Aspects of Eve" from *Aspects of Eve* by Linda Pastan. Copyright © 1970, 1971, 1972, 1973, 1974, 1975 by Linda Pastan. Used by permission of Liveright Publishing Corporation. "At the Loom" from *The Imperfect Paradise* by Linda Pastan. Copyright © 1988 by Linda Pastan. Used by permission of W. W. Norton & Company, Inc. "Journey's End" and "Passover" from *Carnival Evening: New and Selected Poems 1968–1998* by Linda Pastan. Copyright © 1998 by Linda Pastan. Used by permission of W. W. Norton & Company, Inc.

LAURIE PATTON: "Chayei Sarah," "T'rumah," "T'zav," "M'tzora," "Acharei Mot," "Naso," "Sh'lach L'cha," "Balak," "Eikev," and "Korach." Copyright © by Laurie Patton. Used by permission of the author.

HAVIVA PEDAYA: "please with gentleness." Used by permission of Haviva Pedaya and translator Harvey Bock.

JULIE PELC: "Sukkot 2001" from *Joining the Sisterhood*, edited by Tobin Belzer and Julie Pelc (Albany: SUNY Press, 2003). Copyright © 2003 by Julie Pelc. Used by permission of the author.

DEBBIE PERLMAN: "Psalm 5: Lullaby for Courage," "Psalm 32: A Song of Endings and Beginnings," and "Psalm 50," reprinted from *Flames of Heaven: New Psalms for Healing and Praise* (Wilmette, IL: Rad Publishing, 1998). Copyright © 1998 by Debbie Perlman. Used by permission of Reid Perlman.

HARA E. PERSON: "Leah at Benjamin's Brit Milah," and "Tamar's Lament," copyright © 1999 by Hara E. Person, revised and reprinted from *CCAR Journal*, Spring 1999 "Serah bat Asher," "Passover Love Song," "This Night," and "The

Land of the Patriarchs" copyright © 2007 by Hara E. Person. Used by permission of the author.

MARGE PIERCY: "V'ahavta" from *The Art of Blessing the Day* by Marge Piercy, copyright © 1999 by Middlemarsh, Inc.; "How divine is forgiving" from *Available Light* by Marge Piercy, copyright © 1988 by Middlemarsh, Inc.; "Rape poem" from *Circles on the Water* by Marge Piercy, copyright © 1982 by Marge Piercy. "Sometimes while I am chanting" from *Colors Passing Through Us: Poems* by Marge Piercy, copyright © 2003 by Middlemarsh, Inc. Used by permission of Aldred A. Knopf, a division of Random House, Inc.

HAVA PINCAS-COHEN: "The Ineffable Name" from *Dreaming the Actual: Contemporary Fiction and Poetry by Israeli Women Writers*, NY: SUNY Press, 2000. Copyright © Miriyam Glazer. Used by permission of Miriyam Glazer. "A Mother's Morning Prayer," translated by Jules Harlow and Rochelle Furstenberg, reprinted from *Pray Tell: A Hadassah Guide to Jewish Prayer* (Hadassah and Jewish Lights Publishing, 2003). Used by permission of Jules Harlow and Rochelle Furstenberg. All poems used by permission of Hava Pincas-Cohen and ACUM, Israel.

ANDA PINKERFELD-AMIR: "And These Are Hagar's Poems to This Very Day" reprinted from *And Rachel Stole the Idols: The Emergence of Modern Hebrew Women's Writing*, by Wendy Zierler (Detroit, MI: Wayne State University Press, 2004). Used with permission of Wayne State University Press, Wendy Zierler, and ACUM, Israel.

RIV-ELLEN PRELL: "My Entitlement and My Obligation" from *The Jewish Woman's Book of Wisdom*, ed. Ellen Jaffe-Gill (Secaucus, NJ: Birch Lane Press, 1998). Used by permission of Riv-Ellen Prell.

ESTHER RAAB: Excerpt from "Shirat Ishah," reprinted from *Kol HaShirim Shel Esther Raab*, translated by Harold Schimmel, edited by Jules Harlow. Used by permission of Ehud Ben-Ezer; "Age," excerpt from "Thistles," "Like a Poppy Borne by Wind," "Last Prayer" from *Thistles: Selected Poems of Esther Raab*, translated by Harold Schimmel. Jerusalem, Israel: Ibis Editions, 2002. Hebrew-language version copyright © 2002 Esther Raab, Ehud Ben-Ezer. English translation copyright © 2002 The institute for the Translation of Hebrew Literature. Used by permission of Ehud Ben-Ezer; "Requests" translated by Catherine Shaw and Moshe Dor. Reprinted from *After the First Rain: Israeli Poems on War and Peace,* edited by Moshe Dor and Barbara Goldberg (Syracuse, NY: Syracuse University Press, 1998), copyright © 1997 by Dryad Press. Used by permission of Dryad Press.

RAHEL: "Rachel" reprinted from *And Rachel Stole the Idols: The Emergence of Modern Hebrew Women's Writing,* by Wendy Zierler (Detroit, MI: Wayne State University Press, 2004) Used with permission of Wayne State University Press and Wendy Zierler. "My Dead" and "The Messenger Came in the Night" reprinted from *Found in Translation: Modern Hebrew Poets, A Bilingual Edition*, translated by Robert Friend (Milford, CT: The Toby Press, 2006). Translation copyright © Jean Shapiro Cantu. "To My Country," reprinted from *The Defiant Muse: Hebrew Feminist Poems from Antiquity to the Present*, translated by Robert Friend, edited by Shirley Kaufman, Galit Hasan-Rokem, and Tamar S. Hess (New York: The Feminist Press of the City University of New York, 1999). Translation copyright © Jean Shapiro Cantu. "Comfort Me" and "In the Garden" in *The Plough Women: Records of the Pioneer Women of Palestine*, edited and annotated by Mark A. Raider and Miriam B. Raider-Roth. Copyright © 2002 by Brandeis University Press. Reprinted by permission of University Press of New England, Hanover, NH.

NESSA RAPOPORT: "Undo It, Take It Back" from *A Woman's Book of Grieving* (New York: William Morrow, 1994). Copyright © 2007 by Nessa Rapoport. Used with permission of Nessa Rapoport. All rights reserved.

DAHLIA RAVIKOVITCH: "Like Rachel," "Delight," "Magic Spells," "From Day to Night," "Pride," "The Sorrow of Night," "Beheaded Heifer," and "A Pure Whole Memory" from *Hovering at a Low Altitude: The Poetry of Dahlia Ravikovitch*, translated by Chana Bloch and Chana Kronfeld (New York: W. W. Norton, 2009). Used with permission of Chana Bloch and Chana Kronfeld.

BARBARA REISNER: "The Generations Upon Me." Used by permission of the author.

NAOMI REPLANSKY: "When I Melt Down" and "Gray Hairs" reprinted from *The Dangerous World: New and Selected Poems, 1934–1993* (Chicago: Another Chicago Press, 1994). Copyright © 1994 by Naomi Replansky. Used by permission of the author.

CHAVA ROMM: Source unknown.

JUDITH ROSE: "I Know About the Woman Who Sits and Waits" by Judith Rose. Reprinted from *Sarah's Daughters Sing: A Sampler of Poems by Jewish Women*, edited by Henny Wenkart (Hoboken, NJ: KTAV, 1990). Copyright © 1975 by Judith Rose.

SHIRA BRACHA MOTZKIN RUBENSTEIN: "The Other Shore" by Shira Motzkin Rubenstein. Used by permission of the author.

MURIEL RUKEYSER: "Miriam: The Sea," "[untitled]," from "The Way Out," and "This Place in the Ways" reprinted from *The Collected Poems of Muriel Rukeyser,* edited by Janet Kaufman and Anne Herzog (Pittsburgh, PA: University of Pittsburgh Press, 2006). Copyright © Muriel Rukeyser. Used by permission of International Creative Management.

NELLY SACHS: "We Mothers" translated by Ruth and Matthew Mead from *The Seekers and Other Poems* by Nelly Sachs, translated by Ruth and Matthew Mead and Michael Hamburger. Translation copyright © 1970 by Farrar, Straus & Giroux, Inc. Reprinted by permission of Farrar, Straus &

Giroux, LLC; "Fleeing," "If I Only Knew," and "O the Night of the Weeping Children" from *O the Chimneys* by Nelly Sachs, translated by Ruth and Matthew Mead and Michael Hamburger. Translation copyright © 1967, renewed 1995 by Farrar, Straus & Giroux, Inc. Reprinted by permission of Farrar, Straus & Giroux LLC.

ELIZABETH SARAH: "Meditation for Tefillin" by Rabbi Elizabeth Sarah. Originally published in *Dybbuk of Delight: An Anthology of Jewish Women's Poetry* edited by Sonja Lyndon and Sylvia Paskin (Nottingham: England: Five Leaves Publications, 1995). Used by permission of the author.

SANDY EISENBERG SASSO: "First a Spark" by Rabbi Sandy Eisenberg Sasso. Used by permission of the author.

SHELLEY SAVREN: "The Butcher's Wife" reprinted from *Bridges: A Jewish Feminist Journal,* Spring 2007 (Vol. 12, no. 1). Used by permission of Shelley Savren.

GRACE SCHULMAN: "Kol Nidrei, September 2001" and excerpt from "In Place of Belief" from *The Broken String: Poems by Grace Schulman.* Copyright © 2007 by Grace Schulman. "Offerings" from *Paintings of Our Lives: Poems by Grace Schulman.* Copyright © 2001 by Grace Schulman. Reprinted by permission of Houghton Mifflin Company. All rights reserved.

LAYA FIRESTONE SEGHI: "Listen to the Bird," reprinted from *Voices Within the Ark: The Modern Jewish Poets,* edited by Howard Schwartz and Anthony Rudolf (New York: HarperCollins, 1980). Used by permission of Laya Firestone Seghi.

HANNAH SENESH: Excerpts are from *Hannah Senesh: Her Life and Diary: The First Complete Edition* © 2004 by Eitan Senesh, David Senesh, and Ginsora Senesh (Woodstock, VT: Jewish Lights Publishing). $19.95 + $3.95 s/h. Order by mail or call 800-962-4544 or on-line at www.jewishlights.com. Permission granted by Jewish Lights Publishing, P.O. Box 237, Woodstock, VT 05091.

DRORA SETEL: "The Girl's Name Is Forgotten" by Drora Setel excerpted from *Lifecycles Vol. 2: Jewish Women on Biblical Themes in Contemporary Life* © 1997 Debra Orenstein and Jane Rachel Litman. (Woodstock, VT: Jewish Lights Publishing). $19.95 + $3.95 s/h. Order by mail or call 800-962-4544 or online at www.jewishlights.com. Permission granted by Jewish Lights Publishing, P.O. Box 237, Woodstock, VT 05091.

ONA SIPORIN: "there is the river" from *Poems for a Primitive Mythology* (Bloomington, IN: Raintree Press, 1976). Copyright © by Ona Siporin. "Mikveh Mayim" copyright © by Ona Siporin. Reprinted from www.ritualwell.org. Copyright © Ona Siporin. Both used by permission of the author.

RUTH SOHN: "The Song of Miriam" by Rabbi Ruth Sohn. Copyright © Ruth Sohn. Used by permission of the author.

MYRA SOIFER: "The Dance of the Reform Jew" by Rabbi Myra Soifer, excerpted from Torat Chayim, http://urj.org/torah/, a project of the Union for Reform Judaism, 2004, vol. 9, no. 34.

ELAINE MARCUS STARKMAN: "What We Need," by Elaine Marcus Starkman. Copyright © Elaine Marcus Starkman. Used by permission of the author.

PRISCILLA STERN: "We reach for You, our God," reprinted from *Covenant of the Heart: New Prayers, Poems, and Meditations from Women of Reform Judaism* (New York: 1993). Used by permission of Elsie Stern.

YERRA SUGARMAN: Excerpt from "Home Again," reprinted from *Forms of Gone* (Riverdale-on-Hudson, NY: Sheep Meadow Press, 2002). Copyright © 2002 by Yerra Sugarman. Used by permission of the author. "Broken Prayer" used by permission of the author.

SHULAMITH SURNAMER: "The Kohain's Wife," reprinted from *Sarah's Daughters Sing: A Sampler of Poems by Jewish Women,* edited by Henry Wenkart (New York: Jewish Women's Resource Center, A Project of National Council of Jewish Women, 1990). Used by permission of the author.

ANNA SWANSON: "Boiled Beet" reprinted from *Joining the Sisterhood: Young Jewish Women Unite Their Lives,* edited by Tobin Belzer and Julie Pelc (Albany, NY: SUNY Press, 2003). Used by permission of the author.

HENRIETTA SZOLD: "Letter to Haym Peretz," reprinted from *Four Centuries of Jewish Women's Spirituality,* edited by Dianne Ashton and Ellen Umansky (Boston: Beacon Press, 1992).

EVA TÓTH: "Genesis," translated by Peter Jay. Reprinted from *Modern Poems on the Bible,* edited by David Curzon (London, England: Anvil Press Poetry, 1993). Used by permission of Peter Jay.

SOPHIE TRUPIN: Excerpt from *Dakota Diaspora: Memories of a Jewish Homesteader* (Lincoln: University of Nebraska Press, 1988).

MALKA HEIFETZ TUSSMAN: "At the Well," "I Say," "Holy Quiet," from *With Teeth in the Earth: Selected Poems,* Malka Heifetz Tussman, transl. Marcia Falk; Wayne State University Press (1992); copyright © 1992 Marcia Lee Falk. Used by permission of the translator.

MIRIAM ULINOVER: "The Old Prayer Book," translated by Kathryn Hellerstein. Reprinted from *Four Centuries of Jewish Women's Spirituality: A Sourcebook,* edited by Dianne Ashton and Ellen Umansky (Boston: Beacon Press, 1992). Used by permission of Kathryn Hellerstein.

RASHELLE VEPRINSKI: "Widows," translated by David Goldberg. Reprinted from *A Treasury of Yiddish Poetry,* edited by Irving Howe and Eliezer Greenberg (Austin, TX: Holt, Rinehart and Winston, 1969).

SHEILA PELTZ WEINBERG: "A Prayer for the Journey" and "*Aliyah* is Ascent" by Sheila Peltz Weinberg. Used by permission of the author.

ANDREA L. WEISS: "Lech L'cha" by Andrea L. Weiss. Used by permission of the author.

RUTH WHITMAN: Reprinted from Whitman, Ruth, *The Testing of Hanna Senesh, "Poem 21,"* p. 101, used with the permission of Wayne State University Press.

ELEANOR WILNER: "Epitaph" and "Judgment," reprinted from *Reversing the Spell* (Port Townsend, PA: Copper Canyon Press, 1998). Copyright © by Eleanor Wilner. Used by permission of the author. "Miriam's Song," reprinted from *Sarah's Choice* (Chicago: University of Chicago, 1990). Copyright © 1989 by the University of Chicago. Used by permission of the author.

SHULAMIS YELIN: "In Your Image," reprinted from *Seeded in Sinai* (Philadelphia: The Reconstructionist Press, 1974). Copyright © 1974 by Shulamis Yelin.

HANNA ZACKS: Excerpt from "Clothes My Mother Made," reprinted from *Poems That Happened: Making Sense of Daily Life* (iUniverse, 2003). Copyright © 2003 by Hanna Zacks. Used by permission of Hanna Zacks.

NURIT ZARCHI: "She Is Joseph," translated by Shirley Kaufman. Reprinted from *The Defiant Muse: Hebrew Feminist Poems from Antiquity to the Present,* edited by Shirley Kaufman, Galit Hasan-Rokem, and Tamar S. Hess (New York: The Feminist Press of the City University of New York, 1999). Used by permission of Shirley Kaufman.

ZELDA: "With My Grandfather," "Moon Is Teaching Bible," "Each of Us Has a Name," from *The Spectacular Difference: Selected Poems of Zelda,* translated by Marcia Falk; Hebrew Union College Press (2004); copyright © 2004 Marcia Lee Falk. Used by permission of the translator.

ANNA ZIEGLER: "After Fighting All Night We Watch the Sun Rise" and "The Journey" by Anna Ziegler. Copyright © by Anna Ziegler. Used by permission of author.

WENDY ZIERLER: "For Days Miriam Sat Outside" used by permission of Wendy Zierler.

LINDA STERN ZISQUIT: "Posit," "While Three Men Sit in the Next Room Discussing the Talmudic Tractate on How to Prove a Woman Adulterous," and "Elul" reprinted from *Ritual Bath* (Seattle, WA: Broken Moon Press, 1993). Used by permission of Linda Stern Zisquit. "A Word before the Last about Loss" reprinted from *Unopened Letters* (Riverdale-on-Hudson, NY: Sheep Meadow Press, 1996). "No Sign" and "How to Resist Temptation" reprinted from *The Face in the Window* (Riverdale-on-Hudson, NY: Sheep Meadow Press, 2004). Used by permission of Linda Stern Zisquit.

# *Index of Voices Contributors*

# *Index of Voices Titles*

# *Index of Subjects and Cited Authors*

This combined index covers the introductory essays and all commentary sections except for Voices. The cited authors are shown in small capitals.

***Q***



***R***

## *S*